AGE, WEIGHT &

For use with T

CW00541291

Distance	Age	Mar.	Apr.	May						
5f	4	10–0	10–0	10–0	10–0	10–0	10–0	10–0	10–0	10–0
	3	9–0	9–2	9–4	9–6	9–8	9–10	9–11	9–12	9–13
	2	6–8	6–13	7–3	7–7	7–11	8–1	8–5	8–8	8–11
6f	4	9–13	10–0	10–0	10–0	10–0	10–0	10–0	10–0	10–0
	3	8–11	9–0	9–2	9–4	9–6	9–8	9–10	9–11	9–12
	2			6–13	7–3	7–7	7–11	8–1	8–5	8–8
7f	4	9–12	9–13	10–0	10–0	10–0	10–0	10–0	10–0	10–0
	3	8–8	8–11	9–0	9–2	9–4	9–6	9–8	9–10	9–11
	2					7–4	7–8	7–12	8–2	8–5
1m	4	9–11	9–12	9–13	10–0	10–0	10–0	10–0	10–0	10–0
	3	8–6	8–9	8–12	9–1	9–3	9–5	9–7	9–9	9–10
	2							7–9	7–13	8–2
9f	4	9–11	9–12	9–13	9–13	10–0	10–0	10–0	10–0	10–0
	3	8–4	8–7	8–10	8–13	9–2	9–4	9–6	9–8	9–9
1¼m	4	9–10	9–11	9–12	9–13	10–0	10–0	10–0	10–0	10–0
	3	8–2	8–5	8–8	8–11	9–0	9–3	9–5	9–7	9–8
11f	4	9–9	9–11	9–12	9–13	9–13	10–0	10–0	10–0	10–0
	3	8–0	8–4	8–7	8–10	8–13	9–2	9–4	9–6	9–7
1½m	4	9–9	9–10	9–11	9–12	9–13	10–0	10–0	10–0	10–0
	3	7–12	8–2	8–5	8–8	8–11	9–0	9–3	9–5	9–7
13f	4	9–8	9–10	9–11	9–12	9–13	9–13	10–0	10–0	10–0
	3	7–11	8–1	8–4	8–7	8–10	8–13	9–2	9–4	9–6
1¾m	4	9–7	9–9	9–10	9–12	9–13	9–13	10–0	10–0	10–0
	3	7–9	7–13	8–3	8–6	8–9	8–12	9–1	9–3	9–5
15f	4	9–6	9–8	9–10	9–11	9–12	9–13	10–0	10–0	10–0
	3	7–8	7–12	8–2	8–5	8–8	8–11	9–0	9–2	9–4
2m	4	9–6	9–8	9–10	9–11	9–12	9–13	10–0	10–0	10–0
	3	7–7	7–11	8–1	8–5	8–8	8–11	9–0	9–2	9–4
2¼m	4	9–6	9–8	9–9	9–11	9–12	9–13	10–0	10–0	10–0
	3	7–6	7–10	8–0	8–4	8–7	8–10	8–13	9–1	9–3
2½m	4	9–5	9–7	9–9	9–10	9–11	9–12	9–13	10–0	10–0
	3	7–5	7–9	7–13	8–3	8–6	8–9	8–12	9–1	9–3

For 5-y-o's and older, use **10-0** in all cases.

Curragh Bloodstock Agency Ltd.

ENGLAND **IRELAND**

Crossways,
The Avenue,
Newmarket,
Suffolk CB8 9AA.
Tel: (0638) 662620
Telex: 81426

Newbridge,
Co. Kildare.

Tel: (045) 31402
Telex: 25257

A COMPLETE SERVICE
TO THE THOROUGHBRED INDUSTRY

Represented at all major sales

Worldwide buying & selling of
Bloodstock

Represented by Agents in USA, SOUTH AMERICA,
JAPAN, AUSTRALIA, NEW ZEALAND, SOUTH AFRICA

Comprehensive Bloodstock Insurance
Contact us for absolute security and competitive rates

Stallion Syndication & Management

Shares and Nominations

Worldwide Bloodstock Freight
Service

Pedigrees compiled for public &
private Sales

SALES OFFICE Newmarket
Transport (0638) 663538
Sales Ring (0638) 663748
Doncaster (0302) 68075

IRELAND
Goffs (045) 66014/97311
Ballsbridge (01) 683665

**DIRECTORS: P. E. J. McKEEVER (MANAGING),
MAJ. V. McCALMONT, MRS A. D. H. COOKE,
J. HARRINGTON, LT-COL. R. WARDEN,
L. F. SPRING, M. GARRIGAN, D. MINTON**

BRITAIN'S No1 RACING, POOLS & DOGS WEEKLY.

FORM, TIME, SYSTEMS, BETTING . . . we've got the racing scene covered from all angles.

In-depth articles by our team of racing experts, weekly index-linked returns, programmes for seven days, plus special pages for Pools and Greyhound fans.

Add to this informative lot our readers letter-page "Sports Forum" and Split Second's exclusive speed figures, and you will see why the HANDICAP BOOK is the nationwide hot favourite in betting circles.

Sporting Chronicle
HANDICAP BOOK

Every weekend!

Consult the specialists

Even if saving money isn't the most important consideration, there are plenty of other good reasons for buying the SPORTING CHRONICLE.

RACE REPORTS – Unrivalled analysis of the day's racing by Graham Rock, Jon Freeman and Ray Gould.

BLOODSTOCK – Britain's most authoritative page on breeding every Tuesday featuring Peter Willett and Adrian Cook.

WINNERS ON THE CLOCK – For time enthusiasts we publish Split-Second's ratings along with speed figures and standard times for all courses.

TWO-YEAR-OLD RATINGS – Melvin Day's Thursday assessment of the juveniles is highly regarded by owners, trainers and breeders.

COMMENTS FROM PROFESSIONAL BODIES – The Horserace Advisory Council and the Owners' and Jockeys' Associations contribute regular monthly columns, while the bookmakers' spokesman, William Fanshawe, also writes a weekly article. In addition, the paper's Editor, Tom Kelly, unravels racing's politics in his Frankly Speaking column every Friday.

Add Beat The Book, who holds the record for the highest profit on naps in a season, Francis Kelly, our phenomenally successful Fixed Odds expert, a comprehensive form guide, racecards, results, comments, features a lively postbag . . . Yes, the Sporting Chronicle proves that cheapest can also be best.

SPORTING CHRONICLE

The complete racing daily!

Get amongst the winners
with a

CORAL

Credit account!

CORAL RACING LTD

A Division of the Coral Leisure Group

Glebe House, Vicarage Drive, Barking, Essex.

Become a Coral card holder and, wherever you are, you're just a telephone call away from our comprehensive and confidential betting service.

Our highly-trained staff are immediately on hand to record your bets right up to the 'off' and not just on horse racing, as a Coral card holder you can also bet on a wide range of other sports including golf, tennis, cricket, greyhounds, darts, snooker, rugby and football.

To become a Coral card holder, simply telephone **01-591 5151 ext 289** or write to:

CORAL BOOKMAKERS

Glebe House, Barking, Essex IG11 7NS

FOR THE CLASSIC BETTING SERVICE IN THE 80's

For credit and deposit accounts, telephone:

London 01-499 7372/7296
Chatham 0634 577151
North Wales 0492 77551

MECCA BOOKMAKERS

"WILL I GET THE CREDIT I NEED FROM PTS?"
YOU BET.

Just fill in the coupon below and full details of our credit service will be sent to you immediately.

The PTS credit card showing your personal account number enables you to 'phone any of our offices at Leatherhead (London Area), Birmingham, Bristol, Leeds, Liverpool, Manchester, Newcastle and Nottingham.

PTS accept every type of bet at S.P. or Tote with stakes as low as 10p, plus a host of unique money making multiple bets. Ante-post and board prices and race by race results are always available.

POST THIS COUPON NOW TO APPLY FOR A CREDIT ACCOUNT

Name_____

Address_____ (I am over 18)

_____

_____

_____

YOU BET
PTS
NATIONWIDE BOOKMAKERS

Deposit Accounts welcomed (Minimum £25). Send Cash today, start betting tomorrow. *Cheques accepted subject to clearance.*

If you prefer send cash with your bet. (Minimum total stake £3). *Subject to rules.*
P.O. Box 40 Leatherhead.Surrey.Regd.No.1007700 (England). RH/81

AGENCE
FLYING FOX

(Associated with the British Bloodstock Agency)

rectors: Bernard de Saint-Seine, Emmanuel de Seroux

Purchases of thoroughbreds for racing and breeding

International Bloodstock Transactions - Stallion Management - Insurance - Nominations - Breeding Consultation - Shares Transactions

11 RUE ROYALE, 75008 PARIS
Tel. (265) 0936
Telex 290565 F (SOPRODO)

ALL THE BEST...

Board Prices
Ante-Post [all major events]
Weekly Settlement
Results Service
Credit Accounts
(from £50 upwards)

To open a Credit Account telephone or write

STEVENAGE (0438) 61221
PARK PLACE, STEVENAGE, HERTS.

BOOKMAKERS TO LEADING OWNERS AND TRAINERS

Established 1890

HEATHORNS

BOOKMAKERS

OVERSBY HOUSE
ONSLOW STREET
GUILDFORD
SURREY GU1 4SR
Telephone: (0483) 31233

The BRITISH
BLOODSTOCK AG

Established 1911

PURCHASES, SALES, SHARES AND NOMINATIO
VALUATIONS, INSURANCE, TRANSPORT, RESEAR

EUROPE'S LEADING

Managers or Syndicate Secret
30 Stallions

Shares and nominations available upo

HEAD OFFICE:
British Bloodstock Agency
11A ALBEMARLE STREET,   THORMANBY HOUSE
LONDON, W1X 4JB
TELEPHONE: 01-493 9402   TELEPI
TELEX: 27403

Bri

Your best bet for 1983.

The Bradford & Bingley £20,000 Handicap over One Mile at York August 18.

Bradford & Bingley
Head Office, Bingley, West Yorkshire.

We're odds on favourite for all your accountancy personnel.

A Nationwide Answer to Accountancy Recruitment

37 Eastcheap, London EC3
Tel: 01-623 3544.

Birmingham: 021-643 2875
Bristol: 0272 211041
Leeds: 0532 742616
Manchester: 061-832 6708
New Zealand: (Auckland) 771619

dunlop & badenoch

Ever tried catching the 8.15 a.m. flight to Chantilly?

You won't, because there isn't one, from anywhere in the U.K. Which is a pity if your business happens to be in Chantilly. You'll probably have to fly to Paris and then drive.

There is another way of course. A way that can put you down much closer, or at any one of the 2,000 airports in Europe that are not used by the airlines. Airports that are usually nearer to your place of business.

And by way of a bonus, you'll enjoy minimum check-in formalities, an almost total absence of airport hold ups, an extremely comfortable seat, good things to eat (and drink!) and a freedom to travel by your own timetable rather than someone else's.

It's called Eagle Executive Charter. For people who know where they're going.

Please 'fly' me the details of Eagle's executive air charter services.

Name _____

Position _____

Company _____

Address _____

_____

Tel No _____

FLY Eagle

Eagle, Leavesden Airport, Watford, Herts, WD2 7BY
London: Tel: (09273) 79611 Telex: 261502 EAGLE G
Aberdeen: Tel: (0224) 725700 Telex: 739928 EAGABZ G

15

Based on the exciting Jaguar XJS HE, the superb new Lynx Eventer combines extra space with amazing grace and thrilling pace.

The versatile loadspace area is a large 46 cu. ft. with the rear seat folded down – ideal for carrying anything from equipment to furniture.

And yet the estate car styling has the same overall dimensions as the XJS HE and takes nothing away from the breathtaking performance of the incredible V12 5.3 litre engine, now featuring the new high efficiency cylinder head for greater economy.

With top speed of 156 mph the luxurious but totally practical Eventer is not only the fastest estate car money can buy – but also the only one with a legendary sports pedigree.

Patrick Motors are the sole distributors in the UK. Contact your nearest specialist dealer for further information.

PMG **Midlands and North**
Reeve & Stedeford, Berkley Street (off Broad Street), Birmingham. Tel. 021-643 6932
PMG **Sales in the South**
Spink of Bournemouth, Poole Hill, Bournemouth. Tel. 0202 25405

THE RACIEST ESTATE CAR YOU'VE EVER SEEN

The helicopter has come a long way

This is the 1983 Aerospatiale helicopter family for the business and leisure market.

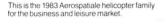

The 4/5 seat single-engined 'Squirrel'.
The 6/8 seat twin-engined 'Dauphin'.
The 4/5 seat twin-engined 'Squirrel'.

Between them the quietest, most sophisticated helicopter range available today and the fastest way for point-to-point travel –
- *business to business*
- *city to city*
- *racecourse to racecourse*
- *home to home*

Typical journey examples		
London (City Helistop) Paris		1hr. 20m.
Swindon	York	1hr. 20m.
Newmarket	Goodwood	50m.
Isle of Man	Troon, Ayrshire	35m.

Today's helicopter represents the ultimate in time saving comfortable travel.
The Aerospatiale range is offered by sole U.K. distributors M Alpine Helicopters in a variety of attractive and flexible schemes – outright purchase, joint-user, management, and charter, to meet clients individual needs. Discuss your requirements with Robin Keith. Managing Director, on 01-848 3522 or Telex: 933286.

McAlpine Helicopters Ltd

Hayes Helicentre. Swallowfield Way. Hayes. Middlesex

-the UK business helicopter company

17

Buying or Selling Gold Coins: Deal Direct
Tel: 0532 468251

Now you can buy or sell Krugerrands, Maple Leafs, USA Twenty Dollars, Sovereigns and Half Sovereigns, quickly and effectively.

Here at Harvey Michael Ross we have many years of bullion coin investment experience with a large international clientele.

We are pleased to deal with clients who wish to buy coins on margin or gold futures. To help holders or potential holders take full advantage of the hyperactive gold market, Harvey Michael Ross publishes a free weekly, Gold Information Bulletin.

To receive your free copy dial (0532) 468251 and ask to be placed on our FREE automatic mailing list.

JERSEY OR ZURICH DELIVERY AVAILABLE

Harvey Michael Ross

Russell House,
St. Paul's Street, Leeds 1, England.
Tel: 0532 454930/455083 Dealing: 0532 468251 (7 lines)
Foreign Exchange and Commodities Room (0532) 450707
Accounts: 0532 458479 Telex: 556373/55207 Cables: Invest Leeds

RACEHORSES
OF
1982

A Timeform Publication   Price £42.00

A Timeform Publication

Compiled and Produced under the direction of
Phil Bull, B.Sc., and Reg Griffin

by members of the Timeform Organisation
G. Greetham, B.A. (Deputy Managing Director), J. G. Clarke (Director), G. F. Walton, Dip.A.D. (Director), J. D. Newton, B.A. (Editor), D. P. Adams, A. M. Caulfield, G. C. J. Dench, B.A., J. P. Early, B.A., A. Elves, B.A., R. M. Gibson, B.A. and C. S. Williams.

Published by Portway Press Limited, Timeform House, Halifax, Yorkshire, and Printed by Walter Pearce & Co., Brentford, Middlesex.

An action heard before Mr Justice Vaisey in the Chancery Division of the High Court in October 1957 established that copyright subsists in Timeform, Timeform Ratings and Race Ratings, and Timeform Commentaries.
No part of this annual volume of "Racehorses" or of any Timeform publication may be stored or recorded in any storage and retrieval system, mechanical, electronic or photographic, or by any other means, and no part of it may be transmitted or reproduced in any form or in any way without permission, in writing, from the publishers.

Registered at Stationers' Hall

Every care is taken in the compilation of this publication, but no responsibility is accepted by the Publishers for errors, omissions or their consequences.

© **Portway Press Limited 1983**

ISBN 0 900599 35 9

CONTENTS

*EVZON (centre) winning
the Queen's Vase (Gp.3), £15,520
Royal Ascot 1982*

EVZON

was bred by

KERR & Co. Ltd.

and sold as a foal for

4,500 Gns.

**For the best advice and guidance on all
Bloodstock matters—contact us at:**

**KERR HOUSE, 2 FITZWILLIAM SQUARE,
DUBLIN 2.**

Tel: 760391. Telex: 24342. Cables: "Bloodstock Dublin"

Foreword

"Racehorses of 1982" deals individually, in alphabetical sequence, with every horse that ran under Jockey Club Rules in 1982, plus a number of foreign-trained horses that did not race here. For each of these horses is given (1) its age, colour and sex, (2) its breeding, (3) a form summary giving details of all its performances during the past two seasons, (4) a rating of its merit, (5) a commentary upon its racing or general characteristics as a racehorse, with some suggestions, perhaps, regarding its potentialities in 1983, and (6) the name of the trainer in whose charge it was on the last occasion it ran.

The book is published with a twofold purpose. Firstly, it is designed to provide the betting man with data for practical use in analysing the racing programmes from day to day, and instructions as to its use in this capacity will be found in the Explanatory Notes which follow this Foreword; and secondly, the book is intended to have some permanent value as a review of the exploits and achievements of the more notable of our thoroughbreds in 1982. Thus, while the commentaries upon the vast majority of the horses are, of necessity, in note form, the best horses are more critically examined, and the short essays upon them are illustrated by half-tone portraits and photographs of the finishes of some of the races in which they were successful.

The attention of foreign buyers of British bloodstock, and others who are concerned with Timeform Ratings as a measure of absolute racing class in terms of a standard scale, is drawn to the section headed "The Level of the Ratings" in the Explanatory Notes on page 37.

February, 1983.

ROBIN McENERY

M.V.B., M.R.C.V.S.

BLOODSTOCK AGENT

FOR ALL
PURCHASING
INSURANCE—**COMPETITIVE RATES**
STALLION SHARES
NOMINATIONS
MANAGEMENT
MATING SELECTIONS
OVERSEAS INSPECTION
HORSES IN TRAINING

Managing:
BALLIOL—Group winning full brother to Balidar, standing at Sheepcote Farm, Denston, Newmarket

and

RHUS—Group winning son of Riva Ridge, out of Bold Pink, standing at Lindenhoff Farm, Beernem, Belgium.

---

1 STABLE COTTAGE
ST. ALBANS, FORDHAM ROAD
NEWMARKET CB8 7AH
Tel: Newmarket (0638) 3260 or 4838
Telex: 817666 TH1 BG1

INDEX TO PHOTOGRAPHS

PORTRAITS & SNAPSHOTS

26

Fire-Thatch	..	2 ch.c.	Thatch–Gigiolina		
			(King Emperor)	*J. Crofts*	322
Fitzpatrick	..	3 b.c.	Oats–Shannon Princess		
			(Connaught)	*Fiona Vigors*	325
Gallant Special	..	2 ch.c.	Gallant Romeo–		
			Special Account		
			(Buckpasser)	*J. Crofts*	341
General Holme	..	3 ch.c.	Noholme II–		
			Generals Sister		
			(Count Fleet)	*P. Bertrand*	346
Glenstal	..	2 b.c.	Northern Dancer–		
			Cloonlara		
			(Sir Ivor)	*Jacqueline O'Brien*	352
Glint of Gold	..	4 b.c.	Mill Reef–Crown Treasure		
			(Graustark)	*W. W. Rouch & Co.*	355
Golden Fleece	..	3 b.c.	Nijinsky–Exotic Treat		
			(Vaguely Noble)	*Jacqueline O'Brien*	363
Gordian	..	2 ch.c.	Grundy–Mrs Tiggywinkle		
			(Silly Season)	*W. W. Rouch & Co.*	369
Gorytus	..	2 b.c.	Nijinsky–Glad Rags		
			(High Hat)	*Fiona Vigors*	373
Grease	..	3 b.f.	Filiberto–Greedy of Gain		
			(Habitat)	*W. Everitt*	378
Great Eastern	..	5 br.h.	Jukebox–Miss Bangkok		
			(Sovereign Path)	*W. W. Rouch & Co.*	379
Green Forest	..	3 ch.c.	Shecky Greene–		
			Tell Meno Lies		
			(The Axe)	*P. Bertrand*	382
Habibti	..	2 br.f.	Habitat–Klairessa		
			(Klairon)	*W. W. Rouch & Co.*	388
Halsbury	..	4 b.c.	Exbury–Wig and Gown		
			(Mandamus)	*Fiona Vigors*	391
Harbour	..	3 ch.f.	Arctic Tern–		
			Heres To You		
			(Molvedo)	*P. Bertrand*	395
Hays	..	3 b.c.	Wolver Hollow–		
			Sing a Song		
			(Sing Sing)	*W. W. Rouch & Co.*	402
Heron Bay	..	2 b.c.	Alleged Foreign Missile		
			(Damascus)	*Jacqueline O'Brien*	409
High Cannon	..	2 b.c.	Cannonade–So High		
			(Sea-Bird II)	*Timeform*	412
Horage	..	2 b.c.	Tumble Wind–Musicienne		
			(Sicambre)	*Fiona Vigors*	422
Indian King	..	4 b.c.	Raja Baba–Protest		
			(Rash Prince)	*W. W. Rouch & Co.*	433
Ivano	..	3 ch.c.	Snow Knight–		
			Smiling Jacqueline		
			(Hilarious)	*J. Crofts*	438
Jacquinta	..	3 b.f.	Habitat–Jacinth		
			(Red God)	*W. W. Rouch & Co.*	440
Jalmood	..	3 b.c.	Blushing Groom–		
			Fast Ride		
			(Sicambre)	*W. W. Rouch & Co.*	443
Kafu	..	2 b.c.	African Sky–		
			Pampered Dancer		
			(Pampered King)	*W. W. Rouch & Co.*	457
Kalaglow	..	4 gr.c.	Kalamoun–Rossitor		
			(Pall Mall)	*W. W. Rouch & Co.*	462
Karadar	..	4 b.c.	Rheingold–Shahinaaz		
			(Venture VII)	*J. Crofts*	465
Kareena	..	3 b.f.	Riverman–Kermiya		
			(Vienna)	*Fiona Vigors*	466
Kind of Hush	..	4 b.c.	Welsh Pageant–Sauceboat		
			(Connaught)	*Fiona Vigors*	475
Lafontaine	..	5 b.h.	Sham–Valya (Vandale)	*J. Crofts*	488

27

L'Emigrant	..	2 b. or br.c.	The Minstrel–Suprina (Vaguely Noble)	*P. Bertrand*	500
Lightning Label		6 br.h.	African Sky– Soie Sauvage (Shantung)	*J. Crofts*	504
Little Wolf	..	4 ch.c.	Grundy–Hiding Place (Doutelle)	*Fiona Vigors*	510
Lomond ..	..	2 b.c.	Northern Dancer– My Charmer (Poker)	*Jacqueline O'Brien*	515
Lords ..	..	3 b.c.	Hoist the Flag– Princessnesian (Princequillo)	*Jacqueline O'Brien*	517
Lyphard's Special		2 b.c.	Lyphard–My Bupers (Bupers)	*W. W. Rouch & Co.*	524
Ma Biche	..	2 b. or br.f.	Key To The Kingdom– Madge (Roi Dagobert)	*P. Bertrand*	528
Maximova	..	2 b.f.	Green Dancer–Baracala (Swaps)	*P. Bertrand*	546
Merlins Charm		3 b.f.	Bold Bidder–Lucky Spell (Lucky Mel)	*Fiona Vigors*	554
Minnelli ..	..	2 b.f.	Dom Racine– Nigella Damascena (St Paddy)	*Jacqueline O'Brien*	560
Mr Fluorocarbon		3 ch.c.	Morston–Western Air (Sound Track)	*J. Crofts*	579
Mubarak of Kuwait	..	3 b.c.	Morston–Dominant (Behistoun)	*W. W. Rouch & Co.*	581
Muscatite	..	2 b.c.	Habitat–Takette (Takawalk II)	*J. Crofts*	584
Noalcoholic	..	5 b.h.	Nonoalco–Alea II (Galivanter)	*J. Crofts*	599
Noalto ..	..	4 ch.c.	Nonoalco–Lyrical (Gratitude)	*Sporting Pictures (UK)*	600
Norwick ..		3 b.c.	Far North–Shay Sheery (A Dragon Killer)	*Sporting Pictures (UK)*	607
Old Country	..	3 b.c.	Quiet Fling–Little Miss (Aggressor)	*J. Crofts*	613
On Stage	..	2 b.c.	Comedy Star–Last Case (Firestreak)	*Laurie Morton Photography*	617
On The House ..		3 b.f.	Be My Guest–Lora (Lorenzaccio)	*J. Crofts*	620
Ore ..	..	4 ch.c.	Ballymore–Minatonka (Linacre)	*J. Crofts*	625
Pas De Seul	..	3 b.c.	Mill Reef–Thereby (Star Moss)	*Jacqueline O'Brien*	638
Peacetime	..	3 b.c.	Nijinsky–Peace (Klairon)	*W. W. Rouch & Co.*	642
Persepolis	..	3 gr.c.	Kalamoun–Perlita (Baldric II)	*P. Bertrand*	648
Polished Silver		2 ch.c.	Try My Best–Mettle (Pretendre)	*J. Crofts*	658
Ponchielli	..	4 b.c.	Pitskelly–Pennycress (Florescence)	*J. Crofts*	660
Prima Voce	..	3 b.c.	Elocutionist–Que Mona (Ribot)	*J. Crofts*	664
Prince Reymo ..		2 b.c.	Jimmy Reppin– Honey Thief (Burglar)	*J. Crofts*	668
Princes Gate	..	5 br.h.	Realm–Consensus (Majority Blue)	*J. Crofts*	670

Prince's Polly ..	3 b.f.	English Prince–Suspicious Polly (Above Suspicion)	*Jacqueline O'Brien*	672
Proclaim ..	2 b.c.	Mr Prospector–Maybellene (Fleet Nasrullah)	*W. W. Rouch & Co.*	676
Punctilio ..	3 b.c.	Forli–Minstrelete (Round Table)	*Jacqueline O'Brien*	679
Rebollino ..	3 b.c.	Nebbiolo–Cloe (Shantung)	*Timeform*	691
Rosananti ..	3 ch.f.	Blushing Groom–Clarina (Klairon)	*W. W. Rouch & Co.*	712
Rose of Montreaux ..	3 ch.f.	Habat–Gliding (Tudor Melody)	*Fiona Vigors*	713
Rutland	2 b.c.	Mummy's Pet–Rennet (King's Bench)	*W. W. Rouch & Co.*	724
Salieri	2 ch.c.	Accipiter–Hogan's Sister (Speak John)	*J. Crofts*	733
Salmon Leap ..	2 ch.c.	Northern Dancer–Fish-Bar (Baldric II)	*Jacqueline O'Brien*	734
Sandhurst Prince	3 ch.c.	Pampapaul–Blue Shark (Silver Shark)	*W. W. Rouch & Co.*	738
Santella Man ..	3 ch.c.	Nebbiolo–Belle Bretonne (Celtic Ash)	*W. W. Rouch & Co.*	741
Sayyaf	5 b.h.	Habitat–Pavello (Crepello)	*Laurie Morton Photography*	744
Sharpo	5 ch.h.	Sharpen Up–Moiety Bird (Falcon)	*W. W. Rouch & Co.*	757
Shearwalk ..	2 gr.c.	Godswalk–Sairshea (Simbir)	*J. Crofts*	759
Sing Softly ..	3 br.f.	Luthier–Melody Hour (Sing Sing)	*J. Crofts*	771
Six Mile Bottom	4 b.c.	Brigadier Gerard–Bamba (Busted)	*J. Crofts*	774
Soba	3 ch.f.	Most Secret–Mild Wind (Porto Bello)	*Timeform*	783
Solford ..	2 b.c.	Nijinsky–Fairness (Cavan)	*Jacqueline O'Brien*	787
Spanish Pool ..	3 b.c.	Gay Fandango–Watermark (Henry the Seventh)	*J. Crofts*	793
Sweet Emma ..	2 b.f.	Welsh Saint–Gang Plank (Tower Walk)	*Jacqueline O'Brien*	816
Swiftfoot ..	3 b.f.	Run The Gantlet–Whitefoot (Relko)	*Fiona Vigors*	821
Tants	3 ch.f.	Vitiges–Hants (Exbury)	*J. Crofts*	826
The Fort ..	2 ch.c.	Sallust–Fortlin (Fortino II)	*J. Crofts*	839
The Noble Player	2 ch.c.	The Minstrel–Noble Mark (On Your Mark)	*W. Everitt*	841
The Wonder ..	4 br.c.	Wittgenstein–The Lark (Lanark)	*E. G. Byrne*	846
Thug	2 ch.c.	Persian Bold–Spring Azure (Mountain Call)	*J. Crofts*	849
Time Charter ..	3 b.f.	Saritamer–Centrocon (High Line)	*W. W. Rouch & Co.*	854
Top O'The North	2 b. or br.c.	High Top–Gold Poulet (Goldhill)	*Timeform*	861
Touching Wood	3 b.c.	Roberto–Mandera (Vaguely Noble)	*J. Crofts*	865
Tres Gate ..	5 b.h.	Thatch–Setsu (Shantung)	*J. Crofts*	870

Triple Tipple		3 b.f.	Raise A Cup–		
			Ameridouble		
			(Nodouble)	*J. Crofts*	871
Tugoflove	..	6 b.h.	Tudor Rhythm–Speyside		
			(Live Spirit)	*Fiona Vigors*	875
Vaigly Star	..	3 b.f.	Star Appeal–Dervaig		
			(Derring-Do)	*J. Crofts*	880
Valentinian	..	4 ch.c.	Morston–Appian Way		
			(Romulus)	*Fiona Vigors*	883
Widaad	..	2 b.f.	Mr Prospector–		
			Attache Case		
			(Diplomat Way)	*J. Crofts*	904
Wind and Wuthering	..	3 br.c.	No Robbery–J. A's Joy		
			(Johns Joy)	*W. W. Rouch & Co.*	907
Woodstream	..	3 ch.f.	Northern Dancer–		
			Rule Formi		
			(Forli)	*Jacqueline O'Brien*	912
Yard Bird	..	3 ch.c.	Busted–Final Orders		
			(Prince John)	*W. W. Rouch & Co.*	915
Zino	..	3 b.c.	Welsh Pageant–Cyriana		
			(Salvo)	*A. Russell*	922
Zoffany	..	2 b.c.	Our Native–		
			Grey Dawn Girl		
			(Grey Dawn II)	*W. W. Rouch & Co.*	925

RACE PHOTOGRAPHS

Duke of Edinburgh Stakes (Ascot)	..	..	*George Selwyn*	605
Duke of York Stakes (York)	..	..	*J. Crofts*	447
Earl of Sefton Stakes (Newmarket)	..		*Sport and General*	459
Esal Bookmakers Handicap (Doncaster)	..		*George Selwyn*	465
Exeter Stakes (Newmarket)	..	..	*A. Russell*	675
Extel Stakes (Handicap) (Goodwood)	..		*J. Crofts*	167
Firth of Clyde Stakes (Ayr)	..	..	*A. Russell*	588
Flying Childers Stakes (Doncaster)	..		*A. Russell*	456
Fred Darling Stakes (Newbury)	..		*Press Association Photos*	777
Fulbourne Maiden Stakes (Newmarket)		..	*E. G. Byrne*	513
Gallinule Stakes (the Curragh)	..	..	*M. Ansell*	97
Garrowby Stakes (York)	..	..	*A. Russell*	151
Geoffrey Freer Stakes (Newbury)	..		*George Selwyn*	90
Gilbey Champion Racehorse Futurity				
(York)	..	..	*A. Russell*	609
Gimcrack Stakes (York)	..	..	*A. Russell*	422
Goffs Irish One Thousand Guineas				
(the Curragh)	..	..	*E. G. Byrne*	671
Gold Cup (Ascot)	..	..	*J. Crofts*	89
Goodwood Cup ..	..	..	*E. G. Byrne*	405
Gordon Stakes (Goodwood)	..	..	*A. Russell*	294
Grand Criterium (Longchamp)	..		*P. Bertrand*	729
Grand Prix de Deauville	..	..	*P. Bertrand*	690
Grand Prix de Paris (Longchamp)	..		*P. Bertrand*	501
Grand Prix de Saint-Cloud	..		*P. Bertrand*	354
Great Voltigeur Stakes (York)	..		*Press Association Photos*	294
Guardian Classic Trial (Sandown)	..		*George Selwyn*	641
Hardwicke Stakes (Ascot)	..	..	*A. Russell*	231
Harry Rosebery Challenge Trophy (Ayr)	..		*A. Russell*	451
Heinz '57' Phoenix Stakes (Leopardstown)	..		*M. Ansell*	816
Henry II Stakes (Sandown)	..	..	*J. Crofts*	88
Highland Spring Derby Trial (Lingfield)	..		*W. Everitt*	442
Hoover Fillies Mile (Ascot)	..	..	*A. Russell*	44
Hungerford Stakes (Newbury)	..	..	*George Selwyn*	636
Hyperion Stakes (Ascot)	..	..	*George Selwyn*	795
Intercraft Solario Stakes (Sandown)	..		*E. G. Byrne*	838
Irish Guinness Oaks (the Curragh)	..		*E. G. Byrne*	819
Irish Sweeps Derby (the Curragh)	..		*E. G. Byrne*	99
Jefferson Smurfit Memorial Irish St Leger				
(the Curragh)	..	..	*Caroline Norris*	864
Jennings The Bookmakers Zetland Stakes				
(Newmarket)	..	..	*J. Crofts*	449
Jersey Stakes (Ascot)	..	..	*J. Crofts*	553
Jockey Club Cup (Newmarket)	..		*A. Russell*	509
Jockey Club Stakes (Newmarket)	..		*A. Russell*	87
Joe McGrath Memorial Stakes				
(Leopardstown)	..	..	*Ruth Rogers*	101
John Barr Scotch Whisky Stakes (Ayr)	..		*A. Russell*	183
John Smith's Magnet Cup (York)	..		*A. Russell*	169
King Edward VII Stakes (Ascot)	..		*J. Crofts*	623
King George Stakes (Goodwood)	..		*A. Russell*	856
King George VI and Queen Elizabeth				
Diamond Stakes (Ascot)	..	..	*A. Russell*	461
King's Stand Stakes (Ascot)	..	..	*A. Russell*	316
Kiveton Park Steel Stakes (Doncaster)	..		*A. Russell*	843
Ladbroke Chester Cup ..	..	..	*Press Association Photos*	252
Ladbrokes (Ayr) Gold Cup Handicap		..	*A. Russell*	309
Ladbrokes Craven Stakes (Newmarket)	..		*J. Crofts*	766
Lancashire Oaks (Haydock)	..	..	*A. Russell*	771
Land of Burns Stakes (Ayr)	..	..	*A. Russell*	188

32

Prix Morny (Deauville)	..	..	..	*P. Bertrand*	255
Prix Niel (Longchamp)	..	..	..	*P. Bertrand*	147
Prix Perth (Saint-Cloud)	..	..	..	*P. Bertrand*	215
Prix Robert Papin (Maisons-Laffitte)	..	..	*P. Bertrand*	526
Prix Royal-Oak (Longchamp)	..	..	*P. Bertrand*	258
Prix Saint-Roman (Longchamp)	..	*E. G. Byrne*	728
Prix Vermeille (Longchamp)	..	..	*P. Bertrand*	61
Quail Stakes (Kempton)	..	..	*Sport and General*	557
Queen Anne Stakes (Ascot)	..	..	*J. Crofts*	577
Queen Elizabeth II Stakes (Ascot)	..	*W. Everitt*	169
Queen Mary Stakes (Ascot)	..	..	*A. Russell*	903
Queen's Vase (Ascot)	..	..	..	*A. Russell*	303
Ribblesdale Stakes (Ascot)	..	..	*A. Russell*	270
Ribero Stakes (Doncaster)	..	..	*A. Russell*	212
Richmond Stakes (Goodwood)	..	..	*A. Russell*	340
Rockfel Stakes (Newmarket)	..	..	*A. Russell*	744
Rosebery Memorial Handicap (Epsom)	..	*J. Crofts*	261
Rous Memorial Stakes (Goodwood)	..	*Sport and General*	731
Royal Hunt Cup Handicap (Ascot)	..	*J. Crofts*	168
Royal Lodge Stakes (Ascot)	..	..	*George Selwyn*	283
Sandwich Maiden Stakes (Ascot)	..	..	*J. Crofts*	482
Scarbrough Stakes (Doncaster)	..	..	*E. G. Byrne*	782
Selsey Maiden Stakes (Goodwood)	..	*E. G. Byrne*	280
Shadwell Maiden Stakes (Yarmouth)	..	*A. Russell*	516
Somerville Tattersall Stakes (Newmarket)	..	*J. Crofts*	657
Star Stakes (Sandown)	..	..	..	*J. Crofts*	855
St Hugh's Stakes (Newbury)	..	..	*George Selwyn*	314
St James's Palace Stakes (Ascot)	..	*A. Russell*	249
St Leger Stakes (Doncaster)	..	..	*A. Russell*	863
Sun Chariot Stakes (Newmarket)	..	..	*J. Crofts*	852
Sussex Stakes (Goodwood)	..	..	*A. Russell*	619
Temple Stakes (Sandown)	..	..	*Press Association Photos*	582
Thirsk Sprint Stakes	..	..	..	*A. Russell*	233
Timeform Race Card Stakes (Thirsk)	..	*A. Russell*	338
Tolly Cobbold Trophy Nursery Handicap					
(Newmarket)	..	..	..	*A. Russell*	529
Tote Cesarewitch Handicap (Newmarket)	..	*A. Russell*	576
Tote-Ebor Handicap (York)	..	..	*A. Russell*	78
Tote European Free Handicap (Newmarket)	..	*A. Russell*	542
Tote Lockinge Stakes (Newbury)	..	..	*George Selwyn*	575
Trusthouse Forte Prix de l'Arc de Triomphe					
(Longchamp)	..	..	..	*P. Bertrand*	53
Two Thousand Guineas Stakes (Newmarket)	*A. Russell*	921
Vernons Sprint Cup (Haydock)	..	..	*A. Russell*	431
Vernons Stakes (York)	..	..	..	*A. Russell*	736
Washington International	..	..	*Laurel Racecourse Inc*	82
Waterford Candelabra Stakes (Goodwood)	..	*E. G. Byrne*	326
Waterford Crystal Mile (Goodwood)	..	*W. Everitt*	737
William Hill Cambridgeshire Handicap					
(Newmarket)	..	..	..	*A. Russell*	194
William Hill Cheveley Park Stakes					
(Newmarket)	..	..	..	*E. G. Byrne*	527
William Hill Dewhurst Stakes (Newmarket)	*A. Russell*	266
William Hill Futurity Stakes (Doncaster)	*A. Russell*	284
William Hill July Cup (Newmarket)	..	*A. Russell*	755
William Hill Lincoln Handicap (Doncaster)	*A. Russell*	477
William Hill Middle Park Stakes (Newmarket)	*E. G. Byrne*	265
William Hill November Handicap					
(Doncaster)	..	..	..	*A. Russell*	277
William Hill Sprint Championship (York)	..	*A. Russell*	756
William Hill Stewards' Cup (Goodwood)	..	*A. Russell*	781
William Hill Trophy (York)	..	..	*A. Russell*	238
Wokingham Stakes (Ascot)	..	..	*A. Russell*	120
Yorkshire Cup (York)	..	..	..	*A. Russell*	88
Yorkshire Oaks (York)	..	..	..	*A. Russell*	108

Whenever you insure a horse

THINK

BGI

MR. JOHN HANCOCK

WILL BE IN ATTENDANCE AT

**ALL PRINCIPAL
BLOODSTOCK SALES
IN ENGLAND, IRELAND, FRANCE
AND THE UNITED STATES
IN 1983**

Bloodstock & General Insurance Brokers Ltd.,
162 High Street, Newmarket.   Tel 61411/3
Telex: 817666 (THIBGI)

1982
ANOTHER VINTAGE YEAR FOR TATTERSALLS WINNERS

71 European and North American
Group Races won by horses
purchased at Park Paddocks, Newmarket

1982 SALES DATES (subject to alteration)

SPRING SALES	April 30
JULY SALES	July 6–7
OCTOBER PREMIER SALES	September 27–30
OCTOBER OPEN SALES	October 10–15
AUTUMN SALES	October 25–28
DECEMBER SALES	November 23–26
	November 28–December 1

Tattersalls

TERRACE HOUSE, NEWMARKET, SUFFOLK, CB8 9BT
Telephone: Newmarket (0638) 665931. Telex: 817582 (Hammer)

Provisional
Sales Programme 1983
Bloodstock Sales

Derby Sale Select Sale of high-class potential chasers & hurdlers	June 23rd-24th
Yearling Sale	August 30th-September 1st
November National hunt Sale	Oct 30th-Nov 5th
December Flat-bred Sale of Horses in Training Yearlings, Mares & Foals	December 5th-8th

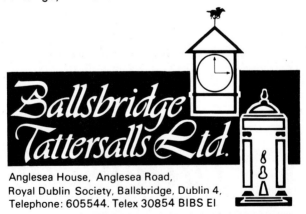

Ballsbridge Tattersalls Ltd.

Anglesea House, Anglesea Road,
Royal Dublin Society, Ballsbridge, Dublin 4,
Telephone: 605544. Telex 30854 BIBS EI

Brindley

36

EXPLANATORY NOTES

TO assess the prospects of any horse in a race it is necessary to know two things about him: first, how good he is; and second, what sort of horse he is. In this book the merit of each horse is expressed in the form of a *rating* (printed on the right); and the *racing character* of the horse given in the commentary.

TIMEFORM RATINGS

The Timeform Rating of a horse is simply the merit of the horse expressed in pounds. More precisely, it is *the number of pounds which, in our opinion, the horse would be entitled to receive in an average Free Handicap.* Thus, a horse which we regard as worth 9 st 7 lb in an average Free Handicap, i.e., 133 lb, would receive a rating of 133: and one regarded as worth 8 st (112 lb) would receive a rating of 112; and so on.

This explains what the ratings are; but of course individual ratings are not actually allocated in this way, merely by "inspection." The rating of any horse is a result of careful examination of its running against other horses. We maintain a "running" handicap of all horses in training throughout the season, or, to be strictly accurate, two handicaps, one for horses aged three years and over, and one for two-year-olds.

THE LEVEL OF THE RATINGS

At the close of each season all the horses that have raced are re-handicapped from scratch, and each horse's rating is revised. It is also necessary to adjust the general level of the handicap, so that the mean of all the ratings is kept at the same standard level from year to year. Left to itself, the general level of the ratings, in each succeeding issue of Timeform, tends to rise steadily. For technical reasons it is desirable to allow it to do so during the season: but, in the winter, when the complete re-handicap is done, the ratings must, of course, be put back on their proper level again.

This explains why, in this book, the ratings are, in general, different from those in the final issue of the 1982 Timeform series.

RATINGS AND WEIGHT-FOR-AGE

These matters, however, are by the way. What concerns the reader is that he has, in the ratings in this book, a universal handicap embracing all the horses in training it is possible to weigh up, ranging from tip-top classic performers, with ratings from 130 to 145, down to the meanest selling platers, rated around the 40 or 50 mark. And what we now have to explain is the practical use of these ratings in the business of weighing up a race.

Before doing so, it is important to mention that all ratings are at weight-for-age, so that equal ratings mean horses of equal merit: perhaps it would be clearer if we said that the universal rating handicap is really not a single handicap, but four handicaps side by side: one for 2-y-o's, one for 3-y-o's, one for 4-y-o's and one for older horses. Thus, a 3-y-o rated, for argument's sake, at 117 is deemed to be identical in point of "merit" with a 4-y-o also rated at 117: but for them to have equal chances in, say, a mile race in June, the 3-y-o would need to be receiving 13 lb from the 4-y-o, which is the weight difference specified in the Age, Weight and Distance Table on the page facing the front cover. However, let us to cases!

USING THE RATINGS

In using Timeform Ratings with a view to discovering which horses in any race have the best chances at the weights, we have two distinct cases, according to whether the horses taking part are of the same age or of different ages. Here is the procedure in each case:—

A. Horses of the Same Age

If the horses all carry the same weight there are no adjustments to be made, and the horses with the highest ratings have the best chances. If the horses carry different weights, jot down their ratings, and to the rating of each horse add one point for every pound the horse is set to carry less than 10 st, or subtract one point for every pound he has to carry more than 10 st. When the ratings have been adjusted in this way the highest resultant figure indicates the horse with the best chance at the weights.

Example (any distance: any month of the season)

2 Good Girl (9-6)	.. Rating 119	.... add 8	....	127
2 Paulinus (9-4)	.. Rating 113	.... add 10	....	123
2 Abilene (8-11)	.. Rating 107	.... add 17	....	124
2 Bob's Joy (8-7)	.. Rating 108	.... add 21	....	129
2 Time Warp (8-2)	.. Rating 100	.... add 26	....	126
2 Eagle Eye (7-7)	.. Rating 92	.... add 35	....	127

Bob's Joy (129) has the best chance; Good Girl (127) and Eagle Eye (127) are next best.

B. Horses of Different Ages

Take no notice of the weight any horse receives from any other. Instead, consult the Age, Weight and Distance Table on the page facing the front cover. Treat each horse separately, and compare the weight it has to carry with the weight prescribed for it in the table, according to the age of the horse, the distance of the race and the month of the year. Then, add one point to the rating for each pound the horse has to carry less than the weight given in the table: or, subtract one point from the rating for every pound he has to carry more than the weight prescribed by the table. The highest resultant figure indicates the horse most favoured by the weights.

38

Example (1½ **miles in July**)
(Table Weights: 5-y-o 10-0; 4-y-o 9-13; 3-y-o 8-11)

6 Nimitz (9-12)	.. Rating 115	.... add	2	 117
4 Red Devil (9-9)	.. Rating 114	.... add	4	 118
6 Sweet Cindy (9-5)	.. Rating 115	.... add	9	 124
3 Jailhouse (8-12)	.. Rating 120	subtract	1	 119
4 Haakon (8-11)	.. Rating 101	.... add	16	 117
3 Fine Strike (8-7)	.. Rating 112	.... add	4	 116

Sweet Cindy (124) has the best chance at the weights, with 5 lb in hand of Jailhouse.

JOCKEYSHIP AND APPRENTICE ALLOWANCES

There is just one further point that arises in evaluating the chances of the horses on the basis of their ratings: the question of jockeyship in general, and apprentice allowances in particular. The allowance which may be claimed by an apprentice is given to enable apprentices to obtain race-riding experience against experienced jockeys. For the purposes of rating calculations it should, in general, be assumed that the allowance the apprentice is able to claim (3 lb, 5 lb, or 7 lb) is nullified by the boy's inexperience. Therefore, the *weight adjustments to the ratings should be calculated on the weight allotted by the handicapper, or determined by the conditions of the race*, and no extra addition should be made to a rating because the horse's rider claims an apprentice allowance.

The above is the general routine procedure. But of course there is no reason why the quality of jockeyship should not be taken into account in assessing the chances of horses in a race. Quite the contrary. Nobody would question that the jockeyship of a first-class rider is worth a pound or two, and occasionally an apprentice comes along who is riding quite as well as the average jockey long before he loses the right to claim. There is no reason whatever why, after the age and weight adjustments have been made to the ratings, small additional allowances should not be made for these matters of jockeyship. This, however, is a matter which must be left to the discretion of the reader.

WEIGHING UP A RACE

It having been discovered, by means of the ratings, which horses in a particular race are most favoured by the weights, complete analysis demands that the racing character of each horse, as set out in the commentary upon it, shall be checked to see if there is any reason why the horse might be expected not to run up to his rating. It counts for little that a horse is thrown in at the weights if he has no pretensions whatever to staying the distance, or is unable to act on the prevailing going.

These two matters, suitability of distance and going, are, no doubt, the most important points to be considered. But there are others. For example, the ability of a horse to accommodate himself to the conformation of the track. Then there is the matter of pace versus stamina: as between two stayers of equal merit, racing over a distance suitable to both, firm going, or a small field with the prospect of a slowly-run race, would favour the one with the better pace and acceleration, whereas dead or soft going, or a big field with the prospect of a strong gallop throughout the race, would favour the sounder stayer. There is also the matter of temperament and behaviour at the start: nobody would be in a hurry to take a short price about a horse with whom it is always an even chance whether he will consent to race or not.

A few minutes spent checking up on these matters in the commentaries upon the horses concerned will sometimes put a very different complexion on a race from that which is put upon it by the ratings alone. We repeat, therefore, that the correct way to use Timeform, or this annual volume, in the analysis of individual races is, first to use the ratings to discover which horses are most favoured by the weights, and second, to check through the comments on the horse to discover what factors other than weight might also affect the outcome of the race.

Incidentally, in setting out the various characteristics, requirements and peculiarities of each horse in the commentary upon him, we have always expressed ourselves in as critical a manner as possible, endeavouring to say just as much, and no whit more than the facts seem to warrant. Where there are clear indications, and definite conclusions can be drawn with fair certainty, we have drawn them: if it is a matter of probability or possibility we have put it that way, being careful not to say the one when we mean the other; and where real conclusions are not to be drawn, we have been content to state the facts. Furthermore, when we say that a horse *may not* be suited by hard going, we do not expect the reader to treat it as though we had said that the horse is *not* suited by hard going. In short, both in our thinking and in the setting out of our views we have aimed at precision.

THE FORM SUMMARIES

The form summary enclosed in the round brackets shows for each individual horse the distance, the state of the going and where the horse finished in each of its races on the flat during the previous two seasons. Performances are in chronological sequence, the earliest being given first.

The distance of each race is given in furlongs, fractional distances being expressed in the decimal notation to the nearest tenth of a furlong.

The going is symbolised as follows: h=hard or very firm; f=firm; fg=fairly good, or on the firm side of good; g=good; d=dead, or on the soft side of good; s=soft, sticky or holding; v=heavy, very heavy or very holding.

Placings are indicated, up to fourth place, by the use of superior figures, an asterisk being used to denote a win.

Thus, 1982 $10s^*$ $12f^3$ 11.7g signifies that the horse ran three times in 1982, winning over ten furlongs on soft going first time out, finishing third over twelve furlongs on firm going next time out, and then unplaced, not in the first four, over 11.7 furlongs on good going. NR means that the horse did not race.

Included in the pedigree details are the highest Timeform Annual ratings during their racing careers of the sires, dams and sires of dams of all horses, where the information is available.

Where sale prices are given F denotes the price in guineas sold as a foal, Y the price in guineas sold as a yearling. The prefix IR denotes Irish guineas.

THE RATING SYMBOLS

The following symbols, attached to the ratings, are to be interpreted as stated;—

p   the horse is likely to make more than normal progress and to improve on his rating.

P   there is convincing evidence, or, to say the least, a very strong presumption that the horse is capable of form much better than he has so far displayed.

+   the horse may be rather better than we have rated him.

d   the horse appears to have deteriorated, and might no longer be capable of running to the rating given.

§   a horse who is somewhat ungenerous, faint-hearted or a bit of a coward; one who may give his running on occasions, but cannot be relied upon to do so.

§§   an arrant rogue or a thorough jade; so temperamentally unsatisfactory as to be not worth a rating.

?   if used in conjunction with a rating this symbol implies that the rating is based upon inadequate or unsatisfactory data, upon form which it is impossible to assess with confidence. The use of a query without a rating implies that although the horse has form, his merit cannot be assessed on the data at present available.

Proposed
SALES DATES FOR
1983

February Mixed Sale
Monday 7th February

August Sale and
National Hunt Show Championship
Sunday 14th August (show)
Monday 15th August (sale)

Autumn Horses in Training and Yearling Sale
Monday 19th September

Invitation and Premier Yearling Sale
Tuesday 4th-Friday 7th October

November Sale Part 1
Monday 7th-Wednesday 9th November

November Sale Part 2
Sunday 20th-Wednesday 23rd November

All enquiries welcome
**Goffs Bloodstock Sales, Kildare Paddocks, Kill, Co. Kildare,
Ireland. Tel: Kildare (045) 9211. Telex: 24227**

RACEHORSES OF 1982

AABORUN 3 gr.c. Run The Gantlet–Aabora (Don II 123) (1981 8d 1982 **86**
11.7f 12fg 13.3f⁴ 12d² 13.1g² 12f* 13.8f* 12fg) rather sparely-made colt; decisively landed the odds in maiden race at Redcar and minor event at Catterick
in summer; suited by 1¾m; seems to act on any going; best in blinkers; sometimes sweats up. *J. Dunlop.*

ABALIGHT 4 gr.g. Abwah 118–Moonlight 101 (Djebe) (1981 7d 8d³ 7f 7f⁴ 7g   —
7f³ 8fg 8.2s⁴ 1982 8f 11.5fg) small gelding; plater; stays 1m; often blinkered
(not in 1982); has worn bandages. *J. Harris.*

ABDOUN 3 b.c. Luthier 126–Afrique (Exbury 138) (1981 NR 1982 12f* **99**
14fg⁴ 14g* 13.3f* 14fg 13.3g⁴ 14g) small, sparely-made colt; good walker and
very good mover; fourth foal; dam, half-sister to Val de Loir and Valoris, won
over 1¼m in France; won maiden race at Doncaster and handicaps at Yarmouth
and Newbury; beat Brevet by 3 lengths in Morland Brewery Trophy on last-
named in July; kept on very gamely to be 2¼ lengths fourth to Fitzpatrick in
Coral Autumn Cup at Newbury in September; will stay 2m; yet to race on a soft
surface; ran moderately fifth start. *M. Stoute.*

ABERFIELD 5 ch.g. Northfields–Abergara (Abernant 142) (1981 15.8s 13d* **91**
12.5g 12g² 12g* 12.3fg³ 12f⁴ 12fg 10f³ 12f² 1982 12fg² 10fg* 10f 11.1g* 12f
10.2g² 10.5f³ 10g* 12f* 13.3g⁴ 10g² 9d 10v 8s³ 12s) leggy, narrow gelding;
middle-distance handicapper; had a very good season and was successful at
Newmarket in April (apprentice ridden), Kempton in May, Ripon in July and
Brighton in August, winning impressively on 3 occasions; possibly unlucky when
½-length second to Charlie's Prospect at Epsom later in August; probably acts
on any going; blinkered once in 1980; suitable mount for an inexperienced
rider; given quite a lot to do fifth outing and was out of his depth tenth start.
P. Kelleway.

ABEROYALE 4 b.f. Nos Royalistes 119–Phyl's Pet (Aberdeen 109) (1981   —
12g 10.1fg 1982 16fg) no sign of ability in maiden and minor races. *D.
Grissell.*

ABERRATION 2 b.c. Abwah 118–Pilamenon 90 (Parthia 132) (1982 7s) May   —
18; 920F, 4,500Y; half-brother to several winners, including useful 1977 2-y-o
of winner My Habibi (by Habitat), dam won over 1m and 1¼m unquoted;
finished eighth of 12 behind Rana Pratap in minor event at Chepstow in October.
M. McCormack.

ABKASSA 2 b.f. Radetzky 123–Authors Correction 68 (Narrator 127) (1982   —
6g 7fg 7d 7g) Apr 11; 6,000Y; rangy, useful sort; half-sister to middle-distance
winner Grade Well (by Derring-Do); dam won 17f amateur riders event; poor
form, including in a seller; sold 520 gns Newmarket Autumn Sales. *C. Brittain.*

ABLE ALBERT 2 gr.c. Abwah 118–Polly Peachum 123 (Singing Strand) **101**
(1982 5s* 5f* 5g* 5f*) Jan 31; rangy, good sort; third foal; dam very genuine
and smart sprinter; justified favouritism in the spring in small races at Haydock
(beat Time's Time 4 lengths), Beverley (by 6 lengths from Eastform), Chester
(had to be hard driven to get the better of Dorset Eagle by a length) and Beverley
again (8/1 on, came home 3 lengths clear of Hardwick Eagle); was next to have
run at Royal Ascot, but reportedly met with a set-back, and was not seen out
again; will be suited by 6f; acts on any going; seemed unsuited by track at
Chester. *M. H. Easterby.*

ABLE SAILOR 2 gr.c. Abwah 118–Shipwrecked 72 (Javelot 124) (1982   —
6d 7fg 6f) Apr 15; small, close-coupled colt; second foal; dam won over 2¼m
and was fair hurdler; behind in maiden company; not seen out after July.
W. Wharton.

ABORIGINE (FR) 2 b.f. Riverman 131–Prima 75 (Alcide 136) (1982 9s*)   **?**
Mar 19; half-sister to several winners, including useful 1¼m winner Laska Floko
(by Thatch) and good Italian performers King Jav (by King Emperor) and
My Royal Prima (by Captain's Gig); dam half-sister to very useful stayer
Saraceno; put up an impressive first effort when beating Lyre d'Or by 3 lengths
in 7-runner newcomers event at Longchamp in October; will stay 1½m; bound
to make a very useful filly. *E. Bartholomew, France.*

ABSENTIA (USA) 3 b.f. Raise A Cup–Cecelia (Royal Levee) (1981 NR **108** 1982 7.5s² 8v* 8s² 8fg³ 8s³ 8s 10f) most attractive filly; fourth foal; half-sister to fairly useful Irish 1978 2-y-o 7f winner Wayfarer (by Apalachee), subsequently successful in USA, and to another winner in USA; dam unraced daughter of half-sister to top-class American horses Chieftain and Tom Rolfe; won maiden race at Longchamp in May in fine style; placed afterwards in 100,000 francs race at Chantilly and Prix d'Astarte (½-length third to Thorough) and Prix Quincey (2¼ lengths third to King James) at Deauville; should be suited by 1¼m; seems to act on any going; sent to USA. *O. Douieb, France.*

ABSTAINER 3 b.g. Abwah 118–Nae Bird 78 (Birdbrook 110) (1981 5d 6d **61** 5g 7fg 1982 5d 8f*) robust gelding; well-backed favourite and dropped in class when winning seller at Bath in April; sold to T. Hallett 1,600 gns afterwards; suited by 1m; acts on firm going. *R. Smyth.*

ABU TORKEY 5 gr.g. Majority Blue 126–Nantgarw (Abernant 142) (1981 — 8v² 12g³ 8g² 8d 8g² 8f 8s 8.2f⁴ 8g 7g 9f* 8f³ 11d⁴ 10.5s 1982 10.2g) big, strong, good-topped gelding; in rear only outing of 1982 (March); acts on any going; suitable mount for an apprentice; blinkered once. *J. Blundell.*

ABWACADABWA 4 br.f. Abwah 118–Jetwitch 56 (Lear Jet 123) (1981 — 8g 7fg 9fg* 8fg⁴ 12d 1982 10f) neat filly; plater; stayed 9f; acted on any going; changed hands 2,300 gns Doncaster June Sales; dead. *J. Blundell.*

ABWAH GIRL 2 b.f. Abwah 118–Romany Girl 103 (Worden II 129) (1982 — 7g 7g.8g 8v) May 2; 1,300F; rangy, workmanlike filly; half-sister to 7f winner Remainder Imp (by Jimmy Reppin) and a winner in Brazil; dam won at up to 13f in Ireland; won fair company at Newbury, Brighton and New-market, and in Criterium Femminile at Rome. *D. Sasse.*

ACADIE (FR) 2 ch.f. Caracolero 131–Djallybrook (Djakao 124) (1982 6f **80** 7fg* 8fg 7g³) Apr 8; $10,500Y; sparely-made filly; first foal; dam won over 11f in French Provinces; won minor event at Doncaster in July by 4 lengths from Dromodan; 2 lengths third of 15 to Killanin's Lass in mixed-aged race at Newmarket three months later, best other effort; out of her depth in Silken Glider Stakes at Leopardstown on third outing; should stay 1½m; acts on a firm surface; is reportedly to race in Florida. *M. Ryan.*

ACANTHA 2 b.f. Prince Tenderfoot 126–Catherine's Sister 96 (Petition 130) **77** (1982 5d³ 5fg* 5f) May 12; IR 27,000Y; well-made filly; good walker; sister to 1978 Irish 2-y-o 5f performer King's Scout, and half-sister to 2 winners; dam 1m winner; won 8-runner maiden race at Newbury in April by 4 lengths from Rumpleteazer, easily best effort; not seen out after May. *P. Cole.*

ACAPULCO GOLD 6 ch.h. Gulf Pearl 117–Capsville (Cyane) (1981 10f³ **57** 10fg² 10fg² 10fg⁴ 10f⁴ 10g 1982 10fg 10f³) strong, well-made horse; stays 1½m; seems to act on any going; blinkered twice at 4 yrs; sold 3,000 gns Ascot October Sales. *A. Pitt.*

ACCLIMATISE 2 b.f. Shirley Heights 130–Habituee (Habitat 134) (1982 7d* **116** 7g² 8g⁴ 8g*)
As a top-class, courageous and attractive son of the brilliant Mill Reef, Shirley Heights had a lot to recommend him when he retired to stud. Not even

Hoover Fillies Mile, Ascot—Acclimatise stays on well to win from Dancing Meg and Alligatrix

his most ardent admirers though would have claimed that precocity and speed, two of today's most sought-after qualities, were among his major attributes: when tried over six furlongs as a two-year-old he finished fifth of six in a minor event at York and went down by five lengths in ordinary maiden company at Doncaster. Consequently it was a pleasant surprise when Shirley Heights's first ever runner, Shirley Reef, won the Premio Norma at Naples on July 1st and when his second, Acclimatise, took the Wayfoong Stakes at Sandown the following day.

Acclimatise's debut was most impressive. After dwelling and still being almost last of the fourteen runners entering the straight, she swept into the lead entering the final furlong and drew away to win very comfortably by four lengths from Ominous. The style of Acclimatise's victory left little doubt that she would develop into one of the leading staying two-year-old fillies, but her rise to the top wasn't so smooth as had seemed likely and two defeats followed. The first, at the hands of Flamenco when giving her 8 lb in the Sweet Solera Stakes at Newmarket in August, was an honourable one. The race was spoilt to a great extent when Bright Crocus swerved badly at the start, causing a fair amount of scrimmaging. Acclimatise wasn't actually hampered but her hind legs seemed to go from under her and she was quickly in last place, where she stayed for over half a mile. Only on meeting the rising ground in the final furlong did she begin to cut into Flamenco's decisive advantage and by then it was too late: Acclimatise, despite making ground hand over fist, was still three quarters of a length behind at the line. Acclimatise emerged with much less credit from her next race, the May Hill Stakes at Doncaster's St Leger meeting for which she started favourite. In her trainer's words 'she just decided to tail herself off in the first half-mile' and then, to make matters worse, she found difficulty obtaining a run. By the time Acclimatise had been switched to the outside with a quarter of a mile to run she was fully ten lengths behind Bright Crocus who was making the best of her way home. Acclimatise never had any prospect of cutting back such a lead and in the end was beaten just under six lengths into fourth place. We thought she would have finished second with a clearer run.

Acclimatise renewed rivalry with Bright Crocus in the Hoover Fillies Mile at Ascot a fortnight later and, with Bright Crocus breaking blood vessels, the outcome was very different. For the first time in her career Acclimatise was able to hold a good position from the start, turning into the straight in third place behind Dancing Meg, the winner of a nursery in remarkable fashion at York on her last start, and Alligatrix, an Alleged filly who had won a twenty-nine-runner maiden race at Newmarket last time out. It took Acclimatise a long time to assert her superiority over these two but she always looked the likely winner and forged steadily clear in the final furlong to beat Dancing Meg by a length and a half. Alligatrix held on to third place a further three lengths behind. In our opinion this was the second-best performance of the season by a staying two-year-old filly in Britain and Ireland.

Acclimatise's main objective is said to be the Oaks but she will also be aimed at the One Thousand Guineas. The way she has run so far suggests she is much more likely to be an Oaks filly than a Guineas filly, but we must point out that we thought the same about a previous winner of the Hoover Fillies Mile, Quick As Lightning, and she went on to win the Guineas before disappointing badly in the Oaks! Quick As Lightning is the only one of the seven earlier winners of the Hoover Fillies Mile (known as the Argos Star Fillies Mile before 1978) to win a classic; five of the seven, Icing ,Miss Pinkie, Cherry Hinton, Formulate and Height of Fashion, never even made it to the start of the Oaks. Hopefully Acclimatise will fare much better. We feel sure she will.

Acclimatise (b.f May 30, 1980)	Shirley Heights (b 1975)	Mill Reef (b 1968)	Never Bend
			Milan Mill
		Hardiemma (b 1969)	Hardicanute
			Grand Cross
	Habituee (b 1971)	Habitat (b 1966)	Sir Gaylord
			Little Hut
		Participator (ch 1960)	Petition
			Participation

Acclimatise, a well-made, very attractive filly, has the looks of a high-class filly and she has a fine pedigree too. She is the third good winner from Habituee's first five foals, following the Bustino filly Ma Femme and the Wollow colt Bruckner. Ma Femme, who was also trained by Hobbs, stayed well, winning the 1981 Galtres Stakes in addition to finishing a close third in the Park Hill

Mr Jocelyn Hambro's "Acclimatise"

Stakes, but the three-year-old Bruckner seems better at much shorter distances; he gained his most important victory in the six-furlong Seven Springs Sprint Stakes soon after finishing a remote seventh in the Irish Sweeps Derby. Habituee raced in France. After showing very useful form at two, when she was second in the Prix d'Aumale, she won a maiden race over a mile at Saint-Cloud as a three-year-old. Habituee's dam Participator also started her racing career in France but she didn't win until she was sent to be trained at Malton as a four-year-old, when she took a mile race at Lanark and mile-and-a-half events at Pontefract and Leicester. Participator was one of eight British winners bred by Participation and among her half-brothers and half-sisters were two smart stayers, Alexis and Partner, and the very useful filly Neutron who bred Court Harwell, the champion sire of 1965. Participation was in turn out of Pretty Polly's granddaughter Arabella, the second-best two-year-old filly of 1928. *B. Hobbs.*

ACCUSED (USA) 2 br.c. Alleged 138–Pas de Nom (Admiral's Voyage) (1982 **93** 7fg² 7fg³ 8g³) Mar 20; $125,000Y; quite well-made, attractive colt; good mover; fourth foal; half-brother to fairly useful 1981 2-y-o 5f winner Ibtihaj (by Raja Baba) and very promising but hard-to-train American winner Danzig (by Northern Dancer); dam very useful sprinter; quite useful maiden, placed at Sandown, Newmarket (length third of 29 to Alligatrix) and Newbury (2½ lengths third of 21 behind Polished Silver); will be suited by 1¼m; should have little difficulty in winning maiden event. *I. Balding.*

ACHERON 2 ch.c. Bay Express 132–River Aire 82 (Klairon 131) (1982 5d* **51** 5fg 6f⁴ 7fg⁴ 8.2d 8s 6s) Mar 19; 270Y; small, well-made colt; first foal; dam placed over 7f and 1m; went down by 20 lengths to 'Flockton Grey' in 9-runner auction event at Leicester in March but was awarded race 4 months later; un-placed afterwards including in sellers; stays 7f; acts on a firm and a soft surface. *C. Wildman.*

ACHIEVED 3 ch.c. Thatch 136–Last Call 74 (Klairon 131) (1981 5fg* 5fg* **125** 7fg* 1982 7s² 7s* 8fg 8g 8f³ 8s³)

Dara Monarch excepted, no Irish horse had better form over a mile than Achieved who ran creditably in several of the top races without being quite good enough to win any of them. Unbeaten in three outings in 1981, including the Gallaghouse Phoenix Stakes and the Laurent Perrier Champagne Stakes, and rated the best Irish two-year-old in the Tote European Free Handicap, Achieved didn't start his second season with much of a flourish. Odds on for the Gladness Stakes and the Tetrarch Stakes, both run at the Curragh in April, he went down by a short head to Kilian in a muddling race for the former and accounted for Exhilarate in workmanlike fashion by a length in the latter. In passing, it is worth remarking on the fact that quite a few of the races in Britain and Ireland named after good horses fail adequately to reflect the particular talents of the performers concerned. Gladness, an outstanding stayer, was at her best at four and five, while The Tetrarch, a brilliant two-year-old, never raced beyond six furlongs and didn't see a racecourse at three. Excellent as it is to recall the giants of the past, it seems slightly odd to have seven-furlong classic trials bearing the names of Gladness and The Tetrarch, just as it is to have a five-furlong two-year-old event at Warwick called after the Oaks and Gold Cup winner Quashed.

To return to Achieved, his form improved after the Tetrarch Stakes even though he didn't again finish in the first two. In the Two Thousand Guineas, for which he started second favourite in an open market, and the Airlie/Coolmore Irish Two Thousand Guineas at the Curragh he ran the same sort of race, being soon under pressure but keeping on steadily under strong riding to be sixth respectively to Zino and Dara Monarch. Probably to make him concentrate more in the early stages, since he lacked nothing in resolution in a finish, Achieved was equipped with blinkers for his last two appearances. In the Sussex Stakes at Goodwood in July he managed to reverse form with Tender King, third at Newmarket and second at the Curragh, and with the Irish Guineas third Red

Mr R. E. Sangster's "Achieved"

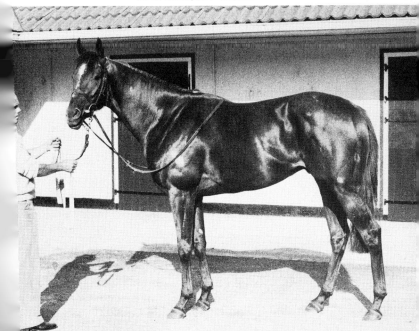

Sunset, but found On The House and Sandhurst Prince too good for him, producing no extra in the closing stages after holding third place virtually from the start and being beaten just over a length. The opportunity of running Achieved in the Pacemaker International Whitehall Stakes, won by his stable-companion Punctilio, or the Desmond Stakes, won by Anfield, in either of which races he would have gone well, was passed over in the interests of a tilt at Dara Monarch, Mr Fluorocarbon and Sandhurst Prince in the Queen Elizabeth II Stakes at Ascot in September. Achieved beat all three but was still six lengths behind the shock winner Buzzards Bay in third place at the post, having kept on without showing the necessary pace to trouble the principals. Not for the first time, he gave the impression he might have stayed beyond a mile if he had been given the chance.

Achieved (ch.c. 1979)	Thatch (b 1970)	Forli (ch 1963)	Aristophanes
			Trevisa
		Thong (b 1964)	Nantallah
			Rough Shod
	Last Call (b 1964)	Klairon (b 1952)	Clarion III
			Kalmia
		Stage Fright (ch 1954)	Big Game
			Bashful

Last Call, who won a one-mile maiden race at Pontefract at three, has produced five winners besides Achieved and most have had well above average ability. To a previous mating with Thatch she foaled Final Straw, successful in the Laurent Perrier Champagne Stakes and Clerical, Medical Greenham Stakes and runner-up in the Sussex Stakes and Prix Jacques le Marois, while her foals by Tudor Melody and Busted, Final Chord and Curtains, were frequent visitors to the winner's enclosure, Final Chord scoring in the Britannia Stakes at Royal Ascot. This is the family of such good performers as Hardiesse (a half-sister to Last Call), Gwen and Pelerin, so it is scarcely surprising that Achieved fetched 162,000 guineas as a yearling.

Achieved, a neat sort, lacked a little of his brother's strength and additionally didn't often impress in the paddock. This didn't stop his running consistently on all types of going, though. Along with his stable-companions Pilgrim and Belted Earl he has been syndicated to stand at the Winfield Farm in Kentucky; his fee is 12,500 dollars. *V. O'Brien, Ireland.*

ACK ACK REGIMENT (USA) 2 b.c. Ack Ack–En Tiempo (Bold Hour) — p (1982 8g) May 7; $110,000Y; second foal; dam, winner twice at up to 1m, is half-sister to smart animals Muse and Never Confuse; unquoted, showed up well for long way in 21-runner £4,200 event won by Polished Silver at Newbury in September; should improve. *P. Cole.*

ACKSTATIC (USA) 3 br.c. Ack Ack–Space Happy (Never Say Die 137) (1981 **92** d 7d* 7d 1982 10f 10fg⁴ 10f² 10g 10f) well-made, attractive colt; fairly useful handicapper; will be suited by 1½m; seems to act on any going; below form last 2 starts. *M. Stoute.*

ACLE 7 br.g. Yukon Eric–Abask (Henry the Seventh 125 or Abernant 142) — (1981 NR 1982 12f 12f) of little account. *W. Stubbs.*

ACORA'S PREDICTION 2 gr. or ro.f. Scallywag 127–Royal Ribston (Ribston — 104) (1982 7fg 7g) first known foal; dam never ran; in rear in September in £3,600 event at Chepstow and £4,500 event (last of 23) at Newbury. *W. R. Williams.*

ACQUISITIVE 2 b.c. Star Appeal 133–Requisition 101 (Petition 130) (1982 — 5g 6f 6fg 8d 10s) May 27; small colt; a twin; bad plater. *C. Austin.*

ACTION 3 br.c. Tower Walk 130–Delayed Action 113 (Jolly Jet 111) (1981 — 6f 6f 7f 1982 6fg 8d 10f) workmanlike colt; plater; best run at 7f on firm going in blinkers. *S. Norton.*

ACTION BELLE 2 b.f. Auction Ring 123–Tavella 98 (Petingo 135) (1982 — 6g 8f) Feb 25; 4,000Y; quite well-made filly; half-sister to 2 winners, including Italian 3-y-o Swing Faster (by Swing Easy), a fairly useful winner at 2 yrs; dam at her best at 2 yrs when 6f winner; in rear in September in £3,500 event at York and in 20-runner maiden auction race at Redcar. *C. Booth.*

ACT PROMPTLY 5 ch.m. Midsummer Night II 117–Impromptu 88 (My — Swanee 122) (1981 NR 1982 12s 16g) won seller at Leicester in 1980; well beaten both outings since; stays 1¼m; acts on a soft surface. *B. Richmond.*

ACUSHLA MACREE 5 ch.m. Mansingh 120–Cannie Cassie 70 (Canisbay 120) **54**
(1981 10f 10.8fg³ 8.2g⁴ 10f 8.3g* 8g 8d* 8s 10.2g 1982 10.2g 8d 10f 10.1fg 10fg
10.6f 10fg³ 8g³ 10d 8fg 10f 10f² 10g² 8fg* 8fg⁴ 10.6s) neat mare; won apprentice
handicap at Chepstow in August; unplaced in sellers on occasions earlier; stays
1⅛m well; acts on any going, except possibly very soft; wears blinkers or a hood;
good mount for an inexperienced rider; sometimes bandaged behind. *F. J.
Houghton.*

ADAM CRAIG 4 b.g. Connaught 130–Karenina 95 (Silver Shark 129) (1981 **56**
12f 10.2fg 10d² 11d³ 12.2g 12s² 1982 12f* 12f⁴ 13g 20fg 20g) lengthy gelding;
won handicap at Redcar in May and ran quite well next time; stays at least 1⅛m
(had stiff task and wasn't disgraced first outing over 2½m); acts on any going;
has sweated up. *M. Naughton.*

ADDERYBURY LAD 3 ch.g. Tachypous 128–Pretty Mall 86 (Pall Mall 132) **—**
(1981 5s 5g 7fg 7f 7d 1982 6s 6s 5fg 10f) strong gelding; little sign of ability;
has been tried in blinkers. *J. Townson.*

ADDISON'S JUBILEE 3 b.f. Sparkler 130–Red Sunset II 105 (High Hat 131) **73**
(1981 6fg 6g 1982 8fg 7.6fg⁴ 8g* 11g² 10g 10g* 10.6f³ 10g 11s) compact, rather
lightly-made filly; won maiden race at Yarmouth in June and handicap at Newcastle in August; stays 11f; acts on firm going. *G. Pritchard-Gordon.*

ADEEBAH (USA) 2 br.f. Damascus–Transylvania (Bold Ruler) (1982 6fg³ **94**
5fg* 5g³ 6g³ 6g 5s² 5g) Mar 1; $150,000Y; close-coupled filly; half-sister to 2
winners, including very useful 1977 Irish 2-y-o 6f winner Santon (by Round
Table); dam, winner over 6f, is sister to high-class stakes winner Jacinto; had to
be driven along when landing odds in poor maiden event at Ayr in August;
running consistently, showed much better form in her other races, on penultimate
appearance finishing good second in nursery at Haydock; appears to need testing
conditions to be seen to advantage at 5f, and stays 6f well; seems to act on any
going. *H. T. Jones.*

ADIRONDACK 7 br.g. Wolver Hollow 126–Palgal (Le Prince 98) (1981 NR **—**
1982 10f³ 11g 12g 14s 18s) lengthy ex-Irish gelding; not the best of movers; fair
maiden when trained by I. Balding as a 2-y-o; won on flat and over hurdles in
Ireland subsequently; third in apprentice handicap at Navan in May, first
outing on flat for a long time; soundly beaten over here afterwards (gambled on
first time); stays 1¾m; seems well suited by firm going; has worn blinkers,
including when successful; formerly trained by T. Gallagher. *A. Bailey.*

ADITI 2 b.f. Kala Shikari 125–Eternity (Never Say Die 137) (1982 6f⁴ 6fg* 6g* **92**
0.) Mar 2½; IR 5,900Y; lengthy, good sort; half-sister to 3 winners, including Al
Burak (by Silver Shark), a useful winner at up to 1¼m; dam never ran; made
most of running when successful in 17-runner maiden race at Folkestone in
August and small race at Hamilton (beating Hot On The Trail 2½ lengths) in
September; racing in Italy. *H. Cecil.*

ADJUSTED 3 ch.g. Busted 134–Angel Row 96 (Prince Regent 129) (1981 **—**
6fg 8d 8.2d 8s 8s 10.2g 1982 7d 8.2v 6f⁴ 5g 6fg³ 6g⁴ 5g 6s) big, strong, plain
gelding; in frame in varied company, including selling; best form at 6f on a sound
surface though is bred to stay further. *R. Hobson.*

ADMIRAL'S CUP 4 b.g. Deep Run 119–Mirror Back (Master Owen) (1981 **—**
NR 1982 12fg) IR 2,600Y, IR 12,400 3-y-o; second foal; half-brother to a
winner over hurdles who also won a bumpers race; dam won over hurdles; 20/1
when ninth of 21 finishers behind Pontin Boy in gentleman riders race at Kempton
in September; winner over hurdles. *F. Winter.*

ADMIRAL'S HEIR (USA) 4 b.c. Crafty Khale–Triggs'z (Successor) (1981 **—**
12.3g 10.1s² 10.6s³ 12f² 12f⁴ 1982 12fg 10f 12s⁴) quite attractive, compact colt;
good walker and mover; didn't win as a 3-y-o but showed useful form nevertheless; subsequently operated on for a wind infirmity; last in John Porter Stakes at
Newbury and handicap at Lingfield in spring and in minor event at Lingfield again
in September; stays 1½m; acts on any going; one to be wary of until showing signs
of recovering his form. *P. Cole.*

ADMIRAL'S PRINCESS (USA) 3 b.f. Groton–Triggs'z (Successor) (1981 **105**
5s³ 5d* 5fg² 5f* 6fg³ 6g³ 7g⁴ 1982 6fg* 6f 6fg⁴ 7g) small, lengthy, good-quartered
filly; came with a strong run to lead on line when beating Celestial Dancer a short
head in valuable handicap at Newmarket in May; respectable 2¼ lengths fourth of
8 to Sylvan Barbarosa in valuable Leisure Stakes at Lingfield in June; has run
creditably over 7f but seems better at shorter distances; probably acts on any

49

going but has shown best form on a sound surface; has run well when sweating up; game. *P. Cole.*

ADMIRAL STEVE 2 ch.c. Home Guard 129–Sardinia (Romulus 129) (1982 **78** 5d 5fg 6s 5g³ 5s⁴ 6s) Apr 25; 5,400Y; rather leggy, quite attractive colt; half-brother to 2 minor winners; dam won over 5f and 1m in Ireland; 3¼ lengths fourth of 15 to Dry Land in maiden event at Sandown in October, best effort; probably stays 6f; acts on soft going. *R. Hannon.*

ADMIRING GLANCE 3 ro.f. Northern Flash–Che Bella (Beau Sabreur 125) — (1981 7f 7f 1982 8g 8fg 8g 10.6s 10s) heavy-topped filly; poor walker; well beaten in maiden and minor races; blinkered final start; sold to A. Bailey 2,000 gns Newmarket Autumn Sales. *H. T. Jones.*

ADONIJAH 2 ch.c. High Line 125–Shadow Queen (Darius 129) (1982 6d³ 6g³) **91** May 12; small, strong, sturdy colt; half-brother to 3 winners, including high-class sprinter Absalom (by Abwah); dam of little account; placed in big fields of maidens at Newmarket in October, favourite on first outing and second favourite on second; stoutly bred (maternal grandam won over 13f) and is certain to win races at 1m or more; acts on a soft surface; sold 38,000 gns Newmarket December Sales. *B. Hobbs.*

ADRANA 2 ch.f. Bold Lad (Ire) 133–Le Melody 102 (Levmoss 133) (1982 5g*) **86 p** May 5; 75,000Y; lengthy, useful-looking, good-quartered filly; fourth foal; half-sister to top-class middle-distance stayer Ardross (by Run The Gantlet) and useful Irish 1m and 1¼m winner Karol (by Kalamoun); dam, half-sister to Irish 1000 Guineas winner Arctique Royale, won both her starts, over 7f and 1¼m; joint-favourite, didn't stride out at all well on way to start of 12-runner maiden race at Sandown in April but came back much better, running on under fairly hard driving to beat Reign a neck; chipped a bone in her knee in process and wasn't seen out again; the type to go on to better things. *C. Brittain.*

AEROLITE (USA) 3 gr.g. Al Hattab–Francie T (Grey Dawn II 132) (1981 — 7fg 1982 7f) rangy gelding; soundly beaten in maiden races; hurdling in France. *H. Cecil.*

Mr W. H. Ponsonby's "Admiral's Princess"

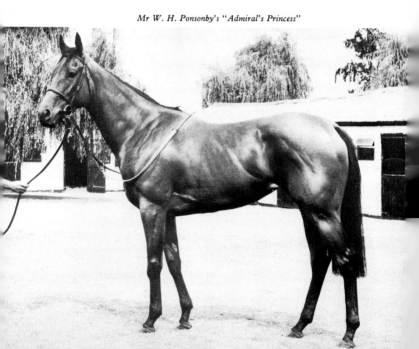

AFDAL 3 b.g. Realm 129–Golden Gorse (Crepello 136) (1981 7g 1982 6fg) —
strong gelding; showed a little ability in maiden race at Newmarket in 1981
but finished last in apprentice event at Nottingham in August after refusing to
race in early stages on only outing at 3 yrs. *W. O'Gorman.*

AFFIANCE 3 b.c. Sassafras 135–Sterna (Neckar) (1981 NR 1982 10s 10f* **97**
11.5fg*) 60,000Y; half-brother to numerous winners, notably Arc de Triomphe
winner Star Appeal (by Appiani II); dam placed 6 times in Germany as a 3-y-o;
landed odds in 14-runner maiden race at Navan in May and got home by a neck
from Gold Exchanged in 11-runner Ulster Harp Derby at Down Royal in July;
broke out of stalls and was withdrawn after galloping full circuit of course before
Jefferson Smurfit Memorial Irish St Leger at the Curragh in October; will stay
1¾m. *T. Curtin, Ireland.*

AFFILIATION ORDER (USA) 3 b.c. Intrepid Hero–Lovers Lane (Raise A **81** d
Native) (1981 6g³ 7fg 7fg⁴ 7fg³ 8g 1982 11f³ 12fg 10fg 12v 8s) rangy colt;
excellent mover; fair maiden at his best but has become disappointing; stays
11f; blinkered final start; sold 6,000 gns Newmarket Autumn Sales. *P. Cole.*

AFGHAN (USA) 3 b.c. The Minstrel 135–Quilly (Bagdad) (1981 5d 7f² 6fg* **107**
7d 7.5d 6g* 1982 6g 8g*) half-brother to Irish 5f winner Rooftree (by
Thatch); dam unraced half-sister to outstanding American filly Revidere;
short-priced favourite when beating Kaksi in workmanlike style by ½ length in
6-runner Sean Graham Extended Handicap at the Curragh in May; stays 1m;
blinkered fourth and fifth starts in 1981; racing in California. *V. O'Brien, Ireland.*

AFRICAN DREAM 2 b.f. African Sky 124–Jabula 99 (Sheshoon 132) (1982 **82**
5f³ 6g 5.8g 8.2d³) Apr 20; IR 35,000Y; rather lightly-made filly; half-sister to 3
winners, including fairly useful 1976 2-y-o 5f and 7f winner The Bowler (by Bold
Lad, Ire); dam winner at up to 1½m; 2 lengths third of 18 to Decorated in nursery
at Nottingham in September, easily best effort; evidently suited by 1m. *P. Cole.*

AFRICANOS 5 b.g. African Sky 124–Welshpool 75 (Henry the Seventh 125) **73** d
(1981 8.2d 7d³ 8g³ 7.2s⁴ 8g 7g² 7g⁴ 8g* 8fg* 7g* 8g 8g² 8g² 8fg⁴ 8d³ 10fg 1982
9fg³ 7fg⁴ 9fg 8fg 8f 8fg³ 7g 8d 8f 8d) strong gelding; didn't recover his best
form but was in frame in 3 handicaps; best at up to 1m; probably acts on any
going; occasionally blinkered (wore them final start); sometimes sweats up;
sometimes wears a tongue strap; usually apprentice ridden; does best when held
up. *H. Bell.*

AFRICAN PEARL 4 b.c. African Sky 124–Stickpin 74 (Gulf Pearl 117) (1981 **84**
7g 7d³ 8g 8g 8 3fg 1982 10g* 10fg* 8f² 9fg³ 9g² 10f²* 10f²*) quite attractive
ex-English colt; won handicaps at Folkestone and Epsom in April, beating
Golden Brigadier by ½ length in City and Surburban on latter course; subsequently ran well in similar events in Ireland and won at the Curragh in August and at
Leopardstown in September; suited by 1¼m; yet to race on very soft going, but
acts on any other; sometimes sweats up; bandaged near-hind second start;
trained until after third start by R. Simpson. *J. Oxx, Ireland.*

AFRICAN TUDOR 2 b.c. African Sky 124–Spare Filly 95 (Beau Sabreur 125) **100**
(1982 5d 6f³ 5g* 5fg* 5g² 5.3g² 6d³) Mar 7; IR 81,000Y; tall, good sort; half-
brother to numerous winners, including fairly useful 1m to 1¼m performer
Manfilia (by Mandamus), herself dam of African Hope and Kilijaro (both by
African Sky); dam soft-ground stayer; successful in minor events at Wolverhampton and Warwick in August; good second to Wiki Wiki Wheels in valuable
nursery at Newbury in September, fifth outing and best effort in 5 other appearances; best form at 5f. *M. Stoute.*

AFSARJAAN 2 gr.c. Nishapour 125–Afariya (Silver Shark 129) (1982 6fg* **110**
7g²) May 3; rather lightly-made, racy colt; second foal; half-brother to French
3-y-o 1m winner Afiyaana (by Brigadier Gerard); dam, daughter of very smart
1967 French 2-y-o Lady Millie, won small races over 7f and 1m in France; won
6-runner newcomers race at Evry in July impressively by 6 lengths from Fresh
Bidder; came out best horse at weights when head second to Etoile de Paques in
5-runner Criterium de Bernay at Deauville the following month (led to closing
stages); should stay 1m. *F. Mathet, France.*

AFTER EDEN (USA) 3 ch.c. Forceten–Impressive Native (Impressive) —
(1981 NR 1982 10fg 11f 14.7f) $58,000Y; big, rangy colt; second foal; half-
brother to a winner in USA by Lt Stevens; dam won 6f claiming race at 2yrs;

sire, son of Forli, was high-class winner at up to 1¼m; soundly beaten in maiden races; sold 775 gns Ascot December Sales. *P. Walwyn.*

AGRELOUI 3 ch.f. Tower Walk 130–Greenhill Lass (Upper Case) (1981 6g **59** 6g 1982 7fg 5fg 5f²) small, lightly-made filly; tended to hang left when 2 lengths second of 12 to Famous Star in maiden race at Nottingham in July; evidently best at 5f on firm ground; went very freely to post at Nottingham and is possibly not easiest of rides. *R. Armstrong.*

AHONAJLA 3 gr. or ro.c. Godswalk 130–Denaneer 78 (Green God 128) (1981 — 5s 5g 1982 6fg 8d) quite attractive, rather leggy colt; good mover; soundly beaten in varied company; sold to Norsk Jockey Club 600 gns Doncaster November Sales. *R. Price.*

AIRBORNE DEAL 3 ch.c. Sandford Lad 133–Acropolita Mia 75 (Acropolis 132) — (1981 7fg 1982 9s³ 11g 8fg 8g 9g 7fg) lightly-built colt; plater; not certain to stay 11f; has worn blinkers; sold 1,350 gns Newmarket Autumn Sales. *N. Callaghan.*

AIR CADET 2 br.c. Air Trooper 115–Modom 81 (Compensation 127) (1982 5s — 5g) Feb 11; quite a useful-looking colt; first living foal; dam middle-distance winner; in rear in maiden races at Chepstow and Newbury (last of 13) in April. *W. Wightman.*

AIR COMMAND 2 ch.c. Air Trooper 115–Snotch (Current Coin 118) (1982 **83** 5f 5fg 5f 5g² 6g⁴ 5d³ 5g² 5s 5g*) workmanlike colt; poor mover; third foal; dam unraced half-sister to 1,000 Guineas and Oaks second Spree and to top-class broodmare Set Free; won 13-runner nursery at Edinburgh in October; stays 6f but is evidently considered better suited by 5f; possibly needs some give in the ground. *D. Smith.*

AIR COUPON 3 ch.f. Air Trooper 115–Gift Coupon 64 (Gift Card 125) (1981 — 8fg 7.6s 1982 8g) behind in maiden races; sold 420 gns Doncaster October Sales. *W. Wightman.*

AIR DISTINGUE (USA) 2 b.f. Sir Ivor 135–Euryanthe (Nijinsky 138) **111** (1982 6g²* 8d* 8s) Apr 30; tall, lengthy filly; second foal; half-sister to winning American 3-y-o Steambath (by Honest Pleasure); dam unraced sister to high-class middle-distance stayer Caucasus and half-sister to several very good performers; finished fast to win newcomers race at Deauville in August by ½ length and easily bettered that effort when favourite for Group 3 Prix d'Aumale at Chantilly the following month, winning in good style by 1½ lengths from Riverba; never looked like taking a hand when 4¼ lengths seventh of 11 to Goodbye Shelley in Prix Marcel Boussac at Longchamp in October; will be suited by 1¼m+; looked past her best for year at Longchamp and will probably leave that form behind. *F. Boutin, France.*

AIREDALE JUNCTION 4 b.g. Karabas 132–Dinant 114 (Abernant 142) **36** (1981 12.2fg 10fg 9s 1982 9f 8fg³ 8.3g) tall, leggy gelding; close third in a poor 1m seller, only form. *G. Toft.*

AIRFIELD 2 ch.c. Northfields–Easy Landing 110 (Swing Easy 126) (1982 6f³ 7s) **92** Mar 19; second foal; dam very useful sprinting 2-y-o; ran well behind useful horses at Kempton in July and Ascot in September; stays 7f; sure to win a race. *J. Tree.*

AIR GIRL 2 ch.f. Air Trooper 115–Bosworth Moll (Henry the Seventh 125) — (1982 5fg 5fg 5.8f 6f 6g) Feb 26; lengthy filly; second foal; dam second over 13f in France; last on 4 of 5 outings, wearing blinkers on last 2; apparently of little account. *W. Wightman.*

AIR POWER 5 gr.g. Supreme Sovereign 119–Queen Of The Winds (Borealis) — (1981 8g 8g 9.4g 8s 10.1fg 12g 1982 10f) no sign of ability in varied company; was tried in blinkers; dead. *A. Moore.*

AIRSHIP 4 br.c. Manado 130–High Sphere (St Paddy 133) (1981 7fg 8.2g **79** 7d 7g 7.2s³ 7f³ 8f³ 7.2f 7g⁴ 1982 7s 7.6g 8f* 8f* 9fg² 8f 9g) rather lightly-made colt; ran best races for a while when short-head winner of handicaps at Wolverhampton in May (from On Edge) and Redcar in June (from Saulann); most disappointing last 2 outings; ideally suited by a strongly-run 1m and stays 9f; acts on any going but seems suited by firm; unreliable in 1981, but reportedly suffered from back trouble. *R. Hollinshead.*

AIRSLEE 4 gr.g. Town Crier 119–Tavaro (Gustav 121) (1981 8s 8fg 10fg —
11.7fg 1982 10f 10.1fg 8.3g 8fg 8f) disappointing plater; often blinkered;
cost 1,550 gns at Ascot March Sales. *P. Butler.*

AIRSPIN 3 gr.g. Jukebox 120–Whispering Breeze (Caliban 123) (1981 6fg³ **79**
7g* 7s 7v 7g² 1982 7g² 7g² 6fg 8d³) workmanlike gelding; good mover; placed
in handicaps at Doncaster, Newmarket and Sandown; stays 1m; probably
unsuited by very soft going. *R. Price.*

AIRSTREAM 4 br.g. Saritamer 130–Midsummertime (Midsummer Night II 117) —
(1981 8fg 8d 10.1d 11.7g⁴ 13.3d 11g 12fg 8h 1982 13.1f 15.5g) compact gelding;
slow maiden; often blinkered; sent to Hong Kong. *D. Arbuthnot.*

AIRWAIR 3 br.g. Godswalk 130–Haunting Melody 96 (Sing Sing 134) (1981 —
7f⁴ 7g* 1982 10f 10g 8f 8.2f 8.2fg⁴ 8f) sturdy gelding; good mover; won
maiden race at Leicester in 1981; soundly beaten in handicaps at 3 yrs; not
certain to stay 1¼m; blinkered fourth and fifth starts, pulling hard on first
occasion. *A. Hide.*

AJAS 2 ch.f. Abwah 118–Pinwave 82 (Pinza 137) (1982 6g) June 2; half-sister —
to useful 1¼m winner Wire Up (by Firestreak), to a winner in Italy and to a
winning hurdler; dam won at up to 13f; 14 lengths sixth of 14 behind Our Katy
in seller at Ripon in July; sold 350 gns Doncaster September Sales. *Miss S.
Hall.*

AKIYDA 3 br.f. Labus–Licata (Abdos 134) (1981 10s* 1982 10.5d⁴ 9.5fg³ **131**
12s* 10.5v² 13.5fg² 12f² 12s*)
  There were many outstanding performances at middle distances in Europe
in 1982 but no dominant performer as Shergar had been the previous year.
Except for Golden Fleece, retired after the Derby, none of the leading horses
possessed an unbeaten record; and the most hotly-contested race of the season,
the Trusthouse Forte Prix de l'Arc de Triomphe, whose field included two horses
that once had threatened to command the middle-distance division in dual-Derby
winner Assert and French Oaks winner Harbour, went entirely on merit to a
three-year-old filly previously without a pattern victory in seven starts. Ideally
suited by prevailing conditions and beautifully ridden, Akiyda showed fine
pace and great courage to prevail, in a very close finish, over the Gold Cup winner
Ardross, the Yorkshire Oaks winner Awaasif and the 1981 Arc third April
Run, becoming the fourth of her sex in a row to win the race and the seventh in
the last eleven runnings following a period of almost twenty years of unbroken
success for the colts.
  As always the Prix de l'Arc de Triomphe set an intriguing puzzle and
promised an exciting contest, though on this particular occasion there was no
general feeling that the middle-distance championship of Europe was at stake
since Golden Fleece had long been retired, Kalaglow, Time Charter, Glint of
Gold and General Holme were also missing and, furthermore, the very soft
ground which had forced Kalaglow's withdrawal threatened to influence the
outcome excessively. Although Assert was heavily backed down to 5/2 clear
favourite ahead of the improving Prix Niel winner Bon Sang and Harbour his

Trusthouse Forte Prix de l'Arc de Triomphe, Longchamp—
Akiyda keeps on strongly and courageously to hold off
Ardross, Awaasif and April Run

form was not so superior that he could afford to be at anything less than his best. And his best form was on top-of-the-ground; he had never raced in public in the mud, and his connections insisted conditions would be against him. Nearly all his sixteen opponents had shown their ability to act on soft but some were better suited than others; four—in betting order Harbour, Bikala (second in 1981), the hardy No Attention and Cadoudal—had shown themselves very well suited by it. Since the nature of the ground was certain to increase the emphasis on stamina, virtually to guarantee a test of stamina, such as Ardross and Akiyda who would have been hard pressed to keep up with Assert on the fast tracks of summer, were brought much more into the reckoning; on the day Ardross started at 25/4, Akiyda at 11/1.

Let's take a look at the record of Akiyda, a full sister to the favourite for the 1981 Prix de l'Arc de Triomphe Akarad and a half-sister to the 1978 French Derby winner Acamas. It was an excellent one despite her relative lack of success, that of a consistent, top-class filly. She'd pursued a typical campaign for a good three-year-old filly in France after easily winning a ten-furlong maiden at Saint-Cloud on her only appearance at two. She ran in the Prix Penelope on the same course in the very early spring, then in the Vanteaux and the Tuileries at Longchamp, the Diane Hermes at Chantilly, the Pomone at Deauville and the Vermeille at Longchamp; she made the frame each time. Her easiest race, the Prix des Tuileries in May, she won by a length and a half from First Water. Akiyda progressed along the right lines afterwards and finished second in all three races, never beaten by more than two lengths, the distance the Vanteaux winner Harbour had to spare in the Prix de Diane Hermes (the French Oaks) in June. The Diane identified Akiyda as a staying type. She came home very strongly in the testing conditions, passing four horses, one of them the Penelope winner All Along, in the final two hundred and fifty yards. The Pomone's thirteen and a half furlongs should have shown her to advantage but unfortunately the race turned into an untidy crawl; Zalataia got first run and just held on in a sprint finish. In contrast the Prix Vermeille, a highly significant Arc trial in recent years, had two efficient pacemakers (one of them Akiyda's stable-companion Kawarah). Akiyda was never far behind and she chased All Along virtually the length of the straight, once the latter had taken over, without ever looking like beating her on the firm ground; in the end Akiyda was a length and a half down having been about the same distance behind on the turn. Harbour finished fourth, Zalataia sixth and Awaasif seventh.

On form there was clearly not a lot to choose between All Along, Harbour and Akiyda. However the radically different conditions three weeks later put paid to All Along's chance in the Arc and she beat only Mariacho and the apparently out-of-place Russian classic winner Kastet home, while Harbour also failed to reproduce her best, dropping away disappointingly in the straight into ninth. As expected the race developed into a thorough test. Bon Sang and Bikala soon became embroiled in a battle for the lead, allowing the others little or no chance to settle as horses of that calibre couldn't be given much rope. Assert and Ardross made moderate starts, among the worst, in consequence having to be pushed along through the first half mile in search of a better position, whereas Akiyda was always able to lie up in third or fourth, eventually joined at the furthest point of the course by Assert. Kastet apart, the runners stayed well bunched to the straight while avoiding the fairly familiar boring and checking on the run down the hill. Bon Sang and Bikala still led the field straightening for home but it was becoming obvious they had practically run themselves out. That fact certainly hadn't escaped Saint-Martin, the near-veteran who almost alone among contemporary French jockeys has been able to stand comparison with Piggott. He quickly slipped Akiyda between the leaders, finding her capable of producing enough to take her two lengths clear and secure a place on the rails. This acceleration of Akiyda's and the finish were the most memorable aspects of the race. As the post drew closer so Ardross, Awaasif and April Run on the outside began to bear down strongly on Akiyda, and in the end she needed reserves of courage as well as stamina to hold on by a head, half a length and a head. A gap of four lengths separated the money earners from the rest headed by the French Derby second Real Shadai, who thus confirmed himself about the best of an undistinguished crop of French three-year-old colts. Then came No Attention, the Hocquart winner Cadoudal, and Critique who ran better than expected on unfavourable ground. Assert like Harbour went out quickly in the straight, and he finished eleventh alongside the moderate Newjdar; the only one still to be mentioned, Last Feather, finished fourteenth.

With 90/1-shot Awaasif and April Run as well as Akiyda in the frame, fillies took three of the first four places in an Arc for the first time since 1972, the year of San San, Rescousse and Regal Exception; at least one filly made the frame in each of the intervening seasons. Fillies haven't quite so good a record over the same period in the other major all-aged middle-distance race of the autumn, the Champion Stakes; nevertheless they have provided six of its eleven winners, the latest of them, Time Charter, one who must have gone close in Paris at her best. Incidentally, Awaasif's forward showing wasn't unforeseen. Although she started at long odds against there were 2,689 winning 'tierce' forecast tickets naming the first three in correct order and another 8,544 naming the first three in any other order.

The pari-mutuel tierce bet forecasting the first three in a selected race each Sunday was established in 1954 and is extremely popular throughout France; it's the French equivalent of the English treble-chance football pool. The amount of money speculated on the tierce alone on the Arc was about eleven and a half million pounds (the largest total amount bet on an English flat race is an estimated eighteen million pounds on the Derby). The deduction from the tierce pool before pay-out was a swingeing 34.28%, a proportion of which will go towards the cost of financing French racing. Racing in France has done extremely well out of pari-mutuel betting; and it still does, though recently fears have been expressed that other lotteries were gaining ground at the expense of the tierce and that central government is taking too big a slice of the cake. The prosperity of French racing as a direct result of income from betting is probably the chief reason for the very small amount of sponsorship to be found in France in the past twenty years, a period which has seen a tremendous increase in the volume of sponsorship in England. There was one outstanding example of commercial sponsorship though, one that surpassed anything in England inasmuch as the race concerned is a classic. From 1978 to 1981 the Prix de Diane acquired the appendage 'de Revlon'; in 1982 the race became a vehicle for advertising French fashion instead of American cosmetics and acquired instead 'Hermes'. In 1982 also, France's greatest race the Prix de l'Arc de Triomphe became sponsored for the first time. The hotel and catering group Trusthouse Forte contracted to support the event for four years with a total contribution of

H.H. Aga Khan's "Akiyda"

almost five million francs, almost £412,000. Including the substantial breeders' prizes a sum of about £350,000 plus trophies was on offer in the latest Arc.

Akiyda's owner the Aga Khan picked up the winning breeder's prize of over £41,000, as a result of his purchase of M Marcel Boussac's bloodstock interests for a sum reportedly between 8.1 million dollars and 9.7 million dollars not long after Acamas had won the French Derby in Boussac's colours. The mare Licata had already been covered by the unfashionable Labus at the time of the sale so, in a way, Akiyda's victory represented a final one in the Arc for Boussac who won the race on six occasions between 1936 and 1949 with Corrida (twice), Djebel, Ardan, Caracalla and Coronation. The fascinating story of the rise and fall of Boussac's bloodstock empire has been told many times, Akiyda's success naturally prompting further retelling. Boussac won virtually everything worth winning on the turf in England as well as France in the period from the first of his successes in the French Derby with Ramus in 1922 and his twelfth with Acamas; he won all the English classics except the One Thousand Guineas. From 1957 his stable went into a decline attributed, wrongly or rightly, to the degree of inbreeding exhibited by the families at his Fresnay-le-Buffard stud. Of Akiyda's grandparents only Busted was not bred by Boussac and of her dam's grandparents only Shantung. The dams of both Labus and Licata descend directly through many generations of the stud's mares to a mare called Banshee who was also the grandam of one of Boussac's famous and most used stallions Tourbillon.

Akiyda (br.f. 1979)			
	Labus (br 1971)	Busted (b 1963)	Crepello
			Sans le Sou
		Cordovilla (b 1957)	Pharis
			Cordova
	Licata (b 1969)	Abdos (br 1959)	Arbar
			Pretty Lady
		Gaia (b 1962)	Shantung
			Gloriana

The story of how financial constraints led to Boussac's using the lightly-raced home-bred stallion Labus on his pattern race winner Licata was outlined in the summary of the Grand Prix de Saint-Cloud winner Akarad in *Racehorses of 1981*. Necessity, the mother of invention, has in this case also been the mother of improbable success. How much share of the credit to award Labus for Akarad and Akiyda is problematical: Licata (due to foal to Shergar in 1983) is obviously an exceptional broodmare, and previously had produced three winners, including Acamas to Mill Reef and the smart filly Licara to Caro. Nevertheless Labus certainly deserves some, and now that he is getting considerably better opportunities he may well turn out to be one of the good stallions that the French bloodstock industry badly needs. So far he has an excellent winner-to-runner ratio. When first transferred from the service of Boussac to that of the French National Stud through the offices of the Aga Khan Labus was so little regarded that he spent two years as a sire of saddle horses, reportedly having no thorough-bred mates. Now, naturally enough, he is in enormous demand from thorough-bred breeders and his fee for 1982 had risen to ten times that of the original £50 or so—still peanuts at today's prices—kept artificially low by deliberate policy of the French National Stud. One last word on the Boussac dispersal: the good news is that Fresnay-le-Buffard continues to exist as a stud farm, having been purchased for that purpose by Stavros Niarchos.

Akiyda, an attractive filly, has been retired. Like Akarad and Acamas she was extremely well suited by a mile and a half, and at that distance she was almost certainly as good as either: to her credit she ran much better in her Prix de l'Arc de Triomphe than the two colts did in theirs. Akiyda acted on any going, but there is no doubt that the arrival of the soft ground of the autumn was very timely for her. She was a very genuine filly and far more consistent than many of her contemporaries. She visits Shergar. *F. Mathet, France.*

AKKA 3 b.f. Malacate 131–Amicable 73 (Bold Ruler) (1981 NR 1982 8f 10.1fg 8fg) fourth foal; half-sister to fair middle-distance handicapper Mickey Tim (by Gay Fandango); dam, placed over 1¼m, is half-sister to Sir Wimborne and Lady Capulet; soundly beaten in maiden races and a minor event; blinkered final start; sold 2,300 gns Newmarket December Sales. *J. Dunlop.*

ALABAMA 4 gr.f. Warpath 113–Montana (Mossborough 126) (1981 10d 10fg 10d 11.7d 12s⁴ 15.8g 18g 12d 1982 10f) strong, deep-girthed, sturdy filly; no form since trotting up in seller at 2 yrs; should stay at least 1½m; suited by a soft surface. *W. Clay.*

AL-ABJAR 2 b.c. Blakeney 126–Glamour Girl (Riverman 131) (1982 8d 8s **73** 10s²) neat colt, lacking in scope; first foal; dam, minor French 7f and 9.5f winner, is half-sister to dam of Gold River (by Riverman); weak in the market, finished second in maiden event at Nottingham in October, first indication of merit; lacks pace, and will be suited by 1½m+; acts on soft going. *P. Walwyn.*

ALAHLI (USA) 3 b.c. What A Pleasure–Jovial Josie (Sea-Bird II 145) (1981 **—** 5g 1982 8.2f⁴ 7.6d 8.2s) strong, attractive colt; plating-class maiden; would have stayed 1¼m; pulled up lame final start; dead. *F. Durr.*

AL AMEEN (USA) 3 b.c. Lyphard 132–Priceless Gem (Hail to Reason) (1981 **79** 7g 1982 7f⁴ 9fg² 10d³ 13g* 12fg 16g* 15d² 16d³ 16.5s³) tall, useful sort; has a round action; stayed on well to win maiden race at Nottingham in July and amateur riders race at Beverley in August; suited by 2m; seems to act on any going; one paced. *H. T. Jones.*

ALANGROVE SOUND (CAN) 4 gr.c. Champagne Charlie–De Soto Queen **—** (Fleet Nasrullah) (1981 12g 12g² 12.5f 14f³ 16f* 14fg³ 16.5f 1982 12g 15.8f 17f 12f 16fg 15g) neat colt; staying handicapper; soundly beaten in 1982, wearing blinkers on last 2 starts; acts on firm going; has worn a tongue strap; sold 1,050 gns Doncaster August Sales. *J. Berry.*

ALAN STUART 2 b.c. Town Crier 119–My Sweet Afton 73 (Javelot 124) **49** (1982 6f 5fg 5d 6f 6fg³ 7f 8fg 8fg) May 28; compact colt; poor plater; stays 6f; blinkered fifth, sixth and final outings; sold 650 gns Doncaster October Sales. *N. Bycroft.*

ALASIA 3 b.f. Thatch 136–Topling 85 (High Top 131) (1981 6g⁴ 1982 8s **—** 8d 9fg⁴ 11d⁴ 10.2f) compact filly; plating-class maiden; possibly doesn't stay 11f; gives impression she will probably do best on a galloping track; ran freely and finished tailed off when blinkered final start; sold 1,500 gns Newmarket December Sales. *G. Pritchard-Gordon.*

ALASTOR O MAVROS (USA) 3 gr.c. Tentam–Carte Noire (Native Charger) **85** (1981 7d 7fg 7g 1982 12fg 12fg 16fg 16d* 16.5f* 16.5fg* 16fg²) rangy sort; not a good mover; won maiden race at Lingfield in June and handicaps at Folkestone in July and August; stays well; seems to act on any going; best in blinkers; refused to enter stalls once. *G. Harwood.*

A LA VAI 4 ch.g. Gay Fandango 132–Solo Stream 106 (Jolly Jet 111) (1981 **—** NR 1982 10d) 2,400F, 2,500Y; second foal; dam stayed 7f; 50/1 when remote eighth of 10 behind My Maravilla in minor event at Nottingham in September. *J. Spearing.*

ALAWIR (FR) 2 br.c. Riverman 131 Reine du Chant 112 (Premier Violon) **—** (1982 6s) Feb 7; $350,000Y; lightly-made colt; half-brother to 2 winners in France, including useful 1m to 1¼m winner Mondino (by Caro); dam won Prix Robert Papin; 20/1, showed speed 3f in maiden race won by Raashideah at Doncaster in November. *H. T. Jones.*

ALBADEEAH (USA) 2 b.f. Nashua–Precious Girl (Intentionally) (1982 6g*) **85** p Feb 18; $240,000Y; strong, rangy filly with scope; sister to a minor winner, and half-sister to another; dam won small 6f race at 3 yrs; second favourite, led 1½f out after travelling well from start when beating Forever Mary by 1½ lengths in 18-runner maiden race at Newmarket in September; will stay beyond 6f; sure to improve. *H. T. Jones.*

ALBERTAT 2 gr.g. Habat 127–Albertina 102 (Great Nephew 126) (1982 5f **70** 5f 5f 7g 7fg 7f 8f 8.2s) Mar 27; 5,000Y; lengthy gelding; half-brother to 3-y-o middle-distance winner Kings Soldier (by Queen's Hussar); dam, daughter of very smart Victorina, won over 1m; quite a moderate maiden; stays 1m; acts on firm going. *D. Smith.*

ALBRIZZI (USA) 5 b.g. Cannonade–Table (Round Table) (1981 NR 1982 **35** 10.1fg³ 12d) compact gelding; plater; stays 1¼m; probably acts on any going; has been tried in blinkers. *J. Jenkins.*

ALCHISE (USA) 2 gr.c. Al Hattab–Beat the Chief (Chieftain) (1982 6f* 7g* **115** 7.2g* 7f 6g²) Apr 8; $60,000Y; neat, rather lightly-made colt; half-brother to winners by Mr Leader and Bold Forbes; dam, half-sister to 3 stakes winners, won over 6f at 4 yrs; not an impressive individual, but very useful nonetheless; won his first three races, maiden at Doncaster in May, minor event at Newcastle in June, and valuable Cock of the North Stakes (made all to beat Shearwalk by length) at Haydock in July; ran creditably afterwards in Lanson Champagne

*Cock of the North Stakes, Haydock—Alchise makes all.   The grey
Shearwalk finishes second with The Noble Player third*

Stakes at Goodwood and Clarence House Stakes at Ascot; better suited by 7f
than by 6f, and will stay 1m; acts on firm going; sold 100,000 gns Newmarket
December Sales and is to race in USA. *H. Cecil.*

ALCONBURY HILL 3 br.g. Pals Passage 115–Varamette (Varano) (1981   —
5g 6fg 7fg 7fg 1982 12g) quite a useful sort; good mover; well behind in
maiden races and a minor event. *J. Gifford.*

ALDENHAM (USA) 4 ch.g. His Majesty–Mama's Silver (Silver King 119)   **71**
(1981 10fg* 12g 10g³ 8f 10fg 10g⁴ 12fg 10fg 11.7g² 10.1fg³ 10f⁴ 11.7d 10d   1982
10f 10g 11.7fg³ 10fg* 12fg 10d 10f³ 10f 12fg² 11.7fg⁴ 10g³ 10fg⁴ 10.2f* 10v* 10v²
10.2d) smallish, fair sort; won handicaps at Goodwood in May, Bath in September (brought wide to race) and Lingfield in October; made running on first 2
courses; stays 1½m; acts on any going; blinkered once in 1981. *G. Balding.*

ALDERN STREAM 2 gr.f. Godswalk 130–Betsy Ross 100 (Petingo 135)   **94**
(1982 5fg* 6s⁴ 6s³) Feb 8; 15,500Y; lengthy, useful-looking filly; has a smooth,
light action; second foal; dam useful at up to 1¼m; very tenderly handled in
10-runner £3,400 event at Goodwood in September but quickened in excellent
style to win by a neck from Misguided; in frame subsequently in Blue Seal
Stakes at Ascot (odds on, beaten nearly 5 lengths by Khaizaraan) and 4-runner
event at York (6 lengths third to Domynsky); will stay beyond 6f; action suggests
she's possibly not at her best on soft going. *H. Wragg.*

ALDERSHAWE HALL 3 b.c. Wollow 132–Hatha 78 (Bold Reason) (1981   **54**
6s 6fg 6fg 6g   1982 8g 8fg 8f² 8f² 8g 9.4fg³ 8g 8.2fg² 8g 8g³ 8f 10fg 8g³ 8d 8g)
smallish, fair sort; poor walker; first past post in maiden race at Beverley in May
on third start but was moved down a place for hampering second; stays 9f; acts
well on firm going; does best when ridden up with pace. *R. Hollinshead.*

ALDINGTON MILL 2 b.g. Legal Eagle 126–Dear Catalpa (Dear Gazelle 113) **72**
(1982 7d 7f 7fg 7f 6g³ 7f 8.2d) May 27; leggy, rather lightly-made gelding;
sixth foal; dam won over hurdles; quite modest form in varied company, including selling; stays 1m; acts on firm going; blinkered final outing; gelded afterwards; sure to win a seller. *Mrs J. Reavey.*

ALEOS (FR) 5 b.g. Faunus–Aphytis (Crepello 136) (1981 12s 1982 10.2f 12d⁴) —
workmanlike gelding; fairly useful in 1980; lightly raced and soundly beaten on
flat since; stays 1½m; acts on firm going; looked ungenuine when blinkered
once in 1980. *J. Old.*

58

ALERTED 2 ch.f. Red Alert 127–Ladies Night 65 (Midsummer Night II 117) **74**
(1982 6fg 6d 6s) Mar 19; strong filly; fourth living foal; dam won over 1m;
nearest finish when 3 lengths fifth to Stephalotus in 12-runner minor race at
Pontefract in October, second start and best effort; will be suited by 7f. *Miss
S. Hall.*

ALERT JOHNNIE 2 ch.c. Red Alert 127–Corbara II (Marino) (1982 5fg 7fg —
8s) Apr 4; 15,000Y; well-grown colt; has a round action; closely related to
3 winners by Red God, including very useful 5f to 9f winner Tickled Pink and
fairly useful 7f performer Red Johnnie, and half-brother to 2 winners; dam
French 9f winner; last in maiden races, on second occasion blinkered. *C.
Brittain.*

ALERT ROSY 2 b.f. Red Alert 127–Spanish Ribbon (Pieces of Eight 128) —
(1982 5.8g 7g) Apr 1; 1,500Y; first foal; dam never ran; in rear in maiden race
at Bath in August and minor event (last of 13) at Brighton in September. *J.
Holt.*

ALETHE 4 br.f. Derring-Do 131–Argitone (Aureole 132) (1981 8g 8d 9.4g³
9f 7d⁴ 8s 8s 1982 10g) quite a well-made filly; showed some ability in 1981;
stays 9f. *G. Pritchard-Gordon.*

ALEV 3 ch.g. Hot Spark 126–St Citrus 108 (Relic) (1981 5s 5g⁴ 5f 5d³ 5g⁴ **84**
1982 6fg 6fg 5f² 5g* 5g 6g 5fg 5g 6v 5s) lengthy, useful-looking gelding; sprint
handicapper; made all to beat Welwyn by 1½ lengths at Sandown in June;
well beaten most subsequent starts; form only at 5f; seems to act on any going;
blinkered 3 of his last 4 outings; sold 6,000 gns Newmarket Autumn Sales. *M.
Masson.*

ALEXANDER NEVSKY 4 b.c. Furry Glen 121–Levanstell Queen (Le Levan- —
stell 122) (1981 10s 11.7g 8fg 10.8fg 1982 12f) rangy colt; behind in varied
company, including selling; sold 610 gns Ascot July Sales. *P. Ransom.*

ALEXANDRIE (USA) 2 b. or br.f. Val de l'Orne 130–Apachee (Sir Gaylord) ?
(1982 8v*) first foal; dam, half-sister to high-class French filly Aryenne, was a
very useful winner at around 1¼m in France; put up a pleasing first effort when
winning 16-runner newcomers event at Saint-Cloud in October by ½ length from
Florenly; will be well suited by 1¼m+; bound to leave this form well behind.
A. Head, France.

ALEX CHOICE 3 ch.g. Gay Fandango 132–Eileen's Choice 106 (Tin Whistle 128) **62**
(1981 7fg 1982 10d² 10.6s 9.4f⁴ 10f³ 12f⁴ 16d 10g³ 10fg² 9g 10s³ 10g² 12f² 10fg
10d² 12d 10.2s) smallish, strong gelding; in frame in maiden races and handicaps; ran poorly in seller final start; stays 1½m; acts on any going; sometimes
blinkered but is effective without. *B. Hanbury.*

ALEXANDRINA 3 ch.f. Gay Fandango 132–Schloss 87 (Busted 134) (1981 6g —
1982 8f 8g 7fg) smallish, workmanlike filly; poor mover; plating-class maiden;
will be suited by 1¼m; sold 5,800 gns Newmarket Autumn Sales. *G. Pritchard-
Gordon.*

ALFIE DICKINS 4 ro.c. Spanish Gold 101–Vila Real 76 (Town Crier 119) (1981 **50**
7s 8d 8fg 7s 8.2g³ 8fg 8.2f⁴ 8fg 9.4g⁴ 7.6s 9g 8d⁴ 9s 1982 8f⁴ 11fg⁴ 12f 12f²
12fg² 12g³ 12d³ 12f 12f 12fg² 12g⁴ 12g⁴ 12fg⁴ 12fg³ 13s⁴ 12g⁴) robust colt;
plating-class maiden; stays 1½m; has run respectably in blinkers; none too
genuine. *R. Hollinshead.*

ALFRED'S CHOICE 3 br.c. So Blessed 130–Scamperdale 81 (French Beige 127) **121**
(1981 5g 5.5d* 8.5v² 8v³ 1982 8s* 10.5d⁴ 10.5fg² 12fg⁴ 12.5d⁴ 12f² 10s 10v²)
15,000F, 9,600Y; rangy, attractive colt; good walker; fourth foal; half-brother
to 2 winners, including Lady Peg (by Young Emperor), fairly useful winner at
up to 1m here and also successful in Norway; dam stayed well; beat Persepolis by
½ length in Prix Omnium at Saint-Cloud in March; ran creditably most subsequent
starts, including when in frame in Prix Greffulhe at Longchamp, Prix Lupin on
same course (2 lengths second to Persepolis), Prix du Jockey-Club at Chantilly
(5¼ lengths fourth to Assert), Grand Prix de Saint-Cloud (about 5½ lengths
fourth to Glint of Gold) and Prix Niel at Longchamp again (6 lengths second
to Bon Sang); stays 1½m; acts on any going; consistent. *E. Bartholomew,
France.*

ALIMONY 2 ch.f. Sallust 134–Constanza 94 (Sun Prince 128) (1982 6f 6g²) **86** p
Mar 10; rangy, quite attractive filly; first foal; dam won over 1½m from 2 starts;
½-length second of 16 to Elysian in maiden race at Newbury in August; will
stay at least 1m; sure to improve and win races. *R. Hern.*

ALISON ROSE 2 b. or br.f. Jaazeiro 127–Tribal Feast 100 (Tribal Chief 125) **58**
(1982 5f 5fg⁴ 5f 5d) Apr 27; 8,400F; third live foal; dam speedy half-sister to
high-class sprinter Runnett; 3½ lengths fifth of 13 to Amber Wind in maiden
race at Folkestone in July, third outing and best effort; looks something of a short
runner. *B. Swift.*

ALIWOOD GIRL 2 b.f. Broxted 120–Tiranica (Tyrant) (1982 5f³ 6f 5g³ **64 §**
5fg² 5f* 5f⁴ 5f⁴ 5f³) Apr 15; compact filly; not a good mover; second foal; dam
never ran; after getting beaten in 4 sellers, came out at Redcar in July and won
maiden race; ran moderately in nurseries afterwards, twice apparently well
handicapped; acts on firm going; not to be trusted. *W. Bentley.*

ALJOTON 3 br.g. Welsh Saint 126–Lydja 75 (Hethersett 134) (1981 NR **71**
1982 7g 8g*) half-brother to winners here and abroad, including Troms (by
Wolver Hollow), a useful winner at up to 1¼m in France and also successful in
USA; dam stayed 1½m; decisively won claiming race at Brighton in June; claimed
£4,220 afterwards and has been sent to Singapore; stays 1m. *C. James.*

AL KHASHAB 5 ch.g. Habat 127–Parlais 101 (Pardao 120) (1981 10g 8d 8d **47 d**
10.6s 9f 10.6f² 8f⁴ 11.5d 10g 10fg² 10g⁴ 12d 10.2g 12s 10.2g⁴ 1982 10d 12g*
12f* 12f 12f 12f 10.6s 12s 10d) workmanlike gelding; successful in handicaps at
Pontefract (won in good style) and Thirsk (made all) in April; rather disappointing
afterwards, but not disgraced penultimate start; stays 1½m; acts on any going.
R. Hollinshead.

ALKIS (USA) 3 b.f. Roberto 131–Lady Mere 118 (Decoy Boy 129) (1981 NR **—**
1982 7fg 10.2g) fair sort; first foal; dam smart from 5f to 1m; behind in newcomers event at Newbury and maiden race at Bath. *M. Smyly.*

AL KUWAIT 6 br.h. Blakeney 126–Camenae 72 (Vimy 132) (1981 13s* 16fg **—**
14fg² 18.4d 16s⁴ 16fg* 14d 14fg 16s² 13s³ 14g² 1982 12g) strong, good-
bodied horse; fair handicapper in 1981; not disgraced when on burly side only
outing of 1982 (September); stays well; acts on any going, but is suited by some
give in the ground; blinkered last 3 outings in 1980; not an easy ride. *F. Winter.*

ALLADO 6 b.g. Crooner 119–Head On (Never Say Die 137) (1981 NR 1982 **—**
10f) 200Y; first foal; dam last on only start; poor hurdler; tailed-off seventh of 8
behind Leopard's Rock in apprentice event at Brighton in May, first outing on
flat. *A. Neaves.*

ALL ALONG (FR) 3 b.f. Targowice 130–Agujita (Vieux Manoir 132) (1981 **129**
8.2g* 1982 10d* 10.5d* 10v² 12f 10.5v 12.5d* 12f* 12s 12f²)
There are over two hundred French Provincial racecourses and while a
number, such as Les Sables-d'Olonne, Cazaubon-Barbotan-les-Thermes and
Montlucon-Neris-les-Bains, have names that sound intriguing to the English
ear, the quality of the horses racing on them is as a rule nothing out of the ordinary. Occasionally, though, these lesser tracks entertain angels unawares as
when All Along, trained by Zilber, dead-heated with Tarbelissima in a twelve-
runner maiden race at Amiens in November, 1981. The subsequent careers
of the two fillies make interesting reading. Joining Tarbelissima's trainer
Biancone for her three-year-old season, All Along developed into one of the best
of her age and sex in Europe, whereas Tarbelissima failed to catch the judge's
eye again and ended up running in a claiming event.
    After her first two starts at three All Along was being widely touted as
another outstanding filly to race in the Wildenstein colours that have been carried
by performers of the calibre of Allez France, Flying Water, Lianga, Madelia,
Paulista and Pawneese. A comfortable success in a minor event at Saint-Cloud in

Prix Maurice de Nieuil, Saint-Cloud—All Along wins from the colts
No Attention and Arc d'Or

Prix Vermeille, Longchamp—All Along accounts for a top-class field.
Akiyda is second, Grease third, Harbour (rails) fourth,
Perlee fifth and Zalataia sixth

February preceded an excellent display in the Prix Penelope on the same course in March in which All Along came with a powerful run from two furlongs out that took her four lengths clear of Paradise by the post. On the strength of this All Along started at odds on for the Prix Saint-Alary on very soft going at Longchamp two months later but her reputation received something of a dent since she finished a very tired second to Harbour, beaten four lengths. All Along next followed in the steps of recent fillies like Pawneese, Fabuleux Jane and Madam Gay by running in both the English and French Oaks, but neither race did anything to salvage her claim to be a top performer. Held up at Epsom presumably because of doubts about her stamina, she probably wasn't particularly well suited to the track and merely stayed on at one pace to be sixth to Time Charter. More enterprising tactics proved no more fruitful in the Prix de Diane Hermes at Chantilly, for All Along could finish only fifth to the impressive two-length winner Harbour after leading briefly a furlong and a half out.

All Along's efforts at Epsom and Chantilly suggested that if there was a deficiency in her make-up it was lack of pace rather than lack of stamina, and in the Prix Maurice de Nieuil at Saint-Cloud in July, Gorli rode her as if he had no doubts about her staying power. Because the Maurice de Nieuil comes in the three-week gap between the Grand Prix de Saint-Cloud and the King George VI and Queen Elizabeth Diamond Stakes, and has fairly stiff penalties for the best pattern-race winners, it is not usually contested by top class fields though some of its winners, notably Homeric, Admetus and Perrault, have proved to be out of the top drawer. The most recent running of the race was no exception to this rule, with All Along meeting the Prix du Jockey-Club fifth Noble Bloom, the Prix Jean de Chaudenay second Le Mamamouchi, the British challenger Diamond Shoal and eight others. Close up from the start, All Along took command at the distance and kept on well to beat the improving four-year-old No Attention a shade cleverly by half a length; Diamond Shoal ran no sort of race in eleventh place.

As is usual with a good French-trained filly All Along was given quite a lengthy rest in preparation for the severe autumn tests of the Prix Vermeille and the Prix de l'Arc de Triomphe. She evidently thrived during this period, for when we saw her in the paddock at Longchamp prior to the Vermeille in September she impressed us enormously as a strong, attractive filly who looked especially well. Even so, she didn't appear to have an obvious chance of winning a contest which had the strongest field assembled for any race restricted to fillies in Europe all year. The twelve other runners consisted of nine pattern-race winners, notably Harbour, Grease, Awaasif and Dish Dash; the Prix de Diane runner-up Akiyda; and two pacemakers put in to assist Harbour and Akiyda. Ridden by Starkey because Gorli had been suspended, All Along was soon lying two or three lengths behind the pacemakers in third, with Akiyda not far away and Harbour, who lost a little ground at the start, towards the rear. As the leaders began to fall away entering the straight Starkey sensibly sent his mount on and the pair quickly opened up a two-length advantage which All Along never looked likely to surrender; staying on resolutely she passed the post a length and a half ahead of Akiyda with Grease a head away third, Harbour, who didn't enjoy an entirely trouble-free run, fourth and Awaasif seventh. The time was **the fastest** for the race since Highest Hopes set the record in 1970.

M D. Wildenstein's "All Along" (G. Starkey)

Creditably as All Along had run on soft ground previously, the Vermeille proved conclusively that a sound surface suited her a great deal better. Her two subsequent starts more than confirmed the point. In very testing conditions for the Trusthouse Forte Prix de l'Arc de Triomphe she failed to reach the front rank and dropped out in the last three furlongs to beat just two of her sixteen rivals home—with Akiyda winning the race and Awaasif finishing third it is fair to assume that on better ground All Along would have been thereabouts at the end. In the Japan Cup at Tokyo towards the end of November All Along returned to form on the very fast ground, weaving her way through to lead less than a furlong out before being caught near the line by the short-neck winner Half Iced; April Run was a further neck behind.

All Along (Fr) (b.f. 1979)	Targowice (b 1970)	Round Table (b 1954)	Princequillo / Knight's Daughter
		Matriarch (b 1964)	Bold Ruler / Lyceum
	Agujita (b 1966)	Vieux Manoir (b 1947)	Brantome / Vieille Maison
		Argosy (b 1950)	Coastal Traffic / Prosodie

Targowice, the best French two-year-old of 1972, has been represented by several good horses in Europe since being sent to Japan in 1980, notably Prince Mab and Ukraine Girl, but All Along is the best of his offspring to date. Ironically, further evidence of the lack of esteem in which All Along was apparently held at two is afforded by the fact that her dam, covered by New Chapter, was sold at the 1981 Newmarket December Sales for just 2,400 guineas, a price which now looks a distinct bargain even though Agujita is sixteen. A daughter of the St Leger runner-up Vieux Manoir, who died in 1981 at the advanced age of thirty-four, Agujita showed smart form over middle distances at three, winning the Prix de Royaumont. All Along is her fifth foal; the previous four included the very useful miler Abala (by Baldric II) and the successful French chaser Angel (by Faraway Son). The grandam Argosy, fourth over seven furlongs at Le Tremblay on her only start, produced two winners besides Agujita including the good middle-distance stayer Autre Prince, while the third dam foaled a total of seven winners on the Flat, six of them after being sent to Brazil.

A notably determined filly who is suited by a mile and a half and enterprising riding tactics, All Along may well stay in training. If so, and she makes normal progress, it doesn't require too vivid an imagination to see her running creditably in races like the Grand Prix de Saint-Cloud, run at a course where she remains unbeaten, and the King George VI and Queen Elizabeth Diamond Stakes, in both of which events the going is likely to be in her favour. *P.-L. Biancone, France.*

ALLAN WELLS 3 ch.g. Queen's Hussar 124–Baggage 86 (Zeus Boy 121) (1981 **51** d 5v 5g 5g 5d 5fg 7fg 7g* 7fg⁴ 7g 8fg 8.2d 7d 8d 1982 8g⁴ 10s 8f³ 7f 8g 7f 8.2g) compact gelding; plater; stays 1m; acts on firm going; usually wears blinkers; trained by T. Craig first 6 starts; sold 550 gns Doncaster October Sales. *M. H. Easterby.*

ALL BRONZE 2 ch.c. Cavo Doro 124–Bronze Princess 72 (Hul a Hul 124) **51** (1982 6g 5.1fg 8d 7.2s 10d) Mar 31; 900 2-y-o; small colt; first foal; dam won twice over 5f at 2 yrs; 8¼ lengths fifth of 24 to Miss Carine in 1m seller at Leicester in September, best effort; suited by 1m. *T. Bill.*

ALLERGIRL 2 ch.f. Some Hand 119–Sweet Illusion (Decoy Boy 129) (1982 **53** 5fg⁴ 5h² 5fg⁴) Apr 28; small, compact filly; first foal; dam never ran; poor plater; not raced after June; sold 390 gns Ascot October Sales. *P. Cole.*

ALLIED BEAUMEL 4 ch.f. Jimmy Reppin 131–Tarmandy (Black Tarquin — 136) (1981 8fg 8s 8g 8d 7fg⁴ 7f 1982 8fg 10.1g 8g 8s) compact filly; has shown a little ability; stays 1m. *S. Harris.*

ALLIED CARDIFF 4 b.f. Import 127–Monday Morning (Royal Record II) **35** (1981 6g 6g 7g³ 8f 8f 8f⁴ 7s 8s⁴ 8.2s² 1982 12fg 12.2g⁴ 12g³ 11g 12d) plater; in frame in non-sellers in 1982; stayed 1½m; went well on soft; wore blinkers; reportedly in foal to Cawston's Clown. *G. Blum.*

ALLIED KINGSWOOD 2 ro.g. Mandrake Major 122–Fair Jacqueline 79 — (Fortino II 120) (1982 6d) May 5; 5,000Y; compact, good-bodied gelding; poor walker; brother to fairly useful 1981 2-y-o 5f winner Major's Affair, and half-brother to 3 winners; dam 6f winner; unquoted and burly, always behind in 22-runner maiden race won by Foil'Em at Doncaster in October. *S. Harris.*

ALLIED LONDON 3 ch.c. Jimmy Reppin 131–Yoñ (Articulate 121) (1981 **57** 5d 5s 5f 6g 1982 7f³ 6f 6fg 8g) strong colt; plating-class maiden; best run at 7f on firm going. *J. Harris.*

ALLIGATRIX (USA) 2 b.f. Alleged 138–Shore (Round Table) (1982 6g⁴ **111** 7fg* 8fg³) May 14; small, close-coupled, quite attractive filly; half-sister to several minor winners in USA; dam, very useful at 2 yrs, won at up to 9f and is sister to very smart animals Cabildo and Canal; came through in good style after dwelling to win going away by a length from Clanrallier in 29-runner maiden race at Newmarket in August; easily bettered that effort in Hoover Fillies Mile at Ascot the following month, finishing 2¼ lengths third of 8 to Acclimatise after having every chance 1f out; stays well, and will be suited by 1¼m+; sure to win more races. *R. Armstrong.*

ALLI-RECO 4 ch.g. Record Run 127–Alli-Bee 57 (Violon d'Ingres) (1981 — NR 1982 9v) strong gelding; seems of little account. *F. Watson.*

ALL IS FORGIVEN 2 b.g. Mummy's Pet 125–Condonna 92 (Constable 119) **82** (1982 6fg 6fg 6g³ 6g 6f³ 6s) May 25; 10,000Y; well-grown, quite attractive gelding; half-brother to 2 winners, including fair 1981 2-y-o 5f winner Bonne Baiser (by Most Secret); dam 5f winner at 2 yrs; thought good enough to take part in Gimcrack Stakes at York on fourth outing, but ended season a maiden, and a disappointing one; beaten off modest marks in nurseries at Newmarket (favourite) and Haydock on last two appearances; has raced only at 6f but should prove effective at 5f; possibly best with give in the ground; sweated up badly second start and was on toes on fourth; gelded after final outing. *D. Thom.*

ALLODIUM 2 gr.g. Dragonara Palace 115–Pepperita 79 (Nelcius 133) (1982 — 6g 6g 7fg 8s) May 27; 5,600Y; compact, good-bodied gelding; fourth foal; brother to 7f and 1m winner Young Daniel and half-brother to another winner;

ALL

dam won over 7.6f at 2 yrs; soundly beaten, including in a £5,000 seller; gelded after final outing. *M. W. Easterby.*

ALL RISKS 3 b.f. Pitcairn 126–Willow Bird 74 (Weepers Boy 124) (1981 —
8fg 8d* 8g 1982 8.5fg 12.2g 10.6f 10.1fg 8s) rangy, attractive filly; stayed on bravely when winning maiden race at Wolverhampton in 1981; well beaten in handicaps at 3 yrs; not certain to stay 1½m; possibly needs some give in the ground; blinkered fourth start; sold 2,000 gns Newmarket December Sales. *P. Cole.*

ALL SEASONS 3 b.f. Silly Season 127–Little Rapide 90 (Rapace 130) (1981 —
NR 1982 10f 12.2f2 12fg 12.2f4) half-sister to fairly useful stayer Petit Pretendre (by Pretendre) and to a winner in USA; dam out-and-out stayer; plating-class maiden; suited by 1½m; bandaged near-hind final start; sold 1,000 gns Doncaster September Sales. *Miss S. Hall.*

ALL SYSTEMS GO 2 ch.c. Bay Express 132–Omnia 80 (Hill Clown) (1982 **119**
6fg2 6d* 7f* 7f* 7g* 7fg)
Gavin Pritchard-Gordon has in the past trained several pattern-race winners: Ardoon won both the Queen Anne Stakes and the Hungerford Stakes in 1976, Court Chad won the Hungerford the year before, Caporello the 1977 Ladbroke Derby Trial at Lingfield, and Record Run was successful in top races in France and Germany as well as winning the 1975 Prince of Wales Stakes. Surprisingly, though, Pritchard-Gordon had never trained a leading two-year-old until All Systems Go came to the fore in 1982.

All Systems Go first looked something out of the ordinary when tried over seven furlongs in the Friargate Stakes at York in July. He'd shaped well on both his previous starts, finishing second to Wassl in a valuable maiden race on Timeform Charity Day before winning in maiden company at Doncaster, but the well-bred Rare Event, successful on his only start, was preferred to him in the betting at York. The betting proved way off the mark; All Systems Go trounced Rare Event, bursting clear in a matter of strides inside the final quarter mile and winning by five lengths despite being eased well before the line. In the process All Systems Go lowered Water Mill's course record for two-year-olds by ·34 of a second.

Naturally All Systems Go had his sights raised afterwards. On his next appearance he took on six other useful winners in the Lanson Champagne Stakes at Goodwood at the end of July, starting co-second favourite behind the unbeaten Lyphard's Special from whom he received 6 lb. Another unbeaten colt, the Cock of the North Stakes winner Alchise, went off in front and maintained his lead until All Systems Go and Lyphard's Special took his measure with a furlong to run. The last two then fought out a splendid battle to the line, where All Systems Go, showing great determination, got the verdict by a head. Although not the best horse at weights carried, All Systems Go showed at Goodwood that he was still very much on the upgrade. He showed further improvement when favourite for the Seaton Delaval Stakes at Newcastle less than two weeks later. After Beldale Concorde had made the running for five furlongs All Systems Go quickened smoothly into a two-length lead and soon had the race sewn up. The strong-finishing Cause Celebre managed to cut back his advantage to half a length as he was eased close home. All Systems Go's progress came to an abrupt end in the Laurent Perrier Champagne Stakes at Doncaster. The betting suggested he was much the likeliest to test Gorytus but he put up a poor effort, trailing in last of five after being beaten by halfway. He was edgy in the paddock and reportedly at the stalls; no doubt he was past his best for the year.

		⎧ Polyfoto	⎧ Polic
	⎧ Bay Express	⎨ (br 1962)	⎩ Brabantia
	⎨ (b 1971)	⎩ Pal Sinna	⎧ Palestine
All Systems Go		(ch 1977)	⎩ Sinna
(ch.c. Mar 14, 1980)	⎨		⎧ Hillary
		⎧ Hill Clown	⎨ Mary Machree
	⎩ Omnia	⎨ (b 1963)	
	(ch 1973)	⎩ You All	⎧ Alcide
		(ch 1965)	⎩ Come On Honey

All Systems Go, a well-made, attractive colt, has proved a very shrewd buy; he cost only 6,200 guineas at the Newmarket Open Yearling Sales and has already won over £30,000, showing yet again that it's not essential to spend vast amounts to buy a good horse. Interestingly one of his joint-owners has bought eight horses in recent years and All Systems Go, the cheapest of the eight, is the first to win.

64

*Lanson Champagne Stakes, Goodwood—the strongly-ridden
All Systems Go battles on gamely to win from
Lyphard's Special (striped cap)*

Although a cheap yearling All Systems Go is by no means badly bred. He's the third foal and third winner bred by Omnia, following the Italian performer Mister Goldrake and the three-year-old stayer Royal Agnes, both of whom are by Royal Palace. Omnia won over a mile and a half and finished a game second, despite breaking down, when tried over a mile and three quarters.

Mr Arno Rudolf's "All Systems Go"

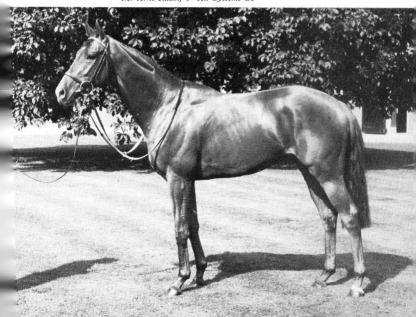

Had she remained sound Omnia would almost certainly have shown she stayed further: her sire Hill Clown's best representatives, May Hill, Mr Kildare and Popsi's Joy, all stayed well, and her dam, the winning Alcide filly You All, was a half-sister to both Attica Meli, who numbered the Doncaster Cup among her seven victories, and Royal Hive, the 1977 Park Hill winner who later finished a creditable second in the Gold Cup. Omnia's great-grandam, the One Thousand Guineas winner Honeylight, was a half-sister to Twilight Alley and Crepello.

All Systems Go is by that excellent five-furlong performer Bay Express. When two such different types are mated together the produce often takes exclusively after one parent. All Systems Go however seems to have inherited a measure of speed and stamina; he possesses an excellent turn of foot and gives the strong impression he'll stay a mile. His targets in the spring are said to be the Greenham Stakes and then the Guineas. Good, game colt though he is, he'll need to improve a fair bit to beat the likes of Diesis, Danzatore and Gorytus. His best performances so far have been on a sound surface but he also won on the only occasion he encountered ground softer than good. *G. Pritchard-Gordon.*

ALL THERE (USA) 3 gr.g. Al Hattab–Luring Dora (Lurullah) (1981 5s 5d — 6g 6d 1982 5d 5g) stocky, short-legged gelding; no worthwhile form; blinkered second start; sold 1,200 gns Ascot May Sales. *B. Swift.*

ALLURED 3 b.f. Decoy Boy 129–Charter Belle 60 (Runnymede 123) (1981 **60** NR 1982 7f 8s 7g 9.4f⁴ 9g 8g⁴ 8fg 8.2g* 10.6s) rangy filly; first foal; dam won 1¼m seller; attracted no bid after winning seller at Hamilton in September; promises to stay 1¼m; blinkered fifth start. *E. Weymes.*

ALLUVIA (FR) 2 br.c. Riverman 131–Alea II (Galivanter 131) (1982 6s³ **113** 7fg* 6.5d 7.5v³ 7s) Apr 7; 580,000 francs Y (approx £53,000); half-brother to several winners, notably high-class 7f to 1¼m winner Noalcoholic (by Nonoalco); dam won Italian 1,000 Guineas; won maiden race at Chantilly in July by 1½ lengths; ran creditably afterwards in pattern races, finishing 4 lengths fifth of 9 to Crystal Glitters in Prix Eclipse at Saint-Cloud, narrowly-beaten third of 9 behind Bal des Fees in Prix Thomas Bryon on same course and just over 3 lengths fifth of 16 to L'Emigrant (who gave 7 lb) in Criterium de Maisons-Laffitte; will be suited by 1m. *R. Collet, France.*

ALLVERTON (USA) 2 b.c. Alleged 138–Royal Honoree (Round Table) (1982 **115** 8f* 10v²) Apr 25; $200,000Y; second foal; half-brother to Irish St Leger runner-up Father Rooney (by Val de l'Orne); dam, winner 3 times at up to 6f, is sister to top 1972 French 2-y-o Targowice; put up a very pleasing first effort when winning 5-runner Prix de Villebon (newcomers event) at Longchamp in September, scoring by a neck from Northern Fashion after being last early on: headed Nile Hawk 1½f out in Prix de Conde on same course the following month but failed by a short head to hold that colt's renewed challenge; will stay 1½m; smart. *F. Boutin, France.*

ALLYANZA 2 ro.f. Swing Easy 126–Sunny Sovereign 85 (Lucky Sovereign) **68** (1982 5fg 5fg 6g 5fg* 6f 5g⁴ 5g*) May 22; 2,400F, 1,100Y; rather sparely-made filly; third foal; half-sister to winning stayer Rising Fast (by High Line); dam 5f sprinter; won seller (bought in 2,100 gns) at Hamilton in July and nursery on same course in September; apparently best at 5f; has raced only on a sound surface; none too well away second and third starts. *P. Rohan.*

ALLYA (USA) 3 gr.f. Little Current–Harrapan Seal 117 (Habitat 134) (1981 — 7g 7f 7fg 7d³ 7g 1982 8d 8.2s 8s) neat filly; only plating class on balance of form; best run at 7f on a soft surface; blinkered final start. *H. T. Jones.*

ALMA ATA (FR) 2 b.f. Rheffic 129–Autorin (Orsini 124) (1982 7.5d* 8s 8s) **111** lengthy filly; sixth foal; half-sister to winners in Germany and France; dam German; ran out an impressive winner of newcomers race at Saint-Cloud in September, coming home 6 lengths clear of Maewo; fifth in pattern races at Longchamp the following month, being beaten only 2¼ lengths by Goodbye Shelley in Prix Marcel Boussac and ¾ lengths by Belka in Prix des Reservoirs; will be suited by middle distances. *M. Zilber, France.*

ALMA-CANDY 2 b.c. Tudor Music 131–Autumn Glory (Silly Season 127) — (1982 6v 8s) May 12; IR 7,600Y; third foal; dam, granddaughter of 1,000 Guineas winner Abermaid, was fourth twice over 1¼m in Ireland; well beaten in maiden events at Folkestone (last of 9) in October and Leicester in November. *J. Bethell.*

AL NASR 4 b.c. Green Dancer 132–Padrona 103 (St Paddy 133) (1981 10.2f **§§** 14g²(dis) 14g² 14fg* 18.8fg³ 14fg² 16g³ 14s² 16s 1982 12.2d² 13f 14fg³ 12f³

12g 12.2s 12s) rangy, good-looking colt; stays very well; probably acts on any going; has been tried in blinkers; has ability but is ungenuine and not to be relied upon. *J. Benstead.*

AL NASR (FR)   4 b.c. Lyphard 132–Caretta (Caro 133)   (1981 11g* 10v* 12d **126** 10g² 10f*   1982 10s* 10v² 10.5g³ 9.7fg* 9.2g* 10f)

    The decision to keep Al Nasr in training as a four-year-old paid off handsomely. It would have been no surprise to have seen him retired to stud upon injuring an ankle on the gallops during his preparation for the 1981 Prix de l'Arc de Triomphe, especially as a quarter share in him was sold to Spendthrift Farm shortly afterwards. At that time he had four wins under his belt, including Group Three successes in the Prix La Force and the Prix de la Cote Normande, and with Lyphard for his sire his future at stud was probably already assured. Three more wins as a four-year-old will have considerably enhanced his value as a stallion though, particularly as one of them was gained in a Group One event, the Prix d'Ispahan at Longchamp.

    Al Nasr ran badly in the Derby on his only outing over here. He trailed in last but one behind Shergar, never having gone well, whereas on his best form he'd probably have been in the frame. Al Nasr's record in France is most impressive—seven wins and three placings from ten starts—and he was better than ever as a four-year-old. His high-class performance in the Ispahan on his last outing in France crowned his career there. He had only five opponents, one of which was his pacemaker Mourtazam; nevertheless he faced a stiff task against the 1981 d'Ispahan winner The Wonder, whom he had beaten narrowly on terms far more favourable in the Prix Dollar, and the Poulains winner Melyno who had been tremendously impressive in the Prix Jean Prat on his last outing. Al Nasr raced in second place behind Mourtazam until slightly outpaced when things hotted up turning for home. The Wonder looked the likely winner at one stage, taking over from Melyno a furlong and a half or so from home, but Al Nasr worked his way through on the far rails and wore him down in the last furlong. Al Nasr finished much the best and beat The Wonder by three quarters of a length with Melyno a neck away third.

    In the Prix Dollar, also at Longchamp, Al Nasr had received 6 lb from The Wonder and had beaten him by a neck, a little more easily in fact than the bare result suggests. His other win, in the Prix Exbury at Saint-Cloud on his reappearance, was gained without any fuss: he outclassed his six opponents and landed the odds very easily from Mbaiki. In Al Nasr's other two runs in France he was placed in the Prix d'Harcourt and the Prix Ganay, both at Longchamp in the spring. In the Harcourt he went down by a neck to Lancastrian in a field of four; he seemed to have every chance although reportedly he lost a shoe. In the Ganay he never threatened to get on terms with all-the-way winner Bikala but snatched third from Vayrann in the last strides.

Al Nasr (Fr) (b.c. 1978)	Lyphard (b 1969)	Northern Dancer (b 1961)	Nearctic Natalma
		Goofed (ch 1960)	Court Martial Barra II
	Caretta (b 1973)	Caro (gr 1967)	Fortino II Chambord
		Klainia (b 1960)	Klafron Kalitka

    Al Nasr was aimed at some of the major turf races in the United States in the second half of the season and was intended to run in the Budweiser Million, the Turf Classic and the Washington International. He was sent over to Chicago five weeks before the Million and given a thorough preparation by all accounts—

Prix d'Ispahan, Longchamp—Al Nasr beats The Wonder again;
Melyno is third, Big John fourth

trainer Fabre flew over six times before the race to supervise. Unfortunately though, for the second time in his career Al Nasr palpably failed to do himself justice. After chasing long-time leader Motavato he weakened quickly on the home turn and trailed in a remote thirteenth of fourteen behind Perrault. Al Nasr was subsequently found to have once again injured an ankle and news of his retirement followed shortly afterwards.

Al Nasr has been syndicated, for a reported eight million dollars, and is to stand at Spendthrift Farm, Kentucky, at a fee of 40,000 dollars, live foal. His sire Lyphard, also standing in the States now, has had a host of high-class runners and in 1982 commanded a stud fee of 150,000 dollars (almost £90,000)—one of the highest in the world. The dam Caretta, whose first foal Al Nasr is, won twice at up to eleven furlongs in the French Provinces. The next dam Klainia, a daughter of the 1957 Prix de Diane second Kalitka, was a useful winner over five furlongs as a two-year-old and has produced numerous other winners, including the smart middle-distance colts Kebah and L'Ensorceleur and the very speedy Klaizia, winner of the Prix du Gros-Chene; Klaizia is herself the dam of the smart Lyphard colt Lypheor who is now at stud.

Al Nasr should do well in his new career. His fashionable pedigree and sound racing record are complemented by his looks—he's a strong, good sort who often impressed in appearance. Al Nasr was a genuine sort, capable of giving his running from nine to eleven furlongs regardless of the state of the ground. He was well handled by his trainer who had hitherto been best known as a trainer of jumpers. *A. Fabre, France.*

ALOA (USA) 3 b.g. Hawaii–C'mon Up (On-and-On) (1981 7g 8g 8.2s 1982 10s) rangy gelding; little worthwhile form, including in a seller; blinkered final start at 2 yrs. *A. Moore.*

ALOE (USA) 3 b.f. Silent Screen–Turning Bold (Turn-to) (1981 7d 6d* 1982 6fg²(dis) 8d³ 6fg² 8v) $275,000Y; third foal; half-sister to Explosivo (by Delta Judge), a very useful stakes winner at up to 1m; dam, stakes-placed winner at up to 7f, is out of half-sister to Red God; placed in Seven Springs Sprint Stakes at the Curragh in July (disqualified after going down by a length to Bruckner), Gilltown Stud Stakes on same course in September (respectable 4½ lengths third of 12 to Mary Mitsu) and Carna Fillies' Stakes at Naas later in September (length second to Molly); stays 1m; acts on a firm and a soft surface. *V. O'Brien, Ireland.* **97**

ALPHA-EL-GRECO 3 gr.g. Abwah 118–Eurolink (Current Coin 118) (1981 5g 5f 7fg 7fg 8.2fg 6fg 6s 1982 10.8fg 7fg 8.2g 7g 9f 7f 7d) small, strong gelding; poor plater; has worn blinkers. *S. Wiles.*

ALPHA OMEGA 3 b.g. Auction Ring 123–Hey Dolly (Saint Crespin III 132) (1981 5s 5s³ 5s³ 5fg⁴ 6s² 7fg 7f 8d 8s 1982 10s² 12s² 12f* 12.3fg* 12f² 12f³ 16fg 12.3d³ 11.7g² 11.5g² 13s² 12v⁴ 12g) workmanlike gelding; good mover; kept on strongly to win handicaps at Ripon in April and at Chester in May; ran respectably most subsequent starts; stays 13f (out of his depth over 2m in Queen's Vase at Royal Ascot); acts on any going but goes well on firm ground; suited by front-running tactics; blinkered once at 2 yrs; genuine and consistent. *R. Williams.* **82**

ALPINE AIR 2 br.g. Sparkler 130–Argitone (Aureole 132) (1982 7fg 7fg 8s) May 4; half-brother to 2 winners, including useful 1974 2-y-o Sassari (by Sassafras); dam unraced daughter of Park Hill winner Collyria; behind in maiden races; gelded after final outing. *J. Cann.* **—**

ALPINE GREAT 2 br.f. Great Nephew 126–Kanvita (Home Guard 129) (1982 5fg⁴ 5g 6f 7g) Apr 4; tall, leggy, rather narrow filly; second foal; dam never ran; ran poorly after finishing fourth in Newmarket maiden in April; should stay 7f. *F. J. Houghton.* **63**

ALPINE ROCKET 5 ch.g. Shiny Tenth 120–Dusty Bluebell (Sky Gipsy 117) (1981 6s 6fg² 6g 6s 6g 6fg 6g³ 6f 6fg 6fg 6f 6fg 6fg 6g² 6fg* 6g 6s* 6s 1982 6d 5g 6g 6f³ 6fg 7fg) lengthy, useful sort; sprint handicapper; best at 6f; acts on any going but is ideally suited by top-of-the-ground; usually wears blinkers; suitable mount for a boy; missed break second outing; sold 640 gns Newmarket Autumn Sales, probably for export to Scandinavia. *D. H. Jones.* **76**

ALPINE SILK 2 b.f. Malinowski 123–Shortia (Shantung 132) (1982 7d 7g) Jan 18; IR 9,400Y; small filly; fifth foal; dam placed over 10.5f and 1¾m in French Provinces on only starts; well beaten in October in minor event at Doncaster and maiden race at Newmarket. *G. Pritchard-Gordon.* **—**

ALPINE WAY 3 gr.c. Dragonara Palace 115–Country Ramble 93 (Kribi **67**
110) (1981 NR 1982 7g² 12fg³ 9s* 12.2d⁴ 8g 12d⁴) short-coupled colt; fourth
reported foal; half-brother to fairly useful middle-distance performer Country
Walk (by Warpath); dam staying sister to very useful Farm Walk; showed
improved form when accounting for Bombshell by 2½ lengths in minor event
at Newcastle in October; possibly doesn't stay 1½m; acts well on soft going.
J. Calvert.

ALTERED STATE 2 gr.c. Godswalk 130–Attitude 116 (Gratitude 130) —
(1982 6f 7g 7fg 7fg) May 11; 9,400Y; big, strong, attractive colt; half-brother
to several winners, including very useful 1970 2-y-o 6f winner Outlook (by
Ballymoss) and fairly useful 7f and 1m winner Rectitude (by Runnymede);
dam smart 2-y-o sprinter; little show in maiden races at Newbury (2), Sandown
and Salisbury; sold BBA 3,000 gns Newmarket Autumn Sales. *R. Laing.*

AL TRUI 2 gr.c. Scottish Rifle 127–Sweety Grey (Young Emperor 133) (1982 **91**
5.1g⁴ 5f* 5g* 5g³ 5d⁴ 5f* 5v²) May 19; small, compact colt; first living foal;
dam ran once; ran well in nurseries after winning seller at Folkestone in July
(bought in 2,600 gns), gaining further successes at Windsor and Edinburgh;
will stay 6f; acts on any going; suitable mount for an apprentice; genuine and
consistent. *W. Musson.*

ALUWHITE HABIT 3 b.c. Hittite Glory 125–Tritonia 69 (Tyrant) (1981 —
6g 1982 7d 8.2fg 7f 8fg 8.2s 6s 7s 7s) quite an attractive colt; has a round
action; well beaten in varied company, including selling; sometimes sweats
up. *W. Holden.*

ALVOR (GER) 3 b.c. Lombard 126–Agora (Pantheon) (1981 7g* 7s² 7g **102**
1982 10.4fg 12fg* 12fg³ 14fg 12fg) lengthy, rather lightly-made colt; got first
run in slowly-run £3,700 event at Beverley in June and kept on strongly to
hold off Boxberger Speed by ¾ length; put up easily best subsequent effort
when 5¼ lengths third of 5 to Lyphmas in Churchill Stakes at Ascot later in
month; suited by middle distances; seems to act on any going. *M. Stoute.*

AL WASHL (USA) 2 b.f. The Minstrel 135–Velvet Flight (Stevward) (1982 **79**
5fg² 6h² 6fg² 6d²) Feb 16; $800,000Y; leggy, quite attractive filly; has a round
action; second foal; dam, winner of 5 sprint races, is half-sister to 3 stakes
winners, including smart Sweet Little Lady, successful at up to 7f; placed in
modest maiden company, on final outing starting 11/2 on when beaten 3 lengths
by sole-opponent Dollar Darling at Nottingham in September; will stay beyond
6f; possibly not at her best on a soft surface. *H. T. Jones.*

ALWAYS EIRLYS 4 ch.f. Toujours Pret 121–Eirlys 90 (Elopement 125)
(1981 7g 8g 8s² 8s* 10.6s* 10.2d 8f 10f³ 12.3s 12fg 1982 10f) rangy filly;
stays 1½m; acts on any going, but is well suited by soft; often apprentice ridden;
sometimes starts slowly; sold privately 1,900 gns Doncaster May Sales. *N.
Callaghan.*

ALWAYS WELCOME 3 b.c. Be My Guest 126–I'll Be Here (Ambiopoise) **91**
(1981 NR 1982 8fg* 10.4g 8fg 10.6g³ 10fg²) IR 36,000F, 56,000Y; strong,
medium-sized, quite attractive colt; fourth foal; half-brother to 3 winners,
including 1980 French 2-y-o 8.5f winner Prunheco (by Bustino); dam, winner
of claiming races at up to 1m in USA, is half-sister to successful broodmare
Peace; beat Top Lady by a neck in 19-runner Wood Ditton Stakes at Newmarket in April; placed in handicaps at Haydock and Sandown (blinkered)
afterwards; stays 1¼m well; sent to Hong Kong. *M. Jarvis.*

ALYS 2 b.f. Blakeney 126–Bessie Wallis 106 (Prince de Galles 125) (1982 — p
6fg) Mar 15; lengthy, attractive filly; second foal; dam won over 7f and
1¼m; 14/1 and decidedly green, soon chased along after missing break when
behind in 20-runner maiden race won by Linklighter at Salisbury in September;
will probably need 1¼m+; should improve; to be trained by J. Pease in France.
P. Walwyn.

ALZAO (USA) 2 b.c. Lyphard 132–Lady Rebecca (Sir Ivor 135) (1982 9s* **110** p
8v*) Feb 28; third foal; half-brother to 3-y-o Faenza (by Forli); dam, half-
sister to top-class American colts Tom Rolfe and Chieftain, was very useful
French middle-distance winner; successful twice in October, winning newcomers
event at Evry in good style by 2½ lengths and then making all to win 70,000-
franc event at Maisons-Laffitte by a length from Jabal Tarik; will make a very
useful middle-distance colt. *F. Boutin, France.*

AMANDA MARY 4 b.f. Wishing Star 117–Marchpane (Parthia 132) (1981 **39**
6g 8fg 5f 6fg⁴ 6g³ 7fg³ 6d² 7s⁴ 6v 6g 6d 1982 6fg 5f 7f 6f² 6f² 6fg 6g 7f⁴ 8.2s
8.2v⁴) lengthy filly; plater; stays 7f; acts on any going, but goes well on firm;

ungenuine, and usually wears blinkers; usually bandaged nowadays; trained until after seventh start by W. Stubbs. *Mrs A. Cousins.*

AMANZI 2 b.f. African Sky 124–Azurn (Klairon 131) (1982 6g 5f² 5fg* 5g³ 6d) Apr 10; sister to good 1978 Italian 2-y-o Nosy Be, and half-sister to several winners, including very useful sprinter Touch Paper (by Roan Rocket); dam half-sister to Blue Wind; made all to win 7-runner maiden race at Leopardstown in August by 3 lengths from Director General; ran well under top weight in nursery at the Curragh later in month, finishing 1¼ lengths third to Lady Earn, but finished only tenth of 15 behind Habibti in Moyglare Stud Stakes on same course the following month; should stay 6f; acts on firm going; fell on debut. *J. Oxx, Ireland.* — 94

AMARACH 4 ch.g. Deep Run 119–Irish Halo (Macherio) (1981 NR 1982 13.8f) half-brother to 7f and 1¼m winner St Rioch's Boy (by Richboy) and a bumpers winner; dam won over 1½m in Ireland; winning hurdler; held up when respectable sixth of 17 behind Blakey Bank in maiden race at Catterick in May, first outing on flat. *R. Fisher.* — —

AMARONE 2 b.c. Realm 129–Misacre 66 (St Alphage 119) (1982 5d* 5fg³ 5f⁴ 5f 7f² 6fg 7v 8.2s) Feb 24; well-made, quite attractive colt; has a round action; second reported foal; won 10-runner minor event at Folkestone in March by 7 lengths from Another Risk; ran consistently afterwards until failing to show off stiffish marks in nurseries on last three appearances; stays 7f; acts on firm going and a soft surface; blinkered sixth outing. *R. Simpson.* — 82

AMAROO 4 ch.f. Bonne Noel 115–Ebullient (Darius 129) (1981 NR 1982 12d 7fg 8f) fourth reported foal; half-sister to minor French 1¼m winner Huso Huso (by Welsh Saint); dam Irish 7f winner; little worthwhile form, including in sellers. *J. O'Donoghue.* — —

AMAZON PRINCE (USA) 2 b. or br.c. Native Royalty–Bright n'Gay (Citation) (1982 6g 6fg 7fg² 7s³) Apr 9; $80,000Y; useful sort; half-brother to numerous winners, including very smart Happy Intellectual (by Wolfram), a stakes winner at up to 9f and subsequently a leading jumper; dam placed at 2 yrs; came to himself steadily, and on last two outings finished good second in maiden event at Salisbury in September and creditable third under 9-7 in well-contested nursery at Doncaster in November; will stay 1¼m; should win a small race. *G. Hunter.* — 95

AMBERATION 2 ch.f. Continuation 120–Amber Anne (Amber X 133) (1982 5f⁴ 6fg 6f 8d) Apr 3; leggy, sparely-made filly; bad plater; blinkered fourth outing; sold 310 gns Doncaster October Sales. *J. Hardy.* — —

AMBER BAY 2 b.g. Orange Bay 131–Amber Flyer 91 (Amber Rama 133) (1982 5fg² 5fg² 5fg 7fg) 1,000Y; tall, lengthy, leggy gelding; second live foal; dam 2-y-o 5f winner; second in May in maiden auction races at Salisbury and Brighton; not seen out after July, and was subsequently gelded. *R. Hoad.* — 63

AMBER PALACE 4 ch.f. Sallust 134–Breide's Wood (Le Levanstell 122) (1981 5fg 6s⁴ 6g 1982 8g 6g) only plating class; runs as though 5f is her trip; sold 800 gns Ascot August Sales. *J. Yardley.* — —

AMBER RAMBLER 3 b.c. Scottish Rifle 127–Jackie's Joy (Skymaster 126) (1981 NR 1982 14.6g 12.3g 14fg 13.5d) big colt; has a round action; half-brother to several winners, including fairly useful middle-distance winners Amber Vale (by Warpath) and Amber Valley (by Forlorn River); dam well beaten all outings; in rear in maiden races and a seller in the North. *J. Hanson.* — —

AMBERUSH 5 ch.m. No Rush–Amberdonna 52 (Amber Rama 133) (1981 7fg 10d 12f⁴ 12g 12g 1982 17.1f 12fg) plater; stays 1½m. *P. Ashworth.* — —

AMBER VALE 5 gr.m. Warpath 113–Jackie's Joy (Skymaster 126) (1981 10.6d 12d 11g 9g 12s 12g 1982 10d 12f 10f 8.2g 12f⁴ 12f² 12f² 10g³ 9g 10fg 10d 11f 8fg 8s) rangy mare; mainly disappointing since 1980 but was placed in small handicaps in summer; stays 1½m; probably acts on any going; blinkered sixth to ninth outings; none too genuine. *D. Chapman.* — 58

AMBER WIND 2 ch.g. Tumble Wind–Super Amber (Yellow God 129) (1982 5f 5f³ 5f* 5d 5g) May 5; 6,200Y; leggy, narrow gelding; third foal; closely related to 1981 2-y-o 5f performer Super Natalie (by On Your Mark) and half-brother to a winning plater; dam never ran; won maiden race at Folkestone in August by ½ length from Sable Princess; transferred from A. Jarvis' stable afterwards, and was in rear in nurseries subsequently, wearing blinkers final start; clearly considered a 5f performer but is bred to stay further; gelded after last outing. *M. Blanshard.* — 71

AMBER WINDSOR 2 ch.f. Windjammer (USA)–Rose Amber (Amber Rama — 133) (1982 7d 7g) May 28; 1,600Y; fair sort; fourth foal; dam ran twice; well beaten in October in maiden race at Leicester and mixed-aged event (moved badly to post) at Newmarket. *N. Callaghan.*

AMBIANCE 3 gr.c. Three Legs 128–Ambient 68 (Amber Rama 133) (1981 **94** 7g 7d⁴ 1982 8s² 9g⁴ 10f* 12f² 12g* 12f 12fg* 12f 14fg⁴ 12.5g⁴) compact, useful-looking colt; good walker; fairly useful performer; won minor event at Brighton and handicaps at Newbury, Kempton and Carlisle; fourth to Broken Rail in Melrose Handicap at York in August and to Ataxerxes (beaten only about a length) in Grote Prijs der Nederlanden at Duindigt in September; stays 1¾m; acts on any going; blinkered sixth start. *M. Jarvis.*

AMBIAN HILL (FR) 3 b.c. Dancer's Image–Joe's Florence (Quadrangle) — (1981 NR 1982 8s) 4,400F, 8,400Y; half-brother to Household Word (by Pan Dancer), a winner of 10 sprint races in USA, including claiming events; dam won over 6f at 3 yrs in USA; unquoted when staying-on sixth of 15 to Bold Hawk, beaten about 12 lengths, in minor event at Warwick in October; sold 15,000 gns Newmarket Autumn Sales and is to be trained by M. O'Toole. *T. Robson.*

AMBOSELLI 2 b.f. Raga Navarro 119–Late Spring 101 (Silly Season 127) **73** p (1982 5g³) May 16; smallish, rather lightly-made filly; half-sister to 4 winners, notably Spindrifter (by Sandford Lad), winner of 13 races at 2 yrs and successful at up to 9f; dam won twice over 5f at 2 yrs; 7/1, shaped promisingly when 5 lengths third of 20 to Ike's Mistress in maiden race at Beverley in August, staying on nicely without being knocked about; will be suited by 6f. *Sir Mark Prescott.*

AMEGHINO 2 gr.g. So Blessed 130–Maruka 70 (Abernant 142) (1982 5.8f³ **95** 5.8f* 6f³ 6d³ 6g⁴) Mar 19; half-brother to 2 winners, including sprinter Rosellio (by Roan Rocket); dam won over 5f at 2 yrs; won 10-runner maiden race at Bath in June by 3 lengths from Maritime England; off course nearly 3 months after next start but ran well in nurseries on return, finishing 4½ lengths fourth of 16 to Prince Spy at Newmarket in October on final appearance; runs as though 7f will suit him; seems to act on any going; genuine and consistent; sold M. McCourt 20,000 gns Newmarket Autumn Sales and subsequently gelded. *J. Dunlop.*

AMELIA HOWARD 2 ch.f. Lepanto–Etoile de Ville (Shoolerville 121) (1982 — 7f 7f 7fg 7d 7g) May 10; sparely-made filly; in rear in valuable seller and maiden races; blinkered third start; of no account. *G. Blum.*

AMENDOLA 2 br.f. Ercolano 118 Crab Apple (Nelcius 133) (1982 7d 7g) **71** Mar 22; big, rangy, useful sort; fourth foal; half-sister to disappointing 3-y-o Growing Wild (by Free State); dam unraced daughter of very useful 1962 2-y-o Tzigane; unquoted and bit backward, ran on steadily when 7¼ lengths sixth of 15 to Miss Bali Beach in maiden race at Leicester in October, first outing and better effort; will be suited by 1¼m+. *R. Baker.*

AMENITY (FR) 3 b.f. Luthier 126–Almyre (Wild Risk) (1981 NR 1982 **76** 7fg 10.4fg* 10.1fg² 8f 11.7s) tall, attractive filly; good mover; sister to high-class middle-distance stayer Ashmore and 1¾m winner Abordage, and half-sister to several winners, notably very smart middle-distance filly Acoma (by Rheffic); dam very useful winner at up to 13f; favourite, showed signs of greenness when holding off strong-finishing Bundu by ¾ length in 11-runner maiden race at Chester in July; needs further than 1m and should be suited by 1¼m+; sold 66,000 gns Newmarket December Sales. *H. Cecil.*

AMERICAN BOY 2 gr.c. Yankee Gold 115–Mollies First 59 (Songedor 116) **78** (1982 5fg 5fg 7g 7fg⁴ 7fg⁴ 7f³ 7g 8fg³ 7g⁴ 8g²) Apr 25; 1,200Y; workmanlike colt; half-brother to several winners here and abroad; dam won at up to 11f; in frame in several races, on final occasion finishing very strongly when ½-length second of 11 to Triple Jump in £2,900 seller at Newmarket in October; will be well suited by 1¼m; has raced only on a sound surface; consistent. *W. Marshall.*

AMERICAN GIRL 3 b. or br.f. Yankee Gold 115–Grannys Whistle (Whistling **70** Wind 123) (1981 7f 1982 8fg 8fg 8.5f⁴ 8g 10.1fg 10.1fg⁴ 10.1d² 12v² 10s²) leggy, lengthy, shallow-girthed filly; runner-up in varied company; suited by 1½m; suited by some give in the ground; has run respectably when sweating up; trained by T. Marshall first 2 starts. *H. O'Neill.*

AMERICAN MINSTREL (USA) 2 b.c. The Minstrel 135–American Legacy **81** (Hail to Reason) (1982 7f 7d³ 7s) Mar 27; $100,000Y; tall, rather narrow colt; second foal; closely related to modest 3-y-o Czar's Bride (by Northern Dancer); dam, unplaced 5 times, is half-sister to top-class filly and broodmare

Fanfreluche; nearest finish when 3 lengths third of 14 behind Bold and Woolly in maiden race at Leicester in September, best effort; will be suited by 1m+. *R. Sheather.*

AMERICAN STRESS (USA) 2 b.c. Sham–Stresa (Mill Reef 141) (1982 5g* **114** 5g* 5.5g⁴ 7.5v) Mar 7; 1,000,000 francs Y (approx £91,000); first foal; dam, half-sister to very smart animals Antrona and Terreno, won over 1¼m in France; won newcomers event at Chantilly in June and was awarded Group 3 Prix du Bois at Longchamp later in month after going down by 2 lengths to Deep Roots; ran well when about 2¼ lengths fourth of 9 to Ma Biche in Prix Robert Papin at Maisons-Laffitte the following month but was then off course until October when 10 lengths seventh of 9 to Bal des Fees in Prix Thomas Bryon at Saint-Cloud; should be well suited by 1m+; possibly unsuited by heavy going. *F. Palmer, France.*

AMERICK 2 ch.c. High Line 125–Paripan (Pardao 120) (1982 7fg) Apr 18; **74 p** 6,200F, 50,000Y; rangy colt; brother to useful 1977 2-y-o 1m winner Economy Drive and to a disappointing maiden; dam never ran; 33/1, ran on steadily without being knocked about when about 9 lengths seventh of 12 to stable-companion Zoffany in minor event at Goodwood in September; will be suited by 1¼m+; sure to do better. *G. Harwood.*

AMERICUS 3 ch.c. Sallust 134–Cat O'Mountaine (Ragusa 137) (1981 6f* **110** 6.3fg² 6.3fg 7d 5g* 5d* 1982 8g 5f 5d4 5g² 5s* 5v³) IR 182,000Y; brother to 2,000 Guineas winner Tap On Wood, and half-brother to 2 winners, including Piping Rock (by Tudor Music), a useful winner from 6f to 9f in Ireland and a good winner in Malaya; dam, half-sister to high-class stayer Bounteous, won over middle distances in Ireland and France; gained second successive win in MacDonagh and Boland Waterford Testimonial Stakes at the Curragh in October, accounting for Mink Goddess by 2 lengths (odds on); also in frame at the Curragh again in Stackallen Stakes (fourth to Royal Hobbit) and Philips Electrical Stakes (Handicap) (neck second to Sweet Side) and in Premio Omenoni at Milan (about a length third to Sun Shines); best at sprint distances; acts on any going; racing in California. *V. O'Brien, Ireland.*

AMIGO ALEGRE 2 ch.c. Great Nephew 126–Pardina 98 (Pardao 120) (1982 — 6fg) Apr 15; 8,000Y; half-brother to several winners here and abroad, including fair 1979 2-y-o 5f winner Swinford Rose (by Upper Case); dam won from 6f to 1¼m; unquoted when behind in 20-runner minor event won by Indian Rajah at Lingfield in September. *P. K. Mitchell.*

AMILA 2 gr.f. Great Nephew 126–Allara (Zeddaan 130) (1982 7.2s*) Apr 4; **89 p** wiry filly; third foal; half-sister to French 3-y-o 9f winner Anilal (by Huntercombe); dam, closely related to Nishapour, won small 7f race in France; easy in market but fit, led approaching last furlong and kept on well despite edging slightly left when winning 9-runner minor event at Haydock in October by ¾ length from Gloria Mundi; will probably stay 1¼m. *M. Stoute.*

AMILLE 2 ch.f. Anax 120–Omi (Hopeful Venture 125) (1982 6fg 7g) Mar 28; — first foal; dam poor maiden; behind in September in maiden race at Salisbury (last of 20) and £4,500 event at Newbury. *M. McCormack.*

AMIRS DRUM 5 b.h. Meldrum 112–Take a Chance 107 (Rockefella) (1981 — NR 1982 5f) fair (rated 85) at 2 yrs; has run only twice on flat since; should stay 1m+. *N. Tinkler.*

AMORATA (USA) 2 b.f. Nordic Prince–Our Taska (Our Native) (1982 5f⁴ 6g **63** 8.2s 7s) May 7; $50,000Y; rather leggy, narrow filly; first foal; dam ran only once; sire, son of Nearctic, was smart winner at up to 1m; plating-class maiden; seems to stay 1m. *S. Norton.*

AMOROUS 4 b.g. Mummy's Pet 125–Maxim's 88 (Major Portion 129) (1981 7g **82** 7g 6f 6fg 6f 6g 1982 7s 8d 6g² 6fg² 6f⁴ 6g* 6fg 6f² 6f* 6f 6f³ 6g 7fg 5s 5s) lightly-made, leggy gelding; ran better than in 1981 and readily won handicaps at Leicester in June and Nottingham in July; placed on several other occasions; suited by 6f; acts well on firm going; blinkered final start in 1981; behaved rather mulishly before fourth outing. *M. McCourt.*

AMPERSAND (USA) 2 b.f. Stop the Music–Quicksand (Mill Reef 141) (1982 **79** 5f² 5g⁴ 5g 7g³ 7d³) Feb 5; short-backed, quite attractive filly; first foal; dam once-raced half-sister to smart 1m and 1¼m winner Leap Lively; in frame in a variety of races, on final occasion finishing in good style when 1¼ lengths third of 14 to Zariya in minor event at Catterick in October; better suited by 7f than 5f and will stay at least 1m. *I. Balding.*

AMPHITHEATRE 2 ch.f. Relkino 131–Drury Lane 83 (Gala Performance) **90** p
(1982 7g²) May 30; lengthy, useful-looking filly; half-sister to 2 winning
platers, including 1980 2-y-o 6f winner Supreme Show (by Supreme Sovereign);
dam won over 1m; 33/1, stayed on well after taking time to warm up when 1½
lengths second of 21 to Ski Sailing in maiden event at Newmarket in October;
will stay 1¼m; should improve and win a race. *M. Jarvis.*

AMRULLAH 2 br.g. High Top 131–Ravenshead (Charlottown 127) (1982 7g **70** p
8g 8s) May 20; 80,000Y; big, strong, good sort; walks and moves well; fourth
foal; half-brother to very useful 1981 staying 2-y-o Ashenden (by Blakeney);
dam poor half-sister to smart sprinter Nevermore; not seen out until late in
season, and ran best race when 11 lengths seventh of 21 behind Rock's Gate in
maiden event at Leicester in November on final appearance; will stay 1¼m.
G. Harwood.

AMSAM 4 b. or br.f. Prince de Galles 125–Lovage (Linacre 133) (1981 8s 8s³ —
7v 1982 7g³ 6g 10f 10fg 8f 10f 6g) narrow, light-framed filly; plater; stays 1m;
sold 750 gns Doncaster August Sales. *A. Smith.*

AMY LOUISE 2 b.f. Le Johnstan 123–Walshaw Minnie 62 (Nice Music 115) —
(1982 5f 5g) first foal; but one and last in maiden
races at Catterick and Hamilton in August. *E. Alston.*

AMYNDAS 4 b.c. Sparkler 130–Gem of Gems 106 (Grey Sovereign 128§) (1981 **118**
12g* 12g² 10.5s* 10.5g* 12fg⁴ 10d⁴ 10g³ 1982 12fg² 12fg³ 10f³ 12f 12f² 12g*
10.5fg³ 12d 10d) strong, compact, attractive colt; not quite so good as in 1981,
when successful 3 times and third in Champion Stakes, but was nevertheless
smart on his day; put up best efforts when neck second to Glint of Gold in John
Porter Stakes at Newbury, about ¾-length third behind Ardross and Glint of Gold
in Jockey Club Stakes at Newmarket, 2 lengths second of 4 to Height of Fashion
in Princess of Wales's Stakes at Newmarket again, and about 6 lengths third of 7

Mrs H. G. Cambanis' "Amyndas"

to Assert in Benson and Hedges Gold Cup at York; gained only success of season when beating Palace Gold by a neck in 5-runner £5,300 event at Lingfield in August; didn't have best of runs fourth start and ran disappointingly last 2; stays 1½m; acts on any going; often gets a bit stirred up in preliminaries. *B. Hobbs.*

ANA GABRIELLA (USA) 3 ch.f. Master Derby–Overland (Sir Gaylord)   —
(1981 NR 1982 9s) $105,000Y; smallish, workmanlike filly; poor mover; third foal; half-sister to 2 minor winners; dam won 6f claiming race; 20/1 when tailed-off last of 15 to Mill Queen in maiden race at York in October. *R. Boss.*

ANATOLIAN ELF 3 b.f. Hittite Glory 125–La Mome 109 (Princely Gift 137)   —
(1981 6fg 1982 10fg 7f 8d 6f 8f 6g 7f) tall, close-coupled filly; poor plater; has been tried in blinkers. *R. Hannon.*

ANCAT 2 b.c. Lochnager 132–Bovick 75 (Compensation 127) (1982 5fg 6d)   **70**
Apr 15; strong, good-bodied colt; second foal; dam won sellers from 6f to 1¼m; backward, showed signs of ability in minor event at Beverley in August and maiden race at Doncaster in October; may improve. *M. W. Easterby.*

ANCESTRAL 2 b.c. Habitat 134–Ampulla 110 (Crowned Prince 128) (1982 6d*   **112+**
6.3g* 6g) Mar 30; 350,000Y; well-made, handsome colt; has a round action; second foal; brother to winning Italian 3-y-o Steel Habit; dam, winner of Cherry Hinton Stakes, is half-sister to high-class sprinter Steel Heart (by Habitat); favourite when winning 11-runner maiden race at the Curragh in July (ran green) and 7-runner Railway Stakes on same course the following month; put up a useful performance when decisively beating Virginia Deer by 2½ lengths in latter; second favourite for William Hill Middle Park Stakes at Newmarket in September but was beaten soon after halfway and finished 5¾ lengths last of 5 to Diesis; yet to race on a firm surface; a very taking individual who is probably a good bit better than his Newmarket running suggests. *V. O'Brien, Ireland.*

AND NOW 2 b.c. English Prince 129–Senama (Sanctus II 132) (1982 7.6v)
May 10; IR 8,400F, IR 20,000Y; fourth foal; half-brother to smart French 8.5f to 1¾m winner Moulouki (by Sassafras); dam French middle-distance winner; ninth of 13 to Joyful Dancer in maiden race at Lingfield in October; sold I. Walker 6,000 gns Newmarket Autumn Sales. *G. Harwood.*

Mr R. E. Sangster's "Anfield"

ANDREX 3 ch.g. Privy Seal 108–Miss Frenchy (Exbury 138) (1981 NR 1982 —
9fg 17f) small gelding; closely inbred to Privy Councillor; second foal; dam poor
maiden; in rear in newcomers race and maiden event at Wolverhampton. *R. Hollinshead.*

'ANDSOME 6 br.g. Some Hand 119–March Stone 84 (March Past 124) (1981 —
NR 1982 8g) compact gelding; winner of seller and 2 apprentice handicaps in
1979; last on only outing of 1982; best form at 1¼m; acts on soft going, but is well
suited by firm; good mount for a boy. *M. Pipe.*

ANDSON 2 ch.g. Sagaro 133–Forty Love 79 (Fortino II 120) (1982 5d 5fg*) **52**
May 11; third foal; dam half-sister to high-class Take a Reef; won 7-runner
seller at Warwick (no bid) in April by ¾ length from Kumu; not seen out again.
P. Cundell.

ANDY LOU 4 b.g. Be Friendly 130–Ribara (Barbare II 128) (1981 6g⁴ 5g* —
5d³ 5f³ 6s³ 5f³ 8g 7fg 7fg 5f³ 5fg 6d 6s 5d 6g 1982 5g 6d 5f 5f) poor handicapper;
poor walker and mover; stays 6f (not disgraced over 1m); acts on any going;
blinkered final outing in 1981; sold 600 gns Doncaster August Sales, and resold
500 gns Ascot December Sales. *G. Toft.*

ANFIELD 3 b.c. Be My Guest 126–Mother 88 (Whistler 129) (1981 7fg* 6.3fg* **117**
8g* 8s⁴ 1982 8g³ 8g⁴ 8fg 8d* 8s²) IR 53,000Y; attractive, medium-sized colt;
closely related to top-class 7f to 11f winner North Stoke (by Northfields) and
half-brother to 3 winners; dam won over 5f at 2 yrs; favourite when beating
Murcot by 3 lengths in Desmond Stakes at the Curragh in September; also in
frame in Coolmore Gay Fandango Stakes at Leopardstown (1¼ lengths third to
Salutely), Airlie/Coolmore Irish 2,000 Guineas at the Curragh (5 lengths fourth
to Dara Monarch) and Prix Perth at Saint-Cloud (4 lengths second to Commodore
Blake); never-dangerous sixth of 9 to Dara Monarch in St James's Palace Stakes
at Royal Ascot on other start; stayed 1m; seemed to act on any going; retired
to King Edward's Place Stud, Wiltshire. *D. O'Brien, Ireland.*

ANGELA EDELSON 3 b.f. Owen Dudley 121–Mauritania 74 (The Brianstan **61**
128) (1981 5s 6g 5d 1982 8g 7s³ 7g 8d) lightly-made filly; poor handicapper;
possibly stays 1m; acts on soft going and has yet to race on a firm surface.
N. Guest.

ANGELO SALVINI 6 br.g. Relko 136–Sweet Sauce (Fr) (Hard Sauce 131)
(1981 18s* 18.4d 16g 15g⁴ 14.7d* 14d 17.4g 16.1s³ 14s³ 1982 14s) narrow,
rather sparely-made gelding; fairly useful handicapper in 1981; far from disgraced
only outing of 1982 (carried quite a lot of condition); suited by a test of stamina;
acts on any going but is very well suited by soft; game and genuine; front runner;
good mount for an inexperienced race-rider. *M. H. Easterby.*

ANGELUS CHIMES 3 b.f. Northfields–Twelve O'Clock (Hardicanute 130) **67**
(1981 5f 6fg⁴ (dis) 7fg 6fg 6g³ 7g² 1982 8.5fg 10fg⁴ 12fg² 12f² 12f⁴ 10fg 11.7s
10s²) quite attractive, lightly-made, lengthy filly; modest maiden; stays 1½m;
acts on any going; trained by D. Whelan most of season. *H. Candy.*

ANGEVIN 4 b.f. English Prince 129–Paddyflower 88 (St Paddy 133) (1981 —
9s³ 10fg 12d 12g 14g 8d 1982 6g 8g 10g 12f 16g) big, well-made ex-English
filly; plating-class maiden; should be suited by middle distances; sometimes
blinkered; trained by D. Ringer first outing. *F. Dunne, Ireland.*

ANGLEPOISE (USA) 5 b.g. Angle Light–Burns' Babe (Fleet Nasrullah) —
(1981 8v³ 9g 10.2g 9d⁴ 8g 8g³ 8g 8g 11d 1982 8g) compact gelding; fair
handicapper in 1981; rather disappointing only outing of 1982 (April); best
at up to 9f; suited by some give in the ground; blinkered when successful once
in 1980; suited by front-running tactics; genuine. *S. Norton.*

ANGLO GREEK 5 b.g. English Prince 129–Orange Sensation 69 (Floribunda —
136) (1981 7g 8g 7.2v 1982 8d 5fg 6f 7.6g 10.6f) compact gelding; no form
for a long time and was well beaten in selling company final start; should stay
beyond 6f; acts on firm going; has been tried in blinkers; sold 680 gns Doncaster
June Sales, probably for export to Norway. *L. Barratt.*

ANGMERING 2 b.f. Raga Navarro 119–Tamarisk Way 92 (Tamerlane 128) —
(1982 5f 5g 5s) Mar 31; 25,000Y; well-made filly; good walker; half-sister to
several winners, notably Nagwa (by Tower Walk), a smart winner of 13 races at
up to 7f at 2 yrs in 1975, and unbeaten 1981 2-y-o sprinter Warm Hearted (by
Steel Heart); dam sprinter; 9 lengths eighth of 20 to Misguided in maiden race at
Newbury in September, second outing (first for over 3 months) and only indication
of merit; will stay 6f. *J. Winter.*

ANGUILLO 2 b.c. Reform 132–Stardom 75 (Hornbeam 130) (1982 6f 6g³ 7.5g* **122**
8s*) Apr 9; 11,500Y; attractive colt; brother to 2 winners, including fairly

useful middle-distance performer Tolstoy, and half-brother to 2 winners; dam, half-sister to Irish Oaks winner Discorea, won over 13f; creditable length third of 16 to Jalmood The Stone in maiden race at Folkestone in June when trained by L. Cumani; was afterwards sent to race in Italy, winning on his debut there in September and then landing an important prize when making all to beat Beldale Concorde 2 lengths in Gran Criterium at Milan in October; stays well, and will be suited by 1¼m+; acts on soft going. *A. Botti, Italy.*

ANGUS PRINCE 2 ch.c. Octavo 115–Jean Armour 88 (Delirium 126) (1982 —
5.8f 6f 6g) May 7; 6,800Y; workmanlike colt; half-brother to winners here and abroad, including fairly useful 7f and 1m winner Shangarry (by Pitskelly); dam middle-distance winner; well beaten in sellers at Bath, Nottingham and Hamilton (blinkered) in the summer. *P. Haslam.*

ANGUS SPRITE 3 b.f. Saulingo 122–Saratoga Springs 92 (Worden II 129) —
(1981 5fg 5fg 6g 6fg 6g 7f² 7.2v* 7g 7d⁴ 7g   1982 6fg 8g 7g 7g 10d 8.2s 7d 13.8d) unfurnished filly; poor plater nowadays; sometimes blinkered; has worn a bandage on off-hind; sold 440 gns Ascot December Sales. *K. Ivory.*

ANIECE 4 br.c. Ballymoss 136–Gay Maria (Tacitus 124) (1981 10g 8d² 11.5f³   **65**
10.1fg³ 12d* 16fg² 12f⁴ 16s* 18g   1982 16.1s 12fg 12f³ 14fg 14fg 16.1s 15d²) well-made colt; rather disappointing, although placed in ladies race at Ripon in June and handicap at Edinburgh in November; very well suited by a test of stamina; probably acts on any going; sometimes coltish in paddock; retained 5,600 gns Newmarket Autumn Sales. *F. Durr.*

ANIKONERI 7 br.m. Yukon Eric–Sayarani 96 (Hard Tack 111§) (1981 7g⁴ —
11g 8fg⁴ 8.2d 1982 8.2g 5g 8d 7g) poor handicapper nowadays; seems to stay 1m; well suited by fast ground; suitable mount for an apprentice. *W. H. H. Williams.*

ANKARA (USA) 2 ch.c. Northern Dancer–Rule Formi (Forli) (1982 7g*) **93** p
May 29; brother to top 1981 Irish 2-y-o filly Woodstream and half-brother to 2

Mr R. E. Sangster's "Ankara"

winners, notably high-class miler Jaazeiro (by Sham); dam never ran; evens favourite, led 1f out when winning 16-runner maiden race at Leopardstown in October by a length from Changed His Mind; will probably stay 1¼m; promising. *V. O'Brien, Ireland.*

ANMIRANDA 3 b.f. Some Hand 119–Miss Miranda (Caliban 123) (1981 NR 1982 7fg) quite well-made filly; second foal; dam ran only 3 times; unquoted and backward when behind in seller won by Mr Sugar at Lingfield in May. *T. Gosling.*   —

ANNAMOE BRAY 2 ch.c. Whistling Deer 114–Evening Sky 74 (Skymaster 126) (1982 5s 5f 5f 6g³ 6g 6g* 7f³ 6fg² 7g³ 6g* 6g 6s* 6s 6v) May 18; IR 1,000F, IR 3,500Y; lengthy, workmanlike colt; half-brother to Irish middle-distance winner Evening in May (by Skymaster); dam placed over 7f at 2 yrs; successful in sellers at Hamilton in July and Doncaster (£5,000 event) in September; bought in both times, at Doncaster for 4,100 gns; also ran well in several nurseries, winning one at Hamilton later in September by ¾ length from Ardrox Lad; better suited by 6f than 7f; acts well on soft going and has run creditably on a firm surface; ran poorly in blinkers fifth start; sweated up quite badly ninth start. *J. Wilson.*   **79**

ANNESLEY 3 b.c. Relkino 131–My Candy 81 (Lorenzaccio 130) (1981 6g* 7fg³ 7g² 7h³ 8fg 1982 10.1fg 10.8fg 11.7fg) well-made, attractive colt; good walker and mover; fair performer in 1981; soundly beaten in handicaps at 3 yrs; should be suited by middle distances; blinkered final outing in 1981. *R. Hern.*   —

ANNIE EDGE 2 ch.f. Nebbiolo 125–Friendly Court (Be Friendly 130) (1982 5f* 5f² 5fg³ 6g³ 7fg²) Mar 24; IR 6,800Y; tall, workmanlike filly; third foal; half-sister to fairly useful Irish 6f and 7f winner Maiacourt (by Malacate) and a winner in USA; dam fairly useful 2-v-o 5f winner in Ireland; won maiden race at Leicester in April by 2 lengths from Ridge Heights; afterwards acquitted herself well in 2 top fillies' races, dead-heating for third place in Queen Mary Stakes at Royal Ascot and finishing third, 4½ lengths behind Habibti, in Lowther Stakes (blinkered) at York; looked hard trained and failed to produce her best form when second to Flamenco in Waterford Candelabra Stakes at Goodwood in August on final appearance; probably stays 7f. *D. H. Jones.*   **108**

ANNIE GO QUICKLY 2 b.f. Anax 120–Miss Swift 79 (Canisbay 120) (1982 6f 5fg 6f) Mar 22; 3,800Y; strong filly; half-sister to fairly useful 6f and 1¼m winner Hiz (by Persian Plan); dam won over 1m and 1¼m; 12 lengths fifth of 7 to Another Risk in minor event at Windsor in July, third outing; started none too well in valuable seller at York on previous appearance; should stay 1m. *N. Callaghan.*   —

ANNIVERSARY TOKEN 2 ch.f. Record Token 128–Josceline (Knightly Manner) (1982 7g 8s 6d) May 16; first foal; dam poor maiden; behind in varied company in the autumn. *R. Hollinshead.*   —

ANOMALY 2 b.f. The Brianstan 128–Aunt Winnie (Wolver Hollow 126) (1982 5g⁴ 6g 5g⁴ 6g) May 2; 1,900F; quite attractive, compact filly; first produce; dam poor maiden; fourth in maiden races at Kempton in May and Sandown in July; should stay 6f; blinkered last 2 starts. *G. Pritchard-Gordon.*   **70**

ANOTHER CITY 3 ch.f. Scallywag 127–Must Improve 47 (Lucky Brief 128) (1981 8g 8d 1982 12fg 12.2fg* 14g 13.8f⁴ 11s) tall filly; made much of running to win minor event at Catterick in July; should stay 1¾m; suited by enterprising riding tactics. *G. Richards.*   **68**

ANOTHER GIFT 2 b.f. Record Token 128–The Danstan 66 (The Brianstan 128) (1982 5g 5fg* 6g 6f 6s 5v) Apr 16; 1,000Y; fair sort; second foal; half-sister to a winning plater; dam won 5f seller at 2 yrs; won maiden auction event at Epsom in April; fifth in selling nursery at Brighton in September, fourth outing and only form afterwards; stays 6f; acts on firm going; sold B.B.A. 1,700 gns Newmarket Autumn Sales. *R. Smyth.*   **60**

ANOTHER HIT 2 b.f. Hittite Glory 125–Partridge 65 (Mossborough 126) (1982 5.1g 6fg 5.1fg⁴ 6fg) Mar 6; 700Y; lightly-made filly; sister to 3-y-o 1¼m winner Glory Bird and half-sister to 1¼m winner Ascot Weather (by Silly Season); dam suited by a test of stamina; poor form in sellers; should be suited by further. *G. Blum.*   **48**

ANOTHER MEMORY 3 br.g. Free State 125–Saxelby Melody 88 (Highland Melody 112) (1981 6fg 6f 6f 7f 7.2v 8.2s 8d 1982 7f 7f 8fg) neat gelding; poor plater; blinkered twice at 2 yrs. *K. Stone.*   —

Tote-Ebor Handicap, York—Another Sam goes comfortably clear of Lusitania

ANOTHER RISK 2 b.c. The Brianston 128–Sally Ann III (Port Corsair 98) **103**
(1982 5d² 5f* 6f² 6fg² 6d² 6fg* 5f³ 6f 5g³ 5g) Apr 24; 2,400Y; robust, deep-
girthed non-thoroughbred colt; half-brother to 1¼m to 2m winner Arctic Rascal
(by Arctic Kanda) and a winning jumper; dam never ran; successful in maiden
race at Doncaster in May and small event at Windsor in July; ran well on most
of his other starts, particularly on last 2, when length third of 4 to Soba in all-
aged Scarbrough Stakes at Doncaster in September and length fifth of 6 to
Jonacris in Harry Rosebery Challenge Trophy at Ayr later in month; effective
at 5f and 6f; seems to act on any going; has run well for apprentice S. Dawson;
consistent. *P. Mitchell.*

ANOTHER RUMBO 4 ch.g. Royben 125–Fiord (Mountain Call 125) (1981
5s 5d 6g 5f 5.8f 7f 8g 6g 1982 5g 8g 8g 8.3g 8.3g 8fg 6g) workmanlike gelding;
very disappointing handicapper; behind in sellers on occasions; stays 6f; acts on
any going; often blinkered nowadays; sold 1,050 gns Ascot December Sales.
G. Hunter.

ANOTHER SAM 5 b. or br.h. Comedy Star 121–Balandra Star 92 (Blast 125) **99**
(1981 13s 16fg 14fg* 14s² 16f 16g² 18.4fg² 14d 14d² 14.6fg² 13.3d 17.1d* 16s
1982 16s 14f 18.4fg² 14fg* 16g⁴ 16.1f² 16fg 16fg² 16g 16fg* 19f 14g* 14.6g 18d)
leggy, narrow horse; useful handicapper on his day; won Tote-Ebor at York in
good style, moving through easily from back of field and going clear when shaken
up to beat Lusitanica comfortably by 3 lengths; had earlier won at Newmarket
(by 5 lengths from Popsi's Joy) and Newbury (shade cheekily from Prince Santiago), each time keeping in closer touch than usual; suited by a test of stamina;
acts on any going; often drops himself out in early stages and is not an easy ride.
R. Hannon.

ANOTHER SPECIAL 4 b.f. Space King 115–Pip's Princess (Border Chief 101) **—**
(1981 NR 1982 12fg 10d⁴ 10s 12d) small filly; sister to 3 winners over jumps;
dam maiden hurdler; 40/1 when about 12 lengths fourth of 10 to My Maravilla
in minor event at Nottingham in September. *D. Francis.*

ANOTHER TEQUILA (USA) 2 ch.c. Restless Wind–Lovely Shelia (Francis **—**
S.) (1982 7g 8d 8g) Mar 1; $48,000Y; leggy; rather narrow colt; brother to
smart 1979 Irish 2-y-o 7f winner Johnny O'Day (by Restless Wind) and half-
brother to numerous winners; dam won 6f claiming race; behind in maiden
races at Yarmouth in September and Newmarket and Edinburgh (hampered)
in October; blinkered at Edinburgh. *J. Hindley.*

ANOTHER THRILL 3 b.c. Morston 125–Another Treat 92 (Derring-Do 131) **70**
(1981 7fg 7g⁴ 1982 12f* 17.1s) attractive colt; readily won maiden race at
Brighton in May; behind in handicap at Bath in October; should stay beyond
1¼m; sold out of M. Stoute's stable only 1,600 gns Ascot July Sales after first
start; resold 400 gns Newmarket Autumn Sales. *Dr A. Jones.*

ANOTHER WAY 3 b.f. Wolverlife 115–Free and Easy (Liberator III) (1981 **64**
5.8f 6fg 5f² 5.8h 5fg 1982 6fg 6g 5fg 6g 6fg² 6f) smallish, useful sort; sprint
handicapper; stays 6f; acts on firm going; often blinkered; sold 620 gns Newmarket Autumn Sales. *N. Vigors.*

ANSTRUTHER 3 b. or br.c. Oats 126–St Tropez 99 (Princely Gift 137) (1981 **93**
6d 6fg* 7.3d 1982 8g 6fg² 6f 6fg 7g 5g 5v⁴ 6d⁴) big, strong, good-bodied colt;
excellent mover; in frame in handicaps at Newmarket in April and Ascot (fourth
to Bri-Eden in Bovis Stakes) and Doncaster in October; soundly beaten most
other starts (virtually pulled up on third); needs further than 5f and stays 7f;
seems to act on any going; trained by D. Ringer first 3 starts. *C. Brittain.*

78

ANTILLA 3 b.f. Averof 123–Anegada 79 (Welsh Pageant 132) (1981 5g* 5s — 5f⁴ 5g³ 5g² 5fg 6s 1982 6h 6g) smallish, fair sort; fair performer in 1981; well beaten in 2 handicaps at 3 yrs; should stay 6f; form only on good ground. *P. Cole.*

ANTIQUE SURPRISE 2 ch.c. Porto Bello 118–Unexpected 84 (Laser Light **72** 118) (1982 5s³ 5f³ 5d 5.8g 6fg) Apr 22; 5,000Y; workmanlike colt; first foal; dam won over 7.6f at 4 yrs; quite a modest maiden; exported to Malaysia. *J. Benstead.*

ANTUM 2 b.f. Hittite Glory 125–Early Rose 61 (Will Somers 114§) (1982 **56** d 5fg⁴ 5f 6g 5f 6g) Feb 15; lightly-made filly; half-sister to several winners, including 1m and 1¼m winner Secateurs (by Sharp Edge); dam of little account; showed ability on debut but ran badly afterwards; evidently failed to train on. *A. Ingham.*

ANVIL INN 4 b.g. Roi Soleil 125–Floor Show 78 (Galivanter 131) (1981 **51** 11v 8g 7g² 7fg 8fg 9d³ 10f* 8g 8.2f 9d³ 11d 12g 1982 12g⁴ 12.3fg 8f² 11g 9g 10fg* 9g³ 10f 13.8d 12g²) compact gelding; bought in 1,050 gns after winning selling handicap at Pontefract in August; stays 1¼m; well suited by a sound surface; inconsistent. *T. Craig.*

ANVIL LARK 4 b.g. Sir Lark 101–Douraine (Doubtless II 111) (1981 NR — 1982 16.5fg 11s 15.8d 8g) of little account. *M. Reddan.*

APANG (USA) 2 b.c. Elocutionist–My Lana (My Host) (1982 6g) Apr 29; — $45,000Y; $50,000 2-y-o; half-brother to 3 winners in USA, notably Current Concept (by Exalted Rullah), a very useful stakes winner at up to 7f; dam won 7 sprint races; 25/1 when behind in 20-runner maiden race won by Asswan at Yarmouth in September; sold 2,500 gns Newmarket Autumn Sales. *H. Cecil.*

APERITIVO 4 ro.c. Sharp Edge 123–Feasting (Sayajirao 132) (1981 8s* **89** 10d* 10fg 10fg 12d 10g⁴ 10g 10s 12g 1982 10s 10f* 10f⁴ 10fg² 12fg³ 10f 10fg 10d³ 8f* 8g 9d 8s) lengthy colt; beat Ditton Wood by 2 lengths in Sunley Sandown Cup (Handicap) in April and got up close home to beat Fandangle by a neck in £4,400 handicap at Goodwood in July; also ran well when 2 lengths second of 6 behind Castle Keep in Clive Graham Stakes at Goodwood and creditably when third to Lafontaine in £7,700 handicap at Sandown, but is inconsistent; stays 1¼m; evidently acts on any going; can produce a useful turn of foot when in the mood but is unpredictable; sold to R. Atkins 16,000 gns Newmarket Autumn Sales. *R. Armstrong.*

APHRA BEHN 3 b.f. Malinowski 123–Masina (Current Coin 118) (1981 7g³ — 1982 8d 10f 10fg 12fg⁴ 11.7g 11.1fg 12v³ 10s) well-made filly; plating-class maiden; stays 1¼m; sold 5,000 gns Goff's November Sales. *R. Price.*

APOLLO DANCER 3 b.c. Runnymede 123–Treasure Flower 67 (Donore 119) — (1981 6fg 7g 6g 5s 1982 5d 7fg 5h⁴) light-framed colt; has a rather round action; plater; sometimes blinkered; sold 400 gns Newmarket July Sales. *P. Haslam.*

APPLE BLOSSOM 3 ch.f. Orange Bay 131–Appleshaw (St Alphage 119) **§§** (1981 6fg 6f 6g² 7g 8fg 7s 1982 10d⁴ 8.5f 7.6f² 7f⁴ 7fg² 7d* 8g 7f 7fg 7g) tall, leggy filly; has a round action; well backed when winning minor event at Salisbury in June; seems to stay 1¼m; gives impression she'll always be suited by some give in the ground; sometimes blinkered (was when successful); has started slowly, put head in air under pressure at Salisbury and refused to race final outing; one to be wary of. *G. Beeson.*

APPLE HONEY 3 b. or br.c. Bold Lad (Ire) 133–Pampalina 116 (Bairam II — 101) (1981 NR 1982 8f 8f) IR 40,000Y; rangy colt; half-brother to 3 winners, notably Irish 2,000 Guineas winner Pampapaul (by Yellow God); dam won Irish Guinness Oaks; behind in maiden race at Thirsk and minor event at Goodwood in the summer. *F. Durr.*

APPLE ORCHARD 2 b.g. Shirley Heights 130–Apple Peel 109 (Pall Mall 132) — (1982 8s 8g) Mar 7; lengthy, rather angular gelding; second foal; half-brother to disappointing 3-y-o Apples of Gold (by Godswalk); dam won 5 times over 1m and 1¼m; backward, showed no worthwhile form in October in maiden race at Warwick (dwelt) and minor event at Newmarket; gelded after. *W. Hastings-Bass.*

APPLES OF GOLD 3 ro.f. Godswalk 130–Apple Peel 109 (Pall Mall 132) — (1981 6fg² 6f² 6d² 1982 8fg² 8f² 8.3g) strong, quite attractive filly; runner-up in 3 good-class races in 1981; didn't run up to that form at 3 yrs; stays 1m; blinkered second start; sold 10,500 gns Newmarket December Sales. *R. Hern.*

APPLE WINE 5 ch.g. Ribston 104–Ruffino 99 (Como 120) (1981 10.2s* 9g — 1982 10d 12fg 10.6s 10.2d) workmanlike gelding; won amateur riders race at Doncaster in 1981; suited by 1¼m; probably acts on any going but revels in the mud; blinkered twice at 2 yrs; suitable mount for an inexperienced rider; trained until after first outing by M. W. Easterby. *D. Chapman.*

APRICOT ROSE 3 ch.f. Mill Reef 141–Jolie Fleur 111 (Exbury 138) (1981 — 7g 1982 11.5f 8g) leggy, unfurnished filly; has shown some ability; bred to stay 1½m but pulled hard when tried at trip. *H. Cecil.*

APRIL LEAVES 5 br.g. March Past 124–Booked (Counsel 118) (1981 NR — 1982 10.1d 12f) first foal; dam never ran; well beaten in minor events at Windsor and Lingfield; sold 540 gns Ascot December Sales. *G. Beeson.*

APRIL LUCKY 9 b.g. St Alphage 119–Susceptible 86 (Supreme Court 135) **61 d** (1981 6s 6g² 6d* 6g⁴ 6f² 6f³ 6fg 6f⁴ 7f 6f⁴ 6d 1982 6f 6fg² 6f⁴ 6fg* 6g 6g 6g⁴ 6g 6f 7.2s) leggy gelding; goes particularly well at Hamilton and gained his seventh win there in a handicap in June; stays 7f; acts on any going; blinkered twice at 3 yrs; sometimes sweats up; good mount for an inexperienced rider; needs to be held up; has occasionally broken a blood vessel; hampered in early stages eighth outing. *C. Crossley.*

APRIL MEMORIES 3 b.f. Rolfe 77–Sweet Memories 58 (Runnymede 123) **58** (1981 6fg 5d 1982 6g 6f² 6fg² 5g² 6fg³ 5d 5fg² 6d) quite attractive, well-made filly; plater; moved down a place after winning at Leicester in June on second start (veered badly right); has run respectably in better company on occasions; will stay 7f; acts well on fast ground; sometimes sweats up; sold 500 gns Ascot December Sales. *N. Vigors.*

APRIL ROSE 2 ch.f. Wollow 132–April Days 75 (Silly Season 127) (1982 7g — 7d) Apr 3; 2,500Y; leggy filly; first live foal; dam, daughter of Oaks second Maina, won over 10.4f; behind in October in maiden races at Newmarket and Leicester (last of 15). *W. Hastings-Bass.*

APRIL RUN 4 b.f. Run The Gantlet–April Fancy (No Argument 107) (1981 **130** 10.3² 12d* 10.5s* 10.5fg³ 12.5g⁴ 13.5f* 12g* 12d³ 12g* 12fg² 1982 12fg⁴ 10.5g 13.5fg³ 12f* 12s⁴ 12f* 12d* 12f³)

For long enough it looked as if the sporting decision to keep April Run in training as a four-year-old would not reap the reward it deserved. April Run had been the outstanding middle-distance filly of her generation in 1981 with wins in the Prix Vermeille at Longchamp and the Turf Classic at Aqueduct and places in the Prix de l'Arc de Triomphe and the Washington D.C. International, but her early efforts as a four-year-old were none too encouraging. Happily, as with many of her sex, April Run just needed time. In the autumn she was as good as ever: she won the Prix Foy and finished fourth in the Trusthouse Forte Prix de l'Arc before embarking on a tremendously successful campaign abroad in which she scored a second Turf Classic success and also won the Washington D.C. International and came third in the Japan Cup. She thus joins a magnificent list of French middle-distance fillies who have raced with distinction as four- or five-year-olds during the last ten years or so, following very much in the tradition of Allez France, Comtesse de Loir, Dahlia, Detroit, Gold River, Ivanjica, Three Troikas and Trillion.

It wasn't until she finished third behind Zalataia and the subsequent Arc winner Akiyda in the Prix de Pomone at Deauville in August, a race which she'd won easily in 1981, that April Run showed signs of returning to form. In a race that was very slowly run and filled with incident she looked unlucky, coming home in very good style after getting into all sorts of trouble. This represented nothing like April Run's best form, of course, but at least she showed a great deal more sparkle here than in either of her races at Longchamp in the spring, the Prix d'Hedouville and the Prix Ganay. In the former, a race which she'd have won without much fuss on her best form, she finished only fourth behind Gap of Dunloe; in the latter, a far more strongly-contested event, she trailed home eighth of ten behind Bikala. Unfortunately April Run returned from Deauville with cuts on both hind legs, a legacy of her having been baulked at least twice, and she had to miss some important work before running in the Prix Foy at Longchamp the following month, a traditional stepping-stone to the Prix de l'Arc. April Run still wasn't right at her best therefore in the Prix Foy, and despite starting at long odds on against six opponents, none of them in the highest class, she only scrambled home. Piggott, who'd ridden her in the spring, adopted different tactics, setting off in front. He slowed the pace running down the hill and April Run had a fight on her hands in the straight before, under hard driving, she forced her nose in front on the line to win from the subsequently-disqualified Mariacho and No Attention.

Frankly we didn't rate April Run's prospects particularly highly on Arc day, certainly nowhere near so highly as the previous season. The French Press didn't give much for her chance either, and she wasn't selected by any of the twenty-seven tipsters featured in *Paris-Turf's* table. Hearing her grind her teeth loudly and regularly in the paddock didn't exactly increase one's confidence in her, though it had been said that the noisier she is beforehand the better form she's supposed to be in. Partnered for the first time by the American Asmussen, recently returned to the saddle after a nasty fall at Evry in July, April Run put up a fine effort. She came with a strong run on the wide outside in the straight and looked for a moment as if she might improve on her previous year's third place. She kept battling away but wasn't quite strong enough in the closing stages and finished fourth behind Akiyda, Ardross and Awaasif, beaten about half a length altogether. In view of how narrowly she was beaten her connections must have been left counting the cost of her interrupted preparation and her hard race in the Prix Foy.

April Run was sent across to North America in mid-October, as she had been in 1981. There are rich pickings to be had for grass horses there in the autumn, and European horses are being sent over in ever-increasing numbers with the Turf Classic, the Washington International and the Canadian International the prime targets. The French pattern of racing is tending to produce a much stronger challenge for these particular types of events than the English pattern, and the French have a superb record in them. April Run's latest win in the Turf Classic was France's third since the Turf Classic was instituted in 1977, following her previous win in the race and that of Anifa in 1979. Her Washington International success was France's eleventh in thirty-one runnings and sixth since the last British winner Karabas in 1969, following on the wins of Dahlia, Admetus, Nobiliary, Youth and Argument. In the latter period Dahlia and Youth also won the Canadian International, as did Exceller.

The conditions of entry for the Turf Classic were altered in 1982 and instead of being purely invitational the race closed to nominations of 100 dollars per horse on February 16th with a combined supplemental nomination and entry fee of 30,000 dollars to be paid on October 23rd, the day before the race, subject to a horse's being selected to start. The change in conditions made no appreciable difference to the size or quality of the field. April Run started favourite in a field of seven in which she seemed outstanding and always looked like justifying the support. She was handily placed throughout as Bottled Water and Sprink set a fairly sedate pace, and Asmussen again brought her with her challenge on the wide outside coming off the home turn. April Run was soon on

Prix Foy, Longchamp—April Run (rails) comes back at Mariacho with No Attention also finishing well

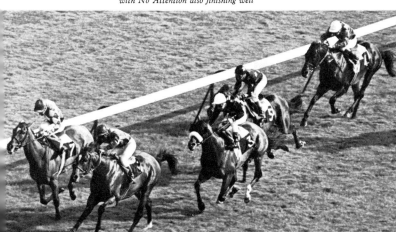

Washington D.C. International, Laurel—April Run romps home

top and went clear in a matter of strides to win very impressively by six and a half lengths from the second favourite Naskra's Breeze, an improved five-year-old gelding who'd won the United Nations Handicap and the Man o'War Stakes but had been only eighth in an international field for the Budweiser Million. In the Washington International at Laurel a fortnight later April Run faced stronger opposition, with the first two in the Canadian International (now known as the Rothman's International), Majesty's Prince and Thunder Puddles, the Arc third Awaasif and Diamond Shoal among her nine opponents. She was no less impressive though, cruising to the front three furlongs from home in a race run at a fast pace on rain-softened going, and pulling right away to win by six and a half lengths once more. Majesty's Prince followed her home with Thunder Puddles a further four and a half lengths back in third, Diamond Shoal fourth and Awaasif fifth. April Run's win marked trainer Boutin's first in the race; previously the trainer had saddled La Lagune for fifth in 1968, Monseigneur for sixth in 1977, Le Marmot for third in 1979, and April Run herself for second in 1981.

April Run (b.f. 1978)	Run The Gantlet (b 1968)	Tom Rolfe (b 1962)	Ribot / Pocahontas II
		First Feather (ch 1963)	First Landing / Quill
	April Fancy (b 1967)	No Argument (b 1960)	Narrator / Persuader
		April Slipper (ch 1962)	Panaslipper / April View

April Run's two wins in the States were impressive enough to suggest she was in even better form there than in the Arc and they would have made a fitting climax to her season; they took her first-place earnings to £469,168. Her season wasn't over yet though. She was sent on to Tokyo for the Japan Cup at the end of November, a valuable race which the organisers had gone to great lengths to promote world wide during the year. The line-up fully justified the organisers' efforts, for in addition to April Run it attracted the top-class American turf specialist John Henry, the Prix Vermeille winner All Along, and runners from several other countries. Possibly April Run's travelling caught up with her. She was beaten in a desperately close finish by the American-trained outsider Half Iced, in the same ownership, and All Along.

April Run was bought for only 11,500 guineas as a yearling at a time when her sire Run The Gantlet, himself a Washington International winner, wasn't particularly fashionable. Run The Gantlet was returned to the States after the covering season of 1980 and, as so often with stallions sent abroad, the achievements of his offspring improved after his departure. He's a prominent sire now, thanks to April Run, Ardross, the Irish Guinness Oaks winner Swiftfoot, and Providential who beat April Run at Laurel in 1981. April Run's dam April Fancy, a half-sister to the 1977 Gladness Stakes winner Rare April and the 1974 Prix du Lys runner-up Hard April, ran only five times and wasn't seen out after finishing last but one behind Black Satin in the 1970 Irish One Thousand Guineas. She won over nine and a half furlongs at Dundalk as a two-year-old—earning a mark 37 lb behind Nijinsky in the Irish Free Handicap—and over seven furlongs at Naas at three. April Fancy has produced two other winners, Northern View (by Northfields), a useful performer who finished fourth in the 1976 Irish Two Thousand Guineas and was subsequently successful in Italy, and Aherlow Boy (by Tudor Music), successful in a mile-and-a-half maiden at Roscommon and over hurdles. April Fancy has since produced a Kashiwa filly Laputa, placed over a mile in Ireland in 1982, and a filly from Run The Gantlet's last covering season in Ireland. It is said that when April Run finishes racing she'll be mated with either Cure The Blues, the second-highest rated two-year-old in the States in 1980, or General Assembly, one of the top middle-distance three-year-olds there in 1979, both of whom are now standing at her owner's Gilltown Stud in Ireland.

If April Run remains in training as a five-year-old, her programme seems sure to be geared principally to an autumn campaign on the same lines as in 1982 with another crack at the Arc high on the agenda. Having already gone close twice in the Arc she seems likely to be thereabouts again in 1983, all

Mrs B. Firestone's "April Run" (L. Piggott)

being well with her. And who's to say she won't win it? Even if she doesn't it will be very surprising if she doesn't win another big prize or two. A big, good-quartered filly who acts on any going, April Run is well suited by a mile and a half or more. Would that there were more as good and as tough as her around. *F. Boutin, France.*

AQABA PRINCE 2 br.c. Sweet Revenge 129–Lady Anita 72 (Como 120) **88** (1982 6g 5fg 6f 6f² 6g⁴ 6fg³ 6g 5d⁴ 6v² 5g⁴) May 27; 1R 1,400F, 1,500Y, 6,400 2-y-o; workmanlike colt; fifth reported living foal; dam sprinter; despite busy time, ran easily best race when under 2 lengths fourth of 13 to Chaplin's Club in nursery at Newmarket in October on final start; stays 6f; probably best on an easy surface; blinkered seventh outing. *R. Hannon.*

AQUA BLUE 5 ch.m. Blue Cashmere 129–Aquanimba (Acropolis 132) (1981 **41** 7s 6g 7g 8g 8.2fg 7f 7f 6fg* 6fg 6fg 1982 6g 6f 6f 6f* 7g 6fg 7f) lightly-made mare; inconsistent plater; well beaten after winning at Catterick in June (no bid); stays 7f; acts on firm going; has been tried in blinkers; unseated rider start on second appearance; sold 780 gns Doncaster October Sales. *D. Yeoman.*

AQUA VERDE 3 b.g. Auction Ring 123–Regal Guard (Realm 129) (1981 — 5g* 1982 5v 6f 8fg⁴ 8g⁴ 7f 5f) plater; seems to stay 1m; sometimes wears blinkers. *J. Berry.*

ARAB ART 3 b.f. Artaius 129–Limbara (Espresso 122) (1981 7f 1982 — 8g 10g 16f) behind in maiden races and a minor event; sold 5,000 gns New-market December Sales. *B. Swift.*

ARABELLA'S CLUB 2 b.f. Full of Hope 125–Chalandy (Alcide 136) (1982 — 5fg 5d) May 8; 1,000Y; second foal; dam never ran; in rear in sellers in the Midlands in April. *J. Fox.*

ARAGON 2 b.c. Mummy's Pet 125–Ica (Great Nephew 126) (1982 5fg* **109** 6fg* 6g² 6f³ 7f 7v² 7s³) Mar 2; 52,000Y; quite attractive, full-quartered, close-coupled colt; second foal; closely related to useful French 1981 2-y-o 5f winner Sun And Shine (by African Sky); dam unraced half-sister to Song; 4-length winner of minor event at Newbury in May (quickened in remarkable style to beat Bold Bob) and of £4,300 race at York in June; put up best sub-sequent efforts when 3½ lengths third of 4 to Gallant Special in Richmond Stakes at Goodwood in July and when close up under top weight in nurseries won by Under the Hammer at Ascot and Timber Creek at Sandown in October; suited by 7f; acts on any going, but is particularly well suited by heavy; genuine. *J. Dunlop.*

ARAS AN UACHTARAIN 2 b.c. Habitat 134–Galletto 111 (Nijinsky 138) **92 p** (1982 6s³ 5s*) Apr 28; second foal; dam, daughter of Irish Guinness Oaks winner Gaia, was very useful at up to 1½m; 2/1 on when beating Last Out ½ length in 19-runner maiden race at the Curragh late in season; had previously finished promising 6½ lengths third of 20 to South Atlantic in another Curragh maiden event; likely to show further improvement over 7f+. *D. O'Brien, Ireland.*

ARC D'OR (USA) 4 b.c. Ack Ack–Arme d'Or (Armistice 131) (1981 11fg² **118** 9s² 10.5v 1982 12d⁴ 12fg 9d* 11s* 12v 12.5d³ 12g 12d) French colt; smart performer at his best; decisively accounted for small fields in minor events at Evry and Longchamp in May; ran best race when 3½ lengths third of 12 to All Along in Prix Maurice de Nieuil at Saint-Cloud in July; stays 1½m; probably acts on any going; bandaged in front nowadays; sent to USA. *J. Cunnington, jnr, France.*

ARCHIMBOLDO 4 b.g. Midsummer Night II 117–Quenilda 101 (Fair Copy) — (1981 6d 6d* 6g² 6g* 6d 6g 1982 5d 6f 8f 8f 7f 6f 6fg 6g 6f 6s 5d 5g) lightly-built gelding; disappointing handicapper; should stay 7f; acts on any going except perhaps very soft; has been tried in blinkers; sometimes sweats up badly. *W. A. Stephenson.*

ARCH MELODY 4 b.c. Arch Sculptor 123–Prophetic Melody (Tudor Melody **77** 129) (1981 6g 6g 6fg 5g² 5.3f² 5fg 5fg 5g 5d⁴ 5s 5d 5s² 5s⁴ 1982 8s 5g 5fg³ 5f³ 5g⁴ 5d 5g 7.5s³ 8g³ 6v) neat, strong ex-English colt; third in handicaps at Chester in May (narrowly beaten by Susarma and Go Total), Leopardstown in June and Punchestown and Leopardstown in October; evidently stays 1m; acts on any going; effective with blinkers and without. *M. Connolly, Ireland.*

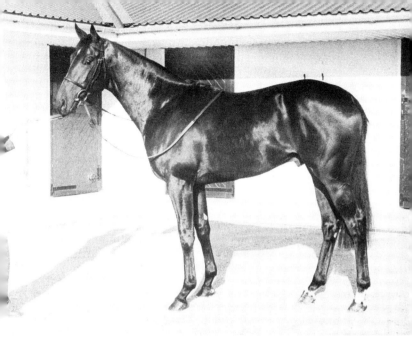

Mrs M. V. O'Brien's "Aras An Uachtarain"

ARCHON 2 b.c. Anax 120–Lutescens (Skymaster 126) (1982 5fg 5g 6g*   **87**
6fg 7fg 6fg) Apr 25; 3,300F; really stocky little colt; half-brother to 2 winning
platers and a winner in Holland; dam once-raced half-sister to Grand Prix
de Paris winner Funny Hobby; made virtually all to win 13-runner maiden
race at Haydock in July by 2½ lengths from Bali Mill, the pair clear; ran on
again after dropping out after 4f to finish 3¼ lengths sixth of 7 to Mac's Palace
in valuable nursery at Newmarket later in month, next start and best subsequent effort; should stay 7f. *B. Hobbs.*

ARCTIC LORD 2 br.c. Lord Gayle 124–Arctic Chimes (Arctic Slave 116)   **88** p
(1982 7d 9v*) May 28; half-brother to several winners, including 3-y-o 1m
and 11f winner Polar Star (by Rarity) and Irish 6f to 1m winner Little Bitty
Tear (by Sterling Bay); dam sister to excellent broodmare Arctic Melody,
the dam of Arctique Royale and grandam of Ardross; odds on, had rest well
beaten off when winning 19-runner maiden race at Gowran Park in October
by a short head from Ragabury; likely to develop into a useful stayer. *P.
Prendergast, Ireland.*

ARCTURA 2 b.f. Comedy Star 121–Uranda 93 (King's Troop 118) (1982   —
5.8g 8s) Apr 3; half-sister to several winners, including useful 1972 2-y-o
Master Sing (by Sing Sing); dam sprinter; soundly beaten in maiden races at
Bath in August and October; sold 920 gns Newmarket Autumn Sales. *P.
Walwyn.*

ARDENT LADY 3 ch.f. Status Seeker–Hello Amy 70 (Forlorn River 124)   **57**
(1981 6g 5fg³ 5g⁴ 5fg 6s⁴ 1982 7fg⁴ 8g 7f² 7f 6f 6fg⁴ 6f) plating-class maiden;
stays 7f; acts on any going; has run respectably when sweating up; trained
by D. Morley part of season. *M. Blanshard.*

ARDENT WARRIOR 3 b.g. Roman Warrior 132–Ardent Belle (Buisson Ardent   —
129) (1981 5s³ 5g 5f 1982 6g 6g) big gelding; little worthwhile form, including
in a seller. *A. W. Jones.*

ARDGOUR 4 b.g. Nonoalco 131–Hecla 117 (Henry the Seventh 125) (1981 —
7fg 8d 8s⁴ 8.3fg 8fg 8fg 8g 1982 8f 10f 10fg) attractive, well-made gelding;
very disappointing and ran deplorably in sellers last 2 starts; stays 1m; gives
impression he needs strong handling; sometimes blinkered; sold 1,400 gns
Doncaster June Sales, and sent to race in Scandinavia. *L. Barratt.*

ARDOONY 4 b.c. Ardoon 124–Linbel (Linacre 133) (1981 7d* 7g 8g² 8.2s **66**
8f 8f* 8g 8fg 8fg 8fg 8d 8.2v 8d⁴ 1982 8fg⁴(dis) 8f 8fg 7fg³ 8g 7.6d² 9d² 8.2f
8d⁴ 10.5s² 10d 10.2d) neat colt; placed in handicaps; stays 10.5f; acts on any
going; suitable mount for an apprentice; sometimes sweats up; has often
disappointed and is none too genuine. *R. Hollinshead.*

ARDROSS 6 b.h. Run The Gantlet–Le Melody 102 (Levmoss 133) (1981 14d* **134**
20f* 21fg* 13.3fg* 12d 15.5v* 1982 12fg* 14f* 16f* 20f* 12f³ 13.3g* 18g* 12s²)
 The end of an era? The retirement of Ardross leaves the Gold Cup, for the
first time for several seasons, without a contender of established championship
class at the distance still in training. The last eight years have seen the emergence
in Europe of at least five Cup horses of exceptional merit in Sagaro, Buckskin,
Le Moss, Ardross and the filly Gold River, a vintage collection whose achievements have generated as much public interest in long-distance racing as in any
period since the 'forties when the status of the Cup races was much higher than it
is today.
 The careers of Sagaro, Le Moss and Ardross in particular—they won seven
of the last eight Gold Cups between them—helped to bring home to the British
turf authorities, who had previously shrugged off criticism of their bias against
stayers, the fine entertainment value of races between high-class Cup horses.
The tremendous interest created by Sagaro's unique hat-trick in the Gold Cup and
by Le Moss's epic struggle with Ardross in 1980 for the so-called stayers' triple
crown has undoubtedly been partly responsible for the end to the repressive
measures that were taken against the stayers in earlier decades. When Sagaro
won his third Gold Cup in 1977 he earned for his owner £17,837, a prize which
put the Gold Cup in twentieth place in the first-prize money league table in
Britain; by 1982 the Gold Cup had climbed to fifteenth place with a first
prize of £42,649. The Goodwood Cup and the Doncaster Cup, the two other legs
of the so-called stayers' triple crown, have also had an injection of prize money.
Although we doubt whether we shall see long-distance racing in Britain restored
to its former status—when the great Alycidon won the Gold Cup in 1949 the
race ranked fifth in Britain in terms of first-prize money and was the most
valuable race open to horses above the age of three—we sincerely hope the
authorities will press on with the policy of upgrading the Cup races. The stakes
for the Goodwood Cup and the Doncaster Cup in particular are still not high
enough to make them automatic targets for the best of the previous season's
staying three-year-olds still in training; they need really big stakes to help to
counteract the stigma which attaches to long-distance races in some quarters.
 No commercial breeder nowadays sets out to breed horses for the Cup races,
horses likely to be at their peak as four-year-olds or five-year-olds over two
and a quarter miles plus, but chance has a large share in the breeding of racehorses and long-distance horses are still being produced and should be catered
for fairly. Long-distance races should be an integral part of the overall pattern
of races. The drift over the past thirty years or so towards breeding for speed
at the expense of stamina may have dangerous consequences for the long-term
welfare of British racing. Sprinters mature earlier than stayers and the breeding
of more and more sprinter-milers seems to be threatening to change the face
of our two-year-old racing. It is arguably becoming increasingly difficult to
win a top two-year-old race with a potential Derby horse, for example. Of the
last ten Derby winners only Grundy and The Minstrel, who both won the Dewhurst, and Shirley Heights, who won the Royal Lodge, succeeded in winning a
pattern race as a two-year-old; of the ten Derby winners between 1963 and 1972
only Relko and Blakeney (both of whom remained in training as four-year-olds,
as did four others in the period under review) failed to win a pattern race or its
equivalent at two and most of the Derby winners of that era were leading two-
year-olds. Racegoers and breeders alike were therefore much better informed
about the capabilities of this earlier group of Derby winners than they have
been about the group in the past decade, all but two of which, incidentally,
have been packed off to stud as three-year-olds. The current view among
most of the top trainers seems to be that training a staying-bred horse nowadays
for the top two-year-old races (with the possible exception of the one-mile Royal

*Jockey Club Stakes, Newmarket—Ardross runs on bravely
to beat Glint of Gold and Amyndas (spots)*

Lodge Stakes and William Hill Futurity) may be harmful to the animal physiologically. Two-year-old racing, with its richly-endowed major races, seems in danger of becoming much more a specialist category than formerly, dominated by horses a greater proportion of whom owe their success not only to their intrinsic merit but also to the fact that they are already, as two-year-olds, more or less mature and very near the zenith of their powers. Would anybody claim that this is a desirable state of affairs? Of course no-one can blame breeders for catering for the demand and filling the sales catalogues with potentially early-maturing sprinter-milers; and if racecourse executives find that races over shorter distances attract bigger fields and provide more competitive races it isn't practical to ask them to promote more long-distance races or more races for slower-maturing young horses. But it is our view that the trend towards breeding for speed at the expense of stamina could and should be reversed. There is a strong case for the reorganisation of the pattern of racing to shift the emphasis on to racing merit at three and four years, when most racehorses are fully mature. We should like to see, as a first step, some of the resources that are given at present to the leading two-year-old races being channelled into good races for four-year-olds and upwards, some of them over long distances. This would be a start towards encouraging a more balanced breeding policy and would help to provide a more rational pattern of racing, one which would enable more horses to be judged when they are the finished product.

Many a true stayer does not reach his best until after three years of age. Without exception, the five long-distance horses mentioned in the opening paragraph all showed their best form after their three-year-old days. Sagaro and Ardross were, in our view, at their very best as six-year-olds; Le Moss was at his peak in his final season, as a five-year-old. Since his last encounter with Le Moss, who beat Ardross in magnificent and memorable races for the Gold Cup, the Goodwood Cup and the Doncaster Cup, Ardross has been beaten only once in twelve races at distances beyond a mile and a half. That defeat, by Gold River in the 1980 Prix Royal-Oak at Longchamp, was avenged twelve months later and Ardross' impressive sequence of victories also includes two Gold Cups, two Yorkshire Cups, two victories in the Geoffrey Freer Stakes, and one each in the Jockey Club Cup, the Goodwood Cup, the Henry II Stakes and the Doncaster Cup. Victory in the Doncaster Cup in September took Ardross' career earnings in first-prize money to £304,371, a remarkable achievement for a stayer and a

Yorkshire Cup, York—a second successive victory for Ardross;
he has to be kept up to his work

sum which put him behind Dahlia (£497,741), Allez France (£493,100), April Run (£469,168), Troy (£415,735), Shergar (£388,970), Youth (£366,624), Glint of Gold (£328,817), Alleged (£327,315), Exceller (£324,694), Three Troikas (£316,676) The Minstrel (£315,212) and Grundy (£312,122) in the list of leading European-based money winners (the totals for Dahlia and Exceller do not include money earned after their permanent transfer to the United States). Interestingly, Ardross is the only one among that list that could not be termed a middle-distance specialist; the rewards in Europe for the top mile-and-a-half horses are much greater than those available to racehorses in other categories. Shergar and Troy, for example, earned more in a single season—as three-year-olds—than did Ardross in a career spanning four seasons.

Ardross' place as Europe's top out-and-out stayer has been threatened only by Gold River since the retirement of Le Moss. In the most recent season he stood head and shoulders above his fellow long-distance horses. As he got older Ardross developed a very relaxed, rather lazy style of racing and in the most recent season it seemed to take Piggott a little longer than formerly to get him fully opened out in his races; Ardross also developed a tendency to idle in front and he usually had to be kept up to his work with hands and heels after taking the lead. That said, there was no real doubting his invincibility at distances beyond a mile and a half. After narrowly winning the Jockey Club Stakes over a mile and a half on his seasonal reappearance at Newmarket in April, Ardross picked up the Yorkshire Cup in May and the Henry II Stakes at Sandown in June on his way to Royal Ascot, resisting the renewed challenges of Capstan and Little Wolf by a length and a short head at York and asserting himself impressively in the final furlong when beating Capstan by two lengths at Sandown, being driven fairly hard in both races before getting into top gear. Ardross conceded weight all round at York and Sandown and no English-trained stayer

Henry II Stakes, Sandown—Ardross wins from Capstan

Gold Cup, Ascot—Ardross is a class apart from French challengers
Tipperary Fixer (right) and El Badr, and the
Irish-trained Noelino (grey)

took him on in the Gold Cup. Only four opposed him, one more than in the previous year which had produced the smallest Gold Cup field for more than sixty years. In spite of the presence of the two best out-and-out stayers in France at that time, El Badr and Tipperary Fixer, who had finished first and second in the Prix du Cadran (French Gold Cup) in May, Ardross started at 5/1 on. The Polish-bred and Swedish-trained 66/1-shot Dzudo went off in front, setting a modest gallop in the early stages, and was followed, passing the stands for the first time, by El Badr, the Irish-trained Noelino, Ardross and Tipperary Fixer. The order remained more or less unchanged, the pace gradually quickening, until Noelino took up the running rounding the home turn with two and a half furlongs to go. Noelino's lead was short-lived. Ardross, looking a class apart from the rest, moved to the front inside the two-furlong marker and won very comfortably by three lengths and a neck from the strong-finishing Tipperary Fixer and El Badr. It was the fourth year in a row that trainer Cecil had saddled the Gold Cup winner and the eleventh winning ride in the race for Piggott.

Ardross ran into a spot of trouble on his next outing, being beaten into third place by Height of Fashion and Amyndas in the Princess of Wales's Stakes over a mile and a half on firm ground at the Newmarket July meeting. But he was back in the winner's enclosure in the one-mile-five-furlong Geoffrey Freer Stakes at Newbury in August, galloping on in great style after slipping through on the inside of the front-running Baffin to beat him four lengths with Easter Sun a short head away third. Ardross' victory gave Lester Piggott, who rode his first winner at the age of twelve in 1948, his 4,000th winner on the flat in Britain, a milestone passed previously by only Sir Gordon Richards who rode 4,870 winners between 1921 and 1954. Piggott stands out today among British jockeys as Richards did in his prime and is the outstanding present-day personality in British racing, a brilliant jockey whose success has been enormous—his twenty-five classic winners put him a clear second in the record books (only two behind Frank Buckle) and he has won the jockeys' championship eleven times, an achievement bettered only by Richards (twenty-six), George Fordham (fourteen) and Fred Archer (thirteen) since the seasonal record of jockeys' winners was first published in 1846. Piggott has every attribute that a great jockey should possess: equable temperament and patience, exquisite hands and balance, first-class judgement of pace, consummate nerve, the ability to ride a strong finish and last but by no means least, an excellent appreciation of the form-book and a thorough comprehension of the peculiarities and racing characteristics of any horse he rides. There has surely never been a better jockey for the big occasion—his eight victories in the Derby is a record—but does Piggott deserve to be regarded as 'the greatest jockey in British racing history' or 'the best jockey in the world', descriptions that are frequently applied to him? It's impossible to prove the validity or otherwise of either claim. If it were simply a matter of consulting the record books, of taking account of the number of winners ridden or number of championships attained, no fair-minded critic could judge Richards, for one, inferior to Piggott. And what of the achievements of the American Willie Shoemaker, who has ridden more than 8,000 winners? It's interesting to record something Piggott himself said as an eighteen-year-old: 'I'm as good as any jockey riding today except Gordon Richards who is out on his own.' Make allowances for the fact that Richards was champion jockey and Piggott was several years away from winning his first championship, but the statement reveals something of the reputation of Richards among his contemporaries. Richards, who rode more than two hundred winners in a season on no fewer than twelve occasions, was a magnificent jockey: he lost fewer races which he ought to have won than any rider in our experience, and there was no-one better for turning a hopeless cause into victory. Not many would disagree that Richards and Piggott are entitled to be regarded as the greatest British jockeys of the last half century. They'll still be remembered a hundred years from now, which is as good a test of greatness as any. But to claim that Piggott is the better is pointless. Bobby Jones, widely regarded as the best golfer of all time, memorably summed up a controversy about his standing in his particular sport. 'All you can do', he wrote, 'is to beat those who are around when you are around. You cannot beat those who came before or those who follow after.'

But let's return to Ardross. He was seen out twice after the Geoffrey Freer Stakes before being retired to the Beech House Stud at Newmarket where he will take up stallion duties in 1983. Heighlin, who took advantage of Ardross' absence to gain a hard-fought victory in the Goodwood Cup, was put in his place when he met Ardross in the Doncaster Cup in September; as had become his wont Ardross did all that was necessary to win—no more, no less—passing the post, pushed along, a length and a half in front of Heighlin with the three-year-old Santella Man a head away third and five others well beaten off. Ardross made his final racecourse appearance on foreign soil, in Europe's most prestigious race the Trusthouse Forte Prix de l'Arc de Triomphe at Longchamp in October, a race in which he had finished fifth twelve months earlier. Our interpretation of Ardross' running on that occasion got us into hot water with some experts. His performance—he came home just under five lengths behind the winner Gold River—clearly marked him as a high-class performer at a mile and a half but we found ourselves at variance with the view that his defeat could be explained away by his outside draw. We thought he had been found wanting for finishing speed—'he lacks that dash of top-class finishing pace that is so often a hallmark of the outstanding mile-and-a-half performer' was how we put it. To blame the draw for a horse's defeat in a race over a mile and a half is, in our view, fanciful and we can't help feeling that some of those who excused Ardross' running in the Arc on this score allowed their almost boundless enthusiasm for the horse to outrun their judgement. We defer to no-one in our admiration for Ardross as a racehorse: he was a magnificent performer, tough and hardy, consistent and courageous, able to show his form on all types of going, and as genuine as it is possible for a racehorse to be. But a mile and a half under anything like normal conditions simply wasn't far enough for him in the very best company. His half-length defeat of Glint of Gold in the Jockey Club Stakes, with Amyndas a neck away third, does not represent tip-top mile-and-a-half form—not the way we read the form-book at any rate (Glint of Gold came

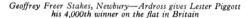

Geoffrey Freer Stakes, Newbury—Ardross gives Lester Piggott his 4,000th winner on the flat in Britain

Doncaster Cup—Ardross records the final victory of his long career

out the better horse at the weights, using our weight-for-age scale); and after Ardross' defeat in the Princess of Wales's Stakes his connections abandoned plans to send him to Ascot for the King George VI and Queen Elizabeth Diamond Stakes, Britain's most important all-aged mile-and-a-half event. The going at Ascot for the King George was on the firm side of good, and we're sure Ardross wouldn't have been at the races against Kalaglow and Assert that day. In *Racehorses of 1981* we stated that there were circumstances—soft ground and a searching end-to-end gallop, both of which would put a premium on stamina—in which we could envisage Ardross' improving on the form he had shown at a mile and a half. The going for the most recent Prix de l'Arc was soft, softer than it had been for the race in 1981, and the gallop set by Bon Sang and Bikala was a cracker (in 1981 the very early pace hadn't been quite so cut-throat as usual). Ardross found the early pace too hot and Piggott was niggling at him soon after the start, he turned for home in the middle of the field, about six or seven lengths off the leaders. But as the gruelling gallop took its toll on some of those in front Ardross, under the strongest driving from early in the straight, stayed on strongly, enjoying an uninterrupted run near the inside rail. In the final furlong Piggott took the whip to Ardross at least a dozen times, riding a tremendous finish reminiscent of his winning efforts on Roberto and The Minstrel in the Derby. Showing wonderful pluck and gameness Ardross forged ahead of Awaasif and April Run and made ground steadily on Akiyda all the way to the line, but he couldn't peg her back and was beaten a head. Ardross went by the post like a train, still full of running and still battling on with determination and gusto; in another few strides he would almost certainly have won. To express disappointment at Ardross' performance in the Prix de l'Arc, as some did, was quite wrong. The way we interpreted it, Ardross ran one of the races of his life at Longchamp. Conditions were in his favour but, on the day, Ardross beat some of the best middle-distance performers in Europe at their own game. Would it be fair to ask how well they would have done against Ardross at his specialist distance? In our view Ardross put up one of the performances of the racing year on Prix de l'Arc day. Coupled with his brilliant record in the long-distance events it earned Ardross our vote in the end-of-season poll of leading racing journalists for the 'Horse of the Year' award, an award made to the horse who, in the opinion of the selected official panel, does the most for British racing during the year.

There is plenty of stamina in Ardross' pedigree. The average distance of races won at three years and upwards by the progeny of his sire Run The Gantlet is a mile and a half and the majority of Run The Gantlet's best progeny in

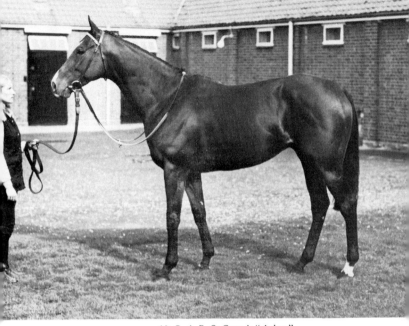

Mr C. A. B. St George's "Ardross"

Europe, including the top fillies April Run and Swiftfoot and the classic-placed Classic Example, have been suited by a mile and a half plus. Run The Gantlet was a top-class racehorse in North America: he won the very valuable Garden State Stakes as a two-year-old and the Man o'War Stakes and the Washington International (by six lengths) as a three-year-old. Ardross' dam Le Melody, who won at seven furlongs as a two-year-old and at a mile and a quarter at three on her only starts, is by Le Moss's brother Levmoss, a strong influence for stamina,

Ardross (b.h. 1976)	Run The Gantlet (b 1968)	Tom Rolfe (b 1962)	Ribot
			Pocahontas II
		First Feather (ch 1963)	First Landing
			Quill
	Le Melody (ch 1971)	Levmoss (b 1965)	Le Levanstell
			Feemoss
		Arctic Melody (b 1962)	Arctic Slave
			Bell Bird

out of the Musidora Stakes winner Arctic Melody, also the dam of the Irish One Thousand Guineas winner Arctique Royale and the Irish Guinness Oaks third Racquette among others. Ardross is Le Melody's first foal and she was represented on the racecourse by two others in the most recent season, the Irish four-year-old Karol (by Kalamoun), winner of a maiden race over a mile at Leopardstown as a three-year-old and the mile-and-a-half Trigo Stakes on the same course in 1982, and the two-year-old Adrana (by Bold Lad) who chipped a bone in her knee when winning over five furlongs at Sandown in April on her only start. Few top performers retire to stud so thoroughly tried and tested on the racecourse as Ardross and the valuation placed on him as a stallion—two million pounds—would have been very much higher had he made his reputation in more fashionable races. Gold Cup winners, in the main, are not well patronised at stud these days and we regard it as essential to Ardross' success as a stallion that he be mated with a good proportion of relatively speedy mares. Unless he proves capable of siring high-class middle-distance performers—as the stayer High Line has done, for example—we fear that commercial breeders will quickly lose interest in him. Ardross should certainly fill the eye as a stallion: he is a big, rangy attractive horse, and we greatly impressed with his appearance on most of his outings as a six-year-old. *H. Cecil.*

ARDROX LAD 2 ch.c. Roi Soleil 125–Petalina 93 (Mummy's Pet 125) (1982 **98** 5f 6fg² 5g* 5fg* 5g² 6fg² 6g 6g* 6fg² 6g² 6s² 6g² 5s⁴) Mar 26: 2,200F; smallish, workmanlike colt; first foal; dam a 2-y-o 5f winner who didn't train on; bought in 3,800 gns after winning seller at Folkestone in June in good style; afterwards ran very well in nurseries, winning 2, at Hamilton in July and Windsor in August, and finishing second in another 4; needs at least 6f and will be suited by 7f; seems to act on any going, but goes particularly well on an easy surface; genuine and most consistent. *M. Blanshard.*

ARDVERIKIE 2 b.f. Red Alert 127–Black Gnat (Typhoon 125) (1982 6d — 6g 7f) Apr 26: IR 6,000Y; smallish, lengthy filly; half-sister to 4 winners here and abroad, including 1977 2-y-o 5f winner The Gate (by On Your Mark); dam won 7 times from 5f to 9f in Ireland; behind in maiden races, one an auction event; blinkered third outing. *D. Morley.*

ARENA 2 b.f. Sallust 134–Melodramatic 112 (Tudor Melody 129) (1982 6d) **86 p** Mar 30; half-sister to 3 winners, all at least useful, including miler Crown Witness (by Crowned Prince) and Irish 8.5f and 11.5f winner Overplay (by Bustino); dam very useful winner at 7f and 9f; 8/1, nearest finish when 3¼ lengths fifth of 21 to Spanish Place in maiden race at Newmarket in October; will be suited by 7f+; bound to improve. *M. Stoute.*

ARIADNE 3 b.f. Bustino 136–Zerbinetta 96 (Henry the Seventh 125) (1981 **79** 8fg 8g 1982 11g 12g 16fg* 16d 13.8f² 13g 16s⁴) good-bodied, attractive filly; good walker and mover; stayed on well to win 11-runner maiden race at Lingfield in May; ran creditably in handicap fifth start; suited by a test of stamina; acts on any going; one paced. *J. Dunlop.*

ARIOS 4 b.g. Manacle 123–Blue Bird 84 (Majority Blue 126) (1981 8g 8g **43** 8fg⁴ 8f 10fg⁴ 12.2g 12s* 1982 12g 12.3fg 14.6g) big, strong gelding; was suited by 1¼m; acted well on soft going; dead. *M. Camacho.*

ARISTOPHON 2 b.c. Averof 123–Fille de Joie 106 (Midsummer Night II — 117) (1982 6fg) May 27; strong, well-grown colt; half-brother to 13f winner Fontainbleau (by Royal Palace) and useful Scandinavian winner Grau du Roi (by Great Nephew); dam, half-sister to Brigadier Gerard, stayed 7f; tailed-off last of 21 behind Coquito's Friend in minor event at Newmarket in August. *W. Holden.*

ARISTO TREAT 3 ch.g. Be My Guest 126–Betsy Ross 100 (Petingo 135) — (1981 NR 1982 8fg 11f 13g² 13f 15.5fg 14fg 12v) 16,500Y; tall, useful-looking gelding; first foal; dam useful at up to 1¼m; plating-class maiden; appears not to stay 1¾m; apparently needs some give in the ground (moved very poorly to post on firm fourth start); wears blinkers; sold to M. Lambert 3,800 gns Newmarket Autumn Sales. *G. Hunter.*

ARITIMA 2 br.c. Manado 130–Westgate Sovereign 89 (Sovereign Path 125) **69** (1982 5s² 5s² 5f² 5f³ 6fg 5d 6d) Mar 11; IR 10,000Y; leggy, fair sort; keen walker; first foal; dam won over 5f at 2 yrs; second in small fields in the spring, twice completely outpointed by Horage, but well beaten afterwards; should stay 6f; probably failed to train on. *K. Ivory.*

ARIZONA SKY 3 b. or br.g. African Sky 124–Daffodil Girl (Blakeney 126) — (1981 NR 1982 8g 8fg 8d 8f) 10,000Y; rather leggy gelding; second foal; dam modest half-sister to smart 6f and 1¼m winner Escapologist; beaten some way in maiden races and a seller; blinkered final start; sold 570 gns Doncaster August Sales. *P. Kelleway.*

ARKAN 4 b.c. Prince Tenderfoot 126–Adamantos 92 (Yellow God 129) (1981 **69** 8.2fg³ 12g³ 11g² 10f* 10.1f³ 10g⁴ 10fg³ 10g* 10fg 10f* 9s⁴ 10g 1982 12fg⁴ 10fg 12.2f* 10f⁴ 11g³ 12g² 12.3fg² 12f³ 13fg⁴ 12.2f*) strong, good sort; not a good walker; stayed on when winning handicaps at Catterick in May and August; suited by 1½m nowadays; acts on a soft surface but is well suited by firm going; iron broke when blinkered on reappearance; probably suited by a strong gallop. *J. Hindley.*

ARKENGARTHDALE 8 b.m. Sweet Story 122–Fortzeno 78 (Fortino II 120) — (1981 16.5g 18g 1982 16g) small mare; lightly raced and no sign of ability on flat though has won over hurdles; bandaged only outing of 1982.   *N. Bycroft.*

ARLINGTON GIRL   3 b.f. Rarity 129–Santa Nan (Santa Claus 133)   (1981   **42**
7f⁴ 7g 7d 10d 8.2s³ 8d   1982 12.2g 10s³ 12.2f⁴ 12f 12fg³ 12d)   narrow, light-
framed filly; plater; best run at 1¼m on soft going; sold 400 gns Newmarket
Autumn Sales and sent to Holland.   *Mrs J. Reavey.*

ARMALITE   2 ch.f. Mansingh 120–Damsel II (Chamier 128)   (1982 5fg 6f)   —
May 17; leggy, lightly-made filly; half-sister to winners in Italy and Norway;
dam won 2 races in Italy; well beaten in sellers at Nottingham in April (blinkered) and Leicester in July.   *D. H. Jones.*

ARMALOU   3 gr.f. Ardoon 124–Sweet Rocket (Roan Rocket 128)   (1981   **54**
5g 5fg 5g⁴ 6fg 6g 7g 6d   1982 6g 7d 7g 8fg 8fg 10v* 12d)   robust filly; plater;
attracted no bid after winning at Lingfield in October; stayed 1¼m; acted on
heavy going; was tried in blinkers but didn't wear them at Lingfield; covered
by Anax.   *D. Sasse.*

ARMENISTIS   3 b.c. Relkino 131–Persian Market 105 (Taj Dewan 128)   (1981   **62**
7fg 7f³ 8g 8g   1982 16f³ 16f* 15.5f 16h 17fg 16fg 14g)   compact, quite useful
sort; not the best of movers; narrowly won 11-runner maiden race at Thirsk
in April; well beaten afterwards, but had stiffish tasks; suited by 2m; yet to
race on a soft surface; blinkered third start; sold to S. Leadbetter 3,100 gns
Newmarket Autumn Sales.   *C. Brittain.*

ARMONIT   2 ch.f. Town Crier 119–Wasdale 97 (Psidium 130)   (1982 5fg   **76**
5g⁴ 5f 5fg 7fg 7fg 6d 7d*)   May 4; 1,000F; tall filly; half-sister to 2 winners,
including 1¼m winner Caspardale (by Frankincense); dam won 5 sprint races;
33/1, won 15-runner maiden race at Leicester in October by a length from Iver
Saga; will stay 1m; suited by a soft surface; trained by Mrs B. Waring first
7 outings.   *R. Hannon.*

ARNAB   2 b.g. Pitskelly 122–Reelin Bridge (New Day)   (1982 5s 5fg³ 5g 5fg   **76**
6g 7fg* 7g³ 7fg 7.6fg²)   Feb 12; IR 9,000F, 700Y; brother to a winner in Belgium, and half-brother to 3 winners, including very useful sprinter Reelin
Jig (by Jukebox); dam won over 1¼m in Ireland; only sixth of 12 in seller on
fifth start but ran out a surprise winner of 10-runner maiden race at Brighton
in July on next appearance, coming through to beat Jayvee 1½ lengths; placed
subsequently in nurseries won by Back'hus Boy at Lingfield; evidently needs
at least 7f; blinkered third start; none too consistent.   *R. Smyth.*

ARNALDO   4 b.g. Upper Case–Flower Petals (Busted 134)   (1981 10fg* 12fg²   —
11.7fg* 12f² 10.4s   1982 10.1d)   neat gelding; plater; stays 1½m; acts on firm
going; usually a front runner; claimed £2,700 after finishing in rear only outing
of 1982 (bandaged).   *N. Callaghan.*

ARNCLIFFE   2 ch.g. Netherkelly 112–Not Suspect 73 (Above Suspicion 127)   —
(1982 9s)   Apr 8; 2,600Y; strong gelding; half-brother to 3 winners; dam appeared to stay 2m; unquoted and backward when last of 15 to Omar Ramsden
in maiden race at Redcar in October.   *I. Vickers.*

ARRAS GIRL   3 br.f. Rapid River 127–Arras Gem 82 (Three Wishes 114)   **47**
(1981 5s⁴ 5g² 5d³ 5f 5f 6g 5f 5f   1982 7g* 6fg 7fg)   neat filly; has a round
action; plater; won at Catterick in March (no bid); ran abysmally next time;
evidently suited by 7f and may stay 1m; possibly needs some give in the ground.
A. Smith.

ARROWOOD BOB (USA)   2 ch.c. Full Pocket–Lauravella 108 (Aureole 132)   **108**
(1982 5fg² 5f* 6f² 6d* 6f⁴ 7fg² 7f² 7g² 7v)   Feb 18; $85,000Y; small, useful-
looking colt; good mover; half-brother to several winners, including minor stakes
winners Dancing Laura (by Duck Dance) and North Marlinn (by Northern
Fling); dam, half-sister to very smart sprinter Creetown, was third in Irish 1,000
Guineas; won 2 of his 9 races, maiden event at Newcastle in May and Chesters
Stakes on same course in June; second in 5 of his other starts, on last 3 occasions
being beaten ½ length or less, by Sheriff Muir in well-contested event at Redcar,
by Northern Secret in Grand Criterium International d'Ostende and by Linda's
Fantasy in nursery under top weight at Yarmouth; suited by 7f; acts on firm
going and a soft surface, and had stiff task when well beaten only outing on heavy
ground; genuine and consistent.   *G. Pritchard-Gordon.*

ARROWOOD DREAM (USA)   3 b.c. Far North 120–Dear Annie (Impressive)   **96**
(1981 7g² 7fg³ 8g* 8s*   1982 7d 10fg⁴ 11g² 11g³ 13fg* 12f 10g 12s)   rather
lightly-made colt; useful performer; long odds on when making all to win small
race at Ayr in July decisively from Misty Halo; in frame most previous starts,

finishing 4½ lengths fourth of 8 to Electric in White Rose Stakes at Ascot, 2½ lengths second to Anno in Grosser Hertie-Preis at Munich and 3¼ lengths third to Rivellino in Grand Prix de Bruxelles at Groenendael; stays 13f; seems to act on any going but goes well on soft; gave trouble at start and ran moderately final outing. *J. Dunlop.*

ARROWOOD JUNCTION (USA) 2 b.c. Junction–Promised Princess (Promised Land) (1982 8g 8g) Apr 30; $65,000Y; strong, compact, attractive colt; half-brother to 2 minor winners in USA; dam won 6f claiming race at 2 yrs; showed promise when eighth of 17 to Oula Owl in maiden race at Newmarket in October, second outing; looks capable of better. *G. Pritchard-Gordon.* — p

ARTISTE 2 b.f. Artaius 129–Val's Girl 113 (Sir Ivor 135) (1982 6g 8f*) June 5; IR 400,000Y; rather lightly-made, quite attractive filly; half-sister to 3-y-o middle-distance winner Valiancy (by Grundy) and fairly useful 1979 2-y-o maiden Val's Mill (by Mill Reef); dam second in Oaks and daughter of Irish 1,000 Guineas and Epsom Oaks winner Valoris; made all and kept on strongly to win 23-runner maiden race at Leicester in September by 1½ lengths from Thessaloniki; likely to develop into a useful middle-distance filly. *J. Tree.* 95 p

ARTIST'S REEL 2 ch.c. Artaius 129–Come Dancing 91 (Northern Dancer) (1982 5f² 6fg 7fg² 7g* 7g⁴ 8g² 8g) Apr 23; 28,000Y; small, fair sort; half-brother to 3 winners, including very smart stayer General Ironside (by Sea Hawk II) and useful 7f to 1½m winner Welsh Dancer (by Welsh Pageant); dam stayed 1m; won 10-runner nursery at Wolverhampton going away by 2½ lengths from Jalmood The Stone; stays well, and will be suited by 1¼m+; yet to race on a soft surface; consistent. *P. Walwyn.* 93

ARUN'S DELIGHT 2 b.g. Furry Glen 121–Aran Jacket (Le Levanstell 122) (1982 5fg 7f) May 15; IR 3,600F, IR 4,000Y; brother to Cool Decision, a fairly useful middle-distance winner, and half-brother to a bumpers winner and chaser Lord Gulliver (by Varano); dam fair Irish middle-distance performer; behind in maiden races at Windsor in May and Brighton (last of 12 after starting slowly) in August; trained by S. Mellor first start. *G. Lewis.*

ASCOT BLUE 9 b.g. Majority Blue 126–Pebble Ridge 107 (Big Game) (1981 5d 5d 5s³ 5.8g 5fg⁴ 5.8d 5fg 5.8f 5.8g 5s³ 5d² 5s 6d³ 1982 5d 5fg 5fg 5g 5fg 5fg 5fg⁴ 5d 5s 6s) sprint handicapper; probably ideally suited by some give in the ground nowadays; suitable mount for an inexperienced rider; has occasionally worn blinkers. *M. Bradley.* —

ASHANTI 2 gr.f. Yankee Gold 115–Ghana's Daughter 93 (Sallust 134) (1982 7d³ 8d*) Mar 28; first foal; dam won over 9f at 2 yrs in Ireland and is half-sister to Irish Oaks winner Gaia; put up a pleasing display to win 20-runner maiden race at Leopardstown in October by 2½ lengths from Joannes Joy, who won her next start by 8 lengths; will stay 1½m; has further improvement in her. *J. Oxx, Ireland.* 96 p

ASHBUD 3 br.f. Ashmore 125–Love-In-The-Mist 78 (Aureole 132) (1981 6g 1982 10.1d 12f 12f 10.1g 9fg 8.2s) light-framed filly; poor maiden; sold 11,500 gns Newmarket December Sales. *G. Hunter.* —

ASHENDEN 3 b.c. Blakeney 126–Ravenshead (Charlottown 127) (1981 111§ 7f² 7fg* 7g² 7fg³ 8d 1982 10f 12.3g 12f⁴ 12f⁴ 21f 12g) lengthy, attractive colt; good mover; very useful performer at his best; made running and stayed on strongly to be 2½ lengths fourth of 11 to Open Day in King Edward VII Stakes at Royal Ascot, third start and easily best effort at 3 yrs; finished last on all subsequent outings; evidently doesn't stay extreme distances; seems to act on any going; blinkered second start; not an easy ride and is doubtful temperamentally; sent to USA. *B. Hills.*

ASHINGTON 3 b.g. Habat 127–Aberangell 96 (Abernant 142) (1981 NR 1982 10f 8s 8d) 5,600Y; sturdy gelding; half-brother to several winners, including 1¼m winner Gelignite (by St Paddy); dam 2-y-o 5f winner; little worthwhile form. *R. D. Peacock.* —

ASH KING 3 b.c. Ashmore 125–Four Queens (Quorum 126) (1981 5d² 5d 6fg³ 8.2s 8d 1982 8g 12f 12f³ 13.8f 10d* 10fg²(dis) 12g² 10g³ 10v 11v* 12g) rather lightly-made colt; plater; won at Beverley in July (no bid) and 2-runner event at Hamilton in October (bought in 880 gns); stays 1½m; acts on any going; best in blinkers. *W. Musson.* 61

ASHLEIGH BOY 5 gr.g. Habat 127–Vimy Line (Vimy 132) (1981 12s 7d 8s 8f 1982 10fg) small gelding; plater; stays 1m; suited by some give in the ground; blinkered once at 2 yrs. *R. Hoad.* —

ASHMOLEAN (USA) 2 ch.c. Vaguely Noble 140–Dona Maya (Reviewer) **101**
(1982 7f⁴ 7fg* 8fg² 8g*) Mar 14; $120,000Y; quite attractive colt; good walker;
first foal; dam, minor stakes winner, won at up to 1m; successful in maiden race
at Warwick in July and 9-runner minor event at Leicester in October; looked in
fine shape and made all to beat Blushing River, who was eased, by 4 lengths on
latter; stays 1m; fought for his head and went to start very freely on debut, and
refused to settle after being taken down very early and very slowly on third
appearance; evidently headstrong; sold BBA (Italia) 20,000 guineas Newmarket
Autumn Sales. *G. Harwood.*

ASHMORE LADY 2 b.f. Ashmore 125–Hasten Slowly (Mark-Ye-Well) (1982 —
6fg) Apr 3; 6,000Y; well-made, good sort; half-sister to useful 5f to 1m winner
Darwood (by Sallust) and 2 other winners; dam won from 6f to 1m in Ireland;
unquoted and rather backward, finished tailed-off thirteenth of 14 behind
Octavia Girl in valuable newcomers event at Ascot in June. *B. McMahon.*

ASHORE 4 ch.g. Ashmore 125–Ornella (Princely Gift 137) (1981 10s 12fg⁴ —
12g 1982 16d 14fg 18.8fg) fair sort; poor maiden; doesn't seem to stay 1¾m.
H. Candy.

ASH RIDGE (USA) 3 b.f. Bold Reason–Favoletta 115 (Baldric II 131) (1981 **93**
6g 6g* 1982 7d 7fg 10.5fg² 10.5v 10fg 10fg³ 8v² 10s²) good-bodied, attractive
filly; did well physically over the winter; very useful on her day, as she showed
when 1½ lengths second to Last Feather in Musidora Stakes at York in May, but
has run her share of disappointing races also; suited by 1¼m; seems to act on any
going; sometimes sweats up; blinkered sixth start; possibly needs to be held
up (didn't find much in front for apprentice rider penultimate start). *H. Wragg.*

ASHTON GATE 5 ch.m. Sovereign Bill 105–Slipaway (Sunny Way 120) —
(1981 NR 1982 8fg) second foal; dam ran once over hurdles; novice selling
hurdler; behind in amateur riders race at Warwick in July. *M. Bradley.*

ASIA MINOR 2 b.g. Hittite Glory 125–Paresseuse 114 (Relko 136) (1982 **80**
6fg 7.2g³ 7d⁴ 8f) Mar 13; strong, good-bodied gelding; brother to 3-y-o Idle
Days and half-brother to 3 winners in France, including useful 1m to 11f winner
Stand Hill (by Mountain Call); dam middle-distance stayer; in frame in August
in minor event at Haydock (started slowly) and maiden race at Chester, on both
occasions putting in all his best work in closing stages; favourite for £5,700 nursery
at Doncaster the following month but was always making heavy weather of it and
finished only seventh of 11 to Axkernish; should be suited by 1m; possibly needs
some give in the ground; seemed unsuited by track at Chester; gelded after
final outing. *W. Hastings-Bass.*

ASIDE 2 ch.f. Bold Lad (Ire) 133–Never A Whisper (Crepello 136) (1982 6g) —
Apr 26; quite attractive filly; half-sister to 1981 Irish 2-y-o 7f winner With
Discretion (by Be My Guest) and a winner in France; dam Irish 9f winner; 14/1
but pretty fit, faded after chasing leaders to halfway when eleventh of 15 to
Miss Thames in maiden race at Yarmouth in June; sold Susan Piggott
Bloodstock 1,600 gns Newmarket Autumn Sales. *H. Cecil.*

ASK THE WIND 2 ch.f. Run The Gantlet–Arburie (Exbury 138) (1982 7v* **103**
10v* 10v 9v) Apr 20; third foal; half-sister to a winner in USA by Kalamoun;
dam, half-sister to very smart French middle-distance winner Armos, won over
13f in Ireland; shaped like a smart filly when winning 16-runner newcomers
event at Saint-Cloud and 70,000-franc race at Evry in October, landing the
odds by 3 lengths from Squadron Leader in latter; only ninth of 12 to Escaline
in Criterium de Saint-Cloud in November next time out; will be well suited by
1½m. *F. Boutin, France.*

ASMALWI 2 gr.f. Averof 123–Sylvanecte 70 (Silver Shark 129) (1982 5g —
5f 8fg 7s) Apr 24; 11,000Y; tall, lengthy filly; half-sister to 3 winners, including
useful Shark Song (by Song), successful from 5f to 9f here and in USA, and
useful 6f and 7f winner Silver Lord (by Abwah); dam won over 1¼m; no worthwhile form in maiden events and a Leicester nursery; should stay 1m; off course
4 months between second and third starts. *W. Musson.*

ASMID 3 b.c. Wishing Star 117–Pouilly Fuse (Tudor Music 131) (1981 NR **65**
1982 8g 8g 8.2g* 8.2fg⁴ 10g³) 2,100Y; lengthy, useful-looking colt; fourth foal;
half-brother to 11f winner Winterreise (by Fine Blade) and to 2 winners in
Malaya; dam never ran; short-priced favourite when winning 7-runner maiden
race at Hamilton in July; ran respectably in handicap final start; stays 1¼m;
seems suited by some give in the ground. *S. Norton.*

ASPERITY 2 b.f. Averof 123–Won't Linger (Worden II 129) (1982 5s) Apr — 15; half-sister to numerous winners, including smart stayer Hazy Idea (by Hethersett); dam unraced half-sister to several good winners, including very smart Heath Rose; weak 16/1-shot when twelfth of 21 behind Holy Day in maiden race at Bath in October; sold CBA 12,000 gns Newmarket Autumn Sales. *H. Candy.*

ASSADAA 2 b.c. Habitat 134–Gallissa (El Gallo 122) (1982 6g 5d 6d 6g⁴) **83** Apr 5; 160,000Y; good-topped colt; half-brother to several winners, including Phoenix Stakes winner Perla (by Young Emperor); dam, fairly useful over 5f at 2 yrs in Ireland, is half-sister to Lorenzaccio; blinkered, kept on steadily when 7 lengths fourth of 19 to Matou in maiden race at Newmarket in October, first indication of merit; moved badly to post here and also on second outing; will stay beyond 6f. *H. T. Jones.*

ASSERT 3 b.c. Be My Guest 126–Irish Bird (Sea-Bird II 145) (1981 8g² **134** 8d* 8d 1982 10fg² 12g* 12fg* 12g* 12fg² 10.5fg* 10fg* 12s)
The emergence of the Irish-trained horse as a force in international competition is a more recent phenomenon than may be generally appreciated. It dates only from the 'fifties and was due mainly to the advent of Paddy Prendergast and Vincent O'Brien as great trainers and to the resources of their patrons. Prendergast, who died in 1980, topped the list of trainers in Britain three years in a row in the early sixties, a remarkable achievement for a foreign-based trainer; there was hardly a major race in Britain and Ireland that he didn't win during a career in which his outstanding horses included Ragusa and Meadow Court, both successful in the King George VI and Queen Elizabeth Stakes, the Oaks winner Noblesse, the Guineas winners Martial and Pourparler, the brilliant sprinter Floribunda and the tip-top two-year-olds Windy City, The Pie King, La Tendresse, Young Emperor and Bold Lad, all of whom headed the Free Handicap. The Derby, a race that eluded Prendergast, has been won six times by Vincent O'Brien who was responsible for the most recent winner Golden Fleece. Ballymoss was O'Brien's first champion: the 1957 St Leger winner won the next year's King George VI and Prix de l'Arc. Since then O'Brien has trained a host of famous racehorses, among them Sir Ivor, Nijinsky, The Minstrel and Alleged, each of whom, like Golden Fleece, was bred in North America. O'Brien has been leading trainer in Britain twice (in 1966 and 1977) and five two-year-olds handled by him have topped the Free Handicap (Nijinsky, Apalachee, Try My Best, Monteverdi and Storm Bird).
In 1982 the exploits of the Irish-trained and Irish-bred Assert thrust Vincent O'Brien's son David, based like his father at Ballydoyle, into the forefront of his profession in only his second season as a trainer. The younger O'Brien has proved thoroughly worthy of the tremendous support he has received—among his owners in his first season were such as Binet, Fluor, Sangster, Schwartz, St George and Wildenstein—and the racing world looks wide open to him. O'Brien sent out Assert to win five of his eight races, the Gallinule Stakes at the Curragh in May, the Prix du Jockey-Club (French Derby) at Chantilly and the Irish Sweeps Derby at the Curragh in June, the Benson

Gallinule Stakes, the Curragh—Assert wins in fine style from Rivellino

and Hedges Gold Cup at York in August and the Joe McGrath Memorial Stakes at Leopardstown in September. The four last-named are Group 1 pattern races and Assert failed by only a neck to add another Group 1 event to his record when beaten by the four-year-old Kalaglow in Britain's most important all-aged middle-distance event, the King George VI and Queen Elizabeth Diamond Stakes at Ascot in July. Assert's poor showing in the Trusthouse Forte Prix de l'Arc de Triomphe on his final outing—he finished eleventh to Akiyda—was the only blot on his record which, taken as a whole, gave Assert a strong claim to recognition as the horse who made the greatest contribution to European racing in the middle-distance category during the year. Unlike the lightly-raced Derby winner Golden Fleece and the Prix de l'Arc winner Akiyda, whose performances at Epsom and Longchamp outstripped all their others, Assert had his merit underlined by a string of top-class performances: he won the Gallinule by ten lengths, the Prix du Jockey-Club by three, the Irish Sweeps Derby by a long-looking eight, the Benson and Hedges by six and the Joe McGrath Memorial by three. In particular, he won the twenty-first Irish Sweeps Derby and the eleventh Benson and Hedges Gold Cup in tremendously impressive fashion, winning on each occasion by the widest margin of victory officially recorded in the race.

Assert was rated only the joint-tenth best two-year-old to race in Ireland in 1981, 7 lb below the top weight in the Irish Classification, Achieved; in the International Classification Assert was joint-thirty-sixth, 13 lb below French-trained Green Forest, officially regarded as Europe's top two-year-old. Assert had only three outings in his first season, on the second of them winning the Beresford Stakes at the Curragh in October by four lengths and six from Longleat and Furry Berg. Later in October Assert finished eighth, hampered two furlongs out, to Count Pahlen in the William Hill Futurity, leaving us with the impression that he was the type to show to better advantage as a three-year-old. However, without being unreasonably optimistic few outside his stable could have expected Assert to reach top classic standard. He opened his three-year-old campaign in somewhat leisurely fashion, very much catching our eye when runner-up to Golden Fleece, who started at 3/1 on, in the Nijinsky Stakes over a mile and a quarter at Leopardstown early in May; Golden Fleece had beaten Assert with ease in a maiden race at the same course the previous September. Two weeks later Assert left his rivals standing in the mile-and-a-half Gallinule Stakes, showing fine acceleration early in the straight to win without being shaken up from Rivellino and Tooska, both winners of maiden races on their previous outings; in fourth place, fourteen lengths behind Assert, came Future Spa who on his previous outing had finished three lengths second to Golden Fleece in the Sean Graham Ballymoss Stakes.

It was evident from his early-season performances that Assert had developed into a high-class three-year-old, a worthy contender for the major middle-distance races. A decision about his next appearance was delayed while Golden Fleece, owned by a syndicate headed by Robert Sangster the controlling shareholder in Assert, recovered from slight lameness which at one point threatened his participation in the Derby. When Golden Fleece was declared fit to take his place in the field at Epsom, Assert was sent to Chantilly for the Prix du Jockey-Club, four days after the Derby. Because of its proximity to the Epsom Derby, the French equivalent attracts very few runners from British or Irish stables. In 1974, Grundy's stable-companion Patch was beaten a head by Val de l'Orne and three years later Artaius, whose stable was represented at Epsom by The Minstrel, Valinsky and Assert's sire Be My Guest, went down by half a length to Crystal Palace. Assert faced no opponent of the calibre of Val de l'Orne or Crystal Palace and, in the absence of the Prix Lupin winner Persepolis who contested the Derby, Assert started favourite for the Prix du Jockey-Club in which the home-based opposition included Alfred's Choice, Sharp Singer and Le Monastere, second, third and fourth in the Prix Lupin, France's most important classic trial, and the first four in the Prix Hocquart, Cadoudal, Noble Bloom, Real Shadai and Newjdar; Criterion represented the Harwood stable which had saddled Recitation for the race twelve months earlier. Roche kept Assert handily placed from the start and moved him into fourth place on the outside rounding the home turn, on to the heels of Real Shadai who was challenging Newjdar and Marcao for the lead. Assert had a short struggle with Real Shadai before forging ahead to win by three lengths, kept up to his work to the line. Next came Bois de Grace, Alfred's Choice and Noble Bloom, none of whom seriously threatened the first two in the straight, with Criterion ninth.

Assert's performance in the Prix du Jockey-Club was inevitably over-shadowed in the public mind at the time by the striking victory of Golden Fleece

Prix du Jockey-Club, Chantilly—Assert becomes the first foreign-trained winner of the French Derby

in the Derby. Assert was stretching out with a will in the closing stages of the Prix du Jockey-Club but he didn't win so spectacularly as the confidently-ridden Golden Fleece who showed tremendous acceleration at Epsom to come from behind to beat Touching Wood by three lengths. For a short time it seemed that Assert and Golden Fleece might meet in the Irish Sweeps Derby but nothing came of it. While Assert went from strength to strength after the Prix du Jockey-Club, Golden Fleece never ran again after Epsom. Three weeks after running at Chantilly, Assert was presented with a relatively simple task in the Irish Sweeps Derby in which only the Derby third Silver Hawk of his nine rivals started at odds shorter than 11/1. Assert's performance at the Curragh was one of the most impressive seen in a classic in recent times. He won with great ease by eight lengths—we made it ten—from Silver Hawk, who had finished four behind Golden Fleece at Epsom. Assert swept into the lead with about half a mile to run and soon after entering the straight had all his rivals off the bridle, vainly trying to keep in touch. Pushed along for a furlong or so he quickened to such purpose that with a quarter of a mile to go he was out on his own with the race won. Throughout the last furlong Assert sailed along hard held with his head in his chest, a remarkable sight in a race of such importance. What caught our eye most of all though was Assert's action. In our experience we doubt whether we have seen a more fluent and impressive mover; the freedom, smoothness and elasticity of his stride were a delight to watch.

Although Assert was impressive at the Curragh, it had to be borne in mind that with the exception of Silver Hawk the opposition in the Irish Sweeps Derby was poor by classic standards: the third Patcher, beaten ten and a half lengths by Assert, had finished only fourth in the Queen's Vase at Royal Ascot on his previous outing and the fourth Favoloso had come seventh in the King Edward VII Stakes. That said, Assert made hacks of the opposition—Silver Hawk included—and the inevitable conclusion to be drawn from his performance was that he would prove a very tough nut to crack in the King George VI and Queen Elizabeth Diamond Stakes in July. Assert started odds on at Ascot in a field which included his French-trained half-brother Bikala, winner of the 1981 Prix du Jockey-Club and of the Prix Ganay at Longchamp in May. Assert, the only three-year-old colt among the nine runners, found one too good for him on the day in Kalaglow, a four-year-old who had gained impressive wins in the Earl of Sefton Stakes at Newmarket and the Brigadier Gerard Stakes and the Coral-Eclipse Stakes at Sandown. In a race run at a cracking gallop Assert moved up a very close third about five furlongs from home and took up the running from Bikala as soon as the field turned into the finishing straight; hard ridden to hold the challenge of Glint of Gold two furlongs out Assert stayed on very strongly, shaking off all his rivals except Kalaglow and losing the lead only close home. Beaten a neck by Kalaglow, Assert finished three lengths in front of third-placed Glint of Gold, the only occasion that the latter was out of the first two in his career. Using our scale of weight for age (which gives a three-year-old 3 lb less to carry against a four-year-old at this stage

Irish Sweeps Derby, the Curragh—Assert bags another classic with this effortless win from Silver Hawk

of the season than do the King George weights) Assert comes out the best horse in the race at the weights.

Assert's connections had announced after the Irish Sweeps Derby that they intended to keep him in training as a four-year-old and with that in mind it had been planned that Assert would contest only one more major race after the King George as a three-year-old, possibly the St Leger, leaving the Benson and Hedges Gold Cup and the Prix de l'Arc de Triomphe as a likely programme for Golden Fleece, provided he recovered from a viral infection. By mid-season, however, it was becoming increasingly clear that all was not well with Golden Fleece and it was Assert who carried the Sangster colours in the Benson and Hedges Gold Cup at York in August. With Kalaglow in reserve for the autumn, Assert's most dangerous opponent appeared to be the Cecil-trained Mr Fluorocarbon who had created a very favourable impression when winning the Queen Anne Stakes over a mile at Royal Ascot. But there was nothing in the Benson and Hedges Gold Cup field that Assert couldn't beat on his King George running and he gave another scintillating performance, making practically all the running and drawing right away when ridden along in the straight. Assert's jockey Eddery, nursing a broken finger sustained in a fall in the previous race, put his whip down inside the final furlong but Assert ran through to the finish without slackening his pace to win by six lengths and a neck from the Derby fifth Norwick and the four-year-old Amyndas, both of whom were ridden out; Mr Fluorocarbon came fifth. Assert's achievement in winning the Benson and Hedges Gold Cup so decisively should not be underestimated. The race comes at an awkward time of the season for a top-class middle-distance three-year-old: Assert, for example, had contested the Prix du Jockey-Club, the Irish Sweeps Derby and the King George in the space of seven weeks in June and July and had had only a little over three weeks to recover from a very hard race in the King George; like most of the best three-year-olds that contest the Benson and Hedges, Assert was also returning to a shorter distance after being campaigned at a mile and a half. The previous ten runnings of the race had provided set-backs for a number of horses who had won or played a leading role in the King George VI and Queen Elizabeth Diamond Stakes, Brigadier Gerard, Rheingold and Grundy being the most famous examples.

As Group 1 races go, Assert's next race the Joe McGrath Memorial Stakes at Leopardstown in September is usually easy pickings: it was instituted in 1976 and is Ireland's most important all-aged middle-distance event but it clashes with a number of important races in England and France and has proved something of a benefit for Ballydoyle stables who, before Assert, had won the

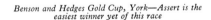

*Benson and Hedges Gold Cup, York—Assert is the
easiest winner yet of this race*

previous four runnings with Inkerman, Fordham, Gregorian and Kings Lake. For ease and impressiveness Assert's victory in the Joe McGrath almost matched that in the Irish Sweeps Derby. There was nothing to touch him and he had little more than an exercise gallop, quickening away from his nine rivals coming into the straight and opening up a lead of about eight lengths before being eased down inside the final furlong; the winning margin of three lengths greatly flattered the runner-up Kind of Hush. The Joe McGrath was Assert's seventh race of the season—victory took his career earnings in first-prize money to £299,409—but he looked as well as ever beforehand and to all appearances seemed to be in the kind of form that would make him a danger to all in the Prix de l'Arc de Triomphe. The going at Longchamp was soft and Assert had never previously raced on ground any softer than dead. His participation in the Prix de l'Arc was in doubt until the eleventh hour, his connections being anxious about the conditions which were worsened by further rain after the runners had been declared. Starting favourite, Assert was in a good position approaching the straight but he was one of the first to come under strong pressure and dropped away quickly two furlongs out; he clearly didn't show his form. The majority of critics put down Assert's performance purely and simply to the state of the going. For our part, we're sure there was more to it than that. Assert was such a glorious mover that we'd have been surprised if soft ground had inconvenienced him—superbly fluent movers, such as Mill Reef and his son Glint of Gold for example, are often as effective in the mud as on firm going. Certainly there was no hint as Assert cantered to post for the Prix de l'Arc that he was ill at ease; he went down beautifully, his action faultless as usual. There are more likely explanations for Assert's defeat. It's possible that the combination of soft ground and the blistering gallop set by Bon Sang and Bikala proved too much for Assert; the Arc was far and away the most searching test of stamina he faced in his career. It's also possible that after going through a full programme of big races in the summer, Assert was past his best. And it should be borne in mind that he might not have been quite good enough to win the Arc at his best in any case. Real Shadai, beaten three lengths by Assert in the Prix du Jockey-Club, confirmed his ranking as the best three-year-old middle-distance colt in France when finishing six places ahead of Assert in the Prix de l'Arc; but Real Shadai finished more than four and a half lengths behind winning filly Akiyda. To have won the Arc Assert would almost certainly have had to give the best performance of his career.

			Northern Dancer		Nearctic
Assert (b.c. 1979)	Be My Guest (ch 1974)		(b 1961)		Natalma
			What a Treat		Tudor Minstrel
			(b 1962)		Rare Treat
	Irish Bird (b or br 1970)		Sea-Bird II		Dan Cupid
			(ch 1962)		Sicalade
			Irish Lass II		Sayajirao
			(b 1962)		Scollata

Assert was retired after the Prix de l'Arc de Triomphe, arrangements for his syndication as a stallion having been completed earlier in the autumn. His syndication put a value on him of 25,000,000 dollars (around £14.7m at prevailing exchange rates) and he is to stand at Windfields Farm, Maryland, United States in 1983. The enormous sums available to secure the best horses for stud, particularly for North America, are often blamed for the haste with which owners rush their top-class three-year-olds off to stud. But the practice in Europe of retiring top-class horses at the end of their three-year-old days is not new, nor is the exporting of stallions to North America. Both have been going on for a very long time. For instance, three of the first sixteen Derby winners were exported to the United States, and so were six of the Derby winners between 1868 and 1886—and that's not counting the first American-bred Derby winner Iroquois, the 1881 winner, who was afterwards repatriated. The plain fact is that however much the European racing public may wish to see more of the very best horses kept in training as four-year-olds, there's little chance of much improvement in the situation so long as the programme of racing continues to offer, as it almost always has, the greatest rewards to horses bred and trained to be successful at two and three years. There is, as the Americans might say, no percentage in keeping a horse like Assert in training as a four-year-old. What fields had Assert left to conquer? His reputation and value were established by classic success as a three-year-old and he could not add materially to his value as a stallion without winning the King George VI and Queen Elizabeth Diamond Stakes *and* the Prix de l'Arc de Triomphe, a very tall order. The prize money for those two races would be a small fraction of the stud fees to be earned by the horse as a four-year-old. The pressure on an owner to retire a three-year-old like Assert is well-nigh irresistible: honour and glory are noble ambitions but they butter no parsnips.

Assert, a big, handsome colt, should make a magnificent-looking stallion. Why he should have fetched only 160,000 francs (approximately £16,000) as a yearling we don't claim fully to understand—evidently Sangster and his partners expected to have to pay at least three times that amount. Assert is well bred, a member of the first crop of the Northern Dancer stallion Be My Guest (also responsible for the One Thousand Guineas and Sussex Stakes winner On The House) out of a winning mare from a well-known family. The year after Assert went through the sale-ring his half-brother Bikala (by Kalamoun) won the Prix du Jockey-Club and finished second in the Grand Prix de Saint-Cloud and the Prix de l'Arc de Triomphe. The dam's only previous foals, Irish Gantlet (by Run The Gantlet) and Shadowbrook (by Dancer's Image) had proved only moderate, however, which could partly explain why Bikala and Assert were bought so cheaply. Assert's dam Irish Bird, by Sea-Bird II out of a very useful sister to the Irish Oaks and Irish St Leger winner Lynchris, is a half-sister to the Irish Sweeps Derby winner Irish Ball and set a then-record French yearling price of 700,000 francs. She won a newcomers race over eleven furlongs at Longchamp before being retired to the paddocks. After producing Irish Gantlet and Shadowbrook, then missing a year, she produced Bikala in 1978 and Assert in 1979. Shortly after Bikala had fetched only 6,000 guineas as a yearling Irish Bird was returned to the Sales by the Moyglare Stud, carrying a foal by Paddy Prendergast's Bold Lad, and fetched 200,000 francs (about £22,000 at the time). After Bikala's three-year-old career and the first-season promise shown by Assert, the Bold Lad colt made 170,000 Irish guineas as a yearling! Named Bold Irish he was in training in France in 1982. Irish Bird had a colt by Northfields in 1981.

Assert and On The House were largely responsible for putting Be My Guest at the top of the sires' list in the most recent season: their combined

Mr R. E. Sangster's "Assert"

first-prize earnings in Britain and Ireland—£340,053—accounted for the bulk of Be My Guest's total. Syndicated at £20,000 a share when he was retired in 1977—he was a high-class miler, gaining his most important victory in the Waterford Crystal Mile—Be My Guest is now a much hotter property. Shares in him reportedly changed hands for up to 500,000 dollars (about £295,000) in 1982 and he will be standing at IR £75,000 (1st October concession) in 1983. Among mares said to be booked to him for 1983 are Arkadina, Favoletta, Glass Slipper, Harmonise, Hogan's Sister, Nasseem, Noiritza, Sorbus, Sutton Place, Swiftfoot, Topsy and Typecast. The careers of both Assert's sire and dam illustrate vividly that fashions in bloodstock breeding can change as quickly as those on the pages of women's magazines! Whether Assert himself will turn out to be worth the enormous sum paid for him by the Americans only time will tell. Certainly he has a lot to recommend him to the breeder, not least his fine racing record. He was of top classic standard and showed himself to be admirably tough, genuine and consistent, as effective at a mile and a quarter as at a mile and a half, able to handle a firm and a soft surface and a particularly zestful galloper who showed unmistakable enthusiasm for the game. *D. O'Brien, Ireland.*

ASSERTER (USA) 3 b.c. Go Go Roger–Laura Dora (Pleiades 115) (1981 7f 1982 10.6s 12f³ 12f 12f² 12f* 12f* 12d² 13g 12.2f 13s 18s) leggy, fair sort; won handicaps at Carlisle and Thirsk in June; not sure to stay extreme distances; seems to act on any going. *S. Norton.*　**76**

ASSWAN 2 ch.c. Sharpen Up 127–Wild Romance 96 (Pirate King 129) (1982 6g*) Mar 7; 20,000F, 50,000Y; half-brother to 1979 2-y-o 5f and 6f winner Tremiti (by Sun Prince) and a winner in Malaya; dam won at up to 7f; 14/1, accounted for some well-bred animals when leading close home to win 20-runner maiden race at Yarmouth in September by a short head from The Minster; will stay 7f; likely to go on to better things. *J. Hindley.*　**94 p**

ASTARA 2 gr.f. Nishapour 125–Astana (Arbar 135) (1982 5g 5fg 5g² 6fg 7f* 6s³ 7d) Apr 25; close-coupled, sharp sort; half-sister to several winners, notably Prix de Diane winner Crepellana (by Crepello); dam, useful stayer, is half-sister to French Derby winner Philius; showed easily best form when winning 17-runner nursery at Leicester in September by 4 lengths from Game Dame; needs further than 6f, and will stay at least 1¼m; probably acts on any going. *M. Stoute.*　**78**

ASTERI (USA) 2 ch.f. Stage Door Johnny–Laughing Allegra (His Majesty) (1982 8s³ 10s*) May 22; $95,000Y; second foal; half-sister to 1981 2-y-o 1m winner Sir John Falstaff (by True Knight); dam closely related to smart 1¼m winner Prince Dantan and half-sister to smart stakes winner Stage Door Betty (by Stage Door Johnny); landed the odds easily by 3 lengths from Messagere du Soir in 16-runner maiden race at Saint-Cloud in October; the type to do well over middle distances at 3 yrs. *F. Boutin, France.*　**104 p**

ASTON 3 b.g. So Blessed 130–Sequoia 87 (Sassafras 135) (1981 NR 1982 5fg 7g 5fg) 1,000Y; lightly-made gelding; first foal; dam 2-y-o 6f winner; well behind in minor event and maiden race at Thirsk; refused to race third start. *L. Barratt.*　—

ATAMAN 2 ch.c. Ashmore 125–Selenis 95 (Huntercombe 133) (1982 8s) Mar 7; first foal; dam winning sprinter; third favourite but green, chased leaders some way when ninth of 14 behind Broad Beam in maiden race at Leicester in November. *F. J. Houghton.*　—

ATHENS STAR 7 b.g. Athens Wood 126–Maushe Joan 78§ (Major Portion 129) (1981 17.1d 16f 1982 10fg) of little account on flat. *M. Bradley.*　—

ATHERSMITH 3 ch.f. Goldhill 125–Tunbridge Lane 77 (Privy Councillor 125) (1981 6s 5g 1982 6s 5fg 5g 5fg 5f 5h 5fg 5f 5fg 6d) sturdy filly; sprint handicapper; well beaten in seller final start; acts on firm going; has twice worn blinkers. *J. Tierney.*　—

ATLANTIC AIR 2 ch.f. Air Trooper 115–Atlantica (Tulyar 134) (1982 5f 7fg) May 4; close-coupled filly; half-sister to a winning plater and a winner in Austria; dam never ran; in rear in maiden race at Newbury in July and £3,600 event at Chepstow in September. *Mrs R. Lomax.*　—

ATLANTIC LEISURE 2 ch.f. Roi Soleil 125–Atlantic Princess 69 (Four Burrow 91) (1982 8g) May 8; workmanlike filly; second foal; half-sister to a winner in Belgium; dam won from 1m to 1½m; 11/1 and green, weakened very quickly in closing stages when ninth of 11 to Triple Jump in £2,900 seller at Newmarket in October. *P. Cole.*

ATLANTIC TRAVELLER (USA) 5 b.h. Noholme II–Mlle Quille (On-and-On) **73** (1981 16s 16g³ 18d² 20fg* 20.4fg* 19fg² 18f³ 17.4g 18g 1982 16s 18.4fg 18f² 20fg 20.4g³ 19f* 20g² 18d 20g) rather sparely-made horse; out-and-out staying handicapper; ran best races when ⅛-length second to Chincoteague at Doncaster in May and when winning Pimm's Goodwood Stakes in July (made all and beat Baron Blakeney decisively by 2 lengths); well suited by top-of-the-ground; seems ideally suited by strong handling; game; sold out of J. W. Watts's stable 10,000 gns Ascot September Sales after seventh start. *M. Naughton.*

ATOM ANT 2 b.c. Crooner 119–Pat's Best (Star Moss 122) (1982 8g) May 8; — fourth foal; dam poor maiden; tailed-off last of 9 in seller won by Jonacris at Warwick in May. *P. Butler.*

ATOSSA 3 ch.f. Artaius 129–Living Free 81 (Never Say Die 137) (1981 6f* 6g* **79** 6fg 5fg 1982 8fg 8fg 7fg⁴ 8g 10fg) neat, strong filly; good walker and mover; quite a modest handicapper; bred to stay middle distances but was well beaten when tried at 1¼m; sometimes sweats up. *F. J. Houghton.*

A.T.S. PRINCE 3 b.g. He Loves Me 120–Miss Holborn (Pall Mall 132) (1981 **61 d** 5g 6d 6fg 7g⁴ 7d 8f 8f* 8.2s 8d* 8.2s 1982 10g 8fg² 8fg³ 12f 9g 12fg) rather lightly-made gelding; plater; should stay 1¼m; acts on any going except perhaps soft; has run moderately when sweating up; none too consistent. *P. Rohan.*

ATTACHED 4 b.g. Thatch 136–Veruschka 101 (Lorenzaccio 130) (1981 8g 8d — 9s 8d³ 8.2s³ 9s 1982 10g 10fg 8h 7fg 8fg) workmanlike gelding; poor maiden; stayed 1m; dead. *R. Hoad.*

AUBURN HILL 2 b.c. Silly Season 127–Molvitesse 75 (Molvedo 137) (1982 **79** 5fg 7f 6g* 7f³ 6g) Mar 25; 2,000Y; short-coupled colt; half-sister to 2 winners by Caliban, including 6f to 1¼m winner Calaburn; dam won over 1m; 50/1, showed first form when beating Romantic Knight a short head in 18-runner maiden race at Thirsk in July; modest third of 7 to Sticky Fingers in auction race on same course later in month; should stay at least 1m; reared as stalls opened on final outing. *Hbt Jones.*

AUCKLAND EXPRESS 2 ch.g. Bay Express 132–Loweswater 74 (Saint Crespin — III 132) (1982 6f 8f) Apr 4; 3,500Y; big gelding; half-brother to winning stayer Village Swan (by My Swanee); dam won over 1¼m; in rear in September in minor race at Pontefract and maiden auction event at Redcar. *D. Smith.*

AUDIT 4 ch.c. Henry The Seventh 125–Red Again (Red God 128§) (1981 10v — 8.2s² 10g³ 9.4g 12g² 12g⁴ 13.8fg 12f³ 12.2fg⁴ 10g 10f 10f² 13.8g* 11g 1982 13.8f) small, stocky colt; plater; stays 1¾m; seems to act on any going; effective with blinkers and without; sold out of J. Parkes's stable 2,500 gns Doncaster June Sales and played up a good deal on only subsequent appearance. *G. Lockerbie.*

AUGUSTA'S PET 3 b.f. Mummy's Pet 125–Aunt Augusta 80 (Counsel 118) **64** (1981 5s 5f 5d³ 5s 6g 1982 5f 5fg* 5fg 6s) big, strong filly; made most when winning 14-runner maiden race at Lingfield in September; best at 5f; acts on a firm and a soft surface; retained 2,300 gns Newmarket Autumn Sales. *G. Huffer.*

AULAIT 2 ch.c. Gay Fandango 132–Rings 104 (Realm 129) (1982 7g 7d) Apr — p 21; hollow-backed colt; second foal; dam 6f sprinter; ran well to 2f out when seventh of 13 to Russian Roubles in Houghton Stakes at Newmarket in October, second outing; should improve. *B. Hills.*

AULD LANG SYNE 3 b.g. Warpath 113–Eternally 85 (Ballymoss 136) **73** (1981 NR 1982 10fg 12d* 16g³ 12g 13d) lengthy, workmanlike gelding; good walker; second living foal; half-brother to 1979 2-y-o 6f winner Countyour-blessings (by So Blessed); dam needed long distances; won maiden race at Beverley in July in good style from Storton; should stay 2m; acts well on soft ground; sold 6,200 gns Doncaster November Sales. *C. Thornton.*

AULD MUNG 4 gr.g. Scallywag 127–Linton Spring 84 (Khalkis 127) (1981 — 11v³ 12s⁴ 16g* 15.8g 12.3fg 1982 15g 15f 12g⁴) rangy gelding; stays 2m; ran best race on final start; sold 850 gns Doncaster August Sales. *D. Smith.*

AURA (USA) 3 ch.f. Vaguely Noble 140–Windy Mama (Windy Sea) (1981 **93** NR 1982 9g* 12f² 12f³ 11.7fg³ 11.1fg³ 14.7fg* 12s* 14s*) \$140,000Y; medium-sized, quite attractive filly; good walker; half-sister to a winner by Royal Champion; dam, half-sister to high-class Royal Owl, was stakes winner at up to 1m; won maiden race at Wolverhampton (apprentice ridden) and handicaps at Redcar (trotted up), York and Sandown; led close home to beat Path of Peace by ¾

Meadowlands Stayers' Limited Handicap, Sandown—Willie Shoemaker on Aura gets the American jockeys off to a winning start in a three-race competition against a team of British jockeys. The British jockeys took the trophy for the second year in a row

length on last-named in October; suited by 1¾m; acts on any going but goes well in the mud; genuine and consistent. *J. Dunlop.*

AURIA 3 b.f. Reliance II 137–Diascia (Dike) (1981 NR 1982 8f 12g 10g 12v) compact filly; second foal; half-sister to fairly useful 2-y-o 5f winner Davinia (by Gold Form); dam probably of little account; behind in maiden races and a handicap. *M. Masson.* —

AUSPICIOUS BOY 2 b.c. Mansingh 120–Liangold (Rheingold 137) (1982 5fg 5f³ 5f³ 6f⁴ 7d*) Feb 16; plain colt; first foal; dam ran once at 2 yrs in France; won 10-runner seller at Beverley (retained 1,550 gns) in July by 4 lengths from Orange City; better suited by 7f than 6f; acts well on a soft surface; exported to Singapore. *J. Etherington.* **62**

AUSPICIUM 2 b.f. Record Token 128–Sultan's Slipper (Saint Crespin III 132) (1982 5f⁴ 5f 5g 5f) May 17; 820F; small filly; poor plater; not raced after July. *E. Weymes.* **40**

AUST FERRY 2 b.c. Welsh Pageant 132–Severn Bridge 81 (Hornbeam 130) (1982 8s 8s²) Feb 6; useful-looking colt; half-brother to several winners, including very useful 1977 2-y-o 5f winner Swing Bridge (by Swing Easy); dam won over 9f; pick of paddock, drew long way clear of remainder when length second of 13 to Kilner in maiden event at Warwick in October; will stay 1¼m; acts on soft going; capable of winning small race. *B. Hills.* **78**

AUTUMN BALLET 3 b.f. Averof 123–Autumn Ballad 75 (Tudor Melody 129) (1981 5g 5.1f⁴ 5f 8d 7g 8g 1982 8f 16d 14.6fg 10fg) big, workmanlike filly; poor maiden; sold 600 gns Doncaster September Sales. *C. Brittain.* —

AUTUMN DAZE 3 gr.c. Sallust 134–Red Roan (Roan Rocket 128) (1981 5d³ 5g⁴ 6fg 7fg 6fg 6f³ 8.2d 6d⁴ 1982 8s 5fg 6f 6f² 6g 6fg 6g) sturdy, compact colt; plating-class maiden; needs further than 5f and stays 1m; seems to act on any going; blinkered once at 2 yrs; sent to Singapore. *W. Elsey.* **54**

AUTUMN GIFT 3 b.f. Martinmas 128–Hung Pao 75 (Cumshaw 111) (1981 NR 1982 14f 16d 14.6fg* 14s) big filly; half-sister to 2 winners in Ireland, including fairly useful 1980 2-y-o 5f winner Happy Reprieve (by Tower Walk); dam placed at up to 1m; won modest 7-runner maiden race at Doncaster in July; stays well. *G. Pritchard-Gordon.* **65**

AUTUMN SUN 5 ch.g. Amber Rama 133–Rainswept (Charlottesville 135) **48** (1981 16d 11.7d 14s 12d 14fg 16fg² 17.1h³ 1982 13.3f² 16fg) poor handicapper; ran well when apprentice ridden at Newbury in June, making running until caught on line by Sandalay; stays well; probably acts on any going; sometimes wears blinkers. *A. Jarvis.*

AUTUMN SUNSET 2 b. or br.c. African Sky 124–Merrie Moira (Bold Lad, **103** Ire 133) (1982 6fg⁴ 5fg² 5d³) Mar 27; IR 13,500Y; second foal; half-brother to Irish 3-y-o Merrie Laughter (by Morston), a fairly useful winner at up to 9f; dam useful winner over 5f and 6f at 2 yrs in Ireland; showed plenty of ability in varied company; beaten less than a length when third of 9 to Virginia Deer in Goffs Stakes at the Curragh in September; will be suited by a return to 6f+; acts on a firm and a soft surface; sure to win races. *J. Oxx, Ireland.*

AUTUMN WALK 2 br.f. Tower Walk 130–Autumn Double 72 (Double Jump **60** 131) (1982 5fg 6g 6g 5d 6g 6s) May 24; leggy filly; plater; sixth of 22 to Blue Nantucket in £3,600 event at York in October, final outing and first indication of ability; acts on soft going; blinkered fifth and sixth starts. *Hbt Jones.*

AVAGO GIRL 2 b.f. Anax 120–Ava (Aggressor 130) (1982 6d 7f) Feb 27; 2,100Y; smallish, plain filly; third foal; dam twice-raced half-sister to smart middle-distance performer Arthur; no form; 50/1 and apprentice ridden, missed break when last of 7 to Dullingham Gold in seller at Redcar in July, second outing. *P. Rohan.*

AVALANCHE WAY (USA) 2 b. or br.c. Bold Forbes–Avalanche Lily (T.V. **90** Lark) (1982 6g* 7g*) May 29; half-brother to several winners, notably very smart American and Japanese middle-distance winner Mairzy Doates (by Nodouble); dam placed at 3 yrs; 1½-length winner from Go Alone in 16-runner maiden race at Naas in June and in 4-runner Hennessy V.S.O.P. Stakes at Leopardstown the following month; not seen out again; will stay 1¼m. *T. Curtin, Ireland.*

AVANOTHER 4 b.f. Averof 123–Another Princess 83 (King Emperor) (1981 — 7g 10fg 10f 8fg 1982 10f 7f 7fg 8f 8g 5fg 6v 6s) rather a lightly-made filly; no worthwhile form; has been tried in blinkers; sold out of C. Brittain's stable 2,000 gns Newmarket July Sales after fourth outing. *C. Austin.*

AVENITA LADY 2 b.f. Free State 125–Square Note 85 (High Top 131) (1982 — 7fg 7g 8s 8g) Apr 17; hollow-backed filly; first foal; dam 2-y-o 6f winner; no sign of ability; last of 11 in seller at Newmarket on final appearance; evidently of no account. *R. Sheather.*

AVERAYR 2 b.c. Averof 123–Mingalles 65 (Prince de Galles 125) (1982 6g 6g) — Feb 20; 2,500Y; neat colt; first foal; dam 1½m winner; beaten some way in minor events at Ripon in August and Hamilton in September. *P. Calver.*

AVERNUS 3 b.g. Averof 123–Lacemaker (Astec 128) (1981 7fg 8g 10g 1982 **56** 12fg 16f⁴ 17f 13.8f⁴ 11.5g² 10v* 10s) compact gelding; bought in 3,000 gns after winning seller at Lingfield in October; seems to stay 2m; acts on any going; sold to T. Forster 3,500 gns Ascot December Sales. *I. Walker.*

AVERON 2 b.c. Averof 123–Reluctant Maid 94 (Relko 136) (1982 5g³ 5g 6f **66** 7.3g) May 23; 2,500Y; tall, workmanlike colt; half-brother to Austrian 2000 Guineas winner Lorencio (by Lorenzaccio); dam won at up to 13f; ridden along all way when 4½ lengths third of 13 to Maariv in maiden race at Newbury in April, only indication of merit; should stay at least 1¼m. *C. Wildman.*

AVILA TOR 3 ch.f. Morston 125–Tortola § (Narrator 127) (1981 NR 1982 — 11d 10fg) 16,000F; 30,000Y; rangy filly; poor walker; half-sister to 4 winners, including useful 1980 2-y-o Doobie Do (by Derring-Do) and fairly useful 6f to 7f winner Avenged (by Sweet Revenge); dam half-sister to high-class stayer Almeria; tailed off in maiden races at Wolverhampton and Salisbury. *T. Robson.*

AVISFORD 2 br.c. Averof 123–Galoprise 88 (Tudor Music 131) (1982 7f 7f 8fg) — Feb 9; strong, well-made, good sort; fifth foal; half-brother to 2 winners, including fair 1979 2-y-o 7f winner Highland Bear (by Scottish Rifle); dam won over 6f; showed no ability, and would seem to be nowhere near so good as he looks. *J. Dunlop.*

AVON BELLE 2 ch.f. Balidar 133–Destiny Girl 112 (Karabas 132) (1982 5f **75** 6g 5.8g³ 5g² 6f 5d 5fg⁴ 7g³ 8s 6s) Feb 23; IR 5,000Y; well-made filly; first foal; dam won 4 times at around 7f at 2 yrs; showed consistent form in modest company until descending to sellers and running poorly on last three outings; evidently best at 5f or 6f; suited by a sound surface; sweated up when blinkered seventh start. *P. Cundell.*

AVONDALE PRINCESS 4 b.f. The Brianstan 128–Roseanne 68 (St Paddy 133) —
(1981 5d 7g 7f 6fg 5.3fg 5g³ 6f 5fg 5g 6s 6s 6d 1982 11.7d 8s) sturdy filly;
poor form on flat, including in sellers; stays 7f; usually blinkered in 1981. *M. McCourt.*

AVON EXPRESS 2 ch.g. Bay Express 132–Mehudenna 77 (Ribero 126) —
(1982 6f 5f) Mar 28; 7,000Y; useful-looking gelding; first foal; dam won over 5f
at 2 yrs; weak 10/1-shot, wasn't knocked about when 6 lengths fifth of 13 finishers
behind Django in maiden race at Salisbury in August, second outing. *P. Cundell.*

AVONMORE WIND 3 b.c. Tumble Wind–Gay Friend (Be Friendly 130) **94**
(1981 5d³ 5s³ 5d* 1982 6d 6g 5f⁴ 5f* 5g* 6f 6f 5g 5s* 5v 5s³ 5s) quite attractive,
useful-looking colt; usually impresses in appearance; won handicaps at Sandown
and Doncaster in June and at Goodwood in September; best at 5f; acts on
any going; sometimes sweats up. *S. Mellor.*

AVRAEAS (USA) 3 b.c. Key To The Mint–Rosewater (Sir Ivor 135) (1981 —
6s 7g 1982 8.2f 8d 11.5f 7s 6s) small, strong colt; soundly beaten in varied
company; blinkered last 3 starts, looking ungenuine on first occasion; sold to
R. Morris 3,000 gns Newmarket Autumn Sales. *H. T. Jones.*

AWAASIF (CAN) 3 b.f. Snow Knight 125–Royal Statute (Northern Dancer) **130**
(1981 6fg⁴ 7g* 1982 8d 10fg* 12f⁴ 12fg* 12f 12s³ 12d)
    None in the field benefited more than Awaasif from the thorough test of
stamina provided by the Trusthouse Forte Prix de l'Arc de Triomphe. In
finishing third at 90/1 she left her previous form well behind. She ended the
race only a head and half a length down on Akiyda and Ardross in a four-
cornered driving finish after producing a sustained run towards the outside in the
straight. This performance led to Awaasif's being kept in training; any repeat,
never mind any improvement on it, would make the exercise well worthwhile but
Awaasif's trainer faces no easy task in getting the best out of her. Opportunities
at middle distances for top-class four-year-old fillies are severely limited, the
more so for Awaasif since her strong suit is stamina and since, also, a galloping
track suits her much better than a sharp one. Predictably, she was unable to
reproduce her Arc running in the Washington International, demonstrating

*Yorkshire Oaks, York—Awaasif just gets there from
Swiftfoot (rails) and Dish Dash*

Sheikh Mohammed's "Awaasif"

perfectly clearly once again her racing character as, in finishing a modest fifth to
the Arc fourth April Run, she couldn't get in a blow at the leaders.

Awaasif, a six-length winner from Dreaming Away in a small race at Lingfield in May, didn't act well on the Epsom course in the Oaks the following month.
Had she come down the hill better she must have gone close, for after looking
out of contention round Tattenham Corner and early in the straight she began
to gain on the leaders inside the two-furlong marker and she finished best of all
in fourth place, about three lengths behind Time Charter. Developing mastitis
cost Awaasif a chance of compensation in the Irish Guinness Oaks and kept her
off the course until August, when she met the Irish Oaks winner Swiftfoot, the
Oaks third Last Feather and seventh Cut Loose (neither of whom had been out
since Epsom), Dancing Rocks (who'd beaten Time Charter in the Nassau Stakes),
the Princess of Wales's Stakes winner Height of Fashion and the Ribblesdale
Stakes winner Dish Dash in the Yorkshire Oaks, a highly competitive affair
worthy of the occasion. The finish lived up to expectations, Awaasif just
getting home from Swiftfoot and Dish Dash, and in so doing giving the distinct
impression she needed every yard of a mile and a half despite enjoying the
benefit of a strong pace on a galloping track.   Long-striding Height of Fashion,
one of Hern's three runners, set off in front as she'd done at Newmarket; stable-
companion Swiftfoot followed, then Last Feather, Awaasif, Cut Loose, Dancing
Rocks and Dish Dash, the last four being held up. The field began to close up
rounding the bottom turn and continued to do so until it could be seen early in the
straight that Height of Fashion would not be able to hold her place much longer.
As Swiftfoot went on, Height of Fashion dropped away pretty quickly, leaving
the others to determine whether Swiftfoot would be caught. All five mustered a
challenge but though Swiftfoot never succeeded in moving far ahead she still held
the lead running into the last furlong. By this stage Awaasif and Dish Dash were
the chief threats, Awaasif having been hard driven to come and do battle. The

109

three fillies, Awaasif between Swiftfoot on the rails and Dish Dash, disputed the issue right to the line. Awaasif went on very narrowly about a hundred and fifty yards out and very gamely maintained her advantage under strong pressure to win by a neck and a head from Swiftfoot and Dish Dash. With hindsight, Awaasif would probably have been more gainfully employed in the Park Hill Stakes next rather than in the selected alternative engagement, the Prix Vermeille. She found them too fast for her on the firm going at Longchamp. Piggott wasn't hard on her when she couldn't get up to challenge, but she finished less than five lengths down on All Along, seventh of the thirteen runners.

		Firestreak	Pardal
	Snow Knight	(br 1956)	Hot Spell
	(ch 1971)	Snow Blossom	Flush Royal
Awaasif (Can)		(br 1957)	Ariana
(b.f. 1979)		Northern Dancer	Nearctic
	Royal Statute	(b 1961)	Natalma
	(b 1969)	Queen's Statute	Le Lavandou
		(b 1954)	Statute

Awaasif is by the 1974 Derby winner Snow Knight; Canadian bred, she was purchased in the United States as a yearling at the Kentucky Summer Sales for 325,000 dollars and is owned by an Arab, Sheikh Mohammed. Snow Knight, standing alongside Awaasif's grandsire Northern Dancer at Windfields Farm (at a fee of 10,000 dollars in 1982), is also the sire of the Dee Stakes winner Ivano. The dam Royal Statute has bred another notable filly to run in England in the One Thousand Guineas second Konafa, and her achievements at stud don't end there. Three of her other foals won in North America, among them a top-class colt called Akureyri (by Buckpasser) who finished second in the Florida Derby and has now been retired after injury to Windfields. The family fortunes have improved dramatically since the second dam Queen's Statute was exported from England to Canada in 1956. Unraced herself, Queen's Statute bred thirteen foals to race; all were winners and six were stakes winners. One of them, Menedict, won the Canadian Oaks but the best was Royal Statute's full brother Dance Act, twice champion handicap horse in Canada; another full brother North Of The Law also won a stakes. Royal Statute won a relatively minor race over five furlongs as a two-year-old.

Awaasif is a good-looking filly; she was easily the highest-priced yearling at her sale. She is a thoroughly genuine filly, too, necessarily so to win and to do well in top-class races run at a distance an absolute minimum for her. She acts on any going but will always be particularly well served by some give in the ground in that it puts a premium on stamina. *J. Dunlop.*

AXKERNISH (USA) 2 br.f. Drone–Cynthiana (Nashua) (1982 5f 7f³ 7f 8f* **94** 8g³) Apr 9; long-backed filly; half-sister to several winners in USA, including 2 stakes-placed winners; dam, who never ran, is closely related to successful sire Bolinas Boy; showed much improved form when winning £5,700 nursery at Doncaster in September by 2 lengths from Conor's Rock; creditable third of 12 to Johnny Nobody in similar race at Newmarket later in month; will stay 1¼m; has raced only on a sound surface. *J. Tree.*

AYMAN (USA) 2 b.c. Raja Baba–I Understand (Dr Fager) (1982 5f* 5f³ **100** 7f² 7fg³) Feb 27; $700,000Y; medium-sized, good-bodied, attractive colt; third foal; half-brother to Seeker's Gold (by Mr Prospector), winner of a good sprint race in Australia; dam, winner 4 times at up to 1m, is half-sister to smart stakes winners Royal and Regal and Regal and Royal; stayed on very strongly to win 9-runner maiden race at Haydock in May by ¾ length from Sheriff Muir; ran well on next 2 outings, finishing 4½ lengths third of 11 to Prince Reymo in Windsor Castle Stakes at Royal Ascot and drawing well clear of remainder when beaten 2½ lengths by Thug in £4,600 event at Newmarket; stays 7f; has raced only on fast ground (scratched down to start when running below his best on fourth start and tended to hang left when pace quickened). *H. T. Jones.*

AYYABAAN 5 b.h. Sun Prince 128–Adayra (Le Haar 126) (1981 16g 20f³ **—** 12g 16fg* 1982 14fg 16d 16d 19s 17.1s) well-made, attractive horse; excellent mover; staying handicapper; in rear all outings in 1982 (not seen out until September); acts on firm going; blinkered once in 1979. *J. Jenkins.*

AZAAM 4 b.c. Mummy's Pet 125–Emperor Star (King Emperor) (1981 5s⁴ **79** 5d⁴ 7d* 8g 7fg³ 6fg² 7f* 7g⁴ 7f 7f 7fg⁴ 7g² 7g² 6g 1982 7f⁴ 7g 6g² 7fg 6fg 8f 6s* 6s 6s² 7d) useful-looking colt; returned to form when beating Kathred by 3 lengths in handicap at Haydock in October; also second at Newmarket and Nottingham, but is none too consistent; best form at up to 7f; acts on any going; below form when tried in blinkers on occasions; sold out of R. Fisher's stable 6,000 gns Ascot June Sales after second start (had won over hurdles for him) and rejoined W. O'Gorman who has trained him most of his career. *W. O'Gorman.*

AZARA 2 b.f. Quiet Fling 124–Alangia 101 (Shantung 132) (1982 7f⁴ 7fg) **67 p**
Mar 24; lengthy, good sort; sister to winning 3-y-o stayer Fallen Angel; dam won from 7f to 1½m; stayed on nicely when 7¼ lengths fourth of 11 behind Moment In Time in maiden race at Sandown in July and when nearly 10 lengths fifth of 19 to Liberty Tree in maiden event at Chepstow the following month; will be very well suited by 1¼m+; sure to improve. *H. Candy.*

AZD 6 ch.g. Be Friendly 130–Portden (Worden II 129) (1981 12s* 12d² 12d³ 12g³ **§§**
12g² 12d* 15.5d* 12g³ 12f 12d 12f 12d* 12d³ 12s 13s 1982 12d² 12fg 12f 12fg) moody handicapper; stays well; acts on any going but seems suited by some give in the ground nowadays; sometimes blinkered; often difficult at start (refused to race last 3 appearances). *M. Masson.*

AZTEC 2 b.c. Jaazeiro 127–Water Frolic 92 (Sir Ivor 135) (1982 5s) Feb 23; **—**
neat, well-made colt; first foal; dam, daughter of 1,000 Guineas winner Waterloo, stayed 1¼m; 8/1 and backward, dropped right out after showing speed to halfway when sixth of 7 to Able Albert in maiden race at Haydock in April. *E. Weymes.*

B

BABYCHAM SPARKLE 2 b.f. So Blessed 130–Effervescence II (Charlottesville **80**
135) (1982 5f* 6g* 7d 5g) Apr 10; 27,000Y; half-sister to several winners, including fairly useful sprinter Clicquot (by Bold Lad, Ire) and smart French middle-distance colt El Famoso (by Ragusa); dam won twice over 1¼m in France and is half-sister to Zeddaan; won minor events at Catterick in September and Edinburgh in October; seems not to stay 7f; acts on firm going. *Sir Mark Prescott.*

BABY LEROY (USA) 2 b.c. Forli–Virginia Green 83 (Nashua) (1982 6fg 7d) **—**
Feb 7; $42,000Y, $76,000 2-y-o; compact, good-bodied colt; half-brother to 2 winners, including fairly useful sprinter Old Dominion (by In Reality); dam, winner over 10.8f, is half-sister to dam of Mill Reef; rather burly when behind in September in minor event at Lingfield and maiden race at Leicester. *J. Sutcliffe.*

BABY'S SMILE 2 b.f. Shirley Heights 130–Two's Company (Sheshoon 132) **—**
(1982 7f) Apr 20; 22,000Y; attractive, well-made filly; second foal; half-sister to quite useful 3-y-o 1½m winner Two High (by High Top); dam useful French 6.5f and 1½m winner; unquoted and backward, soon trailing when last of 11 behind Silk Pyjamas in maiden race at Sandown in July; likely to need long distances. *J. Benstead.*

BACK'HUS BOY 2 b.c. Workboy 123–Knocknashee 70 (Astec 128) (1982 **105**
5g 7d 7fg* 7g* 7fg 7.6fg* 7v) Feb 27; 3,100F, 7,000Y; compact, good sort; half-brother to useful middle-distance winner Mirror Boy (by Pieces of Eight) and to winner in Belgium; dam won over 1m; 4-length winner of maiden race at Warwick in July; subsequently carried top weight to victory in 2 nurseries at Lingfield; co-favourite when remote seventh of 13 to Indian Rajah in another Lingfield nursery in October; will stay 1m; acts on a firm surface and is possibly unsuited by heavy ground. *G. Harwood.*

BACK STAGE 3 b.c. Busted 134–Bold Words (Bold Ruler) (1981 8d 1982 **—**
12fg 14g 13f) big, rangy colt; soundly beaten in maiden races and a minor event. *M. Albina.*

BADACHRO BOY 3 br.g. Import 127–Right Beauty 66 (Right Boy 137) **—**
(1981 NR 1982 7f 7g 6fg 6g 6g 7s) bad plater. *D. Chapman.*

BADAYOUN 3 b.c. Kalamoun 129–Bubunia 122 (Wild Risk) (1981 NR 1982 **88**
9fg³ 10f* 10g 10f* 10f⁴) big colt; good walker; acts on any going, being smart from 9f to 13f, is daughter of top-class Bella Paola; won maiden race at Redcar in May and handicap at Folkestone in July; will stay 1½m; acts well on firm going; ran moderately final start (July). *M. Stoute.*

BAD HABITS 2 b.g. Habat 127–Riboffleur 74 (Ribero 126) (1982 7g 7fg 8s) **—**
Apr 12; robust, sprint type; second foal; half-brother to 3-y-o Takhos (by Tachypous); dam placed from 7f to 1¾m; no form in maiden events. *B. Swift.*

BADINAGE 3 br.f. Brigadier Gerard 144–Adina (Neckar) (1981 6fg 7d⁴ 1982 —
8f⁴ 8fg) rangy filly; good mover; quite a modest maiden; will be suited by 1¼m.
W. Hastings-Bass.

BADRAAN (USA) 2 br.c. Honest Pleasure–Crafty Action (Crafty Admiral) **78**
(1982 5fg 5fg⁴ 5fg² 5f) Apr 16; $50,000Y; strong, sturdy colt; good mover;
half-brother to 2 winners, including useful 1977 French 2-y-o Kutuzov (by Bold
Reason); dam won 8 sprint races, including claiming events; second of 8 to easy
odds-on winner Bid Again in maiden race at Nottingham in June, best effort;
needs further; yet to race on an easy surface. *L. Cumani.*

BADSWORTH GIRL 4 b.f. Arch Sculptor 123–Falcade (Falcon 131) (1981 —
7fg 7fg 5f⁴ 7f 1982 12s 13v) big, rangy filly; not bred to stay 1m+; blinkered
final start; sold 800 gns Doncaster May Sales and has won over hurdles. *G. Toft.*

BAFFIN 4 b.c. Busted 134–Ocean 112 (Petition 130) (1981 10g* 8g³ 12s² **115**
10g 1982 13.4fg 13.3g²) strong, useful-looking colt; decisively won minor
event at Goodwood and finished neck second to Little Wolf in St Simon Stakes
at Newbury as a 3-y-o; ran only twice in 1982, easily better effort when 4 lengths
second of 4 to Ardross in Geoffrey Freer Stakes at Newbury in August (made
running and ran on extremely well under strong driving); suited by 1½m+;
acts on soft going; sold 29,000 gns Newmarket December Sales. *R. Hern.*

BAHHR 2 b.g. Bay Express 132–Sixandahalf (Thirteen of Diamonds 126) (1982 —
7fg 7g 8s 8g) May 15; IR 34,000Y; smallish, lengthy gelding; good walker; half-
brother to several winners here and abroad, including smart 6f to 1½m winner
Charlie Bubbles (by Wolver Hollow); dam won at 1⅛m in Ireland; no worthwhile
form; shuffled down to start and was soon well behind in £2,900 seller at
Newmarket in October on final appearance. *N. Callaghan.*

BAHOOR (USA) 2 br.c. L'Enjoleur–Jalapa 117 (Luthier 126) (1982 7g 8g³) **91**
Mar 8; $350,000Y; strong, good-bodied colt; first foal; dam smart at around 1¼m
in France; co-favourite, had every chance when 2¼ lengths third of 17 to Oula
Owl in maiden event at Newmarket in October; will stay 1¼m; sure to win a race.
G. Harwood.

BAHRAIN PEARLS (USA) 2 ch.c. Annihilate 'Em–My Blue Jay (Royal Note) **75**
(1982 5fg³ 6f³ 6d 6f 7g 10s 7s) May 12; $13,000Y, resold 10,000 gns Y; well-
made colt; third foal; half-brother to a winner in USA; dam won twice at up to
1m; modest form in varied company; should stay 1m; ran very freely in blinkers
on third start; disappointing. *R. Price.*

BAJAN BOY 2 ch.c. Mandao–Cardio-Vanter (Galivanter 131) (1982 5fg 5fg —
6fg 6g 6f) Apr 26; lengthy, lightly-made colt; bad plater. *C. Wildman.*

BAJAN SUNSHINE 3 b.g. Reliance II 137–Nyanga (Never Say Die 137) **96**
(1981 NR 1982 10g² 12f⁴ 12f³ 14g* 14f⁴ 15.5fg* 16fg* 19s² 18d 18d* 18s⁴)
11,500Y; good-topped gelding; half-brother to 3 winners, including high-class
middle-distance stayer Mistigri (by Misti IV) and useful stayer Tanaka (by
Tapalque); dam won twice over 1⅛m in France; successful in maiden race at
Yarmouth, amateur riders race at Folkestone and minor events at Lingfield
and Doncaster; kept on strongly to beat Viennese Waltz by ½ length (pair clear)
on last-named in October; stays very well; acts on any going but is ideally
suited by some give in the ground; tough and genuine. *R. Simpson.*

BAKLAWA 3 b.f. Orange Bay 131–Colonial Cousin (Tom Rolfe) (1981 7fg 6fg **72**
8fg 1982 10f 12fg 12g⁴ 12d³ 10f² 10g* 10g) tall, rangy, plain filly; sweated up
when easily winning maiden race at Epsom in August; bred to stay 1½m but
pulls hard and is likely to prove best at shorter trips. *G. Lewis.*

BAKUNIN (FR) 2 b.c. Riverman 131–Hairbrush (Sir Gaylord) (1982 5f³ 7g **74**
7d⁴ 6s 6s 7v) Apr 28; 25,000Y; quite attractive colt; half-brother to 2 winners,
including middle-distance performer Hymnos (by Luthier); dam, daughter of
top American filly Bug Brush, won twice over 6f in USA; quite a modest maiden;
should stay 1m; blinkered last 2 starts; trained by P. Mitchell first outing.
M. Ryan.

BALANCHINE 3 b.c. Ballymore 123–Ambuscade 77 (Relko 136) (1981 6f² **108**
6fg² 6s* 7g* 1982 10d⁴ 10.6fg³ 11f² 12d³ 12fg* 12f* 12g* 12g³) well-made,
attractive colt; poor walker; good mover; developed into a useful handicapper,
winning at Newmarket (awarded race), Goodwood and Newbury; short-priced
favourite when accounting for Sa-Vegas by 1½ lengths in ATS Trophy on last-
named in August; will stay 1¾m; acts on any going; consistent; sold privately
after final start and is hurdling with D. Nicholson. *M. Stoute.*

BALARUM 3 b.f. Goldhill 125–Balquhidder (Pardao 120) (1981 6d 5f 6g 7.2v —
1982 8fg 7f) leggy filly; poor plater; has worn blinkers. *P. Rohan.*

BALATINA 4 ch.f. Balidar 133–Toccatina 79 (Bleep-Bleep 134) (1981 5f 5fg **78**
5g 6g 1982 5d* 6fg³ 5fg* 5fg³ 5.1f³ 5g* 5.1g* 5.3fg* 5f 5.6f* 6g* 5g 5fg⁴)
fair sort; had a tremendous season and won handicaps at Folkestone, Wolverhampton, Warwick, Yarmouth, Brighton, Doncaster and Lingfield; rider lost
irons ninth start and run can be ignored, but was a shade disappointing last 2
starts; stays 6f; probably acts on any going; suitable mount for an apprentice;
often used to wear blinkers; withdrawn after giving a lot of trouble in stalls
intended final appearance. *H. Westbrook.*

BALAUSTIN 3 b.f. Balidar 133–Princess Log 78 (King Log 115) (1981 5f 7fg
8s 1982 8.5fg 6g) close-coupled filly; little worthwhile form; pulled hard first
start; sold 650 gns Ascot 2nd June Sales. *R. Price.*

BAL-A-VERSAILLS 2 ch.c. Bustino 136–Bedouin Dancer 79 (Lorenzaccio 130) —
(1982 6g 7g) Apr 10; tall colt; second foal; dam won over 1m; last in quite
valuable races at York in August and September. *J. Hanson.*

BALAYER 3 ch.f. Balidar 133–Feather Duster 80 (Tickler 106) (1981 5g 5.8f
6fg³ 7d 6fg 7d 5s 1982 6f⁴ 6fg 7f 6g³ 6g 7f 6fg) rather lightly-made filly;
plater; should stay 7f; possibly unsuited by soft ground; blinkered nowadays.
S. Woodman.

BALCANOONA 3 b.f. Cawston's Clown 113–Duns Tew 70 (Mandamus 120) **70**
(1981 5d³ 5fg 5d* 5s³ 6fg² 6fg 6fg 5d² 7s 6v 6g 1982 6fg 7g 6f² 6f 6f 6f 6g 6s)
lightly-made filly; good mover; suited by 6f but isn't sure to stay 7f; seems to act
on any going; blinkered seventh start. *R. Hannon.*

BALDA 4 br.f. Relko 136–Basilia Dea (Habitat 134) (1981 10fg 12fg 12d⁴ 12fg²
12f* 1982 15.8g) tall, leggy filly; plater; stayed 1¼m; acted on firm going; in
foal to Free State. *S. Norton.*

BAL DES FEES (FR) 2 ch.c. Rheffic 129–Bal Carra (Baldric II 131) (1982 6g* **114**
5.5g 6fg⁴ 8s 7.5v* 7s) Apr 18; half-brother to 3 winners in France, including useful 1981 2-y-o 6f winner Beau Temeraire (by Tennyson); dam, placed at 2 yrs, is
half-sister to very useful French middle-distance filly Arinda; won newcomers race
and Prix Thomas Bryon at Saint-Cloud, coming out best by a head from
Northern Fashion in blanket finish to latter in October; also prominent in Prix
Robert Papin at Maisons-Laffitte (3¼ lengths sixth to Ma Biche), Prix Morny at
Deauville (about 5 lengths fourth to Deep Roots) and Prix des Chenes at Longchamp (1¼ lengths fifth to Pluralisme); will stay at least 1¼m. *N. Pelat, France.*

BALDINGSTONE BOY 4 b.c. Scaepic 100–Vivyiki (Kirtonian 88) (1981 8s
8g 12f* 12f 12g* 13.8fg* 12f 13d 1982 12f 12f 10fg⁴) compact colt; plater;
suited by 1¼m+; acts on firm going; often apprentice ridden; inconsistent. *A.
Balding.*

BALGOWNIE 2 br.f. Prince Tenderfoot 126–Grandee Ann (Cyane) (1982 5f 5f
6f 6s) May 7; 1,000Y; fair sort; half-sister to 1m winner Maris Quest (by Windjammer); dam won 6 times at up to 7f in USA; no sign of ability, including in
sellers; blinkered third start. *M. W. Easterby.*

BALIBURN 2 b.g. Balidar 133–Golden Apple 68 (Athens Wood 126) (1982 7g⁴ **80**
8d 8s) Apr 20; sturdy gelding; good walker; first foal; dam won over 2m and
2¼m; possibly flattered when 3¼ lengths fifth of 13 to Mister Valentino in slowly-
run maiden race at Ayr in September, second outing and best effort; lacks pace,
and will be suited by longer distances. *P. Asquith.*

BALIDAMSEL 2 br.f. Balidar 133–Mam'selle Marron 72 (Quayside 124) (1982 **54**
5fg 5fg³ 6fg³ 6g⁴ 6g² 7g² 7.2s) Feb 27; 310Y; first foal; dam, half-sister to very
smart miler General Vole, won over 1m; ridden by apprentice C. Cox when
second in sellers at Lingfield in August and Wolverhampton in October, best
efforts; stays 7f. *P. Cundell.*

BALI DANCER 3 ch.c. Habitat 134–Miss Bali 95 (Crepello 136) (1981 6fg³ 6g² **107**
1982 8f* 8.2f⁴ 8fg* 8f² 10f² 9g* 10.5g 10g) lengthy colt; good walker; a very
useful colt who had a good year, winning minor event at Ripon and handicaps
at Royal Ascot (beat Nioulargo decisively by 1½ lengths in Britannia Stakes)
and York (beat Reside a length in Falmouth Handicap); also runner-up in valuable handicaps at Newmarket (neck behind Farioffa) and Goodwood (failed by a
neck to peg back Busaco in Extel Stakes); stays 1¼m; acts well on firm going;
best in blinkers; suited by waiting tactics and isn't an easy ride; consistent.
M. Stoute.

BALIDILEMMA 3 ch.f. Balidar 133–Charybdis (Chanteur II 135) (1981 **77**
6fg 6g 7g 1982 8s 9.4fg 12g 10fg 8.2v* 8g*) strong filly; attracted no bid
after decisively winning seller at Hamilton in October; won minor event at
Edinburgh later in month; stays 1m well; acts on heavy going. *Miss S. Hall.*

BALI MILL 2 b.c. Balidar 133–Milly Lass 85 (Bold Lad, USA) (1982 5f² 5fg² **80**
6g²) Apr 20; 7,200Y; lengthy colt; first foal; dam, 2-y-o 7f winner, is half-
sister to smart Kashmir Lass; creditable second in maiden races, finishing well
clear of 11 others when beaten 2½ lengths by Archon at Haydock in July (hung
under pressure) on last outing; stays 6f; sent to Hong Kong. *D. Smith.*

BALINESE 2 b.f. Balidar 133–Gleaming Horn 97 (Hornbeam 130) (1982 **82**
5fg³ 5fg 5fg 7g² 7fg² 7f* 7fg 7.3g 7d) Apr 14; lengthy, rather lightly-made
filly; half-sister to several winners here and abroad; dam miler; had her 11
opponents strung out when making all to win maiden race at Brighton in August
by 6 lengths from River Maiden; beaten in nurseries subsequently; suited by
7f; acts well on firm going. *R. Smyth.*

BALI-ON-BY 2 b.g. Balidar 133–Hurly Burly (Sing Sing 134) (1982 5fg² **77**
6fg⁴ 5g 5fg⁴ 5g³ 6g 6g) Apr 3; strong, fair sort; fourth living foal; dam showed
no worthwhile form; in frame in maiden races and a minor event in Scotland;
probably stays 6f; blinkered fifth and seventh outings. *W. H. H. Williams.*

BALITOU (FR) 3 ch.c. Margouillat 133–Dynamite (Marino) (1981 8.5d⁴ 8v² **121**
1982 10s* 11fg⁴ 12s 10.5f 13.5g 15f* 15.5v 12s*(dis)) lengthy colt; sixth foal;
brother to a modest French maiden and half-brother to 3 minor winners in
France and Spain; dam won 5 times over middle distances in France; won
minor event at Saint-Cloud in March and Prix de Lutece at Longchamp in
September; accounted for Delpour by 4 lengths in latter; also first past post in
Grand Prix de Bordeaux in November but was disqualified; ran respectably in
good company several other starts; suited by a test of stamina; acts on any
going. *P-L. Biancone, France.*

Mr S. S. Niarchos' "Ballydoyle"

BALKAN 2 b.c. Balidar 133–Self Satisfied 100 (Great Nephew 126) (1982 **73**
5fg 6f 5fg 6f 5f² 6fg 5d) Apr 8; strong-quartered, useful-looking colt; third foal;
half-brother to 3-y-o Hand-Rolled (by Sagaro); dam 5f sprinter; quite a modest
maiden; stays 6f; acts on firm going. *W. Wightman.*

BALLADIER 2 b.c. Busted 134–Ring Rose 86 (Relko 136) (1982 7g 7fg) —
Mar 30; tall, useful-looking colt; second foal; dam, winner of 3 middle-distance
races, is daughter of very smart Heath Rose; behind in maiden races at Newbury
in August and Salisbury (ninth of 16) in September; the type to do better with
time and longer distances. *H. Candy.*

BALLAD ISLAND 2 b.f. Ballad Rock 122–Taggs Island 76 (Silly Season 127) **78**
(1982 6f 8s*) Feb 20; 4,000F, 5,800Y; leggy, good-topped filly; fourth produce;
half-sister to 2 winners, including middle-distance winner Tamarin Falls (by
Mount Hagen); dam won over 1m; ran on strongly to win 11-runner maiden
race at Wolverhampton in October by 1½ lengths from Maestrette; suited by
1m; acts on soft going (moved badly to start on firm on debut). *M. Jarvis.*

BALLAGARROW GIRL 2 ch.f. North Stoke 130–Capule (Middleground) —
(1982 5f 8s 7.2s) Apr 27; IR 8,400F; quite well-made filly; half-sister to several
winners, notably smart 6f and 7f winner The Quiet Bidder (by Auction Ring);
dam minor 2-y-o 5f winner in USA; soundly beaten in maiden and minor events;
prominent quite a long way last 2 starts. *R. Hollinshead.*

BALLET CHAMP (USA) 4 ch.g. Dancing Champ–Countess V (Cyane) (1981 —
8s 12.8f* 12f² 12f⁴ 10g² 1982 8g 10d 8fg) $3,200F, $9,000Y; ex-Irish gelding;
second produce; half-brother to a winner in USA; dam won at up to 9f; won
maiden race at Wexford as a 3-y-o; well beaten in amateur riders events over
here; stays 13f; probably acts on any going; blinkered last 2 outings in 1981;
formerly trained by J. Oxx. *J. Jenkins.*

BALLNACARN 3 ch.c. Firestreak 125–Deer Forest (Huntercombe 133) (1981 **60**
5g 5d 5g 5.8f⁴ 5f 1982 8.2d 9f³ 8f² 8fg³ 8.3fg* 8.3g 8fg² 8s² 7d* 7g) leggy
colt; plater; bought in 3,400 gns after winning decisively at Windsor in July;
ran creditably in better company several times and won handicap at Catterick
in October; stays 1m well; acts on any going. *J. Toller.*

BALLYDOYLE (CAN) 2 br.c. Northern Dancer–South Ocean (New Providence) **101**
(1982 6.3fg⁴ 8d² 6s*) Mar 23; $3,500,000Y (world record price for a yearling to
end of 1981); brother to champion 1980 2-y-o Storm Bird and to Northernette,
a very smart filly at 2, 3 and 4 yrs who won at up to 9f, and closely related to
2 winners, one of them very useful; dam won Canadian Oaks; didn't have much
to beat when 5/2 on for 13-runner maiden race at Naas in November and made
all to win by 3 lengths from Glenhurst; had looked sure to win similar event at
Leopardstown the previous month when going clear 1f out but was caught close
home and beaten a neck by Putney Bridge; should stay beyond 1m. *V. O'Brien,
Ireland.*

BALLYDURROW 5 ch.g. Doon 124–Even Tint (Even Money 121) (1981 —
NR 1982 13d) big gelding; third live foal; dam never ran; winning hurdler;
needed run when ninth of 11 behind Chalkey Road in minor event at Ayr in
September. *R. Fisher.*

BALLYFEE 5 br.m. Sovereign Bill 105–Ballyarctic (Arcticeelagh 119) (1981 —
NR 1982 12s) poor novice hurdler; over 20 lengths sixth of 13 behind Misty
Halo in apprentice event at Chepstow in October. *R. Armytage.*

BALLY-GO 5 b.g. Ballymoss 136–Cloudy (Nyrcos 130) (1981 12.5s³ 1982 —
16f) strong gelding; winning hurdler; very lightly raced on flat; looks an out-
and-out stayer; blinkered only outing of 1982. *M. W. Easterby.*

BALLYREEF 2 br.f. Ballymore 123–Belle Reef 98 (Mill Reef 141) (1982 6g —
7d) Feb 16; small filly; first foal; dam, daughter of Prix de Diane winner Belle
Sicambre, won from 6f to 1½m; soon struggling when behind in sizeable fields
of maidens at Newmarket and Leicester late in season. *P. Walwyn.*

BALLYSEEDY HERO 4 gr.g. Supreme Sovereign 119–Knocknagrena (Worden **57**
II 129) (1981 7fg 8g 6fg 6f² 7f³ 6fg 8g 8d 10d 1982 7f 8f³ 10.1g³ 8fg³ 10.2f³
10v) tall, lengthy gelding; third in 2 minor events and 2 handicaps; suited by
1¼m; acts on firm going (well beaten on heavy on only outing); blinkered final
start in 1981; trained until after first outing by D. Whelan. *D. Elsworth.*

BALLYWACKMACROO 5 b.h. Ballymore 123–Mountain Lark (Chamier 128) —
(1981 12g 10g 12d* 12f 12fg² 16f 12f* 12fg 12f 12f² 12fg 1982 12.2f) compact,

well-made horse; bought out of G. Pritchard-Gordon's stable 1,850 gns Doncaster August Sales; bandaged in front when last at Catterick the following month, only outing of 1982; stays 1½m; best form on a sound surface. *J. Parkes.*

BALOYD 3 b.g. Royal Palace 131–Betty Burke 95 (Prince Chevalier) (1981 NR 1982 10d 11g 16f 14g 13.8f) 5,000Y; workmanlike gelding; poor mover; brother to very useful 1m winner Stirling Castle and a winning hurdler, and half-brother to several winners, including very useful stayer Arisaig (by Acropolis); dam won at 5f and 6f; well beaten in maiden races and handicaps; blinkered final start. *W. Musson.* —

BAL ROYAL 2 b.c. Arctic Tern 126–Broadway Dancer 131 (Northern Dancer) **92** (1982 5f* 5f) Feb 21; robust, very attractive colt; third foal; half-brother to 3-y-o Bombshell (by Ashmore) and a fairly useful maiden; dam won Prix Morny by 6 lengths; put up a promising effort when favourite for 13-runner maiden race at York in May, soon racing with leaders, taking a definite advantage 2f out and holding off Cast A Shadow by 1½ lengths despite hanging left; beaten fully 2f out when second favourite for Norfolk Stakes at Royal Ascot the following month; will be much better suited by longer distances; sent to USA. *H. Cecil.*

BALTIC AIR 2 b.c. Stradavinsky 121–Grunhilde 54 (Mountain Call 125) **45** (1982 6d 7d 6f 6f 6fg⁴ 7f 7f 8fg) Apr 9; 780F, 2,400 2-y-o; neat colt; first produce; dam won twice over 1½m in Jersey; poor plater; stays 1m; blinkered fifth and sixth outings. *W. Bentley.*

BALTIMORE BAY (USA) 2 b.f. Banquet Table–Bay of Fundy (Portsmouth) **75** (1982 6d 7d 6s) Feb 29; $33,000Y; workmanlike filly; third foal; half-sister to very useful stayer Castelnau (by Irish Castle); dam, stakes-placed winner at up to 1m, is sister to Brindabella, a very useful winner at up to 1¼m; close up until weakening final furlong when 8 lengths fifth of 13 finishers behind Acclimatise in £4,000 maiden race at Sandown in July, second outing and only indication of merit; dead. *D. Elsworth.*

BAMDORO 3 br.f. Cavo Doro 124–Pat 98 (Ennis 128) (1981 NR 1982 12s) 3,200F, 800Y; half-sister to several winners here and abroad including 1m winner Chrome Mag (by Prince de Galles); dam 5f sprinter; 33/1 and blinkered when bad last in seller at Redcar in October. *J. Mulhall.* —

BANBURY CROSS 4 b.c. Tower Walk 130–Hark Hark 75 (Sing Sing 134) **50** (1981 6fg 6g⁴ 6d 6g 5.3f 5h² 7f 7g 7d 1982 5g 6d 8g⁴ 7f³ 7.6g² 8fg 8f 6g 7fg 7.3g 7.2s 6v 8g) poor handicapper; stays 1m; acts on any going; sometimes blinkered; sold 2,200 gns Newmarket Autumn Sales. *W. Wightman.*

BANCARIO 3 ch.c. Owen Dudley 121–Brescianina (Hugh Lupus 132) (1981 **113** 6g* 7fg² 7d² 7fg² 8.2fg* 8d* 8s* 1982 8.5fg² 12.3g 8g*) medium-sized, well-made colt; having first run for 3 months when driven out to beat Riyahi in 7-runner minor event at Newcastle in August; beaten in 2 pattern races in the spring, finishing 4½ lengths fourth to Count Pahlen in Blue Riband Trial at Epsom and remote sixth to Super Sunrise in Chester Vase; should be suited by middle distances; probably acts on any going; usually makes the running; sent to Hong Kong. *H. Cecil.*

BANCHORY BRIDGE 3 ch.c. Bay Express 132–Renoir Picture 90 (Relko 136) (1981 7d 7d 1982 8g 8f 10fg 8fg 8.2s 7d 8s) strong colt; plating-class maiden; probably stays 1m; sometimes blinkered; sold to M. Pipe 2,100 gns Newmarket Autumn Sales. *J. Bethell.* —

BAND 2 b.c. Blakeney 126–Zither 72 (Vienna 127) (1982 6d² 7g⁴) Apr 10; **80 p** strong, good sort; half-brother to several winners, including smart middle-distance winner Zimbalon (by Ragusa); dam won at 1½m; in frame in the autumn in minor event at Windsor (short-head second to Kwela) and 28-runner maiden race at Newmarket; will be much better suited by 1½m+; sure to win maiden event. *R. Hern.*

BANDELERO 2 br.c. Relkino 131–Siouan 78 (So Blessed 130) (1982 6fg **78** 7fg 8d 8.2s⁴) Feb 8; compact colt; first foal; dam, half-sister to high-class stayer Dakota and very useful Warpath, won over 1½m; modest maiden; will stay 1½m; acts on soft going. *C. Thornton.*

B AND K EMPEROR 5 ro.g. Young Emperor 133–Fiery Clare (Firestreak 125) (1981 10.2d 1982 12fg) leggy gelding; plating-class maiden on flat; stays 1m; probably needs some give in the ground; sometimes blinkered. *M. W. Easterby.* —

BANFF SPRINGS 5 gr.m. Sir Albert 72–Valli 81 (Vigo 130) (1981 10.6d **37** 12f 10f3 10s 1982 8d 11fg2 10f 12f2 10.6f 16.5f4 14.7f 15.8f) plater; ran creditably in a slowly-run non-seller over 2m sixth start; acts on firm going. *Miss L. Siddall.*

BANOCO 4 b.c. Nonoalco 131–Denaneer 78 (Green God 128) (1981 7s 6d **72§** 8g* 7g 8s3 8g 1982 7.5g 6.5fg2 8s 7.5d* 8g 7d 8g 7f 7.2fg 8f 7fg 9fg 8f3 8fg 8fg 8.2g4 10g4 8.2g3 8d2 8d* 8s 7g4 8s) won at Cagnes-sur-Mer in March and Ayr in September, on latter course beating Windpipe by a short head in £4,800 handicap (apprentice ridden); none too consistent however through a busy season; suited by 1m (not entirely disgraced over 1¼m); acts on firm going but is suited by some give underfoot; tends to sweat up; sometimes bandaged on off-hind; has looked none too genuine on occasions (including at Ayr), and is suited by waiting tactics. *T. Craig.*

B. A. POUNDSTRETCHER 3 b.f. Laser Light 118–Grecian Flame (Sound Track 132) (1981 5s* 5d* 5v2 6fg2 6fg 6fg 6fg 6s 1982 5d 6fg 5.8f 6fg 6g) lengthy, workmanlike filly; successful in maiden race at Wolverhampton and minor event at Windsor in 1981; soundly beaten in handicaps at 3 years 6f; seems to act on any going; blinkered last 2 starts; has worn bandages behind. *R. Hannon.*

BARA GILL 2 gr.g. Baragoi 115–Gill Breeze (Farm Walk 111) (1982 5fg4 **75** 6f3 6g 8fg 8f 7.2s*) Mar 11; 1,200Y; lengthy gelding; half-brother to 5 winners, including fair 7f performer Secret Gill (by Most Secret); dam never ran; dropped in class, made virtually all and stuck on well to beat Prince Giovanni by 1½ lengths in 10-runner seller at Haydock (bought in 3,200 gns) in October; should be suited by 1m; appears to act on any going; ran poorly fifth outing. *W. Haigh.*

BARAK (ISR) 2 b.c. Verre Dore–Nooret (Tompion) (1982 8s 10s) Apr — 12; 3,000Y; workmanlike colt; first foal; dam never ran; well beaten in maiden events at Bath and Nottingham in October. *D. Sasse.*

BARASTONE ROSE 3 b. or b.f. Ragstone 128–Barbary Miss (Barbary — Pirate 91) (1981 NR 1982 11.7f 16fg 12f 12g) fifth foal; dam of no account; well beaten in maiden races and a seller in the South; trained part of season by J. Jenkins. *R. Simpson.*

BARBEE (ISR) 2 b.f. Bally Russe 113–Barbara Bee (Sharpen Up 127) (1982 — 6g 7f 7f 7g 8d 6.5s2 8.5s3 9g) Feb 6; lengthy filly; first foal; dam of no account; in rear in varied company, including selling, when trained by G. Blum; sent to Holland after fifth start; has worn blinkers. *H. Wolffers, Holland.*

BARBRANCER 9 b.g. Carnival Dancer 113–Delitta (Saintly Song 128) (1982 **45** 5f4 6f 6f 6g 6d) May 1; compact, plain gelding; poor form in sellers; blinkered last 2 starts. *Mrs A. Cousins.*

BARB'S BEAU 5 b.g. Festino 105–Beauatire 86 (Beau Sabreur 125) (1981 — 10g 12d4 14d2 16d4 16g 19s 1982 16fg 12f) lengthy gelding; staying maiden. *M. Masson.*

BARDAN 2 b.c. Dom Racine 121–That Girl (Breeders Dream 116) (1982 — 7g 7s) Apr 7; 8,200Y; lengthy, rather leggy colt; first foal; dam showed no form; gave indications of a little ability in maiden races, finishing ninth of 28 behind Jungle Romeo at Redcar in October on second start. *R. Armstrong.*

BARDSEY POET 2 ch.f. Monsanto 121–Barlow Fold 99 (Monet 126) (1982 **72** 5f 7fg 7d 7d) Apr 11; 6,800Y; compact filly; half-sister to several winners here and abroad, including useful 1976 2-y-o sprinter Namara (by Pieces of Eight); dam 2-y-o 5f winner; beaten 4½ lengths when seventh of 15 behind Muznah in maiden race at Yarmouth in August, third outing and best effort; sweated up a bit and didn't move particularly well final start. *G. Huffer.*

BARE ESSENTIALS 3 b.g. Streak 119–Gardenia (Cagire II 122) (1981 6fg — 6f 7f2 7g 7f3 7f 8f 1982 8fg 9f 8f) leggy gelding; poor maiden; runner-up in seller at 2 yrs; suited by 7f but has been well beaten over further; blinkered once in 1981. *R. Whitaker.*

BARK 3 b.g. Quiet Fling 124–Crepe Myrtle 80 (Crepello 136) (1981 NR 1982 — 12fg 10.1fg 13g 16s) big, strong gelding; half-brother to 2 winners, including useful 1976 2-y-o Ground Cover (by Huntercombe), subsequently a stakes winner at up to 1¼m in North America; dam won over 1m; beaten some way in varied company; trained part of season by J. Tree. *P. Mitchell.*

BAR

BARLEY BIRCH 4 b.g. Crooner 119–Bella Sandra 88 (Botticelli 129) (1981 **52**
10.1fg 8fg 11.5g 1982 10f² 12f³ 10s⁴ 10fg 9g 10fg⁴ 12f⁴ 12fg) compact, short-
legged gelding; probably stays 1¼m; probably suited by a sound surface; sold to
M. Pipe 3,600 gns Newmarket Autumn Sales. *M. Tompkins.*

BARNABY SAM 3 br.c. Comedy Star 121–Balandra Star 92 (Blast 125) (1981 —
5g 6g³ 7fg 6fg 8fg 1982 12fg 8f 14d 10.1g 10.1g 10.1g 13.1f³ 12v) useful sort;
good walker; quite a modest maiden at his best; seems to stay 13f; sold to P.
Mitchell 3,600 gns Newmarket Autumn Sales. *R. Hannon.*

BARNBROOK 2 br.c. Dom Racine 121–Focal 92 (Faubourg II 127) (1982 5d²)
May 15; 1R 6,200Y; half-brother to 9 winners, including useful 1967 2-y-o The
Industan (by El Gallo); dam won from 6f to 2m; 5½ lengths fourth of 9 to Dorset
Eagle in maiden race at Warwick in April; dead. *D. H. Jones.*

BARNCOURT 2 ch.c. Jolly Me 114–The Suestan 71 (Ballyciptic 122) (1982 —
6fg) May 10; strong, good-looking colt; fourth reported foal; dam won over
1½m; unquoted and backward, never showed in £3,500 race at Goodwood in May.
K. Brassey.

BARNET HEIR 4 ch.g. Great Nephew 126–Right as Rain 96 (King's Bench 132) **80**
(1981 5s 5fg⁴ 5f 5fg⁴ 5.3f³ 6g 5fg⁴ 5.6fg 6g⁴ 6g 1982 6d 6d³ 6fg⁴ 6g* 7f 6g 6fg
5g² 5.3fg² 5f 5g 5g² 5fg² 5d) small, sturdy, very attractive gelding; good mover;
one of only 2 runners to race on far side when beating Amorous by 7 lengths in
£4,700 Greenham Ballast Handicap at Kempton in May; second at Lingfield,
Brighton, Epsom and Goodwood, best subsequent efforts; stays 6f; acts on any
going; has run creditably for an apprentice. *B. Swift.*

BARNEY MILLER 2 b.g. Monseigneur 127–Etta (Umberto 118) (1982 5fg 7f) —
May 30; 10,500Y; big, rangy gelding; half-brother to numerous winners, notably
very useful 5f to 1m performer Majetta (by King's Troop) and useful 7f to 1¼m
winner Etching (by Auction Ring); dam never ran; behind in maiden races at
Windsor in May and Newmarket (looked very green, sweated up and was coltish
in paddock) in July; gelded subsequently. *M. Ryan.*

BARNLOUGH 4 br.f. Blue Cashmere 129–Stick 'Em Up (Burglar 128) (1981 —
6g 5f 6f 7f⁴ 6fg² 5h 5g 1982 7f 6f 5.3g 5fg) compact filly; plating-class maiden;
stays 7f; trained first 3 starts by V. Soane. *D. Thom.*

BARON BLAKENEY 5 gr.h. Blakeney 126–Teleflora 89 (Princely Gift 137) **83 d**
(1981 16fg⁴ 18fg* 18.4d 1982 17f² 18.8fg* 20fg² 16.1g² 16.1f⁴ 19f² 18.8fg 18g⁴
19s 18d 20g) neat horse; won handicap at Warwick in May and was second in
others at Wolverhampton, Royal Ascot (Ascot Stakes), Haydock and Goodwood
(Pimm's Goodwood Stakes); had very stiff task and ran well when about 12
lengths fourth to Ardross in Doncaster Cup eighth start, but disappointed next
time; suited by a test of stamina; acts on any going; suited by strong handling;
blinkered final start at 3 yrs. *M. Pipe.*

BARONET 10 b.g. Huntercombe 133–Chagrin Falls 101 (Polic 126) (1981 8s —
10fg 8g 8s* 8f 10fg³ 8fg 8fg⁴ 8fg² 9g² 10g 1982 10s 8g 8f) lengthy,
attractive gelding; a very useful performer who maintained his form and
enthusiasm really well and was deservedly one of the most popular handicappers of
recent years; had a particularly fine record in William Hill Cambridgeshire at
Newmarket, winning it in 1978 and 1980 and finishing second in 1977 and 1981;
unfortunately had to be put down shortly after pulling up lame at York in May;
stayed 1¼m; acted on any going; usually held up and was suited by a strong
gallop; sometimes sweated up; game. *J. Benstead.*

BARON HOPKINS 8 ch.g. Frankincense 120–Jolie 64 (Jolly Jet 111) (1981 8g —
1982 8.2s 8f 8.2fg 10g 8fg 8.2g 8fg) plater; stays 1m; probably acts on any
going. *A. W. Jones.*

BAROOQ (USA) 3 br.c. Turn and Count–Ballet Pleasure (What A Pleasure) **94**
(1981 5f 6fg² 6fg² 7g² 6fg* 8g 7g 1982 8.2s 8fg 10f 8g² 9d) well-made colt;
good mover; 20/1, returned to form when going down by a short head to Mashin
Time in handicap at Ripon in August, travelling on bridle for most of race and
staying on strongly despite not having clearest of runs; behind in William Hill
Cambridgeshire at Newmarket in October; should stay 1¼m; tends to pull hard.
F. Durr.

BAROWIN 3 br.c. Owen Dudley 121–Garnette Rose 74 (Floribunda 136) (1981 —
7fg 1982 10s 11g 15fg⁴ 16fg 16.5fg) quite well-made colt; plating-class maiden;
stays well; sold to M. Hinchliffe 1,550 gns Newmarket Autumn Sales. *C. Nelson.*

118

BARRA HEAD 2 b.c. Nonoalco 131–Bruntlaw 94 (Bounteous 125) (1982 7g) —
Apr 30; half-brother to 3 winners, including 1981 Irish 2-y-o 6f winner Valley
Law (by Sun Prince); dam won at up to 1¼m; unquoted, finished out of first 9 of
30 behind Mandelstam in maiden race at Newmarket in October. *J. Dunlop.*

BARRERA LAD (USA) 2 ch.c. Barrera–Misty Joy (Misty Day) (1982 5f³ 5f **83 §**
5f 5f⁴ 5s²) Mar 17; $60,000Y; well-made colt; good mover; half-brother to
several winners in USA and Mexico; dam at her best at 2 yrs, when very useful
sprinter; temperamental sprint maiden, placed at Newbury in June and at
Sandown in October; was slowly away first two starts, unseated rider as stalls
opened on third appearance (blinkered) and gave deal of trouble at start on
fourth appearance (also blinkered); one to treat with caution. *D. Elsworth.*

BARRON JULIUS 2 ch.c. North Stoke 130–Golden Gorse (Crepello 136) —
(1982 7.6v 8s) Apr 29; 45,000Y; quite attractive, short-backed colt; half-
brother to 3-y-o Afdal (by Realm) and to winning Irish stayer Quarter Bridge
(by Thatch); dam, winner over 1¼m in Ireland, is half-sister to Derby fourth
Royal Sword; well behind in big fields of maidens at Lingfield (12/1) and
Sandown (33/1) in October; sold 1,050 gns Ascot November Sales. *J. Dunlop.*

BARROW STRAND 2 br.g. Mansingh 120–Vaunt (Hill Rise 127) (1982 6g) —
May 5; IR 2,400F, 1,500Y; well-made gelding; half-brother to 3 winners here
and abroad, including useful 1½m winner Saint Osyth (by Blakeney); dam won
3 races at up to 6f; 66/1 and very backward, soon tailed off in 12-runner maiden
race won by Sir Butch at Epsom in August. *D. Whelan.*

BARRYPHILIPS DISCO 5 br.g. Firestreak 125–Appollo Fourteen 78 (Space —
King 115) (1981 16.5g 1982 18d 12d) strong gelding; winning hurdler; behind
all outings on flat. *R. Whitaker.*

BARTRA 4 b.g. Mandamus 120–Pandomyne 71 (Pandofell 132) (1981 7g* 8g* **52**
6f³ 7.6g 5.3f⁴ 7.6fg 8g 1982 6g 8g³ 7fg 8f⁴ 10f³ 10fg³ 12g 8fg⁴ 10fg* 7f⁴ 10v³)
compact gelding; plater; attracted no bid after winning at Folkestone in
September; stays 1¼m; acts on any going; sometimes dwells at start. *M. Masson.*

BARYSHNIKOVSKY 2 b.c. Manado 130–Neriad (Princequillo) (1982 8s 8.2s²) **83**
Feb 6; IR 26,000Y; tall, leggy, rather narrow colt; half-brother to numerous
winners, including top-class 1½m filly Comtesse de Loir (by Val de Loir) and
smart middle-distance performer Zein (by Zeddaan); dam never ran; had two
races in October, on second occasion staying on strongly when 3 lengths second
of 19 to Holy Spark in minor event at Nottingham; looks sure to win over
middle distances. *R. Boss.*

BARZINI 3 br.g. Baragoi 115–Primeapple (Primera 131) (1981 8d 1982 12fg —
14s) workmanlike gelding; behind in maiden races and an amateur riders
event. *C. Williams.*

BASICALLY BRIGHT 2 b.f. Sparkler 130–Rosetown 84 (Charlottown 127) **74**
(1982 5.8f³ 5.8g³ 7f⁴) Apr 30; 6,200Y; half-sister to 2 winners, including fairly
useful 1980 2-y-o 5f winner Rosewing (by Swing Easy); dam, winner over 1m, is
daughter of 1,000 Guineas second Rosalba; in frame in maiden races, on final
occasion 5¼ lengths fourth of 14 to Zariya at Brighton in September; will stay 1m.
B. Hills.

BASIL BOY 3 b.c. Jimsun 121–Slick Chick 89 (Shiny Tenth 120) (1981 **92**
5s* 5fg² 5d⁴ 5g³ 6fg 6fg 6fg* 7.3d 6g 7g 8.2s 1982 8d 7g⁴ 8f 7f³ 7f³ 6fg 7.2g
7.6g 7f² 7g³ 7fg* 8g³ 8f³ 10g 7s 8v⁴ 8s) strong, sturdy colt; fair handicapper;
won at Sandown in August; didn't have best of runs and looked unlucky when
strong-finishing 2 lengths third to Paperetto in Northern Goldsmiths' Handicap at
Newcastle next time; promises to stay 1¼m; has won on soft ground but has shown
better form on firm; tends to get behind in early stages nowadays. *R. Hannon.*

BASTA 3 b.f. Busted 134–The Woodbird (Tudor Melody 129) (1981 7g **72**
1982 11g³ 12f 12fg 14.7f⁴ 14d² 14g 10s* 12d*) rangy, attractive filly; good
walker; won maiden race at Nottingham and minor event at Edinburgh in the
autumn; stays 1¾m; needs some give in the ground; sold to R. Hollinshead
14,500 gns Newmarket December Sales. *G. Pritchard-Gordon.*

BATIK 4 ch.f. On Your Mark 125–Taffeta 72 (Shantung 132) (1981 6g 8.5d —
8fg 6fg 6g 1982 6fg 6fg) lengthy filly; poor plater; should stay 1m+; usually
wears blinkers. *D. Sasse.*

BATON CHARGE 2 b.c. Garda's Revenge 119–Song Selector (Jukebox 120) **87**
(1982 5g 5fg* 5f 6fg 5f 5fg⁴ 5fg) Feb 27; IR 2,200F, IR 1,000Y; neat, strong
colt; second produce; dam fourth once from 6 starts in Ireland; led throughout

to win auction race at Naas in May by ¾ length from Wraparound Sue; led to past halfway when less than 10 lengths eighth of 11 to Prince Reymo in Windsor Castle Stakes at Royal Ascot on fifth start; a speedy sort but wasn't disgraced when tried over 6f; blinkered final start. *W. Fennin, Ireland.*

BATONI 3 b.c. Realm 129–Marthe Meynet (Welsh Pageant 132) (1981 5g* 5g* (dis) 1982 7f 6f 5s 6s² 6s 5s) lengthy colt; good mover; sprint handicapper; stays 6f; acts on soft going. *M. H. Easterby.* **83**

BATON MATCH 2 ch.c. Royal Match 117–Fado (Ribero 126) (1982 6g 6f 7f) — Mar 22; sturdy colt; in rear in sellers; sold 320 gns Doncaster September Sales. *P. Haslam.*

BATTALION 4 br.g. Bustino 136–True Love 89 (Princely Gift 137) (1981 6g² 8f⁴ 8d² 9s* 8g* 10d² 1982 10.2g² 13d³ 8f² 8f 12f 8f⁴ 8fg 8fg 12f) useful-looking, though rather hollow-backed gelding; placed in 2 amateur riders events and a handicap in the spring; stays 13f, but will possibly prove best at shorter distances; acts on any going, but gave impression in summer he was feeling effects of repeated outings on firm. *D. Chapman.* **68 d**

BATTEN 6 ch.g. Tumble Wind–Darya 104 (Darius 129) (1981 NR 1982 14fg 13.1f³ 12f³) quite a moderate maiden; stays 13f; acts on any going; has worn bandages in front. *B. Palling.* **44**

BATTLE HYMN 3 b.c. Music Boy 124–Wild Words 76 (Galivanter 131) (1981 NR 1982 6g 6fg* 6fg² 8.2f 6fg* 7f 6g 7f⁴) 16,000Y; big, handsome colt; half-brother to 5 winners, including useful 7f and 1m winner Chukaroo (by Kibenka) and fairly useful 1979 2-y-o sprinter Lunar Eclipse (by Hot Spark); dam half-sister to very useful sprinter Sound Barrier; won maiden race at Haydock in May (odds on) and Wokingham Stakes (Handicap) at Royal Ascot; had race won fully 2f out on latter and beat Camisite decisively by 1½ lengths despite hanging badly right; ran respectably in well-contested 7f handicaps at Newmarket and Doncaster afterwards but gave impression both times trip is just too far for him; yet to race on a soft surface; apprentice ridden at Royal Ascot but is probably suited by stronger handling. *G. Harwood.* **100**

BATTLING AGAIN 2 ch.f. Crooner 119–Battling 75 (Pinza 137) (1982 5fg 5g 5.3fg 6g) May 12; half-sister to winning stayer Bean Boy (by Some Hand); dam won sellers over 5f and 1m, and also won a hurdle and point-to-points; behind in maiden races, twice last. *G. Beeson.*

BAUHINIA 3 ch.f. Sagaro 133–Boswellia 109 (Frankincense 120) (1981 8s⁴ 1982 8f 8f 12g 10.6s) strong, good-bodied filly; showed some promise only start in 1981 but was well beaten at 3 yrs, should stay middle distances; sometimes taken early to post. *W. Hastings-Bass.* —

BAY EMANUELLE 2 b.f. Anax 120–Khotso (Alcide 136) (1982 5f³ 5f 5f 5f⁴) Jan 20; 800F; rather lightly-made filly; fourth foal; dam never ran; poor maiden; not raced after June. *Mrs M. Nesbitt.* **46**

Wokingham Stakes, Ascot—a decisive win for Battle Hymn

Mrs Dan Abbott's "Battle Hymn"

BAY FELLA 2 b.g. Bay Express 132–Felipa (Philip of Spain 126) (1982 6s 7.6v 6g) Apr 21; first foal; dam seemingly of little account; no worthwhile form in 3 races in the autumn. *J. O'Donoghue.* —

BAYFORD 3 ch.c. Brittany–Sweet Silhouette 79 (Setay 105) (1981 NR 1982 5f 8f) 1,500F; half-brother to a winner; dam winning hurdler; well behind in maiden races at Bath early in year; blinkered on second occasion. *Mrs B. Waring.* —

BAY GIRL 2 b.f. Persian Bold 123–Dasa Girl (Prince de Galles 125) (1982 5f) May 30; lightly-made filly; second foal; dam French 1m winner; modest sixth of 9 in maiden race at Epsom in April. *P. Ashworth.* —

BAZALI 3 b.g. Native Bazaar 122–Rogali 80 (Royal Avenue 123) (1981 NR 1982 8g 7.6f 8.5f 8g) tall, useful-looking gelding; half-brother to several winners, including fairly useful 1m to 1¼m winner Doogali (by Doon); dam a sprinter; well beaten in varied company, including selling; blinkered final start; sold 540 gns Ascot October Sales. *R. Smyth.* —

BAZ BOMBATI 4 ch.g. Sun Prince 128–Salsafy 81 (Tudor Melody 129) (1981 8g 12g* 12fg³ 12fg 12v³ 12d 12g 1982 15d) well-made, useful-looking gelding; good walker and mover; useful performer as a 3-y-o when trained by G. Pritchard-Gordon; split a pastern on gallops in January and was off course until September, when soundly beaten in amateur riders event at Ayr (looking fairly fit, went reasonably well until straight); suited by 1½m; best form on a sound surface. *S. Mellor.* —

BEACH LIGHT 2 ch.f. Bustino 136–Street Light 120 (St Chad 120) (1982 7g⁴ 7g) Mar 7; IR 50,000Y; lengthy, rather shallow-girthed filly; third living foal; half-sister to 3-y-o 1m winner Mycenaen (by Be My Guest) and useful 5f and 6f winner Highland Light (by Home Guard); dam smart sprinter; unquoted, put up pleasing first effort when 1¼ lengths fourth of 30 to Mandelstam in maiden race at Newmarket in October; ran on well after dwelling when 3 lengths sixth of 22 behind Toveris in similar event on same course later in the month; will stay 1m. *M. Jarvis.* **87**

121

BEACON BOY 6 b.g. Sahib 114–Lucky Pigeon (The Mongoose 108) (1981 —
NR 1982 17f) little sign of ability, including in a seller; has been tried in
blinkers. *P. Burgoyne.*

BEAKER (USA) 2 ch.c. Crow 134–Tucked In (Jim J) (1982 7s⁴) Mar 18; **86 p**
$25,000Y; close-coupled, quite attractive colt; third foal; dam unraced half-
sister to very smart middle-distance performer Big Whippendeal; 33/1 and
just in need of outing, improved steadily after dwelling without being given
hard race when creditable 9 lengths fourth of 8 behind Sackford in minor event
at Leicester in November; will be suited by 1¼m+; sure to do better. *P. Walwyn.*

BEAMING ANNE 2 ch.f. The Go-Between 129–Ann's Beam (Bold and Free **51**
118) (1982 5fg² 5fg 6g 6f 5v 5v) Mar 17; second foal; dam well behind both
starts; neck second in seller at Lingfield in May, only form. *P. K. Mitchell.*

BEAMING LASS 3 b. or br.f. Silly Season 127–Oh Well 61 (Sahib 114) (1981 **50**
5g 5fg 5g 5g⁴ 5f³ 6fg⁴ 5g 6f* 5d 8.2d 1982 6s 8g² 8.2fg 8g⁴ 6fg 7g⁴ 8g 9fg* 9g)
plain filly; plater; attracted no bid after winning at Hamilton in July; stays 9f;
acts on firm going; ran poorly in blinkers once at 2 yrs; sold 550 gns Ascot
September Sales. *J. S. Wilson.*

BEAMOF 3 b. or br.g. Averof 123–Beamless 73 (Hornbeam 130) (1981 5g 6g —
7fg 7.2fg 1982 12g 10s 16d 10d 12fg 10f 12d) strong gelding; poor form,
including in sellers, though has won over hurdles; sometimes blinkered; has
sweated up. *G. Toft.*

BEAMWAM 4 br.g. Bing II–Canute Lady 66 (Hardicanute 130) (1981 12g⁴ —
1982 16.5fg) very lightly raced and little form on flat. *H. Bell.*

BEAN BOY 4 ch.g. Some Hand 119–Battling 75 (Pinza 137) (1981 8s 7v **54**
12.2g² 12g* 9g 12fg 1982 12f⁴ 12.3fg³ 15.8f* 12fg 15.8f*) workmanlike
gelding; won at Catterick in June and July; stays well; acts well on firm going;
blinkered last 3 outings in 1981; suitable mount for an apprentice. *D. Smith.*

BEARS COPSE 2 ch.c. Be Friendly 130–Lunar Queen 96 (Queen's Hussar —
124) (1982 7fg 6g) Mar 12; 3,300Y; big colt; half-brother to 2 winners, including 5f to 7f winner Royal Duty (by Import); in rear in sellers at Chepstow
and Newmarket in the autumn. *Mrs J. Reavey.*

BEAT THE DRUM 2 b.f. Brigadier Gerard 144–Tantara (Pakistan II 84) **104**
(1982 6fg 8.5g* 7g²) Apr 16; half-sister to winning hurdler Roll of Drums
(by Royal Prerogative); dam won 5 times in New Zealand; cost only 720 gns
at 1982 Newmarket May Sales but later proved herself one of the best Irish
staying 2-y-o fillies, winning maiden race at Galway in September by 5 lengths
from Anne's Dance and finishing ¾-length second of 13 to Countess Candy, after
having none too clear a run, when favourite for Park Stakes at Leopardstown;
suited by 1m. *M. Connolly, Ireland.*

BEAUCOUP D'ARGENT 4 b.g. Streak 119–Mona's Own (Entanglement 118) **45**
(1981 7.6g 1982 10fg 13f² 16f 14d 12.2f 12f 12fg* 12d² 12.2s) small, lengthy
gelding; dropped in class when 6-length winner of selling handicap at Lingfield
in September (apprentice ridden); bought in 1,650 gns afterwards; stays 13f;
seems to act on any going; blinkered sixth outing; sold 2,500 gns Doncaster
October Sales. *E. Eldin.*

BEAUDELAIRE (USA) 2 ch.c. Nijinsky 138–Bitty Girl 123 (Habitat 134) **107+**
(1982 5fg* 7fg*) rather short-coupled, attractive colt; has a rather sharp
action; fourth foal; brother to stakes-placed American winner Nijit and half-
brother to useful Irish 3-y-o 7f winner Memento (by Roberto); dam, sister
to Hot Spark, won first 5 starts, all over 5f, and later won at up to 1m in USA;
showed a good turn of foot when landing the odds twice at Leopardstown in
September, winning by 5 lengths from Autumn Sunset in maiden race and by
a length from Gormanstown Prince, who gave 4 lb, after being eased close home
in Coolmore Try My Best Stakes; will stay 1m; still looked a bit green on second
outing and will improve further. *V. O'Brien, Ireland.*

BEAU JULES 3 b.c. Tachypous 128–Asmara 94 (Alycidon 138) (1981 NR —
1982 8fg 8fg 9.4f⁴ 10f) 12,000Y; big, rangy colt; half-brother to several winners, including useful 2-y-o's Tudoron (by Tudor Melody), Ashabit (by Habitat)
and As Blessed (by So Blessed); dam won at 1¼m; only plating class on balance
of form; dead. *P. Walwyn.*

Mr R. E. Sangster's "Beaudelaire"

BEAU PRETENDER (FR) 3 ch.c. Anne's Pretender 124–Belle de Reux **118**
(Diatome 132) (1981 7.5fg 7.5fg⁴ 8d* 10v* 1982 11fg² 12s 12fg 12.5d 12.5g
10fg³ 12f 10v 10v) 30,000 francs Y (approx £3,000); first foal; dam, minor middle-
distance winner, is daughter of smart 1962 French 2-y-o Chesa; smart in 1981
when he won Prix de Conde at Longchamp on final start; didn't win at 3 yrs
but ran creditably to be placed in Prix Noailles at Longchamp (2 lengths second
to Persepolis) and Prix de la Cote Normande at Deauville (just over a length
third to General Holme); well beaten in Prix du Jockey-Club at Chantilly and
Grand Prix de Saint-Cloud on third and fourth starts; stays 11f; seems to act
on any going; suited by forcing tactics. *R. Touflan, France.*

BEAU SAUVAGE 3 gr.g. Warpath 113–Turtle Dove (Gyr 131) (1981 NR —
1982 10.2g 13g) neat gelding; brother to 3 winners, including useful middle-
distance stayer Path of Peace; dam ran only once; tailed off in maiden
races at Doncaster and Nottingham; sold 1,600 gns Doncaster September Sales.
C. Thornton.

BEBE HATTIE 2 ch.f. Gracious Melody 117–Tennis Girl 79 (Ennis 128) —
(1982 7f 8.2d 8s) May 24; sturdy filly; half-sister to some poor animals; dam
won over 7f; in rear in minor event and sellers; bandaged near-hind final
appearance. *J. Doyle.*

BE BE OF KUWAIT 3 br.g. Prince Tenderfoot 126–Spinning Jenny (Timmy —
My Boy 125) (1981 5g 5s² 6fg* 6fg² 6fg* 7fg⁴ 1982 6d 7fg) strong, well-
made gelding; fairly useful at 2 yrs; well beaten both starts early in 1982, in
£3,700 event at Kempton and valuable handicap at Newmarket; should stay 7f;
has run respectably on soft going but has shown best form on a firm surface;
sweated up badly and took a strong hold final start in 1981; to USA. *J. Sutcliffe.*

BEDFORD ROW 2 gr.c. Bruni 132–Mecara 90 (Gulf Pearl 117) (1982 7s) —
Feb 7; 22,000F; fourth foal; dam, half-sister to smart Majetta, won twice over

123

5f at 2 yrs; easy in the market, started slowly when eighth of 12 behind Dabdoub in minor event at Chepstow in October. *G. Lewis.*

BEDFORD (USA) 4 b.c. Nijinsky 138–Drumtop (Round Table)   (1981 10d 12d 10fg 10fg2 11fg* 12f* 13.1g* 14d3 14s   1982 12fg 13.4fg 16.1f4 16fg 13.1f2 12fg* 14g4 12f* 18g 12d) strong, lengthy, quite attractive colt; good mover; landed the odds from Francesco in small races at Pontefract in August and September; also in frame in Lymm Stakes at Haydock and handicaps at Bath and York (Tote-Ebor), but ran disappointingly on his other starts; suited by a test of stamina; acts on any going except possibly very soft; sometimes blinkered (ran well first time but not on either subsequent occasion); races with his tongue tied down; sent to race in USA. *I. Balding.*   **88**

BEE ALIVE (USA) 3 gr.c. Drone–Whirled 116 (Globemaster)   (1981 7g 6s 1982 6d 7f 8g 7.6f* 8f 8g 8f2) big, rangy colt; won maiden race at Lingfield in June; reportedly broke blood vessel when running creditably in handicap on final start; suited by 1m; acts well on firm going; sold to D. Ringer 6,200 gns Newmarket Autumn Sales. *P. Walwyn.*   **62**

BEECHWOOD SEEKER 4 b.g. Status Seeker–Julie's Gi-Gi (Brave Invader)   (1981 10s 12g 12d* 12g 12.5f2 13fg 12.3fg 12.3fg4 16f3 16g* 18f* 17.4g2   1982 16.1g) workmanlike gelding; good walker; did well in handicaps as a 3-y-o (rated 78); needed race on only outing of 1982 (July) and reportedly had a setback afterwards; very well suited by a test of stamina; acts on any going; has run well in blinkers. *K. Stone.*   **—**

BEE-DEE 2 b.g. Mandrake Major 122–Clear Song 67 (Saintly Song 128)   (1982 5g3 5g 5f4 5f2 5f* 5g 5fg 5f 5g 5f 6s) May 10; 5,000Y; leggy, lightly-made gelding; poor mover; second living foal; dam won over 5f at 2 yrs; showed no form after winning maiden race at Catterick in June by 2 lengths from Romantic Knight; acts on firm going; blinkered ninth outing. *D. Smith.*   **70**

BEELEIGH 4 b.g. Sallust 134–Mythical Lady 86 (Track Spare 125)   (1981 7s* 8.2fg* 8fg* 7d4 8.2s 8f 8g 9d 8fg2   1982 8fg4 7fg2 8f4 8fg 8fg 8g 7g) leggy, useful sort of gelding; in frame in Newbury Spring Cup, Autobar Victoria Cup at Ascot (3 lengths second to Indian King) and Thirsk Hunt Cup in spring; disappointing afterwards, including when blinkered; stays 1m; probably acts on any going; has won for an apprentice but used to have a tendency to hang; sometimes sweats up and often fails to impress in paddock; sold to Miss S. Morris 5,200 gns Newmarket Autumn Sales. *N. Callaghan.*   **81**

BEFANA 3 b.f. Persian Breeze 121–Fair Amanda 105§ (Firestreak 125)   (1981 NR   1982 5f 6d 8.2s) half-sister to minor winners by Charlottown and Kalydon and to a winner in Sweden; dam won twice at 6f at 2 yrs; beaten a long way in maiden races and a minor event. *J. Mulhall.*   **—**

BEHIND THE LINES 2 b.c. Brigadier Gerard 144–Oh So Fair (Graustark)   (1982 7g 7fg* 8s 7d) May 4; 11,000Y; tall, rangy colt; brother to smart 6f and 7f winner Etienne Gerard, and half-brother to several winners, notably very smart 5f to 1¼m filly Roussalka and 1000 Guineas runner-up Our Home (both by Habitat); dam won over 1¼m in Ireland; won maiden race at Salisbury in September; had no chance subsequently in Royal Lodge Stakes at Ascot and nursery under 9-7 at Doncaster; should stay 1m. *D. Elsworth.*   **84**

BEKONSCOT 2 b.c. Reform 132–Shorthouse 100 (Habitat 134)   (1982 6d 7g) Mar 7; first foal; dam, daughter of smart middle-distance stayer Guillotina, won twice over 7f at 2 yrs; soundly beaten in maiden races at Doncaster in June and Yarmouth in August; exported to Malaysia. *M. Jarvis.*   **—**

BEL BOLIDE (USA) 4 ch.c. Bold Bidder–Lady Graustark (Graustark)   (1981 7g4 8g3 8s 8fg3 7.3fg   1982 9fg 8f2 8f 8s) quite attractive, if rather lightly-built colt; excellent mover with a long stride; ran well twice at Newmarket in spring 1981, notably when third to To-Agori-Mou in 2000 Guineas; ran best race for quite a while when 1½ lengths second to Tugoflove in Hambleton Stakes (Limited Handicap) at York in May; looked very well and seemed to be carrying a good deal more condition than usual when next seen out in Sussex Stakes at Goodwood in July, and ran most creditably to finish about 2¼ lengths fifth of 13 behind On The House; unsuited by soft going when over 5 lengths seventh of 14 to King James in Prix Quincey at Deauville in August; stays 1m; needs a sound surface; free-running sort; sent to race in USA. *J. Tree.*   **122**

BELDALE CONCORDE (USA) 2 b.c. Super Concorde 128–My Gal Lucky (Gallant Man)   (1982 5f3 7fg* 7g4 8.2fg2 8s2 8d) Jan 23; $70,000 2-y-o; rangy, attractive colt; has a free but round action; first foal; dam third once from 10   **118**

outings; won 8-runner minor event at Sandown in July by 6 lengths from Accused; took on good horses subsequently, and ran particularly well in his three races at 1m in the autumn, running The Noble Player to 1½ lengths in £4,600 event at Haydock, finishing 2 lengths second to Anguillo in Gran Criterium at Milan, and just over 3 lengths fifth of 8, after looking short of room much of way up straight, to Dunbeath in William Hill Futurity Stakes at Doncaster; will stay 1¼m; seems to act on any going. *M. Jarvis.*

BELDALE FLEET (USA) 3 b.c. Fleet Nasrullah–Adjudicate Miss (Traffic Judge) (1981 7fg² 7g⁴ 7f 1982 9fg 12fg) big, good-looking colt; has a round action; fairly useful at 2 yrs; well beaten at Newmarket early in 1982 in Gerry Feilden Memorial Stakes and minor event; not sure to stay 1½m. *M. Jarvis.* —

BELDALE LUSTRE (USA) 3 br.c. Explodent–Added Lustre (Clandestine) (1981 6g³ 6g³ 6g² 6g² 1982 6fg² 7fg² 8f³ 7fg³ 7g² 7fg⁴ 7.3g² 8fg³) $26,000Y $38,000 2-y-o; strong, good sort; fourth foal; half-brother to 3 minor winners in USA; dam, out of half-sister to Kentucky Derby winner Foolish Pleasure, won 5f claiming race at 4 yrs; has plenty of ability but is still a maiden; in frame all starts at 3 yrs, notably when close third in Lockinge Stakes at Newbury (to Motavato), second in Prix de la Porte Maillot at Longchamp (¾ length behind Exclusive Order) and Hungerford Stakes at Newbury (beaten 1½ lengths by Pas de Seul) and 2¼ lengths third to easy winner Sandhurst Prince in Waterford Crystal Mile at Goodwood; subsequently sent to USA; stays 1m; yet to race on a soft surface; best in blinkers; finds little off bridle and is suited by waiting tactics. *M. Jarvis.* **119**

BEL ESPRIT 3 b.f. Sagaro 133–Esprit d'Or 86 (Jolly Jet 111) (1981 6f 5.8f 1982 11.7f 7fg 11.5fg 16fg) dipped-backed, sparely-made filly; behind in varied company, including selling; trained by G. Cottrell first 2 starts. *D. Elsworth.* —

BELFE 3 ch.f. Tachypous 128–Appian Way 89 (Romulus 129) (1981 8d⁴ 8g 8g⁴ 1982 10.6g⁴ 12g 12f 12g 14g² 14fg 16.5fg* 16s 16.5s) rather unfurnished filly; easily won 9-runner minor event at Redcar in September; stays very well. *R. Hollinshead.* **72**

Mr A. J. Kelly's "Beldale Lustre"

Princess Royal Stakes, Ascot—33/1-shot Believer wins from the Irish challenger Santa Roseanna and Tants

BELFRY BOY 3 ch.g. Import 127–Elbeam (Hornbeam 130) (1981 6f 6fg 6g 1982 8f 8.2f) compact, sturdy gelding; beaten long way in maiden races. *H. Wharton.* —

BEL HARBOUR 3 ch.g. Northfields–Rose of Tralee 114 (Buisson Ardent 129) (1981 5g 5g 6fg³ 7fg 5d 8f 8fg 1982 8g 10f 10.6f 10g 10f 10v) small gelding; quite a moderate maiden at his best; well beaten in seller final outing; suited by 1¼m; often pulls hard; usually wears blinkers; sold out of P. Kelleway's stable 3,200 gns Doncaster August Sales after fifth start. *C. Mackenzie.* —

BELIEVER 3 b.f. Blakeney 126–Seein Is Believin (Native Charger) (1981 7d² 1982 10f 12f 12g² 12fg² 12f* 10g² 12v*) well-made, attractive filly; sister to French 1½m winner Prince Blakeney and closely related to fairly useful 13f winner No Evil (by Morston); dam daughter of Prix Morny winner Princeline; put up a vastly improved display when staying on strongly to lead close home and beat Santa Roseanna by ¾ length in Princess Royal Stakes at Ascot in October; had previously comfortably won maiden race at Brighton in September; finds 1¼m on sharp side and will be suited by 1¾m; acts on any going but clearly goes well on heavy ground; best in blinkers; very useful. *J. Dunlop.* **112**

BELINDA BROWN 2 br.f. Legal Eagle 126–Port Meadow 83 (Runnymede 123) (1982 5g* 5g⁴ 5f³ 6d⁴ 5fg 5s 5g) Mar 5; workmanlike filly; half-sister to 3 winners, including 1981 2-y-o 6f winner Steel Choice (by Comedy Star); dam probably stayed 1m; won minor event at Catterick in March by 2¼ lengths from Tennis Tune; 5½ length fourth of 10 to Domynsky in minor 6f event at Ripon in August, first race for 4 months and best subsequent effort; evidently stays 6f. *T. Barron.* **83**

BELKA (FR) 2 b.f. Riverman 131–Kalibella (Barbare II 128) (1982 8s* 8s*) Feb 28; half-sister to 3 winners in France, including middle-distance winner Djebello (by Dike); dam, half-sister to very useful French miler Alik, comes from same family as top-class Irish River; a very promising filly who won newcomers event at Longchamp in September (by a length from L'Empress) and Prix des Reservoirs on same course the following month (led close home to beat Little Meadow by half a length after being held up); will stay 1¼m. *A. Head, France.* **115**

BELLAMONTI 2 br. or gr.c. Godswalk 130–Marta 87 (Aureole 132) (1982 5g 5fg 5g⁴ 6fg) May 5; IR 6,400F, 15,000Y; close-coupled, quite attractive colt; half-brother to minor winners here and abroad; dam, middle-distance performer, is daughter of very smart sprinter Street Singer; quite modest form in varied company, on final outing finishing 5½ lengths fifth of 6 under 7-7 to Gangawayhame in nursery at Goodwood (second favourite) in August; should be well suited by 6f+. *B. Hills.* **73**

BELLARIBO 2 ch.f. Porto Bello 118–Dorriba (Ribero 126) (1982 6fg 6f 7.6v) May 29; small, lengthy filly; first foal; dam never ran; in rear in minor and maiden events. *R. Simpson.*

126

BELLA TRAVAILLE 4 b.f. Workboy 123–Thorganby Bella (Porto Bello 118) **48**
(1981 5d 5s 5fg 5f 5fg 5f 5g 5fg 5fg 5g³ 5fg⁴ 5g 1982 5fg 5fg 5f 5f² 5fg² 5fg²
5.1g⁴ 7f 5f² 5fg* 6fg 5g² 6d 5d 5g 5.8f 5fg 5d 5g) lengthy filly; gained a well-
deserved success when beating Kaimlaw by a length in handicap at Hamilton
in July; speedy and best at 5f; seems best on a sound surface; occasionally
blinkered and has also worn a hood. *R. Hobson.*

BELLBROOK 3 ch.c. Porto Bello 118–Miss Bubbly 78 (Track Spare 125) (1981 —
6g 7fg 5g 7.6s 1982 8d 8d 7.6f 10fg 10.1g 8fg) big, rangy colt; not the best
of movers; only plating class; suited by 1¼m; sold to R. Atkins 3,000 gns
Newmarket Autumn Sales. *W. Wightman.*

BELLE VUE 9 b.g. Track Spare 125–Royal Camp 91 (Sovereign Path 125) **36**
(1981 8fg 1982 8f 7f 10d 7.6fg 8fg 8f³ 8f² 8.2g 8fg 12fg³ 8fg 10d 10.2d⁴) neat
gelding; poor handicapper; stays at least 1¼m; acts on any going; used to wear
blinkers; suitable mount for an inexperienced rider. *R. Hollinshead.*

BELL GREEN 3 b.g. Dragonara Palace 115–Anna Boleyna 84 (Right Royal **67**
V 135) (1981 7d 7fg 1982 10s³ 10f³ 10fg 10d² 9g 10s) well-made gelding;
placed in maiden races and a minor event; stays 1¼m; acts on any going; sold
4,200 gns Newmarket Autumn Sales. *R. Boss.*

BELLINA BENEDETTA 3 b.f. Pablond 93–Benedetta da Castello (St Paddy —
133) (1981 7g 8s 10.2g 1982 16.5f 14.7f) smallish filly; beaten some way
in maiden and minor events. *K. Stone.*

BELL ISLAND 2 b.f. African Sky 124–Salima (Palestine 133) (1982 5g⁴ **69**
5g 5fg 6g) May 24; IR 40,000Y; leggy, close-coupled filly; half-sister to several
winners, including 5f to 1m winner Lady Oakley (by Gulf Pearl), subsequently
a smart winner in USA; dam placed at up to 7f in Ireland; quite a moderate
maiden; had stiffish task in nursery at Windsor in August on final outing;
should stay 6f; sent to USA. *B. Hills.*

BELLITICO 4 ch.g. Politico 124–Hibel (High Table 105) (1981 NR 1982 —
13v) second foal; dam never ran; last of 11 in maiden race won by Selborne
Record at Hamilton in April. *J. Charlton.*

BELLS OF ST MARTIN 2 b.f. Martinmas 128–Trackalady 96 (Track **89**
Spare 125) (1982 5g* 5g⁴ 5fg³ 5d³ 6s 6s) May 9; leggy filly; first foal; dam
fairly useful over 5f at 2 yrs; 50/1-winner of 15-runner maiden race at Windsor
in July, coming through in final 2f to beat Velocidad comfortably by 3 lengths;
creditable 3 lengths third of 12 to Songroid in nursery on same course in September, fourth start; should stay 6f; often ridden by apprentice K. Powdrell.
R. Laing.

BELL-TENT 11 b.g. Bivouac 114–Chilcombe Belle 75 (Robert Barker 125) —
(1981 10g⁴ 10v² 10.8fg 10f 10f 1982 10fg 10d 10f) one-time useful handicapper
but has deteriorated; best at 1¼m; acts on any going but is suited by top-of-
the-ground; usually held up and isn't the easiest of rides. *W. Wightman.*

BELROSE 3 ch.f. Music Boy 124–Red Form (Reform 132) (1981 5g 1982 **51**
6s³ 5g³ 5fg⁴ 6g) fair sort; plater; stays 6f. *S. Norton.*

BELTED EARL (USA) 4 ch.c. Damascus–Moccasin (Nantallah) (1981 **115**
6f* 7fg* 8g* 1982 7.2fg⁴ 6g* 8f) lengthy colt; half-brother to 4 good winners,
notably outstanding 1973 2-y-o Apalachee (by Round Table); dam champion
American 2-y-o filly of 1965 and sister to Ridan and Lt Stevens; most promising
as a 3-y-o and won all his 3 races, including Desmond Stakes at the Curragh
(by short head from Cairn Rouge); put up easily best effort of 1982 in Green-
lands Stakes at the Curragh in May, being pulled to wide outside at halfway,
quickening into lead about 1½f out, and winning by 2 lengths from Jasmine
Star; soon in trouble and was most disappointing when brought over here on
his other 2 starts, finishing fourth of 5 behind Mummy's Game when odds on
for Cold Shield Windows Trophy at Haydock earlier in month and remote
seventh of 10 behind impressive Mr Fluorocarbon when co-favourite for Queen
Anne Stakes at Royal Ascot in June; stayed 1m; raced only on a sound surface;
sold privately after Royal Ascot and is to stand at Winfield Farm, Lexington,
Kentucky. *V. O'Brien, Ireland.*

BELTURBET BRIDGE 2 b.c. Stradavinsky 121–Sandolett (Nimbus 130) —
(1982 7d 7fg) Mar 16; IR 2,000Y; useful-looking colt; half-brother to several
winners here and abroad; dam won twice at up to 6f in USA; not fully wound
up when in rear in maiden races at Chester in August and Salisbury in September.
D. H. Jones.

BE MY DARLING 2 b.f. Windjammer (USA)–Kilcurley Lass (Huntercombe **79**
133) (1982 5d 6fg 6fg³ 5s⁴) Apr 18; IR 8,000F, 28,000Y; quite an attractive
filly; second produce; half-sister to 3-y-o 7f winner Slick Willie (by Red Alert);
dam unraced half-sister to high-class 1969 2-y-o Divine Gift; having first race
for 2 months, ran on nicely in closing stages when eye-catching 2 lengths third
of 18 behind Julia Flyte in maiden race at Salisbury in September, giving
impression she'd have gone very close had her effort started sooner; favourite
when fourth in similar event at Bath next time; probably needs further than 5f,
and promises to stay 7f. *G. Lewis.*

BE MY LADY 2 ch.f. Be My Guest 126–Image Intensifier (Dancer's Image) —
(1982 7g) Feb 24; 43,000F; fourth produce; half-sister to smart 1980 American
2-y-o Toooverprime (by Red Alert), successful at up to 7f; dam Irish 7f winner
and closely related to high-class US sprinter Gaelic Dancer; unquoted and bit
backward, last of 22 in maiden race won by Toveris at Newmarket in October.
P. Haslam.

BE MY LOVE 2 ro.f. Be My Guest 126–Romantic Love (Sovereign Path 125) **94**
(1982 7.9g⁴ 8.5g 6s*) May 17; 19,000F; first produce; dam disqualified winner
of Italian 1,000 Guineas; 14/1, showed much improved form when winning
18-runner maiden race at the Curragh in October by 5 lengths from Persian
Royale; evidently well suited by 6f and soft going; wears blinkers. *K. Prender-*
gast, Ireland.

BE MY NATIVE (USA) 3 br.c. Our Native–Witchy Woman (Strate Stuff) **121**
(1981 6g⁴ 7g² 6g⁴ 7s* 7g² 1982 10f² 10.5f³ 10v* 9fg³ 10fg 10.5fg 10f² 10s³ 12f]
    The second running of the most valuable race in the world, the Budweiser
Million at Arlington Park in August, showed the difficulties inherent in trying to
bring together an outstanding international field of middle-distance performers
even when the first prize money on offer approaches £350,000. Injury, an
understandable unwillingness by American trainers to run dirt specialists on turf
and a lack of readiness by the connections of many of the top European horses
to break away from the entrenched programme of races on this side of the
Atlantic in order to chase what could turn out to be shadows on the other are
always likely to make the organisers' task an extremely tough one. In 1982 the
problems persisted even after the original selection of the fourteen contestants
early in August, for Day Is Done, Silver Hawk, Spence Bay, The Bart and The
Wonder were all ruled out for one reason or another as were the first two
reserves, Open Call and It's The One. Consequently on the day the runners
included several that a month before had appeared to have slim prospects of
participating.
    One of the late-comers was the fourth reserve, Be My Native, and on the
principle that it is an ill wind which blows nobody any good he took full
advantage of the circumstances that allowed him to run, putting up the
performance of his life to finish second. Notwithstanding the absentees, the
field was a strong one, including the good American-trained horses Perrault,
Lemhi Gold, Erins Isle, Rossi Gold and Naskra's Breeze; the Prix d'Ispahan
winner Al Nasr; Duplex, the best horse in South America; and two other
challengers from Britain, Motavato and Noalto. In this company Be My
Native looked to have only an outside chance of success and he started at 72/1;
the 1981 Arc de Triomphe fourth, Perrault, who had already proved his
superiority to most of the American runners in the race, was a warm favourite
coupled with the ex-Irish Erins Isle. Ridden by a local jockey called Earlie
Fires, Be My Native was held up towards the rear as first Al Nasr then Motavato
took them along at a cracking pace. Despite making progress from halfway, he
still had eight to ten lengths to make up with three furlongs left but producing
a strong run up the rails he passed horse after horse and snatched second place
from Motavato in the dying strides, just over two lengths behind the authoritative
winner Perrault. For this admirable effo.t—one very different from his second
run in the States which saw him trail in a poor last of seven to April Run in the
Turf Classic at Aqueduct in October—Be My Native picked up over £100,000,
more than he would have done for winning all four of the European races he
gained places in during the year.
    On his form in Europe Be My Native is a consistent colt almost a stone
below the best. His sole success came in the Prix La Force at Longchamp in
May in which he made his move early in the straight, showing good acceleration
in the heavy ground to draw three or four lengths clear of his rivals, and kept
on well to hold off Magwal by two and a half lengths. His other runs, apart
from a below-par display in the Prince of Wales's Stakes at Royal Ascot, were

Prix La Force, Longchamp—the British-trained Be My Native
gains an impressive win from Magwal
and River Sand

all creditable and only in the Benson and Hedges Gold Cup at York did he fail
to reach the first three.   In the Guardian Classic Trial at Sandown he alone made
a race of it with Peacetime, going down by two lengths after chasing the winner
hard from two furlongs out, while in the Mecca-Dante Stakes at York, the Prix
Jean Prat at Chantilly and La Coupe de Maisons-Laffitte he finished third
respectively to Simply Great, Melyno and Coquelin.   He came closest to success
at Maisons-Laffitte, losing out narrowly in a driving finish that also involved
Bylly The Kid.

		Exclusive Native (ch 1965)	Raise A Native
	Our Native (b or br 1970)		Exclusive
		Our Jackie (gr 1964)	Crafty Admiral
Be My Native (USA) (br.c. 1979)			Rakahanga
		Strate Stuff (ch 1965)	Noholme II
	Witchy Woman (ch 1972)		Lady Vale
		Witchy Norma (ch 1967)	Crimson Satan
			Tomratta

Be My Native is a neat, attractive colt with a look of quality and he was
well bought as a yearling for 45,000 dollars. He is the second foal and first

Mr K. Hsu's "Be My Native"

runner out of Witchy Woman, who won five times over sprint distances in the States; since producing Be My Native she has foaled colts by Full Out and Master Derby, the latter of whom fetched 130,000 dollars at the Keeneland September Sale and will be trained in England. Witchy Woman is a half-sister to Devil's Bluff, a tough performer successful in twelve of one hundred and two starts, out of the unraced Witchy Norma whose dam was a sister to the high-class Chompion from the family of one of America's outstanding horses, Equipoise. Be My Native, who stays a mile and a quarter well, has a fluent though slightly round action; until his fine run at Arlington Park he seemed well suited by some give in the ground, but it is now apparent that he acts on any going. The fact that he wore blinkers once at two in no way reflects upon his courage since he is entirely genuine. *R. Armstrong.*

BE MY PRINCESS 2 b.f. Try My Best 130–Mare D'Erba (Habitat 134) (1982 **68** 7g 6g) Apr 7; IR 51,000Y; fair sort; second foal; half-sister to 3-y-o Irish Grenadier (by Home Guard), fairly useful winner over 6f in 1981; dam unraced granddaughter of smart 1964 2-y-o Unity; nearest finish when 6¼ lengths sixth of 18 behind Albadeeah in maiden race at Newmarket in October, second outing; should stay 1m. *P. Haslam.*

BEN BOW 3 br.c. Lochnager 132–Affirmative 96 (Derring-Do 131) (1981 NR **68** 1982 6g* 8t 8g⁴ 8d 9g 10g⁴ 8.2g² 8d) 7,200Y; big, rangy colt; shows a bit of knee action; second foal; half-brother to fairly useful miler Teamwork (by Workboy); dam won 9 times at around 1m; won maiden race at Hamilton in May; ran creditably in handicaps on occasions afterwards; suited by 1m; suited by some give in the ground. *M. H. Easterby.*

BENEAGLES 2 gr.c. Godswalk 130–Dastina 80 (Derring-Do 131) (1982 5fg) **73** June 4; 19,000Y; big, strong, useful-looking colt; second foal; half-brother to 3-y-o Jean Varon (by Averof), a winner at up to 7f; dam, second over 7f at 2 yrs, is sister to smart 7f performer Tudor Mill; 4 lengths fifth of 8 to Snatch And Run in minor event at Ayr in July; sold German International Bloodstock 2,000 gns Newmarket Autumn Sales. *M. H. Easterby.*

BENFEN 3 ro.g. Lochnager 132–Ensign Steel 57 (Majority Blue 126) (1981 5v² **83** 5d 5g* 5d 5fg⁴ 1982 5fg³ 6g⁴ 6d* 6fg 6f 6g 6g* 6s) sturdy gelding; made virtually all to win handicaps at Newcastle in June and Ripon in August; stays 6f; well suited by some give in the ground; has run respectably for an apprentice; blinkered eighth start. *M. H. Easterby.*

BENGAL LANCER 2 b.g. Mandrake Major 122–Rose Petite 66 (Negotiation) **53** (1982 7fg 6s 8s 8d) May 4; neat gelding; first foal; dam, plater, won at up to 1¼m and seemed to stay 2m; 5½ lengths fifth of 15 to Gunnard in seller at Redcar in October, third outing and best effort; evidently suited by 1m. *Miss L. Siddall.*

BEN JARROW 3 ch.c. Roman Warrior 132–Shady Desire 88 (Meldrum 112) **82** (1981 7f 5d⁴ 5s 7g 5d⁴ 1982 6s³ 7g 6f 6f* 5f⁴ 6fg³ 6f² 6g 5fg² 6f 6fg* 7fg² 6fg 7f* 6d⁴ 7g 7f* 6g 7s 6s⁴ 7d) big, workmanlike colt; good walker; won maiden race at Redcar and handicaps at Hamilton and Redcar (twice); suited by 7f; acts on any going but is ideally suited by top-of-the-ground; usually blinkered; has been ridden by lad in paddock. *T. Fairhurst.*

BENJEYA 2 br.g. Golden Mallard 103–Dearon II (Ron 103) (1982 6fg) Mar **—** 23; non-thoroughbred gelding; fair sort; fourth known foal; dam never ran; 20/1 and green, dropped right out in closing stages when last of 13 to Castanet in newcomers race at Goodwood in September. *J. Holt.*

BEN'S BIRDIE 2 ch.g. Track Spare 125–Gold Topaz 76 (Goldhill 125) (1982 **71** 6g 8.2s⁴) Apr 20; 700Y; plain gelding; second foal; dam 6f winner; showed up well in October in £2,700 seller at Newmarket and minor event at Nottingham, having anything but hard race on second occasion; stays 1m; should have no difficulty in winning seller. *M. Tompkins.*

BEN TRUMAN DRAUGHT 2 b.f. Pampapaul 121–Kazama (Relko 136) **—** (1982 6fg 6f 6g 7fg 8.2d 8s 8d) Mar 15; IR 6,800Y; small, well-made filly; poor walker; sister to fairly useful 1981 2-y-o 7.6f winner Sandwalker and half-sister to winners in Italy and France; no worthwhile form, including in sellers; sold 440 gns Newmarket Autumn Sales for export to Italy. *S. Mellor.*

BEN TRUMAN EXPORT 2 b.c. Persian Bold 123–Mickety Midge (Whistling **63** Wind 123) (1982 5g 5d 7fg 8s 7s) Apr 29; IR 8,000F, IR 5,400Y; neat colt; second produce; dam won twice at around 9f in Ireland; only poor form; sold 1,550 gns Newmarket Autumn Sales. *S. Mellor.*

BE ON TIME 2 b.g. Be My Guest 126–Deep Brook (Wolver Hollow 126) —
(1982 7f 7fg 8s) Mar 16; IR 20,000Y; quite attractive gelding; half-brother to 3
winners, including fairly useful 1981 2-y-o sprinter Petite Realm (by Realm);
dam unraced half-sister to dams of very useful 2-y-o's Hanu and End of the
Line; in mid-division in maiden races; missed break third outing. *P. Walwyn.*

BERENSON (USA) 3 b.c. Empery 128–Rainbow Rose (Ambiorix 130) (1981 **75**
NR 1982 7g⁴ 8fg⁴ 8fg³ 10f⁴ 12f 10f) $60,000Y; short-backed colt; closely
related to Vaguely Familiar (by Vaguely Noble), a very smart winner at up
to 7f at 2 yrs in 1972, and middle-distance winner Rafael Molina (by Ace of
Aces), and half-brother to a useful winner; dam won at 2 yrs and comes from
same family as Miswaki; quite modest maiden; suited by 1¼m and should stay
further; sold to M. Naughton, 1,250 gns Ballsbridge December Sales. *R. Sheather.*

BERESFORD 3 b.g. Great Nephew 126–Hedge Warbler 89 (Sing Sing 134) **57**
(1981 NR 1982 6f 5f 5g³ 6g 5f⁴ 6d 6g) strong, sturdy gelding; third foal;
half-brother to 1980 2-y-o 5f winner Super Smile (by High Top) and to a winner
in Italy by Blakeney; dam won over 6f and 1m; sprint maiden; has run respectably for an apprentice. *A. Hide.*

BE RESOLUTE 3 ch.c. Relko 136–All Hail 112 (Alcide 136) (1981 8d 10s³ **72**
1982 12g 14f³ 16d⁴ 16.9fg 14g⁴) big, rangy colt; good mover; staying maiden;
sweated up fourth start. *M. Stoute.*

BERGENIA 2 ch.f. Shiny Tenth 120–Gunnera (Royal Gunner) (1982 5f **54**
5fg 6fg³ 6fg 5f 6g 7fg³ 8d 7g) Apr 12; close-coupled, unimpressive sort; first
foal; dam never ran; quite a moderate plater; stays 7f; sold 1,000 gns Newmarket Autumn Sales. *D. Whelan.*

BERGERAC 2 ch.g. Sweet Revenge 129–Lady Whistler (Whistling Wind 123) **71**
(1982 6fg 6g 6g⁴ 6f 7fg 6g³) Apr 1; 1,600F, 4,800Y; big gelding; third produce;
dam never ran; blinkered first time, came from good way back when 5½ lengths
third of 15 to Luisa Miller in £2,700 seller at Newmarket in October, best effort;
promises to stay 7f; needs some give in the ground; should win a seller. *J.
Holt.*

BERNARD SUNLEY (USA) 3 ch.c. Rainy Lake–Charling (Charabanc) **78**
(1981 5s 6g 5g³ 5f² 6g² 6s³ 6g 1982 6g* 6fg⁴ 6g 5d³ 6fg 6v² 6d⁴ 6s) strong,
good-bodied colt; not the best of movers; won 6-runner maiden race at Pontefract in April; in frame in handicaps afterwards; suited by 6f; acts on any going;
has run respectably for an apprentice. *G. Hunter.*

BERTHA 2 ch.f. Filiberto 123–Petchora 64 (Le Haar 126) (1982 6fg 7g) **67**
Mar 31; fair sort; first foal; dam, placed over 1m, is half-sister to very smart
1975 French 2-y-o Bynoderm; showed ability in September in maiden race
won by Linklighter at Salisbury and £4,500 event won by Salvinia at Newbury;
will stay 1m. *R. Baker.*

BERTHON GOLD 2 b.c. Averof 123–Buff Beauty 92 (Mossborough 126) —
(1982 5g 5f) of no account. *M. Bradley.*

BERTIDA 4 b.f. Porto Bello 118–Miss Bubbly 78 (Track Spare 125) (1981 **76**
8.2g* 7.2v³ 8d³ 8d 1982 8.2g² 8fg 10f* 10d⁴ 10.2g³ 8g*) useful sort; successful
in handicaps at Nottingham and Yarmouth in August and at Yarmouth again
in September; stays 1¼m; acts on any going; suitable mount for an apprentice.
E. Eldin.

BERTIE ME BOY 7 b.g. Philip of Spain 126–Well Scored 104 (Final Score **70**
113) (1981 12v* 12s 1982 12fg 12fg 10g² 12g 12fg³ 12g 11s) quite a moderate
handicapper nowadays; suited by 1½m; seems to act on any going but is best
on soft; usually ridden up with pace; usually blinkered in 1980. *M. H. Easterby.*

BERTIE'S WISH 3 ch.f. Mr Bigmore 123–Jamaya 71 (Double-U-Jay 120) —
(1981 8s 8d 1982 11.7f 12g) behind in maiden races. *S. Harris.*

BERTOCELLI (USA) 2 ch.c. Roberto 131–Cellist (Bagdad) (1982 6g* 7g⁴ **102**
8d² 7d) Mar 28; fourth foal; half-brother to 3 winners, including 1981 2-y-o
7f winner Crellistovi (by Sir Ivor); dam, smart stakes winner at up to 1m,
is half-sister to top-class Gay Fandango; won maiden race at Yarmouth in
August; good second to Dawn River in nursery at Brighton in October, easily
best subsequent effort; joint-favourite when last of 14 in nursery at Newmarket
on final outing; better suited by 1m than shorter distances, and should stay
further; yet to race on a firm surface. *H. Cecil.*

BE SHARP 4 b.f. Sharpen Up 127–Natasha 87 (Native Prince) (1981 5s **59**
5g² 5d 5f 5f 5fg² 5fg 5g 5fg 5s 1982 5f⁴ 5f* 5g 5fg 5fg) rather leggy, fair sort;

confirmed the promise of her first outing of the season when winning apprentice handicap at Catterick in August unchallenged; shade disappointing afterwards; best at 5f; ran creditably on a soft surface but seemed better on a firm one; blinkered once as a 2-y-o; in foal to Cawston's Clown. *B. McMahon.*

BESIEGED (USA) 4 b.g. Cannonade–Regal Royal (Swoon's Son) (1981 10fg 11g 12fg³ 14fg* 13.1g³ 14g⁴ 1982 18g 16g) strong, attractive, deep-girthed gelding; well beaten in 1982; looks slow and should be suited by 2m; acts on a firm surface; usually wears blinkers. *P. Cundell.* —

BESSIE MARY 2 b.f. Workboy 123–Jury 66 (Lucky Brief 128) (1982 5f 5f 5fg⁴ 5d 5g² 5f) Mar 24; 460Y; poor plater; sold 310 gns Doncaster October Sales. *K. Stone.* **50**

BEST BIDDER 2 b.f. Auction Ring 123–Storming Finish (Arctic Storm 134) (1982 5fg 5fg⁴ 5fg³ 5fg 5g 5g* 5d 5s⁴) Mar 26; 5,400F, 16,000Y; neat, sturdy filly; half-sister to several winners here and abroad; dam maiden Irish sprinter; won modest 8-runner nursery at Beverley in September by ½ length from Vitigeson, the pair 4 lengths clear; will stay 6f. *R. Hollinshead.* **72**

BEST BIZ 2 b. or br.f. Best Turn–That's Show Biz (Promised Land) (1982 5g⁴ 5fg⁴ 7fg) Apr 24; $80,000Y; rather unfurnished filly; half-sister to very useful 1981 2-y-o 5f and 6f winner Take The Floor (by Cornish Prince), subsequently a stakes winner in USA; dam very useful stakes winner over 9f at 5 yrs; poor form in modest company; off course 3 months after second outing; should stay at least 1m; sold 25,000 gns Newmarket December Sales. *G. Hunter.* **57**

BEST BOLD (USA) 3 ch.g. Bold Hour–Couldn't Be Better (Better Bee) (1981 5g 5d⁴ 5d* 6g² 5fg⁴ 6g 6d 1982 7fg 8g 8d 8f³) strong gelding; good mover; made all to win maiden race at Folkestone and finished good second in small race at Catterick at 2 yrs; had stiffish tasks all outings at 3 yrs; should be suited by 7f+; acts on a firm and a soft surface. *M. Jarvis.* **65**

BETH OF HOUNDHILL 2 b.f. Filiberto 123–Teenager 71 (Never Say Die 137) (1982 5g 7fg 6s) Apr 26; second foal; half-sister to 1¼m winner Standon Rock (by Mansingh); dam second over 6f at 2 yrs; in rear in maiden races and a £3,600 event, twice last. *T. Taylor.* —

BETSEY SHANNON 2 b.f. Hittite Glory 125–Solway Bay 86 (Tamerlane 128) (1982 7f 6g 6d 8s) Mar 10; 10,500F, 9,000Y; strong, good-bodied filly; half-sister to several winners here and abroad, including Norsk St Leger winner Halcyon Bay (by Henry the Seventh); dam 1¼m winner; no form in maiden events. *D. Ringer.* —

BETTABET GERAGHTY 4 b.g. Blue Cashmere 129–Piccadilly Etta 76 (Floribunda 136) (1981 7s 7fg 6g* 6g² 7.3g 6s 6f 7fg 1982 6f 6fg³ 6f 6f* 6fg 6f⁴ 6g 6f* 6g⁴ 6d 6d 6fg 7f² 6f) neat, strong gelding; a most frustrating and unreliable character, but was on his best behaviour when winning handicaps at Leicester in June and Redcar in July; won both decisively after making virtually all; stays 7f; acts well on firm going; usually blinkered. *G. Huffer.* **62**

BETTER BID 2 b. or br.c. Auction Ring 123–Wigeon 80 (Divine Gift 127) (1982 5fg 6g 7fg 7f 6g 6fg 6s 8s) Apr 3; 4,400F, 21,000Y; leggy, good-topped colt; second produce; half-brother to 3-y-o Ma Pierrette (by Cawston's Clown), a winner at up to 1m; dam won 5 times at up to 1¼m; little worthwhile form in minor and maiden races; blinkered fifth outing. *T. Gosling.* **62**

BETTER BOY 2 ch.g. Roan Rocket 128–Come On Girl (Sheshoon 132) (1982 5g 6f 7d 7fg) Mar 26; rangy gelding; half-brother to 3 winners, including fairly useful 2-y-o sprint winners City Link Lass and Daikoku (both by Double Jump); dam never ran; unquoted when behind in maiden events; not raced after July. *P. Ashworth.* —

BETTER BUILDER 2 gr.g. Habat 127–Opalina (Tudor Melody 129) (1982 5f 6g 5g 8.2fg) Mar 13; 2,600Y; good-topped gelding; bad plater; wears blinkers. *K. Stone.* —

BETTER PORTION 3 ch.c. Music Boy 124–Shirwani 77 (Major Portion 129) (1981 5d 5fg² 5g* 5g² 5d⁴ 5d 5s² 6s* 6g³ 1982 7d 8g 7g 7fg 7fg 7s 6s 6v) quite a well-made ex-English colt; won minor event at Lingfield and nursery at Newbury in 1981; well beaten all starts at 3 yrs; suited by 6f; yet to race on very firm going but seems to act on any other; blinkered seventh start; sometimes taken early to start; trained by P. Ashworth first 7 outings. *P. Mullins, Ireland.* —

BETTYKNOWES 4 b.g. Satingo 129–Djimbaran Bay (Le Levanstell 122) (1981 11s 10s* 11d² 10fg² 10fg* 10fg⁴ 12fg 1982 10fg 10d² 10f* 12g 10g 10s) **81**

lengthy, workmanlike gelding; split a pastern final outing in 1981; ran best subsequent races when second to Lafontaine in £7,700 handicap at Sandown in July and when beating The Pain Barrier gamely by ¾ length at Salisbury the following month; possibly doesn't stay 1½m; acts on any going; sold to A. Ingham 25,000 gns Newmarket Autumn Sales. *J. Tree.*

BHAIBUNDI CHEWUNJA 3 b.g. Spanish Gold 101–Pensong 84 (Pendragon) **43**
(1981 5fg 6s 6f 5fg 7.2v³ 10d* 8s 1982 8f 9.4f 12f 10d 12g 13.8f⁴ 10f 13.8f⁴ 12s⁴ 13.8d* 12s³) lightly-made, narrow gelding; plater; attracted no bid after winning at Catterick in October; stays 1¾m; best with some give in the ground; blinkered third start; has run respectably for an apprentice. *J. Wilson.*

BIBI BELLE 2 ch.f. Morston 125–Parmesh 105 (Home Guard 129) (1982 7s) **— p**
June 3; compact filly; first foal; dam useful 2-y-o 5f performer; 33/1, slow-starting tenth of 13 finishers behind Sackford in maiden event at Sandown in October; likely to do better. *J. Dunlop.*

BID AGAIN 2 b.c. Auction Ring 123–Another Flutter 75 (Credo 123) (1982 **106**
5fg³ 5fg* 6f* 5fg² 6f* 6d³ 6d²) Apr 11; 35,000Y; neat, good-looking colt; extremely good mover; half-brother to 4 winners, including useful Irish and Italian winner Flying Saint (by St Chad); dam stayed 1¼m; won maiden race at Nottingham, £3,400 event at Leicester and minor race at Thirsk before end of July, scoring comfortably by 2½ lengths from Dick 'E' Bear when ridden by 5-lb claimer at Thirsk; having first race for over 2 months when excellent third of 14 under top weight in £9,000 nursery won by Bumpkin at Newmarket in October; well suited by 6f; probably acts on any going; consistent. *M. Stoute.*

BIDDABLE 3 b.c. Auction Ring 123–Imperial Levee (Levmoss 133) (1981 **54**
5f 5g³ 5f⁴ 5g 5d 1982 7g 6f 5fg³ 5f 6d 5fg 6f⁴ 5fg 6f 6g 6g 6s³ 6s⁴) fair sort; sprint maiden; twice beaten in sellers; stays 6f; acts on any going. *W. Elsey.*

BID FOR BUCKS (USA) 2 b.f. Empery 128–Magnabid (Bold Bidder) (1982 **111 p**
8g³ 8d*) Apr 24; fourth foal; half-sister to 2 winners in USA; dam smart stakes winner at up to 1m; won 20-runner minor event at Maisons-Laffitte in September in fine style by 5 lengths from Tearing with third horse a further 4 lengths behind; likely to improve a good deal further over longer distances. *M. Zilber, France.*

BID FOR FREEDOM 2 b.f. Run The Gantlet–Fothcringay 101 (Right Royal **— p**
V 135) (1982 7g) May 29; half-sister to several winners, notably Ascot Gold Cup winner Ragstone (by Ragusa) and very smart middle-distance stayer Castle Keep (by Kalamoun); dam won at 1m; 25/1, caught our eye travelling strongly on bridle at halfway and was not knocked about at all when out of first 10 of 22 behind Toveris in maiden race at Newmarket in October; will need 1¼m or more; sure to improve. *J. Dunlop.*

BIG BLONDE 3 ch.f. Ballymore 123–Lunar Star (Star Gazer 123) (1981 6g **80**
6g³ 1982 7f² 7fg* 7fg) leggy, narrow filly; stayed on well to win handicap at Yarmouth in August; will be suited by 1m; usually bandaged near-hind; sold to BBA 4,200 gns Newmarket December Sales. *N. Guest.*

BIG-ED 3 ch.c. Sparkler 130–Ours 76 (Yours 125) (1981 7g 7g 1982 7g 7f **79**
8fg 12d* 12f² 10fg³ 12fg⁴ 14fg 14g 16g 14g) tall colt; good walker; stayed on strongly to win amateur riders race at Beverley in July; creditable second to Khairpour in handicap at York next time; stays 1½m (well beaten at 1¾m); seems to act on any going; sold out of P. Kelleway's stable 22,000 gns Doncaster August Sales after seventh start. *R. Hollinshead.*

BIG HITTER 3 br.g. Comedy Star 121–Gold Braid 80 (Martial 131) (1981 **—**
NR 1982 9.4f 10.2g 10s) 2,400Y; half-brother to prolific Italian winner Jonker (by Sassafras); dam in frame at up to 10.5f here and in France; tailed off in maiden races and a minor event; trained by M. Camacho first 2 starts. *T. Kersey.*

BIG JASPER 7 b.h. Sit In The Corner–Bebe Mine (Bleep-Bleep 134) (1981 **—**
NR 1982 10d) lightly-raced plater; stays 1¼m; acts on hard going; usually wears blinkers; has worn bandages. *J. Doyle.*

BIG JOHN (FR) 4 br.c. Gift Card 124–Trelex (Exbury 138) (1981 8v* 8g 9g³ **118**
9s² 10g 8f 1982 8v 8d* 8s² 9.2fg³ 8g* 9.2g⁴ 8d² 9d 7v⁴ 8s) French colt; ran consistently well and won Prix de Ris-Orangis at Evry in April and Prix du Chemin de Fer du Nord at Chantilly in June; showed a good turn of foot when beating Ya Zaman by 1½ lengths in latter; in frame in several other good races, on last 2 occasions in Prix Messidor at Maisons-Laffitte in July (3 lengths second

of 12 to Noalcoholic) and Prix de la Foret at Longchamp in October (about 4½ lengths fourth of 9 to Pas de Seul); stayed 9f; probably acted on any going; standing at Haras du Petit Tellier. *E. Chevalier du Fau, France.*

BIG LAND 3 ch.c. Habitat 134–Bay Triumph (Canisbay 120) (1981 6f 6g   **63** 1982 8g 7f³ 7f³ 9f³ 8g⁴ 10f 8f 8fg 7fg² 7f² 6d³ 6g 6f³ 6g 6s) neat colt; poor walker; best at up to 7f; seems to act on any going; usually blinkered nowadays; has run respectably for an apprentice. *Mrs N. Macauley.*

BIG PAL 7 gr.g. Pals Passage 115–Queen's Honey (Tudor Treasure 119) (1981   **79** 10.2d³ 12d 12fg⁴ 12g 12f³ 12f 12fg² 12f⁴ 10f* 10fg 9g 10s² 10.2g 10g⁴ 1982 10fg 10fg* 8g* 8f* 10fg* 10fg* 10g* 10fg 10d) big, rangy gelding; seemed to take on a new lease of life and was in tremendous form; successful in 2 apprentice handicaps at Goodwood, trainers race at Kempton, 2 handicaps at Sandown (first of them another apprentice race and second of them on disqualification of Irish Keep), and a handicap at Folkestone; stays 1½m, but is probably best at up to 1¼m; acts on any going; a thoroughly genuine front runner who is an excellent mount for an apprentice; credit to his trainer. *G. Harwood.*

BIG SPIEL (USA) 2 b.c. To The Quick–Gorgeous Gay (Blue Gay) (1982   **—** 6f 7fg) Apr 4; $125,000Y; well-made, quite attractive colt; half-brother to 10 winners, including fair 1979 2-y-o 1m winner Torsion Balance (by Torsion) and smart 1970 2-y-o sprinter She Is Gorgeous (by Drop Volley); dam won 2 sprint races at 2 yrs; in rear in £3,400 event at Salisbury in August and maiden race on same course in September; sold 3,100 gns Newmarket Autumn Sales. *P. Cole.*

BIG STEVE 2 b.g. Malinowski 123–Itinerant 69 (Sky Gipsy 117) (1982   **62** 6f 7f 7fg 7g 8s) May 6; IR 8,800Y; lengthy gelding; good walker; fourth foal; dam showed little worthwhile form; plating-class maiden; blinkered final outing. *A. Ingham.*

BIG TROUBLE 3 b.g. Reform 132–Estructura 102 (Gulf Pearl 117) (1981   **80 ?** 6d 6fg² 7g* 7g³ 7fg³ 8g² 10g⁴ 1982 10d*) rangy gelding; has a round action; made virtually all and kept on well to win 15-runner amateur riders race at Lingfield in June; suited by 1¼m and will stay further; game, genuine and consistent; sold 16,000 gns Doncaster August Sales, reportedly to race in Holland. *G. Pritchard-Gordon.*

BIGWOOD CAY (USA) 2 ch.c. Blade–Indyson (Son Ange) (1982 6g⁴ 6f³   **103** 7g* 7f³ 8s⁴ 8s) Mar 5; $40,000Y; quite attractive colt; first foal; dam won 1m claiming race; proved well suited by 7f in 20-runner maiden race at Newmarket in June, staying on strongly to win by ¾ length from Proclaim; in trouble at halfway when giving at least 4 lb to his 5 opponents in £4,600 event on same course the following month but stayed on to finish 10½ lengths third to Thug; sent to race in Italy, and finished creditable fourth in Gran Criterium in October. *M. Jarvis.*

BIKALA 4 b.c. Kalamoun 129–Irish Bird (Sea-Bird II 145) (1981 10v² 9.2fg*   **129** 10.5s⁴ 12g* 12.5g² 10s² 12d² 1982 10.5g* 12fg 10f² 12s)

By the end of the season Bikala's connections must have been left questioning the wisdom of keeping their horse in training as a four-year-old. Bikala gained only the first of his three well-publicised objectives, the Prix Ganay at Longchamp, and demonstrably wasn't so good as in 1981; he failed to reach the frame in either the King George VI and Queen Elizabeth Diamond Stakes or the Trusthouse Forte Prix de l'Arc de Triomphe. For one who so obviously thrived on his racing as a three-year-old Bikala had a surprisingly light season in 1982 and raced on only one other occasion, finishing second. He thus retires with only three wins to his name, a disappointing total for a horse of his ability, though it includes two of France's most important races.

Bikala, a very decisive winner of the 1981 Prix du Jockey-Club, looked set for another good season when winning the Ganay in which he started a short-priced favourite despite meeting strong opposition, including Al Nasr, April Run, Kalaglow, Lancastrian and Vayrann, over a trip one might have thought on the sharp side for him. After his pacemaker Maraway got off to a poor start Bikala made his own running, followed initially by Kalaglow who had recently begun his comeback with an impressive win in the Earl of Sefton Stakes at Newmarket. He drew away from Kalaglow early in the straight, and it was Lancastrian who came out of the pack to trouble him most. Bikala, who looked beforehand to have done plenty of work, was able to keep up the gallop and hold him off by half a length with Al Nasr just snatching third from

Vayrann.   On the face of it Bikala's was a high-class performance, but there's no doubt that Vayrann, Kalaglow (eventually seventh), and April Run (eighth) failed to do themselves justice.

Bikala's preparation for the King George reportedly went well and he travelled over with his companion, the seven-year-old Kariaam, and his own blacksmith to fit Bikala with special protective racing plates, so long is his stride. Bikala looked well in himself in the paddock but was taken down to the start too steadily to see how he would go on the firmish ground. His young rider Gorli, who'd had a ride on Grand Maitre the previous day to familiarise himself with the course, sent him straight off into the lead setting a very strong gallop but being pounced upon by his half-brother Assert as soon as they turned into the straight and thereafter fighting a losing battle.   He faded in the final furlong to finish fifth, less than four lengths behind Kalaglow and beaten a couple of necks for third.   Trainer Bianconne subsequently said that he felt Bikala had travelled too soon—he was in top form when arriving on Wednesday but had gone off the boil by Saturday—and weakly added that Ascot's mile and a half start, which faces downhill and is followed almost immediately by a right-handed turn, isn't ideal for such a big, long-striding colt who isn't particularly quick out of the gate as front runners go.

Bianconne was sufficiently disappointed with Bikala's King George running to change his plans and give Bikala a preparatory race for the Arc in the Prix du Prince d'Orange at Longchamp in September, a race in which Bikala had been second to Vayrann as a three-year-old.   On ground even firmer than at Ascot and ridden by Head in place of Gorli, who had 'flu, Bikala made the running as usual until beaten for finishing speed by the improving three-year-old General Holme, recording his sixth consecutive victory, and going down by a short neck.   On this showing Bikala looked sure to give a good account of himself in the Arc, the more so when the ground turned soft, but he finished down the field.   There was no obvious excuse for Bikala—he had no trouble taking up a good position despite his outside draw, and tracked Bon Sang or else shared the lead with him until weakening quickly early in the straight. Perhaps he and Bon Sang cut each other's throats; they certainly set a strong gallop in the conditions.   In 1981 hardly anything had made ground on Bikala in the straight and the winner Gold River passed him only well inside the last furlong; this time he simply couldn't hold his place and came home twelfth, over ten lengths behind Akiyda.

Bikala (b.c. 1978)	Kalamoun (gr 1970)	Zeddaan (gr 1965)	Grey Sovereign
			Vareta
		Khairunissa (gr 1960)	Prince Bio
			Palariva
	Irish Bird (b or br 1970)	Sea-Bird II (ch 1962)	Dan Cupid
			Sicalade
		Irish Lass II (b 1962)	Sayajirao
			Scollata

We remarked in *Racehorses of 1981* that Bikala must have been one of the outstanding yearling buys of 1979 at 6,000 guineas, a bargain price which some attribute to shortcomings in his conformation.   Bikala lacks some of the quality that one likes to see in a top-class colt, nevertheless he's tall, strong and good-bodied.   He is a very valuable property as a stallion now.   His dam Irish Bird, after a modest start to her stud career—neither of her first two foals won on the flat, though Irish Gantlet (by Run The Gantlet) was a hurdles winner—now bears the remarkable distinction of having produced

Prix Ganay, Longchamp—a successful reappearance for Bikala

consecutive winners of the Prix du Jockey-Club with Bikala and Assert (by Be My Guest). She has since produced Bold Irish (by Bold Lad, Ire) who fetched 170,000 guineas as a yearling in 1981, and a colt by Northfields. Irish Bird won over eleven furlongs and is from a good family—she's a half-sister to the Irish Sweeps Derby winner Irish Ball out of a very useful sister to the top-class Irish staying filly Lynchris. Bikala begins his new career at the Haras du Val Henry. He was a particularly tough and genuine racehorse capable of a really good end-to-end gallop, and when gaining his two most important wins he was sent for home a long way out. He acted on any going, though some give in the ground suited him ideally. *P.-L. Biancone, France.*

BILA SHAKA 4 ch.g. No Mercy 126–Powderhall 81 (Murrayfield 119) (1981 **47** 7s 7fg 7fg* 8d² 6g 7g 1982 8f² 10f³ 8.3fg 10d 8fg 8g) lightly-made gelding; placed in seller and claiming race, best efforts; stays 1¼m; yet to race on very soft going but acts on any other; apprentice ridden; ran moderately in blinkers final start. *W. Hastings-Bass.*

BILDARA 3 br.f. Balidar 133–Dido's Grandaughter (By Thunder! 122) (1981 — 6fg 7fg 8s 10s 1982 8f 10h 10g 10fg) quite attractive filly; little worthwhile form; well beaten in a seller final outing; sold out of H. T. Jones's stable 880 gns Newmarket July Sales after third start. *W. Clay.*

BILLBROKER 6 br.g. Lombard 126–Eastern Blue 84 (Majority Blue 126) (1981 13.4d² 10s⁴(dis) 1982 12d) big, strong gelding; useful performer in 1981, when second in Ormonde Stakes at Chester; pulled up lame at Brighton in October, first outing for nearly 18 months; stayed 2m, but was probably better over shorter distances; acted on any going; sometimes sweated up before his races but was genuine and consistent; suited by front-running tactics; dead. *R. Simpson.*

BILLIEDON 2 ch.g. Young Nelson 106–Skiff 60 (Galivanter 131) (1982 **51** 5g⁴ 7fg 5g 5f) Mar 23; fourth foal; dam plater; poor plater; not sure to stay 7f; blinkered second and third starts; sold for export to Norway 4,600 gns Doncaster November Sales. *T. Taylor.*

BILSBORO LASS 7 b.m. Bilsborrow 85–Whitwitch (Shotley Spa 96) (1981 — NR 1982 16f) half-sister to a point-to-point winner; dam lightly-raced N.H. mare; tailed off in maiden race won by Wippin Crust at Beverley in April, first outing on flat. *G. Harman.*

BINCLEAVES 4 ch.c. Tumble Wind–Pink Doll (Palestine 133) (1981 6.5s **56** 5s 1982 6s 5g²) close-coupled, quite attractive colt; not a good mover in his slower paces; lightly raced since 1980; second in seller at Edinburgh in October, first outing for 6 months; stays 6f. *M. McCormack.*

BINDLOSS (USA) 2 b.f. Nostrum–Swizzle (Nearctic) (1982 6g 8s³) Mar 9; **69** $70,000Y; well-made filly; good mover; third foal; half-sister to stakes-placed winner This One's Mine (by One For All); dam never ran; sire stakes-placed half-brother to Northern Dancer; going very strongly early in straight in maiden race at Wolverhampton in October but seemed to flounder when let down and was beaten 4 lengths into third place behind Ballad Island; sent to USA. *B. Hills.*

BINFIELD 3 b.f. Rheingold 137–White Meadow (Bold Bidder) (1981 7fg **70** 7h 1982 12g³ 12f 12g² 12fg⁴ 13.4g³ 14g) leggy, narrow, sparely-made filly; only plating class; should stay 1¾m. *R. Sheather.*

BIRD ROCK (USA) 2 br.c. Full Out–Colombe (Grey Dawn II 132) (1982 **87** 5fg 5fg* 5g³ 5d) May 1; $80,000Y; lengthy, attractive colt; sixth foal; half-brother to 3 winners, including stayer Port Aransas (by Quack); dam won 4 small sprint races from 8 starts in USA; won minor event at Chepstow in July; odds on when third of five behind Al Trui in nursery at Windsor later in the month; will stay 6f; taken down early final start. *F. J. Houghton.*

BIRDSEDGE (USA) 2 b.c. Giacometti 130–Featheredge 110 (Nashua) (1982 — 7d 8d) tall colt; half-brother to several winners, including very useful Irish 7f and 1m winner Greek Waters (by Summer Tan); dam probably best at around 6f; well beaten in minor event at Doncaster in October and maiden race (last of 6) at Edinburgh in November. *S. Norton.*

BIRTHDAY FROLIC (USA) 3 br.g. Drone–Sailor Frolic (Cap Size) (1981 — 6g 6fg 6fg 6fg⁴ 6g 8d 1982 7f 14g) workmanlike gelding; plating-class maiden; stays 6f; blinkered twice in 1981; trained until after first outing by N. Vigors; sold 440 gns Ascot September Sales *J. Bosley.*

136

BIRTHRIGHT 2 b.c. Free State 125–Oudalia 107 (Gala Performance) (1982   —
6s 6g) Apr 29; third foal; half-brother to 3-y-o Springs Eternal (by Sagaro)
and 1980 2-y-o 5f winner Boganach (by Town Crier); dam best at sprint distances;
no worthwhile form in minor event at Lingfield in September and maiden race
at Newmarket the following month. *J. Benstead.*

BISHEN (USA) 2 b.c. Our Native–Khedija (Jacinto) (1982 5f 5fg 6fg 7d 7d⁴   **73**
6g 7g 6f³) Feb 24; $60,000Y; sturdy colt; second foal; dam useful winner at
up to 9f in USA; 6 lengths third of 10 to Gentle Music under top weight in
selling nursery at Brighton in September; will stay 1m; blinkered fifth to seventh
outings. *G. Lewis.*

BISHOPSPORT (USA) 2 b.g. Amasport–Lil Teresa (Traffic Mark) (1982   —
6g 5d) May 3; $4,200F, $16,500Y; first foal; dam placed third once from
20 starts; sire stakes winner at up to 9f; apparently not fully wound up, behind
in maiden races at Yarmouth and Nottingham (blinkered) in September. *G.
Huffer.*

BISHOPS RIDE 3 ch.g. Hot Spark 126–Montcall (Mountain Call 125) (1981   —
5.8d 6g 6fg 6f 5f 1982 5f 7f 7f 11f 10d 8f⁴ 8.3fg) stocky gelding; poor maiden;
stays 1m; hung violently left for apprentice rider penultimate start. *R. Baker.*

BIT OF A STATE 2 b.f. Free State 125–On A Bit 66 (Mummy's Pet 125)   **68**
(1982 6fg 7d 6f⁴ 7fg 6g 6g² 7fg 7g 7.2s³ 6s 6s) Apr 3; compact filly; second foal;
dam in frame at up to 11f; plater; placed at Yarmouth and Haydock in the
autumn; stays 7f; suited by an easy surface; blinkered last 3 starts. *S. Wiles.*

B. JASKI 3 ch.c. Malinowski 123–Fair Halo (Nimbus 132) (1981 8g 1982   **68**
10.6s 12f 16fg⁴ 12d⁴ 13f 12.2f² 12f² 12.2f* 10.2f) useful sort; good walker;
won maiden event at Catterick in August; suited by 1½m; seems to act on any
going, but goes well on firm. *M. Jarvis.*

BLACK COBRA 2 b. or br.c. Raga Navarro 119–Amana (Relko 136) (1982   **68**
5f³ 5fg 5f 7d 6f*) Apr 22; IR 4,500F, IR 5,600Y; short-backed, sharp sort;
half-brother to smart middle-distance 3-y-o Rajhaan (by English Prince) and
2 winners in France; dam won 4 middle-distance races in French Provinces;
attracted no bid after winning 9-runner seller at Pontefract in July by ½ length
from Water Pistol, the pair clear; stays 6f well; acts on firm going; winner in
Italy. *D. Morley.*

BLACK EARL 5 br.g. So Blessed 130–La Presidente (Primera 131) (1981   —
10.8fg 8d 8f 12f 11.7fg 1982 17.1f) leggy gelding; stays 1m (not certain to
get further); seems to act on any going; blinkered once at 3 yrs. *I. Wardle.*

BLACK FALCON (USA) 2 b.c. Irish Ruler–Sebago (Day Court) (1982   **95**
6f³ 6fg 5d 7g*) Apr 19; quite attractive colt; half-brother to several winners in
USA; dam, half-sister to smart animals Eggy and Juge de Paix, won claiming
races at up to 1m; 33/1 when beating Tetron Bay by a neck in 11-runner maiden
race at Leicester in October; will stay 1m. *P. Cole.*

BLACKFEET 3 b. or br.g. Import 127–Sky Hostess 72 (Skymaster 126) (1981   —
NR 1982 7fg 6g 8.2fg) 1,700F, 2,600Y; fourth living foal; dam won over 6f
and 1m; well beaten in maiden races in Scotland. *J. S. Wilson.*

BLACK GLAZEPTA 2 br.c. Mansingh 120–Kareela (Deep Diver 134) (1982   **97**
5s* 5f* 5fg³ 5f³ 5f³ 5.1f* 5fg³ 5fg³ 5g⁴ 5d⁴ 6d³) Feb 18; 15,000Y; quite
attractive, robust, well-made colt; first foal; dam, half-sister to Prix de l'Abbaye
winner Farhana, won 2 small races at around 9f in France; successful in small
races at Ayr and Ripon early in season and in another at Yarmouth in July; had
much stiffer tasks on most of his other starts but was never out of first four, on
final appearance finishing fair third of 8 behind Boom Town Charlie in slowly-run
minor event at Redcar in November; probably stays 6f; acts on any going;
genuine and consistent. *A. Jarvis.*

BLACK MIKE 7 b.h. Hardicanute 130–Sariette (Barbare II 128) (1981 8s 7s⁴   **75**
7d⁴ 8d 9fg* 10d* 8.5g 8g* 9fg² 10g² 1982 10fg 8fg⁴ 10d² 11.7fg⁴ 12f* 14g 12fg)
smallish, strong sort; stayed on most gamely when beating Gidian by ½ length
in handicap at Beverley in July; evidently suited by 1½m nowadays (had stiffish
task over 1¾m); seems to act on any going; ran badly final start. *P. Haslam.*

BLACK NARCISSUS (USA) 3 b.f. Sham–Scoring Play (Reviewer) (1981 **116**
NR 1982 10d 12s 12.5g 10fg* 10g² 9.2s) $90,000Y; first foal; dam, closely re-
lated to very smart Bold and Brave, won maiden race at Deauville
in July by a length from Teresa Talani and ran well in Prix de la Nonette on
same course following month, going down by 4 lengths to Grease; soundly

beaten in Prix de l'Opera won by Dione at Longchamp in October on final start; stays 1½m; form only on a sound surface. *M. Saliba, France.*

BLACK PIRATE 5 bl.g. Barbary Pirate 91–Fire Fairy 70 (Firestreak 125) — (1981 10d 8g⁴ 10d 12fg 10f 10fg² 8.2s³ 10s 10.2g 1982 10.1fg 10.6f 8f) neat, lightly-built gelding; plater; stays 1½m; probably acts on any going; has worn blinkers; has run respectably for a boy. *A. W. Jones.*

BLACK VEIL 2 br.f. Blakeney 126–Kaftan 68 (Kashmir II 125) (1982 7d) — Mar 25; neat, well-made filly; has a deformed knee; first foal; dam, sister to high-class 5f to 7f performer Blue Cashmere, won over 1¼m; out of first 9 of 18 in maiden race won by Cormorant Wood at Leicester in October; sold M. Blanshard 5,000 gns Newmarket Autumn Sales. *H. Candy.*

BLACK ZENUS (USA) 3 b.f. Bold Forbes–Airman's Lassie (Bold Lad, USA) — (1981 NR 1982 7f 8fg) $110,000Y; robust filly; first living foal; dam, stakes-placed winner at up to 6f, is daughter of champion handicap mare Airmans Guide; well beaten in maiden races at Leicester and Warwick. *M. Albina.*

BLAKESWARE 3 b.f. Home Guard 129–Barbarina (Molvedo 137) (1981 6g 7g — 1982 8f 10f 8fg) quite attractive, well-made filly; well beaten in maiden races. *L. Cumani.*

BLAKESWARE COUNTY 3 b.f. Wolverlife 115–Dream County 78 (Sing Sing 87 134 or Breeders Dream 116) (1981 6fg⁴ 5fg² 6fg² 7f² 7g 7g² 1982 7.6fg 10.6f 7g³ 8f⁴ 7fg* 7.2f¹ 7g² 7g³ 6d) leggy filly; made all to win minor event at Goodwood in August and handicap at Haydock in September; tended to drift right on latter; ran creditably next 2 starts; best at 7f and is unlikely to stay 1½m; possibly unsuited by soft ground; sold probably for export to South Africa 26,000 gns Newmarket December Sales. *M. Jarvis.*

BLAKESWARE DANCER 2 br.f. Dance In Time–Carlton's Girl 87§ (Hotfoot 68 126) (1982 5.1f⁴ 5d⁴ 8f 7.6v 8s) Apr 18; 17,000Y; lengthy filly; first foal; dam middle-distance performer; quite a modest maiden; will stay 1¼m; appears to act on any going. *L. Cumani.*

BLAKESWARE SAINT 3 b.f. Welsh Saint 126–Regency Girl 89 (Right Boy 74 137) (1981 5g 5s 5g³ 5d⁴ 1982 5g³ 5s* 5fg² 5fg* 5.6g 5g 5d) lengthy filly; showed improved form to win handicap at Nottingham and minor event at Edinburgh in April; off course 5 months afterwards and was well beaten on return; seems to act on any going; blinkered final start. *M. Tompkins.*

BLAKEY BANK 3 b.g. Blakeney 126–Be Tuneful 130 (Be Friendly 130) (1981 72 8g 8g 1982 10d³ 10f⁴ 17f² 13.8f* 13.8f* 12f⁴ 17fg² 16fg 16d 15f³ 14g 10.2s) small, strong gelding; not the best of walkers; stayed on well to win maiden race at Catterick in May and handicap on same course in June; stays well; acts on firm going; below form eighth and ninth starts and finished well beaten in seller final appearance; trained most of season by J. Hindley. *Hbt Jones.*

BLAZE OF HONOUR 3 ch.f. Quiet Fling 124–Streak of Honour 102 (Fire- — streak 125) (1981 5g 1982 8f 7fg) big filly; behind in maiden races; has given trouble at start. *Mrs A. Bell.*

BLESSED SILENCE 4 b.g. So Blessed 130–Cease Fire 112 (Martial 131) (1981 63 6fg⁴ 6f 8f 1982 6f 6f³ 7fg 6s 6fg 6g² 6fg* 6f 5d 6s* 6s 6s⁴) fair sort; successful in handicaps at Ayr in August and Redcar in October; had stiff task and ran well final start; not certain to stay 1m; acts on any going; successful with and without blinkers; suited by forcing tactics. *P. Asquith.*

BLESS'EM ALL 3 b.g. So Blessed 130–Misnomer 85 (Milesian 125) (1981 7f 66 8s² 7g 1982 8f 8f³ 10f³ 12f 12f³ 16d² 15fg* 16f³ 17.4d 15f²) strong, lengthy gelding; won maiden race at Edinburgh in July; suited by a test of stamina; acts on any going; blinkered second, third and fourth outings. *W. Elsey.*

BLESS THE MATCH 3 b.f. So Blessed 130–Matloch 70 (Matador 131) (1981 101 5g³ 6fg* 6fg³ 6f 6fg* 6g 1982 7.3g 6g⁴ 6fg) good-bodied filly; good walker and mover; won maiden race at Lingfield and St Catherine's Stakes at Newbury and ran well in William Hill Cheveley Park Stakes at Newmarket in 1981; had stiffish task and didn't break too well when 4 lengths fourth of 16 to Gabitat in valuable handicap at Kempton in May, best effort at 3 yrs; stays 6f well; yet to race on a soft surface; suited by forcing tactics; not seen out after May. *G. Pritchard-Gordon.*

BLITHE BARD (USA) 2 b.c. The Minstrel 135–Silk Hat (Shantung 132) — p (1982 7s) Mar 23; $170,000Y; half-brother to 3 winners, including Bold Chapeau (by Bold Bidder), a smart winner at up to 9f; dam very useful winner at up to 1m in USA; 16/1, never threatened leaders when 8 lengths sixth of 12 behind Rana Pratap in minor event at Chepstow in October; should improve. *F. J. Houghton.*

BLOAK MOSS 4 b.g. Cavo Doro 124–Tabasheer (Indian Chief) (1981 12d 11fg **44** 12.3g 12fg² 12fg 1982 12f⁴ 11.7g) neat, good-topped gelding; plater; stays 1½m; blinkered second start at 3 yrs; bandaged nowadays. *G. Kindersley.*

BLOCHAIRN SKOLAR 4 ch.f. Most Secret 119–Olibanum 61 (Frankincense **50** 120) (1981 5g 5f 5f 5fg³ 5f² 6f 5f 5fg 5s 6d 1982 6f 5f⁴ 5f 5fg* 6g* 5fg³ 6f 6g 5d 6g 8fg 6s 5g²) compact filly; successful in apprentice handicaps at Beverley in June (made all) and Hamilton in July; ran best subsequent race on final start; stays 6f; acts on firm going; occasionally blinkered (has run well in them); trained by V. Mitchell until after Beverley. *N. Bycroft.*

BLOEMFONTEIN 3 ch.g. Free State 125–Belligerent 74 (Roan Rocket 128) **61** (1981 5g 5g 5fg 7fg 8s 1982 7g⁴ 5fg² 6f* 6g⁴ 6f⁴ 6g⁴ 7.2g 7f 8g 7g 6g 7s) neat, strong gelding; won handicap at Carlisle in April; twice beaten in sellers afterwards; stays 7f; acts on firm going. *T. Craig.*

BLONDELLO 3 ch.c. High Line 125–Mink Mini 103 (Martial 131) (1981 — NR 1982 14f) third foal; dam sprinter; unquoted when in rear in 15-runner maiden race won by Rock Ballet at Salisbury in July. *R. Sturdy.*

BLONDIN (USA) 2 ch.c. The Minstrel 135–Fair Renown (Stage Door Johnny) — (1982 7f³ 8g 8s) Mar 6; $325,000Y; has a round action; third foal; dam, placed twice from 4 starts, is half-sister to top-class Little Current and very smart filly Prayers 'n Promises; injured a leg when last of 3 in £5,700 event at Newbury in July and wasn't seen out again until the autumn, when soundly beaten in maiden races at Newmarket and Leicester. *J. Dunlop.*

BLOW MY TOP 3 gr.f. Some Hand 119–Tempered Wind (Fleece 114) (1981 **50** 6s 8d 8s³ 1982 8g 8.2d 9f 10f 10.1d 8g² 9f² 8g⁴ 8g*) plain filly; plater; sold 2,050 gns after winning at Bath in August; stays 9f; acts on any going; suitable mount for an apprentice. *P. Cundell.*

BLOW YOUR MIND 2 b.g. Take a Reef 127–Living For Kicks (Murrayfield — 119) (1982 5f) Apr 29; 1,450Y; lengthy, fair sort; first foal; dam won 2 novice hurdles but was of little account on flat; dwelt and was always tailed off in 5-runner seller at Leicester in April. *W. Musson.*

BLUE AGAIN 3 b. or br.g. Blue Cashmere 129–Pink Garter (Henry the — Seventh 125) (1981 NR 1982 6s 6g 6f 7g 6s) 3,700Y; rangy gelding; good walker; half-brother to 2 winners, including smart sprinter Son of Shaka (by Tribal Chief); dam placed over 6f at 3 yrs in Ireland; behind in varied company, including selling; sold 400 gns Newmarket Autumn Sales. *N. Callaghan.*

BLUE BABY 4 br.f. The Brianstan 128–Le Brillante (Eudaemon 129) (1981 **33** 8.2f 5f 5d 1982 8fg 8g 6fg² 6fg 5fg 5fg 5g 7s) small, sturdy filly; sprint plater. *D. Francis.*

BLUEBIRDINO 3 ch.g. Bustino 136–Blue Bird 84 (Majority Blue 126) (1981 — 8s 1982 8s 8g) big, attractive gelding; has rather a round action; beaten some way in maiden races in the North; chipped a bone in a knee final start (July). *M. Camacho.*

BLUE BREEZE (USA) 2 b.f. Blue Times–Nuturf (Noble Union) (1982 — p 6s) Apr 12; $14,000Y; compact filly; sister to American 3-y-o County Turf, and half-sister to 2 winners, one stakes placed; dam won 2 sprint races at 3 yrs; sire won 12 times at up to 9f, including 2 stakes races; weak in the market and in need of race, stayed on steadily when seventh of 16 to Marzooga in maiden event at Leicester in November; should improve. *S. Norton.*

BLUEBUTTON 2 b.f. Blue Cashmere 129–My Candy 81 (Lorenzaccio 130) **65** (1982 5g 5fg² 5f⁴) neat filly; third foal; half-sister to 2 winners, including fair 1981 2-y-o 6f winner Annesley (by Relkino); dam placed over 7f at 2 yrs; odds on when second in maiden race at Wolverhampton in May; not seen out after May. *N. Gaselee.*

BLUE CAVALCADE 3 b.g. Blue Cashmere 129–Feasting (Sayajirao 132) — (1981 NR 1982 7g 7g) small, quite attractive gelding; good walker; half-brother to numerous winners, including fairly useful 1m and 1½m winner Aperitivo (by Sharp Edge); dam won at 1½m and 11f; soundly beaten in new-comers race at Doncaster and maiden race at Newcastle early in year; sent to Singapore. *E. Eldin.*

BLUE CLOUD 3 ch.f. Blue Cashmere 129–Hill Cloud 60 (El Gallo 122) (1981 **64**
5d 5d 5s³ 5g⁴ 1982 5f 5g 5fg 5fg⁴ 6f² 6g 6fg 5fg 6s 6s 7s²) strong, compact
filly; second in maiden race and selling handicap; stays 7f; acts on any going;
has run creditably for an apprentice. *Mrs R. Lomax.*

BLUE COURTIER 5 ch.h. Blue Cashmere 129–Abercourt 89 (Abernant **117**
142) (1981 6v* 6s 5fg⁴ 6.5fg 6d 7s⁴ 5v 1982 6v* 5s* 5fg⁴ 6f 6d 6g 5s⁴ 5v)
lengthy French horse; very useful as a 2-y-o when trained by T. Marshall;
was trained abroad after, and won twice in Norway in 1980 and once in France
in 1981; probably better than ever in 1982 and won 70,000 francs event at
Maisons-Laffitte in March and Prix de Saint-Georges at Longchamp in May,
latter decisively by 1½ lengths from Kind Music; in rear fourth to sixth outings,
including in William Hill July Cup at Newmarket (sweating), but returned
to form when about 3 lengths fourth of 13 to Sharpo in Prix de l'Abbaye at
Longchamp in October; best at sprint distances; won on firm going but was
much better with plenty of give in the ground; trained until after second start
by D. Becquemin; standing at Haras de Roiville. *J. Piednoel, France.*

BLUE DO 3 b.g. Swing Easy 126–Nylon Pirate (Derring-Do 131) (1981 5v **—**
5d 7fg 7fg 8g² 8.2d⁴ 1982 11s 11g² 9g 9fg⁴ 10f 8.2fg 12f 12g 11fg 12fg 10d
8g 8d) workmanlike gelding; plating-class maiden; stays 11f; sometimes
blinkered. *T. Craig.*

BLUE EMMANUELLE 3 b.c. Lochnager 132–Julie Be Quick (Selari) (1981 **92**
6g³ 7fg 5fg² 5d³ 5g² 6g² 1982 5g 6.5g² 6.5v 6s³ 6s* 6d² 6f 6fg 6g 7f* 6fg³ 7.2g*
7fg* 6g) big, rangy colt; won maiden race at Hamilton and quite valuable
handicaps at Epsom, Haydock (beat Crown a head in Sporting Chronicle
Handicap) and Newcastle; showed a good turn of foot to beat Ben Jarrow
impressively by 3 lengths in Harry Peacock Challenge Cup on last-named in
July; suited by 7f; acts on any going; blinkered third start. *N. Callaghan.*

BLUE FOX 5 ch.g. Apollo Eight–Lady Blue (Majority Blue 126) (1981 **—**
12f 16.5g 10s 1982 15.5f 15f) probably of little account. *A. Bailey.*

BLUE GRASS 2 br.c. Warpath 113–Delphinium 93 (Tin King 126) (1982 **68 p**
7s) Apr 27; strong, good sort; good walker; brother to 3 winners, including
middle-distance winner Gunmetal Blue, and half-brother to a winner; dam
stayed 6f; 10/1, shaped well when running-on 6 lengths fifth of 11 to Ice
Patrol in maiden race at Redcar in October; a taking individual, sure to do
better. *C. Thornton.*

BLUE NANTUCKET 2 b. or br.f. Mansingh 120–Bluets 74 (Hitting Away) **83**
(1982 6fg 6s³ 6s* 7d 7s² 7s⁴) Jan 10; 1,000Y; fair sort; poor walker; half-sister to
a winning plater; dam won over 1¼m; responded very gamely to extremely
hard driving when winning valuable seller at York (bought in 2,700 gns) in
October by head from Luisa Miller; good second in nursery at Leicester the
following month; stays 7f; suited by soft surface. *D. Thom.*

BLUE REALM 3 b.f. Realm 129–Honey Tower 70 (Tower Walk 130) (1981 **52**
5g 1982 6s 8fg 8f 6g* 8f³ 6g 7fg* 10d 8.2s 6s 8s) leggy, close-coupled filly;
plater; won at Hamilton in July (no bid) and Beverley in August (sold out of
G. Richards' stable 1,700 gns); best at up to 7f; suited by a sound surface.
R. Ward.

BLUE RHAPSODY 4 ch.c. Sandford Lad 133–Sovereign Court 87 (Sovereign **—**
Path 125) (1981 6s 5fg 6s 7g 6g 1982 10f) strong, useful sort; plater;
should stay 7f; acts on soft going; has worn blinkers; one to be wary of. *A.
Neaves.*

BLUEROOI 2 b.f. Red Alert 127–Bunch of Blue (Martinmas 128) (1982 **65**
5fg² 5f³ 5g) Mar 22; 27,000Y; sturdy, quite attractive filly; first foal; dam,
winner at up to 13f in France, is half-sister to very smart American horse Czar
Alexander; placed in maiden races in August, at Ayr and Catterick (favourite,
swerved start); will be suited by 6f; wears blinkers and looks none too
enthusiastic. *J. Hindley.*

BLUE SAPPHIRE 3 br.g. Blue Cashmere 129–The Maid (Milesian 125) (1981 **45**
5s 5v 5g⁴ 5s 5fg 5fg 6f 5f 5g² 5g 1982 5s⁴ 5g³ 5f⁴ 5f 5fg³ 5fg 5.3g 5.8g 5f)
leggy gelding; good mover; in frame in varied company, including selling; best
form at 5f; acts on any going; sometimes blinkered; trained part of season by
T. Taylor; sent to Singapore. *M. Haynes.*

BLUES BANK 3 ch.g. Fair Decision 93§–Dazzling Hue (Double Jump 131) **—**
(1981 NR 1982 10f 12f) 625F; half-brother to Irish 1½m winner Northern
Queen (by Northfields); dam unraced half-sister to Cambridgeshire winner King
Midas; behind in seller and maiden race at Folkestone. *B. Wise.*

Mr D. O. McIntyre's "Blue Singh" (W. R. Swinburn)

BLUESHOES 2 ch.f. Blue Cashmere 129–Lady Helen 63 (Majority Blue 126) **63**
(1982 5d 5f* 5fg* 5f) Apr 12; 360Y; leggy, sparely-made filly; sister to a winning
plater; dam best at up to 7f; retained, on second occasion for 2,600 gns, after
winning 5-runner sellers at Leicester in April and Lingfield in June; last of 8
in valuable nursery at Lingfield in July; acts well on firm going. *C. Wildman.*

BLUE SINGH 4 ch.f. Mansingh 120–Great Blue White 73 (Great Nephew 126) **111**
(1981 6fg³ 6g 5s 6d³ 5d 5f³ 5f* 6fg 5fg 5g³ 5f³ 5.6fg 5g 5s 5s* 5g   1982 5fg² 2s 5f
5fg³ 5g 6f 5g² 6g³ 5d⁴) leggy, fair sort; showed vastly improved form when
¾-length second of 12 to Lightning Label in Palace House Stakes at Newmarket
in May, 3 lengths third of 14 to Fearless Lad in King's Stand Stakes at Royal
Ascot in June and 2¼ lengths third to Indian King in Diadem Stakes at Ascot
again in September; also ran creditably third outing, but was favoured by
weights and didn't run up to her best when ¾-length second of 4 to Soba in
Scarbrough Stakes at Doncaster and 1¾ lengths fourth of 11 behind Ferryman
in £4,600 event at Newmarket; ran respectably over 7f but best form at shorter
distances; won on soft going but was very well suited by a sound surface; sold
100,000 gns Newmarket December Sales and retired to South Africa. *R. Boss.*

BLUE TIMES 2 ch.c. Blue Cashmere 129–Oakwoodhill (Habat 127) (1982 **89**
5d 5.1f² 5fg³ 5f² 5d* 5v⁴ 5s) Feb 27; 6,000Y; small, strong colt; first foal;
dam never ran; having first race for 2¼ months (had damaged a cannon bone)
when winning 10-runner nursery at Wolverhampton in October by 3 lengths from
Friendly Bobby; evidently thought best at 5f; best effort on dead ground;
sold 5,800 gns Newmarket Autumn Sales, probably for export to Italy. *W.
O'Gorman.*

BLUEWITCH 3 b.f. Blue Cashmere 129–Jetwitch 56 (Lear Jet 123) (1981 **62**
5g 6f 6g⁴ 7g 7v 1982 8s³ 8.2v 8g 7f* 8f³ 7fg³ 7f 7.2f² 7d⁴ 7g* 7g 7f) long-
backed, unfurnished filly; plater; attracted no bid after winning at Beverley

in April; narrowly won non-selling handicap at Warwick in June; stays 1m; acts on any going; best in blinkers; exported to Algeria. *A. Young.*

BLUKALA 2 b.f. Kala Shikari 125–Blue Bleep (Bleep-Bleep 134) (1982 — 5g 5.3f 5fg) Feb 21; 3,300Y; close-coupled, fair sort; last all starts, including in a valuable seller; sold 370 gns Doncaster September Sales. *S. Matthews.*

BLUSHING NURSE 2 gr.f. Saritamer 130–Red Cape 84 (Matador 131) (1982 — 8g) Mar 5; second living foal; half-sister to modest 1½m winner Ruby Red Dress (by Sparkler); dam, half-sister to Night Nurse, stayed 1m; tailed-off last of 12 in maiden race at Edinburgh in October. *N. Bycroft.*

BLUSHING RIVER 2 ch.c. Blushing Groom 131–Lys River 119 (Lyphard 132) **93** (1982 6f³ 7fg⁴ 7g* 7g² 8g⁴ 8g²) Mar 4; small colt; first foal; dam smart French middle-distance filly; kept on strongly to beat Trigger Point by 4 lengths in 16-runner maiden race at Yarmouth in August; in frame all other starts, on final outing finishing good second of 9 (eased final furlong) to Ashmolean in minor event at Leicester in October; will stay 1¼m; yet to race on soft surface. *H. T. Jones.*

BLYTHSMERE 4 b.g. Blue Cashmere 129–Blesseen 71 (So Blessed 130) (1981 **48** NR 1982 5.8f 7f 8g 8fg² 10fg 8fg 8f² 8s⁴) tall, plain gelding; second in sellers at Warwick and Bath; stays 1m; acts on any going. *M. Pipe.*

B.M.C. SPECIAL 7 gr.h. Supreme Sovereign 119–Agapimou (Great White — Way) (1981 8s 8.2fg 8fg* 8d⁴ 12d 8fg 8g 8.2f 8f 8fg² 10.4s³ 10f 8g 8d 8fg 9s 1982 8fg⁴ 8fg 8f⁴ 8f 15f) plater; suited by 1m; seems to act on any going; blinkered once at 3 yrs; bandaged nowadays. *J. Gilbert.*

BOARDMANS BEAUTY 3 b.g. Lauso–Torbay (Hill Prince) (1981 7fg 8s⁴ — 10s⁴ 1982 12f) quite a useful sort; quite a modest maiden at his best; promises to stay 1½m; acts on soft going. *A. Jarvis.*

BOARDMANS CROWN 3 b.g. Lauso–Taj Girl 68 (Taj Dewan 128) (1981 **76** 8g 1982 12f 16d 14f² 16fg* 18d³ 15d⁴) fair sort; ridden by 5-lb claimer when winning maiden race at Nottingham in August; stays very well; seems to act on any going; tended to hang left final start; sold to C. Mackenzie 15,000 gns Doncaster October Sales. *A. Jarvis.*

BOARDMANS STAR 3 ch.f. Cawston's Clown 113–Weewanda 94 (Cagire II — 122) (1981 5fg³ 5s⁴ 6s 5.3f 6fg 1982 6d 5f 6f) small, lightly-made filly; good mover; poor performer nowadays; form only at 5f. *R. Hannon.*

BOARHUNT 3 ch.g. Queen's Hussar 124–Muninga 108 (St Alphage 119) (1981 — 5s 6fg 6g 5s 1982 6s 5fg 8.3g) tall gelding; behind in varied company, including selling. *Mrs J. Reavey.*

BOATROCKER 3 b.c. African Sky 124–Cheap and Sweet (Rising Market) **84** (1981 5v 5d* 1982 6s³ 6g* 6f² 6f²) quite useful-looking colt; justified favouritism in handicap at Pontefract in April; creditable second in quite valuable handicaps at York and Redcar in May; not seen out again; stays 6f; acts on any going. *S. Norton.*

BOBBY BUSHTAIL 2 ch.c. Porto Bello 118–Rich Harvest (Bounteous 125) **87** (1982 6f 6f* 6d⁴ 8.2d 8s) June 3; smallish, good-topped colt; good walker; half-brother to fairly useful miler Melissa Jane (by No Mercy); dam never ran; finished very fast to win 6-runner maiden race at Brighton in August by ½ length from Timber Creek; again did best work in closing stages when 9 lengths fourth behind Swift To Conquer in minor event at Chester later in month, best of 3 disappointing runs afterwards; should stay beyond 6f; possibly not at his best on a soft surface. *J. Dunlop.*

BOCCACCIO (USA) 2 b.c. Full Out–Mindy's Hurricane (Noble Commander) **76** (1982 6f³ 6f³ 6d) May 6; $70,000Y; strong, attractive, good-quartered colt; good walker; first foal; dam very useful winner of 13 races at up to 7f; third in small race at Haydock in June and 12-runner maiden event at Pontefract in July; looked unsuited by course when always behind in minor event at Chester in August; will stay 7f. *S. Norton.*

BOHEME 2 b.c. Lypheor 118–Sweet Jewel (Will Somers 114§) (1982 7fg 8s 7s) May 23; IR 9,200Y; short-coupled colt; half-brother to 3 winners including very smart miler Ardﻩ (by Track Spare) and fairly useful middle-distance filly Melaleuca (by Levmoss); dam won 4 times at up to 1m in Ireland; behind in maiden races at Redcar (2) and Newcastle in the autumn. *M. W. Easterby.*

BOIS DE GRACE (FR) 3 b.c. Luthier 126–Tafarette (Ballymoss 136) (1981 **122**
8d* 10v³ 1982 10.5d* 12s 12fg³) half-brother to 2 winners in France, including
middle-distance winner Helisara (by Brigadier Gerard); dam, daughter of smart
1962 2-y-o Chesa, was very useful over 1¼m; beat Nabirpour by a head in driving
finish to Prix Greffulhe at Longchamp in April and kept on well to be 5 lengths
third of 14 to Assert in Prix du Jockey-Club at Chantilly in June; below form in
Prix Hocquart at Longchamp in between; suited by 1½m; seems to act on any
going; sent to USA and won 9f allowance race at Hollywood Park in December.
F. Mathet, France.

BOKARAH IN SHALLAH 5 b.g. Forlorn River 124–My Worry 72 (March —
Past 124) (1981 6s² 6d 6f 6f 6fg 6g 6s 6g 1982 6f 6fg⁴ 6v 6s) plater; stays
7f; probably acts on any going; suitable mount for a boy; bandaged second
start. *Peter Taylor.*

BOLD AND WOOLLY 2 br.c. Kashmir II 125–Tarakanova (Bold Lad, **88**
USA) (1982 6g² 7d* 7v⁴ 6v* 7d) Apr 21; 11,000F, 8,400Y; leggy colt; half-
brother to 2 winners, including 6f to 13f winner Teresilla (by High Echelon);
dam won at up to 6f in USA; successful in maiden race at Leicester in September
and 9-runner nursery at Hamilton the following month; also in frame in £5,000
seller at Doncaster and £4,500 nursery at Ascot; will stay 1m; has raced only
on an easy surface. *B. Hanbury.*

BOLD APPAREL (FR) 2 br.f. Bold Forbes–Gay Apparel (Up Spirits) (1982 **?**
6g² 5v 5s* 6.5v* 6v*) first foal; dam very useful Canadian 2-y-o, winning 2
sprint stakes races, and is sister to 2 other stakes winners; in fine form late in
season, winning maiden race at Maisons-Laffitte, 70,000-franc race at Evry and
Group 2 Premio Umbria at Rome, getting home by a neck from Super Sky in
last named, with 15 others well beaten off; will probably stay beyond sprint
distances; acts on heavy going. *R. Collet, France.*

BOLD BOB 2 ch.c. Sharpen Up 127–Finest View 66 (Bold Lad, Ire 133) **117**
(1982 5fg² 5fg* 5f⁴ 5f² 5f⁴ 5g⁴ 5f²) Apr 18; 13,000Y; quite attractive, rangy
colt; half-brother to prolific Italian winner Miss Vermont (by Sandford Lad);
dam stayed 7f; won 10-runner maiden race at Doncaster in May made comfortably by ¾ length from Faites Vite; improved with his races afterwards, and
on last 2 outings finished 1¼ lengths fourth of 8 to Cat O'Nine Tails in Prince
of Wales's Stakes at York in August, and ¾-length second to odds-on Kafu
in Flying Childers Stakes at Doncaster; should stay 6f; yet to race on a soft
surface; genuine. *C. Brittain.*

BOLD FORESTER 3 ch.g. Import 127–Blotie (Misti IV 132) (1981 NR —
1982 10.1fg 11.7d 10s) second foal; dam won from 7f to 1½m in France; poor
form in maiden and minor events; dead. *P. Haynes.*

BOLD FORT 3 b.c. Auction Ring 123–Via Mala 81 (Pall Mall 132) (1981 5s² —
5g³ 5d² 5d* 5f 6fg* 6f² 5d 6f 7s 6g* 6g 7g 1982 8fg 6fg 6f 6g 5s 6d 6s) neat,
sharp sort; good mover; tough and genuine in 1981 when he won 3 times; in
rear most starts at 3 yrs in varied company; better suited by 6f than 5f but has
yet to show he stays 7f; probably acts on any going; blinkered final outing.
R. Hollinshead.

BOLD HAWK 3 br.c. Bold Lad (Ire) 133–Slavissima (Sea Hawk II 131) **92**
(1981 6g⁴ 1982 8g*(dis) 8fg² 10.1fg* 10g² 12d 10d 10fg 10g 8s* 8s²) good-
looking colt; first past post in maiden race at Doncaster in March (subsequently
disqualified) and minor events at Windsor in May and Warwick in October;
also ran creditably in defeat on several occasions; stays 1¼m but not 1½m;
seems to act on any going but goes well on soft; sometimes sweats up; sometimes
pulls hard and is suited by strong handling; sold 19,500 gns Newmarket Autumn
Sales. *G. Harwood.*

BOLDIE 3 b.f. Bold Lad (Ire) 133–Amadina 96 (Great Nephew 126) (1981 **81**
5fg² 6g⁴ 1982 6fg³ 7.6fg 7d 7fg* 8fg* 8.3g³ 9f³ 10.6f* 10.5s* 10.2d) slightly
hollow-backed, fair sort; won maiden race at Chepstow and handicaps at
Wolverhampton, Haydock (awarded race) and York; stays 1¼m well; acts on
any going; suited by waiting tactics. *F. J. Houghton.*

BOLD IMAGE 5 b. or br.h. Balidar 133–Darinda (Darius 129) (1981 6s **69**
6f 6f 7fg 8f² 8fg 8fg 8d 8d⁴ 1982 7.5g* 8s⁴ 8v 7f 7f 8f 8fg⁴ 8.3fg³ 8fg 7g⁴ 7s)
useful-looking horse; shows quite a bit of knee action; won in quite good style
at Cagnes-sur-Mer in February, but has deteriorated and was beaten in valuable
seller tenth start; suited by 1m; seems to act on any going; blinkered ninth and
tenth outings; unseated rider leaving stalls twice in 1981; sold 3,600 gns Doncaster November Sales. *W. Hastings-Bass.*

BOLDLY GO 4 b.c. Realm 129–Kilcarn Lass 74 (Bold Lad, Ire 133) (1981 —
5d³ 5.8g 5.8f³ 6f⁴ 6f⁴ 5fg 5g 6g 1982 6d 6f 5g⁴ 6f 6fg 5g 5f⁴ 6fg 6g 5g 5fg 6g
8fg) hollow-backed colt; plater; stays 6f. *J. Holt.*

BOLD MAID 2 b.f. Persian Bold 123–Gold Pollen 110 (Klondyke Bill 125) **69**
(1982 5f² 5.8f⁴ 7f 6f 5fg 5fg⁴ 5fg 5s) Apr 22; lightly-made filly; half-sister to
several winners, including useful 7f and 1m winner Nugget and very useful
French 5f and 1m winner Gold Nugget (both by Silver Shark); dam sprinter;
disappointing maiden; last in nursery and 21-runner maiden race (blinkered)
last 2 outings; sold 800 gns Newmarket Autumn Sales. *A. Ingham.*

BOLD MAJOR 2 ch.c. Orange Bay 131–Armelle 87 (Tribal Chief 125) (1982 **100**
6f 7g³ 6f² 6g* 6s* 8f⁴ 7s) Apr 28; 5,400Y; useful-looking colt; good walker;
second living foal; dam 2-y-o 5f winner; successful in minor events at Ripon
(easily by 4 lengths from Lahab) and Yarmouth (held off Bold Mover by 1¼
lengths) in August; just over 2 lengths fourth of 11 to Axkernish in £5,700 nursery
at Doncaster in September; stays 1m but gives impression he'll prove better
at shorter distances; acts on any going; goes well for apprentice E. Guest.
E. Eldin.

BOLD MANEUVER (USA) 2 gr.f. Par Excellent–Bold Fascinator 122 —
(Bold Lad, USA) (1982 6fg 6s) May 8; well-grown, workmanlike filly; half-
sister to a winner in USA; dam won French 1,000 Guineas; sire, son of Sea-
Bird II, won a 7.5f race at 2 yrs in France from 33 starts; always behind in
September in 18-runner maiden race at Salisbury and Blue Seal Stakes at
Ascot. *M. Francis.*

BOLD MOVER 2 b.c. Bold Lad (Ire) 133–Short Rations (Lorenzaccio 130) **91**
(1982 6fg* 6s² 7v) Feb 14; quite well-made, attractive colt; good mover;
first foal; dam, winner at 2 yrs in Italy, is half-sister to very smart animals
He Loves Me and Wattlefield and closely related to smart Common Land;
ran on strongly to win 19-runner maiden race at Newmarket in July by ¾ length
from Flying Corps; beaten 1¼ lengths by Bold Major in 6-runner minor event
at Yarmouth the following month; should stay 7f (tailed off in nursery when
tried at trip); possibly unsuited by heavy going. *M. Stoute.*

BOLDON LADY 3 b.f. Broxted 120–Dane Valley (Simbir 130) (1981 5s —
6d 1982 7fg 7.6fg 7fg 10d 7fg 6f 7d 6g) workmanlike filly; well behind in
varied company, including selling; blinkered final appearance; reluctant to
race sixth start. *D. Wilson.*

BOLD PRINT 3 ch.c. High Line 125–Star Story 117 (Red God 128§) (1981 **80**
6d 6fg 1982 10.1fg³ 10.1d* 12fg⁴ 8s) quite attractive, rather lightly-made
colt; favourite when winning 20-runner minor event at Windsor in June; not
disgraced next time; stays 1½m. *F. J. Houghton.*

BOLD QUEEN 2 b.f. Persian Bold 123–Queen of Time (Charlottown 127) —
(1982 6s) Feb 23; 15,000Y; second foal; half-sister to French plater Alheure
(by Manado); dam lightly-raced half-sister to Gold Cup winner Erimo Hawk;
unquoted and very backward, failed to recover from slow start in 19-runner
maiden race won by Hawk Lady at Leicester in November. *G. Lewis.*

BOLD ROWLEY 2 br.c. Persian Bold 123–Lady Rowley 114 (Royal Levee) **88 p**
(1982 6f 6s²) Apr 20; 15,500F; fourth produce; half-brother to 3-y-o 1m
winner King's Holt (by Royal Palace); dam very useful 2-y-o sprinter; 5/1,
had rest well strung out behind when 4 lengths second of 16 to Coquito's Friend
in minor event at Lingfield in September; should improve and win a race.
G. Lewis.

BOLD SARACEN (USA) 3 b. or br.c. Forli–Mohmond (Jaipur) (1981 —
5s 5.8d² 5.3f³ 5f² 7h 5g* 5s² 1982 6s 5g 5f 5.8g) small, lengthy, quite attractive
colt; good mover; fair performer at 2 yrs; well beaten in 1982; suited by 6f
and should stay further (swerved at start when always behind over 7f); best
form with some give in the ground; blinkered final start. *P. Walwyn.*

BOLD SCUFFLE 4 b.g. Bold Lad (Ire) 133–Cloe (Shantung 132) (1981 **§§**
5s 6s* 6fg⁴ 6g 6g 6s* 6fg* 6f² 6g 6d³ 5f 5s 5g*(dis) 1982 5g 5fg 6fg 6g³ 6d 5g²
5f 5.6f 5fg 5fg 5fg) useful-looking gelding; not a good mover; beaten neck by
Touch Boy in handicap at Haydock in July but would probably have won if he
hadn't tried to savage winner; suited by 6f; gives impression he needs some
give in the ground nowadays; blinkered seventh start; moody and thoroughly
inconsistent nowadays. *R. Hollinshead.*

BOLD SECRET 2 b.g. Auction Ring 123–Whispering Star 78 (Sound Track 132)   **81 p**
(1982 6g) May 5; 10,000Y; brother to 2 winners, including 3-y-o French
sprinter Flying Melody, and half-brother to numerous winners, including very
useful performers Seadiver, Pearl Star and Portese (all by Gulf Pearl) and smart
sprinter Blue Star (by Majority Blue); dam won over 5f on only start; 10/1 and
apparently very backward, showed good speed when 1½ lengths fifth of 20 behind
Fiefdom in maiden race at Newmarket in October; sure to improve. *G.
Pritchard-Gordon.*

BOLD SPINNEY 2 ch.f. Bold Lad (Ire) 133–Stunog Wood 98 (Falcon 131)   **81**
(1982 7fg 7g⁴ 7d²) Mar 21; well-grown, workmanlike filly; sister to fairly useful
1980 2-y-o Bold Wood, and half-sister to 2 winners; dam, twice a winner over 5f
at 2 yrs, is half-sister to good French stayer A Chara; beaten length by Super
Sunshine in maiden event at Chester in August, best effort; will stay 1m; capable
of winning small race. *J. Hindley.*

BOLD THOUGHTS 2 b.f. Diamonds Are Trump 108–No Fooling 83 (Narrator   **62**
127) (1982 6g 7f 8f) Mar 31; IR 3,400Y; rangy filly; half-sister to several
winners here and abroad; dam probably best at middle distances; just over 5
lengths sixth of 20 to Figure de Danse in maiden auction event at Redcar in
September, third outing and best effort. *A. Jarvis.*

BOLTRANS 2 br.f. Monsanto 121–Brush's Choice (Robson's Choice 105) (1982   **—**
5d 5fg 6d) Mar 7; 5,000 2-y-o; rather leggy filly; half-sister to 2 winners,
including fairly useful miler Town Farm (by Tycoon II); dam of little account;
poor form in maiden and minor events; should be suited by 7f+. *J. Berry.*

BOLT THE GATE 3 ch.c. Bustino 136–Madame Quickly 80 (Saint Crespin III   **—**
132) (1981 NR 1982 14s⁴ 16.5s⁴) big, rather dipped-backed colt; half-
brother to several winners in France, including useful 1980 6f and 1m winner
Kisty (by Kashmir II); dam won at up to 7f; showed a little ability when well-
beaten fourth in £3,100 event at York and minor event at Redcar in October.
W. Elsey.

BOMBALINI 6 b.g. Ribero 126–Villarrica (Dan Cupid 132) (1981 NR 1982   **52**
12d* 12g* 12f²) won handicaps at Salisbury (amateur riders) and Folkestone
in June (apprentice ridden); should stay beyond 1½m; yet to race on really soft
going but probably acts on any other. *P. Haynes.*

BOMBIL 3 b.g. The Brianstan 128–Bombay Duck 65 (Ballyciptic 122) (1981   **65**
5d 5s⁴ 6fg 7fg² 6g 6g³ 7f* 8f⁴ 7fg 1982 8f 8f 10d 8g 7fg 8.2fg³ 8fg* 9s 10s)
neat gelding; won valuable 25-runner seller at Doncaster in September; surprisingly attracted no bid afterwards; suited by 1m or more; ideally suited by a
sound surface. *P. Rohan.*

BOMBILI 3 ch.g. Native Bazaar 122–Curry Favour 62 (Negotiation) (1981 NR   **70**
1982 7g² 7fg 10.1fg 8fg² 8.2s³ 8g 10s) 2,000Y; workmanlike gelding; fourth foal;
brother to 1978 2-y-o 5f winner Foul Fella; dam plater; runner-up in newcomers race at Doncaster in March and maiden event at Salisbury in September;
stays 1m. *G. Balding.*

BOMBSHELL (FR) 3 b.f. Ashmore 125–Broadway Dancer 131 (Northern   **59**
Dancer) (1981 6d 1982 10g 9s² 10s 10g) lightly-made, leggy filly; lacks scope;
didn't look particularly keen when 2½ lengths second to Alpine Way in minor
event at Newcastle in October, best effort; seems to stay 1¼m; sold 60,000 gns
Newmarket December Sales. *H. Cecil.*

BOND DEALER 5 gr.g. Habat 127–Sounion 69 (Vimy 132) (1981 10d 8d 8v   **62**
8s⁴ 7g³ 7.6fg* 7fg³ 8g² 8fg* 8fg* 10fg 8h³ 10f 10g 1982 8g 7f⁴ 8g 7f* 7g* 8fg² 7f²
8fg* 8f² 8f* 8fg 8fg) good-looking gelding; had a good season and won
apprentice handicaps at Yarmouth, Lingfield, Ascot (by 5 lengths) and Salisbury;
seems best at up to 1m; acts on any going, but clearly goes well on top-of-the-
ground; best in blinkers; usually makes running. *B. Swift.*

BOND HOUSE 3 ch.c. Tumble Wind–Rold Gold (Bold Combatant) (1981 5s   **—**
5fg 8s 7d 6g 1982 10.1fg 7g 8fg) big colt; poor form in varied company;
blinkered final start. *D. H. Jones.*

BONDS AND BANANAS 2 br.f. Mansingh 120–Babanina (Bleep-Bleep 134)   **—**
(1982 5fg 5d) Mar 16; 1,300F; half-sister to 1980 2-y-o 5f winner Supertramp
(by Mummy's Pet); in rear in sellers at Nottingham and Warwick (last of 13) in
April; sold 380 gns Newmarket May Sales. *T. M. Jones.*

BONDY'S BOY 2 b.c. Native Bazaar 122–French Bond (Prince de Galles 125)   **—**
(1982 5d 5fg 5fg) Feb 18; second foal; brother to a poor animal; dam never
ran; little worthwhile form in maiden and minor events; not seen out after
August; blinkered third start. *R. Baker.*

BONJOUR VITESSE 2 b.f. Vitiges 132–So Valiant 80 (So Blessed 130) (1982 **62**
5.1g² 5f*) Apr 12; sturdy filly; has deformed near-fore; fourth foal; half-sister
to 2 winners, including fairly useful but temperamental 1979 2-y-o 5f winner
Heroic Air (by Song); dam 2-y-o 5f winner; bought in 2,400 gns after landing
odds by 2 lengths from Suelizelle in 17-runner seller at Catterick in July; will be
suited by 6f. *Sir Mark Prescott.*

BON MARCHE (USA) 2 gr.c. The Minstrel 135–Nocturnal Spree 121 **93**
(Supreme Sovereign 119) (1982 6.3fg³ 7fg* 7d*) Jan 17; $175,000Y; second
living foal; dam won 1,000 Guineas; odds on when successful twice at Naas in the
autumn, beating Changed His Mind a length in maiden race and Northern Game
3 lengths in 19-runner minor event; had previously finished 4 lengths third of 16
to stable-companion Glenstal when 25/1 for similar event at the Curragh in
July; will be suited by 1m+; a progressive individual. *V. O'Brien, Ireland.*

BONNE BAISER 3 ch.f. Most Secret 119–Condonna 92 (Constable 119) (1981 **76**
5s* 5g* 5d³ 5d 5fg 5d² 5s* 5g² 1982 5v² 6f 5f² 5f) leggy filly; sprint handicapper; stays 6f; acts on any going; suitable mount for an apprentice. *A. Jarvis.*

BONNE CHANCERY 3 b.f. Native Bazaar 122–Mustardflower 68 (Mustang) —
(1981 NR 1982 8fg 8f 10.1d 10fg) sister to Chancery Bloom, successful at up
to 1m; dam won over jumps; poor plater; has worn blinkers. *R. Baker.*

BONNIE BESS 3 b.f. Ardoon 124–Bessborough (Mossborough 126) (1981 NR **95**
1982 7s 7v 10f* 8g 9f* 10d 8g² 10d 10v) IR 26,000Y; half-sister to numerous
winners, including Italian 1,000 Guineas winner Grand Nube (by Faberge II);
dam never ran; easily won maiden race at Navan in May and beat Moreda
decisively by 3 lengths in valuable Ballylinch and Norelands Studs Stakes at
Gowran Park in June; respectable eighth of 24 to stable-companion Prince's
Polly in Goffs Irish 1,000 Guineas at the Curragh in between and ran well to be
1½ lengths second to Pilgrim in Youghal Stakes at Leopardstown; stays 1¼m;
probably needs a sound surface and acts well on firm going. *D. Weld, Ireland.*

Mr R. E. Sangster's "Bon Marche"

Prix Niel, Longchamp—Bon Sang beats his rivals in good style

BONNY BASSETT 3 b.f. Gold Form 108–Lady Cortina 80 (Cortachy 107) — (1981 5g* 5f 6d 5fg 1982 5f 6f) narrow filly; plater; form only at 5f; has worn bandages; exported to Algeria. *D. Garraton.*

BONNY GOLD 4 br.g. Goldhill 125–Politely 55 (Polic 126) (1981 10s⁴ 8g 8g² 9s 8fg 9g⁴ 10f 10fg 8g 8d³ 11d 8s 1982 12s⁴) strong gelding who carries plenty of condition; good walker; seems to stay 1½m; acts on any going. *K. Stone.*

BONNY MUSIC 2 b.f. Music Boy 124–Bonandra 82 (Andrea Mantegna) (1982 6fg 5fg 5f) Apr 9; small, unimpressive sort; first foal; dam won over 6f and 1¼m; behind in maiden and minor events; not raced after August. *W. Hastings-Bass.*

BONNY SHIELDS 2 gr.f. Owen Dudley 121–Saragail (Warpath 113) (1982 **94** 5g* 5g* 5fg³ 5f² 6f⁴ 6d³ 5d³ 7f³ 6fg 6fg 6s 8d 8.2s) Apr 27; 1,200F; well-grown, workmanlike, slightly hollow-backed filly; first produce; dam never ran; successful in early-season events at Doncaster and Pontefract; put up several fair efforts afterwards, best race when 4¼ lengths fifth of 17 to Rare Roberta in valuable nursery at Haydock in September on eleventh start; probably stays 7f; possibly best with some give in the ground; ridden by apprentice M. Beecroft most outings. *T. Fairhurst.*

BONOL 5 b.h. Ridan–Lynda's Own (Schapiro 99) (1981 8s² 8d⁴ 9g 10.2g* **105** d 12g² 10fg 10fg² 11g 1982 10s 10f⁴ 12fg³ 11d) strong, good-bodied horse; good walker; very useful performer at his best; ran respectably in spring and finished 5 lengths fourth to Princes Gate in Westbury Stakes at Sandown in April; well below his best afterwards, including when third in valuable gentlemen riders event at Epsom in August; evidently stays 1½m; ideally suited by some give in the ground; best on a galloping track; blinkered last 3 outings; sold to BBA 7,000 gns Newmarket Autumn Sales. *M. H. Easterby.*

BON SANG (FR) 3 ch.c. Gyr 131–La Caldera (Mourne 126) (1981 7d* **126** 8s* 10v 10s* 1982 10g² 10fg² 12f* 12s) half-brother to successful French stayer Dernier Tango (by Tapalque) and to a winner in France and Sweden; dam ran once at 2 yrs; narrowly beaten in Prix Eugene Adam at Saint-Cloud in July (by What A Guest, who gave 4 lb) and Prix de la Cote Normande at Deauville the following month (by General Holme) before beating Alfred's Choice in good style by 6 lengths in Prix Niel at Longchamp in September, really impressing us with his enthusiasm; led for some way when thirteenth of 17 to Akiyda in Trusthouse Forte Prix de l'Arc de Triomphe at Longchamp again following month; suited by 1½m and would have stayed further; acted on any going; standing at Haras de Meautry at a fee of 60,000 francs (approx £5,500). *M. Saliba, France.*

BONZOLENA 3 ch.f. Air Trooper 115–Aberdeen Lassie 102 (Aberdeen 109) (1981 6fg 5g 7d 7g 1982 9g 7.6f 7d 7.2g 8fg 8.3g) stocky filly; poor plater; sometimes blinkered. *Mrs R. Lomax.*

BOODLEBIRD (USA) 3 b.f. Plenty Old–Curtain Raiser (Duel) (1981 5g 5d 5g 5fg 5fg 1982 5d 5f 5g 6f 6fg⁴) big, rangy filly; poor form, including in an apprentice selling event; will stay 7f; has sweated up. *D. Whelan.*

BOOM TOWN CHARLIE (USA) 2 ch.c. Silent Screen–Serica (Silky Sullivan) **109** (1982 6f 7g* 6f* 7f 6f³ 6d*) Apr 4; $55,000Y; rangy colt; half-brother to 2 minor winners in USA; dam stakes-placed winner of 6 races at up to 7f; won minor events at Yarmouth in June, Kempton in August and Redcar (beating

147

Bid Again decisively by 4 lengths) in November; stays 7f; yet to race on really soft going, but acts on any other; pulled a muscle in his quarters when last on fourth outing; very useful. *W. O'Gorman.*

BOOTEY (USA) 3 b.g. Raja Baba–Precious Silver (Prize Silver) (1981 — NR 1982 6f) $40,000Y; second foal; half-brother to a minor winner in USA by Dancing Dervish; dam unraced half-sister to very smart stakes winner My Gallant; 20/1 when last of 11 to Curve The Wind in maiden race at Brighton in May. *R. Price.*

BOOTH'S TOWN BOY 2 b.g. Decoy Boy 129–Aldbury Girl 79 (Galivanter 75 131) (1982 5g⁴ 6fg 5d⁴ 6s 6s 6v⁴ 5g² 5d²) Feb 24; 2,600Y; workmanlike gelding; first foal; dam won over 5.9f at 2 yrs; quite a modest maiden; second in nursery at Edinburgh in October and seller at Redcar in November; stays 6f; appears suited by some give in the ground; consistent. *J. Berry.*

BOOTIES 2 b.f. Riboboy 124–Step Softly 81 (St Chad 120) (1982 6fg 5g 6g⁴ 42 8.2fg 7g) May 14; 480Y; small filly; second foal; dam 2-y-o 5f winner; a poor plater; sold 320 gns Doncaster November Sales. *J. Wilson.*

BOOZE CRUISE 2 gr.f. Saritamer 130–Brierley Lodge 67 (Lorenzaccio 130) 83 (1982 5f 5d 5fg* 6g 6fg² 5fg* 6d) Feb 13; small, fair sort; first foal; dam ran 4 times at 2 yrs; won maiden race at Warwick in July and nursery at Wolverhampton in September; stays 6f; best form on a firm surface; wears blinkers; sold BBA 10,000 gns Newmarket Autumn Sales. *H. Candy.*

BO-PEEP 2 ch.f. Decoy Boy 129–Picture 98 (Lorenzaccio 130) (1982 5f 78 7g*) May 5; leggy, light-framed filly; first foal; dam, half-sister to Queen's Hussar, won over 6f at 2 yrs; improved greatly on her first effort when successful in £2,800 seller at Newmarket in September, beating Mister Accord easily by 3 lengths after travelling well throughout; sold 16,000 gns afterwards, and raced in Italy; stays 7f well. *W. Hastings-Bass.*

BORDER BALLAD 2 br.f. Broxted 120–Mexican Music 71 (Aztec 128) (1982 — 7d 8s) May 9; lengthy filly; fourth foal; half-sister to 3-y-o 7f and 9f winner Crackhill (by Legal Eagle); dam, half-sister to dam of Pitcairn, was placed over 10.8f; backward, in rear in maiden races at Ayr in September and Newcastle in October; sold for export to Norway 1,700 gns Doncaster November Sales. *J. Haldane.*

BORDER GIRL 3 b. or br.f. Mummy's Pet 125–Kelso Girl (Royal Palm 131) — (1981 6f 8fg 1982 10f 12.2f) small filly; behind in maiden races in the North; sold 470 gns Doncaster September Sales. *W. C. Watts.*

BORDER RIVER 9 b.g. Forlorn River 124–Kelso Girl (Royal Palm 131) — (1981 NR 1982 13s 12g 12f 12f⁴ 12f 12s) strong gelding; poor handicapper; stays 1¼m; seems to act on any going, but has done all his winning on a sound surface; has been tried in blinkers; usually apprentice ridden; usually bandaged nowadays; sold 500 gns Doncaster September Sales. *W. C. Watts.*

BORDER SPOIL 4 b.g. Mummy's Pet 125–Kelso Girl (Royal Palm 131) — (1981 NR 1982 8s 8g 8f 12f 10f³) lengthy gelding; has a round action; plating-class maiden; possibly stays 1¼m; acts on a firm and a soft surface. *W. C. Watts.*

BOREAS 7 br.g. Boreen (Fr) 123–Great Aunt 74 (Great Nephew 126) (1981 — 15.8g 9g 10.6s 10.6s³ 12f 15fg 13.8fg 1982 8.2s 11fg 12.2f 10fg 15.8f 10fg) poor plater; stays 1¾m; acts on any going; usually wears blinkers. *Mrs M. Nesbitt.*

BOREHAM DOWN 3 b.g. High Top 131–Woodwind 103 (Whistling Wind 60 123) (1981 5g 7g 7g 7fg 1982 12fg 12fg 10s*) big, rangy gelding; 20/1-winner of handicap at Chepstow in October; stays 1¼m; acts on soft going; sold to M. Lambert 10,000 gns Doncaster November Sales. *W. Hastings-Bass.*

BORN HERO 3 br.c. Blakeney 126–Regal Lady 93 (Relko 136) (1981 8g* 109 1982 11.1fg 14.6f 10g) robust, attractive colt; fairly impressive winner of maiden race at Newmarket in 1981; not seen out until autumn at 3 yrs (chipped a bone in knee early in year) and put up best effort when leading for 1m and coming home 6 lengths sixth of 7 to Critique in September Stakes at Kempton; well beaten in St Leger at Doncaster and Tia Maria Autumn Handicap at Newmarket afterwards; will be suited by 1½m+. *H. Candy.*

BORN TO STAR 2 b.f. Jimsun 121–Dapple (Jukebox 120) (1982 5f 7g — 7f 7f 7f 8.2d 7d) Apr 19; strong filly; bad plater; blinkered final outing. *Hbt. Jones.*

BOSSANOVA BOY 3 b.c. Rhodomantade 110–Samba 69 (Sammy Davis 129) **67**
(1981 7d 1982 8d 7f* 8f 8g⁴ 10g 10.2d 10d2) lightly-built colt; bought in
5,200 gns after winning seller at Doncaster in May; ran respectably in better
company several subsequent starts; stays 1¼m well; yet to race on very soft going
but acts on any other; ran well in blinkers final start. *P. Makin.*

BOSSEY 2 br.g. Oats 126–Sinful 72 (Grey Sovereign 128§) (1982 8g 6d) Apr —
29; IR 5,400Y; half-brother to numerous winners here and abroad, including
very useful sprinter Adams Pet (by Super Sam); dam ran only at 2 yrs; showed
early speed in maiden race at Beverley and minor event at Catterick in the
autumn. *J. Berry.*

BOTANIST 9 ch.g. Ballymoss 136–Larkspur's Love (Larkspur 128) (1981 NR —
1982 16g 14f 16fg) staying handicapper; lightly raced and no form since 1980;
acts on a soft surface, but has done most of his winning on a firm one; good
mount for an apprentice. *G. Balding.*

BOTH ENDS BURNING (USA) 2 b.g. Nalees Man–Star Game (Pia Star) **90**
(1982 6f 5d2 6f*) Apr 18; $15,000F; lengthy, useful-looking gelding; good
walker; second foal; half-brother to a minor winner in USA; dam third once at 3
yrs; favourite all starts, eventually justifying support when making all to win 11-
runner maiden race at Lingfield in July by 2 lengths from Sedra; gelded after;
suited by 6f and will stay further; seems to act on any going. *H. Candy.*

BOTTESFORD BOY 2 b.g. Record Token 128–Facetious 88 (Malicious) (1982 **92**
5f³ 5fg* 5fg² 7f 5d* 5g³ 6g) May 9; 2,000Y; robust, strong gelding; first foal;
dam disappointing maiden; won 6-runner maiden auction event at Carlisle in
June and 8-runner nursery at Chester in August; best at 5f. *H. Wharton.*

BOTTISHAM 4 ch.c. Moulton 128–Relkalim 102 (Relko 136) (1981 10.5s 8.2s⁴ —
7d 8f³ 8fg³ 8fg 8d 8d 1982 8f 8fg 10.1d) robust, short-legged colt; plater
nowadays; should stay at least 1¼m; seems suited by a sound surface. *W.
Marshall.*

BOUGIE 3 ch.f. Bustino 136–Catherine Wheel 116 (Roan Rocket 128) (1981 **73**
NR 1982 12fg⁴ 12fg 12g 10.1fg² 10.1fg² 10f³ 10.1fg* 10fg 11.5g³) small filly;
half-sister to 2 winners, including Cheshire Oaks winner Hunston (by Blakeney),
also a good winner in USA; dam, smart and tough, stayed at least 1¼m; stayed
on strongly to win minor event at Windsor in August from Singleton; gives
impression she'll be suited by 1¾m; sold 92,000 gns Newmarket December Sales.
B. Hobbs.

BOUKAYR 3 b.g. Kouban–Busarella (Busted 134) (1981 6fg 6g 7fg⁴ 8d2 **71**
1982 12g 12s³ 16f² 17f⁴ 16fg³ 16d3) small gelding; quite a moderate staying
maiden; seems to act on any going; blinkered fourth start; has run creditably for
an apprentice; sold privately after final start and is to be trained by P. K.
Mitchell. *F. J. Houghton.*

BOUNTY BAY 3 b.f. Pitcairn 126–Hark Hark 75 (Sing Sing 134) (1981 5d³ **65**
6s 1982 8fg 7fg⁴ 7.6fg 7d 7fg³ 7f 7.6d* 8f* 8s) smallish filly; all out to win
maiden race at Chester and 5-runner minor event at Brighton in summer; suited
by 1m; seems to act on any going; has run creditably in blinkers. *I. Balding.*

BOURGEONETTE 3 b.f. Mummy's Pet 125–Enlighten (Twilight Alley 133) **81**
(1981 7g² 7g 7f² 7fg³ 1982 9f² 10.2g 8fg* 8fg⁴ 10d* 10d² 10d) smallish,
lengthy filly; won maiden race at Ayr and handicap at Ripon; suited by 1¼m;
acts on any going; blinkered third and fourth starts, sweating up on second
occasion; has run creditably for an apprentice. *G. Pritchard-Gordon.*

BOURIENNE 4 b.f. Bolkonski 134–Blanche Hardy (Ribot 142) (1981 8s 9s 8g² —
8g 8f 9fg² 10h⁴ 9g* 10s⁴ 8s* 7g 1982 8g³ 8d 8fg 8s) small, lightly-made filly;
plater; stays 1¼m; acts on any going; blinkered final start. *D. H. Jones.*

BOURNEMOUTH BELLE 2 ch.f. Roan Rocket 128–Sand Valley 61 (Arabian) —
(1982 10s) Apr 27; half-sister to a minor winner in USA; dam won 3 sellers at
around 1¼m; unquoted, behind in 16-runner maiden race at Nottingham in
October. *W. Turner.*

BOUTADE 2 b.f. Bold Lad (Ire) 133–Turiana (Citation) (1982 6g 6g⁴ 6f 7.6v **76**
7d) Apr 8; 64,000Y; neat, quite attractive filly; half-sister to winning stayer On
Her Own (by Busted); dam, winner at up to 7f, is half-sister to Kentucky Derby
winner Forward Pass; quite a moderate maiden; form only at 6f, but should
stay further. *B. Hobbs.*

BOWIE BOY 2 b.g. Tachypous 128–Miss Poker Face (Raise You Ten 125) —
(1982 6g) Mar 5; 2,200F, IR 7,600Y; third produce; dam fairly useful hurdler;

14/1, showed early pace when twelfth of 22 to Riverside Artist in minor event at Nottingham in July; should be suited by 7f+. *O. Brennan.*

BOWTHATCH 3 br.g. Thatch 136–Sally Bowles 87 (Blakeney 126) (1981 7g — 7g 8s 1982 10d) compact gelding; behind in sizeable fields of maidens; sold 440 gns Doncaster September Sales. *D. Dale.*

BOXBERGER DREAM (HOL) 3 ch.f. My Swanee 122–Dolphinetta 88 (Gulf ? Pearl 117) (1981 6fg 6.5g* 9fg⁴ 1982 10d* 9g* 12fg⁴ 12fg) lengthy, work-manlike filly; successful twice in Dutch 1,000 Guineas in May on second start (beat stable-companion Boxberger Beauty by 1½ lengths); modest fourth of 10 to Cool Decision in amateur riders race at Hamilton in June; possibly stays 1½m; refused to enter stalls intended final outing. *M. Ryan.*

BOXBERGER MELODY (HOL) 2 br.f. Swing Easy 126–Montespan 83 ? (Roi Soleil 125) (1982 5fg 5d³ 6.5g³ 9g⁴) half-sister to 3-y-o Boxberger River (by Ercolano); dam stayed 1m; in frame 3 times in Holland after finishing in rear in maiden race at Windsor in August. *M. Ryan.*

BOXBERGER OSCAR (HOL) 2 ch.c. Filandre–Nancy (Compromise 109) **105** (1982 5fg 6f⁴ 7g 7f² 5d* 6.5g* 9g²) Feb 21; strong, well-developed Dutch-bred colt; dam won 1972 Dutch Oaks and St Leger; won Van Brienens Memoriaal at Duindigt in August by ¾ length and Clingendaalren on same course in September by ½ length, beating Wouter Raaphorst both times; went down by 1½ lengths to same horse in Dutch Criterium in October; had earlier shown useful form over 7f in this country; should stay well. *M. Ryan.*

BOXBERGER RELKO (HOL) 4 br.c. Filandre–Head High 92 (Star Gazer 123) — (1981 10fg 9g² 10f 14.5g 14g 10.7d² 1982 12.5g 14f² 10s³ 12d 9.5s⁴) Dutch-bred colt; fair sort; little worthwhile form here when trained by M. Ryan; stays 11f. *J. Ives, Holland.*

BOXBERGER RIVER 3 b.c. Ercolano 118–Montespan 83 (Roi Soleil 125) ? (1981 6g 5g 5.1d 1982 10.1fg 9g 14f 5fg 12fg) sturdy, compact colt; soundly beaten in varied company, including selling, in England but has won over 9f in Holland; has worn blinkers. *M. Ryan.*

BOXBERGER SPEED (HOL) 3 b.c. Lombard 126–Alison's My Girl 77 **109** (Appiani II 128) (1981 6g 5g* 6.5g² 9fg* 1982 10.4fg³ 9g* 12fg² 11g 12fg* 14.5d*) strong colt; second foal; dam won 1¼m seller at 2 yrs; won 3 classics in Holland, namely 2,000 Guineas, Derby (from Aiglon) and St Leger (beat stable-companion Boxberger Beauty); placed twice over here, running well to be 2¾ lengths third of 11 to Ivano in Dee Stakes at Chester; stays 1¾m; acts on a firm and a soft surface. *M. Ryan.*

BOXBERGER TAMARA (HOL) 2 ch.f. Shiny Tenth 120–Alison's My — Girl 77 (Appiani II 128) (1982 7d 6.5g 9g) Mar 25; well-grown, close-coupled, plain filly; third foal; half-sister to useful 3-y-o Boxberger Speed (by Lombard) winner of 3 Dutch classics; dam won 1¼m seller at 2 yrs; 50/1 and ridden by 7-lb claimer, missed break when last of 15 behind Muznah in maiden race at Yarmouth in August; well beaten in Holland subsequently. *M. Ryan.*

BOXBERGER TRIX (HOL) 2 ch.f. Mount Hagen 127–Lady Alpha (St — Alphage 119) (1982 5.1f) Mar 28; second foal; dam won small 5.5f race in France at 2 yrs; 7/2 but rather in need of race, showed up 3f when 13 lengths fifth of 8 finishers behind Key Wind in maiden race at Yarmouth in June; may be capable of better. *M. Ryan.*

BOX THREE RANGERS 2 b.f. Blue Cashmere 129–Yorkist (Crepello 136) — (1982 7fg) Apr 19; 1,000Y; half-sister to 2 minor winners; dam unraced sister to very useful middle-distance performer Donello; 8/1 when in rear in 15-runner seller won by Viceroy Princess at Chepstow in September. *A. Ingham.*

BOXWOOD LADY 2 br.f. Porto Bello 118–Curry Favour 82 (Negotiation) **54** (1982 6fg 7fg 7fg 7fg⁴ 8d) Apr 3; workmanlike filly; half-sister to 3-y-o Bombili and 1978 2-y-o 5f winner Foul Fella (both by Native Bazaar); 4½ lengths fourth of 15 to Viceroy Princess in seller at Chepstow in September, best effort; not sure to stay 1m. *M. Blanshard.*

BOYD'S PRIDE 2 b.g. Tudor Rhythm 112–River Bell 72 (Divine Gift 127) **44** (1982 5f 5fg 6f 7f 6fg 6g 8d 8.2s 8d) Apr 15; plain gelding; poor form, including in sellers; stays 1m. *T. Craig.*

BOY LEIGH 3 ch.g. Music Boy 124–Playbird (My Swallow 134) (1981 5d — 5g 5fg 1982 6d 6f 7fg 6f 5h 5fg 5f 6fg) sprint plater. *P. K. Mitchell.*

BOY PIPER 3 br.c. Bold Lad (Ire) 133–Pipeline 85 (Gulf Pearl 117) (1981 **65** 6g 1982 8fg 8fg 8g³ 8f⁴ 7fg 7.3g 8s) good-bodied colt; not the best of movers; plating-class maiden; will stay 1¼m; has worn bandages in front; blinkered sixth start; sold to M. Haynes 720 gns Newmarket Autumn Sales. *F. J. Houghton.*

BOY SANDFORD 3 br.g. Sandford Lad 133–Perldia (Diatome 132) (1981 — 5v² 5g 6g 6g 5f 7fg 6fg 1982 6g 6fg 8g 8fg) poor plater. *H. Bell.*

BOY TRUMPETER 2 ro.c. Music Boy 124–La Magna 104 (Runnymede **101** 123) (1982 5fg³ 5fg* 5g³ 5.3g* 6s² 5d*) May 7; 7,200Y; smallish, strong, compact, sturdy colt; very good walker; third foal; brother to good French 3-y-o sprinter Kind Music; dam won twice over 5f at 2 yrs; won maiden race at Windsor and minor events at Brighton and Doncaster; also ran well when 1¼ lengths third to Cat O'Nine Tails in Prince of Wales's Stakes at York in August on third outing and when 2 lengths second (finished very tired after leading for 5f) to Domynsky in Marston Moor Stakes on same course in October; likely to prove best at 5f; probably acts on any going; a likeable individual who should go on and make a very useful 3-y-o. *B. Hobbs.*

BRACADALE 4 b.g. The Brianstan 128–Can't Wait (Eudaemon 129) (1981 **94** 6fg 6f⁴ 6fg* 6g* 5g⁴ 6f 1982 6fg 6fg* 6f² 6g⁴ 6s⁴ 6f* 6f² 6f* 6g 6d² 6g) neat, good-quartered gelding; good mover; successful in handicaps at Goodwood in May (apprentice event), Kempton in July (apprentice ridden) and Brighton in August; second on 3 other occasions, including to Soba in William Hill Stewards' Cup at Goodwood on seventh outing; best form at 6f; acts on a soft surface but is particularly well suited by a firm one; usually held up; best in blinkers in 1981, but didn't wear them in 1982; sent to race in USA. *R. Armstrong.*

BRACKEN GILL 4 gr.c. Ribston 104–Gill Breeze (Farm Walk 111) (1981 **43** 6g 5fg 1982 6s 6s 6fg 7f 5fg 5f³ 6fg 6g 5fg* 5g⁴ 5g) plater; 4-length winner of amateur riders handicap at Edinburgh in July; none too consistent earlier; should stay 6f; best form on a sound surface; blinkered last 3 outings. *Mrs A. Bell.*

BRADAMANTE 6 ch.h. Royal Prerogative 119–Cracker 103 (Court Harwell — 130) (1981 7d 10.4g 8g 10fg* 10fg 11g 1982 10f 11.7g 8g) tall, leggy horse; behind in handicaps in 1982; stayed 1¼m; possibly not at his best on really soft going; inconsistent; sold out of D. Smith's stable 2,000 gns Newmarket July Sales after first outing; dead. *W. Marshall.*

BRADY 3 gr.g. Pitcairn 126–Brenda (Sovereign Path 125) (1981 8g 6g 1982 **111** 8g² 8.2fg² 8g* 10.1fg² 10fg* 10g* 10f* 10f* 12f⁴ 10.5g* 11.7d* 10fg³ 10g² 10g⁴)

Garrowby Stakes, York—Brady runs on well to defeat Dreaming Away (noseband) and Rajhaan (left)

good-bodied gelding; had a splendid year, winning maiden race at Pontefract, handicaps at Newmarket, Kempton, Leicester, Yarmouth and York and £3,900 event at Windsor; gained last 2 successes in September, holding off Dreaming Away by ½ length in Garrowby Stakes at York and accounting for Lafontaine by 1½ lengths at Windsor; ran creditably most other starts; seems to find 1½m too far in a strongly-run race; yet to race on very soft going but acts on any other; has a good turn of foot and is suited by waiting tactics; tough, genuine and consistent and a credit to his trainer; sent to race in Florida. *M. Ryan.*

BRAE TOP 3 ch.g. Import 127–Taj Jahan 77 (Hornbeam 130) (1981 6g 6fg 6g 8g 1982 10d 10f 12.2f 9g 12fg) strong gelding; poor plater; has been blinkered; has worn a bandage on off-fore. *M. W. Easterby.* —

BRANCH LINE 2 ch.c. Dom Racine 121–Sapling 78 (Hornbeam 130) (1982 7fg*) May 15; 19,000Y; half-brother to 2 winners, including useful 1974 2-y-o 7f and 1m winner Estructura (by Gulf Pearl); dam won over 13f and is half-sister to smart miler Prince Midge; did well to win 13-runner maiden race at Leopardstown in August on only start, getting up close home to beat Stirabout a short head after having to be switched in closing stages; had rest well beaten off and should make a useful colt over middle distances. *E. O'Grady, Ireland.* **92 p**

BRANDING IRON 5 ch.g. Hotfoot 126–Caesar's Love 85 (Above Suspicion 127) (1981 NR 1982 16fg 12f4) lengthy gelding; winner over hurdles; lightly-raced maiden on flat; stays 1¼m (had stiff task over 2m). *I. Balding.* —

BRANDO 5 ch.h. Busted 134–Cafe au Lait 97 (Espresso 122) (1981 16s 1982 16fg) leggy, lightly-made horse; fairly useful stayer at 3 yrs; respectable sixth to Radfield in amateur riders handicap at Chepstow in August, only second outing since; probably acted on any going; stud. *G. Thorner.* —

BRANDON CREEK 3 b.f. Be My Guest 126–La Creperie 70 (Crepello 136) (1981 7g2 7g 1982 7fg4 7g 7g 10g2 11d 12f* 11.7s) neat filly; narrowly won 5-runner apprentice handicap at Brighton in September; suited by 1¼m; acts on firm going and is probably unsuited by soft; has twice worn blinkers (ran creditably on first occasion but poorly on second); sold 14,000 gns Newmarket December Sales. *P. Cole.* **68**

BRANKSOME TOWERS 2 b.f. Hotfoot 126–Let Slip 77 (Busted 134) (1982 5fg* 5f 5fg 5g4 5d3 5d) Apr 3; 6,200Y; leggy, quite useful sort; first foal; dam showed some ability at 2 yrs; won 4-runner minor event at Newmarket in May by 2½ lengths from Paddock Princess; in frame subsequently in nurseries at Lingfield in August and Wolverhampton (favourite when 4 lengths third of 10 to Blue Times) in October; evidently thought best at 5f but is bred to stay a good deal further; acts on a firm and a soft surface. *E. Eldin.* **80**

BRANSDALE 2 ch.g. Anax 120–Radio City (Bleep-Bleep 134) (1982 5fg 6g) Apr 23; workmanlike gelding; half-brother to 2 winners, including very useful 6f and 7f winner Welsh City (by Maestoso); no sign of ability in sellers at Nottingham (heavily-backed favourite) in April and Haydock (last of 10 after moving badly to start) in July. *D. Garraton.* —

BRAVADO (GER) 3 b.c. Alpenkonig–Babylon (Priamos 123) (1981 6fg4 6g* 6f2 7g* 1982 10f4 10g 10fg2 10g 10g4 10g 10d4) compact, workmanlike colt; quite a modest handicapper; will be suited by 1½m; best form on a sound surface; ran moderately in blinkers fourth start. *M. Stoute.* **90 d**

BRAVE BRIDGE 3 b.g. Jolly Me 114–Spaniard's Darling (Darling Boy 124) (1981 8g 1982 10f 12fg 14fg 15.8f4 12fg 16s 12g) quite attractive gelding; well beaten in varied company; blinkered last 2 starts. *Miss L. Siddall.* —

BRAVE IVY 2 b.f. Decoy Boy 129–Mauritania 74 (The Brianstan 128) (1982 5fg 6f 5fg2 5g2 5f2 6fg 6fg4 6fg 5fg 5fg 7d) May 9; 2,500F, 3,000Y; small filly; good walker; second foal; dam placed at up to 1m; plating-class maiden; stays 6f, but best form at 5f; acts on firm going; lost chance at start when blinkered ninth outing; sold 2,000 gns Newmarket Autumn Sales. *A. Bailey.* **68**

BRAVE MAIDEN 3 gr.f. Three Legs 128–Julie's Gi-Gi (Brave Invader) (1981 5g3 5s 5d 6f4 7g3 8.2fg2(dis) 8d 1982 10g* 12.2g3 12f2 12f3 12fg3 16.5g2 15.8d 16fg 16d2 16s 16s) lightly-made filly; plater; bought in 1,500 gns after winning at Pontefract in April; placed in better company most subsequent starts; stays well; seems to act on any going; effective with or without blinkers. *J. Bethell.* **61**

BRAVE MEMORY (USA) 2 b.c. Crow 134–Out Of The Past (Olden Times) (1982 7f2 8d3) lengthy colt; half-brother to winners in USA by Noholme II and Nashua; dam, winner of 2 sprint races, is half-sister to high-class Italian colt **96**

Laomedonte; led early in straight and gave odds-on Polished Silver an excellent fight before going down by ½ length in 13-runner Chertsey Lock Stakes at Kempton in September; looked to be going extremely well 2f out when favourite for maiden race at Newmarket the following month but didn't find a great deal under pressure and was beaten 3¾ lengths into third place behind The Liquidator; stays 1m. *J. Hindley.*

BRAVE SONG 3 b.g. Busted 134–Net Call 108 (Song 132) (1981 7fg 7g 7d 1982 10d 12f 13.3f 14d 10.1g 12g) rangy gelding; poor walker; plating-class maiden; best run at 13.3f on firm going; has worn a tongue strap; sold 875 gns Ascot September Sales. *J. Bethell.* —

BRAZEN BID 3 b.f. Auction Ring 123–Parmassia (Pampered King 121) (1981 6s⁴ 5fg 6g 1982 8d 10.4d 12d 15.8d) small, lengthy filly; only plating class; not sure to stay 1½m; best run on soft going; sold 1,200 gns Newmarket Autumn Sales. *B. Hanbury.* —

BREATHING EXERCISE 9 ch.g. Pall Mall 132–Karen Chase 82 (Will Somers 114§) (1981 6s 7d 8d 7g 8v 7fg 7.6g 1982 8g) poor handicapper nowadays; stays 7f; acts on any going; has been tried in blinkers; occasionally sweats up. *J. O'Donoghue.* —

BREEZE HILL 3 b.c. Swing Easy 126–Jester's Girl 71 (Will Somers 114§) (1981 7fg⁴ 7fg³ 7g³ 7d 1982 8d* 7g³ 7g⁴ 10.2f2 12d 8fg 8f) rangy colt; very good mover; favourite when winning 16-runner maiden race at Warwick in April; placed in 2 handicaps afterwards, one of them an apprentice event; stays 1¼m; seems to act on any going; looked light and finished well beaten last 2 starts. *P. Cole.* **75** d

BREEZY GLEN 2 b.g. Furry Glen 121–What A Breeze (Whistling Wind 123) (1982 6f 7fg) May 15; 6,200Y; strong, rangy gelding; good walker; third reported foal; half-brother to fairly useful Irish 3-y-o Mistral Man (by Sweet Revenge), successful at up to 7f; dam in rear in maiden and minor events; not fully wound up, showed no form in maiden events at Newbury in June and Yarmouth (speed 4f) in July; gelded subsequently; has plenty of scope. *A. Jarvis.* —

BRENDAN'S CHOICE 2 ch.c. Flashback 102–Dumette 89 (Dumbarnie 125) (1982 6g 6s) Mar 13; second foal; brother to a poor animal; dam won over 7f and also over hurdles; behind in maiden race at Folkestone in June and claiming event at Nottingham in October. *A. Davison.* —

BRENHINES 3 b.f. Mount Hagen 127–Gay Surrender 70 (Sir Gaylord) (1981 5g 6f 8fg 1982 8g 11f 10f 7f 7s) lightly-made, short-backed filly; poor maiden; sold 4,100 gns Newmarket Autumn Sales. *D. Arbuthnot.* —

BRENIN 7 gr.h. King's Company 124–Cool Melody 65 (Right Boy 137) (1981 NR 1982 12d) lightly raced and disappointing maiden; has worn blinkers. *Dr A. Jones.* —

BRENTEX 4 gr.c. Birdbrook 110–Black Mink 83 (Gratitude 130) (1981 6g 5.8g 5.8g 5f 5g 1982 6fg 5d* 5fg² 5g⁴ 5f³ 5fg 5g 5g 5fg⁴ 5fg⁴ 5.8f³ 5s² 5d 5s² 6s³ 5s) neat colt; sprint handicapper; won at Warwick in April and was placed on several other occasions; shade disappointing sixth and seventh starts; appears to act on any going; occasionally blinkered as a 2-y-o; suited by waiting tactics. *N. Vigors.* **69**

BRETON BANQUET 4 gr.g. Brittany–Nosh (Court Martial) (1981 7s 8s 8g 7g 8.3s 6g³ 8fg 6g* 1982 8.2s 6g 7f 8f 10g 8.3fg 6f² 6g⁴ 8f² 10fg⁴ 8d 8.3g 7g) plater; poor walker and mover; stays 1¼m; often blinkered. *W. Marshall.* **43**

BRETTON PARK 4 b.c. Mummy's Pet 125–Trickster 92 (Major Portion 129) (1981 6g 7.2s 6s* 6f 6f* 7g 7g 1982 6s 7f 8f 8f 8f 8fg 8fg² 8f) strong, fair sort; has a round action; showed only form of year when second in handicap at Carlisle in June; stays 1m; acts on any going but goes particularly well on soft; often blinkered (has worn them when successful); ungenuine; sold 900 gns Newmarket Autumn Sales. *S. Norton.* **§§**

BREVET 3 b.c. Busted 134–Major Barbara 90 (Tambourine II 133) (1981 7g 1982 9fg 10f² 13.3f* 13.3f²) most attractive colt; good walker; quickened up well once he found an opening to beat Deroulede by ¾ length going away in 19-runner maiden race at Newbury in June; improved on that effort when keeping on to be 3 lengths second of 9 to Abdoun in Morland Brewery Trophy (Handicap) on same course in July; not seen out again; will stay 1¾m; has run well on firm **102**

going but gives distinct impression he may do even better on easier ground; useful. *P. Walwyn.*

BREWMASTER 9 br.h. John Splendid 116–Ronelda (Tyrone 130) (1981 10g —
1982 8.2g) poor plater; stays 1¼m; acts on any going; blinkered once; often apprentice ridden. *J. Mulhall.*

BRIANS BRIDGE 3 b.f. The Brianstan 128–Villa Vera (Gilles de Retz 132) **42**
(1981 5g 5s 1982 5f 6f* 5g 6g⁴ 6fg) plater; attracted no bid after winning at Ripon in June; suited by 6f; acts on firm going; has been unruly in paddock. *Miss L. Siddall.*

BRIANS NIPPER 2 br.f. The Brianstan 128–Gay Nipper 70 (Aggressor 130) —
(1982 5g 5.8g 5.3f 6fg 7g) May 15; neat filly; half-sister to 1981 2-y-o 6f winner Gayonara (by Dragonara Palace); dam won over 9f; in rear in varied company, including selling; sometimes starts slowly. *M. Blanshard.*

BRIAN'S STAR 7 br.h. The Brianstan 128–Claral Star 71 (Top Star 96) **46** d
(1981 5s 5s 5g*(dis) 5fg⁴ 5g⁴ 5g* 5fg 5fg 5g⁴ 5d² 5fg³ 5f 5g³ 1982 5d 5fg 5f 5g* 5f 5fg 5g⁴ 5g 5f) workmanlike horse; won apprentice handicap at Edinburgh in May; ran respectably next time; best form at 5f on a sound surface; usually wears blinkers; good mount for an apprentice. *A. Balding.*

BRIAVAN 2 br.f. Saulingo 122–Miss Season (Silly Season 127) (1982 5s³ **71**
5fg² 6f⁴ 5.8g³ 5fg 5d 5s 6g) May 13; IR 2,500Y; small filly; fifth foal; dam never ran; plating-class maiden; stays 6f; seems to act on any going; blinkered sixth and seventh outings. *M. McCourt.*

BRIDLE ROAD 2 b.f. Free State 125–Meadow's Alley (St Paddy 133) (1982 —
8f 7g) May 31; sister to 1981 2-y-o 6f winner Dev, and half-sister to several winners; dam never ran; well behind in maiden race and a seller in the Midlands in the autumn. *W. Wharton.*

Bovis Handicap Stakes, Ascot—Bri-Eden gains his seventh win of the season

BRI-EDEN 8 b.g. The Brianstan 128–Dainty Eden 53 (Orbit 106) (1981 **100**
5fg³ 5g 5g 5g 5s 5g 1982 5g⁴ 5fg 5fg 5f* 5fg³ 5f 5g* 5fg* 5f* 5g² 5fg² 5g* 5g⁴
5f* 5fg³ 5v*) sprint handicapper; has reportedly had a soft palate operation
and been fired; had an excellent year and was better than ever; goes well at
Wolverhampton, and won there in May, June and July; subsequently successful
at Catterick (trainers race, easily), Epsom, Edinburgh and Ascot, beating
Singing Sailor in good style by 5 lengths in Bovis Stakes on last-named in October;
best at 5f; acts on any going; has won for an amateur rider; often wears bandages;
thoroughly game and genuine, and a credit to his trainer. *J. Berry.*

BRIGADIER GREEN 5 b.g. Brigadier Gerard 144–Queen's Parole (Worden —
II 129) (1981 10v 11s 9fg 13d⁴ 12s 13d 1982 12f³ 10.6f 12d 10f 15.8f³) neat
gelding; poor handicapper; stays well; probably acts on any going; ran badly in
blinkers once in 1980. *J. Blundell.*

BRIGADIER HAWK 4 b.c. Brigadier Gerard 144–Flibbertigibbet 97 (Klairon **81 §**
131) (1981 11s 10d³ 10.5s² 12f 14fg* 11g 14.6g 12g² 16s 1982 12d 14f² 16fg
16fg 12f 12fg 12g⁴ 10g 12fg* 14f⁴ 12g 11.7g 14.6g 12d 12s) compact, good-
bodied colt; beat Grand Maitre by 2½ lengths in modestly-contested £4,500
handicap at Ascot in July (held up and was driven out without rider resorting
to whip); has quite often faced stiff tasks; suited by 1¾m; probably acts on any
going; blinkered fifth and sixth starts; races with tongue tied down nowadays;
ran poorly last 5 starts and is none too genuine. *C. Brittain.*

BRIGADO 3 ch.f. Brigadier Gerard 144–Selham 71 (Derring-Do 131) (1981 **75**
5f 6fg 8g* 1982 7g⁴ 8f 9g² 8f³ 9g⁴ 9.4fg 9g³ 9g⁴ 10.4d² 10d) tall filly; in frame
in varied company; stays 1¼m; seems to act on any going; blinkered seventh
start; suitable mount for an apprentice. *D. Smith.*

BRIGHT CONE (USA) 2 gr.f. Giacometti 130–Lovelight 112 (Bleep-Bleep **98**
134) (1982 5fg² 6g* 6f 7fg 8g 6s³ 7d*) Feb 23; big, well-made, quite attractive
filly; good walker; half-sister to disappointing 3-y-o Flicker to a Flame (by
Empery) and very smart 5f to 1m winner Motavato (by Apalachee); dam very
game sprinter; won maiden race at Doncaster in June by a short head from
Super Entente and small race at Catterick in October by a length from Grey
Desire; not disgraced when taking on good-class fillies in between; stays 1m;
appears to act on any going. *B. Hills.*

BRIGHT CROCUS (USA) 2 b.f. Clev Er Tell–Bold Saffron (Bold Hour) **119**
(1982 5fg² 6f* 6g* 6f⁴ 6fg³ 7g⁴ 8g* 8g)
    Henry Cecil told Timeform subscribers before Royal Ascot that Bright
Crocus could 'definitely go a bit' and that she was his fourth- or fifth-top two-
year-old at the time. Perhaps because he felt he had some better fillies for
later on, or perhaps because she didn't appear to possess a great deal of scope
—we described her early in the season as rather leggy, short-backed, as well as
quite attractive—Cecil made hay with Bright Crocus while the sun shone.
She was soon in action and was kept busy. She was the first of the stable's
team of over ninety juveniles to appear and by early-August she had had six
races. Unluckily beaten by Henry's Secret at Windsor in May first time out
Bright Crocus won on her next two appearances, both in fairly valuable events.
After breaking the course record for two-year-olds in great style in the Kingsclere Stakes at Newbury she made full use of her experience against the newcomer Key Tothe Minstrel in the Dance In Time Stakes at Newmarket, rallying
well to score by a length. But when she took on better fillies she was beaten.
In the Cherry Hinton Stakes at Newmarket she finished only fourth, three
and a half lengths behind Crime of Passion; in the Princess Margaret Stakes
at Ascot she faded quickly after leading to the distance and was beaten just
over two and a half lengths into third place behind Royal Heroine; and in the
Sweet Solera Stakes she finished fourth, beaten two lengths by Flamenco,
after swerving badly at the start. Misbehaviour at the start had been a regular
feature of Bright Crocus' appearances and on her third start she had fallen
after rearing over backwards while being loaded into the stalls.
    As autumn approached one might have expected Bright Crocus to be over-
taken by some of the late-developing Cecil fillies but, significantly, when the
runners were declared for the May Hill Stakes at Doncaster it was Bright Crocus
who had been chosen to represent the stable. The May Hill was her first
race for nearly five weeks and she seemed to have benefited both mentally and
physically from her brief break: she gave no trouble at the stalls and, although
still by no means a robust individual, she appeared to have put on some weight.
Bright Crocus' performance was also that of a much improved filly. Piggott

May Hill Stakes, Doncaster—Bright Crocus is well clear of the second horse Silk Pyjamas

rode a masterly race, bouncing her out of the stalls and quickly taking a three-length advantage. After allowing the field to close on her at halfway, he asked Bright Crocus to quicken again coming to the final quarter mile and she quickly shot clear, stretching out impressively to win by five lengths from Silk Pyjamas. Three quarters of a length back in third place came Goodbye Shelley, showing nothing like the form she later produced on soft ground to win the Prix Marcel Boussac. Fourth place went to Acclimatise, who had tailed herself off in the early stages.

The May Hill established that Bright Crocus had few equals among the staying two-year-old fillies and she started favourite for the Hoover Fillies Mile at Ascot a fortnight later. Sadly she trailed in last behind Acclimatise after breaking blood vessels, and her racing career is probably now at an end. She has been sent to Florida in the hope that she will make a complete recovery with the help of the sun. If she does recover it is hoped to return her to England to take her chance in the One Thousand Guineas; if not she will be mated to a leading American stallion. Her future will have been decided by the time this Annual is published.

Bright Crocus (USA) (b.f. Mar 20, 1980)	Clev Er Tell (b 1974)	Tell (b 1966)	Round Table
			Nas-Mahal
		Clever Bird (b 1970)	Swoon's Son
			Sally Catbird
	Bold Saffron (b 1971)	Bold Hour (br 1964)	Bold Ruler
			Seven Thirty
		Meadow Saffron (b 1964)	High Perch
			Meadow Music

Bright Crocus was very well bought for 62,000 dollars as a yearling at the Keeneland Fall Sales. Her sire, Clev Er Tell, isn't well known over here but he was a very good colt; after winning four six-furlong races at the Fair Grounds track as a two-year-old 'he developed into a leading three-year-old, winning two important nine-furlong events, the Arkansas Derby and the Louisiana Derby. He evidently wasn't easy to train though, managing only five starts in each of his first two seasons and then only two (unplaced) at four. Bright Crocus belongs to Clev Er Tell's first crop, as do the American stakes winners How Clever and Say I'm Smart. Bright Crocus comes from a family which has produced several notable European performers. Her great-grandam Meadow Music, a winning daughter of the high-class Argentinian and American mare Miss Grillo, produced nine winners in Britain and Ireland. Meadow Saffron, an Irish mile-and-a-quarter winner, was one of them as was Meadow Court, the runner-up to Sea-Bird II in the 1965 Derby who later won the Irish Sweeps Derby and the King George VI and Queen Elizabeth Stakes. Meadow Saffron was retired to stud in the USA. She has bred five winners, including the 1976 One Thousand Guineas third Kesar Queen, who won the Coronation Stakes, and Bold Saffron, the winner of three sprint races from thirty-seven starts. Bright Crocus is the third winner from Bold Saffron's first tour foals. Her fifth foal, a colt by Poker who was bought for 110,000 dollars at the 1982 Keeneland September Yearling Sales, is now in training with Cecil.

In the unlikely event of Bright Crocus being returned to training, she will probably stay a mile and a quarter. She is a good mover with a smooth action and acts well on fast ground; she has never raced on a soft surface. *H. Cecil.*

BRIGHT HONEY 2 ch.f. Duc D'Orleans 76–Honey Bright 80 (Right Boy 137) —
(1982 5g 7g) Feb 27; small, strong filly; first reported foal; dam best at up to
9f; burly when tailed off in sellers in August and October. *B. Richmond.*

BRIGHT IMP 3 ch.f. Import 127–Star of Light 85 (Counsel 118) (1981 5f 6d **55**
5d³ 1982 6fg 5fg 7d* 8g⁴ 7f² 7.2f 8fg 7s 8g) fair sort; narrowly won 19-
runner handicap at Doncaster in June; stays 1m; acts on firm going but is better
with some give in the ground. *P. Calver.*

BRIGHTON ROAD 3 ch.g. Gulf Pearl 117–Gossamer Wings 73 (The Phoenix) **78**
(1981 7g 8g 8g 1982 8.5fg* 10v³ 10s⁴ 8fg 9fg³ 9f² 10fg² 10fg⁴) strong gelding;
won small race at Cagnes-sur-Mer in spring; placed most subsequent starts; would
have been suited by 1¼m; acted on any going; changed hands 10,500 gns
Newmarket July Sales; dead. *R. Armstrong.*

BRIGHT SPIRIT 2 br.c. Quiet Fling 124–Liberation 63 (Native Prince) (1982 **67**
6fg³ 6s) Apr 21; 4,600F, 8,200Y; fourth live foal; half-brother to 2 winners,
including 1978 2-y-o 6f winner Maryoma (by Rheingold), subsequently successful
abroad; dam half-sister to good sprinter Tudor Grey; plating-class maiden;
placed in newcomers' race at Chepstow in August; will be suited by 7f+. *R.
Baker.*

BRIGHT VIEW 3 ch.f. Hot Spark 126–Gilliflower 90 (Great Nephew 126) **94**
(1981 5d 5g² 5g* 6g² 5fg* 5f³ 6f³ 6f² 5g* 1982 7d³ 7fg 6f 6f 5f) tall filly;
weakened close home when 3 lengths third of 10 to Rose of Montreaux in
Salisbury 1,000 Guineas Trial in April; behind all subsequent starts and wasn't
seen out after July; possibly doesn't quite stay 7f; yet to race on very soft going
but acts on any other. *T. Fairhurst.*

BRIGHT WIRE 3 ch.g. Condorcet–Fairy Tree (Varano) (1981 6g 6f 6f* 1982 **71**
10s* 10g³ 10f 16f 16d 16d 16.1s) lengthy gelding; quite a moderate handicapper;
won at Ayr in March; stays 2m; acts on any going. *A. Jarvis.*

BRILLIANT ROSA 2 b.f. Luthier 126–Raduga (Counsel 118) (1982 7d*) **81 p**
tall, leggy, rather sparely-made filly; half-sister to useful French middle-distance
performer Grand Trianon (by Diatome) and useful French and Italian middle-
distance winner Step to Fame (by English Prince); dam 2-y-o 5f and 6f winner
in France; although looking bit weak, overcame slowish start to win 18-runner
maiden race at Leicester in October going away by 2 lengths from Changatre;
likely to develop into a useful middle-distance 3-y-o. *M. Stoute.*

BRISBANE 4 ch.g. Welsh Pageant 132–Pavello 94 (Crepello 136) (1981 12s —
12fg 12d 1982 11g⁴ 12s 13.4g 12f) poor plater; blinkered last 2 outings in 1981.
M. Cousins.

BRISBANE ROAD 2 b.g. Pitskelly 122–Gamma (Zank) (1982 6d 7d 6f⁴ 6g 8d) **50**
May 5; 5,400Y; short-backed gelding; brother to Royal Whip, a winner over 8.5f
in Ireland at 2 yrs and subsequently successful in Norwegian St Leger; poor
plater; best effort over 6f; blinkered fourth outing; changed hands 440 gns
Doncaster October Sales. *C. Williams.*

BRIT 3 b.f. Pardigras 91–Brighty (Connaught 130) (1981 8d 8s 10s 1982 10s) —
in rear in maiden races in the Midlands; sold 500 gns Ascot September Sales.
W. Turner.

BRITISH CROWN 6 ch.g. English Prince 129–Chapeau Bleue (High Hat 131) —
(1981 12f 12g 1982 11.7g 12fg 10s) strong gelding; has been fired; only plating
class on flat but is fair hurdler; stays middle distances; possibly unsuited by
heavy going; bandaged in front both starts in 1981. *D. Elsworth.*

BRITWELL LAD (USA) 4 b.g. Son Ange–Hurricane Helen (Etonian) (1981 **51**
11s 10d³ 10s 12fg⁴ 11.7h 11.7fg 1982 10d 11.7f³ 12f² 15.5f²) small, sturdy
gelding; good walker; in frame in maiden races and handicaps; seems to stay 2m.
P. Cole.

BROAD BEAM 2 b.c. Averof 123–Angel Beam 115 (Hornbeam 130) (1982 **88 p**
8s*) Apr 27; third living foal; half-brother to fairly useful 1976 2-y-o 5f performer Angelos (by Town Crier); dam, smart winner over 5f and 6f at 2 yrs,
needed 1¼m+ at 3 yrs; 8/1, on backward side and a little green, won 14-runner
maiden race at Leicester in November by length from Errigal, leading 1½f out after
travelling well from start; will stay 1¼m+; sure to improve, and looks a useful
colt in the making. *P. Walwyn.*

BROAD LOOM 6 b.g. Continuation 120–Compatriot (Pindari 124) (1981 NR —
1982 12fg) poor maiden; should stay at least 7f; seems to need a soft surface;
has worn blinkers. *Mrs A. Finch.*

BROADWAY LODGE 3 b.f. The Go-Between 129–Canteen Katie (King's **66** Troop 118) (1981 5s³ 5d* 5g⁴ 5d* 5g 6d⁴ 6d² 6g 6f 6fg 6fg 6s 6s⁴ 1982 6g 6s 7fg³ 6f) leggy, lightly-made filly; fair at her best; stays 7f; seems to act on any going; game; sent to USA. *C. Wildman.*

BROCKLEY BELLE 3 ch.f. Track Spare 125–Just Jolly 80 (Jolly Jet 111) **59** (1981 5g 5fg 6g 6fg² 1982 7f⁴ 7g³ 8fg 7g 8s⁴ 8d 8s³) tall, light-framed filly; not a good walker or mover; stays 1m; acts on any going. *C. Spares.*

BRODI CRYSTAL (FR) 3 gr.c. Crystal Palace 132–Brodie (Bryan G) (1981 **72** 7g 8g 1982 10f² 10d² 10f³ 10fg) runner-up in maiden races; will stay 1½m; sweated up badly third start and wore blinkers on fourth; sold 3,000 gns Newmarket Autumn Sales. *L. Cumani.*

BROGAN (USA) 2 b.c. Nijinsky 138–Drumtop (Round Table) (1982 7fg⁴ **98** 8fg² 8s*) May 24; strong, good-bodied, attractive colt; brother to useful 11f to 13f winner Bedford and stakes-placed winner Kyra's Slipper, closely related to very useful USA sprinter Topsider (by Northern Dancer) and half-brother to 2 winners, including smart 1979 2-y-o stakes winner War of Words (by Arts and Letters); dam top-class American middle-distance filly; after showing promise in useful company, won 11-runner maiden race at Bath in October; will stay 1½m; seems to act on any going; type to make useful 3-y-o. *I. Balding.*

BROKEN BONDS 5 b.g. Bustino 136–Betty Burke 95 (Prince Chevalier) — (1981 NR 1982 13.8f 12.2f 12fg 12g) strong, good sort; very lightly raced and no form in varied races. *M. Naughton.*

BROKENCROSS 2 b.c. The Brianstan 128–Aurelia 68 (Aureole 132) (1982 **73** 6d 7g² 7d 8g 8s) Apr 12; 5,600Y; lightly-built colt; half-brother to a winning plater, to a winner in Brazil and to a winning hurdler; dam stayer; beaten a short head by odds-on Hot Boy in maiden race at Chester in July, only form; had stiff tasks in nurseries last 2 starts; suited by 7f. *J. Douglas-Home.*

BROKEN HABIT (USA) 2 b.f. Habitony–Split Personality 68 (Home Guard **99** 129) (1982 5g² 6d⁴ 5.8g* 5g* 5g² 5g 5s* 5g²) lengthy, quite attractive filly; first foal; dam 1½m winner; successful in maiden race at Bath in July and nurseries at Lingfield in August and Sandown in October; particularly impressive in apprentice event at Sandown, drawing right away in final furlong to win by 5 lengths; bred to stay beyond sprint distances; acts very well on soft going and has yet to race on a firm surface; good mount for apprentice; game and genuine. *I. Balding.*

BROKEN HILL 3 b.g. Bronze Hill 96–Lido Light (Good Light 92) (1981 NR — 1982 11g 11.7f 8fg) 820 2-y-o; compact gelding; second foal; dam staying hurdler; well behind in maiden races; sold 550 gns Ascot November Sales. *P. Cundell.*

BROKEN RAIL 3 b.c. Busted 134–First Huntress 64 (Primera 131) (1981 **111** 8s² 1982 10.4g* 14fg* 14.6f) big colt; poor walker and has a round action; half-brother to several winners, notably very smart middle-distance horse Town and Country (by Town Crier); dam of little account; a smart colt who won £3,200 event at Chester in May and Melrose Handicap at York in August; created a very favourable impression in latter, coming with a good run from rear in straight and staying on strongly to beat Crusader Castle by a length (pair well clear); faded after coming with a chance halfway up straight when ninth of 15 behind Touching Wood in St Leger at Doncaster in September; suited by 1¾m and will stay further; evidently acts on a firm surface but gives impression he'll always be suited by some give in the ground. *R. Hern.*

BROKEN SEAL 3 br.f. Privy Seal 108–Histoun (Behistoun 131) (1981 **75** 5g³ 5fg 5f 8.2d 8g 1982 12.2g² 16f² 16fg* 16d⁴ 15.8f² 19f* 16f⁴ 17.4d) leggy, narrow filly; has a round action; bad plater at 2 yrs; showed much improved form in 1982, winning maiden race at York in June and handicap at Beverley in July; suited by a test of stamina on firm ground. *C. Gray.*

BRONDESBURY 2 br.c. Welsh Saint 126–Whistling Tudor (Whistling Wind **128** 123) (1982 5g* 5fg* 5fg² 5g* 5f* 5f* 5f*) Recent seasons have proved Bill O'Gorman to be highly adept at training sprinters and speedy two-year-olds. He has handled such fast animals as Abdu, Camisite, Gypsy Dancer, Manor Farm Boy, Mummy's Game and Sayyaf, Abdu's nine victories in 1978 and Manor Farm Boy's seven the previous year well illustrating his skill at placing two-year-olds. It was interesting therefore to read an interview in the American magazine *The Thoroughbred Record* in which he detailed some of his training techniques. O'Gorman said of his

*Brocklesby Stakes, Doncaster—Brondesbury is much too good
for typical early-season opposition*

approach to training two-year-olds: 'When I start to work them, it will almost always be on the bridle, seldom more than two and a half furlongs. The idea is to get them to use themselves, but from quite an early stage I will have them competing. If you let them think they can get away with being idle all the time, that's what they'll do.'

Brondesbury, one of O'Gorman's 1982 two-year-olds, learnt his lessons well, perhaps too well. He proved an extremely keen competitor, always eager to gallop as fast as he could for as long as he could and his keenness made him a demanding ride, even in an Australian noseband which holds the bit up in the mouth: 'We can only canter him once a day. Even on his own the second time would always be a gallop. I know they say anyone can train good horses but sometimes it doesn't seem all that easy.' Brondesbury's explosive nature made him an extremely exciting colt to watch, and racegoers had the pleasure of seeing him lead throughout on six of his seven starts, the first of them in the opening race of the British flat season, the Brocklesby Stakes at Doncaster. Brondesbury brought back memories of the 1971 Brocklesbury winner Deep Diver as he trotted up by six lengths, and though top-class two-year-olds are an extremely rare sight on a racecourse in March some of his subsequent displays suggested that he wasn't much inferior to that outstandingly fast colt.

Before May was out Brondesbury had gained further successes in the Granby Stakes at Newmarket, in a £2,500 race at Kempton in which he accounted for the newcomer Kafu by seven lengths, and in a two-runner event at Thirsk. On each occasion he shot out of the gate and had the race sewn up by halfway. He also appeared to be sailing to another victory when five lengths clear at halfway in the Garter Stakes at Ascot on his third outing but on that occasion his stride started to shorten approaching the final furlong and the unbeaten Horage went past for a five-length win. Our interpretation of Brondesbury's defeat was that he had taken too much out of himself on the testing Ascot track, but his trainer believes a contributory factor was Brondesbury's becoming unbalanced after jumping the road which crosses the track.

Brondesbury later proved that his running in the Garter Stakes was nothing like a true reflection of his merit. His display in the Great Surrey Stakes on Derby Day can rarely have been bettered by an early-season two-year-old. His four opponents, all receiving weight, included Dorset Eagle, beaten only once in three starts, and the dual winner Black Glazepta, who had finished just three quarters of a length behind Brondesbury at Ascot. They scarcely saw the way he went. Proving extremely well suited to the sharp course, he pinged out of the stalls and had the race in his pocket in no time at all. He came home fully ten lengths ahead of Dorset Eagle despite being eased, and recorded the exceptionally fast time of 55.42 seconds. His timefigure of 1.36 fast was the best of the year by a two-year-old and was bettered only by Golden Fleece, Sharpo, Assert, Kalaglow and Dara Monarch.

Fifteen days later Brondesbury met pattern-race company for the first time in the Norfolk Stakes at Royal Ascot. He started odds on ahead of Bal Royal, a very well-bred colt who had won his only race in good style, and Krayyan, conqueror of Brondesbury's stable-mate Sayf El Arab in the National Stakes, with the field made up by the Doncaster winner Bold Bob and the twice-successful Maariv. As usual Brondesbury was able to establish a decisive early lead, racing up the centre of the course. Bold Bob did his best to give chase and Bal Royal was pushed along to stay within striking distance but it was clear they had shot their bolt fully two furlongs from home, by which stage Brondesbury had drifted right over to the far rails. Once again the stiff Ascot course began to test Brondesbury's limited stamina and by the distance Krayyan had started to cut into his lead. Ives, appreciating Brondesbury was doing his utmost, sat quietly, trying to nurse him home as the much more powerfully ridden Krayyan drew closer and closer. This time the post came just in time and Brondesbury held on by a neck, lowering the course record for two-year-olds to 60.75 seconds.

With only a third of the season gone and six wins already under his belt Brondesbury looked to have a fine chance of bettering Abdu's nine wins in his first season. Unfortunately nothing went right for him afterwards; he missed his next engagement at Windsor early in July because of a pricked foot; he had to miss the Molecomb Stakes, a race which looked tailor-made for him, because he was coughing. When he didn't recover in time for the Flying Childers Stakes on St Leger day, his connections decided to retire him for the season.

Brondesbury's target is said to be the King's Stand Stakes at Royal Ascot in which he will attempt to join those excellent sprinters Sound Track, Song, Swing Easy and Godswalk as the only animals since the war to win both that race and the Norfolk (formerly New) Stakes. Providing he has made a full recovery from his long bout of coughing and gets the five furlongs against top-class opposition he must stand a good chance. Brondesbury's rider reportedly believes that Brondesbury even has a chance of staying six furlongs if he proves more amenable to restraint, but it's hard to envisage Brondesbury's learning to settle. It's questionable whether he should be taught to settle. Certainly he will stand a better chance of seeing out a stiff five furlongs in top company if he races less freely but blistering early pace was his major asset at two.

Brondesbury (br.c. Feb 6, 1980)	Welsh Saint (b 1966)	St Paddy (b 1957)	Aureole / Edie Kelly
		Welsh Way (gr 1954)	Abernant / Winning Ways
	Whistling Tudor (b 1970)	Whistling Wind (ch 1960)	Whistler / Good As Gold
		Pink Standard (br 1963)	Tudor Melody / Rose Cloud

Purely on pedigree there is no reason why Brondesbury shouldn't stay six furlongs: Welsh Saint was best at that distance and Whistling Tudor, a seven-furlong winner at Sligo, stayed a mile. Whistling Tudor, from three previous

Norfolk Stakes, Ascot—the brilliantly speedy Brondesbury (rails) lasts home from Krayyan

Mr A. Foustok's "Brondesbury"

foals, has also produced the Irish middle-distance winner Exciting Times (by Windjammer), as well as a winner in Belgium. Whistling Tudor is a half-sister to two winners, the mile-and-a-quarter performer Nathaniel and the French seven-furlong and a mile winner Vallina. Their dam, Pink Standard, had the unusual record of finishing second in her six races, all of them over five furlongs, as a two-year-old in England. After being sold for a mere 330 guineas she was sent to Ireland where she raced a further twenty-two times without success, once finishing third over a mile and once over a mile and a quarter. Pink Standard's brother, the Bunbury Cup winner Swinging Minstrel, won five times at up to a mile. Brondesbury's family on his dam's side is distinctly modest in recent generations. He may have inherited much of his ability and his excitable character from Welsh Saint, a grandson of the highly-strung Aureole. Welsh Saint didn't stay nearly so well as one would have expected and, in addition to showing a tendency to sweat up, he had something of an aversion to the stalls, a fault which has appeared in two of his best offspring, the good fillies Welsh Garden and Welshwyn.

Brondesbury, who fetched 7,000 Irish guineas as a foal, was bought as a yearling for 15,000 guineas by his trainer's brother. The O'Gormans explained their purchasing policy in the *Thoroughbred Record* article. 'We don't have the money to buy perfection, or anything like it, so we weigh the pros and cons. Where there is enough pedigree, we may forgive ugliness. If a yearling is good-looking and athletic, we may even forgive total absence of pedigree. What we are concerned about is the way a horse walks and uses himself. What stops us buying a horse is lack of action.' Brondesbury is a perfect example of the good-looking, athletic individual, somewhat lacking in pedigree. He's an extremely strong, muscular individual, very well developed for a two-year-old as his portrait shows, who invariably looks in tremendous shape before his races. He also walks well and has a beautifully smooth, light action which suggests that there must be a doubt about whether he'll be effective on very soft ground; as yet he has raced only on a sound surface and he acts very well on

161

firm going. Let's hope he'll be able to show the same brilliant speed on his return as he showed at Epsom. With Sharpo retired, racing is very much in need of a top five-furlong performer. *W. O'Gorman.*

BRONZAMER 5 gr.m. Saritamer 130–Palmitin 68 (Crepello 136) (1981 8f 8f 8fg 9fg 8f 7g 8.2f 8f 8s* 1982 8f 8f⁴ 8d⁴ 9f 8fg 8fg³ 8g 8d) small, lightly-made mare; stays 1m; acts on any going but is probably ideally suited by soft nowadays; blinkered nowadays; started slowly sixth outing. *P. Asquith.*   **52**

BRONZE MEDAL 4 ch.g. Jimmy Reppin 131–Maroon 92 (Roan Rocket 128) (1981 10.1f² 10.4fg³ 12fg* 1982 10fg 12v) rangy, quite attractive gelding; in rear both outings in 1982; stays 1½m; acts on firm going. *J. Old.*   —

BROOK GREEN 4 b.g. Run The Gantlet–Fortezza 106 (Botticelli 129) (1981 8g 8g 10s 10d 12.3g 1982 15.5g) good sort; well beaten in varied company; blinkered once in 1981; sold 1,000 gns Ascot September Sales. *M. Haynes.*   —

BROOKLINE 3 ch.g. Hotfoot 126–La Lidia 78 (Matador 131) (1981 5g* 5d 7d* 7.6g² 7s 7g³ 1982 8.2s 8f 6fg 8f* 8g² 8f² 8f 8g³ 8d⁴) leggy gelding; quite a moderate handicapper; decisively won at Thirsk in June; will be suited by 1¼m; has won on a soft surface but is ideally suited by top-of-the-ground; tended to hang fifth start but has run well for an apprentice; sent to Hong Kong. *R. Sheather.*   **80**

BROON'S SECRET 8 b.g. Most Secret 119–Vaudaville 77 (Vigo 130) (1981 5g³ 6g 6g* 5fg 6g 5.1f 6f 5g* 5fg⁴ 5h² 6fg* 1982 6fg* 6f* 6f* 6fg 6t³ 6fg* 5g 6fg 6fg*) strong gelding; sprint handicapper; showed improved form and had a good season; won at Nottingham (3 times) and at Ripon (apprentice event) in first half of season, and gained a further success at Thirsk in September on disqualification of Cyril's Choice; acts on any going, but clearly goes well on top-of-the-ground; has twice worn blinkers; is usually ridden by apprentice T. Jarvis who carried overweight at 8-11 final start. *A. Jarvis.*   **91**

BROTHER GEOFFREY 3 b.g. Sheshoon 132–Eilan Aigas 93 (Counsel 118) (1981 NR 1982 10.2g 12g³ 14.6g) 6,000Y; lengthy gelding; brother to successful stayer Mister Geoffrey, and half-brother to 3 winners, including useful miler Geoffrey's Sister (by Sparkler); dam won at 1m and 11f; remote third of 6 to Chalkey Road in minor event at Ripon in July; will stay well. *C. Thornton.*   —

BROUGH'S BOY 3 b.c. Lucky Wednesday 124–Ruffino 99 (Como 120) (1981 6f 7.2d 6f 1982 9s) big, strong colt; well beaten in maiden and minor events. *M. W. Easterby.*   —

BROUGH SCOTT 3 ch.c. Steel Heart 128–Parthian Song (Parthia 132) (1981 6fg 1982 8fg 8fg 7fg 7fg 6v* 6d) useful-looking colt; good mover; 33/1, showed improved form to win handicap at Lingfield in October; ran moderately only subsequent start; suited by 6f; acts on heavy going; blinkered last 4 starts. *R. Price.*   **67**

BROUGHTON STAR 2 ch.g. Mossberry 97–Monet Royal 79 (Monet 127) (1982 8g 8s) May 10; half-brother to 3 winners, including fairly useful middle-distance performer Kentucky Fair (by Crocket); dam won twice over 6.5f in Ireland; soundly beaten in maiden races at Beverley and York in the autumn; gelded after final outing. *J. Etherington.*   —

BROWFOLD 3 ch.g. Realm 129–Trusian (Milesian 125) (1981 5d 5g 6g 6g 6s 5s 1982 5s 6s 5g 5fg 5g 6g) smallish, lightly-made gelding; poor plater. *K. Stone.*   —

BROWN JUG 2 br.g. Kala Shikari 125–Cobble (Major Portion 129) (1982 5f 6f 5d) May 16; 5,400Y; half-brother to 1981 2-y-o 7f winner Sanches (by Sandford Lad) and a winner in Italy; dam Irish 7.5f winner; no form; blinkered in June sellers at Thirsk and Newcastle, last 2 starts. *M. W. Easterby.*   —

BROWN RIFLE 2 bl.c. Scottish Rifle 127–Mother Brown 103 (Candy Cane 125) (1982 6d 6g 7.2s 8d) Apr 5; 700Y; leggy colt; third foal; brother to 1980 2-y-o 1m seller winner Orkney Annie; dam genuine handicapper at up to 1¼m; modest plater; should stay 1¼m. *M. Naughton.*   **56**

BROWN SANDS 2 b.f. Radetzky 123–Double Sands (Double Jump 131) (1982 5g 6g 7g 8fg 5s) May 23; workmanlike filly; first foal; dam tailed off only outing; behind in maiden and minor races; blinkered last 2 starts. *D. Sasse.*   —

BROWN SHADOW 2 b.g. Hittite Glory 125–Pop Gun 85 (King's Troop 118) (1982 5fg² 6fg* 6g³ 8.2s) Mar 22; 4,400 2-y-o; rather dipped-backed gelding; half-brother to 3-y-o Swift Encounter (by Owen Dudley) and 1979 2-y-o 5f winner Hot Gun (by Hotfoot); dam best at 5f; bought in 3,500 gns after winning 14-runner seller at Windsor in June by 2½ lengths from Ardrox Lad; 7 lengths third   **77**

of 10 to On Stage in minor event at Chepstow later in month; well suited by 6f; found to be lame at start when withdrawn from seller at Newmarket in July, and wasn't seen out again until October. *M. Pipe.*

BROWN VELVET 2 b.f. Mansingh 120–Luckhurst (Busted 134) (1982 **68** 5fg 5fg 5.3g⁴ 5g) May 31; 13,000Y; compact, workmanlike filly; fifth foal; half-sister to 2 winners by Owen Anthony, notably smart Stumped, successful at up to 1m; dam unraced daughter of very smart sprinter Lucasland; plating-class maiden; gives strong impression she's a short runner. *B. Swift.*

BROXADELLA 2 br.f. Broxted 120–Addie (Klairon 131) (1982 5d) May 3; — second foal; dam of no account; 33/1 when last of 14 behind Priceoflove in maiden race at Wolverhampton in August. *A. W. Jones.*

BROXBURN 2 b. or br.c. Averof 123–Tomfoolery 73 (Silly Season 127) (1982 — 5d 5fg 6g 6g) June 10; compact, good sort; fourth foal; half-brother to 2 good winners in Belgium; dam ran only at 2 yrs; little worthwhile form; sold BBA 1,400 gns Newmarket Autumn Sales. *D. Whelan.*

BRUCKNER 3 br.c. Wollow 132–Habituee (Habitat 134) (1981 7f 8g 7g **109** 1982 8s⁴ 7g* 7fg 12g 7g⁴ 6fg* 5g⁴) 12,500Y; half-brother to useful 1¼m winner Ma Femme (by Bustino) and 2-y-o Acclimatise; dam French 1m winner; readily beat Toast of the Town by 2 lengths in handicap at the Curragh in May and accounted for subsequently-disqualified Aloe by a length in Seven Springs Sprint Stakes on same course in July; ran respectably most other starts, including in 7f Jersey Stakes at Royal Ascot (2 lengths fifth to Merlins Charm) and 5f Philips Electrical Stakes (Handicap) at the Curragh (1½ lengths fourth to Sweet Side); best at up to 7f; acts on a firm surface; to be trained by H. Cecil. *C. Collins, Ireland.*

BRUMMENDELLE 3 gr.f. Bruni 132–Make Amends 74 (Tutankhamen) (1981 **57** 7g 1982 8d 9g⁴ 11.7f 12f 12f 17.1s) lengthy, plain filly; poor maiden. *D. Wintle.*

BRYMA 2 b. or br.g. Rymer 121–Saucy Walk (Saucy Kit 76) (1982 5d 7fg 6f) — Apr 17; tall, rangy, slightly dipped-backed gelding; second foal; half-brother to 3-y-o Ty-With-Belle (by Pamroy); dam ran once over hurdles; poor form in maiden events; will probably need long distances; gelded after final outing. *B. Palling.*

BUCHANAN (FR) 7 gr.g. Dancer's Image–Fiery Diplomat 120 (Diplomat Way) — (1981 10.2s 5f 1982 8d 13.4g) of little account on flat nowadays; has been tried in blinkers; wears a tongue strap. *M. Chapman.*

BUCHANETTE (USA) 3 b.f. Youth 135–Duke's Little Gal (Duke of Dublin) **117** (1981 NR 1982 10.5fg* 10.5v 10g³ 12g⁴ 13.5fg 12g² 10s⁴ 10v⁴ 10.5v* 12f 9d* 9g²) $70,000Y; quite attractive filly; fifth foal; half-sister to middle-distance winners Commonty (by Empery) and Platinum (by Vaguely Noble); dam won 7 races including 7f Santa Paula Handicap; won newcomers race at Longchamp, Prix de Flore at Saint-Cloud (beat Doubling Time a short head) and California Jockey Club Handicap at Bay Meadows (comfortably from Sweet Maid); ran creditably most other starts, notably when third to Grease in Prix de Malleret at Long-champ and nose second to Super Moment in Bay Meadows Handicap; stays 1½m; best form with some give in the ground; trained by M. Zilber first 10 starts. *M. Whittingham, USA.*

BUCKENHAM BELLE 5 b.m. Royben 125–Dux Girl 99 (Bewildered 102) — (1981 NR 1982 16f) lengthy mare; poor plater; stays 1¼m; acts on any going; often wears blinkers; suitable mount for a boy. *C. Wildman.*

BUCKLAND 6 b.g. Busted 134–Queensferry 81 (Pindari 124) (1981 12.2d — 12.2fg 12g 12d* 1982 12fg) big gelding; good mover; middle-distance handicapper; last on only outing of 1982 (August); probably acts on any going; bandaged in front nowadays. *B. Palling.*

BUCKLES (NZ) 8 b.g. St Puckle 110–Queen of the Clouds (Golden Cloud) — (1981 NR 1982 6f 8g 7g 6f 5g 6fg) ex-New Zealand gelding; novice hurdler; soundly beaten in varied races on flat over here; blinkered or hooded last 3 outings; dead. *J. Webber.*

BUCKLOW HILL 5 b.g. Rheingold 137–Parmassia (Pampered King 121) **86** (1981 12f* 12f* 13.8fg* 12f* 12g² 18g 12g 1982 12fg 12f 12fg² 14.7f* 14g 12fg* 14.6g² 13d 12s) tall gelding; won handicaps at Redcar in July (3 ran) and Beverley in August, on latter course beating Show-A-Leg by a length after being waited with; ran creditably on several other starts and finished ¾-length second to Karadar in valuable handicap at Doncaster in September; stays 1¾m; acts well on firm ground; sometimes sweats up. *J. Fitzgerald.*

BUCKS FIZZ MUSIC 2 ch.f. Be Friendly 130–Hastily 99 (Hornbeam 130)   **74**
(1982 5.8g 5d² 5fg)   May 2; IR 1,500F (privately), 4,400Y; sister to 4 winners here and abroad, including fairly useful 6f and 7f performer Fast Friend, and half-sister to a winner in France; dam 2-y-o 5f winner; quite moderate maiden; will be suited by 6f; acts on a soft surface. *B. Gubby.*

BUCKTON 3 ch.f. Double-U-Jay 120–Remana (Remainder 106)   (1981 5.1f   —
6fg 6d 6g 8g 8g   1982 8s 7f 7fg 8f)   plain filly; poor plater; has worn blinkers. *W. Holden.*

BUD'S GIFT 3 ch.g. Tudor Music 131–Recapped (Sallust 134)   (1981 5.8g   **45**
6fg 6fg⁴ 6s⁴   1982 7d 7f 6f³ 7fg 8g 6fg 7f)   neat gelding; plater; stays 6f; acts on any going; suitable mount for an apprentice; has worn blinkers. *G. Balding.*

BUFFAVENTO 4 b.c. Connaught 130–Duke Street (Lorenzaccio 130)   (1981 **104**
8.2fg³ 10g⁴ 8g* 8fg 8fg⁴ 8f⁴ 8d⁴ 8g   1982 8g² 8g 10f³ 9g* 10g⁴ 10g⁴ 9d 10g)   neat, strong colt; very useful performer; put up a good performance when beating Wauthi 2¼ lengths in Group 3 Grosser Preis von Dortmund in June; also in frame in valuable handicaps at Newcastle (beaten neck by Seven Hearts), Epsom and Newbury and in Land of Burns Stakes at Ayr; ran creditably from a poorish draw when ninth of 29 behind Century City in William Hill Cambridgeshire at Newmarket in October (top weight), better subsequent effort; gives impression he's suited by 1¼m nowadays; yet to race on very soft going, but acts on any other; sold privately to M. Morris. *G. Pritchard-Gordon.*

BUGLE BOY (USA) 3 b.c. Hoist the Flag–Dusky Evening (Tim Tam)   (1981   **67**
NR   1982 11g 10fg 11.7f 16d* 15.5f⁴)   lengthy, good-bodied colt; half-brother to 3 winners in USA by Nijinsky, including stakes winner Javamine, successful at up to 11f; dam won 3 times at up to 1m and is half-sister to top 1968 3-y-o American filly Dark Mirage; stayed on well to win 10-runner maiden race at Newcastle in June; suited by a test of stamina. *J. Dunlop.*

BUILD CARTWRIGHT (USA) 3 ch.c. Try Sheep–Maid of Arc (Knight in   —
Armor)   (1981 7fg   1982 8.2fg 12f 14g 8fg 10.1fg)   compact colt; little worthwhile form; promises to stay 1½m. *B. Hanbury.*

BUKARA 3 ch.c. Red Alert 127–Solar Jinks (Immortality or Delirium 126)   **69**
(1981 6fg 7f 7g   1982 8g 12f⁴ 11.5f 10g² 10g 12f⁴ 12f² 12.2f³ 10fg* 10g²)   plain colt; poor walker; easily won 11-runner maiden race at Yarmouth in August; ran well in minor event on same course following month; stays 1½m; yet to race on a soft surface; suited by forcing tactics; has run respectably when sweating up. *J. Winter.*

BULANDSHAR 3 ch.g. Royal Palace 131–Castle Mona 78 (Sound Track 132)   —
(1981 NR   1982 11.5fg 10.1g)   1,000Y, 760 2-y-o, 4,400 3-y-o; fair sort; half-brother to 3 winners, notably very smart middle-distance performer Ksar and very useful stayer Castle (both by Kalydon); dam sprinter; backward when tailed-off last in maiden races at Sandown and Windsor in August. *D. Jermy.*

BULGING POCKETS 8 br.g. Arctic Kanda 111–Sealac 81 (Sea Wolf 116)   —
(1981 NR   1982 12.2f)   poor maiden; stays 1½m; bandaged on only outing of 1982. *J. Yardley.*

BULLOM 2 b.c. Bustino 136–Romella (Romulus 129)   (1982 7g⁴ 7g⁴ 7fg 8.2d)   **67**
Mar 15; 10,000F, 16,000Y; big, useful-looking colt; good walker; half-brother to 3 winners, including 1981 2-y-o 6f winner Dance in Rome (by Dance In Time), and 2 winning hurdlers; dam never ran; plating-class maiden; looked ungenuine (pulled hard early on and put head in air when let down) when well beaten under low weight in nursery at Nottingham (blinkered) in September; sold to Denys Smith 9,000 gns Doncaster November Sales. *M. H. Easterby.*

BULLRING 3 gr.g. Warpath 113–Loop The Loop 81 (Hopeful Venture 125)   —
(1981 7f 10s² 10.2g   1982 10d 13g 16d³ 16.9fg)   rangy, lengthy gelding; good walker; slow maiden; will be suited by extreme distances; needs some give in the ground; sold to I. Wardle 2,900 gns Doncaster November Sales. *C. Thornton.*

BUMPKIN 2 b.f. Free State 125–The Country Lane 90 (Red God 128§)   (1982 **103**
5f³ 5fg* 5f³ 5fg 6fg* 6g 5fg² 6d*)   Mar 2; 8,000F, 21,000Y; well-made filly; good walker; half-sister to several winners, including prolific 7f to 9f winner On Edge (by Sharp Edge); dam won 4 times over 6f; made all in 17-runner maiden race at Salisbury in May and in 6-runner minor event at Windsor (beating Silk Sari 6 lengths) in July; seemed to be becoming increasingly headstrong in the summer but proved amenable to restraint in 14-runner Martini Trophy (Nursery)

*Martini Trophy, Newmarket—Bumpkin comes clear from Sea Pago (left)
and Bid Again (white sleeves) to win the season's
most valuable nursery*

at Newmarket in October, coming from last place to win by 3 lengths from Sea
Pago; suited by 6f; acts on a firm and a soft surface. *I. Balding.*

BUNCE BOY 6 b.g. King Emperor–All Hail 112 (Alcide 136) (1981 11.7d **63**
12f⁴ 12fg* 12.3fg⁴ 12f* 12f² 12f* 12fg⁴ 12d³ 12v 1982 12f² 12f* 12f 12g 12f³
12g² 12fg 12g⁴ 12g) useful sort; middle-distance handicapper; usually goes well
at Brighton and beat Superior Saint by 4 lengths there in May; ran poorly on
occasions however; ideally suited by top-of-the-ground conditions and forcing
tactics; occasionally blinkered; suitable mount for an apprentice; sold to Miss A.
Sinclair 4,000 gns Ascot December Sales. *A. Hide.*

BUNDABURG 2 ch.c. Creetown 123–Maple Syrup 89 (Charlottown 127) (1982 **72**
5fg 5fg⁴) Mar 2; second foal (first to Northern Hemisphere time); dam, daughter
of 1,000 Guineas and Oaks winner Sweet Solera, was placed over 6f and 1¼m;
4¾ lengths fourth of 8 to Bird Rock in minor race at Chepstow in July; will
be suited by 6f+. *S. Matthews.*

BUNDLE OF KISSES (USA) 3 b.c. Nijinsky 138–Bundler (Raise A Native) **76**
(1981 8d³ 1982 12g² 13g² 12fg² 15.5f* 12f) big, rangy, workmanlike colt;
made much of running and stayed on strongly to land odds in 8-runner maiden
race at Folkestone in August; needs a test of stamina; has run respectably for a
lady rider; sent to USA. *G. Harwood.*

BUNDU (FR) 3 b.f. Habitat 134–No Relation 94 (Klairon 131) (1981 6fg² 7v³ **88**
1982 7g 8fg² 8fg⁴ 10.4fg² 10d² 10fg* 10.6s* 10.6s³ 10.2d) close-coupled filly;
favourite, spreadeagled rivals in maiden race at Salisbury in September and
minor event at Haydock in October; will stay 1½m; probably acts on any going;
sweated up third start and tended to hang on eighth. *H. Wragg.*

BUNTER 4 b.c. Prince de Galles 125–New Flag (Royal Serenade 131) (1981 **—**
8g 8g* 10.6s 8fg 8fg 8fg* 8g* 9g 1982 8g 8fg 7fg 8g) quite an attractive, good
sort; developed into a useful handicapper in 1981; disappointing in good handicaps in 1982 (off course over 2-months before final start); best at 1m; acts on a
firm surface; sold to A. Moore 4,200 gns Newmarket Autumn Sales. *R. Price.*

BURFORD BELLE 4 b.f. Roman Warrior 132–Motionless 109 (Midsummer
Night II 117) (1981 6g 7g 8fg 8.2s 10s 1982 8g 8f 10f 12fg) big, strong,
lengthy filly; plating-class maiden. *W. Wightman.*

BURGLARS BOY 8 ch.g. Burglar 128–Tilt Guard 75 (Crepello 136) (1981 **—**
5s 5d 5g 5g 6fg 5f⁴ 5fg 5f 5f 5f 5h 1982 8.2s 6f) poor handicapper; best at 5f
(not entirely disgraced over 1m in a seller); acts on any going; sometimes wears
blinkers; sometimes sweats up; has a tendency to hang left; has given trouble
at start *L. Barratt.*

BURGLARS WALK 2 b.c. Godswalk 130–Pay Roll 94 (Burglar 128) (1982 **75**
5fg² 6fg 6f⁴) Feb 22; IR 15,000Y; big, rangy individual; second foal; dam won
8 times over 6f and 7f; beaten about 6 lengths when in frame in maiden races
won by Concorde Hero at Newmarket in May and by Prince's Circus at Yarmouth
in July; stays 6f; apprentice ridden at overweight all starts; has scope. *A. Jarvis.*

BURGUNDY 3 b.g. Bustino 136–Land of Fire 99 (Buisson Ardent 129) (1981 **71**
7g 7s 1982 11g³ 12fg 13g³ 15d 14g) tall, lengthy gelding; has shown ability in
maiden races; should stay 1¾m; sold 8,400 gns Newmarket Autumn Sales.
P. Walwyn.

BURKE'S FOLLY 5 ch.g. Shiny Tenth 120–Miss Sousa (March Past 124) —
(1981 8fg 8d 10s³ 7f 9fg 1982 8d) lightly-made gelding; poor mover; plater;
stays 1¼m; suited by soft going; has worn blinkers; suitable mount for a boy;
races with head in air. *K. Bridgwater.*

BURLEY GRIFFIN 2 b.c. Octavo 115–Whispering Breeze (Caliban 123) **83**
(1982 7g⁴ 8d 7d²) Jan 28; IR 4,800F, IR 12,000Y, resold 5,000Y; big, strong
colt; carries plenty of condition; third living foal; half-brother to 1981 2-y-o
7f winner Airspin (by Jukebox), and to Credit Centre (by Tudor Music), a fairly
useful winner at 1½m; dam plater; prominent all outings, running particularly
well when head second of 11 to Ice Patrol in maiden race at Redcar in October;
will stay 1¼m; acts on a soft surface; a likeable individual, sure to win races.
D. Smith.

BURLEY HILL LAD 2 b.c. Anax 120–Home Sweet Home (Royal Palace 131) —
(1982 5f) May 12; 7,000Y; second foal; dam once-raced half-sister to Hays;
50/1 and backward, moved poorly to start and was always outpaced when remote
last of 6 to Cast A Shadow in minor event at Leicester in May. *C. Mackenzie.*

BURLINGTON LAD 3 ch.c. Sweet Revenge 129–Allegretto (Preciptic 122) **53**
(1981 5d 5d⁴ 5f³ 6g 6s 1982 6d 5d 6g 5f 5g 5d 6g 7s*) small colt; plater;
apprentice ridden, attracted no bid after winning at Doncaster in November;
suited by 7f; acts well on soft going; blinkered third start; sold out of C. James's
stable 850 gns Ascot May Sales after fourth outing. *J. Perrett.*

BURNBECK 3 b.c. Music Boy 124–Festival Night 115 (Midsummer Night II **88 d**
117) (1981 5d³ 5g* 5fg² 1982 7.3fg⁴ 6f³ 8d 5g 5fg) good-quartered, quite
attractive colt; good walker; suited by 7f (well beaten over 1m). *P. Cole.*

BURNCROFT 2 br.c. Rapid River 127–Davett 88 (Typhoon 125) (1982 —
5f 6d 7f) May 5; 3,100Y; workmanlike colt; second foal; dam genuine middle-
distance handicapper; little worthwhile form in maiden auction events; exported
to Algeria. *M. W. Easterby.*

BURN UP 3 b.f. Blue Cashmere 129–Stick 'Em Up (Burglar 128) (1981 —
5g³ 5g³ 5g⁴ 5fg* 5g⁴ 5fg 6d² 6fg* 6fg 7g 8d 1982 7f 7f 6g 7s 7d 6s 7s) neat filly;
won maiden race and nursery at Catterick in 1981; soundly beaten most starts
at 3 yrs, including in 2 sellers; possibly stays 7f; acts on a firm and a soft surface;
suitable mount for an apprentice. *P. Asquith.*

BURROW 2 b.g. Homeboy 114–Philmarnie 66 (Klondyke Bill 125) (1982 **54**
5f 5g 6g 7fg 6s) Mar 24; 3,000Y; strong, compact gelding; modest plater; form
only at 5f. *M. W. Easterby.*

BURSLEM 2 ch.c. Nebbiolo 125–Spice Road (Gallant Man) (1982 5g* 5f 7fg* **110**
6.3fg³ 7d² 8s²) Feb 20; IR 66,000Y; half-brother to numerous winners here and
abroad, notably smart 1979 Irish 2-y-o 6f winner Noble Shamus (by Royal
and Regal); dam won at up to 1m in USA; successful in maiden race and valuable
Ardenode Stud Stakes at Leopardstown, putting up a good effort in latter in
August when scoring by 6 lengths from Simmay; placed in pattern races at the
Curragh subsequently, finishing just over 2½ lengths third of 5 to Caerleon in
Ballsbridge-Tattersalls Anglesey Stakes, length second of 9 to Glenstal in National
Stakes and 6 lengths second of 7 to very easy winner Danzatore in Panasonic
Beresford Stakes; stays 1m; probably acts on any going (hampered on only
outing on very firm ground). *K. Prendergast, Ireland.*

BUSACO 3 b.g. Bustino 136–Deed 86 (Derring-Do 131) (1981 6d² 6g⁴ 7fg* **114**
7f* 7.6g³ 7.3s² 1982 10.4fg 8.2f 10g* 10f* 10v⁴ 10s* 10g) strong, compact
gelding; half-brother to 1978 2-y-o 6f winner Super Jack (by Blakeney); dam
won over 5f at 2 yrs; a smart handicapper who won at Newmarket, Goodwood
and Sandown; held off Bali Dancer by a neck in Extel Stakes at Goodwood and
wore down Ricardo to score by ¾ length at Sandown; will stay 1½m; acts on any
going; suited by waiting tactics; sold privately out of R. Hern's stable after
fourth start. *S. Mellor.*

BUSHY BAY 8 b.g. Polyfoto 124–Latest Bird 81 (Pardal 130) (1981 10f —
1982 8g 6g 17f 18.4g) useful performer at up to 1¼m in Ireland in 1979, winner of
Irish Lincolnshire; lightly raced and well beaten on flat since (had stiff tasks
first 2 starts in 1982). *M. Chapman.*

BUSORM 2 ch.c. Bustino 136–Wrekinianne 96 (Reform 132) (1982 5f* 6f²) **98 ?**
Mar 3; 30,000Y; medium-sized, quite attractive colt; brother to 3-y-o Sasol and
fair stayer Sir Gordon, and half-brother to fair miler Staffordshire Knot (by
Welsh Pageant); dam stayed 1m; stayed on well to win 15-runner maiden race
at Thirsk in May by 1½ lengths from Naive, the pair clear; not given hard time

when going down by 5 lengths to odds-on Horage in 4-runner minor event at Haydock the following month; should stay well; sold 12,000 gns Doncaster November Sales. *M. H. Easterby.*

BUSTER BROWN 2 b.g. Record Run 127–Somer's Jewel (Will Somers 114§) —
(1982 7g 7g 6d) Apr 28; IR 6,800Y; big, useful-looking gelding; half-brother to 2 winners, including fair 1979 2-y-o sprinter Video Boy (by Laser Light); dam lightly raced; soundly beaten in maiden races in the autumn; sold J. Toller 2,500 gns Newmarket Autumn Sales. *Sir Mark Prescott.*

BUSTINETO 4 b.c. Bustino 136–Petipa 115 (Habitat 134) (1981 7s 10d 12fg —
7fg 7fg* 7fg 9f⁴ 8d 8g 1982 9f 8f) strong, shapely colt; first foal; dam sprinter; won handicap at Phoenix Park as a 3-y-o; often faces stiff tasks, and did when last of 10 behind Mr Fluorocarbon in Queen Anne Stakes at Royal Ascot in June on final start; should stay beyond 7f; acts on a firm surface; blinkered last outing in 1981; has done well over hurdles. *M. O'Toole, Ireland.*

BUSTING 8 b.h. Busted 134–Yasseen (Charlottesville 135) (1981 12d 14d³ **57**
1982 13.1f 12g 13.1g³) staying handicapper; ran creditably last 2 starts; acts on any going; good mount for a claimer; bandaged nowadays. *A. Turnell.*

BUSTOFF 2 b.c. Bustino 136–Magical 95 (Aggressor 130) (1982 8g) Apr 24; — p
strong, good-topped, attractive individual; good mover; brother to 2 winners, including Coronation Cup winner Easter Sun, and half-brother to 2 other winners; dam won twice over 5f at 2 yrs; 9/1 but decidedly backward, chased leaders until beaten and eased right up in 17-runner maiden race won by Oula Owl at Newmarket in October; will do a lot better in time. *M. Jarvis.*

BUSY BEE (USA) 3 b.f. Drone–Solid Booking (Boldnesian) (1981 7g 1982 —
8fg³) lengthy filly; beaten a long way in maiden race at Leicester and private sweepstake at Newmarket; sold, covered by Monsanto, 8,200 gns Newmarket December Sales. *W. Hastings-Bass.*

BUSY BUBBLE 3 b.f. Red Alert 127–Chanson (Tudor Melody 129) (1981 5g —
5fg 5fg 7fg 1982 8fg) neat, strong filly; no worthwhile form in varied company, including selling. *D. Thom.*

BUT 7 ch.g. Menelek 114–Rain Leagh (Raincheck 114) (1981 NR 1982 12s) —
ex-Irish gelding; second foal; dam never ran; showed some ability in bumpers races in Ireland in 1980 and was a point-to-point winner there; last but one in 13-runner apprentice race at Chepstow in October. *O. O'Neill.*

BUTLERS PET 3 b.g. Mummy's Pet 125–Reluctant Maid 94 (Relko 136) **49**
(1981 5d 5d 6f 6fg 1982 10d 10f⁴ 8f² 8.3g 7.2f³ 7g 7g² 6fg 6g) tall, fair sort; plater; stays 1¼m; acts well on firm going; claimed £2,475 after final start. *M. Blanshard.*

BUTTERFLY BLUE 2 br.f. Goldhill 125–Super Fly (Above Suspicion 127) —
(1982 6fg 5g) Apr 30; robust filly; first foal; dam maiden hurdler; backward when behind in big fields of maidens at Salisbury and Newbury (last of 20) in September. *G. Kindersley.*

Extel Stakes (Handicap), Goodwood—a storming finish with Busaco (rails) holding off Bali Dancer. Century City (No. 4) finishes third with Dreaming Away (noseband) fourth

BUTTON BRIGHT (USA) 2 br.c. Honest Pleasure–Admiring (Hail to — p
Reason) (1982 8g) Feb 2; half-brother to numerous winners, notably very
smart Glowing Tribute (by Graustark), successful at up to 1¼m in USA, and
Irish 1½m winner Courting Days (by Bold Lad, USA), herself dam of Magesterial;
dam, half-sister to top-class fillies Affectionately and Priceless Gem (dam of
Allez France), was smart stakes winner at 2 yrs; unquoted when behind in 21-
runner £4,200 event won by Polished Silver at Newbury in September; will do
better in time. *I. Balding.*

BUXOM LASS 2 br.f. Bustino 136–Lady From Aske 82 (French Beige 127) **56**
(1982 6g 8.2fg 7fg 6s) Mar 19; lightly-made filly; half-sister to 2 fairly useful
2-y-o winners, including 5f to 7f winner Good Tune (by Crooner); dam, second
3 times at 2 yrs, is sister to 2 useful stayers; 2¾ lengths fifth of 20 behind Freedom Glory in seller at Redcar in September, third outing and best effort; should
stay well; sweated up badly final start; sold 1,100 gns Newmarket Autumn Sales.
J. W. Watts.

BUXTON ROAD 5 b.h. Murrayfield 119–Necora 79 (Royal Record II) (1981 —
NR 1982 8.2s) won over 5f as a 2-y-o; lightly raced and no subsequent form
on flat, including in a seller; dead. *I. Vickers.*

BUY BRITISH 2 b.c. Import 127–Empress of Britain 92 (Amber X 133) (1982 —
5.8g) Apr 11; half-brother to smart 5f to 1m winner Pipedreamer (by Breeders
Dream); dam prolific winner at up to 1¼m; 25/1 when last of 13 in maiden race
won by Broken Habit at Bath in July; sold 450 gns Ascot August Sales. *H.
Candy.*

BUY INTERSPORT 2 br.g. Track Spare 125–Last Stop (Charlottown 127) —
(1982 5fg 5fg 8s) second foal; dam poor half-sister to high-class miler Final
Straw; in rear in maiden races; gelded after final start. *J. Etherington.*

BUZZARDS BAY 4 b.c. Joshua 129–Grande Merci 82 (Gratitude 130) (1981 **128 §**
10s³ 10f³ 8f* 8g³ 8g* 8fg* 8.2f* 8d* 9g 8s² 1982 10f³ 10.2f² 8fg* 10d 10.5f*
10fg 11.1fg 8s* 10d)

The section mark '§' is attached to the rating of a horse who may fairly be
regarded as 'somewhat ungenerous, faint-hearted or a bit of a coward; one who
may give his running on occasions, but cannot be relied upon to do so.' The
symbol is awarded only after the most careful consideration of the facts; where
there may be a valid excuse for a horse's in-and-out form we give the horse
the benefit of the doubt. Buzzards Bay is a prime example of a horse
thoroughly deserving the symbol; one about whom the punter should be warned.
On his best behaviour he's a top-notcher—his resounding victory over strong
opposition in the Queen Elizabeth II Stakes at Ascot in September was a high-
class performance, make no mistake, and Soba apart one would be hard pressed
to name any that improved more through the season—but, sadly, he's thoroughly
unpredictable and moody. On several occasions Buzzards Bay hardly ran a
race at all and another time he threw away a decent handicap by giving ten to
fifteen lengths away at the start and hanging at the finish.

Buzzards Bay started at 50/1 for the Queen Elizabeth and caused one of the
turn-ups of the season; even on his very best form he looked to have no chance.
His two wins in midsummer had been in handicap company, albeit in the

*Royal Hunt Cup Handicap, Ascot—Buzzards Bay (nearest camera)
comes wide for a storming victory in Royal Ascot's
most valuable handicap*

*John Smith's Magnet Cup, York—Buzzards Bay races wide again
to account for Cannon King and Aberfield*

Royal Hunt Cup at Royal Ascot and the John Smith's Magnet Cup at York, and on his two most recent outings he'd apparently had his limitations well and truly exposed in the Prix Gontaut-Biron at Deauville and the September Stakes at Kempton. He could hardly have looked better than he did at Kempton and he seemed in a decent enough mood going to the start, but he found nothing under pressure in the straight and finished last of seven behind Critique. We can't subscribe to the view that the distance of eleven furlongs was beyond him as he'd stayed on well when beating Cannon King and company decisively over a distance only fractionally shorter in the Magnet Cup, and the going was on top both times. How then could he have any prospects of winning so tough a race as the Queen Elizabeth II Stakes, opposed by the classic winner Dara Monarch and the pattern race winners Achieved, Mr Fluorocarbon, Noalcoholic and Sandhurst Prince, all well established amongst the season's leading milers? Yet Buzzards Bay treated these good colts almost with contempt. He was quite clearly on good terms with himself beforehand—he went much more smoothly to the start than often he does, and apart from a small bandage on his off-fore he couldn't be faulted in appearance. Amazingly, he was always going easily. He made rapid headway from the back of the field approaching the home turn, swung wide into the straight, and almost as soon as the field had straightened up he could clearly be seen going best of all. He led at least a furlong and a half out and won by three lengths and the same from Noalcoholic and Achieved, nothing ever looking like getting in a blow at him. Quite probably the going was too soft for Dara Monarch, Mr Fluorocarbon and Sandhurst Prince, but Noalcoholic and Achieved both act in the mud and were in good form at the time, especially Noalcoholic who shortly afterwards won the Bisquit Cognac Challenge

*Queen Elizabeth II Stakes, Ascot—one of the upsets of the season.
Noalcoholic finishes second and the
blinkered Achieved third*

Mrs V. M. McKinney's "Buzzards Bay"

Stakes at Newmarket. No doubt Swinburn's sympathetic handling suited Buzzards Bay well as did the tactic of bringing him wide to challenge; he clearly doesn't like to be crowded nowadays and was also brought wide by Mercer and Birch respectively when winning at Royal Ascot and York.

When a horse appears to show such dramatic improvement as Buzzards Bay ideally, for everyone's satisfaction, it should be substantiated as soon as possible. Buzzards Bay had the opportunity to do so in the Dubai Champion Stakes at Newmarket, but was unco-operative. Since he had behaved mulishly on the course in the 1981 Cambridgeshire his trainer went to the trouble of driving him down the motorway to Stansted and back the previous day and stabling him at the racecourse rather than in his own yard in an elaborate attempt to deceive the horse into putting his best foot forward. All to no avail! Buzzards Bay trailed in next to last, dropping out under pressure after getting close to the leaders with three furlongs or so to go. Plans to run him in the Japan Cup were dropped shortly afterwards: it's a long way to travel a horse who may not consent to do his best.

Buzzards Bay (b.c. 1978)	Joshua (b 1967)	Welsh Rake (b 1955)	Abernant / Wayward Belle
		Charybdis (b 1958)	Chanteur II / Brighton Rock
	Grande Merci (b 1963)	Gratitude (ch 1953)	Golden Cloud / Verdura
		Bibi Mah (b 1955)	Tehran / Mulier Magnifica

Buzzards Bay was bought at the bargain-basement level of 880 guineas as a yearling, having fetched slightly less as a foal. His sire Joshua has not been well patronised at stud. He was a thoroughly game and genuine sort who never stopped improving and ended his career as Timeform's Champion Sprinter of 1971, but lacked a top-class pedigree. Besides Buzzards Bay his best winners

170

here have been Leith Lady and Gifford, the latter a winner of around £50,000 in Malaysia but about three stone behind the very best over here. Buzzards Bay's dam Grande Merci was a five-furlong winner who stayed a mile. A daughter of the useful Bibi Mah and a half-sister to Jukebox, she has produced nothing of note besides Buzzards Bay, her sixth foal, although More (by Song) won a Teesside seller and did quite well when exported to Austria.

Both Joshua and Grande Merci were imposing individuals, particularly Joshua who was a big, powerful, really handsome colt, and Buzzards Bay takes after them. He's a strong-topped, good sort who carries plenty of condition. At the time of writing Buzzards Bay remains in training if a suitable offer isn't forthcoming, which is not such good news for the punter as for the non-betting racegoer. Buzzards Bay is so able that he can't safely be ruled out in any company, yet, as we've said, he can't be trusted. Perhaps there's a case here for bringing in the rule they have in Germany whereby such as he can be left out of the betting. We first heard of its implementation in the case of Los Santos, a very smart though thoroughly unreliable character over there, and it could for example have been used to good effect in races contested by the wayward hurdlers Derring Rose and Levaramoss. Los Santos was left out of the betting on the Hessen-Pokal at Frankfurt in July, so after he finished third punters who backed the fourth received place money; if Los Santos had won the second would have been regarded as the winner for betting purposes. Buzzards Bay stays a mile and a quarter well and acts on any going but ran easily his best race over a mile in the mud. He wore blinkers in his last five races. *H. Collingridge.*

BYCLOUGH BOY 5 br.g. The Brianstan 128–Corcyra Beach 60 (Behistoun — 131) (1981 8s 5g 7g 6fg 6g 5d 1982 8s⁴ 11fg) compact gelding; poor plater; sometimes wears blinkers. *R. Allan.*

BY DECREE (USA) 2 gr.c. Caro 133–Lindaria (Sea-Bird II 145) (1982 7fg **113 p** 7s*)

Perhaps Harwood's best two-year-olds didn't quite come up to the standard set by To-Agori-Mou, Recitation and Kalaglow in recent years but the stable nonetheless had a very successful season with its juveniles: they won over forty races between them. Gordian, Kafu, Lyphard's Special and Proclaim all performed well in top races, and were backed up strongly by such as Northern Adventure who looked particularly promising when winning all his starts, Zoffany who put up very useful efforts to win at Newbury and Goodwood, Sackford who won with great authority at Sandown and Leicester, and By Decree who showed himself a colt of great potential when winning the Mornington Stakes at Ascot on his second appearance. Like so many of the stable's two-year-olds By Decree needed the experience when making his debut in a huge field of maidens at Newmarket late in August. He finished out of the first nine behind Alligatrix. Just a month later By Decree left this form a long way behind when a well-supported second favourite at Ascot. He was soon reasonably close up as the favourite, the Hern-trained Tecorno, made the running in the soft ground. He still had a couple of lengths to make up entering the final furlong but he responded so well to very strong pressure that he pipped Tecorno on the line. The eleven other runners, including the Acomb Stakes third Good As Diamonds and the Goodwood winner Castanet, were left toiling a long way behind.

			Fortino II	Grey Sovereign
		Caro	(gr 1959)	Ranavalo
		(gr 1967)	Chambord	Chamossaire
By Decree (USA)			(ch 1955)	Life Hill
(gr.c. Apr 6, 1980)			Sea-Bird II	Dan Cupid
		Lindaria	(ch 1962)	Sicalade
		(ch 1969)	Wendasy	Your Host
			(ch 1955)	Rampart

Although this was a very good effort by By Decree, his appearance and his pedigree both lead us to believe he'll be capable of still better over middle distances as a three-year-old. He looked far from the finished article at two, rangy and rather sparely made, and he's by Caro, a sire whose stock generally improves from two to three. Caro had a splendid record at stud in France. He topped the list of sires in 1977 and sired such good performers as the Prix du Jockey-Club winner Crystal Palace, the Prix de Diane winner Madelia and the high-class middle-distance colts Nebos, Carwhite and Rusticaro.

*Mornington Stakes, Ascot—a game performance from By Decree
who gets up in the last stride to beat
Tecorno (striped cap)*

In the same year as he headed the list he followed those other top French stallions Herbager, Prince Taj and Le Fabuleux to the USA. Unfortunately the achievements of his first two American crops suggest that Caro, like his predecessors, would have been best left in France.

By Decree was bought for 135,000 dollars at the Saratoga Yearling Sales, a very fair price for a colt of his breeding. His dam, the Sea-Bird II mare Lindaria, was placed only twice from eight starts but she is a daughter of the smart 1957 two-year-old Wendasy and is a half-sister to Northern Bay, the winner of three one-mile stakes races, and Indian Guard, a very useful winner at up to nine furlongs in Ireland. Lindaria has done extremely well at stud. Her first foal, Vagaries (by Vaguely Noble), was a good middle-distance performer in France, winning the Prix Juigne and the Grand Prix d'Evry; her second, the Roberto colt Pittsburgh, was a very useful seven-furlong winner at two in France; and her fifth, the Northern Dancer filly Linda North, has won stakes races both in 1981 and 1982. Interestingly her seventh foal, a colt by Lyphard, was bought by James Delahooke for 150,000 dollars at the 1982 Saratoga Sales so he too will be in training over here. *G. Harwood.*

BYE APPEAL 6 ch.g. Busted 134–One Extra 85 (Abernant 142) (1981 15.5d **73** 16g* 16g 16.5f⁴ 16.5f 1982 15.5fg* 16f⁴ 15.5f* 20fg) rangy gelding; staying handicapper; won at Folkestone in April and May, beating Britwell Lad by 6 lengths on second occasion; last in Ascot Stakes at Royal Ascot on only subsequent start; suited by top-of-the-ground; often makes the running; has worn bandages. *J. Winter.*

BYE BYE BLACKBIRD (USA) 3 b. or br.c. In Reality–Bernie Bird (Bolero) **—** (1981 NR 1982 8f 8.2f 8fg) $275,000Y; small, strong colt; not the best of movers; sixth foal; half-brother to 5 winners, including smart stakes winner Proud Birdie (by Proud Clarion), successful from 6f to 1¼m; dam won twice over 6f in USA; behind in maiden race and minor events; blinkered final start; sold 480 gns Newmarket July Sales. *J. W. Watts.*

BYLLY THE KID 6 ch.g. Yours 125–Bycorne (Prominer 125) (1981 10.5v **118** 8d³ 9.7fg* 9.2s 10.5d² 10.5d* 10f⁴ 10s³ 10d² 10v* 12g⁴ 1982 10d 9.7fg⁴ 10.5d³ 9g 9d* 12g 10fg⁴ 10fg 9.7f* 10s² 10g) first foal; dam, who ran only twice, was placed over 6f at 2 yrs; much improved over last 2 seasons and in 1982 won at Evry in July and at Longchamp (handicap) in September; ran well in better company too, notably when close fourth to Great Substence in Prix Gontaut-Biron at Deauville in between and head second of 13 to Coquelin in La Coupe de Maisons-Laffitte later in September; seems best at around 1¼m; acts on any going. *R. Touflan, France.*

BYROC BOY 5 b.g. Runnymede 123–Royal Pat 80 (King's Troop 118) (1981 **61** 7d 8g 6d 5.3f⁴ 6f 5fg³ 5.3f 5fg⁴ 5fg⁴ 6g 1982 5d 6g 5f 5g* 5.8f2(dis) 6f 5.8f 5g²) former plater; won apprentice handicap at Warwick in May and was close second twice (disqualified on first occasion); best at sprint distances; probably acts on any going; sometimes blinkered. *D. Jermy.*

BYRON'S DAUGHTER 3 ch.f. Hot Spark 126–Blak-en-Bloo 72 (Blakeney — 126) (1981 5fg 5fg³ 5f 7fg 5g 1982 7fg 5fg 5g) small filly; poor plater nowadays; has worn blinkers; sold to D. Yeoman 480 gns Doncaster August Sales. *T. Fairhurst.*

BY THE LAKE 4 b.f. Tyrant–Holiday Inn (Le Haar 126) (1981 12fg 12g — 16.5g² 1982 16.5fg 16.5 15.8d) big, lengthy filly; no form in 1982; suited by 2m; has run well in blinkers. *M. Naughton.*

C

CABALLO 3 ch.g. Track Spare 125–Colinetta (Alba Rock 107) (1981 NR **72** 1982 8fg 9g 8fg² 12fg² 10fg² 12v 10s) rangy gelding; first reported foal; dam never ran; second in large fields of maidens at Chepstow and Beverley; stays 1½m; has run respectably for an amateur rider. *K. Brassey.*

CACHUCHA 3 b.f. Gay Fandango 132–Lisabella (Right Royal V 135) (1981 — NR 1982 10s 8fg 7f 10fg 12d 12.2f 10d 10.6s) 5,800F, IR 7,800Y; plain filly; poor mover; sister to 1½m winner Sunningdale Queen, and half-sister to Bellagolo (by Rheingold), a winner at around 9f; dam, daughter of Irish Guinness Oaks winner Aurabella, won over 9f and 1¼m in France; well beaten in maiden and minor events. *P. Haslam.*

CADASI 2 br.f. Persian Bold 123–Beau Darling 100 (Darling Boy 124) (1982 **68** 6f* 6g 7f) Apr 17; 27,000Y; half-sister to several winners, including smart Irish sprinter Back Bailey (by Roi Soleil); dam, daughter of high-class filly Fair Astronomer, stayed 1m at 2 yrs; won 8-runner minor event at Carlisle in June by short head from The Texel; off course three months after next outing; should stay 7f; sold to BBA (Ireland) 17,500 gns Newmarket December Sales. *Sir Mark Prescott.*

CADDAGAT 2 b.c. Be My Guest 126–Merry Mate 109 (Ballymoss 136) (1982 — 8d 10s 8s⁴) May 30; 14,000Y; deep-girthed colt; half-brother to several minor winners; dam won Irish Guinness Oaks and is daughter of top-class stayer Gladness; no worthwhile form in end-of-season maiden events. *D. Sasse.*

CADEM'S LAW 3 b.g. Legal Eagle 126–Alcadem 75 (Alcide 136) (1981 — 8s 10.2g 1982 8g) big, workmanlike gelding; behind in minor events and a maiden race; has been bandaged behind. *J. Wilson.*

CADI HA 3 b.f. Welsh Pageant 132–Super Dancer 72 (Taj Dewan 128) (1981 **109** 7fg 7f* 1982 10.5fg³ 12f 10fg 10d³ 8g* 8s) tall, rangy filly; excellent mover; first foal; dam lightly-raced daughter of half-sister to Blakeney and Morston; favourite when readily accounting for Montekin by 2 lengths in Petition Stakes at Newmarket in September; had earlier run creditably to be third in Musidora Stakes at York (1¾ lengths behind Last Feather) and Virginia Stakes at Newcastle (stuck on gamely to be just over 1½ lengths behind Cut Loose); not disgraced in Oaks, Nassau Stakes at Goodwood and Prix Perth at Saint-Cloud on other starts; promises to stay 1½m; seems to act on any going. *B. Hobbs.*

CADOUDAL (FR) 3 br.c. Green Dancer 132–Come To Sea (Sea Hawk II 131) **122** (1981 NR 1982 10d* 10.5d³ 12s* 12fg 12f 12s 12v⁴) 180,000 francs Y (approx £18,000); third foal; half-brother to French 1¾m winner Come To Reef (by Mill Reef); dam very useful middle-distance performer in France; won newcomers race at Saint-Cloud in March and Prix Hocquart at Longchamp in May, in latter getting on top in last furlong and winning by a length from Noble Bloom; unlucky in running when very close third to Bois de Grace in Prix Greffulhe at Longchamp in between and ran well on sixth outing in Trusthouse Forte Prix de l'Arc de Triomphe at Longchamp in October, keeping on to be about 7 lengths seventh of 16 to Akiyda; stays 1½m; acts well on soft going; bandaged first appearance. *B. Secly, France.*

CAERLEON (USA) 2 b.c. Nijinsky 138–Foreseer (Round Table) (1982 **117** p 6g* 6.3fg*)
Over the years it has become customary for Vincent O'Brien's two-year-old colts to dominate the Irish Free Handicap. Rarely though can they have shown such tremendous strength in depth as in 1982: seventeen of the stable's eighteen individual runners won a race. These seventeen winners accounted for twenty-seven of the eighty-seven races which fell to a two-year-old colt or gelding in Ireland, a remarkable 31·00%. At the top level their striking rate was even higher; of the eight pattern races open to colts one, the Heinz '57' Phoenix Stakes fell to the filly Sweet Emma, another, the Curragh Stakes, went to Virginia Deer

from the small Flynn stable, and the rest were taken by O'Brien colts. The prospects certainly look bleak for many of the other leading stables facing O'Brien in the top three-year-old events in 1983.

One of the O'Brien pattern race winners, Caerleon, was the first of the stable's juveniles to win. Together with his unconsidered stable-companion Treasure Trove he made his debut in the Tyros Stakes at the Curragh on Irish Sweeps Derby day in June. Caerleon justified favouritism in fine style, quickly joining the leaders, taking a definite advantage soon after halfway and then holding the late run of his stable-mate by two lengths. Third, fifth and seventh places went to the previous winners Kimbernic, Jazz Me Blues and Stormy Fellow, all of whom Caerleon met at level weights, so this was a very pleasing first effort, hardly devalued by the fall of three of the field after halfway. Seven weeks later Caerleon reappeared in the Ballsbridge-Tattersalls Anglesey Stakes, a race his stable has won in the past with, among others, Caerleon's sire Nijinsky and Storm Bird. Storm Bird's three-and-a-half-million-dollar brother Ballydoyle was also in the Anglesey field, as were Virginia Deer, who was giving weight all round, Burslem, a six-length winner of the valuable Ardenode Stud Stakes on his last appearance, and Rock 'N' Roller, a well-regarded winner from the O'Toole stable. Caerleon, at 7/4 on, started nowhere near so well as he had on his debut. He stayed at the rear as Rock 'N' Roller and Virginia Deer disputed the lead and it wasn't until the second half of the race that he began to make up the lost ground. Once into his stride he went about his task in style, moving into the lead below the distance and running on well to beat Rock 'N' Roller by two and half lengths. Burslem finished just a head further behind. This wasn't an exceptional performance—Rock 'N' Roller proved no match for Horage in the Gimcrack soon afterwards and Burslem was later thrashed by Danzatore—but there was every reason to think Caerleon would continue improving. He was mentioned as a possible runner in the Prix de la Salamandre but he met with a slight setback. The Anglesey Stakes turned out to be his final appearance so we are still rather in the dark about him.

Caerleon is an attractive colt who cost 800,000 dollars at the Keeneland Select Sale. He comes from a highly successful family. His half-sister, the very

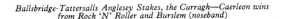

Ballsbridge-Tattersalls Anglesey Stakes, the Curragh—Caerleon wins from Rock 'N' Roller and Burslem (noseband)

Mr R. E. Sangster's "Caerleon"

useful Forli filly Palmistry, won three stakes races at Santa Anita including the Santa Ysabel over eight and a half furlongs; his half-brother Good Thyne, by Herbager, finished second in the Gallinule Stakes, the Queen's Vase, the Irish St Leger and the Queen Alexandra Stakes; and another half-brother, the Reviewer colt Old Testament, is a stakes-placed winner in the USA. Their dam Foreseer

Caerleon (USA) (b.c. Mar 27, 1980)	Nijinsky (b 1967)	Northern Dancer (b 1961)	Nearctic Natalma
		Flaming Page (b 1959)	Bull Page Flaring Top
	Foreseer (b or br 1969)	Round Table (b 1954)	Princequillo Knight's Daughter
		Regal Gleam (b or br 1964)	Hail to Reason Miz Carol

was also very useful, once finishing second to the outstanding filly Susan's Girl in the seven-furlong Santa Ynez Stakes. Foreseer's brother Royal Glint was even better. He became one of the select band to win over a million dollars, amassing the grand total of twenty-one wins. Among his important wins was one in the mile-and-a-quarter Santa Anita Handicap, one of America's most sought-after prizes. Caerleon's grandam Regal Gleam was the champion two-year-old filly of 1966 when successful from five to eight and a half furlongs. She won five of her thirteen starts that year, including the Blue Hen, Frizette and Selima Stakes. Regal Gleam was herself out of a half-sister to the champion handicap mare Straight Deal.

As yet Caerleon's form doesn't match up to that of his stable-companion Danzatore but he is sure to improve a good deal over middle distances. With Danzatore not sure to stay the Derby distance Caerleon could well become the stable's chief Derby hope. We shall watch his progress with interest. *V. O'Brien, Ireland.*

CAERNARVON LAD 3 ch.g. Jimmy Reppin 131–Goldbell (Sovereign Path 125)   —
(1981 5f 6fg 7f 6d   1982 10f 8f 8f 8f 8.2f 10.6h 10.2g 12g 7g 9f 10fg⁴ 10g 10d 8s)
leggy, workmanlike gelding; poor plater; sometimes blinkered.   *R. Hollinshead.*

CAESAR'S GHOST 3 gr.g. Young Emperor 133–Xanthoria (Levmoss 133)   —
(1981 5g 6fg   1982 6fg 6g 6f⁴ 7g 8.3g)   plater; stays 6f; has worn blinkers.
R. Baker.

CAFERANA (BRZ) 5 b.m. Figuron–Ribesia (Jour et Nuit III 123) (1981   —
including 8g   1982 9f 10f 12fg)   compact ex-Brazilian mare; sister to 2 winners
and half-sister to Group 2 winner Adilesa (by Silver); sire won 12 races in Chile
and Brazil, including Grande Premio Sao Paulo; successful from 5f to 1½m in
Brazil where she was one of leading 3-y-o fillies of 1980, winning 4 races, including
Group 1 Grande Premio Jose Guathemozin Nogueira over 1¼m at Sao Paulo;
in rear in minor event at Ripon, Brigadier Gerard Stakes at Sandown (still
burly) and another minor event at Beverley; not beaten all that far when last
of 5 to Alvor in slowly-run race on last-named course in June; stays 1¼m; sold
22,000 gns Newmarket December Sales.   *T. Robson.*

CAJOLERY 6 br.h. Pall Mall 132–Do Please (I Say 125) (1981 7.2fg* 7g⁴   **84**
7.6g* 7g 7f⁴ 8fg 7g 7d   1982 7.2s 7f 7f² 7g⁴ 7g³ 7f 7d)   lightly-made horse;
fair handicapper; in frame at Newmarket in July (neck second to Silver Ruler)
and Lingfield and Brighton in August; best at around 7f; seems to act on any
going.   *I. Walker.*

CAJUN 3 ch.c. Red Regent 123–Ermyn Lass 64 (Ennis 128) (1981 5s⁴ 6f*   **120 §**
6fg 6fg² 7g³ 6fg² 6g*   1982 7fg* 8g 6f³ 5fg 7g³ 6g)   IR 33,000Y; well-made,
attractive colt; good walker; half-brother to several winners, notably smart
sprinter Ubedizzy (by Carnival Dancer); dam won 5f seller; very smart on his
day; always travelling nicely when holding late challenge of Tender King by ½
length in 5-runner Clerical, Medical Greenham Stakes at Newbury in April;
disappointing subsequently, finishing third to Not For Show in Gus Demmy
Memorial Stakes at Haydock (odds on) and to The Quiet Bidder in Kiveton
Park Steel Stakes at Doncaster (found nothing after seemingly going very well),

Mr James H. Stone's "Cajun"

and being well beaten in Airlie/Coolmore Irish 2,000 Guineas at the Curragh, King's Stand Stakes at Royal Ascot and Diadem Stakes at Ascot; took little interest when blinkered in last-named; appeared not to stay 1m; action suggested he'd always be suited by top-of-the-ground; needed to be held up and wasn't one to rely on; retired to Ashleigh Stud, Co. Dublin. *H. Cecil.*

CALAMAN 2 ch.c. Mandrake Major 122–Calaburn 71 (Caliban 123) (1982 52 5fg 5f 5fg 5g³ 5g 6g) Apr 18; 600Y; second foal; dam won 5 times from 6f to 1¼m; moderate plater; not seen out after August; should stay 6f. *Mrs A. Bell.*

CALCUBET 2 b.g. Tower Walk 130–Lucky Deal 93 (Floribunda 136) (1982 — 5g⁴) May 28; 2,500Y; brother to 3-y-o Trade High and half-brother to 3 minor winners; dam 2-y-o 5f winner; 15/8, none too well away when last of 4 in maiden auction event at Ayr in June. *W. Stubbs.*

CALEDONIAN 6 b.h. Philip of Spain 126–Blasllyn 88 (Blast 125) (1981 5s 60 6g 6g 6g³ 5g* 5g* 5f* 5fg 5f⁴ 5f 5f 5f 5fg 5g 5d 1982 5d 5f 5f³ 5f 5f* 5fg 6f² 6d 6g² 6g 5f² 6g 5fg 5d 6f³ 5g 6s 6s 5s) tall horse; sprint handicapper; won at Carlisle in June; acts on any going, but is well suited by top-of-the-ground; wears blinkers; suitable mount for a boy. *J. Calvert.*

CALIBUNDA 7 b.g. Caliban 123–Fairabunda 59 (Floribunda 136) (1981 — 12fg 14d 1982 13d 13f 12f 8fg 12gf 11fg) poor handicapper; stays 13f; suited by a soft surface. *R. E. Peacock.*

CALISOLON 8 b.g. Caliban 123–Solensister 100 (Ennis 128) (1981 8s 12f 47 10s 10s* 14g 1982 12d 10g 12fg 8g 12fg 7g 10g⁴ 10v 10v⁴) plater; stays 2m; acts on any going; has worn blinkers and bandages. *P. K. Mitchell.*

CALLING BIRD 2 b.f. Warpath 113–Hirondelle 86 (Falcon 131) (1982 6fg) — Apr 29; half-sister to 3 winners, including useful 1¼m winner April (by Silly Season); dam won at 1m; 33/1, not in first 9 of 18 to Liberty Tree in minor event at Redcar in September. *C. Thornton.*

CALMACUTTER 5 br.g. Murrayfield 119–Snow Leap 66 (King's Leap 111) — (1981 11s 1982 11g) poor maiden; sometimes wears blinkers; sold 850 gns Doncaster May Sales. *A. W. Jones.*

CALSONG 3 b.c. Song 132–Calspea 81 (Calpurnius 122) (1981 5s 5g² 6s 5g 62 1982 7f² 7f⁴ 7f* 6f² 7f) leggy colt; plater; attracted no bid after winning at Beverley in May; stays 7f; acts on firm going. *J. Hardy.*

CALVINIST 2 b.c. Reform 132–Press Corps 93 (Realm 129) (1982 7f) Mar 5; — neat colt; first foal; dam 2-y-o 6f winner; 25/1, no show in £4,900 event at Kempton in September; sold to P. Burgoyne 725 gns Ascot December Sales. *B. Hanbury.*

CALYPSO BAY 3 b. or br.g. Blue Cashmere 129–Lobster Pot 64 (Silver Shark 60 d 129) (1981 7g 1982 8.2fg 10f 10f² 11.5f 14g 12f 9s) leggy, sparely-made gelding; second in maiden race at Beverley in May; not knocked about in selling handicap sixth start; stays 1½m; acts on firm going; blinkered final outing; sold 2,100 gns Newmarket Autumn Sales. *E. Eldin.*

CAMACHO (USA) 7 b.g. Mickey McGuire–To My Lady (Amber Morn) (1981 71 10d 10g 12f* 11.7fg 10fg² 12h² 10f³ 12s⁴ 10.2d⁴ 1982 8f 12h³ 16fg 12fg² 13.1f* 14f* 13.1g* 13.3g 12g) quite a modest handicapper; in good form in summer and won at Bath (twice) and at Salisbury in between; had stiff task and ran creditably eighth start; stays 1¾m; acts on any going but goes well on top-of-the-ground; goes well for apprentice R. Hills; does best when ridden up with pace; game. *G. Cottrell.*

CAMALOO 4 b.f. Take a Reef 127–Evening Storm (Arctic Storm 134) (1981 — 5fg⁴ 5f 6f 6fg 5g 6s 6g 6d 1982 6d 8d⁴ 7fg 7fg 7g 10.8fg 6fg) compact filly; plater; stays 1m; in rear in blinkers final start. *D. Wilson.*

CAMASUNERIE 2 b.c. Monsanto 121–Fairmist 89 (Skymaster 126) (1982 — 7fg 7.6v) June 6; lengthy, quite attractive colt: good walker; second foal; dam won at up to 7.2f; moderate eighth in big fields of maidens at Salisbury in September and Lingfield (second favourite) in October. *J. Dunlop.*

CAMBERLOT 2 b.c. Solution–Miss Worden 40 (Worden II 129) (1982 6f 65 6fg 6s 6v) May 5; second foal; brother to a poor animal; dam winning hurdler; plating-class maiden; will stay beyond 6f; best form in blinkers final outing. *B. Wise.*

CAMERATA (USA) 3 b.g. Stage Director–Foxy Pam (Tudorich 115) (1981 49 5g⁴ 5g² 5fg³ 6g 6fg 7fg 8f 7d 1982 7g² 8g) compact gelding; plater; stays 7f (well beaten over 1m); has twice worn blinkers. *C. Thornton.*

Mr Andrew Watts's "Camisite"

CAMERONIAN LAD 3 b.g. Bay Express 132–French Maid 89 (Shantung — 132) (1981 NR 1982 12fg) 1,000Y; half-brother to winning Irish stayer Folio (by Jolly Jet); dam, half-sister to good 1¼m filly Bamboozle, won over 1¼m; tailed-off last of 6 to Pottinger in minor event at Edinburgh in May. *J. S. Wilson.*

CAMILLIAN 2 b.c. Prince Tenderfoot 126–Sarphle Wood (St Paddy 133) — (1982 5fg 6f 6fg 7g 10s) Mar 13; IR 6,200F, 13,000Y; smallish, attractive colt; half-brother to a winner in Belgium; dam twice-raced half-sister to several very useful animals; no worthwhile form, including in valuable seller; pulled hard final outing. *N. Callaghan.*

CAMISADO 2 ch.c. Mill Reef 141–Goosie 112 (Sea-Bird II 145) (1982 7s⁴) **82 p** May 9; 60,000Y; half-brother to several winners, including useful middle-distance stayer Lohengrin (by Rheingold) and useful Italian middle-distance 3-y-o Great Boss (by Grundy); dam very useful at around 1m; 3/1, shaped quite well when 3 lengths fourth of 15 to Stratford in maiden race at the Curragh in October; sure to leave this form behind. *D. O'Brien, Ireland.*

CAMISITE 4 ch.c. Hittite Glory 125–Camisole 94 (Psidium 130) (1981 5s³ **118** 5s² 6g 6s² 6d 1982 6fg* 7fg³ 6fg* 6fg² 6d* 6g* 6f 6fg* 6g³ 6g 6d³ 6s*) leggy colt; doesn't impress in his slower paces; improved considerably and had a marvellous season; ran race of his life at end of a busy compaign at Doncaster in November, winning £5,300 Remembrance Day Stakes by 1½ lengths from unlucky-in-running Jester; had earlier won handicaps at Newmarket (2), Doncaster, Nottingham (dead-heated with Winter Wind in Home Ales Gold Tankard) and Ayr (£11,100 Tote Sprint Trophy, from Great Eastern); ran well most other starts, including in Wokingham Stakes at Royal Ascot (second to Battle Hymn) and Ladbrokes (Ayr) Gold Cup (third behind Famous Star); best at 6f; acts on any going; genuine and consistent, and a great credit to his trainer. *W. O'Gorman.*

CAN CAN GIRL 2 ch.f. Gay Fandango 132–Noiritza 114 (Young Emperor 69
133) (1982 6g 6g 6g 5fg) Apr 5; IR 34,000Y; quite attractive, well-made filly;
first foal; dam a speedy 2-y-o who didn't train on; plating-class maiden; stays 6f;
blinkered last 2 outings. *R. Armstrong.*

CANDAULES 4 b.c. Supreme Sovereign 119–Sweet and Naughty 76 (Connaught —
130) (1981 7d³ 5.8d 10f 10f 1982 8f) strong, quite attractive colt; not
certain to stay 1¼m; acts on hard going; sometimes blinkered. *C. James.*

CANDICO 2 b.f. Ancient Monro 89–Proud Sarah (Aggressor 130) (1982 5f³ 47
5f²(dis) 7d 5f 5d) Apr 20; sturdy filly; had a crooked off-fore; poor plater;
dead. *R. Woodhouse.*

CANDIDE 3 gr.f. Bustino 136–Matinee 119 (Zeddaan 130) (1981 7.2d* 7.3d* —
7g 1982 10f 7f) tall, rangy filly; excellent walker; showed useful form at
2 yrs; well beaten in £4,100 event and handicap at Newbury in 1982 and didn't
race after July; should stay 1m+; possibly needs some give in the ground;
has twice been bandaged behind; sold 10,000 gns Newmarket December Sales.
R. Hern.

CANDID PEAL 4 gr.f. Town Crier 119–Angelica (Hornbeam 130) (1981 —
NR 1982 8fg) of no account. *T. Kersey.*

CANDY BURN 2 br.f. Lucky Wednesday 124–Threshoon 81 (Sheshoon 132) —
(1982 5g) May 3; 500Y; third living foal; dam needed long distances; unquoted,
tailed-off last of 7 in minor event at Edinburgh in October; likely to need much
further. *Mrs A. Bell.*

CANDY CASTLE 3 b.f. Habitat 134–Jujube 102 (Ribero 126) (1981 6s³ 58
1982 8d 10f 12f 8.2g* 8.2fg* 9g 9g* 9g 8.2g 8.2s) tall, rangy filly; won apprentice
maiden race and minor event at Hamilton and handicap at Ripon in summer;
should stay 1¼m; ran freely in blinkers third start; has twice run below her best
at Newcastle; trained by P. Walwyn first 3 outings. *E. Weymes.*

CANDY STREET 4 b.f. Streetfighter 120–Sweet Boronia 96 (Mandamus 120) —
(1981 7d 10d 8.3s 8d 10d 8f 7fg 1982 10.8fg 10fg) of no account; has been
tried in blinkers. *W. Charles.*

CANICULAR 2 ch.c. Silly Season 127–Canicule 75 (Canadel II 126) (1982 —
6f 7d 7f 8g 10d) Apr 16; smallish colt; in rear all outings, including in sellers;
sold 300 gns Doncaster Sales. *C. Gray.*

CANIO 5 b.g. Welsh Pageant 132–Nedda 113 (Alcide 136) (1981 10g 12d³ 10g 71
12g 14fg 1982 12d³ 12fg 12fg) lightly-made gelding; hasn't won on flat since
1979 but showed he retained a little ability when third behind easy winner
Capricorn Line in handicap at Kempton in April; suited by 1½m; acts on a firm
and a soft surface; blinkered once at 3 yrs; sold to R. Hodges 3,000 gns Ascot
2nd June Sales. *R. Hannon.*

CANLAS 2 ch.f. Master Sing 109–Blue Oak (Blue and Grey 93) (1982 5fg —
6s) small filly; first known foal; dam of no account; sweated up when well
beaten in maiden races at Wolverhampton (saddle slipped) and Leicester in
the autumn. *K. Bridgwater.*

CANNON KING 6 b.h. Owen Anthony 102–Primmy 56 (Primera 131) (1981 104
10g 1982 10f⁴ 10g³ 10fg⁴ 10f* 12fg² 10.5f² 12g² 11d⁴ 9d 10g*) smallish horse;
won Daily Mirror Handicap at Epsom in June and Tia Maria Autumn Handicap
at Newmarket in October in really good style, beating Lafontaine by 5 lengths
in former and Fine Sun by 3 lengths in latter; also second in good handicaps won
by Spin of a Coin at Royal Ascot, Buzzards Bay at York and Lusitanica at
Newmarket; stays 1½m; acts on any going; suitable mount for an apprentice;
genuine, although was a shade disappointing eighth start. *J. Dunlop.*

CANNON SHELL (USA) 3 ch.c. Torsion–Promise Us (Promise) (1981 102
6g³ 5s* 1982 7f 6fg² 5f) attractive, good-topped, useful sort; good mover;
creditable 3½ lengths third of 6 to Lightning Label in Ladbrokes Abernant
Stakes at Newmarket in April, setting a strong gallop for nearly 5f; not disgraced
when eighth of 13 to Mummy's Game in Temple Stakes at Sandown in May on
only subsequent start; likely to prove best at sprint distances; seems to act on
any going; useful. *M. Albina.*

CANOODLE 4 ch.f. Warpath 113–Turtle Dove (Gyr 131) (1981 8g 12.5f* 65
12fg* 12.5f² 13fg 12.2g 13d³ 16s² 16s³ 18g 1982 13s 15.8f³ 15f* 14.6g³ 16f⁴
16.5g⁴ 16fg 16d* 15.8d² 12d) small, lightly-made filly; won handicaps at

Edinburgh in June and Nottingham in September, latter by head from Brave Maiden when 33/1; stays 2m (didn't seem to get 2¼m on final start in 1981), acts on any going; sold 3,000 gns Doncaster November Sales. *C. Thornton.*

CANTABILE 3 b.f. Bustino 136–Penumbra 99 (Wolver Hollow 126) (1981 — 5g 6g 1982 7fg 7.6fg) sparely-made filly; behind in maiden races; sold 500 gns Ascot 2nd June Sales. *P. Mitchell.*

CANTENAC BROWN (USA) 3 b.g. Sham–Swingster (Bold Ruler) (1981 **61** 6g 7g 7fg 1982 10f 12f 16d 16f 16.5f3 15.5f3 15.5fg2 15.5fg 14g 16s) neat, attractive gelding; staying maiden; acts on firm going. *B. Swift.*

CAN'T SWIM 3 b.f. Bruni 132–Out of Depth 65 (Deep Diver 134) (1981 7g — 7g 7fg 6fg 8.2fg 8g 1982 8d 12f) compact, strong-quartered filly; plater; best run at 6f; blinkered last 3 outings in 1981; has sweated up badly. *P. Mitchell.*

CAP D'AZURE 2 b.f. Majority Blue 125–Fravelot (Javelot 124) (1982 5g4 5g **76** 6s2 6v3) Mar 13; IR 11,000Y; neat filly; third produce; half-sister to The Very Thing (by Jupiter Pluvius), a fair middle-distance winner and useful hurdler; dam won over 1¼m; 4 lengths second to New Coins in maiden event at Hamilton in September, easily best effort; will stay beyond 6f; yet to race on a firm surface. *S. Norton.*

CAPITAL HAND 2 ch.c. Nearly A Hand 115–Florecilla 90 (Matador 131) **77** (1982 5g 7g 6f 6g3 6d3 6g4 7s) Mar 20; 3,600F, 3,000Y; close-coupled colt; half-brother to several winners; dam won over 6f at 2 yrs, and stayed 1m; modest maiden; form only at 6f, but should be suited by 7f+; hung under pressure sixth start. *G. Toft.*

CAP OF FREEDOM 3 b.c. Thatch 136–Parolee 88 (Sing Sing 134) (1981 NR **81** 1982 7fg 8d4 8fg2 7s*) strong, attractive colt; good mover; eighth foal; half-brother to 7 winners, including smart miler Trusted (by Crepello); dam sprinter; apprentice ridden when winning handicap at Goodwood in September; had shown plenty of ability previously; will stay beyond 1m; acts well on soft going. *J. Dunlop.*

CAPRICORN LINE 4 ch.c. High Line 125–Floradora Do 85 (Derring-Do 131) **111** (1981 7fg 10s* 10g2 10d* 10.6s2 13.3g2 12fg2 12g2 14g* 1982 12d* 12s3 12v

Mr Ivan Allan's "Capricorn Line"

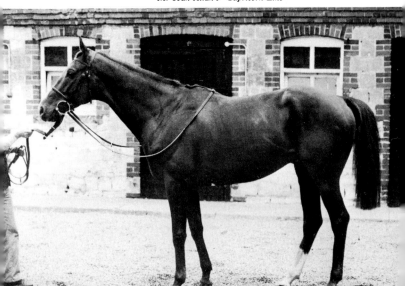

12g² 16g* 12g²) medium-sized, quite attractive colt; has improved steadily through his career and in 1982 developed into a very useful performer, winning handicap at Kempton in April (very easily indeed) and Lonsdale Stakes at York in August; had a very hard race in latter, but responded gamely to pressure and beat Ore by a head after a good battle; looked extremely well and ran another good race when 1½ lengths second of 8 to Khairpour in £5,200 event at Newmarket in September; had stiffish tasks and also ran well abroad on second, third and fourth starts, including when third to Hard To Sing in Grand Prix d'Evry and second to Terreno in Gran Premio di Milano, beaten only about 2 lengths each time; stays well; yet to race on very firm going, but acts on any other; sometimes sweats up; most genuine and consistent. *L. Cumani.*

CAPRICORN SAINT 2 b.f. Welsh Saint 126–January 68 (Aggressor 130) — (1982 5.1f) Feb 1; 3,600Y; sturdy filly; half-sister to 2 minor winners; dam, a plater, won at up to 1m; 50/1 and in need of race, always behind in maiden race at Yarmouth in June. *C. Spares.*

CAPRILI (FR) 4 gr.f. Caro 133–Vivarella (Cambremont 121) (1981 7g 10f 8fg **45** 8.2s 8s 10v 1982 8d 7g 7.6f⁴ 7f* 6s) close-coupled filly; held up when winning apprentice handicap at Folkestone in August; stays 7f well; acts on firm going; blinkered final outing at 3 yrs. *G. Balding.*

CAPSTAN 4 b.c. Welsh Pageant 132–Packet 96 (Royal Palace 131) (1981 10fg **119** 12f⁴ 12fg* 12d³ 14fg* 12fg⁴ 16g² 1982 12fg⁴ 14f² 16f² 12f 12f*) strong, compact, good sort; very smart performer; goes particularly well at Goodwood and was gaining his second win in the race (and breaking his third course record there) when runaway winner of 4-runner Alycidon Stakes in July, beating Lafontaine by 12 lengths; had earlier been no match for Ardross but had nevertheless run very well when second in Yorkshire Cup at York (beaten a length) and Henry II Stakes at Sandown (went down by 2 lengths); suited by a test of stamina; possibly needed a sound surface; wore blinkers; often made running; sold 41,000 gns Newmarket December Sales; stud in India. *R. Hern.*

CAPTAIN BLUE 2 b.c. Captain James 123–Edansa (Majority Blue 126) (1982 **54** 5.8g 7fg 7fg 8s 10d) May 4; 2,100Y; lengthy colt; half-brother to French 1m winner November Rose (by Huntercombe); dam, French 8.5f winner, is sister to French Oaks third Odisea; moderate plater; best run at 1m. *T. Marshall.*

CAPTAIN BRASSBOUND 5 b.g. Brigadier Gerard 144–Hardware 86 (Hard — Sauce 131) (1981 7g⁴ 8.2d 12g² 1982 10g 8.2g⁴ 10g 8.2v 7g) poor handicapper; stays 1½m; seems to act on any going. *R. McDonald.*

CAPTAIN CRAIGTON 4 gr.g. Derwent–Morag (Our Babu 131) (1981 NR — 1982 12f 13.8f 16fg 9f) smallish, lightly-made gelding; first known foal; dam never ran; showed first sign of ability when fifth of 11 to Broken Seal in long-distance handicap at Beverley in July on final start; apprentice ridden. *C. Spares.*

CAPTAIN HENRY 3 ch.g. Bay Express 132–Astraline 97 (Skymaster 126) — (1981 5s 5f³ 6g 6d 6fg* 6d³ 6g 1982 6s 6fg 6g 6g 6fg) small gelding; good mover; won maiden race at Yarmouth in 1981; ran poorly at 3 yrs; stays 6f; probably acts on any going; sold to M. Lambert 880 gns Newmarket Autumn Sales. *R. Armstrong.*

CAPTAIN OATES 3 b.c. Oats 126–Gay Signal (Lord Gayle 124) (1981 5g 6fg **66** 1982 10.1fg 10f 14f⁴ 16fg 15.5fg⁴ 16fg⁴ 16s* 16s) close-coupled, narrow colt; enterprisingly ridden when winning handicap at Warwick in October; suited by a test of stamina; acts well on soft going. *N. Vigors.*

Alycidon Stakes, Goodwood—Capstan gains his second win in the race with a runaway victory from Lafontaine

CAPTAIN'S BIDD 2 ch.c. Captain James 123–Muffet 75 (Matador 130) (1982 — 6g 6s 5d 5g) May 5; 8,600Y; sturdy, workmanlike colt; half-brother to several winners here and abroad, including 3-y-o sprinter Feather Sound (by Be My Guest); dam (known as Matty) won over 5f; no worthwhile form in maiden and minor events; sweated up final start; sold 1,250 gns Ascot December Sales. *G. Huffer.*

CAPTAIN TEMPEST 2 b.c. Manado 130–Calibina 101 (Caliban 123) (1982 **80** 5g 6v* 7s 7s) May 10; 10,000Y; rather lightly-made colt; second foal; dam, winner of Wokingham Stakes and Stewards' Cup, stayed 1m; won 9-runner maiden race at Folkestone in October by 1½ lengths from Aqaba Prince; should stay 1m; acts on heavy going. *G. Hunter.*

CAPTAIN WEBSTER 2 ch.c. Sandford Lad 133–Maynooth Belle (Busted 134) **78** (1982 6f 7fg 8s 8s 10s*) Apr 1; 2,800F, 6,600Y; smallish, lengthy colt; second produce; dam, out of half-sister to Psidium, never ran; finished strongly to win 17-runner maiden race at Nottingham in October by 2½ lengths from Al-Abjar, easily best effort; evidently well suited by test of stamina; acts on soft going. *S. Woodman.*

CAPTIVATE 2 b. or br.f. Mansingh 120–Mildura 98 (Vilmorin) (1982 6s) Apr — p 25; sister to fairly useful sprinter Pontin Lad, and half-sister to speedy animals Gourmet (by Grey Sovereign) and Gauleiter (by Mummy's Pet); dam 5f sprinter; 25/1; prominent throughout without being knocked about when 7 lengths sixth of 16 behind Onaizah in maiden race at Leicester in November; should improve. *A. Hide.*

CAPTIVATING LADY 2 b.f. Averof 123–Sacred Mountain 74 (St Paddy 133) **81** (1982 6f 8f 5s 6g*) Mar 19; 2,100Y; rangy filly; third foal; half-sister to a winner in Norway; dam sister to very smart 1m to 1¼m performer Calpurnius; 66/1 and ridden by 5-lb claimer, won nursery at Newmarket in October by head from Rumz, producing fine turn of foot to lead near finish; bred to stay 1m. *W. Musson.*

CAP TOO 6 b.g. Continuation 120–Merry Thought (Pindari 124) (1981 NR — 1982 18f) small, strong gelding; plater; stays 1m; acts on firm going. *J. Blundell.*

CARABIN 2 b.c. Scottish Rifle 127–Quick Burn 94 (Carnival Dancer 113) (1982 **82** 5f² 5fg³ 6f⁴ 6f 5g³ 5fg 5fg* 5g 5d) May 1; workmanlike colt; has rather a round action; half-brother to 2 winning 2-y-o's, including far 1980 5f winner Miss Quaver (by Averof); dam winning sister to smart sprinter Ubedizzy and half-sister to Cajun; blinkered, showed return to form when winning 17-runner maiden race at Folkestone in September by 5 lengths; best at 5f; none too consistent. *S. Matthews.*

CARA FLORA 2 br.f. Scottish Rifle 127–Aracara (Prince Tenderfoot 126) — (1982 7g 6fg 8fg) June 7; small, close-coupled filly; third foal; dam placed at up to 1½m in Ireland; no form in varied company. *W. Wightman.*

CARALIST 6 ch.g. Traditionalist–Hy Carol (High Hat 131) (1981 NR 1982 — 12s) strong, attractive gelding; stays 1½m; acts on hard going and is probably unsuited by soft; races with his head high; sold out of M. Delahooke's stable 680 gns Ascot July Sales. *Dr A. Jones.*

CARAN D'ACHE 3 ch.g. Huntercombe 133–Alfambra (Nashua) (1981 5s **50** 6s 6g 1982 6s⁴ 5f 6fg 6g⁴ 6g⁴ 7fg² 6fg⁴ 6g³ 7d 6s) quite well-made gelding; plater; suited by 7f; seems to act on any going; suitable mount for an apprentice; didn't find much off bridle sixth start. *G. Balding.*

CARDIFF 5 ch.h. Appiani II 128–Christiana 106 (Double Jump 131) (1981 — 12s² 12d 14d* 14s 16s 16fg 1982 15.5g) lightly-made horse; possibly stays 2m; suited by some give in the ground; bandaged in front final start at 4 yrs; pulled up only outing of 1982; sold 1,100 gns Newmarket July Sales. *R. Hoad.*

CARDINAL FLOWER 5 ch.h. Sharpen Up 127–Ixia 91 (I Say 125) (1981 **87** 10fg 10.2g 8g² 9fg 8fg² 8g² 8fg* 8fg³ 8fg² 1982 8g* 8f 9.4f² 8f³ 8.3fg³ 8fg 8fg²) good sort; good mover; looked exceptionally well when beating Romoss by 1½ lengths in handicap at Pontefract in April; placed at Carlisle (twice), Windsor and Goodwood (amateur riders) afterwards; stays 1¼m; yet to show he can handle very soft going but acts on any other; has run respectably for an amateur; sold to A. Scott 11,000 gns Ascot September Sales. *G. Pritchard-Gordon.*

CARDINAL PALACE 4 ch.f. Royal Palace 131–Early Rose 61 (Will Somers **71** 114§) (1981 9.4g 8g² 9.4fg² 9.4g* 10f 11fg 11d² 11d⁴ 12g* 1982 12.3g 16f⁴

12f⁴ 12d⁴ 12f* 13fg 12fg 11s* 12v* 12s) tall, lightly-made filly; won handicaps at Leicester in July and Hamilton in September and October; suited by 1¼m (possibly doesn't stay 2m); acts on any going; sweating and below form final start; sold 9,400 gns Newmarket December Sales. *R. D. Peacock.*

CARDINALS WALK 4 ch.g. Red Alert 127–Stay Nice 85 (Nice Guy 123) (1981 10d 12g 8.3fg 10.1fg³ 12fg 1982 12fg 11g) poor form, including in selling company; promises to stay 1¼m. *D. Francis.*   —

CARIBBEAN BLUE 4 b. or br.f. Blue Cashmere 129–Dido's Grandaughter (By Thunder! 122) (1981 8g 7.6g 11.5g³ 8.2s⁴ 10s 1982 8f 8.2g³ 10f⁴ 10f 12.2f 10fg 12fg) poor maiden; in frame in 2 handicaps at Nottingham in July; probably stays 11.5f; sometimes blinkered; retained by trainer 820 gns Newmarket July Sales. *J. Winter.*   —

CARIBBEAN DREAM 3 b.g. Saucy Kit 76–Lady Lake (Tennyson 119) (1981 5g 5d 6g 5fg 6fg³ 5g 7g² 7fg 8f 8.2d 1982 7g 8f 9f 8fg 8f) small, non-thoroughbred gelding; poor plater. *T. Barnes.*   —

CARIBIQUE 2 b.c. Mansingh 120–Off The Mark (On Your Mark 125) (1982 6s 6g) Mar 20; 4,100Y; chunky, short-legged colt; third foal; half-brother to a winning plater by Red God; dam won over 1m in France; backward, soundly beaten in minor event at Lingfield in September and maiden race at Newmarket the following month. *G. Lewis.*   —

CARLTON HALL 5 b.g. Club House 110–Donna Lollo 102 (Donatello II) (1981 11s 12d 7g 8fg* 9g* 8fg⁴ 10.5s⁴ 1982 8f⁴ 8f) workmanlike gelding; poor walker; stays 9f; acts on any going and on any track; good mount for an inexperienced rider; sold 2,000 gns Doncaster August Sales. *D. Smith.*   —

CARLTON OPAL 3 gr.f. Godswalk 130–Sirmio 82 (Shantung 132) (1981 NR 1982 7fg 7.6fg⁴ 8fg* 8.5f 8fg 8d³ 7.6g 10.4d 8.2g 8.2s) IR 5,500Y (privately); lengthy, well-made filly; good walker; reportedly split a pastern at 2 yrs; half-sister to fairly useful Irish 6f to 9f winner Exactly (by Red Alert) and a winner in Malaya; dam won over 7f at 2 yrs; easily won 22-runner maiden race at Goodwood in May; creditable third in £5,000 handicap at Beverley in July; stays 1m (well beaten over 1¼m); sold 6,600 gns Newmarket December Sales. *R. Williams.*   **81**

CARNEADES 2 b.c. Homing 130–Connarca (Connaught 130) (1982 7d² 7g* 7g² 8d) Mar 16; workmanlike colt; good mover; fourth foal; half-brother to a winner in Hungary; dam unraced half-sister to Cesarewitch winner Orosio; led inside last to beat Il Pontevecchio by ¾ length in 10-runner maiden race at Ayr in July; good second to Moment In Time in minor event at Redcar the following month; didn't impress in paddock when last of 10 to Quite A Night in nursery at Ayr in September; should stay 1¼m; yet to race on a firm surface. *M. H. Easterby.*   **93**

John Barr Scotch Whisky Stakes, Ayr—the apprentice-ridden Carneades runs on well to beat Il Pontevecchio

CARNIVAL DAN 3 b.g. Carnival Dancer 113–Alegria (Right Boy 137) (1981 —
5g 1982 8fg) robust gelding; last in seller and minor event in the North.
J. Mason.

CARNIVAL PRIZE 2 b.g. Carnival Dancer 113–Bath Miss 83 (Appiani II 128) 51
(1982 5g 5d³ 5g 6d 7fg 8d) June 5; plain, compact gelding; dam won over 7f at
2 yrs; poor plater; no form after second outing; should stay beyond 5f; blinkered
last 3 starts. *D. Yeoman.*

CAROLINE FISHER 3 b.f. English Prince 129–Travelling Fair 95 (Vienna 127) —
(1981 6fg 6s 6d 1982 10d 6fg 7fg 7.6fg 7f 6fg 7fg 6d) lengthy filly; poor plater;
sometimes blinkered. *A. Jarvis.*

CAROL'S COMEDY 2 b.f. Cawston's Clown 113–Welsh Carol (Singing Bede 61
122) (1982 5g 5g 5fg 5fg 5g 5.1g 5fg* 5g 5v) Mar 6; reportedly 1,600Y (privately), resold 500Y; lengthy filly; first foal; dam never ran; won maiden auction
event at Folkestone in August by a head from Creme d'Or; in rear in sellers
subsequently; acts on a firm surface; does best when held up; blinkered third
outing; sold 1,250 gns Newmarket Autumn Sales. *G. Blum.*

CAROLSIDE 2 br.f. Music Maestro 119–Primrose Bank 91 (Charlottown 127) 108
(1982 5fg* 5f* 5fg³ 6f² 6fg 6g) Apr 15; lengthy, quite attractive filly; good
walker and mover; second foal; half-sister to 3-y-o 1¼m winner Primrolla (by
Relko); dam middle-distance filly; useful at her best, but appeared not to progress
after failing by only head to overhaul Crime of Passion in 8-runner Cherry
Hinton Stakes at Newmarket in July, running moderately in St Catherine's
Stakes at Newbury and just a fair race in Lowther Stakes at York; earlier had
won small races at Wolverhampton and Brighton and had dead-heated for third
place, 3 lengths behind Widaad, in Queen Mary Stakes at Royal Ascot; may
stay beyond 6f. *P. Walwyn.*

Susan Lady Chetwode's "Carolside"

CARO NOME 3 b.f. Jolly Good 122–Gilda 65 (Connaught 130) (1981 NR 62
1982 14g 14d 12fg* 16fg³) 4,400Y, 540 2-y-o; second foal; dam won 1m seller;
dropped in class and apprentice ridden when winning seller at Thirsk in September; bought in 1,750 gns afterwards; creditable third to Bajan Sunshine in
minor event at Lingfield later in month; stays well; acts on a firm surface.
A. Bailey.

CAROUSER 5 b.g. Warpath 113–Brandy (Busted 134) (1981 12g 12g⁴ 12fg 37
12g 12.2fg 12f⁴ 1982 12g 12g 8f 11fg 8f² 11g 10d 12fg⁴ 19f 12g) lightly-made,
lean gelding; plater; stays 1½m; acts on a firm and a soft surface; has run creditably for an inexperienced rider; has worn bandages; blinkered eighth start.
D. Chapman.

CARPENTER'S BOY 4 b.g. Steel Heart 128–Grandee Ann (Cyane) (1981 6s —
6g 7g 6d 6d 5f 1982 6fg⁴ 5g⁴ 6f 5f) neat, strong gelding; poor sprint plater;
blinkered last 3 outings. *M. Naughton.*

CARPET GENERAL 6 b.g. Sallust 134–Red Val 110 (Red God 128§) (1981 —
8d 12d 8f 8g³ 8fg 8g 1982 10fg 8f) strong gelding; poor mover nowadays;
useful handicapper at his best but seems to have lost his enthusiasm; stays 1m
well; acts on any going but is possibly suited by some give in the ground; suitable
mount for an apprentice; blinkered final start; sold 950 gns Ascot June Sales.
W. Wharton.

CARREG CENNEN 3 ch.g. Native Bazaar 122–Cennen-Olive (Wolver Hollow 61
126) (1981 5g 5s⁴ 5.8g³ 5f 5g 1982 6d 5fg² 5.8f² 5f 5h 5g 5.3f³ 5fg 5f² 6fg 6g 5d)
tall, leggy gelding; sprint maiden; acts on any going; usually bandaged off-fore.
Dr. A. Jones.

CARRIAGE WAY 8 br.h. Track Spare 125–Polyandrist 92 (Polic 126) (1981 71
8s* 8v² 7d 8g 8fg 8fg 8d* 8d 8s 8v 8g 1982 8g 8.2v³ 8d* 8f⁴ 8g 8f 8fg 8.2f 8g 8fg*
7.2s² 7s 9s* 8.2s³ 8.2s³ 8s) won handicaps at Warwick in April, Redcar
(apprentices) in September and York in October; awarded race after going down
by a head to Lion City in apprentices' event on last-named; best form at around
1m; acts on any going, but is very much at home with give in the ground;
blinkered once in 1979; good mount for a boy. *W. Stubbs.*

CARRY ON AGAIN 4 ch.g. Swing Easy 126–Hi-Conkers 86 (Sica Boy 132) —
(1981 6fg 6g 8g 1982 12fg 12f) rangy gelding; lightly raced and poor form
since 1980; yet to prove he stays middle distances; looked temperamental when
blinkered once in 1980. *G. Fletcher.*

CARRY OVER 4 b.g. Some Hand 119–Hardella 60 (Hard Ridden 131) (1981 43
8d 8fg 8fg³ 7f³ 8fg 8f² 8g 7d 1982 8f⁴ 8f 8h 8f 10d⁴ 10g 10g 8fg⁴ 8g) lengthy,
workmanlike gelding; poor walker; plater; ran respectably in non-sellers on
occasions in 1982, but is none too consistent; stays 1m; acts on firm going.
G. Balding.

CARTERS WAY 2 b.c. Farm Walk 111–Darling Do (Derring-Do 131) (1982 —
7d) June 8; neat, sturdy colt; brother to 3 winners, notably very useful 1m
to 1¾m winner Move Off; dam unraced half-sister to high-class miler Quorum;
unquoted and in need of race, chased leaders 4f in 18-runner minor event won
by Northern Adventure at Doncaster in October. *Miss S. Hall.*

CARTHAGENA 2 b.f. Royalty 130–Roman Meeting (Quorum 126) (1982 —
7d 8fg) Apr 9; small, fair sort; sixth foal; dam unraced half-sister to high-
class chaser Spanish Steps; little worthwhile form in maiden races at Yarmouth
(33/1) in August and Beverley (10/1) in September. *W. Hastings-Bass.*

CARTRON 4 b.g. Military 112–Belle Tack (Hard Tack 111§) (1981 10.6d 5fg —
1982 9g 6g 5g) little worthwhile form in varied races, including seller. *B.
McMahon.*

CASA ESQUILLINA (USA) 4 b.c. Key To The Kingdom–Missile Miss —
(Cyclotron) (1981 8g 7g³ 7fg² 6f* 8g 6g² 6g 6d 1982 6fg 7fg 6fg 7g 6g) workmanlike, slightly hollow-backed colt with a round action; didn't run up to his
best in 1982; best at distances short of 1m; yet to race on very soft going, but
acts on any other; rather headstrong, and wore blinkers last 2 starts (ran wide
into straight on first occasion); sold 1,600 gns Newmarket July Sales. *P. Cole.*

CASAL ROYALE 4 b.f. Netherkelly 112–Composite 61 (Compensation 127) —
(1981 NR 1982 8fg) 720 3-y-o; first foal; dam won over 1m and was also
successful over hurdles; poor form over hurdles; in rear in amateur riders race
at Warwick in July. *D. McCain.*

CASANNA 3 b.f. Star Appeal 133–Try-Gun (Combat 123) (1981 NR 1982 **62**
10.2g 12.3g⁴ 12fg² 12fg⁴ 12fg 15.8d) fair sort; half-sister to several winners
here and abroad; dam of no account; only plating class; stays 1½m. *A. Hide.*

CASE HISTORY 4 gr.c. Track Spare 125–Petite Path 106 (Sovereign Path 125) **70 d**
(1981 5d* 6d⁴ 6g 6fg 6fg 5s 6s 1982 6g 6f³ 6fg⁴ 7fg 5g 6g 5.8f 5g 5fg) lightly-
made, fair sort; sprint handicapper; third to Gabitat at Newbury in May,
easily best effort of 1982; probably acts on any going; often wears a bandage
on his off-fore; sold 420 gns Ascot November Sales. *R. Hannon.*

CASE THE JOINT 4 b.f. Upper Case–Ribo Pride 77 (Ribero 126) (1981 **—**
10s 10fg 10fg 8.2s 1982 7fg 10.1d) poor plater; has worn blinkers. *J. Cann.*

CASHEL BAY 3 ch.g. Riboboy 124–Beech Tree 67 (Fighting Ship 121) (1981 **66**
5s³ 5d 5d³ 6d 5d 6g 7g 8g 7g 8s 10s 1982 12d³ 10d 16.5fg² 14fg⁴ 19s) workmanlike gelding; good mover; staying maiden; acts on a firm and a soft surface;
has sweated up; has twice worn blinkers; suitable mount for an apprentice;
sold out of G. Beeson's stable 5,000 gns Ascot January Sales. *Mrs. N. Smith.*

CASHEL EXPRESS 2 b.g. Bay Express 132–Damaring (Saidam) (1982 **57**
5f 5f 6g 5g³) May 15; 2,200Y; sturdy, compact, quite attractive gelding; half-
brother to several winners, including smart 1980 French 2-y-o Mont Pelion
(by Luthier); dam 2-y-o 6f winner in USA; plater; blinkered when creditable
third at Ripon in August; should stay 6f. *M. W. Easterby.*

CASHEL PRINCE (USA) 3 b.c. Exclusive Native–Semi Princess (Semi-Pro) **93**
(1981 NR 1982 12s* 12fg² 12fg² 12fg² 14fg⁴ 11.7fg* 12g 12g) $70,000Y; tall colt;
not the best of movers; third foal; half-brother to a minor stakes winner in USA
by Prince John; dam, minor stakes winner, won from 4f to 6f; won maiden race
at Haydock in April and handicap at Windsor in July; in frame in minor event
and 2 handicaps in between; seems to stay 1¾m; has won on a firm surface but
gives impression he'll always do better with some give in the ground; one paced.
G. Harwood.

CASHMOOR 4 b.g. Ashmore 125–Go Friendly (Be Friendly 130) (1981 **78**
8g 8fg 10f 11.7h 10fg³ 12g 12f 1982 8d³ 10f 8g² 8f⁴ 10fg 10f 12d* 12g 12.2fg*
11.7g* 11.7fg*) strong, close-coupled gelding; much improved and won handicaps at Lingfield, Warwick and Windsor (twice); won both races at Windsor
in good style after making all; stays 1½m; yet to show he acts on extremes of
going. *R. Baker.*

CASH OR CARRY (USA) 2 b.c. Naskra–Pay Cash (Whistler 129) (1982 **84**
5fg⁴ 6fg³ 6g 8.2s² 7.6v⁴ 7s 7s) Apr 24; quite an attractive colt; half-brother
to winners in USA by Cougar II and Grey Dawn II; dam, winner 6 times from
4.5f to 7f in France and USA, is half-sister to Oaks winner Pia; in frame in
maiden races, being beaten just over 2 lengths when fourth of 13 to Joyful
Dancer at Lingfield in October; stays 1m; seems to act on any going; off course
3 months before third outing; wore tongue strap final start. *B. Hanbury.*

CASSIO LIL 3 b. or br.f. Scottish Rifle 127–Solway Bay 86 (Tamerlane 128) **58**
(1981 5d 5fg 5g 6f 7g 6d⁴ 1982 12g 10d² 13.8f* 12fg³ 12g 12.2f² 12g³ 13.8d)
leggy, lightly-made filly; plater; bought in 2,500 gns after winning at Catterick
in July; stays 1¾m; seems to act on any going but goes well on firm; effective
with or without blinkers; has worn bandages; has sweated up. *D. Morley.*

CASSLEY RIVER 3 b.f. Relkino 131–Strathoykel 94 (Aberdeen 109) (1981 **—**
6f³ 7fg* 7d* 7fg* 8g⁴ 7g 1982 7f 7.2g⁴ 8fg) leggy, rather narrow filly; good
mover; successful 3 times in varied company in 1981; didn't really find her form
at 3 yrs; suited by 7f and 1m; acted on a firm and a soft surface; dead. *Sir
Mark Prescott.*

CASTANET 2 ch.c. Green Dancer 132–Pampas Flower 80 (Pampered King 121) **86**
(1982 6fg* 7s) Feb 18; rangy colt; half-brother to several winners, including
useful 6f and 7f winner Evita (by Reform); dam, half-sister to top-class performers Gratitude and Highest Hopes, won at 1m; just in need of race, looked
inexperienced in paddock but showed no signs of greenness in race when second
favourite for 13-runner newcomers event at Goodwood in September, disputing
lead throughout and running on well to win by ½ length from Fatih; 9/1, disappointed in stronger company on different ground at Ascot later in month,
being towards rear most of way in 13-runner race won by By Decree; should be
suited by 7f and 1m. *P. Walwyn.*

Doublet Ltd's "Castelnau"

CAST A SHADOW 2 b.c. Welsh Saint 126–Predestination 73 (Premonition **87**
130) (1982 5fg 5f² 5f* 6f 6g⁴ 6fg 6s) Apr 24; well-grown, rather leggy, lengthy
colt; brother to useful Irish 5f to 1m winner La Samanna; dam won over 1m;
won 6-runner minor event at Leicester in May; ran consistently in his other
races until failing to show under 8-6 in Golden Gates Nursery at Ascot in September on final start; promises to stay 7f; bit coltish on second outing, was on toes
on third and sweated up on subsequent appearances. *A. Jarvis.*

CASTAWAY (FR) 3 ch.f. Filiberto 123–Castania (Orsini 124) (1981 6fg 6s —
6d 1982 5fg 6g 7fg 6fg 7fg 7f⁴ 8g 5fg 7g) workmanlike filly; plating-class
maiden; promises to stay 7f. *C. Austin.*

CASTELNAU (USA) 4 b.c. Irish Castle–Bay of Fundy (Portsmouth) (1981 **111**
12fg² 12s 16d² 16.9fg* 16f² 19fg* 18g 1982 16fg* 18.4fg 16f 22.2fg² 21f) strong,
good-looking colt; has a good, long stride; made an impressive reappearance
when winning Mono Sagaro Stakes at Ascot in April, finding a tremendous turn
of foot and winning by 1½ lengths from Heighlin; stayed on when 1½ lengths
second to Ore in Queen Alexandra Stakes at Royal Ascot in June but was among
first beaten when 8 lengths fifth of 7 finishers behind Heighlin in Goodwood Cup
the following month (co-favourite); given a great deal to do in slowly-run Chester
Cup and had stiff task in Henry II Stakes at Sandown on second and third starts;
stays extremely well; has run creditably on a soft surface but is very well suited
by top-of-the-ground; can produce an excellent turn of foot for a stayer; sent
to USA. *P. Cole.*

CASTLE DOUGLAS 2 b.g. Amboise 113–Linguistic 95 (Porto Bello 118) —
(1982 8.2s) Apr 19; rangy gelding; second foal; dam won twice over 5f at 2
yrs; unquoted, on backward side and green, made some late headway when
eleventh of 19 behind Holy Spark in minor event at Nottingham in October.
Sir Mark Prescott.

CASTLE GUARD 2 br.c. Home Guard 129–Perldia (Diatome 132) (1982 **111**
6fg³ 7d* 6f* 7f 8s) Mar 24; well-made, useful-looking colt; superb mover;
second foal; dam won over 4.5f at 2 yrs in France; kept on strongly to win 19-
runner maiden race at Salisbury in June by 1½ lengths from Jackdaw; made all
to beat Stop Talking 2 lengths in 4-runner £3,800 event at Lingfield the following
month; good fifth to Dunbeath, after setting strong gallop to distance, in Royal
Lodge Stakes at Ascot, final outing and easily better subsequent effort; acts on
any going; sent to France. *R. Price.*

CASTLE KEEP 5 b.h. Kalamoun 129–Fotheringay 101 (Right Royal V 135) **117**
(1981 12g 12f⁴ 12f² 12fg² 13.3fg² 13.5f² 11g* 10g 1982 10fg* 12f⁴ 10fg³ 10g*
11f* 10.5fg⁴ 11g³)
The Grand Prix Prince Rose at Ostend has received a lot of publicity since
its inception in 1978, and rightly so. The prize money was extremely generous
from the start and the race was won by three good French-trained colts, Dom
Alaric, Noir et Or and Argument, in its first three years. Since then the value
of the race has shown a relative decline and in the last two runnings the French
challenge has not been so strong; even so, in 1982 the prize money picked up
by Castle Keep, the first British-trained winner, was only slightly less than
that for the Coronation Cup, a race in which Castle Keep could finish only fourth.
The field Castle Keep beat was a truly international one, including runners
from Ireland, France, Britain and Germany as well as Belgium, without being
a particularly strong one, the sole previous pattern-race winner being the French-
trained Vidor. In the event Vidor ran poorly as Castle Keep registered his
third comfortable success of the year, leading over two furlongs from home
and drawing five lengths clear of Spin of a Coin. The Grand Prix Prince Rose
does not qualify for pattern status since Belgian racing itself is not included in
the European pattern; nevertheless the race does provide a very good opportunity
for middle-distance horses just below the top class like Castle Keep, and is surely
rewarding enough to risk subsequently becoming subject to the arbitrary pattern
rule that the winner of an event worth £12,000 in a country outside the pattern
system is liable to the same penalties as a Group 1 winner.
Castle Keep's two earlier victories came in the Clive Graham Stakes at
Goodwood in May and the Land of Burns Stakes at Ayr in July. He took
them in similar style, coming with a smooth run after being held up to beat
Aperitivo by two lengths and Say Primula by three lengths respectively. His
Goodwood success represented a particularly fine piece of training, for not long
prior to it Castle Keep had been undergoing faradic treatment for the lameness
that had plagued him throughout the winter, and by the time of the Clive Graham
Stakes he had reportedly been back in training only three weeks. Neither the
Clive Graham Stakes nor the Land of Burns Stakes enjoys pattern status, so
although Castle Keep had a successful year he failed to achieve the main object in
his being kept in training. As in 1981, he ran well enough in his pattern races
without being good enough to beat the best middle-distance performers. In
the Coronation Cup he never really looked like getting to the front and was beaten

Land of Burns Stakes, Ayr—a smooth win for Castle Keep

five and a half lengths into fourth by Easter Sun; in the Prince of Wales's Stakes at Royal Ascot and the Benson and Hedges Cup at York he seemed to find little off the bridle, although in the former he did appear to be caught in the face by a whip; and at San Siro, Milan, on his final appearance Castle Keep was a rather disappointing seven-length third to Haul Knight in the Premio Federico Tesio, though again there may be a valid excuse—that he was unsuited by the ridiculously slow pace.

Castle Keep (b.h. 1977)	Kalamoun (gr 1970)	Zeddaan (gr 1965)	Grey Sovereign Vareta	
		Khairunissa (gr 1960)	Prince Bio Palariva	
	Fotheringay (b 1964)	Right Royal V (br 1958)	Owen Tudor Bastia	
		La Fresnes (ch 1953)	Court Martial Pin Stripe	

Castle Keep has been retired, and takes up stallion duties at the Lavington Stud, Graffham, Sussex at £2,000, no foal no fee. He is one of four winners out of his dam, a useful miler out of the very smart sprinter La Fresnes, the best of the others being the Gold Cup winner Ragstone (by Ragusa). Castle Keep's sire Kalamoun died young, leaving behind such as Kalaglow, Bikala (who has the same fifth dam as Castle Keep) and Dom Racine, the last-named already making a name for himself as a stallion with Deep Roots among his first crop. Castle Keep, a neat, strong, good sort of horse, was a good mover. He stayed a mile and three quarters but was raced mainly at shorter distances and only once tackled further than eleven furlongs in his final season. He never raced on soft ground and was said by connections not to be suited by it, but he acted on any other. Invariably held up, he wasn't an easy ride. *J. Dunlop.*

CASTLE RISING 2 b.c. Blakeney 126–Christchurch 88 (So Blessed 130) **76** p (1982 10.2s) Mar 26; attractive colt; third foal; half-brother to smart 6f to 10.5f winner Church Parade (by Queen's Hussar) and 3-y-o 1½m winner Glastonbury (by Grundy); dam, 1½m winner, is half-sister to 1,000 Guineas and Oaks winner Highclere; 33/1 and in need of race, made headway from rear until finding no extra in last 2f when 11 lengths fifth of 15 behind Whitstar in minor event at Doncaster in November; will do better. *W. Hastings-Bass.*

CASWELL ROAD 4 b.g. Tycoon II–Cherry Brandy (Tenerani 135) (1981 **—** 9d 1982 10.2g 13d 9fg) seemed of little account; dead. *T. Taylor.*

CATHERINE PEG 2 ch.f. Star Appeal 133–Brazen Faced 84 (Bold and Free **85** 118) (1982 7fg³ 6g* 7g 7fg 6s 7.2s 6s) Mar 4; 5,000Y; quite attractive, well-made filly; first foal; dam 2-y-o 5f winner; wore down odds-on Misguided inside final furlong to win 15-runner maiden race at Windsor in July by a neck; generally out of her depth subsequently, but ran creditably when 3 lengths fifth of 8 behind Flamenco in Sweet Solera Stakes at Newmarket in August, third outing; stays 7f well. *C. Brittain.*

CAT O'NINE TAILS 2 b.c. Le Johnstan 123–The Dupecat 75 (Javelot 124) **118** (1982 5fg³ 5f* 5g* 5fg² 5g* 6f³ 6.5d³ 7s)
The inaugural Select Invitational Session of the Doncaster St Leger Yearling Sales in 1981 created a lot of interest and most of the Sales records were broken. However there were some excellent buys to be had in the ordinary sessions: Horage was the best of them and the smart Cat O'Nine Tails was well bought for 15,500 guineas, rather less than the average for the Select Invitational Session. Cat O'Nine Tails's best effort was his strong-finishing third in the Prix Eclipse at Saint-Cloud in October. He was beaten half a length and two and a half by Crystal Glitters and Drumalis, both of whom received 9 lb. The previous month he'd disappointed when last of three to Orange Squash in the Bonusprint Sirenia Stakes at Kempton but before that he'd won three of his five races and shown himself a game and progressive individual. His victories in a maiden race at Epsom and a minor event at Sandown in June were gained by wide margins but he had to work much harder for his success in the Prince of Wales's Stakes at York in August, contested as usual by some useful animals. Cat O'Nine Tails was taken off his feet early on but stayed on best of all from two furlongs out and led inside the last furlong to beat Jonacris by a length.
Cat O'Nine Tails's dam won over a mile and a half and has produced three other winners on the flat, one subsequently successful over jumps, and a winning hurdler; best of them is Cat O'Nine Tails's full sister Lightning Record, fairly

189

Prince of Wales's Stakes, York—Cat O'Nine Tails (nearest camera)
leads inside the final furlong to win
from Jonacris (centre)

useful at up to a mile and a quarter. Cat O'Nine Tails's grandam Alley Cat and great grandam were both useful two-year-old winners. Alley Cat is the dam of nine winners over a variety of distances, including Coventry Stakes winner Doleswood and Cork and Orrery Stakes runner-up Ma-Shema. Cat O'Nine

Cat O'Nine Tails (b.c. Jan 24, 1980)	Le Johnstan (b 1968)	El Gallo (ch 1959)	Matador / Discipliner
		Garden Green (b 1964)	Pinturischio / Focal
	The Dupecat (b 1967)	Javelot (b 1956)	Fast Fox / Djaina
		Alley Cat (ch 1962)	Alycidon / Mistress Ann

Tails has plenty of speed and is unlikely to stay so well as his sister. He ran a little below his best over seven furlongs in the Criterium de Maisons-Laffitte but should stay that far. The going was firm when he disappointed at Kempton and he's probably suited by some give in the ground. A quite well-made, useful-looking colt, Cat O'Nine Tails is a good walker and mover. *R. Price.*

CAUSE CELEBRE 2 gr.c. Habitat 134–Canton Silk 108 (Runnymede 123) **113** (1982 5f² 5fg* 5f⁴ 7g² 6g² 7g² 7s) Apr 15; 91,000Y; lengthy, attractive colt; half-brother to several winners, including very useful 5f to 8.5f winner Royal Pinnacle (by High Top) and fair 1981 2-y-o 5f winner Justicia (by Nonoalco); dam 5f performer; had plenty in hand when ½-length winner of maiden race at Ayr in May; ran most creditably in good company afterwards, particularly when second to comfortable winner All Systems Go in Seaton Delaval Stakes at Newcastle on fourth outing, and when going down by head to Polished Silver in Somerville Tattersall Stakes at Newmarket on sixth appearance; outpaced by Shicklah at Baden-Baden in between; needs at least 7f; genuine. *J. Hindley.*

190

CAVA ALTA 4 b.g. Upper Case–Spring Exploit (Exploitation 108) (1981 9.4g
12d 15.5g 1982 12fg 12g 16.5fg⁴) fair sort; showed signs of a little ability;
ran best race of year on final start; dead. *N. Crump.* —

CAVALIER SERVENTE 4 gr.c. Barbaro–Quoro Star (Quorum 126) (1981
10s 10v 10fg 10fg³ 11d 8g 10d² 8g 1982 12s 12.2f² 12f² 10fg² 12f⁴ 13.8f³ 16g
16fg 12g⁴ 12s² 12s) strong colt; close second in 3 handicaps and a minor event
but is none too genuine; stays 1¾m; acts on any going; has worn bandages. *P.
Wigham.* **50§**

CAVALINGO 4 b.f. Rustingo 94–Cavalry Cloak (Queen's Hussar 124) (1981
NR 1982 8fg 8g) lightly-raced plater; blinkered once. *D. Wintle.* —

CAVARADOSSI (USA) 3 b.c. Vaguely Noble 140–Nalee (Nashua) (1981 NR
1982 12fg 12f² 13f* 12f³ 10g² 12s⁴ 12v* 10.6s) $280,000Y; well-made colt;
half-brother to numerous winners, notably high-class middle-distance stayer
Meneval (by Le Fabuleux) and very useful stakes winners Nalees Man (by Gallant
Man) and Nalees Folly (by Tom Fool); dam, smart winner at 2 yrs and 3 yrs in
USA, is sister to champion American mare Shuvee; long odds on when winning
maiden race at Nottingham in July and minor event at Lingfield in October; ran
respectably in between; will stay 1¾m; acts on any going; gives impression he
needs strong handling. *H. Cecil.* **95**

CAWARRA LAD 3 b.c. Sovereign Spitfire 81–Spanish Coin (Matador 131)
(1981 NR 1982 7.6fg 6f⁴ 8.2fg 7fg 6d 6v 6s) half-brother to 2 winning
hurdlers; dam never ran; poor form, including in a seller; blinkered sixth start.
R. Simpson. —

CAWSTONELLA 3 b.f. Cawston's Clown 113–Lantao Lady 63 (King's Troop
118) (1981 5d 5fg 6f² 6f³ 1982 8g 12.2g 6s 7f 9f 8f 9f 8.2g 7fg 8d) small,
lightly-made filly; plater; yet to prove she stays beyond 6f; acts on firm going;
sometimes blinkered. *J. Wilson.* —

CAWSTON STAR 3 br.f. Comedy Star 121–Telouet 90 (Sing Sing 134) (1981
5.1f 5.1fg 6g 5f³ 5f² 5fg⁴ 5fg 5g 5g 1982 5fg 5f 5f 5fg 5.3f⁴ 5f³ 5fg 5g² 5g)
smallish, fair sort; sprint plater; blinkered fourth to seventh starts; has twice
started slowly. *H. Collingridge.* **46**

CAYMAN RUNNER 3 b.c. Blakeney 126–Bella Canto 82 (Crooner 119) (1981
NR 1982 7d 10s 8fg 10d² 10d 10.2g³ 11.5fg³ 10g 11.5fg³ 9g³ 10d³ 10.1d⁴ 8f 10g⁴)
medium-sized, lengthy colt; has a round action; second foal; half-brother to 6f
winner Dibbinsdale Lass (by Amber Rama); dam won over 1m and 1¼m; placed
in handicaps and a ladies race; will be suited by 1½m; suitable mount for an
inexperienced rider; ran badly fifth start. *R. Armstrong.* **65**

CEANDARO 2 b.c. Free State 125–Katie Gay 65 (Royben 125) (1982 5d 6g 7d)
May 8; 10,000Y; first foal; dam half-sister to very smart Hillandale; behind in
maiden and minor events; sold 920 gns Newmarket Autumn Sales. *P. Walwyn.* —

CECCHETTI 3 gr.c. Kalamoun 129–Kinharvie 63 (Abernant 142) (1981 8g
1982 7g² 6fg 9fg 7g) ex-English colt; seems only plating class; needs further
than 6f and will stay 1¼m; trained by R. Price first 2 starts; sold 2,400 gns Goffs
November Sales. *C. Collins, Ireland.* —

CECILE 2 b.f. Captain James 123–Spring Again (Primera 131) (1982 5f³ 5fg*
5d² 5fg³ 5g 6g) Mar 7; 8,200F, 1,450Y; rather leggy, narrow filly; half-sister
to a 2-y-o winner by Will Somers; dam behind in maiden races; made virtually
all to win maiden auction race at Redcar in June by 2½ lengths from Melowen;
placed following month in minor event at Beverley (ridden by 7-lb claimer) and
nursery at Hamilton; bred to stay at least 1m; acts on a firm and a soft surface.
J. Fitzgerald. **82**

CEDAR PRINCESS 2 b.f. Mount Hagen 127–Running Cedar (Bryan G) (1982
5f 5fg 6fg⁴ 6g 7fg 7g* 7g 6g 6g 7f³ 6g) May 10; IR 4,000Y; small, compact filly;
good mover; half-sister to 2 minor winners and a winner abroad; dam won at up
to 1m in USA; bought in 3,900 gns after winning seller at Newmarket in August
by 2½ lengths from On Tour; 5 lengths third of 15 behind Bo-Peep in another
Newmarket seller in September; suited by 7f, and will stay 1m; yet to race on a
soft surface; wears blinkers. *R. Hannon.* **71**

CEDEES 2 b.f. Habat 127–Water Rat 83 (Hard Tack 111§) (1982 5g 5g 5fg)
Apr 18; 4,000F; sturdy filly; half-sister to winning sprinter Ratamataz (by Shiny
Tenth) and winning stayer Baby Rat (by Reliance II); dam won at up to 9f;
soundly beaten in minor and maiden events. *M. Tompkins.* —

CEDRELLA 3 b.f. Averof 123–Maria Da Gloria (St Chad 120) (1981 6f 5f³ 6fg³ **64**
5g² 5fg² 5f* 5g³ 5d 1982 7f 6f 5f 6f* 6f 6g) lightly-made filly; not a good
mover; won handicap at Carlisle in June; stays 6f (had stiffish task when behind
over 7f); best form on a sound surface. *E. Weymes.*

CEEDEE REVENGE 2 b.g. Garda's Revenge 119–Fiddle Myree 69 (Frankin- —
cense 120) (1982 8fg 8d 6g) Apr 8; 10,500Y; strong, well-made gelding; third
live foal; dam won sellers over 5f and 7f; backward, behind in big fields of
maidens at Goodwood in September and Newmarket (2) in October; subsequently
gelded. *P. Haslam.*

CELESTIAL BRIDE 2 b.f. Godswalk 130–Light Diamond (Florescence 120) —
(1982 6f 6fg) Apr 2; IR 9,600F, 26,000Y; fair sort; half-sister to 3 winners,
including successful 7f and 1m performer Paterno (by Young Emperor); dam
won over 5f at 4 yrs in Ireland; little sign of ability in maiden races at
Newmarket (20/1) in July and Nottingham (8/1) in August. *G. Pritchard-
Gordon.*

CELESTIAL CITY 3 gr.f. Godswalk 130–Nibbler 66 (Primera 131) (1981 5g* —
5g* 5g* 5f 1982 6fg) lengthy, attractive filly; won maiden race at Newmarket,
Wilkinson Memorial Stakes at York and Uplands Park Acorn Stakes at Epsom
early in 1981; in rear in valuable handicap at Newmarket only start at 3 yrs in
May (favourite); possibly unsuited by firm going; twice showed a distinct
tendency to hang left at 2 yrs. *H. Cecil.*

CELESTIAL DANCER 3 b.c. Godswalk 130–Oulanova (Nijinsky 138) (1981 **115**
7d 6fg 6g* 6g³ 6s³ 7g 1982 6fg² 6fg*(dis) 5fg² 6f* 6f³ 6g* 6d⁴ 6g) big, strong,
rangy colt; carries plenty of condition; very useful colt who was first past post
in William Hill Trophy at York (beat Cyril's Choice by ¾ length but was
subsequently disqualified), quite valuable handicap at Newmarket (wasn't
extended to beat Master Cawston by 1½ lengths) and Northumberland Sprint
Trophy at Newcastle; got up to beat Soba by a short head on last-named in
August; in frame most of season, including when close fourth to Great
Eastern in Prix de Meautry at Deauville; suited by 6f; acts on any going; needs
to be held up, has a tendency to hang and isn't an easy ride; consistent. *A. Hide.*

CELESTIAL PATH 3 gr.f. Godswalk 130–Princess Hattab (Al Hattab) (1981 **101**
5g* 6f* 6f* 5d 1982 7s* 8fg 5f) IR 3,200Y; rather narrow, fair sort; poor
walker; second foal; dam never ran; won 10-runner Athasi Stakes at the Curragh
in April by a short head from Miss Lilian; by no means disgraced when seventh
of 15 to On The House in 1,000 Guineas at Newmarket later in April but finished
in rear behind Longleat in Ballyogan Stakes at Leopardstown in June; not seen
out again; not certain to stay 1m; acts on any going; sold 50,000 gns Newmarket
December Sales. *J. Bolger, Ireland.*

CELTIC BIRD 2 b.f. Celtic Cone 116–Bird Cherry 61 (Falcon 131) (1982 **60**
5f 5f² 5f* 5g* 5fg 5d⁴ 5s) May 2; 420Y; small, strong filly; first foal; dam won
over 1m; 5-length winner of sellers at Beverley (no bid) and Hamilton (bought in
2,100 gns) in May; best race afterwards when fourth of 10 to Blue Times in
nursery at Wolverhampton in October; will stay 6f; acts on firm going and a soft
surface. *A. Balding.*

CELTIC HALO 6 b.h. Welsh Saint 126–Levanswood 74 (Le Levanstell 122) **78**
(1981 6g³ 6d 6g² 6s² 6f 6fg 7f 6fg 8g² (dis) 10.8s 8v 7s 1982 7.2s⁴ 6fg 8f 8f 8fg³
6fg 8fg² 7f 8fg*) neat horse; didn't run all that consistently, but won handicap
at Ayr in August by ½ length from Windpipe; stayed 1m; acted on any going;
ideally suited by strong handling; successful with blinkers and without; dead.
S. Norton.

CELTIC PROMISE 2 b.g. Martinmas 128–Irish Bride (Track Spare 125) **78 p**
(1982 7s⁴) May 12; 13,000Y; third foal; half-brother to fairly useful 1981
2-y-o 5f and 7f winner Major Irish (by Malinowski) and winning Irish miler Cut
The Cake (by Fine Blade); dam never ran; 12/1, every chance until outpaced
final furlong when 6½ lengths fourth of 12 behind Dabdoub in minor event at
Chepstow in October; gelded afterwards; sure to improve. *I. Balding.*

CELTIC STORY 2 b.g. Celtic Cone 116–Coxmoor Maid 60 (Royal Pennant 112) —
(1982 8.2fg 7.2s) May 12; smallish gelding; second foal; dam won over hurdles
and fences; in rear in 2 sellers at Haydock in the autumn; subsequently gelded.
W. Wharton.

CELTIC TARA 6 b.m. Welsh Saint 126–La Sarmate (Hard Sauce 131) (1981 **47**
12d² 18d³ 12g 16f³ 1982 16s³ 13d² 16f⁴) neat mare; placed in handicap and
amateur riders event at Nottingham in April; stays well; probably acts on any
going. *C. Booth.*

CENTIMETER 2 b.c. Thatch 136–Millimeter (Ribocco 129) (1982 7g 8g) —
Apr 29; 22,000Y; sturdy, attractive colt; third foal; half-brother to Italian
winner Milanese Mill (by Claude); dam, unplaced in Italy, is half-sister to very
speedy Peterhof; carrying a fair bit of condition when out of first 9 at long odds
in large fields of maidens at Newmarket in October. *L. Cumani.*

CENTRAL CARPETS 3 b.f. Garda's Revenge 119–Homecomings (Primera 131) **60**
(1981 5d³ 5s³ 5fg 5g³ 5fg³ 5fg 6fg³ 7.2fg 6f 6d⁴ 6g 5d² 5g 1982 6g 5s 5fg 6fg
6fg³ 5f 5f* 6fg 6f 6h 6g 5fg 6g 5fg 5d 5d² 5g 5s) lightly-made filly; poor mover;
sprint handicapper; won at Pontefract in May; beaten in a seller thirteenth start;
seems to act on any going; has run well for a 7-lb claimer; blinkered twelfth
outing. *W. Stubbs.*

CENTROLINE 4 b.c. High Line 125–Centro 86 (Vienna 127) (1981 8d⁴ 12g³ **119**
13.3d* 15.5f* 14fg² 14g* 14.6g* 16g* 1982 12fg⁴ 14f) small, lightly-made
colt; brother to 3 winners, notably Nicholas Bill and Centrocon, latter dam of
Time Charter; improved with virtually every race as a 3-y-o, and developed into a
very smart colt, winning 5 races, notably Jockey Club Cup at Newmarket;
looked very well indeed and ran an excellent race when just over a length fourth
behind Glint of Gold in John Porter Stakes at Newbury in April, racing in touch
all way and keeping on strongly in closing stages, despite looking short of room;
ran very disappointingly when second favourite for Yorkshire Cup at York the
following month, proving difficult to settle, finding nothing when asked to
quicken over 3f out, and trailing in last of 6 behind Ardross; wasn't seen out again;
stays very well; possibly not at his best on very firm going; suited by a strong
gallop; a genuine sort who responds well to driving. *H. Candy.*

CENTRUST (USA) 2 b. or br.c. Mr Prospector–Rock Fever (Hawaii) (1982 **94**
5g* 5g⁴ 5f² 6fg⁴ 6fg) Feb 20; $150,000Y; neat, attractive colt; first foal; dam
won at up to 1m, including a minor stakes; landed odds by 3 lengths from Off
The Cuff in maiden race at Wolverhampton in April; ran well in nurseries last 3
starts, twice when apprentice ridden; stays 6f; acts on firm going. *P. Walwyn.*

CENTURION 7 ch.g. Connaught 130–Calleva (Worden II 129) (1981 NR —
1982 13.3f) big, strong, heavy-topped gelding; very useful stayer at 3 yrs,
winner of 5 races, including Tote Cesarewitch; broke down in 1980 Newmarket
Challenge Whip and was last of 7 behind Sandalay in handicap at Newbury in
June on only outing since (bandaged in front and needed race); acts on any
going. *I. Balding.*

CENTURION PRINCE 3 b.c. Martinmas 128–Cobblers Daughter 84 (Right —
Boy 137) (1981 5s 1982 8d⁴ 8.2fg⁴ 7fg⁴ 8fg 7f) fair sort; plating-class maiden;
stays 1m; blinkered last 2 starts, missing break on second. *P. Feilden.*

CENTURIUS 4 ch.c. Great Nephew 126–Word from Lundy 93 (Worden II 129) ?
(1981 8.5g* 10.5s 12f²(dis) 12f³ 12fg² 10.5g⁴ 12fg 1982 12f*(w.o.) 10fg* 12f 12f)
rangy, attractive ex-English colt; good walker; brother to Derby winner Grundy;
gained sole success of 1981 in Ladbroke Blue Riband Trial at Epsom; in frame
in top company most subsequent starts but looked ungenuine several times;
walked over in minor event at Pontefract in May, and wasn't over impressive,
despite his winning margin of 8 lengths, when accounting for 3 modest opponents in
a similar race on same course later in month; left M. Stoute's stable after
finishing poor seventh of 8 behind Critique in Hardwicke Stakes at Royal Ascot
in June, and finished in rear in Japan Cup at Tokyo in November; suited by
1½m; seemed to need a sound surface; had a lot of ability but was no battler;
stud in Australia. *L. Browne, Ireland.*

CENTURY CITY 3 br.c. High Top 131–Pearl Wedding 83 (Gulf Pearl 117) **118**
(1981 7g² 1982 7d* 8.5fg² 7f* 10.6h* 10f³ 10g² 9d*)
In winning the William Hill Cambridgeshire under 9-6 Century City broke
the weight-carrying record for a three-year-old in the race set by Sayani who
scored with 9-4 in 1946. Such record-breaking achievements are almost a
commonplace nowadays and in fact a glance at the history of the Cambridgeshire
reveals that because of changing circumstances it doesn't necessarily require an
exceptional horse to win this or any other competitive handicap under a high
weight now. From 1839 to 1945, thirty-five winners carried under 7-0, including eight with less than 6-0, and in 1856 Malacca won with just 5-5; Sayani
was only the second horse to succeed with over 9-0. Since 1946 however, with
such factors as alterations in the weight range and conditions of the event coming
into play, only four winners have carried under 7-7 and no fewer than six have
won with more than 9-0. To give an indication of how things have changed, in

1877 the Grand Criterium, French Derby and French St Leger winner Jongleur won with 8-4 while in 1892 the One Thousand Guineas, Oaks and St Leger winner La Fleche did so under 8-10; in 1982 such as Miramar Reef and Mou-Ferni-Tychi carried more than both these classic winners.   Hence admirable as Century City's display was, it does not make him an outstanding colt.

Nonetheless, Century City is undoubtedly both smart and consistent, and since he stays in training there's a chance he will progress even further. His six starts before the Cambridgeshire was run in October had resulted in three wins and three places.   The first two successes, in a maiden race at Leicester and a minor event at Catterick in which he started at long odds on, were nothng out of the ordinary, but his four-length defeat of Mailman in the valuable Stones Best Bitter Handicap at Haydock in June was altogether more significant. Travelling well throughout, he led a quarter of a mile from home and quickened clear for a decisive success.   Following this improved display Century City ran creditably in two more valuable handicaps, the Extel Stakes at Goodwood and the Peter Hastings Stakes at Newbury, finishing under two lengths third to Busaco in the former and a length second to Oratavo, after showing a tendency to hang left, in the latter.

Though evidently on the upgrade, Century City still looked to have no more than an average chance in the twenty-nine-runner Cambridgeshire for which he started at 20/1 behind Commodore Blake, Fine Sun, Indian Trail, Dreaming Away, Barooq, King's Glory, Mou-Ferni-Tychi and Oratavo.   Not for the first time on the course, the draw played a part in proceedings for of the first eight to finish only one was drawn in the high numbers.   Century City lay plumb last of his group on the favoured stand side at halfway but began to make strong headway from there to reach a challenging position a furlong and a half out as Oratavo and Fine Sun battled for the lead.   Maintaining his momentum, Century City soon hit the front and galloped on powerfully to hold off the fast-finishing Indian Trail by a neck with Oratavo a length and a half away third and Fine Sun fourth.   After this brave effort Century City was put away for the season; he should start 1983 a fresh horse and it will be interesting to see how he fares in the pattern races which are said to be his objective.

Century City (br.c. 1979)	High Top (br 1969)	Derring-Do (br 1961)	Darius
			Sipsey Bridge
		Camenae (b 1961)	Vimy
			Madrilene
	Pearl Wedding (b 1972)	Gulf Pearl (ch 1962)	Persian Gulf
			Nan
		Miss Mandy (br 1967)	Mandamus
			Zarapido

Century City is the second foal and first winner out of the genuine and consistent middle-distance performer Pearl Wedding, whose dam won at a mile and has produced two other winners, notably the useful 1976 two-year-old Le Chat, successful over five and six furlongs.   The third dam, a half-sister by the Gold Cup winner Zarathustra to Florescence and Prince Poppa, ran second in two of her three starts over one and a half miles in Ireland.   There is a reasonable amount of stamina in the pedigree—a fair proportion of the sire High

William Hill Cambridgeshire Handicap, Newmarket—a smart display by Century City who holds off Indian Trail by a neck

Mr Ivan Allan's "Century City"

Top's progeny stay beyond ten furlongs—and it is conceivable that Century City will get a mile and a half at four. A rangy colt who cost 10,000 guineas as a yearling, Century City has a round action; though his best run came on a soft surface he showed at Haydock that hard going is no inconvenience to him. He gives the impression he will always be best with strong handling. *L. Cumani.*

CEREMONIOUS 4 ch.f. Queen's Hussar 124–Queen's Keys 84 (Right Royal V 135) (1981 12.2s 8d 12.2g* 12g³ 12g 12fg 12.5f 15.8g 12fg 12g⁴ 13.8g³ 16.5f 13.8g⁴ 11s³ 10d 1982 10fg) small, unfurnished filly; plater; stays at least 1¾m; often apprentice ridden; blinkered once in 1981; sold out of R. Whitaker's stable 1,350 gns Doncaster March Sales. *D. Weeden.* —

CEREZA 3 b.f. High Line 125–Aera Fair (Aera) (1981 NR 1982 10fg 11.7fg⁴ 16fg³ 16fg² 15.5fg* 18.8fg) 1,000Y; smallish, wiry filly; not the best of movers; half-sister to several winners abroad; dam prolific winner of minor events in USA; won maiden race at Folkestone in August; stays well; yet to race on an easy surface. *H. Candy.* **63**

CERTAIN SOMETHING 2 b.f. Solinus 130–Taotl (Yellow God 129) (1982 6fg* 6f* 7g) Mar 3; IR 96,000Y; first living foal; dam, who never ran, is bred on same lines as Irish 2,000 Guineas winner Pampapaul; successful in maiden race at the Curragh in July and 14-runner Oldtown Stud Stakes at Naas the following month, beating Top Rated a short head in latter; third favourite for Park Stakes at Leopardstown in October but finished only twelfth of 13 to Countess Candy; possibly doesn't stay 7f; acts on firm going. *K. Prendergast, Ireland.* **102**

CHADLEIGH LASS 2 br.f. Mansingh 120–Silvera 73 (Ribero 126) (1982 5s 6g 7f 7f 6fg 6d) Apr 6; 8,000Y; good-topped filly; first foal; dam won over 1m; no worthwhile form in maiden and minor races; blinkered last 4 outings; sold 1,000 gns Newmarket Autumn Sales. *C. Brittain.* —

CHADS GAMBLE 7 ch.g. St Chad 120–Another Flutter 75 (Credo 123) (1981 8g² 7g 7g 7f 7f² 8h⁴ 7f² 7h* 6f³ 1982 6f³ 7h² 7fg 8fg 6f 7fg⁴ 6f⁴ 7g 7f³) poor **59**

handicapper nowadays; stays 1m; appears to act on any going but is suited by a sound surface; often blinkered nowadays; has run creditably for an apprentice. *J. Bethell.*

CHAIN OF REASONING (USA) 8 b.g. Hail to Reason–Daisy Chain 103 — (Darius 129) (1981 NR 1982 16s 12g 12s) lightly-raced staying handicapper nowadays; acts on a firm surface; used to wear blinkers; often bandaged. *S. Harris.*

CHALET WALDEGG 2 ch.f. Monsanto 121–Glistening 84 (Aureole 132) — (1982 5fg 7fg 7fg) Apr 6; rather unfurnished filly; half-sister to 11f winner Glitter (by Reliance II) and a winner in Italy; dam winning stayer and half-sister to high-class Proverb; 8 lengths fifth of 15 to Ashmolean in maiden race at Warwick in July, final outing; will be suited by 1m+. *D. Gandolfo.*

CHALKANIAN FIGA 3 ch.c. French Chalk–Cigamarosa (March Past 124) — (1981 NR 1982 12fg 13.3f) good-topped colt; second foal; dam never ran; tailed-off last in maiden races at Salisbury and Newbury. *D. Sasse.*

CHALKEY ROAD 3 b.f. Relko 136–Feather Bed 111 (Gratitude 130) (1981 **100** 7d 6g 7g⁴ 1982 10d 12d* 12f³ 12g* 12g⁴ 13d* 18d 12s³) rangy filly; successful in maiden race at Beverley and minor events at Ripon and Ayr; also ran creditably in 2 races at York, coming home 3¾ lengths fourth to Sans Blague in Galtres Stakes on second occasion, and in William Hill November Handicap at Doncaster (¾-length third to dead-heaters Double Shuffle and Turkoman); apparently doesn't stay extreme distances; acts on any going; has run creditably when sweating up. *H. Wragg.*

CHALKIES PET 2 b.f. Reliance II 137–Solentown 72 (Town Crier 119) (1982 **57** 6d 8f 8.2d 7g 8s³ 10d) May 17; 3,400Y; 1,600 2-y-o; leggy filly; bad mover; first foal; dam winning jumper; plater; should stay 1¼m. *D. Marks.*

CHALLANGING 2 b.f. Mill Reef 141–Vital Match 113 (Match III 135) (1982 **95** 7f* 7f⁴ 7fg²) Apr 9; 66,000Y; small, close-coupled filly; nice, easy mover; sister to 3-y-o middle-distance winner His Turn and quite useful 5f and 1½m winner Soldiers Point, and half-sister to 2 winners, including useful middle-distance stayer Vital Season (by Silly Season); dam miler; put up an impressive first effort in 16-runner maiden race at Yarmouth in August, being ridden clear to win unchallenged by 6 lengths from Monongelia; took on better opposition afterwards, finishing 4¼ lengths fourth of 6 to Muscatite in £6,700 race at Newmarket and 1½ lengths second of 12 to Silk Sari in £3,600 event at Chepstow; will be suited by longer distances, and should stay at least 1½m; acts on firm going. *B. Hobbs.*

CHALON 3 ch.f. Habitat 134–Areola 114 (Kythnos 126) (1981 7g³ 7g* 1982 **125** 7fg* 7fg* 8g* 8fg* 8f* 7f* 7.3g 7g)
This big, strong, even-tempered filly was an important absentee from the One Thousand Guineas line-up. Surprisingly, following her defeat of Merlins Charm and Triple Tipple in very fast time in the Ladbrokes Nell Gwyn Stakes at the Craven meeting when backward, Chalon missed the big race in favour of the Ward Hill Handicap at Newmarket later in Guineas week, duly winning with ease in course-record time on a very lenient mark (even penalized 5 lb and carrying 2 lb over she received weight from four opponents, a stone from Be Be Of Kuwait). The manner of her victory on each occasion suggested that Chalon was a high-class filly, and subsequently she showed herself among the best fillies of her generation at up to a mile, winning another four races before she met her first defeat of the season against the colts in the Hungerford Stakes at Newbury in August.

Report had it that Chalon missed the Guineas because of a doubt about her stamina. Her breeding, by Habitat out of a very speedy mare who never raced beyond seven furlongs, provided grounds for such a doubt but she ran like a horse who would be suited by a mile; even as a two-year-old she stayed on really well up the hill when making all over seven furlongs in a big field of maidens at Newmarket at the back-end. Before very long Chalon indeed proved well suited by a mile, for her three races following the Ward Hill Handicap were all over that distance and she won the lot with authority. She didn't have a great deal to beat in the first of them, the International Fillies Stakes at Kempton in May; Wink chased her home at two and a half lengths. The Coronation Stakes at Royal Ascot and the Child Stakes at Newmarket, both pattern races, set her much more difficult tasks, the former attracting an international field with Grease from France and Woodstream and Kazankina from Ireland. The race

*Coronation Stakes, Ascot—Chalon makes all the running to
beat Grease (rails) by three lengths*

for the Coronation Stakes was one of the most interesting of the whole meeting.
Chalon and Piggott dictated affairs from start to finish. The seven other jockeys
seemed content to allow Chalon to give them a lead at a steady pace to the bend,
remaining nicely bunched in what no doubt appeared to each of them a handy
covering position. However when Piggott made his move early in the straight
and Chalon quickened appreciably, none of the other horses could respond
swiftly enough to prevent her opening up a substantial gap; and once in the clear
she never looked like being caught. She won in really good style by three lengths
from Grease who put in a strong run up the inside. Woodstream and Circus Ring,
two of the best fillies of the previous season, filled the last two places and never
ran again. On The House finished only fifth, below her best probably as a result
of the way the race had been run, though connections, we know, think she might
have needed a short rest by then. It's a pity she was below top form, for this
was the second time Chalon beat her (the Nell Gwyn being the occasion of the
first).

Chalon received 4 lb from On The House in the Coronation Stakes, and from
the other Group 1 winners Grease and Woodstream. In the Child Stakes at
Newmarket in July she herself had to concede weight to her three-year-old
opponents—the Coronation Stakes third and fourth Dancing Rocks and Rose of
Montreaux, the Guineas third Dione who had been a shade disappointing since
the spring, and the Ascot winners Merlins Charm (Jersey Stakes) and Kareena
(Fern Hill Handicap). The six-year-old Lasani, a 500/1 chance, completed the
field. Chalon started at 15/8 on. She looked magnificent, the pick, really
thriving physically as the season approached the halfway mark. As had become
her custom she made the running, and she was never headed as she beat Kareena
by a length. Kareena quickened with the winner two furlongs out and both
she and Merlins Charm gave the winner a good chase to the line, but Chalon was
too strong, keeping on very resolutely under hands-and-heels driving.

Missing the Guineas may have been a boon to Chalon, in more than one
respect. Had she run and had a hard time she might not have developed so well
as she did; had she run and won she would have been penalized more heavily
in some races (the Coronation Stakes for example) and would have been ineligible
to run in others. The conditions of her next race, the Oak Tree Stakes for three-
year-old fillies over seven furlongs at Goodwood in July, excluded any of the
year's Group 1 winners. That didn't leave many who could be guaranteed to
extend Chalon, and when Merlins Charm went out overnight she was left facing
only four opponents—Wink, Travel On and the handicappers Lucayan Lady and

Apple Blossom. It was a gift for Chalon. Though she was said not to have travelled well from Newmarket she won cruising by three parts of a length from Wink, Piggott able to afford several backward glances as she maintained her long-held advantage through the last furlong.

Later that week On The House won the Sussex Stakes from Sandhurst Prince and Achieved. Chalon hadn't met any of the colts up to that time. She got the opportunity of taking some on at Newbury in August in the Hungerford Stakes, and started a hot favourite against a less strong field than turned out for the Sussex Stakes. Unfortunately for those interested in comparing their relative merits, Chalon was in little or no better form in this important test against the colts than On The House had been in her two races against Chalon and was beaten nearly five lengths into fifth place behind Pas de Seul, beaten for fourth by the maiden Mean Francine. There was no obvious explanation for her modest showing. Beforehand she looked as well as ever and she moved down satisfactorily. In the race she wasn't so quickly into her stride as usual, at any rate she couldn't immediately strike the front, and settled two or three lengths behind the leaders. Once they turned for home she saw daylight and looked to have every chance but it was perfectly obvious before long that she wasn't going all that well—she was tending to hang to her left—and eventually when Piggott really got at her there was very little forthcoming. Possibly she had simply 'gone' for the season; a break until the Bisquit Cognac Challenge Stakes at Newmarket in October failed to restore her form. Although she again looked keen and well in the paddock, and this time had had no travelling to do, she was never moving comfortably in the race. Piggott had said goodbye to any chance of being concerned in the finish halfway through the penultimate furlong.

Chalon (ch.f. 1979)	Habitat (b 1966)	Sir Gaylord (b 1959)	Turn-to
			Somethingroyal
		Little Hut (b 1952)	Occupy
			Savage Beauty
	Areola (ch 1968)	Kythnos (b 1957)	Nearula
			Capital Issue
		Alive Alivo (ch 1963)	Never Say Die
			Fluorescent

Chalon cost only 46,000 guineas as a yearling at Goffs. She is out of a mare who in her day was an even bigger sales bargain, one who fetched 720 guineas as a foal and 1,200 guineas when resold as a yearling. Areola went on to run four times over five furlongs as a two-year-old: she won a maiden race at the Curragh, and the Emily Persse Cup and the Phoenix Stakes at Phoenix Park, and finished second to Cawston's Pride in the Queen Mary Stakes at Royal Ascot. She ran only once at three, unplaced in the Athasi Stakes which is an early-season classic trial at the Curragh. Areola's first foal Areonative (by Raise A Native) won a small race in the United States as a three-year-old after being raced in France at two. Her only other winner besides Chalon is also an American one, Chalfont Place (by Little Current); she won four races there and was placed in a stakes. Since producing Chalon, Areola has foaled colts by Be My Guest and Homing and she is reportedly in foal to Northfields. Areola is the first foal and only important winner of the maiden racemare Alive Alivo. The next dam Fluorescent, a daughter of the 1948 One Thousand Guineas runner-up Ariostar, won

Child Stakes, Newmarket—Chalon gives weight to Kareena, Merlins Charm and Dancing Rocks

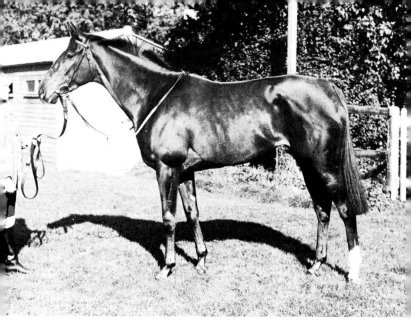

Mr Michael Doyle Riordan's "Chalon"

the Imperial Produce Stakes in 1953. One further notable aspect of Areola's pedigree is the close inbreeding to Nasrullah, the sire of both Nearula and Never Say Die.

Chalon's last two performances have almost certainly booked her a place in the paddocks in 1983. At her best she was a good miler, in the top two or three of her sex in the country, and a pleasure to watch on the racecourse. She was, as we said, very well suited by a mile. A filly with a smooth, easy action, she never raced on ground softer than good and she acted extremely well on firm. *H. Cecil.*

CHALUMINUM 3 gr.f. Town Crier 119–Tudor Top 104 (Tudor Minstrel 144) (1981 NR 1982 7g) 1,400Y; wiry filly; half-sister to several winners, including very useful 1m to 1¼m performer Atopolis (by Acropolis); dam useful but disappointing at up to 7f; dropped out from halfway when last of 11 to The Grass in newcomers race at Doncaster in March. *W. O'Gorman.* —

CHAMBESY 3 br.g. Moulton 128–Verdun 82 (Relic) (1981 6f 7g 8d 1982 12f 17f* 15.5f 16.1h 16d 15.8f 18d 16fg) tall, rather leggy gelding; stayed on well to win 14-runner maiden race at Wolverhampton in May; soundly beaten in handicaps afterwards, including when tailed off last 2 starts; well suited by a test of stamina; blinkered seventh start; one to be wary of; sold to W. Clay 4,000 gns Ascot September Sales. *D. Morley.* **71** d

CHAMPAGNE CHARLIE 5 br.h. Charlottown 127–The Guzzler 69 (Behistoun 131) (1981 14fg 14d 14s⁴ 14d³ 16f³ 16fg* 16fg 19fg 14d 16h⁴ 16fg 16s 18g 1982 17f³ 16fg³ 16fg 16.9fg²) compact horse; staying handicapper; appears to act on any going; suitable mount for an inexperienced rider; not particularly consistent. *N. Gaselee.* **58**

CHAMPAGNE DOLLY 3 b.f. Grey Mirage 128–Santa Marta 51 (Lavandin 128) (1981 5s 5fg 5fg 5.8f 8.2s 8s 1982 5f 6f 7g 6g 6fg* 7fg) lengthy filly; plater; attracted no bid after winning apprentice selling handicap at Windsor in August; stays 6f; acts on a firm surface; sold 550 gns Ascot October Sales. *P. M. Taylor.* **57**

CHAMPAGNE GLORY 3 b.c. Hittite Glory 125–Tilt Guard 75 (Crepello 136) —
(1981 7fg 7fg 7g 7g 8s 1982 10g) short-backed colt; poor plater. *M. Bradley.*

CHAMPAGNE MANDY 2 b.f. Mandrake Major 122–Champagne Party 65
(Amber Rama 133) (1982 5f⁴ 5f 5g 5fg⁴ 7g³ 7.2s 8d) Mar 24; 750Y; lightly-
made, plain filly; first foal; dam poor maiden; fair plater; well beaten in selling
nurseries last two starts; best run at 5f, but probably stays 7f; appears to need
a sound surface. *R. Hollinshead.*

CHAMPAGNE PRINCESS 3 b.f. Welsh Pageant 132–Campagna (Romulus 62
129) (1981 6fg 7fg⁴ 8fg 1982 10f 12f 10f⁴ 8.2g 8fg³ 8fg³ 8fg³ 8g 9s 8g⁴)
medium-sized, fair sort; plating-class maiden; stays 1¼m; sometimes blinkered;
sold 4,000 gns Newmarket December Sales. *M. Jarvis.*

CHAMY'S-GIRL 3 ch.f. Roman Warrior 132–Chamolive 56 (Poaching 115) —
(1981 NR 1982 15.8d) half-sister to fair 1977 2-y-o 5f winner Cham-Ol Bazaar
(by Native Bazaar) and 1m winner Rolleston (by Communication); dam winning
jumper; behind when unseating rider at halfway in minor event won by Prince
Elo at Catterick in October. *W. Wharton.*

CHANCELER 2 b.c. Homing 130–Deed 86 (Derring-Do 131) (1982 6s 7.6v² 86
8.2s) May 9; 46,000Y; medium-sized, well-made, quite attractive colt; excellent
walker; half-brother to 2 winners, including very useful 3-y-o Busaco (by
Bustino), successful at up to 1¼m; dam won over 5f at 2 yrs; 1½ lengths second
of 13 to Joyful Dancer in maiden race at Lingfield in October, easily best effort;
should be suited by 1m. *G. Harwood.*

CHANEY 4 b.g. Sparkler 130–Anippe 102 (Aggressor 130) (1981 7g 7d 7d 7fg 40
6fg 8d 1982 9fg 10f³ 10.6f 14.6g) strong, compact gelding; bad mover;
third in seller at Pontefract, only form; stays 1¼m. *G. Fletcher.*

CHANGAN 2 ch.f. Touch Paper 113–Tin Tina 72 (Tin Whistle 128) (1982 59
5s³ 5g 6fg 7.2f 7f) May 5; IR 8,000Y; sparely-made filly; good walker; sister
to very useful 1977 5f and 6f winner Ludstone; dam won 5f seller at 2 yrs; plating-
class maiden; stays 7f; acts on any going. *R. Hollinshead.*

CHANGATRE 2 ch.f. Malinowski 123–Good Reliance (Good Bond 122) (1982 76
6f 6g 8f 7d² 10s⁴ 7g) Apr 15; small, rather shallow-girthed filly; fourth foal;
half-sister to 2 fairly useful winners by Touch Paper, namely 5f to 1m winner
Changabang and 1981 2-y-o 5f and 6f winner Changatu; dam never ran; quite
a modest maiden; stays 1¼m; acts on any going. *R. Hollinshead.*

CHANNING GIRL 3 b.f. Song 132–Maternal 93 (High Top 131) (1981 6fg 72
6f³ 6f 7f 8.2fg³ 7.6g³ 8d 7g 1982 6g 8.5fg 8f² 8fg 8d² 10fg 10.1g³ 12g* 12g 14.7fg³
16g² 14g² 16s) lengthy filly; trotted up in modest 5-runner maiden race at
Redcar in August; creditable second in 2 handicaps at Newmarket afterwards;
stays well; probably acts on any going; blinkered twice at 2 yrs. *C. Brittain.*

CHANTAGE 3 b.f. Sweet Revenge 129–Wedding March (March Past 124) 60
(1981 7g 1982 7f 8fg 8g³ 8d* 8fg 8.2fg³ 10f* 8.2s* 8s) big, rangy filly; plater;
won at Yarmouth (bought in 1,000 gns), Leicester (bought in 1,700 gns) and
Haydock (no bid); stays 1¼m; acts on any going; genuine; sold 4,600 gns
Newmarket Autumn Sales. *Sir Mark Prescott.*

CHANTRY 2 b.f. Habitat 134–Chappelle Blanche 96 (Olden Times) (1982 5s) — p
Apr 29; rangy filly; second foal; half-sister to 3-y-o 11f winner Escapist (by
Run The Gantlet); dam, half-sister to Beldale Flutter, won over 6f and stayed
1m; 10/1 and in need of race, soon behind when 7¾ lengths eighth of 15 to Dry
Land in maiden race at Sandown in October; has scope and will do better in time.
G. Harwood.

CHAPLINS CLUB (USA) 2 ch.c. Parade of Stars–Nautical Rose (Henrijan) 94
(1982 5fg² 5g³ 6g³ 6g 6d² 5v* 5g*) Apr 9; $10,000Y; small, well-made colt;
third foal; half-brother to a minor winner by Three Quarters; dam won 8 small
sprint races in USA; won nurseries at Folkestone and Newmarket in October;
best form at 5f, but stays 6f; acts well on heavy going; game and genuine. *I.
Walker.*

CHARADE (USA) 3 ch.f. Exclusive Native–Clairvoyance (Round Table) 68
(1981 6fg 6fg 7.3s 1982 10h⁴ 10g³ 11.7f² 14fg 11.7s) well-made, attractive
filly; has shown some ability in maiden races; stays 11.7f; acts on firm going;
sold 42,000 gns Newmarket December Sales. *J. Tree.*

CHARBONNEL (USA) 3 b.c. Roberto 131–Chocolate Beau (Beau Max) 81
(1981 6h* 7g² 6g 1982 10f 8f⁴ 9g³ 8g 8.3g² 7f² 8f 7f³ 7f) quite attractive colt;

modest handicapper; stays 1m well; acts on hard going; has run creditably for an apprentice; didn't run particularly well in blinkers final start; trained part of season by P. Walwyn and R. Laing. *G. Huffer.*

CHARLES BOOT 3 ch.g. Sun Prince 128–Tudor Gal 106 (Henry the Seventh **46** 125) (1981 6g 6fg 6f⁴ 8.2s 6s 8g 8d 1982 8g³ 10s 8fg* 8.3g⁴ 7d 10d 8d 8f 8.2s) compact gelding; plater; sold out of M. Tompkins' stable 1,300 gns after winning at Wolverhampton in April; stays 1m; best form on a sound surface; has twice worn blinkers. *K. Bridgwater.*

CHARLES STREET 5 ch.g. Huntercombe 133–Limerick Queen (Whistling **66** Wind 123) (1981 7fg 1982 5d³ 6g³ 7.6g 6fg 5.3g* 6g 5s 5s) neat gelding; beat Kassak by 7 lengths in handicap at Brighton in June; stays 6f; acts on any going but is well suited by some give in the ground; often blinkered. *P. Haynes.*

CHARLES STUART (FR) 3 b.c. Anne's Pretender 124–Kerline (Spy Well **—** 126) (1981 7.6s 7d 1982 8fg 10fg 8g 8d 10.8fg⁴ 12f 12g 11.7fg 12fg⁴) big, rangy colt; little worthwhile form in varied company. *R. Baker.*

CHARLIE KILGOUR 3 b.g. Pitskelly 122–Nuageuse (Prince Regent 129) **—** (1981 7fg 8d 7d 1982 10f³ 10.8fg 12g 12v) plating-class maiden; best run at 1¼m on firm going; blinkered final start; sold to A. Pitt 6,000 gns Newmarket Autumn Sales. *H. Candy.*

CHARLIE'S PROSPECT (USA) 3 ch.c. Prove Out–Chill (Nearctic) (1981 **84** 6f 8g 1982 10d* 10f* 9fg* 10f* 12f 10f⁴ 10g* 10d* 10v) smallish colt; much improved and won maiden race at Folkestone and handicaps at Nottingham, York, Epsom (2) and Ayr; stays 1¼m; possibly unsuited by very soft going but acts on any other; suited by waiting tactics; genuine; ran well below his best final outing. *G. Pritchard-Gordon.*

CHARLIE'S SUNSHINE 5 b.m. Jimsun 121–Dracaena 62 (Double Jump **—** 131) (1981 11s⁴ 12g 12g 1982 12.2fg) small mare; poor performer; stays 11f; acts on soft going; has sweated up. *J. Townson.*

CHARLOTTE AMALIE 3 br.f. No Mercy 126–Penhill Point 84 (King's **—** Leap 111) (1981 NR 1982 8g 12fg) 2,500F, 3,200Y; first produce; dam 2-y-o 5f winner; behind in varied company, including selling. *A. Smith.*

CHARLOTTE'S CHOICE 7 b.g. Blakeney 126–Queendom 109 (Quorum **64** 126) (1981 12s 12fg 12g 16s 13.8g* 12g 16fg 12g³ 12d³ 12.3s* 14f* 13.3d 1982 12.2d 16fg² 13.1f 13.3f³ 16.1g 16fg⁴ 12fg³) neat, attractive gelding; ran best races of year when placed in handicaps at Lingfield, Newbury and Chepstow; stays well; acts on any going; has been tried in blinkers; sometimes bandaged in front. *W. Wightman.*

CHARLOTTE'S DUNCE 2 br.c. Sit In The Corner–Bollin Charlotte 79 **86** (Immortality) (1982 5fg 6f* 6fg⁴ 7f² 7f² 7g* 8fg*) May 13; compact colt; brother to a plater and half-brother to 2 winners, including useful 6f to 9f winner Immortal Knight (by Midsummer Night II); dam miler; won seller (retained 3,100 gns) at Thirsk in June; proved well worth the money, going on to successes in nurseries at Beverley in August and Thirsk (made light of 5 lb penalty) in September; will probably stay 1¼m; has raced only on a sound surface; genuine. *M. H. Easterby.*

CHARMED CIRCLE 2 b.f. Comedy Star 121–Freia 91 (Rheingold 137) (1982 **—** 5f 6g 6fg 7.6v 8s) Apr 3; 15,000Y; small, quite well-made filly; first foal; dam, 1m winner, is sister to Lancashire Oaks winner Rhein Bridge and half-sister to very smart Connaught Bridge; behind in maiden races, one at Folkestone. *A. Ingham.*

CHARMED LIFE TOO 2 ch.f. Dominion 123–Party Girl 96 (Pardao 120) **65** (1982 5f 6g 7fg 7.6v 7d) Apr 15; quite well-made filly; good walker; third foal; half-sister to useful hurdler Norfolk Dance (by Blakeney); dam, daughter of very useful sprinter Eternal Goddess, showed best form at sprint distances; plating-class maiden; best run at 7f on a firm surface. *J. Bethell.*

CHARMING CHARLES 3 ch.g. Welsh Pageant 132–Orapa 88 (Aureole 132) **—** (1981 8g 10g 1982 12s 12fg 14fg 10.6f 16s) rather lightly-made gelding; good walker; poor maiden; blinkered fourth start; sold out of P. Kelleway's stable 2,200 gns Doncaster August Sales after fourth outing. *D. Morrill.*

CHASE THE WIND (USA) 3 ch.c. King's Bishop–Tempest Flower (Crafty **—** Admiral) (1981 6fg⁴ 7fg* 7fg 7g 1982 8.2s 8f 12f 10fg 11.7fg 10.1d 8s) strong, good-bodied, quite attractive colt; fairly useful at 2 yrs; well below his best most starts in 1982; probably stays 1¼m; has run respectably when sweating up badly; ran poorly in blinkers fifth outing; sold 3,300 gns Newmarket Autumn Sales. *G. Hunter.*

CHASTE LADY 3 ch.f. Sandford Lad 133–King's Chase (King's Leap 111) **59** (1981 5s 6g 7f² 6g³ 7h 7fg 8.2d⁴ 1982 8d 8f² 8g 9.4f* 9g² 10.2g* 9g⁴) fair sort; good mover; won maiden race at Carlisle in June and apprentice handicap at Bath in July; stays 1¼m well; yet to show she acts on very soft ground but acts on any other; suitable mount for an apprentice; sold 4,000 gns Newmarket Autumn Sales. *C. Nelson.*

CHAUFFEUSE 2 b.f. Gay Fandango 132–Home Glo (Globemaster) (1982 **76 p** 5g*) Feb 19; leggy, narrow filly; closely related to fairly useful 6f winner Berry Island (by Thatch) and half-sister to 3 winners abroad; dam, twice a winner at up to 6f at 2 yrs in USA, is half-sister to high-class sprinters Home Guard and Boone's Cabin; very fit and wearing tongue strap, ran on gamely to lead close home when winning modest 12-runner maiden race at Wolverhampton in October by a head from Hartburn Reliance; will be suited by 6f. *H. T. Jones.*

CHEEKY MONKEY 3 ch.f. Shiny Tenth 120–Evvoia 53 (Khalkis 127) (1981 **—** 5fg 5g⁴ 5d³ 6g 6fg 6f³ 6g 1982 8d 8f 8fg 8g 8fg 8g 7g 8d⁴ 7g) plater; stays 1m; sometimes blinkered; sold 840 gns Newmarket Autumn Sales. *G. Blum.*

CHEF MARCEL (USA) 4 b.g. Personality–Raise A Big Peach (Raise A **—** Native) (1981 11s³ 16s* 13fg 19fg 18.1d 1982 18d) lengthy gelding; no form on flat since winning maiden event at York in 1981; stays well; shows a lot of knee action and probably needs some give in the ground; blinkered final start in 1981. *N. Bycroft.*

CHEHO (USA) 3 b.c. Parade of Stars–Flower Basket (Mr Leader) (1981 **—** NR 1982 8g 13.3f 13g 10fg 14fg 10s) $10,000Y; medium-sized, fair sort; fourth foal; half-brother to 3 minor winners in USA; dam won claiming race over 7f at 2 yrs; poor maiden; sold to R. Akehurst 3,900 gns Ascot November Sales. *I. Walker.*

CHEKA (USA) 6 b.g. Russian Bank 110–Sweet Seventeen (County Delight) **83 d** (1981 17.1g* 18d* 20fg 17.1d 18g 1982 18g* 16s* 16fg* 18.4fg 16g 14fg 16d 16.1s 18d) strong gelding; good walker; out-and-out staying handicapper; in fine form in spring and won in good style at Doncaster and Kempton (from Halsbury in Queen's Prize) and gamely at Newmarket; didn't run particularly well afterwards, but was off course over 3 months after fifth start; seems to act on any going; genuine and versatile (also a winner over hurdles and fences). *I. Balding.*

CHEKIKA 2 gr.c. Warpath 113–Border Honour 76 (Above Suspicion 127) **79** (1982 7g 7f 7fg 8d) Apr 26; big colt; third reported foal; brother to 7f and 1¾m winner Border Squaw; dam, who stayed 1½m, is half-sister to very useful Border Bounty, the dam of Pitcairn; beaten less than 4 lengths when seventh of 13 to Mister Valentino in slowly-run 1m maiden race at Ayr in September, best effort; will stay 1¼m; the type to do much better in time. *C. Gray.*

CHELLASTON PARK 3 b.f. Record Token 128–Acquire 105 (Burglar 128) **117** (1981 5s² 5s* 5g* 5g* 5f² 5fg* 5g* 5d² 5fg² 1982 5s* 6f³ 5s³ 5f² 5fg² 5f 5g² 5g²)
Fillies occupied second place in no fewer than seven of the ten British pattern races for three-year-olds and upwards over sprint distances, with Blue Singh runner-up in the Palace House, Vaigly Star in the Cork and Orrery and July Cup, Soba in the Diadem and Chellaston Park in the Temple, King's Stand and William Hill Sprint Championship. At the top of their form there wasn't much between the four fillies concerned, and for sheer consistency Chellaston Park matches Soba or any other horse in training. Only once in seventeen starts over two seasons on all types of going has she failed to finish in the first three and even then, in the King George Stakes at Goodwood, she had the excuse of starting none too well and not enjoying the best of runs in the closing stages.
Though a five-furlong performer pure and simple—on her sole outing over further she patently failed to get the trip—Chellaston Park does not show blinding speed from end to end, needing rather to be held up and brought with a late flourish. Her reappearance in the Field Marshal Stakes at Haydock

in April showed how effective she can be when everything goes right, for after accelerating to lead a furlong out she wasn't troubled to hold off the Irish colt Cooleen Jack by two and a half lengths. This was Chellaston Park's only success of the year but since she raced mainly in top company thereafter that was no disgrace. Well as she ran when third to Blue Courtier in the Prix de Saint-Georges at Longchamp and second, beaten three quarters of a length, to Mummy's Game in the Temple Stakes at Sandown, it was Chellaston Park's performances at Royal Ascot and the York August meeting which revealed her true merit. At Royal Ascot she came with her usual run to challenge for the lead entering the final furlong, but though too good for the rest, including Blue Singh, Jester, Cajun and Lightning Label, she was swamped by Fearless Lad who strode clear to win by two lengths. In the William Hill Sprint Championship she kept on well to get the better of Kind Music by a neck in the battle for second place, two lengths behind Sharpo who outclassed his opponents. Chellaston Park's final outing, in a minor event at Newbury, looked to offer her a fine chance of gaining due reward for her consistency, but starting at 5/1 on she was comfortably outpointed by Special Pleasure. It is safe to assume that her arduous season had taken some of the shine off Chellaston Park for this contest—at her best she would have had little trouble coping with the winner.

There were two notable bargains to be had at the Ascot December Sales in 1979 when Acquire, covered by Record Token, and her filly foal by the same sire sold as successive lots for 925 guineas and 2,200 guineas. The filly, resold at Newmarket the following year for 3,500 guineas, was Chellaston Park and the foal Acquire was carrying, now called Sir Butch, won a six-furlong race at Epsom in 1982. The family hasn't produced any top horses in the past few years but there has been no shortage of winners from it. Acquire won twice over five furlongs at two and her first foal, Lady Acquiesce (by Galivanter), also won over the minimum trip in her first season. The second and third dams both won and Acclio, a useful sprinter, foaled seven winners on the flat

Mrs C. M. Smalley's "Chellaston Park"

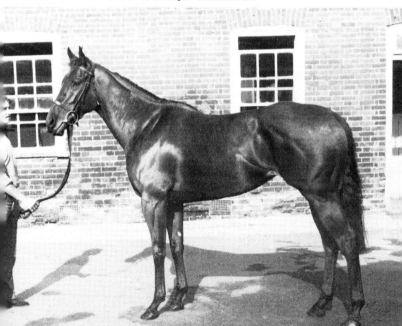

and over hurdles, notably the smart sprinter Acquit, the very useful miler and William Hill Imperial Cup Hurdle winner Acquaint and Accelerate, useful at up to a mile and a quarter.

Chellaston Park (b.f. 1979)	Record Token (ch 1972)	Jukebox (b 1966)	Sing Sing / Bibi Mah
		Bare Costs (b 1965)	Petition / Bootless
	Acquire (br 1973)	Burglar (b 1966)	Crocket / Agin the Law
		Acclio (b 1958)	Acropolis / Clio

Chellaston Park, a good mover, stays in training and we assume she'll pursue a similar campaign to that of 1982. There may be some doubt about her being able to maintain her form—though well made, she is on the small side and doesn't always particularly impress in the paddock—but if enthusiasm for the job is any criterion she won't be disgraced however good the company. *B. Hobbs.*

CHEMIN DE GUERRE 5 gr.m. Warpath 113–Flying Florrie 74 (I Say 125) (1981 12f 12.2fg³ 19g* 12f* 16f² 16s⁴ 18g* 1982 12fg* 14g³ 18d² 16g² 16.1s³ 18d 18s) rangy, workmanlike mare; good walker; having first race since cracking a cannon bone in November, 1981, when making all to win handicap at Ripon in August virtually unchallenged by 1½ lengths from Alfie Dickins; ran well afterwards when placed in handicaps at Haydock (amateur riders and apprentice events), Ripon and Beverley after; effective at 1½m when enterprising tactics are employed and stays very well; acts on any going; game and genuine. *M. H. Easterby.* **78**

CHEM (USA) 3 b. or br.c. The Minstrel 135–Banning (Crafty Admiral) (1981 NR 1982 10.5d⁴ 12g³ 12s* 15fg* 15g² 12.5g* 14.6f 15.5v) 170,000Y; small, robust, full-quartered, attractive colt; half-brother to several winners here and abroad, notably good French middle-distance stayer Balompie (by Pardao); dam ran only 3 times; a smart colt who won minor event at Evry, Prix de l'Esperance at Longchamp (beat Le Nain Jaune a short neck) and Prix de Menneval at Deauville (accounted for Brezzo by a short head); also ran very well in Grand Prix de Paris at Longchamp, going down by 2 lengths to Le Nain Jaune (eased in closing stages when clearly held by winner); well beaten on final 2 starts in St Leger at Doncaster (tenth of 15 to Touching Wood) and Prix Royal-Oak at Longchamp (last of 13 to Denel); stays very well; probably acts on any going; sent to USA. *O. Douieb, France.* **118**

CHENKYNOWA 2 b.f. Connaught 130–Paperwork (Brigadier Gerard 144) (1982 5f 5fg² 5fg 6g) Mar 17; small filly; first foal; dam minor winner over 8.5f in France and won over hurdles in this country; neck second of 9 to Rapid Lady in seller at Beverley in June, only form; not raced after June; bred to need 7f+. *A. Smith.* **48**

CHEQUERED LIFE 2 b.f. Wolverlife 115–The Chequer (Majetta 115) (1982 6fg 7s) Mar 31; IR 3,300Y, 2,300 2-y-o; lengthy, shallow-girthed filly; second foal; dam third over 9f in Ireland; in mid-division in maiden races at Salisbury and Sandown in the autumn. *R. Laing.* **—**

CHERCHEZ LA FEMME 6 b.m. Mon Fils 124–Angele 98 (Match III 135) (1981 8d³ 10f 8f 1982 8d 8f 7f 10.6h 8g) plater; best run at 1m on a soft surface; blinkered third and fifth starts; sold 625 gns Ascot 2nd June Sales. *M. Pipe.* **—**

CHERI BERRY 3 b.f. Air Trooper 115–Diorina 91 (Manacle 123) (1981 5fg 5d³ 5.8h* 6fg* 7s 1982 6fg 6f³ 6fg 6f² 6g 5fg 6d 6s* 5s) small, lengthy filly; sprint handicapper; won at Nottingham in October; stays 6f; acts on any going; blinkered last 3 starts. *W. Wightman.* **78**

CHERRY SEASON 2 gr.f. Silly Season 127–Tudor Gus 64 (Gustav 121) (1982 6g 7fg 6g 7fg² 8s 8d) May 6; leggy filly; has a round action; half-sister to useful plater Cherry Corner (by Sit In The Corner), successful at up to 1m, and a winner in Denmark; dam won 7f seller; ½-length second of 20 behind Freedom Glory in seller at Redcar in September, only form of note; should stay 1m; possibly requires sound surface; inconsistent. *Hbt Jones.* **62**

CHESTNUT PALE 3 ch.f. Record Token 128–Whitestake 74 (Compensation 127) (1981 5fg 5fg 5f⁴ 7g 6f³ 6fg 7f 6s 5g⁴ 1982 6fg 6f 7fg 10f⁴ 10d⁴ 13.8d **48**

12s³ 12g 12s) stocky filly; poor mover; plater; stays 1½m; suited by some give in the ground; usually wears blinkers. *Hbt Jones.*

CHE TESORO 2 ch.c. Gay Fandango 132–Deluge 74 (Primera 131) (1982 — 7g 8s 8g) May 4; 12,000Y; strong, compact colt; half-brother to 3 winners, including useful 5f and 6f winner Adam's Well (by Reform); dam, winner at 1¼m, is half-sister to Hotfoot; well beaten in maiden and minor events; off course 4 months after debut; sold 4,000 gns Newmarket Autumn Sales. *M. Jarvis.*

CHEUNG SING 3 b.c. Vitiges 132–Singing Witch 71 (Sing Sing 134) (1981 — NR 1982 5f 8g) 3,400Y; small, compact colt; half-brother to 1980 2-y-o 5f winner La Belle Sorcière (by Sparkler) and 1978 2-y-o 5f and 6f winner Rose of Shenfield (by Upper Case); dam half-sister to smart sprinter Vilgora; behind in maiden races at Sandown in April and Kempton in May. *P. K. Mitchell.*

CHEVELEY STAR 3 b.c. Roman Warrior 132–Tipsy Rider 60 (Hard Ridden 71 131) (1981 7g 6s³ 1982 7f 7g² 8f² 7g 7fg 8.2s 8s) sturdy colt; suited by 1m; acts on any going; blinkered sixth outing. *C. Spares.*

CHEVINGTON 5 b.g. Moulton 128–Joey 110 (Salvo 129) (1981 NR 1982 — 11.1g) strong, attractive, deep-bodied gelding; fairly useful at 3 yrs; no show only outing of 1982; stays 1¼m; blinkered final outing in 1980; sold privately 10,000 gns Ascot June Sales. *J. Gifford.*

CHEVRULLAH 3 gr.f. Grisaille 115–Princess Zarina (Prince Chevalier) (1981 — NR 1982 7fg 9f) sparely-made filly; half-sister to 2 winning sprint platers; dam never ran; tailed off in maiden race at Chepstow and minor event at Wolverhampton. *D. C. Tucker.*

CHICANERY 3 ro.c. Abwah 118–Chiana (Compensation 127) (1981 5d 5fg — 6fg² 6f⁴ 6d³ 6f² 8fg 7.2v⁴ 6s 1982 7d 7fg⁴ 7fg 7g 7g 8g 10.8fg⁴) small colt; poor walker; plater; stays 7f but isn't sure to get 1m; acts on any going; sold 400 gns Ascot August Sales. *T. Marshall.*

CHIC BOUTIQUE (USA) 2 ch.c. Wajima–Chain Store (Nodouble) (1982 69 p 7g) Apr 14; quite a useful-looking colt; second foal; dam, sister to very smart Double Discount, was very useful winner at up to 9f; 33/1 and in need of race, unruly in stalls when respectable eighth of 13, 8 lengths behind Cock Robin, in Ribero Stakes at Doncaster in September; will stay 1m; sure to do better. *B. Hanbury.*

CHICKEN AGAIN 5 b.g. Royalty 130–Dust Sheet (Silly Season 127) (1981 — 7.2g 7.2s 6fg³ 7fg³ 7g 7d 6s³ 6s 1982 6d 6s 6s) tall gelding; well beaten in 1982, beat ⁿt up to 7f; probably acts on any going; sometimes sweats up; often blinkered but is effective without; suitable mount for an apprentice. *C. Crossley.*

CHICKWEED 3 b.g. Porto Bello 118–Groundsel 72 (Reform 132) (1981 NR — 1982 7f 8g 7f 6g 8fg) small gelding; first foal; dam third over 9f at 2 yrs; well beaten in varied company; has twice been blinkered. *M. Smyly.*

CHIEF HABIT 2 b.c. Habat 127–Jeldi 58 (Tribal Chief 125) (1982 5f3 5g 59 6f⁴) Feb 18; 3,100Y; sturdy colt; half-brother to a winning plater and a winner in Malaya; dam ran only at 2 yrs; moderate plater; not raced after June; best form at 5f; blinkered last 2 starts. *A. Jarvis.*

CHIEF SPEAKER 4 b.c. Nonoalco 131–Anice (Crepello 136) (1981 9fg 76 12.3g³ 12fg⁴ 10d² 9s* 8d* 1982 7d 8fg² 8g 8f⁴ 8fg 10d⁴ 9f³ 8fg 8g 8s) tall colt; modest handicapper; in frame at Newbury (twice, including ½-length second to Molon Lave in Spring Cup), Sandown and York, but became rather disappointing; stays 1¼m, but not 1½m; acts on any going; reportedly struck into himself third outing. *R. Sheather.*

CHIKALA 2 br.f. Pitskelly 122–Ballychord (Ballymoss 136) (1982 5f² 5d* 81 5fg³ 6g⁴ 6f² 6fg) Feb 5; IR 6,600F; strong filly; carries plenty of condition; sister to 1¼m winner Miner's Song and half-sister to 3 winners, including prolific Italian winner Brilli Peri (by Windjammer); dam reportedly won in Denmark; overcame difficulties in running when winning 9-runner minor event at Beverley in July, in good style by 2½ lengths; creditable second in nursery at Catterick the following month; will be suited by longer distances; seems to act on any going; wore a tongue strap fourth outing; blinkered last 2 starts. *Miss S. Hall.*

CHILCOMBE 3 b.f. Morston 125–Parvati 82 (Paveh 126) (1981 8d 1982 — 12fg 16d) big, deep-girthed filly; behind in maiden races. *G. Balding.*

CHILDOWN (USA) 2 b.c. Sadair–Swoonson Gal (Swoon's Son) (1982 7g) — p
Mar 31; $24,000F, 44,000Y; well-grown, deep-girthed, good sort; half-brother
to 2 winners in USA by Angle Light, including minor stakes winner Hit A Gusher,
successful at up to 7f; dam a minor winner at up to 6f in USA; favourite although
in need of race and rather green, struggling soon after halfway and not given
hard time when remote sixth of 9 behind Boom Town Charlie in minor event
at Yarmouth in June; sure to be better for the experience. *M. Stoute.*

CHIMANGO 4 b.g. African Sky 124–Cockatoo (Indiana 129) (1981 7s 7fg³ —
8fg 6f 1982 6d 6fg⁴ 7f 8g 8.2g 6s 8.2v) lightly-made gelding; poor handicapper;
should stay 1m; blinkered final outing in 1980. *K. Stone.*

CHINA GOD 9 b.g. Cumshaw 111–White Goddess 65 (Red God 128§) (1981 **62**
NR 1982 10.6f* 12s 12d 11fg³ 12fg* 12.3d² 11f 10.6s) quite a useful hurdler
at his best; held up when winning amateur riders handicaps at Haydock in
June and Doncaster in July, being well ridden by Mr D. Browne both times;
stayed 1½m; probably acted on any going; dead. *D. Francis.*

CHINA GOLD 3 b.g. Blue Cashmere 129–China Girl 76 (Shantung 132) (1981 —
NR 1982 5fg 5fg 8fg 6s) 4,800F, 4,600Y; lengthy gelding; half-brother to a
winning plater and to winners in Spain and Brazil; dam placed over 5f and
6f at 2 yrs; poor form in maiden and minor events; sold 620 gns Doncaster
October Sales. *Miss L. Siddall.*

CHINA PEAK (USA) 2 ch.c. Key To The Mint–Another Treat (Cornish —
Prince) (1982 7g 7d) May 4; $175,000Y, $95,000 2-y-o; half-brother to
Creative Plan (by Sham), a stakes-placed winner of over $100,000; dam, unplaced
in 5 starts, is half-sister to dams of Be My Guest and Golden Fleece; unquoted,
behind at Newmarket in October in 30-runner maiden race and 13-runner
Houghton Stakes. *B. Hills.*

CHINA RUN 4 ch.g. Chingnu 99–Gay Runner (Clear Run 109) (1981 5f —
9d 10s 1982 5g 8.3fg 7fg 8g) small gelding; only poor form, including in
sellers; stays 1¼m; changed hands for 1,300 gns Doncaster June Sales and
680 gns Ascot August Sales after final start. *J. Yardley.*

CHINCOTEAGUE 5 b.g. Gulf Pearl 117–Sheila's Pearl (Javelot 124) (1981 **72**
NR 1982 18f* 20fg³) out-and-out staying handicapper; having first race
since 1980 when getting up in last 100 yards to beat Atlantic Traveller by
½ length at Doncaster in May; never stopped fighting and ran most creditably
when 4 lengths third to Popsi's Joy in Ascot Stakes at Royal Ascot the following
month; acted on any going; usually sweated up; had been fired; thoroughly
game and genuine; dead. *M. Stoute.*

CHINOOK 3 b.f. Tumble Wind–Papoosette (Raise You Ten 125) (1981 5s —
5d³ 1982 5f 6fg 5f 6f) lengthy, good sort; plating-class maiden; has worn
blinkers; sold 550 gns Doncaster September Sales, resold 370 gns same venue in
November. *N. Guest.*

CHIPTOWN BOY 3 gr.g. Town Crier 119–Sparkation (Communication 119) **47**
(1981 6f 5v 5s 1982 6fg 7f 9s 5g⁴) neat gelding; plater; best run at 5f; sometimes blinkered. *S. Norton.*

CHIQUITITA 5 b.m. Reliance II 137–Marcida 85 (Alcide 136) (1981 NR —
1982 12fg) neat mare; plater in 1980 (rated 44); stays 1¼m; suited by fast
ground. *D. Arbuthnot.*

CHLOSTERLI .2 ch.f. Wollow 132–Anadyomene 101 (Sea Hawk II 131) (1982 —
6g) Apr 16; well-grown, lengthy filly; third foal; dam, daughter of Cheveley
Park winner Lalibela, won over 11f and 13f; unquoted but very fit, soon behind
and chased along when out of first 9 of 19 behind What Lake in maiden race
at Newmarket in September; likely to need further. *G. Hunter.*

CHOIR 2 br.f. High Top 131–Land of Song 82 (Sing Sing 134) (1982 7fg 7g —
8s) Mar 30; 35,000Y; lengthy filly; good mover; sister to 2 winners, including
1m and 9f winner Hand Made, and half-sister to 2 winners; dam, half-sister
to out-and-out stayer Celtic Cone, won over 5f; behind in maiden races, starting
25/1 or more each time. *B. Hobbs.*

CHOOSY MISS 3 br.f. Warpath 113–Discernment 66 (Pan II 130) (1981 **43**
NR 1982 7fg 12g 16.5s 12s 12g³) fair sort; closely related to promising but
lightly-raced Declamation (by Town Crier) and half-sister to 2 minor winners;
dam lightly-raced half-sister to very useful 1½m horse Buff's Own; plater;
will stay 1¾m; best run in blinkers final start; trained part of season by W.
Crawford. *J. Fitzgerald.*

CHRISANTHY 5 b.m. So Blessed 130–The Ambion 113 (Henry the Seventh —
125) (1981 NR 1982 6g) no form since a 2-y-o; should stay 6f; probably
acts on any going; has shown signs of temperament. *R. Hollinshead.*

CHRIS'S LAD 3 ch.c. Sandford Lad 133–Perfect Bid (Baldric II 131) (1981 **102**
5s² 5g² 5g* 5g* 6d* 6fg² 6fg 6f² 6d 6g 1982 7fg 6f³ 6d 6f 6f 6fg 6g 6g⁴ 7f³
7.3g 8g⁴ 8g² 8s*) good sort; good walker; useful performer; beat Macmillion
decisively by 1½ lengths in minor event at Doncaster in November; in frame
several other starts, notably when running on strongly after dropping himself
out in early stages to be neck second to Mighty Fly in handicap at Newmarket;
suited by 1m; acts on any going; used to sweat up; has run creditably for an
apprentice; blinkered sixth and eighth outings; trained by V. Soane first 4
starts; sent to race in Florida. *M. Ryan.*

CHRISTMAS COTTAGE 4 br.g. Lochnager 132–Nelski 83 (Skymaster **80**
126) (1981 7s 8s² 8s² 7g³ 7g² 6fg 8f² 8d² 7g² 8d* 8d² 1982 8g² 7d* 8fg 8f
6d 7d 7s⁴) workmanlike gelding; ran very well when 2 lengths second of 26
behind King's Glory in William Hill Lincoln Handicap at Doncaster in March
and beat Indian King gamely by a neck in McEwan's Lager Handicap at Newcastle the following month; ran best subsequent races last 2 outings (was off
course 3 months after fourth start); gives impression 7f is an absolute minimum
for him nowadays and stays 1m well; acts on any going; blinkered fourth and fifth
outings as a 3-y-o. *J. Mason.*

CHRISTMAS CRACKER (USA) 3 b.g. On The Warpath–Virginia Cracker **42**
(Crackpot) (1981 NR 1982 8g 8d 8fg⁴ 8fg 16g 10.8fg 9fg³ 12s) sturdy gelding;
plater; should be suited by middle distances. *D. Wintle.*

CHRISTMAS GREETING 4 ch.g. Bonne Noel 115–Princess Mea (Meadow —
Court 129) (1981 12.2fg³ 16f* 16.5f³ 16s 15.8g* 1982 16d) strong gelding;
will be suited by extreme distances; acts on firm going; possibly ran a bit too
freely when blinkered once in 1981; pulled himself up on only outing of 1982.
M. H. Easterby.

CHROME MAG 4 br.f. Prince de Galles 125–Pat 98 (Ennis 128) (1981 7v⁴ **43**
8g 7g⁴ 7d⁴ 8.2f 8f² 8fg* 9f⁴ 8.2g 8f² 8f³ 8g 1982 8f 8f 8f 10fg 8fg 8fg 8f 8g 8d
10g² 8fg 8.2s⁴ 8d*) leggy, rather sparely-made filly; ran best races in selling
company, and won at Edinburgh in November (no bid); stays 1¼m; acts on
any going; blinkered sixth and seventh outings; looked none too genuine tenth
start. *W. Bentley.*

CHUMMY'S BOY 2 ch.g. Cawston's Clown 113–Barbara Bryce (Yellow God —
129) (1982 5.8f) May 11; 3,800F, 13,000Y; fourth foal; half-brother to
1979 2-y-o 5f winner Willing To Learn (by Balliol); dam never ran; unquoted,
last of 11 in maiden race won by Razor Sharp at Bath in July. *R. Hannon.*

CHURCHES GREEN 3 b.g. Sassafras 135–Alice Johnston (Majetta 115) **65**
(1981 7g 10s 1982 12g 12fg 10.1fg 10.1fg 11.7fg⁴ 12fg²) good sort; quite
a modest maiden; stays 1½m; best form on fast ground; ran creditably for amateur
rider final outing; has given trouble at start. *S. Mellor.*

CHURRA 3 b.f. Realm 129–Venus of Stretham 107 (Tower Walk 130) (1981 —
5s² 5s⁴ 6d 1982 6d⁴ 7f 7.2s) only plating class; stays 6f. *F. J. Houghton.*

CIDER QUEEN 3 b.f. Oats 126–Damascus Sky (Skymaster 126) (1981 6fg —
7d 7.6s 1982 10d 8.5fg 8g 10f) strong, rangy filly; good walker; plating-class
maiden; stays 1m. *R. Smyth.*

CIEL D'ARGENT 2 b.f. African Sky 124–La Tirelire (Run The Gantlet) (1982 **79**
6g 6g* 6fg³ 7g 7f⁴) Apr 17; IR 5,600F, IR 15,500Y; lightly-made filly; second
produce; half-sister to minor French 1981 2-y-o 1m winner Plaidoirie (by
Malacate); dam, from good family, won twice at around 1m at 2 yrs in France;
won 9-runner maiden race at Ayr in July by 1½ lengths from Parissaul; ¾-length
third of 7 to Mac's Palace in valuable nursery at Newmarket later in month,
easily best subsequent effort; should stay 7f. *J. Hindley.*

CIELO-AZZURRO 3 b.f. He Loves Me 120–Blue Plover (Majority Blue 126) —
(1981 NR 1982 10.1fg 10fg 12v⁴ 12s) 8,200Y; fair sort; half-sister to fairly
useful 7f performer Protectress (by Auction Ring) and a winner in South Africa;
dam half-sister to smart sprinter Vatellus; beaten some way in varied company.
R. Boss.

CILERNA JET 3 b.f. Lear Jet 123–Cilerna Rock (Coliseum 116) (1981 NR —
1982 8fg 8s 8s) second foal; dam never ran; behind in maiden races and a
minor event. *R. Baker.*

CIMA 4 br.g. High Top 131–Lemon Blossom 83 (Acropolis 132) (1981 12s* **100** 12d* 10d 12g* 12d* 12f³ 12fg 16s 1982 12.2d* 12fg² 12f 12s⁴ 12s* 12s) quite well-made gelding; good mover; won handicaps at Warwick in May and Haydock in October, beating Cavalier Servente by 2 lengths on latter course; in frame at Epsom (¾-length second to Lafontaine) and Ascot (first outing for over 3½ months) in between, but ran poorly final start; suited by 1½m; acts on any going but was never going well on really firm ground on third start and is ideally suited by some give underfoot; doesn't seem to find much off bridle. *J. Old.*

CIMARRON 4 ch.f. Carnival Dancer 113–Duresme 76 (Starry Halo 122) (1981 — 8fg³ 8g 10g³ 10.2f 10f 10g 1982 8fg 9f 9fg³ 8f³ 10.8fg 8g 7f 8f 9g 9g 8g) leggy filly; plating-class maiden; stays 1¼m; behind when hooded second start. *Mrs N. Macauley.*

CIRCASSIAN CIRCLE (FR) 2 b.g. Dance In Time–Circlet 97 (Baldric II **80** 131) (1982 6f 6d² 5s) Mar 15; sturdy, full-quartered, good sort; excellent walker; second foal; half-brother to 3-y-o middle-distance winner Round Tower (by High Top); dam, half-sister to 1,000 Guineas and French Oaks winner Highclere, stayed 1½m; having first race for 2 months when 2 lengths second of 14 to Dawn's Dream in maiden race at Brighton in October, best effort; bred to need further than 5f; gelded at end of season. *W. Hastings-Bass.*

CIRCUS RING 3 b.f. High Top 131–Bell Song 101 (Tudor Melody 129) (1981 — 6fg* 6fg* 6g* 1982 8fg)
    Following the retirement of Shergar and Marwell Stoute's stable wasn't so strong in 1982 as in other recent years although it enjoyed a fine season, topping the hundred mark for the second year in three. At the end of 1981 the stable did at least seem to have a natural successor to Marwell in Circus Ring, outstandingly the best of her age and sex at two years and a hot ante-post favourite for the One Thousand Guineas, who had gained wide-margin wins in a large maiden race at Newmarket and the Princess Margaret Stakes at Ascot, and a facile two-length win in the Lowther Stakes. In the event the Guineas went by without Circus Ring, withdrawn following a disappointing gallop less than a fortnight before the race, and although Circus Ring was saddled for the Coronation Stakes at Royal Ascot she trailed in last of eight behind Chalon after travelling well for a long way; it was announced afterwards that she wouldn't race again. There had been doubts about Circus Ring's prospects for quite some time before her withdrawal from the Guineas. In some quarters it was questioned whether she would stay a mile; in others whether she would train on, since neither of the two previous winning fillies out of the dam, the pony-sized Great Paul and the excitable Great Tom (each by Great Nephew) had done so. But perhaps the most serious question mark against Circus Ring during the winter was that concerning injury. A bout of lameness had caused her to miss the Cheveley Park Stakes and although she reportedly was cantering well at the beginning of February her poor showing on the gallops prior to her withdrawal from the Guineas was put down by connections to her feeling the ground due to her injury. After Royal Ascot Stoute was again quick to draw attention to Circus Ring's injury problems, although confirming that he had felt she would go very well. Our impression of Circus Ring at Ascot was that she looked very fit and well while appearing not to have grown very much since her two-year-old days. She showed little of her former sparkle in the race, but it would be unfair to assert that she failed to train on without mentioning in the same breath her possible unsoundness.

			Derring-Do		Darius
	High Top		(br 1961)		Sipsey Bridge
	(br 1969)		Camenae		Vimy
Circus Ring			(b 1961)		Madrilene
(b.f. 1979)			Tudor Melody		Tudor Minstrel
	Bell Song		(br 1956)		Matelda
	(b 1966)		Campanette		Fair Trial
			(b 1948)		Calluna

    The Snailwell Stud will no doubt be pleased to have Circus Ring joining its broodmares, particularly as it no longer owns her dam Bell Song. Bell Song was sold for 19,000 guineas at the December Sales in 1979 in foal to Sassafras, and was sent to France. Her new owners have done very nicely out of Circus Ring's success, selling Your Song, the Sassafras yearling, to Guy Harwood at Deauville for 1,050,000 francs (almost £100,000) and Arctic Song (by Arctic Tern), the next produce, at the same venue in 1982 for 1,250,000 francs. As well as the three winners already mentioned Bell Song has produced Night Porter (by Connaught), successful over nine furlongs at three years, and Wimsey (by Run The Gantlet), who won a two-mile private sweepstakes at four. Bell Song was herself useful at up to a mile and a quarter and is a half-sister to the Dante Stakes winner Lucky Finish and the broodmares Priddy Fair (grandam of Dibidale, Shellshock and Cracaval) and Belle of Athens (dam of Athens Wood and the good middle-distance filly Sleat). Circus Ring, a quite attractive filly, moved particularly well. *M. Stoute.*

CITRUS ˙3 ch.c. Orange Bay 131–Lady Lowndes 97 (Tamerlane 128) (1981 — 7fg 1982 10g 12d) well-made, good sort; good walker; little worthwhile form in maiden races and a minor event; sold to D. McCain 2,500 gns Ascot December Sales. *P. Walwyn.*

CITY LINK EXPRESS 5 ch.g. Dubassoff–Chaddy (St Chad 120) (1981 7.6g — 8.3fg⁴ 8.3g 8.3g 1982 10g) leggy gelding; plater; best at around 1m; acts on any going; sometimes wears blinkers; ran creditably for a boy. *D. Wilson.*

CITY LINK LAD 6 ch.g. Jimmy Reppin 131–Aleta 71 (Montaval 129) (1981 — 8fg 8g 8f 7fg 8fg 10g 10fg 8fg 8s 1982 8g 8g 10fg) big, strong gelding; poor handicapper; stays 1m; acts on a firm surface; suitable mount for an apprentice; sometimes blinkered. *D. Wilson.*

CITY'S SISTER 4 ch.f. Maystreak 118–Must Improve 47 (Lucky Brief 128) **72** (1981 8s 9s 8g 6g* 7.2s* 8g⁴ 7fg 8g² 9.4fg³ 10f 10.6fg 7g 8.2v³ 8d 11d² 1982 6f 8f 8fg 10fg² 12.2f² 12g* 12.2f 13s* 12g 12s² 12v² 12s) lengthy, rather lightly-made filly; second twice, including in a seller, before winning handicaps at Hamilton in August and September, latter by 12 lengths; suited by 1¼m+ nowadays; acts on any going, but is very well suited by plenty of give in the ground; sometimes sweats up; usually apprentice ridden; lost place when running wide ninth start. *G. Richards.*

CIVILITY 2 b.f. Shirley Heights 130–Makeacurtsey (Herbager 136) (1982 7g) — p Apr 7; half-sister to smart 1976 2-y-o 5f performer Piney Ridge (by Native Prince) and very useful 1¼m winner Hill's Yankee (by Thatch); dam, placed in USA, is half-sister to 3 good stakes winners, including very smart grass horse Knightly Manner; 16/1 and in need of race, out of first 9 in 30-runner maiden event won by Mandelstam at Newmarket in October; should do better. *J. Tree.*

CLACHAN 2 ch.c. Habitat 134–Padrona 103 (St Paddy 133) (1982 6fg 7g²) **91 p** Feb 21; compact, attractive colt; closely related to high-class middle-distance colt Pelerin (by Sir Gaylord) and half-brother to 2 winners; dam won over 5f and 6f at 2 yrs; second favourite, challenged from 2f out when promising ¾-length second of 13 to Cock Robin in Ribero Stakes at Doncaster in September; will stay 1m; sure to make a useful performer and looks a ready-made winner. *H. Wragg.*

CLANGERWINSTANLEY 2 ch.c. Homing 130–Lady of Chalon (Young **76** Emperor 133) (1982 6d 7d 7f 7f² 8d) Apr 9; 6,000Y; quite attractive, smallish colt; a twin; closely related to smart sprinter Enchantment (by Habitat) and half-brother to a winner and to disappointing 3-y-o maiden Wongchoi (by Bustino); dam minor winner at up to 6f in USA; dead-heated for second place with Liberty Tree, 1½ lengths behind Helium, in 18-runner event at Catterick in August, best effort; last of 19 in Pontefract nursery next time; stays 7f; acts on firm going; wears blinkers. *R. Laing.*

CLANJOLLY 4 gr.c. Pals Passage 115–Olanrose (Kythnos 126) (1981 6v³ **105** 7s² 6g² 5g* 5s* 5d* 5f* 5fg 5g³ 1982 6fg² 5f⁴ 5fg) Irish colt; fourth foal; brother to very smart Jellaby, successful at up to 11f, and half-brother to 2 winners, including useful 1977 Irish 2-y-o 5f winner Te Igitur (by King's Leap); dam unraced half-sister to very smart sprinter The Brianstan; did well in 1981 and won 4 races in succession; went down by a short head to Princess Seal in Castleknock Sprint Stakes at Naas in May; short-priced favourite when very close fourth to Longleat in Ballyogan Stakes at Leopardstown the following month; ninth of 14 behind Fearless Lad in King's Stand Stakes at Royal Ascot on only subsequent outing; stays 7f, but is speedy and probably better at shorter distances; acts on any going; genuine. *M. Connolly, Ireland.*

CLANRALLIER 2 b.g. Captain James 123–Mary Campbell (Mossborough 126) **87** (1982 7f⁴ 7fg² 8d³ 8s⁴) Mar 6; 32,000F, 27,000Y; well-grown, good sort; has a long, raking stride; half-brother to minor French middle-distance winner Bamboleo (by Welsh Pageant) and a winner in Belgium; dam won from 9f to 1¾m in Ireland and France; beaten favourite in maiden races at Newmarket in July and August, Ayr in September and Newcastle in October; went down by a length to Alligatrix (who raced on opposite side of the course) in 29-runner event on second start, best effort; one paced, and will be suited by 1¼m+; possibly not at his best on a soft surface; doubtful temperamentally; gelded after final outing. *J. W. Watts.*

CLAP IN TIME 3 b.f. Dance In Time–Little Claude (Claude) (1981 NR 1982 7g 8f⁴ 10f²) lightly-made, quite attractive filly; good walker; third foal; dam second in Italian Oaks; second in maiden race at Beverley in May; not seen out again; will stay 1½m. *L. Cumani.* **67**

CLARE ISLAND 3 b.f. Connaught 130–Island Lore 100 (Court Martial) (1981 7fg* 8g² 8fg 1982 8.5f* 10fg) rangy, attractive filly; half-sister to several winners, notably very smart 1½m horse Caliban (by Ragusa); dam 2-y-o 5f winner; didn't have much luck in running in 9-runner Princess Elizabeth Stakes at Epsom in April and was awarded race after going down by ¾ length to Mary Mitsu; made much of running when seventh of 11 to Dancing Rocks in Nassau Stakes at Goodwood in July; should have stayed 1¼m; acted well on fast ground and never raced on soft; stud. *H. Cecil.* **108**

CLARENDON 5 gr.g. Brigadier Gerard 144–France (Milesian 125) (1981 12s 16s 12d 15.8g 1982 12s) poor performer nowadays; should stay middle distances; possibly needs some give in the ground; bandaged in front only outing of 1982. *J. Yardley.* —

CLARES LOCH 3 br.f. Lochnager 132–Aberklair 72 (Klairon 131) (1981 5d 5g 6fg 6f 5s⁴ 5s 1982 5g 6g 5h³ 5fg 8.3fg 6fg⁴) sprint plater; blinkered final start. *K. Brassey.* **38**

CLASS AGENT (USA) 2 b.f. Mr Leader–Millinery Lady (In Reality) (1982 7fg 6fg 5f⁴ 6d⁴ 6g) Mar 19; $70,000Y; rather leggy filly; third foal; half-sister to Fancy Hatter (by Prove Out), a very useful winner at up to 9f; dam, half-sister to 2 smart animals, won at up to 1m; plating-class maiden; promises to stay 7f; seems to act on any going. *H. T. Jones.* **74**

CLASSY COLLEEN 2 b.f. St Paddy 133–Dinamarsh (Nelcius 133) (1982 5s 5f) Apr 16; leggy filly; fourth foal; dam probably of no account; in rear in maiden races at Nottingham in April. *D. Leslie.* —

CLAUDIUS CROZET (USA) 3 b.c. Halo–Ima Roan (Determine) (1981 5fg 6fg 6g 6fg⁴ 6g² 8s 7g 1982 8fg 12f⁴ 14f⁴ 12g* 11.5fg* 14s² 12g* 14g) neat, strong cost; good mover; blind in near eye; won minor event at Leicester and ladies race at Yarmouth in August and handicap at Wolverhampton in October; suited by 1½m or more; seems to act on any going; suited by front-running tactics; wears an eye shield; tailed off final start. *G. Huffer.* **87**

CLAVERHAM MANOR 3 br.c. Saulingo 122–Edissa 66 (Honeyway 125) (1981 5fg 6fg 8d 7.6s 1982 8fg 8fg) lightly-made colt; soundly beaten in varied company, including selling; sold 420 gns Ascot November Sales. *R. Hannon.* —

CLEOBURY KATE 2 gr.f. The Brianstan 128–Sovereign Comment (Sovereign Path 125) (1982 5fg 5fg 6s) May 21; small filly; half-sister to fairly useful 7f to 1½m winner Fiery Copper (by Lord Gayle); dam won over 1m in Ireland; behind in maiden races and a seller. *J. Tierney.* —

CLEWISTON 6 b.g. Manacle 123–Blue Bird 94 (Majority Blue 126) (1981 7g* 7g³ 8fg 7.2v 7g³ 1982 6d 8fg) leggy gelding; well beaten in 1982, on second occasion in a valuable seller; stays 1m; suited by top-of-the-ground; sometimes sweats up; sold 720 gns Doncaster October Sales. *M. Camacho.* —

CLINKER 2 gr.c. Saritamer 130–Burning Deck 56 (Fighting Ship 121) (1982 8g) Apr 24; half-brother to 2 winners, including fairly useful 1m to 1½m winner Cinderwench (by Crooner); dam poor half-sister to 4 smart animals, including Bivouac; 11/1, soon well behind when eighth of 10 to Statesmanship in maiden race at Beverley in September. *Sir Mark Prescott.* —

CLIPHOME 4 gr.g. Sandford Lad 133–Seamyside (Sea Hawk II 131) (1981 10fg³ 10.6d² 10g 10g 9.4fg* 8g 1982 10d 10.2g 10.5s) quite a moderate handicapper; well beaten in 1982 (blinkered final start); stays 1¼m; probably acts on any going. *M. H. Easterby.* —

CLOCK TOWER 3 b.g. Tower Walk 130–Cappuccilli 111 (Lorenzaccio 130) (1981 8g 8d 8s 1982 10d 8fg 10f 10f³ 12f 16fg 10s 10.2s) sturdy gelding; poor form, including in sellers; has had tongue tied down. *S. Wiles.* —

CLOSE TO YOU 2 b.f. Nebbiolo 125–Etoile Freda (Florescence 120) (1982 —
6fg 5.8g 6s) June 2; IR 3,000Y (privately); half-sister to Irish and Belgian
winner Superb (by Roi Soleil); dam never ran; well beaten in maiden events;
off course over 2 months after second outing. S. Matthews.

CLOUDED VISION 3 b.f. So Blessed 130–Bundling (Petingo 135) (1981 5.8g **68**
7d 7v 1982 6g³ 6f 6fg 6f* 6f³ 7fg⁴ 6f 6d) rangy filly; blind in near eye; made
all to win 11-runner maiden race at Lingfield in July; not sure to stay beyond 7f;
acts on firm going. I. Balding.

CLOUDS HEAVEN 3 ch.f. Import 127–Fragrant Cloud 69 (Balidar 133) (1981 —
6f 6s 6d 6d 1982 8f 7f³ 9fg 8f 7fg 8fg 10.8fg) strong filly; poor plater; has twice
been blinkered; sold out of W. Elsey's stable 760 gns Doncaster June Sales after
fifth start. K. Bridgwater.

CLOUDWALKER 4 gr.g. Dragonara Palace 115–Misfired 101 (Blast 125) (1981
7g 7d 7s* 7g 8fg 7f 7fg 8g* 7g 8d 1982 8.2v 8f 10.4d) leggy, sparely-made
gelding; didn't run well in 1982; stays 1m; seems to need some give in the
ground; often blinkered (has worn them when successful); suitable mount for
an apprentice. M. Lambert.

CLUB CLASS (USA) 3 b.f. Roberto 131–Queen of the Sky (Bold Ruler) (1981 **88**
7g 10g 1982 10f⁴ 12.3fg³ 14fg 14f⁴ 13g³) medium-sized, quite well-made filly;
creditable 6 lengths third of 6 to Swiftfoot in Cheshire Oaks in May on second
start; didn't run up to that form subsequently; best run at 1½m on fast ground.
J. Hindley.

COAL BUNKER 4 ch.c. On Your Mark 125–Powder Box (Faberge II 121)
(1981 8d 8g 8.3fg 8fg 7f 8.3fg⁴ 10fg 10f* 10f 11.7d⁴ 10d 1982 10d 12.2s 10s)
workmanlike colt; shows a lot of knee action; probably stays 11.7f; has run
creditably on soft ground, but best form on a sound surface; blinkered third
outing in 1980. R. Hannon.

COASTING BREEZE 4 br.g. Windjammer (USA)–Etoile Freda (Florescence
120) (1981 6fg 6g 5fg 5g 1982 10.1d 10.1fg 6g 6s) tall, leggy gelding; showed
only sign of ability in 6f apprentice handicap on third outing (wore a tongue strap)
J. Bosley.

COASTLINE 3 b.g. So Blessed 130–Coaster 61 (Right Tack 131) (1981 5g 6g **46**
5g 6g 6g 8d 1982 8d 7d 7g³ 8f 7fg³ 7.6g 10f) robust gelding; poor handicapper;
stays 7f; exported to Malaysia. J. Benstead.

COCKFOSTERS 3 b.g. Music Boy 124–Sunny Bloom 71 (Forlorn River 124) —
(1981 5s 5s 1982 6s 5fg 5fg 6f) lengthy gelding; little worthwhile form in
varied company, including selling; sold, probably for export to Norway, 840 gns
Doncaster June Sales. H. Westbrook.

COCKIE 3 b.f. Queen's Hussar 124–Mountain Rescue 95 (Mountain Call 125) —
(1981 NR 1982 8f 7fg) first foal; dam 2-y-o 6f winner; beaten some way in
minor event at Warwick and maiden race at Chepstow. N. Gaselee.

COCK ROBIN (USA) 2 gr.c. Raise A Native–Flyingtrip (Vaguely Noble 140) **122**
(1982 7fg* 7g* 8d²)
    Colonel and Mrs Hue-Williams, the owners of the Woolton House and
Rathasker Studs, have long been staunch supporters of racing and breeding in
Britain, Ireland and France. They have done extremely well too, between them
winning a King George VI and Queen Elizabeth Stakes with Supreme Court,
a St Leger with Aurelius, an Irish Sweeps Derby with English Prince, a One
Thousand Guineas, Oaks and Irish Guinness Oaks with Altesse Royale and a
Prix du Cadran with Rock Roi (who was also twice disqualified in the Gold Cup).
Among their other good representatives were the classic-placed animals Radio-
therapy, Imperial Prince, Classic Example and Seraphima. Recently the flow
of winners has slackened somewhat but steps have been taken to remedy matters
through the purchase of three mares, for a total of 834,000 dollars, at the 1979
Keeneland Breeding Stock Sale. Ribofilio's sister Belle Sorella, the In Reality
mare Amatilla and the well-bred Flyingtrip, a winner of four races as a three-
year-old in Italy, were obtained for that sum. The 300,000-dollar investment in
Flyingtrip already looks money well spent, for the Raise A Native foal she was
carrying at the time, Cock Robin, proved himself a smart colt when second to
Dunbeath in the William Hill Futurity Stakes at Doncaster in October.
    Cock Robin didn't have much luck in running at Doncaster. He was always
fairly close up as Muscatite and Shackle Pin disputed the lead. Perhaps his
rider hoped to gain a run through when the 100/1-shot Shackle Pin, who was

*Ribero Stakes, Doncaster—odds-on favourite Cock Robin
runs on well to hold off Clachan*

directly in front, began to weaken; if so he was to be disappointed. Shackle Pin
and Muscatite managed to hold on to the lead until the distance and by then
Cock Robin had nowhere to go, with Beldale Concorde challenging to his left and
both Lyphard's Special and Dunbeath to his right. While Cock Robin was being
switched to the outside, dropping back to sixth place in the process, Dunbeath
was sweeping into a three-length advantage. Cock Robin, to his credit,
quickened so well that he overtook four of those in front of him but he was still
a length and a half adrift of Dunbeath at the line. His rider subsequently
voiced the opinion that he would nearly have won had he been able to get out
in time. This seems an optimistic assessment to us and it also overlooks the
fact that Dunbeath eased up about a length close home. Nonetheless this was a
fine effort by Cock Robin. He had won both his previous starts, starting
favourite each time. He overcame his obvious inexperience to get the better
of Hawa Bladi by a length and a half in a minor event at Sandown in August
and then made virtually all under top weight when beating Clachan by three
quarters of a length in the thirteen-runner Ribero Stakes at Doncaster the
following month. Incidentally he impressed as a particularly good walker in
the paddock before his races.

Cock Robin (USA) (gr.c. Apr 24, 1980)	Raise A Native (ch 1961)	Native Dancer (gr 1950)	Polynesian Geisha
		Raise You (ch 1946)	Case Ace Lady Glory
	Flyingtrip (gr 1973)	Vaguely Noble (b 1965)	Vienna Noble Lassie
		Flying Legs (gr 1966)	Palestine Alona

Judged purely on pedigree it would have been no great surprise had Cock
Robin turned out a sprinter. His sire Raise A Native possessed tremendous
speed; he started his career winning a three-furlong maiden race in the February
of his two-year-old days and ended it five months later when breaking the track
record in the Great American Stakes over five and a half furlongs, the longest
distance he tackled. Cock Robin's grandam Flying Legs was a very speedy
animal too. Only once did she race over a distance longer than five furlongs in a
fourteen-race career during which she won both the Molecomb Stakes and the
Lowther Stakes. Also Cock Robin, a third foal, is a half-brother to a five-
furlong winner by The Minstrel, the 1981 North American two-year-old
All In Mist.

Cock Robin doesn't look like a sprinter—he's a rather finely-made, medium-
sized colt—and he most certainly isn't one. He was very well suited by a mile
at two and runs as though he'll stay further. How much further isn't easy to
say. Among Raise A Native's previous good European winners were the

212

Ribblesdale winner Gallina, the Oaks runner-up Where You Lead and the good Italian middle-distance stayer Laomedonte. Cock Robin, with a dam by Vaguely Noble and a great-grandam by Alycidon, must have reasonable prospects of staying a mile and a quarter or more. If he can continue improving at the rate he did at two he's sure to win a good prize. *M. Stoute.*

CODRINGTON 3 b.c. Malinowski 123–Manfilia 95 (Mandamus 120) (1981 6fg* 6fg² 7d² 7g⁴ 1982 8g 8.5fg 10.4fg) strong, good-looking colt; very useful at 2 yrs; didn't run up to his best in 1982, finishing sixth of 9 to Silver Hawk in Ladbroke Craven Stakes at Newmarket, moderate last to Count Pahlen in Blue Riband Trial at Epsom (pulled hard in blinkers) and well-beaten sixth of 11 to Ivano in Dee Stakes at Chester; should stay middle distances; best form on an easy surface; sent to USA. *B. Hills.* **94**

COJ 4 b.g. Copte–Warm Springs 67§ (Mid-day Sun) (1981 10s 10d 10s 1982 12s 15.8f) small gelding; well beaten in varied company, including selling. *D. Leslie.* **—**

COLANDER 2 gr.f. Roan Rocket 128–Couloir 114 (Court Martial) (1982 5fg 6h 6fg 6fg² 7d) May 10; neat, well-made filly; has a sharp action; half-sister to numerous winners, including useful 5f to 1m winner Collapse (by Busted) and useful miler Coulomb (by Crepello); dam at her best at 2 yrs when very useful over 5f; ¾-length second of 17 to Aditi in maiden race at Folkestone in August, best effort; not certain to stay 7f; possibly not at her best on a soft surface; sold BBA (Ireland) 16,500 gns Newmarket Autumn Sales. *H. Candy.* **77**

COLARO 4 b.f. Tennyson 124–Montcall (Mountain Call 125) (1981 12.2s 1982 15.5g 10fg² 8.3g 10f⁴ 10fg 8.3fg 7.6f 10f 10f 10fg³ 10g) maiden plater; stays at least 1¼m; has worn blinkers. *P. K. Mitchell.* **40**

COLD FOURPENNY 3 ch.g. Scallywag 127–Raver 71 (Runnymede 123) (1981 8g 1982 7g 8fg⁴ 12f 8f 8g 15fg 11g³ 9fg⁴ 11g 8g) fair sort; plater; stays 11f; best in blinkers. *T. Craig.* **50**

COLD JUSTICE 9 br.g. Arctic Judge 94–Rimelo (Richard Louis 116) (1981 10g 16d 16g⁴ 1982 10d 16s) moderate hurdler; very lightly raced on flat nowadays; stays well. *J. Benstead.* **—**

COLEBROOK FOLLY 3 b. or br.g. Hittite Glory 125–Pahlavi Line 65 (Young Emperor 133) (1981 7fg 6g 7.6s 10.2g 1982 12s 11.7f 10fg 10f 12fg) poor plater; blinkered third and fourth starts. *T. Gosling.* **—**

COLEY 3 b.c. Morston 125–Consistent 90 (Connaught 130) (1981 5s 5d⁴ 6g 6g 6f 6d 7d³ 1982 11s 9g³ 8f³ 8f 9fg³ 8g* 8g 9g 8d 10s 8.2s 10d) neat colt; won maiden race at Edinburgh in May; soundly beaten in handicaps afterwards; should stay 1¼m+; seems to act on any going; sometimes blinkered (was at Edinburgh). *D. Smith.* **70** d

COLLATION 2 ch.f. Wollow 132–Collapse 107 (Busted 134) (1982 5.8g* 7fg) Mar 24; first foal; dam admirably tough winner from 5f to 1m; led last strides when beating Fairlawne by a neck in 11-runner maiden race at Bath in August; ridden by 7-lb claimer when eighth of 12 to Silk Sari in £3,600 event at Chepstow the following month; should stay 1m; sold 9,000 gns Newmarket Autumn Sales. *H. Candy.* **83**

COLLECTORS GIRL 2 br.f. Mr Bigmore 123–Peace of Mind 81 (Midsummer Night II 117) (1982 7d) May 5; smallish, lengthy filly; first foal; dam won over 5f and 11f and also won over hurdles; 20/1 and backward when behind in 18-runner maiden race won by Cormorant Wood at Leicester in October. *M. Ryan.* **—**

COLLEGE ARM'S 2 b.f. Decoy Boy 129–Her Worship 61 (Privy Councillor 125) (1982 5f⁴ 5fg 5fg⁴ 6fg 6f³ 6g 6fg 7g 6s) Jan 29; 1,000F, 250Y; lengthy, light-framed filly; half-sister to a minor winner and to a winner in Malaya; dam placed over 9f; poor plater; best form at 6f. *S. Matthews.* **49**

COLONEL MAD 3 gr.c. Town Crier 119–Golden Thoughts 86 (Golden Cloud) (1981 5s³ 6fg⁴ 6fg 6fg 7.3d 6g 1982 8.2s) leggy, narrow colt; good walker; plater; best run at 5f on soft ground; blinkered once at 2 yrs. *J. Spearing.* **—**

COLONEL MONCK 4 b.g. Connaught 130–Mwanza 93 (Petition 130) (1981 NR 1982 12d) 31,000Y, resold 3,100 and 850 gns as a 3-y-o; half-brother to 3 winners, notably very smart 1969 2-y-o Tribal Chief (by Princely Gift); dam won at 1m; backed at longish odds but looking in need of race when remote **—**

seventh of 12 behind Starawak in maiden race at Redcar in November. *M. McCormack.*

COLONIAL LINE (USA) 4 ch.f. Plenty Old–Es Cabalistica (Eslavo) (1981   **52** 6v⁴ 5g² 5s* 1982 5g² 5f² 5g⁴ 5.3g³ 6g⁴ 5f* 5g) lengthy filly; beat Quae Supra by ¾ length in apprentice handicap at Lingfield in July; in frame all previous starts; evidently regarded as best at 5f but is bred to stay further; acts on any going; blinkered last 2 starts (well beaten in them second occasion). *P. Cole.*

COLORADO FALLS 3 b.c. Rapid River 127–Long Drop 78 (Tower Walk 130)   — (1981 5d 5d⁴ 5g 6f⁴ 7f 1982 7g 10.8fg) small, good-bodied colt; plater; not sure to stay 7f; sold 310 gns Ascot August Sales. *T. Marshall.*

COLUMNIST 5 b.h. Swing Easy 126–Namecaller 83 (Malicious) (1981 6g³   — 7d* 6g² 7s 6f 8fg 6d⁴ 7s 1982 6fg 6g) lengthy horse; good mover; smart performer on his day in 1981, winner of Autobar Victoria Cup at Ascot and placed in high-class company; dwelt and ran a sour sort of race when fifth of 6 behind Lightning Label in Ladbrokes Abernant Stakes at Newmarket in April; never got into race when eleventh of 12 behind Indian King in Diadem Stakes at Ascot in September on only subsequent start; suited by 7f (well beaten over 1m); possibly not at his best on very soft ground; wears blinkers; sold 6,000 gns Newmarket Autumn Sales. *J. Tree.*

COMASCAN 2 b.c. Cawston's Clown 113–Duns Tew 70 (Mandamus 120) (1982   **69** 5f 5fg 5d 6s) Mar 10; well-made colt; good walker; second reported foal; brother to fair 1981 2-y-o 5f winner Balcanoona; dam won over 5f at 2 yrs; 8 lengths seventh of 15 to Solar Rock in maiden race at Salisbury in June, third outing and only indication of merit; off course for 3 months afterwards; sold 380 gns Ascot November Sales. *R. Hannon.*

COMEDIAN 4 b.g. Comedy Star 121–Ruetina 74 (Rugantino 97) (1981 10g   — 12fg* 12fg* 11.5d² 12d³ 1982 12fg) small, quite attractive gelding; good mover; middle-distance handicapper; well beaten only outing of 1982 (April); suited by 1½m; acts on a firm and a soft surface. *D. Nicholson.*

COMEDY BAY 2 b.c. Comedy Star 121–Errichel (Sweet Revenge 129) (1982   **47** 5fg 5fg 6fg 6g⁴ 8fg 6g³ 5d 5g 8.2s 7g) Apr 30; 850Y; sturdy colt; first foal; dam never ran; plater; suited by 6f; wears blinkers. *T. Craig.*

COMEDY CROFT 5 b.g. Comedy Star 121–Twyford Ridge (Schapiro 99)   — (1981 12fg 13s 12g 12g 1982 12g 16f) poor handicapper nowadays; doesn't stay 2m; probably acts on any going; sometimes wears blinkers, but didn't when successful; sold 1,550 gns Doncaster June Sales, probably for export to Norway. *D. Ancil.*

COMEDY FAIR 2 b.g. Comedy Star 121–Fair Saint 79 (Bleep-Bleep 134)   **82** (1982 6fg 6fg 6g⁴ 6g² 8f) Mar 19; 8,200F, 27,000Y; big, strong colt; third foal; half-brother to a winner in Jersey; dam won over 5f at 2 yrs; 1½ lengths second of 9 to Diana's Pet in £5,300 maiden event at York in August, best effort; no show when running moderately in nursery at Doncaster the following month; stays 6f; possibly requires some give in the ground; gelded at end of season; capable of winning in the North. *M. H. Easterby.*

COMEDY LADY 4 b.f. Comedy Star 121–Sayida 65 (Kalydon 122) (1981   **46** 7g 10.1fg 10fg 8fg 8fg 6g 1982 7fg² 8.3g* 7h⁴ 8d 8fg 8f 10fg⁴ 10fg 10.2f 8.2s) compact filly; favourite when readily winning selling handicap at Windsor in May; bought in 4,200 gns afterwards; ran respectably in non-sellers on occasions; seems to stay 1¼m; best form on a sound surface. *P. Makin.*

COME ON THE BLUES 3 b.c. Blue Cashmere 129–Floral Gift 84 (Princely   **101** Gift 137) (1981 5s 5.1f² 5f 6fg* 6fg³ 6g⁴ 6f² 6f² 6g 6s² 1982 6s* 7fg 8fg 7f 7g* 8.5d 7fg 7g³ 8f³ 7fg 7g 7f⁴ 7g 7s⁴ 6g) quite attractive, lengthy colt; good walker; won minor event at Nottingham in April and 7-runner Heron Stakes at Kempton in May; came with a strong run to catch weakening Mirabeau close home and win by a neck in latter; ran creditably several other starts, notably when 2½ lengths third to Noalcoholic in 7f Van Geest Stakes at Newmarket; stays 1m; acts on any going but seems ideally suited by some give in the ground; blinkered third and thirteenth starts; has shown a tendency to hang, is suited by strong handling and goes well for W. Carson. *C. Brittain.*

COME PLAY WITH ME 7 b.g. Jukebox 120–Compatriot (Pindari 124)   — (1981 14d 7g 12fg 11.7fg 1982 8fg 10g) poor handicapper; suitable mount for a boy; has been tried in blinkers; has worn bandages. *R. Atkins.*

COMING AND GOING (USA) 2 b.f. Roberto 131–Honor An Offer (Hoist **105 ?** the Flag) (1982 8g* 8v²) May 9; $85,000Y; big, rangy filly, with plenty of scope; second foal; dam unraced half-sister to 2 stakes winners; 8/1 but apparently backward, held on well after leading 2f out when winning 19-runner minor event at Newmarket in October by ½ length from Rodners; creditable 3½ lengths second of 14 to Tajwind in Criterium Femminile at Rome in November; will be suited by 1¼m or more; should make very useful 3-y-o. *M. Jarvis.*

COMMAND RESPECT 2 ch.g. Brigadier Gerard 144–Nedda 113 (Alcide 136) **?** (1982 6fg⁴ 6f⁴ 6f 7g* 8f) Apr 7; 11,500F, 30,000Y; quite attractive, well-made gelding; brother to 2 winners, including Cheshire Oaks and Lancashire Oaks winner Princess Eboli, and half-brother to 3 more; dam stayed 1½m; led near finish when beating Kuwait Desert by ¾ length in 9-runner nursery at Bath in August; afterwards showed improved form to win over 1¼m in Italy; suited by some give in the ground. *I. Balding.*

COMMITTED (USA) 2 b.f. Hagley–Minstinguette (Boldnesian) (1982 6.3fg **97** 7f* 7fg* 6d³) Feb 26; $52,000Y; second foal; dam once-raced half-sister to Miss Toshiba, a very smart winner over 9f in USA who won at up to 1½m here; accounted for 4 previous winners when getting better of Moral Leader by a neck in minor event at Galway in July and put up quite a useful effort to win 7-runner race at Leopardstown the following month by ½ length from Persian Polly; excellent 3 lengths third of 15 to Habibti in Moyglare Stud Stakes at the Curragh in September; will stay 1m. *D. Weld, Ireland.*

COMMODORE BATEMAN 2 br.c. Tarboosh–Hellspear (Breakspear 11) **81** (1982 6f 7d⁴ 7f* 6fg² 8g 7g) Feb 2; IR 620F, IR 4,000Y; fair sort; half-brother to 1975 Irish 2-y-o 5f winner Devil Woman (by Prince Regent); dam second twice over 5f in Ireland; won 9-runner maiden auction event at Catterick in July by 3 lengths from Enbyar Dan; 2 lengths second to Wiki Wiki Wheels in minor event at Hamilton later in month, only subsequent form; stays 7f; seems to act on any going; blinkered final start. *I. Walker.*

COMMODORE BLAKE 5 br.h. Blakeney 126–Ribamba 82 (Ribocco 129) **123** (1981 10g* 12f 10.5g⁴ 10g* 8fg* 8d⁴ 10.2g* 9g 1982 12g 11.1fg² 10f³ 9d 8s* 8v*) Commodore Blake's resounding win in the Prix Perth at Saint-Cloud in November would have come as a bitter blow to most of those who had backed him in the William Hill Cambridgeshire at Newmarket the previous month. Commodore Blake was clear favourite for the Cambridgeshire having been placed in two pattern races after the weights were framed, and on the evidence of his neck second to Critique in the September Stakes at Kempton and his four-length third behind the high-class French middle-distance colts General Holme and Bikala in the Prix du Prince d'Orange at Longchamp he was thrown in at the weights with only 9·5. Yet after showing up on the outside early on

Prix Perth, Saint-Cloud—Commodore Blake leaves his Cambridgeshire form well behind; Anfield and Tres Gate (No. 1) make it a good day for the visitors

he was beaten by halfway and trailed in last of twenty-nine behind Century City. As things turned out he was not well drawn, but that on its own can't excuse his running. Neither jockey nor trainer could offer an explanation to the stewards, save that the horse had run in similar fashion in the Cambridgeshire the year before. He finished last then too, and on that occasion was said to have returned lame.

The Prix Perth attracted a big field as usual and Commodore Blake was virtually ignored in the betting at 32/1, the longest priced of any of the five runners sent over from England or Ireland. After being held up near the back of the field until the straight he was brought steadily over to the stand rail in search of the best ground and as soon as he arrived on the scene it was clear he was going best of all. He was well on top in the last furlong and won by four lengths from Anfield, Tres Gate and Dom Donizetti. Ten days later Commodore Blake started a short-priced favourite for the Premio Ribot at Rome, run in similar conditions. He again won easily, beating Montekin by five lengths.

Commodore Blake (br.h. 1977)	Blakeney (b 1966)	Hethersett (b 1959)	Hugh Lupus
			Bride Elect
		Windmill Girl (b 1961)	Hornbeam
			Chorus Beauty
	Ribamba (b 1970)	Ribocco (b 1964)	Ribot
			Libra
		Bombazine (b 1963)	Shantung
			Whimsical

Commodore Blake is a late-developing type who didn't see a racecourse until towards the end of his three-year-old days. Since getting off the mark at Stockton as a four-year-old he's gone from strength to strength; he won three more races that year, including the Chesterfield Cup at Goodwood and the Holsten Pils Handicap at Doncaster, in both of which he beat Easter Sun, another who graduated successfully from handicap company relatively late in his career. Judged on his pedigree—by Blakeney out of the Ribocco mare Ribamba—one would expect Commodore Blake to be well suited by a mile and a half, but whenever he has tried that distance he has given the impression he's found it a shade too far. Interestingly Ribamba, a daughter of the 1966 Oaks and Ribblesdale fourth Bombazine, didn't stay so far as one would have expected either; she was second over a mile and nine furlongs in the North. Commodore Blake is Ribamba's second foal. In 1981 the dam produced a colt by the sprint handicapper Laxton, her first foal since.

Commodore Blake is likely to remain in training. A neat, attractive horse—a typical son of Blakeney—he is effective from a mile to eleven furlongs and acts on any going. He seems ideally suited by waiting tactics and can produce a fine turn of foot on his day. *M. Stoute.*

COMMONTY (USA) 4 b.c. Empery 128–Duke's Little Gal (Duke of Dublin) **65**
(1981 11s 10d* 12s⁴ 10d² 10fg⁴ 10fg⁴ 10d 10g 10.6s* 12s² 11s² 1982 10d 10.6s 10.4g 10fg³ 10fg² 10s³ 10.6g³ 8.2s⁴ 10fg 10s* 8v 10s⁴) well-made, quite attractive colt; runs his share of disappointing races, but was on his best behaviour in handicap at Goodwood in September and beat Mills High decisively by 4 lengths; stays 1½m, but races over shorter distances nowadays; acts on any going but has shown most of his best form with some give underfoot; often blinkered (not on last 4 starts). *J. Bethell.*

COMPACTOR 3 br.c. Rubbish (Major Portion 129) (1981 —
7fg 7.2fg 8g 8g 10.2g 1982 12f 12f 13g 12f) workmanlike colt; poor plater; has worn blinkers. *R. Hobson.*

COMPOSER 4 ch.c. Music Boy 124–Contadina (Memling) (1981 6g² 6s³ 7.2f⁴ **66**
6f⁴ 6g 6g 6s² 1982 8.2v⁴ 8g 6fg 7g² 7f 8d) big, lengthy colt; disappointing handicapper; stays 7f; acts on soft going; blinkered sixth outing in 1981; trained until after fourth start by W. Marshall. *H. O'Neill.*

COMPOUND 8 b.g. Siliconn 121–Compose 94 (Compensation 127) (1981 **54**
8d 7g² 6f 7f 8.3g 6fg⁴ 8fg 8d³ 6d 1982 7f 8g 7f³ 8f* 7g⁴ 8fg 8f* 7fg 8.3g⁴ 7g* 8g) plater; bought in after winning decisively at Yarmouth in June (900 gns) and August (1,600 gns); attracted no bid after being awarded a race on same course in September; stays 1m; acts particularly well on firm going; has won for a boy, but was ridden by L. Piggott when successful in 1982; sometimes starts slowly; has run respectably in blinkers. *Mrs N. Kennedy.*

COMRA 3 b.g. Moulton 128–Armelle 87 (Tribal Chief 125) (1981 7fg 8d 8s —
1982 8d 8f 16d 17f) lengthy gelding; staying maiden. *H. Candy.*

COMTEC PRINCESS 3 ch.f. Gulf Pearl 117–Miss Hart 75 (Track Spare 125) **60**
(1981 5g 5f 6g 8d* 1982 8.2d* 8f 9.4fg 8fg 8.3g 8.2g 8.2s 10s* 10.2s) leggy,
lengthy filly; plater; won in better company at Nottingham in April and Redcar
in October; suited by 1¼m; needs some give in the ground. *P. Rohan.*

COMTINA 2 gr.f. Comedy Star 121–Quortina 88 (Quorum 126) (1982 6g 6fg —
7d) Apr 3; quite attractive filly; half-sister to 1978 2-y-o 6f seller winner Ben's
the Boy (by Burglar); dam successful middle-distance handicapper; behind in
maiden and minor events, on final outing tailed off. *J. Holt.*

CONA 4 br.g. Connaught 130–Lowna 120 (Princely Gift 137) (1981 7fg 10.2f —
12g 11g 11d⁴ 12d 1982 8g) useful sort; showed some ability in 1981; stays 11f;
has a tendency to hang; ran freely in blinkers once. *D. Francis.*

CONCANNAN 5 ch.g. Malicious–Six Wives 80 (Royal Record II) (1981 NR —
1982 15d) sturdy gelding; winner over hurdles and has also shown a little
ability in NH Flat races; needed run and wasn't altogether disgraced when
remote sixth of 11 behind Path of Peace in amateur riders race at Ayr in
September. *M. Lambert.*

CONCAVE 2 b.f. Connaught 130–Aberangell 96 (Abernant 142) (1982 8s) — p
Mar 4; strong, good-topped filly; half-sister to several winners, including 1¼m
winner Gelignite (by St Paddy); dam 2-y-o 5f winner; weak in market, prominent
until 3f out when distant eighth of 11 behind Running Melody in maiden event
at Wolverhampton in October; should improve. *Sir Mark Prescott.*

CONCERT HALL 6 ch.g. Connaught 130–Hello Honey 105 (Crepello 136) —
(1981 NR 1982 14f) well-made, good sort; fairly useful handicapper in 1980
(rated 90); bandaged in front when reportedly breaking down at Sandown in
April, only outing since; stays 1¾m; acts on a firm and a soft surface. *G. Lewis.*

CONCERT PITCH 3 ch.g. Royal Match 117–Ballychord (Ballymoss 136) **68**
(1981 7fg 8g 7g² 1982 7g 7g 8f³ 12.2f³ 9g* 9.3fg³ 11fg* 8g³ 9g 10g 9s 10s)
strong, dipped-backed, lengthy gelding; narrowly won maiden race at Hamilton
in June and overcame difficulties in running when scoring in handicap at Ayr in
July; seems to stay 1½m; best form on top-of-the-ground. *Miss S. Hall.*

CONCORDE HERO (USA) 2 b.c. Super Concorde 128–Method Actress (Round **101**
Table) (1982 5fg* 6g* 6f⁴ 6f⁴) Apr 11; $120,000Y; attractive colt; good
walker and mover; half-brother to several winners, including French 1m and 1¼m
winner Methane (by Never Bend); dam won 2 sprint races; easy odds-on winner
of 10-runner maiden race at Newmarket and 7-runner minor event at Kempton
in May; favourite for 8-runner Coventry Stakes at Royal Ascot the following
month but ran disappointingly, coming home nearly 10 lengths fourth behind
Horage; not seen out again until September when 3½ lengths fourth (eased when
beaten) to Fenny Rough in well-contested event at Pontefract; will stay 7f;
possibly not at his best on very firm ground; sold 21,000 gns Newmarket
Autumn Sales to race in Barbados. *H. Cecil.*

CONDELL 3 ch.c. Condorcet–Liberty Nell (Weavers' Hall 122) (1981 6.3fg **105**
8g⁴ 9g² 8d² 8s* 1982 10s³ 14f* 13f* 14g* 12g) first foal; dam, an unraced
twin, is half-sister to top-class mare Park Top; favourite when winning handicaps at Navan in May and Leopardstown and Navan again in June; eased
considerably in closing stages when landing odds by ¾ length from Five Star
Final for final success; respectable fifth of 10 to runaway winner Assert in Irish
Sweeps Derby at the Curragh later in June on only subsequent start; will stay
2m; acts on any going. *J. Bolger, Ireland.*

CONDOR 3 gr.g. Warpath 113–Hirondelle 86 (Falcon 131) (1981 NR 1982 —
10.2g 13g) half-brother to 9f winner So Swiftly (by So Blessed) and 2 others,
including useful 1¼m winner April (by Silly Season); dam won at 1m; behind in
maiden races at Doncaster and Nottingham; sold 800 gns Doncaster October
Sales. *C. Thornton.*

CONERTON (USA) 2 br.c. Super Concorde 128–Jolie Sirene 114 (Timmy My **111**
Boy 125) (1982 7.5fg⁴ 8g² 8v*) Apr 21; $200,000Y; first foal; dam, very
useful winner at around 1m in France, is sister to Water Boy, a very smart
performer at up to 10.5f; blinkered, made all to win 7-runner maiden race at
Longchamp in October easily by 4 lengths from Toujours Lucky, best effort;
will stay 1¼m; the type to do better at 3 yrs. *F. Boutin, France.*

CONGO EXPRESS 4 b.c. Bay Express 132–Congola (Bold Lad, Ire 133) —
(1981 8g 5d² 6g⁴ 1982 5g 6fg 6fg 6fg 6d) tall, quite attractive colt; ran very
well in autumn, 1981, but was well beaten in 1982, including in good-class events;

stays 6f; moved down scratchily second and last starts; sold 1,200 gns Doncaster August Sales. *C. Brittain.*

CON JEM 3 gr.g. Dragonara Palace 115–Barbara Bryce (Yellow God 129) — (1981 NR 1982 7g 7f 11g 8fg) 5,200F, 5,100Y; rangy gelding; third foal; half-brother to 1979 2-y-o 5f winner Willing To Learn (by Balliol); dam never ran; beaten some way in newcomers race and maiden events. *T. Craig.*

CONNAUGHT KING 5 b.g. Connaught 130–Ruling Class 92 (King Emperor) — (1981 12f 10s 10.6s 1982 10g 8fg) of little account; has worn bandages. *M. James.*

CONNAUGHT RANGER 8 ch.g. Connaught 130–Franconia 83 (Charlottesville — 135) (1981 NR 1982 12fg) won 3 times at Cagnes-sur-Mer in 1977 when trained by C. Milbank in France; having first outing on flat since when eighth of 11 behind Glint of Gold in John Porter Stakes at Newbury in April; better known nowadays as a high-class (but somewhat ungenerous) hurdler and a winning chaser; should stay 1½m; acts on soft going; below his best when tried in blinkers once at 3 yrs. *R. Simpson.*

CONNECTOR 3 ch.c. Red Alert 127–Polana 68 (Silver Shark 129) (1981 5fg **70** 5d² 5d 6fg 6fg 6fg 6g 1982 8g 7d 9s 8d³ 8f 10f 8fg 9g⁴ 12f* 14s) small colt; poor mover; plater; springer in market when decisively winning at Newmarket in July; bought in 3,600 gns afterwards; suited by 1½m; seems to act on any going. *W. Marshall.*

CONOR'S ROCK 2 br.c. Rheingold 137–Captains Queen (Captain's Gig) (1982 **85** 6f 7g 7fg² 8f² 8g³) May 26; small, useful-looking colt; first foal; dam won over 6f at 3 yrs in USA; showed no form until finishing good second in minor event at Sandown in August; placed following month in two nurseries, looking unlucky after bad run at Doncaster on first occasion, but disappointing at Yarmouth on the second; stays 1m; acts on firm going. *R. Armstrong.*

CONRAD HILTON 2 b.c. Be My Guest 126–Bentinck Hotel 74 (Red God 128§) **91 p** (1982 6g³) Feb 24; first foal; dam 2-y-o 5f winner; third favourite, shaped well when length third of 20 to Asswan in maiden race at Yarmouth in September, making running until closing stages; will make a useful colt and is sure to be placed to advantage. *H. Cecil.*

CONSCRIPTION 2 ch.c. Gunner B 126–Needless 81 (Petingo 135) (1982 7d) **75 p** Apr 26; strong, lengthy, useful-looking colt; second foal; half-brother to useful 3-y-o 1m winner Telephone Man (by Record Token); dam middle-distance winner; 12/1, shaped quite nicely when 9½ lengths seventh of 18 behind easy winner Northern Adventure in minor event at Doncaster in October, keeping on fairly well in closing stages; will be suited by 1m+; has plenty of scope and is sure to improve. *F. J. Houghton.*

CONSORTIUM 5 b.h. Targowice 130–Annerbelle 108 (Aureole 132) (1981 7d **42** 8.3s³ 6f 5f 8g 7v 8s 1982 10.1fg 10fg 10g² 10g³ 11.7g² 14f 10g 12fg 8g⁴ 10v 9g 7s) strong horse; plater; stays 1½m; suited by some give in the ground; front runner; often blinkered; suitable mount for a boy; retained by trainer 440 gns Ascot March Sales. *K. Ivory.*

CONS PAL 4 b.f. Connaught 130–Palotra 86 (Palestine 133) (1981 8s 12g⁴ 10f **69** 12f 14fg 12f 10.6v* 12.2g⁴ 10.2d² 1982 11f* 10.5f 9.4f⁴ 10fg³ 10d 11fg² 10g 11s³ 10.2d² 10d*) lean filly; has a round action; won handicaps at Redcar in May and November and was in frame 5 times in between; possibly doesn't stay 1¾m; evidently acts on any going, but gives impression she's suited by some give in the ground; usually held up; sometimes gives trouble at stalls. *R. D. Peacock.*

CONTESTER 2 ch.c. Connaught 130–Mitigation 91 (Milesian 125) (1982 5fg **87** 5.8f³ 7f⁴ 7g 8fg 8f³ 8.2s* 7g⁴ 8.2v³) Mar 26; well-made, good sort; closely related to fairly useful 1975 2-y-o 6f and 7f winner Conciliation (by St Paddy) and half-brother to several winners, including smart middle-distance performer Colum (by Santa Claus); dam won at up to 1m; won 11-runner nursery at Hamilton in September; in frame in similar events at Edinburgh and Hamilton the following month; suited by 1m, and will stay further; acts on any going; blinkered first 2 outings; sold out of R. Hern's stable 3,700 gns Ascot Second June Sales after second start. *F. Watson.*

CONVEYOR BELLE 2 ch.f. Gunner B 126–Thorganby Bella (Porto Bello 118) **57** (1982 5fg³ 5g² 5f³ 5d* 6f 6fg⁴ 5g) Apr 16; 1,500Y; leggy filly; third foal; half-sister to winning 5f handicapper Bella Travaille (by Workboy); placed in maiden auction events prior to making virtually all to win 13-runner seller at Newcastle (no bid) in June easing up by ½ length from Hot Potato; no form afterwards; should stay 6f. *J. Berry.*

CONWAG 4 gr.g. Scallywag 127–Confident Girl 66 (Quorum 126) (1981 NR 1982 12f 14.6fg³ 12fg³ 13.8f 12g) strong gelding; first foal; dam suited by 7f and 1m; only poor form on flat, but is a winner over hurdles; looks temperamental. *G. Toft.* —

CONWAY GROVE 2 b.g. Pongee 106–Sherry (King's Coup 108) (1982 6fg 7g 7g 8.2s) May 21; small, plain gelding; brother to a winning chaser; dam of little account; behind in minor events and a nursery. *N. Chamberlain.* —

COOL CLEAR WATER 2 b.f. Imperial Crown 96–Moonstream 62 (Forlorn River 124) (1982 5.8f 6g) Mar 3; fifth foal; dam plater; in rear in maiden races at Bath and Folkestone in June. *B. Swift.* —

COOL DECISION 5 b.g. Furry Glen 121–Aran Jacket (Le Levanstell 122) (1981 10g³ 12g² 11.5fg* 10f² 12.3fg² 12g⁴ 10g² 10.2g 1982 10.2g 12fg 12f² 12fg* 13fg² 12d⁴ 12f* 12f⁴ 14g 12fg* 11d³ 9s⁴ 10g 12s) lengthy gelding; seemed to show improved form when 33/1-winner of Moet and Chandon Silver Magnum (gentleman riders) at Epsom in August, beating Muslab in good style by 5 lengths; had earlier won similar event at Hamilton and minor race at Pontefract by wide margins and subsequently beat Say Primula by a neck in 5-runner Ladbroke Ayrshire Handicap at Ayr; suited by middle distances; acts on any going; good mount for an inexperienced rider; ran badly second and eighth outings. *Miss S. Hall.* 88

COOLEEN JACK 4 b.c. Targowice 130–Polyxo (Polyfoto 124) (1981 6d³ 6s 5s* 5f⁴ 6fg 5g 5d 1982 5s² 5fg 6g 5f 5d) medium-sized, quite attractive Irish colt; possibly needed race when creditable 2½ lengths second of 5 to Chellaston Park in £3,600 event at Haydock in April, staying on well; ran best subsequent race when about 2 lengths fifth of 11 behind Longleat in Ballyogan Stakes at Leopardstown in June on fourth start; stays 6f; acts on any going; sent to USA. *E. O'Grady, Ireland.* 104

COOLIDGE 3 b.f. Northern Flash–Miss Twights (Hopeful Venture 125) (1981 7g³ 7f 8fg 8g 1982 10fg 10g³ 10f) small, workmanlike filly; plater; will stay 1½m; usually sweats up. *M. Jarvis.* 58

COOL WIND 3 ch.f. Windjammer (USA)–Cool Mistress 59 (Skymaster 126) (1981 5d 5g² 5fg* 6g 6fg* 6d 5fg 5d³ 5d 1982 5s 5v* 5g* 5f³ 5f 5f³ 5h 5fg 5fg 5fg 5d 5d) neat filly; won handicaps at Hamilton and Wolverhampton in April; stays 6f; seems to act on any going; has run creditably when sweating up; ran moderately towards end of season; sold 750 gns Doncaster October Sales. *J. Berry.* 64

COOMBE SPIRIT 2 ro.c. Grundy 137–Dame Clara 95 (Manacle 123) (1982 7fg 8s) Apr 6; 36,000Y; neat colt; good walker; second foal; dam, who stayed 7f, is half-sister to very smart 1977 2-y-o John de Coombe; very weak in market, ran green early on when about 9 lengths fifth of 15 to Gallic Wit in maiden race at Salisbury in September; well-beaten second favourite in similar event at Bath the following month. *H. Candy.* —

COPPER BEECHES 5 b.g. Owen Anthony 102–Primmy 56 (Primera 131) (1981 6f 6g 6g⁴ 6fg* 6fg² 6fg⁴ 6g³ 6fg 5s 1982 6f 6f 5g² 6g² 6fg⁴ 5d) quite attractive, lightly-made gelding; sprint handicapper; ran best races when second at Newbury and Goodwood in August; stays 6f; acts on any going; often blinkered, but best form without in 1982. *J. Holt.* 69

COPT AGAIN 4 ch.f. Copte–Annie 65 (Damremont 120) (1981 9s 16g 12d 10.6s 8f 12f² 13.8f* 15.8fg 12fg 12f 13.8g 12d 1982 12f⁴ 10d 15g 10.8fg³ 10fg³ 12d) compact filly; plater; stays 1¾m; acts well on firm going; has run creditably in blinkers; sold to T. Fairhurst 2,700 gns Ascot December Sales. *R. Hollinshead.* 32

COQUELIN (USA) 3 ch.c. Blushing Groom 131–Topolly (Turn-to) (1981 8s 1982 9fg² 10d* 10fg 12v* 10g³ 10s* 12v) 220,000Y; half-brother to Turn Back The Time (by Youth), successful at up to 1¼m, and French 1½m winner Meg's Pride (by Sparkler); dam, French 9f winner, is granddaughter of top-class filly Bella Paola; won minor event at Evry in May, Prix du Lys at Chantilly in June (beat My Midway by ½ length) and La Coupe de Maisons-Laffitte in September; got the better of Bylly The Kid by a head in last-named; also ran well to be ½-length third of 10 to What A Guest in Prix Eugene Adam at Saint-Cloud in July; below form final start; stays 1½m; revels in the mud; smart. *F. Boutin, France.* 121

COQ

COQUITO'S FRIEND 2 b.c. Owen Dudley 121–Kissin' Cousin (Be Friendly **105**
130) (1982 6fg* 6fg² 6s* 6g³) Apr 25; 4,000F, 6,800Y; good-bodied colt;
second produce; brother to 1981 2-y-o 6f seller winner Super Sunset; dam twice-
raced sister to very useful sprinter As Friendly; accounted for sizeable fields in
£3,100 event at Newmarket in August (beat Kalyoub ¼ length) and minor race
at Lingfield in September (won easily by 4 lengths from Bold Nowhere); also ran
well when 2½ lengths second of 25 to Orixo in minor event at Doncaster and
when 2½ lengths third of 16 to Prince Spy under top weight in £4,700 nursery at
Newmarket; will stay 7f; seems to act on any going; has a good turn of foot.
B. Hanbury.

CORAL LEISURE 5 b.g. Welsh Saint 126–Bessborough (Mossborough 126) —
(1981 8g 1982 7s) lengthy, good sort; very lightly raced on flat nowadays;
best form at 1m; acts on a firm and a soft surface; blinkered nowadays. *G.
Balding.*

CORALLIE REEF 3 ch.f. Sandford Lad 133–French Oyster (Gulf Pearl 117) —
(1981 5g 5g 5fg 7g 6d 8.2d 1982 5g 6g 8.2g 7s) compact, lightly-made filly;
poor plater; sold 500 gns Doncaster October Sales. *G. Richards*

CORBALLY 2 br.f. Wolverlife 115–Grindelwald 76 (Le Levanstell 122) (1982 —
7.6v 8s 6g) Apr 5; tall, shallow-girthed filly; half-sister to 2 winners, including
6f and 7f winner Movement (by Daring Display); dam won at up to 13f; soundly
beaten in maiden races in the autumn, but did show up for long way on last
2 occasions. *A. Ingham.*

CORBIE LYNN 4 b.g. Supreme Sovereign 119–Sarum Lady 97 (Floribunda —
136) (1981 8.2s 9.4g 8.2s 9fg 9d² 11d 8d 1982 8fg 8f 8.2g⁴ 8.2g 9g) good-
topped gelding; poor mover; maiden plater; stays 9f; has been tried in blinkers;
seemed to have too much use made of him final outing. *G. Richards.*

CORDITE SPEAR (USA) 3 br.c. Explodent–Lovely Lance (Assagai) (1981 **96**
7g 6g³ 7.2fg² 7g⁴ 7.6s* 7g* 7d³ 1982 7g³ 8.2s* 8f² 10f³ 10.6h³ 10g 8fg³ 8g 8g²
8s* 8v² 8s) well-made colt; very good mover; won handicaps at Haydock in
April (beat Spanish Pool 3 lengths) and Goodwood in September (held off Dem
An Doze by a short head); ran creditably most other starts; stays 11f; acts on
any going but goes well on soft; suited by a strongly-run race; sold 31,000 gns
Newmarket Autumn Sales and is to be trained by D. Nicholson. *G. Harwood.*

CORDUROY 6 ch.h. Hotfoot 126–Twill 89 (Crocket 130) (1981 12s² 10.5d* —
12fg* 12fg⁴ 12fg 1982 12s 10v 12v 12s) rangy horse; middle-distance handicapper; well beaten in 1982 (autumn); acts on any going; needs strong handling.
H. Beasley.

CORINNE'S GOLD 4 b.f. Gold Rod 129–Beaute Royale (Duc de Gueldre 129) —
(1981 5f 6g 1982 5g 8fg) small filly; little worthwhile form, including in
sellers; bred to stay 1¼m. *A. Davison.*

CORKED 3 b.c. Tumble Wind–Bristol Milk 88 (Raise You Ten 125) (1981 7fg² **96**
7f 8s³ 8g² 1982 12fg 10.5f* 10g*) well-made, attractive colt; made all and
ran on strongly to win 4-runner Glasgow Stakes at York in May by 1½ lengths
from Noble Gift and well-contested minor event at Kempton later in month by
a length from Ricardo; reared over backwards in stalls and was withdrawn at
Haydock in June; not seen out again; gives impression he'll stay 1½m (not fully
fit when tried at trip); suited by a sound surface; game. *B. Hobbs.*

CORMORANT WOOD 2 b.f. Home Guard 129–Quarry Wood 89 (Super Sam **88** p
124) (1982 6g 7d*) Mar 6; big, rangy, good sort, with plenty of scope; second
reported foal; dam won at up to 1¾m; ran on strongly to win 18-runner maiden
race at Leicester in October by ½ length from Cristalga; will be suited by 1m+;
likely to improve further. *B. Hills.*

CORN BELLE 6 b.m. Cornuto 111–Ballabeg 61 (Typhoon 125) (1981 12.2g —
1982 16.5g) no worthwhile form on flat, though has won selling hurdles. *A.
Smith.*

CORNISH ECHO 3 ch.g. Oats 126–Blue Echoes 105 (Mountain Call 125) (1981 —
7g⁴ 7fg 7fg 1982 8.5fg 8f 9v 8g) well-made ex-English gelding; poor maiden;
trained by J. Sutcliffe first 2 starts. *M. O'Toole, Ireland.*

CORNISH GEM 3 br.c. Cornish Prince–Jeanie Duff 83 (Majestic Prince) **79**
(1981 6g 1982 7d³ 7fg² 8fg 10g³ 7fg³ 8fg³ 8g) compact colt; not the best of
movers nowadays; placed in varied company, best effort when just over 3
lengths third to Hays in Salisbury 2,000 Guineas Trial on reappearance; will be
suited by a return to 1¼m; suited by some give in the ground; blinkered fifth
start. *P. Haslam.*

CORNISH GRANITE 4 gr.g. Ragstone 128–Pasty 122 (Raffingora 130) (1981 8d² 8d³ 8s² 8d* 8g³ 10.2f 8h 8.2g 8g 1982 13.1f) small gelding; quite a moderate handicapper; stays 1m (never in race when well beaten over 13f on only outing of 1982); best form with some give in the ground; has worn blinkers. *M. Pipe.* —

CORNISH HEROINE (USA) 3 b.f. Cornish Prince–Pomade (Prince John) (1981 7f 8fg* 1982 10fg² 12fg³ 10.6h⁴ 12.2g*) lengthy, attractive filly; good mover; got up on line to beat Dreaming Away by a head in 7-runner Warwick Oaks in June; placed earlier in Pretty Polly Stakes at Newmarket (2½ lengths second of 9 to Sing Softly) and Esal Bookmakers Oaks Trial at Lingfield (7 lengths third of 9 to Tants); stays 1½m; blinkered third start; sent to USA. *M. Stoute.* **101**

CORNISHMAN 4 ch.c. Connaught 130–Alley Cat 100 (Alycidon 138) (1981 12d³ 12g² 12g* 12.3d⁴ 12d 16f 12fg 14s 14g 12g 1982 16.1fg* 17f) big, strong, long-striding colt; showed first form on flat for a long time when winning 5-runner handicap at Haydock in May, making all and coming home 7 lengths clear of High Rainbow; disappointed only subsequent start; stays well; acts on a firm and a soft surface. *R. Hollinshead.* **71**

CORNISH MINER 3 ch.c. Jimmy Reppin 131–Wheal Harmony (Song 132) (1981 7g 1982 8d 10.1fg 10fg 10d⁴ 8fg 9g) plain colt; plating-class maiden; best run at 1¼m on soft ground. *C. James.* **57**

CORN STREET 4 ch.g. Decoy Boy 129–Diamond Talk (Counsel 118) (1981 6g² 6s² 6g² 6f² 7f⁴ 6fg 7g³ 6s⁴ 8s* 8s² 7d² 1982 7s⁴ 8d³ 8f 7fg 8g 8fg* 8g* 8g 8g* 8v* 8s* 8s) workmanlike gelding; in particularly good form in second half of season and won 5 of his last 7 races, last of them a handicap at Sandown by a head from Cob Gless after being held up; had earlier won amateur riders race at Warwick, Esal Credit Handicap at Newbury and 2 fairly valuable handicaps at Ascot; suited by 1m; acts on any going but is particularly well suited by some give; suitable mount for an apprentice; genuine; didn't have best of runs eighth start. *J. Bosley.* **95**

CORNY STORY 3 b.f. Oats 126–Twaddle II (Tim Tam) (1981 7d 8s 1982 11f* 12f⁴ 12g 14f 12fg) big, well-made, attractive filly; stayed on strongly to win 13-runner maiden race at Newbury in July; ran respectably next time but had some stiff tasks subsequently; stays 1½m; acts on firm going; blinkered fourth outing. *R. Baker.* **75**

COROMUS 5 br.m. Sit In The Corner–To Rome (Romulus 129) (1981 NR 1982 10s) small, dipped-backed, rather lightly-made mare; poor plater; possibly stays 1m. *B. McMahon.* —

CORSKY 3 b.f. Pitskelly 122–Corsuedei (King's Troop 118) (1981 6fg* 8fg 1982 6fg 7f 7fg 8d 7g) well-made filly; fair handicapper on her day; bolted on intended reappearance and was withdrawn; should stay 1m; tends to pull hard; sold 6,200 gns Newmarket December Sales. *G. Harwood.* **86**

CORSTON LAD 2 ch.c. Orange Bay 131–Corston Lass (Menelek 114) (1982 7g) May 15; useful-looking colt, with plenty of scope; first foal; dam placed over hurdles; 50/1, came through in good style from back of field when 12 lengths sixth of 23 to The Fort in maiden race at Newmarket in August; will be much better suited by longer distances; sure to improve. *J. Winter.* — p

CORVELLE 2 ch.f. Reliance II 137–Corvette (Biarritz 115) (1982 6fg 7fg 8fg) Mar 23; first foal in this country; dam Australian; little worthwhile form. *P. Cole.* —

CORVEN 5 b. or br.g. Owen Anthony 102–Cameo 114 (Como 120) (1981 8s³ 8fg 7d* 8d 6f 11.7fg 1982 6d⁴ 10f* 10f 10f) plater; attracted no bid after winning at Brighton in April; stays 1¼m; acts on any going; blinkered when successful; inconsistent. *D. Grissell.* **43**

COSHLEA 2 ch.f. Red Alert 127–White Legs (Preciptic 122) (1982 6fg 8fg) May 1; strong, compact filly; closely related to Musidora Stakes winner Princess of Man (by Green God) and half-sister to numerous winners, 2 very useful; dam placed in Ireland; no form in September in minor event at Doncaster and maiden race (seventh of 13) at Beverley. *J. W. Watts.* —

COSTAPLENTY 4 ch.f. Ribston 104–Forlorn Leap (Forlorn River 124) (1981 NR 1982 10f 8fg 6g) strong filly; behind in varied company, including selling; sold out of M. Blanshard's stable 620 gns Doncaster March Sales; dead. *D. Chapman.* —

Mr J. Whelan's "Countess Candy"

COTTAGE STYLE 3 ch.f. Thatch 136–Toast Record (El Gallo 122) (1981 **65**
NR 1982 7d⁴ 7.2g 7d⁴) 76,000Y; good-topped filly; half-sister to 1½m winner
Waleed (by Tudor Melody) and Irish middle-distance winner Lavache (by Levmoss), subsequently a good winner in Australia; dam, winner over 5f at 2 yrs, is
half-sister to Lorenzaccio; fourth in minor events at Salisbury in June and Ayr
in September; will stay 1m; sold 20,000 gns Newmarket December Sales.
T. Robson.

COTTAM EXPRESS 3 b.f. Runnymede 123–Royal Bit (King's Troop 118) —
(1981 5s 5s³ 5d* 5g 6f 5f 6f 1982 8f 8f) leggy filly; poor plater; possibly needs
a soft surface; sold 410 gns Doncaster October Sales. *H. Bell.*

COUGH 3 ch.g. Most Secret 119–Outburst 57 (Articulate 121) (1981 5fg 6fg **47**
6f⁴ 8g 8.2d⁴ 8d 7g² 8d 1982 8g* 7f 9f⁴ 8fg² 9g 8g² 8g 8g⁴) plater; attracted
no bid after winning at Edinburgh in April; stays 9f; seems to act on any going.
T. Craig.

COUNTACH 3 br.g. Balidar 133–Fiji Express (Exbury 138) (1981 6fg 6f **75** d
6fg* 5d 5s 1982 5d* 6s³ 5g⁴ 5fg* 5f* 5fg* 5h⁴ 6fg⁴ 7f 6f 5d) quite attractive
gelding; won handicaps at Leicester, Wolverhampton (2) and Brighton; stays
6f; seems to act on any going; has won 3 times for apprentice T. Quinn; below
form last 2 starts. *P. Cole.*

COUNT DERRY 2 ch.c. Derrylin 115–Noble Countess (Mossborough 126) **90**
(1982 7fg 8g 8.2s²) Apr 14; 14,000Y; big, workmanlike colt; closely related to
1m winner Daring Dame (by Derring-Do) and half-brother to several minor
winners; dam closely related to Oaks winner Noblesse; showed ability on all
starts, on last 2 finishing 4 lengths fifth of 21 to Polished Silver in £4,200 event
at Newbury in September and 3 lengths second of 11 to Mitilini in maiden race
at Haydock in October; will probably stay 1½m; should win at one of the smaller
meetings. *R. Hannon.*

COUNTESS CANDY 2 b.f. Great Nephew 126–Zoomie 78 (Pinza 137) (1982 **106**
8.5g* 8fg 7g*) Apr 13; 25,000Y; rather leggy, attractive filly; half-sister to
several winners, including very useful Irish middle-distance filly Countess Tully
(by Hotfoot); dam, half-sister to smart animals Pithiviers and Blinis, won over
1m and 9f; a very useful filly who won maiden race at Galway in September
and Park Stakes at Leopardstown in October, holding off unlucky-in-running
Beat The Drum by ¾ length in latter; favourite for Silken Glider Stakes at
Leopardstown in between but missed break and was beaten 3½ lengths into
fifth place behind Impudent Miss, giving distinct impression she wasn't at ease
on firmish ground; will stay 1¼m. *L. Browne, Ireland.*

COUNT FERNANDO 5 b.g. Connaught 130–Ankole 85 (Crepello 136) (1981 —
10d 10.6f 10.5g 10f 12f 1982 15.8g) smallish, lengthy gelding; stayed 1½m;
was possibly unsuited by soft ground; was tried in blinkers; dead. *I. Vickers.*

COUNT MIDAS 3 gr.g. Dragonara Palace 115–Native Nymph 97 (Indigenous —
121) (1981 NR 1982 7f 8fg 7g 8fg 12.2d) leggy gelding; poor plater; sold out
of J. Tierney's stable 900 gns Doncaster August Sales after fourth start. *A.
Watson.*

COUNT MORPHEUS 2 ch.g. Morston 125–Sovereign Gate 81 (Sovereign —
Path 125) (1982 6f 6g 7fg) Mar 8; good-bodied gelding; behind in maiden and
minor events; sold 550 gns Ascot October Sales and subsequently gelded. *R.
Baker.*

COUNT OF SICILY 3 b.c. Dubassoff–Sicilia (Die Hard 127) (1981 8s 8s **62**
1982 13g 15fg³ 14.6g 16.5fg² 15.8d 18d) neat colt; staying maiden; best form
on a firm surface. *P. Calver.*

COUNT PAHLEN 3 gr.c. Hotfoot 126–Tanara 93 (Romulus 129) (1981 **115**
7fg³ 7g³ 8d 7g* 8d* 1982 8.5fg* 10.5f⁴ 12f 10s 10d) strong, good sort who
carries plenty of condition; brother to useful 1977 2-y-o 1m winner Schumann;

Mrs A. Villar's "Count Pahlen"

dam 1¼m winner; put up a high-class display to win William Hill Futurity at Doncaster in 1981; didn't run up to that form at 3 yrs though won Blue Riband Trial at Epsom (beat Steel Bay a neck) and ran respectably to be fourth in Mecca-Dante Stakes at York (behind Simply Great), ninth in Derby (to Golden Fleece) and seventh in Dubai Champion Stakes at Newmarket (behind Time Charter); promises to stay 1½m; has won on a firm surface but is ideally suited by some give in the ground. *B. Hobbs.*

COUNTRYCLASS LAD   3 b.c. Track Spare 125–Ring True 80 (Gulf Pearl 117)   **65**
(1981 7fg 8.2d   1982 8f 8f³ 8g³ 10f² 10fg³ 11g 11g* 10.1d)   fair sort; won maiden race at Hamilton in August; needs a strongly-run race at 1¼m and will stay 1½m; acts on firm going; sold to K. Bailey 11,000 gns Ascot October Sales. *Sir Mark Prescott.*

COUNTRY MONARCH   2 b.c. Scottish Rifle 127–Double Mint 82 (Double-U-   **51**
Jay 120)   (1982 5f 5f 6f² 6h 6fg)   small, rather lightly-made colt; fourth foal; dam won at 1½m and also over hurdles; staying-on 5 lengths second of 7 to Time Is Time in seller at Yarmouth in June, only form; bred to be much better suited by longer distances, and should stay at least 1½m; blinkered second outing. *B. Hanbury.*

COUNTRY SQUIRE   5 b.g. Galivanter 131–Esquire Maid 86 (Aureole 132)   —
(1981 NR   1982 8f 8fg)   small gelding; only poor form, including in a seller as a 3-y-o. *S. Wiles.*

COUNT TOLSTOY   5 ch.g. Sir Ivor 135–Vaguely Mine 90 (Silly Season 127)   —
(1981 NR   1982 16.5s)   big, lengthy gelding; very backward when tailed-off last behind Viennese Waltz in minor event at Redcar in October. *H. Fleming.*

COUNTY BROKER   2 b.c. Kashiwa 115–Ardrionn (Wolver Hollow 126)   (1982   **101**
5fg* 5g* 5f4 6d³ 6f³ 6g 5fg³(dis) 5g 5v)   Feb 6; IR 8,200Y; strong, good sort; first foal; dam poor Irish maiden; impressive winner of maiden race at Nottingham in April and minor event at Windsor in May; good third in New Ham Stakes at Goodwood in July, fifth outing and best of several mixed efforts afterwards; apparently better suited by 6f than 5f; acts on firm going, and wasn't disgraced on heavy; best with strong handling. *A. Jarvis.*

COURAGEOUS BUZBY   6 b.g. Communication 119–Courageous Chic 75   **63**
(Cash and Courage 116)   (1981 6f 5g* 7.2v 6s* 5g³   1982 6f² 6f 5fg4 6fg 6g 6f 5d* 6s 6s 5s)   workmanlike gelding; sprint handicapper; won at Pontefract in October; stays 6f; acts on any going; occasionally sweats up; has been taken down early; wears a tongue strap nowadays. *B. McMahon.*

COURTESY CALL   3 ch.f. Northfields–Makeacurtsey (Herbager 136)   (1981   —
NR   1982 10f 10.4d³ 11d4)   80,000Y; smallish, quite well-made filly; half-sister to smart 1976 2-y-o 5f performer Piney Ridge (by Native Prince) and very useful 1¼m winner Hill's Yankee (by Thatch); dam, placed in USA, is half-sister to 3 good stakes winners, including very smart grass horse Knightly Manner; 2 lengths third of 14 to Fair Fantasia in maiden race at Chester in August, best effort; will be suited by 1¼m; sold to BBA 70,000 gns Newmarket December Sales. *T. Robson.*

COURT GATE   2 ch.f. Hell's Gate 99–Court Amour 76 (Irish Ball 127)   (1982   —
5g 7fg)   Apr 5; 310Y, 1,000 2-y-o (privately); first foal; dam placed over 6f and 1m; in rear in sellers at Wolverhampton in August and Chepstow in September. *D. Wintle.*

COURT KING   2 gr.c. Hotfoot 126–Virginia Wade 116 (Virginia Boy 106)   **66**
(1982 5d 5fg 7d)   Feb 3; sturdy, non-thoroughbred colt; third foal; brother to 1980 2-y-o 5f winner Court Queen, and half-brother to 3-y-o 6f winner Princess Virginia (by Connaught); dam won 5 times over 5f; plating-class maiden; showed form only on second outing. *P. Cole.*

COURT PLAY   8 br.g. Prince Regent 129–Hobby (Falcon 131)   (1981 16d4   —
14f³ 16.5f*   1982 8g)   ex-Irish gelding; won amateur riders event at Killarney in 1981; well beaten in trainers race in May; stayed well; probably acted on any going; dead. *D. Jermy.*

COURT PROCEDURE (USA)   2 b.c. Valid Appeal–New Hat (Tim Tam)   **87**
(1982 5d³ 5fg² 5.8f² 6fg 6d³ 6v² 6g)   Feb 1; $102,000F, $375,000Y; smallish, deep-girthed, quite attractive colt; closely related to 4 winners by In Reality and half-brother to several other winners, including Kentucky Derby second Francie's Hat (by Francis S.) and smart 1m to 1¼m horse Hat Full (by Prince Taj); dam won 3 times at 2 yrs; placed 5 times in maiden events, and ran well, though unplaced, in 2 nurseries; should stay beyond 6f; acts on any going; most consistent. *J. Tree.*

COVENANT 5 ch.m. Good Bond 122–Concession Day 79 (Will Somers 114§) — (1981 NR 1982 10fg⁴ 15f) poor performer nowadays; stays 1½m; acts on any going, but best form on soft; has worn blinkers. *J. Gilbert.*

COVERGIRLS CHOICE 5 b.h. Red Alert 127–Singe (Tudor Music 131) (1981 — 5s* 6s⁴ 5fg 5g² 5g² 6g² 6g* 6g 6f 6f³ 7fg 6g 6fg³ 6s 6s 6d 1982 5d 6f 5g) slightly hollow-backed horse; poor mover; sprint handicapper; best with some give in the ground and revels in the mud; good mount for a boy; has run respectably in blinkers; sold 680 gns Doncaster October Sales and resold 800 gns Newmarket Autumn Sales. *N. Callaghan.*

COWDENBEATH (USA) 5 b.h. Buffalo Lark–Intervene (Prince John) (1981 66 10.2s 14g 12g 12d 12.3fg* 12f* 12fg* 12f² 12d 12f³ 14f⁴ 14.6fg 12.2g 16g* 1982 18g⁴ 14g 18.4g 14f³ 16.1f 17f* 16.5g 18.8fg 16.9fg³ 16g 18d 20g) good-bodied, attractive horse; good mover; beat Dark Proposal by 5 lengths in slowly-run handicap at Wolverhampton in August; stays well; probably acts on any going but goes well on a sound surface; ran well in blinkers once in 1980; inconsistent. *R. Hollinshead.*

COXWELL EAGLE 2 ch.c. Mandrake Major 122–My Bushbaby 100 (Hul a Hul 81 124) (1982 5g 6g* 7fg 6g 6v) Apr 8; 10,500Y; big, strong colt; fourth foal; half-brother to 2 winners, including fairly useful 1978 2-y-o 6f winner Bushwhacker (by No Mercy); dam won over 5f at 2 yrs and is half-sister to smart Panomark; kept on well to beat No Remission by ½ length in 8-runner maiden race at Hamilton in July; no form in nurseries subsequently, on final outing tried in blinkers; not certain to stay 7f; yet to race on a firm surface. *C. Nelson.*

COYOR (USA) 2 b. or br.c. Clev Er Tell–Bee's Oro (Ben Lomond) (1982 — 6g) Mar 30; $30,000Y; third foal; half-brother to 2 winners, including very useful Bee A Scout (by West Coast Scout); dam won 6 small races at up to 1m; 10/1 when never-dangerous 9 lengths eighth of 22 to Riverside Artist in minor event at Nottingham in July; sold D. Arbuthnot 3,000 gns Newmarket Autumn Sales. *M. Stoute.*

CRACKERJILL 5 b.m. Sparkler 130–Token Girl 116 (Bolinas Boy) (1981 NR 37 1982 8f 8f 7d 8g³ 8fg 8v³ 6s) poor maiden; stays 1m; trained by M. Tompkins most of season. *W. Wightman.*

CRACKHILL 3 b.g. Legal Eagle 126–Mexican Music 71 (Astec 128) (1981 6f 88 d 6fg 7.2fg⁴ 8.2d² 7g² 7g 1982 7fg* 9g* 8fg 8f² 8d 8d 9s) lengthy, good sort; won maiden race at Edinburgh and landed odds readily in minor event at Hamilton in May; good second to Rekal in handicap at York in July; may stay 1¼m; seems to act on any going; sold privately to Miss S. Hall 7,000 gns Doncaster October Sales. *J. Hanson.*

CRADLE OF JAZZ (USA) 2 b.c. Verbatim–Louisiana (Nadir) (1982 7fg 7g³) 91 good-topped, quite attractive colt; half-brother to 3 minor winners in USA; dam, a minor winner, is half-sister to outstanding fillies Levee, Bayou and Delta; showed promise in good-class races, finishing 11½ lengths fifth of 13 to Gorytus in Acomb Stakes at York in August and 3¾ lengths third to Cock Robin in 13-runner Ribero Stakes at Doncaster in September; will be well suited by 1m+; sure to win in maiden company. *J. Hindley.*

CRAY 2 b.g. Mummy's Pet 125–Kiara (Great Nephew 126) (1982 6fg 6g 5g 7f 69 7s) May 9; compact gelding; good mover; first foal; dam of little account on flat and over hurdles; plating-class maiden; stays 7f; suited by an easy surface; hung under pressure when tried in blinkers on final appearance; subsequently gelded. *J. W. Watts.*

CREATIVE STAR 4 b.g. Wishing Star 117–Rag Flowers (Tarqogan 125) — (1981 8.2s 10s* 12d 16.5f 16s 16s 1982 12.3g) big gelding; poor walker; suited by middle distances; seems suited by plenty of give in the ground. *J. Fitzgerald.*

CREE BAY 3 b.g. Bay Express 132–Porsanger (Zeddaan 130) (1981 5d 5fg² 88 5g² 5d 6d 6g 1982 5f 5f 5f 5f* 5fg* 5g³ 5g* 5fg* 5f* 5fg* 5.8f³ 5g² 5.6g 5g 5s* 5s) useful-looking gelding; has proved a rare bargain since being bought for 420 gns at Ascot November Sales in 1981, winning minor event at Chepstow, handicaps at Catterick, Beverley, Carlisle, Leicester and Wolverhampton and another minor event at Haydock; beat Path to Glory unchallenged by 5 lengths in last-named in October; best at 5f; acts on any going; blinkered once at 2 yrs; tough, genuine and consistent and a credit to his trainer. *J. Spearing.*

CREE SONG 6 b.h. Song 132–Gentle Gael 97 (Celtic Ash) (1981 6v² 5g 6d 5g **82**
6fg 5g⁴ 5g⁴ 5g 6d 6g 1982 6fg 5fg³ 6f* 6fg⁴ 6d 5f² 5fg⁴) strong horse; poor
mover in his slower paces; sprint handicapper; gained first win since 1980 when
beating Polly's Brother by a short head at Ripon in May (got up close home);
also placed twice at York; stays 6f; acts on any going; sometimes blinkered.
P. Calver.

CREG-NA-BAA 3 b.c. Imperial Crown 96–Rose of France 83 (Grand Roi 118) —
(1981 NR 1982 10d 8d 7fg) small, lightly-made colt; second foal; dam won
over 1¼m at 3 yrs and over 11f at 9 yrs, latter after birth of first foal; behind in
2 maidens and a seller. *D. Jermy.*

CREMATION 2 b.c. Ashmore 125–Sacred Ibis (Red God 128§) (1982 5g² 5f* **97**
6g² 6fg² 7fg⁴ 6f³ 7fg² 8s² 8g⁴(dis)) Apr 6; IR 11,000Y; third foal; half-brother
to fairly useful 1980 2-y-o 5f winner Sybaris (by Crowned Prince); dam, sister
to very useful 1969 2-y-o Red Velvet, looked a short runner; made virtually all
to win 6-runner maiden race at Navan in May by 2½ lengths from Bective Baby;
second in 5 of his other races, notably going down by ¾ length to Virginia Deer
in 18-runner event at the Curragh on third outing, by 6 lengths to Danzatore at
Leopardstown on seventh and by a neck to Le Java under top weight in nursery
at the Curragh on eighth; stays 1m well; acts on any going; genuine and
consistent. *M. Connolly, Ireland.*

CREME D'OR 2 ch.f. Roan Rocket 128–Tudor Cream 72§ (Tudor Melody 129) **65**
(1982 5fg 5fg⁴ 6fg 5fg² 5fg 6fg 5.3g 5s 6s) Apr 1; 3,000Y; compact filly; half-
sister to several winners here and abroad; dam disappointing; in frame in maiden
auction events; form only at 5f; acts on a firm surface. *G. Beeson.*

CRESTA SWALLOW 2 ch.f. Hittite Glory 125–Cresta 84 (Ribero 126) (1982 **66**
5g⁴ 5fg* 5fg) Apr 14; 1,200Y; small filly; first foal; dam, half-sister to very
good 3-y-o Electric, won over 7f on only start at 2 yrs; bought in 1,500 gns after
winning seller at Wolverhampton in May by 4 lengths from Patsy Pennall; had
to be destroyed at Beverley the following month. *D. Dale.*

CRESTBOY 3 ch.g. Scottish Rifle 127–Ginger Puss (Worden II 129) (1981 5.8g **52**
6g 7f 8s 1982 8.3g² 8.3fg 8fg 8.3g) smallish, plain gelding; plater; bred to
stay middle distances; has worn blinkers. *K. Cunningham-Brown.*

CRESTED LARK 6 ch.h. Crowned Prince 128–Bird of Dawning (Sea-Bird II **78**
145) (1981 12d* 12g² 14s 12g* 12g* 12d² 12g 12g 1982 12d* 12d 13fg* 12f*
12g 12fg) big, rangy horse; had a good season and won at Folkestone, Ayr and
Salisbury; beat Bombalini by 2 lengths on last-named course in July; stays 13f
(pulled hard when well beaten over 1¾m); acts on firm and a soft surface; genuine
front runner. *M. Smyly.*

CREST WINDOWS 7 ch.g. Levanter 121–Midsummer Magic (Midsummer —
Night II 117) (1981 12s 13fg 8d 6f 7f 1982 7h 7fg 10d) probably of little
account. *T. Gosling.*

CRESUN 3 b.c. Sunyboy 110–Credo's Daughter (Credo 123) (1981 NR 1982 —
14d 16f 15.5fg 16fg) lengthy, workmanlike colt; second foal; dam won 4 middle-
distance races, 1 hurdle and 9 chases; well beaten in varied company; pulled up
third start. *S. Woodman.*

CRICKETERS CLUB 5 gr.h. Touch Paper 113–Mairi's Love (His Highness) —
(1981 5g 6f 6g 5d³ 5fg 5g 1982 5d 5f 5g 5f) small horse; poor handicapper;
best run at 5f on a soft surface; sold 430 gns Ascot September Sales. *M. Haynes.*

CRICKET FIELD 3 b.f. Northfields–Emma Canute 93 (Hardicanute 130) **77**
(1981 6d⁴ 6fg 6fg* 6f 1982 8f 10fg*) attractive, shapely filly; excellent mover;
made all and kept on well to beat Singleton by ½ length in 4-runner minor event
at Chepstow in August; stays 1¼m. *B. Hobbs.*

CRIME OF PASSION 2 b.f. Dragonara Palace 115–Catriona 96 (Sing Sing 134) **115**
(1982 5g* 5f* 5fg² 6f* 5.5g³ 5g²)
For trainer Laing the 1982 season was easily his most successful since he
took out a licence in 1978. His useful handicapper Tugoflove had a remarkably
good year, picking up three highly competitive races worth over £32,000, his
two-year-old filly Dancing Meg developed into a very useful stayer and another
two-year-old filly, Crime of Passion, credited the stable with its first success in a
pattern race when she took the Cherry Hinton Stakes at Newmarket in July.

226

Cherry Hinton Stakes, Newmarket—a driving finish with Crime of Passion (No. 6) just getting the better of Carolside (nearest camera) and Silk Pyjamas

Crime of Passion started at 12/1 for the Cherry Hinton, a very generous price considering her previous record. She had won twice in May, getting home narrowly in a maiden race at Kempton on her debut and then holding off the strong-finishing Annie Edge by a neck in a £2,600 event at Newbury. And on her third start she had put up a fine display in the Queen Mary Stakes at Royal Ascot. After showing excellent speed to lead her opponents, twelve of them previous winners, for nearly four furlongs she kept on to retain second place, a length and a half behind Widaad. Crime of Passion was one of five Queen Mary runners to reappear in the Cherry Hinton. Strictly on form she appeared to have a good chance: she was meeting Widaad on terms 6 lb better, and she had at least a length and a half in hand of the others, Carolside, Deportment and Shicklah. However there was strong doubt about Crime of Passion's ability to get the sixth furlong at Newmarket and Widaad again started favourite, with the Kingsclere Stakes winner Bright Crocus and Deportment next in the betting at 2/1 and 9/2. If Crime of Passion's connections had any plans to conserve her stamina, the filly soon put paid to them, breaking very quickly and immediately striding into the lead. Coming to the final furlong she looked about to be swamped as Carolside moved up to challenge on her right with Silk Pyjamas looking equally dangerous on her left. Crime of Passion wouldn't be denied though and battled on tremendously well up the final hill to hold them off by a head and a neck.

Nearly three weeks later Crime of Passion started third favourite behind Deep Roots and Ma Biche in the nine-runner Prix Robert Papin at Maisons-Laffitte. She put up a very bold show before going under to both, leading for much of the way and giving best only in the last two hundred yards where Ma Biche quickened away. In fact in finishing third, beaten one and a half lengths and a short neck, Crime of Passion put up her best effort—Ma Biche later won the Cheveley Park and Deep Roots both the Prix Morny and Prix de la Sala-mandre. Unfortunately Crime of Passion was seen out only once subsequently, when a beaten favourite in the St Hugh's Stakes at Newbury in August. The nature of her task that day wasn't apparent until afterwards; she had to give 4 lb to Favoridge and was made to look almost ordinary as that filly quickened in brilliant style to beat her six lengths. Crime of Passion was then to have run in the Flying Childers Stakes but she wrenched a joint in training and was retired for the year, having shown herself a smart, tough and game performer. She also showed she acts well on firm going; she has yet to race on a soft surface.

Mr Christopher Wright's "Crime of Passion"

Crime of Passion cost 12,500 guineas as a yearling after changing hands for only 4,600 guineas as a foal. She's a lengthy, workmanlike individual with more scope than many precocious two-year-old fillies; she must have good prospects of training on even though both her parents were at their best at two. Dragonara Palace gained four of his five successes at that age, notably winning the July Stakes and the Richmond Stakes, and it is largely as a sire of speedy two-year-olds that he has made his name at stud. In 1982 he sired ten individual winning juveniles, including the other very useful performer Mac's

	Dragonara Palace (gr 1971)	Young Emperor (gr 1963)	Grey Sovereign
			Young Empress
		Ruby's Princess (b 1962)	Fidalgo
Crime of Passion (b.f. Apr 11, 1980)			Persian Ruby
	Catriona (b 1967)	Sing Sing (b 1957)	Tudor Minstrel
			Agin the Law
		Paphos (ch 1961)	Vilmorin
			Royal Myth

Palace. Catriona, Crime of Passion's dam, was a splendidly consistent filly at two, winning three five-furlong events and never finishing out of a place in nine starts. She disappointed the following year but has made amends at stud, producing the Ayr Gold Cup winner Primula Boy (by Sallust) and winners in France and Barbados from four previous foals. Catriona's sister Singing Girl was also a fairly useful sprinter, as was their dam Paphos, and Crime of Passion is most unlikely to stay beyond six furlongs. Indeed she may prove best at five. Some of her relatives have stayed quite well though: Catrina's half-brother Playboy Jubilee won the Dee Stakes, Paphos' half-brother Tudor Tale was a very useful stayer, and Paphos' close relative Quarrymaster won the Great

228

Metropolitan Handicap. This is also the family of the Horris Hill Stakes winner Fair Season and the Oaks d'Italia winner Val d'Erica. *R. Laing.*

CRIMSON CARGO 2 ch.f. Import 127–Golden Ears 94 (Gratitude 130) (1982 — 5v 5g 5f) Feb 16; sturdy filly; sister to a poor animal and half-sister to several winners, including smart 1977 2-y-o sprinter Fire Angel (by Sharpen Up); dam best at 7f; no form in modest company; not seen out after July. *E. Weymes.*

CRIMSON KNIGHT 3 b.c. Blushing Groom 131–Sirnelta (Sir Tor) (1981 **75** 6fg 7d* 7.6g 1982 7.2h 10s³) rather lightly-made colt; excellent mover; fairly useful in 1981; put up better effort at 3 yrs when under a length third to Whenyourtrainsgone in minor event at Leicester in November; suited by 1¼m; acts well on soft ground. *F. J. Houghton.*

CRIMSON LAKE (FR) 3 b.f. Mill Reef 141–Maroon 92 (Roan Rocket 128) **71** (1981 NR 1982 10fg 9f³ 8f² 8g² 8f³ 10.1g² 10.2f 9s² 10s) small, rather lightly-made filly; doesn't always impress in appearance; good walker and mover; second foal; half-sister to 1½m winner Bronze Medal (by Jimmy Reppin); dam, daughter of smart stayer Mulberry Harbour, won over 1¾m and 2m; runner-up in maiden races; a stoutly-bred filly who will be suited by 1½m; acts on any going; didn't look keen eighth start and pulled hard in blinkers final appearance. *I. Balding.*

CRIMSON LINE 3 ch.c. High Line 125–Crimson Belle 80 (Red God 128§) — (1981 NR 1982 11f 10.1g 10.1fg 11.5fg 16fg) big, tall, short-backed colt; brother to middle-distance winner Crimson Royale, very smart 1¼m horse Crimson Beau and a winner in Belgium, and half-brother to several winners; dam won at 7f; in rear in maiden and minor races; wears bandages. *P. Cole.*

CRIMSON ROYALE 4 ch.f. High Line 125–Crimson Belle 80 (Red God 128§) **75 d** (1981 10fg 9d³ 8f⁴ 10.1fg² 10.2h² 10fg* 12f⁴ 10.1g* 12g 11.7d* 1982 10f³ 11f 12fg³ 12d³ 11.7fg 13.1f 12g⁴ 14fg 16.1s) small, fair sort; below her best in 1982, but was third in handicaps at Lingfield (2) and Leicester; stays 1¾m; acts on any going, except perhaps very soft; often sweats up. *P. Cole.*

CRIMSON SILK 8 ch.g. Counsel 118–La Muleta (Matador 131) (1981 7.2fg **55** 6g² 7fg² 7fg 7.6fg 8g⁴ 7fg⁴ 6g 7s 1982 6s 7f² 7fg 8fg 8fg) poor handicapper nowadays; unplaced in sellers last 2 starts; stays 7f; appears to act on any going; often blinkered; trained first 3 starts by A. Jarvis. *J. Hardy.*

CRINGLEFORD 5 b.g. Sterling Bay–Paludamentum (Royal Palm 131) (1981 **51** 10d 8v 8g³ 8f³ 8fg 8g* 10fg 8.3g² 8g³ 8s³ 1982 8g⁴ 8g 8f* 8f* 8fg 7.6fg 8f 8.3fg) workmanlike gelding; made most when winning apprentice event and a handicap at Carlisle in June; stays 1m; acts on any going; sold to BBA (Italia) 3,000 gns Newmarket Autumn Sales. *C. Spares.*

CRISTALGA 2 br.f. High Top 131–Coralivia (Le Levanstell 122) (1982 6fg **87** 7g³ 7d²) Mar 9; medium-sized, good-bodied, quite attractive filly; half-sister to 2 winners, including 7f and 1½m winner Countess Olivia (by Prince Tenderfoot); dam, half-sister to very smart Ballyhot, won over 1½m in Ireland; placed in big fields of maidens at Newmarket and Leicester (favourite) in October; should stay at least 1¼m; sure to win in ordinary maiden company. *G. Pritchard-Gordon.*

CRISTINA TIMES 4 b. or br.f. Will Somers 114§–Reina Cristina 84 (Tamerlane **52** 128) (1981 8d 6d 1982 10g 10f* 8g* 8fg* 10g) lightly-made filly; plater; in fine form in May, and was bought in after winning at Pontefract, Edinburgh and Pontefract again, on last occasion for 1,400 gns; soundly beaten in a non-seller final start (June); stays 1¼m; acts on firm going; often blinkered but not when successful. *B. McMahon.*

CRITERION 3 b.c. Royal Palace 131–Climbing Rose 81 (Pirate King 129) **119** (1981 7fg² 1982 10.6s* 12g* 12fg⁴ 12fg 10g³ 10fg* 11.1fg³ 10fg⁴ 12d² 10d) 13,000Y; tall, quite attractive colt; half-brother to several winners, including smart 1m to 1½m performer Saint Jonathon (by Welsh Saint) and useful 6f to 1m winner Rocket Symphony (by Roan Rocket); dam 2-y-o 5f winner; a smart performer who won maiden race at Haydock in April, minor event at Kempton in May and Trident Chesterfield Cup at Goodwood in July; responded gamely to strong pressure to get up in final strides and beat Oratavo a head in last-named; in frame most other starts, and was beaten only ½ length by Critique when third in September Stakes at Kempton on seventh and a neck by Lafontaine in Cumber-

Mr A. E. Bodie's "Criterion"

land Lodge Stakes at Ascot on ninth; stays 1½m; seems to act on any going; has run well when sweating up; often impresses in appearance. *G. Harwood.*

CRITICAL PATH 3 ch.g. Shiny Tenth 120–Tamaqua 69 (Tamerlane 128) **68** (1981 6fg 5d 6g 1982 8d 10f 12f* 12fg² 13d 12v² 12d) big, strong gelding; plater; bought in 3,000 gns after winning at Newmarket in August; twice second in better company afterwards; suited by 1½m; acts on any going; suitable mount for an inexperienced rider. *G. Balding.*

CRITIQUE (USA) 4 br.c. Roberto 131–Cambrienne 95 (Sicambre 135) (1981 **124** 8d⁴ 10s⁴ 10d 8fg* 10fg* 12fg* 10g 1982 12fg³ 13.4fg² 13.3f² 12f³ 12f* 12fg⁴ 11.1fg* 12d³ 12s)
Flat racing has lost one of its characters with Critique's retirement to stud. Critique never quite reached the heights that were entertained for him after his close second in the Grand Criterium and could never be trusted implicitly, but he was undoubtedly a high-class middle-distance colt on his day. The Vanian brothers, who bought him in mid-1981 when his reputation had sunk to its lowest and who passed him on to stand at Stone Farm, Lexington, Kentucky, at a fee of 15,000 dollars (live foal), have good reason to be well pleased with their purchase. There are many examples of an entire's enthusiasm for racing fading in its third season, and with Critique, whose interest had needed rekindling less than halfway through his second season, trainer Cecil faced an unenviable task. Cecil proved equal to it though, and Critique kept both form and enthusiasm quite well through a fairly busy season. Indeed the only time he was out of the frame was in the Trusthouse Forte Prix de l'Arc de Triomphe at Longchamp on his final start when, on ground much softer than is ideal for him, he finished a creditable eighth of seventeen to Akiyda.
Critique was ridden in all but two of his races after joining Cecil from Vincent

O'Brien by Piggott, who clearly struck up a good understanding with him. When Critique won the Cumberland Lodge Stakes at Ascot in 1981 with Piggott in the saddle he didn't start running until half a mile from home and made up a remarkable amount of ground from last place to win, in the end, quite impressively. In 1982 similar tactics paid off with thrilling wins in two good races, the Hardwicke Stakes at Royal Ascot and the September Stakes at Kempton. Even to those used to watching the horse run, Critique's prospects looked slim in the Hardwicke as he turned for home at the rear of the field and came under fairly strong pressure almost as soon as the field of eight had straightened up. Piggott brought Critique with his effort on the outside and, after tending for a moment to hang in behind the Irish filly Stanerra, Critique really began to run. He hit the front well inside the last furlong and won by a length from Glint of Gold, from whom he received 5 lb. In the September Stakes, granted pattern-race status for the first time, Critique had a simpler task although neither the sharp course nor the slightly shorter distance of eleven furlongs were to his advantage. A heavily-backed odds-on shot, Critique raced in closer touch than usual until eased back on the turn and was then produced with a strong run again on the outside. His supporters had an anxious moment or two when Critique veered sharply right under pressure at around the furlong marker, but once straightened up he had the speed to win rather cleverly from Commodore Blake and Criterion in a finish of necks.

Of Critique's other performances his fourth to Kalaglow in the King George VI and Queen Elizabeth Diamond Stakes, beaten about three and a half lengths, and his half-length second to Easter Sun in the Aston Park Stakes at Newbury were particularly meritorious. Although it wasn't apparent at the time Critique faced an extremely stiff task conceding 7 lb to Easter Sun in the latter event since Easter Sun went on to win the Coronation Cup at Epsom in which Critique himself was a three-length third at level weights. Critique's display in the Ormonde Stakes is also noteworthy; this, however, because it reveals another side to his nature. Long odds on and looking to have a simple task in a field of six, Critique hardly took hold of his bridle at any stage. He was soon twenty lengths behind and being chased along and Piggott tried a variety of tactics to make him go, to little avail. Critique was beginning to get on terms when becoming rather boxed in on the turn into the straight, and only close home did Piggott manage to coax him into second behind the easy winner Six Mile Bottom. Frankly we thought Critique behaved thoroughly mulishly. Cecil told us that Critique had hated the track; with an outside rail all the way round, he explained, Critique seemed to think he was heading into a cul-de-sac and didn't want to race at all. Critique is genuine enough, he said, but is a character who does have his days.

Critique's sire Roberto had an exceptionally successful year in 1982 and was also represented in Europe by Real Shadai, Silver Hawk, Slightly Dangerous and Touching Wood. The dam Cambrienne, from a top-class family, un-

*Hardwicke Stakes, Ascot—Critique comes with a late run
to beat Glint of Gold (noseband), Stanerra and
Lafontaine (rails) in the rain*

Mr Garo Vanian's "Critique"

fortunately died in April shortly after her premature foal by Northern Dancer had also died. Critique is easily the best of Cambrienne's produce to reach the racecourse so far but she bred several other winners, including the fillies Cambretta (also by Roberto) and Rose Red (by Northern Dancer). Cambretta

Critique (USA) (br.c. 1978)	Roberto (b 1969)	Hail to Reason (br 1958)	Turn-to
			Nothirdchance
		Bramalea (b 1959)	Nashua
			Rarelea
	Cambrienne (br 1969)	Sicambre (br 1948)	Prince Bio
			Sif
		Torbella III (br 1955)	Tornado
			Djebellica

has made a fine start to her own career at stud, her first foal Pluralisme winning the Prix des Chenes at Longchamp in September. Rose Red, sent to stud after winning as a two-year-old for O'Brien in 1981, was reported in August in foal to Mr Prospector. In 1983 O'Brien will have in his stable Cambrienne's three-year-old colt by The Minstrel, named Silurian, as well as her two-year-old by Alleged.

A neat, attractive colt who did well from three to four, Critique was suited by a mile and a half and did all his winning on a sound surface, although he acted on any going. Right-handed courses seemed to bring out the best in him and he went particularly well at Ascot. Critique was occasionally blinkered and won in them at Leopardstown as a two-year-old, but he didn't wear them after he joined Cecil. He possessed an excellent turn of foot. *H. Cecil.*

CROFTHALL 5 ch.h. Native Bazaar 122–Woodland Promise 76 (Philemon **110** 119) (1981 6s 7d 6fg* 6g³ 6g* 6fg⁴ 6fg² 5d* 5g* 6f² 6fg² 7g 5g³ 6s² 6d³ 1982 6f² 5fg⁴ 6f³ 6f* 5fg 6f 5f 5fg) compact horse; first foal; dam unplaced on flat and over hurdles; gained first 2 wins of his career in sellers as a 3-y-o but improved considerably; developed into a fair handicapper at 4 yrs and made dramatic progress in 1982, running well in top company; looked in tremendous shape when gaining a well-deserved win in Thirsk Sprint Stakes in May, beating Lucky Hunter by a length, and acquitted himself with great credit afterwards; had earlier finished in frame in Thirsk Hall Stakes, Palace House Stakes at Newmarket and Duke of York Stakes, in last-named event finishing about 1½ lengths third to Jester; stayed 7f but best at shorter distances; acted on any going but clearly went well on firm; suitable mount for a boy; sometimes gave a bit of trouble at start and reportedly severed an artery when kicking out at rails on last intended appearance; most consistent and a credit to his trainer; retired to Melbourne Hall Stud, York, fee £600 (Oct. 1st). *R. Whitaker.*

CROFT RISE 3 br.g. Sit In The Corner–Como Queen (Como 120) (1981 5f 5g 8g 6s 1982 8g) compact, fair sort; poor form, including in a seller. *E. Weymes.* —

CROGHAN HILL 7 b.h. Lord Gayle 124–Good Report (Golden Cloud) (1981 10d* 16d* 12v 12g 12g 12d 1982 10d 16fg⁴ 12g² 16fg⁴ 11.5g* 11d 12g 12s) tall, leggy Irish horse; useful performer; beat Polisteppin by a short head, pair well clear, in quite valuable handicap at Galway in September; always struggling when remote last of 6 behind Fine Sun in Doonside Cup at Ayr next time; had run respectably earlier, and been in frame at Leopardstown and the Curragh (twice); effective from 1¼m to 2m but doesn't stay extreme distances; acts on any going. *D. Weld, Ireland.* 97

CROONING BERRY 3 ch.c. Crooner 119–Strawberry Ice (Arctic Storm 134) (1981 NR 1982 8fg) 1,050Y; tall, close-coupled colt; half-brother to 13f winner South Georgia (by Ballymoss); dam Irish 1m winner; unquoted when in rear behind Relkina in 11-runner maiden race at Sandown in August. *S. Matthews.* —

CROSBY COIN 2 br.g. Crooner 119–Moneywise (Hook Money 124) (1982 5g 5d 6s) Mar 4; 150Y; neat gelding; well behind all outings, including in a £2,000 seller; off course 6 months after second start. *T. M. Jones.* —

CROSBY EMPEROR 3 gr.g. Young Emperor 133–Lady Whistler (Whistling Wind 123) (1981 5d 5g 6fg 7f 8s 1982 9g 12f 8f) lightly-made gelding; in rear in varied company, including selling; has worn blinkers; sold, probably for export to Norway, 920 gns Doncaster June Sales. *J. Calvert.* —

CROSSWAYS 3 b.c. Habitat 134–Silky 112 (Nijinsky 138) (1981 5g 6s 7g 1982 9fg³ 10fg² 10f* 8f 11g 12g 10d 10g) strong, good-bodied, good-looking colt; had outstanding chance at weights when landing odds decisively by 1½ lengths from Meeka Gold in slowly-run 8-runner XYZ Handicap at Newcastle in May; ran creditably several other starts, including when length second of 9 to Electric in White Rose Stakes at Ascot and 4½ lengths last of 5 to Jalmood in Mecca Bookmakers Scottish Derby at Ayr in July on fifth; needs further than 1m and should stay 1½m; acts on firm going; blinkered last 2 outings, sweating up and running moderately on second occasion. *H. Wragg.* 97

Thirsk Sprint Stakes—Crofthall gains a well-deserved win from Lucky Hunter

CROWEBRONZE 4 ch.f. Huntercombe 133–Frances Louise 88 (Saint Crespin III 132) (1981 5d⁴ 6g 6s 5d 5s 5f* 6f 5fg² 5f³ 5fg⁴ 6f 5g 5fg³ 5g 5s 6g 5s 6d 1982 5fg⁴ 6f³ 5f 6g* 6fg 6s² 6fg 6f⁴ 6f² 6g³ 6d⁴ 6f 6f) compact filly; sprint handicapper; beat Amanda Mary a short head at Carlisle in May; acts on any going; sometimes starts slowly; apprentice ridden. *R. Hollinshead.*   **46**

CROWECOPPER 3 b.g. Netherkelly 112–Cammy 75 (Sing Sing 134) (1981 NR 1982 8s 12d) second foal; dam best at sprint distances; backward when well behind in minor event at Warwick and maiden race at Redcar in the autumn. *R. Hollinshead.*   **—**

CROWN 3 b.c. Realm 129–Moneycashen 72 (Hook Money 124) (1981 5s² 5fg² 5g 6g 5s⁴ 5g 1982 8g 8s³ 8d* 7g* 8.2d⁴ 7fg* 8fg³ 7.2g² 7fg 8s* 8v) sturdy, compact colt; won small race at Cagnes-sur-Mer in spring; subsequently ran well in handicaps, winning fairly valuable events at Doncaster, Chester and York (battled on well to beat Transient a head in October) and being placed in Britannia Stakes at Royal Ascot (5½ lengths third to Bali Dancer) and Sporting Chronicle Handicap at Haydock (head second to Blue Emmanuelle); stays 1m well; acts on a firm surface but is ideally suited by some give in the ground; blinkered once at 2 yrs; sometimes makes the running; game and consistent. *C. Booth.*   **88**

CROWN COUNSEL 3 ch.g. Simbir 130–Edie's Court (Barron's Court) (1981 NR 1982 12fg 14fg 11g 8fg* 8fg³ 8fg 10.6s 8s) lengthy gelding; poor walker; second foal; dam never ran; won ladies race at Redcar in June; suited by 1m; acts on a firm surface; suitable mount for an inexperienced rider. *P. Feilden.*   **60 d**

CROWN FLIRT 3 ch.c. Sharpen Up 127–Saucy Flirt 102 (King's Troop 118) (1981 NR 1982 8fg) 19,000Y; good sort; good walker; half-brother to Prix de Diane winner Madam Gay (by Star Appeal), to a winner in Brazil and a winning plater; dam stayed 6f; kept on in closing stages without being punished unduly when eighth of 19 to Always Welcome in Wood Ditton Stakes at Newmarket in April; not seen out again. *L. Cumani.*   **—**

CROWN JULES 4 gr.f. Abwah 118–Charville 73 (Town Crier 119) (1981 8f 10.1fg 8.3fg 12fg 10f 12g 1982 12f) neat filly; poor plater; sometimes blinkered. *P. Cundell.*   **—**

CRUMBLE 2 b.f. Thatch 136–Small Dessert (Derring-Do 131) (1982 5g² 5g²) Mar 19; 7,200Y; neat filly; first foal; dam never ran; went down by 3 lengths to all-the-way winner Dance In May in maiden race at Leicester in June but would have been closer but for swerving badly over 2f out; short-priced favourite, every chance when beaten 2 lengths by Mydella in similar event at Wolverhampton later in month; should stay 1m. *B. Hobbs.*   **77**

CRUNCHER 2 b.c. Tachypous 128–Marphousha (Only for Life 126) (1982 6f 6g⁴ 6g³ 7f³ 8.2fg² 8.2d 10d³) Apr 28; 2,000Y; big colt; has a growth above off-fore knee; half-brother to 1974 2-y-o 5f winner Desert Fire (by Sky Gipsy) and a winning hurdler; in frame in sellers; stays well; yet to race on really soft going but acts on any other; consistent. *W. Wharton.*   **64**

Prix Eclipse, Saint-Cloud—Crystal Glitters holds off the British-trained Drumalis

CRUSADER CASTLE (USA) 3 ch.c. The Minstrel 135–Mille Fleurs 100 **97**
(Jacinto) (1981 7s 10g³ 1982 11g 12f² 14g² 14d* 12f² 14f² 14fg² 14.6g 14v* 14v)
big, handsome colt; half-brother to a winner in USA by Damascus and to a
winning hurdler; dam, successful over 7.6f, is half-sister to Mill Reef; decisively
won 21-runner maiden race at Sandown in July and showed much improved
form when trotting up by 8 lengths from Bater in St Leger Italiano at Milan
in September; ran creditably most other starts, on seventh going down by a
length to Broken Rail (pair well clear) in Melrose Handicap at York; suited by
a test of stamina; acts on any going but revels in the mud; sometimes bandaged
off-hind. *I. Balding.*

CRYMLYN 2 b.f. Welsh Pageant 132–Cribyn 96 (Brigadier Gerard 144) (1982 — p
6g) Mar 1; lengthy, useful-looking filly; first foal; dam, winner of both her
starts over 7.2f and 1m at 3 yrs, is half-sister to 1,000 Guineas winner Caergwrle
and good miler St Chad; 16/1 and in need of race, showed good speed until
beaten and eased right up after 4f in 19-runner maiden event won by What Lake
at Newmarket in September; the type to do better. *W. Hastings-Bass.*

CRYSTAL GLITTERS (USA) 2 b.c. Blushing Groom 131–Tales To Tell **121**
(Donut King) (1982 6g* 7f³ 6.5d* 7s³) May 30; $105,000Y; half-brother
to several minor winners in USA; dam, smart winner at up to 1m, is half-sister
to dam of Danzatore; made a promising debut when successful in newcomers
race at Deauville in August, beating L'Emigrant by a short neck, and landed a
valuable prize when beating Drumalis by ½ length in Prix Eclipse at Saint-Cloud
in October (swerved at distance); also ran well in Prix de la Salamandre at Longchamp in between, finishing 3 lengths third of 6 to dead-heaters Deep Roots
and Maximova, and put up a good display when 2 lengths third of 16 to L'
Emigrant in Criterium de Maisons-Laffitte late in October; will be suited by 1m;
acts on any going; sure to win more races. *M. Saliba, France.*

CRYSTAL VISION 3 ch.f. Sagaro 133–Deep Blue (Deep Diver 134) (1981 —
NR 1982 8d) 540Y; first foal; dam well beaten both starts; 20/1 when out
of first 9 of 20 behind Dame de Fer in maiden race at Warwick in April. *H.
Candy.*

CUBIC ZIRCONIA 2 b. or br.g. Averof 123–Whistling Waltz (Whistler 129) **83**
(1982 5fg² 5g³ 5fg* 5fg³ 6f³ 7g⁴ 7g 8.2g 8g) Mar 2; 5,000Y; rather leggy gelding;
half-brother to 3-y-o 10.4f winner Fair Fantasia (by Tachypous) and to 2
winners in Scandinavia; dam Irish 5f winner; made virtually all when winning
maiden auction event at Haydock in May; ran creditably several times afterwards, on seventh start being beaten little more than 2 lengths when fifth of 10
to Shadan in nursery at Yarmouth; best form up to 7f; has raced only on a
sound surface; blinkered when last on final outing. *R. Williams.*

CUDGEL 9 br.g. The Brianstan 128–Pelta (Border Chief 101) (1981 6g 5f **84**
6fg 6fg 5g 6g² 6fg 6fg² 6v* 1982 6f⁴ 5fg³ 6g 6f⁴ 6fg 6d³ 7g³ 8f⁴ 7s 6s) fairly
useful handicapper at his best; third at Beverley, Chester and York; stays
1m but has done all his winning at shorter distances; acts on any going; ideal
mount for an inexperienced rider; has won 5 times at Redcar. *P. Rohan.*

CUEVAS (USA) 3 b.c. Caro 133–Strip Poker (Bold Bidder) (1981 6g⁴ 6g⁴ **70**
1982 6s⁴ 6g² 7fg³ 7d 7g³ 7f³ 7fg² 7.6d 7fg² 8f) lengthy, lightly-made, quite
attractive colt; in frame in varied company; should stay 1m; best form on a
sound surface; blinkered last 2 starts; looks none too genuine. *P. Walwyn.*

CUILLIN GAEL 3 ch.f. Scottish Rifle 127–Gentle Gael 97 (Celtic Ash) (1981 —
6g 1982 11.7d 12f 12v) well-made filly; behind in maiden and minor races.
J. Dunlop.

CUMANA 2 b.g. Sparkler 130–Gentle Gael 97 (Celtic Ash) (1982 5fg 6f 7f —
7fg) May 20; 9,600Y; workmanlike gelding; has a rather round action; brother
to 1980 2-y-o 1m winner Crystal Gael and half-brother to winners here and
abroad, including useful sprinter Cree Song (by Song); soundly beaten, including
in valuable sellers at York. *P. Rohan.*

CUMREW 2 b.c. Gunner B 126–Almadena 73 (Dairialatan 111) (1982 7d **76**
7fg 7g) May 3; useful-looking colt; good walker; third foal; half-brother to
very useful 6f and 7f winner Scarrowmanwick (by Tickled Pink); dam placed
at 2 yrs; having first race for over 2 months, put up easily best effort when
7½ lengths ninth of 30 to Mandelstam in maiden race at Newmarket in October,
final start; will stay 1¼m. *N. Vigors.*

CUMULUS 4 br.c. Relko 136–Nuageuse (Prince Regent 129) (1981 5g 5g* **81**
6v³ 6d* 6f* 6fg 6fg 6g) 1982 6fg4 6f* 7g³ 7fg* 7g 7fg³ 7d 7f³ 7.2s³) strong,
compact, good-bodied colt; poor walker; favourite when winning handicaps at
Thirsk in April and Doncaster in July; stays 7f; acts on any going; has run
creditably for an apprentice; sold to R. Atkins 14,000 gns Newmarket Autumn
Sales. *H. T. Jones.*

CURALE 5 ch.g. Le Johnstan 123–Last Sensation (Compensation 127) (1981 **39**
5g 7f 6fg 6g 5f 5g 10s 1982 6f 6f 6f³ 6fg 8fg 6g 6s) hollow-backed gelding;
plater; third at Catterick in June, first placing of his career; stays 6f; has worn
blinkers and bandages. *R. Ward.*

CURRAVILLA 2 gr.c. Nishapour 125–Domination (Luthier 126) (1982 5f* **98**
8d³ 8s4) Mar 1; IR 10,000Y; half-brother to Irish 6f and 1¼m winner Ascending
Star (by Ballymore); dam unraced daughter of sister to Match III and Reliance
II; 5/4 favourite when winning 8-runner maiden race at Leopardstown in June
by 1½ lengths from Gormanstown Prince; not seen out again until the autumn
when in frame behind Danzatore in 2 races at the Curragh, beaten 5¾ lengths
in Ashford Castle Stakes and 11½ lengths in Panasonic Beresford Stakes; may
stay 1¼m. *J. Oxx, Ireland.*

CURRENT PATTIE (USA) 3 ch.f. Little Current–Proud Pattie (Noble **—**
Commander) (1981 6g 6g4 1982 10fg 7g 8s) attractive, lengthy filly; good
mover; ran well to be fourth of 13 to Woodstream in William Hill Cheveley
Park Stakes at Newmarket in 1981; favourite all 3 starts at 3 yrs in varied
company but finished well beaten each time; bred to stay middle distances.
B. Hills.

CURRENT RAISER 2 b.f. Filiberto 123–Miss Budock Vean (Never Say Die **89**
137) (1982 6g 7fg 7g 6d 7g²) May 12; well-grown filly; second foal; dam poor
maiden; length second of 22 to Toveris in maiden race at Newmarket in October,
easily best effort; finds 6f on sharp side and will be suited by 1m+. *C. Brittain.*

CURVE THE WIND 3 b.c. Windjammer (USA)–Caught In The Rye 97 **89 d**
(Manacle 123) (1981 5fg³ 5g 5g 1982 5fg³ 6f* 7f* 7fg 6g³ 5fg4 5.3f) tall,
rather lightly-made colt; won maiden race at Brighton in May and minor event
at Epsom (made all) in June; needs further than 5f and stays 7f; acts well on
firm going and has yet to race on soft; does best when ridden up with pace.
P. Haslam.

CURZON HOUSE 5 ch.m. Green God 128–Laburnum Grove 70 (Pall Mall **37 d**
132) (1981 5s 5s4 6s 5d 7fg 5f 6g 7f 1982 6d 5d 5fg³ 5f4 6f 5g 6fg 5g 5fg 5.8f)
short-coupled mare; sprint plater; probably acts on any going; used to wear
blinkers. *J. Perrett.*

CUSTER (USA) 3 b.c. Chieftain–La Chunga (Bolero) (1981 6f* 5f* 5.1d* **—**
6d* 6fg* 6fg4 1982 6fg) strong, good-bodied, attractive colt; unbeaten in
his first 5 starts at 2 yrs, gaining most important successes in Chesterfield Stakes
at Newmarket and Washington Singer Stakes at Newbury; top weight and not
fully wound up, never placed to challenge when in rear behind Admiral's
Princess in valuable handicap at Newmarket in May; not seen out again; stays
6f; seems to act on any going. *H. Cecil.*

CUTACROSS (USA) 2 b.c. Cutlass–Mother Superior (Bold Ruler) (1982 **72 p**
5fg 7fg) Apr 16; $75,000Y; quite attractive, well-made colt; good walker;
third foal; dam, closely related to smart King of the Castle, won twice at up to
1m; not given unnecessarily hard time when eighth of 11 behind dead-heaters
Kuwait Tower and Muscatite in maiden event at Ascot in July, second outing;
should do better. *G. Harwood.*

CUT A DASH 3 b.g. Bold Lad (Ire) 133–Rosalie II 66 (Molvedo 137) (1981 **64**
6s 1982 12fg 16fg² 14s²) quite attractive, well-made gelding; poor mover;
staying maiden; seems to act on any going; sold out of R. Hern's stable 2,300 gns
Ascot 2nd July Sales after first start; useful young hurdler. *Mrs N. Smith.*

CUTE FACE 2 ch.c. High Award 119–Consequently 101 (Con Brio 121) (1982 **—**
5fg 5d 5d) Feb 9; sturdy, compact colt; half-brother to a winning plater;
dam stayed 1m; no form in maiden races. *D. Leslie.*

CUT LOOSE 3 b.f. High Top 131–Cutle 86 (Saint Crespin III 132) (1981 **118**
7fg 1982 10.5fg* 12f 12fg 10d* 10fg² 10g)
Sir John Astor must bless the day in 1960 when he arranged to exchange
his mare Indian Twilight for a three-year period with Mr Dick Hollingsworth's

Middleton Stakes, York—Cut Loose is not troubled to beat Mirkan Honey

Cutter. Both mares had been good racehorses, Cutter winning the Park Hill Stakes, John Porter Stakes and Yorkshire Cup, Indian Twilight winning the Yorkshire Oaks. For some years it seemed as though the exchange had benefited neither party significantly: Indian Twilight produced one fair winner for Mr Hollingsworth but died in 1961 whilst Cutter, barren in her first year, produced a poor colt in 1962 and then Cutle. Cutle won at up to thirteen furlongs and showed just fair form. But at stud she was to make a name for herself, producing two classic winners in the Astor colours, Sharp Edge (by Silver Shark), who took the 1973 Irish Two Thousand Guineas, and the 1981 St Leger winner Cut Above (by High Top). Cutle has produced three other winning colts, the useful pair So Sharp (by So Blessed) and Murat (by Brigadier Gerard), and the hurdler and point-to-pointer Scar (by Relic), whilst her first daughter, Cut Above's full sister Cut Loose, proved herself a smart performer in the latest season.

	High Top (br 1969)	Derring-Do (br 1961)	Darius / Sipsey Bridge
Cut Loose (b.f. 1979)		Camenae (b 1961)	Vimy / Madrilene
	Cutle (ch 1963)	Saint Crespin III (ch 1956)	Aureole / Neocracy
		Cutter (b 1955)	Donatello II / Felucca

Cut Loose served notice that she might be something out of the ordinary when winning the nine-runner Middleton Stakes at York on her reappearance in May. A promising fifth in a Newmarket maiden race on her only outing at two years, she started a strong second favourite. Held up in a slowly-run race, still at the back of the field turning for home, she enjoyed a far from clear run when asked to improve. When she finally managed to get through she quickened in fine style and ran on strongly to beat Mirkan Honey going away by three quarters of a length despite edging to her left. It wasn't until August, when she took Newcastle's Virginia Stakes, that Cut Loose managed to win again, but she was far from disgraced in the Oaks and the Yorkshire Oaks in the meantime. At Epsom she was beaten under eight lengths into seventh behind Time Charter, racing with the leaders as they turned for home, then finding the pace too hot. In the Yorkshire Oaks, in which she was the longest-priced of the trio competing from her stable, Cut Loose looked to be going really well on the home turn but found little and drifted to her left when let down, eventually finishing a six-length fifth of seven to Awaasif. Conditions suited Cut Loose down to the ground in the Virginia Stakes and she showed her best form to win going away by a length and a half from Dancing Rocks. The evidence suggested a mile and a quarter was Cut Loose's ideal trip; some give in the ground appeared to suit her well too (her two-month absence from the racecourse after the Oaks had been ascribed to sore shins after racing on the firm ground); and the two rivals which appeared to present the greatest opposition, Dancing Rocks and Dish Dash, were giving her 3 lb. Cut Loose looked tremendously well and was always going strongly in another slowly-run race. With three furlongs to travel the leaders quickened away and caught Cut Loose rather flat footed but, roused along, she wore them down inside the last furlong and won with something in hand. Appearances in the Valdoe Stakes at Goodwood in September and in the Sun Chariot Stakes at Newmarket the following month brought Cut Loose no further success; she started favourite for both. At Goodwood she did well to finish second to Peacetime, beaten three parts of a length, after experiencing difficulty in obtaining a run. At Newmarket she was beginning to go in her coat and ran her one poor race; she could manage no better than sixth, twelve lengths behind Time Charter.

Cut Loose's family is a stout one. Cutle would have stayed further than thirteen furlongs, and Cutter was one of three half-sisters to win the Park Hill Stakes, the others being Ark Royal and Kyak (the last-named grandam of Oaks winner Bireme and St Leger runner-up Buoy, and great-grandam of the out-and-out stayer Sea Anchor). Nevertheless Cut Loose showed her best form at a mile and a quarter, and she ran as though not quite seeing out the distance of the Yorkshire Oaks. A compact, good-bodied filly with a round action, Cut Loose has been retired and will be covered by Final Straw. She should prove another valuable broodmare for her owner. *R. Hern.*

CUT'N DRY 2 b.c. Dubassoff–Dissipation 83 (Disciplinarian) (1982 6f 7f³ — 8d) Jan 26; 7,000Y; brother to 6f and 7f winner Winged Beauty, and half-brother to 2 winners; dam won over 5f at 2 yrs; in rear all outings, twice last. *G. Pritchard-Gordon.*

CUT THROAT 4 br.c. Sharpen Up 127–Zantedeschia 91 (Zimone) (1981 **102** 7d 8g⁴ 7f⁴ 7fg² 6g 7.3fg 8fg² 1982 7f 7.2fg² 8f 7.2h³ 6g⁴ 7fg) lightly-made, quite attractive colt; good mover; hasn't won since his 2-y-o days and has become rather disappointing; placed twice at Haydock in 1982 however, finishing length second to Mummy's Game in Cold Shield Windows Trophy in May and 2 lengths third behind impressive Indian King in John of Gaunt Stakes in June; stays 1m; possibly needs a sound surface; ran poorly when blinkered once as a 2-y-o; sent to race in USA. *H. Candy.*

CUTTING COMMENT 7 b.g. Sharpen Up 127–Mrs Hauksbee 102 (Pindari **§§** 124) (1981 10.4g 1982 13s 11s 12d 7.6fg 12g⁴) disappointing and ungenuine handicapper; stays 11f; probably acts on any going; usually wears blinkers. *M. James.*

William Hill Trophy, York—the most valuable event on Timeform Charity Day which raised a record £93,445 for cancer charities. Celestial Dancer is first past the post but the race is awarded to Cyril's Choice

CWMYREITHIN 6 b.m. Roxy–Whitney (Venture VII 129) (1981 16fg⁴ — 18fg 12f 12f 17.1h² 14.6f 16h 12g 1982 16.9fg) staying handicapper; acts on hard going; suitable mount for an apprentice. *M. Tate.*

CYNICAL SAM (USA) 3 gr.g. Grey Dawn II 132–Cool Mood (Northern — Dancer) (1981 NR 1982 10d 10.1fg 10f 10fg 11.7d 12f) $37,000F, 6,200 gns 2-y-o; big, strong gelding; half-brother to several winners, including good 1980 Canadian 2-y-o Passing Mood (by Buckpasser); dam won Canadian Oaks; behind in varied company; blinkered last 4 starts; sometimes bandaged. *J. O'Donoghue.*

CYPRUS GARDEN 4 ch.f. Wishing Star 117–French Furze (Hard Tack — 111§) (1981 7fg 7g 6v 7s² 7f 8f⁴ 1982 10d 10fg 12d) lengthy, plain filly; plater; well beaten in non-sellers in 1982; stays 1m; usually blinkered; often bandaged behind nowadays; sold 400 gns Doncaster October Sales. *M. Chapman.*

CYPRUS SKY 5 ch.g. Redundant 120–Palestra 92 (Palestine 133) (1981 **73** 8d 9g* 10g⁴ 8fg² 8fg* 10fg⁴ 12f² 15.5f² 8s³ 12s* 1982 12f 12f⁴ 10d² 12d 7.6f 16g³ 12v³) tall, close-coupled gelding; placed in amateur riders races at Lingfield (head second to Big Trouble), Beverley (distant third) and Ascot; stays at least 1½m; acts on any going; usually owner ridden. *R. Smyth.*

CYRIL'S CHOICE 3 b.c. Malicious–Saran (Le Levanstell 122) (1981 5f **107** 5fg* 5f⁴ 5g* 7g* 6f³ 7f³ 7.2fg 6d³ 1982 8.2d 6f* 6g⁴ 5fg² 6fg* 5.8g 6f² 6f 6g³ 6g* 6fg*(dis) 6s² 6d) neat colt; showed improved form, winning handicaps at Ripon and York (2); awarded William Hill Trophy on disqualification of Celestial Dancer on first occasion at York and accounted for On Return by 2½ lengths on second; also first past post in handicap at Thirsk but was disqualified for hampering third; ran well most other starts; best at 6f; acts on any going; genuine and consistent though has a tendency to hang and isn't an easy ride. *S. Mellor.*

CZAR'S BRIDE (USA) 3 b.f. Northern Dancer–American Legacy (Hail **72** to Reason) (1981 5.8h⁴ 8fg 7g² 1982 8.5fg 10.2f⁴ 12fg³ 12fg² 12.2f⁴ 11d) quite an attractive filly; quite a modest maiden; will stay 1¾m; blinkered last 2 starts. *P. Walwyn.*

D

DABDOUB 2 ch.c. Habat 127–No Cards 109 (No Mercy 126) (1982 7fg³ 7fg² **98** 8s³ 7g² 7s* 7s⁴) Mar 27; 5,600Y; tall, strong colt; first foal; dam won at up to 1m; won 12-runner minor event at Chepstow in October by 4 lengths; in frame all other starts, on final one finishing good fourth behind Holloway Wonder in nursery at Leicester; best form at 7f; seems to act on any going; genuine and consistent. *P. Cole.*

DAGEEGAH (USA) 3 b.c. Timeless Moment–Pia's Lady (Pia Star) (1981 **88** 5g 5g⁴ 7fg⁴ 6fg² 7fg* 7.3d³ 8.2s* 7s² 8.2s⁴ 1982 10f⁴ 12f 10g 12g⁴ 10fg 13d 10.2s* 12g) strong, attractive colt who carries plenty of condition; good mover; showed first form at 3 yrs when winning apprentice race at Bath in October; should stay 1½m; probably acts on any going but seems particularly well suited by soft ground; ran abysmally third start. *F. Durr.*

DAGENHAM 2 b.f. Captain James 123–Castletimon (Tudor Music 131) (1982 — 5d) Feb 4; IR 7,400Y; small, lightly-made filly; third living produce; half-sister to a prolific winner in Italy; dam lightly-raced half-sister to very useful middle-distance performer Shamsan; 8/1 and very fit, eighth of 17 to Wayward Polly in seller at Ripon in August. *H. T. Jones.*

DAHA (USA) 2 b.f. What A Pleasure–Mostly (Grey Dawn II 132) (1982 **70** 6fg 6g 6g) Jan 29; $155,000Y; half-sister to winners in North America and France, including Bude (by Cornish Prince), a smart sprint stakes winner at 2 yrs; dam, sister to a stakes winner, won at up to 7f; plating-class maiden; not raced after July. *J. Dunlop.*

DAISY TREADLIGHT 3 b.f. Tachypous 128–Princess's Time (Arctic Time — 127) (1981 NR 1982 9fg 11.7f) 5,000Y; half-sister to 3 winners, including middle-distance stayer Lousy Time (by Lauso); dam half-sister to Irish St Leger winner Allangrange; always behind in newcomers race at Wolverhampton and maiden event at Bath early in year. *C. Nelson.*

DALBREAC 3 br.f. Bustino 136–Corriefeol 102 (Jaipur) (1981 6fg 8fg⁴ 8d 6d — 1982 7f 10fg 10g) rather leggy, lightly-made filly; plating-class maiden; stays 1¼m; sold 900 gns Ascot November Sales. *J. Dunlop*.

DALBURY 4 b.g. Royal Palace 131–Tikki Tavi 92 (Honeyway 125) (1981 NR **69** 1982 8fg³ 10f* 12f 10.2g* 10fg 10g) sparely-made gelding; half-brother to several winners, including useful 1m to 1½m winner Duration (by Only for Life); dam a sprinter; having only his second outing when beating Orange Tip by 2½ lengths in maiden event at Redcar in May; beat Aberfield by ¾ length in slowly-run 4-runner handicap at Doncaster the following month but was very disappointing afterwards; stays 1¼m; yet to race on a soft surface; possibly isn't one to trust implicitly; sold to P. Haynes 6,600 gns Newmarket Autumn Sales. *J. W. Watts*.

DALEGARTH 4 ch.g. Laser Light 118–Inkflash (Hul a Hul 124) (1981 5d* **86** 5g³ 5fg³ 5d 5d 5f⁴ 5fg 5fg 5d³ 5g 1982 5.1f 5f 5fg* 5g 5g 5fg⁴ 5fg 5d) compact, sturdy gelding; good mover; none too reliable these days but made all and held off Telegraph Boy by a neck in handicap at Sandown in July; very speedy and unlikely to stay beyond 5f; possibly not at his best on very soft ground; blinkered once as a 2-y-o; often bandaged; reared leaving stalls second outing and dwelt fifth start; sold 5,200 gns Newmarket Autumn Sales, for export to Italy. *K. Ivory*.

DALMALLY 3 ch.f. Sharpen Up 127–Victa 79 (Northfields) (1981 6d* 1982 8g **80** 8.5f* 8fg) rangy, good sort; good mover; made much of running and kept on well to beat Wink by ½ length in NMT Ebbisham Stakes (Handicap) at Epsom in June; stays 1m well; seems to act on any going; swishes her tail under pressure; sold to BBA 36,000 gns Newmarket December Sales. *R. Price*.

DALMANE 2 br.c. So Blessed 130–Opium 97 (Espresso 122) (1982 6f² 7g⁴ 7g) **83** May 10; tall, rather leggy, attractive colt; half-brother to quite useful 1976 2-y-o winner Mecanopsis (by Major Portion); dam won at up to 1½m; prominent in maiden races, on final outing finishing 5 lengths sixth of 30 to Mandelstam at Newmarket in October; will stay 1m. *P. Burgoyne*.

DALTRA 4 ch.g. Majority Blue 126–Pretty Breezy (Signal Light) (1981 8.2s — 1982 7g 9f) compact gelding; lightly raced and no worthwhile form, including in a seller. *J. Toller*.

DAMASCUS PRINCE (USA) 2 b.c. Damascus–Durga (Tatan) (1982 8g) — p Apr 28; $130,000Y; attractive colt; brother to 2 winners, including very smart 1m filly Sarsar, and half-brother to numerous winners, 3 of them of stakes, including Santa Anita Derby winner An Act (by Pretense); dam never ran; 8/1, not knocked about when behind in 18-runner maiden race won by Holy Spark at Newmarket in October; sure to do better. *M. Stoute*.

DAME ASHFIELD 2 b.f. Grundy 137–African Dancer 116 (Nijinsky 138) **83 p** (1982 7d 8fg⁴ 7g³) Feb 23; good-bodied filly; second foal; half-sister to fairly useful middle-distance filly On Show (by Welsh Pageant); dam won Cheshire Oaks and Park Hill Stakes; showed plenty of promise when 50/1 for £3,600 event at Goodwood in September, making excellent late headway from last place after starting slowly to finish 4 lengths fourth of 12 to Ghaiya; kept on well when creditable third to Ski Sailing in big field of maidens at Newmarket the following month; likely to continue improving, and looks sure to win races over middle distances. *H. Wragg*.

DAME DE FER 3 b.f. Nonoalco 131–Hardware 86 (Hard Sauce 131) (1981 **81** 6f² 6fg² 7f³ 7d² 1982 8d* 10.2f² 10.2f² 10.1fg) rather leggy, lightly-made filly; kept on well to win maiden race at Warwick in April; second in 4-runner handicaps at Bath and Doncaster following month; stays 1¼m; probably acts on any going; lacks scope; sold 10,000 gns Newmarket December Sales. *H. Cecil*.

DAME PEGGY 2 gr.f. Comedy Star 121–Peggy Wig 55 (Counsel 118) (1982 — 5g 6f) Mar 28; compact filly; first foal; dam won sellers over 7f and 1m at 4 yrs; last in July in maiden race at Pontefract and valuable seller at York. *K. Stone*.

DAME SUE 6 b.m. Mandamus 120–Catherine Rose 59 (Floribunda 136) (1981 **55** 12f 12.2fg² 12g* 16f⁴ 12h³ 14fg 1982 12f* 11g 12d) strong mare; won apprentice handicap at Leicester in May; stays 2m; acts on any going. *S. Mellor*.

DANCE CARD 2 ch.f. Be My Guest 126–Ivor's Honey 91 (Sir Ivor 135) (1982 — 7g) May 13; 56,000Y; neat, quite attractive filly; first foal; dam, 1¼m winner, is sister to Irish Guinness Oaks third I've A Bee; 9/1, eighth of 15 behind Killanin's Lass in mixed-aged race at Newmarket in October. *M. Jarvis*.

DANCE IN MAY 2 br.f. Hotfoot 126–Cambus O'May 100 (Sing Sing 134) **81** (1982 5g² 5f⁴ 5f² 5g* 6fg 5fg³ 6fg 6g 5v)   Feb 26; 7,600Y; rather lightly-made filly; good mover; half-sister to fairly useful 1977 2-y-o 5f winner Gruinard (by Amber Rama); dam 6f winner; disappointing (beaten favourite in sellers last 2 starts) after winning maiden event at Leicester in June; headstrong and doesn't stay 6f; acts on firm going; blinkered eighth outing. *P. Cole.*

DANCE OF LIFE 3 b.g. Green Dancer 132–Petrovna (Reliance II 137)   (1981 **63** 5.8d 5.8f* 7s 7g 1982 7fg 6g 8g 10f 8.2f² 8.3g 7s 8.2s)   sturdy gelding; quite a modest handicapper on his day; will be suited by a return to 1¼m; acts on firm going and is probably unsuited by soft; blinkered nowadays. *M. Smyly.*

DANCE OF THE NILE 2 br.f. Quiet Fling 124–Spice Berry 63 (Tutankhamen) **59** (1982 6f 7fg 8f 7.6v 8s)   Apr 1; 5,000F, 3,000Y; rather lightly-built, fair sort; half-sister to 1m winner Scotsezo (by Scottish Rifle); dam half-sister to smart animals Red Berry and Big Bead; little worthwhile form in maiden events. *A. Ingham.*

DANCE ON WATER 2 b.g. Rapid River 127–Royal Bally 71 (Bally Russe **—** 113)   (1982 6fg 7fg 8s)   May 15; lengthy gelding; first foal; dam won over 10.6f and was quite a useful hurdler; well beaten in maiden and minor events; gelded after final outing. *W. A. Stephenson.*

DANCER'S EMULATION 2 gr.c. Dancer's Image–Mossinella 69 (Ballymoss **—** 136)   (1982 5f 7fg 7.6v 6s)   Mar 30; 3,000Y; robust, workmanlike colt; fourth foal; half-brother to winning stayer Spark Off (by Sparkler) and a winner in Trinidad; dam won over 1¼m; little worthwhile form in maiden and minor events. *M. Masson.*

DANCING ADMIRAL 2 b.c. Julio Mariner 127–Autumn Ballad 75 (Tudor **—** Melody 129)   (1982 7fg 8d)   Apr 21; big colt; half-brother to winning stayer Karminski (by Pitskelly); dam second twice over 6f; outpaced in Ribero Stakes (ninth of 13) at Doncaster in September and in maiden race (tenth of 23) at Newmarket in October; likely to do better in time. *C. Brittain.*

DANCING COAT 3 ch.f. Carnival Dancer 113–Coatham 81 (Divine Gift **—** 127)   (1981 NR 1982 7g 7fg)   small filly; second foal; sister to headstrong plater Singapore Sue; dam won 5f seller at 2 yrs; in rear in 2 sellers. *D. Smith.*

DANCING DAUGHTER 2 b.f. Dance In Time–Timur's Daughter 103 **79** (Tamerlane 128)   (1982 6g³ 6g³ 6g⁴ 7v)   Apr 13; small, lengthy filly; grand walker; half-sister to 3 winners, including useful 6f to 1½m winner Heir Presumptive (by Habitat); dam stayed at least 9f; in frame in maiden and minor events, running well when length third to Super Sioux at Chester in July on second outing; should be suited by 7f (had very stiff task and was having first race for 2 months when tried at trip). *F. J. Houghton.*

DANCING DEVIL (DEN) 6 gr.h. Dancing Lad–Prascovia (Welsh Saint 126) **?** (1981 9s² 8d⁴ 10s 8g 9g 7g² 5g 6f 6d 6g* 1982 8g 6s 8g 8g 6g² 8g² 8.5g 8g⁴ 7.5g 9g³ 6g² 7g 7v 8s)   big, strong horse; in rear twice over here in spring when trained by G. Fletcher; placed several times in Scandinavia afterwards for trainer B. Olsson, including when ½-length second of 15 to Doc Marten in SAS First Class Open Sprint at Taby in September; well beaten in good company last 3 outings, on first occasion in Bisquit Cognac Challenge Stakes at Newmarket; effective at 6f and stays 9f; acts on any going; has won for an apprentice. *J. Piednoel, France.*

DANCING DISPLAY 2 gr. or ro.f. Dancer's Image–No Display 92 (Meadow **114** Court 129)   (1982 5s³ 6fg* 7g⁴ 8s³)   Mar 19; half-sister to winners in France and Malaysia and to useful chaser Reldis (by Relko); dam, daughter of top-class filly Display, won over 7f; won minor event at Evry in July; later ran creditably when 4½ lengths fourth of 12 to Maximova in Prix du Calvados at Deauville in August and when close-up third of 9 to Belka in Prix des Reservoirs at Longchamp in October; will probably stay 1¼m. *C. Bartholomew, France.*

DANCING FEVER 3 br.f. Sweet Revenge 129–Great Emerald 75 (Great **—** Nephew 126)   (1981 5s 5g⁴ 5g 6s 6f 6f 7fg 7d 1982 8fg 7f 12.2f 8f 9g)   poor plater; sometimes blinkered; has been bandaged on near-fore. *J. Mason.*

DANCING KATE 7 ch.m. Jukebox 120–Epee (Cranach)   (1981 12g 13.4fg **30** 10f 10.6d⁴ 12g 1982 12s 10.6f 10fg² 12fg 12fg 10.8s)   workmanlike mare; plater; stays 1¾m; probably acts on any going; used to wear blinkers; suitable mount for an apprentice; bandaged behind final start. *A. Arnold.*

DANCING LIGHTS (USA) 2 b.c. Northern Dancer–My Great Aunt (Bold   **72 p**
Ruler) (1982 6d) Apr 9; $525,000Y; close-coupled, good-topped colt; fourth
foal; half-brother to a minor winner in USA by Grundy and a poor animal
by Youth; dam smart French middle-distance performer and daughter of top
filly Aunt Edith; had only one race, showing good speed until fading after
4f in Champagne Stakes at Salisbury in June. *J. Tree.*

DANCING MEG (USA) 2 b.f. Marshua's Dancer–Coxwain's Meg (Sailor) **113**
(1982 5fg 6g* 6fg 7f² 8g* 8g²) Apr 1; $88,000Y; rangy filly; good mover with
a lovely long stride; fourth foal; half-sister to very useful 1981 American 2-y-o
Michelle Mon Amour (by Best Turn); dam, half-sister to smart Cathy's Reject,
won twice at up to 4f at 2 yrs in USA; ran best race on final outing, when
excellent second, 1½ lengths behind Acclimatise, in 8-runner Hoover Fillies
Mile at Ascot in September; won twice previously, maiden event at Lingfield
and nursery at York; did extremely well to win at York, having to make up
tremendous amount of ground in straight after being hampered early on; stays
really well; yet to race on a soft surface; genuine. *R. Laing.*

DANCING NYMPH 3 ch.f. Dance In Time–Constant Nymph 85 (Venture   **64**
VII 129) (1981 6d 6g 6g 1982 12.2f 12g⁴ 12.2f² 12d² 10d³ 10.6s 12d²) strong,
deep-girthed filly; runner-up in maiden races in the North; stays 1½m; acts on
firm going and a soft surface; tended to wander and found little under pressure
fourth start. *J. Fitzgerald.*

DANCING ROCKS 3 b.f. Green Dancer 132–Croda Rossa (Grey Sovereign   **118**
128§) (1981 5fg* 6s* 1982 8d 8f² 8fg³ 8f⁴ 10fg* 12fg⁴ 10d² 10g)
Sir Philip Oppenheimer had considerable strength in depth with his three-
year-old fillies, all of whom were trained by that master of the art of training
three-year-old fillies Harry Wragg. On The House proved herself one of the
best milers of the year with victories in the One Thousand Guineas and Sussex
Stakes, Zinzara showed smart form over middle distances, picking up the Sir
Charles Clore Memorial Stakes and the Prix de Psyche, and Dancing Rocks
put up a scintillating display to win the Nassau Stakes besides finishing in the
frame in three more pattern races. Sir Philip is on record as saying that he is
more enthusiastic about breeding than racing—'anticipation is much better than
fact'—but with mares of this calibre eventually entering his Hascombe Stud
it isn't difficult to envisage the fact matching, if not surpassing, the anticipation
in future.
By the time she came to Goodwood for the Nassau at the end of July
Dancing Rocks had run four times in the current season. Her campaign could
hardly have got off to a worse start, for in the Masaka Stakes at Kempton
she became upset at the start and at no stage looked like preserving her unbeaten
record, being pulled up soon after halfway and coming back very distressed.
Her trainer was as mystified as everyone else about this dismal run, since an
hour afterwards Dancing Rocks was apparently in good shape again and a
private dope test revealed nothing untoward. Apparently the Kempton
stewards, though they inquired into Dancing Rocks's running, failed to call
for a dope test, a decision which takes some fathoming given that the filly
started a well-backed favourite.
Dancing Rocks recovered from whatever ailed her at Kempton during a
seven-week break immediately afterwards, and ran creditably in each of her
next three starts. Her best effort came in the Coronation Stakes at Royal
Ascot in which she beat her stable-companion On The House and finished
three lengths third to the impressive Chalon, losing second to Grease close home.
Yet Chalon beat Dancing Rocks even more readily into fourth in the Child
Stakes at Newmarket, and since the eleven runners for the Nassau included
the Oaks winner Time Charter, shouldering a 7 lb penalty, and the Ribblesdale
Stakes winner Dish Dash and Lancashire Oaks winner Sing Softly, both also
penalized, Dancing Rocks looked to have her work cut out. She rose to the
occasion splendidly. Held up, she made a forward move a quarter of a mile
out and quickened in tremendous fashion to take the lead off Time Charter;
gamely as the latter struggled on Dancing Rocks drew clear to score by two
lengths with Triple Tipple a length and a half away third and Sing Softly a
well-beaten fourth.
It is obvious that the Time Charter Dancing Rocks beat at Goodwood
was not in the same form as the filly who later trounced her rivals in the Dubai
Champion Stakes, and that Sing Softly and Dish Dash really needed further
to be seen to best advantage, but Dancing Rocks's victory was still a good one
and clear-cut enough to suggest she would be a force to be reckoned with during

Nassau Stakes, Goodwood—Dancing Rocks quickens in tremendous style to beat Time Charter and Triple Tipple

the rest of the year. In fact Dancing Rocks failed to win again. Though suited by a mile and a quarter she seemed to find the mile and a half of the Yorkshire Oaks a shade too far; her promising challenge petered out as she finished fourth to Awaasif, albeit beaten only about three lengths. Back to ten furlongs for the Virginia Stakes at Newcastle, Dancing Rocks couldn't match Cut Loose's late turn of foot, going down by a length and a half, while in the Sun Chariot Stakes at Newmarket she trailed in a sorry seventh to Time Charter—like so many other fillies that have failed to do themselves justice in the latter event, Dancing Rocks was evidently over the top.

Dancing Rocks (b.f. 1979)	Green Dancer (b 1972)	Nijinsky (b 1967)	Northern Dancer
			Flaming Page
		Green Valley (br 1967)	Val de Loir
			Sly Pola
	Croda Rossa (b 1967)	Grey Sovereign (gr 1948)	Nasrullah
			Kong
		Crenelle (b 1960)	Crepello
			Mulberry Harbour

Dancing Rocks, who commences her stud career with a visit to Kris, has a good pedigree. The get of her sire Green Dancer includes such pattern-race winners as Aryenne, The Dancer and Maximova—all fillies—and her dam, bought privately in 1973, comes from a good Anglo-Italian family. Dancing Rocks is the fifth live foal and second winner out of Croda Rossa—the first, Cragador (by Hoist the Flag), had training troubles but still showed himself a very useful colt on his day, winning the City of York Stakes. Since producing Dancing Rocks, Croda Rossa has foaled colts by Blakeney and Grundy in 1981 and 1982. Croda Rossa had plenty of ability, winning three of her four races in Italy, notably the mile-and-a-quarter Premio Lydia Tesio in which she beat the Italian Oaks winner; her half-brother Cerreto won the Italian Derby and a half-sister, Croda Alta, won ten races in Italy including the Premio Chiusura. The second dam ran only at three when she carried the Royal colours into third place in the Musidora Stakes before being exported to Italy, while the third dam, who foaled eight winners, won the Cheshire Oaks and was a half-sister to the Hunt Cup winner Alexander.

Each time we saw Dancing Rocks we were very taken with her—she is a good-bodied, most attractive filly and a good mover. Unfortunately she sometimes slightly spoiled her looks by sweating up and seemed a rather nervous type, but she showed no lack of pluck in her races and proved capable of running well on both firm and soft ground. *H. Wragg.*

DANCING SOVEREIGN 3 b.c. Dance In Time–Golden Treasure 106 (Crepello 136) (1981 7fg 7fg 7fg3 1982 11f 12f 11.7fg4 12f* 12f2 11.1fg 16.9fg 12g 12g) quite well-made colt; has a rather round action; won maiden race at Folkestone in July; ran respectably next time but moderately most subsequent starts; will stay 1¾m; acts on firm going; trained part of season by J. Dunlop. *M. Bolton.* **73**

DANCING VALERINA 2 br.f. Comedy Star 121–Polyandrist 92 (Polic 126) (1982 6f 6g 5.8g 7g 7d) May 27; quite attractive filly; half-sister to 3 winners, including very useful 5f performer Trigamy (by Tribal Chief); dam best at up to **60**

1¼m; poor maiden; showed form only on third outing; should stay at least 7f. *R. Price.*

DANCING WIND 2 b.f. Dance In Time–Winden (Worden II 129) (1982 7g) — p
Apr 5; big, lengthy filly; half-sister to winners in Italy by Great Nephew and Ribero and to Gran Premio d'Italia winner Wale (by Ardale); dam never ran; 16/1 and bit backward, ran well until weakening and eased right up in closing stages in 22-runner maiden event won by Toveris at Newmarket in October; sure to improve. *P. Walwyn.*

DANDANA (USA) 3 br.c. Stop The Music–Arctic Image (Fathers Image) **92 d**
(1981 NR 1982 7f* 7.6fg² 7.3fg 8fg 8.2s 8g) $70,000Y; medium-sized, lengthy, attractive colt; second foal; half-brother to a minor winner in USA; dam won at up to 7f; decisively won maiden race at Leicester in April; short-head second of 6 to Gavo in minor event at Chester in May; soundly beaten in handicaps afterwards; should stay 1m; pulled hard in blinkers final outing. *F. J. Houghton.*

DANGEROUS MOONLITE 3 gr.f. Warpath 113–Midsummer Madness 66 **71**
(Silly Season 127) (1981 6f 7g 8d⁴ 1982 8fg 12.2f² 12.2f* 13.8f² 12g³ 14g)
leggy, lightly-made filly; good walker; has rather a round action; made all and was eased in closing stages when narrowly winning maiden race at Catterick in July; ran respectably next 2 starts but badly on final one; stays 1¾m; acts on firm going; sold 3,600 gns Newmarket December Sales. *C. Thornton.*

DANISH EXPRESS 3 ch.c. Music Boy 124–Ptarmigan 75 (Hill Clown) (1981 **70**
5s 6g 6fg³ 6fg⁴ 6fg⁴ 6f 7d* 6s 7d³ 1982 6fg 8.2fg³ 8g 8d 8s* 8d 7d 8s) powerful, deep-girthed colt; apprentice ridden when keeping on well to win handicap at Bath in October; stays 1m well: ideally suited by some give in the ground. *W. Hastings-Bass.*

DANNY LA RUE 5 ch.g. Sharpen Up 127–Oceania (Aureole 132) (1981 8g —
6g 6g 6f 8g 6fg³ 5fg³ 6f 5f 5d 1982 7f 6f 6fg 10fg 7f) plater; stays 7f; blinkered nowadays. *A. Potts.*

DAN ZAKI (USA) 2 b.c. Accipiter–Patrina (Olympia) (1982 7d 6s) Apr 16; — p
$20,000Y; well-made colt; half-brother to numerous winners, including 1¼m winner Secret Harbour (by Ribot), herself dam of St Leger second Secret Man; dam ran twice; had two races at Doncaster in autumn, on second occasion finishing eighth of 25 behind Raashideah in maiden event; will stay 1¼m. *P. Haslam.*

DANZATORE (CAN) 2 b.c. Northern Dancer–Shake A Leg 106 (Raise A **127+**
Native) (1982 7fg* 8d* 8s*)

Bearing in mind the eclipse at three years of the recent champion Irish two-year-olds Storm Bird, Monteverdi and Try My Best, it's with some trepidation that we come to assess the prospects of the 1982 champion, Danzatore. Danzatore like his predecessors is trained by Vincent O'Brien; like the others he is unbeaten; and like Storm Bird and Try My Best he is a son of Northern Dancer (Monteverdi is a grandson). Unlike the others he raced exclusively in Ireland. Whereas Storm Bird, Monteverdi and Try My Best all won the William Hill Dewhurst Stakes, Danzatore ducked a confrontation with Gorytus and Diesis at Newmarket in favour of the Panasonic Beresford Stakes at the Curragh six days earlier. The decision to run at the Curragh was understandable—why risk spoiling a potentially top-class three-year-old by giving him an inevitably hard race when there were much easier pickings at home? Understandable though it was, the decision deprived Danzatore of a chance of gaining valuable experience in highly-competitive company; it also made the assessment of his merit and potential that much more difficult.

When Assert won the Beresford in 1981 he collected only IR £10,025 but with sponsorship the race's value was boosted in 1982 to IR £26,137.50, a very worthwhile sum even if some way short of the first prize offered by the Dewhurst. The extra prize money didn't raise the overall standard of the field though and only three of Danzatore's six opponents were winners, Burslem and Homeowner the best supported of them. Burslem, who had looked a good colt when running out a six-length winner of the valuable Ardenode Stud Stakes at the beginning of August, had since been beaten by two of Danzatore's stable companions, finishing third to Caerleon in the Anglesey Stakes and second to Glenstal in the National Stakes. Homeowner, trained by David O'Brien, had scraped home by a short head from another of Danzatore's stable-mates, South Atlantic, on his only appearance. The other winner, Curravilla, had already been thrashed by Danzatore so it was no great surprise to see Danzatore start as short as 4/1 on. Danzatore was tremendously impressive, even allowing for the fact that there wasn't

*Ashford Castle Stakes, the Curragh—an impressive performance
by Danzatore who finishes well clear*

a Diesis or a Gorytus among his opponents. He lobbed along in front, dictating
the pace from the start, and clearly had the others in trouble early in the straight.
His jockey Eddery allowed himself a look round approaching the distance,
relaxed his hold slightly and just sat there as Danzatore strode effortlessly
clear to win by six lengths from Burslem with Homeowner a further half a
length behind. Just how far Danzatore could have won had he been ridden
out is anyone's guess.

Danzatore had been similarly impressive in both his previous races, a
minor event at Leopardstown early in September and the Ashford Castle Stakes
at the Curragh three weeks later. Despite the presence in the field at Leopardstown of the previous winners Persian Poet, Kimbernic, Spending Cut, Cremation,
Dorconcet and Piccadilly Prince, Danzatore started at 9/4 on. He didn't
give his supporters a moment's worry. After holding a narrow advantage
from the start he burst clear in the straight to win very easily by six lengths
from Cremation who was beaten only a neck under top weight in a nursery at the
Curragh on his next appearance. Danzatore started at even shorter odds in the
Ashford Castle Stakes in which all five of his rivals were winners. Red Rudy,
having his first race since finishing sixth to Prince Reymo at Royal Ascot, went
into the lead with Danzatore seemingly cantering in second place. With two
furlongs to go Danzatore swept into the lead in breathtaking fashion and but for
being eased would probably have doubled his five-length winning margin over
Red Rudy. So Danzatore's first season amounted to three effortless victories
over second-rate opposition. With so little evidence to go on we haven't been
able to rate him the top-class colt he almost certainly is.

As can be seen from his posed portrait Danzatore is a big, rangy, imposing
individual, reminiscent of another O'Brien-trained son of Northern Dancer,
Nijinsky, and possessing more physical scope than many of Northern Dancer's
good sons. Like Nijinsky he was bred by E. P. Taylor who offered him for sale
at the Keeneland Select Sale where the BBA (Ireland) outbid Harry Thomson
Jones to secure him for 1,000,000 dollars. Danzatore's dam Shake A Leg was

245

Panasonic Beresford Stakes, the Curragh—yet another effortless victory for the unbeaten Danzatore

Mr D. Schwartz's "Danzatore"

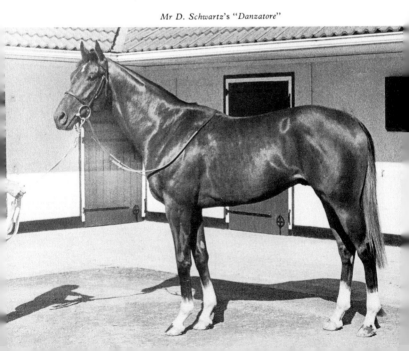

also trained by O'Brien before being sent to race in the USA, as was another of her sons, London Bells. Shake A Leg, a fine, big, strong, lengthy filly, proved well worth the 50,000 dollars she cost as a yearling. English racegoers may not have fond memories of her—she finished only twelfth when second favourite for the 1972 Queen Mary Stakes on her only start here—but she did well in Ireland, winning two five-furlong races including the Waterford Testimonial Stakes. She also proved very useful on her return to the States, winning seven sprint races from fourteen starts and finishing second in three more. When successful in the six-furlong Miss Woodford Stakes at Monmouth Park she beat the champion three-year-old filly Desert Vixen into second place. As a son of Nijinsky London Bells is a close relative of Danzatore. After finishing second in the Coventry Stakes he broke the six-furlong two-year-old course record at the Curragh but he never lived up to his reputation, finishing a beaten favourite in four of his six races at two, including the Gimcrack. When returned to the States he won three times from eleven starts as a three-year-old, scoring twice over seven furlongs and once over eight and a half. His only placing in a stakes race was his second under 7-5 in the Rochester Cup at the little-known Finger Lakes track. London Bells returned to Ireland for the 1981 and 1982 stud seasons and has now crossed the Atlantic yet again. Danzatore is a half-brother to two other winners, notably the Vaguely Noble filly Vaguely Modest whose most important victory came in a division of the Selene Stakes over eight and a half furlongs at Woodbine as a three-year-old in 1979. His yearling sister fetched the fourth-highest price for a filly at the 1982 Keeneland Select Sale when bought by the Aston Upthorpe Stud for 1,400,000 dollars.

Danzatore (Can) (b.c. Mar 4, 1980)			
	Northern Dancer (b 1961)	Nearctic (br 1954)	Nearco Lady Angela
		Natalma (b 1957)	Native Dancer Almahmoud
	Shake A Leg (b 1970)	Raise A Native (ch 1961)	Native Dancer Raise You
		Fleeting Doll (b 1961)	Fleet Nasrullah Chinese Doll

That good French two-year-old Crystal Glitters, winner of the Prix Eclipse, is out of Shake A Leg's half-sister Tales To Tell, who won the California Oaks over a mile. Modern Spirit, a brother to Tales To Tell, won a six-furlong stakes race. Their dam Fleeting Doll won two sprints from twenty starts as a three-year-old and was a half-sister to the smart Mr America, winner of the Argonaut Stakes over eight and a half furlongs in 1961. A further interesting aspect of Danzatore's pedigree is that he is inbred in the third generation to that outstanding American performer Native Dancer. Native Dancer won all but one of his twenty-two starts, scoring over all distances from five furlongs to a mile and a half, and he has since proved a major influence at stud. Through his son Raise A Native he is the grandsire of two of America's foremost stallions, Mr Prospector and Exclusive Native; through his daughter Natalma he is the grandsire of Northern Dancer; his son Dan Cupid sired Sea-Bird II, the best European horse in our experience; and another son Atan is himself the grandsire of Kris and Diesis.

Estimating how far Danzatore will stay is very difficult. He hasn't the pedigree of a Derby horse and if it weren't for his obviously placid temperament we shouldn't have given much for his chances of staying a mile and a half. He strikes us as yet another American-bred who will prove best at up to a mile and a quarter. One thing we are sure of is that he will put up a very bold show in the Guineas. So far as his going requirements are concerned—he has yet to encounter very firm but seems at home on any other. V. O'Brien, Ireland.

DANZIG 5 b.g. Wolver Hollow 126–None-So-Pretty (Never Say Die 137) (1981   **47** d
12g 10.5d 8g 12f   1982 6g⁴ 6s 6g² 8.5f 8g 8fg 11.5f 7fg)   compact gelding; plater nowadays; stays 1½m, but seems reasonably effective at sprint distances; acts on firm going; claimed out of M. Lambert's stable £2,200 after third outing. D. Sasse.

DARA MONARCH 3 b.c. Realm 129–Sardara 106 (Alcide 136) (1981 6f 7g²   **128** d
6.3fg* 6.3fg³ 8g   1982 7g* 8fg 8g* 8fg* 8fg 8s⁴ 7v)
Quantity rather than quality was a distinctive feature of the latest Two Thousand Guineas: twenty-six ran, not an exceptional miler among them, and of the first ten home only eighth-placed Dara Monarch and tenth-placed Vin St Benet managed to win subsequently. As a guide to the merits of the contestants

the race proved misleading in one important respect, since the first and second clearly weren't so superior as their domination of the greater part of affairs suggested at the time; indeed they cannot now be regarded as the best in the field. Dara Monarch turned the form inside out with a very convincing victory in the Airlie/Coolmore Irish Two Thousand Guineas two weeks later and followed up with an equally convincing performance in the St James's Palace Stakes. Unfortunately, to all intents and purposes that was the end of him for the season. He was brought back after illness to run in another three races, when really it would have been better to have retired him.

There was no reason for regarding odds of 20/1 about Dara Monarch's chance in the Irish Two Thousand Guineas at the Curragh in May as over-generous. He had been beaten more than nine lengths at Newmarket after dropping away in the last furlong, and was reopposed by Wind and Wuthering (second), Tender King (third) and Achieved (sixth). His form up to that time fell short of top class. He had won two of his six other races, the Ballsbridge-Tattersalls Anglesey Stakes at the Curragh from Americus as a two-year-old and the McCairns Trial Stakes at Fairyhouse by a length from the maiden race winner Senior Citizen in April; his best other run had been his excellent third to Anfield in the Ashford Castle Stakes, again as a two-year-old. Yet Dara Monarch won the Irish Two Thousand hands down by three lengths from Tender King; Anfield finished fourth, Wind and Wuthering fifth, Achieved sixth. In winning he showed an impressive turn of speed over the last furlong after being waited with, and there lies the clue to explaining his improvement. As his trainer said, to be seen to best advantage he needed covering up more than he had been at Newmarket where, drawn on the same side as Zino and Wind and Wuthering, he had attempted to take them on from halfway. His regular jockey Kinane didn't ride him that day but was back in the saddle at the Curragh. The good gallop set by Full Extent and Wind and Wuthering suited Kinane's purpose well; Dara Monarch dropped in nicely towards the rear of the fourteen-runner field, remaining there until switched outside with two furlongs to go. When he made his challenge running into the last furlong it was impossible to envisage him or any of the others an eventual three-length winner; Anfield, Tender King, Wind and Wuthering and Red Sunset were still neck-and-neck inside him. It says a great deal for Dara Monarch, then, that he should so quickly go so far clear of so many horses in a classic as he did; he looked far and away the best in the race passing the post.

Impressive as it was Dara Monarch's performance did not convince everyone that he could win the St James's Palace Stakes at Royal Ascot, for Ivano started favourite ahead of him, 2/1 against 7/2. Ivano, dropping back to a much shorter distance here, was said to have beaten the Queen Anne Stakes winner Mr Fluorocarbon in a recent home gallop. Dara Monarch had met the majority of the field before. Except for Ivano, My Dad Tom and Riyahi the runners had taken part in the Two Thousand Guineas or the Irish Two Thousand Guineas, or both. With Wind and Wuthering present Kinane was, at the outset, able to adopt similar tactics to those employed at the Curragh, but Wind and Wuthering didn't last so long in front on this firmer ground, giving way over two furlongs out to Red Sunset and Ivano who hadn't the pace to stay there for long themselves. Dara Monarch swept by on the outside into a clear lead with at least a furlong and a half still to travel, leaving the others at such a rate at this point that he was able to get away with diving sharply inside. Nothing threatened to catch him, though ultimately, probably because he'd been in front much longer than last time, he had to be pushed out to hold off Tender King by a length and a half. Ivano finished third, Hays fourth, Red Sunset fifth, Anfield sixth and Wind and Wuthering only seventh, ahead of My Dad Tom and Riyahi. Not a

Airlie/Coolmore Irish Two Thousand Guineas, the Curragh—
Dara Monarch sprints clear on the outside

*St James's Palace Stakes, Ascot—Dara Monarch
beats Tender King again*

vintage St James's Palace Stakes by any means—a fact which necessarily moderates enthusiasm for what was, to watch, an exhilarating performance by the winner.

Dara Monarch caught a viral infection afterwards and did not reappear on the racecourse until the last Saturday in August. In the meantime a two-thirds share in him had been sold to stallion owner Tim Rogers, whose Airlie Stud is part-sponsor of the Irish Two Thousand Guineas. Four races were planned for Dara Monarch before his retirement, starting with the Waterford Crystal Mile at Goodwood; then the Prix du Moulin de Longchamp, the Queen Elizabeth II Stakes at Ascot and the Dubai Champion Stakes at Newmarket. Some horse had he won all four! In fact he ran in only the first and third of them, without much distinction, and ended his career in France in the Prix de la Foret. Dara Monarch finished plumb last of eight to the Sussex Stakes second Sandhurst Prince at Goodwood, the short life of his initially-promising challenge (plus the readiness of his jockey to accept defeat) suggesting he hadn't fully recovered from the effects of his illness. Any chance of re-establishing his reputation was almost certainly denied him by the conditions he encountered in his two remaining races. In our opinion he was a top-of-the-ground performer. If we are right he could not be expected to run up to his best at Ascot, where the going was soft, or at Longchamp, where the going was practically the heaviest of the season. He finished fourth of ten to Buzzards Bay at Ascot, fifth of nine to Pas de Seul at Longchamp, on neither occasion reaching a higher position during the race than he held at the line.

Dara Monarch's sire Realm was exported to Japan as a twelve-year-old in 1979. The same year his dam Sardara was sold out of the Citadel Stud (the stud which bred Zino) for 7,200 guineas at the December Sales, carrying Dara Monarch. Twelve months later Dara Monarch himself was sold at the same venue for 6,400 guineas, only to be passed on as a yearling at the Houghton Sales for 1,400 guineas less. That he represented a tremendous bargain is axiomatic now. In 1980, though, Realm was regarded primarily as a sire of two-year-olds and Sardara had bred nothing worthy of note from three previous foals (Dara Monarch remains her only winner from four runners, the latest the 1982 two-year-old filly Pure Perfection). The most persuasive selling point in Dara Monarch's entry in the Houghton catalogue was the fact of Sardara's being a

Capt. A. D. D. Rogers' "Dara Monarch"

winning half-sister to the St Leger winner Intermezzo (by Hornbeam). She, like her half-brother, stayed well, on her penultimate outing as a three-year-old beating the subsequent Jockey Club Cup winner Irvine in tremendous style in the Eglinton and Winton Memorial Handicap over a distance of almost two and a quarter miles at Ayr. Sardara's dam Plaza, a winner apparently best at a mile, was out of a winning sprinter.

		Princely Gift	Nasrullah
	Realm	(b 1951)	Blue Gem
	(b 1967)	Quita II	Lavandin
Dara Monarch		(b 1962)	Eos
(b.c. 1979)		Alcide	Alycidon
	Sardara	(b 1955)	Chenille
	(ch 1969)	Plaza	Persian Gulf
		(b 1958)	Wild Success

Dara Monarch has been retired to the Grangewilliam Stud in Ireland, one of the studs that make up the Airlie complex. The fees for all the Airlie stallions except Habitat, by the way, have been reduced by 20% to 30% on their 1982 values. Dara Monarch, a neat, attractive colt, will be standing alongside Habitat. As a miler he wasn't in the class of that horse; he was clearly, though, among the best of his generation when everything was right. *L. Browne, Ireland.*

DARINE 4 b.f. Nonoalco 131–Be Noble (Vaguely Noble 140) (1981 9.4g[2] **90** 12fg[3] 10g* 13.3d[3] 11.7d[2] 10.8s[3] 1982 12d* 13d 12f[4] 15g 12g[3] 11.7g* 10fg* 8f 12d* 10g[4] 12v 10.2d[4]) strong, good sort; improved and had a fine season, winning minor event at Folkestone in March and handicaps at Windsor and Newmarket in August and at Ascot in September; gained last 2 wins in good style in apprentice events, putting up a particularly impressive performance when beating Perchance by 10 lengths at Ascot; had stiff tasks and ran well eighth and tenth starts, on latter staying on to finish about 6 lengths fourth of 10 behind Time Charter in Sun Chariot Stakes at Newmarket in October; best at up to 1½m; probably acts on any going; genuine, although ran well below her best final outing. *F. Durr.*

DARK MYSTIQUE (USA) 3 b. or br.f. Fleet Allied–Zerosa (Silky Sullivan) —
(1981 6f 6d 1982 6f 7f³ 6f 5fg³ 7fg 6f³ 6g 6f⁴) compact filly; third in minor
event and 2 handicaps; stays 7f; acts on firm going; blinkered last 2 starts;
sold 2,400 gns Newmarket Autumn Sales. *P. Haslam.*

DARK PROPOSAL (USA) 4 b.c. Blood Royal 129–Lady Gertrude (Mr **76 d**
Leader) (1981 16s 10.2f 10fg 13f* 12.3g² 13fg³ 16.5f 1982 13fg 14g 16fg*
17f* 18.8fg⁴ 16f 17f² 18d 18.1g² 19s 20g) rather leggy, quite useful sort; won
handicaps at Lingfield (by 5 lengths) and Wolverhampton (beat Baron Blakeney
by ¼ length), both in May; none too consistent however; a thorough stayer
who is suited by a strong gallop; suited by firm going; needs plenty of driving
and gives impression he's not an ideal mount for an apprentice; has raced with
tongue tied down. *B. Hanbury.*

DARRONIUS 3 ch.g. Windjammer (USA)–Hot Baby (Tropique 128) (1981 —
NR 1982 12f 14f 16d) 7,200Y; leggy, sparely-made gelding; half-brother
to several winners, including fairly useful 7f to 1¼m winner Sure Loser (by
Falcon); dam of little account; beaten some way in maiden races; collapsed
and died at Nottingham in June. *P. Kelleway.*

DARTCAN 3 ch.f. Streak 119–Canamour (Canisbay 120) (1981 NR 1982 —
7fg 8fg⁴ 10.1g 8fg) second living foal; dam never ran; plating-classs maiden;
stays 1m. *D. C. Tucker.*

DARTING GROOM (USA) 2 ch.c. Blushing Groom 131–Mystery Mood **91**
(Night Invader) (1982 7fg 7fg² 7d² 8d² 8g* 8g) Apr 22; $55,000Y;
lengthy, good-bodied, strong-quartered colt; third foal; half-brother to smart
1981 American 2-y-o filly Mystical Mood (by Roberto); dam at her best at 2
yrs when smart stakes winner at up to 1m; blinkered first time, led well inside
final furlong to win 10-runner maiden race at Beverley in September by ¾
length from Full Rainbow; had previously gone down by a neck to Monetarist
at Ayr, by a short head to Rich Benefit at Chester and by a neck to Mister
Valentino at Ayr again; will stay 1¼m; acts on a firm and a soft surface; probably
needs to be brought very late. *S. Norton.*

DARYMOSS 5 b.m. Ballymoss 136–Darlinda 85 (Darius 129) (1981 NR —
1982 8h 8f 10g³ 12f³) workmanlike mare; third in ladies race and a maiden
event at Brighton; probably stays 1½m. *A. Turnell.*

DASHING DEANO 3 b.g. Full of Hope 125–Lillima 73 (Crooner 119) (1981 —
NR 1982 11.7f) 4,100Y, 480 2-y-o; third foal; half-brother to 8.5f winner
Sea Miss (by Matahawk); dam 6f winner; unquoted when remote seventh of
12 to Date Palm in maiden race at Bath in April. *T. Hallett.*

DASSEERA 4 b g. Prince Regent 129–Red Laser 95 (Red God 128§) (1981 —
NR 1982 8d 8g 10g) robust, good sort; lightly raced and little worthwhile
form, including when blinkered in a seller final start. *J. Sutcliffe.*

DATA JUDGE 3 ch.c. Shiny Tenth 120–Justify 74 (Jefferson 129) (1981 —
NR 1982 6fg 5fg 7g 10g 10fg) lengthy, lightly-made colt; first foal; dam
disqualified winner of 1m seller; poor plater; sold 400 gns Doncaster September
Sales. *W. Holden.*

DATATEXT 2 b.c. Raga Navarro 119–Ribara (Barbare II 128) (1982 5fg **64**
6f 5.8f 6f 6fg 7fg 8s 8d*) Apr 29; 3,100Y; workmanlike colt; blinkered, showed
first form when winning 27-runner selling nursery at Doncaster (bought in
2,900 gns) in October by 1½ lengths from Fashion Lover; evidently suited by
1m; acts on a soft surface. *T. Marshall.*

DATE PALM (USA) 3 br.f. Damascus–Oraza (Zank) (1981 7v 1982 11.7f* **68**
11.7g 13fg⁴) well-made filly; 25/1 when narrowly winning 12-runner maiden
race at Bath in April; seems to stay 13f; not raced after June. *H. Candy.*

DAVENPORT BOY 6 b.h. Workboy 125–Sea Tycoon 80 (Tycoon II) (1981 **94**
6g 6fg 6g 6s 6s 6g 6g 6s² 1982 6d 6fg* 6f² 6g³ 6g³ 6d) strong horse; landed
a gamble in £3,200 handicap at Epsom in April, beating Lord Wimpy readily
a length; ran well when placed at Newbury, Kempton, and Newmarket (first
outing for almost 5 months) afterwards, but disappointed final start; best form
at 6f; acts on any going; sent to USA. *R. Pitt.*

DAVIDGALAXY AFFAIR 5 b.h. Tower Walk 130–Lady's Walk (Pall Mall —
132) (1981 8s³ 10s 8s 7.2d³ 12.3d 5fg 6f³ 8f 6f 6f 1982 13.1f 10d 10g 8g 5fg)
poor handicapper nowadays; best at up to 1m; acts on any going; sometimes
blinkered; suitable mount for a boy. *R. Keenor.*

DAVID'S ISOPON 3 b.f. Saulingo 122–Better Than None (Compensation —
127) (1981 5fg 6fg 6fg 6g 1982 12d) strong, lengthy, dipped-backed filly;
behind in varied races, including a valuable seller. *H. O'Neill.*

DAWNBALLET (USA) 3 ch.c. Nijinsky 138–Dauntu (Grey Dawn II 132) **71** (1981 7fg⁴ 8s 1982 11g⁴ 12g 16fg³ 16fg³ 17.1s) big, rangy colt; poor walker but good mover; staying handicapper; best form on fast ground; sweated slightly when running moderately final start; sold 6,000 gns Newmarket Autumn Sales. *H. Candy.*

DAWN BOY 2 ch.g. Amboise 113–Dawn Affair 77 (Entanglement 118) (1982 **—** 7fg 7g 7.6v) Mar 3; rather lightly-made gelding; third foal; dam ran 49 times without success on flat and over hurdles; behind in maiden and minor events. *S. Woodman.*

DAWN DITTY 3 ch.f. Song 132–Chick 106 (My Swanee 122) (1981 5d 6fg⁴ **80** 6fg* 6d³ 7g 1982 7fg 6fg 7f 5.3f² 6f² 5fg* 5s) big, rangy, useful sort; made all and was eased near finish when landing odds in minor event at Redcar in September; runner-up in 2 similar events at Brighton earlier; yet to prove she stays 7f; seems to act on any going; blinkered last 4 starts. *H. T. Jones.*

DAWN JOHNNY (USA) 5 gr.h. Grey Dawn II 132–Door Star (Stage Door **90** Johnny) (1981 16fg² 18.4d 16s 20fg² 16g* 16.1g 19fg⁴ 14d 16.1fg³ 16fg³ 1982 16s 18.4fg* 16g³) well-made horse; fair handicapper on his day, winner of Northumberland Plate at Newcastle in 1981 and Ladbroke Chester Cup in 1982; always well placed and got on top inside last furlong when beating Dragon Palace a length in latter race in May; injured a tendon when 2½ lengths third to Heighlin at Kempton later in month, and was subsequently retired; stayed well; needed top-of-the-ground; was best in blinkers. *M. Stoute.*

DAWN RAID (USA) 3 ch.c. Hail The Pirates 126–Shy Dawn (Grey Dawn **82** d II 132) (1981 7.6s² 1982 11g⁴ 12fg² 14g⁴ 10f 10fg 8g 8fg 10v) small, fair sort; in frame in maiden races; well beaten in seller final outing; needs further than 1m and stays 1¾m; blinkered seventh start. *P. Cole.*

DAWN RIVER (USA) 2 b.c. Grey Dawn II 132–Relifordie (El Relicario 124) **106** (1982 6f³ 7f 8fg* 8d* 10g) Feb 2; $250,000Y; rangy, attractive colt; not the best of walkers; brother to 3 stakes winners, notably top-class middle-distance horse Vigors, and half-brother to several winners; dam won from 4.5f to 1m in France; won maiden event at Goodwood in September and nursery under top weight at

Ladbroke Chester Cup—the grey Dawn Johnny is on top at the finish. Dragon Palace finishes second with the partially-hidden Another Sam third

Brighton in October; well below form races immediately before (moved poorly) and after; should stay 1¼m; possibly not suited by really firm ground. *G. Harwood.*

DAWN'S DELIGHT 4 b.g. Dawn Review 105–Bird of Passage (Falcon 131) (1981 6s* 7v³ 6g* 6d* 6s* 6s⁴ 6g* 6fg⁴ 6g² 6f² 6fg³ 6d 5g 6g 1982 6s* 6d³ 6f 7f 6fg³ 7g 6g⁴ 6g 6fg 6g³ 6d 6s 6v 6g 6d*) leggy, lightly-made gelding; former plater; won handicaps at Ayr in March and Doncaster in October, on latter course beating Sparkling Boy by ½ length in £6,400 Yorkshire Bank Handicap; none too consistent in between; best form at 6f; acts on any going, but has done all his winning when there's been some give underfoot; blinkered once at 2 yrs; often apprentice ridden when successful; sometimes bandaged; very tough. *K. Ivory.* **86**

DAWN'S DREAM 2 ch.f. Sandford Lad 133–Humble Portion 73 (Mossborough 126 or Major Portion 129) (1982 5f³ 5f⁴ 6d* 7s) Mar 23; quite well-made filly; keen walker; half-sister to 2 minor winners; dam placed over 5f at 2 yrs; having first race since May, showed improved form when running on well to win 14-runner maiden race at Brighton in October by 2 lengths from Circassian Circle; creditable sixth off stiff mark in nursery at Doncaster the following month; stays 7f; suited by a soft surface. *R. Price.* **82**

DAY AFTER 6 b.g. High Top 131–Bisley (Polic 126 or Punchinello 97) (1981 10.6s⁴ 12g² 10f* 12g 12f³ 11.7fg² 12fg² 12f* 10.4s* 12fg⁴ 1982 12fg 11.7fg 12f² 10d 10g³ 11.7fg 12fg³ 10g) middle-distance handicapper; ran best races when placed at Ripon, Chepstow and Doncaster, twice in amateur riders events; acts on any going; usually wears blinkers. *S. Mellor.* **64**

DAYARA (USA) 3 ch.f. Empery 128–Diriyya (Ribocco 118) (1981 7fg* 1982 10.6f) small, fair sort; won maiden race at Warwick in 1981; not seen out after running moderately in handicap at Haydock in May; should stay 1¼m+; sold to BBA 3,800 gns Newmarket December Sales. *M. Stoute.* **—**

DAY IS DONE 3 ch.c. Artaius 129–Headin' Home 105 (Habitat 134) (1981 5s* 5s* 5f* 6.3fg² 7d* 1982 7g³ 8fg³ 8s 9fg 8d³) strong, good sort; fourth foal; **115**

Mr B. R. Firestone's "Day Is Done"

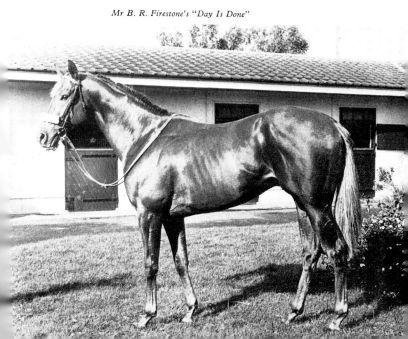

half-brother to a winner in Belgium; dam won over 7f and 1m; third in McCairns Trial at Fairyhouse, Poule d'Essai des Poulains at Longchamp (ran very well to be beaten 1¼ lengths by Melyno) and Desmond Stakes at the Curragh (blinkered when 4 lengths behind Anfield); not disgraced on other starts, in Prix Quincey at Deauville (under 4 lengths fifth to King James) and Pacemaker International Whitehall Stakes at Leopardstown (under 3 lengths fifth to Punctilio); will stay 1¼m; has won on firm going but gives impression he's better suited by some give in the ground; genuine. *D. Weld, Ireland.*

DAY OF JUDGEMENT 2 b.c. Bay Express 132–Whip Finish 77 (Be Friendly **97** 130) (1982 5f⁴ 5f³ 5f* 5fg³ 5f² 5fg 5fg) Apr 19; strong, good sort; good walker; second foal; dam won twice over 5f at 2 yrs; ran on strongly to beat Red Cedar by 3 lengths in 7-runner maiden race at Thirsk in May; gave at least 14 lb to his 8 opponents in nursery at Leicester in July and in circumstances ran a fine race to finish 2½ lengths second to Jonacris; below his best afterwards, finishing last of 5 behind Jonacris when meeting him on terms 29 lb better at Ripon three weeks later; yet to race on an easy surface; has shown a tendency to hang right and needs strong handling. *R. D. Peacock.*

DAY OUT 5 b.g. Reliance II 137–Ming Vase 84 (Princely Gift 137) (1981 NR **—** 1982 5fg 8g 5fg 7.6fg 5g) small, strong gelding; poor maiden; often bandaged in front nowadays. *R. E. Peacock.*

DAYTON LEGACY 3 b.c. Auction Ring 123–Mansi (Pardao 120) (1981 6fg **56** 1982 6fg 5fg 6fg³ 8g 6s) rangy colt; plating-class maiden; suited by 6f and should stay further; sold 4,400 gns Ascot December Sales. *I. Walker.*

DAZARI 2 b. or br.c. Relkino 131–Damosa (Abdos 134) (1982 8g²) Apr 6; **92 p** strong, good sort; third foal; dam French 11f winner; 10/1, shaped very well in maiden race at Newmarket in October, making up lot of ground from halfway on apparently slower ground on outside to finish highly creditable 2 lengths second of 17 behind easy winner Oula Owl; has makings of useful middle-distance performer. *M. Stoute.*

DEAL ON 3 b.g. Quiet Fling 124–Remould 83 (Reform 132) (1981 7f 7fg **73** 7fg² 7f 8f⁴ 8d³ 1982 10f³ 11.5f 14g 12fg² 11.5g* 10 6s 11s² 12g) useful sort; easily won 9-runner maiden race at Yarmouth in September; ran creditably in handicap penultimate start; stays 1¾m; acts on any going. *W. Hastings-Bass.*

DEAR ALICIA 4 gr.f. Runnymede 123–Dibby's Cousin (Be Friendly 130) **—** (1981 6f 6f 6fg 5fg 1982 10f 8g) workmanlike filly; poor maiden; well beaten after being bought out of J. Bosley's stable 1,700 gns Doncaster March Sales; not certain to stay beyond sprint distances; has worn blinkers. *C. Williams.*

DEAR JEM 4 b. or br.f. Dragonara Palace 115–Czar's Diamond 66 (Queen's **—** Hussar 124) (1981 5d 5g 5.8g 5s² 6f 5g 5g 6f 6s 1982 5.3fg 5f) lightly-made filly; stays 6f; probably acts on any going; usually apprentice ridden; inconsistent; has worn blinkers; retained, covered by Roman Warrior, 2,100 gns Newmarket December Sales. *A. Bailey.*

DEBACH RIVER 3 b.c. Forlorn River 124–Debach Game 69 (Darius 129) **—** (1981 7.6s 6g 1982 8.5f 8g³ 10f 10g 12fg 10v 7d) well-made colt; plater; stays 1m; sometimes blinkered; sold to M. Chapman 560 gns Newmarket Autumn Sales. *P. K. Mitchell.*

DEBAJ 2 b.c. Blue Cashmere 129–Floral Palm 69 (Floribunda 136) (1982 **92 p** 7fg 5s*) May 5; 10,500Y; lengthy, quite attractive colt; half-brother to 3 winners, including very useful Italian sprinter Dublin Taxi (by Sharpen Up); dam won 5f seller at 2 yrs; held up when beating Sheldan by ½ length in 19-runner maiden event at Haydock in October; speedy and likely to prove best at 5f or 6f; type to win more races. *P. Walwyn.*

DEBIAN 3 ch.f. Relko 136–Brightelmstone 105 (Prince Regent 129) (1981 **54** 5g 5d* 6fg 6fg³ 5g³ 5s³ 6s 1982 8f 7fg² 7d 7d⁴ 7f 7f 7fg 8f 8g 6v) fair sort; poor handicapper; stays 7f; seems to act on any going; blinkered last 2 starts; tends to pull hard; sold 7,200 gns Newmarket December Sales. *D. Ringer.*

DEBUTINA PARK 2 b.f. Averof 123–Debutante 78 (Silly Season 127) (1982 **87** 5fg² 5f³ 6f⁴ 7d 6fg* 6g³ 6g* 6s) Mar 5; 5,400Y; lengthy filly; first foal; dam 7f winner; successful in maiden race at Nottingham in August and in £3,500 event (beating Quilting a short head in blanket finish) at York in September; should stay 7f (never in race and was possibly unsuited by softish ground when tried at trip); acts well on a sound surface; genuine. *E. Eldin.*

DECORATED 2 ch.f. Gunner B 126–New Ribbons 79 (Ribero 126) (1982 **83** 5f 5f³ 5s 7fg⁴ 8.2d* 8.2s) Apr 28; leggy, rather close-coupled filly; poor walker;

second foal; half-sister to a winner in Italy by Connaught; dam won twice over 1¼m; ridden by a girl apprentice and having first race for nearly 3 months, put up easily best effort when winning 18-runner nursery at Nottingham in October by ⅛ length from Jendor despite wandering badly; stays well, and will be suited by 1¼m+; acts on a soft surface. *F. J. Houghton.*

DECORATIVE 5 b.h. Martinmas 128–War Ribbon (Anwar 120) (1981 10.6g* **79** d 10.2g 11s² 11.1s* 10.5g 12fg 10fg 10d 1982 10f 10fg 10g⁴ 10.6g 10.5s) compact, attractive horse; quite a useful handicapper at his best; ran respectably second outing; stays 11f; ideally suited by an easy surface; usually blinkered nowadays; sold out of D. Kent's stable 7,200 gns Doncaster March Sales. *C. Mackenzie.*

DEEP ROOTS 2 b. or br.c. Dom Racine 121–La Paqueline (Sassafras 135) **124** (1982 5d* 5g³ 5.5g² 6fg* 7f* 8s⁴)
There are very few two-year-old races of consequence in France before August. The Prix du Bois, run at Longchamp towards the end of June, has often been one of the exceptions. Since the end of the 'sixties the race has fallen to My Swallow, Daring Display, Lianga, Irish River and Maelstrom Lake, all of whom later took at least one of the Group 1 races for two-year-olds, while the 1979 Prix d'Arenberg winner Adraan also won the Prix du Bois. Among those beaten in the race during the same period were Green Forest and the 1972 Prix de la Salamandre winner Zapoteco. This splendid record encouraged the authorities to elevate the Prix du Bois to pattern-race status in 1982, nearly doubling the prize money in the process. The race again attracted a leading two-year-old, Deep Roots, who was one of six previous winners in a field of eight. Deep Roots had made an impressive debut at Maisons-Laffitte in May, running out an eight-length winner of a newcomers race, and he put up another excellent effort at Longchamp, winning by two lengths from the favourite American Stress with the filly Targhese a further two lengths back in third place. Unfortunately Deep Roots's jockey Dubroeucq lost his whip and was unable to prevent the colt from veering towards the rail in the final one and a half furlongs, hampering Targhese quite badly in the process and American Stress to a lesser extent. The stewards decided to move Deep Roots down to third place even though he was clearly the best horse on the day.
Deep Roots raced exclusively in Group 1 events afterwards, starting with the Prix Robert Papin at Maisons-Laffitte a month later, in which he was reopposed by both American Stress and Targhese. He started an even-money favourite with the betting suggesting that he had more to fear from the fillies Ma Biche, a good seven-furlong winner on her last start, and Crime of Passion, winner of the Cherry Hinton Stakes. This proved to be so, with Deep Roots going down by a length and a half to Ma Biche. The riders of the first two put up sharply contrasting displays. Head, on the winner, came in for a deal of criticism

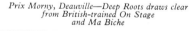

*Prix Morny, Deauville—Deep Roots draws clear
from British-trained On Stage
and Ma Biche*

for the way he drove out Ma Biche in the last furlong and a half, using his whip about a dozen times, whereas Saint-Martin, riding Deep Roots for the first time, seemed more intent on keeping the colt straight than anything else; once Ma Biche had gone clear Deep Roots was asked to do only enough to beat Crime of Passion narrowly for second place. The results of their different handling showed, we think, when the two met again in the Prix Morny at Deauville four weeks later: Deep Roots easily turned the tables on a below-par Ma Biche. After being given plenty of time to find his stride he came to challenge in between Ma Biche and On Stage, one of the English challengers, with two furlongs to run. He quickly took a decisive advantage and by the line had stretched it to three lengths over On Stage, who had earlier gone down by only half a length to Horage when receiving 6 lb in the Anglia Television July Stakes. Just behind On Stage came Ma Biche and the strong-finishing Bal des Fees who later won the Prix Thomas Bryon. Incidentally Deep Roots's victory here was the first in a pattern race for his young trainer, a former assistant to Boutin who has held a licence for only three years.

Deep Roots reappeared in the Prix de la Salamandre at Longchamp in September, starting co-favourite with Ma Biche's stable-companion Maximova, an unbeaten filly who had gained the last of her four successes in the Prix du Calvados at Deauville. Making up the field were the stable-mates Soigneuse and Interco, runners-up respectively to Maximova at Deauville and to Go Jogging in the Prix d'Arenberg, the Blushing Groom colt Crystal Glitters, who had beaten the subsequent Prix La Rochette winner L'Emigrant when winning his only start, and Ginger Brink, a colt with only one win to his name from twelve starts. Deep Roots provided his trainer with a second pattern-race success but he had to share the spoils with Maximova and was rather lucky to do so. While Maximova was running into all sorts of trouble on the rails, Deep Roots came with a steady run on the outside in the straight to join Crystal Glitters in the lead with a furlong to go. Soon afterwards Deep Roots looked certain to be beaten as Maximova shot between the leading pair to take a half-length advantage but he battled on very gamely under Carson's strenuous driving. Deep Roots may have been fortunate but he nonetheless did very well to draw three lengths clear of Crystal Glitters, the subsequent winner of the Prix Eclipse. Deep Roots next attempted to win the Grand Criterium and thereby join the select band, Grey Dawn II, My Swallow, Blushing Groom and Green Forest, to have won three or more of France's four top juvenile events. The task proved beyond him but he wasn't disgraced in finishing fourth, three lengths behind Saint Cyrien, when looking past his best for the season.

			Kalamoun	Zeddaan
		Dom Racine	(gr 1970)	Khairunissa
		(br 1975)	La Ferte Milon	Timmy Lad
Deep Roots			(b 1968)	Salamine III
(b. or br.c. Mar 25, 1980)			Sassafras	Sheshoon
		La Paqueline	(b 1967)	Ruta
		(b 1973)	Etari	Taboun
			(b 1963)	Erica

Deep Roots is a rather workmanlike colt and when he appeared in the sales ring at Deauville as a yearling his appearance wasn't improved by a swollen tendon, caused by his striking into himself a few days earlier. He fetched only 80,000 francs, or approximately £7,300, but even that was 30,000 francs more than he'd fetched as a foal. His dam La Paqueline has also twice changed hands for small sums. After running once as a three-year-old, when fourth of five at Longchamp, and once as a three-year-old, when fifth of fifteen at Cagnes-sur-Mer, she was sold at Goffs in November 1976 for 3,000 guineas. The following year she was covered by Home Guard, producing a colt, Malcolm, who later won three middle-distance events in the French Provinces. In November 1978 she was resold for as little as 6,500 francs, falling to the bid of agents Horse France. At about this time Horse France arranged the sale of the Prix Jean Prat winner Dom Racine to stand at the Greenmount Stud and were given a nomination to the stallion which they used on La Paqueline, with Deep Roots the result. Dom Racine's first crop also includes the very useful Irish filly Minnelli. He now stands at the Haras du Logis; he was never very popular in Ireland and was sent to France when the Greenmount Stud ceased to stand stallions after the 1981 season.

La Paqueline was very cheap for a mare of her breeding. Both her dam Etari and grandam Erica won as two-year-olds and Etari was very useful, winning sprint events at Maisons-Laffitte and Deauville before finishing a

Prix de la Salamandre, Longchamp—a thrilling finish with
Deep Roots sharing the spoils with Maximova.
Crystal Glitters finishes third

creditable fourth in the Criterium de Maisons-Laffitte. Etari has produced five
winners in France, including the very useful middle-distance stayer Queribus and
Hagerstown, a winner at up to seven furlongs who later produced the smart mile
to one-and-a-quarter-mile filly Daeltown. Incidentally when Daeltown came up
for auction in 1981 she fetched 2,200,000 francs, a far cry from the 6,500 francs
paid for La Paqueline only three years before. Animals from this family have
won over all sorts of distances and Deep Roots has already shown he possesses a
degree of speed and stamina. He had probably gone over the top when running
a little below his best over a mile and he should be well suited by that distance
at three. Indeed he may well stay further since Dom Racine won at up to a
mile and a quarter and La Paqueline is a daughter of the Arc winner Sassafras.
Deep Roots is such a tough, game colt that he seems sure to win more races but
whether he'll do quite so well at three is questionable; Saint Cyrien and
L'Emigrant, two of the colts who beat him in the Grand Criterium, strike us as
having greater room for improvement. Unlike many French colts he has shown
he acts very well on firm ground and he has also won on a soft surface. *P. Bary,*
France.

DELIGHTFUL TERN 2 ch.f. Towern 96–Mossy's Delight 44 (Mossy Face 98) —
(1982 7f 7fg 8s) May 9; lightly-made filly; sister to tough 1981 2-y-o 5f to 7f
performer Mosswern; dam poor plater; behind in sellers at Redcar. *P. Wigham.*

DELIRAH 2 ch.f. Mansingh 120–Joie de Galles 72 (Welsh Pageant 132) (1982 **61**
5g 6g 6fg⁴ 6g 7d² 7d 7g 8s 8s) May 13; 3,400Y; rather lightly-made filly; first
foal; dam 1½m winner; plating-class maiden; suited by 7f and 1m; appears to
act on any going. *W. Elsey.*

DEL MAR 3 ch.f. Orange Bay 131–Stolen Love 85 (Alcide 136) (1981 NR —
1982 12f 17f) 4,200Y; fair sort; half-sister to 6f winner What Heaven (by So
Blessed) and a winning hurdler; dam placed at up to 1½m; behind in maiden
races at Doncaster and Wolverhampton in May; blinkered on latter; sold 900 gns
Ascot June Sales. *J. W. Watts.*

DELOS 2 gr.c. Dancer's Image–Some Dame (Vieux Manoir 132) (1982 5f 6fg —
7g 8f) Apr 24; compact, attractive colt; good walker; half-brother to 3 winners
in France, including smart 1978 2-y-o 4.5f to 5.5f winner Some Guy (by Blue
Tom); dam minor 2-y-c winner over 8.5f; cost 36,000 gns as a yearling but is only
a poor maiden; blinkered second and third outings. *P. Walwyn.*

DELTA QUEEN 3 gr.f. Warpath 113–Shenandoah 88 (Mossborough 126) **63**
(1981 NR 1982 10fg 12.2f 12d 14.7f² 15.8f² 15.8d 18d⁴ 20g²) lengthy filly;
fourth produce; sister to 1½m seller winner Rolling River and to winning stayer
Do Or Die; dam won over 14.7f, and is half-sister to very useful Sovereign
Edition; second in maiden races and a handicap; suited by a test of stamina; acts

257

on firm going; pulled hard fifth outing; bandaged in front final appearance; sold to T. Taylor 9,000 gns Doncaster November Sales. *C. Thornton.*

DEM AN DOZE 3 b.c. Malacate 131–Cinquapace 61 (Tudor Melody 129) (1981 **56** 7g 6fg 5g 5fg 5d 5.3d⁴ 5s 1982 8d 7fg 10f 7.2f 6f⁴ 7g 7g³ 7g 8.3fg² 10.1g 8fg* 8s² 10v) stocky colt; poor mover; plater; bought in 2,000 gns after winning at Kempton in September; ran creditably in better company next time; suited by 1m; seems to act on any going; trained part of season by R. Hannon. *P. Ashworth.*

DEMMY MANCHESTER 3 gr.g. Red Alert 127–Noaxe To Grind (The Axe **45 d** 115) (1981 5s 5f 5f 7.2fg 7.2v 5s 8d 1982 8d 8fg² 7f 7g 8fg 5f 8fg 10g 10s) workmanlike gelding; plater; stays 1m. *J. Smith.*

DENDROLIVANO 2 b.f. Pitskelly 122–Sara's Star 70 (Sheshoon 132) (1982 — 5g) Apr 2; 6,600F, 7,200Y; small, fair sort; half-sister to several winners, including useful and very tough 5f to 1m winner Venus of Stretham (by Tower Walk); dam quite moderate at 2 yrs; ninth of 10 to Favoridge in maiden race at Sandown in July; sold following week 6,000 gns Newmarket July Sales. *D. Marks.*

DENEL (FR) 3 ch.c. Devon III 125–Vernel (Lionel 128) (1981 8v 9d³ 8v* **126** 1982 10.5s³ 11fg 12d³ 12d⁴ 12fg 12s⁴ 15.5v* 15.5v*) 30,000 francs Y (approx £3,000); leggy colt; fourth foal; half-brother to a minor winner in France by Phaeton; dam French middle-distance maiden; showed himself very well suited by a thorough test of stamina on very soft going when decisively winning valuable handicap at Longchamp and Prix Royal-Oak on same course in October; got the better of stable-companion Ideal Point by a neck, with such as No Attention, Little Wolf and Zilos further behind, in latter; had earlier been in frame in varied company, best effort when 3 lengths third to Oui Mon Capitaine in 1½m 80,000 francs event at Saint-Cloud; genuine; trained by N. Pelat first 2 starts; clearly a very smart stayer when conditions are in his favour. *B. Secly, France.*

DENMORE 6 ch.h. Moulton 128–Dugo 90 (Dumbarnie 125) (1981 6s 6fg* **82 d** 6g 7g³ 6f 6fg³ 6fg 6f 6fg⁴ 1982 6d 6fg 6g 6f* 6f 6g 6g² 6f 6f 6f⁴ 5.8f 6s 7s) sturdy, good-bodied horse; fair handicapper; made all and held on by ¾ length from Bracadale at Brighton in May; ran creditably on occasions afterwards; best form at 6f and 7f; acts on any going; sometimes blinkered, but not when successful. *C. Nelson.*

DENTAL BOUTIQUE 4 ch.f. Simbir 130–Roman Rocket 84 (Aggressor — 130) (1981 NR 1982 10d) 1,400Y; half-sister to several minor winners here and abroad; dam placed at 1m; of no account over hurdles; last of 15 in amateur riders race at Lingfield in June, first outing on flat; sold 410 gns Ascot August Sales. *H. O'Neill.*

DENVER 2 b.c. Welsh Saint 126–Indian Runner (Sallust 134) (1982 7fg 7s **76** 8s) Apr 19; IR 13,500Y; good sort; second foal; half-brother to 3-y-o Mandriano (by Manado); dam never ran; quite a modest maiden; stays 1m. *B. Hills.*

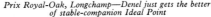

Prix Royal-Oak, Longchamp—Denel just gets the better of stable-companion Ideal Point

DENVER ROYAL 2 b.g. Royal Match 117–Wilden (Will Somers 114§) (1982 — 6g 8s) Mar 30; IR 7,000Y; third foal; half-brother to two 2-y-o winners; dam Irish 2-y-o 6f winner; backward, well beaten in minor event (tailed off) at Windsor in August and maiden race at Leicester in November. *M. McCourt.*

DEPORTMENT 2 b.f. So Blessed 130–Lady's Walk (Pall Mall 132) (1982 99 5fg* 5fg* 5fg 6f 6f) Mar 6; 36,000Y; attractive filly; has a round action; half-sister to several winners, including prolific 1979 2-y-o 5f winner David-galaxyaffair and useful 6f and 7f winner Scott Joplyn (both by Tower Walk); dam lightly raced; came to hand early and won 2 small races at Newmarket in April before going on to finish creditable fifth, 3 lengths behind Widaad, in Queen Mary Stakes at Royal Ascot; lost her form afterwards, finishing last in both Cherry Hinton Stakes at Newmarket and New Ham Stakes (unimpressive in paddock) at Goodwood; should be suited by 6f; possibly not at her best on very firm going; sold to BBA 68,000 gns Newmarket December Sales. *B. Hobbs.*

DEPUTY HEAD 2 b.c. Tower Walk 130–Ista Jil 97 (Gratitude 130) (1982 76 6f 6g4 5fg* 6fg) May 13; 7,800Y; good-bodied, quite attractive colt; half-brother to several winners, including fairly useful miler Strathfillan (by Hotfoot); dam 2-y-o 5f winner; won 6-runner minor event at Windsor in August; out of first 12 of 25 behind Orixo in minor race at Doncaster the following month but had difficulty finding a run when beginning to make progress after halfway; promises to stay 7f. *J. Holt.*

DEROULEDE 3 b.c. Blakeney 126–Set Free 90 (Worden II 129) (1981 NR 78 d 1982 11f 13.3f2 14d 14fg4 12f 14s) attractive, rangy colt; good walker; brother to 4 winners, including Oaks and Irish Guinness Oaks winner Juliette Marny, St Leger winner Julio Mariner and smart middle-distance stayer Saviour, and half-brother to 2 winners, including Oaks winner Scintillate (by Sparkler); dam won at 1m; ¾-length second of 19 to Brevet in maiden race at Newbury in June; failed to reproduce that form; stays 1¾m; blinkered fourth and fifth starts; trained by J. Tree first 5 outings. *G. Balding.*

DERRING PRINCE 4 b. or br.g. Derring-Do 131–Native Fleet (Fleet Nasrullah) 43 (1981 7fg 6d 6g 6fg 6f 7f 7fg 1982 6d 6g2 7f 6f 7g 6g) plater; stays 6f; blinkered final outing; fractious in preliminaries on several occasions; trained first 3 starts by P. Mitchell. *W. Charles.*

DERRYNSON 2 ch.g. Derrylin 115–Lovely Evening 85 (Henry the Seventh — 125) (1982 7s) June 2; fourth reported foal; half-brother to a winner in Brazil; dam showed ability at 2 yrs; unquoted, last of 12 in minor event at Chepstow in October. *L. Kennard.*

DERWENT RIVER 3 b.f. Another River 89–Aldy (Varano) (1981 5g 5d2 — 5fg4 5g 6fg 6g4 6d 8.2fg 8g 8.2d2 1982 6d 7f 8f 9g 6fg) narrow, lightly-made filly; plater; well beaten at 3 yrs; stays 1m; acts on a firm and a soft surface; has been tried in blinkers. *T. Barnes.*

DESERT AIR 3 b.g. St Columbus 98–Lady Impeccable (Dalesa 109) (1981 — NR 1982 6d 7f 8f 11.7f 8.2g) short-backed gelding; first reported foal; dam never ran; well beaten in varied company. *K. Bridgwater.*

DESERT ISLAND (USA) 2 b.f. Roanoke Island–Savage Call (Jungle Savage) — (1982 6g) Jan 27; $25,000Y; quite a well-made, attractive filly; second foal; half-sister to Lady Jove (by Northern Jove), a stakes winner at up to 6f; dam won two 6f claiming races; weak in market and just in need of race, no show in 19-runner maiden event won by What Lake at Newmarket in September. *L. Cumani.*

DESERT ROCK 2 ch.g. Grey Mirage 128–Green Diamond (Green God 128) — (1982 5f 6f 6g) behind in maiden races and a seller; dead. *N. Vigors.*

DESERT STAR 5 ch.h. Hot Spark 126–Ice Ballet 87 (Ballymoss 136) (1981 47 13fg2 12d 12g3 10f2 12g 12d 12g 1982 10fg 12g 10f 10fg* 12fg) attractive, well-made horse; dropped in class when winning poorly-contested seller at Folkestone in August (no bid); stayed 13f; was suited by a sound surface; blinkered and bandaged once in 1980; was good mount for an inexperienced rider; dead. *S. Woodman.*

DESTROY (USA) 3 b. or br.c. Annihilate 'Em–Nun Better (Bupers) (1981 — NR 1982 7.6fg 12f 11f 10f 9g 8g2 8.2s 8g 7g) $4,300F, $18,000Y; tall, rather narrow colt; third foal; brother to a minor winner at up to 1m in USA; dam won 5 races up to 1m in USA, including claiming events; poor maiden on balance of form; best run at 1m; blinkered fifth start; sold to R. Akehurst 5,000 gns Ascot November Sales. *I. Walker.*

DETENTE 2 ch.f. Dominion 123–Dove 92 (Sea Hawk II 131) (1982 7d 10s)   – p
June 10; 8,000Y; good-topped filly; third foal; closely related to useful 1980
2-y-o 5f winner Palumba (by Derring-Do) and half-sister to 3-y-o 1½m winner
Fitzwarren (by Busted); dam, winner of 6f winner; noted staying on strongly when
just behind first six in big fields of maidens at Leicester and Nottingham (slowly
away after getting upset in stalls) in October; likely to improve. *P. Kelleway.*

DEUTSCHMARK 2 b.c. Nebbiolo 125–Santa Luciana (Luciano) (1982 6d   **84** p
6s) Jan 28; IR 12,500Y; strong, lengthy colt; third foal; half-brother to
Sabrine (by Mount Hagen), a winner at up to 1½m in Ireland; dam, winner at
2 yrs in Ireland, comes from excellent German family; backward, never-dangerous
eighth of 21 to Spanish Place in maiden race at Newmarket in October, first
outing and better effort; needs further than 6f, and will stay at least 1¼m:
should improve. *H. Wragg.*

DEV 3 b.c. Free State 125–Meadow's Alley (St Paddy 133) (1981 7d 7fg 7fg   –
6d* 6g 1982 6s 8fg 8fg 8fg 11f⁴ 10d 10f 7s 8d) well-made colt; good mover;
quite a moderate handicapper; possibly stays 11f; sold 3,900 gns Newmarket
Autumn Sales. *G. Harwood.*

DEVIL MAY CARE 5 b.g. Galivanter 131–Taffimai (Never Say Die 137)   **64**
(1981 7.5g² 8.5d² 7.5g² 8s 7g² 7fg³ 8d³ 8fg 8g 8s³ 10.2g 1982 8fg 8fg⁴ 7fg²
8.3g 8g² 8fg³ 7s² 7g 8.2s) strong, good sort; ran best races when placed in
handicaps; stays 1m well (beaten in valuable seller over 1¼m final start in 1981);
seems to act on any going; has run well for an apprentice. *W. Hastings-Bass.*

DEVIL QUEEN 2 ch.f. Queen's Hussar 124–God Sent 75 (Red God 128§)   **53**
(1982 5d⁴ 5d³ 5f 5f⁴ 6s 6g 7f 6fg 6f³ 6g 6d 7g) Mar 19; 700Y; leggy filly; half-
sister to 2 winners, including 1¼m winner Marguerite Gerard (by Rheingold);
poor plater; stays 7f; sometimes wears blinkers; none too consistent. *D. Dale.*

DEVILS ALTERNATIVE 3 br.f. Hotfoot 126–Heaven Knows 113 (Yellow   **67**
God 129) (1981 5d 6fg 1982 7.6fg 12fg 10g 12f⁴ 12g³ 10g 12fg) strong,
short-legged filly; plating-class maiden; suited by 1½m; ran badly final start.
R. Smyth.

DEVISDALE 3 b.c. Swing Easy 126–Miss By Miles 91 (Milesian 125) (1981   – §
5d 5g² 6fg 5d 6d 1982 7g 10f⁴ 8f⁴ 7.2f⁴ 6fg 9fg³ 8g⁴) most attractive colt;
good walker; only plating class; seems to stay 1¼m; acts on firm going; blinkered
fourth to sixth starts, looking sour on final occasion. *J. Fitzgerald.*

DEVON AIR 3 b.f. Sparkler 130–Vicomtesse 97 (Relko 136) (1981 6fg 7fg²   –
8fg⁴ 1982 12fg⁴ 12fg 12f 10f³ 11.5fg³ 12fg 8v) big, rangy, deep-girthed filly;
poor walker; useful performer at her best; below form most starts at 3 yrs;
one paced and is suited by 1½m; acts on firm going. *J. Cann.*

DEWBERRY 4 b.f. Bay Express 132–Rosaberry 94 (Rockefella) (1981 6fg²   **52**
6s² 6g² 5f⁴ 6f* 6fg 7fg 6fg³ 5.8g 1982 5.8f² 5.8f 5.3g) compact, well-made filly;
good mover; hampered and moved up a place after finishing third to Lord
Wimpy in handicap at Bath in May; stayed 6f; acted on any going; reportedly in
foal to Monsanto. *C. Nelson.*

DHANTERAS 4 b.g. Nonoalco 131–Classic Tune (Ribero 126) (1981 8d   –
8.5fg⁴ 9s⁴ 7g 1982 8s) rangy gelding; lightly raced but has shown signs of
ability, including in 1981 Ladbrokes Blue Riband Trial at Epsom; 20/1 when
eighth of 15 behind Heart of Steel in minor event at Folkestone in October on
only outing of 1982; best form on a firm surface. *G. Lewis.*

DHOFAR 2 ch.g. Octavo 115–Cress (Crepello 136) (1982 5g 6fg³ 6fg³ 7fg⁴   **89**
8g³ 8fg²) Mar 29; IR 5,200F, IR 18,000Y; well-made, good sort; half-brother to
2 winners, including speedy 1976 2-y-o Self Portrait (by Jukebox); dam ran
only 3 times; in frame in maiden and minor events, on final occasion finishing 5
lengths second of 12 to Onslow at Newcastle in October; will stay beyond 1m;
best form with some give in the ground. *G. Pritchard-Gordon.*

DHUARD 5 br.h. Perdu 121–High Fidelyty (Hautain 128) (1981 6s² 5s* 6g*   **72**
5s 5d 7d 7g 1982 6g² 6g* 6d* 6s) good-topped horse; ran well first 3 outings
and was successful in seller at Pontefract in April (bought in 1,550 gns after
winning comfortably) and in 5-runner handicap at Chester in August (made
nearly all); seems to stay 7f; acts well on soft going; sometimes sweats up;
has worn blinkers. *D. Hanley.*

DIAMOND CHARM 3 b.f. Sparkler 130–Molly Morgan 91 (Pirate King 129)   –
(1981 5d 5fg 6fg 1982 12f) compact filly; behind in maiden races. *R. Smyth.*

DIAMOND CUTTER 3 b.c. Song 132–Lucinda Anne (Abernant 142) (1981 **115**
5g* 5d 7g 7g 1982 5f 6g* 6f* 6f⁴ 6f 5f* 6d² 6d) strong, good-topped colt;
won handicap at Kempton in May from Lindsey, minor event at Lingfield in June
from El Mansour and small race at Beverley in July from Hello Cuddles (odds on);
also ran creditably to be 3¾ lengths fourth of 18 to Indian King in Cork and
Orrery Stakes at Royal Ascot and equal second of 7, a head behind Great Eastern,
in Prix de Meautry at Deauville in August; suited by 6f; seems to act on any
going; used to give trouble at start; very useful. *R. Williams.*

DIAMOND GALLERY 4 ch.f. Record Token 128–Stroppy Lou (Shantung 132) —
(1981 10f 8.2s 8s 1982 8d 8f 7g) unfurnished filly; poor maiden; showed
a little ability in handicap on first outing. *R. Boss.*

DIAMOND HILL 2 b.f. High Top 131–Montania 68 (Mourne 126) (1982 7g) **82** p
May 10; good-topped filly; sister to 3-y-o Farseeing and closely related to middle-
distance winner Base Camp (by Derring-Do); dam won over 7f; 8/1; stayed on
nicely in closing stages when just over 5 lengths sixth of 21 behind Ski Sailing in
maiden race at Newmarket in October; will stay 1¼m; sure to be better for the
experience. *J. Winter.*

DIAMOND HORSESHOE 4 b.g. Some Hand 119–Hammerwood (Combat 123) —
(1981 5s 5d 6fg 5v 5fg 6g 5s² 6d 1982 6d 7fg 7f) maiden plater; stays 6f;
well suited by soft going; seems best in blinkers. *S. Woodman.*

DIAMOND KING 3 ch.c. Music Boy 124–Long Valley 71 (Ribero 126) (1981 **55**
5s 6d 5g² 5fg 5fg 5d 6g 1982 6s⁴ 5f 7d 6fg 6fg 7s 6s² 6d 6s) strong, sturdy
colt; carries plenty of condition; has a round action; appears not to stay 7f;
needs some give in the ground; ran badly in blinkers final start. *J. Benstead.*

DIAMOND SHOAL 3 b.c. Mill Reef 141–Crown Treasure (Graustark) (1981 **121**
5.8d* 7g² 7f* 7g⁴ 7s 8s 1982 12f* 12f 12fg² 12.5d 12s² 12s² 14.6f³ 12v³ 12d4)
When the Washington International was first staged by John D. Schapiro
in 1952 it was claimed in the American Press that a 'whole new era in racing'
had begun. Schapiro undertook the redoubtable task of bringing together
horses from different countries, even different hemispheres, to compete with
some of the best North American thoroughbreds at Laurel each November.
Entry was by all-expenses-paid invitation so that theoretically the best horses
in the world had the opportunity of meeting; and Schapiro bent over backwards
to see to it that the European horses, particularly those from England, had a
fair chance by staging the race on grass and by having a 'walk-up' start instead
of using stalls. The inaugural running, which attracted a record crowd to
Laurel, was won by the English-trained Wilwyn whose success at least proved,
to the surprise of many sceptics in Europe, that good horses could retain their
form after being flown across the ocean. Of the thirty subsequent winners
of the race, fifteen have represented the United States, eleven have represented
France and there has been one winner each for England, Ireland, Australia and
Venezuela. The French have supported the Washington International with
fervour, particularly since the early-'seventies when other top races on turf,
such as the Turf Classic, the Man o'War Stakes and the Canadian International
Championship, also began to attract French runners in increasing numbers.

*Rosebery Memorial Handicap, Epsom—a winning reappearance for
Diamond Shoal (left), who just gets up from Fitzpatrick
with Alpha Omega (blaze) third*

Tackling American horses in their own back yard has proved highly remunerative but, for some reason, campaigning top horses in North America in the autumn seems to be frowned upon by most of the leading English trainers. Schapiro's efforts to attract the best English-trained middle-distance performers to Laurel have met with only a small measure of success; the majority of horses originally invited to run in the race over the years have stayed at home. Perhaps the race is run too late in the year, perhaps the prize money is not high enough (the 1982 Washington International was worth £89,286 to the winner), perhaps the tight Laurel circuit is unsuitable, but whatever the reason the Washington International is not achieving the purpose for which it was designed. The filly Awaasif and the St Leger third Diamond Shoal represented England in the Washington International in 1982, only the third year in the last eight that there has been an English challenge for the race. Diamond Shoal's creditable fourth to the French-trained April Run was the best by an English-trained runner since Scottish Rifle came third in 1973.

Diamond Shoal was typical of the type that has represented England in the Washington International, several pounds behind the best middle-distance horse of his year trained in England. He won only one of his five races in Britain during the season, the Rosebery Memorial Handicap at the Epsom Derby meeting, but never ran badly, finishing runner-up in the Welsh Derby at Chepstow (to Touching Wood) and in the Great Voltigeur Stakes at York (to Electric), being beaten a length and a half and two and a half by Touching Wood and Zilos in the St Leger, and finishing less than three lengths behind the winner Open Day when fifth in the King Edward VII Stakes at Royal Ascot. Diamond Shoal didn't always get the opportunity in his races to display his full merit. He was usually held up among the backmarkers in the early stages, giving the impression that doubts were entertained about his stamina, and on at least two occasions we thought the tactics contributed to his defeat.

Mr Paul Mellon's "Diamond Shoal"

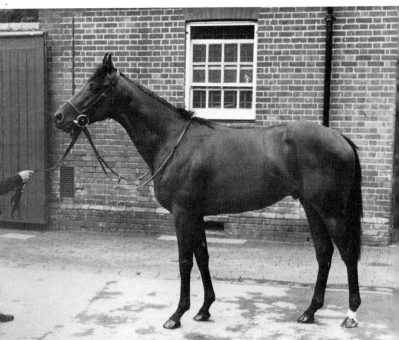

At Royal Ascot his rider elected to make his run on the inside and got badly pocketed; in the St Leger Diamond Shoal, who had only one behind him with half a mile to go, seemed to be set with too much ground to make up and, although he got within striking distance of the leaders and looked dangerous for a few strides, his run petered out in the final furlong. After Diamond Shoal's performance in the Great Voltigeur we had expected him to be ridden in the St Leger in the manner appropriate to a horse whose stamina was not in doubt: Diamond Shoal was beaten for speed, not for stamina, at York, being outpaced by Electric early in the straight when the race began in earnest but staying on the better in the closing stages and going down by only three quarters of a length, with Touching Wood seven lengths away third. As we have said before, Diamond Shoal's trainer is quick to identify opportunities for winning races abroad and Diamond Shoal was sent to contest valuable events in France and Germany during the season. He didn't manage to win from three starts but picked up place money in the Bayerisches Zuchtrennen at Munich and the Preis von Europa at Cologne.

		Never Bend	Nasrullah
	Mill Reef	(b 1960)	Lalun
	(b 1968)	Milan Mill	Princequillo
Diamond Shoal		(b 1962)	Virginia Water
(b.c. 1979)		Graustark	Ribot
	Crown Treasure	(ch 1963)	Flower Bowl
	(b 1973)	Treasure Chest	Rough 'n Tumble
		(b 1962)	Iltis

The Preis von Europa was one of the races won as a three-year-old by Diamond Shoal's full brother Glint of Gold. As his record suggests Diamond Shoal isn't so good a racehorse as his brother, nor is he so imposing an individual in appearance, lacking the size and substance of the magnificent-looking Glint of Gold. Diamond Shoal is an attactive individual nonetheless and, like Glint of Gold, a good mover. Glint of Gold and Diamond Shoal are the first two foals of the very useful Crown Treasure who was also represented on the racecourse in the most recent season by Emerald Reef, a sister to Glint of Gold and Diamond Shoal, who was also in training at Kingsclere. Diamond Shoal stays a mile and three quarters and acts on any going. He is a genuine and consistent colt with the ability to pick up a good race or two as a four-year-old. If he were ours he would be aimed initially at the John Porter Stakes and the Jockey Club Stakes, the conditions of which favour horses that haven't won pattern events. Diamond Shoal is by no means devoid of finishing pace but, with the doubt about his stamina resolved, we can't help feeling his chances of success in pattern-race company would be improved if he were ridden more enterprisingly, making his challenge from a position nearer the front line than has become the habit with him. *I. Balding.*

DIANA'S PET 2 b.c. Mummy's Pet 125–Charonne 87 (Charlottown 127) **104** (1982 5d 6fg² 6f⁴ 6g* 6f⁴ 7fg⁴ 6s) Apr 24; 1,600F, 7,200Y; shallow-girthed, fair sort; good walker and mover; third produce; brother to a poor animal; dam showed promise on second start but never ran again; won 9-runner Moore-style Convivial Maiden Stakes at York in August by 1½ lengths from Comedy Fair; showed better form in most other races, on fifth outing finishing good fourth under 10-0 in nursery at Newmarket, and on final appearance creditable sixth under 9-4 in Golden Gates Nursery at Ascot; apparently best at 6f; appears to act on any going. *P. Kelleway.*

DIBBINSDALE LASS 4 ch.f. Amber Rama 133–Bella Canto 82 (Crooner — 119) (1981 6g 7.6d 5g³ 6d* 7f 6f 7.2fg 6g 6d 1982 5f) leggy, unfurnished filly; stays 6f; acts on any going, but best form with some give in the ground; unruly at start and tailed off throughout on only outing of 1982. *K. Stone.*

DICK 'E' BEAR 2 gr.g. Rupert Bear 105–Silent Swindler 59 (Tacitus 124) **89** (1982 5g² 6f² 6g* 7d 6fg³ 8d) Apr 28; fair sort; half-brother to 5f winner Fiddler (by Song); dam won 1¼m seller; didn't have a lot of room but kept on gamely to catch Mister Valentino close home when winning maiden race at Haydock in August by a neck; put up easily best subsequent effort when 2¼ lengths third of 10 to Hunters Grove under top weight in nursery on same course in September; not sure to stay beyond 6f; acts on firm going. *M. Jefferson.*

DICK'S FOLLY 3 b.c. Martinmas 128–No Princess (Prince Regent 129) (1981 **66** 5g 6g² 6fg² 6s 1982 10.4fg 9fg 8fg² 8fg* 8d³ 8d⁴ 8.2s 8s) quite attractive colt; won handicap at Wolverhampton in September; often pulls hard and isn't certain to stay 1¼m; acts on a firm and a soft surface; sold 3,800 gns Ascot December Sales. *W. Elsey.*

DIDIER 3 ch.c. Relkino 131–French Fern 118 (Mossborough 126) (1981 NR 1982 11f 12g 10fg 7.6d) lengthy colt; half-brother to several winners, including Gold Cup winner Shangamuzo (by Klairon); dam won 1960 Ribblesdale Stakes; well beaten in maiden races; blinkered final start. *J. Bethell.* —

DIDIMO 3 ch.c. Grundy 137–Anchor 106 (Major Portion 129) (1981 NR 1982 8g 12f 14.7f) 5,600Y; compact colt; twin brother to Sea Harrier and half-brother to several winners, notably high-class stayer Sea Anchor (by Alcide); dam won Nell Gwyn Stakes and is half-sister to Oaks winner Bireme (by Grundy); behind in maiden races; sold 1,200 gns Doncaster September Sales. *C. Brittain.* —

DIDO 2 b.f. Full of Hope 125–Current Approach 77 (Right Tack 131) (1982 5fg³ 5fg* 6g* 5f 6fg 6g² 6fg 6d) May 14; leggy, useful-looking filly; second foal; half-sister to fairly useful 1981 2-y-o plater O Solo Mio (by Porto Bello); dam at her best at 2 yrs; successful in sellers at Goodwood (no bid) in May and Lingfield (bought in 3,500 gns) in June, making virtually all both times; ran best subsequent race when failing by only a short head to hold off Ardrox Lad in nursery at Windsor in August; stays 6f well; acts on a firm surface; ridden by 7-lb claimer third to fifth outings. *P. Cole.* **70**

DIE ROYA 2 b.g. Anax 120–Catherine Street (Pall Mall 132) (1982 5f) May 17; 300F; second produce; dam poor maiden; unquoted; tailed-off last of 17 in seller at Catterick in July. *R. Whitaker.* —

DIESIS 2 ch.c. Sharpen Up 127–Doubly Sure 59 (Reliance II 137) (1982 6f 6g* 6g* 7g*) **133**

The *Aeneid's* 'fortune sides with him who dares' rings as true today as in Virgil's time after Diesis' victory in the William Hill Dewhurst Stakes at Newmarket in October. The presence in the field of Gorytus, universally acclaimed as the most exciting two-year-old for years, was enough to frighten off most of the opposition. The Irish colt Danzatore, also spoken of as a potential champion, was aimed instead at the Panasonic Beresford Stakes at the Curragh six days earlier and as usual the French entrants, which had included Deep Roots and L'Emigrant, stayed at home for the Grand Criterium. The only horses to stand their ground against Gorytus were the 200/1-shot Tough Commander, still a maiden after three runs, the 33/1-chance Gordian and the William Hill Middle Park Stakes winner Diesis, who started at 2/1. Even running Diesis attracted some criticism. He had still been patently immature when winning the Middle Park and the suggestion was that a race against the more precocious Gorytus would not only prove fruitless but damaging, very possibly. His owner took a different view, believing it to be jumping the gun a little to regard Gorytus as invincible on the evidence of only two races, and he was keen to take him on. The decision whether or not to run was left ultimately to Diesis' trainer, and Cecil had his mind made up for him when Diesis turned in a spectacular gallop against some of the stable's other top juveniles. As things turned out Diesis had anything but a hard race. Gorytus, running inexplicably badly, was beaten soon after halfway where Diesis was in last place, as he'd been from the start. As Gorytus began to drop out Diesis came to challenge, impressing enormously as he moved from last to first in a matter of strides and quickened right away up the hill, putting five lengths between himself and the long-time leader Gordian in no time at all. Diesis thereby became the first horse to win both the Middle Park and Dewhurst since the subsequent Derby winner Lemberg did so in 1909.

In the blaze of publicity surrounding Gorytus' defeat Diesis' performance tended to be overlooked, or even dismissed on the grounds that he had had only Gordian and Tough Commander to beat. This seems most unfair. Certainly one would have wished for more testing opposition but Gordian is no slouch. On his previous start he had appeared unlucky to be beaten by those smart colts Polished Silver and Cause Célèbre after getting boxed in in the Somerville Tattersall Stakes, yet Diesis left him standing. Diesis' time was highly respectable, producing a timefigure of 1.14 fast, the third best of the season by a two-year-old. And, all in all, Diesis has done quite enough to convince us that he is a very worthy favourite for the Two Thousand Guineas.

The first intimation that Diesis might prove out of the ordinary came from his trainer in the spring. He told us: 'Diesis is a full brother to Kris. He was a rather thin, narrow yearling and didn't do particularly well when turned out,

William Hill Middle Park Stakes, Newmarket—Diesis keeps on gamely under pressure to account for Orixo (spots) and Krayyan (left)

but he's really thriving now and looks more and more like his full brother. He's a very good mover with a much more placid temperament than Kris had, and I'm very keen on him—I don't think it's because of Kris, but rather on his own merits!' Considering that Kris won fourteen of his sixteen starts, including the Sussex, Lockinge and Queen Elizabeth II Stakes, Diesis was clearly an exciting prospect. Kris didn't tackle top company until the autumn of his two-year-old days and Diesis too was brought along steadily, making his debut in the Fulbourne Maiden Stakes at Newmarket in July. He started none too well, then didn't find much room when making good progress from the distance and in the circumstances showed plenty of promise in finishing fifth of fifteen, only three lengths behind Lofty. A month later he reappeared on his home course in the Rhys-Jenkins and Standing Stakes, starting at 7/4 on in a field of eleven. He quickly showed the enormous benefit he'd derived from his previous run. This time he broke well and was soon striding out powerfully in the lead. All Is Forgiven managed to stay in touch until one and a half furlongs out but then Diesis produced a magnificent burst of speed, sprinting away without any apparent effort. After being fully ten lengths clear at one stage, Piggott began pulling Diesis back and they crossed the line seven lengths ahead of Swift To Conquer, a winner at Chester on her next start.

Diesis still looked immature and narrow at this stage, and he wasn't to be rushed; eventually it was announced that Diesis' next target was the Burr Stakes at Lingfield on September 21st. As things turned out Diesis missed Lingfield, partly because it was feared the ground would be too firm (ironically the race was eventually run on soft ground) and partly because his stable found need for a substitute for Salieri in the Middle Park Stakes since that horse had less than a fortnight to recover after his win in the Mill Reef Stakes at Newbury. Diesis, who had reportedly been working well with Salieri, was the obvious replacement.

The Molecomb Stakes and Flying Childers Stakes winner Kafu and the National Stakes winner Krayyan, the two colts who had chased Salieri home at Newbury, also took the field in the Middle Park. Diesis' other opponents at Newmarket were the unbeaten Railway Stakes winner Ancestral, who was testing the strength of the British two-year-olds for the Vincent O'Brien stable, and Orixo, an improving sort who had made all in a big field at Doncaster on his last appearance. Diesis, perhaps the least appealing individual in a very good-looking field, started odds on and put up a splendid display. Again he

265

quickly took the lead, racing towards the outside, with Krayyan and Orixo giving chase. In this much stronger company he was never travelling so easily as on his previous start and Piggott began to push him along fully two furlongs out. Diesis responded most gamely, lengthening his stride and battling on well to beat Orixo by two and a half lengths. One particularly impressive aspect of Diesis' performance here was the tremendous action he displayed; he strode out like a really good horse, just as he did in the Dewhurst.

		⎧ Atan	⎧ Native Dancer
	⎧ Sharpen Up	⎨ (ch 1961)	⎨ Mixed Marriage
	⎪ (ch 1969)	⎩ Rocchetta	⎧ Rockefella
Diesis	⎨	(ch 1961)	⎩ Chambiges
(ch.c. Apr 23, 1980)	⎪	⎧ Reliance II	⎧ Tantieme
	⎩ Doubly Sure	⎨ (b 1962)	⎨ Relance III
	(b 1971)	⎩ Soft Angels	⎧ Crepello
		(ch 1963)	⎩ Sweet Angel

Diesis' emergence makes Sharpen Up's exportation to the States look even more regrettable. Diesis belongs to Sharpen Up's penultimate British crop which also includes the very useful colts Bold Bob and Fine Edge. Thankfully Kris is already at stud here and Sharpo is to stand his first season at the Woodlands Stud, Newmarket, in 1983 so breeders at least have the services of two top-class sons of Sharpen Up. Diesis unfortunately won't be increasing that figure to three. His owner, feeling he can't stand him in this country in direct competition with Kris, has sold a quarter share and Diesis will eventually stand at Mill Ridge Farm, Kentucky. Lord Howard will eventually face a similar dilemma if reports of Diesis' younger brother Keen are to be believed. Keen, another chesnut, is said to be a far better-looking yearling than was either of his brothers. Incidentally all three sons of Sharpen Up and Doubly Sure are well named, particularly Kris (a double-edged Malaysian dagger) and Diesis (the double dagger character used in musical notation and printing).

Diesis is the first winner bred by Doubly Sure since Kris. Of her three foals in between, the first died as a yearling, the second, the Priamos filly Pris, was retired to stud without racing (she produced her first foal, a colt by Manado, in 1982) and the third, the Reform colt Risk, has proved very disappointing. Doubly Sure wasn't covered after producing a late foal, a colt, by General Assembly in 1982 but she is to visit Mill Reef in 1983. Doubly Sure's dam Soft Angels has had a chequered career as a broodmare. She bred three fillies in her first four years: the first, the very useful Dulcet, died as a four-year-old, the second, Wolfing, broke her pelvis as a two-year-old and the third, Doubly Sure, achieved next to nothing on the racecourse. Soft Angels wasn't covered the year Doubly Sure was foaled, and since then she has been barren six times and slipped her foal on three other occasions. It must therefore have been a great relief to her owner when Sancta, Soft Angels' only foal in the last eleven years, won her first three starts as a three-year-old in 1982. Soft Angels was a high-class two-year-old, winning both the Princess Margaret and the Royal Lodge Stakes but she became very troublesome at the start and proved most disappointing. Kris also proved troublesome at the start on occasions, obstinate at any rate, but Diesis appears to have an excellent temperament.

Diesis is a rangy, attractive colt. His portrait, taken late in the season, shows his distinct resemblance to Kris at the same age, although Diesis is perhaps slightly lengthier. Kris later filled out into a very attractive individual, improving a good deal in the process. If Diesis makes similar physical progress—and we see no reason why he shouldn't—he will surely be a very formidable miler. His form at two was better than Kris's and he must have a splendid chance of improving on his brother's second in the Two Thousand Guineas. His trainer is

William Hill Dewhurst Stakes, Newmarket—Diesis strides away from Gordian for his second Group 1 victory of the season

Lord Howard de Walden's "Diesis"

particularly keen to give him a preliminary race, believing that Diesis improves a great deal with a run, and his initial target is said to be the Greenham Stakes, a race Kris won by three lengths. If he proves as courageous and consistent as his brother we are in for some wonderful races in 1983. *H. Cecil.*

DIFFERENT CLASS 2 b.c. The Brianstan 128–Acknowledgement (Fleet Nasrullah) (1982 6fg 5d) Apr 16; 1,700F; leggy colt; half-brother to 3-y-o 6f winner Musical Score (by Music Boy) and a winner in Italy by My Swallow; dam unraced daughter of $122,000-earner Tinkalero; no sign of ability in newcomers race at Chepstow in August and maiden event at Nottingham (unruly in paddock) in September. *Mrs B. Waring.* —

DIGNIFIED AIR (FR) 2 b.f. Wolver Hollow 126–Dismantle 77 (Aureole 132) (1982 6s³) half-sister to 3-y-o Hotmantle (by Hotfoot) and 7f winner Triple Bar (by Jimmy Reppin); dam, winner over 7f at 2 yrs, is half-sister to very smart Joking Apart; second favourite but apparently in need of race, had to be chased along at halfway and was not unduly punished in closing stages when 4 lengths third of 16 to Marzooga in maiden event at Leicester in November; will stay 7f+; sure to improve. *M. Jarvis.* **70** p

DIJLA 3 ch.f. Hittite Glory 125–La Meme 90 (Pall Mall 132) (1981 6fg 7fg³ 7fg³ 7h* 7.3d 8.2d 1982 7g⁴ 7g 7f 8fg⁴ 8f* 7f⁴ 8fg*) close-coupled filly; successful in handicaps at Leicester and Chepstow; runs as if she'll be suited by 1¼m; acts well on firm ground. *H. T. Jones.* **77**

DI LITHO (USA) 2 b.f. Forli–Clear Copy (Copy Chief) (1982 7.6v 7s) Mar 21; quite attractive filly; fourth foal; half-sister to a winner by Riva Ridge; dam smart at 3 yrs in USA when winner 8 times at up to 1m; behind at long odds in maiden races in October at Lingfield and Sandown. *J. Dunlop.* —

DIMITRI 3 ch.c. Sharpen Up 127–Doushiska 78 (Hornbeam 130) (1981 7g 1982 8fg² 11f 10fg² 10.1d³ 10.1fg⁴ 10g*) well-made, attractive colt; short-priced favourite when winning 9-runner maiden race at Brighton in August; will probably stay 1½m. *C. Nelson.* **77**

DINGLE BELLE 2 ch.f. Dominion 123–Temple Wood 105 (Sweet Revenge 129)   **72** p
(1982 6d) Apr 8; neat filly; first foal; dam, winner from 5f to 1m, is half-sister
to very smart Town and Country; 14/1 and fit, stayed on after dwelling and
being outpaced when about 4 lengths sixth of 12 behind Stephalotus in minor
race at Pontefract in October; will stay 1m. *W. Hastings-Bass.*

DINNER TOAST (USA) 2 b. or br.f. Raise a Cup–Dinner Meeting (Bold   — p
Ruler) (1982 6g) Feb 6; \$77,000Y; well-grown, useful-looking filly; fourth
foal; sister to a winner and half-sister to another; dam, unraced twin, is half-
sister to Nostalgia, a very smart stakes winner at up to 1m; unquoted and
ridden by apprentice unable to claim his 7-lb allowance, wasn't knocked about
when never-dangerous seventh of 19 to What Lake in maiden race at Newmarket
in September; has plenty of scope and is sure to do better. *R. Armstrong.*

DINSLEY 3 ch.f. Morston 125–Noirmont Girl 95 (Skymaster 126) (1981 NR   **66**
1982 8fg 10.5fg 8g 8.2fg³ 8fg 10fg 10.6s³ 12v⁴ 12d²) 45,000Y; tall, workmanlike
filly; half-sister to 5 winners, including very useful 1977 2-y-o 5f performer
Noiritza (by Young Emperor); dam ran only over 5f; quite modest; stays 1½m;
seems to act on any going; well beaten in blinkers third start. *J. W. Watts.*

DIONE 3 gr.f. Mill Reef 141–La Speroana 68 (Roan Rocket 128) (1981 7g³ **119**
1982 7g* 8fg³ 12f 12fg 8f 10fg 10f* 9.2s*)
    While the simultaneous duplication of names among racehorses is now
more prevalent and at times more confusing than ever, it is not just a recent
phenomenon. Admittedly, in 1982 there were such examples as Al Nasr and
Al Nasr (Fr) and Indian King (Fr) and Indian King (USA), but in 1835, for
instance, two colts called Ibrahim ran in the Derby and in 1944 a pair of three-
year-olds named Sirius won races on the same day in Melbourne and Kentucky.
In fact consideration of the incidence of name repetition over a long period
reveals that originality in naming thoroughbreds is no easy matter. There
were colts called Nijinsky foaled in the States (two), England and France before
the 1970 Triple Crown winner saw the light of day, and to take an extreme
example there have been twenty-three fillies named Cinderella in the *General
Stud Book* plus a number abroad. Given this, the name of one of Zeus's wives in
classical mythology, Dione, carried by fillies foaled in Britain in 1824, 1845,
1867, 1893, 1908, 1925 and 1979—two of them were subsequently renamed—has
a long way to go before it reaches a challenging position in the popularity stakes.
    The most recent Dione enjoyed a three-year-old career that was solid at either
end but distinctly unsteady in the middle. Her reappearance in a sixteen-
runner maiden race at Newmarket in April saw her finish strongly to peg back
Vadrouille and win by three quarters of a length. Dione moved up markedly
in class for her next assignment in the One Thousand Guineas on the same
course later in the month and acquitted herself well, keeping on courageously
despite being outpaced by the first two to be four and a half lengths third to
On The House, decisively outpointing her better-fancied stable-companion
Stratospheric in sixth. Four comprehensive defeats followed this excellent
display and by September, when she took part in the Twickenham Stakes at
Kempton, Dione looked for all the world like a filly who had failed to progress.
Two of the defeats came at a mile and a half, a trip which on breeding ought to
have suited Dione but in the event proved beyond her. In the Oaks she dropped
right out in the last three furlongs to be tenth to Time Charter and in the Ribblesdale Stakes at Royal Ascot she led for ten furlongs before weakening quickly
to finish sixth to Dish Dash. Yet when brought back to shorter distances
Dione still failed to reproduce her Guineas running, making little show in the
Child Stakes at Newmarket, in which she ended up fifth to Chalon, and disputing
the lead for a mile but only plugging on at one pace to be eighth to Dancing
Rocks in the Nassau Stakes at Goodwood.

			Never Bend		Nasrullah
	Mill Reef		(b 1960)		Lalun
	(b 1968)		Milan Mill		Princequillo
Dione			(b 1962)		Virginia Water
(gr.f. 1979)			Roan Rocket		Buisson Ardent
	La Speroana		(ro 1961)		Farandole II
	(gr 1969)		La Speranza		Princely Gift
			(ch 1962)		The Accused

    Hence when she arrived at Kempton Dione was relatively unfancied,
starting fourth favourite in a five-runner field completed by the odds-on favourite
Zinzara, fresh from a success in the Prix de Psyche, the Galtres Stakes winner

Prix de l'Opera, Longchamp—Dione is all out to beat Unknown Lady

Sans Blague, Top Hope and Mirkan Honey. Sent on immediately they left the stalls, she set a fast pace and had a three-length lead entering the straight; maintaining the gallop well Dione never looked like surrendering the advantage and at the line had three lengths to spare over Zinzara who didn't manage to pose a serious threat after being given plenty to do. Even allowing for the possible over-confidence of Zinzara's jockey, it was evident that Dione had returned to something like her best, and she started second favourite for the Group 2 Prix de l'Opera at Longchamp on Arc day. Opposed by such as the Prix d'Astarte winner Thorough, the Prix de Royaumont winner Vidor, Parannda, successful in the Prix de Sandringham, and Unknown Lady and Black Narcissus, each of whom had smart form in pattern races to her name, Dione soon lay at the head of affairs setting a strong gallop. As at Kempton she kept up

Mr D. D. Prenn's "Dione"

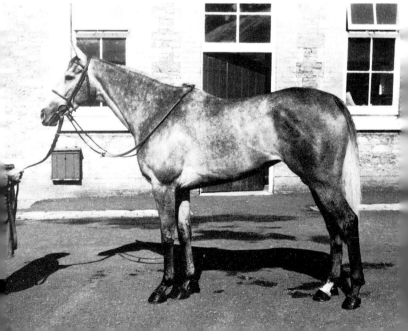

the good work to the end, battling on with commendable resolution to hold off Unknown Lady by a length with Vidor a further length and a half away third. This was the second success in the race for an English-trained filly since its inception in 1974—Cistus had won in 1978.

Dione, who has been sent to California to be trained by Gosden, is the third winner produced by La Speroana, successful in a mile maiden race at three. Both the others have also been by Mill Reef, and both stayed further than Dione— Beau Reef showed smart form at up to two miles before being killed in Australia and Madigan Mill won over eleven and a half furlongs as a four-year-old. The second dam, a once-raced half-sister to the top-class miler The Creditor (dam of Owen Dudley and Abwah) and the Royal Lodge winner Pinched, has foaled three other winners, two of them sprint winners in England by Song. Dione is a small, well-made filly who stays a mile and a quarter and acts on any going. Ideally suited by forcing tactics, she's most genuine. *J. Dunlop.*

DIONYSUS 3 ch.g. Red God 128§–Queen's Keys 84 (Right Royal V 135) (1981 5d 8s³ 8d 1982 12f 10.1fg 15.5f³ 16s) big, well-made, attractive gelding; only plating class; not sure to stay 2m; blinkered third start; sold out of P. Walwyn's stable 2,700 gns Ascot January Sales. *H. Beasley.* —

DISCO 4 ch.g. Jukebox 120–Only A Game (Whistling Wind 123) (1981 6s* 6s⁴ 7d³ 7s 7fg 7g 1982 7fg 5.8f 6f) strong gelding; soundly beaten in 1982; stays 7f; acts on soft going; often blinkered; sold 1,600 gns Ascot September Sales. *L. Kennard.* —

DISCO FEVER 4 br.f. Workboy 123–Gin A Go Go 72 (Cash and Courage 116) (1981 5s 6g 5d 6g 5f 5f 5fg³ 7fg 6f 5d² 1982 6f 6f 5fg 6fg) strong, compact filly; plater; best form at 5f; blinkered final start in 1981. *J. Mason.* —

DISH DASH 3 b.f. Bustino 136–Loose Cover 106 (Venture VII 129) (1981 **118** 6fg² 7d² 6d* 1982 8f* 12fg* 10fg 12fg³ 10d⁴ 12f 10g³)

Bustino's career as a stallion has so far taken an entirely predictable course. Retired in 1976 he is now established among the leading sires in England, an influence for stamina, tending strongly to get the slower-developing type. Each of his first three crops has contained at least one pattern winner: this became so upon Easter Sun's victory in the Coronation Cup. Bustino had two other pattern winners in the latest season, the three-year-old fillies Dish Dash and Height of Fashion, the former the more typical of her sire in that she improved considerably from two years to three.

Ribblesdale Stakes, Ascot—Dish Dash (left)
holds off Sing Softly by a neck

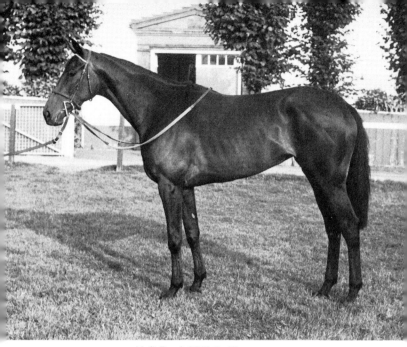

Mr J. Bryce's "Dish Dash"

As a two-year-old Dish Dash took until the last of her three races to get off the mark, in a six-furlong maiden at Nottingham in the autumn, having been second in a minor event at Newmarket and a maiden at Newbury. She gave the impression that she found six furlongs very much on the sharp side. A hard-gained win over Dancing Rocks in the Chequers Stakes over a mile at Sandown in June was her only additional racecourse experience before she faced much the strongest field and tackled much the longest distance of her career to that point in the Ribblesdale Stakes at Royal Ascot two weeks later. While much the strongest Dish Dash had faced, the Ribblesdale field was nothing out of the ordinary by its own standards. Main Sail started favourite ahead of Top Hope who hadn't run since 1981, and there were only two from the Oaks, Dione and Tants; Dish Dash started co-third favourite with Sing Softly in a field of ten. That which Dish Dash had to do she accomplished very well, racing into the lead from Dione and Tants below the distance and staying on sufficiently strongly never to appear in danger of being overtaken by Sing Softly whom she held by a neck in the end. Subsequently Dish Dash regularly took on the best of the three-year-old fillies, including the French in the Prix Vermeille, without further success. She was well beaten behind All Along in the Vermeille but by then had confirmed that a distance of a mile and a half suited her well with a splendid performance in the Yorkshire Oaks, a very close and game third to Awaasif and Swiftfoot. Three races over a mile and a quarter brought place-money on two occasions—through her fair fourth to Cut Loose in the Virginia Stakes at Newcastle and her equally fair third to Time Charter in the Sun Chariot Stakes.

Dish Dash's dam was a miler, a useful one; she won four handicaps in a row, equalling the course record at Brighton on one occasion. She has had a long and highly successful career in the paddocks, producing six winners besides Dish Dash, of whom the miler Silk and Satin (by Charlottown), the middle-

271

distance horse Feliciano (by Alcide) and the American stakes winner Canterbury Tale (by Exbury) were well out of the ordinary, and a fourth, the versatile Smoggy (by Run The Gantlet), was on the verge of classic standard in France and later won a Grade 2 Handicap in the United States. The next dam Nymphet was a winning sprinter and so was her dam Circassia, the latter a

			Busted		Crepello
	Bustino		(b 1963)		Sans le Sou
	(b 1971)		Ship Yard		Doutelle
Dish Dash			(ch 1963)		Paving Stone
(b.f. 1979)			Venture VII		Relic
	Loose Cover		(br 1957)		Rose O'Lynn
	(b 1963)		Nymphet		Nearula
			(ch 1958)		Circassia

half-sister to the One Thousand Guineas winner Zabara. Dish Dash is a lengthy filly, and excellent walker. She is more effective on a softish surface than was her dam but, as was Loose Cover, she is particularly well suited to top-of-the-ground conditions. She is a genuine sort. *R. Armstrong.*

DISTANT THUNDER 2 b.c. Wolver Hollow 126–Trusted Maiden (Busted 134)   **71 p**
(1982 7g 8g) May 8; IR 56,000Y; well-made, attractive colt; half-brother to 1980 Irish 2-y-o 1m winner Nulla Bona (by Realm); dam placed at up to 1¼m in Ireland; 20/1 although pick of paddock, unable to quicken after going well at halfway when 11 lengths sixth of 17 behind Oula Owl in maiden race at Newmarket in October, second outing; will do better if looks count for anything. *B. Hills.*

DISTINCTION 3 br.g. Star Appeal 133–Love Resolved (Dan Cupid 132)   (1981   **—**
7g 7.6s 10s   1982 12f 16h 16g⁴ 13.4g 13f) strong, compact gelding; good mover; beaten some way in varied company, including selling; blinkered last 3 outings; has given trouble at start. *D. H. Jones.*

DITTON WOOD 5 b.h. Moulton 128–Fortezza 108 (Botticelli 129)   (1981 10s   **84**
12v 8g* 8fg* 9fg³ 8g² 9d³ 8v   1982 8g 10f² 8g) big, strong horse; blinkered first time when 2 lengths second to Aperitivo in 5-runner handicap at Sandown in April; in rear without blinkers only subsequent start (May); stays 1½m but is better at shorter distances; acts on a soft surface but goes well on top-of-the-ground; suitable mount for a boy; sold 4,400 gns Newmarket Autumn Sales. *H. Wragg.*

DIVINE MADNESS 3 gr.g. Godswalk 130–Crash Helmet 77 (Crocket 130)   **80**
(1981 5s 6f 6fg 6fg³   1982 6.5g* 8s 5s 6g² 7f* 7f* 7g 7f 7g⁴) smallish, lengthy gelding; carries plenty of condition; won small race at Cagnes-sur-Mer and handicaps at Warwick and Doncaster; not seen out after August; stays 7f but is a free-running sort and isn't certain to get 1m; suited by a sound surface; hung left fourth start; changed hands 26,000 gns Newmarket July Sales; sent to Hong Kong. *R. Armstrong.*

DIVINE TRUTH 3 b.c. So Blessed 130–False Evidence 53 (Counsel 118)   (1981   **79**
5g 6g 6g   1982 6g 7f² 8fg 8.2f³ 10.2g² 11.7fg² 12.3g* 11.7g 12fg⁴ 11.7s) good-looking colt; good mover; placed in varied company before winning 8-runner maiden race at Newcastle in August; stays 1½m well; acts on firm going; suitable mount for an apprentice; sold to P. Haynes 10,000 gns Newmarket Autumn Sales. *G. Harwood.*

DIVO (CHI) 5 b.g. Decano–Miti Miti (Monterrico 128)   (1981 NR   1982 8g*   **51**
10d 11.7g) Chilean-bred gelding; won 4 times over 6f in Chile; led on post to beat Frank Berry a head in 25-runner amateur riders race at Warwick in June; stays 1m; sold 480 gns Doncaster November Sales. *P. Haynes.*

DIZZY HEIGHTS 4 b.f. Daring Display 129–Balholm 61 (Le Levanstell 122)   **—**
(1981 7v 8g* 8f 9f 10fg³ 10f* 8d 10f 10fg 7s 10s³ 10.2g   1982 10.1fg 10f 8fg 10fg 10d 10g 10f 8g 10g⁴) small, lengthy filly; disappointing plater; stays 1¼m; acts on any going; occasionally blinkered; suitable mount for an apprentice. *H. Fleming.*

DJANGO 2 br.c. Music Boy 124–Young Mementa (Young Christopher 119)   **90**
(1982 5f* 5g² 5g) Mar 10; rangy colt; brother to useful 1980 2-y-o 5f and 6f winner Mementa Mia and half-brother to several winners; dam never ran; won 14-runner maiden race at Salisbury in August in good style by 2½ lengths from Balkan; ran well afterwards, giving 10 lb to winner when ½-length second

to Play Our Song in £3,600 event at Goodwood and finishing 2¾ lengths fifth of 15 to Wiki Wiki Wheels in valuable nursery at Newbury; may stay 6f. *K. Brassey.*

D'LO 4 b.g. Sovereign Path 125–Blaskette 99 (Blast 125) (1981 10s 10.1f **67** 11g* 10f* 12fg 10f 10d 1982 11f³ 12fg* 12fg⁴ 12.2fg² 12.2fg³ 12f* 13.1g 12fg) rangy, quite attractive gelding; won poorish handicaps at Pontefract in May and Redcar in August; not all that consistent however; stays 1½m; acts well on firm going; best in blinkers; sold to R. Holder 7,200 gns Newmarket Autumn Sales. *J. Bethell.*

DOC MARTEN 4 b.c. Hotfoot 126–Rockney 84 (Roan Rocket 128) (1981 **97** 7g 6g 1982 7fg 7f³ 7f³ 6fg 6g³ 7f⁴ 6fg³ 6f³ 6fg⁴ 6fg 6g*) quite useful sort; picked up a good prize when beating Dancing Devil by ½ length in £14,200 SAS First Class Open Sprint at Taby, Sweden, in September; usually thereabouts in his handicaps earlier and was in frame at Lingfield (twice), Newcastle, Newmarket (twice), Newbury and Nottingham; stays 7f; acts on any going, except perhaps heavy; often used to be bandaged behind; broke out of stalls and was withdrawn on one occasion. *A. Hide.*

DOCTOR FAUSTUS 4 gr.g. Martinmas 128–Pampatamy 75 (Immortality) — (1981 6fg* 7f* 6d² 8g⁴ 8f 7g 8fg 7fg 1982 8g 10f) small, sturdy gelding; probably stayed 1m; won on a firm surface but seemed suited by some give in the ground; was tried in blinkers; dead. *Mrs J. Pitman.*

DOCTOR PANGLOSS 3 ch.c. Sheshoon 132–Palouci 59 (Palestine 133) — (1981 8d 7g 1982 14g) well-made, attractive colt; showed signs of ability in 2 races in 1981 but finished tailed off in minor event at Newmarket on only outing at 3 yrs in October. *M. Stoute.*

DOCUMENTARY 7 b.g. Pontifex–All England 93 (St Paddy 133) (1981 — 8d³ 10g 8g 8f 8f 7fg 8fg 8fg 10f 8s 1982 8fg) poor performer; needs further than 7f and stays 13f; acts on a soft surface; ran freely in blinkers final start in 1981; sold 950 gns Ascot July Sales. *S. Woodman.*

DODGY FUTURE 2 b.c. Nebbiolo 125–Taking Silk (Shantung 132) (1982 **72+** 5fg 7d⁴ 6f) Apr 22; IR 9,200Y; big, quite well-made colt; half-brother to several winners, including disqualified 1978 Italian 1,000 Guineas winner Romantic Love (by Sovereign Path); dam never ran; looked promising by manner of his performances in maiden and minor events in first part of season, but wasn't seen out after July; will be suited by 1m+; one to keep an eye on. *S. Mellor.*

DOGBERRY 4 ch.c. Sassafras 135–Ombra Del Sol (Ballymoss 136) (1981 12d² **90** 12g⁴ 12g³ 12s* 10.5f* 12f* 13.3g 10.5f² 1982 12fg 13.4fg³ 12fg 12fg 12g) tall, quite well-made colt; good walker; useful front-running handicapper as a 3-y-o; had stiff task and ran well when about 4 lengths third of 6 behind stable-companion Six Mile Bottom in Ormonde Stakes at Chester in May; didn't show much afterwards, although looked on backward side next time; will stay 1¾m; acts on any going but is well suited by firm; sold 13,000 gns Newmarket Autumn Sales. *H. Wragg.*

DOGWALK 6 b.g. Ribero 126–Country Path 101 (Mossborough 126) (1981 — NR 1982 12s) strong, good-bodied gelding; good mover; modest handicapper in 1980 (rated 84); bandaged in front when last of 20 only start since (October); stays well; acts on any going. *O. Brennan.*

DO IT NOW 3 b.g. Deep Diver 134–Pim-Pam (Acropolis 132) (1981 5v² — 5s⁴ 5g 5fg 6g 1982 6s) poor form, including in a seller; dead. *J. Berry.*

DOLLAR DARLING 2 ch.f. Record Token 128–Readies (Red God 128§) **80** (1982 5fg 5f² 6fg³ 6f² 6fg⁴ 7g 6d* 6v) Apr 3; 7,200Y; useful-looking filly; fifth foal; half-sister to fairly useful 1981 2-y-o 5f to 6f winner Bolivar Baby (by Gay Fandango); dam ran once; beat long odds-on Al Washl 3 lengths in 2-runner maiden race at Nottingham in September; best form at 6f, but probably stays 7f; seems to act on any going, with possible exception of heavy; consistent. *N. Callaghan.*

DOLLYMIXTURE BOY 4 b.g. Connaught 130–Country Niece (Great Nephew **68** 126) (1981 8d 10g² 10d 10f 10f 8fg² 8.3fg³ 8.2f⁴ 10fg 8fg³ 9f² 8.2s 7g 1982 12f* 12fg* 10f* 10f* 12f* 12g 10g 10g⁴ 10f 10d⁴ 10d) small, sturdy gelding; good walker and mover; improved after being gelded and won his first 5 starts; adopted front-running tactics when winning 2 handicaps at Brighton in runaway style by 12 lengths (second of them an apprentice event), similar races at Ripon and Yarmouth, and minor race at Thirsk, all in first half of season; suited by middle distances and top-of-the-ground; often blinkered at 3 yrs, and has also worn a hood, but didn't wear either in 1982; successful 3 times for apprentice S. Dennison; off course almost 8 weeks after sixth outing and didn't recover his form. *R. Armstrong.*

DOMICILE 2 b.f. Dominion 123–Siliciana 113 (Silly Season 127) (1982 5g 5.8g 8s 7d) Feb 28; strong, stocky, good-bodied filly; half-sister to 3-y-o Kikkuli (by Hittite Glory) and 3 winners, including useful 7f and 11f winner Junta (by Brigadier Gerard); dam won 1973 Cambridgeshire; no worthwhile form in maiden events; may do better in time. *I. Balding.* —

DOMINION GIRL 2 ch.f. Dominion 123–Blue Book 101 (Majority Blue 126) (1982 6fg 7s) Mar 20; 2,100Y; small filly; half-sister to 4 winners, all successful at 2 yrs, including useful La Voleuse (by Burglar) and fairly useful Blues Swinger (by Swing Easy); dam, winner twice over 5f at 2 yrs, stayed 1m; behind in maiden races at Salisbury and Sandown in the autumn. *K. Cunningham-Brown.* —

DOM PERIGNON 7 b.g. Sparkler 130–Breathalyser (Alcide 136) (1981 NR 1982 13f⁴ 12f⁴ 12f 15f) middle-distance handicapper; acts on any going; sold to Mrs R. Lomax 980 gns Newmarket July Sales. *W. Elsey.* —

DOMYNSKY 2 ch.c. Dominion 123–My Therape 112 (Jimmy Reppin 131) **110** (1982 5g² 5f* 6f* 5fg² 6g* 7fg² 6d* 6f² 7f² 6s*) Feb 22; 4,700Y; useful-looking colt; turns his off-fore out slightly; first foal; dam won 7 times at up to 1m; a splendidly tough colt, never out of first 2 in 10 starts; put up very useful effort in 4-runner Marston Moor Stakes at York in October on final appearance, wearing down Boy Trumpeter inside final furlong to win by 2 lengths; had earlier won minor events at Ripon, in May, June and August, and £3,100 race at Pontefract; beaten only a neck under 9-8 in nursery at Catterick on ninth outing; stays 7f well; acts on any going; thoroughly genuine; a credit to his trainer; sent to USA. *M. H. Easterby.*

Mr David Slater's "Domynsky"

DON AVANTI 2 br.c. Dom Racine 121–Injection 94 (On Your Mark 125)   **72**
(1982 5fg 7g 7g) Feb 29; 19,000Y; robust colt; first foal; dam, half-sister to
Night Nurse, won over 1m at 2 yrs; quite a modest maiden; will stay 1m;
off course 3 months after first outing. *A. Jarvis.*

DONEGAL PRINCE 6 b.g.Prince de Galles 125–Serena Rose 76 (Hethersett   **88**
134) (1981 18s² 16.1fg* 16d⁴ 18.4d* 14d⁴ 20fg³ 22.2f* 16g⁴ 21fg² 16d* 18fg³
20s⁴ 16g³ 18g⁴ 1982 18g 16fg 18.4fg 16f⁴ 22.2fg 16.1f 18g 16d⁴ 16v 18s) quite
attractive gelding; a tough customer who won 4 races in 1981, including Chester
Cup and Queen Alexandra Stakes at Royal Ascot; didn't run particularly well
in 1982, although was beaten only 8 lengths after making running when fourth
of 5 behind Ardross in Henry II Stakes at Sandown in June and wasn't entirely
disgraced when fourth to easy winner Mubarak of Kuwait in handicap at Ascot
in September; needs a thorough test of stamina; acts on any going; effective
with or without blinkers; suited by a strong gallop; smart hurdler. *P. Kelleway.*

DONE GOOD 3 gr.g. Jolly Good 122–Donna Julia 79 (Don II 123) (1981   **—**
6g 7fg 7fg 7g 7f² 7d 7d³ 1982 7g 10f 10f 8f² 8fg 8fg 10fg 8.2s³ 10.6s 10g 12d³
10.2s) big, lengthy gelding; good walker; plater; possibly doesn't quite stay
1½m; acts on any going; blinkered nowadays; sold to J. Parkes 1,550 gns
Doncaster November Sales. *R. Whitaker.*

DON GIOVANNI 3 b.g. Dance In Time–Magic Flute 124 (Tudor Melody 129)   **89**
(1981 6g 7g* 1982 8f⁴ 8f 8f 8f 10fg) deep-girthed, quite attractive gelding;
good walker; kept on well to be under a length fourth of 12 to Spanish Pool in
Esher Cup (Handicap) at Sandown in April; well beaten in similar events afterwards; should stay 1¼m. *H. Cecil.*

DONNA BELLINA 3 b.f. Porto Bello 118–Camina 55 (Don Carlos) (1981   **—**
NR 1982 10s 10f 16g) lengthy filly; first foal; dam won 1¼m claiming race and
poor novice hurdle; poor maiden; has given trouble at start. *R. Sturdy.*

DONNA CANDELABRA 3 b.f. Don Carlos–Lantern (Relic) (1981 NR   **—**
1982 7d 10.2g 9f 7.6d 8fg 6fg) lightly-made filly; sister to 3 winners, including
fair 7f and 9f winner Dras Lass; dam unraced twin; poor maiden. *S. Mellor.*

DONNA GREY 2 gr.f. Joshua 129–Empress Donna 48 (Don II 123) (1982 5fg   **—**
7.2s 6s) Mar 18; half-sister to winning sprint plater Secret Express (by Most
Secret); dam poor plater; behind (twice last) in maiden races and a seller.
W. Stubbs.

DON PRESTO (FR) 8 b.g. Presto–Donna Speranza (Stani) (1981 NR   **87 d**
1982 9f² 16.1f 12fg³ 12g 12f³ 10g 11.7fg 12fg 12d³ 12s) strong ex-French gelding;
won 3 races in France in 1980; placed in 1982 minor events at Ripon and Beverley,
handicap at Leicester and amateur riders race at Brighton; stays middle distances;
probably acts on any going; suitable mount for an amateur rider. *D. Morley.*

DON'T WALK BY 3 b.g. Bustino 136–Via Tritus 103 (Sovereign Path 125)   **—**
(1981 NR 1982 10g 12fg 8fg 7s) 9,200Y; workmanlike gelding; third foal;
half-brother to 5f seller winner La Rue Royale (by Realm) and a winner in Belgium;
dam won twice at around 1m; behind in varied company, including selling.
M. W. Easterby.

DON VOLANTE 3 b.g. Free State 125–Moben 73 (Counsel 118) (1981 NR   **—**
1982 11g 8g 10d 10d 8g) 35,000F, 33,000Y, 400 2-y-o; half-brother to Teacher's
Pet (by Mummy's Pet), a very useful 5f to 1m performer in Europe and a stakes
winner in USA; dam, 7f winner, is half-sister to high-class stayer Grey Baron;
well beaten in maiden and minor races; has been tried in blinkers. *G. Lockerbie.*

DOONALLY 6 b.g. Gold Rod 129–Bust 93 (Tenerani 135) (1981 10.6s 12g 10f   **—**
1982 11.7f) small, stocky gelding; poor maiden on flat though has won over
hurdles; has been tried in blinkers; bought out of C. James's stable 4,600 gns
Ascot June Sales. *L. Kennard.*

DORA MAAR (USA) 2 gr.f. Native Charger–Pan Shot (Northern Dancer)   **68**
(1982 6f 6g) Mar 28; $102,000Y; quite attractive, well-made filly with scope;
third foal; dam, daughter of champion 2-y-o filly Process Shot, was stakes-placed
winner at up to 6f; showed good speed without being knocked about when 6½
lengths seventh of 18 to Albadeeah in maiden race at Newmarket in September,
second outing; may improve. *L. Cumani.*

DOREE MOISSON (FR) 2 ch.f. Connaught 130–Bombazine 110 (Shantung   **84**
132) (1982 8f³ 8f³ 8f³) small, fair sort; good mover; half-sister to 3 winners,
including St Leger winner Bruni (by Sea Hawk II) and smart middle-distance
winner Royal Blend (by Crepello); dam fourth in 1966 Oaks; placed in maiden

events at Leicester in September and Wolverhampton in October, running well first time and not so well second; will stay 1½m; hasn't a lot of scope but should win a race. *J. W. Watts.*

D'ORLEANS 5 b.m. Duc D'Orleans 76–What A Performance (Gala Performance) (1981 7g 1982 8d 6g 12d 12f 16g) of no account; sold out of B. Richmond's stable 640 gns Doncaster May Sales after second outing. *R. Ward.* —

DOROTHY BREWIS 3 ch.f. Gulf Pearl 117–Dubarry (Quisling 117) (1981 6g 1982 9.4f³ 9f 10.4d) leggy, sparely-made filly; poor maiden. *G. Richards.* —

DOROTHY JANE 3 b.f. He Loves Me 120–Merette 63 (Runnymede 123) (1981 5g 5fg 6s 5fg⁴ 6g 6fg⁴ 7fg 1982 9fg 8s) neat filly; of little account. *D. Wintle.* —

DORSET EAGLE 2 br.g. Condorcet–Sans Sabots (Whistler 129) (1982 5d* 5g² 5f* 5f² 5fg² 5d* 5f) Apr 22; 5,400Y; smallish, useful-looking gelding; half-brother to numerous winners, including fair miler L'Eveque (by St Chad); dam never ran; won maiden race at Warwick in April and minor events at Folkestone in May and Beverley in July; second on 3 other outings, going down by a length to Able Albert at Chester, by 10 lengths to Brondesbury in Great Surrey Stakes at Epsom and by 1½ lengths to Time's Time in well-contested race at Ayr; not raced after July; will be suited by 6f; seems to act on any going; often sweats up; gelded after final appearance; sent to Hong Kong. *K. Brassey.* **90**

DOUBLE DISCOUNT 4 b. or br.g. Double-U-Jay 120–Quick Sort (Henry the Seventh 125) (1981 7d 11.5f 8s 10d 10f⁴ 8fg 10d* 10d³ 1982 10f 10d) leggy, lightly-made gelding; very lightly raced in 1982; stays 1¼m; probably acts on any going; tends to pull hard. *C. James.* —

DOUBLE FLORIN (USA) 5 b.g. His Majesty–Stamp and Cash (Roi Rouge) (1981 16f* 16fg⁴ 21fg 16.1d 16fg 17.4g 1982 14f 17.1f 16g 16f³ 20fg 14fg 14f 18.8fg 16d) small gelding; good mover; staying handicapper; ran respectably third and fourth starts; needs a sound surface; sometimes sweats up; tends to pull hard and needs straightforward handling. *A. Turnell.* —

DOUBLE-HEADER 7 b.g. Double-U-Jay 120–Hi Tess 65 (Supreme Court 135) (1981 NR 1982 7f) poor plater; stays 1¼m; wears blinkers; good mount for a boy; sold 500 gns Ascot July Sales. *D. Jermy.* —

DOUBLE JET 3 ch.g. Double Jump 131–Aleta 71 (Montaval 129) (1981 5s 5g 7g 8s 1982 8fg) workmanlike gelding; in rear in varied company, including selling. *Miss A. Hill-Wood.* —

DOUBLE MEANING 6 gr.g. High Top 131–Pseudonym 110 (Acropolis 132) (1981 8s 8g 8g 8h⁴ 9fg³ 8g 1982 8.2s 8f 8g⁴) plater nowadays; should stay beyond 9f; acts well on a sound surface; has won for an apprentice. *A. Bailey.* —

DOUBLE SHARP 4 gr.g. Sharp Edge 123–Florintina 104 (Floribunda 136) (1981 8s³ 8d 10s 1982 10fg³ 10g² 10fg 10.2g³ 10.6g 9f) useful-looking gelding; not the best of movers; ran best races when placed in handicaps; stays 1¼m; sometimes blinkered (seems better without). *E. Eldin.* **60**

DOUBLE SHUFFLE 3 b.f. Tachypous 128–Ali Drake (Dicta Drake 126) (1981 8g 1982 10f² 11f⁴ 12d* 12fg² 16g² 14.6g 12s* 12v⁴ 12s*) big, rangy filly; successful in maiden race at Lingfield in June, 4-runner minor event at Lingfield in September (from Lafontaine) and William Hill November Handicap at Doncaster; just held on to dead-heat with Turkoman in last-named; ran creditably most other outings, including when over 6 lengths fourth to Believer in Princess Royal Stakes at Ascot; stays 2m; acts on any going but goes well on soft; blinkered last 4 starts; game. *G. Pritchard-Gordon.* **103**

DOUBLE STITCH 2 b.f. Wolver Hollow 126–Tactless 91 (Romulus 129) (1982 6d²) Mar 27; strong, attractive filly; half-sister to 2 winners, including very useful Padro (by Runnymede), a winner at up to 7f; dam won at 1¼m; second favourite, kept on to finish 2 lengths second of 12 to very easy winner Misguided in minor event at Pontefract in October; will be suited by 7f+; a likeable individual, sure to win at one of the minor meetings. *Sir Mark Prescott.* **74 p**

DOUBLE VIE (FR) 3 br.f. Brigadier Gerard 144–Blondinette (Zeddaan 130) (1981 5f* 5fg³ 6fg³ 7d 1982 7f 5fg 6f 6g 5d) lightly-built filly; fair performer in 1981; well beaten most starts at 3 yrs; stays 6f; acts on firm going. *Sir Mark Prescott.* —

*William Hill November Handicap, Doncaster—a thrilling finish
to the last big race of the season. Double Shuffle (blinkers)
and Turkoman share the spoils*

DOUBLING TIME (USA) 3 ch.f. Timeless Moment–Lodeve (Shoemaker 121) **117**
(1981 NR 1982 9fg³ 10fg* 10g² 10g³ 10.5v² 10v² 10v²) $34,000Y; second foal;
sister to minor stakes-placed 6f winner Space of Time; dam unraced half-sister
to Faraway Son and Liloy; won well-contested minor event at Longchamp in
May by a length from Absolute; placed all other starts, putting up an excellent
effort on fifth outing when beaten a short head by Buchanette in Prix de
Flore at Saint-Cloud in October; stays 1¼m well; seems to act on any going.
O. Douieb, France.

DOUBTFUL 3 br.c. Pitskelly 122–Mistrust (Rustam 127) (1981 5fg 6d 7d **63**
1982 6f 5fg 7.2f⁴ 7f* 7g⁴ 8g*) sturdy colt; plater; won at Catterick in June
(bought in 4,100 gns) and Redcar in August (bought in 1,900 gns); suited by 1m;
acts on firm going; exported to Malaysia. *Sir Mark Prescott.*

DOUBTWASH GIRL 4 b.f. Hot Spark 126–Arodstown Alice (Sahib 114) **60**
(1981 6g 5g 6f⁴ 5fg 5f 5g* 5g 1982 5f* 5fg 6f) small filly; 33/1-winner at
Thirsk in July, beating Caledonian in a desperate finish; in rear both subsequent
outings; speedy and best at 5f; acted on firm going; reportedly in foal to
Lochnager. *M. W. Easterby.*

DOUMAYNA 3 b.f. Kouban–Delsy (Abdos 134) (1981 5fg 6f³ 6fg 1982 10s³ **77**
12g² 12f³ 12f³ 16d 13.4g 13f² 16fg* 16f² 15.8d 18.8fg⁴ 16g 16.1s⁴) neat, well-
made filly; good walker and excellent mover; won maiden race at Warwick in
July; stays well; acts on any going; best in blinkers; lacks pace. *F. J. Houghton.*

DOVER FORT 3 br.g. High Top 131–Idover 95 (Fortino II 120) (1981 7g³ **—**
7g 1982 10s 8fg⁴ 8f 8.5f) lengthy, useful sort; plater; not certain to stay 1¼m;
blinkered last 3 starts; sent to Malaysia. *J. Sutcliffe.*

DO WE KNOW 2 ch.f. Derrylin 115–Who Can Tell 109 (Worden II 129) **—**
(1982 6g 7fg 7f) lengthy, useful sort; good walker; half-sister to
numerous winners, notably high-class 1¼m horse Rarity (by Hethersett); dam
won Fred Darling Stakes; prominent 2f out when remote eighth of 19 to Liberty
Tree in maiden race at Chepstow in August, second outing and only indication
of ability; sold 12,500 gns Newmarket Autumn Sales. *H. Candy.*

DOWN FLIGHT 2 ch.c. Run The Gantlet–Feather Bed 111 (Gratitude 130) **—**
(1982 7g 7fg 7g) May 15; well-made, quite attractive colt; brother to useful
stayer Popaway, and half-brother to several winners, including 3-y-o 1½m and
13f winner Chalkey Road (by Relko) and smart middle-distance filly Cheveley

277

Princess (by Busted); dam second in Irish 1,000 Guineas; unquoted, soundly beaten in large fields of maidens at Newmarket; looks the type to do better in time. *H. Wragg.*

DOWN TO DARKIE 7 ch.g. Shantung 132–Nutting Grove 95 (Crepello 136) — (1981 16s² 18fg³ 14d 14s 16g 16f 16g* 18.4fg* 16fg 16fg 14fg⁴ 12fg³ 16g 18g 1982 18g 16d 18f 14fg 16g) staying handicapper; poor form in 1982; acts on any going; suitable mount for a lady rider; seemed reluctant to race when blinkered fourth start. *M. Haynes.*

DOWN TO ME 5 b.g. Swing Easy 126–Royal Deb (Flush Royal 127) (1981 — NR 1982 12f) 2,000F, 1,850Y; half-brother to 2 winners, including 1¼m seller winner Soloning (by Solon Morn), subsequently a smart jumper; dam never ran; always behind when last of 8 in maiden race won by Believer at Brighton in September. *H. Westbrook.*

DOYLE'S FOLLY 3 b.f. Rheingold 137–Belidra (Prince Taj 123) (1981 5g — 7g 8g 1982 14f 16.5f 12f 12fg) rather lightly-made filly; poor form, including in sellers. *G. Fletcher.*

DRAGARA 2 gr.f. Dragonara Palace 115–Femme Fatale 67 (King's Leap 111) **48** (1982 5g 5d 5f² 5f 5f 6g) May 17; 2,000Y; leggy filly; poor plater; exported to Malaysia. *M. W. Easterby.*

DRAGON FIRE 3 b.f. Dragonara Palace 115–Firella 56 (Firestreak 125) **54** (1981 5s 6f² 7f³ 6g 7g⁴ 6d 1982 8g² 7f 7f 10f³ 11.5f 11.5f⁴ 8.3g* 9g³ 8d 8.3g⁴ 8fg³ 8fg 8.2s³ 8s) lightly-made filly; plater; bought in 820 gns after easily winning at Windsor in July; stays 1¼m; acts on any going; blinkered third start; doesn't always impress in appearance. *M. Ryan.*

DRAGONIST 4 b.f. Dragonara Palace 115–Tzu-Hsi 66 (Songedor 116) (1981 — 6g² 5g² 6s 6fg 6fg 6fg 5.8g* 5s 5d 1982 7.2s 6s 6s 7s) tall, quite well-made filly; sprint handicapper; not seen out until October; probably acts on any going but is ideally suited by some give in the ground; blinkered final start. *M. Camacho.*

DRAGONLEA 2 gr.f. Dragonara Palace 115–Murton Crags 81 (No Argument **90** 106) (1982 5f⁴ 5f* 5d 6f² 6f* 7d⁴ 6g³ 6fg 7s³) May 31; 1,000Y; leggy, light-framed filly; half-sister to Miss Murton (by Mummy's Pet), a minor 2-y-o 5f winner here who subsequently did well in Italy; dam stayed 13f; surprisingly failed to attract a bid after winning 9-runner seller at Doncaster in May by 4 lengths from Leandros; afterwards ran creditably in non-selling company, winning a nursery at Redcar in August and also finishing 1½ lengths third to John French in 7f nursery at York in October; stays 7f well; acts on any going; has worn a bandage on off-hind. *W. Haigh.*

DRAGON PALACE (USA) 4 ch.c. Le Fabuleux 133–Barbara Longhi (Ribot **92** 142) (1981 10.6d 12s 11.7f 16fg* 16fg² 14fg* 14g² 14.6fg³ 16g³ 1982 14f³ 18.4fg² 16g² 16g² 16.1f² 19f³ 14g 16d 18d) compact colt; quite a useful handicapper; placed most outings, including in Ladbroke Chester Cup in May (length second to Dawn Johnny) and Pimm's Goodwood Stakes in July (about 2 lengths third to Atlantic Traveller); ran disappointingly seventh and eighth starts but creditably in Tote Cesarewitch at Newmarket on final outing; suited by a test of stamina; acts on a soft surface, but has run most of his best races on a sound one; quite often sweats up; sold to D. Elsworth 25,000 gns Newmarket Autumn Sales. *M. Jarvis.*

DRAGON PRINCE 2 ch.c. Nishapour 125–Nanno (Busted 134) (1982 5f **87** 6g³ 7g⁴ 6g³ 7s) Apr 30; 12,000Y; big, strong colt; half-brother to 2 winners, including 1981 1-y-o 1m winner Mrs Currie (by He Loves Me); dam unraced half-sister to Gulf Pearl; fair maiden; third in minor events at Newcastle in August and Ayr in September; should stay 1m; looked headstrong on third outing and was taken down early last 2. *J. Etherington.*

DRAGON ROCKET 2 gr.c. Dragonara Palace 115–Running Firework 106 — (Runnymede 123) (1982 5d 7.2s 6s) Apr 15; well-grown colt; cost 9,200 gns as a yearling but showed no sign of ability, including in sellers. *M. W. Easterby.*

DRAGUNN 3 ch.g. Dragonara Palace 115–Maria Bicknell (Jolly Jet 111) (1981 **70** 5fg* 5d⁴ 5g⁴ 5f³ 5f 5d 6s 1982 5g⁴ 5s³ 5f* 6fg 5f⁴ 5f³ 5h 5g 5fg³ 5fg 5f 6g 5d⁴ 5d⁴ 5d 5g 5s) rather sparely-made gelding; sprint handicapper; won at Thirsk in April; best at 5f; acts on any going; wears blinkers; has worn a bandage on his near-fore; not the heartiest of battlers. *R. Hollinshead.*

DRAKE'S LADY 4 b.f. Pieces of Eight 128–Bally Tudor 75 (Henry the Seventh — 125) (1981 8f 12fg 10.6v 12.2g 1982 10fg) fair sort; well beaten in maiden and minor events and a seller; refused to enter stalls twice in 1981; changed hands 430 gns Doncaster June Sales; dead. *D. Chapman.*

DRAW THE LINE 3 b.g. High Line 125–Minibus 77 (John Splendid 116) (1981 5g 6g 7g 1982 11s 11g) leggy, close-coupled gelding; poor maiden. *G. Richards.* —

DR BRODIE 2 ch.c. Monseigneur 127–Power Girl 77 (Tyrant) (1982 6s) Apr 25; IR 4,800Y; second foal; dam won over 5f and 6f; soundly beaten in 16-runner minor event won by Larionov at Lingfield in September. *A. Jarvis.* —

DREAM AGAIN 2 b.f. Blue Cashmere 129–Sundream (Petingo 135) (1982 5v² 5f* 5fg* 5f⁴ 5g 5g 5fg) Apr 5; 5,600Y; lengthy, useful-looking filly; good mover; third live foal; half-sister to a winning plater; dam unraced half-sister to speedy Song of Songs; put up a very smooth display when winning maiden race at Epsom in April; very fortunate winner of minor event at Goodwood the following month, being left to win by a length from Reign after Pearl's Diamond came down in lead 100 yds out; subsequently ran well, though unplaced, against useful fillies at Epsom in June on fourth outing and at Salisbury in September on final appearance; will probably stay 6f; acts on firm going. *A. Jarvis.* **88**

DREAMING AWAY (USA) 3 ch.f. Sir Ivor 135–Northern Gem 121 (Northern Dancer) (1981 6fg 7d³ 8fg² 8fg 1982 8d³ 10f³ 10fg² 10fg² 12.2g² 10.2g* 10f⁴ 10.5g² 10.5g* 9d 10.5v) strong, well-made, attractive filly; very good mover; successful in maiden race at Bath in July and 7-runner Grosser Preis der International Harvester at Neuss in September; dead-heated with Kaiserblume on latter, but was awarded race outright as she'd been hampered; ran well most other outings, notably in Sir Charles Clore Memorial Stakes at Newbury (2½ lengths second to Zinzara), Garrowby Stakes (Limited Handicap) at York (½-length second to Brady), William Hill Cambridgeshire at Newmarket (about **115**

Mr George Strawbridge's "Dreaming Away"

2½ lengths fifth of 29 to Century City) and Prix de Flore at Saint-Cloud (had little luck in running when length sixth of 13 to Buchanette); stays 1½m; acts on any going; consistent. *I. Balding.*

DROMODAN 2 b.c. Dance In Time–Wordrone (Worden II 129) (1982 7fg² 85
7g³ 8d⁴ 9s⁴) Apr 21; lengthy, slightly dipped-backed colt; half-brother to useful 1981 2-y-o sprint winner Mydrone (by Mummy's Pet) and smart Lady Mere (by Decoy Boy), a winner from 5f to 1m; dam ran once; in frame in minor and maiden events, coming closest to success when 1¾ lengths fourth of 13 to Mister Valentino over 1m at Ayr in September; one paced and will be suited by middle distances. *M. H. Easterby.*

DROMOLAND CASTLE 3 b.c. Joshua 129–Westmead Lady 60 (King's Troop 49
118) (1981 5s 5.8g 7fg 8g 8s³ 8.2s² 8d 1982 10s² 8d 10.1fg) lightly-made colt; plater; possibly doesn't quite stay 1¼m; revels in the mud. *J. Spearing.*

DRONACHARYA (USA) 6 gr.h. Nijinsky 138–Belle de Nuit (Warfare) (1981 —
9g⁴ 13g 10g 6.5g 10g 9.5g 9g 8.5g 10.5g⁴ 10.5d 1982 12fg 6g 5.8f 8g) good-bodied horse; has run tubed; disappointing maiden over here in 1980 (trained by A. Breasley at time); raced mainly in Holland in 1981 (also ran once in Belgium) and showed little worthwhile form; bought by present owner at end of 1981 and was sent to Israel where he reportedly covered 8 mares; reportedly finished lame when distant last in King George VI and Queen Elizabeth Diamond Stakes at Ascot in July on his return to this country; soundly beaten afterwards, including in a seller; should stay middle distances; has been tried in blinkers; has given impression on occasions that he's none too genuine; trained first 2 starts by A. Netser of Israel. *D. Sasse.*

DR PAVLICK 2 ch.c. Gunner B 126–Startop 72 (Divine Gift 127) (1982 7d 7f) —
Apr 25; 2,600F; workmanlike colt; second foal; dam quite moderate; unquoted, in rear in 19-runner maiden races at Salisbury in June and July. *R. Hannon.*

DRUMALIS 2 b.c. Tumble Wind–Virna (Coursing) (1982 6f 6f* 6.5d² 7s²) 117
It was announced in midsummer that trainer Hastings-Bass would leave Britain at the end of the year to pursue a new training career in Australia. Hastings-Bass has done well in his six years at Newmarket with more than 170 winners, the best of them the 1978 Queen Mary Stakes and Molecomb Stakes winner Greenland Park. Unfortunately he was prevented from enjoying a particularly successful final season by sickness in his stable although his horses were in good form by the autumn and Drumalis twice came close to giving him a pattern-race success.

Drumalis first gave an indication of his merit in the Selsey Maiden Stakes at Goodwood in July. On his only previous outing at Newmarket earlier in the month he'd caught our eye in the paddock, being an attractive, strong, well-made colt, but he'd also been backward and had finished towards the rear. At Goodwood he was a different proposition when starting third favourite in a field of eighteen. Confidently ridden, he was sent after the leader Northair with a

Selsey Maiden Stakes, Goodwood—Drumalis (No. 13)
wears down Northair inside
the final furlong

furlong to run and was then pushed right out to win by three quarters of a length. Drumalis wasn't in any of the top English two-year-old races (they closed before his ability became apparent), so he was sent to France for his final two outings. In the Prix Eclipse at Saint-Cloud in October he found the odds-on Crystal Glitters, third in the Prix de la Salamandre on his previous start, too strong at level weights. Nevertheless he stuck to his guns and went down by only half a length with the third horse, Cat O'Nine Tails, two and a half lengths behind. In the Criterium de Maisons-Laffitte later in October Drumalis again finished second to an odds-on favourite, this time the Grand Criterium runner-up L'Emigrant. Well though he finished Drumalis was still a length behind L'Emigrant, who won comfortably, at the line with Crystal Glitters a further length behind in third; both L'Emigrant and Crystal Glitters gave Drumalis 7 lb, but this was a smart performance nevertheless.

Drumalis (b.c. Apr 25, 1980)	Tumble Wind (b 1964)	Restless Wind (ch 1956)	Windy City
			Lump Sugar
		Easy Stages (b 1953)	Endeavour II
			Saturday Off
	Virna (b 1972)	Coursing (b or br 1963)	Fleet Nasrullah
			Miss Rabbit
		Snowy Owl (b 1964)	Hillary
			Mother Wit

Drumalis, the fourth foal of his dam, was very well bought as a foal for 8,000 guineas. At the time of the sale Virna had bred one winner, Lead The Floor (by Dancer's Image), successful over a mile in Ireland as a two-year-old; her second foal Crowned Hare (by Crowned Prince) has since won over a mile and a quarter in Ireland. Virna won from six furlongs to nine furlongs in France and comes from a good family. Her dam was an unraced half-sister to 100,000-dollar earners Ready Wit and Ask Father and the very smart Quicken Tree, winner of fifteen races including the Jockey Club Gold Cup, the Santa Anita Handicap and the San Juan Capistrano Handicap. Virna's sire Coursing isn't a particularly well-known name over here. His later career was blighted by injury but he won all his five races at two years, all over six furlongs, and was rated only 3 lb below Buckpasser and 1 lb below Graustark in the 1965 Experimental Handicap. Drumalis acts on any going and judging from the style in which he finished at Maisons-Laffitte he'll stay a mile. He is to be trained by Ian Balding. *W. Hastings-Bass.*

DRUMCROON 3 br.c. Crooner 119–Cuddly Toy (Sovereign Lord 120) (1981 5g 5f 6g 7.6s 6g 1982 10d 8g 7fg) neat colt; has a sharp action; well beaten in varied company, including selling; blinkered final start; sold 540 gns Ascot 2nd June Sales. *P. K. Mitchell.*   —

DRUM MAKER 2 br.c. Scottish Rifle 127–Ardice 91 (Hard Tack 111§) (1982 7f 7g⁴ 7s) Mar 14; 7,400Y; quite attractive colt; half-brother to 2 winners, including 1¼m winner Morice (by Morston); dam 6f to 1m performer; quite a modest maiden; will stay 1m; acts on firm going; off course for 3 months after first outing. *N. Vigors.*   70

DRUMMOND STREET 3 ch.g. Ragstone 128–Scottish Lullaby 92 (Aberdeen 109) (1981 8.2d 8s 8.2d 1982 11s 12s 12f 14fg 16s 16s) lengthy gelding; little worthwhile form. *A. Jarvis.*   —

DRUMNADROCHIT (USA) 3 ch.c. Nijinsky 138–Quadruple (Fleet Nasrullah) (1981 NR 1982 10fg⁴ 12fg* 10.5fg 12f⁴ 16d) $250,000Y; lengthy, quite attractive colt; fourth foal; brother to stakes winner La Jalouse, successful at up to 1m at both 2 yrs and 3 yrs, closely related to stakes winner Stephanie Leigh (by Northern Dancer) and half-brother to French 1¼m winner First Quadrant (by Vaguely Noble); dam won at up to 9f; decisively beat Dawn Raid in 18-runner maiden race at Goodwood in May; ran respectably in handicap fourth outing; promises to stay 2m; gives impression he'll always be suited by strong handling; blinkered final start. *R. Hern.*   92

DRY LAND 2 b.f. Nonoalco 131–Land Ho (Primera 131) (1982 5s 5s*) Apr 16; good-topped filly; half-sister to several winners, including very useful 1976 2-y-o 5f winner Easy Landing (by Swing Easy); dam daughter of very smart sprinter Lucasland; made virtually all and held on to win by 1½ lengths from Barrera Lad in 15-runner maiden race at Sandown in October; the type to make a useful sprinter. *J. Tree.*   84 p

DUAL INVESTMENT 2 b. or br.c. The Brianstan 128–Charlies Double **76**
(Fighting Charlie 127) (1982 5g 6f 6g 5s) Mar 27; 3,500Y; quite attractive,
lengthy colt; good walker; half-brother to 3 winners, including stayer Shooting
Butts (by Tycoon II); dam never ran; showed first sign of ability when staying-
on 3¾ lengths fifth of 15 to Dry Land in maiden race at Sandown in October,
fourth outing; should be suited by 6f; possibly needs a soft surface. *P. Mitchell.*

DUBAI RUBY (USA) 2 ch.f. The Minstrel 135–Kesar Queen 117 (Nashua) —
(1982 6s 6d) rather small filly; second foal; half-sister to fair 1981 2-y-o 5f
winner Kesarini (by Singh); dam won Coronation Stakes and was third in 1,000
Guineas; showed early speed in Blue Seal Stakes at Ascot and minor event at
Pontefract in the autumn. *P. Walwyn.*

DUBASSOFF MAID 3 br.f. Dubassoff–Fahal Saya (Stupendous) (1981 —
6g 6d 1982 14g 12.2f 12g 16fg 12v) useful-looking filly; behind in maiden
and minor events; trained by A. Jarvis first 2 starts. *P. K. Mitchell.*

DUBLIN JARVEY 2 ch.c. Dublin Taxi–Nikali 89 (Siliconn 121) (1982 5fg) —
Mar 15; third foal; dam second twice over sprint distances at 2 yrs; 8/1, started
slowly when tailed-off last of 6 in seller at Wolverhampton in May. *J. Berry.*

DUBLIN ROCK 2 b.f. Dublin Taxi–Demi Rock (Double-U-Jay 120) (1982 —
5fg 5g 6fg 5g) Apr 21; first foal; dam second in 2 bumpers races and won over
hurdles in Ireland; unquoted, in rear in maiden races. *R. Hannon.*

DUDLEY WOOD (USA) 3 ro.g. One For All–Aglimmer (Grey Dawn II 132) **98**
(1981 7g 8g 8g* 1982 12fg 12.3d 12fg 14s* 14g* 13g* 17.4d² 13d⁴ 16g* 16.1s²
14s) attractive gelding; fairly useful handicapper on his day but runs atrociously
on occasions; decisively won at Yarmouth in August and York, Nottingham and
Newmarket in September; suited by a test of stamina; suited by some give in
the ground and revels in the mud; sometimes blinkered but seems better without;
usually brought wide to race alone; sent to Hong Kong. *B. Hanbury.*

DUKE OF BRITTANY 4 gr.c. Saritamer 130–Belle Bretonne 90 (Celtic —
Ash) (1981 12s 12s 12d 12g³ 1982 12s) compact colt; quite a moderate
maiden; will stay beyond 1½m; probably needs some give in the ground. *S.
Woodman.*

DUKE OF DOLLIS 3 b.g. Condorcet–Evening Primrose (Varano) (1981 **74**
8g³ 9g* 1982 7d 8f 10fg² 16fg 12d 12f² 12fg 12f³ 11.1fg) IR 1,100F, IR 2,500Y;
workmanlike ex-Irish gelding; first produce; dam won over 7f at 2 yrs in Ireland;
runner-up at Lingfield in ladies race and handicap in the summer; stays 1½m;
best form on a sound surface. *D. Elsworth.*

DUKE OF WELLINGTON 2 b.c. Wollow 132–Lady Dacre 86 (Queen's —
Hussar 124) (1982 6g) June 14; rather lightly-made colt; third foal; dam,
placed over 6f at 2 yrs, is sister to Brigadier Gerard; 20/1, and in need of race,
not in first 10 in 20-runner maiden event won by Fiefdom at Newmarket in
October. *W. Holden.*

DUKE'S HEIR 3 gr.g. Saritamer 130–La Pitore (Will Somers 114§) (1981 **45**
6f³ 6d 6fg⁴ 7g 7g 1982 11.5fg 12f 12fg³ 10v 12s) useful-looking gelding;
plater; stays 1½m; acts on a firm surface; retained 4,000 gns Newmarket July
Sales. *W. Musson.*

DULLINGHAM GOLD 2 b.c. Anax 120–Midriff 62 (Busted 134) (1982 **54**
5g 7fg 7f* 7g 8fg 8g) May 28; 2,000Y; lengthy, useful-looking sort; has a
round action; won by a short head from Stately Maiden in 7-runner seller at
Redcar (no bid) in July; in rear in nurseries subsequently; needs at least 7f;
sold 1,500 gns Doncaster October Sales. *N. Callaghan.*

DULLINGHAM LAD 4 gr.g. Saulingo 122–Ambient 86 (Amber Rama 133) —
(1981 6fg³ 6g 7.6g 7f 6f 1982 6d 6g) lengthy, dipped-backed gelding; disappointing sprint maiden; last in a seller when blinkered on reappearance.
H. Collingridge.

DUNBEATH (USA) 2 b.c. Grey Dawn II 132–Priceless Fame (Irish Castle) **127**
(1982 7f² 7f* 7g* 8s* 8d*)
  When Dunbeath swept through to win Europe's richest two-year-old race,
the William Hill Futurity at Doncaster in October, he took trainer Henry Cecil's
earnings for the season past Dick Hern's record total of £831,964 set in 1980.
Cecil ended the year as leading trainer with earnings of £872,614, his fourth title
in the last seven years, during which time he also twice finished runner-up.
Cecil's total is particularly remarkable considering that, of England's eleven
races with £60,000 or more added money, he didn't have a runner in seven—the

*Royal Lodge Stakes, Ascot—Dunbeath is kept up to his work
to account for Lyphard's Special (left)
and The Noble Player*

One Thousand Guineas, Two Thousand Guineas, Derby, Coral-Eclipse, Sussex, St Leger and Dubai Champion Stakes—and didn't win any of the other four—the Coronation Cup, the Oaks, the King George VI and Queen Elizabeth Stakes and the Benson and Hedges Gold Cup. What Cecil did win, primarily, was twenty-four of England's remaining eighty-nine pattern races, with fourteen different animals, and he became the first trainer since Bernard van Cutsem in 1971 to win all three Group 1 races open to two-year-old colts, the Middle Park, Dewhurst and William Hill Futurity.

Dunbeath came to the Futurity the winner of his last three races. He had been brought along steadily since making his first appearance in the Plantation Maiden Stakes at Newmarket early in July, where he had shaped very promisingly to divide two other potentially smart colts, St Boniface and Muscatite. One of the lasting memories of his debut was his comportment in the preliminaries: in the pre-parade ring he gave the strong impression of being a very lazy, relaxed individual, having virtually to be dragged round. His subsequent performances proved this to be so. In the Foxhall Maiden Stakes at Goodwood later in July he landed the odds easily by two lengths from Morcon, doing little more than was necessary after leading some way out, and in a £3,600 race at York in September he barely came off the bridle to win easing up by four lengths from Tobina's Guest after quickening away impressively two furlongs out. Although Dunbeath's form up to this stage was nothing out of the ordinary the manner of his victories left little doubt that he was capable of a great deal better. Not surprisingly he was made favourite on his first appearance in pattern-race company, in the Royal Lodge Stakes at Ascot towards the end of September. Judging by the betting he had most to fear from Lyphard's Special and St Boniface, who on their latest appearances had finished second and fourth respectively to All Systems Go in the Lanson Champagne Stakes at Goodwood. The only other runners to start at shorter than 20/1 were The Noble Player, an improving colt with a good win over a mile already to his name, and Kuwait Tower, a respectable second to Dunbeath's stable-companion The Fort in the

William Hill Futurity Stakes, Doncaster—a smooth display by Dunbeath who gives Henry Cecil his sixth two-year-old pattern race of the season

Intercraft Solario Stakes. Once again Dunbeath proved himself a very placid individual, settling willingly at the rear of the field as Castle Guard set a strong pace. As the field bunched up coming to the straight it was obvious that Dunbeath was going extremely well. When finally asked to quicken he moved up very smoothly to lead a furlong and a half from home and from then on had the race sewn up, keeping on well to win by one and a half lengths from Lyphard's Special. A similar distance back in third came The Noble Player who ran well without, in our opinion, showing such good form as that which later brought him third place behind Saint Cyrien in the Grand Criterium.

As one writer put it, the Royal Lodge was staged again at Doncaster a month later, this time called the William Hill Futurity. Dunbeath, at 7/4 on, and Lyphard's Special, a 6/1-chance, again took the field, joined by the good-class seven-furlong winner Muscatite, the unbeaten Cock Robin, the Italian Gran Criterium runner-up Beldale Concorde, the once-raced maidens Neorion and Stratford Place, and the 100/1-shot Shackle Pin. Dunbeath was ridden with even greater confidence than at Ascot and was last of the eight at halfway, where Muscatite and Shackle Pin were still disputing the lead as they'd done from the start. Although there were still five in front of Dunbeath passing the two-furlong post he quickened so well, without Piggott's resorting to the whip, that he'd taken the lead within a furlong. Dunbeath increased his advantage to three lengths as a desperate struggle developed for the minor places but he then appeared to decide he'd done enough and eased himself close home. At the line he had a length and a half to spare over the strong-finishing Cock Robin, who'd had to be switched at the distance, with Lyphard's Special a fraction behind. It was revealed afterwards that Dunbeath had nearly missed the race. Reportedly his hind legs had become swollen only two days previously, a reaction it is thought to a new consignment of Australian oats. The swelling soon subsided and, since his temperature was normal, he was allowed to take his chance.

Dunbeath became his trainer's fourth Futurity winner, following Approval, Take Your Place and Hello Gorgeous (the first two won the race when it was known as the Observer Gold Cup). Interestingly Dunbeath and Hello Gorgeous are the only colts ever to win both the Royal Lodge and the Futurity during the latter's twenty-two-year history. With the Guineas favourite Diesis also in the stable, Dunbeath is likely to have the Derby as his main target. Cecil has said that Dunbeath compares very favourably with his previous Futurity winners. Hopefully he's right; Take Your Place proved very disappointing and both Approval and Hello Gorgeous finished unplaced in the Derby after winning the Dante Stakes. In our opinion Dunbeath's form as a two-year-old was better than that of Hello Gorgeous but he still needs to improve if he's to justify his position as winter favourite for the Derby. He may well do so—his posed portrait shows he still has room to strengthen—and he has already shown he possesses a first-class turn of foot. Perhaps a more important question about his Derby prospects at this stage is whether he will get the trip. We think he probably will.

Dunbeath's sire Grey Dawn II never won beyond eight and a half furlongs.

He showed his best form at two, winning the Prix Morny, Prix de la Salamandre and the Grand Criterium, becoming the only horse to beat his stable-companion Sea-Bird II when winning the Grand Criterium. He later won two seven-furlong races from six starts at three and then two more races, one of them a division of the Brandywine Turf Handicap, from ten outings in America. Grey Dawn was retired to stud in 1967 at a fee of 3,000 dollars and he has met with regular success, finishing third on the list of American sires in 1977 and 1978. Only once since 1975 has he sired the winners of less than 1,000,000 dollars in a season and by 1982 his fee had risen to 35,000 dollars. Grey Dawn's sire Herbager proved a strong influence for stamina but his dam, Polamia, was a speedy half-sister to those fast animals Takawalk II and Sly Pola. It was therefore to be expected that Grey Dawn would sire all types of animals and he has done so. Several of his best performers have shown a fair amount of stamina: Vigors, a top-class colt, won the Hollywood Invitational Handicap over a mile and a half; Cloudy Dawn won the Arlington Park Handicap over the same distance; Mr Redoy's wins included the ten-furlong Charles H. Strub Stakes; Christmas Past won the CCA Oaks over a mile and a half in 1982; and the Canadian filly Bye Bye Paris twice won the Maple Leaf Stakes over a mile and a quarter. In Britain and Ireland he has had six individual winners over the age of two and of these Dawn Johnny, Grand Maitre, Green Dawn, My Sunny and Tender Angus have all won over a mile and a half or more.

Dunbeath (USA) (b.c. Mar 23, 1980)	Grey Dawn II (gr 1962)	Herbager (b 1956)	Vandale Flagette
		Polamia (gr 1955)	Mahmoud Ampola
	Priceless Fame (b 1975)	Irish Castle (b 1967)	Bold Ruler Castle Forbes
		Comely Nell (b 1962)	Commodore M. Nellie L.

Dunbeath is the first foal of Priceless Fame who gained both her successes over sprint distances. Priceless Fame's sire Irish Castle never won after two years but he had the pedigree of a middle-distance horse; and her brother Bold

Mr Michael Doyle Riordan's "Dunbeath"

Forbes, the champion three-year-old of 1976, numbered the mile-and-a-quarter Kentucky Derby and the mile-and-a-half Belmont Stakes among his successes. Dunbeath's grandam Comely Nell was an unraced daughter of the Acorn Stakes and Kentucky Oaks winner Nellie L., herself a sister to the champion handicap mare Mar-kel. This is a good American family and Priceless Fame's filly by Best Turn fetched 550,000 dollars at the 1982 Saratoga Yearling Sale, falling to the bid of H. T. Jones. Surprisingly Dunbeath fetched only 100,000 dollars as a yearling, a small sum these days for a well-bred animal; after the Futurity he was purchased by Sheikh Mohammed for a reported six million pounds. Dunbeath is an attractive, deep-girthed colt, and an impressive, loose-limbed walker. He also gallops with a nice, easy action which seems effective both on firm and soft going. He could become the first William Hill Futurity winner to go on to success in the Derby. *H. Cecil.*

DUNCOMBE PRINCE 3 b.g. Dragonara Palace 115–Disarmament (Busted — 134) (1981 NR 1982 10d 13d 14s 12v) 4,400Y; fair sort; first foal; dam well beaten both starts; slow maiden. *M. Jefferson.*

DUNDONNEL 3 b.f. Roan Rocket 128–All Love 83 (No Argument 107) (1981 — NR 1982 10s 12f 12f 16fg⁴ 19f) workmanlike filly; turns her off-hind out; has shown only a little ability in maiden races; stays well; lacks pace. *W. Wharton.*

DUNEANY 3 b.c. Free State 125–Rosalina 71 (Porto Bello 118) (1981 7fg⁴ — 7fg 1982 8d⁴ 12g 13.3f 14d 14f 12g 14fg) 5,100F, 10,500Y; neat ex-Irish colt; second produce; half-brother to fair 1980 2-y-o 5f performer Fire Mountain (by Dragonara Palace); dam won over 7f and 1m; quite a modest maiden; seems to stay 1¾m; a winner over hurdles. *D. Nicholson.*

DUNFELL 2 br.f. Tower Walk 130–Queen Donna (Thatch 136) (1982 5f 6g 57 5g 5g 7fg 7g 6s 5d) Feb 26; 2,100Y; leggy filly; first foal; dam unraced half-sister to smart Irish colt Cobblers Cove; poor plater; stays 7f. *W. Haigh.*

DUNFORD 2 b.f. Legal Eagle 126–Ol Arabel (Relic) (1982 5g 5fg) Apr 18; — half-sister to several winners, including very useful 1967 sprint 2-y-o The Rift (by Major Portion); dam moderate at sprint distances; last in seller and maiden race at Wolverhampton. *M. James.*

DUNGEON GHYL 4 ch.f. Roman Warrior 132–Birdcage 78 (Manacle 123) 63 (1981 5.8g* 6d 5fg² 5.8f³ 5fg* 1982 6fg 6g 5.8f 5fg³ 6f 5f 6g 5fg 8fg⁴ 8g) big, well-made filly; ran best races when in frame in handicaps at Wolverhampton in July (missed break) and Beverley in September; needs a strongly-run race at 5f and seems to stay 1m; acts well on fast ground; sold 2,000 gns Newmarket Autumn Sales. *D. Gandolfo.*

DUNHAM PARK 5 b.g. Manacle 123–Sweet Reproach 94 (Relic) (1981 78 8g² 8fg⁴ 8fg⁴ 8f² 8g² 8f⁴ 8g² 8f 8.2fg⁴ 7.2v* 7s 1982 7f* 7f³ 8g³ 7f³ 8fg² 7g* 7g⁴ 7f 7g 7s⁴ 8s³) tall, useful sort; beat Miss Twiggy when winning handicaps at Catterick in June and Newcastle in August; stays 1m; acts on any going; blinkered twice at 2 yrs; sometimes sweats up; doesn't find a great deal in front. *J. Fitzgerald.*

DUNSYRE 4 b. or br.f. Lorenzaccio 130–Black Fire 92 (Firestreak 125) (1981 49 8g 12.2g⁴ 10d³ 12d 12g 1982 10g³ 15.8f³ 11g 13.8f⁴ 12.2f 10f* 12d 10d 10.2s) small filly; bought in 1,050 gns after making all in seller at Pontefract in September; ran poorly next time; effective at 1½m and possibly doesn't quite stay 2m; possibly not at her best on really soft going, but acts on any other. *J. Fitzgerald.*

DUO NARA 2 ch.f. Dragonara Palace 115–Two For Joy 77 (Double-U-Jay — 120) (1982 6fg 8s 6d) June 2; tall, lengthy filly; third foal; half-sister to 3-y-o High Poppa (by Mummy's Pet); dam, 2-y-o 7f seller winner, also won over hurdles and fences; in rear in minor event and maiden races in the autumn. *S. Norton.*

DURANDAL 5 br.h. Bay Express 132–High Ransom 88 (High Treason 126) 68 (1981 6fg 5g 6d⁴ 6g 5f 5fg 5g 5fg² 5fg 5.3f 5f 5g 5s 6d 1982 6f 6fg 5.8f² 5g 5g 5fg³ 5fg⁴ 5g 5g³ 5fg 5fg 5.8f 8d 5s) strong, good sort; sprint handicapper; hasn't won since his 2-y-o days but ran creditably on several occasions in 1982; yet to show he can handle very soft going, but acts on any other; sometimes blinkered. *D. Wilson.*

DUREL 4 b.c. Reliance II 137–Dugo 90 (Dumbarnie 125) (1981 8f 5f 6v 1982 — 5.8f 7h) compact, workmanlike colt; in rear in minor events as a 3-y-o and 2 handicaps in May. *D. H. Jones.*

DURUN 3 b.f. Run The Gantlet–Duboff 120 (So Blessed 130) (1981 5f 7fg **89** 7h³ 8s⁴ 1982 12f² 12.2g* 10.6f* 10fg* 12g 10d) small, well-made, quite attractive filly; good mover; won handicaps at Warwick, Haydock and Newbury; held off Safe House by ¾ length on last-named in July; respectable staying-on fifth to Sans Blague in 1½m Galtres Stakes at York in August; will stay 1¾m; seems to act on any going; has shown a tendency to hang. *H. Candy.*

DUSTY FARLOW 3 b.g. Jukebox 120–Reelin Bridge (New Day) (1981 **51** 5s 5s 6d 6g 1982 7fg 7f 9g 6g² 8.2g³ 8fg 8.2s) plater nowadays; stays 1m well; blinkered once in 1981; has worn bandages. *R. Morris.*

DUSTY ISLES 4 gr.g. Saritamer 130–Scilly Isles 54 (Silly Season 127) (1981 **—** 9d² 8g 7g³ 9.4g² 10.2d 8fg 8f² 8d 12s 1982 8d 10f 10fg 10g 12.2fg⁴ 12f⁴) leggy gelding; disappointing maiden; stays 9f; has worn blinkers. *T. Marshall.*

DUSTY PATH 4 gr.g. Warpath 113–The Squeeze 85 (Bing II) (1981 8d **—** 12.5fg 12.2fg 13g² 12f² 10fg 12.2fg 12.3g 15.5g 16s 13.8g 12s 1982 12f 16d 15.8f 13.8f 12fg 12d) workmanlike gelding; poor maiden; stays 13f; often wears blinkers. *W. Bentley.*

DUTCH GIRL 5 b.m. Workboy 123–Dutch Gold 117 (Goldhill 125) (1981 **66** 6g⁴ 5fg 6f⁴ 5fg* 5f* 5g² 5f³ 5d 5f 5fg* 5g 5g⁴ 1982 5f 5fg 5f⁴ 5fg 5g² 5fg³ 5f 5g⁴ 5d 5fg⁴ 5d) strong, compact mare; slight handicapper; ran creditably several times; best at 5f; ideally suited by fast ground; had a poor run seventh start. *M. W. Easterby.*

DUTCH MAID 3 b.f. Souvran 98–Moonstream 62 (Forlorn River 124) (1981 **—** NR 1982 6g) last in 5f maiden race at 2 yrs and in 21-runner seller at Windsor in July; only outings. *B. Swift.*

DUTCH PRINCESS 4 b.f. Royalty 130–Miss Wilhemina 84 (Quorum 126) **60** (1981 10s⁴ 10fg 12g 12s² 15.5s² 1982 12d⁴ 15.5g² 16g) workmanlike filly; staying maiden; seems suited by some give in the ground. *Miss A. Sinclair.*

DUTCH ROMANTIC 3 ch.c. Tachypous 128–Top Line 99 (Saint Crespin III **—** 132) (1981 6g 7g 6s⁴ 7g 1982 8g 10fg⁴ 12g 10f⁴ 10.1g 12fg) strong, well-made colt; plating-class maiden; suited by 1¼m and should stay further. *W. Wightman.*

DUTY WATCH 3 ch.f. Import 127–Radar Girl 75 (Bleep-Bleep 134) (1981 **—** 5fg 5f 5fg 6g 5f 5d 1982 5g⁴ 6f 6f 7f 5fg 5g) small filly; poor form, including in sellers. *W. C. Watts.*

DWIGHT 3 b.g. Reform 132–Limerick Queen (Whistling Wind 123) (1981 5d **—** 1982 8fg 9fg 13.8f) of no account; blinkered final outing; sold out of P. Cundell's stable 775 gns Ascot May Sales after first start; resold 360 gns Doncaster September Sales. *C. Pinkham.*

DZUDO (POL) 5 bl.h. Conor Pass 115–Dzuni (Antiquarian 102) (1981 **?** won twice and placed 4 times from 8 starts in Poland 1982 10g³ 10g 20f 11g 12g 10g 12g) big, lengthy, workmanlike Polish-bred Swedish horse; sire won Irish St Leger; brother to 4-y-o Dzim, successful in Poland and several times in Sweden; won twice in Poland in both 1980 and 1981 and was reportedly also placed in classics there; gained his last success over 2m at Warsaw; trained in Sweden in 1982 and finished 6 lengths third of 11 behind his brother Dzim at Taby in May; had very stiff task and was by no means disgraced when last of 5 behind Ardross in Gold Cup at Royal Ascot in June on third start, making running and dropping out only in home straight; stays well; trained by D. Persson when running at Royal Ascot. *H. Doria, Sweden.*

E

EAGLE COURT 2 b.g. Legal Eagle 126–Privy Court 73 (Adropejo 114) (1982 **—** 5.8g 5.8f 7fg 8s 6s) Apr 1; first foal; dam showed ability at 2 yrs; in rear in maiden race and sellers. *M. Pipe.*

EAGLE ISLAND 7 b. or br.g. Tower Walk 130–Musaka (Guard's Tie 131) (1981 **61** 9g 9d 6g 10.2fg 10f 10f 10fg² 10g⁴ 10f⁴ 11fg* 12d 11d⁴ 1982 10fg² 10d⁴ 12fg 10f 11.7fg⁴ 10f) strong, compact gelding; has been fired; in frame in handicaps; stays 1½m; seems to act on any going; has been bandaged on near-fore; trained until after fourth start by P. Calver. *N. Gaselee.*

EAGLESFIELD 5 ch.h. Mountain Call 125–Rubella (Buisson Ardent 129) **75** (1981 6fg⁴ 6g 6g* 6fg³ 6fg 6fg 1982 7f 6f 6g 6fg 7f³ 7f³ 7fg² 7g⁴ 7f) good mover; placed in handicaps at Goodwood, Salisbury and Sandown in summer; suited by

7f nowadays; acts on any going; blinkered once in 1981; bandaged second start. *C. Nelson.*

EAGLE'S QUEST 4 b.f. Legal Eagle 126–My Cervantes (Hill Clown or Nulli **52** Secundus 89) (1981 6fg 6g 5g² 5f 5fg² 5f² 6f⁴ 5fg* 6f⁴ 1982 5d³ 5fg 5g 5g 6g² 6f 6f⁴ 5g) leggy, unfurnished filly; sprint handicapper; yet to race on very soft going, but acts on any other. *J. Holt.*

EARL'S COURT 6 ch.h. Lord Gayle 124–Paddy's Rose 81 (St Chad 120) **65** (1981 12f 12f² 12.3fg 11d 10.6d³ 12.3s² 16.1fg 12v³ 13s* 12d³ 1982 12.3fg³ 12f* 12fg² 12fg³ 12g² 18.4g⁴ 10.6g² 12.3d 12fg 12s 12s⁴) small horse; held off Sheba's Glory by a short head in handicap at Thirsk in May; also placed at Chester, Doncaster, York and Haydock (twice); best form at middle distances; acts on any going; suitable mount for a boy; suited by front-running tactics (unable to dictate affairs and ran moderately eighth start); tough and genuine. *C. Crossley.*

EARLY PROMOTION 2 ch.c. High Echelon–Endeavorer (Forward Pass) — (1982 7.6v 8g) Jan 15; 8,000F, IR 14,500Y; useful-looking colt; first foal; dam, Irish 7f and 1¼m winner, is half-sister to Dragonara Palace; well beaten in maiden race at Lingfield and minor event at Newmarket (tailed off) in October. *G. Hunter.*

EARLY SUPRISE 2 b. or br.f. Oats 126–Dawn (Moutiers 127) (1982 6g 6fg 6s³) **73** Apr 19; IR 3,800F, 7,000Y; half-sister to numerous winners, including Irish 6f and 7f winner Sallawn (by Sallust); dam, from same family as Larkspur, won over 5.5f at 2 yrs in France; staying-on 3 lengths third of 19 behind Hawk Lady in maiden race at Leicester in November, first indication of merit; will be much better suited by 7f+. *D. Ringer.*

EASBY EXCHANGE 4 b.f. Import 127–Easby Flirt (Royal Levee or Nelcius 133) — (1981 NR 1982 8g 12.2f) first known foal; dam lightly-raced half-sister to good jumper Easby Abbey; behind in seller at Ayr in May and minor event at Catterick in June; sold 460 gns Doncaster August Sales. *G. Lockerbie.*

EASTBROOK 2 b. or br.c. Lochnager 132–Lush Gold 91 (Goldhill 125) (1982 **76** 5d 5g³ 5d² 5f 6fg 6s 6s) Mar 26; strong colt; good walker and mover; third foal; dam won over 5f and 1m, and is sister to very useful sprinter Lush Park; placed in maiden races at Newcastle in August, best efforts; only seventh of 22 to Blue Nantucket in valuable seller at York in October on seventh outing; best form at 5f; disappointing. *M. H. Easterby.*

EAST COAST GIRL 3 ch.f. Relko 136–Starboard Belle 85 (Right Tack 131) — (1981 5v 5fg 5s 6f 8fg 7.2f 7f 7fg 7d 7f 10d 1982 8.2fg 12fg⁴ 12f 13.8f 16d) lightly-made filly; plater; suited by 1½m; has worn blinkers; has been bandaged. *J. Gilbert.*

EASTER JANE 2 b.f. Palm Track 122–Jane Again (Spartan General 109) (1982 — 6f 7f 8.2fg 8s 10.2s) Apr 7; compact filly; first reported foal; dam fair hurdler; poor plater. *W. Haigh.*

EASTER LEE 2 b.c. Idiot's Delight 115–Stacy Lee 95 (French Beige 127) (1982 **78** 5fg 7d 7f⁴ 7fg³ 8s⁴ 7s⁴) Apr 6; tall, leggy, lightly-made colt; half-brother to 1m to 1½m winner Morning Lee (by Arctic Judge), also a fairly useful hurdler; dam, winner over 6f and 8.5f at 2 yrs, stayed 1¼m; modest maiden; will stay beyond 1m; acts on any going. *D. Elsworth.*

EASTERLY GAEL 2 b.f. Tudor Music 131–Rathcoffey Deer (Pal's Passage 115) **65** (1982 6g 6fg 7f 7fg 8f) Mar 12; IR 1,600F, 5,800Y; first foal; dam ran only once; plating-class maiden; stays 7f. *C. Nelson.*

EASTERN PALACE 8 gr.g. Habitat 134–Al Burak 103 (Silver Shark 129) — (1981 8g 10d 17.1d 1982 10f) lengthy gelding; has shown no form for a long time; stays 1¼m; needs top-of-the-ground; best in blinkers; suitable mount for an apprentice; often starts slowly nowadays. *G. Beeson.*

EASTERN SHORE 3 ch.f. Sun Prince 128–Land Ho (Primera 131) (1981 7g **70** 1982 7fg³ 7g³ 10.1fg³ 10fg⁴ 11.7g⁴ 10g) lengthy, attractive filly; quite a modest maiden; stays 11.7f; wore a brush-pricker on near-side of her bridle only start at 2 yrs; sold 29,000 gns Newmarket December Sales. *J. Tree.*

EASTERN TREASURE 3 b.f. Flashback 102–Eastern Lullaby (Zulu 94) — (1981 NR 1982 9f 11d 8.2s 8s 8s) tall, rather leggy filly; first foal; dam novice hurdler; well behind in maiden and minor events. *J. Smith.*

EASTERN VALLEY 3 b.g. Mansingh 120–Wolver Valley 72 (Wolver Hollow — 126) (1981 6g 7f 1982 8f 8s 8f) fair sort; well beaten in maiden races; exported to Malaysia. *Miss S. Hall.*

EASTER SUN 5 b.h. Bustino 136–Magical 95 (Aggressor 130) (1981 10g* **122**
10d* 10.5g 10g² 9d² 10.2g² 9g⁴ 1982 13.3f* 12f* 12fg 13.3g³ 13.5g)

Easter Sun looked one of the most optimistic of the thirty-seven original
entries for the Coronation Cup; his form at the time they were published (before
the start of the season) was nowhere near good enough to win the race in a poor
year, and was upwards of 25 lb behind that of the race's best recent winners,
Bustino, Ile de Bourbon, Mill Reef and Roberto.   Easter Sun's standing in the
spring is accurately illustrated by the weights published for the Daily Mirror
Handicap, a race also run at Epsom in Derby week and won by Easter Sun
himself in 1981.   He was allotted 9-12—only 3 lb more than Show-A-Leg who
got a place in the Coronation Cup field only as pacemaker for the favourite
Glint of Gold.   Yet Easter Sun won the Coronation Cup fairly and squarely
from the biggest field the race has attracted since Oncidium's success in 1965.
His vast improvement, surprising in a five-year-old, was chiefly the result of his
being moved up in distance to a mile and a half or more.   As a three- and four-
year-old Easter Sun had generally been regarded as a mile-and-a-quarter
specialist, but after the horse finished fourth in the 1981 Cambridgeshire (carrying
8-13) his regular jockey Raymond was adamant that he had come to need a
mile and a half.   Easter Sun, too, benefited from the opportunity of racing
on firm ground again for the first time since his three-year-old days: he was in
his element.   Furthermore he had developed, says his trainer, both mentally
and physically.   As a youngster Easter Sun had been the type who wouldn't
travel and it took him a long time to overcome his nervousness.

By the time the Coronation Cup came around Easter Sun had fully justified his entry by beating Critique and Prince Bee in the six-runner Aston Park
Stakes at Newbury in May, a thirteen-furlong event run on firm going.   Surprising though it was, there seemed no fluke about his win; he was always going
well and produced a telling burst when asked to quicken which took him to the
front inside the last furlong.   He beat Critique, who gave 7 lb, by half a length
with Prince Bee seven lengths back in third.   Easter Sun met both Critique
and Prince Bee again in the Coronation Cup less than three weeks later and his
starting price of 20/1—the other two were both 7/1—suggested that by no
means all were convinced of his improvement.   Once again he was always
going well, held up, as Show-A-Leg set the pace for Glint of Gold until Tattenham
Corner.   He was switched to the outside coming to the last quarter mile and
quickened to get the better of Glint of Gold by half a length, striking the front

*Coronation Cup, Epsom—a high-class performance from Easter Sun who
wears down Glint of Gold (noseband) close home;
Critique (right) finishes third*

Lady Beaverbrook's "Easter Sun"

well inside the last furlong. No doubt the runner-up would have been a more formidable opponent on easier ground, but the merit of the winner's performance shouldn't be underestimated.

The remainder of the season was disappointing for Easter Sun. His opportunities were limited, and he ran just three more times. In the King George VI and Queen Elizabeth Diamond Stakes at Ascot in July he looked his usual bonny self but never promised to take a hand in the finish, coming home around fourteen lengths behind Kalaglow in sixth place. The Geoffrey Freer Stakes at Newbury the following month saw him struggling halfway up the straight against Ardross at level weights; he was beaten around four lengths, and just lost second in the four-runner race to Baffin, who received 8 lb. Finally in the Grand Prix de Deauville later in August he could finish only sixth of twelve behind the French Derby second Real Shadai, beaten about seven lengths; he lost his place on the final bend, possibly through being hampered, and although running on at the finish he couldn't get back to the leaders.

		Busted	Crepello
	Bustino	(b 1963)	Sans le Sou
	(b 1971)	Ship Yard	Doutelle
Easter Sun		(ch 1963)	Paving Stone
(b.h. 1977)		Aggressor	Combat
	Magical	(b 1955)	Phaetonia
	(b 1970)	Rosebid	Whistling Wind
		(ch 1965)	Amber Slipper

Easter Sun is a compact, useful sort, bred by his owner Lady Beaverbrook. He's a son of Bustino, the best horse she's owned, and Magical, who was quite useful as a two-year-old. Magical won over five furlongs at Epsom and Goodwood before she trained off; the next dam, Rosebid, was another five-furlong winner as a two-year-old who failed to train on. Easter Sun is Magical's third foal. Her first Hurakan (by Seaepic) was a fair middle-distance winner, her second Atataho (by Royalty) was a useful winner over a mile as a two-year-old and later a fair but unreliable hurdler. Magical has since produced two more colts by Bustino, the fair middle-distance handicapper Magikin, now known as Top Champ and winner of the 1982 Queen Mother's Cup in Hong Kong, and Bustoff. The latter, a stable-companion of Easter Sun, showed some promise at Newmarket in October on his first outing and looks the sort to do much better in time. *M. Jarvis.*

EASTFORM 2 b.g. Reform 132–Nip in the Air 114 (Northern Dancer) (1982 **95** 5f2 5f* 5f 6fg2 6d4 6g3 6fg2 8g3 7s) Mar 10; 5,400Y; strong gelding; has a round action; third foal; half-brother to French 3-y-o Grunip (by Grundy) and a winner in Italy; dam stayed 1¼m; landed the odds by 6 lengths from Final Set in maiden race at Carlisle in April; in frame most of his subsequent starts, on eighth finishing excellent 1¾ lengths third of 7 to Dancing Meg in £4,000 nursery at York in September; will stay 1¼m; seems to act on any going with possible exception of very soft; consistent; gelded after last outing. *M. H. Easterby.*

EAST MEON 3 b.g. Gulf Pearl 117–Palgal (Le Prince 98) (1981 6g 7fg 7fg — 7g 8d 1982 11fg 17f 12fg 16d 12g 13.8f4) compact gelding; plater; stays 1¾m; sometimes blinkered; sold 500 gns Ascot September Sales. *J. Douglas-Home.*

EASY AIR 2 b.c. Mummy's Pet 125–Kushi 65 (Paridel 112) (1982 6fg 6g 7g — 6d) Apr 7; 8,000Y; rangy colt; half-brother to several winners, including fair sprinter Friendly Annie (by Be Friendly); dam miler; little worthwhile form in maiden and minor events; may do better in time. *R. Armstrong.*

EASY GO 4 b.g. Targowice 130–Easy Can (Tudor Music 131) (1981 6d 8g — 7s3 1982 8f4 12f 10.2g 8.2g) strong ex-Irish gelding; first reported foal; dam won over 5f and 1¼m in Ireland; well beaten after finishing fourth in apprentice race at Carlisle in June; stays 1m (always behind over 1½m); blinkered final start; sold to M. Pipe 1,000 gns Ascot November Sales. *M. Naughton.*

EASY STAR 2 ch.c. Red Alert 127–Jantu 81 (Deep Diver 134) (1982 5f 6fg **77** 6fg4 5g 5.1d2 6d2 6g 6s3 6d3 5s 5g) Mar 25; neat colt; second foal; dam 6f winner; placed in sellers, 1¾m quite valuable events, and in a maiden race; needs at least 6f; acts well on a soft surface; ran very freely in blinkers fourth start; bandaged fifth and sixth outings; has worn a tongue strap; sweated up sixth and seventh appearances. *B. Hanbury.*

EBONY GUARD 3 bl.f. Home Guard 129–Bouboulina (Hornbeam 130) (1981 — 6s 7d 1982 12.2f 9fg 12fg) big, rangy filly; well beaten in maiden races and a seller; blinkered final start; sometimes bandaged. *G. Lockerbie.*

EBONY HILL 4 br.f. Bronze Hill 96–Sweet Electra (Straight Cut 103) (1981 — 8f 11f 1982 11g) tailed off in minor and maiden events. *R. Allan.*

ECONOMY GIRL 2 b.f. Scottish Rifle 127–Choralist 77 (Polyfoto 124) (1982 **64** 7fg 8d2 8.2d 8d) May 2; 420F; small, lightly-made filly; half-sister to a winner in Hungary; dam second over 5f on only start; 1¼ lengths second of 24 to Miss Carine in seller at Leicester in September, only form; stays 1m. *Mrs J. Reavey.*

ECSTATICA (USA) 3 b.f. Damascus–Fantastic Review (Reviewer) (1981 **81** 6fg2 1982 7.3g3 7.6fg* 8g 8fg 7g 7fg4 7g) rather lightly-built, quite attractive filly; poor walker; good mover; creditable 2¼ lengths third of 5 to Slightly Dangerous in Fred Darling Stakes at Newbury prior to narrowly winning 16-runner maiden race at Chester in May from Larla; well beaten most subsequent starts, including in good-class company; should stay 1m; yet to race on a soft surface. *F. J. Houghton.*

EDGEDALE 4 gr. or ro.c. Sharp Edge 123–Queen's Penny (Queen's Hussar — 124) (1981 6g 7d* 8g 8s4 7d 8.2g 10d 10s4 13.3s 1982 10g 11.7fg 10fg4) lightly-made colt; rather disappointing since winning at Salisbury (apprentice ridden) as a 3-y-o; stays 1¼m; acts on soft going; blinkered final start. *T. Marshall.*

EGERTON 2 ch.g. Welsh Pageant 132–Visite Royale (Dapper Dan) (1982 7g) — Apr 27; 210Y; rather lightly-made gelding; fourth foal; half-brother to 3 winners here and abroad, including Garter Star (by Star Appeal), successful at around 1¼m; dam ran only twice; unquoted, ninth of 10 behind Moment in Time in minor event at Redcar in August. *W. Haigh.*

EGNOUSSA 3 b.f. Swing Easy 126–Devon Night 100 (Midsummer Night II **76** 117) (1981 5f 6g 5f 5s 5s4 1982 8.5f 7g2 8fg4 7fg* 7f 7fg* 7fg* 7g4) fair sort; won maiden race at Chepstow in July and handicaps at Epsom in August and Lingfield in September; best at 7f; acts well on fast ground; blinkered twice at 2 yrs; has sweated up. *C. Brittain.*

EGRI LEANYKA 2 gr.f. Dragonara Palace 115–Red April 59 (March Past 124) **56** (1982 5g 5d 6f 5f 5fg³ 6s 5s) Mar 22; 2,000Y; workmanlike filly; second foal; dam won 6f seller; poor maiden; apparently best at 5f; sold Mrs G. Forbes 400 gns Newmarket Autumn Sales. *P. Bailey.*

EIGHT FOLD 2 ch.f. Octavo 115–Lucerne 76 (Gun Shot) (1982 5fg 7fg) — Apr 8; IR 4,400Y; neat filly; half-sister to several winners, including fairly useful 1981 2-y-o 6f winner Tickletimes (by Home Guard); dam won at up to 11f; soundly beaten in sellers at Goodwood (well-backed favourite, didn't stride out at all well to start) in May and Redcar (easy in market) in September. *A. Jarvis.*

EIGHT ROSES 5 ch.m. Pieces of Eight 128–Miss Rosy (Quorum 126) (1981 **53** 16.9s 15.5d 17.1d³ 15.5fg 17.1h 16.5f³ 12g* 12g² 12.2s² 12d 1982 12s⁴ 12g 15.8f 12g* 14s⁴ 18.1g³ 16g³ 17.1s 13.8d² 20g) small, narrow mare; plater; won claiming race at Newmarket in August and was subsequently in frame in better company; stays well; seems to act on any going; often sweats up. *M. Tompkins.*

ELARIM 3 br.c. Meldrum 112–Souriciere 73 (Count Albany 99) (1981 6fg 6f **55** 7g³ 6g³ 6f 6fg 6d 7f 7s 1982 8f 8f² 8fg 10g⁴ 11fg² 10fg 10d⁴ 9s) compact, workmanlike colt; poor handicapper; suited by middle distances; tended to hang and didn't look an easy ride second start. *J. Carr.*

ELA ZINA MOU 3 b. or br.f. Prince de Galles 125–Reine d'Etat 53 (High Hat — 131) (1981 6g 5g 1982 7g⁴ 7g 8fg) fair sort; poor plater; has been tried in blinkers. *D. Ringer.*

EL BADR 7 b.h. Weavers' Hall 122–Indian Maid 117 (Astec 128) (1981 15.5d **111** 15.5g 20v 14d* 20s² 15.5v⁴ 1982 15.5v* 15.5fg² 20v* 20f³) rangy French horse; has been fired; won Prix de Barbeville at Longchamp in April (by a nose from Kelbomec) and Prix du Cadran on same course in May; gaining his second win in latter when holding off Tipperary Fixer by a short head (moved easily into lead early in straight but only just held on); also placed in Prix Jean Prat on

Mr M. Fustok's "El Badr"

ELE

same course in between (½-length second to Starski) and Gold Cup at Royal Ascot in June (had no chance with 3-length winner Ardross but lost second place to Tipperary Fixer by only a neck); well suited by a thorough test of stamina; acts on any going. *M. Saliba, France.*

ELBURY COVE 3 ch.g. Kashiwa 115–Passing Glory 68 (Majority Blue 126) — (1981 NR 1982 8.2fg) IR 840F, IR 6,600Y; first foal; dam poor maiden; unquoted and burly when last of 15 to Tawfiq in maiden race at Nottingham in April. *W. Wharton.*

EL CITO 5 b.h. Ridan–Airgead Beo (Hook Money 124) (1981 10.4s 15.5f 10f — 10d 1982 8fg 12d 12s) lengthy, rather lightly-made ex-Irish horse; placed in varied company in 1980; soundly beaten since; stays 1¾m; acts on any going; good mount for an apprentice; has worn blinkers, including when successful on only outing at 2 yrs; sold 480 gns Ascot November Sales. *G. Balding.*

EL CUBANO 4 b.g. Pitskelly 122–Aurorian (Rise 'N Shine II) (1981 8g — 12.2g³ 12d 1982 12s) workmanlike gelding; poor form, including in a valuable seller; suited by 1½m; blinkered final start at 2 yrs; bandaged only outing of 1982 (October). *M. Hinchliffe.*

EL DJEM 3 br.g. Mansingh 120–Mumtaz (Sheshoon 132) (1981 5s 6g 7fg⁴ 6f — 7f 7s 1982 10f 9fg 9g 12fg⁴ 12fg 12fg 13.8d) neat gelding; poor plater, possibly stays 1½m; has been bandaged in front. *P. Wigham.*

ELECTRIC 3 b.c. Blakeney 126–Christiana 106 (Double Jump 131) (1981 **126** 7fg² 7.2fg 1982 9fg² 10fg* 12f³ 12f 12f* 12g* 14.6f)

Some of the pleasures and pitfalls of a trainer's life are clearly illustrated in the three-year-old career of Electric. On his day he was a very good racehorse, a match for any English-trained three-year-old at a mile and a half, but he was bedevilled by a muscular injury in his quarters and twice came back tailed-off last in important races, including the St Leger on his final outing when he started favourite. Surprisingly, the Doncaster stewards didn't inquire into Electric's running but trainer Stoute found himself in front of the Goodwood stewards in July after Electric won the Gordon Stakes from the Derby runner-up Touching Wood. The stewards inquired into the improvement in form of Electric compared with the King Edward VII Stakes at Royal Ascot when he was tailed off; they accepted Stoute's explanation that when Electric returned from Ascot he was found to have muscular trouble in his hind quarters. If Electric could be relied upon to reproduce the form he showed in the Gordon Stakes—and in the Great Voltigeur Stakes at York in August—he would be one to follow in 1983. At his best, he is that most desirable of thoroughbreds from a flat-racing owner's point of view: a mile-and-a-half horse with pace, the type that earns most of the prestige and the prize money. Whether Electric can overcome his unsoundness only time will tell but when a horse has a recurrent injury it necessarily undermines confidence in his future and we'd advise readers against falling over themselves to take short odds about him, at least until we have seen how he performs in his first few races as a four-year-old.

Electric began the most recent season still a maiden, having had two outings in minor company as a two-year-old, creating a favourable impression on the first and running most disappointingly when odds on on the second. As so often with a slow-maturing middle-distance three-year-old, the Derby came too soon for Electric. After running encouragingly on his reappearance and then putting up a sound performance to win the White Rose Stakes at Ascot in April, Electric showed in the Highland Spring Derby Trial at Lingfield that he wasn't quite ready to tackle the very best company. He was quoted at 20/1 for the Derby after winning at Ascot but was wisely put by after his performance at Lingfield where he was ridden for stamina, taking up the running before the home turn, but was convincingly beaten by Jalmood and Mr Fluorocarbon. Apart from the fiasco at Royal Ascot, Electric wasn't seen out again until the Gordon Stakes. What an impressive performance he gave that day! With stable jockey Swinburn out of action with a broken wrist, Starkey took the mount on Electric who started at 25/1. Starkey rode a waiting race and Electric showed easily the best turn of foot at the end of a fairly slowly-run race to win by three lengths from Touching Wood with the odds-on Jalmood, who had won the Mecca Bookmakers Scottish Derby after running below his best at Epsom, a length away in third. Electric was striding out with tremendous enthusiasm in the closing stages and was a most decisive winner. His excellent pace was again in evidence in the more truly-run Great Voltigeur Stakes. With three furlongs to go at York only two of the seven runners, Electric and Diamond Shoal, were still on the bridle. Electric quickened away from his field soon afterwards and with Diamond Shoal,

293

*Gordon Stakes, Goodwood—Electric strides clear from
Touching Wood and Jalmood (rails)*

who couldn't keep up at first, cutting steadily into his lead inside the final furlong Electric got home by three quarters of a length; Touching Wood finished seven lengths behind Diamond Shoal in third place with the rest of the field well strung out.

A well-made, quite attractive colt and a good walker, Electric was a 32,000-guinea yearling. His sire the Derby winner Blakeney improved greatly between two and three years and showed his best form as a four-year-old when he finished second to Nijinsky in the King George and fifth to Sassafras in the Prix de l'Arc, beating the older horses home in both races; he also went very close to winning the Gold Cup. Blakeney has been a very successful stallion and almost

*Great Voltigeur Stakes, York—Electric keeps on well to beat Diamond Shoal,
with Touching Wood in third place this time*

Mr R. C. Clifford-Turner's "Electric"

always imparts a fair degree of stamina to his offspring. Electric's dam Christiana, a half-sister to the very smart mile to mile-and-a-quarter performer Calpurnius, did not race after showing useful form over five furlongs as a two-year-old. Christiana bred five winners before Electric: to High Top and Luthier, both of

Electric (b.c. 1979)	Blakeney (b 1966)	Hethersett (b 1959)	Hugh Lupus
			Bride Elect
		Windmill Girl (b 1961)	Hornbeam
			Chorus Beauty
	Christiana (ch 1967)	Double Jump (ch 1962)	Rustam
			Fair Bid
		Mount Rosa (ch 1957)	Hill Gail
			Vestal Virgin

whom showed high-class form at a mile, she bred the French mile-winner High Hopper and the smart English miler Chalet respectively; to the middle-distance stayers Ribero, Appiani II and Reliance II she foaled Cresta, who dead-heated in a seven-furlong maiden race at Warwick as a two-year-old on her only start, the moderate Cardiff and the fair Courchevel, the two last-named winners at up to a mile and three quarters. How far Electric stays is of only academic interest: it would be a major surprise if he were to be campaigned at distances beyond a mile and a half as a four-year-old. He acts well on firm going and has yet to race on a soft surface. One final point: Electric moved to post magnificently before the Gordon Stakes, in marked contrast to several other occasions when we saw him, and it could be worth paying particular attention to the way he strides out before his races in 1983. *M. Stoute.*

EL GITANO 2 ch.c. Wollow 132–Welsh Miniature 85 (Owen Anthony 102) **93**
(1982 7f 8f 8s*) Apr 10; 12,000Y; lengthy, shallow-girthed colt; first foal; dam, half-sister to top-class Raffingora, won over 5f at 2 yrs; 25/1, won 14-runner

maiden race at Leicester in November by 1½ lengths from Nestor, the pair coming well clear; suited by 1m; acts on soft going. *R. Boss.*

ELISETTA 2 b.f. Monsanto 121–Silette 84 (Siliconn 121) (1982 6g 5.8g 5fg) — Apr 12; 8,200Y; compact filly; first foal; dam top-of-the-ground 1¼m performer; no show in maiden races; needs further. *M. Blanshard.*

ELITE PETITE 4 b.f. Welsh Saint 126–Super Amber (Yellow God 129) (1981 47 5d 6g 7v 7d 7f 8.3f 10f* 10f² 8.3g 10s 10s* 1982 10fg 10d 11.7fg 10f³ 10fg² 10fg 10fg 10g 10s) light-framed filly; plater; ran moderately after fifth outing and is one to leave alone; suited by 1¼m; acts on any going; sold out of M. Haynes's stable 620 gns Ascot September Sales after seventh start. *D. Wintle.*

ELITE SYNCOPATION (USA) 2 ch.c. Lyphard 132–Zaire (Sir Gaylord) 93 (1982 6fg 6d* 7s³) Apr 15; $65,000Y; quite attractive colt; third foal; dam, winner twice at up to 1m, is half-sister to smart 1966 American 2-y-o Pepperwood; landed the odds by a head from Chaplin's Club in 9-runner maiden event at Brighton in October; creditable third behind impressive winner Sackford in 8-runner minor event at Leicester the following month; will stay 1m. *H. Cecil.*

ELIZABETH HOWARD 4 ch.f. Sharpen Up 127–Molly Flo (Paveh 126) (1981 — 7g 12d 14f 14.6fg³ 11f² 12f² 11.5g* 12g* 10.6v 12g 1982 12.2fg 12fg 12fg 12s) strong, fair sort; no form in 1982; gives impression she doesn't stay 1¾m; blinkered second start in 1980. *S. Harris.*

ELIZA DE RICH 5 b.m. Spanish Gold 101–Dumb Kathy (Dumbarnie 125) 50 (1981 8g 8g⁴ 7f* 7fg² 8fg 6fg² 8.2g 8f² 8fg⁴ 8.2s 7s 7g 1982 8s 8f 8f* 7fg 7g⁴ 8fg* 8f 8.2g* 8d³ 8fg 8fg 7g) lightly-made mare; plater; bought in when successful at Carlisle in June (1,600 gns) and Edinburgh in July (780 gns) but attracted no bid after winning rather comfortably in a big field at Haydock in August; stays 1m; suited by a sound surface; occasionally sweats up; usually held up and has a fair turn of foot for a plater. *R. Hollinshead.*

ELLARON 4 gr.f. Abwah 118–Smartie Pants 68 (Galivanter 131) (1981 NR 45 1982 10g 10fg 12s 12v 8g 8f 10f⁴ 10fg 10g*) lengthy filly; plater; attracted no bid after winning by 4 lengths at Nottingham in September; stays 1¼m; trained by T. Craig early in season. *W. Holden.*

ELLERENE 3 b.c. Hot Spark 126–My Cecilia 83 (Prevailing) (1981 5g 5d² 6s* 92 1982 7g 5f* 6f³ 5g⁴ 5fg 6d 6f 7fg) small, close-coupled, quite attractive colt; kept on well to win handicap at Sandown in April; in frame in similar races at York and Sandown afterwards; stays 6f; acts on any going; blinkered seventh start; has worn bandages; sent to Hong Kong. *P. Mitchell.*

EL MANSOUR 3 b.g. Tower Walk 130–Gay Amanda 75 (Counsel 118) (1981 — 5s⁴ 6d⁴ 6f* 6fg* 6f² 6fg* 6f 6s² 1982 7fg 6fg 6g 6f² 6g) leggy gelding; useful at his best; below form most starts at 3 yrs; may stay 7f (needed run when tried at trip); acts on any going but put up best effort on soft; blinkered last 2 starts, running moderately on second occasion. *N. Gaselee.*

ELMAR 3 b.f. Lord Gayle 124–Regal Step 101 (Ribero 126) (1981 NR 1982 82 7g 7g³ 7g* 8f² 7g* 8.5fg² 8g² 9s²) IR 9,600Y; quite attractive, small, lightly-made filly; first living produce; dam stayed well; always prominent and stayed on strongly to win maiden race at Thirsk in July and handicap at Newbury in August; ran creditably most other starts; will stay 1¼m; acts on any going. *J. Dunlop.*

ELMDON 2 b.g. Hittite Glory 125–Margaret's Ruby (Tesco Boy 121) (1982 78 7d 6g) Mar 21; 4,200Y; attractive gelding; half-brother to several winners, including fairly useful 1976 2-y-o 5f performer Yes Love (by On Your Mark); dam Irish 2-y-o 5f winner; 8¾ lengths sixth of 19 behind Matou in maiden race at Newmarket in October, second outing. *J. Winter.*

EL PATO 3 br.f. Moulton 128–Black Mink 83 (Gratitude 130) (1981 5s*(dis) — 5s 5g 5fg 6fg 5s 5s 1982 6g 5s 8fg⁴ 9g 10d) workmanlike filly; plater; stays 1m; blinkered second start; sold 480 gns Newmarket Autumn Sales. *W. Wharton.*

EL PRESIDENTE 4 b.g. Bold Lad (Ire) 133–Inquisitive Girl 97 (Crepello 136) 53 (1981 5s² 5s 5s² 5d³ 7d 6g⁴ 6s⁴ 6g⁴ 6f 5g³ 6fg 6f² 6g 6g 5s 1982 5g 6fg 5f³ 5f 7h 5fg³ 5fg 6g) strong gelding; ran best races when third twice at Beverley; stayed 6f (not disgraced over 7f); acted on any going; sometimes blinkered; sold 950 gns Ascot September Sales; dead. *K. Ivory.*

ELSELL 7 ch.m. Grey Mirage 128–Mary's Twiggy (Queen's Hussar 124) (1981 31 12s³ 13s² 1982 16d² 16f 12s) narrow, lightly-made mare; plater; second in better company at Warwick in April; stays well; acts on soft going. *M. Eckley.*

ELYSIAN 2 b. or br.f. Northfields–Elizabethan 89 (Tudor Melody 129) (1982 **93**
6fg² 6g* 8fg³) Feb 21; neat filly; second foal; dam, from excellent family, won
over 1m on only start; in front rank throughout and kept on strongly to win
16-runner maiden race at Newbury in August by ½ length from Alimony; 2
lengths third of 12 to Ghaiya in £3,600 race at Goodwood the following month;
stays 1m. *P. Walwyn.*

EMAD 2 ch.c. Hot Spark 126–Sky Miss (Skymaster 126) (1982 5d 6f 8s) May 25; **66**
half-brother to two 2-y-o winners, including 1980 Irish 5f winner Azurette (by
Owen Anthony); dam poor half-sister to very smart Sexton Blake; plating-class
maiden; unlikely to stay 1m; off course 3 months after second start. *R. Hannon.*

EMANDAR 3 b.g. Abwah 118–Double Bank 80 (Double Jump 131) (1981 NR **—**
1982 12fg 10d 16.5s 12.2d) robust gelding; brother to a poor maiden; dam won
twice over 5f at 2 yrs; behind in varied company. *H. Wharton.*

EMERALD REEF 2 b.f. Mill Reef 141–Crown Treasure (Graustark) (1982 **104**
7f 8g 8g) May 2; well-grown, lengthy, attractive filly; third foal; sister to top-
class middle-distance stayer Glint of Gold and St Leger third Diamond Shoal;
dam very useful at 2 yrs in USA when winner over 5f; 50/1, showed plenty of
promise when running-on 6 lengths sixth of 8 to Bright Crocus in May Hill Stakes
at Doncaster in September on second outing; 8/1, moderate sixth of 8 to
Acclimatise in Hoover Fillies Mile at Ascot later in month; the type to make
a much better 3-y-o. *I. Balding.*

EMLYN PRINCESS 2 ch.f. Julio Mariner 127–Rotondo (Royal Buck) (1982 **—**
7f 7fg) Mar 29; good-bodied filly; excellent mover; half-sister to several winners
here and abroad, including 3-y-o middle-distance winner Sa-Vegas (by Star
Appeal); dam Irish 1½m winner; not fully wound up, well beaten in maiden
events at Salisbury (recovered from slow start to show prominently 2f out) and
Newmarket in August; may do better. *B. Swift.*

EMMA ALISON 2 ch.f. Mansingh 120–Tanzanite (Mongo) (1982 6g 5.1fg 7g) **—**
of no account; sold 380 gns Ascot November Sales. *K. Ivory.*

EMMA LA DOUCE 3 b.f. Shiny Tenth 120–Four Lawns 77 (Forlorn River 124) **—**
(1981 5s 5s³ 6d 1982 5g 5fg 5g⁴ 6g 5fg 5f 6d⁴ 7d) fair sort; plater; stays 6f;
suited by some give in the ground; sold 400 gns Ascot November Sales. *D.
Marks.*

EMMA ROYALE 3 b.f. Royal and Regal–Moment To Remember (Assagai) **69**
(1981 7f 8.2fg 1982 10s 12g 12fg 13.8f 10f⁴ 10.6s 12.2d³ 12d* 12g) fair sort;
made all and battled on well to win valuable selling handicap at Doncaster in
October; bought in 2,000 gns afterwards; stays 1½m; suited by some give in the
ground; has run respectably for an apprentice. *R. Hollinshead.*

EMMA'S STAR 2 b.f. Comedy Star 121–Dancin In The Wind 61 (Aureole 132) **—**
(1982 8s) Mar 14; leggy, close-coupled filly; fourth foal; half-sister to a winner
in Italy; dam placed over 1¼m; needed race and went badly to post when distant
tenth of 11 behind Running Melody in maiden race at Wolverhampton in October.
M. Blanshard.

EMPERADOR 4 ch.c. Empery 128–Stogumber 96 (Habitat 134) (1981 NR **87**
1982 10d³ 9g⁴ 9.4fg* 10g* 10g 8s³ 10s²) 43,000Y; workmanlike colt; second
foal; half-brother to a winner in Italy by St Paddy; dam, 2-y-o 6f winner, comes
from same family as Great Nephew; didn't have his first race until the spring;
quickened clear to beat Jacinto Times in good style by 6 lengths in minor event
at Carlisle in July and beat Warm Wind decisively by a length after being held
up in similar race at Nottingham in September; probably found 1m too sharp
and stayed 1¼m; best form on a sound surface; had a fair turn of foot; sold
20,000 gns Newmarket Autumn Sales and exported to Trinidad as a stallion. *T.
Robson.*

EMPEROR NAPOLEON 5 gr.g. Young Emperor 133–Polly Charlot (Charlot- **—**
town 127) (1981 NR 1982 14fg) tall gelding; placed at up to 7f as a 2-y-o;
well beaten since; acts on any going. *N. Mitchell.*

EMPEROR'S PALACE 2 gr.c. Dragonara Palace 115–Emperor Star (King **77 p**
Emperor) (1982 7g) Mar 5; 9,000Y; strong colt; third foal; half-brother to 2
winners by Mummy's Pet, including very useful 3-y-o Not For Show, a winner
at up to 7f; dam of little account; 40/1 and on backward side, always behind
when 11 lengths last of 6 to Polished Silver in Somerville Tattersall Stakes at
Newmarket in October; should improve. *M. Jarvis.*

EMPRESS JEANNIE 5 b.m. Young Emperor 133–Jean Armour 88 (Delirium — 126) (1981 10s 10.8d⁴ 12f 12f 10f 10.1g 10s 10g 1982 10fg) compact mare; behind in a seller only outing of 1982; stays 11f; acts on a firm and a soft surface. *H. Collingridge.*

ENBYAR DAN 2 ch.c. Porto Bello 118–Alleyn (Alcide 136) (1982 5fg 5.1g⁴ 87 7f² 7f* 7g² 7fg) Apr 1; 3,800Y; well-grown, workmanlike colt; first foal; dam showed no form on flat or over hurdles; put up a game effort to win 3-runner nursery at Yarmouth in August by a short head from Boxberger Oscar; again kept on most genuinely when ½-length second of 8 to clever winner John French in another nursery at Newmarket later same week; suited by 7f; yet to race on a soft surface. *M. Tompkins.*

ENDOW 2 b.f. Mr Bigmore 123–Fulfilment (David Jack 125) (1982 6f) Feb — 3; sister to 3-y-o Junior Trustee and half-sister to quite useful middle-distance winners Westminster Abbey (by Royalty) and Stephen's Day (by Bonne Noel); dam ran only twice; 50/1 and backward, moved very poorly to start when well behind in 19-runner maiden race won by Gangawayhame at Leicester in May. *F. Durr.*

ENERGY PLUS 7 b.h. Tyrant–Reformed Maid (Reform 132) (1981 6g⁴ 6g³ — 6g* 6d 5fg 6fg 6fg⁴ 6f 6s 6d 6d 1982 6fg 6d 7g 6f 6s) neat, strong horse; poor mover; poor handicapper; stays 6f; acts on any going; has been tried in blinkers; often bandaged nowadays. *W. Wharton.*

ENGLISH MASTER (USA) 2 b.c. Master Derby–Final Quote (Minnesota — Mac) (1982 7g) Mar 2; $50,000Y; first foal; dam, out of half-sister to Derby third Hunza Dancer, won at up to 7f; unquoted, out of first 9 behind Mandelstam in 30-runner maiden race at Newmarket in October. *J. Sutcliffe.*

ENGLISH MUFFIN 2 gr.f. Owen Dudley 121–Pure Honey 94 (Don II 123) 63 (1982 5g³ 5fg³ 6g 6f² 5.8f² 6d 5d⁴ 6s) May 29; 1,150F, 2,600Y; third foal; half-sister to a winner in Belgium by High Line; dam 5f performer; narrowly-beaten second in maiden auction event at Kempton and seller at Bath (odds on) in July; not seen out again until October; stays 6f; seems to act on any going; has run well for an apprentice. *R. Laing.*

ENGLISH STAR 2 gr.c. English Prince 129–Scargill's Girl 56 (St Alphage 119) 80 (1982 5fg³ 5fg² 5fg 5g 7g 6d⁴ 5g 5fg* 5s 5g) Feb 10; IR 2,000F, 11,000Y; work-manlike colt; first foal; dam half-sister to Decoy Boy; won 11-runner nursery at Redcar in September; fourth of 14 in £3,000 seller at Newcastle on sixth start; best form at 5f, but had very stiff task when tried over 7f; best form on a sound surface; swerved 2f out and finished in rear when blinkered fourth outing; inconsistent. *A. Jarvis.*

ENGULF 4 b.g. Gulf Pearl 117–Primrose 86 (Primera 131) (1981 10.6fg⁴ 12.3g 77 1982 8g 10fg 12fg 14f⁴ 12g 13g 14g 10d) strong, compact, deep-girthed gelding; good walker and mover; useful performer as a 2-y-o, but was brought down final start and doesn't seem to have recovered fully; promises to stay 1¾m; probably acts on any going but goes well in the mud; blinkered final start in 1981. *J. W. Watts.*

ENMAR 4 b.g. Acrania 110–Tamblast (Tamerlane 128) (1981 12s 10v 1982 — 12s 14fg) lengthy gelding; lightly raced and well beaten in varied company. *D. Elsworth.*

ENTHRALMENT (USA) 3 b. or br.f. Sir Ivor 135–Trevisana (Aristophanes — 116) (1981 6fg* 6s 1982 8.5f 11g) lengthy, attractive filly; excellent mover; won maiden race at Salisbury in 1981; in rear all subsequent starts; should stay middle distances; has given trouble in preliminaries. *J. Tree.*

EPETIOS 2 b.c. Wolver Hollow 126–Treechka (Reform 132) (1982 7s⁴) Mar 88 p 31; 23,000Y; strong, good sort; second foal; dam Irish 1½m winner; 50/1 and on burly side, put up a pleasing first effort when 9 lengths fourth of 6 to The Fort in £4,700 event at Goodwood in September, keeping on well without being knocked about after running a bit green at halfway; likely to leave this form well behind. *G. Harwood.*

EPITHET 3 b.f. Mill Reef 141–Namecaller 83 (Malicious) (1981 6fg 5g* 6fg* 105 6s³ 1982 8d² 12.3fg² 10.5fg² 12g³ 12fg) small, quite attractive, lightly-made filly; good mover; ran creditably most starts, going down by 5 lengths to Time Charter in Masaka Stakes at Kempton, by 3 lengths to all-the-way winner Swift-foot in Cheshire Oaks and by 2 lengths to Vidor in Prix de Royaumont at

Beckhampton Ltd's "Epithet"

Chantilly, and coming home 1¾ lengths third to Sans Blague in Galtres Stakes at York; will stay 1¾m; seems to act on any going; ran disappointingly final start. *J. Tree.*

EPOCH 3 b.f. Wolver Hollow 126–Darling Bud (Whistling Wind 123) (1981 9d 1982 8f) IR 8,200Y; medium-sized, attractive ex-Irish filly; good walker; half-sister to 3 winners, including fairly useful 5f to 7f winner A Star is Born (by Tudor Music); dam useful Irish 2-y-o; well beaten in maiden race at Gowran Park at 2 yrs and minor event at Newmarket in July (just needed run when last of 13 to Singleton). *Sir Mark Prescott.* —

EPRYANA 2 b.f. English Prince 129–Ayana (High Flown 117) (1982 7fg 8f 7d) Mar 22; 2,500Y; rather unfurnished but useful-looking filly; half-sister to Italian winner Hit (by Hittite Glory); dam won in Sweden at 2 yrs; no form in maiden events. *P. Makin.* —

EPSOM IMP 9 br.g. St Alphage 119–Sarah Jane 80 (Pardao 120) (1981 5g 5fg 5.3f² 6f³ 5g² 5s 5s 1982 5s 5f 5.8f⁴ 5g⁴ 5g 5f 5fg 5.3f 5g) modest handicapper nowadays; hasn't won since 1979; best at 5f; acts on any going; blinkered once at 2 yrs; good mount for an apprentice. *J. Holt.* —

EQUANAID 2 b.c. Dominion 123–Jungle Queen (Twilight Alley 133) (1982 7g 8.2s* 8.2s) Mar 24; 24,000Y; tall, fair sort, but rather unfurnished; third living produce; half-brother to 2 winners, including fairly useful 1980 2-y-o 1m winner Jungle Jim (by Hotfoot); dam ran 3 times; second favourite, led 3f out and wasn't troubled to beat Cash Or Carry by 4 lengths in 11-runner maiden race at Hamilton in September; again second favourite, failed to recover after being badly hampered on turn in nursery at Nottingham the following month; will stay 1½m; acts on soft going. *C. Nelson.* **92**

ERCOL BELLE   2 b. or br.f. Ercolano 118–Belle Year (Quorum 126)   (1982 5d   **61**
5fg² 5fg 5h² 7f 6g 6s 5v)   Apr 13; useful-looking filly; half-sister to 2 winners,
including 1979 2-y-o 5f winner Monkland Glen (by Runnymede); second in small
races at Folkestone in April and Chepstow in May; soundly beaten in sellers last
2 starts; should be suited by 6f + ; blinkered sixth outing.   *R. Hoad.*

ERIC'S WISH   2 b.g. Cawston's Clown 113–Sirette (Great Nephew 126)   (1982   **39**
7fg 6fg 6s)   May 21; 240Y; leggy, close-coupled gelding; first living foal; dam
poor plater; bad plater; best run at 6f on a firm surface.   *A. W. Jones.*

ERITREA (USA)   2 ch.f. Upper Nile–Foxyphyllis (Minnesota Mac)   (1982 7g)   —
Mar 27; $135,000Y; second foal; dam, half-sister to 3 stakes winners, won 6 times
at up to 1m; sire, son of Nijinsky, was very smart winner at up to 1¼m at 4 yrs;
16/1, and bit backward, out of first 10 of 22 in maiden race at Newmarket in
October.   *I. Balding.*

ERMAC   4 br.g. Balidar 133–Sateen 83 (High Treason 126)   (1981 8s³ 7d⁴ 8.2fg 7g   **63**
1982 8fg 6f 7g³ 7.6d 8.2s* 7d 7s)   tall gelding; nothing like the force he was but
managed to win seller at Haydock in October (no bid); stays 1m; acts very well
on soft going; unseated rider when hampered second outing; bandaged nowadays.
G. Richards.

ERNEL   8 ch.g. Sassafras 135–Belaying Pin (Iron Peg **§§**)   (1981 15.5d 16g   —
18.8fg 12g 15.5fg 10fg 17.1h   1982 16g 12f 12fg)   poor staying handicapper;
suited by top-of-the-ground conditions; suitable mount for an amateur; well
beaten in a seller when blinkered final start.   *R. Atkins.*

EROS   2 gr. or ro.c. Brittany–Sweet Silhouette 79 (Setay 105)   (1982 5g 5fg⁴ 5d²   **54**
5f* 5fg² 5f 6fg 5.1g 5f 5f)   Apr 30; hollow-backed colt; half-brother to winner;
dam winning hurdler; won seller at Beverley (no bid) in April; should stay 6f;
seems to act on any going; usually blinkered; exported to Algeria.   *K. Ivory.*

ERRANTRY   7 br.g. Sterling Bay–Burletta (Derring-Do 131)   (1981 10g   1982   **34**
10f³ 7f⁴)   compact gelding; plater; stays 1¼m; suited by a sound surface;
blinkered once at 2 yrs; has run respectably for a lady rider.   *D. Wilson.*

ERRIGAL   2 b.g. Guillaume Tell 121–Levrosa (Levmoss 133)   (1982 8.2s 8s²)   **83**
Feb 27; IR 2,000F, 7,400Y, 1,300 2-y-o; rather sparely-made gelding; second
foal; half-brother to 3-y-o Mean Francine (by African Sky); dam never ran;
staying-on length second of 14 to Broad Beam in maiden event at Leicester in
November; will be suited by 1¼m.   *R. Hollinshead.*

ERROLL'S BOY   3 b.c. Bay Express 132–Brave Sally (Sallymount 125)   (1981   **90**
5g 5g* 5g³ 5f 5fg 5fg* 5g   1982 5f 5f² 5f* 5h* 5fg³ 5g 5f* 5fg 5g³)   big, strong,
well-made colt; did well over the winter; successful in handicaps at Redcar,
Haydock and Goodwood; made all and held off Street Market by a neck in
Singleton Handicap on last-named in July; also ran well when third in valuable
events at Ascot and York; acts well on firm going and has yet to race on a soft
surface; has twice run well in blinkers; sent to USA.   *M. W. Easterby.*

ERROLL'S ELITE   4 b.f. Saulingo 122–Silly Sue 55 (Great Nephew 126)   (1981   —
5g 5g 6g   1982 6g 8fg)   leggy filly; not a good mover; plater; blinkered once in
1980.   *T. Craig.*

ESCALINE (FR)   2 ch.f. Arctic Tern 126–Esdee (Hail to Reason)   (1982 8f² 8s*   **118**
10v*)   Mar 11; 90,000 francs Y (approx £8,200); fourth reported foal; half-sister
to 3-y-o French middle-distance winner Escalibur (by Caracolero); dam second
over 1¼m in France; put up a smart display when successful in 12-runner
Criterium de Saint-Cloud in November, drawing away from distance to beat
White Spade 1½ lengths; had earlier quickened well to win maiden race at
Longchamp; will stay 1½m; acts well on heavy going; sure to win more good
races.   *J. Fellows, France.*

ESCAPE CLAUSE   3 gr.f. Godswalk 130–Bethlehem (Santa Claus 133)   (1981   —
5v 5s²   1982 6f 8f 7f 8g 8fg⁴ 10fg)   rather lightly-made filly; quite a modest
maiden at her best; stays 1m; blinkered first start.   *W. Wharton.*

ESCAPE FROM HELL   3 b.c. Nonoalco 131–Border Bounty 113 (Bounteous   **61**
125)   (1981 7g 5s 6s   1982 10s 8.2v² 11fg³ 12f 8g 9g 10g 11.5f² 16fg 12v)   strong,
good-bodied colt; poor walker; middle-distance maiden; acts on any going;
blinkered eighth and ninth starts; changed hands 28,000 gns Doncaster September
Sales.   *N. Callaghan.*

ESCAPISM (USA)   3 b.c. Native Royalty–Dont Wanta Hear It (Dead Ahead)   **72**
(1981 7fg³ 7fg² 7fg(dis) 8d 7.6s² 7d² 8g   1982 7d⁴ 10f 10fg 8f 8g⁴ 10.5fg⁴ 11g²
10.2f° 10.6s⁴ 10.2d* 8s)   strong, rangy, good-looking colt; excellent mover;

genuine front-running handicapper who won at Doncaster in September (beat Field Lady a neck in valuable event) and October; will stay 1½m; acts on any going; sold out of G. Harwood's stable 2,600 gns Ascot 2nd June Sales after third start. *R. Whitaker.*

ESCAPIST 3 b.g. Run The Gantlet–Chappelle Blanche 96 (Olden Times) **74** (1981 7.2fg 8g 1982 11s* 12.3fg 16.1h³ 16fg³) attractive gelding; stayed on strongly to win maiden race at Ayr in March; third in 2 handicaps afterwards; one paced and stays very well; acts on any going. *J. W. Watts.*

ESCART BAY 2 ch.c. Stradavinsky 121–Succeed 85 (Parthia 132) (1982 5s³ **99** 5g² 5f² 5g* 5fg* 6fg² 6fg* 6d) Mar 28; 3,000F, 3,500Y; compact colt; half-brother to 3 winners, all successful at 2 yrs, including quite useful 1978 7f winner Arizona Pie (by Averof); dam, winner at 1m from 3 starts, is half-sister to Observer Gold Cup winner Approval; improved with racing, winning maiden race at Edinburgh in May, 8-runner minor event at Beverley in June and truly-run 2-runner nursery at Ayr in August; put up his most notable effort at Beverley, striding away in final furlong to beat Jonacris by 5 lengths; not seen out after August; will stay 7f; suited by a firm surface; hung second and third starts; sweated up quite badly third outing. *D. Smith.*

ESKVIEW LAD 4 br.g. Abwah 118–Safe Anchorage 63 (Quayside 124) (1981 **38** 7v³ 9.4g 8g 1982 8s 11g 7fg 8f 11fg 10f⁴ 7g 8fg³ 11fg³ 12.3g 13d 10d 12g³ 12g) small gelding; plater; stays 1¼m; probably acts on any going; often apprentice ridden; has run creditably in blinkers. *T. Craig.*

ESPANITA 2 b.f. Riboboy 124–L'Aventura 65 (Elopement 125) (1982 6fg 8s **64** 7d) Apr 28; half-sister to several winners here and abroad, including quite useful sprinter Chin-Chin (by Sing Sing); dam won at 1m and 1¼m; plating-class maiden; will stay 1¼m; appears to act on any going. *T. Gosling.*

ESPIGA 2 ch.f. English Prince 129–Estructura 102 (Gulf Pearl 117) (1982 **78 p** 7g 7d²) Feb 3; robust filly; third foal; half-sister to 3-y-o Big Trouble (by Reform), a winner at up to 1¼m; dam useful staying 2-y-o; 25/1, stayed on when 4 lengths second of 15 to Miss Bali Beach in maiden race at Leicester in October; will be suited by 1¼m+; likely to improve further. *G. Pritchard-Gordon.*

ESPRIT DU NORD (USA) 2 b.c. Lyphard 132–Rajput Princess 118 (Prince **103 p** Taj 123) (1982 8v*) Apr 5; half-brother to several winners, notably Irish Guinness Oaks winner Regal Exception (by Ribot); dam won Poule d'Essai des Pouliches; 7/2, outclassed his 16 opponents in newcomers race at Saint-Cloud in October, winning by 5 lengths and 4 lengths; has all the makings of a smart middle-distance 3-y-o. *J. Fellows, France.*

ESSAM 4 b.g. Sallust 134–Bold Words (Bold Ruler) (1981 8.2s 10fg 8g 8g² **58 §** 8.2g² 7fg 8.2f⁴ 8g⁴ 8f² 8f* 8f* 8f 8g 8d 1982 8f 8f* 8fg 8.2g 8g 8fg 8g) strong, compact ex-Irish gelding; not a good mover; won apprentice handicap at New-castle in May by a short head from Pause For Thought; little other form in 1982 and ran badly last 3 starts; stays 1m; acts on firm going; usually blinkered; has run well when sweating up; not entirely genuine. *A. Hide.*

ESTERE (FR) 4 b.f. Targowice 130–Eastern Silk 88 (Zeddaan 130) (1981 **108** 10v³ 1982 10s* 9.5fg² 8g 9d) 150,000 francsY (approx £15,000); leggy, rather lightly-made filly; second foal; dam won over 1m; decisively won maiden race at Saint-Cloud in March; ran next start to be ½-length second of 6 to Harbour in Prix Vanteaux at Longchamp; soundly beaten in Poule d'Essai des Pouliches at Longchamp and Prix Chloe at Evry afterwards; stays 1¼m; seems to act on any going. *P-L. Biancone, France.*

ESTIMA 3 b.f. Lucky Wednesday 124–Safe Anchorage 63 (Quayside 124) (1981 — 7g 8.2d 8g 1982 8g) soundly beaten in maiden company; sold 1,000 gns Doncaster March Sales. *T. Craig.*

ETCETERA 2 ch.f. High Line 125–Word Perfect (Worden II 129) (1982 7d — 10s) Apr 27; fair sort; half-sister to several winners, including very useful English and French 5f to 7f winner Giriama (Tribal Chief); dam never ran; well beaten in big fields of maidens at Leicester and Nottingham in October; sold BBA (Italia) 3,000 gns Newmarket Autumn Sales. *J. Hindley.*

ETOILE-DE-MANOIRE 3 b.f. Comedy Star 121–Polly Buckle 97 (Polic 126) — (1981 5f 6fg 5d 1982 8f 8f 9g) fair sort; of no account. *T. Hallett.*

ETOILE D'OR 3 b. or br.g. Comedy Star 121–Burdigala (Tudor Music 131) — (1981 6f 5fg 6f 6fg 5f 5g 5g² 5s⁴ 1982 5d⁴ 5v 5fg 5f) fair sort; poor mover; plater; best at 5f; wears blinkers; sold 660 gns Doncaster September Sales. *R. Hobson.*

ETONIAN 7 ch.h. Majority Blue 126–Gilded Egg (Faberge II 121) (1981 —
7g⁴ 7fg* 6fg 1982 11.7fg 8fg) poor handicapper nowadays; stays 7f; probably
acts on any going; suitable mount for an apprentice. *G. Thorner.*

EUGENE BOUDIN 2 b.c. Pampapaul 121–Ludhiana (Faraway Son 130) §§
(1982 5.1f⁴ 6g 5.8f 7f 6f) Apr 17; IR 8,600F, 2,500Y, 9,000 2-y-o (privately);
rangy colt; showed more temperament than ability; refused to race fourth outing
and reluctant to race final appearance; usually blinkered; sold 460 gns Newmarket Autumn Sales. *E. Eldin.*

EUGENES CHANCE 2 b.f. Flashback 102–Mingwyn Wood (Pirate King 129) —
(1982 5v 6s) Mar 24; half-sister to 1979 2-y-o 5f winner Lawrence-Lee (by Grey
Mirage); dam ran only twice; behind in October in maiden race (last of 14) at
Folkestone and claiming event at Nottingham. *J. Long.*

EURODANCER (USA) 3 b.c. Caucasus 127–Tumbling Dancer (Dancer's 101
Image) (1981 6fg⁴ 7g³ 7f³ 1982 10.4g 10f* 10.5fg³ 10g*) good-topped colt;
won maiden race at Epsom (made most) and minor event at Brighton in June;
subsequently sent to race in Canada and ran second in a minor stakes race at
Woodbine in October; stays 1¼m well; acts on firm going; sweated up at Epsom;
apprentice ridden at Brighton. *B. Hills.*

EVEN BANKER 3 ch.c. Lombard 126–Eventura 87 (Huntercombe 133) (1981 88
5g 5d⁴ 5f 6fg 7g 8g 8d⁴ 8s* 7d 1982 8d² 8.2d² 7fg² 8fg² 10.1fg³ 10d⁴ 10f* 10fg
10g⁴ 10.2g* 10g³) workmanlike colt; won handicaps at Kempton in July and
Doncaster in September; suited by 1¼m; acts on any going; sweated up and
pulled hard third start; suited by waiting tactics; consistent. *R. Hannon.*

EVENING BELLE (USA) 2 b. or br.f. Damascus–Belle O'Belgium (Amarullah) 97
(1982 7fg* 6g 7d² 7d²) May 3; $180,000Y; rangy, quite attractive filly; has a
round action; sister to 3 winners, including stakes winner Daring Damascus,
successful at up to 1m, and half-sister to a winner in Italy; dam stakes winner
at up to 1m; creditable second in two races in October, going down by a neck
to Hole In The Wall in minor event at Naas and by a length to slow-starting
Heron Bay in Larkspur Stakes at Leopardstown; had earlier landed the odds in
maiden race at Naas and finished about 13 lengths last of 9 to Ma Biche in William
Hill Cheveley Park Stakes at Newmarket; will be suited by 1m; the type to train
on. *T. Curtin, Ireland.*

EVENING STANDARD 2 b.f. Realm 129–Evening Blaze (Soderini 123) (1982 72 d
5fg⁴ 6f² 5fg 6fg) Mar 7; 1,900Y; shapely, attractive filly; half-sister to fairly
useful 1978 Irish 2-y-o 5f and 6f winner Windy Sunset (by Tumble Wind); dam
placed over 1¼m in Ireland; beaten at odds on in maiden auction events on
second and third outings, running badly at Folkestone in August on latter
occasion; needs further than 5f; disappointing; sold BBA 400 gns Newmarket
Autumn Sales. *R. Smyth.*

EVENOS 2 b. or br.c. Rheingold 137–Edelliette (Edellic 124) (1982 10.2s) —
Apr 21; 10,000Y; big colt; half-brother to several winners, including very useful
1980 French 2-y-o 5f winner Enigma (by Habitat) and very useful middle-distance
performer Eddystone (by Barbare II); dam won over 1¼m and 1½m in French
Provinces; unquoted, tailed off in 15-runner minor event won by Whitstar at
Doncaster in November; sold 800 gns Ascot December Sales. *R. Laing.*

EVE OF TROY 3 b.f. Willipeg 112–Pontesbury (Falls of Clyde 126) (1981 NR —
1982 7f 8fg 7fg) half-sister to 2 winners, including quite useful sprinter Mino
Boy (by Decoy Boy); dam ran only at 2 yrs; in rear in maiden races. *Mrs B.
Waring.*

EVER GREAT 3 b.c. Grundy 137–Forever 68 (Never Say Die 137) (1981 8g 77
1982 12s 12g³ 14fg³ 14f 13d⁴ 16g) compact, strong colt; quite a modest maiden;
one paced and is suited by a test of stamina; sold 7,000 gns Newmarket Autumn
Sales. *P. Walwyn.*

EVERSEAL 2 ch.g. Patch 129–Dunstells (Saint Crespin III 132) (1982 6fg 7g 76
7f² 8s) Apr 2; IR 6,000F, IR 20,000Y; useful-looking gelding; half-brother to 3
winners, including 1981 Irish 2-y-o 5f winner Red Jersey (by Red Alert); dam
ran only twice; length second of 6 to odds-on Flying Corps in maiden race at
Brighton in September, best effort; should stay at least 1¼m; acts on firm going,
and is possibly not suited by soft. *G. Hunter.*

EVERWARM 2 br.f. Hot Grove 128–Aunt Eva 99 (Great Nephew 126) (1982 70
5fg³ 5fg⁴ 7g) Apr 5; lengthy filly; third foal; half-sister to 1978 2-y-o 5f winner
Evasive (by Song); dam won over 1m and 1¼m, and is half-sister to Cesarewitch

winner Centurion; disappointed after finishing promising 4½ lengths third of 10 to Reign in maiden race at Salisbury in May; should stay at least 1¼m; sold BBA 1,700 gns Newmarket Autumn Sales. *I. Balding.*

EVERYMAN 3 ch.g. Porto Bello 118–Fiery Comet 82 (Star Moss 122) (1981 **55** 6g 5f 6f 5g³ 1982 6fg³ 6g³ 5f* 6fg* 5f² 6g) plater; attracted no bid after winning at Catterick (well backed) and Ayr in summer; stays 6f; acts on firm going; blinkered nowadays; sweated up at Catterick; has run respectably for an apprentice. *G. Richards.*

EVESTONE 3 ch.f. Ragstone 128–Crockeve 77 (Crocket 130) (1981 NR 1982 — 8f 8f) lengthy, short-legged filly; second foal; dam, placed over 5f and 6f, is closely related to Queen Mary winner Farfalla; beaten some way in maiden race at Sandown and minor event at Newmarket (went very freely to post) in July; sold 400 gns Doncaster September Sales. *J. Winter.*

EVZON 4 ch.c. English Prince 129–Spanish Empress 64 (Don II 123) (1981 10s **102** 12g* 12fg 1982 10s 12.3fg⁴ 14f* 16fg* 16.1f) leggy, useful-looking colt; improved considerably and put up an excellent performance to beat Santella Man by 1½ lengths in Queen's Vase at Royal Ascot in June, leading a furlong out and staying on resolutely under strong driving; had beaten Whitworth gamely by 2 lengths in small handicap at Haydock earlier in month after making all; suited by a test of stamina; acts well on firm going (has also run respectably on soft); genuine; reportedly finished lame final start (July). *C. Brittain.*

EWEN'S ROCK 8 b.g. Stephen George 102–Bravadora (Cash and Courage 116) — (1981 NR 1982 10fg) plater; stays 7f; suited by heavy ground; has worn blinkers; often bandaged. *M. Bradley.*

EXCAVATOR BOY 2 b.g. Roman Warrior 132–Forgets Image 87 (Florescence **70** 120) (1982 7d 6g 6d 5fg 6fg 7fg) Apr 16; 8,000Y; workmanlike gelding; second foal; half-brother to 3-y-o 9f winner Excavator Lady (by Most Secret); dam, half-sister to smart Millingdale Lillie, won 3 times over 1m; plating-class maiden; stays 6f; acts on firm surface. *Mrs. M. Nesbitt.*

EXCAVATOR EXPERT 2 gr.g. Celtic Cone 116–Dardanella Lady 66 (Samo- **59** thraki 108) (1982 6g 7.2s 8s³ 8d) Jan 18; 2,400F, plain, well-grown gelding; first foal; dam won 5f seller at 2 yrs, two races in Jersey and 7 hurdle races, most of them sellers; moderate plater; will be suited by 1¼m+; acts on soft going. *Mrs M. Nesbitt.*

EXCAVATOR LADY 3 b.f. Most Secret 119–Forgets Image 87 (Florescence 120) **53** (1981 5fg 5f³ 5g⁴ 5f 5d 6d 6s 1982 6g 7f 7f² 7f² 8f 8.2g³ 11g² 11g 9.4f* 11fg⁴ 13.8f 8d 8f³ 8.2g 8.2s²) compact filly; plater; sometimes runs creditably in better company, and won maiden race at Carlisle in July; stays 11f; acts on any going; blinkered last 2 starts, running well on second occasion. *Mrs M. Nesbitt.*

EXCITEMENT 3 ro.c. Sagaro 133–Belinda Mede 86 (Runnymede 123) (1981 — 5g 5s³ 6d² 7fg 5d 1982 8f 7f 10f 10fg 8s 8fg 8fg) small colt; poor walker; plating-class maiden; appears not to stay 1¼m; acts on soft going; blinkered and wore a hood final outing; has been bandaged. *R. Laing.*

Queen's Vase, Ascot—an excellent performance by Evzon who stays on resolutely under strong driving to beat Santella Man (right) and Karadar (left)

*Prix Maurice de Gheest, Deauville—Exclusive Order wins
from British-trained Indian King*

EXCLUSIVE ORDER (USA) 3 ch.f. Exclusive Native–Bonavista (Dead Ahead) **120**
(1981 6f* 7f* 7s⁴ 1982 8d² 8fg 7g* 6.5fg* 8g⁴ 6g² 5s) most attractive, strong,
good-bodied filly; sister to Teddy's Courage, a smart winner at up to 9f in USA,
closely related to 2 stakes-placed winners by Raise A Native, and half-sister to
3 minor winners; dam won 3 times at up to 4f, and is half-sister to 2 minor stakes
winners; wore down Beldale Lustre in determined style when ¾-length winner of
Prix de la Porte Maillot at Longchamp in June and led in last 100 yds to account
for Indian King by a length in Prix Maurice de Gheest at Deauville in August;
also ran well when in frame in Prix de la Grotte at Longchamp (2½ lengths second
to River Lady), Prix Jacques le Marois at Deauville (3¾ lengths fourth to The
Wonder) and Prix de Seine-et-Oise at Maisons-Laffitte (moved up a place after
coming home 3½ lengths third to Sayyaf); below her best when eighth of 15 to
On The House in 1,000 Guineas at Newmarket on second outing; needs further
than 5f and stays 1m; seems to act on any going but goes well on fast ground;
genuine. *J. Cunnington, jnr, France.*

EXHILARATE 3 b.c. Wolverlife 111–Rachel Ruysch 81 (Skymaster 126) **94** d
(1981 5d³ 6fg 6fg² 6f² 6d* 6g 5s² 1982 6d 6g³ 7s² 8f 7g 6fg 6g³) IR 2,400F,
IR 2,000Y; workmanlike ex-Irish colt; half-brother to 2 winners in Ireland,
including 5f winner Ruysch (by Polyfoto), also successful in USA; dam showed
ability at 2 yrs; placed in Coolmore Godswalk Race at Fairyhouse (2 lengths third
to Hay Habit), Tetrarch Stakes at the Curragh (excellent length second of 7 to
Achieved) and minor event at Brighton; well beaten most other starts; suited by
7f; acts on any going but is ideally suited by some give in the ground; trained by
N. Meade first 3 outings; sold 8,200 gns Newmarket Autumn Sales. *I. Balding.*

EXPEDITIOUS 2 b.c. Tachypous 128–My Own II (El Relicario 124) (1982 **91**
6f⁴ 7g³ 7fg³ 7d) Mar 26; 14,500Y; big, rangy colt; half-brother to 3 winners,
including 3-y-o 1½m winner Honriette (by Henry the Seventh) and very smart
middle-distance performer Haul Knight (by Firestreak); dam won from 1m to
11f; ran well in big fields of maidens on first 3 starts, and was not disgraced
when seventh of 14 in valuable nursery at Newmarket in October; will be suited
by 1m+; sure to win a race. *R. Hannon.*

EXPLETIVE 2 ch.f. Shiny Tenth 120–Pemba (Sodium 130) (1982 5fg* 5fg* 6f² **77**
6g³ 6fg) Mar 16; 530Y, resold 450Y, 1,800 2-y-o; lengthy filly; second reported
live foal; sister to a poor animal; dam won over 11f in France; won seller (bought
in 3,300 gns) at Wolverhampton in July and weakly-contested nursery on same
course in August; will be suited by 7f; has raced only on sound surface; never
going well when blinkered on final appearance. *D. H. Jones.*

EXPRESS BOY 2 b.c. Averof 123–Tory Island (Majority Blue 126) (1982 5.1g **—**
6g) Apr 27; 1,900Y; poor mover; second foal (first to Northern Hemisphere
time); dam poor sister to useful miler Votecatcher; in rear in maiden auction race
at Yarmouth (bandaged near-hind) in June and minor event at Ayr in September;
sent to Malaysia. *W. Stubbs.*

EXPRESS EMPRESS 2 b.f. Young Emperor 133–Hot-As-Hell (Firestreak 125) **56**
(1982 5g³ 5fg² 5fg³ 5f⁴ 5fg 5.3f⁴) May 26; IR 1,350F, 2,000Y; lengthy filly;

half-sister to several winners here and abroad; dam, Irish 2-y-o 5f winner, is half-sister to smart Welsh Rake; in frame in a variety of races, including sellers; not seen out after early August; disappointing. *P. Haslam.*

EXPRESSIONIST (USA) 3 b.g. Exclusive Native–Lady's Prerogative **69** (Nashua) (1981 6s 1982 10fg³ 12fg³ 13g⁴ 11.5f* 10.1fg³ 11.5fg⁴ 10.6f) strong, rangy gelding; won amateur riders race at Yarmouth in July; suited by 1½m; acts on firm going; one paced and is suited by enterprising riding tactics; sold 3,600 gns Ascot December Sales. *P. Walwyn.*

EXPRESSLY YOURS 3 ch.f. Bay Express 132–Never Part (Never Say Die **71** 137) (1981 5g 5g 6fg⁴ 6g³ 6g 6fg 5f⁴ 5d 1982 6fg³ 6f 7d 6f* 6g* 7fg⁴ 6g) lengthy filly; poor mover; won handicaps at York and Ayr in July; stays 6f; acts well on firm ground. *P. Asquith.*

EXPRESS MISS 2 b.f. Bay Express 132–Miss Portal (St Paddy 133) (1982 — 5d 6g 6s) Apr 1; 1,600F, 4,400Y, resold 1,700Y; neat, strong filly; first foal; dam poor maiden; little form in maiden events; may do better in sellers. *G. Toft.*

EXTROVERT (FR) 10 b.g. Bon Mot III 132–Exhibition 109 (Nearula 132) — (1981 NR 1982 8g) of little account. *D. Jermy.*

EXTRUDE 2 b.c. Grey Mirage 128–Casadina (Right Tack 131) (1982 6f 6g 7d — 7fg 8d) May 12; compact colt; bad plater. *R. Cambidge.*

EYE DAZZLER (USA) 2 ch.f. Nijinsky 138–First Squaw (First Landing) **90** (1982 6f 7g 7s²) May 14; $175,000Y; strong, rangy filly; nice easy mover; second living foal; dam, daughter of CCA Oaks winner Cherokee Rose, won at up to 1m; put up easily best effort when 1½ lengths second of 11 to New Coins in £3,700 event at York in October; should stay at least 1¼m; likely to make quite a useful 3-y-o. *R. Hern.*

EYELIGHT 5 gr.g. Roan Rocket 128–Pie Eye 88 (Exbury 138) (1981 8fg 7.2s **58** 6fg 7.6fg 8fg⁴ 9fg³ 8g³ 8f² 8f 8g* 8d² 8fg⁴ 8.2s 7f 1982 8f* 8f 8f 8f⁴ 7f 8fg⁴ 7.6fg 8fg³ 8f³ 8f 7g² 8fg 10g 9g² 8.2s 8s) robust, short-legged gelding; usually goes well at Beverley and won handicap there in April, showing more resolution than usual; sometimes runs in sellers; stays 1¼m; seems to act on any going; effective with or without blinkers; suitable mount for an inexperienced rider. *R. Hollinshead.*

F

FABULOSA (USA) 2 ch.f. Mateor–Fabulous Native (Le Fabuleux 133) (1982 **77** 5f² 6g 8g 8g⁴) Apr 26; $25,000Y; workmanlike filly; first foal; dam lightly-raced half-sister to useful Irish 6f to 9f winner Muscovite; sire very useful winner from 5.5f to 9f in France and USA; quite a moderate maiden; will stay 1¼m. *N. Guest.*

FABULOUS DUNCE (USA) 4 b.c. Le Fabuleux 133–Dulia (Dunce) (1981 **50** 10d⁴ 10fg* 12f² 1982 10g² 10fg 10fg 12d 10f² 10fg 10v) rangy colt; second in handicaps at Folkestone in April (apprentice ridden) and July (amateur riders), best efforts; should stay 1½m; blinkered last 3 starts. *A. Pitt.*

FABULOUS PRINCE (USA) 5 b.g. Le Fabuleux 133–Call The Queen (Hail — to Reason) (1981 10s⁴ 11s³ 10.5g 11v* 10.5d 12g² 12d³ 12g 1982 8s) ex-French gelding; trained in 1981 (rated 109); tailed off throughout in minor event at Doncaster in November, only outing of 1982 (bandaged); stays 1½m; suited by plenty of give in the ground. *G. Balding.*

FACET 2 b.c. Star Appeal 133–Balista 86 (Baldric II 131) (1982 7f 6s⁴ 6d 6d) **68** Apr 23; useful sort; half-brother to 2 winners, including very speedy 1980 2-y-o Labista (by Crowned Prince); dam stayed 7f; quite moderate form in maiden and minor events; sold 1,400 gns Ascot November Sales for export to Italy. *B. Hobbs.*

FACING 3 b.f. Quiet Fling 124–Facade 99 (Double Jump 131) (1981 7g 8g **47** 1982 12d³ 8fg³ 10f 10f 8g⁴ 10.1fg 8fg 10d 10.8s⁴) leggy, lengthy, slightly hollow-backed filly; plating-class maiden; best at around 1m; blinkered sixth start. *D. Dale.*

FAHRENHEIT 3 ch.f. Mount Hagen 127–Fair Darling 93 (Darling Boy 124) **69** (1981 NR 1982 8g³ 7f³) 13,500F; rather leggy filly; half-sister to several winners, including fairly useful 1980 2-y-o 6f winner Paradise Bird (by Sallust); dam, best at up to 1m, is daughter of very good filly Fair Astronomer; third in maiden races at Yarmouth in July; will be suited by 1¼m; bandaged both outings. *W. O'Gorman.*

FAI LA BELLA (USA) 3 b.f. Fifth Marine–No Need Askin (Reflected Glory) —
(1981 7f 7d 7.6s 1982 8fg 10d) quite attractive filly; excellent mover; only
plating class; stays 1m. *L. Cumani.*

FAIRBEN 2 b.f. Royben 125–Fairabunda 59 (Floribunda 136) (1982 5fg) May
4; 440Y; strong, plain filly; half-sister to 2 winners, including prolific 1m to
1½m winner Fairman (by Manacle); dam stayed at least 7f; slow-starting when
last of 12 in maiden auction event at Epsom in April. *D. Jermy.*

FAIR CITY 5 b.g. Charlottown 127–Fair Amanda 105§ (Firestreak 125) (1981 —
13v 12g 18.4d 13fg 12g 12fg³ 12g 15g 12.2g 1982 12d 10g) leggy gelding; poor
performer; stays 13f; suited by some give in the ground; has run creditably for a
boy; blinkered last 2 starts in 1981. *T. Kersey.*

FAIRDALE 4 gr. or ro.g. Roan Rocket 128–Catalonia 97 (Abernant 142) (1981 **47**
5d 5fg 5.8g⁴ 5g 6f³ 5.8f⁴ 6fg 6fg³ 8h 8fg 1982 6fg 6g 5d 5s³ 6s) small, stocky
gelding; plating-class maiden; stays 6f; acts on any going. *G. Cottrell.*

FAIR DUEL 5 b.g. Status Seeker–Double Irish (Dual 117) (1981 10d 10s³ 10v —
8f 10f 1982 10fg) strong, well-made gelding; stays 1¼m; acts on any going:
sometimes wears blinkers. *P. Makin.*

FAIR FANTASIA 3 b.f. Tachypous 128–Whistling Waltz (Whistler 129) **70**
(1981 NR 1982 9g⁴ 10.4d* 10g³ 11s³ 12v³) third living foal; half-sister to 2
winners in Scandinavia; dam Irish 5f winner; stayed on well to win 14-runner
maiden race at Chester in August (behaved rather mulishly beforehand); third in
3 minor events afterwards; stays 1½m; yet to race on a firm surface; sold 4,200 gns
Newmarket December Sales. *R. Williams.*

FAIRFIELD LADY (USA) 3 b.f. North Sea–Kitten Too (Tamao) (1981 5g —
5v 5f 5g 5.3d 5s 1982 8g 6g) in rear in varied company, including selling; has
twice been blinkered. *G. Lewis.*

FAIRGREEN 4 b.g. Music Boy 124–Sunny Bloom 71 (Forlorn River 124) (1981 **66**
5s* 6fg 6g 5fg 5fg 8f 1982 6d 5fg⁴ 5d 5g 6s² 5s² 6s 5d* 5s) big, strong gelding;
bad walker and mover; ran creditably, including in a seller, before winning
handicap at Catterick in October; better at 5f than 6f; acts on a firm surface,
but is very well suited by soft going; missed break fourth start; sold out of
H. Westbrook's stable 500 gns Doncaster March Sales. *D. Chapman.*

FAIR GROVE 2 ch.f. Hot Grove 128–Panto 71 (Ben Novus 109) (1982 5fg) —
Apr 8; second foal; dam won in Norway; tailed-off last of 8 in seller at Lingfield
in May; sold 310 gns Ascot 2nd June Sales. *A. Davison.*

FAIRHAM 2 ch.f. Porto Bello 118–Impromptu 88 (My Swanee 122) (1982 5d **72**
5g⁴ 6h 5fg 6g³ 6g⁴ 7g 6fg² 6fg² 6g 5g 7g* 7.2s* 7s) Apr 10; 1,400F, 5,200Y;
lengthy filly; half-sister to a winning plater; dam won over 7f and 1¼m; stood
up well to a busy season, winning sellers in October at Wolverhampton (bought
in 1,450 gns) and Haydock (no bid); suited by 7f; has run creditably on a firm
surface but is better with some give in the ground; wears blinkers; slipped up
tenth start; trained by B. Hills first 6 outings; changed hands 1,400 gns Doncaster October Sales before final start. *E. Carter.*

FAIR HEROINE (USA) 2 b.f. Our Hero–Fair Diplomacy (Diplomat Way) **74**
(1982 5fg 5g* 5fg³ 5d⁴) Feb 27; $47,000Y; leggy filly; first foal; dam 2-y-o 6f
winner; odds on, led inside last to beat Navarino Bay a neck in 5-runner minor
event at Ayr in May; in frame afterwards in similar race at York in June and
nursery at Chester in August; will stay 6f; lacks scope. *J. Hindley.*

FAIR LAVINIA 3 ch.f. Oats 126–For Keeps 57 (Track Spare 125) (1981 7f 6g —
1982 10f 9f 6g) 2,900Y; leggy ex-Irish filly; second foal; dam, placed over 1m
and 1¼m, is sister to very smart Record Run; soundly beaten in maiden races
and a minor event; ran very freely first start; brought down final outing; sold
2,400 gns Newmarket Autumn Sales. *J. Bethell.*

FAIRLAWNE 2 b.f. Northfields–Isobelline (Pronto) (1982 6g 5.8g² 5f* 5fg³ 6g) **99**
May 13; quite attractive filly; carries quite a lot of condition; fourth foal;
closely related to 3-y-o Gleeman (by The Minstrel) and half-sister to high-class
1980 staying 2-y-o Robellino (by Roberto); dam Irish 7f winner; routed her 10
opponents in maiden race at Haydock in September, drawing away to beat
Private Label 5 lengths; ran very well later in month when close-up third of
10 to Aldern Stream in £3,400 event at Goodwood and about 8 lengths seventh
of 9 to Ma Biche in William Hill Cheveley Park Stakes at Newmarket; will stay
7f; acts on firm going. *F. J. Houghton.*

FAIR MADAME 2 b.f. Monseigneur 127–Fair Mark 95 (On Your Mark 125) **88**
(1982 5f 5f 5g⁴ 5f* 5g² 5g⁴ 5f² 5f³ 6fg² 6g 6s³ 6d* 6g) Apr 17; 6,800Y; rather

leggy filly; first foal; dam 2-y-o 6f winner; successful in maiden race at Edinburgh in July and 12-runner minor event at Catterick in October; ran well in several nurseries in between; stays 6f; acts on any going; consistent; wears blinkers and on sixth start also wore a hood. *C. Booth.*

FAIR MOUNT LAD 3 ch.c. Mount Hagen 127–Jabula 99 (Sheshoon 132) **78**
(1981 5fg 5d* 6fg 6fg 6fg 7s² 8fg 7s   1982 8d 10d² 10f² 10g⁴ 12d 11.7fg² 12g³ 12fg²
12s³ 12s)   close-coupled colt; suited by 1½m; acts on any going; blinkered once
at 2 yrs; sent to Malaysia. *R. Price.*

FAIR PATRICK 3 b. or br.c. St Paddy 133–Fire Fairy 70 (Firestreak 125)   —
(1981 NR   1982 12fg 10f 16g 14f 10s⁴)   neat colt; second foal; half-brother to a
winning plater by Barbary Pirate; dam won over 1m and 1¼m; little worthwhile
form, including in a seller; has sweated up; has given trouble at start (broke loose
and was withdrawn before intended final outing). *D. C. Tucker.*

FAIR SUNSET 2 ch.f. Porto Bello 118–Town Girl 99 (Town Crier 119)   (1982   —
6s)   May 20; poor mover; second foal; dam won twice over 6f; unquoted, slow-
starting last of 16 in maiden race at Leicester in November. *D. C. Tucker.*

FAIRWEATHER FRIEND (USA) 3 ch.f. Forli–Weatherwise (Arts and **69**
Letters)   (1981 NR   1982 11f 12f 12fg³ 15.8d² 16s)   tall, lengthy filly; poor
mover; first foal; dam, winner 4 times at up to 1m, is sister to high-class American
gelding Winter's Tale; staying maiden. *I. Balding.*

FAIRY TERN 3 b.f. Mill Reef 141–Elegant Tern 102 (Sea-Bird II 145)   (1981 **109**
5g* 6fg 5d³ 5fg* 5g³   1982 7d⁴ 7fg² 7f⁴ 7f³ 7g² 7fg* 8g² 8v³)   quite attractive,
rather lightly-made filly; third foal; sister to a moderate filly; dam won 3 times
at around 1m and stayed 1½m; stayed on strongly to beat Love Tangle by 1¼

Mr Paul Mellon's "Fairy Tern"

lengths in 5-runner £4,400 event at Goodwood in September; in frame all other starts, including Strensall Stakes at York (second to Triple Tipple) and Grosser Kaufhof Preis at Cologne (third to Mister Rock's); bred to stay at least 1¼m; acts on any going; consistent; very useful. *I. Balding.*

FAIT ACCOMPLI 3 ch.g. Sagaro 133–Fell Swoop 66 (Falcon 131) (1981 NR 1982 10s) first foal; dam fairly useful hurdler; backward when well-beaten eighth of 18 to Whenyourtrainsgone in minor event at Leicester in November. *R. Hollinshead.* —

FAITES VITE 2 b.c. So Blessed 130–Terre Promise (Soderini 123) (1982 5fg³ 5fg² 6fg⁴ 6d³ 6f²) Apr 16; leggy, narrow, short-backed colt; good walker; half-brother to winners here and abroad, including 1980 2-y-o 6f winner Miss St Mawes (by Derring-Do); dam ran once; placed in maiden races, going down by ¾ length to Bold Bob at Doncaster in May on second outing and failing by a short head to hold off Gaygig at Pontefract (odds on) in July on final appearance; will stay 7f; seems to act on any going; consistent. *B. Hobbs.* 80

FAITHFUL DON (USA) 3 br.c. Dawn Flight–Always Faithful 103 (Super Sam 124) (1981 7fg 7d 7fg 7g 7d 1982 10.1fg 10f³ 10g 10g 10.1g 9fg 10v² 10.2s³) useful-looking colt; plater; will be suited by 1½m; acts on any going, but goes well in the mud. *G. Balding.* 57

FAITHFUL LOVER 2 b.c. Wolver Hollow 126–Semper Fi (Above Suspicion 127) (1982 5d 5g 6s³) May 12; IR 6,800F; fair sort; half-brother to 2 minor winners; dam Irish 2-y-o 7f winner; hard driven at halfway and gave impression of needing further when 7½ lengths third of 18 to Hopeful Waters in claiming race at Nottingham in October; has ability to win a seller. *G. Lewis.* 69

FALABELLA 3 ch.f. Steel Heart 128–Farfalla 115 (Crocket 130) (1981 NR 1982 5g 6s) workmanlike, smallish filly; first live foal; dam, speedy 2-y-o, is half-sister to top-class sprinter Matatina and high-class miler Showdown; beaten a long way in maiden race and apprentice event at Nottingham. *R. Price.* —

FALAKA 3 ch.f. Sparkler 130–Falassa (Relko 136) (1981 5g² 5fg² 6fg⁴ 5g³ 6d² 5d² 1982 8f* 7f* 8fg³ 7f 9.4fg² 10f 10f 11.7g⁴ 11f) small, quite attractive filly; won maiden race at Beverley in April and handicap at Thirsk in May; promises to stay 1¼m; seems to act on any going. *D. Morley.* 83

FALA KALIMA 2 b.f. Sousa 97–Ukundu 60 (Tudor Treasure 119) (1982 5f 5f 5f) Apr 3; fair sort; third foal; dam placed over 5f at 2 yrs and ran over hurdles after having first foal; poor plater; not raced after May. *J. Fitzgerald.* 44

FA LAMPI 2 b.f. Reform 132–Senta 103 (Chanteur II 135) (1982 8f 8s) May 1; lengthy, good-bodied filly; poor walker; sister to 1971 Gimcrack Stakes winner Wishing Star, and half-sister to winners here and abroad; dam won at up to 2m; no worthwhile form in maiden events at Leicester (seventh of 23) in September and Wolverhampton (eleventh of 18) in October. *R. Boss.* —

FALASION DREAM 2 br.f. Dragonara Palace 115–Double Reception (Siliconn 121) (1982 6f 5g⁴ 6fg² 6f 6s) Mar 10; 960F; small filly; first living foal; dam never ran; plater; in frame twice at Windsor in August, gambled on on first occasion; stays 6f; badly hampered fourth start. *Mrs J. Reavey.* 53

FALCON'S HEIR (USA) 3 b.c. Accipiter–Famous Princess (Diplomat Way) (1981 6d 6g⁴ 5fg⁴ 1982 7g 8.2s 7f³ 8f* 7fg² 7f* 8f 7fg 8.2s* 8s³ 8s) lengthy, quite attractive colt; won maiden race at Beverley in May, minor event at Edinburgh in June (made all) and handicap at Haydock in October; stays 1m well; acts on any going; has won twice for apprentice T. Quinn. *P. Cole.* 80

FALCON'S REVENGE 5 b. or br.g. Sweet Revenge 129–Grey Falcon (Falcon 131) (1981 NR 1982 14d) plain gelding; plater as a 3-y-o; stays 1m well; acts on any going; blinkered final start in 1980. *J. Jenkins.* —

FALCON'S TARTAR 5 b.g. Mr Mainwaring–Tartar Ash 89 (Celtic Ash) (1981 NR 1982 10fg 12fg) poor performer; blinkered in 1982. *J. Scallan.* —

FALGORA 2 gr.g. Algora 110–Court Flower (David Jack 125) (1982 6g 6fg³ 6s 8s) June 5; second foal; dam of little account; moderate plater; gelded after final outing. *B. Palling.* 53

FALKLAND SOUND (USA) 2 b.c. Plotting–Alamosa Kitty (Cougar) (1982 6fg 8d) Apr 5; $23,000 2-y-o; sparely-made colt; first foal; dam won 1m claiming race; sire, son of Bagdad, won 3 small races at up to 1m at 3 yrs; 50/1 when behind in big fields for minor event at Doncaster in September and maiden race at Newmarket (speed to past halfway) in October. *P. Haslam.* —

*Ladbrokes (Ayr) Gold Cup Handicap—a stirring finish with Famous Star (No. 18)
just holding on from Polly's Brother and Camisite (No. 4);
the blinkered horse is Murillo who finished sixth*

FALLEN ANGEL 3 b.f. Quiet Fling 124–Alangia 101 (Shantung 132) (1981 7fg **88**
6fg 7fg 8fg² 8d 1982 12g* 10f 12fg² 16.1h* 17fg* 19f⁴ 16fg* 16fg³ 18d⁴) quite
attractive, lengthy filly; has a round action; won maiden race at Folkestone and
handicaps at Haydock, Wolverhampton and Sandown; ran well most other starts,
on final one coming home 6½ lengths fourth to Mountain Lodge in Tote Cesarewitch at Newmarket; stays very well; has run creditably on soft ground but goes
very well on firm; genuine and consistent. *H. Candy.*

FALLIG SCHNELL 6 ch.g. King's Leap 111–Sea Melody 79 (Tudor Minstrel 144) **—**
(1981 10.6s 8g 7fg 1982 8.2s) workmanlike gelding; poor plater; has worn
bandages; sold 500 gns Doncaster October Sales. *S. Wiles.*

FAMOUS STAR 3 ch.c. Sharpen Up 127–Hecla 117 (Henry the Seventh 125) **97**
(1981 5f 6s² 1982 5f* 6d* 6fg³ 5.6g² 6g* 5v) strong, close-coupled colt; won
maiden race at Nottingham and handicaps at Yarmouth and Ayr; apprentice
ridden at 3-lb overweight when all out to beat Polly's Brother by a head in 14-
runner Ladbrokes (Ayr) Gold Cup in September; ran well on his other starts,
including when just over a length third of 14 to Vorvados in Portland Handicap at
Doncaster (afterwards moved up to second); stays 6f; acts on any going; sweated
up badly and was coltish in paddock at Nottingham. *M. Albina.*

FANDANCE 3 ch.f. Gay Fandango 132–Clariden 82 (Hook Money 124) (1981 **57**
5d³ 6f 5fg³ 5g 6d 6s 1982 6g 6f 8g² 8d) sturdy filly; only plating class;
evidently suited by 1m; has run respectably for an apprentice. *W. Wharton.*

FANDANGLE 4 ch.c. Gay Fandango 132–Sandra II (Le Haar 126) (1981 7fg **85**
6g* 6g 6fg 7fg³ 7fg³ 7.3d² 8s⁴ 1982 8d² 8f 8fg* 8f* 8fg 8f² 8g² 8.2f* 8d 8s⁴)
well-made, quite attractive colt; has been hobdayed; successful in handicaps at
Goodwood in May (quickened up well and won in good style), Newbury in June
(apprentice event) and Haydock in September; beat Seven Hearts by ½ length in
£6,000 event on last-named course; ran well most other starts, although disappointed second and ninth outings, hanging badly on former occasion; stays 1m;
probably acts on any going. *J. Tree.*

FANDANGO TIME 4 ch.c. Gay Fandango 132–Sapho 59 (Raeburn II) (1981 **97**
8d² 10d* 10.5f² 8g² 8g* 8fg* 8d 1982 8f 8g⁴ 8d³ 10.2g² 8g 9d 12s) lengthy, rather
lightly-made colt; not seen out until quite late, but ran respectably when in frame
in quite valuable handicaps at Newbury, Ripon and Doncaster and when seventh
of 29 behind Century City in William Hill Cambridgeshire at Newmarket; stays
1¼m; seems to act on any going; blinkered on reappearance; hasn't always looked
the easiest of rides. *B. Hills.*

FANFARE MAID 3 b.f. Swing Easy 126–Just Jenny 88 (Ennis 128) (1981 5g **—**
6g 1982 6f 5f 6h) workmanlike filly; little worthwhile form in varied company;
dead. *R. Hollinshead.*

FAN-LOI-SING 3 ch.c. Dragonara Palace 115–Trespassing (Poaching 115) (1981 NR 1982 8g 6f 6fg 8.2g 8fg) 3,600Y; poor walker; half-brother to a winning jumper; dam won over hurdles and fences; behind in varied company; blinkered final start. *W. Clay.* —

FANNY'S COVE 3 b.f. Mill Reef 141–Honeypot Lane 91 (Silly Season 127) (1981 NR 1982 10d*) leggy, lightly-built filly; first foal; dam middle-distance winner; 12/1 when coming with a steady run to beat odds-on Bundu by a length (pair clear) in 24-runner maiden race at Ripon in August; not seen out again; will stay 1½m+. *W. Hastings-Bass.* **89 ?**

FAN THE FLAME 2 b.f. Grundy 137–Cendres Bleues (Charlottesville 135) (1982 8s) Apr 16; tall, lengthy filly; half-sister to several winners, including very smart 1m to 1½m filly Calderina (by Lyphard) and very useful middle-distance filly Cattarina Ginnasi (by Tierceron); dam very useful Italian middle-distance filly; 12/1, showed distinct promise when 11 lengths sixth of 26 to Magic Rarity in maiden race at Sandown in October, making very significant progress in closing stages; will be well suited by 1¼m+; bound to do a good bit better. *I. Balding.* **69 p**

FARASI 3 b.g. Shiny Tenth 120–Cecilia Gallerani (Pinturischio 116) (1981 7g 7.6s⁴ 7g³ 1982 8f 8f 8.2fg 8s² 10d³ 8g³) strong, compact gelding; quite a modest maiden; stays 1¼m; needs some give in the ground. *G. Huffer.* **72**

FARIDELLA 4 gr.f. Silly Season 127–Fair Fabiola 94 (Acropolis 132) (1981 12d 12.2g 16f 12.2g² 12.2fg* 12f³ 11g² 10s* 12d³ 10.2g³ 1982 11.7fg 10.6h³ 11g 11fg⁴ 12g 10fg³ 10d 10fg³ 12d³) leggy, rather unfurnished filly; third at Haydock (valuable seller), Folkestone (twice) and Leicester (claiming race); stays 1½m; acts on any going; wears blinkers; ungenuine and by no means the easiest of rides; sold, probably for export to Italy, 310 gns Ascot November Sales. *I. Walker.* **51 §**

FARIOFFA 3 gr.c. Hotfoot 126–Lapis Lazuli 84 (Zeddaan 130) (1981 8g* 1982 7fg 10g⁴ 8f* 10fg 8g 10g* 10s*) 7,000Y; big, rangy colt; half-brother to a winner in Malaya; dam won over 5f at 2 yrs and is half-sister to smart Bas Bleu; a smart colt who beat Bali Dancer a neck in £7,700 handicap at Newmarket in **112**

Mr P. De Bour's "Farioffa"

July, Nikiforos a length in £4,800 handicap at Newmarket again in September and Phebis by ½ length in Group 3 Premio Carlo Porta at Milan in October, on each occasion finishing strongly; suited by 1¼m and may get further; acts on any going; often sweats up; suited by strong handling and goes well for B. Raymond. *L. Cumani.*

FARM LANE 3 b.f. Moulton 128–Country Path 101 (Mossborough 126) (1981 6g 1982 7g 10f 12.3fg 9f 10.2f³ 12fg³ 12g 9g 11.5g 9s 12g) quite attractive filly; stays 1½m; has run respectably for an apprentice; has twice worn blinkers, pulling hard on first occasion; sold 4,000 gns Newmarket December Sales. *H. Wragg.* **63**

FAROLITO (USA) 3 b.c. Foolish Pleasure–Dotty Jay Jay (Lurullah) (1981 6g⁴ 6fg⁴ 1982 10f 11f 12fg) big, strong, lengthy colt; good walker; ran respectably in quite valuable events at Doncaster and Ascot in 1981; blinkered when soundly beaten in maiden races at 3 yrs; should stay middle distances; sweated up second start; sold to R. Hollinshead 5,600 gns Newmarket Autumn Sales. *R. Hern.* **—**

FAR SAHARA (USA) 3 b.c. Far North 120–Rare Relish (Johns Joy) (1981 5fg 7fg 7f 8g 1982 10d³ 8d² 10f 10f⁴) small, rather leggy colt; best run at 1m on soft ground; blinkered last 3 starts; sent to Malaysia. *R. Smyth.* **65**

FARSEEING 3 b.f. High Top 131–Montania 68 (Mourne 126) (1981 7g 1982 9.4f) lengthy filly; well beaten in maiden races at Newmarket and Carlisle. *W. Hastings-Bass.* **—**

FARSOUND 4 b.f. Wolver Hollow 126–Farfisa 86 (Sassafras 135) (1981 11.5f 13f³ 13g⁴ 16g* 16s* 16s² 1982 16g 16d 16.1g² 14fg⁴ 18.8fg 19s 16.1s) leggy, lightly-made filly; staying handicapper; seems to act on any going. *I. Walker.* **63**

FAR TOO MUCH 3 b.g. Windjammer (USA)–Sweet Princess (Prince Regent 129) (1981 8g 1982 12fg* 12f 13.1g 13.3f³ 13.1g 13g) big, rangy gelding; kept on strongly to win maiden race at Salisbury in May; made much of running when creditable 4½ lengths third of 9 to Abdoun in Morland Brewery Trophy (Handicap) at Newbury in July (flashed tail under whip); well beaten afterwards; will stay 1¾m; yet to race on a soft surface. *M. Smyly.* **74**

FASCADALE 8 br.g. Frankincense 120–Straight Off 88 (Straight Deal) (1981 10v³ 12fg 12s² 12g 12f* 11fg² 12f³ 12d³ 11g* 11d³ 12g 1982 12fg 12fg 12g 12fg⁴ 12g 11d³ 11s* 10d) fair handicapper; led close home to beat Deal On by a neck at Redcar in October (pair 5 lengths clear); stays 1½m; acts on any going; suitable mount for a boy; sometimes sweats up; needs to be held up and is suited by a strong gallop. *J. W. Watts.* **78**

FASHION LOVER 2 ch.f. Shiny Tenth 120–Glencora (Ribero 126) (1982 6g 7g 8d³ 8.2d 7g² 8s 8d²) Mar 28; smallish filly; third foal; dam unraced twin; placed in sellers, best race when going down by 1¼ lengths to Datatext in 27-runner nursery at Doncaster in October on final outing; suited by 1m; yet to race on a firm surface. *M. Ryan.* **70**

FAST AND HIGH 2 gr.f. Roan Rocket 128–Moeru Bara 107 (Firestreak 125) (1982 5d 5f 5f⁴) Apr 6; 3,000Y; half-sister to several winners, including very useful middle-distance stayer Fire Red (by Salvo); poor plater; not raced after May. *C. Booth.* **46**

FAST AND LOOSE 2 ch.f. Relkino 131–Scarlet Woman (Red God 128§) (1982 7f) Apr 29; small, close-coupled filly; second foal; dam poor maiden; last of 14 in valuable seller at Newmarket in July; sold 280 gns Ascot August Sales. *J. Hindley.* **—**

FAST AND SURE (USA) 3 gr.g. Tudor Grey 119–Miss Adorable (Ramsinga 115) (1981 7g 1982 8fg 8g 7f⁴ 8g² 8.2g⁴) tall, lengthy gelding; plating-class maiden; stays 1m; blinkered last 2 starts. *G. Pritchard-Gordon.* **58**

FAST DANCER 2 ch.f. Hotfoot 126–Mixed Melody 82 (Alcide 136) (1982 5f 5f 5g 8f 8.2s 7g 7d) Apr 25; neat filly; first foal; dam, sister to smart stayer Flagon, won over 13f and won Victor Ludorum Hurdle; apprentice ridden, 3¾ lengths fifth of 20 to Figure de Danse in maiden auction event at Redcar in September, fourth outing and only indication of merit; will stay 1½m; acts on firm going. *G. Richards.* **60**

FAST LAD 3 b.c. No Loiterer 90–Young Rowette 99 (Delirium 126) (1981 5g³ 5fg² 6f 6g³ 6d 5s* 6d 1982 5s² 5s² 5f 6g 5fg 5f³) small, sturdy colt; sprint handicapper; best form at 5f; acts on any going but is suited by some give in the ground; has run respectably in blinkers; trained part of season by A. Jarvis. *H. Collingridge.* **79**

FASTNET ISLAND 5 b.g. Young Emperor 133–Long Shadow 77 (Royal Palm —
131) (1981 10s 15.5d 14s³ 14d 12.3g 12f 1982 12fg) lengthy gelding; staying
handicapper; acts on soft going; usually blinkered nowadays. *P. Kelleway.*

FAST PEACH 2 b.f. Firestreak 125–Peregrine Peach 79 (Falcon 131) (1982 **63**
5fg 5g 5f² 5fg 6fg* 7g 6f* 7f³) Apr 30; 700Y; workmanlike filly; half-sister to 3
winners abroad; dam stayed 7f; plater; successful in 8-runner event at Nottingham (bought in 1,500 gns) in June and 11-runner race at Doncaster (no bid) in
July; stays 7f; possibly best on a firm surface; exported to Algeria. *G. Blum.*

FAST SERVICE 3 ch.g. Sharpen Up 127–Ginnies Pet 106 (Compensation 127) **61**
(1981 5.8f 5fg³ 5fg 5g 1982 5d 5fg³ 5fg³ 5f 5f 5g 5fg) small, strong, close-
coupled gelding; sprint handicapper; will be suited by 6f; blinkered twice at
2 yrs. *J. Holt.*

FAST TORPIDO (USA) 2 ch.c. Wajima–Morelle (Vitelio) (1982 6g 7fg 7fg² **81**
7d) Apr 6; tall, quite attractive colt; dam best sprinting mare of 1971 generation in Argentina; best effort when length second of 16 to Behind The Lines in
maiden event at Salisbury in September, making running and sticking on well;
gives impression he'll stay 1m; possibly unsuited by soft surface. *M. Albina.*

FAST YIELD 2 b.f. Streak 119–Crop (Acropolis 132) (1982 5fg 5h⁴ 6fg 5f³ 5g 5s) **43**
Mar 9; 1,500Y; half-sister to 2 winners, including fair sprinter Spanish Issue (by
Philip of Spain); poor plater. *D. Elsworth.*

FATENAH 2 b.f. Emboss 112–Tumble Judy (Tumble Wind) (1982 6g 7g) —
May 3; compact filly; first foal; dam never ran; 50/1, in rear in maiden races at
Yarmouth in June and September. *A. Hide.*

FATHER GUEST 2 b. or br.c. Be My Guest 126–Side Step (Double Jump 131) **68**
(1982 7f 7f 7d 8s) Apr 1; tall, close-coupled colt; fourth foal; half-brother to
3-y-o Saysaban (by Sassafras); dam placed at up to 1½m in Ireland; plating-
class maiden; showed form only on third outing. *R. Sheather.*

FATHER ROONEY (USA) 3 b.c. Val de l'Orne 130–Royal Honoree (Round **124 §**
Table) (1981 7g² 7g 1982 10f* 12.3g² 12f 10g 10.5fg² 14f² 12fg² 12d 14s²)
Had Father Rooney won only half as often as he'd threatened to win, a
paragraph would have been wholly inadequate space in which to deal with his
career. However, the fact is he's won only one race in his life, a minor affair at
Bath in April by a length and a half from Brevet; more often than not he's finished
second. Father Rooney possesses a good deal of ability. Much of his time has
been spent tackling good-class opposition, and two of his seconds were gained in
pattern races—behind Super Sunrise in the Chester Vase in May and behind
Touching Wood in the Jefferson Smurfit Memorial Irish St Leger at the Curragh
in October. His biggest failing is that he lacks resolution. All too often he has
found little or nothing in a finish after moving very smoothly into a challenging
or winning position, nowhere more manifestly than at Goodwood in August
where he went under by a short head to the hard-driven Santella Man in the
March Stakes: he had the race won, then threw it away. At the Curragh Father
Rooney began his run half a mile out and made such good progress through the
field that he had gone second to Touching Wood at the distance, passing Swiftfoot
on the inside in the style of a very good horse. For a while as he sat on the
leader's tail he made Touching Wood appear ordinary too, but in the end
Touching Wood ran on the stronger and won by two lengths, Father Rooney never
quite getting to grips when switched outside again. Cauthen never went for the
whip. As Father Rooney finished eight lengths clear of Swiftfoot in the Irish
St Leger and two lengths clear of third-placed Zilos in the March Stakes, both
races run at a strong pace, there's no doubt that he stays the trip. His performance in Ireland was unquestionably his best so far, though he has gone nearer to
winning on four occasions—at Chester and Goodwood, in the High Line Stakes at
York in August (Yard Bird beat him three parts of a length) and in the Troy
Stakes at Doncaster in September (Sabre Dance beat him a length).

		{ Val de Loir	{ Vieux Manoir
	{ Val de l'Orne	(b 1959)	{ Vali
	(b 1972)	{ Aglae	{ Armistice
Father Rooney	{	(b 1965)	{ Aglae Grace
(USA)		{ Round Table	{ Princequillo
(b.c. 1979)	{ Royal Honoree	(b 1954)	{ Knight's Daughter
	(b or br 1973)	{ Matriarch	{ Bold Ruler
		(b 1964)	{ Lyceum

For all that Father Rooney was bred in the United States he has a familiar
enough pedigree to European eyes. His sire beat Patch in the French Derby while

his grandam Matriarch is the dam of the leading French two-year-old of 1972 Targowice. Father Rooney's dam, whose first foal he is, is Targowice's full sister and also full sister to a very useful racemare in the States called Rondeau. She herself won three times at distances up to six furlongs. Royal Honoree has since produced the very promising French two-year-old Allverton (by Alleged) and a filly by Sir Ivor. In November she realized the world-record price for a broodmare of 3.8 million dollars, when sent up to Keeneland in foal to Northern Dancer. Father Rooney fetched 70,000 dollars as a yearling. An attractive, tall, rangy colt, he acts on any going. He needs to be held up and is the type on whom Cauthen usually excels. He has been sent to the USA. *B. Hills.*

FATIH (USA) 2 b.c. Icecapade–Native Nurse (Graustark) (1982 6fg² 5s⁴)   **85**
Mar 22; $650,000Y; strong, close-coupled, quite attractive colt; good mover; half-brother to high-class American middle-distance filly Love Sign (by Spanish Riddle); dam placed at 2 yrs and 3 yrs; 7/1, ran on well after being scrubbed along at halfway when ½-length second of 13 to Castanet in newcomers event at Goodwood in September; favourite, chased along all way when never-dangerous 4½ lengths fourth of 7 to Prince Spy in £4,500 race at Ascot later in month; much better suited by 6f than 5f, and will be suited by 7f+; capable of winning maiden event. *H. T. Jones.*

FATOUM 2 ch.f. Sassafras 135–Swift Protectress (Court Martial) (1982 6fg)   **— p**
Apr 13; IR 23,000Y; rather unfurnished filly; half-sister to 3 winners, including very useful middle-distance colt Fast Frigate (by Sea Hawk II); dam won 3 small races at around 1m in France; 20/1, apprentice ridden and very green, didn't realise what was required until closing stages when remote seventh of 13 to Debutina Park in maiden race at Nottingham in August; will do better over longer distances. *F. Durr.*

FAVOLOSO 3 b.c. Sun Prince 128–Lovely Clare 106 (Sing Sing 134) (1981 6fg   **104**
7fg 8s² 8d 1982 12fg* 10fg 12fg 12f 12g4) rangy, quite attractive colt; led near finish to beat Prince Santiago by ¾ length (pair well clear) in 16-runner maiden race at Newmarket in April; faced stiffer tasks afterwards but wasn't disgraced, putting up a good display when fourth of 10 to runaway winner Assert in Irish Sweeps Derby at the Curragh in June; not seen out again; will stay 1¾m; seems to act on any going. *R. Boss.*

FAVORIDGE (USA) 2 b.f. Riva Ridge–Favoletta 115 (Baldric II 131) (1982   **122**
5g* 5f² 5g* 6g²)
    Harry Wragg trained some excellent two-year-old fillies in his thirty-six years as a trainer, the Queen Mary Stakes winners Cynara, Sovereign and Amaranda among them, but surprisingly he never won the William Hill Cheveley Park Stakes. Favoridge, who appeared to have a good chance in the race, was beaten into second place in 1982, just after her stable-companion On The House had filled the same position. Favoridge started favourite for the Cheveley Park largely on the strength of a tremendously impressive performance in the St Hugh's Stakes at Newbury in August. Her opponents there included the Cherry Hinton winner Crime of Passion, an excellent third to Ma Biche in the Prix Robert Papin on her last appearance, and Misty For Me, the winner of three of her last four races including a nursery under 10-0 at Goodwood, but Favoridge made them look third-rate. She soon held a good position as the favourite Crime of Passion disputed the lead with Sparkling Suzie and was clearly cruising two furlongs out. Cauthen, riding Favoridge for the first time, waited another furlong before asking her for her effort and his confidence wasn't misplaced; she quickened in the style of a top-class filly, putting six lengths between herself and Crime of Passion by the line. The Cheveley Park, run at Newmarket late in September, was Favoridge's first race over six furlongs and Eddery was keen to conserve her stamina by making her settle, succeeding to the extent that he had Favoridge in last place at halfway though not very far behind. Unfortunately for Favoridge the French challenger Ma Biche was already in full flight ahead of her by the time Eddery asked her to challenge running into the Dip and she had to use her splendid acceleration to reach a challenging position. After looking likely to swamp Ma Biche Favoridge faltered in the closing stages and went down by three quarters of a length. A fine effort nonetheless.
    Favoridge had stamped herself a potentially high-class filly as soon as she set foot on a racecourse. She won the Kingston Maiden Stakes at Sandown early in July most impressively, leading throughout and then sprinting right away in the final one and a half furlongs to win very easily by six lengths. So impressive was she that she started at 7/4 on against better animals in the Star Stakes

*St Hugh's Stakes, Newbury—Favoridge quickens away
from Crime of Passion in brilliant style*

on the same course nearly three weeks later. She looked sure to keep her unbeaten record as she came through on the bridle to tackle the top-weighted Time's Time approaching the final furlong but Time's Time, with five consecutive wins to his credit, proved a formidable opponent. Although Favoridge quickened under the strongest pressure she couldn't peg him back and was still a neck down at the finish.

Favoridge (USA) (b.f. Apr 7, 1980)	Riva Ridge (b 1969)	First Landing (b 1956)	Turn-to / Hildene
		Iberia (ch 1954)	Heliopolis / War East
	Favoletta (b 1968)	Baldric II (b 1961)	Round Table / Two Cities
		Violetta III (b 1958)	Pinza / Urshalim

Favoridge's trainer will no doubt be more than happy if she goes on to do as well as On The House at three. Her first-season form was a good bit better than On The House's but there must be a chance that she won't train on so well —although quite an attractive filly she's small and rather lacking in scope (incidentally she's also a good walker and she has a nice, smooth action). There's also the question of whether she'll stay well enough for the Guineas. On the face of it there seems no reason why she shouldn't. Her half-sisters Pipina (by Sir Gaylord) and Ash Ridge (by Bold Reason) both stayed a mile and a quarter; her half-brothers Good Fellow (by Queen's Hussar) and Audley End (by Nijinsky) won at up to at least a mile; her sire Riva Ridge won ten stakes races over a mile or more, including the Belmont Stakes over a mile and a half; her dam Favoletta won the Irish One Thousand Guineas; and her grandam Violetta III dead-heated in the Cambridgeshire. There is another side to the story though. Easily the best of Favoletta's five previous winners was Amaranda (by Bold Lad, Ire), an exceptionally speedy filly who gained all her wins over five furlongs and only once tried a longer trip. Also, Favoridge is bred on the same lines as the sprinter Court Barns who was by Riva Ridge out of Violetta's half-sister Sovereign, a high-class winner at up to a mile. Favoridge is much more amenable to restraint than Amaranda was so she may stay beyond sprint distances but we doubt whether she will. If she trains on her unusual powers of acceleration look sure to bring her more good prizes but even if she doesn't she must be worth a small fortune: those excellent performers Topsy, Furioso, Lacquer, Bright Finish, Shining Finish and Lucky Sovereign all come from this family and when Clarista,

314

a filly by Riva Ridge out of Furioso, was sold in 1981 still a maiden after ten runs she fetched 96,000 guineas. *H. Wragg.*

FAWG (USA) 2 b.c. Hagley–One Spot (Cavan) (1982 7d) Apr 17; $220,000Y; **81 p** strong colt; brother to 3 winners, including very useful sprinter Spot Two and stakes winner Rolling Mill, successful at up to 1m, and half-brother to 2 winners; dam won claiming races at up to 7f; 16/1, ran on without looking dangerous when 7 lengths sixth of 13 to Russian Roubles in Houghton Stakes at Newmarket in October; will probably stay 1m; bound to benefit from the experience. *G. Harwood.*

FEALTY (FR) 2 b. or br.c. Blakeney 126–Noble Duty (Reliance II 137) (1982 **—** 8s) Mar 4; 35,000Y; big colt; third foal; half-brother to useful stayer Sentry Duty (by Sparkler); dam won over 13f in France; 12/1 and backward, always in rear and was ridden along most of way in 26-runner maiden race won by Magic Rarity at Sandown in October; will need long distances. *J. Sutcliffe.*

FEARLESS LAD 3 ch.c. Import 127–No Fear 91 (Quayside 124) (1981 6g 5f* **126** 6d² 5g* 1982 6f 6f⁴ 5fg* 5fg* 5f 5g 6f³ 5s²)

Northern-trained horses have not met with great success in pattern races at Royal Ascot in recent years, winning an average of one every other season since 1962. An event in which their scoring rate has been relatively high is the King's Stand Stakes, one of the two Group 1 races run at the meeting. Goldhill, Roughlyn and Lochnager won this five-furlong test in 1965, 1966 and 1976 respectively, and in 1982 Fearless Lad, whose trainer had sent Tudor Melody down to Royal Ascot to score in the 1958 Chesham Stakes, added his name to the list with a decisive victory.

Fearless Lad's very useful form as a two-year-old had marked him down as a colt with a bright future over short distances, but his first two outings at three scarcely suggested he would develop into one of the best sprinters in training. Needing the run in the Duke of York Stakes in May he came home sixth of eleven to Jester after showing speed to halfway and in the Thirsk Sprint Stakes a fortnight later he found little in the closing stages when fourth to Crofthall. Much better followed and in a minor event at Beverley nine days before the King's Stand Fearless Lad, reverting to the minimum trip, put up a highly impressive display to beat Special Pleasure easing up by five lengths after showing devastating acceleration. Fearless Lad was obviously now in fine fettle, but even in a rather substandard field at Royal Ascot he seemed to have no more than each-way prospects and started at 10/1. His thirteen opponents included the favourite Jester, the Palace House winner Lightning Label, the Temple Stakes runner-up Chellaston Park and the smart four-year-old Tina's Pet. Drawn on the stand rail, Fearless Lad was settled in behind Tina's Pet who took a narrow advantage over the others at about halfway, where there were apparently several still in with an excellent chance. The position soon changed as Hide switched Fearless Lad outside the leader and brought him with a powerful run that took them to the front a hundred and fifty yards out. So strongly was Fearless Lad travelling that the result stood in little doubt from this point and he drew away in fine style to defeat Chellaston Park and Blue Singh by two lengths and one.

		Porto Bello	Floribunda
	Import	(ch 1965)	Street Song
	(ch 1971)	Immortelle	Never Say Die
Fearless Lad		(ch 1960)	Thunder
(ch.c. 1979)		Quayside	London Gazette
	No Fear	(ch 1967)	Wong
	(ch 1973)	My Plucky Lady	Cash and Courage
		(gr 1963)	Blue Robe

His next three starts saw Fearless Lad failing to reproduce this form, and by the time he ran in the Prix de l'Abbaye de Longchamp in October his reputation was at a fairly low ebb. In the King George Stakes at Goodwood he carried a hefty penalty and ran disappointingly, sweating up, pulling hard, showing a tendency to hang and finishing in the rear behind Tina's Pet. Probably the sharp track didn't favour him here, but this excuse couldn't be used for his display in the William Hill Sprint Championship at York in which he found little in the way of acceleration and managed only sixth place behind Sharpo, beaten also by Chellaston Park and Tina's Pet. Similarly, in the Vernons Sprint Cup at Haydock Fearless Lad never looked like troubling Indian King and lost second near the finish to Great Eastern, a horse demonstrably some way short of top class.

King's Stand Stakes, Ascot—a decisive win for Fearless Lad who gives his trainer the most valuable win of his career

As usual, the Abbaye brought together nearly all the best five-furlong sprinters in Europe. To all intents and purposes it appeared to be a less a question of who would win—Sharpo had outstanding credentials—than of who would finish second, and it was in fact the struggle for the minor placings which provided the most excitement. Fearless Lad broke well and soon lay a close fourth to Blue Courtier, Kind Music and Music Streak. By the time Sharpo produced his decisive run over a furlong out Fearless Lad looked likely to finish no better than fourth, but running on just as strongly as at Royal Ascot he put in a renewed challenge

Mr G. Soulsby's "Fearless Lad"

which took him past first Blue Courtier then, in the dying strides, past Kind Music. At the line he had a head to spare over the latter, a length behind Sharpo: in our opinion this represented an improvement even on his King's Stand form and entitles him to be regarded as the best three-year-old sprinter of the season.

With the retirement of Sharpo and Indian King Fearless Lad ought to be vying with such as Soba, Kind Music and the three-year-olds Brondesbury, Kafu and Krayyan for top sprint honours in 1983. He needs to improve a bit to become true championship material in a normal year, but if he follows the example of his sire Import he may well do so. Useful at three and four, Import improved out of all recognition as a five-year-old when he won the Wokingham Stakes under 9-4 and finished an excellent third to Lochnager and Three Legs in the July Cup. Fearless Lad comes from his second crop and is easily the best of his progeny so far though Wiki Wiki Wheels showed useful form at two in 1982. Import stood at the Hunsley House Stud in Yorkshire for five seasons before being sold to make way for Nicholas Bill; he is now at the Stanlake Park Stud in Berkshire. On the dam's side Fearless Lad is the first foal of the mile-and-a-quarter winner No Fear, a sister to a winner in England and Belgium and a half-sister to several other successful performers here and abroad. Her dam won three races, two of them sellers, from five furlongs to a mile and was one of three winners out of the Hunt Cup third Blue Robe. Fearless Lad, a big, strong colt, is a typical sprinter in appearance. Though he showed at Haydock that he stays six furlongs, his best form is unquestionably over five and he acts on any going. *R. D. Peacock.*

FEARLESS MOVER 2 gr.c. Dragonara Palace 115–Ash Fell 83 (Bleep-Bleep 134) (1982 6s 6d) Mar 26; 10,000Y; fair sort; brother to fair 1980 2-y-o 5f winner Trytravelscene, and half-brother to 2 winners, including very useful 1974 2-y-o 5f and 6f winner Lady Rowley (by Royal Levee); dam 5f sprinter; behind in autumn minor events at Lingfield and Leicester. *R. Hannon.* —

FEATHERED (USA) 3 gr.c. Al Hattab–Miss Plumage (Bold Legend) (1981 7g 8s³ 10s 1982 11fg⁴ 12f 10g) close-coupled, useful-looking colt; one paced and should be suited by 1½m+; blinkered nowadays. *P. Walwyn.* —

FEATHER SOUND 3 ch.g. Be My Guest 126–Muffet 75 (Matador 131) (1981 5fg 5g 5fg³ 6fg 7.3d⁴ 7s 7g 7d 6g⁴ 1982 5g* 5s⁴ 5g² 6f* 5.1f 6fg³ 8g 6fg 6d) quite attractive, well-made gelding; won race at Cagnes-sur-Mer in February and handicap at Brighton in April; best at sprint distances; seems to act on any going; blinkered 4 times at 2 yrs; takes a good hold; inconsistent; exported to Malaysia. *R. Armstrong.* 77

FEELING GREAT 3 b.c. Tyrant–Palace Gold (New Chapter 106) (1981 NR 1982 9fg² 10f 11g³ 10f 10g² 10d³ 9s³) 13,500Y; big, useful-looking colt; good walker; first foal; dam, minor winner over 6f and 11.5f in France, is half-sister to smart animals Pale Ale and Polynikis; placed in varied company; stays 11f; lacks pace; sold to L. Cumani 9,000 gns Newmarket Autumn Sales. *M. Jarvis.* 81

FEELINGS (FR) 5 b.h. Green Dancer 132–Fast Iron (Iron Peg §§) (1981 12g* 12g* 13g 12.3fg² 12fg² 15g 14.7d² 14d 13d 1982 14.7f³ 14g 12.2f³ 14g 12fg 13d 12g²(dis) 15.8d) well-made, quite attractive horse; modest handicapper; stays well; seems to act on any going; blinkered nowadays; has often made running; sold to T. Craig 5,800 gns Doncaster October Sales. *J. Hanson.* 69

FELIPA 8 b.m. Philip of Spain 126–City Carriage 88 (Counsel 118) (1981 8fg 7f 7g 8s 1982 7g 7f 8fg 12v 7s) of little account; has been to stud. *J. O'Donoghue.* —

FELIXSTOWE LAD 3 br.g. Pongee 106–The Squeeze 85 (Bing II) (1981 7fg 6fg 8d 1982 8.2fg 9g 8fg) poor plater; has been bandaged. *R. Johnson.* —

FELTHORPE MARINER 3 b.c. Be My Guest 126–Sea Horse 98 (Sea-Bird II 145) (1981 6f 5f⁴ 7fg⁴ 7fg* 7d⁴ 7fg 7g³ 6d 1982 8d* 8.2s³ 8f 8d* 8f 8fg⁴ 8s) quite attractive, lengthy colt; not the best of movers; stayed on well to win handicaps at Salisbury in April and Sandown (beat Transient by 2½ lengths in £5,500 event) in July; will stay beyond 1m; seems to act on any going but is ideally suited by some give in the ground. *C. Brittain.* 95

FELTWELL (USA) 4 b.c. Habitat 134–Reload 119 (Relko 136) (1981 10s 10v² 10.6d* 10g⁴ 12g² 10.6s* 12f* 12fg 11g 1982 10d 10g⁴ 11f² 10f⁴ 12fg 10.2g 10g³ 12s 10.2d) good-bodied colt; blinkered first time, ran best race for a while when just over a length third to Oratavo in Peter Hastings Handicap at Newbury in September; ran poorly afterwards, with blinkers and without; suited by 1¼m; 84 has won on firm going but gives impression he's ideally suited by some give underfoot; suitable mount for an apprentice; unreliable; sold to BBA 7,000 gns Newmarket December Sales. *H. Wragg.*

FENKIN 4 b. or br.g. Swing Easy 126–Path of Pride (Sovereign Path 125) — (1981 10s 10fg 10s 12d 1982 10g4) rangy gelding; showed first form on only outing of 1982, when dropped to selling company; stays 1¼m; sold 1,700 gns Ascot 2nd June Sales. *M. Ryan.*

FENNY ROUGH 2 br.f. Home Guard 129–Geraldville (Lord Gayle 124) (1982 **101** 5f* 6fg4 6f2 6f* 6g4) Mar 23; IR 10,000Y; tall, lengthy filly; good walker; first foal; dam Irish middle-distance winner; put in best work in closing stages when winning maiden race at Kempton in July and well-contested minor event (beating Domynsky a length) at Pontefract in September; also fourth in 2 good-class fillies races, Princess Margaret Stakes at Ascot in July and Firth of Clyde Stakes at Ayr in September; will stay 7f; has raced only on a sound surface. *B. Hills.*

FERRIBY HALL 5 ch.g. Malicious–Gallic Law 91 (Galivanter 131) (1981 6g **84** 5d 6g 7fg3 6f3 5fg* 6fg 6g 5.6fg 6d 6s 5d 1982 5f* 5f 5fg 5fg 5fg 5g) strong gelding; 20/1-winner of handicap at Beverley in April, beating Miss Poinciana a short head; stays 6f; acts on any going; used to wear blinkers; sometimes sweats up; has run well for an apprentice. *A. Smith.*

FERRYBOAT 2 ch.f. Silly Season 127–Aberklair 72 (Klairon 131) (1982 5f3 **50** 5fg2 6s) Apr 30; 900Y; lengthy filly; second foal; dam, best at up to 1m, is half-sister to smart sprinter Blue Courtier; plater; disappointing favourite at Pontefract in June on final outing, weakening quickly inside final furlong; bred to stay 1m. *J. Hardy.*

FERRY LANE 2 ch.f. Dom Racine 121–Nana's Girl 109 (Tin Whistle 128) — p (1982 5fg) May 12; IR 11,500Y; compact filly; half-sister to several winners, including Royal Boy (by Realm), a smart performer at up to 7f, and good 1977 2-y-o Aythorpe (by Ridan); dam useful at up to 1m and sister to very smart Tin King; 25/1 on and backward side, didn't stride out at all well to start when seventh of 10 behind Aldern Stream in £3,400 event at Goodwood in September; should do better over longer distances. *A. Jarvis.*

FERRYMAN 6 b.g. Forlorn River 124–La Miranda 80 (Miralgo 130) (1981 **94** 5fg2 5d 5g3 6fg2 5d4 5fg3 5g 5s2 6v3 1982 5f4 6g 5f3 6fg 5g 6f 5g 5g 5fg2 5d 5d* 5v 5s* 5s) small gelding; appeared to put up an extraordinarily good performance when faced with a very stiff task in £4,600 event at Newmarket in October, producing a strong burst from Dip and winning by ½ length from Vaigly Star; has no other form of comparable merit, although won handicap at Sandown later in month by 1½ lengths from Singing Sailor; stays 6f; acts on any going, but is apparently well suited by some give underfoot; occasionally blinkered; sometimes sweats up. *D. Elsworth.*

FESTAL SPIRIT 3 b.f. Jimmy Reppin 131–Celebrate 85 (Rockavon 120) **81** (1981 7g 1982 10f 10.5fg 12f4 12d2 12f 12.3fg3 12d 13d3 14g* 15g3 15d*) big, strong filly; enterprisingly ridden when winning minor event at Newmarket and handicap at Edinburgh in the autumn; suited by a test of stamina; well suited by some give in the ground; game. *W. Elsey.*

FICKLE FORTUNE 3 ch.f. Mount Hagen 127–Coumfea (Gulf Pearl 117) — (1981 5g 1982 7fg 8f 10f 8s 7s) quite well-made filly; little worthwhile form in varied company, including selling; has been tried in blinkers; trained part of season by C. Nelson. *A. Jarvis.*

FIDALCO (FR) 3 br.c. Nonoalco 131–High Fidelyty (Hautain 128) (1981 6g **70** 1982 10s 10s 12g4 10.6s 7f2 6g3 7f3 7.2f3 7fg 7g2 6f 7g 9g 7g2 8s) big, useful-looking colt; poor walker; placed in varied company here and in France; should stay 1m; acts on firm going; blinkered fourth and fifth outings; looked a very difficult ride third start but ran well for 5-lb claimer on fifth; trained most of season by C. Brittain. *C. Austin.*

FIDURI 3 b.f. Wolver Hollow 126–Sans Blague (Above Suspicion 127) (1981 — 5d 7f 1982 10.1d 8fg 10.1g 13d) behind in varied company; trained part of season by J. Toller. *C. James.*

FIEFDOM 2 ch.c. Home Guard 129–Eastwood Bounty 87 (Bounteous 125) **85** p (1982 6g*) Mar 18; 16,500Y; attractive colt; half-brother to 3 winners, including smart Woodsome (by Runnymede), a winner at up to 8.5f in England and USA; dam effective from 5f to 1¼m; 7/1, overcame slow start and distinct signs of greenness when winning 20-runner maiden race at Newmarket in October by ¾ length from Follow The Stars; will stay 1m; sure to improve, and seems to have makings of quite a useful 3-y-o. *B. Hobbs.*

FIELD LADY 3 ch.f. Habitat 134–Meadow Pipit 103 (Worden II 129) (1981 6g **71**
1982 7.6fg 8fg 7d³ 7.2g² 8f³ 8fg² 8g⁴ 10.2f² 10.6s) strong, well-made filly; runner-up in maiden races and a handicap; suited by 1¼m; possibly unsuited by soft going. *B. Hills.*

FIERY AMBER 3 ch.f. Streak 119–Crop (Acropolis 132) (1981 5s 5fg 5fg 6f 5f⁴ **35**
6g 1982 7f 7fg⁴ 8g 8f⁴ 8fg⁴ 8f³ 8g 7g 8s) neat filly; plater; stays 1m; acts on firm going; has been tried in blinkers. *C. James.*

FIESTA FUN 4 br.f. Welsh Pageant 132–Antigua 100 (Hyperion) (1981 10g **89**
10d* 12g 10f* 10.1fg* 10g 12g³ 12s 1982 10f 10fg⁴ 10f 12f³ 12g³ 8fg* 8f) workmanlike filly; enterprisingly ridden when beating Cardinal Flower by 2 lengths in £3,700 amateur riders event at Goodwood in August; went too fast for her own good only subsequent outing; stays 1½m; probably acts on any going; blinkered last 2 outings. *P. Cole.*

FIFI 3 ch.f. Rheffic 129–Crespinall 110 (Saint Crespin III 132) (1981 NR 1982 **—**
10fg) rather sparely-made filly; half-sister to 3 winners, notably very useful middle-distance performer Son Fils (by Mon Fils); dam won Princess Elizabeth Stakes and Nassau Stakes; backed at 16/1 though in need of run when behind in 15-runner maiden event won by Bundu at Salisbury in September. *M. Pipe.*

FIGHETTA (FR) 3 b.f. Free Round 127–Lean On (Turn-to) (1981 7f 1982 8g **—**
8f) tall, leggy, close-coupled filly; excellent mover; behind in maiden races and a minor event; exported to Algeria. *R. Sheather*

FIGHTER PILOT 2 gr.c. Warpath 113–Brief Flight 108 (Counsel 118) (1982 **69 p**
7s 8.2s) Apr 27; smallish, lengthy colt; brother to 3 winners, notably Derby fourth Shotgun, and half-brother to several winners, including smart Aviator (by Frankincense); dam won Northern Free Handicap; not seen out until October, and ran easily better race when 9½ lengths sixth of 19 behind Holy Spark at Nottingham on second appearance; will be suited by 1¼m+. *C. Thornton.*

FIGHTING FALCON 2 b.c. Sallust 134–Sweet Chupatti (Rustam 127) (1982 **94 p**
7fg²) May 6; IR 30,000Y; half-brother to numerous winners, including fairly useful 1m winner Winning Hand (by Majority Blue); dam won twice over 5f in Ireland; 20/1, had rest well beaten off when creditable ¾-length second of 13 to all-the-way winner Treasure Trove in maiden race at Naas in September; will probably stay 1m; should win races. *M. O'Brien, Ireland*

FIGHT THE FIRE 3 b.c. Firestreak 125–Fighting Winnie (Fighting Charlie 127) **—**
(1981 5s 5s 5s³ 1982 8d 12.2f 10f 10f 9g 12g) plain, rather lightly-made colt; poor plater; has been tried in blinkers. *W. Holden.*

FIGURE DE DANSE (FR) 2 b.f. Dancer's Image–Figure de Proue (Petingo 135) **74**
(1982 5fg³ 5fg³ 6d³ 6f³ 7f 7g 6g 8f* 8s³ 10f) Mar 25; 775Y; well-grown, useful sort; first foal; dam fourth over 5f in France at 2 yrs on only start; won 20-runner maiden auction event at Redcar in September by 1½ lengths from Mick's Star; suited by 1m; acts on any going; blinkered seventh, eighth and tenth outings. *R. Sheather.*

FILABEG 3 br.c. Swing Easy 126–Chantal 74 (Charlottesville 135) (1981 NR **—**
1982 8.2f 9.4fg 10g) tall, leggy colt; half-brother to Derby third Scintillating Air (by Sparkler); dam placed twice over 1¼m; well beaten in varied company, including selling; dead. *J. Fitzgerald.*

FILAO (USA) 3 ch.g. Fleet Allied–Space Odyssey (Promised Land) (1981 6fg **—**
6g 1982 11.5fg) rangy gelding; beaten some way in varied company; blinkered second start at 2 yrs; sent to France. *R. Hern.*

FILARIO (FR) 3 b.g. Filiberto 123–Escaria (Right Royal V 135) (1981 6h 1982 **58**
8d 8g* 8fg* 9g²) strong, lengthy gelding; attracted no bid after winning seller at Bath in July (well backed); won in better company at Warwick later in month; will stay 1¼m; has run creditably for an apprentice. *M. Pipe.*

FILLETTS FARM 8 b.g. Stephen George 102–Markeeba (March Past 124) **48**
(1981 12.3g 12f 12f 16g* 15.8fg* 18.8fg² 16.1fg 1982 16f 18f 15.8f² 16fg) strong gelding; staying handicapper; ran best race when second at Catterick in June; yet to race on a softer surface. *J. Etherington.*

FIMI 3 br.f. Tachypous 128–Chequered Flag 70 (King's Troop 118) (1981 5g³ **—**
5fg² 5s* 5f² 6d* 5f* 6f* 1982 7f) good-quartered, well-made filly; good mover;

most genuine and consistent in 1981 when she won 4 times; had stiff task and probably needed run only start at 3 yrs in May; stays 6f well; acts on any going. *B. Hobbs.*

FINAL CAST 3 b.f. Saulingo 122–Speyside 84 (Live Spirit 121) ˙ (1981 NR 1982 — 7.6f 6f 6g 8fg 6s) half-sister to 2 winners, including useful 6f to 1m winner Tugoflove (by Tudor Rhythm); dam placed over 5f at 2 yrs; soundly beaten in maiden races and an apprentice event; has worn bandages in front; sold 1,000 gns Ascot December Sales. *R. Laing.*

FINALE SEPT 2 b.g. Malinowski 123–Desertville 92 (Charlottesville 135) **71** (1982 7g 7fg 6fg*) Feb 26; IR 20,000Y; strong, medium-sized gelding; good walker and mover; half-brother to several winners, including very useful stayer New Jerusalem (by Reform) and smart 1975 French staying 2-y-o Empty Jest (by Bon Mot III); dam, half-sister to Tiger and Berber, won over 1m at 2 yrs; sold 4,600 gns to join M. H. Easterby's stable and was subsequently gelded after winning 8-runner seller at Ayr in August easing up by 2½ lengths from Fairham; should stay 1m; ran poorly in blinkers second outing. *J. Hindley.*

FINAL SET 2 b.f. Tumble Wind–Papoosette (Raise You Ten 125) (1982 5f2 **74** 5f* 5fg 5fg* 5g 5f2 5fg2) Mar 7; good-bodied, workmanlike filly; good mover; second living foal; dam ran only twice; made all in maiden race at Catterick in June and in seller (retained 3,600 gns) at Sandown in August; creditable second in 2 nurseries at Redcar in September; bred to stay at least 6f but is a free runner and most unlikely to do so; yet to race on a soft surface; goes well for apprentice K. Williams. *Sir Mark Prescott.*

FINAL STRIKE 3 b.c. Artaius 129–Cape Race 88 (Northern Dancer) (1981 5g **108** 5d* 5s3 5g3 6fg4 6f3 7f4 8fg2 7s3 7g* 7g 1982 7d 8fg 7g) small, compact colt; useful performer who ran respectably all starts, finishing about 5 lengths fifth of 14 to Hays in Salisbury 2,000 Guineas Trial in April (short of room in closing

Mr K. Abdulla's "Fine Edge"

stages), over 8 lengths seventh of 26 to Zino in 2,000 Guineas at Newmarket in May and about 3 lengths fifth of 7 to Come On The Blues in Heron Stakes at Kempton later in May; not seen out again; needs further than 7f and will be suited by middle distances; seems to act on any going. *F. Durr.*

FINE ASSET 3 b.f. Hot Spark 126–Omentello 91 (Elopement 125) (1981 6s 6s — 1982 7fg 12f) good-bodied, useful-looking filly; in rear in varied company; fractured a splint bone in off-fore and has been retired to stud. *R. Laing.*

FINE EDGE 2 ch.c. Sharpen Up 127–Metair 118 (Laser Light 118) (1982 5fg* **105+** 5f* 6g) Mar 30; medium-sized, attractive colt; a good walker and a smooth, easy mover; first foal; dam game winner of 7 races over 5f and 6f; looked very promising when winning with plenty in hand at Newmarket (maiden event) in April and at Newbury (Berkshire Stakes) in June; off course subsequently until mid-September, and possibly needed race when 4¾ lengths last of 5 to Salieri, after holding every chance at distance, in Mill Reef Stakes also at Newbury; stays 6f; may be capable of improvement. *J. Tree.*

FINE SEASON 6 ch.g. Silly Season 127–Floral Palm 69 (Floribunda 136) — (1981 NR 1982 6f) strong gelding; quite a moderate handicapper; always behind at Ripon in May, first outing on flat since 1980; stays 1m; appears to act on any going; sometimes blinkered. *Hbt Jones.*

FINE STYLE 3 b.f. Fine Blade 121–Deagloss (Green God 128) (1981 NR 1982 — 7.6fg 7g) 960F; leggy, narrow filly; first produce; dam won over 6f in Ireland; beaten some way in maiden races at Lingfield in May and Thirsk in July; unruly at start when withdrawn in between. *V. Soane.*

FINE SUN 5 ch.g. Fine Blade 121–All Sunshine (Miralgo 130) (1981 10.2g 9d* **114** 10d³ 12f 10.5g 12f⁴ 10.2g³ 11g² 8g 9s*(dis) 10g² 1982 11d* 9d⁴ 10v* 10g² 11.2d³) fair sort; reportedly acid-fired after injuring himself early in 1982; didn't reappear until September, but was better than ever; won Doonside Cup at Ayr (beat Meeka Gold by a neck) and £7,800 handicap at Ascot (by similar distance from Ricardo); beat Rouge Oiseau and Judd in close finish in Premio Unire at Naples in December, but was relegated to third; also in frame twice at Newmarket, finishing less than 2 lengths fourth of 29 to Century City in William Hill Cambridgeshire (possibly hit front too soon) and 3 lengths second to Cannon King under 10-1 in Tia Maria Autumn Handicap; stays 11f; probably acts on any going; often sweats up; genuine, but seems to need holding up. *M. Lambert.*

FIONAS PRIDE 3 gr. or ro.f. Runnymede 123–Crowberry (Crozier 117) (1981 — § 7f 7f 7g 1982 10s 10s) compact filly; temperamental plater. *E. Carter.*

FIORENZO 2 b.g. Filiberto 123–Guiletta 63 (Runnymede 123) (1982 6d 6g 6fg) — Mar 19; lightly-built gelding; half-brother to 2-y-o winners here and in France; dam ran only 3 times; no worthwhile form; off course 2 months after second outing. *M. Camacho.*

FIOSSA 2 ch.f. Sweet Revenge 129–Roman Rocket 84 (Simbir 130) (1982 6g) — Apr 30; half-sister to several minor winners here and abroad; dam stayed at 1m; 50/1, behind in 15-runner maiden race at Windsor in July. *D. H. Jones.*

FIRBECK 6 ch.m. Veiled Wonder–Highview Jill 73 (Proud Chieftain 122) (1981 — 5g³ 5s 5f 5f 5.6f 5f 5f 5fg 1982 5fg 5g 5g) strong mare; lightly raced and well beaten in handicaps in 1982, but probably needed first 2 outings; yet to show she stays 6f; acts on any going except perhaps very soft; usually wears blinkers. *A. Balding.*

FIRDALE FLYER 3 gr.f. The Go-Between 129–Cullen 80 (Quorum 126) (1981 — 5s 5fg 5fg 5g 5f 1982 5f 5f) compact, rather narrow filly; poor maiden. *W. Wharton.*

FIRDALE ROSIE 3 gr.f. Town Crier 119–Hethabella 62 (Hethersett 134) (1981 — 5s* 6f 7g 7g 6s 7d 1982 8.2d 8f 7f 8g 8.2g 9g 13.8d) lightly-made filly; won maiden race at Wolverhampton in 1981; soundly beaten in handicaps at 3 yrs; not sure to stay 13f; acts on any going; blinkered fifth start. *W. Wharton.*

FIRE BUS 2 br.g. Firestreak 125–Follow the Sun (Kythnos 126 or Saint **53** Crespin III 132) (1982 5f⁴ 5f³ 5f³) Mar 27; 700Y; small, lightly-made gelding; fourth foal; dam ran only once; plater; not seen out after May; exported to Malaysia. *K. Stone.*

FIRE OFF 2 b.f. Averof 123–Fiery Kiss 82 (Floribunda 136) (1982 5fg 5f) — Apr 17; lightly-made filly; half-sister to 3 winners, including fair 1979 2-y-o

1m winner Swift Kiss (by Sparkler); dam won over 6f; well beaten in maiden events at Warwick (auction) and Catterick in July. *W. Stubbs.*

FIRESPARK 3 ch.f. Hot Spark 126–Kari Simbi 63 (Galivanter 131) (1981 **64** 6g 6g 5v 6d 1982 5f² 6h 7d 6fg² 6g* 6g* 7.2f 6s) strong, compact filly; won 2 sellers at Newcastle in August, attracting no bid on first occasion and being bought in 2,500 gns on second; runner-up in better company earlier; stays 6f; suited by top-of-the-ground; best in blinkers; retained 2,300 gns Doncaster November Sales. *M. Camacho.*

FIRE-THATCH 2 ch.c. Thatch 136–Gigiolina (King Emperor) (1982 5.1f* **109** p 5f² 5f*)
A facile five-length success over four rivals when long odds on for a maiden race at Yarmouth in June told us little about newcomer Fire-Thatch, other than that he was well regarded and possessed above-average ability.   Much more informative was his performance in the Windsor Castle Stakes at Royal Ascot later in the month, for which he started second favourite in a field of eleven that included nine previous winners.   Fire-Thatch made much of the early running after a fast start and kept on well when passed two furlongs out by the more-experienced Prince Reymo, going down by a length and a half with the third horse three lengths behind.   This was a most promising effort by Fire-Thatch, who confirmed himself a very useful performer in the Chesterfield Stakes at Newmarket in July.   Starting at long odds on he beat his two rivals in fine style and in a fast time.   He led on the bridle at halfway and, despite changing his legs when meeting the rising ground, quickened well without being hard ridden to beat Bold Bob by three lengths.   Unfortunately he struck into himself during the race and returned with a cut on his near-hind; the horse had tended to strike into himself earlier, and experiments with boots and shoes had failed to remedy matters.   Subsequently it was announced that Fire-Thatch would be rested to give him an opportunity to strengthen and mature.   We had noted at

Mr C. d'Alessio's "Fire-Thatch"

Ascot that he was still on the weak side and slightly lacking in quality, and we shall be interested to see how he's progressed when he reappears.

Fire-Thatch (ch.c. Apr 1, 1980)	Thatch (b 1970)	Forli (ch 1963)	Aristophanes / Trevisa
		Thong (b 1964)	Nantallah / Rough Shod
	Gigiolina (b 1973)	King Emperor (b 1966)	Bold Ruler / Irish Jay
		Goddess (br 1968)	Immortality / Virtuous

Fire-Thatch was bought for 32,000,000 lire (about £14,600) as a yearling. He is the second foal of Gigiolina, who was placed in Italy. His grandam Goddess won over a mile in England, and was a half-sister to the French Derby winner Hard to Beat and the good mile-and-a-half to two-and-a-half mile performer Authi. Thatch was a versatile racehorse and has produced winners at distances of five furlongs to upwards of a mile and three quarters. There's little doubt that Fire-Thatch, a short-coupled colt who has been raced exclusively at five furlongs on firm ground, will prove best at sprint distances. He'll stay six furlongs and has the makings of a smart performer. *H. Cecil.*

FIRMAMENT 2 b.c. Relkino 131–Lady Of The Moon 89 (Crepello 136) (1982 7g 7d) Apr 14; big colt; good mover; second foal; dam, sister to Derby fourth Great Wall, won 3 times over 1¼m; showed up most of way when 13½ lengths seventh of 28 to Tolomeo in maiden race at Newmarket in October and when about 7 lengths fifth of 13 to Russian Roubles in Houghton Stakes on same course later in month; was a bit gangly at the time, and is the type to do better at 3 yrs. *P. Walwyn.* **81 p**

FIRM EVALUATION (USA) 3 ch.g. Vaguely Noble 140–Valmara 104 (Fleet Nasrullah) (1981 8g 10s 1982 12fg 12f² 12f* 14f 12f) big, rangy gelding; short-priced favourite when narrowly winning handicap at Wolverhampton in May; respectable staying-on sixth of 20 to Mubarak of Kuwait in King George V Stakes (Handicap) at Royal Ascot on final start; stays 1¾m; acts well on firm going; retained 7,000 gns Newmarket Autumn Sales. *J. Hindley.* **79**

FIRM FOUNDATIONS 5 br.g. Pieces of Eight 128–Streetcar 87 (Crocket 130) (1981 15.5d³ 16g 1982 17.1f 12d³ 12fg³ 12g²) plater; good second in claiming race at Brighton in August; stays well; acts on a firm and a soft surface; blinkered at 4 yrs. *M. Hinchliffe.* **34**

FIRST APPEAL 2 b.f. Star Appeal 133–Brazilian Beauty (Busted 134) (1982 6f) Apr 14; 25,000Y; good-topped, quite attractive filly; half-sister to 1m winner Dawn Redwood (by Mummy's Pet); dam sister to useful Colourful and closely related to smart stayer Pink Gem; 25/1 and in need of race, soon pushed along when tenth of 11 to Sharp Sea in maiden race at Yarmouth in August; looks capable of better in time. *M. Albina.* **—**

FIRST DEGREE 4 b.g. Balliol 125–Barbara Bryce (Yellow God 129) (1981 8fg 9s 8d 7g 1982 8g) strong, lengthy gelding; gave signs of a little ability at 3 yrs; in rear in seller in 1982. *C. Booth.* **—**

FIRST IMAGE (USA) 2 ro.c. Caucasus 127–Image's Sister (Native Dancer) (1982 7fg) Mar 6; $110,000F, $150,000Y; quite a well-made colt; half-brother to several winners in USA; dam unraced sister to disqualified Kentucky Derby winner Dancer's Image; unquoted and green, ran on nicely in closing stages when about 5 lengths sixth of 16 to Behind The Lines in maiden race at Salisbury in September; will improve. *J. Benstead.* **72 p**

FIRST KNIGHT (USA) 3 ch.g. Roberto 131–Showyourself (Sir Gaylord) (1981 6fg⁴ 7g 7s 1982 8fg 8f 7f 7g 7fg 8f) tall, lengthy gelding; poor handicapper; should stay 1m; blinkered nowadays. *R. Armstrong.* **59**

FIRST MINT (NZ) 3 gr.c. Sovereign Edition 109–La Douce (Le Filou 110) (1981 8g³ 1982 10d* 12f* 14f⁴ 14fg* 15fg² 14f* 16g) rather sparely-made, useful sort; good walker; very useful colt who won maiden race at Nottingham, minor event at Beverley (odds on) and quite valuable handicaps at York and Goodwood; beat Layal by 2 lengths at York in June and responded well to strong driving to account for Crusader Castle by 1½ lengths at Goodwood in July; didn't **108**

Michael Sobell Handicap, York—First Mint
stays on well to beat Layal

run up to his best final start; suited by a test of stamina; seems to act on any going; has a tendency to hang left but is genuine; consistent. *M. Stoute.*

FIRST MOVEMENT 4 b.c. Music Boy 124–Lunar Princess 109 (King's Bench 132) (1981 6g 6g 6g 6f* 6d* 1982 6fg³ 6fg 6g 6fg 6s) strong, good sort; won Ladbrokes (Ayr) Gold Cup as a 3-y-o; very disappointing after finishing 2¾ lengths third to Camisite in £5,400 handicap at Doncaster in May; stays 6f; acts on any going. *G. Huffer.* **92 d**

FIRST PHASE (USA) 3 b.c. Cannonade–Precious Elaine (Advocator) (1981 6fg 7g³ 8s 1982 7g* 8.2fg* 8.2f² 10.6h 8f* 8fg* 10f) small, quite attractive colt; not the best of movers; much improved and won amateur riders race at Haydock and handicaps at Wolverhampton, Salisbury and Newmarket; always going well and beat Perang Tejam a shade comfortably by a length in Food Brokers Trophy on last-named in July; also ran well to be ½-length second to Spanish Pool in Cecil Frail Handicap at Haydock; kicked in stall and finished lame when below form fourth start and had a poor run final outing in July; bred to stay middle distances; acts well on firm ground; usually held up. *G. Hunter.* **95**

FIRST VERSE 2 br.f. Rymer 121–Sunmaid (Sunny Way 120) (1982 7d 7fg 6fg) Feb 13; smallish filly; second foal; dam poor half-sister to Bolkonski; behind in maiden races. *S. Mellor.* **—**

FIRSYJABS 3 b.f. Saritamer 130–Miss Osprey 93 (Sea Hawk II 131) (1981 6g 7fg 7fg² 7d⁴ 1982 10f 12fg 10fg 12f⁴) lengthy, well-made filly; showed fair form in 1981; didn't run up to her best at 3 yrs; possibly stays 1¼m; sold 2,600 gns Ascot August Sales. *B. Hobbs.* **—**

FIT FOR A KING 3 b.f. Royalty 130–Confidante (Gulf Pearl 117) (1981 5g 6fg 6fg 7d 1982 8d⁴ 10f³ 8.5f 8g 7f 7f) smallish, unfurnished filly; plating-class maiden; stays 1¼m; seems to act on any going; suited by enterprising riding tactics. *J. Winter.* **59**

FITZPATRICK 3 b.c. Oats 126–Shannon Princess (Connaught 130) (1981 7g **95**
7g 1982 11g 12f² 14fg³ 12f² 12f³ 12fg* 12f* 12g 12g⁴ 13.3g* 12g) close-coupled,
robust colt; good mover; successful in amateur riders race at Newmarket, minor
event at Salisbury and 14-runner Coral Autumn Cup Handicap at Newbury;
always prominent and stayed on well to hold Sa-Vegas by a neck in last-named
in September (apprentice ridden); will probably stay 2m; yet to race on a soft
surface; genuine. *P. Walwyn.*

FITZROY 4 b.g. Furry Glen 121–Miss Wittington (Red God 128§) (1981 8g³ **70**
8fg 10d 12g 1982 8f 10fg 10d² 12fg* 10fg² 10.6s* 12v) lengthy, hollow-backed
gelding; has rather a round action; improved and won handicaps at Kempton in
September (very comfortably) and Haydock in October, on latter course beating
Warflight by 2½ lengths in a quite valuable amateur riders event; good second to
Rose Du Soir at Goodwood in between; suited by middle distances; seems to act
on any going, with exception of heavy; sold 10,500 gns Newmarket Autumn
Sales. *M. Smyly.*

FITZWARREN 3 ch.c. Busted 134–Dove 92 (Sea Hawk II 131) (1981 8d 7s 8g **79**
1982 12fg 12fg³ 12fg* 12f 12f) strong colt; went on some way out and kept on
strongly to win 11-runner maiden race at Salisbury in May; creditable though
never-dangerous tenth of 18 to Golden Fleece in Derby following month; behind
in King George V Stakes (Handicap) at Royal Ascot later in June; not seen out
again; will stay 1¾m. *G. Balding.*

FIVE JACKS 2 ch.c. Hot Spark 126–Every Blessing 110 (Parthia 132) (1982 **64**
5fg 5g 5fg⁴ 7f⁴ 6fg* 6f² 5d) Apr 4; 5,000Y; small colt; half-brother to 3 winners,
including fairly useful 1½m winner Pine Tree Hill (by Sir Ivor); dam, half-sister to
high-class stayer Die Hard, won at up to 8.5f; plater; bought in 3,200 gns after
winning at Yarmouth in July by 1½ lengths from Roman Beach; needs at least 6f;
acts on firm going; blinkered last 3 outings; sold Susan Piggott Bloodstock
3,000 gns Newmarket Autumn Sales. *N. Callaghan.*

Mr A. D. G. Oldrey's "Fitzpatrick"

FIZZER 2 ch.c. Roi Soleil 125–Caught Speeding (Psidium 130) (1982 8s 8.2s) **70**
Apr 24; 1,000F, 5,800Y; useful-looking colt; half-brother to a winner in Algeria;
dam half-sister to smart miler Miletus; showed ability behind quite useful horses
at Sandown (eighth of 26) and Nottingham (fifth of 19) in October; stays 1m.
T. Gosling.

FIZZICAL 2 b.f. Filiberto 123–Sky Jenny (Sky Gipsy 117) (1982 5v² 5d 5f 5g* **54**
5fg³ 5f 5fg) Mar 23; 500Y; small filly; first foal; dam poor maiden; moderate
plater; blinkered first time when successful at Hamilton (no bid) in June; exported
to Algeria. *A. Young.*

FIZZMASTER 2 ch.c. Porto Bello 118–Taranari (Grand Roi 118) (1982 5fg —
6v 5s 6g) Apr 23; small, useful-looking colt; fourth reported foal; dam of little
account; soundly beaten in maiden and minor events. *T. Gosling.*

FLAMENCO (USA) 2 b.f. Dance Spell–Santiago Sweetie (Boldnesian) (1982 **114**
6f* 7g* 7fg* 7g⁴)
    Sheikh Mohammed's horses won over £140,000 in 1982 but he certainly
had his disappointments. Jalmood started second favourite for both the Derby
and St Leger and finished unplaced in each; Minshaanshu Amad ended the year
a maiden, having repaid the princely sum of £196.80 towards the 700,000 dollars
he cost as a yearling; the good French two-year-old filly Air Distingue, bought by
Sheikh Mohammed after winning the Prix d'Aumale in good style, was only
seventh in the Prix Marcel Boussac; and another of the Sheikh's purchases,
Flamenco, the winner of her first three starts in excellent style, was beaten at
odds on in the Rockfel Stakes at Newmarket in October when carrying his
colours for the first time. Flamenco's performance at Newmarket was well below
par. She went straight into the lead but never managed to build up much of an
advantage over the maiden Thessaloniki and was clearly in trouble well over a
furlong out. Thessaloniki then started to edge ahead and the pair were made
to look one paced when the newcomer Saving Mercy, receiving only 4 lb from
Flamenco, sailed past in the closing stages. Flamenco even lost third place close
home and in the end was beaten just over three lengths. She looked well enough
beforehand but possibly needed the run after being off the course for seven weeks;
equally possibly, she might simply have been past her best for the season.
    Flamenco had previously proved herself one of the best staying two-year-old
fillies, much to her trainer's surprise. He told us that 'early on she looked, quite
frankly, useless–so much so that I was half inclined to send her home in April.'
Apparently she began to show some sign of ability in May but she hadn't shown
anything out of the ordinary before making her debut in a thirteen-runner minor
event at Salisbury in July. She started at 20/1. Her performance proved once
again that too much reliance shouldn't be placed on home gallops: she cruised up
to the leaders inside the last two furlongs, then burst clear in the closing stages to
win by seven lengths from another well-bred newcomer, Northair. Flamenco
reappeared a month later unpenalized in the Sweet Solera Stakes at Newmarket,
receiving 8 lb from Acclimatise, another winner of her only start, and from the
Kingsclere Stakes winner Bright Crocus. She made full use of her advantage,
setting a steady pace ahead of the favourite Montrevie and then quickening clear
from two furlongs out, stealing a march on Acclimatise and Bright Crocus. She
kept on well enough up the final hill to hold Acclimatise's strong late run by three
quarters of a length but her trainer believes she wasn't fully fit; she had missed
some work after jarring herself at Salisbury and had had a rushed preparation.

*Waterford Candelabra Stakes, Goodwood—Flamenco quickens
in really good style to beat Annie Edge (stars) with
Octavia Girl (rails) third*

Balding had been particularly keen for Flamenco to meet her Newmarket engagement, not just to take advantage of the favourable conditions but to boost interest at the Saratoga Yearling Sales four days later in her half-sister by Damascus who eventually fetched only 100,000 dollars, a comparatively modest amount for a filly of her pedigree.

Flamenco was given a lot of work before her next race, the Waterford Candelabra Stakes at Goodwood three weeks later in which she started co-second favourite with the Queen Mary Stakes and Lowther Stakes third Annie Edge behind the improving Silk Pyjamas. She looked extremely well and showed improved form, racing in third or fourth place until she moved up strongly to take a decisive advantage entering the last two furlongs. She was particularly impressive in the closing stages, sprinting away in excellent style to win un-challenged by four lengths from Annie Edge who received 3 lb. Flamenco's trainer was then left with the problem of where to run her next. Her eye-opening first appearance hadn't come until July 10th, three days after the closing date of the May Hill Stakes and the Hoover Fillies Mile, and she hadn't been entered for either race. Her target was said to be the Prix Marcel Boussac, which has a much more sensible closing date less than four weeks before the race, but she ran instead in the Rockfel Stakes.

Flamenco (USA) (b.f. Apr 16, 1980)	Dance Spell (b 1973)	Northern Dancer (b 1961)	Nearctic
			Natalma
		Obeah (b 1965)	Cyane
			Book of Verse
	Santiago Sweetie (b 1974)	Boldnesian (b 1963)	Bold Ruler
			Alanesian
		Santiago Lassie (b or br 1967)	Vertex
			Aysha

Flamenco has an interesting pedigree. Her great-grandam Aysha was the champion three-year-old filly of her year in Chile, winning Las Oaks and El Ensayo, and was then sent to the USA where she was placed in stakes races at around nine furlongs. The Chilean correspondent in the *Bloodstock Breeders' Review*, commenting on Aysha's exportation, said 'she may not be a serious loss to the country for her female line is not impressive'. He was probably wrong. She did well at stud in the States, producing eight winners including the smart sprinting two-year-old Santiago Road and the useful Irish filly Aysha Road, as well as Flamenco's grandam Santiago Lassie, a stakes-placed winner at up to seven furlongs. Santiago Lassie has done even better; her daughter Syria was a leading three-year-old filly in 1981, winning the Mistletoe Handicap over eight and a half furlongs; and her son Bold Laddie was a very smart two-year-old in 1975. Bold Laddie won six of his fifteen starts that year, finishing second in another four, and he also won the Hibiscus Stakes as a three-year-old. The longest distance he won over was six and a half furlongs but he ran second in the Kentucky Jockey Club Stakes over a mile at two. Flamenco is the second foal of Santiago Sweetie, a sister to Bold Laddie who gained her only success over six furlongs as a three-year-old. Flamenco's sire Dance Spell isn't very well known here. He was a well-bred colt, a son of Northern Dancer and the very smart Obeah, and he was also a high-class performer at two and three years, winning seven times at up to a mile including the Saranac Stakes and the Jerome and Jamaica Handicaps. Dance Spell's death after only two seasons at stud looks highly regrettable; his first crop included the smart American two-year-old Dancing School, the useful English colt Triple Axel and the very good American filly Broom Dance, winner of the Alabama Stakes over a mile and a quarter and the Gazelle Handicap over nine furlongs; and among his two-year-olds are Flamenco and two colts, Encourager and Fortnightly, who were highly ranked in the Experimental Free Handicap.

Flamenco is a strapping, robust individual and she looks the type to train on. The distance of the Guineas will suit her well—indeed she will probably stay further—but she needs to improve if she's to win that race; she will also need to come to hand earlier than she did in her first season. Her trainer believes she'll prove well suited by softish ground; as yet she has raced only on a sound surface. *J. Balding.*

FLAME OF TARA 2 b.f. Artaius 129–Welsh Flame 106 (Welsh Pageant 132) **105** (1982 6f* 6fg* 6d* 5fg⁴) Apr 20; third foal; half-sister to fair middle-distance maiden Fruition (by Rheingold) and useful 1981 French 2-y-o 7f winner Nacibi (by Nonoalco); dam won 4 times over 1m; a useful filly who won maiden and minor events at Naas and 12-runner Irish Chorus Stakes at Navan before end of

June; accounted for several other previous winners in good style under top weight at Navan, winning by 2 lengths from Hot Princess with rest at least 4 lengths further behind; probably found 5f too sharp when 4¼ lengths fourth of 11 to Sweet Emma in Heinz '57' Phoenix Stakes at Leopardstown in August; will be suited by 1m; seems to act on any going. *J. Bolger, Ireland.*

FLAMINGO GARDENS 3 b.f. Ercolano 118–Foolhardy 101 (Sicambre 135)   —
(1981 NR 1982 9fg 12f) lengthy filly; half-sister to several winners, notably very smart 6f to 1m winner Jan Ekels (by Derring-Do); dam, a stayer, is half-sister to smart long-distance horse Shatter; in need of race when well beaten in newcomers event at Wolverhampton in April and well-contested maiden event at Haydock in May. *J. Etherington.*

FLASH LAMP 3 b.g. Maystreak 118–Alumia (Great Nephew 126) (1981 5d   —
6fg 6fg 5s 1982 8g 6.5g 8f 10.8fg 6fg 7g) fair sort; poor plater; sometimes sweats up; trained by D. Leslie part of season. *M. Chapman.*

FLASH MINT 3 ch.c. Streak 119–Treasury (Henry the Seventh 125) (1981   —
7d 1982 7fg 8g 10fg 12f) well beaten in maiden and minor events; sold 300 gns Ascot August Sales. *R. Atkins.*

FLASHPOINT 2 b.f. Red Alert 127–Snow Path (Warpath 113) (1982 5d 5f3   **70**
5fg*) Apr 15; useful-looking filly; good mover; first foal; dam of no account; held on by a neck from Pamya after making all in 12-runner maiden race at Warwick in May; troublesome at start on other occasions, and was twice withdrawn; wears blinkers; sent to Trinidad. *B. Swift.*

FLASHRAY 4 ch.c. Flashback 102–Dumette 89 (Dumbarnie 125) (1981 10s   —
8g 6d 8.3s 6v 6g 1982 10fg 7fg) poor plater; possibly stays 1¼m; has been tried in blinkers. *J. Long.*

FLASHY GAL 2 b.f. Continuation 120–Hillset (Hill Clown) (1982 5f 6g)   —
May 2; leggy, narrow filly; sister to a winning 2-y-o plater and half-sister to two 2-y-o winners; dam of no account; 7 lengths fifth of 7 behind Mummy's Apple in minor event at Thirsk in May; not seen out again until September when out of first 10 of 26 to Annamoe Bray in £5,000 seller at Doncaster. *J. Hardy.*

FLASHY VYNZ 2 ch.c. Whitstead 125–Noaxe To Grind (The Axe 115) (1982   **65**
6f 7.2s4 8g) Apr 25; 5,400Y; workmanlike colt; has a round action; fourth foal; dam plating-class novice hurdler; 7 lengths fourth of 11 behind Under The Hammer in seller at Haydock in October, only indication of merit; should stay at least 1¼m. *W. Haigh.*

FLATTERY'S CAP 2 b.f. Tarboosh–Flattery (Atan) (1982 7g) Feb 2;   —
plain filly; sixth foal; dam won over 5f at 2 yrs in Ireland; unquoted, behind in 21-runner maiden race at Newmarket in October. *G. Beeson.*

FLAVELLS RECORD 3 b. or br.g. Record Token 128–Hascombe Lady 70   —
(Galivanter 131) (1981 5s 5g 5g 6g 7g 5s 10.2g 1982 5d 7f 5fg 6f) rather leggy gelding; poor plater; has worn blinkers; sold 340 gns Doncaster November Sales. *G. Fletcher.*

FLEET BAY 2 gr.g. Bay Express 132–Porsanger (Zeddaan 130) (1982 5g4   **82**
5f3 5f* 6f3 6g4) May 25; lightly-made gelding; brother to prolific 3-y-o 5f winner Cree Bay and 1980 2-y-o 5f winner Royal Blood; dam from family of Grey Dawn II; led close home to win 10-runner maiden race at Thirsk in June by a neck from Harleyford Maid; good fourth in nursery at Ayr in September; stays 6f; yet to race on a soft surface; wears blinkers; gelded after final appearance. *J. W. Watts.*

FLEETING KNIGHT 2 b.c. Artaius 129–Fleet Wahine 121 (Fleet Nasrullah)   —
(1982 7g) May 19; IR 26,000Y; well-made colt; half-brother to useful Irish 7f and 1½m winner Fleet Serenade (by Lorenzaccio); dam won Ribblesdale Stakes and Yorkshire Oaks; 14/1 and backward, no show in mixed-aged event at Newmarket in October. *J. Dunlop.*

FLEET REVIEW 2 b.f. Artaius 129–Fleet 123 (Immortality) (1982 6g2) Apr   **84** p
20; 25,000 gns F, $220,000Y; lengthy filly; good walker; half-sister to 2 winners, including smart American stakes winner Heloise (by Dr Fager), successful at up to 9f; dam won Cheveley Park Stakes and 1,000 Guineas; 6/4 favourite and very fit indeed, rallied well after leading to inside final furlong when head second of 15 to Miss Thames in maiden race at Yarmouth in June; should stay 1¼m. *H. Cecil.*

FLEMING 2 ch.c. Royalty 130–Zulaika 75 (Worden II 129) (1982 6g) Apr   —
14; brother to 1½m winner Zulaika Hopwood, and half-brother to 2 winners;

dam won at 1½m; unquoted, thirteenth of 22 to Riverside Artist in minor race at Nottingham in July. *W. Holden.*

FLICKER TO A FLAME (USA) 3 ch.f. Empery 128–Lovelight 112 (Bleep- **65** Bleep 134) (1981 6g³ 1982 7g⁴ 8.5f 7d³ 8fg³ 10g) big, well-made, attractive filly; good walker and mover; quite a modest maiden; stays 1m; acts on a firm and a soft surface. *B. Hills.*

FLIGHT OF TIME 2 b.g. Stradavinsky 121–Kelso's Niece (Herbager 136) **62** (1982 6f 6g 5fg⁴) Feb 26; IR 16,000Y; neat gelding; second foal; dam very useful French middle-distance filly; strong-finishing fourth in valuable seller at Sandown in August; gelded subsequently; will be suited by 7f+; acts on a firm surface. *B. Hills.*

FLIGHTY FRIEND 4 ch.g. Be Friendly 130–Glimmer of Light (Only for Life — 126) (1981 10fg 9s³ 8g 8g 1982 12.3g 14g 18d) workmanlike gelding; best run at 9f on soft going. *R. Woodhouse.*

FLINDERS RANGE 2 ch.c. Native Bazaar 122–Hedonist 74 (Mandamus 120) **63** (1982 5s⁴ 5d³ 5fg* 5f² 6fg³) Feb 5; well-grown, lengthy, rather plain colt; second foal; dam sprint plater; won valuable seller at Newbury in May by 3 lengths from Eros; bought in 3,000 gns afterwards; claimed for £7,600 after finishing 2½ lengths third of 10 to Shadan at Brighton the following month; stays 6f; acts on firm going; to race in Italy. *R. Hannon.*

FLOATING CHARGE 4 ch.g. Hotfoot 126–Loweswater 74 (Saint Crespin III — 132) (1981 12fg 12g 11.7d 1982 16fg 12fg) big, tall gelding; no form since 2 yrs; should stay middle distances. *M. McCourt.*

FLOATING PETAL 2 ch.f. Wollow 132–Fallen Rose (Busted 134) (1982 6g) **90 p** Apr 30; 13,000Y; smallish, well-made filly; first foal; dam, half-sister to high-class filly First Bloom, won small 11.5f race in France; 12/1, recovered from slow start and ran very well until fading in closing stages when 6 lengths fifth of 19 behind What Lake in maiden race at Newmarket in September; will be much better suited by 7f+; sure to improve. *H. Wragg.*

FLOCKTON GREY 2 gr.g. Dragonara Palace 115–Misippus (Green God 128) June 5; 900F; 1,700Y; a 'ringer', allegedly 3-y-o Good Hand, reportedly masqueraded as this gelding in maiden auction event at Leicester in March, and won it by 20 lengths; 4 months later the race was awarded to runner-up Acheron on grounds that the winning horse had not been under care of its trainer for period of 14 days immediately prior to the race, thereby contravening rule 184(a); the race has been subject of inquiry by Humberside Police Fraud Squad, and a report has been sent to Director of Public Prosecutions. *S. Wiles.*

FLOGERA 3 b.f. Owen Dudley 121–Argentina 115 (Nearco) (1981 6fg 7f 8g — 1982 10f 13fg³ 15fg 16fg) smallish, rather unfurnished filly; slow maiden; best run at 13f on firm ground; blinkered final start. *C. Brittain.*

FLOPSY (FR) 3 b.f. Brigadier Gerard 144–Miss Slip 107 (Coursing) (1981 NR — 1982 10s 8fg) useful-looking filly; fourth foal; half-sister to minor French 8.5f winner False Move (by Malacate); dam won Molecomb Stakes; in rear in maiden race at Chepstow and £5,100 event at Ascot in April. *C. Austin.*

FLORAL ELEGANCE 3 b.f. Martinmas 128–Our Duck (The Go-Between 129) **43** (1981 5s⁴ 5d* 5fg 5g 6fg 6fg 6fg 5g 5d 6v 6s 1982 5d 5s 6f² 6fg 5g 5f⁴) small, lightly-made filly; good mover; plater; seems to act on any going; has worn blinkers; sold 500 gns Newmarket Autumn Sales; sent to Holland. *Mrs J. Reavey.*

FLORENCIA 3 b.f. Moulton 128–Spanish Sail 113 (Matador 131) (1981 6g⁴ **65** 1982 6g³ 6g 6fg⁴ 5g⁴ 6f 6g³ 6d* 6s) leggy filly; won modest maiden race at Nottingham in September; in frame in similar events and a seller earlier; will stay 7f; suited by some give in the ground; blinkered last 2 starts; sold 2,800 gns Newmarket Autumn Sales. *G. Pritchard-Gordon.*

FLORENLY (FR) 2 ch.f. Pharly 130–Florentia (Relic) (1982 8v² 10v³) Jan 27; **?** 520,000 francs Y (approx £47,300); half-sister to 3 winners, including very smart French middle-distance filly Floressa (by Sassafras) and very useful French middle-distance colt Talis Filius (by Sanctus II); dam won over 1m in France at 4 yrs; in frame twice at Saint-Cloud late in season, notably going down by ½ length to Alexandrie in 16-runner newcomers event; should stay 1¼m; entered in Oaks. *F. Boutin, France.*

FLORIANO (USA) 3 b.c. Turn and Count–Lock Box (No Robbery) (1981 5d* **116** 5s 1982 8s* 8d* 8d²) $30,000Y; fourth foal; half-brother to 3 winners in USA, including minor stakes winner Spice Isle (by Fiddle Isle); dam never ran; made all to win minor events at Saint-Cloud and Maisons-Laffitte in the spring; again made running but was caught in final strides when good short-head second to What A Guest in Prix de la Jonchere at Longchamp in May; subsequently sent to USA and won allowance race at Santa Anita in November; stays 1m; yet to race on a sound surface. *F. Boutin, France.*

FLORIDA DANCER 3 b.f. Realm 129–Cambus O'May 100 (Sing Sing 134) — (1981 5fg 1982 6fg) good sort; soundly beaten in maiden event and £3,700 race. *Peter Taylor.*

FLORIDA SON 3 b.c. Busted 134–Peach Stone (Mourne 126) (1981 6g 8g 8s* — 1982 10.5f 12f 14fg 8s) big, strong colt; made much of running and kept on to win maiden race at York in 1981; well beaten all starts at 3 yrs but was twice out of his depth, including in Derby; will stay well; acts on soft going. *J. Hanson.*

FLORITA 2 br.f. Lord Gayle 124–Golden Moss 91 (Sheshoon 132) (1982 7g³) **86 p** May 12; 53,000Y; workmanlike filly; sister to fairly useful Irish middle-distance performer Loriot, and half-sister to 2 winners, notably smart Irish 1m to 1½m winner Orchestra (by Tudor Music); dam Irish middle-distance winner; 33/1, kept on well after being pulled along some way out when 2 lengths third of 22 to Toveris in maiden event at Newmarket in October; looks sure to win in maiden company at 1¼m or more. *G. Pritchard-Gordon.*

FLORI WONDER 2 b.f. Floriana 106–Greek Wonder 52 (Veiled Wonder) **59** (1982 6f 6f 6g 6fg 7g² 8g 8d) Mar 31; lightly-built filly; bad mover; first foal; dam plater; 3 lengths second of 11 to Incarnadine in seller at Wolverhampton in October; stays 1m; suited by some give in the ground. *T. Marshall.*

FLOTSKY 2 b.g. Radetzky 123–Phlox 101 (Floriana 106) (1982 5f 5fg 5fg 5f 6g — 7fg 8d 8.2d 8s 10.2s) bad plater; has worn blinkers. *R. Hoad.*

FLOUT (USA) 2 ch.c. Bold Bidder–Manta (Ben Lomond) (1982 6f) Apr 1; **85 p** $150,000Y; rangy, good sort; half-brother to 3-y-o 1m to 1½m winner Tawfiq (by Blushing Groom) and a winner in USA; dam high-class winner of 18 races at up to 11f; showed plenty of promise in £3,400 event at Salisbury in August, making up a lot of ground in final 2f to finish 2¾ lengths fifth of 14 to Naar after getting well behind through inexperience; moved moderately to start beforehand; will be very well suited by middle distances; sure to improve and win races. *J. Tree.*

FLOWERFARM 2 b.g. The Brianstan 128–Hope Baggott (Hopeful Venture 125) **68** (1982 6f⁴ 6f⁴ 7g 6f⁴ 7g) May 8; 5,800Y; rather leggy gelding; second foal; dam never ran; plating-class maiden: form only at 6f, but had stiff tasks at 7f. *D. Smith.*

FLUELLA 2 br.f. Welsh Pageant 132–Ya Ya 84 (Primera 131) (1982 6d 7g) — Apr 11; sister to smart 7f and 10.6f winner Fluellen, and half-sister to winning 3-y-o stayer Master Boatman and 7f and 11f winner Seven Seas (both by Riverman); dam staying half-sister to Park Hill winner African Dancer; well beaten in large fields of maidens at Newmarket in October. *H. Wragg.*

FLUID MECHANICS (USA) 2 ch.f. Sir Ivor 135–Envidiada (Con Brio 121) **76** (1982 6g⁴ 7d⁴ 7g) Apr 5; lengthy American-bred filly; dam good winner in Argentina; quite a modest maiden; should stay 1¼m. *M. Albina.*

FLUKE (USA) 2 b.f. Sham–Scoring Play (Reviewer) (1982 7g) Apr 10; **82 p** $110,000Y; big filly; second foal; sister to smart French 1¼m winner Black Narcissus; dam, closely related to very smart 7f and 1m winner Bold and Brave, won 2 sprint races; second favourite, stayed on nicely from halfway without being punished when promising 5 lengths fifth of 21 behind Ski Sailing in maiden event at Newmarket in October; will be suited by further; sure to improve. *J. Dunlop.*

FLY BABY 3 b.f. African Sky 124–Gay Bird 111 (Birdbrook 110) (1981 5d 5g* **101** 5d³ 5f* 6fg 5g³ 1982 5f 6fg 5g 5f³ 5fg 5g³ 5d³ 5v) workmanlike filly; useful sprinter; creditable third in Singleton Handicap at Goodwood in July on fourth start (behind Erroll's Boy) and in £4,600 event at Newmarket in October on seventh (to Ferryman); best at 5f; seems to act on any going but goes well on firm; genuine; sold to Horse France 30,000 gns Newmarket Autumn Sales. *R. Hannon.*

FLYING CORPS (USA) 2 b.c. Ack Ack–Flutter Away (Double Jay) (1982 **89** 7fg³ 6fg² 7f* 7g²) Apr 1; $60,000Y; close-coupled, workmanlike colt; excellent mover; brother to 2 winners, including Shackles, a stakes winner at up to 9f, and half-brother to 2 winners; dam won at up to 1m; led well inside final furlong when winning 6-runner maiden race at Brighton in September by a length from

Everseal; favourite when going down by 1½ lengths to Rana Pratap in minor event on same course later in month; will stay 1m; sent to Trinidad. *G. Harwood.*

FLYING DISC 2 br.c. Record Token 128–Supremelos (Supreme Sovereign 119) **87**
(1982 5f 5fg* 5f² 5f³ 5f⁴ 5fg 5g) Mar 27; 4,200Y; quite attractive colt; second foal; dam never ran; made all in 15-runner maiden race at Lingfield in May; cocked jaw and forfeited chance by running wide into straight when odds on in two-horse race at Brighton on next outing; didn't show much afterwards, but was given stiff tasks by handicapper on last 2 appearances; sold BBA 3,800 gns Newmarket Autumn Sales. *A. Pitt.*

FLYING DREAMER 4 b.g. My Swallow 134–Forgotten Dreams 82 (Shoemaker —
121) (1981 8d 12d 12d 11.7fg⁴ 10f 11.7fg 16g 13.1h 10.1fg 10.2g 1982 12fg 17.1f) leggy gelding; good walker; stays 1¼m; acts on a firm and a soft surface; ran creditably in blinkers once; inconsistent. *M. Blanshard.*

FLYING EASY 2 b.f. Swing Easy 126–Flying Sovereign 74 (Sovereign Bill 105) —
(1982 5fg 6fg 7f) Feb 22; big, rangy filly; good walker; first foal; dam 2-y-o 5f winner; soundly beaten in maiden races at Salisbury, Lingfield and Sandown; not seen out after July. *R. Hannon.*

FLYING FANTASY 2 b.f. Habitat 134–Formentera (Ribot 142) (1982 5fg⁴) — p
Mar 1; $310,000Y; small, strong, quite attractive filly; sister to 1,000 Guineas and Champion Stakes winner Flying Water, and half-sister to a winner in USA; dam, in frame over 1m at 2 yrs, is half-sister to high-class French colt Felicio II; 7/1, made steady progress from slowish start when 5¾ lengths fourth of 10 to Myra's Best in maiden race at Sandown in June; will be much better suited by 6f+. *H. Candy.*

FLYING FRIEND (USA) 2 br.f. Accipiter–Friendly Neighbour (Deck Hand) —
(1982 6fg) Apr 19; $65,000Y; well-made filly; second foal; half-sister to fair 1981 2-y-o 7f winner Neighboring (by Herculean); dam won 2 sprint claiming races; 12/1 and bit backward, slowly into stride when last of 9 in £6,000 new-comers event at Ascot in July. *F. J. Houghton.*

FLYING HALO 2 ch.g. Dom Racine 121–Naval Artiste (Captain's Gig) (1982 **50**
5g 6fg 5s) Apr 11; 3,000Y; fourth foal; dam Irish 2-y-o 5f winner; poor plater; sold 340 gns Ascot November Sales. *R. Hannon.*

FLYING LANCER 2 gr.c. Runnymede 123–Torlonia 63§ (Royal Palace 131) **68**
(1982 5d 7g 8s) Apr 9; sturdy, workmanlike colt; first reported foal; dam, placed at up to 2m, was most unsatisfactory temperamentally; little form in autumn maiden events in the Midlands; blinkered first outing. *Mrs R. Lomax.*

FLYING MAIL 3 b.f. Pretty Form 97–Miss Little 78 (Dunoon Star 110) (1981 —
5d² 5g³ 5d 6d 5f 1982 6g 6fg 8d) leggy filly; sprint plater; best form at 5f with some given in the ground; sold 520 gns Doncaster November Sales. *A. W. Jones.*

FLYING MEMBER 2 gr.g. New Member 119–Golden Columbine (Column) —
(1982 8s 8s) first reported foal; dam poor hurdler; backward, behind in maiden races at Bath and Warwick in October. *J. Brennan.*

FLYING OFFICER 5 b.g. Warpath 113–Rosie Wings 102 (Telegram II 120) **63**
(1981 12s 14f² 16g 12g 14s⁴ 15.8g 1982 12f* 15g 14f 20fg 16d* 20.4g² 16fg⁴ 16d* 16.9fg 16.1s 14s³ 18s) neat, rather lightly-made gelding; good walker; successful at York in May (apprentice event), Beverley in July and Newcastle in August; stays very well; acts on any going; sold to M. Pipe 6,800 gns Doncaster November Sales. *C. Thornton.*

FLYING PALACE 2 b.c. North Stoke 130–Splosh (Silly Season 127) (1982 6g) **71** p
May 30; second foal; half-brother to 3-y-o Hithermoor Lass (by Red Alert); dam poor sister to smart Idiot's Delight; 10/1, never-dangerous 6¾ lengths sixth of 17 to Indian Rajah in minor event at Windsor in August; will do better over 7f+. *W. Hastings-Bass.*

FLYING ROSE 2 b.f. Welsh Saint 126–Ardara Rose (Tudor Music 131) (1982 —
6f 6fg 6f) Feb 8; IR 3,200F, IR 3,500Y; rather lightly-made filly; well beaten in maiden company, twice last; blinkered third start; sold 320 gns Ascot July Sales. *I. Walker.*

FLYING RUPEE (USA) 3 br.g. Marshua's Dancer–Treasury Maid (Prince of —
India) (1981 NR 1982 9g 8g 8g 8s) $17,000Y; tall, leggy, close-coupled gelding; fourth foal; half-brother to 2 minor winners in USA; dam, sister to a stakes winner, won 8 times at up to 9f including claiming events; soundly beaten in maiden races and a minor event. *B. Hanbury.*

FLYING SAUCE 2 b.f. Sauce Boat–Fly To Post (Assagai) (1982 6g* 8g* 6.5d) **107**
third foal; half-sister to 3-y-o 1m winner Fly the World and American winner
Queen of Cheeses (both by Empery); dam won over 7f at 2 yrs in France; won
newcomers race at Saint-Cloud in July and 9-runner Prix Herod at Evry in
September, justifying favouritism by 2 lengths from Faraona in latter; second
favourite for Prix Eclipse at Saint-Cloud in October but ran disappointingly,
finishing only sixth of 8 to Crystal Glitters; suited by 1m. *F. Boutin, France.*

FLYING SCOTSMAN (DEN) 2 b.c. Tower Walk 130–Scotch Thistle 73 **78**
(Sassafras 135) (1982 6f 5f 6g 5f 5d² 5s) Mar 26; strong, workmanlike colt;
first foal; dam placed at up to 1½m; quite a modest maiden; best race at 5f, but
was not disgraced at 6f, and may well be suited by that distance as 3-y-o; acts
on soft going. *R. Hollinshead.*

FLYING SISTER 4 b.f. St Paddy 133–Quick Aim (Pardal 130) (1981 12d 12fg —
8fg 8fg 10d 12g⁴ 1982 16s 15.8d) tall, lightly-made filly; plating-class maiden;
should stay beyond 1½m; blinkered final start. *A. Jarvis.*

FLYING TYKE 7 ch.h. Huntercombe 133–Maid of Iron (Crozier, USA) (1981 —
6s 5s² 5d* 6s 6d 5fg 5fg 5g³ 5d 5g 6s 5g 1982 5s⁴ 5d 6s 5s) useful-looking sort;
not a good mover; sprint handicapper; not seen out until October; stays 6f;
suited by some give in the ground nowadays; sometimes blinkered; sometimes
bandaged in front. *A. Smith.*

FLYNN 3 ch.g. Malacate 131–Army Court (Court Martial) (1981 6fg 8s 8s 1982 —
10f 10d) rangy, rather plain gelding; well beaten in varied company in the
North; blinkered final start. *J. Mason.*

FLY THE WORLD (USA) 3 b.f. Empery 128–Fly To Post (Assagai) (1981 **74**
NR 1982 8g* 8g) 7,800Y; small filly; has a slight enlargement of off-fore
knee; not the best of movers; second foal; sister to American winner Queen of
Cheeses; dam won over 7f at 2 yrs in France; easy in market when running on
strongly to beat Crimson Lake by 1½ lengths going away in 19-runner maiden
race at Pontefract in July; went very freely to post and ran badly in handicap on
same course in August; will be suited by 1¼m+; sold 20,000 gns Newmarket
December Sales. *B. Hills.*

FOIL 'EM (USA) 2 ch.f. Blade–Spookem Joanne (Skookum) (1982 6d*) **82 p**
Apr 7; $30,000Y, $37,000 2-y-o; first foal; dam won claiming races at up to 4.5f;
14/1 and apparently in need of race, put up promising display in 22-runner
maiden event at Doncaster in October, producing strong finish to get up on line
from Happy Season; will stay beyond 6f; certain to improve. *M. Jarvis.*

FOLEY'S FOLLY 2 ch.f. Legal Tender 94–Get In Touch (Communication 119) —
(1982 5f 5g) June 21; small filly; first foal; dam never ran; tailed-off last in
seller at Doncaster in May and maiden race at Leicester in June; of no account.
D. Weeden.

FOLLOW THE STARS 2 ch.f. Sparkler 130–St Citrus 108 (Relic) (1982 5g **80**
5f³ 7.6v 6g²) May 31; short-backed filly; half-sister to numerous winners, including smart sprinter Florestan (by Petingo) and very useful French 9f to
1¼m winner Schoeller (by Nashua); dam miler; placed in maiden events at
Kempton in July (off course 3 months afterwards) and Newmarket in October;
should stay 1m; acts on firm going. *D. Elsworth.*

FOOLISH WAYS 3 b.c. Comedy Star 121–Susie Hall (Gold Rod 129) (1981 **78**
6g 5fg 6g⁴ 7f 8s 8d 1982 10s 8.2fg 8f⁴ 8f⁴ 8f² 8g² 8.2fg* 7fg⁴ 8.2g* 8.2g* 8.2fg³
9g) strong, deep-girthed colt who carries plenty of condition; won maiden race
and handicap at Hamilton in June and quite valuable handicap on same course
in July; stays 1m well; acts on firm going; consistent. *A. Balding.*

FOOL'S TESTIMONY 5 ch.g. High Line 125–Lady Advocate 116 (King's —
Bench 132) (1981 10.1fg² 12f³ 12fg⁴(dis) 1982 16f) well-made, good sort;
poor maiden; stays 1½m. *G. Thorner.*

FOOTWORK (USA) 2 ch.c. Dance Spell–Laraka (Impressive) (1982 7fg³ 7g **81 d**
7fg 7d) Feb 8; $85,000Y; sturdy, short-legged colt; good walker; half-brother
to a winner by Stage Door Johnny; dam very useful sprinter; disappointed after
promising third in maiden race at Newbury in July; had his card marked for
unsatisfactory stalls behaviour on one occasion; doubtful temperamentally.
F. J. Houghton.

FORESTERS BOY 5 br.g. Swinging Junior 118–Wilden (Will Somers 114§) —
(1981 7g 7f 1982 7fg 7f 8f 7f) leggy, lop-eared gelding; only plating class; not
certain to stay 1¼m; probably acts on any going; usually blinkered nowadays.
W. Haigh.

FORESTERS LAD 4 gr.g. Porto Bello 118–Raffinata (Raffingora 130) (1981 —
6g 7d 7g 7.2s⁴ 6g⁴ 6d 7.2g 6g 7.2v 1982 7f 7fg) leggy gelding; best at 6f; acts
well on a soft surface; sold out of W. Haigh's stable 2,100 gns Doncaster May
Sales after first outing. *J. Spearing.*

FOREST RIDE (USA) 3 gr.c. Al Hattab–Papamiento (Blade) (1981 5g³ —
6g² 6fg 1982 8fg 8fg 8d 8g 10.1fg) neat, short-backed colt; good mover;
placed in maiden races at Salisbury and Newmarket in 1981; didn't reproduce
that form at 3 yrs; bred to stay 1½m; blinkered nowadays; possibly none too
genuine; sold 1,750 gns Ascot August Sales. *R. Hern.*

FOREVER MARY 2 ch.f. Red Alert 127–Calamarie (Deep Diver 134) (1982 **81**
6fg 6g² 5v²) Mar 29; lengthy filly; good walker; first foal to Northern Hemisphere time; dam, half-sister to very smart Greenland Park, won over 6f in
Ireland; favourite when second in autumn maiden events at Newmarket and
Folkestone; stays 6f; acts on heavy going. *W. O'Gorman.*

FORGET ME NOT 2 br.f. Mansingh 120–Marita (Right Royal V 135) (1982 **73 §**
5g³ 5f* 5fg³ 7d 6g 6f) Apr 3; 5,700Y; small filly; half-sister to several winners
in France, notably very useful 1979 2-y-o 5.5f to 7f winner Koboko (by Balidar);
dam won over 9f and 10.5f; dead-heated with Student Venture in 3-runner minor
event at Pontefract in May; showed signs of going wrong way afterwards; went
to post very freely fourth and sixth outings and put up temperamental display
in preliminaries on fifth; sold 2,200 gns Ascot September Sales, probably for
export to Italy. *B. Hobbs.*

FORLORN RAIDER 3 gr.g. Forlorn River 124–Vicki Ann (Floribunda 136) —
(1981 5d 5d 6f 1982 6g 7f 7g) leggy, narrow gelding; poor plater; sold, probably for export to Norway, 820 gns Doncaster June Sales. *W. Holden.*

FORT GARRY 3 b.c. Relkino 131–Partridge Brook 109 (Birdbrook 110) (1981 **74**
5g 6d⁴ 6g² 7g 7h² 8s* 8s 1982 7g 8fg 12fg 10f 10.2g 10.8fg*) small, quite attractive
colt; dropped in class when easily landing odds in seller at Warwick in July; sold
3,600 gns afterwards, reportedly to race in Switzerland; not certain to stay
1½m; acts on any going. *B. Hills.*

FOR THE RECORD 3 ch.c. Record Token 128–Pirana (High Hat 131) (1981 **65**
7fg 7g 1982 7.6f 7fg³ 8f 8d 8f 7f⁴ 7fg 8g² 7fg) medium-sized, attractive colt;
excellent mover; plating-class maiden; stays 1m; has run respectably for an
apprentice; blinkered last 2 starts; sold 4,300 gns Newmarket Autumn Sales.
B. Swift.

FORT LAMY 3 b.c. African Sky 124–Mayfield Girl (Le Prince 98) (1981 6fg **67**
5g 7d⁴ 1982 8g 8g 7f 8d² 7g) sturdy, well-made colt; quite a modest maiden;
possibly finds 1m on soft ground just too far. *B. Hills.*

FORT LAUDERDALE (USA) 2 br.c. Holy War–Sis Gallamar (Royal Dorimar) —
(1982 6fg) Feb 3; lengthy, good-topped colt; third foal; half-brother to a winner in Puerto Rico; dam ran 3 times; sire, brother to Accipiter, won 3 times at
up to 7f from 51 starts; unquoted, very burly and green, remote ninth of 13 to
Castanet in newcomers race at Goodwood in September. *M. Francis.*

FORT NAYEF 2 b.c. Sharpen Up 127–Sacred Way 88 (Milesian 125) (1982 **73 p**
7g) Mar 14; 37,000Y; tall colt; half-brother to 2 winners, including very useful
1m and 1½m winner Highway (by High Top); dam 2-y-o 5f winner; 7/1, stayed
on nicely when never-dangerous 5 lengths fifth of 15 to Killanin's Lass in £3,600
mixed-aged race at Newmarket in October; sure to improve. *J. Dunlop.*

FORWARD (USA) 3 b.c. Caro 133–Tipping Time (Commanding II) (1981 **104 d**
7d 7fg 8.2fg³ 8g² 1982 8.2fg 8g 10f² 12f* 12f³ 13g* 12f 12fg⁴ 13d 12g) well-
made colt; good walker; has a round action; useful handicapper at his best;
showed a good turn of foot to win at Thirsk in May and Ayr (odds on) in July;
made astonishing late progress to be length third of 20 to Mubarak of Kuwait in
King George V Stakes (Handicap) at Royal Ascot in between; will be suited by
1¾m; acts on firm going; ran moderately towards end of season. *J. Dunlop.*

FOR YOUR EYES 2 b.f. Gay Fandango 132–Miller's Lass 103 (Mill Reef 141) **85**
(1982 6fg 7fg² 7f) Mar 31; IR 92,000Y; quite attractive, good-topped filly;
second foal; half-sister to 3-y-o 11f winner Mistress Kipling (by Nonoalco); dam,
half-sister to Play It Safe and Providential, won at up to 11.5f in Ireland; made
much of running and kept on gamely when neck second of 12 to Game Dame in
maiden race at Wolverhampton in July; second favourite, scratched down to
start when 12 lengths fifth of 16 behind Challanging in similar event at Yarmouth the following month; should stay 1¼m. *P. Walwyn.*

FOUR FOR MUSIC 3 ch.c. Music Boy 124–Visitation 84 (Tarqogan 125)   **79**
(1981 5s 5f 5.3f 5fg⁴ 6g² 7d 6fg³ 6fg 5d² 5g²   1982 5d 7d² 6fg* 6fg 6fg 5fg 6f 6g
6fg) compact, fair sort; stormed clear in final furlong to beat Anstruther comfortably in handicap at Newmarket in April; well beaten most subsequent
starts; best form at sprint distances though probably stays 7f; acts on a firm
and a soft surface; best in blinkers. *P. Haslam.*

FOUR OF A KIND 6 b.g. Levmoss 133–Alauda (Shantung 132) (1981 NR   —
1982 10fg 12g) big, rangy gelding; staying maiden; very lightly raced since his
3-y-o days; best form with some give in the ground; has been tried in blinkers.
W. Musson.

FOX 3 ch.c. Free State 125–Red Velvet 114 (Red God 128§) (1981 6fg 6g   1982   **84**
7fg³ 8g³ 8fg³ 8f³ 8fg² 8fg² 10g* 10.1g) big, rangy colt; good walker; placed in
varied company before winning 14-runner maiden race at Newmarket in August;
stays 1¼m; gives impression he may prove best with some give in the ground
(looked unhappy on firm ground fifth start); sold 12,000 gns Ascot September
Sales. *P. Walwyn.*

FOXHOLLOW 2 b.f. Pampapaul 121–Pendula 76 (Tamerlane 128) (1982 5d 5f   **54**
5g 5g 7g³) Mar 12; IR 5,800Y; small filly; half-sister to a winning plater and a
winner in Sweden; dam won at up to 1¼m; 2¼ lengths third of 12 to Fairham in
seller at Wolverhampton in October, first sign of ability; sold 1,150 gns Doncaster
October Sales, probably for export to Scandinavia. *W. Wharton.*

FOXTROT TANGO 4 ch.g. Patch 129–Gallant Breeze (Mongo) (1981 9f   1982   —
9f 10fg² 12d 9f 10d⁴ 13f 10d⁴ 14v 16s) strong gelding; in frame in minor event at
Pontefract, ladies race at Tralee and handicap at Leopardstown; probably
stays 2m; trained by Mrs J. Pitman first 3 outings. *Miss J. Morgan, Ireland.*

FOXY QUEEN 3 b.f. Simbir 130–Riboellina (Ribero 126) (1981 NR 1982   —
10.1fg) second foal; half-sister to 6f and 7f winner Lady of the Isle (by Pitskelly);
dam never ran; unquoted when behind in 12-runner minor event won by Sabre
Dance at Windsor in June. *G. Blum.*

FRANCA 8 b.m. Frankincense 120–Maltese Cat 58 (Pall Mall 132) (1981 NR   —
1982 8fg) very lightly-raced mare; won handicap at Chepstow at 5 yrs (rated 73);
prominent for a long way before finishing tailed off in ladies race at Ascot in July,
first outing since; stays 1m; well suited by top-of-the-ground conditions and a
sharp track; has been to stud. *J. Thorne.*

FRANCESCO 6 b.h. Royal and Regal–Rising Lark (Ballymoss 136) (1981   **87**
14f² 12f* 12f³ 14fg* 12g*   1982 12g² 13f* 14fg 12f² 14f* 14f 13f³ 12fg² 14fg³
12f² 12g) strong, deep-girthed, round-barrelled horse; fair handicapper; won
very easily at Nottingham in April and Yarmouth (only 2 ran) in June; stays
well; acts on any going; sometimes sweats up; good mount for an inexperienced
rider; has won 4 times at Yarmouth. *H. Cecil.*

FRANCISCUS 5 br.h. Lord Gayle 124–Frances Jordan 102 (Prince Regent 129)   **57**
(1981 16s 18fg 14g 13fg 12g 14f 14g³   1982 12d² 13fg³ 12fg) neat ex-Irish horse;
ridden by 7-lb claimer when placed in handicaps at Folkestone and Nottingham
in spring, best efforts for a while; stays 1¾m; ideally suited by some give in the
ground; blinkered sixth start at 4 yrs. *A. Jarvis.*

FRANCIS FURY 2 ch.c. Touch Paper 113–Dinar (Grey Sovereign 128§)   **79** d
(1982 5f³ 5f² 5f 5fg 7.9f 6s) small, workmanlike colt; poor walker but excellent
mover; half-brother to a winner in Spain; dam ran once; placed twice in maiden
races at Down Royal in May, notably going down by a head to Atan Rose in
14-runner event; last on subsequent starts, including in Windsor Castle Stakes at
Royal Ascot, and seems to have deteriorated. *J. Scott, Ireland.*

FRANK BERRY 4 ch.c. Lorenzaccio 130–Bora Bora 91 (Hethersett 134) (1981   **43**
7s 7fg 7d 11.7s 7fg³ 8g* 8.2d² 7f³ 7g 8s 7g⁴   1982 7g 8g² 7g³ 7.6f 8.2fg 7f 7fg 7g²
8s) lengthy, attractive colt; good walker; placed in varied races, including
amateur riders event; soundly beaten in selling handicap final start; bred to stay
at least 1¼m; acts on any going except possibly soft; best in blinkers. *G. Lewis.*

FRANKIE 9 br.g. Crooner 119–Old Dutch 91 (Fastnet Rock 123) (1981 NR   —
1982 12fg) poor handicapper nowadays; stays 1¼m; acts on firm going; has worn
blinkers. *A. W. Jones.*

FRANTONIOS 2 ch.g. Thatch 136–Slavissima (Sea Hawk II 131) (1982 8g 8g³)   **96**
May 6; IR 35,000Y; useful-looking gelding; has a round action; half-brother to
3 winners, including 3-y-o 1m and 1¼m winner Bold Hawk (by Bold Lad, Ire) and

Irish 1¼m to 2m winner Rommels Star (by Arratos); dam never ran; 33/1 and apparently still in need of race, was always prominent and kept on well when 1½ lengths third of 19 to Coming And Going in maiden event at Newmarket in October; will stay 1¼m; gelded at end of season. *J. Hindley.*

FRAYLAND 2 b.f. Sallust 134–Flying Escape 74 (Hook Money 124) (1982 5f 5f 5v) Apr 22; 7,200Y; compact filly; half-sister to 2 winners, including fairly useful miler Chop-Chop (by Birdbrook); dam at her best at 2 yrs; behind in maiden races, one at Folkestone. *J. Benstead.* —

FREDERIC THE GREAT 2 b.g. Ballymore 123–Bold Words (Bold Ruler) (1982 7g 7d) May 10; 8,000Y; half-brother to 1m winner Essam (by Sallust); dam won twice at up to 9f in USA; ridden by 7-lb claimer, last in maiden races at Yarmouth in August. *M. Ryan.* —

FREEBIE 2 ch.f. Free State 125–Mehir 71 (King's Company 124) (1982 6g 6fg 6g 7g 5v 6g) May 29; 1,250F, 1,250Y; stocky, short-legged filly; moderate plater; best run on final outing. *M. Haynes.* 58

FREEDOM GLORY 2 ch.f. Hittite Glory 125–Liberty Light 82 (Henry the Seventh 125) (1982 5f³ 5f² 5f 5fg⁴ 5f 5fg 6g 6g⁴ 6f⁴(dis) 6fg 6d⁴ 8.2fg⁴ 8fg⁴ 7fg* 8s) Mar 21; 4,100Y; neat filly; second foal; dam won at up to 1m; won 20-runner seller at Redcar (no bid) in September; best form at 7f; seems to act on any going, with possible exception of soft; blinkered eighth to tenth outings. *T. Fairhurst.* 63

FREEDOM KEY (NZ) 5 br.m. Dusky Hunter–Superform (Clarification 110) (1981 NR 1982 8g) New-Zealand bred mare; sister to very useful jumper Narribinni; soundly beaten in amateur riders race at Warwick in June on first outing over here. *D. Elsworth.* —

FREEFALL 2 ch.f. Air Trooper 115–Rota 58 (Reliance II 137) (1982 6fg) Apr 7; second foal; dam won 1¼m claiming race; unquoted and backward, no show in 18-runner maiden race won by Julia Flyte at Salisbury in September. *W. Wightman.* —

FREEMANTLE PARK 3 gr.f. Royal Palace 131–Charter Island 88 (Runnymede 123) (1981 NR 1982 8.2fg 10f 10.6s 12d) big, lengthy filly; half-sister to very useful Watership Down (by Murrayfield), a winner at up to 1m in France, and to a winner in Italy; dam stayed 7f well; behind in varied company; sold 510 gns Doncaster November Sales. *E. Incisa.* —

FREE PRESS 3 b.g. Free State 125–Miss McWorden 75 (Worden II 129) (1981 6g 7fg⁴ 7fg³ 8d 1982 10s* 10g* 10.6fg* 10fg 10f³ 10.1fg²) lengthy gelding; successful in maiden race at Nottingham and handicaps at Pontefract and Haydock in the spring; placed in 2 more handicaps afterwards; not raced after June; will stay 1½m; acts on any going; usually sweats up. *I. Balding.* 80

FREE RANGE 3 gr.f. Birdbrook 110–Micky Goleah (Quorum 126) (1981 5d 5fg 5.3f 5fg⁴ 6g 6g³ 1982 5h 6g 6fg* 5fg² 5g* 6fg² 5g 5fg 5g⁴ 6g 5fg) leggy, lengthy filly; plater; bought in 4,000 gns after narrowly winning apprentice seller at Windsor in July; raced creditably in better company several times afterwards, including when scoring in handicap at Windsor again later in month; stays 6f; good mount for an inexperienced rider. *J. Holt.* 62

FREEWAY FOLLY (USA) 3 ch.f. One For All–Forliane (Forli) (1981 8d 1982 11g² 10.5fg⁴ 12fg² 10.5g³ 12f 9g² 9fg³ 8g 9s³) lengthy filly; in frame in varied company, putting up easily best effort when 2½ lengths third to Vidor in Prix de Royaumont at Chantilly in June on fourth start; stays 1½m; seems to act on any going; blinkered eighth outing. *B. Hills.* 82

FRENCH CURRENT (AUS) 3 b.c. Without Fear 128–Cap D'Antibes (Better Boy 91) (1981 6fg 1982 8fg 8f* 10.5f³ 8f) strong, rangy, attractive colt; usually impresses in appearance; lightly raced but is fairly useful; always going nicely and ran on well to beat Silly Steven impressively by 3 lengths going away in 11-runner minor event at Sandown in April; not disgraced in £4,200 race at York in May next time but finished behind in valuable handicap won by Farioffa at Newmarket in July; may prove best at distances short of 1¼m; yet to race on an easy surface; returned to Australia. *B. Hills.* 96

FRENCH GEMMA 2 b.f. Manado 130–French Cracker (Klairon 131) (1982 7f 8fg 8fg) Feb 22; IR 10,000Y; small filly; first foal; dam won over 1¼m in Ireland; in rear in maiden and minor events. *P. Kelleway.* —

FRENCH GENT 3 b.c. Sassafras 135–Nom de Plume 70 (Aureole 132) (1981 **105**
5d* 6g* 6f 7g 7s* 1982 12.3g 12fg³ 8fg² 10g⁴ 12g 10g⁴) compact colt; doesn't
always impress in paddock; useful handicapper on his day; put up best effort
when strong-finishing 4¼ lengths fourth of 17 to Cannon King in valuable event at
Newmarket in October on final start; suited by middle distances and some give
in the ground; takes a strong hold; trained by M. H. Easterby first 2 starts.
G. Harwood.

FRENCH GREY (USA) 2 gr.g. Al Hattab–Francie T (Grey Dawn II 132) —
(1982 8s 8s) May 10; $15,000Y; well-made, robust gelding; third foal; brother
to a winner in USA; dam unraced granddaughter of champion handicap mare
Mar-kell; soundly beaten in maiden events at Sandown (dwelt) in October and
Leicester in November. *H. Candy.*

FRENCH KNOT 4 b.g. Take a Reef 127–Merette 63 (Runnymede 123) (1981 **62**
10v* 10s* 9.4g³ 11fg² 10g⁴ 11g 10.5s 11d* 12d 1982 13s³ 10.6s³) neat gelding;
quite a moderate handicapper; probably stays 13f; acts on a firm surface but is
well suited by plenty of give in the ground; wears blinkers; sold 1,600 gns
Ascot 2nd June Sales. *J. W. Watts.*

FRENCH PLEAT 2 b.f. Take a Reef 127–Boudoir 95 (Klairon 131) (1982 **101**
6g⁴ 6f³ 7fg³ 7d²) Apr 10; lightly-made, racy filly; third foal; half-sister to
two 2-y-o winners, including fairly useful 1978 6f winner Lady's Slipper (by
Hotfoot); dam won at up to 1m and stayed 1¼m; in frame in each of her 4 races,
putting up by far her best performance when chasing home easy winner Travelguard in well-contested nursery at Doncaster in October; will stay 1¼m; has
little scope. *B. Hobbs.*

FRENCH SCRIBE (USA) 3 ch.f. Arts and Letters–Chez Elle (Mongo) (1982 **64**
7fg 7g² 7v 1982 10fg 8.5f 9g³ 11g³ 10s* 12.2f³ 12g⁴ 20g³) lengthy filly; ran on
dourly to win maiden race at Yarmouth in August; third in 2 handicaps afterwards; stays very well; acts on any going. *J. Hindley.*

FRENCH SPRING 3 ch.g. Roi Soleil 125–May Double 54 (King's Bench 132) —
(1981 NR 1982 10g 8g 10d 8.2s) 3,200F; strong gelding; half-brother to
fairly useful 5f to 7f winner Double River (by Forlorn River) and a winner in
Brazil; dam won 7f seller; well beaten in minor event and 3 maiden races in the
North. *M. W. Easterby.*

FRENCH TOUCH 5 ch.m. Dieu Soleil 111–Fabric 77 (Sheshoon 132) (1981 **45**
5s 6g 6g 6fg 5g 6g 5fg 5f 5d* 5g 1982 6g⁴ 5fg 6f 5f* 7g 5g⁴ 5fg) neat mare;
plater; bought in 950 gns after winning at Edinburgh in June; stays 6f (never in
race over 7f); acts on any going. *A. Balding.*

FRESH FORD 3 b.f. Pampapaul 121–Independence 64 (Runnymede 123) —
(1981 7fg 7f 8fg 7g 1982 8fg 8f 12d) lightly-made filly; in rear in maiden and
minor events; blinkered second start; sold 460 gns Newmarket July Sales.
B. Hanbury.

FRIDAY STREET 3 ch.g. Town Crier 119–Honey Palm 86 (Honeyway 125) **69**
(1981 5fg⁴ 5s 6g³ 7g 6f³ 6g 7fg⁴ 5.3d³ 6d* 1982 7fg 7.3fg 6f² 7f³ 7d⁴ 10.2g⁴ 8.3g
8.3g) quite attractive gelding; promises to stay 1¼m; seems to act on any going;
sweated up but ran respectably fifth start. *R. Smyth.*

FRIENDLY ANAX 2 b.c. Anax 120–Friendly Queen 73 (Be Friendly 130) —
(1982 5s 6g) Apr 17; 520 2-y-o; second foal; dam, best at 5f on flat, stayed 2½m
over hurdles; always behind in maiden events at Sandown (tailed off) and Newmarket in October. *O. Jorgensen.*

FRIENDLY BOBBY 2 b.g. Coded Scrap 90–Friendly Jester 90 (Be Friendly **80**
130) (1982 6f 6fg 5f* 5g 5g⁴ 5d² 5g) Feb 23; tall, leggy, rather narrow gelding;
first reported foal; dam, half-sister to the dam of Jester, won twice over 5f; won
maiden race at Catterick in July; ran well in nurseries subsequently until failing
to show in race won by Air Command at Edinburgh in October on final appearance; evidently best at 5f; seems to act on any going. *T. Fairhurst.*

FRIENDLY FUN 7 ro.g. Be Friendly 130–Primerva (Primera 131) (1981 5s 5s 5d **73**
5d³ 5d 6d 5g 5fg 5f³ 6fg⁴ 5f³ 5g 5g 5g⁴ 5d 6d 5g 1982 5g 5d² 6fg 6g² 6f 5g 6g 5g
5fg³ 5d* 5d 5s 6s 6d 5s³) sprint handicapper; beat Westering Breeze by a length
at Ripon in August (made all) and was placed on several other occasions; stays 6f;
acts on any going, but is well suited by some give in the ground; effective with or
without blinkers (usually wears them nowadays). *N. Crump.*

FRIENDLY GLEN   4 b.f. Furry Glen 121–Gay Friend (Be Friendly 130)   (1981   —
NR 1982 8fg 10f 13.8f)   750F, 1,900Y; big, rather plain filly; has a round
action; first foal; dam placed over 5f and 7f in Ireland at 2 yrs; towards rear in
maiden races. *J. Parkes.*

FRIENDLY HENRY   2 ch.g. Be Friendly 130–Henry's Lady 64 (Henry the   —
Seventh 125)   (1982 5d 5g 8s)   Apr 8; big, plain, good-bodied gelding; poor
walker; first live foal; dam won over 15f; in rear in autumn maiden races in the
Midlands. *B. Richmond.*

FRIENDLY LASS   2 ch.f. Be Friendly 130–Friston Mist (Silver Cloud 121)   —
(1982 5g 7.6v)   small, useful-looking filly; first foal; dam winning hurdler; in
rear in £3,400 event at Sandown in July and maiden race at Lingfield in October.
P. Mitchell.

FRIGHTENING   2 ch.g. Habat 127–Well Off (Welsh Pageant 132)   (1982   —
5fg 5fg)   May 14; 800Y; compact gelding; half-brother to good Belgian winner
Sharpset (by Sharpen Up); towards rear in sellers at Beverley in June; exported
to Malaysia. *K. Stone.*

FRIVOLOUS RELATION (USA)   4 b. or br.f. Buckpasser–Aunt Edith 128   ?
(Primera 131)   (1981 10f 10f 12.3g² 1982 12d* 12v 12s)   attractive filly; not
the best of movers; won 18-runner event at Cagnes-sur-Mer in February; was
suited by 1½m and some give underfoot; in foal to Kings Lake. *J. Dunlop.*

FROGMORE SWEET   2 ch.f. Morston 125–Sweet Relief 90 (Sweet Revenge 129)   —
(1982 5fg 5f 5g 7f 10d)   Mar 30; 1,600Y; neat filly; first foal; dam won three
6f races; soundly beaten, including in a 1¼m seller. *R. Thompson.*

FRONTLET   2 b.f. Moulton 128–Facade 99 (Double Jump 131)   (1982 5fg 5g 5fg   60
5fg 5fg 6g 6fg 7fg² 7g⁴)   Apr 29; 700Y; compact filly; half-sister to a winner in
Malaysia; dam stayed 6f; plater; put up best effort when 2 lengths second of 15
to Viceroy Princess at Chepstow in September; suited by 7f and should stay 1m;
blinkered seventh outing. *M. Bolton.*

FRUITBERRY   2 ch.f. Filiberto 123–Wimberry 78 (Hotfoot 126)   (1982 6g 6g³   44
7f⁴ 8.2fg)   Mar 22; 1,350F; fair sort; second foal; dam stayed well; poor plater;
will stay 1½m; acts on firm going. *P. Rohan.*

FUDDLED   3 br.f. Malacate 131–Egualita 111 (Democratic 124)   (1981 7g 8s   72
7g 1982 8fg³ 12fg¹ 12b⁴ 11fg³ 12.2f)   neat, attractive filly; readily justified
favouritism in 14-runner maiden race at Redcar in June; suited by 1½m; below
form final start (July). *B. Hills.*

FUEGO LAD   2 b.g. Legal Eagle 126–Conyer (Connaught 130)   (1982 5fg 6f   —
8d)   May 26; lightly-made gelding; behind in maiden races and a seller; sold
320 gns Ascot November Sales. *P. Taylor.*

FUGACIOUS   4 ch.c. Sallust 134–Phantasmagoria 65 (Le Haar 126)   (1981 6fg   —
7d 6g 5v 7fg 5g 6f 9g 1982 7g⁴ 12fg 10.1g)   small, stocky colt; little worthwhile
form in 1981, including in a seller; ran respectably first 2 starts in 1982, on
second occasion in amateur riders race at Newmarket in July; promises to stay
beyond 1½m; seems to act on any going; sometimes blinkered. *M. Hinchliffe.*

FULL BRIGADE   2 b.c. Full of Hope 125–Leaplet (Alcide 136)   (1982 7d 7f 8s)   —
Mar 25; 3,000Y; lengthy colt; poor walker; first foal; dam unraced half-sister to
very useful King's Leap; no worthwhile form in maiden and minor events. *R.
Hannon.*

FULL EXTENT (USA)   3 b.c. Full Out–Mary Biz (T. V. Lark)   (1981 5g⁴   103
6fg* 6fg* 7fg* 6d* 7fg 1982 8f* 8fg 8g) $67,000Y; strong, sturdy colt; excellent
mover with a long, raking stride; third foal; half-brother to 1m and 9f winner
Angle Fire (by Angle Light) and a winner by Shecky Greene; dam, unplaced 4
times, is half-sister to smart Terrible Tiger; very useful performer at his best;
having first outing since chipping a bone in near-fore on final start at 2 yrs, made
all and never looked in danger of defeat when beating Knave of Trumps by ¾
length in 5-runner Timeform Race Card Stakes at Thirsk in April; reportedly
suffering from a trapped nerve when dropping out in closing stages to finish in
rear behind Zino in 2,000 Guineas at Newmarket and behind Dara Monarch in
Airlie/Coolmore Irish 2,000 Guineas at the Curragh following month; subse-

*Timeform Race Card Stakes, Thirsk—Full Extent makes all
to defeat Knave of Trumps in this classic trial*

quently had trouble with his back and has been retired; stayed 1m; seemed to act on any going; genuine. *S. Norton.*

FULL NIGHT (USA) 2 b.c. Full Out–Nuit Blanche (Gray Phantom) (1982 6g⁴ 6g³ 6f* 6g) Mar 9; $52,000Y, $60,000 2-y-o; half-brother to 2 winners, including smart 1979 American 2-y-o Nuit d'Amour (by Restless Native); dam stakes-placed sprint winner at 2 yrs; won 4-runner maiden race at Ostend in August; will stay 7f. *M. Jarvis.* **77**

FULL OF FORTUNE 3 b.f. Full of Hope 125–Alisma II (Alizier 131) (1981 8s 10s 1982 9f 12f 12f 9g) poor form, including in a seller; wears blinkers; sweated up badly third start. *C. James.* **—**

FULL OF LOVE 3 br.f. Full of Hope 125–Lovage (Linacre 133) (1981 7g 6d 1982 11g 8g 8.5f 12.2g 10.1d 10.8fg⁴) tall, lengthy filly; plater; stays 1¼m; claimed £1,510 after final start and subsequently sold 775 gns Ascot September Sales. *D. Elsworth.* **—**

FULL OF STARS 2 b.c. Tennyson 124–Full of Courage (Bold Ruler) (1982 9d⁴ 8s*) Apr 12; tall, rangy colt; half-brother to 2 winners, including very smart 1975 French staying 2-y-o Four Spades (by Sassafras), subsequently successful in USA; dam lightly-raced daughter of champion American 2-y-o and 3-y-o filly Doubledogdare; always well placed when winning maiden race at Longchamp in October by a neck from Mille Balles; has plenty of scope and will improve over middle distances. *F. Boutin, France.* **?**

FULL RAINBOW (USA) 2 b.c. Forli–Loop (Round Table) (1982 7g³ 8g² 8s* 8d²) Mar 10; $150,000Y; good-topped, quite attractive colt; third foal; half-brother to a minor winner; dam, minor stakes winner at up to 1m, is sister to 3 stakes winners, including very smart 5f to 1¼m winner Duel; stayed on strongly when winning 19-runner maiden race at Warwick in October by 2 lengths from Trusty Troubadour; beaten short head by High Cannon in 16-runner minor event at Redcar the following month; will stay beyond 1m; acts on soft going and has yet to race on a firm surface; a progressive sort, likely to make a useful 3-y-o. *M. Stoute.* **97**

FULVIO (USA) 2 b.c. Full Out–Instant Beauty (Pronto) (1982 7f⁴ 7d⁴ 6v⁴) Apr 7; $132,000Y; strong, well-made, quite attractive colt; third foal; dam unraced half-sister to St Leger winner Boucher; fourth in varied company in the autumn, on final occasion beaten 3½ lengths by Joy Hour in maiden race at Folkestone; will stay beyond 7f. *P. Walwyn.* **82**

FUN FAIR 2 br.c. Comedy Star 121–Equal Chance 95 (Hitting Away) (1982 6f 6s 6v) Mar 5; 19,000Y; brother to a poor animal and half-brother to several winners here and abroad, including useful 1979 Irish 2-y-o 5f performer Jay Bird **65**

(by Hot Spark); dam sprinter; plating-class maiden; best race in blinkers final start; sold German International Bloodstock 4,200 gns Newmarket Autumn Sales. *I. Balding.*

FUNNY SPRING 7 b.g. Rheingold 137–Lotus 79 (Aureole 132) (1981 10g² 10g³ 11s 10s 10g 1982 10s* 10f³ 10g 10d) stocky gelding; carries a lot of condition; fair handicapper; won Rosebery Stakes at Kempton in April in quite good style by 3 lengths from King's Ride; about 2 lengths third of 5 behind Aperitivo at Sandown later in month, easily best subsequent effort (off course almost 5 months before final outing); best form at up to 1¼m; acts on any going, but is well suited by soft; genuine but needs strong handling and seems to go particularly well for W. Carson; trained over hurdles and first start of 1982 by G. Pritchard-Gordon. *L. Cumani.* **81**

FUNTLEY 2 b.g. Streak 119–Belinda Pocket 84 (Pampered King 121) (1982 5g⁴ 5fg 5fg 6d* 7f 6fg 7d) May 12; 480F, 1,450Y; big, workmanlike gelding; closely related to fair 1975 2-y-o 5f winner Shernden (by Runnymede) and half-brother to 2 more 2-y-o winners; dam won over 5f at 2 yrs; disputed lead throughout when winning 21-runner maiden auction event at Nottingham in June by 1½ lengths from Miss Annie; 4½ lengths fifth of 8 to The Quiet Don in minor event at Leicester the following month, next outing and only subsequent form; stays 7f; appears to act on any going; gelded after final appearance. *B. Palling.* **73**

FURRY FRIEND (USA) 2 b.f. Bold Bidder–Funny Cat (Tom Cat) (1982 6g) Jan 8; $495,000F; rangy, short-legged filly; first produce; dam, smart winner at up to 9f, comes from a very successful family; second favourite although on backward side, outpaced until running on nicely in closing stages when 7 lengths fifth of 16 to Jemeela in maiden race at Newbury in August; will be suited by 7f+; sure to improve. *R. Hern.* **72 p**

FUTURE SPA 3 b.c. Ballymore 123–Breakage (Breakspear II) (1981 8s 8.5s* 1982 10s² 12g⁴ 11.5fg⁴ 13d* 14s⁴) 10,000Y; brother to Irish 7f and 1¼m winner Bennaunmore and half-brother to a winner; dam won over 6f at 2yrs in Ireland; beat Double Wrapped by 1½ lengths in valuable handicap at Tralee in September; ran creditably most other starts, notably when 3 lengths second of 15 to easy winner Golden Fleece in Sean Graham Ballymoss Stakes at the Curragh and remote fourth of 10 to Touching Wood in Jefferson Smurfit Memorial Irish St Leger on same course; stays 1¾m; acts well on soft ground. *P. Prendergast, Ireland.* **95**

G

GABITAT 4 ch.c. Arch Sculptor 123–Golden Hostess (Kythnos 126) (1981 6d 6v* 6s 6f 6fg³ 6f³ 6fg* 7g³ 6fg² 6g 6d 6g 8s 6g 1982 6f* 6g* 6f 6f 6f 6d 6d³ 6g 5v) useful-looking colt; has been hobdayed; successful in handicaps at Newbury and Kempton in May, on latter course making all up favoured far rails and holding on by a length from Worlingworth in Victor Wild Stakes; subsequently ran well in much better company in Cork and Orrery Stakes at Royal Ascot, William Hill July Cup at Newmarket (less than 3 lengths fifth of 16 behind Sharpo), Prix de Meautry at Deauville and Goldene Peitsche at Baden-Baden (1¾ lengths third to Tina's Pet); best at 6f; acts on any going but goes particularly well on firm; blinkered nowadays; ran moderately last 2 outings. *B. Gubby.* **108**

GABLES FLIGHT 2 gr.f. Tack On 114–Gables Grey 66 (Colonist II 126) (1982 5d 5g) Mar 5; sister to Gables Star, a winner of 5f seller here and subsequently successful in Belgium; dam moderate winning hurdler; in rear in 10-runner minor events at Folkestone in the spring. *R. Smyth.* **—**

GADINA 2 ch.f. Gay Fandango 132–Danova (Dan Cupid 132) (1982 5f⁴ 6g 7fg) Feb 12; IR 3,100F, IR 6,000Y; compact filly; half-sister to 2 winners in France by Labus, including 1981 2-y-o 7f winner Dannyour; dam French 10.5f winner; no sign of ability, including in a seller; blinkered third start; sold 400 gns Doncaster October Sales. *D. Morley.* **—**

GAELIC HARP 7 ch.g. Paddy's Birthday 110–Condicote Lane (Sunny Way 120) (1981 16f 16fg 16.5fg 1982 16f) workmanlike gelding; winner over jumps; behind in poor maiden races; bandaged only outing of 1982. *G. Lockerbie.* **—**

GAELIC JEWEL 2 br.f. Scottish Rifle 127–Red Ruby 113 (Tudor Melody 129) (1982 7g) Mar 21; rather lightly-made, quite attractive filly; second foal; half- **— p**

339

sister to 3-y-o 1m winner The Ripleyite (by Northfields); dam, half-sister to smart sprinter Laser Light, was very useful miler; 16/1, ran on steadily without being given hard race when never-dangerous ninth of 22 behind Toveris in maiden event at Newmarket in October; will stay 1m; sure to improve. *J. Dunlop.*

GAINFORD 2 b.c. The Brianstan 128–Queen Swallow 58 (Le Levanstell 122) (1982 5d 5fg 5f⁴ 5f* 5f* 6f³ 6f²) Feb 8; 3,600Y; small, strong colt; first reported foal; dam, closely related to My Swallow, was unplaced from 5f to 2m; won sellers at Thirsk (no bid) and Carlisle (bought in 3,000 gns) in May; not seen out after June; stays 6f; acts on firm going; wears blinkers. *C. Spares.* **71**

GALA FERIA 3 b.f. Native Bazaar 122–Galactic 52 (Star Moss 122) (1981 NR 1982 8fg) first foal; dam plater on flat and over hurdles; 20/1 and in need of run when last of 13 to Over the Limit in maiden race at Salisbury in September. *G. Balding.* **—**

GALA GIRL 2 b.f. Welsh Pageant 132–Damiana 84 (Mourne 126) (1982 7f 7g 8f) Apr 18; tall, lengthy filly; fourth live foal; dam 1m winner; behind in maiden and minor events. *P. Cole.* **—**

GALA LAD 8 ch.g. Gala Performance–Land 62 (Baldric II 131) (1981 12g 12s 12s 12v 12d 1982 12g 13g 15.8d) poor middle-distance handicapper; blind in right eye; acts on any going; suitable mount for a boy; has worn blinkers. *N. Bycroft.* **—**

GALA RAG 5 b.m. Ragstone 128–Gala Premiere § (By Thunder! 122) (1981 NR 1982 12d 13.4g) leggy, sparely-made mare; half-sister to several winners here and abroad; dam ran only twice; looked rather lean when remote sixth of 15 behind Big-Ed in amateur riders race at Beverley in July, first outing. *D. Francis.* **—**

GALE BOY 2 b.g. Bay Express 132–Morning Cloud 79 (Hard Tack 111§) (1982 5fg 5g 5g 6g 5s 6s⁴ 8s) Apr 19; fair sort; half-brother to fair 1978 2-y-o 7f winner River Canyon (by Rheingold); dam placed at up to 9f in England and Ireland; plating-class maiden; stays 6f; acts on soft going; gelded after final outing. *J. Berry.* **71**

GALETZKY 2 br.f. Radetzky 123–Gallant Bid 109 (Galivanter 131) (1982 6fg 6g³ 7f 6fg⁴ 6fg) Mar 12; 4,600Y; big, well-made filly; second live foal; half-sister to 1m winner Rebid (by Jimmy Reppin); dam, half-sister to Peleid and Coup de Feu, stayed 1½m; in frame in maiden race at Redcar in August and nursery at Haydock in September; should stay at least 1m. *C. Brittain.* **77**

GALLANT NATIVE 2 b.c. Pitskelly 122–Nativity 91 (Native Royalty) (1982 7d 6d) Apr 6; 11,500Y; useful-looking colt; first foal; dam lightly-raced 2-y-o 5f winner; no worthwhile form in maiden events at Leicester in September and Doncaster (ninth of 22) in October. *J. W. Watts.* **—**

GALLANT RELIC (USA) 7 ch.g. Gallant Man–Relieve (Relic) (1981 NR 1982 10f 17.1f) plating-class maiden in 1979; not disgraced in a seller on first outing of 1982. *B. Forsey.* **—**

GALLANT SPECIAL (USA) 2 ch.c. Gallant Romeo–Special Account (Buckpasser) (1982 6f² 6fg* 6f* 6fg) Apr 27; quite attractive, well-made colt; has a nice, easy action; third foal; brother to American 3-y-o Bank On Love; dam, winner over 1m, is sister to champion 2-y-o filly Numbered Account and 2 other stakes winners; looked a very useful colt when trouncing a small field in Black Duck Stakes at York in July and when comfortably beating his 3 opponents (Solar Rock, Aragon and Think On) in £25,000 Richmond Stakes at Goodwood later in month; never looked likely to take a hand and was rather disappointing when last of 6 to Deep Roots in Prix Morny at Deauville in August, but reportedly **114**

Richmond Stakes, Goodwood—Gallant Special coasts to victory over Solar Rock and Aragon

Mr W. R. Hawn's "Gallant Special"

coughed and had a temperature afterwards; will stay 7f; yet to race on an easy surface; sent to USA. *R. Armstrong.*

GALLEA 4 b.g. Prince de Galles 125–Russellia (Red God 128§) (1981 10s 10s 10s 10.8fg 10fg 8.3fg 8f* 8d³ 7f* 8fg* 8f 8g* 7g 8d⁴ 8.2s 1982 8.2g 8fg 8f 8f 6g 7f 8fg³ 7.2s⁴ 8v) leggy, narrow gelding; ran best races of 1982 when in frame in handicaps at Redcar in September (apprentices) and Haydock in October (apprentice ridden); stays 1m; evidently acts on any going. *N. Guest.* **55**

GALLIC WIT (USA) 2 ch.c. Roberto 131–Gallina 120 (Raise A Native) (1982 7d 7fg² 7g 7fg* 8d³) May 13; strong, good sort; carries plenty of condition; half-brother to 1¼m and 2m winner Brave The Reef (by Mill Reef); dam won Ribblesdale Stakes; made much of running and rallied splendidly under very strong driving when winning 15-runner maiden race at Salisbury in September by a head from Dabdoub, the pair clear; respectable 4½ lengths third of 11 to Dawn River in nursery at Brighton the following month; stays well, and will be suited by 1¼m+; acts on a firm and a soft surface; suited by forcing tactics. *I. Balding.* **85**

GALLIUM (FR) 2 ch.g. Be My Guest 126–Gadfly 108 (Le Fabuleux 133) (1982 6f⁴ 8.2fg 5g 6d 6g) Mar 31; 11,000Y; fair sort; third foal; half-brother to 2 winners in France, including 7.5f winner Fly Round (by Free Round); dam, daughter of smart Chatter Box, won over 1m at 2 yrs in France; little worthwhile form in varied company; blinkered and gave trouble at stalls final start. *R. Hollinshead.* **—**

GAMBLERS DREAM 5 b. or br.g. Prince Regent 129–Red Laser 95 (Red God 128§) (1981 6fg 6g 6s⁴ 6f 6f² 6fg 6fg⁴ 6fg* 6fg* 6d 6g 5s 6v 1982 6f 6g 6fg⁴ 6d 5fg 6f 6f 6g³ 5.6g⁴ 6g 5d 6g 5s⁴) strong, attractive gelding; good mover; fair handicapper; ran respectably several times; stays 7f; acts on any going; effective with or without blinkers. *D. Wilson.* **85**

GAMBLING LORD 3 b.c. Lord Gayle 124–Gambling Queen 80 (Pretendre 126) (1981 NR 1982 8g 10d 8fg 7.6f* 8fg 8.2f) IR 30,000Y; quite attractive colt; third foal; half-brother to 9f to 1½m winner Cloneash Emperor (by Young

341

Emperor); dam showed some ability at 2 yrs; well backed when winning valuable 25-runner maiden race at Lingfield in May from Apple Blossom; stays 1m; not raced after May. *P. Haslam.*

GAME DAME (USA) 2 ch.f. Gummo–Miss Damascus (Damascus) (1982 6f² **99** 7fg* 7g* 7.2f* 7f² 8g) Mar 18; $50,000Y; workmanlike filly; good walker; half-sister to 2 winners, including smart stakes winner Damas (by Montparnasse II); dam unraced half-sister to smart Fascinating Girl, a winner at up to 9f; successful in maiden race at Wolverhampton in July, well-contested minor event (by 1½ lengths from Sheriff Muir) at Leicester in August and £4,400 nursery (beating Nothing Blue decisively by 2 lengths) at Haydock in September; suited by 7f; yet to race on a soft surface; usually ridden by apprentice T. Quinn; genuine. *P. Cole.*

GAME ON 2 ch.c. Continuation 120–Eve Darlin 50 (Arcticeelagh 119) (1982 **57** 7f⁴ 8.2fg³) Mar 25; good-bodied colt; sixth foal; brother to a poor animal; dam poor plater; in frame in sellers at Redcar in July (bandaged) and Haydock in September; suited by 1m. *J. Hardy.*

GAME ROCKET 2 ch.g. Roan Rocket 128–Debach Game 69 (Darius 129) **81 p** (1982 7s⁴) May 26; 2,000Y; brother to fair 1978 2-y-o 6f winner Jenny's Rocket and half-brother to 3 other winners; dam stayed 1¼m; 33/1 and in need of race, tended to hang left when 6 lengths fourth of 6 behind easy winner Northern Adventure in slowly-run minor event at Doncaster in November. *Hbt Jones.*

GAMON 2 b.c. Be My Guest 126–Au Revoir 79 (Ballymoss 136) (1982 5f³ 6f³ **80** 7.2g) Mar 26; 104,000Y; tall, close-coupled colt; good walker; half-brother to 2 winners, including 1m winner Abide (by Habitat); dam, 1½m winner, comes from good staying family; moderate form in varied company, on final outing finishing 8 lengths fifth of 6 to Alchise in Cock of the North Stakes at Haydock in July; will stay 1¼m. *M. H. Easterby.*

GANGAWAYHAME 2 b.f. Lochnager 132–Silbadora 67 (Don II 123) (1982 **91** 5d² 5g³ 5g³ 6f* 6g² 6fg* 6s) Mar 17; IR 5,000Y; small filly; third foal; half-sister to fair 1978 2-y-o 5f winner Mister Tino (by Saulingo); dam ran only at 2 yrs; won 19-runner maiden race at Leicester in May (off course 2½ months afterwards) and weakly-contested nursery at Goodwood in August; suited by 6f; acts on firm going and is possibly unsuited by soft; game and genuine. *G. Balding.*

GAP OF DUNLOE (FR) 4 b.c. Sassafras 135–Absaretch (Dancer's Image) **107** (1981 12fg* 12s 12g³ 12fg 11fg² 12d 12v 1982 12fg* 12s 12g³ 11g⁴ 12.5d 15g 12f) well-made, attractive colt; made a successful reappearance in 8-runner Prix d'Hedouville at Longchamp in April, beating Protection Racket by a short neck; ran creditably afterwards, including when length third of 8 behind Little Wolf in Prix Jean de Chaudenay at Saint-Cloud in May; stays 1½m; best form on a sound surface; usually blinkered at 3 yrs but showed best form in 1982 without; sold to BBA 60,000 gns Newmarket December Sales. *P.-L. Biancone, France.*

GARFUNKEL 3 b.g. Music Boy 124–First Court 82 (Primera 131) (1981 6g **—** 6fg⁴ 6f² 7f* 7f 8g 7d² 1982 8g 8f 8fg 10f 10fg 11.7d 8fg⁴) big, good-topped, quite attractive gelding; good mover; modest performer in 1981; well beaten most starts at 3 yrs; promises to stay 1m; seems to act on any going; blinkered third, fifth and sixth starts; often sweats up. *P. Mitchell.*

GARN GIRL 3 b.f. Rustingo 94–Truquita (Mosquito II 110) (1981 NR 1982 **—** 8.3g) fourth reported foal; dam never ran; tailed-off last in seller at Windsor in July. *Dr A. Jones.*

GARSTANG 2 ch.f. Swing Easy 126–High Density 66 (Pall Mall 132) (1982 **65 d** 5fg⁴ 5g³ 5f³ 6f 6d) May 10; 2,700Y; rather lightly-made filly; sister to fair 1981 2-y-o sprint winner Knight Security, and half-sister to a winner in Hungary; dam won 1m seller; disappointed, including in sellers, after finishing 2 lengths third of 5 behind Fair Heroine in minor event at Ayr in May on second outing; sold 400 gns Newmarket Autumn Sales; sent to Holland. *J. Berry.*

GARTHLAND ARMS 3 b.g. Lucky Wednesday 124–Katebird 89 (Birdbrook **43** 110) (1981 5g³ 6g 7fg² 6fg* 6f 6fg 1982 9fg 8f 8.2g³ 6g 7fg 7g 8.2g 6g 9s⁴) workmanlike gelding; plater; will stay 1¼m; seems to act on any going; often wears blinkers; showed a tendency to hang sixth start. *J. S. Wilson.*

GARY SHAW 2 br.c. Wolver Hollow 126–Early Release (Prince Regent 129) **79 p** (1982 7g³) Apr 3; IR 10,500Y; first foal; dam won 3 times at around 9f in

France; 66/1, kept on well in closing stages when promising 6 lengths third of 16 behind Blushing River in maiden event at Yarmouth in August; will stay 1m; should improve. *I. Walker*.

GAS ONLY 2 ch.f. Northfields–Coquette (St Paddy 133) (1982 6fg) Apr 13; — p 41,000Y; rather leggy, quite attractive filly; sister to 7f and 1m winner Poles Apart; dam won over 9f in Ireland; 12/1 but pretty fit, unable to sustain effort after being shaken up vigorously 2f out, when 7 lengths sixth of 13 to Castanet in newcomers event at Goodwood in September; should do better over 7f+. *F. J. Houghton*.

GATEMASTER (USA) 2 b.c. L'Enjoleur–Sun Gate (Bull Lea) (1982 7d³ 6s) 81 Mar 2; $111,000F, $205,000Y; small colt; half-brother to several winners, including 6f stakes winner Harry's Secret Joy (by What A Pleasure) and 1978 2-y-o 1m winner Cougar's Surprise (by Cougar); dam, placed at 3 yrs in USA, is half-sister to dam of Champion filly Davona Dale; blinkered, ran on to finish 3¾ lengths third of 19 behind Bon Marche in minor event at Naas in October; soon struggling when out of first 9 behind Raashideah in 25-runner maiden race at Doncaster the following month; will be suited by 1m; trained when in Ireland by D. Weld. *F. Durr*.

GATHER NO MOSS 5 ch.h. Ballymoss 136–Swoop (Pandofell 132) (1981 — 12s 12d 14g 10.1g 16g 19s³ 18g 1982 18g 15.5g 15.5fg 15.5fg) lengthy horse; staying maiden; best run on soft going; blinkered second and third starts (ran respectably first time); pulled up when saddle slipped final outing. *G. Beeson*.

GAVO 3 b.g. Windjammer (USA)–Eleanor Clare 89 (Petingo 135) (1981 6f⁴ 95 6g⁴ 5f² 6f 7g 10v 1982 7g 6g² 7fg* 7.6fg* 7f* 8.2f³ 7.6f³ 8fg 7g 7f) neat, strong, good-bodied gelding; has an excellent smooth action; won maiden race at Epsom, minor event at Chester and Norwest Holst Trophy (Handicap) at York; made running and battled on most genuinely once headed to regain lead close home and beat Match Winner a short head in last-named in May; twice ran respectably afterwards; stays 1m; gives impression he will always be suited by top-of-the-ground; blinkered final start; suited by front-running tactics; tough and game. *P. Kelleway*.

GAWAINE 3 gr.g Three Legs 128–Fei-Hoo 65 (Dionisio 126) (1981 NR 1982 48 6d 6g 8.3g 6g 7fg 8fg 10v³ 10v* 12s³) 1,100Y; half-brother to several winners, including useful miler Thrifty (by Continuation); dam of little account; plater; won non-selling apprentice handicap at Lingfield in October; suited by 1¼m+; revels in the mud; suitable mount for an apprentice. *J. Holt*.

GAWNMYSUN 4 br.c. Furry Glen 121–Fair Colleen (King Emperor) (1981 6fg — 6d 6g 6v² 6f 6s 1982 5d 6g 7g) neat colt; should stay 7f; suited by some give in the ground. *A. Pitt*.

GAY BROAD 2 ch.f. Gay Fandango 132–Broad River 75 (Chieftain) (1982 78 5d 5g 6g 5.8g³ 6d 7d³) May 13; small, well-made filly; good walker and mover; half-sister to 5 winners, including useful 1976 Irish 2-y-o Laughing River (by Dike); dam placed over 5f at 2 yrs; third in maiden races at Bath in August and Leicester in October; suited by 7f; yet to race on a firm surface. *R. Hannon*.

GAYGIG 2 b.c. Lord Gayle 124–Gig (Dionisio 126) (1982 6fg⁴ 6f* 6g) Mar 4; 80 6,800£, 13,000Y; useful-looking colt; half-brother to winners here and abroad; dam unraced half-sister to Aggressor and High Perch; got up on line to win 12-runner maiden race at Pontefract in July by a short head from odds-on Faites Vite; found nothing after pulling hard early on when last of 6 behind Shaves You Close in nursery at Haydock the following month; should stay 1m; sold to D. Chapman 5,900 gns Doncaster November Sales. *M. H. Easterby*.

GAYGO LADY 2 ch.f. Gay Fandango 132–Bally Keys 72 (Bally Russe 113) 91 (1982 6f 6fg³ 7g² 7s) Mar 17; IR 7,200F, 41,000Y; useful-looking filly; second living foal; half-sister to 1980 2-y-o 5f winner Ballylingo (by Saulingo); dam ran only at 2 yrs; length second of 23 behind Salvinia in £4,500 event at Newbury in September, best effort; disappointing favourite in race won by New Coins at York the following month; should stay 1m; possibly not at her best on soft going. *B. Hills*.

GAY HERALD 7 ch.h. Dike–Daisy June (Epaulette 125) (1981 12d 1982 — 10fg 11f⁴ 12.2f) lightly-raced middle-distance handicapper; acts on any going; blinkered twice at 3 yrs; suitable mount for an apprentice; usually bandaged nowadays. *D. Ringer*.

GAY LEMUR 2 b.c. Lord Gayle 124–Coming-of-Age 93 (Majority Blue 126) 91 (1982 6f⁴ 7g² 7s²) Mar 20; 20,000Y; strong, good-bodied colt; half-brother to

2 winners, including fairly useful 5f to 1½m winner Oriental Star (by Falcon); dam 2-y-o 6f winner; second in maiden races in October, going down by ¾ length to Mandelstam in 30-runner event at Newmarket (hung quite badly in closing stages) and by 4 lengths to Sackford in 14-runner race at Sandown; will stay 1m; has plenty of scope and is sure to win races. *B. Hobbs.*

GAY MEADOW   3 b.c. Goldhill 125–Dumb Kathy (Dumbarnie 125)   (1981   — 6fg   1982 10f 9g 10g 10d 8d 8.2s 8s)   tall, strong colt; plating-class maiden; best runs at 1m on soft ground. *R. Hollinshead.*

GAY MINSTREL   4 br.g. Tudor Music 131–Belen (Milesian 125)   (1981 5fg 8g   **49** d 7f 7fg⁴ 8fg* 8g³ 8g   1982 12fg³ 11.7fg 10fg 8.3fg 8.3g 8fg 10d 10v)   good-topped gelding; plater; evidently stays 1½m; acts on a firm surface; blinkered final start; sold 1,000 gns Newmarket Autumn Sales. *A. Ingham.*

GAYONARA   3 ch.f. Dragonara Palace 115–Gay Nipper 70 (Aggressor 130)   — (1981 6s 6f* 6fg² 6fg   1982 7fg 7d 7f)   rather lightly-made filly; good mover; won maiden race at Stockton in 1981; soundly beaten in handicaps at 3 yrs; will stay 1m; blinkered once at 2 yrs; sold 4,000 gns Newmarket Autumn Sales. *B. Hanbury.*

GAY PATRICIA   3 b.f. Gay Fandango 132–Moon Cake (Red God 128§)   (1981   **63** 6fg 7d   1982 7fg⁴ 7.6f 7fg³ 8.5f 8d 8fg 8fg 6v)   small, lengthy filly; in frame in maiden races; stays 7f; trained part of season by A. Pitt. *H. O'Neill.*

GAY SHORE (FR)   2 ch.f. Gay Fandango 132–Meadow Shore (Bold Reason)   **68** (1982 6f 5f⁴ 6fg 8.2g 7fg 8g)   Apr 11; 42,000 francs Y (approx £3,800); small, lengthy filly; second foal; half-sister to useful French 3-y-o Meandre (by Wollow), a winner at up to 9f; dam won twice at up to 7f in USA; plating-class maiden; ran well when facing stiff tasks in nurseries on last 2 starts; stays 1m; acts on firm going; sold 1,500 gns Newmarket December Sales. *R. Armstrong.*

GAYTHORN   4 b.f. Laser Light 118–Olivia Staypleton 88 (Road House II)   — (1981 7g 8fg 7s 6g 5g   1982 10.1fg 8.3g)   plater; should stay 1m. *A. Davison.*

GAY TROUBADOUR   3 b.c. Song 132–First Delight 80 (Primera 131)   (1981   — 5g 5.8f 7g   1982 6s 7g 6fg)   good sort but has shown only poor form, including in a seller; sometimes blinkered; sold 350 gns Ascot August Sales. *J. Bethell.*

GAY WHISTLER   4 b.c. Gay Fandango 132–Tin Saint 99 (Tin Whistle 128)   — (1981 9d 8g 7g⁴ 8fg 6g 7f   1982 8s 6g)   smallish, lengthy colt; stays 7f; sometimes blinkered; bandaged when well beaten in 1982; sold 320 gns Doncaster October Sales. *H. Fleming.*

GAZAAN   4 ch.g. Margouillat 133–Goldena (Relko 136)   (1981 12g² 12f³ 15.5f⁴   — 16g   1982 22.2fg 15.5f)   lightly-built gelding; plating-class maiden; stays well. *T. Gosling.*

GEMMA STAR   3 b.g. African Sky 124–Stevia (Supreme Court 135)   (1981   — NR   1982 6f³ 7.6f 5f 6f³)   IR 6,200F, 4,000Y; unfurnished gelding; brother to useful sprinter Laudon, and half-brother to 3 winners; dam poor French maiden; has shown only a little ability; promises to stay 1m; sold 1,250 gns Doncaster August Sales. *P. Kelleway.*

GEM-MAY   2 ro.f. Mansingh 120–Unclaimed Treasure 61 (Nice Guy 123)   **71** (1982 5f³ 5fg³ 5f 6g² 6g 5f 6g 7d 6s⁴ 5v)   Apr 18; lengthy filly; sister to successful 7f to 1¼m performer Manstrove and half-sister to 2 winners in Spain; dam plater; placed in maiden races; suited by 6f (had stiffish task when tried over 7f); probably acts on any going; blinkered final start. *T. Fairhurst.*

GEMSBOK   4 br.g. Redundant 120–Duiker 81 (Sovereign Lord 120)   (1981 6s   — 5d 5fg   1982 11.7f)   leggy gelding; sprint maiden; well beaten in blinkers final start in 1981. *C. V. Miller.*

GENERAL ANDERS   3 ch.c. Habat 127–Camenae 72 (Vimy 132)   (1981 7fg²   **106** § 6g² 7f³ 7g* 8d   1982 10g 12fg⁴ 12f³ 10.6g 10g)   big, rangy, quite attractive colt; carries plenty of condition; good walker and mover; useful at his best; suited by 1½m; acts on firm going; blinkered last 2 starts, running atrociously on second occasion; possibly temperamental and is best left alone. *R. Hern.*

GENERAL BREYFAX   4 ch.g. Sweet Revenge 129–Perbury 88 (Grisaille 115)   — (1981 8s 7d 11.7s 12s 10fg   1982 17.1s)   strong, workmanlike gelding; little worthwhile form on flat since 1980, but is a useful hurdler; acts on soft going. *M. McCourt.*

GENERAL CONCORDE   2 b.c. Radetzky 123–Concorde Lady 66 (Hotfoot 126)   **87** (1982 5g 5fg 7fg 6f⁴ 8fg* 8f 8s² 8.2s² 7s)   Apr 5; useful-looking colt; first foal;

dam of little account on flat and over hurdles; showed much improved form when winning 11-runner nursery at Warwick in August by 5 lengths from Miss Annie; creditable second in similar events at Warwick again and Nottingham in October; suited by 1m; acts on any going; blinkered fifth, sixth and eighth outings but goes as well when not; game and genuine.   *R. Hannon.*

GENERAL HOLME (USA)   3 ch.c. Noholme II–Generals Sister (Count Fleet) **128**
(1981 NR   1982 8d* 10fg* 10.5s* 9d* 10fg* 10f*)
   The unbeaten General Holme is an interesting prospect.   He came gradually to the fore in France as a three-year-old during a run of six wins, and by September had put himself into the reckoning for the Trusthouse Forte Prix de l'Arc de Triomphe and the Dubai Champion Stakes as a result of his defeats of Bon Sang in the Prix de la Cote Normande at Deauville in August and Bikala in the Prix du Prince d'Orange at Longchamp in September.   Connections at this stage decided, probably wisely, against testing him to the limit and they set him aside until 1983 when his early objectives will be the Prix d'Harcourt and the most important race in France for older horses in the first half of the season, the Prix Ganay.
   General Holme wouldn't need to be substantially better than he showed as a three-year-old to be up to winning the Ganay in an average year, and it's doubtful whether we have seen the best of him.   For one thing he was still improving at the time of his last appearance; for another, he was winning his races in a manner that suggested he had a certain amount in reserve.   General Holme possesses a fine turn of speed and is never asked to produce it until late on —that's probably the only reason why his winning margins have been largely unexceptional.   He won a maiden race at Saint-Cloud by a length, a small race at Longchamp by the same distance, the Prix Tourbillon at Maisons-Laffitte by four lengths, the Prix Daphnis at Evry by three parts of a length and both the Cote Normande and Prince d'Orange by a neck or so.   Although the Prix Daphnis is Group 3 category just as the Cote Normande and Prince d'Orange, his defeat of What A Guest in that event was of less significance than his defeats of Bon Sang and Bikala who were among the best middle-distance horses in Europe.   General Holme gave 5 lb and a fair amount of start to front-running Bon Sang, who was admittedly making his way back to top form after illness and injury, and beat him cleverly.   The English-trained Prima Voce finished fourth in this race, by the way, two lengths behind the winner at level weights.   There were two English-trained runners in the field of six for the Prince d'Orange which, unlike the Cote Normande, is open to horses above the age of three years.   One of them, Lobkowiez, chased Bikala until dropping away early in the straight; the other, Commodore Blake, was only two lengths down on Bikala and a length down on General Holme at the distance but at that point he was going back whereas General Holme was improving his position to some purpose.   General Holme led Bikala throughout the final hundred yards, and at the finish had drawn four lengths clear of Commodore Blake who took third place by a margin of five lengths.   The first two met virtually at weight for age, while Commodore Blake and Lobkowiez met the winner on terms more favourable than weight for age; General Holme started at odds on.
   Should General Holme win the Ganay or run well in it he is bound to come into the reckoning for the King George VI and Queen Elizabeth Stakes and

Prix du Prince d'Orange, Longchamp—the unbeaten General Holme gains his sixth victory of the season with this defeat of Bikala

Mr K. Abdulla's "General Holme" (A. Lequeux)

other of the year's big races at a mile and a half. He hasn't yet attempted the distance. The probability is that he'll stay—both his relaxed style of racing and his strength at the finish of ten-furlong races suggest as much, and his pedigree is as encouraging for stamina as an American pedigree normally can be. His sire Noholme II stayed a mile and a half, and so did his dam's sire Count Fleet. That none of his dam's numerous other winners has won over the distance can probably be ascribed to their being trained in the United States where a very small proportion indeed of the racing strength is tested over distances beyond a mile and

General Holme (USA) (ch.c. 1979)	Noholme II (ch 1956)	Star Kingdom (ch 1946)	Stardust Impromptu
		Oceana (b 1947)	Colombo Orama
	Generals Sister (b 1960)	Count Fleet (br 1940)	Reigh Count Quickly
		Cigar Maid (br 1949)	Pavot Never Again

a quarter. The ex-Australian Noholme II has recently been retired after a long and successful period at stud in the States. He never looked back after siring a remarkable number of individual two-year-old winners in his first full crop—twenty-four from thirty-three starters—and among his runners were the champion handicap horse Nodouble (sire of the top-class middle-distance performer Mairzy Doates), the champion sprinter Shecky Greene and the Italian Oaks winner Carnauba (now safely established at stud after her lucky escape from horse thieves and the knacker's yard). General Holme's dam, a minor two-year-old winner in the States, produced eight previous winners including a full brother called Secret Treaty and the smart stakes winner Commissary (by To-Market). The third dam Never Again, by Pharos, was also a good broodmare; she foaled four stakes winners, among them the champion two-year-old Oil Capitol and the very useful

346

two-year-old Cigar Maid. She was imported from France where she won as a two-year-old.

Such was General Holme's promise in the autumn that between his last two races he changed hands for around 6.5 million dollars. He is now the property of Serge Fradkoff and Khaled Abdulla, each noted for his shrewd dealings in the bloodstock market. At that price General Holme probably represents good value; he will certainly do so if he succeeds in capturing one or more of the top middle-distance events in 1983. He acts on any going. *O. Douieb, France.*

GENERAL WADE 7 b.h. Bold Lad (Ire) 133–Zerbinetta 96 (Henry the Seventh **74** 125) (1981 5s 6g⁴ 6fg* 6f 6f⁴ 6fg 6g 5h* 6f⁴ 5.8g³ 6d³ 1982 6f⁴ 6f² 6fg⁴ 6f³ 6fg⁴ 6g⁴ 5fg⁴ 5fg⁴ 5fg 6fg 5.8f 6s*) strong, good sort; sprint handicapper; claimed £3,200 after winning claiming handicap at Nottingham in October; acts on any going; wears blinkers; sometimes sweats up. *P. Makin.*

GENERAL WOOD 6 gr.g. Precipice Wood 123–Lady C (Princely Gift 137) — (1981 NR 1982 9s 16.5s) selling hurdler; behind in minor events in autumn. *D. Chapman.*

GENEROUS HEART 2 b.c. Connaught 130–Manoeuvre 105 (Mountain Call 125) — (1982 6g 7fg 7f 5v) Apr 25; 3,000F, 6,000Y; good-bodied individual; beaten some way, including when top weight in selling nursery. *R. Baker.*

GENNARO 2 gr.c. Dance In Time–Landed Lady 89 (Realm 129) (1982 6g 6d 6g) — Jan 30; 18,000F; rangy, good sort; nice, easy mover; third produce; dam, sister to smart Another Realm, won over 5f at 2 yrs; no worthwhile form; off course 5 months after first outing. *J. Dunlop.*

GENTLE DOWN (USA) 2 ch.f. Naskra–First Fluff (Olden Times) (1982 7g 7d³) **76** Mar 28; $115,000Y; second foal; dam, winner of 6f maiden race, is half-sister to smart 1m stakes winner Moontee; 10/1 and on burly side, showed up throughout when just over 2 lengths third of 18 to Brilliant Rosa in maiden race at Leicester in October; will stay 1m. *G. Hunter.*

GENTLE MUSIC 2 b.f. Gentilhombre 131–French Music (French Beige 127) **62** (1982 5fg 5f² 5f² 5s 7g³ 6f 6f* 5s³) May 12; 6,000Y; rather leggy, short-backed filly; half-sister to fair 1981 2-y-o 6f and 7f winner Lively Rhythm (by Sharpen Up) and 2 minor winners; dam ran only once; attracted no bid after winning 10-runner selling nursery at Brighton in September by a head from Repitch, the pair clear; ran creditably in blinkers next outing; best form at 5f or 6f; acts on any going; has sweated up; sold 2,300 gns Newmarket Autumn Sales. *B. Hills.*

GENTLE RHYTHM 2 ch.f. Ballad Rock 122–Super Restless (Restless Wind) — (1982 6fg) May 18; 6,000F, 28,000Y; strong, full-quartered filly; half-sister to winners in USA and Ireland, including 1981 2-y-o 5f winner Moon Rocket (by Kalamoun); dam, sister to On Your Mark, won over 5f in Ireland; 50/1 and backward, made no show in 19-runner maiden race won by Bold Mover at Newmarket in July. *F. Durr.*

GENTLE STAR 3 b. or br.f. Comedy Star 121–Super Princess 85 (Falcon 131) **57** (1981 5d⁴ 6fg 6fg 5f 6d² 6v 6d⁴ 1982 5g 5d 6f 6f 10.1fg 7g 6f* 6fg³ 6fg* 6f² 6fg 6g³ 6f 6f 6d³ 6s) lightly-made filly; plater nowadays; attracted no bid after winning at Yarmouth in July and held on gamely to score in claiming race at Newmarket later in month; best form at 6f; acts on firm going; effective with or without blinkers; has run well for an apprentice; retained 1,300 gns Newmarket Autumn Sales. *K. Ivory.*

GENTLE WARRIOR 3 b.f. Warpath 113–Gentle Spring 118 (Gentle Art 121) — (1981 5.1f 1982 8f 10.1fg 10fg) compact filly; bad plater. *J. Gilbert.*

GENTLY DOES IT 10 b.g. Le Levanstell 122–Soft Fall 85 (Chamossaire) — (1981 17.1h 1982 13.1f) poor handicapper on flat. *L. Kennard.*

GEOMANCER 3 gr.c. Shiny Tenth 120–Future Chance 86 (Hopeful Venture **55** 125) (1981 5fg 5s³ 5d 1982 6s² 6f² 7.2f 6g) fair sort; plater; stayed 7f; acted on any going; dead. *P. Makin.*

GEORDIE LAD 4 b.g. Track Spare 125–Silesca (Silent Screen) (1981 8g 9d 12fg³ — 12g⁴ 16fg 16s 1982 13v³ 15.8f 12fg³) workmanlike gelding; looked slow; dead. *D. Smith.*

GEORGE'S SONG 2 ch.c. True Song 95–Sassy Lady (Philemon 119) (1982 6s) — Apr 21; second foal; dam never ran; unquoted; tailed-off last of 9 in claiming race at Nottingham in October. *D. Wintle.*

GERARDINA'S BOY 3 ch.c. Music Boy 124–Solace (Floribunda 136) (1981   **46**
5d³ 5d* 5g 5f 5d   1982 5fg 5f 5s⁴ 6d)   good-quartered, workmanlike colt; sprint
handicapper; best at 5f; needs some give in the ground; blinkered last 2 outings;
trained first start by V. Soane. *D. Thom.*

GETTING PLENTY 3 b.f. Oats 126–Allander Girl (Miralgo 130) (1981 6d 8fg   —
8s² 10g*   1982 12f 17fg 12f 12g 10v³ 13.8d⁴)   sparely-made filly; middle-
distance plater; acts well on soft going and is possibly unsuited by firm; has worn
a tongue strap; sold 960 gns Newmarket Autumn Sales. *G. Hunter.*

GHAIYA (USA) 2 b.f. Alleged 138–Proud Pattie (Noble Commander) (1982   **93 p**
7g 8fg*)   Apr 17; $310,000Y; quite attractive, rangy filly; second foal; half-
sister to 3-y-o Current Pattie (by Little Current); dam, half-sister to dam of
Nonoalco, won 6 times at up to 7f; short-priced favourite, made much of running
and was ridden right out when winning £3,600 event at Goodwood in September
by 1½ lengths from Northern Script; had acquitted herself with credit in Sweet
Solera Stakes at Newmarket the previous month; will stay beyond 1m; type to
improve with experience. *J. Dunlop.*

GHAWAR 3 b.g. Malacate 131–Gulf Bird 71 (Gulf Pearl 117) (1981 5g⁴ 5fg² 5s   **65**
5.3f² 6fg² 5f* 5fg* 5d 6s   1982 5g 6s 7fg 6fg 5f 5g⁴)   quite attractive, good sort;
good mover; sprint handicapper; stays 6f; yet to show his form on very soft
ground but acts on any other; sent to Malaysia. *R. Smyth.*

GHAZAL 6 br.g. Averof 123–Vilswitch 93 (Vilmorin) (1981 NR   1982 18g   —
15.8g)   dipped-backed gelding; poor performer nowadays; not certain to stay
2¼m (although not disgraced over trip, despite pulling hard); acts on any going;
blinkered once at 3 yrs. *J. Hardy.*

GIANLORENZO 10 ch.g. Lorenzaccio 130–Turkhan Law (Turkhan) (1981 NR   —
1982 10fg)   winning hurdler; lightly raced on flat and was behind in a seller on
only outing of 1982. *J. Perrett.*

GIDDY ANN 3 br.f. Dubassoff–Giddy Lyn (Relko 136) (1981 5g 5s 6fg 7g   1982   —
8g 10f 10g 10fg³ 12f⁴)   lightly-made filly; middle-distance plater; exported to
Algeria. *G. Blum.*

GIDIAN 5 ch.h. Brigadier Gerard 144–Jovian 88 (Hardicanute 130) (1981 NR   **52**
1982 10fg 10g 10d⁴ 10f² 12f² 12fg 12g 10fg² 10g⁴ 10s)   lengthy horse; middle-
distance handicapper; stays 1½m; acts on any going. *C. Brittain.*

GIGGLE 3 gr.f. Sagaro 133–Joking 81 (Ribero 126) (1981 6fg 8fg   1982 10fg   **51**
12g 12d⁴ 13.8d³ 12d 12s²)   smallish, lightly-made filly; plater; stays 1¾m; acts
on soft going; blinkered fourth and fifth starts; sold 3,400 gns Doncaster
November Sales. *W. Hastings-Bass.*

GIGONDAS 3 b.f. Brigadier Gerard 144–Gingerale (Golden Horus 123) (1981   —
6g   1982 7.6fg 10g 8.5fg⁴ 7g)   smallish filly; has shown a little ability; seems to
stay 1m. *W. Holden.*

GILDED CHIEF 5 br.g. Gilded Leader 75–Seminole Squaw 66 (Seminole II)   **51**
(1981 NR   1982 12s 12g² 16fg)   strong gelding; backed at long odds when 3
lengths second to Sandalay in minor event at Pontefract in April; 200/1, had
some useful performers behind him and seemed to run very well when 12 lengths
fifth to Castelnau in Mono Sagaro Stakes at Ascot later in month; suited by a test
of stamina. *B. McMahon.*

GILDED STRACOMER 2 b.c. Averof 123–Peta's Bay 67 (I Say 125) (1982   **56**
5fg 5g⁴ 5fg 7fg 6f 6fg 6g 9v 7s)   Feb 29; good-topped ex-English colt; brother to
useful 5f performer Haditos, and half-brother to 2 winners; dam, half-sister to
high-class Gold Rod, won over 7f; only plating class; trained by G. Beeson first
7 starts. *T. Gallagher, Ireland.*

GILDORAN 2 b.c. Rheingold 137–Durtal 121 (Lyphard 132) (1982 7v 7d⁴)   **83 p**
June 6; well-made colt; first foal; dam, half-sister to Arc winner Detroit, won
Cheveley Park and Fred Darling Stakes; 6 lengths fourth of 8 behind easy winner
Northern Adventure in minor event at Doncaster in October, staying on to be
second-best of stand-side group; will be suited by longer distances, and should
stay 1½m; likely to improve. *B. Hills.*

GIL (ISR) 2 br.c. Verre Dore–Gil-Ad (Shoolerville 121) (1982 5f 5f 5fg 5fg 7fg   —
7d 7g)   Feb 2; 2,400Y; lengthy, plain Israeli-bred colt; good walker; dam never
ran; poor form in varied races, including a valuable seller; trained by Mrs B.
Waring first 5 starts. *D. Sasse.*

GILLIES PRINCE 3 b. or br.c. Furry Glen 121–Rosy O'Leary (Majetta 115)   **60**
(1981 5f 6f 7f 6fg⁴ 6fg 7.2v⁴ 8g   1982 7fg 9g³ 8f² 9f* 12f⁴ 9f* 8d 10d)   leggy,

lightly-made colt; has a round action; plater; successful at Wolverhampton in August (bought in 1,550 gns) and Redcar in September (attracted no bid); stays 1½m but seems best at around 9f; probably acts on any going but goes well on firm. *P. Rohan.*

GIMITA 3 b.f. Blue Cashmere 129–Gimima 54 (Narrator 127) (1981 6fg 6fg — 5g⁴ 7fg 5g 1982 6g⁴ 5fg³ 5f 5f 6f 6f) lengthy filly; plating-class maiden; by no means sure to stay 7f; blinkered final outing; exported to Algeria. *E. Eldin.*

GIMRI 7 ch.g. Quayside 124–Conita 94 (Constable 119) (1981 7d³ 8g 7d² 7g 7v⁴ — 7fg 7.6g 7fg 7fg 7fg 7g 7s* 7s 7d 1982 7s 8d⁴ 8g 7.6g 7g 7s 8g 7s) workmanlike gelding; stays 1m; acts on any going, but is particularly well suited by some give in the ground; excellent mount for an apprentice. *J. Benstead.*

GIN GAME 5 b.g. Red Alert 127–Watermark 83 (Henry the Seventh 125) (1981 — 6s 7d 7g² 7v 6f³ 6f 6g² 7fg⁴ 7fg 6fg 6f² 5.8g 6s³ 6d* 1982 8fg) neat, strong, attractive gelding; quite a modest handicapper in 1981; needed race only outing of 1982; stays 7f; acts on any going; blinkered once at 3 yrs. *M. Tate.*

GINGER BRINK (FR) 2 ch.c. Brinkmanship 125–La Roussiere (Le Fabuleux **117** 133) (1982 5g⁴ 5.5g 5.5d² 7g 7g² 7fg³ 7.5g 8g³ 7.5fg⁴ 8s² 7g* 8f 7f 8s⁴ 8s 8.5v* 7s⁴ 10v) Apr 25; 100,000 francs Y (approx £9,000); fourth foal: half-brother to 2 winners, including middle-distance performer Tarsiere (by Tarbes); dam won 2 small middle-distance races; had an extremely busy season but stood up to it well, winning minor event at Evry in September and Prix Herbager at Maisons-Laffitte in October, latter by 1½ lengths from Ice Hot; also ran well in pattern events, notably finishing 4½ lengths fifth to L'Emigrant in Prix La Rochette at Longchamp on twelfth outing, close-up fourth to Pluralisme in Prix des Chenes on same course on fourteenth and 3 lengths fourth of 16 to L'Emigrant in Criterium de Maisons-Laffitte on seventeenth; should stay 1¼m; acts on any going. *R. Collet, France.*

GIN N' LIME 8 ch.g. Divine Gift 127–Fruit Cup 72 (Silver Shark 129) (1981 — 11.7f⁴ 1982 12.2fg 11.7f) poor maiden on flat; has been tried in blinkers. *C. V. Miller.*

GIORSAL 3 b.f. Tudor Rhythm 112–Mary Newall 69 (Coronation Year 124) **37** (1981 5s 1982 7f 7f 6f 8f³ 9g 10d³ 8g 10fg 12fg) leggy, lightly-made filly; plater; stays 1¼m; seems to act on any going; sold 575 gns Ascot December Sales. *T. Fairhurst.*

GIPSY ROAD (FR) 3 b.f. Trepan 133–La Route Millard (Busted 134) (1981 **118** 8v 8v⁴ 10g³ 10v² 1982 12g² 12s* 10g⁴ 12fg² 12f⁴ 12s* 12.5s* 12s*) 100,000 francs F (approx £10,000); fifth foal; half-sister to minor winners in France by Nonoalco and Caracolero; dam won over 1¼m and 1⅜m in France; developed into a smart filly and on penultimate outing beat Gold Bird decisively by 1½ lengths in Prix de Royallieu at Longchamp in October; also won minor event and Prix Joubert at Evry and Grand Prix de Bordeaux, dead-heating for second with Welsh Term behind subsequently-disqualified Balitou in last-named; stays 1½m well; acts on any going but goes well on soft; consistent. *F. Boutin, France.*

GIRL ON A SWING 3 br.f. High Top 131–Gilwanigan (Captain's Gig) (1981 **79** NR 1982 7fg² 7.6fg³ 7.6fg 7g) 101,000Y; smallish, lengthy filly; good mover; has been pin-fired; first foal; dam, half-sister to Irish Guinness Oaks winner Pampalina and Free Handicap winner Short Commons, was fairly useful winner over 6f and 7f at 2 yrs in Ireland; placed in newcomers race at Newbury in April and maiden event at Chester in May; will stay 1m; off course 5 months before final start. *H. Candy.*

GLAD TIDINGS (FR) 3 b.f. Pharly 130–Gaily 121 (Sir Gaylord) (1981 7d³ 7v **85** 1982 8f 10f² 10.1g* 10fg* 12v) attractive, well-made filly; successful in 22-runner maiden race at Windsor (odds on) and 4-runner minor event at Goodwood; stays 1¼m; possibly unsuited by very soft going but acts on any other. *R. Hern.*

GLANCING 3 b.f. Grundy 137–Splashing 123 (Petingo 135) (1981 6fg³ 5g* 6f* — 5fg* 1982 8fg 6g) compact, short-legged, quite attractive filly; very useful at 2 yrs when she won Champion Two Yrs Old Trophy at Ripon and Prix d'Arenberg at Chantilly on last 2 starts; faded quickly in closing stages when soundly beaten in 1,000 Guineas at Newmarket in April and Diadem Stakes at Ascot in September on only outings in 1982; moved moderately to post and was withdrawn second intended outing, and moved very badly at Ascot; not certain to stay 1m; yet to race on soft ground. *W. Hastings-Bass.*

GLASGOW CENTRAL 5 gr.h. Roan Rocket 128–Nettlebed 84 (Hethersett — 134) (1981 8d 10fg⁴ 10g 10s³ 10d² 12g* 10fg² 12fg³ 12.3fg* 12f⁴ 13.3d² 12s* 12g

1982 13.3f) short-backed horse; good mover; fair handicapper; won amateur riders race at Salisbury, ladies race at Newcastle and handicap at Ascot in 1981; had stiff task on only outing of 1982 (May); suited by 1½m or more; suited by some give in the ground; possibly best on galloping track. *M. Scudamore.*

GLASTONBURY 3 ch.f. Grundy 137–Christchurch 88 (So Blessed 130) (1981 NR 1982 10.2g 12g*) small, lightly-made filly; second foal; half-sister to smart 6f to 10.5f winner Church Parade (by Queen's Hussar); dam, 1½m winner, is half-sister to 1,000 Guineas and Oaks winner Highclere; stayed on very well to get up close home and beat Rheinza by a neck in 13-runner maiden race at Haydock in August; will be suited by 1¾m; sold 70,000 gns Newmarket December Sales. *R. Hern.* **73**

GLAVERS 2 ch.f. Red Regent 123–Shepherds Bush 80 (Shooting Chant) (1982 7g⁴ 7f 7f 8fg³ 8s⁴ 10d) May 4; neat filly; first foal; dam won from 6f to 11.5f in Ireland; poor plater; should stay beyond 1m; acts on any going; sold 800 gns Doncaster November Sales. *E. Carter.* **55**

GLEEMAN 3 ch.c. The Minstrel 135–Isobelline (Pronto) (1981 6fg 7fg² 1982 8.5fg³ 10.4g 10.1fg 9g) neat, attractive colt; has had a soft palate operation; quite a modest maiden; will stay 1½m. *J. Tree.* **—**

GLEN AIR 4 b.g. Furry Glen 121–Mountain Air 74 (Tudor Melody 129) (1981 10fg³ 10.1d³ 10g 10f 10g 11.5g 8d 10d 1982 10s 7f 8fg 8.2fg 10fg) neat, lightly-made gelding; plater; stays 1¼m; acts on soft going; blinkered final outing in 1981. *T. Taylor.* **—**

GLENANNA 2 b.f. Furry Glen 121–Annatown 68 (Charlottown 127) (1982 7.6v⁴ 7d) May 14; 1,950Y; fair sort; half-sister to a winner in Algeria; dam placed at up to 13f; not disgraced in maiden races in October at Lingfield (fourth of 18 to Keyboard) and Leicester (fifth of 15 to Miss Bali Beach); will stay 1¼m. *R. Price.* **71**

GLENBOUR 6 ch.g. Campaigner 55–Hill Sixty (Slippered 103) (1981 NR 1982 12f) winner over jumps; sweating and blinkered when behind in amateur riders event at Thirsk in May, first outing on flat; sold 1,650 gns Doncaster June Sales. *M. James.* **—**

GLENFIELD PORTION 2 b.f. Mummy's Pet 125–Shirwani 77 (Major Portion 129) (1982 5g² 5g 5g 5d³ 5fg* 5fg 5f* 5d³ 5g³) Apr 4; small filly; half-sister to useful 1981 2-y-o sprinter Better Portion (by Music Boy); dam 2-y-o 5f winner; quite speedy; made all in maiden race at Chester in July and in 6-runner nursery at Redcar in August; excellent third of 15 to Wiki Wiki Wheels in valuable nursery at Newbury in September on final appearance; unlikely to stay beyond 5f; yet to race on very soft going; sweated up on occasions, including once when successful. *P. Brookshaw.* **86**

GLENHAWK 6 b.g. Furry Glen 121–Genazzano (Shantung 132) (1981 NR 1982 18g 15.5fg³) strong, rangy gelding; good walker and mover; quite a modest stayer nowadays; better known as a jumper; acts on any going. *R. Price.* **53**

GLENRIEFFE 4 b. or br.g. Scottish Rifle 127–Jendean 68 (Florescence 120) (1981 8fg 8fg 8.2s 8s 8d 1982 12.2f 8fg² 12d 8.3fg⁴ 10fg 8fg 8.3g 10fg² 8.3g² 10g³ 8fg 8g) workmanlike gelding; in frame in an apprentice race and 4 sellers; stays 1¼m; occasionally blinkered. *S. Matthews.* **50 d**

GLENSIDE LADY 3 b.f. So Blessed 130–Croomedale (Alcide 136) (1981 5fg 8d³ 7g³ 8g 1982 7d 7g 8g 6f 8g 10v² 10d 8s⁴ 7s) short-backed filly; poor walker; quite moderate at her best; second in seller at Lingfield in October; stays 1¼m; suited by some give in the ground; wears blinkers; trained part of season by F. Durr. *K. Ivory.* **50**

GLENSTAL (USA) 2 b.c. Northern Dancer–Cloonlara 130 (Sir Ivor 135) (1982 6.3fg* 7d*) **112 p**
Vincent O'Brien has in the past met with enormous success with the off-spring of Northern Dancer, winning pattern races with Nijinsky, Minsky, The Minstrel, Be My Guest, Try My Best, Storm Bird, Magesterial and Woodstream. It's therefore not surprising that his string nowadays is dominated by descendants of that brilliant stallion. Of O'Brien's seventeen individual two-year-old winners in 1982 Treasure Trove is by Try My Best, Bon Marche is by The Minstrel, Beaudelaire, Caerleon and Solford are sons of Nijinsky and seven, Ankara, Ballydoyle, Danzatore, Glenstal, Lomond, Salmon Leap and Taoiseach, are by Northern Dancer himself. Danzatore is obviously the most promising of the Northern Dancer colts seen out but a lot more is likely to be heard of some

National Stakes, the Curragh—14/1-shot Glenstal springs a surprise, beating Burslem (noseband) by a length with odds-on stable companion Lomond third

of the others. Four won on their debut: Ankara, a brother to Woodstream, won nicely at Leopardstown in October on his only appearance; Salmon Leap, a close relative of Kings Lake, also won on his only start, looking particularly promising when trouncing the opposition in another Leopardstown maiden event later the same month; Lomond, a half-brother to the American triple crown winner Seattle Slew, trotted up by six lengths in a twenty-one-runner race at the Curragh in August; and Glenstal got home by a short head in a maiden event at the Curragh in July, beating Najran who next time out finished second in the Heinz '57' Phoenix Stakes.

Glenstal and Lomond each had one more outing, both taking the field in the National Stakes at the Curragh in September. Eddery, originally scheduled to partner Lomond, was side-lined by a fall at Doncaster the previous day and Hogan, Glenstal's intended rider, was switched to Lomond who started at 7/2 on. Rossiter, principally a work rider nowadays, took the mount on Glenstal who drifted out to 14/1 from half those odds. Both colts held every chance as the second favourite Burslem led entering the final quarter mile but it was Glenstal, not Lomond, who was going the better and he wore down Burslem inside the final furlong to win a shade comfortably by a length, with Lomond a short head back in third place. The six other runners were well beaten off. Despite the result it's far from certain that Glenstal will eventually prove better than Lomond. He might have been flattered by his defeat of his stable companion. The trainer was initially at a loss to explain the outcome of the National Stakes; it later transpired that Lomond was suffering from a throat infection.

Glenstal (USA) (b.c. Apr 6, 1980)	Northern Dancer (b 1961)	Nearctic (br 1954)	Nearco / Lady Angela
		Natalma (b 1957)	Native Dancer / Almahmoud
	Cloonlara (b 1974)	Sir Ivor (b 1965)	Sir Gaylord / Attica
		Fish-Bar (b 1967)	Baldric II / Fisherman's Wharf

Glenstal, like Salmon Leap, is closely related to Kings Lake, the winner of the Irish Two Thousand Guineas, Sussex Stakes and Joe McGrath Memorial Stakes: he is by Kings Lake's paternal grandsire out of Kings Lake's half-sister Cloonlara. Readers who have a copy of *Racehorses of 1980* will be able to compare Kings Lake's portrait as a two-year-old with Glenstal's. The photographs show them to be very similar types, and it will be intriguing to see whether Glenstal can make anything like the progress Kings Lake did. If he can he'll make an excellent three-year-old. Glenstal is Cloonlara's second foal, following the 1981 two-year-old six-furlong winner Chivalry (by Nijinsky). Unfortunately Cloonlara had only one more foal, a Lyphard colt, before being killed by lightning in August 1981 when again in foal to Northern Dancer. Cloonlara was a brilliant

Mr R. E. Sangster's "Glenstal"

two-year-old, winning all her three starts including the Phoenix Stakes by six lengths from Godswalk, but she proved temperamental at three, at which age her best effort was her fourth in the One Thousand Guineas. In addition to Salmon Leap and Kings Lake, Cloonlara was a half-sister to the smart sprinter Denizen. Fish-Bar, Cloonlara's dam, was also very useful, winning at up to a mile and a half in France, and the next dam Fisherman's Wharf was a daughter of the One Thousand Guineas and St Leger winner Herringbone. Cloonlara had far more speed than stamina but Glenstal will be suited by a mile and may well stay a mile and a quarter. *V. O'Brien, Ireland.*

GLENVARA 5 b.g. Furry Glen 121–Varamette (Varano) (1981 13v 16g 13.8fg 1982 15d) useful-looking gelding; staying handicapper; possibly unsuited by very soft ground; has run creditably for a boy; needed race and was bandaged only outing of 1982; sold 560 gns Doncaster October Sales. *T. Craig.*   —

GLEN VINE 2 b.f. Artaius 129–Charlotteen 96 (Charlottown 127) (1982 7g) useful-looking filly; half-sister to Irish 3-y-o 7f winner Wollotteen (by Wollow) and 1m seller winner Longridge (by Derring-Do); dam, middle-distance performer, is half-sister to dam of Homing and Water Mill; 25/1, ran creditably for a newcomer when 6 lengths sixth of 7 to Saving Mercy in Rockfel Stakes at Newmarket in October, showing speed for 5f; should win in maiden company. *R. Hollinshead.*   **82 p**

GLIDE PATH 4 b.f. Sovereign Path 125–Falcon Bess (Falcon 131) (1981 9d 8fg 7f 10f* 9f³ 10.1g³ 10g* 10s 11d 12g³ 1982 10fg⁴ 11.1fg⁴ 12f³ 12g* 10g* 10fg* 11.5f* 12f⁴ 12fg* 13.3g³ 12v) sparely-made filly; middle-distance handicapper; had a fine season and won at Brighton, Yarmouth (twice), Sandown and Epsom; got up close home and beat Haresceugh by a neck on last-named course in August; finished well when 1¾ lengths third to Fitzpatrick in Coral Autumn Cup at Newbury in September; had stiff task final start; acts on firm going (well beaten on soft); most genuine. *J. Winter.*   **91**

GLINT OF GOLD 4 b.c. Mill Reef 141–Crown Treasure (Graustark) (1981 **127**
12fg* 12g* 12d² 15s* 12d* 14.6g² 12v* 1982 12fg* 12fg² 12f² 12f² 12.5d*
12fg³ 12g*)

The news that Glint of Gold would be unable to run in the Trusthouse Forte
Prix de l'Arc de Triomphe at Longchamp in October came as one of the disappointments of the season. Glint of Gold was a top-priced 10/1-chance in the
ante-post lists when his trainer announced nine days before the Arc that Glint of
Gold had shown some heat in a tendon followed by a slight temperature. The set-
back couldn't have come at a less opportune moment. Conditions in Paris were
ideal for him—he hadn't been beaten on a soft surface since his second to Shergar
in the Derby—and given that the race was run at the customary good pace he
would surely have been in the firing line at the finish, and he might even have won
an Arc contested by a field of no more than average strength. It was all the
more disappointing since Glint of Gold had until then been marvellously hardy
and he might have been all right on the day had he been risked. Understandably
though, Balding felt he couldn't send Glint of Gold for so demanding a race having
missed two important pieces of work and it was decided to retire him forthwith.
Glint of Gold retires with a magnificent record of ten wins and six seconds from
seventeen starts and first-place earnings of £328,817 which places him seventh
among the leading European-based money winners, listed in the commentary on
Ardross. He achieved six Group 1 wins from six outings abroad, including his
sole classic success in the Derby Italiano at Rome, a remarkable record which
illustrates his wonderful temperament as well as his trainer's enterprise.

Glint of Gold won three of his seven races as a four-year-old, the John Porter
Stakes at Newbury in April, the Grand Prix de Saint-Cloud in July and the
Grosser Preis von Baden at Baden-Baden in September. In a way his John
Porter win was as meritorious as any, because he looked and ran as though he
needed the race. He's a strong, well-made colt—among the biggest sons of
Mill Reef yet seen—and it was clear from the condition he was carrying that he'd
done very well through the winter. In the end his lack of peak fitness very
nearly cost him the race, for having been nicely placed throughout and looking
as if he might win well when leading over a furlong out he drifted to the right
across the course throughout the last furlong and needed to be hard ridden to
hold on. He won by a neck and a length from Amyndas and Critique who
received 6 lb and 3 lb respectively, the latter finishing particularly well, and it
was Glint of Gold's courage as much as anything that saw him home.

Glint of Gold was beaten on each of his next three starts: by Ardross in the
Jockey Club Stakes at Newmarket later in April, by Easter Sun in the Coronation
Cup at Epsom in June and by Critique, who received 5 lb, in the Hardwicke Stakes
at Royal Ascot, each time failing narrowly to hold the winner's late thrust. The
Hardwicke Stakes was the last race in which Glint of Gold was ridden by Matthias,
who'd been on him in all his races; the week after Royal Ascot a statement was
issued to the effect that, as a result of pressure from some of the stable's owners,
Matthias wouldn't be retained as stable jockey in 1983. Whether or not Matthias' riding of Glint of Gold had anything to do with this we can't be sure. However, he did come in for criticism from some quarters after both the Coronation
Cup and the Hardwicke Stakes. At Epsom, where Glint of Gold looked in tremendous shape and was the pick of the paddock, the pace-maker Show-A-Leg,
bought specially for the purpose at the Autumn Sales, was unable to provide a
strong enough gallop. Glint of Gold, always travelling easily behind him, moved
smoothly past rounding Tattenham Corner and held a clear advantage much of
the way up the straight, but in the closing stages he was outpaced by the top-of-
the-ground specialist Easter Sun and beaten half a length. Arguably Matthias,
on seeing that Show-A-Leg wasn't up to his job, should have kicked for home
sooner; ridden more enterprisingly Glint of Gold might well have taken the edge
off Easter Sun's finish. At Ascot, where the going was once again firm, Lafontaine
set a strong pace from the start and Glint of Gold was held up in mid-field until
taking closer order approaching the home turn. Once in the straight his inability
to quicken decisively on this sort of ground was all too obvious and he had a long,
hard struggle before mastering Lafontaine, Stanerra and Amyndas, all four at
times coming extremely close to one another. In the closing stages he was unable
to hold Critique who challenged on the outside and avoided the trouble.

Whether the decision to take Matthias off Glint of Gold was justified or not
the horse's partnership with Eddery bore immediate fruits in the Grand Prix de
Saint-Cloud, Glint of Gold's first opportunity of the year of racing on softish
ground. In the absence of Show-A-Leg and any obvious pacemaker Eddery sent
Glint of Gold off in front and set such a gallop that most of the opposition were
struggling before the home turn. The good French five-year-old Lancastrian

proved an exceptionally tough nut to crack though and challenged persistently up the straight. For a moment or two Lancastrian looked to be getting the better of the argument but, as we'd seen before, there are few hardier, more resolute battlers than Glint of Gold who kept pulling out more under severe pressure until he got home by a head. Paul Mellon, voted Owner of the Year in the annual Derby Awards, was one of those lucky enough to be present for one of the season's most thrilling finishes; he was paying his first visit to Saint-Cloud since 1927. At Ascot later in July Glint of Gold faced a stiffer task in the King George VI and Queen Elizabeth Diamond Stakes and started fifth favourite in a field of nine. As usual he gave everything, showing no sign of his hard race at Saint-Cloud, but he was outpaced by Kalaglow and Assert and beaten about three lengths. He just held off Critique and Bikala for third in a finish of necks; it was the only time in his career in which he failed to finish in the first two. Glint of Gold made his only subsequent appearance in the Grosser Preis von Baden, in which his principal opponent in a field of seven was Orofino, the outstanding German four-year-old. Glint of Gold had possibly the easiest win of his career, making the running, being firmly in control in the last couple of furlongs, and coming in two and three quarter lengths clear of Orofino. Eddery was subsequently fined about £120, as Glint of Gold had carried Orofino into the centre of the course. Sensibly, as the result was not affected, the placings remained unaltered. Had the race taken place in Britain Glint of Gold would have had to be relegated to last place under the terms of the now-infamous rule 153!

		Never Bend	Nasrullah
	Mill Reef	(b 1960)	Lalun
	(b 1968)	Milan Mill	Princequillo
Glint of Gold		(b 1962)	Virginia Water
(b.c. 1978)		Graustark	Ribot
	Crown Treasure	(ch 1963)	Flower Bowl
	(b 1973)	Treasure Chest	Rough 'n Tumble
		(b 1962)	Iltis

Glint of Gold is to stand alongside the top-class miler Posse at the Derisley Wood Stud, Newmarket, his owner retaining five shares and another twenty-one being offered for sale at £95,000 each. He retires to stud with a pedigree to match the many qualities he displayed on the racecourse.

Glint of Gold's sire Mill Reef was one of the very best racehorses in our experience and he has fortunately been a great success at stud. Among Mill Reef's best winners have been the Derby winner Shirley Heights, the French Derby winner Acamas and the One Thousand Guineas winner Fairy Footsteps; his 1982 winners included the Mecca-Dante winner Simply Great, the high-class miler Pas de Seul, the One Thousand Guineas third Dione and Glint of Gold's very promising young stable-companion Special Leave. The distaff side of Glint of Gold's pedigree is first-rate too. He's the first foal of the very useful Graustark mare Crown Treasure who won over five furlongs and was third in the Grade 3 Schuylerville Stakes as a two-year-old. Crown Treasure has since produced Diamond Shoal and the promising Emerald Reef to Mill Reef, a yearling filly by Troy, and a colt foal by Shirley Heights; she's due to Mill Reef again in 1983. The next dam Treasure Chest was another very useful performer who won ten races from two to five years, including the six-and-a-half-furlong Lottie Wolf Memorial Stakes at Hazel Park and a division of the mile Modesty Handicap at Arlington Park. Treasure Chest has produced several other winners besides Crown Treasure, including Diomedia and Gold Treasure, both winners of more than 100,000 dollars and the former already a successful broodmare. The third dam Iltis won five times and produced the champion two-year-old filly of 1959 My Dear Girl, herself the dam of the top-class racehorse and successful sire In Reality.

It is to be hoped that the decision to stand Glint of Gold in this country in the

Grand Prix de Saint-Cloud—another Continental triumph for Glint of Gold who rallies gamely to beat Lancastrian

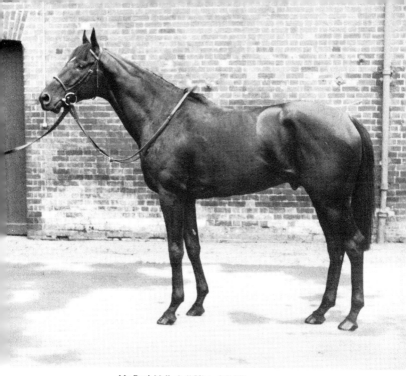

Mr Paul Mellon's "Glint of Gold"

face of tempting offers from the States meets with the success it deserves. A really attractive colt with a fine temperament and just about as fluent a mover as you'll see, Glint of Gold was a top-class performer and an extraordinarily tough and genuine one too. We wish him well. *I. Balding.*

GLISSEEN 5 b.m. Shiny Tenth 120–Blesseen 71 (So Blessed 130) (1981 NR 1982 8.2s 8f) fair sort; plater; stays 9f; acts on soft going; wears blinkers; sold 720 gns Doncaster May Sales. *M. James.* — —

GLITTERING GEM 2 b.f. Silly Season 127–Arrival 102 (Henry the Seventh 125) (1982 6g 7fg 7f2 7.6v) Apr 25; strong filly; half-sister to several winners here and abroad; dam, a sprinter, at her best at 2 yrs; 4 lengths second of 14 to Zariya in maiden race at Brighton in September, only form; stays 7f; acts on firm going. *K. Brassey.* 77

GLOMACH (USA) 3 ch.f. Majestic Light–Seven Locks (Jacinto) (1981 NR 1982 7fg 7d 7fg2 7g* 9f) quite well-made filly; half-sister to 3 winners in USA; dam unraced half-sister to top-class American horses Fort Marcy and Key to the Mint; sire high-class winner from 1m to 1¼m; favourite when winning maiden race at Thirsk in July; had shown ability all previous starts; should stay beyond 7f but ran poorly at 9f. *J. Dunlop.* 73

GLORIA MUNDI 2 b.f. Blakeney 126–Final Orders (Prince John) (1982 7fg3 7f 7.6v2 7.2s2 8d3) Apr 30; small, close-coupled filly; half-sister to several winners, including useful middle-distance 3-y-o Yard Bird (by Busted) and very useful stayer Hans Brinker (by Dike); dam ran only twice; placed in maiden and minor events, on final outing finishing long way clear of remainder when going 87

355

down by short head and a head to High Cannon and Full Rainbow in 16-runner race at Redcar in November; will stay well; appears to act on any going; hung left last 2 starts; hasn't a lot of scope. *B. Hobbs.*

GLORIOUS   4 ch.g. Hittite Glory 125–Cathays Park (Reliance II 137)   (1981 6s   **61**
6g 6s 5g⁴ 7fg* 7g 1982 8fg 7.2s 6s 7d* 7g³)   strong gelding; plater; 33/1 when
beating Sitica a neck in non-seller at Doncaster in October; promises to stay
1m; yet to race on really firm going, but probably acts on any other. *M. W.*
Easterby.

GLORIOUS JANE   2 b.f. Hittite Glory 125–Westmoreland Jane 76 (Vimy 132)   **83**
(1982 6fg 7g² 6g² 6v²)   Apr 26; quite attractive filly; half-sister to several
winners, including good Brazilian winner Bac (by Sharpen Up); dam placed at up
to 17f when named Ciboulette; second in maiden races at Ayr and Hamilton, and
in minor event at Ripon in between; temperamental in paddock and reluctant to
go to post at Ripon; sold H. de Bromhead 7,600 gns Newmarket Autumn Sales.
J. W. Watts.

GLORIOUS SPRING   2 ch.f. Hittite Glory 125–Primrose Day 64 (The Brianstan   **41**
128)   (1982 5fg⁴ 6f 6s 5.1g³ 5fg)   May 14; 700Y; small, light-framed filly; bad
plater; blinkered last 2 starts; sold 420 Newmarket July Sales. *G. Blum.*

GLORY BIRD   3 ch.c. Hittite Glory 125–Partridge 65 (Mossborough 126)   (1981   **56**
5d 5s 6fg 6d 7d 7g 8d⁴ 1982 10s* 10d³ 10f 10d 12d 12d⁴)   useful-looking colt;
plater; attracted no bid after winning decisively at Nottingham in April; stays
1½m; best form on a soft surface; ran respectably in blinkers once at 2 yrs.
P. Rohan.

GLORY GIRL   2 b.f. Hittite Glory 125–Ribots Affair 100 (Ribot 142)   (1982   **42**
5g⁴ 5f)   Apr 10; 460Y; fourth foal; half-sister to a winner in France; dam Irish
2-y-o 6f winner; bad plater; not raced after May. *Miss L. Siddall.*

GLORY ISLE   3 ch.f. Hittite Glory 125–Island Woman 76 (King's Troop 118)   **60**
(1981 5fg 1982 7d⁴ 7.2g 8.2g³ 9f* 8.3g 10d 10s)   7,600Y; tall, close-coupled
filly; half-sister to several winners, including fairly useful stayer Iona (by
Kalydon); dam, a sprinter, comes from same family as Park Top and Ksar;
stayed on to win minor event at Redcar in August (sweated up); suited by 9f;
acts on firm going. *A. Bailey.*

GLORY ME   2 br.c. Hittite Glory 125–Mummy's Darling 114 (Mummy's Pet 125)   —
(1982 5fg 5d)   Apr 12; 6,400F; strong colt; first foal; dam won five 5f races;
well beaten in sellers; dead. *M. W. Easterby.*

GLOWING HALO   3 ch.f. Grundy 137–Blessed Again 90 (Ballymoss 136)   (1981   **82**
7g 1982 10s* 12f* 13.3f 14f)   useful-looking filly; easily won maiden race at
Chepstow in April and held persistent challenge of Aura by ¾ length in minor
event at Salisbury in May (pair 8 lengths clear); well beaten in quite valuable
handicaps at Newbury (finished sore after spreading a plate) and Goodwood in
July; should stay 1¾m; acts on any going. *H. Candy.*

GLYNDEBOURNE (USA)   4 ch.c. Annihilate 'Em–Worthy Charm (Boldnesian)   —
(1981 7s 7g 6g 6d 8g 1982 8g 7s)   robust, useful sort; has plenty of ability, but
usually faces stiff tasks; probably stays 7f. *G. Balding.*

GOBLIN   7 ch.h. Sun Prince 128–Rocelle 101 (Sodium 128)   (1981 12f 12f⁴ 12f   —
1982 11f 12fg 13.1f)   poor handicapper nowadays; suited by 1½m; needs a sound
surface; has worn bandages in front. *M. Bradley.*

GOD BLESS   3 b.f. So Blessed 130–Lady Gaylord (Double Jump 131)   (1981 6g   **85**
1982 10s 8fg 7fg* 7.2f² 7fg 7f 10f⁴ 10fg 10g 10g 8v⁴ 8s² 8.2s 7d)   strong filly;
sometimes raced out of her depth; decisively won maiden race at Goodwood in
May; second afterwards in handicaps at Haydock and Sandown; stays 1¼m;
acts on any going but is ideally suited by some give in the ground; has run
respectably when sweating up; has shown a tendency to hang; sold 8,000 gns
Newmarket December Sales. *H. Collingridge.*

GO DIANA   5 gr.m. The Go-Between 129–My Diana 94 (Sovereign Path 125)   —
(1981 NR 1982 8f 8fg⁴ 5.3fg)   leggy mare; poor plater; fourth in apprentice race
at Brighton in June; stays 1m; often blinkered. *J. Jenkins.*

GODLORD   2 gr.c. Godswalk 130–Gay Pariso 82 (Sir Gaylord)   (1982 5f²)
Jan 27; 12,000F, 27,000Y; half-brother to 3-y-o Independentia (by Home Guard);
dam, daughter of Musidora winner Jakomima, won over 1m; 5/2 on, went
down by 8 lengths to Jonacris in 4-runner minor event at Ripon in May, only
outing; sold 4,400 gns Doncaster November Sales. *M. H. Easterby.*

GODLY   3 ro.c. Godswalk 130–Desert Pet 77 (Petingo 135)   (1981 6g   1982 6s* **83** d
8.2fg 6d 7fg* 6fg² 6g 7g 8g 8d 8d 6s 6s 7d)   strong colt; won maiden race at
Ayr in March and handicap on same course in July (made most); ran creditably
next time but finished well beaten most subsequent starts; stays 7f; seems to
act on any going; blinkered tenth and eleventh outings; sold to Miss A. Sinclair
6,200 gns Ascot December Sales.   *W. Elsey.*

GODOLPHIN   2 gr.c. Godswalk 130–Lilgarde 83§ (Hugh Lupus 132)   (1982   **75**
5f⁴ 5f⁴ 5f³ 5f² 5f⁴ 5f² 5g)   May 18; 15,000Y; strong, short-coupled colt; half-
brother to several winners, including very useful 1972 2-y-o sprinter Laylock (by
Fortino II); dam won at 1¼m; ran best race when second to Glenfield Portion in
nursery at Redcar in August on penultimate appearance; disappointed in valuable seller at York (bandaged near-fore) the following month; gives impression
5f is his trip; blinkered third and sixth starts; ridden by jockey in spurs on third.
M. W. Easterby.

GOD'S IMAGE   3 gr.g. Godswalk 130–Pink Larkspur (Ragusa 137)   (1981 NR   **65**
1982 6g 7.6f⁴ 8fg⁴ 7f 7f* 8g)   11,000F, 8,800Y; sparely-made, workmanlike
gelding; third living foal; dam, placed over 9f at 2 yrs in Ireland, comes from a
very successful family; outsider of 7 when winning handicap at Yarmouth in
August; may stay 1¼m.   *I. Walker.*

GODSRUN   2 b.f. Godswalk 130–Eranos (Arts and Letters)   (1982 5g 5f³ 5f 6f   **47**
7f 8fg 8d 10d)   May 26; 8,000Y; leggy filly; poor walker; second foal; dam, out
of half-sister to Northern Dancer, ran only once; poor form, including in sellers;
sent to India.   *Mrs M. Nesbitt.*

GODSTRUTH   3 gr. or ro.c. Godswalk 130–Light Opera 101 (Vienna 127)   (1981   **69**
5g 5g 5f² 5f³ 5fg² 5.1d² 5g 5s²   1982 6d* 6f 5g 6fg 6v⁴ 6d 6g)   small, strong colt;
good walker and mover; won maiden event at Nottingham in April; not disgraced in handicaps several subsequent starts; suited by 6f; acts on any going;
blinkered nowadays.   *H. T. Jones.*

GOING GOING   3 b.g. Auction Ring 123–Whitethorn (Gulf Pearl 117)   (1981   **72**
NR   1982 8fg³ 8fg 10f 10.2s² 10d 12s²)   IR 21,000Y; compact, attractive
gelding; good walker; first foal; dam Irish 1½m winner; placed in varied company;
stays 1½m; gives impression he'll always be suited by some give in the ground;
has run creditably for an apprentice.   *H. Candy.*

GOING WELL   3 b.f. Dance In Time–Little Firefly (Bold Ruler)   (1981 5s 5g   **—**
5d 5g 6f   1982 9.4fg 8g⁴ 6g 6g)   leggy, rather lightly-made filly; little worthwhile
form, including in a seller; suited by 1m; blinkered once at 2 yrs; trained first 3
outings by M. W. Easterby.   *T. Craig.*

GO JOGGING (FR)   2 b.f. Go Marching–Tanit (Blanc Bleu 124)   (1982 5.5d²   **120**
5.5d* 5d* 5g* 5v³)   half-sister to several French middle-distance winners, including 1½m winner Ribit (by Sir Ribot); dam won at around 1m at 4 yrs in
France; one of the best two-year-old sprinters in France and won 3 of her 5
starts, a minor event at Evry in July, 7-runner Prix de la Vallee d'Auge at

Prix d'Arenberg, Chantilly—Go Jogging wins from Interco.   Dona
Gaylord finishes third with Sevruga (No. 5) fourth

Deauville in August (by 4 lengths from Dona Gaylord) and Prix d'Arenberg at Chantilly in September (long odds on, had to struggle to beat Interco ¾ length); also ran very well against older horses in Prix du Petit Couvert at Longchamp in October, finishing 1¼ lengths third to Kind Music after showing up throughout; will stay 6f. *J. Cunnington, jnr, France.*

GOLD BIRD (FR)   3 b.f. Rheingold 137–Orange Bird (Sea-Bird II 145)   (1981 **115** NR   1982 10d² 12g³ 10.5d* 12g² 13.5fg 12f 12.5s² 12v)   260,000 francs Y (approx £26,000); third foal; dam, winner over 1m in France, is half-sister to very smart performers Duke of Marmalade and Aladancer; won valuable handicap at Longchamp in May by ½ length from Kazatska; placed most other starts, running well to be second in Prix de la Porte de Passy at Longchamp in June and Prix de Royallieu on same course in October, going down by 1½ lengths to Gipsy Road in latter; stays 1½m well; ideally suited by some give in the ground. *J-C. Cunnington, France.*

GOLD BREEZE   4 b. or br.f. Persian Breeze 121–Gold Poulet 84 (Goldhill 125)   — (1981 6v 5d 5g³ 5g 6g   1982 5f 6g)   strong filly; poor handicapper; well beaten in sellers on occasions; unlikely to stay 6f; has run badly when tried in blinkers. *Mrs A. Bell.*

GOLDEN ALRAY   4 br.f. Ballynockan 112–Mollie (I Say 125)   (1981 10f 12g   — 10s³ 11d* 12d   1982 8.2s 10f 11f)   leggy filly; stayed 11f; dead. *B. McMahon.*

GOLDEN BRIGADIER   4 b.c. Brigadier Gerard 144–Golden Fez (Aureole 132)   **80 §** (1981 8s* 10fg² 12.3g 12g² 12d 12f 12f³ 10g 12fg 10.5g³ 12g 10d 10d 10v 12g 12g 1982 10.6s² 10fg² 10.4g 11f* 10f 12g 12fg)   strong, good sort; by no means the heartiest of battlers and was ridden superbly by W. Newnes when winning London Gold Cup (Handicap) at Newbury in May by ¾ length from Feltwell; stays 1½m; seems to act on any going; occasionally blinkered, and has won in them; sometimes bandaged behind; often apprentice ridden; pulled himself up final start and can't be relied upon. *J. Old.*

GOLDEN DECOY   2 b.f. Decoy Boy 129–Nina's Gold 55 (Nina's Boy)   (1982 **70** 5.8g 8s 7d 6s)   May 12; first foal; dam poor plater; 4 lengths fifth of 16 behind Marzooga in maiden race at Leicester in November, final outing and first indication of merit; suited by 6f. *D. C. Tucker.*

GOLDEN FLAIR   3 b.g. Golden Dipper 119–Floral 82 (Floribunda 136)   (1981   — NR   1982 7g 8f 8fg 9fg 13d)   900Y; fair sort; good walker; half-brother to 6f winner Floral Dance (by Record Token) and a winner by Runnymede; dam 2-y-o 7f winner; only plating class. *S. Mellor.*

GOLDEN FLEECE (USA)   3 b.c. Nijinsky 138–Exotic Treat (Vaguely Noble **133** 140)   (1981 8g*   1982 10s* 10fg* 12f*)

It is probably true to say that there is rarely a moment in the running of the Derby when there are not at least half a dozen jockeys who would be pleased to be sailing along in front, if only their mounts were capable of getting to the front. One reason is that the Derby is the biggest occasion of the flat-racing year in Britain and big occasions often engender eagerness and sometimes impatience on the part of jockeys, especially when there is a big field as there usually is for the Derby. But there's a much more important reason: it is more desirable in the Derby than in any other major race of the same distance to be well placed throughout and usually of paramount importance to hold a good position on the steep descent to Tattenham Corner. The three-and-a-half-furlong run-in at Epsom continues on a gradually decreasing downhill gradient until approaching the final furlong and prospects of recovering lost ground on this part of the Derby course are much worse than on flat, galloping courses such as York, Newbury and Doncaster or on courses such as Ascot and Sandown where races are very much against the collar in the straight. We can count on the fingers of one hand the horses in the past forty years or so that have won the Derby after being among the backmarkers at Tattenham Corner. The latest winner Golden Fleece is one of them: he came from fifteenth-of-eighteen position at the entrance to the straight, achieving victory in a manner which can rarely have been seen in the entire history of the race. No Derby winner in the previous twenty years had overtaken so many horses after Tattenham Corner.

In one respect at least the victory of Golden Fleece was more dramatic and remarkable than that of the 1961 winner Psidium who passed more than twenty horses in the straight, getting up inside the final furlong. Psidium's position approaching Tattenham Corner created little stir at the time—his chance of winning appeared so forlorn that he started at 66/1—but Golden Fleece was favourite for the Derby and to see him so far behind coming down Tattenham

*Nijinsky Stakes, Leopardstown—Golden Fleece is eased before
the finish when beating Assert and Lords*

Hill—he was at least a dozen lengths behind the leaders at one stage—was little
short of astonishing, especially since his rider appeared quite unconcerned and was
making no attempt to improve his position after purposely dropping Golden
Fleece to the back of the field at the start. Troy had been a similar distance
behind at Tattenham Corner in his Derby but through no choice of his rider who
had had to work hard to maintain a place in the middle of the field. We have
never seen a Derby favourite ridden with the degree of confidence that Eddery
displayed on Golden Fleece: he was coolness personified. The nearest parallel
in our experience is Breasley's handling of Santa Claus in 1964: Santa Claus had
only three behind him at halfway and rounding the final bend, where there were
eight in front of him, he had a dozen lengths to make up on the leaders. But
Santa Claus needed practically all the length of the straight to get in front;
he took the lead in the last hundred yards and had only a length to spare at the
finish. By contrast, Golden Fleece, steered to the outside as the field straightened
out for home, showed phenomenal acceleration for a middle-distance performer
to get himself into a good position in the space of little more than a furlong.
With about two furlongs to go he had only to pass Norwick, Peacetime and
Touching Wood to win and so strongly was he travelling that it was obvious he
was going to do so. Sweeping into the lead approaching the final furlong
Golden Fleece drew away, drifting towards the rails, for a victory which, on the
face of it, could only be described as astounding.

It has been said that Golden Fleece outclassed the opposition in the Derby.
As usual, however, there were hard-luck stories after the race, the two most
notable concerning the third Silver Hawk and the fourth Persepolis both of whom
finished strongly, the latter even more strongly than Golden Fleece. Silver
Hawk's rider reported that his mount was baulked at the top of the hill and for
the French-trained Persepolis the race was a chapter of misfortunes. Having lain
even further back than the winner until after Tattenham Corner, Persepolis' rider
tried to make progress along the inside and met with the trouble that so often
attends such a manoeuvre at Epsom. By the time Persepolis got clear his
position was hopeless. Had he enjoyed as good a run as Golden Fleece he would
almost certainly have finished second and might have troubled the winner.
Golden Fleece won by three lengths from the resolute stayer Touching Wood
who had to be pushed along throughout the last mile to hold a prominent position
and was strongly ridden in the straight; Silver Hawk finished a length behind
Touching Wood with Persepolis a head away. Norwick, well placed all the way
and the leader from early in the straight until just before Golden Fleece surged
past, tired in the closing stages and finished fifth with Palace Gold, like the
runner-up a maiden at the time of the Derby, in sixth place. Of the others,
Jalmood, a decisive winner of the Highland Spring Derby Trial at Lingfield
and the pick of the paddock at Epsom, and Peacetime, who had won both the
Guardian Classic Trial at Sandown and the Schroder Life Predominate Stakes at

Goodwood, were the biggest disappointments; Jalmood was prone to muscular trouble as a three-year-old which probably explained his Derby running, while Peacetime had been affected by coughing and had had an incomplete preparation for the race. Golden Fleece himself had missed a few days work just before the Derby because of slight lameness in a hind leg.

The tradition of the Derby and the immense publicity that attends its running leads to most winners of the race being the subject of exaggerated plaudits, at least for a time. Golden Fleece was no exception, hailed by most critics who witnessed his performance as an outstanding top-class horse, possibly another Nijinsky or Alleged for his trainer. But the Derby is run early in the season—before some of the best middle-distance performers have reached their full powers—and it seldom turns out to be the most significant middle-distance race in Europe. It happens as often as not that the best middle-distance three-year-old of the year is not even in the Derby field. For a Derby winner to prove himself a good Derby winner he ideally has to go on and beat the best of those of his generation that for one reason or another missed the Derby and to beat the best of the older horses that have remained in training. Unfortunately there was no such opportunity for Golden Fleece; like Psidium, and a more recent Derby winner Morston, he never ran afterwards. Golden Fleece became a source of ceaseless worry to his trainer in the time after Epsom, contracting a viral infection which was slow to clear and then being held up in his work because of lameness in the same hind leg that had caused trouble before the Derby. In August it was announced that Golden Fleece had been retired to the Coolmore Stud in Ireland, his trainer saying there wasn't enough time to get a full preparation into him for his major autumn objective, the Prix de l'Arc de Triomphe. It is on his Derby performance that Golden Fleece has therefore primarily to be judged.

What was the Derby form worth? Well, before giving an appraisal of the strength of the field, let us make one thing clear. Although Golden Fleece achieved victory in striking manner and showed most impressive acceleration, we cannot agree with those who labelled him an easy Derby winner. To hold that he treated the opposition with contempt, as some did, was not our reading of things at all. Golden Fleece was ridden hard after taking the lead, Eddery cracking him with the whip at least five times in the last furlong, and it would be a mistake for anyone to assume that he had much, if anything, in hand at the finish beyond the three lengths by which he defeated Touching Wood. Perhaps

Derby Stakes, Epsom—rounding Tattenham Corner, Florida Son leads from Norwick with Touching Wood on his inside. Peacetime (striped sleeves) is also close up with Reef Glade (light colours), the grey Count Pahlen and on the wide outside Super Sunrise and Father Rooney (breastgirth). Golden Fleece (noseband) has only three behind him including the French-trained Persepolis (rails)

Derby Stakes, Epsom—a striking victory for Golden Fleece who draws clear of Touching Wood. The fast-finishing Silver Hawk and Persepolis (striped sleeves) are third and fourth and Norwick (rails) fifth

if Eddery had secured a better place approaching the final turn and had not used up so much of Golden Fleece's reserves to reach a challenging position the horse would have won by a wider margin. But, of course, that's conjecture. In any case, there was no cause for complaint at the time about Eddery's handling of Golden Fleece: he received instructions to ride a waiting race and his job was primarily to see that the horse won, not to see that he showed the full measure of his superiority over the field on the day.

Only five of the eighteen runners in the Derby were subsequently successful and most of them were beaten often enough to show that, as three year olds at any rate, they could not be regarded as a vintage collection judged by normal Derby standards—the manner alone of Golden Fleece's victory suggested as much. In the months that followed the only real compliments paid to the Derby form came from Touching Wood who almost certainly needed a longer distance to show to best advantage later in the season and won the St Leger in September and its Irish equivalent in October after defeats in the Gordon Stakes at Goodwood and the Great Voltigeur Stakes at York. Silver Hawk injured a cannonbone in the summer which kept him off the course after he had finished second to Assert in a modest field for the Irish Sweeps Derby, beaten twice as far by Assert at the Curragh as he had been by Golden Fleece at Epsom. Persepolis ran moderately in his only subsequent race. Norwick didn't win as a three-year-old but ran creditably on a number of occasions, notably when runner-up to Assert in the Benson and Hedges Gold Cup, beaten six lengths—about the same distance that separated him from Golden Fleece on Derby Day—and fourth in the St Leger, finishing a couple of lengths or so further behind Touching Wood than he had at Epsom. Of the others in the Derby field that won afterwards, Peacetime won the Valdoe Stakes at Goodwood, Jalmood the Mecca Bookmakers Scottish Derby at Ayr, and the rank outsiders Tidworth Tattoo and Reef Glade a maiden race at Sandown and a handicap at Ripon respectively.

A strict reading of the form-book suggests that Golden Fleece is little better than such recent run-of-the-mill Derby winners as Shirley Heights and Henbit. It was a great pity that Golden Fleece never had a chance to show his worth in the big open-aged middle-distance races. The Derby was only his fourth race and there was almost certainly improvement in him. In none of his three races before the Derby was Golden Fleece extended. He won his only start at two, a maiden event at Leopardstown in September in which we were greatly taken with his performance, and the Sean Graham Ballymoss Stakes at the Curragh in April and the Nijinsky Stakes at Leopardstown in May, both over a mile and a quarter. Golden Fleece beat Assert easing up by two and a half lengths in the Nijinsky Stakes and, although Assert was tenderly handled that day, it is probably reasonable to accept that at that time Golden Fleece was the better horse at a mile and a quarter. Whether Golden Fleece would have won the Derby, particularly ridden the way he was, had Assert been in the field—he won the Prix du Jockey-Club four days after Derby Day—no-one can know. The argument about which was the better could only have been solved satisfactorily by another meeting between them when both were fully fit and in a race of more importance than the Nijinsky Stakes.

Interestingly, Eddery who rode both Golden Fleece and Assert to a big-race victory, had no doubts about their respective merits. His considered view was that Golden Fleece was the best horse he had ridden, high praise indeed considering the quality of some of the other horses with which he has been associated, including Grundy. Trainer Vincent O'Brien, who has now saddled more Epsom Derby winners than any man this century, was reported to have said after the Derby that he ranks Golden Fleece with those he regards as the best of his five other winners of the race, Nijinsky and Sir Ivor. 'He has such speed', O'Brien said, explaining that his greatest worry before the race had been whether Golden Fleece would get the trip. Apparently he harboured no doubts about the ability of Golden Fleece to act on the Epsom course. A big, well-made, most attractive colt—the biggest in the Derby field—Golden Fleece didn't strike everyone as the ideal type for Epsom, but then neither had such as Pinza, Crepello, Golden Fleece's sire Nijinsky, or more recently, Snow Knight, Morston and Henbit, none of whom found their above-average size a bar to Derby success. Except for becoming a little unbalanced in the closing stages, which could have been as much a result of tiredness or greenness as of inability to handle the camber of the track, Golden Fleece negotiated the turns and gradients of Epsom with dexterity. Although the effect on the Derby runners of the so-called Epsom 'ordeal'—the mobbing in the crowded paddock, the lengthy parade and the long trail in Indian file across the course to the start—is generally much over-estimated, some also thought that Golden Fleece might be upset by the Derby preliminaries. He was reputedly a highly-strung animal, a nervous character said to be subject to claustrophobia when confined in a horse box or starting stalls. He did break into a sweat during the parade but was one of the last to be loaded into the stalls and gave no trouble.

Fears that Golden Fleece might not possess the necessary stamina to win a strongly-run Derby proved ill-founded: he stayed the trip very well. Golden Fleece's time—2m 34.27 sec—was the fastest for the race since Mahmoud set the record of 2m 33.80 sec (hand-timed) in 1936, indicating not only that the ground was riding fast but also that the pace was a hot one from start to finish. Incidentally, the time record for Epsom's mile-and-a-half course is held by Bustino who recorded 2m 33.31 sec in the 1975 Coronation Cup. One other thing the Derby showed: although he moved short in his slower paces on the way to post Golden Fleece acted well on the very firm going. As the going for the Sean Graham Ballymoss Stakes was soft it seems safe to conclude that Golden Fleece acted on any going.

		Northern Dancer (b 1961)	Nearctic
	Nijinsky		Natalma
	(b 1967)	Flaming Page	Bull Page
Golden Fleece (USA)		(b 1959)	Flaring Top
(b.c. 1979)		Vaguely Noble	Vienna
	Exotic Treat	(b 1965)	Noble Lassie
	(ch 1971)	Rare Treat	Stymie
		(ch 1952)	Rare Perfume

In the light of the massive value that is usually put on a Derby winner as soon as he has passed the post many readers may be surprised to learn that only six Derby winners in the past forty-six years have been sired by a former winner of the race. Sandwiched between Mahmoud, who was by the 1930 winner Blenheim, and Golden Fleece came two horses who won war-time substitutes at Newmarket, Owen Tudor (by Hyperion) and Ocean Swell (by Blue Peter), followed by Never Say Die's son Larkspur in 1962 and Mill Reef's son Shirley Heights in 1978. Hyperion, Mill Reef and Nijinsky are among the Derby winners to become outstanding stallions but a Derby victory does not guarantee success at stud. Seven post-war Derby winners have finished up in Japan and two,

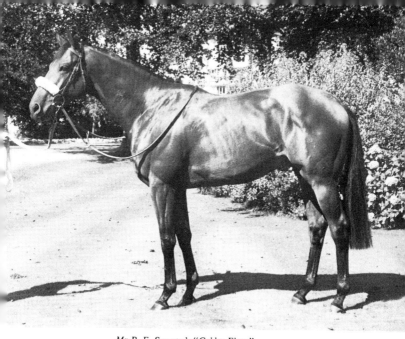

Mr R. E. Sangster's "Golden Fleece"

including Psidium, were eventually sold to Argentina. Although some sired good horses in Europe—Psidium sired the Irish Sweeps Derby and St Leger winner Sodium—there is no evidence that their exportation represented a serious loss to our bloodstock breeders. Of course, Derby winners are among the best horses to breed from—it would be absurd to suggest otherwise—but the enormous value put on the Derby winner each year for stud purposes would seem to have no rational basis. Golden Fleece's fee is IR 100,000 guineas.

Golden Fleece's value as a stallion is not, of course, based solely on the prestige attached to his success at Epsom. He has good looks and an extremely fashionable pedigree. The eighth American-bred Derby winner in the last fifteen runnings of the race, he is the first English classic winner sired by the triple crown winner Nijinsky whose sons and those of his sire Northern Dancer are nowadays the most sought-after commodities in the yearling market—a Nijinsky colt fetched a world record 4,250,000 dollars (about £2,500,000 at prevailing exchange rates) at Keeneland in 1982, bought by a syndicate headed by Robert Sangster whose colours were carried to success in the English, French and Irish Derby in 1982, a sequence of victories without precedent. Golden Fleece was also a Keeneland yearling purchase, costing Sangster and his associates 775,000 dollars, a sum which placed him among the ten highest-priced yearling colts of the year in the United States. Golden Fleece is the third living foal of Exotic Treat, an unraced half-sister to the champion three-year-old filly of 1965 in the United States What A Treat. What A Treat, once the world's record-priced broodmare, is the dam of several winners, notably Be My Guest, a high-class miler in his racing days and the champion sire in Britain and Ireland in 1982. Golden Fleece's grandam Rare Treat, who also bred a very smart North American middle-distance performer in Ring Twice, was one of the hardiest race-mares of her day, winning sixteen races and finishing in the first three on fifty of her hundred-and-one starts. Before Golden Fleece, Exotic Treat bred Northern Treat (by Northern Dancer), a winner in the United States as a three-year-old and now at stud in France, and the smart Secretariat racemare Office Wife who won the Modesty Handicap, a stakes race over nine and a half furlongs, at Arlington Park in 1982. Exotic Treat foaled a full brother to Golden Fleece shortly before the Derby. What must he be worth? *V. O'Brien, Ireland.*

GOLDEN GREEN 3 gr.c. Godswalk 130–Kentucky Green 100 (One For All) **93**
(1981 5f³ 5s   1982 5f* 5fg 6g 5.8g² 6f³ 5.8f² 5f² 5g 5fg³ 5f⁴) well-made, good sort; favourite when winning maiden event at Bath in May; placed most subsequent starts, running race of his life on seventh to be 2 lengths second of 12 to Tina's Pet in King George Stakes at Goodwood in July, but isn't the most reliable of animals; stays 6f; acts well on firm going; blinkered fifth and final appearances. *J. Bethell.*

GOLDEN LADDIE 3 ch.c. Northern Flash–Annalie (Crepello 136) (1981 5fg **65**
5g 7d 7fg 7fg 1982 10d⁴ 8.5fg 8g 10fg* 11.7fg 10d² 10f) compact, short-legged colt; made most of running to win handicap at Lingfield in June; should stay 1½m; acts on a firm and a soft surface. *M. Haynes.*

GOLDEN LEICESTER 6 br.g. Workboy 123–Snow Rum (Quorum 126) —
(1981 7s 12d 8fg³ 10f 10fg⁴ 1982 11s) strong gelding; stays 1¼m; acts on any going; blinkered twice in 1981; sometimes sweats up; has worn bandages; needed race when tailed off on only outing of 1982 (October). *P. Wigham.*

GOLDEN LIBRA 7 b.g. Goldhill 125–Lush Pool 70 (Dumbarnie 125) (1981 —
NR 1982 6f 8f 8fg) strong gelding; has been hobdayed; poor performer nowadays; probably acts on any going. *T. Cuthbert.*

GOLDEN LISLE 3 br.c. Pieces of Eight 128–Lisle's Filly (Burglar 128) (1981 **52**
5fg 5f 6g 7g* 6f 8.2fg 8fg² 7d 8g⁴ 1982 9.4f 8fg 8f* 9g³ 10f² 8f³ 8fg⁴ 7g) strong, compact colt; plater; won at Carlisle in June (bought in 1,950 gns); twice ran creditably in better company subsequently; suited by 1¼m; acts on firm going; wears blinkers; sent to Holland. *J. Etherington.*

GOLDEN MATCH 4 ch.g. Royal Match 117–Hunea (Hornbeam 130) (1981 —
10fg 10f 1982 12f 12d 10.1d) big gelding; poor maiden; blinkered last 2 starts. *M. Hinchliffe.*

GOLDEN PIN 3 b.f. Golden Dipper 119–Pin Hole 83 (Parthia 132) (1981 6d —
5d 1982 6s 6f 6g 7g 7fg) sturdy filly; poor plater. *E. Carter.*

GOLDEN REEF 5 b.g. Mill Reef 141–Photo Flash 119 (Match III 135) (1981 —
9s² 10g 12fg 1982 8g 10fg⁴ 11s² 12f* 12fg) well-made, attractive sort; won at Cagnes-sur-Mer in March; broke a leg at Newmarket the following month; would have stayed well; acted on any going; dead. *W. Hastings-Bass.*

GOLDEN RHYME 2 ch.f. Dom Racine 121–Silly Song (Silly Season 127) **87**
(1982 7fg⁴ 7.2s³) Apr 26; IR 15,500Y; fourth foal; half-sister to 3-y-o Korypheos (by He Loves Me) and Irish 1980 2-y-o 5f winner Keep Chanting (by Auction Ring); dam, half-sister to 3 very useful animals, won over 7f in Ireland; looked unlucky when third, beaten less than a length, to Amila in minor event at Haydock in October, racing on the inside and not finding an opening until well inside last furlong; acts on soft going; should have little difficulty in winning. *G. Hunter.*

GOLDEN SHERRY 3 b.f. Golden Sammy–Sherry Bird (Sherry Netherland —
113) (1981 7g 8d 1982 10fg 8fg 15.5fg) lightly-made, plain filly; behind in maiden races and a minor event. *J. Scallan.*

GOLDEN SOUVENIR (USA) 2 b.c. Damascus–Mysterious 127 (Crepello 136) **95** p
(1982 6s*) Mar 20; $500,000Y; fourth foal; half-brother to a winner in USA by Brigadier Gerard; dam, half-sister to top-class J. O. Tobin, won 1,000 Guineas and Oaks; co-favourite, shaped well when winning 13-runner maiden race at Naas in November by ¾ length from Saracen, the pair clear; will do much better over 1m or more and will win more races. *V. O'Brien, Ireland.*

GOLDEN WILKIE 3 b. or br.g. Averof 123–Royal Handful (Some Hand 119) **45**
(1981 5d* 5f⁴ 6f 6f 5f 5f 7f 1982 7g² 6g 7f³ 7f 5f 6fg 7fg² 9f 7f⁴) leggy gelding; good mover; plater; stayed 7f; seemed to act on any going; blinkered once in 1981; trained by B. Wilkinson first 4 starts; dead. *J. Parkes.*

GOLD FLOOR 5 b.g. Goldhill 125–Floor Show 78 (Galivanter 131) (1981 —
NR 1982 8fg) small gelding; little sign of ability. *M. Bradley.*

GOLD GROUND 4 ch.c. Grundy 137–Paltrasse 84 (Palestine 133) (1981 —
11.7g* 12s³ 12s 1982 14f 12g) well-made colt; lacks pace and will stay well; sold 2,000 gns Newmarket July Sales and exported. *P. Butler.*

GOLD HARMONY 3 ch.f. Goldhill 125–Bishop's Song 67 (Bishop's Move 92) —
(1981 NR 1982 10fg) fourth foal; dam 1¼m winner; unquoted, backward and
apprentice ridden at overweight when last of 8 to Steel Glow in maiden race at
Ripon in August. *J. Parkes.*

GOLD HEART 2 ch.g. Roman Warrior 132–Pickling Spice 79 (Frankincense **68**
120) (1982 6f 6g 7g 7fg 6s 6g⁴ 5d) May 14; short-backed, plain gelding;
fair plater; best form at 6f; wears blinkers. *A. Bailey.*

GOLD HUNTER 2 b.c. Rheingold 137–Mothers Girl (Huntercombe 133) —
(1982 8g) Apr 11; 24,000Y; good walker; first foal; dam unraced half-sister to
top-class middle-distance colt North Stoke; 14/1 and on backward side, made no
show in 17-runner maiden race won by Oula Owl at Newmarket in October. *J.
Sutcliffe.*

GOLD INLAY (USA) 2 ch.c. Le Fabuleux 133–Pamlisa (What A Pleasure) —
(1982 8g 10s) Apr 25; $37,000Y; leggy, close-coupled colt; second foal; dam
unraced sister to a stakes-placed winner; little worthwhile form in maiden events
at Newmarket and Nottingham (dwelt) in October. *W. Hastings-Bass.*

GOLD KEY 3 b.f. Lochnager 132–Gold Cheb 88 (Chebs Lad 120) (1981 5s³ **63**
5g* 6fg 5g 6d 6s⁴ 1982 6fg³ 5f³ 6g 8fg 7d 7s) strong-quartered filly; plater;
stays 6f; seems to act on any going. *M. W. Easterby.*

GOLDLINER ABBEY 4 b. or br.g. Abwah 118–Bright and Early (Rise 'N —
Shine II) (1981 10s⁴ 12d 12.5f 10f* 12.2g 12d 1982 10g) plater; stays 1¼m;
acts on firm going; wears blinkers. *J. Hardy.*

GOLD MEASURE 5 br.h. Goldhill 125–Fair Measure (Quorum 126) (1981 16f —
17.1h 14g⁴ 16f* 16g 15.8g 1982 16f 16fg) lengthy horse; soundly beaten in 1982;
suited by a test of stamina; acts on firm going. *J. Spearing.*

GOLDORATION 7 b.g. Gold Rod 129–Fair Jinks 65 (Tudor Jinks 121) (1981 **34**
6s³ 8fg² 8f 7g 1982 8s² 10fg⁴) plater; needs further than 6f and stays 1¼m;
probably acts on any going. *H. O'Neill.*

GOLD PHOENIX 2 b.c. Gold Rod 129–Princess Feola (South Pacific 87) (1982 —
5fg 6g 6s 8s) Feb 24; small, sturdy colt; no sign of ability, including in sellers;
blinkered third and fourth starts. *P. Burgoyne.*

GOLD RIFLE 3 br.c. Scottish Rifle 127–Bar Gold 80 (Lucky Brief 128) (1981 **76**
5g 6g 6fg⁴ 7f² 7f 7f⁴ 8f³ 8.2d³ 8.2s 1982 10g² 12f⁴ 12f* 12f³ 12fg² 12f² 12g 12.3fg
14g⁴ 12g² 12g 15d⁴) neat colt; quite a modest handicapper; won at Redcar in
May; suited by 1½m and wasn't disgraced over 15f; probably acts on any going;
sometimes blinkered; consistent. *J. Etherington.*

GOLD SPRING 2 gr. or ro.c. Goldhill 125–Another Spring 66 (Town Crier 119) —
(1982 5g 5d 7fg 8s) Jan 16; 3,500F, 1,800Y; neat colt; behind in sellers; of no
account. *J. Mason.*

GOLDWATER 2 b.c. Rheingold 137–Niltava (Habitat 134) (1982 7g) Apr 28; — p
27,000Y; rangy colt; first foal; dam, half-sister to Champion Stakes winner
Giacometti, ran twice in Germany; 8/1, prominent over 5f in 21-runner maiden
race won by Zoffany at Newbury in August; the type to do better. *B. Hobbs.*

GOLFERS DREAM 3 b.f. Carnoustie 132–Dream (Hornbeam 130) (1981 5d² —
5fg* 7fg 7fg⁴ 7f 1982 10fg⁴ 10.1d 8d) small, workmanlike filly; won small race
at Hamilton in 1981; well beaten at 3 yrs; should stay 1¼m+. *G. Thorner.*

GOLF GIRL (USA) 2 b.f. Vigors–Caption (Riva Ridge) (1982 5g) Mar 16; —
$75,000Y, $80,000 2-y-o; first foal; dam, from excellent family, was very useful
sprint stakes winner at 2 yrs; 25/1, none too well away when behind in 20-runner
maiden race won by Misguided at Newbury in September; likely to need further.
G. Hunter.

GOLLYNO 5 b.g. Giolla Mear 115–Nonnie (Dumbarnie 125) (1981 8d 13.3s 10g —
1982 7s 10f) tall, narrow, short-backed gelding; soundly beaten in varied company since 1980; stays 1½m; acts on any going; sold 1,000 gns Ascot June Sales.
I. Wardle.

GONE SAILING 3 b.f. Malacate 131–Go Surfing (Go Marching) (1981 7fg —
1982 10s⁴) big, lengthy, unfurnished filly; excellent mover; showed ability in
maiden race at Newmarket at 2 yrs; beaten a long way in similar event at
Chepstow in April. *L. Cumani.*

GONE WITH THE WIND 3 gr.g. Warpath 113–Bubbles 76 (Ballymoss 136) —
(1981 NR 1982 10g 12.3g) rangy gelding; first foal; dam won at up to 1¾m, and

is half-sister to Derby fourth Shotgun (by Warpath); behind in minor event at Ripon and maiden race at Newcastle in August; sold 1,500 gns Doncaster November Sales. *C. Thornton.*

GOOD AS DIAMONDS   2 b.c. Persian Bold 123–Aliceva (Alcide 136)   (1982   **95** 6d⁴ 7fg³ 7g² 7s⁴)   Apr 25; IR 35,000Y; smallish, well-made, attractive colt; half-brother to several winners, notably Irish 2,000 Guineas winner Nikoli (by Great Nephew), very smart Captain James (by Captain's Gig) and Coronation Stakes winner Sutton Place (by Tyrant); dam won over 1¼m and is half-sister to dam of Levmoss, Sweet Mimosa and Le Moss; ran in races, mainly of good class, won by All Systems Go, Gorytus, Muscatite and By Decree, and acquitted himself well each time; will stay 1m; fought for his head on third outing; sure to win in ordinary maiden company. *B. Hills.*

GOODBYE SHELLEY (FR)   2 b.f. Home Guard 129–Filiform 76 (Reform 132)   **116** (1982 6h 7d* 7fg³ 7g² 8g³ 8s*)

Enterprise reaped a rich reward when 36/1-outsider Goodbye Shelley won the Prix Marcel Boussac at Longchamp in October. Sending Goodbye Shelley all the way from Yorkshire to take on what, by record or reputation, were some of France's leading two-year-old fillies seemed the height of optimism since she'd been beaten in her last three races in England, on the latest occasion failing to get on terms with Bright Crocus and Silk Pyjamas in the May Hill Stakes at Doncaster, a contest in many respects similar to the Prix Marcel Boussac. She was up against Maximova who had dead-heated with the Prix Morny winner Deep Roots, a colt, in the Prix de la Salamandre; the unbeaten pattern race winner Air Distingue and eight other runners, all except one at shorter odds than Goodbye Shelley. In the event the stiff mile and soft going suited her extremely well, but ultimately the critical factor was the riding of her jockey, Lowe, every bit as enterprising an effort on his part as that of his patrons in sending her over. Goodbye Shelley had only a short head to spare in the end, and she would not have had that if Lowe, on his first ride in France, had delayed a second longer in sending her for home. The winner, almost the pick of the paddock and keenly on her toes, broke smartly and took up a good position straight away, pulling hard in third place as far as the home turn. Making the turn she was dashed into a two-length lead and for a long time looked as though she would maintain that sort of advantage, but gradually the best of the others began to close, forcing her to undergo a very hard race indeed for a two-year-old filly. The runner-up Mysterieuse Etoile, too, had a very hard race; she stayed on very strongly but paid for her jockey's underestimating the leader's ability, having been left with four lengths to make up and four horses to pass in the last furlong and a half. Maximova finished a disappointing third, a length down, and was subsequently relegated to fourth place for hampering L'Attrayante; Air Distingue, a tall, lengthy filly who'd gone in her coat, never threatened to take a hand, eventually finishing out of the first six.

The result provided all the justification needed for Goodbye Shelley's presence in the field. There remains, though, to explain the confidence behind her. It occurs to us that this was grounded largely in two related things—her breeding and her character. Goodbye Shelley, a half-sister to horses whom time and distance improved substantially in the Goodwood Cup winner Heighlin and his brother the Spanish St Leger winner El Pais, is over 16 hands; as the season had progressed so she had been growing to her frame and becoming more mature. When she first began to run she was backward and very green, and she remained green for quite a while, up to the May Hill Stakes in fact. When she gained her only previous win, in a small race over seven furlongs at Beverley in July, she ran all over the track before beating Carneades a length; so too at Redcar later in July where she finished third to Sheriff Muir. And in the Gilbey Champion Racehorse Futurity at York in September she ran in snatches before finishing strongly for a very close second place to Now and Again. She wore blinkers at York, wore them again at Doncaster and again at Longchamp. At Doncaster she kept an encouragingly straight course, running on well to get within a length of Silk Pyjamas though Bright Crocus beat her more than five lengths. Further to her character—her trainer did tell us shortly after Beverley that he anticipated she would be suited by some give in the ground, the type of going she didn't encounter between Beverley and Longchamp.

Some very good fillies have run in the Prix Marcel Boussac and its predecessor the Criterium des Pouliches, subsequent classic winners among them. What bearing on the classics the latest race will have remains to be seen; we doubt that the result will prove as significant as some of its predecessors.

Prix Marcel Boussac, Longchamp—the hard-ridden British-trained Goodbye Shelley (blinkers) just holds on from Mysterieuse Etoile

Goodbye Shelley may not often find conditions so favourable to her as they were at Longchamp in October; given a wet summer she may get her best chance of winning a classic in the French Oaks. The probability is that as a three-year-old she will be well suited by a longer distance than a mile, and we don't at this stage envisage her winning the Guineas.

		⌠Forli	⌠Aristophanes
	⌠Home Guard	⌡(ch 1963)	⌡Trevisa
	⌡(bl 1969)	⌠Stay at Home	⌠Bold Ruler
Goodbye Shelley (Fr)		⌡(br 1961)	⌡Alanesian
(b.f. Mar 30, 1980)		⌠Reform	⌠Pall Mall
	⌠Filiform	⌡(b 1964)	⌡Country House
	⌡(br 1970)	⌠Filigrana	⌠Niccolo Dell'Arca
		⌡(b 1953)	⌡Gamble in Gold

Goodbye Shelley's sire Home Guard stayed a mile and a quarter (he finished third to Brigadier Gerard in the Eclipse) though he was best at six furlongs. So far he hasn't set the world alight as a stallion and in 1981 he was transferred from Coolmore to stand in France. Goodbye Shelley came up for sale in France, at the Deauville Yearling Sales, being extremely well bought for 420,000 francs (around £38,000) by her present trainer. The dam Filiform has now produced four significant winners, for her first foal Fillaline (by High Line, as also are Heighlin and El Pais) went on to make a name in Hong Kong after winning as a two-year-old in this country. Filiform, a modest middle-distance winner, is from an excellent family, since she is a half-sister to the high-class filly Magic Flute and the very smart middle-distance performer Entanglement and a grand-daughter of the very speedy Gamble in Gold. The family had another important runner recently, the Queen Mary Stakes winner Pushy, whose great grandam is out of Gamble in Gold.

Goodbye Shelley had made up into a strong, quite attractive filly by the end of the season; she should train on, unless her very hard race at Longchamp spoils her. She obviously acts very well on soft going, possibly she even needs some give in the ground. *S. Norton.*

GOOD HABIT 4 ch.g. Habat 127–Parlais 101 (Pardao 120) (1981 10d 10s 12g 1982 7h 7fg 8fg 10.1d 10fg) small, fair sort; poor maiden. *G. Beeson.* —

GOOD MAN FRIDAY (USA) 3 b.g. Noble Commander–Tinker Jet (Hi-Hasty) (1981 6fg 7g³ 5d³ 8g 7d 1982 10s 8f⁴ 10g 10f 10.1fg 13g 9s³ 16s 10s 10.2s⁴) small, lightly-made gelding; poor performer nowadays; beaten in a seller final start; stays 1¼m; acts on soft going. *D. Thom.* 62

GOOD ON YOU 5 br.m. Virginia Boy 106–Mini Skirt (Bald Eagle 119) (1981 8.2d² 9fg⁴ 7g 8f* 7fg 8.2d 8s 8.2s* 1982 8f³ 8fg) small mare; poor mover; plater; ran creditably in non-sellers in 1982; stays 9f; acts on any going. *R. Johnson.* 43

GOOD PERFORMER 3 b.g. Sun Prince 128–Haymaking 115 (Galivanter 131) (1981 6d 6fg³ 7g⁴ 8s³ 7d 1982 8g⁴ 10s⁴ 8d 11s 8.5f⁴ 7g* 7g 7f 7fg) leggy, work-manlike gelding; plater; bought in 4,200 gns after justifying favouritism at Ayr in June; has worn blinkers; sold to D. Yeoman 1,900 gns Doncaster August Sales. *N. Callaghan.* 51

GOOD SCOUT 2 b.c. Prince Tenderfoot 126–Set Right (Never Bend) (1982 6g 6g³ 5d) May 18; small, active sort; second live foal; half-brother to French 3-y-o All In Order (by Tudor Melody or Riboboy), successful over 7f at 2 yrs; 75

dam, winner over 6f in Ireland, is sister to very smart stakes winner Triple Bend; 5½ lengths third of 19 to Return To Paris in minor event at Windsor in August, easily best effort; will stay 7f; hasn't much scope; sold 5,000 gns Newmarket Autumn Sales; sent to Malaysia. *R. Hern.*

GOOD TO FOLLOW 3 b.f. Wollow 132–Pavello 94 (Crepello 136) (1981 NR   **82** 1982 7fg* 8fg 8.5f⁴ 8fg) 33,000Y; small, quite attractive filly; third foal; half-sister to very smart sprinter Sayyaf (by Habitat); dam 1m winner and half-sister to smart Rymer; came with a strong run to beat Girl On A Swing by a head in 18-runner newcomers race at Newbury in April; put up easily best subsequent effort when keeping on to be just over 2 lengths fourth of 10 to Dalmally in valuable handicap at Epsom in June; stays 1m well. *P. Walwyn.*

GO ON GREEN 3 br.g. On Your Mark 125–Catilina (Sallust 134) (1981 5s 5s   — 5g² 5g³ 5g 6g 6fg 5fg 5f² 5g 1982 6f 6fg 6fg 5fg 5g 5f 7fg) fair sort; plater nowadays; speedy and is unlikely to stay 7f; evidently needs a sound surface. *D. Smith.*

GOOSE GREEN 2 ch.f. Celtic Cone 116–Fanny Green 68 (Space King 115)   — (1982 6s) Apr 17; lightly-made filly; first live foal; dam plating class on Flat and over hurdles; 20/1, faded in last 2f when behind in 19-runner seller at Haydock in October; will need much further. *P. Rohan.*

GORDIAN 2 ch.c. Grundy 137–Mrs Tiggywinkle 109 (Silly Season 127) (1982 **117** 6f⁴ 7fg* 7g³ 7g²)

Despite winning only one of his four starts Gordian managed to accumulate over £20,000 in prize money and can be said to have enjoyed a highly satisfactory season, especially as he runs like a colt who will be well suited by longer trips. By far the lion's share of his earnings came in the William Hill Dewhurst Stakes at Newmarket. Opposed by Diesis, Gorytus and Tough Commander, on form he didn't look likely to trouble the first two in the betting but appeared in the nature of a good thing to gain third prize worth in excess of £8,000. In the event, with Gorytus running inexplicably badly Gordian collected £17,505 for finishing second, thus proving that boldness sometimes receives its due reward. Sent on immediately they left the stalls, Gordian stayed in front until Diesis moved past him with ease less than two furlongs out; keeping on well, albeit at one pace, Gordian went down by five lengths, two lengths ahead of Tough Commander.

When we interviewed Guy Harwood for the Timeform Black Book in September he told us the plan for Gordian was to 'run him in a maiden and then probably a maidens-at-closing before asking him to tackle pattern-race company. You don't want to give them hard races before they have got their confidence'. He followed this programme almost to the letter. Odds on for a nineteen-runner maiden race at Salisbury in September after showing distinct promise on his debut in a £3,400 event on the same course the previous month, Gordian appropriately tied his rivals in knots, drawing clear in the final furlong to beat Amazon Prince driven out by five lengths. He moved up in class for his next outing in the Somerville Tattersall Stakes at Newmarket a fortnight before the Dewhurst. Favourite to beat Polished Silver, Cause Celebre, Mac's Palace and two others, Gordian looked none too lucky in finishing about one and three quarter lengths third to Polished Silver, finishing well but all too late after seeing very little daylight in the last quarter mile.

Gordian (ch.c. May 21, 1980)	Grundy (ch 1972)	Great Nephew (b 1963)	Honeyway
			Sybil's Niece
		Word from Lundy (b 1966)	Worden II
			Lundy Princess
	Mrs Tiggywinkle (ch 1971)	Silly Season (br 1962)	Tom Fool
			Double Deal
		My Enigma (ch 1964)	Klairon
			Land of Hope

Grundy, Gordian's sire, has got several good performers, notably Bireme, Kirtling, Little Wolf and Zilos, but to date his stud career has hardly been an unqualified success. After occupying eighth place in the sires list in 1980, he dropped to twentieth the following year and finished much further down in 1982. On the dam's side, Gordian is the second live foal of the One Thousand Guineas third Mrs Tiggywinkle who is a half-sister to the smart six-furlong and eight-and-a-half-furlong winner Mystic Circle out of the useful My Enigma, successful four times at up to a mile. My Enigma's dam produced four other winners, one of whom bred Merry Madcap, successful in the July Cup. Gordian, quite a well-made colt and a good walker and mover, cost 28,000 guineas as a yearling. We

Mr S. S. Niarchos' "Gordian"

think it will pay to start him off over a mile and a quarter at three since the specialist milers will almost certainly have too much pace for him, and in so far as his career has been one of steady improvement it is on the cards that he'll be up to running creditably in the sort of races those good colts Rankin and Newick contested for Harwood in their second season. *G. Harwood.*

GORMANSTOWN PRINCE 2 br.c. Windjammer (USA)–Finesse 87 (Miralgo **107**
130) (1982 5g 5g³ 6f² 5f² 5fg* 5fg² 6fg 7fg² 9d 7d) Mar 4; IR 19,000Y;
strong, good sort; half-brother to 3 winners, including very useful 3-y-o Irish
sprinter Princess Seal (by Prince Tenderfoot); dam won over 1¼m; won a bit
cleverly by a neck from odds-on Cat O'Nine Tails in 6-runner Erroll Stakes at
Ascot in June; also second 4 times in Ireland, on last 2 occasions going down by
short head to Virginia Deer in Curragh Stakes in July and by a length to comfortable winner Beaudelaire in Coolmore Try My Best Stakes at Leopardstown
in September; 6¾ lengths fourth of 6 to Danzatore in Ashford Castle Stakes at
the Curragh later in September; stays 1m; yet to race on really soft going but
acts on any other. *M. Cunningham, Ireland.*

GORSKY 6 b.g. Dubassoff–Artistically (Ribot 142) (1981 13d² 16d 12g 1982 **§§**
16g 14g) small gelding; inconsistent maiden; stays 2m; seems to act on any
going; used to wear blinkers; not resolute. *B. Richmond.*

GORYTUS (USA) 2 b.c. Nijinsky 138–Glad Rags 118 (High Hat 131) (1982 **132**
7fg* 7fg* 7g⁴)
The defeat of Gorytus in the William Hill Dewhurst Stakes at Newmarket
in October caused a sensation. Widely acknowledged as a two-year-old of
exceptional merit and hailed as an outstanding prospect for the 1983 classics
after impressive victories in the Acomb Stakes and the Laurent Perrier Champagne Stakes, Gorytus trailed in a distant last of four behind Diesis, beaten

369

in a matter of strides three furlongs from home and falling further and further behind until being virtually pulled up before the final furlong. When brought back to the unsaddling enclosure Gorytus was shaking badly and appeared both distressed and exhausted. What could possibly have caused such a reaction? His rider, Carson, reportedly thought the colt was choking, so could Gorytus have swallowed his tongue, a common enough occurrence? It was noticeable that Carson looked down at Gorytus' hind legs one and a half furlongs out, so had Gorytus rapped a nerve as sometimes happens, causing a temporary loss of action? Neither of these possibilities was ultimately accepted by Gorytus' connections. Was Gorytus coughing? This seemed the most likely explanation since some of Gorytus' stable-companions had also run below form recently and the stable hadn't had a winner since Little Wolf in the Jockey Club Cup two weeks earlier. Indeed there had been strong rumours before the Dewhurst that Gorytus was coughing—because of them the sponsors of the race temporarily suspended betting on it. When pressed the trainer denied there was any truth in the rumours, declaring Gorytus 100% fit and pointing out that his blood had been tested at the Equine Research Station on the Monday and Wednesday preceding Friday's race, producing perfectly normal results both times. There was emphatically nothing in Gorytus' appearance in the paddock to suggest that anything was amiss—he looked in superb condition, absolutely magnificent—and we can't believe that a trainer of Hern's skill and experience would risk jeopardising Gorytus' future by running him when under the weather. It turned out that coughing wasn't to blame either. Gorytus was reported 'perfectly normal' the following day and just a week after the race Hern made the following statement: 'He looks a picture in the box and he's so well I've had to give him some good exercise. I've got quite a few horses that are coughing, and even those are well in themselves. But Gorytus is showing no signs of a cough, and even if he did have a virus he should not have stopped as quickly as he did at Newmarket.'

So, if Gorytus' distress wasn't the result of a natural physical ailment, was it caused by something more sinister? An announcement was made at the end of October that Gorytus' dope test had proved negative, followed in December by a statement from Racecourse Security Services that they had found no evidence of foul play. One of Carson's post-race reactions had been that Gorytus 'had run like a horse that had been got at' and even before the results of the dope test were known there was a great deal of speculation that Gorytus had been the victim of some form of malpractice which wouldn't show up

Acomb Stakes, York—a scintillating debut from Gorytus who quickens away in breathtaking style to beat the odds-on Salieri

in a dope test. There were similarities between Gorytus' performance and Ribofilio's when a beaten favourite in the 1969 Two Thousand Guineas. *Racehorses of 1969* had this to say of Ribofilio: 'Ribofilio's extraordinary performance in the Two Thousand Guineas is never likely to be explained, for an official dope test proved negative. He looked bright and well in his coat beforehand, walked into the paddock as though he meant business, and gave no hint that anything might be wrong with him on the way down to the post. In the race he held a place among the backmarkers from the start and began to lose touch by halfway. He soon became tailed off and Piggott, his rider, eased him up to a canter over the last two furlongs. Ribofilio appeared to pull up sound, but Piggott reported "he could not raise a gallop at any stage" and neither jockey nor trainer was able to offer any explanation of Ribofilio's running at the stewards' inquiry.'

The Guardian's racing correspondent Richard Baerlein, reviewing the performance of Gorytus in the Dewhurst, reported that Piggott had told him he was positive that Ribofilio had been 'got at'. Baerlein also related the story of how Pinturischio, the 1961 Derby favourite, was 'got at'. According to him, a substance was administered to Pinturischio which 'was not a dope but an exceedingly strong purgative known as croton oil. This is used on constipated elephants and Pinturischio was given a double dose. . . . It worked like a charm and a similar dose could have been given to Gorytus'. Baerlein had reported the day after the Dewhurst that 'Gorytus had been scouring and appearing uncomfortable as he was led from the parade ring onto the course'. This brought to light new evidence 'that the colt dropped a large excreta as he was led towards the parade ring. A vet standing nearby said that no horse could possibly win after such an excretion and would be lucky if he was not finished for life'. However, Hern has said that Gorytus lost only 10 lb in the Dewhurst which scarcely seems consistent with the colt's being given a dose of elephant laxative!

The theory was expounded in the *Daily Star*, under a headline 'Nobbled!' in two-inch letters, that Gorytus had been exposed to a broken capsule of irritant vapour, similar to the type of anti-personnel spray developed in America for use against rapists or muggers. Gorytus' jockey Carson raised his eyebrows at such a suggestion saying 'I find it hard to believe the horse was tampered with while I was on board. Only two stalls handlers got near me'. For our part, we regret the sensationalist manner in which some sections of the media, apparently oblivious to the serious implications arising for the image of racing, dealt with the so-called 'Gorytus affair'. To those who will apparently settle for nothing less than that Gorytus was 'got at' we say: where is the proof? It is possible that no-one will discover what caused Gorytus to run so badly in the Dewhurst. We certainly do not have the evidence at the time of writing to offer a satisfactory explanation for his performance.

Gorytus' performance was an extremely sad conclusion to an otherwise faultless first season. He had first appeared in the Acomb Stakes at York in August, a race won by the stable in three of the previous five years, most recently with the newcomer Height of Fashion who became the top staying two-year-old filly of 1981. The St Leger winner Bustino had also made his debut in the Acomb so the chances were that Gorytus, the son of two classic winners, was highly regarded. It was easy to see why as soon as he appeared in the parade ring—he proved to be an exceptionally handsome individual, a good walker and a grand mover. And yet he started at 5/1 in a market dominated by the unbeaten Salieri, reputedly the best of the Cecil two-year-olds at that time. Gorytus quickly showed he had the ability to match his looks and pedigree. He was soon close up as Salieri went straight into the lead, and moved up on Salieri's outside early in the straight. Gorytus steadily got on top and then, when shaken up inside the final two furlongs, he was most impressive, lengthening his stride in tremendous style and drawing away to win by seven lengths from Salieri who was conceding 7 lb. Salieri wasn't at all hard ridden once Gorytus had his measure but there was no denying the enormous promise of Gorytus' performance; his time of 1m 23.73sec knocked more than a second off All Systems Go's short-lived course record.

Gorytus followed this display with an even better one in the Laurent Perrier Champagne Stakes at Doncaster less than a month later. He started at 13/8 on although opposed by the Lanson Champagne Stakes and Seaton Delaval Stakes winner All Systems Go, the highly-regarded Proclaim from the Harwood stable, the tough On Stage, who had finished a highly respectable second to Horage in the July Stakes and to Deep Roots in the Prix Morny, and the sole Northern challenger Top o' the North who had looked a smart colt when winning the Champion Two Yrs Old Trophy at Ripon on his last appearance.

Gorytus was always going well, racing on the heels of the leader On Stage, and took command of the race when he quickened away two furlongs out. He was particularly impressive in the final furlong, where Carson pushed him out with hands and heels, and by the line they had drawn five lengths clear of Proclaim with the others, headed by On Stage, well beaten off. Once again Gorytus' time was excellent, producing a timefigure of 1.24 fast, the second best of the year by a two-year-old.

When asked for his plans Hern replied succinctly 'The William Hill Dewhurst, the Two Thousand Guineas and the Derby'. Hills immediately made Gorytus a 4/1-favourite for the Guineas and a 5/1-chance for the Derby, incredibly short odds for races still over seven and eight months ahead. We now know Gorytus' fate in the Dewhurst and his puzzling failure there makes it impossible to assess his classic prospects with any sort of confidence. If some physical problem was responsible for his dismal display is it likely to recur? And if he was indeed 'got at', will he ever be the same again? Only time will tell. All we can say is that, up to the Dewhurst, Gorytus had proved to our complete satisfaction that he had all the qualities which go to make an outstanding three-year-old.

Gorytus (USA) (b.c. Feb 7, 1980)	Nijinsky (b 1967)	Northern Dancer (b 1961)	Nearctic
			Natalma
		Flaming Page (b 1959)	Bull Page
			Flaring Top
	Glad Rags (ch 1963)	High Hat (ch 1957)	Hyperion
			Madonna
		Dryad (ch 1950)	Panorama
			Woodside

Gorytus' portrait shows just how handsome and commanding he is: he's beautifully-proportioned, combining size, strength and quality, and he has splendid limbs and quarters in addition to a noble head. Only very rarely does one see an individual like him, the more rarely as a two-year-old, of course. Gorytus' pedigree is also first rate. Nijinsky has proved an outstanding success and he was represented by a particularly promising group of two-year-olds in 1982, headed by Gorytus. In Ireland he had the unbeaten colts Beaudelaire, Caerleon and Solford, in England there was also the Houghton Stakes winner Russian Roubles and in North America Bemissed established herself among the leading fillies with a win in the Selima Stakes, a Grade 1 event worth 136,050 dollars to the winner. Gorytus was bred by his owner Mrs Alice Mills, of the Hickory Tree Farm in Virginia, from her One Thousand Guineas winner Glad Rags, one of the first fillies owned by Mrs Mills. The American magazine *The Blood-Horse* published the story of how she acquired her:

'Captain Tim Rogers of Ireland had a High Hat filly for sale and he and Vincent O'Brien called to see if Mrs Mills was interested. "Well over the phone of course I could not know what she looked like, and I did not know a thing about High Hat or anything in the female family, so I thought it did not seem like such a good idea. Then a little later, Bill (William Haggin) Perry called and said he thought I should take the filly and that he would if I didn't. So, I bought her without even seeing her, which usually is a mistake".'

Glad Rags did in fact come from a successful family. Her grandam Wood-

Laurent Perrier Champagne Stakes, Doncaster—Gorytus has only to be pushed along for a five-length victory over Proclaim

Mrs J. Mills's "Gorytus"

side won seven races, all over five furlongs, while her dam Dryad won four times
at up to seven furlongs from three to five years in Ireland. Dryad had already
met with plenty of success by the time Glad Rags came on the market as a yearling in 1964; her first foal Victorina won five times as a two year-old and then
showed very smart form to take the Stewards Cup and the Goldene Peitsche
at three; her second won the fairly useful sprinter Sylvan Ash; her third, Doney,
was unbeaten at two in Italy in 1963, winning the Premio Primi Passi; and her
fourth, Kubera, was a useful two-year-old winner. Glad Rags cost her owner
6,800 guineas and Mrs Mills must be extremely grateful that she was persuaded
to buy her. Glad Rags won the Railway Stakes at two before finishing third
to Soft Angels in the Royal Lodge Stakes (ironically Soft Angels is the grandam
of Diesis). The Guineas proved to be her only success in four starts at three
but she also ran well when a most unlucky loser in the Coronation Stakes. She
gave every indication she would not have stayed beyond a mile. Dryad later
produced six more winners and had her last foal at the age of twenty-six.

Glad Rags has spent her stud career in the States, producing foals by such
outstanding runners as Native Dancer, Buckpasser, Raise A Native, Hoist the
Flag and Nijinsky. Her latest, foaled when she was nineteen, is a colt by
Alydar. The first of her six winners, the Buckpasser filly Better Begin, was
nothing out of the ordinary but she was sold, in foal to Seattle Slew, for 725,000
dollars at the Keeneland November Sales in 1982. Glad Rags's first notable
performer was the Raise A Native filly Mirthful Flirt who was initially trained
by van Cutsem at Newmarket, winning the Kingsclere Stakes and finishing
second in the Cherry Hinton. She was then returned to the States where she
won the seven-furlong Golden Rod Stakes at two and the six-furlong Flirtation
Stakes at three. Interestingly Mirthful Flirt's two-year-old What's Dat was
also a good winner in 1982, winning the Grade 2 Cowdin Stakes in September

373

but he then disappointed in the Champagne Stakes, just six days before Gorytus' defeat. Although none of Glad Rags's first four winners won over further than a mile, her fifth, Gorytus' sister Terpsichorist, proved well suited by longer distances. Terpsichorist, a big, rangy filly, was unraced at two but she made up for lost time as a three-year-old, winning eight of her sixteen starts, including stakes races over ten, eleven and twelve furlongs on grass. At the end of the season she was rated 10 lb inferior to the top grass filly Waya. As a four-year-old she ranked third in the handicap for grass fillies, 5 lb behind the French mare Trillion, after winning the Sheepshead Bay Handicap over a mile and a quarter and the Violet Handicap over an extended mile. As well as stamina Terpsichorist possessed an excellent turn of foot. Gorytus certainly isn't lacking in speed and we think he too possesses a fair amount of stamina; middle distances will suit him well. Let's hope he comes back and confirms his exceptional promise. *R. Hern.*

GO SANDICLIFFE 3 b.c. Saulingo 122–Animated (Anamnestes 118) (1981 NR 1982 7fg 8fg 8fg 8fg 8g 8s) 31,000Y; close-coupled colt; good walker; half-brother to winners here and abroad, including useful middle-distance performer Hardatit (by Hard Ridden), subsequently a top-class hurdler in France; dam of little account; well beaten in varied company; sold to T. Craig 2,000 gns Newmarket Autumn Sales. *B. Hills.* —

GO SPECTRUM 2 br.c. Malinowski 123–Alli-Bee 57 (Violon d'Ingres) (1982 5f² 5f 5f⁴ 7d 6s) Feb 29; IR 4,400F, IR 5,500Y; neat, useful-looking colt; fourth foal; dam plater; in frame in May in 4-runner fields at Ripon and York; off course 3 months afterwards and had stiffish tasks in nurseries on return; should stay 7f; trained by J. Mason first 3 outings. *A. Jarvis.* **74**

GO TO SLEEP 2 b.c. Ercolano 118–Precious Light 90 (Psidium 130) (1982 7g 7g 7fg 8g) Apr 28; 6,200Y; well-grown, close-coupled colt; half-brother to 2 winners abroad; dam won over 1m; ran badly after finishing promising sixth (worth a rating of 78) in maiden race at Newmarket in June on first outing; one to leave alone. *A. Jarvis.* **— §**

GO TOTAL 6 br.h. Philip of Spain 126–Lazy Time (Linacre 133) (1981 6g 5d 5fg 5g⁴ 5f 5fg 5g 6g⁴ 5g³ 6g² 5g 5d 5s 5s 1982 5d 5f⁴ 5fg² 5fg⁴ 5.3g 5g⁴ 5g 5s) robust, short-coupled horse; sprint handicapper; beaten a head by Susarma at Chester in May; stayed 6f; acted on any going; blinkered occasionally at 3 yrs; had run respectably for an apprentice; dead. *P. Makin.* **79**

GOUMI 3 b.c. Grundy 137–Gay Trinket 72 (Grey Sovereign 128§) (1981 7g 1982 10f² 12f* 12d*) well-made, quite attractive colt; successful in maiden race at Doncaster in May (battled on well to beat Crusader Castle by ½ length) and minor event at Leicester in June (eased in closing stages when accounting for stable-companion Miguel Clement by 4 lengths); looked like developing into a useful performer but wasn't seen out again; stays 1½m; yet to race on very soft going but acts on any other. *M. Stoute.* **96**

GOUVERNO 3 b.c. Star Appeal 133–Gundula (Mercurius) (1981 6g 6fg 8d² 8s 8g² 8d 1982 10fg 10.4fg 8g 12f² 10fg² 12s 10g 8fg 8fg³ 8fg* 9s* 9s⁴) good mover with a long stride; decisively won maiden race at Salisbury in September and landed odds readily in minor event at Hamilton later in month; occasionally faced much stiffer tasks; stays 1½m; didn't look at ease on very firm ground fourth start; doesn't usually impress in appearance. *F. Durr.* **75**

GOVERNMENT PROGRAM (USA) 4 ch.c. Secretariat–Northern Gem 121 (Northern Dancer) (1981 8.2s³ 9d* 10.4g 12g³ 12d⁴ 10f* 10d² 10f* 10fg² 10g⁴ 10g² 10s 10g³ 1982 10f 10g) strong colt; did well in 1981 and won 4 times; disappointed both starts over here in 1982 and returned to race in USA, where he was stakes-placed; stays 1½m; probably acts on any going; usually blinkered. *H. T. Jones.* **—**

GRACEFUL BOY 7 b.g. Prince de Galles 125–Only By Chance (Golden Cloud) (1981 6fg⁴ 6g 7g 6d⁴ 1982 6fg 8d³ 6fg 7.6fg* 8g 7fg⁴ 8fg) poor handicapper; third in a seller before winning apprentice handicap at Chester in July in really good style; stays 1m; acts on a firm and a soft surface; used to wear blinkers; has been fired; has often worn bandages. *D. H. Jones.* **55**

GRADILLE 2 br.f. Home Guard 129–Gradiva 110 (Lorenzaccio 130) (1982 5.8g 6fg 6d 6s⁴) Mar 4; rather lightly-made, quite attractive filly; second foal; half-sister to disappointing 3-y-o Gravina (by Godswalk); dam, half-sister to top sprinter Double Form, won from 5f to 1m; blinkered when 3 lengths fourth **73**

of 19 behind Hawk Lady in maiden race at Leicester in November, best effort; acts on soft going. *F. J. Houghton.*

GRAF METTERNICH 7 b.h. High Top 131–All Shy 64 (Alcide 136) (1981 — 11fg 13.8g 12g* 12d 1982 10s) shapely horse; stays 1½m; acts on any going; has worn blinkers; has run respectably for a boy; needs to be held up; sold 650 gns Doncaster May Sales. *Miss S. Hall.*

GRAFTING 2 b.c. Grundy 137–Paddyflower 88 (St Paddy 133) (1982 7s) **74 p** Feb 24; half-brother to Fastpad (by Hotfoot), a useful winner from 6f to 11f in England and France and a winning hurdler; dam 2-y-o 5f winner; weak in the market, never threatened when 8 lengths fifth of 12 to Dabdoub in minor event at Chepstow in October; likely to improve. *P. Walwyn.*

GRAFTON 2 b.c. Great Nephew 126–Hazy Idea 118 (Hethersett 134) (1982 7g) May 14; lightly-made colt; half-brother to several winners, including very smart 1975 2-y-o Hittite Glory (by Habitat); dam won from 6f to 1¾m; 33/1 and apprentice ridden, didn't impress on way to start when making no show in 15-runner maiden race won by Herodote at Leicester in October. *H. Candy.*

GRAFTY GREEN 7 ch.g. Traditionalist–Crusheen (Typhoon 125) (1981 10f — 10f⁴ 12f 12fg 10fg 10f 1982 10f 8fg 10fg 7f 10f 10fg) poor handicapper; stays 1½m; probably acts on any going; has worn blinkers; sometimes sweats up; suitable mount for a boy. *D. Dale.*

GRANADOS KING 2 b.c. Whitstead 125–Esquinade 84 (Silly Season 127) — (1982 7d 8s 10s 8s) Apr 17; workmanlike colt; second foal; dam 2-y-o 6f winner; well beaten in autumn maiden races; blinkered last 2 starts. *W. Turner.*

GRAND ALLIANCE 5 b.g. Sweet Revenge 129–Lima 105 (Abernant 142) — (1981 8s 6g 7g 7f² 8f 10f 8f 7v 1982 8g 6g 5f 8.2fg 6f 5f) strong gelding; has had a soft palate operation; plater; stays 7f; acts on firm going; sometimes sweats up; has raced with his tongue tied down; blinkered last 2 outings. *K. Stapleton.*

GRANDE CUVÉE 2 b.c. Saulingo 122–Islay 75 (Parthia 132) (1982 7f 7fg 8s) — Mar 26; lengthy, attractive colt; half-brother to Irish middle-distance winner Hilton York (by Right Tack) and a winner in France; dam half-sister to 1000 Guineas and Oaks second Spree and top-class broodmare Set Free; no worthwhile form in big fields of maidens; led to halfway final start. *M. Jarvis.*

GRAND GRUNDY 3 ch.c. Grundy 137–Dudinka (Mossborough 126) (1981 NR — 1982 14f 14fg) fourth foal; half-brother to 2 winners in Italy; dam useful winner in Italy; well beaten in maiden races at Salisbury and Sandown in July. *J. Dunlop.*

GRAND HARBOUR 2 br.c. Dragonara Palace 115–Top Of The Tree 66 **87** (Lorenzaccio 130) (1982 5d⁴ 5g 5fg² 6f 6g⁴ 5g³ 6fg³ 7g²) May 2; workmanlike colt; third foal; half-brother to French 3-y-o 1m and 9.5f winner Ma Gonzesse (by Quiet Fling); dam daughter of smart filly Top of the Milk; in frame in a variety of races, on final occasion finishing 6 lengths second of 13 behind Jalmood The Stone in nursery at Wolverhampton in October; needs further than 5f and runs as though 1m will suit him; acts on firm going. *R. Baker.*

GRAND LEGACY 4 ch.f. Relko 136–Grandpa's Legacy 102 (Zeus Boy 121) — (1981 11s 11.7g³ 8.3s 11.7d 10s⁴ 1982 13f³ 12g 12fg³ 12h 11.7fg 10f 11.7g 12.2g) smallish filly; plating-class maiden; suited by 1½m+; well beaten in blinkers seventh start. *P. M. Taylor.*

GRAND MAITRE (USA) 3 gr.c. Grey Dawn II 132–Broken Promise (Majestic **92** Prince) (1981 NR 1982 12f⁴ 13.4f 13g* 12g 12fg² 11.1fg* 11.5g) $90,000Y; tall, close-coupled, workmanlike colt; third foal; half-brother to a winner in Puerto Rico by Prove Out; dam, unplaced in 6 starts, is half-sister to 3 stakes winners; landed odds in maiden race at Nottingham in July and accounted for Perchance by ½ length in handicap at Kempton in September; stays 13f but seems better at shorter distances; yet to race on a soft surface; sent to France. *H. Cecil.*

GRAND MARCH 4 b.g. Song 132–Calleva (Worden II 129) (1981 NR 1982 — 10fg 10d) strong, well-made, quite attractive gelding; good walker and mover; fairly useful (rated 91) as a 2-y-o; has run only twice since, and wasn't fully wound up either occasion; will probably stay middle distances; sold to K. Cunningham-Brown 3,000 gns Newmarket Autumn Sales. *I. Balding.*

GRAND PALACE 3 b.f. Royal Palace 131–Grand Central 79 (Grand Roi 118) **54** (1981 6fg 8fg 8fg² 7g³ 1982 11.7f³ 10f 13g⁴ 11.7g 12v 12s⁴ 12d) big, rangy filly;

placed in maiden races; stays 1½m; acts on firm going; blinkered final start. *R. Laing.*

GRANDREAMS 2 ch.f. Some Hand 119–Scottish Peace (Aberdeen 109) (1982 — 7d 8s) Apr 17; 1,500Y; third foal; dam of no account; well beaten in autumn in minor event at Doncaster and maiden race (tailed off) at Leicester. *J. King.*

GRAND UNIT 4 b.c. Home Guard 129 -Silken Topper (High Hat 131) (1981 **81** 8g² 8.2s² 8fg 1982 10d 10d* 10g² 11.1g² 12fg* 12f⁴ 12.3g 10f* 12f* 10g² 10g* 12fg 10d) strong colt; had a tremendous season and won handicaps at New-castle, Doncaster, Leicester, Thirsk and Yarmouth; beat Tai Lee by 1½ lengths on last-named course in August; stays 1½m; acts on any going; has worn bandages. *E. Eldin.*

GRANOBLE 3 br.g. Perdu 121–Grand Slam 65 (Fidalgo 129) (1981 6g 7.6s 8s — 10g 7g 1982 10g 8f⁴ 8f 8g 10v 12s 13.8d) rather leggy gelding; plater; seems to stay 1m; sometimes blinkered; sold 650 gns Ascot November Sales. *C. Austin.*

GRAPHICS SOLAR 4 b.c. Royal Palace 131–Tina Fort (Fortina) (1981 10s **52** 12s 12g 13fg 12f 14g⁴ 16f 14fg 1982 16s* 16d 17.1f² 17f 16fg 16fg) leggy colt; won handicap at Nottingham in April; showed only other form 2 outings later; stays well; acts on any going; usually ridden up with pace nowadays. *B. McMahon.*

GRAVINA 3 gr.f. Godswalk 130–Gradiva 110 (Lorenzaccio 130) (1981 5fg² — 1982 6fg 5g 5g 7f 11d² 10fg 10g⁴ 10s 12d⁴) small, lengthy filly; disappointing maiden; suited by middle distances; blinkered final start. *F. J. Houghton.*

GRAY HEAT 4 b.g. Ribston 104–Petoria 74 (Songedor 116) (1981 NR 1982 — 10d) light-framed gelding; second foal; dam won over 5f at 2 yrs and stayed 13f; springer in market despite looking backward when tailed-off eighth of 11 behind Philip Henry in modest maiden race at Newcastle in April, first outing. *W. Haigh.*

GREASE 3 b.f. Filiberto 123–Greedy of Gain (Habitat 134) (1981 5v* 5g* 5g* **125** 6g* 5.5d³ 6v* 8s* 1982 7.5s² 10v 8fg² 10g* 9d* 10g* 12f³)

Francois Boutin has come a long way since setting up as a public trainer in 1966 after spending one year training privately for Marcel Boussac. He commenced operations with just two horses which won two races; nowadays he has about one hundred and seventy in his string, averages ninety wins per season and has been champion French trainer in terms of money won five times in the past seven years. He didn't top the list in 1982, finishing second to Mathet, but his stable still contained ten individual pattern-race winners, two of whom, River Lady and Zino, won classics and another three of whom, Persepolis, Terreno and April Run, also won Group 1 or Grade 1 races. Boutin's most prolific pattern-race winner in Europe turned out to be Grease, the top Italian two-year-old of 1981. Bought privately out of Benetti's yard at the end of her first season, Grease fully justified the decision to campaign her in France, showing high-class form and collecting three top fillies' races in a two-month spell in mid-season.

The Coronation Stakes at Royal Ascot provided the first indication in 1982 that Grease might be capable of making her presence felt in the best company. Carrying a penalty for her success in the Gran Criterium at Milan the previous October, she was held up in last place until the three-furlong marker and then came with a strong run up the rails that took her past six of her rivals to snatch second place on the line from Dancing Rocks, three lengths behind the impressive winner Chalon. This represented a distinct improvement on Grease's first two starts—a length second to Dom Donizetti in the Prix Montenica at Maisons-Laffitte and a well-beaten fifth to Harbour in the Prix Saint-Alary at Longchamp —and it suggested that given the opportunity of racing over a little further she wouldn't be long in picking up a good prize. Eleven days later Grease lined up for the Prix de Malleret at Longchamp, opposed by six fillies including the Prix de Sandringham winner Parannda and the English challenger Zinzara, the latter starting favourite. Grease had little difficulty coping with them in a slowly-run race, producing an excellent turn of foot to sweep past Parannda and win by two lengths with Zinzara back in fourth. The Prix de Malleret was the fifth French pattern race won by the American jockey Asmussen after he joined Boutin's stable in May with nearly nine hundred successes in the States behind him. Allowing for the misfortune he had in picking up a leg when Unknown Lady fell in the Prix de Minerve, an injury which kept him out of the saddle for a couple of months, Asmussen did well in his first season in France, averaging a

*Prix de Malleret, Longchamp—Grease shows a fine turn of foot
to beat Parannda by two lengths*

winner every four rides or so. He and Grease were too strong a combination
for their opponents in the Prix Chloe at Evry in July; the filly justified short-
priced favouritism in great fashion, cutting down the front-running Rudolfina well
inside the last furlong to gain a clever three-parts-of-a-length success. Grease
faced a better field in the Prix de la Nonette at Deauville the following month,
when Moore had the mount, but her bright acceleration and the outcome were
the same as at Evry. Breezing past Rockfest and Play It Safe at the distance,
Grease won by an effortless four lengths from Black Narcissus with Sham's
Princess third and Paradise fourth.

These smashing victories behind her, Grease appeared to have a fine chance
of providing her trainer with a second successive winner of the Prix Vermeille at
Longchamp in September—April Run had won the previous year—and she
started second favourite to Harbour. While her run of success came to an end,
Grease put up the best performance of her career in a race contested by most of the
top middle-distance fillies in Europe. Held up as usual, she lay no better than
eighth of the thirteen runners turning into the straight, but finding a good run
towards the far side she swiftly accelerated into third place and for a moment
looked a serious danger to All Along who had struck the front two furlongs out
and was galloping on resolutely. Grease's momentum faltered in the last
hundred and fifty yards, however, and in the end she was beaten a length and a
half and a head by All Along and Akiyda. The way Grease had run suggested
to us that the trip had been possibly a shade too far—apparently Boutin also
thought this—but there is no need to look for excuses when a horse has run the
race of its life, and in beating such as Harbour and Awaasif and finishing much
further ahead of Paradise and Sham's Princess than in their previous encounter
that is exactly what Grease had done. She did not race again, despite being
spoken of as a likely contender for the Dubai Champion Stakes—an event in
which she would probably have gone well—and has been sent to the States.

Grease (b.f. 1979)		Filiberto (b 1970)		Ribot (b 1952)		Tenerani
						Romanella
				Fast Line (b 1958)		Mr Busher
						Throttle Wide
		Greedy of Gain (b 1971)		Habitat (b 1966)		Sir Gaylord
						Little Hut
				Gently (gr 1962)		Grey Sovereign
						Be Careful

Given her style of racing—she was a strong puller, albeit one suited by
waiting tactics—Grease could not be regarded as certain to stay the Vermeille
trip; moreover, her breeding is not that of a mile-and-a-half performer. The
sire, Filiberto, had sufficient pace to win the six-furlong Prix Morny in a three-
race career curtailed by injury, and the dam won four times over sprint distances
in Italy. Greedy of Gain has produced three other winners in Italy including
Godot (by Canisbay), successful in the Criterium Nazionale and Premio Umbria,
and Great Race, a sister to Grease. The grandam Gently won the Nell Gwyn
Stakes and has foaled seven winners, notably Godzilla, a very useful two-year-old
and dam of the good French miler Phydilla, while the third dam won the Gimcrack
Stakes and Champagne Stakes. A workmanlike filly who didn't usually impress

Mrs J. Abercrombie's "Grease" (P. Paquet)

in appearance, Grease fetched 38,000,000 lire, or approximately £17,700, as a yearling at Milan. Six yearlings went for more at the Sale, but on the track none of them would have been able to hold a candle to Grease whose turn of foot was a formidable weapon, whatever the going. *F. Boutin, France.*

GREAT BLISS 2 b. or br.c. Great Nephew 126–Sheer Bliss 76 (St Paddy 133) —
(1982 7g 7fg 7d) Feb 1; 2,000Y; fair sort; half-brother to several winners, including useful Irish middle-distance winner Sheringham (by Blakeney); dam showed only a little ability; little worthwhile form in varied company; not seen out after August. *W. Marshall.*

GREAT DEVELOPER 5 br.g. Royalty 130–Spring Music (Silly Season 127) —
(1981 16s* 16.1fg 16g⁴ 1982 18g) lengthy gelding; good walker; staying handicapper; acts on any going but is particularly well suited by the mud. *D. Nicholson.*

GREAT EASTERN 5 br.h. Jukebox 120–Miss Bangkok (Sovereign Path 125) **116**
(1981 6g 5d³ 6f* 6fg 6fg³ 6d 6g* 1982 6g² 6d 7fg 6f 6f³ 6g² 6f 6d* 6f² 7s³) leggy horse; good mover; smart performer; won Wokingham Handicap at Royal Ascot in 1981; favourite and favoured by race conditions when winning slowly-run 7-runner Prix de Meautry at Deauville in August, leading about a furlong out and holding on by a head from dead-heaters Try To Smile and Diamond Cutter in a blanket finish; excellent 2 lengths second to Indian King in Vernons Sprint Cup at Haydock the following month, running on well; placed earlier in Cammidge Trophy at Doncaster (½-length second to Sayyaf), Cork and Orrery Stakes at Royal Ascot (2¾ lengths third of 18 to Indian King) and Tote Sprint Trophy at

378

Prix de Meautry, Deauville—a blanket finish with Great Eastern holding on by a head from dead-heaters Try To Smile (striped cap) and Diamond Cutter. Celestial Dancer (noseband) finishes fourth and Gabitat (No. 2) fifth

Mrs A. Struthers' "Great Eastern"

Ayr (second to Camisite); ideally suited by a strongly-run 6f, although not entirely disgraced either outing over 7f; probably acts on any going; tends to get behind in early stages; game; sent to race in USA. *J. Dunlop.*

GREATEST HITS 5 b.g. Derring-Do 131–Vallota 85 (Klairon 131) (1981 10s⁴ **51**
9d 10d 10v* 10f² 10g 10g 1982 10fg 8d² 10f⁴ 8f 10g⁴ 10.6g 10.6s) attractive, well-made gelding; poor handicapper; stays 1¼m; has run creditably on firm going but is ideally suited by some give in the ground; best in blinkers; has run creditably for an apprentice; sold out of R. Laing's stable 1,250 gns Newmarket July Sales after sixth start. *R. Holder.*

GREAT GUNNER 3 ch.g. Ercolano 118–Joan of Arc 94 (Never Say Die 137) **74**
(1981 6f 8.2fg 1982 12f 12d³ 13f⁴ 16fg⁴ 12fg 12f* 15.5fg³ 12fg 12s) compact gelding; trotted up in 12-runner maiden race at Brighton in August; stays 2m; seems to act on any going; sweated up badly third start; has run respectably for an amateur rider; retained 6,000 gns Doncaster August Sales. *P. Kelleway.*

GREAT LIGHT 4 ch.g. Great Nephew 126–Failing Light 70 (Ballymoss 136) —
(1981 10s³ 10s* 9d⁴ 12g 12g 10.2d⁴ 10.2d 12d* 13.3s 12d² 1982 12v) rangy gelding; won maiden race at Nottingham and apprentice handicap at Pontefract in 1981; had stiffish task only outing of 1982; suited by 1½m; acts well on soft going. *J. Jenkins.*

GREAT PRETENDER 2 ch.g. Anne's Pretender 124–Pampas Miss (Pronto) **81**
(1982 5fg 6f² 6d 8g) Mar 25; 30,000Y; rangy gelding; grand walker and mover; first foal; dam lightly-raced daughter of top-class American filly Bayou; completely outpointed when beaten 5 lengths by Prince Reymo in £4,500 race at Epsom in June, only indication of merit; appeared to race too freely when tried in blinkers on last outing; should be suited by 1m; looks and moves like a very useful horse, but evidently only moderate; gelded after final outing. *P. Kelleway.*

GREAT SHADOW 2 ch.g. Grundy 137–Plant at Dusk 83 (Crepello 136) (1982 —
8g 8s) Mar 6; fair sort; turns his near-fore out; first foal; dam won over 6f at 2 yrs; well beaten in end-of-season maiden races at Newmarket and Leicester. *P. Walwyn.*

GREAT SUBSTENCE (USA) 4 br.c. Pretense–Gay Northerner (Northern **117**
Dancer) (1981 8d⁴ 10.5s 8fg 10.5s 10.5v* 1982 10s³ 9g³ 8d 10fg* 10s² 8s) neat, attractive colt; very useful performer; won 8-runner Prix Gontaut-Biron at Deauville in August, beating Ranapour by ¾ length; also placed 3 times, on first occasion finishing 3 lengths third to Al Nasr in Prix Exbury at Saint-Cloud in March; by no means disgraced when 7 lengths sixth of 18 to Commodore Blake in Prix Perth, also at Saint-Cloud, in November; stays 1¼m; probably acts on any going. *M. Saliba, France.*

GREENE NORMANDY (USA) 2 b.c. Shecky Greene–Bold French (Jim **97**
French) (1982 5f* 6d² 7f⁴ 5g³ 7.6s 6d 6d² 6g 7s²) Feb 25; 30,000Y; medium-sized, useful sort; not a good mover; third foal; dam twice-raced half-sister to very useful French animals Lady Jane Grey and Rhus; won maiden race at Brighton in May; in frame in variety of races afterwards, putting up best efforts when length third of 6 to Jonacris in Harry Rosebery Challenge Trophy at Ayr in September and 1½ lengths second to Travelguard, clear of remainder, in 13-runner nursery at Doncaster in November; ran some moderate races, finishing last of 12 when blinkered in Newmarket nursery on eighth outing; stays 7f; best form with some give in the ground; sent to race in Florida. *M. Ryan.*

GREEN FOREST (USA) 3 ch.c. Shecky Greene–Tell Meno Lies (The Axe 115) **134**
(1981 4s* 5s⁴ 5.5d² 6f* 7s* 8s* 1982 8fg⁴ 9fg 8g² 8f*)
On balance the leading colts in the French Handicap Libre have done very well at three over the past few years, rather better than their counterparts in the Free Handicap. Since 1977 Blushing Groom, Pharly, Acamas, Irish River, Recitation, Green Forest and Zino have all won Group 1 races in their second season—Nureyev was disqualified from one—and only Dragon and Nice Havrais have failed to show the form expected of them. Yet for much of the year Green Forest, successful in the Prix Morny, Prix de la Salamandre and Grand Criterium at two, threatened to be going the way of Dragon, who raced in the same colours, and it wasn't until late summer that he recaptured top form in the two most important mile races in France, the Prix Jacques le Marois and the Prix du Moulin.

It took a long time for Saliba's stable to reach its best in 1982 and the blame for this, as well as for the low striking rate of Mr Fustok's horses trained in England by Albina, has been ascribed to excessive doses of a worming vaccine

Prix du Moulin de Longchamp—a sparkling performance by Green Forest who runs on strongly to account for The Wonder and Sandhurst Prince

administered to both strings early in the year which caused colic and a number of other problems. Before the Poule d'Essai des Poulains at Longchamp in April there were rumours that Saliba had not been entirely happy with Green Forest—he hadn't managed to give him a preparatory race—and though a short-priced favourite the colt was not the odds-on shot his two-year-old form entitled him to be. In finishing under two lengths fourth to Melyno, beaten also by Tampero and Day Is Done, he hardly ran badly, albeit the best part of a stone below his best, yet his evident failure to produce the powerful finish that had been so noticeable the previous year could only be described as disappointing. Admittedly plausible excuses were put forward—that Green Forest needed the run after taking time to come to himself, and that he was struck into during the contest—but a poor showing in the Prix Jean Prat at Chantilly in June cut deeply into optimism about his future. Held up in a small field as Zino set a strong gallop, he found little when asked to make progress over two furlongs out and ended up last of five behind Melyno again, beaten seven lengths.

The general view, that Green Forest had not trained on, was supplemented in some quarters by the theory that by not running on and apparently downing tools he had shown himself ungenuine. It didn't take him much more than two months to disprove this allegation and illustrate the folly of making hasty judgements on such matters. Horses are, by and large, genuine, and if one fails to find much off the bridle the reasons can be physical rather than mental. In the light of subsequent events this evidently applied to Green Forest, and certainly the revelations about the after-effects of the vaccination make it easier to come to terms with the contrast between his Chantilly run and his last two performances. The transformation was little short of stunning. The Prix Jacques le Marois at Deauville brought together a typically strong field headed by Melyno, The Wonder, What A Guest, Zino and the British challenger Noalcoholic. Green Forest, only sixth favourite, lay close up as Zino's pacemaker Spoleto and Noalcoholic took them along; he seized the initiative fully three furlongs out, Spoleto having weakened rapidly, and made the best of his way home. Keeping on strongly he still led two hundred yards out but by this time The Wonder had begun to wear him down and in the drive to the line Green Forest just came off worse, going down by three quarters of a length. Zino, slightly hindered by Green Forest's drifting left in the closing stages, finished well to be third, half a length away, while Melyno, who met with a mishap during the race, was virtually tailed off.

Green Forest had clearly advertised his chances of playing a major part in the best races to come. Even so, he didn't head the market for the Prix du Moulin de Longchamp at the start of September; that honour went to the impressive Waterford Crystal Mile winner Sandhurst Prince with The Wonder second choice. The six remaining runners included Melyno once more, the Prix d'Astarte winner Thorough, the 1,700,000-dollar yearling Lichine and a pacemaker put in for Green Forest because Saliba believed his charge had hit the front a little soon at Deauville. With the overall form of the milers somewhat confusing the way was clear for one of the main contenders to stamp himself as the best in Europe with an authoritative victory. Authoritative Green Forest's display undoubtedly was. Sandhurst Prince went off at such a fast pace that the pacemaker proved incapable of performing his allotted task as the English runner bowled along with Melyno and Green Forest not far behind. Entering the straight Sandhurst Prince still led, Melyno showed signs of wilting in the face of the unremitting gallop and Green Forest, travelling smoothly, was making relentless progress. Green Forest got to the leader's quarters less than two furlongs out and settled the issue in a few strides as he produced a brilliant turn of foot that left Sandhurst Prince standing; while The Wonder made late headway to deprive a tired Sandhurst Prince of second place, Green Forest was away and gone, keeping on powerfully to run out a decisive three-length winner with a length and a half between second and third and Melyno fourth. Though Pas de Seul (who wouldn't have been suited by the ground anyway), Wind and Wuthering, Zino and On The House were absentees, and though Sandhurst Prince might have reduced his chances of success by setting so furious a gallop—a gallop which resulted in Northjet's course record being broken—we see no reason to conclude other than that this was an outstanding performance, quite good enough to mark Green Forest down as the top miler of the season.

Green Forest (USA) (ch.c. 1979)	Shecky Greene (b 1970)	Noholme II (ch 1956)	Star Kingdom / Oceana
		Lester's Pride (b 1957)	Model Cadet / Meadow Flower
	Tell Meno Lies (gr 1971)	The Axe (gr 1958)	Mahmoud / Blackball
		Filatonga (b 1960)	Count of Honor / Blarney Castle

In the aftermath of the Moulin three possible targets were mentioned for Green Forest. His trainer reportedly favoured running him in the Prix de la Foret while the general consensus seemed to be that the Dubai Champion Stakes might provide a fitting climax to a distinguished career. In the event Green Forest wasn't entered for the Foret and his name appeared in the list of scratchings from the Champion over two weeks before the race. The third possible engagement broke new ground. Mr Fustok, stating that Green Forest had nothing further to prove at home, proposed a 2,000,000 dollars a side match at around a mile between his colt and any American-trained colt to be run in two legs, the first at Longchamp and the second, on dirt if necessary, at Belmont Park. The 4,000,000 dollars at stake would go to the horse who won both races or, should each win once, to the one beaten by the smaller margin. Since it had been arranged at the end of 1981 that once he had finished racing Green Forest would be retired to the stud where he was bred, the Jonabell Farm in Kentucky, Mr

Mr M. Fustok's "Green Forest"

Fustok's plan clearly aimed at letting American breeders know a little more about Green Forest's capabilities. Hopes, or fears, of another match like that of 1923 when the Derby winner Papyrus met the Kentucky Derby winner Zev and was trounced on dirt at Belmont were not fulfilled. Despite an initially favourable response from the connections of the ill-fated Timely Writer, one of the best colts in the States at two and three, the plan proved still-born and Green Forest was retired to stud without racing again, syndicated for a sum stated to be not less than 14,000,000 dollars.

Green Forest's pedigree will be familiar enough to American breeders. His sire Shecky Greene won fifteen races at up to eight and a half furlongs and was champion sprinter at three; at stud he has been a prolific sire of two-year-old winners and in 1982 his progeny won well over a million dollars in the States. Green Forest is the second foal of his dam, following the good filly Honest and True (by Mr Leader) who won the eight-and-a-half-furlong Fair Ground Oaks and ran third in the Kentucky Oaks over the same trip. Green Forest cost 100,000 dollars as a yearling. Tell Meno Lies's next two foals, colts by Full Out and Vigors, sold for 55,000 dollars and 300,000 dollars at the same age. The latter, incidentally, was knocked down to Mr Fustok's Buckram Oak Farm at the Keeneland Selected Yearling Sale in July. Successful in small races at five furlongs and a mile, Tell Meno Lies is a half-sister to five winners, the best of them the minor stakes winners Emerald Landing and Energy Boy, out of the modest Filatonga who comes from the family of such good American performers as Ruffian, Castle Forbes and Icecapade. Green Forest, a compact, quite attractive colt and an excellent mover, stayed a mile well and acted on any going. Though he pulled hard on occasions and was clearly regarded as highly strung—his connections usually took great care to prevent his becoming excited in the preliminaries—he lacked for nothing in courage. *M. Saliba, France.*

GREEN LUCIA 2 ch.f. Green Dancer 132–Cockade 104 (Derring-Do 131) **102** (1982 6g* 6f⁴ 8fg²) Apr 30; 31,000Y; second foal; dam, 1m winner, is sister to High Top and Camden Town; ran out an impressive 6-length winner from El Kantaoui in 14-runner maiden race at Navan in June; narrowly beaten subsequently when fourth of 14 to Certain Something in Oldtown Stud Stakes at Naas in August (beaten 3 short heads) and when second to Impudent Miss in Silken Glider Stakes at Leopardstown the following month; will stay 1¼m; useful. *J. Oxx, Ireland.*

GREEN MEADOWS INN 3 b.c. Saulingo 122–Just Alice (Worden II 129) — (1981 5v 5g 5f 1982 6s 6s 8f 7fg 8g 11g) poor plater; sold 400 gns Doncaster September Sales. *Mrs A. Bell.*

GREEN REEF 2 ch.f. Mill Reef 141–Infra Green 121 (Laser Light 118) (1982 **93 p** 8g²) Mar 7; second foal; dam won from 6f to 1¼m, including Prix Ganay-favourite, led it out but was caught close home when ½-length second of 13 to Dame Blanche in newcomers race at Evry in September; very well bred and is sure to win races over middle distances; entered in Oaks. *J. Cunnington, jnr, France.*

GREENSWARD BLAZE 3 ch.f. Sagaro 133–Uragano 101 (Buisson Ardent 129) **50** (1981 6fg 6g 6fg 7.6s 1982 10h 7fg 8fg² 8f*) plater; bought in 3,300 gns after winning at Bath in September; should stay at least 1¼m; acts on firm going. *M. Blanshard.*

GREENWOOD BELLE 2 ch.f. Gay Fandango 132–Matty (Sailor) (1982 5.8g **64** 6g 8f) Apr 14; 5,000Y; lengthy filly; seventh foal; dam unplaced 8 times in USA; showed some ability, on final outing finishing eighth of 23 to Artiste in maiden race at Leicester in September; retained by trainer 1,000 gns Ascot December Sales. *G. Hunter.*

GREENWOOD STAR 5 gr.h. No Mercy 126–Golden Palermo 70 (Dumbarnie **98** 125) (1981 8d 8g* 8s 8f² 7fg 7f 1982 8g³ 7.2h⁴ 8fg 9d⁴ 10g 8g⁴ 9d) strong, robust horse; useful handicapper; reportedly fractured his pelvis on final start in 1981 and was off course afterwards for 10 months; in frame several times on his return, notably when third to Tugoflove in Jubilee Stakes at Kempton in May and fourth to Indian King in John of Gaunt Stakes at Haydock in June on next outing and to Corn Street in handicap at Ascot in September on sixth start; also ran creditably when sixth to Buzzards Bay in Royal Hunt Cup at Royal Ascot; not certain to stay 1¼m (reportedly hampered in early stages however when tried at trip for second time on fifth start); needs a sound surface; invariably held up and is sometimes rather slow into his stride; gave trouble at stalls at Royal Ascot and raced from flag start next time; sent to race in USA. *G. Hunter.*

GRENFELL BOY 2 b.c. Sharpen Up 127–Maternal 93 (High Top 131) (1982 **83**
5s* 5fg* 5fg² 5g² 6f³ 6d⁴) Apr 9; 6,000Y; lightly-made colt; second foal; half-
brother to 3-y-o 1¼m winner Channing Girl (by Song); dam won over 5f and
6f at 2 yrs; won 2 races in April, maiden at Chepstow and minor event at Thirsk;
stays 6f; acts on any going; exported to Singapore. *G. Hunter.*

GREY CHARTER 2 gr.f. Runnymede 123–Lovely Beak (Counsel 118) (1982 **58**
5fg 6g 5g 5g 6s) Feb 21; 4,000Y; compact, sturdy filly; half-sister to 2 winners,
including useful 1m to 1¼m winner Starfen (by Comedy Star), also smart winner
over jumps; dam ran once; plater; best runs at 5f; hung quite badly left final
start. *P. Rohan.*

GREY DESIRE 2 gr.c. Habat 127–Noddy Time 97 (Gratitude 130) (1982 **105**
5fg 5g* 5g³ 5fg* 8fg³ 5f* 7d²) Apr 18; 3,800Y; workmanlike colt; half-brother
to several winners, including smart 1¼m performer The Dunce (by High Hat);
dam stayed 1m; successful in maiden race at Edinburgh in July, minor event
at Beverley the following month and in nursery at Redcar in September; creditable length second of 4 to Bright Cone in minor event at Catterick in October;
best form at up to 7f; yet to race on very soft going but acts on any other.
M. W. Easterby.

GREY HUNTER 4 gr.c. Warpath 113–Janabelle 101 (Gentle Art 121) —
(1981 12g 12d 12.5f 13fg³ 16.1f² 14d³ 16.5g 1982 16d 16f 16fg) tall, rather
leggy, narrow colt; poor form in 1982 (didn't come round bend well at Beverley
second start); stays well; acts on any going; blinkered second outing in 1980;
has worn bandages. *E. Eldin.*

GREY MERCY 3 gr.c. No Mercy 126–Queens To Open 75 (Darius 129) (1981 **76**
5d³ 5s 5g* 6g⁴ 6f⁴ 7.2f² 7fg² 6d² 7f 7fg⁴ 8.2s 7s 1982 7g 7g 8f⁴ 10.6f⁴ 12d 7.2g³
8fg 7f² 7f* 7.6d 7fg) leggy, long-striding colt; good walker; made virtually all
and battled on gamely to win handicap at Wolverhampton in August; best at
around 7f; acts on any going; looked unsuited by Chester track tenth start;
genuine; sold 4,200 gns Newmarket Autumn Sales. *S. Mellor.*

GREY TWIG 2 gr.f. Godswalk 130–Akimiski (Deep Diver 134) (1982 5d 5g **68**
5d 5f⁴(dis)) Apr 7; IR 10,000Y; workmanlike filly; first foal; dam placed twice
over 1m in Ireland; plating-class maiden; looks a short runner. *R. Hannon.*

GRIZABELLA 2 b.f. Bustino 136–Hurdy-Gurdy 90 (Espresso 122) (1982 8g) **76 p**
Feb 22; strong, lengthy, slightly hollow-backed filly; half-sister to 3 winners,
including 3-y-o 1¼m winner Pianola (by Welsh Pageant) and very smart middle-
distance filly Vielle (by Ribero); dam won at up to 1¼m; bit backward, showed
definite ability without being knocked about when eighth of 19 behind Coming
and Going in minor event at Newmarket in October; will stay 1¼m+; certain
to improve. *B. Hobbs.*

GROAT 4 b.g. Connaught 130–Grisbi 96 (Grey Sovereign 128§) (1981 12fg³ **67**
12.3fg* 1982 12d 12f³) big, good-topped gelding; has rather a high knee action;
very lightly raced; moved poorly to start when 5 lengths third to High Old Time
in handicap at Leicester in June; will stay beyond 1½m; gives impression he'll
be suited by some give in the ground (pulled a muscle when behind on reappearance, only outing on softish ground so far). *B. Hobbs.*

GROSZEWSKI 2 gr.c. Godswalk 130–Claddie (Karabas 132) (1982 5g⁴ 5f² **86**
6g 7g 6g 6s* 6g² 6s* 7s) Mar 16; 6,400F, 30,000Y; fair sort; third produce; half-
brother to Irish 3-y-o Class (by Malinowski); dam, from good family, never ran;
spreadeagled a big field in £2,000 seller at Goodwood (bought in 4,200 gns)
in September, leading inside final furlong to win by 5 lengths from Star of Anax;
4-length winner of 16-runner nursery at Nottingham the following month; best
form at 6f; has run respectably on firm going but revels in soft ground; blinkered
last 4 starts. *J. Sutcliffe.*

GROWING WILD 3 b. or br.f. Free State 125–Crab Apple (Nelcius 133) (1981 **77**
7d 7.6s 1982 8fg 10fg 10fg 10fg 11.7f⁴ 12g 8fg⁴ 8fg) big, rangy filly; has a
round action; only plating class; stays 1½m; sold 1,100 gns Newmarket Autumn
Sales. *R. Baker.*

GRUB 2 b.f. Be My Guest 126–Table Rose (Round Table) (1982 6f² 6fg 5.8g² **80**
5fg* 6fg³ 5s) May 7; IR 70,000Y; rather lightly-made filly; half-sister to several
winners, including Centre Piece (by Tompion), herself dam of Greenland Park;
dam 2-y-o 4f winner in USA; won 14-runner maiden race at Wolverhampton
in September by a short head from Yafefia; good third to Liberty Tree and Indy
in minor event at Redcar later in the month; better at 6f than 5f; acts on firm
going. *G. Harwood.*

GRYLOS 4 b.g. Dubassoff–Nevilles Cross 67 (Nodouble) (1981 7g 14g 16g — 15.5fg 6f 10f 7f 1982 8fg 14d 10f 12f 10fg⁴ 10g) poor form in varied races, including selling; has been tried in blinkers. *O. Jorgensen.*

GUERRIERO 2 b.c. Hittite Glory 125–Mantua 80 (Ballyciptic 122) (1982 5.1f **70** 6g*) May 12; well-made colt; good walker; half-brother to 3 winners, including useful middle-distance performer Amber Town (by Amber Rama); dam stayer; sold 3,600 gns after winning 10-runner seller at Doncaster (blinkered) in June by a length from Lemelasor; exported to Malaysia. *M. Stoute.*

GUERRIER (USA) 3 b.c. Forli–Brown Hare (Coursing) (1981 6s 1982 8fg **78** 8fg 10.4fg 8f 7f 6g²) well-made colt; seemed to show improved form in blinkers, despite hanging badly left, when ¾-length second of 16 finishers in apprentice maiden race won by Havara at Newbury in August. *F. J. Houghton.*

GUESS WHO 2 b.f. Be My Guest 126–Tulalanee (Habitat 134) (1982 7g 7g **74** 8s) Mar 20; 11,500Y; leggy, sparely-made filly, lacking in scope; first foal; dam, half-sister to Derby runner-up Cavo Doro, showed only a little ability; prominent in three autumn races in fair company; stays 1m. *P. Kelleway.*

GUEST SPEAKER 3 ch.c. Honoured Guest 113–Spring Gipsy 75 (Sky Gipsy **70** 117) (1981 7fg 7g 1982 11f 12f⁴ 10fg 12f³ 11.7f³) rangy, quite attractive colt; good mover; quite modest; gives impression he may prove best at around 1¼m; sold 3,900 gns Newmarket Autumn Sales. *G. Harwood.*

GUN 5 b.h. Ribero 126–Mafia (Milesian 125) (1981 9s 13d 8f 7fg³ 8.2f 8d 7g — 1982 6g 5g 5f 6s) ex-Irish horse; poor maiden on flat, though has won over hurdles; stays 1¼m; suited by a sound surface; blinkered first start in 1981. *R. Fisher.*

GUN-CARRIAGE 2 b.g. Gunner B 126–Miss Little 78 (Dunoon Star 110) — (1982 8g 8d) fourth known foal; dam stayed 1½m; in rear in maiden race at Edinburgh and minor event at Redcar in the autumn. *A. W. Jones.*

GUNGA DIN 2 br.g. Mansingh 120–Mow Meadow (Acropolis 132) (1982 6g) — May 21; 3,100Y; half-brother to Irish 1m winner Our David (by Great Nephew); tailed-off last of 13 in maiden race at Haydock in July; sold 580 gns Doncaster September Sales. *J. Fitzgerald.*

GUNNARD 2 ch.f. Gunner B 126–La Conistrano 86 (Capistrano 120) (1982 6h **62** 7d 7g 7g 8s*) Apr 14; plater; showed first form when winning 15-runner event at Redcar (no bid) in October by neck from Just Gunner; will be suited by 1¼m; acts on soft going. *K. Stone.*

GUNS OF NAVARONE 2 b.c. Bold Lad (Ire) 133–Busted Flush 103 (Busted **90** 134) (1982 6f⁴ 6f²) Feb 19; 98,000Y; big, well made, quite attractive colt; third living foal; half-brother to smart 1979 staying Irish 2-y-o Cobbler's Cove (by Realm), subsequently a winner over 1¼m; dam, half-sister to many winners, won over 6f at 2 yrs; in frame in July in maiden race at Newmarket (1½ lengths fourth of 16 to Lofty) and minor event at Kempton (favourite, went down by 2 lengths to Boom Town Charlie); will stay 1m. *C. Brittain.*

GUNTRIPS CENTENARY 2 br.c. Manado 130–Bantam 64 (Combat 123) — (1982 5s 6g) Apr 2; half-brother to several winners, notably high-class 1m to 1¼m performer Gold Rod (by Songedor); dam won 5f seller at 2 yrs; behind in £4,500 event at Ascot (tailed off) in September and maiden race at Newmarket in October. *G. Hunter.*

GUYWOOD 4 b.g. Tudor Rhythm 112–Smokey Dawn 68 (March Past 124) — (1981 8fg 8.3fg 8fg 1982 10f) lengthy gelding; behind in varied company, including selling, on flat; winner over hurdles; blinkered only outing of 1982. *P. M. Taylor.*

GWYNPRIDE 2 b.f. Val de l'Orne 130–Foresighted Lady (Vent du Nord) — (1982 6fg 5g 7g 7g) Feb 2; 8,000F; first produce; dam won 3 sprint races in USA; poor form in maiden and minor events. *D. Marks.*

H

HABANNE 2 gr.g. Habat 127–Sister Anne 74 (Mourne 126) (1982 7s 8d) — Mar 9; 3,000Y; sturdy gelding; half-brother to 2 winners, including fair 1978 2-y-o 5f winner Carrie Red (by Scottish Rifle); dam, half-sister to smart King Log, stayed extremely well; backward, little worthwhile form in maiden race at Redcar in October and minor event (eighth of 16) on same course in November. *J. Etherington.*

HABATASHIE 4 gr.f. Habat 127–Shenachie 79 (Sheshoon 132) (1981 7s —
6g 6g⁴ 6g 7fg 8fg 7f 1982 6fg 6g 8g) strong filly; maiden plater; has run
creditably in blinkers; sold 660 gns Doncaster October Sales. *A. Smith.*

HABIBTI 2 br.f. Habitat 134–Klairessa 88 (Klairon 131) (1982 6fg* 6g* 6d*) **120** p
    Although England's major two-year-old events close later than they used
to the system still demands a great deal of foresight from trainers. Of the
twelve pattern races confined to juveniles which take place in September and
October, eleven closed as early as July 7th in 1982, the exception being the
Cornwallis. Interestingly Gorytus, Salieri and Diesis, the winners collectively
of the Laurent Perrier Champagne Stakes, Mill Reef Stakes, William Hill
Middle Park and William Hill Dewhurst Stakes, hadn't even appeared on the
racecourse by July 7th while Acclimatise, the Hoover Fillies Mile winner, had
made her debut only five days before and Dunbeath, the winner of both the
Royal Lodge Stakes and the William Hill Futurity, had had his first race on
July 6th. Some trainers are less selective in making big race entries than
others. Some feel it necessary, understandably, to enter their two-year-olds
virtually en bloc: Peter Walwyn for example had nineteen in the Royal Lodge,
twenty-two in the Cheveley Park, seven in the Middle Park, twenty in the
Dewhurst and twenty in the Futurity, none of whom took part in the end.
The initial cost of making these entries, leaving aside the money paid at subsequent declaration stages, amounted to £11,060. Those who practise greater
selectivity, in the interests of economy or whatever, run the risk of leaving a late-
maturing animal without any suitable engagements. John Dunlop had the
misfortune to find himself in such a position with Habibti in 1982. He told us:
'We had a little problem with her joints in the early spring and I thought she
was going to be rather difficult to train because she's a typical Habitat—rather
heavy-topped and not the very best of forelegs. Time improved those though
and we've had no problems recently. She was, and is still, rather sleepy, and
not an obviously fast filly at all in her slower paces. Indeed when we first
started working her she didn't show very good speed.' Because of this Dunlop
left Habibti out of the autumn pattern events, no doubt believing he was saving
her owner unnecessary expense. However he soon had reason to regret his
decision: Habibti made an impressive debut to win the Virginia Water Stakes, a
valuable newcomers race at Ascot on July 23rd, showing no lack of speed. She
was soon prominent, moved into second place behind Lebanese Song with two
furlongs to run, and though for a while she ran a little green in the end she
quickened well to win convincingly by a length and a half from Elysian.
    Luckily for Habibti's connections the Lowther Stakes at York in August
didn't close until July 28th so they were able to enter her. Dunlop admitted
that he was in two minds as to whether to run her, thinking it might be 'a bit
sharp for her against some of those very fast professional sprinting fillies.'
Eventually he let her take her chance, and she started second favourite to
Royal Heroine, who had accounted for another Lowther runner, the St Catherine's Stakes winner Henry's Secret, when an impressive winner of the Princess
Margaret Stakes at Ascot. Making up the field were Bumpkin, a six-length

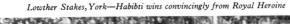

Lowther Stakes, York—Habibti wins convincingly from Royal Heroine

Moyglare Stud Stakes, the Curragh—the unbeaten Habibti proves much too good for these Irish fillies

winner of her last race, Annie Edge, the Queen Mary third, Carolside, a close second in the Cherry Hinton, and the winners Myra's Best and The Babe. For a long time it looked doubtful whether anything would peg back the very speedy Bumpkin but she had shot her bolt below the distance and Habibti quickened past, hotly pursued by Royal Heroine. Habibti soon began to assert her authority and lengthened her stride to win decisively by a length and a half, with Annie Edge coming through to take third place a further three lengths behind. Habibti's timefigure was extremely good, 1.15 fast, the best of the season by a two-year-old filly.

Normally the Lowther winner ends her first season by running in the Cheveley Park; Habibti hadn't even been entered for it. Strangely enough she did hold a suitable alternative engagement. Way back in March, before the British season had begun and presumably before her trainer had much idea of her capabilities, she had been entered along with two hundred and eighty-nine others in the Moyglare Stud Stakes at the Curragh. By September 11th the two hundred and ninety had been reduced to fifteen with Habibti starting favourite ahead of two other unbeaten fillies, Minnelli, an impressive six-length winner of her only previous start four months earlier, and the Heinz '57' Phoenix Stakes winner Sweet Emma. The twelve remaining runners included only three other previous winners, Amanzi, Committed and High Style, and it's surprising that no other British trainer decided to challenge for the valuable prize. Eddery, who had been engaged to partner Habibti, was forced to miss the ride because of a fall the day before and Gillespie, a Dunlop apprentice in the mid-'seventies, stood in. Gillespie handled her with plenty of confidence, taking her up to dispute the lead after only a quarter of a mile, and he received an immediate response when he asked her to quicken two furlongs later. Habibti soon shook off Sweet Emma, who appeared to run out of stamina, and it was left to Minnelli to chase her home at a distance of one and a half lengths. The 20/1-shot Committed took third place the same distance further back. Habibti thereby earned her owner Mohammed Mutawa, a Kuwaiti who owns the Sussex Stud, the task of giving a speech at the Moyglare dinner. The story goes that when Mr Mutawa asked in what language he would have to address the company one wag told him 'in Gaelic or, if need be, in English'. Mr Mutawa, deciding to rise to the challenge, then left, with the suspicion of a smile, to find a Gaelic-Arabic grammar! On a more serious note the Moyglare shows the reason why the majority of pattern races have early closing dates. Although it carried only IR £25,000 added money, of which IR £12,500 was given by the sponsor, the race carried a first prize of IR £40,484 with nearly IR £65,000 going to the owners of the first three. Around IR £35,900 had come from the pockets of the owners of the huge number of original entrants which didn't even make it to the start. Had the race closed much nearer its running date it would have attracted far fewer entrants who would consequently have had to pay a much higher entrance fee to maintain the same level of prize money. Surely on balance this would be preferable though, as then no horse would have to miss a race because its trainer had been unaware of its merit months before the race and no owner would have to waste money entering animals which turn out to be moderate, backward or unsound.

Habibti comes from a fine family. Her great-grandam Tessa Gillian, a sister to the highly influential stallion Royal Charger, was a high-class performer

Mr M. A. A. Mutawa's "Habibti"

in her own right, meeting only one defeat in five starts at two, when short-headed by Bebe Grande in the Cheveley Park. She later finished a creditable second in the One Thousand Guineas. Tessa Gillian also made her mark at stud, producing among others the very smart sprinting two-year-old Gentle Art and the 1960 Gimcrack Stakes winner Test Case who gained all his wins at two. Habibti's grandam Courtessa was a sister to Test Case. She was a twin and never raced but she too has produced a high-class winner, D'Urberville, whose successes included the King's Stand Stakes, Prix du Petit Couvert and the Norfolk (now Flying Childers) Stakes. Klairessa, Habibti's dam, is a sister to D'Urberville and she is also closely related to On The House's dam Lora, who is by Klairon's son Lorenzaccio out of Courtessa. Although nowhere near so good as D'Urberville Klairessa did win a race, a handicap at Wolverhampton over a little less than six furlongs. Habibti is the third of her foals to win, following the Great Nephew filly Great Klaire, who won at three and four years in Australia, and the Habat colt Khedive, a close relative of Habibti who was a fairly useful sprinter.

Habibti (br.f. Mar 29, 1980)	Habitat (b 1966)	Sir Gaylord (b 1959)	Turn-to
			Somethingroyal
		Little Hut (b 1952)	Occupy
			Savage Beauty
	Klairessa (b 1969)	Klairon (b 1952)	Clarion III
			Kalmia
		Courtessa (b 1955)	Supreme Court
			Tessa Gillian

Many of Habibti's relatives were speedy animals. With Habitat as her sire, she can't be considered certain to stay a mile, but fortunately she possesses an excellent, relaxed temperament which should help and to our mind she represents England's best chance of beating Ma Biche in the Guineas. Her form at two wasn't quite so good but she had an easier first season and may well make the greater improvement. She is a well-made, strong-quartered filly with plenty of scope, altogether a grand type, worth every penny of the 140,000 guineas she cost as a yearling. *J. Dunlop.*

HABITASSA 2 b.f. Habitat 134–Sassabunda 108 (Sassafras 135) (1982 6g 7d) — Mar 16; $425,000Y; strong, rangy filly; has a round action; second foal; half-sister to 3-y-o middle-distance winner Nauteous (by Nonoalco); dam short-head second in Irish Guinness Oaks; little worthwhile form in autumn maiden events at Newmarket and Leicester (sixth of 15). *B. Hills.*

HABIT FORMING 2 gr.f. Habat 127–Hi Jay (Double-U-Jay 120) (1982 6g 6g) Apr 24; 2,500Y; workmanlike filly; third live foal; dam won 5 times from 9f to 1¾m in Ireland; no worthwhile form in sellers at Lingfield (fifth of 15) in August and Doncaster in September. *D. Ringer.*

HABIT ROUGE 2 b.c. Habitat 134–Bombshell 76 (Le Levanstell 122) (1982 8d) May 18; strong colt; fifth foal; closely related to poor 1¼m winner Miss Minefield (by Northfields) and half-brother to 1¾m winner Orlandoland (by Reliance II); dam won over 8.5f; unquoted and in need of race, always struggling in 16-runner minor event won by High Cannon at Redcar in November. *J. Hanson.*

HABITUALLY DANCING 3 b.f. Habitat 134–Come Dancing 91 (Northern 73 Dancer) (1981 NR 1982 5g 7.2g4 7f2 8fg3) 43,000Y; strong, heavy-bodied filly; carries plenty of condition; sister to 6f and 7f winner Hab Dancer, and half-sister to very smart stayer General Ironside (by Sea Hawk II) and useful 7f to 1½m winner Welsh Dancer (by Welsh Pageant); dam stayed 1m; quite moderate form in varied company; stays 1m. *A. Bailey.*

HABOOB (USA) 3 b.g. Graustark–Angenora (Two Relics) (1981 7f 7g 7g — 1982 11fg 10f 8f 10fg 10fg4 7g 9.4fg 8g 8.2s4 8s) smallish, strong, quite attractive gelding; quite modest; will stay 1½m; acts on soft going; sometimes blinkered; has run respectably for an apprentice; sold to J. Douglas-Home 5,000 gns Newmarket Autumn Sales. *F. J. Houghton.*

HABUS 4 b.c. Habitat 134–Rebus 97 (Busted 134) (1981 10s 10d4 10.2f* 12f3 — 14fg3 14g 1982 10fg 12fg3 11.1g 10fg 10fg 12d 12g 12s 12s) compact colt; poor walker; poor handicapper nowadays; stays 1¾m; acts on firm going; apprentice ridden when successful; blinkered last 2 outings. *C. Brittain.*

HADAJAR 7 b.g. Royalty 130–Sea Gal (Sea Hawk II 131) (1981 16.9s4 18.8fg2 **40** 12.2s 12d4 1982 16d3 17f) strong gelding; suited by a test of stamina; acts on a firm and a soft surface. *M. Tate.*

HADA RANI 2 ch.f. Jaazeiro 127–Fast Line (Klairon 131) (1982 6fg) Apr 5; — IR 28,000Y; first foal; dam, sister to smart Klairvimy, won over 9f and 1½m in Ireland; 33/1, failed to recover from slow start when last of 7 behind stable-companion Indian Lady in minor event at Epsom in August. *G. Lewis.*

HADDFAN 7 ch.g. Lorenzaccio 130–Golden Windlass 79 (Princely Gift 137) — (1981 8g 8f 8fg 8f* 8fg3 8f4 8.3g4 1982 7f 8fg) quite a moderate handicapper; soundly beaten in 1982; stays 1¼m; acts on any going; suitable mount for an apprentice. *J. Dunlop.*

HADERA 7 ch.m. Northfields–Flat Impulse 75 (Meadow Court 129) (1981 8fg **62** 8.3fg 8h3 8.3g 8.3g 8.3g2 10.8s 8g 1982 8g 8d 8.3fg 8fg 8.3fg2 8.3fg* 8.3g*) quite a moderate handicapper; in good form in August and won twice at Windsor; stayed 1m; possibly wasn't at her best on very soft ground but acted on any other; suitable mount for an apprentice; in foal to Song. *B. Gubby.*

HADI'S HOPE (USA) 2 b.c. Run Dusty Run–Engaged (Promise) (1982 5f4 **87** 6f2 5fg* 7f4 7fg 7fg 6fg) Mar 16; $30,000Y; lengthy, long-striding colt; good walker; second foal; dam, half-sister to smart 1978 French 2-y-o Ice Cool, won 6 times at up to 1m, including claiming events; odds on, ran on strongly to beat Bali-On-By a neck in 9-runner maiden race at Hamilton in June; fair fifth of 8 to Sheriff Muir in well-contested race at Redcar in July, fifth outing; stays 7f; sold 4,200 gns Doncaster October Sales. *M. H. Easterby.*

HADITOS 3 b.f. Averof 123–Peta's Bay 67 (I Say 125) (1981 5s 5fg3 5.8g 6fg2 **92** 5fg* 5g4 5d* 5d4 5fg2 1982 7d 5f 5g3 5fg 5g 5fg2 5fg* 5f 5g) big, workmanlike filly; sprint handicapper; beat Red Rosie by a neck at Newmarket in July; best at 5f; acts on a firm and a soft surface; ran creditably in blinkers sixth start; tends to swish her tail. *G. Beeson.*

HADRAS 2 b.c. Brittany–My Duty 70 (Sea Hawk II 131) (1982 5d 5fg 6g 6fg — 8.2d 8s 10d) May 29; useful-looking colt; half-brother to a winner in Brazil; dam showed ability at 2 yrs; behind in maiden races and sellers; sold 480 gns Ascot December Sales. *J. Holt.*

HAEMAVITE 3 b.g. Swing Easy 126–Katira 83 (Paveh 126) (1981 6d 6fg³ 5s — 6g 1982 8f 7f 8fg 7g 8g) workmanlike gelding; plater nowadays; probably stays 1m; sometimes blinkered. *A. Jarvis.*

HAGEN QUEEN 3 b.f. Mount Hagen 127–Fenland Queen (King's Troop 118) **65** (1981 7v 7g 1982 8f 10.6f⁴ 11fg² 12g² 10.6f 14.7fg 12s³ 12s) fair sort; middle-distance handicapper; seems to act on any going. *C. Crossley.*

HAGEN'S BARGAIN 2 ch.f. Mount Hagen 127–Titmouse (Petingo 135) **62** (1982 5fg 5d 5g* 5f³ 5f 7fg 7g 6s² 6s³) May 11; 1,000Y; rather leggy, lightly-made filly; first foal; dam never ran; plater; sold out of P. Haslam's stable for 2,450 gns after showing improved form to win at Wolverhampton in April; creditable 4 lengths second to Star of Anax at Haydock in October; will probably stay 1m; best form with some give in the ground. *J. Yardley.*

HAGEN'S PEAK 2 ch.c. Mount Hagen 127–Mayfield Girl (Le Prince 98) (1982 **66** 6fg³ 6g³ 6g* 7f 7d³ 7.6fg 8.2s) Mar 12; 4,400Y; fair sort; half-brother to 3-y-o Fort Lamy (by African Sky); dam useful Irish 2-y-o; won 10-runner seller (bought in 3,600 gns) at Haydock in July by a length from Mel Mira; beaten 4½ lengths in nurseries on next 2 outings, on second occasion running on well after a slow start; stays 7f; suited by some give in the ground. *Mrs J. Reavey.*

HAGEN STAR 2 b.c. Mount Hagen 127–Blue and Silver (Blue Tom 127) — (1982 6f) May 21; 6,000Y; strong, workmanlike colt; fourth foal; half-brother to middle-distance winner Southfields (by Northfields); dam, half-sister to Irish Guinness Oaks winner Aurabella, won 3 small middle-distance races in France; 13/2 and on backward side, 4½ lengths fifth of 10 to Alchise in maiden race at Doncaster in May. *A. Jarvis.*

HAIL THE BRAVE 2 b.c. Solinus 130–Coming About 99 (Right Tack 131) — (1982 6g 5s) Feb 12; well-grown, lengthy colt; third foal; half-brother to useful 1980 2-y-o 6f and 7f winner Cavalry Twill (by Queen's Hussar) and useful 7f to 1¼m winner Atlantic Boy (by Busted), subsequently a winner in Scandinavia; dam won twice over 5f at 2 yrs; in rear in maiden races at Haydock in July and October; looks capable of better. *D. Garraton.*

HALCYON AGE 2 b.f. Silly Season 127–Wax Fruit 91 (John Splendid 116) **64** (1982 5g 5fg⁴ 5f² 6f 6fg 6g 6f 5g 5f 5fg 6d) May 6; leggy, light-framed filly; second living foal; half-sister to fair 1981 2-y-o 5f performer Drago (by Dragonara Palace); dam won twice over 6f at 2 yrs; plating-class maiden; maintained her form through the season; stays 6f; probably acts on any going; blinkered last 3 outings. *Mrs M. Nesbitt.*

HALE LANE 3 br.f. Comedy Star 121–King's Fillet (King's Bench 132) (1981 — 5s 6g³ 6fg 6fg 6fg 8.2fg 6g 7g 1982 8.2fg 10f 10fg 7.6f) compact, well-made filly; poor plater. *T. M. Jones.*

HALF CHANCE 2 ch.f. Sandford Lad 133–Anoda (Amber Rama 133) (1982 **65** 5d 5g 5f* 6fg) May 11; 3,800Y; fair sort; second foal; dam, placed in Italy, is half-sister to smart 1977 2-y-o Bolak; backed from 13/8 to 6/5 on, showed much improved form when winning 8-runner seller (bought in 2,000 gns) at Wolverhampton in May by 3 lengths from Fast Peach; well beaten under 7-12 in nursery at Windsor in August; should stay 6f; well suited by firm going. *P. Haslam.*

HALLEL (USA) 3 b.c. Shecky Greene–Escondidas (Better Self) (1981 6fg — 7g 1982 12fg 10f 13.1g) lengthy colt; soundly beaten in varied company; sold 1,700 gns Doncaster November Sales after winning over hurdles for D. Nicholson. *R. Hannon.*

HALLO ROSIE 2 gr.f. Swing Easy 126–Mary Crooner 57 (Crooner 119) (1982 **67** 6fg⁴ 5g³ 6s) second foal; dam sprint plater; put up a pleasing effort after being squeezed out at start when 3½ lengths third of 12 to Pip'em in valuable seller at York in September; favourite, moved poorly to post when well beaten in similar event at Goodwood later in month; best run at 5f. *J. Holt.*

HALSBURY 4 b.c. Exbury 138–Wig and Gown (Mandamus 120) (1981 9d* **106** 10d² 12g* 12s³ 16f 16f³ 15g² 21fg³ 15d* 18g* 1982 16s² 16fg³ 20v³ 22.2fg⁴ 15fg⁴ 21f³ 16d² 18d) big, well-made colt; ran well most starts and was in frame on 7 of his 8 outings; put up particularly good efforts in Prix du Cadran at

Mr A. D. G. Oldrey's "Halsbury"

Longchamp in May (about 2 lengths third to El Badr and Tipperary Fixer), Goodwood Cup in July (dead-heated for third, 2 lengths behind Heighlin) and Jockey Club Cup at Newmarket in October (stuck on well after being held up to finish 6 lengths second of 8 to Little Wolf); shade disappointing when attempting to win Tote Cesarewitch at Newmarket later in October for second successive year, finishing about 8 lengths sixth of 28 behind Mountain Lodge after having every chance; stays very well; acts on any going; usually blinkered, but didn't wear them sixth and seventh starts; suited by strong handling. *P. Walwyn.*

HALSEYS FLUTTER 2 ch.f. Some Hand 119–Lynella (Clear Run 109) (1982 6fg) Apr 4; sixth foal; dam of no account; last of 14 in seller at Windsor in June. *B. Forsey.* —

HAL'S JOY (USA) 3 b.g. L'Heureux–Majestic Flight (Majestic Prince) (1981 7fg 8d 1982 12fg 12f 12f 14f 14.7fg 12v⁴ 14s³ 15.8d³ 18d³) smallish, good-bodied gelding; staying maiden; suited by some give in the ground; sold to M. Pipe 8,400 gns Newmarket Autumn Sales; promising hurdler. *M. Jarvis.* 70

HALYARD 2 gr.g. Gaberdine 106–Cabotage 54 (Sea Hawk II 131) (1982 7f 7g 10d 10d⁴) May 15; useful-looking gelding; good walker; 5 lengths fourth of 13 to Pierrot August in seller at Leicester (blinkered) in October; will stay 1½m; sold out of B. Hobbs's stable 1,300 gns Ascot September Sales after second outing. *A. Young.* 58

HALYUDH (USA) 6 ch.h. Herbager 136–Swapsetta (Swaps) (1981 placed 3 times from 9 starts in USA 1982 form figures include 12f 8.5f 8.5f⁴ 11.7fg 12fg⁴ 12f 11.7g) big, well-made horse; useful handicapper in 1980 (rated 103); was in USA afterwards and was placed 3 times in 1981, including when third in a stakes race at Saratoga; also ran 5 times there early in 1982, on last occasion finishing fourth in $32,500 claimer at Gulfstream in April; made running when 12 lengths fourth of 5 behind Brigadier Hawk in handicap at Ascot in July, easily —

best effort on his return; effective at middle distances and stayed well; acted on any going but was well suited by top-of-the-ground; standing at Quillet Stud, Shaftesbury, £350 n.f.n.f. *R. Armstrong.*

HAMPSHIRE 8 b.g. Silly Season 127–Pirate Queen 77 (Pirate King 129) **57**
(1981 NR 1982 10g 10fg 10f³ 10fg² 12g⁴ 10fg² 10f³ 10g 10f⁴) middle-distance handicapper; placed at Brighton (3 times) and Leicester; acts on any going but has done all his winning on a sound surface; wears blinkers; usually bandaged in front. *A. Pitt.*

HAMPTON BAY 3 b.f. Habitat 134–Petocracy 102 (Petingo 135) (1981 **88**
5fg³ 5g* 7g 1982 6s 5fg³ 6g 5fg 6f 6g 6g 6g⁴ 7.3g 6g⁴ 6d) big, deep-girthed filly; fairly useful handicapper on her day; needs further than 5f nowadays; blinkered seventh start; sold 27,000 gns Newmarket December Sales. *R. Armstrong.*

HANABI 3 b.g. Hittite Glory 125–Derry Willow (Sunny Way 120) (1981 **68**
6h 7fg 6g 6g 1982 7d 7d 11f 8f⁴ 8d³ 8fg 8.3g 7fg 7fg³ 8d* 7s²) quite attractive gelding; made virtually all to win handicap at Leicester in September; stays 1m; suited by some give in the ground; blinkered nowadays. *W. Wightman.*

HANADI 2 b.f. Blakeney 126–Upanishad 85 (Amber Rama 133) (1982 8fg **—**
7s) Mar 4; 54,000Y; neat filly; second foal; half-sister to modest middle-distance winner Diwali (by Great Nephew); dam, 1¼m winner, is half-sister to smart Bas Bleu and very useful Primerello; in rear at long odds in races won by very promising animals at Goodwood in September. *J. Dunlop.*

HANCOCK'S HALFHOUR 2 b.f. Comedy Star 121–Coaster 61 (Right Tack **72**
131) (1982 6g 6f) Apr 16; 13,000Y; good-quartered, quite attractive filly; half-sister to 1m and 1¼m winner We'll Meet Again (by Song) and fairly useful 1980 2-y-o 5f winner Gandoorah (by Record Token); dam, half-sister to top-class sprinter Roman Warrior, won over 1m; 3½ lengths sixth of 18 to Shareef Dancer in maiden race at Newmarket in August, second outing; dead. *R. Williams.*

H AND K GAMBLER 3 b.f. Rheingold 137–Chapeau Bleue (High Hat 131) **—**
(1981 NR 1982 11g 12v) 5,600F; third foal; half-sister to 2 winners, including fairly useful 1980 2-y-o 6f and 7f winner Mr Gus (by Tower Walk); dam won twice over 9f in Ireland; showed a little ability in maiden race won by Step Dance at Newbury in April but was well beaten in minor event at Lingfield in October. *D. Gandolfo.*

HAND MAID 2 b.f. Some Hand 119–Chatter Girl (Beau Brummel) (1982 **68**
5g 6fg 5fg³ 5g 5v) Mar 23; lengthy, quite attractive filly; second foal; dam placed over hurdles; plating-class maiden; headstrong, and better at 5f than 6f; acts on a firm surface; broke out of stalls when withdrawn at Sandown in October; trained by A. Pitt first 3 starts. *M. Haynes.*

HAND OF THE LAW 2 ch.g. Garda's Revenge 119–Jillette (Fine Blade **56**
121) (1982 5f 6f 7f 7g 7fg⁴ 7f³) Mar 20; IR 3,000F, IR 10,000Y; compact gelding; first produce; dam Irish 1½m winner; a modest plater; exported to Malaysia. *J. W. Watts.*

HAND-ROLLED 3 b.f. Sagaro 133–Self Satisfied 100 (Great Nephew 126) **—**
(1981 6d 1982 8fg 10g 7.6fg 7d² 7.2g 6g 7.6d⁴ 7d) useful sort; good mover; plating-class maiden; best at around 7f; acts on a soft surface; sold 800 gns Newmarket December Sales. *W. Wightman.*

HANDSOME BLAZE 7 b.g. Some Hand 119–Court Whisper 83 (Queen's **47**
Hussar 124) (1981 8.2g* 8g* 8f⁴ 8g 8.2g* 1982 8g 8fg 10fg 8.2g² 8.3g) plater; ran on well when 3 lengths second to Eliza de Rich at Haydock in August and would have gone close to winning if he hadn't been given so much to do; disappointing only subsequent start; stays 1m; acts on any going but is suited by some give in the ground; sometimes sweats up and is taken down early. *C. Booth.*

HANDSOME KID 6 b.g. Polyfoto 124–Helen Maire (Queen's Hussar 124) **58**
(1981 10fg 8.3g 10g 10.2g 1982 8f 10f 10fg 10g* 12fg) quite attractive gelding; ran best race of 1982 when 50/1-winner of handicap at Chepstow in June; stays 1¼m; possibly needs some give in the ground and acts on soft going; suitable mount for an apprentice; blinkered twice in 1980; usually held up; sold out of S. Harris' stable 2,000 gns Ascot 2nd June Sales after fourth start. *T. Bill.*

HANDSOME TRAILBOSS 4 ch.c. Some Hand 119–Cedez Cela (Bleep- **—**
Bleep 134) (1981 7fg⁴ 7g 7g 8d² 7g 7f 8f 10f 9d 8f 10s⁴ 10d 1982 8s 8d 10f 8f) workmanlike colt; plater; stayed 1¼m; blinkered fifth start at 3 yrs; sold 550 gns Ascot July Sales; dead. *B. Forsey.*

HANDY GRAY 4 gr.g. Grey Mirage 128–Ishka 58 (Tribal Chief 125) (1981 **48**
6fg 6s 6d 7fg 8fg 9d 8s 6d 1982 6fg² 9f⁴ 8d 6g 5g* 6s) big, rangy gelding;
bought in 1,050 gns after winning seller at Edinburgh in October (apprentice
ridden); best form at sprint distances, but not disgraced at 9f. *R. Cambidge.*

HANDYLAD 3 b.g. Mandamus 120–Rosie Crucian (Polkemmet 91) (1981 —
7fg 7d 7fg⁴ 7fg 8d 1982 10fg) robust, good sort; quite modest at his best;
well beaten only start at 3 yrs in September; should stay 1m+. *W. Wharton.*

HANHAM ROAD 4 b.c. Shiny Tenth 120–Prompt Delivery (Catullus) (1981 **56**
8.2s 7fg 7d 7d² 7s³ 8g² 8g⁴ 7fg 7f 7f² 10.8s 6d 1982 7s² 7f 8g 7h³ 8f² 8fg 8fg 8fg
8s⁴ 8g) lengthy colt; placed in handicaps at Chepstow (2) and Newbury
(apprentice event); stays 1m; acts on any going; often blinkered, but has run
well without. *D. Marks.*

HANLEY AFFAIR 3 b.f. The Brianstan 128–Lucky Affair 83 (Stephen George —
102) (1981 NR 1982 9g 8fg) third foal; half-sister to fair 6f to 1m winner
Havon Cool (by Celtic Cone); dam won 3 times at up to 6f at 2 yrs; behind in
large fields of maidens at Wolverhampton and Warwick in August. *J. Spearing.*

HANNAH LIGHTFOOT 3 b.f. Royalty 130–Gay Charlotte 95 (Charlottown **72**
127) (1981 NR 1982 12f 12fg*) 2,700 2-y-o; leggy, sparely-made filly;
second reported foal; half-sister to fairly useful 1¼m to 1½m winner High Gait
(by High Top); dam, winner over 7.5f at 2 yrs in Ireland and over 1m at 3 yrs
in USA, is daughter of Irish Guinness Oaks winner Merry Mate; heavily backed
when beating Casanna in good style by 6 lengths in 10-runner maiden race at
Beverley in August; will stay 1¾m. *R. Boss.*

HANOVIA HAUT GIRL 4 b.f. Roman Warrior 132–Last Report 96 (Demo- —
cratic 124) (1981 6g 8fg 1982 7fg 10fg 10fg) tall filly; poor maiden; evidently
stays 7f; blinkered final start. *M. Haynes.*

HANS BRINKER 7 ch.g. Dike–Final Orders (Prince John) (1981 18s 16s 18fg —
16.1s 13.3g 17.1h 1982 16g) poor handicapper nowadays; stays well; probably
acts on any going; occasionally blinkered in 1981; bandaged only outing of 1982.
I. Wardle.

HANSE 2 ch.f. Mount Hagen 127–Kissing 98 (Sing Sing 134) (1982 7d) Apr —
12; 20,000Y; workmanlike filly; half-sister to several winners, including fairly
useful 1981 Irish 2-y-o 7f winner Karissima (by Kalamoun); dam won twice
over 5f at 2 yrs; 12/1, behind in 18-runner maiden race at Leicester in October.
G. Pritchard-Gordon.

HANUMAN (FR) 4 ch.c. Giacometti 130–Stereo (Ribero 126) (1981 10.1fg —
10.1g 1982 12s 12g 18.8fg) no worthwhile form in varied races; dwelt when
blinkered second outing; sold 280 gns Ascot July Sales. *C. Austin.*

HAPPY ALWAYS 2 br.f. Lucky Wednesday 124–Mary of Scots 84 (Relic) **48**
(1982 5f 5f³ 6fg⁴ 7f 8fg 7g⁴ 8s) May 18; 600F; half-sister to 2 winners, including
smart French miler King James (by English Prince); poor plater; best form
at up to 7f, but should stay 1m; bandaged near-hind final start. *W. Haigh.*

HAPPY EATER 2 b.g. Furry Glen 121–Barby Road 62 (Tin Whistle 128) **55**
(1982 5fg 6d 5f 6d 7fg) May 9; IR 2,400Y, 3,200 2-y-o; rather dipped-backed
gelding; half-brother to several winners, including fairly useful 5f to 1m winner
Sunny Jim (by Super Sam); dam poor maiden; soundly beaten in maiden races
and sellers. *D. Smith.*

HAPPY EVENT 5 b.h. High Top 131–Blessed Again 90 (Ballymoss 136) —
(1981 NR 1982 11.7f) quite moderate (rated 73) at 2 yrs; well beaten only
outing since. *T. M. Jones.*

HAPPY MOO 3 b.f. Williamston Kid–Tartarbee 72 (Charlottesville 135) —
(1981 NR 1982 8fg) half-sister to 7f to 1½m winner Made My Day (by
Double Jump); dam, a plater, stayed 1m; unquoted, fell after 1½f in 17-runner
maiden race won by Rossett at Warwick in May. *J. Peacock.*

HAPPY RHYTHM 2 b.g. Tudor Rhythm 112–Happy Donna 106 (Hunter- —
combe 133) (1982 5fg 5g 8.2s 6s 8.2v³) Feb 26; first foal; dam won 3 times over
5f at 2 yrs; well beaten in varied company, including plating; gelded after final
outing. *J. S. Wilson.*

HAPPY SEASON 2 b.c. Silly Season 127–My Shoon (Sheshoon 132) (1982 **85**
6f 6d 6g 7s 6d² 6s) Feb 27; lengthy colt; first foal; dam never ran; short-headed
on line by Foil 'Em in 22-runner maiden race at Doncaster in October, best
effort; should stay 1¼m; acts on soft going. *J. Etherington.*

HAPPY STORY 2 br.f. Relko 136–Novelista 101 (El Gallo 122) (1982 7d 7f) —
Mar 15; 1,600Y; quite attractive, well-made filly; half-sister to 9f winner Noble
Legend (by Noble Decree) and a winner in Australia; dam successful 2-y-o 5f
performer; not fully wound up, always in rear in July in maiden race at Sandown
and seller at Beverley. *M. Blanshard.*

HAPPY WONDER 2 ch.c. Levanter 121–Gretna Wonder 46 (Elopement 125)
(1982 6fg 5f 7fg) Mar 18; lengthy filly; half-sister to 2 minor winners, including
Walnut Wonder (by Crozier) who is also a fairly useful jumper; dam plater;
soundly beaten in £3,500 event at Goodwood and maiden races at Newbury and
Warwick; not seen out after July. *D. Elsworth.*

HARBOUR BAZAAR 2 gr. or ro.c. Native Bazaar 122–Overseas 48 (Sea Hawk —
II 131) (1982 5fg 7g 8d 5g⁴ 8s 6d 6s) Mar 23; leggy, shallow-girthed colt;
first foal; dam poor maiden; 2½ lengths fourth of 12 to Chauffeuse in weakly-
contested maiden race at Wolverhampton in October, only form, including in
sellers; not sure to stay 7f; bandaged off-hind and blinkered final start. *M.
Chapman.*

HARBOUR BRIDGE 2 b.c. Blakeney 126–Solar 120 (Hotfoot 126) (1982   **80 p**
7f 7fg³ 7s) Feb 4; good sort; good walker and mover; third foal; half-brother to
useful 1980 2-y-o 5f winner Ashbrittle (by Great Nephew), subsequently successful in USA; dam, half-sister to smart fillies Walk By and Smarten Up, was one
of leading 2-y-o fillies in 1975 and stayed 1¼m; apparently still far from fully fit,
ran on strongly from rear when promising 1½ lengths third of 16 to Behind The
Lines in maiden race at Salisbury in September; unquoted, ran a similar race
when seventh of 13 to By Decree in £5,900 event at Ascot later in month; promises
to make up into quite a useful stayer. *W. Wightman.*

HARBOUR (FR) 3 ch.f. Arctic Tern 126–Heres To You (Molvedo 137) (1981   **129**
8.5s³ 8s* 1982 9.5fg* 10v* 10.5v* 12f⁴ 12s)
    Although French fillies have had a magnificent record in the last dozen
runnings of the Prix de l'Arc de Triomphe only Allez France has completed the
Arc-French Oaks double in that period, and even she took two years to achieve
it; in the same period eight others have finished in the first three in both, one of
them Akiyda who improved on her French Oaks second in the Arc while the
filly who beat her at Chantilly, Harbour, finished only ninth of seventeen.
Harbour ran some way below her best at Longchamp: she held a good position
on the home turn and had every chance early in the straight, but she went out
quickly in the last two furlongs eventually to be beaten around nine lengths,
running as though she didn't quite stay the distance in a testing race. The
somewhat improbable explanation that Harbour ran out of stamina is one of
two we've heard advanced for her disappointing showing on soft ground that,
all else equal, should have suited her ideally. The other (her trainer's), that she
fretted away her chance down at the start, is much more feasible: she was
sweating when loading-time arrived, having previously impressed in the paddock.
What made her performance the more disappointing was that three weeks
earlier she'd run a splendid trial in the Prix Vermeille. On that occasion she'd
been a strong-finishing fourth behind the firm-ground filly All Along, Akiyda and
Grease, about two and a half lengths behind the winner, despite encountering
difficulties in obtaining room to challenge.
    In the first half of the season Harbour had a record the equal of any French
three-year-old filly and superior to all except that of River Lady, who was an
impressive winner of the Prix de la Grotte and the French One Thousand Guineas,
the Poule d'Essai des Pouliches. As River Lady won both her starts so too
did Harbour: she won the Prix Vanteaux at Longchamp in April from Estere
and Akiyda, and the Prix Saint-Alary at Longchamp in May from All Along and
Perlee. The Prix Saint-Alary, a Group 1 race, has fallen to Pistol Packer,
Dahlia, Comtesse de Loir, Nobiliary and Three Troikas during the palmy days

*Prix de Diane Hermes, Chantilly—Harbour gains her third win of
the season with this defeat of Akiyda in the French Oaks*

Ecurie Aland's "Harbour"

since 1971, and seldom goes to one who fails subsequently to leave her mark on the season. Harbour had four lengths to spare over All Along, so much on top once she took over from the runner-up halfway up the straight that she was never touched with the whip. The French One Thousand Guineas second Typhoon Polly and third Vidor never managed to get into the race, and the Newmarket fourth Play It Safe finished well back.

After this the French Oaks, the Prix de Diane Hermes, presented all the appearance of a match between Harbour and River Lady, though the race attracted a field of fourteen, the same as in the two previous years. Harbour coupled with her pacemaker Santa Musica started favourite at 12/10, River Lady with her two pacemakers Ninoushka and Pasadoble started at 2/1; Akiyda was third favourite at 31/4. Next in the betting came the Prix Cleopatre winner Paradise and her owner's other runner Vidor, who since the Saint-Alary had beaten a fair-sized field in the Prix de Royaumont over the course and distance, then All Along, sixth to Time Charter at Epsom. The only English representative, the Musidora Stakes second Ash Ridge, started among the outsiders at 21/1. Sadly, the eagerly-anticipated test between Harbour and River Lady did not materialise. There seemed every prospect that it would when the pacemakers dropped away on the home turn, leaving River Lady moving easily in front, a length up on All Along and about two up on Harbour just ahead of the pack. Two and a half furlongs out River Lady pulled up sharply, injured beyond hope of saving. On her departure from the race Harbour soon got on top of the rest though All Along, Vidor and Paradise stuck close on her heels until running into the final furlong where Akiyda came through strongly to finish a clear second, two lengths down on Harbour who won easily; Ash Ridge finished among the back three. At this stage of the season Harbour was unquestionably the best middle-distance filly of her age in France, arguably the equal of Time Charter. With an autumn campaign in mind she was subsequently given a long break from racing until the Prix Vermeille. During her absence the next four home at Chantilly soldiered on, fifth-placed All Along achieving the best result through winning the Prix Maurice de Nieuil at Saint-Cloud from the colts. Akiyda was beaten in the Prix de Pomone at Deauville (second to Zalataia), Paradise in the Prix de la Nonette at Deauville (fourth to Grease) and Vidor in the Grand Prix Prince Rose at Ostend (eighth to Castle Keep).

Harbour (Fr) (ch.f. 1979)	Arctic Tern (ch 1973)	Sea-Bird II (ch 1962)	Dan Cupid	Sicalade
		Bubbling Beauty (ch 1961)	Hasty Road	Almahmoud
	Heres To You (b 1970)	Molvedo (br 1958)	Ribot	Maggiolina
		Naila (ch 1960)	Swaps	Nasrina

Harbour's sire and dam both stayed a mile and a half; the sire never won over the distance but the dam did, in maiden company at Deauville shortly before her sale in 1973 for 240,000 francs at the Howell Jackson dispersal in 1973 (the equivalent of £21,250 in sterling at that time). Arctic Tern beat a very strong field in the Prix Ganay in 1977. Consistency wasn't his strong point, possibly as a result of a nervous temperament or even as a result of his having sight in only one eye, but he had several high-class performances to his credit, including seconds to Youth in the Prix Lupin and Prix Niel. Harbour and the very useful English-trained stayer Khairpour are members of his first crop. Harbour is the third reported foal of Heres To You and her second runner, following the useful miler Heresty (by Tyrant) who won three races in France and the Group 3 Premio Royal Mares in Italy. The next dam Naila won in the United States prior to her import to France. She won a minor event from fourteen starts there, in contrast to her dam Nasrina, rated equal-best two-year-old American filly in 1955 as a result of victories in the Frizette Stakes and the Gardenia Stakes. Nasrina was imported to France at the age of ten, and like Naila bred minor winners there.

Harbour is set to make the reverse crossing of the Atlantic, for she has been retired and is booked to visit Raja Baba; there was little in her final run to encourage keeping her in training another year. A lightly-made filly, she was ideally suited by plenty of give in the ground. It speaks volumes for her as a racehorse that her least satisfactory performance should be ninth of seventeen in Europe's most strongly-contested event. *Mme C. Head, France.*

HARBOUR MUSIC 2 br.g. Tudor Music 131–Sark (Chamier 128) (1982 —
6g 6g 7fg 6d) May 8; 2,000F, 7,800Y; strong, compact gelding; half-brother to several winners, including Irish 1m to 1½m winner Sarcastic (by Ballyciptic); dam never ran; little worthwhile form; gelded after final outing. *R. Whitaker.*

HARD BOILED 3 gr.c. No Mercy 126–Bird in the Hand 82 (Major Portion 129) —
(1981 5s 6g 6g 1982 6g 8f 8g 8g⁴ 6d 10g) lengthy colt; plater; stays 1m. *W. Holden.*

HARD FROST 6 br.h. Right Tack 131–Broken Blossoms (Breakspear II) **38**
(1981 NR 1982 8.2s 8f 10.6f³ 10d 8fg 10fg 5g) strong, robust horse; poor walker; plater nowadays; stays 1¼m; seems to act on any going; often wears blinkers. *P. Bevan.*

HARDIHOSTESS 2 b.f. Be My Guest 126–Hardiemma 81 (Hardicanute 130) **104**
(1982 5g 7fg³ 7fg* 7fg* 8f) Apr 25; rather angular, good-backed, good-quartered, smallish filly; has a sharp action; sister to 3-y-o 11f winner Inviting and half-sister to 3 winners, notably Derby and Irish Sweeps Derby winner Shirley Heights (by Mill Reef); dam won at up to 11f; won 17-runner maiden race at Warwick in July by 2½ lengths from Balinese and valuable nursery at York the following month by 2 lengths from Riverside Artist; will stay at least 1¼m; acts on firm going. *M. Stoute.*

HARD KINGDOM 2 b.c. Realm 129–Hard To Tell 68 (Buckpasser) (1982 **84 p**
6fg⁴ 6fg) Mar 4; good-bodied colt; good walker; first living foal; dam, half-sister to Derby third Freefoot and high-class Moulton, was second over 10.6f; favourite for newcomers race at Ascot in July but found lack of condition telling after leading briefly in straight and faded to finish 4¾ lengths fourth of 5 to Naar; 8/1, showed good speed on stand side 4f when 9 lengths ninth of 25 to Orixo in minor event at Doncaster 2 months later; a likeable individual, certain to do better. *H. Wragg.*

HARDSTONE 6 b.g. Ragstone 128–Hard to Catch 59 (Hardicanute 130) (1981
NR 1982 15f 12fg) poor maiden on flat though is a winning plater over hurdles; blinkered on reappearance. *R. Morris.*

HARD TO SING (FR)   6 b.g. Hard to Beat 132–Concord Hymn 107 (Emerson) **117**
(1981 NR   1982 10g* 12s⁴ 12s² 12d* 15.5v⁴ 12g* 12s* 12v² 12g*) big French
gelding; broke down in 1980 and didn't race in 1981, but returned to his best in
1982 and added 5 wins to the 9 he'd achieved at 3 and 4 yrs; won small race at
Cagnes-sur-Mer, 2 races at Maisons-Laffitte, Grand Prix d'Évry (beat Two Step by
a short neck in 15-runner event) and Grand Prix de la Ville de Toulouse; beat
No Attention by ½ length in last-named event in June on final start; also ran
well when neck second to Terreno in La Coupe at Chantilly on penultimate
start; effective at middle distances and stays well; acts on heavy going; wears
blinkers; most genuine and consistent; very smart. *C. Milbank, France.*

HARDWICK EAGLE   2 b.f. Legal Eagle 126–Keenland (Weensland 121)   **63**
(1982 5f² 6g 5fg⁴ 6g 5g 5g) Apr 23; second foal; dam bad hurdler; in frame in
5-runner events at Beverley and Ayr; should be suited by 6f; blinkered fifth
start. *M. Jefferson.*

HARDWICK SUN   4 ch.f. Dieu Soleil 111–Hyper Rose 62 (Pinza 137)   (1981   **—**
12.2s 9s   1982 12v) narrow, leggy filly; little better than plating class on
flat but is a winner over hurdles; should stay 9f. *M. Jefferson.*

HARESCEUGH   4 b.g. Andrea Mantegna–Mertola (Tribal Chief 125)   (1981   **78** d
10s³ 10fg² 10d³ 12d* 12s* 12g* 12f 13.3g 12g 12fg 12d   1982 12s 12g* 12f 11.7fg
11.7g⁴ 12fg² 13d 12g⁴ 12d³ 12s) strong, workmanlike gelding; beat Leopard's
Rock by ¾ length in handicap at Brighton in July; in frame on 4 other occasions
but isn't all that consistent; suited by 1½m; acts on a firm surface, but has done
all his winning with some give in the ground; quite often blinkered nowadays.
N. Vigors.

HARI-HARI-MOU   2 b.c. Malinowski 123–Shangara (Credo 123)   (1982 6f*   **91**
6g³ 8.2g 8.2d 8s 8.2s³) Mar 28; 4,200Y; smallish, fair sort; half-brother to useful
middle-distance stayer Pal's Bambino (by Pals Passage) and 3-y-o 9.4f winner
Secret Pursuit (by Ardoon); dam won twice over 5f at 2 years in Ireland; won
maiden race at Carlisle in July; ran well in blinkers in nurseries at Warwick
and Nottingham in October, last 2 outings; will stay 1¼m; acts on any going.
E. Eldin.

HARLESTON LASS   3 ch.f. Bold Lad (Ire) 133–Court Sensation 73 (Appiani II   **43**
128)   (1981 5g 5v³ 5.1f 6f 6fg 6g   1982 8fg 7g 8fg 7f 8g 8fg 8fg 8.2v²) leggy, fair
sort; plater; stays 1m well; acts on heavy going; sometimes blinkered; has
sweated up; sold out of G. Blum's stable 1,300 gns Doncaster September Sales
after seventh start. *M. Cousins.*

HARLEW   4 b.f. Fine Blade 121–Jillaroo 79 (Javelot 124)   (1981 8.2s 10g   **—**
12d* 12d 11fg 10.8fg 12d 12g   1982 11s 13d) small filly; stays 1½m; acts on a
soft surface. *A. W. Jones.*

HARLEYFORD MAID   2 gr.f. The Go-Between 129–Comprella 54 (Compensa-   **72**
tion 127)   (1982 5f 5f² 5g 5fg⁴ 5f³ 5f 5g² 5g³ 5v⁴) Apr 19; close-coupled filly;
half-sister to 1m winner First Vote (by Royal Prerogative), also a very good
winner over hurdles in France, and to Triumph Hurdle winner Shiny Copper
(by Shiny Tenth); dam won 11f seller; beaten neck in maiden race at Thirsk in
June and in nursery at Hamilton in September; unlikely to stay beyond 5f; acts
on any going. *D. Smith.*

HARLOW MILL   3 b.c. Artaius 129–Celina 115 (Crepello 136)   (1981 NR   **—**
1982 11.7f 16g² 14f) 28,000Y; half-brother to 3 winners, including fairly useful
middle-distance filly Calf of Man (by Derring-Do); dam won 1968 Irish Guinness
Oaks; seems only plating class; best run at 2m on an easy surface. *M. Pipe.*

HARLOWS BOY   2 b.g. Ercolano 118–No Man's Land (Salvo 129)   (1982 7fg   **67**
7fg 7g 7d 8.2fg 8g⁴) May 10; lengthy gelding; first foal; dam poor half-sister to
very useful middle-distance stayer No Bombs; plating-class maiden; will stay
at least 1½m; wears blinkers; gelded after final outing. *P. Brookshaw.*

HARLY (FR)   2 b.c. Pharly 130–Helvetique (Val de Loir 133)   (1982 7d 7g*   **97**
8d⁴ 8g) May 23; 44,000Y; small, fair sort; third foal; half-brother to a minor
winner in France by Forli; dam, half-sister to smart Hamada, won twice in
France; improved tremendously on first effort when wearing
down Hot Boy to win 16-runner minor event at Lingfield in August by ½ length,
the pair clear; nearest finish when creditable fourth of 10 to Quite A Night in
nursery at Ayr in September, easily better subsequent effort; will stay 1¼m.
J. Dunlop.

HAROME   3 b.f. Workboy 123–Roxanne (Sheshoon 132)   (1981 NR   1982 10fg)   **—**
sixth foal; sister to a poor performer; dam well behind in maiden races; tailed

off virtually throughout in 18-runner maiden race won by Traviata at Beverley in September. *K. Stone.*

HARPERS BAZAAR 3 ch.g. Native Bazaar 122–French Salute (Salvo 129) **80**
(1981 6f 6fg³ 5f* 1982 5d⁴ 6fg² 6fg 5g 5.3g 5fg² 5.3f* 5g 6f³ 5s⁴) narrow, lightly-made gelding; sprint handicapper; made all to win easily at Brighton in August; stays 6f; acts well on firm going and wasn't disgraced on soft final outing; blinkered fifth start. *R. Smyth.*

HARP SONG 2 b.f. Auction Ring 123–Destiny's Daughter 75 (Manacle 123) **64**
(1982 5f⁴ 5.1fg* 5f 5d) Mar 30; IR 4,500Y; small filly; second foal; dam won 6f seller; won 8-runner seller (bought in 1,400 gns) at Yarmouth in August; will be suited by 6f; acts on firm going; sometimes sweats up, but races consistently. *D. Morley.*

HARRIET WALK 3 ch.f. Ampney Prince 96–Pennings Road (Zarathustra 131) —
(1981 NR 1982 6g 10.1fg 8fg) half-sister to 2 winning jumpers; dam of no account; behind in maiden races and a minor event. *P. Burgoyne.*

HARRY HASTINGS (USA) 3 b.c. Vaguely Noble 140–Country Dream —
(Ribot 142) (1981 7g 1982 11f 13.3f 10f⁴ 8s 8.2s) big, rangy colt; heavily backed when 4½ lengths fourth of 16 to Miramar Reef in maiden race at Newmarket in July, best effort; should stay 1½m+; sold to J. S. Wilson 9,000 gns Newmarket Autumn Sales. *G. Harwood.*

HARTBURN RELIANCE 2 b.g. Reliance II 137–Helgonet (Soueida 111) **79**
(1982 6g³ 6g 5g² 5d³) Feb 27; 2,800Y; sturdy, good-bodied gelding; half-brother to 2 winners, including 5f to 7f winner Portogon (by Porto Bello); dam won in Sweden and Denmark; placed in maiden races, notably head second to Chauffeuse at Wolverhampton in October; should be well suited by 7f+; capable of winning small maiden event. *I. Vickers.*

HARTBURN ROYALE 2 b.c. The Brianstan 128–Aequanimitas (Infatuation —
129) (1982 8s) June 5; 800Y; strong colt; turns off-fore out; brother to a poor animal, and half-brother to a winning plater; dam won over 1½m in Ireland; 50/1 and backward, tailed-off last of 12 in maiden race at Newcastle in October. *I. Vickers.*

HARTFIELD LAD 3 br.g. Jimsun 121–Julita 87 (Rockavon 120) (1981 **44**
5g 5d 6d 8g 8d 10g 8d³ 1982 10g 10f 10.1fg 10g² 10d) neat gelding; plater; stays 1¼m; has worn blinkers; trained part of season by A. Pitt. *J. Hardy.*

HARTNELL DREAM 3 b.f. Grundy 137–Scarlet Thread 80 (Joshua 129) —
(1981 NR 1982 12f 12d 12v 10s 12s) deep-girthed, quite attractive filly; second foal; half-sister to a winner in Belgium; dam won over 9f and 1¼m; beaten some way in varied company. *P. Makin.*

HARTSFIELD 5 ch.h. Grundy 137–Omentello 91 (Elopement 125) (1981 **55**
12fg 12g 12s³ 12fg⁴ 11.7d⁴ 12f³ 12s 1982 12s 12d 12g³ 12fg 15.5f 12g⁴ 12f⁴ 10fg 10fg) big, dipped-backed horse; not the best of movers; middle-distance handicapper; acts on any going; often blinkered nowadays; seems to need strong handling. *R. Laing.*

HARVEST 2 ch.c. Continuation 120–Polly Bellino 56 (Dadda Bert 95) (1982 —
7fg) Mar 10; brother to 3-y-o 1m winner Tinterello and half-brother to a successful plater; dam won at 1¼m; unquoted, remote tenth of 18 in maiden race at Warwick in July. *J. Hardy.*

HARVEST BOY 2 gr.g. Oats 126–Madlin 102 (Sovereign Path 125) (1982 **88**
6f² 6f⁴ 6f⁴) Feb 14; tall, quite attractive gelding; half-brother to 3 winners, including 1978 Irish 2-y-o 7.5f winner Sassalin (by Sassafras); dam won over 6f at 2 yrs; fair form in varied company, best effort when 4½ lengths fourth of 10 to Right Dancer in Chesham Stakes at Royal Ascot on second outing; will be suited by 7f+; sent to Hong Kong. *N. Vigors.*

HARVESTER GOLD 2 gr.c. Rheingold 137–Colloquy (Quorum 126) (1982 **87**
7fg 8fg⁴ 8d) Mar 25; IR 13,500Y; quite attractive, lightly-made colt; half-brother to several winners, including useful sprinter Takawin (by Takawalk II); dam of little account; had none too clear a run when creditable fourth of 18 to Dawn River, beaten about 5 lengths, in maiden race at Goodwood in September; 7/1 when ninth of 23 in similar race won by The Liquidator at Newmarket the following month. *M. Jarvis.*

HARVESTER LAD 2 gr.g. On Your Mark 125–Miss Vicki 94 (Roan Rocket —
128) (1982 5g 6g) May 12; 7,400Y; strong gelding; brother to a moderate

2-y-o 5f winner, and half-brother to 2 winners; dam won twice over 5f at 2 yrs; 14/1 and having first race since June, modest eighth of 15 to Luisa Miller in £2,700 seller at Newmarket in October; sold BBA 1,400 gns Newmarket Autumn Sales. *M. Jarvis.*

HARVEST FORTUNE 2 b.c. Oats 126–Fortellina (Fortino II 120) (1982 7f 7d 8s) May 5; IR 2,200F; rangy colt; half-brother to Irish 1¼m and 13.5f winner Uncle Walter (by Ballyciptic); dam, placed in Ireland, is half-sister to Supreme Sovereign; showed early speed when behind in varied company. *H. Collingridge.*

HARWOOD BAR 3 br.f. Wollow 132–Princess Ayesha (Bold Lad, Ire 133) — (1981 NR 1982 7d 6s 8g) 3,000Y; useful sort; first foal; dam Irish 1¼m winner; poor form in minor events; has given trouble at start and looks highly strung. *M. Naughton.*

HASTY DALE 3 ch.f. Hasty Word 84–Severndale (Bounteous 125) (1981 — 6fg 6fg 5f 5fg² 5fg 5.8f 5f 5g⁴ 5s 1982 7g 8d 5g) neat filly; bad mover; plater; should stay at least 6f; acts on firm going. *K. Bridgwater.*

HASTY FLIRT (USA) 2 b.c. Vitriolic–Lucky Flirt (Lucky Debonair) (1982 7g⁴ ? 7g⁴ 7f* 7fg 8g 8g* 8g² 8d² 8g*) Apr 13; $37,000Y, $33,000 2-y-o; quite attractive colt; third foal; half-brother to 3-y-o 1m winner Torsion Prince (by Torsion); dam, half-sister to good filly Copano, won at up to 1m; lucky winner of 17-runner maiden race at Newmarket in July, leading near finish to beat Zoffany ½ length after runner-up veered badly left when clear inside final 2f; ran well in nurseries in the autumn, winning one at Yarmouth, and put up a splendid effort in Group 2 Premio Tevere at Rome in November, leading at halfway and drawing right away in final two furlongs to win by 7 lengths from Mount Fire; will probably stay 1¼m; seems to act on any going; lost all chance at start fourth outing; genuine; very useful judged by his Italian display (101 on form here). *B. Hanbury.*

HASTY GODDESS 3 ch.f. Nebbiolo 125–No Delay 72 (Never Say Die 137) 72 (1981 5d 1982 10s³ 12fg² 13f³ 14.7f 12d³ 14.7f⁴ 14.7fg) plating-class maiden; stays 13f; acts on any going; often races with head in air and doesn't look particularly genuine; sold to W. A. Stephenson 2,000 gns Newmarket December Sales. *T. Robson.*

HASTY IMPORT 3 ch.g. Import 127–Isis Rapide (I Say 125) (1981 5d — 6g 1982 10d) leggy gelding; in rear in minor events and a maiden race. *J. Mason.*

HATHAWAY 3 ch.f. Connaught 130–Ragirl (Ragusa 137) (1981 NR 1982 — 10fg 10fg 12fg 16f) 14,500F, 27,000Y; lightly made filly; closely related to useful 1¼m winner Il Padrone (by St Paddy) and half-sister to several winners, including very speedy 1974 2-y-o Fats Waller (by Sing Sing); dam never ran; behind in maiden races in the South. *A. Ingham.*

HAT HILL 3 ch.f. Roan Rocket 128–La Colline 97 (Acropolis 132) (1981 NR — 1982 7f 7g 7d 10.1g) small, useful-looking filly; half-sister to numerous winners, including 7f and 1m winner Sobhia (by Silly Season); dam won over 7f and 1m at 2 yrs; beaten some way in maiden and minor events. *R. Baker.*

HATS OFF 3 ch.f. Manado 130–Golden Fez (Aureole 132) (1981 NR 1982 52 7fg 8d 10f⁴ 8f⁴) 16,500F; quite well-made filly; half-sister to 7f to 11f winner Golden Brigadier (by Brigadier Gerard) and useful French middle-distance stayer Marriageable (by Great Nephew); dam, daughter of 1,000 Guineas winner Zabara, won over middle distances in France; has shown a little ability in varied company; will probably stay 1¼m. *J. Dunlop.*

HAUGHTINESS (USA) 3 ch.f. Top Command–Snobishness (Forli) (1981 54 raced in USA 1982 10fg 8.5f 8d 13f 12g) deep-girthed filly; fourth foal; sister to Oh So Choosy, successful 3 times at around 1m; dam smart French middle-distance performer; raced 4 times unplaced in USA at 2 yrs; showed little worthwhile form over here; blinkered third outing. *I. Balding.*

HAUTE HAT (USA) 2 b.f. Exclusive Native–Lady Marguery (Tim Tam) — (1982 7fg 8f) May 14; rangy, good-bodied filly; half-sister to numerous winners in USA, including Kentucky Derby third Partez (by Quack); dam, placed at 3 yrs, is half-sister to dam of top-class Trillion; no form; weakened quickly 2f out when tenth of 23 in maiden race at Leicester in September, second outing; looks capable of better. *S. Norton.*

HAVANEZA 4 b.f. Simbir 130–Lucindale (Ballyciptic 122) (1981 8fg 1982 — 15.8d 12f 12fg) leggy, workmanlike filly; showed a little ability at 2 yrs; should be suited by a test of stamina. *E. Eldin.*

HAVARA 3 b.f. African Sky 124–Arriva (Disciplinarian) (1981 NR 1982 5fg² 82
5g² 6g* 7fg³ 7.3g² 7s) big, well-made filly; fourth foal; half-sister to 3 winners,
including fairly useful 2-y-o 5f winners King's Consort (by King's Company) and
Quiana (by Huntercombe); dam unraced daughter of California Oaks winner
Renova; finished very strongly when winning 18-runner apprentice maiden event
at Newbury in August; placed most other starts in varied company; will stay
1m; best form on a sound surface. *J. Sutcliffe.*

HAVE BLESSED 2 b.c. Averof 123–As Blessed 101 (So Blessed 130) (1982 71
5fg⁴ 6f⁴ 7g⁴ 7fg 8d 8d) Apr 22; compact colt; second foal; dam, 2-y-o 5f winner,
stayed 1m; 3¾ lengths fourth of 7 to Stay Sharp in Woodcote Stakes at Epsom
in June, second outing and best effort; should stay 1m; blinkered final start.
C. Brittain.

HAVE FORM 2 b.f. Haveroid 122–Good Form 54 (Deep Diver 134) (1982 6g —
7g 7fg) Feb 29; 3,200Y; first foal; dam, a plater, stayed 1¼m; little worthwhile
form; blinkered in maiden race at Wolverhampton in July on final outing.
D. H. Jones.

HAVEN BLESSED 2 b.f. So Blessed 130–Haven Bridge 88 (Connaught 130) —
(1982 7g) Apr 28; 5,000Y; good-bodied filly, slightly hollow-backed; first foal;
dam 2-y-o 6f winner; unquoted, never-dangerous tenth of 22 in maiden race at
Newmarket in October. *C. Nelson.*

HAVEN CENTURION (USA) 3 ch.c. Giacometti 130–Indialucie (Sir Ivor 135) —
(1981 7f 8d 10s 1982 8f 10f 13.1g 14f³ 14g 11.7d) fair sort; good mover; poor
maiden; best run at 1¾m on firm going; sold 1,200 gns Newmarket Autumn Sales.
P. Cole

HAVEN'S PRIDE (USA) 3 b.c. Dewan–Victoire (Crafty Admiral) (1981 5f 69
6fg⁴ 7g 7d⁴ 7h 7fg 8d³ 8s⁴ 8d² 1982 7fg 7.6f 8f² 10.6h* 12d 10.8fg 12fg 14g 8g*
8.2g 8fg 8d 10.6s) small colt; plater; won at Haydock in June; sold out of P.
Cole's stable 5,800 gns afterwards; successful in better company at Wolverhampton in August; stays 1¼m; acts on any going; has twice been blinkered;
goes well for apprentice T. Quinn. *W. Charles.*

HAVENWOOD 3 br.c. Relko 136–Pepin (Midsummer Night II 117) (1981 5fg 72 d
6f 7fg 8s 1982 10f* 12fg 10f 12g 10d 10d) leggy colt; made all and floored
odds laid on Indulgence by 8 lengths in 3-runner race at Ripon in June; well
beaten afterwards; should stay 1½m; acts on firm going; has been bandaged on
near-hind; trained most of season by P. Felgate. *K. Stone.*

HAVERHILL LAD 6 ch.g. Queen's Hussar 124–Court Sensation 73 (Appiani II 48
128) (1981 8g 10g² 10d³ 10f 10fg³ 10d³ 10fg 10fg² 12g 1982 11.7fg 10fg 10f
12g 10d⁴ 10fg 10fg) middle-distance handicapper; acts on any going; has worn
blinkers but does better without. *G. Blum.*

HAVERHILL LASS 3 b.f. Music Boy 124–March Queen 88 (March Past 124) 62
(1981 5s* 5s 5g³ 5d 5fg 6g 5fg* 5g² 5g² 5f 5s 5g 1982 6fg 6g 5f² 5g 5.1g 6f 5f³
5d* 6g 5d 5g) sturdy filly; sprint handicapper; won at Wolverhampton in
August; best at 5f; acts on any going; often blinkered. *G. Blum.*

HAVERING HILL 4 b.g. So Blessed 130–Heaven and Earth (Midsummer Night —
II 117) (1981 7fg 8g³ 9s 8fg³ 10fg² 9s⁴ 1982 10.1d 10f) fair sort; placed in
maiden races as a 3-y-o; stays 1¼m. *J. Jenkins.*

HAVOC 4 br.c. Swing Easy 126–Bobelle 62 (Pirate King 129) (1981 8d 8fg² 81
8g* 7g* 7.6g 7.6fg⁴ 7g 7g 7g 1982 7f³ 7fg 7fg² 8fg 8fg⁴ 7g 8f³) big, rangy colt;
placed in £7,400 event at Leicester in April (had very stiff task) and handicaps at
York in June and Kempton in July; stays 1m; acts on firm going; blinkered fifth
and sixth outings; a front runner who possibly needs things his own way; carries
his head high and is a difficult ride; sold 4,600 gns Newmarket Autumn Sales. *C.
Brittain.*

HAVON COOL 6 b.h. Celtic Cone 116–Lucky Affair 83 (Stephen George 102) 80
(1981 7.6g³ 8d³ 7.2s³ 8.5g² 6f* 6fg* 7fg 6g 6s 7s 6d 7d 1982 8g 7.2s* 7.2fg³ 7.6g²
7f 6d 6g⁴ 8.3fg⁴ 7f² 7.6d 9d 7fg 6s⁴ 6s 7s) neat, strong horse; poor mover; beat
Prince Reviewer in really good style by 7 lengths in handicap at Haydock in
April; placed subsequently in Cold Shield Windows Trophy at Haydock (had
stiff task) and handicaps at Chester and Wolverhampton; needs further than 6f,
and is best at up to 1m; acts on any going; usually wears blinkers; suitable
mount for a boy. *Mrs M. Rimell.*

HAWA BLADI 2 gr.c. Nishapour 125–Nofertiti (Exbury 138) (1982 7fg³ 7fg² 87
8fg³) Mar 2; 30,000Y; quite well-made colt; first foal; dam, second over 1¼m

in France, is half-sister to high-class 1m to 1¼m performer Nadjar; placed in good-class company at Ascot, Sandown and Goodwood; should stay beyond 1m; sure to win a race. *P. Walwyn.*

HAWAIIAN HEIR (USA) 3 b.c. Hawaii–Madam Fox (Rising Market) (1981 7fg 10s² 1982 12g⁴ 14fg 12f 12f 10.2g 16fg 12f 12f 10f) quite attractive, useful-looking colt; modest maiden at his best; blinkered when soundly beaten in selling handicaps last 2 starts; probably stays 1½m; best run on soft going; sold 1,800 gns Newmarket Autumn Sales. *P. Cole.* —

HAWALI 5 b.m. Gay Fandango 132–Gentle Way 74 (Gentle Art 121) (1981 7fg² 7fg* 7fg⁴ 1982 7fg³ 7g) quite attractive mare; most creditable third to Paulager in handicap at York in June, staying on after having to be checked; didn't run up to her best in blinkers only subsequent start; stays 7f; acts on firm going; tends to sweat up. *W. O'Gorman.* **69**

HAWKBARROW 4 br.g. Appiani II 128–Glistening 84 (Aureole 132) (1981 12g 10.1fg 1982 12s⁴ 16fg³) staying maiden on flat; in frame at Haydock and Lingfield; blinkered nowadays. *D. Gandolfo.* **53**

HAWK LADY (USA) 2 b. or br.f. Accipiter–Nova Miss (Great McGow) (1982 6fg 6g 6s*) Apr 10; $32,000Y; first foal; dam won 11 races in USA, including 2 minor stakes races at up to 1m at 5 yrs; 25/1, and having first race for over 2 months, made steady progress after dwelling to lead on bridle 1f out when winning 19-runner maiden event at Leicester in November ridden out by length from Lady Gerard; will stay 1m; acts on soft going. *Mrs R. Lomax.* **81**

HAWKLEY 2 br.c. Monsanto 121–Varvel (Falcon 131) (1982 5f² 5fg² 5g* 6g² 6g³ 6d 7fg³ 7v) Apr 9; fair sort; good walker; first foal; dam not of much account on flat or over jumps; made heavy weather of landing odds by ½ length from John Doyle in maiden race at Wolverhampton in June; ran creditably most subsequent starts; suited by 7f; seems to act on any going; had stiff task and was slowly into stride when well beaten in blinkers sixth start. *K. Brassey.* **96**

HAWKS NEST 3 b.f. Moulton 128–Good Try 92 (Good Bond 122) (1981 5fg 5fg² 1982 5fg² 5h² 6g⁴ 5g 6f 6d 6v* 6d² 6s) neat filly; decisively won apprentice handicap at Folkestone in October; will stay 7f; acts on any going; best in blinkers. *A. Hide.* **66**

HAWTHORN ARCH 4 b.f. Wishing Star 117–River Leaves (Varano) (1981 7v 8d⁴ 9.5s 12g⁴ 9fg² 11.2f⁴ 12f* 12f³ 10g 1982 12s 9.5g 12f² 13g⁴ 10.2s²) 1,400Y; lightly-built ex-Irish filly; second foal; dam Irish 7f winner; middle-distance handicapper; favourite when 1½ lengths second of 20 to Record Wing in well-contested seller at Doncaster in November, first outing over here; acts on any going; formerly trained by F. Ennis. *J. Fox.* **59**

HAYAKAZE 3 ch.c. Hotfoot 126–Sugar Cookie 71 (Crepello 136) (1981 7fg 7fg* 8d 1982 8f 10g 10.6g 10fg* 10f 10fg) well-made colt; showed a good turn of foot in slowly-run handicap at Newcastle in July; stays 1½m; blinkered last 4 starts; sometimes sweats up. *G. Pritchard-Gordon.* **93**

HAYCOMBE BARN 3 ch.c. Hittite Glory 125–Jolisu 110 (Welsh Abbot 131) (1981 6fg 6g 5s* 1982 6s 7f 7f 7g) good-bodied, fair sort; good mover; won maiden race at Nottingham in 1981; well beaten in handicaps and a valuable seller at 3 yrs; should have stayed 6f +; was clearly well suited by soft going; dead. *W. Hastings-Bass.* —

HAY GUINNESS 4 b.f. Birdbrook 110–Molvitesse 75 (Molvedo 137) (1981 8g 9s 8.2fg 8.2d 1982 11s 12fg 11f) little worthwhile form, but has yet to run in a seller. *T. Craig.* —

HAY HABIT 3 ch.c. Habitat 134–Hayrake 98 (Galivanter 131) (1981 6s³ 6d* 7g² 8g 7d 1982 6g* 7g⁴ 6g* 7fg² 6.3g³ 7g 7fg³ 7g 7g 8g³ 6s⁴ 6d) 21,000Y; close-coupled ex-Irish colt; half-brother to very useful 1977 Irish 2-y-o Thunor (by Green God); dam stayed 1¼m; won Coolmore Godswalk Race at Fairyhouse in April by ½ length from Rue Royale and justified favouritism by ¾ length from Wolverbee in 11-runner handicap at the Curragh in May; ran creditably several other starts; stays 1m; yet to race on very firm going but acts on any other; trained part of season by S. Murless. *M. Jarvis.* **102**

HAYMAN 2 b.g. Habitat 134–Paddy's Princess (St Paddy 133) (1982 7fg 8f² 8g) Apr 7; 91,000Y; third foal; half-brother to useful 3-y-o Padalco (by Nonoalco), successful at up to 1m; dam good French middle-distance stayer; 1½ lengths second of 10 to Riv d'Ao in maiden race at Edinburgh in September, best effort; stays 1m; blinkered final outing; subsequently gelded. *J. Hindley.* **76**

Mr A. Salman's "Hays"

HAYS 3 b.c. Wolver Hollow 126–Sing a Song 115 (Sing Sing 134) (1981 5fg* **117**
6f* 6fg 7fg² 6d* 6g 1982 7d* 8fg 8fg⁴ 7.3g³ 7s* 7g) 15,000Y; tall, good-looking
colt; did very well over the winter; half-brother to 2 winners, including fairly
useful 1976 2-y-o 5f performer Red Shield (by So Blessed); dam very speedy;
smart performer on his day but runs some unaccountably modest races; favourite
when winning Salisbury 2,000 Guineas Trial in April in good style by 3 lengths
from Sabutai and Harroways Stakes at Goodwood in September a shade comfortably by ½ length from Tres Gate; also ran respectably in St James's Palace
Stakes at Royal Ascot (fourth of 9 to Dara Monarch) and Hungerford Stakes at
Newbury (3 lengths third of 10 to Pas de Seul); stays 1m; seems to act on any
going but goes well on soft ground; has a good turn of foot; possibly does best
when fresh; finished distressed final start. *G. Harwood.*

HAYSTACK (USA) 3 ch.f. Farewell Party–Firecracker Love (Crackpot) **62**
(1981 8fg 8fg 8d² 1982 10d 12f 16fg³ 14fg 16s) sturdy filly; carries plenty of
condition; staying maiden; sold 2,500 gns Newmarket Autumn Sales; resold
1,500 gns Ascot December Sales. *I. Balding.*

HAZARDOUS 2 br.g. Idiot's Delight 115–Fool 'Em 49 (Dadda Bert 95) (1982 —
7f 6d) Mar 27; 500Y; leggy, lightly-made gelding; first foal; dam second in
3 middle-distance sellers; no show in maiden events at Doncaster (auction)
in July and Nottingham in August. *J. Hardy.*

HAZEBOROUGH 3 ch.c. Morston 125–Eringa 101 (Saint Crespin III 132) —
(1981 NR 1982 10f 11.5fg) compact, attractive colt; fifth live foal; closely
related to 1½m winner Bewick (by Blakeney) and half-brother to a winner;
dam disappointing half-sister to Huntercombe; beaten some way in maiden races
at Newmarket and Sandown in summer; dead. *J. Bethell.*

HAZEL BANK 3 gr. or ro.f. Pongee 106–Petoria 74 (Songedor 116) (1981 NR **54**
1982 8f³ 8g 12f⁴ 12.3g 12g 12f) half-sister to a winning hurdler; dam won over
5f at 2 yrs; plating-class maiden; stays 1½m; yet to race on a soft surface. *R.
Allan.*

HAZEL BUSH 2 b.f. Sassafras 135–Selham 71 (Derring-Do 131) (1982 8s) — p
Apr 9; rangy filly; second foal; half-sister to fair 1981 2-y-o 1m winner Brigado
(by Brigadier Gerard); dam won over 1m; 16/1 and backward, chased leaders
until beaten and eased after 6f when ninth of 18 to Oranella in maiden race at
Wolverhampton in October; has scope and looks capable of quite a lot better.
Sir Mark Prescott.

HAZEL HOLT 2 b.f. Monsanto 121–Sylvan Path 69 (Sovereign Path 125) —
(1982 5fg 5fg 7d) Apr 6; 2,800Y; close-coupled filly; half-sister to 3 winners
here and abroad; dam won over 2m; no form; had to be destroyed at Sandown
in July after breaking down. *R. Hannon.*

HAZIM 3 b.c. Mill Reef 141–Angel Chile (Herbager 136) (1981 6f 5fg² 6d 5d 86
5d* 1982 6s³ 5f³ 8f 5d* 5s) neat, attractive colt; good mover; beat Miss
Trilli a shade cleverly by ½ length in handicap at Wolverhampton in October;
bred to stay at least 1m but is evidently best at sprint distances; acts on any
going. *H. T. Jones.*

HEADWAY 3 b.f. Pieces of Eight 128–Horns Dilemma (Quadriga 97) (1981 —
6fg 7fg 6s 7fg 6g 1982 7g 10f) small, lightly-made filly; seems of little account;
has worn blinkers. *J. Gilbert.*

HEART OF STEEL 3 ch.c. Steel Heart 128–Tetrazzini 70 (Sovereign Path 77
125) (1981 6g 1982 8.2fg 8g³ 8fg 8fg 8fg 8g³ 8s² 8s* 8.2s) strong, useful-
looking colt; made much of running to win minor event at Warwick in October
readily; stays 1m; ideally suited by some give in the ground; suited by forcing
tactics. *M. Albina.*

HEART'S CONTENT 3 ch.c. Some Hand 119–Can't Wait (Eudaemon 129) —
(1981 8s 7d 1982 8g 8fg³ 9f 8fg 8f 10d 9f 8.2g 7fg 6f) small colt; plater; stays
1m; sometimes wears blinkers; sold out of C. Williams' stable 360 gns Doncaster
January Sales. *R. Ward.*

HEARTWOOD 2 b.f. Hittite Glory 125–Cursorial 115 (Crepello 136) (1982 82
6fg² 5.8g* 7.3g) Mar 9; fair sort; half-sister to several winners, including very
smart 1970 2-y-o Fine Blade (by Fortino II) and French 1,000 Guineas third
Curtain Bow (by Jimmy Reppin); dam won Park Hill Stakes; won maiden event
at Bath in August; ran well in Newbury nursery the following month; will
stay 1m; sold 31,000 gns Newmarket Autumn Sales. *H. Candy.*

HEARTY HUNTER 3 gr.g. Huntercombe 133–Quantity 77 (Quorum 126) 44
(1981 5d 5d 5v 5g 6fg* 6fg 6g* 1982 8.2d 7f 7fg³ 8.3g) quite well-made gelding;
plater; stays 7f; best form on a sound surface; best in blinkers; claimed £2,400
after final start and has been sent to Singapore. *J. Sutcliffe.*

HEATED DEBATE 4 br.g. Politico 124–Lady Phoenix (Lorenzaccio 130) —
(1981 16.9fg 16.5fg 1982 10.8fg) big gelding; behind in varied races including
in a seller in July (last of 12). *J. Gilbert.*

HEAT HAZE (USA) 2 b.f. Jungle Savage–Bold Betty (Bold Commander) 66
(1982 5d 6fg⁴ 7g) Mar 16; $18,000Y; workmanlike filly; second foal; sister
to American 3-y-o Nancy the Queen; dam won small races over 5f and 6f in
USA; plating-class maiden; not seen out after August. *H. Candy.*

HEATHEN PRINCE 4 ch.g. Sun Prince 128–Heather Grove (Hethersett 134) 45
(1981 5d 7d 6d 1982 6d* 6g⁴ 7.6g 6v 6v 6s 7s 7s) small, strong gelding; good
walker; dropped in class and gambled on when winning selling handicap at
Folkestone in March (bought in 2,000 gns); bred to stay at least 7f; best form
with some give in the ground; occasionally blinkered. *R. Simpson.*

HEATHER CROFT 2 bl.f. Kala Shikari 125–Asail (Atan) (1982 5fg 5fg² 79
5f* 5h² 5f 5f 5d 5fg* 5g 5s) Mar 29; 5,400F, IR 3,900Y; useful sort; half-
sister to 5f winner Land of Point (by Pontifex); dam sister to prolific 1971 2-y-o
winner Sea Music; won 4-runner minor event at Brighton in April and 10-runner
nursery at Chepstow in August; evidently considered a 5f performer; acts on
firm going and didn't move at all well on soft on final start; not particularly
consistent. *R. Hannon.*

HEATHER PRINCE 2 b.g. Lochnager 132–Gym Slip 64 (Mummy's Pet 125) —
(1982 6g 5g 5f 5s) Apr 1; light-framed gelding; first foal; dam second in 5f
seller at 2 yrs; behind in maiden races; gelded after final outing. *A. W. Jones.*

HEATHER'S REEF 3 b.f. Mill Reef 141–Heatherside 80 (Hethersett 134) 81
(1981 8g 1982 11g² 10fg⁴ 12fg 12f³ 12d² 12fg* 13d) rangy filly; good walker;
favourite when winning maiden race at Carlisle in June; in frame most previous

starts, including when 5 lengths fourth of 9 to Sing Softly in Pretty Polly Stakes at Newmarket; will stay 1¾m; flashed her tail repeatedly under the whip first start; tends to hang and is not an easy ride. *G. Huffer.*

HEAVENLY RULER (CAN) 5 b.h. Riva Ridge–Heavenly Power (Bold — Ruler) (1981 7s² 8v 12.5g 10.6s 12g 10s 8.2s 1982 10g 10f 10f 8.2g) good-bodied horse; bad mover; plater nowadays; not certain to stay 1½m; has worn bandages in front; blinkered final start. *A. Smith.*

HECKLEY HINNY 2 b.f. Decoy Boy 129–Heckley Surprise (Foggy Bell 108) **76** (1982 6g 6fg³ 7d 7g) Mar 12; rangy filly; first foal; dam won over hurdles and fences; just over 2 lengths third of 20 to Linklighter in maiden race at Salisbury in September, best effort. *G. Balding.*

HEIGHLIN 6 b.g. High Line 125–Filiform 76 (Reform 132) (1981 18fg² 16fg² **111** 18g² 1982 16fg² 14f⁴ 16g* 16f³ 22.2fg 21f* 16g⁴ 18g² 16d² 18d)
    One of several outstanding dual-purpose horses of the last few years, Heighlin added an achievement to his record in 1982 that eluded even the redoubtable Sea Pigeon during his career: victory in a pattern race on the flat. Sea Pigeon won a listed race, giving weight all round to a good-class field in the Doonside Cup at Ayr, but Heighlin's record now boasts a victory in the Goodwood Cup, as well as two seconds in the Doncaster Cup, a third in the Henry II Stakes and a fourth in the Yorkshire Cup. In the most recent season Heighlin took his total of victories on the flat to thirteen, adding the fairly valuable H. S. Persse Memorial Handicap at Kempton in May and the Goodwood Cup in July to earlier successes which included the Ascot Stakes and the Goodwood Stakes, two of Britain's most famous long-distance handicaps. Like Sea Pigeon, Heighlin can produce a telling burst of speed at the end of his races but he is a tricky ride and his challenge has to be delayed, desirably, until the last possible moment. Cauthen rode him in most of his races in the most recent season and did a difficult job well, bringing Heighlin very late at both Kempton and Goodwood to lead almost on the post; Heighlin won the Goodwood Cup by half a length from the Queen Alexandra Stakes winner Ore, hardly coming off the bridle. Keeping a horse covered up until precisely the right moment is always liable to present difficulties (Heighlin might have won the Mono Sagaro Stakes at Ascot in April had he not hit the front a shade too soon and he also looked unlucky in the Lonsdale Stakes at York's August meeting on his seventh outing when he got shut in and didn't get a clear run until the race was almost over) but where Heighlin is concerned there is an additional problem for his jockey: on several occasions in 1982 Heighlin appeared to race as if he wasn't enjoying it and Cauthen's skill in producing him at the right moment wasn't always matched by a resolute response from the horse. At his best, however, Heighlin is a very useful stayer on the flat—he was beaten only a length and a half by Ardross in the Doncaster Cup in September—and he should continue to pick up races for as long as he remains fit and well. As things stand, however, he will not be able to contest Britain's most prestigious long-distance event, the Gold Cup, because he is a gelding. Geldings are barred from the Gold Cup as they are from other Group 1 pattern races, an absurd prohibition which has been challenged on several occasions in editions of this Annual. Almost everyone now acknowledges that, as in North America, the top races should be open to the best horses, whether they be entires or not. The stubborn refusal to end discrimination against geldings is another example of the Jockey Club's unwillingness to accept any change if they themselves don't agree with it, however strong the case might be.

Heighlin (b.g. 1976)	High Line (ch 1966)	High Hat (ch 1957)	Hyperion
			Madonna
		Time Call (b 1955)	Chanteur II
			Aleria
	Filiform (br 1970)	Reform (b 1964)	Pall Mall
			Country House
		Filigrana (b 1953)	Niccolo Dell' Arca
			Gamble in Gold

    Heighlin's breeding has been discussed in earlier editions of *Racehorses* and *Chasers & Hurdlers*. His dam was also represented on the racecourse in the most recent season by the good two-year-old filly Goodbye Shelley (by Home Guard) whose pedigree is discussed in greater detail in this Annual. Heighlin stays extremely well and acts on any going. He is up to championship standard as a hurdler. *D. Elsworth.*

Goodwood Cup—the well-ridden Heighlin finishes strongly to beat Ore (noseband).
Sheer Grit (left) and Halsbury (right) dead-heat for third place

HEIGHTEN 4 b. or br.c. High Top 131–Curtains 113 (Busted 134) (1981 8d 11d 11.7f* 10.1g* 10.1fg* 10f* 10.2fg* 1982 12f² 12f 10.5f 12fg³ 12fg³ 11d³ 12g) well-made, good sort; developed into a useful colt as a 3-y-o and won 5 times; ran really well when length second to More Harmony in quite valuable handicap at Epsom in June; rather disappointing next 3 starts, but finished creditable third to Khairpour in similar race at Haydock and to Fine Sun in Doonside Cup at Ayr in September; stays 1½m; acts on a soft surface but is well suited by a firm one; often makes running; sold 40,000 gns Newmarket Autumn Sales, and sent to race in Italy. *R. Hern.* **99**

HEIGHT OF FASHION (FR) 3 b.f. Bustino 136–Highclere 129 (Queen's Hussar 124) (1981 7g* 8g* 8fg* 1982 12fg* 12f* 12fg 12fg) **124**
Height of Fashion's season took rather a different course from that generally predicted during the winter. Long-time favourite for the Oaks largely on the strength of an unbeaten run as a two-year-old in the Acomb Stakes, the May Hill Stakes and the Hoover Fillies Mile, she was pulled out of the big race after her performance at Goodwood on her reappearance made pretty plain that Epsom wouldn't suit her even if she were good enough for the event. She ran only three times subsequently, only once up to her capabilities; her retirement coincided, possibly significantly, with her furnishing evidence that she was losing interest in the game.

Compared with her later tasks, that facing Height of Fashion in the Lupe Stakes at Goodwood in May was ridiculously easy. Only Devon Air and Tetarose took her and her pacemaker Round Tower on, the size of the field an affront to the executive's enterprise in staging a classic trial. Little worthwhile information could realistically be expected from such a trial, yet even after what remained of the contest was almost ruined by the fall of second-placed Devon Air directly in front of Height of Fashion five furlongs out we saw enough to conclude that Height of Fashion would not represent her powerful stable at Epsom. She was a big filly with an enormous stride, and though sufficiently nimble to clear the faller she never managed to get back on an even keel; she struggled all the way, looking about a bit, to make up fifteen lengths on the tenderly-ridden pacemaker in the last two and a half furlongs. The Newmarket Summer course turned out to be the scene of Height of Fashion's next appearance, in the Princess of Wales's Stakes in July. She wore blinkers and was ridden in front, most intelligently ridden in front, by Carson who made full use of the advantages offered him. Height of Fashion received 10 lb more than weight-for-age from the odds-on favourite Ardross, who by no stretch of the imagination could be expected to be seen at his best in a four-horse race at a mile and a half on firm going, and she also had the better of the weights with Amyndas and the three-year-old colt Ashenden. Ardross never came close. Amyndas was the only one that did, reducing her lead to about a length over

405

a furlong from home after being ridden along from three furlongs out. Height of Fashion went off at such a strong pace that she broke the course record set by her half-brother Milford in the same race in 1979. She had to be ridden along with more than two furlongs left but she stayed on strongly and never looked like going under; she doubled her advantage over Amyndas on the run up the hill to the line.

Shortly afterwards it was announced that Height of Fashion had been sold to Hamdan Al-Maktoum; reports of the sum paid over varied from £1.8 million to £1.4 million. Since she is a filly, judgement must be reserved on the wisdom of the purchase until the end of her productive career at the very least. She stood little chance of recouping a significant part of her cost on the racecourse unless she won the St Leger or the Prix de l'Arc de Triomphe. In winning the Princess of Wales's Stakes Height of Fashion had given the impression she would be a live contender for the Leger. However, before the Leger came round she had been retired. What chance she had in her next race, the King George VI and Queen Elizabeth Diamond Stakes at Ascot later in July, disappeared when she dwelt, losing three lengths in relation to the others; without the lead she looked a different filly from the one at Newmarket and she never got near the front. Nevertheless she underwent a very hard race, and this seemed to have its repercussions when she ran in the Yorkshire Oaks the following month, the middle-priced of the three challengers from her stable (one of them, Swiftfoot, started favourite). Height of Fashion held the lead until early in the straight, she couldn't have had things more in her favour, yet she lasted a very short time once Swiftfoot and the others tackled her; she ultimately finished last of seven behind Awaasif. In both of her races since Newmarket she had again been equipped with blinkers.

Height of Fashion (Fr) (b.f. 1979)	Bustino (b 1971)	Busted (b 1963)	Crepello
			Sans le Sou
		Ship Yard (ch 1963)	Doutelle
			Paving Stone
	Highclere (b 1971)	Queen's Hussar (b 1960)	March Past
			Jojo
		Highlight (b 1958)	Borealis
			Hypericum

In 1982 there were at the Royal Studs five mares out of Highlight (Highclere, Light Duty, Christchurch, Circlet and Blaze of Glory) and a full sister to Height of Fashion (Beacon Hill). Height of Fashion's sale should not therefore be felt for a year or two at least, if at all. Some of the mares in this family are too young to have made their mark; others, like Christchurch (dam of Church Parade), Light Duty (dam of Paradise Bay and the two-year-old Special Leave) and Highclere are old enough to have proved themselves. Highclere is the dam of Height of Fashion, Milford (by Mill Reef) and the mile-and-three-quarter winner Burghclere (by Height of Fashion's grandsire Busted) who sold for 460,000 guineas at the 1981 Newmarket December Sales. Highclere was the Queen's best winner to come along since Aureole: she won the One Thousand Guineas and French Oaks and was runner-up in the King George. She is a granddaughter of the One Thousand Guineas winner Hypericum, and a great granddaughter of one of the Royal Stud's best-known mares Feola.

Height of Fashion would have been well suited by distances further than a mile and a half; possibly a more testing surface than she ever encountered would also have suited her well, though this might be disputed as she showed such an impressive action on firm, one of the most impressive, long actions we've seen since Rock Roi's. She is, as we said, a big filly. At her best she was

*Princess of Wales's Stakes, Newmarket—Height of Fashion
gallops on relentlessly to account for Amyndas and Ardross*

quite good looking, but eventually she grew lengthier and more lean, and towards the end of her career she became far from impressive in appearance, a plain Jane. It will be interesting to see how she fares at stud. *R. Hern.*

HELANDY 5 br.g. Downstream 105–Steak House 68 (Road House II) (1981 — 9g 9fg⁴ 8g³ 8s* 10f 8.2g⁴ 8g 8fg 1982 8s 8.2v 12f³ 9.4f) neat, strong gelding; not a particularly good mover; poor handicapper; last in a seller second outing; stays 1m (not disgraced in small race over 1¼m); acts on any going but is ideally suited by some give in the ground; suitable mount for a boy; trained early in season by J. Berry. *T. Barnes.*

HELAPLANE (USA) 2 b.f. Super Concorde 128–Dihela (Hitting Away) — (1982 5g 7g) Apr 2; $80,000Y; close-coupled filly; half-sister to numerous winners, one of them stakes placed; dam at her best at 2 yrs when smart stakes winner at up to 7f; behind in autumn maiden events at Newbury and Newmarket (ninth of 21). *H. T. Jones.*

HELDIGVIS 2 b.f. Hot Grove 128–Twin-Set (Double Jump 131) (1982 5g 63 5g 5fg 7fg 6g³ 6g 8.2s* 7g*) May 22; 500 2-y-o; small filly; half-sister to a bumpers winner; dam poor maiden; plater; attracted no bid after winning by 4 lengths at Hamilton in September; beat Vindication by a head in nursery at Edinburgh the following month, despite not having the best of runs and carrying 5 lb more than long handicap weight; stays 1m; acts on soft going. *H. Bell.*

HELEWISE 2 ch.f. Dance In Time–Wether Fell (Klairon 131) (1982 6f 76 6f 7g 8d*) May 9; lightly-made filly; half-sister to several winners, including French 1m winner La Rouquine (by Silly Season); dam once-raced half-sister to 1,000 Guineas second Marisela; showed no form until winning 6-runner maiden race at Edinburgh in November by 1½ lengths from Suwaina; suited by 1m; acts on a soft surface. *R. D. Peacock.*

HELEXIAN 5 b.h. Song 132–Permutation 79 (Pinza 137) (1981 7d* 7fg 76 d 7g 7v* 7d² 7fg² 8f 7.3d 6s 1982 7s 7g 7.6g⁴ 7g² 7f³ 7g 7fg 8fg 8s 8s) compact, good sort; good mover; looked ungenuine when placed in handicaps at Sandown (apprentice ridden) and Newbury in July, giving both races away in tight finishes; best at up to 7f; acts on any going but goes well in the mud; has worn blinkers but does at least as well without; out of his depth ninth start; sold to N. Tinkler 3,000 gns Newmarket Autumn Sales. *A. Ingham.*

HELIUM 2 br.c. Wollow 132–Helcia 86 (Habitat 134) (1982 7g 7fg² 7f² 7f*) 83 Apr 22; medium-sized, rather leggy, quite attractive colt; good walker and excellent mover; third foal; brother to American 6f winner Hippodrome and half-brother to useful 1980 2-y-o 6f winner Chirk Castle (by Welsh Pageant); dam runner-up 5 times from 6f to 11.5f; favourite and pick of paddock, had to thread his way through after breaking none too well when winning 18-runner maiden event at Catterick in August by 1½ lengths from dead-heaters Clangerwinstanley and Liberty Tree; will stay 1¼m; sold to race in Italy and is a winner there. *H. Cecil.*

HELLESYLBAR 3 b. or br.c. Sovereign King–Ballyhardtack 77 (Ballyciptic 122) — (1981 NR 1982 7f) strong colt; first foal by a thoroughbred stallion; dam won 1m seller at 2 yrs; unquoted and distinctly behind when last of 16 in minor race won by Queen of Scots at Leicester in June. *A. Potts.*

HELLO CAMPERS 2 ch.g. Wolverlife 115–Forever Wild (Eighty Grand) — (1982 5d 5fg) June 2; IR 1,800F, 2,000Y; half-brother to a winner in Singapore; dam won 3 times at up to 7f in USA; unquoted, behind in maiden races at Windsor in June and July. *S. Mellor.*

HELLO CUDDLES 3 b.f. He Loves Me 120–Royal Sensation 103 (Prince Regent 99 129) (1981 5d*(dis) 5s 5g² 5g³ 5g² 5f 6f 5fg 5fg* 5fg³ 5s³ 1982 8g 8fg 5fg 5f² 5fg* 6f 5f³ 5d 6s) quite a well-made filly; useful on her day but isn't too consistent; beat Sanu a length in 3-runner race at Chepstow in August; form only at 5f; acts on any going; tended to hang fourth start. *R. Hollinshead.*

HELLO SONNY 2 ch.c. Blue Cashmere 129–Saucy Jane 82 (Hard Sauce 131) — (1982 6g 6fg 6s 8d) Mar 11; lengthy, shallow-girthed colt; brother to a minor 2-y-o winner and half-brother to fair stayer C'est Afrique (by Behistoun); dam sprinter; behind in minor events and sellers; sold 420 gns Ascot December Sales. *J. Holt.*

HELLO SUNSHINE 3 b.c. Song 132–Tropical Fruit (Tropique 128) (1981 84 6f 6fg 5d 6s* 6g* 7g* 1982 6s 7fg 6d³ 6f 7f³ 7g 7f* 7s* 7d² 8g) small, well-made colt; came with a strong run to beat Jade Ring a length in handicap at

Newmarket in August and held on to dead-heat with Lucky Man in valuable handicap at Ascot in September; stays 7f; acts on any going but revels in the mud; goes well for apprentice S. Dawson. *J. Holt.*

HELVIC (USA) 4 b. or br.g. Angle Light–Red River (Diatome 132) (1981 7g² **52** 6g 9.4g⁴ 8g 9s⁴ 8.2f 8fg* 8.2g 8f* 8.2f⁴ 8f 7g 1982 8g² 7f 8fg 7f 7fg 7fg² 7g 7.6f³ 8fg 7f⁴ 8.3fg 8g²) poor handicapper; second in seller at Brighton on final outing; will stay 1¼m; best on a sound surface; successful with blinkers and without; has worn a tongue strap. *M. Haynes.*

HENCEFORTH 2 b.f. Full of Hope 125–Ergo 82 (Song 132) (1982 5d² 5f² 5g*) **58** Apr 6; small, fair sort; first foal; dam won once over 5f from 3 starts at 2 yrs; won 7-runner maiden race at Warwick in May by a neck from Ominous; will be suited by 6f. *H. Candy.*

HEND 2 b.f. Dominion 123–Deodar 88 (Hopeful Venture 125) (1982 5fg 5g 6f — 7f) Feb 20; 2,800Y; well-grown, fair sort; third foal; dam won over 7f and 1m; soundly beaten in maiden races; not seen out after August. *D. Thom.*

HENRY GEARY STEELS 2 br.c. Connaught 130–Halkissimo 61 (Khalkis 127) — (1982 5g 7f) Feb 10; rather leggy colt; half-brother to 9f to 1½m winner Mac's Delight (by Scottish Rifle) and 2 other winners; dam won over 1m; outpaced in minor events won by Able Albert at Chester in May and by All Systems Go at York in July. *D. Smith.*

HENRY GREEN 5 b.g. Brigadier Gerard 144–La Grange 105 (Habitat 134) — (1981 NR 1982 12s) big gelding; placed in maiden races and a handicap as a 3-y-o; should stay 1½m; probably acts on any going. *B. Palling.*

HENRY SHOESTRING 3 b.c. Eastwood Prince–Osheanna (Easter Island 101) — (1981 NR 1982 10.1g) first foal; dam never ran; unquoted when remote seventh of 10 to Manntika in minor event at Windsor in August. *M. Haynes.*

HENRY'S SECRET 2 b.f. Solinus 130–Katie Cecil 120 (Princely Gift 137) **108** (1982 5fg* 5fg* 6fg* 6fg² 6g 6g³) Mar 26; 33,000F; neat filly; good mover; half-sister to Irish 3-y-o 7f winner Hav-A-Heart (by Steel Heart) and a winner in France; dam very smart miler; won minor event at Windsor and Hilary Needler Trophy at Beverley on first 2 outings; did well in good-class fillies' races subsequently, winning St Catherine's Stakes at Newbury, finishing 2½ lengths second, conceding 3 lb, to Royal Heroine in Princess Margaret Stakes at Ascot, and ¾-length third, again conceding 3 lb, behind Myra's Best in Firth of Clyde Stakes at Ayr; will probably stay 7f; yet to race on a soft surface; lacks scope. *M. Stoute.*

HENRY'S WENCH 3 b.f. Tudor Rhythm 112–Pretty Asset 100 (Galivanter 131) — (1981 6fg 5g 8d 1982 8f 5h 8g 8g) small, lengthy filly; poor plater; has been tried in blinkers. *G. Cottrell.*

HENRY'S WISH 4 b.g. Wishing Star 117–Tudor Story 96 (Henry the Seventh — 125) (1981 7s 7fg 8g 8.5d 1982 8f 8g 14g 14d 14fg 10v) tall, rangy gelding; poor plater; bred to stay middle distances; possibly unsuited by softish ground. *R. Atkins.*

HERBIE QUAYLE 4 b.c. Thatch 136–Bella Carlotta (Charlottesville 135) **84 §** (1981 7s⁴ 10.4d⁴ 8.2s* 8g² 8g⁴ 12fg 9d 8fg³ 7.3d⁴ 8g 1982 8g 8g³ 10fg³ 10.4g³ 11f 10f 8fg³ 8g* 7f³) big, strong colt; third in 3 quite valuable handicaps and an amateur riders race before comfortably winning apprentice race at Bath in July; stays 1¼m; probably acts on any going; finds little off the bridle and is ungenuine; sent to USA. *B. Hills.*

HERE COMES HARRY 2 b.g. Mandrake Major 122–Ritratto (Pinturischio **68** 116) (1982 6f 6fg³) May 10; useful-looking gelding; half-brother to 7f and 8.2f winner Italian Master (by Workboy); dam never ran; 25/1 and blinkered, made good headway final 1½f when 3¾ lengths third of 9 to House Guest in maiden race at Pontefract in August; gelded afterwards; will be suited by 7f. *M. H. Easterby.*

HERE'S SUE 3 b.f. Three Legs 128–Gaino (Chaparral 128) (1981 5fg* 5d* **63** 5g³ 1982 5f 6f 5fg 6g³ 6fg 6f 6g 6g* 7d 6g) rather lightly-made filly; won seller at Ayr in September (no bid); stays 7f; acts on a firm and a soft surface; usually blinkered nowadays; often apprentice ridden. *A. Jarvis.*

HER EXCELLENCY 5 b.m. Dragonara Palace 115–My Paddy 83 (St Paddy **36** 133) (1981 5s 5fg 6g 7f 6fg 7fg⁴ 8fg 7f 7f 1982 8f 6f 8f 10g 8fg² 8f 8.2g 8fg) plater; well beaten after finishing good second at Edinburgh in July; stays 1m; acts on firm going; has run respectably for a boy; blinkered final start in 1981. *R. Morris.*

HERODOTE (USA) 2 b.c. Super Concorde 128–Heiress (Habitat 134)   (1982   **98**
6f3 7s3 8d2 7g*)   Feb 24; well-grown, deep-girthed, quite attractive colt; first
foal; dam unraced half-sister to top-class animals Saraca and Simbir; always
going easily and was asked to do no more than necessary when winning 15-runner
maiden race at Leicester in October by a head from Dabdoub, the pair clear; had
run creditably on previous starts, notably going down by 3 lengths to The
Liquidator in 23-runner maiden event at Newmarket in October; stays 1m; sure
to win more races.   *H. Cecil.*

HEROIC JAMES 3 b.c. Bold Lad (Ire) 133–Elm 88 (Realm 129)   (1981 7f 7fg4   **68** d
7fg 7d   1982 8s3 10.6fg 12f 10.2g 12d)   strong colt; poor mover; only plating
class; evidently stays 1m but has been well beaten over further.   *R. Williams.*

HEROIC SAGA   4 ch.g. Hittite Glory 125–Who Can Tell 109 (Worden II 129)   —
(1981 8d   1982 7g 8g 6g)   small, strong gelding; lightly raced and no worthwhile
form, including in sellers in 1982.   *P. Haynes.*

HERON BAY (USA) 2 b.c. Alleged 138–Foreign Missile (Damascus)   (1981 **109** p
7d* 7d*)

As the dual Prix de l'Arc de Triomphe winner Alleged was a late-maturing
colt—with a two-year-old career limited to an impressive victory in an end-of-
season maiden race—it seemed fair to expect him to make a relatively quiet
start as a stallion. Consequently it was a pleasant surprise when several of
his first runners showed plenty of promise in 1982: in England Alligatrix was
a good third in the Hoover Fillies Mile after defeating a huge field of maidens
at Newmarket; Ghaiya, another English-trained filly, looked a splendid prospect
when successful at Goodwood; in France Allverton won a newcomers race at
Longchamp before being touched off by Nile Hawk in the Group 3 Prix de
Conde; in America his million-dollar son Chumming showed a great deal of
potential, finishing second in the Grade 1 Remsen Stakes, while his daughter
Carambola also won there; and in Ireland Heron Bay became Alleged's first

Mr D. Schwartz's "Heron Bay"

pattern-race winner when landing the Larkspur Stakes at Leopardstown in October.

The Larkspur was Heron Bay's second outing following a pleasing debut at the Curragh in September. He started favourite to beat twenty-four others in a seven-furlong maiden race and had done everything that could be expected of him in winning by three lengths from Mr Big John, the rest well beaten off. The O'Brien stable had a near-monopoly on good staying two-year-old colts in Ireland and Heron Bay started at 3/1 on at Leopardstown. The only others to start at less than 20/1 in an eleven-strong field were Nadasdy, the winner of a maiden race and a nursery at Galway, Gormanstown Prince, an Ascot winner who had had his limitations exposed by Heron Bay's stable-companions Beaudelaire and Danzatore on his last two outings, Iron Leader, an improving colt who had won a twenty-one-runner maiden race last time out, and Changed His Mind, who'd had the misfortune to be beaten into second place in all four of his races, three times behind O'Brien colts. In landing the odds Heron Bay gave his supporters plenty of anxious moments. After starting slowly he turned into the short straight with only one or two behind him, then ran into trouble as Eddery tried to save ground by sticking to the inside. He did well to quicken through a small gap when switched entering the final furlong, and once clear he finished strongly on the dead ground to catch Evening Belle close home. His winning margin of a length doesn't reflect his superiority, which is just as well since the bare form looks distinctly modest by pattern-race standards. Evening Belle, a winner on her debut, had since finished last in the Cheveley Park and second in a minor race at Naas; third, beaten only three lengths, was the front-running The Cable Rock, who had finished out of the first three in his four previous races. The Cable Rock later finished only seventh of twenty-three in ordinary company at the Curragh. Still, Heron Bay proved he has a good turn of foot and also gained experience which will stand him in good stead at three.

Heron Bay (USA) (b.c. April 6, 1980)	Alleged (b 1974)	Hoist the Flag (b 1968)	Tom Rolfe / Wavy Navy
		Princess Pout (b 1966)	Prince John / Determined Lady
	Foreign Missile (b 1973)	Damascus (b 1964)	Sword Dancer / Kerala
		Queen of the Sky (b 1967)	Bold Ruler / Misty Morn

Heron Bay was sold for 610,000 guineas at the Newmarket Premier Sales, providing his consignors with a spectacular profit on the 210,000 dollars they'd paid for him at Keeneland less than a year before. Whether he will prove worth 610,000 guineas is hard to say but he has only to win another pattern race or two to become a valuable stallion prospect, coming as he does from one of America's finest families. His third and fourth dams are the champion three-year-old filly Misty Morn, who won at up to thirteen furlongs, and the outstanding broodmare Grey Flight. Both mares met with tremendous success with their offspring by Bold Ruler; Grey Flight produced three stakes winners by him, including the champion sire What A Pleasure, and also the allowance winner Clear Ceiling who bred Quick As Lightning; and Misty Morn produced two stakes-winning fillies, Bold Consort and Beautiful Day, and two champion two-year-old colts, Bold Lad (USA) and Successor. One of Misty Morn's other daughters by Bold Ruler was the unraced Queen of the Sky whose eight winners include the English stayer Consenting and the seven-furlong winner Foreign Missile. Heron Bay is Foreign Missile's second winner from her first three foals, following the claiming race performer Denali Ridge (by Riva Ridge). Foreign Missile is a daughter of Damascus, who won at up to two miles, so Heron Bay will probably prove well suited by middle distances. He's sure to leave his two-year-old form well behind. *V. O'Brien, Ireland.*

HERON'S ROSE 3 ch.f. Leander 119–Heron's Strike (Combat 123) (1981 — 5s 7fg 7fg 1982 12g) leggy filly; in rear in maiden and minor races. *J. Peacock.*

HERON'S PARADE 3 br.c. Queen's Hussar 124–Changing Tides (Swaps) **50** (1981 7g 7.6s 6s 1982 10d 10f 10f 10.1fg 11.7g 9g^2 10f* 7f^3) useful-looking colt; won amateur riders handicap at Folkestone in July; runner-up in seller previous start; stays $1\frac{1}{4}$m; acts on firm going; sold 3,000 gns Newmarket Autumn Sales. *P. Mitchell.*

HERR CAPITAN 6 ch.g. Lombard 126–Ista Jil 97 (Gratitude 130) (1981 NR 1982 10.6s 12v) modest handicapper as a 3-y-o; soundly beaten both starts in 1982 (October); stays 1¼m; acts on any going; has worn blinkers; fair jumper. *J. Old.* —

HERRING 3 br.f. Comedy Star 121–Fiery Romance (Fighting Don) (1981 NR 1982 6s 8f 7fg³ 10f 10.6h 11fg 8g 6f 7d) 3,000Y; lightly-made filly; half-sister to 1m winner Incensed (by Frankincense); dam lightly-raced half-sister to Irish 2,000 Guineas winner Mistigo; plater; stays 7f; sold 460 gns Ascot December Sales. *W. Elsey.* —

HESHAM (USA) 2 b.c. Annihilate 'Em–Rule Me Lucky (Lucky Debonair) (1982 6f 7g³ 7s) Mar 18; $15,000F, $45,000Y; big, rangy, quite attractive colt; half-brother to 2 winners by Mito; dam third once from 9 starts; staying-on 9 lengths third of 28 to Tolomeo in maiden race at Newmarket in October; joint favourite, never really got into race after being hampered at start, and was eased in closing stages, when tenth of 28 behind Jungle Romeo in similar event at Redcar later in month; should stay 1¼m. *G. Harwood.* **80**

HETTIE-HEN 2 br.f. Some Hand 119–Wontell 90 (Buisson Ardent 129) (1982 6f) Apr 14; 300 2-y-o; lengthy filly; half-sister to very useful sprinter Mummy's Darling (by Mummy's Pet) and a winner in Belgium; dam ran only at 2 yrs; moved very poorly to start when last of 12 to Fenny Rough in minor event at Pontefract in September. *R. Johnson.* —

HEXGREAVE STAR 4 b. or br.g. Comedy Star 121–Double Grand (Coronation Year 124) (1981 8s⁴ 8v 7d 6g³ 6g 6f 5fg 1982 6f 6g 7g 5fg 5g* 5fg 5s) strong, compact gelding; ran poorly after winning handicap at Hamilton in September; best at sprint distances; acts on any going; has worn bandages; often blinkered. *D. Garraton.* **66**

HIAT 3 gr.f. High Line 125–Atonement 109 (Palestine 133) (1981 NR 1982 6g 8v 10.2d) 1,150F; very small, lightly-made filly; half-sister to 5 winners, 4 of them at 2 yrs, including useful Fresh Start (by Busted); dam, speedy 2-y-o, is sister to Pall Mall; tailed-off last in quite valuable events at Taby in Sweden, Ascot and Doncaster (blinkered) in the autumn and is apparently of little account. *A. Davison.* —

HI-BUCK 2 ch.g. Runnymede 123–Pibroch III (Specific 103) (1982 5s 5d Jfg⁴ 6f 5ff) non-thoroughbred gelding; closely related to 1980 2-y-o 5f winner Flash Gordon (by Sucaryl) bad plater. *P. Burgoyne.* —

HI EASTER 2 ch.c. High Line 125–Decked Out 77 (Doutelle 128) (1982 7fg 7g 8f² 7.6v³) Mar 30; smallish, useful sort; brother to disappointing maiden Hi Friday; dam middle-distance maiden; placed in the autumn in maiden races at Brighton and Lingfield; will stay at least 1¼m; acts on any going. *H. Candy.* **85**

HIGH AFFAIR 4 b.f. High Line 125–Lucky Affair 83 (Stephen George 102) (1981 NR 1982 12s) lengthy, strong, plain filly; second foal; half-sister to fair 6f to 1m winner Havon Cool (by Celtic Cone); dam won 3 times at up to 6f at 2 yrs; tailed off in maiden race won by Cashel Prince at Haydock in April. *J. Spearing.* —

HIGHAM GREY 6 gr.g. Warpath 113–Jackies Joy (Skymaster 126) (1981 8g* 10.5d 8g² 10f2 12f² 16g³ 10f* 11fg* 10g* 10g 13fg³ 12f 11g 8s 18g 1982 10d 10f 10.2f⁴ 12.3fg 13fg 12.3g* 12d* 11g³ 13g 14.6f* 13fg³ 12g 12fg 17.4d 12fg* 16.1s 18s) useful-looking gelding; not all that consistent, but won handicaps at Newcastle, Beverley and Doncaster and an amateur riders race at Redcar; 20/1 when beating Pontin Boy by ¾ length in last-named race in September; suited by 1¼m+ nowadays and stays 2m; seems to act on any going; effective with or without blinkers. *D. Chapman.* **81**

HIGHAM HILL 3 b.g. High Line 125–Beychevelle (Sir Herbert 106) (1981 NR 1982 11g) leggy, lengthy, lightly-made gelding; first foal; dam won up to 9f in Ireland, and also won over hurdles; 20/1 when behind in 15-runner maiden event won by Oration at Newbury in April. *D. Gandolfo.* —

HIGH AUTHORITY 3 b.f. High Award 119–Elia (Narrator 127) (1981 5s² 5fg 5d 5d 5g* 6g⁴ 5f 6f 7fg 5g³ 5d² 5g* 5g 6s 1982 5g 6.5v 6g 5g 5fg 5d⁴ 7f 5f 5d 6f 5s) workmanlike filly; good mover; inconsistent sprint handicapper; best form with some give in the ground; sometimes troublesome at start; has sweated up. *D. Leslie.* —

HIGH CALORY 2 ch.f. High Line 125–Calloo 99 (Ballyciptic 122) (1982 **82** p
6g 8s*) Apr 16; robust, good sort; good mover; fourth foal; half-sister to
1977 2-y-o 5f winner Friendly Baker (by Be Friendly); dam 2-y-o 6f and 7f
winner; favourite, showed herself well suited by a test of stamina when winning
13-runner maiden race at Bath in October by 6 lengths from Sonic Meteor;
acts on soft going; promises to make a useful stayer. *J. Tree.*

HIGH CANNON (USA) 2 b.c. Cannonade–So High (Sea-Bird II 145) (1982 **100**
8f 8.2s 8s* 8.2v* 8d*) June 3; $25,000Y; useful-looking colt; fourth foal;
half-brother to 2 winners by Dynastic; dam, granddaughter of Park Hill Stakes
winner Moon Star, won 6f maiden race; showed marked improvement with
each race after finishing last of 10 behind stable-companion Riv D'Ao in maiden
event at Edinburgh in September on first appearance, on last 3 outings winning
maiden race at Newcastle and minor events at Hamilton and Redcar; will stay
1¼m; acts on heavy going; worth following. *S. Norton.*

HIGH CLASS BUILDER 4 ch.f. Flair Path 122–Holly (Chamossaire) (1981
10s 9g4 8d 10f 9d4 8g 10g 9g 13.8g 1982 10g 10fg 7f) compact filly; plater;
will stay 1½m; seems to act on any going; occasionally blinkered. *A. Young.*

HIGHER AND HIGHER 3 b.f. High Award 119–Tide And Time (Easter
Island 101) (1981 6f 1982 8d 7f 8fg) compact filly; seems of little account.
D. Leslie.

HIGH FANDANGO 2 b.c. Gay Fandango 132–Miss Africa (African Sky 124) **78**
(1982 7.6v 7s) Feb 12; 16,000Y; first foal; dam never ran; 8½ lengths sixth of 12
behind Dabdoub in minor event at Chepstow in October, second outing. *B.
Hills.*

HIGH GROUND (FR) 2 b.f. Shirley Heights 130–Crofting 102 (Crepello 136) —
(1982 7g) Feb 25; second foal; dam stayed 1¼m; unquoted, eleventh of 13
in minor event at Brighton in August; sold BBA 4,100 gns Newmarket Autumn
Sales. *I. Balding.*

Mr N. Granata's "High Cannon"

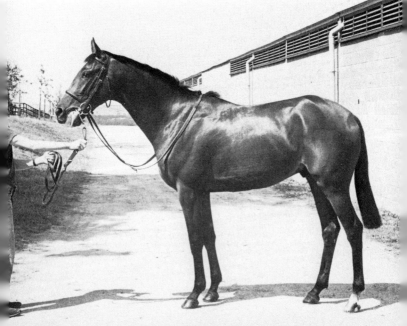

HIGH HAWK 2 b.f. Shirley Heights 130–Sunbittern 112 (Sea Hawk II 131) **74**
(1982 7g 8s⁴) Mar 17; 31,000Y; light-framed, quite attractive filly; half-sister
to 3 winners, including useful miler Heron's Hollow (by Wolver Hollow); dam
6f and 7f winner at 2 yrs, subsequently temperamental; 2/1 on for 18-runner
maiden race at Wolverhampton in October, following a promising debut at
Newbury, but had to be driven along throughout after dwelling and was beaten
3¾ lengths into fourth place behind Oranella; ridden by 5-lb claimer here and
possibly needs stronger handling. *J. Dunlop.*

HIGH HILLS 8 gr.g. High Top 131–Charity Walk (Sovereign Path 125) (1981 **42**
13v² 14s 1982 18g³ 16.1s 16fg² 16f 15g 15f⁴ 16.1g 15g³ 18d) staying handicapper; acts on any going; often blinkered; suitable mount for an apprentice;
none too consistent. *T. Craig.*

HIGH IMP 2 ch.c. Import 127–High Walk (Tower Walk 130) (1982 5f 5f) **—**
Apr 24; second foal; brother to 1981 2-y-o 1m winner High Port; dam bad
plater; burly, in rear in minor event at Redcar and maiden race at Newcastle
in May. *G. Toft.*

HIGHLAND BEAUTY 3 ch.f. High Line 125–Fire Queen (Prince Hansel **—**
118) (1981 8d 10s 1982 13g 14g 12v) short-backed, quite attractive filly;
well beaten in maiden races and a minor event. *D. Thom.*

HIGHLAND BERRY 3 br.f. Scottish Rifle 127–Spice Berry 63 (Tutankhamen) **—**
(1981 6g 1982 8fg⁴ 10g 9g 10g 10fg) workmanlike filly; only plating class;
best run at 1m on fast ground; sold 840 gns Newmarket Autumn Sales. *P.
Walwyn.*

HIGHLAND LINNET 5 b.g. Highland Melody 112–Golden Linnet 96 (Sing **—**
Sing 134) (1981 10fg 9s 1982 10f) leggy gelding; little worthwhile form in
maiden and minor events; not certain to stay middle distances. *B. Richmond.*

HIGHLAND ROSSIE 2 b.f. Pablond 93–Highland Lassie 62 (Highland **67**
Melody 112) (1982 5fg 6fg 8.2fg 7fg 8d 8.2d⁴ 7g* 6s 7s) Apr 16; sturdy filly;
plater; well handled by 7-lb claimer B. Hayes when winning by a neck from
Fashion Lover at Wolverhampton (no bid) in October; stays 1m. *R. Hollinshead.*

HIGHLY POLISHED 2 b.f. High Top 131–Brilliantine 109 (Stage Door **79** p
Johnny) (1982 7f⁴) Mar 20; lengthy, attractive filly; third foal; half-sister
to 1m winner Neat (by Wollow); dam, winner over 7f and 1¼m, is half-sister to
Bright Finish and Shining Finish; 12/1, looked very dangerous when moving
up on bridle 2½f out in 16-runner £3,700 event at Salisbury in August but
couldn't maintain progress and was beaten 7 lengths into fourth place behind
Sailor's Dance; sure to improve and win a maiden race. *J. Tree.*

HIGH OLD TIME 6 ch.h. Mount Hagen 127–Witch of Endor 80 (Matador **79**
131) (1981 NR 1982 12g 10fg* 12f* 12fg*) big horse; quite a character,
but was in great form in summer, winning handicaps at Salisbury, Leicester
and York; effective at 1¼m and stayed at least 1¾m; acted on any going, but
seemed suited by firm; suited by a strongly-run race; used to wear blinkers;
standing at Manor Farm Stud, Tring, Herts. *S. Mellor.*

HIGH PITCHED 3 ch.g. Crooner 119–Lucky Run 101 (Runnymede 123) **79**
(1981 7f 7d² 8g³ 1982 8g* 8fg³ 8.2fg² 7s 7s* 8.2s* 8s² 8s) useful sort; narrowly
won valuable seller at Doncaster in March (sold out of R. Smyth's stable 6,400
gns); subsequently showed himself better than a plater, winning handicaps at
York (apprentices) and Haydock; stays 1m well; seems to act on any going
but goes well on soft; has run respectably when sweating up; good mount for
a boy. *I. Walker.*

HIGH POPPA 3 b.c. Mummy's Pet 125–Two For Joy 77 (Double-U-Jay 120) **—**
(1981 7fg 6g 5g² 5s⁴ 1982 5f 6f 8fg 6s 7g) lengthy, lightly-made colt; in frame
in maiden events in 1981; well beaten at all outings at 3 yrs; not sure to stay
1m; possibly needs some give in the ground; blinkered final start; trained part
of season by P. Cundell. *S. Norton.*

HIGH PORT 3 b.c. Import 127–High Walk (Tower Walk 130) (1981 5g **68**
6s 6f 6f 6fg⁴ 6g³ 8f* 6d² 7d 7g 1982 8fg 8f 10f 7f 6g 7f 6f² 6g² 6g² 6f 7f 6s 6s
6s³ 6s 7d³) compact, quite attractive colt; good mover; stays 1m; acts on
any going; suited by enterprising riding tactics; sometimes goes very freely
to post. *G. Toft.*

HIGH RAINBOW 5 b.g. High Line 125–Darwin Tulip (Campaign 106 or **70**
Pirate King 129) (1981 12g 10.6s² 11g³ 11d² 13fg* 12d 1982 12g 16.1s*
16.1fg² 12fg 16.1g) useful-looking gelding; proved well suited by trip when

beating Worth Avenue by 3 lengths in 2m handicap at Haydock in April; second to easy winner Cornishman on same course in May; acts on any going; sometimes sweats up; not the easiest of rides. *J. Etherington.*

HIGH REALM   3 b. or br.c. Realm 129–Melodramatic 112 (Tudor Melody 129)   **63** (1981 5d⁴ 5s   1982 6g⁴ 5f² 6fg 6g 7d) lengthy, quite attractive colt; good mover; in frame in maiden races; stays 6f; pulled very hard third start. *M. Albina.*

HIGH RENOWN (USA)   2 br.c. Raise A Bid–Starlet O'Hara (Silent Screen)   **– p** (1982 8s 8s) Mar 15; $42,000Y; strong, good-topped colt; third foal; brother to useful 1981 2-y-o 7f winner Beldale Bid and half-brother to a winner; dam, placed 3 times, is half-sister to Kentucky Oaks winner Blue Norther; no form; 12/1, well there long way when remote tenth of 26 to Magic Rarity in maiden race at Sandown in October, second outing; looks capable of a good bit better in time. *B. Hills.*

HIGH RIDGE   3 b.g. High Top 131–Naughty Party (Parthia 132) (1981   **–** 7fg   1982 14d) well-made gelding; in rear in maiden races; blinkered only start at 3 yrs in July; sold to R. Holder 1,000 gns Ascot July Sales. *G. Hunter.*

HIGH RISER   3 b.f. Connaught 130–Absent 66 (Abernant 142) (1981 6f   **–** 6g 6d 8s   1982 10f 7f 10g) leggy filly; poor form, including in a seller; sold 300 gns Doncaster October Sales. *C. Brittain.*

HIGH STATE   2 b.f. Free State 125–High Society 96 (So Blessed 130) (1982   **72** 5fg 7f 6g² 6fg³ 6f³ 6g² 7g 6d 8fg² 7.2s³ 7.2s⁴ 8d³ 5d)   Apr 2; 2,500Y; neat filly; third foal; dam 2-y-o 5f winner; second in seller at Ripon, nursery at Leicester and selling nursery at Beverley during busy season; needs further than 5f, and stays 1m; seems to act on any going; blinkered seventh and eighth outings (seems better when not); has worn bandage on near-fore. *M. W. Easterby.*

HIJAZIAH   3 ch.f. High Line 125–Keadby Bridge (Petition 130) (1981 8d   **69** 1982 11.5f 14g³ 14.7f* 16.5fg 14g) fair sort; sweated up slightly when comfortably winning maiden race at Redcar in September; should stay 2m; acts on firm going. *A. Hide.*

HILLSDOWN GOLD   5 b.g. Goldhill 125–Dumana 96 (Dumbarnie 125) (1981   **80** 10s 10.6g 10.2fg 10f 8fg* 10g³ 8fg 8fg² 9g 8.2s 8g   1982 10f 8f 10f 8fg 8.2g⁴ 8fg* 8fg⁴) neat gelding; returned to form when well backed in handicap at Doncaster in July, making all and beating Dunham Park decisively by 3 lengths; didn't reproduce that form at Newmarket 3 days later and wasn't seen out again; best at around 1m; probably acts on any going; has won in blinkers; sometimes sweats up; sold to I. Vickers 2,000 gns Newmarket Autumn Sales. *G. Huffer.*

HILLSDOWN LAD   4 b.c. Forlorn River 124–Alchorus 78 (Alcide 136) (1981   **67** 8.2s² 8g⁴ 8d 6g   1982 6f 7f 7f² 7f* 7d) rangy colt; good mover; got off mark at last in apprentice handicap at Doncaster in May, beating Miss Twiggy by 2½ lengths; off course afterwards until October (last of 16); stays 1m; acts on any going; blinkered last 2 starts in 1981 (found little under pressure on first occasion). *G. Huffer.*

HILL'S GUARD   3 br.g. Home Guard 129–Ballinkillen (Levmoss 133)   (1981 7d   **63** 1982 8.2fg 8fg² 7fg 8g) quite attractive gelding; blinkered when second in maiden race at Edinburgh in April; well beaten afterwards, including in a selling handicap; stays 1m; sweated up first start; sold out of M. Stoute's stable 2,600 gns Ascot June Sales after third start. *J. Dodds.*

HILL'S PAGEANT   3 b.c. Welsh Pageant 132–Reita 87 (Gilles de Retz 132)   **91** (1981 7fg 7.2fg³ 7g   1982 8g 8f³ 9fg 10fg* 10.1fg* 10f* 10fg* 10f 10g³ 9d) good-looking colt; shows quite a bit of knee action; won maiden race at Brighton and handicaps at Windsor, Newmarket (beat Mill Plantation ¾ length in £5,200 event) and Sandown; will stay 1½m; acts well on firm ground; game. *P. Walwyn.*

HILL VIXEN   3 b.f. Goldhill 125–Foxy Fanny 66 (Space King 115) (1981 6f⁴   **67** 6g 7d   1982 12.2g³ 12f* 12g* 12g* 12g² 12fg 12v) neat filly; won seller at Thirsk in May (no bid); subsequently showed herself better than a plater, winning handicaps at Doncaster (apprentices) and Hamilton; stays 1½m; suited by a sound surface and acts on firm going. *P. Rohan.*

HI LOVE   2 b.f. High Top 131–Love Story 79 (Aureole 132) (1982 6fg 7d)   **70 p** Mar 25; fair sort; third foal; half-sister to 3-y-o Storton (by Morston) and modest 1½m winner Rheingold's Gift (by Rheingold); dam won twice over 1m; second favourite but still not fully wound up, made steady late progress without being punished unnecessarily when 4¾ lengths sixth of 18 to Brilliant Rosa in maiden race at Leicester in October; should do better over middle distances. *B. Hills.*

HIMORRE 3 b.c. Song 132–Monagram 77 (Mon Fetiche 120) (1981 6g² 7g³ 7.6s³ 1982 7fg⁴ 8g* 7.3fg³ 10g 9g* 8f) lengthy, good-quartered, attractive colt; good walker; won maiden race at Kempton in May and Noble Dancer Norwegian Jockey Club Jubilee Stakes at Ovrevoll in June; beat Danish-trained The Tinker by a length in latter; stays 9f; gives impression he's a top-of-the-ground performer; not raced after July. *R. Price.* **83**

HINNENI 2 br.c. Lypheor 118–Emarbee § (Will Somers 114§) (1982 6f 7d 6f 6f⁴) May 12; IR 5,000Y (privately), 9,200Y; close-coupled, useful-looking colt; half-brother to winners here and abroad; dam, half-sister to Deep Diver and King's Company, won 10 races in Scandinavia; 50/1, 6 lengths fourth of 7 to Boom Town Charlie in minor race at Kempton in July, best effort. *R. Hannon.* **79**

HINTONADO 3 b.c. Manado 130–Sea Dog (Sea Hawk II 131) (1981 6fg 6fg 7g² 8d³ 10s 1982 10f 10f² 12g² 12f³ 16d² 16.9fg) neat, compact colt; runner-up in maiden races and a handicap; stays 2m; seems to act on any going; does best when ridden up with pace; moved badly to post final start; sold to M. Lambert 3,100 gns Newmarket Autumn Sales. *P. Cole.* **75**

HINTSBROOK 4 b.c. Upper Case–Leisure Hour (Persian Gulf) (1981 8d 8.2s 10fg 8f 1982 12g) winner over hurdles; well beaten in maiden and minor races on flat; has twice started slowly. *B. McMahon.*

HIP HIP HIP (USA) 2 ch.c. To The Quick–Sugarberry (King's Bishop) (1982 5f³ 6s⁴) Feb 25; $160,000Y; attractive, full-quartered colt; first foal; dam won twice over 5f in USA; in frame in maiden race at Salisbury in August and minor event at Lingfield in September; stays 6f; seems to act on any going. *G. Lewis.* **75**

HIPPARION 10 gr.g. Sayfar 116–Grecian Palm 78 (Royal Palm 131) (1981 NR 1982 13d 12d 12fg) fair jumper; does little racing on flat nowadays; stays 2m; appears to act on any going; has been tried in blinkers; good mount for an inexperienced rider. *S. Mellor.* **—**

HIPPO DISCO 3 b.c. Wollow 132–Yell Aloud (Laugh Aloud) (1981 7g 8s² 8d 1982 10f² 11.7g* 12f* 11.7d 11.7fg² 11.5fg² 13f) well-made colt; good mover; won handicap at Windsor in May and minor event at Carlisle in June (odds on); suited by 1½m; acted on any going; best in blinkers; broke a leg at Nottingham in July and was destroyed. *M. Stoute.* **81**

HIS HONOUR 2 b. or br.c. Busting 136–Honerko 112 (Tanerko 134) (1982 7g) May 20; good sort; good walker and mover; third foal; half-brother to high-class middle-distance winner Prince Bee (by Sun Prince) and smart 1970 French staying 2-y-o Balteus (by Baldric II); dam very useful middle-distance winner here and in France; weak in market, showed up to past halfway in 30-runner maiden race won by Mandelstam at Newmarket in October; has scope and is sure to do a lot better. *R. Hern.* **— p**

HIS TURN 3 b.c. Mill Reef 141–Vital Match 113 (Match III 135) (1981 NR 1982 12g² 14fg 11.5f*) 43,000Y; attractive colt; brother to quite useful Soldiers Point, a winner at 5f and 1½m, and half-brother to 2 winners, including useful middle-distance stayer Vital Season (by Silly Season); dam miler; favourite when running on well to beat Sectori by 2½ lengths (pair clear) in 14-runner maiden race at Yarmouth in June; subsequently sent to USA; possibly doesn't stay 1¾m. *M. Stoute.* **82**

HITHERMOOR LASS 3 b.f. Red Alert 127–Splosh (Silly Season 127) (1981 5g³ 5fg³ 6fg 5.8f⁴ 6fg² 6g³ 6fg 6d 6g 1982 7.6fg 7d 5.8g 6f 7g³) quite well-made filly; third in seller at Leicester in August; stays 7f; has run poorly in blinkers and is not particularly consistent. *C. Williams.* **44**

HI-TOPSY 3 b.f. High Top 131–Noble Countess (Mossborough 126) (1981 7f 7.6s⁴ 1982 10.1fg 12fg 12f 9s) fairly prominent in maiden races in 1981; soundly beaten at 3 yrs; should stay middle distances; bandaged off-fore final start; sold 3,000 gns Newmarket Autumn Sales. *P. Cole.* **—**

HITRAVELSCENE 3 b.f. Mansingh 120–Kassiope 54 (Sir Gaylord) (1981 5d 5g 5s 1982 6fg 5fg 7g 7g 10g) small, lightly-made filly; poor plater; has worn blinkers; sold to A. Balding 420 gns Doncaster September Sales. *K. Stone.* **—**

HIT RECORD 4 ch.g. Record Token 128–Silk Willoughby (Pirate King 129) (1981 6g⁴ 7d* 7g 7d² 7f⁴ 7g² 6g³ 8d 7g 7s* 7d 8g³ 1982 7s 7f⁴ 7fg 7f) quite an attractive, well-made colt; quite a modest handicapper; stays 1m; acts on any **65**

going, but is well suited by some give underfoot; sold 2,100 gns Newmarket Autumn Sales. *F. Durr.*

HIT THE ACE (USA) 2 ch.c. Stop the Music–Audace (Tom Fool) (1982 7f³   **80** 7d⁴ 7g) Mar 10; $185,000Y; strong, attractive colt; half-brother to 2 winners by What A Pleasure; dam won 6f maiden race; in frame in maiden races at Yarmouth in August and Leicester in September; stays 7f. *M. Albina.*

HIT THE HAMMER 5 b.g. Blakeney 126–Guessing Game 87 (Doutelle 128)   — (1981 12d 12f³ 16s³ 1982 16fg 12fg) strong, quite attractive gelding; staying maiden; well beaten in 1982; suited by some give in the ground; bandaged in front nowadays. *D. Elsworth.*

HIT THE LINE 3 br.f. Saulingo 122–Speed Easy (On Your Mark 125) (1981   **59** 5fg 6fg² 6d³ 1982 8d 7fg 6f* 7f 6f 5fg³ 5.3fg⁴ 5fg 6f 5.3f 7fg) lengthy filly; made running and rallied gamely to win handicap at Brighton in May; well beaten most subsequent starts; best at sprint distances; seems to act on any going; has run respectably when sweating up. *R. Simpson.*

HITTITE PRINCE 3 b.g. Hittite Glory 125–Lady R. B. (Gun Shot) (1981   **50** 5g 5d³ 5g 5f² 6g⁴ 6g² 7g 7f* 6fg 1982 8fg 7g³ 8g 7g 7g) compact gelding; plater; suited by 7f; seems to act on any going; has run respectably in blinkers; sent to Malaysia. *B. Hanbury.*

HITTITE WARRIOR 2 b.c. Hittite Glory 125–Celeste 83 (Sing Sing 134)   **66** (1982 5g² 5fg 5fg³ 5fg 6s 6v) May 13; 1,900F, 3,300Y; neat colt; half-brother to several winners, including 5f and 7f winner Sharp Celeste (by Sharpen Up); dam stayed at least 6f; placed in seller at Ripon in August and maiden race (ridden by 7-lb claimer) at Folkestone in September; form only at 5f; acts on a firm surface. *C. Spares.*

HIYA JUDGE 4 b.c. Ashmore 125–Grey Home 110 (Habitat 134) (1981 7g   **60** 7fg 8g* 8.3g 8f 7g 8s 7v² 8d 1982 8g 7f 7fg² 8g⁴ 8f² 8fg² 8f² 7fg* 8g⁴ 8fg³ 7fg³ 8g) rather plain colt; second 4 times, including in a lady riders race, before winning handicap at Folkestone in August decisively; stays 1m; acts on any going; usually apprentice ridden. *A. Bailey.*

HIZ 4 gr.g. Persian Plan–Miss Swift 79 (Canisbay 120) (1981 8s³ 8d 10d² 10g⁴   — 10d⁴ 10d* 1982 10.6s) big, strong gelding; fair performer as a 3-y-o; ran moderately only outing of 1982 (April); stays 1¼m; acts on a firm surface, but is well suited by soft ground. *R. Hannon.*

HLA TUN 3 b.g. High Top 131–Clippie 99 (Nimbus 130) (1981 5d 7g 7fg²   **73** 1982 12g 8fg 7f 7fg* 7f 7f² 7f⁴ 7f*) strong gelding; successful in handicaps at Sandown in June (awarded race on disqualification of Red Fantastic) and Brighton in August (made all); best form at 7f on fast ground; blinkered last 2 starts; sent to Hong Kong. *P. Cundell.*

HOBA SUPREME 4 br.g. Sit In The Corner–Open Arms 77 (Dignitary 121)   — (1981 5d² 5g 5s 6f 5fg 6fg 8fg 7g 1982 8fg 8g) compact gelding; plater; should stay 6f; possibly needs some give in the ground. *W. Storey.*

HOBOURNES LAD 3 ch.c. Palm Track 122–Magic Garden (Florescence 120)   — (1981 5d 5f 6g 7.2v 5g 1982 8s³ 6s 7f 6f 6fg 6fg 6fg) neat colt; plater; stays 1m; acts on soft going. *R. Hollinshead.*

HODAKA (FR) 5 b.h. Sir Gaylord–Chigusa 89 (Skymaster 126) (1981 8s 8s   — 9fg 8d⁴ 10fg 8d² 8.5v 8s 1982 9.1g* 9.2g* 8d³ 9s⁴ 7g 10g 10f 8.2f 9g 10d) small, strong ex-French horse; first foal; dam won twice over 5f as a 2-y-o; successful in minor events at Rouen (dead-heated) and Le Croise-Laroche, both in March; little form over here, but had particularly stiff tasks in first 2 races; stays 9f; acts on soft going; sometimes blinkered (has won in them); formerly trained by F. Palmer. *I. Walker.*

HO HOI SHUM 2 b.g. Roman Warrior 132–Moon's Lass 70 (Prince de Galles   — 125) (1982 5f 5fg 6d 6f 6g) Apr 15; 1,100Y; plater; of no account; dead. *R. Ward.*

HOLDALL 4 ch.f. Manacle 123–Berostina 88 (Ribero 126) (1981 6f 6f 6fg 6f   **53** 7g 6d 7g 7s⁴ 7g 1982 6s⁴ 6f 7f* 6f³ 7f 6d⁴ 6f 6f 6g 7g 7f 8.2s 7s 7d) compact filly; bought in 2,300 gns after winning seller at Redcar in May; in frame in non-sellers afterwards; stays 7f; acts on any going; sometimes blinkered; has often hung badly; sweated and missed break seventh start. *P. Asquith.*

HOLD THAT TIGER 3 ch.g. Warpath 113–Indian Error 64 (Seminole II)   — (1981 NR 1982 10f 12f) brother to useful 6f to 1¼m performer Indian Brave; dam, half-sister to numerous winners, was of little account; seems of little account; sold 900 gns Ascot July Sales; resold 820 gns at Doncaster in September. *C. Thornton.*

HOLD TIGHT 3 b.c. Reform 132–Silk Rein 107 (Shantung 132) (1981 8d 7g⁴ 8g³ 1982 12fg 10f 12f* 12g⁴ 12g 12fg* 12s³) big, handsome colt; has a round action; successful in maiden race at York and £4,700 handicap at Goodwood; ran on really well to beat Lyphard's Pride by a length in latter in September; will be suited by 1¾m; acts on any going; blinkered last 2 starts; sold to R. Whitaker 17,000 gns Newmarket Autumn Sales. *R. Hern.* **96**

HOLE IN THE WALL 2 b.f. Windjammer (USA)–Just A Glimmer 75 (Dumbarnie 125) (1982 7f 7fg 6g² 6d* 7.5s³ 7d*) Mar 22; IR 3,600Y; third foal; half-sister to 5f and 6f winner Welsh Noble (by Welsh Saint); dam won over 5f and 6f, and stayed 1m; won maiden race at Navan in September by a neck from Crimson Crest, the pair clear of 12 others, and had same margin to spare over Evening Belle when winning minor event at Naas the following month; will probably stay 1m; acts on soft going. *P. Prendergast, Ireland.* **98**

HOLLERING 2 gr.c. Wolver Hollow 126–Princess Ayesha (Bold Lad, Ire 133) (1982 5f* 6d 6g) Apr 17; 5,400Y; big, lengthy colt; second foal; dam Irish 1¼m winner; moved very badly to start and ran very green in early stages when odds on for 6-runner minor event at Thirsk in April but came through in good style to win by 5 lengths; off course for long time afterwards and finished last on both outings on return (had very stiff task under top weight in nursery on final start); should stay at least 6f; sold 4,600 gns Doncaster October Sales. *M. H. Easterby.* **79**

HOLLINGREEN 2 ch.g. Malinowski 123–Laconia 58 (Great Nephew 126) (1982 6g 6d) May 30; IR 10,000Y; smallish, lengthy gelding; half-brother to 2 winners, notably Italian Oaks winner Val d'Erica (by Ashmore); dam half-sister to very useful stayer Tudor Tale; in rear in minor events at Ayr in September and Catterick in October; subsequently gelded. *E. Weymes.* **—**

HOLLOWAY WONDER 2 bl. or br.f. Swing Easy 126–Laconsu (Blakeney 126) (1982 6fg 7g4 5s* 7s*) Mar 1; 1,000Y; fair sort; first foal; dam never ran; easy 5-length winner from Manlight in 20-runner maiden auction event at Warwick in October; won well-contested nursery at Leicester the following month by length from Blue Nantucket, going well when leading 1f out but having nothing in hand at finish; stays 7f, but may prove best at 6f; seems to act on any going. *B. McMahon.* **93**

HOLLOWELL 2 b.g. Wolver Hollow 126–Shooting Season 91 (Silly Season 127) (1982 6g 7f 7fg 8g 8d³) Apr 8; good sort with plenty of scope; good mover; second foal; dam stayed 1m well; ran best races in Edinburgh maiden events on last 2 starts; suited by 1m; acts on a soft surface; ridden by lad in paddock first start; gelded after second outing. *Sir Mark Prescott.* **72**

HOLLOW HEART 3 b.f. Wolver Hollow 126–Shortwood 90 (Skymaster 126) (1981 5fg 5fg* 6g 1982 5fg³ 5f 6f 6fg² 6f) big, rangy filly; good mover; fairly useful performer; sometimes has stiff tasks; creditable 2 lengths second of 7 to Lucky Hunter in £4,000 race at Newbury in July; suited by 6f; yet to race on a soft surface; sometimes sweats up. *G. Lewis.* **87**

HOLLY BUOY 2 b.c. Blind Harbour 96–Holly Doon (Doon 124) (1982 5g 5d 7g* 7f 6f 8fg 7f) lightly-made colt; second foal; half-brother to a winning plater; dam poor plater; rallied well when beating Royal Export a length in 13-runner seller (no bid) at Thirsk in July; last in nurseries on last 2 appearances. *G. Harman.* **60**

HOLLYWOOD PARTY 3 ch.g. Be My Guest 126–Western Goddess 95 (Red God 128§) (1981 5s* 5fg* 5d³ 5g³ 6fg 6f* 7fg 7g 6d* 1982 6g 6g 7f² 6fg 6f 5fg 6g 6g 6g) strong, quite attractive gelding; good mover; 1¼ lengths second of 5 to Blue Emmanuelle in quite valuable handicap at Epsom in June; well beaten most afterwards; suited by 7f; acts on any going but put up best effort on a soft surface; blinkered once in 1981; has won for an apprentice; highly strung and has shown signs of temperament. *B. Hills.* **97§**

HOLMBURY LAD (USA) 4 gr.g. Al Hattab–Fairly Faithful 87 (Prove It) (1981 7s 6fg 6g 6d 6d 10g 8s 8d 12.2g 1982 10g 6g) poor performer nowadays; behind in a seller and a claiming event (seemed reluctant to race) in 1982; has been tried in blinkers; sold 620 gns Ascot December Sales. *K. Ivory.* **—**

HOLMBURY (USA) 2 ch.c. Quack–Riganda (Ribot 142) (1982 5fg 7fg² 8d) Mar 6; $40,000Y; rangy, useful-looking colt; half-brother to several winners including fairly useful 5f to 7f winner Ritruda (by Roi Dagobert) and a minor stakes winner by Delta Judge; dam useful winner at up to 7f; first to finish on **77**

far side but had no chance with 4-length winner Zaheendar in 26-runner maiden race at Redcar in September; chased leaders throughout when seventh of 23 to The Liquidator in maiden race at Newmarket the following month; stays 1m; has plenty of scope and is sure to win at one of the minor meetings. *G. Huffer.*

HOLY DAY 2 b.f. Sallust 134–Red Letter Day 100 (Crepello 136) (1982 5f 6f **82** 5d 6fg⁴ 5s*) Apr 4; neat, quite attractive filly; first foal; dam won over 6f and 1m; ran creditably most starts and on final one ran out a length winner from Lady Emily in 21-runner maiden race at Bath in October; should stay beyond 6f; acts on any going. *P. Walwyn.*

HOLY SPARK 2 b.c. Sparkler 130–Saintly Miss 63 (St Paddy 133) (1982 **99** 8g* 8.2s* 10.2s²) May 23; 6,000Y; quite well-made colt; excellent mover; half-brother to fair 1¼m winner Virgin Soldier (by Queen's Hussar) and a winning sprint plater; dam stayed 1½m; 20/1 and on backward side, with leaders throughout and rallied well under very strong driving to win 18-runner maiden race at Newmarket in October by a short head from Stride; won minor event at Nottingham later in the month; 9/4 on, outpaced from 2f out and eased close home when 4 lengths second of 15 to Whitstar in minor event at Doncaster in November; will stay 1½m; acts on soft going; has plenty of scope, and looks sure to win more races. *G. Harwood.*

HOLYWELL BAY 3 ch.g. The Go-Between 129–Highly Paid (Compensation — 127) (1981 5d 5d 5g 7fg 7fg 7g 1982 8f 10fg 11f 11.7f 8d 10f 8fg 12d) stocky gelding; poor maiden; beaten in seller seventh start; stays 1m; has been tried in blinkers. *R. Hannon.*

HOME COMING (FR) 4 gr.c. Habitat 134–Zeddera (Zeddaan 130) (1981 **105** 6g* 8fg* 7fg³ 7s* 8g⁴ 1982 8g 10s 8g* 8s 9d) strong, well-made colt; good walker and mover; developed into a very useful colt as a 3-y-o; didn't run well either outing in spring and was subsequently off course until September, when putting up an excellent performance to beat Mighty Fly by a neck in £6,000 handicap at Doncaster (always going well); ran poorly afterwards, although had stiff task next time; stays 1m well; probably acts on any going, but is well suited by some give underfoot; sold 35,000 gns Newmarket December Sales. *G. Harwood.*

HOME COMMAND 2 ch.c. Home Guard 129–Fleurie 81 (Reliance II 137) **75** (1982 7fg 7f 8g 6d⁴ 5g) Mar 4; IR 32,000Y; quite well-made colt; first foal; dam, half-sister to top-class 1971 French staying 2-y-o First Bloom, won over 6f in France at 3 yrs; quite a moderate maiden; stays 7f; blinkered last 2 outings. *C. Williams.*

HOME DAN 3 b.g. Homeric 133–Dance All Night 106 (Double-U-Jay 120) — (1981 7.6s 8d 1982 10.1g 8d 8s 10s) poor maiden; sold to M. Hinchliffe 1,200 gns Newmarket Autumn Sales. *M. Smyly.*

HOME LEAVE 2 b.c. Riboboy 124–The Wrekin Joy 68 (Reform 132) (1982 — 5f) Feb 15; 1,400Y; first foal; dam stayed 1½m; well beaten in maiden auction event at Redcar in May; sold 900 gns Doncaster August Sales. *M. H. Easterby.*

HOMEOWNER (USA) 2 b.c. L'Enjoleur–Zeal (Round Table) (1982 8fg* 8s³) **108** May 6; $95,000F, IR 72,000 gns Y; lightly-made colt; brother to 3-y-o American winner Coaxing and half-brother to several winners in USA and France, including French 1m and 1¼m winner Zarinia (by Right Royal V); dam twice-raced sister to top-class American mare Drumtop and Observer Gold Cup winner Take Your Place; 2/1 and fairly fit, looked green early on in 14-runner maiden race at Leopardstown in September but led 2f out and responded well to strong pressure, winning by a short head from odds-on South Atlantic; 7/1 when 6½ lengths third of 7 to Danzatore in Panasonic Beresford Stakes at the Curragh the following month; will stay 1¼m; useful but lacks scope. *D. O'Brien, Ireland.*

HOME SECRETARY 2 ch.c. Homing 130–Albany 120 (Pall Mall 132) (1982 **85 p** 6fg 7fg⁴) Mar 29; good-looking colt; half-brother to 4 winners, all at least very useful, including stayer Buttress (by Busted) and middle-distance performer English Harbour (by Mill Reef); dam, daughter of high-class stayer Almeria, was smart at 1¼m; 2 lengths fourth of 29 to Alligatrix in maiden race at Newmarket in August, racing with leaders on far side all the way and keeping on well; will be suited by 1m or more; a sure winner in maiden company. *R. Hern.*

HOMEWARD 2 b.g. Homing 130–Whitefoot 108 (Relko 136) (1982 8g) Feb — 10; well-made gelding; good walker; half-brother to several winners, including

Irish Oaks winner Swiftfoot (by Run The Gantlet) and useful 1979 2-y-o 6f
winner Neenah (by Bold Lad, Ire); dam stayed at least 1½m; third favourite and
looking fit and well, ridden along fully 3f out and showed little promise when
ninth of 17 to Oula Owl in maiden race at Newmarket in October; gelded
subsequently. *R. Hern.*

HONEST TOKEN 3 b. or br.g. Record Token 128–Be Honest 95 (Klairon 131)   —
(1981 6g 6g 6s 1982 7g 7g) compact gelding; only plating class. *C. Thornton.*

HONEY MAY 3 b.f. Artaius 129–Honeystar (Primera 131) (1981 NR 1982   65
7g 10f 8g 5f³ 7g 7fg 10fg 6d² 8g 6v) 29,000Y; robust ex-English filly; half-
sister to useful 1975 2-y-o 7f winner Heraclius (by Don II), subsequently successful
in France, and to 3 other winners here and in France; dam, winner over 9f in
France, is daughter of 1,000 Guineas winner Honeylight; placed in maiden race
at Bellewstown in July and handicap at Navan in September; best at sprint
distances though is bred to stay further; trained part of season by G. Huffer.
P. Norris, Ireland.

HONEY STAGE (USA) 2 ch.f. Stage Door Johnny–Honey Pot (Drone) **106 p**
(1982 7v³ 8s*) Apr 1; $235,000Y; third foal; half-sister to very useful 1981
French 2-y-o 7f winner Honeyland (by Stop the Music); dam, stakes-placed
winner over 5f at 2 yrs, is out of half-sister to top-class broodmare Alanesian;
accounted for some well-bred fillies in good style when winning 10-runner maiden
race at Saint-Cloud in November by 3 lengths from subsequently-successful
Stephany's Dream; will be suited by 1¼m+; entered in Oaks; promising.
Mme C. Head, France.

HONORA 2 b. or br.f. Saulingo 122–Cigarette 61 (Miralgo 130) (1982 5fg   —
5f 5f) Mar 17; 4,000Y, 480 2-y-o; neat filly; half-sister to 2 winners, including
useful 1974 Irish 2-y-o Say Cheese (by Polyfoto); dam plater; bad plater;
exported to Algeria. *D. Weeden.*

HONRIETTE 3 ch.f. Henry the Seventh 125–My Own II 96 (El Relicario 124)   **74**
(1981 7v² 7g 1982 12g⁴ 11f³ 12g*) tall, lengthy filly; won 11-runner maiden
race at Lingfield in August; suited by 1½m; acts on any going. *G. Harwood.*

HOOD HILL 6 ch.g. Silly Season 127–Whatawind (Typhoon 125) (1981   —
8d 8f 1982 10g) close-coupled gelding; plater; stays 1¼m; best in blinkers.
G. Fletcher.

HOODWINK 4 br.g. No Mercy 126–Rose Blanche 89 (French Beige 127) (1981   **53**
7fg² 7d 8g 7f 8f³ 7fg² 8.3fg 10f⁵ 0g³ 8f³ 8fg² 1982 8d 10f² 7fg⁴ 8f 8g 8.3fg³ 10.1fg
10f⁴ 10fg) plater; stays 1¼m; acts on firm going, often blinkered and probably
isn't entirely genuine. *N. Vigors.*

HOOFER 2 ch.g. Hotfoot 126–Frivolity 70 (Varano) (1982 10s) Mar 8;   —
5,000Y; good-bodied gelding; second foal; half-brother to 3-y-o 2m winner
Radfield (by Connaught); dam, 2m winner, is half-sister to Irish 1,000 Guineas
and Irish St Leger winner Pidget; 16/1, failed to recover from slow start in 17-
runner maiden race at Nottingham in October; sold 620 gns Newmarket
Autumn Sales. *J. Hindley.*

HOOLIGAN 2 br.c. Mummy's Pet 125–Trickster 92 (Major Portion 129) (1982   **88**
5f 5g⁴ 6g³ 7s³) Apr 14; fair sort; brother to fair 6f winner Bretton Park, closely
related to smart 3-y-o sprinter Jester (by Song) and half-brother to 2 winners,
one useful; dam sprinter; first to finish on far side when length third of 28 to
Jungle Romeo in maiden race at Redcar in October, final outing and easily best
effort; evidently stays 7f; acts on soft going; started slowly first 2 starts; refused
to enter stalls when withdrawn at Newbury intended first outing, and gave
trouble at start on debut. *P. Rohan.*

HOPE COVE 3 b.f. High Top 131–Greek Gift (Acropolis 132) (1981 6fg 7f   **65**
1982 10f 7g 7f 12d 8f 9f 10g³ 12fg) strong, lengthy filly; only plating class; best
run at 1¼m. *D. Whelan.*

HOPEFUL ANN 3 b.f. Abwah 118–Hopeful Subject 82 (Mandamus 120) (1981   —
5f 6fg 6fg 7f 1982 6s 7g 8f 7fg 7f 12d) workmanlike filly; poor form, including
in a seller; trained most of season by T. Craig. *C. Thornton.*

HOPEFUL WATERS 2 br.f. Forlorn River 124–Hopeful Way 72 (Hopeful   **66**
Venture 125) (1982 5f 6g 6fg 6fg² 7g 6s 6s 5s 5d⁴ 6s*) Mar 20; lightly-made
filly; first foal; dam won 1½m seller; ran easily best race when winning 18-runner
claiming event at Nottingham in October pushed out by 6 lengths from Maestro
Lady; evidently acts well on soft going. *J. Spearing.*

*Coventry Stakes, Ascot—Horage shows great determination to
hold off Kafu with the others well beaten*

HORAGE   2 b.c. Tumble Wind–Musicienne (Sicambre 135)   (1982 5s* 5g* 5fg* **123**
5f* 6f* 6f* 6f* 6g* 6g* 6g⁴)

Is the Walt Disney company, we wonder, aware of Horage's story?   It tells
of a heart-warming victory for courage and endeavour in the face of tremendous
difficulties, and at times stretches credulity to the limits: struggling trainer Matt
McCormack, with only a handful of winners to his name in his first two seasons,
visits the Doncaster Sales and buys eight yearlings for £42,000, including a
Tumble Wind colt for 8,000 guineas; McCormack then finds himself in dire
straits when the people for whom he'd bought back out of the deal, leaving him
to foot the bill; Lebanese businessman Abed Rachid visits the stable to look at
another horse but ends up buying the Tumble Wind colt purely on a whim; and
then the colt, named Horage, not only solves his trainer's financial problems by
landing a gamble on his debut but proceeds to win nine races off the reel,
including three of the best six-furlong events for two-year-olds.   It's too soon
to say whether all concerned will live happily ever after but McCormack will no
doubt receive much better opportunities because of his handling of Horage,
Mr Rachid has already received a return of £105,916 on his investment and
Horage, as tough and courageous a colt as one could wish to see, is guaranteed
a place at stud if he never wins another race.

Following an impressive trial against the fair three-year-old Shiny Hour
Horage was dispatched to Ayr before the season was a week old and appeared
in the six-runner Hillhouse Stakes.   He won well, drawing away in the final
furlong to win by three lengths, and if his subsequent exploits made his starting
price of 6/1 look remarkably generous so too did the exploits of his opponents—
all five of them ended the season still maidens.   Incidentally this was the only
time Horage was to encounter ground softer than good.   His first test of any
consequence came at Ascot a month later on his third outing.   By then he had
accounted for four newcomers, including Domynsky, with the minimum of fuss
in a small race at Pontefract but he started only third choice in the Ascot
betting, behind two other colts who were unbeaten in two starts, Brondesbury
and Black Glazepta.   Horage staked his claim to be considered the best two-
year-old seen out, running on so well from halfway that by the furlong pole he'd
wiped out Brondesbury's lead, which for a long time had looked unassailable.
The further they went the further Horage drew clear and he crossed the line
five lengths clear of the odds-on Brondesbury.   Excellent though Horage's
performance was, Brondesbury later proved that he hadn't shown his true form.

By the time Horage took on pattern company for the first time in the
Coventry Stakes at Royal Ascot he had landed the odds in two more races, a
three-runner affair at Salisbury in May in which his rivals hardly got him out
of a canter, and a four-runner event at Haydock in June.   The most notable
features of his display at Haydock were his sweating up badly and his pulling
hard early on; he'd never behaved in such a way before and he didn't do so again.
He would have had every excuse had he done at Royal Ascot, for the blacksmith pricked his foot when shoeing him the day before the race, causing slight
lameness.   The horse appeared to recover but Eddery was given orders to with-
draw him if things didn't seem right on the way to the start.   In the end
Horage was able to line up alongside the six other previous winners in an eight-
strong field.   He extended his winning sequence to six with a first-class display,
making the running, going comfortably within himself, until Kafu threw down
a very threatening challenge coming to the final furlong.   Horage then showed
his great determination, beating off Kafu's challenge to win by a length and a
half despite appearing to be feeling his foot—he changed his legs a couple of
times and edged right.   Horage was reportedly very sore in the evening but he
was back to normal within a couple of days and reappeared just over three

weeks later in the Anglia Television July Stakes at Newmarket. Here he had to give 6 lb to Kafu and the pair started co-favourites ahead of the Windsor Castle Stakes winner Prince Reymo. Once again Horage's footwear threatened his chance. This time he nearly lost his near-fore plate in the early stages—our photograph of the finish shows just how badly it was twisted—which surely explains why he appeared to become outpaced as Kafu and Prince Reymo disputed the lead. Horage was nevertheless just as game for a battle as ever. He deprived Kafu of the lead at the distance then fought off On Stage, who was also receiving 6 lb, to win under very strong driving by half a length. As at Royal Ascot the third horse was well beaten.

Thirty-eight days elapsed before Horage reappeared in the Washington Singer Stakes at Newbury in August, the longest time between any of his races. Horage looked very well indeed, carrying plenty of condition, the main object of the exercise being to sharpen him up for his next major target, the Gimcrack Stakes at York just five days later. He was ridden for the first time by Murray as Eddery was claimed to ride in Ireland. He tended to run lazily in front and he must have given his rider a few anxious moments coming to the final furlong; he had to be really rousted as The Noble Player, who received 6 lb, came at him and only then did he quicken away to win by two and a half lengths. This was a good effort from Horage, although The Noble Player wasn't yet in the form he showed over a mile in the autumn. The Gimcrack rarely attracts a top-class field these days and the latest field was certainly substandard. Sayf El Arab, the second favourite, was having his first race for over eleven weeks; the third favourite Rock 'N' Roller had received 4 lb and a two-and-a-half-length beating from Caerleon at the Curragh only five days earlier; and the other four runners started at 33/1 or more. Horage started at 13/8 on and made all to win comfortably by four lengths from Rock 'N' Roller, again showing signs of becoming lazy, needing to be pushed along for a furlong before he quickened away in the last quarter mile. Horage's record now read nine wins from nine starts, a truly remarkable achievement. There have been several other amazingly tough two-year-olds since the war—Nagwa and Spindrifter both won thirteen races, with Spindrifter winning ten in a row, Kursaal won the last nine of her ten races in 1967 and Abdu won nine times in 1978—but none of these won a pattern race. The only animals we can think of whose achievements compare with Horage's are Sky Gipsy and the French filly Texana: Sky Gipsy's ten wins in 1965 included those in the Windsor Castle, July and Richmond Stakes (as well as a walk over); and Texana won all her eleven starts in 1957, including the Prix d'Arenberg and Prix de l'Abbaye de Longchamp.

After the Gimcrack report had it that Horage was to be tried over seven furlongs, in either the Fitzroy House Stakes at Newmarket, which would be his final race of the season, or in a small race followed by the Dewhurst. Nevertheless when Horage reappeared it was over six furlongs in the Mill Reef Stakes at Newbury, starting favourite. Unfortunately he lost his unbeaten record, managing to lead for only four furlongs and finishing fourth of the five runners,

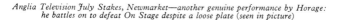

Anglia Television July Stakes, Newmarket—another genuine performance by Horage: he battles on to defeat On Stage despite a loose plate (seen in picture)

Gimcrack Stakes, York—Horage gains his ninth win of the season

beaten just under four lengths by the winner Salieri and three lengths by his old rival Kafu. He could simply have been feeling the effects of his long, hard season but the trainer later reported that Horage had returned home with very sore shins, adding that Horage had since made a complete recovery and that he would reappear in the Salisbury Two Thousand Guineas Trial in preparation for the Guineas itself.

While admitting to immense admiration for Horage at two we're not sure he'll be so effective at three. Hopefully he'll prove us wrong but it was noticeable in his first season that some of his contemporaries made much greater physical progress. Early in the year we described him as a strong, useful-looking colt and a good mover, but by July one of our paddock critics commented

Mr A. R. Rachid's "Horage"

that Horage seemed to be 'steadily melting away' and by the Gimcrack he definitely looked on the small side against the later developers. Who knows though, perhaps his exceptional courage will continue to see him through?

			Windy City
	Tumble Wind	Restless Wind	Lump Sugar
	(b 1964)	(ch 1956)	Endeavour II
Horage		Easy Stages	Saturday Off
(b.c. Feb 20, 1980)		(b 1953)	Prince Bio
	Musicienne	Sicambre	Sif
	(ch 1968)	(br 1948)	Prince Chevalier
		Musical II	Musidora
		(ch 1961)	

Horage should prove well suited by seven furlongs and a mile; indeed a case can be made out for his staying further. His sire Tumble Wind won the Hollywood Derby over a mile and a quarter and the San Luis Obispo Handicap over a mile and a half, and his dam Musicienne is by the Prix du Jockey-Club and Grand Prix de Paris winner Sicambre. Musicienne, who ran only once, had a modest record at stud until Horage came along. Only one of her three reported foals had won, the Faraway Son colt Music Box whose single success came in a nine-furlong race at La Capelle. In view of this record it's not so surprising that Horage cost only 8,400 guineas as a foal and 8,000 guineas as a yearling (his yearling brother sold better in 1982, fetching 82,000 guineas at Doncaster, and he is to be trained by David O'Brien). Musicienne comes from an excellent family. Her half-brother by Relko, Master Guy, won the nine-furlong Prix Jean Prat before finishing third to Nijinsky in the Irish Sweeps Derby and her half-sister by Right Royal V, Musique Royal, reached the frame in the Prix de Pomone over thirteen and a half furlongs and the Prix de Royallieu over a furlong less. Their dam Musical II was a useful filly, winning the Prix du Rond-Point over seven furlongs, and she was in turn a daughter of the One Thousand Guineas and Oaks winner Musidora. This is also the family of the top-class miler Homing. *M. McCormack.*

HORKEY 5 ch.m. Shoolerville 121–Omnia Opera 83 (Major Portion 129) (1981 10.1d 10d³ 12.2fg 12f 10fg⁴ 10f 10f² 11.5d 1982 10f) leggy mare; plater; stays 1¼m; seems to act on any going. *J. Harris.* —

HORRORS 3 ch.g. Gay Palm 111–Calamint (Punchinello 97) (1981 NR 1982 10.1fg 11.7f 12g) brother to winning chaser The Herb; dam of little account; well beaten in minor event and maiden races. *D. Oughton.* —

HORSESHOE BAY 2 ch.f. Duc d'Orleans 76–Wall Street 82 (Cash and Courage 116) (1982 5f 5g) Mar 26; bad maiden; sold 420 gns Doncaster September Sales. *J. Leigh.* —

HOSSAM 2 b.c. Artaius 129–Shebeen 124 (Saint Crespin III 132) (1982 6fg* 6s) Feb 21; 52,000Y; second live foal; half-brother to disappointing 3-y-o Pedometer (by Great Nephew); dam very smart middle-distance performer; 5/4 favourite, made much of running and had his 11 opponents well strung out when winning newcomers event at Chepstow in August by 3 lengths from Tournament Leader; soundly beaten when favourite for minor event won by Larionov at Lingfield the following month; will be suited by longer distances, and should stay at least 1¼m; acts on a firm surface. *P. Walwyn.* **83**

HOSTESS 3 b.f. Be My Guest 126–Ginger 90 (Red God 128§) (1981 6f 7f* 7fg 1982 8.2d 8f* 8.5f) small, close-coupled filly; has an excellent, smooth action; beat Channing Girl in handicap at York in May; poor last in valuable handicap won by Dalmally at Epsom in June; not seen out again; stays 1m; acts well on firm going; needs strong handling; sold 12,000 gns Newmarket December Sales. *H. Cecil.* **73**

HOT ANNA 3 ch.f. Hotfoot 126–Lantana 74 (St Paddy 133) (1981 5g⁴ 5g 6g 6fg² 6g 7f 8.2fg 1982 7d 11.5f 10g⁴ 11d 12d 12g 10g) tall filly; good mover; disappointing maiden; quite stoutly bred but has yet to show she stays beyond 6f; blinkered final start. *P. Feilden.* —

HOT BETTY 2 b.f. Hotfoot 126–Sunstrucks Betty (Sunstruck) (1982 7g) Apr 28; 1,300F, 6,400Y; fourth reported foal; half-sister to a winner in Belgium; dam won 1m claiming race in USA at 2 yrs; unquoted and backward, best work in closing stages when seventh of 22 behind Toveris in maiden race at Newmarket in October; will stay 1m; sure to improve. *L. Cumani.* **75 p**

HOT BOY 2 b.c. Hot Grove 128–Gloria Maremmana (King Emperor) (1982 6d 7g* 7g² 7f 7d* 7.2f³ 8s) Feb 5; lengthy, attractive colt; good walker; **107**

second foal; dam won at 2 yrs in Italy; won 7-runner maiden race at Chester in July and 6-runner nursery on same course in August; also ran well under top weight when ½-length second to Harly in minor event at Lingfield and when 2 lengths third of 11 to Game Dame in £4,400 nursery at Haydock; should be suited by 1m+ (had very stiff task when seventh of 9 in Royal Lodge Stakes); seems to act on any going; will win more races. *F. J. Houghton.*

HOT CAPTAIN   3 b. or br.g. Roi Soleil 125–Telling 91 (High Treason 126)   — (1981 5g 6g 7fg 8.2d   1982 11g 9.4fg 11fg 13.8f 9s)   neat gelding; in rear in varied company, including selling. *G. Richards.*

HOT GOLD   2 b.c. Hot Grove 128–Lumiere 56 (Siliconn 121)   (1982 6fg 8.2s)   — Mar 22; 8,200F, 5,400Y; first produce; dam poor daughter of very smart sprinter Lucasland; backward, behind in maiden race at Newmarket (backed at long odds) in July and minor event (pulled hard) at Nottingham in October. *H. Collingridge.*

HOT JACKIE   3 b.f. Hot Spark 126–Miss Jack 97 (Pampered King 121)   (1981   — 5s   1982 10s 12g 10fg 14d)   good-bodied filly; beaten a long way in maiden races. *M. Ryan.*

HOTMANTLE   3 b.g. Hotfoot 126–Dismantle 77 (Aureole 132)   (1981 5fg   **66** 5g³ 7d 6d 6g 8s   1982 7g 8fg⁴ 7f² 10fg 8g 7f⁴ 8.3g 8.3fg³)   sturdy gelding; suited by 1m; sweated up badly fifth start; exported to Malaysia. *J. Benstead.*

HOT ON THE TRAIL   2 b.c. Garda's Revenge 119–Hot Baby (Tropique   **81** 128)   (1982 6g 6g 6g² 8.2s 7s)   May 29; small colt; half-brother to numerous winners here and abroad, including fairly useful 7f and 1¼m winner Sure Loser (by Falcon); dam of little account; 2½ lengths second of 15 to Aditi in minor race at Hamilton in September, best effort; possibly doesn't stay 1m. *N. Guest.*

HOT POTATO   2 ch.g. Class Distinction–Cateryne (Ballymoss 136)   (1982   **73** 5d² 6d* 7s⁴ 7d)   May 3; lengthy, workmanlike gelding; first foal; dam ran only once; bought in 3,100 gns after leading inside final furlong to win £3,000 seller at Newcastle in August by a length from Easy Star, first race for 2 months; good fourth of 10 to John French in nursery at York in October, better subsequent effort; will stay 1¼m; has raced only on a soft surface. *C. Booth.*

HOT PRINCESS   2 ch.f. Hot Spark 126–Aspara 58 (Crimson Satan)   (1982 **101** 5g 5fg 5f* 6d² 5fg 6f* 5s 6d)   Apr 3; half-sister to 7f winner Varuna (by Luthier); dam placed over 5f in Ireland and England; successful in maiden race at Leopardstown in June and minor event at Navan in September, scoring by 2 lengths from Burrow Hill in latter; creditable 3 lengths fifth of 13 to Treasure Trove in valuable nursery at Naas in October on final outing; stays 6f well; acts on firm going and a soft surface; none too well away first 2 starts and subsequently wore blinkers. *D. Weld, Ireland.*

HOT PROPERTY   3 br.f. Hot Spark 126–Klairette (Klairon 131)   (1981   — 5fg 6fg 7d   1982 6f 6g)   quite attractive, well-made filly; behind in maiden races and handicaps. *J. Sutcliffe.*

HOT SPICE   4 b.f. Hotfoot 126–Persian Market 105 (Taj Dewan 128)   (1981   — NR   1982 13.8f 12f² 12.2f⁴ 12d 18d)   lengthy filly; first living foal; dam awarded 1975 Princess Elizabeth Stakes; in frame in minor events at Pontefract and Catterick in July; off course 3 months afterwards; stays 1½m. *D. Morley.*

HOT STONE   4 br.f. Hotfoot 126–Quarry Wood 89 (Super Sam 124)   (1981   — 11f 13.4g 12d³ 14.7fg   1982 12fg 13.4g)   big, rangy filly; poor maiden; probably stays 1½m; usually apprentice ridden. *D. Francis.*

HOTTER THAN JULY   2 b.f. Gay Fandango 132–Ophalia (Aforethought)   **71** (1982 5s 6s⁴)   June 7; 700Y; reportedly second foal; dam placed at up to 1m in French Provinces; blinkered, one-paced fourth, beaten 3½ lengths, behind Marzooga in 16-runner maiden race at Leicester in November; will be better suited by 7f+. *H. Candy.*

HOT TOUCH   2 b.c. Moulton 128–Fairly Hot 109 (Sir Ivor 135)   (1982 8d⁴)   **87** p May 13; second foal; half-brother to 3-y-o middle-distance performer Mill Plantation (by Northfields); dam, daughter of 1,000 Guineas winner Full Dress II, was useful but temperamental performer at up to 1¼m; 33/1 and on backward side, made up a lot of ground in final 2f and kept on strongly when promising 7¾ lengths fourth of 23 to The Liquidator in maiden race at Newmarket in October; will be suited by 1¼m+; sure to win races. *H. Wragg.*

HOTWAVE 4 ch.f. Hotfoot 126–Pinwave 82 (Pinza 137) (1981 7f 10f⁴ 9f **49** 8d 9s⁴ 1982 8fg² 8f) compact, fair sort; good mover; ran well when second in maiden race at Thirsk in April and respectably in a handicap only subsequent start; stays 1¼m; tends to sweat up. *Miss S. Hall.*

HOUGHTON WEAVER 3 b.g. Warpath 113–Broughton Flyer (Huntercombe **73** d 133) (1981 5d*(dis) 5fg* 6f³ 5d* 6g* 7s³ 6fg⁴ 6d³ 1982 7g 7g² 9fg 8.2f 8.2g⁴ 8.2g 6f 6d 8.2s 6s 7g) leggy, rather narrow gelding; poor walker; length second to Wibis Range in Northern Free Handicap at Newcastle in April, best effort; behind in seller ninth start; stays 7f; probably acts on any going; blinkered penultimate outing. *J. Berry.*

HOUSE GUEST 2 b.f. Be My Guest 126–Plum Fool (Silly Season 127) (1982 **75** 5fg⁴ 6fg² 6fg* 7d 6s) Apr 18; IR 24,000Y; leggy, lightly-made filly; fourth foal; sister to 3-y-o Plum Bold, a winner over 6f in 1981, and half-sister to 1980 2-y-o 5.8f winner Plum Lane (by Thatch); dam half-sister to top-class 1969 French 2-y-o Breton; having first race for 2 months, led inside final furlong to win 9-runner maiden race at Pontefract in August by 3 lengths from Red Minstrel; soundly beaten in nurseries afterwards; should be suited by 7f (had stiff task when tried at trip); acts on a firm surface. *B. Hanbury.*

HOUSE SPARROW 3 gr.f. Hotfoot 126–Guinea Sparrow 119 (Grey Sovereign **—** 128§) (1981 NR 1982 6s 8g) rangy filly; half-sister to 3 winners, including Ascot 1,000 Guineas Trial winner Gilding (by Kauai King) and a winner in Austria; dam sprinting 2-y-o; 17/2, made some late headway after starting slowly when 7½ lengths sixth of 16 to Sparkling Form in minor event at York in October, first start and better effort; sold 7,200 gns Newmarket December Sales. *W. Hastings-Bass.*

HOYDEN 3 b.f. English Prince 129–Kelfresco 59 (Kelly 122) (1981 5f⁴ 6g **53** 6d 1982 5fg⁴ 6fg 6f 6fg 5g² 6fg 6g) stocky filly; sprint maiden; beaten in sellers last 2 outings; best at 5f; blinkered last 4 starts; suitable mount for an apprentice. *A. Jarvis.*

H. R. MICRO 4 br.f. High Award 119–Crusheen (Typhoon 125) (1981 6s **53** 6fg 6g 6f 5f* 6fg 5.3fg³ 6fg 5f 5f 5f 7d 6s 6g⁴ 1982 6g 6fg 5f 5f² 5g² 6s² 6g² 5g³ 6f 5f³ 5fg 7f 8fg 6s) small, lengthy filly; won apprentice handicap at Edinburgh in May; second on 5 other occasions, including in a seller; stays 6f; probably acts on any going, but is suited by firm; occasionally blinkered; good mount for an apprentice. *M. Lambert.*

HULA RULER (USA) 3 b.f. Chieftain Native Go-Go (Raise A Native) (1981 **94** 6fg³ 7g* 7f* 1982 10fg³ 10fg³ 12fg 7f) big, rangy, attractive filly; very good walker and mover; creditable third in Pretty Polly Stakes at Newmarket in April (4 lengths behind Sing Softly) and Sir Charles Clore Memorial Stakes at Newbury in May (beaten 5 lengths by Zinzara); well beaten in Ribblesdale Stakes at Royal Ascot and £6,100 handicap at Newmarket afterwards; needs further than 7f and should stay 1½m; yet to race on a soft surface but gives impression one may suit her; usually makes the running. *L. Cumani.*

HULDA (FR) 7 ch.g. Linden Tree 127–Mapiona (Tompion) (1981 NR 1982 **—** 10.2s 12s) poor middle-distance handicapper; acts on a firm surface; well beaten when tried in blinkers. *O. O'Neill.*

HUMBLE BLUE 4 ch.c. Some Hand 119–Papillon Rouge 80 (Klairon 131) **66** (1981 5s² 5s* 5g* 6d 5f⁴ 5fg² 5g* 5g 5fg 6fg 5d⁴ 5g 1982 5d² 5fg 5fg⁴ 5f 5.1f² 6g² 5fg* 6g 5.6f 6d 5fg 5fg) sprint handicapper; second 3 times before beating Rambling River by 1½ lengths at Beverley in June; races mainly at 5f but stays 6f; acts on any going; has run creditably in blinkers; saddle slipped second outing. *G. Fletcher.*

HUMBLE SUPPLIER 2 b.c. Mummy's Pet 125–Creolina 72 (Quorum 126) **—** (1982 5g 6s) Mar 22; 5,400F, 6,400Y; workmanlike colt; closely related to a winning plater and a winner in Belgium (both by Song); dam placed over 6f at 2 yrs; well beaten in maiden race at Kempton in May and £2,000 seller at Goodwood in September; sold 300 gns Ascot November Sales. *R. Hannon.*

HUNGARIAN PRINCE 2 b.c. Monseigneur 127–Magyar Melody (Prince **85** Tenderfoot 126) (1982 8fg³ 8.2s*) Apr 24; 17,000Y; strong, compact, good sort; carries plenty of condition; first live foal; dam won over 5f and 1m at 2 yrs in Ireland; having first race for over 3 months, made virtually all to land the odds very easily by 2½ lengths from Philpride in 8-runner maiden race at Haydock in October; previously promising 4½ lengths third of 10 to Rocky Marriage in maiden race at Sandown; stays 1m well; sold R. Sheather 12,500 gns Newmarket Autumn Sales. *G. Harwood.*

HUNGRY HEART 3 b.c. English Prince 129–Sheila's Tarquin 111 (Black **87**
Tarquin 136) (1981 7.9f 8s 1982 8s 10s 13g* 16fg 12fg 14f³) half-brother
to several winners, including useful Silent Call (by Continuation); dam very
useful winner over 5f at 2 yrs; accounted for Red Sandal by 2 lengths in 14-
runner maiden race at Dundalk in May; soundly beaten subsequently, including
in Queen's Vase at Royal Ascot fourth start; should stay well. *S. McGrath,
Ireland.*

HUNTER HAWK 3 ch.c. Huntercombe 133–White Legs (Preciptic 122) (1981 **53**
6fg 6fg 6d 6g 5f⁴ 5v 5s 6d 1982 10d 6f³ 6g 5g 5g² 6f³ 5f 5f) neat, strong colt;
poor maiden; unlikely to stay 1¼m; acts on firm going; sometimes blinkered
but is effective without. *A. Balding.*

HUNTERS GROVE 2 b.f. On Your Mark 125–Invisible (King Emperor) **97**
(1982 5g⁴ 5fg* 5fg* 5g³ 6g³ 5d⁴ 5fg 6g 5fg³ 5fg³ 6fg* 6g⁴ 6g 6s) Mar 4; 960Y;
neat filly; first foal; dam ran 3 times; trained on well after winning 2 maiden
auction events in good style within a week in April and won nursery at Haydock
in September; better suited by 6f than 5f; acts well on firm ground; genuine;
good mount for an apprentice; sold 10,000 gns Newmarket Autumn Sales and
exported to Trinidad. *A. Bailey.*

HUNTING LAD 3 b.c. Huntercombe 133–Pot de Creme 68 (Candy Spots) —
(1981 7d 6d 6s 1982 8.2fg 6fg 7d 6fg 8fg) tall colt; little sign of ability in
varied company, including selling; blinkered third start; sold 740 gns Doncaster
October Sales. *S. Matthews.*

HUNT THE THIMBLE (USA) 3 b.f. Turn and Count–Esprit Belle (Ack Ack) —
(1981 6f⁴ 6fg³ 6fg³ 1982 8g) rather unfurnished filly; showed fair form in
1981; well beaten in maiden race at Yarmouth in June on only outing at 3 yrs;
may prove best at distances short of 1m; has run well when sweating up. *L.
Cumani.*

HUNZA 2 ch.c. Habat 127–Amaryllis 92 (Tudor Melody 129) (1982 5g 5g 6s) **44**
Apr 25; 1,400F, 4,200Y; workmanlike colt; half-brother to minor winners here
and in Belgium; dam won over 5f at 2 yrs; poor form in varied company; sold
2,100 gns Newmarket Autumn Sales. *S. Mellor.*

HURWORTH HOUSE 6 ch.g. Habitat 134–Light Opera 101 (Vienna 127) —
(1981 6fg 6g³ 6d² 6s 6s 6s 1982 6d 6g) smallish, sturdy gelding; sprint handicapper; in rear both outings in 1982; acts on a firm surface but is particularly
well suited by some give in the ground; best in blinkers; suitable mount for an
apprentice; sold to BBA 1,400 gns Newmarket Autumn Sales. *H. T. Jones.*

HUTTON GLORY 2 b.g. Hittite Glory 125–Divided 74 (Busted 134) (1982 —
5g 7g 8s) Feb 25; 5,000Y; neat gelding; second foal; half-brother to 1979
2-y-o 7f winner Marita (by Great Nephew); dam stayed 1½m well; little worthwhile form; off course 5½ months after first outing. *I. Walker.*

HUTTON MISS 2 b. or br.f. Joshua 129–Siciliana 77 (Sicilian Prince 126) —
(1982 7fg 8s) May 31; rather leggy filly with a round action; half-sister to a
winning plater and a winning hurdler; dam stayer; in rear in seller and maiden
race (last of 9) in the autumn. *R. Robinson.*

HYDE 5 b.g. Royalty 130–Impatience (Kibenka 119) (1981 NR 1982 13v⁴) —
quite a moderate maiden as a 3-y-o; has run only once on flat since; should stay
1¼m+; suited by some give in the ground. *M. W. Easterby.*

HYDRANGEA 3 br.f. Warpath 113–Hitesca 110 (Tesco Boy 121) (1981 **73**
NR 1982 8fg 12fg 15fg² 16.5f* 16g³ 16.1s 16.1s 16s* 18s) small, rather
sparely-made filly; good walker; half-sister to fairly useful middle-distance
colt Rodeo (by Bustino) and miler Referendum (by Reform); dam, very game
filly, stayed 1¼m; won maiden race at Redcar in July and handicap at Nottingham in October; lacks pace and is suited by a test of stamina; acts on any going;
sold to D. Chapman 4,000 gns Doncaster November Sales. *C. Thornton.*

HYMNOS (FR) 5 ch.g. Luthier 126–Hairbrush (Sir Gaylord) (1981 12s³ **58**
12g³ 9g⁴ 10d 12f* 10fg* 13g² 12fg² 11.7d 12f² 12g 1982 12g 13.3f 12g³ 12f
12f 13.1f⁴ 10f³ 10g 10fg* 11f 12v³) workmanlike gelding; narrowly won handicap at Folkestone in September; stays 13f; acts on any going, but seems suited
by a sound surface; best in blinkers; has run respectably for an amateur rider;
none too genuine; sold to D. Elsworth 6,000 gns Newmarket Autumn Sales.
J. Bethell.

HYPERION PRINCESS 3 gr.f. Dragonara Palace 115–Hyperion Girl 59 —
(Royal Palm 131) (1981 8fg 1982 10.6s 12.2d) well behind in varied company. *W. Wharton.*

HYPNOSIS (USA) 3 ch.c. Unconscious–Puzzesca (Law and Order) (1981   **75**
5d 7g 7fg 1982 8g 10f² 12fg 10d 10.2g 11f² 15.5f² 11.5fg⁴ 14fg⁴ 12fg² 16s)
strong, deep-girthed colt; runner-up in £4,500 event and 3 maiden races; stays
well; acts well on firm going and is probably unsuited by soft. *D. Elsworth.*

I

IBTIHAJ (USA) 3 b.f. Raja Baba–Pas de Nom (Admiral's Voyage) (1981   **87**
5f 6fg⁴ 5fg* 5g³ 5f 1982 5f⁴ 5g 5f 5fg) well-made filly; sprint handicapper;
stays 6f; yet to race on a soft surface; ran moderately last 2 starts (blinkered
on second one). *H. T. Jones.*

ICE 4 b.g. Northfields–Carmine City 104 (Charlottesville 135) (1981 12s 12d   **55**
12d³ 10g² 10v 1982 10fg 10fg 10fg 10g 10fg* 10f³ 10f² 10fg³) well-made,
attractive gelding; got off mark in minor event at Brighton in July, beating
Hampshire by 5 lengths; will possibly stay beyond 1½m; yet to show he acts
on really soft going, but acts on any other; ran rather freely in blinkers third
outing. *I. Balding.*

ICE GALAXIE (USA) 2 b.f. Icecapade–High Galaxie (Irish Castle) (1982   **—**
6fg 6s 7d) Mar 7; small filly; first foal; dam won 6f claiming race at 4 yrs;
no worthwhile form in varied company. *R. Laing.*

ICEN 4 b.g. Tycoon II–Pepstep 88 (Polic 126) (1981 7fg² 8g⁴ 8fg² 8f² 8fg² 8fg*   **89**
9s² 1982 10s 10g* 8fg* 9g 8f) well-made, quite attractive gelding; won handicaps at Kempton in May (made all) and Ascot in July, on latter course putting up
a most courageous display when getting home from Silver Season and Teamwork
in a very close finish; not disgraced fourth start but was rather disappointing
final outing; stays 1¼m; suited by a sound surface. *M. Smyly.*

ICE PATROL (USA) 2 b.c. Far North 120–Mary Biz (T. V. Lark) (1982   **84**
7fg 8s 7s*) May 4; $325,000Y; smallish, close-coupled, quite attractive colt;
half-brother to 3 winners, notably 1981 Gimcrack winner Full Extent (by
Full Out); dam, unplaced 4 times, is half-sister to smart Terrible Tiger; got
up after none too clear a run to win maiden race at Redcar in October by head
from Burley Griffin; acts on soft going. *S. Norton.*

I-CHING 4 gr.f. No Mercy 126–China Girl 76 (Shantung 132) (1981 8s 8f   **—**
10.1fg 10.8fg² 10f 10fg* 10d 1982 8s) unfurnished filly; plater; suited by
1¼m+; acts on a firm surface (tailed off on soft on only outing of 1982); sometimes wears blinkers or a hood; has worn a tongue strap; has won for a 7-lb
claimer; tends to dwell at start; sold 900 gns Doncaster May Sales. *B. Richmond.*

IDEAL POINT (USA) 3 b.c. Val de l'Orne 130–Larkswing (Nasrullah) (1981 **125**
8v 10d³ 1982 10.5v* 10v 12fg 12s* 12v 12.5d 12f⁴ 12v 15.5v²) $60,000Y;
half-brother to several minor winners in USA; dam, sister to champion 2-y-o
filly Leallah, won twice at 3 yrs in USA; won maiden race at Maisons-Laffitte
in March and Prix de l'Avre at Longchamp in May; accounted for Le Nain
Jaune by 2 lengths in latter; also ran respectably in Prix du Lys at Chantilly,
Prix Maurice de Nieuil at Saint-Cloud and Prix Niel at Longchamp, and did
very well in Prix Royal-Oak at Longchamp again in October, going down by
a neck to stable-companion Denel; suited by a test of stamina; acts on any
going but clearly revels in the mud. *B. Secly, France.*

IDLE DAYS 3 b.f. Hittite Glory 125–Paresseuse 114 (Relko 136) (1981 5g²   **66**
1982 7g 10.6g³ 9g³ 8.2s 9s) compact, sturdy filly; split pasterns at 2 yrs;
third in maiden races at Haydock in August and York in September; will be
suited by a return to 1¼m or more. *W. Hastings-Bass.*

IDYLLIC GLEN 3 br.f. Furry Glen 121–Idylle (Dan Cupid 132) (1981 10.2g   **70**
1982 10s⁴ 12fg 17f 12f 12g³ 11.5f³ 12fg 14f² 14.6g 14g) narrow filly; plating-
class maiden; suited by 1¾m; acts on firm going, blinkered ninth start; suitable
mount for an inexperienced rider. *W. Marshall.*

IKE'S MISTRESS (USA) 2 b.f. Master Derby–Ike's Gamble (Correlation)   **85**
(1982 7f 5g* 5g 5s³) Apr 7; $75,000Y; workmanlike filly; good walker; half-
sister to 2 minor winners; dam stakes-placed winner of 8 sprint races; won
20-runner maiden race at Beverley in August by 3 lengths from Kynaston;
2½ lengths third of 7 to Prince Spy in £4,500 race at Ascot the following month,
better subsequent effort; bred to stay beyond 5f. *J. Hindley.*

ILAKAN 4 b.f. Forlorn River 124–Nikali 89 (Siliconn 121) (1981 8g 8d 1982 8s   **—**
8.2s 5f) plater; unlikely to stay 1m. *J. Berry.*

427

ILLICIT 3 b.g. He Loves Me 120–Princess Parthia (Parthia 152) (1981 6fg — 6g 5s² 5s* 1982 6fg⁴ 7fg 6g 8g 7fg 6g⁴) tall, sparely-made gelding; has a round action; fourth in £4,700 handicap at Newmarket in April and seller at Ayr in September; should stay 7f; acts well on soft going; blinkered third and final outings; sold out of J. Hindley's stable 2,900 gns Newmarket July Sales after third outing; sold to J. Harris 1,800 gns Doncaster November Sales. *W. Musson.*

I'LL SEE YOU 4 b.c. Averof 123–Keeps (Roan Rocket 128) (1981 8fg² 8fg 8fg² **100** 8d⁴ 1982 7d 8g 7fg 8f 8.5f 8fg* 8g* 8fg* 8f* 7.3g 8s 8fg²) rangy colt; good mover; improved considerably once raced with his tongue tied down and made most to win 4 successive handicaps at Brighton; beat Smokey Shadow decisively by 2 lengths on last occasion in August; also most unlucky at Epsom on fifth start, having race won when saddle slipped and jockey was unseated; stays 1m; acts on firm going; hasn't run well when tried in blinkers; had stiff tasks last 3 outings (no match for Mr Fluorocarbon in 2-horse race at Goodwood on final start); goes well on switchbacked tracks. *C. Brittain.*

IL PONTEVECCHIO 2 b.c. Tumble Wind–Netherside 73 (Alcide 136) (1982 **97** 6fg 7g 7g² 7g³ 7.3g 7s²) Apr 29; 13,500Y; neat, strong, quite attractive colt; half-brother to 3 minor winners; dam lacked pace; made much of running when close second in maiden race at Ayr in July and nursery (beaten a head, keeping on very gamely) at Sandown in October; will stay 1¼m; acts on soft going. *B. Hobbs.*

IMAGINATION 3 b.f. Relko 136–Romancing 82 (Romulus 129) (1981 7f* **89** 7g 7g² 1982 8.5fg² 12.3fg⁴ 9f* 8.5f 8fg³ 8f 8g 8g) small filly; won minor event at Wolverhampton in May; in frame several other starts; will stay 1¼m but appears not to stay 1½m; acts on firm going. *L. Cumani.*

I'M COMINGYOURWAY 2 ch.g. Music Boy 124–Observation 81 (Corona- — tion Year 124) (1982 5s 6d 6d) Apr 21; 11,500Y; tall, lengthy gelding; half-brother to fairly useful 1979 2-y-o 5f winner Ayoub (by The Go-Between) and a winner in Trinidad; dam stayed 1m; soundly beaten in varied company in the autumn. *N. Callaghan.*

I'M HOT (USA) 3 ch.f. Dike–Royal Hula (Raise A Native) (1981 6g* — 7.3s³ 1982 8.5f 8fg 7g) rather lightly-made filly; has a round action; fairly useful at 2 yrs; last in varied company in 1982; bred to stay 1¼m but is unlikely to unless she learns to settle; possibly needs some give in the ground. *M. Albina.*

IMMACULATE GIRL 2 b.f. Habat 127–Irish Elegance 60 (French Beige 127) **67** (1982 6g⁴ 6g) Mar 4; fair sort; poor walker; half-sister to 3 winners, including fairly useful 1976 2-y-o 6f winner Pasaguarda (by Runnymede); dam 1¼m winner; unquoted and distinctly backward, stayed on quite nicely when 4½ lengths fourth to No Remission in 14-runner maiden race at Redcar in August, easily better effort; will stay 7f. *R. D. Peacock.*

IMPECCABLE LADY 3 br.f. Silly Season 127–Gorse Bush (Hallez 131) (1981 **51** 6fg 5.8h 7.6s 7g 1982 10.1d 8g 8f³ 7f 7g* 7fg⁴ 10f² 10g) leggy, rather lightly-made filly; not the best of movers; plater; bought in 1,000 gns after winning at Leicester in August; stays 1¼m; acts on firm going; has been tried in blinkers. *C. Williams.*

IMPERIAL LANTERN 2 gr.c. Import 127–Eternal Triangle 55 (The Brianstan — 128) (1982 6d) May 9; sturdy colt; second foal; dam plater; 50/1 and in need of race, always behind in minor event won by Domynsky at Ripon in August. *J. Calvert.*

IMPERIAL ROSE 3 b.f. Imperial Crown 96–Rosie Glow (Royben 125) (1981 — 5fg 5f 6g 1982 6d 10g 8f 10.1fg 12fg 12fg 10.1fg 8.3g) poor plater. *R. Hoad.*

IMPERIUM 5 ch.g. Mount Hagen 127–Idea (Ragusa 137) (1981 14fg 12g — 1982 10fg) well-made gelding; stays 1¼m (well beaten over further at 4 yrs); yet to race on a soft surface; blinkered once in 1980. *J. Old.*

IMPLICATION (USA) 3 b.c. Tentam–Caught in the Act (Nijinsky 138) **88** (1981 7g 10g² 10s² 10fg* 12.3f* 12fg³ 16s 17.1s) rangy colt; successful in maiden race at Salisbury (odds on) and 4-runner minor event at Newcastle in May; off course 3 months before fifth start and finished well beaten on return;

stays 1½m; acts on any going; sold to A. Moore 3,200 gns Newmarket Autumn Sales. *G. Harwood.*

IMPORT EXPORT (FR) 4 b.g. Import 127–Lucy 83 (Sheshoon 132) (1981 — 12s 9.4g 12g³ 12g* 16.1f 13fg⁴ 14d 12f³ 18f 15g⁴ 16s³ 1982 12fg 16.1s) very big gelding; well beaten in 1982; stays well; usually a front runner; usually blinkered as a 3-y-o. *J. Wilson.*

IMPROVING RUN 3 b.g. Run The Gantlet–Well Rowed (Delta Judge) — (1981 NR 1982 12g) 1,300Y; lengthy gelding; fourth foal; dam lightly-raced sister to Swing Easy; bad last of 6 to Chalkey Road in minor event at Ripon in July (moved poorly to post). *W. A. Stephenson.*

IMPUDENT MISS 2 ch.f. Persian Bold 123–Pavello 94 (Crepello 136) (1982 **105** 5g⁴ 5g* 6f* 7f⁴ 6f³ 8fg* 7g) June 7; smallish filly; half-sister to 3-y-o 7f winner Good To Follow (by Wollow) and very smart sprinter Sayyaf (by Habitat); dam 1m winner and half-sister to smart Rymer; successful in maiden race at Tralee in June, minor race at Naas in July and 14-runner Silken Glider Stakes at Leopardstown in September; 14/1, led on line to beat Green Lucia and Top Rated by a head and a short head in last-named; also ran well when beaten 2 short heads by Certain Something in Oldtown Stud Stakes at Naas in August but finished only tenth of 13 to Countess Candy under top weight in Park Stakes at Leopardstown in October; suited by 1m; yet to race on a soft surface; game. *L. Browne, Ireland.*

I'M VEXED 3 b.c. High Top 131–Sassalya (Sassafras 135) (1981 5g² 5v 1982 — 8.2s 9v) strong, quite useful sort; ran creditably first start at 2 yrs; well beaten all subsequent outings; should stay 1m+; possibly unsuited by very soft going. *M. W. Easterby.*

INCANDESCE 3 b.c. Wolver Hollow 126–Lavington 64 (Ratification 129) **71** (1981 6g² 7fg² 8d³ 10g² 1982 12f 10g³ 12f 10.1g⁴ 12g 11.5fg² 10g) strong, rangy, good sort; good mover; useful performer at his best; below form most starts at 3 yrs; stays 1½m; blinkered fourth and final starts, running badly on latter. *P. Cole.*

INCARNADINE 3 ch.f. Hot Spark 126–Scarlet Thread 80 (Joshua 129) (1982 **66** 6s⁴ 7g*) May 21; short-coupled filly; third foal; half-sister to 3-y-o Hartnell Droom (by Grundy) and a winner in Belgium; dam won over 9f and 1¼m; bought in 2,000 gns after winning 11-runner seller at Wolverhampton in October by 3 lengths from Flori Wonder; suited by 7f. *P, Makin.*

INCA THIEF (USA) 3 b.g. Chieftain–Native Cindy (Raise A Native) (1981 **62** 6g 6g 7f³ 8d 1982 7.6d³ 8g 10fg) strong, useful sort; quite a modest maiden at his best; should stay 1¼m; sold 4,000 gns Newmarket Autumn Sales. *S. Norton.*

INCENSE 2 b.g. Martinmas 128–Cabochard (Nelcius 133) (1982 7f⁴ 7f 7.2s³) **65** Mar 5; 1,700Y; fair sort; half-brother to winners here and in Norway by Royben; dam of little account; in frame in maiden auction race at Catterick in July and seller at Haydock in October; will stay at least 1m; gelded after final outing. *J. Etherington.*

INCESTUOUS 3 b.g. Mummy's Pet 125–Autumn Breeze (King's Bench 132) **59 d** (1981 6g 6fg 1982 6s 7f² 7g 6g 8f 7g 6d 6s 7s) fair sort; good walker; plater nowadays; suited by 7f; acts on firm going; blinkered fourth and fifth starts; sold out of J. Hindley's stable 2,000 gns Newmarket July Sales after sixth outing. *B. McMahon.*

INCHGOWER 5 b.g. Ribero 126–Lutine Bell 82 (Luthier 126) (1981 NR **66** 1982 10.2g 8f 10f² 10fg* 12fg 11.7g* 12g* 12fg 12g²) workmanlike gelding; led well inside last furlong when first past post in handicaps at Brighton (3) and Windsor; hung left and was moved down a place after beating Pieroth by 2½ lengths on former course on last occasion in September; stays 1½m; acts on firm going; rather disappointing eighth start. *W. Wightman.*

INCH HIGH 3 ch.f. Starch Reduced 112–Billie Franks (Goldhill 125) (1981 — 5fg⁴ 5d⁴ 5s 5f² 5f³ 6f* 6g 1982 6f 6f) small, stocky filly; sprint plater; seems to act on any going; sold 490 gns Ascot October Sales. *V. Soane.*

IN CONFIDENCE 4 ch.f. Most Secret 119–Isis Rapide (I Say 125) (1981 — 7d⁴ 7f³ 8fg 1982 8f 8g) lightly-raced plater; probably stays 1m; has worn bandages in front. *D. Gandolfo.*

INDADO 4 b.g. Manado 130–Indian Beauty 93 (Indiana 129) (1981 14f 10fg — 1982 12d) little worthwhile form in maiden races and an amateur riders event; blinkered nowadays; sold 825 gns Ascot July Sales. *N. Kernick.*

INDEPENDENTIA 3 br.f. Home Guard 129–Gay Pariso 82 (Sir Gaylord) **52** (1981 6d 6g 1982 7fg 7f² 8fg 7d 8.2s⁴ 8s) well-made filly; quite modest; stays 1m. *B. Hills.*

INDIAN 2 ch.c. Great Nephew 126–Ardneasken 84 (Right Royal V 135) (1982 — p 7d 8d) May 16; neat, quite attractive colt; half-brother to several winners, including 3-y-o stayer Red Injun (by Mill Reef), high-class stayer Dakota (by Stupendous) and very useful middle-distance performer Warpath (by Sovereign Path); dam out-and-out stayer; showed up well until outpaced final 2f when seventh of 16 behind High Cannon in minor 1m event at Redcar in November, easily better effort; will be suited by 1¼m+; probably capable of improvement. *C. Thornton.*

INDIAN CALL 3 br.f. Warpath 113–Sing High 85 (Sound Track 132) (1981 **56** 6g 6g 6g 8fg 8g* 1982 8f 10d 7fg* 8g³ 7fg³ 7s) useful sort; good walker; plater; attracted no bid after winning at Newcastle in July; stays 1m; best in blinkers; has worn a tongue strap. *J. Fitzgerald.*

INDIAN DANCER 4 ch.f. Streak 119–Crop (Acropolis 132) (1981 NR 1982 — 13d 10.1fg) small filly; in rear in varied races, including a seller; has worn blinkers. *R. Sturdy.*

INDIAN GIVER 2 b.f. Prince Tenderfoot 126–Belaying Pin (Iron Peg **§§**) **99** (1982 6d 7fg* 7.5f* 6f* 8fg 5d⁴ 6d) Mar 1; IR 6,400F, IR 9,000Y; good-quartered filly; half-sister to 2 winners, including quite useful 5f performer Steel Charger (by Steel Heart); dam won at up to 7f in USA; gained her third win in succession in 8-runner nursery at Naas in August; had earlier won maiden race at Down Royal (easily) and 8-runner nursery at Gowran Park (by a neck from Sept); stays 7f well (in rear in Group 3 Silken Glider Stakes at Leopardstown when tried over 1m); probably acts on any going. *K. Prendergast, Ireland.*

INDIAN KING (USA) 4 b.c. Raja Baba–Protest (Rash Prince) (1981 8g* **128** 7fg² 7g* 7s 7g 1982 8g³ 7d² 7fg* 7fg* 7.2h* 6f* 6f³ 6.5fg² 6f* 6g*)
Guy Harwood had another outstandingly successful season in 1982, sending out one hundred and twenty winners in Britain, a total bettered in modern times only by Henry Cecil (one hundred and twenty-eight in 1979) and Peter Walwyn (one hundred and twenty-one in 1975). Harwood's success was broadly based but his strike-rate with the handful of older horses he trained was particularly notable. Five of them had a full season and between them they won twenty races. The game front-running handicapper Big Pal, reportedly invaluable as a lead-horse, won six races in succession; the miler Home Coming returned from a lengthy lay-off to win a fairly valuable handicap at Doncaster; Kalaglow won four of his six races, including the Coral-Eclipse Stakes and the King George VI and Queen Elizabeth Diamond Stakes; the modest Silver Ruler was well

Cork and Orrery Stakes, Ascot—Indian King wins from Vaigly Star with Great Eastern in third place

Vernons Sprint Cup, Haydock—a splendid performance from Indian King. Great Eastern (hidden by winner) finishes second, Fearless Lad (blaze) third, Sayyaf (right) fourth and Sharpo (left) fifth

placed to win three times; and Indian King won six good races from ten starts. The last-named's success must have given particular satisfaction as Indian King had more than his share of problems in his younger days. A really big, rangy colt who was one of the stable's most expensive purchases when bought for 130,000 dollars at Keeneland as a yearling, he was a contemporary of To-Agori-Mou and Recitation and gave the impression in his homework as a two-year-old that he, like them, was in the top flight. However his problems began on his very first outing, when odds on for a minor event at Newmarket: he ran into trouble and returned home injured, apparently with a pulled muscle in a shoulder. Indian King reportedly recovered from the injury quite quickly but had several other setbacks which kept him off the racecourse for nearly a year. On his return he quickly made up for lost time, winning the Surplice Stakes at Goodwood and the valuable Battle of Britain Handicap at Doncaster from only five outings, but it wasn't until 1982 that he fully realised his potential.

Indian King thrived on racing as a four-year-old and became a formidable opponent for the very best. After being placed in the Doncaster Mile on the first day of the season, over a distance a shade too far for him in good company, and a handicap at Newcastle, where the ground was softer than ideal, he hardly looked back. He got off the mark for the season with an impressive win over Beeleigh in the Autobar Victoria Cup at Ascot and then made the step up from handicap company without any difficulty, adding wins in the Prix du Palais Royal at Longchamp, the John of Gaunt Stakes at Haydock and the Cork and Orrery Stakes at Royal Ascot before meeting his next defeat. He impressed each time with his zest for racing, and at Haydock and Ascot he broke course records; on extremely fast going on the former course, when having his second outing in a week, he beat the record set by Kris without having to be ridden out. Such strides was Indian King making that three weeks after the Cork and Orrery he started a well-backed favourite for the William Hill July Cup at Newmarket, one of the most strongly-contested sprints of the season. Indian King's run was halted temporarily at Newmarket: he was beaten one and three quarter lengths into third behind Sharpo (widely expected to find the going

431

too firm) and Vaigly Star, who'd been second in the Cork and Orrery. He made unusually heavy weather of getting to the front and was overhauled on the hill. He also ran a little below his best on his next outing, when going down by a length to the French filly Exclusive Order in the Prix Maurice de Gheest at Deauville, but after a well-deserved rest of just over a month, his longest all season, he returned in September to win the Vernons Sprint Cup at Haydock and the Diadem Stakes at Ascot.

Indian King didn't receive all due credit for his win in the Vernons; some reports on the race concentrated on the failure of the odds-on favourite Sharpo whose jockey claimed he'd lost his chance through being barged on the home turn. If there was interference Indian King had no part in it, and he won most convincingly, on merit. Looking big and well after his rest—his trainer was reportedly afraid that he might need the race—Indian King was always going well, pulling keenly as he often did, and he was sent after the pace-setting Sayyaf two furlongs from home. He had his race won in a matter of strides, forged clear, and won easing down by two lengths from the strong-finishing Great Eastern. At Ascot he had to fight quite a bit harder as the magnificent Northern filly Soba, another tremendously popular sprinter, proved a tenacious rival. Soba, having her first outing in pattern-race company, was soon bowling along in front as usual and Indian King tracked her until asked to quicken over a furlong out. Indian King was soon on top and looked for a moment as though he'd come clear, but Soba made him fight nearly all the way before Indian King prevailed by a length and a half. It was said afterwards that Indian King might have one more race in the Bisquit Cognac Challenge Stakes at Newmarket. It would have been interesting to see him tried over seven furlongs again, a distance which for a time had seemed his best, but the race went by without him. He would have faced two worthy opponents in Noalcoholic and Motavato.

	Raja Baba	Bold Ruler	Nasrullah
	(b 1968)	(b 1954)	Miss Disco
Indian King (USA)		Missy Baba	Tulyar or My Babu
(b.c. 1978)		(b 1958)	Uvira
	Protest	Rash Prince	Prince John
	(bl 1970)	(b 1960)	Prompt Impulse
		Dynamis	Sailor
		(b 1959)	Dynamite

Indian King looks a most promising stallion proposition for he has a pedigree to match his racecourse record, his physique and his admirable temperament. The sire Raja Baba, a son of Bold Ruler, was a smart performer at his best and won seven times over six furlongs during four seasons. He was leading sire of two-year-olds in the States in 1976 with his first runners and in 1980 he was the top sire overall and the leading sire of two-year-olds again. The 1978 Middle Park winner Junius is Raja Baba's best winner over here apart from Indian King; in 1982 he was represented also by Indian King's useful stable-companion Silk Sari. The dam Protest is from the family of the successful stallions Ack Ack, Chieftain, Sham and Tom Rolfe, all of whom descend from Indian King's fourth dam Minnewaska. Protest is the best of four winners produced by Dynamis, an unraced half-sister to the smart stakes winner Toluene.

Diadem Stakes, Ascot—Indian King holds on well from Soba.
Blue Singh finishes third

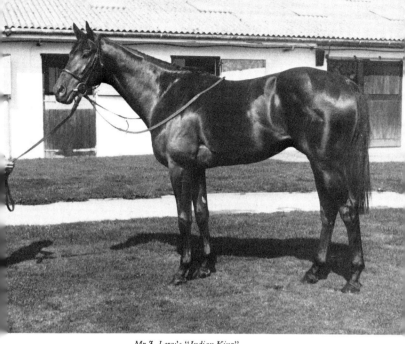

Mr J. Levy's "Indian King"

Protest was a very useful stakes winner at two and three, successful five times at up to a mile. Indian King is her third foal; her first, the Nodouble filly No Test, won twice at up to six furlongs as a two-year-old.

Indian King is to stand at the Irish National Stud alongside such as African Sky, Ahonoora, Lord Gayle, Sallust, and Tap On Wood at a fee of IR £6,500 with the October 1st concession. He was purchased by Stallion Investments Ltd shortly after the Cork and Orrery and leased back to the owner for racing; the Irish National Stud later took a half share. Two hundred and fifty applications were received for 1983 nominations and he's obviously going to be a popular stallion. *G. Harwood.*

INDIAN LADY 2 b.f. African Sky 124–Engage (Whistling Wind 123) (1982 **90** 5fg 5f 5.3fg³ 5g 5f³ 5f⁴ 5d* 6fg* 5fg) Mar 11; 28,000Y; well-made, quite attractive filly; second foal; dam won from 5f to 1m in Ireland; made all in maiden race at Chester and minor event at Epsom in August; better suited by 6f than by 5f; yet to race on very soft going, but acts on any other; blinkered fifth and sixth starts, on latter occasion being disqualified from second place in Goodwood nursery after failing to keep a straight course. *G. Lewis.*

INDIAN MOONSHINE 2 ch.f. Warpath 113–Midsummer Madness 66 (Silly **—** Season 127) (1982 6d 9s) Feb 18; lengthy filly; good walker; third foal; sister to 3-y-o 1½m winner Dangerous Moonlite and half-sister to a winner; dam won over 1½m; no worthwhile form in 2 autumn races, in first slowly away; looks the sort to do better in time. *C. Thornton.*

INDIAN RAJAH 2 b.c. Sallust 134–Light House (Primera 131) (1982 6g* **106** 6fg* 7v*) Apr 4; 3,400F, IR 35,000Y; half-brother to Irish 5f winner Sea Maiden (by Windjammer) and a winning hurdler; dam half-sister to top-class German horse Luciano; unbeaten in 3 races at Windsor and Lingfield (2), on final outing taking advantage of lenient mark to win valuable John Sutcliffe Trophy Nursery at Lingfield in October by 8 lengths under 7-7; will stay 1m; acts on a firm surface, but clearly goes extremely well in the mud. *J. Sutcliffe.*

INDIAN TRAIL (USA) 4 b.c. Apalachee 137–Majestic Street (Majestic Prince) **102** (1981 8d* 8.2fg² 10.4g² 8d⁴ 10fg* 10fg* 10d³ 10.2fg⁴ 9g 1982 10.5f² 10f³ 8fg 10.5f⁴ 10fg³ 8g* 9d² 10g) neat colt; good mover; led over a furlong out and ran on strongly to beat Cordite Spear by 2½ lengths in £7,400 Rose of York Handicap at York in August; also in frame on same course (twice), Redcar (Zetland Gold Cup), Goodwood (Trident Chesterfield Cup) and Newmarket, finishing strongly when neck second to Century City in 29-runner William Hill Cambridgeshire on last-named in October; effective at 1m and stays 1¼m; probably acts on any going but is suited by some give underfoot nowadays; sent to USA. *B. Hills.*

INDULGENCE 3 ch.f. Prominer 125–Perennial Twinkle (Continuation 120) **83** (1981 8d² 1982 8f* 10f² 10g* 12g* 12s* 10d³) successful in maiden race at Carlisle, handicaps at Beverley and Edinburgh and apprentice race at Chepstow; stays 1½m; acts on any going; tended to hang final start. *Sir Mark Prescott.*

INDY 2 ch.f. Indigenous 121–Dracula's Daughter (Hook Money 124) (1982 5f **77** 5g 5fg 5f² 6fg² 5s 5s 6g) Apr 10; workmanlike filly; fourth reported foal; dam poor performer; runner-up in minor events at Catterick and Redcar in September; stays 6f; best form on top-of-the-ground; has worn bandages in front. *A. Bailey.*

IN FAVOUR 2 b.f. Bustino 136–Grazia 90 (Aureole 132) (1982 7fg³ 7f) Apr **73** 19; sister to Irish 3-y-o 7f winner Graziano and half-sister to 2 winners, including useful 6f and 7f winner Faiz (by Prince Tenderfoot); dam 2-y-o 6f winner; came out clear best of newcomers when 4½ lengths third of 19 to Liberty Tree in maiden race at Chepstow in August; favourite, only seventh of 14 to Zariya in similar event at Brighton the following month. *P. Walwyn.*

INFINITE STAR 2 ch.c. St Columbus 98–Bloomsbury Girl 63 (Weepers Boy — 124) (1982 6f 8.2s) good-bodied colt; third foal; brother to quite modest 1m winner T.V. Star; dam won 5f seller; backward, well behind in autumn minor events at Pontefract and Nottingham. *T. Taylor.*

INGHAM 10 ch.g. Silver Shark 129–Australe (Sicambre 135) (1981 NR 1982 — 9fg) of little account on flat nowadays; quite a modest jumper. *Mrs M. Nesbitt.*

INHABITED 3 b.c. Habitat 134–Infra Green 121 (Laser Light 118) (1981 NR — 1982 8fg) 102,000Y; strong, good-bodied colt; first foal; dam won from 6f to 1½m, including Prix Ganay; 12/1 and very burly, chased along throughout when tailed-off last of 19 to Always Welcome in Wood Ditton Stakes at Newmarket in April; sent to USA. *G. Lewis.*

INITIAL TRY 3 b.g. Jimsun 121–Demta (Astec 128) (1981 NR 1982 8d — 11.7f 7g) second live foal; brother to seemingly poor animal; dam won from 6f to 1¼m in France; well behind in maiden races and a seller; blinkered final start. *K. Brassey.*

IN MOTION 2 br.f. Monsanto 121–Thorganby Melody (Highland Melody 112) **91** (1982 5s³ 5s 5fg* 5f² 5fg³ 5g 5g) Mar 2; 4,400F, IR 7,200Y; small ex-Irish filly; first foal; dam never ran; soon had race sewn up when winning 7-runner maiden event at Chester in May by 2½ lengths from Miami Dolphin; unsuccessful subsequently in better company but confirmed herself speedy, failing by 1½ lengths to hold off Shicklah in Uplands Park Acorn Stakes at Epsom, finishing 3½ lengths third to Jonacris in £3,850 event at Ripon and 4 lengths sixth of 8 to Cat O'Nine Tails in Prince of Wales's Stakes at York; always likely to be best over sharp 5f; has run respectably on soft going but is probably better served by a sound surface; trained by P. Doyle in Ireland first 3 starts. *J. W. Watts.*

IN RHYTHM 5 b.h. Gay Fandango 132–Procession 118 (Sovereign Path 125) **62** (1981 6s 6s 6d⁴ 6d³ 7fg⁴ 6g* 6fg 6fg 7v 7s 7d 1982 6d⁴ 6f² 7f 7fg 6g* 6g* 6fg² 6fg³ 7fg 6g² 6fg³ 7s 6s²) strong horse; successful in handicaps at Ayr (apprentices) and Hamilton in June; best at 6f; probably acts on any going; good mount for an apprentice; blinkered last 3 starts in 1981; lost chance at start third outing. *P. Makin.*

IN SLIPS 3 b.g. Mount Hagen 127–Get Ready 91 (On Your Mark 125) (1981 **66** 5g² 6s 6f* 6d⁴ 6g⁴ 6fg 5g 1982 6f² 6g* 6f 5fg 6f 8g² 8fg 8.2g³ 8d 8fg) narrow, rather leggy gelding; awarded 24-runner handicap at Windsor in May; suited by 1m; apparently needs a sound surface; sold 4,700 gns Newmarket Autumn Sales. *Sir Mark Prescott.*

INSPIRED 2 ch.c. Star Appeal 133–Easy Swinger (Swing Easy 126) (1982 6f **66**
7f³ 7f 7g⁴) Apr 23; compact colt; fourth foal; dam never ran; plating-class
maiden; will be suited by 1m. *P. Kelleway.*

INTERCO (USA) 2 ch.c. Intrepid Hero–Yale Coed (Majestic Prince) (1982 **113**
5.5s* 7g³ 5.5g 7g 8fg³ 5g² 7f⁴ 7.5v⁴) Apr 21; $200,000Y; attractive colt; third
foal; half-brother to a winner in USA by Triple Bend; dam, very useful winner
at up to 6f at 2 yrs in USA, is granddaughter of outstanding broodmare
Exclusive; won newcomers race at Maisons-Laffitte in June by 5 lengths;
subsequently ran well over a variety of distances, finishing about 3 lengths fifth
to Ma Biche in 5.5f Prix Robert Papin on same course, ½-length third to Sherbaz
in 1m Prix des Foals at Deauville, ¾-length second to Go Jogging in 5f Prix
d'Arenberg at Chantilly, 4½ lengths fourth to dead-heaters Deep Roots and
Maximova in 7f Prix de la Salamandre at Longchamp and ½-length fourth to
Bal des Fees in 7.5f Prix Thomas Bryon at Saint-Cloud; stays 1m; acts on any
going; slipped at start and took no part fourth outing. *F. Boutin, France.*

INTONE 2 br.c. Relkino 131–Singing (Petingo 135) (1982 5g²) Feb 15; **75 p**
19,000Y; big, strong, rangy colt; third foal; half-brother to winning miler
Smashing Fellow (by Dragonara Palace) and a winner in Italy; dam never ran;
4/1 but green and definitely backward, shaped extremely well in circumstances
when beaten 8 lengths by odds-on Cat O'Nine Tails in 6-runner £3,300 event at
Sandown in June; certain to do much better at 7f+. *G. Harwood.*

IN TOP FORM 3 br.f. Lochnager 132–Lady Jester 108 (Bleep-Bleep 134) (1981 **—**
NR 1982 5f) 8,500Y (privately); lengthy filly; half-sister to 3 winners, including
fairly useful sprinter Friendly Jester (by Be Friendly); dam won seven 5f races;
10/1, moved poorly to post when last of 17 to Soba in maiden race at Thirsk in
May. *R. Boss.*

INTREPIDORA (USA) 3 b.f. Intrepid Hero–Cantadora II (Canthare) (1981 **—**
NR 1982 8d 12g 11d 12fg) $160,000Y; half-sister to numerous winners,
including stakes winners Loved (by Jaipur) and Struck Out (by Nashua), and
useful 1m and 1¼m filly Rock Gold (by Fleet Nasrullah); dam won 4 races in
Argentina, including Argentine Oaks; beaten some way in maiden races; pulled
up final start. *G. Harwood.*

INUVIK 2 b.c. Ashmore 125–Star Relation (Star Gazer 123) (1982 7g 7fg* 8s) **82**
Apr 21; IR 2,800F, 9,400Y; attractive, shapely colt; good walker; has a nice,
easy action; half-brother to fairly useful 1976 2-y-o 5f and 6f winner Star
Attention (by Northfields); dam Irish maiden: despite having plenty to do at
halfway and despite hanging left in closing stages, got up to win 7-runner minor
event at Chester in July by neck from Miss Sinclair; favourite when eighth of 18
in nursery won by Moon Jester at Warwick 3 months later; should stay 1m; acts
on a firm surface. *B. Hills.*

INVER BRAE 2 ch.c. Vitiges 132–Brookfield Miss 73 (Welsh Pageant 132) **—**
(1982 8s) Apr 25; strong, close-coupled colt; first foal; dam showed a little
ability at 2 yrs; unquoted and burly, dwelt and soon pushed along when behind
in 19-runner maiden race at Warwick in October; sold German International
Bloodstock 1,600 gns Newmarket Autumn Sales. *I. Balding.*

INVERSALE 2 b.g. Touch Paper 113–Hello Amy 70 (Forlorn River 124) (1982 **66**
5s⁴ 5f³ 6f 7fg 6g) Feb 12; IR 7,800F, 22,000Y; well-grown, quite attractive
gelding; brother to useful sprinter Touch Boy; dam placed over 5f at 2 yrs;
6½ lengths third of 12 to Ridge Heights in maiden race at Salisbury in May,
best effort; not certain to stay 7f; blinkered final outing. *A. Jarvis.*

INVINCIBLE SHADOW 2 b.f. Abwah 118–Pardilly 71 (Pardao 120) (1982 **—**
5fg 7g 8s 10s) May 3; big, well-made filly; half-sister to 2 minor winners;
dam stayed 1½m; behind in maiden races and a £4,500 event; blinkered final
start. *D. Sasse.*

INVITED (USA) 3 ch.c. Vaguely Noble 140–Exotic Age (Olden Times) (1981 **—**
NR 1982 10d) third foal; dam very useful sprinter; well beaten in 18-runner
maiden race won by First Mint at Nottingham in April. *J. Dunlop.*

INVITING 3 b. or br.c. Be My Guest 126–Hardiemma 81 (Hardicanute 130) **90 ?**
(1981 NR 1982 9fg 11g* 10.1fg⁴ 12f² 13.8f) IR 70,000Y; leggy colt; poor
mover; half-brother to 3 winners, including 1¼m and 13f winner Regal Heiress
(by English Prince) and Derby and Irish Sweeps Derby winner Shirley Heights
(by Mill Reef); dam won at up to 11f; decisively won maiden race at Ayr in

May; fine neck second to Yard Bird in £3,400 event at Newmarket in July but ran very disappointingly in handicap at Catterick following month (never striding out well and possibly unsuited by course); suited by 1½m; yet to race on a soft surface. *F. Durr.*

IOWA 3 br.c. So Blessed 130–Montana (Mossborough 126) (1981 6s⁴ 1982 76 8s* 9f 8f 10f² 9g⁴ 10d³ 11s⁴) leggy, narrow colt; won maiden race at Ayr in March; placed afterwards in Andy Capp Handicap at Redcar (good 4 lengths second to Mill Plantation after being hampered on turn) and £5,200 handicap at Ayr; suited by 1¼m; acts on any going. *C. Thornton.*

IRENE'S CHOICE 2 gr.c. Young Emperor 133–Brontewood (Proud Clarion) — (1982 7fg 7f 7g 7g 7fg) May 15; 1,500Y; small colt; second foal; dam never ran; well beaten in maiden and minor events; sold Norsk Jockey Club 2,300 gns Doncaster November Sales. *S. Wiles.*

IRENE'S PRIDE 2 b.f. The Brianstan 128–Zip Flip (Bleep-Bleep 134) (1982 63 5g 5f⁴ 5f⁴ 5.8f* 5g⁴ 6fg 6g³ 8.2g 6s) Mar 26; leggy filly; sister to fairly useful 5f performer Brianston Zipper; dam well beaten in 3 outings; bought in 2,200 gns after winning seller at Bath in July by a short head from odds-on Muffin; respectable third of 5 in nursery won by Linda's Fantasy at Leicester the following month; stays 6f but isn't bred to get 1m; acts on firm going; blinkered second start; said to be a difficult ride but goes well for apprentice G. Thomas. *A. Bailey.*

IRISH BAR (USA) 2 ch.c. Barrera–Lady Regan (King of the Tudors 129) — (1982 6d) May 7; $75,000Y; quite attractive colt; third foal; half-brother to a minor winner by Go Marching; dam never ran; 20/1 and in need of race, chased leaders to halfway in 21-runner maiden race won by Spanish Place at Newmarket in October. *L. Cumani.*

IRISH CLIPPER 2 b.f. Windjammer (USA)–Rachel Rose (King's Company — 124) (1982 5d) June 11; IR 4,400Y; sparely-made filly; second living produce; dam unraced twin; backed at long odds, chased leaders throughout, pushed along hands and heels, when about 8½ lengths sixth of 17 to So True in maiden race at Salisbury in June. *P. Cole.*

IRISH COMMANDMENT 5 ch.g. Shiny Tenth 120–Ritruda 95 (Roi Dagobert — 128) (1981 6g 7fg 6g⁴ 7g 7.2s 8fg³ 6f⁴ 7.6fg 7fg 6f 7fg 6g 7g 1982 7f 7.6g 6g 6v 5s 6s) sturdy gelding; good mover; disappointing handicapper; stays 1m; seems to act on any going; sometimes blinkered; has worn bandages in front; inconsistent. *D. Elsworth.*

IRISH CORN 2 b.f. Oats 126–Belleek (Never Say Die 137) (1982 8fg) Mar — 10; IR 9,200Y; sister to 3-y-o Markenfield and half-sister to 3 winners, including useful 1972 Irish 2-y-o 5f and 6f winner Sancerre (by Golden Horus); dam placed at up to 1m; last of 13 in maiden race at Beverley in September. *P. Haslam.*

IRISH FLAX 3 b.g. Connaught 130–Blue Linnet 96 (Habitat 134) (1981 — 5g 6fg 7.6s 10s 1982 10d 12g 10f) strong, good-quartered gelding; poor form, including in a seller; probably stays 1¼m; has been bandaged in front. *A. Ingham.*

IRISH GRENADIER 3 b.c. Home Guard 129–Mare D'Erba (Habitat 134) 72 (1981 6g⁴ 6g³ 6f* 7g 7g⁴ 1982 8.2d 8f 10d 8f³ 8.3g⁴ 10fg² 8.3g 10.1d) attractive, rangy colt; in frame in handicaps; stays 1¼m; acts well on firm ground; blinkered seventh start; sold 1,000 gns Goffs November Sales. *J. Dunlop.*

IRISH KEEP 4 b.c. Connaught 130–Golden Keep 77 (Worden II 129) (1981 95 d 8g 12g 12s² 14s² 12.3g² 10fg* 12fg² 10d² 10.2fg⁴ 1982 12s 10g³ 10fg³ 10fg* 10d 11.5f⁴ 11d 10.5s 10d⁴) strong, sturdy colt; finished first in handicaps at Sandown and Redcar, but was relegated to third after hanging badly at Sandown; mainly disappointing afterwards; best form at around 1¼m nowadays, but has run respectably at up to 1¾m; acts on any going; seems best when held up; none too genuine and was blinkered last 3 outings; sold 22,000 gns Newmarket Autumn Sales. *H. Wragg.*

IRISH RIFLE 5 b.h. Scottish Rifle 127–Sunsaly 75 (Sallymount 125) (1981 46 18s 12.2fg³ 12v⁴ 12f 14d 12fg³ 10.1fg 11.7fg 12f³ 1982 13fg 11.7f² 12f 10.1d 11.7fg 11.5f) well-made horse; middle-distance handicapper; suited by firm going; has been tried in blinkers; has worn bandages in front; pulled up lame final start. *R. Laing.*

IRISH WILLIAMS 2 ch.g. Shiny Tenth 120–Tweetie Pie (Falcon 131) (1982 — 6g) May 12; fifth foal; brother to 7f winner My Sylvia and 1m seller winner

Marshgate; dam never ran; 66/1, behind in 19-runner minor event at Windsor in August. *D. Marks.*

ISHKOMANN 3 b.c. Faunus–Irova (Iron Liege) (1981 6f 7f$_g^2$ 7g^2 7d 8.2d 1982 10s 9g 11.7f^4 11.7f^4 11.7f* 16h 12d^3 12g^3 12f^3 10.1d 12f$_g$ 11.7s 13.8d^4) **68** strong, good-looking colt; excellent mover; won maiden race at Bath in May; stays 13f; seems to act on any going; sold 10,500 gns Newmarket Autumn Sales. *T. Robson.*

ISLA 3 b.f. Reform 132–Krafty Kate 73 (Klairon 131) (1981 6f$_g$ 1982 7f — 6f$_g$ 6f$_g$) well-made filly; poor plater. *C. Pinkham.*

ISLAND WALK 4 b.f. Palm Track 122–Ladyfold 60 (Never Dwell 89) (1981 **47** 7s* 7v 7f$_g$ 7g^3 7f$_g$ 6g* 6f$_g$* 6d 6g^3 7g* 1982 6s* 6f^4 6d 6f$_g$ 8f 8.2s) small filly; did very well in sellers in 1981; narrowly won non-selling handicap at Hamilton in April; stays 7f; acts on any going. *W. Haigh.*

ISLE OF HALF 2 b.g. Monsanto 121–Quick Half (Quorum 126 or Caliban — 123 (1982 8s 8.2s) May 19; well-grown, close-coupled gelding; second foal; dam won over hurdles; backward, always behind in maiden races at Newcastle and Haydock (tenth of 11) in October. *D. McCain.*

ISLE OF SHONA 3 b.g. Connaught 130–Abbot's Isle 116 (Welsh Abbot **62** 131) (1981 NR 1982 10f 10g 12g^3 15.8d 12s^2 12g*) strong, workmanlike gelding; not a good mover; half-brother to 1978 2-y-o 5f winner Abbotsinch (by Bold Lad, Ire); dam very speedy; reportedly cracked a cannon bone at 2 yrs; plater; bought in 1,200 gns after winning at Edinburgh in October; stays 1½m; acts on soft going; sold to M. Pipe 2,600 gns Newmarket Autumn Sales. *Sir Mark Prescott.*

ISMORE (USA) 2 b.c. Libra's Rib 121–Lesse (Noblesse Oblige 99) (1982 **85** 5f$_g$ 6f 6f 7f 5f$_g^3$ 5g* 5g^4 5g 6s^2 7v^3) Apr 10; compact, sturdy colt; half-brother to 3 winners in USA; dam never ran; made all in 15-runner maiden race at Hamilton in August; in frame afterwards in £3,600 event at Goodwood (blinkered) and valuable nurseries at Haydock and Ascot; will stay 1m; has run respectably on firm ground but goes particularly well in the mud; good mount for an apprentice. *N. Guest.*

ISOM DART (USA) 2 b.c. Bold Forbes–Shellshock 110 (Salvo 129) (1981 **68** 6g 7f$_g^4$ 7f$_g$ 8s 1982 12f 11.7f 14g^2) neat, well-made, attractive colt; good walker; quite modest; stays 1¾m. *B. Hills.*

ITALIAN MASTER 5 b.g. Workboy 123–Ritratto (Pinturischio 116) (1981 **44** 8.2g 8f$_g^2$ 8g^4 8f$_g$ 8.2s 1982 10f 8f 8.2f$_g$* 8f^4 8f) big gelding; plater nowadays; bought in 1,800 gns after winning at Hamilton in May; stays 1m; acts on firm going and is possibly unsuited by soft; wears bandages; sold 650 gns Ascot October Sales. *D. Garraton.*

ITALIAN SUNRISE 2 b.c. The Brianstan 128–Roman Dawn 87 (Neron **76** 121) (1982 7.6v 8s 8s) Apr 25; well-made, good sort; half-brother to 3 winners here and abroad; dam won at up to 1¼m; staying-on 9 lengths fifth of 26 to Magic Rarity in maiden race at Sandown in October, second outing and best effort. *R. Price.*

IT'S A PLEASURE 2 gr.f. Runnymede 123–Ginger Puss (Worden II 129) **85** (1982 5f$_g$ 5f$_g$ 5d^2 5f^2 5f 5f$_g^2$ 5f^3 5s^3 5v^3) Apr 24; compact filly; good walker; half-sister to 2 minor winners; dam never ran; placed in maiden events and a nursery; has raced only at 5f, but gives impression will be suited by 6f; acts on any going; consistent. *W. Wightman.*

ITS FOR SURE 2 br.f. Ardoon 124–Schull (Yorick II 127) (1982 5g 5f^4 **63** 5s) Mar 31; 9,400Y; quite attractive filly; good walker; half-sister to several winners, including very useful 6f to 7f performer Step Ahead (by Continuation); dam never ran; little worthwhile form; off course 3 months after second outing. *B. Gubby.*

IT'S FOR YOU 2 gr.g. Town Crier 119–Flora Day 92 (Floribunda 136) (1982 **85** 5f$_g^4$ 6f 6g^2 6g) Mar 2; 4,200Y; well-grown, fair sort; sixth foal; dam stayed 1m; in frame twice at Windsor, better effort when 1½ lengths second of 17 to Indian Rajah in minor event (blinkered) in August; suited by 6f and should stay 7f; out of his depth in Moet and Chandon Zukunfts-Rennen on final start. *B. Gubby.*

Mr C. d'Alessio's "Ivano"

IT'S HEAVEN 2 b.f. African Sky 124–Coumfea (Gulf Pearl 117) (1982   **74**
5g 5fg⁴ 6f³ 6g) Mar 28; 4,600Y; tall, close-coupled filly; second foal; dam ran
only once; ran easily best race when 2½ lengths third of 18 to Shareef Dancer
in maiden event at Newmarket in August, weakening only in final furlong;
always struggling in nursery at Ayr the following month; suited by 6f; sweated
up very badly second start. *R. Hollinshead.*

IT'S KELLY 2 b.g. Pitskelly 122–Reelin Star (Star Gazer 123) (1982 5fg⁴   **77**
5fg 5f⁴) Jan 22; IR 7,000Y; useful-looking gelding; brother to 1981 Irish 2-y-o
5f winner Reelin Elly and half-brother to a winner in Malaya; dam unraced
half-sister to very useful sprinter Reelin Jig; fourth in 7-runner newcomers
race won by Rutland at Goodwood in May, best effort; not raced after June.
G. Balding.

IT'S MAGIC 6 b.m. Miracle 116–Tammy's Princess 78 (Tamerlane 128) (1981   **—**
NR 1982 8f 7f) bad plater; has sweated up; has worn blinkers. *W. Elsey.*

IT'S ONLY ME 3 b.f. The Brianstan 128–Toplady 85 (Rockavon 120) (1981   **—**
5s 6d 1982 8g 6fg 8.3g) fair sort; bad mover; little worthwhile form in varied
company, including selling. *Mrs B. Waring.*

IVANO (CAN) 3 ch.c. Snow Knight 125–Smiling Jacqueline (Hilarious) (1981 **119**
7g* 1982 9fg* 10.4fg* 12fg³ 8fg³)
    The name of Ivano had become almost forgotten by the season's close,
for he hadn't been seen out since running in the St James's Palace Stakes
at Royal Ascot. He's a very useful horse, though, and if he returns fit and well
he should win more good races. Ivano started a heavily-backed favourite for
the St James's Palace, partly as a result of reports that he'd finished ahead of
the Queen Anne Stakes winner Mr Fluorocarbon in a recent gallop, but he was
beaten seven and a half lengths into third place behind Dara Monarch; the

winner and Tender King were much too sharp for him over the last two furlongs, and on this showing Ivano needs further than a mile to be seen to best advantage. Ivano had been running well over longer trips earlier, winning the nine-furlong Gerry Feilden Memorial Stakes at Newmarket by a neck from Electric and the ten-and-a-half-furlong Dee Stakes at Chester by three parts of a length from Spanish Pool, and finishing third of nine in the Schroder Life Predominate Stakes, a classic trial over a mile and a half at Goodwood. Ivano's trainer thought the horse didn't stay the mile and a half; we thought he did stay it and put up probably his best performance in going down by only half a length and the same behind one of the Derby favourites Peacetime and Touching Wood (the latter received 8 lb). The course Ivano's future programme follows will be interesting to note.

Ivano (Can) (ch.c. 1979)	Snow Knight (ch 1971)	Firestreak (br 1956)	Pardal
			Hot Spell
		Snow Blossom (br 1957)	Flush Royal
			Ariana
	Smiling Jacqueline (b 1969)	Hilarious (b 1950)	Bimelech
			Laughter
		Fulfiliole (ch 1960)	Beau Gar
			Filiole

Ivano is a strong, good-bodied, attractive colt, the first foal of his dam, an American mare. By American standards the dam stayed well, since she managed to win at up to a mile and a quarter, and looking at the pedigree there's not much in it that would lead one to suppose that Ivano wouldn't stay a mile and a half, though it's true that his dam's sire Hilarious was a sprinter. In his all-too-short career to date Ivano has encountered only top-of-the-ground conditions. *H. Cecil.*

IVER SAGA 2 ch.f. Sagaro 133–Florrie Ford 79 (Kelly 122) (1982 7d² 6s)   **74** May 6; sparely-made filly; half-sister to 2 winners, including fairly useful 1m winner Rheinford (by Rheingold); dam won over 6f at 2 yrs; 33/1 and in need of race, finished very fast when length second of 15 to Armonit in maiden event at Leicester in October; again finished well when seventh of 19 behind Hawk Lady in similar race on same course in November; will be better suited by 1m+. *R. Williams.*

IVORY KEYS 2 ch.f. Octavo 115–Whitewood 74 (Worden II 129) (1982 5fg   — 5f 6s 6g) Apr 29; fair sort; half-sister to several winners, including quite useful out-and-out stayer Amberwood (by Amber Light); in rear in maiden races and quite valuable sellers; sold 740 gns Newmarket Autumn Sales; sent to Holland. *J. Benstead.*

IVY THORNE 3 b.f. Relko 136–Calling The Tune 94 (Tudor Melody 129)   — (1981 7fg 8fg 7g 1982 10h 14fg 14g 9v³ 10g) strong, useful-looking filly; plating-class maiden; should stay at least 1¼m. *F. Durr.*

IZOBIA 3 br.f. Mansingh 120–Ibozia 73 (Mossborough 126) (1981 NR 1982   — 12fg 8f 8g 10fg) small filly; sister to 7f and 1¼m winner Tenoria, and half-sister to a winner; dam won over 1¼m; well beaten in maiden races. *K. Stone.*

J

JACINTO TIMES (USA) 3 b.c. Olden Times–Jacinto Rose (Jacinto) (1981   **70** 7g 1982 8fg² 9.4fg² 10fg⁴ 12.3d 11.5g) lengthy colt; kept on well to win maiden race at Ayr in July; should stay 1½m; sold 2,100 gns Newmarket Autumn Sales. *J. Hindley.*

JACKDAW (USA) 2 b.c. Crow 134–Lycabette 64 (Lyphard 132) (1982 6fg   **84** 7d²) Apr 13; $80,000Y; neat, strong colt; first foal; dam, daughter of Prix Morny winner Revoquee II, was placed over sprint distances in France and England before winning over 7f at 4 yrs in USA; appeared to show plenty of promise in 19-runner maiden race at Salisbury in June going down by 1¼ lengths to Castle Guard after making much of running, but was not seen out again; sold 13,500 gns Newmarket Autumn Sales. *G. Harwood.*

JACK RAMSEY 2 b.c. Tudor Rhythm 112–Top Soprano 89 (High Top 131)   — (1982 6g) lengthy, good-topped, short-legged colt; good walker; second foal; dam 2-y-o 5f winner; unquoted, no show in 20-runner maiden race at Newmarket in October. *M. McCormack.*

JACK'S LAD 2 gr.c. Dragonara Palace 115–Spring Girl (Crowned Prince 128) —
(1982 6d) Apr 28; 1,500F, 450Y; tall, leggy colt; first foal; dam never ran;
behind in 14-runner £3,000 seller at Newcastle in August; sold 420 gns Doncaster
November Sales. *G. Toft.*

JACK SPLENDID 7 b.h. John Splendid 116–Grace (Gratitude 130) (1981 —
5fg 5d 5g 5.3f 5d 5h 5g 1982 5f 5g 5fg 5fg) big, strong horse; sprint handicapper;
acts on any going; has twice been tried in blinkers; sometimes sweats up. *M.
Blanshard.*

JACOLETTA 3 b.f. Artaius 129–Jarama (Amber Rama 133) (1981 7g 7d —
7f³ 7d 1982 8g 9f 11d) small filly; has shown a little ability; should stay
1¼m; possibly needs firm ground; sold 3,100 gns Newmarket December Sales.
P. Cole.

JACQUINTA 3 b.f. Habitat 134–Jacinth 133 (Red God 128§) (1981 6fg 95
6g³ 1982 8.2fg² 7g³ 6g* 6fg* 6f 6g* 6f) deep-girthed, attractive filly; made
virtually all to win £3,300 event at Kempton, £3,700 race at Newbury (odds
on) and fairly valuable handicap at Newmarket; held on by short head from
Lucayan Lady in last-named in June; best at distances short of 1m; has won
on a firm surface but is ideally suited by some give in the ground. *B. Hobbs.*

JAD 2 b.g. Riboboy 124–Jawhara 93 (Upper Case) (1982 7fg⁴ 7f* 7fg² 7g³ 92
6g³ 7g³ 6d³ 7g²) Feb 26; strong, compact gelding; first foal; dam won from
5f to 7f; won 9-runner minor event at Catterick in July; never out of first 3
in varied company afterwards, being claimed after finishing apparently unlucky
neck second to Luigi's Glory at Yarmouth in September on final appearance;
needs further than 6f, and will stay 1m; seems to act on any going; blinkered
sixth and seventh starts; sent to Italy and is a winner there. *W. O'Gorman.*

JADE AND DIAMOND 4 ch.g. Bold Lad (Ire) 133–Tegleaze 81 (Galivanter —
131) (1981 10fg⁴ 9s 7f 1982 10d 11.7fg) compact gelding; stays 1¼m;
seems to act on any going. *D. Elsworth.*

Sir Kenneth Butt's "Jacquinta"

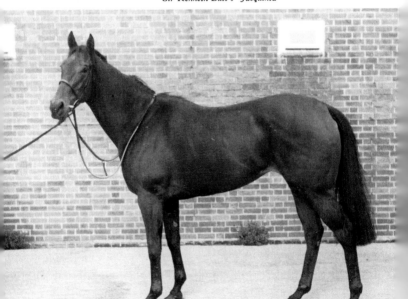

JADE RING   3 b.f. Auction Ring 123–Msida (Majority Blue 126)   (1981 6g² 6s²   **75**
1982 6f² 5g 7f² 7.2f³ 7d* 7g)   neat, attractive filly; poor mover; won minor
event at Ayr in September; will be suited by 1m; acts on any going.   *J. Toller.*

JAIN   2 b.f. Condorcet–Surfacing (Worden II 129)   (1982 5f 6fg 5f 5fg 5fg 7f   **—**
7.6v)   May 7; 2,500Y; small, lightly-made filly; apparently of no account.
R. Hoad.

JALABAD   4 b.c. Kalamoun 129–Wenduyne 113 (Moutiers 127)   (1981 10g   **—**
10d 10g   1982 10g 8s 7.5d 10s⁴ 8g 10f 8f 8fg)   lightly-made colt; good mover;
disappointing handicapper; should stay 1m; seems to act on any going; blinkered
seventh start (finished last).   *R. Baker.*

JALAIN   3 b.f. Pitcairn 126–Dutch Bells (The Scoundrel)   (1981 7g   1982   **82**
12d 12g* 10.1fg⁴ 11.7d⁴ 12g* 12fg⁴ 16.5s²)   fair sort; successful in maiden
race at Newbury in August and minor event at Hamilton in September; stays
very well; suited by some give in the ground; sold 5,000 gns Newmarket
December Sales.   *R. Williams.*

JALMOOD THE STONE (USA)   2   br.c.   Herculean–Tish   (Porterhouse)   **100**
(1982 5fg² 6g* 7g⁴ 7g² 7d* 7.3g² 7g* 7d*)   Mar 27; fair sort; good walker;
half-brother to Ascender (by Cougar II), a stakes winner at up to 9f, and to
3 stakes-placed winners; dam unraced half-sister to On Your Mark; had excellent
season, winning maiden event and 3 nurseries from 8 starts; gained his nursery
successes by 4 lengths and by 6 lengths at Wolverhampton and by ½ length,
very cheekily indeed, at Edinburgh; suited by 7f; genuine and consistent;
goes well for apprentice T. Quinn.   *P. Cole.*

JALMOOD (USA)   3 b.c. Blushing Groom 131–Fast Ride (Sicambre 135)   (1981   **124**
7g 7fg 7.2fg* 8g* 8s* 8d³   1982 10f³ 12f* 12f 11g* 12f³ 14.6f)
Injury curtailed Jalmood's activity and affected his form as a three-year-old;
like those of another of his contemporaries Electric, Jalmood's performances were
a mixture of the high class and the mediocre and he must be a frustrating horse
to train.   Jalmood and Electric were, on balance of form, probably the two
best three-year-olds in England at a mile and a half but both are suspect on the
score of soundness and it is impossible to be emphatic about their prospects as
four-year-olds.   Of the pair Electric, lightly raced as a two-year-old and a
slower-maturing three-year-old than Jalmood, could fairly be regarded as the
better by the end of the season and is more the type to progress in his third
season.   But in the spring it was a different story: Jalmood, a very good two-
year-old who had finished third in the William Hill Futurity, confirmed his
standing as a leading contender for the Derby with good performances in the
Guardian Classic Trial at Sandown in April and the Highland Spring Derby Trial
at Lingfield in May.   A strained muscle in his groin hampered Jalmood's early-
season preparation, causing his connections to abandon ideas of a tilt at the
Two Thousand Guineas, and he was some way short of peak fitness when third,
running on late, to Peacetime in the Guardian Classic Trial a week before the
Guineas.   At Lingfield Jalmood still wasn't fully wound up but he ran a
thoroughly satisfactory trial for the Derby, carrying right through to the end
without faltering, after leading two furlongs out, to beat Mr Fluorocarbon and
Electric by two and a half lengths and two.   It is easier now to discount the
value of what Jalmood accomplished at Lingfield—Mr Fluorocarbon turned out
to be better at shorter distances and Electric wasn't the horse he became later
in the season—but there was strong support at the time for Jalmood in the ante-
post market on the Derby and he started joint-second favourite.   No winner of
the Lingfield Derby Trial had gone on to success at Epsom since Parthia in 1959
but Jalmood seemed a good bet at least to emulate Pardao and Black Prince II
who were both placed in the Derby after winning at Lingfield.   Lingfield's mile-
and-a-half course bears quite close resemblance to the Epsom Derby course and
is a good testing ground for leading Derby contenders; regrettably, there have
been several disappointing turn-outs for the Lingfield Derby Trial in recent
seasons, due no doubt to the race's having lost ground to such as the Mecca-
Dante Stakes at York, which was worth more than double the value of the
Lingfield trial in 1982.

Jalmood's performance in the Derby was dismal: looking extremely well, in
our view the pick of the paddock, he trailed in fourteenth of eighteen, beaten
more than twenty-five lengths by the winner Golden Fleece.   On his return home
Jalmood was found to have muscular problems in his quarters, an injury which
recurred in the Gordon Stakes at Goodwood in July when, starting odds on, he
finished third to Electric.   Jalmood's performances at Epsom and Goodwood

*Highland Spring Derby Trial, Lingfield
—Jalmood stays on well to beat Mr
Fluorocarbon and Electric*

led to speculation that perhaps he was ill-suited to tracks with pronounced gradients. Jalmood has rather a round action and horses that display 'knee-action' are often at a disadvantage on such courses, especially when the going is firm as it was for both the Derby and the Gordon Stakes; but to excuse Jalmood's performances on such grounds was to fly in the face of the evidence of his impressive display at Lingfield where the going was also firm. Jalmood returned home with similar, though less serious, muscular trouble after finishing sixth in the St Leger on his final outing—the Doncaster track is quite flat except for a slight hill about a mile and a quarter from the finish. Arguably Jalmood's best performance came at Ayr, a course which is relatively flat but has gentle undulations throughout. In the fourth running of the Mecca Bookmakers Scottish Derby in July he reversed Epsom placings with Norwick (fifth in the Derby), Rocamadour (eighth) and Palace Gold (sixth). Held up, Jalmood came with a steady run in the straight to win decisively by two lengths from Norwick who, like the other runners, received 6 lb from Jalmood.

Jalmood showed in the strongly-run St Leger, in which he finished well after being hemmed in for much of the straight, that he stays a mile and three quarters which might be thought a little surprising for a son of Blushing Groom, a top-class miler who was found out by the trip in the Derby. Blushing Groom was syndicated before the 1977 Derby for 6,000,000 dollars, a sum that seemed hard to justify at the time (he was rated 1,000,000 dollars ahead of the already-proven young stallion Lyphard, for example). Jalmood is one of Blushing Groom's first crop of three-year-olds, an outstanding crop which also includes the Italian

*Mecca Bookmakers Scottish Derby, Ayr—Jalmood comes with
a steady run to cut down long-time leader Norwick*

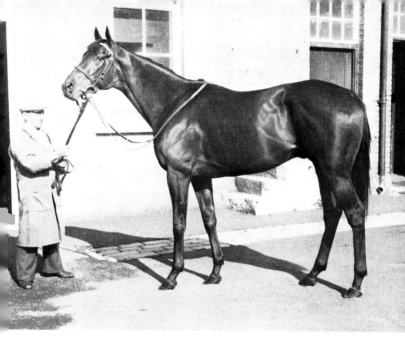

Sheikh Mohammed's "Jalmood"

One Thousand Guineas winner Rosananti, the smart French middle-distance performer Coquelin, and several good horses in North America including Runaway Groom (Travers Stakes, Grade 1), Blush With Pride (Kentucky Oaks and Santa Susana Stakes, both Grade 1), Too Chic (Maskette Stakes, Grade 1) and Shy Groom (New York Derby). In the light of such success Blushing Groom's fee has been raised to 150,000 dollars (about £90,000) for 1983, putting him on the same mark as Gainesway Farm's most expensive stallion Lyphard.

Jalmood (USA) (b.c. 1979)	Blushing Groom (ch 1974)	Red God (ch 1954)	Nasrullah
			Spring Run
		Runaway Bride (b 1962)	Wild Risk
			Aimee
	Fast Ride (br 1966)	Sicambre (br 1948)	Prince Bio
			Sif
		Fast Lady II (b 1948)	Fastnet
			Charbonniere

Jalmood's dam Fast Ride was a smart racemare, winner of the Prix Vanteaux at Longchamp over nine and a half furlongs as a three-year-old, and she has done well at stud, breeding three winners before Jalmood including Flaunter (by High Echelon), a stakes winner at up to a mile and a quarter in the States, and the stakes placed Prestissimo (by Bold Reasoning) whose first foal is the filly Vidor, a smart winner in France and North America. A well-made, attractive colt, Jalmood acts on any going. *J. Dunlop.*

JALNA 3 br.f. Free Boy 96–Khanum 81 (Soueida 111) (1981 NR 1982 7fg 8fg) third reported live foal; half-sister to 7f to 1¼m winner Malvan (by Decoy Boy); dam won over 1m and 1¼m; in rear in 2 maiden races at Chepstow in summer. *A. Turnell.*

JAMESTINO 4 ch.c. Bustino 136–Miss Wrekin 97 (Pardao 120) (1981 12.3g 77
12g⁴ 10.6s 12f* 13g* 14d⁴ 16f⁴ 12g⁴ 1982 12d² 13g⁴ 14.7f² 16g² 14g 14.6g)
strong colt; rather disappointing, although was second at Beverley (2 amateur
riders events) and at Redcar (3 ran) in between; possibly doesn't truly stay 2m;
evidently acts on any going; occasionally blinkered; retained by trainer 3,600
gns Doncaster October Sales. *M. H. Easterby.*

JAMSHID 5 b.h. Dragonara Palace 115–Never Lonely (Never Say Die 137) 56
(1981 10.2d 12.5g 11.7d⁴ 12d⁴ 12g² 12fg 12f* 12g 12f² 12f³ 12fg² 12g³ 13f³ 14.7d⁴
12f³ 12f³ 16.1fg⁴ 16s 13s 1982 15.8g 16.1s 16f 16fg* 17.1f 16f* 15.5f⁴ 16fg³ 16fg
16d 16f² 16g 15f 16.1s 15.8d 15d) compact horse; staying handicapper; won at
Ripon and Beverley (by 6 lengths) in May; suited by top-of-the-ground;
suitable mount for a boy; sometimes blinkered; didn't find a great deal off
bridle and was usually held up; well beaten last 5 starts; dead. *R. Hollinshead.*

JAN CAN 4 br.f. Palm Track 122–Ivy Dee 68 (Meldrum 112) (1981 7fg 8.2f —
7f 11f 1982 8.2fg 6f 9.4fg 7g) in rear in varied races, including sellers. *T.
Barnes.*

JANES JET 5 b.m. Another River 89–Jolly Jane (Jolly Jet 111) (1981 NR —
1982 5g 12d) showed a little ability as a 2-y-o; behind in the autumn, including
in a 5f seller. *G. Harman.*

JANINE 3 b.f. Dance In Time–Ankole 85 (Crepello 136) (1981 NR 1982 —
8s 8g 7g 10.6s) 13,000Y; strong, useful-looking filly; half-sister to numerous
winners, including useful miler Horbury (by Sing Sing); dam won at up to 13f;
behind in maiden races and a minor event; sold 7,200 gns Newmarket December
Sales. *M. Camacho.*

JANIVY 3 b.f. Legal Eagle 126–Poliwog (Polic 126) (1981 5s 5d* 5g² 5g* 66
5d³ 6fg 1982 10s³ 10g 8f* 8f* 8f⁴ 8f³ 8f 8g) deep-girthed, useful sort; good
mover; won seller at Thirsk (bought in 3,700 gns) in April; successful in better
company at Wolverhampton in May; not certain to stay 1¼m; seems to act on
any going but goes well on firm; didn't look happy in blinkers final start; genuine.
A. Young.

JANLARMAR 3 b.f. Habat 127–Princess Caroline 68 (Sovereign Path 125) 41
(1981 5g 5s⁴ 5f 6g 5d 5d 5s⁴ 5g 7d 7g 1982 10d 7f 7f 6f 5fg 5fg 5f³ 6fg*
5f 6d 7f 6f 7g 7s³ 6s 6s) plain filly; plater; attracted no bid after winning at
Redcar in July; stays 7f; seems to act on any going; usually wears blinkers;
has run creditably for an apprentice. *A. Bailey.*

JANNDAR 3 b.c. Queen's Hussar 124–Gedera 80 (Palestine 133) (1981 5s³ 96 d
5d* 7fg³ 1982 7s² 7fg 8f 10g 10d) small, lightly-built, quite attractive colt;
fairly useful performer; good ¾-length second to clever winner Mirabeau in
strongly-contested though slowly-run £3,000 race at Leicester in March; ran
respectably in £4,900 handicap at Newmarket in June on fourth start; had stiff
task when blinkered final outing; stays 1¼m; suited by some give in the ground.
F. J. Houghton.

JANUS 4 ro.g. Ragstone 128–January (Sigebert 131) (1981 13.3d 10fg³ 12fg —
14fg⁴ 12d³ 15.5s³ 1982 12fg⁴ 11.7fg) strong, workmanlike gelding; fit from
hurdling, made running when fourth to Perdiccas in apprentice handicap at
Ascot in April; stays 2m. *Mrs N. Smith.*

JARALL 2 b.f. Le Johnstan 123–Compro 66 (Como 120) (1982 5fg 7g 7f 8.2fg —
8.2d) May 18; bad plater. *K. Stone.*

JARB 2 gr.f. Bruni 132–Make Amends 74 (Tutankhamen) (1982 7fg) Mar 9; —
quite an attractive, deep-girthed filly; half-sister to 2 winners by The Brianstan,
including useful 1977 2-y-o 6f winner Reparation; dam won over 5f at 2 yrs
and stayed well; never really going when last of 10 behind Cock Robin in minor
event at Sandown in August; had been withdrawn on intended first appearance.
D. Wintle.

JARDY 2 b.f. Auction Ring 123–Majesta (Majority Blue 126) (1982 5fg 5fg —
5fg 6g 7.6v) Apr 5; 2,500F, 4,000Y; neat, sharp, active sort; first produce;
dam second over 6f and 7f in Ireland; no worthwhile form in maiden and minor
events. *D. Morley.*

JASMINE STAR 6 ch.h. Ridan–Gay Cloud 99 (Golden Cloud) (1981 5g 5d* 108
5s² 5f 6fg³ 5fg* 6g 5fg 5g 1982 5s³ 6s 5fg* 6g² 6fg 5d 6fg 5fg² 6f* 5g 5fg 6g)
tall horse; won handicap at Leopardstown in May and Herbertstown Stakes
at Naas in August, latter by 1½ lengths from Southern Music; second in Green-
lands Stakes at the Curragh (beaten 2 lengths by Belted Earl) and handicap

at Leopardstown in between; sweated up badly when towards rear in Woking-ham Handicap at Royal Ascot; stayed 6f; acted on any going; standing at Mylerstown Stud, Co Kildare, fee IR £1,000 (Oct 1st). *M. Connolly, Ireland.*

JASPER 2 ch.c. Busted 134–Riboreen 116 (Ribero 126) (1982 8s²) Mar 6; **95 p** rangy colt; second foal; dam won Oaks Trial at Lingfield; 15/2, led inside final furlong until close home when short-head second of 26 to Magic Rarity in maiden event at Sandown in October; sure to win races, and looks useful stayer in the making. *J. Dunlop.*

JASPER'S MOUNT 2 b.c. Sparkler 130–Fratini 69 (Reliance II 137) (1982 **—** 7f) Mar 23; rangy colt; good walker; first foal; dam placed over 2m; 50/1 and backward, soon tailed off in £4,900 event at Kempton in September; will need plenty of time. *N. Vigors.*

JASSIM (USA) 4 b.g. Cyane–Lady Bellaston (Tudor Minstrel 144) (1981 **—** 10d⁴ 11g⁴ 14.6fg² 12d³ 15.5fg* 1982 10.2g 12d 16fg 15.5fg) quite attractive, strong, well-made gelding; suited by a test of stamina; seems best on a sound surface. *P. Cundell.*

JAT 2 ch.c. English Prince 129–Sweet Rocket (Roan Rocket 128) (1982 7d) **—** May 3; IR 2,400Y, IR 6,400Y; strong colt; half-brother to 2 winners, including 6f and 7f winner Astral Suite (by On Your Mark); dam lightly-raced half-sister to very smart sprinter Harem; unquoted and backward, no show in minor event won by Northern Adventure at Doncaster in October. *R. Hollinshead.*

JATIJAYA 2 ch.g. Monseigneur 127–Singing Girl 96 (Sing Sing 134) (1982 **64** 6g 6f 6fg 6f 6d 8f 8fg³ 8s 8d) Apr 11; 3,600F, 4,200Y; unfurnished gelding; 2 lengths third of 10 to Rustic Track in selling nursery at Redcar in September; stays 1m; usually blinkered. *J. Fitzgerald.*

JAVA TIGER 4 gr.c. Saritamer 130–Country Music (Red God 128§) (1981 **58** 6v² 5g² 6fg* 6s 6f* 6f³ 6fg² 6fg* 6f 6g 1982 6f 6f³ 6f 6fg⁴ 6f) strong, good-bodied colt; sprint handicapper; third at Pontefract in May, best effort; seems well suited by firm going; ran moderately in blinkers once; needs to be held up; ridden by apprentice N. Connorton on last 2 occasions when successful; broke a blood vessel final start. *J. W. Watts.*

JAY ELLE THAW 2 b.g. Owen Dudley 121–Pure Magic 94 (Pinza 137) (1982 **58** 5s⁴ 5fg 5f 8.2s² 7.2s) Feb 6; 1,500Y; workmanlike gelding; 4 lengths second to Heldigvis in seller at Hamilton in September, first race for nearly 5 months and best effort; never dangerous when co-favourite for 16-runner selling nursery at Haydock the following month; suited by 1m, and will stay further; blinkered third outing. *T. Fairhurst.*

JAYVEE 2 b.g. Monsanto 121–Festival Night 115 (Midsummer Night II 117) **72** (1982 7g 7fg²) Feb 26; 8,000Y; third foal; half-brother to 1981 2-y-o 5f winner Burnbeck (by Music Boy) and a winning hurdler; dam won from 6f to 1¼m; 50/1, recovered from slow start to finish 1½ lengths second of 10 to Arnab in maiden race at Brighton in July; gelded subsequently; will stay 1m. *P. Cole.*

JAZZ BAND (USA) 3 b.c. Quack–Dixieland Jazz (Royal Serenade 132) **80** (1981 7fg 8g 8d⁴ 8s* 8.2d³ 10g 1982 12d² 12f⁴ 12f³ 11.7g 11.7fg³ 16f* 16f³ 16f2) big, rangy colt; staying handicapper; won at Lingfield in July; acts on any going; blinkered fifth outing; needs strong handling; sent to USA. *G. Harwood.*

JAZZ FORTESCUE 3 gr.f. Song 132–Porto Novo (Sovereign Lord 120) (1981 **—** 5d 5fg 5f 5g 1982 10g) quite a well-made filly; poor maiden. *A. Pitt.*

JAZZ ME BLUES 2 b.c. Jaazeiro 127–La Grange 105 (Habitat 134) (1982 6f* **85** 6g 7fg⁴) Feb 7; 16,500F, 13,000Y; third foal; dam won from 7f to 2m; won 15-runner maiden race at Naas in May by a length from Butler's Bridge; not disgraced when 4¾ lengths fifth behind Caerleon in Tyros Stakes at the Curragh the following month nor when 7 lengths fourth of 7 to Burslem in Ardenode Stud Stakes at Leopardstown in August; will stay 1¼m. *J. Bolger, Ireland.*

J C SPECIAL 2 ch.g. Tachypous 128–Florabette (Floribunda 136) (1982 6fg) **—** Apr 12; 5,200Y; useful sort; half-brother to 3 winners, including 9f to 1½m winner Target Path (by Scottish Rifle); dam never ran; chased leaders until beaten and eased after halfway in 21-runner minor event won by Coquito's Friend at Newmarket in August; gelded subsequently. *M. Jarvis.*

JEALOUS MOOR 4 b. or gr.g. Hotfoot 126–Eleanor Bold 81 (Queen's Hussar **—** 124) (1981 7d 9g* 8g 9fg³ 7s² 12d 1982 10.6f 8f 10d 9g) lightly-made gelding; plater; wears a bandage on his off-fore. *I. Jordon.*

445

JEANJIM 3 b.f. Homeric 133–Dance Mistress (Javelot 124) (1981 6f 6g⁴(dis) —
7d 8s² 8.2s⁴ 8d 1982 10s 8d 9f 12.2f 10g) lightly-made filly; plater; well
beaten at 3 yrs; should stay middle distances; acts on soft going; has run creditably for an apprentice; has worn blinkers. *K. Bridgwater.*

JEAN PROSPER 3 ch.g. Sparkler 130–Julie De Fortisson (Entanglement 118) —
(1981 NR 1982 10.1g) first foal; dam poor novice hurdler; unquoted when
behind in 22-runner maiden race won by Glad Tidings at Windsor in August.
D. Elsworth.

JEAN VARON 3 b.g. Averof 123–Dastina 80 (Derring-Do 131) (1981 5fg 5d **58**
5s 5s 5d 5fg* 6fg³ 7fg* 8f⁴ 1982 6s 6fg 6f 7g 5fg 7f* 7f 7fg³) compact gelding;
won handicap at Folkestone in July; suited by 7f; best form on fast ground;
has won both with and without blinkers; sometimes starts slowly; exported to
Malaysia. *G. Lewis.*

JECKEL 4 ch.g. High Award 119–Reina Isabel 69 (St Alphage 119) (1981 **47**
8s 5fg² 5fg⁴ 6d³ 6d² 6d² 1982 6g 6g 6fg² 5f 6f 6v 6g) sprint handicapper;
apprentice ridden; usually bandaged in front; didn't handle turn well at Catterick
on reappearance; behind in blinkers final start. *E. Eldin.*

JELLY BEAN 2 br.f. Rapid River 127–Princess Chesnut (King Chesnut 120) —
(1982 6g 5g 5d 5d 5f 5s 5d) May 8; 320Y; small filly; in rear all outings, including
in sellers. *J. Wilson.*

JEMEELA 2 b.f. Windjammer (USA)–King's Darling (King of the Tudors 129) **90**
(1982 6g 6g* 6fg³ 6s⁴ 6s) Mar 23; IR 5,000F; 45,000Y; tall, lengthy filly; half-
sister to numerous winners, including Just A Dutchess (by Knightly Manner),
successful 7 times at up to 1m in USA and dam of Miami Springs; dam never ran;
showed vast improvement on first effort when winning 16-runner maiden race at
Newbury in August by ¾ length from Shore Line; ran well next 2 starts, better
effort when fourth of 16 to Worrell, beaten short head, neck and short head, in
valuable nursery at Ascot in September; will stay 7f; seems to act on any going.
J. Dunlop.

JENDOR 2 b.f. Condorcet–Windy Lady (Whistling Wind 123) (1982 5s* 5fg **82**
6f 6fg 6f 8.2d² 8d 8.2s) Mar 25; fair sort; has a round action; second foal;
half-sister to Irish 3-y-o 5f winner Hi Little Gal (by Ardoon); dam lightly-raced
Irish maiden; won maiden race at Haydock in April by 3 lengths from Queen's
Glory after dwelling at start; strong-finishing ½-length second of 18 to Decorated
in nursery at Nottingham in September, easily best subsequent effort; ran badly
when co-favourite for nursery at Brighton in October; well suited by 1m;
inconsistent. *R. Hannon.*

JENNY DUVAL 2 br.f. Record Token 128–Rosia Steps 98 (Red Pins 114) **59**
(1982 5fg 6g 7fg 6g² 6d 7.2s 8d) Mar 18; 4,600Y; small filly; half-sister to 2
winners, including fair 1980 2-y-o 7f winner Sausolito (by Relko); dam won
over 5f and 7f at 2 yrs; moderate plater; stays 7f; acts on soft going; blinkered
last 2 starts, on final one hooded as well; sold 370 gns Ascot December Sales.
D. Arbuthnot.

JENNYJO 3 b.f. Martinmas 128–Judy O'Grady (Whistler 129) (1981 6f 7v **64**
1982 8.2fg 7f² 7f* 8f³ 7f 7.6g 7f³ 7f 7fg) rangy, attractive filly; good walker;
won maiden race at Redcar in May; barely stays 1m; acts on firm going; behaved
mulishly before going down final start; sold 800 gns Newmarket Autumn Sales,
resold 700 gns Ascot December Sales. *W. Wharton.*

JENNY LOU 4 ch.f. Sunyboy 110–Necora 79 (Royal Record II) (1981 12.2fg —
11f 1982 12s 12.2f) behind in maiden races. *I. Vickers.*

JE REVIENS 2 b.f. Streak 119–Bodicea (King's Troop 118) (1982 5fg 6fg 5fg —
5s) May 2; lengthy filly; third foal; sister to 5f winner Miss Worth; dam never
ran; soundly beaten in maiden races. *C. James.*

JESTER 3 b.c. Song 132–Trickster 92 (Major Portion 129) (1981 5g* 5g* 6fg⁴ **119**
5d* 5g* 6s* 1982 6fg² 6f* 5fg 6f 6f 6g 5s 7v 6s²) rangy, attractive colt; usually
a good mover; fourth foal; closely related to 6f winner Bretton Park (by Mummy's
Pet) and half-brother to 2 winners, including 5f to 7f winner Jebb Lane (by
The Brianstan); dam sprinter; beat Sweet Monday by 1½ lengths in 11-runner
Duke of York Stakes in May; didn't get going until too late when 1¼ lengths second
to Camisite in £5,300 event at Doncaster in November; not disgraced most starts
in between including in King's Stand Stakes at Royal Ascot, Vernons Sprint
Cup at Haydock, Diadem Stakes at Ascot and Prix de l'Abbaye de Longchamp;
about 3 lengths fifth to Sharpo in last-named; has given impression he would be
suited by 7f but finished tailed off when tried at trip in Prix de la Foret at Long-

Duke of York Stakes, York—Jester runs on well to beat Sweet Monday (stripes) with Crofthall (left) third and Mummy's Game fourth

champ; acts on any going except possibly heavy; suited by waiting tactics; has a tendency to hang left. *B. Hills.*

JESTER'S BOY 5 b.h. John Splendid 116–Jester's Girl (Will Somers 114§) (1981 7d⁴ 7g⁴ 6f 7g 6g 8f 8d 8v 1982 7fg 6f 6fg³ 7fg 6f 8.3fg) rather leggy, good sort; quite a modest handicapper nowadays; stays 1m but races mainly at shorter distances; acts on any going; has worn blinkers but is better without; has run creditably for an apprentice; sold 2,500 gns Ascot September Sales. *C. James.* **66**

JE T'AIME 2 ch.f. Ballad Rock 122–Pipeline 85 (Gulf Pearl 117) (1982 6fg) Apr 26; IR 15,000Y; rangy filly; closely related to winning sprinter Bold Polly (by Bold Lad, Ire) and half-sister to 2 winners, including useful 1978 staying 2-y-o Messenger of Peace (by Simbir); dam 2-y-o 6f winner; third favourite but in need of race, made good headway from slow start to have every chance until weakening at distance when promising 5 lengths equal sixth of 21 behind Coquito's Friend in minor event at Newmarket in August; sure to improve. *R. Williams.* **73 p**

JIBARO 3 b.f. Crooner 119–Bella Sandra 88 (Botticelli 129) (1981 NR 1982 10s) strong, stocky filly; sister to fair middle-distance performer Bella Canto and half-sister to a winner in Norway; dam won over 13f; backward when behind in 18-runner minor event won by Whenyourtrainsgone at Leicester in November. *J. Old.* **—**

JIMJAMS 2 b.c. Jimsun 121–Gamlingay (Daring Display 129) (1982 5f 7d 7g 7g⁴ 7g³ 7fg⁴ 8fg² 7.3g* 7v) Apr 21; well-grown, lengthy colt; second foal; half-brother to useful 1981 2-y-o sprint plater First Connection (by Bay Express); dam never ran; got up close home to win 13-runner nursery at Newbury in September by a neck from Jalmood The Stone; stays 1m; acts on a firm surface. *R. Hannon.* **89**

JIMMY RAINE 2 b.c. Jimmy Reppin 131–La Raine 93 (Majority Blue 126) (1982 5s⁴ 5fg² 5f 5g³ 5f 5d) May 5; neat, strong colt; first foal; dam at her best at 2 yrs when 5f winner; placed in minor races at Thirsk in April and Edinburgh in July; will stay 6f; moved badly to start final outing. *T. Barron.* **70**

JIM'S TRICKS 5 b.g. Jimsun 121–Floral Palm 69 (Floribunda 136) (1981 8fg 10g 8s⁴ 10d 10g 8fg* 8g³ 8fg 9fg⁴ 8.2fg 9g 8s 1982 8g 8g) lengthy, good-looking gelding; good mover; fair handicapper in 1981; in rear both starts in 1982; stays 1¼m; probably acts on any going; has run creditably in blinkers; has worn bandages; suited by front-running tactics. *Mrs J. Pitman.* **—**

JIRETTA 3 b.f. Jimmy Reppin 131–Robhetta (Track Spare 125) (1981 7fg* 7.2fg 7g 8.2s 1982 8fg 8f 10d) fair sort; won minor event at Doncaster in 1981; last in handicaps at 3 yrs; stays 1m; seems to act on any going; sometimes sweats up. *G. Toft.* **—**

JOANNE'S JOY 2 ch.f. Ballymore 123–Fiona's Joy (High Top 131) (1982 7fg 7g 8.5g 7fg⁴ 8d² 7v*) May 3; second foal; dam Irish 9f winner; improved late in season and ran out an impressive winner of 16-runner maiden race at the Curragh in October, making all to win by 8 lengths from Calvino; had previously finished 2½ lengths second of 20 to Ashanti in similar event at Leopardstown; will stay 1¼m; acts very well on heavy ground. *C. Collins, Ireland.* **95**

447

JOBROKE 2 b.c. Busted 134–Joey 110 (Salvo 129) (1982 6g) Apr 22; half- —
brother to fairly useful 1m and 1¼m winner Chevington (by Moulton); dam,
winner over 5f and 7.6f, stayed 1¼m; 33/1, tenth of 11 to Diesis in maiden race
at Newmarket in August; will need further. *H. Wragg.*

JOELLA 4 ch.f. Porto Bello 118–Jolisu 110 (Welsh Abbot 131) (1981 8.2s 7d —
1982 8g 10.1fg 8d 8.3g) lightly raced and no worthwhile form, including in
sellers; blinkered final start; sold 300 gns Ascot November Sales. *M. Ryan.*

JOG 5 b.g. Mount Hagen 127–Strolling Sweetly (Le Levanstell 122) (1981 12g⁴ —
12f 1982 9f) ex-Irish gelding; winner over hurdles; has also shown some
ability on flat, but is still a maiden; stays 1½m; probably acts on any going; has
worn blinkers. *W. Musson.*

JOHARA (USA) 3 b.f. Exclusive Native–Never Linger (Never Bend) (1981 —
6fg* 7d 6fg 1982 8g) well-made filly; useful in 1981; dropped out in closing
stages when sixth of 7 to Chalon in International Fillies Stakes at Kempton in
May, only start at 3 yrs; should stay 1m. *H. T. Jones.*

JOHN CLARE 4 b.c. Derring-Do 131–Madam Clare 66 (Ennis 128) (1981 7.3g   **66**
7g 8g 10d 7fg 1982 13f 8f 8h² 8fg* 8d 8fg 8.2fg⁴ 8f³ 8.3fg⁴ 7fg 8fg) strong,
shapely colt; quite a moderate handicapper nowadays; won decisively at Beverley
in June; promises to stay beyond 1m; yet to race on very soft going, but acts on
any other; blinkered final start in 1981; sold to BBA (Italia) 3,000 gns
Newmarket Autumn Sales. *M. Blanshard.*

JOHN DOYLE 2 b.g. Import 127–September Fire (Firestreak 125) (1982 5f³   **79 §**
5g² 5d 5f² 6g 5.3g 5s 6s) Apr 7; 1,050Y (privately), 10,000 2-y-o; big, rangy
gelding; half-brother to 5f to 15f winner Autumn Glow (by Pongee) and a winner
in Belgium; dam never ran; showed modest ability in first half of his season, and
no ability at all in second, when last in 3 races; might not be suited by soft
ground, but is obviously not to be trusted. *M. Pipe.*

JOHN FEATHER 3 b.g. Gulf Pearl 117–Galtee Princess (Varano) (1981 NR   **69**
1982 9s* 12.3d 13g 16g⁴ 13s³) 5,000Y; third foal; dam ran only 4 times; kept
on well to win 5-runner maiden race at Hamilton in April; quite soundly beaten
in handicaps afterwards; may stay 2m. *J. W. Watts.*

JOHN FRENCH 2 ch.c. Relko 136–Anegada 79 (Welsh Pageant 132) (1982 **115**
7g⁴ 7fg* 7g* 7s* 10g*)
     British racing would benefit from having an equivalent of France's mile-
and-a-quarter pattern races for two-year-olds, the Prix de Conde and the
Criterium de Saint-Cloud. These two French races usually throw up a high-
class performer and in the last dozen years such good colts as Margouillat,
Pevero, Top Ville, Rheffic, Providential and The Wonder have won one or both
of them. The nearest Britain has to the Prix de Conde and the Criterium de
Saint-Cloud is the Zetland Stakes at Newmarket at the end of the season.
Although worth considerably less it too has been won by some good animals,
including Scallywag, Crimson Beau and Many Moons, and those top-class stayers
Proverb and Grey Baron are among those to have been placed in the race.
Perhaps the Zetland will eventually be raised to listed-race or pattern-race
status. It is certainly going the right way and in 1982, with sponsorship from
Jennings The Bookmakers boosting the first prize to over £8,300, it attracted
a field of promising young stayers. Dawn River, Ring of Greatness and Mitilini
all had useful wins over a mile to their names but evens favourite was John
French, the winner of the last three of his four races. Two of the runners,
Figure de Danse and Media Man, went off far too fast, leaving the seven others
a long way behind. Both had been swallowed up by the final three furlongs
where John French was travelling strongly on the heels of the leaders. When
finally asked to take the lead running into the Dip he quickened very smoothly.
His rider then tended to take things easy, so much so that he briefly had to
roust him to repel Swift Service's challenge, but by the line John French was
well on top, winning rather cleverly by half a length. The rest, headed by
Mister Prelude, were at least six lengths further back.
     John French's previous wins had been cleverly gained. After landing
the odds in a maiden race at Yarmouth in July he showed surprising acceleration
for one of his breeding in a slowly-run nursery at Newmarket; he had that race
won entering the final furlong, after being at the back of the field when the pace
quickened suddenly three furlongs out, and was then asked to do the minimum
amount to hold off Enbyar Dan by half a length. He carried 9-7 there and

Jennings The Bookmakers Zetland Stakes, Newmarket—John French wins cleverly from Swift Service

also to a further victory in a nursery at York in October. Once again he was settled at the rear but this time he encountered a lot of problems moving through the field and he had to wait for a gap to appear. Luckily one came in time and he ran on strongly to win most decisively by a length from Sharp Sea, beaten only a short head in a valuable race on her previous start and receiving 12 lb here. Incidentally John French showed at York that he acts well on soft going; he has also won on firmish ground.

John French (ch.c. Apr 20, 1980)	Relko (b 1960)	Tanerko (br 1953)	Tantieme La Divine
		Relance III (ch 1952)	Relic Polaire
	Anegada (ch 1974)	Welsh Pageant (b 1966)	Tudor Melody Picture Light
		Antigua (ch 1958)	Hyperion Nassau

John French, a rangy colt, almost certainly has the improvement in him to make a smart performer over a mile and a quarter or more. Although like many of Relko's offspring he's not a particularly attractive individual, he was sufficiently attractive to fetch 27,000 guineas as a yearling. He comes from a very successful family. His great-grandam Nassau was a very smart two-year-old, winning five sprint races, and she later bred six winners all named after Caribbean islands. Several were at least useful: St Lucia won the Lancashire Oaks and Coronation Stakes, Andros won the Houghton Stakes and Antigua, John French's grandam, won the Galtres. Antigua also did well at stud, producing five winners including Derrylin, who won both the Horris Hill and Greenham Stakes, and the useful middle-distance filly Fiesta Fun, who finished an excellent third in the Yorkshire Oaks. John French's dam Anegada, a less-talented sister to Fiesta Fun, finished fourth in a large field of maidens at Newbury. John French is her second foal; her first, the Averof filly Antilla, was a fair five-furlong winner at two. *H. Cecil.*

JOHN HUNTER 2 b. or br.g. Majestic Streak–Misty Belle (Foggy Bell 108) — (1982 8fg 7.6v) Apr 29; good-topped gelding; fourth foal; dam of no account; behind in autumn maiden races at Goodwood and Lingfield; subsequently gelded. *M. Bolton.*

JOHNNIE HUSSAR 4 b.c. Queen's Hussar 124÷Corbara II (Marino) (1981 7d **55** 8g² 7fg² 8fg² 10fg 10f² 10fg* 12s 11d 1982 12.3fg⁴ 12g⁴ 9fg⁴ 11g² 12g) workmanlike colt; seemed to stay 1½m; acted on firm going; dead. *W. H. H. Williams.*

JOHN NORTH 2 b.g. Pongee 106–Norgill (Keren 100) (1982 6g 6f 8.2fg 8fg) — June 5; small gelding; first foal; dam poor hurdler; well beaten in maiden race and sellers. *N. Chamberlain.*

JOHNNY NOBODY 2 b.c. Derrylin 115–Crystallize (Reliance II 137) (1982 **115** 5d² 6fg* 6f³ 7g 7f⁴ 6f* 6d² 6f³ 8d² 8g*) Apr 14; 6,600Y; small, deep-girthed, sturdy colt; first foal; dam unraced half-sister to very smart miler Greengage; put up a splendid effort under 9-7 in Rowley Mile Nursery at Newmarket in September, running on strongly after being held up to win decisively by 2 lengths from Hasty Flirt; previously successful in £3,500 event at Goodwood in May and nursery under top weight at Catterick in August; disappointed immediately after his first success, but was most consistent once winning again; better suited by 1m than shorter distances; seems to act on any going; best with strong handling but has run well for apprentice T. Jarvis; to be trained by H. Blackshaw. *A. Jarvis.*

JOHN O'GROATS 5 b.h. Welsh Pageant 132–Romany 87 (King's Bench **84** 132) (1981 12fg 10.2g 12g 12f 12f³ 15g 12d³ 14d⁴ 14.6fg⁴ 18g 1982 14f* 14fg² 13fg⁴ 12fg 14f³ 14f² 14.6f² 14fg* 14.6g 16s³ 14s) well-made horse; made running when winning handicaps at Sandown in April and Yarmouth in August, latter by 8 lengths from Miguel Clement; placed several other occasions, but ran moderately in a more strongly-contested race ninth start; best at around 1¾m; not at his best on really soft going, but acts on any other; wears blinkers; suited by strong handling and forcing tactics nowadays. *J. Winter.*

JOHNS PRESENT 4 b.g. Gift Card 124–Kirmeen (Charlottesville 135) (1981 — 7.6g⁴ 8fg 8fg 8fg 7fg 8fg² 8d³ 10v² 1982 12.2d⁴ 8s) robust, hollow-backed gelding; respectable fourth to Cima in handicap at Warwick in April; off course subsequently until October; promises to stay 1½m; probably acts on any going; tended to wander under pressure final outing in 1981. *R. Holder.*

JOHN'S SECRET 2 bl.c. Town Crier 119–Spring Secret 71 (Hillary) (1982 5d) — Apr 23; 1,500F (privately), 800 2-y-o; half-brother to a winner in Italy; dam 1m winner; 66/1, last of 24 in maiden race at Windsor in June. *K. Bridgwater.*

JOIN THE CLUB 2 ch.f. Dance In Time–Micklemere 82 (Blakeney 126) **67** (1982 5fg⁴ 5g* 5fg 7g) Mar 28; 880Y; first foal; dam won over 1½m; won maiden auction event at Warwick in June by 2½ lengths from Trumpery; last in nurseries subsequently. *B. McMahon.*

JOLIE COURTISANE 2 b.f. Owen Dudley 121–Oh Well 61 (Sahib 114) **85 ?** (1982 5fg⁴ 5g* 5g* 6fg 5f) Feb 27; 1,250F, 1,000Y; workmanlike, good-quartered filly; third foal; half-sister to a winning plater; dam stayed 1m; won 4-runner auction race at Ayr in June and 7-runner minor event at Hamilton in July; ran badly last 2 outings, on final one when apparently leniently handicapped in July nursery at Thirsk; should be suited by 6f+; possibly needs some give in the ground; trained by J. S. Wilson first 4 starts. *P. Haslam.*

JOLLIDEE 3 ch.f. Jolly Good 122–Sugadee 69 (Vimadee 120) (1981 NR — 1982 16fg 16d 12fg) smallish, lengthy filly; third living foal; half-sister to Richdee (by Richboy), a smart performer over jumps; dam, placed from 6f to 1½m, won over hurdles and fences; in rear in maiden races. *W. Wharton.*

JOLLIFFE'S DOUBLE 6 b. or br.g. Pamroy 99–Miss Dunoon 83 (Dunoon — Star 110) (1981 9g 12d 12fg 12d² 16s⁴ 1982 10.2g 12fg² 10g) long-backed gelding; good second in amateur riders handicap at Doncaster in July; disappointing only subsequent outing; suited by 1½m. *A. Bailey.*

JOLLY BURGLAR 3 b.g. Jolly Good 122–Moaning Low 75 (Burglar 128) **58** (1981 5s 5g 6g 6f 6f² 1982 6f 8f 7f⁴ 7f² 7g* 7g 6fg 7fg 9f 9s² 7s 6s³) small, workmanlike gelding; plater; bought in 1,700 gns after winning at Leicester in June; stays 9f; acts on any going; wears blinkers; suitable mount for an apprentice. *G. Toft.*

JOLLY MARJIM 5 ch.g. Jolly Me 114–Rose's Leader (Damremont 120) — (1981 10v 12g²² 12g 1982 12g 10f 10fg) workmanlike gelding; well beaten in 1982, on final occasion when blinkered in a seller; stays 1½m; acts on any going; sold 1,500 gns Doncaster June Sales. *E. Weymes.*

JOLLY SARA 2 ch.f. Jolly Good 122–Sarasingh 93 (Mansingh 120) (1982 — 6s) Apr 13; 1,500Y; second foal; sister to a plater; dam 2-y-o 6f winner; unquoted, no show in 16-runner maiden event at Leicester in November. *M. McCormack.*

Harry Rosebery Challenge Trophy, Ayr—Jonacris makes all and keeps on strongly to withstand the challenge of the grey Mac's Palace

JONACRIS 2 ch.c. Broxted 120–Squires Girl (Spanish Gold 101) (1982 5fg **115** 5g* 5f* 5fg² 5f* 5fg* 5fg* 5g² 5fg² 5g*)

Over the years the name Paul Felgate has become fairly well known to supporters of National Hunt racing; since taking out a permit in 1967, followed by a trainer's licence in 1972, he had sent out a total of fifty-three winners over jumps to the end of the 1981/2 season. To followers of flat racing only his name wasn't nearly so familiar—his only success before 1982 had come when Tshainik won a poor maiden race at Beverley in 1980—but it has now been put firmly before the flat-racing public by the exploits of the wonderfully tough two-year-old Jonacris.

Jonacris' rise from rags to riches almost rivals Soba's. His rise even started from lower down the scale, his first success coming in the Stonebridge Selling Stakes at Warwick early in May when he made all to win by seven lengths from Leandros with the others at least five lengths further back. Considering the ease of his win his connections were lucky to retain Jonacris for as little as 1,700 guineas and by the time of his next race, at Ripon in June, appeared luckier still: Leandros had gone on to win at Salisbury, the Warwick third, Shadan, had won a seller at Bath and a non-seller at Hamilton and the fifth, Half Chance, had picked up a seller at Wolverhampton. Jonacris quickly proved he was much better than a plater, winning his race at Ripon by eight lengths from the odds-on Godlord, breaking Pisces' thirteen-year-old course record in the process. Further wins soon followed in nurseries at Leicester and Warwick, the latter by four lengths under a 10-lb penalty, and Jonacris then put up a splendid effort under top weight in the Horn Blower Stakes at Ripon in August. He appeared to have a stiff task, set to concede 13 lb to the speedy In Motion, 3 lb to the Uplands Park Acorn Stakes winner Shicklah, and 10 lb to Day of Judgement whom he'd beaten two and a half lengths when receiving 19 lb at Leicester. He started the outsider of five and showed just how much progress he'd made, running on strongly to win by two lengths from Shicklah after being in the lead, as he'd been when gaining all his previous successes, coming to the final two furlongs.

Jonacris got the chance he deserved against some of the best young sprinters in the Prince of Wales's Stakes at York in August, starting second favourite to Time's Time, the winner of his last six races. He ran well, battling on under strong pressure to have every chance inside the final furlong, only to have Cat O' Nine Tails sail past on the outside and beat him a length. Jonacris put up a fine effort nonetheless, beating Boy Trumpeter, Bold Bob (both of whom received 7 lb) and Mac's Palace. After another honourable defeat at the hands of Sayf El Arab in the Highflyer Stakes at Thirsk early in September, where he went down by only a length giving the winner 12 lb, Jonacris ended his first season on a high note in the Harry Rosebery Challenge Trophy at Ayr later the same month. His appearance in the paddock reflected great credit on his trainer—he looked tremendously well despite his hard season—and his performance was equally praiseworthy. He made all, fighting off one challenge after another in typically courageous fashion, and kept on strongly to win by three quarers of a length from Mac's Palace. The first prize of nearly £11,000 took his earnings, including place money, to over £25,000, a remarkable achievement for a former plater.

451

Jonacris' pedigree is more typical of a selling plater than a leading two-year-old. He comes from a very poor female line and it's not surprising that he failed to reach a modest reserve as a yearling at the Doncaster October Sales. The mediocrity of his family was well demonstrated by his pedigree details in the Doncaster catalogue; they took up only about a third of the page allocated to him. He is the first foal of the unraced Squires Girl, who was injured as a yearling and covered as a three-year-old. According to the catalogue his grandam Squire's Lady was also unraced. This is far from the truth. She ran five times as a two-year-old, abysmally, had a further four outings at three and then had eleven races over hurdles in the 1965/66 season. She once finished fourth on the flat and on another occasion filled the same position over hurdles.

Jonacris (ch.c. Apr 29, 1980)	Broxted (gr 1973)	Busted (b 1963)	Crepello
			Sans le Sou
		Luciennes (gr 1964)	Grey Sovereign
			Courtship
	Squires Girl (ch 1976)	Spanish Gold (ch 1967)	Whistling Wind
			Matrisse
		Squire's Lady (ch 1962)	Lord of Verona
			Kings Mills

Squire's Lady was the only foal of Kings Mills, a middle-distance plater who retired a maiden after nineteen races, and produced only five foals herself. None of them won and the catalogue again paints a false picture by saying that Squires Girl's brother Spanish Squire 'ran very promisingly in his only two races on the flat'. He did in fact run three times as a two-year-old, finishing tailed off each time. Squires Girl and Spanish Squire are by Spanish Gold, a tough and useful sprint handicapper who gained most of his ten wins over six furlongs. So far he has sired the winners of only ten races in Britain and Ireland and he was sold for as little as 1,400 guineas in February 1979. Broxted, Jonacris' sire, is now at stud in Saudi Arabia. He gained all his three wins over six furlongs and took after his dam, the speedy Grey Sovereign filly Luciennes, rather than his sire Busted. Jonacris, a strong, compact colt and a good mover, is obviously a sprinter too; he has so far raced only over five furlongs (and only on a sound surface come to that). Although he gave the impression that a stiff five furlongs was beyond him when beaten at Beverley on his fourth outing, he ran on so strongly in his later races that the possibility of his staying six furlongs can't be ruled out. He was as tough and consistent a two-year-old as one could wish to see and hopefully he'll continue to do well. Unfortunately he'll probably find races a good deal harder to come by at three; he's unlikely to be leniently handicapped and he needs to improve still further if he's to hold his own in pattern-race company. *P. Felgate.*

JONDALE 5 b.g. Le Johnstan 123–Levandale 102 (Le Levanstell 122) (1981 8s 7.2fg 8g 10fg 10.6d⁴ 9d* 8.2fg 8g³ 9g 9s³ 8g 1982 8g 7.2s³ 7.6g 9fg 10d 8f 9g 7g 9s 10.2d 8.2s) workmanlike gelding; fair handicapper at his best but is inconsistent and unreliable; stays 1¼m; seems to act on any going but is ideally suited by some give in the ground; has run creditably for an apprentice; suited by front-running tactics; blinkered ninth outing. *A. Smith.* —

JO NDI 6 b.g. The Parson 119–Miss Sunblest 87 (Whistler 129) (1981 18fg 10g³ 13.3g4 12g* 15.5fg³ 10fg³ 12g 15g* 16d³ 16d³ 1982 12fg 16s) good-looking gelding; unreliable handicapper; stays well; acts on any going; sometimes wears blinkers but does just as well without; sometimes sweats up; bandaged when behind both outings in 1982. *P. Mitchell.* —

JONI 3 ch.f. Ruy Lopez 84–Early Summer (Silly Season 127) (1981 NR 1982 10.2g) small filly; second foal; dam of no account; unquoted when tailed-off last in maiden race at Doncaster in June. *D. Morrill.* —

JOPHIL 2 gr.f. Town Crier 119–Sounding Star 71 (Bleep-Bleep 134) (1982 7fg 6f 7g) May 18; 290F; workmanlike filly; poor walker; in rear in maiden race and sellers in the Midlands. *J. Tierney.* —

JORDAN 3 b.c. Moulton 128–Jibuti 114 (Djebe) (1981 8g 8g 1982 8.2fg³ 8f 10d⁴ 10s* 12s³ 11v) well-made, attractive colt; readily won 18-runner maiden race at Sandown in October; stays 1¼m; acts on soft going; sold 16,000 gns Newmarket Autumn Sales and later ran in France. *P. Walwyn.* **80**

JORGE MIGUEL 3 b.c. Welsh Pageant 132–Smeralda 105 (Grey Sovereign 128§) (1981 7d 7fg² 8g² 1982 9s² 10f³ 12fg4 10fg³ 10g* 10fg² 10fg 10s³ 10s³) **85**

well-made, good sort; landed odds readily in 12-runner maiden race at Folkestone in June; ran respectably several times afterwards, including in amateur riders event; stays 1½m; acts on any going but goes well on soft; has run creditably when sweating up; game; promising hurdler. *G. Pritchard-Gordon.*

JOSE COLLINS 5 b.m. Singing Bede 122–Piccadilly Etta 76 (Floribunda 136) **79** (1981 5g 5g⁴ 6d 5g* 6g 5g³ 6g 5fg 5.6fg 5.8g⁴ 5s* 5s³ 5s 5g 1982 5g 5g 5g 5fg 5fg³) sturdy mare; not the best of movers; sprint handicapper; best at 5f; best served by an easy surface; suitable mount for an inexperienced rider. *F. Durr.*

JOTA 6 gr.g. Dragonara Palace 115–Aspiration 53 (Roan Rocket 128) (1981 **57** 12s³ 12s 9f² 12fg² 10f³ 12g 12d 1982 12f 12f² 12f* 12f² 12s* 12d 12fg⁴ 12d) short-coupled gelding; poor walker; middle-distance handicapper; successful at Beverley in May and Pontefract in June; acts on any going; good mount for for an inexperienced rider. *W. Wharton.*

JOUCAS 3 b.c. High Top 131–Alezan Dore 82 (Mountain Call 125) (1981 **79** 6fg 6g 1982 7fg 10f³ 10g 7f⁴ 8g* 8f* 7fg⁴ 8f 8s) quite attractive colt; won minor event at Bath and handicap at Kempton in July; suited by 1m; suited by top-of-the-ground. *J. Winter.*

JOURNEY HOME (USA) 2 b.f. Windy Sands–Carry Me Home (Coursing) **85** (1982 6fg 7s 7g⁴) rather leggy filly; has a round action; sister to 3 winners in USA, including 1981 2-y-o stakes winner Journey Ahead, and half-sister to 5 more; dam ran only 3 times; not seen out until the autumn, running best race when 2½ lengths fourth of 22, chased along throughout, to Toveris in maiden event at Newmarket; will stay 1m. *H. Wragg.*

JOVENITA 3 gr.f. High Top 131–Jovian 88 (Hardicanute 130) (1981 5fg 6g **—** 1982 5g 5f 6g 11d) small filly; behind in varied company. *C. Brittain.*

JOWOODY 2 b.c. Tudor Rhythm 112–Strawberry Ice (Arctic Storm 134) **76** (1982 5d⁴ 7g³ 7.2g 7f 7fg 8f 8.2d 8s) May 20; well-grown, lengthy colt; half-brother to 13f winner South Georgia (by Ballymoss); dam Irish 1m winner; quite a modest maiden; best form at 7f but stays 1m. *J. Gilbert.*

JOYFUL AFFAIR (USA) 3 ch.g. One For All–Happy Ending (Groton) **52** (1981 7fg 7fg 1982 12g 12fg 16f³) rangy gelding; plating-class maiden; stays 2m; sent to Singapore. *E. Eldin.*

JOYFUL DANCER 2 ch.c. Gay Fandango 132–Sheer Joy (Major Portion 129) **89** (1982 7s 7.6v*) Feb 29; IR 9,200Y; brother to fairly useful 7f and 1m winner Sheer Delight, and half-brother to 3 winners, including smart 1m and 1¼m handicapper Jumpabout (by Double Jump); dam never ran; 33/1, won 13-runner maiden race at Lingfield in October by 1½ lengths from Chanceler; will stay 1m. *P. Cole.*

JOY HOUR (USA) 2 b.c. Bold Hour–J. A's Joy (Johns Joy) (1982 7g 7g⁴ **100** 7d³ 6v* 6d* 6g⁴ 6v) Mar 4; $37,000Y; $100,000 2-y-o; lengthy colt; has a round action; half-brother to numerous winners, notably 2000 Guineas second Wind and Wuthering (by No Robbery); dam placed at 3 yrs; successful in October in maiden race at Folkestone and 10-runner minor event (beating Greene Normandy a head) at Leicester; good fourth in nursery at Newmarket later in the month; better suited by 6f than 7f; yet to race on a firm surface. *M. Jarvis.*

JOY OF MUSIC 2 b.c. Music Maestro 119–Blak-En-Bloo 72 (Blakeney 126) **65** (1982 6f 6g 6d 8f) May 26; 3,700Y; quite well-made colt; third foal; dam stayed 1½m; poor maiden; stays 6f. *P. Rohan.*

JOZANDA'S DELIGHT 3 gr.f. Jozanda 80–Sovereigns Delight (Sovereign **—** Lord 120) (1981 NR 1982 5g) first foal; dam placed in point-to-points; unquoted when last of 13 to Cree Bay in minor event at Chepstow in June. *N. Kernick.*

JUBILEE KING 4 ch.g. Farm Walk 111–Fiametta (High Hat 131) (1981 **—** 12.2f⁴ 14.7fg 12.3g 10f 10f 1982 12.2fg) leggy gelding; little sign of ability in varied races. *M. Chapman.*

JUBILEE PRINCE 7 ch.g. Sun Prince 128–Theban Queen (Pindari 124) **—** (1981 11s 8f 10f 8f 10.2fg 10fg 10fg 10g 1982 10f 12fg 14f³ 13g 12fg 8g) poor handicapper nowadays; probably stays 1¾m; acts on any going but goes very well on top-of-the-ground; often starts slowly; good mount for an apprentice; *F. Durr.*

JUBILEE SAINT 6 ch.g. Saintly Song 128–Saint-Cyr 73 (Set Fair 129) (1981 **58**
NR 1982 12g 10d 12fg³ 12f 10.6f 12fg³ 15g* 13.8f² 15d) big gelding; readily
won handicap at Edinburgh in July; stays well; acts on any going but is well
suited by some give in the ground; held up nowadays; has won for an amateur;
bandaged last 2 starts. *Miss S. Hall.*

JUDD 4 b.c. Sparkler 130–Poppy Day 78 (Soleil II 133) (1981 8f 8f 8g³ 10f* **86**
12f² 1982 12g³ 12f³ 12fg* 12d² 14f⁴ 12.3d⁴ 14g² 13d 16v⁴ 14s³) leggy,
lightly-made colt; had opponents well strung out at finish, despite having
wandered once in front, when winning handicap at Leicester in June; in frame
most other starts, on last occasion finishing close third to Aura in handicap at
Sandown in October (hung badly right under pressure and didn't look all that
keen); stays 2m; acts on any going; one paced; sold 10,000 gns Newmarket
Autumn Sales and subsequently did well in Italy. *C. Brittain.*

JUDY CONKERS 2 b.f. Swing Easy 126–Sally Conkers (Roi Lear 126) (1982 **80**
5f 6g² 6fg* 6g 6fg) Feb 18; rangy filly; first foal; dam in rear all outings;
well beaten in nurseries, on final outing last of 12, after winning minor event
at Windsor in July by head from Luck Penny; stays 6f; acts on a firm surface;
sold 5,400 gns Newmarket Autumn Sales; sent to Trinidad. *G. Harwood.*

JUJU 3 b.f. Dragonara Palace 115–Go Too 78 (Goldhill 125) (1981 5fg* 5g⁴ **—**
6g 6f⁴ 5fg³ 5fg 1982 6f 7f 7f 5d) very leggy filly; quite modest in 1981; well
beaten in handicaps at 3 yrs; probably stays 6f; ran moderately in blinkers
once in 1981. *W. Haigh.*

JUKEBOX KATIE 3 ch.f. Jukebox 120–Castaway Katie 80 (Never Say Die **—**
137) (1981 5f 5f⁴ 5fg 6f 1982 8.2fg 10d 12fg 8f) lengthy filly; only plating
class; not certain to stay 1½m. *R. Hollinshead.*

JULARD 6 b.g. Golden Mallard 103–Jury 66 (Lucky Brief 128) (1981 12.2g **—**
1982 12s 13d) poor maiden; stays 1½m; possibly unsuited by firm ground;
bandaged in front on first outing and blinkered only subsequent start. *J.
Leigh.*

JULIA FLYTE 2 gr.f. Drone–Miss Upward 77 (Alcide 136) (1982 6g³ 6fg* **91**
7g) Feb 14; IR 100,000Y; well-made filly; half-sister to 4 winners, including
very useful middle-distance filly Miss Petard and useful 1m winner Master
Petard (both by Petingo); dam won at 1¼m; beat Al Washl by 2 lengths in 18-
runner maiden race at Salisbury in September, travelling well throughout and
running on strongly; second favourite, 4 lengths fifth of 7 to Saving Mercy in
Rockfel Stakes at Newmarket the following month; will stay 1m. *G. Harwood.*

JUMAIREH (USA) 2 b.f. Cornish Prince–Glad To Get (Absurd) (1982 5fg **76**
6g³ 7fg³ 7f⁴ 7g 8.2d 8s) Feb 19; $45,000Y; smallish, shallow-girthed filly,
first foal; dam won 1m claiming race; quite a modest maiden; well beaten in
nurseries last 3 starts; should stay 1m. *H. T. Jones.*

JUMANA 2 ch.f. Windjammer (USA)–How Much (Palestine 133) (1982 **—**
5g 5g) Apr 22; 18,000Y; half-sister to several winners, including fairly useful
5f to 7f winner Flower Man (by Floribunda); dam of little account; towards
rear in minor event at Bath in July and modest maiden race at Wolverhampton
in October; sold 1,000 gns Newmarket Autumn Sales. *G. Hunter.*

JUMP JAR 3 b.g. Lochnager 132–Light Jumper 100 (Red God 128§) (1981 **90**
5s* 6s* 5g³ 6g* 6g 6s 1982 7g³ 7f) rangy, good sort; good walker and mover;
creditable 1½ lengths third to Wibis Range in Northern Free Handicap at
Newcastle in April; last of 11 to Gavo in valuable handicap at York in May;
subsequently gelded and didn't race again; stays 7f; needs some give in the
ground; sold to D. Chapman 1,700 gns Doncaster November Sales. *M. H.
Easterby.*

JUNGLE ROMEO (USA) 2 b.c. Jungle Savage–Baby Louise (Exclusive **90 p**
Native) (1982 7s*) Mar 7; $85,000Y; lengthy, rather sparely-made colt;
half-brother to 3 winners, including very smart 1981 American 2-y-o filly Proud
Lou (by Proud Clarion); dam minor sprint stakes winner at 2 yrs; 5/1, always
prominent, led 2f out and held on by a short head from Major Don in 28-runner
maiden race at Redcar in October; should improve. *M. Stoute.*

JUNIOR TRUSTEE 3 ch.g. Mr Bigmore 123–Fulfilment (David Jack 125) **—**
(1981 7fg 8g 10s 1982 16f) strong, good-bodied gelding; carries plenty of
condition; has a rather round action; poor maiden; sold 620 gns Newmarket
Autumn Sales. *F. Durr.*

JUNIPER 3 ch.g. Morston 125–Windflower 77 (Crepello 136) (1981 NR 1982 — 10f³) half-brother to 3 winners, including useful 1978 2-y-o 6f and 7.3f winner Bluebell (by Town Crier); dam, half-sister to Queen's Hussar, seemed to stay 1¾m; not seen out after staying on strongly without being knocked about to finish 10 lengths third of 16 to The Dice Man in maiden race at Nottingham in April; will stay 1½m+. *W. Hastings-Bass.*

JUPITER EXPRESS 4 ch.g. Jupiter Pluvius 119–La Perla 81 (Majority Blue — 126) (1981 NR 1982 12g) promising winner over hurdles; 33/1, pulled hard when 11 lengths fifth of 7 behind Two High in minor event at Beverley in September, first outing on flat. *J. Fitzgerald.*

JUPITER ISLAND 3 b.c. St Paddy 133–Mrs Moss 81 (Reform 132) (1981 94 6fg 7f 1982 10.5f⁴ 10g 10t 12fg* 12g⁴ 12fg³ 11.5g* 12s* 10v³ 12s) close-coupled, quite attractive colt; good mover; won minor event at Wolverhampton and handicaps at Yarmouth and Ascot; beat Polar Star unchallenged by 8 lengths on last-named in September; suited by 1½m; has won on a firm surface but evidently revels in the mud; does best when ridden up with pace. *C. Brittain.*

JUPITER'S GEM 4 b.f. Jupiter Pluvius 119–Parry (Pampered King 121) 44 (1981 14.6fg 1982 10f 14g 12fg 11.7fg³) lengthy filly; ran respectably in handicaps on last 2 starts, first form; stays 1¾m. *R. Thompson.*

JURY PALACE 3 b.f. Dragonara Palace 115–Reppeve 45 (Jimmy Reppin — 131) (1981 5fg⁴ 5fg 5g 5d⁴ 6d 7g 5g 1982 5f 6h 5fg 7.2g 7f) useful sort; quite moderate form in varied company at 2 yrs; ran poorly in 1982; best form at 5f. *R. Hollinshead.*

JUST A KINSMAN 6 b.g. Great Nephew 126–Carcosa 103 (Sovereign Lord — 120) (1981 NR 1982 10.6f) poor form, including in a seller; sold 2,600 gns Doncaster November Sales. *Mrs S. Cousins.*

JUST A SPARK 3 b.f. Sparkler 130–Pontresina 70 (Ballymoss 136) (1981 — 7g 7g 1982 8fg 9f 12.2f 16fg) small filly; poor mover; of no account. *N. Bycroft.*

JUST GORGEOUS 2 b. or br.f. Home Guard 129–Mia Cosa 78 (Ragusa 60 137) (1982 5d 5f⁴ 5g 7g 7fg 6g 6fg 5fg) Apr 1; 7,400Y; good-bodied, quite attractive filly; good mover; sister to 3-y-o 6f seller winner Reluctant Hero and half-sister to a winner in Italy; dam, half-sister to smart 1971 Irish 2-y-o Open Season, won 3 times in Italy; plating-class maiden; stays 6f; blinkered last 3 starts. *B. Swift.*

JUST GRAYLE 3 gr. or ro.g. Habat 127–Tomboy 95 (Sica Boy 132) (1981 — 7fg 7fg 10s 1982 11.7f 10.1fg 7.2f 9g 8g⁴ 10.1fg 10.8fg²) fair sort; bad walker; plater nowadays; should stay 1¼m; blinkered final start; has run creditably for an apprentice; claimed £1,550 after final outing. *P. Cole.*

JUST GUNNER 2 ch.c. Gunner B 126–Lady Tarcherio 65 (Pontifex) (1982 64 6fg 8.2fg 6g 7.2s⁴ 8s² 8d 10s 10.2s) Apr 16; small colt; first foal; dam won over 7f; plater; best race when neck second of 15 to Gunnard at Redcar in October; suited by 1m; acts on soft going; often blinkered. *S. Norton.*

JUSTINIANI (USA) 4 b.g. Kentuckian–Light Verse (Reverse) (1981 8d 64 8fg 10d² 12s³ 10fg² 9s 8g 1982 10fg 12fg* 11.7f 13.5g⁴ 14g 16.5d 14fg² 14fg 14fg 12d) rangy ex-English gelding; ran best race when beating No-U-Turn by 2 lengths in handicap at Folkestone in April; stays 1¾m; acts on any going; ran poorly last 3 starts, wearing blinkers on final occasion; trained until after third start by R. Price; sold 1,900 gns Ballsbridge November Sales. *C. Collins, Ireland.*

JUST MAGGIE 2 b.f. So Blessed 130–Balnespick 101 (Charlottown 127) — (1982 5f) Apr 14; 17,500Y; sister to 3-y-o 1¼m winner Kaukas; dam stayed at least 13f; 12/1 and backward, seventh of 13 to Widow Bird in maiden race at Nottingham in April. *J. Bosley.*

JUST MARTIN 4 b.g. Martinmas 128–Just Alice (Worden II 129) (1981 58 5s 5d 7fg³ 8d 1982 10d⁴ 8d 10f 10f 11.7fg 8g³ 10fg) leggy colt; quite a moderate handicapper; set a strong gallop and ran well when 5 lengths third to Bancario in minor event at Newcastle in August; ran badly only subsequent start; stays 1¼m; acts on a firm and a soft surface; headstrong; sold out of R. Price's stable 4,000 gns Doncaster August Sales after sixth start. *R. Champion.*

JUST ONE MORE TIME 2 ch.f. Bonne Noel 115–Dialectic (Red God 71 p 128§) (1982 6g) Feb 8; IR 1,500F, 3,700Y; sparely-made filly; half-sister to several winners, including very useful 7f and 1m horse Lucky Monkey (by Le Levanstell); dam from same family as Karabas; unquoted but fairly fit, kept on nicely when 5¼ lengths fifth to stable-companion Albadeeah in 18-runner maiden race at Newmarket in September; will be well suited by further; should improve. *H. T. Jones.*

JUST QUEEN 2 b.f. Runnymede 123–Just Janie 84 (John Splendid 116) (1982 5fg⁴) Jan 29; 1,450Y; first foal; dam sprinter; poor fourth in maiden auction event at Salisbury in May; dead. *W. Wightman.* —

JUST RAIN 2 b.f. Blue Cashmere 129–Aqua Nimba (Acropolis 132) (1982 6fg) May 17; sister to 6f seller winner Aqua Blue and half-sister to fair 1978 2-y-o miler Top Stream (by Highland Melody); dam poor sister to smart stayer Acrania; unquoted and bit backward, twelfth of 13 in maiden race at York in July. *P. Asquith.* —

JUST WISHING 4 b.f. Wishing Star 117–Lepe 65 (Exbury 138) (1981 8.3fg 1982 10f² 10f* 10f 12g 12f² 11.7g³ 10g² 12fg² 12fg 10f) workmanlike filly; bought in 2,600 gns after winning seller at Leicester in May; placed in non-sellers afterwards; stays 1½m; acts on firm going; sold 2,000 gns Newmarket Autumn Sales. *J. Winter.* **47**

K

KABOUR 4 b.c. Habitat 134–Kermiya (Vienna 127) (1981 8g 6s 5f* 5s 1982 6d 6fg* 7f 6s 5f 6f³ 6g 5g 5g) strong, quite attractive colt; has an enlarged off-fore joint and is a poor mover; short-head winner at Thirsk in April on only outing in a seller (no bid); ran respectably fifth and sixth outings; stays 6f; acts on any going; bandaged second and third starts; retained 760 gns Doncaster November Sales. *D. Chapman.* **57**

KACHELA 3 br.f. Kalamoun 129–Cheshunt 102 (Relic) (1981 NR 1982 8fg 8.2g 8fg 9g 9s) IR 13,000Y; neat, well-made filly; poor walker; half-sister to a winner in Italy and smart French 7f to 10.5f winner Hether (by Hethersett); dam 2-y-o 5f winner; well beaten in varied company; blinkered final start. *C. Nelson.* —

KAFU 2 b.c. African Sky 124–Pampered Dancer (Pampered King 121) (1982 5g² 5g* 6f² 6f³ 5f* 5f* 6g² 6g⁴) **120**

If the intention behind the re-opening of the Molecomb Stakes to colts was to produce larger fields and more competitive events, then the move has

Flying Childers Stakes, Doncaster—Kafu gains his second pattern-race success with a comfortable win from Bold Bob

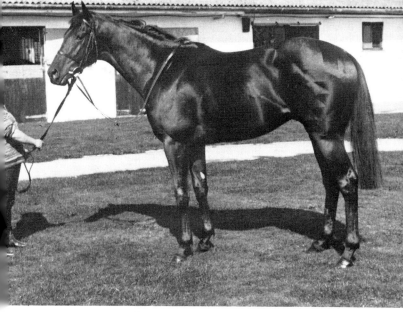

H. H. Yazid and Ahmed Ltd's "Kafu"

not so far been a success. In 1981 a field of six contested the race with Prowess Prince the winner. The latest running went to a better horse in Kafu but lost much of its appeal when a bout of coughing forced the late withdrawal of Brondesbury leaving a field of four, the smallest since 1974, with the outcome apparently resting between odds-on favourite Rutland, winner of his three races, and Kafu, placed in the Coventry Stakes and Anglia Television July Stakes on his last two appearances. The result was never in doubt from the moment that Kafu was sent on two furlongs out; he quickly went clear and had three lengths to spare over Rutland despite being eased. Kafu's win in the Molecomb was one of three for the horse as a two-year-old, all comfortably gained over five furlongs. At Kempton in May he'd won a maiden race and at Doncaster in September he took the Flying Childers Stakes, thus adding a second pattern race to his tally. At Doncaster he again accounted for a small field, only four rivals opposing him, this time starting at odds on himself with Widaad second favourite, followed by Sayf El Arab, Bold Bob and Irish challenger Virginia Deer. Held up in the rear early on, Kafu quickened well to lead a furlong out and had considerably more in hand over Bold Bob than the three-quarter-length margin might suggest, for Starkey rode at his cheekiest on him. Kafu spent just as much of his season racing in good company at six furlongs and usually did well. His best efforts came in the Coventry Stakes at Royal Ascot, in which he kept on well and went down by a length and a half to Horage, and the Mill Reef Stakes at Newbury in September, when a strong late surge saw him a runner-up by three quarters of a length to Salieri who received 4 lb. Kafu ran slightly below that form when fourth of five to Diesis in the William Hill Middle Park Stakes at Newmarket later in September; his only seriously below-par performance was when third to Horage in the Anglia Television July Stakes, also at Newmarket.

Kafu, purchased for 52,000 guineas in Ireland as a yearling, was one of two British pattern-race winners in 1982 by African Sky, the other being the sprinter

Lightning Label. His dam Pampered Dancer raced once and is a granddaughter of One Thousand Guineas winner Dancing Time and half-sister to Irish One Thousand Guineas winner Royal Danseuse, herself a good broodmare. Four of Pampered Dancer's six foals to race have been colts and all four have won, the pick besides Kafu being Moomba Masquerade (by Gay Fandango), winner of the Land of Burns Stakes, and the quite useful sprinter Captain Irish (by

Kafu (b.c. Feb 17, 1980)	African Sky (b 1970)	Sing Sing (b 1957)	Tudor Minstrel / Agin the Law
		Sweet Caroline (b 1954)	Nimbus / Lackaday
	Pampered Dancer (b 1969)	Pampered King (b 1954)	Prince Chevalier / Netherton Maid
		Star Dancer (br 1954)	Arctic Star / Dancing Time

Green God). Kafu should continue to run well in the top sprint races but we should favour his prospects more if he looked keener on racing than he sometimes does: he tends to race with his ears laid back. Furthermore he looked a difficult ride at Kempton, where he also gave trouble at the start; he hung left in the closing stages of the July Stakes and in the Middle Park Stakes he found very little off the bridle after making smooth progress over a furlong out. He needs things his own way to be seen at his best. A big, well-made, quite attractive colt, Kafu has yet to race on a soft surface. *G. Harwood.*

KAIMLAW 8 ch.g. Native Prince–Misty Morn 70 (Worden II 129) (1981 **72** 5g* 5g4 5fg 5fg2 5f2 5g2 5g4 5f 5g* 5f 5f) 1982 5fg* 5fg 5g4 5g 5f4 5fg2 5fg 5g 5d3 5g 5d* 5fg) sprint handicapper; has run tubed; made all at Hamilton in May and Ayr in September; best at 5f; acts on any going, except perhaps really soft; used to wear blinkers; suitable mount for an apprentice; tough and genuine. *H. Bell.*

KALAGLOW 4 gr.c. Kalamoun 129–Rossitor 78 (Pall Mall 132) (1981 9fg* **132** 10.5s 12d 1982 9fg* 10.5g 10f* 10g* 12fg* 10d)
Switching and confusion of identity among racehorses has been a vexing problem for the turf authorities down the centuries. Several Derby winners had lain under suspicion of being older than they ought to have been before the disqualification in 1844 of Running Rein who was proven to be a four-year-old named Maccabaeus. Since then many other 'ringers' have raced on the turf and recently this undesirable aspect of racing has come once more into the public eye. In March 1980 a National Hunt trainer was given a suspended prison sentence and ordered to pay £3,000 after being convicted at Exeter Crown Court for his part in an alleged betting coup involving the winner of a selling handicap hurdle at Newton Abbot's Bank Holiday fixture in August 1978; the prosecution claimed that the one-time useful hurdler Cobbler's March was run masquerading as In The Money, a gelding who had been off the track for two seasons and had not previously completed the course over hurdles. The most recent season saw the Jockey Club call in the police to investigate another suspected ringer after a substantial gamble on the two-year-old Flockton Grey in an auction event at Leicester in March; Flockton Grey, disqualified in July on a technicality, slammed his field by twenty lengths but it is now alleged that the winner was a three-year-old called Good Hand and the matter is in the hands of the Director of Public Prosecutions at the time of writing. The publicity given to such cases is naturally greater than that to cases of accidental confusion which, nevertheless, can be potentially almost as serious. For example, the identity of the four-year-old sprinters Sanu and Steel Pass became muddled when they were returned from the United States in 1982 and Sanu, the better of the pair, ran in error as Steel Pass before the mistake was discovered. Even more alarming, in some of its aspects, was the revelation that the four-year-old Kalaglow, a winner of the Coral-Eclipse Stakes and the King George VI and Queen Elizabeth Diamond Stakes, two of Britain's most valuable and prestigious events, raced under an erroneous pedigree as a two-year-old and three-year-old.
Soon after Kalaglow's first race as a four-year-old, the Earl of Sefton Stakes at Newmarket which he won impressively by three lengths, it became known that Kalaglow's supposed dam Aglow had been confused with another mare Rossitor. Incredibly, the mix-up over the identities of Aglow and Rossitor, both of whom were chestnuts, had gone undetected for at least ten years, the muddle having originated either before or during the time when the pair were

Earl of Sefton Stakes, Newmarket—Kalaglow makes all to win in impressive style from Ring The Bell (rails) and Kind of Hush

transferred from the Someries Stud at Newmarket where they were bred to trainer Gordon Smyth as yearlings or, less likely, while they were two-year-olds. It was established that Aglow and Rossitor raced in their wrong names as three-year-olds, Rossitor (racing as Aglow) winning a maiden race over thirteen furlongs at Bath and a handicap at Newmarket over a mile and three quarters in her only season to race, and Aglow (racing as Rossitor) failing to reach a place in six outings. Although a correction to the racing records of Aglow and Rossitor as three-year-olds was published in *The Racing Calendar* in July, no mention was made of the true identity of the filly who ran unplaced under the name of Rossitor in a maiden race at Newbury as a two-year-old. At the end of their racing careers Rossitor (under the name Aglow) was returned to the Someries Stud and Aglow (under the name Rossitor) was sent up to the Newmarket December Sales where she fetched 800 guineas and was exported to South Africa. The mistaken identity of Rossitor and Aglow came to light when Rossitor (under the name Aglow) was visiting the Irish National Stud in 1982 when it was noticed that the mare's markings did not tally with the particulars on her passport. If reports be true, the mare in question had three white legs whereas Aglow's passport showed her as having one! How such a blatant discrepancy could have remained undetected for so long is baffling. Since 1974 Rossitor (under the name Aglow) had visited Roan Rocket, Queen's Hussar, Kalamoun, Wolver Hollow and Nebbiolo (twice); on each occasion a covering certificate was issued and signed by the stallion owner or his representative confirming, among other things, that 'I examined the mare's passport and satisfied myself as to her correct identity.'

Kalaglow is not the only British pattern-race winner to have run under a wrong pedigree in recent years. The winner of the 1974 Coventry Stakes Whip It Quick, who subsequently won pattern events in Germany, raced until towards the end of his three-year-old career with his dam described as being by Eborneezer or Ritudyr. Blood-typing revealed that neither stallion could have sired Whip It Quick's dam and it was established that Indian Ruler, a stallion at the same stud as Eborneezer and Ritudyr, was in fact her sire. These examples, coupled with cases of ringers and innocent mistakes involving horses in training, have led to the efficiency of the system of identification used in this country being called into question. Identity in Britain begins within four months of birth when a foal has to be examined by an independent vet

Coral-Eclipse Stakes, Sandown—Kalaglow is never in any danger from his nearest pursuer Lobkowiez; Peacetime is third

who checks the mare's passport and completes an identification certificate for the foal, describing such details as its sex, colour, markings and exact positions of whorls (changes in the hair-pattern). This document, which includes diagrams, must be sent to Weatherbys for the foal to be registered in the *General Stud Book*. The original document is retained—and a copy kept on film—until such time as the animal is named (names are not accepted for foals) when it is re-examined by a vet and another identification document submitted to the Racing Calendar Office. The colour, markings and whorls of the horse are compared with those described on the foal identification certificate before the trainer is issued with a passport, containing the details taken at naming, which must accompany the horse and be available for official inspection throughout its racing and breeding life (the passport must be endorsed by the Stud Book authority when a broodmare or stallion enters stud). Trainers, breeders and bloodstock and shipping agents are required by the *Rules of Racing* to check the identity of any horse which is in their care against its passport and notify the authorities of any discrepancy in age, colour or markings.

Is there a better alternative to the present system? Racing in the United States is not controlled by a single body as it is in Britain, but most of the authorities in that country have adopted a system of lip tattooing, an index number being tattooed with permanent and unchangeable dye on the upper lip of every yearling and the number being added to the horse's record in the Stud Book. The New York Racing Association use a system which incorporates details of the chesnuts, horny growths appearing on the inside of each leg about halfway up; when experiments in using chesnuts were first conducted it was found that in fifty thousand horses not one duplication occurred. Heat branding is used in New Zealand and Australia, a number or a code being branded on the shoulder. This last-named system and another suggested alternative, the freeze branding of a number or code on the neck underneath the mane, apparently find no favour with the British turf authorities who claim that the present system is *in theory at least* sound and reliable. Tattooing, branding or using chesnuts for identification purposes might prove a stronger deterrent to those considering using a ringer because, for one thing, it would make it practical to employ a check on all runners as they enter the paddock; but tattooing or branding would be no guarantee against one horse being crossed with another through confusion of identity as foals or yearlings. In our view the biggest problem about preserving the accuracy of the identity of horses while they are in training and the accuracy of the *General Stud Book* lies not with the system but with the human element upon which it relies for efficient operation. It seems clear that there are trainers, breeders and stallion owners who patently fail to carry out passport checks with any degree of thoroughness, so why should anyone believe they would check tattooed or branded numbers or chesnuts? Stiffer penalties for those found guilty of error would almost certainly help to reduce the number of mistakes in identification and authentication. The prevention of criminal fraud and the preservation of the accuracy of racing and stud records are too important to allow slip-shod mistakes to go virtually unpunished, as they apparently do at present. Had Kalaglow not seriously injured himself in the usual first-mile scrimmaging during Shergar's

Derby—an injury which kept him off the course for ten months until the Earl of Sefton Stakes in April—he might have achieved his potential as a three-year-old. There would have been possible legal repercussions if he had been syndicated as a stallion in a multi-million-pound deal before the error in his pedigree had been brought to light.

Kalaglow had been a strong second favourite behind Shergar for the Derby before running badly on soft going in the Mecca-Dante Stakes; he started third favourite on Derby Day and finished thirteenth of eighteen. Kalaglow's all-the-way win in the nine-furlong Earl of Sefton Stakes at Newmarket augured well for his four-year-old campaign and he finished a fairly close seventh to Bikala in the Prix Ganay at Longchamp in May on his next appearance. Kalaglow hardly looked back afterwards, winning the Brigadier Gerard Stakes at Sandown at the end of May, the Coral-Eclipse Stakes at Sandown in early July and the King George VI and Queen Elizabeth Diamond Stakes at Ascot towards the end of July. Throughout the season he impressed with his general fitness and well being and appeared to have progressed physically each time we saw him. He slammed a very useful field of four- and five-year-olds in the Brigadier Gerard Stakes, winning comfortably by eight lengths and two from Silver Season and Amyndas, taking the lead about two furlongs from the finish after being waited with just behind the leaders most of the way. Kalaglow set a time record for Sandown's mile-and-a-quarter course when winning the Brigadier Gerard Stakes, one of several new marks set at Sandown in the most recent season following the completion of course modifications. Silver Season was one of eight opponents for Kalaglow in the Coral-Eclipse Stakes over the same course and distance five weeks later. The Coral-Eclipse had been a reported objective of the Derby winner Golden Fleece but when he had to miss the race Kalaglow started a hot favourite. The field for the Coral-Eclipse contained five representatives of the classic generation including three who had finished behind Golden Fleece at Epsom—Peacetime (seventh), Rocamadour (eighth) and Lobkowiez (fifteenth). Kalaglow was chased home by Lobkowiez, who had been beaten a short head at Royal Ascot by another Coral-Eclipse runner Kind of Hush in the Prince of Wales's Stakes over the Eclipse distance. Rocamadour finished third in the Eclipse and Peacetime fourth, all three Derby runners finishing closer to Kalaglow at Sandown than they had to Golden Fleece at Epsom. Kalaglow won a shade cleverly by four lengths, quickening in fine

King George VI and Queen Elizabeth Diamond Stakes, Ascot—Kalaglow puts up the performance of his life to beat Assert. Glint of Gold (stripe on cap) finishes third, Critique fourth and Bikala (left) fifth

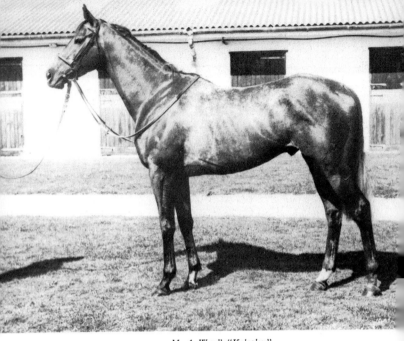

Mr A. Ward's "Kalaglow"

style in the straight after being in the front rank throughout, but his form did not look good enough to give him an outstanding chance in the King George VI and Queen Elizabeth Diamond Stakes. His stamina had also to be taken on trust, the Derby being his only previous race over a mile and a half.

As usual, the King George VI and Queen Elizabeth Diamond Stakes attracted a top-class line-up. The Irish-trained dual Derby winner Assert and the unbeaten filly Height of Fashion were the only three-year-olds among the nine runners but among the older horses were Assert's half-brother Bikala, the previous year's Prix du Jockey-Club winner who had not run since the Prix Ganay, and the tough-as-teak Glint of Gold, runner-up in Shergar's Derby and winner of the Grand Prix de Saint-Cloud on his latest outing. Critique, winner of the Hardwicke Stakes, and Easter Sun, winner of the Coronation Cup, were also in the field which was completed by the 100/1-shot Lafontaine and the Israeli-trained Dronacharya at 750/1. Assert started at 11/10 on, with Bikala (11/2) and Kalaglow (13/2) next in the betting. Bikala set a blistering gallop —the smart Lafontaine, an habitual front runner, was off the bridle soon after the start vainly trying to keep up with him—and Kalaglow, on the rails in fourth place, was among those being pushed along vigorously approaching the home turn, apparently outpaced by Bikala and Assert who was on the heels of the leader. Assert passed Bikala early in the short straight but was soon challenged by Glint of Gold on his outside. Kalaglow, who had slipped through on the inside of the weakening Lafontaine entering the straight, was kept to the rails and, under pressure, steadily improved into a challenging position. The hard-driven Assert proved too strong for Glint of Gold to pass but Assert couldn't shake off Kalaglow who forged ahead close home to win by a neck in a stirring finish. Kalaglow and Assert were drawing away from the others as the post was reached and Glint of Gold finished three lengths away third, just ahead of Critique and Bikala who were well clear of the remainder. Needless to say, Kalaglow's performance removed the question mark against both his ability and his stamina. Our scale of weight-for-age gives a three-year-old 3 lb less to carry against a four-year-old at this stage of the season than do the King George weights and on straightforward handicapping principles Assert came out the best horse in the race at the weights; but Kalaglow gave a tip-top display on King George day, the best of his life. Kalaglow's win at Ascot took his career record to ten victories from thirteen starts—his defeat in the Dubai Champion Stakes (in which he was badly hampered when apparently beaten running into the Dip) on his only outing after the King George made it ten from fourteen and he ended his racing career with first-prize earnings of £274,260.

One of the ironies of the result of the King George VI and Queen Elizabeth Diamond Stakes was that, with yearling prices reaching record levels at Keeneland earlier in the week, Britain's most prestigious open-aged race was won by a horse who cost only 11,500 guineas at public auction at that age from another who fetched approximately £16,000. Spending freely on fashionably-bred yearlings can be a successful mode of operation but Kalaglow's trainer has enjoyed remarkable success in recent seasons with relatively cheaply-bought yearlings. The 4,500 guineas purchase Ela-Mana-Mou, who completed the Eclipse-King George double as a four-year-old when trained by Hern, was bought out of Harwood's yard for £500,000 at the end of his three-year-old days after winning the King Edward VII Stakes and finishing in the frame in the Derby, the Grand Prix de Saint-Cloud and the King George. In the same year that he acquired Kalaglow, Harwood struck two other notable bargains, picking up To-Agori-Mou for 20,000 guineas and Recitation for 35,000 dollars; To-Agori-Mou was the best two-year-old colt in England and went on to win the Two Thousand Guineas and other good races as a three-year-old while Recitation won the Grand Criterium, the most important race for two-year-olds in France, and the Poule d'Essai des Poulains (French Two Thousand Guineas).

		Zeddaan	Grey Sovereign
	Kalamoun	(gr 1965)	Vareta
	(gr 1970)	Khairunissa	Prince Bio
Kalaglow		(gr 1960)	Palariva
(gr.c. 1978)		Pall Mall	Palestine
	Rossitor	(ch 1955)	Malapert
	(ch 1970)	Sonia	Worden II
		(ch 1965)	Sonsa

The death of Kalaglow's sire Kalamoun at the early age of nine was a considerable loss to European breeders. In spite of fertility problems—Kalamoun was one of only fifteen reported live foals by him in 1978—Kalamoun turned out to be a top-class stallion. He has sired good winners in England, including Castle Keep and Kampala, but, except for Kalaglow, his most notable offspring have been trained in France including Bikala, Persepolis, Shakapour and Kenmare, each of whom won Group 1 pattern races. Kalamoun himself won three Group 1 pattern races, the Poule d'Essai des Poulains, the Prix Lupin and the Prix Jacques le Marois but he didn't last out the trip in the French Derby; he came from a very speedy family and although speed was his main asset—he had an excellent turn of foot—he proved his ability to stay a stiff ten furlongs in the Prix Lupin and we went on record as saying that we expected him to do very well as a stallion. Kalaglow's dam Rossitor possessed plenty of stamina winning at up to a mile and three quarters, as has been detailed earlier, and being placed at two miles. Rossitor, who has been represented so far by Kalaglow and the Irish two-year-old Glowing Embers (by Nebbiolo), was by the Two Thousand Guineas winner Pall Mall out of the fair mile-and-a-half winner Sonia. Rossitor's grandam Sonsa was a very useful racemare who won the Ebbisham Stakes at Epsom on her racecourse debut and was probably best at a mile to a mile and a quarter. Sonsa, who was also the grandam of Aglow, was out of a half-sister to Daily Double, the dam of Meld. At one time Kalaglow took after his sire and dam in conformation: both were lightly made and Kalaglow, although much improved in physique as a four-year-old, still looked somewhat lacking in substance at the side of some of his rivals in the King George parade; this could not be said however when he lined up for the Champion Stakes by which time he had developed into a tall, useful-looking colt. In another respect, however, Kalaglow seemed to favour neither his sire nor his dam, both of whom handled a soft surface well. Kalaglow's smooth, light, flowing action is the type often associated with a top-of-the-

ground performer and he seemed ideally suited by a sound surface, although
he won the Horris Hill Stakes as a two-year-old on dead going. He was a
genuine racehorse and his four-year-old career in particular was a great tribute
to the skill and judgement of his trainer. It had looked, at one time, as if
the leg injury sustained in the Derby might end Kalaglow's racing days but
Harwood and a group of his owners reportedly bought a half share in him from
Kalaglow's original owners during the winter, a gamble which paid off in no
uncertain manner: Kalaglow was retired with a valuation on him of £5,000,000,
comprising forty shares at £125,000 each. He will stand his first season at
the Brook Stud, Newmarket, in 1983. *G. Harwood.*

KALAMAIDAN 2 b.f. Kala Shikari 125–Buttermilk Sky (Midsummer Night II **56**
117) (1982 5fg 5fg³ 6g 5fg 6f⁴ 6s 5v) Mar 9; 2,800F, 7,000Y; lightly-made filly;
half-sister to Glideaway (by Gay Fandango), successful at up to 1¾m in Ireland;
moderate plater; best form at 5f; appears to need a firm surface; disappointing.
G. Hunter.

KALIFI (USA) 3 gr.c. Caro 133–Hasten On (Fleet Nasrullah) (1981 NR **75**
1982 9fg⁴ 14fg) $205,000Y; tall, leggy colt; half-brother to several winners,
including French 1m winner Exclusive Kid (by Exclusive Native) and Hasty
Tudor (by King of the Tudors), a smart winner at up to 9f; dam won 5f maiden
race; made running and kept on at one pace when 3¾ lengths fourth of 12 to
Rel Tiger in newcomers race at Wolverhampton in April, better effort; not seen
out after May. *H. Cecil.*

KALKUS 3 b.c. Strongheart 65–Right On (Right Tack 131) (1981 7f 8d 8s⁴ 10g **55**
1982 8f² 12h 9g* 10.2g 10.2s) small colt; plater; bought in 1,900 gns after
trotting up at Wolverhampton in June; should stay 1¼m; acts on any going.
M. Pipe.

KALLISTA ANTARTIS 2 ch.c. Jimmy Reppin 131–Cuddly Toy (Sovereign **64**
Lord 120) (1982 5fg⁴ 5fg 5fg 6fg) Apr 13; tall, narrow colt; half-brother to 5f
to 11f winner Keira (by Keren); dam of little account; poor maiden; not seen
out after August; better suited to 6f than by 5f, and will stay further. *P. K.
Mitchell.*

KALYOUB 2 ch.c. Sallust 134–Khadaeen (Lyphard 132) (1982 6fg² 5g⁴) **89**
Mar 6; robust, deep-girthed, chunky colt; good walker but has a round action
and is not a particularly good mover; first foal; dam placed over 1m in France;
½-length second of 21 to Coquito's Friend in minor event at Newmarket in August,
better effort; needs at least 6f, and will stay 1m. *F. J. Houghton.*

KAMENEV 5 b.g. Ribero 126–Welsh Mistress 113 (Abernant 142) (1981 **—**
6v 8s 9g 6g 6fg 10fg 12fg 13.8fg 12.3fg 6d 8s 1982 6f 8fg 8.2fg 8g) short-backed
gelding; good mover; poor plater nowadays; stays 7f; best form on a firm surface;
blinkered third start; bandaged final outing; trained until after third outing by
D. Chapman. *W. Barrett.*

KANO FLOWER (USA) 3 b.c. Far North 120–Flower Vase (Round Table) **65**
(1981 NR 1982 7.6f 10f 10fg² 10s² 10.2f 12fg 9v² 10.2s) $20,000Y; small,
useful-looking colt; second foal; dam did not run; runner-up in maiden races;
blinkered when well beaten in seller final start; stays 1¼m; seems to act on any
going. *I. Walker.*

KANSU 7 b.g. Caliban 123–Jolisu 110 (Welsh Abbot 131) (1981 NR 1982 **—**
12d 16f) won 4 times from 1½m to 2m in 1979 (rated 71); acts on any going;
has won for an amateur rider. *M. Ryan.*

KAPRIELIAN (USA) 2 b.c. The Minstrel 135–Rainbow's Edge (Creme dela **—**
Creme) (1982 7g) Apr 29; $130,000Y; third foal; half-brother to French
3-y-o 9f winner Vadsa (by Halo); dam, half-sister to smart middle-distance
fillies Sweet Rhapsody and Sisterhood, won over 5f at 2 yrs; 100/1, failed to
recover from slow start when tailed off in maiden race at Yarmouth in September.
M. Stoute.

KARABLAKE 2 b.c. Blakeney 126–Karenina 95 (Silver Shark 129) (1982 **81** p
7fg³) Feb 29; 39,000Y; rangy colt; half-brother to 3 winners, including smart
1976 staying 2-y-o Sultan's Ruby (by Royal Palace); dam won twice from 4
starts at 2 yrs; stayed on well without being knocked about when 4½ lengths
third of 10 behind Cock Robin in minor event at Sandown in August; will be
suited by 1¼m+; sure to improve and win a race. *G. Harwood.*

KARADAR 4 b.c. Rheingold 137–Shahinaaz (Venture VII 129) (1981 12g **99**
11s² 10s⁴ 10fg² 12fg* 12fg* 12g* 12v* 12g⁴ 1982 14g² 12fg* 16.1f* 16fg³ 14g³
14.6g* 16d) quite an attractive, well-made colt; ran consistently well again

*Esal Bookmakers Handicap, Doncaster—Karadar stays on magnificently under pressure
to hold off Bucklow Hill (centre) and Morgan's Choice (left)*

H. H. Aga Khan's "Karadar"

and put up a typically game performance when beating Bucklow Hill by ¾ length in £18,600 Esal Bookmakers Handicap at Doncaster in September, going on fully 4f out and responding magnificently to pressure; had earlier won at York (dead-heated with Keelby Kavalier in a handicap) and Haydock (beat Another Sam easing up by a length in Lymm Stakes); also placed at Newmarket, Royal Ascot (Queen's Vase) and York (Tote-Ebor); suited by a test of stamina nowadays; acts on any going; usually sweats up; thoroughly genuine; had stiffish task final start. *M. Stoute.*

KARAMAZOV 6 b.g. High Top 131–Over The Water II (Doutelle 128) (1981 —
NR 1982 12fg 12fg 16f) apparently of little account. *Mrs C. Lloyd-Jones*

KARDAMYLA 3 br.f. Mummy's Pet 125–Copacabana 67 (Petingo 135) (1981 —
NR 1982 7g 10f⁴ 8fg³ 8fg 7f 9g) third foal; half-sister to 1m winner Mar del Plata (by Crowned Prince); dam slow half-sister to very smart animals Averof and Falkland; quite a modest maiden; promises to stay 1¼m; blinkered final start. *B. Hanbury.*

KAREENA 3 b.f. Riverman 131–Kermiya (Vienna 127) (1981 6fg⁴ 6g³ 1982 **110**
8d* 8d⁴ 8.5fg* 8fg* 8.5f³ 8fg* 8f² 8fg 8fg⁴ 8v²) smallish, close-coupled, attractive filly; second foal; half-sister to 5f and 6f winner Kabour (by Habitat); dam won over 9f and 1¼m in France; had a good year and won maiden race at Leicester, minor event at Epsom, £5,100 race at Ascot (beat Bundu) and Fern Hill Stakes (Handicap) at Ascot again (from Loup de Mer); also ran well in pattern races on occasions, going down by a length to Chalon (gave 6 lb) in Child Stakes at Newmarket, coming home fifth to Thorough in Prix d'Astarte at Deauville and keeping on to be 3¼ lengths fourth to easy winner Sandhurst Prince in Waterford Crystal Mile at Goodwood; will stay 1¼m; acts on any going but is ideally suited by fast ground; suited by waiting tactics; game and consistent. *F. J. Houghton.*

H. H. Aga Khan's "Kareena"

KARENA PARK 2 b. or br.f. Hot Spark 126–Dunmore Lass II 94 (Nashua) (1982 5g) Feb 14; 8,200Y; closely related to very useful 6f and 1m winner Dun Habit (by Habitat) and half-sister to 2 other winners; dam won at up to 9f; 16/1, prominent to past halfway when seventh of 14 in maiden race at Leicester in June. *M. Ryan.* —

KAREN'S BIRTHDAY 3 br.f. The Brianstan 128–Alexa (Runnymede 123) (1981 5d⁴ 5g⁴ 5fg 5fg 5g 5g 5g 5s³ 5s 5s³ 6d 1982 6d 6fg 6fg 5s 7s) compact filly; plater; possibly needs some give in the ground; looks a short runner. *S. Matthews.* —

KAREN'S GEM 3 b.g. Workboy 123–Colate 59 (Como 120) (1981 5v 5g² 5g 5f 5fg³ 5f 5g³ 5f 1982 7g 6fg 7f 6f 5fg) small gelding; bad plater; has worn blinkers and bandages; sold, probably for export to Norway, 620 gns Doncaster June Sales. *J. Doyle.* —

KAREN'S STAR 5 b.g. Aglojo 119–Colate 59 (Como 120) (1981 6v 6s 5d 5s 5fg⁴ 5fg³ 5f 5.1fg² 5g² 5f⁴ 5g⁴ 5f³ 6f 6f² 5g² 5g 5s 5d² 5g 1982 6f 6f 5f 5fg 5fg⁴ 5g 5g 6f* 5.6f² 5f⁴ 6g* 5fg 6d 5d 5fg 5s 6s 5s⁴) lightly-made gelding; bad mover; sprint handicapper; made all at Carlisle in July and Ripon in August; veered right across course when ridden by 7-lb claimer on latter course, but for which he'd have won by a wide margin; suited by a sound surface; has twice been tried in blinkers; sold 1,025 gns Ascot December Sales. *Mrs M. Nesbitt.* 65

KARKOUR (FR) 4 b. or br.c. Relko 136–Koblenza 118 (Hugh Lupus 132) (1981 10g* 12d 12g* 12s* 1982 12fg 12s 12.5v² 12g⁴ 15g 12g* 13.5g⁴ 12f 12v³ 12v) French colt; smart performer; won 3 of his 4 races in 1981; gained only win of 1982 in 12-runner Grand Prix de Vichy in August, beating No Attention by a length; in frame subsequently in Grand Prix de Deauville later in month (less than 2 lengths fourth of 12 to Real Shadai) and Gran Premio del Jockey Club at Milan in October (8 lengths third of 6 to Friendswood); had also run creditably in varied races earlier, including when 3½ lengths fourth of 8 to Little Wolf in Prix Jean de Chaudenay at Saint-Cloud; possibly stays 15f; seems best with some give in the ground and acts on heavy going. *J. Audon, France.* 120

KARLIAN 2 br.g. Ercolano 118–Madam Jane 58 (No Mercy 126) (1982 8s 8s 10s 8s) compact gelding; first known foal; dam third over 6f and 1¼m, and also over hurdles; plating class maiden; will stay 1m. *R. Hannon.* 61

KARMINSKI 4 b.f. Pitskelly 122–Autumn Ballad 75 (Tudor Melody 129) (1981 12.2s² 10g³ 12d² 12d 12fg² 13g* 13.8fg² 16fg³ 18.1d 1982 12h 16f² 13fg 16f 13f² 16.1g* 18.8fg² 16.9fg* 18d 18s) won handicaps at Newmarket in August and Wolverhampton in September; made most both times and on latter course beat Champagne Charlie by 4 lengths; rather disappointing third and fourth starts; stays very well; acts on any going. *C. Brittain.* 63

KAROL 4 b.c. Kalamoun 129–Le Melody 102 (Levmoss 133) (1981 8d* 1982 10s 14f³ 14fg⁴ 14fg² 12g*) second foal; half-brother to top-class stayer Ardross (by Run The Gantlet); dam, daughter of Musidora Stakes winner Arctic Melody, won both her starts over 7f and 1¼m; put up a good performance when beating Festive Lady by 5 lengths in 10-runner Trigo Stakes at Leopardstown in October; also in frame in 2 minor events and a handicap on same course; will stay 2m; probably acts on any going. *D. O'Brien, Ireland.* 107

KARYOBINGA 4 b.f. So Blessed 130–Pine Ridge Gal (Arturo A) (1981 7g 7g 8.2s 8d 10.2g 1982 8f³ 7f⁴ 8.2fg² 8f² 8g³ 8g 8.3g⁴ 8d 7g³) rangy, quite attractive filly; plater; stays 1m; usually wears blinkers; ungenuine. *P. Makin.* 41

KASCINA 5 b.m. Midsummer Night II 117–Tavaro (Gustav 121) (1981 NR 1982 10f) well-made mare; poor maiden; should stay beyond 1m; acts on firm going and is possibly unsuited by soft; blinkered once at 3 yrs. *H. O'Neill.* —

KASH-IN 3 b.f. Kashiwa 115–Deviation (Petingo 135) (1981 5fg 5d² 6g² 5d* 5s⁴ 5g 1982 6s 6f 5g² 6fg³ 6g 6d² 6f 6f 6g³ 6fg 6f³ 6s³ 6s² 6s) good-quartered, useful-looking filly; runner-up in handicaps and an apprentice race; drifted quite badly left in latter and probably needs stronger handling; stays 6f; ideally suited by some give in the ground; ran poorly in blinkers eighth start; sent to Trinidad. *R. Hannon.* 82

KASSAK 6 gr.g. Dragonara Palace 115–Dauphiness 74 (Supreme Sovereign 119) (1981 5s³ 6g 5d 6d* 5.3f* 6g* 6fg² 5fg³ 6fg⁴ 6fg⁴ 6fg 6s 1982 6s 6fg 6g 6f⁴ 6f³ 6f 5.3g² 6g 6g³ 5.3fg³ 5.8f⁴ 6v 6v 6s) leggy gelding; sprint handicapper; acts on any going; has worn blinkers but does as well without; sometimes bandaged off-fore; has run well for an amateur rider; trained most of season by H. O'Neill. *P. Ashworth.* 60

KATAYUN 3 b.f. Busted 134–King's Gem 88 (King's Troop 118) (1981 NR — 1982 10g) sister to a plating-class maiden and half-sister to fairly useful 1972 2-y-o African God (by Runnymede) and 2 winners in France; dam sprinter; 33/1 when behind in 14-runner maiden event won by Fox at Newmarket in August; sold 5,200 gns Newmarket December Sales. *J. Dunlop.*

KATE KIMBERLEY 3 b.f. Sparkler 130–Ma Griffe (Indian Ruler 89) (1981 **55** NR 1982 8f 8fg 8s³ 10g) deep-girthed filly; good walker; half-sister to numerous winners, notably very smart English and German winner Whip It Quick (by Philemon); dam never ran; staying-on 4½ lengths third of 15 to Bold Hawk in minor event at Warwick in October; should stay 1¼m; acts on soft going. *H. Candy.*

KATE'S WISH 3 ch.f. Wishing Star 117–Kay's Hour 93 (Bleep-Bleep 134) **41** (1981 5s 5d³ 6f³ 6d⁴ 8.2s 1982 8g 6s³ 9f 8g³ 6g 7s³) leggy, light-framed filly; plater; stays 1m; suited by some give in the ground. *J. Fitzgerald.*

KATE THE SHREW 2 b.f. Comedy Star 121–Fiery Romance (Fighting Don) — (1982 5fg 5g 5.8g) May 14; sister to 3-y-o Herring and half-sister to 1m winner Incensed (by Frankincense); dam lightly-raced half-sister to Irish 2,000 Guineas winner Mistigo; in rear in August in maiden races and a seller. *C. James.*

KATHANCO 4 ch.f. Panco 91–Dumb Kathy (Dumbarnie 125) (1981 16.9fg — 12d 1982 12f 18f 14.6g) strong filly; soundly beaten in varied races, including an amateur riders event. *R. Hollinshead.*

KATHLEEN'S MONEY 2 b.f. My Swanee 122–Philanderess (Philemon 119) **58** (1982 5f² 6g 5fg 8s) Apr 24; quite well-made filly; half-sister to a winning plater and a winner in Belgium; neck second in seller at Lingfield in July, only form. *J. Fox.*

KATHRED 4 b.f. Starch Reduced 112–Kathy King (Space King 115) (1981 **87** 6g² 6g 6d* 6s* 7f⁴ 6f 6s* 6f³ 6d* 5g 5s⁴ 6g* 6d 1982 6s² 6d 6fg² 6f⁴ 6fg 6d⁴ 6f² 6f 6fg 6g⁴ 6fg 5.6g 6s* 5v³ 6s² 6d) sprint handicapper; beat Cyril's Choice decisively by 1½ lengths in 18-runner £8,400 Otis Handicap at Haydock in October; ran creditably on a number of other occasions, including when second at Ayr, Newmarket, Kempton and Haydock; acts on any going but has done most of her winning on an easy surface; suitable mount for a boy. *R. Hollinshead.*

KATHYS GIRL 2 b.f. Hasty Word 84–Stretton Queen 52 (Grey Mirage 128) — (1982 5fg 5d) first foal; dam poor plater; behind in maiden races at Wolverhampton in August. *R. Morris.*

KATIE BOURNE 2 br.f. Jimsun 121–Wilsome (Will Somers 114§) (1982 **51** 5g 5v³ 5f 7g 8fg 8.2g 9s 8s) Apr 8; fair sort; second foal; dam probably of no account; only poor form; slowly away from flag start fifth outing. *E. Carter.*

KATIE KOO 2 br.f. Persian Bold 123–Gwendolyn (Bagdad) (1982 7g) Mar — 27; rangy, useful-looking filly; half-sister to 7f winner Copt Hall Princess (by Crowned Prince) and a winner in Belgium; dam, placed 3 times in USA, comes from a good family; 16/1, no show in 22-runner maiden race at Newmarket in October. *B. Hills.*

KATRICK 3 b.f. Sparkler 130–Marbella II 64 (Match III 135) (1981 5d 7f — 1982 8d 5fg 7fg 8f 8.5f 7g) well-made filly; plater; stays 1m; sold 620 gns Newmarket July Sales. *R. Smyth.*

KAUKAS 3 b.g. So Blessed 130–Balnespick 101 (Charlottown 127) (1981 **73** 5g⁴ 5s 5.8d 5g 6g⁴ 6fg 6fg 8g 6d 1982 8fg 10f⁴ 10.1fg 10.2g² 10f⁴ 10f* 10fg* 10d* 10s) well-made gelding; won claiming race at Brighton and handicaps at Chepstow and Leicester; stays 1¼m; seems to act on any going. *G. Balding.*

KAYELLA 3 b.f. Fine Blade 121–Peregrine Peach 79 (Falcon 131) (1981 5s³ — 5d 5s 6f 7fg 6d 1982 8.2fg 8d 12f 10f) plating-class maiden; promises to stay 1¼m; blinkered once in 1981. *W. Wharton.*

KAYSARIYYA 2 br.f. Shirley Heights 130–Kermiya (Vienna 127) (1982 **74** p 7.6v⁴) May 19; third foal; half-sister to 2 winners, including smart 3-y-o 1m winner Kareena (by Riverman); dam won over 9f and 1¼m in France; 6/1, came out best of newcomers when 6¾ lengths fourth of 21 to wide-margin winner Woodcote Belle in maiden race at Lingfield in October; will be suited by middle distances; sure to do better. *F. J. Houghton.*

KAYUDEE 2 ch.g. Nebbiolo 125–Wet Powder (Above Suspicion 127) (1982 **78** 5f 7g 8s⁴) Mar 16; IR 16,000Y; sturdy gelding; half-brother to 3 winners, including very useful 1976 2-y-o 5f winner No Conventions (by Balidar) and very useful hurdler Seldom Dry (by Rarity); dam won at up to 13f in Ireland; quite a modest maiden; will stay beyond 1m; gelded after final outing. *J. Fitzgerald.*

KAZANKINA 3 ch.f. Malinowski 123–Berserk 68 (Romulus 129) (1981 7s **107**
1982 8d* 7g 10g⁴ 10fg* 8g⁴ 8fg 10g² 12fg⁴ 12d 8d² 8d) IR 6,400Y; half-sister to a winner in Norway; dam 2-y-o 5f winner; won maiden race at Navan in March and handicap at Leopardstown in May; ran creditably afterwards at the Curragh to be 1½ lengths fourth of 24 to Prince's Polly in Goffs Irish 1,000 Guineas, ¾-length second of 13 to same filly when receiving 4 lb in Pretty Polly Stakes and 3 lengths second to Mary Mitsu in Gilltown Stud Stakes; dropped out in closing stages when sixth of 8 to Chalon in Coronation Stakes at Royal Ascot on sixth start; best at up to 1¼m; acts on a firm and a soft surface; blinkered last 2 starts; sold 82,000 gns Goffs November Sales. *N. Meade, Ireland.*

KEADEEN 5 b.g. Martinmas 128–Medaea 90 (Darius 129) (1981 8fg) 1982 **—**
10fg 10g 10f 10f) sturdy gelding; very lightly raced and no form in sellers since 1980; should stay 1¼m; acts well on heavy going; blinkered once at 3 yrs. *W. Clay.*

KEELBY KAVALIER 4 b.c. Ardoon 124–Elegant Lady 69 (Round Table) **88**
(1981 12g* 12d² 11g⁴ 12fg* 13.3g⁴ 14g 13fg² 12fg* 14g² 1982 12f* 12fg⁴ 12fg* 12fg 12g 12g³ 14g 12fg² 12fg³ 12g² 12s) leggy colt; poor walker; fair handicapper; battled on well when beating Regal Steel by a neck at Thirsk in April and when getting on line to dead-heat with Karadar at York in May; ran creditably afterwards and was placed at Newmarket (twice), Doncaster and Redcar (amateur riders); stays 1¾m; acts on firm going and a soft surface; occasionally blinkered (wore them last 2 starts); genuine. *J. Etherington.*

KEELBY KERNEL 2 b.c. Averof 123–Rising Star (St Paddy 133) (1982 5f⁴ **57**
5f 8f 8g 7.2s) Apr 30; 4,700Y; neat colt; second foal; half-brother to 3-y-o Startling (by Vitiges), a useful winner in Belgium; dam temperamental half-sister to very useful animals Riot Act and Laurentian Hills; poor maiden; tailed-off last of 16 in selling nursery at Haydock in October on final appearance; stays 1m; evidently not suited by soft ground; sold Norsk Jockey Club 4,200 gns Doncaster November Sales. *J. Etherington.*

KEEP BELIEVING 3 ch.f. Sweet Revenge 129–The Star of Sharon 73 (Mid- **—**
summer Night II 117) (1981 7.2v 1982 8fg 12fg) lightly-made filly; poor plater. *H. Fleming.*

KEEP IT DARK 2 b. or br.g. Welsh Pageant 132–Rotisserie 106 (Tesco Boy **—**
121) (1982 7g) Apr 10; 9,400F, 9,200Y; neat gelding; half-brother to 3 winners, including useful 1½m and 1¾m winner Rowlandson (by Blakeney); dam won Fred Darling Stakes; eighth of 11 in maiden race at Leicester in October. *H. Candy.*

KEEP ME WAITING 2 gr.c. Malinowski 123–Gay Charmaine 103 (Charlottes- **83**
ville 135) (1982 6g² 7fg³ 7fg 8.2g² 8f⁴ 8d⁴) Mar 4; 4,200Y; compact, quite attractive colt; half-brother to 1976 2-y-o 5f winner My Angel (by St Alphage), 7f Irish winner Brancusi (by Arch Sculptor), and a winner in France; dam won over 6f at 3 yrs; second in maiden race at Folkestone in June and nursery at Nottingham in September; better suited by 1m than shorter distances, and will stay further; blinkered last 3 outings. *R. Price.*

KEEP SHINING (USA) 2 ch.f. Stage Door Johnny–Carolina Moon 116 **77** p
(Grey Dawn II 132) (1982 8s⁴) Feb 11; rangy filly; first foal; dam smart winner from 5f to 9f in France and later showed very useful form at around 1m in North America; not fully wound up and very green, handled gently after disputing lead briefly 3f out when 4½ lengths fourth of 13 behind Ring of Greatness in maiden race at York in October; certain to derive considerable benefit from the experience, and should win races. *J. Tree.*

KEEP SILENT 3 b.f. Balidar 133–Thieves Honour (Hook Money 124) (1981 **—**
6f 6fg 6g* 6g² 6d⁴ 7g 1982 6s) rather leggy, workmanlike filly; won seller at Yarmouth (made all) and finished creditable second in minor event at Redcar in 1981; sweated up and looked unimpressive when below form only start at 3 yrs in April; not sure to stay 7f; apprentice ridden all outings. *A. Jarvis.*

KEEP SMILING 3 b.g. Tumble Wind–Retiro (Pardal 130) (1981 5fg 5fg² **—**
6fg 6fg 6d 1982 7g 7g⁴ 8fg 10f 8g³ 8fg 10fg⁴) quite attractive gelding; plater; possibly stays 1¼m; trained by N. Callaghan first 4 starts; sold 1,950 gns Ascot October Sales. *J. Jenkins.*

Prix Gladiateur, Longchamp—Kelbomec wins the race for the second successive year

KELBOMEC (FR) 6 b.g. Direct Flight–Piqueuse (Piqu' arriere) (1981 15.5d* **114** 15.5g³ 12s³ 12d² 15f³ 13.5f 20s* 1982 15.5v² 15.5fg⁴ 12s 15g³ 15fg² 20s*) French gelding; won Prix Gladiateur at Longchamp in September for second successive time, beating The Neurologist by 2 lengths; placed earlier on same course in Prix de Barbeville in April (beaten a nose by El Badr) and Prix du Carrousel in June (had anything but a clear run when 1½ lengths third to Marasali) and at Deauville in Prix Kergorlay in August (kept on strongly when 1½ lengths second to all-the-way winner Valentinian); stays very well; acts on any going but goes well in the mud; consistent. *J. C. Cunnington, France.*

KELLY'S DAUGHTER 3 b.f. Pitskelly 122–Muraka (Off Key 121) (1981 **58** 6fg 1982 10d 8fg 7g² 8g 10.1d* 10fg⁴) useful sort; plater; easily won at Windsor in June (bought in 4,100 gns); stays 1¼m; exported to Algeria. *P. Haslam.*

KELLY'S SHADOW 2 b.f. Bruni 132–Palesa (Palestine 133) (1982 6s⁴ 6s) — Mar 30; 1,500Y; leggy, short-backed filly; sixth living foal; sister to Belgian winner Sea Bomb; dam won over 7.5f in France; moderate fourth in 18-runner claiming race at Nottingham in October; will be better suited by 7f+. *R. Price.*

KELLY THORPE 2 ch.f. Le Johnstan 123–Pinzica (Pinza 137) (1982 6s 5d) — Apr 27; 400Y; fifth foal; dam apparently of little account; well beaten in autumn sellers at York and Redcar. *C. Gray.*

KENNINGHALL (USA) 3 ch.c. Riva Ridge–Reload 119 (Relko 136) (1981 **100** 7f 6d³ 6f 7s 7d⁴ 1982 10.4g³ 9fg* 10g⁴ 10.5fg² 11.7fg* 10f 10.5fg) smallish, good sort; smoothly justified favouritism in 6-runner maiden race at Newcastle in May and accounted for Divine Truth by 2½ lengths in 7-runner handicap at Windsor in July; ran creditably in between; will stay 1½m; seems to act on any going; broke 2 blood vessels and fell final start. *H. Wragg.*

KENTUCKY 4 b.f. Warpath 113–Shenandoah 88 (Mossborough 126) (1981 **35** 8f 10fg 1982 15.8g 13v 12f 15g² 15.8f 12f³ 12.2f⁴ 15f⁴ 12fg⁴) big, strong filly; good walker; in frame in handicaps and an amateur riders race; suited by a test of stamina; sold to BBA 3,400 gns Doncaster November Sales. *C. Thornton.*

KENTUCKY KID 3 ch.c. On Your Mark 125–Purple Heron (Great Heron 127) **81** (1981 6f³ 7f² 7g⁴ 6g² 7d 1982 8s² 12g² 12f* 12f⁴ 12d* 11.5f 12fg* 12fg³ 12fg 12fg* 12fg) IR 9,000Y; third foal; brother to 2 winners, including Irish middle-distance winner Colonel Sanders; dam never ran; successful in maiden race at Limerick Junction and handicaps at Killarney, Leopardstown and Naas; modest fifth of 8 to Cool Decision in valuable gentleman riders race at Epsom ninth start; suited by 1½m; acts on any going. *T. Curtin, Ireland.*

KEROINE 2 b.f. Keren 100–Ribera (Ribston 104) (1982 6d) Apr 16; first — foal; dam pulled up in hurdle race on only start; last of 14 in £3,000 seller at Newcastle in August. *N. Chamberlain.*

KESARINI (USA) 3 ch.f. Singh–Kesar Queen 117 (Nashua) (1981 5g² 5v* **66** 5.8g⁴ 7.2f 7d³ 1982 8.2s 8fg 7d³ 8d) compact filly; quite a modest handicapper; should stay at least 1m; needs some give in the ground and acts on heavy going; sold 46,000 gns Newmarket December Sales. *G. Hunter.*

KESHOON 4 b.f. Sheshoon 132–Matt's Colleen 105 (Epaulette 125) (1981 — 6fg 8fg 8.2s 9d* 8s 10d 1982 12s 12s) compact filly; trotted up in a seller in 1981; lightly raced since; probably stays 1¼m; acts on a soft surface. *P. Bevan.*

470

KEVELA 2 b.f. Radetzky 123–Jim's Bellinna (Cavo Doro 124) (1982 6f 6g **40** 7d⁴ 7f 7f 8fg 8.2s 10d) Apr 1; 1,000Y; fair sort; bad plater; often blinkered; sold 310 gns Doncaster October Sales. *K. Stone.*

KEVINSFORT 4 b.g. Will Somers 114§–Hinemoa (Connaught 130) (1981 NR — 1982 12f 15.8d) second foal; dam won at 7f to 1½m in Ireland; behind in maiden race at Beverley in May (ridden by 7-lb claimer) and minor event at Catterick in October. *J. Fitzgerald.*

KEYBOARD 2 br.f. High Top 131–Happy Music 84 (Hethersett 134) (1982 **88 p** 7g³ 7.6v*) Apr 7; neat, good sort; half-sister to very useful middle-distance winner Galveston (by Sir Ivor) and a winner in France; dam staying daughter of Park Hill winner Cursorial; favourite, led close home to win 18-runner maiden race at Lingfield in October by ½ length from Gloria Mundi; will be suited by 1¼m+; likely to improve further. *W. Hastings-Bass.*

KEY SONG 3 ch.f. Crooner 119–The Keys 71 (Major Portion 129) (1981 — 5.3f 7f 8d 8s⁴ 8.2s 1982 7fg 9g 10g) plater; best run at 1m on soft going; has worn blinkers. *M. Hinchliffe.*

KEY TOTHE MINSTREL (USA) 2 ch.f. The Minstrel 135–Seven Locks **108** (Jacinto) (1982 6g² 6f* 7fg 8g⁴) Apr 7; $350,000F; medium-sized, lengthy, attractive filly; good walker; half-sister to 3-y-o 7f winner Glomach (by Majestic Light) and winners in France and USA, including stayer Georgetown (by Tom Rolfe); dam unraced half-sister to top-class animals Fort Marcy and Key To The Mint; landed odds of 11/4 on by 2½ lengths from Leslie Stone in 3-runner John Courage Stakes at York in July; took on very useful fillies in her other races, on final outing finishing good fourth to Acclimatise in Hoover Fillies Mile at Ascot in September; will stay beyond 1m; has raced only on a sound surface. *M. Stoute.*

KEY WIND 2 b.f. On Your Mark 125–Key Note (Kythnos 126) (1982 5fg **81** 5f² 5.1f* 6g⁴ 5f³ 5fg² 5g 5d 5g) May 9; 5,800Y; rangy, useful sort; half-sister to 2 winners, including Irish stayer Moonlight 'N Roses (by Bonne Noel); dam, moderate Irish maiden, is daughter of very smart 1957 Irish 2-y-o Vestogan; won maiden race at Yarmouth in June; none too lucky in nurseries on fifth and sixth outings, being badly hampered at distance when going well at Goodwood in July and failing by a short head to hold off Sidab after wandering under pressure at Nottingham in August; better suited by 5f than 6f; acts on firm going. *A. Jarvis.*

KHAIRPOUR 3 gr.c. Arctic Tern 126–Khayra (Zeddaan 130) (1981 8g 1982 **116** 8g² 12f* 10fg* 11f* 12f² 12f* 13.3f 12.3d* 12fg* 14.6f 12g*) medium-sized, quite attractive colt; good walker and mover; first foal; dam unraced sister to Kalamoun; developed into a smart colt, winning minor events at Wolverhampton and Doncaster (made all), handicaps at Newbury, York (odds on), Chester and Haydock and £5,800 event at Newmarket; accounted for Capricorn Line by 1½ lengths in last-named in September; also ran well to be ¾-length second to Mubarak of Kuwait in King George V Stakes (Handicap) at Royal Ascot and seventh, just over 7 lengths behind Touching Wood, in St Leger at Doncaster; stays 1¾m; yet to race on very soft going but acts on any other; genuine though tends to idle in front nowadays; consistent. *F. J. Houghton.*

KHAIZARAAN (CAN) 2 br.f. Sham–Beautiful Sister (Hail to Reason) (1982 **97 p** 6s*) Mar 29; $150,000Y; big, well-made filly; really good mover; first foal; dam, unplaced 4 times, is half-sister to smart animals Pass the Word and Rube the Great; 10/1 and apparently not fully wound up, put up very promising performance in 11-runner Blue Seal Stakes at Ascot in September, winning by 1½ lengths from Sun Princess after going well throughout; will stay 1m; has plenty of scope, and could prove very useful. *H. T. Jones.*

KHALEEL 4 br.g. Lochnager 132–Vital Error 105 (Javelot 124) (1981 5d 5d³ — 5d 5fg³ 5fg 5f³ 5g³ 6g² 6fg² 5fg 6d 6s 1982 6f 5fg 6g 7f 7f) disappointing sprint maiden; no form in 1982, including in a seller; has run creditably for an apprentice; has been tried in blinkers. *A. Hide.*

KHYBER 2 b.c. Oats 126–Mahlene (Pontifex) (1982 7f 8s⁴ 8s⁴ 10s³) Apr 6; **78** IR 14,500Y; well-made colt; poor walker; first foal; dam placed from 5f to 7.5f in Ireland; in frame in October maiden events at Bath, Warwick and Nottingham; stays well; acts on soft going. *G. Lewis.*

KICKING LADY 2 ch.f. Take a Reef 127–Suku 80 (Light Thrust 114) (1982 **39** 5f 5g⁴ 5f 7f) Mar 20; 840F; workmanlike filly; bad plater; blinkered second outing; sold out of O. Jorgensen's stable 420 gns Newmarket May Sales after first start. *C. Pinkham.*

KIKALONG 2 gr.f. Runnymede 123–Scoop (Bleep-Bleep 134) (1982 5fg 6d —
5s 7g) Mar 30; 1,600F, 1,900Y; strong, compact filly; poor maiden. *R. Simpson.*

KIKKULI 3 b.c. Hittite Glory 125–Siliciana 113 (Silly Season 127) (1981 —
7g 7v³ 1982 8d 8fg) big, well-made colt; has a round action; soundly beaten
both outings at 3 yrs; should stay 1m; needs some give in the ground; blinkered
final start; sold to L. Cumani 2,200 gns Newmarket Autumn Sales. *I. Balding.*

KILDARE 3 ch.c. Tachypous 128–Crisalgo 83 (Miralgo 130) (1981 NR 1982 —
7g 8d) 4,500F, IR 14,000Y; dam won Chester Cup; showed a little ability in
newcomers event at Doncaster in March; dead. *G. Harwood.*

KILFORD 2 b.c. Northfields–Ashaireez (Abernant 142) (1982 6fg 7fg 10d 10d) —
May 24; 6,200F, 5,800Y; quite attractive colt; brother to 1975 2-y-o 6f winner
Taiseera, and half-brother to 2 winners; dam twice-raced daughter of Irish
Oaks winner Amante; no form, including in 1¼m sellers; blinkered third outing;
sold BBA 760 gns Newmarket Autumn Sales. *W. Hastings-Bass.*

KILIAN 4 br.c. Thatch 136–Fortunal (Fortino II 120) (1981 8s* 10f* 1982 **108**
7s* 9fg 8g³ 8d⁴ 8s* 8v⁴) Irish colt; tall, good sort; won in fairly modest company
at Leopardstown and Navan as a 3-y-o; successful in 1982 in 7-runner Gladness
Stakes at the Curragh in April (put up a good performance when beating odds
on 3-y-o Achieved by a short head) and 10-runner Group 2 Premio Vittorio di
Capua at Milan in October (won by ½ length from Charlo Mio); also in frame in
Coolmore Hello Gorgeous Stakes (4 lengths third to Senior Citizen) and Desmond
Stakes (8 lengths fourth to Anfield), both at the Curragh, and in Premio Ribot
(nearly 11 lengths fourth to Commodore Blake) at Rome; disappointing last
of 8 behind Kalaglow in Earl of Sefton Stakes at Newmarket on his only other
start; effective at 7f and stays 1¼m; acts on any going, but is clearly well suited
by plenty of give in the ground. *D. O'Brien, Ireland.*

KILLANIN'S LASS (USA) 3 b.f. Olympiad King–My Violet (Warfare) **82**
(1981 6d² 1982 8g 8.2s² 7g* 7s) rangy filly; split a pastern early in year;
always going well when beating Wongchoi in good style by 1½ lengths in 15-
runner £3,600 event at Newmarket in October; stays 1m well; yet to race on a
firm surface; sold 8,000 gns Newmarket December Sales. *G. Pritchard-Gordon.*

KILLIFRETH 2 ch.f. Jimmy Reppin 131–Spring River 66 (Silly Season 127) —
(1982 5g 6g) Mar 3; first foal; dam in frame over 1½m and 2m; 33/1, prominent
to 2f out when 11 lengths eighth of 20 to Rare Roberta in maiden race at Lingfield
in August, second outing. *H. Candy.*

KILLINEY BAY 2 b.f. Stradavinsky 121–Game Laura (Relic) (1982 5g 6g² **62**
5.1g* 7f³ 7f) Mar 23; IR 4,700F; leggy, angular filly; half-sister to 3 winners,
including useful Caven Mill (by Clever Fella), successful here and in Belgium;
dam half-sister to The Go-Between; bought in 3,000 gns after winning 8-runner
seller at Yarmouth in June by short head from Bonjour Vitesse; strong-finishing
3 lengths third of 14 to Miss Annie in valuable seller at Newmarket the following
month; suited by 7f; wears blinkers; exported to Algeria. *W. O'Gorman.*

KILLINGHOLME CLAY 3 b.c. Targowice 130–Patricia (Sovereign Path 125) **86 ?**
(1981 5g 5g² 6fg²(dis) 7fg* 1982 8.2s 8fg² 8fg 10f² 8fg 10d) leggy colt; has a
round action; runner-up in handicaps; below form on several occasions, running
as though something was seriously wrong with him on fifth start (off course
2 months afterwards); stays 1¼m; suited by a sound surface; hung very badly
once in 1981. *G. Pritchard-Gordon.*

KILNER 2 ch.c. Relkino 131–String Along 77 (Crepello 136) (1982 6fg 8s³ 8s* **80**
8.2v²) Apr 14; 8,200Y; big, rangy, workmanlike colt; third foal; half-brother
to 1¼m winner Mr Argentina (by So Blessed); dam 1¼m winner and half-sister to
top 1977 2-y-o filly Cherry Hinton; won 13-runner maiden race at Warwick in
October; odds on when 6 lengths second to High Cannon in 3-runner minor event
at Hamilton later in month; will stay 1¼m; sold BBA, for export to Hong Kong,
25,000 gns Newmarket Autumn Sales. *G. Harwood.*

KILROE'S CALIN 3 ch.f. Be Friendly 130–Miss Soundly (Maelsheachlainn 117) —
(1981 8fg 8s 8d 1982 6s 8f) tall, leggy filly; soundly beaten in maiden and
minor events. *J. Fitzgerald.*

KILSYTH 3 b.f. Jolly Good 122–Harmony Thyme 73 (Sing Sing 134) (1981 —
5fg 5g 5f⁴ 1982 7g 8g³ 8f 9g 8fg 7d 10.6s 9s 8g) compact filly; poor maiden;
stays 1m; blinkered sixth and seventh starts. *C. Booth.*

472

KIMBIA 2 b.f. Never Return 121–Palencia (Palestine 133) (1982 6fg) Apr 22; —
workmanlike filly; half-sister to several winners, including very useful 1976 Irish
2-y-o 5f winner Haraka (by Hul a Hul); dam sister to very useful sprinter Coney
Island; unquoted and backward, behind in 20-runner maiden race at Salisbury
in September. *W. Wightman.*

KIMBLE GIRL 2 ch.f. Some Hand 119–Tacoma 89 (Hard Tack 111§) (1982   **80**
5g 5d² 5g²) Mar 15; 820F; lengthy filly; half-sister to fair 1978 2-y-o 5f winner
Tigertamer (by Saritamer); dam won twice over 5f at 2 yrs; second in maiden
events at Nottingham in June and Sandown in July. *R. Baker.*

KINCS 2 b.f. Comedy Star 121–Miss Merida 64 (Midsummer Night II 117)   —
(1982 7d) Apr 24; big, strong filly; fourth foal; dam seemed to stay 1¼m;
unquoted and backward, no show in 15-runner maiden race at Leicester in
October. *G. Balding.*

KIND MUSIC 3 gr.c. Music Boy 124–La Magna 104 (Runnymede 123) (1981 **125**
5g* 5s³ 5g² 5f 5f* 6s 5g³ 1982 7s⁴ 7.5s 5s² 6s* 5fg* 6f 5g³ 5s³ 5v*)
The departure of Maelstrom Lake to the States at the end of 1981 left no
obvious heir apparent to the title of best French sprinter, a title that hasn't
always been difficult to gain in recent years. Not surprisingly, given the now
usual weakness of French-trained horses in this department, sprinters from
England enjoyed a good season across the Channel, picking up the Prix de
l'Abbaye, Prix de Meautry and Prix de Seine-et-Oise, while the best of the
home defence turned out to be the ex-English Kind Music. Successful for
Stoute in a minor event at Kempton and Redcar in 1981, Kind
Music improved by well over a stone and proved up to taking on the best in
England as well as in France.
Kind Music's only moderate performance on returning to sprint distances
after a short-lived attempt to turn him into a miler came in the William Hill
July Cup at Newmarket in which he led to halfway before dropping out to finish
well back behind Sharpo. Besides winning a 70,000 francs six-furlong event at
Maisons-Laffitte, Kind Music contested all four of the French pattern races
open to him over five furlongs plus the William Hill Sprint Championship at
York, finishing no worse than third in any of them and being beaten by just four
horses. His victories in the Prix du Gros-Chene at Chantilly and the Prix du
Petit Couvert at Longchamp were gained in similar style. Breaking quickly he
took a definite advantage at the distance and kept on well to score authoritatively
by a length from Ponchielli at Chantilly, where he broke the course record, and
by half a length from Sky Lawyer with the Prix d'Arenberg winner Go Jogging
third at Longchamp. In both these races Kind Music had Blue Courtier behind
him, thus exacting handsome revenge for a length-and-a-half defeat at the hands
of the older horse in the Prix Saint-Georges at Longchamp earlier on. The three
other horses that beat Kind Music over the minimum trip were all, predictably
enough, trained in England. At York, where he became the first French challenger for the Sprint Championship since Hittite Glory in 1976, Kind Music came
in third to Sharpo and Chellaston Park, beaten two lengths and a neck, while
in the Prix de l'Abbaye he lost second place in the dying strides by a head to
Fearless Lad, a length behind Sharpo again. Each time Kind Music showed
the excellent initial pace that is his hallmark, and with this style of racing he
will presumably be aimed almost exclusively at five-furlong tests in 1983.
Unless a good three-year-old turns up in France Kind Music should add more
races to his tally when the best of the English are absent.
Kind Music is the second produce of the speedy 1974 two-year-old La Magna

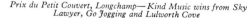

Prix du Petit Couvert, Longchamp— Kind Music wins from Sky
Lawyer, Go Jogging and Lulworth Cove

whose first foal, Rival (by Forlorn River), has won several times over hurdles. La Magna's two-year-old Boy Trumpeter, a brother to Kind Music, cost 7,200 guineas as a yearling—Kind Music cost 25,000 guineas—and has the makings of a very useful five-furlong sprinter after scoring in three of his six starts in 1982 including the Doncaster Stakes. The second dam stayed much further than her

Kind Music (gr.c. 1979)	Music Boy (ch 1973)	Jukebox (b 1966)	Sing Sing Bibi Mah
		Veronique (b 1961)	Matador Narcisse
	La Magna (gr 1972)	Runnymede (gr 1961)	Petition Dutch Clover
		La Garoupe (gr 1965)	Pirate King Corn Beam

daughter, winning at up to seventeen furlongs, and her only other winner on the flat, the useful handicapper Chokwaro, stayed a mile and three quarters well. Kind Music is a neat, well-made colt and an excellent mover who acts on any going. *R. Collet, France.*

KIND OF HUSH 4 b.c. Welsh Pageant 132–Sauceboat 120 (Connaught 130) **118** (1981 8g* 8g 12d 10.5g 11.1f* 10g³ 10g 1982 9fg³ 10f² 10fg* 10g 10fg² 10d)

Steve Cauthen has won a great many friends and admirers since his arrival from America in 1979 to ride over here. He got off to the best possible start when his very first ride Marquee Universal won at Salisbury, he won his first classic here on Tap On Wood only four weeks later, and each season he has significantly improved on his previous winning total, at the same time developing in his strength and adapting his style. Cauthen started 1982 with an outside chance of the jockey's title and although that had virtually gone by midsummer his year certainly wasn't without its highspots. Riding five winners in an evening at Doncaster in June was one, reaching the one hundred-winner mark for the first time on Triple Jump at Newmarket in October another, and riding his first Royal Ascot winner on Kind of Hush in the Prince of Wales's Stakes a third.

Cauthen was seen at his best in the Prince of Wales's Stakes. Kind of Hush was very keen and full of himself before the race, having been off the course for nearly two months since being placed behind Kalaglow in the Earl of Sefton Stakes at Newmarket and Princes Gate in the Westbury Stakes at

Prince of Wales's Stakes, Ascot—Cauthen and Kind of Hush (right) get up in the last strides to touch off Eddery and Lobkowiez

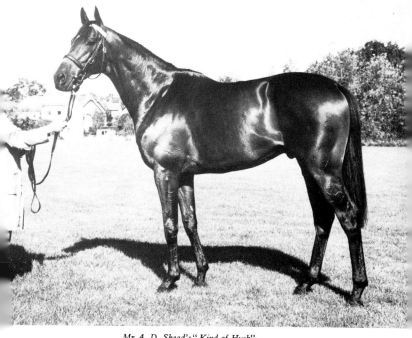

Mr A. D. Shead's "Kind of Hush"

Sandown in the spring. As usual he pulled hard early on but Cauthen soon had him nicely settled towards the back of the field. Kind of Hush turned for home with only one behind him, quickened well under pressure and moved through to challenge when a gap opened up between Lobkowiez and Be My Native. In a thrilling battle with Lobkowiez, ridden by Eddery who put up 8 lb overweight, Cauthen was seen at his strongest, and in the last few strides he forced the resolute Kind of Hush in front for a short-head victory. We've seldom been more impressed by Cauthen's dash and will to win. It had taken him forty-three rides to notch his first Royal Ascot winner but before the meeting was over he'd also won on Merlins Charm and Prince Reymo.

Kind of Hush (b.c. 1978)	Welsh Pageant (b 1966)	Tudor Melody (br 1956)	Tudor Minstrel / Matelda
		Picture Light (b 1954)	Court Martial / Queen of Light
	Sauceboat (b 1972)	Connaught (b 1965)	St Paddy / Nagaika
		Cranberry Sauce (gr 1964)	Crepello / Queensberry

The Coral-Eclipse Stakes at Sandown the following month possibly came a bit too soon for Kind of Hush—he always seemed to do best when fresh—and he didn't do himself justice in finishing sixth of nine, nearly eight lengths down on Kalaglow. After another lay-off he returned in the autumn for the Joe McGrath Memorial Stakes at Leopardstown and the Dubai Champion Stakes at Newmarket which had also been his last two races as a three-year-old. As in 1981 Kind of Hush put up easily his better performance in the Joe McGrath, on this occasion finishing a creditable three-length second to Assert, immensely flattered by his proximity to the winner yet having some very useful Irish runners well strung out behind him.

It was announced in August that Kind of Hush was being syndicated at £8,000 a share to stand at the Britton House Stud, near Crewkerne, Somerset; he replaces another Prince of Wales's Stakes winner Crimson Beau who died in March. His fee is £3,000 with the live foal concession. Although not from the very top drawer Kind of Hush was a smart top-of-the-ground middle-distance performer at his best and he has the looks and pedigree to make a stallion. An attractive colt, he's by Welsh Pageant, whose reputation was revived considerably when Zino won the Two Thousand Guineas, out of Sauceboat, a very well-bred pattern race winner. Kind of Hush is Sauceboat's first foal; her 1982 filly by Dance In Time was her first subsequent foal. *B. Hills.*

KINDRED SPIRIT 3 ch.f. Relkino 131–Cavalier's Blush 75 (King's Troop 118) (1981 6s 1982 10f 12f) big filly; little worthwhile form in maiden races; dead. *W. Wightman.* —

KING BILLY 4 br.g. Sovereign King–Co-Co Mo (Como 120) (1981 12s 1982 16fg) tall gelding; in rear in maiden events and is probably of little account; sold 1,600 gns Ascot August Sales. *D. Garraton.* —

KING CHARLEMAGNE 3 gr.g. Habat 127–Calibina 101 (Caliban 123) (1981 NR 1982 8g 8.2g 9fg 8g 8.2g 8d 8.2g 12v 12s) 9,200Y; strong gelding; first foal; dam, winner of Wokingham Stakes and Stewards' Cup, stayed 1m; poor form, including in a seller; blinkered seventh start; has worn bandages; trained part of season by F. Watson. *D. Smith.* —

KINGFORD 3 ch.g. Supreme Sovereign 119–Florrie Ford 79 (Kelly 122) (1981 6g 1982 8.2fg 10.1fg 12d 13.4g 12g) compact gelding; not the best of movers; poor form, including in a seller. *R. Williams.* —

KING JAMES 5 b.h. English Prince 129–Mary of Scots 84 (Relic) (1981 8s³ 8s 9s 8g* 6.5d* 6s³ 5fg³ 5fg³ 6f* 6d 9s⁴ 1982 6v 9s 8d* 8d* 7s 7fg⁴ 9g 8g* 8s* 9d 8s) strong, workmanlike horse; very useful handicapper as a 3-y-o when trained by R. Price, winner of a well-contested race at Kempton; was sold out of Price's stable for only 2,600 gns at Newmarket Autumn Sales later that year and has raced in France since, proving himself a rare bargain; successful 7 times in France, gaining his 1982 wins in handicap at Saint-Cloud, gentleman riders event at Compiegne, 21-runner Grand Handicap de Deauville and 14-runner Prix Quincey on same course; gained last 2 wins in August, beating Pampabird smoothly by ¾ length after being held up in Prix Quincey; best at up to 1m; acts on any going; genuine. *G. Bonnaventure, France.* **119**

KINGLAKE 4 ch.g. Gulf Pearl 117–Spring Blossom 85 (Queen's Hussar 124) (1981 5g 8g 8f 8fg 1982 10fg 10.1d 8.2g) poor maiden; dead. *H. Candy.* —

KING OF MAN 3 gr.g. Three Legs 128–Auld Rogue (Tarqogan 125) (1981 5f 5f 5d 1982 8fg 9.4fg 11g² 12.3fg² 12g² 9s 12v⁴ 12d) neat, quite attractive gelding; runner-up in maiden races and a handicap; stays 1½m; one paced. *C. Thornton.* **65**

KING OF ROCK 2 ch.c. Music Boy 124–Visitation 84 (Tarqogan 125) (1982 5fg 5fg 5g 7g⁴) Apr 11; 10,000Y; robust, well-made colt; brother to winning 3-y-o sprinter Four For Music and 1980 2-y-o 5f winner Merely Mozart, and half-brother to a winner; dam stayed 1½m; plating-class maiden; sweated up and disappointed when tried in blinkers in valuable seller at Newmarket in September on final appearance; may prove better suited by 6f than 7f; should win an ordinary seller. *P. Haslam.* **70**

KING OF SPEED 3 b.c. Blue Cashmere 129–Celeste 83 (Sing Sing 134) (1981 5s⁴ 5f 5g 6g² 6fg⁴ 6g* 1982 6s 7fg 7f* 7.3fg 7d 8f⁴ 8g 7d* 7fg 7s 7d) lengthy, quite attractive colt; won handicaps at Salisbury in May and Yarmouth in August; best at 7f; seems to act on any going; good mount for an apprentice; trained by A. Pitt first 6 starts. *D. Weeden.* **70**

KING RAGAPAN 5 b.g. Ragapan 118–At The Kings Side (Kauai King) (1981 13.3s 8fg 12g 10fg 1982 12d 14f 12fg) big, good sort; ex-Irish gelding; well beaten since 1980; stays 1¾m; trained first outing of 1982 by P. M. Taylor. *R. Atkins.* —

KING'S BIDDER 4 b.g. Lochnager 132–Ruling Class 92 (King Emperor) (1981 5d 5v 1982 7f 7fg 6g 5fg) narrow, lightly-made gelding; lightly raced and no worthwhile form since 1980, including in sellers; should stay 6f. *B. Gubby.* —

KING'S COLLEGE BOY 4 b.g. Andrea Mantegna–The Guzzler 69 (Behistoun 131) (1981 12g 12g 12g 13.3g 14fg 16g² 18.8fg* 18.1d⁴ 19s* 16s* 1982 18.4fg 16g 20fg 22.2fg 18.4g³ 19f 16.1g³ 18.8fg* 17.4d 19s* 18d 20g⁴ 18s³) big, rangy gelding; fair handicapper; inconsistent, but won decisively at Warwick in August **86**

and Goodwood (from Bajan Sunshine) in September; suited by a stiff test of stamina; acts on a firm surface but is well suited by some give in the ground; seems best in blinkers (didn't wear them in his 4 races before Warwick); not one to rely on. *N. Vigors.*

KING'S FOREST 3 b.g. Realm 129–Pardina 98 (Pardao 120) (1981 6g 6g 6fg **74**
6g 5g 1982 5f³ 6g 7f³ 7g* 7.6g³ 7fg³ 10fg 8g 8s) big, well-made, attractive gelding; good mover; always going well when winning maiden race at Newcastle in June; third in handicaps at Chester and Newcastle in July; well beaten afterwards; not sure to stay 1¼m; acts well on firm going; sold privately out of H. Wragg's stable after fifth start. *R. Hollinshead.*

KING'S GLORY 4 br.c. Royal and Regal–Dazzling Light 116 (Silly Season 127) **90**
(1981 12.3g 10.6s 8f 8fg 10g 12fg 10g* 1982 8g* 10s 8fg 7f² 8f³ 9d) compact, good-bodied colt; won 26-runner William Hill Lincoln Handicap at Doncaster in March in good style, leading fully 2f out and being pushed clear to beat Christmas Cottage by 2 lengths; ran easily best subsequent races at Newmarket, finishing neck second to Paterno in Ward Hill Bunbury Cup in July and just over a length third to Royaber in August; by no means disgraced considering his poorish draw when in mid-field behind Century City in William Hill Cambridgeshire, also at Newmarket, in October; effective at 7f to 1¼m; acts particularly well on firm going and is possibly unsuited by really soft; seems to do well when fresh; blinkered third and fifth outings in 1981 (not running at all well at time). *P. Mitchell.*

KING'S GRANGE 2 b.c. English Prince 129–Gisela 94 (Queen's Hussar 124) **74**
(1982 5fg³ 5fg* 6fg 6f 7f 7g³ 7.2f 6fg) Mar 28; IR 1,800Y; good-bodied, fair sort; poor mover; second foal; dam 2-y-o 5f winner; won 11-runner maiden auction event at Salisbury in May; 1¼ lengths third to Command Respect in 9-runner nursery at Bath in August, best subsequent effort; stays 7f; possibly unsuited by really firm ground; blinkered sixth and seventh outings; sold 1,500 gns Newmarket Autumn Sales. *Mrs J. Reavey.*

KING'S HOLT 3 b.c. Royal Palace 131–Lady Rowley 114 (Royal Levee) (1981 **77**
6fg 8g⁴ 8g 7g³ 1982 10d 7fg 8g* 8s⁴ 7g⁴) big, rangy colt; won maiden race at Edinburgh in October; stays 1m but isn't sure to get further unless he learns to settle; trained by A. Jarvis first 2 starts. *M. McCormack.*

KING SINBAD 2 ch.c. Dublin Taxi–Richo's Melody 57 (Double Jump 131) **68**
(1982 5fg 5fg³ 5g⁴ 5d) May 17; 8,000Y; useful-looking colt; first foal; dam won 6f seller; in frame in valuable sellers at Sandown in August and York in September; always struggling when last in nursery at Wolverhampton in October; will stay 6f; possibly unsuited by a soft surface; should win in ordinary plating company. *P. Haslam.*

KING'S LINE 2 ch.c. High Line 125–Soverena 98 (Sovereign Lord 120) (1982 **—**
7g 7g 7fg) May 2; 6,000Y; small, sturdy colt; particularly good walker; half-brother to 4 winners, including very useful middle-distance performer So Royal (by Tudor Melody) and very smart 1975 French staying 2-y-o Luna Real (by Roan Rocket), subsequently successful at up to 1¼m; dam, a sprinter, is half-sister to top-class sprinter Set Fair; soundly beaten in big fields of maidens; blinkered final outing; sold 2,000 gns Newmarket Autumn Sales. *H. Candy.*

*William Hill Lincoln Handicap, Doncaster—King's Glory
scores in good style*

KING'S MARCH 3 b.g. Moulton 128–Walk By 113 (Tower Walk 130) (1981 **51** 7g 8g 8d 1982 8g 10s⁴ 10g⁴) lengthy gelding; plater; stays 1¼m; acts on soft going; sold 1,800 gns Ascot May Sales. *W. Musson.*

KINGS OFFERING 7 b.g. Frankincense 120–Ribble Girl 96 (Trouville 125) **44** (1981 5d³ 5d⁴ 5d 5fg 5f* 5f⁴ 6fg 5fg 6g 5f 5g 5d 5s 5g 7d 1982 5g 5fg 5fg 5f 5fg 5g⁴ 5g³ 5fg 5d) strong, good-topped gelding; sprint handicapper; best at 5f; acts on any going; good mount for an inexperienced rider; effective with or without blinkers; goes well on a sharp track. *R. Ward.*

KINGS PARADE 4 ch.c. Realm 129–La Lidia 78 (Matador 131) (1981 10fg **83** 10g 10g* 10.1d* 10.1g³ 10g 1982 12f²) strong, well-made colt; good walker and mover; ran very well when length second to Valentinian in Newbury Summer Cup (Handicap) in June, only outing of year on flat; stays 1½m well; yet to race on very soft going, but acts on any other; useful hurdler. *G. Thorner.*

KING'S RIDE 6 b.h. Rarity 129–Ride 71 (Sovereign Path 125) (1981 8d 10fg **71** 12g² 11s 12g 12d² 12g* 16g 1982 10s² 12fg) tall, attractive horse; fair handicapper at his best, winner of 1980 William Hill Lincoln; ran only twice in 1982, easily better effort when 3 lengths second to Funny Spring in Rosebery Stakes at Kempton in April; stayed 1½m (out of depth over 2m); acted on any going, but was very well suited by some give in the ground; was tried in blinkers; standing at Russellstown Stud, Mullingar, Co. Westmeath. *W. Wightman.*

KINGS SOLDIER 3 b.g. Queen's Hussar 124–Albertina 102 (Great Nephew **80** 126) (1981 6fg 7.6s 1982 8fg 10fg³ 10f² 10d* 10f 11g* 11.1fg 12f²) lengthy, useful-looking gelding; good walker; won maiden race at Folkestone in June and handicap at Wolverhampton in August; stays 1½m; seems to act on any going; sold to J. Jenkins 14,500 gns Newmarket Autumn Sales. *P. Walwyn.*

KINNIGGER 4 b.g. Rapid River 127–Princess Gretel 97 (The Phoenix) (1981 **55** 8s* 7g 8fg 8fg 10d 8s 1982 12fg⁴ 12g² 11f 12fg⁴ 12fg⁴ 12g² 12fg 12fg) lengthy gelding; middle-distance handicapper; probably acts on any going; sometimes sweats up. *M. Francis.*

KIR ROYALE 3 b.c. So Blessed 130–Borana 105 (Aureole 132) (1981 5s 6g 7g **62** 7fg 7.6s³ 8d² 1982 8f 7fg 10f 10f 8d⁴ 7g 7f⁴ 7fg 8s) rangy colt; stays 1m; best form with some give in the ground; best in blinkers and with forcing tactics; probably none too keen. *B. Swift.*

KIR ROYALE (USA) 2 b.f. Ack Ack–Old Gypsy (Olden Times) (1982 7f 7g **83** 7d⁴) May 3; $30,000Y; rangy filly; fifth foal; half-sister to 2 winners in USA and smart 3-y-o Zinzara (by Stage Door Johnny), a winner at up to 1¼m; dam minor stakes winner at up to 1m; 2 lengths fourth of 18 to Cormorant Wood in maiden race at Leicester in October, best effort; will stay 1m. *M. Stoute.*

KISRA'S DAUGHTER 3 ch.f. Native Bazaar 122–Persian Poem 58 (Darius 129) **—** (1981 NR 1982 5s) small filly; half-sister to winners here and abroad, including fairly useful 1974 2-y-o 6f winner Double Nap (by Double Jump); dam poor plater; 50/1, dwelt when last of 7 to Cree Bay in minor event at Haydock in October. *R. Baker.*

KISSIMMEE 2 b.f. Abwah 118–Boston Flyer 57 (Mansingh 120) (1982 5fg **—** 5.3fg 6s 5d) May 26; 5,200Y; second foal; half-sister to 1981 2-y-o 5f winner She's My Girl (by Mandamus); dam won over 5f at 2 yrs; no worthwhile form; favourite for 17-runner Catterick seller final outing; looks a short runner; sent to Holland. *G. Hunter.*

KITHAIRON 11 br.h. Klairon 131–Gin-Ginger 82 (Happy Monarch 109) (1981 **62** 8.2d 7.6g 8fg 8g³ 8g 8fg³ 9d 8g 8.2d⁴ 8s⁴ 8.2d 8g 1982 8.2v* 9fg 8fg 8.2g 8d 8fg 8.2s) a grand old horse who won 21 of his 144 races on flat, last of them at Hamilton in April; best at around 1m; acted on any going but was ideally suited by some give in the ground; excellent mount for an apprentice; used to wear blinkers; usually got well behind in early stages; dead. *J. W. Watts.*

KITSON (USA) 4 b.c. Secretariat–Gunite (Crozier USA) (1981 12fg 12g 1982 **—** 12g⁴ 14fg 12f⁴ 14.6fg⁴) well-made colt; chipped a bone in a knee as a 3-y-o; lightly raced and rather disappointing in 1982; sold 800 gns Newmarket Autumn Sales. *P. Walwyn.*

KITTY COME HOME 2 b.f. Monsanto 121–Fair Kitty 73 (Saucy Kit 76) **71** (1982 5fg 7fg 7fg 8.2d 8s) Mar 28; 4,000Y; deep-girthed filly; first foal; dam won 8 times from 5f to 2m and also won 8 races over jumps; no form until showing up in Nottingham nursery and Leicester maiden race on last 2 starts; will stay beyond 1m; apparently suited by some give in the ground. *D. Dale.*

KITTY FRISK 2 b.f. Prince Tenderfoot 126–Claremont Girl (Will Hays) (1982 7s 7s) May 15; IR 6,200F; quite well-made, attractive filly; second produce; dam Irish 1½m winner; in rear in October in £3,700 event at York and 11-runner maiden race at Redcar. *J. W. Watts.* —

KITTY RIVERS 2 b.f. Rapid River 127–Kitty H (Takawalk II 125) (1982 5f 5f³ 5fg 6f 6fg) Apr 6; second live foal; dam fourth of 11 on first of 2 starts on flat; bad plater; not seen out after August. *M. Camacho.* **40**

KIVA (USA) 3 b.f. Tom Rolfe–Befuddled (Tom Fool) (1981 6fg 6fg* 7fg² 7d 1982 8f³ 8f³ 8fg) neat, attractive filly; good mover; third in June in £3,800 event at Sandown (5 lengths behind Dish Dash) and in £4,000 race at Newbury (didn't have best of runs but could only keep on at one pace when beaten just over a length by Silly Steven); below form final start; will be suited by 1¼m+; best form on a sound surface. *R. Hern.* **95**

KIWIETTE 2 b.f. Thatch 136–Domani 106 (Mourne 126) (1982 6fg 6g³ 6g³ 7f 6fg 5v* 5g) Apr 22; $65,000Y; neat filly; closely related to a minor winner by Home Guard and half-sister to fairly useful 3-y-o sprinter Sonseri (by Prince Tenderfoot) and very useful 6f to 1m winner Apres Demain (by King Emperor); dam, winner over 6f and 7f, is half-sister to Showdown, Matatina and Duke Ellington; won 9-runner maiden race at Hamilton in October; possibly doesn't stay 7f; best form with give in the ground, and acts on heavy going; blinkered fifth start. *M. Jarvis.* **79**

KLAIROVE 3 b.f. Averof 123–Klaire 85 (Klairon 131) (1981 6g 8fg³ 7g 1982 10.1g 10g 8s 8.2s) lightly-made filly; plating-class maiden; should stay 1¼m; sold to B. McMahon 1,750 gns Doncaster November Sales. *D. Dale.* —

KLIL A HORES (ISR) 3 b.c. Verre Dore–Goshreia (Grey Mirage 128) (1981 NR 1982 6g 8fg 9fg) first foal; dam won in Israel; sire won Kenyan Derby; well behind in varied company, including selling; bandaged final outing. *Mrs B. Waring.* —

KNAVE OF TRUMPS 3 b.c. Great Nephew 126–Clean Canasta 95 (Silly Season 127) (1981 6d 6fg² 6g* 6g* 1982 8f² 10.1g* 10.5fg) useful-looking colt; good walker and mover; had simple task when winning 3-runner race at Windsor in May; had previously stayed on without promising to get to the winner when ¾-length second of 5 to Full Extent in Timeform Race Card Stakes at Thirsk; well beaten in £5,700 race won by Yard Bird at York in August; stays 1¼m; tends to go to post keenly; sold 6,400 gns Newmarket Autumn Sales. *H. Cecil.* **95**

KNIGHTHALL (USA) 4 b.c. King's Bishop–Midnight Hush (Sunrise Flight) (1981 8d 10.1f⁴ 13.1f⁴ 10g 10f³ 9g² 10d⁴ 9s⁴ 10s² 1982 10.2s³ 10fg 12g 10.4g 10f⁴ 8g³ 8fg³ 12.3g 9g) plating-class maiden; in frame in varied races, including an amateur riders event and a lady riders race; stays 1¼m. *A. W. Jones.* **46**

KNIGHTSBRIDGE BOY 3 gr.g. Be Friendly 130–Immaculate (Sovereign Path 125) (1981 6g 7g 7.6s 1982 8d 11.7g 12g 10v⁴) compact gelding; poor plater. *D. Wilson.* —

KNIGHTSBRIDGE GAME 3 gr.g. Abwah 118–Turnstone 83 (Sea Hawk II 131) (1981 5d 6f 7g 7.6s 8s 8.2s* 8d² 1982 8.2d 6f 8.3fg 8fg 10d² 8s 10g² 10s 10s* 10.2s) plain gelding; plater; bought in 2,900 gns after winning decisively at Leicester in November; suited by 1¼m; acts well on soft ground. *D. Wilson.* **54**

KNIGHT'S CUCKOO 3 ch.f. Birdbrook 110–Voleuse 65 (Burglar 128) (1981 NR 1982 5fg) first foal; dam won 5f seller at 2 yrs; unquoted when in rear in 13-runner maiden race won by Premier Lass at Folkestone in April; dead. *R. Smyth.* —

KNIGHT SECURITY 3 b.f. Swing Easy 126–High Density 66 (Pall Mall 132) (1981 5g² 5d⁴ 5s 5f* 6f⁴ 6d* 6fg 6fg 6d 6s* 1982 6g 6g⁴ 6f⁴ 6fg 6g³ 6fg 6fg 6s 7s 6s) leggy, narrow filly; stays 6f; acts on any going but is ideally suited by some give in the ground; has twice been blinkered; retained 2,800 gns Ascot August Sales. *J. Berry.* **69**

KNOCKIN 3 ch.c. Relkino 131–Knocknagrena (Worden II 129) (1981 8s 8s 1982 10d 10f 13.8f) lengthy colt; little worthwhile form, including in sellers; blinkered final start; sold 400 gns Doncaster September Sales. *J. Etherington.* —

KOCHIA 4 b.f. Firestreak 125–Lead Me On (King's Troop 118) (1981 5s 6g⁴ 6fg³ 6d 5f 6g 5d 1982 8g 8f³ 8f² 8f³ 10f² 10fg³ 8fg² 8fg³ 8.3fg² 8fg* 8g² 8fg² 8s) small, stocky filly; in frame most starts and won decisively when dropped to **54**

selling company at Salisbury in September (bought in 3,800 gns); ran creditably in better company afterwards; suited by 1¼m; acts on any going, but goes particularly well on firm; sweated badly eighth start. *J. Toller.*

KOHINOOR DIAMOND 2 ch.f. Roman Warrior 132–Czar's Diamond 66 —
(Queen's Hussar 124) (1982 5h⁴ 6s) May 7; big, workmanlike filly; sister to a bad plater and half-sister to 3 winners; dam plater; well beaten in minor event (last of 4) at Chepstow in May and maiden race at Leicester in November. *G. Kindersley.*

KOMATCH (USA) 3 ch.c. Apalachee 137–Zambezi River (Pretendre 126) 72
(1981 8g 7g 1982 14fg 16fg² 16d² 16f⁴ 16.9fg 12f² 10.1s² 16s²) plain colt; good mover; second in varied races, including a selling handicap at Newmarket; stays very well; acts on any going; blinkered fourth and fifth starts, sweating up on latter; trained by J. Hindley part of season. *M. Pipe.*

KONDAIR 2 b.c. Record Run 127–Milk and Honey 102 (So Blessed 130) (1982 71
7f³ 7s) Apr 20; 5,000Y; lightly-made colt; first foal; dam won over 5f and 6f at 2 yrs but didn't train on; showed ability in autumn maiden events at Brighton and Redcar; will stay 1m. *D. Arbuthnot.*

KOOKABURRA 3 br.g. Cawston's Clown 113–Lindy Ann (King's Leap 111) —
(1981 6fg 7f⁴ 8g 1982 10.1fg 12fg) unfurnished gelding; good mover; plating-class maiden; unlikely to stay 1¼m; sold 800 gns Ascot August Sales. *G. Pritchard-Gordon.*

KORYPHEOS 3 b.g. He Loves Me 120–Silly Song (Silly Season 127) (1981 65
7fg² 7.6s³ 1982 7.6f 8fg³ 7f 6g 6s) leggy, lightly-made gelding; stays 1m. *P. Mitchell.*

KOTOR 3 gr.g. Welsh Pageant 132–Tirana 101 (Ragusa 137) (1981 NR 1982 —
11f 12fg 12fg) big gelding; half-brother to fairly useful middle-distance performer Brave Hussar (by Brigadier Gerard), winning middle-distance stayer Scutari (by St Paddy) and a winner in Austria; dam won over 6f and 7f at 2 yrs; well beaten in maiden races and a gentleman riders event; bandaged in front first start; sold out of H. Candy's stable 3,700 gns Ascot 2nd June Sales after first appearance. *P. Mitchell.*

KRACON MISON 2 b.g. Le Johnstan 123–Food For Thought 76 (Frankincense —
120) (1982 5fg 6fg) Apr 29; 450F, 980Y; small, well-made gelding; first produce; dam winning sprinter; in rear in valuable seller at Sandown in August and minor event at Lingfield in September. *G. Balding.*

KRAKOW 2 b.f. Malinowski 123–Fighting 105 (Aggressor 130) (1982 6f 6g 78
6fg) Mar 16; 36,000Y; lengthy filly; good walker and mover; half-sister to 3 winners, including Irish 7f and 1m winner Kri Kri (by Karabas) and fairly useful 1978 2-y-o Balilla (by Balidar); dam miler; quite a modest maiden; disappointing favourite in maiden race won by Julia Flyte at Salisbury in September on final appearance; will stay 1m; possibly requires some give in the ground. *M. Stoute.*

KRAYYAN 2 ch.c. Tower Walk 130–Mrs Moss 81 (Reform 132) (1982 5fg* 5f* 117
5f² 6g³ 6g³)
The commentary on Pushy in *Racehorses of 1980* sings the praises of Mrs Moss, bought at the bargain price of 2,100 guineas by the Marchioness of Tavistock at the 1975 December Sales. Since then the story has continued to run, and in the latest season two of Mrs Moss's sons won races, giving her the remarkable record of seven winners from as many foals of racing age. Both sons showed well above-average ability, Jupiter Island (by St Paddy) proving a useful middle-distance performer whilst Krayyan, sold for 150,000 guineas as a yearling, developed into one of the best two-year-old sprinters in training.

Krayyan made his debut in the Royal Crown Derby Stakes at Haydock in May and became the third winner of the race in succession from his stable. Despite a slow start he was in command by halfway and had only to be shaken up to win in good style by two lengths from Sheldan. He had to work considerably harder for his success in the five-runner National Stakes at Sandown the following month; although he always looked like getting the better of his tussle with Sayf El Arab he needed fairly hard driving to hold on by a head. Krayyan stepped up to pattern-race company afterwards and put up a game and smart performance to run Brondesbury to a neck in the Norfolk Stakes at Royal Ascot, sticking to his task so well after being taken off his legs early on that in the end he would have needed only a few more strides for victory. A twisted ankle and a bout of ringworm kept Krayyan off the course for three

National Stakes, Sandown—Krayyan holds on under fairly strong driving from Sayf El Arab (left)

months after Ascot. He returned to show good form in the Mill Reef Stakes at Newbury and the William Hill Middle Park Stakes at Newmarket. At Newbury he gave Salieri a good fight throughout the last two furlongs before going down by just over a length, losing second place to Kafu in the closing stages; at Newmarket he was again third, beaten four lengths by Diesis.

			High Treason		Court Martial
		Tower Walk	(ch 1951)		Eastern Grandeur
		(b 1966)	Lorrikeet		Pearl Diver
Krayyan			(b 1955)		Parakeet
(ch.c. Mar 5, 1980)			Reform		Pall Mall
		Mrs Moss	(b 1964)		Country House
		(ch 1969)	Golden Plate		Whistler
			(ch 1964)		Good as Gold

Krayyan impresses both in his style of racing and in his appearance; he's a well-made, most attractive colt. There's plenty of speed in his pedigree. Mrs Moss won a five-furlong maiden race at two years from only four starts. Of her produce only Jupiter Island has stayed particularly well whilst Pushy (by Sharpen Up) was very speedy, Pit Stop (by Pitskelly) won five races over five furlongs and all the wins of Socks Up (by Sharpen Up) have been gained over sprint distances. Mrs Moss's dam Golden Plate was a sister to the unbeaten Whistling Wind, who topped the Irish Two-Year-Old Free Handicap in 1962; her great-grandam is Gamble in Gold, the speediest two-year-old filly in England in 1950, great-grandam also of Goodbye Shelley and grandam of Magic Flute as well as Whistling Wind. Krayyan is a genuine and consistent performer. Although he stays six furlongs he gives the impression he may prove best at five. He has yet to race on a soft surface. *G. Hunter.*

KRISCHINA 3 ch.f. Music Boy 124–Alchorus 78 (Alcide 136) (1981 6fg⁴ 1982 — 7.6fg 8g) leggy filly; has shown some ability in maiden races; promises to stay 1m; sold 9,800 gns Newmarket December Sales. *J. Hindley.*

KRISTALLINA 3 b.f. Homeric 133–Go Friendly (Be Friendly 130) (1981 72 6g 6d 1982 8d 8.5f 10fg² 10f³ 10fg 10g² 12f 13.8f* 14f 14g 14s 15.5fg) lengthy filly; came with a strong run to win handicap at Catterick in July; stays 1¾m; needs a sound surface; blinkered sixth and seventh starts; bolted on way to start and was withdrawn intended third outing and dwelt fifth outing; sold 4,000 gns Newmarket December Sales. *A. Bailey.*

KRISTEN 3 ch.f. Sheshoon 132–Sweet Boronia 96 (Mandamus 120) (1981 44 6g 7.6s 10.2g 1982 12g⁴ 10.1fg 10f 9g 10.1d³ 10.8fg* 10.1fg³ 12g⁴ 10f 10v) small filly; middle-distance plater; bought in 1,600 gns after winning at Warwick in July; acts on a firm and a soft surface. *R. Hoad.*

KRUGERAMA 4 br.g. Amber Rama 133–Krugerrand 74 (Goldhill 125) (1981 38 8g 8g⁴ 8g 6f 7f 6d 6f 6fg 6f 8fg 8.2v 12.2g 12d³ 1982 10s 8.2g 8g 8fg 8.2v³ 8d³) plater nowadays; seems to stay 1½m; probably acts on any going; occasionally wears blinkers. *E. Weymes.*

KRUIDTVAT 2 gr.c. Broxted 120–Pinnacle 70 (High Perch 126) (1982 5fg³ **68**
5f 5g) May 11; 3,800Y; sturdy colt; good walker; half-brother to 3 winners,
including 3-y-o 1m winner Top Lad (by Town Crier) and Senator Sam (by
Meldrum), a winner 9 times from 6f to 1¼m; dam best at up to 1½m; 3¼ lengths
third of 15 to Flying Disc in maiden race at Lingfield in May, best effort; not
seen out after June; probably needs further than 5f. *R. Price.*

KUMU 2 b.f. Streak 119–Fleur d'Amour 85 (Murrayfield 119) (1982 5d 5fg² **50**
5fg 5.8f 5g 5v⁴ 5s) Apr 7; 400Y; second foal; dam won over 6f and 7f; poor
plater; seems to act on any going; swerved badly at distance when apprentice
ridden on final start. *M. Bradley.*

KUSHSHOON 2 b.g. Sheshoon 132–Kushbehar 80 (Behistoun 131) (1982 **—**
7g 8.2d) Apr 22; big gelding; second foal; dam at her best at 2 yrs when 6f
winner; in rear in minor event at Newcastle in August and seller at Nottingham
(last of 17) in September. *S. Wiles.*

KUWAIT BEACH (USA) 2 gr.c. Grey Dawn II 132–Horsing Around (Ad- **—**
vocator) (1982 6s 7g) Mar 16; $45,000Y; big colt; first foal; dam very useful
winner at up to 1m; backward, behind in the autumn in minor event at Lingfield
and 28-runner maiden race (speed 4f) at Newmarket. *J. Sutcliffe.*

KUWAIT DESERT 2 ch.c. Dominion 123–Kadsai 90 (Lorenzaccio 130) (1982 **86**
5g³ 7g* 6f³ 7g² 8.2g 7.3g 8s) Mar 8; neat colt; first foal; dam 2-y-o 6f and 1m
winner; won maiden race at Brighton in July; ran creditably subsequently
until finishing in rear in nurseries on last 2 starts; stays 1m; possibly unsuited by
soft going; sold BBA 10,500 gns Newmarket Autumn Sales. *G. Harwood.*

KUWAIT SUN 2 gr.c. Bruni 132–Countess Decima (Sir Gaylord) (1982 7fg) **— P**
Apr 12; 35,000Y; close-coupled, useful-looking colt; half-brother to 4 winners,
including fairly useful 1m to 1¼m winner Countess Lor (by Lorenzaccio) and
useful French sprinter Miliar (by Thatch); dam never ran; very weak in the
market, caught the eye making strong and significant headway after being settled
at rear and nearly last at halfway, when eighth of 16 in maiden race won by
Behind The Lines at Salisbury in September; certain to do much better, and is
one to note. *G. Harwood.*

KUWAIT TEAM (USA) 2 ch.c. Graustark–D'Arqueangel (Raise A Native) **83**
(1982 7g 8s³) Feb 7; $300,000Y; quite useful-looking colt; good walker; first
foal; dam, winner over 6f, is closely related to very smart fillies Native Street
and Street Dancer; 5 lengths third of 21 behind Rock's Gate in maiden race at
Leicester in November; will be suited by 1¼m+. *G. Harwood.*

KUWAIT TOWER (USA) 2 gr.c. Little Current–Gris Vitesse (Amerigo 116§) **116**
(1982 7fg* 7fg² 8s⁴) Apr 24; $55,000Y; attractive, well-made colt; half-brother
to several winners, including Derby third and Irish Sweeps Derby runner-up
Silver Hawk (by Roberto) and very useful French 1m to 11f winner Blast Off
(by Graustark); dam won Prix Jacques le Marois; dead-heated with Muscatite in
11-runner £5,300 Sandwich Maiden Stakes at Ascot in July, leading 1f out until
swerving quite sharply left near finish; co-favourite for 6-runner Intercraft
Solario Stakes at Sandown the following month but ran green once again when

*Sandwich Maiden Stakes, Ascot—the inexperienced Kuwait Tower (right)
swerves near the finish and has to share the spoils
with Muscatite*

pulled out to challenge and finished 3 lengths second to The Fort; still bit green when 4 lengths fourth of 9 to Dunbeath in Royal Lodge Stakes at Ascot in September; should stay 1½m; appears to act on any going. *J. Sutcliffe.*

KWA ZULU (USA) 2 ch.c. Naskra–Sweet Nothings (Promised Land) (1982 6fg 6v 6d) May 9; $70,000Y, $52,000 2-y-o; half-brother to 2 winners, including Sweet Sad (by Sadair), successful over 1m and also over jumps in France; dam stakes-placed sprint winner; quite modest form in varied company in the autumn; will stay 7f; may do better. *G. Hunter.* **77**

KWELA 2 b.f. Dance In Time–Jujube 102 (Ribero 126) (1982 5fg⁴ 6fg* 6d* 6s 6g) Apr 13; sturdy filly; fourth foal; half-sister to 1m and 9f winner Candy Castle (by Habitat) and fairly useful 1m to 1½m winner Maintop (by High Top); dam, a stayer, won 5 of her 6 races; made all when winning maiden race at Lingfield in June by a length from House Guest and minor event at Windsor in September by a short head from Band; soundly beaten subsequently in minor event at Goodwood and nursery at Newmarket; bred to stay much further than 6f; possibly not at her best on very soft going; sold to BBA 12,500 gns Newmarket December Sales. *P. Walwyn.* **83**

KYLE-HELEN 3 b.f. Orange Bay 131–Kyle Keep 73 (Ballymoss 136) (1981 8d 1982 13.1f 10.2s 8s 12s) little worthwhile form in varied company, including selling. *Dr. A. Jones.* **—**

KYNASTON 2 b.f. Pals Passage 115–Kelly Green (Kelly 122) (1982 5fg³ 5g² 6s 6d 5d² 6s) Apr 2; 2,900Y; lengthy filly; not a good mover; half-sister to several winners, including very useful 5f to 1m winner Super Kelly (by Supreme Sovereign); dam won over 5f at 2 yrs in Ireland; quite a moderate filly; evidently best at 5f *J. Berry.* **75**

KYOTO 4 b.g. Averof 123–Klondyke Fire (Klondyke Bill 125) (1981 8.2s 6g 8g 10fg⁴ 10.2f 10d 11f 10fg² 10f 9f³ 9g* 8.2d 9s 1982 8f 10f 8d 8.2g) big, lengthy gelding; behind in handicaps, going too fast for his own good on third start; stays 1¼m; sometimes blinkered; inconsistent. *H. Collingridge.* **—**

KYROOTA 2 b. or br.c. Reliance II 137–Anna Barry 76 (Falls of Clyde 126) (1982 7g 7fg⁴) Mar 28; strong, workmanlike colt; half-brother to 3 winners, including useful 5f performer Heywood Hardy (by Tribal Chief) and sprinter Swan Ann (by My Swanee); dam 5f sprinter; 33/1, 7 lengths fourth of 5 behind very easy winner On Stage in £4,100 race at Newmarket in July. *M. Tompkins.* **—**

L

LA BANDERA 4 ch.f. Morston 125–Patois (I Say 125) (1981 10s 1982 9g 12d⁴ 11g² 10.1g⁴ 11.7d* 10v⁴) good-bodied filly; ran respectably all starts, and beat 7/1-on Round Tower by ¾ length in minor event at Windsor in September; stays 1½m; acts on heavy going (yet to race on a firm surface); sold 15,000 gns Newmarket December Sales. *T. Robson.* **60**

LA BANEZA 4 ch.f. Balidar 133–Abanilla 115 (Abernant 142) (1981 5d 6d² 7.6g 7fg* 6f 1982 8f 6f 6fg 5.3f⁴ 6g 6s 5d) ex-Irish filly; half-sister to numerous winners, including useful middle-distance filly Evvia (by Sir Ivor); dam very useful at 2 yrs; won maiden race at Phoenix Park at 3 yrs; bought out of K. Prendergast's stable 10,000 gns Newmarket December Sales, and ran best subsequent race when fourth to Sanu in minor event at Brighton in August; stays at least 7f; acts on firm going and a soft surface; sweated up in blinkers final start (ran poorly). *B. Hanbury.* **—**

LA BIRD 3 b.f. Le Johnstan 123–Bird 80 (Firestreak 125) (1981 6fg 7fg 8.2d* 8.2s 8.2s 1982 12g 13.8f 12g 13.8f³ 12f³ 10d) lengthy filly; poor mover; plater; probably stays 1¾m; seems to act on any going; sometimes bandaged behind *K. Stone.* **35**

LA CASTELLANA 3 b. or br.f. Sparkler 130–Jeanina (Congolese 109) (1981 5g 7fg 8fg* 7v⁴ 7d* 1982 12s) rangy filly; won maiden race at Beverley and nursery at Leicester in 1981; virtually pulled up lame in handicap at Chepstow in April, only start at 3 yrs; stays 1m well and will get 1¼m; seems to act on any going *F. Durr.* **—**

LACKBRIDGE 2 ch.g. Mansingh 120–Talsaana (Crepello 136) (1982 6f 6f 6g 6s) Mar 23; 6,400GY; half-brother to a winner in France by Relko; dam unraced daughter of top-class 2-y-o filly Opaline II; staying-on 5 lengths fifth of 25 behind Raashideah in maiden race at Doncaster in November, first indication of merit; will be suited by 7f; acts on soft going. *G. Balding.* **79**

LA COMEDIENNE 3 gr.f. Comedy Star 121–Ruetina 74 (Rugantino 97) (1981 —
6fg 5.8h 7g 1982 7.6f 8g) lengthy, lightly-made filly; soundly beaten in varied
company, including claiming. *J. Dunlop.*

LA CONGA 2 b.f. Dance In Time–Pop Music (Val de Loir 133) (1982 6s) —
Mar 14; a twin; half-sister to winners in France and Italy; dam unraced daughter
of smart 2-y-o Runnello; 25/1, dwelt when twelfth of 13 in maiden race at
Hamilton in September. *E. Incisa.*

LAC ROYALE 2 b.f. Lochnager 123–Jubilee Year 63 (Red God 128§) (1982 8s) —
Mar 2; 700Y; first foal; dam 1m winner; unquoted, no show in maiden race at
Leicester in November. *D. Arbuthnot.*

LACY RIVER 2 gr.c. Forlorn River 124–Grey Blossom 67 (Grisaille 115) (1982 —
5fg 5f⁴ 5g 6s) Mar 25; 900F; workmanlike colt; of no account; blinkered last
outing; sold 400 gns Newmarket Autumn Sales. *O. Jorgensen.*

LADENDA 2 b.f. Bold Lad (Ire) 133–Brief Agenda (Levmoss 133) (1982 71
7d 8g³) May 11; smallish, lengthy filly; second foal; sister to Irish 1¼m winner
Bold and Brief; dam, placed in small 9.5f race in France, is daughter of 1,000
Guineas winner Pourparler; quite moderate form in autumn in maiden races at
Ayr and Edinburgh; stays 1m. *J. W. Watts.*

LA DI DA 2 b.f. Cawston's Clown 113–Leylandia 69 (Wolver Hollow 126) 65
(1982 5g⁴ 5s³ 5fg 5fg 5fg⁴ 6d² 5g 5d²) Mar 3; leggy filly; first reported foal;
dam won over 2m at 4 yrs; second in sellers at Ripon (nursery) in August and
Catterick in October; stays 6f; probably needs some give in the ground. *J.
Fitzgerald.*

LADOUCETTE 4 b.f. Bustino 136–Sunblast 108 (Roan Rocket 128) (1981 102
10f* 14f* 12fg 12f² 11.5d² 12g 1982 12s 16fg³ 22.2fg 16g* 14f⁴ 16f* 14fg²
16s 12g³) lengthy, sparely-made filly; second foal; half-sister to quite useful
7f winner Carlyle (by Wolver Hollow); dam won at up to 1m; successful in
minor event at Limerick Junction in July (won easily when long odds on)
and in handicap at Clonmel in August; also placed 3 times at Leopardstown
in Savel Beg Stakes (third to Steel Duke), a minor event (4 lengths second to
Patcher) and Trigo Stakes (5 lengths third to Karol); ninth behind Ore in Queen
Alexandra Stakes at Royal Ascot on third start; stays well; probably acts on
any going. *D. Weld, Ireland.*

LADY ARPEGE 4 b. or br.f. Swing Easy 126–Giglet (Frankincense 120) 50
(1981 6g 7g⁴ 7g 7f 8.2f 5f 6d 1982 6s 7fg 8f 7g² 6fg³ 6fg² 6g⁴ 8g* 8fg⁴ 8s 8g³)
plater nowadays; attracted no bid after beating Whangarei by 5 lengths at
Beverley in August; not disgraced in better company last 2 starts; suited by 1m;
blinkered fifth and seventh outings; sold out of P. Calver's stable 780 gns
Doncaster September Sales after ninth start. *W. Musson.*

LADY ASTIR 4 b.f. Abwah 118–Ma Mitte (Faristan 123) (1981 9s 6g 7fg —
7fg 5fg² 6fg 6fg 6fg 5g 1982 5fg) fair sort; maiden plater; last on only outing
of 1982; best at sprint distances; acts on a firm surface; blinkered once; sold
410 gns Doncaster November Sales. *T. Taylor.*

LADY BLANROID 2 b.f. Haveroid 122–Blandford Lady (Blandford Lad —
96) (1982 7s) Mar 5; lengthy non-thoroughbred filly; half-sister to 1981
2-y-o 6f and 1m winner Blandor (by Le Coq d'Or); dam ran over hurdles in
Ireland; 20/1, made some late headway when eleventh of 28 in maiden race at
Redcar in October. *J. W. Watts.*

LADY BOUNTY 3 ch.f. Hotfoot 126–Donnarose (Fighting Don) (1981 52
6fg 6g² 7f³ 7g 7fg⁴ 8g⁴ 8d² 8.2s 1982 7f⁴ 8f² 9g 8fg 7d 8.2s² 9s⁴) lengthy,
rather lightly-made filly; quite a modest maiden; second in seller on sixth
start; suited by 1m or more; acts on any going; sold 2,000 gns Doncaster October
Sales. *J. Etherington.*

LADY CARA 2 br.f. Lochnager 132–Gold Cheb 88 (Chebs Lad 120) (1982 77
6g 5fg 5g) May 2; 3,400Y; shallow-girthed filly; second living foal; sister to
modest 1981 2-y-o 5f winner Gold Key; dam won three 7f races; ridden by
7-lb claimer, 5½ lengths fifth of 11 to African Tudor in minor event at Wolverhampton in August, final outing and best effort; should stay 6f. *J. Berry.*

LADY CLEMENTINE 2 b.f. He Loves Me 120–In The Clover (Meadow Mint —
120) (1982 6g 6fg 7f) Apr 17; 15,000Y; second foal; half-sister to 3-y-o
6f winner Music Lover (by Gay Fandango); dam won over 7f at 2 yrs in Ireland;
behind in maiden races. *B. Swift.*

LADY COX 3 b.f. Sun Prince 128–Lady Rowe 97 (Sir Ivor 135) (1981 6s 6d2 1982 8d 5.8g4 6s 6s) lengthy, attractive filly; poor walker; quite moderate at her best; will be suited by 7f; yet to race on a firm surface. *B. Hills.* **81**

LADY CYNTHIA 2 ch.f. Welsh Pageant 132–Petulant (Petingo 135) (1982 6f 7fg 7fg 8.2d) Feb 13; well-grown, leggy, lengthy filly; third foal; dam never ran; beaten some way in maiden races and when blinkered in nursery. *P. Cundell.* **—**

LADY DARA 2 b. or br.f. Lord Gayle 124–Tanndara (Venture VII 129) (1982 7fg4 7fg* 7d) Mar 24; IR 28,000Y; half-sister to 2 winners, including fair 7f and 1m winner Park Place (by Royal and Regal); dam, French middle-distance winner, is half-sister to outstanding New Zealand stallion Pakistan II; 5/4 favourite, finished well to win 12-runner maiden race at Leopardstown in September by ¾ length from Safe Process; also started short-priced favourite when giving weight to most of her rivals in minor event at Naas the following month but never got in a blow, finishing 8½ lengths sixth of 11 to Persian Polly; will be suited by 1¼m+; acts on a firm surface; evidently quite well thought of. *M. O'Toole, Ireland.* **93**

LADY DONARO 2 br.f. Ardoon 124–Lady Kasbah (Lord Gayle 124) (1982 5g 5g 5g 5f 6s) Mar 23; 4,600Y; compact filly; first foal; dam never ran; plating-class maiden; will be suited by 7f and 1m; acts on any going. *G. Toft.* **63**

LADY EMILY 2 b.f. Auction Ring 123–Village 91 (Charlottesville 135) (1982 5s2 7d) June 6; IR 14,500Y; half-sister to 2 winners, notably useful miler Yamadori (by Mountain Call); dam, half-sister to Parthia, best at up to 1¼m; length second of 21 to Holy Day in maiden race at Bath in October; favourite, weakened below distance when 9½ lengths sixth of 14 to Zariya in minor event at Catterick later in month; should stay 7f; sold to BBA 15,000 gns Newmarket December Sales. *W. Hastings-Bass.* **79**

LADY EN DOUCE 3 gr.f. Ballynockan 112–Clare Blue 83 (Blue Streak 106) (1981 5d 1982 8fg 8f 8fg 8f) of little account; blinkered final start. *Peter Taylor.* **—**

LADY EVER-SO-SURE 4 ch.f. Malicious–Time of Hope 98 (Matador 131) (1981 8g 8d 7.2s2 8fg 7fg 10f2 9g2 9f 12f4 12.2g 11g* 12d3 1982 10d 11s 12g 10.2s) strong, compact filly; fairly useful plater at her best, but ran moderately in 1982; stays 1½m; acts on any going; usually wears blinkers. *J. Etherington.* **—**

LADYFISH 2 ch.f. Pampapaul 121–Tuna 63 (Silver Shark 129) (1982 6g 6f 6g 8fg* 8.2s 7d) Feb 22; IR 6,800F, 6,000Y; quite attractive filly; sister to Irish 3-y-o 9f and 1¼m winner Exclusive Romeo, and half-sister to 3 winners, including useful 1m and 1¼m performer Brother Kempinski (by Right Tack); dam poor performer; showed improved form when winning 13-runner maiden race at Beverley in September by a length from Perovskia; well beaten in nurseries subsequently, once last of 11; will stay 1¼m; acts on a firm surface and is evidently unsuited by soft going. *B. Hanbury.* **79**

LADY GERARD 2 b.f. Brigadier Gerard 144–Sirnelta (Sir Tor) (1982 7d 6fg4 6s2) Mar 15; quite attractive filly; third reported foal; half-sister to fairly useful 1981 2-y-o 7f winner Crimson Knight (by Blushing Groom); dam, daughter of sister to top-class Sanctus II, won from 1m to 1¼m in France; prominent in maiden races, on final outing finishing length second of 19 to Hawk Lady at Leicester in November; should stay at least 1¼m. *F. J. Houghton.* **78**

LADY GREENE 4 br.f. No Mercy 126–Sea Tycoon 80 (Tycoon II) (1981 7fg 8g 7v 8.5g 8.3fg 8g 1982 8f 8fg 7fg 8fg* 8g) well-backed favourite and dropped in class when winning selling handicap at Warwick in July (bought in 3,500 gns); soundly beaten in similar company only subsequent start; stays 1m; acts on a firm surface. *A. Pitt.* **47**

LADY GREENHAM 3 b.f. Wolverlife 115–Miltonia (Star Moss 122) (1981 5g 6g 6d 1982 7s4 7g* 8d 8d 8g 8g) IR 780F, IR 1,500Y; half-sister to 3 winners here and abroad; dam lightly raced; showed improved form when finishing under 2 lengths fourth of 14 to Miss Lilian in April Fillies Stakes at the Curragh in April and winning 11-runner Mulcahy Stakes at Fairyhouse later in month by 2 lengths from Petite Realm; not seen out again until September and put up best subsequent effort when 4½ lengths fifth to Pilgrim in Youghal Stakes at Leopardstown on fifth start; stays 1m; yet to race on a firm surface; sold 42,000 gns Newmarket December Sales. *L. Browne, Ireland.* **94**

LADY JUSTICE 4 ch.f. Status Seeker–Alldyke (Klondyke Bill 125) (1981 8g 1982 10f* 10fg4 10g3 10f* 11.7g2 10fg* 10.2g 10g 10g 10d* 10g3 8s) workmanlike filly; had a good season and was gaining her fourth win when beating Two **90**

High by ½ length in £6,400 Webster's Yorkshire Bitter Stakes at Doncaster in October (20/1 and appearing to face a very stiff task); good third of 17 to Cannon King in Tia Maria Autumn Handicap at Newmarket afterwards; had earlier won a maiden race and handicap at Beverley and a handicap at Nottingham; best form at 1¼m; acts on any going, except perhaps really soft. *R. Boss.*

LADY KAMINA 3 gr.f. Dragonara Palace 115–Miss Carvin (Carvin 127) (1981   **60** 6g 6fg 7g 1982 9g 8g 10f* 10.6h⁴ 8fg 8g 8.3g² 10fg³ 8g* 8g* 7d³ 10s⁴) workmanlike filly; plater; won at Folkestone in May (bought in 2,600 gus) and Brighton in August and September (attracted no bid either time); stays 1¼m; acts on any going; blinkered eighth outing; good mount for an apprentice; trained by D. Kent first 3 starts. *P. Haynes.*

LADY KNIPHOFIA 3 b.f. Sparkler 130–Flora Day 92 (Floribunda 136) (1981   **—** 5d 1982 7fg 8fg 10fg 9s 10s) robust, good sort; poor form, including in a seller. *P. Makin.*

LADY LIANGA (USA) 2 gr.f. Secretariat–Lianga 133 (Dancer's Image) (1982   **81** 6f4 6f) Apr 19; rather short-backed, fair sort; good mover; fourth foal; closely related to 2 winners by Reviewer, namely useful sprinter Long Legend and very useful 1979 2-y-o 5f and 6f winner La Legende; dam top-class winner from 4.5f to 1m; modest form in maiden events at Leicester (7/2 on, ran very green) in May and Goodwood (jockey fined £150 for not persevering) in July; sent to USA. *H. Cecil.*

LADY LILY 3 ch.f. Quiet Fling 124–Tambresi 89 (Tamerlane 128) (1981 5fg   **—** 6f 7fg⁴ 1982 9g 10f⁴ 12f 16h 7fg 10d 13.8f) light-framed filly; plater; stays 1¼m; sold out of R. Hollinshead's stable 960 gns Newmarket July Sales after sixth start. *W. Storey.*

LADY LORRAINE 3 gr.f. Three Legs 128–Happy Evening 89 (Hethersett 134)   **36** (1981 7fg 8fg 7g 1982 10s 12.2f⁴(dis) 12f⁴ 12.2f 10f) sturdy filly; plater; suited by 1¼m; best in blinkers; sold 540 gns Doncaster October Sales. *W. Wharton.*

LADY LUAN 3 ch.f. Hot Spark 126–Disa 55 (Dike) (1981 5g 5g 5f 1982 5g)   **—** small, short-backed filly; well beaten in maiden races and an apprentice handicap; sold 480 gns Ascot March Sales; resold 500 gns Newmarket July Sales. *D. Weeden.*

LADY MANTEGNA 5 b.m. Andrea Mantegna–Grand Central 79 (Grand Roi   **—** 118) (1981 16s* 16fg³ 1982 16s⁴) leggy mare; staying handicapper; ran respectably only outing of 1982 (bandaged); seems to act on any going but goes well on soft. *R. Laing.*

LADY MOON 2 b.f. Mill Reef 141–Moonlight Night 112 (Levmoss 133) (1982   **83 p** 7g⁴) Apr 19; quite attractive filly; third foal; dam, third in Oaks, is half-sister to high-class Main Reef (by Mill Reef); weak in the market, always prominent without being given hard race when 4½ lengths fourth of 21 behind Ski Sailing in maiden event at Newmarket in October; sure to do better over middle distances. *H. Cecil.*

LADY MURFAX 3 b. or br.f. Ercolano 118–Golden Storm 95 (Golden Cloud)   **59** (1981 5s 5g 7f 6f 1982 7.2g 8g⁴ 6fg 6g 7fg⁴ 8d⁴ 8.2g² 7f² 7s² 8s* 10d) leggy filly; good mover; plater; made most of running and kept on gamely to win at Warwick in October (bought in 1,750 gns); stays 1m; acts on any going; effective with or without blinkers. *S. Norton.*

LADY MUSKOKA (USA) 2 b.f. Majestic Prince–Sensual (Sensitivo) (1982   **66** 5fg 5f⁴ 7fg) Apr 2; $50,000Y; compact, quite attractive filly; second foal; dam placed at 2 yrs; plating-class maiden; best run at 5f; sent to USA. *B. Hills.*

LADY NIRAN 3 b.f. Supreme Sovereign 119–Lovelorn 56 (Forlorn River 124)   **—** (1981 NR 1982 9fg) leggy, sparely-made filly; half-sister to a minor winner; dam stayed 7f; 33/1, always struggling when in rear in 14-runner minor event won by Photo at Wolverhampton in September. *R. Laing.*

LADY OF IRELAND 2 ch.f. Be My Guest 126–Lantern Light 86 (Le Levanstell   **72** 122) (1982 6g 6g 5fg³ 6s) Feb 21; 1R 62,000Y; quite attractive filly; second foal; dam, half-sister to very smart sprinter Street Light, was placed over sprint distances; quite moderate form in varied company; should stay beyond 6f; seems to act on any going; has run creditably for 5-lb claimer. *M. Stoute.*

LADY OF RENOWN (USA) 3 b.f. His Majesty–Fair Renown (Stage Door   **56** Johnny) (1981 7g 1982 10d 9f 12f⁴) lightly-made filly; poor maiden; stays 1½m. *J. W. Watts.*

LADY ORYX 2 b.f. Hotfoot 126–Hum 69 (Crooner 119) (1982 8s 7d) Apr 20; —
5,000Y; rangy, useful sort, with plenty of scope; second foal; half-sister to 6f
winner Opal Lady (by Averof); dam stayed 1¼m; backward, no form in October
maiden events at Wolverhampton and Leicester. *S. Mellor.*

LADY REEF 3 gr.f. Mill Reef 141–Reap The Wind 110 (Roan Rocket 128) —
(1981 NR 1982 10f) 1R 29,000Y; useful-looking filly; first foal; dam won 7f
National Stakes; unquoted, stayed on well after getting behind early on to be
seventh of 12 to Noble Gift in well-contested maiden race at Sandown in June;
not seen out afterwards. *M. Albina.*

LADY SAPPHIRE 2 b.f. Amboise 113–Lady Advocate 116 (King's Bench 132) —
(1982 6fg 6fg 5s) May 29; half-sister to several winners here and abroad, including 1976 2-y-o 5f performer Docket (by Swing Easy); dam smart sprinter; behind
in varied company, including selling. *R. Simpson.*

LADY SAXON 3 b.f. Track Spare 125–Il Regalo (Meadow Mint 120) (1981 5s —
7g 1982 7fg 6f 7s 7d) fair sort; behind in varied company, including selling;
trained part of season by T. Gosling. *P. Mitchell.*

LADYSHIP 3 b f. Windjammer (USA)–Just A Dutchess (Knightly Manner) **76**
(1981 6g 6fg 6fg 8d 6d 1982 8fg 10f4 16d 10f 8fg2 8fg4 8g 8s*) strong, compact
filly; won maiden race at Goodwood in September; best form at 1m; acts well
on soft going; sold 33,000 gns Newmarket December Sales. *F. Durr.*

LADY SIAN 2 b.f. Tycoon II–Super Sian (Supreme Sovereign 119) (1982 **77**
5f 7f 6fg 5g 5v2) Feb 22; 900Y; neat filly; first foal; dam never ran; showed
much improved form when going down by ¾ length to Kiwiette in 9-runner
maiden race at Hamilton in October, leading 1½f out until near finish; should
stay 6f+; evidently suited by heavy going. *G. Lockerbie.*

LADY TUT 2 b.f. Fine Blade 121–Tutty 62 (Hotfoot 126) (1982 7fg* 7f **61**
7.2s) Apr 4; 350F, 420 2-y-o; fair sort; third foal; dam ran only at 2 yrs;
showed little in nurseries after running away with 12-runner seller at Wolverhampton (bought in 2,800 gns) in July; will stay 1m; acts on a firm surface;
bandaged near-fore final start; gave lot of trouble at Wolverhampton entering
stalls. *T. Bill.*

LADY TYCOON 3 br.f. No Mercy 126–Sea Tycoon 80 (Tycoon II) (1981 **67**
7g 1982 7.6fg 10.1g 10fg3 10fg*) tall, quite attractive filly; kept on well
to win 17-runner maiden race at Beverley in September from Numismatist;
stays 1¼m; yet to race on a soft surface. *G. Harwood.*

LA FEMME 2 ch.f. Brittany–Whiphand 83 (Supreme Court 135) (1982 **59**
5fg 5.1g 5fg3 5g 6fg 5.1fg3 6s) May 4; 1,800F, 1,700Y; small filly; half-sister
to several minor winners; dam disappointing half-sister to Connaught; modest
plater; should stay 6f; ran creditably in blinkers sixth outing. *W. Marshall.*

LAFONTAINE (USA) 5 b.h. Sham–Valya (Vandale) (1981 8d3 8.5d 8d **117**
10fg* 10.2g 10d 10f* 12f2 10g* 12f2 10.5g 14d 10f3 12fg2 12g 9g 12g 12v3 10g
12g* 1982 10.6s 12fg* 10f3 10.2f* 10f2 12f4 10d* 10.5f 12fg 12f2 11.7d2 12s2
12d*)
    Lafontaine's win in the Cumberland Lodge Stakes at Ascot in September
was richly deserved in that it rewarded two long seasons of endeavour in which

*Cumberland Lodge Stakes, Ascot—another game front-running performance
by Lafontaine who holds the challenge of
Criterion and Critique*

he was called upon to race far more often than most. He ran twenty times in 1981 (gaining his fourth and most important victory of that year in the William Hill November Handicap), and thirteen times in 1982. His win was also the reward for a tremendously game front-running performance on the day. The combined efforts of Critique, Amyndas, Criterion, Father Rooney, Super Sunrise and Telephone Man were not enough to deprive him of his lead, and in the end he held on by a neck and three parts of a length from Criterion and Critique in a driving finish. But Lafontaine's win caused considerable surprise (he started at 22/1), although it's true he had shown to advantage in two of his three previous ventures in pattern company—when third to Princes Gate in the Westbury Stakes and fourth to Critique in the Hardwicke Stakes. Only two days prior to the Cumberland Lodge he'd been beaten four lengths by the three-year-old filly Double Shuffle in a small race at Lingfield, and his recent record had been generally uninspiring, with a defeat by the handicapper Brady in another small race at Windsor and a twelve-length defeat by Capstan in the Alycidon Stakes at Goodwood included in it.

Lafontaine (USA) (b.h. 1977)	Sham (b 1970)	Pretense (br 1963)	Endeavour II Imitation
		Sequoia (b 1955)	Princequillo The Squaw II
	Valya (b 1965)	Vandale (b 1943)	Plassy Vanille
		Lilya (b 1955)	Clarion III La Fougueuse

If Lafontaine is charged fully for his performance in the Cumberland Lodge he will find winning handicaps much harder in future than in the past. He led throughout in three handicaps in 1982, at Epsom, Doncaster and Sandown, picking up a valuable prize on the two last-named courses in the Sporting Chronicle Spring Handicap and the Royal Hong Kong Jockey Club Trophy respectively; he gave Buzzards Bay 5 lb and beat him almost a length at

Mrs J. Bigg's "Lafontaine"

Doncaster, he gave Bettyknowes 19 lb and beat him two lengths at Sandown. Lafontaine cost 14,000 guineas as a yearling. Although American bred, he is from a very good French family. His dam Valya was a smart winner of three races including the Prix de Pomone and is out of Lilya, whose seven victories included the Prix du Moulin and the Prix d'Astarte. The third dam was a full sister to French Two Thousand Guineas winner Mistral. Valya has done very well when sent to Sham with three winners from as many foals including Beau Sham, a smart stakes winner at up to nine furlongs, and Lafontaine. She has also produced Sassalya (by Sassafras), a useful winner over seven furlongs and a mile and a quarter in Ireland. Both Lafontaine's grandam and great-grandam were very successful broodmares, the former producing six winners and the latter eight, including the dam of the Arc winner Topyo. Lafontaine, a big, strong horse, stays a mile and a half. He is not at his best on really soft ground but acts on any other. He benefits from strong handling and is suited by forcing tactics. *C. Brittain.*

LA GAVINA 3 b.f. Sagaro 133–Private Collection 70 (Whistling Wind 123) — (1981 8d 1982 11g 12f 12fg 10g) big, rangy filly; beaten a long way in maiden races and a minor event. *W. Wightman.*

LA GRIGIA 2 ch.f. Habat 127–Wimosa 92 (Mossborough 126) (1982 6g⁴) **72 p** May 29; 1,900F, 7,000Y; well-grown filly; half-sister to fairly useful 7f and 1m winner Master Golfer (by Swing Easy); dam suited by 1½m+; unquoted and backward, broke smartly and kept on well despite being green when 5 lengths fourth of 18 behind Albadeeah in maiden race at Newmarket in September; will be better suited by 7f and 1m; sure to improve. *R. Boss.*

LAGSKONA 2 ch.f. Be Friendly 130–Super Anna (Super Sam 124) (1982 — 6g) May 8; half-sister to 2 winners, including smart 3-y-o 7f and 1m winner Silly Steven (by Silly Season); dam won at up to 1⅛m in Ireland and also won over hurdles; unquoted, soon tailed off in 18-runner maiden race at Newmarket in September. *D. Morrill.*

LAHAB (USA) 2 ch.c. The Minstrel 135–Playmate (Buckpasser) (1982 5g **86** 6g² 7d³) Apr 15; $1,000,000Y; narrow, short-backed, active sort; first foal; dam, placed once from 5 starts, is sister to best 1977 American 2-y-o filly Numbered Account and smart middle-distance colt Cunning Trick; placed in August in minor event at Ripon and maiden race (beaten 2 short heads) at Chester; will be suited by 1m+; acts on a soft surface. *F. Durr.*

LA HOUGUE 4 br.f. Matahawk 127–Carrouges (Klairon 131) (1981 12d² **111** 12g² 12.5d* 1982 12d 12d* 10.5g* 10s 12.5d 12.5g 10.5v) French filly; 42,000 francs Y (approx £4,000); half-sister to numerous winners; dam won over 1¼m; ran easily best races at Saint-Cloud in April, beating Swift Arrow by ½ length in an 80,000 francs event and Votre Altesse and La Pompadour by a neck and a head in 6-runner Prix Corrida; stays 1½m well; acts on a soft surface. *G. Bonnaventure, France.*

LAKENHEATH (USA) 4 ch.c. Northfields–Cheveley Princess 120 (Busted **93** 134) (1981 12g 12g 12d³ 11.5f* 11d 12g 1982 12g 12fg³ 12.3fg² 12.3g⁴ 12.3fg* 13g* 12s 12d) quite an attractive colt; in good form in summer and won handicaps at Chester, Ayr and Leicester; stayed 13f; ran respectably on a soft surface but was much better on a sound surface; wore blinkers when successful in 1981; stud in New Zealand. *H. Wragg.*

LAMBAY 4 ch.f. Lorenzaccio 130–Treasure Island 80 (Whistling Wind 123) — (1981 7fg 8g² 8f 8.2d 8d 10s⁴ 1982 8d 7s) close-coupled filly; stays 1m; best form with some give in the ground. *E. Incisa.*

LAMBWATH FLYER 3 b.g. Red Alert 127–Powder Box (Faberge II 121) **52 ?** (1981 10d 1982 8f 5f⁴ 8g 7fg 7s* 6s) big gelding; plater; showed improved form when winning at Newcastle in October (attracted no bid); stays 7f; acts well on soft going; sometimes blinkered (was at Newcastle). *A. Smith.*

LAMBWATH HALL 5 b.h. Caliban 123–Golden Dolly 76 (Golden Horus **47** 123) (1981 NR 1982 10d³ 12f 8fg) lengthy horse; has a round action; plater; ran well in non-seller on reappearance; stays 1¼m; possibly unsuited by firm going; suitable mount for a claimer; often blinkered. *A. Smith.*

LAMLASH 3 gr.c. Habat 127–Iona 92 (Kalydon 122) (1981 6fg 6fg 6fg⁴ **78 d** 6g 6fg² 7g² 7.6g 1982 7g² 7fg 8f* 7f 8fg* 7f² 9fg 8g 9f 8f 8.2g 8fg 8s³ 8d) strong, round-barrelled colt; good walker but poor mover; made all to win 2 handicaps at Doncaster in May; twice ran respectably afterwards; stays 1m; acts on any going but goes particularly well on fast ground; sold 6,000 gns Newmarket December Sales. *C. Brittain.*

LANCASTRIAN 5 b.h. Reform 132–Rosalie II 66 (Molvedo 137) (1981 12fg* **126** 12s* 12f³ 12.5g³ 12g² 12d 12v 1982 10v* 10.5g² 12f 12.5d²)

We haven't seen anything like the best of Lancastrian in his three races here. In the 1980 St Leger he was uncharacteristically troublesome before the start and finished a well-beaten fifth behind Light Cavalry, possibly finding the distance too far; in both the 1981 Hardwicke Stakes, when he was a soundly-beaten third behind Pelerin, and the 1982 Coronation Cup, when he finished only sixth to Easter Sun, the going was too firm for him, and on the latter occasion the course didn't suit him either. In France Lancastrian has held his own in top company for three seasons. He's regarded there, justifiably, as a notably tough and courageous horse. He's been involved in numerous tight finishes—none of his six wins has been gained by more than three quarters of a length—yet even as a five-year-old he raced as genuinely as ever.

Lancastrian appeared to do well through the winter and he showed the best form of his career on his return, though only lightly raced. He faced a stiff task when making a successful reappearance in the mile-and-a-quarter Prix d'Harcourt at Longchamp in April, the shortest race he'd ever run in (he didn't race as a two-year-old when trained by Hern), for although only four turned out his opponents included Al Nasr and The Wonder, both already winners. He tracked the pace-setting outsider Bobiffic until taking over early in the straight and stayed on most gamely to hold off Al Nasr by a neck; The Wonder ran no sort of a race and was virtually pulled up. A month later Lancastrian gave everything again in the Prix Ganay on the same course and put up an excellent effort to finish second to the front-running Bikala, beaten only half a length; he had some really good performers well strung out behind him. His only other run in France was in the Grand Prix de Saint-Cloud in July in which he faced another stiff task. Glint of Gold, who'd finished well in front of him when the pair were second and sixth respectively in the Coronation Cup the previous month, the Champion Stakes winner Vayrann and the three-year-olds Alfred's Choice, Beau Pretender, Persepolis and Real Shadai were all preferred in the betting. Lancastrian moved up to challenge early in the straight and was soon pressing Glint of Gold, in front from the start, the pair having the finish to themselves. For a moment or two Lancastrian seemed to be getting the better of Glint of Gold, another renowned for his fighting spirit; in the end he was denied by a head, with the French Derby second Real Shadai three lengths away in third. This was the third time Lancastrian had finished in the frame in the Grand Prix de Saint-Cloud, following on his fourth behind the dead-heaters Dunette and Shakapour in 1980 and his third to Akarad in 1981. Owing to a setback Lancastrian missed the Trusthouse Forte Prix de l'Arc de Triomphe, and talk of his being campaigned in the States and running in the Washington D.C. International came to nothing. At the time of writing whether he'll be in training as a six-year-old is undecided.

Lancastrian (b.h. 1977)	Reform (b 1964)	Pall Mall (ch 1955)	Palestine Malapert
		Country House (br 1955)	Vieux Manoir Miss Coventry
	Rosalie II (b 1965)	Molvedo (br 1958)	Ribot Maggiolina
		Lovely Rose III (b 1956)	Owen Tudor Galatina

Lancastrian, a big, strong horse, was bred at the Ballymacoll Stud and is the product of the mating between two horses who raced in the Sobell colours. Reform was a grand little character, one of the most popular of his time. He won eleven of his fourteen races, including the St James's Palace Stakes, the Sussex Stakes and the Champion Stakes, and was out of the first two only on his debut. The dam Rosalie, bought for around 10,000 guineas as a yearling at Deauville, was by contrast raced only three times. She scraped home by a short head in a maiden race at Salisbury but was considered good enough to run in the Prix Vermeille, finishing down the field. Rosalie produced three winners before Lancastrian, notably the Sun Prince filly Cistus who won four good races in 1978, including the Nassau Stakes and the Prix de l'Opera, and was second in the Prix de Diane de Revlon. Rosalie has since produced three foals by Bold Lad (Ire), including Cut A Dash, a promising winner over hurdles; in 1982 she had a colt by Posse. The second dam Lovely Rose III dead-heated in the Prix de la Salamandre and subsequently showed useful form over middle distances at three. *D. Smaga, France.*

LANCE OF ST GEORGE 3 b. or br.g. Warpath 113–Step Softly 81 (St Chad 120) (1981 5f 6f 1982 8g 12.2f 12f 13.8f 16g) neat gelding; bad plater; blinkered last 2 starts. *J. Townson.* —

L'ANCRESSE LODGE 4 ch.f. National Trust 89–Rosy Moll (Vermeil II 104) (1981 NR 1982 10f 16.5f 7fg) small, fair sort; soundly beaten in varied races. *J. Long.* —

LANDING LANE 2 b.f. Hittite Glory 125–Noor Jehan (Taj Dewan 128) (1982 6fg 6s 6d 6s 6d) Apr 13; first foal; dam never ran; plater; not disgraced in non-sellers third and fifth outings; stays 6f. *M. Lambert.* 60

LANDSAVER 2 ch.c. Continuation 120–Stevie 79 (The Phoenix) (1982 5fg 6f) Mar 14; hollow-backed colt; half-brother to several winners; dam sprinting half-sister to Deep Diver; beaten some way in sellers at Wolverhampton in May and Pontefract (missed break) in July. *J. Hardy.* —

LANDSEER 2 br.c. Lochnager 132–Parlais 101 (Pardao 120) (1982 6fg2 6f* 6f 6f4 7.3g 6d) Feb 7; 10,000Y; well-made colt; half-brother to 2 winners, including useful 5f winner Mi Favorita (by Mummy's Pet); dam sprinter; landed the odds by ½ length from Hadi's Hope in 13-runner maiden race at Redcar in June; off course over 2 months after next outing and soundly beaten in nurseries on return; not sure to stay 7f. *D. Sasse.* 88

L'ANGELO DI CARLO 3 ch.f. Record Token 128–Emanuela (Lorenzaccio 130) (1981 5f 5g 6g 1982 6f 6fg 7.2f 7g2 7d 6fg4 6g 7.2f 6g) sturdy filly; plater; stays 7f; has worn blinkers; has run respectably for an apprentice. *C. Crossley.* 46

LANGLEY COURT 3 gr.g. Saritamer 130–Marypark 93 (Charlottown 127) (1981 6g 7d4 7fg 7.6g 8d 1982 12f 12f 16d 7fg3 8g 7g 8d 7d) big, leggy gelding; good walker; plater; stays 7f; wears blinkers; sold 1,400 gns Newmarket Autumn Sales. *D. Morley.* —

LANGTON LAD 2 br.c. Tudor Rhythm 112–Golden Linnet 96 (Sing Sing 134) (1982 6fg 7g 6g) May 21; brother to 1981 2-y-o 6f winner Virgi and half-brother to 3 winners, including fairly useful 5f performer Blue Linnet (by Habitat); dam won over 5f and 6f and is half-sister to good sprinter Monet; in rear, twice last, in July maiden and minor events in the North. *T. Craig.* —

LANTIC BAY (USA) 3 b. or br.c. Cornish Prince–Nit Flit (Tom Fool) (1981 6g3 7.6s2 1982 8d* 8fg 8d 8s) smallish, workmanlike colt; narrowly won maiden race at Warwick in April despite veering left; soundly beaten in handicaps most subsequent starts; stays 1m; blinkered final outing. *P. Walwyn.* 65

LAOIS PRINCESS 2 ch.f. Crash Course 128–Laois Lady (Windjammer) (1982 7.5f* 7g 7d3 7d4) Feb 26; first foal; dam placed over 5f at 2 yrs in Ireland; got the better of Dwynwen by a neck to win 16-runner maiden race at Gowran Park in July, the pair 12 lengths clear; fairly prominent in 2 pattern races at Leopardstown, finishing 5 lengths fifth of 13 to Countess Candy in Park Stakes and 7 lengths fourth of 11 to Heron Bay in Larkspur Stakes; will probably stay middle distances. *L. Browne, Ireland.* 94

LA PAILLE 3 ch.f. Thatch 136–La Carrageen 59 (Levmoss 133) (1981 NR 1982 8d* 8g2 8d3 8fg2 8v) 54,000Y; second foal; dam, half-sister to Champagne Stakes winner Breeders Dream, placed over 1m; accounted for Kalamont by a length in 16-runner newcomers race at Evry in May; placed afterwards in Prix de Sandringham at Chantilly (½-length second of 7 to Paran) and 80,000 francs event at Saint-Cloud and Prix de la Calonne at Deauville (½-length second to Pasadoble); stays 1m; acts on a firm and a soft surface. *O. Douieb, France.* 113

LA PERRICHOLI (FR) 2 b.f. Targowice 130–Belle Margot (Counsel 118) (1982 5f 6g 6g3 7g2 6f 7f 6d* 8d) tall, leggy, workmanlike filly; sixth reported foal; dam won over 1½m at 5 yrs in France; won 7-runner maiden race at Nottingham in September by a length from Princess Irina; should stay 1m; acts on a soft surface and has run respectably on firm going. *D. Marks.* 80

LA PICCOLINA 6 b.m. Tudor Rhythm 112–The Guzzler 69 (Behistoun 131) (1981 12.2d2 12.2fg 11s 10.8fg4 13.3g 10.2g 10s3 12.2s4 11s 1982 12.3fg 11f 12f 12s 12fg 12.2fg4 12.3s) small mare; rather disappointing in 1982; appears not to stay beyond 1½m; acts on any going but seems ideally suited by some give in the ground nowadays; often apprentice ridden. *N. Vigors.* —

LA PIROUETTE (USA) 3 ch.f. Kennedy Road–Nedancer (Nearctic) (1981   **68**
5fg 6f² 6fg 6d² 6d 1982 7f 8f⁴ 8f² 8.2f 8d 8g³ 7f* 7f 7fg* 7s⁴ 7g 7s) big, workmanlike filly; successful in handicaps at Doncaster in July and September;
ran moderately in between; stays 1m but may prove best at 7f; seems to act
on any going but goes well on firm; seemed unsuited by Beverley track fifth
outing. *D. Morley.*

LA REINE ROSE (USA) 2 b.f. King Pellinore 127–M'lle Cyanne (Cyane)   **80**
(1982 5fg 6g⁴ 7f³ 7g³ 7fg⁴ 8f 8s⁴) Apr 16; $240,000Y; lengthy, good-quartered
filly; good mover; fourth foal; dam smart winner of 11 races at up to 1m; in
frame in varied races, including nurseries; stays 1m; probably acts on any going;
ran well for 7-lb claimer on final start. *F. J. Houghton.*

LARIONOV 2 br.c. Balidar 133–Double Finesse 97 (Double Jump 131) (1982 **100 ?**
6f 6fg 6s* 6g) Apr 19; rangy, quite attractive colt; first foal; dam 2-y-o 6f
winner; showed first form (backward previously) when winning 16-runner
minor event at Lingfield in September by 6 lengths from Telephone Numbers;
favourite, eleventh of 12 in nursery at Newmarket the following month; possibly
requires soft ground; obviously not easy to weigh up, but has scope and could
train on into useful 3-y-o. *J. Winter.*

LARLA 3 b.f. He Loves Me 120–Croque Madame 107 (Crocket 130) (1981   **81**
6f 6d 6g 1982 7fg 7.6fg² 6f 10g* 11.5g⁴ 11.5g*) lengthy ex-English filly;
good mover; successful in minor event and Grand Prix du Lion d'Angers at
Le Lion d'Angers in August, beating Grand Comte by 4 lengths in latter; had
previously been caught close home when short-head second of 16 to Ecstatica
in maiden race at Chester; suited by middle distances; trained by J. Hindley
first 3 starts. *D. Sepulchre, France.*

LA ROSIAZ 2 b.f. Riboboy 124–Fleeting Image 90 (Dancer's Image) (1982   **82**
6g 6fg 7fg 6g 7g 8f) Feb 14; small, close-coupled filly; third foal; half-sister
to a minor 2-y-o winner by Sparkler; dam won 3 times at around 7f; put up
best effort, despite being hampered, when 3¾ lengths fifth of 12 to Walton
Heath in 1m nursery at Bath in September; evidently suited by 1m; blinkered
fourth outing. *R. Baker.*

LARWOOD (USA) 2 b.c. Vigors–All Serene 104 (Le Levanstell 122) (1982   —
7g 7g) Feb 11; $100,000Y; deep-girthed, good sort; first foal; dam, useful
6f and 7f winner at 2 yrs in Ireland, is half-sister to very useful animals Kilian,
Card Game and Festive Morn; behind in sizeable fields of maidens at Newmarket
in June and Leicester in October; sold 9,200 gns Newmarket Autumn Sales.
G. Harwood.

LASANI (FR) 6 b.m. Appiani II 128–Ballast (Polic 126) (1981 10s 11s² 10.5d   —
8s² 8g* 10f* 10f 10d 9.7v 8s 1982 9fg 10f 10fg 8f 10fg) big ex-French mare;
third living foal; half-sister to a winning plater; dam placed over 11f in France;
won handicaps at Evry and Deauville (valuable event) in 1981 when trained
by J-P. Pelat; behind in goodish company over here; stays 11f; acts on any
going; blinkered final start; bandaged in front first 3 outings. *C. Austin.*

LA SEINE 4 b.f. Blue Cashmere 129–Snap (Snob 130) (1981 7s 7d 7d 6f   —
7g 10.1g 8fg 10d 12d 12.2g 1982 17.1f 16fg 12d) workmanlike filly; won
2m private sweepstakes at Plumpton in April; blinkered fourth and fifth starts
in 1981; has worn bandages behind; sold 610 gns Doncaster October Sales.
S. Matthews.

LASKA FLOKO 6 b.h. Thatch 136–Prima 75 (Alcide 136) (1981 12fg 10g   **73**
12d⁴ 10fg* 10.2g 12g 10.2g 10g 1982 12fg 12fg⁴ 22.2fg 14.6g⁴ 16f³ 11.5f 12g)
strong, heavy-topped, good sort; moody and inconsistent handicapper latterly;
probably stayed 1¾m; seemed to act on any going except very soft; often
wore blinkers; was a suitable mount for an apprentice; sold 15,000 gns
Newmarket Autumn Sales, reportedly for stud in South Africa. *C. Brittain.*

LAST ACT 4 b.f. Gala Performance–Gweedore (Prince Hansel 118) (1981   **51**
11g 9d 12s 9g 8.5f³ 8s 9s 1982 8f 8f³ 8fg 7fg 8g⁴ 8f⁴ 8f 8g² 8.5g² 12g³ 10d⁴
12g³) lightly-made ex-English filly; has shown ability in varied races, including
in a seller on eighth start; stays 1¼m; sometimes sweats up; bandaged off-
fore seventh outing; trained until after eighth start by B. McMahon. *J.
Kavanagh, Ireland.*

LAST DEVICE 5 b.g. Grey Mirage 128–Gorgeous Device 88 (Falls of Clyde   **63**
126) (1981 8g³ 7.6g 8g 7.6fg³ 8f² 8fg² 8f 8f 8.2fg 8f 1982 8f* 7.6g* 8f 8.5f*
8fg² 8f 8f⁴ 7.6d 8.2f 7d) compact gelding; improved and won handicaps at

Thirsk (apprentice event), Chester and Epsom; made all and won on merit on first 2 courses but was left in lead after a fall inside last furlong at Epsom in June; stays 1m; probably acts on any going; suitable mount for an apprentice; sometimes used to be blinkered. *C. Crossley.*

LAST FEATHER (USA) 3 b.f. Vaguely Noble 140–Quill (Princequillo) (1981 **120** 7fg⁴ 7g² 7.3s* 1982 10.5fg* 12f³ 12fg 12s)

Last Feather started at 58/1 for the Trusthouse Forte Prix de l'Arc de Triomphe, fourteenth of seventeen in the betting, and she came home four-teenth of seventeen behind Akiyda after showing prominently to halfway. She was a much better filly than that, but hadn't given any recent evidence to suggest she might be in the form to trouble the best in Europe. Whereas Akiyda had been second to All Along in the Prix Vermeille on her previous appearance Last Feather had been only sixth of seven behind Awaasif in the Yorkshire Oaks on hers, hardly a performance to recommend her as an Arc candidate. Prior to the Yorkshire Oaks Last Feather had made only two starts all season, her latest in the Oaks ten weeks back.

In contrast to her status at Longchamp Last Feather was one of the better fancied in the thirteen-strong field at Epsom, preferred to Slightly Dangerous as a mount by stable-jockey Cauthen. A beautifully-bred filly who could be anticipated making a much better three-year-old than two-year-old, she'd won her last race in 1981 by six lengths and on her reappearance had led through-out to win the Musidora Stakes at York in May by a length and a half from Ash Ridge. As an Oaks trial the Musidora Stakes left a lot to be desired (the five-horse contest developed into a sprint over the last two and a half furlongs, Last Feather got first run and poached an advantage which was never seriously threatened); but Last Feather showed the confidence behind her for the Oaks not entirely misplaced. For a while the race promised to go very much as the Musidora for Last Feather. Always up there running freely she went for home with about three furlongs left, only to find her lead strongly challenged by four or five of the others at the distance. Having quickened once, she couldn't quicken again and by the line had been overtaken by Time Charter and Slightly Dangerous; she held on well enough under pressure to remain within three lengths of the winner, and she kept Awaasif out of third place by three parts of a length.

		Vaguely Noble (b 1965)	Vienna (ch 1957)	Aureole
Last Feather (USA) (b.f. 1979)				Turkish Blood
			Noble Lassie (b 1956)	Nearco
				Belle Sauvage
		Quill (ch 1956)	Princequillo (b 1940)	Prince Rose
				Cosquilla
			Quick Touch (ch 1946)	Count Fleet
				Alms

Last Feather was sold privately before the Arc and was retired to the United States after it. She visits Nijinsky. Any issue from the union will be closely related to two extremely well-known racehorses, for Last Feather's dam Quill produced to Nijinsky the Irish St Leger winner Caucasus (who later became one of the best grass horses of his time in the United States); and to Nijinsky's

Musidora Stakes, York—Last Feather is never headed and readily accounts for Ash Ridge, Cadi Ha and Sing Softly (rails)

sire Northern Dancer she produced the champion Canadian horse One For
All, a winner of thirteen races at up to two miles. In an extraordinary career
as a broodmare Quill threw yet another good horse, the Arc sixth Riboquill
(by Ribot), between the arrival of her first foal First Feather (dam of Run
The Gantlet) in 1963 and that of the aptly-named Last Feather in 1979. Quill
was already a celebrity when she was retired to stud. By the time she finished
racing at the age of five she had amassed a total of 382,041 dollars in prize
money and had won fourteen races including four that could be regarded in
Group 1 category—the Delaware Handicap, the Acorn Stakes, the Matron
Stakes and the Mother Goose Stakes; she also finished second in the CCA
Oaks, and in 1958 was the champion two-year-old filly in the States. Nor
was Quill the only good racemare out of her dam Quick Touch: her half-sisters
Sorceress and Capelet won stakes races, too. And her half-brother Count
Amber finished second in the important Withers Stakes. Quick Touch's dam
was a half-sister to the Kentucky Derby winner Twenty Grand. What a family!
Last Feather made little physical progress from two to three; we should
describe her as a smallish, lengthy filly. She was a good walker and mover who
acted on any going. A free runner, inclined to pull for her head, she gave the
impression that a mile and a half was the limit of her stamina. *B. Hills.*

LASTING HOPE 2 ch.f. Full of Hope 125–Shipshape (Shantung 132) (1982 —
7f 7g) Mar 30; strong, well-made filly; third foal; dam never ran; behind in
maiden race at Sandown in July (backward) and minor event at Brighton
in August; sold 800 gns Newmarket Autumn Sales. *D. Whelan.*

LA TAJARAH (USA) 2 b.c. Elocutionist–Queens Turf (Round Table) (1982 —
7g 8s) Apr 24; $50,000Y; neat colt; half-brother to a minor winner; dam,
placed twice from 9 starts, is half-sister to high-class 1975 American 2-y-o
Hang Ten; behind in maiden races at Sandown (backward) in July and Leicester
in November. *J. Bethell.*

LA TAKAROSE 3 ch.f. Le Johnstan 123–The Rose Royale (Takawalk II —
125) (1981 NR 1982 5fg) 3,400Y; third foal; sister to modest 1978 2-y-o
5f winner Bart; dam once-raced half-sister to smart miler My Drifter; 33/1
when last of 18 finishers behind Turtle Hill in maiden race at Warwick in August.
S. Matthews.

LATE HOUR 3 br.f. Reform 132–Midnight Melody 92 (Linacre 133) (1981 **73**
6g 7h⁴ 6d² 6d* 1982 8fg² 7f 8.2fg 8g 7s 6d 6s) small filly; reportedly broke
a blood vessel when length second to Polar Star in handicap at Thirsk in April;
well beaten subsequently; will stay 1¼m; acts on a firm and a soft surface;
blinkered fourth to sixth starts. *A. Jarvis.*

LATEST LOVE (FR) 4 b.c. Roi Dagobert 128–Love Lasting (Prince Regent **48**
129) (1981 8fg 8g 8g³ 8g² 9d 9s 1982 13v² 12f 13.8f 15.8f 12.3g 10d) ex-
French colt; second in maiden race at Hamilton in April; stays 13f; often
blinkered nowadays; trained by A. Jarvis first start. *J. Mason.*

LATIN FORT 2 br.c. Comedy Star 121–Rosy Glow 60 (Hotfoot 126) (1982 **91 ?**
5g 5fg 7s²) May 6; 3,600F, 5,400Y; attractive colt; very poor walker; second
foal; dam, moderate plater at 2 yrs in England, subsequently did well in Norway;
off course since May, finished creditable second behind easy winner Northern
Adventure in slowly-run 6-runner minor event at Doncaster in November;
will stay 1m; difficult to assess. *R. Hollinshead.*

LATIN GUEST 3 ch.f. Be My Guest 126–Keep Right (Klairon 131) (1981 NR —
1982 7f 7g 10.1fg 8g) 48,000Y; small, quite well-made filly; half-sister to 2
winners, including William Hill Futurity winner Sandy Creek (by Petingo); dam
unraced daughter of very useful Narrow Escape; little worthwhile form in maiden
races and a minor event in the South. *R. Price.*

LATIN LIGHT 3 b.f. Roman Warrior 132–Spanish Lantern 92 (Don Carlos) —
(1981 5d 5g 5f² 5fg³ 6f² 1982 7f 7g 8.3g 8fg 8s) useful sort; second in maiden
races at Wolverhampton and Brighton in 1981; well beaten in varied company
at 3 yrs; not sure to stay 1m; acts on firm going. *G. Lewis.*

L'ATTRAYANTE (FR) 2 br.f. Tyrant–Camerata (Klairon 131) (1982 5.5d* **112**
7.5g* 7.5fg² 7g³ 8s³) Mar 8; 130,000 francs Y (approx £11,800); sister to minor
French 11f winner Camerante and half-sister to numerous winners, notably very
smart long-distance performer Campo Moro (by Bel Baraka); dam won over 5.5f
at 2 yrs; had a fine season, winning minor event at Evry in July (by neck from
Go Jogging) and Prix des Yearlings at Deauville the following month (by ½

length); also ran well in 2 more races at Deauville, finishing neck second to Tarte Chaude, who received 4 lb, in Prix de l'Agence Francaise and 2½ lengths third of 12 to Maximova in Prix du Calvados; promoted to third place after finishing 1¾ lengths fourth of 11 to Goodbye Shelley in Prix Marcel Boussac at Longchamp in October; will probably stay 1¼m. *O. Douieb, France.*

LAUBALL 4 b.f. Lauso–Ballyputt (Ballymoss 136) (1981 NR 1982 11.7fg — 11.7g 8.3fg) poor form in sellers as a 2-y-o; in rear in handicaps at Windsor in 1982. *M. Bolton.*

LAUDERHILL 3 ch.g. Status Seeker–Purple Cuckoo (Continuation 120) (1981   **38** 6fg 7f⁴ 7fg 7f 8f 8g 8.2d 8d 1982 10g 12f 12f³ 10f 16d) compact gelding; plater; possibly stays 1½m; usually blinkered; ran badly fourth start; sold 1,050 gns Ascot August Sales. *K. Stone.*

LAUGHING LAD 2 br.c. Bold Lad (Ire) 133–Laughing Girl 110 (Sassafras 135)   **— p** (1982 7d 8g) Feb 28; strong, good-bodied, attractive colt; good walker; third foal; dam, fourth in Oaks, is half-sister to Furioso and Favoletta; well beaten at Newmarket in October in Houghton Stakes (very backward) and a minor event; certain to do better if looks mean anything. *H. Wragg.*

LAUGHING LEE 3 br.f. Cawston's Clown 113–Lindylee 99 (Grey Sovereign 128§) (1981 5g 1982 6fg 6f 9g) lengthy, rather lightly-made, quite attractive filly; poor maiden; sold to BBA 1,650 gns Newmarket Autumn Sales. *G. Pritchard-Gordon.*

LAURA'S PRIDE 5 ch.g. Midsummer Night II 117–Flashlight 88 (Firestreak   **—** 125) (1981 12d 1982 12g 13.1g 12fg 16s) bad plater; has worn blinkers and bandages. *C. Wildman.*

LAURENCE MAC 3 gr.g. Grey Ghost 98–Mactavish 90 (St Alphage 119) (1981   **68** 6d 7f 5d 1982 6s⁴ 7g³ 6g⁴ 6f* 5g² 6g³ 5fg⁴) compact gelding; made virtually all to win minor event at Thirsk in April; creditable second in handicap at Doncaster in June; best at sprint distances; acts on firm going. *T. Barron.*

LAUTREC 4 b.g. Wolver Hollow 126–Night Vision 100 (Yellow God 129) (1981   **—** 10fg³ 8g 8fg⁴ 10f 8g³ 8s* 8d³ 1982 10.2g 13d 10.6f) tall, good-looking gelding; soundly beaten in amateur riders races in 1982 (blinkered and carrying considerable overweight at 11-11 second start); stays 1¼m; probably acts on any going; sold 1,800 gns Ascot October Sales. *R. Smyth.*

LAVENDER GRAY 3 b.f. Bay Express 132–Ma Belle Amie (Never Say Die 137)   **65** (1981 5g 5d² 7f 6fg 6d⁴ 1982 7d* 8f⁴ 8f* 8f⁴ 8.2g 8f³) useful-looking filly; won handicaps at Warwick in April and Brighton in May; stays 1m; seems to act on any going. *J. Winter.*

LAW BIRD 3 b. or br.g. Legal Eagle 126–Altarnun (Alcide 136) (1981 5s 5d   **—** 1982 15.5v) small gelding; seems of little account; has worn blinkers; sold 390 gns Doncaster March Sales; resold 525 gns same venue in November. *D. Weeden.*

LAWERS 3 ch.c. Hot Spark 126–Aspara 58 (Crimson Satan) (1981 5s 5g 5fg   **—** 5g² 5fg 5d 1982 6fg 6g 5g 6g 5fg 8.3g 6v 6g) compact colt; sprint handicapper; sometimes blinkered; sold to Mrs N. Smith 370 gns Ascot November Sales. *J. Benstead.*

LAWNSWOOD CUTTER 2 b.c. Dragonara Palace 115–My Paddy 83 (St Paddy   **52** 133) (1982 5d 5g 5f 5g 7f 7d 8g 8d⁴) Mar 20; 1,000F; neat colt; brother to a plater and a winner in Belgium; dam won over 7.5f and is daughter of Cheveley Park winner My Goodness Me; poor maiden; appears to stay 1m; sold Norsk Jockey Club 1,600 gns Doncaster November Sales. *R. Hollinshead.*

LAWNSWOOD MISS 4 b.f. Grey Mirage 128–Lor Darnie 65 (Dumbarnie 125)   **—** (1981 8s 10d 10fg 9g 12s* 13fg⁴ 16.9fg 12fg⁴ 13.8fg 12g³ 1982 12g) narrow filly; won seller as a 3-y-o; stays 13f; probably acts on any going; suitable mount for an apprentice. *R. Hollinshead.*

LAYAL 3 b.c. Blakeney 126–Queen of Twilight 107 (Off Key 121 or Twilight Alley   **94** 133) (1981 7fg 7fg 7fg³ 8.2s 1982 8d 10d 12fg⁴ 14fg² 15.5g* 16f 16.5fg⁴ 16d) attractive colt; creditable 2 lengths second of 8 to First Mint in £5,400 handicap at York in June before easily winning handicap at Folkestone later in month; suited by a test of stamina. *J. Dunlop.*

LAZI BEAM 2 gr.c. Track Spare 125–Moonlight 101 (Djebe) (1982 5f 5f² 5fg³)   **49** Feb 26; 1,000F, 2,200Y; leggy colt; plater; placed at Carlisle in May and Beverley in June; dead. *J. Berry.*

LEADENHALL LAD 2 b.c. Comedy Star 121–Swaynes Lady 76 (St Alphage   **84**
119) (1982 5d² 5fg³ 5f³ 5fg² 5g² 6f* 5fg² 5d² 5g⁴ 5g⁴)   May 7; 6,400Y; leggy,
sharp sort; first foal; dam 2-y-o 5f winner; surprisingly cost only 2,600 gns to
buy in after winning valuable seller at York in July; showed form way above
plating class in non sellers, on seventh and ninth outings being beaten only
¾ length in nurseries at Sandown and Newbury; barely stays 6f; yet to race on
really soft going but acts on any other; consistent; sold 12,000 gns Newmarket
Autumn Sales; sent to Trinidad. *R. Boss.*

LEAH'S PEARLS 3 gr. or ro.f. Sea Wolf 116–Patterdon (Precipice Wood 123)   —
(1981 NR 1982 12g 11.5fg 11d) leggy filly; first foal; dam poor novice
hurdler; poor maiden. *T. Taylor.*

LEANDROS 2 b.c. Lepanto–Annes Gift (Ballymoss 136) (1982 5d² 5fg 5f³ 5g²   **67**
5f² 5fg* 5f² 5g 7f 7fg² 7g) May 12; 480Y; fair sort; second foal (first by a
thoroughbred stallion); dam of no account; plater; beat Sax 2 lengths in 7-
runner event at Salisbury (no bid) in May; made much of running when short-
head second of 8 to Prince Concorde at Newcastle in July on penultimate
appearance; stays 7f; acts well on firm ground; wears blinkers; exported to
Algeria. *R. Hannon.*

LEAP BRIDGE 4 b.g. King's Leap 111–The Tower (High Treason 126) (1981   **55**
5g 6d 6fg 7g² 7s 7g 1982 7g* 6f 8f 7f⁴ 7f 6f 7f) small gelding; bought in 5,200
gns after winning seller at Edinburgh in July by 8 lengths; ran well in non-
sellers fourth and sixth starts; stays 7f; acts on firm going; often sweats up;
brought down final start. *Miss L. Siddall.*

LEASE OF LIFE 2 ch.f. Tower Walk 130–Voucher Book 96 (Good Bond 122)   **84 ?**
(1982 5s 7d³ 8d³) Mar 17; smallish, fair sort; first foal; dam won 8 times at up
to 13.8f; ran on strongly without being knocked about unnecessarily when 1½
lengths third of 18 to Cormorant Wood in maiden race at Leicester in October,
best effort; beaten at odds on in similar event at Edinburgh the following month.
C. Thornton.

L'EAU VERT 2 br.c. Tachypous 128–Myna Tyna 85 (Blast 125) (1982 6fg   **62**
7g 7g 7g) Feb 5; 13,000Y; small colt; half-brother to 2 winners, including 1979
2-y-o 5f winner Another Venture (by Roan Rocket); dam won over 5f at 2 yrs,
and is half-sister to good stayer Lomond; poor maiden; blinkered final start;
sold 800 gns Newmarket Autumn Sales for export to Scandinavia. *J. Hindley.*

LEBANESE SONG (USA) 2 b.f. Shecky Greene–Gambrel (A Gambler)   **75**
(1982 6fg³ 6g 5d² 5d 5f 6v*) Mar 12; $40,000Y, resold 28,000 gns Y; small,
rather sharp sort; first foal; dam, out of half-sister to top-class Olden Times, won
twice at up to 7f; disappointed after finishing third in newcomers' race at Ascot
in July until struggling home by ¼ length in 3-runner maiden at Hamilton in
October; stays 6f; seems to act on any going. *J. Hindley.*

LE BARON ROUGE 2 b.g. Hittite Glory 125–Gem Wood Betty (Sailor Beware)   —
(1982 7fg 8g) May 16; 1,700F, 4,000Y; workmanlike gelding; half-brother to
Irish 1½m winner Royal Tiara (by Royal and Regal) and a winner in Algeria;
dam stakes-placed winner of 6 races at up to 9f; well behind in September
maiden races at Salisbury and Beverley; subsequently gelded. *J. Douglas-
Home.*

LE BEAU 4 b.g. Hot Spark 126–La Meme 90 (Pall Mall 132) (1981 8d 10d⁴   —
12d² 12g⁴ 14fg³ 16.9fg* 1982 17f 18.8fg 15.5g) quite well-made gelding;
soundly beaten in 1982; suited by a test of stamina; acts on a firm and a soft
surface; has worn bandages in front. *P. Cole.*

LEBENSTANZ 2 b.f. Lypheor 118–Strawberry Blonde II (Red God 128§)   — p
(1982 5f 7d) May 14; 20,000Y; quite well-made filly; half-sister to 4 winners,
including fair 1979 Irish 2-y-o 5f winner Racing Blonde (by On Your Mark);
dam, sister to smart French middle-distance horse Red Vagabonde, won in
France; 66/1, close up for long way when seventh of 13 finishers behind Acclimatise in £4,000 maiden race at Sandown in July, second outing. *H. Candy.*

LEEKMORE 3 b.c. Welsh Saint 126–Carnmore (Breakspear II) (1981 5d 5fg   **68**
6g 5fg³ 5fg 5d 5s 5g³ 5g 1982 5d 5d* 5f³ 5f* 5f 5g 5s 5s) rather a lightly-made
colt; won handicaps at Salisbury in April and Redcar in May; probably acts on
any going; used to wear blinkers; had stiffish tasks last 3 starts. *S. Matthews.*

LEFRAK LADY 5 b.m. Starch Reduced 112–Misty Morn 70 (Worden II 129)   —
(1981 8.3s 7fg 1982 6f) bad plater; has been tried in blinkers. *J. Long.*

LEGAL GAMBOL 4 ch.g. Double-U-Jay 120–Absuleno 78 (Above Suspicion —
127) (1981 10s* 12g 16f² 16.9fg³ 1982 13fg 12f 15d) no form in 1982, being
pulled up lame on reappearance and finishing last on both subsequent starts,
including in a seller; suited by 2m; acts on any going; sold 600 gns Doncaster
October Sales, probably for export to Scandinavia. *D. Chapman.*

LEGAL LAIRD 8 ch.h. Murrayfield 119–Legal Mistress (Counsel 118) (1981 —
8g 10s* 10g 10f 8g 1982 8g 10fg 10d 12fg) poor handicapper; soundly beaten
in a seller final start; stays 1¼m; suited by some give in the ground; wears
blinkers; good mount for an inexperienced rider; sometimes starts slowly. *S.
Woodman.*

LEGAL LOVER (USA) 2 b. or br.f. Good Counsel–Sleepy Sis (Advocator) —
(1982 10s) Apr 6; $8,300Y, resold 13,500 gns Y; third foal; half-sister to French
3-y-o Clarinette (by Proud Clarion), a winner at up to 1m; dam 2-y-o 6f winner;
7½ lengths sixth of 17 behind Captain Webster in maiden race at Nottingham
in October; sold BBA (Ireland) 6,200 gns Newmarket Autumn Sales. *W.
Hastings-Bass.*

LEGAL SOUND 3 b.f. Legal Eagle 126–Sound Recordo 95 (Sound Track 132) **67**
(1981 NR 1982 6f 7f 6fg* 6fg⁴ 6g³ 6s² 6d* 6s³) smallish filly; half-sister to
3 winners, including modest 5f to 1¼m winner Coriace (by Prince Consort);
dam won over 5f at 2 yrs; springer in market when winning seller at Carlisle in
June (no bid); ran creditably in better company afterwards and won handicap
at Leicester in October; stays 6f; seems to act on any going; has run respectably
for an apprentice. *J. Etherington.*

LEGENDARY QUEEN 2 b.f. Wolver Hollow 126–Miss Legend (Bold **66 p**
Legend) (1982 5fg 6g) Mar 29; 31,000Y; well-made, attractive filly; half-
sister to useful 1978 Irish 2-y-o 5f performer Devilish (by Red God); dam won
twice over 6f in USA; showed signs of ability, on second start 7 lengths eighth
of 18 to Albadeeah in maiden race at Newmarket in September; should stay
7f; looks capable of better. *G. Lewis.*

LEGEND OF FRANCE (USA) 2 b.c. Lyphard 132–Lupe 123 (Primera 131) **80 p**
(1982 6v) Feb 21; rather small, quite attractive colt; half-brother to 3 winners,
including smart 1m to 11f winner Leonardo da Vinci (by Brigadier Gerard)
and very useful middle-distance filly L'Ile du Reve (by Bold Lad, USA); dam
won Oaks and Coronation Cup; evens favourite and looking to have done plenty
of work, soon in trouble after moving up threateningly 2f out, when 10 lengths
fifth of 10 behind Northern Adventure in Duke of Edinburgh Stakes at Ascot in
October; almost certainly capable of a good deal better, especially over further.
H. Cecil.

LE GRAN BRUN (USA) 4 b.g. Our Native–Summary Procedure (Court **63 d**
Martial) (1981 11s 10s 11.5f⁴ 12g 10d² 10fg 10f² 10f* 10g² 10d³ 1982 16g³
14f⁴ 16fg³ 16fg 16d) strong, attractive gelding; fit from a successful spell over
hurdles when beating Morgan's Choice on merit by a length in handicap at
Newbury in April; hampered another runner when drifting to his left however,
and was relegated to third; in frame at Sandown and Ripon (odds on rather
disappointing) afterwards; stays well; acts on any going, except possibly very
soft; sold to S. Cole 5,000 gns Ascot December Sales. *P. Cundell.*

LEGS OF MAN 3 ch.c. Hotfoot 126–Colony 93 (Constable 119) (1981 5f² 5f⁴ —
6g 7s* 6d 7s 1982 10s⁴ 7f⁴ 8f 11fg 8.2g 11g 11fg 12.3fg 8g 8.2g 8.2v) sturdy
colt; has a round action; quite a modest handicapper at his best; stays to stay
11f; has run respectably on firm going but is evidently best on soft; suitable
mount for an apprentice; has twice run moderately in blinkers; ran poorly
towards end of year. *D. Smith.*

LEIGHMOR 2 b.f. Connaught 130–Lidmoor (Caerdeon 98) (1982 6d) Feb 14; **77 p**
deep-girthed, attractive filly; second foal; dam unraced half-sister to 3-y-o
Lowna; unquoted, weakened after having chance at distance when ninth of
21 to Spanish Place in maiden race at Newmarket in October; will be better
suited by 7f+; certain to do better. *C. Brittain.*

LEIOS 2 ch.g. Singh–Smooth Siren (Sea-Bird II 145) (1982 7d 7f 7fg) Apr —
11; close-coupled gelding; half-brother to 3-y-o 1¼m winner Seabattle (by Cannonade) and very useful 1¼m performer Sirenivo (by Sir Ivor); dam won over 6f
at 3 yrs in USA and is daughter of Swift Lady, a good-class stakes winner at
up to 1m; little worthwhile form in maiden races; gelded after final outing. *H.
Candy.*

LEIOTRICHOUS 3 b.c. Nonoalco 131–Helmsdale 107 (Habitat 134) (1981 **52**
6d 8s 8g 6g 1982 8fg 8fg 7f³ 7.6f 7.2g 7.6g⁴ 7fg 7f 7fg² 7fg 8g 10d 10s) strong,
compact, good-bodied colt; poor walker and mover; plating-class maiden;
should stay 1m; blinkered eighth start; sold out of C. Brittain's stable 5,000 gns
Doncaster September Sales after eleventh outing. *T. M. Jones.*

LEITH SPRING 3 b.f. Silly Season 127–Jane Escart (Escart III) (1981 **62**
6s 6s 6s 1982 6g 6fg² 6f 6g 6fg 6d⁴) rather lightly-made filly; bred to stay 1m;
acts on a firm and a soft surface; blinkered third start. *M. Francis.*

LE LEVADOR 3 br.g. Levanter 121–Adored (Aggressor 130) (1981 6g 1982 —
11g 13.3f) workmanlike gelding; beaten some way in maiden races. *M.
Blanshard.*

LE MAMAMOUCHI (FR) 4 b.c. Tennyson 124–Adèle Toumignon (Zeddaan **119**
130) (1981 10v 12fg 12s* 12v 15fg* 15s⁴ 15f 1982 14d* 15.5v³ 15.5fg 12g²
12.5d 12.5g) first foal; dam, half-sister to Preis von Europa winner Acacio
D'Aguilar, won over 9f; won 18-runner handicap at Saint-Cloud in March by a
neck from Hand Beau; ran easily best subsequent races when about ½-length third
of 11 behind El Badr and Kelbomec in Prix de Barbeville at Longchamp in April
and when going down by a neck to Little Wolf in Prix Jean de Chaudenay at
Saint-Cloud in May; stays well; seems to act on any going; often blinkered,
but effective without. *G. Bridgland, France.*

LE MAXIMUM (USA) 3 ch.f. Giacometti 130–Maximova 88 (Sensitivo) —
(1981 NR 1982 7fg 7fg 10g 8g) $43,000Y; big, tall ex-English filly; first
reported foal; dam one-paced half-sister to useful 1980 2-y-o Chateau Dancer
(by Giacometti) and top American chaser Zaccio; showed a little ability in
newcomers race at Newbury in April but subsequently finished in rear in maiden
and minor events, 2 of them in French Provinces; trained by R. Price first 2
starts. *R. Chastin, France.*

LEMELASOR 2 ch.f. Town Crier 119–Broadway Lass 70 (March Past 124) **75**
(1982 5d* 6g² 5f⁴ 6g² 6g⁴ 7d² 7g) Mar 29; 640Y; small, lightly-made filly; poor
mover; half-sister to 3-y-o Warrenice Lad (by Abwah), successful in sellers
at up to 1½m; dam ran only at 2 yrs; bought in 2,450 gns after putting in a strong
late run to win seller at Warwick in April by 1½ lengths from Eros; second
afterwards in another seller at Doncaster and in nurseries at Windsor and
Chester; suited by 7f: genuine. *D. H. Jones.*

L'EMIGRANT (USA) 2 b. or br.c. The Minstrel 135–Suprina (Vaguely Noble **126**
140) (1982 6g² 8f* 8s² 7s*)
Vaguely Noble's sons have so far proved rather disappointing at stud.
The unraced Noble Bijou, a great success in Australasia, is a notable exception,
and Royal and Regal has sired the high-class miler Hilal and the Irish One
Thousand Guineas winner Arctique Royale, but Empery, Ace of Aces, Mississipian
and Noble Decree have failed badly. Perhaps Exceller and Gay Mecene will
make amends when their first runners appear in 1983. Even if they don't
Vaguely Noble's influence will be extended through his daughters. His daughters
were only sparsely represented as broodmares in Britain and Ireland in 1982 but
between them they produced the Derby winner Golden Fleece, the St Leger
winner Touching Wood and the William Hill Futurity second Cock Robin; and
in France the Prix d'Astarte winner Thorough, the very useful two-year-old Le
Voleur and the highly talented L'Emigrant, who promises to rise to similar
heights as Golden Fleece and Touching Wood, were all out of Vaguely Noble
mares.
We were most impressed with L'Emigrant when we first saw him in the
Prix La Rochette at Longchamp in September. There were some handsome
individuals among the eight runners but none more handsome than L'Emigrant
who started at odds on on the strength of a fine debut at Deauville a month
earlier, where he'd failed by only a short neck to hold off Crystal Glitters in a
newcomers race. L'Emigrant also proved to be a most impressive mover, with
a smooth, flowing action, and his performance in the race was just as taking.
He won in the manner of a high-class colt, moving easily into the lead two
furlongs out and then striding out in great style to win by three lengths from
Le Voleur, with the Prix des Foals winner Sherbaz a short neck away third.
Although L'Emigrant was receiving weight from both placed horses there was no
doubting his superiority. He would clearly take a lot of beating whatever the
company and only Saint Cyrien started shorter in the Grand Criterium four

Prix La Rochette, Longchamp—L'Emigrant strides out in
great style to beat Le Voleur (No. 7) and Sherbaz

weeks later. L'Emigrant was accompanied to post by a pacemaker Midford who, like many of his kind, was virtually ignored by the others as he built up a substantial lead. After racing in second place L'Emigrant took over once his stablemate ran himself out inside the final quarter mile, hotly pressed on his left by the Morny and Salamandre winner Deep Roots and on his right by the English raider The Noble Player. L'Emigrant managed to hold off both of these but he had no answer to Saint Cyrien's impressive burst in the final furlong and went down by a length. His trainer, while acknowledging that L'Emigrant had been beaten by a colt of enormous potential, added his opinion that L'Emigrant hadn't been suited by the testing conditions; on good ground, he said, Saint Cyrien would have found it much more difficult to beat him and perhaps wouldn't have done so. Interestingly, our race-reader had said after the Prix La Rochette that L'Emigrant 'has a most impressive action and it is hard to believe that he will be so effective on soft ground as he is on the firm going he encountered today.'

However L'Emigrant's final performance makes it exceedingly difficult at this stage of his career to argue that the ground is a material factor with the horse. In conditions very similar to those for the Grand Criterium he beat fifteen others in fine style in the Criterium de Maisons-Laffitte at the end of October. The winners of the Prix Eclipse and the Prix Thomas Bryon, Crystal Glitters and Bal des Fees, were in the field as were the English challengers Cat O'Nine Tails, Cause Celebre and Drumalis. L'Emigrant was made an odds-on favourite despite the strength of the opposition. He fully justified the support, leading one and a half furlongs out and holding the late run of Drumalis, who received 7 lb, by a length without much trouble. Crystal Glitters took third place a length further behind. L'Emigrant's victory extended his trainer's remarkable record in the Criterium de Maisons-Laffitte to five wins in as many years, following those of Crowned Music, Viteric, Cresta Rider and Zino, and had Cosmopolitan not been disqualified in 1977 Boutin's total would be six. L'Emigrant is reportedly likely to follow the same programme at three as Zino, starting with the Prix Djebel at Maisons-Laffitte and then the Two Thousand Guineas. Presumably one of the reasons for his being aimed at the Guineas is to avoid

Criterium de Maisons-Laffitte—odds-on L'Emigrant comfortably
accounts for Drumalis and Crystal Glitters

Mr S. S. Niarchos' "L'Emigrant" (L. Piggott)

another clash with Saint Cyrien in the Poule d'Essai des Poulains but the opposition at Newmarket will probably be even tougher with Diesis, Danzatore and possibly Gorytus in the field. Nevertheless L'Emigrant's chance must be respected; he probably still has improvement in him and his trainer certainly knows what is required to win the Guineas, having sent out Nonoalco and Nureyev as well as Zino in the last nine years.

L'Emigrant (USA) (b. or br.c. Apr 26, 1980)	The Minstrel (ch 1974)	Northern Dancer (b 1961)	Nearctic Natalma
		Fleur (b 1964)	Victoria Park Flaming Page
	Suprina (b 1970)	Vaguely Noble (b 1965)	Vienna Noble Lassie
		Perfecta (bl 1965)	Swaps Cosmah

Stavros Niarchos bought L'Emigrant at the Keeneland Select Sale on the same day as he paid 2,950,000 dollars for Fulmar, a colt by Northern Dancer out of Bernie Bird. Fulmar didn't race at two but he has been entered for the Derby so his name may prove worth remembering. L'Emigrant cost much less than Fulmar—'only' 360,000 dollars—and he already looks a bargain. His connections were no doubt attracted by the fact that his dam Suprina had already produced an excellent winner, Salpinx, by L'Emigrant's grandsire Northern Dancer. Salpinx, who was also trained by Boutin, never stopped improving and ended her career with a couple of sterling efforts over a mile and a half, running Three Troikas to a short head in the Prix Vermeille and winning the Prix du Conseil de Paris. All three of Suprina's other living foals are winners. Suprina herself never raced and her dam Perfecta managed only three appearances, winning over seven furlongs as a three-year-old, but L'Emigrant's great-grandam Cosmah was a smart and tough performer, winning nine of her thirty starts. Cosmah bred eight other winners besides Perfecta, several of them very good: Tosmah, the best three-year-old of 1964, won twenty-three times from thirty-nine outings; Maribeau won the Fountain of Youth Stakes over eight and a half furlongs;

Father's Image, a brother to Perfecta, was a high-class two-year-old in 1965; and Halo was a very smart middle-distance performer on grass. Another of Perfecta's half-sisters, Queen Sucree, bred the Kentucky Derby winner Cannonade. Interestingly Cosmah is a half-sister to Natalma who appears in the top half of L'Emigrant's pedigree as the dam of Northern Dancer

Although some of The Minstrel's offspring, such as Peterhof and Longleat, have proved surprisingly short of stamina, others have stayed well; Chem won the fifteen-furlong Prix de l'Esperance and Crusader Castle the St Leger Italiano. L'Emigrant should eventually be suited by a mile and a half but he has surprisingly been entered for only the Guineas and not the Derby. He has, however, been entered for the Irish Sweeps Derby so perhaps it's not his stamina which is in doubt, rather his ability to handle the Epsom course. Significantly his rider said after the Criterium de Maisons-Laffitte that 'he seems to act well on a straight track'. *F. Boutin, France.*

LEMON CURD (FR) 3 b. or br.f. Gay Fandango 132–Jam Treacle (Jaipur)   **77**
(1981 NR 1982 7fg³ 8g³ 10f² 8fg³ 8g² 10fg³ 10.6s*) rather lightly-made filly; half-sister to 3 winners, including smart French 1977 staying 2-y-o Orange Marmelade (by Aureole); dam French 1¼m winner; always going well when beating Emperador by 5 lengths in minor event at Haydock in October; placed all previous starts, on second finishing 5½ lengths third to Chalon in International Fillies Stakes at Kempton; stays 1¼m well; acts on any going but revels in the mud; sold 40,000 gns Newmarket December Sales. *B. Hills.*

LEMON PIE 2 b.c. Saulingo 122–Stop Thinking (Divine Gift 127) (1982 6s)   **—**
Mar 24; 7,400Y; third foal; half-brother to 2 winners, including Santellas (by Arch Sculptor), a fair winner at around 1m; dam never ran; tailed off in claiming race at Nottingham in October. *P. Feilden.*

L'EMPEREUR 5 b. or br.g. Prince de Galles 125–Reine d'Etat 53 (High Hat 131)   **—**
(1981 NR 1982 10.1fg) little worthwhile form, including in a seller. *A. Moore.*

LE NAIN JAUNE (FR) 3 ch.c. Pharly 130–Lady Berry 121 (Violon d'Ingres)   **121**
(1981 NR 1982 12d* 12fg* 12s² 15fg² 15g* 14.6f 15.5v) lengthy colt; excellent walker; has a round action; fourth foal; closely related to French 1¼m and 1½m winner Featherhill (by Lyphard) and half-brother to 2 winners in France; dam won Prix Royal-Oak; showed himself suited by a thorough test of stamina when leading 4f out and staying on resolutely to beat Chem by 2 lengths in Grand Prix de Paris at Longchamp in June; had previously won maiden race at Saint-Cloud and minor event at Evry and finished second in Prix de l'Avre and Prix de l'Esperance (short neck behind Chem), both at Longchamp; well beaten last 2 starts in St Leger at Doncaster won by Touching Wood and Prix Royal-Oak at Longchamp won by Denel; stays well; has run creditably on a firm surface but action suggests he will always be suited by some give. *F. Mathet, France.*

LENTON PALACE 2 gr.f. Dragonara Palace 115–Street Vendor 60 (High Perch   **—**
126) (1982 5½g 6f 7f 5g) Mar 28; tall, lengthy filly; bad walker; half-sister to 6f winner Star Venture (by Swing Easy) and 2 winners abroad; dam won 5f seller at 2 yrs; in rear all outings, including in sellers; not seen out after August; blinkered final start. *P. Ashworth.*

LENYGON 7 b.g. Le Levanstell 122–Nanette 100 (Worden II 129) (1981 18s   **—**
8g 12v 12v 18g 1982 16s 12f³) rangy gelding; fair handicapper at his best; soundly beaten on flat since 1980, including when third in amateur riders race at Redcar in June; stays well; acts on a firm surface but has done all his winning on a soft one; suitable mount for an inexperienced rider. *P. Rohan.*

Grand Prix de Paris, Longchamp—Le Nain Jaune
turns the tables on old rival Chem

LEODEGRANCE (USA) 6 b.g. King's Bishop–Reasonably (Hail to Reason) **67**
(1981 12g 14fg² 14fg* 12s 1982 14fg* 12g 12f³ 16fg³ 14f² 13.1g²) well-made
gelding; made all and beat Spin of a Coin by 1½ lengths in 5-runner handicap at
Sandown in June; ran creditably most subsequent starts; stays 1¾m; ideally
suited by firm ground; blinkered once at 3 yrs. *G. Balding.*

LEONIDAS (USA) 4 ch.g. Exclusive Native–Double Think (Double Jay) (1981 **59 §**
8g 8d 10.1fg 10f 10d* 9f² 10d 10g 10.8s 1982 10.2g⁴ 10g 12.2d 10f* 11.7fg
10fg² 10fg 10fg⁴ 10fg) workmanlike gelding; won handicap at Beverley in April
but is inconsistent and not the heartiest of battlers; stays 1¼m; acts on any
going, except possibly very soft; often races with his tongue tied down; blinkered
seventh start. *F. J. Houghton.*

LEOPARDO 2 b.c. Busted 134–Naughty Party (Parthia 132) (1982 8g) Mar —
17; robust, deep-bodied colt; brother to 1m winner Bustellina; dam, 7f winner
in Ireland, is half-sister to Whistling Wind; unquoted and decidedly backward,
always well behind in 19-runner minor event at Newmarket in October. *B.
Hobbs.*

LEOPARD'S ROCK 8 b.g. Huntercombe 133–Reina Cristina 84 (Tamerlane **70**
128) (1981 12g 12f² 12fg³ 10f 11.7d 10fg³ 10fg⁴ 10g³ 10d 1982 10f* 10.8fg*
12fg* 12g² 12f* 11.7g 12g² 12f³ 12d 10d) middle-distance handicapper; in
excellent form in summer and won at Brighton (apprentice event), Warwick,
Lingfield and Folkestone; acts on any going but goes extremely well on top-of-the-
ground; very good mount for an inexperienced rider. *J. Dunlop.*

LEPARDA 2 ch.f. Lepanto–Balisarda 82 (Ballymoss 136) (1982 6fg) Mar 29; —
1,000Y; leggy filly; half-sister to 2 winners in France, including 1971 2-y-o 1m
winner Balking (by Charlottown); dam staying half-sister to Derby runner-up
Alcaeus; always behind in 12-runner seller at Ripon in August. *W. Haigh.*

LERINA 3 b.f. Oats 126–Coole Park (Wolver Hollow 126) (1981 5.1f² 5f 5fg —
1982 6g) small, lightly-made filly; only plating class; bred to stay at least 1m.
B. Hanbury.

LES DANCER 3 b.c. Northern Flash–Aracara (Prince Tenderfoot 126) (1981 —
5fg 5d⁴ 5d³ 6g 6fg 7fg 6f 7fg 7.6s 5s 8g 1982 10g 10f 14g 16d 12f⁴ 12f) sturdy
colt; plating-class maiden; promises to stay 1½m. *D. Jermy.*

LESLIE STONE (USA) 2 br.f. Bold Bidder–Drop the Pigeon (No Robbery) **100**
(1982 5fg³ 5f 6fg* 6f² 6g* 7g 7d³) Apr 24; $140,000Y; lengthy filly; first foal;
dam very useful stakes winner at up to 1m; successful in maiden race at Ayr in
June and nursery at Windsor in July; best form at 6f; hampered at start on
penultimate appearance. *J. Hindley.*

LE SOLEIL 8 ch.h. Roi Soleil 125–Mayo Blues 73 (Abernant 142) (1981 12s⁴ **75 d**
12fg* 12g³ 12v* 12g 12f³ 12f 12fg 12g² 12fg 12v² 12g 1982 12d² 12g³ 11.1g³
12f 12fg 12fg³ 12fg⁴ 13.1g⁴ 12fg 12s 12g) middle-distance handicapper; edged
right and was moved down to third after beating More Harmony by a neck at
Kempton in May on second start; acted on any going; had been tried in blinkers;
good mount for an inexperienced rider; stud. *R. Price.*

LE TOUQUET 3 b.g. Town Crier 119–Stella Roma (Le Levanstell 122) (1981 —
5v 6f 6g 1982 10f) leggy gelding; probably of little account; retained 850 gns
Ascot October Sales. *R. Hartop.*

LETSGOMO 3 b.g. Royben 125–Veinarde (Derring-Do 131) (1981 5v 5d 5g³ **46 d**
5fg* 6f 5fg 5.1d⁴ 6f 5g⁴ 5d 1982 5d 5d 6fg⁴ 7f 7fg 6f* 5fg 6g 6fg 6f 6d) workmanlike gelding; plater; awarded race at Leicester in June; stays 6f; suited by a
sound surface; has run respectably when sweating up; has given trouble in
preliminaries; sold 800 gns Doncaster September Sales. *B. Richmond.*

LE VOLEUR (USA) 2 b.c. Super Concorde 128–Noble Georgia (Vaguely Noble **109**
140) (1982 7.5fg* 8f²) Jan 31; $40,000 Y, $50,000 2-y-o; big, good-looking
colt; half-brother to a winner in USA by Cannonade; dam, half-sister to champion 3-y-o filly Lamb Chop, won twice at up to 9f in USA; made much of running
and battled on well to win newcomers race at Deauville in August by a short
head from Pluralisme; 6/1, finished well when 3 lengths second of 8 to L'Émigrant
in Prix La Rochette at Longchamp the following month; will stay middle
distances; returned to USA. *C. Beniada, France.*

LEW HEATH LADY 2 br.f. Roman Warrior 132–Samia 73 (Galivanter 131) —
(1982 5s) Feb 23; 700Y; half-sister to a winner in Malaya; dam poor maiden;
tenth of 21 in maiden race at Bath in October. *J. Bosley.*

LEX (FR) 5 ch.g. Tarbes 125–Toranquine (Right Royal V 135) (1981 18s 15.8s⁴ —
16s⁴ 1982 18g) big gelding; staying handicapper; acts on any going; has run
creditably for an amateur rider; possibly best on a galloping track. *N. Callaghan.*

LEYANI (USA) 3 ch.f Hagley–Uranie II (Again II) (1981 NR 1982 10fg —
8g 12.2f 12fg 10.1fg 12fg) 700Y; third foal; half-sister to a minor winner in
USA by Hawaii; dam, a winner in Argentina at 4 yrs, is sister to smart Zografos,
stakes winner at up to 9f, and to Niarkos, high-class performer in both Argentina
and USA; plating-class maiden; possibly stays 1½m; usually apprentice ridden;
sold to BBA 800 gns Newmarket December Sales. *R. Sheather.*

L'HAWAIENNE (USA) 3 b.f. Hawaii–Saracen Song (Khaled) (1981 NR —
1982 8fg 10f) 300,000 francs F (approx £33,500), IR 48,000 gns Y; slightly
dipped-backed, lengthy filly; fourth foal; half-sister to Irish 1½m winner Saracen
Glory (by Barbizon Streak) and to a minor winner in USA; dam, minor 1m
winner, is half-sister to dams of Derby second Hawaiian Sound (by Hawaii)
and Italian Oaks winner Maria Waleska; behind in Wood Ditton Stakes at
Newmarket in April and minor event at Salisbury in May. *B. Hills.*

LIANA LOUISE 2 b.f. Silly Season 127–Red Ranger 102 (Red God 128§) —
(1982 6f 7g 7d) Apr 15; 3,500F, 525 2-y-o; fair sort; sister to a winner in
Trinidad, and half-sister to 3 winners; dam sprinter; no worthwhile form,
including in a seller; not seen out after August. *D. Weeden.*

LIAR-DICE 2 b.f. Pretty Form 97–Eleonora 70 (Falcon 131) (1982 5g³ 5g —
5f 5g⁴) Mar 28; good-topped filly; fifth foal; dam, placed at up to 1m, reportedly
won in Greece; soundly beaten in small race and 3 sellers; not seen out after
May; of no account. *A. W. Jones.*

LIBBY JAYNE 3 ch.f. Tumble Wind–Ardrose (Pakistan II 84) (1981 5g³ —
5d⁴ 5s⁴ 6f 6f³ 5.1fg² 6f 6f 6d 1982 6d 5fg 7g 5g 5d 6d) ex-English filly; plating-
class maiden; best run at 6f; possibly suited by really soft going; blinkered
last 2 outings; trained part of season by G. Huffer. *P. Norris, Ireland.*

LIBERATED LADY 3 b. or br.f. Tycoon II–Queens Folly (King's Bench 132) —
(1981 NR 1982 8s 10s) first foal; dam quite a moderate hurdler; tailed off
in minor event at Warwick and maiden race at Nottingham in October. *A.
Arnold.*

LIBERTY TREE 2 ch.f. Dominion 123–Enlighten (Twilight Alley 133) (1982 **96**
7f² 7fg* 6fg* 6g* 6fg* 8g⁴) Apr 13; 13,500Y; useful-looking filly; good walker;
half-sister to 3-y-o 1m and 1½m winner Bourgeonette (by Mummy's Pet) and
fairly useful 1¼m winner Godoliero (by Green God); dam poor maiden; not seen
out until August, and then had 6 races within space of 8 weeks, running moderately (possibly feeling effects of her races) only when fourth of 12 behind Johnny
Nobody in nursery at Newmarket in September on final appearance; won maiden
event at Chepstow, all-aged race at Folkestone, and minor events at Ayr (dead-
heated with Sangrador) and Redcar; should stay 1½m; has raced only on a
sound surface; game and genuine. *Sir Mark Prescott.*

LIBERTY WALK 3 b.g. Free State 125–Path Of Pride (Sovereign Path 125) **63**
(1981 7fg 7g 1982 8f 8fg 10f 10d 11.5fg* 12f⁴) attractive, well-made gelding;
very good walker; made all to beat Hippo Disco by 7 lengths in 4-runner handicap at Yarmouth in July (apprentice ridden); suited by 1½m; blinkered third
start; suited by forcing tactics; sold to H. Wharton 3,600 gns Doncaster November Sales. *J. Winter.*

LICHEN GREEN 4 b.f. Welsh Saint 126–Lichen 93 (Tyrone 130) (1981 **55**
8g² 8f* 8g⁴ 10f 8g² 8s 1982 8g 9fg 8.2g 8d³ 8s 8g⁴) rather unfurnished filly;
poor mover; third in handicap at Ayr in September; stays 1m (well beaten over
1¼m); probably acts on any going; sold to Mrs C. Lloyd-Jones 1,600 gns Newmarket Autumn Sales. *J. W. Watts.*

LICHINE (USA) 3 b.c. Lyphard 132–Stylish Genie (Bagdad) (1981 NR **117**
1982 9d* 11g* 10v 9d³ 10fg 8f 8s⁴) $1,700,000Y (the most expensive yearling
sold at auction up to end of 1980); smallish, wiry colt; second foal; dam, stakes
winner, won at up to 9f and is half-sister to top-class 1m to 1½m colt Artaius; won
newcomers race at Evry in April and Prix de Suresnes at Longchamp in May;
came with a steady run to beat Nabirpour by ¾ length in latter; also ran creditably
in Prix Daphnis at Evry (length third to General Holme), 1m Prix du Moulin
de Longchamp (7 lengths fifth to Green Forest) and Prix du Rond-Point at
Longchamp again (6 lengths fourth to Ya Zaman); stays 11f but is better at
shorter distances; acts on any going. *F. Boutin, France.*

LIDO ISLE (USA) 2 b. or br.f. Far North 120–She Is Gorgeous (Drop Volley) —
(1982 7d) Mar 2; $110,000Y; tall, leggy filly; half-sister to 3 winners, including
stakes winner Diamond Lover (by Shecky Greene); dam, small stakes winner,
won at up to 7f; 11/2 but in need of race, never better than mid-division in 15-
runner maiden event won by Muznah at Yarmouth in August. *M. Stoute.*

LIFESTYLE 4 br.f. Jimmy Reppin 131–Cave Girl 67 (Pindari 124) (1981 **52**
8s 8f² 9.4fg⁴ 9f 8g 8.2v 1982 10s⁴ 9fg 8fg⁴ 10.6g 9g 10g³ 10fg) lightly-made
filly; didn't have best of runs when third in handicap at Newmarket in August;
stays 1¼m; acts on any going; blinkered final outing at 3 yrs; often races with
her tongue tied down; dwelt fourth start. *D. Francis.*

LIFT HIGH 3 gr.g. Town Crier 119–Make A Turn (Turn-to) (1981 5s³ 6d **53**
1982 8.2v⁴ 8f 8f 11g⁴ 8s 8s) strong, lengthy, useful-looking gelding; quite a
modest maiden at his best; stays 11f; possibly needs some give in the ground;
blinkered last 4 starts; sold 1,250 gns Doncaster November Sales. *J. W. Watts.*

LIGHT AND SHADE 3 ch.f. High Line 125–White Light (Amber Light 114) **66**
(1981 6fg 5g³ 7g 8s 1982 11.7f 12f² 13.8f² 16h³ 17.1f 14f* 14fg 12fg² 14fg)
fair sort; staying handicapper; made all and kept on gamely to win 3-runner event
at Sandown in July; acts on hard going; does best when ridden up with pace;
has run creditably for an apprentice. *K. Brassey.*

LIGHTLY POACHED 2 ro.f. Runnymede 123–Monumental Moment 91 **63**
(St Paddy 133) (1982 5f³ 5fg² 5f³ 5fg 5fg³ 5fg 5f 5fg 5f 5d 5g⁴) Apr 27; 1,400Y;
lightly-made filly; second foal; sister to 5f winner Kent's Pride; dam second 4
times from 7.2f to 11.1f and won over hurdles; plating-class maiden; not sure
to stay beyond 5f; ran creditably in blinkers last 2 outings. *N. Bycroft.*

LIGHTNING JANE 2 b.f. Morston 125–Grain of Truth 84 (Mill Reef 141) —
(1982 6d) first foal; dam stayed 1½m; 33/1, 12½ lengths sixth of 9 to Kwela in
minor event at Windsor in September; will need much further. *R. Laing.*

Mr R. Mandell's "Lightning Label"

LIGHTNING LABEL 6 br.h. African Sky 124–Soie Sauvage (Shantung 132) **116**
(1981 6g² 1982 6g³ 5s* 6fg* 5fg* 5fg 5s) leggy, rather lightly-made horse;
smart performer; spent much of 1981 in USA but didn't run there; in fine form
in spring, 1982, winning £7,200 handicap at Chepstow (made virtually all),
Ladbrokes Abernant Stakes at Newmarket (led last furlong and went clear on hill
to beat Scarrowmanwick by 2½ lengths) and Palace House Stakes at Newmarket
again; came with a storming late run to beat Blue Singh by ¾ length in last-
named event in May; towards rear in King's Stand Stakes at Royal Ascot in
June and Prix de l'Abbaye at Longchamp in October on his only subsequent
outings; best at sprint distances, though stayed 1m; acted on any going; blinkered
3 times in 1980; most genuine; standing at Hamilton Stud, Newmarket, fee
£1,000 n.f.n.f. *P. Kelleway.*

LIGHT OF EIRE (USA) 3 b.f. Majestic Light–Irish Manor (Bold Ruler) **—**
(1981 NR 1982 8fg 8g) half-sister to 3 minor winners; dam, winner at up to
1m, is sister to very smart stakes winners Irish Castle and Alpine Lass; well
behind in maiden races at Warwick in August and Yarmouth in September.
R. Boss.

LIGHT SHOW 2 b.g. Swing Easy 126–Laser Song 69 (Laser Light 118) (1982 **77**
7d³ 7fg 7g 7s) Feb 24; 5,000Y; strong, lengthy, heavy-bodied gelding; half-
brother to 1978 2-y-o 5f winner Lisa Laser and to winners in Malaya and Italy
(all by Comedy Star); dam won over 1¼m at 2 yrs; showed no form after finishing
¾-length third of 18 to The Quiet Don in maiden race at Salisbury in June;
stays 7f. *R. Laing.*

LILAC CHARM 2 b.f. Bustino 136–Rose Dubarry 127 (Klairon 131) (1982 **78 p**
7d) Apr 12; rather lightly-made filly; fourth foal; half-sister to 1976 2-y-o 5f
winner Scented Air (by Derring-Do); dam fastest 2-y-o filly of 1971; 14/1 and
backward, prominent 6f when 7 lengths fifth of 18 behind easy winner Northern
Adventure in minor event at Doncaster in October; likely to do better. *H.
Cecil.*

LILAC LADY 6 b. or br.m. Fair Turn–Reine de Saba (No Argument 107) **—**
(1981 10f 10s 1982 12d) no worthwhile form. *R. Thompson.*

LINANHOT 2 ch.f. Hot Spark 126–Anatevka (Privy Councillor 125) (1982 **46**
5v⁴ 5f 6f 6f 5d) May 25; lightly-made filly; half-sister to several winners,
including useful Pittencrieff (by Manacle), successful from 7f to 1¾m; poor form,
not seen out after June; blinkered in sellers last 2 starts. *A. Young.*

LINBURY LADY 3 b.f. Royal Palace 131–Shooting Season 91 (Silly Season 127) **—**
(1981 NR 1982 10d) first foal; dam stayed 1m well; unquoted when tailed-off
last of 12 to Kings Soldier in maiden race at Folkestone in June. *B. Wise.*

LINCOLN'S REALM 3 ch.c. Realm 129–Lindera 71 (Linacre 133) (1981 **51**
NR 1982 6f⁴ 6fg² 8.2fg⁴ 6f 7g 6f) 6,400Y; sturdy, colt, half-brother to 2
winners, including Iron Ruler (by Lyphard), a very useful winner at up to 7.5f in
France and Germany; dam stayed 1¾m; in frame in maiden races; possibly
stayed 1m; dead. *Miss S. Hall.*

LINDA BEARD 3 b.f. Pitskelly 122–Wavy Navy (Hardicanute 131) (1981 **—**
6fg 6fg 6g* 1982 6fg 6g 7.2f 7d 7f 8.3fg 7d) strong filly; apprentice ridden when
winning maiden race at Newmarket as a 2-y-o; disappointing most starts in
1982 and moved appallingly to post third outing; should be suited by 7f+;
blinkered last 3 outings. *R. Armstrong.*

LINDA DUDLEY 2 gr.f. Owen Dudley 121–Tanara 93 (Romulus 129) (1982 **81**
5g 6fg 8f 7g) Jan 24; sturdy, short-legged, attractive filly; half-sister to 2
winners by Hotfoot, notably William Hill Futurity winner Count Pahlen, and a
winning hurdler; dam 1¼m performer; moderate form in varied company; will
stay 1¼m. *B. Hobbs.*

LINDA'S ECSTASY 2 b.f. Martinmas 128–Crassatella (Epaulette 125) (1982 **—**
6g 7d) Apr 15; 4,100F, IR 8,000Y; half-sister to numerous winners here and
abroad, including fairly useful 1m to 1½m winner Promote (by Hard Tack);
dam never ran; showed no merit in maiden race at Newmarket in September and
minor event at Catterick in October. *R. Armstrong.*

LINDA'S FANTASY 2 ch.f. Raga Navarro 119–Loch Leven 87 (Le Levanstell **100**
122) (1982 5fg 5g⁴ 6fg 6fg* 6g* 6g* 7g* 7f*) Mar 5; IR 1,500F, IR 5,000Y
(privately); smallish, well-made filly; good walker; fifth foal; half-sister to
3-y-o 1½m winner Migoletty (by Oats); dam disqualified 2-y-o 6f winner; failed
to get within 8 lengths of winner in maiden and minor events on first 3 outings,
and then had the remarkable record of 5 successive wins in nurseries, at Windsor,

Leicester, Doncaster, Yarmouth and Catterick, in the space of around 6 weeks in August and September; defied penalties on 3 occasions, one of 9 lb when narrowly beating Domynsky in £3,500 race at Catterick; stays 7f; has raced only on a sound surface; has a useful turn of foot; genuine. *R. Armstrong.*

LINDA'S ROMANCE (USA) 2 b.f. Restless Restless–Red Skies 84 (Sky-master 126) (1982 7d 8.2s 6s) May 12; lengthy filly; half-sister to 2 winners by King's Company; dam won over 6f; sire, son of Restless Wind, was at his best at 2 yrs when very smart sprinter; well beaten in late-season maiden and minor events, twice tailed-off last. *R. Armstrong.* —

LINDSEY 3 b. or br.f. Mummy's Pet 125–Merchantmen's Girl 58 (Klairon 131) (1981 5v⁴ 5fg 5d² 5.3f 5fg* 5fg 5fg 5g 1982 6g 6fg² 6g² 5fg⁴ 6g² 6f⁴ 6f 6f* 5g⁴ 6g 7d³ 6g 5s) small, quite attractive filly; fairly useful handicapper; ridden with more restraint than usual when decisively winning from Cheri Berry at Salisbury in August; stays 7f; seems to act on any going; consistent. *D. Elsworth.* 90

LINDY BAY 5 br.g. Bay Express 132–Lindylee 99 (Grey Sovereign 128§) (1981 5s³ 5g* 5g 5g 5f 5.6f 5fg 5fg 5g² 5s⁴ 5g 7g 7s 7g³ 1982 6g 5f 7f 7fg 7f 6g* 7fg 6g 5fg 6s 6s 7d) strong, good sort; returned to form in handicap at Thirsk in July, beating Blessed Silence by a head; stays 7f, but probably best at shorter distances; acts on any going; wears blinkers or a hood nowadays. *Hbt Jones.* 49 d

LINE ABREAST 3 b.f. High Line 125–Filiform 76 (Reform 132) (1981 NR 1982 10fg 11.7f 16.9fg⁴ 15.5fg² 16s³) small, lightly-made filly; poor mover; sister to 3 winners, including Heighlin and Spanish St Leger winner El Pais, and half-sister to 2-y-o Goodbye Shelley (by Home Guard); dam, half-sister to very smart animals Magic Flute and Entanglement, won over 1¼m; staying maiden; seems to act on any going; has run respectably for an apprentice; sold to S. Norton 35,000 gns Newmarket December Sales. *H. Candy.* 62

LINE SLINGER 3 b.f. High Line 125–Snow Tribe 94 (Great Nephew 126) (1981 6g 8d 1982 10f 12f 12fg² 12.2f³ 16g² 16.5f² 14.6g* 12g² 12g² 14s² 14g* 18s) fair sort; not the best of movers; stayed on stoutly to win maiden race at Ripon in August and £4,100 handicap at Newmarket in October; beat Channing Girl emphatically by 5 lengths in latter; ran creditably in between; suited by a test of stamina; ideally suited by some give in the ground; game. *W. Elsey.* 88

LINGDALE 5 b.g. Crooner 119–Dream (Roan Rocket 128) (1981 8d 8s 8d 11g 8g 7d 9s 1982 10.4g 12f 12g 10d 10g⁴ 5f⁴ 10f) disappointing handicapper; poor mover; ran in sellers fourth and fifth starts (not disgraced in latter); stays 1¼m; acts on firm going but is ideally suited by some give in the ground; has worn blinkers. *M. Naughton.*

LINGEH 2 gr.f. Persian Bold 123–Pearl Grey (Gulf Pearl 117) (1982 6g) Apr 29; IR 12,000Y; sturdy filly; half-sister to 3-y-o Love Tangle (by Wollow) and a winner in USA; dam, Irish 1¼m winner, is half-sister to Belmont Stakes winner Celtic Ash; unquoted and backward, tailed off in 18-runner maiden race at Newmarket in September. *B. Hanbury.* —

LINGIA LIL 4 br.f. Mandamus 120–Tecclyn 97 (Technion 96) (1981 5fg 6f 6fg 6fg 6f 5s 6g 1982 8f 7g⁴ 5f 6g³ 7f 8fg 7s) strong, workmanlike filly; in frame at Lingfield (apprentice handicap) and Windsor (seller) in summer; probably stays 7f; acts on firm going; inconsistent; blinkered once in 1981; changed hands 675 gns Ascot October Sales before final start. *Mrs R. Lomax.* 45

LINGRETA 3 b.f. Pitskelly 122–Sheralanth (Pontifex) (1981 5fg 5s² 5d 6fg 6v² 6s 1982 7f 7f⁴(dis) 8.3fg 7fg 8.2s 7d 8d) narrow filly; not the best of movers; plater nowadays; stays 7f; has run respectably on firm going but is ideally suited by plenty of give in the ground; has been tried in blinkers; good mount for an apprentice. *Peter Taylor.* 66

LINKLIGHTER 2 b.f. Busted 134–Gay Trinket 72 (Grey Sovereign 128§) (1982 7d 6fg* 6g) Apr 23; well-made, good sort; half-sister to several winners here and abroad, including 3-y-o 1¼m winner Goumi (by Grundy) and useful sprinter Nusantara (by Lorenzaccio); dam headstrong half-sister to French Derby second Patch; always going well when winning 20-runner maiden race at Salisbury in September most decisively by 2 lengths from Princess Zita; 10/1 when tenth of 16 to Prince Spy in £4,700 nursery at Newmarket the following month; should be well suited by 7f and 1m; acts on a firm surface. *G. Harwood.* 82

LINPAC BELLE 3 ch.f. Steel Heart 128–Prima Bella 76 (High Hat 131) (1981 5s 5g 6g⁴ 7fg 6f 6d 5f 6d 6s 1982 7.6fg 6fg 6fg⁴ 5fg⁴ 7g 7.2g 8s 6s 7s) robust filly; poor form, including in a seller. *W. Elsey.* —

506

LINPAC GOLD 3 b.f. Rheingold 137–Purple Goddess 69 (Red God 128§) **62** (1981 6d 6d 7g 1982 10.5fg 12fg 12.2f² 12f³ 12g 15d 16s⁴ 12s 12d 12d) sturdy filly; stays 1½m; acts on firm going; one paced; has twice started slowly; sold 550 gns Ascot December Sales. *W. Elsey.*

LINPAC RED 3 ch.g. Red Alert 127–Flotilla 64 (Alcide 136) (1981 6fg **—** 7fg 8.2d 10.2g 1982 11s 12fg 10f 11fg 12.3g) strong gelding; carries plenty of condition; little worthwhile form in varied company, including selling; has worn blinkers and is probably temperamental; sold 540 gns Ascot December Sales. *W. Elsey.*

LINRO CHARLIE 3 b.g. Happytown 89–Lesley's Fil (Right Boy 137) (1981 **—** 5s 7fg 6fg 6f 7f 6s 5g⁴ 5s 1982 12.2d) lengthy gelding; of little account; has twice been blinkered. *Mrs M. Nesbitt.*

LIN SLIPPER 9 b.g. Linacre 133–Tartan Slipper (Panaslipper 130) (1981 **—** NR 1982 12g 16g) of little account on flat; has worn blinkers. *M. Reddan.*

LION CITY 3 b.g. Simbir 130–Fille Sifflante §§ (Whistler 129) (1981 6fg **81** 7f 1982 10s 12fg 10.6fg² 10f 8fg* 8fg⁴ 8f* 9fg³ 8g⁴ 8.2g* 8d* 9s² 8s²) close-coupled gelding; won maiden race at Ayr and handicaps at Carlisle (apprentices), Nottingham and Ascot (apprentices); also first past post in valuable apprentice handicap at York in October on penultimate start but was moved down a place for hampering runner-up; best at up to 9f; acts on any going; best in blinkers; suitable mount for an apprentice; suited by waiting tactics. *E. Eldin.*

LISA GREENE (USA) 3 br.f. Shecky Greene–Hail Lisa (Hail to Reason) **—** (1981 6g 6g 1982 7.6f 7f 7.2g 6f⁴) small filly; shows traces of stringhalt; only plating class; sent to Singapore. *L. Cumani.*

LISAILY (USA) 2 ch.c. Raja Baba–Controlled Landing (First Landing) **— p** (1982 7d) Mar 16; $200,000Y; tall, good-looking colt; fifth foal; half-brother to 3 minor winners; dam very useful stakes winner at up to 1m; 8/1, showed early speed in 13-runner Houghton Stakes at Newmarket in October; looks capable of better. *H. T. Jones.*

LISARDA 3 b.c. Moulton 128–Alisarda (Aureole 132) (1981 7f 6g 6g 1982 **54** 7d 8g 8fg 11.7g 12f² 9g⁴ 11g 12g 8.2f⁴ 8.2g 8.2s) rangy colt; plating-class maiden; suited by 1½m and will stay further; acts on firm going. *N. Guest.*

LISTEN TO ME 3 b.f. He Loves Me 120–Karen Chase 82 (Will Somers 114§) **46** (1981 5d 5fg 8d 5s 1982 10fg 5f 5fg² 5g 5.8f) well-made filly; good walker; sprint handicapper; best at 5f on fast ground and in blinkers; sold 480 gns Ascot September Sales. *L. Kennard.*

LITTLE ANGELIQUE (USA) 3 ch.f. Son Ange–Robadan (Prince John) **—** (1981 NR 1982 5fg 6d) $28,000Y; half-sister to Chief Admiral (by Chief-tain), successful at up to 1m, and several winners in USA; dam very useful stakes winner at up to 1m at 2 yrs; soundly beaten in maiden races at Warwick in August and Nottingham in September. *S. Norton.*

LITTLE ATOM 5 gr.h. The Go-Between 129–Native Nymph 97 (Indigenous **52** 121) (1981 5s 5g⁴ 5g² 5fg 5g 5fg³ 5f 5fg⁴ 5.8f 6f* 5f 6f 6f 6g 1982 6f 6f⁴ 6f 6f³ 6g³ 6d³ 5f³ 6f 7f 6f⁴ 6g 5fg 5d 7f³ 7d) poor handicapper; stays 7f; goes well on top-of-the-ground; has worn blinkers. *D. Yeoman.*

LITTLE BEN 2 gr. or ro.c. Old Lucky 113–Sovereigns Delight (Sovereign **—** Lord 120) (1982 7fg 5f 6g 5f 8s) Apr 7; fair sort; second foal; dam placed in point-to-points; no worthwhile form in maiden and minor events. *N. Kernick.*

LITTLE BLUE 2 b.g. Blue Cashmere 129–Petitt 60 (Mummy's Pet 125) **—** (1982 8s) Apr 18; small gelding; first foal; dam sprint plater; tailed-off last of 15 in seller at Redcar in October; dead. *P. Asquith.*

LITTLE BOUNDER 2 b.c. Averof 123–Parthian Glance 120 (Parthia 132) **64** (1982 7fg 7fg 7fg⁴) May 13; 5,000Y; half-brother to French 3-y-o William Blake (by Blakeney) and 2 winners, including useful stayer Knight Templar (by King Log); dam best 3-y-o staying filly of 1966; 8 lengths fourth of 9 to Acadie in minor event at Doncaster in July, only indication of merit. *P. Brookshaw.*

LITTLE BOY 2 b.g. Free Boy 96–Sousocks (Soueida 111) (1982 5fg 7d **—** 7fg) May 25; compact gelding; of little account; has worn blinkers. *P. Burgoyne.*

LITTLE CHANGE 2 ch.f. Grundy 137–Pennycuick 101 (Celtic Ash) (1982 **70** 5f⁴ 5g³ 6f 7d) May 25; neat filly; half-sister to 3 winners, including very useful 1978 2-y-o 5f winner Penny Blessing (by So Blessed); dam sprinting half-sister to Mummy's Pet, Arch Sculptor and Parsimony; in frame in June in maiden events at Newbury and Wolverhampton; not raced after August. *F. J. Houghton.*

LITTLE FLOSS 2 b.f. Streak 119–Flossie's Girl (Current Coin 118) (1982 — 5g) May 1; first foal; dam of no account on flat and over hurdles; last of 8 in seller at Folkestone in June. *G. Beeson.*

LITTLE GINGER 3 ch.f. Cawston's Clown 113–Henrietta Georgina 72 (Rustam 127) (1981 5fg 6fg 6fg 1982 10s) tall, leggy filly; of little account and is possibly temperamental. *B. McMahon.*

LITTLEGOOD JILL 5 b.m. Military 112–Littlegood Belle (Ron 103) (1981 NR 1982 8g) tailed off in amateur riders event at Warwick in June. *J. Webber.*

LITTLE GRIMALDI 2 b.c. Cawston's Clown 113–Coymount (Goldhill 125) — (1982 5.3g 5d 5fg 5f 5fg 7g) May 3; 2,800F, 7,000Y; close-coupled colt; first produce; dam, half-sister to very smart Sir Montagu, showed no worthwhile form on flat or over hurdles; no worthwhile form in maiden and minor events; should be suited by further than 5f; may do better in sellers. *S. Matthews.*

LITTLE LONDON 3 br.g. Pieces of Eight 128–Whistler's Princess (King — Emperor) (1981 6g 6f 6f³ 6f 6g 8g 1982 8d 10f 10f 10fg 10d 8fg) neat gelding; plater; stays 1m; sometimes blinkered. *T. M. Jones.*

LITTLE MADAM 2 ch.f. Habat 127–Obedience (Reliance II 137) (1982 5g **66** 5fg* 5g 5g 5f² 6fg⁴ 5fg³ 6s) Mar 7; 2,300Y, 4,000 2-y-o; small filly; half-sister to 2 winners, including 3-y-o sprinter Premier Lass (by Lochnager); dam ran only 3 times; ran 8-runner seller at Lingfield (no bid) in May by a neck from Beaming Anne; in frame in nurseries subsequently; not disgraced over 6f but is possibly better suited by 5f. *D. Wilson.*

LITTLE MEADOW (FR) 2 b.f. Carmarthen 130–Andelle (Spy Well 126) **114** (1982 6s 6.5g* 7.5g³ 7.5fg 8fg⁴ 8g 8d 8d³ 9d 8s² 8v³) Mar 19; 28,000 francs Y (approx £2,500); rangy, workmanlike filly; half-sister to a minor 2-y-o winner by Carvin; dam won over 6f and 1m in France; claimed out of P. Bartholomew's stable for 68,888 francs after winning claiming race at Evry in July; improved subsequently and ended season gaining places in Group 3 Prix des Reservoirs at Longchamp in October (went down by ¼ length to Belka) and Group 3 Criterium Femminile at Rome in November (3¾ lengths third to Tajwind); will stay 1¼m. *R. Collet, France.*

LITTLE MERCY 4 gr.f. No Mercy 126–Petite Rock (Goldhill 125) (1981 8.2s³ **81** 9s 10g 1982 8fg* 8f* 8g² 8fg* 8f² 8g² 7g* 7f* 8g³ 7g²) big, strong, good-topped filly; good walker and mover; showed improved form and had an excellent season; won maiden event at Thirsk (dead-heated with Mary Burns) and handicaps at Warwick, Brighton, Yarmouth and Brighton again, making running for last 3 wins; also ran well on her other starts; best at 7f or 1m; probably acts on any going, but is ideally suited by a sound surface; very game and genuine. *J. Winter.*

LITTLE MILLS 4 ch.g. Tumble Wind–Gamma (Zank) (1981 10g 7s 7d⁴ 6d⁴ — 8fg 7.9f² 8f 1982 10f4¹) strong ex-Irish gelding; looking fairly fit but weak in market when 8 lengths fourth of 6 behind Trendbucker in maiden race at Redcar in May, first outing on flat over here; stays 1m; probably acts on any going. *G. Lockerbie.*

LITTLE MUFF 3 br.f. Potent Councillor 98–Kyle Valley (Barbin) (1981 NR — 1982 16.5fg) non-thoroughbred filly; first live foal; dam never ran; unquoted when tailed-off last of 11 to Lucky Ivor in minor event at Redcar in September. *A. Young.*

LITTLE RED HUT 3 ch.f. Habitat 134–Redowa 60 (Red God 128§) (1981 — NR 1982 7fg 7.6fg 6fg 6fg 5g 10f 10s) sturdy filly; half-sister to several winners, including very smart middle-distance performer Red Regent (by Prince Regent) and fairly useful sprinter Ballydowa (by Ballymoss); dam sister to St Alphage and Yellow God; well beaten in varied company. *P. Walwyn.*

LITTLE ROBERT 3 br.g. Wolver Hollow 126–La Lola (Le Levanstell 122) — (1981 5fg² 5g³ 6d² 6g² 6fg* 6fg³ 6fg 7d³ 6fg 5fg 5g 6s 1982 6s 6fg 7g 6fg 10f⁴ 10fg 12g) well-made, attractive gelding; fairly useful in 1981; below form at 3 yrs; stays 1¼m; seems to act on any going; blinkered third and fourth starts, pulling hard on first occasion; exported to Malaysia. *A. Ingham.*

LITTLE SMASHER 3 b.f. Jimsun 121–Metis 55 (Be Friendly 130) (1981 5s —
5fg³ 6g 6fg 6f 6f* 6g² 6fg 1982 7fg 8fg 6f) neat filly; quite modest at her best;
last in 3 handicaps in 1982; should stay 7f; acts on firm going; sold 640 gns Ascot
September Sales. *M. Haynes.*

LITTLE SPEEDY 2 b.f. Starch Reduced 112–Misty Morn 70 (Worden II 129) —
(1982 5fg 5f) Apr 13; 1,300Y; small, leggy, lightly-made filly; sister to fair
sprinter Little Starchy and half-sister to another winner; dam stayed 11f; not
raced again after finishing poor sixth in seller at Folkestone in July; probably of
no account. *A. Pitt.*

LITTLE STARCHY 4 b.c. Starch Reduced 112–Misty Morn 70 (Worden II 129) 76
(1981 5d² 5fg*(dis) 6d 6s 5d 1982 5s³ 5g² 5fg 5.3g⁴ 5g 5fg² 5fg 5.3f³ 5g 5fg
5fg* 5s³ 5s²) fair sort; placed on several occasions before and after beating
Barnet Heir by ¾ length in handicap at Goodwood in September; best at 5f; acts
on any going. *J. O'Donoghue.*

LITTLE STEEL 3 ch.c. Steel Heart 128–Nagin 120 (Pretense) (1981 5v 5v —
5fg 1982 5f) neat, dipped-backed colt; well beaten in varied company,
including selling. *B. Gubby.*

LITTLE VAGABOND 2 ch.c. Ampney Prince 96–Lady Jay 61 (Double Jump 62
131) (1982 5g 5fg 5d 5fg² 5fg 5f³ 5g 5d² 5v) Mar 24; smallish, chunky colt;
first foal; dam second in two 1m sellers; placed in sellers, being caught in final
furlong when second at Wolverhampton in July and Ripon in August; bred to
stay beyond 5f but races very freely and may not do so; seems to act on any
going with possible exception of heavy; blinkered last 2 outings. *S. Matthews.*

LITTLE VEE 3 ch.g. Roi Soleil 125–Lynella (Clear Run 109) (1981 5v⁴ 5s 6fg —
5f 1982 6s 6s 5g) lengthy gelding; no worthwhile form, including in sellers;
headstrong; dead. *J. Berry.*

LITTLE WOLF 4 ch.c. Grundy 137–Hiding Place 109 (Doutelle 128) (1981 124
10g³ 11g* 12d² 12fg³ 12s* 1982 14f³ 12g* 12g² 16d* 15.5v)
   Little Wolf's failure in the Prix Royal-Oak at Longchamp in October
concluded a season that had more than its usual share of disappointments for
his stable. It came only a day after Hern's 1980 record for prize money won
in a season had been beaten by Cecil as a result of Dunbeath's Futurity win and
only nine days after Gorytus' mystifying flop in the Dewhurst. The stable's
total of forty-four winners in Britain was its lowest since 1972. Little Wolf
started favourite for the Royal-Oak, won by Hern with Niniski in 1979, and
looked a worthy one, too, in a substandard field. His record over three seasons
was one of steady improvement and he was beginning to be looked upon as a
possible successor to Ardross among the stayers. But in the Royal Oak he
never held out much hope. Racing on possibly the worst going seen all year in
Paris, Little Wolf dropped towards the rear of the field on the far side and five
furlongs out was last of thirteen, being pushed along. He took closer order

Jockey Club Cup, Newmarket—Little Wolf
is well on top at the finish

Lord Porchester's "Little Wolf"

coming into the turn and was produced on the outside in the straight, but the effort of getting a good position was taking its toll. Little Wolf had nothing left in the last two furlongs and finished sixth to Denel, beaten about five lengths; it was the first time he'd been unplaced.

Little Wolf (ch.c. 1978)	Grundy (ch 1972)	Great Nephew (b 1963)	Honeyway
			Sybil's Niece
		Word from Lundy (b 1966)	Worden II
			Lundy Princess
	Hiding Place (ch 1963)	Doutelle (ch 1954)	Prince Chevalier
			Above Board
		Jojo (gr 1950)	Vilmorin
			Fairy Jane

Little Wolf won two of his four races before the Royal-Oak, the Prix Jean de Chaudenay at Saint-Cloud in May and the Jockey Club Cup at Newmarket in October. The Jean de Chaudenay, over a mile and a half, attracted only a modest field—the only three-year-old in the race was the English handicapper Turkoman—and Little Wolf won by a neck from Le Mamamouchi. The runner-up came with quite a good run in the straight but Little Wolf always looked like holding him. The rider of third-placed Gap of Dunloe objected unsuccessfully to Little Wolf for interference coming out of the bend. In the Jockey Club Cup, over two miles, Little Wolf was much more impressive. The distance, the longest he'd been over, clearly suited him admirably for at no stage did he look better than in the last couple of furlongs. Early in the long straight Little Wolf looked in a bit of trouble—he was in a poorish position and making fairly heavy weather of things. However, he improved steadily, came through to take up the running about three furlongs out and, after a brief struggle with Karadar, he got on top and strode clear to win by six lengths from Halsbury. Since he gave weight away all round this was a particularly good effort, and so strongly did he finish that we were left in no doubt that he'll get extreme distances in 1983, given the chance. On his other two starts Little Wolf was placed in the Yorkshire Cup at York, in which he put up a determined effort to finish only about a length behind Ardross in third, and the Grosser Preis von Berlin at Dusseldorf, in which the outstanding German colt Orofino beat him decisively by a length and a half. He looked rather tapped for speed at York, and at Dusseldorf Carson reported that Little Wolf had found the course too sharp and that he'd be suited by a return to distances longer than a mile and a half.

The last two generations of Little Wolf's family have produced over twenty individual winners. Hiding Place has produced nine from ten foals to reach the racecourse so far, including the Royal Hunt Cup winner Camouflage (by March Past), the Horris Hill winner Disguise (by Klairon) and the Yorkshire Cup winner Smuggler (by Exbury). Hiding Place was a useful winner herself, and is a half-sister to Brigadier Gerard's sire Queen's Hussar.

Despite his performance in the Royal-Oak there are few with as good prospects in the Cup races as Little Wolf. Whether he'll run in them remains to be seen. Little Wolf's half-brother Smuggler spent most of his career racing over distances too short to show him at his best and Lord Porchester reportedly said of the Gold Cup at the time that 'it even devalues a horse to enter him.' In our opinion Little Wolf's talents will be wasted if reverting to middle distances, and in any case winning good races with him over them will be difficult. He's unlikely to meet such weak opposition in a mile-and-a-half pattern race again as he did in the Jean de Chaudenay, and he lacks the speed for races like the Coronation Cup and Hardwicke Stakes. A strong, close-coupled, quite attractive colt, Little Wolf acts on any going except really heavy. He's thoroughly genuine. *R. Hern.*

LITTLE WORKER 2 br.f. Workboy 123–Little Singer (Sing Sing 134) (1982 **47** 5g 5f² 6f 5d 5f 6fg⁴ 5g⁴ 6d 8fg) Mar 16; 370Y; small filly; half-sister to successful sprinter Two Ronnies (by Carnival Dancer); bad plater; stays 6f but is unlikely to get 1m; acts on firm going; blinkered fifth outing. *P. Calver.*

LIVELY ROSE 3 ch.f. Wolverlife 115–Baby Rose (Our Babu 131) (1981 **—** 5fg 5d* 5g 6fg 6fg² 6g* 6fg 5d 1982 5f 5.8f 6g) leggy filly; winner of maiden race at Wolverhampton and nursery at Windsor in 1981; behind in handicaps at 3 yrs; suited by 6f; acts on a firm and a soft surface. *N. Vigors.*

LIZMOR 3 gr.c. Morston 125–Elizabeth Wales 95 (Abernant 142) (1981 8g **64** 1982 11g 14fg 16fg² 12.3g³ 16fg 16s⁴) fair sort; suited by a test of stamina; has run respectably for an apprentice; sold to R. Champion 8,400 gns Newmarket Autumn Sales. *I. Balding.*

LOBKOWIEZ 3 b.c. Radetzky 123–Fulcrum Miss (Fulcrum) (1981 6fg 6g **119** 7fg 7fg³ 8f* 8fg* 8s³ 1982 7fg 8.5fg 12.3g³ 12f 10fg² 10g² 12f⁴ 12g 10f 10d) Any horse beaten a short head in a Group 2 race carrying 8 lb overweight, as was Lobkowiez in the Prince of Wales's Stakes at Royal Ascot, deserves some sympathy. Given the shortage of light-weight jockeys and the tendency for apprentices generally to be heavier than they were going back twenty years, a small amount of overweight is an everyday occurrence despite there being what is, by past standards, a relatively high minimum mark in handicaps of 7-7; in the Tote Cesarewitch, for instance, seven of the twenty-eight runners, including the winner Mountain Lodge, carried more than they were set to. Such a state of affairs may be inevitable, but it is also regrettable since any overweight lessens a horse's chances of success and does little service to the animal concerned, its connections or the off-course punter. Consequently to have a horse humping 8 lb above his allotted weight is verging on the suicidal, however good the jockey involved, and any claim that the rider is worth the extra weight flies in the face of logic and fact. The facts with Lobkowiez are that his original weight at Royal Ascot stood at 7-10, but with Eddery on board he carried 8-4; in going down by the minimum margin to the four-year-old Kind of Hush he ran the race of his life and lost the best chance he had of winning a good prize in a campaign which saw his taking on the best almost all the time. Fine jockey as Eddery is, no one can persuade us that Lobkowiez would have done anything other than win had he run off his correct weight.

The Prince of Wales's Stakes and the Coral-Eclipse Stakes were the twin peaks of Lobkowiez's season. A smart two-year-old with a good third to Norwick in the Royal Lodge to his credit, Lobkowiez came to Royal Ascot with only one respectable piece of form behind him in the current season, namely a staying-on third behind Super Sunrise in the Chester Vase. His other starts had resulted in sound defeats in the Salisbury Two Thousand Guineas Trial, the Blue Riband Trial and the Derby, and in the light of this, plus the overweight Eddery had to put up, the pair understandably started 20/1-outsiders of seven. Settled in behind his stable-companion Silver Season, Lobkowiez took over halfway up the straight and, battling on with admirable tenacity all the way to the line, lost out only in the last few strides to Kind of Hush. With Be My Native running well below form and several of the others suffering in what looked a rough race, the Prince of Wales's Stakes was a rather unsatisfactory contest, but Lobkowiez's performance was still a great advance on his four previous runs and, considering the added burden he carried, a splendid effort.

Lobkowiez confirmed his status with a good second in the Coral-Eclipse at Sandown in July. He avenged the Royal Ascot defeat by comfortably out-pointing fifth-placed Kind of Hush but had no chance with the four-length winner Kalaglow whom he chased with enthusiasm from three furlongs out. Lobkowiez's form progressively tapered off after the Eclipse. A respectable fourth to Electric in the Gordon Stakes at Goodwood, he then proceeded to run moderately in the Great Voltigeur, the Prix du Prince d'Orange and the Dubai Champion Stakes, beating just four out of a total of twenty-four opponents home in the three events. We hope this loss of form indicated nothing more serious than that Lobkowiez had gone over the top for the year: it would be a great shame if his regular struggles against very good horses had soured him for at his best he's as game as any horse in training.

	Radetzky (br 1973)	Huntercombe (b 1967)	Derring-Do / Ergina
		Selina Fair (b 1964)	Hugh Lupus / Raggoty Ann
Lobkowiez (b.c. 1979)	Fulcrum Miss (b 1967)	Fulcrum (ch 1955)	Spy Song / Fulmar
		Unicrose (br 1953)	Bey / Rose of Bengal

Lobkowiez's third dam was a half-sister to the Irish Derby winner Hindostan out of a half-sister to Umiddad, but the family hasn't enjoyed spectacular success since that time. Rose of Bengal foaled four winners, among them Lobkowiez's grandam Unicrose who won over nine furlongs in France and bred seven minor winners in the States including Fulcrum Miss, successful in four sprint claiming events. Lobkowiez is Fulcrum Miss's sixth foal; the best of the others was his close relative Von Erlach (by Huntercombe), a fairly useful winner over six furlongs and a mile. Lobkowiez, a neat colt who didn't grow much from two to three, stays a mile and a half but has shown his best form at a mile and a quarter. He acts on any going. *C. Brittain.*

LOCH ARD 3 b.c. Music Boy 124–Caesar's Love 85 (Above Suspicion 127) (1981 6g 1982 10.2g4 10f 10f4 12g2 10s 14g4 12f4) rangy colt; seems to stay 1¾m; gave trouble at start fifth outing; possibly ungenuine, and was blinkered final start. *B. Hobbs.*   **63**

LOCHBOISDALE (USA) 2 b.c. Stage Door Johnny–Blue Law (Tom Rolfe) (1982 8s4) Mar 31; third foal; half-brother to fair 1981 2-y-o 5f winner Leixlip (by Drone); dam unraced daughter of very smart 1962 American 3-y-o filly Firm Policy; easy in market, kept on one pace when 7 lengths fourth of 21 behind stable-companion Rock's Gate in maiden race at Leicester in November; should do better at 1¼m+. *J. Tree.*   **79 p**

LOCH EARN 4 bl.g. Undulate–Citrine 77 (Meldrum 112) (1981 NR 1982 12f 16g) 3,500 3-y-o; big, rangy gelding; second foal; dam, lightly raced, was placed over 6f at 2 yrs; behind in minor event at Pontefract in July and maiden race at Beverley (still backward) in August.   **—**

LOCHLINNHE 3 b.g. Lochnager 132–Sunbird II (River Chanter 121) (1981 6g 1982 10g 12.3g4 14.7f 12v3 12d3) good-topped gelding; plating-class maiden; stays 1½m; suited by soft ground; has sweated up. *Miss S. Hall.*   **65**

LOCH PEARL 2 b.c. Lochnager 132–Dusky Pearl 68 (Gulf Pearl 117) (1982 6fg 5s4) Mar 27; rangy colt; has a good, long stride; second living foal; half-brother to a winner in Belgium; dam won over 1m; promising 6½ lengths seventh of 25 to Orixo in minor event at Doncaster in September, racing in front rank until fading inside final 2f; ran quite well but seemed to flounder in the soft   **81**

ground when about 4 lengths fourth of 7 to Private Label in minor race at York the following month; may prove suited by a sound surface. *M. H. Easterby.*

LOCHRANZA 11 br.g. Highland Melody 112–Earall (Khalkis 127) (1981 12s 12.5s 12s 13g 12fg 14.6f 13fg⁴ 12fg 12v 12s 1982 15.8g² 15g 13.8d) fairly useful and very genuine front-running handicapper at his best but deteriorated; retired after finishing lame at Catterick in October; stayed 2m; was ideally suited by some give in the ground; acted on any track; sometimes wore blinkers; was a good mount for an inexperienced rider. *J. Carr.* **36**

LOCHTILLUM 3 b.c. Song 132–Spring Storm 74 (March Past 124) (1981 6d 6g 7g 1982 5d 6d 5fg⁴ 5fg⁴ 5fg 5g* 5fg³ 5g 6d 5d 6fg 5s) good-quartered colt; sprint handicapper; won at Bath in July; best at 5f. *J. Douglas-Home.* **64**

LOCKED TOWER (USA) 3 br.c. Key To The Kingdom–Royal Cage (Royal Willow) (1981 NR 1982 8fg 10fg 7g 9fg 10.6g) $100,000Y; rangy, good-topped colt; closely related to 2 winners, including Bold Trap (by Bold Commander), a smart winner at up to 9f, and half-brother to 2 winners; dam won 3 sprint races; poor maiden; sold out of G. Harwood's stable 2,400 gns Ascot 2nd June Sales after second start; dead. *R. Whitaker.* **—**

LODDON MUSIC 2 gr.f. Music Boy 124–Spanish Chestnut (Philip of Spain 126) (1982 5g 5g 5g* 5v 6s) Mar 31; 2,600F, 5,200Y; first produce; dam poor plater; having first race for 12 weeks (had a soft palate operation in meantime) when showing improved form to win 12-runner seller at Windsor (sold out of G. Hunter's stable 1,850 gns) in August; not sure to stay 6f; dwelt fourth outing. *R. Hannon.* **59**

LOFTY 2 b.c. High Top 131–Enchanted 116 (Song 132) (1982 5g² 6f* 7fg⁴ 7fg³ 8fg* 7v² 7s²) Apr 13; strong, good-bodied colt; carries plenty of condition; third foal; half-brother to fair 1981 2-y-o 5f performer Pleasant Dream (by Sharpen Up); dam smart sprinting 2-y-o; won maiden race at Newmarket in July and 4-runner minor event (beating Ashmolean) at Goodwood in September; ran well all other starts, particularly when 7 lengths third of 6 behind The Fort in Intercraft Solario Stakes at Sandown and when second of 13 behind runaway winner Indian Rajah in valuable John Sutcliffe Trophy Nursery at Lingfield; stays 1m well; acts on any going; game and consistent. *H. T. Jones.* **105**

LOGAN 5 b.g. Biskrah 121–Amber Star (Amber Rama 133) (1981 8fg 10d⁴ 10f 7f 1982 10g 14f 12g⁴ 12fg⁴ 16d 16f² 16.5f⁴ 16g* 16.5fg³ 16fg) rather lightly- **46**

Fulbourne Maiden Stakes, Newmarket—Lofty narrowly beats the grey Timber Tycoon

made gelding; made all in handicap at Lingfield in August; stays 2m; acts on firm going; usually blinkered nowadays; ran moderately final start. *M. Masson.*

LOLLY GIRL   2 b. or br.f. Swing Easy 126–Goldmine 58 (Goldhill 125)   (1982   **32** 5f 5fg 6fg)   Mar 5; 2,100F; fair sort; third foal; dam won 1m seller; bad plater; not raced after July.   *P. Rohan.*

LOMOND (USA)   2 b.c. Northern Dancer–My Charmer (Poker)   (1982 6g*   **109+** 7d³)   Feb 3; half-brother to several winners, notably brilliant American triple crown winner Seattle Slew (by Bold Reasoning); dam minor stakes winner at up to 1m; 3/1 on, made a very promising debut when winning 21-runner maiden race at the Curragh in August by 6 lengths from Changed His Mind; again long odds on in National Stakes on the same course the following month but was beaten a length into third place behind stable-companion Glenstal; reportedly had a throat infection after National Stakes and is probably better than his running these suggests; will stay at least 1¼m; sure to win more races.   *V. O'Brien, Ireland.*

LONDON BLITZ   2 b.f. Home Guard 129–Quatemala (Welsh Saint 126)   —
(1982 7d)   Feb 6; 3,700F, IR 2,500Y; big, strong filly; first foal; dam useful winner over 5f and 6f at 2 yrs in Ireland; 16/1 and badly in need of run, last of 18 in maiden race at Leicester in October.   *M. McCourt.*

LONELY DAWN (USA)   3 b.f. Plenty Old–Dueling Time (Duel)   (1981 6g   **63** 1982 8d 8f 8f* 7.2f* 8g 8fg)   lengthy filly; won sellers at Brighton (bought in 2,200 gns) and Haydock (no bid) in May; suited by 1m; acts on firm going; sold to L. Barratt 640 gns Newmarket Autumn Sales.   *B. Hills.*

LONE RAIDER   5 b.g. Shantung 132–Love Resolved (Dan Cupid 132)   (1981 NR   1982 14fg⁴ 18.8fg)   big, workmanlike gelding; won maiden race at Edinburgh and amateur riders event at Newmarket in 1980; has run only twice since; stays 2m; acts on firm going and is probably unsuited by very soft; sold 560 gns Newmarket July Sales and resold 825 gns Ascot in October.   *R. Boss.*

LONGCLIFFE   7 br.g. Mandamus 120–Pepin (Midsummer Night II 117)   (1981   **48** 10s10s² 10g 12.2s   1982 10.5s 10d⁴   big gelding; middle-distance handicapper; acts on any going; bandaged in front on reappearance.   *K. Stone.*

LONGLANDS LADY   4 ro.f. Grey Mirage 128–Ursula 78 (Songedor 116)   **41** (1981 5d* 6g³ 5g 5fg 5fg* 5g 5g 6fg 6f 5f   1982 6s⁴ 5f 5fg 5fg 5g³ 5f 6g² 5fg⁴ 5fg 6fg)   sturdy filly; sprint plater; acts on a firm and a soft surface; sold 480 gns Doncaster October Sales.   *J. Berry.*

LONGLEAT (USA)   3 ch.c. The Minstrel 135-Fair Arrow (Turn-to)   (1981 **109** 6fg* 7g* 8d²   1982 6g 5f* 6f) $250,000Y; smallish, strong, attractive colt; half-brother to 2 winners, one a stakes winner, and to dam of high-class filly Alma North (by Northern Dancer); dam, placed at 2 yrs, is out of half-sister to champion 2-y-o filly Diableretta; blinkered, came with a strong run to lead near finish when beating subsequently-demoted Princess Seal a short head in 11-runner Ballyogan Stakes at Leopardstown in June; again blinkered, never going pace when eighth of 18 to Indian King in Cork and Orrery Stakes at Royal Ascot; not seen out again; stayed 1m but was clearly regarded as a sprinter; probably acts on any going; retired to Collin Stud, Newmarket, at £3,000 live foal.   *V. O'Brien, Ireland.*

LONGTOFT   3 gr.c. Tachypous 128–Donrae 106 (Don II 123)   (1981 5g³   **56** 1982 5f³ 6f⁴ 7g 8f)   workmanlike colt; good walker; only plating class; should stay 7f+; blinkered final start; exported to Algeria.   *M. H. Easterby.*

LOOKALIKE   2 br.c. Dancer's Image–Without Reproach 102 (Above Suspicion   **87** 127)   (1982 7f 8d 8s)   Mar 5; 5,400Y; strong, workmanlike colt; half-brother to several winners, including useful stayer Hikari (by Petingo); dam won Lancashire Oaks; showed up in large fields of maidens at Newmarket and Sandown in October on second and third outings; will stay beyond 1m.   *P. Haynes.*

LOOKING GLASS   3 b.c. Lochnager 132–Arodstown Alice (Sahib 114)   (1981   **81** NR   1982 7fg 8fg³ 7f 8fg³ 8fg 7g 6fg* 6f* 6fg² 6d² 6g 6g 5fg)   2,750Y; big, strong colt; not the best of walkers; half-brother to 5f winner Doubtwash Girl (by Hot Spark); dam ran only 3 times; won handicaps at Yarmouth in July and August; made all on second occasion; ran respectably next 2 starts, but was below form afterwards; better suited by 6f than longer trips; yet to race on very soft going but acts on any other; moved very badly to post when withdrawn on intended third outing; usually blinkered; suited by strong handling.   *W. O'Gorman.*

514

Mr R. E. Sangster's "Lomond"

LOOK NO HANDS 2 ch.c. Some Hand 119–Juristicia (Supreme Court 135) — (1982 5fg 5fg 6fg) May 6; of no account; sold 300 gns Doncaster October Sales. *S. Matthews.*

LOOKS A MILLION 2 b.f. Wollow 132–Grange Fire (Allangrange 126) — (1982 7.6v 8g) Apr 4; 7,000Y; leggy, lengthy filly; first foal; dam unraced half-sister to Deep Run; beaten some way in October maiden races at Lingfield and Newmarket. *W. Musson.*

LORA DEL RIO 2 b.f. Riverman 131–Lora (Lorenzaccio 130) (1982 6g) Apr 5; big, rangy filly; half-sister to 2 winners, including 1,000 Guineas winner On The House (by Be My Guest); dam closely related to high-class sprinter D'Urberville; no show in maiden race at Newbury in August; dead. *H. Candy.*

LORDAVILLE 3 b.g. Lord Nelson 107–Vaudaville 77 (Vigo 130) (1981 5s 1982 8g 12f4) lengthy gelding; good walker; soundly beaten in maiden races and a minor event; sold 900 gns Doncaster October Sales. *R. Fisher.*

LORD CHANTICLEER 2 ch.g. Oats 126–Linbel (Linacre 133) (1982 7f **61** 7fg 7f4 7g 8fg 8d 8d) Apr 15; IR4,000Y; short-coupled gelding; has no near eye; half-brother to 3 winners, including 5f to 1m winner Ardoony (by Ardoon); dam Irish 9f winner; only poor form, including under top weight in selling nursery; sold CBA 400 gns Newmarket Autumn Sales and subsequently gelded. *D. Morley.*

LORD CLEWES 4 ch.c. Status Seeker–Calcine 75 (Roan Rocket 128) (1981 — 10s3 10.6d 12.3d 1982 10d) workmanlike colt; stays 1¼m; acts on any going but is possibly best on soft. *D. Francis.*

LORD JOHNSTAN 2 b.g. Le Johnstan 123–Pamora (Blast 125) (1982 — 6g 6g 6f 5g 6s 5d) Feb 22; 350Y; tall gelding; bad plater; became very upset in stalls third start; gelded after final outing. *R. Whitaker.*

*Shadwell Maiden Stakes, Yarmouth—a successful debut by the much-vaunted
Lord Protector who is not hard pressed to hold off Tolomeo*

LORD NORTH 5 gr.g. Zeddaan 130–Laria (Silver Shark 129) (1981 13fg* — 1982 12d) ex-Irish gelding; won amateur riders race in 1981; behind on only outing of 1982; stays 13f; acts on a firm surface. *A. Pitt.*

LORD OF MISRULE 8 gr.h. Supreme Sovereign 119–Mirth (Tamerlane — 128) (1981 12d 1982 12g 12fg⁴ 10f⁴ 12f) poor handicapper; stays 1½m; acts on any going; usually wears blinkers; suitable mount for an inexperienced rider. *M. Haynes.*

LORD OF THE REALM 4 ch.c. Realm 129–Suir-Delight (Precipitant 113) — (1981 7s 7fg² 7.6d³ 7g 6s* 5.8d 6fg 7fg 6fg 7g 6s 1982 7.5g 6.5v 5d 5d 5fg 7f 7g 6v) small colt; soundly beaten since winning handicap at Kempton as a 3-y-o, including in a seller on sixth start; stays 7f; probably acts on any going; blinkered fourth outing. *G. Beeson.*

LORD PROTECTOR (USA) 2 b. or br.c. Vaguely Noble 140–April Bloom **102** p 108 (Bold Lad, Ire 133) (1982 7g* 7v³) May 19; $135,000Y; attractive, rangy colt; brother to smart French 3-y-o Noble Bloom, and half-brother to 2 American winners by The Axe, including April Axe, a smart stakes winner at up to 1m; dam won twice over 5f at 2 yrs and was in frame in good races at up to 1m; appeared with a big reputation when 2/1 on for 12-runner maiden race at Yarmouth in September and did all that could be expected of him, leading below distance and not being hard pressed to hold off more-experienced Tolomeo by ½ length; again 2/1 on, appeared to be going extremely well until drifting badly right inside last 2f when 4 lengths third of 6 behind Special Leave in Hyperion Stakes at Ascot the following month; will stay 1¼m; possibly not at his best on heavy ground; worth another chance. *H. Cecil.*

LORD SCRAP 6 ch.g. Tower Walk 130–La Concha (Le Levanstell 122) (1981 **62** 6s 6fg 5g 6d 6g 6fg³ 6f 5.8f² 6fg 5h⁴ 6fg 1982 5d⁴ 6fg 6f² 6f 6fg² 6g* 6f 6g² 5fg* 5.8f* 5d² 6s) good-looking gelding; sprint handicapper; won at Brighton in July and at Chepstow (apprentices) and Bath in September; stays 6f; acts on any going, except possibly really soft; has won in blinkers but is better without; excellent mount for a boy; started slowly second start. *B. Swift.*

LORDS (USA) 3 b.c. Hoist the Flag–Princessnesian (Princequillo) (1981 **119** 8d* 1982 10s² 10fg³ 12f² 12fg* 12fg*)
    The Keeneland Summer Select Yearling Sale has become the most important talent-spotting arena for the world's richest racehorse owners. Vincent O'Brien's principal owner Robert Sangster, with BBA (Ireland) doing his bidding, has been among the sale's leading buyers each year since the early 'seventies. Among the lots purchased for syndicates headed by Sangster at the 1980 sale were three of the six highest-priced lots: Pilgrim (1,250,000 dollars), Lords (1,050,000 dollars) and Golden Fleece (775,000 dollars), all of whom went into training with O'Brien. Sangster claims to have made money on almost every horse bought on his behalf at Keeneland, the end product being the stallions and broodmares which are sold or syndicated. The Sangster racing interests

516

enjoyed another successful year in Europe in 1982, notably with the relatively cheaply-bought French-bred Assert, who won the French and the Irish Sweeps Derby, and Golden Fleece who won the Epsom Derby. The purchase of Lords also paid dividends: racing in the colours of one of Sangster's partners, the American Danny Schwartz, Lords won two mile-and-a-half pattern races in Ireland, the Royal Whip Stakes at the Curragh in July and the Blandford Stakes on the same course in August, and was sold in the autumn to stand at Spendthrift Farm, Kentucky, at a fee of 12,000 dollars live foal.

The commercial logic of relatively early retirement is inescapable where expensive yearlings are concerned—the books have to be balanced—and the careers of so many horses of Lords's type are often all too short. Lords raced six times, only once outside Ireland, and a training set-back kept him out of the field for the St Leger, by some way the most important challenge he would have faced in his career and a race for which, at the time of his withdrawal, he was ante-post favourite. Lords won a maiden race at Leopardstown on his only appearance at two but needed time to come to himself—'He needs to improve on his homework of last year', his trainer told us in an interview in April—and he was beaten on each of his first three outings as a three-year-old, in the third of them going down by three quarters of a length to Open Day in the King Edward VII Stakes at Royal Ascot. Lords gave the distinct impression at Royal Ascot that he would be suited by further than a mile and a half, staying on strongly in the straight after being pushed along before the turn to hold his place. His victories in the Royal Whip Stakes and the Blandford Stakes, in both of which he started odds on, confirmed him as a good-class middle-distance performer: the Irish Sweeps Derby third Patcher was runner-up in the Royal Whip, beaten five lengths, but Lords had to work much harder to hold off the very useful handicapper Steel Duke by a neck in the Blandford.

A tall, lengthy son of Alleged's sire Hoist the Flag, Lords is the ninth foal of the Princequillo mare Princessnesian, a high-class winner of eleven races at up to a mile and a quarter including the Hollywood Gold Cup, the Santa Margarita Invitational Handicap and the Santa Barbara Handicap. Lords

Mr D. Schwartz's "Lords"

is the best racehorse produced by Princessnesian. Two of her earlier winners, the fillies Bold Enchantress (by Bold Ruler)—the dam of Fordham—and Passing Fancy (by Buckpasser), were also trained by O'Brien: Bold Enchantress won a maiden event over six furlongs and was second in the Park Stakes at Phoenix Park as a two-year-old, her only season to race; Passing Fancy didn't run at two and was very lightly raced at three, winning a maiden event over a mile and a quarter at Phoenix Park. Considering that Princessnesian hadn't exactly hit the highspots as a broodmare it seemed a little surprising at the time that Lords fetched such a high price as a yearling, although Princessnesian certainly had the pedigree to match her racing record, being a half-sister to the Santa Anita Derby winner Boldnesian and to the unraced Stay at Home,

Lords (USA) (b.c. 1979)	Hoist the Flag (b 1968)	Tom Rolfe (b 1962)	Ribot Pocahontas II
		Wavy Navy (b 1954)	War Admiral Triomphe
	Princessnesian (b 1964)	Princequillo (b 1940)	Prince Rose Cosquilla
		Alanesian (b 1954)	Polynesian Alablue

the dam of the brothers Boone's Cabin and Home Guard, high-class performers with whom O'Brien did particularly well in the seventies. Although Lords has a rather round action, the type often associated with the soft-ground performer, he did most of his racing on a firm surface. *V. O'Brien, Ireland.*

LORD WIMPY 4 gr.g. Dragonara Palace 115–My Worry 72 (March Past 124) (1981 8s² 7s² 7fg*(dis) 7g² 7d² 7d 7d 8f 7f 7f* 7fg 8g 6g 1982 6fg² 5fg 6f* 5.8f* 7f* 6f*) strong, sprint type; not seen out after June, but was in tremendous form during his short season; won handicaps at Pontefract, Bath and Epsom (two), making all for both his wins on last-named course; best at up to 7f; acts on any going but is very well suited by firm; blinkered once; has sometimes tended to hang and is not the easiest of rides. *J. Bethell.* **76**

LOR MOSS 2 ch.g. Mossberry 97–Lor Darnie 65 (Dumbarnie 125) (1982 8.2s 8d) Apr 12; tall, narrow, close-coupled colt; half-brother to a winning plater and a winning jumper; dam won sellers over 7f and 1m; well in rear in maiden race at Haydock in October and minor event at Redcar in November. *J. Etherington.* **—**

LOTHIAN EMPRESS 4 ch.f. Broxted 120–Lothian Countess (New Brig 120) (1981 NR 1982 11g 8fg) second foal; dam fair hurdler; soundly beaten in maiden races at Edinburgh in April. *W. Crawford.* **—**

LOTRA-SHACA 2 b.f. Ercolano 118–Thimothea 43 (Timmy My Boy 125) (1982 5f 5g 5fg⁴ 6g 7g 6fg) Apr 4; 4,300Y; first foal; dam well bred but of little account; poor maiden; not raced after July; sold BBA (Ireland) 700 gns Newmarket Autumn Sales. *T. Craig.* **50**

LOTTIE'S FOLLY 2 b.c. Royben 125–Josilu (Caliban 123) (1982 5f² 5g⁴ 5g 5fg² 5.3f* 5fg 5d 5s) May 30; neat colt; half-brother to 2 winners, including 5f and 1m winner Rollin Hand (by Some Hand); dam of no account; proved well suited by course when making all to win 8-runner claiming race at Brighton in August by 10 lengths from Mrs Chandler; not sure to stay beyond 5f; acts on firm going; sent to Malaysia. *P. Cole.* **72**

LOTUS DANCER 3 b.f. Midsummer Night II 117–Kushbehar 80 (Behistoun 131) (1981 6f 6f 1982 8f 7g 8f 5g 5.3f 6fg 5fg 10d 12v) small, lightly-made filly; poor plater; has worn blinkers; trained part of season by J. Jenkins. *R. Simpson.* **—**

LOUISA ANNE 2 b.f. Mummy's Pet 125–Lucinda Anne (Abernant 142) (1982 6h 6g 5g 5f³ 6d) Apr 30; narrow filly; closely related to very useful 3-y-o sprinter Diamond Cutter (by Song) and half-sister to 3 winners; dam lightly-raced maiden; 6 lengths third of 11 to Fairlawne in maiden race at Haydock in September, only form. *P. Rohan.* **73**

LOUP DE MER 3 b.f. Wolver Hollow 126–Milveagh 92 (Milesian 125) (1981 6f² 7fg³ 6d³ 7g* 1982 8fg* 8fg² 8d 10f 10fg) lengthy, sparely-made filly; kept on well to win handicap at Pontefract in May; 1½ lengths second to Kareena in quite valuable handicap at Ascot in June; suited by 1m (well beaten over 1¼m); has twice worn blinkers. *M. Stoute.* **86**

LOU PIGUET (FR) 4 b.c. Habitat 134–Tuneria (Tanerko 134) (1981 8d **116**
11fg 8s* 9g 10g 8g⁴ 8s⁴ 7v² 1981 8v³ 8d 8s³ 7fg² 7g 6.5fg³) French colt;
brother to successful Italian colt Hagg Hagg, subsequently a winner in USA,
and half-brother to a winner by Thatch; dam French middle-distance winner;
won Prix de la Jonchere at Longchamp as a 3-y-o and ran extremely well when
4 lengths second to Moorestyle in Prix de la Foret on same course on final
start; placed in 1982 in Prix Edmond Blanc at Saint-Cloud, Prix du Muguet
and Prix du Palais Royal at Longchamp, and Prix Maurice de Gheest at Deauville; beaten a neck by shade comfortable winner Indian King (pair clear) in
Palais Royal and finished 3½ lengths third to Exclusive Order in Maurice de
Gheest; showed best form at up to 1m; acted on a firm surface but was very
well suited by the mud; usually blinkered; wasn't particularly consistent;
standing at Haras du Camp Benard. *J. C. Cunnington, France.*

LOUVIERS 4 br.g. Vitiges 132–Vive la Reine (Vienna 127) (1981 10.1d⁴ **65**
10s* 10fg 11g⁴ 1982 10s² 12.3g) compact, good-bodied gelding; second to
easy winner Rage Glen in apprentice handicap at Ayr in March; promises
to stay 1½m; acts on soft going (didn't run particularly well on a firm surface
third start in 1981); blinkered final start in 1981. *G. Richards.*

LOVABLE CLOWN 2 b.f. Cawston's Clown 113–Lovable 84 (Miralgo 130) **51**
(1982 5fg 6f² 6f² 6g 7fg⁴ 8fg) May 8; 1,000F; leggy, close-coupled, lightly-
made filly; half-sister to 2 winners, including fairly useful 1½m winner Sungold
(by Royalty); dam stayed 2m; second in sellers at Leicester in July and
Nottingham in August; probably stays 7f. *R. Hollinshead.*

LOVE EXPRESS 2 ch.c. Bay Express 132–Sweet Season (Silly Season 127) **70**
(1982 5d 5d³ 6g) Apr 7; IR 19,500Y; medium-sized, good-topped colt; first
foal; dam ran 3 times at 3 yrs; plating-class maiden; should stay 6f. *B. Hills.*

LOVELY DANCER 2 b.c. Green Dancer 132–Janthina 118 (Petingo 135) **115**
(1982 7.5fg 8s* 7.5s 9d⁴ 10v³ 10v⁴) Apr 13; second foal; half-brother to useful
1981 French 2-y-o 9f winner Quouki (by Zeddaan); dam second in Prix Morny;
in frame in pattern races late in season, finishing 5½ lengths fourth of 9 to Saint
Cvrien in Prix Saint-Roman at Longchamp, being beaten only a short head and
a head by Nile Hawk in Prix de Conde on same course and over 4½ lengths when
fourth to Escaline in Criterium de Saint-Cloud; had earlier won maiden race at
Deauville; will stay 1½m; acts well on heavy going. *O. Douieb, France.*

LOVELY LEANA 2 gr.f. Town Crier 119–Set Piece 69 (Firestreak 125) (1981 **66**
5.8f 5g 6f 6g⁴ 7f⁴ 6s 7.2s) Apr 30; leggy, lightly-made filly; third live foal
in this country; dam prolific winner in Norway; fair plater; suited by 7f; acts
on firm going; blinkered final outing. *C. Williams.*

LOVELY LUCY 2 ch.f. Grundy 137–Romany 87 (King's Bench 132) (1982 **69** p
6d 6s) Apr 17; fair sort; half-sister to several winners, including fairly useful
stayer John O'Groats (by Welsh Pageant); dam beaten at sprint distances;
nearest finish when 4 lengths fifth of 16 behind Onaizah in maiden race at
Leicester in November, second outing; got loose in paddock on debut; will be
much better suited by 7f+; should improve. *J. Winter.*

LOVE MATCH (USA) 2 b.f. Affiliate–Nanny Tammy (Tim Tam) (1982 **73**
7d 7d⁴) Mar 18; $45,000Y; well-made filly; third foal; half-sister to 2 winners
in USA; dam, out of sister to top German horses Neckar and Naxos, never
ran; sire top-class winner at up to 9f at 3 yrs; quite modest form in maiden
races at Yarmouth in August and Leicester (odds on) in October; will stay 1¼m.
H. Cecil.

LOVE ME DO 3 b.f. He Loves Me 120–Gang Plank 84 (Tower Walk 130) **62**
(1981 6fg 7d 7g⁴ 1982 8f 6f² 6fg⁴ 6fg* 6f⁴ 7fg² 7s 7g) lengthy, deep-girthed
filly; made all to win minor event at Brighton in July despite hanging badly
right (apprentice ridden); stays 7f; acts well on fast ground; effective with or
without blinkers; sold 14,000 gns Newmarket December Sales. *M. Smyly.*

LOVE ME LADY 3 b.f. He Loves Me 120–Lady Relka (Relko 136) (1981 **—**
7g 1982 10fg 10h) leggy, shallowed-girthed filly; behind in maiden races;
blinkered final start. *J. Sutcliffe.*

LOVE ME TRUE 3 b.f. He Loves Me 120–Lady Lambourn 82 (Habitat 134) **—**
(1981 5g 1982 5fg⁴) neat filly; good walker; poor form in a £3,200 event
and maiden race in South. *B. Hills.*

LOVE POEM 3 br.f. Orange Bay 131–Affection 110 (Compensation 127) **—**
(1981 NR 1982 9f) 4,500Y, 500 2-y-o; big, lengthy filly; half-sister to fairly

useful 5f performer Cockney Rebel (by Sparkler) and to a winner in Italy; dam very useful sprinting 2-y-o and later won over 1m; 50/1 and bandaged, moved poorly to post and always behind in 9-runner minor event won by Glory Isle at Redcar in August. *N. Tinkler.*

LOVE'S DREAM (FR) 3 b.f. Rheingold 137–Glass Slipper 100 (Relko 136) **58** (1981 NR 1982 13.3f 16d 12g⁴ 16g) tall, quite well-made filly; half-sister to 3 winners, including St Leger winner Light Cavalry (by Brigadier Gerard) and 1,000 Guineas winner Fairy Footsteps (by Mill Reef); dam staying half-sister to Royal Palace; little worthwhile form in maiden races; sold to BBA 46,000 gns Newmarket December Sales. *H. Candy.*

LOVE TANGLE 3 gr.f. Wollow 132–Pearl Grey (Gulf Pearl 117) (1981 6g⁴ **68** 1982 7.6fg 7fg² 7.6fg² 7g⁴ 10.4d² 10fg² 7fg² 8s 8g 8g³) well-made filly; runner-up in maiden races and a £4,400 event; stays 1¼m; possibly unsuited by very soft ground; blinkered nowadays; often wears bandages behind; sold 12,500 gns Newmarket December Sales. *M. Smyly.*

LOVING CUP 2 b.f. He Loves Me 120–Time Bomb (Supreme Court 135) **93** (1982 6fg 6g 6g* 6s⁴ 7v 6g 7s) Feb 12; rangy filly; half-sister to several winners, including Smokey Rockett, a useful winner at up to 7.6f; dam sister to dam of good animals Good Bond and Roll of Honour; won 16-runner minor event at Ripon in August by 1½ lengths from Glorious Jane; 2½ lengths seventh of 12 behind Captivating Lady in 6f nursery at Newmarket in October, best subsequent effort; should stay 7f; acts on soft going. *W. Hastings-Bass.*

LOVING DOLL 2 gr.f. Godswalk 130–Le Levandoll 92 (Le Levanstell 122) **72** (1982 5g 5fg 6s³) May 24; sturdy filly; half-sister to a minor 2-y-o winner; dam won from 6f to 1½m; 3 lengths third of 16 behind Marzooga in maiden event at Leicester in November, easily best effort; will stay beyond 6f. *A. Hide.*

LOVING EVE 6 b.m. Sir Nulli 87–Little Weed 48 (Lord of Verona 120) (1981 — NR 1982 9v) pulled up in juvenile hurdle in 1979; tailed-off last of 8 behind Time Wind in maiden race at Hamilton in October. *M. James.*

LOWTHER STREET 4 gr.f. Grey Mirage 128–Sherbet (Zarathustra 131) — (1981 8s 8fg 12d 14s⁴ 16g⁴ 1982 17.1s) strong filly; has shown a little ability. *D. Ancil.*

LOYAL SUPPORTER 3 b.g. Scottish Rifle 127–Miss Moss Bros 69 (Sparkler **67** 130) (1981 NR 1982 10.1g³ 11.7g³ 10.2s³ 10d³) first foal; dam placed over 6f at 2 yrs; third in varied races, including an apprentice event; will stay 1½m+; yet to race on a firm surface; pulled hard final start. *G. Harwood.*

LUAN CAUSCA 3 b.f. Pampapaul 127–Tintale (Tin Whistle 128) (1981 **61** 5f 5f* 5g 5g 1982 5g² 5g⁴ 5f 5f 8fg 8fg 8.2g) small, workmanlike filly; not sure to stay 1m; blinkered fourth start. *W. Wharton.*

LUCAYAN LADY 3 b.f. Swing Easy 126–Mary Mullen 88 (Lorenzaccio 130) **78** (1981 5g 5s³ 6d* 6g 1982 6g² 6f³ 7f³ 6g 6g² 7s³ 7s² 6s) sturdy filly; fair handi-capper; stays 7f; acts on any going; has run creditably for an apprentice. *R. Sheather.*

LUCINSKI 3 b.f. Malinowski 123–Lucindale (Ballyciptic 122) (1981 7g 1982 — 10s 11.7f) lightly-made filly; well beaten in maiden races. *R. Hollinshead.*

LUCK PENNY 2 b.f. Bustino 136–Thrifty Trio 116 (Groton) (1982 6fg² 6f 6fg **80** 5s) Mar 28; IR 30,000F, IR 41,000Y; close-coupled filly; first foal; dam smart sprinter; showed little worthwhile form after finishing head second of 20 to Judy Conkers in minor event at Windsor in July; possibly unsuited by soft going. *I. Balding.*

LUCKY APPEAL 2 b.f. Star Appeal 133–Lucky Omen 99 (Queen's Hussar 124) — (1982 7d) May 28; quite well-made filly; second foal; half-sister to very useful 3-y-o sprinter Lucky Hunter (by Huntercombe); dam 2-y-o 5f and 6f winner; 7/1 and in need of run, soon chased along when in mid-division in 18-runner maiden race at Leicester in October. *C. Brittain.*

LUCKY CHOICE 3 br.c. Lucky Wednesday 124–Pams Choice 87 (Mandamus **63** 120) (1981 5s 6g 7g⁴ 7fg⁴ 8f² 8g 8s³ 7d⁴ 1982 8s 9.4fg 9fg² 8g⁴ 9g² 10fg³ 10d 10.2f⁴) strong, good-bodied colt; stays 1¼m; acts on any going; one paced and needs to lie up with leaders; best in blinkers; has run respectably for an apprentice; not the heartiest of battlers. *M. H. Easterby.*

LUCKY DUTCH 3 b.c. Lucky Wednesday 124–Dutch May 109 (Maystreak 118) **66** (1981 5g 5fg* 6f 6s 7g 1982 8f 8g 5d2) fair sort; heavily-backed favourite, showed first form for a long time when 5 lengths second of 8 to Sew Nice in handicap at Beverley in July; not raced again; best at sprint distances; sometimes sweats up. *M. W. Easterby.*

LUCKY FIDDLER 3 b.g. Old Lucky 113–Semi-Quaver (Seminole II) (1981 —
5.8f 5fg 5fg 1982 8g 8f 7f) lengthy gelding; poor maiden. *A. Turnell.*

LUCKY FINGERS 2 ch.f. Hotfoot 126–Tilt Guard 75 (Crepello 136) (1982 **81 p**
7d⁴) Apr 1; well-made filly; half-sister to 3 winners, including 7f and 1m
winner Minibank (by Saritamer); dam ran only 3 times; 33/1, made a lot of
late ground when 8 lengths fourth of 13 finishers behind Acclimatise in £4,000
maiden race at Sandown in July; will stay at least 1¼m. *C. Brittain.*

LUCKY FRIEND 3 ch.f. Galivanter 131–Jolly Jane (Jolly Jet 111) (1981 —
NR 1982 10.2g 12.2f) fifth reported foal; dam never ran; well behind in
maiden races at Doncaster and Catterick in summer. *M. Lambert.*

LUCKY HUNTER 3 b.c. Huntercombe 133–Lucky Omen 99 (Queen's Hussar **107**
124) (1981 5g⁴ 5g* 5d⁴ 5f 5g 5g² 6d⁴ 5g 6g² 1982 6g⁴ 5s⁴ 5fg 6f² 6f⁴ 5fg* 5fg
6f 6fg* 6f 5g 5g 6g) strong, compact, good sort; very useful sprinter; beat
Havara by 3 lengths in Alington Stakes at Sandown in June and wasn't troubled
to account for Hollow Heart by 2 lengths in Hackwood Stakes at Newbury in
July; creditable fifth to Sharpo in William Hill Sprint Championship at York in
August on eleventh start; stays 6f; seems to act on any going; often blinkered
but is effective without; sweated up badly eighth start and moved poorly to
start on final appearance; not particularly consistent. *C. Brittain.*

LUCKY IVOR (USA) 3 b.c. Sir Ivor 135–Carnival Queen (Amerigo 116§) **83**
(1981 7d⁴ 1982 12g 14g* 16.5fg* 14g⁴ 16.5s 18d) big, rangy colt; won maiden
race at Yarmouth and minor event at Redcar (odds on) in September; stays well;
possibly unsuited by very soft going; gave trouble going into stalls and ran rather
in snatches first outing. *J. Dunlop.*

LUCKY JENNIE 2 b.f. Lucky Wednesday 124–Miss Cameron 76 (Decoy Boy **59**
129) (1982 5d 5g 6fg 6d 6g) Apr 17; leggy, rather narrow filly; first foal;
dam won over 5f; poor maiden; stays 6f; sold 330 gns Ascot December Sales.
N. Vigors.

LUCKY JOKER 3 br.f. Cawston's Clown 113–Charlie's Double (Fighting **47**
Charlie 127) (1981 5g 5s⁴ 6s² 6f 7fg* 6fg 7s 7g 1982 12d 12f 8f 10d 10f³ 12fg⁴
11g 10.4d⁴ 10.6f⁴ 13d 12d 10.2s) lengthy, rather dipped-backed filly; won
maiden race at Wolverhampton at 2 yrs; showed poor form in 1982, including in
a seller; possibly stays 1½m; acts on any going; has run respectably for an
apprentice. *R. Hollinshead.*

LUCKY KNIGHT 2 b.c. Rarity 129–Emerin 85 (King Emperor) (1982 7fg) —
May 4; 3,200Y; useful-looking colt; first foal; dam won twice over 6f; unquoted,
backward and green, last of 19 in maiden race at Salisbury in September. *B.
Swift.*

LUCKY LUCY 3 gr.f. Comedy Star 121–Lovely Beak (Counsel 118) (1981 —
6s 6fg 6f 7fg 1982 8d 12d) fair sort; poor maiden; wears bandages. *C. Gray.*

LUCKY MADAM 2 b.f. Lucky Wednesday 124–Polistina 106 (Acropolis 132) —
(1982 6g) June 22; 600Y; quite a useful sort; half-sister to 3 winners, including
fairly useful 1m winner Polisteppin (by Jimmy Reppin); dam stayed 7f; slow-
starting last of 9 in maiden race at Haydock in July. *D. H. Jones.*

LUCKY MAN 6 b.g. Manacle 123–Quite Sweet 100 (Super Sam 124) (1981 **98**
8s 7d 7d³ 7g 7fg 7fg 7g 7fg² 7fg² 7fg³ 7s² 6s* 7d 1982 7f 7fg³ 7f⁴ 6f 7g 7f* 7f²
7f⁴ 7.3g 7s*) workmanlike gelding; fairly useful handicapper who maintains
his form and enthusiasm well; battled on well when beating Basil Boy by a
neck at Newbury in July and when dead-heating with Hello Sunshine after
disputing lead throughout in valuable Pearce Duff Handicap at Ascot in September; finds 6f on fast ground too sharp and stays 1m; acts on any going; good
mount for a boy; started slowly ninth outing; tough and genuine, although
soundly beaten fourth and fifth starts. *P. M. Taylor.*

LUCKY MISTAKE 5 gr.m. Averof 123–Kingdom Come 77 (Klondyke Bill 125) **49**
(1981 10.2s 7d 8g 7d 8d 7d 8g³ 8f 7f 8f 10g 8f 1982 10.2g 8g 8fg² 12f² 11.5fg
10g) strong mare; plater; good second in amateur riders races at Warwick
and Redcar; stays 1½m; acts on hard going; blinkered twice in 1980; has worn
bandages, sometimes sweats up; sold 5,800 gns Ascot December Sales. *W.
Marshall.*

LUCKY ORPHAN 2 b.f. Derrylin 115–Sinkit (Sing Sing 134) (1982 6fg 6fg³ 8s) **73**
May 14; close-coupled, lightly-made filly; half-sister to 3-y-o 8.2f winner Sparkling Sin (by Sparkler) and 1980 2-y-o 6f winner Sea Aura (by Roi Soleil); dam
never ran; quite a modest maiden; stays 6f. *R. Boss.*

LUCKY OXTON 3 b.g. Lucky Wednesday 124–Oxton Lady 81 (Chebs Lad —
120) (1981 5g 5g 5g 5f 7fg 1982 7fg) leggy, narrow non-thoroughbred gelding;
poor maiden. *M. W. Easterby.*

LUCKY SEASON 3 br.f. Lucky Wednesday 124–Honey Season 66 (Silly —
Season 127) (1981 5g⁴ 5d⁴ 5g* 6f² 1982 8f 8f 7g 8s) rather leggy filly; plater;
bred to stay 1¼m; has been tried in blinkers; sold 680 gns Doncaster November
Sales. *P. Felgate.*

LUCKY TUESDAY 3 ch.f. Lucky Wednesday 124–Lady Phoenix (Lorenzaccio —
130) (1981 5g² 5g 6g 7f 7.2v 5g 1982 7f 8f 9f) lightly-made filly; poor plater.
D. Yeoman.

LUCKY WEDDING 3 b.f. Lucky Wednesday 124–Lilmi Love 82 (Miralgo 130) **52**
(1981 5s 6fg 5g 5d 5s⁴ 1982 8f³ 7g 8.3fg 8g 8fg 10fg) plater; stays 1m; has
twice been blinkered; trained part of season by V. Soane. *S. Matthews.*

LUCY PLATTER (FR) 2 br.f. Record Token 128–Luciennes 108 (Grey **74**
Sovereign 128§) (1982 5s 5s 5v³) June 1; 23,000Y; half-sister to 3 winners,
including very smart sprinter Broxted (by Busted); dam won her first 2 starts
at 2 yrs; 1¾ lengths third of 9 to Kiwiette in maiden race at Hamilton in October;
will stay 6f; yet to race on a sound surface. *M. W. Easterby.*

LUCY RAYNALDS 2 b. or br.f. So Blessed 130–Ciao (Mandamus 120) (1982 **79**
6fg 7f² 7g 7fg) Mar 11; 10,000Y; leggy, quite attractive filly; good mover;
second living foal; dam Irish 5f winner; moderate maiden; stays 7f; acts on
firm going. *P. Kelleway.*

LUIGI'S GLORY 2 b.g. Hittite Glory 125–Glengarry 72 (High Hat 131) (1982 **72**
5d 5fg 6g 5fg 7g* 8.2v²) May 23; 3,000F, 10,000Y; seventh foal; dam half-
sister to numerous winners; claimed out of B. Hills's stable after winning 11-
runner race at Yarmouth in September by a neck from unlucky-in-running
Jad; good second to Sea Reppin in nursery at Hamilton the following month;
stays 1m; acts on heavy going. *R. Williams.*

LUISA MILLER 2 b.f. Wollow 132–Marthe Meynet (Welsh Pageant 132) **83**
(1982 6g 6fg 6s² 6g*) May 1; neat filly; second foal; half-sister to fair 1981
2-y-o 5f winner Batoni (by Realm); dam never ran; very useful in selling company and ran out a 4-length winner from Saleaf in £2,700 event at Newmarket in
October; sold 8,000 gns afterwards, for export to Italy; will stay 1m; acts on
soft going. *M. H. Easterby.*

LULAV 4 br.g. Prince Regent 129–Scarletta 103 (Red God 128§) (1981 12s **80**
12d* 10f 12fg³ 14g⁴ 12fg* 10fg³ 10fg 11.1fg³ 10g² 9g³ 12g 1982 8g 10fg 12fg²
10fg² 12f³ 10d 10d) well-made gelding; placed in handicaps at Goodwood and
Salisbury in May and Newbury in June, probably best efforts; probably finds
1m too sharp for him and stays 1½m; yet to show he can handle very soft going,
but acts on any other; useful hurdler. *R. Hannon.*

LULUWA (USA) 3 ch.f. Secretariat–Krassata 114 (Nijinsky 138) (1981 —
NR 1982 12f 16d) $400,000Y; fair sort; first foal; dam fourth in Irish 1,000
Guineas and Irish Guinness Oaks, and was also a very useful winner at up to 9f
in USA; beaten a long way in minor event at Salisbury in May and maiden
race at Nottingham in June; sold 60,000 dollars Keeneland November Sales.
J. Tree.

LUMEN 7 br.g. Prince Tenderfoot 126–Bright Match 73 (Match III 135) (1981 —
16d 12fg 18g 1982 19s⁴) compact, deep-girthed gelding; useful hurdler;
lightly raced on flat nowadays, but retains some ability and finished respectable
fourth to King's College Boy in handicap at Goodwood in September; stays
well; acts on any going but goes well on a sound surface; used to wear blinkers;
suitable mount for an inexperienced rider. *J. Gifford.*

LUMINEUX (USA) 3 b.c. Majestic Light–Imperial Spirit (Never Bend) (1981 **101**
8v³ 1982 8s* 9.2d 11fg* 12s³ 8.5f) $155,000Y; neat, quite attractive colt;
fourth foal; half-brother to 3 winners in USA, 2 of them stakes-placed; dam
never ran; won 10-runner maiden race at Saint-Cloud in March and 19-runner
handicap at Longchamp the following month, latter decisively by 1½ lengths
from Premier Concert; led over 5f when well-beaten fifth of 8 to Prima Voce in
Diomed Stakes at Epsom in June; not seen out again; stays 1½m; seems to act
on any going. *F. Boutin, France.*

LUNAR HARVEST 2 b.f. Whitstead 125–Moon Lover (Forlorn River 124) —
(1982 8.2s) Apr 16; first foal; dam, well beaten both starts, is sister to 3 winners;
last of 11 in seller at Hamilton in September. *B. Hanbury.*

LUNAR WIND 7 ch.g. Windjammer (USA)–Lunar Star (Star Gazer 123) (1981 **63** 9f* 8fg* 8fg 8f* 9d 8.2f² 7g³ 8fg* 1982 7fg 8f 8f 8f² 9fg 8fg) leggy, narrow gelding; ran best race when second in handicap at Beverley in May; best at up to 9f on top-of-the-ground; has worn blinkers; good mount for an apprentice. *J. Parkes.*

LUSITANICA 5 b.m. Pieces of Eight 128–Auspice 84 (Aureole 132) (1981 **89** 10g 8d⁴ 10g* 10fg 10.2fg 10d² 10g* 10fg* 10fg³ 11g⁴ 12g 12s 12g² 10.2d⁴ 1982 10f 16g 16.1f* 15fg* 12g* 14g² 14.6g⁴ 13.3g 18d) lengthy mare; much improved and put up a good performance when beating Cannon King by 2 lengths in Owens Group of New Zealand Handicap at Newmarket in August; ran a fine race when 3 lengths second to Another Sam in Tote-Ebor at York later in August and was by no means disgraced most subsequent outings; had won 2 rather slowly-run handicaps in July, beating Dragon Palace gamely by 1½ lengths at Newmarket and First Mint by ½ length in £10,800 Tennent Trophy at Ayr; effective at 1¼m and clearly stays pretty well; acts on any going; goes particularly well for apprentice A. Mackay; usually held up and has a fair turn of foot; tough, genuine and consistent; wore bandages in front when pulled up lame final start. *M. Tompkins.*

LUSTRE LINE 3 ch.c. High Line 125–Palmyrrha 98 (Palestine 133) (1981 NR 1982 8f 10.1fg 10g 12fg 12v) 7,400F, 15,000Y; half-brother to 3 winners; dam 2-y-o 5f winner; soundly beaten in maiden and minor events; sold out of T. Robson's stable 4,200 gns Ascot July Sales after fourth start. *G. Kindersley.*

LUXURIATE (USA) 5 b.g. Tom Rolfe–Dee Dee Luxe (Cavan) (1981 14fg — 1982 16.1g 17.1g³) staying maiden; acts on firm going; usually blinkered in 1980. *I. Wardle.*

LUXURY 3 b.f. Ragapan 118–Vanessa's Queen (Faberge II 121) (1981 5g³ 5d **73** 6g³ 7fg² 7f 7fg² 8fg 8g³ 8fg² 8s⁴ 10s* 10.2g³ 1982 12fg 12f 16.1h⁴ 13.8f² 13.8f³ 14g 14.7fg² 16s² 15.8d* 16s³ 15d) lightly-made filly; staying handicapper; won at Catterick in October; acts on any going but is ideally suited by some give underfoot; sometimes sweats up and rarely impresses in paddock. *J. Carr.*

LYDIEN 3 gr.f. Sandford Lad 133–Purissima (Walhalla) (1981 NR 1982 14g — 14s) lengthy filly; fourth reported living foal; dam never ran; well beaten in minor event at Newmarket and maiden race at Sandown in October. *R. Boss.*

LYMINSTER 2 gr.c. Hittite Glory 125–January (Sigebert 131) (1982 7g 8fg **91** 8s² 8s 9s²) Apr 30; compact colt; half-brother to 1m winner Rifle Green (by Scottish Rifle) and useful hurdler Janus (by Ragstone); dam placed twice at around 11f in France; second twice in the autumn, to very easy winner Proclaim in £3,400 event at Goodwood and to Omar Ramsden, beaten neck after looking to have race won, in maiden event at Redcar; possibly best at 1m; acts on soft going. *J. Dunlop.*

LYMOND 3 b.c. Rapid River 127–Gill Breeze (Farm Walk 111) (1981 5s 5g⁴ **58** 6f⁴ 6f 6fg 6fg 5s 1982 7fg 6f 7f² 8f 8f 6f 8fg 10d 8fg³ 8.2g 9s⁴ 8.2s² 8s 8s⁴) fair sort; plating-class maiden; possibly stays 1¼m; acts on any going; blinkered last 2 outings at 2 yrs. *J. Calvert.*

LYNESS DETECTIVE 3 b.g. Most Secret 119–Whistlewych 40 (Whistler 129) — (1981 5g 5g 7f 1982 7g 7.2f 9g 7fg 8.2g 7s⁴ 8d 8d) workmanlike gelding; plater; best run at 7f on soft going. *Mrs M. Nesbitt.*

LYNETZKY 2 br.f. Radetzky 123–Nellykelly (Polyfoto 124) (1982 5fg 6g 7g — 6fg 7d 6g) Apr 27; 4,500Y; smallish, lengthy filly; no sign of ability, including in a seller; sold 330 gns Doncaster November Sales. *P. Brookshaw.*

LYNN LIGHTFOOT 3 b.f. St Paddy 133–Quick Half 60 (Quorum 126 or — Caliban 123) (1981 5g 7.2v 1982 12.2f 12f 8f) leggy filly; has stringhalt; of little account; sold to W. Turner 660 gns Doncaster June Sales. *D. McCain.*

LYPHARD'S PRIDE (USA) 3 b. or br.c. Lyphard 132–Maidsmorton (Bold **85** Ruler) (1981 7fg² 8g 1982 10f² 10f* 12f 12.3fg³ 11.7fg³ 12f² 12g² 12fg² 12g³ 12.2s 12.2d*) neat, attractive colt; landed odds in maiden race at Brighton in May and apprentice event at Catterick in October; placed in handicaps in between; suited by 1½m; probably acts on any going; ran freely in blinkers third start. *M. Stoute.*

LYPHARD'S SPECIAL (USA) 2 b.c. Lyphard 132–My Bupers (Bupers) **122** (1982 6f* 6d* 7f* 7f² 8s² 8d³)
At 450,000 dollars Lyphard's Special was the most expensive yearling bought by the Harwood-Delahooke partnership up to the end of 1981. Why

Lady Harrison's "Lyphard's Special"

they had been prepared to pay so much was easy to see when Lyphard's Special first appeared at Newbury in June in a division of the Kennett Maiden Stakes. He proved to be a splendid individual, rangy, good-bodied and very attractive; at the same time he looked very much as though the race was needed, a view supported by the way he drifted out from 2/1 to 9/1. In the circumstances he did extremely well to win, running on very strongly to catch another newcomer, Gallant Special, in the closing stages, getting home by half a length without being hard ridden. Lyphard's Special also looked decidedly green at Newbury and Harwood quickly gave him two more runs to further his education in the Champagne Stakes at Salisbury and a three-runner event at Kempton. He won both in fine style, scoring particularly impressively at Salisbury. After being steadied behind the leaders he lengthened his stride to take the lead soon after halfway and had built up a four-length lead by the last two hundred yards. Starkey then began looking round and easing him up, completely unnecessarily, and his advantage over Greene Normandy had been reduced to two and a half lengths by the post.

The one slightly worrying aspect of Lyphard's Special's performance at Kempton, afterwards discounted by his trainer, was his behaviour in the paddock: he was very full of himself. When Lyphard's Special reappeared in the Lanson Champagne Stakes at Goodwood later in July he was ridden by a lad in the paddock and bounced around on very good terms with himself. He faced a stiff task, having to give 6 lb to all except the Cock of the North Stakes winner Alchise, and met his first defeat. His chance didn't look bright when he came under the whip over two furlongs out but he kept on very well and, together with All Systems Go, moved past the long-time leader Alchise entering the final furlong. After a splendid fight to the line Lyphard's Special came off the worse by a head. Lyphard's Special was also beaten in both his subsequent starts, the Royal Lodge Stakes at Ascot at the end of September and the William

Hill Futurity at Doncaster a month later. He ran well in both. At Ascot he finished second, beaten one and a half lengths by Dunbeath, after moving through with the winner two furlongs out; at Doncaster he was again made to look one paced as Dunbeath quickened away in the final furlong, and this time he lost second place close home to the strong-finishing Cock Robin.

		Northern Dancer	Nearctic
Lyphard's Special (USA) (b.c. Feb 17, 1980)	Lyphard (b 1969)	(b 1961)	Natalma
		Goofed (ch 1960)	Court Martial
			Barra
	My Bupers (b or br 1967)	Bupers (b 1961)	Double Jay
			Busanda
		Princess Revoked (br 1959)	Revoked
			Miss Muffet

Lyphard's Special is a half-brother to six winners, including the useful 1981 French two-year-old Embarrassed (by Blushing Groom). Easily best of the six was the Gallant Romeo filly My Juliet who dominated the year-end voting for the champion American sprinter in 1976, having won six of her eight starts that year including the seven-furlong Vosburgh Handicap. We have pointed out before that the American concept of a sprinter varies somewhat from the European. My Juliet is a fine example—only two of her victories in 1976 were gained over as short a distance as six furlongs and she later won the Michigan Mile and One Eighth Handicap. In all she won twenty-four of her thirty-six starts and retired with earnings of 548,859 dollars, a far cry from the 1,581 dollars amassed by her dam My Bupers in thirteen starts. My Bupers was herself a half-sister to four winners, including the minor sprint stakes winner Readyfourshoes and the fairly useful 1979 English two-year-old five-furlong performer Stormont. The next dam Princess Revoked won eight times and was once third in a stakes race over six furlongs. Lyphard's Special stayed a mile well at two; it's not easy to say how much further he will stay but he'll probably get a mile and a quarter. He's consistent, acts on any going and is such a good sort that he looks sure to train on. *G. Harwood.*

LYPHMAS (USA) 3 b.c. Lyphard 132–Christmas Belle (Santa Claus 133) **108** (1981 7g* 1982 10f 12fg* 12f) attractive colt; half-brother to 11f and 1¾m winner Tom Noel (by Tom Rolfe); dam, Irish middle-distance winner, is half-sister to smart Royal Sword; very strongly ridden to lead in final strides and beat Rajhaan by a neck in 5-runner Churchill Stakes at Ascot in June; not disgraced in Guardian Classic Trial at Sandown previous start; dropped away in closing stages to be last of 6 to Electric in Gordon Stakes at Goodwood in July on only other start; suited by 1½m; sent to USA to be trained by C. Whittingham. *H. Cecil.*

LYPHNAP (USA) 2 b.f. Lyphard 132–Smooth 111 (Bound I Pack 132) (1982 **96** 5g⁴ 6g³) Mar 6; $450,000V; smallish, strong, good-bodied, attractive filly; half-sister to several winners, including very useful 1979 2-y-o 6f performer Suavity (by Personality); dam game sprinter; in frame in 8-runner St Hugh's Stakes at Newbury in August and 19-runner maiden race (second favourite) at Newmarket in September; stays 6f. *J Tree.*

LYRE D'OR (FR) 2 b.f. Lyphard 132–Arme d'Or (Armistice 131) (1982 **?** 9s² 10v*) half-sister to several winners including smart French middle-distance colts Arc d'Or (by Ack Ack), Caron (by Caro) and Oreste (by Luthier) and good North American stakes winner Morold (by Sir Gaylord); dam smart at around 1½m; odds on when winning 11-runner maiden race at Saint-Cloud in October by a neck from Clem; will stay 1½m; a very well-related filly who will go on to better things. *J. Cunnington, jnr, France.*

M

MAARIV 2 b.c. Godswalk 130–Catilina (Sallust 134) (1982 5s⁴ 5g* 5fg* 5fg² **97** 5f 5f³) Apr 7; IR 4,700F, IR 17,000Y; workmanlike colt; second produce; dam lightly-raced daughter of sister to Wolver Hollow; came to hand early, winning at Newbury and Epsom in April, and not seen out again after finishing creditable third (blinkered) behind Brondesbury and Krayyan in Norfolk Stakes at Royal Ascot; will stay 6f; acts on firm going; sent to USA. *R. Hannon.*

MABELLA 2 b.f. Julio Mariner 127–Dorabella 88 (Rockefella) (1982 7g) **—** May 1; 6,000F, 5,000Y; half-sister to several winners here and abroad, including useful 1977 staying 2-y-o Fiordiligi (by Tudor Melody); dam, winner over 9f and 1½m, is half-sister to Anamnestes and Arietta; 33/1 and backward, no show in 21-runner maiden race at Newmarket in October. *W. Elsey.*

MA BICHE (USA) 2 b. or br.f. Key To The Kingdom–Madge (Roi Dagobert **123** 128) (1982 5s³ 5.5g* 7g* 5.5g* 6fg³ 6g*)

The French filly Ma Biche had a family tradition to uphold when she lined up alongside six home-trained fillies and two Irish challengers in the William Hill Cheveley Park Stakes at Newmarket in September: her dam Madge is a half-sister to the 1968 winner Mige, and her grandam Midget II was an impressive winner of the race in 1955. Ma Biche didn't let her predecessors down. When a narrow gap appeared between the long-time leader Sweet Emma, winner of the Phoenix Stakes, and her nearest pursuer Super Entente, Ma Biche burst through to lead running into the Dip, getting first run on the favourite Favoridge in the process. After looking likely to be beaten when Favoridge drew up to her quarters entering the final furlong, Ma Biche stayed on strongly to keep her at bay, crossing the line three quarters of a length to the good. Favoridge is a high-class filly, she'd shown that by slamming Crime of Passion in the St Hugh's Stakes at Newbury the previous month, so this was a splendid effort. Among those further behind were Widaad, the Queen Mary Stakes winner, Myra's Best, who'd accounted for a good field in the Firth of Clyde Stakes on her last outing, and Shicklah, a clear-cut winner of Germany's most valuable two-year-old race, the Zukunfts-Rennen.

Ma Biche had come to the Cheveley Park with a more impressive record than either Mige, the winner of a newcomers race on her only appearance, or Midget who, from two runs, had been placed in the Prix Yacowlef and Prix Morny. Ma Biche had won three of her five races, gaining the last of her wins in the Prix Robert Papin at Maisons-Laffitte late in July. Considering that the Papin usually attracts some of Europe's speediest juveniles Ma Biche had an unusual preparation. After winning a minor race at Evry in June she returned to the same course for the Prix La Fleche, a fairly valuable seven-furlong race which drew seven other previous winners. She showed she was very much on the upgrade, catching the front-running Sevruga at the distance and drawing away to beat her by two and a half lengths with the rest, headed by the very useful Interco, three lengths further back. Naturally enough Ma Biche found the likes of the Cherry Hinton winner Crime of Passion and the demoted Prix du Bois winner Deep Roots much tougher nuts to crack when brought back to five and a half furlongs in the Papin. Both were in front of her entering the final furlong but Ma Biche's jockey was already applying very strong pressure and she gamely forged past to win by a length and a half from Deep Roots. Perhaps Ma Biche hadn't fully recovered from her hard race when she and Deep Roots renewed rivalry in the Prix Morny at Deauville four weeks later; she couldn't quicken after showing up throughout and Deep Roots gained his revenge

Prix Robert Papin, Maisons-Laffitte—Ma Biche keeps on well to win from Deep Roots (No. 1) and the British-trained Crime of Passion

*William Hill Cheveley Park Stakes, Newmarket—a second Group 1
pattern race success for Ma Biche. Favoridge
finishes second*

by three lengths. The English colt On Stage also beat her, pipping her by a
short head for second. Possibly the firmish going was a contributory factor
to her slightly below-par performance: she has a short, round action, the type
often best suited by some give in the ground.

			Bold Ruler	Nasrullah
			(b 1954)	Miss Disco
	Key To The Kingdom		Key Bridge	Princequillo
	(b or br 1970)		(b 1959)	Blue Banner
Ma Biche (USA)			Roi Dagobert	Sicambre
(b. or br.f.			(b 1964)	Dame d'Atour
Jan 23, 1980)	Madge		Midget II	Djebe
	(b 1975)		(gr 1953)	Mimi

Ma Biche's prospects are much easier to assess than many a Cheveley Park
winner's. She is a taking individual, big, rangy and good bodied, who seems
certain to train on; and we see nothing in her pedigree or temperament to suggest
she won't be suited by a mile. Her sire Key To The Kingdom is a half-brother
to two top-class performers at up to a mile and a half in the States, the dual
Washington International winner Fort Marcy and the champion 1972 three-
year-old Key to the Mint, and to the very smart Key to Content who won at up
to nine furlongs. Key To The Kingdom also won at up to nine furlongs, gaining
his only stakes victory over that trip. He wasn't so good as his half-brothers
but he was nonetheless very useful and fetched 730,000 dollars when sold in
1975, a world record price for a horse in training. His other 1982 two-year-olds
include the American filly For Once'n My Life, winner of the Grade 1 Arlington-
Washington Lassie Stakes over seven furlongs.

Ma Biche is Madge's first foal. Madge, after winning a newcomers race over
a little less than eleven furlongs, spent most of her time acting as a pacemaker
for her stablemates Reine de Saba and Dancing Maid when they won the Prix
Saint-Alary, the Prix de Diane de Revlon and the Prix Vermeille. Madge was
the last of Midget's twelve foals, born when her dam was twenty-two, and
became her ninth winner. Mige wasn't the only smart performer among them:
Midou, a sister to Mige, finished a good fourth in both the Poule d'Essai des
Pouliches and the Prix de la Foret. Neither, however, was so good as her dam.
Midget didn't stay so well as one of her half-brothers, the King George VI and
Queen Elizabeth Stakes winner Vimy, but she stayed well enough to finish
third in the Prix de Diane over ten and a half furlongs and later showed an

Mme A. Head's "Ma Biche"

admirable versatility, winning the one-mile Coronation Stakes, the six-furlong Prix de Seine-et-Oise and the seven-furlong Prix de la Foret. Both Ma Biche and her stable-companion Maximova are entered in the One Thousand Guineas. Reports suggest that Ma Biche is the likelier to come; if she does run she must have a first-rate chance of succeeding where Midget (second to Honeylight) and Mige (fifth to Full Dress II) both failed. *Mme C. Head, France.*

MACMILLION 3 br.c. So Blessed 130–Salsafy 81 (Tudor Melody 129) (1981 **99 ?** 6d 6g² 6fg 7fg* 6f² 6d² 7s 1982 7fg³ 8fg 6d 8g² 7.3g 7g 8s²) workmanlike colt; ran well to be placed in Clerical, Medical Greenham Stakes at Newbury (1¼ lengths third of 5 to Cajun), £5,600 handicap at Sandown (apprentice ridden when 2 lengths second to Sauvage) and minor event at Doncaster (second to Chris's Lad); soundly beaten in 2,000 Guineas at Newmarket and Hungerford Stakes at Newbury on 2 of his other starts; suited by 1m; acts on any going; usually ridden up with pace; trained by Mrs B. Waring first 5 starts. *A. Bailey.*

MACPHAIL 2 b.g. Captain James 123–Sadie Thompson 82 (Sheshoon 132) — (1982 6g) May 20; 5,000F, IR 5,000Y; tall, well-made gelding; third produce; dam 11f winner; 40/1 and in need of race, in trouble before halfway when distant last of 5 to On Stage in £5,200 event at Ascot in September. *P. Walwyn*

MAC'S DELIGHT 5 ch.g. Scottish Rifle 127–Halkissimo 61 (Khalkis 127) — (1981 12.3d³ 12s⁴ 12g² 10g² 11g² 10.2fg³ 12.3fg* 10f³ 12f² 15.8g 1982 13fg) strong gelding; stays 1½m; acts on any going but goes well on top-of-the-ground; often blinkered but is effective without; suitable mount for a boy; doesn't always find much off bridle. *R. Carter.*

MAC'S GIFT 2 ch.g. Anax 120–Mini Pie 61 (Dike) (1982 5f 6fg 7fg 6g) Mar — 22; leggy gelding; good walker; first foal; dam 1m winner at 4 yrs; behind in maiden and minor events; not seen out after August. *D. Smith.*

MAC'S MELODY 2 br.f. Wollow 132–Salsafy 81 (Tudor Melody 129) (1982 — 6g) Jan 20; 8,200Y; third foal; half-sister to very useful 3-y-o Macmillion (by So Blessed) and to Baz Bombati (by Sun Prince), a very useful winner at up to 1½m; dam won over 12.2f; 20/1, behind in 19-runner minor event at Windsor in August. *Mrs B. Waring.*

MAC'S PALACE 2 gr.c. Dragonara Palace 115–Swan Ann 84 (My Swanee 122) **113** (1982 5f³ 5fg* 5fg* 6fg* 5g 6f² 5g² 7g 5v² 5d³) Apr 16; 4,200Y; rangy, useful-looking colt; half-brother to useful 6f and 7f winner Poyle Crusher (by Sweet Revenge) and speedy Swan Princess (by So Blessed); dam won over 6f; won maiden race at Leicester in June, minor event at Windsor the following month, and Tolly Cobbold Trophy (nursery) at Newmarket in August; placed in very useful company subsequently, including short-head second to Orange Squash in Bonusprint Sirenia Stakes at Kempton, ¾ length second to Jonacris in Harry Rosebery Challenge Trophy at Ayr, and 1½ lengths runner-up to Tatibah in Cornwallis Stakes at Ascot; effective at 5f and 6f; acts on any going; bandaged in front last 5 starts; thoroughly game and consistent. *W. O'Gorman.*

MAC'S TREASURE 5 ch.h. Pieces of Eight 128–Taurette (Major Portion 129) — (1981 NR 1982 13.1g 16fg 17.1s) small, strong horse; plater in 1980; lightly raced and no form on flat since; stays 1¼m; best form on a sound surface; has been tried in blinkers. *J. Old.*

MADAGASCAR 2 ch.g. Warpath 113–Jasmin (Frankincense 120) (1982 6g **71** 6g 7g) May 20; workmanlike gelding; good walker; third foal; dam unraced half-sister to very useful sprinter High Sun; quite a modest maiden; disappointing favourite in £2,800 seller at Newmarket in September on final appearance; should be suited by 7f. *C. Thornton.*

MADAM BREEZE 2 br.f. Tumble Wind–Golda (Red God 128§) (1982 5fg⁴ **58** 6g 6fg 6g) Feb 24; IR 7,000F, IR 12,000Y; well-grown, leggy filly; fourth foal; half-sister to fairly useful Irish 1975 2-y-o 5f winner Harford Belle (by Track Spare); dam moderate half-sister to Oaks winner Ginevra; plating-class maiden; no form after first outing. *R. Hollinshead.*

MADAM DIX PER CENT 3 b.f. Import 127–Yolancar 65 (Kibenka 119) — (1981 7fg 8fg 1982 8d 10f) plain, leggy filly; in rear in Northern maiden races; dead. *Mrs M. Nesbitt.*

MADAME BLEU 3 gr.f. Bruni 132–La Sinope (Thatch 136) (1981 6f 6f **44** 1982 13g 12.2f 12d 9s*) fair sort; dropped in class, attracted no bid after winning seller at Hamilton in September; had looked temperamental on occasions previously; should have stayed 1¼m; acted on soft going; blinkered third start; injured foot at Hamilton and has been retired. *K. Stone.*

Tolly Cobbold Trophy Nursery Handicap, Newmarket—Mac's Palace gets home from the hanging Solar Rock

MADAME MIM 2 b.f. Artaius 129–Spring Valley (Val de Loir 133) (1982 —
· 6g 7d) Mar 3; $25,000Y; fair sort; second foal; dam won small 9f race in
France; unquoted, little show in maiden races at Newmarket in September and
Leicester (eighth of 15) in October. *B. Hanbury.*

MADAME NON 3 gr.f. My Swanee 122–Aunt Jane (Le Levanstell 122) (1981 —
NR 1982 10s 10g) strong filly; half-sister to 3 winners, including useful 1973
staying 2-y-o Uncle Cyril (by I Say); dam poor sprint maiden; tailed-off last
in maiden races at Sandown and Newmarket in October. *Peter Taylor.*

MADAM FLUTTERBYE 2 ch.f. Quiet Fling 124–Balgreggan (Hallez 131) **75**
(1982 7fg 8f⁴) Mar 6; second foal; half-sister to useful 5f performer Street
Market (by Porto Bello); dam twice-raced half-sister to smart stayer Golden
Love; 6¼ lengths fourth of 23 to Artiste in maiden race at Leicester in September;
stays well, and will need 1¼m+. *N. Vigors.*

MADAM IMPORT 2 ch.f. Import 127–Chinese Falcon 81 (Skymaster 126) **63**
(1982 5s³ 5g⁴(dis) 5f 5g 5g) May 25; fair sort; carries plenty of condition;
second foal; sister to successful 5f performer Miss Import; dam 2-y-o 6f winner;
plating-class maiden; best run on first appearance; blinkered on final one.
T. Barron.

MADISON STYLE 4 b.g. Crowned Prince 128–Monte Rosa (Crepello 136) **48**
(1981 8g 7g 7f 7g³ 6f 8fg² 7.2g 9f 8f 8g 1982 8f³ 7f 10f³ 7f 7g) leggy, lightly-
made gelding; rather a disappointing maiden; possibly stays 1¼m; yet to
race on a soft surface; often bandaged; ran poorly in blinkers once, exported to
Malaysia. *F. J. Houghton.*

MAD MONEY 4 br.g. Silly Season 127–Generous Thought 81 (Compensation **48**
127) (1981 8fg 12g 10fg 10d 12fg 1982 8.2s³ 10f 8g* 11g 9f 8.2f 8.2s 10s) big
gelding; attracted no bid after winning seller at Ayr in May; stays 1m well;
sometimes bandaged nowadays; sold 2,000 gns Ascot November Sales, reportedly
for export to Italy. *D. Garraton.*

MADONA 3 ch.f. Manado 130–Light Diamond (Florescence 120) (1981 5s **56**
5.3f 5fg³ 5g 5d 1982 6fg³ 6f 5fg³ 6d³ 7d) small, rather lightly-made filly;
sprint maiden; acts on a firm and a soft surface; trained part of season by P.
Haslam. *G. Lewis.*

MADRIGAL MAID 2 b.f. Tudor Rhythm 112–Whistler's Princess (King **54**
Emperor) (1982 6f 5s⁴ 5g) Apr 3; small filly; second foal; dam poor maiden;
plating-class maiden; not seen out after July. *W. Wharton.*

MAESTRETTE 2 b.f. Manado 130–Camogie (Celtic Ash) (1982 6fg³ 7g³ **75**
8s² 8d²) Mar 1; IR 24,000Y; leggy, lightly-made filly; half-sister to very
useful Never A Lady (by Pontifex), a winner over 5f and 1m; dam unraced
daughter of leading 1963 2-y-o Mesopotamia; placed in maiden events, appearing
to improve with her races; off course 3 months after second outing; will be suited
by 1¼m; seems to act on any going. *S. Norton.*

MAESTRO LADY 2 b.f. Music Maestro 119–Silver Peggie 61 (Song 132) (1982 **47**
5d 6s²) June 2; small filly; first foal; very closely inbred to Song; dam won 5f
seller at 2 yrs; claimed to race in Sweden after finishing 6 lengths second to
Hopeful Waters at Nottingham in October. *M. Tompkins.*

MAFOO'S MESSAGE 2 gr.g. Moulton 128–Queens Message 93 (Town Crier —
119) (1982 8s) Mar 21; 5,800Y; workmanlike gelding; third foal; brother to a
disappointing animal; dam speedy 2-y-o; tailed-off last of 13 after starting
slowly in maiden race at Warwick in October. *J. Bethell.*

MAGELKA 3 ch.f. Relkino 131–Magical 95 (Aggressor 130) (1981 7g 7f⁴ 8fg —
1982 7fg 10g) good-topped filly; has shown ability but ran as though something
was wrong with her final start; should be suited by 1¼m. *M. Jarvis.*

MAGIC EARS 3 ch.f. Mandrake Major 122–Burning Ears 87 (Firestreak 125) —
(1981 6f 7g 7fg 7g 1982 9.4fg 12.2f 12f) smallish, workmanlike filly; behind
in maiden races and a minor event; blinkered last 2 starts. *E. Weymes.*

MAGIC MINK 2 ch.c. Record Token 128–Cowbells (Mountain Call 125) (1982 **72**
7d 7fg 7fg 8g) Apr 5; 6,000Y; lengthy, useful-looking colt; good walker;
first foal; dam never ran; quite moderate maiden; dwelt when blinkered final
outing. *C. Nelson.*

MAGIC RARITY 2 b.c. Rarity 129–Magic Shoes (Henry the Seventh 125) **95** p
(1982 8s*) Apr 10; IR 44,000Y; tall, short-backed, quite attractive colt;
third foal; half-brother to 2 winners, including Maria Stuarda (by Royal and

Regal), winner of Group 2 Premio Tevere over 1m at 2 yrs in 1981; dam ran only 4 times; without being given hard race, recovered from bump entering last furlong to win 26-runner maiden event at Sandown in October at 33/1 by short head from Jasper; will stay at least 1¼m; bound to improve. *G. Harwood.*

MAGIC SOVEREIGN 4 gr.g. Young Emperor 133–Magic Lady (Gala Per- — formance) (1981 NR 1982 10.1fg 8.3fg 7f 5.3g) lightly-raced plater; showed some ability over 5f at 2 yrs; blinkered third start; sold 1,000 gns Ascot July Sales. *H. Beasley.*

MAGJOY 5 b.f. Le Johnstan 123–Rockfire 65 (Epaulette 125) (1981 5g 5f — 1982 7f) leggy, lightly-made filly; well beaten in maiden events and a seller. *R. Woodhouse.*

MAGNAMALA 3 ro.g. Runnymede 123–Mala Mala (Crepello 136) (1981 **52** 5g 5s 5fg³ 6fg 6f 5f³ 5fg 5g 1982 5f 5f 5f² 7f 5fg² 5fg 5g* 6fg³ 5f⁴ 5d 6s 5d⁴ 5d) lengthy, quite useful sort; good walker; won maiden race at Nottingham in July; best at 5f; seems to act on any going; usually wears blinkers. *J. Etherington.*

MAGNETIC FIELD 2 b.c. Northfields–Maid of Iron (Crozier USA) (1982 **105** 6f* 7g²) June 8; 52,000Y; well-made, quite attractive colt; half-brother to several winners, including speedy 1974 2-y-o Amazing Maid (by Amazing) and useful 6f to 1m winner Iron Lad (by Petingo); dam never ran; ran a little green after leading at halfway when winning 12-runner maiden race at Nottingham in July decisively by 2½ lengths from Bold Major; 5/2 on, clear of remainder when head second to 100/1 Wargame in 18-runner sponsored event at Newcastle the following month; should stay 1m. *H. Cecil.*

MAGNETO 5 b.m. John Splendid 116–Magibbillibyte 77 (Constable 119) (1981 — 6v* 6s 6g 6d 7s² 6fg² 6g² 6fg³ 6fg 5f 6d 6g 7g 1982 7fg 7g) plater; stayed 1m; was well suited by some give in the ground; occasionally wore blinkers; dead. *D. Garraton.*

MAGONIS 3 b.f. Blakeney 126–Ribaria (Ribero 126) (1981 8d⁴ 1982 11.7f — 11.7f 12fg) showed ability in maiden race at Leicester in 1981 but finished soundly beaten in similar events at 3 yrs; will be suited by a test of stamina; possibly needs some give in the ground. *P. Cole.*

MAGWAL (FR) 3 b.c. Dictus 126–Val Gardena (Val de Loir 133) (1981 NR **112** 1982 7.5s² 10d* 10v² 9d 10fg 9.5s 12v³ 12v³) 36,000 francs Y (approx £3,600); second live foal; half-brother to French 4f and 6.5f winner Prince de Conty (by Filiberto); dam never ran; won maiden race at Saint-Cloud in April decisively from Strong Blake; ran creditably several subsequent outings, notably when 2½ lengths second to Be My Native in Prix La Force at Longchamp and 4 lengths third to Marasali in Prix du Conseil de Paris on same course on penultimate start; stays 1½m; acts well on soft going; trained by F. Palmer first 3 outings. *M. Saliba, France.*

MAHABBA (USA) 3 ch.f. Elocutionist–Amphora 110 (Ragusa 137) (1981 **65** 6fg 7g⁴ 6d³ 1982 8.2f² 8d² 10f⁴ 12f* 11g³ 14s) well-made filly; made all and stayed on well to win handicap at Brighton in August; suited by 1½m but appears not to stay 1¾m; seems to act on any going. *H. T. Jones.*

MAHARALI (USA) 2 ch.c. Sauce Boat–Princess Grundini (Prince John) **90** (1982 5fg 5f* 7f⁴ 5d 6g*) Feb 3; $110,000Y; stocky colt; half-brother to numerous winners, including 3 stakes-placed animals by Executioner; dam, half-sister to smart miler Reverse, ran 4 times; made all in maiden race at Leicester in June and nursery (blinkered) on same course in October; speedy, and possibly does not stay 7f. *R. Smyth.*

MAHCRIB 2 ch.c. Meldrum 112–Jacine Tudor (Henry the Seventh 125) (1982 — 5f 5g 5f) May 13; small colt; in rear in maiden races; blinkered third start; dead. *Mrs M. Nesbitt.*

MAIDA VALE 3 br.f. Furry Glen 121–Gifted Samanta (Divine Gift 127) **48** (1981 5.3fg³ 7f³ 6s 1982 10f 11.7g 10f 12fg 10.1d 8g 8fg³ 10f² 12g³ 10fg² 10fg 10fg² 12fg² 7d² 8s 10s²) small, lightly-made filly; plater; stays 1½m; acts on any going. *S. Woodman.*

MAIDEN'S DANCE 2 b.f. Hotfoot 126–Rhine Maiden 106 (Crepello 136) **65** p (1982 5fg 6g) Mar 16; lengthy, quite attractive filly; half-sister to 3 winners, including very useful 1m to 1¼m winners Tudor Rhythm and Rhineland (both by Tudor Melody); dam genuine middle-distance performer; showed a little ability, on second outing breaking well and chasing leaders for some way when 7½ lengths ninth of 18 to Albadeeah in maiden race at Newmarket in September; likely to need 7f+. *P. Walwyn.*

MAIDIGA (USA) 3 ro.c. Tumiga–Mobile Maiden (Prince John) (1981 7g — 8g 1982 7fg 10f 12fg) short-backed colt; beaten some way in maiden races; blinkered final start; sold to K. Morgan 1,850 gns Newmarket July Sales. *J. Hindley.*

MAID OF MILAN 2 ch.f. Home Guard 129–Farfisa 86 (Sassafras 135) (1982 **78** 7f 7d 8s²) Jan 25; quite attractive filly; has a round action; second foal; half-sister to winning stayer Farsound (by Wolver Hollow); dam won at up to 1¼m; 16/1, with leaders throughout when 2 lengths second of 18 to Oranella in maiden race at Wolverhampton in October, best effort; suited by 1m and will stay further; should win a race. *M. Stoute.*

MAILMAN 3 ch.g. Malacate 131–Sallail (Sallust 134) (1981 6d 7f³ 7f 8d² 1982 **84** 8.2fg⁴ 8g² 11.7f² 9f* 10.6h² 10.1fg* 8f² 8fg⁴ 8g* 10fg² 9d* 9d) tall, useful-looking gelding; good mover; had a fine season and won minor event at Windsor and handicaps at Wolverhampton (2, one an apprentice event) and Pontefract; a free-running sort who is best at up to 1¼m; seems to act on any going; good mount for an apprentice; consistent. *I. Balding.*

MAIN SAIL 3 b.f. Blakeney 126–Fluke 117 (Grey Sovereign 128§) (1981 **104** NR 1982 7fg* 8.2f* 12fg 12g⁴ 10fg 8fg* 8f³) very attractive filly; sixth foal; sister to an apparently poor animal, and half-sister to useful middle-distance filly Sextant (by Star Appeal); dam won from 5f to 7f, and is half-sister to high-class Buoy and Oaks winner Bireme; won maiden race at Goodwood and minor event at Haydock (odds on) in May and £4,400 race at Sandown in August; drew clear in last 2f to beat Wink unchallenged by 8 lengths in last-named; best at around 1m though wasn't disgraced in Ribblesdale Stakes at Royal Ascot, Lancashire Oaks at Haydock and Nassau Stakes at Goodwood over further; blinkered last 3 starts; reportedly awkward at home and sweated up and looked highly strung at Ascot; stud. *R. Hern.*

MAINTOP 5 b.g. High Top 131–Jujube 103 (Ribero 126) (1981 10fg 10g 10d³ **85** 10g 10f* 10g 10d 10fg* 10f 10g 1982 10f² 12fg* 12f⁴ 10d 12fg* 14g 13.3g 12g) strong gelding; ran moderately after accounting for small fields in handicaps at Goodwood in May and July; stays 1½m; acts on a soft going, but is much better suited by top-of-the-ground; blinkered last 4 starts as a 4-y-o. *M. Smyly.*

MAJESTIC FLIGHT 2 ch.c. Royal and Regal–Black Butterfly 78 (Prince — Tenderfoot 126) (1982 6f 6g) Mar 28; 7,000Y; compact, deep-girthed, quite attractive colt; first foal; dam, sister to very smart 5f and 7f winner Duke Ellington, won over 5f; behind in maiden races at Newmarket in August and Yarmouth (showed up long way) in September. *E. Eldin.*

MAJESTIC NURSE 7 br.m. On Your Mark 125–Bristol Milk 88 (Raise You **66** Ten 125) (1981 8s 8f³ 8.5fg 8.5fg 8d* 10s 8s³ 8d 10d³ 12g 1982 8g 8g 8fg 8f³ 10f³ 9.4f 9fg⁴) rather lightly-made mare; running-on third in Thirsk Hunt Cup in May (won by Teamwork) and handicap at Ripon in June; stays 1½m; acts on any going; suitable mount for an apprentice; inconsistent. *S. Norton.*

MAJESTIC STAR 5 b. or br.g. Star Appeal 133–Vivante 87 (Bold Lad, Ire **110** 133) (1981 NR 1982 10s 8d* 7fg 8d* 8d 8s² 10v) neat, strong, good sort; good walker; fairly useful at 3 yrs; apprentice ridden when winning 2 handicaps at the Curragh, beating Red Realm by a neck under top weight in Irish Cambridgeshire on second occasion in September (25/1, made most of running and put up a very useful performance); last in between and was soundly beaten when facing stiffish task fifth outing (tailed-off last in Derby only attempt at 1½m); acts on any going; trained first outing by R. Simpson. *C. Collins, Ireland.*

MAJESTIC TOWER 3 ch.c. Tower Walk 130–Tzu-Hsi 66 (Songedor 116) **60** (1981 5v 1982 8g 5fg⁴ 6f 6g⁴ 6f 7g 6f⁴ 6g 6g² 5g) workmanlike colt; second in seller at Newcastle in August; stays 6f; acts on firm going; blinkered seventh to ninth starts; retained 500 gns Doncaster October Sales. *C. Gray.*

MAJICA 2 b.f. Morston 125–Seein Is Believin (Native Charger) (1982 7g 6g) **73** p Apr 28; sister to fairly useful 13f winner No Evil, and closely related to Princess Royal Stakes winner Believer and French 1¼m winner Prince Blakeney (both by Blakeney); dam daughter of Prix Morny winner Princeline; seventh of 20, beaten 3¾ lengths, in maiden race won by stable-companion Fiefdom at Newmarket in October, second outing; should improve over middle distances. *B. Hobbs.*

MAJOR ANTHONY 2 b.c. Dublin Taxi–Chiltern Miss 85 (Hook Money 124) **82** (1982 6fg 6g³ 6fg 7v) May 22; big, strong, well-made colt; poor walker; closely related to 1m winner White Domino (by Sharpen Up) and half-brother to a winner; dam won over 1m; outpaced until running on well closing stages when 5 lengths third of 7 behind Concorde Hero in minor event at Kempton in May, only indication of merit; off course for over 3 months afterwards; will be suited by 1m; may be capable of improvement; to be trained by J. Bosley. *R. Hannon.*

MAJOR BREW 2 b.g. Brigadier Gerard 144–Light Lager 91 (Crepello 136) —
(1982 6f) May 13; 720Y; first foal; dam, who stayed 2m, is half-sister to very smart hurdler Major Thompson (by Brigadier Gerard); well beaten in maiden race at Redcar in June; sent to Barbados. *P. Rohan.*

MAJOR DOMO 3 br.c. Mandrake Major 122–Queezy 86 (Lear Jet 123) (1981 —
6fg* 1982 9fg) strong, good sort; easily won maiden auction event at Newcastle at 2 yrs; last of 14 to Ivano in Gerry Feilden Memorial Stakes at Newmarket in April on only outing in 1982 (didn't move to post at all well); not certain to have stayed middle distances; has been retired. *D. Smith.*

MAJOR DON 2 ch.g. Mandrake Major 122–Kindling (Psidium 130) (1982 **90**
6fg 7s²) Mar 24; strong, good-bodied gelding; half-brother to 3 winners, including fairly useful 1¼m to 13f winner Timber Track (by Palm Track); dam ran only 3 times; apparently still burly, finished well and failed by only a short head to catch Jungle Romeo in 28-runner maiden race at Redcar in October; will stay 1m; has plenty of scope and is sure to win a race. *E. Weymes.*

MAJORIAN 4 b.g. Majority Blue 126–Tinker Lass (Tin Whistle 128) (1981 —
8s² 8g 10.1f* 10f 10fg 10g 11s⁴ 1982 11s⁴ 10.2f 9fg 5fg 8f 11s 10.6s 8.2v) poor handicapper nowadays; stays 1¼m; evidently acts on any going; inconsistent and possibly needs things his own way; hooded final start; sold to J. Harris 480 gns Doncaster October Sales. *W. H. H. Williams.*

MAJOR OAK 3 br.g. Arctic Wood 93–Levajok (Andrea Mantegna) (1981 —
NR 1982 10.4fg 10f) smallish, sturdy, short-legged gelding; fourth reported foal; half-brother to a winner in Norway; dam unraced; in rear in maiden races at Chester and Nottingham in July. *R. Ward.*

MAJOR ROCK 3 ch.g. Mandrake Major 122–Rock Snake 76 (Rockefella) —
(1981 6s 6s 1982 8fg 6fg 6f 7d) fair sort; poor plater; sometimes blinkered; sold 680 gns Doncaster October Sales. *S. Matthews.*

MAJORS CAST 2 gr. or ro.c. Morston 125–Be Easy 110 (Be Friendly 130) **83 p**
(1982 6f 6g³) Mar 15; 15,000Y; close-coupled, workmanlike colt; first foal; dam best at up to 7f; off course since July, finished very strongly after taking long time to warm up when ¾-length third of 20 to Fiefdom in maiden race at Newmarket in October; sure to improve over further. *H. Wragg.*

MAJOR SETBACK 3 b.c. Brigadier Gerard 144–Bedfellow 104 (Crepello 136) —
(1981 6g³ 6fg 1982 11.5fg) strong, good-bodied colt; good mover; promising third in Ribero Stakes at Doncaster at 2 yrs; soundly beaten both subsequent starts, including in maiden race at Sandown in August; bred to stay middle distances; sold 3,900 gns Newmarket Autumn Sales. *P. Walwyn.*

MAJOR SINCLAIR 3 b.g. Mandrake Major 122–Stroppy Lou (Shantung 132) — §
(1981 5d 5s 6f 5f 7fg³ 7g⁴ 7.2fg 1982 7fg 7.2f 9g⁴ 8g 9g) rangy gelding; plater; may prove best at 1m; has been tried in blinkers and didn't look keen final start; sold 420 gns Doncaster October Sales. *M. H. Easterby.*

MALADHU 3 b.c. Malacate 131–Mhairi Dhu 88 (Great Nephew 126) (1981 —
5v 6s 1982 8g 10.1g 8fg 13.1f⁴) fair sort; plating-class maiden; best run at 1m on a firm surface though should stay further. *T. Robson.*

MALAPERT 3 gr.c. Three Legs 128–Miss Julie 75 (Babur 126) (1981 NR —
1982 8fg 8fg 11.5f) 5,800Y; attractive colt; carries plenty of condition; good walker; half-brother to 3 minor winners; dam won 6f seller at 2 yrs; soundly beaten in maiden races. *L. Cumani.*

MALEVOLENT 2 b.f. Bustino 136–Namecaller 83 (Malicious) (1982 6v) — p
Apr 6; rangy, quite attractive filly; fourth foal; half-sister to useful middle-distance 3-y-o Epithet (by Mill Reef) and smart 6f and 7f performer Columnist (by Swing Easy); dam won over 1m; weak 12/1-shot, showed lot of promise although only ninth of 10 in Duke of Edinburgh Stakes at Ascot in October, racing with leaders long way and being tenderly handled when weakening; sure to do lot better over longer distances. *J. Tree.*

MALIN HEAD 2 b.f. Malinowski 123–Lady At Leisure 64 (Never Bend) (1982 —
5g 5s 5f) Mar 17; 4,100F; small, leggy, close-coupled filly; third foal; dam placed over sprint distances here and in Ireland; bad plater; blinkered at Thirsk in May on final appearance; sent to Holland. *N. Tinkler.*

MALINISSA 3 ch.f. Connaught 130–River Severn 96 (Henry the Seventh 125) — (1981 NR 1982 8g 9f 12g 10.4d) 6,200F, 1,600 2-y-o; fair sort; half-sister to quite useful Irish sprinter Arun River (by Runnymede); dam stayed 1¼m; behind in maiden and minor events. *D. McCain.*

MALLARD SONG 8 b.g. Tudor Melody 129–Romping (Sir Gaylord) (1981 **32** 16g 16.9s 13.1g 10f 16fg 16h² 12f 19s⁴ 18g 1982 12d 12f 16fg² 17.1s) staying handicapper; second in amateur riders event at Chepstow in August, easily best effort; goes well on top-of-the-ground; has worn bandages. *Dr A. Jones.*

MALMAR 3 ch.f. Palm Track 122–Wicker (Pinza 137) (1981 5g 6s 5d 6d 1982 — 10d 6g 7fg 6g 9f 7s 6s) light-framed filly; poor plater; sometimes blinkered. *J. Mulhall.*

MALORS 3 ch.f. Malicious–Orseniga 97 (Privy Councillor 125) (1981 5fg 5d **46** 7fg 10d 10d 8g 8d 1982 10s 10g 12.2f³ 12f* 12f 12.2f* 13.8f 10g) rangy filly; plater; won at Thirsk (no bid) and Catterick (bought in 1,700 gns) in May; stays 1¼m; acts on firm going; effective with or without blinkers; ridden by apprentice E. Guest when successful. *N. Guest.*

MALSEEDY 4 ch.f. Malicious–Ballyseedy 73 (Dicta Drake 126) (1981 12s³ — 12s² 12.3d 12g 12d³ 12.5f 12fg 12fg⁴ 13fg 10fg 11g 10d⁴ 10.2g 1982 10s 10g 11fg 10fg 10g 10.8fg 15d 12fg 10.6s 7s) small filly; plater; stays 1½m well; acts on any going; occasionally blinkered; sometimes bandaged behind; suitable mount for an apprentice; trained until after sixth start by W. Stubbs. *R. Ward.*

MALTESE PET 2 b.f. Dragonara Palace 115–Miss Carvin (Carvin 127) (1982 — p 7d) June 1; second produce; sister to 3-y-o 1m and 1¼m seller winner Lady Kamina; dam ran 4 times unplaced; in need of run, stayed on steadily when 6 lengths fifth of 15 to Armonit in maiden race at Leicester in October. *R. Baker.*

MALVAN 6 b. or br.g. Decoy Boy 129–Khanum 81 (Soueida 111) (1981 8s² **61** 9d* 8d* 11s⁴ 10s 10d⁴ 10g 8f 10g 8s² 11s³ 1982 11f 10fg 12f 8d⁴ 8g² 8fg³ 8fg² 10g* 8fg 8fg 12.2s²) quite a moderate handicapper; gained a well-deserved success at Leicester in August, showing far more resolution than Scarlet Town and beating him by a head; stays 1½m; acts on any going, but is well suited by some give underfoot; effective with or without blinkers; good mount for a boy. *A. Turnell.*

MAMA LEONE 2 b. or br.f. Young Emperor 133–London Spin 86 (Derring- **87** Do 131) (1982 5g⁴ 5f* 5fg 6fg³ 6fg 6fg³) May 2; IR 6,400F, IR 10,000Y; quite attractive, lengthy filly; second foal; dam stayed 1m; easily landed the odds in maiden race at Haydock in May; blinkered when third in nursery at Goodwood in August, final outing and best subsequent effort; suited by 6f; yet to race on a soft surface. *G. Hunter.*

MAMIE 2 ch.f. Roman Warrior 132–Shady Desire 88 (Meldrum 112) (1982 — 5f 5s 7f 5s 6s) May 17; strong, sturdy filly; second foal; sister to 3-y-o 6f and 7f winner Ben Jarrow; dam won from 5f to 1m; in rear in maiden and minor events; blinkered last 2 starts. *T. Fairhurst.*

MAMUNIA (USA) 2 b.f. Cutlass–Sparkling Spear (Raise A Native) (1982 **95** 6f 7fg* 7g* 7fg³ 6d) May 21; $48,000Y; lengthy, slightly slightly-girthed filly; third foal; half-sister to a minor winner; dam, sister to smart sprinter Sparkling Native, won over 6f at 3 yrs; won 16-runner maiden race at Yarmouth and 13-runner minor event at Brighton in August; creditable 3½ lengths third of 12 to Silk Sari in £3,600 event at Chepstow the following month; needs at least 7f. *L. Cumani.*

MANAGERESS 2 br.f. Mandamus 120–Fire Hawk 70 (Firestreak 125) (1982 **74** 5.1g 6f* 6g 8.2s) Mar 30; 1,600F, 3,300Y; close-coupled, workmanlike filly; half-sister to a winning plater; dam, placed at 2 yrs, is half-sister to prolific 6f to 1¼m winner Mandalus (by Mandamus); won 8-runner maiden auction event at Folkestone in July at 50/1; no form in nurseries afterwards; should stay 1m. *P. Feilden.*

MANAL (FR) 3 b.f. Luthier 126–Top Twig (High Perch 126) (1981 7g 1982 — 7.6fg 5fg) good sort; well bred but seems only plating class; quite stoutly bred and almost certainly needs further than 5f. *H. T. Jones.*

MANCHESTERSKYTRAIN 3 b.g. Home Guard 129–Aswellas 93 (Le Levans- — tell 122) (1981 7fg 6fg² 6fg* 1982 5d 5f 6f 8fg 8fg) strong, well-made geld-ing; good mover; in mid-division in handicaps and an amateur riders race; gives impression 5f is too sharp for him and promises to stay 1m; sold 2,300 gns Newmarket Autumn Sales. *R. Smyth.*

MANDELSTAM (USA) 2 b.c. Vaguely Noble 140–Abergwaun 128 (Bounteous **93** p
125) (1982 7g* 7d⁴) Mar 17; useful-looking colt; half-brother to fairly useful
1981 2-y-o 5f and 6f winner Algardi (by Avatar); dam top-class and courageous
sprinter; showed good speed throughout and kept on well when winning 30-
runner maiden race at Newmarket in October by ¾ length from Gay Lemur;
favourite for Houghton Stakes on same course later in month but weakened
after disputing lead for long way, finishing 4¾ lengths fourth of 13 to Russian
Roubles; will stay 1m. *H. Cecil.*

MANDRAKE BELLE 3 ch.c. Mandrake Major 122–Janabelle 101 (Gentle Art **57**
121) (1981 5d 5v³ 5f⁴ 5f 1982 5f 5fg 5g 5fg 5g 5fg² 5d 5d) compact colt;
poor performer nowadays; acts on any going; usually blinkered; has run respectably for an apprentice; wore a brush-pricker on near-side of bridle final outing;
taken down early fourth start. *B. Gubby.*

MANDRAKE MINI 2 br.f. Mandrake Major 122–Tipsy Rider 60 (Hard Ridden —
131) (1982 5fg⁴ 6s 5g) Apr 26; 2,000Y; lightly-made filly; well beaten in
sellers; blinkered third start; of no account. *J. Douglas-Home.*

MANDRIANO 3 ch.g. Manado 130–Indian Runner (Sallust 134) (1981 5g⁴ —
6fg⁴ 1982 8fg 8fg 8g) workmanlike gelding; showed some ability in 1981 but
finished soundly beaten in maiden races and a seller (blinkered) at 3 yrs; should
stay 1m; sold 600 gns Ascot September Sales. *G. Pritchard-Gordon.*

MANDY'S TIME 6 b.m. High Time 96–Mandy's Melody (Highland Melody —
112) (1981 10.2s² 11.5fg 1982 10.2g) poor performer; will be suited by
1½m; acts well on soft going; has run respectably for an amateur rider. *J.
Harris.*

MANILOW 5 ch.h. Singing Bede 122–Lease Lend 96 (Cash and Courage 116) **81**
(1981 6g 5g 5.3f² 5g 5f* 5g* 5fg 1982 6d 6g 5f³ 5fg² 5f 5.1f* 5g 5f³ 5g 5fg 5fg)
strong, good sort; sprint handicapper; beat Humble Blue by 4 lengths at Yarmouth in June; needs a sound surface; has run well for an apprentice; rather
slow into stride fifth outing. *B. Swift.*

MANIMSTAR 2 b.c. Martinmas 128–Reddish Radish (Red God 128§) (1982 **85**
6f 6fg 6g⁴) Apr 27; 19,000Y; rangy, good sort; half-brother to 2 winners, including 3-y-o sprinter Preparation (by On Your Mark); dam ran once; promising
sixth, beaten little more than 3 lengths, behind Lofty in 16-runner maiden event
at Newmarket in July; well beaten in races won by Salieri and On Stage subsequently; will probably do better in time. *M. Jarvis.*

MAN IN THE MIDDLE 6 ch.g. Good Bond 122–Sharp Work 110 (Beau **74**
Sabreur 125) (1981 10.2d 8d 10s 8.5g 8fg 8d² 8.2d* 8.2s* 1982 7.5g 8s 10v³
9.5g* 10d 8g 10.4g* 10g⁴ 8f 8g 8v³ 8.2s* 8s⁴) big gelding; won ladies event at
Lyon in March and handicaps at Chester in May and Nottingham in October;
not all that consistent however; stays 1¼m well; suited by some give in the
ground and acts well in the mud; effective with and without blinkers; sometimes
starts slowly; off course nearly 4 months after ninth start; reportedly injured a
hip final start. *D. Sasse.*

MANISH 3 br.c. Mansingh 120–Pinwave 82 (Pinza 137) (1981 NR 1982 —
8fg 10.1fg 10.4fg 10g 12s) 1,300F, 2,300Y; sturdy colt; half-brother to useful
1¼m winner Wire Up (by Firestreak) and a winner in Italy; dam won at up to
13f; soundly beaten in varied company, including selling; has twice been blinkered. *J. Toller.*

MANLIGHT 2 b.c. Manado 130–Lady Habitat (Habitat 134) (1982 5g³ 5s²) **76**
May 1; IR 4,000Y; smallish, sparely-made colt; first foal; dam, winner 4 times
in Italy, is half-sister to smart 1m and 1¼m performer Understudy; placed in
autumn maiden events at Wolverhampton and Warwick; will be suited by
6f+. *L. Cumani.*

MANNTIKA 3 gr.f. Kalamoun 129–Manushka (Sheshoon 132) (1981 6g⁴ **77**
1982 10fg 10f 10.1g* 10g² 10g³ 10g) lightly-made filly; ran on strongly to win
minor event at Windsor in August; will stay 1½m; possibly went too fast early
on for own good when well beaten final start. *F. J. Houghton.*

MAN OF SPIRIT 3 b.g. Vitiges 132–Dauphine 102 (Pampered King 121) **88**
(1981 7g 7fg 7fg 1982 10f 13fg* 12g³ 13.8f* 16f* 15.8d 19s³ 16v*) attractive,
well-made gelding; won handicaps at Nottingham, Catterick, Thirsk and Ascot;
accounted for Salora Lady by ½ length on last-named in October; stays very well;
acts on any going; has run respectably for an apprentice; genuine. *J. Dunlop.*

MANOLA (SPA) 2 b.f. Brabant 118–Rosette (Tenerani 135) (1982 including **114** 6.5g* 7g* 8g* 7s) Mar 3; Spanish filly; sire won 1969 Austrian Derby, showed smart form over 1m here and in France at 4 yrs and later won in USA; unbeaten in 5 races in Spain, including Group 3 Premio Carlos Sobrino by 8 lengths in September and Group 2 Gran Criterium by 3½ lengths in October; proved herself a good filly by anyone's standards in Criterium de Maisons-Laffitte later in October, finishing 4½ lengths sixth of 16 to L'Emigrant, ahead of such as Cat O'Nine Tails and Cause Celebre, both of whom received weight; will stay middle distances. *F. Sanchez Y Jabardo, Spain.*

MANOR FARM LAD 3 ch.c. Free State 125–Ranjita 84 (Ballylinan 118) — (1981 7fg 6g 1982 8d 8f 6g) leggy, sparely-made colt; plating-class maiden; not certain to stay 7f; blinkered final start; sold 820 gns Newmarket July Sales. *W. O'Gorman.*

MANOR FARM ROCKER 2 ch.f. Shiny Tenth 120–Mixed Up Kid 53 (Track — Spare 125) (1982 6fg 6f) May 14; fair sort; first foal; dam won 3 times at up to 1m at 4 yrs; little worthwhile form in sellers at Yarmouth and Doncaster in July; exported to Algeria. *M. Tompkins.*

MANOR FARM TOOTS 3 br.f. Royalty 130–Winklepicker (Hotfoot 126) — (1981 NR 1982 8fg 10g 10g) leggy filly; poor mover; third live foal; dam last on only start; soundly beaten in maiden races and a seller. *M. Tompkins.*

MANSERIN 2 b.g. Mansingh 120–Kaiserin (Carapalida) (1982 5fg 5fg 6g 8.2fg) **47** Apr 6; 2,400F, IR 7,000Y; smallish, workmanlike gelding; half-brother to several winners here and abroad, including useful 1977 2-y-o 6f winner Kayseri (by Brigadier Gerard); dam won 5 times in Argentina; poor form, including in a seller; blinkered final start; gelded subsequently. *J. Bethell.*

MANX SWALLOW 3 b.c. Habitat 134–Swallow (Forli) (1981 NR 1982 — 6s 8fg 8fg 7g 7.2g 7fg 8f 7s) 43,000Y; useful sort; third foal; half-brother to 1980 2-y-o 6f winner Down The Hatch (by Relko); dam ran 3 times; poor maiden; best run at 7f on a firm surface. *R. Hollinshead.*

MA PIERRETTE 3 b.f. Cawston's Clown 113–Wigeon 80 (Divine Gift 127) **77** (1981 6f 6g 5.1fg* 6f⁴ 5g 1982 6fg 6g 7fg⁴ 7d* 7d 7f⁴ 8f* 8g 8g⁴ 8g⁴ 9s³ 8g 8s) leggy, light-framed filly; not the best of movers; won handicaps at Leicester in June and Redcar in July; stays 9f; acts on any going; has run creditably for an apprentice and when sweating up. *D. Dale.*

MAPRANG 2 b.c. Mill Reef 141–First Huntress (Primera 131) (1982 7f 8g **97** 7g⁴) Apr 2; 58,000Y; well-made, attractive colt; half-brother to 5 winners, 4 at least useful, including very useful 3-y-o 1¼m and 1¾m winner Broken Rail (by Busted) and very smart middle-distance horse Town and Country (by Town Crier); dam of little account; ran easily best race when blinkered for first time in Somerville Tattersall Stakes at Newmarket in October, coming from hopeless position at halfway to finish creditable fourth of 6, only 3 lengths behind Polished Silver; will be suited by 1¼m+. *R. Hern.*

MAPUTO PRINCESS 2 b.f. Raga Navarro 119–Buggles 66 (Kelly 122) — (1982 5g 6f) Apr 3; 4,000Y; half-sister to several winners, including fair 1980 2-y-o sprinter Southern Swanee (by My Swanee); dam won 6f seller at 2 yrs and stayed 1¼m; behind in maiden races at Pontefract (dwelt) in July and New-market in August. *P. Rohan.*

MARACAS BAY 3 b.g. Simbir 130–Valiretta (Go Marching) (1981 7fg 8d — 1982 8g 12.2f) well beaten in maiden races and a seller; has worn bandages; sold 1,000 gns Newmarket May Sales. *P. Brookshaw.*

MARALINGO 2 br.g. Saulingo 122–Rose Marullah 104 (Valerullah 113) (1982 **61** 5s³ 5f 5fg³ 5f* 7f² 5fg⁴ 6f³ 6g³ 6d) Apr 26; 1,000Y; rather leggy, close-coupled gelding; half-brother to several winners, including fair sprinter Whistling Fool (by Whistling Wind); dam won over 5f at 2 yrs in Ireland; won 7-runner maiden auction race at Carlisle in May; placed subsequently in good-class sellers; stays 7f; acts well on firm going. *R. Hollinshead.*

MARASALI (FR) 4 b.c. Tennyson 124–Monique (Tanerko 134) (1981 12s³ **118** 12d² 12s* 15s² 12.5d 15s² 12v 1982 12d 12d³ 12fg 10.5g 12s 15g* 15fg³ 13.5g 20s 12v* 15.5v) strong, deep-girthed, good-bodied colt; won Prix Nimbus at Saint-Cloud and was subsequently second to Tipperary Fixer twice at Long-champ as a 3-y-o; successful twice at Longchamp in 1982, beating Sardos by ½ length in Prix du Carrousel in June and holding off No Attention by a length after making much of running in 11-runner Prix du Conseil de Paris in October; also ran creditably when 2 lengths third to Valentinian in Prix Kergorlay at

Deauville in August; one paced and needs a test of stamina; yet to race on really firm going, but seems to act on any other; blinkered fifth outing; acted as a pacemaker for Protection Racket on third and fourth outings; trained by F. Mathet until after second start. *O. Douieb, France.*

MARCH FANDANGO 3 b.g. Gay Fandango 132–March Wonder 99 (March — Past 124) (1981 NR 1982 6fg 8.2fg 8fg) 7,000F, 12,000Y; half-brother to several winners; dam won 5 races at 1¼m; beaten some way in maiden races and a seller; sold out of C. Thornton's stable 2,500 gns Ascot July Sales after second start. *S. Pattemore.*

MARCH SPARK 6 b.g. Sparkler 130–March Malona 88 (Derring-Do 131) — (1981 8g 8g² 1982 9g 10g) lightly raced and fairly moderate nowadays; on burly side when in rear at York and Newcastle in August; stays 11f; acts on a firm surface but is well suited by soft ground; has been fired and is reportedly difficult to train. *C. Thornton.*

MARDI GRAS 3 gr.c. Martinmas 128–Miss Pimm 88 (Gentle Art 121) (1981 74 d 5fg⁴ 5d 5d³ 5f³ 5fg³ 6fg³ 6fg² 1982 6s² 6d 7.6fg³ 8fg 10fg⁴ 8.2fg 5fg 6f⁴ 6v 6d) neat, strong colt who carries plenty of condition; in frame in varied company; seems to stay 1¼m but races mainly at sprint distances; acts on any going; has shown a tendency to hang and may need strong handling; sometimes blinkered; sold 5,200 gns Newmarket Autumn Sales. *B. Hobbs.*

MARDI SONG 3 ch.g. Song 132–Impregnable 66 (Never Say Die 137) (1981 — NR 1982 5fg 6fg 7f 7g 8fg 6fg) close-coupled gelding; little worthwhile form in varied company, including claiming. *J. Holt.*

MARDY 4 b.g. Mummy's Pet 125–Tackard 87 (Hard Tack 111§) (1981 9s — 1982 8d 13.8f) fair sort; quite a moderate maiden; not sure to stay beyond sprint distances; sold 560 gns Doncaster September Sales. *W. C. Watts.*

MARECHAL (FR) 5 b.h. Bolkonski 134–Miss Univers (Le Fabuleux 133) 49 (1981 12d⁴ 12d⁴ 14g 12v 13.3g 12f 12fg³ 16g 12s³ 1982 10g*) workmanlike horse; attracted no bid when 4-length winner of selling handicap at Folkestone in April (blinkered); stays 1¾m; probably acts on any going. *V. Soane.*

MARGUERITE GERARD 5 b.m. Rheingold 137–God Sent 75 (Red God 128§) — (1981 10.2s 13fg³ 12g³ 12f 12f⁴ 1982 13g) workmanlike mare; stays 13f; probably acts on any going; suitable mount for an inexperienced rider. *W. Elsey.*

MARIACHO 4 b.c. Mariacci 133–Sea Queen (Le Fabuleux 133) (1981 10.5fg³ 117 12s³ 12g 1982 10.5fg* 10.5d³ 9s* 9g* 12g* 12.5g 12.5d² 12f³ 12s 10s 12s³) French colt; won both his starts as a 2-y-o but was lightly raced and a little disappointing at 3, although in frame in Prix Greffulhe and Prix Hocquart at Longchamp; spent much of 1982 in more modest company and won 3 races at Evry (including one restricted to inexperienced jockeys and apprentices, and an amateur riders event) and one at Saint-Cloud; beat Dalal by a length in 70,000 francs event on latter course in July when gaining last success; ran creditably in better company afterwards and particularly well when going down through down by a nose to April Run in Prix Foy at Longchamp in September (subsequently moved down a place); stays 1½m well; acts on any going. *M. Zilber, France.*

MARIAKOVA (USA) 2 ch.f. The Minstrel 135–Mofida 115 (Right Tack 131) 84 p (1982 6f³) strong-quartered, attractive filly; first foal; dam very tough winner of 8 races at up to 7.2f at 2 yrs and 3 yrs; ran on well after dwelling slightly when close-up last of three behind Key Tothe Minstrel in John Courage Stakes at York in July; will be suited by 7f+; sure to improve. *B. Hills.*

MARIBAN 3 b.f. Mummy's Pet 125–Gay Ribbon (Ribero 126) (1981 6s 6fg 63 1982 8.2f³ 8fg 12d 10g 8s) leggy, sparely-made filly; good walker; poor maiden on balance of form; best run at 1m on firm going; sweated up second start; sold out of W. Elsey's stable 2,400 gns Ascot August Sales after fourth outing. *O. O'Neill.*

MARIBO 2 b.g. Ribston 104–Sanandrea (Upper Case) (1982 5f 5fg 6fg) May — 6; 400Y; lightly-made gelding; first foal; dam ran 3 times; no worthwhile form in maiden auction events; blinkered second start; sold 520 gns Doncaster August Sales. *D. Smith.*

MARILENA 3 b.f. Rolfe 77–Nevilles Cross 67 (Nodouble) (1981 5s² 5fg 5g² 59 6f 6g* 5f⁴ 7s⁴ 7g 1982 9.4f² 10g 12.2f⁴) lightly-made filly; second in handicap at Carlisle in April; should stay 1½m (pulled hard when tried at trip); acts on any going; sold 820 gns Doncaster August Sales. *D. Smith.*

MARINA BAILEY 2 br.f. Julio Mariner 127–Orange Sensation 69 (Floribunda **79** 136) (1982 7f 7d² 8fg 7.6v) Feb 20; 14,000Y; small, fair sort; good walker and mover; half-sister to numerous winners here and abroad, including useful 1976 2-y-o Swift Sensation (by My Swallow); dam placed at up to 7f at 2 yrs; ¾-length second of 15 to Muznah at Yarmouth in August, best effort; should stay at least 1m. *M. Jarvis.*

MARINERA 2 b.f. Julio Mariner 127–Mimika 85 (Lorenzaccio 130) (1982 — 7f 8s) Feb 18; big, well-made filly; third foal; dam won over 5f at 2 yrs; in rear in maiden races at Sandown in July and Wolverhampton in October. *C. Brittain.*

MARIO MARINI 2 ch.c. Whitstead 125–Charites (Red God 128§) (1982 — 5fg 6g 6d) Feb 22; second foal; dam poor sister to top-class sprinter Green God; behind in minor events; sold 360 gns Doncaster September Sales. *R. Price.*

MARITIME ENGLAND 2 b.c. Tumble Wind–Summer's Lease (Soderini 123) **85** (1982 5.8f² 5.8f² 5g* 6fg) Apr 13; IR 24,000Y; quite attractive, well-made colt; half-brother to useful 1977 2-y-o 5f winner Pingat Mas (by Polyfoto) and a winner in Malaya; dam won over 1¼m in Ireland; finished strongly after rearing as stalls opened to win 10-runner minor event at Bath in July by 1½ lengths from Leadenhall Lad; ran poorly in nursery at Goodwood later in month; stays 6f. *C. Nelson.*

MARJOEMIN 2 b.f. Import 127–French Joy (French Beige 127) (1982 7s) Apr — 26; big, backward-looking filly; half-sister to a minor 2-y-o winner; dam poor NH performer; last of 11 in maiden race at Redcar in October. *J. Etherington.*

MARJORAM 3 ch.f. Warpath 113–Jasmin (Frankincense 120) (1981 NR **40** 1982 7f 8f 7fg² 8.2g 7f 7s) lightly-made filly; second foal; dam unraced half-sister to very useful sprinter High Sun; plater; should stay 1m; blinkered last 2 starts. *C. Thornton.*

MARJORIE DAW 2 br.f. Manado 130–Singing Away 66 (Welsh Pageant 132) **78** (1982 6f 7fg² 6d³) Apr 24; IR 11,000Y; smallish, lengthy, shallow-girthed filly; second foal; dam, from excellent family, ran only at 2 yrs; 2½ lengths second of 19 to Liberty Tree in maiden race at Chepstow in August; odds on, probably found 6f too sharp when 1½ lengths third of 7 behind Princess Irina in similar event at Nottingham the following month; will be suited by 1m. *J. Hindley.*

MARJORIE'S WISH (USA) 2 ch.f. Avatar–Trick Maneuver (What A **84** Pleasure) (1982 6h* 6f 6g) Jan 28; lengthy, quite attractive filly; good walker; first foal; dam stakes-placed winner at up to 1m; led virtually throughout when winning 13-runner maiden race at Haydock in June decisively by 5 lengths from Al Washl; failed to impress in paddock when well beaten subsequently in Chesham Stakes at Royal Ascot and nursery at Pontefract in July; bred to stay at least 1m. *M. Jarvis.*

MARKENFIELD 3 b.c. Oats 126–Belleek (Never Say Die 137) (1981 8s **70** 1982 11g³ 12f 12g² 13g³ 12g² 12s 12d) small, attractive colt; quite modest; well beaten in valuable selling handicap final start (blinkered); will be suited by 1¾m; has run respectably for an apprentice; sold to L. Cumani 5,200 gns Newmarket Autumn Sales. *J. W. Watts.*

MARKET MELODY 5 b.m. Highland Melody 112–Sandalshoon 103 (Red — God 128§) (1981 8g⁴ 8g⁴ 10.2f 8f 8s 9s 8s 1982 12f 8g 9fg² 12f 10g³ 10d² 9g 11s) lengthy mare; good walker; placed in varied races, but is still a maiden; stays 1¼m; doesn't always impress in paddock. *J. Carr.*

MARKET ROSE 3 b.f. Most Secret 119–Rosemarkie 75 (Goldhill 125) (1981 — 5d 5fg⁴ 5g 5fg⁴ 6g⁴ 5f 6f⁴ 6d 7.2v* 1982 8fg 9.4fg 7d) neat filly; shows plenty of knee action; won seller at Haydock in 1981; behind in handicaps at 3 yrs; stays 7f well; acts well on heavy going; has been bandaged; retained 520 gns Doncaster October Sales. *C. Gray.*

MARKET ROYAL 2 gr.c. Supreme Sovereign 119–Greek Bazaar 49 (Philemon **91** 119) (1982 6f 6f 6fg³ 6f²) Apr 15; 4,500Y; big colt; half-brother to a winning plater; dam stayed 1¼m; split a pastern when head second of 4 to Nothing Blue in maiden race at Yarmouth in August and had to be destroyed. *W. O'Gorman.*

MARKET STREET 2 b.c. Dragonara Palace 115–Coral Flower (Quorum 126) ? (1982 5g 5f*) May 3; 2,500F, 5,600Y; sturdy colt; brother to a winner in

Trinidad, and half-brother to several minor winners; dam of little account; favourite and blinkered, won 6-runner seller at Beverley (bought in 1,500 gns) in May by 2½ lengths from Romany Boy; won in Italy afterwards. *W. O'Gorman.*

MARKIE 6 br.g. On Your Mark 125–Jeannette (Whistler 129) (1981 8fg 7.6fg   **43** 10f 8fg 10g 10f³ 8g 10g² 13.8g³ 12g 12d 1982 10.2g 12g³ 10f² 12f³ 12fg 12f 12fg 8fg) well-made, attractive gelding; poor handicapper nowadays; possibly best at distances short of 1½m; acts well on firm going; sometimes blinkered; usually apprentice ridden nowadays; usually wears bandages. *R. E. Peacock.*

MARKIMLEEKAR 2 gr.c. Cavo Doro 124–Fishwife 96 (Right Boy 137) (1982   **–** 7d 7f 7f) Mar 23; 1,800Y; tall, leggy colt; last in sellers; blinkered last 2 outings; of no account. *N. Tinkler.*

MARK OF RESPECT 2 ch.c. North Stoke 130–Scarcroft 66 (King's Bench   **–** 132) (1982 7g 8s) May 28; IR 12,000Y; leggy, rather lightly-made colt; half-brother to several winners, including useful 1976 2-y-o King Croesus (by Green God) and useful sprinter Last Tango (by Be Friendly); dam won at 7f; soundly beaten in late-season maiden races at Newmarket and Leicester. *R. Armstrong.*

MARK'S HALL 3 gr.f. No Mercy 126–Hi Tess 65 (Supreme Court 135) (1981   **–** NR 1982 8g 8g) half-sister to 3 winners by Double-U-Jay; dam plating class; behind in maiden races at Beverley and Yarmouth. *P. Haslam.*

MARLEYCOMBE HILL 3 b.c. Sagaro 133–L'Anguissola 102 (Soderini 123)   **59** (1981 8g 8s 10s 1982 10s 6fg 16d 15.5f 15.5fg³ 15.5fg³) smallish colt; staying maiden; blinkered fourth start; has twice sweated up. *W. Wightman.*

MARLOWSWOOD 2 ch.g. Hittite Glory 125–Thieves Honour (Hook Money   **75** 124) (1982 7fg 8g) May 29; half-brother to 1981 2-y-o 6f winner Keep Silent (by Balidar); dam ran once; 5 lengths fifth of 26 behind Zaheendar in maiden race at Redcar in September; ran poorly in similar event at Edinburgh the following month. *Sir Mark Prescott.*

MARNET 3 ch.g. Sweet Revenge 129–Tra-La-La (Penhurst) (1981 7g 1982   **–** 11s 16f) sturdy gelding; in rear in £4,100 event and 2 maiden races; sold 1,150 gns Ascot June Sales. *K. Ivory.*

MARNIE'S GIRL 3 br.f. Crooner 119–Philmarnie 66 (Klondyke Bill 125)   **–** (1981 NR 1982 8f 8s 8f 8g 10d 10fg 10d) lengthy, workmanlike filly; first foal; dam, plater, stayed 1½m; poor form, including in a seller. *A. Smith.*

MAROUKHY 3 b.f. Queen's Hussar 124–Maroukh (Kashmir II 125) (1981   **–** 6f 7g 1982 7fg) leggy, sparely-made, rather narrow filly; behind in maiden and minor events; ran very freely in blinkers only start at 3 yrs in June; sold 380 gns Doncaster September Sales. *C. Brittain.*

MARQUESSA D'HOWFEN 3 br.f. Pitcairn 126–Fire-Screen 92 (Roan Rocket 128) (1981 6d⁴ 7f* 1982 8fg 10.6f 8g 8.2s 9s) small, lightly made filly; doesn't usually impress in appearance; won Gilbey Champion Racehorse Futurity at York in 1981; soundly beaten in handicaps most starts at 3 yrs; promises to stay 1½m; bandaged second start; troublesome at start first outing. *W. Hastings-Bass.*

MARSHALLA 2 b.f. Cawston's Clown 113–Abbey Rose 84 (Lorenzaccio 130)   **–** (1982 6h) Feb 29; 700Y; tall, leggy, lightly-made filly; first foal; dam second over 7f and 1m at 2 yrs; twelfth of 13 in maiden race at Haydock in June. *J. Wilson.*

MARSHAL OSTHOFF 3 ch.c. Royal Match 117–Compliment (Tudor Music   **–** 131) (1981 6fg 7f 7g⁴ 7d 1982 8.2fg 8f 10f) small, useful sort; plating class nowadays; should stay 7f; best form with some give in the ground; sold 410 gns Ascot December Sales. *I. Walker.*

MARSHGATE 4 b.g. Shiny Tenth 120–Tweetie Pie (Falcon 131) (1981 8d*   **–** 7f 8f 10fg 10d 1982 8.2s⁴ 12g) lengthy gelding; plater; disappointing since winning at Brighton as a 3-y-o; stays 1m; trained first outing by D. Marks. *W. Charles.*

MARSH TRACK 2 br.g. Palm Track 122–Miss Warwick (Stupendous) (1982   **62** 6fg³ 6d 6g 7fg 6s) Apr 7; leggy gelding; moderate plater; suited by 7f; acts on firm going; missed break fourth outing. *W. Haigh.*

MARSTAIN 5 ch.g. Porto Bello 118–Florecilla 90 (Matador 131) (1981 8d   **–** 6d⁴ 5.8g⁴ 6f 6fg 6f 7fg 7fg 7h 6f 10s⁴ 1982 11.7g) poor handicapper; suited by 7f or more; probably acts on any going; sometimes blinkered but does at least as well without. *R. Hoad.*

MARTELLI 4 b.f. Pitskelly 122–Martita 99 (Tacitus 124) (1981 8.3fg 8f 8.3g — 1982 12d 18f) poor performer nowadays; not disgraced over 1½m on reappearance; sometimes blinkered. *R. Smyth.*

MARTHA SPANKS 2 br.f. Home Guard 129–Amazer (Mincio 127) (1982 79 5f 5.3fg* 6fg⁴ 5f 6fg 6fg⁴ 7g) May 18; leggy, fair sort; half-sister to several winners, including very useful 1m to 1½m filly Astonished (by Connaught) and very useful French middle-distance filly Button Up (by Busted); dam won over 6f at 2 yrs in France and is half-sister to 3 very useful animals; 33/1, led close home to win maiden race at Brighton in June by ½ length from Rivetting; creditable fourth afterwards in minor event at Windsor and 6-runner nursery (sweated up) at Goodwood; suited by 6f. *J. Benstead.*

MARTIAL FITZGERALD 2 b.c. Tower Walk 130–Capsville (Cyane) (1982 73 5s 5s) Mar 8; IR 3,600Y; sturdy, good-bodied colt; brother to a prolific winner in Italy, and half-brother to winners here and abroad; dam, placed in USA, is sister to smart stakes winner Pinch Pie; showed quite modest form in October maiden events at Haydock and Warwick; will stay at least 6f. *S. Norton.*

MARTIALIS 3 b.c. Martinmas 128–Adamay (Florescence 120) (1981 5f 66 5.8f* 6g² 7g³ 7f* 6g⁴ 1982 8fg 8f 7d 7d 7.6f 7g 8g 8.3g 7s) compact colt; not disgraced in handicaps on occasions; stayed 7f well; acted on firm going; ran poorly eighth start; dead. *S. Mellor.*

MARTINEAU 3 br.c. Martinmas 128–Romardia 75 (Romulus 129) (1981 7g 81 1982 8fg 10.2g² 10f 12f* 11.7fg³) attractive, well-made colt; stayed on well to beat odds-on Silk Screen a shade comfortably by ½ length in 5-runner maiden race at Kempton in July; well suited by 1½m; yet to race on a soft surface. *B. Hobbs.*

MARTON BOY 4 br.g. Tycoon II–Marton Lady 103 (March Past 124) (1981 36 6g 5g 5d⁴ 6g 6f 5s 5g 1982 5g³ 6f 6f 5f 7g 8fg 8fg 8g) robust gelding; plater nowadays; probably stays 1m; acts on a firm and a soft surface; has run moderately in blinkers. *S. Wiles.*

MARTON MAID 2 b.f. Silly Season 127–Marton Lady 103 (March Past 124) 74 (1982 6g 6fg 7s 6d⁴ 6s) Mar 25; neat filly; half-sister to several winners, notably very smart sprinter Haveroid (by Tycoon II); dam sprinter; 3 lengths fourth of 22 behind Foil 'Em in maiden race at Doncaster in October, only indication of merit. *S. Wiles.*

MARTYNIA 3 b.f. Simbir 130–Mary Paddy 100 (St Paddy 133) (1981 NR — 1982 8fg 12v) half-sister to 2 winners, including prolific 6f to 9f winner Paddy's Luck (by Cumshaw); dam 2-y-o 7f winner; behind in maiden race at Warwick and minor event at Lingfield; sold 840 gns Newmarket Autumn Sales. *J. Benstead.*

MARY BURNS (USA) 3 b. or br.f. Advocator–Burns' Babe (Fleet Nasrullah) 66 (1981 6g 6f² 6d 1982 8fg* 10.5fg 10.6f² 8f 12g 9g 10f 8.2g) leggy, rather narrow filly; good mover; favourite, hung and didn't look too keen when getting up on post to dead-heat with Little Mercy in maiden race at Thirsk in April; stays 1¼m and wasn't disgraced when having very stiff task over 1½m; possibly not at her best on a soft surface; blinkered seventh start; takes a strong hold. *S. Norton.*

MARY MAGUIRE 5 b.m. Rapid River 127–Flicka (Balidar 133) (1981 68 5s⁴ 5s 5g 6g 6fg 6fg² 6g² 6f* 5f* 5fg 6s 6v 6s 1982 5d 6f³ 6f² 6f 5fg² 5fg⁴ 6fg 6d² 6g* 6f² 6fg³ 6g² 6d 6f² 5g³ 6s* 6s 6s) strong-quartered mare; sprint handicapper; won at Pontefract in July and Hamilton in September, on latter course beating Fairgreen by 4 lengths; acts on any going; usually blinkered at 3 yrs; sometimes sweats up; suitable mount for a claimer. *Mrs M. Nesbitt.*

MARY MITSU 3 br.f. Tarboosh–Misty Hill (Hill Clown) (1981 5g* 5f² 110 1982 8.5f² 8g 8f² 8d*) IR 9,400Y; workmanlike ex-Irish filly; second foal; half-sister to a winner in USA by Prince Tenderfoot; dam won over 13f and 1⅜m in France; moved down to second for hampering runner-up after beating Clare Island by ¾ length in 9-runner Princess Elizabeth Stakes at Epsom in April; gained compensation in 12-runner Gilltown Stud Stakes at the Curragh in September, beating Kazankina smoothly by 3 lengths; creditable 4 lengths fifth of 24 to Prince's Polly in Goffs Irish 1,000 Guineas at the Curragh, easily better effort in between; stays 1m well; yet to race on really soft going, but acts on any other; racing in USA. *J. Dunlop.*

MARZIE 3 b.f. Silly Season 127–Terran Royal (Right Royal V 135) (1981 6fg 47 7f 8d 8d 1982 9f 8fg 12.2f 8fg 10d³ 10f* 10g 10g 10s) neat filly; plater; attracted no bid after winning at Nottingham in July; stays 1¼m; acts on firm going; has worn blinkers; trained part of season by P. Asquith; sent to Cyprus. *J. Harris.*

MARZOOGA 2 ch.f. Bold Lad (Ire) 133–Lady Astronaut (Polly's Jet) (1982   **84** p
6g 6s*) Apr 10; 78,000Y; good-quartered filly; good walker; half-sister to
Star Bound (by Crowned Prince), a useful winner at up to 9f in Ireland, and
Great Oak (by Athens Wood), a useful 2-y-o in 1976 and subsequently a good
winner in Norway; dam, placed at 2 yrs in France, is sister to high-class performer
Turbo Jet and half-sister to Fabergé II; third favourite, won 16-runner maiden
race at Leicester in November easing up by 2½ lengths from Rainbow Springs;
will stay beyond 6f; acts on soft going; has makings of useful 3-y-o. *J. Dunlop.*

MASAKARI 2 b.c. Anax 120–Mary Mine 102 (Infatuation 129) (1982 5g   **67**
6f 7fg 6fg 6d 8s) Apr 21; 3,500F, 8,000Y; well-made colt; half-brother to
1976 2-y-o 7f winner Do Better (by Derring-Do); dam won from 1m to 1½m and
is half-sister to Cheveley Park winner Pasty; little worthwhile form in maiden
and minor events; blinkered final outing; sold 1,200 gns Newmarket Autumn
Sales. *R. Smyth.*

MASH 3 gr.g. Warpath 113–Piccalilli 78 (Klairon 131) (1981 NR 1982 10g   **57**
12fg⁴ 16.5fg⁴ 16s) workmanlike gelding; brother to 3 minor winners; dam
seemed to stay 1¾m; staying maiden; sold 5,400 gns Doncaster November Sales.
C. Thornton.

MASHIN TIME 3 b.f. Palm Track 122–Baggin Time 91 (Pinsun 108) (1981   **73**
6f 6f² 6fg* 7f⁴ 1982 9f 7f⁴ 8f* 8g* 8fg* 8g* 8g*) narrow, leggy filly; not the
best of movers; beaten in sellers on first 2 starts but subsequently showed herself
much better than a plater, winning handicaps at Carlisle, Ripon, Pontefract,
Newcastle and Ripon again; suited by 1m; yet to race on a soft surface; genuine
and consistent. *M. H. Easterby.*

MASKELL GOLD 2 br.c. On Your Mark 125–Mulattin (Henry the Seventh 125)   **—**
(1982 6v) Mar 4; IR 15,000F, 21,000Y; compact colt; half-brother to very
smart and tough 1979 2-y-o Sonnen Gold (by Home Guard) and middle-distance
winner Cooks Corner (by Martinmas); dam never ran; tailed-off last of 10 in
Duke of Edinburgh Stakes at Ascot in October. *C. Nelson.*

MASKELL LAD 2 b.c. The Brianstan 128–Abeville (Charlottown 127) (1982   **75**
5d³ 5s² 5fg* 5f* 5fg*) Mar 22; 5,600Y; compact colt; good mover; first foal;
dam unraced half-sister to very useful Sheer Grit; bought in 7,200 gns after
winning good-class seller at York in June by 1½ lengths from Leadenhall Lad;
successful in non-sellers at Warwick and Brighton on 2 previous outings, being
presented with second one when only opponent cocked his jaw and ran hopelessly
wide into straight; will stay 6f; best form on a firm surface; reportedly sold
privately to race in Hong Kong. *C. Nelson.*

MASSIMO 3 b.c. Blakeney 126–Never a Fear 121 (Never Say Die 137) (1981   **80**
8g 10g 1982 10fg² 10f² 12f³ 10fg⁴ 12f 8fg⁴ 9g* 10fg² 10g* 9s) stocky, strong,
attractive colt; all out to win maiden race at York and minor event at Yarmouth
in September; stays 1½m; unsuited by soft going. *L. Cumani.*

MASTER ABBOT 2 b.c. Whitstead 125–Elton Abbess 86 (Tamerlane 128)   **—**
(1982 8.2s) Apr 11; 1,800Y; small, quite well-made colt; first foal; dam won 3
sprint races; 33/1 and bandaged off-hind, no show in 19-runner minor event at
Nottingham in October. *R. Boss.*

MASTER-BLOW 3 ch.g. Roi Soleil 125–Surfacing (Worden II 129) (1981   **67**
6d³ 6s² 7f 6d 5v* 6s 1982 6f 5f 5g⁴ 6g 6g* 7d⁴ 7s) leggy gelding; won handicap
at Ayr in September; stays 7f; suited by some give in the ground. *W. Elsey.*

MASTER BOATMAN 3 ch.g. Riverman 131–Ya Ya 84 (Primera 131) (1981   **89**
6d 7f⁴ 7g³ 1982 10.6s³ 12fg³ 12.2f² 14fg² 12g 14fg² 15d⁴ 14g²) quite a useful
sort; good walker; battled on well to win 7-runner minor event at Ayr in September from Sunny Look; also runner-up in varied company; will be suited by
2m+; seems to act on any going. *H. Wragg.*

MASTER BOON 3 b.g. Sagaro 133–Miss Boon 84 (Road House II) (1981   **—**
NR 1982 10.1fg 14f 12f) first foal; dam won twice over 1½m and also won over
hurdles and fences; beaten some way in minor event and maiden races in the
South; will need a test of stamina. *H. Candy.*

MASTER BROKER 2 b.c. Mummy's Pet 125–Ardent Runner 94 (Runnymede   **76**
123) (1982 5f 5fg 6g 6s 5d*) Mar 27; 4,700Y; workmanlike colt; has been
tubed; showed no form until winning 20-runner seller at Redcar (no bid) in
October by ½ length from Booth's Town Boy; acts on a soft surface. *W.
Hastings-Bass.*

MASTER CARL 3 b.c. Pitskelly 122–Lepello (Le Levanstell 122) (1981 **84**
5d² 5g³ 6f 7f⁴ 7d³ 7.3d 7f 1982 10d² 10fg² 12f 12fg* 12fg³) strong colt who
carries a lot of condition; landed odds in maiden race at Hamilton in July;
suited by 1¼m; seems to act on any going but goes well on a soft surface; has
run respectably for inexperienced riders but gives impression he's suited by
stronger handling. *P. Rohan.*

MASTER CAWSTON 3 ch.c. Cawston's Clown 113–Teresa Way 66 (Great **87**
White Way) (1981 6fg³ 6g* 6s 6g 1982 6fg 6fg⁴ 6f² 6f 6g 6g⁴ 5s 6s) tall,
useful sort; good mover; in frame in 3 handicaps at Newmarket; stays 6f;
probably needs a sound surface; blinkered sixth and final starts; sometimes
apprentice ridden but gives impression he's suited by strong handling. *H.
Wragg.*

MASTER LOCKWOOD 2 b.c. Mummy's Pet 125–Tzu-Hsi 66 (Songedor 116) **81**
(1982 5d 5.8g 6fg² 6d) Apr 28; 12,000Y; half-brother to winning sprinter
Dragonist (by Dragonara Palace); dam 6f winner; ran Indian Rajah to ¾ length
in 20-runner minor event at Lingfield in September, best effort; favourite when
only eighth of 14 to Dawn's Dream in maiden race at Brighton the following
month; promises to stay 7f; possibly not at his best on a soft surface. *G. Hunter.*

MASTERS 6 br.g. Swing Easy 126–Visitation 84 (Tarqogan 125) (1981 NR **—**
1982 10s) quite modest (rated 77) on flat in 1979; stays 7f (last over 1¼m on
only outing of 1982); acts on any going; wears blinkers; has worn a bandage
on near-hind. *D. Ringer.*

MASTER THIEF 11 ch.g. Pieces of Eight 128–Tudor Song (Tudor Minstrel **—**
144) (1981 15.5d² 16d⁴ 15.5d 16.9s 1982 16d 15.5fg) poor stayer; acts
on any going; suitable mount for an apprentice; used to wear blinkers. *P.
Makin.*

MATARANY 2 ch.g. Mansingh 120–Nelion 102 (Grey Sovereign 128§) (1982 **80**
7fg 7s²) May 5; 11,000Y; attractive, rangy gelding; half-brother to several
winners here and abroad, notably high-class stayer Recupere (by Reliance II);
dam won at 6f and 1m at 2 yrs; 2½ lengths second of 12 to Rana Pratap in minor
event at Chepstow in October; gelded subsequently; will stay 1m. *I. Balding.*

MATAWA 2 ch.f. Royal Match 117–Dance Away (Red God 128§) (1982 **—**
6fg 6g 6g 8fg) Apr 1; IR 1,700F, IR 7,400Y; small filly; half-sister to several
winners, including useful 1981 2-y-o 6f winner Risk Taker (by Auction Ring)
and Irish 7f to 1¼m winner Maculata (by Right Tack); dam fairly useful Irish
2-y-o 5f winner; behind in maiden and minor events. *D. Morley.*

Tote European Free Handicap, Newmarket—a tremendous finish
as Match Winner, Rebollino (noseband, left) and
Mirabeau (noseband, right) are
driven to the line

MATCH MASTER 3 ch.g. Roman Warrior 132–Giglet (Frankincense 120) —§
(1981 5fg 6f² 6fg⁴ 6d³ 6g   1982 7fg 7.6f⁴ 7f³ 8g² 6fg 6g³ 6f² 8g) quite well-made, good sort; carries a lot of condition; good walker and mover; disappointing maiden; stays 1m; seems to act on any going; sometimes blinkered; possibly ungenuine, has a tendency to hang left and isn't an ideal mount for an apprentice. *C. Nelson.*

MATCH WINNER (FR) 3 br.c. Dancer's Image–Mosstown (Mossborough 126) **113**
(1981 6g³ 6fg* 7g* 7.3s³ 1982 7fg* 7f² 7fg) good-topped, useful sort; fifth foal; half-brother to smart middle-distance performer Masked Marvel (by Hard to Beat); dam won at up to 9f in France; favourite, battled on magnificently under very strong pressure to beat Rebollino a short head in 13-runner Tote European Free Handicap at Newmarket in April; failed to hold Gavo's renewed challenge by a short head when second of 11 in Norwest Holst Trophy (Handicap) at York in May; dropped out in last 2f when behind in Jersey Stakes won by Merlins Charm at Royal Ascot on only other start; will stay 1m; acts on any going; sent to USA. *H. Cecil.*

MATHEMAGICIAN (USA) 2 b.c. Minnesota Mac–Margaritaville (Tom Rolfe) —
(1982 7.9f 7s) Apr 12; $60,000Y; smallish ex-Irish colt, lacking in scope; first foal; dam unraced half-sister to smart Dancing Blade, a winner up to 1m; behind in maiden race at Dundalk in September (trained by D. Weld) and minor event (last of 6) at Doncaster in November. *F. Durr.*

MATLOVA 3 b.f. He Loves Me 120–Matty (Sailor) (1981 NR 1982 7fg 7f) —
IR 1,200Y; sixth foal; dam unplaced 8 times in USA; behind in sellers at Lingfield and Beverley in May; sold 780 gns Ascot June Sales. *S. Mellor.*

MATOU 2 b.c. Mummy's Pet 125–Great Optimist 55 (Great Nephew 126) **101**
(1982 6f 6fg³ 6d 6g*) Apr 2; well-made colt; first foal; dam in frame over middle distances; confidently ridden, won 19-runner maiden race at Newmarket in October going away by 3 lengths from Shining Out; will stay 7f; seems likely to make useful handicapper. *G. Pritchard-Gordon.*

MATTABOY 4 ch.c. Music Boy 124–Green Chartreuse 91 (French Beige 127) **115**
(1981 7g 8g 8g² 8s⁴ 8fg 9g 1982 5fg 6f) strong, compact colt; good walker; successful in William Hill Middle Park Stakes as a 2-y-o; didn't win in 1981 but ran a fine race and was possibly unlucky when neck second to To-Agori-Mou in 2,000 Guineas at Newmarket; didn't have best of runs and wasn't disgraced when seventh of 12 to Lightning Label in Palace House Stakes at Newmarket in May on reappearance; very disappointing when favourite for Duke of York Stakes later in month, trailing home last but one behind Jester after showing early speed; reported a few weeks latter to have pulled check ligaments in his off-fore; stays 1m; well suited by a sound surface; tends to pull hard in early stages and seems to do best when he can be covered up. *R. Armstrong.*

MATTS MUSIC 2 ch.f. Music Boy 124–Ventrex 95 (Henry the Seventh 125) —
(1982 6g 5v 5s) Mar 11; 4,100Y; workmanlike filly; first foal; dam won over 1¾m and 2m; beaten about 8 lengths when ninth of 15 to Dry Land in maiden race at Sandown in October, third outing. *K. Cunningham-Brown.*

MATURE 3 b.f. Welsh Pageant 132–Material 107 (Song 132) (1981 5g 5fg 6g —
7g 1982 8fg 8fg 11s) leggy, lightly-made filly; not a particularly good mover; only plating class; best run over 7f. *E. Weymes.*

MAUJENDOR 2 b.c. Rose Laurel 125–Mark My Word (On Your Mark 125) **83**
(1982 7g 6g⁴ 7fg 7v 7d) Mar 9; 6,000Y; small, stocky colt; third foal; half-brother to French 9f winner Jetstream (by Direct Flight); dam placed over 4.5f at 2 yrs in France; just over 2 lengths fourth of 17 to Indian Rajah in minor event at Windsor in August, only form; blinkered fourth outing. *C. Brittain.*

MAURICE'S TIP 4 b.g. Jolly Me 114–Spaniard's Darling (Darling Boy 124) —
(1981 8s² 7v² 8.2s 8g 8g³ 7f 8f² 8f 8.3fg² 8.2s 7s 8.2s 1982 8s) compact gelding; plater; stays 1m; acts on any going; usually blinkered nowadays. *J. Jenkins.*

MAURISH LAD 2 b.c. Double Jump 131–Darts Lane 80 (Javelot 124) (1982 **67**
5fg 5f⁴ 6fg 5g² 5.8g 7g 6fg 8d 10s) Apr 15; 4,000Y; workmanlike colt; has rather a round action; half-brother to a winner in Jersey; dam won over 5f at 2 yrs; plating-class maiden; stays 1¼m; usually blinkered; sold 4,000 gns Newmarket Autumn Sales. *S. Mellor.*

MAURITZFONTEIN 3 b.c. Habitat 134–Reine Dagobert 76 (Roi Dagobert 128) **82**
(1981 7g 7g⁴ 1982 8fg³ 7f² 7.3fg² 7f* 8fg) neat, attractive colt; well-backed

favourite when getting up in dying strides to beat Off The Hook by a head in 15-runner maiden race at Sandown in May (showed a tendency to hang); runner-up earlier in maiden race at Leicester and quite valuable handicap at Newbury; seems to find 7f on sharp side and stays 1m; gives impression that he'll be suited by some give in the ground; not seen out after June. *H. Candy.*

MAURMAX 2 b.g. Dragonara Palace 115–Lochness Lass (Track Spare 125)   **77**
(1982 5fg² 5g 5g⁴ 5f⁴ 7g 6fg 5fg 6s⁴) Mar 21; 4,400Y; good-bodied gelding; second foal; dam well beaten in 3 outings at 2 yrs; quite a modest maiden; suited by 6f; acts on any going; gelded after final appearance. *P. K. Mitchell.*

MAVOURNEEN (USA) 3 ch.f. Hail The Pirates 126–Blaheen (Beekeeper)   **65**
(1981 6g 6g 7g 1982 8fg 12g⁴ 13.8f* 11.7fg* 13g 11.5g⁴ 12.2s) tall, narrow filly; led near finish to win handicaps at Catterick and Windsor in August; stays 1¾m; acts on firm going and is possibly unsuited by soft; suited by waiting tactics. *R. Armstrong.*

MAVOURNSKI 2 b.f. Malinowski 123–Judy Green (Green God 128) (1982   **81**
6g 6f⁴ 6f² 7fg 8fg 7.6v² 8.2s⁴ 7g) Apr 23; IR 6,000Y; good-bodied filly; second foal; dam, third over 7f and 1m in Ireland, is half-sister to very smart David Jack; second in maiden races at Yarmouth in August and Lingfield in October; ran moderately in between; stays 1m; seems to act on any going. *B. Hanbury.*

MAWATEA 2 ch.f. Meldrum 112–Bon Feu 75 (Blason 109) (1982 8.2fg² 7.2s   **57**
10d 10.2s) May 13; smallish, workmanlike filly; half-sister to a winning plater; dam, plater, stayed 1m; moderate plater; stays 1¼m; probably acts on any going. *K. Stone.*

MAWJ 3 b.f. Sharpen Up 127–Village 91 (Charlottesville 135) (1981 6fg 5g   **—**
6d³ 5d 1982 8f) lightly-made filly; plating-class maiden; should stay 1m; has run respectably for an apprentice. *F. Durr.*

MAXIMAIN 2 ch.c. Monsanto 121–Long Valley 71 (Ribero 126) (1982 6f 8.2fg   **—**
7fg 8d 6s 7g) May 4; good-bodied colt; bad plater; blinkered second outing. *P. Burgoyne.*

MAXIMOVA (FR) 2 b.f. Green Dancer 131–Baracala (Swaps) (1982 6s* 6d*   **121**
6fg* 7g* 7f* 8s⁴)
When Maximova dead-heated in the Prix de la Salamandre at Longchamp in September she became only the third filly to win the race in the last twenty years, following Delmora in 1974 and Princesse Lida in 1979. Her record so far is very similar to Princesse Lida's. Princesse Lida, a daughter of Nijinsky trained by Alec Head, maintained her unbeaten record by winning the Salamandre, only to lose it when an odds-on favourite for another Group 1 race on her next start; Maximova, a granddaughter of Nijinsky trained by Head's daughter Criquette, extended her unbeaten run to five in the Salamandre and then ended her first season with a defeat at odds on in a Group 1 event. Both fillies were admirable two-year-olds and in our opinion Maximova was marginally the better. She faced a very tough opponent in the Salamandre in Deep Roots, who had dealt out a three-length beating to the Robert Papin winner Ma Biche, a stable-mate of Maximova's, and the English colt On Stage in the Prix Morny a month before. Maximova and Deep Roots were inseparable both in the betting at Longchamp and at the finish, but Maximova would certainly have won outright with a clearer run; she became trapped on the rails behind the front-running Interco as she moved up to challenge two furlongs out and had to be snatched up and pulled to the outside to find an opening. She nevertheless managed to find an excellent turn of foot, bursting through between Crystal Glitters and Deep Roots to take a half-length lead inside the final furlong. Unfortunately her exertions began to take their toll, her stride shortened and she was caught by the very determined Deep Roots. Crystal Glitters, later successful in the Prix Eclipse, was the next to finish, three lengths behind. Whereas Princesse Lida subsequently reopposed the colts in the Grand Criterium Maximova took on her own sex in the Prix Marcel Boussac on Arc day, starting at 2/1 on. The soft ground seemed to blunt her turn of foot and all she could do was stay on steadily in the straight to finish third, beaten one length behind the close finishers Goodbye Shelley and Mysterieuse Etoile. In the process she drifted quite badly right, hampering fourth-placed L'Attrayante, and the placings were later reversed.
By French standards Maximova had had quite a busy time for a two-year-old before the Prix de la Salamandre, racing four times in little more than two months. After gaining her first two victories by less than a length in a new-comers race at Chantilly and a minor event at Maisons-Laffitte, she showed her

Prix du Calvados, Deauville—highly-regarded Maximova (No. 2)
lands the odds from Soigneuse

true ability when racing on a sound surface for the first time in the Prix de Cabourg on the opening day of the Deauville meeting. Her four opponents, three of them winners of their last race, were quite unable to get her off the bridle; she quickened away most impressively inside the last two furlongs to win by eight lengths from Sevruga, who last time out had run Ma Biche to two and a half lengths. Not surprisingly Maximova started at odds on for the Group 3 Prix du Calvados later in the Deauville meeting, even though she was opposed by eleven other winning fillies including Miss Jonquiere and Palitana, the two who had run her close on her first two starts. She won well, making all and comfortably holding off Soigneuse, who received 3 lb, by half a length. L'Attrayante was two lengths further back in third.

Maximova (Fr) (b.f. Apr 16, 1980)	Green Dancer (b 1972)	Nijinsky (b 1967)	Northern Dancer Flaming Page
		Green Valley (br 1967)	Val de Loir Sly Pola
	Baracala (ch 1972)	Swaps (ch 1952)	Khaled Iron Reward
		Seximee (ch 1966)	Hasty Road Jambo

Will Maximova fare better at three than Princesse Lida, who gained her single success from six starts at that age in a race of no great importance? We think she will. She's a fine, big filly with plenty of scope and her dam Baracala, a late-maturing animal who didn't race until she was three, was a very different type from Princesse Lida's dam, the precocious two-year-old Princesse Lee. Maximova is Baracala's second reported foal and second winner following the lightly-raced Disco Girl, a sister who won over a mile and a half. Although Baracala didn't win until her eighth attempt she was a useful performer, accounting for a good field in the Prix Coronation over a mile at Saint-Cloud on her

545

Haras d'Etreham's "Maximova"

ninth and final appearance. She was sold two years later, carrying Disco Girl, for 800,000 francs (approximately £93,000), a reasonable figure for a winning half-sister to the Two Thousand Guineas winner Nonoalco. Baracala's sale price looked even more reasonable a year later in 1978 when her half-brother Stradavinsky won the nine-furlong Whitehall Stakes and reached the frame in the King Edward VII, Coral Eclipse and Queen Elizabeth II Stakes. Maximova is bred on the same lines as Stradavinsky, being a granddaughter of his sire Nijinsky and his dam Seximee, the latter the winner of two small sprint races in the USA. Seximee's dam Jambo was a winning half-sister to the smart Nancy Jr., who won the Kentucky Oaks over eight and a half furlongs.

The fact that Maximova has been entered for the One Thousand Guineas and not the Oaks suggests her connections have doubts about her staying a mile and a half, even though many of Green Dancer's offspring, including Disco Girl, have done so. Certainly Maximova showed plenty of pace at two and distances up to a mile and a quarter will probably suit her best. She can produce a splendid turn of foot, at least when the ground isn't soft, and she should prove just as hard to beat at three as she was at two. *Mme C. Head, France.*

MAYBEHANDY 4 b.f. Some Hand 119–Unpredictable 103 (Pardal 130) (1981 **58** 7s⁴ 8s⁴ 8g* 8g³ 8fg 9fg 7g² 8g 7fg* 7s³ 1982 7.2s 7fg³ 7f 7fg³ 7f* 7fg² 7g) leggy filly; plater as a 3-y-o; won handicap at Catterick in July and ran well next time; saw far too much daylight when running poorly final start; suited by 7f and 1m; probably acts on any going; needs holding up. *M. Camacho.*

MAYBELLA 3 b.f. Quiet Fling 124–July Mist 79 (High Treason 126) (1981 NR **62** 1982 10.2g 14.6fg² 14.6g 16g² 16s) 5,800F; lengthy filly; half-sister to minor winners here and abroad; dam won 1¼m claiming race; second in maiden races at Doncaster in July and Beverley in August; suited by a test of stamina. *J. Etherington.*

546

MAYBURY 3 ch.f. Manado 130–Lady Exbury 111 (Exbury 138) (1981 NR **81**
1982 10fg 10g³ 12fg 12g² 9g³ 8g³ 8fg* 10.1d* 10fg³ 10g* 8s) IR 7,200F, 13,000Y;
strong, most attractive filly; second foal; dam, half-sister to very smart Boreen,
stayed 1½m well; won maiden race at Warwick, handicap at Windsor and minor
event at Brighton in summer; best at up to 1¼m; acts on a firm and a soft surface
(ran badly on very soft going final start); suited by forcing tactics; sold to BBA
12,000 gns Newmarket December Sales. *G. Harwood.*

MAYGATE 4 gr.f. Malicious–Sovereign Gate 81 (Sovereign Path 125) (1981 —
10fg 12d 16.9s 14f 10fg 12fg 12g 10s 10d² 1982 10.6g 18.8fg) strong filly;
temperamental plater; tailed off both starts in 1982; stays 1½m; usually blinkered
as a 3-y-o. *D. H. Jones.*

MAYO BOY 2 b.g. Decoy Boy 129–Hethabella 62 (Hethersett 134) (1982 **82**
5f 6g² 5fg⁴ 6g 6d⁴ 6g) Apr 30; fair sort; half-brother to 1981 2-y-o 5f winner
Firdale Rosie (by Town Crier) and a winning hurdler; dam won over 1½m;
moderate maiden; will stay 7f; acts on a firm and a soft surface; consistent.
W. Wharton.

MAYOTTE 7 ch.m. Little Buskins 118–Jill Scott (Jock Scot 121) (1981 NR **79**
1982 14g 11.7d 12fg³ 16.1s* 16.1s* 20g* 18s²) smart staying hurdler; only
lightly raced on flat, but was winning her third handicap of the month when
trotting up by 8 lengths from Delta Queen at Newmarket in October; had
earlier been successful twice at Haydock, on first occasion in an apprentice
event; 1½ lengths second to Tea-Pot at Doncaster in November; suited by a
thorough test of stamina; probably acts on any going, but is well suited by
soft; genuine. *R. Holder.*

MAYPOLE LANE 3 ch.f. Grundy 137–Lauretta 111 (Relko 136) (1981 NR **64**
1982 7fg⁴ 10.5fg 9fg*) tall filly; third foal; half-sister to fairly useful 1¼m
winner Brinkley (by Moulton); dam won over middle distances; not raced again
after justifying short-priced favouritism in 11-runner maiden race at Newcastle
in July; will be suited by 1¼m. *H. Wragg.*

MAZERAT 3 b.f. Ballynockan 112–Cissac (Indian Ruler 89) (1981 6f 7fg —
1982 8d² 9g 10fg 13g 12fg 9s 8g) small filly; plating-class maiden; best run at
1m on soft ground; blinkered final start. *D. Ancil.*

MCCARTHY 4 b.c. Steel Heart 128–Chevy Chase (Raise You Ten 125) (1981 **80**
8.5fg 8g 6fg 6g 8d 10.2fg 10.8s⁴ 1982 8g³ 8d 10.4g) strong, quite attractive
colt; very useful performer at 2 yrs; disappointing since, but ran respectably
when third in apprentice handicap at Doncaster in March; probably stays 11f;
probably needs some give in the ground; has worn blinkers. *W. O'Gorman.*

MEADEWAY 2 b.f. Roi Soleil 125–Cotillion 73 (Gala Performance) (1982 **64**
5.3fg 5fg 5fg² 6f⁴) Apr 4; 1,200Y; second foal; dam 2-y-o 5f winner; plating-
class maiden; stays 6f. *H. Westbrook.*

MEAN FRANCINE 3 b.f. African Sky 124–Levrosa (Levmoss 133) (1981 6s **83**
1982 8g⁴ 7.3g⁴ 7g⁴ 8f 10g) tall, good-topped filly; put up a highly creditable
effort on second outing when finishing strongly to be just over 3 lengths fourth
of 10 to Pas de Seul in Hungerford Stakes at Newbury in August; didn't
reproduce that form; should stay 1m. *P. Kelleway.*

MEAUME 2 b.c. High Line 125–Cissac (Indian Ruler 89) (1982 8s 8.2s) May **75**
9; strong, close-coupled colt; half-brother to 5f winner Tou Fou (by Royben);
dam of little account; backward; in mid-division in October in maiden race at
York and minor event at Nottingham; will be suited by 1¼m+. *D. Ancil.*

MEDAALA 2 b.f. Owen Dudley 121–Mathilde 84 (Whistler 129) (1982 5g* **74**
5g* 5f² 5f⁴) Apr 8; 2,600F, 2,000Y; light-framed filly; half-sister to numerous
winners, including speedy 1974 2-y-o Material (by Song); dam at her best early
on at 2 yrs; successful twice in April, in 4-runner event at Edinburgh and in
small race at Newcastle; broke a knee bone at Redcar early the following month.
K. Stone.

MEDIA MAN 2 ch.c. Northfields–Awakening Rose (Le Levanstell 122) (1982 **85**
8d 10g 7s) Feb 25; 37,000Y; small colt; first foal; dam, French 10.5f winner, is
half-sister to Rose Laurel and Rambling Rose; ran moderately after finishing
promising sixth of 23 behind The Liquidator in maiden race at Newmarket in
October on first outing; backed from 12/1 to 15/2 to beat useful horses on second
appearance (went off much too fast). *W. Hastings-Bass.*

MEEKA GOLD (USA) 3 b.c. Ward McAllister–Locklear (First Landing) **109**
(1981 6g* 6g² 7f* 8g* 1982 7g 7g 10.4fg⁴ 10f² 10f² 10g 10f 10.4d* 10.5g⁴ 11d²
10g 10.8s*) strong, good sort; had little trouble landing odds in apprentice

race at Chester in August and beat odds-on Montekin unchallenged by 6 lengths in minor event at Warwick in October; in frame several other starts, including in Dee Stakes at Chester (2¾ lengths fourth of 11 to Ivano), XYZ Handicap at Newcastle (1½ lengths second to well-handicapped Crossways), Zetland Gold Cup Handicap at Redcar (caught on line and beaten a short head by Sav Primula) and Doonside Cup at Ayr (creditable neck second to Fine Sun); stays 11f; acts on any going; genuine; sent to USA. *S. Norton.*

MEGGIES DENE 6 b.m. Apollo Eight–Singing Hinny (Melody Maker 116) — (1981 NR 1982 16f 13.8t) winning hurdler; tailed off in maiden races at Beverley and Catterick. *W. Barrett.*

MEHRAGAN 2 gr.f. Dance In Time–First Watch (Primera 131) (1982 7d 7s) — June 2; 2,100Y; good-bodied filly; sister to a poor animal and half-sister to a winner in Ireland; dam half-sister to dam of Nocturnal Spree and Tootens; last at Leicester in the autumn in maiden race and minor event, getting very stirred up in preliminaries on first occasion. *R. Hollinshead.*

MEIKLEOUR 3 b.g. Reliance II 137–Videmanette (High Perch 126) (1981 NR 65 1982 12fg⁴ 14.6g³ 14fg 16s) good-bodied gelding; half-brother to fairly useful middle-distance stayer Almond Valley (by Jimmy Reppin) and very useful out-and-out stayer Mountain Cross (by French Beige); dam quite useful hurdler; in frame in maiden races at Redcar in June and Ripon in August; should stay long distances; a strong puller. *J. W. Watts.*

MELASH 2 br.f. Meldrum 112–Kailash 78 (Mandamus 120) (1982 6f) Apr 17; — first foal; dam won 4 times over 1¼m and also won over hurdles; slow-starting seventh of 9 in maiden race at Carlisle in July. *E. Weymes.*

MELBA TOAST 8 br.g. Meldrum 112–Ivory Coast 90 (Poaching 115) (1981 — 7g 6g* 5s 6s 5g² 5g* 6fg 5fg* 5fg² 5d⁴ 5f 5fg 6f³ 5f² 6d³ 5g 5g 1982 5fg 6g 5fg² 5g 5fg 5fg) strong gelding; plater; stays 6f; acts on hard going; suitable mount for an inexperienced rider; often wears blinkers. *T. Taylor.*

MELCAIRN 3 br.g. Pitcairn 126–Karatha (Mossborough 126 or Tamerlane — 128) (1981 7f 8s 8s 1982 12g 9g 9.4fg 10g 9f³) leggy gelding; plater; promises to stay 1¼m; blinkered fourth start (ran badly). *K. Stone.*

MELCHESTER 5 b.g. Supreme Sovereign 119–Two on a Tower 89 (Nulli — Secundus 89) (1981 NR 1982 8g 10.1d 10fg) probably of little account. *R. Hodges.*

MELCOMBE REGIS 2 b.c. Red Alert 127–Alcinea 93 (Sweet Revenge 129) 70 (1982 5g 5f³ 5s) Feb 20; 2,600F, 3,800Y; small, good-bodied colt; first foal; dam won twice over 5f at 2 yrs; 3¼ lengths third of 7 to Town Star in maiden auction event at Beverley in April, only form: not seen out again until October. *M. McCormack.*

MELINDRA 3 b.f. Gold Form 108–Welsh Spear (Welsh Saint 126) (1981 64 5fg 5g 1982 5f³ 5g 5g 7d 5g² 5f* 5.8f) strong, lengthy, workmanlike filly; made virtually all to win maiden race at Kempton in September; will stay 6f; acts on firm going. *D. Elsworth.*

MELISSA JANE 4 gr.f. No Mercy 126–Rich Harvest (Bounteous 125) (1981 80 8d³ 8f* 8.2f* 8g² 8.5fg* 8g³ 8g⁴ 1982 7f 8f 8f 7.6f* 6fg 8g 8g 7s⁴ 8v 8s 7d) lengthy filly; good mover; returned to form in 4-runner £11,600 Queen Elizabeth Stakes (Handicap) at Lingfield in June, getting up inside last furlong and beating Ta Morgan by 1½ lengths; off course 2 months before finishing about 5 lengths fourth behind dead-heaters Lucky Man and Hello Sunshine in another valuable race at Ascot in September, best subsequent effort; stays 1m well and finds 6f too short; seems to act on any going, but clearly goes well on firm; has given trouble at start. *R. Thompson.*

MELLOW MOOD 3 b.f. Badedas 81–June Clare (Fairwell) (1981 5.8f 7fg — 8d 1982 10s 8fg 12s 8s) of little account. *J. Edmunds.*

MEL MIRA 2 ch.f. Roi Soleil 125–Hei'land Mary 76 (Highland Melody 112) 68 (1982 6g 6g² 6d³ 8f 8.2d) May 26; 300F, 700Y; good-bodied filly; first foal; dam a sprinter; plating-class maiden; better suited by 1m than 6f. *D. H. Jones.*

MELODIE MYSTIQUE 3 ch.f. Record Token 128–Sweet Sauce (High Perch 52 126) (1981 NR 1982 8fg 8f²(dis) 8g² 10.1fg²) 1,500F, 4,600Y; very big filly; half-sister to fair 1978 2-y-o 5f winner Sweetboy (by Richboy); dam poor plater; stays 1¼m; claimed £2,550 after final start and has reportedly been sent to Switzerland. *P. Haslam.*

MELODY MOON 7 b.m. Philip of Spain 126–Cry For The Moon (Town Crier **44**
119) (1981 NR 1982 8.2v² 8f) fair handicapper at her best; very lightly
raced nowadays; stays 1m; appears to act on any going, but is well suited by
some give in the ground; suitable mount for an apprentice; missed break final
start (April); has been to stud and in 1981 had a filly by Mandrake Major.
D. Smith.

MELOWEN 2 ch.f. Owen Dudley 121–Gambit (King's Troop 118) (1982 **75**
5fg 5f² 6f³ 5fg² 7f 7f² 6g² 7fg 7d² 8f 6v² 7d⁴) Mar 13; 1,600Y; leggy filly;
half-sister to 6f winner Migrant (by My Swallow); dam closely related to outstanding sprinter Floribunda; second in 3 maiden auction events, a maiden race
and 2 nurseries; stays 7f well; acts on any going; blinkered seventh outing.
M. W. Easterby.

MEL'S CHOICE 4 b. or br.g. Birdbrook 110–Port Meadow 83 (Runnymede **69**
123) (1981 5g 5f 5f 6d⁴ 5d⁴ 6f⁴ 5f 5g 7g 7v 1982 5f² 5f⁴ 5fg³ 5fg* 5fg* 5s³)
good-topped gelding; had successful season and was heavily backed when
winning handicaps at Beverley in May (blinkered for only time) and at Haydock
(£4,000 event) and Redcar in September; made most of running and rallied
well when beating Rambling River a neck on last-named course; seems best
at 5f; acts on any going; genuine; started slowly second outing. *M. W.
Easterby.*

MELTHEMI (USA) 2 ch.c. Restless Wind–Surfboard Betty (Bold Commander) **101**
(1982 5fg 5fg⁴ 5fg³ 5f* 6g* 6f² 6g 5g) Mar 13; useful-looking colt: good mover;
half-brother to minor winners here and in USA, including 6f winner J. E. B.
Stuart (by Turn to Reason); dam never ran; showed much improved form when
winning maiden race at Beverley in July; readily defied 7 lb penalty in nursery
at Pontefract the following month; good second to Nagarro in valuable Newmarket nursery 3 weeks later, easily best subsequent effort; suited by 6f;
acts on firm going; trained by D. Ringer first 3 starts. *M. H. Easterby.*

MELTING SNOWS 3 b.f. High Top 131–Midsummertime (Midsummer Night **—**
II 117) (1981 7d* 7g 1982 12.2g⁴ 12g 12g 10s) well-made filly; won
maiden race at Newbury in 1981; soundly beaten all subsequent starts; should
stay middle distances; blinkered final outing; sold BBA 10,000 gns Newmarket
December Sales. *F. J. Houghton.*

MELTON ROSS 2 br.g. Dawn Review 105–Boudella 101 (Rockefella) (1982 **65**
6d 6fg⁴ 7f 7fg 5g 5g 7d 7s) May 28; 500Y; leggy, rather close-coupled gelding;
closely related to 11.7f winner By Command (by March Past) and half-brother
to a winner in Norway; dam, half-sister to smart middle-distance filly In
Command, won over 6f at 2 yrs; plating-class maiden; will stay 1m; bolted
after final appearance. *D. Morrill.*

MELVIN 3 br.f. Quiet Fling 124–Clarity 98 (Panaslipper 130) (1981 NR **—**
1982 9g 10d) half-sister to numerous winners, including quite useful 1979
2-y-o 5f winner Loyal Manacle (by Manacle), and fairly useful stayer Amity
(by Amber Rama); dam, winner at up to 1¼m, is half-sister to Santa Claus;
behind in maiden races at Wolverhampton in April and Lingfield in June.
P. Walwyn.

MELYNO 3 b.c. Nonoalco 131–Comely (Boran) (1981 5.5g 6f³ 6.5f* 6.5s 7.5s* **130** d
1982 8v* 8fg* 9fg* 9.2g³ 8g 8f⁴)
April the twenty-fifth turned out to be something of a red letter day for
Stavros Niarchos. Involved in racing on and off for over twenty-five years,
he has invested a prodigious amount of money in bloodstock and although
Pipe of Peace was a close third in the 1957 Two Thousand Guineas and
Nureyev won that race in 1980 only to be disqualified, Melyno's victory in the
Poule d'Essai des Poulains at Longchamp on the last Sunday in April provided
Mr Niarchos with his first classic success. Ironically Melyno, bought for the
equivalent of £92,000 as a yearling at Longchamp, was by no means the most
expensive of his owner's purchases that year. A dozen or so colts cost more,
notably Lichine who set a world record when sold for 1,700,000 dollars and
has yet to win a pattern race despite possessing ability well above average.
For part of the season Melyno looked like developing into a brilliant miler.
Rated about a stone behind Green Forest in the Handicap Libre chiefly on the
basis of his success in the Prix Thomas Bryon—a race Nureyev had won—he
followed a typical route for a colt being aimed at the Poule d'Essai des Poulains
by contesting the Prix de Fontainebleau over the course and distance earlier in
the month. He didn't face a particularly exacting task but still impressed

observers by the way he justified favouritism with a three-length success from Welsh Term, effortlessly drawing clear after leading a quarter of a mile out. With Green Forest the subject of various rumours, Melyno started a well-backed second favourite in a field of nine for the classic three weeks later; the other runners included the Fontainebleau fourth Tampero, the Irish colt Day Is Done and the British challenger Telephone Man. Melyno kept taking our eye in the paddock and his performance matched his appearance. Always travelling strongly in behind the leaders as Day Is Done set a good gallop, he produced a powerful run in the straight, swept past Day Is Done and Green Forest a furlong from home and drew clear under hand riding to gain a length-and-a-half win from the strong-finishing Tampero. Day Is Done and Green Forest were close up in third and fourth.

On the face of it the form of the French Guineas wasn't outstanding—Green Forest had evidently run below his best—and the Prix Jean Prat at Chantilly on French Derby day in June presented Melyno with an apparently stiffer assignment. The four remaining participants consisted of Tampero and Green Forest again, the Two Thousand Guineas winner Zino and the good English colt Be My Native. Melyno put up a devastating display. Following Zino, who set a cracking pace, from the outset, he unleashed a tremendous turn of foot immediately Saint-Martin asked him to improve with a furlong and a half to go, rapidly eliminating a three-length deficit and storming away for a resounding four-length success with Zino holding on to second by half a length from Be My Native. The time bettered Night Alert's course record by over two seconds.

After this win it seemed that Melyno needed only to prove his superiority against the older horses, none of whom had revealed exceptional merit, to take the palm as the best miler in Europe. Rather surprisingly he failed to win again. Odds on to beat Al Nasr, The Wonder, Big John and two others in the Prix d'Ispahan at Longchamp later in June, Melyno didn't find the expected turn of foot in the closing stages, losing out by three quarters of a length and a neck to Al Nasr and The Wonder, while in the Prix Jacques le Marois at Deauville he finished tailed off behind The Wonder. A comprehensive attempt to discover the reason for this dismal run, involving several specialists, a dope test and an electrocardiogram, came up with the explanation that Melyno had suffered from a painful sprain in a testicle soon after the start. We assume this unfortunate experience had no lasting effect on Melyno; if so, his final appearance in the Prix du Moulin de Longchamp in September, seemed to reveal his limitations conclusively. Close up as Sandhurst Prince led them into the straight, he was left behind once the back-to-form Green Forest mastered the English runner, coming home six lengths behind the champion two-year-old of 1981 in fourth, beaten also by The Wonder and Sandhurst Prince.

Nonoalco hasn't enjoyed so much success at stud as his attractive pedigree and excellent form suggested he would. The best European miler of 1974, he has sired such good performers as Noalcoholic, Noalto and Nonoalca but Melyno is his only Group 1 winner to date; following a drop in the average sale price of his yearlings from 49,000 guineas in 1978 and 1979 to 34,000 guineas in 1980 and 1981 he was exported to Japan. If Melyno had been by a more popular stallion it is possible he would have fetched a much higher price as a yearling for his dam's record is a fine one. Her six other winners include Comeram (by Amber Rama), a good miler who ran second in the Grand Criterium and Irish Two Thousand Guineas, and Pharly (by Lyphard), a tip-top colt who had successes in the Prix de la Foret, Prix Lupin and Prix du Moulin to his name. Comely won only one race but showed very useful form over middle distances, finishing in the frame in the Prix Chloe and Prix Cleopatre; she was out of a half-sister to the Grand Prix de Paris winner Armistice and the very smart American middle-distance performer Twice Worthy. Melyno will be at his owner's Haras de Fresnay-le-Buffard in 1983, alongside Persepolis. A good-looking colt who stayed nine furlongs and would have got further, he acted on any going. *F. Mathet, France.*

Poule d'Essai des Poulains, Longchamp—a clear-cut victory for Melyno; Tampero (No. 1) just gets the best of Day Is Done and the favourite Green Forest for second

MEMENTO (USA) 3 b. or br.c. Roberto 131–Bitty Girl 123 (Habitat 134) **105**
(1981 NR 1982 7g⁴ 6g⁴ 8f² 7fg⁴ 8g² 7g* 8d³ 10s) $300,000Y; rangy, attractive colt; good walker and mover; third foal; half-brother to stakes-placed American winner Nijit (by Nijinsky); dam, sister to Hot Spark, won first 5 starts, all over 5f, including Queen Mary, Molecomb and Lowther Stakes, and later won at up to 1m in USA; accounted for Southern Music by ½ length in 12-runner Ballycorus Stakes at Leopardstown in July; placed most other starts, notably when length second to Tellurano in Kilruddery Stakes at Leopardstown, 2 lengths fourth of 21 behind Merlins Charm in Jersey Stakes at Royal Ascot and 2¼ lengths second to Senior Citizen in Coolmore Hello Gorgeous Stakes at the Curragh; stays 1m; seems to act on any going; blinkered last 5 starts; racing in California. *V. O'Brien, Ireland.*

MEMORANDA (USA) 3 br.g. Verbatim–Gallihad Rose (Hafiz II 136) (1981 — NR 1982 8fg 8fg) $70,000Y; strong, stocky gelding; fifth foal; half-brother to 2 winners, including stakes-placed Wonder Bowl (by Greek Money); dam won 6f claiming race; soundly beaten in Wood Ditton Stakes and maiden race at Newmarket in April; sent to Singapore. *E. Eldin.*

MEMORIA IN ETERNA 2 br.c. Rheingold 137–Fighting Lady 104 (Chebs **75** Lad 120) (1982 7fg⁴ 7g) May 6; 14,000Y; fair sort; first foal; dam won over 5f and 7f; backward, 6 lengths fourth to very easy winner Proclaim in 19-runner maiden race at Newbury in July, better effort; should stay 1¼m. *R. Baker.*

MENANDER (USA) 3 ch.c. Honest Pleasure–Curvature (Gallant Man) (1981 — NR 1982 8fg 10fg 12fg) $120,000Y; robust colt; third foal; dam unraced sister to 2 stakes winners and daughter of Dotted Line, a high-class filly at up to 2m; sire, champion 2-y-o of 1975, won 12 times from 5½f to 1¼m; behind in Wood Ditton Stakes at Newmarket in April and 2 maiden races at Salisbury in May. *B. Swift.*

MENDALEAK 5 b.g. Hipster 101–Potter's Wheel (Aureole 132) (1981 NR — 1982 8.2fg 10fg) light-framed gelding; plater; stays 1¾m; acts on any going; often blinkered. *V. Thompson.*

MEND IT 4 ch.g. Patch 129–Startop 72 (Divine Gift 127) (1981 10g 9f 11.5g⁴ — 14s 12.2g 10d 1982 9f 10f 8f 10fg 12fg) leggy, close-coupled gelding; poor plater; blinkered fourth outing; trained until after third start by V. Mitchell. *N. Bycroft.*

Prix Jean Prat, Chantilly—Melyno leaves Zino, Be My Native and Tampero standing

MEN

MENJOU 3 b.g. He Loves Me 120–Goldwyn Princess 72 (Native Prince) (1981 —
6g 1982 8g⁴ 10f 10f 8f 8f 8g 11.7d) lengthy, workmanlike gelding; plating-
class maiden; stays 1m; blinkered sixth start; sold 500 gns Ballsbridge December
Sales. *R. Sheather.*

MENNEA (USA) 3 ch.c. Wajima–Had My Way (Summer Tan) (1981 NR **112**
1982 8fg* 8fg* 8fg* 8f*) $100,000Y; quite attractive, leggy, rather lightly-made
colt; good walker and mover; closely related to 2 winners by Cornish Prince,
namely very useful 6f and 7f winner Ackermann and very smart 1975 American
2-y-o Imacornishprince, and half-brother to several other winners, 2 of them
stakes winners; dam sister to high-class 2-y-o Eudaemon; a smart colt who won
all 4 of his starts, namely maiden race at Newbury, minor event at Goodwood
(odds on) and handicaps at Sandown and Kempton; showed an excellent turn
of foot and outclassed his opponents when beating Miss Longchamp by 3 lengths
in £4,700 event on last-named in September; will stay 1¼m; yet to race on an
easy surface. *R. Price.*

MENTON 2 b.c. Relkino 131–Antimacassar 86 (Tudor Melody 129) (1982 7fg —
7g 8g) May 23; well-made, quite attractive colt; second foal; dam, second over
7f and 1m, is half-sister to smart animals Smoggy and Dish Dash; no worthwhile
form in fair company at Newmarket. *R. Armstrong.*

MERCI 7 ch.g. No Mercy 126–Rose Blanche 89 (French Beige 127) (1981 NR —
1982 10.6f) won over 6f as a 3-y-o and stayed further; acted on any going;
sometimes wore blinkers; dead. *J. Cann.*

MERCIA SOUND 3 b.c. Wishing Star 117–Audition (Tower Walk 130) (1981 **67**
5d 5s 5fg² 5f³ 6g³ 7f² 8f 7fg 8d 8s   1982 12g³ 12s 12f³ 10.6fg⁴ 12f⁴ 12f⁴) useful
sort; middle-distance handicapper; acts on firm going. *R. Hollinshead.*

MERCIFUL SUN 4 gr.f. No Mercy 126–Follow the Sun (Kythnos 126 or Saint **37**
Crespin III 132) (1981 7fg 7g 8fg 10fg 10f⁴   1982 8s² 10g 8d) compact filly;
plater; stays 1¼m; blinkered once as a 3-y-o. *M. Haynes.*

MERCREDI 3 b.g. Mount Hagen 127–Amorce 81 (Le Levanstell 122) (1981 6s —
6g   1982 8d 10fg 11f 10f 11.7d) lengthy gelding; beaten some way in maiden
races and a handicap; has given trouble at start. *J. Holt.*

MERCY CURE 6 gr.m. No Mercy 126–Sinecure (Parthia 132) (1981 5fg 5d **60**
5.1fg³ 5fg² 5f² 5fg* 5.6f* 5g 5f* 5fg⁴ 5g 5g   1982 5f 5g³ 5f 5f 5f* 5.1f⁴ 5fg 5.3fg
5f 5g) sprint handicapper; won £3,900 event at Redcar in June; acted on firm
going; blinkered once at 3 yrs; sometimes sweated up; suitable mount for an
apprentice; genuine; reported in foal to Manado. *D. Dale.*

MERCY LESS 3 b.g. No Mercy 126–Pink Moss 82 (Ballymoss 136) (1981 NR **58**
1982 10f 12f 13.3f 16d⁴ 15.5f² 15.5f 11.7d⁴ 12v) lengthy, fair sort; fifth foal;
dam won over 1¾m; only plating class; suited by a test of stamina. *R. Smyth.*

MERE GAMBLER 5 b.g. Jimmy Reppin 131–Stormy Gal 71 (Rockavon 120) —
(1981 NR   1982 10d 7s) compact gelding; seems a poor performer nowadays;
bred to stay at least 7f; probably acts on any going; blinkered once at 3 yrs.
M. Eckley.

MERELY A SECRET (USA) 2 ch.c. Secretariat–Lady Mere 118 (Decoy Boy **80**
129) (1982 6f 7d 7g* 7g 8g² 7.6fg⁴) Apr 3; robust, short-legged, good-looking
colt; second foal; half-brother to 3-y-o Alkis (by Roberto); dam smart from 5f
to 1m; won maiden race at Ayr in July; good second to Dancing Meg in nursery
at York 2 months later; lacks pace, and will be suited by 1¼m. *P. Walwyn.*

MERIKA 2 gr.f. Morston 125–Mariko (Dancer's Image) (1982 6s) Apr 15; —
first foal; dam Irish 5f winner; unquoted, behind in 16-runner maiden race at
Leicester in November. *D. Whelan.*

MERINGUE 3 ch.f. Ballymore 123–Icing 112 (Prince Tenderfoot 126) (1981 **88**
7g³   1982 7fg³ 8g⁴ 8d* 9fg² 9f* 12g² 8d 10g 12d⁴ 10s⁴) first foal; dam won
from 5f to 1m at 2 yrs; won minor event at Navan in June by ¾ length from
Sleepy Hollow and accounted for Kraal by 1½ lengths in 4-runner handicap at
Mallow in August; excellent ¾-length second to Miraflora in Brownstown Stakes
at the Curragh later in August (caught near finish); suited by 1¼m; acts on any
going; consistent; sold to BBA 32,000 gns Newmarket December Sales. *K.
Prendergast, Ireland.*

MERITOUS 7 b.g. Decoy Boy 129–Welsh Huntress 106 (Big Game) (1981 6d **69**
6g 6fg³ 6f 6f 6fg 6g 5fg 6d 5d 6s   1982 6d 6f 7.6g 5fg 7g⁴ 6f 6g 7.6fg 7f² 8g² 6d²
7g* 7g* 7d³ 6s) big, lengthy gelding; second 3 times before winning handicaps
at Beverley in August and York in September; stays 1m; acts on any going but
is suited by some give in the ground; has worn blinkers and bandages; ran
poorly final outing. *T. Taylor.*

552

*Macallan Malt Whisky Trophy Handicap, Sandown—Mennea (right)
continues unbeaten, very narrowly from Royaber*

MERLANE / b.g. Tamerlane 128–Harry's Daughter (Will Somers 114§) (1981 —
  9g 12s 12s² 12.8s⁴ 12g² 10fg 11.5d 12g 1982 10.2g) sturdy ex-Irish gelding;
  well beaten in amateur riders event over here; stayed 1½m; acted on soft going;
  dead. *G. Balding.*

MERLINS CHARM (USA) 3 b.f. Bold Bidder–Lucky Spell (Lucky Mel) **113**
  (1981 6f⁴ 7d 6g* 1982 7fg² 8fg 7fg* 8f³ 8f 7g² 7s) $130,000Y; leggy, quite

*Jersey Stakes, Ascot—Merlins Charm quickens up very well to win going
away from Silly Steven, Beldale Lustre, Memento
(almost hidden) and Bruckner*

Mr R. E. Sangster's "Merlins Charm"

attractive filly; not the best of movers; second foal; dam very smart winner of 12 races at up to 9f; quickened up well to beat Silly Steven by ½ length going away in Jersey Stakes at Royal Ascot; also placed behind Chalon at Newmarket in Ladbrokes Nell Gwyn Stakes (½-length second of 12) and Child Stakes (over a length third of 7 after not having best of runs), and behind The Quiet Bidder at Doncaster in Kiveton Park Steel Stakes (sweating, finished ½-length second); will stay 1¼m; apparently needs a sound surface. *B. Hills.*

MERMAID 2 br.f. Furry Glen 121–Wavy Navy (Hardicanute 131) (1982 7fg **70** 7g 8s) Apr 26; angular filly; third foal; half-sister to 2 winners, including very useful Irish middle-distance stayer Red Invader (by Brave Invader); dam won 3 times at up to 1m in Ireland; backward, ran on strongly after being outpaced when 7 lengths fifth of 29 to Alligatrix in maiden race at Newmarket in August, first outing and easily best effort; should stay 1m. *D. Ringer.*

MERRY KING 5 ch.g. King's Equity 106–Paramatta 85 (Pardal 130) (1981 — NR 1982 13.8f) fair sort; half-brother to Irish 13f winner Mirarja (by Miralgo); dam raced only at 2 yrs; beat only one home in 17-runner maiden race won by Blakey Bank at Catterick in May on only outing (unquoted); sold to W. Clay 780 gns Doncaster October Sales. *N. Callaghan.*

MERRY TASSE 2 ch.c. Rymer 121–Fragrant Coffee 80 (Frankincense 120) **67** (1982 5g 5f² 5g²·5fg* 6fg 5f 5fg⁴ 5g* 5g 5f 5g³ 6d 5g) Apr 18; compact, lightly-made colt; doesn't impress in his slower paces; first foal; dam placed over 5f at 2 yrs; always front rank when successful in sellers at Beverley (bought in 1,550 gns) in June and Ripon (bought in 2,700 gns) in August; should stay further than 5f; none too consistent. *W. Bentley.*

MESA KID (USA) 3 b.c. Jig Dancer–Double Princess (Prince Blessed) (1981   **67** d
NR 1982 8fg³ 8f 10g⁴ 12f 8fg 10fg 10s) $13,500Y, $50,000 2-y-o; half-brother
to 6 winners by Hempaces, including stakes winners Tonto Basin and Tonto Rim;
dam, winner of claiming races at up to 7f, is half-sister to smart stakes winner
Bahia Key; in frame in maiden races at Warwick and Folkestone; stays 1¼m;
blinkered fifth start. *P. Cole.*

METCALFE MERCURY 2 b. or br.g. Workboy 123–Sovereign Melody 89§   **65**
(Fortino II 120) (1982 5fg 5fg 6f 6f⁴ 5f 6g) Mar 27; strong, good-bodied
gelding; poor mover; fifth foal; dam 2-y-o 5f winner; plating-class maiden;
suited by 6f; acts on firm going; blinkered final appearance; exported to Malaysia.
M. W. Easterby.

METRO MAID 3 ch.f. Connaught 130–Relza 91 (Relko 136) (1981 7g 1982   **—**
10f 16fg 17fg⁴ 15fg 12g) strong, lengthy filly; poor maiden; blinkered fourth
start; changed hands 1,800 gns Newmarket July Sales; sold to W. Clay 2,700
gns Ascot August Sales. *Sir Mark Prescott.*

METUCHEN 2 ch.f. Star Appeal 133–Merchantmen's Girl 58 (Klairon 131)   **82**
(1982 5f 6f 7f 7f 8fg 7v⁴) Apr 12; sturdy, quite attractive filly; excellent
mover; half-sister to winning 3-y-o sprinter Lindsey (by Mummy's Pet); dam
placed over 5f; showed ability in good-class company, on final outing finishing
9 lengths fourth of 5 to Special Leave, after leading 5f, in Hyperion Stakes
at Ascot in October; stays 1m; good enough to win ordinary maiden race.
D. Elsworth.

MIAMI DOLPHIN 2 br.f. Derrylin 115–Maggibillibyte 77 (Constable 119)   **85**
(1982 5fg³ 5fg² 5f² 5f 7g² 6f⁴ 5fg⁴ 7fg) June 2; 7,000Y; workmanlike filly;
good walker; half-sister to several winners, including fairly useful 1977 2-y-o
5f performer Maggydamus (by Mandamus); dam 7f to 1¼m selling handicapper;
had 8 races without winning, but was second 3 times, and almost invariably
close up; creditable sixth in Waterford Candelabra Stakes at Goodwood in
August on final outing; stays 7f; acts on firm going; genuine and consistent.
P. Kelleway.

MIANALCO 3 br.g. Nonoalco 131–La Mia Raggazza 76 (Alcide 136) (1981   **—**
6f 1982 7.2f) robust gelding; has an enlarged off-fore knee; tailed off in
maiden race and valuable seller at Haydock; sold 490 gns Ascot 2nd June Sales.
M. Naughton.

MIANDRA 2 ch.f. Porto Bello 118–Moral (Aureole 132) (1982 5fg 6f 5f 7fg   **52**
7f*(dis) 8.2fg 8.2s) Apr 14; 850F; sturdy filly; usually carries plenty of condition; half-sister to 2 minor winners and 2 winners over jumps; came out best
in desperate finish to 15-runner seller at Catterick in August, beating Too
Familiar a head, but hung left in closing stages and was disqualified; showed
nothing in her other races; suited by 7f, acts on firm going. *N. Tinkler.*

MICKLETON STAR 2 b.c. Comedy Star 121–Gingermede 76 (Runnymede   **74**
123) (1982 6fg 6s 6d 6v³ 6d) Apr 12; small colt; second foal; dam 2-y-o
sprint winner; blinkered first time when 2½ lengths third of 9 to Captain
Tempest in maiden race at Folkestone in October, best effort. *J. Dunlop.*

MICKS BABY 2 b.f. Roi Soleil 125–Andy's Girl 65 (Court Feathers 120)   **59**
(1982 5g 6g 5fg⁴ 5g 5s 5s) Feb 24; 480F; compact filly; half-sister to a winning
plater; dam showed a little ability at 2 yrs; 8 lengths fourth of 15 to Boy Trumpeter in maiden race at Windsor in August, only form; possibly requires a firm
surface. *D. Ancil.*

MICK'S RITUAL 3 ch.g. Malacate 131–Aurabella 113 (Aureole 132) (1981   **—**
6fg⁴ 6fg 6g⁴ 8fg 8.2d) leggy, lengthy gelding; plating-
class maiden; bred to stay 1¼m; blinkered final outing in 1981. *M. W. Easterby.*

MICK'S STAR 2 br.g. Orange Bay 131–Starboard Belle 85 (Right Tack 131)   **81**
(1982 6g 7f 8f² 8d*) Apr 4; 3,000Y; big, rather leggy gelding; has rather a
round action; fourth foal; dam won over 6f and 7f at 2 yrs; showed improved
form when winning 19-runner nursery at Pontefract by 3 lengths from Hasty
Flirt; gelded afterwards; will stay 1¼m; seems to act on any going but may
prove best with some give in the ground; good mount for an apprentice.
M. W. Easterby.

MIDDLETON SUE 3 ch.f. Rugantino 97–Twyford Ridge (Schapiro 99)   **—**
(1981 6d⁴ 6fg³ 5d 8g⁴ 1982 10f 12fg 12g 8.3g 12fg 8f³ 10v 15.5v 12s) close-
coupled, plain filly; plater; should stay at least 1¼m; ran badly in blinkers
third start; sold 490 gns Ascot November Sales. *R. Hannon.*

MIDDLIN THRANG 4 b.g. Farm Walk 111–Darling Do (Derring-Do 131) **68**
(1981 9s 8g* 8.2s⁴ 10.6s 12.3g 8f³ 8.2f² 8g⁴ 8d 8.2d 1982 8fg⁴ 9g² 11fg* 12g*
12g² 12fg 11f² 12.2f* 10.6s 11s 12s) small, workmanlike gelding; won handicaps
at Hamilton in July, Ripon in August and Catterick in September, being waited
with each time; stays 1½m; acts on any going, but is ideally suited by a sound
surface; has a fair turn of foot, but has sometimes looked none too resolute.
Miss S. Hall.

MIDNIGHT FLIT 2 b.f. Bold Lad (Ire) 133–Tawny Owl 123 (Faberge II **88**
121) (1982 6f 7fg² 7s⁴ 7s⁴) Mar 30; neat, attractive filly; excellent walker;
sister to useful 1m winner Bold Owl, and half-sister to a winner; dam won
at up to 1m in France and was placed in Poule d'Essai des Pouliches; beaten
short head in 19-runner maiden race at Chepstow in August; ran well at York
next time, and moderately at Redcar the time afterwards; will stay 1m; seems
to act on any going. *H. T. Jones.*

MIDNIGHT MOUSE (USA) 2 gr.f. Silver Series–Hada Say (Sadair) (1982 **69**
5g³ 5fg³ 6fg² 6g 8.2g³ 8f 7g) Feb 10; $15,000Y; small filly; half-sister to 3
winners in USA; dam stakes-placed winner of 9 sprint races; placed in varied
races, including a good-class 6f seller and 1m nursery; better suited by 1m
than shorter distances. *P. Cole.*

MIDRIDGE DRIFT 4 ch.f. Most Secret 119–Lyn's Pride 85 (Star Moss 122) **—**
(1981 5g 5g 6g 1982 10.1fg 10f 8f) sturdy filly; poor plater; sometimes
blinkered; sold to W. Charles 525 gns Ascot September Sales. *K. Ivory.*

MIDWEEK SPECIAL 2 b. or br.f. Lucky Wednesday 124–Cherry Cake **—**
(Pieces of Eight 128) (1982 6f 7f 7g 8f) Mar 22; 960F, 3,100Y; first foal;
dam poor maiden; 8½ lengths ninth of 20 to Figure de Danse in maiden auction
event at Redcar in September, final outing; will be suited by 1¼m. *G. Pritchard-
Gordon.*

MIGELITTO (FR) 10 ch.g. Lorenzaccio 130–Vivien 66 (Nearco) (1981 **—**
18s 16g 1982 16s) out-and-out staying handicapper; acts on any going
but is suited by firm; has worn blinkers; suitable mount for an apprentice;
sold 820 gns Doncaster June Sales and resold 480 gns Doncaster August Sales.
M. Chapman.

MIGHTY FLY 3 b.f. Comedy Star 121–Lettuce 60 (So Blessed 130) (1981 **85**
5fg 5d 5f³ 5.8h⁴ 1982 7fg 10.1fg 8d* 8g* 8fg⁴ 8fg³ 8fg⁴ 8g² 8g⁴ 8g* 8s) strong
filly; won maiden race at Salisbury in June and handicaps at Bath in July
and Newmarket in October; gamely held off Chris's Lad by a neck on last-
named; ran creditably most other starts; stays 1m; seems to act on any going;
genuine and consistent. *D. Elsworth.*

MIGHTY MONOCLE 2 b.c. Free State 125–Forest Flower 91 (Fine Blade **51**
121) (1982 6fg 7f 6g³) Apr 22; 1,500Y; strong, compact colt; first foal;
dam 2-y-o 5f winner; plater; exported to Algeria. *W. Musson.*

MIGHTY STEEL 2 b.c. High Top 131–Shortwood 90 (Skymaster 126) (1982 **—**
6g 7g) Apr 18; strong colt; half-brother to several winners, including smart
middle-distance handicapper Royal Match (by Sovereign Path) and very useful
1974 2-y-o Tranos (by Caliban); dam sprinter; well beaten in minor events
at Ripon and Newcastle in August; sold to T. Craig 4,600 gns Doncaster October
Sales. *Miss S. Hall.*

MIGOLETTY 3 b.f. Oats 126–Loch Leven 87 (Le Levanstell 122) (1981 **59**
8g 8fg 8d 1982 12.2g* 12.2g 16h 16f) lightly-made filly; narrowly won modest
maiden race at Catterick in March; behind in handicaps afterwards, wearing
blinkers on third start and looking reluctant to race on fourth; should stay
beyond 1½m; one to be wary of. *P. Haslam.*

MIGRATOR 6 b.g. My Swallow 134–Houbichka (Swoon's Son) (1981 12f* **63**
1982 14fg⁴ 12fg 12fg⁴) rangy ex-Irish gelding; won ladies race at Chepstow
in 1981; not disgraced in 1982; stays 1½m; acts on any going; smart hurdler.
L. Kennard.

MIGUEL CLEMENT (USA) 3 ch.c. Avatar–Harvest Girl (Herbager 136) **86**
(1981 7f³ 7g³ 1982 12d² 12g* 12f* 12f* 12g² 14fg² 14fg² 16g) rangy colt;
won apprentice maiden race at Newmarket and minor events at Lingfield and
Leicester (made all); ran creditably several other starts; stays 1¾m (below form over
2m); seems to act on any going but goes well on firm; sweated up at Leicester;
gives impression he will always be suited by a galloping track. *M. Stoute.*

MIKRO POULAKI 2 b.f. Julio Mariner 127–Sandfly (French Beige 127) —
(1982 7d) May 26; 13,000Y; smallish, close-coupled, quite attractive filly;
half-sister to useful 5f to 1¼m winner Ippolyti (by Derring-Do) and a winner in
Trinidad; dam, French 1½m winner, comes from good family; unquoted and on
backward side, behind in 15-runner maiden race at Leicester in October. *C.
Brittain.*

MILANION 3 ro.g. Roman Warrior 132–Fleora 61 (Fleece 114) (1981 5s 5fg —
6g⁴ 5f 5g 6d 7.2v² 6d 8g 8d* 7g³ 1982 6g 7d 10.6fg 8f 9g 9.4fg) compact gelding;
won seller and finished good third in nursery at 2 yrs; beaten some way in handicaps in 1982; stays 1m well; needs some give in the ground and acts on heavy
going. *J. Wilson.*

MILETRIAN 3 b.f. Music Boy 124–Chaddy (St Chad 120) (1981 NR 1982 —
7f 8g 8g 10.1fg 10fg⁴ 8g) third foal; half-sister to a winner in Sweden; dam won
in Norway; poor plater. *H. O'Neill.*

MILITARY BAND (FR) 4 b.c. Sassafras 135–Melody Hour 105 (Sing Sing 134) **99**
(1981 14fg* 12f3 14fg* 16f* 14g* 18g3 1982 14g* 16fg4 12fg4 12g2 12fg2 14g)
tall, fair sort; head winner of handicaps at Newmarket in April (from Karadar
after a good battle) and July (from Balanchine), but hampered runner-up
and placings were reversed on latter occasion; stuck on well when ¾-length
second to Valentinian in Old Newton Cup at Haydock in between; had every
chance when seventh of 15 to Another Sam in Tote-Ebor at York in August
on final start (favourite); may prove best at around 1¾m although stays further;
acts on firm going; ridden by apprentice N. Day twice when successful. *H.
Cecil.*

MILITARY MERCHANT 2 b.g. Tower Walk 130–Nasty Niece (Great Nephew —
126) (1982 8g 7g) May 20; 7,000Y; good-bodied, workmanlike gelding;
second foal; half-brother to 3-y-o 1m winner Tender Niece (by Prince Tenderfoot);
dam won over 7f at 2 yrs in Canada; tailed off in maiden race at Beverley and
seller at Newmarket in September; gelded subsequently; retained by trainer
800 gns Newmarket Autumn Sales. *P. Haslam.*

MILK HEART 3 ch.c. Steel Heart 128–Cafe au Lait 98 (Espresso 122) (1981 **96**
5s⁴ 5s 5g⁴ 6fg 6d 8.2d 6d² 1982 5d² 6d* 7fg⁴ 6g 7f 6g⁴ 6f* 6f 6d² 6g) compact,
quite attractive colt; won minor event at Warwick (heavily backed) and handicaps at Epsom and Salisbury; seemed to improve considerably on these efforts
when excellent ¾-length second of 11 to Tina's Pet in Goldene Peitsche at Baden-
Baden in September, but didn't run up to that form when about 3 lengths fifth
of 14 to Famous Star in Ladbrokes (Ayr) Gold Cup later in month; stays 7f;
seems to act on any going; used to wear blinkers. *G. Lewis.*

MILK OF THE BARLEY 5 b.h. Mummy's Pet 125–Tots (Dual 117) (1981 **111**
6d³ 9d² 7.2s² 6g 7g* 7.3fg⁴ 5d 8fg 8s 6g³ 1982 8g⁴ 6d* 6fg⁴ 8f 6f 6f 6g 8fg² 8s 7g⁴
6s³) tall, short-backed horse; very smart performer on his day; didn't have

*Quail Stakes, Kempton—Milk Of The Barley wins
impressively from the grey Vorvados*

best of runs when 2¾ lengths fourth to Princes Gate in Doncaster Mile on reappearance in March; beat Vorvados impressively by 3 lengths in £3,700 event at Kempton the following month; usually had stiff tasks afterwards, and did when running race of his life to finish 1½ lengths second to impressive Sandhurst Prince in Waterford Crystal Mile at Goodwood in August (150/1, was flattered by proximity to easy winner, but had some really good animals behind); evidently effective at 6f and stays 9f; seems to act on any going; gives impression he needs to be held up; dwelt third start; often blinkered nowadays (was at Kempton); sold privately, reportedly to race in California. *W. O'Gorman*.

MILLE BALLES (FR) 2 b.c. Mill Reef 141–Elezinha (Tourangeau 99) (1982 **106**
6g³ 8s² 7v*) first foal; dam, half-sister to very smart French 1m to 1½m performer Solicitor, was smart winner from 4f to 7.5f; landed the odds easily by 1½ lengths from Stephany's Dream in 14-runner maiden race at Maisons-Laffitte in November, the pair 6 lengths clear; had gone down by only a neck to Full of Stars in similar event at Longchamp the previous month; will stay 1¼m; a progressive colt who should make a very useful 3-y-o. *F. Mathet, France*.

MILLERS GOLD 3 gr. or ro.g. Gold Form 108–The Merrickstan 66 (Klondyke —
Bill 125) (1981 NR 1982 12f) first foal; dam plating-class novice hurdler; 33/1 when tailed-off last of 12 to Dancing Sovereign in maiden race at Folkestone in July. *P. K. Mitchell*.

MILLFIELD LAD 5 b.g. Jimmy Reppin 131–Alexa (Runnymede 123) (1981 —
NR 1982 8f 10fg³ 10g 10g) quite a moderate handicapper nowadays; stays at least 1m (seemed to run quite well in slowly-run race over 1¼m on second outing); ideally suited by some give in the ground; has run respectably in blinkers; has run creditably for a claimer; trained by M. H. Easterby until after first outing. *J. Charlton*.

MILLIARD 2 b.c. Mill Reef 141–Fascinating Trick (Buckpasser) (1982 8f* 9d) **105**
Apr 28; half-brother to 2 winners, including useful 1981 2-y-o 7f winner Skytrick (by African Sky); dam twice-raced sister to best 1971 American 2-y-o filly Numbered Account; odds on, put in a good run in straight to win 5-runner Prix de Fontenoy (newcomers race) at Longchamp in September by ½ length from Two Minutes Hero; never-dangerous 6½ lengths seventh of 9 to Saint Cyrien in Prix Saint-Roman on same course the following month (not given a hard time once chance had gone); will be suited by 1¼m+; entered in Derby. *F. Boutin, France*.

MILLISLES 2 gr.f. Pongee 106–Growing Leisure 81 (Constable 119) (1982 —
5f 6fg 6g) Apr 17; leggy, unfurnished filly; half-sister to 2 minor winners; dam a plater, best at 5f; in rear in varied company, including selling; not seen out after July; invariably starts slowly. *N. Chamberlain*.

MILL PLANTATION 3 b.c. Northfields–Fairly Hot 109 (Sir Ivor 135) (1981 **90**
7g 1982 8g³ 9g* 9if 11f³ 12f 10f² 12f² 10f* 12g³ 10g 12s) neat, attractive colt; favourite when winning maiden race at Newcastle in April and 8-runner Andy Capp Handicap at Redcar in August; beat Iowa decisively by 4 lengths in latter; ran rather in snatches seventh outing; stays 1½m; acts on firm going; blinkered nowadays. *H. Wragg*.

MILL QUEEN 3 b.f. Mill Reef 141–Passer Queen (Buckpasser) (1981 NR **86**
1982 10g 14.6g 12d 9fg² 8.2s³ 9s* 7g*) lengthy, quite attractive filly; second foal; dam won over 1m in Ireland at 2 yrs, and is sister to very useful Buckstopper; decisively won maiden race at York in October and held off subsequently-disqualified Minmax by short head in £5,800 handicap at Newmarket later in month; best at up to 9f; seems to act on any going but best form with some give in the ground. *F. Durr*.

MILLS HIGH 4 b.f. High Top 131–Iona 92 (Kalydon 122) (1981 9s³ 10fg⁴ **57**
8s 10fg* 10.6v² 12.2g* 10.2d 1982 10fg* 12s 12f³ 12.2g 12f 10s 10fg³ 12f⁴ 10g² 10d 8f 10s² 11s 10.2d³) small, fair sort; won at Cagnes-sur-Mer in February; ran best subsequent races when placed in handicaps and in a £6,400 event, facing a very stiff task in last-named on final start; stays 1½m; acts on any going, but best form with some give in the ground; sometimes starts slowly. *C. Brittain*.

MILLS MARAUDER 2 b.c. Oats 126–Maride (Ridan) (1982 5fg 5f 6f⁴ 6f **77**
7g 8fg⁴ 8g³ 8d⁴) Mar 14; 5,200Y; quite attractive colt; half-brother to 2 winners in USA; dam won 6f claiming race; quite a moderate maiden; will be suited by 1¼m+. *E. Eldin*.

MILLY MONROE 3 b.f. Lochnager 132–Polly Peachum 123 (Singing Strand) **56**
(1981 5fg 5f 5f³ 6g 7g 6d 1982 7f 7f 5fg⁴) useful sort; good walker; only plating
class; not certain to stay 7f. *J. Fitzgerald.*

MINAGE 3 gr.f. Prince de Galles 125–Mellormoor (Forlorn River 124) (1981 —
5d 5fg³ 5g 6fg 6g 6g 5g 8s 1982 6d 8fg 8f 10f 5fg 9g 7g 6fg 6g) leggy, lightly-
made filly; poor plater; has worn blinkers. *R. Hoad.*

MIND OUT 2 br.f. Gay Fandango 132–Deer Leap 106 (Deep Diver 134) (1982 —
6fg 5s) Jan 30; first foal; dam Irish 5f winner; little worthwhile form in autumn
races at Lingfield and Bath. *N. Vigors.*

MINE AT LAST 2 gr. or ro.f. Nishapour 125–Mrs Binks (Whistling Wind 123) —
(1982 6fg) Mar 6; 11,000Y; useful-looking, compact filly; half-sister to several
winners, including smart sprinter Divine King (by Divine Gift); dam unraced;
eighth of 9 in £6,000 newcomers event at Ascot in July. *J. Bethell.*

MING VILLAGE 2 b. or br.c. Persian Bold 123–Wild Orchid (Sassafras 135) **77**
(1982 5fg 6f 7g 7fg 7g) Mar 30; IR 3,000F, IR 10,000Y; well-made, quite
attractive colt; first foal; dam never ran; quite modest form in maiden events;
will stay 1m; acts on a firm surface; may be capable of some improvement.
R. Armstrong.

MINIBANK 4 b.c. Saritamer 130–Tilt Guard 75 (Crepello 136) (1981 6fg —
7s 7f² 7fg* 8f³ 8fg³ 8.3fg 8f⁴ 8.2fg* 8g⁴ 8g 1982 7s 8fg 8g) good-topped,
workmanlike colt; in rear all outings in 1982; stays 1m; acts on firm going; successful with blinkers and without. *M. Bradley.*

MINICA 5 ch.m. Prince des Loges 73–Mink Mini 103 (Martial 131) (1981 NR —
1982 8fg 10fg 5.3f 6s⁴) second foal; dam sprinter; fourth of 18 behind Pusey
Street in handicap at Chepstow in October, best effort. *R. Sturdy.*

MINIE O'NEILL 2 b.f. Pitskelly 122–Karlaine 86 (Tutankhamen) (1982 **67**
5s 5d* 5f³ 6f 7g) Apr 22; small filly; half-sister to a winner in Italy and to a
bumpers winner who went on to win over hurdles; dam won over 1¼m; won
maiden race at Warwick in April by 1½ lengths from Henceforth; off course 3
months before final start; should stay 1m. *W. Wharton.*

MINIFORM 3 ch.f. Reform 132–Minarika (Djakao 124) (1981 NR 1982 7.6fg —
10g 10.4d⁴) neat filly; third foal; dam dead-heated in small 9f race in France
and is out of half-sister to Habat; little worthwhile form; best run at 1¼m on
soft ground. *P. Walwyn.*

MINK GODDESS 2 b.f. Godswalk 130–Ermyn Lass 64 (Ennis 128) (1982 **90**
5g² 5s²) Apr 24; IR 41,000Y; half-sister to several winners, including 1981
Middle Park winner Cajun (by Red Regent) and smart sprinter Ubedizzy (by
Carnival Dancer); dam 5f winner; ran creditably in 12-runner maiden race at
Leopardstown in May, finishing 4 lengths second to High Style after leading for
4f; not seen out again until October when excellent 2 lengths second of 7 to
3-y-o Americus in Macdonagh and Boland Waterford Testimonial Stakes at
the Curragh; sure to win races. *E. O'Grady, Ireland.*

MINMAX 4 b.c. Record Run 127–Paddy's Tickle (Shooting Chant) (1981 **79**
7fg³ 8g² 7fg* 7g* 8fg 7.6g² 1982 8d 7fg 7f 7f⁴ 7fg 7fg 7fg³ 8v 7g²(dis) 7d)
leggy, good-topped colt; returned to form when going down by a short head to
Mill Queen in handicap at Newmarket in October, but was disqualified for
edging left under pressure and impeding another runner; rather disappointing
only subsequent start; stays 1m; probably acts on any going but gives impression
he'll possibly prove best with some give underfoot; suitable mount for an
apprentice; wears blinkers nowadays. *P. K. Mitchell.*

MINNELLI 2 b.f. Dom Racine 121–Nigella Damascena 101 (St Paddy 133) **107** p
(1982 6g* 6d²)
In 1980 one of Ireland's best two-year-old fillies, Blue Wind, was sold
for 180,000 Irish guineas at the Goffs November Sales, a record price for a
two-year-old filly at auction in the British Isles. In 1981 she won the Oaks
by seven lengths and then took the Irish Guinness Oaks for her new trainer
Dermot Weld. Weld will be hoping that lightning can strike twice in the same
place: at the 1982 Newmarket December Sales he paid another record price,
240,000 guineas, for one of the past Irish two-year-old fillies, Minnelli. Minnelli had
run only twice in her first season, making her debut in a ten-runner maiden
race at Naas in May. Judging by her starting price of 7/4 on she must have
shown plenty at home and she justified the support in great style, quickening

right away inside the last quarter mile to win by six lengths. Four months elapsed before she was seen out again in the very valuable Moyglare Stud Stakes at the Curragh in which the English-trained Habibti, winner of both her starts including the Lowther Stakes, was an odds-on favourite. Minnelli, at 4/1, was the best supported of the fourteen Irish fillies, ahead of her former stable-companion Sweet Emma, another unbeaten filly who had run out a clear-cut winner of the Phoenix Stakes. Minnelli looked well despite her long absence and put up a fine effort although no match for the length-and-a-half-winner Habibti; she stayed on well to finish a clear second ahead of the 20/1-shot Committed and Sweet Emma after holding a good place throughout.

			Kalamoun		Zeddaan
	Dom Racine		(gr 1970)		Khairunissa
	(br 1975)		La Ferte Milon		Timmy Lad
Minnelli			(b 1968)		Salamine III
(b.f. Feb 3, 1980)			St Paddy		Aureole
	Nigella Damascena		(b 1957)		Edie Kelly
	(ch 1972)		Sally Loveridge		Alycidon or Nearco
			(ch 1956)		Crawley Beauty

Minnelli's sale for 240,000 guineas represents a spectacular profit, for she cost only 10,500 Irish guineas as a yearling. Her sire Dom Racine wasn't particularly popular at that time and none of his first-crop yearlings sold for more than 19,000 guineas. Since then the emergence of Minnelli and the Prix Morny and Prix de la Salamandre winner Deep Roots has established Dom Racine as a sire of great promise, a fact reflected in the prices paid for some of his 1982 yearlings. Minnelli is the second foal and first winner bred by Nigella Damascena, who won over seven furlongs on her only start at two and then showed useful form at up to two miles the following year, winning once over a mile and a half. Nigella Damascena was one of four winners on the flat

Mrs D. M. Solomon's "Minnelli"

produced by Sally Loveridge, a maiden who gained both her placings over five furlongs. Loveridge, a very useful two-year-old sprinter, was best of the others but Miss Loveridge, a winner over a mile and a half, has since bred the smart middle-distance stayer Riboreen. Crawley Beauty, Minnelli's third dam, won the Molecomb Stakes and did very well at stud, producing ten winners here and abroad. Crawley Beauty was a very well related filly. Her sister Flirting bred the Eclipse winner Arctic Explorer; her half-sister Forecourt the King George VI and Queen Elizabeth Stakes winner Supreme Court; her half-brother The Cobbler, a top-class colt, finished second in the Two Thousand Guineas; and her half-sister Sea Symphony won the Irish One Thousand Guineas. The Irish Guineas is a likely target for Minnelli—Blue Wind went for the race, finishing a short-head second—and she looks Ireland's best hope of keeping the prize at home. She should later prove effective over middle distances. *M. Connolly, Ireland.*

MINNE LOVE 3 ch.f. Homeric 133–Late Love 107 (Great White Way) (1981 **49** 5fg 5.8h 5g 6g* 6fg³ 5d⁴ 6g 1982 6f 6g² 5fg² 5g³ 6fg 6f 6d 10v) small filly; plater; should stay 1m+; has run respectably when sweating up. *C. Nelson.*

MINSDEN 3 ch.g. Habitat 134–Moon Min (First Landing) (1981 6g 1982 **67** 7fg 6f³ 6f² 8f⁴ 6fg) strong, compact, good sort; good walker; in frame in varied company; stays 7f; acts on firm going; blinkered third and fourth starts; exported to Malaysia. *J. W. Watts.*

MINSHAANSHU AMAD (USA) 3 br.c. Northern Dancer–Tappahannock **69 §** (Chieftain) (1981 8s 7.3s 1982 9fg 11.7f⁴ 10f³ 8fg 16g) small, attractive colt; good walker and mover; disappointing maiden; stays 1¼m; blinkered second outing and didn't look too genuine on third. *F. J. Houghton.*

MINTALA (USA) 2 ch.c. Key to the Mint–Tatallah (Tatan) (1982 6g 7fg) **72** May 23; $140,000Y; well-grown, quite attractive colt; brother to 2 winners, including 1978 2-y-o sprint stakes winner Joi'ski and half-brother to 2 winners; dam stakes-placed daughter of high-class filly Leallah; disappointing favourite in maiden race won by Behind The Lines at Salisbury in September on second start; should stay 1m. *P. Walwyn.*

MINUS MAN 4 b.g. Firestreak 125–Cheb's Honour 70 (Chebs Lad 120) (1981 **47** 7d 6g 8f* 8fg⁴ 1982 8.2s 7fg 10f 10fg 8g 8f 8f 8d² 8fg² 8g³ 7s⁴) lengthy gelding; plater; stays 1m; probably acts on any going. *W. Holden.*

MIO MEMENTA 3 b.f. Streak 119–Young Mementa (Young Christopher 119) **—** (1981 6g 5d⁴ 1982 5f 7.6fg 6fg 5g 5fg 6f) plating-class sprint maiden; has been tried in blinkers. *K. Brassey.*

MIRABEAU 3 ch.c. Sharpen Up 127–La Mirabelle 92 (Princely Gift 137) **111** (1981 6g 6g² 6g* 6s* 1982 7s* 7fg³ 8fg 7g² 7fg 7fg³ 7g*) leggy, quite attractive colt; good mover; brother to smart 6f and 7f winner Jeroboam and half-brother to 2 winners; dam won over 6f; smart colt; won £3,000 race at Leicester in March and City of York Stakes in August; blinkered, accounted for Tony Tan by ½ length in latter; placed in between in Tote European Free Handicap at Newmarket (battled on splendidly to be very close third to Match Winner), Heron Stakes at Kempton (neck second to Come On The Blues) and Beeswing Stakes at Newcastle (2 lengths third to Silly Steven); should stay 1m; seems to act on any going but goes well on soft; has a tendency to hang and is suited by strong handling; game; sold privately and sent to USA. *H. Wragg.*

MIRADELL 3 b.f. Wolver Hollow 126–Miralife 103 (Miralgo 130) (1981 NR **—** 1982 6g 8fg) IR 50,000Y; lightly-made, lengthy filly; very good walker; sister to smart Irish 5f to 1m performer Wolverlife and half-sister to 3 other winners, notably Irish 1,000 Guineas winner Miralla (by Allangrange); dam, third in Irish 1,000 Guineas, stayed at least 9f; soundly beaten in £3,300 event at Kempton in May and maiden race at Salisbury in September. *H. Candy.*

MIRAFLORA (USA) 3 ch.f. Forli–Salvatico (Sir Ivor 135) (1981 7s 1982 **102** 9g* 7d* 8fg* 12g*) first foal; dam unraced daughter of Arkadina, placed in Irish 1,000 Guineas and Oaks and Epsom Oaks; developed into a very useful filly and won all 4 of her starts, namely minor events at Mallow and the Curragh, Cornelscourt Stakes at Leopardstown (landed odds by ½ length from Karissima) and Brownstown Stakes at the Curragh; came with a steady run to beat Meringue by ¾ length in last-named in August; suited by 1½m; acted on a firm and a soft surface; in foal to Northfields. *V. O'Brien, Ireland.*

MIRAMAR REEF   3 b.c. Mill Reef 141–Thalassa 94 (Appiani II 128)   (1981 **100**
7fg 7f   1982 9fg⁴ 10fg 10.4fg 12fg 10fg² 12f 10f* 10f 10.5fg 10.5g 12fg 10g 9d)
strong, good sort; good mover; superbly ridden when accounting for Voracity
by 2½ lengths in 16-runner maiden race at Newmarket in July; often faced stiff
tasks on his other starts but wasn't disgraced on occasions; should stay at least
1½m; acts on firm going; possibly none too genuine and is suited by waiting
tactics. *C. Brittain.*

MIRKAN HONEY   3 b.f. Ballymore 123–Honey Bend (Never Bend)   (1981 NR   **83**
1982 10.5fg² 10f 10f 10f 10.6s⁴ 12s⁴)   IR 46,000Y; sturdy, compact filly; half-
sister to 4 winners, including useful Italian 1½m performer Choco Air (by Sassafras); dam won twice over 6f in Ireland; promising ¾-length second of 9 to Cut
Loose in £4,200 race at York in May; put up best subsequent effort on fourth
outing when 6 lengths last of 5 to Dione in Twickenham Stakes at Kempton in
September; possibly stays 1¼m; lacks pace. *W. Wharton.*

MIRROR BOY   5 ch.h. Pieces of Eight 128–Knocknashee 70 (Aztec 128)   (1981   **79**
12fg² 12d 13.3s² 10d 10g 10g   1982 12g 16s⁴ 14f 16fg)   well-made horse; fairly
useful handicapper at his best; possibly stays 2m; probably acts on any going
but is suited by some give in the ground; ran poorly in blinkers once at 2 yrs;
usually held up and is suited by a strongly-run race. *R. Price.*

MIRTHFUL   5 b. or br.m. Will Somers 114§–French Line 98 (Set Fair 129)   **55**
(1981 8.2d⁴ 8g³ 9fg³ 9.4g* 11g² 10.6f* 10f 10g⁴ 10g³ 10f*   1982 10.4g 10.5f⁴
10fg² 10.5s)   sturdy mare; made all in 3 handicaps in 1981; caught on post by
Kaukas at Chepstow in September, first outing for 4 months; gave impression
she'd stay 1½m; acted on any going; sometimes wore blinkers but was better
without; suitable mount for a boy; in foal to Free State. *W. Elsey.*

MISDIRECTED   2 ch.f. Ardoon 124–Grecian Palm 78 (Royal Palm 131)   (1982   **76**
5fg 5f³ 5g² 5g⁴ 5g 6d⁴)   Feb 21; small, good-bodied filly; has a short, sharp
action; sister to 3-y-o 5f winner Miss Trilli and half-sister to several winners,
including useful sprinter Trillium (by Psidium); dam temperamental 5f sprinter;
placed in maiden races at Wolverhampton in May and Pontefract (favourite,
beaten head) in July; probably stays 6f; yet to race on really soft going but
seems to act on any other. *G. Pritchard-Gordon.*

MISGUIDED   2 b.f. Homing 130–Miss By Miles 91 (Milesian 125)   (1982 6f   **106**
6g² 5fg² 5g* 6s* 6d*)   Mar 11; well-made, attractive filly; good mover; half-sister
to 3-y-o Devisdale (by Swing Easy) and smart 6f and 1m winner Missed Blessing
(by So Blessed); dam game miler; showed improved form September onwards,
winning 20-runner maiden race at Newbury, 9-runner minor event at Goodwood
and 12-runner race at Pontefract; most impressive at Goodwood, hacking up by
2½ lengths from Sedra after being 6 lengths clear at one stage; will stay 1m; acts
very well on soft going; likely to hold her own in useful company. *H. Cecil.*

MISINSKIE (USA)   2 b.f. Nijinsky 138–Kankakee Miss (Better Bee)   (1982   **84**
6g⁴ 7f² 6f³ 7fg³)   May 7; $300,000Y; attractive, well-made filly; half-sister to
several winners, including high-class sprinter/miler Clever Trick (by Icecapade);
dam stakes-placed winner at up to 1m; in frame in maiden races, on final occasion
¾-length third of 19 to Tiger Scout at Chepstow in August; needs further than 6f;
has quite a lot of scope and should win a small race. *P. Walwyn.*

MISS ABWAH   3 b.f. Abwah 118–Ladies Night 65 (Midsummer Night II 117)   **47**
(1981 7fg 6f 6f 6s 5d   1982 6f 5d 7f⁴ 8fg 9f² 10f³ 10d 8.2v 10s 7s)   fair sort;
has a round action; plater; stays 1¼m; acts on firm going; has worn blinkers;
races with head in air; sold 1,300 gns Doncaster November Sales. *M. Camacho.*

MISS ACROW   3 b.f. Comedy Star 121–Queen's Penny (Queen's Hussar 124)   —
(1981 7.6s   1982 8d 7f 10fg 11.7f)   workmanlike filly; beaten some way in
maiden races. *D. Elsworth.*

MISS ADMIRAL   2 ch.f. Native Admiral–Running Mate (Track Spare 125)   —
(1982 5v)   Apr 20; first foal; dam ran once; 20/1, eighth of 14 in maiden race at
Folkestone in October. *R. Simpson.*

MISS ANAGRAM (USA)   2 b.f. Hurok–Added Attraction (Double Jay)   **108**
(1982 5fg* 5g² 5fg* 5g² 5v)   smallish, quite well-made filly; good walker; half-
sister to several minor winners in USA; dam never ran; sire, closely related to
smart animals De La Rose and Upper Nile, ran only at 4 yrs when winner of 2
small races over 8.5f; produced a fine turn of foot when successful in maiden race
at Wolverhampton in August and £3,100 event (beating Bumpkin 1½ lengths) at
Salisbury in September; good second to Prince Spy under 10-0 in nursery at

Newmarket later in September; speedy, and not certain to stay 6f; possibly unsuited by heavy going. *H. Candy.*

MISS ANNIE 2 b. or br.f. Scottish Rifle 127–Ryoanji 100 (Lyphard 132) **73** (1982 6d² 7f* 7f 8fg² 7.6fg³) Apr 23; 1,500Y; useful-looking filly; good mover; second foal; dam ran only at 2 yrs when winner twice over 7f; cost 11,200 gns to buy in after winning by 3 lengths from Maralingo in valuable 14-runner seller at Newmarket in July (showed a marked reluctance to get on with things once in front and swished tail repeatedly); ran well when placed subsequently in nurseries at Warwick and Lingfield; will stay beyond 1m; consistent. *P. Haslam.*

MISS BALI BEACH 2 b.f. Nonoalco 131–Miss Bali 95 (Crepello 136) (1982 **88** p 7d*) Mar 14; lengthy, attractive filly; good mover; half-sister to very useful 3-y-o 1m and 9f winner Bali Dancer (by Habitat) and to a winner in Italy; dam won over 1½m and is half-sister to smart Welsh Harmony; 7/1 and apparently green and in need of race, showed deal of promise and looked potentially useful when winning 15-runner maiden event at Leicester in October by 4 lengths from Espiga, clearly having measure of her field from halfway and drawing away in final furlong; will stay 1m; sure to improve, and win more races. *M. Stoute.*

MISS BLACK GLAMA 2 br.f. Derrylin 115–Decatullus (Catullus) (1982 **63** 7f 7.6v 7d) Feb 17; 3,800F, 10,000Y; third live produce; half-sister to 9f winner Wesscam (by Scottish Rifle); dam won claiming races at up to 9f in USA; little worthwhile form in autumn maiden events. *N. Callaghan.*

MISS CARINE 2 b.f. Cawston's Clown 113–Lucy 83 (Sheshoon 132) (1982 **67** 7g 8d* 8s 8d) May 9; lightly-made filly; half-sister to 3 winners, including 1976 2-y-o 5f winner Hone (by Sharpen Up), subsequently winner of Les Guineas in Belgium; dam won over 1¼m; 25/1, bought in 1,500 gns after winning 24-runner seller at Leicester in September by 1½ lengths from Economy Girl; suited by 1m. *J. Wilson.*

MISS CAWSTON 3 b.f. Cawston's Clown 113–Cornage 82 (Candy Cane 125) **—** (1981 NR 1982 6fg) 1,800Y; smallish, fair sort; second foal; dam won over 7f; unquoted and in need of race when tenth of 11 behind Mummy's Pleasure in apprentice event at Nottingham in August. *R. Hollinshead.*

MISS CHESSY 4 ch.f. Swing Easy 126–Tassel (Ragusa 137) (1981 6v⁴ 5g³ **41** 5g³ 6fg² 6g 6f 5fg 6d 7fg 6fg³ 6d 7s 1982 7g 6fg² 7f 8fg² 7g 8fg⁴ 8g² 8f 8.2g 8d) lightly-made filly; poor mover; plater; ran best races when second at Thirsk, Edinburgh and Ayr; stays 1m; acts on any going; blinkered once as a 3-y-o. *J. Berry.*

MISS CONNAUGHT 3 ch.f. Connaught 130–Breathalyser (Alcide 136) **103** (1981 9d⁴ 7d 8d 7s 1982 12f* 12fg² 14f*) 8,000Y; half-sister to 3 winners, including smart middle-distance stayer Major Green (by Double-U-Jay); dam showed only poor form; showed much-improved form to win maiden race at Thurles in June and handicap at Gowran Park in July (trotted up by 8 lengths from Anglesea Lace); ran well in between to be 8 lengths fourth of 10 to Swiftfoot in Irish Guinness Oaks at the Curragh; stayed 1¾m; acted well on firm going; dead. *L. Browne, Ireland.*

MISS COUTURE 5 br.m. Tamerlane 128–Tragara (Buisson Ardent 129) **52** (1981 15.8g 18g 1982 15.8g* 16fg⁴ 15g⁴ 15.8f 17.4d⁴) won handicap at Catterick in March by 2½ lengths from Lochranza; stays well; acts on a firm surface, although is possibly best with some give underfoot; wears blinkers. *J. W. Watts.*

MISS DIAWARD 5 br.m. Supreme Sovereign 119–Gay Pretendre (Pretendre **82** 126) (1981 10.8d 12fg³ 11d* 12d* 1982 13s* 12f³ 13fg* 12fg 13g² 13fg* 12fg 14.6g 13d 12s³ 14s* 18s) quite attractive, lengthy mare; good walker, but poor mover; successful in handicaps at Ayr in March, May and August, and at York in October; led 1½f out and ran on strongly to beat Path of Peace by 2½ lengths on latter course; stays 1¾m; acts on any going; usually bandaged nowadays; has a good turn of foot. *Miss S. Hall.*

MISS DUNSTER (USA) 2 b.f. Nizon 120–Janie V. (Dewan) (1982 7d 7g* 7s) **88** Apr 22; quite attractive, smallish, rather lightly-made filly; first foal; dam won 6f maiden race at 3 yrs; won 15-runner maiden race at Yarmouth in September by 2½ lengths from New Coins; 5 lengths fifth of 11 to same horse in minor event at York the following month; will stay 1m. *L. Cumani.*

MISS FANDANGO 3 ch.f. Gay Fandango 132–Nana's Girl 109 (Tin Whistle **56** 128) (1981 5fg 5f 5g 5g 1982 7f 7.2g 7f² 7f 7g 7d) strong, good sort; good walker; poor handicapper; will probably stay 1m; blinkered once at 2 yrs; sold 9,200 gns Newmarket December Sales. *G. Pritchard-Gordon.*

MISS FLASH 2 b. or br.f. Scottish Rifle 127–Flashing Light (Sky Gipsy 117)   **57**
(1982 5f⁴ 5g⁴ 5fg 6g)   May 20; 5,800Y; fair sort; half-sister to quite moderate
1981 2-y-o Kenson Venture (by Most Secret); dam unraced half-sister to smart
Vibrant; poor maiden; should stay at least 6f.   *W. A. Stephenson.*

MISS FLIRT 3 ch.f. Welsh Pageant 132–Flirtigig 96 (Silly Season 127)   (1981   —
NR 1982 10h 12g 13.1t)   workmanlike filly; third foal; half-sister to fairly
useful 1976 2-y-o 5f and 6f winner Miss Pert (by Roan Rocket) and a winner in
Holland; dam won at 1m and 1¼m; soundly beaten in maiden and minor events;
sold 4,200 gns Newmarket Autumn Sales.   *P. Walwyn.*

MISS GALLANT 3 ch.f. Gallo Gallante 96–Miss Me (Pinturischio 116)   (1981   —
5d 5g 7fg 7fg 7fg   1982 8fg 15.8f)   leggy, rather unfurnished filly; poor maiden.
T. Barnes.

MISS GENEROUS 5 b.m. Bronze Hill 96–Generous Device 69 (Bounteous 125)   —
(1981 12g 15.8g   1982 13v 11fg⁴ 12f 10.6f)   strong mare; plater; stays 1½m;
acts on firm going; has been tried in blinkers.   *M. Camacho.*

MISS HENRY 2 b.f. Blue Cashmere 129–Rhodia (Parthia 132)   (1982 6g 5fg 5g)   —
Mar 4; lengthy filly; half-sister to 3 winners by Blast, including very useful 7f
to 1m performer Rhodomantade; dam once-raced half-sister to Champion Hurdle
winner Saucy Kit; little form in maiden events; blinkered final outing.   *J.
Benstead.*

MISS HIBERNIAN 3 br.f. Ascendant 96–Ladyrullah (Bluerullah 115)   (1981   —
5fg 5d 5v 7g 8.2s 8d   1982 8fg 5f 10f 8f)   small, lightly-made filly; of no
account.   *K. Ivory.*

MISS HOT FOOT 2 b.f. Hotfoot 126–Petite Case 76 (Upper Case)   (1982 6s)   —
May 19; lengthy filly; second foal; dam stayed 7f; unquoted, no show in 16-
runner maiden race at Leicester in November.   *M. McCourt.*

MISSILE MISS 4 ch.f. Firestreak 125–Flora Leigh 94 (Floribunda 136)   (1981   **30**
7f 7fg 7fg 12g 12d   1982 11s² 15.5fg⁴ 12.2g 11.7g 12g 12fg)   lengthy filly;
plater; ran best race when second in apprentice handicap at Hamilton in April;
stays 11f.   *W. Holden.*

MISS IMPORT 4 ch.f. Import 127–Chinese Falcon 81 (Skymaster 126)   (1981   **83**
5g* 5g 5d 5fg* 5g 5fg 5.6f 5d* 5fg 5f 5g* 5d   1982 5g² 5d⁴ 5f 5fg 5f³ 5f* 5g³ 5g*
5g* 5fg* 5fg 5d)   workmanlike filly; sprint handicapper; improved and won at
Thirsk, Edinburgh, Ripon and Pontefract in summer, making all on last 3
occasions; speedy and is likely to prove best at 5f; yet to race on really soft going
but acts on any other; sometimes sweats up badly; sometimes slowly away;
successful with blinkers and without; won 3 times for E. Hide in 1982.   *T. Barron.*

MISS INIGO 3 b.f. Sagaro 133–Parradell 104 (Pandofell 132)   (1981 NR   —
1982 10h 10.2g)   half-sister to 2 minor winners; dam 1¼m winner and sister to
very smart stayer Piaco; well beaten in maiden races at Chepstow in June and
Bath in July.   *P. Walwyn.*

MISSISSIPI BLUES (USA) 3 b.g. Mississipian 131–Conga (Sword Dancer)   —
(1981 NR   1982 10s 10s) $30,000Y, 2,800 gns 3-y-o; half-brother to 4 winners,
including Conga Miss (by Dewan), a smart stakes winner at up to 1m; dam
lightly-raced half-sister to 2 stakes winners; well beaten in maiden race at
Sandown and minor event at Leicester in the autumn.   *K. Ivory.*

MISS KATIE 3 b.f. Porto Bello 118–Serein (Prince Chevalier)   (1981 5d 5d 6fg   —
1982 8fg)   lightly-made filly; no worthwhile form; has been tried in blinkers;
sold 420 gns Ascot July Sales.   *Mrs J. Reavey.*

MISS LILIAN 3 b.f. Sandford Lad 133–Bustina (Busted 134)   (1981 5s 5g² 6s²   **98**
5s² 5fg³ 6fg² 6f* 7.9f* 6d⁴ 5g³ 7d 6g   1982 7s 7s* 7s² 8g 10g)   IR 3,200F, IR
5,800Y; second foal; half-sister to Irish 6f winner Wintina (by Tumble Wind);
dam ran once in France; won quite valuable April Fillies Stakes at the Curragh
by a length from Legal Expertise; just failed to get up when short-head second
of 10 to Celestial Path in Athasi Stakes on same course later in month; creditable
seventh of 24 to Prince's Polly in Goffs Irish 1,000 Guineas at the Curragh again
in May; stays 1m; acts on any going; blinkered nowadays; not raced after June.
P. Norris, Ireland.

MISS LONGCHAMP 3 ch.f. Northfields–Miss Paris 111 (Sovereign Path 125)   **94**
(1981 6g   1982 7.2s* 8f* 8fg³ 8f² 8g 8g)   smallish, strong, lengthy, attractive
filly; won maiden race at Haydock and handicap at Goodwood in July; placed
in handicaps won by Mennea at Sandown and Kempton afterwards; will stay
beyond 1m; acts on any going.   *M. Stoute.*

MISS MALINOWSKI 2 ch.f. Malinowski 123–Vaguely Related (Pall Mall 132) **77**
(1982 6fg 6fg 7fg 7g 7.2s 8g⁴ 8d*) Apr 22; 4,600 2-y-o; leggy filly; half-sister to
winners here and abroad, including fairly useful 5f and 7f winner Primonato
(by Native Prince); dam poor maiden; won 6-runner maiden race at Edinburgh
in November; suited by 1m; possibly requires a soft surface; has worn bandages
behind. *N. Guest.*

MISS MAPLELEAF 2 b.f. Shiny Tenth 120–Prompt Delivery (Catullus) (1982 —
6fg 7fg 7g) May 21; sister to 3-y-o 6f and 7f winner Webbs Jewel and half-sister
to a winner in USA; dam won over 5f and 6f in USA; behind in sellers; sold
330 gns Ascot November Sales. *D. Marks.*

MISS MAREMMA 3 b.f. Ashmore 125–Mismaloya 116 (Emerson) (1981 6fg⁴ —
6fg⁴ 7fg 8fg 7d 1982 10f) lightly-made filly; plating-class maiden; should stay
middle distances. *R. Hollinshead.*

MISS MARSTAIN 3 ch.f. Song 132–Insurance 106 (Yellow God 129) (1981 —
5g 5fg 6fg 5g 5s⁴ 5s 1982 5d 6g 8g 6f⁴ 5h 7g 7g 7f 8.3g 10v 6g 8d) plater; stays
7f; acts on any going; often blinkered; sold 450 gns Ascot December Sales and
sent to Cyprus. *R. Hoad.*

MISS MATILDA 2 b.f. Jimmy Reppin 131–Ysemeopit 64 (Town Crier 119) —
(1982 6fg 5fg 6d 6s) Apr 20; small, lightly-made filly; first foal; dam won 5f
seller at 2 yrs; behind in varied races, final one a claimer. *W. Clay.*

MISS MONITA 2 b.f. Monsanto 121–Llynian 81 (Ballylinan 118) (1982 —
5d 5fg 5.8f 5g 6fg 7fg 5f) Feb 28; half-sister to 2 minor winners; in rear in
maiden races and sellers; of no account; blinkered final outing. *P. Burgoyne.*

MISS NELSKI 5 ch.m. Most Secret 119–Nelski 83 (Skymaster 126) (1981 **48**
6g 5d 5fg 5f 6f 7f² 5g* 8f 6f 5f 5fg³ 5g³ 5g⁴ 5d* 5g 5g 1982 5fg 5fg 5g 5f 5g
5fg 5fg 7f 5g⁴ 5fg 5d 5d⁴ 5g³) small, strong mare; mainly disappointing in
handicaps in 1982, although ran creditably last 2 starts; effective at 5f on a stiff
track and stays 7f; seems to act on any going; usually blinkered. *J. Etherington.*

MISS OLDHAM 2 b.f. Lochnager 132–Hi Baby 102 (High Treason 126) **73**
(1982 6h 5g⁴ 6g 5g 6d⁴ 5d) May 8; 4,600Y; smallish, lengthy filly; half-sister
to several winners, including good Italian winners Travolta (by Porto Bello)
and Hoche (by Celtic Ash); dam won over 5f and 6f at 2 yrs; 50/1, 2 lengths
fourth of 7 to La Perrichole in 6f maiden race at Nottingham in September;
suited by a soft surface. *J. Fitzgerald.*

MISS PATCH 2 ch.f. Patch 129–Compatriot (Pindari 124) (1982 5fg 5fg⁴ **51**
5fg 8d) Apr 22; IR 2,000F, 2,300Y; neat filly; half-sister to 2 winners by Jukebox, including fair 5f to 1m winner Come Play With Me; poor form, including
in a seller; sold 560 gns Ascot October Sales. *S. Mellor.*

MISS PERFECT 6 ch.f. Beau of Paree–Perfect Harmony (Darling Boy 124) —
(1981 5g 6fg 8fg 8.2d 8s 1982 8g 10.1d) good-bodied individual; bad plater;
has worn blinkers. *T. M. Jones.*

MISS POINCIANA 5 br.m. Averof 123–Miss Twomey (Will Somers 114§) **78**
(1981 5s* 5g³ 5g 5f 5fg* 5g⁴ 5fg² 5f⁴ 5f 5fg 5f² 5g* 1982 5g* 5f² 5fg* 5f⁴
5g⁴ 5fg 5fg⁴ 5d⁴ 5fg² 5d 5d) strong mare; in great form in spring and won
handicaps at Edinburgh, Newcastle and Haydock in good style; ran well when
½-length second to Mel's Choice at Haydock in September, but was a shade
disappointing last 2 starts; stays 6f but races exclusively at 5f nowadays;
acts on any going; often sweats up; usually held up; missed break tenth start
and was blinkered afterwards. *M. Camacho.*

MISS POSY 3 b.f. Pitskelly 122–Pushpa Ji Rao (Sayajirao 132) (1981 6fg* **35**
6fg 5d 7f 8g 7g 1982 7f 6g 6f 9g 10.1d 10.8fg² 10f⁴ 10fg³ 10fg) workmanlike
filly; plater; stays 1¼m well; best form on firm ground; sometimes blinkered;
sold 1,000 gns Doncaster October Sales. *J. Douglas-Home.*

MISS REALM 2 b.f. Realm 129–Saltana 101 (Darius 129) (1982 5fg* 5f* 5fg³ **86**
6fg 6f⁴) Apr 3; 4,800F; 6,200Y; compact, quite attractive filly; good walker;
half-sister to winner in France; dam won over 6f and 7f at 2 yrs and stayed 1¼m;
won 11-runner maiden race at York in May and 4-runner event at Ripon a week
later; 5 lengths third to Henry's Secret in 4-runner £3,800 race at Beverley in
June, best subsequent effort; not seen out after running poorly at Thirsk in July;
should stay beyond 5f; blinkered fourth start. *M. H. Easterby.*

MISS SHAMROCK 2 br.f. Saritamer 130–Miss Osprey 93 (Sea Hawk II 131) —
(1982 5.8g 5fg 5f) May 4; 3,000F, 2,800 2-y-o; third foal; sister to 3-y-o
Firsyjabs; dam suited by extreme distances; no show in maiden races; probably
needs much further than 5f. *K. Brassey.*

MISS SHAPE   4 ch.f. Reliance II 137–Shipshape (Shantung 132)   (1981   —
NR   1982 8g 8fg 10fg 8g 12.2d³ 12d)   first foal; dam never ran; showed a little
ability last 2 starts, on first occasion in an amateur riders event; will stay well.
G. Fletcher.

MISS SINCLAIR   2 br.f. Warpath 113 Lush Pool 70 (Dumbarnie 125)   (1982   **78**
7fg² 7.2g² 7d)   Apr 4; 3,600Y; fair sort; half-sister to numerous winners,
including very useful sprinter Lush Park and speedy 1977 2-y-o Golden Libra
(both by Goldhill); dam won over 6f; second in minor events at Chester in
July and Haydock in August, on latter course going down by a neck to Shackle
Pin after a good battle; stays 7f; doesn't have much scope.   *M. H. Easterby.*

MISS ST ANDREWS   3 ch.f. Sassafras 135–Miss Scotland 111 (Henry the
Seventh 125)   (1981 NR   1982 10g)   third foal; sister to 1¼m winner Stuart
King; dam won at up to 7f; third favourite, chased leaders to past halfway
when eighth of 14 behind Fox in maiden race at Newmarket in August; sold
920 gns Newmarket Autumn Sales.   *W. Hastings-Bass.*

MISS STARCHY   3 b.f. Starch Reduced 112–Anthela 76 (Acropolis 132)   (1981   —
5fg 5f   1982 7fg 6fg 10.1fg 12g)   light-framed filly; poor plater; has worn
blinkers.   *B. Gubby.*

MISS TANTAN   2 gr.f. Native Admiral–Tantanoola 75 (Swing Easy 126)   —
(1982 6s)   May 10; rather lightly-made filly; first foal; dam won 3 sellers over
7f; unquoted, no show in 25-runner maiden race at Doncaster in November.
R. Simpson.

MISS TETO   2 b.f. African Sky 124–Texly (Lyphard 132)   (1982 6f 6f 6g²   **76**
5d⁴ 6g 6d)   Apr 14; IR 13,000Y; strong, deep-girthed, sturdy filly; second
produce; half-sister to 3-y-o Lycia (by Targowice), successful at up to 9f in
Ireland; dam, granddaughter of brilliantly speedy Texana, showed no form
in France, including in claiming races; 5 lengths second of 20 to Rare Roberta
in maiden race at Lingfield in August, best effort including in nurseries; will
probably stay 7f.   *J. Toller.*

MISS THAMES   2 b.f. Tower Walk 130–Ebb and Flo 82 (Forlorn River 124)   **84**
(1982 5.1f² 6g*)   Apr 8; lengthy, rather sparely-made filly; third foal; half-
sister to 2 winners, including fairly useful 1981 2-y-o 7f winner Connaught
River (by Connaught); dam 2-y-o 6f winner and stayed 1¼m; won 15-runner
maiden race at Yarmouth in June in very close finish with Fleet Review, Sharp
Sea and French Pleat; suited by 6f.   *M. Stoute.*

MISS TRILLI   3 ch.f. Ardoon 124–Grecian Palm 78 (Royal Palm 131)   (1981   **79**
5g 5s² 5g* 5fg² 5g² 5f³ 5g³ 5g   1982 5g³ 5g 5f 5.1g 5fg 5f* 5fg⁴ 5d² 5d³)   smallish,
attractive filly; sprint handicapper; made all to win at Redcar in June;
acts on any going; has run respectably when sweating up; game.   *G. Pritchard-
Gordon.*

MISS TWIGGY   4 gr.f. Tycoon II–Golden Herb 80 (Goldhill 125)   (1981   **53**
5s 5fg 5g 5fg⁴ 5.1fg 6f³ 7f   1982 6fg 5d 6f 7g³ 7f² 7f² 7fg 7g 7f* 7g² 7f⁴ 7d 7f)
compact filly; held up, beat Secret Gill decisively in handicap at Catterick in
July; didn't have best of runs next 2 outings; stays 7f; acts on firm going;
ran badly when blinkered once; usually apprentice ridden.   *Mrs N. Macauley.*

MISS WHIZZ   2 ch.f. Artaius 129–Dame Buckle (Buckpasser)   (1982 5g)   —
Apr 18; 13,000F, 29,000Y; lengthy, rather lightly-made, shallow-girthed filly;
second foal; sister to useful French 3-y-o 1m and 9f winner Sabr Ayoub; dam,
who showed ability at around 7f at 2 yrs in Ireland, is half-sister to smart
1977 Irish 2-y-o Octavo; weak in market, no show when seventh of 12 in maiden
race at Wolverhampton in June; needs further.   *P. Cole.*

MISS WINTERFOLD   3 br.f. Jolly Good 122–Pamsam 67 (Constable 119)   —
(1981 NR   1982 9fg 8s)   second foal; half-sister to a winning plater; dam won
on flat and over hurdles; beaten a long way in minor events at Wolverhampton
and Warwick in the autumn.   *M. Tate.*

MISS ZHIVAGO   2 b.f. Gay Fandango 132–Jilly Winks (Blakeney 126)   (1982   **78**
6f 6f)   May 1; lengthy, good-bodied filly; fourth foal; half-sister to Irish 1m
winner Heather's Dream (by My Swanee); dam poor Irish maiden; ran on
strongly after slow start when 8½ lengths fifth of 12 behind Magnetic Field in
maiden race at Nottingham in July, second outing; will be much better suited
by 7f+.   *N. Callaghan.*

MISTER ACCORD   2 ch.c. Nishapour 125–Welshpool 75 (Henry the Seventh   **74**
125)   (1982 5f 8f 7g²)   Apr 18; 3,100Y; lengthy, quite attractive colt; half-
brother to 3-y-o 1m winner Seven Bridges Road (by Malinowski) and 3 other

winners here and abroad, including 7f and 1m winner Africanos (by African Sky); dam ran in England and Ireland; stayed on well after having lot to do at halfway when 3 lengths second of 15 to Bo-Peep in £2,800 seller at Newmarket in September; stays 1m; trained by R. Hollinshead on debut; sold to H. Bell 900 gns Doncaster October Sales. *M. Jarvis.*

MISTER AVATAR (USA) 2 ch.c. Avatar–Bitter Boredom (Nearctic) (1982 7g 6g) May 13; $45,000Y; good-topped colt; poor walker; fifth foal; half-brother to 3 minor winners in USA; dam unraced half-sister to very smart Riboboy and Sea Sands; prominent some way in maiden races at Leicester and Newmarket in October. *M. Albina.* —

MISTER CHAS 3 ch.g. Dragonara Palace 115–Dauphiness 74 (Supreme Sovereign 119) (1981 5f 6g 1982 6fg 6fg³ 6g 7fg 8g 7d⁴) workmanlike gelding; plater; stays 7f; has run respectably for an apprentice. *J. Holt.* 54

MISTEREFF 5 b.g. Track Spare 125–Ring True 80 (Gulf Pearl 117) (1981 6fg 7f 8.3fg 8g 8fg 1982 8.2g 16g) very small gelding; poor plater; seems to stay 1m; blinkered final start; sold 370 gns Ascot October Sales. *K. Bridgwater.* —

MISTER GOLDEN 2 ch.c. Diamonds Are Trump 108–St Pet (St Chad 120) (1982 6g³ 7d²) May 14; IR 1,800F, 36,000Y; tall, useful-looking colt; half-brother to two 2-y-o winners, including 1980 5f winner Advertrack (by Arch Sculptor); dam never ran; favourite when placed in minor event at Windsor in August and maiden race (second to Vaisseau) at Leicester in September; will stay 1m; sure to win a race. *G. Harwood.* 94

MISTER LORD (USA) 3 b.g. Sir Ivor 135–Forest Friend (Linacre 133) (1981 NR 1982 12s 14f 9fg³ 12.8fg* 12d*) ex-English gelding; half-brother to several winners, including smart Irish stayer Moss Trooper (by Levmoss) and 1980 2-y-o 7f winner Free Forester (by Bold Bidder); dam half-sister to Vaguely Noble's dam; easily landed odds in 10-runner maiden race at Wexford in July and justified short-priced favouritism by 4 lengths from Hill of Howth in 6-runner handicap at Killarney later in month; suited by 1½m+; trained by R. Price first start; sold 19,000 gns Ballsbridge November Sales and is to be trained by S. Mellor. *C. Collins, Ireland.* 79

MISTER LUCKY 5 br.g. Royalty 130–Fair Songstress 100 (Compensation 127) (1981 10s³ 12d 11.7fg 12f 13.3d 12d 12g 12d 1982 10fg 12f 12v⁴) middle-distance handicapper; acts on any going; suitable mount for a boy; changed hands 2,400 gns Ascot July Sales. *D. Jermy.*

MISTER PITT 3 b.c. Pitskelly 122–High Command (High Hat 131) (1981 5f 6fg 7fg⁴ 7s 8s² 1982 10d 8fg⁴ 8g 7.6d 8fg 8fg 8s 12v) compact, quite attractive colt; plating-class maiden; should stay 1¼m; best run on soft going; blinkered nowadays; sold out of G. Hunter's stable 3,200 gns Ascot September Sales after sixth start. *T. M. Jones.* 66

MISTER PRELUDE 2 gr. or ro.c. Warpath 113–Mitsuki 79 (Crowned Prince 128) (1982 8.2s 10g³) May 23; fair sort; first foal; dam 2-y-o 5f winner; creditable third behind John French in 9-runner £8,300 event at Newmarket in October; stays well; capable of winning maiden race. *M. Jarvis.* 91

MISTER VALENTINO 2 b.g. Wollow 132–Bernice Clare 68 (Skymaster 126) (1982 6fg 6g² 6g 7g 8d* 7d⁴) Apr 3; smallish, useful-looking gelding; good walker; second foal; dam won over 1m at 4 yrs; won 13-runner maiden event at Ayr in September; had stiff tasks on several of his other outings; suited by 1m; acts on a soft surface; gelded after final appearance. *J. Hanson.* 87

MISTIGORA 3 ch.f. Algora 110–Pink Slip (Indigenous 121) (1981 6f 5f 1982 8f 8fg) plating-class maiden; not sure to stay 6f let alone 1m. *B. Palling.* —

MISTOFFOLEES 2 b.g. Solinus 130–Poquito (Major Portion 129) (1982 5fg⁴ 5f 5f 6g 7fg 8d³) Apr 12; 6,200Y; strong, compact gelding; half-brother to 3 winners, including very useful 6f and 1¼m winner Senorita Poquito (by Connaught); dam won from 5f to 1¼m in Ireland; quite a moderate maiden; suited by 1m; best form with some give in the ground but has run respectably on a firm surface; gelded after final appearance. *J Fitzgerald.* 75

MISTRESS KIPLING 3 b.f. Nonoalco 131–Miller's Lass 103 (Mill Reef 141) (1981 6fg 5fg⁴ 6fg³ 5.8h³ 8s 1982 10fg⁴ 10g⁴ 10.2g 11.7g² 11d* 13.1f² 12s) tall, rangy, quite attractive filly with a long stride; won maiden race at Wolverhampton in August; stays 13f; seems to act on any going. *B. Hills.* 67

MISTY FOR ME   2 gr.f. Roan Rocket 128–Rana (Welsh Pageant 132)   (1982 **102**
5fg 5fg³ 5fg 5d* 5fg² 5fg* 5f* 5g³ 5v)   Apr 25; 1,700F, 4,600Y; big, workmanlike
filly; second foal; dam, from family of Raffingora, never ran; at her best in the
summer, winning maiden race at Nottingham, minor event at Wolverhampton
and nursery under 10-0, after overcoming difficulties in running, at Goodwood;
out of her depth subsequently behind Favoridge in St Hugh's Stakes at
Newbury and behind Tatibah in Cornwallis Stakes at Ascot; has raced only
over 5f; has won on a soft surface but goes really well on firm ground; game.
M. McCourt.

MISTY GLEN   6 b.m. Leander 119–Tudor Style 98 (Owen Tudor)   (1981   —
12f 17.1d² 16f² 16.1f   1982 16d⁴ 15.5fg 16f)   strong, lengthy mare; suited by a
test of stamina; probably acts on any going; has run creditably for an apprentice.
M. Bradley.

MISTY HALO   3 b.f. High Top 131–Ringed Aureole 77 (Aureole 132)   (1981   **93**
8fg 8d* 8.2d* 8s   1982 12fg² 13fg² 14g³ 10g* 15.5fg² 10f* 12d* 12.2d* 12s*)
lengthy filly; had a splendid year, winning ladies race at Brighton, apprentice
events at Leicester and Chepstow and amateur riders races at Brighton again
and Catterick; stays well; acts on any going; splendid mount for an inexperienced rider; consistent.   *Sir Mark Prescott.*

MISTY LIGHT   3 gr.f. Bustino 136–France (Milesian 125)   (1981 NR   1982   **65**
9g 12f 16.9fg 11.5g³ 12s⁴ 12s)   6,000Y; workmanlike ex-English filly; half-
sister to several minor winners here and abroad; dam placed twice over 5f at
2 yrs in France; 1¾ lengths third of 17 to Regal Promise in maiden race at
Galway in October, best effort; stays 1½m; trained by H. Candy first 3 outings.
J. Oxx, Ireland.

MITILINI   2 ch.c. Julio Mariner 127–Charming Thought (Stage Door Johnny)   **96**
(1982 7g 7g 8g 8.2s* 10g)   Apr 16; 16,000F, 28,000Y; strong, short-coupled colt;
fourth foal; dam disappointing maiden; won maiden race at Haydock in October
by 3 lengths from Count Derry; ran creditably behind John French in £8,300
event at Newmarket later in the month; stays well; acts on soft going.   *R. Boss.*

MIYSAM   3 b.f. Supreme Sovereign 119–Enniscrone 73 (Royal Palm 131)   —
(1981 5g* 5g 5f   1982 7f 5f)   neat, lightly-made filly; good mover; made all to
win maiden race at Haydock early in 1981; in rear all subsequent starts, including
in a seller.   *C. Spares.*

MIZZENHEAD (USA)   7 br.g. Mill Reef 141–Black Satin 114 (Linacre 133)   —
(1981 12s* 12s   1982 10d)   strong, lengthy gelding; stayed 13f; acted on soft
going; dead.   *M. W. Easterby.*

MOAT HOUSE   3 ch.g. Sun Prince 128–Stickpin 76 (Gulf Pearl 117)   (1981   **57**
5s 5fg 7fg 7g³ 7.6s 6d³ 8.2s 6g   1982 7d 6f 7g* 7d² 8.3g 8g 8.3g⁴ 7d² 8.2s)   small,
strong gelding; plater; wel-backed favourite when successful at Kempton in
May; bought in 3,100 gns afterwards; ran respectably in better company several
times afterwards; stays 1m; best form with some give in the ground.   *D. Thom.*

MODUPE (USA)   2 b. or br.c. Bold Hour–Lost For Words (Verbatim)   (1982   —
6f 7g)   Apr 25; leggy, close-coupled colt; second foal; dam third once from
7 starts; 50/1, eleventh of 20 in June maiden races at Newbury and Newmarket.
I. Walker.

MOLLINGTON   3 b.g. Decoy Boy 129–Aces High 62 (Acer 123)   (1981 NR   **69**
1982 6f⁴ 8f⁴ 6f 7s* 8.2s)   strong gelding; second foal; half-brother to a winning
plater; dam won 6f seller; finished very strongly to win handicap at Wolverhampton in October; stays 7f; clearly revels in the mud.   *J. Webber.*

MOLLISON   2 b.c. Anax 120–Puss Moth (Hotfoot 126)   (1982 5fg³ 5.3g⁴ 6f   **48**
6g⁴ 7fg)   Mar 9; 1,350F, 5,000Y; well-made, attractive colt; poor plater; should
stay 7f; sold 600 gns Newmarket Autumn Sales.   *G. Hunter.*

MOLLY (USA)   3 b.f. Christopher R–Evening Kiss (Saggy)   (1981 6d³ 1982   **100**
6fg* 7fg 6f 6fg 6f³ 5g³ 6fg*)   rangy, good sort; sister to stakes-placed winner
Kiss Chris and half-sister to several winners in USA, including Mac Corkle (by
Jig Time), a very useful winner at up to 1m; dam second once from 9 starts;
sire, one of best American sprinters as a 4-y-o and 5-y-o, won at up to 9f; won
maiden race and Carna Fillies' Stakes at Naas, in latter beating Aloe by a length
in September; also ran respectably to be eighth of 21 to Merlins Charm in 7f
Jersey Stakes at Royal Ascot (faded in closing stages) and third in Herbertstown
Stakes at Naas (1¼ lengths behind Jasmine Star) and Philips Electrical Stakes
(Handicap) at the Curragh (½ length behind Sweet Side); in rear in William Hill

July Cup at Newmarket and Seven Springs Sprint Stakes at the Curragh on other starts; possibly doesn't quite stay 7f; acts well on fast ground. *N. McGrath, Ireland.*

MOLOKAI 2 b.f. Prince Tenderfoot 126–Cake (Never Say Die 137) (1982 **81** 6fg⁴ 6g³ 7d*) May 7; IR 58,000Y; smallish, lengthy, good-quartered filly; none too good a walker; sister to very useful 1975 Irish 2-y-o 5f to 1m winner Icing, and half-sister to 2 winners; dam of little account; won maiden race at Ayr in September; will stay 1m. *J. Hindley.*

MOLON LAVE 5 b.g. Welsh Pageant 132–Another Princess 83 (King Emperor) **72** (1981 7.6g* 6g 7fg 7g⁴ 7fg² 6fg³ 8fg* 8g³ 7.6s 8fg* 8fg² 1982 8g 8fg* 7.6g 7fg² 8fg² 7f⁴ 7f 8fg 8fg² 8g 8fg 7fg 7g 7s⁴) big, strong gelding; quite a modest handicapper; beat Chief Speaker a shade cheekily by ½ length (pair clear) in Newbury Spring Cup in April; second at Newmarket (twice) and Goodwood; stays 1m; ideally suited by top-of-the-ground; sweated up badly when blinkered once in 1980; had a poorish run sixth start. *C. Brittain.*

MOLOVE 2 ch.f. Cawston's Clown 113–Charmelaine (Sheshoon 132) (1982 6s) May 20; sixth reported foal; dam lightly-raced half-sister to very useful Fleece; unquoted, always behind from slow start in 16-runner maiden race at Leicester in November. *J. Edmunds.*

MOMENT IN TIME 2 b.f. Without Fear 128–Heavenly Bounty (Captain's **91** Gig) (1982 6f 7f* 7g* 8g⁴ 8g) Mar 15; leggy, lightly-built filly; conceived in Australia; dam useful winner of 5 races from 9.5f to 1¼m in Ireland in 1977; successful in 11-runner maiden race at Sandown in July and 10-runner minor event (beating Carneades a neck) at Redcar in August; had stiff tasks afterwards in nurseries; stays well; usually sweats up and did so particularly badly last 2 starts. *M. Stoute.*

MOMENT OF WEAKNESS 5 b.m. Pieces of Eight 128–Glimmer of Hope **42** 90 (Never Say Die 137) (1981 NR 1982 10.8fg 12fg 10fg 10g 10f² 10f² 10f⁴ 10fg) small, well-made mare; good walker; second in 2 sellers at Nottingham in July; stays 1½m; acts on any going; suitable mount for an apprentice. *A. Ingham.*

MONACO DANCER 3 b.g. Ampney Prince 96–Molly Cockell (Wynkell 88) — (1981 5fg 6d 5fg 1982 7g) bad plater; sold 320 gns Ascot July Sales. *D. Elsworth.*

MONARCHS MISS 3 ch.f. Royal Match 117–Fyjia (Hul a Hul 124) (1981 — NR 1982 7fg 8g) 450Y; third foal; dam Irish 2-y-o 5f winner; always behind in seller at Beverley in August and maiden race at Edinburgh in October; blinkered first start. *Mrs N. Macauley.*

MON BEAUX 8 ch.g. Continuation 120–Affectionately 82 (Mark-Ye-Well) — (1981 10.6s 1982 12s 10fg) lightly raced nowadays and is probably of little account. *J. Yardley.*

MONCLARE TROPHY 3 ch.c. Sandford Lad 133–Blue Warbler (Worden **45** II 129) (1981 5g 6fg 5fg³ 6g 1982 6s 5f 6f 6g 6g 6d² 6f 8s) lightly-made colt; plater nowadays; stays 6f; acts on a firm and a soft surface; blinkered third and fourth starts. *A. Pitt.*

MONDAY BLUES 2 b.g. Workboy 123–Monday Morning (Royal Record II) **— §** (1982 5g 5g4 6fg 5f 6f 6g 6d) Jan 29; 1,100F, 3,800Y; sturdy gelding; half-brother to 2 winning platers; dam ran only at 2 yrs; bad plater, temperamental into the bargain; blinkered last 2 starts; gelded after final appearance. *R. Whitaker.*

MONETARIST 2 ch.c. Monseigneur 127–Elated 80 (Sparkler 130) (1982 **98** 7d 7f² 7fg* 7fg⁴ 7d 7.3g³ 8d 7d) Apr 17; 11,000Y; big, lengthy colt; good walker; first foal; dam won over 1m at 2 yrs; got up close home to win maiden race at Ayr in August by a neck from Darting Groom; excellent third in nursery at Newbury in September, best subsequent effort; should be suited by 1m; not particularly consistent. *J. Dunlop.*

MONIAR (USA) 3 ch.c. Silent Screen–Mademoiselle Molly (Nashua) (1981 **87** NR 1982 8fg* 8f 10.1fg 10fg 10fg³ 12fg 11.7s) $175,000Y; quite attractive colt; second foal; half-brother to American 4f winner Dramatist (by Elocutionist); dam, half-sister to very useful 1974 2-y-o Highest Trump, won over 6f at 4 yrs; beat Off The Hook by 2 lengths in 21-runner maiden race at Newmarket in May; not disgraced most subsequent starts though ran badly final outing; stays 1⅛m; probably needs a sound surface; sold to A. Moore 6,400 gns Ascot December Sales. *P. Walwyn.*

MONKS GOLD 2 b.g. Habat 127–Golden Dolly 76 (Golden Horus 123) (1982 **62 §**
5f 5f 6f 7d³ 6fg* 7f 5g 6d) Mar 29; 1,700F, 1,100Y; neat gelding; half-brother
to a winning plater by Caliban and a winner in France; dam won 5f seller at 2
yrs; plater; quickened clear in good style to win by 4 lengths from Fairham at
Ripon (no bid) in August; showed a little form in race either side of that
win, but absolutely nothing otherwise; wears blinkers; unreliable. *J. Carr.*

MONMOUTH (FR) 4 ch.c. Welsh Pageant 132–Cockade 104 (Derring-Do 131) —
(1981 8.2s 10.1f 12.3g 1982 10g 13.4g⁴ 13fg³ 12fg 16fg) workmanlike colt;
has shown a little ability; sold 3,800 gns Newmarket Autumn Sales. *T. Robson.*

MONNOW MILL 3 b. or br.g. Kambalda 108–Well of Dreams (Military 112) —
(1981 5.8g 5f 7fg 1982 10.2g) well beaten in varied company. *N. Kernick.*

MONONGELIA 2 ch.f. Welsh Pageant 132–Bird of Dawning (Sea-Bird II 145) **84**
(1982 7f² 7fg² 7g³) Mar 25; 29,000Y; lengthy filly; half-sister to 2 winners,
including quite useful Irish 7.5f to 1¼m winner Mice Bird (by Busted); dam,
daughter of Argentinian 1,000 Guineas and Oaks winner Sweet Sue, won over 6f
at 3 yrs in USA; placed in maiden races at Yarmouth, twice favourite; will be
better suited by 1m+. *H. Cecil.*

MONSANTO LAD 2 br.c. Monsanto 121–Swallow of Flandre (Flandre II 83) **74**
(1982 5f 5f 5f³ 6f 7f 7d 8g 7g 8g² 8d⁴) Apr 8; short-backed colt; second foal; dam
never ran; best effort when ½-length second of 12 to Real Monty in maiden race
at Edinburgh in October; suited by 1m and will stay further. *K. Stone.*

MON'S BEAU 7 b.g. Mon Plaisir 121–Beauatire 86 (Beau Sabreur 125) (1981 —
16fg 16.1s* 16s 16g 21fg 16d 16fg 18g 1982 15.5g⁴) out-and-out staying
handicapper; suited by some give in the ground; suitable mount for a boy;
occasionally sweats up; game. *D. Grissell.*

MONS LAD 2 ch.c. Manado 130–Cabermaid (Shoemaker 121) (1982 8g 8.2s) —
Feb 18; IR 7,000F, IR 11,500Y; first produce; dam won small 1¼m race in
France; well beaten in October in maiden race (last of 8) at Edinburgh and
minor event at Nottingham. *C. Nelson.*

MONTE ACUTO 8 ch.g. Mountain Call 125–Island Woman 76 (King's Troop **52**
118) (1981 8s 7fg 8g 7g 8d 8f 8fg³ 8f² 8g³ 8d³ 8s⁴ 1982 8f 8fg 8h³ 8g 8fg⁴ 8g
8g² 8fg² 10.2f 9g) strong, well-made gelding; in frame in handicaps at Chepstow
(3) and Bath; best at 1m; acts on any going; has twice run below form in blinkers;
good mount for an apprentice. *G. Cottrell.*

MONTEKIN 3 b.c. Mount Hagen 127– Sweet Relations (Skymaster 126) **117**
(1981 6fg² 7fg* 7f² 7d* 7.3s* 1982 7fg 8fg 10.5f 8g² 10.8s² 10d⁴ 8s 8v²)
strong, very attractive colt; very good mover; second foal; half-brother to a
winner in Italy by Lochnager; dam lightly-raced daughter of 1,000 Guineas winner Night Off; very smart on his day; well below form first 3 starts in Clerical,
Medical Greenham Stakes at Newbury, 2,000 Guineas at Newmarket and Mecca-
Dante Stakes at York; injured himself in last-named in May and was off course
4 months afterwards but showed himself back to something like his best when
9 lengths fourth to Time Charter in Dubai Champion Stakes at Newmarket after
having every chance 2f out (hung left) and 5 lengths second to Commodore
Blake in Premio Ribot at Rome; suited by 1¼m and may get further; has won on
a firm surface but needs some give in the ground to show his best form; usually
impresses in preparation; not the easiest of rides. *J. Dunlop.*

MONTEREEF 2 b.c. Take a Reef 127–Montage 64 (Polyfoto 124) (1982 7g 7fg —
7d) Apr 13; small, close-coupled colt; first foal; dam won 7f seller at 2 yrs
and several hurdle races; soundly beaten in maiden races. *C. Spares.*

MONTICELLI 2 b.c. Radetzky 123–Sovereigns Whistle 67 (Sovereign Path 125) —
(1982 7g 6g 6g) Mar 5; 10,000Y; fair sort; brother to 3-y-o Val de Ponce and
half-brother to useful sprinter The Sandford (by Sandford Lad); dam poor
and temperamental plater; poor form in maiden and minor events. *C. Brittain.*

MONTREVIE 2 b.f. Monseigneur 127–Tack 88 (Tacitus 124) (1982 6f² 7g³ **89**
8.2fg³ 7s) May 8; 9,000Y; leggy, narrow filly; half-sister to several winners,
including smart 6f to 1m winner Trevita (by Tyrant), subsequently a stakes
winner in USA; dam stayer; ran well in races won by Royal Heroine, Flamenco
and The Noble Player on first 3 starts, but flopped badly when presented with
relatively simple task in maiden event at Redcar in October; stays 1m; possibly
not suited by soft ground. *H. T. Jones.*

MOONBAT 3 gr.g. Habat 127–Lady Of The Moon 89 (Crepello 136) (1981 6s **64** 1982 7f 7.6f 7f³ 8d 8g 7fg 8f) robust gelding; has shown only a little ability; should stay 1m; blinkered last 3 starts; sold 1,600 gns Newmarket Autumn Sales and sent to Holland. *M. Smyly.*

MOONDUSTER 3 b.f. Sparkler 130–Go Gracefully 85 (Jolly Jet 111) (1981 **65** 7g 1982 8d⁴ 9fg 12.3g³ 16g* 15d³ 16.1s) leggy filly; stayed on well to win maiden race at Beverley in August; ran creditably next start; suited by a test of stamina; sold 4,600 gns Doncaster November Sales. *C. Thornton.*

MOON JESTER 2 gr.c. Comedy Star 121–Castle Moon 79 (Kalamoun 129) **85** (1982 7fg 7g 7fg 8g⁴ 8s*) Mar 28; 3,100F, 4,000Y; fair sort; first foal; dam, winner from 1m to 13f, is sister to very smart middle-distance stayer Castle Keep and half-sister to Gold Cup winner Ragstone; put up best effort when winning 18-runner nursery at Warwick in October by a neck from General Concorde; will be suited by 1¼m+; acts on soft going. *T. Marshall.*

MOONLIGHT BAY 2 ch.f. Palm Track 122–Moonbay (Ovid 95) (1982 6g **46** 8.2fg 7g 6s) May 11; plain, short-legged filly; first foal; dam poor plater; bad plater. *M. Lambert.*

MOONLIGHTING 2 b.f. Workboy 123–Ashen Light 76 (Shiny Tenth 120) — (1982 6s) May 17; 1,400Y; first foal; dam won over 5.9f and 1¼m; eleventh of 13 in maiden race at Hamilton in September. *P. Calver.*

MOON MARINER 2 ch.c. Julio Mariner 127–Maroukh (Kashmir II 125) **89** (1982 8fg 8s 10s* 10.2s⁴) Apr 3; 9,400Y; well-made, quite attractive colt; third foal; half-brother to a winner in Barbados; dam ran only twice; won 16-runner maiden race at Nottingham in October by ¾ length from Only A Pound; needs a good test of stamina; acts on soft going. *C. Brittain.*

MOORES METAL 2 b.c. Wolverlife 115–Torino (Firestreak 125) (1982 **94** 6g³ 6fg 6g³ 6d 6d⁴ 7d⁴ 7s) May 19; IR 7,200Y; neat, quite attractive colt; first foal; dam won over 9.5f in Ireland; in frame in maiden races and a nursery; will stay 1m; acts on a soft surface. *R. Hollinshead.*

MOOR FARM 6 ch.g. Grey Mirage 128–Lor Darnie 65 (Dumbarnie 125) — (1981 NR 1982 10.8fg) well beaten in maiden races and a handicap. *G. Thorner.*

MOORLAND GAL 3 br.f. Baragoi 115–Vetsera (Hopeful Venture 125) (1981 — NR 1982 11.7f) third foal; half-sister to winning stayer Right Regent (by Kambalda); dam never ran; tailed-off last of 17 finishers behind Taffy Jones in maiden race at Bath in July. *W. R. Williams.*

MOOR MOUSE 3 ch.f. Lombard 126–Grill Room 79 (Connaught 130) (1981 — NR 1982 7g 10h 12g 10g 16fg 12f) workmanlike filly; poor mover; third foal; dam ran only twice; soundly beaten in maiden races and a seller; trained first start by B. Hanbury. *G. Thorner.*

MOOR VIEW 3 b.c. Mansingh 120–Sicalaine 52 (Sica Boy 132) (1981 5v — 5s 5d 1982 5fg 5g 5g 6f 6f) rangy colt; poor sprint maiden; sold 350 gns Doncaster October Sales. *J. Etherington.*

MOPSY LOVEJOY 2 b.f. Tudor Rhythm 112–Friendly Sylvan (Be Friendly — 130) (1982 5fg 5fg⁴ 6g 7g 6g) Mar 27; plain filly; second foal; dam well behind in maiden races; well beaten in maiden races and a seller; sold 400 gns Ascot August Sales. *J. S. Wilson.*

MOQUETTE 3 b.f. Moulton 128–Miss Tweedie 114 (Aberdeen 109) (1981 — 6g 8g 1982 12d⁴ 13.4g 16.9fg 12g) lengthy filly; poor maiden; sold to L. Barratt 720 gns Newmarket Autumn Sales. *R. Hollinshead.*

MORALITY STONE 5 b.h. Ragstone 128–Miss Casanova 84 (Galivanter **64** 131) (1981 12fg 12g 11s* 12d* 12fg* 12fg³ 12.5fg² 14d 10d² 12g 12v 1982 10.2f 11.5f³ 12g 11.7g³ 11.5g 10v 10s) robust, well-made horse; middle-distance handicapper; has won on a firm surface but is ideally suited by some give in the ground; has run creditably for an amateur rider. *P. Mitchell.*

MORAL LEADER 2 gr.c. Guillaume Tell 121–Miss Sarah (The Axe 115) **98** (1982 5f 7.5f* 7f² 7fg² 7fg² 7g²) Feb 27; half-brother to 2 winners, including useful 1980 Irish 2-y-o Master Thatch (by Thatch), subsequently a stakes winner at up to 1m in USA; dam, placed over 6f at 2 yrs in France, is sister to smart stakes winner Foggy Note; won maiden race at Gowran Park in July by a neck; second on all subsequent starts, notably going down by a neck to Committed at Galway in July on third start, by a short head to Solford in minor event at Leopardstown in September on fifth and by a neck to Academy Award under top weight in nursery at Limerick in September on sixth; will stay middle distances; has raced only on a sound surface; sent to USA. *K. Prendergast, Ireland.*

MORAVIA 2 ch.f. Morston 125–Abstract 73 (French Beige 127) (1982 6f) — Mar 12; medium-sized, quite attractive filly; fourth foal; half-sister to 2 winners, including useful 1979 2-y-o 7f performer Summary (by Mandamus); dam won over 10.8f; refused to race in maiden event at Yarmouth in August; dead. *B. Hobbs.*

MORAYSHIRE 5 b.h. Royal Palace 131–Outward Bound 79 (Sing Sing 134) — (1981 9g2 8fg 10fg4 8fg 10.2g 9g 1982 8g) lengthy horse; good mover; very useful at his best; stayed 9f; acted well on firm ground; dead. *W. Musson.*

MORCON 2 ch.c. Morston 125–Conciliation 98 (St Paddy 133) (1982 7f2) **87 p** Mar 17; third foal; half-brother to 2-y-o winners by Brigadier Gerard and Wollow; dam, half-sister to smart middle-distance horse Colum, won over 6f and 7f at 2 yrs; 7/2 and looking particularly fit and well, shaped like a certain future winner when 2 lengths second of 10 to comfortable winner Dunbeath in valuable maiden race at Goodwood in July, leading to past halfway and keeping on nicely; should stay at least 1¼m. *R. Hern.*

MOREDA 3 ch.f. Mount Hagen 127–Woo 72 (Stage Door Johnny) (1981 **93** 5s 5g 5d3 5s 6s 7.5f4 7f* 7.5f 7f 8d 1982 10g* 10g3 9f2 9fg 8fg 8d4 8s) 5,400F; workmanlike filly; half-sister to fairly useful 1980 Irish 2-y-o 5f winner Ring of Steel (by Steel Heart); dam middle-distance maiden; showed improved form in 9-runner Azalea Stakes at Leopardstown in May, accounting for Quite Shy by a length; ran creditably afterwards in valuable race at Gowran Park (3 lengths second to Bonnie Bess) and Gilltown Stud Stakes at the Curragh (4½ lengths fourth of 12 to Mary Mitsu); finds 1m on sharp side and will be suited by 1½m; seems to act on any going; not disgraced in blinkers final start at 2 yrs; sold 64,000 gns Newmarket December Sales. *L. Browne, Ireland.*

MORE FOR ENGLAND 2 b.g. Ballymore 123–Kiyofuji 98 (Grey Sovereign — 128§) (1982 8.2s) Apr 4; 2,500Y; tall, good-topped gelding; fifth foal; dam won twice over 5f at 2 yrs; 50/1 and distinctly burly, soon tailed off when last of 8 in maiden race at Haydock in October. *D. McCain.*

MORE HARMONY 4 br.c. Morston 125–Melody Maid (Tudor Melody 129) **82 d** (1981 12fg 11.7g3 10fg* 12g4 13.3g 12fg* 11f2 12fg 11.7d 1982 12fg3 12g* 11f4 12f* 12g 15fg 12f 14g 12fg 13.3g) quite attractive, rather lightly-made colt; ran moderately after winning handicaps at Kempton in May (on disqualification of Le Soleil) and Epsom in June (beat Heighten a length in £6,900 Northern Dancer Stakes); stays 1½m; very well suited by a firm surface; blinkered once; sold 15,000 gns Newmarket December Sales and sent to India. *J. Bethell.*

MORE HASTE 3 ch.f. Morston 125–Fly For Home 78 (Habitat 134) (1981 **74** 7g 1982 11.7f 16fg2 12d4 16.9fg* 14fg 16.9fg 17.1s* 16.1s) leggy filly; won maiden race at Wolverhampton in July and handicap at Bath in October; needs a thorough test of stamina; has won on a firm surface but better form on soft; often sweats up; sold to BBA 12,500 gns Newmarket December Sales. *J. Bethell.*

MORE KISSES 3 ch.f. Morston 125–Buss 102 (Busted 134) (1981 NR 1982 **86** 10fg* 10f* 12g 10f3 10fg 10s) narrow, rather lightly-made filly; half-sister to 3 winners, including fairly useful miler Imperial Ace (by Derring-Do); dam game performer at up to 11f; won maiden race at Salisbury in May and £4,100 event at Newbury in June; beat Shooting High by 1½ lengths going away in latter; should stay 1½m (last of 8 in Lancashire Oaks when tried at trip); acts on firm going and is possibly unsuited by soft; suited by waiting tactics. *H. Candy.*

MORE WIT 2 ch.f. Whitstead 125–Misty Echo (Mountain Call 125) (1982 — 6g 5g 7d) May 20; third foal; dam ran only at 2 yrs; backward, behind in maiden and minor events. *P. M. Taylor.*

MORGAN'S CHOICE 5 ch.h. Reliance II 137–Piave (Alcide 136) (1981 **79** 12.2fg 11.7d 11.1s 12.2fg 13.1f 14fg* 13.1h* 14fg 1982 7s 16g* 18.4fg 17.1f* 17f4 17.1f* 16fg* 16.1g3 17.1g* 16fg4 14.6g3 13.3g 17.1s 18d) small, well-made horse; had a most successful season and won handicaps at Newbury, Bath (3) and Ascot; disappointed tenth and twelfth starts, but finished good third to Karadar in valuable handicap at Doncaster in September in between (came from a long way back); needs a test of stamina; acts on any going; has won in blinkers, but didn't wear them after third start; genuine. *J. Hill.*

MORGAN'S PEARL 5 ch.g. Gulf Pearl 117–Morganette (Tudor Music 131) §§
(1981 14g⁴ 16g 1982 18.8fg 16d) useful sort; not a good mover in his slower
paces; fair handicapper at his best, but has become temperamental at start
and is one to be wary of; stays well; acts on any going with possible exception
of very soft; bandaged nowadays. *G. Blum.*

MORICE 4 b.g. Morston 125–Ardice 91 (Hard Tack 111§) (1981 8d³ 10d* —
12s⁴ 10d* 1982 10s 12fg 13.3g) well-made gelding; ran creditably when about
6 lengths sixth of 15 behind Funny Spring in Rosebery Stakes (Handicap)
at Kempton in April on reappearance; stays 1½m; acts on soft going. *R.
Hannon.*

MORKULLA (SWE) 7 ch.m. Royal Park 114–Canary Bird 79 (Bleep-Bleep —
134) (1981 10.2s 8d 12s³ 10.8fg 8fg⁴ 10fg 10f 10g 10.6s 10s³ 1982 10.2g 10f
10fg) leggy mare; inconsistent plater; stays 1½m; seems to act on any going;
often wears blinkers; good mount for an inexperienced rider; hampered in early
stages on final outing. *G. Fletcher.*

MORNING AFTER 3 gr.c. Busted 134–Flying Nelly 107 (Nelcius 133) (1981 93
7g 8g 1982 12s³ 14fg* 14f* 12s) strong, well-made, quite attractive colt;
stayed on well to win maiden race at Newmarket (beat Muslab) and handicap
at Sandown (accounted for Protos by 1½ lengths) in May; off course 4 months
afterwards; suited by 1¾m and will stay further; acts on firm going; sold 6,800
gns Newmarket Autumn Sales. *G. Harwood.*

MOROCCO BOUND 3 gr.g. Roan Rocket 128–Hoppity 72 (Negotiation) —
(1981 7d 1982 10d 8g) behind in minor event and maiden races. *S. Woodman.*

MORON 7 ch.g. Morston 125–One Extra 85 (Abernant 142) (1981 NR 1982 —
17.1s) quite a moderate handicapper; won 4 times in 1979; last of 22 on only
outing since; stays well; needs some give in the ground; has been tried in blinkers.
R. Hodges.

MORSE PIP 3 b.c. Bay Express 132–Code of Love 99 (Bleep-Bleep 134) (1981 80
5g 5s³ 1982 5g* 6fg² 5fg 5g⁴ 5d³ 6s*) fair sort; not the best of movers; won
apprentice maiden race at Lingfield in August and apprentice handicap at
Leicester in November; suited by 6f; suited by some give in the ground; good
mount for an apprentice. *S. Woodman.*

MORSTONS MAID 3 ch.f. Morston 125–Dairy Queen 76 (Queen's Hussar 124) —
(1981 5fg 6fg 7fg 6d 1982 12f 12.2f⁴ 12fg 15fg 12g 12.2f⁴) lightly-made filly;
plating-class maiden; stays 1½m; blinkered second to fourth starts. *S. Norton.*

MORTAR 8 ch.g. Firestreak 125–Chance Shot 86 (Hornbeam 130) (1981 NR —
1982 10d) plater; suited by 1½m; acts on any going; used to wear blinkers;
bandaged only outing of 1982. *P. Bevan.*

MORVERN 3 b.c. Thatch 136–Sleat 112 (Santa Claus 133) (1981 NR 1982 66
10.4g 12f 11.5f⁴ 14g³ 16.5fg³ 15.8d⁴) strong, compact colt; half-brother to fairly
useful stayer Sligo Bay (by Sassafras) and French middle-distance winner Deep
Snow (by Amber Rama); dam, half-sister to St Leger winner Athens Wood, won
over 6f and 1¼m; staying maiden; acts on a firm and a soft surface; blinkered
final start; sold to J. Jenkins 8,000 gns Newmarket Autumn Sales. *B. Hobbs.*

MORWRAY BOY 2 b.g. Workboy 123–Lyn's Pride 85 (Star Moss 122) (1982 79
5f 6fg 5.8f³ 6g² 7f³ 7fg⁴ 6g² 6f 6s³ 6v 6g) May 2; 4,800Y; useful-looking gelding;
excellent mover; half-brother to a winning plater and a winning hurdler; dam
stayed 7f; in frame in most of his races; stays 7f; acts on any going; blinkered
penultimate outing; gelded after final appearance. *D. Wilson.*

MOSES SAMPSON 4 b.g. Bold Lad (Ire) 133–Countess Decima (Sir Gaylord) 64
(1981 5fg 8g 6fg 6f 7f* 7fg³ 6g 5s⁴ 5s 1982 6f 8.3g 7f* 8fg 7g² 7g 7.6f* 7f⁴ 7f 7g
7fg) stocky gelding; readily won selling handicap at Brighton in May (no bid)
and amateur riders race at Lingfield in July; stays 7f well; acts on any going;
seems best in blinkers; missed break first and fourth outings; sold 3,700 gns
Doncaster November Sales. *N. Callaghan.*

MOSHI-MOSHI 3 ch.c. Cawston's Clown 113–Copthorne Polly (Double-U-Jay —
120) (1981 7g 1982 10.1g 11.7g 8fg) good-topped colt; in rear in maiden
races and a minor event. *Dr A. Jones.*

MOSSBLOWN 2 b.f. Warpath 113–Montana (Mossborough 126) (1982 5f 7d 70
8fg⁴) May 3; fair sort; third foal; sister to a winning plater and half-sister to
3-y-o 1m winner Iowa (by So Blessed); dam poor maiden on flat and over
hurdles; 8 lengths fourth of 13 to Saba in maiden race at Beverley in September;
will be suited by 1¼m+. *C. Thornton.*

MOSSO 3 b.f. Ercolano 118–Mossy 95 (Mossborough 126) (1981 5.8g* 6d* 7.3s —
1982 7fg 10fg 8f) well-made filly; good walker; won maiden race at Bath and
Kingsclere Stakes at Newbury in 1981; behind all starts at 3 yrs, in Ladbrokes
Nell Gwyn Stakes at Newmarket, Sir Charles Clore Memorial Stakes at Newbury
and handicap at Newmarket again; bred to stay middle distances. *J. Toller.*

MOSS WALK 4 b.f. Private Walk 108–Moss Ville (Levmoss 133) (1981 NR —
1982 10.1g) ex-Irish filly; fourth foal; half-sister to a winner in
Belgium by Wind Drift; dam never ran; soundly beaten in maiden race at
Galway as a 2-y-o and minor event at Windsor in August (last of 10). *J. King.*

MOSSWERN 3 ch.f. Towern 96–Mossy's Delight 44 (Mossy Face 98) (1981 **77**
5s² 5s*(dis) 5g² 5s 6g 6f* 7fg² 7g² 7f² 5f 7g 8d 1982 10f² 8f² 8fg) leggy,
lightly-made filly; stays 1¼m; acts on any going; genuine. *G. Toft.*

MOSSY MANOR 2 ch.c. Habitat 134–Milly Moss 112 (Crepello 136) (1982 6g —
7d 7s) Feb 26; good-bodied, attractive colt; good walker; half-brother to 3
winners, including smart Kashmir Lass (by Kashmir II), a winner from 6f to 1m;
dam won Cheshire Oaks and is sister to very smart Mil's Bomb; well beaten in
maiden races at Haydock (favourite), Yarmouth and Redcar; sold to BBA
(Italia) 5,600 gns Newmarket December Sales. *H. Cecil.*

MOST FUN 4 b.c. Morston 125–Darling Bud (Whistling Wind 123) (1981 10f⁴ —
12g* 12g² 1982 22.2fg 8fg 8fg 16fg) ex-Irish colt; compact, good sort; third
foal; half-brother to 2 winners, including fairly useful 5f and 7f winner A Star Is
Born (by Tudor Music); dam useful Irish 2-y-o; won maiden race at Sligo and
ran creditably on both his other starts as a 3-y-o when trained by J. Oxx; poor
form on flat over here, probably best effort over 2m; bandaged behind on first
outing. *J. Old.*

MOTAVATO (USA) 4 b.c. Apalachee 137–Lovelight 112 (Bleep-Bleep 134) **120**
(1981 7g* 8g 8.5d³ 8g* 7g³ 1982 7f² 8f* 8f 10f³ 7g²)
    Some indication of the glaring disparity in the levels of prize-money here
and in the United States can be gleaned from the fact that Motavato virtually
doubled his career earnings by finishing third in the Budweiser Million at
Arlington Park, Chicago, admittedly an exceptionally valuable race even by
American standards. He earned 110,000 dollars in that one run there (£63,953
at prevailing exchange rates) compared to the £64,324 he'd accumulated during
nearly three seasons in top company over here. Motavato ran remarkably well
in the Budweiser Million, an international event run over a mile and a quarter
in August. He seemed to face a stiff task—he started at 49/1 coupled with the
good ex-English filly Star Pastures—and his stamina had to be taken on trust.
Surprisingly, since he'd nearly always been waited with over shorter distances,
Motavato was in front by the first turn and remained bowling along at the head
of affairs until Perrault passed him turning into the home straight. Instead of
dropping back as one might have expected Motavato kept on strongly and he
lost second to Be My Native by only a neck, the pair finishing just over two
lengths behind Perrault. The new tactics obviously suited Motavato well. He
was sent off in front again in the Bisquit Cognac Challenge Stakes at Newmarket
in October on his only subsequent outing, at such a pace that the favourite
Noalcoholic, whose jockey had intended to lead, was unable to match him and
the whole field was soon struggling. Motavato maintained his advantage until
joined by Noalcoholic running into the Dip and he put up such a good fight that
he was eventually beaten by only three quarters of a length.
    Motavato had put up his best previous efforts against Noalto in the spring,
going down by a length to him in the Philip Cornes Trophy at Leicester and
narrowly taking his revenge in the Tote Lockinge Stakes at Newbury. At
Leicester Motavato took such a strong hold that Reid, substituting for Cauthen
who was riding at Sandown, had great difficulty restraining him. He was left
in front two and a half furlongs from home and was unable to answer the
winner's late challenge. In the Lockinge, the most important win of Motavato's
career, the field crawled for the first three furlongs, and Motavato again gave
his rider an uncomfortable time. In the inevitable sprint finish Motavato
responded most generously to Cauthen's vigorous riding and produced a
tremendous late surge to force his head in front on the line.
    Motavato is the best of Apalachee's runners seen over here. He's the third
foal and first winner produced by the very game sprint handicapper Lovelight,
a winner of the Northumberland Sprint Trophy and runner-up in the Stewards
Cup. Lovelight has since bred Flicker to a Flame (by Empery), a very disappointing filly considering the high hopes held out for her after her only run at

Tote Lockinge Stakes, Newbury—Motavato's late surge carries the day after Noalto (blaze) and the blinkered Beldale Lustre had each been in front

two, and Bright Cone (by Giacometti), a fairly useful six- and seven-furlong two-year-old winner in 1982. We understand that Motavato is to continue his racing career in the United States: very sensible, too. He will do well there, and if he reproduces his Budweiser Million running he'll be a contender for major

Motavato (USA) (b.c. 1978)	Apalachee (b 1971)	Round Table (b 1954)	Princequillo Knight's Daughter
		Moccasin (ch 1963)	Nantallah Rough Shod
	Lovelight (gr 1971)	Bleep-Bleep (b 1956)	Hard Sauce Curtsey
		Lovely Beam (gr 1956)	Infatuation Port Beam

honours. A big, attractive, powerful colt, an exceptionally good mover with a really long stride, he is evidently effective from seven furlongs to a mile and a quarter and he acts on any going. He's altogether a grand sort, and we shall continue to follow his career with interest. *B. Hills.*

MOTORWAY MADNESS 2 b.f. Thatch 136–Ringed Aureole 77 (Aureole 132) **60** (1982 6s* 7f 7g 8f 8d) Mar 17; 1,300Y; well-grown, leggy filly; second foal; half-sister to fairly useful 1m to 1¼m winner Misty Halo (by High Top); dam won from 1½m to 2m; won auction seller at Pontefract (bought in 2,000 gns) in June; showed nothing in nurseries last 3 starts; should stay 1¼m. *J. Berry.*

MOTT THE HOOPLE 4 gr.g. Goldhill 125–Belligerent 74 (Roan Rocket 128) **58** (1981 5s 5d² 7d² 7g* 7.2s³ 6g² 8.2f² 7.6fg 6d 8.2f³ 7g² 6d* 8.2d 1982 6g 6s⁴ 8g 7fg 6fg² 6g² 7g² 7.6fg³ 6g² 8.2g² 7fg⁴) strong, compact gelding; second in handicaps at Hamilton (4) and Lingfield (apprentices); stays 1m; acts on any going, except possibly very soft; best in blinkers. *P. Haslam.*

MOU-FERNI-TYCHI 3 br.c. Royal and Regal–Vesper Bell (Larkspur 128) **102** (1981 6fg² 7fg³ 6fg 6g 1982 6s² 7fg² 7f⁴ 7fg* 7f² 8fg 8.3g* 8.3fg* 9d) handsome colt; good mover; successful in minor event at Brighton in May and handicaps at Windsor in July and August; stays 1m well; acts on any going; races with head held high and doesn't always look particularly keen; ran badly sixth start. *G. Harwood.*

MOUFIDE 3 b.g. African Sky 124–Supreme Punishment (King of the Tudors **64** 129) (1981 5s 1982 5g 6f² 8g 6f* 6f² 7s) fair sort; won apprentice maiden race at Pontefract in September; stays 6f; acts well on firm going and is possibly unsuited by soft. *A. Hide.*

575

*Tote Cesarewitch Handicap, Newmarket—Mountain Lodge
defies a penalty and overweight, beating the
1980 winner Popsi's Joy*

MOUHANNED 4 b.c. Ashmore 125–French Bird (Guersant 129) (1981 8.2s* —
10d 9s 8g 8f 8.2f 1982 12d) compact, good sort; mainly disappointing on flat
since winning maiden event at Nottingham as a 3-y-o; stays 1¼m; evidently acts
well on soft going; usually a front runner. *J. Old.*

MOUHRA (USA) 2 b.f. Night Invader–Fiery Kiss (Irish Ruler) (1982 6fg) —
Mar 15; sister to a minor winner in USA; dam won 1m claiming race; sire high-
class winner from 5f to 8.5f; 8/1, ninth of 12 in maiden race at Lingfield in
June. *P. Cole.*

MOUNTAIN LODGE 3 b. or br.f. Blakeney 126–Fiddlededee 94 (Acropolis 132) 97
(1981 6g 1982 11.7f³ 16fg² 16d* 16g* 14fg 17.4d* 18d*) smallish filly; a progressive type who won maiden race at Nottingham, minor event at Thirsk
(trotted up), Eglinton and Winton Memorial Handicap at Ayr (held off Dudley
Wood by a neck) and Tote Cesarewitch Handicap at Newmarket; led over 2f out
and ran on strongly to beat Popsi's Joy decisively by 3 lengths in last-named in
October; needs a stiff test of stamina; suited by some give in the ground;
consistent though ran below her best fifth start. *J. Dunlop.*

MOUNTAIN MONARCH 5 b.g. Royal and Regal–Sally of the Hills 80 (Sally- —
mount 125) (1981 15.5d⁴ 18fg⁴ 16g² 16g³ 16s 16f² 16g 19fg 16d 19s 1982 18f⁴
16fg) staying handicapper; acted on any going; suitable mount for a boy; wore
blinkers; dead. *S. Woodman.*

MOUNTCOUT 3 ch.f. Manado 130–Beaume (Faraway Son 130) (1981 5v 6f —
8d 1982 10v 12s) leggy, lightly-built filly; bad plater. *T. Gosling.*

MOUNT EATON 9 b.g. Florescence 120–Golden Pumpkin 86 (Monet 127) —
(1981 13fg 9g 13f 12f 12i 10.5s 1982 12.2f) strong ex-Irish gelding; has been
fired; poor performer nowadays; stays 7f; acts on any going; usually wears
blinkers; has won for an apprentice. *P. Asquith.*

MOUNT ELIZA 4 b.f. Welsh Saint 126–Shantung Lassie (Shantung 132) (1981 50
6s 6fg⁴ 6g⁴ 6g⁴ 7fg 6fg² 7g 1982 7f 7fg* 7f 7f* 7f 7d 8fg) sparely-made filly;
plater; won at Leicester in June (bought in 1,550 gns) and Brighton in August
(no bid); stays 7f; acts on firm going; sold 2,500 gns Newmarket Autumn Sales.
G. Blum.

MOUNT KELLETT 2 b.c. Pitskelly 122–Belmullet (Bold Lad, Ire 133) (1982 76
6d 5g 6fg² 7g 6fg 5d³ 6d) Mar 30; IR 9,500Y; lengthy colt; grand walker; first
foal; dam Irish 5f winner; placed in minor event at Windsor in July and maiden
race at Nottingham in September; not certain to stay 7f; acts on a firm and a
soft surface. *R. Armstrong.*

MOUNT MAGIC 6 ch.g. Mount Hagen 127–Magical Music (Sing Sing 134) 48
(1981 11fg* 12s 8g 10fg* 11g³ 10f 12fg⁴ 9g 12.2fg 11d 12d 12g 1982 10s³ 12g*
12fg² 10.4g² 11fg² 12g 10g) leggy gelding; former plater; won handicap at

Edinburgh in April; stays 1½m; ideally suited by top-of-the-ground; good mount for an apprentice; usually makes running; off course 3 months after fifth outing and was bandaged when below his best on his return. *R. Allan.*

MOUNT RULE 2 b.c. Manado 130–Angkor Vat (Vienna 127) (1982 5f 6g 5s 6d) Mar 14; 27,000F; strong colt; fourth live foal; dam, winner over 1¼m in France, is sister to prolific winner Kursaal; little form in maiden and minor events; wears blinkers. *R. Hollinshead.*   —

MOUNT ST MARY'S 3 gr.f. Lochnager 132–Kingdom Come 77 (Klondyke Bill 125) (1981 NR 1982 10.2g 12d) 3,600Y; big filly; half-sister to several minor winners; dam 6f winner; well behind in maiden races at Doncaster in June and Ripon in August. *M. Camacho.*   —

MOURNDYKE 10 ch.g. Klondyke Bill 125–Moura (Mourne 126) (1981 16s 1982 16g 16fg 16g 16f) poor staying handicapper; often bandaged nowadays. *R. Atkins.*

MOURWARA 2 b.f. Wolver Hollow 126–Miss Melody 110 (Tudor Melody 129) (1982 6f 5d³ 5d) Mar 19; attractive, good-quartered filly; half-sister to 3 winners, including French 3-y-o 1m winner Mabira (by Habitat) and very useful middle-distance winner Maiymad (by Rheingold), latter also a very successful jumper; dam, half-sister to good 1m to 1¼m horse Lord David, was very useful over 5f at 2 yrs; disappointing favourite in maiden company on each of her 3 appearances; blinkered final outing. *M. Stoute.*   **64**

MOUSLAT (USA) 2 b.c. Golden Ruler–Fleeing Countess (Count Amber) (1982 7f 7fg) Mar 8; second foal; half-brother to a winner; dam unplaced 10 times; showed little form in July maiden events at Salisbury and Warwick. *P. Cole.*   **64**

MOVE AGAIN 2 b.g. Continuation 120–Final Girl (Dadda Bert 95) (1982 5fg 5f) Mar 13; small gelding; in rear in maiden race at Nottingham in June and seller at Catterick in July. *J. Hardy.*   —

MOYSPRUIT 3 br.g. Import 127–River Moy (Niagara Falls 104) (1981 6d 5v³ 1982 7g 6fg³ 8fg 8g 10d 8.2s) big, strong gelding; plating-class maiden; gives impression he'll be suited by a return to sprint distances (by no means certain to stay 1¼m); refused to enter stalls once in 1981. *G. Richards.*   **50**

MR FABULEUX (USA) 3 ch.g. Le Fabuleux 133–Miss Blue Norther (Pronto) (1981 NR 1982 10fg) rangy gelding; has a round action; third foal; half-brother to a minor winner in USA by Olympiad King; dam, placed twice from 7 starts in USA, is half-sister to very smart French middle-distance winner Beau Buck; 10/1, always struggling in last position in 6-runner minor race won by Khairpour at Doncaster in May. *R. Armstrong.*   —

MR FLUOROCARBON 3 ch.c. Morston 125–Western Air 101 (Sound Track 132) (1981 6s 1982 8fg* 10fg* 12f² 8f* 10.5fg 8fg* 8s)   **126**
   Royal Ascot opened with a bang. Nothing that followed during the rest of the four days of top-class racing surpassed Mr Fluorocarbon's performance in winning the Queen Anne Stakes, a performance as striking in its manner of

Queen Anne Stakes, Ascot—Mr Fluorocarbon opens the meeting with a highly impressive win from Noalcoholic and Spanish Pool

achievement as in its merit. Mr Fluorocarbon hadn't the slightest difficulty lying up in a very strongly-run race, and after sitting on the tail of front-running Noalcoholic for six furlongs or so, ridden with great confidence, he brushed him aside and quickly went clear to leave a field of good horses well and truly strung out. He beat the runner-up Noalcoholic by four lengths, Spanish Pool by six, Prima Voce by six and a half, and Motavato, the only other remotely concerned in the finish, by eight and a half. This display would have graced an even more important setting than the Queen Anne Stakes. How regrettable, therefore, that Mr Fluorocarbon didn't occupy instead his stable-companion Ivano's place in the St. James's Palace Stakes later on the card, and how fortunate, probably, for those who ran: he would have put Dara Monarch to the test.

Mr Fluorocarbon never did win a race of the calibre of the St James's Palace Stakes. The only race of any description that went his way after Ascot was the Crown of Crowns Stakes at Goodwood in September, disputed by only himself and I'll See You. His challenge for the Benson and Hedges Gold Cup at York in August and the Queen Elizabeth II Stakes at Ascot later in September saw him a well-beaten fifth behind Assert and a disappointing sixth behind Buzzards Bay. The soft going beat him in the Queen Elizabeth II Stakes, no doubt about that; we always suspected it might. He couldn't have looked fitter, and in the race none went better until the time arrived for him to be let down early in the straight; he soon lost his action then. His defeat at York isn't so easily explained, or rather his failure to account for Castle Keep, Amyndas or Norwich isn't. Maybe the distance was his undoing: it certainly seemed that way. Assert and Eddery set out at a pace calculated to search out any weak spots in the opposition. Mr Fluorocarbon settled in second place once Assert denied him the lead (Piggott can't have had too many reservations about Mr Fluorocarbon's stamina, seeing he had been prepared to go out in front), and travelled fairly smoothly in second until Piggott became uneasy almost three furlongs from home. When asked for more Mr Fluorocarbon responded sufficiently to hang on to his place until inside the distance but well before he gave way to Norwich it was obvious he was so tired that he would do well to make the frame. Mr Fluorocarbon had won over a slightly shorter trip in the Heathorn Stakes at Newmarket in the spring, though his task on that occasion did not begin to compare with the one in the Benson and Hedges, and his clear-cut defeat of Touching Wood and Paternoster Row, two staying horses making their seasonal reappearance in a fairly slowly-run race, falls some way short in merit of his Royal Ascot win. We should say that Mr Fluorocarbon was undoubtedly best at a mile. He certainly found a mile and a half too far for him. He had Jalmood at his mercy in the Highland Spring Derby Trial at Lingfield in May, only to be outstayed by two and a half lengths and promptly disappear from the Epsom entries; he had stood at around 10/1 in the betting on the Derby. Mr Fluorocarbon easily won his only other race of the season, a maiden over a mile at Newbury in April. This was his first for the stable since his transfer from Laing, for whom he had run once unplaced as a two-year-old.

Mr Fluorocarbon (ch.c. 1979)	Morston (ch 1970)	Ragusa (b 1960)	Ribot
			Fantan II
		Windmill Girl (b 1961)	Hornbeam
			Chorus Beauty
	Western Air (ch 1967)	Sound Track (ch 1957)	Whistler
			Bridle Way
		Peggy West (ch 1956)	Premonition
			Oola Hills

Mr Fluorocarbon's sire Morston is a very strong influence for stamina; his best previous runners, Whitstead and More Light, were both staying types. The dam's family is a very speedy one. Every horse shown in her pedigree except Premonition was a sprinter, all except Bridle Way best at five furlongs. The outstanding sprinter in this family is the brilliant Pappa Fourway, a half-brother to Peggy West, but Western Air herself was useful as a two-year-old and her second foal Western Jewel (by Tower Walk) won five races over five furlongs as a two-year-old in 1975 including the Cornwallis Stakes. Not all Western Air's other foals before Mr Fluorocarbon were speedy. Apart from her first, Western Goddess (by Red God) who won three races at up to six furlongs in Ireland as a four-year-old, they showed form at a distance of at least seven and a half furlongs. One of them Western Star (by Alcide) won the Lupe Stakes at Goodwood and ran well in the Nassau Stakes and the Oaks, another, Western Knight (by Grundy), won at a mile and a quarter and ran well in the King George

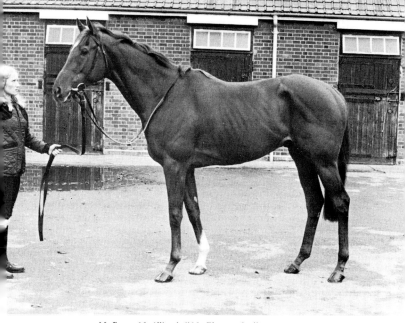

Mr James McAllister's "Mr Fluorocarbon"

V Handicap at Royal Ascot; a third, Western Gem (by Sheshoon), stayed a mile and a half.

Mr Fluorocarbon is a well-made attractive colt (his portrait barely does him justice) and a good mover, very well suited by top-of-the-ground conditions. On his best form he was a top-class miler, one possessing a fine turn of foot. He has been retired to the Ballykisteen Stud, Tipperary, at a fee of IR £3,000 (October 1st). *H. Cecil.*

MR GOLD SPUR   3 ch.c. Windjammer (USA)–Everlasting Rose (Continuation 120)   (1981 5s 6fg² 6f³ 5f 6fg 5d   1982 6s 5fg 5h 6f 6f⁴ 5g)   small colt; poor form, including in a seller; will probably stay 7f; has worn blinkers. *A. Jarvis.*   —

MR KEEPS   3 b.c. Orange Bay 131–Keeps (Roan Rocket 128)   (1981 8s 10.2g   1982 10fg 13.3f 10.1fg 10.1d)   workmanlike colt; in rear in varied company. *D. Marks.*   —

MR LINNET   10 b.g. Linacre 133–Fine Mesh (Match III 135)   (1981 NR 1982 8fg 12d)   of no account. *P. Butler.*   —

MR MUSIC MAN   8 br.g. March Past 124–Merry Melody 68 (Counsel 118)   (1981 NR   1982 10.2g 12g 8f 10.6f² 8f 12fg* 11.7g⁴ 10fg⁴ 12g⁴ 12f⁴ 12s)   plater nowadays; attracted no bid after winning at Brighton in July; stays 1½m; acts on any going. *Mrs J. Reavey.*   **44**

MR PERFECT   3 b.g. Mummy's Pet 125–River Palace (Royal Palace 131)   (1981 7fg)   leggy gelding; tailed off in minor event and maiden race in the North. *E. Weymes.*   —

MR PETIT   5 gr. or ro.g. Zeddaan 130–Balholm 61 (Le Levanstell 122)   (1981 13s 11s³ 12g 10d 10g 12f 12.2fg² 12f   1982 12fg 13.8d)   narrow, lightly-made gelding; poor plater; stays 1½m; probably acts on any going; has been tried in blinkers; has worn bandages; races with head held high. *P. Asquith.*   —

MR PORTIA   2 gr.g. The Go-Between 129–Saucy Councillor 64 (Privy Councillor 125)   (1982 5d 6d)   May 27; half-brother to 3 winners, including fairly useful   —

1981 2 -y-o sprinter Plagal (by Music Boy); dam placed over 1¼m; well beaten in maiden race at Nottingham in September and minor event at Redcar in November; subsequently gelded. *A. W. Jones.*

MR ROLFE (USA) 3 b.c. Tom Rolfe–Glamourie (White Gloves 120) (1981 — NR 1982 10d 11.5g³) $62,000Y; good-bodied colt; third foal; half-brother to a minor winner; dam never ran; beaten some way in minor event at Nottingham in April and maiden race at Yarmouth in September; sent to Italy. *H. Cecil.*

MR ROSE 2 b.c. Whistlefield 118–Berganza 83 (Grey Sovereign 128§) (1982 — 6fg 5fg 6d) June 14; 1,200Y; half-brother to several winners, including smart French middle-distance winner Tonito Pitti (by Sea Hawk II); dam 2-y-o 7f winner; little worthwhile form in maiden races, at Chepstow in August on first outing backed from 8/1 down to 15/8; possibly needs further. *R. Price.*

MRS BUZBY 3 b.f. Abwah 118–Ardeur (Roan Rocket 128) (1981 NR 1982 — 7g 8fg 7d) compact filly; first foal; dam poor maiden; little worthwhile form. *Miss S. Hall.*

MRS CHANDLER 2 b.f. Decoy Boy 129–Perfect Lady 85 (Sovereign Lord **59** 120) (1982 5d 5d⁴ 5f³ 5f* 5.3f²) May 19; reportedly 1,500Y (privately), resold 480Y; small, lengthy, quite good-quartered filly; half-sister to 2 winning platers and a winner in Malaysia; dam won over 5f at 2 yrs; bought in 1,380 gns after winning seller at Folkestone in July by ½ length from Star of Anax; not sure to stay 6f; acts well on firm going; sold 1,100 gns Doncaster September Sales. *G. Blum.*

MRS CULLUMBINE 3 ch.f. Silly Season 127–Prime Thought 69 (Primera **60** 131) (1981 NR 1982 8g 8f 9s² 10s² 12d⁴) fair sort; fifth foal; half-sister to useful 6f winner Chantry Bridge (by Porto Bello) and bumpers winner; dam comes from good family; runner-up in minor event at Hamilton and handicap at Redcar in the autumn; stays 1½m; acts on soft going. *J. W. Watts.*

MRS LOVE IT 3 b.f. Rapid River 127–Fibeel 72 (Most Secret 119) (1981 **61** 5s 5d² 5g³ 5fg 5fg 6d⁴ 6g 6d 1982 5s* 5v⁴ 5f⁴ 5f 5fg 6g⁴ 6g⁴ 5fg⁴) workmanlike filly; sprint handicapper; won at Ayr in March; stays 6f; acts on any going, but is suited by some give in the ground; sometimes blinkered. *G. Lockerbie.*

MR SUGAR (USA) 3 b.g. Sadair–Bird Guide (Sunrise County) (1981 6fg **51** 6fg 6d 1982 7d 7fg 7fg* 7g 8fg) well-made gelding; plater; heavily-backed favourite when winning at Lingfield in May (bought in 1,600 gns); stays 7f (tailed off in blinkers over 1m); sold 2,300 gns Newmarket Autumn Sales. *J. Sutcliffe.*

MRS WILLIE 3 b.f. St Paddy 133–Theodelinda 63 (Lombard 126) (1981 — 5f 5.3f 6g 7fg 8s 7.6s 1982 12f 7.6g) workmanlike filly; behind in varied company. *M. Masson.*

MUBARAK OF KUWAIT 3 b.c. Morston 125–Dominant 86 (Behistoun 131) **108** (1981 NR 1982 11.7f* 12f² 12f* 16g* 15fg 16d*️ 18d) good-bodied, quite attractive colt; good mover; third foal; half-brother to a winner in USA by Derring-Do; dam, winner at 1½m, is half-sister to very smart English and American horse Dominion; developed into a very useful handicapper after winning maiden race at Bath, gaining successes at Royal Ascot (beat Khairpour ¾ length in King George V Stakes), Sandown and Ascot again; sweated up when beating Heighlin impressively by 5 lengths easing up in Gordon Carter Handicap on last-named in September; stays well, but has a good turn of foot; yet to race on really soft going but acts on any other; often coltish in paddock; below form in Tote Cesarewitch at Newmarket final start. *G. Harwood.*

MUBHEDJ (USA) 3 b.c. Key To The Mint–Colombade 89 (Boldnesian) **90** (1981 6f³ 6fg 6fg² 6g* 6fg⁴ 5.3d 1982 6s 7fg 8fg² 8f⁴ 8d 8f³ 8f* 8fg³ 8f* 8g⁴ 8s⁴ 8s) fair sort; successful in minor event and handicap at Brighton in summer; suited by 1m; acts well on firm ground and isn't at his best on soft; blinkered nowadays; sometimes sweats up; best on a turning track; sometimes taken down early; has run respectably for an amateur rider. *H. T. Jones.*

MUCK ABOUT 2 b.f. Sweet Revenge 129–Messie (Linacre 133) (1982 6g — 7s) Apr 7; 2,400Y; rather lightly-made filly; half-sister to a winning 2-y-o plater; dam ran twice; eighth of 20 to Asswan in maiden race at Yarmouth in September, better effort; sweated up next time. *G. Pritchard-Gordon.*

MUDSLINGER 4 gr.g. Roan Rocket 128–Galosh 86 (Pandofell 132) (1981 — 16.9s⁴ 1982 13fg⁴ 14g 16fg 14.7f) big, rangy gelding; slow maiden; sold 5,200 gns Newmarket Autumn Sales. *W. Elsey.*

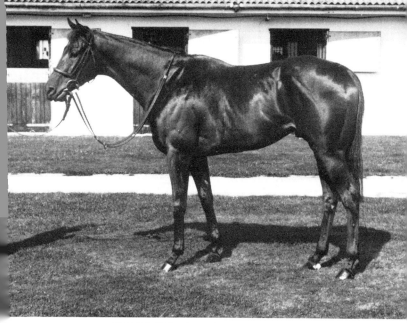

Sheik Fahad's "Mubarak of Kuwait"

MUJIB (USA) 3 b.c. L'Enjoleur–Native Street (Native Dancer) (1981 7g 1982 8fg 8g) strong, useful-looking colt; good walker and mover; has shown a modicum of ability in £4,100 event and maiden races; will stay 1¼m; blinkered final start (May). *J. Tree.* —

MUKIIULI 2 b.c. Nonoalco 131–All Beige (Ballyciptic 122) (1982 7fg 7fg 8s⁴ 10s) Mar 15; IR 33,000Y; good-topped, strong colt; second produce; half-brother to 11f winner All Moss (by Prince Tenderfoot); dam unraced daughter of Yorkshire Oaks winner Feevagh and half-sister to dam of Levmoss, Sweet Mimosa and Le Moss; well beaten in maiden races. *I. Balding.* 58

MULATA 3 gr.g. Mandrake Major 122–Raffinata (Raffingora 130) (1981 6g 1982 6s 7g 6fg 11g⁴ 12f 12fg 12g) strong gelding; plating-class maiden; stays 1½m; winning hurdler. *G. Lockerbie.* 62

MULLET 2 b.f. Star Appeal 133–Grandpa's Legacy 102 (Zeus Boy 121) (1982 6g³ 7g) Feb 2; half-sister to 3 winners, including very smart 7f to 13.3f winner Consol (by Reliance II); dam stayed 1½m; came out best of newcomers when promising 5¼ lengths third of 20 to Rare Roberta in maiden race at Lingfield in August; disappointing ninth of 13 behind Mamunia in minor event at Brighton later in month; should stay at least 1¼m. *P. Walwyn.* 75

MULTICOMPUTER 2 ch.c. Nebbiolo 125–No Surtax 112 (Never Say Die 137) (1982 5.1g 6f 5fg 5f 5fg 7fg³ 10d³ 8d) May 29; 3,000Y; stocky colt; third living foal; dam, half-sister to Busted, won twice over 1½m; placed in sellers at Redcar and Leicester in the autumn; stays well; acts on a firm and a soft surface; sold 2,000 gns Newmarket Autumn Sales. *G. Huffer.* 64

MULTI GUARANTEE 2 b.g. Riboboy 124–Prudent (Silly Season 127) (1982 7.6v 7s 6s) Mar 29; 7,000F, 13,000Y; quite well-made, useful-looking gelding; second foal; dam poor half-sister to very smart Silver Cloud and Jupiter Pluvius; behind in end-of-season maiden events, twice last. *J. O'Donoghue.* —

MUMMY'S ANGEL 3 br.f. Mummy's Pet 125–Charonne 87 (Charlottown 127) —
(1981 5d 5s 5fg 5.8f³ 6g 7f 1982 8f 8.3g) poor plater; has been tried in blinkers;
sold to S. Pattemore 800 gns Ascot July Sales. *T. Marshall.*

MUMMY'S APPLE 2 b.c. Mummy's Pet 125–Apple Queen (Behistoun 131) **76**
(1982 5f⁴ 5f* 6f⁴ 6f 5d 5f) June 6; compact, rather lightly-made colt; half-
brother to a winning plater; dam bad plater; won minor event at Catterick in
May; ran well in similar race next time, but not so well (once tailed off) in
nurseries afterwards; stays 6f; acts on firm going; blinkered fifth start; sent to
Malaysia. *M. H. Easterby.*

MUMMY'S BOY 2 b.g. Mummy's Pet 125–Jebs Junior (Huntercombe 133) —
(1982 5g 5f 6fg 6g) Apr 23; 7,000Y; small, compact gelding; twice last, including
in a seller; blinkered third start; of no account; sold A. Neaves 400 gns
Newmarket Autumn Sales. *I. Walker.*

MUMMY'S GAME 3 b.c. Mummy's Pet 125–Final Game 83 (Pardao 120) **120**
(1981 6fg³ 6fg* 6fg* 7fg⁴ 6fg³ 5fg* 6g 6g² 6s⁴ 1982 7fg⁴ 6fg* 7.2fg* 6f⁴ 5f* 6f)
  The season didn't start or end ideally for Mummy's Game but at least he had
the chance in between to show himself a tough, courageous and smart colt,
winning three of his six races in a fairly hectic two-month spell from April to
June. The climax of his career came in the five-furlong Temple Stakes at
Sandown in May, an event which provided trainer O'Gorman with a first pattern-
race winner after a number of placings over the years with such as Abdu and
Sayyaf. On his previous form Mummy's Game looked to have as good a chance
as any in an open race and in a field of thirteen he headed the market from
Chellaston Park, Mumruffin and Ponchielli. It was Chellaston Park who gave
the favourite most to do. Quickly away, Mummy's Game accelerated into the
lead from Tina's Pet a furlong out and battled on well to hold the filly's strong
late challenge by three quarters of a length.
  Apart from putting up an uncharacteristically modest display in the Cork
and Orrery Stakes at Royal Ascot, one that can be excused on the grounds that
he chipped a bone in a knee, Mummy's Game was a model of consistency on his
other appearances. His experience in the Tote European Free Handicap at
Newmarket, in which he got no sort of run and was hit in the face by the winning
jockey's whip when fourth to Match Winner, might have temporarily soured a
few horses we can think of, but not Mummy's Game. Wearing blinkers for the
only time, he came out fresh as paint to pick up a well-contested minor event
at Folkestone from Jester and promptly followed up this success with an emphatic length victory over Cut Throat in the Cold Shield Windows Trophy at
Haydock, his pace proving too much for his older opponent. His only other
start, in the Duke of York Stakes, saw Mummy's Game making much of the
running before finishing under two lengths fourth to Jester.

*Temple Stakes, Sandown—versatile Mummy's Game reverts to
five furlongs and beats Chellaston Park and Tina's Pet*

The injury Mummy's Game sustained at Royal Ascot necessitated his retirement and he is to stand at the Barleythorpe Stud in Leicestershire alongside his highly successful sire Mummy's Pet and Free State. Interestingly, in one of several concessions made to breeders by stud owners in Britain and Ireland for the 1983 season it was announced in October that all veterinary fees would be waived for mares being covered at the Barleythorpe. Mummy's Game is the

Mummy's Game (b.c. 1979)	Mummy's Pet (b 1968)	Sing Sing (b 1957)	Tudor Minstrel / Agin the Law
		Money for Nothing (br 1962)	Grey Sovereign / Sweet Nothings
	Final Game (ch 1970)	Pardao (ch 1958)	Pardal / Three Weeks
		Ankole (ch 1960)	Crepello / Sun Path

second foal out of Final Game, who won over a mile and a quarter; the first, the five-furlong winner Boldwin, is closely related to Mummy's Game, being by Song. The second dam Ankole has foaled a number of successful performers, including the useful milers Horbury and Lady Rhapsody and Duke Street, the dam of Buffavento. Mummy's Game, quite an attractive colt, stayed seven furlongs and put up his best performances on a sound surface. His fee is £1,000 + £1,500. *W. O'Gorman.*

MUMMY'S GLORY 2 b. or br.f. Mummy's Pet 125–Maria Da Gloria (St Chad 120) (1982 5g² 5g* 5fg² 5f³ 5g 5fg) May 20; neat filly; fourth foal; closely related to winning 3-y-o sprinter Cedrella (by Averof) and half-sister to a winner in Italy; dam never ran; won maiden race at Pontefract in July; ran well next 2 starts, but not so well after that; acts on firm going; not certain to train on. *E. Weymes.* **82**

MUMMY'S PLEASURE 3 b.c. Mummy's Pet 125–Par Bloom (Pardal 130) (1981 7g⁴ 6g² 1982 7d³ 6f* 6h⁴ 6g³ 5.8g³ 5fg⁴ 6f⁴ 6fg* 5.6g 6g) tall, rather leggy colt; favourite when winning maiden race at Folkestone in May (trotted up) and apprentice event at Nottingham in August; in frame in handicaps most other starts, including when fine 5 lengths fourth of 30 to Soba in William Hill Stewards' Cup at Goodwood in July on seventh; suited by 6f; acts on firm going. *P. Haslam.* **91**

MUMMY'S STAR 8 br.g. Mummy's Pet 125–Dycord 81 (Royal Record II) (1981 12s² 12f 10fg 12fg⁴ 12f 16d 16f³ 16h³ 1982 12fg 19fl) poor staying handicapper nowadays; best form on a sound surface; suitable mount for an amateur rider; wears blinkers. *J. Blundell.* **—**

MUMMY'S TREASURE 4 b.c. Mummy's Pet 125–Gold Bloom 72 (Klondyke Bill 125) (1981 5fg 5fg 5fg* 5f₆* 0fg 5g 5g 5d 1982 5.8f 5g 5fg 6g² 5g² 5g 5fg* 5fg* 5f² 5s) compact colt; caught near finish when second twice at Windsor in July, on first occasion in a seller; subsequently won handicaps at Beverley in August and Salisbury in September and finished good second to Bri-Eden in minor event at Edinburgh; speedy and probably doesn't quite get 6f; needs a sound surface; genuine, although is blinkered nowadays; claimed out of Mrs J. Reavey's stable £3,000 fourth start. *C. Spares.* **74**

MUMRUFFIN 3 b.f. Mummy's Pet 125–Java Sparrow 96 (Mossborough 126) (1981 5d* 5g* 5fg⁴ 5fg³ 5g 5s 1982 5f² 5g* 5f 5fl) small, useful-looking filly; creditable ½-length second to Pontin Lad in handicap at Epsom in April prior to making all to beat Kash-In by 4 lengths in similar event at Chester in May; in rear in Temple Stakes at Sandown later in May and King George Stakes at Goodwood in July; barely stays up and is highly strung; very speedy and needs a sharp track. *F. J. Houghton.* **101**

MUMTAZ WAY 4 gr.f. Sovereign Path 125–Thaya (St Paddy 133) (1981 8g 8f 8fg 1982 10fg 12fg 12g) small, short-backed filly; behind in varied races; sold 800 gns Newmarket December Sales. *T. Robson.* **—**

MURDIF (USA) 2 b.c. Bold Bidder–Typha (Tantieme 136) (1982 7g) May 11; $80,000Y; compact, quite attractive colt; none too good a walker; half-brother to 2 winners in France by Sheshoon, including Criterium des Pouliches winner Oak Hill; dam, winner of 7f claiming race, is half-sister to Sassafras; third favourite, showed up for long way when about 6 lengths eighth of 30 to Mandelstam in maiden race at Newmarket in October; will be suited by 1m or more; bound to do better. *H. T. Jones.* **79 p**

Mr Kais Al Said's "Muscatite"

MURILLO 6 b.g. Windjammer (USA)–Fuiseog (Eudaemon 129) (1981 6v* **99**
7d* 7d³ 6s* 6f 6fg 6fg 6d 1982 7d⁴ 6fg 7fg³ 6fg³ 6g³ 6g 6s 6d 8s) neat gelding;
useful handicapper; finished well when third at Ayr, Royal Ascot (Wokingham
Stakes) and Ayr again (Tote Sprint Trophy); best at up to 7f; acts on any
going but is very well suited by some give in the ground; wears blinkers, and a
small bandage on his off-fore. *J. W. Watts.*

MURIMANI 2 b.c. African Sky 124–Ardbraccan (Tower Walk 130) (1982 **72**
5f 6f 7d 8s) Apr 28; IR 20,000Y; rather leggy, close-coupled colt; has a round
action; second foal; half-brother to Irish 3-y-o Meisha (by On Your Mark);
dam unraced sister to very useful middle-distance winner Tower-Bird; best effort
when 3 lengths seventh of 18 to The Quiet Don in maiden race at Salisbury in
June on third start; not seen out again until October; sold 3,000 gns Newmarket
Autumn Sales. *P. Cole.*

MUSANDAM 3 ch.g. Mount Hagen 127–Trekker 86 (Grey Sovereign 128§) **—**
(1981 8g 1982 10d 12s 7.6g 16s 14g) poor maiden; blinkered final start. *M.
Masson.*

MUSCATITE 2 b.c. Habitat 134–Takette (Takawalk II 125) (1982 7f³ 7fg* **118**
7f* 8d⁴) Apr 25; 40,000F, 132,000Y; lengthy colt; half-brother to 3 winners,
including very useful middle-distance performer and very smart hurdler Decent
Fellow (by Rarity); dam 6f 2-y-o winner; got up to force dead-heat with Kuwait
Tower (who had swerved sharply left close home) in Sandwich Maiden Stakes at
Ascot in July; gave very useful display under top weight in Fitzroy House
Stakes at Newmarket the following month, leading throughout to win easing up
by 2½ lengths from Good as Diamonds; good fourth, only 3 lengths behind
Dunbeath, in William Hill Futurity Stakes at Doncaster 2 months later; stays
1m; seems to act on any going. *J. Hindley.*

MUSIC AFFAIR 2 ch.f. Music Boy 124–Linden Lea 91§ (Hornbeam 130) **45**
(1982 5g 5.1g 5g 5fg 5g 5.1d 5d) May 28; 2,800F, 3,600Y; well-grown, fair

sort; half-sister to 2 winning platers; poor form in varied company, including selling; blinkered final outing; sold 440 gns Newmarket Autumn Sales. *K. Ivory.*

MUSICAL MINX 4 b.f. Jukebox 120–Battling Bessie (Typhoon 125) (1981 **61** 5s³ 5d⁴ 6d³ 5.8g 5s³ 5d⁴ 6f² 7f⁴ 7f² 6d 6g² 6f² 6f² 6d 1982 5.8f⁴ 6fg 6s* 6g) useful sort; made virtually all when winning handicap at Pontefract in June; stayed 7f; acted on any going; sometimes blinkered; reportedly in foal to Monsanto. *C. Nelson.*

MUSICAL PRINCESS 5 b. or br.m. Cavo Doro 124–Toccata (Kythnos 126) **66** (1981 12g 12g 12g 10.2f 10f³ 10g 12.3fg⁴ 10fg³ 12f 1982 12f 12f* 12f² 16fg* 13fg 16d² 16fg* 16.5g³ 16d 16g*) strong, useful-looking mare; had a good season and won at Beverley (maiden race and 2 handicaps) and Newcastle (slowly-run handicap); beat Chemin de Guerre by ½ length on former course in September on final start; clearly suited by a test of stamina; has run respectably on soft going, but is ideally suited by a sound surface; genuine. *E. Weymes.*

MUSICAL SCORE 3 ch.c. Music Boy 124–Acknowledgement (Fleet Nasrullah) **99** (1981 7g² 7g 1982 7fg 6g* 7g³ 6f* 6fg⁴ 8d) attractive ex-English colt; short-priced favourite when easily beating Dance Empress by 5 lengths in maiden race at Naas in June and landed odds by ¾ length from Hunters Delight in minor event on same course in July; 1½ lengths third of 12 to Memento in Ballycorus Stakes at Leopardstown in between; stays 7f; trained by G. Pritchard-Gordon first start. *M. Kauntze, Ireland.*

MUSIC CITY 4 gr.c. Town Crier 119–Floating Melody 101 (Tudor Melody 129) — (1981 6g³ 7d² 6fg⁴ 7.6s* 7fg 7.3d³ 7s⁴ 6g* 6s 1982 7s 8d 8g 8g 10s) well-made colt; ran respectably over 1m on second start; not disgraced on a firm surface, but clearly acts well on soft going. *M. Bradley.*

MUSIC LOVER 3 b.c. Gay Fandango 132–In The Clover (Meadow Mint 120) **92** (1981 6fg⁴ 6g* 1982 6fg* 6f 6fg 5g 7d 8v) quite attractive colt; good mover; fairly useful handicapper; always going well when decisively beating Harpers Bazaar by 2 lengths at Newmarket in April; stays 7f; acts on a firm and a soft surface; blinkered final start (ran poorly); sold 8,000 gns Newmarket Autumn Sales. *P. Walwyn.*

MUSIC NIGHT 5 ch.h. Jukebox 120–Directrice (Zank) (1981 6g⁴ 6fg² 6f **68** 6f² 5g³ 5g 6f* 7fg 5f 6f 5g* 5fg 6s 6d 5g 1982 5fg 5g* 5fg 5fg³ 6fg 6g 6d 6fg 5g 5fg 5s 6s³ 6s*) sturdy horse; former plater; won handicaps at Hamilton in July and Redcar in October and ran creditably on occasions in between; stays 6f; acts on any going; best in blinkers; has run respectably for an apprentice and an amateur; suited by enterprising riding tactics. *D. Chapman.*

MUSIC'S DESIRE (USA) 2 br.c. Stop the Music–Emperor's Desire (Young **88** Emperor 133) (1982 7fg⁴ 7d² 8s³) May 4; $135,000Y; tall, attractive colt; third foal; half-brother to 2 winners in USA; dam very useful 2-y-o sprinter; in frame in autumn maiden races at Salisbury, Leicester (beaten short head) and Warwick; seems to stay 1m but may prove better over 7f. *G. Harwood.*

MUSIC SEASON 2 ch.g. Baragoi 114–Tide and Time (Easter Island 101) — (1982 6fg) May 24; half-brother to 5f winner Tampa Bay (by Ickford); dam never ran; unquoted and backward, tailed-off last of 22 in minor race at Leicester in June. *D. Leslie.*

MUSKOKA 3 b.f. Hotfoot 126–Miss Dallas 89 (March Past 124) (1981 6d — 1982 8f 10fg 10g 12f 8v 8s 7s) lightly-made, smallish filly; poor form, including in a seller; trained part of season by G. Harwood. *R. Simpson.*

MUSKY 3 ch.f. Owen Dudley 121–Camusky 77 (Charlottown 127) (1981 — 8d 7g 1982 16fg 15.8d) robust filly; in rear in maiden and minor events. *W. Wharton.*

MUSLAB (USA) 3 ch.c. Stage Door Johnny–Forever Amber (Bold Lad, Ire **90** 133) (1981 8d 1982 10s⁴ 12f³ 14fg² 14f 16fg 14f² 13f* 14g* 14fg 12fg² 14.6f 14s 15.5v) good-bodied colt; quite comfortable winner of handicaps at Notting-ham in July and Haydock (amateur riders race) in August; ran in much better company most subsequent starts, including when twice making pace for stable-companion Touching Wood, and wasn't at all disgraced in Jefferson Smurfit Memorial Irish St Leger at the Curragh and Prix Royal-Oak at Longchamp; suited by a test of stamina; acts on firm going; blinkered nowadays; should win a staying handicap or two at 4 yrs. *H. T. Jones.*

MUZNAH 2 b.f. Royal and Regal–Ballinavail (Rarity 129) (1982 6f² 7.2g 7d* **81** 7fg 7.2s) Mar 5; IR 56,000Y; good-bodied, fair sort; first living foal to Northern

Hemisphere time; dam, winner over 1m in Ireland, is half-sister to dam of high-class miler Hilal (by Royal and Regal); won 15-runner maiden race at Yarmouth in August; will stay 1m; seems to act on any going. *H. T. Jones.*

MY ADRIANA 3 ch.f. Roman Warrior 132–La Melodie 77 (Silly Season 127) **71** (1981 6g 6g 1982 7g 8f 9.4f* 10d² 11.5fg⁴ 10v 10s² 10s) big, strong filly; good mover; kept on well to win maiden race at Carlisle in May; twice ran creditably in handicaps afterwards; stays 1¼m; acts on any going. *G. Pritchard-Gordon.*

MY ANNASSAR 4 b.f. Queen's Hussar 124–My Polyanna 81 (Polyfoto 124) — (1981 11.5f 12fg⁴ 14g³ 14fg² 14fg² 15.5g 10s³ 10g 1982 11.7fg 12f 10g 11.5f) very lightly-made filly; poor maiden; stays 1¾m; sometimes blinkered; hung badly when amateur ridden final start. *M. Ryan.*

MY BLUE HEAVEN 3 br.f. Blue Cashmere 129–Christmas Pageant (March — Past 124) (1981 5d 5g 1982 7fg 8s) rather leggy filly; of no account; sold out of S. Matthews' stable 470 gns Ascot August Sales after first start. *K. Bridgwater.*

MYCENAEN 3 ch.g. Be My Guest 126–Street Light 120 (St Chad 120) (1981 **80** 6g 5fg 7fg⁴ 7g 8s² 1982 8g 8f* 8fg* 8fg² 8fg 8f) neat, strong gelding; won handicaps at Bath in April (made most) and Salisbury in May; suited by 1m; acts on any going; best in blinkers. *J. Tree.*

MY CONNOISSEUR 3 b.c. Connaught 130–Honerone 85 (Sammy Davis 129) — (1981 6s⁴ 1982 8fg 8fg 8g 6g 7f) quite attractive, good sort; carries plenty of condition; only plating class on balance of form; best run at 6f on soft going; sweated up badly final start. *J. Holt.*

MY DAD TOM (USA) 3 b.c. My Dad George–His Lady Fair (Tom Fool) **103** d (1981 5d 5d* 5d 6g* 5f* 6f* 5f* 6fg 5g* 7fg³ 7s 6g 1982 8f⁴ 7f 7.2h² 8fg 8fg 8fg 6f 7f) smallish, useful sort; good mover; a very tough individual who won 6 times in 1981; put up easily best effort at 3 yrs in John of Gaunt Stakes at Haydock in June, running on in good style to snatch second, 2 lengths behind Indian King; soundly beaten on his other starts; probably doesn't stay 1m; seems to act on any going but is well suited by top-of-the-ground; blinkered seventh start; has won 3 times for apprentice K. Willey. *B. Hills.*

MY DEAR FELLOW 3 ch.c. Tower Walk 130–Righteous Girl 93 (Right Boy **96** 137) (1981 5s* 5d² 5g 5f³ 5s 5g⁴ 1982 6s 6fg 6fg 6f⁴ 5fg 6g 5.6g²(dis) 5fg²) small, strong, useful sort; doesn't always impress in slower paces; fairly useful handicapper on his day; ran best race when neck second of 14 to Vorvados in Portland Handicap at Doncaster in September but hampered another runner 1f out after setting a good pace and was disqualified; suited by 6f; acts on any going; showed little enthusiasm in blinkers second outing. *N. Vigors.*

MYDELLA 2 b. or br.f. Rymer 121–Mydel Field 66 (Abwah 118) (1982 5f 5g* **83** 6g) Apr 11; fair sort; first foal; dam won 5f seller at 2 yrs; won 12-runner maiden race at Wolverhampton in June at 40/1; 6½ lengths fifth of 9 behind Princely Fighter in minor event at Ripon the following month; stays 6f. *J. Berry.*

MY DESTINY (USA) 3 b.f. L'Enjoleur–Carlese (Proud Clarion) (1981 — 5d 6fg 6f⁴ 6g² 7d* 7v* 1982 10f) strong, well-made, quite attractive filly; fairly useful in 1981; ran miserably in handicap at Yarmouth only start at 3 yrs in August (needed run); should be suited by 1¼m; evidently needs some give in the ground. *M. Albina.*

MYDRONE 3 b.c. Mummy's Pet 125–Wordrone (Worden II 129) (1981 5d* **82** (dis) 5fg* 6f* 6d³ 6f³ 6g 6s² 7g⁴ 1982 8.2fg² 8f 8g 8g 8d 8s) workmanlike colt; first past post 3 times at 2 yrs; beaten a length by First Phase in amateur riders race at Haydock in May; below form most subsequent starts, running poorly on second and third; stays 1m; acts on any going. *M. H. Easterby.*

MY FAIR ORCHID 3 ch.f. Roan Rocket 128–Cama 85 (Pardao 120) (1981 — 5fg⁴ 5g³ 6fg 7g 5fg 5g⁴ 6fg 5fg 5d 5g 5d⁴ 5s³ 6d 1982 8d 5f 6f 5fg 5fg 5g 6d) small, lightly-made filly; plater nowadays; yet to prove she stays 6f; probably acts on any going; has worn a tongue strap; has twice worn blinkers. *S. Matthews.*

MY FANCY 3 ch.f. Roi Soleil 125–Pat's Fancy 82 (Falcon 131) (1981 6d 5g² **62** 5v 5d* 5g 1982 5g 5f² 5g³ 5fg 5f 5g 6g 6g 7d) workmanlike filly; sprint handicapper; probably acts on any going. *J. Berry.*

MY GAZAL (USA) 2 gr.f. Wing Out–Lin's Cherub (Linmold) (1982 5fg⁴ **65** 7f 7f 8fg) Mar 11; close-coupled filly; half-sister to 3 winners in USA, one a minor stakes winner; dam second once from 6 starts; plating-class maiden; stays 7f. *P. Cole.*

MY GODDESS 3 ch.f. Palm Track 122–Captain Frances (Captain's Gig) — (1981 5g 5g 6g⁴ 6f 6g 7g 1982 12f 15.8f 16.5f 10.4d 12fg) plain filly; plating-class maiden; not certain to stay 1½m; blinkered fourth start; trained part of season by J. Calvert. *K. Stone.*

MY HABAT 3 gr.g. Habat 127–Wake Island 101 (Relic) (1981 6g 6fg 6d 7f 52 7g 6s⁴ 8g 1982 8g 11g 8f⁴ 8.2g⁴ 7f*) strong gelding; poor mover; plater; almost threw race away by hanging right when successful at Edinburgh in September (no bid); unlikely to stay 11f; acts on firm going; has worn blinkers, including when successful. *F. Watson.*

MY JOKER 2 ch.c. Diamonds Are Trump 108–Jamar 81 (Kashmir II 125) — (1982 5g) May 24; useful sort; fourteenth of 15 in seller at Ripon in August; sold 330 gns Doncaster September Sales. *C. Booth.*

MY LADY BLUE 3 gr.f. Import 127–Supremelos (Supreme Sovereign 119) — (1981 6f 1982 8g 7g) tall, plain filly; well beaten in a minor event and 2 sellers; sold 400 gns Ascot September Sales. *D. Ancil.*

MY LOVER 3 br.c. Pitskelly 122–Miss Wittington (Red God 128§) (1981 5f 5f² 105 5fg* 5d* 5g* 5s* 1982 5fg 5fg⁴ 5fg) attractive, lengthy colt; showed very useful form at 2 yrs, winning 4 races, including Cornwallis Stakes at Ascot; didn't run up to his best in 1982 in Palace House Stakes at Newmarket, well-contested minor event at Beverley (fourth of 8 to Fearless Lad) and King's Stand Stakes at Royal Ascot (blinkered, last of 14 to Fearless Lad again); won on a firm surface but was possibly better with some give in the ground; sent to South Africa. *M. Jarvis.*

MY MARAVILLA (USA) 3 b. or br.f. Blushing Groom 131–Monade 129 (Klai- 94 ron 131) (1981 5g⁴ 6fg 1982 10fg 10.6f³ 12fg* 12f³ 10f* 12fg⁴ 10d* 12s) small, compact filly; good mover; won maiden race at Brighton in June (odds on), minor event at Salisbury in August and another minor event at Nottingham in September (again odds on); also ran well to be about 3 lengths fourth to Sabre Dance in well-contested minor event at Doncaster; stays 1½m; seems to act on any going. *R. Hern.*

MY MIDWAY (FR) 3 b.c. Trenel–Mirlifique (Le Haar 126) (1981 5.5g* 7d 116 7fg⁴ 8fg 9s⁴ 9s 10v 1982 10s* 11v* 12d 12d³ 12g* 12v² 15g 10fg 12s 11.5s 12s³) half-brother to 3 minor winners in France; dam won over 8.5f in French Provinces; won minor events at Cagnes-sur-Mer and Maisons-Laffitte early in year and Derby du Midi at Bordeaux in May; beat Buggy Lane by 4½ lengths in last-named; also ran well to be ½-length second to Coquelin in Prix du Lys at Longchamp in June and 2½ lengths fourth to subsequently-disqualified Balitou in Grand Prix de Bordeaux in November; stays 1½m; well suited by plenty of give in the ground; blinkered last 3 starts at 2 yrs. *G. Bonnaventure, France.*

MY MONRO 3 b.f. Ancient Monro 89–Mi Lu 80 (Gilles de Retz 132) (1981 6f 46 6f 5d⁴ 6f 5fg 8fg 8d 8s 1982 8f 8fg* 8fg 10d) plater; attracted no bid after winning at Newcastle in May; sweated up and ran moderately next time; stays 1m. *Mrs M. Nesbitt.*

MY MUSIC 2 b.f. Sole Mio–Brazen 83 (Cash and Courage 116) (1982 5f⁴ 6fg 68 5fg² 5fg 5d 5g) May 28; lengthy filly; half-sister to winners abroad, including 1977 French 2-y-o 5f to 7.5f winner Moonduster (by Green God); dam won from 6f to 11f; in frame in maiden races at Haydock in May and Chester in July; ran badly in nursery at Newcastle in August on final appearance; should be suited by 6f+. *W. Elsey.*

MY MY MARIE 3 b.f. Artaius 129–Raffmarie 78 (Raffingora 130) (1981 7g — 1982 12fg) compact, attractive filly; well behind in maiden races; sold 5,000 gns Newmarket December Sales. *B. Swift.*

MY NAUTILUS 2 ch.g. Free State 125–Naiche (Tribal Chief 125) (1982 7fg) — Mar 25; strong, rangy gelding; second foal; brother to 3-y-o Positron, a 7f winner at 2 yrs; dam 4 times unplaced at 3 yrs; last of 15 in maiden event at Salisbury in September. *B. Swift.*

MY PARTY 2 b.f. Music Maestro 119–Dame Fortune 84 (Kashmir II 125) 72 (1982 5fg 6f⁴ 6g 5.8g 7fg* 8s 6s³ 7s) May 29; 5,000; neat, active sort; half-sister to fair 1978 2-y-o 7f winner Avanti Carlo (by Lorenzaccio); dam won over 9f; short-priced favourite and dropped in class, made all to win 13-runner seller at Chepstow (bought in 4,100 gns) in September by 3 lengths from Typeset; good third in 16-runner nursery at Nottingham the following month; best form at 6f, and seems not to stay 1m; acts on any going; wears blinkers; sold 3,000 gns Ascot December Sales. *R. Laing.*

*Firth of Clyde Stakes, Ayr—a good fight back by Myra's Best (rails)
lands her the race from Super Entente and Henry's Secret*

MYRA'S BEST 2 ch.f. Pampapaul 121–Matcher (Match III 135) (1982 5f² **107**
5fg* 5g* 6fg4 6g* 6g) Mar 18; IR 8,400F, IR 13,000Y; well-made filly; sister
to Irish 3-y-o Pampamatch and half-sister to several winners, including useful
1977 French 2-y-o 5f winner Oncle Riton (by Daring Display); dam daughter of
smart miler Lachine; developed into useful filly, winning 2 races at Sandown,
the second worth £3,400, and £8,600 Firth of Clyde Stakes at Ayr; also ran well
against top fillies in Lowther Stakes at York and William Hill Cheveley Park
Stakes at Newmarket, being beaten only around 5 lengths each time; should
stay 1m; has raced only on a sound surface; genuine. *R. Williams.*

MY SCOTCH ARMS 2 b.f. Red Alert 127–Levandia 84 (Le Levanstell 122) **49**
(1982 5d 5f 5fg 5f 5.1fg) Apr 1; 2,100Y; rather lightly-made filly; second
reported foal; dam won twice over 1½m; well beaten, including in a seller; wears
blinkers, and on final start was hooded as well. *C. Spares.*

MYSOTIS (USA) 2 ch.f. Barrera–Mercy Mine (Court Martial) (1982 5fg³ 5d³ **79**
5d) Jan 22; $240,000Y; strong, lengthy filly; closely related to very useful
Native Lovin (by Exclusive Native), winner of 5 sprint races from 6 starts at 2 yrs
in 1976; dam never ran; third in two 17-runner maiden races at Salisbury, disappointing at odds on on second occasion; not seen out after June; sold to NBA
28,000 gns Newmarket December Sales. *J. Tree.*

MYSTERIEUSE ETOILE (USA) 2 b.f. Northern Dancer–Gulanar (Val de **116**
Loir 133) (1982 6.5g* 8s²)
Mahmoud Fustok's collection of European-bred broodmares consists largely
of daughters of Val de Loir. He explained to readers of *Pacemaker* that 'when
I started buying broodmares in 1975, I told somebody in France to find out how
many Val de Loir mares there were in Europe. At that time Val de Loir was not
a very popular broodmare sire. He told me there were something like forty, so
I said let's try and buy the forty.' The upshot of the conversation was that
Fustok's agents managed to buy him 'something like fifteen' of them, not,
unfortunately for Fustok, the dams of the top-class performers Dancing Maid,
Shergar and Vayrann, but he has already been rewarded with one very promising
performer, Mysterieuse Etoile.
Mysterieuse Etoile had two races in her first season. She made her debut
on the final day of the Deauville meeting in a maiden event and won by half a
length from Lyphard's Princess, who on her previous start had gone down by
the same margin to the subsequent Prix d'Aumale winner Air Distingue.
Mysterieuse Etoile herself came up against Air Distingue when the pair were
considered the main threats to the odds-on Maximova in the Prix Marcel
Boussac at Longchamp in October. Mysterieuse Etoile managed to beat all her
compatriots but she failed by a short head to catch the 36/1-shot from Yorkshire, Goodbye Shelley. We thought her a little unlucky not to win. While
Goodbye Shelley was being driven clear early in the straight Mysterieuse Etoile's
jockey, Gibert, seemed to take a long time getting her going and she was still

only fifth, four lengths behind, with three hundred yards to run. She then responded very genuinely to hard riding, finishing so well that she must have won in another few strides. Gibert later explained that his mount had run a little green and had changed her legs before coming to challenge—understandable behaviour for a once-raced filly who hadn't previously raced round a bend. Clearly Mysterieuse Etoile will be all the better for this experience and she looks sure to make her mark in France's top fillies events at up to a mile and a half.

Mysterieuse Etoile (USA) (b.f. Feb 16, 1980)	Northern Dancer (b 1961)	Nearctic (br 1954)	Nearco / Lady Angela
		Natalma (b 1957)	Native Dancer / Almahmoud
	Gulanar (b 1974)	Val de Loir (b 1959)	Vieux Manoir / Vali
		Gulab (b 1966)	Prince Bio / Esmerald

Mysterieuse Etoile is the first foal of Gulanar who, at 120,000 francs, was the cheapest of the six Val de Loir yearlings sold at auction in France in 1975. She was sent to Italy where she won five races, including the Premio Alberto Zanoletti di Rozzano over a mile and a quarter at Milan as a three-year-old and the Premio Agnano over a slightly shorter trip at Naples at four. She was also twice placed in the Group 3 Premio Legano. Gulanar was the only winner from the three living foals produced by Gulab, a fairly useful handicapper at up to a mile and a quarter in France. Gulab died aged nine and her dam, the unraced Esmerald, was even more short lived, dying as a seven-year-old. Esmerald came from one of the Aga Khan's best families. Her half-brother Faristan was a leading staying two-year-old in France in 1964 and her dam Star of Shiraz was a half-sister to Petite Etoile, the One Thousand Guineas and Oaks winner of 1959. Mysterieuse Etoile is engaged in both those races in 1983 but her trainer doesn't often send his horses here and she's more likely to remain in France. *M. Saliba, France.*

MYSTERY TRAIN 2 b.f. Bay Express 132–Baffle 87 (Petingo 135) (1982 6g 6fg⁴ 7.6v) Apr 11; first foal; dam won over 13.3f and comes from good staying family; plating-class maiden; sold 4,100 gns Newmarket Autumn Sales. *J. Dunlop.* —

MYSTIC MARGARET 3 b.f. Realm 129–Primed (Primera 131) (1981 6fg 7f 1982 10d 12f 9g 10.1d⁴ 10f* 10g 11.1fg 12fg² 10d) strong filly; poor walker; plater; bought in 1,350 gns after easily winning at Nottingham in July; stays 1½m; acts well on firm going; has run creditably for an apprentice. *A. Hide.* 61

MYSTIC PRINCESS 3 ch.f. English Prince 129–Ornella (Princely Gift 137) (1981 6d 1982 10f 12fg 15.5f 12g 10fg 12fg) lightly-made filly; poor plater; has worn blinkers; sold out of W. Musson's stable 720 gns Newmarket May Sales. *H. Beasley.* —

MYTHOLOGY (USA) 3 b.c. Norcliffe–Proud N'Happy (Proudest Roman) (1981 5.5fg⁴ 6fg² 6fg² 8.3s³ 8.3fg 1982 8.5fg⁴ 10g 10g) $155,000 2-y-o; close-coupled ex-American colt; third foal; half-brother to 2 winners in USA, notably high-class stakes winner Proud Appeal (by Valid Appeal), successful at up to 9f; dam never ran; placed 3 times in USA at 2 yrs; soundly beaten in varied company over here; should stay middle distances. *J. Dunlop.* —

MYTINIA 2 b.f. Bustino 136–Mineown 85 (Roan Rocket 128) (1982 7g) Jan 28; sister to very smart 1½m winner Bustomi; dam, placed over 5f and 6f, is half-sister to top Italian horse Weimar; well-backed favourite, swerved at start and was hampered early on when never-dangerous seventh of 23 behind Salvinia in £4,500 race at Newbury in September; will be suited by further; sure to do better. *R. Hern.* — p

MY TONY 2 ch.c. Be My Guest 126–Pale Gold (New Chapter 106) (1982 7fg 7fg 7s) Apr 23; 20,000Y; rangy, good-bodied colt; second foal; dam, minor winner over 6f and 11.5f in France, is half-sister to smart animals Pale Ale and Polynikis; well beaten in maiden and minor events; looks the type to need plenty of time. *G. Lewis.* —

MZURI 2 b.f. Captain James 123–Mrs Bee 74 (Sallust 134) (1982 5d* 5fg⁴ 5s) Mar 30; IR 16,000Y; quite well-made filly; second foal; half-sister to 3-y-o Petite Mielle (by Hot Spark); dam 1½m winner; raced wide of most of field when winning 24-runner maiden race at Windsor in June by a head from Stop Talking; off course 3 months after next outing; should stay at least 1m. *C. Nelson.* 84

N

NAAR 2 b.c. North Stoke 130–Kye-Hye 61 (Habitat 134) (1982 6fg* 6f* 7fg) **97**
Mar 11; IR 32,000Y; neat, strong, attractive colt; first foal; dam placed at up to
1¾m; made much of running and battled on well when winning 5-runner Granville
Stakes at Ascot in July by a neck from Northern Secret; again showed plenty of
determination in £3,400 event at Salisbury the following month, rallying to
win by a length from Fenny Rough; 8 lengths fifth of 6 behind The Fort in
Intercraft Solario Stakes at Sandown later in August; should stay at least 1¼m.
P. Walwyn.

NABIRPOUR (USA) 3 b.c. Blushing Groom 131–Alama (Aureole 132) (1981 **122**
8fg 8d³ 8s* 1982 8v* 10.5d² 11g² 10fg) half-brother to French 2,000 Guineas
winner Nishapour (by Zeddaan); dam won over 13f in France and is closely
related to good French stayer Misyaaf; beat Bakst a short neck in 70,000 francs
event at Maisons-Laffitte in March; creditable second in Prix Greffulhe at
Longchamp in April (head behind Bois de Grace) and Prix de Suresnes on same
course in May (went down by ¾ length to Lichine); soundly beaten in Prix de
la Cote Normande at Deauville in August on other start; will stay 1½m; seems
to need some give in the ground. *F. Mathet, France.*

NADASDY 2 br.c. Queen's Hussar 124–Marcrest (On Your Mark 125) (1982 **98**
6g 6d 8.5g* 8.5s* 7d) Apr 29; 8,400Y; first foal; dam won 5 races in Italy;
won at Galway in September and October, having opponents well strung out
when successful in maiden race and making nearly all to win nursery by 5 lengths
from Taj El Arab; second favourite for Larkspur Stakes at Leopardstown later
in October but finished only eighth of 11 to Heron Bay; suited by 1m; yet to race
on a firm surface. *C. Collins, Ireland.*

NAGALIA 3 br.f. Lochnager 132–La Gallia 70 (Welsh Saint 126) (1981 5s³ **63**
5d⁴ 5g³ 5g² 5f² 5fg 6d³ 5f³ 6fg* 5g* 6d* 6d 1982 6s 6g 6f² 6h² 6d) lengthy,
lightly-made filly; not the best of movers; runner-up in 2 handicaps at Haydock;
stays 6f; probably acts on any going; ran moderately in blinkers once at 2 yrs.
K. Stone.

NAGARRO 2 b.c. Raga Navarro 119–Kimin (Kibenka 119) (1982 6g 5f³ 6f³ **93**
6f* 6g*) Apr 11; 1,100F; leggy, close-coupled, fair sort; third produce; dam
won over 7f and 9f at 5 yrs in Ireland; finished well, despite hanging quite badly,
when neck winner of valuable nurseries at Newmarket in August and Ayr
(sweated up badly) in September; suited by 6f and should stay further; acts on
firm going. *W. Musson.*

NAHANE 5 b.m. Porto Bello 118–Hillsquaw (Hillary) (1981 10f 10f 16.1f 12g³ —
1982 10.6f) compact, quite attractive mare; no form for a long time and was
tailed off in a seller on only outing of 1982; stays 1¼m; suited by a sound surface;
has worn bandages in front. *P. Bevan.*

NAHAWAND 2 b.f. High Top 131–Welsh Jewel 72 (Welsh Pageant 132) (1982 —
6g) Mar 13; second foal; half-sister to 3-y-o Sallwah (by Balidar); dam in frame
in 5f maiden events at 2 yrs; unquoted, ninth of 16 in maiden race at Newmarket
in June. *P. Cundell.*

NAIF 4 b.c. Nonoalco 131–Ashavan 114 (Persian Gulf) (1981 7g 7g 8f 10fg' **56**
8g² 8fg² 11fg 12g 10fg 9s 1982 8s 9f⁴ 12f 12f² 12f³ 15g* 15f² 16.1g⁴ 20.4g⁴ 16f²)
big, good-topped colt; has a round action; in frame most outings and won
handicap at Ayr in May; stays 2m; often bandaged. *G. Lockerbie.*

NAISHAPUR 3 b.g. Mansingh 120–Pladda (Reliance II 137) (1981 NR 1982 **69**
7g 8.2fg 6d⁴ 8.2fg² 9g* 10f) 5,800F, 9,400Y; quite attractive gelding; half-
brother to 1979 2-y-o 5f winner Lady Ember (by Hot Spark) and a winner in Italy;
dam won 3 times over 1½m in Ireland; heavily-backed favourite when narrowly
winning handicap at Hamilton in June; stays 9f; sold 5,000 gns Newmarket
Autumn Sales. *P. Haslam.*

NAIVE 2 ch.f. Royal Match 117–Saintly (St Alphage 119) (1982 5f⁴ 5f² 5f² 5fg* **75**
5f 5d) Feb 13; IR 3,600F, IR 3,500Y; smallish filly; second produce; dam Irish
2-y-o 5f winner; won maiden auction event at Brighton in May; not raced after
early July; acts on firm going. *D. Morley.*

NAJAM (USA) 3 b.c. Graustark–Spring Adieu (Buckpasser) (1981 NR **65**
1982 7.6f 10g 10.2g³ 10fg⁴ 10g) $155,000Y; quite attractive, well-made, robust
colt; first foal; half-sister to Northern Dancer, won 3 times at up to 6f at 3
yrs; kept on at one pace when just over 2½ lengths third of 17 to Woolf in maiden
race at Doncaster in June; will be suited by 1½m; yet to race on a soft surface;
wears blinkers. *H. T. Jones.*

NAJMA 2 ch.f. Stradavinsky 121–Garrucha 117 (Prince Taj 123) (1982 6g) —
Apr 28; 10,000Y; half-sister to numerous winners, including top 1975 Italian
2-y-o Northern Spring (by My Swallow) and useful sprinter Peranka (by Klairon
or Palestine); dam sprinter; no show in maiden race at Windsor in July. *F. Durr.*

NAJRAN 2 b.c. Nishapour 125–Diamond Spray 82 (Roan Rocket 128) (1982 **102**
6.3fg² 5fg² 6.3fg³) Apr 11; IR 7,800F, 6,000Y; third produce; dam in frame
twice over 6f at 2 yrs; placed all 3 outings, namely maiden race at the Curragh in
July (beaten a short head by Glenstal), 11-runner Heinz '57' Phoenix Stakes
at Leopardstown in August (3 lengths second to Sweet Emma) and Railway
Stakes at the Curragh again later in August (under 3 lengths third of 7 behind
Ancestral); bred to stay at least 1m; yet to race on a soft surface; certain to win
races. *J. Oxx, Ireland.*

NAKTERJAL 2 b.f. Vitiges 132–Kilavea 92 (Hawaii) (1982 6g 6d 6s) May 25; —
first foal; dam, half-sister to Nureyev, won over 5f on only start; little worthwhile form in autumn maiden events. *J. Dunlop.*

NANUSHKA 3 b.f. Lochnager 132–Monashka 73 (Sica Boy 132) (1981 6fg **53**
7fg 6d 7v 1982 7.2g 8g 6d 6g 6d 5g* 6s) workmanlike filly; won handicap at
Edinburgh in October; well beaten most previous starts, including in a seller;
stays 6f. *R. Hobson.*

NAPA VALLEY 3 b.f. Wolver Hollow 126–Frondia 76 (Parthia 132) (1981 —
7d 8fg* 8.2d² 1982 9fg 10.6f 9s) leggy, sparely-made filly; ran badly at 3 yrs in
1981; should stay at least 1¼m; sold 8,600 gns Newmarket
December Sales. *F. Durr.*

NARBERTH 2 b.f. Swing Easy 126–Spotty Bebe 83 (Credo 123) (1982 5.8g 7fg) —
May 24; third reported foal; dam sprinter; last in maiden events at Bath and
Chepstow in August. *T. Marshall.*

NARBORO BOY 2 gr.g. Dragonara Palace 115–Judolyn 87 (Canisbay 120) —
(1982 5d 8s) May 12; brother to a poor animal and half-brother to 2 sprint
winners; dam won at up to 1m; tailed-off last in autumn maiden events at
Nottingham and Leicester. *A. Fisher.*

NARROW AND SHORT (USA) 2 b.c. Riva Ridge–Waltz Me Sue (Olden **70**
Times) (1982 7fg 5d) May 15; $80,000Y; smallish, quite attractive colt;
first foal; dam won 2 sprint races in USA; backed from 8/1 to 9/2, led 4f when
4¾ lengths fifth of 17 to Seven Clubs in maiden race at Nottingham in September,
second outing; should stay beyond 5f. *M. H. Easterby.*

NARSINH (USA) 3 b.c. Avatar–Fizz (Idle Hour 121) (1981 7fg 1982 8.2g **60**
10f 10f³ 16h⁴ 16d 16.5f² 14.6g⁴ 15.8f³) neat colt; staying maiden; needs top-of-
the-ground; has sweated up; sold to D. Ringer 6,600 gns Newmarket Autumn
Sales. *J. Dunlop.*

NASHAAB 2 ch.c. Sharpen Up 127–Falcon Bess (Falcon 131) (1982 5fg 7s) —
Apr 4; 25,000Y; brother to fairly useful 1977 2-y-o 6f winner Beldale Ball, and
half-brother to prolific middle-distance winner Glide Path (by Sovereign Path);
dam useful winner over 7f and 1¼m in Ireland; well behind in small race at
Warwick in August (flag start) and £5,900 event at Ascot in September; refused
to enter stalls on intended first appearance. *J. Benstead.*

NASHWANE 2 br.f. Balidar 133–Juhayna 78 (Diplomat Way) (1982 5g⁴) —
Apr 3; first foal; dam in frame twice over 7f from 3 outings; 8½ lengths fourth of
10 to Palace Beau in minor event at Folkestone in April; withdrawn not under
orders after playing up in stalls at Brighton the following month; sent to USA.
G. Lewis.

NASSIPOUR (USA) 2 ch.c. Blushing Groom 131–Alama (Aureole 132) (1982 — p
8s) Apr 23; quite attractive colt; brother to French 3-y-o Nabirpour, a very
smart performer at up to 11f, and half-brother to French 2,000 Guineas winner
Nishapour (by Zeddaan); dam won over 13f in France; 13/2, in touch to straight
in maiden race at Sandown in October; will do better. *M. Stoute.*

NATHANIEL 5 b.g. Shantung 132–Pink Standard 81 (Tudor Melody 129) **69** d
(1981 7s 8g 8g 10f⁴ 10f³ 10g* 12f² 12fg 1982 10f 12f 10s* 12g² 10d 10g* 10fg
10g 10.6s 10d) sturdy gelding; won handicaps at Pontefract in June and July
decisively; has run creditably over 1½m but is probably best at around 1¼m; acts
on any going, but is well suited by give in the ground. *M. W. Easterby.*

NATION WIDE 9 b.g. Irish Ball 127–Misylda 100 (Faubourg II 127) (1981 **64**
16s² 14fg 18.4d² 18d 16g 16fg 16.1d* 15.8g* 1982 16.1s³ 14f 18.4fg 16.1g

15.8d³ 16d² 17.4d³ 16d 18s) quite a modest handicapper nowadays; suited by a strong gallop and stays really well; acts on any going but seems suited by some give in the ground; has been tried in blinkers; often gets himself well behind in early stages and is not the most genuine of animals. *H. Wragg.*

NATIVE GUEST 3 b.f. Be My Guest 126–Native Soil 71 (Herbager 136) **75** (1981 6g 6f 7f 7g 6d³ 7g 1982 7g* 8f² 8f³(dis) 8f⁴ 8f* 8g⁴ 9.4fg⁴ 8.2g* 8s⁴ 8s) compact filly; won maiden race at Edinburgh in April and handicaps at Ripon in June and Hamilton in September; will stay 1¼m; acts on any going; sold to BBA 19,000 gns Newmarket December Sales. *N. Tinkler.*

NATIVE RECORD 2 ch.f. Record Token 128–Friendly Native (Native Dancer) — (1982 7.6v 5v) Apr 18; half-sister to several minor winners in France; dam won over 1½m in France; unquoted, behind in maiden races at Lingfield and Folkestone in October. *O. Jorgensen.*

NATIVE SON (FR) 3 b.c. Faraway Son 130–Noble Native 98 (Indigenous 121) — (1981 6g 7fg³ 6fg 8s 8g⁴ 1982 7d 8g 10f 7f 6f⁴) fair sort; poor walker; quite moderate at his best; sometimes raced out of depth; stays 1m; blinkered first, fourth and fifth starts; has run respectably when sweating up. *C. Austin.*

NATIVE TIMES (FR) 2 b. or br.f. Faraway Times 123–Noble Native 98 **80** (Indigenous 121) (1982 5g 8fg 7.6v³ 6d) Apr 2; tall, leggy filly; half-sister to 3-y-o Native Son, and half-sister to 3 winners at up to 1m; dam stayed 1m; quite a modest maiden; suited by 1m; probably acts on any going. *C. Brittain.*

NATURALLY ORIS 2 b.f. Lypheor 118–Scarletta 103 (Red God 128§) (1982 5f 6s) May 20; IR 3,000Y; leggy filly; half-sister to 4 winners, including fairly useful 1½m winner Lulav (by Prince Regent); dam at her best at 2 yrs; poor form in maiden event at Redcar in July and claiming race at Nottingham in October. *C. Booth.*

NAUGHTY TWINKLE 3 b.f. Red Alert 127–Sapphire Lady (Majority Blue 126) **49** (1981 5fg 5fg⁴ 5g 5f 1982 7d³ 5fg 6fg 7fg 6d 5g³ 6s 6s⁴) stocky filly; placed in handicaps, including a selling race; suited by 7f; suited by some give in the ground; trained part of season by D. H. Jones, Mrs A. Bell and W. H. H. Williams. *A. Balding.*

NAUTEOUS 3 b.g. Nonoalco 131–Sassabunda 108 (Sassafras 135) (1981 6g 7g **83** 7f 1982 8f² 10f* 10f³ 12d⁴ 12f* 12fg* 12g² 12g 12s) deep-girthed, quite attractive gelding; won handicaps at Salisbury, Lingfield (odds on) and Wolverhampton; suited by 1½m and will stay further; acts on firm going and is probably unsuited by soft; blinkered final start at 2 yrs. *P. Walwyn.*

NAUTICAL WAY 2 ch.f. Captain James 123–Keep Walking (Continuation 120) — (1982 6fg) Apr 13; 1,850Y; third foal; half-sister to French 3-y-o Mount Keeper (by Mount Hagen), a winner at up to 1¼m; dam fairly useful winner over 5f at 2 yrs in Ireland; 33/1 and in need of run, ninth of 18 in maiden race at Salisbury in September. *M. Smyly.*

NAVAJO BRAVE (USA) 4 br.c. Navajo–Rosy Lark (T. V. Lark) (1981 12s² — 12g 16s³ 12d² 16.9fg⁴ 15.5f² 1982 16d) tall colt; placed in varied company at 3 yrs; stays 2m; acts on any going; sold 430 gns Ascot July Sales. *G. Hunter.*

NAVARINO BAY 2 br.f. Averof 123–Black Fire 92 (Firestreak 125) (1982 **102** 5fg* 5g² 6f²) Feb 22; strong filly; third foal; half-sister to a winning plater; dam middle-distance handicapper; won 6-runner maiden race at Newcastle in May; placed both subsequent starts, on second of them finishing excellent second to Bright Crocus in Kingsclere Stakes at Newbury in June; much better suited by 6f than 5f, and will be even better suited by 7f+; yet to race on a soft surface. *J. W. Watts.*

NAVIGATIONAL AID 5 b.g. Blind Harbour 96–Tiny Clanger 73 (Sky Gipsy — 117) (1981 12s 12g 14.6f* 16f* 15g 14d 15g 1982 14g) big, rangy gelding; fair handicapper at his best; backward when well beaten only outing of 1982; stays 2m but not 2½m; acts on any going; blinkered once in 1980; suited by strong handling. *W. Holden.*

NAWAB 3 b.c. Young Emperor 133–Tokara (Hard Tack 111§) (1981 5g 6g 5fg* **79** 5fg⁴ 6s⁴ 1982 8d 7fg 6fg⁴ 6g 7d 7d² 7f) neat, close-coupled colt; modest handicapper; promises to stay 1m; acts on a firm and a soft surface; ran poorly in blinkers fifth start. *I. Balding.*

NAWARA 2 ch.f. Welsh Pageant 132–Bright Decision 108 (Busted 134) (1982 **75** 6fg 8fg³ 8s³) Apr 13; 14,000Y; smallish, lightly-made, fair sort; second foal; dam won 8 races at up to 1¼m, 7 at 4 yrs; third in maiden races at Beverley in September and Wolverhampton in October; will stay 1¼m; seems to act on any going. *P. Walwyn.*

NAZARETH 3 ch.f. Roi Soleil 125–Suku 80 (Light Thrust 114) (1981 5g 5g 5g 1982 7f 9g) plain filly; poor form in sellers. *Miss S. Hall.*

NEAR STOKE 2 ch.c. North Stoke 130–Idle Thoughts (Bold Ruler) (1982 8g) Apr 19; IR 10,000Y; half-brother to 5 winners, one of them disqualified, including fair stayer May Week (by Herbager); dam won over 6f; tailed off in 9-runner minor event at Leicester in October; sold Norsk Jockey Club 1,500 gns Doncaster November Sales. *R. Hollinshead.*

NEAT 4 ch.g. Wollow 132–Brilliantine 109 (Stage Door Johnny) (1981 8d* 8fg³ 10.1s³ 1982 10f) tall, lengthy gelding; useful performer on his day as a 3-y-o, but appeared none too genuine; had stiff task when in rear in valuable handicap at Epsom in June only outing of 1982 (led 7f); should stay at least 1¼m; possibly not at his best on a firm surface; blinkered final start as a 3-y-o. *J. Tree.*

NEBIHA 2 ch.f. Nebbiolo 125–Roses 103 (Ribero 126) (1982 6fg 7f 7fg 8fg²) **85** Feb 17; 60,000Y; well-made filly; first foal; dam stayed 1¼m; 1½ lengths second of 13 to Saba in maiden race at Beverley in September, easily best effort; needs at least 1m, and will stay 1¼m; acts on a firm surface. *J. Dunlop.*

NEEDWOOD 4 b.g. Averof 123–The Doe 87 (Alcide 136) (1981 NR 1982 12g 17f) rangy gelding; little worthwhile form, including in a seller at 2 yrs; sold 675 gns Ascot 2nd June Sales. *B. Morgan.*

NEGLIGEE 2 ch.f. Some Hand 119–Princess Sahib (Sahib 114) (1982 5fg 5d 5fg) Mar 26; workmanlike filly; first foal; dam ran once over hurdles; no worthwhile form, on last outing (July) blinkered in a seller. *P. Cole.*

NEILAH (CAN) 3 b.c. Knightly Dawn–Main Saggy (Saggy) (1981 5g 5fg 5f 5g 8s 1982 7g 8f) good sort; poor form, including in sellers; had worn blinkers; sold 825 gns Ascot September Sales; dead. *R. Hannon.*

NELDAMUS 3 b. or br.c. Mandamus 120–Nelodor 69 (Nelcius 133) (1981 NR 1982 8f 12g) small colt; good walker; first foal; dam winning hurdler; in rear in maiden races at Doncaster and Redcar in summer; sold 500 gns Doncaster August Sales. *M. H. Easterby.*

NEORION 2 ch.c. Busted 134–Ship Yard 107 (Doutelle 128) (1982 8s² 8d) **111** May 16; 145,000Y; big, strong colt; brother to 2 winners, notably St Leger winner Bustino, and half-brother to 3 winners, including very smart French stayer Oarsman (by Aureole); dam won over 7f and 1m at 2 yrs; looked backward when 20/1 for maiden race at York in October and in circumstances did extremely well to finish ½-length second to Ring of Greatness, battling on in fine style in last 2f; good seventh, beaten only 6 lengths, behind Dunbeath in William Hill Futurity Stakes at Doncaster later in month; stays well; has scope and should win races if not tried too highly. *C. Brittain.*

NEOTERIC 3 ch.f. Some Hand 119–Neophyte II (Never Say Die 137) (1981 5f 8d 7g 1982 10f 13.3f 12d 14d) plain, strong filly; soundly beaten in a minor event and maiden races; often sweats up. *D. Elsworth.*

NEPOTISM 5 b.h. Great Nephew 126–Lantana 74 (St Paddy 133) (1981 7d 11.1s⁴ 10.8fg³ 10g 12.2fg* 12fg² 12f³ 14fg³ 12fg* 12h* 12.5g 1982 12fg 11f 13.3f 12.2fg 11.7g⁴) big, strong horse; fair handicapper in 1981 (rated 90); ran badly in 1982; stays 1¾m; probably acts on any going; blinkered twice in 1980. *G. Balding.*

NERAIDA 2 br.f. Royalty 130–Run The Risk (Run The Gantlet) (1982 7.6v) Apr 20; 2,500Y; first foal; dam once-raced daughter of Cambridgeshire winner Siliciana; unquoted, behind in 18-runner maiden race at Lingfield in October. *I. Walker.*

NERVOUS PASSENGER 3 b.c. Prince Tenderfoot 126–Splendidly (Luminary 132) (1981 NR 1982 7fg 8g 8d 8.2g) 10,000F, 10,500Y; strong, good-bodied, attractive colt; half-brother to several winners, including very useful milers Tack On (by Hard Tack) and Sotto Il Vulcano (by Right Tack); dam half-sister to very useful middle-distance stayer Shackleton; beaten some way in varied company, including selling. *L. Cumani.*

NESTOR 2 gr.c. Nishapour 125–Meadow Rhapsody (Ragusa 137) (1982 7fg **90** 7.6s 8s²) Apr 19; IR 48,000Y; strong colt; half-brother to several winners, including Irish 7f and 1m winner Elegy (by Prince Tenderfoot); dam won over 6f and is half-sister to Meadow Court; favourite, finished well clear of remainder when 1½ lengths second of 14 to El Gitano in maiden race at Leicester in November; will stay beyond 1m; acts well on soft going. *G. Lewis.*

NETHER REGIONS 3 ch.g. Netherkelly 112–Polly Jinks (Ron 103) (1981 —
8g 8.2d 10g 1982 13g 10.8fg) rather leggy gelding; plater; probably stays
1¼m; wears blinkers. *D. Ringer.*

NEVER ENOUGH 4 b.f. Sandford Lad 133–Suffice 84 (Faberge II 121) (1981 67
10fg 10d 10d 8.3fg 1982 8d 10fg* 10f 10.8fg 10f* 10g) strong, well-made
filly; good walker; bought in after winning sellers at Folkestone in April (1,200
gns) and August (820 gns), best efforts: stays 1¼m; acts on firm going. *A.
Ingham.*

NEVER SO BOLD 2 b.c. Bold Lad (Ire) 133–Never Never Land (Habitat 134) 71 p
(1982 6g) Apr 26; 28,000Y; big, rangy, good-looking colt; good walker; third
foal; dam unraced half-sister to Bruni's dam; 20/1, shaped nicely, running on well
under hand riding, when under 6 lengths eighth of 20 behind Fiefdom in maiden
race at Newmarket in October; sure to do better if looks mean anything. *R.
Armstrong.*

NEVER SO LUCKY 3 b.c. So Blessed 130–Lucky Janie 87 (Dual 117) (1981 89
5f* 5f4 6fg2 6g 6fg3 7g4 6g 6s* 7g 1982 6fg 6fg 6h3 6d 6fg 7f3 7f* 8.3g3 7fg4
8f 7d) attractive colt; particularly good mover; hampered in closing stages and
awarded race after finishing short-head second to Swinging Rhythm in handicap
at Salisbury in August; stays 1m; acts on any going; sold 7,400 gns Newmarket
Autumn Sales and sent to Italy. *G. Harwood.*

NEVER TALK 3 br.c. Most Secret 119–To Rome (Romulus 129) (1981 5fg* 101
5g* 5d3 5g2 5fg3 6f 5g3 5g 1982 5fg 5f2 5fg4 6fg 5fg) workmanlike colt; good
walker and mover; useful handicapper; in frame at Doncaster (stayed on strongly
after breaking slowly to be 2 lengths second to Steel Charger) and York (about
1¾ lengths fourth of 14 to Susarma in £7,400 event) in May; best form at 5f;
gives impression a sound surface suits him best; usually apprentice ridden;
ran respectably in blinkers final start (June); sent to USA. *A. Jarvis.*

NEWARK 7 br.g. Folkestone–Street Hawker 74 (Ben Hawke 94) (1981 12s —
1982 15.5fg) rangy gelding; poor handicapper; stays 1½m; acts on any going.
H. O'Neill.

NEW COINS (USA) 2 b.f. New Prospect–Estaciones (Sonny Fleet) (1982 99
6h4 7f3 7d3 7g2 6s* 7s*) Mar 22; $34,000F, $45,000 2-y-o; close-coupled, fair
sort; good mover; first foal; dam, 1m winner, is daughter of very useful Estacion;
sire, son of Never Bend, won stakes races from 6f to 1m; improved in the autumn,
winning maiden race at Hamilton and £2,700 event (beating Eye Dazzler 1½
lengths, conceding 5 lb) at York; will be suited by 1m; acts well on soft going.
B. Hanbury.

NEW CONTINENT (USA) 4 ch.g. Son Ange–Clover Blossom (Green Ticket)
(1981 10s 10fg 11.7s 10f3 13.1f3 8fg 12g2 12g2 12d3 12d4 1982 12d 18f 12.2fg) —
rangy gelding; seems to stay well; acts on any going, except possibly very soft;
exported to Malaysia. *E. Eldin.*

NEW EMBASSY (USA) 5 b.g. Dynastic (USA)–Joys Will (Yes You Will) 76 d
(1981 6f 5s 6d 5g2 1982 5g* 5s4 5f 5fg 5g) strong, well-made, good-quartered
gelding; sprint handicapper; rather disappointing after beating Miss Poinciana
decisively by 2 lengths at Doncaster in March; acts on any going; slowly into
stride third outing. *G. Balding.*

NEW EXPRESS 3 br.c. Bay Express 132–Natasha 87 (Native Prince) (1981 92
6g 1982 5fg* 5fg* 6g4 5f 5g) strong, lengthy colt; poor walker; not the best of
movers; chipped a bone in a knee at 2 yrs; won maiden race at Wolverhampton
in April (well-backed favourite) and found an excellent turn of foot to account
for Celestial Dancer by 1½ lengths going away in James Lane Handicap at
Ascot in June; ran respectably next 2 starts; seems to find 6f too far; yet to race
on a soft surface. *G. Huffer.*

NEW FARM LADY 3 b.f. Native Bazaar 122–So Unlikely 60 (Blast 125) —
(1981 NR 1982 5f 6fg 5f 5h 6fg) fair sort; poor plater. *P. Taylor.*

NEWGATE 9 b.g. Blakeney 126–Set Free 90 (Worden II 129) (1981 12.3d 39
12d 15g* 16g 16g 12fg 13.8fg3 14.7fg3 16fg4 17.4g 13d 1982 15f 12s3 15g4)
staying handicapper; acts on any going; has been tried in blinkers. *A. Scott.*

NEWJDAR (FR) 3 ch.c. New Chapter 106–Ardja (Djakao 124) (1981 9.2g* 118
10s3 1982 10.5v* 10.5d 12s4 12fg 12v3 11f 13.5g 12s 12v 10.5s) French colt;
second foal; half-brother to minor 1m winner Ardyson (by Tennyson); dam
placed over 6.5f as a 2-y-o from only 2 outings; won at Rouen at 2 yrs; beat
Flayosc ¾ length in 70,000 francs event at Maisons-Laffitte in March; in frame

subsequently in Prix Hocquart at Longchamp (about 3 lengths fourth to Cadoudal) and Prix du Lys at Chantilly (about ½-length third of 8 to Coquelin); also ran respectably to be tenth of 17 to Akiyda in Trusthouse Forte Prix de l'Arc de Triomphe at Longchamp in October on eighth start; stays 1½m; acts on heavy going. *P. Biancone, France.*

NEW JERUSALEM 5 b. or br.g. Reform 132–Desertville 92 (Charlottesville 135) — (1981 13.3s 1982 16g 16g) very useful stayer at his best, but deteriorated markedly; dead. *A. Smith.*

NEWLIFE CONNECTION 3 b.g. Rapid River 127–Weirdi 76 (Yrrah Jr) — (1981 6fg 6g 6fg4 7f 8d 7d 1982 7g 7g 8f 10g 10d 12f) leggy, narrow gelding; plating class; stays 1¼m; tends to sweat up; has worn a bandage on off-fore. *W. A. Stephenson.*

NEW MORNING 3 b.f. Wolverlife 115–Carol Barnett (Frigid Aire) (1981 5d — 1982 9.4f 9g) leggy filly; poor form, including in a seller; sold privately 1,400 gns Doncaster October Sales. *G. Richards.*

NEWSTEAD 4 b.g. Hector 88–Norfolk House (Cantab 94) (1981 NR 1982 — 16.5f 16g) novice hurdler; behind in maiden events at Redcar in July (last) and Beverley in August. *M. Jefferson.*

NEXT DECADE 3 gr.g. Shiny Tenth 120- Follow The Brave 68 (Owen Anthony — 102) (1981 5g2 6f2 6fg* 6fg 7f 6s3 6f 5g 1982 7f 5f 6g 5f) small gelding; poor plater nowadays; sold 320 gns Doncaster September Sales. *A. Balding.*

NIALAN 2 b.c. North Stoke 130–Buffy (French Beige 127) (1982 8g 8g3) **99** Feb 29; 15,500Y; well-made, quite attractive colt; half-brother to disappointing Miss Markey (by Gay Fandango) and 2 winners, including fairly useful 1976 2-y-o 5f winner Royal Hand (by Realm); dam, Irish 6f winner, is half-sister to very smart El Mina; 10/1 and apparently still not fully wound up, made up a tremendous amount of ground in closing stages when narrowly-beaten third of 18 to Holy Spark in maiden event at Newmarket in October; will stay beyond 1m; sure to win races. *J. Sutcliffe.*

NIBABU (FR) 2 b.f. Nishapour 125–Noah's Acky Astra (Ack Ack) (1982 6v3) **92 p** strong filly; first known foal; dam, half-sister to high-class Irish and American filly Swingtime, won over 6f at 2 yrs in Ireland and over 10.5f at 3 yrs in France; weak in market and ridden by an apprentice unable to claim his 5-lb allowance, stayed on well when 5½ lengths third of 10 to Northern Adventure in Duke of Edinburgh Stakes at Ascot in October; will stay at least 1m; bound to improve. *B. Hills.*

NICALINE 4 b.f. High Line 125–Ardema 63 (Armistice 131) (1981 NR 1982 — 21f 12s) plain filly; first foal; dam stayed well; not entirely disgraced in Goodwood Cup and apprentice race at Chepstow; had given trouble at start earlier in season (raced from flag start at Goodwood). *R. Sturdy.*

NICE FELLA (USA) 2 ch.c. Raise A Cup–Imalulu (Black Beard) (1982 7.6v **83** 8s) Apr 16; $42,000Y; well-made colt; closely related to 3-y-o middle-distance winner Tirawa (by Majestic Prince) and half-brother to 3 winners in USA; dam, sister to a stakes winner, won 3 times at up to 6f; ran on to finish 3 lengths fifth of 13 to Joyful Dancer in maiden event at Lingfield in October; favourite, beaten and eased right up final 1½f when out of first 10 of 26 behind Magic Rarity in similar event at Sandown later in the month. *M. Jarvis.*

NICE N NAUGHTY 2 b.f. Blue Cashmere 129–Donna Do 56 (Derring-Do 131) — (1982 5g 5fg 5fg) Mar 26; 700Y; lengthy, useful sort; of no account; sold 390 gns Ascot Second June Sales. *R. Hannon.*

NICE VALUE 8 ch.g. Goldhill 125–Sinecure (Parthia 132) (1981 6v 6s 5g 6d4 — 5.8g 6f 6f 6fg4 5fg* 6g 5.8g 6d 7d 1982 5fg 5fg 6fg 6s4) sprint handicapper; acts on any going but is well suited by some give in the ground; blinkered once in 1979. *R. Hollinshead.*

NICKADVENTURE 6 ch.g. On Your Mark 125–High Gloss (Super Sam 124) — (1981 7g3 8.2g 10.4s 10f2 12.3fg 10.6s 1982 11fg) workmanlike gelding; plater; stays 1¼m; acts on any going; suitable mount for an inexperienced rider; doesn't look particularly enthusiastic; bandaged nowadays. *N. Tinkler.*

NICK NICK 2 br.f. Garda's Revenge 119–Prancer 70 (Santa Claus 133) (1982 **67** 5fg3 5g3 5f3 6g 6fg 6fg 6g) Apr 3; leggy filly; closely related to winning Irish sprinter Imagem (by Dancer's Image) and half-sister to winners in Belgium and Italy; dam middle-distance maiden; plating-class maiden; best form early in season, but had little chance in nurseries on last 3 appearances; stays 6f; blinkered final outing. *D. Dale.*

NIGHT CLOWN 3 b.g. Cawston's Clown 113–Night On (Narrator 127) (1981 **64**
6d   1982 5g 5g* 5.8f* 6f⁴ 6f 6fg 5fg³ 6f 5g 5s) rangy, useful sort; won apprentice
race at Edinburgh and handicap at Bath in July; stays 6f; acts on firm going;
has run respectably in blinkers; retained 1,550 gns Newmarket Autumn Sales.
A. Bailey.

NIGHT WATCH (USA) 8 br.g. Stage Door Johnny–Lucretia Bori (Bold Ruler) **58 d**
(1981 12g 12s³ 14g⁴ 1982 13fg 16d 12fg 14fg 12fg* 12d 12g 13.8d) strong,
good-looking gelding; not the force he was, but won apprentice handicap at
Salisbury in September; stays well; appears to act on any going; very good
mount for an inexperienced rider. *I. Balding.*

NIKIFOROS 3 ch.c. Music Boy 124–Contadina (Memling) (1981 6g 7g 1982 **87**
8fg 10fg* 10fg³ 10g* 12f 10g² 10f³ 14f 12fg* 13.3g 10g² 10g) rangy, quite
attractive colt; not the best of movers; won maiden race at Salisbury in May
and quite valuable handicaps at Sandown in June (from Bold Hawk) and Newmarket in August (beat Polar Star); not disgraced most other starts; stays 1½m;
yet to race on a soft surface; has run creditably when sweating up; does best
when ridden up with pace; suited by strong handling; game. *C. Brittain.*

NILE HAWK (USA) 2 b.c. Sham–Trevisana (Aristophanes 116) (1982 8f³ **115**
9d² 10v*)
    In recent years the Prix Saint-Roman, run over nine furlongs at Longchamp
in the autumn, has been a reliable guide to the furlong-longer Prix de Conde on
the same course.   Both have Group 3 status and are usually contested by good
two-year-olds.   In 1977, 1978 and 1979 both races were won by the same horse—
Pevero, Top Ville and Corvaro respectively—whilst the next Prix de Conde winner
The Wonder had been a strong-finishing third in the Saint-Roman.   The latest
running failed to attract the Saint-Roman winner Saint Cyrien but Nile Hawk,
second to Saint Cyrien, landed the spoils in the latter's absence.
    Nile Hawk wasn't seen on a racecourse until September, when he finished
under a length third to Milliard in a newcomers' event at Longchamp.   His two-
and-a-half-length second to Saint Cyrien in the Prix Saint-Roman early in
October was a big improvement and a good performance for one so inexperienced—Saint Cyrien and Milliard had also raced only once but the remaining
six contestants each had at least three outings behind them.   Nile Hawk set off
in front, as he had done on his previous start, and although he had no answer
to Saint Cyrien in the closing stages he kept on powerfully to the finish.   Front-
running tactics were again adopted with Nile Hawk in the Prix de Conde and
once again it looked as though he'd be beaten when tackled in the straight by
the favourite Allverton, winner of a newcomers' race at Longchamp, and the
Prix Saint-Roman fourth Lovely Dancer.   Allverton went nearly a length up
at the distance, then Nile Hawk battled back to beat him a short head with
Lovely Dancer a head further back.   Some observers thought that Allverton
had run a little green, others that his jockey had been a little over-confident; be
that as it may, Nile Hawk showed himself resolute, if perhaps a shade lacking
in pace.

		Pretense	Endeavour II
	Sham	(br 1963)	Imitation
	(b 1970)	Sequoia	Princequillo
Nile Hawk (USA)		(b 1955)	The Squaw II
(b.c. Feb 7, 1980)		Aristophanes	Hyperion
	Trevisana	(ch 1948)	Commotion
	(ch 1966)	Trevisa	Advocate
		(ch 1951)	Veneta

    Nile Hawk, a strong, lengthy, attractive colt, was sold for 110,000 dollars
as a yearling and resold for 270,000 dollars, the third-highest price of the
California Thoroughbred Breeders Association Two-Year-Olds in Training Sales.
Among the graduates from these sales in recent years are Alleged, Beldale Flutter
and the outstanding American filly Bold 'N Determined.   Nile Hawk is a half-
brother to three winners including Enthralment (by Sir Ivor), a two-year-old
six-furlong winner in England in 1981, and the very useful Sifounas (by Secretariat), successful in France and Italy (in the Group 2 Premio Ellington) and
now a sire in the United States.   Nile Hawk's dam Trevisana won in Argentina.
She is a half-sister to a winner and sister to three more including the outstanding
Forli and Argentinian stakes winner Tirreno.   Veneta, Nile Hawk's third dam,
was also a winner in Argentina and is the fourth dam of Crow.   Nile Hawk,
a resolute galloper with a round action, acts well on heavy going.   He should

make a more than useful middle-distance performer, though whether he has the pace to trouble the best remains to be seen. *M. Zilber, France.*

NINEVEH 4 ch.f. Import 127–Catamaran 82 (Lauso) (1981 8fg 10d 8g³ 11g 8f⁴ 8fg 12g³ 10s* 12.2g 10s 10d 10.2g 1982 8s 8d 10g 10f 10f) neat, strong filly; poor plater nowadays; stays 1½m; acts on any going, but seems suited by soft; has been tried in blinkers. *A. Balding.*
—

NIOULARGO 3 b.c. Pitskelly 122–Morzine (On Your Mark 125) (1981 6fg 7d² 7f* 7g* 8g* 1982 8g² 8fg 8fg* 8fg² 7g 8f 10.5g 10g* 10g) quite attractive colt; good mover; successful in £5,600 race at Ayr in May (beat sole opponent That's My Son a head) and 5-runner £4,900 handicap at Yarmouth in September (accounted for Cavaradossi by a length); also ran well on other occasions, including in Ladbrokes Craven Stakes at Newmarket (1½ lengths equal second to Silver Hawk) and Britannia Stakes at Royal Ascot (beaten 1½ lengths by Bali Dancer under top weight); stays 1¼m; wore small bandages in front seventh outing; genuine. *R. Armstrong.*
104

NIP LASS 2 b.f. Ercolano 118–Sherry Girl 81 (Appiani II 128) (1982 5f 7d 7f³ 7f⁴) Apr 9; 2,600Y; fair sort; good walker; third foal; dam 2-y-o 5f winner; plater; sent to Algeria. *P. Rohan.*
49

NOAH'S ARK 2 ch.g. Habat 127–Rainbow's End 83 (My Swallow 134) (1982 6fg) Mar 14; first foal; dam 2-y-o 6f winner; well beaten in newcomers race at Chepstow (blinkered) in August; sold A. Neaves 440 gns Newmarket Autumn Sales. *R. Hern.*
—

NOALCOHOLIC (FR) 5 b.h. Nonoalco 131–Alea II (Galivanter 131) (1981 10.5d² 10.5v² 9.7s 8fg³ 9d² 10f 10fg* 10s 1982 9.2s* 8f² 7g* 8d* 8g 8s² 7g*)
122

A fortuitous combination of factors led to the emergence of the ex-French horse Noalcoholic among the season's leading lights. He came to England in the first place only to comply with quarantine regulations before taking up stud duties in Australia, but he worked so well with the useful Buffavento that the owner was persuaded to allow him to run a couple of times during his stay. Noalcoholic won his races in France at nine or ten furlongs, usually coming from behind. In the time before he was due to leave for Australia there were no races for him at that kind of distance, so it was decided to run him at a slightly shorter trip and send him on to make full use of his stamina. The step down to seven furlongs and a mile combined with the different tactics brought about so dramatic an improvement in Noalcoholic's form that his trip to Australia was postponed, and he spent the rest of the season in training at Newmarket.

Noalcoholic had a mixed career in France, where he was trained by Douieb. He looked most promising as a three-year-old, unbeaten in two races at Evry and the Prix de la Ville de Trouville at Deauville, but at four he was rather disappointing and was once tried in blinkers, his only success coming in a small race at Deauville; he was officially assessed nearly 20 lb behind the best of his age both years. As a five-year-old he won his race before leaving for England, carrying top weight impressively in a tierce handicap at Longchamp in May.

The Queen Anne Stakes at Royal Ascot, a far cry from a handicap, was Noalcoholic's first race in England; in it he belied his starting price of 33/1 with

Prix Messidor, Maisons-Laffitte—Noalcoholic beats Big John

a splendid showing. After breaking fast he led until the impressive four-length winner Mr Fluorocarbon joined him about two furlongs out, and he kept on so well that he always had second place in safe-keeping. We didn't have to wait long for confirmation of Noalcoholic's improvement as he gave another resolute display of front-running in the Van Geest Stakes at Newmarket the following week and won easing up by two and a half lengths from Scarrowmanwick. Since both the Sussex Stakes and the Waterford Crystal Mile closed before Noal-coholic's arrival here he was sent back to France for his next two races, the Prix Messidor at Maisons-Laffitte in July and the Prix Jacques le Marois at Deauville in August, and he dominated the former event to such an extent that French racegoers can hardly have recognised him. He was in no danger whatsoever from halfway and came home three lengths clear of Big John. At Deauville Noalcoholic didn't fare quite so well in a far stronger field, finishing fifth to The Wonder, but he returned to his best with a three-length second to the 50/1-chance Buzzards Bay in the Queen Elizabeth II Stakes at Ascot in September and an extremely game victory over Motavato in a strongly-run Bisquit Cognac Challenge Stakes at Newmarket in October. Motavato foiled Noalcoholic's attempts to lead in the Challenge Stakes and, although Noalcoholic's jockey Duffield reportedly thought he had Motavato's measure by the three-furlong marker, the two horses had a long, hard struggle before Noalcoholic prevailed by three quarters of a length. His win provided owner William Du Pont with some timely consolation for the loss of his stallion Tromos who died in the States earlier in the week after being operated on for colic.

Noalcoholic (Fr) (b.h. 1977)	Nonoalco (b 1971)	Nearctic (br 1954)	Nearco
			Lady Angela
		Seximee (ch 1966)	Hasty Road
			Jambo
	Alea II (ch 1967)	Galivanter (br 1956)	Golden Cloud
			Lycia
		Alleged (ch 1959)	Alycidon
			Plain Justice

Noalcoholic is by Nonoalco, now in Japan, out of Alea II, the only classic winner sired by the July Cup winner Galivanter. Alea was the leading filly of her generation as a two-year-old in Italy and at three won the Italian One Thousand Guineas quite readily. After appearing not to stay the distance in the Italian Oaks, she reverted to five furlongs in the Prix de l'Abbaye only to finish last behind Balidar. Alea produced three winners in Italy before Noalcoholic: his sister Amiel, the very useful Alceo (by Molvedo) and Alato (by Bold Lad, USA); the last two are highly prolific winners with over thirty races between them. In 1982 she was represented in France by the very useful two-year-old Alluvia

Bisquit Cognac Challenge Stakes, Newmarket—an inappropriately-named winner from the sponsor's point of view: Noalcoholic fights off Motavato

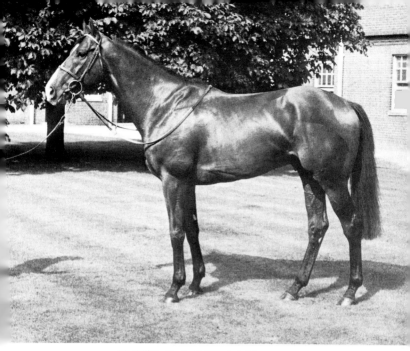

Mr William Du Pont's "Noalcoholic"

(by Riverman), a winner over seven furlongs at Chantilly and a close third in the Prix Thomas Bryon.

Noalcoholic will eventually stand in Australia; just when isn't certain since he will again be in training with Pritchard-Gordon for at least the first half of the 1983 season. Noalcoholic seems bound to play a prominent part in such races as the Queen Anne Stakes, and he may also be worth trying over further again. A strong, good sort who is clearly indifferent to the state of the going, Noalcoholic is thoroughly genuine and consistent. Reportedly he doesn't need a lot of work, and so is likely to be ready early on. *G. Pritchard-Gordon.*

NOALTO 4 ch.c. Nonoalco 131–Lyrical 110 (Gratitude 130) (1981 8fg* 8g 6s³ **120** 7f³ 7f 8fg³ 7.3fg³ 8fg⁴ 10g² 8s⁴ 10g 1982 9fg² 7f* 8f² 8.5f² 8f 10f 10d³)

The Al-Maktoums, the ruling family of Dubai, were numerically well represented in the Dubai Champion Stakes at Newmarket in October, which they sponsored for the first time. Their three runners Noalto, Princes Gate and Rajhaan seemed to have little chance and started at 22/1 or over, but finished third, fifth and sixth respectively. The Al-Maktoums were no doubt well pleased. They have invested heavily in British racing, for apart from their sponsorship of the Champion Stakes—from which they can't benefit commercially—they have over a hundred horses in training and extensive stud interests. Their attitude to racing is refreshingly sporting and their support in the current economic climate is welcome.

Noalto was obviously on very good terms with himself before the Champion Stakes and ran accordingly. He had no chance with the seven-length winner Time Charter but ran on so well from the back of the field in the closing stages that he failed by only a neck to snatch second from Prima Voce. Despite his stable's being badly out of form for most of the season Noalto had been more consistent than as a three-year-old, when outstandingly his best form was a close third behind Kings Lake and To-Agori-Mou in the Sussex Stakes at Goodwood. As a four-year-old he beat Motavato by a length in the Philip Cornes Trophy at Leicester in April on his second outing and finished second in the Tote-Lockinge Stakes at Newbury, in which Motavato very narrowly had his revenge in a race run at a crawl to halfway, and the Diomed Stakes at Epsom, in which the 33/1-chance Prima Voce beat him by two and a half lengths. The only occasions on which he was out of the frame were in the Sussex Stakes, in which he had no sort of a run, and the Budweiser Million at Arlington Park, Chicago. In the latter, his last race before the Champion, he started the outsider of fourteen at 132/1 and finished a most respectable nine lengths seventh to Perrault, ridden by Piggott for the first time.

Noalto (ch.c. 1978)	Nonoalco (b 1971)	Nearctic (br 1954)	Nearco / Lady Angela
		Seximee (ch 1966)	Hasty Road / Jambo
	Lyrical (ch 1966)	Gratitude (ch 1953)	Golden Cloud / Verdura
		Sweet Sonnet (b 1958)	Honeyway / Verse

Noalto is a big, robust colt by Nonoalco out of the tough and genuine sprint handicapper Lyrical. He's a half-brother to several winners, notably the Queen's smart middle-distance performer Rhyme Royal. Noalto, who has already been ridden by nine different jockeys employing a wide variety of tactics, and has been tried in blinkers, has never been an easy horse to weigh up. There was a

Sheikh Mohammed's "Noalto" (W. Carson)

time when we thought he was better at a mile than a mile and a quarter, and ideally suited by fast going and a sharp track; his performance over a mile and a quarter on softish going at Newmarket showed that well wide of the mark. He is reportedly to continue his career in the United States. *F. Durr.*

NO ATTENTION (FR) 4 b.c. Green Dancer 132–No No Nanette 118 **124** (Sovereign Path 125) (1981 10s⁴ 8.5d 9fg 10.5g² 12g³ 12d* 12.5fg³ 12g 12s² 10.5v³ 1982 14d³ 12d² 12v³ 12g² 13.5g* 12.5d² 12g² 12.5g* 13.5g² 12f² 12s 12v² 12v² 15.5v⁴) French colt; first foal; dam won 4 races at up to 10.5f, including Prix de Flore, and is closely related to high-class miler Nadjar; changed hands for 250,000 francs (approx £23,000) late in 1981 and proved a good buy; ran consistently well as a 4-y-o and developed into a very smart performer; successful in Grand Prix de Marseille-Vivaux in July (beat Dhaubix by a length) and in Prix de Reux at Deauville in August (won by 2 lengths from Moulouki); second on 8 other occasions, on last 6 in Prix Maurice de Nieuil at Saint-Cloud (beaten ½ length by All Along), Grand Prix de Vichy (went down by length to Karkour), Grand Prix de Deauville (beaten 1½ lengths by Real Shadai), Prix Foy at Longchamp (promoted from third when beaten very narrowly by April Run), Preis von Europa at Cologne (¾ length behind Ataxerxes) and Prix du Conseil de Paris at Longchamp (length second to Marasali); put up another good effort in Trusthouse Forte Prix de l'Arc de Triomphe at Longchamp in October, making very good headway from back of field in straight to finish less than 6 lengths sixth of 17 behind Akiyda; was suited by 1½m+; showed plenty of form with some give in the ground; seemed none too genuine in a finish and usually wore blinkers; won for an amateur rider and was also successful over hurdles; changed hands privately shortly before Prix de l'Arc de Triomphe; stud in Japan. *R. Collet, France.*

NOBELLION 3 gr.f. No Mercy 126–Tabellion 79 (Tabbas 99) (1981 5fg — 6g 6f 5fg 1982 8f 7g 6fg) leggy filly; poor form, including in a seller; has worn blinkers. *J. Mason.*

NOBLE BLOOM (USA) 3 b.c. Vaguely Noble 140–April Bloom 108 (Bold **120** Lad, Ire 133) (1981 8v 8v* 1982 10v 12fg² 12s² 12fg 12.5d⁴) $200,000Y; half-brother to 2 winners by The Axe, including April Axe, a smart stakes winner at up to 1m; dam won twice over 5f at 2 yrs and was in frame in good races at up to 1m; runner-up in minor event at Evry in April (½ length behind Le Nain Jaune) and Prix Hocquart at Longchamp in May (beaten a length by Cadoudal); also ran creditably in Prix du Jockey-Club at Chantilly (just over 6 lengths fifth of 14 to Assert) and Prix Maurice de Nieuil at Saint-Cloud (5½ lengths fourth to 12 to All Along); suited by 1½m; seems to act on any going. *M. Saliba, France.*

NOBLE GIFT (USA) 3 br.c. Vaguely Noble 140–Queenly Gift (Princely **107** Gift 137) (1981 7b² 7g⁴ 1982 10.5f² 10f* 10.5fg*) attractive colt; good walker and very good mover; won well-contested maiden race at Sandown and 6-runner £5,600 event at York in June; always going well in latter and had more in hand than 1½-length winning margin over Kenninghall suggests; looked

Daniel Prenn Royal Yorkshire Stakes, York—improving Noble Gift is too good for Kenninghall (centre) and Eurodancer

like developing into a very useful performer but wasn't seen out again; will be suited by 1½m; yet to race on a soft surface. *M. Stoute.*

NOBLE LEGEND 4 b.g. Noble Decree 127–Novelista 101 (El Gallo 122) — (1981 9s 12g 10.6d 8g 9s* 1982 8g 8.2fg 10f 10d) lengthy, dipped-backed gelding; no form in 1982 (last on first 3 outings); should be suited by middle distances; acts on soft going; blinkered third start; sold out of M. H. Easterby's stable 1,750 gns Doncaster May Sales after first outing and out of C. Pinkham's stable 1,300 gns Doncaster September Sales after third. *J. Doyle.*

NOBLE PATIA (USA) 2 b.f. Vaguely Noble 140–Patia 119 (Don II 123) — p (1982 7g) Apr 20; 230,000Y; rangy filly; first foal; dam, half-sister to outstanding middle-distance filly Pawneese, won over 1m and 1½m; 12/1 and in need of race, ran creditably after dwelling when 13 lengths sixth of 28 to Tolomeo in maiden race at Newmarket in October; sure to do better. *J. Hindley.*

NOBLE PERRY 4 b.f. Perdu 121–Noble Nugget (Klondyke Bill 125) (1981 6s⁴ 6fg³ 6g 6g 1982 6s 8.2s 7f 6fg 5f 6g 5g) leggy filly; plater; should stay 1m; blinkered final start. *Mrs A. Bell.*

NOBLEU 5 ch.g. Blue Cashmere 129–Palanna 87 (Pall Mall 132) (1981 10.5d 10f³ 10f⁴ 8f 8fg 8f 9d 10fg 8g 8g² 8s* 11d 8g 1982 8.2g 8f 10f 10g⁴ 10fg 10g 12s) compact gelding; poor handicapper; stays 1½m; acts on any going; suitable mount for an apprentice; behind in a seller when blinkered once; usually bandaged in front nowadays. *P. Asquith.*

NOBLE WAY 2 b.c. Monsanto 121–Marble Alley (Psidium 130) (1982 6g 5fg 6g 6g) Apr 11; sturdy colt; half-brother to Marshalsea (by Manacle), successful from 6f to 1½m here and in Ireland; dam of little account; no form; last of 14 under 8-0 in nursery at Leicester in October. *W. Holden.*

NOBLISSIMO (FR) 5 ch.h. Sanctus II 132–Nobla (Dicta Drake 126) (1981 — 10g*(dis) 14g² 12s 20g² 14g 13g* 20d 12g⁴ 15g 14d 12g 11.5g² 12s² 16.7g* 1982 16.1s⁴ 16v 12d 18s) close-coupled, good-looking horse; first past post 3 times in French Provinces in 1981 but was disqualified on first occasion; well beaten after finishing fourth to High Rainbow in handicap at Haydock in April (not seen out again until autumn); probably ideally suited by a thorough test of stamina; acts well on soft going; trained by A. Geraghty in Ireland on first outing. *N. Guest.*

NO BOMBS 7 b.g. St Paddy 133–Land of Fire 99 (Buisson Ardent 129) (1981 **91** 12fg* 12g 1982 12fg 16.1f) big, useful sort; a most versatile performer who is very useful over jumps and a prolific winner on flat; lightly raced on flat nowadays, better effort of 1982 when creditable fifth to dead-heaters Karadar and Keelby Kavalier at York in May on reappearance; effective at 1½m and stays 2m; acts on any going; tough and genuine and has a good turn of foot; used to give trouble at start on occasions; goes well for apprentice K. Hodgson. *M. H. Easterby.*

NO BUTTS 2 b.c. Monsanto 121–Lay Aboard (Sing Sing 134) (1982 8.2s 8s) Mar 10; 950F, 6,200Y; quite well-made colt; poor walker; half-brother to very useful 3-y-o Super Sunrise (by Sagaro), a winner at up to 1½m; dam never ran; well beaten in autumn maiden events at Haydock and Leicester. *R. Hollinshead.*

NO CLOWN 3 b.g. Cawston's Clown 113–Sweet Hortense 71 (King's Troop **74** 118) (1981 5g⁴ 6f⁴ 6fg 6f⁴ 5fg* 6fg 6d 1982 6f³ 8f 7f* 8d) strong, sprint type; narrowly won handicap at Beverley in May; stays 7f but not 1m; acts on firm going; hung when blinkered once in 1981; sent to Singapore. *M. H. Easterby.*

NO CONTEST 3 ch.c. Nonoalco 131–Never So Lovely 87 (Realm 129) (1981 **89** 5g 5g⁴ 6f 6g 7d 7g⁴ 6g⁴ 6s* 6s 1982 8.2d 7fg 8f² 8fg³ 7.2f* 7d* 6g* 6.5fg² 6f³ 6f⁴ 6fg⁴ 7fg* 7fg 7s 7s) workmanlike colt; good mover; made virtually all and kept on gamely to win handicaps at Haydock, Salisbury, Yarmouth and Kempton; best at distances short of 1m; acts on any going; hung badly ninth start; sent to race in Florida. *M. Ryan.*

NO DEFECT 3 ro.g. No Mercy 126–Ruby's Chance 71 (Charlottesville 135) **48** (1981 6g 6f 6fg 6fg 7.2v 8g 1982 10s 7f³ 7f² 7f³ 7f³ 7f* 8g 7fg² 7f 6g 9f³ 7s) lengthy, rather unfurnished gelding; good mover; plater; attracted no bid after winning at Redcar in June (short-priced favourite); possibly stays 9f; acts on firm going; has worn blinkers; consistent. *Hbt Jones.*

NO DOUBLE 2 ch.f. Double Jump 131–Leitha (Vienna 127) (1982 5d 5fg³ **35** 5fg³ 5g 7g 5s) May 4; plain filly; bad plater. *D. Wintle.*

NOELINO 6 gr.h. Bonne Noel 115–Little Fuss (Sovereign Path 125) (1981 **103** 9d 10.5g² 10.5v⁴ 12g⁴ 12g⁴ 1982 10s* 10s 13.4fg⁴ 20f⁴ 21f 12fg 18g) lengthy horse; smart performer at his best; ran below form in France in 1981; made a successful reappearance in 13-runner Mooresbridge Stakes at the Curragh in March, beating Stanerra by ¾ length; wasn't disgraced when about 7 lengths fourth of 6 behind Six Mile Bottom in Ormonde Stakes at Chester in May and appeared to run very well when just over 3 lengths fourth of 6 behind very comfortable winner Ardross in Gold Cup at Royal Ascot in June; has raced mainly over middle distances but seems suited by a test of stamina nowadays; acts on any going; slipped up fifth start; looked very hard trained and ran moderately final outing; sold 28,000 gns Newmarket December Sales. *K. Prendergast, Ireland.*

NOEL STREET 2 b.c. Tumble Wind–Rosy O'Leary (Majetta 115) (1982 6d 7f) May 20; IR 1,900F; second produce; half-brother to a winning plater; dam never ran; last and last but one in 2 races in modest company in September; sold 900 gns Doncaster November Sales. *G. Lewis.* —

NO EXCUSES 5 b.g. Tamerlane 128–Lady Talisman (Continuation 120) (1981 NR 1982 10d) novice hurdler; well beaten on flat. *N. Crump.* —

NO FLUKE 2 br.c. Averof 123–Daisy Warwick 91 (Ribot 142 or Sir Gaylord) (1982 5fg 5.8f* 6f² 6fg 6g 6g) Apr 10; 3,100Y; fair sort; first living foal; dam placed twice over 5f at 2 yrs; won 6-runner maiden race at Bath in May; beaten short head in valuable seller at York in July, only subsequent form; blinkered final start; will stay 7f; acts on firm going; sold 650 gns Ascot October Sales. *M. Smyly.* **71 d**

NO HACK 3 ch.c. High Line 125–Cut and Thrust 78 (Pardal 130) (1981 7fg 8d 1982 12g 14g) tall, lightly-made colt; well beaten in varied company; sold to A. Moore 3,500 gns Newmarket Autumn Sales. *H. Candy.* —

NO HYST (USA) 2 ch.c. No Robbery–Forest Echo (Tompion) (1982 6f 5fg⁴) Mar 4; $150,000 2-y-o; half-brother to a minor winner; dam, winner of claiming races at up to 1m, is half-sister to dam of smart Replant (by No Robbery); quite modest form in July in minor event at Kempton and maiden race at Sandown. *J. Sutcliffe.* **72**

NO ILLUSION 5 ch.m. Grey Mirage 128–Leitha (Vienna 127) (1981 10s* 10f 12f 12d 10s³ 10s⁴ 1982 12f) plater; stays 1¼m; acts well on soft going; often bandaged. *D. Wintle.* —

NO INK 3 b.f. No Mercy 126–Inklet (Never Say Die 137) (1981 5g 6fg 5g 1982 7.6f 5.3f² 5f 5fg 6g) fair sort; sprint handicapper; acts on firm going. *D. Grissell.* —

NOIRIANNA 2 ch.f. Morston 125–Noirima 110 (Right Tack 131) (1982 6s 5f) Jan 8; small, close-coupled, rather leggy filly, lacking in scope; second foal; closely related to 3-y-o 1m and 1¼m winner Noirio (by Blakeney); dam very useful at up to 1m; 3 lengths sixth of 13 to Babycham Sparkle in minor event at Catterick in September, second outing; not bred to sprint. *H. T. Jones.* **71**

NOIRIO 3 b.c. Blakeney 126–Noirima 110 (Right Tack 131) (1981 5g 6f 7g 1982 7f⁴ 8fg* 10f* 11f 11.7d 8.2g) neat colt; won private sweepstakes at Newmarket in April and maiden race at Leicester in May; stays 1¼m; acts on firm going; does best when ridden up with pace; sold to BBA (Italia) 8,400 gns Newmarket Autumn Sales. *P. Cole.* **72**

NOISY BOYSIE 2 br.c. Supreme Sovereign 119–Black Mink 83 (Gratitude 130) (1982 5fg⁴) Apr 21; 1,000F, 5,800Y; compact, fair sort; half-brother to several winners here and abroad, including fairly useful sprinter Brentex (by Birdbrook); dam won twice over 5f at 2 yrs; 3¼ lengths fourth of 8 to easy winner Bid Again in maiden race at Nottingham in June; will stay 6f. *M. Blanshard.* **71**

NOKURU 2 ch.c. Simbir 130–Polly Duckins (Dike) (1982 7s³) Feb 20; IR 2,300F, IR 8,200Y; first produce; dam poor half-sister to smart animals Crozier and Monatrea; gambled on from 5/1 to 6/4 favourite for 15-runner maiden race at the Curragh in October but ran in snatches and was beaten 2 lengths into third place behind Stratford; will be suited by 1¼m+; evidently well thought of and will win races. *L. Browne, Ireland.* **84 p**

NONSTOP 3 ch.g. Nonoalco 131–Fast Motion 86 (Midsummer Night II 117) (1981 7g 8g 8s 1982 8g 8f*(dis) 8f⁴ 8fg 8fg 8.2g³ 8.2s* 8s 7d) tall, rangy gelding; not the best of movers; first past post in handicap at Redcar in May (disqualified for hampering another runner) and maiden race at Haydock in October; stays 1m well; acts on any going; has shown a tendency to hang; blinkered sixth and final starts. *J. Etherington.* **74**

NON-WET 2 b.c. Sallust 134–Maggie's Pet 74 (Coronation Year 124) (1982   77
5d² 6v² 6g) May 24; 30,000Y; strong, good-bodied colt; half-brother to 3
winners, including useful 5f to 7f winner Maxi's Taxi (by Klondyke Bill); dam
won 5f seller at 2 yrs; runner-up in maiden races at Nottingham in September
and at Hamilton (odds on) in October; will stay beyond 6f. *W. Hastings-Bass.*

NORDAN CENTRE 2 b.f. Saulingo 122–Sapphire Red (Red Alert 127) (1982   78
5fg 5f 5s² 5g³ 5fg* 5f⁴ 5f 5g² 5g* 5fg³ 5s*) Mar 17; IR 560F, 4,200Y; strong,
good-bodied filly; first foal; dam never ran; successful in maiden race at Edinburgh in July and in nurseries at Ayr (apprentices) in September and Haydock
in October; only just stays 5f; seems to act on any going; missed break seventh
start. *M. Camacho.*

NORDIC HAWK (DEN) 2 b.c. Shantung 132–Nordic Rose (Drumhead 122)   —
(1982 5fg 8d 8s) fair sort; Danish-bred colt; dam, daughter of smart 1955
2-y-o The Rose of Sharon, finished in rear in 3 maiden races at 2 yrs; behind in
maiden events. *G. Fletcher.*

NO REMISSION 2 b.f. He Loves Me 120–Full Stretch 103 (Sing Sing 134)   79
(1982 5fg⁴ 6g 6g² 6g* 7d⁴ 7.3g) Apr 6; IR 3,700F, IR 9,000Y; lightly-made
filly; half-sister to Irish 7f to 1¼m winner Parole (by Don II); dam won twice
over 6f from 3 starts at 2 yrs; won 14-runner maiden race at Redcar in August by
2 lengths from Melowen; stays 7f. *G. Pritchard-Gordon.*

NORFOLK FLIGHT 5 br.g. Blakeney 126–First Light 82 (Primera 131)   76
(1981 8g³ 11s 10.6s³ 10f² 10f* 10.2fg⁴ 10f³ 10d* 11f⁴ 10fg 10fg* 10g* 9g 10g
1982 10f 10d 10fg⁴ 10fg 12f 10d³ 10g³ 10fg 10f² 10s 10d 8s) strong gelding;
front-running handicapper; none too consistent in 1982; suited by middle
distances; acts on any going but is ideally suited by top-of-the-ground; suitable
mount for an inexperienced rider; ran creditably when blinkered ninth outing;
trained until after tenth outing by W. Hastings-Bass. *R. Carter.*

NORFOLK PAGEANT 3 b.c. Welsh Pageant 132–Norfolk Light 86 (Blakeney   —
126) (1981 NR 1982 8fg 10fg 8fg 10.1fg 10g 12f 10.8fg 10g) 16,000Y; neat,
attractive colt; second foal; half-brother to Norfolk Realm (by Realm), a winner
at up to 1m; dam, half-sister to 1,000 Guineas third Yanuka, won over 7f at
2 yrs and stayed 1½m; soundly beaten in varied company; usually blinkered.
B. Swift.

NORFOLK REALM 4 b.c. Realm 129–Norfolk Light 86 (Blakeney 126) (1981   62
7d 8.2fg 8g* 10g³ 8fg² 8fg 8fg⁴ 8g 8g 8.2v² 8v⁴ 1982 8fg² 8g⁴ 9fg² 8fg³ 7.6g*
8fg 8fg 8d³ 9g 8g² 7s) rangy colt; led near line when beating Banbury Cross
in handicap at Lingfield in June (edged right in closing stages); ran moderately
next 2 outings; stays 1¼m; probably acts on any going; blinkered once in 1981.
P. Makin.

NORFOLK SERENADE 2 b.f. Blakeney 126–Brave Ballard (Derring-Do   76 p
131) (1982 6s⁴) Apr 21; well-made filly; good walker; second foal; dam
unraced half-sister to very smart middle-distance colt Norfolk Air (by Blakeney);
20/1, shaped promisingly after a slow start when strong-finishing fourth of 9
behind very easy winner Misguided in minor event at Goodwood in September; sure to be seen to better advantage over middle distances. *J. Bethell.*

NORMAN'S BOY 4 ch.g. Tarboosh–Flattery (Atan) (1981 8d 1982 10d)   —
plater at 2 yrs; very lightly raced since; should stay 1m; has worn blinkers;
sold 600 gns Ascot December Sales. *D. Hanley.*

NORROY 5 ch.g. Northfields–Tzaritsa 113 (Young Emperor 133) (1981   63
7g* 7.6fg 8fg* 8f³ 7fg⁴ 10g 8s 1982 8f³ 8g³ 8d 8f² 8g³ 8fg² 8fg³ 8d) robust
gelding; placed in handicaps; suited by 1m and is worth another chance over
further; seems to act on any going; blinkered once in 1980; trained early in
season by R. Baker. *D. Elsworth.*

NORSEL 3 ch.g. Hot Spark 126–Primrose Day 64 (The Brianstan 128) (1981   43
NR 1982 6f 6fg 8s 6g³ 7s) 3,000Y; good-bodied gelding; second foal; dam
in frame in early-season events at 2 yrs; little worthwhile form, including in
a seller. *J. Benstead.*

NORTHAIR (USA) 2 b.c. Northern Dancer–Bold Melody (Bold Reason) (1982   97
6f² 6f² 7f³ 6g* 6d) Feb 19; $440,000Y; quite attractive colt; first foal; dam,
winner 5 times at up to 1m at 3 yrs, is half-sister to Prix Morny winner Broadway
Dancer (by Northern Dancer) and high-class Broadway Forli; made all in
7-runner maiden race at Nottingham in September; seems better at 6f than 7f;
best form on a sound surface. *P. Walwyn.*

NORTHBOURNE 2 b.c. Moulton 128–Alisarda (Aureole 132) (1982 7d — 7g 6s 8.2fg) May 3; 440F; lengthy, workmanlike colt; of no account; blinkered final outing; trained first 2 starts by R. Woodhouse. *G. Fletcher.*

NORTH BRITON 3 b.c. Northfields–Juliette Marny 123 (Blakeney 126) **57** (1981 6d 8g 1982 11g 10fg[4] 8f 7fg[4]) neat, attractive colt; well bred but apparently has only a modicum of ability; will stay 1½m; blinkered last 3 starts; sold to C. Brittain 6,000 gns Newmarket Autumn Sales. *J. Tree.*

NORTHERN ADVENTURE (USA) 2 b.c. Far North 120–Liz Piet (Piet) **113** p (1982 6v* 7d* 7s*) May 13; $180,000Y; good-looking colt; half-brother to numerous winners, including Father Hogan (by Dewan), a smart winner at up to 1¼m; dam stakes-placed winner; won Duke of Edinburgh Stakes at Ascot in October by 1½ lengths from Ski Sailing; had little to beat in 2 minor events at Doncaster subsequently, and won easily both times; should stay 1¼m; acts on heavy going; a smart performer in the making, and sure to win more races. *G. Harwood.*

NORTHERN BEAU 2 b.c. North Stoke 130–Beaume (Faraway Son 130) **70** (1982 8d 8g 10s[3]) Mar 25; 10,500Y; lengthy colt; second foal; dam unraced granddaughter of 1,000 Guineas and Oaks winner Sweet Solera; apparently still not fully wound up, finished strongly when 4½ lengths third of 17 behind Captain Webster in maiden race at Nottingham in October; will stay 1½m; acts on soft going. *J. Hindley.*

NORTHERN BREEZE 2 br.f. Persian Breeze 121–Quartette Royale 65 — (Jukebox 120) (1982 5fg) Mar 17; small filly; first foal; placed over 5f at 2 yrs; last of 9 in seller at Beverley in June; dead. *M. W. Easterby.*

NORTHERN CONQUEST (USA) 3 b.g. Far North 120–Easy Conquest — (Royal Charger) (1981 NR 1982 8f) $28,000Y; half-brother to several winners, including stakes-placed Expletive Deleted (by Cornish Prince); dam ran only twice; 7/1, started slowly and always behind when eleventh of 15 to Falcon's Heir in maiden race at Beverley in May; sold to L. Barratt 1,500 gns Newmarket Autumn Sales. *F. Durr.*

NORTHERN ECLIPSE 5 b.h. Derring-Do 131–Haunting Melody 96 (Sing **59** Sing 134) (1981 5g[2] 5g 5f[4] 6g 5g* 1982 6d 5d 5f 5fg[2] 5f 5f 6g) leggy, fair sort; best at 5f; acts well on firm going; has run well for an apprentice; trained first 2 outings by N. Mitchell; sent to race in Belgium and won there. *D. Garraton.*

NORTHERN FASHION (USA) 2 b.c. Northern Dancer–Fashionable Trick **114** (Buckpasser) (1982 8f[2] 7.5v[2]) Apr 12; third foal; half-brother to 1981 American 2-y-o 8.5f stakes winner House Speaker (by King Pellinore); dam unraced daughter of smart 1962 2-y-o sprint stakes winner Fashion Verdict; finished well when neck second of 5 to Allverton in newcomers race at Longchamp in September; had none too clear a run when head second of 6 to Dal des Fnoo in Prix Thomas Byron at Saint-Cloud the following month; will stay 1¼m; very useful and is sure to win races. *J. Fellows, France.*

NORTHERN INTEREST 3 gr.c. My Swanee 122–Frisky Molly 64 (Dumbarnie 125) (1981 7fg 1982 7fg 8fg 8g 8g 7g[4] 8g 7f 8g 7d) lightly-made colt; poor mover; plater; stays 1m; blinkered nowadays. *M. Tompkins.*

Duke of Edinburgh Stakes, Ascot—Northern Adventure makes a fine start to his career

NORTHERN RELISH 3 br.g. Relko 136–Northern Lady 95 (The Brianstan — 128) (1981 7f 1982 12d 10fg 10d 10fg 12g 12d) big gelding; little worthwhile form in varied company, including selling; looked ungenuine final start. *P. Calver.*

NORTHERN REPORT 3 b.g. Northern Flash–Last Report 96 (Democratic — 124) (1981 NR 1982 7f 7fg 8fg 8f⁴ 8.5f 8d 8.3fg 10s) small, strong gelding; good mover; plater; stays 1m; trained part of season by D. Kent; sold 600 gns Doncaster November Sales. *P. Haynes.*

NORTHERN SCRIPT (USA) 2 br.f. Arts and Letters–My Nord (Vent du **90** Nord) (1982 5f 8fg² 7s³) Mar 2; $180,000Y; quite attractive, lengthy filly; third foal; dam won 2 sprint claiming races; having first outing for 3 months, stayed on nicely when 1½ lengths second of 12 to Ghaiya in £3,600 event at Goodwood in September; creditable 1¾ lengths third of 11 to New Coins in similar race at York the following month; will stay middle distances; probably acts on any going; sure to win a race. *J. Tree.*

NORTHERN SECRET (USA) 2 ch.c. Northern Jove–Clandestly (Clandestine) **109** (1982 6fg² 6g* 7f* 8s) Mar 30; $30,000Y, $60,000 2-y-o; rangy, full-quartered, good sort; half-brother to several winners, notably Secret Lanvin (by Lanvin), a very useful stakes winner at up to 1m; dam never ran; won minor event at Newcastle in August and Grand Criterium International d'Ostende (beating Arrowood Bob ½ length) later in the month; little out of his depth in Royal Lodge Stakes at Ascot in September; should stay 1m; acts on firm going. *M. Jarvis.*

NORTHERN TRIAL 2 ch.c. North Stoke 130–Bare Costs (Petition 130) **76 ?** (1982 5f 5g 7fg) May 22; 9,000Y; rangy colt; half-brother to several winners, notably high-class 6f to 1m winner Record Token (by Jukebox); dam unraced sister to dam of very smart Delmora; unplaced, but not discredited, in good-class races won by Krayyan, Cat O'Nine Tails and Gorytus; may be capable of some improvement. *P. Kelleway.*

NORTHERN TRIP 2 ch.c. North Stoke 130–Tripoli 70 (Great Heron 127) **76** (1982 7fg 8fg 7fg³) Apr 4; IR 16,000Y; tall, close-coupled, quite attractive colt; second living foal; dam lightly raced; second favourite, kept on well when 4½ lengths third of 26 behind Zaheendar in maiden race at Redcar in September; will stay 1¼m. *G. Harwood.*

NORTHGATE LODGE 4 b.g. Warpath 113–Pall Nan 86 (Pall Mall 132) (1981 — 16.5fg* 15.8fg 18f 1982 16fg) leggy gelding; no form in handicaps since winning maiden race as a 3-y-o, but has had stiff tasks; stays well; acts on a firm surface; sold 650 gns Doncaster August Sales. *M. H. Easterby.*

NORTH KEY 2 ch.g. North Stoke 130–Pukekohe (Larkspur 128) (1982 **64** 7g 7fg 8.2fg) Apr 21; 7,400F, 8,000Y, 7,000 2-y-o; good-topped gelding; not a good walker; half-brother to a winner in USA; dam lightly-raced half-sister to very useful animals April Bloom and Rare Gold; little worthwhile form in varied company; gelded after final outing. *M. Naughton.*

NORTH LADY 2 b.f. Northfields–Larosterna (Busted 134) (1982 6g 7g) — Feb 18; 16,000Y; small filly; first foal; dam unraced daughter of Molecomb Stakes winner Lowna; backward, behind in 2 autumn maiden races at Newmarket. *P. Haslam.*

NORTHLEIGH 3 ch.c. Reform 132–Sarsgrove 70 (Hornbeam 130) (1981 **87** 6fg 6fg³ 7g* 7d² 7d 7d² 1982 7g 8fg 8f⁴ 8d 8s³ 8g) quite attractive, well-made colt; has a round action; fair handicapper; will be very well suited by 1¼m+; suited by some give in the ground; blinkered last 2 starts; sold to BBA (Italia) 10,000 gns Newmarket Autumn Sales. *J. Dunlop.*

NORTH LIGHT 3 b.c. Northern Flash–Shortigal (Galivanter 131) (1981 7g — 1982 8fg 10f 8g⁴ 8f⁴ 10.1fg 10fg) strong colt; plating-class maiden; should stay 1¼m; sold to W. A. Stephenson 1,700 gns Newmarket Autumn Sales. *P. Walwyn.*

NORTHORPE 3 b.g. Mummy's Pet 125–Jaragua (Flaneur 109§) (1981 6f² **83** 6f 6g 1982 6g 7f³ 6g⁴ 6fg* 6fg 6d⁴ 6g² 6fg* 6g 6g* 6g 6g³ 6g 6s) big, rangy gelding; poor walker; won maiden race at Ayr and handicaps at Ripon and Nottingham (apprentices); best at 6f; seems to act on any going but goes well on fast ground; sometimes sweats up. *G. Huffer.*

NORTH STOKE BOY 2 b.c. North Stoke 130–My Grace (Sahib 114) (1982 — 5.8f 5fg 6g 7fg) May 23; 3,000Y; lengthy colt; third foal; dam won in Norway; no worthwhile form in maiden and minor events. *K. Cunningham-Brown.*

NORTH WEST   7 ch.g. Welsh Pageant 132–Heather Grove (Hethersett 134)   **53**
(1981 15.5d* 16g² 15.5d³ 13.3g² 12f 15.5fg* 16fg² 16.5f* 16fg   1982 12d 15.5g*
15.5fg² 18f² 16fg 15.5f³ 14fg⁴ 16.5f)   tall, short-backed gelding; staying handicapper; goes well at Folkestone and won there in April; seems to act on any
going; used to wear bandages; genuine and consistent.   *M. Masson.*

NORTON CROSS   4 gr.g. Realm 129–Zameen (Armistice 131)   (1981 5s   —
7d⁴ 8g*(dis) 8g* 10d⁴ 8f 8s   1982 8f)   sturdy gelding; good mover; modest
handicapper; below his best only outing of 1982 (May); probably stays 1¼m;
possibly needs some give in the ground; does best when ridden up with pace.
M. H. Easterby.

NORWICK (USA)   3 b.c. Far North 120–Shay Sheery (A Dragon Killer)   (1981 **120**
5g⁴ 5.8g* 6fg* 6f* 7.2f* 7fg² 8s* 8s² 8g⁴   1982 8g 12fg 12f 12f 11g² 10.5fg²
14.6f⁴ 12v⁴(dis))
        The British climate usually provides ample opportunities each season for
horses that require some give in the ground to show their best form.   The unusually dry summer in 1982, resulting in a long period of firm going, must have
been frustrating for the connections of Norwick and others like him.   Norwick's
victory in the Royal Lodge Stakes as a two-year-old had shown him to be well
suited by the distance of a mile, the longest he had tackled up to that time
and also by the soft ground which he met for the first time; forcing tactics were
employed in the Royal Lodge and subsequently in the Grand Criterium (in
which Norwick finished second to Green Forest) and the William Hill Futurity
(in which Norwick came fourth).   Except on his final outing in the Preis von
Europa at Cologne, where he hung badly and was disqualified after finishing
fourth, Norwick encountered top-of-the-ground conditions in all his races as a
three-year-old.   He acts on firm going but such conditions highlight his lack of
a decent turn of finishing speed; other things being equal, soft ground favours
the one-pacer because it takes the edge off the speed of his opponents.   Norwick
ran his best races when fifth in the Derby, second in the Benson and Hedges
Gold Cup and fourth in the St Leger, all of which were run at a hot pace throughout.   Starkey's handling of Norwick in the Derby was a particularly fine example

Mr J. E. Bodie's "Norwick" (G. Starkey)

of vigorous, opportunist jockeyship: never far behind, he sent Norwick to the front soon after Tattenham Corner, driving him along for all he was worth, a move which for most of the length of the straight looked as if it would secure Norwick at least a place. Somewhat surprisingly in the light of his subsequent performance in the St Leger, Norwick gave the impression in the closing stages of the Derby that he barely got the mile and a half. However, his six-length second to Assert in the Benson and Hedges Gold Cup over ten and a half furlongs was probably at least as good as any of his other form as a three-year-old and we shouldn't be surprised to see him campaigned mainly at around that distance as a four-year-old; ridden with more restraint than usual, he never posed a serious threat to the front-running Assert at York but held off the four-year-old Amyndas by a neck and had Castle Keep, Mr Fluorocarbon, Be My Native and Say Primula further behind. Norwick gained his only other placing in the Mecca Bookmakers Scottish Derby at Ayr in July when Jalmood, who gave him 6 lb, came from behind to beat him by two lengths in a small field.

				Nearctic
Norwick (USA) (b.c. 1979)	Far North (b 1973)	Northern Dancer (b 1961)		Natalma
		Fleur (b 1964)	Victoria Park	
				Flaming Page
	Shay Sheery (b or br 1969)	A Dragon Killer (b 1955)		Roman Scandal
				Lutza
		Annie K. (b 1963)		Jester
				Sic Sic

A smallish, well-made, good-looking colt, Norwick is not the best of movers and has rather a sharp action, not the type usually associated with the stayer. Norwick's sire Far North, a full brother to The Minstrel, apparently stayed a mile and a half—he finished fifth in the Irish Sweeps Derby in his only race at the trip—but Norwick's dam gained her four victories over sprint distances and her two foals before Norwick, Irish Amy (by O'Hara) and On The Phone (by Selari), both minor winners, showed speed in excess of stamina, neither being successful at distances longer than nine furlongs. A tough and genuine colt, Norwick would be aimed initially at the Westbury Stakes and the Brigadier Gerard Stakes as a four-year-old if he were ours: winners of pattern races after 1981 are penalized in both; and the races are run at Sandown, a galloping track very much against the collar in the last half mile or so which would suit Norwick's style of racing admirably. Out in front, setting a strong pace, he could run very well, especially given a soft surface to race on. *G. Harwood.*

NO SALE 3 b.c. Nonoalco 131–Salote 109 (Forli) (1981 7fg 8d 1982 10.1d 10.1fg 11.7f 10v 10.8s) neat, well-made, attractive colt; poor maiden; sold out of R. Hern's stable 3,600 gns Ascot August Sales after third start. *R. Atkins.* **57**

NOSEY'S DAUGHTER 3 b.f. Song 132–Roman Nose 95 (Nosca) (1981 5d 6fg 1982 5g) poor maiden. *J. Holt.* **—**

NOSTER PUER (USA) 2 ch.g. Quid Pro Quo–Rose Cloud (Toulouse Lautrec) (1982 7d3 7g2 7fg) Mar 19; $20,000Y; rangy gelding; brother to 2 minor winners; dam won 6f maiden race at 2 yrs; placed in maiden races at Salisbury in June and Sandown in July; got rather stirred up and gave a lot of trouble at stalls at Ascot later in July, and was subsequently gelded; will stay 1¼m. *D. Elsworth.* **86**

NOT A MURMER 4 br.f. Murrayfield 119–Lost in Silence (Silent Spring 102) (1981 NR 1982 8g) first living foal; dam never ran; soon well behind when tailed off in apprentice race at Bath in July. *J. Old.* **—**

NOT AT HOME 3 gr.f. Homeric 133–Desert Nymph (Silver Shark 129) (1981 7d 7g4 1982 8g4) small, lengthy filly; good walker; lightly raced but has definite ability as she showed on only outing at 3 yrs in May when finishing well after being outpaced to be under 6 lengths fourth of 7 to Chalon in International Fillies Stakes at Kempton; will be suited by 1¼m. *R. Hern.* **—**

NOT FOR SHOW 3 b.c. Mummy's Pet 125–Emperor Star (King Emperor) (1981 6g* 7g* 1982 7fg 6fg4 6f* 6f 6f 6f) rangy, good-looking colt; carries plenty of condition; good walker and mover; ran on strongly to beat Vaigly Star by 1¼ lengths in 8-runner Gus Demmy Memorial Stakes at Haydock in May; put up best subsequent effort on fifth start when seventh of 16 to Sharpo in William Hill Cup at Newmarket; stays 7f; yet to race on a soft surface; sold to BBA 17,000 gns Newmarket December Sales and sent to India. *G. Harwood.* **111**

NOTHING BLUE (USA) 2 ch.c. Cyane–Rienza (Graustark) (1982 6f* 7.2f2) Mar 10; $250,000Y; attractive colt; good walker and mover; first foal; dam, **93**

608

granddaughter of excellent broodmare Juliets Nurse, won 4 sprint races; disputed lead throughout with odds-on Market Royal in 4-runner maiden race at Yarmouth in August and prevailed by a head after his rival broke down in final furlong; creditable second to Game Dame in nursery at Haydock the following month; will stay 1m. *H. T. Jones.*

NOTRE FLEUR 2 br.f. Mummy's Pet 125–Sicalaine 52 (Sica Boy 132) (1982 5f 5f 6g) May 7; lengthy, useful-looking filly; half-sister to a winning plater; dam placed at up to 1m; soundly beaten in maiden races at Thirsk (2) and Catterick in the summer. *J. Fitzgerald.*   —

NOT TO WORRY (USA) 2 b.f. Stevward–Lovely Barbizon (Barbizon) (1982 7g 6d) 2-y-o; second foal; dam stakes-placed winner at up to 7f; well beaten at Yarmouth and Pontefract in the autumn. *B. Hanbury.*   —

NOUMAYR 3 b.c. Mount Hagen 127–Noureen (Astec 128) (1981 5fg 7fg 7d* 7g 8d 1982 8d³ 8g³ 10.6fg) compact, quite attractive colt; third in handicaps at Salisbury and Newbury in April; cracked a bone in a leg in similar event at Haydock in May; would have stayed 1¼m; needed some give in the ground; dead. *F. J. Houghton.*   **84**

NOUR EL HAYAT 2 ch.f. Monseigneur 127–Metrovision (Golden Vision 105) (1982 6g 7g 7d² 8fg 7s) Apr 24; 8,200Y; good-bodied filly; half-sister to several winners, including Ebor winner Anji (by Gulf Pearl); dam poor middle-distance maiden; 1½ lengths second of 11 finishers behind Molokai in maiden race at Ayr in September, best effort; saddle slipped on next outing; will stay 1m; sent to France. *S. Norton.*   **77**

NOURIYYA 2 b.f. North Stoke 130–Noureen (Astec 128) (1982 5fg 5fg 6fg 7g 8.2s) Mar 18; small, fair sort; third foal; half-sister to 2 winners, including very useful 5f to 1m winner Nasseem (by Zeddaan); dam unraced half-sister to very smart Tajubena, a winner at up to 1⅓m; quite a moderate maiden; should stay 1¼m; acts on a firm surface. *F. J. Houghton.*   **72**

NO-U-TURN 4 b.g. Nonoalco 131–Raffmarie 78 (Raffingora 130) (1981 7g 8f³ 8f 10f 10fg 10f² 10.4s 10fg² 10d 11d 12g 10s* 1982 10.2g 12fg² 9fg* 12f² 10fg³ 8g³ 10fg 8g 10fg⁴ 9g 10g² 12fg³ 10d) attractive, well-made gelding; in frame most starts and landed odds by a neck from Summary in amateur riders handicap at Ripon in May (always going well but tended to idle in front); stays 1½m; acts on any going. *S. Mellor.*   **68**

NOW AND AGAIN (USA) 2 b.c. Ack Ack–My Violet (Warfare) (1982 6f* 7g* 8s³) Mar 20; $109,000Y; tall, quite attractive colt; excellent mover;   **109**

Gilbey Champion Racehorse Futurity, York—Now and Again (right)
rallies bravely to beat Goodbye Shelley (blinkers) and Special Leave

half-brother to 7f winner Killanin's Lass (by Olympiad King) and a winner in USA; dam won 1m maiden race; gave strong impression of being somewhat immature; nevertheless won his first 2 races, maiden event at Nottingham in August and 5-runner Gilbey Champion Racehorse Futurity (beating Goodbye Shelley and Special Leave in excellent finish) at York in September; struggling from 3f out (possibly not suited by the soft ground) when third of 9 behind easy winner Proclaim in minor event at Goodwood later in September; should stay 1m; sure to win more races. *H. Cecil.*

NOW GERALDINE 2 ch.f. Tarboosh–Estee Lauder (Petingo 135) (1982 5f **75** 5f 5fg 5f 6f² 5g 5d) Feb 29; smallish filly; second foal; dam poor Irish maiden; moderate filly; 1¼ lengths second to Indian Giver under 7-7 in 8-runner nursery at Naas in August; fifteenth of 16 to Widaad in Queen Mary Stakes at Royal Ascot in June on third outing; should stay beyond 6f; acts on firm going (ran poorly on dead); blinkered fourth and final starts. *P. Canty, Ireland.*

NUAGES 2 ch.c. Sallust 134–Arenaria 102 (Aureole 132) (1982 7s) Mar 8; **—** 33,000Y; lengthy colt; half-brother to several winners, notably very useful 7f to 1¼m performer Redesdale (by Bold Lad, Ire); dam, winner at 7f and 1m, is closely related to Parnell and Miralgo; 20/1, no show in 28-runner maiden race at Redcar in October. *F. Durr.*

NUDGE NUDGE 2 br.g. Windjammer (USA)–Veneziana 91 (Tiger 125) (1982 6d 6g 7d) Mar 22; 7,400Y; neat gelding; brother to disappointing Venetian Joy and useful 1977 2-y-o 6f to 1m winner Sicalu, subsequently a good winner in Norway; dam stayed 1¼m; little worthwhile form in maiden and minor events; not seen out after August. *S. Mellor.*

NULLAH 3 b.f. Riverman 131–Tuck In (Princequillo) (1981 NR 1982 10h³) **71** half-sister to 3 winners, including Bolide (by Bold Lad, Ire), a smart winner at up to 1¼m; dam never ran; easy in market when 4 lengths third of 16 to Off The Reel in maiden race at Chepstow in June; not seen out again; will stay 1½m. *R. Hern.*

NUMERATE 3 b.g. Paddy's Stream 80–Flying Music (Little Buskins 119) **—** (1981 NR 1982 13d 8.2s) IR 840Y; good-bodied gelding; good walker; first foal; dam never ran; well beaten in minor event at Ayr and maiden race at Haydock in the autumn. *R. Fisher.*

NUMISMATIST 3 b.g. Vitiges 132–Mile By Mile 92 (Milesian 125) (1981 NR **62** 1982 7.6f 8fg 8d 8f³ 8fg⁴ 9g 7fg⁴ 10fg² 11.7s) IR 8,200Y; lengthy, attractive gelding; half-brother to fairly useful 1977 2-y-o 5f winner Speedometer (by Sharp Edge); dam won over 6f at 2 yrs; showed a little ability in maiden races; stays 1¼m; blinkered fifth and sixth starts; sold to J. Bosley 5,200 gns Newmarket Autumn Sales. *J. Dunlop.*

NUNSWOOD 2 ch.c. Solinus 130–Cafe au Lait 98 (Espresso 122) (1982 5g **80** 7fg 8g) Apr 15; 14,500Y; good-topped colt; half-brother to several winners, including fairly useful stayer Brando (by Busted); dam stayed 1¼m; 8½ lengths ninth of 21 behind Polished Silver in £4,200 event at Newbury in September, final outing and best effort; suited by 1m. *P. Cole.*

NUROSE 7 ch.g. Tobrouk–Gondolina (Aggressor 130) (1981 12s 1982 12f **—** 10g) poor middle-distance handicapper; seems to act on any going; has worn bandages; usually blinkered; finished lame when last in seller final start. *A. Hide.*

NYPUS 2 b.c. Lypheor 119–Lady Kyth (Kythnos 126) (1982 6f 7fg 6s 7g⁴ 7g 10g) **78** Apr 2; IR 5,600Y; smallish colt; half-brother to several winners here and abroad, including useful Irish 1m winner Lady North (by Northfields); dam stayed 1½m; 4 lengths fourth of 13 to Rana Pratap in minor event at Brighton in September, best effort; will stay 1m. *D. Wilson.*

O

O AGAPITOS MOU 2 b.c. High Top 131–Princess Anglaise (Crepello 136) **—** (1982 6fg 10s) Apr 12; second foal; half-brother to a minor winner in France by Run The Gantlet; dam unraced half-sister to Irish Sweeps Derby winner English Prince; behind in newcomers race at Chepstow in August and maiden event (tailed off) at Nottingham in October. *T. Marshall.*

OAKAPPLE 3 ch.f. Connaught 130–Syringa 98 (Set Fair 129) (1981 NR 1982 **77** 8d³ 12fg 10d* 11s² 14g) strong filly; half-sister to several winners, including quite useful 1968 2-y-o 5f winner Galtonia (by Galivanter); dam stayed 1½m; won minor event at Ayr in September; ran creditably in similar event at Hamilton later in month; should stay 1½m+; suited by some give in the ground. *J. W. Watts.*

OAKERTHORPE LAD 3 ch.g. Abwah 118–Wordellow (Yellow God 129) — (1981 NR 1982 10.1d 8f) small, lightly-made gelding; well beaten in 2 sellers, gave trouble at start once; dead. *A. Madwar.*

OAK RUN 2 br.g. Wolfsbane 91–Precious Love (Precipice Wood 123) (1982 5g 7d) first live foal; dam never ran; in rear in small race at Wolverhampton in August and maiden event at Leicester in September. *J. Smith.*

OBADIAH 3 b. or br.c. Joshua 129–Ripatip 68 (Indigenous 121) (1981 6f 6fg 7f 7g 7g 1982 8g 10fg 11.5fg) big, rangy colt; bad mover; poor maiden. *H. Westbrook.*

OCEAN DREAM 3 ch.g. Meldrum 112–Bon Feu 75 (Blason 109) (1981 7g 8d — 1982 12f) strong gelding; poor plater. *Mrs A. Cousins.*

OCH AYE 4 br.f. Lochnager 132–Daisy Knot 81 (Acer 123) (1981 7d 9d 8.5fg 7d² 7g³ 7d 8d 1982 7f 7f 6fg³ 7fg 6s 10fg 5.8f 7g 8fg) big filly; mainly poor form at 4 yrs; stays 7f and wasn't disgraced over 9f; sold out of J. Bethell's stable 1,800 gns Ascot 2nd June Sales after fifth outing. *C. Wildman.*

OCHIL HILLS STAR 9 b.g. Chebs Lad 120–Turkish Maid 58 (Menelek 114) **33** (1981 8v 7g 8.2d 8g* 9fg 1982 8s 11s 11fg 8fg* 8g 8f 7g) plater; attracted no bid after winning poor race at Edinburgh in May; stays 1¼m; acts on any going; has been tried in blinkers; good mount for an inexperienced rider. *Mrs A. Bell.*

OCTAVIA GIRL 2 b.f. Octavo 115–Jane Shaw (Galivanter 131) (1982 6fg* **104** 6fg³ 7fg³ 8g 8g) Feb 13; IR 4,300F, 9,800Y; sturdy filly; half-sister to several winners, including fairly useful 6f and 7f winner Priory Lane (by Martinmas); dam poor maiden; finished very strongly to win 14-runner Fenwolf Stakes (valuable newcomers race) at Ascot in June by a neck from Rare Roberta; ran well afterwards in good-class fillies races, on third and fourth outings finishing 5 lengths third of 9 to Flamenco in Waterford Candelabra Stakes at Goodwood in August and 6 lengths fifth of 8 to Bright Crocus in May Hill Stakes at Doncaster in September; stays 1m; yet to race on a soft surface. *D. Elsworth.*

OCTOBER GIRL 3 gr or ro.f. Roan Rocket 128–Alumina 86 (Fortino II 120) — (1981 NR 1982 10g 10.4d 6d) 10,000Y; third living produce; half-sister to 7f winner That's Magic (by Bay Express); dam miler; behind in maiden races. *J. Toller.*

OFF THE CUFF 2 b.c. The Brianstan 128–Mystic Halo (Aureole 132) (1982 **77** 5g² 5fg³ 6fg 6g 5fg⁴) Mar 29; 10,500Y; fair sort; fourth foal; brother to 1981 2-y-o 5f winner Sy Oui; dam of no account; in frame in maiden and minor events; form only at 5f. *I. Walker.*

OFF THE HOOK (USA) 3 b.c. Full Out–Incommunicado (Double Jay) (1981 **102** 6g² 7fg 8fg² 7f² 6fg 6f* 6f* 6fg² 6f* 6fg* 6g² 6g²) rangy, good-looking colt; developed into a useful performer, winning maiden race at Folkestone, minor event at Brighton (odds on both times) and handicaps at Pontefract and Goodwood; ridden by 7-lb claimer when making all to beat Roman Ruler a head on last-named; good second afterwards in handicaps at Newmarket won by Purnima and Vorvados; best at distances short of 1m; acts on firm going; usually sweats up and also went very freely to post first 2 starts; consistent; sent to USA to be trained by E. Gregson. *G. Harwood.*

OFF THE REEL (USA) 3 b.f. Silent Screen–Harbour Queen (Young Emperor **81** 133) (1981 6g 6g 1982 8g² 8fg⁴ 10h* 11fg 10f* 10f* 10g) big filly; won maiden race at Chepstow in June and handicaps at Pontefract in July and Yarmouth in August; suited by 1¼m; acts on hard going; has won for an apprentice; sold 16,000 gns Newmarket December Sales. *J. Hindley.*

OFFUN 2 ch.f. Octavo 115–Fun (Jukebox 120) (1982 5fg 6fg 5g) Apr 16; IR 1,600Y, 2,500 2-y-o (privately); lightly-made filly; second foal; dam last on only outing; of no account; exported to Algeria. *N. Callaghan.*

OFF YOUR MARK 2 ch.c. On Your Mark 125–Sparkling Diamond (Thirteen **63** of Diamonds 126) (1982 5g⁴ 5f³ 6d) Apr 20; IR 9,600Y; lightly-made colt; half-brother to 3 winners in Ireland, including quite useful stayer Diomedes (by Boreen); dam won over 5f and 1½m in Ireland; plating-class maiden; not raced after June. *J. Mason.*

OH SUGAR 2 b.f. Monseigneur 127–Rogan Honey (Abernant 142) (1982 5fg 6g 7fg) May 17; IR 2,500F, 3,200Y; half-sister to several winners, including fairly useful 6f to 7.6f winner Honey Barron (by Pitcairn); dam placed over sprint distances at 2 yrs in Ireland; soundly beaten in maiden and minor events; not raced after August. *K. Brassey.* —

O. I. OYSTON 6 b.g. Martinmas 128–Last Lap 75 (Immortality) (1981 6v 7s 7.2s 7g 10.6g 7.6fg 8f⁴ 9g³ 8f 7.6s* 7d 7.2v⁴ 7v³ 7g 1982 8g* 7.2s 7.6g 8g 8d 7.6fg 13g 8f⁴ 7.6d* 8f 8fg 7.2s 8.2s⁴ 7d³ 7g* 7d² 8s*) leggy gelding; a tough old character who won at Doncaster at first and last meetings of the season (apprentice event on former occasion) and at Chester (for third successive year) and Edinburgh in between; stays 9f; acts on any going, but is very well suited by some give underfoot; has worn blinkers but is better without; suited by front-running tactics, but has occasionally gone too fast for his own good; ideally suited by a turning track. *J. Berry.* **85**

OKAVANGA GIRL 3 gr.f. Three Legs 128–Rolling Seasons (Road House II) (1981 NR 1982 15.5v⁴) 2,600Y; fourth living foal; dam Irish 2-y-o 5f winner; over 4 lengths fourth of 8 to Scot Bennett in seller at Folkestone in October; sold 700 gns Newmarket Autumn Sales and sent to Holland. *J. Toller.* —

OKLAHOMA CITY 3 b. or br.c. Tachypous 128–Exeat (Quartette 106) (1981 NR 1982 6f⁴) second foal; half-brother to fairly useful 7f winner Singwara (by Blue Cashmere); dam well beaten on flat and over hurdles; tailed-off last of 4 to Off The Hook in minor event at Brighton in August; will need further. *R. Simpson.* —

OLD COUNTRY 3 b.c. Quiet Fling 124–Little Miss 92 (Aggressor 130) (1981 7f² 7fg* 7d³ 1982 12fg* 12v* 12f³) **121**
The Italian turf authorities, who formerly gave a large measure of protection to Italian-bred horses in pattern races, have now opened all but a handful of their major races to international competition. This long-overdue change—which the Germans, who restrict about a third of their pattern races to home-breds, should also adopt—has led to a rise in the status of Italy's top races. The last two runnings of the Derby Italiano have been won by very good British-bred colts, Glint of Gold and Old Country, the latter providing trainer Cumani with his first success in a Group 1 pattern race, appropriately in the land of his birth. Old Country followed the path to Rome taken by Glint of Gold, winning the Warren Stakes at Epsom's spring meeting. The Warren Stakes second and third, Yard Bird and Rajhaan, neither of whom enjoyed the best of runs at Epsom, were also sent for the Derby Italiano but Old Country beat them and the nine home-trained runners most decisively, running on strongly after taking over from Yard Bird in the straight to win by three lengths from the British-bred Teofane with Bater two lengths away third; Yard Bird came fourth and Rajhaan sixth.

Conditions for the Derby Italiano were extremely testing—Old Country's connections reportedly considered withdrawing him on the morning of the race—but they were near the other extreme for Royal Ascot's King Edward VII Stakes which was a somewhat surprising choice for Old Country's next race. As a winner of a Group 1 race Old Country was penalized 10 lb and he appeared to be set a very stiff task indeed, especially as all his rivals bar Electric, including the Derby fifth Norwick, carried the minimum weight. Old Country ran a tremendous race, surpassing his performance in the Derby Italiano, to finish third, beaten three quarters of a length and the same by Open Day and Lords. What's more he looked unlucky, finishing very strongly after being short of room and having to be checked at one point in the straight. We marked down Old Country as a natural for the St Leger: his pedigree and the way he'd finished in all his races as a three-year-old put his ability to stay a mile and three quarters at racing pace beyond question; he possessed a reasonable turn of foot, a highly desirable attribute in a high-class stayer, and the going at Doncaster was most unlikely to be a decisive factor since he had shown good form on heavy and very firm. Unfortunately, nothing went right for him afterwards. He contracted bronchitis a week before York's August meeting and had to miss the Great Voltigeur Stakes, his intended preparatory race for Doncaster. Soon after resuming training Old Country was found to have a high white cell count and it was decided not to risk him in the St Leger.

Old Country stays in training and, assuming he recovers full health, he is just the lightly-raced, progressive type one would expect to continue to train on. Planning a suitable campaign for him is going to present problems though. His Derby Italiano success means that he will have to concede weight to almost

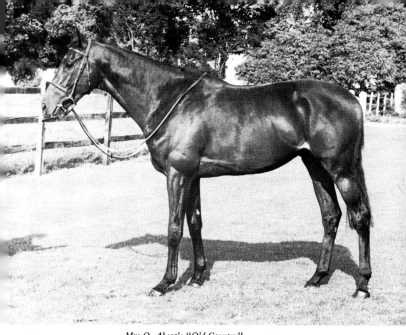

Mrs O. Abegg's "Old Country"

all his rivals in Group 2 and Group 3 pattern races. What's more, the lack of balance in the pattern of racing means, almost inevitably, that he will be campaigned in the big mile-and-a-half races, in spite of giving the overwhelming impression as a three year old that he would be a better proposition, especially with another year on him, at a mile and three quarters than at a mile and a half. That said, we shall be surprised if he fails to enhance his reputation, particularly if he gets soft ground and a strong gallop, conditions which would bring his stamina into play.

Old Country (b.c. 1979)	Quiet Fling (b 1972)	Nijinsky (b 1967)	Northern Dancer
			Flaming Page
		Peace (ch 1966)	Klairon
			Sun Rose
	Little Miss (b 1963)	Aggressor (b 1955)	Combat
			Phaetonia
		Violetta III (b 1958)	Pinza
			Urshalim

A tall colt, and a good mover in all his paces with a long, sweeping action, Old Country is from the first crop of Quiet Fling, a Coronation Cup winner and a good-class horse over a distance of ground; Quiet Fling began his stud career in England but now stands at Mint Lane Farm, Kentucky. Old Country is bred on the same lines as the very smart brothers Bright Finish and Shining Finish who were by Quiet Fling's sire Nijinsky out of Lacquer, a daughter of Old Country's third dam Urshalim; Bright Finish was a stayer who gained his most important victories on a soft surface, as did Shining Finish who was best at a mile and a half. Bright Finish, Shining Finish and Old Country are among a seemingly-endless stream of winners produced in the past thirty years by descendants of Horama, the famous foundation mare of the Moller brothers' White Lodge Stud. Speed has been the dominant characteristic of most of Horama's descendants including Urshalim and her illustrious daughters Lacquer, Sovereign and Violetta III. Old Country's dam Little Miss was Violetta's first foal. Little Miss was a fairly useful racemare, winner of a mile-and-a-half maiden event at Catterick and mile-and-a-quarter handicaps at Windsor and Beverley in her only season to race, but she was small and fetched only 1,200 guineas at the Newmarket December Sales as a three-year-old. When Little Miss next appeared in the sale-ring, as an eight-year-old, she made 10,000 guineas, her half-sister Favoletta having won that season's Irish One Thousand Guineas. Violetta maintained the family tradition by breeding an Oaks runner-up, Furioso, three years later but Little Miss realized only 2,000 guineas, in foal to Balliol, when sent to the sales again that year. Old Country, who fetched 13,500 guineas as a foal and 20,000 guineas when submitted again as a yearling, is easily the best of the five flat-race winners bred by Little Miss, all of whom have won at a mile and half, including Queen of the Brush and Sheba's Glory, both of whom are by Averof whose best performances were at a mile. *L. Cumani.*

OLD DOMINION (USA) 5 b.g. In Reality–Virginia Green 83 (Nashua) **92** (1981 6s 6fg⁴ 6g⁴ 6s⁴ 6g* 5.8d² 6f³ 6fg 6fg 5.6fg 6g 6v 1982 6d 6fg³ 6fg⁴ 6fg² 6g 6f² 5.8f* 6fg* 6f² 6g 5fg² 6g⁴ 6g) strong, good sort; good mover; fairly useful handicapper; won at Bath in June (£3,500 event) and Newcastle in July, putting up an excellent performance when beating In Rhythm in good style by 4 lengths in apprentice race on latter course; suited by 6f and may well stay further; acts on any going; genuine and consistent. *I. Balding.*

OLD JOCUS 3 b. or br.c. Comedy Star 121–Archaic 65 (Relic) (1981 7.6s⁴ — 7d 1982 7g 7s 8s 8s) tall colt; ran respectably in maiden race at Lingfield on debut at 2 yrs but has been soundly beaten all subsequent starts; will be suited by further; often bandaged in front. *D. Elsworth.*

OLD KNOCKER 6 b.h. Mummy's Pet 125–The Keys 71 (Major Portion 129) **51** (1981 11s 10fg² 10f 11.7g² 10fg 11.7g³ 12d 1982 10d 12f³ 12f⁴ 10.6g⁴) attractive horse; middle-distance handicapper; acts on any going, except perhaps very soft; usually wears blinkers; often sweats up; suitable mount for a boy; has worn bandages; inconsistent. *R. Laing.*

OL DONYO 5 b.h. Nonoalco 131–Limuru 83 (Alcide 136) (1981 NR 1982 10f — 8g 12g 12f 12g 12.3g 12d) 74,000Y; big horse; brother to useful Scandinavian filly Nonoartica and half-brother to 5 winners, including Derby runner-up Cavo Doro (by Sir Ivor); dam 1m to 1¼m handicapper; behind in varied company, including an amateur riders event; still looked burly sixth start; blinkered final outing. *D. Leslie.*

OLD ROWLEY 4 b.c. Copte–Cennen-Olive (Wolver Hollow 126) (1981 7g — 8g 1982 12d 12g³ 12f 15.5f) narrow colt; poor maiden; should stay beyond 1½m. *Mrs J. Pitman.*

OLE FAITHFUL 3 bl.g. Warpath 113–Truly Yours 93 (So Blessed 130) (1981 **59** 6g 7f 1982 8g 11g 8g 10fg* 12f² 12g³) lengthy, sparely-made gelding; good walker; plater; attracted no bid after winning at Ayr in July; stays 1½m; yet to race on a soft surface. *C. Thornton.*

OLOVO 3 gr.g. Nonoalco 131–Courting (Quorum 126) (1981 NR 1982 7fg 8g — 12g) IR 21,000Y, 1,400 2-y-o; big, strong, workmanlike gelding; behind in varied company, including claiming; wears blinkers and has also worn a hood; sold out of I. Walker's stable 740 gns Newmarket July Sales after second start. *M. Chapman.*

OLYMPIC CARNIVAL (USA) 3 b.c. Greek Answer–Streamer (Jet Jewel) — (1981 6g 6g² 6fg 1982 6f 6fg) quite well-made colt; has shown no form since second outing in 1981; taken down early final start at 2 yrs; trained by H. Westbrook first outing; sold 680 gns Ascot October Sales. *S. Mellor.*

OLYMPIC CHARM 2 ch.c. Filiberto 123–Pink Goddess (Yellow God 129) **82** (1982 5g³ 5f* 5fg⁴ 6fg² 7f² 7f³ 6f 7g 6fg 6v³) May 13; 1,000Y; well-grown colt; second foal; dam unraced twin; won maiden auction event at Redcar in May; ran well several times subsequently, including in nurseries; stays 7f; acts on any going; ran very wide on bend at Catterick on seventh appearance. *D. Smith.*

OMAR RAMSDEN (USA) 2 b.c. Tentam–Mantra (Herbager 136) (1982 **92** 8d 9s*) Mar 16; $50,000Y; compact, quite attractive colt; second foal; dam, unplaced in 4 races, is daughter of high-class middle-distance mare Manta; after struggling long way out, came through close home to win 15-runner maiden race at Redcar in October by neck from Lyminster; will be suited by 1¼m; sold 10,000 gns Newmarket Autumn Sales and sent to Malaysia. *G. Harwood.*

OMINOUS 2 ch.f. Dominion 123–Safety Measure 68 (Home Guard 129) (1982 **91**
5g 5f³ 5g² 5f⁴ 7d² 7fg⁴ 7g* 7g³) Mar 12; 4,400Y; tall, quite attractive filly;
first foal; dam won over 1m; made all and galloped on strongly to win 8-runner
minor event at Epsom in August by 2 lengths from Blushing River; 3 lengths
third of 23 behind Salvinia in £4,500 event at Newbury the following month;
much better suited by 7f than 5f, and will stay 1m; seems to act on any going but
is possibly best with some give in the ground; sweated up sixth outing. *R.
Smyth.*

ONAIZAH (USA) 2 b. or br.f. Bold Bidder–Forest Friend (Linacre 133) (1982 **80**
6fg 6s*) Apr 16; $475,000Y; strong, good-bodied, sturdy filly; sister to fair
1980 2-y-o 7f winner Free Forester, and half-sister to 4 winners, including Irish
3-y-o middle-distance winner Mister Lord (by Sir Ivor) and smart Irish stayer
Moss Trooper (by Levmoss); dam half-sister to Vaguely Noble's dam; favourite
though having first outing since July, won 16-runner maiden race at Leicester
in November in good style by 2¼ lengths from Saqqara, after leading all the
way; will stay 1m. *H. T. Jones.*

ONE DEGREE 3 b.f. Crooner 119–Rhythm 64 (Bleep-Bleep 134) (1981 **72**
6fg 6fg 5g² 5d³ 5d 6s 6g* 1982 8f 7fg 8f³ 8g² 8.3g 7fg 7.2f² 7g) small, strong,
sturdy non-thoroughbred filly; stays 1m; seems to act on any going; has run
well for an apprentice. *F. Durr.*

ON EDGE 7 gr.g. Sharp Edge 123–The Country Lane 90 (Red God 128§) **87**
(1981 9d 8fg* 8g* 8d² 8g* 8f* 9fg* 8f* 8f* 8fg 9fg* 8.2fg 8v⁴ 9s 1982 8d 8fg³
8g 8f 8f² 8f³ 8.5fg 8fg³ 8.3fg² 8fg²) smallish gelding; fair handicapper; ran
consistently well again but didn't manage to win; stays 9f; suited by top-of-the-
ground; blinkered once at 2 yrs; suitable mount for a claimer; usually held up
but made running final start; tough and genuine. *J. Spearing.*

ONE MORE DANCE 3 b.f. Dance In Time–First Watch (Primera 131) (1981 **—**
NR 1982 7g 9f 8g 12d 6d) plain filly; half-sister to Irish 9f winner Cindy's
Spec (by Shantung) and a winning hurdler; dam from same family as 1,000
Guineas winner Nocturnal Spree; behind in varied company, including claiming.
P. Feilden.

ONE O'CLOCK JUMP 2 b. or br.c. Hotfoot 126–Chiltern Red (Red God **93**
128§) (1982 6fg 7g 7.6v² 7g³ 6g) Apr 28; 52,000Y; well-made, attractive colt;
good walker; brother to 1980 2-y-o 6f and 1m winner Chilblains, subsequently
a winner in Italy, and closely related to very useful 1981 2-y-o sprint winner
Travel On (by Tachypous); dam poor sister to Red Alert; placed in maiden
races at Lingfield (beaten a head by Telephone Numbers) and Leicester in
October; will stay 1m; acts on heavy going. *F. Durr.*

ONESSILOS 2 ch.c. Saint Paul 106–Turnbeam (Hornbeam 130) (1982 6g **66 p**
7f⁴ 8s) Mar 28; fair sort; half-brother to several winners, including very useful
sprinter Oscilight (by Swing Easy); dam won at 2 yrs in Sweden; shaped with
promise in maiden events; worth noting in handicap company. *J. Dunlop.*

ONLY A POUND 2 ch.c. Sharpen Up 127–Double Lock 104 (Home Guard **88**
129) (1982 8g 10s²) Apr 30; rangy colt; first foal; dam won over 1¼m; ran
green under pressure when ¾-length second of 16 (clear of remainder) to Moon
Mariner in maiden event at Nottingham in October; suited by 1¼m and may
stay further; sure to win races. *J. Hindley.*

ONLY GORGEOUS 3 b. or br.f. King's Equity 106–Helenium (Khalkis 127) **—**
(1981 NR 1982 11.7g 12fg 12v 14s) small, short-backed filly; second foal;
dam won on flat and over hurdles in Ireland; soundly beaten in varied company.
P. M. Taylor.

ON MANOEUVRES 2 br.f. Mandrake Major 122–Wandering On (Klairon 131) **68**
(1982 5f² 5fg⁴) June 6; 800Y; lengthy filly; fourth foal; dam of little account;
in frame in late-spring 8-runner maiden auction events at Redcar; should stay
6f. *Miss S. Hall.*

ON RETURN 3 gr.f. On Your Mark 125–Magnificent Return 94 (My Swanee **100**
122) (1981 6fg 6g³ 5f* 5g 1982 6s 6fg⁴ 5.8f* 6fg 6fg⁴ 5f 6g² 5g*) lengthy,
useful-looking ex-Irish filly; useful sprint handicapper; won at Bath in May
and York in September; beat Cree Bay a length in £7,100 event on latter; stays
6f; best form on a sound surface; sweated up first start; sent to USA. *B. Hills.*

ONSLOW (USA) 2 b.c. Banquet Table–Hi Tam (Bold Tactics) (1982 7f³ **100**
8s* 8g⁴) May 5; $10,000Y; neat colt; third foal; half-brother to a winner; dam

won 4 sprint claiming races; swerved violently left before going on to win maiden race at Newcastle in October by 5 lengths from Dhofar; wandered badly when 2½ lengths fourth of 19 behind Coming and Going in minor event at Newmarket later in the month; stays 1m; evidently not an easy ride. *J. Dunlop.*

ON STAGE 2 b.c. Comedy Star 121–Last Case 109 (Firestreak 125) (1982 **123** 6fg² 6g* 6d* 6f² 7fg* 6f* 6fg² 7fg³ 6g*)

On Stage won five races as a two-year-old, but never one in which he had to fight. He's genuine enough though, and wears blinkers solely as an aid to concentration, since he was rather a flighty, nervous sort in his early days. On Stage's record throughout his first season was one of improvement interrupted only by his well-beaten third to Gorytus in the Laurent Perrier Champagne Stakes at Doncaster on his penultimate outing. On his other two defeats after his debut On Stage showed plenty of resolution: in the Anglia Television July Stakes at Newmarket he battled on splendidly under strong driving to run Horage to half a length with the remainder well beaten off; in the Prix Morny at Deauville he kept on gamely to finish a three-length second to Deep Roots.

The pick of On Stage's victories was his five-length defeat of Alchise in the Clarence House Stakes at Ascot in September on his final start. He won it in decisive style, quickening two furlongs out and keeping on strongly to the line. His timefigure, 1.04 fast, confirmed that this was a very smart performance. He had earlier picked up minor events at Chepstow and Windsor in the space of three days in June and two quite valuable races in July, the Limekilns Stakes at Newmarket and the New Ham Stakes at Goodwood. On the last two courses he had an easy task and on both occasions won as an odds-on shot should; he wasn't extended to beat Rasa Singapura by four lengths at Newmarket and was eased near the finish when accounting for Secret Miracle by three lengths at Goodwood.

On Stage (b.c. Apr 17, 1980)	Comedy Star (b 1968)	Tom Fool (b 1949)	Menow / Gaga
		Latin Walk (br 1960)	Roman Tread / Stall Walker
	Last Case (ch 1963)	Firestreak (b 1956)	Pardal / Hot Spell
		Court Case (b 1949)	Court Martial / La Petite

On Stage's sire was a good and genuine racehorse who often wore blinkers. The dam Last Case was another game and consistent performer of well above average ability. She finished third in the Nassau Stakes but was better over shorter distances and won nine races including the St Catherine's Stakes at Newbury, the Brighton Mile and the Newbury Spring Cup. Last Case is a half-sister to four other winners, two of them useful, including Light Case, herself the dam of two good horses by Last Case's sire Firestreak, the White Rose Stakes winner Light Fire and the smart Bright Fire, winner of fourteen races in eleven seasons of racing. Another of Last Case's winning half-sisters, Court Star, is the dam of two very good winners in India. On Stage's grandam was placed

Clarence House Stakes, Ascot—fifth win for the tough On Stage, this one at the expense of Alchise

Mr A. Foustok's "On Stage"

over sprint distances and his third dam La Petite, a sister to Coronation Stakes winner Saucy Sal, won twice at a mile and a quarter. One of La Petite's three winning foals, Canardeau, possessed a record similar to Bright Fire's: he won nineteen races between 1952 and 1960. Last Case has proved a very useful broodmare with three winners besides On Stage, the best of them Court Clown (by Silly Season), a winner over six furlongs as a two-year-old and over a mile and a quarter at three. Unfortunately Last Case hasn't been particularly fertile: On Stage is her sixth foal in twelve years at stud. On Stage was bought as a foal for 9,000 guineas. He is a strong, compact colt and a good mover. He has yet to race on very soft ground. Comedy Star has sired winners over a wide variety of distances; he is known principally for his sprinters, though, including Solinus, Cawston's Clown, Sparkling Boy and Jon George, and On Stage looks as though he'll prove best over sprint distances too. *W. O'Gorman.*

ONTARIO 2 ch.c. Nebbiolo 125–Pink Doll (Palestine 133) (1982 5fg) Apr 20; 10,000Y; robust colt; half-brother to several minor winners; dam placed over 5f and 6f in Ireland; last of 10 in maiden event at Newmarket in May; exported to Singapore. *E. Eldin.* —

ON THE BEACH 4 ch.c. Sandford Lad 133–Curragha (Le Levanstell 122) (1981 8d 8fg 8d 12.2g⁴ 12d 1982 12fg 11.5f 12fg) rangy, good sort; good mover; poor form since 1980, including in a valuable seller; stays 1½m; sold 950 gns Ascot September Sales. *R. Smyth.* —

ON THE HOUSE (FR) 3 b.f. Be My Guest 126–Lora (Lorenzaccio 130) (1981 6fg 5fg* 6f* 6g² 1982 7fg 8fg* 8g³ 8fg 8f* 8fg) **125**
On The House was a surprisingly decisive winner of the One Thousand Guineas. On the eve of the race few gave much for her chance, for although her

form as a two-year-old sufficed to send her into winter quarters third favourite in the ante-post market her performance behind Chalon in the Ladbrokes Nell Gwyn Stakes on her reappearance cost her a deal of support, persuading at least two leading jockeys to turn elsewhere for their mount. On The House lost her next two races after the Guineas but that led up to another very fine effort: her becoming the first filly since Humble Duty, and only the second since Petite Etoile, to beat the colts in the Sussex Stakes. We should put her a few pounds behind the lesser of those other dual winners of the One Thousand Guineas and the Sussex Stakes, Humble Duty, who won by seven lengths at Newmarket and succeeded where On The House failed in the Coronation Stakes, the Wills Mile (now the Waterford Crystal Mile) and the Cheveley Park Stakes. That is to say we rate her an average Guineas winner, in a year when the mile fillies came up to standard while the colts did not.

On The House went down by a length and a half to Woodstream in the William Hill Cheveley Park Stakes on her final outing as a two-year-old, and was allotted 8-7 in the Tote European Free Handicap, 5 lb less than the weight allotted to the three leading fillies Circus Ring, Height of Fashion and Play It Safe. In the absence of Circus Ring, Height of Fashion and Woodstream, Play It Safe arrived for the Guineas with excellent prospects of giving the French their first success since Flying Water's in 1976. Her win in the Prix Marcel Boussac in 1981 had proved her ability to stay a mile and shown her of classic standard, while her ready defeat of Balance in the Prix Imprudence in April showed she'd trained on. She started 5/2 favourite. Where the main danger lay was difficult to identify. Five of the fifteen runners besides On The House and Play It Safe had appeared in the Two-Year-Old Free Handicap, Stratospheric (8-11), Glancing (8-10), Warm Hearted (8-7), Merlins Charm (8-6) and Slightly Dangerous (8-4); another three, Time Charter (Masaka Stakes), Celestial Path (Athasi Stakes) and Dione (Newmarket maiden), had shown significant improvement on their two-year-old form when winning in the spring. Like Play It Safe, the second French challenger Exclusive Order had revealed her well-being, through her second to the very highly regarded River Lady in the Prix de la Grotte. All the runners except the speedy Glancing, who'd been forced to miss the Cheveley Park because of a blood disorder, had had the benefit of an outing during the current season. On their latest form perhaps the stable-companions Slightly Dangerous and Merlins Charm held the best chances of beating Play It Safe; the market suggested as much. The unbeaten Slightly Dangerous had won the Fred Darling Stakes from On The House's stable-companion Zinzara with Stratospheric only fourth of five; Merlins Charm had finished a very promising second to Chalon in the Nell Gwyn, comfortably ahead of another Guineas entry Triple Tipple with On The House only fifth and Warm Hearted only seventh. On The House's running increased substantially the doubts about her ability to stay a mile: she weakened through the last furlong to finish about five lengths down after racing with the leaders from about halfway. Her rider Eddery switched

One Thousand Guineas Stakes, Newmarket—On The House springs a surprise; Time Charter (right) is second, ahead of the grey Dione and Play It Safe

Sussex Stakes, Goodwood—On The House keeps on strongly from the colts Sandhurst Prince and Achieved (blinkers)

to Merlins Charm after this, his place eventually filled by Reid who hadn't ridden On The House in a race before.

On The House's trainer had an outstanding record of success in the One Thousand Guineas, having saddled Full Dress II and Abermaid and having ridden Sun Stream, Herringbone and Campanula. On The House always held out the promise in running of improving that record provided she stayed. Curiously, in view of the doubts about her stamina, none of Wragg's winners was longer in front than On The House who took the lead around two furlongs out, at roughly the same point as Campanula back in 1934, and established a much more commanding advantage over the subsequent Oaks winner Time Charter than Campanula managed over Light Brocade. The pace was a strong one, too strong for Slightly Dangerous, thanks to the work of the sprinter Hello Cuddles and Time Charter; yet On The House, never more than three lengths behind the leaders, had enough in reserve to pull quickly clear then to hold on by two and a half lengths and two lengths from Time Charter and Dione. Play It Safe, just as well placed as the winner approaching the Bushes, failed to produce any acceleration on the firmish going and was beaten a neck by Dione. At 33/1 On The House was the second longest-priced winner of the One Thousand Guineas in fifty years; Enstone Spark started at 35/1 in 1978.

In the weeks between the Guineas and the Sussex Stakes On The House lost ground to Chalon in the public's esteem. She was beaten in the Goffs Irish One Thousand Guineas at the Curragh and the Coronation Stakes at Royal Ascot, and couldn't match Chalon for consistency, though she could be excused her run in the Nell Gwyn on account of a lack of fitness (apparently she'd been held up in her preparation), and might have her modest fifth in the Coronation Stakes explained on one of two counts, the slowness of the pace dictated by Chalon or, as favoured by her trainer, the toll taken by her exertions in Ireland. Probably she ran below her best in Ireland but, if so, not sufficiently below to warrant criticism. She finished third of twenty-four, a length and a short head behind Prince's Polly and Woodstream, fading towards the end after taking a slight lead from Prince's Polly at the distance.

On The House's performance in the Sussex Stakes at Goodwood in July supports to some degree either explanation for her showing at Royal Ascot: she won a very strongly-run affair on her return from a six-week break from racing. The status of the Sussex Stakes has been raised since Petite Etoile's day. As the only Group 1 race in England run over the distance now open to three-year-olds and upwards it should, and often does, attract as strong a field of milers as any seen in the country in the course of the season; it has required a very good horse indeed to win in most recent years, and in the 1977 running neither of the Guineas winners, Nebbiolo nor Mrs McArdy, succeeded in making the slightest impression. The field against On The House was not so strong, apart from numerically, as we have come to expect. She was the only classic winner among the thirteen runners in a wide-open race for which the French four-year-old The Wonder, the Two Thousand Guineas third Tender King and the one-time Guineas favourite Sandhurst Prince, returning after a long absence, shared market call at 4/1. At 14/1 On The House stood five points longer than the only other filly in the field, Merlins Charm. Silver Season's presence ensured a cracking pace and there was no let-up as he gave way to the free-running Bel Bolide early in the straight, for the latter quickly established a threatening advantage of two or three lengths. Bel Bolide lasted in front until the furlong pole; as he weakened he forced Sandhurst Prince to be checked and switched in order to get by. On The House met no such problem. She began her run in fourth place after the turn, came strongly on the outside to lead from Achieved, Sandhurst Prince and Tender King inside the last furlong, and she kept going very strongly to win by half a length from the slightly-unlucky Sandhurst Prince.

The Waterford Crystal Mile on the same course in August brought On The House's racing career to a close. Her finish deserted her in another strongly-run event, and she dropped back in the last furlong from second to sixth-of-eight place behind Sandhurst Prince; she wasn't at her best at a time when she needed to be against the winner who had a pull of 7 lb from their last meeting. She has been retired to stud and first visits Shergar; perhaps we can also look forward to a foal by her owner's fine horse Ile de Bourbon in due course.

On The House's owner-breeder sells some of his yearlings at the Houghton Sales. Fortunately for him On The House, as Pelerin a few years earlier, failed to reach reserve price. Why she should have failed to make a modest reserve can only be guessed at: because she came right at the end of the catalogue perhaps, or more likely because she failed to impress if at that time she no more took the eye than she usually did in the preliminaries to her races. Her pedigree was an attractive one even before her sire's merit as a stallion became known. The third dam Tessa Gillian, out of a half-sister to Nasrullah, made her name

Sir Philip Oppenheimer's "On The House"

both as a racemare and broodmare. She finished second in the One Thousand Guineas and Coronation Stakes, besides winning the Molecomb Stakes and finishing second in the Cheveley Park at two. At stud she foaled six winners including the leading two-year-olds Test Case and Gentle Art. On The House's grandam Courtessa, a sister to Test Case, was a twin and did not race. She produced five winners, one of them at least as good a racehorse as either Test Case or Gentle Art in D'Urberville, a high-class sprinter. On The House's dam is three-parts sister to D'Urberville and to Klairessa, another sprinter. She, Lora, never made the grade on the track but produced a winner first time of asking in Loralane (by Habitat), successful from twenty-two opponents in a seven-furlong maiden at Newmarket as a three-year-old in 1980. On The House is her second foal. Her third, Lora del Rio (a filly by Riverman), had the misfortune to break a leg cantering back after running at Newbury in August.

		Northern Dancer	Nearctic
	Be My Guest	(b 1961)	Natalma
	(ch 1974)	What a Treat	Tudor Minstrel
On The House (Fr)		(b 1962)	Rare Treat
(b.f. 1979)		Lorenzaccio	Klairon
	Lora	(ch 1965)	Phoenissa
	(b 1972)	Courtessa	Supreme Court
		(b 1955)	Tessa Gillian

All Be My Guest's first-crop winners in Britain and Ireland in 1982 except for the hard-pulling Feather Sound won over a distance of at least a mile. We now have a much deeper insight into Be My Guest's nature as a stallion, of course, than when On The House was a Guineas candidate. Though her dam was closely related to two sprinters On The House proved to stay a mile very well; she was suited by the distance. A lengthy filly with an excellent turn of foot, she did all her racing on a sound surface and acted well on firm going. *H. Wragg.*

ON THE SPOT 3 gr.g. Town Crier 119–Creolina 72 (Quorum 126) (1981 **50** 6f 6fg 6g 6f 6fg 7f 6g 6d 1982 8.5fg 6.5v 8d 7f⁴ 7g² 7fg⁴ 8g⁴ 10fg 10.1fg 9fg 10g² 10fg 10g 9fg⁴ 10f 8v 10.2s) quite attractive gelding; good walker; plater; stays 1¼m; sometimes blinkered. *C. Brittain.*

ON THE SPREE 2 b.f. Wolverlife 115–Red Lark (Larkspur 128) (1982 7d — 7g) Apr 20; IR 5,600Y; half-sister to 3 winners in Ireland; dam half-sister to high-class miler Red Slipper; soundly beaten in minor event at Doncaster in October and maiden race at Newmarket later in the month. *D. Morley.*

ON THE WARPATH 3 ro.g. Bustino 136–Cheyenne 83 (Sovereign Path 125) — (1981 7.2fg 8g 10s 1982 11s⁴ 16f 12.3g 16g⁴ 14fg 16s) rangy gelding; staying maiden. *C. Thornton.*

ON TOUR 2 b.f. Queen's Hussar 124–Phaedima 76 (Darius 129) (1982 6g **60** 7d 7g²) Feb 20; 2,000Y; compact filly; has a round action; fifth living foal; dam winner at up to 2m and half-sister to Coup de Feu and Peleid; dropped in class and well-backed favourite, comfortably accounted for 7 others when 2½ lengths second to Cedar Princess in seller at Newmarket in August; will stay 1m. *W. Haigh.*

ONWARDLEE (USA) 2 b.c. Ward McAllister–Stride Out (Impressive) (1982 **77** 6f³ 6f 7d 8d 8g² 9s) May 19; $10,000Y; sturdy colt; third foal; closely related to a winner by Jacinto; dam won 2 sprint claiming races; placed in small race at Thirsk in July and maiden event at Edinburgh in September; suited by 1m; form only on a sound surface. *S. Norton.*

ON YOUR BRIDGE 3 b.f. Scottish Rifle 127–Off The Mark (On Your Mark **41** 125) (1981 5fg 6fg 8g² 8.2d 10d 1982 12f² 12f 12g³ 13.8f 12g* 13.8f³ 12s 12g) lightly-made filly; plater; changed hands 975 gns after winning at Pontefract in August; stays 1¾m; acts well on firm going; ran moderately in blinkers second start; has run respectably when sweating up; has worn a bandage on near-fore; sold to Norsk Jockey Club 840 gns Doncaster November Sales. *Miss L. Siddall.*

OO-LA-LA 3 b.g. Warpath 113–Croisette 95 (Sunny Way 120) (1981 NR **64** 1982 10.2g 12.2f³ 10d 12fg) compact, quite well-made gelding; has a round action; second foal; dam won 9 times from 6f to 11f; little worthwhile form; will stay well. *C. Thornton.*

OOLYWIG 4 b.f. Copte–Dotonlok (Quadrangle) (1981 NR 1982 14d 16.5f — 10.1g) compact non-thoroughbred filly; in rear in maiden races and a handicap. *D. Hanley.*

OOPS-A-DAISY 3 br.f. Warpath 113–Sunflower 96 (Paveh 126) (1981 7g — 10.2g 1982 10.2g 12.2f 12g³ 12fg) useful-looking filly; good walker; poor form, including in sellers; trained part of season by C. Thornton; sold to R. Hartop 2,100 gns Doncaster September Sales. *D. Smith.*

OPAL LADY 4 b.f. Averof 123–Hum 69 (Crooner 119) (1981 6g² 6g 6d 5fg — 6f³ 6f⁴ 6f* 7h 7g 1982 7fg 8h) quite a well-made filly; well beaten both outings at 4 yrs; should be suited by 7f; acts on firm going; usually blinkered; has worn bandages in front. *M. Bradley.*

OPARAU (NZ) 7 br.g. Stipulate–Hokonui Gold (Lomond 124) (1981 NR — 1982 12f) New Zealand-bred gelding; winner over hurdles; remote fifth to The Friend in amateur riders race at Redcar in August, first outing on flat in this country. *P. Felgate.*

OPEN DAY 3 ch.c. Northfields–Knighton House 113 (Pall Mall 132) (1981 **113+** 8g 1982 11f* 12f*)
  Since the victories of Convamore, Pretendre, Connaught and Great Wall in the six-year period between 1965 and 1970, the King Edward VII Stakes has been won only once by a horse which has contested the Epsom Derby. The 'Ascot Derby', as the King Edward VII Stakes is known, usually goes nowadays to a later-developing type, one for whom Epsom has come a little too soon. West Ilsley Stables, which concentrate mainly on producing second- and third-season horses, have won three of the last eight runnings of the King Edward VII Stakes with horses whose programme up to Royal Ascot has taken them into much calmer waters than those middle-distance performers who have had a full Derby preparation. The latest winner Open Day went to Royal Ascot still virtually a novice at the game, his racing experience comprising an outing largely for educational purposes at the back-end of his two-year-old days and a hard-fought victory in a twenty-runner maiden event over eleven furlongs at Newbury in May. The field for the King Edward VII Stakes, a good one judged on looks, included the Derby fifth Norwick, who started favourite, but Open Day's closest challenger at the time was the Irish-trained Lords, another relatively lightly-raced colt who had needed time to develop into a good-class performer. While Open Day enjoyed an uninterrupted run on the outside in the straight, hitting the front approaching the final furlong and winning ridden out by three quarters of a length, some of his rivals were less fortunate, notably third-placed Old Country and fifth-placed Diamond Shoal who both had a rough passage. Hern's previous King Edward VII Stakes winners Sea Anchor and Bustomi trained on into St Leger contenders but Open Day wasn't entered for the St Leger, which closed on July 7th, and in fact didn't race again after taking a little time to recover after jarring himself on the firm ground at Royal Ascot. Plans to race him in the autumn were shelved because of the unusually long spell of firm going. Open Day stays in training but we didn't see enough of him as a three-year-old to be able to assess him thoroughly and we shall have to leave it to the future to show how good he is. He certainly couldn't have made a more promising start to his career.

		Northern Dancer	Nearctic
	Northfields	(b 1961)	Natalma
	(ch 1968)	Little Hut	Occupy
Open Day		(b 1952)	Savage Beauty
(ch.c. 1979)		Pall Mall	Palestine
	Knighton House	(ch 1955)	Malapert
	(b 1966)	Country House	Vieux Manoir
		(br 1955)	Miss Coventry

  Open Day's sire Northfields, who is at stud in Ireland, has followed his half-brother Habitat into the ranks of the leading stallions of the day: the outstanding miler Northjet is Northfields' best winner so far but Northfields is a fair influence for stamina and has sired such good middle-distance performers as North Stoke, Nanticious, Northern Treasure, Tootens and Oats, the last-named possessing enough stamina to win the Ormonde Stakes at Chester and finish in the frame in the St Leger. Open Day's dam Knighton House, a sister to that grand little character Reform, won the Prix de la Calonne over a mile at Deauville and finished second in the Coronation Stakes at Royal Ascot and the Fred Darling Stakes at Newbury; on her final racecourse appearance she ran well to finish third in the Sun Chariot Stakes over a mile and a quarter, the longest distance over which she was raced. Knighton House has bred several other winners, including the smart 1977 French two-year-old River Knight

King Edward VII Stakes, Ascot—lightly-raced Open Day repels the strong challenge of Lords and Old Country (checks)

(by Riverman), who did most of his racing at a mile to a mile and a quarter as a three-year-old, the quite useful miler School Bell (by Baldric II) and the quite useful mile-and-a-quarter filly Sea Venture (by Diatome). Open Day, quite an attractive, well-made colt, seems well suited by a mile and a half; he has yet to race on a soft surface. *R. Hern.*

OPEN THE BOX (USA) 3 b.g. Key To The Kingdom–T.V. Miss (T.V. Lark)   **81**
(1981 5g³ 5.8g² 6fg 6f 6s² 1982 8.2s 7d 5.8g 6f 6f 6g 6g 6v 6d 7s*) smallish, workmanlike gelding; made virtually all when wide-margin winner of handicap at Leicester in November; should stay 1m; needs some give in the ground and revels in soft going; best in blinkers; changed hands 2,500 gns Doncaster October Sales. *G. Balding.*

OPERATION CYRIL 4 ch.g. Jimmy Reppin 131–Western Vale (Milesian   **—**
125) (1981 7s 8s 9d² 9.4g² 8g 1982 8fg 10fg 10.6h 10fg 12g) fair sort; still a maiden, and was behind in a valuable seller third start; stays 9f. *D. Sasse.*

OPINEBO 2 b.f. Nebbiolo 125–Ops (Welsh Saint 126) (1982 6g³ 6d³ 6d 7g)   **73**
Apr 16; lightly-made filly; first foal; dam won 3 middle-distance races in Ireland; placed in minor events at Doncaster in June and Pontefract in October; will stay 1m. *D. Morley.*

OPTIMISTIC DREAMER 3 b.c. Full of Hope 125–La Crima (Runnymede   **63**
123) (1981 7fg 7fg² 7g 1982 7f 8fg⁴ 7fg* 7f 7fg 7d 7d) leggy colt; won maiden race at Folkestone in August; stays 1m; acts on a firm surface; blinkered fifth start; pulled hard fourth outing. *I. Walker.*

ORANELLA 2 ch.f. Orange Bay 131–Quick Dream (Crepello 136) (1982   **82**
7g 8s*) Apr 20; IR 3,000F; well-grown, workmanlike filly; half-sister to 1¼m winner Dream Dancer (by Sword Dancer) and a winner in Italy; dam useful winner in Italy; made up ground hand over fist in closing stages to win 18-runner maiden race at Wolverhampton in October by 2 lengths from Maid of Milan; will be suited by 1¼m; acts on soft going. *G. Pritchard-Gordon.*

ORANGE BLOSSOM 2 b.f. Orange Bay 131–Aggrapina 79 (St Alphage 119)   **69**
(1982 7g 8s⁴ 8d) Mar 28; 6,200Y; tall, leggy filly; first foal; dam showed form only over 5f; backed from 6/1 to 5/2 favourite, under the whip from 3f out when just over 4 lengths fourth of 11 to Ballad Island in maiden race at Wolverhampton in October, best effort; slow. *J. Etherington.*

ORANGE CITY 2 br.c. Orange Bay 131–Golden City 82 (Skymaster 126)   **55**
(1982 5f⁴ 5f 7d² 7fg³) Apr 23; 3,100F; tall colt; half-brother to useful 1977 2-y-o 6f winner Hillbrow (by Swing Easy); dam 7f winner; placed in sellers at Beverley and Newcastle in July; exported to Algeria. *M. W. Easterby.*

ORANGE COUNTY 3 ch.g. Reform 132–Bedouin Dancer 79 (Lorenzaccio 130)   **39**
(1981 NR 1982 8f 8g 8d 8fg 8g 8.2g 9s³ 8.2v 12d) 1,100 2-y-o; compact gelding; first foal; dam won over 1m; poor plater. *W. Bentley.*

ORANGE ROSE 2 ch.f. Orange Bay 131–Garnette Rose 74 (Floribunda 136)   **?**
(1982 5g⁴ 5fg³ 5f² 5f³ 6f³ 6s⁴) May 25; 1,600Y; leggy filly; half-sister to 1977
2-y-o 5f winner Superior Class (by Decoy Boy); dam seemed to stay 1m; plater
in this country; did much better subsequently in Belgium, her wins including
Grade 3 event at Ostend; acts on any going; consistent. *G. Toft.*

ORANGE SILK 3 ch.f. Moulton 128–Orange Sensation 46 (Floribunda 136)   **—**
(1981 5s 5d² 6fg 5d 6fg 7g 6s² 6g 1982 6f 6fg) small filly; plater at 2 yrs;
well beaten in handicaps in 1982; should stay 7f; best form with some give in
the ground; ran creditably in blinkers last 2 starts in 1981. *J. Winter.*

ORANGE SORBET 3 b.f. Orange Bay 131–Sandfly (French Beige 127) (1981   **—**
7g 7.2d⁴ 7fg 8g² 8.2d 10s 1982 12.2f 13g 12fg) leggy filly; plating-class maiden
over here; finished first over 1¼m in Holland after being sold 1,400 gns Doncaster
August Sales; has worn blinkers. *M. H. Easterby.*

ORANGE SQUASH (USA) 2 ch.c Unconscious–Doveland (Jet Man) (1982 **113**
5f⁴ 5fg* 6f 5f* 6fg* 5fg* 6f* 5v) Apr 9; 10,500Y; good-bodied, quite attractive
colt; first foal; dam minor stakes winner at up to 1m; had excellent season and
boosted his earnings almost to £20,000 when running on really well under pressure
to beat Mac's Palace a short head in 3-runner Bonusprint Sirenia Stakes at Kempton in September; had earlier won maiden race at Lingfield and nurseries at
Lingfield, Goodwood and Sandown; weakened quickly after holding every
chance at distance when 7½ lengths fifth of 9 to Tatibah in Cornwallis Stakes at
Ascot in October; stays 6f well; acts well on fast ground and possibly isn't at
his best on heavy going; genuine. *R. Smyth.*

ORANGE TIP 3 b.f. Orange Bay 131–Blessed Beauty 97 (Rustam 127) (1981   **71**
8g 1982 9g² 10f² 12f 10f* 10.1fg³ 10g⁴ 10d) rangy filly; won maiden race at
Yarmouth in August; should stay 1½m but ran badly when tried at trip; acts
on firm going. *G. Pritchard-Gordon.*

ORANGE VALLEY 4 br.f. Alto Volante 109–Noaxe To Grind (The Axe 115)   **—**
(1981 10s 9d⁴ 12d 10.1fg³ 10fg 8f⁴ 8d² 8fg 7fg 8 2s 1982 6d 10fg) in frame in
varied company, including selling; should stay at least 1½m; has worn blinkers.
J. Scallan.

ORATAVO 4 br.g. The Brianstan 128–Nimble Star (Space King 115) (1981   **92**
10d 10.2d³ 10.2f* 10f* 10.8fg² 10g* 10d* 10fg 10d⁴ 10s* 10.2g 1982 10fg 10fg²
10f* 12fg 10d* 8fg³ 10fg² 8fg 10g* 9d³ 10g) lightly-made gelding; successful
in handicaps at Lingfield in May, Salisbury in June and Newbury in September;
beat Century City by a length in Peter Hastings Stakes on last-named course;
ran an excellent race under a penalty when 1¾ lengths third of 29 behind Century
City in William Hill Cambridgeshire at Newmarket in October; stays 11f;
acts on any going; often apprentice ridden but hung when ridden by an inexperienced boy eighth start. *J. Sutcliffe.*

ORATION 3 gr.g. Rouser 118–Declamation 93 (Town Crier 119) (1981 NR   **86**
1982 11g* 12fg⁴ 10.1fg 10f² 10s 10g 12s) useful sort; first foal; dam second of
26 over 6f on only start; beat Freeway Folly by ½ length in 15-runner maiden
race at Newbury in April; creditable second in handicap at Leicester in June;
stays 1½m; probably needs a sound surface; sold to C. Thornton 5,200 gns
Newmarket Autumn Sales. *B. Hobbs.*

ORBITSIR 4 b.c. Sir Albert 72–Orbenita (Orbit 106) (1981 NR 1982 8d   **—**
8f 10.6g 10f) of no account; has been tried in blinkers. *J. Mulhall.*

ORCHESTRATE (USA) 4 ch.c. Northern Dancer–Directoire (Gun Bow)   **—**
(1981 10g 8d 1982 10d 8f 10fg 7f) small, strong, stocky colt; a very well bred
colt, but is little better than plating class; blinkered final start. *G. Harwood.*

ORE 4 ch.c. Ballymore 123–Minatonka (Linacre 133) (1981 7g³ 8g⁴ 8s 12v³ **116**
16f* 12fg 14d⁴ 1982 10s 10s⁴ 16fg2 22.2fg* 21f² 16g² 20s 16d³) big, strong,
workmanlike ex-Irish colt; looked particularly well and stayed on strongly
when beating Castelnau by 1½ lengths in Queen Alexandra Stakes at Royal
Ascot in June; second afterwards in Goodwood Cup in July (couldn't answer
Heighlin's extremely late finish and went down by ½ length) and Lonsdale Stakes
at York in August (beaten a head by Capricorn Line after a hard battle); didn't
run up to his best but kept plugging on when 8½ lengths third to Little Wolf in
Jockey Club Cup at Newmarket in October, better subsequent effort; suited by
a stiff test of stamina; very well suited by firm going, although has run respectably
on heavy; blinkered third start as a 3-y-o (Irish 2,000 Guineas); sold privately in
June (trained by K. Prendergast in Ireland first 4 starts). *W. Musson.*

624

Mr O. Zawawi's "Ore"

OREGON TRAIL 2 b.c. Auction Ring 123–Oriental Star 94 (Falcon 131) — p
(1982 8.2s) Mar 27; strong, lengthy, slightly hollow-backed colt; first foal;
dam won 7 times from 5f to 1½m; unquoted, showed some promise when seventh
of 19, after dwelling, in minor event won by Holy Spark at Nottingham in
October. *D. Arbuthnot.*

ORIENTAL-SAINT 3 ch.g. Mandrake Major 122–Saint-Cyr 73 (Set Fair 129) —
(1981 NR 1982 10g) strong, good-bodied gelding; half-brother to several
winners; dam, a plater, stayed 9f; unquoted and very backward, moved badly in
post when tailed-off last of 18 to Steel Kid in minor event at Ripon in August;
sold 600 gns Doncaster September Sales. *Miss S. Hall.*

ORIENTATE 3 ch.f. Hotfoot 126–Guiding Light 78 (Crepello 136) (1981 NR §§
1982 7fg 6g 10g 12g) 10,000Y; lengthy, good sort; good walker; half-sister to 4
winners, including useful 1m to 1½m filly La Dolce (by Connaught); dam middle-
distance maiden; beaten some way in varied company; refused to race when
blinkered final start. *N. Vigors.*

ORIGINAL STEP 7 ch.g. New Linacre 82–Paddy's Walk (Admiral's Walk) —
(1981 NR 1982 12s) fair hurdler; sixth of 13 behind Indulgence in apprentice
event at Chepstow in October, first outing on flat. *T. Hallett.*

ORIXO (USA) 2 ch.c. Our Native–Bold Fluff (Boldnesian) (1982 6f 6d⁴ **122**
6fg* 6g²)
   The Dollanstown Stud of Mr and Mrs Arpad Plesch once housed a broodmare
band of around sixty, and produced such excellent performers as the Derby
winner Psidium, the Prix Vermeille winner Saraca and the Prix de l'Arc de Triomphe
winner Sassafras before its dispersal following Mr Plesch's death in 1974. Mrs
Plesch now owns only a couple of broodmares but she has nevertheless continued
to enjoy considerable success through colts bought as yearlings in the United

Mining Supplies Stakes, Doncaster—Orixo shows much improved form

States—she won the 1980 Derby with Henbit, the 1980 Prix de la Salamandre with Miswaki and now has Orixo, officially rated the fifth-best two-year-old in Britain.

There was nothing in either of Orixo's first two performances to indicate that he would take such high rank: he was beaten nearly ten lengths when sixth to Tatibah in a maiden race at Newbury in June on his debut and could manage only fourth place behind Lyphard's Special, beaten over six lengths, in the Champagne Stakes at Salisbury a fortnight later. After a break of eleven weeks a very different Orixo appeared in the twenty-five-runner Mining Supplies Stakes at Doncaster. He looked extremely well and the way he advanced in the betting from 8/1 to 7/2 suggested that he had improved a great deal during his absence. So it turned out. After disputing the lead from the start he began to go clear of the far-side group from halfway and quickened right away from the distance. His winning margin was cut to two and a half lengths by Coquito's Friend's strong late run in the centre of the course. Wearing a tongue strap probably contributed to Orixo's improved display, and he again wore one on his final appearance, in the William Hill Middle Park Stakes at Newmarket later in September. This time the betting suggested that his chance was remote—he started the outsider of the five runners at 16/1—but he showed he was still very much on the upgrade with a fine effort. He chased the odds-on Diesis from the start and, although outpointed from the Dip, stuck to his task so well that he comfortably held on to second place ahead of Krayyan, Kafu and Ancestral. He was beaten two and a half lengths by Diesis.

Orixo (USA) (ch.c. Apr 11, 1980)	Our Native (b or br 1970)	Exclusive Native (ch 1965)	Raise A Native, Exclusive
		Our Jackie (gr 1964)	Crafty Admiral, Rakahanga
	Bold Fluff (ch 1969)	Boldnesian (b 1963)	Bold Ruler, Alanesian
		Cherry Fluff (ch 1962)	Cohoes, Cherry Puddin'

Orixo, a good-bodied, attractive colt, cost 180,000 dollars as a yearling, 98,000 dollars more than he'd changed hands for as a foal. He's a half-brother to four winners in the USA, including the stakes-placed Le Grand Charles (by Champagne Charlie) and the very useful Bold Rendezvous (by Hold Your Peace), a tough filly who won thirteen races including five stakes events over six and seven furlongs. His dam Bold Fluff, the winner of five races, was nothing out of the ordinary and the only other notable performer produced by the family in recent generations is the smart two-year-old filly of 1969, Cherry Sundae, a half-sister to Orixo's grandam Cherry Fluff. Neither Cherry Fluff nor Bold Fluff won over further than six furlongs and it's hard to imagine Orixo's staying well enough for the Derby, for which he's been entered. He will stay beyond a mile though. His sire Our Native won three valuable races over nine furlongs; Bold Fluff is by Boldnesian, winner of the Santa Anita Derby over the same distance; and Cherry Fluff was a daughter of Cohoes whose successes included one in the Brooklyn Handicap over nine and a half furlongs. Orixo needs to improve further if he's to make his mark at classic level but it's not out of the question that he'll do so—he was improving rapidly in the autumn and his trainer's horses usually improve from two to three. Although it is not yet possible to come to any conclusions on his going requirements, it's worth pointing out at this stage that he has a markedly round action. *R. Hern.*

ORLANDOLAND 3 br.c. Reliance II 137–Bombshell 76 (Le Levanstell 122) **82** (1981 6g 1982 12fg 12fg 10f² 14fg* 12f) strong, good-bodied colt; sweating, looked a useful stayer in the making when leading throughout and battling on in good style to win 8-runner minor event at York in May by a length from Rushbeds; had a heart attack and died during handicap at Thirsk later in month. *J. Hanson.*

ORMOLU (USA) 3 b.g. Val de l'Orne 130–Donna Chere (Conestoga) (1981 8d **67** 1982 11s³ 12s 9f³ 9.4f 10f 12fg 11g³ 11g* 11g³ 11g 9fg) tall, rather leggy gelding; poor mover; hasn't always looked genuine or an easy ride but did little wrong when winning maiden race at Hamilton in June; should stay 1½m; has been tried in blinkers; ran atrociously fifth outing; sold to O. O'Neill 5,500 gns Doncaster August Sales and retained by him 2,700 gns Newmarket Autumn Sales. *W. Elsey.*

OROFINO (GER) 4 br.c. Dschingis Khan–Ordinale (Luciano) (1981 4 wins **125** from 6 starts, including 8f* 11g* 12d* 12g² 12f⁴ 1982 12g* 11g* 11g* 12g* 12d* 12fg²) German colt; first foal; dam, from an excellent family, was joint top-rated 2-y-o filly in Germany in 1974 and was third in Prix de Flore as a 3-y-o; an outstanding performer in his native country where he's won 10 of his 13 races; won 4 races as a 3-y-o, notably Henckel-Rennen (German 2,000 Guineas) at Gelsenkirchen-Horst and Deutsches Derby at Hamburg, latter very impressively by 12¾ lengths from Winslow; successful in his first 5 races as a 4-y-o and won Group 1 events on last 2 occasions, beating Little Wolf by 1½ lengths (pair clear) in Grosser Preis von Berlin at Dusseldorf in July and Ataxerxes by 3 lengths in 12-runner Aral-Pokal at Gelsenkirchen-Horst in August; had earlier won Gerling-Preis at Cologne (from Wauthi), Grosser Preis von Dusseldorf and Grosser Hansa Preis at Hamburg; met only defeat of year in Grosser Preis von Baden in September, going down by 2¾ lengths to all-the-way winner Glint of Gold; stays 1½m well; probably acts on any going; most genuine and consistent; clearly a very smart colt. *S. von Mitzlaff, Germany.*

O-ROSE FORTUNATA 3 b.f. Hot Spark 126–Pandomyne 71 (Pandofell 132) **—** (1981 5d* 7.2f³ 6g³ 8f 6fg 6g 1982 6g 6g 7f 8g 7g) light-framed filly; fair performer in 1981; well beaten at 3 yrs but had stiffish tasks most outings; stays 7f; sold 5,000 gns Doncaster November Sales. *R. Hollinshead.*

ORP BALTIC 3 ch.g. Some Hand 119–Cedez Cela (Bleep-Bleep 134) (1981 **44** 5g 5g 5d 5fg 6d² 5f 6s 6d 1982 7g 8.2s² 6g 8fg² 7f 8g³ 8f) small gelding; plater; stays 1m; seems to act on any going; has been tried in blinkers. *J. Townson.*

ORRIN 3 ch.c. Bustino 136–Never Can Tell (Tambourine II 133) (1981 7f **78** 7fg² 8g 1982 10f 8fg 8g³) quite a useful sort; third in seller at Newmarket in August; subsequently sent to Italy and won at Turin in the autumn; will stay 1½m. *F. J. Houghton.*

ORYX MAJOR 2 ch.g. Sandford Lad 133–You Never Can Tell (Never Say Die **63** 137) (1982 7d 7g 8fg 8g) Apr 20; IR 6,000F; good-topped gelding; half-brother to a minor winner in France; dam never ran; plating-class maiden; showed form only on second outing; sweated up third start; sold 1,500 gns Ascot December Sales. *S. Mellor.*

ORYX MINOR 2 br.g. Music Maestro 119–Minor Chord 88 (Major Portion 129) **76** (1982 5fg 5fg 5d 5fg² 5fg 6fg 5d) June 13; 7,200Y; compact, fair sort; half-brother to 5.8f and 1¼m winner Aldeburgh Festival (by Club House); dam 2-y-o 5f winner; blinkered first time when beaten a head by Deputy Head in 6-runner minor event at Windsor in August; ran poorly over 6f; acts on a firm surface; sold 2,000 gns Ascot December Sales. *S. Mellor.*

OSCAR'S PRINCESS (USA) 2 ch.f. Stage Door Johnny–Eastern Princess   —
(Nasrullah) (1982 8s) May 6; $400,000Y; strong, lengthy, workmanlike filly;
sister to useful Irish 9f and 1½m winner Vanishing Act, and half-sister to numerous winners, including smart stakes winner Shady Character (by Graustark);
dam stakes-placed sister to outstanding racehorse and sire Bold Ruler; 16/1,
always among backmarkers in 18-runner maiden race at Wolverhampton in
October. *P. Cole.*

OTTERHILL 2 b.f. Brigadier Gerard 144–Lowna 120 (Princely Gift 137) (1982   **67**
5fg⁴ 6g 6fg 5g) May 1; neat, well-made filly; half-sister to several winners,
including Gospill Hill (by Crepello), a smart performer at up to 1¼m; dam won
Molecomb Stakes; plating-class maiden; trained first start by D. Ringer. *C.
Brittain.*

OUI MON CAPITAINE (USA) 3 b.c. Majestic Prince–Misty Light 112   **111**
(Ribot 142) (1981 NR 1982 8.5v⁴ 8s⁴ 10.5d* 12d* 12g* 15g 12g 12f) fifth
foal; half-brother to 3 winners in France and America, including very useful
French miler Come Up Smiling (by Amber Rama); dam won 5 times from 1m to
1½m; won maiden race at Saint-Cloud in April, 80,000 francs event on same
course in May (beat Flower Prince by 1½ lengths) and Gran Premio d'Italia at
Milan later in May; accounted for Bater decisively by 3 lengths in last-named;
soundly beaten in Grand Prix de Paris, Gran Premio di Milano and Prix Niel
afterwards; suited by 1½m. *J. Fellows, France.*

OUI MONSIEUR 8 b.g. Levanter 121–Melody Call 55 (Tudor Melody 129)   —
(1981 15.5d 12d³ 12g* 12v³ 12g⁴ 16f 12fg 16d 12fg 1982 12d 15.5fg 12fg 12f)
poor handicapper; stays 2m; acts on any going; suitable mount for an inexperienced rider. *M. Haynes.*

OULA OWL 2 b.c. Tachypous 128–Oula-Ka Fu-Fu 67 (Run The Gantlet)   **96**
(1982 7g 8g* 8g) May 3; 14,000Y; well-made, attractive colt; good mover;
first foal; dam, daughter of very smart Tawny Owl, won over 1m; co-favourite,
quickened clear over 2f out, after disputing lead from start, and won easing up
by 2 lengths from Dazari in 17-runner maiden race at Newmarket in October;
only fifth behind very easy winner Hasty Flirt in Premio Tevere in Rome the
following month; suited by 1m. *L. Cumani.*

OUR BARA BOY 5 b.g. Baragoi 115–Primeapple (Primera 131) (1981   —
16fg 16.1s³ 18d 18.1d³ 16s* 18g 1982 16v 18d) workmanlike gelding; staying
handicapper; acts on any going with possible exception of very firm; effective
with or without blinkers; suitable mount for a boy. *F. Winter.*

OUR BARACUDA 2 ch.f. Baragoi 115–Sea Green 93 (Meadow Court 129)   —
(1982 7g) Mar 4; fourth living foal; half-sister to a winner in Holland; dam
won over 1½m; 16/1, remote sixth of 13 in seller at Chepstow in September;
should stay well. *C. Williams.*

OUR BIRTHDAY 6 b.h. Great Nephew 126–Renoir Picture 90 (Relko 136)   **53**
(1981 9d⁴ 8fg⁴ 8d 8d⁴ 8v 8.3g 8.3g⁴ 10f 8s 1982 10d 10fg³ 10fg* 10d 8fg* 10f
10g 8fg 9g 8g) neat horse; good mover; won handicaps at Leicester and Chepstow in summer but ran poorly afterwards; stays 1¼m; acts on any going; wears
blinkers; sometimes starts slowly. *J. Benstead.*

OUR CHOICE 2 ro.c. Bustino 136–Betty Burke 95 (Prince Chevalier) (1982   **69+**
7.2g 8d) Apr 15; 5,400Y; tall, narrow, leggy colt; half-brother to several
winners, including very useful miler Stirling Castle (by Royal Palace) and very
useful stayer Arisaig (by Acropolis); dam won at 5f and 6f; 5½ lengths sixth
of 11 to Shackle Pin in minor race at Haydock in August, first outing. *R.
Hollinshead.*

OUR DAY (USA) 2 b.c. Judgable–Spanish Wind (Gushing Wind) (1982   **62**
6fg 7fg 5.8f⁴ 7f) robust, quite attractive colt; dam won 6 sprint races, including
claiming events; plating-class maiden; not raced after August. *P. Cole.*

OUR GRACIE 3 ch.f. Star Appeal 133–Tinkling Sound 93 (Sound Track 132)   **52**
(1981 NR 1982 10h 9.4g⁴ 12f² 12v) half-sister to quite useful 1977 2-y-o
sprinter Sounding Brass (by Philip of Spain); dam sprinter; second in minor
event at Edinburgh in September; stays 1½m; probably unsuited by heavy
going; sold 2,700 gns Newmarket December Sales. *Sir Mark Prescott.*

OUR KATY 2 gr. or ro.f. Dragonara Palace 115–Clouds of Gold (Goldhill 125)   **68**
(1982 5.1f 6g 6g* 7g 6g 6g 5s) May 1; 1,400Y; lengthy filly; half-sister to 1m and
1½m winner Farthing (by Maystreak); dam never ran; made all in 14-runner

seller at Ripon (bought in 4,200 gns) in July; little chance in nurseries subsequently; not certain to stay 7f. *K. Ivory.*

OUR LAL   6 b.m. Levmoss 133–Oola Rose (Breakspear II)   (1981 17.1g 16.9s §§ 1982 16.5f)   poor performer; has gone the wrong way temperamentally and refuses to race nowadays. *S. Harris.*

OUR MAGGIE   3 ch.f. Tickled Pink 114–Thundersquall 109 (Roi de Navarre — II 123)   (1982 NR   1982 7.6fg 8d)   small, workmanlike filly; half-sister to a winner in Malaya; dam a stayer; well behind in maiden races at Lingfield in May and Salisbury in June. *R. Thompson.*

OUR MOLLY   2 gr.f. Dragonara Palace 115–Molly Flo (Paveh 126)   (1982 5f*   80 5f 5fg 6g* 6g³ 6g 6d⁴ 6g 5s)   Mar 12; 1,500F; tall, fair sort; half-sister to middle-distance winner Elizabeth Howard (by Sharpen Up); dam never ran; won minor events at Redcar in May and Doncaster in June; better suited by 6f than 5f; probably acts on any going; blinkered sixth outing; inconsistent; sold 7,000 gns Newmarket Autumn Sales. *W. Wharton.*

OUR MOMENT   2 b. or br.c. Garda's Revenge 119–Crimson Velvet 89 (Above   67 Suspicion 127)   (1982 5fg⁴ 5g 5g 5s)   May 1; 6,000Y; lengthy colt; brother to 1981 2-y-o 5f winner Crimson Court, and half-brother to several winners, including useful middle-distance colt Grain Race (by Windjammer); dam stayer; little worthwhile form in maiden and minor events; blinkered final appearance; sold CBA 1,300 gns Newmarket Autumn Sales. *B. Swift.*

OUTLAW   3 ch.c. Morston 125–Heathfield 99 (Hethersett 134)   (1981 7g 7fg³ — 8.2fg² 8g* 8g   1982 12fg 14fg 12f)   quite a well-made colt; good walker and mover; won maiden race at Ayr in 1981; soundly beaten in handicaps at 3 yrs; should stay 1½m+; blinkered last 2 starts; sold to W. Clay 6,200 gns Ascot August Sales. *R. Hern.*

OUT OF HAND   3 ch.c. Some Hand 119–Crusheen (Typhoon 125)   (1981 6g   79 7f 7.2fg³ 7g 7g   1982 7g* 8f 7fg⁴ 7f³ 6fg⁴(dis) 6f 6g* 6g 6g)   lengthy, useful sort; successful in handicaps at Warwick in May and Yarmouth in September; stays 7f well; yet to race on a soft surface; wears a bandage on near-hind; has run creditably for an apprentice. *D. Dale.*

OUT OF THE QUESTION   2 gr.c. Captain James 123–La Grisette (Fortino **104** II 120)   (1982 7g 7.5f 7fg⁴ 7d 8g* 8s²)   Feb 21; IR 12,000Y; half-brother to fairly useful 1979 2-y-o 6f winner Viva L'Armour (by Gay Fandango) and a winner in Malaya; dam won at up to 1¾m in Ireland; ran well in nurseries at Leopardstown towards end of season, winning one by ¾ length from Anne's Dance and finishing 1½ lengths second of 19 to Natingo under top weight in another; had previously shown ability in good company; will stay 1¼m; acts well on soft going and has run respectably on firm. *M. O'Toole, Ireland.*

OUTWITTED   2 b.c. Whitstead 125–Dereta 92 (Aggressor 130)   (1982 7d 7g   60 8f 8g 9s)   Apr 5; compact, attractive colt; half-brother to 3 minor winners; dam stayer; only plating class; should stay well; wore blinkers third and fifth starts; sold 1,400 gns Newmarket Autumn Sales. *C. Brittain.*

OUTWOOD LASS   4 br.f. Most Secret 119–Birgeen (Bing II)   (1981 NR   1982 — 12d 10fg 12fg 12f 16g)   520 3-y-o; fourth foal; dam poor maiden on flat and over hurdles; beat only one home in her 5 outings (4 of them amateur riders events). *K. Bridgwater.*

OVER AND OVER   3 b.g. Tumble Wind–Olvera (Molvedo 137)   (1981 5fg 5f³ — 6g⁴ 5d   1982 8fg 6f 7g 6g)   lightly-made gelding; good walker; plater nowadays; should stay 1m; blinkered final start. *J. Hindley.*

OVERNITE EXPRESS (USA)   2 ch.c. Noholme II–Attacker (Bold Com-   66 mander)   (1982 5fg 5fg 6d 7fg 7g 8d 7s)   Feb 15; $50,000F, 27,000 gns Y; rather lightly-made colt; first foal; dam won 2 small 1½m races in Ireland; plating-class maiden; best race when blinkered for first time in nursery at Leicester in November on final outing; should stay 1¼m; acts on soft going. *G. Balding.*

OVER THE LIMIT   3 b.f. High Top 131–Green Chartreuse 91 (French Beige   70 127)   (1981 NR   1982 9f⁴ 8fg*)   40,000Y; rangy filly; half-sister to 2 winners, notably William Hill Middle Park winner and 2,000 Guineas second Mattaboy (by Music Boy); dam won over 5f and 7f at 2 yrs; ran on strongly to beat Sir Blessed by ¾ length in 13-runner maiden event at Salisbury in September; will be suited by 1¼m; sold 41,000 gns Newmarket December Sales for export to South Africa. *W. Hastings-Bass.*

OVER THE RAINBOW 5 b.g. Song 132–Lady Matador 108 (Matador 131) **81**
(1981 5¹g³ 5d⁴ 5fg 5.1f⁴ 6r⁴ 5fg 6f 6fg 5.6fg 5g 1982 5d² 6f* 6f 6fg 5.1g² 6f³ 6f 6f)
strong, compact gelding; has an enlarged near-fore; sprint handicapper; won
at Catterick in April; well beaten last 2 starts (reportedly jarred himself up) and
wasn't seen out after August; acts on any going; blinkered once in 1981;
sometimes sweats up. *J. Winter.*

OWEN HERBERT 2 br.g. Owen Anthony 102–Invisible Romance 79 (Roman- —
cero 100) (1982 5f) Apr 23; 700Y, resold 620Y; fourth foal; dam won over
1m at 2 yrs; unquoted, last of 9 finishers in auction event at Ripon in April.
M. Lambert.

OWEN ROCK 3 ch.c. Owen Dudley 121–Gillycan (Rockavon 120) (1981 6fg —
6g 7fg 8g 1982 12.2f 12.3g 12fg 16.5s) compact colt; poor form, including in
a seller; has worn blinkers. *I. Jordon.*

OWNIA STAR 3 br.f. Wishing Star 117–Paulownia (Palestine 133) (1981 5s —
1982 7g) leggy, narrow filly; probably of little account. *E. Eldin.*

OXSLIP 3 b.f. Owen Dudley 121–Opencast 97 (Mossborough 126) (1981 6fg **106**
7fg* 1982 8g* 10fg⁴ 10f 12f⁴ 12g² 11.7g* 13d* 12v) strong, good sort; excellent mover; a useful filly who won handicaps at Newbury in April, Windsor in
August and Ayr in September; held on by a neck from Regal Steel in Bogside
Cup on last-named; ran creditably most other starts, notably when ¾-length
second to Sans Blague in Galtres Stakes at York; stayed 13f; seemed to act on
any going; game; visits Mr Leader. *G. Pritchard-Gordon.*

OXTON TREASURE 2 br.f. Lucky Wednesday 124–Oxton Lady 81 (Chebs **40**
Lad 120) (1982 5f⁴ 5f⁴ 5f) Mar 21; smallish non-thoroughbred filly; sister to
a poor animal; dam useful sprint plater; bad plater. *M. W. Easterby.*

OYSTON ESTATES 6 gr.g. Goldhill 125–Port Relic 90 (Relic) (1981 6g 6s **53**
8.2d 1982 6g³ 6fg* 6g⁴ 8f² 6g³ 8.2g 7d 8.2s 6s) strong gelding; won handicap
at Carlisle in June; has run creditably over 1m but is probably better at shorter
distances; probably acts on any going; effective with and without blinkers;
good mount for an apprentice; has won 5 times at Hamilton; sold out of T.
Robson's stable 3,100 gns Ascot July Sales after fourth start. *J. S. Wilson.*

OYSTON IDOL 6 b.m. Continuation 120–Lissome Lisa (Sir Ribot) (1981 —
12.2fg 12.2g 8g 1982 12.3g) poor plater; sometimes wears blinkers. *J.
Charlton.*

OYSTONS WINDMILL 3 b.g. Silly Season 127–Westmoreland Jane 76 (Vimy —
132) (1981 7g 7.2v 7g 1982 11s 12f) tall, leggy gelding; soundly beaten in
sellers and a maiden race. *J. Berry.*

OZRA 2 b.f. Red Alert 127–March Malona 88 (Derring-Do 131) (1982 6fg 6s) —
Apr 22; half-sister to fairly useful 1m winner March Spark (by Sparkler) and
quite useful 1979 2-y-o 6f and 7f winner Sun of Schweppes (by Roi Soleil); dam
middle-distance handicapper; no form; backed at long odds when ninth of 22 to
Blue Nantucket in £3,600 seller at York in October, second outing. *C. Booth.*

P

PABLEU 3 b.c. Blue Cashmere 129–Palanna 87 (Pall Mall 132) (1981 7f⁴ 7g **59**
1982 7g 8f² 8f 8f* 8g³ 8d 8g 8s⁴ 8d 10s) well-made colt; not the best of walkers;
awarded 11-runner maiden race at Beverley in May after being hampered by
short-head winner Aldershawe Hall; stays 1m; acts on firm going; blinkered
seventh start; sold 6,800 gns Newmarket Autumn Sales and sent to Malaysia.
P. Asquith.

PACIFIC SPARKLER 3 ch.c. Sparkler 130–Shanghai Lady 87 (Crocket 130) **71** d
(1981 6d 6g³ 7fg³ 5fg² 5fg³ 7s 7d² 7d) small,
strong colt; stays 9f; seems to act on any going; pulled hard for his apprentice
rider third start; not particularly consistent; sold to J. Thorne 3,700 gns Newmarket Autumn Sales. *P. Cole.*

PACIFIC SPENDOUR 3 gr. or ro.c. Roan Rocket 128–Fir Tree 90 (Santa —
Claus 133) (1981 7fg 7fg 1982 12fg) plain colt; behind in maiden races and
a minor event. *H. Bell.*

PACIVAL 2 b.g. Saulingo 122–Sweet Miss (Silver Cloud 121) (1982 6f 5fg 7g **61**
5d 8d 6s) Mar 19; IR 6,000Y; lengthy gelding; plating-class maiden; best run at
5f; blinkered final appearance; trained by Mrs A. Bell first 3 starts. *M. W.
Easterby.*

PADALCO 3 ch.c. Nonoalco 131–Paddy's Princess (St Paddy 133) (1981 **108**
6d³ 6fg* 7fg* 7fg 8g³ 1982 9fg 8f* 8.5f³ 12f 8f*) lengthy, quite attractive
colt; very good mover; won minor events at York in May (beat That's My
Son by ¼ length) and July (odds on when accounting for Cheveley Star by ¾
length); also ran creditably on first and third starts, coming home about 5
lengths fifth of 14 to stable-companion Ivano in Gerry Feilden Memorial Stakes
at Newmarket and 5½ lengths third of 8 to Prima Voce in Diomed Stakes at
Epsom; will stay 1½m but found 1½m too far fourth start; acts well on firm going;
sent to South Africa. *H. Cecil.*

PADANG 4 ch.g. Patch 129–Tragara (Buisson Ardent 129) (1981 12.5s 1982 —
12.3g) good-bodied, compact gelding; very lightly raced and no worthwhile
form; has given trouble at stalls. *T. Fairhurst.*

PADDLE WHEEL 6 b.m. Huntercombe 133–Paddle Boat 98 (St Paddy 133) —
(1981 7d 6fg 7.6g 5s 6f 7.6fg 6fg³ 7f⁴ 6g 8fg 1982 7f 7f) smallish mare; plater;
best form at distances short of 1m; acts on firm going; suitable mount for a boy;
often badgered thereafter. *C. Wildman.*

PADDOCK BAR 3 ch.f. Roman Warrior 132–Motionless 109 (Midsummer —
Night II 117) (1981 5g 5g 7g 1982 8.3g) fair sort; little worthwhile form in
maiden races and a selling handicap; sold 550 gns Ascot 2nd June Sales and has
been sent to USA. *G. Kindersley.*

PADDOCK PRINCESS 2 gr.f. Dragonara Palace 115–Lady Eton 106 (Le **80**
Dieu d'Or 119) (1982 5d* 5fg² 5h* 5fg 5.1f³ 5g 6g) Apr 9; workmanlike filly;
first foal; dam won over 5f and 6f at 2 yrs; won 6-runner maiden race at Kempton
in April and 4-runner minor event at Chepstow in May; had lot to do, but nevertheless ran poorly, in nurseries at Newmarket in September (blinkered) and
October on last 2 appearances; probably acts on any going; unlikely to train on.
R. Hannon.

PADDYS BELLE 2 b.f. St Paddy 133–Tycoons Belle 47 (Tycoon II) (1982 —
5f 7fg 6g 7fg 8s) May 22; small filly; first living foal; dam poor half-sister to very
smart Crimson Beau; poor form in minor and maiden races. *D. C. Tucker.*

PADINGO 3 b.c. Saulingo 122–Paduia (St Paddy 133) (1981 5g 5s² 5g 5g 5s **39**
1982 6s 6f 5fg 6f⁴ 5fg) plater; stays 6f; acts on any going but goes well on soft;
sometimes sweats up. *D. Garraton.*

PADRELO 3 b.c. Relkino 131–Expadeo 82 (St Paddy 133) (1981 7g 7fg 7fg —
7g⁴ 7d 1982 7.6f 8fg 7f 8d 11.1fg) small, quite well-made colt; good mover;
poor maiden. *A. Pitt.*

PADSKI 9 ch.g. St Paddy 133–No Relation 94 (Klairon 131) (1981 18s 16s³ —
16.1fg³ 16.1s 16.9s 18d⁴ 18.8fg 22.2f 16fg² 16.1f³ 16fg 16g 18f 16.5g² 16.1s⁴ 18g⁴
1982 18g 16s 16d 16f) poor staying handicapper; acted on any going; tried in
blinkers and was none too enthusiastic; dead. *R. Hollinshead.*

PAGAN DEITY 3 ch.f. Brigadier Gerard 144–Criminelle (Crepello 136) (1981 **88**
6fg² 1982 7fg 8f 10g* 10.1fg* 10.1g* 10.1g² 13.5fg 10.6f² 10f) quite well-made
filly; good walker and mover; won maiden race at Brighton and 2 minor events
at Windsor, all in July; ran creditably in handicap penultimate start; will stay
1½m (out of her depth over 13.5f); yet to race on a soft surface; usually makes the
running; game. *J. Dunlop.*

PAGAPAS BAY 5 br.g. Welsh Saint 126–Cherry Plum (Primera 131) (1981 **72**
6s* 6s* 6g* 6d² 6g² 5.1fg* 6g 1982 6g³ 5g 5fg 6f) lengthy gelding; sprint
handicapper; seems to act on any going but goes well on soft; occasionally
blinkered (ran creditably in them final start); sometimes sweats up; suitable
mount for a boy. *A. Jarvis.*

PAGEANTRY 2 b.f. Welsh Pageant 132–Norfolk Light 86 (Blakeney 126) **83**
(1982 5fg³ 6f 6g² 8fg 7.6v) Apr 16; well-made filly; third foal; sister to a winning
hurdler and half-sister to 7f and 1m winner Norfolk Realm (by Realm); dam,
half-sister to 1,000 Guineas third Yanuka, won over 7f at 2 yrs and stayed 1½m;
placed in small fields at Newcastle in May and August; should stay 1¼m; possibly
not at her best on heavy ground. *B. Hobbs.*

PAINTHORPE HOUSE 3 br.g. Tycoon II–Marton Lady 103 (March Past 124) **38**
(1981 6f 7d 1982 7g 6s 6g⁴ 6f 8fg 7f³ 8d 8g⁴ 10fg⁴ 7fg) quite attractive gelding;
plater; stays 1¼m; acts on firm going. *D. Chapman.*

PAIR-OF-DEUCES 3 b.f. Some Hand 119–Lost in Silence (Silent Spring 102) **73**
(1981 5g 5d 6fg 6fg 6s* 8d* 8s 1982 8f³ 7f³ 8d 8g³ 8fg² 8.3fg 8fg³ 7.2f 7.3g* 7s
8s 8s³) fair sort; narrowly won handicap at Newbury in September; stays
1m; acts on any going but goes well in the mud; genuine. *R. Hannon.*

PAIS DE GALES 4 b. or br.g. Mummy's Pet 125–Regal Artist 72 (Breakspear — II) (1981 8fg 7fg 7f 1982 7.2s 7.6g) lightly-made gelding; little worthwhile form; gave trouble at start and was withdrawn not under orders on third intended appearance; sold 800 gns Ascot 2nd June Sales. *Mrs C. Lloyd-Jones.*

PAJALSKI (FR) 2 ch.c. Bolkonski 134–Polly's Harde (Lyphard 132) (1982 **100** 7.5d* 7v*) first foal; dam, out of sister to 2,000 Guineas winner Right Tack, won over 1m in France; won both his starts, scoring by 2 lengths from Godefroi in 11-runner newcomers race at Saint-Cloud in September and holding on by a short head from Olrek in Prix de Martinvast at Longchamp the following month; will be suited by 1m; engaged in 2,000 Guineas and Derby. *F. Boutin, France.*

PALACE BEAU 2 ch.g. Dragonara Palace 115–Hotazur 52 (Hotfoot 126) **79** (1982 5d* 5g* 5fg* 5g 5g) Apr 15; close-coupled, workmanlike gelding; second foal; dam, poor plater, comes from good family; successful 3 times before end of April, landing a gamble in maiden race at Leicester and then making all in 2 small events at Folkestone; not raced after May; has won on both a firm and a soft surface but seems best with some give in the ground; gelded after final start; exported to Hong Kong. *P. Ashworth.*

PALACE GENIE 4 br.g. Royal Palace 131–My Ginny 83 (Palestine 133) — (1981 10.2f 1982 7g 12f 7g) lengthy gelding; poor plater; slowly away when blinkered final start; dead. *Miss S. Hall.*

PALACE GOLD 3 b.c. Rheingold 137–Palace Rose 88 (Aureole 132) (1981 **115** 7d⁴ 8s 1982 10.6s² 10fg³ 10.5f² 12f 11g⁴ 12g² 12g 14.6f) 6,400F; strong, workmanlike, good-bodied ex-French colt; third produce; dam won over 1¼m and comes from same family as Royal Palace; still a maiden but has plenty of ability and ran particularly well on third and fourth starts, keeping on strongly to be 2½ lengths second of 6 to Simply Great in Mecca-Dante Stakes at York in May and under 9 lengths sixth of 18 to Golden Fleece in Derby in June; in frame most other outings, including when 3¼ lengths third of 8 to Electric in White Rose Stakes at Ascot and 4½ lengths fourth of 5 to Jalmood in Mecca Bookmakers Scottish Derby at Ayr; stays 1¾m (reportedly finished lame but ran creditably nevertheless when eighth of 15 behind Touching Wood in St Leger when tried at trip); acts on any going but goes well on firm; blinkered last 3 starts. *W. O'Gorman.*

PALACE OF LOVE 2 ch.f. Dragonara Palace 115–Lovelorn 56 (Forlorn River **68** 124) (1982 6g 7fg 8s) Apr 29; half-sister to a minor winner; dam stayed 7f; quite a modest maiden; no form after first outing; not sure to stay beyond 6f. *R. Laing.*

PALACE PET 3 br.f. Dragonara Palace 115–On A Bit 66 (Mummy's Pet 125) — (1981 NR 1982 8f) 380 2-y-o; first foal; dam in frame in all 4 races at up to 11f; unquoted and in need of run when in rear behind Pallomere in 16-runner maiden race at Doncaster in July. *A. Watson.*

PALACE TRAVEL 3 b.f. High Top 131–Palava (Pall Mall 132) (1981 6g — 1982 10.4g 8fg) lengthy, good sort; well beaten in 2 maiden races and a £3,200 event. *G. Hunter.*

PALEMON 7 b.h. Busted 134–Seaswan 104 (Sea-Bird II 145) (1981 NR **64** 1982 11.7fg 10.8fg⁴ 10fg² 12fg⁴) quite a modest middle-distance handicapper nowadays; appears to act on any going; has been tried in blinkers. *S. Harris.*

PALE ORANGE 3 b.f. Orange Bay 131–Palatch 120 (Match III 135) (1981 **74** NR 1982 10.5fg 10f 12d³ 12f) lengthy, fair sort; half-sister to top-class middle-distance performer Patch (by St Paddy); dam won Musidora Stakes and Yorkshire Oaks; 4½ lengths third of 13 to Double Shuffle in maiden race at Lingfield in June; pulled up only subsequent start; will stay 1¾m; sold to BBA 10,000 gns Newmarket December Sales. *P. Walwyn.*

PALESTINIAN GUARD 2 ch.f. Home Guard 129–Witch of Endor 80 (Matador **69** 131) (1982 6fg 6d) Feb 13; 16,000Y; good-bodied filly; half-sister to 4 winners here and abroad, including 1m to 1¾m winner High Old Time (by Mount Hagen); dam won over 9f; never threatened in maiden race at Salisbury in September and minor event at Pontefract (5 lengths seventh of 12 behind Stephalotus) in October. *P. Walwyn.*

PALLAVICINA 2 b.c. Radetzky 123–Fulcrum Miss (Fulcrum) (1982 6f 7g 7fg **81** 7fg 7g 8g) Apr 17; compact, sturdy colt; brother to smart 3-y-o Lobkowiez and closely related to fairly useful 6f and 1m winner Von Erlach (by Huntercombe); dam won sprint claiming races in USA; modest maiden; best runs on fourth and sixth outings; stays 1m; not particularly consistent. *C. Brittain.*

PALLAX 2 b.c. Laxton 105–Pallmonta 82 (Pall Mall 132) (1982 6d) Apr 16; —
strong colt; half-brother to 1m seller winner Maymonta (by Maystreak); dam
placed several times at 2 yrs; backed from 33/1 to 14/1, behind in 18-runner
maiden race at Doncaster in June; second favourite for seller at Beverley the
following month but sweated up and was withdrawn after being very unruly at
start. *J. Blundell.*

PALLOMERE 3 b.f. Blue Cashmere 129–Pallona 62 (Royal Palm 131) (1981 **64**
6s 7g³ 1982 7fg 8f* 10f 7g 7s 7s³ 7d² 8s³) lengthy, lightly-made filly; made all
and kept on strongly to win maiden race at Doncaster in July; not disgraced
several subsequent outings; stays 1m; acts on any going; often takes a strong
hold. *E. Eldin.*

PALM THE ACE 4 b.g. Palm Track 122–Aces High 62 (Acer 123) (1981 **46**
6s 10s 8fg 7d⁴ 8g 5v³ 5fg 6fg 8s 6g 1982 6d² 8d* 8g 7fg* 7f 6fg 8g 8fg 7f 8g 8s
8g² 8d² 7s) small gelding; plater; successful at Warwick in April (bought in
950 gns) and Lingfield in May (no bid); stays 1m; probably acts on any going.
R. Hoad.

PALOS HEIGHTS 3 b.f. Lochnager 132–Ruling Class 92 (King Emperor) **36**
(1981 6g 6g⁴ 6f 6d 7fg 6f² 8fg 8d 7g 1982 8fg³ 8fg) lightly-made filly; plater;
stays 1m; acts on firm going; has been bandaged on off-hind. *J. Fitzgerald.*

PAMELA'S JET 2 b.f. The Brianstan 128–Brighton Jet 69 (Jolly Jet 111) **64**
(1982 5f² 5fg² 5f 5fg 5fg⁴ 5fg 5fg² 5f² 5d) Apr 17; 1,250Y; sturdy filly; good
walker; third foal; dam won sellers over 6f and 7f; plating-class maiden; second
in maiden maiden events in the spring and in nurseries in September; seems to
need an easy 5f; well served by firm going and ran poorly only outing on a soft
surface; has run well for apprentice; slowly away fourth appearance. *R.
Hollinshead.*

PAMKINS HART 6 b.m. Pamroy 99–Regal Buskin (Little Buskins 119) —
(1981 NR 1982 17f) well beaten on flat but is a winner over hurdles. *M. Tate.*

PAMPABIRD 3 b.c. Pampapaul 121–Wood Grouse 56 (Celtic Ash) (1981 **114**
5g* 5s³ 5.5d⁴ 1982 7s² 8.5d³ 8v 7s* 6.5g³ 8d² 8g⁴ 8s² 7s) IR 29,000F, 25,000Y;
half-brother to 2 winners, including Great Sound (by Meadow Mint), successful
at up to 7f at 2 yrs in Ireland and subsequently a very useful stakes winner in
USA; dam, half-sister to Pitskelly, stayed 13f; won minor event at Evry in June
from Katerina the Great; placed most other starts, running creditably to be 6
lengths second to Zino in Prix Djebel at Maisons-Laffitte on first and ¾-length
second to King James in Prix Quincey at Deauville on eighth; stays 1m; yet to
race on a firm surface; often bandaged. *J. Cunnington, jnr, France.*

PAMPACHRIS 2 b.g. Pampapaul 121–Ragwort 68 (Ragusa 137) (1982 —
7g 7g) Apr 30; IR 21,000Y; third living foal; dam, daughter of smart Turf,
needed a test of stamina; last in big fields of maidens at Newmarket in June
and August (blinkered). *N. Callaghan.*

PAMPALAD (USA) 3 b.c. Naskra–Retirement (Royal Gem) (1981 5g 5d 8s⁴ **65**
1982 10.4g⁴ 13.8f³ 13.8f³ 13g 12.3g² 11g³ 12.3g* 12f* 13d 13.8d) neat, attractive
colt; not the best of movers; won stakes race at Newcastle and minor event at
Edinburgh (made all); stays 1¾m; acts on firm going; sold 7,000 gns Newmarket
Autumn Sales. *W. Elsey.*

PAMPAS 2 b.f. Pampapaul 121–Ribotingo 78 (Petingo 135) (1982 6f 6g) —
Mar 14; IR 6,000F, 22,000Y; quite well-made, lengthy filly; second foal; dam
best at sprint distances; 9½ lengths fifth of 16 to Dancing Meg in maiden race at
Lingfield in June, second outing; will stay beyond 6f. *J. Dunlop.*

PAMPERED GIPSY 3 b.g. Pampapaul 121–Gipsy Heart (Skymaster 126) **64**
(1981 7f 6fg 8s 6g 7d 6g 1982 6f 7fg 7f 6g 6f 7f² 7f³ 6g⁴ 6g⁴ 7fg² 7.3g³ 8d 8fg
7.2s 7s⁴ 6d) poor walker and mover; stays 7f; acts on any going; wears blinkers;
good mount for an apprentice. *A. Bailey.*

PAMRULLAH 2 gr.f. Pals Passage 115–Framboise 67 (Nasram II 125) (1982 **59**
6f 7g) sparely-made filly; fourth reported foal; half-sister to a winning jumper;
dam suited by long distances; showed up in maiden race at Yarmouth in July
and minor event at Leicester in August; worth noting in sellers. *C. Spares.*

PAM'S PROMISE 2 ch.f. Arab Chieftain 79–Signal Time (Umberto 118) **42**
(1982 5g 6g 6fg³ 7f) Mar 18; neat filly; third reported foal; dam of little account;
no worthwhile form in maiden races and a seller. *C. Pinkham.*

PAMYA (USA) 2 b.f. Bold Forbes–Pause 76 (Aureole 132) (1982 5f 5fg² **73** 5g 5f 5d⁴ 5f) Mar 13; $75,000Y; neat filly; fourth foal; dam, sister to good miler Saintly Song, showed ability at 2 yrs; only quite modest form; not bred to be a 5f performer. *J. Dunlop.*

PANATELLA 3 br.f. Firestreak 125–Chebs Lass 84 (Chebs Lad 120) (1981 — 5fg 6f* 7d³ 6g⁴ 1982 6s 8fg 6f 6f 6g 6g) light-framed filly; quite modest in 1981; soundly beaten in varied company at 3 yrs, including when out of depth in 1,000 Guineas at Newmarket; should stay 1m; hung badly first start; trained by V. Soane first 3 outings. *S. Matthews.*

PANDAN 2 br.c. Blue Cashmere 129–Pakpao 77 (Mansingh 120) (1982 5g³ **67** 5s 5f 5f* 5f* 6g 5f) Mar 31; leggy, lightly-made colt; has a round action; first foal; dam 2-y-o 5f winner; won 2 sellers at Redcar in May without attracting a bid; not raced after July; acts on firm going; best in blinkers; sold to K. Morgan 520 gns Doncaster September Sales. *T. Fairhurst.*

PANDORAS GOLD 3 b. or br.f. Wishing Star 117–Moss Girl 59 (Star Moss 122) **49** (1981 5fg⁴ 6fg 5d 5s 5g* 5g 1982 6f 7f 8f* 7fg 8fg 8s 10g* 10s) narrow, un-furnished filly; plater; won at Carlisle in July (no bid) and Leicester in October (bought in 1,500 gns); stays 1¼m; acts on firm going. *P. Taylor.*

PANGULO 2 ch.c. Realm 129–Blue Draco (Majority Blue 126) (1982 5g² **66** 5s³ 5fg⁴ 5fg³ 6f³ 6g⁴ 6g 6g 7g) Feb 13; 6,000Y; smallish colt; second foal; dam unraced half-sister to very useful French miler Welsh Game; plating-class maiden; best form at 5f, but usually had little chance over further; wears blinkers. *T. Fairhurst.*

PANI FELICIA 3 b.f. Import 127–Bouchette 76 (Current Coin 118) (1981 NR — 1982 7f 10.1fg) 3,100Y; second foal; dam, half-sister to smart Lordedaw, won two 7f sellers; last of the finishers in maiden race at Leicester in July and minor event at Windsor in August. *J. Holt.*

PAPERACER 3 ch.g. Jukebox 120–Almanac 89 (London Gazette 117) (1981 **68** 5d 5s 5s 6g 6fg 5d 5s⁴ 5s 6s 1982 7d 7f 9g 8fg³ 8s 10s) robust, close-coupled gelding; stays 1m; appears to act on any going; ran poorly in blinkers once in 1981. *D. Elsworth.*

PAPERETTO 3 br.c. Godswalk 130–Goosie-Gantlet 63 (Run The Gantlet) (1981 **93** 6g 6fg² 7fg* 1982 8s³ 7tg⁴ 8f³ 10g 8d⁴ 8f 7g² 8g* 8f 7d* 7g) useful-looking colt; fairly useful handicapper; made most of running to hold off Vin St Benet by a short head in Northern Goldsmiths' Handicap at Newcastle in August and Hello Sunshine by ¾ length at Newmarket in October; best at up to 1m; acts on any going; suited by forcing tactics. *B. Hills.*

PAPER RICH 9 ch.g. Richboy 117–Paperback 94 (Hard Ridden 131) (1981 NR — 1982 12d⁴) poor staying handicapper; acts on any going; used to wear blinkers; winner over hurdles and fences. *G. Blum.*

PARABEMS 3 b.f. Swing Easy 126–Lunar Queen 96 (Queen's Hussar 124) **61** (1981 6f 6f 5fg² 7f 6d² 6g² 5s 5s* 1982 6g² 5d² 5s⁴ 6f⁴ 6g 5d² 6fg 5d 6d) lengthy filly; poor mover; sprint handicapper; stays 6f; acts on any going but is ideally suited by some give in the ground; has run creditably for an apprentice; has shown a tendency to hang; trained first 6 starts by C. Williams; sold 1,600 gns Newmarket Autumn Sales. *K. Brassey.*

PARADISE (FR) 3 br.f. Brigadier Gerard 144–Orsa Maggiore 117 (Ruysdael II **121** 122) (1981 9d³ 10v 8s* 1982 8s⁴ 10.5d² 10.5g* 10.5v³ 10g⁴ 12f 13d³ 11f) second foal; dam outstanding filly in Italy, winner of Oaks d'Italia, Gran Premio di Milano and Premio Roma; won Prix Cleopatre at Saint-Cloud in May by ½ length from Zalataia; ran well to be placed in Prix Penelope on same course (4 lengths second to All Along), Prix de Diane Hermes at Chantilly (4 lengths third behind Harbour) and Rothmans International at Woodbine, Canada (under 5 lengths third to Majesty's Prince); stays 13f; ideally suited by some give in the ground. *G. Bonnaventure, France.*

PARADISE REGAINED 2 ch.f. North Stoke 130–All Souls 96 (Saint Crespin — III 132) (1982 6fg 8s) May 27; 5,000Y; tall, shallow-girthed filly; half-sister to winners here and abroad, including 9f to 11f winner Regal Steel (by Welsh Pageant); dam won twice at around 1¼m; in rear in minor event at Windsor in July and maiden race at Wolverhampton (last of 18) in October. *T. Marshall.*

PARADISE STRAITS 2 ch.f. Derrylin 115–Flaming Peace 104 (Queen's Hussar — 124) (1982 7g 7fg 7fg 7.6v) Apr 19; 3,000Y; third foal; half-sister to 1980

2-y-o 6f winner Sovereign Flame (by Supreme Sovereign); dam won twice over 7f at 2 yrs; poor form in maiden races. *S. Woodman.*

PARADIS TERRESTRE (USA) 3 b.c. Empery 128–Pixie Tower 116 (Songedor 116) (1981 7s* 8d² 1982 7g⁴ 8s) lightly-made, narrow ex-English colt; has a nice, easy action; trotted up in Hyperion Stakes at Ascot and looked unlucky when strong-finishing ½-length second to Count Pahlen in William Hill Futurity at Doncaster at 2 yrs; didn't run up to his best in 1982, sweating up when about 2½ lengths fourth of 7 to Come On The Blues in Heron Stakes at Kempton in May and coming home well-beaten ninth of 13 to Ya Zaman in Prix du Rond-Point at Longchamp in September; gives impression he needs further than 7f and will probably stay 1¼m; yet to race on a firm surface; trained by H. Cecil first start. *P.-L. Biancone, France.* —

PARANNDA 3 b.f. Bold Lad (Ire) 133–Polana (Botticelli 129) (1981 6fg² 6.5d* 8v 1982 6d* 8g⁴ 8fg³ 8g* 10g² 9d³ 9.2s) deep-girthed filly; half-sister to 3 winners, including smart French and American middle-distance colt Dancing Master (by Dancer's Image) and very smart French 1m to 1¼m filly Pollenka (by Reliance II); dam won at up to 1m in France; won minor event at Evry early in year and Prix de Sandringham at Chantilly in June; beat La Paille ½ length in latter; also ran creditably in Poule d'Essai des Pouliches at Longchamp (fourth to River Lady), Prix de Malleret on same course (2 lengths second to Grease) and Prix Chloe at Evry (2¼ lengths third to Grease again); stays 1¼m; acts on a firm and a soft surface. *F. Mathet, France.* **117**

PARENT 9 br.g. Great Nephew 126–Piragua 85 (Petition 130) (1981 8.2d 1982 10d) lightly-raced handicapper nowadays; stays 1¼m well; acts on any going; has been pin-fired and has worn bandages in front. *E. Weymes.* —

PARISIO (USA) 3 b.g. Sham–Miralla 120 (Allangrange 126) (1981 7g 1982 11g 12fg 16h² 16fg* 14g² 15.5f*) rather narrow, lengthy gelding; has a rather round action; made virtually all and stayed on strongly to land odds decisively in maiden race at Beverley and minor event at Folkestone in summer; ran creditably in between; suited by a test of stamina; yet to race on a soft surface; sold 4,100 gns Newmarket Autumn Sales. *J. Hindley.* **83**

PARIS NORTH (CAN) 2 gr.c. Lucky North Man–Bye Bye Paris (Grey Dawn II 132) (1982 8fg 8s) Apr 25; 10,000Y; sturdy colt; second foal; dam won 13 races, including Canadian Oaks; not fully wound up, ran on without being hard ridden when sixth of 9 behind easy winner Proclaim in £3,400 event at Goodwood in September, second outing; sure to do better. *J. Sutcliffe.* **76 p**

PARISSAUL 2 b. or br.f. Saulingo 122–Varinessa (Varano) (1982 5fg³ 6g² 8d) May 25; IR 47,000Y; strong, compact filly; third reported produce; half-sister to 2 winners, including Musidora and Yorkshire Oaks winner Condessa (by Condorcet); dam, half-sister to Irish St Leger winner Allangrange, was second twice over 1½m in Ireland; second in maiden race at Ayr in July, easily best effort; off course for almost 4 months subsequently. *S. Norton.* **75**

PARK BRIDGE 5 ch.g. Park Lawn 111–Asa-Bridge 77 (Como 120) (1981 6fg 8d 7s 8g 8f³ 8.3fg³ 8.3fg³ 8.2g² 8h* 7h 8g² 1982 6fg³ 10.6h 8g 8fg 9f 8.3g³ 8d² 8fg 8g) compact gelding; plater; stays 1m well; possibly not at his best on very soft going, but acts on any other; has worn bandages; fell fifth outing. *M. Pipe.* **48**

PARKDALE 4 ch.c. Swing Easy 126–Miss McWorden 75 (Worden II 129) (1981 7g 8g 5d 6g 10.2g 8g⁴ 1982 10f³ 10.2f 8fg³ 10g⁴ 10fg² 10g 12g 12fg 12fg 12g 8s) big, strong, well-made colt; excellent mover; mainly disappointing since his 2-y-o days but was in frame in 4 handicaps in 1982; seems to stay 1½m; seems to act on any going; sometimes blinkered. *J. Fitzgerald.* **79 d**

PARLOUR PRINCESS 2 ch.f. Gentilhombre 131–Dairy Queen 76 (Queen's Hussar 124) (1982 5fg 7f 7f 6g 7.6v) Apr 1; workmanlike filly; half-sister to 2 winners by Birdbrook, including very useful Parlour Game, successful at up to 8.5f; dam placed from 6f to 1¾m; plating-class maiden; stays 7f. *R. Smyth.* **60**

PAR PAK 3 b.c. Maystreak 118–Rugby Princess 82 (El Gallo 122) (1981 6fg 5f 6f² 6g 6f 6d 5f² 5.1f* 5f⁴ 5g 1982 5f 6fg⁴ 5fg 7f* 6d 8s) tall, rather leggy colt; former plater; won handicap at Catterick in September; should stay 1m; best form on firm ground; has worn bandages. *J. Spearing.* **55**

PARRE TRIA 3 b.g. Sparkler 130–Flotsam 67 (Rustam 127) (1981 6g 7fg 7d 8.2fg² 7f² 7g 1982 8g 8f⁴ 10f 12f 14g 13.1g⁴ 12.3fg) fair sort; poor form, including in a seller; probably stays 13f; acts on firm going; blinkered fourth start; has worn bandages. *D. Sasse.* **49**

PART-EX 9 b.g. Star Moss 122–Eilan Aigas 93 (Counsel 118) (1981 12g³ — 12g³ 12g* 15g² 1982 15f) former plater; stays 1½m; acts on a soft surface. *R. Allan.*

PARTHIA'S PICTURE 3 b.c. He Loves Me 120–Parthia's Image 92 (Parthia 132) (1981 5s 5g 6f³ 6fg³ 8g³ 7d* 7g² 1982 8d 8g 8f 6g 8fg 8.2g 8fg 7fg) shapely, attractive colt; not disgraced in handicaps at Newbury on second start and Royal Ascot on fifth (heavily backed in Britannia Stakes); ran moderately last 3 starts, wearing blinkers on second occasion; needs further than 6f and may well stay 1½m; probably acts on any going. *G. Lewis.*

PARTICULAR MISS 3 b.f. Luthier 126–One Over Parr 114 (Reform 132) **70** (1981 6g 6fg⁴ 1982 8g* 10.6f 8fg) smallish, quite attractive filly; narrowly won maiden race at Warwick in May; soundly beaten in handicaps afterwards, but didn't look happy on very firm ground on first occasion; should be suited by middle distances. *P. Walwyn.*

PARTON GEORGE 3 b.g. Streetfighter 120–Larullah (Lorenzaccio 130) — (1981 5d 5s 5.8g 6d 5.8f 6g 7d 1982 8d 5fg 8.3g 5h) sturdy gelding; bad plater; has worn blinkers. *D. Wintle.*

PARTY TRICK 3 br.f. Streak 119–Belle Mere (Tacitus 124) (1981 5d 5g **47** 5f² 7f 8s 1982 8f 8g* 8.3fg 8fg 8f⁴ 8.2s 8s) plater; attracted no bid after winning at Ayr in July; stays 1m; has worn blinkers; sold 420 gns Ascot December Sales. *T. Marshall.*

PAS DE SEUL 3 b.c. Mill Reef 141–Thereby 99 (Star Moss 122) (1981 6f² **133** 6.3fg* 6.5s* 1982 7.3g* 8fg 7v*)

Except on the occasions two-year-olds have won the race, the Prix de la Foret at Longchamp has seldom been so effective or useful in establishing merit as in 1982 when Pas de Seul trounced his field. Usually by the time the Foret is run in late-October the capabilities of the great majority of older horses are well exposed, as they certainly were in regard to the winner in the two previous years, Moorestyle, and in regard to the favourite and second favourite in Pas de Seul's race, The Wonder and Ya Zaman, two of France's best milers. But injury had severely limited Pas de Seul's opportunities. A hairline fracture of the off-fore cannon bone which required pinning kept him off the course eleven months between his victories in the Prix Eclipse at Saint-Cloud as a two-year-old and in the Hungerford Stakes at Newbury in August; and he ran only once between Newbury and Longchamp, in the Waterford Crystal Mile at Goodwood. He could not be assessed with any degree of confidence before the Foret. Without that race we should have been reduced almost to writing in generalities about him, having to guess how much better he might be than his running at Newbury (where, despite the proximity of the maiden Mean Francine in fourth place, he put up an excellent performance considering his long absence to win staying on by a length and a half and the same from Beldale Lustre and Hays) and at Goodwood (where he finished three and a half lengths fifth of eight to Sandhurst Prince on firmish ground that might well not have suited him).

It transpired that Pas de Seul was significantly better than he had so far

Hungerford Stakes, Newbury—a successful return from injury for Pas de Seul; Beldale Lustre is second

*Prix de la Foret, Longchamp—another Group 1 winner for Mill Reef
as Pas de Seul easily beats The Wonder*

shown: he was a top-class horse, probably as good as any at his distance trained
outside France. He proved much too good for The Wonder. The race takes
little describing since only three of the nine contestants played any serious part.
Tres Gate, ridden by Piggott, made the running until The Wonder, ridden by
Eddery, moved up from second after the turn into a clear advantage halfway up
the straight. Pas de Seul, held up by stable-jockey Roche, looked like winning
from the moment he made his move and in the last furlong The Wonder, Tres
Gate and Big John, who put in some good work from the turn, were powerless to
prevent his drawing further and further away. Pas de Seul won by three
lengths; he had four and a half to spare over Tres Gate and slightly more over
Big John, a good second to Noalcoholic in the Prix Messidor. We see no reason
to discount the value of the form, though fifth-placed Dara Monarch's showing
can be ignored on account of the very heavy ground, and sixth-placed Ya Zaman's
on account of his being badly hampered at the start. The Wonder had looked
exceptionally well beforehand; the going suited him, and the criticism levelled at
Eddery that he came too soon seems no more than a pretty lame attempt at an
excuse. No-one could complain about the gallop—a strong one, guaranteeing a
fair test, set by a very smart in-form horse also known to be suited by the ground.

Pas de Seul (b.c. 1979)	Mill Reef (b 1968)	Never Bend (b 1960)	Nasrullah
			Lalun
		Milan Mill (b 1962)	Princequillo
			Virginia Water
	Thereby (br 1965)	Star Moss (ch 1960)	Mossborough
			Star of France
		Besides (b 1952)	Naucide
			Bees Knees

Pas de Seul's trainer has made a brilliant start to his career. The Prix de la
Foret was the third pattern race won by him in France with just five runners,
and with Assert, Pas de Seul and Anfield in his team he has never been in the
shadow of his famous father. All three animals were bought as yearlings at public
auction, Assert for around £16,000, Anfield for 53,000 Irish guineas and Pas de
Seul for 80,000 guineas at the Houghton Sales. Pas de Seul, a neat, attractive
colt typical of his sire, turned out by far the best of the ten Mill Reef yearlings
sold in 1980, three of whom cost more. Some had a more imposing pedigree
but his is solid enough, his dam's family one that did plenty of winning for the
man who built it up, the late T. H. Farr. The dam Thereby was a useful
handicapper at up to nine furlongs, the daughter of another useful handicapper
Besides whose distance was five, six or seven furlongs, and the granddaughter
of the sprinter Bees Knees. Besides and Bees Knees each won five races and
produced five winners; among the former's winners were the remarkable racemare
Costmary and Okeover, the dam of the Goodwood Cup winner Girandole. Since
her sale at the end of her three-year-old days Thereby has surpassed the winner-
producing efforts of her two predecessors—seven so far including the useful
sprinter Captive Dream (by Sing Sing) and tough middle-distance filly Major
Concession (by Major Portion).

Pas de Seul was retired after the Prix de la Foret to the Longfield Stud at
Cashel in Tipperary, a part of the Coolmore set-up, at a fee of IR 9,000 guineas.

Mr R. E. Sangster's "Pas de Seul"

While to be deprived of further opportunity of assessing him is disappointing, the decision to retire him is perfectly understandable and reasonable. To get one top race out of a horse that has suffered the type of injury Pas de Seul suffered is no mean feat. The chances of improving on that, of his finding suitable going, of his staying clear of injury, had to be weighed against the benefits of standing him as a stallion right away. Unseasonably dry weather, and the year would be as good as wasted. There seems little doubt that Pas de Seul needed some give in the ground to be seen to best advantage. His distance is more open to argument since in his all-too-short career he was only once tried beyond seven furlongs, that on the firmish ground in the Waterford Crystal Mile. His best run was at seven furlongs but he would surely have stayed a mile and a quarter. He had a good turn of foot. *D. O'Brien, Ireland.*

PASQUIER 3 b.g. Shiny Tenth 120–Tweetie Pie (Falcon 131) (1981 5s 5g 1982 10s) poor maiden. *H. O'Neill.* —

PASSING MOMENT (USA) 3 ch.c. Parade of Stars–Thelma Dear (Ballydonnell) (1981 5.1f 6fg 7g⁴ 6g 6f³ 5fg 7g 1982 6s 10f 8f 9g 10d 12fg) lightly-built colt; good walker; plater nowadays; isn't sure to get 1¼m; blinkered fifth start; trained first 5 outings by G. Pritchard-Gordon. *J. Jenkins.* —

PASSING THROUGH 2 br.f. Be My Guest 126–Angel Row 96 (Prince Regent 129) (1982 6d) May 15; 7,200F, 39,000Y; third foal; half-sister to fair 1979 2-y-o 5f performer Welcombe (by Mountain Call); dam, winner over 1m, is daughter of Irish 1,000 Guineas winner Front Row; unquoted and in need of race, behind in 21-runner maiden event at Newmarket in October. *G. Hunter.* —

PASSIONNEL 2 br.c. So Blessed 130–Gallic Law 91 (Galivanter 131) (1982 5g 5fg³ 6fg²) Apr 25; 8,200Y; stocky colt; half-brother to 3 winners, including fairly useful sprinter Ferriby Hall (by Malicious); dam won twice over 7f at 2 yrs; quite a modest maiden; unable to get Salieri out of a canter in 3-runner event at Goodwood in July on final appearance; probably stays 6f. *D. Marks.* **75**

PASS NO REMARKS 3 b.f. Wolverlife 115–Place To Place (No Robbery) **68**
(1981 5s⁴ 5g* 5fg⁴ 6f 5f² 5g* 5d³ 5h 1982 6f 5fg 5fg 5fg⁴ 7f 7g 7.2f 5d) lengthy,
lightly-made filly; won twice at 2 yrs; well beaten most starts in 1982; best
form at 5f. *B. McMahon.*

PASS TO PARADISE (USA) 3 gr.f. Key To The Kingdom–Duke's Duchess **67**
(The Axe 115) (1981 NR 1982 10g 12.3g² 14g³ 12v 10g² 12d²) $24,000Y;
leggy, narrow filly; first foal; dam won over 1m in USA; quite a modest maiden;
stays 1¾m. *G. Pritchard-Gordon.*

PASTAPEAL 3 b.c. Star Appeal 133–Countess (Shantung 132) (1981 NR —
1982 8f 12d 11g 8g 9s 12.2d⁴) 1,700Y; compact, sturdy colt; half-brother to
winners in Italy by Veronese and Viani; dam won at 3 yrs in Italy and is half-
sister to Italian Derby second Camigliatello; poor maiden; sold 360 gns Ascot
December Sales. *F. Watson.*

PATAUDI (USA) 2 b.c. Apalachee 137–Bonavista (Dead Ahead) (1982 **82**
8g 8s⁴) May 9; $145,000Y; strong, good-bodied colt; half-brother to numerous
winners, including Teddy's Courage (by Exclusive Native), a smart winner at
up to 9f, and very smart French 3-y-o 6f and 7f winner Exclusive Order (also by
Exclusive Native); dam stakes-placed winner over 4f at 2 yrs and 3 yrs; 6½
lengths fourth of 9 to easy winner Proclaim in minor event at Goodwood in
September; will do better in time. *G. Lewis.*

PATCHER 3 b.c. Patch 129–Alace (Rapace 130) (1981 8d 1982 8s⁴ 12f² **109**
10g* 16fg⁴ 12g³ 12fg² 16g³ 14fg* 14s) 11,000Y; leggy colt; half-brother to
several winners, including Irish 1,000 Guineas third Arctic Lace (by Arctic
Chevalier), herself the dam of Oats; dam unraced half-sister to Bold Lad's
dam Barn Pride; made all and drew clear to beat Patroon by 6 lengths in maiden
race at the Curragh in May and accounted for Ladoucette decisively by 4 lengths
in minor event at Leopardstown in September; in frame in between in Queen's
Vase at Royal Ascot (6 lengths fourth of 14 to Evzon), Irish Sweeps Derby
at the Curragh (10½ lengths third of 10 to Assert), Royal Whip Stakes at the
Curragh again (5 lengths second of 9 to odds-on Lords) and Lonsdale Stakes
at York (just over 3 lengths third to Capricorn Line); stays well; acts on firm
going and is probably unsuited by soft; consistent. *K. Prendergast, Ireland.*

PATCHINIA 4 b.f. Patch 129–Tapia (Tanerko 134) (1981 10v³ 12s 12g —
10.5s⁴ 13.8fg 11d 12d 10d 1982 13.8d) tall, leggy filly; bred to stay 1½m,
but pulls hard; acts on heavy going; taken down early to start as a 2-y-o. *G.
Richards.*

PATCHIT 3 b.f. Patch 129–Milonia (Tambourine II 133) (1981 6s 5fg³ 7f —
7f 8d 1982 10s 16f 12s) light-framed ex-English filly; only poor form in
sellers and a maiden race; has worn bandages; trained by J. Doyle first 2 starts.
M. Browne, Ireland.

PATCHWORK SAINT 4 ch.g. Patch 129–Cimaroya (Right Royal V 135) —
(1981 NR 1982 16f 16g) fair sort; second foal; dam never ran; in rear in
maiden races at Beverley in April and August. *F. Watson.*

PATERNO 4 ch.c. Young Emperor 133–Light Diamond (Florescence 120) **97**
(1981 8.2s 8d 6g 10fg 8.3fg* 8g² 8.3g* 8f* 8fg² 8f* 8.2fg* 9g 8g 1982 8fg 8fg⁴
8f 7fg* 8fg² 8g³ 7f* 8fg⁴ 6.5fg 8g 7g 7f) close-coupled, good sort; useful handicapper on his day, as he showed when winning at Lingfield in June (ridden by
7-lb claimer) and Newmarket in July; beat King's Glory gamely by a neck in a
blanket finish when winning Ward Hill Bunbury Cup on latter course; also
ran very well when length second to Buzzards Bay in 20-runner Royal Hunt
Cup at Royal Ascot, but was occasionally disappointing; best at 7f or 1m;
has won on heavy going but needs top-of-the-ground to show his best form;
has a good turn of foot but has sometimes shown a tendency to idle once in
front; sent to race in USA. *R. Armstrong.*

PATERNOSTER ROW 3 b.c. Godswalk 130–Abergara (Abernant 142) **104**
(1981 7g 7g 10g* 1982 10fg³ 12fg 12g 12g⁴ 12fg³) big, rangy colt; good mover;
in frame 3 times at Newmarket, including when third in Heathorn Stakes in
April (6 lengths behind Mr Fluorocarbon) and £4,100 handicap in August (kept
on at one pace to be beaten 3 lengths by Nikiforos); will stay 1¾m; sold 10,000
gns Newmarket Autumn Sales. *B. Hobbs.*

PATH OF PEACE 6 br.g. Warpath 113–Turtle Dove (Gyr 131) (1981 12s **95**
12d* 16d* 12g² 12f 14f 13d⁴ 14s 12g³ 1982 18.4fg 12fg 15d* 13d³ 14s² 14s²
12s) small gelding; useful handicapper; beat Al Ameen a shade comfortably
by ¾ length in amateur riders race at Ayr in September; placed in Bogside

Cup on same course later in week (close third to Oxslip) and handicaps at York and Sandown in October; stays 2m; well suited by plenty of give in the ground; genuine, although rather disappointing final start. *C. Thornton.*

PATH TO GLORY 3 ch.g. Habitat 134—Garvey Girl (Princely Gift 137) **79** (1981 5fg² 5d* 5g² 5s² 1982 6g 6f⁴ 5f 6g 5fg 6f³ 6s 5s²) neat, attractive gelding; has rather a high knee action; not disgraced on several occasions, including when placed in minor events at Brighton in September (third to Vaigly Star) and Haydock in October (5 lengths second to Cree Bay); stays 6f; acts on any going; blinkered fifth start. *M. Jarvis.*

PATINATION 2 br.f. Monsanto 121–Miss Brecqhou 58 (Linacre 133) (1982 — 6g 7fg 6s) Apr 10; good-topped filly; third reported foal; dam second over 9f and 1¼m; well beaten in maiden and minor events, twice last. *Mrs B. Waring.*

PAT ON THE BACK 2 b.f. Mummy's Pet 125–Kalopia 80 (Kalydon 122) **59** (1982 5g² 5fg 6d 6f 6fg 6d 8fg) Apr 30; 4,100F; leggy, lightly-made filly; has a round action; half-sister to 2 minor winners; dam won over 1¼m; placed in a maiden auction event in the spring; showed form only once afterwards, although descending to sellers; not sure to stay 1m; suited by some give in the ground; blinkered last 3 outings. *G. Blum.*

PAT PONG 3 b.f. Mummy's Pet 125–Caught-At-It 77 (Poaching 115) (1981 **59** 5g⁴ 5g 5g³ 5f 5f 5g 6g 1982 6g³ 6s 8d 6fg⁴ 7.6fg 5fg 8fg 7fg) strong filly; bad mover; only plating class; suited by 6f; blinkered fourth and fifth starts. *T. Fairhurst.*

PATSY PENNALL 2 ch.f. Celtic Cone 116–Clyde Bush 59 (Bullrush 106) **54** (1982 5fg² 5d³ 5g² 5fg² 6g³ 7d 6f 5g³ 6d 5v) Apr 2; small, sturdy filly; half-sister to a winning plater by Pinza; plater; appears not to stay 7f; best form on a sound surface; blinkered fourth, eighth and tenth outings; trained by P. Cundell first 3 starts. *J. Yardley.*

PAULAGER 4 b.g. Lochnager 132–Hopeful Subject 82 (Mandamus 120) (1981 **90** 8g 7g 7.2s* 7.6fg* 8fg 7.2g 7g 7d 7g 1982 7d³ 7f* 7fg² 7fg* 7f) strong gelding; quite useful handicapper; set a strong gallop and rallied very well under pressure when beating Secret Gill a neck in 4-runner P.T.S. Racing Handicap at Newcastle in May; beat Havoc by ¾ length at York the following month; also placed at Newcastle and Ayr; suited by a strongly-run 7f but seems to find 1m too far; acts on any going; thoroughly game and genuine, although was soundly beaten final start (July); sold to D. McCain only 2,500 gns Doncaster October Sales. *M. H. Easterby.*

PAUL MARINER 2 ch.c. Julio Mariner 127–Aruba 77 (Amber Rama 133) — (1982 7g 7s 8s) May 14; useful-looking colt; first foal; dam 7f winner; no form in maiden and minor events. *C. Brittain.*

PAUSE FOR THOUGHT 5 ch.g. Jukebox 120–Madlin 102 (Sovereign Path **58** 125) (1981 8f 8f 7g³ 9fg³ 9fg* 8g⁴ 8f⁴ 8.2f³ 8f⁴ 8g 8.2d² 8s² 8.2d 7s 1982 8f² 7fg² 8fg 8f⁴ 8fg⁴ 8f⁴ 8.2g²) tall gelding; beat Windpipe by ¾ length in handicap at Ayr in May; stays 9f; acts on any going; has occasionally worn blinkers; sometimes sweats up; possibly best on a galloping track; suitable mount for an apprentice. *D. Smith.*

PAVILION 4 gr.g. Habitat 134–Game All 109 (Alcide 136) (1981 6g* 6g — 6g 6fg 6f* 6f 7g 6d 1982 8d 10g 10.8fg 7.6g 6s 7s) attractive gelding; good mover; fair performer as a 3-y-o but has become most disappointing; should stay at least 7f; probably acts on any going; blinkered last 4 starts. *G. Hunter.*

PAWAN 2 ch.c. Tumble Wind–Berne (Preciptic 122) (1982 5fg 5fg) Feb 5; — IR 3,600F, 16,000Y; strong colt; half-brother to 2 minor winners; dam won twice at 1m in Ireland; in rear in maiden races at Lingfield in May, in second blinkered; exported to Algeria. *J. Sutcliffe.*

PAWNBROKER 4 ch.g. Lombard 126–Italian Sky 94 (Skymaster 126) (1981 — 9g 10d 1982 10.2g 5fg) tall, rangy, narrow gelding; well beaten in maiden races; looks a plater. *G. Harman.*

PAY THE FARE 2 ch.g. Dublin Taxi–Lizzylin 84 (Tower Walk 130) (1982 — 5f 5fg 5f) May 2; 6,200Y; sturdy, robust gelding; second foal; half-brother to winning 3-y-o sprinter Shiny Hour (by Shiny Tenth); dam won over 5f at 2 yrs; though well beaten, showed measure of promise in maiden events at York and Doncaster in May and at Haydock in September; may be capable of improvement. *M. Camacho.*

PEACEFUL RUN 2 ch.f. Grundy 137–Peaceful 95 (Crepello 136) (1982 6s)   — p
May 25; quite attractive filly; half-sister to several winners, including useful 7f
and 1m winner Romara (by Bold Lad, Ire); dam won at up to 1¼m; favourite,
made headway from slow start until beaten and eased in closing stages when
ninth of 16 behind Marzooga in maiden event at Leicester in November; sure
to do better. *H. Wragg.*

PEACETIME (USA) 3 b.c. Nijinsky 138–Peace 113 (Klairon 131) (1981 **125**
7g³ 1982 10f* 12fg* 12f 10g⁴ 10fg*)
Those with faith in the ability of history to repeat itself were not slow to
grasp the significance of Peacetime's impressive victory in the Guardian Classic
Trial at Sandown in April. Each of the four previous Derby winners, Shirley
Heights, Troy, Henbit and Shergar, had made his seasonal reappearance in the
Sandown Trial and three of them, Troy, Henbit and Shergar, had won. Looking
a gallop or two short of peak fitness, Peacetime was always travelling strongly at
Sandown and had only to be hand ridden to win by two lengths from the William
Hill Dewhurst runner-up Be My Native with the William Hill Futurity third
Jalmood four lengths further behind in third place. Peacetime came in for
strong support in the ante-post betting market on the Derby and in truth he
looked a very good prospect for the race at the time of his Sandown victory:
his imposing appearance in the paddock—he had grown into a magnificent-
looking colt over the winter—and his splendidly fluent display gave the racing
writers plenty to enthuse about. The Guardian Classic Trial was only Peacetime's second outing—he was a promising third in the Houghton Stakes at
Newmarket the previous October—and the experience seemed sure to bring
him on.

Peacetime's preparation for the Derby was seriously interrupted by
coughing and between the Guardian Classic Trial and his next race, the Schroder
Life Predominate Stakes at Goodwood, a period of three and a half weeks, he
reportedly had only one serious gallop and one half-speed. He was carrying
plenty of condition at Goodwood but started favourite and, moving through
the field in fine style to take the lead entering the final furlong, won by half a
length and the same from Touching Wood and Ivano, the former in receipt of
8 lb from the first and third. In the light of his performances at Sandown and
Goodwood—Troy won the same two races before his Derby triumph—Peacetime
was a big disappointment at Epsom. Looking well and moving beautifully on
the way to post, he weakened rapidly after holding a perfect position at Tattenham Corner to finish seventh, beaten more than a dozen lengths by Golden
Fleece. His trainer, in an interview published in *Timeform* shortly after the
Derby, offered a number of possible explanations for Peacetime's showing at
Epsom, among them the interesting one that 'a horse who has been hobdayed,

*Guardian Classic Trial, Sandown—Peacetime comes into the
Derby reckoning by beating Be My Native comfortably*

however successfully, will always be found out in top-class company.' Peace-time had had the operation during the winter after confirming in the Houghton Stakes his trainer's suspicion that he was making 'a slight noise.' Peacetime's next race after the Derby was the Coral-Eclipse Stakes over a mile and a quarter at Sandown. Rocamadour, who had finished a place behind Peacetime at Epsom, reversed the form with him at Sandown, the pair finishing third and fourth to the four-year-old Kalaglow. Peacetime again faded when the pressure was put on, after looking a danger to all at one point in the straight, his performance bearing a striking resemblance to that in the Derby. Peacetime was off the course for ten weeks after the Coral-Eclipse during which time he was operated on for a soft palate. He won the Valdoe Stakes, a listed race at Goodwood, on his return: the race was slowly run and while Eddery gave Peacetime a very clever ride, dictating the pace and allowing Peacetime a breather rounding the home turn, Carson on the favourite Cut Loose found himself pocketed at the moment Eddery decided to strike for home; Peacetime, eased a little before the line, won by three quarters of a length from Cut Loose with the four other runners close behind. Incidentally, Peacetime was fitted with a tongue strap at Goodwood but the strap worked its way loose before the start.

Peacetime stays in training. He is one to treat with caution until he has given stronger evidence than that provided by the Valdoe Stakes that his soft palate operation has been a complete success. At his best he is capable of winning good races but his history of physical problems obviously undermines confidence in his future. Peacetime's registration was transferred into the name of Beckhampton Ltd before the start of the most recent season, his owner-breeder John Hay Whitney having died in February at the age of seventy-seven. The Whitney colours—pink, black and white striped sleeves, white cap—have become very familiar to followers of flat-racing and jumping in Britain over the

Beckhampton Ltd's "Peacetime"

last half century. Whitney was United States Ambassador to Britain during the Eisenhower administration. Paintings, as well as racehorses, were a consuming pastime during his years in Britain and he was particularly proud of his collection of Impressionist and Post-Impressionist works. He liked particularly to relate the story of the visiting senator who, having done a tour of the paintings, turned to him and said: 'Jock, I really had no idea you were an amateur painter.'

Peacetime (USA)
(b.c. 1979)

Nijinsky	Northern Dancer	Nearctic
(b 1967)	(b 1961)	Natalma
	Flaming Page	Bull Page
	(b 1959)	Flaring Top
Peace	Klairon	Clarion III
(ch 1966)	(b 1952)	Kalmia
	Sun Rose	Mossborough
	(ch 1960)	Suntime

Whitney had kept horses with Jeremy Tree since the mid-'fifties and Tree paid him this tribute: 'No-one could ever have asked for a better owner, one more appreciative of success or more understanding of the many disappointments.' Much was written in the obituaries of Whitney as a philanthropist—which he was—but we shall remember him most as the epitome of the sporting owner: he won, and he lost, with grace and as one American writer put it: 'For Whitney, the sport in racing was its only worthwhile ingredient.' Peacetime is the sixth winner bred by Whitney's 1968 Blue Seal Stakes winner Peace whose earlier winners were: the very useful middle-distance stayer Peaceful (by Crepello), the Coronation Cup winner Quiet Fling (a full brother to Peacetime), the Cambridgeshire winner Intermission (by Stage Door Johnny), the good-class middle-distance stayer Armistice Day (by Rheingold) and End of War (by Bustino), a useful performer at around a mile and a half. A lengthy, most attractive colt, Peacetime stays a mile and a half; he acts well on firm going and has yet to race on a soft surface. *J. Tree.*

PEACE TREATY 2 gr.g. Warpath 113–Country Ramble 93 (Kribi 110)   —
(1982 8s) May 30; 1,500Y; fifth reported foal; brother to fairly useful middle-distance performer Country Walk, and half-brother to 3-y-o 9f winner Alpine Way (by Dragonara Palace); dam staying sister to very useful Farm Walk; 50/1, last of 21 in maiden race at Leicester in November. *R. Stubbs.*

PEACH SUNDAE 2 ch.f. Rarity 129–Peach Melba 96 (So Blessed 130) (1982   — p
6v) Feb 25; 35,000Y; useful-looking filly; first foal; dam won over 5f at 2 yrs; second favourite, close up 4f when seventh of 10 to Northern Adventure in Duke of Edinburgh Stakes at Ascot (bandaged near-hind) in October; should do better. *W. Hastings-Bass.*

PEACOCK CHARM 6 ch.g. Crisp and Even 116–Besselsleigh Lass (Quorum   —
126) (1981 15.8s3 15.8g2 16g 12s2 1982 15.8g) staying handicapper; acts on soft going. *J. Mason.*

PEAK CONDITION 6 ch.m. Mountain Call 125–Saffron Hill 101 (Gulf Pearl   —
117) (1981 NR 1982 12f) apparently of no account. *H. Beasley.*

PEAK TOWER 3 br.c. High Top 131–Malossol 62 (Gulf Pearl 117) (1981   —
NR 1982 9g 10.2g) good-bodied colt; first foal; dam plating-class sister to top-class sprinter Deep Diver; soundly beaten in maiden races at Hamilton and Doncaster; sold 700 gns Doncaster August Sales. *B. Hanbury.*

PEARLPIN 2 ch.c. Grundy 137–Pearlesque 88 (Gulf Pearl 117) (1982 6g   82
7fg 8s 10s) well-made colt; half-brother to 3 winners, including Pearlescent (by My Swallow), a smart winner at up to 1m; dam, sister to numerous winners, won over 5f; 5 lengths fifth of 12 to Zoffany in minor event at Goodwood in September, second outing and best effort; sweated up next time; sold 7,200 gns Newmarket Autumn Sales. *P. Walwyn.*

EARLS DIAMOND 2 br.f. Home Guard 129–Limerick Lace (Pall Mall   ?
132) (1982 5fg 5fg) May 2; IR9,400Y; useful-looking filly; half-sister to a minor winner in France by Royal Palace; dam Irish 1¼m winner; had race won when breaking a shoulder and falling 100 yards out in 8-runner minor event at Goodwood in May; dead. *D. Elsworth.*

EARL THYME 2 b.f. Gulf Pearl 117–Wild Thyme 63 (Galivanter 131)   78
(1982 5.1f 6f 6s3 7f 8d 8.2s) Apr 19; 1,000F, 6,400Y; leggy filly; half-sister to 3 winners, including useful 1975 2-y-o sprinter Rampion (by Pall Mall);

dam won 7f seller at 2 yrs; quite a modest maiden; stays 1m; acts on soft going; stumbled at start and unseated rider on debut. *B. Hobbs.*

PEARLY STEPS   3 ch.c. Gulf Pearl 117–Step You Gaily 71 (King's Company 124)   (1981 NR   1982 8fg 10fg 12g⁴ 11.7f 16g 12fg)   1R 4,500F, 15,500Y; rangy colt; first foal; dam at her best at 2 yrs; only plating class; stays 1½m. *P. Haslam.*   —

PEAR SUNDAE   3 b.f. Shiny Tenth 120–Alice Perrers (Twilight Alley 133)   (1981 7d 7g   1982 12f 12g 12g² 12fg 14g 14.6g 12fg)   leggy filly; plater; stays 1½m; blinkered fourth and sixth starts; sold 510 gns Ascot December Sales. *W. Elsey.*   53

PEDOMETER   3 b.g. Great Nephew 126–Shebeen 124 (Saint Crespin III 132)   (1981 8g²   1982 10f² 12fg 12g)   attractive gelding; good mover; has plenty of ability, as he showed when second to Noble Gift in maiden race at Sandown in June, but has become disappointing; should stay 1½m but pulls hard and may prove best at around 1¼m. *J. Tree.*   94

PEG'S PETAL   2 ch.f. Ardoon 124–Abrill (Laser Light 118)   (1982 5g 5f 5fg 5f² 5f* 5d 5fg⁴ 5fg 5f 5s)   May 1; 1,100Y (privately); lengthy filly; second foal; dam never ran; ran poorly in nurseries after winning maiden event at Catterick in August; evidently considered a 5f performer; acts on firm going; blinkered final outing; not one to trust. *J. Gilbert.*   69 §

PEKING DANCER   2 ch.f. Orbit Dancer–Flying Bridge 71 (Bleep-Bleep 134)   (1982 5d 5fg 5fg³ 5fg 6g 5g⁴ 5f 6f 5v)   May 12; 140Y; strong, lengthy filly; bad plater. *P. K. Mitchell.*   38

PELHAM LINE   2 ch.f. High Line 125–Pelham Wood 59 (Marmaduke 108)   (1982 7f 7fg)   Mar 31; quite well-made filly; first foal; dam winning staying hurdler; well beaten in maiden events at Sandown in July and Chepstow (last of 19) in August. *R. Baker.*   —

PELION (FR)   2 b.g. Sassafras 135–Pallakis (Narrator 127)   (1982 7g 8.2s)   Apr 5; 28,000Y; well-made gelding; half-brother to numerous winners in France, including smart 1978 staying 2-y-o Polynikis and smart middle-distance winner Pale Ale (both by Shantung); dam, a twice-raced twin, is sister to 1,000 Guineas winner Night Off; in rear in September in Ribero Stakes at Doncaster and maiden event at Hamilton; subsequently gelded. *Sir Mark Prescott.*   —

PELLINORE'S POINT (USA)   2 b.c. King Pellinore 127–Bronze Point (Tobin Bronze)   (1982 6fg² 7fg)   May 9; quite attractive, well-made colt; second foal; half-brother to very smart American 3-y-o Air Forbes Won (by Bold Forbes); dam very useful winner of 9 races at up to 1m; shaped promisingly in maiden race (beaten a length) at Doncaster in July and behind Gorytus in Acomb Stakes at York in August; will stay 1m; sure to win in ordinary maiden company. *S. Norton.*   84

PELOPONNESE (USA)   2 b.c. Bold Forbes–Snow Lady (Raise A Native)   (1982 5fg 6fg 7f³ 8f⁴ 8d)   Apr 2; smallish, strong colt; second foal; dam, winner over 9f and 10.5f in France, is out of half-sister to Artaius; quite a modest maiden; will stay 1¼m; acts on firm going and on a soft surface; troublesome at start on second and third outings. *H. T. Jones.*   75

PEMELIA   2 b.f. Monsanto 121–Julie Be Quick (Selari)   (1982 5s 8g 6s⁴)   May 20; half-sister to fairly useful 3-y-o 6f and 7f winner Blue Emmanuelle (by Lochnager) and quite useful 1980 2-y-o 5f performer Queen of Prussia (by Bay Express); dam won at up to 1m in USA; chased along throughout when 4 lengths fourth of 16 behind Onaizah in maiden race at Leicester in November, best effort; co-favourite, prominent when hampered halfway in similar event at Edinburgh on previous appearance; should be well suited by 1m; sent to France. *W. Hastings-Bass.*   69

PENARKSEA   2 ch.f. Privy Seal 108–The Festival Chat (Saucy Kit 76)   (1982 5g 6s)   May 23; workmanlike filly; first foal; dam bad hurdler; last in back-end maiden races at Wolverhampton and Leicester. *A. Fisher.*   —

PENCHETTA   2 gr.f. Sharpen Up 127–What A Picture 80 (My Swanee 122)   (1982 5d⁴)   Apr 24; IR 7,000Y; second foal; dam a 5f performer from a speedy family; favourite, led to below distance when 5 lengths fourth of 12 behind Minie O'Neill in maiden race at Warwick in April. *C. Williams.*   —

PENLLYNE TROOPER   2 b.g. Tachypous 128–Fodens Eve 80 (Dike)   (1982 5fg⁴ 5.8g² 6f 6s 6d⁴ 6g 6s²)   Apr 16; well-grown gelding; second foal; half-brother to a winner in Italy; dam 2-y-o 5f winner; best effort when second of   88

16 behind easy winner Groszewski in nursery at Nottingham in October; ran poorly on third outing; stays 6f well; acts on soft going, and is apparently not suited by firm. *W. Hastings-Bass.*

PENNILESS DANCER 3 b.g. Impecunious–La Tango (Sailing Light 119) (1981 NR 1982 10.1fg⁴ 10.1fg 10.1fg) first foal; dam won several point-to-points; little worthwhile form; possibly stays 1¼m. *J. Benstead.* —

PENNY'S DREAM 3 b.g. Dawn Review 105–Orabella II 111 (Set Fair 129) (1981 5d 5g 5d 6g 6f 8g³ 8.2d 8g 8g* 7d 1982 12fg 10fg 10d³ 10.1d2) leggy non-thoroughbred gelding; plater; claimed £2,600 after final start; not certain to stay 1½m. *P. K. Mitchell.* **56**

PENSCYNOR 6 br.g. Lord Gayle 124–I Will (I Say 125) (1981 8s⁴ 12g 9d 9fg 9fg 1982 8d 9fg⁴ 9g⁴) lengthy ex-Irish gelding; poor performer nowadays; stays 1½m; acts on any going; sometimes blinkered and has worn a hood as well. *M. Lambert.* —

PENSEUR (FR) 3 br.g. Luthier 126–Sweet and Lovely (Tanerko 134) (1981 6f 6g 7fg 1982 8g 7fg 7fg 14f) lengthy gelding; poor form in maiden races and a selling handicap; sold 540 gns Newmarket July Sales. *B. Hanbury.* —

PENTAGRAM 3 b.f. Wishing Star 117–Olivia Stapleton 88 (Road House II) (1981 5d 7f³ 7fg 7g 7fg 7g 8.2s 1982 12f 10f 11g 8s 10g 8fg 8s 7s) strong filly; poor form, including in a seller; stays 11f; blinkered last 3 starts; sold 520 gns Ascot December Sales. *W. Elsey.* —

PENTAX 3 bl.c. Tickled Pink 114–Friendly Gift (Be Friendly 130) (1981 5g 5.8g 5f 5f 5f 5fg 5g 1982 5s 6s) small colt; good walker; sprint maiden; has twice worn blinkers. *Mrs N. Macauley.* —

PENTLAND JAVELIN 2 b.c. Solinus 130–Georgian Girl 92 (Prince Tenderfoot 126) (1982 5g² 5g* 5f⁴ 5f³ 6fg³ 6fg* 6f² 6d 6g 6fg* 6d) Feb 25; 10,000Y; attractive, good-bodied colt; carries a lot of condition; first foal; dam won from 1¼m to 1¾m; successful in maiden race at Newmarket in April, 6-runner Strathclyde Stakes at Ayr in July and £5,500 nursery at Redcar in September; will stay 7f; best form on a firm surface; not particularly consistent. *R. Hollinshead.* **103**

PENWOOD 7 b.m. Precipice Wood 123–Penview 73 (Pendragon) (1981 13s 18g2 1982 18g) staying handicapper; revels in the mud; suitable mount for an apprentice. *N. Hall.* —

PENYBONT 2 ch.f. Welsh Pageant 132–Currency (Crepello 136) (1982 7g² 7fg) Mar 25; rather lightly-made filly; second foal; half-sister to very useful 1¼m filly Fee (by Mandamus); dam never ran; 4 lengths second of 23 to The Fort in maiden race at Newmarket in August; joint-favourite, faded after having every chance at halfway when disappointing eleventh of 29 behind Alligatrix in similar event on same course 3 weeks later. *B. Hobbs.* **81**

PEPINA 6 ch.m. Shoolerville 121–Pepstep 88 (Polic 126) (1981 7f 7f 8.2d 1982 8d 7f) small, stocky mare; in rear in all starts since 1980; best at 7f; acts on firm going and is possibly not at her best on a soft surface; pulled up lame final start (bandaged in front). *M. Haynes.* —

PEPPERWOOD 2 br.g. Tudor Rhythm 112–Calibre (Caliban 123) (1982 8s) second foal; brother to a poor animal; dam won selling hurdles; 50/1 and blinkered, prominent 5f in 21-runner maiden race at Leicester in November. *S. Matthews.* —

PEPPERY 5 b.h. Red God 128§–Powder Box (Faberge II 121) (1981 10.2d 10.6g³ 12d⁴ 12s² 12g* 12f 12v 12g 1982 12g 12fg 12fg 12f⁴ 12g 14g³ 12fg 12d³ 12v) neat, attractive horse; good mover; quite a modest handicapper nowadays; stays 1¾m; probably acts on any going but seems suited by some give in the ground; suitable mount for a claimer; unseated rider seventh outing. *P. Rohan.* **71**

PERANG TEJAM 3 b.f. Sharpen Up 127–Carcosa 103 (Sovereign Lord 120) (1981 6g⁴ 6g* 1982 7fg 7f* 8fg² 8f² 8g* 8v³) useful-looking filly; beat Queen of Scots by 1½ lengths in £6,100 handicap at Newmarket in July and accounted for Fairy Tern impressively by 5 lengths in £7,700 handicap at Ascot in September; also ran well to be placed in valuable handicap at Newmarket, £11,900 event at Doncaster and Premio Bagutta at Milan; stays 1m; acts on any going; does best when ridden up with pace; sold to BBA, probably for export to South Africa, 76,000 gns Newmarket December Sales. *W. Hastings-Bass.* **108**

PERCA 3 ch.g. Royalty 130–The Perch 109 (King's Bench 132) (1981 5d 6g 7fg 7fg 8s 1982 12fg) rather leggy, lengthy gelding; poor maiden; has been blinkered. *M. Masson.* —

PERCASE 3 b.g. Tachypous 128–Pertinacity 106 (Aggressor 130) (1981 5fg **76**
5g 6g 1982 10d⁴ 11.7f² 12fg³ 13.1g³ 14f 11.7g* 12fg 12fg³ 11.7s³ 12s⁴) neat
gelding; apprentice ridden when winning maiden race at Bath in August; ran
respectably afterwards; stays 1½m; acts on any going; sweated up and moved
badly to start third outing; suited by waiting tactics; best in blinkers. *I.
Balding.*

PERCHANCE 3 ch.f. Connaught 130–Mey 78 (Canisbay 120) (1981 7d 7g* **77**
8.2s³ 1982 10g⁴ 10.8fg³ 10fg* 12g 11.1fg² 12g² 11.7s 12s*) smallish, fair sort;
won handicaps at Ayr in August (made all) and Leicester in November; suited
by 1½m; seems to act on any going; has run creditably for an apprentice; game.
W. Hastings-Bass.

PERCOL 3 b.f. Silly Season 127–Sea-Hit 85 (Bleep-Bleep 134) (1981 5g 6g 6d —
1982 8d⁴ 7f 7.6fg 7fg 7fg) leggy, rather lightly-made filly; poor maiden; best
run at 1m on a soft surface; sold to A. Neaves 400 gns Newmarket Autumn Sales.
M. Haynes.

PERDICCAS 4 br.g. Perdu 121–Requisition 101 (Petition 130) (1981 7s **55** d
7fg 7d³ 6d² 7.6g 8.3fg 6f 7f 8f² 8fg 7g 7d² 6g² 6g 1982 7s 8.2s 12fg* 12fg 12fg
10fg 11.7fg 12d 10d 8v 10g 6g 7s) compact gelding; 33/1 when winning 1½m
apprentice handicap at Ascot in April; well beaten all other starts, including in
sellers, but wasn't entirely disgraced over 6f penultimate start; probably acts
on any going; has often worn blinkers but seems better without; often bandaged
behind. *C. Austin.*

PERGODA 4 b.g. High Top 131–Saint Joan 63 (Grey Sovereign 128§) (1981 **55**
5f 5fg³ 1982 5f 6f 5fg 5f² 5g² 5fg 5fg² 5g² 5fg² 5s 5d) plater; second 5 times,
3 times in non-sellers; best at 5f; seems to act on any going, except perhaps
very soft; doesn't find much off bridle; has been tubed; trained much of season
by M. W. Easterby. *I. Vickers.*

PERICULO LUDUS (FR) 6 ch.g. Timmy My Boy 125–La Beuvriere (Right **44**
Royal V 135) (1981 11s² 10.4g 11.7d 8f 10f 10f 10f 1982 8f 8f⁴ 10d⁴ 10g³)
workmanlike gelding; not a good mover; plater nowadays; stays 11f; seems to act
on any going; sometimes wears blinkers. *J. Harris.*

PERLEE (FR) 3 b.f. Margouillat 133–Zirconia 105 (Charlottesville 135) (1981 **122**
8g* 8d³ 1982 10.5d 9fg* 10v³ 10.5v 12d* 13.5fg 12f) 130,000 francs Y (approx
£13,000); wiry filly; second foal; half-sister to 2-y-o winner by Roi Lear; dam
useful at up to 1m in France; beat Vidor by ¾ length in Prix Finlande at Evry
in April and got the better of Zalataia by short head (pair clear) in Prix de
Minerve on same course in July; also ran creditably to be 5½ lengths third of
8 to Harbour in Prix Saint-Alary at Longchamp, under 3 lengths fifth of 13
to Zalataia in Prix de Pomone at Deauville on sixth start, and 3 lengths fifth
to All Along in Prix Vermeille at Longchamp again on final appearance; suited
by 1½m+; acts on any going. *C. Milbank, France.*

PERMABOS 3 b.g. Dubassoff–Blue Ann 60 (Road House II) (1981 6fg 1982 —
12v) rangy gelding; has shown only a little ability in maiden races; seems
to stay 1½m. *K. Stone.*

PEROVSKIA 2 b.f. Sagaro 133–Deep Blue (Deep Diver 134) (1982 5fg 6fg **77**
8f 8fg² 9s) Apr 5; 520F, 3,100Y; neat, strong filly; second foal; dam well beaten
both starts; quite a modest maiden; poor form until ridden by 7lb-claimer
G. Brown on last 2 appearances; suited by test of stamina; acts on soft going
and a firm surface. *J. Fitzgerald.*

PERPLEX 3 ch.c. Be My Guest 126–Catherine Linton (High Echelon) (1981 **65**
6g 5g 7fg 7g 7fg² 7g 8g 8.2d² 8d 1982 8s⁴ 9s⁴ 8fg* 10.4g 8d) rather leggy
colt; poor mover; won maiden race at Edinburgh in April; had stiffish tasks
afterwards; should stay 1¼m; acts on a firm and a soft surface; wears blinkers;
suitable mount for a boy; sent to Malaysia. *D. Smith.*

PERSEPOLIS (FR) 3 gr.c. Kalamoun 129–Perlita (Baldric II 131) (1981 **127**
6fg³ 7.5f* 8g* 8s 1982 8s² 11fg* 10.5fg* 12f⁴ 12.5d)
According to one Eastern legend the Persian city of Persepolis was construc-
ted as a hiding place by the jinn, the equivalent of the fallen angels in western
culture, and in some respects the career of the racehorse Persepolis resembled
that of a fallen angel. Praised to the skies for his successes in the Prix Noailles
and Prix Lupin, he fell from grace with a lack-lustre display in the Grand Prix
de Saint-Cloud and failed to race again. Yet this unfortunate conclusion to

Prix Lupin, Longchamp—Persepolis' turn of foot gets him out of trouble; Alfred's Choice and Sharp Singer follow him home

his campaign should not be allowed to detract from Persepolis' achievements, for at his best he was a match over middle distances for any three-year-old colt trained in France.

Persepolis' chief asset was a formidable turn of foot which proved most effective with waiting tactics, though it wasn't until he had gone down by half a length to Alfred's Choice in the Prix Omnium at Saint-Cloud in March that his connections perceived he would do best if held up. In that race Persepolis led some way from home only to be run out of it near the finish, as had almost happened when he narrowly won the Prix La Rochette the previous year. Waiting tactics demand considerable expertise in any country; in France, where a significant number of good middle-distance events are run at a false pace each season, the problems can be even greater owing to bunching in the last half mile as the runners simultaneously try to quicken. Persepolis' next two races, in each of which Piggott had the mount, provided copybook examples of the hazards involved. In the Prix Noailles at Longchamp in April it was a joy to watch the champion jockey calmly manoeuvre the colt to obtain a clear run after being blocked on the outside with two furlongs to go. Weaving his way through, in the course of which action he was struck on the head by the whip of one of his opponents' riders, Persepolis accelerated in grand style to peg back the front-running Beau Pretender a hundred yards out and score by two lengths. While the form of the Noailles appeared far from easy to assess, with Rienzi third and Balitou fourth, the style of success couldn't be faulted and in a field of ten for the Group 1 Prix Lupin on the same course a month later Persepolis started second favourite to the Prix de Guiche winner Sharp Singer. The remaining runners included Alfred's Choice, the French Guineas second Tampero and Welsh Term, second to Melyno in the Prix de Fontainebleau. Persepolis had to put up a remarkable performance to win, such were the difficulties he encountered in running. Held up with just two behind him entering the straight, he received a severe buffeting when trying to make headway through the middle of the field and momentarily looked in danger of slipping up. He stayed on his feet but by this time, with less than a quarter of a mile left, had lost his initial impetus and dropped back to last but one, albeit only about six lengths off the leader. All was far from lost; coolly pulled to the outside, Persepolis produced an electrifying turn of speed to leave his rivals virtually standing, cutting down the leader Alfred's Choice well inside the last furlong to win, easing up, by two lengths with Sharp Singer third, beaten another half length.

The question promptly arose as to what Persepolis' next objective would be. At first he appeared likely to run in the Prix du Jockey-Club; in the event, and largely because of his owner's preference, he followed the Lupin winners of 1970 and 1975, Stintino and Green Dancer, by contesting the Derby, becoming the shortest-priced French challenger in the last few years. With Piggott marked down to ride Simply Great for his retaining stable, Saint-Martin was booked for Persepolis and duly had the mount on the day—Simply Great having injured himself, Piggott ended up without a ride. Saint-Martin's record at Epsom is easily the most distinguished of any French jockey currently riding, including as it does successes in the Derby on Relko, the Oaks on Monade and

647

Pawneese, and the Coronation Cup on Dicta Drake and Relko again. Unfortunately his ride on Persepolis cannot be called one of his best. After lobbing along in last place in the early stages Persepolis, tracking Golden Fleece, lay ahead of only two of the other seventeen runners with five furlongs to travel. Whereas Golden Fleece moved out to begin his run turning for home, Saint-Martin stuck to the rail and consequently faced a wall of horses as he tried to bring his mount through. The task was impossible; Saint-Martin had to sit and suffer until Persepolis finally saw daylight a furlong and a half out, by which time the leader Golden Fleece had an eight-length advantage over him with five other colts in between. As at Longchamp, Persepolis ate up the ground once clear, showing he stayed the trip well by passing Palace Gold, Peacetime and Norwick and failing by a head to snatch third place from Silver Hawk, four lengths behind Golden Fleece. How much closer Persepolis would have finished ridden more judiciously is a matter of opinion, but it is indisputable that he ought to have finished closer and by virtue of this has to be regarded as unlucky.

After his ill-luck at Epsom there was reason to hope Persepolis' meeting with Glint of Gold, Lancastrian, Real Shadai and Vayrann in the Grand Prix de Saint-Cloud in July might provide conclusive proof of his merit and show precisely where he stood in the European middle-distance hierarchy. Regrettably the race did nothing to clarify matters. Though he had reportedly galloped well in his final work-out, Persepolis never looked to be travelling particularly smoothly and trailed in a distant seventh to Glint of Gold; Alfred's Choice finished almost twelve lengths ahead of him in fourth. Persepolis' best form had unquestionably been on fast ground and conditions were on the soft side at Saint-Cloud, but it is unlikely that the going was the only reason behind this decidedly disappointing display—Boutin inclined to lay the blame on the trip to Epsom and Persepolis' exertions there. Either way little more was heard of Persepolis until the announcement in September that he had been retired to the Haras de Fresnay-le-Buffard because of leg trouble.

The presence of Persepolis, Bikala, Melyno, Vayrann and Zino at stud in France in 1983 will give a welcome boost to that country's stallion ranks since in 1982 almost three quarters of the top twenty sires in the French list

Mr S. S. Niarchos' "Persepolis" (L. Piggott)

were either abroad or dead. One of four good sons of Kalamoun retired at the end of the year—Bikala, Castle Keep and Kalaglow are the others—Persepolis has a distaff side packed with good winners and it isn't surprising that he cost 1,600,000 francs, or approximately £163,000, as a yearling. His dam, placed at up to one mile in France, fetched 315,000 francs in 1976 carrying the Rheingold filly Perliere, subsequently successful over nine furlongs; her 1980 foal is a filly by Luthier. Perlita's dam Pola Bella showed top-class

Persepolis (Fr) (gr. c. 1979)	Kalamoun (gr 1970)	Zeddaan (gr 1965)	Grey Sovereign
			Vareta
		Khairunissa (gr 1960)	Prince Bio
			Palariva
	Perlita (b 1972)	Baldric II (b 1961)	Round Table
			Two Cities
		Pola Bella (b 1965)	Darius
			Bella Paola

form, picking up the French One Thousand Guineas and the Prix du Moulin besides running second in the French Oaks and Prix Vermeille, and her three winning foals include Val Divine, dam of Vayrann. The third dam, Bella Paola, needs no introduction since she was outstanding on the track, winning the One Thousand Guineas, Oaks, Prix Vermeille and Champion Stakes, and highly successful as a broodmare, producing five winners of well above average ability of whom Pola Bella was best. With this pedigree and his good looks—he is a well-made, attractive colt—Persepolis should do well in his new career. *F. Boutin, France.*

PERSIAN GLORY 2 ch.c. Persian Bold 123–Painted Glen (Pall Mall 132) **108** (1982 6d² 6fg* 7fg³ 7d⁴) Feb 8; IR 23,000Y; attractive, short-coupled colt; closely related to 2 winners by Bold Lad, Ire, including the exceptionally useful 1971 2-y-o 5f performer Pert Lassie, and half-brother to 2 winners; dam never ran; short-priced favourite, did not get on top until close home when winning 13-runner maiden race at York in July by ½ length from Diana's Pet; showed better form afterwards, on final outing finishing good fourth under top weight in quite valuable nursery at Newmarket in October; evidently better suited by 7f than by 6f, and will stay 1m; acts on a firm and a soft surface. *J. W. Watts.*

PERSIAN POLLY 2 ch.f. Persian Bold 123–Polyester Girl (Ridan) (1982 **99** 7fg² 8fg 7g³ 7d*) Apr 21; first foal; dam, winner over 6f at 4 yrs in Ireland, is half-sister to very good Italian colt Northern Spring; won minor event at Naas in October by 2½ lengths from Manhattan Miss after making much of running; also ran well in 2 races at Leopardstown, finishing ½-length second to Committed in small race in August and ¾-length third of 13 to Countess Candy in Park Stakes in October; should stay 1m. *J. Murphy, Ireland.*

PERSIAN PRINCESS 5 ch.m. Palm Track 122–Persian Silver 61 (Cash and **57** Courage 116) (1981 10g 8s 10.6f⁴ 9fg² 8.2d² 8.2f 8.2d* 1982 9fg 9fg³ 8d 8.2g³ 8.2fg* 8.2g 8.2f 8.2v³) robust mare; has gained all her wins at Hamilton and beat Star Heading by a neck in handicap there in July; soundly beaten next 2 starts; stays 1¼m; acts on any going; has run creditably for an apprentice. *C. Crossley.*

PERSONAL CALL 9 b.g. Personality–Damaring (Saidam) (1981 12g 8s **—** 16fg 12d 1982 10g 10f) no longer of any account; sold 200 gns Ascot 2nd June Sales. *R. Atkins.*

PETE AND DUD 3 ch.g. Owen Dudley 121–Athena Royale 80 (Athens Wood **—** 126) (1981 5d² 5s⁴ 6f 7d 8.2fg 8fg⁴ 10d² 10g 1982 10s 10.1d) compact gelding; plater; will be suited by 1¼m; said to be unsuited by really soft ground; claimed £2,400 after final start. *W. Musson.*

PETER ALLAN 2 br.c. Undulate–Foggy Park (Foggy Bell 108) (1982 8s 9s) **—** Apr 15; leggy colt; first foal; dam tailed off in novice hurdles; well behind in maiden races at York and Redcar in October. *W. Wharton.*

PETERHOF (USA) 3 b.c. The Minstrel 135–Millicent (Cornish Prince) (1981 **106** 5d² 5fg* 6d 5g* 6g 1982 5fg 5f² 5fg) neat, strong, shapely colt; has a short, sharp action; half-brother to 3 winners, including 1982 2-y-o 5f winner Lacework (by In Reality); dam unraced half-sister to Mill Reef; successful in Curragh Stakes and Flying Childers Stakes at Doncaster in 1981; ran respectably last 2 starts at 3 yrs, finishing close third (subsequently moved up to second) behind stable-companion Longleat in Ballyogan Stakes at Leopardstown in June and seventh of 14 to Fearless Lad in King's Stand Stakes at Royal Ascot; last in Palace House Stakes at Newmarket on other start; best at 5f; seems to need a sound surface; sent to USA. *V. O'Brien, Ireland.*

PETE ROCKET 3 ch.g. Roan Rocket 128–Devadara 73 (Royal Levee or Hill 77 Clown) (1981 5s 5fg² 5fg* 6g 6fg 7fg 7g⁴ 8.2d 7g 1982 8s 5g 6g³ 6f* 7fg* 5fg* 7g 7s 7s) sturdy gelding; justified favouritism in handicaps at Folkestone (apprentice event), Warwick (odds on) and Hamilton (unseated rider and bolted beforehand); effective from 5f to 7f; acts well on firm ground and is unsuited by soft; trained until after seventh start by P. Haslam. *J. Jenkins.*

PETER THE BUTCHER 5 br.g. Autre Prince 125–Circumstance 72 (Bleep- — Bleep 134) (1981 8g 10f* 10f 10f 11fg 1982 16fg) poor handicapper on flat but is a fairly useful hurdler; yet to show he stays beyond 1¼m; acts on any going; blinkered once in 1980. *Mrs M. Nesbitt.*

PETE'S FOLLY 2 b.g. Streak 119–Alice (Parthia 132) (1982 5fg 6g² 5fg 5d 67 8f³ 8fg² 8s² 7s) Apr 30; 560F, 4,400 2-y-o; lengthy gelding; half-brother to several winners, including fairly useful 2-y-o 6f winner Surface Heat (by Hot Spark) and 1m winner Winart (by Scottish Rifle); placed in sellers and a nursery; suited by 1m; acts on any going; often blinkered but does at least as well when not. *D. Arbuthnot.*

PETE THE MEAT 2 b.g. Baragoi 115–Young May (Firestreak 125) (1982 55 5f 5f⁴ 6fg 7g) May 11; fair sort; first foal; dam poor plater; only plating class; trained by W. Wharton first 3 starts, and off course 4 months afterwards. *Mrs N. Macauley.*

PETICIENNE 3 b.f. Mummy's Pet 125–Maid In Love (Sky Gipsy 117) (1981 — NR 1982 7fg 8s 9f) 2,300F, 3,300Y; rangy filly; has an enlarged near hock; first foal; dam never ran; tailed off in varied company, including selling. *W. Wharton.*

PETITA (USA) 3 ch.f. Nashua–Petit Rond Point (Round Table) (1981 NR 61 1982 8f³ 9g 10d³ 12d³ 10s 12d³) $85,000Y; neat, sturdy filly; third foal; half-sister to a minor winner by Creme dela Creme; third in maiden races and a handicap; suited by middle distances; blinkered fifth start. *D. Arbuthnot.*

PETITE AIRE 2 ch.f. Tobique 116–Grandaire 65 (Grand Roi 118) (1982 44 5f⁴ 5g 5f⁴ 6g⁴ 5fg⁴ 6f 8.2fg 10d) Apr 21; small filly; poor walker; dam won 6f seller at 2 yrs; poor plater; stays 6f. *B. McMahon.*

PETITE HESTER 4 b.f. Wollow 132–Lady Hester (Native Prince) (1981 81 8.2s 7d 7s 7fg² 7g 7f² 7f* 7.2fg³ 7g³ 7g* 1982 8f 7.6g 7fg 7g* 7f* 7f 7fg² 7g³ 7f 7.3g) small, lengthy, quite attractive filly; returned to form in summer and won handicaps at Brighton and Kempton (apprentice event), latter by a short head from Bond Dealer; had stiff task when very good third to Triple Tipple in Strensall Stakes at York in September, but didn't run up to her best last 2 starts; best at 7f; needs a sound surface and acts well on firm going; didn't have a clear run sixth start. *I. Balding.*

PETITE JOIE (ITY) 3 b.f Canisbay 120–Melancolie (Petingo 135) (1981 62 5fg 7g 6g 6d 6d 1982 8f⁴ 10d 8.2fg 8g* 8d³ 8.2g² 8fg³ 9g³ 9s 8.2s) well-made filly; narrowly won maiden apprentice race at Yarmouth in August; ran credit-ably in handicaps afterwards; will be suited by a return to 1¼m; has run creditably on a firm surface, but is suited by some give in the ground; blinkered final outing in 1981. *R. Armstrong.*

PETITE MIELLE 3 b.f. Hot Spark 126–Mrs Bee 74 (Sallust 134) (1981 6fg — 6g 1982 7.6fg 7fg 7fg 7fg⁴ 7fg 6d 10v) lengthy, workmanlike filly; excellent mover; plater; stays 7f; sometimes blinkered; sold 720 gns Newmarket Autumn Sales. *R. Williams.*

PETITE POMME 2 b.f. Be Friendly 130–Lady Phoenix (Lorenzaccio 130) 51 (1982 5f³ 5f 6g 5f³ 5f 5g 5d 5fg 5s) Apr 7; sturdy filly; third foal; dam unraced half-sister to very speedy Lady Rowley; poor form, including in a seller. *D. Garraton.*

PETITE REALM 3 b.f. Realm 129–Deep Brook (Wolver Hollow 126) (1981 92 5fg³ 5fg* 5d* 5g 6fg² 6fg³ 5fg⁴ 6g 1982 6s² 7g² 8g 6fg⁴ 10g 8fg 8d 5s) neat ex-English filly; runner-up first 2 outings, going down by 2 lengths to Noble Monk in handicap at the Curragh in March and by same margin to Lady Green-ham in Mulcahy Stakes at Fairyhouse in April; 5¼ lengths fourth of 6 to Princess Seal in Castleknock Sprint Stakes at Naas in May; not certain to stay 1m, let alone 1¼m; seems to act on any going; sold 35,000 gns Newmarket December Sales. *J. Bolger, Ireland.*

PETIT MONTMORENCY (USA) 3 ch.c. Stage Door Johnny–Roast Duck **111**
(Sea-Bird II 145) (1981 8v 10d 1982 10.5v 10d* 11fg⁴ 12fg* 15s* 15g 15fg 15f)
third foal; half-brother to 2 minor winners in USA; dam placed over 11f in
France; won handicaps at Evry in March and Longchamp in May and Prix
Berteux at Chantilly in June; accounted for Ekaha by a length in last-named;
soundly beaten afterwards; suited by a test of stamina; acts well on soft going;
blinkered seventh start. *J. Fellows, France.*

PETONG 2 gr.c. Mansingh 120–Iridium 78 (Linacre 133) (1982 7g 6d 6g⁴) **82**
Mar 26; 15,000Y; strong, compact colt; brother to 2 winners, including 5f and
7f winner Miss Cindy, and half-brother to a winner abroad; dam stayed 1¼m;
blinkered, ridden along throughout when length fourth of 20 behind Fiefdom
in maiden race at Newmarket in October, best effort; evidently lacking in pace,
and should be well suited by 7f or more. *M. Jarvis.*

PETROLIC (USA) 4 b. or br.g. Dynastic–Maryland Queen (Piave) (1981 **—**
8s 8g 12d 1982 6fg) ex-French gelding; in rear in varied company, including
selling; blinkered only outing of 1982 (didn't look keen). *A. Jarvis.*

PETTISTREE 4 ch.g. Sallust 134–Kokuwa (Klairon 131) (1981 5s 6g 6g 5d² **70**
5g 6f 5g 5s 6g 6d 1982 6s³ 5s³ 6d⁴) fair sort; in frame in handicaps at Ayr,
Chepstow and Nottingham in spring; stays 6f; acts well on soft going; blinkered
once as a 3-y-o; sold 660 gns Newmarket July Sales. *N. Callaghan.*

PETUNIA 2 b.f. Ballymore 123–Bold Caress 104 (Bold Lad, Ire 133) (1982 7d) **—**
Mar 10; IR 35,000Y; neat, quite attractive filly; good walker; first foal; dam
creditable sixth in Irish Guinness Oaks; 20/1 and in need of run, soon driven
along when behind in 15-runner maiden race at Leicester in October. *P. Cole.*

PETWICE 2 b.f. Mummy's Pet 125–Twice Shy (Lord of Verona 120) (1982 5g) **—**
Mar 21; compact filly; half-sister to 2 winning platers; dam of little account;
unquoted, seventh of 8 in maiden race at Newcastle in June. *W. Haigh.*

PETWORTH 2 b.g. Mummy's Pet 125–Gambela 88 (Diplomat Way) (1982 **— p**
5d) Feb 20; 9,200Y; good-quartered, quite attractive gelding; second foal;
dam won over 1m; 25/1 and far from fully fit, moved nicely to start and chased
leaders for long way without being knocked about when 7 lengths sixth of 17
to Seven Clubs in maiden race at Nottingham in September; gelded afterwards;
sure to do better. *M. Camacho.*

PETWORTH PARK 3 br.f. Mummy's Pet 125–Lancashire Lass 73 (King's **—**
Troop 118) (1981 6g³ 6f 5fg* 1982 5d) lightly-made filly; good walker;
has ability, as she showed when winning maiden race at Wolverhampton in
1981, but is clearly temperamental and races only from flag start; well beaten
in handicap at Wolverhampton only outing at 3 yrs in August; stays 6f. *S.
Woodman.*

PHALABORWA 3 b.f. Oats 126–Marble Chip (Raise You Ten 125) (1981 **—**
7.9f³ 9d 1982 12fg 14s) IR 8,800Y; lengthy ex-Irish filly; second living
foal; half-sister to 1980 Irish 2-y-o 1m winner Lohunda Lady (by Ballymore);
dam Irish 1½m and 13.5f winner, also won over hurdles; only plating class;
should stay middle distances. *W. Wharton.*

PHANJO 2 b.c. Record Token 128–Silk Willoughby (Pirate King 129) (1982 **58**
5f 6f 7fg 10s) Apr 10; 6,000Y; brother to 3-y-o Sister Resista and 7f winner
Hit Record, and half-brother to fair 7f performer Marston (by Tribal Chief);
dam unraced sister to smart stayer Avast; poor maiden; best race on final
outing; will be better off in sellers. *J. Hardy.*

PHAROS RAAPHORST (HOL) 3 br.c. Tyrant–Selina Fair 94 (Hugh Lupus **—**
132) (1981 5d⁴ 5fg 5g⁴ 6.5fg 6.5v* 1982 8f 9g² 10fg 12fg⁴ 9d) lengthy, useful-
looking colt; in frame behind Boxberger Speed in Dutch 2,000 Guineas and
Dutch Derby, both at Duindigt; behind in minor event at York and handicap
at Lingfield on 2 of his other starts; stays 1½m; acts on heavy going. *R. Price.*

PHILATELIST 2 b.g. Dubassoff–Chaddy (St Chad 120) (1982 5f 7g 5g 6s) **—**
June 7; tall, leggy, lengthy gelding; brother to winning hurdler City Link Express
and half-brother to a winner in Sweden; dam won in Norway; no worthwhile
form, including in sellers; gelded after final outing. *C. Williams.*

PHILIPPA JANET 2 ch.f. Roan Rocket 128–Immatation 67 (Polyfoto 124) **53**
(1982 5.8f 5d 5fg⁴) Apr 1; 2,000F, 1,700Y; first live foal; dam won 4 races at
4f and 5f; modest fourth of 11 in maiden auction event at Warwick in July.
G. Kindersley.

PHILIPS HUSSAR 2 ch.c. Queen's Hussar 124–Princess Story 64 (Prince de — Galles 125) (1982 8s 8s 7s) May 12; 1,700F, 2,000Y; small, workmanlike colt; second foal; dam won sellers at around 1m; unquoted, behind in October maiden and minor events. *K. Cunningham-Brown.*

PHILLIP HENRY 3 b.g. Scottish Rifle 127–Galoprise 88 (Tudor Music 131) **63** (1981 6s 7f 6f 7g³ 6f 1982 10d* 12f⁴ 12f⁴ 14fg 10fg 10d 13.8f 10g 10fg 8fg) small gelding; 50/1 when winning modest maiden race at Newcastle in April; well beaten most subsequent starts, including in a valuable seller; stayed 1½m; seemed to act on any going; ran respectably in blinkers; dead. *C. Gray.*

PHILPET 2 b.c. Blue Cashmere 129–Petploy 82 (Faberge II 121) (1982 5d **57** 5d* 5f² 5g³ 5f⁴ 5d 6fg² 6f 5fg 6f 5g 5g 5d) Apr 15; leggy, lightly-made colt; has a very round action; half-brother to a minor winner and a winner in Malaya (both by Crooner); dam won over 6f and 7f; attracted no bid after winning seller at Newcastle in April; kept his form well subsequently; suited by 6f; seems to act on any going. *T. Fairhurst.*

PHILPRIDE 2 br.c. Rheingold 137–Canelle (Sassafras 135) (1982 8d 8.2s²) **68 p** Mar 18; 17,000Y; strong, useful-looking colt; third foal; dam half-sister to smart stayer Irvine; second of 8 behind very easy winner Hungarian Prince in maiden race at Haydock in October; will be well suited by 1¼m+; likely to improve. *W. Elsey.*

PHOTO 3 b.f. Blakeney 126–Photo Flash 119 (Match III 135) (1981 6fg 7fg² **83** 1982 9g 8g 11.5f³ 12g 9f² 9g* 8fg* 9fg* 8d² 9s) quite attractive, smallish filly; successful in maiden race and minor event at Wolverhampton and another minor event at Thirsk in between; gives impression 1m is too short for her and will be suited by 1¼m; possibly unsuited by really soft going but acts on any other; genuine. *H. Cecil.*

PHYDILLA (FR) 4 b.f. Lyphard 132–Godzilla 106 (Gyr 131) (1981 8fg 7s **107** 8g² 8fg* 8g⁴ 1982 8s 7fg³ 6.5fg⁴ 8g) French filly; second foal; half-sister to French 1¼m winner Aristarque (by Rheingold); dam won 5 times at up to 7.5f at 2 yrs in Italy and showed form over 6f at 3 yrs in England; high-class performer as a 3-y-o, winner of Prix Quincey at Deauville and excellent fourth to North-jet (despite being struck into) in Prix du Moulin de Longchamp; fairly lightly raced again in 1982, best effort when 2¾ lengths third of 10 behind Indian King in Prix du Palais Royal at Longchamp in May and 3½ lengths fourth of 9 behind Exclusive Order in Prix Maurice de Gheest at Deauville in August; difficult to settle and by no means certain to stay beyond 1m; acts on any going; blinkered third outing. *O. Douieb, France.*

PHYLJAN 3 ch.f. Flashback 102–Headliner (Pampered King 121) (1981 — 5f 6g 5.3d 1982 6d 10g) poor plater; dead. *M. Bolton.*

PIA FORT 3 b.c. He Loves Me 120–Gammon (Pia Star) (1981 5g* 6d 1982 — 16fg 16fg) tall, lengthy colt; quite moderate at his best; sometimes raced out of his depth; not certain to stay beyond 1m; has twice given considerable trouble at start; pulled up lame final outing. *R. Hollinshead.*

PIANOLA 3 b. or br.f. Welsh Pageant 132–Hurdy-Gurdy 90 (Espresso 122) **68** (1981 8g 1982 9fg 12g 10g*) robust, good-quartered, short-legged filly; won maiden race at Newmarket in October; had faced stiffer tasks previously; stays 1¼m; sold 32,000 gns Newmarket December Sales. *B. Hobbs.*

PIASTRE 3 b.f. Royal Palace 131–Astoria 92 (Derring-Do 131) (1981 6fg — 7d 1982 12f 10h 10.2g 10.4d 10fg) strong, good sort; poor maiden; blinkered final start; sold to BBA 3,600 gns Newmarket December Sales. *I. Balding.*

PICKET LINE 2 ch.c. Run The Gantlet–Calleva (Worden II 129) (1982 — 8g 7s) May 27; half-brother to numerous winners, including Cesarewitch winner Centurion (by Connaught) and very useful 7f winner Piper (by Song); dam of little account; last and last but one in 12-runner races at Newbury and Chepstow in the autumn. *I. Balding.*

PIEMONTE 3 ch.f. Nebbiolo 125–Airgead Beo (Hook Money 124) (1981 NR **75** 1982 7fg 7.6fg 10h 10f⁴ 12.2g 10.2g 9s) IR 10,000Y; quite well-made filly; good walker; fourth living foal; half-sister to fairly useful Citissima (by Simbir), successful at up to 1¼m in Ireland, and to 2 winning Irish stayers; dam never ran; 2 lengths fourth of 10 to More Kisses in £4,100 event at Newbury in June, easily best effort; stays 1¼m; sold 7,000 gns Newmarket December Sales. *T. Robson.*

PIENCOURT 4 br.c. Averof 123–French Bugle 71 (Bleep-Bleep 134) (1981 **82** d
6g 7fg* 7g³ 7d⁴ 6f 6f 7fg 7f 5d 5g² 6g 6g 1982 5g³ 5s² 6fg³ 5f* 6fg³ 6fg 6f 6s⁴
5s) compact, quite attractive colt; beat Pusey Street by 2 lengths in £3,700
handicap at Lingfield in May; placed on 4 other occasions; effective from 5f
to 7f; acts on any going; had stiff task when blinkered once. *C. Austin.*

PIEROTH 4 b.g. Averof 123–Terex (Khalkis 127) (1981 10s 7fg 8fg³ 8g⁴ **68**
8fg⁴ 8g³ 8d 1982 7fg⁴ 10.8fg³ 7f² 8g 8fg⁴ 10f⁴ 12f² 10g³ 10fg 12g* 12v* 12d*)
fair sort; successful in handicaps at Brighton in September (finished second
but was awarded race) and at Folkestone and Leicester in October; put up game
performances in last 2 events, and at Leicester beat Voice of Progress by ½
length; stays 1½m; acts on any going, but is clearly suited by some give underfoot; blinkered eighth and ninth starts (ran creditably first occasion); sold
to G. Kindersley 10,500 gns Newmarket Autumn Sales. *J. Winter.*

PIERROT AUGUST 2 b.c. Cawston's Clown 113–Canty Day 87 (Canadel **77**
II 126) (1982 7g 8s 10d* 10.2s) May 3; 1,000Y, 1,550 2-y-o; tall, leggy,
lightly-made colt; brother to a poor filly, and half-brother to a minor winner;
dam 2-y-o 5f winner; won 13-runner seller at Leicester (bought in 2,500 gns)
in October by neck from Pledgdon Green; good sixth in minor event at Doncaster
(blinkered) the following month; suited by 1¼m. *R. Simpson.*

PIETRU (FR) 2 br.c. Arctic Tern 126–Agila (Sicambre 135) (1982 7.5g² **114**
7.5fg 8d² 10v* 10v³) Feb 10; 270,000 francs Y (approx £24,500); half-brother
to 3 winners, including very useful French middle-distance winner Assita (by
Caro); dam, winner twice at around 1¼m, is granddaughter of high-class 1m
to 1¼m filly Arbele; put up 2 good efforts over 1¼m at Saint-Cloud late in season,
winning 12-runner maiden race by 6 lengths and finishing 4½ lengths third of
12 to Escaline when favourite for Criterium de Saint-Cloud; will be suited by
1½m. *F. Boutin, France.*

PIG TAIL 2 ch.f. Habitat 134–Plencia (Le Haar 126) (1982 6g⁴) Mar 16; **80** p
rather lightly-made filly; good mover; sister to useful 6f and 8.5f winner Petrol-
euse and half-sister to 3 winners, including outstanding middle-distance filly
Pawneese (by Carvin) and smart French 1¼m winner Patia (by Don II); dam
useful at around 1¼m in France; favourite and looking hard and well, stayed on
strongly under hard driving when beaten 2 short heads and neck in 7-runner
minor event won by Debutina Park at York in September; will be suited by
7f+; sure to win in maiden company. *H. Cecil.*

PILGRIM (USA) 3 b.c. Northern Dancer–Fleur (Victoria Park) (1981 6d* **108**
1982 9s² 8g 6.3g* 8g*) $1,250,000Y; brother to Derby winner The Minstrel
and smart French 1m and 9f winner Far North, and half-brother to 2 winners;
dam, stakes-placed winner at up to 1m, is half-sister to Nijinsky (by Northern
Dancer); beat Southern Music by ½ length in valuable handicap at the Curragh
in June and accounted for Bonnie Bess by 1½ lengths in Youghal Stakes at
Leopardstown in October; best at up to 1m; retired to Winfield Farm, Kentucky.
V. O'Brien, Ireland.

PILOT FLYER 3 br.f. Saulingo 122–Terina (Bold Lad, Ire 133) (1981 6fg **—**
6fg³ 6d 1982 5f 6f 6g 6fg 6fg 6f³ 6fg⁴ 6d 6d) workmanlike filly; plater nowadays; stays 6f; possibly unsuited by soft ground; blinkered fourth and fifth
outings; possibly needs strong handling; trained part of season by C. Nelson;
sold 380 gns Ascot December Sales and sent to Cyprus. *Mrs J. Reavey.*

PILTON 4 ch.g. Record Token 128–Wordless 74 (Worden II 129) (1981 **—**
10v 1982 12s 16f 12f) big, strong gelding; very lightly raced and no form;
blinkered last 2 starts; sold 2,900 gns Ascot July Sales. *T. Robson.*

PINE RIDGE 2 b.f. High Top 131–Wounded Knee 78 (Busted 134) (1982 **72** p
7d⁴) Apr 6; 12,000Y; well-grown, attractive filly; turns front feet out; third
produce; dam won over 1¼m and 1¾m; third favourite but just in need of race,
3¾ lengths fourth of 18 to stable-companion Brilliant Rosa in maiden event
at Leicester in October; will be much better suited by 1m+; should win races.
M. Stoute.

PINGARO 2 b.f. Sagaro 133–Pin Hole 83 (Parthia 132) (1982 5fg 6g) Mar **—**
25; small filly; half-sister to a winner in Trinidad; dam 1¼m winner; last in
maiden race at Warwick in May and minor event at Ripon in August. *P.
Felgate.*

PINKERTON'S MAN 6 br. or bl.h. Will Hays–Miss Pinkerton (Above **48**
Suspicion 127) (1981 8.2d 8s 8.2d 7s 1982 8fg 8fg³ 8fg) neat, well-made

horse; poor handicapper nowadays; stays 1m; acts on any going; has worn blinkers. *J. Berry.*

PINK MEX 3 b.f. Tickled Pink 114–Mexilhoeira 66 (Bleep-Bleep 134) (1981 —
NR 1982 8g 6d) plain filly; second foal; dam plater; in rear in maiden races
at Yarmouth in June and Nottingham in September. *Mrs N. Macauley.*

PINK PATH 3 b.g. Warpath 113–Darwin Tulip (Campaign 106 or Pirate King —
129) (1981 7g 1982 10fg 12.3g 16.5fg 12v) compact gelding; has rather
a round action; poor maiden. *J. Etherington.*

PINTIMES (FR) 2 b. or br.f. Faraway Times 123–Queen Pin (Sovereign Path —
125) (1982 6fg 7g 7g 5fg 6s 6s) Apr 11; big, tall filly; half-sister to 1978 French
2-y-o winner Pin Up Boy (by Faristan); dam second in 2 small 1¼m races in
France; little worthwhile form here and in France, including in claiming races;
blinkered final outing. *C. Austin.*

PINXTON 3 b.g. Free State 125–Belinda Pocket 84 (Pampered King 121) —
(1981 5fg 6f³ 7g 7fg* 7fg⁴ 7fg² 8f 1982 8fg 10.6fg 10f 10.6h 12g 11g) narrow
gelding; moves well; has shown no form for a long time, including in a valuable
seller; should stay 1m+; blinkered last 2 starts. *K. Stone.*

PIP 2 b.c. Captain James 123–Where Is It (Wolver Hollow 126) (1982 7d³) **84 p**
Apr 20; IR 10,000Y; leggy, narrow colt; second foal; dam never ran; 14/1
and looking as though run would do him good, ran on very well without being
knocked about when 5½ lengths third of 18 to Northern Adventure in minor
event at Doncaster in October; will be suited by 1m+; should be capable of
winning a small race. *J. Dunlop.*

PIP'EM 2 ch.f. Jimmy Reppin 131–Marock Morley 59 (Most Secret 119) (1982 **77**
6fg 5g² 5g* 5f 5s⁴ 6v) May 14; 2,900Y; small, good-bodied filly; first foal; dam
won over 5f at 5 yrs; bought in 5,400 gns after winning valuable seller at York
in September; form only at 5f; suited by a sound surface; blinkered at York
and on final outing. *S. Norton.*

PIPINIA 3 b.f. No Mercy 126–Pepperita 79 (Nelcius 133) (1981 7g 1982 —
7.2f 8f⁴ 6fg 8g) strong, fair sort; plater; stays 1m; sometimes blinkered. *S.
Norton.*

PITRASI 3 br.g. Pitskelly 122–Princess Ru (Princely Gift 137) (1981 6g **61**
7f³ 7g 6f* 6g 1982 7d 7g 6f 7.2f 7f³ 8fg² 8g² 8.3g³ 11.1fg 8fg³) smallish, fair
sort; plater; stays 1m; acts on firm going; blinkered last 3 starts; sold 1,300 gns
Newmarket Autumn Sales. *P. Haslam.*

PITROYAL 2 br.f. Pitskelly 122–Regal Way (Sovereign Path 125) (1982 6g **72**
7f³ 7g⁴ 7g 7.6v 7d) Mar 26; IR 11,500Y; well-made filly; second foal; sister to
Irish 3-y-o middle-distance winner Regal Promise; dam, sister to useful 7f
performer Oldstock, won over 1¾m in Ireland; quite a moderate maiden; will
stay at least 1m; acts on any going except perhaps heavy; ran creditably in
blinkers final start. *R. Smyth.*

PIT STOP 6 b.g. Pitskelly 122–Mrs Moss 81 (Reform 132) (1981 5s 5s² 5d —
5f 5fg⁴ 5f 5.1fg 5fg 5f 5f 5g 5s 5d 5s³ 5g 1982 5g 5g 6g 5fg 5s 5d) narrow,
leggy gelding; poor mover; inconsistent handicapper; best form at 5f but
probably stays 6f; acts on any going, but is particularly well suited by soft;
effective with or without blinkers; has worn bandages; suitable mount for an
apprentice; sold 1,200 gns Newmarket Autumn Sales. *W. Stubbs.*

PITSYCATO 3 b.c. Pitskelly 122–Movement 79 (Daring Display 129) (1981 —
6fg 7g 1982 7fg 10.1fg 10g⁴ 10d 10g) quite attractive colt; good mover; has
shown only a modicum of ability; not certain to stay 1¼m; sold to D. McCain
3,300 gns Doncaster September Sales. *R. Price.*

PITTENCRIEFF 7 ch.g. Manacle 123–Anatevka (Privy Councillor 125) (1981 —
12g 12g 12d⁴ 13fg 11g⁴ 12f³ 12.2fg⁴ 12.2g* 12v⁴ 13.8g* 1982 12.2f 12g) workmanlike gelding; poor mover nowadays; stays 1¾m; acts on any going; ran
moderately when tried in blinkers; sometimes bandaged in front; suited by a
strong gallop; goes well at Catterick. *E. Weymes.*

PITTER PAT 3 b.f. Pitskelly 122–Tudor Saint (Tudor Music 131) (1981 — §
5d 5s³ 5g* 5g⁴ 5g⁴ 5s³ 5f* 5f 5d⁴ 5g 5g⁴ 5d 5f 5fg* 5fg 5g 5h
5fg 6fg 6f 6g 8f 6g) small, lightly-made filly; inconsistent sprint handicapper;
twice well beaten in sellers; blinkered final start; sold 1,000 gns Newmarket
Autumn Sales. *T. Fairhurst.*

PITTSFIELD 2 br.c. Pitskelly 122–Ida 95 (Jukebox 120) (1982 7g) Mar 14; — p
IR 21,000Y; first foal; dam did most of her racing over 5f; 25/1, ran on in eye-
catching style without being knocked about when in mid-division in 30-runner
maiden race won by Mandelstam at Newmarket in October; sure to do much
better, and is one to watch out for in maiden company. *B. Hills.*

PIT YOUR WITS 6 b.h. Pitskelly 122–Sweet Chupatti (Rustam 127) (1981 70 d
9d 10.4g 8d* 8v² 10s 8d³ 7.6s² 8.3g 7.3d 12d* 12.2s* 10.2g 1982 12.2d 12g*
10.4g 14.6g 12g* 11.7fg² 12.3d 12fg² 12fg 12g 12.2s) well-made horse; successful in handicaps at Wolverhampton in April and Haydock in July; stays 1½m, but
isn't certain to get 1¾m; acts on any going except perhaps very firm; has worn
blinkers; bandaged nowadays; suitable mount for an apprentice; below his
best last 3 starts. *D. H. Jones.*

PLACER QUEEN 3 ch.f. Habitat 134–Santa's Sister 104 (Middle Brother) ?
(1981 7v 1982 8.5f 12.3fg) leggy, useful-looking filly; respectable 5¾ lengths
fifth of 9 to subsequently-demoted Mary Mitsu in Princess Elizabeth Stakes
at Epsom in April prior to finishing remote last of 6 to Swiftfoot in Cheshire
Oaks in May; subsequently did well in Canada, winning a maiden race at Woodbine and a division of 9.5f Tattling Stakes at Greenwood, trained by C. Hopmans;
not sure to stay 1½m. *B. Hills.*

PLATO'S RETREAT 3 b.f. Brigadier Gerard 144–Acte 80 (Alycidon 138) 73
(1981 NR 1982 10fg³ 12fg² 10.6s 12v* 12g) fair sort; poor mover; sister to very
useful French 1¼m winner Actal, and half-sister to several winners, including
French middle-distance performer Exact (by Exbury); dam won at 1¼m and
stayed well; ran on strongly to win maiden race at Hamilton in October; will
stay 1¾m; acts on heavy going. *W. Elsey.*

PLAYBOY BUNNY 4 b.f. African Sky 124–Spa Track (Track Spare 125) (1981 —
8f 8fg 8f 1982 16s) leggy filly; soundly beaten in maiden races and a handicap.
Mrs N. Macauley.

PLAYFUL PADDY 6 br.g. St Paddy 133–Toccata (Kythnos 126) (1981 57
10.5d² 10g³ 8fg 10g⁴ 10f² 10f 10g 10.2g 1982 12f* 12.2f 12fg² 12d 12f² 12fg)
middle-distance handicapper; 6-length winner at Beverley in May; probably acts
on any going, but seems suited by firm; may be best held up till late; found
little off bridle second outing and is inconsistent. *J. Bethell.*

PLAY IT SAFE 3 ch.f. Red Alert 127–Prudent Girl 92 (Primera 131) (1981 115
5fg³ 7s* 7f² 8d* 8d* 1982 7s* 8fg⁴ 10v 8fg² 10g 8v³ 8s*) tall, rather leggy,
close-coupled filly; has a round action; fourth foal; half-sister to 2 winners,
including high-class middle-distance performer Providential (by Run The
Gantlet), successful in France and USA; dam, half-sister to Proud Chieftain,
Hethersett and Royal Prerogative, won over middle distances; landed odds
readily by 3 lengths from Belange in Prix Imprudence at Maisons-Laffitte in
April and accounted for Albala by a short neck in Prix Coronation at Saint-
Cloud in November; in frame in 1,000 Guineas at Newmarket (4¼
lengths fourth to On The House), Prix d'Astarte at Deauville (run out of it close
home when ½-length second to Thorough) and Prix de Saint-Cyr at Longchamp;
possibly doesn't stay 1¼m; ideally suited by some give in the ground; very well
suited by front-running tactics; game. *F. Boutin, France.*

PLAY OUR SONG 2 br.f. Persian Bold 123–Scented Air 92 (Derring-Do 131) 97
(1982 5g* 6g) Mar 2; 43,000Y; lengthy, useful-looking filly; first foal; dam,
2-y-o 5f winner, is daughter of fastest 1971 2-y-o filly Rose Dubarry; put up a
promising display in 4-runner £3,600 event at Goodwood in August, running
on strongly under pressure after being outpaced to beat Django (gave 10 lb) by
½ length; raced more freely when creditable 3¾ lengths fifth of 8 to Myra's Best
in Firth of Clyde Stakes at Ayr the following month; suited by 6f. *J. Dunlop.*

PLAZA TORO 3 ch.g. Ashmore 125–Duke Street (Lorenzaccio 130) (1981 58
7g 7fg 8s³ 10s⁴ 1982 12f* 12fg² 12f3) lengthy gelding; stayed on strongly to
win minor event at Carlisle in April; placed in similar events at Edinburgh and
Carlisle afterwards; suited by 1½m and will stay further; acts on any going; sold
to S. Pattemore 4,100 gns Ascot July Sales. *Sir Mark Prescott.*

PLEASANT DREAM 3 b.f. Sharpen Up 127–Enchanted 116 (Song 132) —
(1981 5fg⁴ 5g² 5f² 5fg* 5g⁴ 5d 5fg 1982 5d) leggy, rather lightly-made filly;
fair at her best; well beaten only start at 3 yrs in March; unlikely to stay 6f;
usually blinkered; hung badly right when apprentice ridden once in 1981;
sometimes brought to race alone and seems temperamental; sold 15,000 gns
Newmarket December Sales. *H. T. Jones.*

PLEASURE WIND 3 b.c. Tumble Wind–Pleasure Boat 91 (Be Friendly 130)　**70**
(1981 NR　1982 8fg 10f 12f² 10.6h 9g* 8fg 8g² 8g 8d* 8d)　IR 7,000F, 8,400Y;
quite attractive colt; third produce; half-brother to fairly useful 1979 2-y-o 5f
winner Launch, subsequently a winner in Malaya; dam won over 5f at 2 yrs and is
half-sister to useful stayer Blueroy; plater; won at Newcastle in June (bought in
4,300 gns); ran creditably in better company afterwards and made all to score in
handicap at Ripon in August; stays 1½m but is better at shorter distances;
suited by some give in the ground; blinkered fourth start; has worn bandages;
sent to Hong Kong. *B. Hanbury.*

PLEDGDON GREEN 2 gr.g. Broxted 120–Lynn Regis (Ballymoss 136)　**71**
(1982 5g³ 6d 8f 8.2d² 10d* 10d²)　Mar 21; 1,500Y; workmanlike gelding; fifth
foal; dam ran only once; plater; bought in 1,400 gns after winning at Pontefract
in October; claimed by D. Thom £3,000 at Leicester later in month; suited by
a test of stamina; acts on a soft surface; gelded after final outing. *N. Callaghan.*

PLEDGE 9 br.g. Rarity 129–Boucle 86 (Princely Gift 137)　(1981 11.7d 10s　—
12s 13.1g² 8d 12.2fg 11.7g 10fg 10.2d　1982 12.2d 10fg 10g 11.7fg)　poor
handicapper nowadays; seems to stay 1¾m; appears to act on any going; below
his best when tried in blinkers; good mount for an apprentice; often makes the
running. *H. Candy.*

PLUM BOLD 3 b.f. Be My Guest 126–Plum Fool (Silly Season 127)　(1981　**82**
6d* 6g　1982 8.5fg³ 7fg 8fg³ 8fg⁴ 8d 10f)　attractive, rather lightly-made filly;
good mover; modest handicapper; should stay 1¼m; acts on a firm and a soft
surface; ran respectably in blinkers fourth start. *F. J. Houghton.*

PLURALISME (USA) 2 b.c. The Minstrel 135–Cambretta (Roberto 131)　**116**
(1982 7.5fg² 8g* 8s*)　Apr 9; 130,000Y; first foal; dam, winner over 9f in Ireland,
is sister to high-class 1m to 1½m winner Critique; evens favourite, made virtually
all to win Prix des Chenes at Longchamp in September by a short neck and a
head from Prince Kebir and Insolent; wore a brush pricker on his off side here
and looked rather a difficult ride: had previously had difficulty negotiating turn
into straight when winning 4-runner maiden race at Chantilly in September by
4 lengths from Conerton; will stay 1½m; likely to make a very smart 3-y-o;
engaged in the Derby but will need to become more manageable if he's to
negotiate Tattenham Corner. *A. Head, France.*

POINT NORTH 4 b. or br.c. Lorenzaccio 130–Off Scent 92 (Faberge II 121)　**63**
(1981 8g⁴ 11fg 10fg² 13g³ 11d⁴ 12.3g 10.6fg 10d　1982 13v 12fg 12f² 12.3fg*
13g³ 15g³ 12f² 13fg² 12g* 13fg* 13fg² 12g⁴ 13d 11s⁴ 16d)　strong colt; won
handicaps at Newcastle in May and Hamilton (2) in July; was possibly
unlucky when second at Carlisle on seventh start; stays 15f; acts well on firm
going. *W. H. H. Williams.*

POKERFAYES (USA) 3 b.c. Poker–Faye's Delight (Barbs Delight)　(1981　**50**
5fg 5s⁴ 6s 6g³ 7g 8g³ 8d　1982 8f 9.4f 8fg 7g 6g³ 7.2g 5fg 6fg 6fg 6d 6fg 5g³ 5s* 6s)
neat colt; narrowly won handicap at Warwick in October; third in seller previous
start; best at sprint distances; suited by some give in the ground; has sweated
up; best in blinkers. *B. McMahon.*

POLAR STAR 3 b.c. Rarity 129–Arctic Chimes (Arctic Slave 116)　(1981　**77**
6g³ 6fg² 7g　1982 8fg* 8f 10.1fg⁴ 10f³ 12fg² 11f* 12s² 12v⁴)　leggy colt; excellent
mover; well-backed favourite when winning handicaps at Thirsk in April and
Redcar in September; stays 1½m; acts on any going; blinkered last 2 starts;
needs holding up. *H. T. Jones.*

POLAR TREK 3 b.f. Decoy Boy 129–Polar Cloud (Crisp and Even 116)　(1981　—
NR　1982 6g 7g 7fg 7g 10g)　320Y; smallish filly; second foal; dam never ran;
poor plater; has worn blinkers; sold 460 gns Newmarket July Sales. *G. Blum.*

POLEMISTIS 3 b.g. Hittite Glory 125–Swing The Cat (Swing Easy 126)　**65** d
(1981 NR　1982 7fg 7f 8fg³ 8fg* 12f³ 9g 10d 8fg² 7s 9s 10s)　rangy, quite
attractive gelding; poor walker and mover; second foal; half-brother to 6f and
7f winner Tamdown Flyer (by Hotfoot); dam never ran; plater; enterprisingly
ridden when winning at Doncaster in May (bought in 2,100 gns); stays 1m but
not 1½m; best form on fast ground; sometimes sweats up; virtually pulled up
seventh start. *C. Brittain.*

POLISHED SILVER 2 ch.c. Try My Best 130–Mettle 107 (Pretendre 126)　**116**
(1982 7d* 7f* 8g* 7g*)
In *Racehorses of 1980* we commented on the depressingly low fertility statistics of some of the stallions which covered their first mares in 1979. According to

the *Statistical Record* Acamas, the champion French three-year-old of 1978, achieved a figure of 14.29%, Gentilhombre, the champion sprinter of 1977, 21.74% and Try My Best, the champion two-year-old of 1977, 42.86%. Gentilhombre was quickly packed off to Japan but the other two were persevered with, with contrasting results; Acamas sired only a handful of foals in 1981 and 1982 and was dispatched to the 1982 Newmarket December Sales where he fetched 125,000 guineas, a fraction of his value a few years before; and Try My Best, after returning a figure of only 53.57% with the twenty-eight mares he covered in 1980, now appears to have normal fertility: he got at least thirty-one of his forty-one mares in foal in 1981, and in 1982 there are reportedly at least forty-seven mares carrying to him. It looks, therefore, as though Try My Best will eventually have sufficient representatives to have a chance of making his mark as a sire. He has already started encouragingly, for although only six of his ten two-year-olds raced he finished quite high up the list of first-season sires, thanks to Sheriff Muir, Treasure Trove, who took the valuable Birdcatcher Nursery under top weight, and the smart Polished Silver.

Polished Silver is unbeaten after four races. Easily his most important win came in the Somerville Tattersall Stakes at Newmarket in October on his final start, in which he gave 3 lb to two other well-fancied colts, the favourite Gordian, a five-length winner in a big field of maidens on his last start, and Cause Celebre who had finished second in two pattern events, the Seaton Delaval Stakes and the Zukunfts Rennen. When Gordian became pocketed on the rails inside the last two furlongs Polished Silver, travelling strongly towards the outside, looked about to win in style. In the end, though, he got home by only a head after taking much longer to wear down Cause Celebre than had seemed likely; he appeared to run lazily, doing no more than was necessary. He had shown a similar tendency when landing the odds in his previous races. In a maiden event at Yarmouth in August, when a 7/2-on chance despite being patently green, he had to be shaken up vigorously to hold off Tolomeo by half a length; in the Chertsey Lock Stakes at Kempton eleven days later he looked about to draw right away from his twelve opponents, all newcomers, when moving up to challenge but eventually had to be thoroughly rousted to get the better of Brave Memory by half a length; and in the Haynes, Hanson and Clark Stakes at Newbury later in September, a race won in the last three years by Henbit, Shergar and Super Sunrise, he'd no sooner deprived Shanipour of the

Somerville Tattersall Stakes, Newmarket—the grey Cause
Celebre just fails to end Polished Silver's unbeaten run

Mr M. Fustok's "Polished Silver"

lead about a furlong out than he decided he'd done enough and started to ease off, winning by a length. Because of Polished Silver's disinclination to do more than the bare minimum it's possible that the best has still to be seen of him; he may yet develop into a fancied classic contender alongside his stable-companions Diesis, Dunbeath, The Fort and Salieri.

	Try My Best (b 1975)	Northern Dancer (b 1961)	Nearctic / Natalma
Polished Silver (ch.c. Feb 11, 1980)		Sex Appeal (ch 1970)	Buckpasser / Best in Show
	Mettle (ch 1969)	Pretendre (ch 1963)	Doutelle / Limicola
		Summer Mark (b 1963)	Summer Tan / Mrs Mark

After fetching 40,000 guineas as a foal Polished Silver was resold as a yearling for 88,000 guineas. He's a strong, rangy colt, and like his sire has a smooth, easy action. It isn't easy to say how much further than a mile he will stay; his sire never won over further than seven furlongs in his short career and his dam, Mettle, gained both her wins over five furlongs as a two-year-old. Mettle did show though that she stayed a mile and a quarter and, of her four other winners, the Lord Gayle fillies Castlemaine and Melody were fairly useful winners at up to nine furlongs and a mile and a half respectively. Mettle is herself a half-sister to six winners, the best of them the smart filly Sound of Summer, who was a stakes winner at up to eight and a half furlongs. Polished Silver's second and third dams Summer-Mark and Mrs Mark both won and Mrs Mark, a stakes winner over a mile, was a sister to Invigorator, a very good stakes winner at up to a mile and a quarter who finished third in the Kentucky Derby. Polished Silver holds the Derby engagement so his connections must be hopeful he'll stay a mile and a half. His style of racing should help him do so. He has won both on firm going and dead ground. *H. Cecil.*

POLITBURO (USA) 2 b.c. Maribeau–Lovely Guinevere (Round Table) (1982 — 6s) big, useful-looking colt; second foal; dam unraced half-sister to dam of Jaazeiro and Woodstream; 12/1, always struggling in 25-runner maiden race at Doncaster in November. *B. Hills.*

POLKA PRINCESS 2 ch.f. Gay Fandango 132–Princess Biddy 86 (Sun Prince **94** p 128) (1982 6d2) Apr 21; 16,000Y; tall, sparely-made filly; first foal; dam, half-sister to top-class animals Double Jump and Royalty, won over 5f at 2 yrs; 33/1 but very fit, made up ground hand over fist after taking long time to warm up when neck second of 21 to Spanish Place in maiden race at Newmarket in October; will be suited by 7f+; sold 12,500 gns Newmarket December Sales. *W. Hastings-Bass.*

POLLY ROYAL 4 ch.f. Music Boy 124–Royal Tactic 62 (Right Tack 131) (1981 **69** 6s 5g 5fg 6f* 6f 7g* 7g 7d4 7s 8g 1982 6s 6f 7f 5g 5fg 6f 5d 6g 6s) small filly; stays 7f; probably acts on any going; sold 4,000 gns Newmarket December Sales. *R. Boss.*

POLLY'S BROTHER 4 ch.c. Roi Soleil 125–Polairia 66 (Polic 126) (1981 7s3 **97 ?** 8d4 11.7g 7fg2 8f3 7g3 7g* 7g* 6g* 7g* 7s 1982 6fg 6f2 6g* 8fg2 6g4 6g2 6d3 6g2 6s) smallish, fair sort; not a good mover; beat Friendly Fun by 1½ lengths in handicap at Ayr in May; in frame afterwards in 5 quite valuable handicaps, on last occasion running race of his life to finish head second of 14 to Famous Star in Ladbrokes (Ayr) Gold Cup in September after struggling to go pace early on; stays 1m, but best form at up to 7f; acts on any going, but is ideally suited by some give in the ground; sometimes tends to hang; genuine and consistent. *M. H. Easterby.*

POLLYS TREASURE 3 b.f. Golden Passenger 98–Pollytooky (Polic 126) — (1981 NR 1982 8f 16g 7fg) second reported foal; dam of little account; bad maiden. *W. R. Williams.*

POLO BOY 2 ch.g. Red Alert 127–Bermuda 81 (Doutelle 128) (1982 5g 6f 6f **75** 7s3) May 28; IR 3,300F, IR 5,200Y; compact, useful-looking gelding; half-brother to numerous winners in Ireland and abroad, including Swedish 1,000 Guineas winner Kreta (by Acropolis); dam won over 1m and 1¼m; blinkered and having first race for over 2 months, finished 4½ lengths third of 12 behind Rana Pratap in minor event at Chepstow in October; evidently suited by 7f; acts on soft going; gelded at end of season. *G. Balding.*

POLWICK 5 b.g. Red Alert 127–Gay Sylvia (Sayajirao 132) (1981 9d2 10d2 8g3 11.7d* 11.7g 10f4 12f 12.2g 1982 8g 12s) well-made gelding; well beaten in 1982 (needed race on reappearance in October); stays 11.7f; acts on a soft surface; sometimes blinkered; has run creditably for an apprentice; has been bandaged in front. *R. Champion.*

POLYLOOM 2 b.f. Cawston's Clown 113–Cashmere Shawl (Ballyciptic 122) — (1982 5f 7g) Mar 29; 950F, 700Y; well-grown, leggy filly; half-sister to several winners, including fairly useful 1979 Irish 2-y-o 7f winner Castlemara (by Virginia Boy); last in maiden auction event at Doncaster in May and claiming race at Yarmouth in September. *Mrs N. Macauley.*

POMEGRANATE (USA) 3 b.f. Damascus–Caspian 122 (Bold Bidder) (1981 **96** 6fg* 6g 6f* 1982 8f4 7f 6g) short-coupled, quite attractive filly; fairly useful performer; ran respectably first 2 starts, coming home about 6 lengths fourth of 5 to Dish Dash at Sandown in June and about 3½ lengths fifth of 8 to Perang Tejam in £6,100 handicap at Newmarket in July; ran moderately final start; stays 1m; acts on firm going; highly strung; sent to USA. *H. Cecil.*

POMPONETTE 3 b.f. Fine Blade 121–Daisy 92 (Abernant 142) (1981 NR — 1982 8fg) big, lengthy filly; half-sister to several winners, including fairly useful 1m and 1¼m winner Darda (by Darius); dam, fairly useful at 2 yrs, is sister to smart sprinter Camille; unquoted and in need of run, showed up 4f when behind in 21-runner maiden race won by Moniar at Newmarket in May. *M. Jarvis.*

PONCHIELLI 4 b.c. Pitskelly 122–Pennycress 99 (Florescence 120) (1981 7g **102** 6s 6s 6f2 5fg* 5fg3 6fg 5d3 5fg* 5f4 5.6fg 1982 6g3 5fg2 5f 5fg2 5g 5f3 5f3 6d 6g 6g) smallish, strong, good sort; useful sprinter; placed in handicaps at Kempton and York (2) and in better company at Chantilly (excellent length second of 10 to

Mr A. I. Donaldson's "Ponchielli"

Kind Music in Prix du Gros-Chene) and Goodwood; chased leaders and kept on well when dead-heating for third, 3 lengths behind Tina's Pet, in King George Stakes on last-named course in July; probably best at 5f; acts on any going but best form on a sound surface; occasionally disappoints and did so on last 2 starts. *R. Armstrong.*

PONTCHARTRAIN (USA) 2 b.c. Lyphard 132–Mauna Loa (Hawaii) (1982 6d³) **72** p
Apr 12; $75,000Y; small, lightly-made colt; lacks scope; second foal; dam, half-sister to top-class middle-distance stayer Exceller, won 7f claiming race at 2 yrs; 3/1, kept on steadily after dwelling when 7 lengths third of 10 behind Joy Hour in minor event at Leicester in October; will be suited by 7f+. *H. Cecil.*

PONTIN BOY 3 b.c. Prince Tenderfoot 126–Buenaventura II (Celtic Ash) **76**
(1981 NR 1982 8.2f 8d 10.1fg⁴ 10f² 12fg* 12fg² 12fg² 12s) IR 21,000Y; strong, lengthy colt; brother to useful 1980 2-y-o 5f winner Brooklyn Prince and half-brother to winners here and in Italy; dam placed at up to 1¼m in France; made all and kept on well to win gentleman riders race at Kempton in September; suited by 1½m; acts on firm going and is apparently unsuited by soft. *H. T. Jones.*

PONTIN LAD 4 br.g. Mansingh 120–Mildura 98 (Vilmorin) (1981 5g⁴ 5g 5fg **101**
5.3f* 5fg³ 5d² 5s 1982 5f* 5f⁴ 5f² 5g* 5f³ 5g) neat, strong, attractive gelding; good mover; useful handicapper; won at Epsom in April (by ½ length from Mumruffin) and at Lingfield in June (beat Barnet Heir a head in £6,300 John Rogerson Handicap); unlikely to stay 6f; acts on any going, except possibly very soft; needs strong handling; ran moderately final start. *H. T. Jones.*

PONTOS 3 b.g. Averof 123–Filandria 90 (French Beige 127) (1981 6f² 6fg² —
6fg 8.2s⁴ 8g⁴ 1982 8g 8.2fg 9fg 11.5f 11.5fg 10.1g 10fg) leggy gelding; poor

performer nowadays; should stay middle distances; acts on any going; sold to Miss S. Morris 800 gns Newmarket Autumn Sales. *C. Brittain.*

POOL PLAYER 2 ch.g. Warpath 113–Snow Goose (Santa Claus 133) (1982 7g) — Jan 14; 6,200Y; brother to 2 winners on flat, including Obergurgl, successful over 1¼m and 13f, and to 2 over hurdles; dam never ran; unquoted, eleventh of 16 in minor event at Lingfield in August. *K. Brassey.*

POP A LONG (USA) 8 b.h. Baldric II 131–Popkins 120 (Romulus 129) (1981 — 7.6fg 1982 8g) poor handicapper; stays 1¼m; often wears bandages; has worn blinkers; usually apprentice ridden. *H. Wragg.*

POPSI'S HOPE 4 b.g. Mandamus 120–Popsie's Pride (Border Legend 119) — (1981 12g 10v 1982 8f 12f 12fg) small gelding; in rear in maiden and minor races and a ladies event; sold out of M. Haynes's stable 440 gns Ascot 2nd June Sales after second start. *R. Morris.*

POPSI'S JOY 7 b.g. Hill Clown–Popsie's Pride (Border Legend 119) (1981 **88** 18s⁴ 16fg³ 16g* 16f⁴ 16g 21fg⁴ 16d⁴ 14d 14.6fg 16fg 1982 18g² 14g³ 18f³ 18.4fg 14fg² 20fg* 16fg 16g 19f 16d 18d² 20g) big, strong gelding; staying handicapper; had an excellent chance on his best form when winning Ascot Stakes at Royal Ascot in June with a bit in hand by 2 lengths from Baron Blakeney; ran easily best subsequent race when 3 lengths second of 28 behind Mountain Lodge in Tote Cesarewitch at Newmarket in October; acts on any going; invariably held up; unreliable nowadays. *M. Haynes.*

PORCUPINE 4 ch.g. Sharp Edge 123–Padora 60 (Pardao 120) (1981 NR — 1982 10.6h 8g 8g) seems of little account. *M. Pipe.*

PORTER 3 b.g. Mummy's Pet 125–Morelia 76 (Murrayfield 119) (1981 5f 5f⁴ **60** d 6g 7f 8s 1982 7d 8.2v³ 8fg 10fg 8.2g² 9g³ 11g 10d 12g⁴ 12fg 10s) leggy gelding; poor mover and has a round action; poor maiden; beaten in sellers on occasions; stays 1¼m; acts on heavy going; has run respectably in blinkers. *F. Carter.*

PORTERS PRIDE 2 gr.c. Lord Henham 110–Blue Friend 61 (Blue Streak 106) — (1982 7.2g 8.2fg) May 19; small, lightly-made colt; fourth live foal; dam plater; tailed off in minor event and a seller at Haydock. *J. Townson.*

PORTETTE 3 gr.f. Wolver Hollow 126–Portden (Worden II 129) (1981 6fg — 8fg³ 8d* 8s 1982 10f⁴ 10fg 10d 8f 8d) rather lightly-made filly; won maiden race at Bath in 1981; below form most starts at 3 yrs; stays 1¼m; seems to act on any going; sold 2,400 gns Newmarket December Sales. *C. Spares.*

PORT MOULTON 3 ch.f. Moulton 128–Safe Port (Above Suspicion 127) — (1981 5s 1982 10s 12g) poor maiden; retained 640 gns Newmarket May Sales; sold 360 gns Doncaster November Sales. *P. Duggins.*

PORTOGON 4 gr.c. Porto Bello 118–Helgonet (Soueida 111) (1981 5s 6fg² **75** 5fg 7.3g⁴ 7f 6f* 6fg³ 7f* 7fg 7fg² 7fg² 7g 7s³ 1982 8g 6.5fg 6.5v² 7.5d³ 7s 8fg 7fg⁴ 8g 7f 8f 7f³ 7g* 7fg² 7fg* 7d² 7s) big, strong, workmanlike colt; won handicaps at Lingfield in August and Salisbury in September narrowly, latter from Rawlinson End after disputing lead throughout; stays 7.5f; acts on any going. *T. Marshall.*

PORTO IRENE 2 ch.f. Porto Bello 118–Irene Louise 65 (Match III 135) **73** (1982 6fg 5fg 5.8g⁴ 5f 5s) Apr 17; small, compact filly; half-sister to 2 minor winners; dam poor half-sister to high-class sprinter Import (by Porto Bello); quite moderate maiden; stays 6f; acts on any going. *D. C. Tucker.*

PORTO LOUISE 3 ch.f. Porto Bello 118–Irene Louise 65 (Match III 135) — (1981 6fg 7h 8fg 8s 1982 7fg 8.5f 10g) compact filly; no worthwhile form in maiden races and sellers. *D. C. Tucker.*

PORT SAIGON (USA) 2 ch.c. What A Pleasure–Sierra Morena (Canisbay **94** p 120) (1982 9s 10s*) Mar 1; first foal; dam, second in Oaks d'Italia and Gran Premio del Jockey Club, is closely related to 1974 Derby Italiano winner Suffolk; had his 14 opponents quite well strung out when winning maiden race at Saint-Cloud in October by 3 lengths from Jeu de Paille; will stay 1½m; the type to make a very useful middle-distance 3-y-o. *J. Cunnington, jnr, France.*

POSHTEEN 7 ch.m. Royal Smoke 113–Camlet 60 (Fleece 114) (1981 7d — 5.8g³ 1982 5g 5fg 5f) strong mare; one-time fair sprinter; acts well on firm going; has worn blinkers; has been to stud. *O. O'Neill.*

POSITANO 2 b.c. Star Appeal 133–Port Ahoy 93 (Petingo 135) (1982 6g **83** 7g³ 7d³ 8d 8s²) Jan 24; 17,000Y; compact colt; good walker; second foal; half-brother to very useful 1981 2-y-o 7f winner Top Hope (by High Top);

dam 2-y-o 6f and 7f winner; placed in maiden races at Newmarket, Chester (looked unsuited by course) and Bath; will stay 1¼m; yet to race on a firm surface. *P. Walwyn.*

POSITRON 3 br.f. Free State 125–Naiche (Tribal Chief 125) (1981 5d 5f 5fg 8fg³ 7g* 8.2s 1982 8fg² 8f³ 8d 9fg 8g 10d⁴ 10g 8g) small filly; stays 1¼m; best form on a sound surface; has run moderately when sweating up. *W. Wharton.* **77**

POTTINGER (FR) 3 b.c. Vitiges 132–Pot Pourri 97 (Busted 134) (1981 NR 1982 10.6s 10f* 12fg* 12f 10.5g² 12g² 12f* 10.5g⁴ 10.5v³) well-made, attractive, good-bodied ex-English colt; fifth foal; half-brother to 1½m winner Potshot (by Roan Rocket); dam stayer and half-sister to very smart Almiranta; won maiden race at Beverley, minor event at Edinburgh and handicap at Ripon early in year; subsequently sent to France and ran second in races at Mont-de-Marsan (blinkered) and Bordeaux prior to winning 45,000 francs race at Nantes in November; will stay beyond 1½m; acts well on firm going; trained by E. Weymes first 5 starts. *M. Laborde, France.* **96**

POUNENTES 5 b.g. Tumble Wind–La Chanteuse 81 (Hethersett 134) (1981 12g² 13fg 11g⁴ 12d 11fg 12g 1982 13s) workmanlike gelding; stays 1¼m; seems to act on any going; best in blinkers; has run well for an apprentice. *G. Richards.* **—**

POWER EYE (USA) 2 b.c. Run Dusty Run–Rebrook (Reneged) (1982 7d) Mar 14; $62,000Y; rather leggy colt; half-brother to 3 winners; dam unraced sister to Recall, a smart stakes winner at up to 1m; 20/1 and in need of race, 10 lengths eighth of 18 behind easy winner Northern Adventure in minor event at Doncaster in October; likely to improve. *M. Jarvis.* **73 p**

POWERSAVER LADY 2 b. or br.f. Auction King 123–Singing Blues 78 (Paveh 126) (1982 5f² 5g³ 6fg* 8fg) Mar 3; 8,000Y; quite attractive filly; half-sister to fairly useful 7f and 1m winner Jazz King (by Roi Soleil); dam won over 6f at 2 yrs but didn't train on; easily landed the odds in 3-runner maiden event at Hamilton in July; had stiff task under top weight when sixth of 11 behind General Concorde in nursery at Warwick the following month; probably stays 1m; yet to race on a soft surface; sent to India. *M. Jarvis.* **63**

POWERSCOURT (USA) 5 b.g. Buckpasser–Irish Manor (Bold Ruler) (1981 8d 1982 12g 7.2s 7f 6f 5f) robust gelding; rather a disappointing maiden; sometimes blinkered; dead. *J. Edmunds.* **—**

PRAETORIAN 5 gr.g. Home Guard 129–Song In The Air 83 (Tudor Melody 129) (1981 8.3fg 1982 12d 12g 16.5f) behind in varied company, including selling; has worn blinkers and bandages. *J. Jenkins.* **—**

PRAIRIE GOD 2 ch.c. Pampapaul 121–Prairie Oyster (Alarich) (1982 6fg 5.8f 7fg 7d 7f³) May 15; IR 13,000Y; sturdy, good-bodied colt; half-brother to several winners in Germany and Ireland; dam won twice in Germany; placed under a low weight in nursery at Leicester in September; will stay 1m; sold CBA 1,500 gns Newmarket Autumn Sales. *N. Vigors.* **62**

PRAIRIE SAINT 2 b.f. Welsh Saint 126–Prairie Bar (Ballymore 123) (1982 5.3fg 5.1g² 5fg² 5f*) Feb 13; IR 1,000Y; sparely-made filly; first foal; dam won over 1½m in Ireland; won maiden race at Catterick in July easing up by 4 lengths from Unbeknown; apprentice ridden when second in auction events earlier; will stay 6f; acts on firm going. *A. Jarvis.* **74**

PRAJAI 3 b.c. Sun Prince 128–Anice (Crepello 136) (1981 5s³ 5v³ 5fg 6s 8.2s 1982 8g 10.6fg 11g³ 12f 16fg 16d 8.2f³ 9fg 10fg) leggy colt; plating-class maiden; stays 11f; has worn blinkers; sold 650 gns Doncaster October Sales. *W. Elsey.* **—**

PRASLIN 3 ch.f. Sweet Revenge 129–Solinda (Soleil II 133) (1981 NR 1982 8d³ 8d* 10fg 8f⁴ 7f⁴ 7d) 2,800Y; plain filly; half-sister to 2 winners, including fairly useful 7f winner Unicorn's Fancy (by Virginia Boy); dam unraced daughter of high-class 1958 2-y-o Lindsay; stayed on well to win maiden race at Newcastle in April; not disgraced in handicaps fourth and fifth starts; suited by 1m (tailed off in Pretty Polly Stakes at Newmarket over further); yet to race on very soft going but acts on any other. *B. Hanbury.* **73**

PREACHER MAN 5 b.h. Gulf Pearl 117–Miss Etta (King's Troop 118) (1981 10s 12s 13fg 10.6s 11d 12d 12d 1982 13d) poor form, including in a valuable selling handicap; was tried in blinkers; sometimes bandaged; dead. *T. Kersey.* **—**

PRECIOUS MOMENTS 4 b.c. Furry Glen 121–Contourno (Continuation 120) (1981 7d 7.6g 6fg 8g 10d 1982 6s 6g 11g 7f 9fg²) rangy colt; second in seller at Hamilton in July; stays 9f; has been tried in blinkers; sold out of D. Smith's stable 1,450 gns Doncaster May Sales after second outing. *C. Pinkham.*

PRECIS (USA) 3 b.g. Pretense–Vaguely Familiar (Vaguely Noble 140) (1981 **89** NR 1982 7g* 6g² 8fg* 8f² 9d) $150,000Y; big, strong, rangy gelding; has a slightly round action; second foal; dam a leading American 2-y-o filly in 1972 when winner at up to 7f; won maiden race at Newcastle in June and impressively beat Molon Lave in 5-runner handicap at Newmarket in July; suited by 1m; gives impression he will always do best on a galloping track; pulled hard fourth start; gelded at end of season. *J. W. Watts.*

PREMIERE DANSEUSE 3 ro.f. Saritamer 130–First Round 97 (Primera **72** 131) (1981 NR 1982 7g 8g³ 6f² 7fg 7g² 6f³ 6g 7g* 7d) quite attractive filly; half-sister to 4 winners, notably very useful sprinters Glenturret (by Habitat) and Rollahead (by Tower Walk); dam won at up to 1½m; beat Blakesware County by 1½ lengths in 19-runner handicap at Newmarket in October; suited by 7f or more; acts on firm going; ran moderately fourth and seventh starts. *B. Hills.*

PREMIER LASS 3 b.f. Lochnager 132–Obedience (Reliance II 137) (1981 **78** 5d 6fg 5f² 7fg 6fg 6fg 5s³ 6v⁴ 6d⁴ 1982 5fg* 6g⁴ 6fg* 6g² 6fg* 6fg) small, active filly; won maiden race at Folkestone in April and handicaps at Windsor and Lingfield in May; also first past post in another handicap at Windsor but was moved down to second after stewards inquiry; best at sprint distances; acts on any going; consistent; sent to USA. *P. Mitchell.*

PREPARATION 3 ch.f. On Your Mark 125–Reddish Radish (Red God 128§) **72** (1981 5g 5g³ 5fg 6f³ 6fg* 5fg 6g 5s* 5g* 1982 6g 5g 5.8f 7g 5fg 6f² 6fg⁴ 6fg² 6f* 6v³ 6s) fair sort; has a nice smooth action; won handicap at Leicester in September; suited by 6f; acts on any going; has run respectably in blinkers; sent to India. *R. Smyth.*

PRESS BARON 3 b.c. Touch Paper 113–Miss Dorothy 87 (Major Portion 129) — (1981 6fg 5.8f³ 6g 6fg 1982 6s 6d 7f 6f) only plating class; best run at 5.8f on firm going; blinkered final outing; sold to R. Akehurst 775 gns Ascot August Sales. *J. Dunlop.*

PRESS GANG 7 gr.g. Precipice Wood 123–Beige Etoile 54 (French Beige 127) — (1981 9s 1982 13d 9s) winner over hurdles and fences; behind in maiden and minor events on flat. *J. S. Wilson.*

PRESTON MANOR 3 b.g. Riboboy 124–Amatitlan (Amber Rama 133) — (1981 7.2d 7fg 8g* 8d 1982 10g) neat, lightly-made gelding; plater; has ability but more than his share of temperament; bred to stay 1¼m+; sold, probably for export to Norway, 1,400 gns Doncaster June Sales. *Mrs. M. Nesbitt.*

PRETENCIOSA (FR) 3 ch.f. Anne's Pretender 124–Denosa 109 (Worden II — 129) (1981 6d 1982 10fg 8d 5g 12g) small filly; poor maiden. *C. Williams.*

PRETTY MISS 3 br.f. So Blessed 130–Molly Polly (Molvedo 137) (1981 NR — 1982 7d) quite attractive filly; half-sister to 3 winners, including useful 1974 2-y-o Fair Parrot (by Sahib); dam won 5 races in Italy; 25/1 and backward when in rear in 12-runner minor event won by Triple Tipple at Salisbury in June. *J. Bethell.*

PRETTY PICTURE 3 ch.f. Grundy 137–Miss Pinkie 121 (Connaught 130) **81** (1981 6d 1982 12f² 12.2f* 14g⁴ 12fg³) smallish, lengthy filly; comfortably landed odds in maiden race at Catterick in June; not disgraced in minor events at Yarmouth and Wolverhampton afterwards; stays 1¾m; acts on firm going; sold 31,000 gns Newmarket December Sales. *H. Cecil.*

PREVAIL 3 b.c. Steel Heart 128–Lavendula Rose 108 (Le Levanstell 122) **90** (1981 5fg 5fg³ 7g⁴ 6fg⁴ 6d² 6g³ 1982 6s* 6fg* 6f* 6f* 6fg² 7.2g 6g⁴ 6g 7g 7d) neat, strong, attractive colt who often impresses in appearance; good mover; won maiden race at Leicester in March and took valuable handicaps at York in May (from Boatrocker) and Newbury in June (beat Princess Virginia); stays 7f but gives impression 6f is his optimum trip; acts on any going but goes well on firm; suited by waiting tactics; refused to enter stalls once; below form towards end of season. *W. Elsey.*

PRICEOFLOVE 2 b.c. Blue Cashmere 129–Gay Donna (Tudor Jinks 121) **92** (1982 5fg 5f⁴ 5d* 5g 6d* 6g) May 19; 6,000F, 17,500Y; quite attractive, well-made colt; brother to 3 winners, including fairly useful 2-y-o 5f winners Blue Lass and Childown Blue, and half-brother to 2 winners; dam of little account; put up easily best efforts when clear-cut winner of maiden race at Wolverhampton in August and nursery at Nottingham in September; stays 6f well; suited by a soft surface; blinkered third and fourth starts. *R. Laing.*

PRICE OF PEACE 4 gr.g. Averof 123–Kingdom Come 77 (Klondyke Bill 125) —
(1981 8s⁴ 7fg* 6s⁴ 8f 7f³ 7g³ 7.2g 8f⁴ 8f 7g 9d² 8d² 11d³ 1982 13fg 10d 8f 10g)
big gelding; poor form in 1982; stays 11f; seems to act on any going; sometimes
hangs under pressure and isn't an easy ride; has run creditably in blinkers;
has worn bandages in front. *J. Doyle.*

PRICE'S PRINCE 3 br.g. Free State 125–Repel (Hardicanute 130) (1981 —
NR 1982 10.1fg 13g 16.9fg 16fg³ 12g⁴ 13.1g) 2,800 2-y-o; stocky gelding;
fifth living foal; half-brother to a winning hurdler; dam never ran; only plating
class; possibly stays 2m. *B. Palling.*

PRIDE OF FAIRFIELD 3 b.f. Evanavitch 87–Lingala (Pinturischio 116) **43**
(1981 5d 6g 6f 6f 7g² 7fg² 8fg 8.2d 1982 12.2f² 12.3f³ 12g 12g 10.8fg) small
filly; bad mover; plater; suited by 1½m; acts on firm going; suitable mount for
an apprentice; sent to Algeria. *P. Rohan.*

PRIMA VOCE (USA) 3 b.c. Elocutionist–Que Mona (Ribot 142) (1981 5g* **121**
6f* 6g 1982 7fg 8fg 8.5f* 8f⁴ 10g 10fg⁴ 11.1fg 10fg 10d²)
   Prima Voce's departure at the overnight stage from the Tia Maria Autumn
Handicap at Newmarket after he'd worked disappointingly removed one of the
more important elements in a fascinating puzzle. Not every day does a Champion
Stakes second make his very next appearance in handicap company.
Whether he'd have improved on Haul Knight's fourth in the race three years
earlier is problematical. He had 10-0, 1 lb less than the eventual runner-up
Fine Sun; even so he had an excellent chance on his best form as represented by
his seven-length second to Time Charter in the Dubai Champion Stakes and his
game two-and-a-half-length defeat of Noalto in the Diomed Stakes at Epsom in
June. He wouldn't have been out of it, either, on his six-and-a-half-length
fourth to Mr Fluorocarbon in the Queen Anne Stakes at Royal Ascot nor his
two-length fourth to the highly promising French three-year-old General Holme
in the Prix de la Cote Normande at Deauville. But the rest of Prima Voce's

Captain J. Durham-Matthews' "Prima Voce"

form is not quite so good. His two races leading up to the Champion Stakes had seen him fifth of seven behind Critique in the September Stakes at Kempton and fifth of six behind Peacetime in the Valdoe Stakes at Goodwood, hardly the sort of performances to recommend him. And in another two important races he'd seemed out of his depth, when twelfth in the Two Thousand Guineas and when seventh of nine to Kalaglow in the Coral-Eclipse Stakes. There is a certain inconsistency about Prima Voce's record which is reflected by his starting price in the Diomed Stakes and the Champion Stakes: he was allowed to start at 25/1 at Epsom and 50/1 at Newmarket. We can't as yet explain it satisfactorily. There's nothing wrong with his temperament; and he's been raced at distances within his capabilities on ground that events have proved suitable for him. Perhaps an easier task now and again would not have gone amiss.

Prima Voce (USA) (b.c. 1979)	Elocutionist (b 1973)	Gallant Romeo (b 1961)	Gallant Man Juliets Nurse
		Strictly Speaking (b 1967)	Fleet Nasrullah Believe Me
	Que Mona (b 1969)	Ribot (b 1952)	Tenerani Romanella
		Monade (br 1959)	Klairon Myrmyre

Prima Voce is American bred and was picked up at the Keeneland September Yearling Sale very reasonably for 25,000 dollars. His grandam, the Oaks winner Monade, needs little introduction. She has been at stud in the United States since her racing days and has bred numerous winners, notably the stakes winner Pressing Date who finished second in the Delaware Oaks. Monade is also the grandam of the good American three-year-old filly Too Chic. Prima Voce's sire Elocutionist requires very little more introducing than Monade, since he's also the sire of Recitation. He won the Preakness Stakes in 1976. The dam Que Mona was one of Monade's winners, a minor one over six furlongs as a four-year-old. She produced the stakes-placed Que Appeal (by Star Appeal), a winner of five races and over 90,000 dollars, and the two-year-old winner Reasonable Mona (by Bold Reason) before Prima Voce.

Prima Voce, a well-made colt and a good mover, has yet to race on very soft going but acts on any other. Nowadays a distance of a mile and a quarter suits him well. While he won't be easy to place as a four-year-old he is too good a horse to go through the season empty handed. *R. Armstrong.*

PRIMROLLA 3 b. or br.f. Relko 136–Primrose Bank 91 (Charlottown 127) **64**
(1981 NR 1982 8d 10s* 10f 12d 12f 11.1fg 13d 12d 16s) lengthy, lightly-made filly; first foal; dam, 1½m winner, is half-sister to Rodman (by Relko), a smart jumper at his best; apprentice ridden, trotted up in maiden race at Chepstow in April; well beaten most starts afterwards; possibly stays 2m; acts well on soft going; sometimes pulls hard; useful young hurdler. *D. Nicholson.*

PRIMSIDE 6 b.g. Connaught 130–Never Alone 86 (Never Say Die 137) (1981 —
19s 17.1d 1982 15.8g) small gelding; poor stayer nowadays; probably acts on any going; sometimes blinkered; refused to race on only outing of 1982; sold 500 gns Ascot May Sales. *C. Wildman.*

PRIMULA BOY 7 ch.g. Sallust 134–Catriona 96 (Sing Sing 134) (1981 6g **84**
6g 6g 6f 6f* 6fg 6fg 6g4 6f3 6fg 5.6fg 6d 1982 6d 6f 5fg 6g 6f 6fg 6d3 6g 6g 7d* 6f 6fg 7f 6g 6s 7s) fair handicapper on his day; made all in apprentice race at Catterick in July; had run best previous race when third at Nottingham; stays 7f; acts on any going; has worn blinkers but is better without; not particularly consistent; broke a blood vessel eleventh start. *W. Bentley.*

PRINCE AMADEO 2 ch.c. Sallust 134–Flaring Angel (Nentego 119) (1982 **70**
6s 8s3 6d) Apr 28; IR 22,000F, IR 10,500Y; medium-sized, close-coupled colt; half-brother to 1981 Irish 2-y-o 6f winner Sunny South (by Be My Guest); dam won twice at up to 6f at 2 yrs in North America; plating-class maiden; best run on first outing; weakened badly closing stages when 9 lengths third of 13 to Kilner in maiden race at Warwick in October; seemingly does not stay 1m; acts on soft going. *F. J. Houghton.*

PRINCE APALACHEE (USA) 3 b.c. Apalachee 137–Splendid Spree (Damas- **75**
cus) (1981 NR 1982 12g 11.5g 12v2 10.6s4) $110,000Y; well-made, attractive colt; good mover; fifth foal; brother to stakes winner Splendid Way, and half-brother to 3 winners, including very good American 1981 3-y-o Splendid Spruce (by Big Spruce), winner of Santa Anita Derby; dam unraced half-sister to smart

middle-distance colt Manitoulin; quite a modest maiden; will be suited by 1¾m; yet to race on a firm surface. *J. Dunlop.*

PRINCE BARRINGTON 2 b.c. Hotfoot 126–My Princess (King Emperor) **84** (1982 7g 6d) Apr 10; deep-girthed colt; fourth foal; dam, 2-y-o winner in Italy, is out of half-sister to Bold Lad, Ire; unquoted and looking wintry, ran on steadily when seventh of 21 to stable-companion Spanish Place in maiden race at Newmarket in October, second outing; will stay 1m. *B. Hills.*

PRINCE BEE 5 b.h. Sun Prince 128–Honerko 112 (Tanerko 134) (1981 **109** 12d² 12.5g 10g* 12d 10g⁴ 1982 13.3f³ 12f) strong, attractive horse; good mover; second foal; half-brother to smart 1976 staying 2-y-o Balteus (by Baldric II); dam very useful middle-distance winner; high-class performer at his best; won 4 races as a 3-y-o, including Great Voltigeur Stakes at York and Prix Niel at Longchamp, and was second to Tyrnavos in Irish Sweeps Derby; less successful as a 4-y-o, winning 4-runner Valdoe Stakes at Goodwood from 5 starts, and disappointed both starts in 1982; finished 7½ lengths third behind Easter Sun in Aston Park Stakes at Newbury in May (odds on) and 6½ lengths fifth of 8 to same horse in Coronation Cup at Epsom in June (blinkered first time); was suited by 1½m; acted on any going; standing at Dowdstown Stud, Maynooth, at a fee of IR 3,500 gns n.f.n.f. (1st October terms). *R. Hern.*

PRINCE CONCORDE 2 b.c. Condorcet–Barstown Princess (Seminole II) **82** (1982 5g⁴ 5f 7f⁴ 7f 7fg* 8f* 8d³ 8d) Mar 20; IR 6,200F, 5,000Y; rather leggy colt; half-brother to 2 winners in Ireland, including 7.5f and 1¾m winner Prince Tammy (by Tamerlane), and a winner in Holland; dam never ran; won seller (bought in 1,600 gns) at Newcastle in July and nursery at Pontefract in September; excellent third under penalty in nursery at Ayr later in September; will stay 1½m; has won on firm, but best form on a soft surface. *E. Carter.*

PRINCE ECHO 4 ch.c. Crowned Prince 128–Dawn Echo (Don II 123) (1981 — 7s* 8g 8s³ 5s*(dis) 8fg 6g⁴ 6fg⁴ 6fg 6fg 7g 1982 6g⁴ 7g 6f) strong, good-quartered ex-Irish colt; showed smart form at 3 yrs when trained by L. Browne, putting up best efforts when excellent third behind Kings Lake and To-Agori-Mou in Airlie/Coolmore Irish 2,000 Guineas at the Curragh and fourth to Marwell in William Hill July Cup at Newmarket; disappointing in 1982, best effort probably on reappearance when fifth of 6 to Motavato in very slowly-run Tote Lockinge Stakes at Newbury in May; not seen out after finishing last of 16 behind Sharpo in William Hill July Cup at Newmarket; effective from 5f to 1m; possibly needs some give in the ground and acts well on soft going; sometimes blinkered (ran well in them only on first occasion). *H. Cecil.*

PRINCE ELO (USA) 3 b.c. Elocutionist–Family Planning (Cyane) (1981 **77** 7g 7g 1982 8f 10fg² 10fg 12.3d³ 12fg 15.8d*) attractive, lengthy colt; poor walker; showed himself suited by a test of stamina when keeping on strongly to win minor event at Catterick in October; acts on a firm and a soft surface; sold to BBA 13,500 gns Newmarket Autumn Sales. *J. Dunlop.*

PRINCE FANDANGO 4 ch.c. Gay Fandango 132–Procession 118 (Sovereign — Path 125) (1981 8fg 1982 8fg 8g 8d) of little account; dead. *R. Morris.*

PRINCE FELIX 2 b.c. Filiberto 123–Ramuk's Queen 65 (Queen's Hussar 124) — (1982 6fg) May 7; first living foal; dam won 1m seller and was a useful hurdler; 33/1, remote ninth of 12 in newcomers event at Chepstow in August. *J. Cann.*

PRINCE GIOVANNI 2 b.c. So Blessed 130–Lucky Janie 87 (Dual 117) (1982 **72** 6d 5f 7fg 7.2s²) Mar 8; 8,200F; well-grown, attractive colt; brother to 3-y-o Never So Lucky, a winner at up to 7f, and half-brother to several winners; dam won from 5f to 1m; favourite, seemed none too keen when 1½ lengths second of 10 to Bara Gill in seller at Haydock in October, best effort; stays 7f. *D. Garraton.*

PRINCE GUARD 3 ch.c. Home Guard 129–Crassula (Canisbay 120) (1981 **83** 8d 8s 1982 12f 8f⁴ 8s 8s⁴ 8s* 8s) big, fair sort; made all when easily winning minor event at Redcar in October; stays 1m; acts on any going but goes well on soft; blinkered last 2 starts. *S. Matthews.*

PRINCE HELEN 6 b.g. Status Seeker–Lucky Poem (Lucky Guy 121) (1981 — NR 1982 10fg) won maiden race at Lingfield in 1978; behind on only outing on flat since; best form at up to 1¼m; acts on firm going; usually blinkered. *G. Huffer.*

PRINCE HENRY 2 ch.c. Whitstead 125–Concern 63 (Brigadier Gerard 144) — (1982 7g 7fg) Mar 21; small, strong colt; first foal; dam, from good family, won over 9.4f; soundly beaten in maiden races won by The Fort and Alligatrix at Newmarket in August. *M. Tompkins.*

PRINCE LAFITE 2 gr.g. English Prince 129–Haut Lafite (Tamerlane 128) —
(1982 7g 7fg 7fg) Apr 13; IR 4,500Y; fair sort; half-brother to Irish 11.5f winner
Maryville Bick (by Malacate); dam won at up to 1m in Ireland; unquoted and
apprentice ridden, behind in maiden races in June and July. *A. Jarvis.*

PRINCE LEONARDO 2 br.c. Rarity 129–Social Smash (Social Climber) —
(1982 7fg 7fg 8s 8s 10s) Feb 15; IR 13,000Y; attractive colt; half-brother to
winners here and in USA, including 1981 2-y-o 5f winner Queen of the Blues
(by Steel Heart); dam, placed in USA, is half-sister to Belmont Stakes winner
Sherluck; well beaten in minor and maiden events. *F. J. Houghton.*

PRINCELY FIGHTER (USA) 2 b. or br.c. Fifth Marine–Sharon A. (Princely **97**
Gift 137) (1982 6f* 6g⁴ 6g* 6g) Feb 21; $45,000Y; attractive colt; half-
brother to 2 minor stakes winners and several other winners; dam won 8 sprint
races from 2 yrs to 6 yrs; successful in minor events at Yarmouth (by 10 lengths)
in June and at Ripon in August; last of 4 when odds on at Doncaster in between,
and in rear under top weight in nursery at Leicester in October; should stay
beyond 6f; acts well on firm going. *M. Stoute.*

PRINCELY GEM 3 ch.c. Sun Prince 128–Rockeater 94 (Roan Rocket 128) —
(1981 7fg 7f 8g 8.2d* 1982 8g 10g) small, compact colt; plater; should stay
1¼m; possibly needs some give in the ground; sold 1,200 gns Doncaster June
Sales. *J. Etherington.*

PRINCE MAJ (USA) 4 b.c. His Majesty–Lady Rosse (Hail to Reason) (1981 **91**
11s⁴ 10d⁴ 10d³ 12.3g* 12.2f* 12.3g* 14f³ 1982 12d⁴ 12.3fg 16g 16f* 16fg*
14g² 18.8fg³ 18.1g⁴ 16d³ 18d) well-made, attractive colt; awarded race after
going down by a head to Protos in handicap at Kempton in July; won 6-runner
£4,600 event at Ascot later in month very easily indeed by 5 lengths from Sligo
Bay; placed subsequently in handicaps at Haydock (amateur riders, finishing
very strongly after being virtually tailed off), Warwick and Ascot; well suited
by a test of stamina; has run creditably on softish going but is better on a sound
surface; usually wears blinkers; probably needs strong handling; sold to M.
Pipe 19,500 gns Newmarket Autumn Sales. *M. Stoute.*

PRINCE NONO 4 br.g. Nonoalco 131–Kissing 98 (Sing Sing 134) (1981 —
10d 11.5d³ 12d² 12f* 12fg⁴ 12d 1982 12.2s) rangy gelding; well beaten only
start as a 4-y-o; gives impression he'll be very well suited by further than 1¼m;
probably acts on any going; occasionally blinkered in 1981. *R. Hartop.*

PRINCE OF BLADES 5 b. or br.g. Fine Blade 121–Princess Irmgard 83 —
(Delirium 126) (1981 NR 1982 8g 8f 8fg) lengthy gelding; plater; possibly
best at distances short of 1m; acts on firm going; best in blinkers; said by
trainer to be ungenuine. *P. Rohan.*

PRINCE OF CAPRI (USA) 3 br.c. Cornish Prince–Queen of Capri (Forli) **61**
(1981 6g³ 1982 6d³ 8f 7fg 6f) quite a well-made colt; quite moderate; should
stay 1m; ran abysmally in blinkers final start. *M. Jarvis.*

PRINCE OF KASHMIR 3 ch.c. Blue Cashmere 129–Matala 65 (Misti IV —
132) (1981 6h³ 6s 1982 8fg 10fg 8fg 8f³ 10.2g 10fg³ 8fg 10.1d) good-bodied
colt; stays 1¼m; acts on hard going. *P. M. Taylor.*

PRINCE OF LIGHT 10 b.g. Laser Light 118–Royal Escape 94 (King's Bench —
132) (1981 8g 8g 10.6s 10g* 9f 8fg⁴ 12fg* 10fg³ 10g 10f 12.2g 12fg 1982 11s³
12fg⁴ 10f 11fg 8f 9fg⁴ 9.4f 10fg 12fg 12.2f 11s) poor handicapper; stays 1¼m;
acts on any going except heavy; good mount for an apprentice; suited by an
uphill finish and has won 5 times at Carlisle. *D. Smith.*

PRINCE OF PERSIA 2 b.g. Persian Breeze 121–River Rose 97 (Clear River —
114) (1982 6fg 6g 5g) May 30; 1,350Y; compact gelding; behind in varied
races, including a maiden auction event; sold 300 gns Doncaster September
Sales. *D. Smith.*

PRINCE OF PRINCES 3 br.c. Bustino 136–Princess Runnymede 108 (Runny- **89**
mede 123) (1981 7g⁴ 7d³ 8g 1982 12f 11.7g⁴ 12f 11.7fg⁴ 16f* 16.5f² 16f*
16f* 15d) tall, rangy colt; successful in maiden race at Lingfield and handicaps
at Thirsk (apprentices) and Nottingham in summer; suited by a test of stamina;
acts well on firm going and ran below his best on soft ground final start. *J.
Dunlop.*

PRINCE OF SPAIN 7 b.h. Philip of Spain 126–Miss Meryl 80 (River Chanter **69**
121) (1981 7d⁴ 8fg 8d² 7g 7v² 8f³ 7f 8f 7.6fg⁴ 8fg⁴ 8h³ 8h 8fg⁴ 1982 5s* 7h*
8g⁴ 7f 7fg 7fg³ 8fg⁴) quite a modest handicapper; successful at Chepstow in
April and May; stays 1m; acts on any going; suitable mount for an apprentice;
blinkered once in 1980; sometimes bandaged nowadays; soundly beaten fourth
and fifth starts. *P. M. Taylor.*

Mr R. L. Emmitt's "Prince Reymo"

PRINCE REGAL 3 b.c. Reliance II 137–Basilea Dea (Habitat 134) (1981 —
NR 1982 10f 16d 12v) useful-looking colt; closely related to 1¼m seller
winner Balda (by Relko) and half-brother to very useful 1979 2-y-o 1m winner
Gagliardo Umbro (by Green Dancer); dam placed at 2 yrs in Italy; well beaten
in maiden races and a minor event; dead. *M. Masson.*

PRINCE REVIEWER (USA) 4 b.g. Reviewer–Belle Sorella 99 (Ribot 142) 60
(1981 8g 8fg 10.1fg³ 8s² 8s 8.2s 8d⁴ 1982 7.2s² 8fg 10.6g 8fg 8fg 7g 8f 7d⁴
10.6s⁴ 7s³ 8.2s 10.2d) quite a moderate maiden; ran well in handicaps on
occasions; stays 1¼m, but is probably better at shorter distances; sometimes
faces stiff tasks in ladies and amateur races; sometimes sweats up; never going
well when blinkered eleventh start. *A. W. Jones.*

PRINCE REYMO 2 b.c. Jimmy Reppin 131–Honey Thief 77 (Burglar 128) 113
(1982 5fg² 5f* 6f* 5f* 6f) Feb 26; 940F, 9,800Y; neat, strong-quartered colt;
excellent mover; third foal; dam won over 5f at 2 yrs; was one of the very best
early 2-y-o's and seemed destined to take high rank until flopping badly (dropping
right away inside final 2f) in Anglia Television July Stakes at Newmarket on
final appearance; had accounted for Fire-Thatch by 1½ lengths when ready
winner of Windsor Castle Stakes at Royal Ascot on previous outing, and had
hacked up earlier from small fields in Tattersalls' Yorkshire Stakes at York
and Staff Ingham Stakes at Epsom; possibly better at 5f than 6f; yet to race
on an easy surface. *R. Armstrong.*

PRINCE SANTIAGO (USA) 3 b.g. Cougar II–Hasty Aysha (Hasty Road) 87
(1981 8g 1982 12fg² 12fg 14f³ 14g* 14g* 16fg² 14f 16g³ 15d³ 16d) tall, attractive gelding; has a round action; won maiden race at Sandown and minor event
at Yarmouth (odds on) in June; stays well; possibly best with some give in
the ground; best in blinkers; ungenuine and doesn't find much off bridle; sold
to D. Smith 9,000 gns Newmarket Autumn Sales. *J. Dunlop.*

PRINCE'S CIRCUS (USA) 2 b.c. Circle Home–Consanguineous (Connaught, USA) (1982 5fg⁴ 6f*) Jan 24; $14,000Y, resold 20,000 gns Y; well-made colt; half-brother to 3 winners, including American winner Blade's Ruler (by Blade), successful in 1981; dam minor winner at up to 6f in USA; won 7-runner maiden race at Yarmouth in July by ½ length from Sharp Sea; dead. *H. T. Jones.* **88**

PRINCES GATE 5 br.h. Realm 129–Consensus (Majority Blue 126) (1981 8s 8.5g³ 8f³ 8g 8fg* 8fg³ 8fg 8fg 8g 8s* 8v* 8s* 1982 8g* 9fg 10f* 9g² 10f 8d² 8d* 10d 8v) **119**

International jockeys' invitation races used to be promoted mostly in countries which did not have top-class riders but they are also staged regularly nowadays in some of the major racing countries, including Britain and the United States. It is difficult to measure the success of ventures on these lines in Britain. A competition between teams of American and British jockeys has been put on by the Sandown executive in each of the past three years but the fixture failed to attract a sponsor in 1982 and its future looks in some doubt. And just how much did the charity meetings at Newbury in May and Ascot in September benefit from the matches between Carson and Asmussen and Piggott and Shoemaker? Both contests engendered publicity but neither provided much excitement, Carson winning easily on Turn Back The Time at Newbury and Shoemaker making all on Princes Gate at Ascot, stretching Piggott's mount Spanish Pool from the start and having him beaten some way from home. Nevertheless, such events have at least provided opportunities to study and compare the standards and methods of jockeyship at the highest level in Britain and North America. And Ascot and Sandown racegoers had the additional pleasure of seeing again the legendary Willie Shoemaker. First impressions of the tiny Shoemaker are that he does not look to have the strength to pick up the axe, never mind chop down the beanstalk! Yet seeing him in action it is easy to perceive why he has ridden more than 8,000 winners, a world record. His judgement of pace on Princes Gate—and on the patiently-ridden Rose Du Soir

Long John Scotch Whisky Challenge, Ascot—Princes Gate and Shoemaker (left) beat Spanish Pool and Piggott

Mr Hamdan Al-Maktoum's "Princes Gate"

later the same afternoon—was impeccable. Shoemaker also won one of the three races in Sandown's competition in October.

Princes Gate (br.h. 1977)	Realm (b 1967)	Princely Gift (b 1951)	Nasrullah / Blue Gem
		Quita II (b 1962)	Lavandin / Eos
	Consensus (br 1967)	Majority Blue (ch 1961)	Major Portion / Gorm Abu
		Mutual Consent (b 1950)	Fairwell / Sans Reproche

The genuine Princes Gate has shown most of his best form when there has been some give underfoot, as there was at Ascot and also when he won the Doncaster Mile decisively in March, when he was beaten half a length by Spanish Pool in the Oettingen-Rennen at Baden-Baden in August and when he came a creditable fifth to Time Charter in the Dubai Champion Stakes in October. But Princes Gate does not *need* easy going; he won the Westbury Stakes at Sandown in April on firm, beating Kind of Hush by two lengths after being held up. It is good news that Princes Gate remains in training: he is a very smart performer at a mile and a mile and a quarter and should again pay to follow. He is a strong, workmanlike horse by Dara Monarch's sire Realm out of the six-furlong winner Consensus whose first four foals to reach the racecourse have all won, including the good Italian horse Mispy (by Pall Mall). *H. T. Jones.*

PRINCE'S HEIR (USA) 2 ch.c. Princely Native–Lady Bencraft (Crafty **71** Admiral) (1982 5f4 5g3 5.8f4 7d 7fg4 6fg) Mar 25; $12,000Y; small, quite well-made colt; good mover; fifth foal; half-brother to 3 minor winners; dam won several sprint claiming races; quite a moderate maiden; not raced after August; best form at up to 5.8f, but probably stays 7f; acts on firm going; blinkered fifth outing. *P. Cole.*

PRINCE'S POLLY 3 b.f. English Prince 129–Suspicious Polly (Above Sus- **113**
picion 127) (1981 7fg* 7fg² 7fg² 8d* 7d³ 1982 10g³ 8g* 10g* 12fg² 12g)

    No English-trained filly has won the Irish One Thousand Guineas since
Gaily in 1974. It's not for want of trying, and recent results give ample warning
that the race has grown out of being an easy alternative to Newmarket even
though the prize, boosted by sponsorship from Goffs, usually lags well behind
its English counterpart. There has been a challenge from England in
each of the last three years resulting in second and third places for Millingdale
Lillie and Mrs Penny behind Cairn Rouge in 1980, nothing for Star Pastures
or Vocalist behind Arctique Royale in 1981, and third place for On The House
behind Prince's Polly in 1982. On The House appeared to have sound prospects
of stopping the rot, since she'd recently won the One Thousand Guineas very
decisively whereas the undefeated Woodstream, the second favourite, hadn't
been out since beating On The House in the Cheveley Park Stakes the previous
autumn and precious few of the other twenty-two runners possessed form
within a stone of hers; in fact, eleven in the field were so little regarded that they
started at odds of 50/1 or above, seven of them at 100/1. In the event On
The House and Woodstream ran well enough to be almost inseparable for
second but were beaten on merit by 12/1-shot Prince's Polly, an unlucky
third in the Azalea Stakes at Leopardstown on her seasonal reappearance,
who had a great tussle with On The House over the last two furlongs or so.
For the better part of the last two furlongs On The House and Prince's Polly
had the race between them, the latter finally getting on top in the last hundred
and twenty yards and holding on well by a length from the strong-finishing
Woodstream, with On The House, probably not quite the filly we saw at Newmarket, a short head further back.

    Prince's Polly was English Prince's first classic winner: he has been rather
a disappointing sire and is now in Japan. Most of his progeny stay, so a logical
objective for Prince's Polly, a daughter of a middle-distance mare and one of
the leading staying two-year-old fillies in Ireland in 1981, winner of the Silken
Glider Stakes at Leopardstown, was the Irish Guinness Oaks. Before that she
didn't come to Epsom or to Royal Ascot; instead she ran in the Pretty Polly
Stakes at the Curragh later in June, giving the Irish Guineas fourth Kazankina
4 lb and a three-quarter-length beating after holding on stoutly to the lead
over the last three furlongs. She started at even money for the Irish Oaks,
opposed principally by the Italian Guineas winner and Italian Oaks runner-up
Rosananti, and the Cheshire Oaks winner Swiftfoot who'd finished last behind
Time Charter at Epsom. The improving Swiftfoot beat her three lengths.
Prince's Polly gave the impression that she didn't get the trip so well as the
winner, but she finished three lengths clear of Rosananti in a field of ten and
the probability is that Swiftfoot was simply the better filly. Prince's Polly moved
into second behind the front-running Swiftfoot a quarter of a mile out and made
her challenge under strong pressure without quite getting to grips. On her
running here Prince's Polly had the winning of the Brownstown Stakes over the
same course and distance in August; she started at odds on against fourteen
other Irish-trained fillies. However, she finished only a moderate sixth behind
the three-year-old Miraflora, failing to hold on to her lead at the two-furlong
pole for very long. She never ran again.

    Prince's Polly was trained by her owner-breeder T. Nicholson as a two-year-
old. Besides the Silken Glider Stakes she won him a maiden race at Leopardstown and ran well on all her other appearances, notably when she finished

*Goffs Irish One Thousand Guineas, the Curragh—Prince's Polly (noseband) stays
on strongly from Woodstream and On The House (left)*

Mr K. Fitzpatrick's "Prince's Polly"

second to Woodstream in a relatively minor event at Leopardstown and when third in the Park Stakes, a pattern race, at the Curragh. She was transferred to Weld's stable after a half-share in her had been sold during the winter. The dam Suspicious Polly was also owned and trained by Nicholson; she won a maiden over a mile and a quarter at Phoenix Park and mile-and-a-half handicaps at the Curragh and Mallow, the last-named as a four-year-old. Prince's Polly is her third foal and her first winner; the first foal broke a leg,

Prince's Polly (b.f. 1979)	English Prince (b 1971)	Petingo (b 1965)	Petition
			Alcazar
		English Miss (b 1955)	Bois Roussel
			Virelle
	Suspicious Polly (b 1970)	Above Suspicion (b 1956)	Court Martial
			Above Board
		Polly Flinders (ch 1962)	Polly's Jet
			Dedica

the second Sky Above (by African Sky) isn't much good. Until Prince's Polly's arrival the family could be described as workaday, with the fairly useful Suspicious Polly typical of it. The grandam Polly Flinders was one of eight winners produced by Dedica at distances between five furlongs and two miles. Polly Flinders' four wins at seven furlongs to nine furlongs was surpassed in total only by the five of her half-brothers Fray Bentos and Anglo Scot. She herself produced a horse to win seven races between five furlongs and fifteen furlongs—Suspicious Polly's half-brother Franc Flinders.

Prince's Polly, a lengthy, deep-girthed filly, never raced on extremes but showed her form on good to firm and good to soft. She stayed a mile and a half. Her consistency was such that in two seasons and ten races she gave only one moderate performance, her last. She would have been at stud in 1983 but unfortunately she died in the United States early in the year. *D. Weld, Ireland.*

PRINCE SPY 2 b.c. Ballad Rock 122–Bay Laurel (Habitat 134) (1982 **103** 5g² 5f² 5d⁴ 5s* 5g* 6g*) Feb 15; 25,000Y; robust, well-made colt; first foal; dam won over 7f at 2 yrs in France; in splendid form in the autumn, winning £4,500 race at Ascot, and easily and impressively defying penalties (showing excellent turn of foot) in 2 good-class nurseries at Newmarket; stays 6f well; acts on soft going; sure to make a very useful sprinter. *J. Sutcliffe.*

PRINCESS ALOHA 3 b.f. Brigadier Symboli–My Path (Sovereign Path 125) — (1981 NR 1982 10g 10g 10.1fg) half-sister to a winner in Holland; dam well beaten on 4 outings; seems of little account; has worn blinkers. *A. Davison.*

PRINCESS BRIONY 3 b.f. The Brianston 128–Mernian 100 (Counsel 118) — (1981 NR 1982 5fg 6d 8s) 3,300Y; half-sister to 4 winners here and abroad, including middle-distance stayer Apple Of My Eye (by Silver Cloud); dam genuine and consistent miler; in rear in maiden races and a minor event, twice finishing last. *C. James.*

PRINCESSE TIMIDE (USA) 2 br.f. Blushing Groom 131–Rigid Princess **107** (Never Bend) (1982 7.5d* 7s² 8v) Apr 27; $127,000Y; second foal; dam, winner over 6f in USA, is half-sister to smart 1978 French 2-y-o Crowned Music; won newcomers race at Deauville in August and finished creditable second to Lyphard's Princess in Prix de l'Obelisque at Longchamp the following month; favourite for 10-runner Premio Dormello at Milan in October but ran disappointingly, finishing 14 lengths seventh to Stemegna; should stay 1m; engaged in 1,000 Guineas and Oaks. *F. Boutin, France.*

PRINCESS HENHAM 2 bl. or gr.f. Record Token 128–Bog Oak (Sassafras **96** 135) (1982 5fg 6fg³ 6g 7fg 7fg⁴ 8.2g* 8.2d 8d 8d 8.2s* 7s) May 1; workmanlike filly; first reported foal; dam, half-sister to 3 very useful animals, ran only once; won nurseries at Nottingham in September and October, showing useful turn of foot on each occasion; needs at least 1m; well suited by soft ground; suitable mount for an apprentice. *N. Callaghan.*

PRINCESS IRINA 2 b.f. Abwah 118–Empress of Russia 79 (Royal Palace 131) **75** (1982 5f 7fg⁴ 6d² 7d) Mar 10; good-topped, useful sort; second foal; dam, half-sister to Connaught, won over 1½m at 4 yrs; in frame in maiden races at Chepstow in August and Nottingham in September; stays 7f; sold German International Bloodstock 3,600 gns Newmarket Autumn Sales. *H. Candy.*

PRINCESS KINI 3 ch.f. Sun Prince 128–Scarcroft 66 (King's Bench 132) — (1981 5d 5g 5d 1982 6g) leggy filly; only plating class; has given trouble on way to start. *N. Guest.*

PRINCESS MARTINA 3 b.f. English Prince 129–Tyronera 82 (Tyrone 130) **64** (1981 NR 1982 11.7f 12d 15.8f* 16.5fg) 6,800F; half-sister to fairly useful middle-distance winner Tyrondero (by Derring-Do) and to 2 winners in France; dam won over 1½m; won modest maiden race at Catterick in September; stays well; acts on firm going; sold 3,500 gns Newmarket December Sales. *Sir Mark Prescott.*

PRINCESS MONA 3 br.f. Prince Regent 129–Monaspear (Breakspear II) **56** (1981 6g 6s 7g 1982 8fg 7d 7fg 8fg 8g 8f² 8d) quite robust filly; plating-class maiden; best run at 1m on firm going; has sweated up; retained 2,100 gns Newmarket Autumn Sales. *J. Benstead.*

PRINCESS NAVARRO 2 ch.f. Raga Navarro 119–Gorgeous Gael (Atan) (1982 **71** 5g 5d 6g 5g 5v³ 5g) May 30; IR 580F, IR 1,000Y; neat filly; good walker; half-sister to 2 minor winners in Ireland; 1¼ lengths third of 11 behind Nordan Centre in nursery at Haydock in October, first time outside sellers and easily best effort; should stay 6f; acts well on soft going; blinkered last 3 outings. *W. Stubbs.*

PRINCESS SALUKI 3 gr.f. Broxted 120–Misplanted (Hul a Hul 124) (1981 **43** 5g 6g 5g 6f 8fg 6g 7v 6s 1982 8g 12.2g 8fg 8fg³ 9f 8g² 8fg 6g 7g 12d 12fg² 13.8f* 14s) compact, sturdy filly; plater; bought in 3,200 gns after making all at Catterick in September; stays 1¾m; acts on firm going and is possibly unsuited by soft; has worn blinkers; seems to need strong handling; changed hands 1,400 gns Doncaster September Sales. *R. Whitaker.*

PRINCESS SEAL 3 b.f. Prince Tenderfoot 126–Finesse 87 (Miralgo 130) **108** (1981 5g 5s* 5d* 5f² 7d 1982 6s⁴ 7g 6fg* 6f 5f³ 6f 5d²) strong, rangy, quite attractive filly; half-sister to 2 winners, including fair 6f to 1½m winner Zarzaitine (by Murrayfield); dam won over 1½m; beat Clanjolly a short head in Castleknock Sprint Stakes at Naas in May; placed subsequently in Ballyogan Stakes at Leopardstown (moved from a place after going down by short head to Longleat) and Stackallen Stakes at the Curragh (length second to Royal Hobbit); ran respectably in 2 outings in this country, on second finishing 4½ lengths fifth of 18 to Indian King in Cork and Orrery Stakes at Royal Ascot; best at sprint distances; acts on any going; blinkered nowadays. *M. Cunningham, Ireland.*

PRINCESS VIRGINIA 3 br.f. Connaught 130–Virginia Wade 116 (Virginia **79** Boy 106) (1981 8d³ 7g⁴ 1982 10f 8g 5f² 6h* 6f² 6d 6f 6f 6v² 6d) rangy non-thoroughbred filly; good walker; sprint handicapper; won at Chepstow in June; acts on any going; suitable mount for an apprentice; blinkered last 2 starts; sold to R. Hollinshead 4,000 gns Newmarket December Sales. *P. Cole.*

PRINCESS VRONSKI 4 b.f. The Brianstan 128–Vron 91 (Anwar 120) (1981 — 5g 5d 1982 5d 7f) little worthwhile form, including in sellers. *C. Spares.*

PRINCESS ZITA 2 ch.f. Manado 130–Karmala (Tanerko 134) (1982 €g **77** 6fg²) Apr 13; tall, rather narrow filly; good mover; fourth foal; dam placed at up to 12.5f in French Provinces; 11/2, kept on quite strongly without being punished unduly when 2 lengths second of 20 to Linklighter in maiden race at Salisbury (sweated up) in September; will be suited by 7f+. *J. Dunlop.*

PRINCE WARREN 5 b.g. Pieces of Eight 128–Bobelle 62 (Pirate King 129) **46** (1981 10v 10s 11s 10g 9d 8d 10f 10f 10fg 12v 1982 12d 8.2s⁴ 10fg³ 10.1fg 12d 10g* 12fg 8fg) plater nowadays; bought in 1,500 gns after winning at Yarmouth in June; suited by middle distances; acts on any going but is particularly well suited by soft; sometimes sweats up; has worn blinkers; sometimes bandaged in front. *D. Wilson.*

PRINGLE 3 ch.g. Blue Cashmere 129–Word Perfect (Worden II 129) (1981 **74** NR 1982 8fg⁴ 8d³ 8fg* 7.6d 8fg) 12,500Y; lengthy, rather sparely-made gelding; half-brother to several winners, including very useful English and French 5f to 7f winner Giriama (by Tribal Chief); dam never ran; won maiden race at Ayr in August; stays 1m; acts well on firm ground; has shown a tendency to put head in air, and wore blinkers when in rear in valuable seller final start; retained 2,600 gns Newmarket Autumn Sales. *J. Hindley.*

PRINTAFOIL 2 b.f. Habat 127–Breathalyser (Alcide 136) (1982 6s) Mar — 23; half-sister to several winners, including smart middle-distance stayer Major Green (by Double-U-Jay) and Irish Guinness Oaks fourth Miss Connaught (by Connaught); dam showed only poor form; 13/2, no show in 16-runner maiden race at Leicester in November. *M. Jarvis.*

PRIONSAA 4 ch.c. Crowned Prince 128–Frame Up 66 (Alycidon 138) (1981 **48** 9fg 8g² 8fg 6fg² 6fg* 6f 6g⁴ 8d 1982 7fg⁴ 8f⁴ 8g 8f² 6g² 11g⁴ 9g 5d² 6s³ 5d 5g) quite a modest handicapper; second 3 times, appearing to run particularly well after missing break at Ayr in September on last occasion; evidently effective at 5f and stays 1m (not disgraced in rather slowly-run 11f race); acts on any going; has run creditably for a boy; has raced with his tongue tied down; saddle slipped seventh start. *W. H. H. Williams.*

PRIORS CUTIE 2 b.f. Mr Bigmore 123–Cute 75 (Hardicanute 130) (1982 — 8g) May 8; lengthy filly; half-sister to 1978 2-y-o 5f winner Scoot (by Double Jump); dam disqualified winner over 6f at 2 yrs; unquoted, never-dangerous tenth of 19 behind Coming And Going in minor event at Newmarket in October. *A. Madwar.*

PRIORS MISTRESS 2 b.f. Sallust 134–Malmsey (Jukebox 120) (1982 **71** 6fg⁴ 7fg 8s) 15,000Y; strong, well-made filly; second foal; half-sister to 1981 2-y-o 5f winner Lockwood Girl (by Prince Tenderfoot); dam won over 1½m and 1¾m in Ireland; disappointed after finishing 3¾ lengths fourth to Habibti in 9-runner £6,000 newcomers race at Ascot in July; should stay beyond 6f. *I. Balding.*

PRIORY GREY 2 gr.f. Town Crier 119–Star Silk 83 (Counsel 118) (1982 — 5fg 5d 6f 5fg) Mar 12; leggy, narrow, lightly-made filly; closely related to 1979 2-y-o 7f winner Starlitpath (by Warpath) and half-sister to 2 winners; dam placed over 5f at 2 yrs; no worthwhile form, mainly in sellers; dead. *P. Brookshaw.*

PRIVATE AUDIENCE   6 b.h. So Blessed 130–Private View 74 (Derring-Do 131)   **48**
(1981 14fg 14d 11.1s³ 12g 12fg 12f 10f² 1982 12f* 12f 14fg⁴ 12fg⁴)   tall, rather
narrow horse; middle-distance handicapper; well beaten after winning at Brighton
in April; acts on any going.   *G. Beeson.*

PRIVATE BENJAMIN   3 br.f. Queen's Hussar 124–Beguiling 66 (Tower Walk   **—**
130) (1981 6s 6g 1982 8fg)   well beaten in sellers; ran very wide into straight
only outing at 3 yrs and trainer stated he would not run her again.   *C. Nelson.*

PRIVATE LABEL (USA)   2 ch.c. Silent Screen–Summer Time Music (What A   **101**
Pleasure) (1982 6g 5f² 6s³ 5g* 5s* 5d² 5g³)   Feb 13; $37,000Y, $60,000 2-y-o;
lengthy, quite attractive colt; not a good walker; first foal; dam, winner of 3
sprint races, is daughter of very smart 1972 American 2-y-o Natural Sound;
won maiden race at Wolverhampton in Oct ber and minor event at York the
same month; narrowly beaten subsequently in well-contested minor event at
Doncaster and nursery at Newmarket; best form at 5f; suited by some give in the
ground; likely to make a useful sprinter.   *M. Jarvis.*

PROBABILIST   3 gr.g. Mount Hagen 127–Tiara III (Persian Gulf) (1981   **—**
5.8g 7fg 1982 11g 15.5f 16fg)   useful sort; poor maiden on balance of form;
sold to W. Clay 1,070 gns Ascot July Sales.   *B. Hills.*

PROCERUS   2 ch.g. Roman Warrior 132–Pretty Girl 78 (Double-U-Jay 120)   **58**
(1982 6s 5d 6s⁴)   Apr 15; first foal; dam placed at up to 1¼m; modest fourth in
19-runner claiming event at Nottingham in October; stays 6f.   *H. Westbrook.*

PROCLAIM (USA)   2 b.c. Mr Prospector–Maybellene (Fleet Nasrullah) (1982   **120**
7g² 7fg* 7fg* 7fg² 8s*)
      The Horris Hill Stakes at Newbury, which had to be abandoned after
heavy rain, had all the makings of an informative contest with Proclaim, Cause
Celebre, Beldale Concorde, Lofty and Indian Rajah among those declared to
take on the Mill Reef Stakes winner Salieri.   We were especially interested in
Proclaim, who'd had three very easy wins, starting at 7/4 on each time.   His
first two victories came in July in a nineteen-runner maiden race at Newbury and
a minor event at Newmarket; he had only a length and a half to spare over
Gallic Wit at Newbury, after cruising along with the leaders throughout, but
he would have won by at least four lengths had he not been eased; and at Newmarket, after leading from the start, he won by a length and a half from Jad with
his jockey spending most of his time looking around in the closing stages.   It
was much the same story in the Kinrara Stakes at Goodwood in September in
which his opponents included the useful Now and Again: he led throughout,
drew six or seven lengths clear in the straight, without any apparent effort from
his rider, and was then eased right down in the last one hundred yards to cross
the line two and a half lengths ahead of Lyminster.   He seemed extremely well
suited by the soft ground here; he had also put up good efforts on firmish going.
      Proclaim has only two other runs on which to assess him and the first of
them, when he was beaten through inexperience in a maiden race at Newmarket,
tells us little.   His other, against Gorytus in the Laurent Perrier Champagne
Stakes at Doncaster in September, was much more informative—there was no
taking things easy in this company.   Proclaim tracked On Stage on the rails for a
long way until being pulled out to challenge as Gorytus moved into the lead

Exeter Stakes, Newmarket—Proclaim makes all;
Jad is second, Ayman third

Mr S. S. Niarchos' "Proclaim"

with a quarter of a mile to run. Proclaim hung on well for the next furlong but in the closing stages he was completely outpointed and crossed the line five lengths adrift.

Proclaim (USA) (b.c. Apr 25, 1980)			
	Mr Prospector (b 1970)	Raise A Native (ch 1961)	Native Dancer
			Raise You
		Gold Digger (b 1962)	Nashua
			Sequence
	Maybellene (b 1971)	Fleet Nasrullah (b 1955)	Nasrullah
			Happy Go Fleet
		Linstar (b 1965)	Dark Star
			Lindra

Proclaim's sire Mr Prospector has developed into one of America's most popular stallions since starting his stud career in Florida in 1975 at a fee of 7,500 dollars; by 1982 his fee had risen to 100,000 dollars and he now stands at the Claiborne Farm in Kentucky. His fee will no doubt increase even further following his splendid season in 1982. His American runners earned over two million dollars and his son Conquistador Cielo provided him with his first classic success when romping home fourteen and a half lengths clear of the Kentucky Derby winner Gato del Sol in the Belmont Stakes over a mile and a half. Conquistador Cielo showed unusual stamina for a son of Mr Prospector, who never won beyond seven furlongs, and it comes as no surprise that Proclaim hasn't been entered for the Derby. He clearly stays a mile well, and may eventually get a mile and a quarter, but most of his relatives showed more speed than stamina. His dam Maybellene, whose second foal he is, won six of her eleven starts as a three-year-old, including the Rockette Stakes over six furlongs and a division of the Test Stakes over seven; and his grandam Linstar won three sprint races as a three-year-old from five starts. Linstar produced only two foals and interestingly the other one, the winning sprinter Bold Linstar, has also been mated with Mr Prospector, producing the stakes-placed Star Prospector, who won at up to a mile, and the smart stakes-winning sprinter Star Valentine. Linstar was

herself a half-sister to the very useful Ironside, winner of the nine-furlong
Mimosa Stakes, and her dam Lindra was an unraced sister to Itsa Great Day, a
very smart two-year-old of 1960 who won his first five starts, all sprint events.
    Proclaim was well bought for 100,000 dollars as a yearling at the Saratoga
Sales, a figure over 60,000 dollars below the Sales' average. He's a rangy,
rather sparely-made colt—not a particularly taking individual and he also has a
rather odd tail carriage when racing—but he improved physically during the
season and may have further improvement in him. He'll make a very smart
miler. *G. Harwood.*

PRODIGIOUS GIRL 3 ch.f. Windjammer (USA)–Scarletta 103 (Red God **35**
128§) (1981 5g³ 5g⁴ 5f 1982 7g 7f 7g 7fg* 6d 7s) narrow filly; plater; won
at Beverley in August (no bid); stays 7f; often blinkered (was when successful).
J. Etherington.

PROFESSOR'S CHOICE 3 b.f. Mount Hagen 127–Nishat (Sayajirao 132) **75**
(1981 6g² 7d* 7d⁴ 1982 7fg 10fg³ 10d 8g 7s 8d) quite an attractive filly;
good mover; fair at 2 yrs; soundly beaten in varied company in 1982; should
stay 1¼m; blinkered final start. *H. T. Jones.*

PROFIT WARRANT 3 b.c. Ashmore 125–Stipa (Silver Shark 129) (1981 **78**
6fg 6fg 6f 6d* 6f 6s 6g 6v 1982 12fg 10f 11.7g² 10f* 10fg² 11.7fg* 10d* 11.7fg
10fg 11.1fg 12s) tall, lengthy colt; former plater; won handicaps at Folkestone
in May and Windsor and Lingfield in June; stays 1½m; acts on any going; sometimes sweats up; retained 2,300 gns Newmarket Autumn Sales. *P. K. Mitchell.*

PROLIFIC MAJOR 2 ch.g. Mandrake Major 122–Lochville 83 (Charlottesville **67**
135) (1982 5fg 6f 7f 7g 8.2fg* 8d 8d 8.2s) May 9; 2,600Y; workmanlike
gelding; brother to a poor performer and half-brother to 3 winners here and
abroad, including 1971 2-y-o 5f winner Renard Rouge (by Kashmir II), subsequently a useful winner at up to 1½m in France; dam won over 8.7f; landed
a gamble (backed from 10/1 to 3/1 favourite) in 15-runner seller at Haydock
(bought in 3,800 gns) in September; stays 1m well; acts on a firm and a soft
surface; worth keeping an eye on in sellers. *K. Stone.*

PROMINDANTE 2 ch.g. Prominer 125–Hot Penny 105 (Red God 128§) (1982 **72**
7fg⁴ 7d 7d 7g) May 1; IR 35,000Y; strong, heavy-bodied gelding; brother to
fairly useful French 1981 2-y-o maiden Princely Penny and useful 7f winner
Smelter and half-brother to a winner; dam useful maiden at 2 yrs; quite moderate
maiden; best run on third outing; stays 7f; sold CBA 9,600 gns Newmarket
Autumn Sales and subsequently gelded. *J. Hindley.*

PROMISE OF SPRING 2 b.f. Ampney Prince 96–Wynter (Wynkell 88) (1982 —
5fg 5d 5fg 5g) Apr 1; neat filly; third reported foal; dam of little account;
bad plater, not raced after August. *P. Burgoyne.*

PROPOSITIONING (USA) 2 ch.f. Mr Prospector–Stay Over (Prove It) **105**
(1982 7g* 8s) Apr 2; half-sister to a minor winner in USA; dam won at up to
1m and is sister to 1969 American 2-y-o With Evidence; short-priced
favourite created a favourable impression when winning 18-runner newcomers
race at Maisons-Laffitte in September by a length from Louvine; 5/1 when
4½ lengths sixth of 9 to Belka in Prix des Reservoirs at Longchamp the following
month; should stay 1m; engaged in 1,000 Guineas. *O. Douieb, France.*

PROSERPINE 5 ch.m. Proverb 127–Aucuba 98 (Hornbeam 130) (1981 **49**
11.1s 12f 14fg 16fg 17.1h⁴ 16g 14fg 16g² 1982 16fg 16d* 16f³ 17.1s) rangy
mare; made all when 8-length winner of handicap at Lingfield in June; didn't
reproduce that form (off course nearly 3 months after next outing); suited by 2m;
suited by some give in the ground; bandaged in front on reappearance; usually
apprentice ridden. *P. M. Taylor.*

PROTECTION RACKET (USA) 4 b.c. Graustark–Protectora (Prologo) **117**
(1981 12g² 12.3d³ 14g* 16f² 14fg* 14d* 18fg* 14d* 1982 12fg² 10.5g 12f
12.5g⁴) strong, rangy colt; has a round action; developed into a very smart
performer as a 3-y-o when trained by J. Hindley and won 5 races, including
Tote-Ebor (Handicap) at York, Doncaster Cup and Irish St Leger at the Curragh;
was raced over middle distances in 1982 and didn't manage to win; went down
by short neck to Gap of Dunloe (rec 7 lb) in a driving finish to Prix d'Hedouville
at Longchamp in April, was far from disgraced over a trip too short when about
3½ lengths sixth of 10 behind Bikala in Prix Ganay on same course in May,
and ran respectably when about 3 lengths fourth of 8 behind No Attention in
Prix de Reux at Deauville in August; bandaged and blinkered when well-
beaten seventh of 8 behind Easter Sun in Coronation Cup at Epsom in June

on only other start (ran a bit freely early on and was no danger in straight); a relentless galloper who stays very well and lacks the pace to be fully effective over middle distances; probably acts on any going; thoroughly genuine; returned to England after final outing. *O. Douieb, France.*

PROTOS 3 b.c. Tumble Wind–Naughty Lass 82 (Run The Gantlet) (1981 **92**
7fg 7fg 7g 10s³ 1982 12g* 12fg⁴ 12.3fg² 14f² 16f*(dis) 13f 16g³ 14s* 11.2d) strong, close-coupled, quite attractive colt; good mover; first past post in maiden race at Doncaster in March, handicap at Kempton in July (disqualified for interfering with runner-up) and £3,100 event at York in October (odds on); ran creditably most other starts; stays well; acts on any going; gives impression he may be suited by waiting tactics; sold 21,000 gns Newmarket Autumn Sales and is racing in Italy. *B. Hobbs.*

PROUDEST DIANA (USA) 2 b.f. Proudest Roman–Time For Beauty —
(Diplomat Way) (1982 7fg 6fg 6s) Apr 18; $10,500F, $21,000Y; good-topped filly; first foal; dam won 6f claiming race at 4 yrs; no form in maiden and minor events; off course over 2 months after second outing. *I. Walker.*

PROUD LUCY 3 b.f. Dubassoff–Dissipation 83 (Disciplinarian) (1981 6fg —
7g 5fg 5g 5s 1982 5fg 8f 7f 5g 6f 6fg 6d 8g 8s) fair sort; poor plater; best run at 7f on firm going; blinkered last 2 starts; sold 700 gns Doncaster October Sales. *H. Collingridge.*

PROUD SUE 3 b.f. Owen Anthony 102–Primmy 56 (Primera 131) (1981 —
7fg 7f 1982 7.6fg 12g 10g 16.9fg) poor maiden. *D. Sasse.*

PROVANHILL GIRL 2 ch.f. Gentilhombre 131–Lucky Pigeon (The Mongoose —
108) (1982 5fg 5fg 5g) April 27; leggy filly; half-sister to 2 winners, including fair 1973 2-y-o 7f winner Jolly Lucky (by Jolly Jet); dam Irish 1m and 1¼m winner; no show in maiden races. *T. Taylor.*

PROW 5 ch.h. Hotfoot 126–Bedeni 100 (Parthia 132) (1981 12.5s* 12v² **69**
12.3d² 16g* 16d⁴ 15.8g* 16g 15g 14.7d³ 14d 18fg⁴ 16g⁴ 16.1s 1982 12f⁴ 16.1fg³ 18f³ 20fg 16d) good-topped, good-looking horse; staying handicapper; in frame at Thirsk, Haydock and Doncaster; acts on any going; occasionally blinkered; game; pulled up lame final start (July); sold 450 gns Ascot December Sales. *Mrs M. Nesbitt.*

PUESDOWN 3 ch.f. Gay Fandango 132–Pewsey 96 (Appiani II 128) (1981 **66**
5g 5fg 6f 7g 6d⁴ 6s* 1982 7d 7fg³ 7fg⁴ 8.5f 8fg 7d³ 8fg 7fg⁴ 8g 9s⁴ 7g 7s) small, workmanlike filly; good walker; stays 9f; seems to act on any going; sometimes blinkered; sold to N. Tinkler 3,400 gns Newmarket December Sales. *N. Guest.*

PUFF OF SMOKE 3 b.g. Godswalk 130–Bay Tree (Relko 136) (1981 5.8g —
5.8d 6fg² 7g* 7d 7fg 1982 8g) rather lightly-made gelding; has a round action; won maiden race at Salisbury in 1981; behind in handicap at Newbury, only start at 3 yrs in April; suited by 7f; best form on a sound surface; racing in USA. *J. Sutcliffe.*

PUFF PASTRY 2 ch.f. Reform 132–Shortbread 104 (Crisp and Even 116) **78**
(1982 5g 5s* 6f 5f 7v 8d) May 17; 6,400Y; compact filly; has a round action; second foal; half-sister to a winner in Italy by Vitiges; dam winner over 7f here and 1½m in Norway; won maiden race at Pontefract in June by 2½ lengths from Nordan Centre; ran best subsequent races in nurseries in the autumn; stays 1m; appears to need plenty of give in the ground. *D. Morley.*

PUNCTILIOUS 4 b.g. Prince Tenderfoot 126–Heure de Pointe (Le Fabuleux —
133) (1981 NR 1982 10g 8fg 12f 8f 10d 7.6fg 8.2v 12g) plater; should stay middle distances; has worn blinkers and bandages. *R. E. Peacock.*

PUNCTILIO (USA) 3 b.c. Forli–Minstrelete (Round Table) (1981 7g* 1982 **116**
8g² 9f* 9fg* 10fg³) $185,000Y; rather narrow colt; second foal; half-brother to a winner in USA; dam, winner over 1m, is half-sister to top-class Gay Fandango (by Forli); decisively landed odds in minor event at Naas in August and got the better of Royal Rendevouz by a neck in Pacemaker International Whitehall Stakes at Leopardstown in September; not disgraced on other starts, including when 4½ lengths third to very easy winner Assert in Joe McGrath Memorial Stakes at Leopardstown; stays 1¼m; acts on firm going and has yet to race on soft; racing in California. *V. O'Brien, Ireland.*

PUNTERS LAD 2 br.c. Home Guard 129–Arioza (Tambourine II 133) (1982 —
7f 7s) Mar 16; 8,000F, 8,000Y; tall, useful-looking colt; good walker; half-brother to a winner in France; dam never ran; little worthwhile form in minor events at Goodwood in July and Sandown in October. *R. Price.*

Mr D. McCarthy's "Punctilio"

PURE LUST 3 ch.c. Sallust 134–St Rosalie (Aureole 132) (1981 5g 5f 6g 7f — 7g 8g³ 8g² 1982 10.2g 8fg 9v⁴ 10.2s) compact colt; useful plater at his best; no worthwhile form in 1982, but caught our eye second start; should stay 1¼m; blinkered last 2 outings. *P. Rohan.*

PURE PERFECTION 2 b.f. So Blessed 130–Sardara 106 (Alcide 136) (1982 — 5g) Mar 23; 4,000Y; quite well-made filly; good walker; closely related to Irish 2,000 Guineas winner Dara Monarch (by Realm); dam staying half-sister to St Leger winner Intermezzo; weak 12/1-shot, had very stiff task for a newcomer when seventh of 8 behind Favoridge in St Hugh's Stakes at Newbury in August; will be better suited by 6f+. *D. H. Jones.*

PURNIMA 3 b.g. Prince Tenderfoot 126–Chandravati (Hard Tack 111§) (1981 89 6g 5g⁴ 5fg⁴ 6s² 6s* 1982 6s 7g² 6g* 6fg 6fg 6g* 6f 6f 6g* 6s³ 6g) strong, good-bodied, attractive gelding; won handicaps at Kempton in May, Nottingham in July and Newmarket in September; stays 7f; ideally suited by some give in the ground; suited by strong handling. *J. Sutcliffe.*

PURPLE EMPEROR 2 b.g. Red Alert 127–Sea Sovereign (Sea Moss) (1982 — 5g 6fg 6d) May 26; 3,000Y (privately); narrow gelding; tailed off in minor events; sold 380 gns Ascot July Sales. *G. Kindersley.*

PUSEY STREET 5 ch.m. Native Bazaar 122–Diamond Talk (Counsel 118) 80 (1981 6s 6s 5.8g 5.8d³ 6f 6g 6f⁴ 5.8f* 5d* 5fg 5h 5fg 5.8g 5d 5s 1982 6f 5f² 5fg 5g³ 5f⁴ 5fg⁴ 5.8f 5g³ 5fg³ 5.8f 5d* 5d³ 6s* 5s) leggy, light-framed mare; sprint handicapper; in frame most starts and won at Ascot in September (£6,000 Villa Blanca Handicap, by short head from Young Inca) and Chepstow in October (by 5 lengths); acts on any going; genuine; good mount for a boy. *J. Bosley.*

PUTERI EMAS 2 b.f. Radetzky 123–Soft Chinook (Hitting Away) (1982 52 5fg⁴ 5f 5fg⁴ 5g 6d 5g⁴ 5g) May 11; 4,000Y; small, leggy, lightly-made filly; half-sister to 3 winners here and abroad, including fair 1980 2-y-o 5f winner Swinging

Rhythm (by Swing Easy); dam French plater; poor plater; stays 6f; blinkered fourth outing. *B. Hanbury.*

PUTNEY BRIDGE 2 b.c. North Stoke 130–Splash Down 103 (Sicambre 135) **102 p** (1982 8d*) Apr 18; 29,000F, IR 27,000Y; big colt; fourth foal; half-brother to 2 winners; dam won Galtres Stakes; 16/1, finished strongly, after showing signs of greenness, when winning 14-runner maiden race at Leopardstown in October by a neck from odds-on Ballydoyle, the pair clear; will probably stay 1¼m; has scope and should make a useful 3-y-o. *E. O'Grady, Ireland.*

PUTT WOOD 3 ch.f. Record Token 128–Orma (Double Jump 131) (1981 **52** 6fg 5fg 6fg⁴ 7.6g 1982 8g 10f² 12fg 10f 10f 10fg) leggy filly; plating-class maiden; suited by 1¼m; acts on firm going. *J. Winter.*

PYJAMAROUS 3 b.f. He Loves Me 120–Night Attire 77 (Shantung 132) (1981 **—** NR 1982 7.6f) IR 98,000Y; closely related to 1,000 Guineas winner Nocturnal Spree (by Supreme Sovereign) and half-sister to 3 winners, including good French 1¼m winner Tootens (by Northfields); dam sister to smart 1972 staying 2-y-o Setsu; second favourite, never promised to take a hand when out of first 10 of 15 behind Bee Alive in maiden race at Lingfield in June; not seen out again. *J. Dunlop.*

PYKESTAFF 5 b.h. Giacometti 130–Miss Melanie (Hard Ridden 131) (1981 **39** 10s 10s 6fg 12d 7g⁴ 7s 7g 6fg 6f² 6fg 7f² 6f⁴ 6g 8d 6d 8g 1982 7fg² 7h 6f 7g 7g 8fg³ 7f 7f 7fg 6g 7fg) leggy horse; plater; placed in 2 non-sellers; best at up to 7f; suited by firm going; often wears blinkers; sometimes sweats up. *C. Austin.*

Q

QEMLAS 2 gr.c. Town Crier 119–Grecian Charter (Runnymede 123) (1982 **90** 6f⁴ 5f³ 7fg⁴ 6v* 7d²) Feb 28; 15,500Y; small colt; second live foal; half-brother to winning stayer Ribo Charter (by Ribero); dam never ran; won 4-runner maiden race at Hamilton in October; good second in nursery at Edinburgh the following month; stays 7f; best form on a soft surface. *M. Masson.*

QUADRAPHEN 2 br.c. Raga Navarro 119–Guiltrack 99 (Track Spare 125) **64** (1982 5g* 5fg⁴ 5g 6g 5g) May 10; IR 880F, IR 1,500Y; compact colt; first reported foal; dam won 3 sprint races at 2 yrs; won 5-runner maiden auction event at Hamilton in May; apparently best at 5f; ran well in blinkers in valuable seller on final outing; sent to Malaysia. *W. Stubbs.*

QUADRILLION 3 gr.c. Bruni 132–Quantas 91 (Roan Rocket 128) (1981 **64** NR 1982 10.2g 14.6fg 10.6g² 12fg 12g 12fg⁴ 16s² 16s 12d³) 2,900Y; tall colt; has rather a round action; half-brother to 2 winners, including sprinter Stepping Gaily (by Gay Fandango); dam won over 6f at 2 yrs; quite moderate; stays well; suited by some give in the ground; has run creditably for an apprentice. *R. Hollinshead.*

QUAESTOR 4 b.g. Track Spare 125–Syltung (Shantung 132) (1981 9d 8f **73** 10.2f 12f* 12f* 12fg 1982 12g³ 13g² 16d 14s) fair sort; won at Thirsk (seller) and Leicester as a 3-y-o when trained by J. Hardy; subsequently sent to France and won over jumps there; placed in handicaps at Leicester in August and Nottingham in September on his return; stays 13f; probably acts on any going; often sweats up. *B. Hobbs.*

QUAE SUPRA 5 ch.m. On Your Mark 125–Lunar Star (Star Gazer 123) (1981 **54** 6s 5f² 5f 5f³ 5h 5fg² 5g 5d 1982 5g 5f² 5g³ 6g⁴ 6g² 5fg³ 6fg 5d 6v⁴) sprint handicapper; best at 5f; probably acts on any going; usually wears blinkers. *R. Laing.*

QUAKER STAR 6 b.g. Blast 125–Star of Bethlehem 77 (Arctic Star) (1981 **—** 8v 8fg 8.2f 8f 8g 10g 8s 8.2d 1982 10fg) neat gelding; poor handicapper; seems to stay 1¼m; acts on any going; ran poorly in blinkers once; has shown a tendency to hang; bandaged only outing of 1982. *T. Kersey.*

QUALITAIR PRINCE 3 b.c. Saulingo 122–Sabra's Star 65 (Midsummer **—** Night II 117) (1981 5g 5g 6g 7f 6g⁴ 7g 8d* 1982 8.2d 8fg⁴ 10d⁴ 8g⁴ 10d 12.3fg 9f⁴ 8g 8fg 8fg 8.2s 12d) rangy colt; poor walker; plater; suited by 1¼m; acts on a firm and a soft surface; has been tried in blinkers; trained part of season by P. Rohan. *G. Toft.*

QUALITY SUPREME 7 gr.g. No Mercy 126–Stolen Love 85 (Alcide 136) **—** (1981 10s 12g 9d 8fg³ 10.6s 9g 8fg 9g³ 8g⁴ 10.4s 8g 1982 15.8g 16f 15.8f 12f) poor maiden; seems to stay 2m; well suited by top-of-the-ground; has worn blinkers; suitable mount for an inexperienced rider. *D. Smith.*

QUAYSIDE BATTLE 5 ch.g. Quayside 124–Candy Stripe (Wrekin Rambler 120) (1981 NR 1982 12fg) winner over hurdles; last of 15 behind Yeled in ladies race at Chepstow in September, first outing on flat. *J. Webber.* —

QUAZAR LIGHT 5 ch.g. Hot Spark 126–Wrong Call 63 (High Perch 126) (1981 NR 1982 11.7f) neat gelding; very lightly raced on flat; not certain to stay middle distances; seems to act on any going; blinkered once at 2 yrs; has won over hurdles. *L. Kennard.* —

QUDESA 3 ch.c. Swing Easy 126–Gambit (King's Troop 118) (1981 5d 8g 1982 7g 8f 10d 11g 12fg² 16d 14.7fg) rangy colt; poor maiden; best run at 1½m on a firm surface; blinkered final start. *J. Mason.*

QUEEN OF MACEDON (USA) 3 b.f. An Act–Little Corrie (Exclusive Nashua) (1981 5fg 1982 7d 7g 9f 10fg) good-topped filly; plating-class maiden; should stay 1¼m. *M. Albina.* —

QUEEN OF SCOTS 3 b. or br.f. Steel Heart 128–L'Ecossaise (Dancer's Image) (1981 NR 1982 6g² 6f* 7f* 6g 7f² 6f² 6g 6g 6g) quite attractive, well-made filly; second living foal; half-sister to disappointing Liberta (by Mill Reef); dam won over 9f and 1½m in Ireland; landed odds in fine style in minor events at Redcar in May and Leicester in June; creditable second in 2 handicaps at Newmarket in July; may stay 1m. *M. Stoute.* 84

QUEEN OF THE KOP 4 b.f. Queen's Hussar 124–Bound Over (Taj Dewan 128) (1981 12g 12d⁴ 12f³ 16fg 14fg³ 16f 14g⁴ 16.5g⁴ 10s³ 1982 16d 16f 17.1f 18.8fg 12s) small filly; seems not to stay 2m. *P. Kearney.* —

QUEEN'S BIDDER 5 br.m. Auction Ring 123–Stormy Queen 64 (Typhoon 125) (1981 5fg 5fg 5fg 5.8g 1982 5f) sprint handicapper; acts on firm going and is possibly unsuited by soft. *B. Gubby.* —

QUEENSBURY BUBBLES 3 ch.f. Kashiwa 115–Crossboyne (Polyfoto 124) (1981 5d 5.1f 6fg 5g 1982 5s 5f 5f 5fg 6fg) stocky filly; poor plater; has been tried in blinkers. *D. Dale.* —

QUEENSBURY JOE 2 b.c. Rheingold 137–Strike on the Box 62 (Busted 134) (1982 8d 8g 10.2s) Mar 3; 1,500Y; leggy colt; first foal; dam disappointing maiden; behind in autumn maiden and minor events, on second outing last of 18. *D. Dale.* —

QUEENSBURY LADY 5 b.m. Undulate–Dream Shared (Majority Blue 126) (1981 12s 10d 10g 1982 10.2g 10g 13d 10f) poor maiden; well beaten in sellers occasionally; best run at 1¼m on soft going; sold 700 gns Ascot May Sales. *P. Feilden.* —

QUEENSBURY SAM 3 b.g. Cavo Doro 124–Dream Shared (Majority Blue 126) (1981 7g 8g 1982 8.2fg 12fg 13.8f 16.9fg 18d) compact, good sort; behind in varied company; blinkered last 3 starts. *D. Dale.* —

QUEENSBURY STAR 3 b.f. Wishing Star 117–Silent Mover (Burglar 128) (1981 5s 5s 5g³ 5d⁴ 5.1fg 6f* 6g* 6fg 5fg³ 6g² 6d 5g 1982 6g 7f 6fg 6g 6h 7g) small, fair sort; won seller at Doncaster and nursery at Windsor in 1981; well beaten in handicaps at 3 yrs; stays 6f; acts on firm going. *D. Dale.* —

QUEEN'S CHAMPION 3 ch.c. Run The Gantlet–Royal Saint 117 (Saint Crespin III 132) (1981 6g 7s 1982 8f 11.7f) rangy, quite attractive colt; has shown a little ability in varied company; should stay 1½m. *P. Walwyn.* —

QUEEN'S CHASE 2 b.f. Manado 130–King's Chase (King's Leap 111) (1982 6g 8s) Mar 8; 3,000Y; well-made, attractive filly; fourth foal; half-sister to 3-y-o 9f and 1¼m winner Chaste Lady (by Sandford Lad); dam ran only twice; unquoted, behind in maiden races at Newbury in August and Wolverhampton in October. *M. McCourt.* —

QUEEN'S EQUERRY 5 b.g. Hotfoot 126–Queendom 109 (Quorum 126) (1981 10fg 10d² 12fg⁴ 12f 10fg* 10fg 10f 10s 10d 1982 10fg) small gelding; good mover; well beaten since winning at Brighton in 1981; best at 1¼m; probably acts on any going; sold 575 gns Ascot October Sales. *A. Ingham.* —

QUEEN'S GLORY 2 b.f. African Sky 124–Miss Millicent (Milesian 125) (1982 5s² 5f) Feb 26; narrow, rather leggy filly; half-sister to 2 winners in Ireland, including 1m and 1¼m winner Finsbury (by Levmoss); dam won at around 9f in 70

Ireland; favourite, tired after being clear below distance when 3 lengths second of 5 to Jendor in maiden race at Haydock in April; not seen out again until September when seventh in similar event at Bath. *C. Spares.*

QUEEN'S HOME 3 b.c. Royal Palace 131–Come On Honey 94 (Never Say Die **97** 137) (1981 7d 7fg³ 8g* 10g 1982 12fg⁴ 12f 10f² 10f 10fg⁴) deep-girthed, attractive colt; did well over the winter; ran creditably most starts, including when 3½ lengths fourth of 6 to Old Country in Warren Stakes at Epsom and 8½ lengths fifth of 20 to Mubarak of Kuwait in 1½m King George V Stakes (Handicap) at Royal Ascot (stayed on well); needs further than 1¼m and is bred to stay at least 1¾m; acts on firm going. *H. Cecil.*

QUEEN'S SPRITE 3 ch.f. Queen's Hussar 124–Sprightly Sprite 80 (Babur 126) — (1981 7d 1982 10f) fair sort; in rear in maiden races; sold to M. McCausland 480 gns Newmarket July Sales. *D. Elsworth.*

QUEENSWAY ROSE 4 b.f. Crooner 119–Maizenrose 89 (Rustam 127) (1981 — 8f 8f* 8fg 10f 8.2f 1982 7f 7f 8fg 8f 10g) neat filly; soundly beaten in 1982; probably stays 1¼m; acts on firm going; sold to R. Akehurst 675 gns Ascot November Sales. *J. Harris.*

QUEEN TO BE 2 ch.f. Nebbiolo 125–Petrovna (Reliance II 137) (1982 6g³) **76 p** Mar 31; 68,000Y; good walker; half-sister to several winners, including useful French sprinter Peymour (by Habitat); dam, daughter of French 1,000 Guineas winner Pola Bella, won over 1m in France; 10/1, ran green and wasn't punished unduly when promising 3½ lengths third to Albadeeah in 18-runner maiden race at Newmarket in September; will be suited by 7f and 1m; sure to improve. *M. Albina.*

QUELLINEY 3 ch.f. High Line 125–Quelle Pas (Kelling 122) (1981 6g 6f — 6fg⁴ 8d³ 8s³ 8d 1982 11fg 16f 12fg) small, narrow, lightly-made filly; has a round action; plating-class maiden; should stay 1½m+; best form with some give in the ground. *D. Gandolfo.*

QUEST (USA) 3 ch.f. The Minstrel 135–Belle Pensee (Ribot 142) (1981 **84** 5f³ 6f 6fg 8fg³ 7d³ 7g² 1982 7fg² 8.5f² 8d 7f³ 9f* 10.1fg² 10f* 10d* 10d) neat, attractive filly; good walker; won minor event at Wolverhampton (apprentice ridden) and 2 handicaps at Brighton; suited by 1¼m; seems to act on any going. *G. Harwood.*

QUETIVEL 3 b.f. Supreme Sovereign 119–Mossy Girl (Ballymoss 136) (1981 — 6fg 7d 6d 1982 7d 8.3fg 6d) big, close-coupled filly; poor plater. *P. M. Taylor.*

QUICKENING DAWN (USA) 2 b.f. to The Quick–Coral Dawn (Turn To **92 p** Mars) (1982 7g 7d³) Apr 8; $190,000Y; big, strong, good-topped, attractive filly; first foal; dam, stakes placed, won 6 times at up to 1m; backward, shaped well in 2 races at Newmarket in October, particularly when very strong-finishing ¾-length third of 13 to Russian Roubles in Houghton Stakes; will be suited by 1m; impresses greatly as an individual and is sure to show to advantage as a 3-y-o. *J. Hindley.*

QUICK OFF THE MARK 3 ch.f. On Your Mark 125–Skimmer 86 (Skymaster **38** 126) (1981 5g 5d 5f 6f³ 6f⁴ 5f 6f 5g 5s 1982 5f 5f 5fg 5f⁴ 6f³ 5fg⁴ 6g 8.2g 5g) small, strong filly; plater; stays 6f; often blinkered. *D. Chapman.*

QUICKTHORN 6 b.m. Owen-Kiz–Hawthorn III (Prince Bio) (1981 NR — 1982 15.5fg 12d) winner over hurdles and has shown a little ability in NH Flat races; beaten some way in amateur riders events. *R. Hartop.*

QUIET CANNON 5 b.g. Connaught 130–Green Chiffon 83 (Crepello 136) — (1981 10.6g 12d 13fg 13g 12f 15fg 12v 1982 13s 11s 12g 12f) good-bodied gelding; poor performer nowadays; stays 1½m; needs some give in the ground; sometimes blinkered; bandaged last 2 outings; sold to K. Bailey 2,500 gns Doncaster May Sales. *J. Berry.*

QUIET JUSTICE (USA) 3 b.g. Stop the Music–Around The Court (Illustrious) — (1981 7fg 7.2fg 7d 1982 11fg 17f) fair sort; little worthwhile form in varied company; blinkered final start. *G. Hunter.*

QUIET STYLE 2 b.f. Oats 126–Cuba Libre (Rum) (1982 6f 7g 8f) May 7; — useful-looking filly; second foal; dam ran 3 times in Ireland; in rear in maiden races and a claiming event. *M. Tompkins.*

QUILTING 2 b.f. Mummy's Pet 125–Questa Notte 104 (Midsummer Night II **78** 117) (1982 6g² 6s) Apr 17; wiry filly; third foal; half-sister to 1981 2-y-o 1m winner Sent For You (by Moulton) and a winner in Italy; dam 6f performer;

beaten short head by Debutina Park, after wandering in lead inside final furlong, in minor event at York in September; tailed off in similar race at Goodwood later in the month; probably not suited by soft going. *B. Hobbs.*

QUI SON (USA) 2 ch.c. To The Quick–Chief Song (Chieftain) (1982 7g 7fg)   **79 p**
Mar 12; $275,000Y; attractive, good-looking colt; good mover; closely related to a winner by Majestic Prince, and half-brother to several winners, including American Trader (by Swaps), a smart performer at up to 9f; dam never ran; second favourite, ran well until beaten and eased in final furlong when 7 lengths sixth of 12 behind Zoffany in minor event at Goodwood in September, second outing; will probably prove better suited by 6f; bound to do a good deal better in time and win races. *J. Dunlop.*

QUISTADOR 6 ch.h. Le Johnstan 123–Little Bo Bleep 71 (Bleep-Bleep 134)   —
(1981 16s 10f³ 1982 12s 13fg 8.3fg 8.3fg) poor performer nowadays; possibly stays 1¼m; acts on a firm and a soft surface; has been tried in blinkers. *M. Chapman.*

QUITE A NIGHT 2 b.c. Midsummer Night II 117–Quaranta 83 (Hotfoot 126)   **96**
(1982 5fg² 6f² 6g 8d* 7d) Mar 3; 8,000Y; lengthy colt; first foal; dam, 2-y-o 5f winner, is half-sister to smart 5f to 7f performer Quy (by Midsummer Night II); won Jack Jarvis Memorial Nursery at Ayr in September by 2½ lengths from Johnny Nobody; suited by 1m; best form on a soft surface. *B. Hobbs.*

QUITE HOT 3 ch.g. Hotfoot 126–Quite Sweet 100 (Super Sam 124) (1981   **84**
5d 5g 7fg 1982 8.2f 12fg 13.4g* 12.3fg⁴ 15.8d⁴ 14.7fg 16s*) strong, rangy gelding; won maiden race at Chester in July and handicap at Newcastle in October; evidently suited by a test of stamina; suited by some give in the ground and revels in the mud. *P. Rohan.*

QUITE LUCKY 5 ch.m. Precipice Wood 123–Quite Sweet 100 (Super Sam 124)   —
(1981 14d⁴ 14fg 10.2d 12s 1982 12d) strong mare; staying maiden; acts on hard going; has run creditably for an amateur rider. *P. M. Taylor.*

QUITE SHY 3 b.f. Quiet Fling 124–All Shy 64 (Alcide 136) (1981 7s 1982   **87**
7s³ 7s 10g² 8g 9f 12fg) 11,000Y; quite attractive filly; half-sister to 3 winners, including middle-distance performer Graf Metternich (by High Top); dam stayed at least 1½m; ran well first 3 starts, finishing 1¾ lengths third of 14 to Miss Lilian in April Fillies Stakes at the Curragh, just over 2 lengths fifth of 10 to Celestial Path in Athasi Stakes on same course and length second of 9 to Moreda in Azalea Stakes at Leopardstown; not disgraced when tenth of 24 to Prince's Polly in Goffs Irish 1,000 Guineas at the Curragh on fourth outing but finished well beaten behind Dish Dash in Ribblesdale Stakes at Royal Ascot on final appearance; should stay 1½m; acts on soft going. *K. Prendergast, Ireland.*

QUIVER BRIGHT 2 ch.f. Thriller 77–Merry Bright (Festive 107) (1982   —
10d) May 12; tall, lengthy filly; third foal; dam well beaten only outing over hurdles; 50/1, always tailed off in 14-runner seller at Pontefract in October. *T. Kersey.*

QUONSET 3 ch.c. Steel Heart 128–Belinda (Ragusa 137) (1981 NR 1982   —
8fg 11g 13.3f 16d⁴ 10.6g⁴ 12fg⁴ 12v² 13.8d) IR 20,000Y; heavy-topped colt; third foal; dam won 1½m maiden race by 10 lengths in Ireland on second of 2 starts; middle-distance maiden; acts on heavy going; sold to Mrs N. Smith 5,600 gns Newmarket Autumn Sales. *B. Hanbury.*

R

RAASHIDEAH 2 b.f. Dancer's Image–Monaco Melody 103 (Tudor Melody 129)   **88**
(1982 6g 6fg 6s*) Mar 20; attractive, deep-girthed filly; second foal; half-sister to winning 5f performer Brassy (by Bold Lad, Ire); dam useful 6f winner; won 25-runner maiden race at Doncaster in November by short head from Sheldan; disappointing favourite in similar event at Salisbury on previous outing; will stay 7f; acts well on soft going and is possibly not suited by a firm surface. *H. T. Jones.*

RABEEB 2 b.f. Home Guard 129–Mariinsky 69 (Nijinsky 138) (1982 7fg 8fg)   **64**
Feb. 25; unfurnished filly; first foal; dam suited by a test of stamina; 11 lengths fifth of 13 to Saba in maiden race at Beverley in September, second outing. *M. H. Easterby.*

RABOOSH 2 b.c. Tarboosh–Royal Performance 57 (Klairon 131) (1982 5g)   —
Mar 12; IR 260F, IR 1,600Y; first produce; dam won over 8.6f in Ireland; last of 7 in minor event at Hamilton in July; sent to Malaysia. *W. Stubbs.*

RACONTEUR (USA) 3 ch.c. The Minstrel 135–Bubbling (Stage Door Johnny) **107**
(1981 6d² 7g* 7g 1982 10s* 8g 8.5f 12g) $285,000Y; fine, big, handsome colt;
very good mover; first living foal; dam, half-sister to high-class 6.5f to 1¼m
winner Effervescing, was a smart stakes winner over 1m; won well-contested
minor event at the Curragh in April by 3 lengths from stable-companion Lords;
soundly beaten afterwards in Airlie/Coolmore Irish 2,000 Guineas at the Curragh
(seventh of 14 to Dara Monarch), Diomed Stakes at Epsom and Irish Sweeps
Derby at the Curragh again; bred to stay 1½m but is headstrong and is unlikely
to do so; acts on soft going; trained by V. O'Brien first 3 starts. *D. O'Brien,
Ireland.*

RADAR TRAP 2 ch.g. Some Hand 119–Wonderful One 90 (Princely Gift 137) —
(1982 5g 6g 6s 6s 8d) Mar 26; 1,000F, 3,600Y; big gelding; poor walker;
brother to 1979 2-y-o 5f and 6f winner Man-O-War Bay, and half-brother to
several winners; no form in sellers; gelded after final outing. *J. Berry.*

RADFIELD 3 ch.f. Connaught 130–Frivolity 70 (Varano) (1981 NR 1982 10d⁴ **58**
12g 11g 12fg⁴ 16d 12f⁴ 12fg 16fg* 19s) big, strong filly; first foal; dam, 2m
winner, is half-sister to Irish 1,000 Guineas and Irish St Leger winner Pidget;
won amateur riders race at Chepstow in August; suited by a test of stamina;
blinkered seventh start (sweated up badly); gave trouble at start third outing.
P. Cundell.

RAGA 6 b.g. Ragapan 118–Suspension (Arctic Time 127) (1981 10s 12g* 10s² **53**
10d³ 12fg 11.5f 11.5fg 12g 10d⁴ 1982 12f 12fg 22.2fg 11.7fg 11.7g 10f⁴ 10g*
10v 10v) ex-Irish gelding; ran best race since arriving over here when strong-
finishing fourth to Bettyknowes in handicap at Salisbury in August; successful
over 1¼m in Jersey the same month; stays 1½m; probably acts on any going;
has won for an apprentice; sold out of A. Redmond's stable 24,000 gns
Ballsbridge December (81) Sales. *G. Balding.*

RAGAFAN 5 ch.g. Ragstone 128–Hi-Baby 102 (High Treason 126) (1981 8fg —
10fg⁴ 11.5d 12g³ 12fg 1982 8fg) compact gelding; successful twice in Belgium
before running respectably on his return in September; stays 1½m; sold 3,500 gns
Ascot October Sales and won over fences afterwards. *R. Smyth.*

RAG DANCER 5 br.h. Ragstone 128–May Day Follies 80 (Bleep-Bleep 134) **50**
(1981 10s⁴ 11g* 12d 12g* 12fg 13g 12f 11fg 11d³ 12d³ 12g³ 1982 12.3g³ 12f
13fg³ 11g⁴ 12g 13d) lightly-made horse; middle-distance handicapper; acts on a
firm surface but has shown most of his best form with some give in the ground;
had stiff task final outing. *W. Elsey.*

RAGE GLEN 5 gr.m. Grey Mirage 128–Septieme Ciel (Welsh Abbot 131) (1981 **48**
8v 8g 7d³ 7g 7g 7g 8g 10.2f 10fg 7g 7d³ 7v 7g 7g 7s 7g 1982 10s* 8.2s* 10f⁴ 8f)
compact mare; won apprentice handicap at Ayr (by 7 lengths) and
selling handicap at Haydock in April (no bid); stays 1¼m; acts on any going but
is particularly well suited by some give in the ground; has worn blinkers;
headstrong. *M. Lambert.*

RAGFLINT 3 b.g. Ragstone 128–Graceful Scot (Aberdeen 109) (1981 6f 10s —
1982 12 17f) in rear in maiden events; has worn blinkers; sold to Mrs N. Smith
420 gns Ascot December Sales. *P. Feilden.*

RAG-ON-FIRE 3 gr.f. Dragonara Palace 125–Farida Jinks 106 (Tudor Jinks **44**
121) (1981 5.1fg³ 5fg³ 5fg 5d 1982 5v 7f 7f³ 6fg⁴ 6fg 6g) small, lightly-made
filly; plater; stays 7f; acts on firm going; exported to Algeria. *W. Musson.*

RAGTIME BLUES 2 b.f. Netherkelly 112–Blue Mountain (Mountain Call 125) —
(1982 5s 5d 5d) May 19; third foal; dam never ran; in rear in maiden race and
sellers in the autumn. *A. Potts.*

RAGTIME ROSE 3 b.f. Ragstone 128–Miss Venus (Comedy Star 121) (1981 —
6g 7g 1982 7d) quite attractive, lightly-made filly; little worthwhile form.
E. Eldin.

RAGUSTAR 2 b.c. Dance In Time—Bamburi 93 (Ragusa 137) (1982 7fg 7fg —
8d) May 23; 7,000Y; robust colt; half-brother to useful 6f and 1m winner
Eldoret (by High Top); dam won twice at 1m; backward, soundly beaten in
autumn maiden races at Salisbury and Redcar (2). *A. Jarvis.*

RAHERE HUSSAR 2 ch.c. Queen's Hussar 124–Rahere Blackie (Richboy 117) **69**
(1982 5g² 6g² 5fg³ 6fg* 6fg 6g) Apr 10; first foal; dam never ran; 5-length
winner of 21-runner seller at Windsor (bought in 3,800 gns) in August; will
stay 7f; yet to race on a soft surface. *C. Nelson.*

RAINBOW SPRINGS 2 b.f. Silly Season 127–Hod On 67 (Decoy Boy 129) **82**
(1982 6g⁴ 6d³ 6s²) Apr 18; well-grown filly; second foal; dam won 7f seller;

placed in late-season maiden events at Pontefract (beaten 2 short heads) and Leicester; will stay 7f; acts on soft going. *M. Camacho.*

RAIN DANCER 3 gr.c. Dancer's Image–Marala (Sir Khalito) (1981 5g 6d 6fg **48**
1982 7fg 7g 5fg² 5.1g³ 5fg 5fg³ 5f 6fg 5fg⁴ 6d³) strong, good-bodied colt; plater;
stays 6f; acts on a firm and a soft surface; blinkered nowadays. *W. O'Gorman.*

RAISE A HAND 4 b.g. Auction Ring 123–My Fawn 67 (Hugh Lupus 132)   —
(1981 10.5f 13.4fg 13f³ 16.5f³ 16f² 15.5s 1982 13v 12fg) tall, good sort;
staying maiden; blinkered first outing. *P. Makin.*

RAISE THE BID 5 b.g. Auction Ring 123–Karen Chase 82 (Will Somers 114§)   —
(1981 NR 1982 12fg 10.2s) ex-Irish gelding; won 1m apprentice race in
Ireland in 1980 and promised to stay further; behind in ladies race and an
apprentice event in 1982; acts on firm going; usually blinkered in Ireland. *O.
O'Neill.*

RAISE THE OFFER 3 b.f. Auction Ring 123–Raise The Roof (Raise You Ten **76**
125) (1981 5fg 7f 8d 1982 12fg 17f³ 12f³ 16h* 12fg* 14g³ 17fg³ 14f 13g⁴ 12f³
16g 12g² 12g) rangy filly; favourite when winning handicaps at Chepstow and
Beverley (odds on) in June; ran creditably penultimate outing but badly on final
one; stays well; acts on hard going; blinkered seventh and tenth starts;
inconsistent. *M. Ryan.*

RAJA MUDA (USA) 3 br.c. Raja Baba–Aurilla (Winged T) (1981 5g 5s   —
1982 5fg 7.6f 12f 10.2g 9.4fg⁴) strong, well-made colt; only plating class;
blinkered last 2 starts; sent to Malaysia. *F. J. Houghton.*

RAJHAAN 3 br.c. English Prince 129–Amana (Relko 136) (1981 6g 7fg* 8d **116**
8s² 1982 12d² 12fg* 12fg³ 12v 12fg² 12fg³ 10f 10.5g³ 10fg 8s* 10d) IR 11,000F,
14,000Y; smallish, well-made colt; half-brother to French middle-distance
winner Akabor (by Taj Dewan) and winning French stayer Azfazar (by Exbury);
dam won 4 middle-distance races in French Provinces; comfortably won minor
events at Thirsk in April (from Sagamore) and York in October (landed odds
from Romoss); also ran well in Warren Stakes at Epsom, Churchill Stakes at
Ascot (caught close home and beaten a neck by Lyphmas), Welsh Derby at
Chepstow, Garrowby Stakes (Limited Handicap) at York and Dubai Champion
Stakes at Newmarket; about 11 lengths sixth of 14 to Time Charter in last-
named on final start; stays 1½m; seems to act on any going; genuine and
consistent; racing in USA. *F. J. Houghton.*

RAMADA 5 ch.g. St Alphage 119–Strathclair (Klairon 131) (1981 5g 10f 6fg **45**
6g 1982 6g² 6f) strong, compact gelding; plater; stays 6f; acts on any going;
often wears blinkers; sold 800 gns Doncaster September Sales. *B. Richmond.*

RAMBLING RIVER 5 b.h. Forlorn River 124–Who-Done-It 98 (Lucero 124) **80**
(1981 5g 5g 5f 5f 5fg³ 6f² 5g⁴ 5f* 5g³ 6f⁴ 5f⁴ 5fg² 5fg³ 5fg 5d³ 5g 5g 1982 6f 5fg⁴
5fg³ 5f³ 5fg 5fg² 5g³ 5f 5g³ 5fg* 5fg² 5fg² 6d* 6fg⁴ 5fg² 5s⁴ 6g⁴ 6d 5s) strong,
useful sort; sprint handicapper; gained well-deserved wins in quite valuable
races at Newcastle in July (beat Bri-Eden a head) and August (won by a length
from Bracadale); possibly not at his best on really soft going, but acts on any
other; blinkered nowadays; has worn a bandage on his near-fore; missed break
eighth start. *W. A. Stephenson.*

RAMIANA (USA) 3 ch.f. Blushing Groom 131–Irish Meadow (St Paddy 133) **68**
(1981 7fg 7fg 7d 1982 11fg* 12.3fg) leggy, narrow filly; stayed on well to
win handicap at Wolverhampton in April; last in similar race at Chester following
month; not seen out again; should stay 1½m; sold 40,000 gns Newmarket
December Sales. *J. Hindley.*

RAMJAK 3 b.g. Mandrake Major 122–Melanesia (South Pacific 87) (1981   —
5g 5fg 6f 1982 8f 7f) leggy, workmanlike gelding; has a round action; poor
plater. *J. Etherington.*

RAMO'S LADY 3 ch.f. Malinowski 123–Romp 67 (Romulus 129) (1981 6fg   —
7fg 8fg 7g 1982 10s) fair sort; little worthwhile form, including in a seller.
A. Bailey.

RAMPAGING 2 b.c. Bold Lad (Ire) 133–Eleanor Clare 89 (Petingo 135) (1982   —
8d) Apr 26; IR 23,000Y, 1,200 2-y-o; third foal; half-brother to 2 winners,
notably quite useful 3-y-o 7f winner Gavo (by Windjammer); dam disappointing
maiden; 33/1, always struggling in 23-runner maiden race at Newmarket in
October. *G. Fletcher.*

RAMPANT 3 br.g. Reliance II 137–Glimmer of Hope 90 (Never Say Die 137) **65**
(1981 NR 1982 14fg 12f 16fg 14d 15.5fg⁴ 16g 14.7f³ 12g² 14g 14s) 5,200Y;

big, rangy gelding; second foal; half-brother to 6f to 1½m winner Moment of Weakness (by Pieces of Eight); dam stayed well; plating-class maiden; stays well; sold 7,200 gns Newmarket Autumn Sales. *C. Brittain.*

RAMWADASH 4 ch.g. Jukebox 120–Country Court 81 (Meadow Court 129) — (1981 NR 1982 10f) neat gelding; won at Bath as a 2-y-o (rated 75); tailed off only outing on flat since; not certain to stay 1¼m; probably acts on any going; has run well in blinkers. *G. Thorner.*

RANAMAR 2 b.f. Fine Blade 121–Green Marvedo (Green God 128) (1982 **56** 5f² 5f 5fg 6fg) May 6; 1,500Y; tall, leggy filly; second foal; dam second over 7f in Ireland; 1½ lengths second of 6 to Time's Time in auction event at Redcar in May, best effort; not seen out after August; should be suited by 6f; lost all chance when badly hampered at start third outing. *J. Hardy.*

RANA OF COOMBE 2 gr.f. Moulton 128–Madam Clare 66 (Ennis 128) — (1982 5.8g 6g 6fg) Mar 27; sister to Prix de la Salamandre winner John de Coombe; of no account; blinkered final outing. *M. Blanshard.*

RANAPOUR 4 ch.c. Tyrant–Rojika (Tantieme 136) (1981 9s 8.5d* 8.5s* **115** 10v⁴ 8fg² 10g 1982 8d² 10.5s* 10.5d* 10fg² 10g) strong, handsome colt; half-brother to several winners, including smart French middle-distance stayer Goldiko (by Rheingold); dam, winner over 8.5f in France, is sister to Match III and Reliance II and closely related to Relko; decisively won minor events at Evry and Saint-Cloud, on latter course in July beating Hayel by 4 lengths; second in amateur riders event at Compiegne (to King James) and Prix Gontaut-Biron at Deauville (beaten ¾ length by Great Substence); stays 1¼m well; probably acts on any going; genuine; very useful. *F. Mathet, France.*

RANA PRATAP (USA) 2 b.c. Faliraki 125–Dodo S (Nagea) (1982 5fg 6g⁴ **93** 6g⁴ 7g* 7d³ 7s*) May 8; $130,000Y; good-looking colt; good walker; fourth foal; brother to American 3-y-o Irisher, winner of a 6f stakes race at 2 yrs, and half-brother to 2 stakes-placed winners, including Son of a Dodo (by Son Ange), a smart winner at up to 1m; dam never ran; won minor events at Brighton (backed from 12/1 to 7/2) in September and Chepstow in October; excellent third in nursery at Newmarket in between; better suited by 7f than 6f, and will probably stay 1m; acts on soft going. *G. Lewis.*

RANBY 3 ch.g. Tower Walk 130–Town House 91 (Pall Mall 132) (1981 NR — 1982 8f 8fg 7f) leggy, rather plain gelding; well beaten in Northern sellers. *M. H. Easterby.*

RANGEFINDER 2 ch.c. On Your Mark 125–Battling Bessie (Typhoon 125) **76** (1982 5g⁴ 6fg⁴ 5g 5s⁴) Apr 10; 9,600F; well-made, quite attractive colt; half-brother to several winners, including French miler Miss Bessie (by Pitskelly); dam, half-sister to Roman Warrior, placed over 6f at 2 yrs in Ireland; quite a moderate maiden; best runs on first and last outings; none too well away third start. *B. Hills.*

RANNDAKA 2 b.f. Godswalk 130–Ravela II (Tanerko 134) (1982 5s 6f) **61** Apr 16; lightly-made filly; half-sister to several winners, including 3-y-o Riyahi (by Red God), a very useful 6f and 1m winner at 2 yrs in France; dam, half-sister to high-class sprinter Fortino II, won at up to 13f; in mid-division in maiden races at Pontefract in June (favourite) and Carlisle in July; sold 8,200 gns Newmarket December Sales and sent to France. *M. Stoute.*

RA NOVA 2 ch.c. Ragstone 128–Miss Casanova 84 (Galivanter 131) (1981 — 7d 1982 10fg 14d 12f³ 14f 16g) small, quite well-made colt; poor maiden on balance of form. *P. Mitchell.*

RANSOM (FR) 3 br.c. Rose Laurel 125–Cup Cake (Dan Cupid 132) (1981 **77** 7fg 7fg 8d 1982 10s 12f* 12f² 14fg 13.1g* 12f³ 14fg 14fg³,14g) small, close-coupled colt; good mover; won handicaps at Leicester in April and Bath in July; suited by further than 1½m; acts on firm going; game; sold to L. Cumani 12,500 gns Newmarket Autumn Sales. *P. Walwyn.*

RANT AND RAVE 2 ch.c. North Stoke 130–Libonia (Le Haar 126) (1982 — 7f) Mar 25; IR 36,000Y; small, well-made colt; half-brother to 3 winners, including useful 1981 2-y-o 5f performer Fool's Dance (by Gay Fandango); dam never ran; 33/1, remote eighth of 13 in £4,900 event at Kempton in September. *J. Sutcliffe.*

RAPID BEAT 2 b.g. Rapid River 127–On Wings Of Song 51 (Jolly Jet 111) **61** (1982 5f 5f 6g 5g 5g 6d 8.2fg 8fg⁴ 7.2s) Mar 14; leggy, unfurnished gelding; third foal; dam poor maiden; moderate plater; best form at 6f. *W. A. Stephenson.*

RAPID CASH 2 br.c. Rapid River 127–Cashalaika (Cash and Courage 116) **61** (1982 7g 7fg 8.2fg*) Apr 30; compact, fair sort; fourth foal; dam tailed off both outings; backed at long odds and blinkered, showed much improved form when winning 13-runner seller at Haydock (bought in 2,100 gns) in September by ½ length from Mawatea; clearly well suited by 1m. *W. A. Stephenson.*

RAPID KNOT 3 b.g. Rapid River 127–Love-Knot (No Mercy 126) (1981 6f **88** 6f 6fg² 7fg* 7.2fg* 8g 7s 1982 7f 8f* 8d*) strong, plain gelding who carries plenty of condition; poor walker and has a round action; kept on gamely to win handicaps at Redcar in May and Beverley in July; beat Steel Venture ½ length in £5,000 event on latter; stays 1m; seems to act on any going; sent to Hong Kong. *Miss S. Hall.*

RAPID LAD 4 b.c. Rapid River 127–Seacona (Espresso 122) (1981 5f 5g⁴ **57** 6fg 6f 7g 7g 5g⁴ 1982 7s³ 8g 10.8fg² 8fg² 8fg* 8.2g 8f) compact colt; former plater; won apprentice event at Brighton in June; evidently stays 1¼m; acts on any going with possible exception of very firm; occasionally blinkered (ran moderately in them sixth start). *J. Spearing.*

RAPID LADY 2 b.f. Rapid River 127–Princess Gretel 97 (The Phoenix) (1982 **63** 5g 5d² 5fg⁴ 5f 5f 5fg* 5d⁴ 6f 5g² 5g 6g 5d 5d) May 25; 400Y; leggy filly; sister to 1m winner Kinnigger and half-sister to several winners; dam miler; bought in 1,700 gns after winning seller at Beverley in June; form only at 5f, but should stay further; probably acts on any going; blinkered seventh outing. *Mrs M. Nesbitt.*

RAPID MISS 2 gr. or ro.f. Rapid River 127–Zellamaid 54 (Runnymede 123) **70** (1982 6f 6f 5.1d³ 6g* 5g² 5s) Mar 14; small, lengthy filly; first foal; dam plater on flat and over hurdles; plater; won 6-runner event at Yarmouth (retained 950 gns) in September; 2 lengths second of 7 to Babycham Sparkle in non-seller at Edinburgh the following month; stays 6f; possibly unsuited by very soft going. *Mrs N. Macauley.*

RARE EVENT 2 ch.c. Jaazeiro 127–Royal Saint 117 (Saint Crespin III 132) **102** (1982 6fg* 7f² 7fg* 7fg⁴ 7.6s⁴) Apr 27; neat, well-made colt; good mover; half-brother to several winners, including Irish Sweeps Derby and Doncaster St Leger third Classic Example (by Run The Gantlet) and smart middle-distance performer Illustrious Prince (by Le Levanstell); dam smart miler and sister to Altesse Royale; won 22-runner minor event at Leicester in June and 5-runner Heronslea Stakes (beating Domynsky a neck) at Ayr in August; creditable fourth of six behind The Fort in Intercraft Solario Stakes at Sandown later in August, next outing and better subsequent effort; will be suited by 1m. *M. Stoute.*

RARE FRIENDSHIP 2 b.f. Rarity 129–Hidden Hand (Ribocco 129) (1982 **– p** 9s) Apr 29; IR 9,000F, IR 8,000Y; big filly; half-sister to 2 winners, including fair 6f and 1m winner Hugo di Tours (by African Sky); dam, daughter of high-class Hidden Meaning, won 7f claiming race in USA; 25/1 and burly, never-dangerous seventh of 15 to Omar Ramsden in maiden race at Redcar in October; should improve. *E. Weymes.*

RARE GIFT 3 b.c. Rarity 129–Awash (Busted 134) (1981 7fg 7fg² 7.6g⁴ **95** 1982 8s* 8fg 10f 8g 8fg) tall, lengthy, useful-looking colt; good mover; strode clear in fine style to beat Risk by 8 lengths in 6-runner Easter Stakes at Kempton in April; behind in varied company afterwards; will stay 1½m; evidently acts well on soft going; winner over hurdles for N. Callaghan. *J. Sutcliffe.*

RARE HONOUR 2 br.f. Artaius 129–Honorary Member (Never Bend) (1982 **– p** 7.6v) Feb 29; 40,000Y; half-sister to 2 winners in France, including useful 1m winner Hind (by Vaguely Noble); dam, daughter of Kentucky Oaks winner Hail to Patsy, was placed twice from 4 starts in France; 6/1, showed up to past halfway in 21-runner maiden race at Lingfield in October; should do better. *P. Cole.*

RARE REIGN 2 b.f. Rarity 129–Raindrops (King's Troop 118) (1982 7d) **– p** Apr 9; IR 9,000F, 9,000Y; fair sort; half-sister to 2 winners in Ireland, including fairly useful 1980 2-y-o sprinter Indian Splash (by Prince Tenderfoot); dam never ran; 20/1, not knocked about when eighth of 15 in maiden race at Leicester in October; should do better. *J. Sutcliffe.*

RARE ROBERTA (USA) 2 b. or br.f. Roberto 131–Marketess (To Market) **101** (1982 6fg² 7d³ 6g* 6d 6s*) Mar 31; $58,000Y; big, strong filly; first foal; dam won 6 small races at up to 6f; successful in maiden race at Lingfield in August and 17-runner Buggins Farm Nursery at Haydock in October; dis-appointing favourite, running very poorly, at Chester in between; should stay 1m; yet to race on really firm going, but acts on any other. *P. Cole.*

RARFY JAMES 3 ch.c. Gay Fandango 132–Gold Court 79 (Gentle Art 121)   **73**
(1981 8g 6g   1982 7f 7f² 7fg² 7fg 7g² 8g* 7f 10.1fg 10fg* 10g* 10f 10g⁴) strong
colt; beaten 3 times in sellers early in year but subsequently showed himself
better than a plater, winning maiden race at Edinburgh and 2 handicaps at
Newmarket; suited by 1¼m; yet to race on a soft surface; ran a bit freely in
blinkers fourth start. *G. Huffer.*

RASA SINGAPURA 2 b.c. Reform 132–Penitent 85 (Sing Sing 134)   (1982   **77**
7f 7fg² 7f³ 7.3g 8g 8d 8.2s)   Mar 25; 6,000Y; medium-sized, quite well-made
colt; half-brother to 3 winners, including fairly useful sprinter Penumbra (by
Wolver Hollow); dam closely related to top sprinter Song; placed at Newmarket
and Goodwood in July in races won by On Stage and Dunbeath; little form
afterwards off stiff marks in nurseries; acts on firm going. *R. Armstrong.*

RASHANA 3 ch.f. Sharpen Up 127–Hunter's Melody 70 (Off Key 121)   (1981   —
5fg⁴ 5g³ 5g³ 6f* 5g 6g 6v   1982 7fg 7f⁴ 7d)   quite useful sort; quite moderate;
may be suited by a return to 6f; acts on firm going; blinkered once in 1981.
C. Spares.

RASHERCAP 4 br.g. Home Guard 129–Ciotog (Varano) (1981 12s   1982   —
12f⁴ 16d) big, rangy gelding; showed promise on only outing at 2 yrs; well
beaten since; not certain to stay 2m. *J. W. Watts.*

RATAMATAZ 8 b.g. Shiny Tenth 120–Water Rat 83 (Hard Tack 111§) (1981   —
5d 5fg 7g 5f 5fg 7s 5s   1982 6g) poor handicapper; stays 6f; acts on any going;
has worn blinkers; good mount for a boy. *D. Marks.*

RA TAPU 5 ch.h. Sun Prince 128–Bracey Bridge 115 (Chanteur II 135) (1981   —
12d³ 14fg⁴ 18.4d 15.5d² 14fg   1982 18g 10fg 12s 12v) tall horse; mainly
poor form in 1982; stays well; probably acts on any going; has run respectably
for an apprentice; has worn bandages; trained until after first start by P.
Mitchell. *R. Atkins.*

RATHDOWNEY MAY 2 ch.f. Derrylin 115–Angelica (Hornbeam 130) (1982   **47**
5fg 5d 5fg 5.8f⁴ 7f 7g)   Mar 18; small, lengthy filly; plater: showed ability
only when 6 lengths fourth of 12 to Irene's Pride at Bath in July; should stay
7f. *Mrs J. Reavey.*

RATTLING WIND 4 b.f. Youth 135–Rocked Ribbed (Ribot 142) (1981   —
including 8g* 10g* 11s² 10g* 9d⁴ 10s* 10v² 8s²   1982 10f 9.2g 12v) $50,000Y;
lengthy ex-Italian filly; half-sister to several winners, including Piuma al
Vento (by Gyr), successful from 1¼m to 1¾m in France; dam, useful winner in
Italy, is daughter of Irish Oaks winner Garden State; one of the leading fillies
in Italy as a 3-y-o when winning 4 races at Milan, including Premio Baggio
and Group 3 Premio Legnano; also in frame several times, including in Oaks
d'Italia at Milan (2 lengths second to Val d'Erica), Prix Chloe at Evry and
Premio Lydia Tesio at Rome (short-head second to Oraston); well beaten in
1982 in Brigadier Gerard Stakes at Sandown in May (staying-on 15 lengths
fifth of 8 behind Kalaglow), Prix d'Ispahan at Longchamp in June (last of
6) and Princess Royal Stakes at Ascot in October (blinkered, finished last of
14); should stay 1½m; acts on heavy going; formerly trained by A. Botti. *C.
Nelson.*

RAVENS TOWER 5 gr.h. Tower Walk 130–Grey Mink 86 (Double Jump 131)   —
(1981 8d 8d 8f   1982 8fg) quite a moderate handicapper at his best; best
form at up to 1m; was suited by some give in the ground; dead. *M. Pipe.*

RAVISSANT 2 br.c. On Your Mark 125–Andara (Hugh Lupus 132) (1982   —
5g 6f) Apr 1; IR 10,500Y; half-brother to 3 winners here and abroad; dam
won 3 times from 1m to 11.5f in French Provinces; little worthwhile form;
trained by S. Mellor first start; dead. *G. Lewis.*

RAWLINSON END 4 b.c. Song 132–Wong Way Girl 99 (Kibenka 119) (1981   **63**
6s 6fg⁴ 7s² 7d* 7.2s 7g³ 7g 7g 8d 7d⁴   1982 8fg 8g* 7f² 8g 8f 8fg 8fg 8.3g 7fg²
7.3g 8g* 8g) neat, strong colt; good walker; ran best races when winning
handicaps at Warwick in June and Brighton in September and when second
twice in between; stays 1m; acts on any going; ran very badly in blinkers once.
R. Laing.

RAY CHARLES 4 gr.g. Sun Prince 128–Ivory Gull 70 (Sea Hawk II 131)   —
(1981 10s* 11.7f⁴ 11.7fg² 11.7fg² 12fg³ 10fg 10d³ 10.6s³ 11d   1982 12d) tall,
narrow gelding; none too good a walker or mover; ran consistently well as a
3-y-o and showed fairly useful form; behind only outing on flat since; suited by
1½m; acts on any going. *D. Nicholson.*

RAZOR SHARP 2 ch.c. Sharpen Up 127–Pearl Star 110 (Gulf Pearl 117) **92**
(1982 6f 6d 5fg³ 5.8f* 6s²) Apr 4; 40,000Y; good-topped colt; half-brother to 3
winners, including 11f to 13f winner Star Burst (by Busted); dam game performer at up to 7f; showed much improved form when blinkered, winning 11-
runner maiden race at Bath in July by 1¼ lengths from Court Procedure, and
running Worrell to short head, after catching a bump inside final furlong, in
valuable nursery at Ascot in September; better suited by 6f than 5f and will
probably stay further; acts on any going. C. Nelson.

RAZOR SUN (USA) 3 b.f. Blade–Summer Hill (Sir Gaylord) (1981 5g² 5fg⁴ **73**
6s³ 6fg³ 7f* 7d² 7.2fg 8.2s 1982 8.5fg⁴ 10fg 10f 8.3fg 8.3g 7fg² 8f) neat, good-
quartered filly; good walker and mover; quite a moderate handicapper; stays
1m; seems to act on any going; sweated up second start; takes a good hold. B.
Hills.

REAL COOL 2 ch.f. Record Token 128–Balante 90 (Balidar 133) (1982 5s **—**
6d 6d) Apr 8; 5,400F, 12,000Y; first produce; dam effective at up to 1m;
well beaten in maiden and minor events in the autumn. P. Asquith.

REAL MONTY 2 ch.g. Monsanto 121–Vila Real 76 (Town Crier 119) (1982 **75**
5g 5f 5f⁴ 6f⁴ 6fg 6g² 7fg 8f² 8.2s³ 8g*) Apr 28; sturdy, compact gelding; good
walker; third reported foal; dam won 4 sellers over 7f and 1m; gelded after
winning maiden race at Edinburgh in October by ½ length from Monsanto Lad;
suited by 1m; seems to act on any going; withdrawn at Pontefract in October
after twice unseating rider. R. Hollinshead.

REALMS REASON 3 ch.f. Realm 129–Countess Eileen 111 (Sassafras 135) **?**
(1981 6fg 7fg² 7f² 8d² 7g⁴ 1982 8g² 8s³ 8d² 8s² 7d) big, rangy filly; fairly
useful at 2 yrs; didn't run up to that form when placed in 4 races at Cagnes-sur-
Mer in spring but subsequently did well in USA, winning 3 times over middle
distances and running good second to Middle Stage in Athenia Handicap at
Aqueduct in October; stays 1½m; seems to act on any going. W. Hastings-Bass.

REAL SHADAI (USA) 3 b.c. Roberto 131–Desert Vixen (In Reality) (1981 8v **126**
10d² 1982 12fg* 12s³ 12fg² 12.5d³ 13.5g* 12s)
   The average sale price of Roberto's yearlings in 1982, over 228,000 dollars,
was well up on the figures for the previous two years, 178,000 dollars and
152,000 dollars. Even allowing for the bullish nature of the American bloodstock market at the highest levels, this is a substantial increase, one that a glance
at the sires list covering earnings gained by progeny in Europe and North
America during the current season does something to explain. Roberto is near
the top of the table, his offspring having picked up over 2,500,000 dollars.
Represented in the States by performers of the order of the Lexington Stakes
winner Royal Roberto and the Pan American and Dixie Handicap winner
Robsphere, Roberto enjoyed by far his best season to date in Europe where he
had the four-year-old Critique and an excellent crop of three-year-olds. Touching
Wood won the St Leger and Irish St Leger, Silver Hawk, Slightly Dangerous
and Real Shadai all gained places in classics and the last-named has strong
claims to be regarded as the top colt of his generation in France at a mile and a
half.
   Lightly raced in 1981, Real Shadai wasted little time giving notice of his
ability at three, comfortably winning an eight-runner maiden race at Longchamp
in April and finishing strongly after not having the smoothest of passages to be
three lengths third to Cadoudal in the Prix Hocquart on the same course the
following month. Normally this form wouldn't have been sufficient to encourage serious thoughts of success in the Prix du Jockey-Club, but in a substandard field for the Chantilly classic Real Shadai started third favourite to
Assert and Cadoudal and he showed the confidence well founded. In the leading
half dozen most of the way, he hit the front just after rounding the home turn
and though left behind by the three-length winner Assert in the final furlong
and a half he proved too good for the remainder, decisively beating third-placed
Bois de Grace by two lengths. The Prix du Jockey-Club indicated that in the
best company Real Shadai would probably always do best ridden in an enterprising manner on account of his lack of a top-class turn of foot. This failing was
very apparent in the Grand Prix de Saint-Cloud in July; a close second to the
front-running Glint of Gold for much of the race he came under pressure fully
half a mile out and could only plug on at one pace to be third to the British horse
and Lancastrian, beaten a head and three lengths.
   The Grand Prix de Saint-Cloud did little to settle arguments about which

*Grand Prix de Deauville—a smooth win for Real Shadai
over No Attention, Oak Dancer and Karkour*

was the best three-year-old colt in France since Persepolis performed miserably back in seventh and didn't run again. Real Shadai, on the other hand, did his cause no harm whatsoever during the rest of the year and on the point of adaptability to prevailing conditions—he has good form on both firm and soft ground—he has the measure of Persepolis. The Grand Prix de Deauville provided him with a fine opportunity of gaining a valuable reward for his consistency since the conditions let him in on the basic weight for one of his age whereas the older Easter Sun, Karkour and Valentinian, three of his toughest opponents, all carried penalties. Real Shadai took full advantage of the favourable circumstances, moving through from the rear to be fourth entering the straight and finding little difficulty in seeing off No Attention by one and a half lengths after leading at the distance. Neither Easter Sun nor Valentinian did himself justice.

There haven't been more than six French three-year-old colts contesting the Prix de l'Arc de Triomphe in any year since 1978 and in the last two runnings there have been four each time. Besides Real Shadai, who started at 22/1, the others in 1982 were Bon Sang, Cadoudal and Newjdar. Real Shadai came out best of the group, running creditably without managing to make the frame and again giving the impression that a mile and a half is a minimum trip for him. Pushed along at the back almost as soon as they left the stalls, he had the best part of a dozen ahead of him with three furlongs left; well as he ran on to reach fifth place with under a furlong to travel, the first four had drawn clear and at the line Real Shadai was beaten almost five lengths by Akiyda.

	Roberto (b 1969)	Hail to Reason (br 1958)	Turn-to / Nothirdchance
Real Shadai (USA) (b.c. 1979)		Bramalea (b 1959)	Nashua / Rarelea
	Desert Vixen (br 1970)	In Reality (b 1964)	Intentionally / My Dear Girl
		Desert Trial (ch 1963)	Moslem Chief / Scotch Verdict

If Touching Wood heads Roberto's crop of three-year-olds in terms of ability, Real Shadai is undoubtedly one of the best bred on the dam's side. He is the second foal of Desert Vixen, an outstanding performer successful in thirteen of her twenty-eight starts at up to a mile and a quarter, including the Beldame Stakes (twice), Alabama Stakes and Monmouth Oaks; she was voted champion filly at both three and four. Real Shadai, a compact colt, fetched 360,000 dollars as a yearling, her yearling colt by Damascus went for 400,000 dollars at the same age and her colt foal by Northern Dancer must now be worth a small fortune. Unfortunately Desert Vixen, in foal to Lyphard, had to be destroyed in September owing to complications that set in after surgery on a twisted colon. The grandam Desert Trial, who had the rare distinction of being produced when her dam was three, won eleven races, notably the Ramona Handicap twice and Del Mar Oaks over nine furlongs; she had six other winners, the best of them the very smart miler Valid Appeal, while her five successful half-brothers and half-sisters included the Monmouth Oaks winner Kilts N

690

Kapers. Bred as he is, the consistent Real Shadai ought to be an attractive proposition as a stallion when he retires, especially if he wins another good prize or two in 1983 when he will be racing in the States with Charlie Whittingham. Whittingham, whose yard usually contains plenty of ex-European horses, trained the previous Grand Prix de Deauville winner Perrault to win several top races during 1982, and notwithstanding Real Shadai's relative lack of pace the colt could easily do well on the other side of the Atlantic. *J. Cunnington, jnr, France.*

REAR ACTION 2 br.c. Home Guard 129–Matoa (Tom Rolfe) (1982 7g 7fg 7.6v) — lengthy colt; brother to 3-y-o 1½m winner Zimbabwe, and half-brother to Prince Spruce (by Big Spruce), a fairly useful 1m to 13f winner, and to a winner in Italy; dam won twice at up to 1m in USA; no form; prominent to 2f out when remote seventh of 17 to Telephone Numbers in maiden race at Lingfield in October, third outing. *R. Smyth.*

REBELLO 2 b.c. Duc D'Orleans 76–Nina D'Oro (Jimmy Reppin 131) (1982 5d 6f) — May 2; neat colt; second foal; dam of no account; in rear in maiden race at Newcastle (last of 9) in August and minor event at Pontefract in September. *D. Smith.*

REBOLLINO 3 b.c. Nebbiolo 125–Cloe (Shantung 132) (1981 5g² 6g* 7f² **112** 5g² 1982 7fg² 8fg 7fg 8f⁴ 7fg²) 8,200Y; big, rangy colt; none too good a mover; half-brother to winning sprinter Bold Scuffle (by Bold Lad, Ire) and 2 winners in Italy; dam won at 2 yrs and 3 yrs in Italy; runner-up in Tote European Free Handicap at Newmarket in April (short head behind Match Winner) and Beeswing Stakes at Newcastle in July (beaten short head by Silly Steven), on each occasion being caught in final stride; not disgraced in between; stays 1m; yet to race on a soft surface; game and consistent. *T. Fairhurst.*

C. H. Newton Jnr Ltd's "Rebollino"

RECONQUEST 4 ch.c. Red Alert 127–La Concha (Le Levanstell 122) (1981 —
6g 6fg 6fg 6g 6s⁴ 6g³ 6d 5g 1982 6g 6fg 7f 6fg 6fg) small colt; soundly beaten
in 1982, including in a seller on final start (slowly away and tailed off); should
stay 7f; acts on any going; sometimes sweats up; sold 380 gns Ascot September
Sales. *J. Harris.*

RECORD ANSWER 3 b.f. Record Token 128–Tender Answer 80 (Prince **88**
Tenderfoot 126) (1981 5.1f 7fg⁴ 8fg⁴ 8fg 7g 1982 8.2fg 12fg* 11.7fg² 12g* 12d
12g 12g 12g* 12g) leggy, lightly-made filly; won maiden event at Hamilton in
May, minor event at Wolverhampton in June and 4-runner apprentice handicap
at Epsom in August; also ran respectably in better company on occasions,
including in Prix de Minerve at Evry and Galtres Stakes at York; stays 1½m.
R. Williams.

RECORD BREAKER 6 b.h. Jukebox 120–Bare Costs (Petition 130) (1981 —
7d 7d 7d³ 10g 8d 8g⁴ 8f 8f 7fg⁴ 7.6s 7h² 6d 6g 1982 6f 5g 7f⁴) lengthy horse;
stays 1m; seems to act on any going; blinkered once in 1980; has run well for an
apprentice. *B. McMahon.*

RECORD CLEAN 3 ch.g. Record Run 127–Maryfield (Hul a Hul 124) (1981 —
5s 5g 5g 5g 5fg 7g 1982 7g) compact gelding; bad plater; has been blinkered.
J. Mason.

RECORD DANCER 2 b.g. Dancer's Image–Treacle 85 (Hornbeam 130) (1982 **89**
8s³ 8s²) Apr 19; close-coupled, useful-looking gelding; half-brother to 3-y-o
Tequilla Sunrise (by Nonoalco) and several winners, including useful Ivory Girl
(by Sir Ivor), a winner at up to 1½m; dam, half-sister to very useful Darling
Boy, won twice at 1¼m; placed in late-season maiden events at Sandown (3
lengths third of 26 to Magic Rarity) and Leicester (length second of 21 to Rock's
Gate); will stay 1¼m; sure to win a race. *G. Pritchard-Gordon.*

RECORD HANDFUL 2 ch.c. Record Token 128–Royal Handful (Some Hand —
119) (1982 5s 6g 7f 8.2fg 5g) Mar 27; 3,300F, 8,000Y; leggy, fair sort; in rear
in maiden races and sellers; blinkered last 2 outings; sold 410 gns Doncaster
October Sales. *E. Carter.*

RECORD REVIEW 3 b.f. Record Token 128–Right View 75 (Right Tack 131) **49**
(1981 5s* 5g² 6d 8d 1982 6s 7d 7g 8g 7fg³ 8.2s) neat, strong filly; good walker;
plater nowadays; not sure to stay 1m. *W. Wharton.*

RECORD STAR 4 ch.g. Jukebox 120–St Rosalie (Aureole 132) (1981 7fg **55**
6d 6v 7f³ 9d* 10f³ 10f* 10fg* 8f³ 8fg 1982 10.1fg* 10fg² 10fg⁴ 10d 12f⁴ 8f 8fg
9g⁴ 10s² 12s) compact gelding; good walker; well-backed favourite when winning
25-runner selling handicap at Windsor in May (bought in 5,000 gns); subsequently ran creditably in non-sellers on occasions; by no means disgraced at
1½m but probably better at shorter distances; probably acts on any going; wears
blinkers; pulled too hard for his own good fourth start; sold 5,900 gns Ascot
November Sales, reportedly to race in Italy. *G. Lewis.*

RECORD TREASURE 3 ch.f. Record Token 128–Legal Treasure 46 (Quorum —
126) (1981 6s 6d 1982 6fg 8f) beaten some way in varied company, including
selling; sold 460 gns Newmarket July Sales. *J. W. Watts.*

RECORD WING 4 b.g. Record Run 127–O'Flynn (Prince Regent 129) (1981 **65**
NR 1982 10.1fg 8.3g³ 10f 7fg² 10d* 8g* 8.3fg 8.3fg⁴ 12fg³ 10s⁴ 10.2s*) plater;
has been fired; won decisively at Nottingham in June, Bath in July and Doncaster
in November; bought in first 2 occasions but attracted no bid on third; not disgraced over 1½m but best form at shorter distances; acts on a firm surface but
seems ideally suited by some give in the ground; blinkered third outing; has
worn bandages in front. *D. H. Jones.*

RED 2 ch.g. Jimmy Reppin 131–Talis 79 (Tamerlane 128) (1982 5g 7d 7.2s 7g) —
May 13; medium-sized, good-topped gelding; third living produce; half-brother
to a winning chaser; dam 2-y-o 7f winner; little worthwhile form, including in
a seller; gelded after final outing. *W. Wharton.*

REDALCO 2 b.f. Nonoalco 131–Redowa 60 (Red God 128§) (1982 6fg 6f **77**
6d³ 6s) Mar 29; good-bodied filly; half-sister to several winners, including
very smart middle-distance performer Red Regent (by Prince Regent); dam
sister to St Alphage and Yellow God; off course since July, 2 lengths third
of 22 to Foil 'Em in maiden event at Doncaster in October, best effort; will stay 7f.
J. Winter.

RED AND GOLD 3 b.g. Red Alert 127–Aucuparia (Celtic Ash) (1981 7fg⁴ —
1982 10.1fg 10f³ 13g 10g 8g 8d 10g) compact gelding; poor plater; stays 1¼m;
trained by M. Jarvis part of season. *P. Haslam.*

RED ARTIST 6 ch.g. Red Alert 127–Lane House 68 (Bounteous 125) (1981 **38**
10.2s 13fg 10d³ 10.8fg 12d 10fg 11.5d 10f³ 12fg 1982 10d 12fg⁴ 11.7fg 10.6f⁴
12fg²) neat, fair sort; plater; suited by 1½m; probably acts on any going;
blinkered sixth start in 1981; has worn bandages. *J. Perrett.*

RED CARD 3 b.g. Red Alert 127–The Game 80 (Petition 130) (1981 7g 1982 **48**
10f 13.8f 12fg 13.8f² 12f³ 10fg* 10s) tall, strong, fair sort; plater; won at Nottingham in August; stays out of J. Etherington's stable 2,300 gns afterwards; stays
1¾m; acts well on fast ground; often blinkered nowadays; suited by strong
handling. *A. Balding.*

RED CEDAR 2 b.c. Monsanto 121–Sombrilla (Big Game) (1982 5f² 5f² 5f **66**
7d 6g⁴ 5f 5g 6g 5f) May 27; 2,100F, 5,200Y; tall colt; half-brother to several
minor winners; dam never ran; plating-class maiden; showed little form, including
in valuable sellers, after fifth outing; stays 7f; often sweats up, and gives
impression of being somewhat nervous; blinkered third start, and on final
appearance hooded as well. *T. Fairhurst.*

RED CLIP 8 b.g. Double Red 122–Barnstables 72 (Pay Up) (1981 8g 10g 8f —
1982 8d 8f 8fg 5f) plater; stays 1m; has sweated up; has worn blinkers. *J.
Gilbert.*

REDDEN 4 ch.g. Red God 128§–Portden (Worden II 129) (1981 7s 7g 7.3g* **85**
7.6g 7f 7g⁴ 8.3g 10fg² 10fg 1982 8g 10s 10fg⁴ 8g 10f* 8.5f² 10f³ 10fg² 12f 10f
10f* 10g 10g 10f³ 10d) attractive, well-made gelding; won handicaps at
Brighton in May and August; stays 1¼m; needs a sound surface; has worn
blinkers, but seems better without; has worn a tongue strap. *B. Swift.*

RED DUSTER 2 br.c. Luthier 126–Maroon 92 (Roan Rocket 128) (1982 7fg) **71** p
Apr 14; tall, lengthy colt; third foal; half-brother to 1½m winner Bronze Medal
(by Jimmy Reppin); dam, daughter of smart stayer Mulberry Harbour, won
over 1½m and 2m; second favourite, ran on nicely when promising 8 lengths
sixth of 19 behind easy winner Proclaim in maiden event at Newbury in July;
will stay 1¼m; sure to improve. *R. Hern.*

RED ELLETTE 3 ch.f. Red Alert 127–Ellette 105 (Le Levanstell 122) (1981 **55**
5s³ 5d 5s 6fg² 6fg² 5f* 5fg⁴ 6fg 5fg 6g 5d 1982 7d 7f⁴ 6f³ 6fg² 6g 6g 5g 7d)
fair sort; good mover; in frame in handicaps; beaten some way in seller final
outing; stays 7f; best form on a firm surface; blinkered sixth start; sold 1,000
gns Newmarket Autumn Sales. *S. Mellor.*

REDENHAM 6 b.g. Brigadier Gerard 144–Secret Ray 114 (Privy Councillor 125) **30**
(1981 8fg 8f 9g 10g 10f 11fg 12.2g³ 1982 12f² 11f² 11fg) big gelding; poor
handicapper; stays 1½m; acts on any going, except possibly very soft; often
blinkered, but not in 1982; none too genuine; has worn a bandage on near-hind;
sold to L. Kennard 3,200 gns Ascot June Sales. *W. A. Stephenson.*

RED FANTASTIC 3 b.c. Red God 128§–Amablai (Levmoss 133) (1981 7g 7fg **66**
8g 7g 10g 1982 7fg 8.5fg 10f 11.7g 10fg 7f*(dis) 8fg² 8fg⁴ 8.3g 8.3fg) sturdy,
quite attractive colt; hung very badly right and was disqualified after winning
handicap at Sandown in June; suited by 7f and 1m; acts on firm going;
blinkered nowadays; has sweated up; trained by P. Mitchell first 6 outings. *C.
James.*

RED FIELD 4 b.c. Tudor Rhythm 112–Glebe 83 (Tacitus 124) (1981 8.2s⁴ 12d² **56**
12d³ 12g 12d³ 16f 12f 16f 13d 16s 1982 16fg² 14.6g* 18.4g* 16fg⁴ 18.1g* 16d)
strong, lengthy colt; in good form and won handicaps at Doncaster, Chester and
Yarmouth; held on in a very close finish from Dark Proposal and 2 others in a
very slowly-run race on last-named course in September; stays very well; seems
best on a sound surface; winner over hurdles. *W. Holden.*

RED FLYER 2 ch.c. Red Alert 127–Sepulchra (Luthier 126) (1982 7g 8.2fg 7g **49**
7fg) Mar 5; IR 1,900F, 3,000Y; lengthy, workmanlike colt; first foal; dam
never ran; moderate plater; best run on third outing; stays 7f; possibly requires
some give in the ground; sold 1,000 gns Newmarket Autumn Sales and sent to
Malaysia. *P. Haslam.*

RED FORT 3 ch.g. Mansingh 120–Ixia (Le Fabuleux 133) (1981 5.8g 6f 6d —
6g 1982 8f) strong, good sort; good mover; well beaten in maiden races and
and apprentice event; blinkered last 2 starts in 1981. *R. Hollinshead.*

RED GARLAND 3 gr.c. Town Crier 119–Aga Lass 75 (Agamemnon 91) (1981 —
NR 1982 11.7g) 50/1 when soon tailed off and virtually pulled up in maiden
race at Bath in August. *A. Andrews.*

REDGRAVE CREATIVE 2 b.f. Swing Easy 126–Fair Sarita 95 (King's Troop **64** 118) (1982 6g 5g⁴ 5fg 6fg² 6f³ 6g) Apr 2; 2,700Y; big, leggy filly; second foal; dam a sprinter; placed in 10-runner maiden auction event at Newcastle in July and 4-runner nursery at Redcar in August; suited by 6f; blinkered final start. *R. Whitaker.*

REDGRAVE DESIGN 2 b.f. Nebbiolo 125–Ribocana (Molvedo 137) (1982 **77** 5fg 5f³ 5g* 5d 5f 6g³ 6fg) Apr 27; 5,000 (privately); smallish, fair sort; half-sister to 2 winners, including fairly useful 5f to 7f winner Soul Singer (by Saulingo); dam won over 1¼m in Ireland; raced on possibly faster side of course when winning maiden race at Newcastle in June by 3 lengths from Mummy's Glory; 4 lengths third of 6 behind Shaves You Close in nursery at Haydock in August, best subsequent effort; suited by 6f and should stay further; often on toes in paddock and sweated up fifth and seventh starts. *R. Whitaker.*

REDGRAVE GRAPHICS 3 b.g. Welsh Saint 126–Born Friendly (Takawalk II – 125) (1981 6g 8g 5s 8s 1982 10.1fg) big, strong gelding; poor form in maiden and minor events; has worn bandages; sold 800 gns Ascot 2nd June Sales. *R. Whitaker.*

RED INJUN 3 b.c. Mill Reef 141–Ardneasken 84 (Right Royal V 135) (1981 **80** 7.2fg² 8g 1982 12f 14.7f* 18d* 17.4d) medium-sized, quite attractive colt; won maiden race at Redcar and handicap at Ripon in August; suited by a thorough test of stamina; yet to race on very soft going but acts on any other; reportedly pulled a muscle when below form final start. *C. Thornton.*

RED LADY 4 gr.f. Warpath 113–Whisky Lima 82 (Midsummer Night II 117) – (1981 8g 13g* 15.8g 16f 1982 10.2g 15.5g 13.1f⁴ 16f 15.5g² 12f) narrow, lightly-made filly; second in handicap at Folkestone in June; stays 15.5f. *M. Haynes.*

RED LANCE 3 ch.g. Red Alert 127–Shonna (Carlemont 132) (1981 6g 7g 7fg – 7fg 7fg 10s 1982 10s 16f) lengthy gelding; poor maiden; blinkered once in 1981. *Mrs J. Reavey.*

RED MINSTREL 2 b.c. Averof 123–Red Jade 82 (Red God 128§) (1982 7d **75** 7f 6fg² 7f 7f 6fg) Mar 27; 6,000Y; useful-looking colt; first foal; dam 2-y-o 5f winner; quite a modest maiden; probably stays 7f; acts on firm going; ran very freely in blinkers fourth outing; sometimes sweats up. *M. McCormack.*

RED NORTH 2 ch.c. Dublin Taxi–Aberdeen Lassie 102 (Aberdeen 109) (1982 **74** 6f 5d 6s³) May 14; 3,500F, 7,000Y; rather sparely-made, fair sort; third foal; dam won from 5f to 7f at 2 yrs; co-favourite, seemed to find 6f just beyond him when 2¾ lengths third of 22 to Blue Nantucket in seller at York in October; sold 6,200 gns Newmarket Autumn Sales. *P. Haslam.*

RED ROMAN 2 ch.f. Solinus 130–Danger Signal 106 (Red Cod 128§) (1982 **87 p** 6g 5v*) Apr 11; 52,000Y; sturdy, good-quartered, quite attractive filly; good mover; first foal; dam, speedy 2-y-o, is half-sister to dam of Roland Gardens; won 14-runner maiden race at Folkestone in October by 2 lengths from Forever Mary; probably capable of further improvement. *J. Dunlop.*

RED ROSIE 3 ch.f. Red Alert 127–Benita 94 (Roan Rocket 128) (1981 5d 5g⁴ **91** 5.3f* 6fg³ 6fg⁴ 6tg³ 5fg² 1982 6d 5fg² 5f⁴ 6f² 6f⁴) neat, quite attractive filly; sprint handicapper; second at Newmarket in July and Folkestone in August; acts on firm going; has run well for an apprentice. *R. Smyth.*

RED RUDY 2 ch.c. Red Alert 127–Riot Girl (Right Boy 137) (1982 5g* 5f 8d² **99** 6s³) May 2; IR 5,600F, IR 6,600Y; big, rangy colt; half-brother to 3 winners in Ireland, including 5f performer Meeson Girl (by Tyrant); dam Irish 11f winner; made most of running when winning 11-runner maiden race at the Curragh in May by 1½ lengths from Virginia Deer; off course 3 months after finishing 7 lengths sixth of 11 to Prince Reymo in Windsor Castle Stakes at Royal Ascot, putting up easily better subsequent effort when 5 lengths second of 6 to Danzatore in Ashford Castle Stakes at the Curragh; evidently suited by 1m; acts on a soft surface. *J. Oxx, Ireland.*

RED RUFFLES 3 ch.f. Red Alert 127–Repose (Relko 136) (1981 NR 1982 **56** 8fg 8f 9f² 10g 8.2g 7g 8g) tall, rather sparely-made filly; third living foal; dam half-sister to high-class sprinter Sammy Davis and very smart middle-distance colt Super Sam; plating-class maiden; promises to stay 1¼m; blinkered final outing; raced with head in air third start. *B. Hanbury.*

RED SANDERS 2 ch.f. Red Alert 127–Santarelle 78 (Jim French) (1982 5g **71** 5fg³ 5f 6fg 7.6v) Mar 15; IR 6,200F; neat filly; first produce; dam won twice over 1½m; 3½ lengths third of 7 finishers in minor event won by Dream Again at Goodwood in May, best effort; should stay at least 6f; off course nearly 3 months before fourth start and wore blinkers on fifth. *R. Price.*

RED SKY ROSE 2 b.f. Radetzky 123–Bridal Rose 61 (My Swanee 122) **47** (1982 5v* 5d 5g3 5f3 5f 6f 6g) May 17; small filly; second foal; dam poor on flat and over hurdles; poor plater; attracted no bid after beating sole opponent by 12 lengths at Hamilton in April; should be suited by 6f; exported to Algeria. *R. Williams.*

RED STRAND 3 ch.f. Deep Diver 134–Algue Verte (Red Vagabonde 116) **—** (1981 NR 1982 8fg 8f) 1,600Y; fifth foal; dam placed in Italy; behind in maiden race at Chepstow in August and seller at Bath in September. *D. Hanley.*

RED SUNSET 3 b.c. Red God 128§–Centre Piece 73 (Tompion) (1981 5g **120** d 5g* 5s2 6fg* 6fg 7fg2 7f3 7fg4 1982 7s4 8g 8g3 8f2 8fg 8f 7.3g) strong ex-English colt; good walker and has an excellent, smooth action; brother to very smart sprinter Greenland Park, and half-brother to a winner; dam ran 4 times at 2 yrs; excelled himself in Airlie/Coolmore Irish 2,000 Guineas at the Curragh in May, keeping on very well to be 3½ lengths third of 14 to stable-companion Dara Monarch; had earlier finished respectable 2 lengths fourth of 7 to Achieved in Tetrarch Stakes at the Curragh; well beaten in St James's Palace Stakes at Royal Ascot, Sussex Stakes at Goodwood and Hungerford Stakes at Newbury (tailed-off last) final 3 outings; suited by 1m; acted on soft going but was ideally suited by a sound surface; blinkered third to fifth outings; retired to Milford Stud, Co. Carlow, fee IR£4,500 (Oct 1st). *L. Browne, Ireland.*

RED TOFF 5 b.g. Red God 128§–Hit It Off (Hardicanute 130) (1981 12d **45** d 16g 12v 16g2 16g 16fg 16fg 14g 10f 12f 14g 10.2g 1982 10g4 12fg3 10g 10fg 10.8fg 12fg 12g3 12g 12fg 16fg 10f 12g3 10d 16d 13.8d 15.8d) strong gelding; good mover; poor handicapper; stays well; suited by top-of-the-ground; sometimes blinkered but is better without; started slowly fifth and sixth outings; sold 525 gns Ascot November Sales. *C. Austin.*

RED TUESDAY 3 ch.g. Lucky Wednesday 124–Cordon Rouge 99 (Never **—** Say Die 137) (1981 6f 7f 7fg 7g 7.6s 1982 12fg 12f 17f 16d) rangy gelding; plating-class maiden; bred to stay 1¼m+; sold to Norsk Jockey Club 680 gns Doncaster November Sales. *H. Collingridge.*

RED ZEPHYR 2 b.c. Red Alert 127–Paduia (St Paddy 133) (1982 6f 5d **—** 5d) Mar 30; 27,000Y; compact, deep-girthed colt; third foal; dam ran once in Italy; behind in sizeable fields of maidens; off course 3 months before final outing. *T. Gosling.*

REEDMACE 4 b.c. Thatch 136–Pampas Flower 80 (Pampered King 121) **71** d (1981 8fg3 8f* 10f3 8d3 8g 1982 8f* 8f3 9fg 8f2 8fg 8fg 9g) big, rangy colt; beat Wahed by a head in handicap at Redcar in May; subsequently disappointed on occasions, including when blinkered fifth and sixth starts; possibly doesn't stay 1¼m; probably acts on any going; sold 5,200 gns Newmarket Autumn Sales. *E. Weymes.*

REEF GLADE 3 b.c. Mill Reef 141–Green Glade (Correspondent) (1981 **84** NR 1982 7g3 12s2 11.7f* 12f 12f 13.1g 9fg* 9g 9d) 50,000Y; medium-sized, fair sort; brother to useful 1980 staying 2-y-o Wicked Will, subsequently a stakes-placed winner at up to 13f in USA, and half-brother to 3 winners; dam smart stakes winner at up to 9f in USA, and is half-sister to very useful Morris Dancer and Kew Gardens; landed odds in maiden race at Bath in May and made all and battled on well to win handicap at Ripon in August; stays 1½m; acts on any going. *P. Haslam.*

REEMAN 4 b.g. Star Appeal 133–Mary Morison (Ragusa 137) (1981 10fg **—** 10fg 1982 16.1s 15.8d) small gelding; showed a little ability in maiden races as a 3-y-o; sold 440 gns Ascot December Sales. *J. Wilson.*

REFRESHMENT 4 br.f. Nonoalco 131–Intermission 117 (Stage Door Johnny) **46** (1981 8fg 8fg2 1982 8fg4 8f) lengthy, quite attractive filly; very lightly-raced maiden; stays 1m; pulled hard and finished soundly beaten in blinkers final start (sweated up); sold 37,000 gns Newmarket December Sales. *J. Tree.*

REGAL GIFT 2 ch.f. Royal Smoke 113–Friendly Gift (Be Friendly 130) **—** (1982 5g 5d) Mar 13; third foal; dam never ran; well beaten late in season in maiden race (last of 12) at Wolverhampton and seller at Redcar. *R. Thompson.*

REGAL MAN 3 ch.g. Manado 130–Naiad Queen (Pampered King 121) (1981 **74**
6fg 7f 8g 1982 8.2s⁴ 8f 10g³ 12fg³) quite attractive, useful-looking gelding;
quite a modest maiden; probably stays 1½m. *M. Jarvis.*

REGAL MAY 2 b.f. Royal and Regal–Park Paddocks 92 (Hopeful Venture **—**
125) (1982 5fg 6f 7g 7fg) Apr 28; neat, lightly-made filly; poor mover; first
foal; dam won twice over 5f at 2 yrs; behind in maiden races and sellers. *P.
Rohan.*

REGAL MINNIE 3 ch.f. Royal Match 117–Hillberry Corner 70 (Atan) (1981 **49**
5fg 1982 10g⁴ 10s 10fg* 9fg⁴) sturdy filly; dropped in class when winning
seller at Chepstow in August; sold out of R. Williams' stable 1,900 gns afterwards; seems to need at least 1¼m; has given trouble at start. *D. H. Jones.*

REGAL STEEL 4 ch.c. Welsh Pageant 132–All Souls 96 (Saint Crespin III 132) **85 §**
(1981 7d 12g 9s* 10d³ 10.6s 11d* 12f³ 10fg* 10fg 10d 14g³ 12fg³ 12g³ 12v 12g
1982 12g⁴ 12f² 12fg² 12fg³ 12fg³ 12fg 12g⁴ 12fg³ 10.6g⁴ 12g 12fg⁴ 12fg⁴ 13d²
12s⁴ 14s⁴ 12g⁴ 14s⁴ 12s) compact colt; ran more consistently than in 1981
but invariably found at least one or two too good for him; stays 1¾m; acts on
any going; usually comes from behind and is suited by a strongly-run race;
none too genuine and isn't one to rely on. *R. Hollinshead.*

REGAL STEP (USA) 2 b.c. Northern Dancer–Treat Me Nobly (Vaguely **?**
Noble 140) (1982 8v*) Mar 10; $500,000Y; fourth foal; brother to French
1½m winner Faten, closely related to a winner by The Minstrel and half-brother
to another winner; dam unraced half-sister to high-class miler Be My Guest
(by Northern Dancer); justified favouritism in good style in 11-runner newcomers event at Saint-Cloud in October, coming through in straight to win
by 1½ lengths from Mr Paganini; will be suited by 1¼m+; the type to go on
to much better things; engaged in 2,000 Guineas and Derby. *F. Boutin, France.*

REGAL TOUCH 4 b.g. Royal Match 117–Msida (Majority Blue 126) (1981 **67**
8s*(dis) 7g⁴ 8d² 10g 8f 10.2fg 9d* 8v² 10.2g² 8s² 1982 12.3g² 13g* 13fg) big,
strong gelding; good walker; has a round action; ran creditably in handicaps
first 2 starts, and won at Hamilton in May; suited by 1½m+ and some give in
the ground nowadays; has run creditably in blinkers; has raced in a tongue
strap. *M. H. Easterby.*

REGENT GIRL 3 b.f. Ardoon 124–Lady Gregory (Manacle 123) (1981 **—**
5g 5f 6f 6f 5g 6d 5s 1982 8fg 8f 8f 10.2s) strong, compact filly; bad mover;
poor plater; sometimes blinkered; trained part of season by J. Doyle. *P.
Asquith.*

REGENT LEISURE 3 b.c. Undulate–Happy Families 64 (Swaps) (1981 7f **70**
1982 8fg 10f³ 8fg 11.7fg) well-made colt; quite moderate; should stay 1½m.
R. Simpson.

REGGAE 2 b.c. Gay Fandango 132–Some Dame 72 (Will Somers 114§) (1982 **85**
5fg 5f⁴ 5fg³ 5s² 5s³) May 19; 10,500Y; strong, lengthy colt; poor mover; half-
brother to a winning plater in France; dam, half-sister to very smart Espresso,
won at up to 11f; ran best races when placed in fair company at Ascot in September
and Haydock in October on last 2 outings; will be suited by 6f+; well suited
by soft ground. *R. Hannon.*

REHOBOAM 4 b.c. Mummy's Pet 125–La Mirabelle 92 (Princely Gift 137) **§§**
(1981 5d⁴ 5g⁴ 6g 9fg 8g 5g 8g 7fg⁴ 7f⁴ 6f³ 6fg² 6d⁴ 6d 1982 10g 6.5v 7.5d 6s 7fg
7f 6f 6fg 5f⁴ 6g 6fg⁴) lengthy, narrow colt; good mover; has been hobdayed;
plater; stays 7f; has been tried in blinkers; ungenuine and is one to be wary of;
sold 480 gns Newmarket Autumn Sales. *T. Craig.*

REIDOR 4 br.g. Roi Soleil 125–Bella Musica (Sing Sing 134) (1981 6s 6g 6g 7f⁴ **—**
8.2s 1982 7g⁴ 6g) compact gelding; plater; stays 7f; has raced with his tongue
tied down and has also raced in a muzzle. *W. Haigh.*

REIGN 2 gr.f. Mansingh 120–Lune Royale 77 (Sovereign Path 125) (1982 **85**
5s² 5fg* 5fg² 6f) Mar 23; 7,000Y; lengthy filly; half-sister to 3 winners, including
Irish 1975 2-y-o 6f and 7f winner Royal Vanity (by Gala Performance), subsequently successful in USA; dam showed ability at 2 yrs; won 10-runner maiden
race at Salisbury in May; had no chance off 9-7 when last of 9 in nursery on same
course in August; probably acts on any going; exported to Trinidad. *H. Candy.*

REJUVENATOR 6 bl. or br.g. Reliance II 137–Juvenescence 87 (Golden Horus **46**
123) (1981 15.8g 1982 15.8g 15f³ 20.4g* 19f⁴) strong gelding; showed

improved form when facing a thorough test of stamina in handicap at Ayr in July, beating Flying Officer by 2 lengths; rather disappointing only subsequent outing; has worn blinkers. *T. Barron.*

REKAL 4 gr.c. Busted 134–Idover 95 (Fortino II 120) (1981 12d⁴ 10d 10f* 12f **77** 10fg² 10g 11.1fg 10.2fg² 10g 1982 8g 10f* 10.4g⁴ 10fg² 8f* 8g⁴ 8d 8f* 8fg 8f 8fg 10.2g⁴ 10d) quite well-made colt; held up when winning handicaps at Leicester in April, Sandown in May (Whitsun Cup) and York in July; beat Crackhill a head in Harp Lager Handicap on last-named course; best at up to 1¼m; well suited by top-of-the-ground. *C. Brittain.*

RELATIVE EASE 11 ch.g. Great Nephew 126–Glider 83 (Buisson Ardent 129) **49** (1981 6g² 6g 5g² 6g 5f 6f 5fg 5f 5f* 5fg 5fg 5g 5d 5g 5g 5g 1982 6g³ 5d 6f⁴ 5f⁴ 5f 5fg 5g 5g 5.6f³ 5f 5g* 5fg 5d 5d 5d) sprint handicapper; inconsistent nowadays but won amateur riders handicap at Wolverhampton in July for second successive year; probably best at 5f nowadays; acts on any going but is particularly well suited by top-of-the-ground; has worn blinkers; splendid mount for an inexperienced rider; has worn a tongue strap; best on an easy course. *D. Chapman.*

RELDA 2 b. or br.f. Relko 136–Rhodie (Rasper) (1982 6f² 7f) Mar 23; well- **67** p grown filly; half-sister to numerous winners, including very smart middle-distance performers Jolly Good (by Jolly Jet) and Roscoe Blake (by Blakeney); dam a leading American 2-y-o filly; ran with promise in minor event at Yarmouth in June and maiden race (hampered start) at Newmarket in July; will be suited by 1¼m +; likely to improve. *B. Hobbs.*

RELETA 3 b.f. Relkino 131–Dereta 92 (Aggressor 130) (1981 NR 1982 — 12.2f 16d 16d) half-sister to 3 minor winners; dam stayer; poor form in maiden races, blinkered final start; sold to D. Wintle 520 gns Newmarket July Sales. *C. Brittain.*

RELIABLE VYNZ 2 b.c. Reliance II 137–Mazurka 70 (Hotfoot 126) (1982 — 8s 9s) May 29; 1,200Y; quite a useful-looking colt; first foal; dam placed over 1¾m and 2m; in rear in maiden races at Newcastle and Redcar in October. *W. Haigh.*

RELINKA 3 b.f. Reliance II 137–Darlingka 77 (Darling Boy 124) (1981 — 5fg 5fg 6f 8fg 8d 1982 8f 10f 7f 8f 12g⁴ 7fg 12fg 9f 13.8d) leggy, lightly-made, narrow filly; poor plater; trained by G. Lockerbie part of season. *D. Chapman.*

RELKILIA 3 ch.f. Relkino 131–Russellia (Red God 128§) (1981 6fg 6g 6g 6g — 6s² 5s 1982 7f 7fg 8g 7g) tall, useful-looking filly; plater; bred to stay 1¼m; acts on soft going; trained part of season by N. Callaghan; racing in Holland. *N. Tinkler.*

RELKINA (FR) 3 b.f. Relkino 131–Grizel 113 (Grey Sovereign 128§) (1981 **85** 6fg⁴ 6g 6g⁴ 1982 7d 8fg² 8fg* 8g³ 8v³) quite attractive filly; stayed on well to beat Zoiros by ½ length in 11-runner maiden race at Sandown in August; third afterwards in quite valuable events at Ascot won by Perang Tejam (handicap) and Vadrouille (Marlborough House Stakes); will be suited by 1¼m; seems to act on any going. *R. Hern.*

RELKOTINA 3 b.f. Relko 136–Tartown 89 (Gratitude 130) (1981 6fg 7g — 1982 7.6f 10f 11g 12g³ 11s 12v 10s) small, well-made filly; plating-class maiden; will be suited by further than 1½m; blinkered fifth and final starts; sold 800 gns Newmarket December Sales. *N. Guest.*

RELMAND 2 b.c. Relkino 131–On Demand 80 (Mandamus 120) (1982 7f 8fg⁴) — Mar 4; quite attractive colt; half-brother to useful miler Seasurf and to a dis-qualified winner (both by Seaepic); dam stayed 1½m; well beaten both outings, on second last of 4; sold 480 gns Newmarket Autumn Sales. *R. Hern.*

REL TIGER 3 b.g. Relkino 131–Maltese Cat 58 (Pall Mall 132) (1981 NR **90** 1982 9fg* 8f* 8f² 8fg 8f* 8fg 8g³) 7,600Y; lengthy, fair sort; not the best of movers; half-brother to several winners, including 1980 2-y-o 1m winner Rosie Black (by Roan Rocket) and fairly useful fillies Franca (by Frankincense) and Pitiless Panther (by No Mercy); dam poor performer; won newcomers event at Wolverhampton in April and handicaps at Ripon in May and Pontefract in July; will stay 1¼m; yet to race on a soft surface; genuine; sold 3,600 gns Newmarket Autumn Sales. *J. Hindley.*

RELUCTANT HERO 3 br.g. Home Guard 129–Mia Cosa 78 (Ragusa 137) **52** (1981 5g 5g³ 6f 7.2fg 1982 10f 8f 6f 7g 6g* 7fg⁴ 6fg 6g² 6g) leggy, quite useful sort; plater; springer in market, bought in 1,600 gns after narrowly winning at Ayr in July; should stay 1m; wears blinkers; sold 2,600 gns Doncaster September Sales. *J. Etherington.*

REMAINDER LINE 2 b.c. High Line 125–Farida Jinks 106 (Tudor Jinks 121) — (1982 6fg 5s) May 28; 1,300Y; strong, deep-bodied colt; half-brother to several winners, including useful 5f performers Faridina (by Sky Gipsy) and Faridetta (by Good Bond); dam 5f sprinter; behind in newcomers race at Goodwood and maiden auction event at Warwick in the autumn. *P. Mitchell.*

REMANDED 3 gr.c. Garda's Revenge 119–Farmers Daughter (Red Slipper 99 126 or Javelot 124) (1981 5g 5g 6s 7.5f 7fg 7.5f² 7f³ 7.9f* 8g 7.5d² 8d* 7d³ 1982 9s⁴ 10s 9f 16fg 12g 9g 11.5fg³ 12fg 12fg 9fg) IR 10,500F, 10,000Y; robust, useful sort; half-brother to speedy 1979 2-y-o Titauri (by Wishing Star) and 3 winners abroad; dam ran only 3 times; often raced out of his depth; close third of 11 to Affiance in Ulster Harp Derby at Down Royal in July, best effort at 3 yrs; well beaten in Queen's Vase at Royal Ascot on fourth start; unlikely to stay 2m; seems to act on any going; blinkered sixth to eighth starts. *M. O'Toole, Ireland.*

REMODEL 3 b.f. Continuation 120–Touch It Up (Trojan Monarch) (1981 — 5f 6g² 6fg² 7g 7g³ 6s 1982 6fg 6f 7f 5f 5fg 5f 7fg 6g 13.8f 12g) lightly-made filly; plater; possibly stays 1¾m; needs top-of-the-ground; sometimes blinkered; sold out of J. Hardy's stable 900 gns Doncaster June Sales after fifth start; resold 980 gns same venue in November. *W. Storey.*

REMORSELESS (USA) 2 b.c. Accipiter–Joyeux Noel (Happy New Year) 84 (1982 7g 7g³) Mar 1; $140,000Y; quite attractive, long-striding colt; second foal; half-brother to a winner; dam won 3 claiming races at up to 1m; 1½ lengths third of 13 to Rana Pratap in minor event at Brighton in September; heavily-backed favourite when fifth of 23 in maiden race won by The Fort at Newmarket on previous outing; will stay 1m; capable of winning a small race. *W. Hastings-Bass.*

RENDSLEY GIRL 3 ch.f. Hot Spark 126–Singing Girl 96 (Sing Sing 134) — (1981 5fg 6g⁴ 6fg 5s 1982 7fg 7.6fg 10g 10d 7f 10g) useful-looking filly; poor maiden; blinkered last 3 starts. *M. Masson.*

RENOVATE 5 ro.h. The Go-Between 129–Touch It Up (Trojan Monarch) 62 (1981 8d 7.2fg⁴ 7d 6g² 6d² 6g* 6f 6f 6f 6g 5d 6d⁴ 6s 5g 1982 6g 6d 6f 6fg³ 6d 6g 6f 10fg) sturdy horse; poor mover in his slower paces; close third to Broon's Secret in handicap at Nottingham in June, best effort; best at 6f though seems to stay 1m; acts on any going; often blinkered. *J. Hardy.*

REPEATER 5 br.g. Blast 125–Keep At It (Larkspur 128) (1981 NR 1982 — 12fg) temperamental novice hurdler; last of 12 behind Higham Grey in amateur riders race at Redcar in September, first outing on flat. *M. James.*

REPITCH 2 br.g. On Your Mark 125–Rosapenna (King's Leap 111) (1982 70 5g 5d⁴ 5g⁴ 6d 5.8g 5.3f 5fg² 6fg 6f² 6v) Apr 19; IR 600Y, resold 4,700Y; sturdy, compact gelding; closely related to a bumpers winner by Windjammer; strong-finishing second in valuable seller at Sandown in August and selling nursery at Brighton in September; stays 6f; suited by a firm surface; gelded after final outing. *R. Hannon.*

REPOUSSEE 3 b.f. Jimmy Reppin 131–Rose Blanche 89 (French Beige 127) — (1981 NR 1982 12f⁴) half-sister to 3 minor winners by No Mercy; dam 2-y-o 7f winner; 20/1, nearest finish when 15 lengths fourth of 12 to Dancing Sovereign in maiden race at Folkestone in July. *N. Vigors.*

REQUEST 4 b.g. Extra–Qahve Khaneh (Tenterhooks 128) (1981 NR 1982 — 16d) third reported foal; dam of little account; last of 21 in maiden race at Lingfield in June; dead. *T. Gosling.*

RESCUE 2 b.c. Kinglet 98–Haw Lass (Paniko) (1982 5g 5g 5fg) Apr 22; 39 350Y; dam won a poor point-to-point; no worthwhile form in sellers; not seen out after July; sold 460 gns Doncaster September Sales. *A. Balding.*

RESEEKER 2 ch.f. Status Seeker–Fine Mesh (Match III 135) (1982 5g 5g) Mar — 30; IR 900F, IR 3,200Y; half-sister to 3 winners, including useful 1976 Irish 2-y-o 5f and 6f winner Jeremy Fisher (by Prevailing); dam ran only 3 times; in rear in maiden races at Wolverhampton in April and Windsor in July. *M. McCourt.*

RESIDE 6 ch.g. Quayside 124–Resurgence (Runnymede 123) (1981 10.6g 10g 88 9fg 8fg² 8fg* 9fg* 8g 10.6d 9d 8f² 7g⁴ 9g 8v 1982 8f³ 8f² 9.4f* 8fg 8f* 10.6g 9g² 8d 8g 8d) strong gelding; won handicaps at Carlisle in June and Beverley in July, beating Romoss by ¾ length on latter course; ran well on several other occasions; has won over 1½m but is best at 1m or 9f nowadays; best served by a sound surface; invariably held up and often starts slowly nowadays; didn't get best of runs ninth start. *E. Carter.*

RESISTER   2 br.f. Monsanto 121–Irresistable (Siliconn 121)   (1982 5f 5d 7fg   **50** 6fg 7f³ 6g² 8.2fg)   May 13; 3,500 Y; leggy filly; second live foal; dam ran twice; poor plater; stays 7f.   *J. Berry.*

RESOLUTE MISS   3 br.f. Averof 123–Persevering 95 (Blakeney 126)   (1981   — NR   1982 12v 9s 7g)   9,200F, 11,500Y, 5,000 3-y-o; sturdy filly; first living produce; dam won 4 times at up to 2m; no sign of ability in minor events and a maiden race.   *D. Morley.*

RESTLESS CAPTAIN   4 ch.g. Sandford Lad 133–Kirkwall 74 (Sheshoon 132)   **45** (1981 9d 7d 8fg 8d 7g 9s⁴   1982 6s² 6s 8f 7f)   workmanlike gelding; good mover; second in seller at Ayr in March, only form of 1982; has run respectably over 9f but is possibly better at shorter distances; probably needs some give in the ground; blinkered second outing; sold 1,600 gns Doncaster May Sales.   *G. Richards.*

RETAINER   8 ch.g. Gay Pilot 92–Most Precious (Matador 131)   (1981 10.4s   — 1982 10.2g)   poor maiden; has worn blinkers.   *J. Leigh.*

RETORT   2 b.f. Reform 132–Hardware 86 (Hard Sauce 131)   (1982 6g 6g 6g   — 7d 6s)   Feb 29; medium-sized, fair sort; sister to useful 1977 5f and 6f winner Sarissa, and half-sister to 2 winners, including 3-y-o 1m winner Dame de Fer (by Nonoalco); dam won at up to 1m; little worthwhile form; unseated rider leaving stalls fourth outing; sold 520 gns Newmarket Autumn Sales.   *E. Weymes.*

RETSEL   3 ch.c. Scottish Rifle 127–Once For All (Quorum 126)   (1981 6d³ 6fg   **69 d** 8d 8.2s   1982 11fg 8f 8g* 8fg 10f 8s 10v)   fair sort; 50/1 when showing improved form to win handicap at Chepstow in June; should stay middle distances; suited by some give in the ground; blinkered second start.   *R. Baker.*

RETURN MATCH   2 br.c. Sweet Revenge 129–Primrose 86 (Primera 131)   **76 p** (1982 6fg)   Apr 17; IR 12,000 Y; strong, good-bodied colt; good walker; half-brother to 2 winners, notably useful 1980 2-y-o 7f winner Engulf (by Gulf Pearl); dam 2-y-o 5f winner; 20/1 and on backward side, shaped promisingly when 6½ lengths seventh of 9 to Wassl in valuable maiden race at York in June; should do better.   *J. W. Watts.*

RETURN TO ME   3 b.g. Music Boy 124–Perkasa 74 (Huntercombe 133)   **78** (1981 6g 6g   1982 5fg* 5fg* 5fg 5g 6s 5d 5s)   stocky gelding; won minor event at Thirsk in April and 5-runner handicap at Warwick in July; best at 5f on fast ground; sold to M. McCourt 8,600 gns Newmarket Autumn Sales.   *J. Toller.*

RETURN TO PARIS (FR)   2 br.f. Riverman 131–Two to Paris 124 (Sir Ribot)   **93** (1982 6f* 6g* 5fg² 6g)   Apr 20; $125,000 Y; small, rather lightly-made filly; half-sister to 2 winners in France, including 1½m winner Paris Encounter (by Green Dancer); dam, sister to very smart Riot In Paris, won Criterium des Pouliches; successful in maiden race at Nottingham in July and 19-runner minor event at Windsor in August; respectable 4 lengths sixth of 8 to Myra's Best in valuable Firth of Clyde Stakes at Ayr in September; finds 5f on the sharp side and will stay at least 1m; yet to race on a soft surface.   *H. Cecil.*

REVELS END   3 br.f. Welsh Pageant 132–Curfew 76 (Midsummer Night II 117)   — (1981 6fg 8d³   1982 9f 12fg 16.9fg)   deep-girthed, quite attractive filly; showed ability second start in 1981 but was well beaten all outings at 3 yrs; should stay middle distances; sold to M. Ryan 3,700 gns Newmarket December Sales.   *P. Walwyn.*

REVES CELESTES (USA)   3 b.f. Lyphard 132–Tobira Celeste (Ribot 142)   **82** (1981 7g   1982 8f* 8g 9fg² 9g 8f* 10f² 8d*)   small filly; won maiden race at Bath and 2 handicaps at Pontefract; stays 1¼m; yet to race on very soft going but acts on any other; sold 150,000 gns Newmarket December Sales.   *B. Hills.*

REWIRE   2 ch.f. Record Token 128–Miss Eliza 101 (Mountain Call 125)   (1982   — 5fg 5fg 6g 6fg 8fg)   Apr 15; 2,600 Y; first foal; dam stayed 1m well; little sign of ability, mainly in sellers; blinkered second start; sold 320 gns Doncaster October Sales.   *S. Matthews.*

REXRIBO   3 b.c. Riboboy 124–Expresso 76 (Roan Rocket 128)   (1981 8d 8g   **75** 1982 12fg³ 14fg 14d 12g³ 14d* 14.7fg⁴ 14g)   rangy colt; poor walker; won maiden race at Yarmouth in August; will be suited by 2m; acts on a firm and a soft surface; sold 6,200 gns Newmarket Autumn Sales.   *M. Jarvis.*

RHADI BOY 4 b.g. New Model 129–Nagaradhi (Pardal 130) (1981 5fg 7g 6g⁴ —
6f 8fg 8s 8d 1982 8g 6fg 6fg 6g 8g) big, rangy gelding; plater; blinkered
nowadays; sold 850 gns Doncaster September Sales. *D. Smith.*

RHAKI 2 ch.f. Relkino 131–Lady Rhapsody 101 (Northern Dancer) (1982 7d **64**
6fg 7.6v) Apr 28; 6,200Y; strong filly; good walker and mover; second foal;
dam won over 1m and 1¼m; 7 lengths seventh of 20 to Linklighter in maiden
race at Salisbury in September, second outing and only indication of merit;
should stay at least 1¼m; acts on a firm surface. *R. Laing.*

RHAPSODIEN 2 b.c. Habitat 134–Sweet Rhapsody (Sea-Bird II 145) (1982 **115**
6g* 8s) May 13; IR 150,000Y; third foal; half-brother to French 9f to 13f
winner Melody King (by Nonoalco); dam very smart French middle-distance
filly; odds on, put up a pleasing first effort when making all to win valuable 14-
runner newcomers race at Chantilly in September by a length from Bold
Apparel; gave weight all round when creditable 2 lengths sixth of 7 to Pluralisme
in Prix des Chenes at Longchamp later in month; may stay 1¼m; should make
a smart 3-y-o. *F. Boutin, France.*

RHEFFANOSA (FR) 3 gr.f. Rheffic 129–Zeddenosa (Zeddaan 130) (1981 NR —
1982 10s) 3,400F, 4,600Y; lengthy filly; first produce; dam French middle-
distance winner; needed run and gave trouble at start when staying-on seventh
of 18 to Whenyourtrainsgone in minor event at Leicester in November. *Miss A.
Sinclair.*

RHEINFORD 6 gr.g. Rheingold 137–Florrie Ford 79 (Kelly 122) (1981 NR **48**
1982 12s 12g⁴ 16f² 17.1f⁴ 14f 16fg³ 17.1s⁴ 16.1s⁴) staying handicapper;
evidently acts on any going; blinkered twice at 3 yrs. *J. Old.*

RHEINGOLD'S GIFT 4 b.c. Rheingold 137–Love Story 79 (Aureole 132)
(1981 10s² 12s* 12g* 12g³ 13.8fg 11.5d³ 13.8fg² 14fg 12fg 13d 16s 1982 17f 14f)
small colt; has become disappointing; suited by 1¾m; probably acts on any going;
ridden by claimer when successful; sold 620 gns Ascot December Sales. *M. Pipe.*

RHEINHEART 2 b.g. Rheingold 137–Bradden 77 (King Emperor) (1982 6f 6d **81**
7fg⁴ 6f⁴ 6d² 6fg 6fg 7s) May 8; 2,600Y; big, rangy gelding; first foal; dam won
over 1¼m and 2m; ½-length second to Swift To Conquer in minor event at
Chester in August, best effort; should be suited by 7f+ but usually races freely;
seems suited by some give in the ground; gelded after final outing. *P.
Brookshaw.*

RHEINIEKEN 5 b.g. Rheingold 137–Priddy Maid 111 (Acropolis 132) (1981 —
10g 1982 13.8f) strong gelding; well-beaten in modest maiden races; winner
over hurdles. *E. Weymes.*

RHEIN SILVER 2 b.f. Lypheor 118–Athene 64 (Supreme Court 135) (1982 7g)
Apr 30; 15,000Y; half-sister to numerous winners, notably top-class middle-
distance colt Rheingold (by Faberge II); dam ran only at 2 yrs; 33/1, prominent
to halfway in 21-runner maiden event at Newmarket in October. *B. Hanbury.*

RHEINZA 3 b.f. Rheingold 137–Royal Escape 94 (King's Bench 132) (1981 NR **66**
1982 12g² 10.4d 12d 8.2s 12s 10g⁴) small, light-framed filly; half-sister to several
winners, notably high-class miler Belmont Bay (by Auction Ring) and very
useful miler Mendi (by Gratitude); dam 2-y-o 7f winner; middle-distance maiden;
ran as though something was wrong with her when tailed-off last on second start.
B. Hanbury.

RHINE LANE (FR) 2 br.f. Rheingold 137–Double Lane (Nodouble) (1982 8v*) **?**
first foal; dam, winner over 7.5f and 1¼m in France, is out of half-sister to very
smart animals Marble Arch and Dealer's Ace; bandaged, slammed her 8
opponents in newcomers race at Maisons-Laffitte in November, winning by
6 lengths from Flower Parade; will stay 1½m; promises to make a good filly;
engaged in Oaks. *P. Lallie, France.*

RHINESTONE COWBOY 3 br.c. On Your Mark 125–Jeannette (Whistler 129) **58**
(1981 5fg 5s 5g 1982 6s 7fg 6fg 6f³ 5fg² 7f⁴ 7.6g) strong, rangy, good sort;
plating-class maiden; stays 7f; acts well on firm ground; sold 1,200 gns
Newmarket Autumn Sales. *P. K. Mitchell.*

RHOBLUSH 3 b.f. Rhodomantade 110–Tamblush 74 (Tambourin) (1981 NR —
1982 11d 13.1f 12s 12s) half-sister to a winning plater; dam stayer, also won
over hurdles; poor form, including in a seller; blinkered final start. *P. Makin.*

RHODIEMM 2 b.f. Rhodomantade 110–Taj Emma (Taj Dewan 128) (1982 6g —
7fg 6fg 8d 8s) May 3; sparely-made filly; bad plater; changed hands 210 gns
Ascot September Sales after third outing. *W. Turner.*

RHODODENDRON 3 ch.f. Warpath 113–Delphinium 93 (Tin King 126) (1981   **50**
NR 1982 7.2g 10g 9g 10fg 12s³ 11v² 12s* 12s) tall, lengthy filly; sister to 2
winners, including middle-distance winner Gunmetal Blue, and half-sister to a
winner; dam stayed 6f; plater; bought in 1,050 gns after winning at Redcar in
October; stays 1¼m; acts on soft going; sold to T. Taylor 4,100 gns Doncaster
November Sales. *C. Thornton.*

RHODOKOMOS 2 br.c. Rhodomantade 110–Comedy Flo (Comedy Star 121)   **—**
(1982 5fg 7f 7f) Apr 15; 800Y; good-topped colt; no sign of ability, including
in a Catterick seller; sold 360 gns Doncaster September Sales. *S. Matthews.*

RHODONNA 2 b.f. Rhodomantade 110–Susan 88 (Hard Tack 111§) (1982 6g   **64**
7fg 7f 6s 6s⁴ 6s) Feb 12; small, lengthy filly; half-sister to 3 winners, including
quite useful 1977 2-y-o 7f and 1m winner Suetown (by Charlottown); dam 5f
sprinter; modest plater; ran respectably in maiden events on first and final
appearances; form only at 6f; acts on soft going; blinkered fifth outing. *R.
Hannon.*

RHOECUS (FR) 3 b.c. Rheingold 137–Polly Cotton (Vaguely Noble 140) **115**
(1981 10v 1982 12d² 12d² 12g² 11g* 15g³ 12.5g 12d 8v 12v* 12s³ 11.2d⁴)
200,000 francs Y (approx £20,000); tall, quite attractive colt; second reported foal;
half-brother to smart French 4-y-o 1m to 1½m winner Thorough (by Thatch);
dam, unplaced twice in France, is half-sister to high-class Real Good Deal,
winner of Hollywood and California Derbys; runner-up in 3 maiden races at
Saint-Cloud prior to narrowly winning similar event at Chantilly in June; subsequently finished good 4 lengths third to Le Nain Jaune in Grand Prix de Paris
at Longchamp later in June and accounted for Delpour by 2 lengths in minor
event at Saint-Cloud in November; suited by a test of stamina; yet to race on
a firm surface. *A. Fabre, France.*

RHONA'S ROCKET 2 b.c. Roan Rocket 128–Bellinor (Le Levanstell 122)   **—**
(1982 7f 6f) Apr 25; 3,200Y; neat colt; half-brother to a winner in Malaya;
dam won over 1m and 1½m in Ireland; well beaten in maiden race at Newmarket
in July and seller at Nottingham in August. *P. Haslam.*

RHUS (USA) 5 b.h. Riva Ridge–Bold Pink (Bold Bidder) (1981 10fg 9d   **—**
12g³ 10fg 12d 1982 10.6s 10d 10.2s) attractive, well-made ex-French horse;
smart at 3 yrs and ran well third outing as a 4-y-o, but became disappointing;
stayed 1½m; possibly needed some give in the ground; tailed off and looked
sour in blinkers final start in 1981; sold 600 gns Ascot November Sales and is
to stand at stud in Belgium. *J. King.*

RHYMARC 2 ch.f. Rymer 121–Lady Marcia (Arctic Slave 116) (1982 5f) May   **—**
2; half-sister to winning chaser Bell Colleen (by Deep Run); dam never ran;
unquoted, prominent to past halfway in maiden race at Carlisle in April; bred to
need much further. *G. Richards.*

RHYME 2 b.g. Rymer 121–Tucute (Eastern Venture 107) (1982 7s 7g) June   **—**
8; workmanlike gelding; seventh foal; half-brother to 2 winning point-to-
pointers, including fairly useful Major Star (by Starry Halo); dam won point-to-
points; well beaten in minor events at Goodwood (last of 6) and Newmarket in
the autumn. *R. Baker.*

RHYME ROYAL 7 ch.g. Crepello 136–Lyrical 110 (Gratitude 130) (1981   **—**
10fg² 10.2g³ 12f 10.4s* 11g⁴ 9s 12g 1982 10fg) rangy gelding, who carried a lot
of condition; smart handicapper in his prime and a notably genuine one too,
winner 8 times on flat and also successful once over hurdles; needed further
than 9f and stayed 1½m; appeared to act on any going, but went very well in the
mud; was usually ridden up with leaders; dead. *R. Hern.*

RHYMING 2 b.f. Rymer 121–Dunoon Court (Dunoon Star 110) (1982 5f 5f)   **—**
Apr 22; half-sister to a winning plater over hurdles; dam novice hurdler; well
beaten in sellers at Beverley and Carlisle in May. *A. W. Jones.*

RHYTHMIC PASTIMES 2 ch.c. Dance In Time–Pass The Hat 88 (High Hat   **— p**
131) (1982 7f) Mar 22; 8,400Y; well-made, quite attractive colt; half-brother
to 3 minor winners here and abroad; dam stayed 11f; 50/1, ran on strongly
after getting well behind early on when seventh of 17 to Hasty Flirt in maiden
race at Newmarket in July; will stay 1¼m; should do better. *R. Williams.*

RHY-YAN TUDOR 3 b. or br.g. Tudor Rhythm 112–Tudor Yan 72 (Tudor   **51**
Bar 91) (1981 5g 5g 5f 7fg 7fg 7.2g 6s 1982 5v 5g² 5fg 6f 7f 7.2f 6f²(dis)
7f 6g 8g 7fg 6g 8s 6s 7s) neat gelding; plater; should stay 1m; acts on firm
going. *T. Fairhurst.*

RIBBLE ROUSER 9 ch.g. Marcus Brutus 108–Ribble Reed 75 (Bullrush 106) **50** d
(1981 15.8g 15g⁴ 15.8g 16f³ 16f³ 18f 1982 15.8g⁴ 15.8f* 16f² 16fg 15.8f 19f
15.8f⁴ 16g) staying handicapper; won at Catterick in April; acts on any going;
sometimes wears blinkers; suitable mount for an apprentice; inconsistent.
W. C. Watts.

RIBERA (FR) 3 b.f. Wittgenstein 123–Romagnola (Tenerani 135) (1981 NR —
1982 12f 14fg 16fg⁴ 16d 14f³ 14g 10g) big filly; half-sister to several winners
abroad, including French stayer No Roman (by Aureole); dam sister to Ribot;
staying maiden. L. Cumani.

RIBERION 5 ch.g. Ribston 104–Golden Pistol 69 (Goldhill 125) (1981 NR —
1982 12g) well beaten in NH Flat races and a maiden event at Newmarket
in June. M. Ryan.

RIBMIS 4 b.f. Simbir 130–Miss Parsons (Welsh Abbot 131) (1981 14fg 10s **41**
1982 8s 6g³ 8f 8fg 10f² 8.2fg³ 8fg² 10fg 11g 10f³ 10fg 10fg 8g 10g 10f) plater;
stays 1¼m; poor mover; virtually pulled up twelfth start. G. Harman.

RIBODEN 4 b.g. Ribero 126–True Dresden 58 (Vilmoray 126) (1981 10s³ —
12g 7g* 7f 7fg 8d 8s 1982 8f) plain gelding; plater; probably stays 1¼m;
in rear when blinkered final start as a 3-y-o. G. Fletcher.

RIBOT STAR 3 b.c. Star Appeal 133–Ribo Pride 77 (Ribero 126) (1981 —
7fg 7fg 7fg 10s 10.2g 1982 12d 12s⁴ 12fg 17f 14f) neat colt; good walker;
plating-class maiden; best run at 1½m on soft ground. J. Fox.

RIBY TIARA 2 b.f. Imperial Crown 96–Sudden Surrender (The Brianstan 128) —
(1982 7f) Apr 6; first foal; dam of no account; twelfth of 14 in seller at Redcar in
August. P. Rohan.

RICARDO 3 b.c. Sallust 134–Keep Going 113 (Hard Sauce 131) (1981 7fg **103**
1982 8fg* 10g² 10.5fg⁴ 12g 12fg 12fg⁴ 12s* 10v² 10s²) tall, attractive colt; has
a round action; won maiden race at Newmarket in April and handicap at Goodwood in September; made running and came again once headed to beat The Pain
Barrier by 2 lengths in latter; ran creditably in handicaps at Ascot and Sandown
last 2 starts; stays 1½m well; seems to act on any going but revels in the mud;
reared as stalls opened and was left fourth start; sold to N. Bycroft 21,000 gns
Newmarket Autumn Sales. G. Harwood.

RICH BENEFIT 2 b.f. Star Appeal 133–Grand Velvet 83 (Grand Roi 118) **83**
(1982 7d* 8d) Mar 31; compact, quite attractive filly; good walker; sister
to very smart 6f to 1¼m winner Go Leasing, and half-sister to a winner in Belgium;
dam stayed well; produced a strong burst in straight after missing break to win
14-runner maiden race at Chester in August by a short head from Darting
Groom; not disgraced in nursery at Ayr the following month; will stay 1¼m; may
be capable of improvement. J. W. Watts.

RICH LANDING 4 b.g. Communication 119–Cabarita 88 (First Landing) —
(1981 7d 1982 6g) unfurnished gelding; missed break when sixth of 14 to
Dhuard in seller at Pontefract in May. R. Cambidge.

RICHMEDE 9 gr.g. Runnymede 123–Scilly Isles 54 (Silly Season 127) (1981 —
13.3d 1982 10fg 13.3g) probably no longer of any account on flat. M.
Stephens.

RICH VIRGINIA 6 b.g. Tycoon II–Smokey Joe (My Smokey 125) (1981 12g —
1982 8f 8g⁴ 7.6fg² 8fg⁴ 8.2g 6d 7fg 7f) compact, good-quartered gelding; poor
handicapper; fifth of 18 in a seller at Haydock on fifth outing; gives impression
he'll stay beyond 1m; suitable mount for an inexperienced rider. J. Tierney.

RIDARRAGH 8 b.g. Ridan–Relegere (Relic) (1981 12g 12.2g 1982 10.6f) —
poor form, including in a seller. J. Yardley.

RIDGEFIELD 4 br.g. Firestreak 125–Chebs Lass 84 (Chebs Lad 120) (1981 **79** §
10s* 10fg² 10d² 12g 10g 12f 10fg² 1982 10d³ 10s³ 8g 12fg 11.7fg* 10fg³ 12fg
11.7g 11.7g 10d 11f³ 10.6s³ 11s) tall gelding; won handicap at Windsor
in May but often disappoints; stays 1½m; acts on any going; sometimes blinkered
and is none too genuine. D. Thom.

RIDGE HEIGHTS (USA) 2 ch.c. Riva Ridge–Wonderful Gal (The Axe **92**
115) (1982 5g⁴ 5f² 5f* 5fg⁴ 6d 6fg³ 7fg* 6d 7s⁴) Feb 23; sturdy colt; good
walker; half-brother to minor stakes winner Hattab Voladora (by Dewan);
dam, winner at up to 1m, is sister to very smart American colt Al Hattab; winner
of maiden race at Salisbury in May and of nursery at Goodwood in September;

will stay 1m; acts on any going; sweated up sixth and seventh outings; has worn a bandage on off-hind; sold German International Bloodstock 5,600 gns Newmarket Autumn Sales. *H. Candy.*

RIDGEWAY GIRL 2 ch.f. Mr Bigmore 123–Starfold (Ratification 129) (1982 7.6v 7d) Mar 30; sturdy filly; half-sister to 3 winners, including quite useful 7f and 1m winner Elf-Bolt (by Elf-Arrow); dam never ran; unquoted and backward, behind in maiden races at Lingfield and Leicester (moved badly to start) in October. *P. Burgoyne.*   —

RIENZI (FR) 3 b.c. Ben Trovato 128–Princesse Flor (Florin) (1981 8g 10v² 10s 10v* 1982 12s* 11fg³ 11g³ 15fg³ 11.5s³ 15.5v³) useful-looking colt; second foal, brother to a modest maiden; dam won over 1¼m in France; won 70,000 francs event at Saint-Cloud in March by a nose from Le Monastere; subsequently showed himself a smart colt, finishing third in 5 races at Longchamp, notably Prix Noailles (behind Persepolis), Prix de Suresnes (to Lichine), Prix de l'Esperance (behind Chem) and Prix Royal-Oak (bandaged when beaten just over 3 lengths by Denel); stays well; seems to act on any going; consistent. *P. Biancone, France.*   **122**

RIFLE SHOT 3 bl.g. Scottish Rifle 127–West Shaw 101 (Grey Sovereign 128§) (1981 5g 5f 1982 8f 10f) heavy-topped gelding; poor maiden. *A. Smith.*   —

RIGBY LANE (USA) 3 ch.c. Transworld 121–Sea Grey 91 (Sea Hawk II 131) (1981 5s 6d 6fg 7d 1982 12s 11.7g 8.5f 10d⁴ 11g⁴ 10fg 12g* 10fg* 12fg 15.5fg) quite well-made colt; plater; won at Lingfield (no bid) and Folkestone (bought in 4,200 gns) in August; stays 1½m; blinkered third start; suited by front-running tactics. *G. Lewis.*   **60**

RIGHT DANCER 2 b.f. Dance In Time–Right Mall (Pall Mall 132) (1982 5f* 6f* 6fg4) May 16; 15,500Y; big, attractive filly; good walker; third foal; half-sister to a winner in Italy; dam, closely related to Sallust, won 3 times at 3 yrs in Italy; not seen out again after finishing disappointing fourth (hanging badly left inside final 2f) in St Catherine's Stakes at Newbury in July; had revealed considerable potential earlier, winning Wilkinson Memorial Stakes at York after swerving at start, and just holding on to beat The Noble Player by short head in Chesham Stakes at Royal Ascot; has plenty of scope, and has only to learn to settle down and race smoothly to be certain of winning more races. *P. Kelleway.*   **97**

RIGHT DIAMOND 5 b.g. Right Tack 131–Garzoni (Ribot 142) (1981 12.2d 16fg 14d 12v² 12d 1982 12s 12d) good-bodied gelding; poor walker and mover; fairly useful handicapper at his best but is on the downgrade; stays 1¾m; suited by some give in the ground. *G. Balding.*   —

RIGHT REASON 3 gr.c. Morston 125–Rosy Ribbon 83 (Donore 119) (1981 NR 1982 10fg 8fg 12f 14d 13f) 6,200Y; rangy colt; half-brother to numerous winners, including useful sprinter La Rosee (by Reform); dam won over 5f and is sister to very smart sprinter Dondeen; plating-class maiden; stays 1½m. *Mrs R. Lomax.*   —

RIGHT REGENT 4 ch.c. Kambalda 108–Vetsera (Hopeful Venture 125) (1981 12d² 13.3d² 16d* 13.3g 16fg³ 16g 16s 18g 1982 18f* 18.4fg 16f* 20fg 16g) small colt; ran best races when winning handicaps at Epsom in April (Great Metropolitan) and Lingfield in June, making all and beating Karminski by 5 lengths on latter track; suited by a test of stamina; probably acts on any going. *D. Elsworth.*   **79**

RIG STEEL 2 ch.c. Welsh Pageant 132–Fir Tree 90 (Santa Claus 133) (1982 7g 8s 7s³) Apr 11; 4,400Y; strong colt; fifth foal; half-brother to a winner in Malaya; dam, half-sister to smart stayer Celtic Cone, stayed 1¾m; greatly flattered, and therefore difficult to assess, when 3½ lengths third of 6 behind very easy winner Northern Adventure in slowly-run minor event at Doncaster in November; should stay 1½m; wears a boot on near-hind. *R. Hollinshead.*   **88 ?**

RIKA MIA 3 ch.f. Cavo Doro 124–Mimika 85 (Lorenzaccio 130) (1981 8d⁴ 1982 12f 12fg⁴ 16fg 16d 12fg) strong, lengthy filly; plating-class maiden; appears not to stay 2m; sold out of C. Brittain's stable 1,800 gns Newmarket July Sales after fourth start. *D. Ringer.*   —

RIKKI TAVI 2 b.c. Monsanto 121–Goosie-Gantlet 63 (Run The Gantlet) (1982 6f 7g⁴ 8g 8s) Apr 13; fair sort; second foal; half-brother to fairly useful 3-y-o Paperetto (by Godswalk), a winner at up to 1m; dam, daughter of very useful Showdown, stayed well; quite a modest maiden; will stay 1¼m; acts on soft going. *B. Hills.*   **70**

RIMAAL 2 b.f. Averof 123–Mamzelle 85 (King's Troop 118) (1982 6fg⁴ 6fg⁴ **75**
7g⁴ 6d) Mar 12; 24,000Y; lengthy filly; closely related to fairly useful sprint
winner Nor Bars (by Sing Sing) and half-sister to numerous winners, including
smart 6f to 1m performer Gwent (by Welsh Pageant) and smart 1976 French
2-y-o Haneena (by Habitat); dam won over 5f at 2 yrs; fourth in maiden and
minor events, best effort when beaten 5 lengths by Miss Dunster at Yarmouth
in September on third outing; evidently better suited by 7f than 6f. *H. T.
Jones.*

RING BIDDER 4 b.c. Auction Ring 123–Miss Holborn (Pall Mall 132) (1981 **87**
8.5fg³ 8d⁴ 10s 8s 8.2fg* 8g³ 7g 7d² 8f 8fg² 8fg 8f 8.5fg² 8g² 8d 9s 1982 8g 7.2s
8fg⁴ 10fg 8f 7fg* 7.2f* 7fg 8fg* 8d² 7f 8fg³ 8fg⁴ 8g 8g 8f 7.3g⁴ 8g) useful sort;
fair handicapper on his day; won at Newmarket and Haydock (despite edging
badly left in front) in May, and at Ayr in June; rather disappointing on occasions;
suited by a stiff 7f or 1m (didn't stay 1¼m fourth start); acts on any going but
seems ideally suited by top-of-the-ground; does best when held up; well beaten
when blinkered once. *R. Hollinshead.*

RING OF GREATNESS 2 b.c. Great Nephew 126–Fairy Ring 91 (Quorum **95**
126) (1982 7f 8fg³ 8s* 10s⁴) May 8; compact, quite attractive colt; good walker
and mover; brother to 1¼m winner Stonehenge and half-brother to 3 winners,
including very useful miler Fair Season (by Silly Season); dam stayed 1¼m;
won 13-runner maiden race at York in October; creditable fourth behind John
French in £8,300 event at Newmarket later in the month; evidently stays 1¼m;
probably acts on any going. *J. Dunlop.*

RING THE BELL (NZ) 5 b.h. Rangong 123–Witchcraft (Mystery 125) **121 ?**
(1980/1 won 8 out of 15 starts from 7f to 1½m in Australasia 1981 8fg³ 10s 12d
1982 9fg² 10f) big, strong horse; third foal; dam won over 1m in New Zealand;
the top 3-y-o in New Zealand in 1980/1 when he earned a record NZ$217,725;
won New Zealand Derby, Alison Stakes, Avondale Champion Stakes and Avondale Guineas; also ran very well in Australia and won Canterbury Guineas;
wasn't seen to full advantage in his 3 races in Europe in 1981 and ran only twice
here in 1982; had stiffest task conceding weight all round in Earl of Sefton Stakes
at Newmarket in April and finished excellent 3 lengths second to all-the-way
winner Kalaglow, running on well without finding the pace to threaten winner;
dropped out as if something was wrong with him after helping to set a good pace
when last of 9 to Princes Gate in Westbury Stakes at Sandown later in month
(reportedly returned sound); stays 1½m well. *H. Cecil.*

RINGTINGO 3 b.g. Rustingo 94–Ringers Girl (Varano) (1981 8d 1982 **—**
8.2fg 8d 7f 9f 12.2d) workmanlike gelding; of little account; has twice worn
blinkers. *K. Bridgwater.*

RINGWAY CUTHBERT 2 b.c. Spanish Gold 101–Linloskin (Hard Sauce 131) **—**
(1982 6f 7fg 7s) Apr 5; strong, rangy colt with plenty of scope; half-brother to
a winning plater; dam of little account; behind in the autumn in minor event at
Pontefract and maiden races at Redcar. *W. Elsey.*

RIO DEVA 4 b.c. Spanish Gold 101–Deva Rose 80 (Chestergate 111) (1981 7d⁴ **65**
8g 8g³ 8.2s 9g⁴ 8f² 10fg 10f 11.5d 9g² 10f³ 10f³ 10.4s 10f 10d⁴ 8.2s 11d 10d⁴
1982 10fg* 10f² 10.4g 12f 12f⁴ 12f 12fg 10fg* 10s² 10g² 12.2fg³ 10f² 10f² 12f)
smallish colt; successful in handicaps at Nottingham in April and Beverley in
June; stays 1½m; probably acts on any going, except possibly very soft; finds
little off bridle and is probably best in a strongly-run race. *R. Hollinshead.*

RIPCORN (USA) 5 b.g. Cornish Prince–Ripit (Relko 136) (1981 10g 11.1s **—**
12fg* 12f² 12f* 12fg² 11.7g⁴ 12s 1982 15.8f 13.8f 16d) most attractive gelding;
good mover; suited by 1½m and should stay further; acts on any going. *N.
Tinkler.*

RISING FAST 5 b.g. High Line 125–Sunny Sovereign 85 (Lucky Sovereign) **—**
(1981 11s 14d 16.9s 18.8fg* 17.1d* 16g⁴ 16fg 19fg³ 19s² 17.1d² 18g 1982 16g
12.2s 12d) lengthy, good sort; staying handicapper; probably acts on any
going; usually blinkered at 4 yrs, but didn't wear them in 1982; has sweated up;
sold out of D. Elsworth's stable 740 gns Newmarket May Sales before first outing
of year. *M. Chapman.*

RISK 3 b.c. Reform 132–Doubly Sure 59 (Reliance II 137) (1981 6g 7g³ 8g³ **—**
1982 8s² 12fg 11g) elegant colt; has shown a fair measure of ability, including
when 8 lengths second to Rare Gift in 6-runner Easter Stakes at Kempton in
April, but ran moderately last 2 starts; should stay 1½m; possibly needs some
give in the ground; blinkered final outing; sold to BBA (Italia) 6,000 gns
Newmarket Autumn Sales. *P. Walwyn.*

RISK TAKER 3 b.g. Auction Ring 123–Dance Away (Red God 128§) (1981 — 6g² 7.6s² 6s* 6s* 7d³ 1982 6fg 8.2f 8d 7f 7.3g) quite attractive, short-backed gelding; has a round action; useful at his best; well beaten at 3 yrs; best form at 6f on soft going; sweated up badly fourth outing; sold to BBA 4,500 gns Newmarket Autumn Sales. *G. Harwood.*

RITARIUS 3 ch.g. Wollow 132–Mellifont (Hook Money 124) (1981 6g 1982 5fg 7f³ 7g 7fg 7d) lightly-made, fair sort; plater; will stay 1m; ran poorly when blinkered once. *C. James.*

RITSON 3 ch.g. Record Token 128–Florabette (Floribunda 136) (1981 5fg 5d — 7f 7g 8.2d 1982 8f 8d 7g) smallish, workmanlike gelding; poor plater; sold 370 gns Doncaster September Sales. *C. Spares.*

RITUAL DANCE 3 gr.f. Godswalk 130–Faith Lift (Nearctic) (1981 5g 5d 5s* 81 5g 1982 5g⁴ 5f 6f³ 6h* 6fg² 6fg⁴ 6f) neat filly; good mover; sprint handicapper; won virtually unchallenged at Haydock in June (brought wide to race alone in straight); stays 6f; acts on any going; well beaten in blinkers second start; sweated up sixth outing; sent to USA. *B. Hanbury.*

RIVAL 4 b.g. Forlorn River 124–La Magna 104 (Runnymede 123) (1981 10.1d⁴ 10.1fg 10.8fg 10g 1982 12f) compact gelding; plater; stays 1¼m; sold 2,800 gns Ascot October Sales, resold 660 gns Ascot December Sales. *W. Charles.*

RIVALRY 4 b.g. Murrayfield 119–Collina 88 (Matador 131) (1981 NR 1982 — 5fg 6fg 6g 8g) strong, good-bodied gelding; lightly-raced plater. *W. Haigh.*

RIV D'AO (FR) 2 b. or br.c. River Knight 118–Moon Song 96 (Sing Sing 134) 79 (1982 6g⁴ 6fg³ 7d 8f* 7fg 8.2s 7.5v) Apr 8; 300,000 francs Ý (approx £27,000); robust colt; half-brother to French 3-y-o 1¼m winner Moao (by Card King) and 3 other winners, including fair 7f performer Lorenzo Monaco (by Lorenzaccio); dam at her best at 2 yrs; blinkered first time, won 10-runner maiden race at Edinburgh in September by 1½ lengths from Hayman; behind in claiming race at Saint-Cloud final start; stays 1m; suited by a sound surface. *S. Norton.*

RIVELLINO 3 b.c. Rheingold 137–Nothing On (St Chad 120) (1981 NR 1982 102 8s 10s 10g* 12g² 11g* 11f⁴ 12s 14.6f) IR 13,500Ý; leggy colt; second foal; brother to fairly useful 1¼m winner Amal Naji; dam unraced half-sister to 1,000 Guineas winner Nocturnal Spree; easily won maiden race at Leopardstown in May and picked up a valuable prize when accounting for Action King by ¾ length in Grand Prix de Bruxelles at Groenendael in June; no match for winner but ran creditably to be 10 lengths second of 7 to Assert in Gallinule Stakes at the Curragh in between; stays 1½m (thirteenth of 15 to Touching Wood in St Leger when tried over further). *J. Oxx, Ireland.*

RIVENSKY 2 ch.c. Maystreak 118–Come North 72 (Track Spare 125) (1982 6d) — Mar 19; 1,800F, 3,600Ý, resold privately 3,000Ý; second living foal; dam best at up to 1m; unquoted, last of 21 in maiden race at Newmarket in October. *H. Westbrook.*

RIVERBA (FR) 2 br.f. Riverman 131–Barbotine (Tanerko 134) (1982 6.5g* 108 7g 8d²) 460,000 francs Ý (approx £41,800); third foal; half-sister to 2 winners, including 1980 2-y-o 1m winner Barbotte (by Direct Flight); dam, useful winner over 9f in France, is out of half-sister to Prix de Diane winner Barquette; won newcomers event at Evry in July by 2½ lengths; ran in pattern races afterwards, putting up better effort when strong-finishing 1½-length second of 7 to Air Distingue in Prix d'Aumale at Chantilly in September; will be suited by 1¼m; very useful. *C. Milbank, France.*

RIVER BREEZE 4 b.f. Rapid River 127–Groovy 86 (Sound Track 132) (1981 — 5fg 1982 5fg 5f 5d 5fg) poor sprinter nowadays; very lightly raced; probably unsuited by soft ground; bandaged only outing of 1981. *D. Chapman.*

RIVERHILL BOY 4 b.g. Manacle 123–My Grace (Sahib 114) (1981 8fg 12g — 10.1f 8f 8.3fg 8.3g 8.3fg 8.3g 8fg³ 7d 1982 8d) plater; stays 1m; has worn blinkers. *C. Wildman.*

RIVER ISLE 2 b.c. Rheingold 137–Salote 109 (Forli) (1982 7fg 8d) Apr 1; 80 smallish, quite well-made colt; good walker; second foal; half-brother to 3-y-o No Sale (by Nonoalco); dam suited by 1½m; second favourite, struggling from before halfway when 3½ lengths sixth of 13 to Mister Valentino in slowly-run 1m maiden race at Ayr in September; sent to France. *R. Hern.*

RIVER JORDAN 7 b.g. Crowned Prince 128–Pantoufle 86 (Panaslipper 130) — (1981 NR 1982 12d) lightly-raced maiden; stays 1¼m; has worn blinkers. *J. Scallan.*

Poule d'Essai des Pouliches, Longchamp—odds-on favourite River Lady impressively accounts for Typhoon Polly and Vidor

RIVER LADY 3 ch.f. Riverman 131–Prudent Miss 120 (Prudent II 133) (1981 **126** 6fg* 6g* 6f³ 8d² 1982 8d* 8g* 10.5v)

For obvious reasons flat racing sees many fewer horses killed in action than its sister sport over the jumps. One consequence of this is that when a fatal injury occurs the shock caused is arguably more marked, particularly when the animal involved is a good one, and there is little doubt that River Lady's accident in the Prix de Diane Hermes at Chantilly cast a grave shadow over Harbour's decisive victory in the race. Second favourite behind Harbour, River Lady had the benefit of two pacemakers and after lying fifth most of the way she moved through to lead soon after the home turn. As All Along and Harbour came to challenge her, River Lady, still travelling smoothly, suddenly faltered; in a matter of moments she came to a halt and Piggott dismounted. Whatever the cause of the accident, its result was devastating, for River Lady had fractured her pelvis and near-hind femur. Her connections made every effort to save her but with injuries so severe, plus internal haemorrhaging, the prognosis seemed hopeless and River Lady was mercifully put down at a local veterinary clinic. In a year which saw each of them enjoying notable success, this was the blackest day by far for River Lady's joint owners, Robert Sangster and Stavros Niarchos.

While talk of what might have been is seldom helpful, on the evidence of her first two starts it seems likely that River Lady would have played a big part in top fillies' races during the rest of the year had not her career been so sadly cut short. Assisted by the pacemaker Pasadoble she had toyed with her opponents in the Prix de la Grotte and the Poule d'Essai des Pouliches, both at Longchamp, starting odds on each time. In the former she beat Exclusive Order with the minimum of fuss by two and a half lengths and in the latter she led over two furlongs from home and accounted for the strong-finishing Typhoon Polly easing up by the same margin with Vidor third.

River Lady (ch.f. 1979)	Riverman (b 1969)	Never Bend (b 1960)	Nasrullah / Lalun
		River Lady (USA) (b 1963)	Prince John / Nile Lily
	Prudent Miss (b 1967)	Prudent II (ch 1959)	My Babu / Providence
		Miss Glasso (br 1961)	Ratification / Tulip II

The harshest critic would have had difficulty faulting River Lady on breeding or looks. An attractive filly, she set a record price of 1,800,000 francs as a yearling at Deauville though since her breeder Robert Sangster kept half of her this sale might have been rather misleading. Yet another top winner for her sire Riverman, whose progeny also includes Policeman, Detroit and Gold River, River Lady was a half-sister to two winners out of the very smart miler Prudent Miss, easily the better of them No Lute (by Luthier), successful in the Prix Lupin. Sharpman, Mot D'Or and Lydian also come from this family. River Lady would have stayed a mile and a quarter and seemed to act on any going; like Boutin's other good three-year-old filly Grease she had an excellent turn of foot. *F. Boutin, France.*

RIVER MAIDEN (FR) 2 b.f. Riverman 131–Naughty Marcia 97 (Connaught **83** 130) (1982 7d 7f⁴ 7f² 7d 7d² 7s) Mar 22; 84,000Y; small, well-made, very attractive filly; has a sharp action; second foal; half-sister to 1981 French 2-y-o 6f winner Harold's Girl (by Northfields); dam won over 11f and 1½m in France; beaten short head by Zariya in minor event at Catterick in October, fifth outing and best effort; will be suited by 1¼m+; capable of winning small race. *J. Dunlop.*

RIVER OF KINGS 2 b.c. Sassafras 135–Miss Bangkok (Sovereign Path 125) **85** (1982 8g 8s²) Mar 24; third foal; half-brother to 2 winning sprinters, including smart Great Eastern (by Jukebox); dam never ran; good second in maiden event at Bath in October; stays 1m; to be trained by G. Wragg; capable of winning a maiden race. *W. Hastings-Bass.*

RIVERS EDGE 4 b.g. Sharpen Up 127–Ebb and Flo 82 (Forlorn River 124) **66** (1981 6s 6fg² 7g* 7d 1982 8f 7f 8.2g² 7f⁴ 7f* 7f 8.2s* 8s³ 8.2s² 8.2s²) workmanlike gelding; won handicaps at Catterick in August and Hamilton in September; stays 1m well; acts on any going; has worn a muzzle; has been tried in blinkers; usually apprentice ridden; gave trouble at stalls at Catterick. *D. Smith.*

RIVERSIDE ARTIST 2 br.c. Ashmore 125–Sea Music 108 (Atan) (1982 **98** 5d 6g* 6f³ 7fg² 7fg* 7.3g⁴ 7d) May 13; IR 15,000F, IR 7,800Y; good-bodied colt; half-brother to several winners, including fairly useful 1m and 1¼m winner Combine Harvester and useful 9f winner Rule Britannia (both by English Prince); dam won 8 sprint races at 2 yrs; successful in 22-runner minor event at Nottingham in July and 9-runner nursery (apprentice ridden) at Epsom in August; suited by 7f; best form on a sound surface. *N. Vigors.*

RIVETTING 2 b.f. Sweet Revenge 129–No Princess (Prince Regent 129) (1982 **68** 5f 5fg⁴ 5.3fg² 6f³ 6f 6g) May 9; lengthy, full-quartered, fair sort; second foal; half-sister to 3-y-o Dick's Folly (by Martinmas); dam won over 1¼m in Ireland; placed in maiden race at Brighton in June and valuable seller at York in July; suited by 6f; yet to race on a soft surface; sent to Trinidad. *K. Brassey.*

RI-WINE 3 b. or br.f. Free State 125–My Cousins 54 (My Swallow 134) (1981 **38** 5d 5fg 6fg 5.8f* 6g 1982 6f 8fg³ 7fg 9f 8d³ 8fg 7g) small, close-coupled filly; plater; stays 1m; seems to act on any going. *P. Feilden.*

RIYAHI 3 b.c. Red God 128§–Ravela II (Tanerko 134) (1981 5g⁴ 6fg* 8g* **109** 1982 7g³ 8fg 8f 8g² 8fg 8g) strong, heavy-topped, quite attractive ex-French colt; has a round action; half-brother to several winners in France; dam, half-sister to high-class sprinter Fortino II, won at up to 13f; placed in Heron Stakes at Kempton in May and minor event at Newcastle in August; put up best effort when 4 lengths eighth of 13 to On The House in Sussex Stakes at Goodwood on third outing; suited by 1m, and will probably stay 1¼m; probably needs very strong handling (hung badly at Newcastle) and isn't one to trust implicitly; sent to India. *M. Stoute.*

RIZLA GREEN (USA) 2 b. or br.f. Iron Warrior–Sweet Molasses (Snow Fight) **59** (1982 5s² 5f 5f 5.3f) Feb 27; $27,000Y; small, rather short-backed filly; half-sister to numerous winners in USA, including a minor stakes winner; dam won at up to 1m, including claiming races; ran badly, including in a claiming event, after finishing second in maiden race at Nottingham in April; blinkered third outing; sold BBA 1,100 gns Newmarket Autumn Sales. *G. Hunter.*

ROAD TO THE TOP 2 b.f. Shirley Heights 130–Silken Way 103 (Shantung **– p** 132) (1982 6fg) Mar 30; third foal; half-sister to 3-y-o 13f winner Silk Screen (by Relkino) and very useful 1980 staying 2-y-o Silken Knot (by Nonoalco); dam, daughter of smart Boulevard, won over 1¼m from 3 starts; well-backed favourite, lost chance by dwelling but kept on nicely without being knocked about when 5 lengths sixth to Habibti in 9-runner £6,000 newcomers event at Ascot in July; sure to do much better over 1¼m or more. *R. Hern.*

ROAN MIST 4 b.g. Roan Rocket 128–Barchessa 67 (Prince Chevalier) (1981 **85** 8g 1982 7s 7fg* 8fg 7f² 8d² 10g* 8fg 10fg 10s) good-topped gelding; good mover; won handicaps at Salisbury in May and Lingfield in August, on latter course making all and beating Just Wishing by 1½ lengths; stays 1¼m; possibly not at his best on really soft going, but acts on any other. *P. Haynes.*

ROANOKE RIVER 3 ch.f. Roan Rocket 128–Warrior Queen 95 (King's Bench **77** 132) (1981 7g 8d* 1982 9.4f* 11g² 11fg* 10d 10f³ 11.5fg² 12fg 11s) big filly; middle-distance handicapper; won at Carlisle in April and Ayr in June; seems to act on any going; has run respectably for a lady rider; sold 17,500 gns Newmarket December Sales. *Sir Mark Prescott.*

ROBAND 2 br.c. Royal Smoke 113–Nushka (Tom Fool) (1982 7.6v 7g 8s) **—** June 9; big colt; half-brother to Jolly Jeff (by Merger), a winner at up to 1m in USA; dam won over 7f at 3 yrs in USA; soundly beaten in end-of-season maiden races at Lingfield and Leicester (2). *C. James.*

ROBB 3 b. or br.c. Bustino 136–Altiora 100 (Taj Dewan 128) (1981 NR 1982 — 14g 12v) medium-sized colt; good walker; fourth foal; dam won over 7f at 2 yrs; well beaten in minor event at Newmarket and maiden race at Hamilton in October. *M. Jarvis.*

ROBBOE'S PET 2 b.f. Mummy's Pet 125–Regal Trial 93 (High Treason 126) **57** (1982 5f 5f 5g³ 5fg 5fg 5s) May 10; 3,500Y; leggy filly; half-sister to 2 winners, including 1½m winner Dromderrig (by Tribal Chief); dam best at 6f and 7f; poor maiden. *J. Tierney.*

ROBERT ADAM 7 ch.g. Mansingh 120–Pritillor 93 (Privy Councillor 125) (1981 10f 1982 12d 10g³ 10fg 8g) plater; stays 1½m; acts on any going; sometimes wears blinkers; suitable mount for an inexperienced rider. *P. K. Mitchell.*

ROBERTA STAR (USA) 4 b.f. Roberto 131–Starmount Belle 110 (Nantallah) — (1981 12d 10fg⁴ 12fg⁴ 15.5s 1982 10f) leggy, fair sort; in frame in varied company; best form at up to 1¼m. *C. Brittain.*

ROBOUT (USA) 3 b.c. Full Out–Robustious (Rambunctious) (1981 5g 5.1f — 6g 7f⁴ 7fg 7f² 7s 7fg 7g* 8d 7g 1982 12g 10d) smallish, compact colt; quite modest at 2 yrs; well beaten in 2 handicaps in 1982; suited by 7f and forcing tactics; possibly not at his best on very soft going; goes well for an apprentice; blinkered 4 times in 1981; trained part of season by N. Callaghan; sold 1,600 gns Doncaster October Sales. *A. Jarvis.*

ROCAMADOUR 3 b.c. Royal Match 117–Blakeney Belle (Blakeney 126) (1981 **117** 7fg² 7g* 7v* 1982 8fg⁴ 12f 10g³ 11g³ 14.6f 13d) 7,000Y; quite attractive, full-quartered colt; second foal; half-brother to Irish 5f and 7f winner Doon Belle (by Ardoon); dam poor half-sister to smart Daring Boy and Daring March; smart colt who stayed on strongly to be about 4¾ lengths fourth to Zino in 2,000 Guineas at Newmarket in May and 5 lengths third to Kalaglow in Coral-Eclipse Stakes at Sandown in July, and ran well to be 6¾ lengths fifth of 15 to Touching Wood in St Leger in September; not disgraced when eighth of 18 to Golden Fleece in Derby and 4 lengths third to Jalmood in Mecca Bookmakers Scottish Derby at Ayr; stays 1¾m; probably acts on any going; ran in Canada final outing. *A. Pitt.*

ROCK BALLET (USA) 3 b.c. Riva Ridge–Tally Round (Round Table) (1981 **78** 8g 1982 11f 14g³ 14d⁴ 14f* 14g² 16fg 15.5fg) lengthy, attractive colt; made much of running and kept on strongly to win maiden race at Salisbury in July; stays 1¾m; acts on firm going; one paced; blinkered last 2 starts; sold 4,400 gns Ascot December Sales. *P. Walwyn.*

ROCKETONE 4 gr.c. Roan Rocket 128–Sweetstone (Honeyway 125) (1981 8d **39** 10.1d 10.1v⁴ 10.1f 10g 10.1fg 11g 8fg 10.1g³ 10.1fg³ 1982 11.1g 17.1f⁴ 15.5g⁴ 16f⁴ 16.5f) robust colt; staying maiden; ran respectably in handicaps. *J. Benstead.*

ROCKET SONG 4 gr.g. Roan Rocket 128–Our Song 70 (Song 132) (1981 9.4g* **69** 11fg* 8g² 10d³ 10fg 10.6fg* 12f³ 11d* 10.2d* 11d 1982 11fg³ 12g² 12f) fair handicapper and a most genuine one too; placed twice at Edinburgh in May; seemed to stay 1½m; acted on a firm and a soft surface; was suitable mount for an inexperienced rider; dead. *Sir Mark Prescott.*

ROCKFEST (USA) 3 ch.f. Stage Door Johnny–Rock Garden 86 (Roan Rocket **100** 128) (1981 6d³ 7fg³ 7g² 7g* 8fg* 8s² 1982 8.5f⁴ 12fg² 12fg 10g) lightly-built, attractive filly; favourite when in frame in Princess Elizabeth Stakes at Epsom in April (fourth to subsequently-demoted Mary Mitsu) and Esal Bookmakers Oaks Trial at Lingfield in May (4 lengths second to Tants); put up better subsequent effort on final start when 5 lengths fifth of 6 to Grease in Prix de la Nonette at Deauville in August; stays 1½m; acts on any going; genuine. *J. Tree.*

ROCK 'N' ROLLER (USA) 2 br.c. Marshua's Dancer–Shirley Bock (Sir Gay- **105** lord) (1982 7fg⁴ 7fg* 6.3fg² 6g² 5d²) Feb 9; $40,000Y; well-made colt; half-brother to a winner by Gummo; dam, unplaced in 4 starts, is half-sister to smart 7f stakes winner Suteki; favourite for 12-runner maiden race at Leopardstown in August and improved greatly on first effort, winning by 1½ lengths from Piccadilly Prince; second in 3 good races afterwards, namely Ballsbridge-Tattersalls Anglesey Stakes at the Curragh (beaten 2½ lengths by Caerleon, who gave 4 lb), Gimcrack Stakes at York (4 lengths behind Horage) and Goffs Stakes at the Curragh (went down by a head to Virginia Deer); effective from 5f to 7f, and should stay 1m; acts on a firm and a soft surface. *M. O'Toole, Ireland.*

ROCK'S GATE 2 b.c. Lord Gayle 124–Roxboro (Sheshoon 132) (1982 8s*) **94** ₁ Mar 14; IR 82,000Y; second living produce; brother to very useful Irish 1m to

1½m winner Aristocracy; dam Irish 1½m winner; weak in market, led 2f out and kept on well when winning 21-runner maiden race at Leicester in November by length from Record Dancer; likely to make quite a useful middle-distance performer. *J. Tree.*

ROCKY GREEN (USA) 3 b.c. Shecky Greene–Flower O'Kings (Day Court)   **43**
(1981 6d 5v 1982 6s 6s⁴ 7g 6g 7g 7f³ 7f³ 6g³ 6s 6s) strong, compact colt; plating-class maiden; suited by 7f; acts on firm going; blinkered nowadays; has run respectably for an apprentice. *P. Haslam.*

ROCKY MARRIAGE (USA) 2 b.c. Riva Ridge–Exciting Devorcee (Candy   **95 +**
Spots) (1982 7g* 7f* 7g) Feb 20; $40,000F, $60,000Y, resold 17,000 gns Y; lengthy, lightly-built colt; brother to a winner in USA and half-brother to 3 others; dam, sister to stakes winner Belle Marie, won at up to 6f; came out in July and won 2 races, maiden at Sandown and 3-runner Donnington Castle Stakes at Newbury, very easily from weak opposition; dropped away quickly in final 2f when last of 5, beaten 13 lengths, in Seaton Delaval Stakes at Newcastle in August; stays 7f; difficult to assess. *R. Price.*

RODDY 3 b.g. Gold Rod 129–Miss Dike (Dike) (1981 6d 1982 8.2g) sturdy   **—**
gelding; probably of little account. *A. W. Jones.*

RODNERS 2 b.g. Relko 136–Collateral 99 (Compensation 127) (1982 7fg   **98**
7g*(w.o.) 8g²) Apr 24; 5,000Y; quite attractive gelding; half-brother to 3 winners, including 6f to 1m winner Praiselien (by So Blessed); dam effective at 6f to 1m; walked over for Newmarket Challenge Cup in October; excellent second to Coming And Going in 19-runner minor event on same course later in the month; will stay 1¼m; promises to make useful 3-y-o. *G. Pritchard-Gordon.*

RODWELL (USA) 2 b.c. Roberto 131–Queen of the Sky (Bold Ruler) (1982   **101**
8f³ 7.5s³ 8v*) Apr 16; $150,000Y; brother to disappointing Club Class, closely related to 2 winners by Hail to Reason and half-brother to 5 others, including Heron Bay's dam Foreign Missile (by Damascus); dam unraced sister to champion 2-y-o's Bold Lad (USA) and Successor; ran well all starts, finishing ¾-length third to Allverton in newcomers race at Longchamp and to Un Monsieur in maiden event at Saint-Cloud before landing the odds by a head in 16-runner event at Maisons-Laffitte in November; engaged in Derby. *F. Mathet, France.*

ROEBUCK RUNNER 4 b.f. Maystreak 118–Rabelle (Rabirio) (1981 NR   **—**
1982 12d 16.5f) good-bodied filly; half-sister to a winning hurdler; dam moderate hurdler/chaser; behind at Beverley (amateur riders) and Redcar (maiden event) in July; still needed race on latter course. *Miss L. Siddall.*

ROESSA 3 b.f. Relkino 131–Rose Red 95 (Ballymoss 136) (1981 6fg 8s 7g   **—**
1982 8d 8f³ 8f 11.7fg 8f 8.3g³ 15.5fg 10g 12fg⁴) neat, quite attractive filly; plater; bred to stay at least 1¼m; blinkered fifth start; has worn bandages; sold 600 gns Ascot October Sales. *D. Arbuthnot.*

ROGER BACON 7 gr.g. Comedy Star 121–Tinsel 95 (Right Boy 137) (1981   **—**
5g 6.5fg 6.5s³ 7.5g⁴ 5s² 5g² 5s² 6s 6fg 6g³ 6s 5.8d 6f 6f 6g 5fg 6fg 5fg 5.8g² 5g 5s 1982 5g 5g 6g⁴ 7fg 5fg 5.8f) strong, compact gelding; carries plenty of condition; poor mover; sprint handicapper; ran respectably on occasions; acts on any going; usually wears blinkers. *Mrs B. Waring.*

ROGER NICHOLAS 3 b.g. Immortal Knight 103–Lovesome Hill 57 (Murray-   **62**
field 119) (1981 8g 7g 1982 10f 9.4f 5d 12f* 10g⁴ 12g 12.2f 10.6s 11s⁴ 13.8d) lightly-made gelding; attracted no bid after easily winning seller at Thirsk in July; not disgraced in better company on occasions afterwards; suited by 1½m; acts on any going. *J. Calvert.*

ROLLER BOY 3 b.g. Grey Ghost 98–Senior Warden 78 (Eudaemon 129)   **—**
(1981 NR 1982 10d) fourth living foal; dam won over 5f at 2 yrs and stayed well over hurdles; unquoted and backward when last of 24 to Fanny's Cove in maiden race at Ripon in August. *J. Mason.*

ROLLER END 3 ch.g. Red Alert 127–Good Court (Takawalk II 125) (1981   **47**
NR 1982 6s 8s 6g 6f 6g³) IR 6,000F, IR 6,800Y; second produce; half-brother to 1980 2-y-o 1m winner Santella Ascot (by Furry Glen); dam poor Irish maiden; well-backed favourite when third in seller at Hamilton in July; had twice shown a little ability in maiden races at Naas previously; should stay 1m; trained part of season by M. O'Toole. *J. S. Wilson.*

ROLLFAST 3 ch.f. Ragstone 128–Skiboule (Boulou) (1981 NR 1982 10f   **94**
11f 12f² 12.2f* 12.3fg* 12fg 12fg⁴ 13d² 14g⁴ 12fg²) small, lengthy filly; second foal in this country; sister to very useful middle-distance filly Rollrights; dam won in Belgium; won maiden race at Catterick and handicaps at Newcastle

and Folkestone in summer; probably stays 1¾m; yet to race on really soft going but acts on any other; has run respectably for an apprentice; reportedly swallowed tongue when below form sixth start; sold 38,000 gns Newmarket December Sales. *J. Dunlop.*

ROLLIN HAND 4 b.g. Some Hand 119–Josilu (Caliban 123) (1981 6fg 7d⁴ **55**
8s³ 7d² 7f³ 7.2f² 7g 7g 8s² 7d · 1982 6d² 7d 7f 6fg 7fg 8d* 8f 7s 6s) plater nowadays; bought in 3,100 gns after winning narrowly at Wolverhampton in August; stays 1m; acts on any going; has run well for an apprentice; blinkered third and fourth starts; taken down early nowadays; trained until after sixth start by P. Cole; sold 2,300 gns Newmarket Autumn Sales. *D. Arbuthnot.*

ROMACINA 2 b.f. Roman Warrior 132–Pilicina (Milesian 125) (1982 5f —
6g 7fg 7g) Mar 14; rangy filly with scope; half-sister to 5f and 1m winner Handy Sinner (by Some Hand); dam of little account; in rear in maiden and minor races. *P. M. Taylor.*

ROMANA MIA 3 ch.f. Roman Warrior 132–Granny Smith 76 (Tiger 125) —
(1981 NR 1982 10.1fg 12g 10g) 1,050 3-y-o; half-sister to out-and-out stayer Golden Apple (by Athens Wood); dam needed long distances; well behind in varied company. *P. Haynes.*

ROMANARD 3 ch.g. Roman Warrior 132–Tackard 87 (Hard Tack 111§) —
(1981 NR 1982 8f 8d 7g 10.6g 10g 8fg 9s) sturdy, compact gelding; poor walker; half-brother to useful 5f performer Petard (by Mummy's Pet) and a winning plater; dam 2-y-o 6f winner; beaten some way in maiden and minor events; blinkered last 3 starts. *W. C. Watts.*

ROMAN BEACH 2 b.c. Averof 123–Lovage (Linacre 133) (1982 6fg² 7f* **90**+
7d*) May 31; 700Y; well-grown colt; closely related to speedy filly Chain Lady (by Manacle) and half-brother to another winner; dam of little account; claimed out of W. Musson's stable for £3,300 after finishing promising second in seller at Yarmouth in July; improved considerably afterwards, winning 17-runner maiden auction event at Doncaster the same month by 3 lengths, and £4,300 nursery at Newcastle in August impressively by 5 lengths easing up; will stay 1m; seems to act on any going but goes very well on a soft surface; will win more races. *M. Tompkins.*

ROMAN MARINER 3 b.g. Roman Warrior 132–Another Wave (Haris II —
93) (1981 NR 1982 16.5fg 14s 15.8d) workmanlike gelding; half-brother to 2 winning jumpers; dam fair staying hurdler; well beaten in minor events in the North. *S. Norton.*

ROMAN QUEST 3 b.c. Roman Warrior 132–Miss Richton 80 (Lauso) (1981 **67**
5v⁴ 5fg³ 5g* 5f 6f* 5fg 6fg² 6fg 1982 5fg 6s* 6fg 6f 6f³ 7f 6fg 7.2g 6g 7fg³ 7.2g² 6g 8f 6g 8fg) big, useful sort; won handicap at Haydock in April; ran respectably in similar events on occasions afterwards; gives impression he needs 7f nowadays; acts on any going but put up best effort on soft; good mount for an apprentice; sometimes blinkered; didn't look entirely keen eleventh start; sold 6,600 gns Newmarket Autumn Sales and is to be trained by P. Rohan. *T. Fairhurst.*

ROMAN REALM 3 b.c. Realm 129–Breide's Wood (Le Levanstell 122) (1981 **86**
NR 1982 7fg 7g 7fg² 7g⁴ 8g*) 8,200Y; quite attractive, rather lightly-made colt; not the best of movers; half-brother to 5f winner Out of Depth (by Deep Diver); dam Irish 6f winner; well backed when easily winning maiden race at Yarmouth in September; had previously shown plenty of ability, including when creditable 3¾ lengths fourth of 9 to The Quiet Bidder in Kiveton Park Steel Stakes at Doncaster; stays 1m; yet to race on a soft surface. *W. O'Gorman.*

ROMAN RULER 3 br.c. Roman Warrior 132–Broken Blossoms (Breakspear **68**
II) (1981 NR 1982 6s 6d 6fg 5g⁴ 6f* 6f² 7g 7fg 6fg²) big, strong, good-bodied colt; half-brother to 6f and 1m winner Hard Frost (by Right Tack) and 2 winners in Italy; dam Irish middle-distance winner; tended to hang left when getting up in last stride to win maiden race at Nottingham in July; twice ran creditably afterwards; suited by 6f (soundly beaten over further); acts on firm going; gives impression he'll always be best with strong handling. *W. Wightman.*

ROMANTIC KNIGHT 2 b.c. Immortal Knight 103–Young Romance (King's **79**
Troop 118) (1982 5f³ 5f² 6g² 6g) Jan 20; leggy, narrow colt; third foal; dam pulled up only outing; placed in maiden and minor races, being caught on line and beaten a short head by Auburn Hill at Thirsk in July on third start; off course 2 months afterwards; should stay 1m. *M. H. Easterby.*

ROMANTIKI (USA)   2 b.f. Romeo or Giboulee–Dodge Me (The Doge) (1982   — p
7g)   June 1; $200,000Y; half-sister to numerous winners in USA, 4 of stakes,
including Barely Even (by Creme dela Creme), a high-class filly at up to 1m;
dam won 5.5f stakes race at 2 yrs; weak 14/1 chance, showed up well for nearly
5f in £4,500 event won by Salvinia at Newbury in September; sure to improve.
H. Candy.

ROMANY BOY   2 b.g. Continuation 120–Mia Chico (Royal Palm 131) (1982   **51**
5f 5f² 5f⁴)   May 11; smallish, strong gelding; in frame in sellers at Beverley
and Redcar in May. *J. Hardy.*

ROMMEL'S STAR   4 gr.g. Arratos–Slavissima (Sea Hawk II 131) (1981   —
8f³ 9f 11.5g 12g³ 12f* 10g* 16d* 12g* 1982 12g 12g 16g)   strong ex-Irish
gelding; second foal; half-brother to a winner in Germany and to 3-y-o 1m and
1¼m winner Bold Hawk (by Bold Lad, Ire); dam never ran; won maiden race
at Clonmel and handicaps at Listowel (2) and Thurles in the space of a
fortnight in 1981 when trained by L. Browne; well beaten in small race at
Pontefract and well-contested events at Lingfield and York over here; effective
at middle distances and stays 2m; acts on firm going and a soft surface; has
won for an apprentice. *A. Jarvis.*

ROMOSS   4 ch.g. Royal Match 117–Pamela Rose 107 (Vilmorin) (1981 8g²   **75**
8d³ 10.2f4 10fg* 10fg 9f 10.5f4 10fg² 11fg 10d   1982 8g 8g² 8fg 8f 8f* 8f* 9.4f
9fg 8fg4 8g* 8f² 8fg³ 9g³ 8d4 10.2g 10d³ 8s² 7s 8s)   strong, rangy gelding;
waited with when winning handicaps at Beverley and Thirsk in May and at
Thirsk again in July; good 4 lengths second to Rajhaan when having very
stiff task in minor event at York in October on seventeenth start; ran a few
moderate races however; stays 1¼m; probably acts on any going; has a fair
turn of foot. *R. Whitaker.*

ROMSAL   3 ch.g. Roman Warrior 132–Salambos (Doon 124) (1981 7g 1982   —
9g 11g)   useful sort; behind in maiden races and a minor event; sold 4,000 gns
Doncaster October Sales. *H. Bell.*

RONAN'S CABLES   2 b.g. Dublin Taxi–Sweet Sauce (High Perch 126) (1982   **83**
5g 5fg 6f* 6g 5fg² 5f 7f² 6fg4 7d 7s³ 7s)   Apr 27; 1,500Y; robust, close-coupled
gelding; half-brother to fair 1978 2-y-o 5f winner Sweetboy (by Richboy); dam
poor plater; showed much improved form when winning maiden auction event at
Epsom in June; put up best subsequent efforts when placed in minor event at
Windsor and nurseries at Brighton and Leicester; stays 7f; acts on any going;
ran poorly in blinkers final outing; gelded afterwards; inconsistent. *R. Hannon.*

RONNIYA   2 b.c. Home Guard 129–Palace Rose 88 (Aureole 132) (1982   —
6fg 7g)   Mar 30; good sort; good walker; half-brother to very useful 3-y-o
Palace Gold (by Rheingold); dam won over 1½m; 33/1, behind in big fields
at Newmarket in August and October. *R. Armstrong.*

RONSHOPE   2 br.c. Sayfar 116–Miss Cornwall 69 (Brother 116) (1982 6g)   —
Mar 23; sixth foal; dam poor half-sister to smart jumper Soloning; unquoted,
in rear in 22-runner minor event at Nottingham in July. *W. Barrett.*

RONYSOL   3 b. or br.g. Solar Topic 97–Peach Fair (Lord of Verona 120) (1981   —
NR 1982 10.2g 14.6fg)   half-brother to 9f winner Josmoll (by Golden Mallard);
dam apparently of little account; in rear in maiden races at Doncaster in June
and July. *K. Stone.*

ROODEYE   3 b.c. Porto Bello 118–Deva Rose 80 (Chestergate 111) (1981   —
NR 1982 6s 7f 8.2fg 9.4fg 10fg 12.2f 12fg)   3,000Y; good-bodied colt; second
foal; half-brother to 1¼m winner Rio Deva (by Spanish Gold); dam won 4 times
over 5f; well beaten in varied company. *R. Hollinshead.*

ROPPA   2 b.c. Hotfoot 126–Cake Popper 103 (Connaught 130) (1982 6f³   **68**
6g 6fg4 7d 7f)   Mar 23; lightly-made colt; first foal; dam won from 6f to 1½m;
quite a moderate maiden; should stay 1¼m; trained by D. Ringer first 2 outings;
changed hands 1,050 gns Newmarket Autumn Sales; sent to Italy. *C. Brittain.*

RORKE'S SUN   3 b.g. No Loiterer 90–Julie's Dream (Bleep-Bleep 134) (1981   —
NR 1982 8fg 9g 8d)   behind in maiden races and a seller in the Midlands.
J. Smith.

ROSACEAE   3 b.f. Sagaro 133–Floradora Do 85 (Derring-Do 131) (1981 5d   **99**
6fg² 1982 10d² 10.2f* 12fg* 12d* 13.3f4 12g 12g 14.6g4 12v)   strong filly;
won handicaps at Bath, Lingfield and Salisbury; also ran well when blinkered
on eighth start, staying on to be 2½ lengths fourth of 6 to Swiftfoot in Park
Hill Stakes at Doncaster; suited by 1¾m; possibly unsuited by very soft going
but acts on any other. *I. Balding.*

711

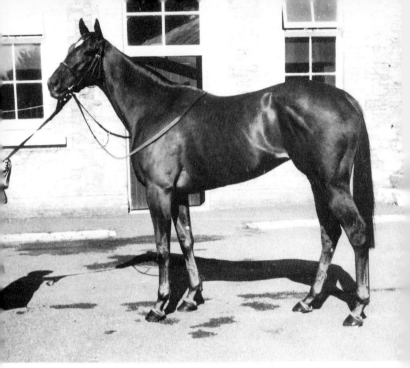

Mr R. More O'Ferrall's "Rosananti"

ROSAGORE 2 ch.g. Bay Express 132–Monjenayr (Jukebox 120) (1982 **63**
5d² 5d³ 5fg 5f 5fg 5g 5f 5fg⁴ 5d 6d 5v 5d) May 30; lengthy, rather unfurnished
gelding; placed in early-season maiden events but is a moderate plater on
balance of form, and was well beaten in sellers (one a nursery) on last 2 outings;
acts on a soft surface. *B. Richmond.*

ROSANANTI 3 ch.f. Blushing Groom 131–Clarina (Klairon 131) (1981 **107**
6fg 6fg² 6fg* 6d* 7s² 1982 7d² 8g* 11g² 12fg³ 9fg) quite attractive, well-
made filly; half-sister to 2 winners, including good English and German performer Claddagh (by Bold Lad, Ire); dam won twice over 1¼m in Ireland;
came with strong run to beat Ilenia by 2½ lengths in Premio Regina Elena
(Italian 1,000 Guineas) at Rome in April; placed most other starts, going down
by 2 lengths to Rose of Montreaux in Salisbury 1,000 Guineas Trial and by a
length to Ilenia in Oaks d'Italia at Milan, and making up a deal of ground in
straight without looking like troubling principals when 6 lengths third of 10
to Swiftfoot in Irish Guinness Oaks at the Curragh in July; stays 1½m; acts
on any going; usually held up. *J. Dunlop.*

ROSA REEF 2 b.f. Take a Reef 127–Daisy Harvey (Calpurnius 122) (1982 **—**
7fg 6g) May 1; first live foal; dam never ran; behind in maiden races at
Yarmouth in August and September. *C. Spares.*

ROSE CHARTER 5 gr.g. Runnymede 123–Tavel (Tabriz 111) (1981 5s **47**
5s 7d 6g 12f* 10f² 1982 12f 13g 12f 11g⁴ 12g 12fg² 13fg² 12f 12.2f 12g 13.8d)
strong gelding; middle-distance handicapper; acts on any going; ran moderately
in blinkers once at 3 yrs. *W. Bentley.*

ROSE DU SOIR (USA) 3 ch.f. Dewan–Pembroke Lane (Olden Times) **88**
(1981 7f⁴ 6g² 6g² 1982 6g 6g 6fg² 8f* 8f³ 8g* 10fg* 10g* 10g) lengthy, quite
attractive filly; won handicaps at Yarmouth (2), Goodwood and Ascot; quickened
well to beat Brady comfortably by 2½ lengths in £5,800 event on last-named
in September; stays 1¼m; acts on firm going; sweated up second start; has
a good turn of foot. *J. Hindley.*

ROSEFOX 5 ch.m. Owen Anthony 102–Sovereign Bracelet (Manacle 123) —
(1981 7f 10f 8f 8.3fg 8.3d 1982 10.1fg) small, quite well-made mare; poor
plater; has worn blinkers. *M. Bradley.*

ROSE GERARD 2 br.f. Brigadier Gerard 144–Sombreuil 95 (Bold Lad, Ire —
133) (1982 6g 8f 6g) Mar 30; first foal; dam best at 1m; little worthwhile form
in maiden and minor events. *H. O'Neill.*

ROSE GLOW 2 ch.f. Moulton 128–Blakewood 75 (Blakeney 126) (1982 5d **70**
7fg 7f² 8.2fg³ 8fg* 8.2d* 8.2v) Mar 21; small filly; first foal; dam winning
stayer; attracted no bid after winning 16-runner selling nursery at Beverley
and 17-runner seller at Nottingham in September; stays well; best form on soft
surface; veered right across course when ridden by 7-lb claimer on second
start. *J. Fitzgerald.*

ROSEMORE 3 ch.f. Ashmore 125–Rosenkavalier 89 (Vienna 127) (1981 —
NR 1982 10s² 12g⁴ 12g³ 14fg⁴ 16f 13g 16v 12s⁴) IR 2,800F, 500Y, resold
1,850 2-y-o (privately); ex-English filly; half-sister to 2 winners, including
fair 1974 2-y-o 7f winner Rofrano (by Wolver Hollow); dam, daughter of Irish
1,000 Guineas winner Northern Gleam, won over 1½m in Ireland; in frame in
maiden races and a handicap; should stay 1¾m; blinkered penultimate start;
trained by R. Simpson first outing. *J. Bolger, Ireland.*

ROSE OF MONTREAUX 3 ch.f. Habat 127–Gliding 94 (Tudor Melody **109**
129) (1981 6d³ 1982 7d* 8.5f³ 8fg⁴ 8f 7fg³) 15,000Y; rangy, robust filly;

Mr F. N. Sahadi's "Rose of Montreaux"

did well over the winter; second foal; half-sister to useful 7f and 8.5f winner Bay Street (by Grundy); dam, winning sprinter, is half-sister to very smart 1973 2-y-o Splashing; made much of running and stayed on well to beat Rosananti comfortably by 2 lengths in Salisbury 1,000 Guineas Trial in April; ran well next 2 starts to be in frame in Princess Elizabeth Stakes at Epsom (didn't seem suited by track when 1¾ lengths third of 9 to subsequently-demoted Mary Mitsu) and Coronation Stakes at Royal Ascot (4½ lengths fourth of 8 to Chalon); stays 1m; seems to act on any going. *P. Cole.*

ROSE OF THE NORTH 2 b.f. Sparkler 130–Twinkling Toes 70 (Prince Tenderfoot 126) (1982 6g 6fg 7.2g 6d 7g 8.2s) Mar 19; 650Y; lengthy filly; poor walker; first foal; dam ran only 3 times; bad maiden. *R. Ward.* —

ROSETTA STONE 4 ch.f. Guillaume Tell 121–Lady Clodagh 113 (Tyrone 130) (1981 11s⁴ 14s* 12d² 13g³ 16.1d² 14.6g 16g 1982 16.1s 12.3g) lengthy filly; has a rather round action; fair performer as a 3-y-o; ran only twice in 1982, better effort on first outing; suited by a test of stamina; acts on soft going. *G. Pritchard-Gordon.* —

ROSIER 3 br.f. Hotfoot 126–Pink Sky 86 (Midsummer Night II 117) (1981 6fg* 6g 6fg* 6f² 6g 1982 8.5fg 8f⁴ 9fg) lengthy, good-quartered, attractive filly; fairly useful at her best; had stiff tasks at 3 yrs; will stay 1¼m; yet to race on a soft surface. *B. Hobbs.* —

ROSIE'S SECRET 5 b. or br.g. Most Secret 119–Rose Palm 73 (Bleep-Bleep 134) (1981 NR 1982 8f 10fg³ 10f³) fair sort; plater; stays 1¼m; probably acts on any going, but has shown most of his form when there's been some give in ground; sometimes has his tongue tied down; sold out of A. Smith's stable 2,200 gns Doncaster June Sales after second outing and to G. Lockerbie 1,600 gns Doncaster September Sales after his next. *R. Whitaker.* —

ROSNI 3 b. or br.f. Blakeney 126–Dash On 93 (Klairon 131) (1981 7fg 1982 10f³) workmanlike filly; kept on to be under a length third of 9 to Orange Tip in maiden race at Yarmouth in August; will be suited by 1½m+; sold 28,000 gns Newmarket December Sales. *H. Cecil.* 66

ROSSETT 3 ch.g. Jukebox 120–Flo Kelly (Florescence 120) (1981 6g 1982 6g 8fg 8fg* 8f 8g⁴ 7.6g² 8f 7.6d⁴ 8.2g 8g 8.2s³ 8d³) fair sort; won maiden race at Warwick in May; ran respectably in handicaps several times afterwards; suited by 1m; probably acts on any going; sold to T. Craig 6,000 gns Newmarket Autumn Sales. *J. Toller.* 70

ROSSETTI (FR) 2 b.f. Bolkonski 134–Contarini Fleming 68 (Abdos 134) (1982 5fg 6s) well-made, quite attractive filly; third foal; dam second over 1½m at 4 yrs; not seen out until September, running better race when 10 lengths sixth of 11 behind Khaizaraan in 6f Blue Seal Stakes at Ascot; will be better suited by 7f+; may improve. *B. Hills.* 75

ROSTRA 3 b.f. Legal Eagle 126–Oca (O'Grady) (1981 5fg 1982 6g) compact filly; in mid-division in maiden races at Windsor and Newmarket. *M. Smyly.* —

ROTHERLEIGH 2 b.c. Workboy 123–Pickwood Sue 74 (Right Boy 137) (1982 5f* 5fg⁴ 5d) Apr 23; leggy, quite useful-looking colt; second foal; dam 5f winner; won 9-runner minor event at Beverley in May by 5 lengths at 33/1; not raced after July. *J. Leigh.* 71

ROUAULT 4 b.c. Wollow 132–Rossellina (Tenerani 135) (1981 10s 10d 10v 1982 10.1g 16s) tall, lightly-made colt; has a badly enlarged off-fore knee; behind in varied races; bandaged final start as a 3-y-o. *D. Arbuthnot.* —

ROUGH PATH 3 ch.f. Warpath 113–Groovy 86 (Sound Track 132) (1981 6g 5.8h 5fg 7g 1982 7g 10g) poor plater; sold 400 gns Ascot August Sales. *O. Brennan.* —

ROUND AGAIN 2 b.g. Decoy Boy 129–Shilly Shally 89 (Sallymount 125) (1982 5d 5g³ 5.8g 6d 6s) Apr 15; half-brother to 2 winners, including fair middle-distance winner Equivocal (by I Say); dam ran only 3 times; quite a modest maiden; off course for almost 3 months after third outing, and showed little worthwhile form on return; stays 5.8f. *A. Turnell.* 78

ROUND TOWER 3 b.f. High Top 131–Circlet 97 (Baldric II 131) (1981 6fg 8fg 7g 1982 12fg² 10.6g* 10.1fg* 11.7d²) quite attractive, lengthy filly; won maiden race at Haydock and minor event at Windsor (odds on) in August; also ran well on reappearance in Lupe Stakes at Goodwood, making running and only being worn down in last furlong when beaten 2 lengths by stable-companion Height of Fashion; stays 1½m. *R. Hern.* 93

ROUTE MARCH 3 ch.g. Queen's Hussar 124–Wide Of The Mark 91 (Gulf —
Pearl 117) (1981 NR 1982 11.7f) second foal; half-brother to 6f winner
Audacity (by Zeddaan); dam 1¼m winner; remote fifth of 11 to Mubarak of
Kuwait in maiden race at Bath in April; sold 800 gns Ascot July Sales. *R. Hern.*

ROWLEY'S MISTRESS 3 b.f. Free State 125–Kirmidian (Bold Bidder) —
(1981 6s 1982 12fg) smallish, good-topped filly; in rear in maiden races;
sold 10,500 gns Newmarket July Sales and has been sent to USA. *G. Hunter.*

ROYABER 6 ch.g. Sandford Lad 133–Honeymoon II (Ballymoss 136) (1981 77
8fg 7g* 7fg⁴ 7f³ 7fg³ 7g² 7fg 7fg³ 8fg⁴ 8fg³ 7g³ 7s 8s⁴ 7d 1982 8d 8f 7fg 7fg³
8.5f⁴ 7f⁴ 8d* 8g³ 8.3fg* 8fg 10g³ 8fg² 8f* 8g³ 10g) big, strong gelding; won
handicaps at Salisbury, Windsor and Newmarket, on last-named course in
August getting up well inside last furlong when beating Precis by a neck;
probably stays 1¼m; acts on any going; consistent; sold to D. H. Jones 7,000 gns
Ascot December Sales. *J. Benstead.*

ROYAL AGAMEMNON 3 gr. or ro.c. Royal Palace 131–Abergrove 103 —
(Abernant 142) (1981 6g 6g 1982 8g 6fg 6fg 5fg) robust colt; well beaten in
varied company; blinkered final start. *A. Pitt.*

ROYAL AGNES 3 ch.f. Royal Palace 131–Omnia 80 (Hill Clown) (1981 68
6fg⁴ 7 2d³ 7fg⁴ 6d 1982 10f 10f 12.2f 12v² 14s* 12g⁴) sturdy filly; comfortably
won maiden race at Sandown in October; suited by 1¾m; acts well on soft
going. *G. Pritchard-Gordon.*

ROYAL AND LOYAL 4 ch.g. Queen's Hussar 124–Lake of the Woods (Never 55
Say Die 137) (1981 7g 8f 8fg 11.5d 14g² 16.5g* 16.1s² 16s 1982 16s 17.1f³
16d 14s³ 18d⁴ 16d 16.1s) compact gelding; staying handicapper; acts on any
going; wears blinkers; sold 1,800 gns Newmarket Autumn Sales. *E. Eldin.*

ROYAL BAIZE 4 b.g. Supreme Sovereign 119–Green Velvet (Epaulette 125) —
(1981 8.2s⁴ 10fg* 12g³ 12g 12.3fg⁴ 13.8g* 16f 13.8fg* 12fg 12fg* 13s⁴ 1982 14f)
lightly-made, quite attractive gelding; good walker; won 4 times as a 3-y-o;
needed race only outing of 1982 (August); stays 1¾m; best form on a sound
surface. *J. Baker.*

ROYAL BRIGADIER 2 ch.c. Brigadier Gerard 144–Royal Pancake 104 77 p
(Crepello 136) (1982 6d 6f) Apr 10; 3,300Y; deep-girthed colt; half-brother to
a winner in Norway; dam won Pretty Polly Stakes; shaped encouragingly when
sixth in good-class events at Salisbury in June and August; will stay 1¼m;
likely to improve. *G. Balding.*

ROYAL BROXTED 3 ch.g. Broxted 120–Smokey Princess 83 (My Smokey 75
125) (1981 6s 6g 1982 8f 8f 7fg 7g² 8fg* 8fg 7.2g* 7.6d³ 9d 8fg² 8d* 8.2s)
lengthy non-thoroughbred gelding; won handicaps at Wolverhampton in July,
Haydock in August and Ayr in September; stays 1m; acts on a firm and a soft
surface; goes well for apprentice J. McLean; has sweated up. *A. W. Jones.*

ROYAL CARNIVAL 3 b.f. Carnival Dancer 113–Royal Escapade 87 (Galivanter —
131) (1981 5f 6fg* 7f 8d 1982 9f 13.8f) lightly-made filly; plater; promises
to stay 1¼m. *W. A. Stephenson.*

ROYAL CHALLENGE 3 ch.c. Gracious Melody 117–Smooth River (Forlorn —
River 124) (1981 NR 1982 10d) first foal; dam well beaten over hurdles;
100/1 when tailed-off last in minor event won by My Maravilla at Nottingham
in September. *R. Ward.*

ROYAL CONDOR 2 b.f. Moulton 128–Condora 99 (Matador 131) (1982 —
7d) Apr 25; 1,100F; half-sister to a winner in France and a winning hurdler;
dam won 4 times over 6f; unquoted, behind in 18-runner maiden race at Leicester
in October. *J. Spearing.*

ROYAL DAUGHTER 2 b.f. High Top 131–Pirate Queen 77 (Pirate King 129) —
(1982 7d) Apr 15; strong, deep-girthed filly; closely related to fairly useful
1¼m winner General Custer (by Derring-Do) and half-sister to 2 winners, notably
Goodwood Cup winner Tug of War (by Reliance II); dam placed over 7f at 2
yrs; unquoted and decidedly burly, in rear in 15-runner maiden race at Leicester
in October. *D. Whelan.*

ROYAL DIPLOMAT 3 ch.g. The Go-Between 129–Grace (Gratitude 130) 67
(1981 6fg 6s 6d 5.8g* 6fg 5s² 6s* 6s² 6s²(dis) 1982 6d 5d⁴ 6fg 5g 6g 6g³ 5g* 6fg
5fg 5s 5s* 6s³ 5s) attractive gelding; sprint handicapper; won at Newbury in
August (from stable-companion Copper Beeches) and York in October (from
Fairgreen); has won on firm going but seems much better with some give underfoot; suitable mount for an apprentice. *J. Holt.*

ROYAL DUTY 4 b.g. Import 127–Lunar Queen 96 (Queen's Hussar 124) **72**
(1981 5g 6f⁴ 5f 8f⁴ 7fg² 7f* 7d 7f 7f 7g 1982 7f 7fg* 6f* 6f 6g* 7g⁴ 6f 7f) lengthy
gelding; good mover; won handicaps at Beverley in June and Pontefract in
July and August; needs a stiffish track when racing over 6f and stays 7f; probably acts on any going, but is well suited by firm; sometimes blinkered; ridden
by apprentice P. Eddery on every occasion when successful. *E. Weymes.*

ROYAL EXPORT 2 b.f. Import 127–Rivachet (Forlorn River 124) (1982 **55**
5f³ 7g² 6f* 5g⁴) Mar 17; lightly-made filly; first foal; dam never ran; won
13-runner seller at Nottingham (no bid) in August by 1½ lengths from Lovable
Clown; modest fourth in nursery at Beverley the following month; probably
needs further than 5f and stays 7f; has shown a tendency to hang. *W. C. Watts.*

ROYAL FIRST 3 b.f. Royal Match 117–January 68 (Aggressor 130) (1981 **58**
5s 5s 5g³ 5d 7g² 6d* 7f 1982 8fg 10.2f³ 8g 8d 7f 8g 7f 10g) quite
modest at her best; well beaten in seller final start; possibly stays 1¼m; suited
by some give in the ground; sold to Norsk Jockey Club 880 gns Doncaster
November Sales. *C. Spares.*

ROYAL GALA 4 b.f. Royal Palace 131–Sweet Alyssum (Gala Performance) —
(1981 5d 7f 1982 6fg 6f 8f 8fg) neat filly; lightly raced and no sign of ability,
including in sellers; sometimes blinkered; dwelt second outing. *L. Barratt.*

ROYAL GLOW 3 ch.g. Royal Match 117–Morning Glow (Grey Dawn II 132) —
(1981 5s 7fg 1982 11g 8.3fg) plain gelding; in rear in varied company,
including selling; sold 625 gns Ascot August Sales. *M. McCourt.*

ROYAL GRANT 3 b.f. Royalty 130–Gold Pension 76 (Compensation 127) **62**
(1981 5s² 5g² 6f 6d 1982 8.2v* 9.4f 7g 6g³ 7fg 6fg⁴ 6g 8.2g 6g) lightly-made
filly; won maiden race at Hamilton in April; soundly beaten in seller final start;
stays 1m well; ideally suited by some give in the ground; sold to M. Cousins
1,000 gns Doncaster October Sales. *W. H. H. Williams.*

ROYAL HERITAGE (FR) 4 b.g. Welsh Pageant 132–Escorial 110 (Royal **46**
Palace 131) (1981 8d 8f 1982 8.2fg 8fg 10f 10d 11s³ 12s⁴ 8s) lengthy gelding;
ran best races since 1980 when in frame in handicaps at Hamilton in September
and Haydock in October; stays 1½m; acts on any going. *E. Incisa.*

ROYAL HEROINE 2 br.f. Lypheor 118–My Sierra Leone (Relko 136) (1982 **116**
6g⁴ 6f* 6fg* 6g²)
In view of the ever-increasing popularity of the Northern Dancer sire line
the Baroda Stud must have had some regrets that they sold their young stallion
Lypheor, a grandson of Northern Dancer, to Japan after only one season; the
more so now that Lypheor's first runners have reached the racecourse. Lypheor's
runners include the Newmarket winner Tolomeo, a highly-regarded colt who
looks sure to make a smart three-year-old, and Royal Heroine, one of the best
two-year-old fillies in England. Royal Heroine, a tall, good-quartered filly,
first looked something out of the ordinary when winning the twenty-runner
Princess Maiden Stakes at Newmarket in July. She showed a splendid turn
of foot in the final furlong, quickening away in a few strides to win easily by

*Princess Margaret Stakes, Ascot—a clear win for Royal Heroine
over Henry's Secret (rails), Bright Crocus
and Fenny Rough*

three lengths from Montrevie. Better still was to follow in the Princess Margaret Stakes at Ascot later in July when she came up against the unbeaten Henry's Secret, fresh from a good win in the St Catherine's Stakes, and the useful Bright Crocus. After tracking Bright Crocus from the start she drew alongside coming to the last furlong and forged steadily clear to win by two and a half lengths. Henry's Secret got up close home to pip Bright Crocus for second. Even allowing for the fact that she was receiving 3 lb from both placed horses, this performance established Royal Heroine as one of the best juvenile fillies, and soon afterwards she was sold out of Mick Ryan's stable for a 'six-figure sum'. Her new owner, Robert Sangster, sent her to be trained by Michael Stoute who had trained the 1981 Princess Margaret Stakes winner Circus Ring. Circus Ring had gone on to success in the Lowther Stakes at York's August meeting and Royal Heroine was made favourite to do the same. She proved unequal to the task but nonetheless ran well, going down by a length and a half to Habibti after looking very dangerous at the distance, and she comfortably accounted for those useful fillies Annie Edge, Myra's Best, Henry's Secret and Carolside. Like Habibti Royal Heroine hadn't been entered for the Cheveley Park; the Lowther turned out to be her last race.

		Lyphard	Northern Dancer
	Lypheor	(b 1969)	Goofed
	(b 1975)	Klaizia	Sing Sing
Royal Heroine		(b 1965)	Klainia
(br.f. May 12, 1980)		Relko	Tanerko
	My Sierra Leone	(b 1960)	Relance III
	(ch 1971)	Smeralda	Grey Sovereign
		(gr 1966)	Brilliant Stone

Although Royal Heroine's races so far have all been over six furlongs (and all on a sound surface come to that), she's sure to stay further. Her connections considered it worthwhile entering her in the Oaks as well as the Guineas. A mile will suit her but whether she'll stay further is impossible to say at this stage. When assessing the stamina potential of her useful half-sister Betsy Red, a daughter of the mile to mile-and-a-half performer Mount Hagen, we confidently predicted that she would stay a mile and a quarter; she proved us wrong, and gained all her three successes as a three-year-old over six furlongs. Betsy Red and Royal Heroine, the first two living foals of My Sierra Leone, were both inexpensive yearlings, costing 3,200 guineas and 5,600 guineas respectively, and My Sierra Leone, at 2,800 guineas, was also a cheap yearling. My Sierra Leone finished behind in both her races, maiden events over seven furlongs and a mile, but she was quite a well-bred filly, the product of two very different types of animal, the Derby winner Relko and the useful sprinter Smeralda who reached the frame in those competitive handicaps, the Great St Wilfrid and the Portland. Among Smeralda's five winners are the three-year-old Jorge Miguel and the French filly Swing Is Back, both successful over a mile and a quarter, and the French mile winner Brittany who spent several years at stud over here. The next dam Brilliant Stone won the Blue Seal Stakes. Royal Heroine, already the best winner produced by the family in recent generations, looks certain to add to her achievements at three. She could well run into a place in the Guineas. *M. Stoute.*

ROYAL HOBBIT 4 b.c. Habitat 134–Royal Danseuse 111 (Prince Chevalier) **112** (1981 5v* 5d* 5g2 5d3 5s* 5s4 5f 5fg 5g 1982 5s2 5g* 5f4 5d* 5f 5g 5fg4 5g4) hollow-backed Irish colt; half-brother to several winners, including smart middle-distance performer Bog Road (by Busted); dam won Irish 1,000 Guineas; won handicap at Navan in April (by 4 lengths from Princess Seal a length) and Stackallen Stakes at the Curragh in July (beat Princess Seal a length); showed good speed throughout when less than 2 lengths fourth of 13 behind Mummy's Game in Temple Stakes at Sandown in between; best form at 5f, but not disgraced over further; acts on any going, but has won only when there's been some give in the ground; blinkered nowadays; consistent (hampered when well beaten at Goodwood fifth start). *S. McGrath, Ireland.*

ROYAL HOME 3 ch.f. Royal Palace 131–Home Fire 99 (Firestreak 125) **69** (1981 7g 6g 1982 8d3 8fg 10.2g 9fg* 9g) useful-looking, good sort; readily won modest maiden race at Newcastle in July; promises to stay 1¼m; blinkered last 2 starts; sold to M. Ryan 1,650 gns Newmarket December Sales. *J. Dunlop.*

ROYAL INSIGHT (USA) 3 ch.c. Majestic Prince–Foresight (Forli) (1981 **78** 8g 1982 11f 10f2 10fg 12fg* 10g 12fg2 12g 12d* 12.2d2) attractive colt;

not the best of movers; decisively won maiden race at Beverley in August and apprentice race at Pontefract in October; suited by 1½m; seems to act on any going; ran badly in blinkers third start; has run respectably for an amateur rider; goes well on courses with an uphill finish; sold 16,000 gns Newmarket Autumn Sales. *M. Stoute.*

ROYAL INVITATION 3 ch.f. Be My Guest 126–Supremely Royal (Crowned **75** Prince 128) (1981 5fg 5f 5f³ 6fg* 6d⁴ 6g 1982 8.2d 8f² 10.2f* 8g 7g³ 8g⁴) small, fair sort: quite a modest handicapper; impressively won 4-runner event at Doncaster in May; needs further than 7f and stays 1¼m; seems to act on any going but goes particularly well on firm; has sweated up; sold 15,000 gns Newmarket December Sales and sent to France. *L. Cumani.*

ROYAL KINGDOM 5 b.h. Saritamer 130–Derring May (Derring-Do 131) — (1981 6s 6fg 6g 6fg 5.8f 6d* 6g³ 6g 6s 1982 6f 5g 6fg 6fg 5.8f 6v 6s) small, strong horse; sprint handicapper; stays 6f; seems ideally suited by some give in the ground; has worn blinkers; sold 700 gns Newmarket Autumn Sales, probably for export to Scandinavia. *M. Smyly.*

ROYAL LYNN 2 ch.f. Runnymede 123–Royal Bit (King's Troop 118) (1982 — 5fg 5fg 6fg 5s) Mar 10; plain filly; sister to a winning plater and half-sister to a winner; dam never ran; well behind in maiden races. *P. Kearney.*

ROYAL MARINE (USA) 3 b.g. Hoist the Flag–Nijana (Nijinsky 138) (1981 **64** NR 1982 11.7f 15fg³ 16d 16.9fg 16g³) tall, plain gelding; first foal; dam smart stakes winner at up to 1m at 2, 3 and 4 yrs; staying maiden; dead. *I. Balding.*

ROYAL MERLIN 3 gr.g. Young Emperor 133–Magic Lady (Gala Performance) — (1981 5d 7d 6g 1982 7f 10fg 6g 7.6d 9s) close-coupled gelding; well beaten in varied company. *D. Hanley.*

ROYAL NECKLACE 3 b.f. Royal and Regal–Daisy Chain 103 (Darius 129) **67** (1981 6g 1982 7g 10g 8.3fg) quite attractive, well-made filly; has shown some ability in varied races; gives impression she'll stay beyond 1¼m. *G. Lewis.*

ROYAL OPPORTUNITY 2 b.g. Royal Palace 131–La Mome 109 (Princely — Gift 137) (1982 7g) Apr 29; 1,500F; robust gelding; half-brother to fairly useful 5f to 10.2f winner La Lutine (by My Swallow) and winners in Italy and Sweden; dam stayed 1¼m; unquoted and in need of race, always behind in 15-runner maiden event at Leicester in October. *M. McCourt.*

ROYAL POWER 5 b.g. Runnymede 123–Alangia 101 (Shantung 132) (1981 — 12g 9s 12d 1982 11fg) neat gelding; little worthwhile form in varied company, including selling; blinkered only outing of 1982. *G. Richards.*

ROYAL QUESTION 3 ch.f. Grey Ghost 99–Royal Raintree (Royal Duet) **65** (1981 6f* 6f 6fg 5f 1982 6g 5fg⁴ 5g 5fg* 5fg³ 5f* 6g* 5g 5s) neat non-thorough-bred filly; plater; attracted no bid after winning at Redcar in June; subsequently ran well in better company, winning handicaps at Nottingham and Hamilton; stays 6f; best form on a sound surface; has run creditably for an apprentice. *T. Barron.*

ROYAL REALM (USA) 4 ch.f. Blood Royal 129–Tomboy Tamele (Verbatim) — (1981 10.6s³ 12fg³ 12f* 12f² 12f* 12g 12f* 14.6g⁴ 1982 12fg⁴) strong, fair sort; won 3 times as a 3-y-o and was in frame in Lancashire Oaks and Park Hill Stakes; needed run and was unsuited by slow pace when fourth of 5 behind Alvor in £3,700 event at Beverley in June (sweated up); had a minor setback afterwards and wasn't seen out again; stayed well; acted on any going but was very well suited by firm; genuine; stud. *S. Norton.*

ROYAL RENDEVOUZ 3 b.c. Artaius 129–Ruta (Ratification 129) (1981 **103** 6f* 7fg⁴ 1982 7s 8fg 12g 10fg 9f³ 9fg² 10fg 8g⁴ 8s) attractive colt; put up best effort when going down by a neck to Punctilio in Pacemaker International Whitehall Stakes at Leopardstown in September; soundly beaten in Group 1 races second (2,000 Guineas), third and seventh starts; should stay 1¼m+; probably needs a sound surface; has had tongue tied down. *T. Curtin, Ireland.*

ROYAL REVENGE 3 ch.g. Sweet Revenge 129–Charley's Aunt 80 (Will **81 §** Somers 114§) (1981 5v* 5d² 5d² 5f³ 7fg 6s 1982 6g 6f 6f⁴ 8g* 7fg⁴ 8g 8d 8.2s 8s 10s⁴) rangy, good sort; excellent mover; won handicap at Ayr in June; stays 1¼m; ideally suited by some give in the ground; blinkered nowadays; didn't seem suited by Catterick track third outing; inconsistent; sold 4,400 gns Newmarket Autumn Sales. *E. Weymes.*

ROYAL REX 6 b.h. Royal Prerogative 119–Ballynulta 91 (Djebel) (1981   **52**
10d* 10.4g⁴ 10v⁴ 10f 9fg 10g 10.2g 12d 1982 10d² 10fg 10f 10.6h 10fg⁴ 10g
12fg 12.3fg⁴ 12.2fg² 12fg) small horse; middle-distance handicapper; ran
creditably on occasions but was always struggling in a valuable seller fourth
start; seems to act on any going; occasionally blinkered. *J. Tierney.*

ROYAL RHAPSODY 3 b.f. Royal Palace 131–Lady Rhapsody 101 (Northern   **57**
Dancer) (1981 7fg 8g 1982 12.2g⁴ 11fg² 11g 10fg 10.2g) small filly; middle-
distance handicapper; yet to race on a soft surface; often blinkered; has shown
a tendency to hang; sold out of J. W. Watts's stable 1,550 gns Newmarket
May Sales after second outing. *W. Stubbs.*

ROYAL TALK 3 b. or br.f. Royal Smoke 113–Diamond Talk (Counsel 118)   —
(1981 5f 5.8h 5g 7g 1982 8f 6f) behind in varied company. *J. Bosley.*

ROYAL TROUPER 3 b.g. Comedy Star 121–Dancing Class 75 (Compensation   **77**
127) (1981 5s 6g⁴ 6g 1982 6f 7d³ 7f² 7fg⁴ 7fg* 7s² 8g³) big, rangy gelding;
good mover; won maiden race at Epsom in August; ran creditably in 2 handicaps
afterwards; acts on any going. *A. Hide.*

ROYALTY MISS 3 b. or br.f. Royalty 130–Blue Delphinium 75 (Quorum   —
126) (1981 5fg 5f 1982 16fg 10fg 12fg 15.5v) of little account. *A. Neaves.*

ROYAL VALEUR 2 b.c. English Prince 129–Valeur (Val de Loir 133) (1982   **91**
6fg* 6d⁴ 6d² 6g) Apr 2; IR 6,800Y; tall, useful-looking colt; first foal; dam
second over 10.5f in France; won 7-runner maiden race at Ayr in July; beaten
head by Fair Madame in 12-runner minor event at Catterick 2 months later;
will be suited by 7f and 1m; acts on a firm and a soft surface. *A. Jarvis.*

ROYAL WRITER 3 b.g. Lochnager 132–Pronuba (Sica Boy 132) (1981   —
5fg 5fg 6fg 7g 5s 1982 6d 7d 7fg 6g 5g) lengthy gelding; of little account;
trained part of season by A. Pitt; sold 700 gns Newmarket Autumn Sales. *J.
Berry.*

ROYLSUN 2 br.c. Royalty 130–Sunbird 103 (Tudor Melody 129) (1982 8g)   —
May 26; narrow, unimpressive colt; third foal; dam, 2-y-o 6f winner, stayed 1m;
20/1, tailed off in 19-runner minor event at Newmarket in October. *M. Jarvis.*

ROYSIA BOY 2 b.g. African Sky 124–For Keeps 57 (Track Spare 125) (1982   —
6g) May 28; workmanlike gelding; third foal; dam, placed over 1m and 1½m,
is sister to very smart Record Run; 12/1, no show in 20-runner maiden race at
Newmarket in October. *G. Pritchard-Gordon.*

RUBABAY 2 b.g. Bay Express 132–Rubella (Buisson Ardent 129) (1982 6s)   —
Mar 21; 14,000Y; half-brother to numerous sprint winners, including speedy
1975 2-y-o Alacriter (by Mountain Call); dam ran once; beaten some way in
16-runner minor event at Lingfield in September; retained 1,400 gns Newmarket
Autumn Sales and subsequently gelded. *H. Candy.*

RUBBER GLOVES 3 b.g. Some Hand 119–Galosh 86 (Pandofell 132) (1981   —
NR 1982 8fg 10.2g) big, strong gelding; half-brother to 3 winners, including
very useful 5f to 1m winner Silly Prices (by Silly Season); dam needed long
distances; backward when in rear in maiden races at York and Doncaster in
June; sold 4,000 gns Doncaster August Sales. *W. Elsey.*

RUBBINO 3 b.g. Red Alert 127–Lucasta (High Hat 131) (1981 6f 8.2d 10.2g   **61**
1982 8g 10s 10g² 11fg 12.2f*) plater; has a round action; won in good style
at Catterick in April; sold 2,800 gns afterwards, reportedly for export to Sweden;
stays 1½m; has worn blinkers; sometimes sweats up. *S. Norton.*

RUBLINK 3 ch.c. Swing Easy 126–Femme Fatale 67 (King's Leap 111) (1981   **64**
5fg 5g² 1982 7d 7g 7g 7g 6g⁴ 6fg² 6fg² 6d* 6g 6s) plater nowadays; bought
in 1,450 gns after winning at Windsor in September; not certain to stay 7f;
acts on a firm and a soft surface; effective with or without blinkers; has run
creditably for an apprentice; sold, probably for export to Italy, 3,400 gns
Newmarket Autumn Sales. *C. Nelson.*

RUBY AND SAPPHIRE 3 b.c. Manado 130–Festal 72 (Alcide 136) (1981   —
7f 8s⁴ 1982 8g 12f⁴ 12f 13g³ 16.9fg 13d 12g 12d) rangy colt; staying maiden;
beaten in valuable seller final start; suited by some give in the ground; usually
blinkered nowadays; sold 2,500 gns Newmarket Autumn Sales. *E. Eldin.*

RUBYLINE 3 b.f. Silly Season 127–Jewel Tower 91 (Double-U-Jay 120)   —
(1981 5d 5s 5d 6d 1982 8d 6f 8g 10f 7g 7.6g 6g 6g 7g) leggy, unfurnished
filly; poor plater; sometimes blinkered; dead. *K. Bridgwater.*

RUBY RED DRESS 5 b.m. Sparkler 130–Red Cape 84 (Matador 131) (1981 **45**
12s³ 12g* 13g² 12g² 11fg⁴ 13fg² 12.3s 11fg 12d² 12g² 1982 12.3g 12g* 12f
12s 12fg³ 12f³ 10g⁴ 9g 11f) big, well-made mare; made all in small handicap
at Edinburgh in May; stays 13f; probably acts on any going; suitable
mount for an apprentice. *M. Camacho.*

RUBY RIVER 3 ch.f. Red God 128§–River Craft (Reliance II 137) (1981 —
NR 1982 8g) 5,200 2-y-o; third foal; half-sister to 1979 Irish 2-y-o 5f winner
Private Craft (by Private Walk); dam, sister to very smart 1m and 1¼m winner
Rymer, was last on only start; 12/1 when behind in 16-runner maiden race
won by King's Holt at Edinburgh in October. *R. Williams.*

RUCKLEY 2 b.g. Free State 125–Avahra 108 (Sahib 114) (1982 8.2fg 7fg) —
May 9; brother to 3-y-o 11f and 13f winner Savahra, and half-brother to fairly
useful sprinter Pavahra (by Mummy's Pet); dam stayed 6f; well beaten in
September in seller (slowly away) at Haydock and maiden race at Redcar.
P. Rohan.

RUDOLFINA 3 b.f. Pharly 130–Rojanya (Petingo 135) (1981 NR 1982 **120**
10.5d² 10s* 12s⁴ 10g* 9d² 10g) fourth foal; half-sister to 3 winners in France,
including useful middle-distance performer Rubino (by Gyr); dam never ran;
won maiden race at Longchamp in May and minor event on same course in
June; beat Doubling Time by ¼ length in latter; also ran well to be ¾-length
second to Grease in Prix Chloe at Evry in July; probably stays 1½m; yet to
race on a firm surface. *J. C. Cunnington, France.*

RUDRY PARK 3 gr.f. Blue Cashmere 129–Lenana (Never Say Die 137) (1981 —
5s 5s 6f 6f⁴ 6d 6fg 8g 1982 10h 7fg 8f 8fg 9f) lengthy filly; plater; probably
stays 1m; has worn blinkers; pulls hard; retained 800 gns Doncaster October
Sales. *D. H. Jones.*

RUEDIGER 2 b.c. Radetzky 123–Settebello (Hul a Hul 124) (1982 7d 7g —
7fg 7fg) Feb 17; 8,600F; robust, stocky colt; second produce; dam never ran;
behind in maiden and minor events; blinkered final outing; sold 620 gns
Newmarket Autumn Sales and sent to Holland. *C. Brittain.*

RUFFORD LINE 3 b.c. High Line 125–Thorganby Bella (Porto Bello 118) —
(1981 7fg 7g⁴ 7fg 6fg 6fg 7fg 8d 10.2g 1982 10d 11g⁴ 12fg³ 12f 12g 17fg 12f
10f 9f) lightly-made colt; plater; stays 1½m; blinkered twice at 2 yrs; has
worn bandages; sold 340 gns Doncaster October Sales. *R. Hobson.*

RUFFO (USA) 3 b.c. Riva Ridge–Brave Lady (Herbager 136) (1981 7fg³ **72**
8d 1982 6g 7.6f³ 7d³ 8s³ 8s) big, rangy colt; has a capped hock; none too
good a walker or mover; third in maiden races and a handicap in the South;
bred to stay middle distances; acts on any going; blinkered final start; sold
6,000 gns Newmarket Autumn Sales. *R. Price.*

RUKOTSO 3 b.g. Gay Pilot 92–Impatience (Kibenka 119) (1981 NR 1982 —
14fg 16.5fg) compact gelding; third foal; half-brother to a winner over hurdles;
dam of little account; well beaten in maiden race at Haydock and minor event
at Redcar in September. *W. Wharton.*

RULA HULER (USA) 2 b.c. Chieftain–Native Go Go (Raise A Native) (1982 **78** p
7g⁴ 6fg) Apr 11; $37,000Y; big, rangy, good sort; brother to a placed animal
in USA and to 3-y-o Hula Ruler, a fairly useful 7f winner at 2 yrs; dam, very
useful 2-y-o, won at up to 1m; showed ability in maiden race at Yarmouth
and minor event at Newmarket in August, on latter course sticking on well
when 5 lengths fifth of 21 behind Coquito's Friend; has plenty of scope and should
win a small race. *L. Cumani.*

RUMASA 4 b.g. Lochnager 132–Sparkling Jewel (Faberge II 121) (1981 NR —
1982 8s 9f 12f) big gelding; poor maiden; probably stays 1m. *T. Barnes.*

RUMMELD 3 br.f. Meldrum 112–Ivory Coast 90 (Poaching 115) (1981 5fg⁴ **54**
1982 6fg⁴ 6fg) compact, fair sort; sprint maiden; pulled up lame final start;
dead. *D. Chapman.*

RUMPLETEAZER 2 ch.f. Mount Hagen 127–Caerinion 76 (Royal Palace 131) **65**
(1982 5fg² 5f 6fg 7g 8fg) May 9; IR 12,500Y; rather lightly-made, sharp sort;
good walker; second foal; dam, daughter of 1,000 Guineas winner Caergwrle,
was placed over 1m; showed no form after finishing second in maiden race at
Newbury in April; should stay at least 1m; sold Mrs G. Forbes 2,000 gns
Newmarket December Sales. *G. Hunter.*

RUMPOLE 3 b.g. Mandamus 120–Thunder Bay 64 (Canisbay 120) (1981 6fg 7fg 1982 8d 8g 11.7f 8fg) good-topped individual; behind in varied company; trained part of season by M. Blanshard. *F. Walwyn.* —

RUM RIVER 2 b.f. Forlorn River 124–Gilead 90 (Quorum 126) (1982 6g) May 24; fifth foal; half-sister to a winner in Holland; dam, a plater, placed at up to 9f; unquoted, behind in 20-runner maiden race at Yarmouth in September. *D. Ringer.* —

RUMZ 2 ch.c. Gay Fandango 132–Double Eagle 71 (Goldhill 125) (1982 6fg 6g⁴ 5f² 5d³ 6g 6g²) May 15; IR 19,000Y; workmanlike colt; half-brother to 3 winners, including useful Irish sprinters Flaming Eagle (by Green God) and Do The Hustle (by Sun Prince); dam won 5f seller at 2 yrs; ridden by 7-lb claimer, beaten head by Captivating Lady in 12-runner nursery at Newmarket in October, final outing and best effort; stays 6f; suited by a sound surface. *N. Callaghan.* 91

RUNAROUND SUE 3 b.f. Porto Bello 118–Fair Camilla 81 (Tiger 125) (1981 6f 5.3f² 6fg* 6g 1982 6f 7g 6f³ 7g 5fg 6fg) workmanlike filly; plater; best at 6f; acts on firm going; sold 660 gns Newmarket Autumn Sales. *P. Cole.* 45

RUNASCA 2 b.f. Runnymede 123–Nasca 81 (King's Bench 132) (1982 5f 5f⁴ 5f⁴ 5fg⁴ 5d 6d 5d) May 31; small filly; half-sister to several winners, including useful 5f performer Superb Lady (by Marcus Superbus); dam won 5.8f seller at 2 yrs; poor plater; off course over 3 months after fifth outing; acts on firm going. *Mrs M. Nesbitt.* 49

RUN DEEP 6 b.g. Deep Run 119–Tilly 64 (Le Levanstell 122) (1981 12g 12s² 17.1d 14.6f 16g⁴ 18.8fg 1982 15.5fg) smallish gelding; plater on flat; stays well; acts on soft going; soundly beaten in blinkers only outing of 1982. *D. Gandolfo.* —

RUN HARD 7 b.g. Run The Gantlet–Isola D'Asti 106 (Court Harwell 130) (1981 18.4d⁴ 16.9s² 16s³ 16fg 1982 16g 12g 13.3f⁴ 13.1f²) quite a modest handicapper; stays well; acts on any going; sometimes bandaged in front; sold 9,600 gns Ascot June Sales and subsequently won in Italy. *A. Turnell.* 71

RUN LIKE MAD 3 b.f. Silly Season 127–Powderhall 81 (Murrayfield 119) (1981 5g² 5fg² 5f* 5fg³ 5.3d² 6g 1982 5g 5fg 5.6g 5s 5g) small filly; made all when winning minor event at Wolverhampton in 1981; well beaten in handicaps at 3 yrs; form only at 5f; possibly unsuited by very soft going but acts on any other. *W. Hastings-Bass.* —

RUNNING MELODY 2 b. or br.f. Rheingold 137–Fleet Serenade (Lorenzaccio 130) (1982 7fg 8fg³ 8s* 8.2s) May 22; second foal; dam, daughter of very smart Fleet Wahine, won over 7f and 1¼m in Ireland; only just lasted home but had remainder well strung out when beating Trendy Philly by a neck in 11-runner maiden race at Wolverhampton in October; favourite, disappointing fifth of 19 in nursery at Nottingham later in the month; should stay 1½m; probably acts on any going. *M. Stoute.* 86

RUN NORTH 3 b.c. Run The Gantlet–Eranos (Arts and Letters) (1981 NR 1982 8g 10.6s 12f³ 12f⁴ 14f* 14g 16f 14fg) IR 6,000Y; strong colt; good walker but poor mover; first foal; dam, out of half-sister to Northern Dancer, ran only once; stayed on well to win maiden race at Yarmouth in June; below form subsequently; suited by 1¾m and should get further; acts on firm going. *R. Sheather.* 73

RUN RECORD RUN 4 ch.f. Record Run 127–Firecrest 58 (Firestreak 125) (1981 8f 8g 10s 1982 8fg 8f 8fg 7fg 10g 8d 12fg⁴ 12f⁴ 13s 13.8d 12d) lengthy filly; poor maiden; stays middle distances; has worn blinkers and bandages; trained until after fourth start by V. Mitchell. *N. Bycroft.* —

RUNS LIKE FURY 2 b.f. Prince Tenderfoot 126–Inter Alia (Diatome 132) (1982 5fg 6f 8f 8g) Apr 18; 26,000Y; fair sort; first foal; dam, half-sister to smart French 1¼m performer Discretion, won over 11f in France; beaten 5 lengths in maiden race at Edinburgh in October, final outing and best effort; off the course for almost 4 months after second appearance; stays 1m. *M. Jarvis.* 61

RUSHBEDS 3 b.g. Ercolano 118–Lichen Lady 70 (Pardao 120) (1981 NR 1982 12fg 12fg* 14fg² 16fg 14f³) 8,600Y; big, strong gelding; second foal; half-brother to 14.7f winner Blakeney Point (by Blakeney); dam won over 1½m; made all to win 11-runner minor event at Newmarket in May by 1¼ lengths from

Cashel Prince; ran respectably in varied company afterwards; stays well; yet to race on an easy surface; lacks pace and is suited by forcing tactics. *B. Hobbs.*

RUSHMOOR 4 br.g. Queen's Hussar 124–Heathfield 99 (Hethersett 134) (1981 7g⁴ 8g² 8g² 8fg* 10.5s² 10.2g* 1982 10.6s) strong, useful-looking gelding; quite useful at 3 yrs; didn't show any sparkle and finished well beaten at Haydock in April on only outing of 1982 (fit from a successful spell over hurdles); stays 1¼m; probably acts on any going; sometimes wears blinkers and isn't the heartiest of animals. *G. Richards.* —

RUSSELL UP 3 b.g. Reliance II 137–My Dearest Sarah 79 (Anwar 120) (1981 8d 1982 11.7g) in rear in 2 maiden races. *G. Balding.* —

RUSSETING 3 b.f. Mummy's Pet 125–Rennet 109 (King's Bench 132) (1981 6fg 5g* 1982 7.2g³ 6f) strong filly; won maiden race at Beverley in 1981; soundly beaten in 2 handicaps at 3 yrs; appears not to stay 7f. *W. Hastings-Bass.* —

RUSSIAN DEBONAIR 3 b.f. Balidar 133–Cala Na Sith (Reform 132) (1981 NR 1982 6d 5fg³ 5f⁴ 5f⁴ 5f 5g 5.3fg 6f⁴ 5f⁴ 5f) 3,500Y, 600 2-y-o; sturdy, compact filly; first foal; dam ran only once; in frame in maiden races; best run at 5f on firm going. *D. Weeden.* **51**

RUSSIAN FLAME (CAN) 2 ch.f. Sevastopol–Flaming Tan (Tentam) (1982 6g) Mar 31; $20,000Y; tall, lengthy filly; second foal; dam, unraced half-sister to Canadian Derby winner All For Victory, comes from same family as Nijinsky; sire, unraced son of Nijinsky, is half-brother to Storm Bird; unquoted, behind in 19-runner maiden race at Newmarket in September; has plenty of scope but looks the type to need time and long distances. *B. Hills.* —

RUSSIAN ROUBLES (USA) 2 b.c. Nijinsky 138–Squander (Buckpasser) (1982 7.6s 7d*) **97 p**

John Dunlop didn't mince words when he told us about Russian Roubles in the summer. 'He's a grand horse and a lovely mover. He gives every sign of making a very high-class horse. He's done some work and did it extremely well . . . I like him immensely'. He added that because of Russian Roubles' size, he doubted whether he would run the colt more than twice. Russian Roubles did indeed run twice, making his first appearance in the Burr Stakes at Lingfield in September. His reputation preceded him; he started favourite in a field which included the useful winners Rare Event, Greene Normandy, Sharp Sea and Spindle Berry. With a quarter of a mile to run he appeared likely to justify the support but he then began to tire in the very testing conditions and was quickly eased, crossing the line only seventh of eight behind Ultimate Pride. Dunlop is very sparing with the entries he makes. That he considered it worthwhile entering Russian Roubles for the Prix de la Foret, a highly-competitive all-aged event, suggested strongly that his confidence in the colt hadn't been shaken. In the end Russian Roubles missed the Foret to take on his contemporaries a week earlier in the Houghton Stakes at Newmarket, where he started second favourite behind Mandelstam, the winner of a thirty-runner maiden race at the previous Newmarket meeting. Russian Roubles showed distinct signs of inexperience as Carson pushed him along, and for a while it looked as though his rider's urgings were having no effect. The picture changed rapidly as the field met the rising ground. Russian Roubles suddenly found his stride, producing a whirlwind finish to catch Vaisseau on the post as the latter wandered off a true line. Although this was no more than a useful effort by Russian Roubles—he was receiving 7 lb from Vaisseau—there's no denying his promise and he could well justify his trainer's opinion of him.

		Northern Dancer	Nearctic
Russian Roubles (USA) (b.c. Mar 30, 1980)	Nijinsky (b 1967)	(b 1961)	Natalma
		Flaming Page	Bull Page
		(b 1959)	Flaring Top
	Squander (b 1974)	Buckpasser	Tom Fool
		(b 1963)	Busanda
		Discipline	Princequillo
		(b 1962)	Lady Be Good

Russian Roubles is an extremely well-bred colt, coming from the same family as the top-class miler Posse, a former stable star who, incidentally, took second place in the 1979 Houghton Stakes. His grandam Discipline and Posse's dam In Hot Pursuit are both out of the very useful 1958 two-year-old Lady Be Good. Discipline was a high-class filly, winning the Demoiselle Stakes over a mile at two, the Test Stakes over seven furlongs at three and the Molly Pitcher Handicap over eight and a half furlongs at four. Besides being a half-sister to In Hot Pursuit, one of the best two-year-old fillies of 1973, Discipline was a half-sister to the very smart six- and seven-furlong performer Disciplinarian and the very useful filly Full of Hope, who won at up to a mile. In addition to Posse, Lady Be Good's daughters have produced the very smart sprinter Highest Regard, the Del Mar Oaks winner French Charmer, the good 1982 three-year-old Wavering Monarch and Squander, the dam of Russian Roubles. Squander was the best of Discipline's four winners. She was rated inferior only to Sensational among the two-year-old fillies of 1976 when she won the Astoria Stakes over five and a half furlongs and the Sorority Stakes over six. After winning three of her four starts at two she failed to win again in ten outings. Russian Roubles is her second foal. Many of Russian Roubles' relatives in the USA were speedy animals but we expect him to stay at least a mile and a quarter. *J. Dunlop.*

RUSSIAN SALAD 3 ch.g. Malinowski 123–Bordelaise 96 (Above Suspicion 127) (1981 6g 7.2fg 8g 8g 1982 8.2fg⁴ 10g) rangy, good-topped gelding; plater; should stay 1¼m (reportedly finished lame when tried at trip); claimed £2,415 after final start. *Sir Mark Prescott.*   **45**

RUSSIAN WINTER 7 b.g. King Emperor–Am Stretchin (Ambiorix 130) (1981 6s 5d* 5fg* 5g² 5f 6f 5fg 5d 5fg 5f 5fg 5fg⁴ 5g 6d 1982 6f 5fg² 6f 5f 5fg 5fg* 5f 5.8f 5.1g 5fg 6fg² 5g² 5fg* 6d 5fg 5d³ 6s 5g) lengthy gelding; sprint handicapper; won at Ayr in May (amateur riders event, from Cyril's Choice) and York in August (by short head from Rambling River); disappointed on quite a few occasions; probably unsuited by really soft going; usually wears blinkers; excellent mount for an inexperienced rider; possibly best on a galloping track. *A. W. Jones.*   **74**

RUST FREE 3 gr.f. Free State 125–Iridium 78 (Linacre 133) (1981 6g 5g 5s 6g 1982 6.5s 8s 10d 8d 7fg 7.6fg 7g 10g³ 10.4fg⁴ 11f 9g) workmanlike filly; plating-class maiden; stays 1¼m; sometimes blinkered. *G. Beeson.*   **58**

RUSTICARA 3 b.f. Tachypous 128–Ranikhet (Tanerko 134) (1981 5fg 6fg 8fg 1982 8fg 6f 7f⁴) workmanlike filly; plater; stays 7f; often bandaged. *M. W. Easterby.*   **—**

RUSTIC ART 2 b.c. Thatch 136–Bravour II (Birkhahn) (1982 5fg 5.8f² 7fg 7g³) Apr 11; fair sort; half-brother to winners here, in France, and in USA, including very useful 1976 2-y-o sprinter Brave Lass (by Ridan); dam best 2-y-o filly of 1965 in Germany and won German 1,000 Guineas; in frame in maiden race at Bath in May and 9-runner seller at Newmarket in August; stays 7f; sold 4,000 gns Ascot August Sales; winner in Italy. *A. Ingham.*   **67**

RUSTIC CHARM 4 br.g. Palm Track 122–Polly-Ann Tanja (Cletus) (1981 8s 8g 7fg 7g* 8fg* 10fg⁴ 9s 8s 7g 1982 7g 8f 8g² 8g³ 10fg³ 12f⁴ 8g⁴ 8fg 8fg 8.2s) smallish, workmanlike gelding; plater; possibly stays 1¼m; acts on a firm surface; usually blinkered nowadays; below form last 3 starts. *J. Carr.*   **52 d**

RUSTIC TRACK 2 b.g. Palm Track 122–Polly-Ann Tanja (Cletus) (1982 5f 5f 5f 5fg³ 6f⁴ 7f 5f 8fg* 8s⁴ 8d) Apr 12; smallish, lengthy gelding; brother to 7f and 1m winner Rustic Charm; plater; won 10-runner selling nursery under 7-7 at Redcar (no bid) in September by 1½ lengths from Pete's Folly; effective at 5f and stays 1m; seems to act on any going; blinkered third to sixth starts. *J. Carr.*   **63**

RUSTLE OF SPRING 3 ch.f. Leander 119–Geraghty Girl 54 (Frankincense 120) (1981 5s 6d 1982 5h) poor form, including in a seller. *G. Price.*   **—**

RUSTY ROCKET 2 gr. or ro.g. Roan Rocket 128–Dariana (Reform 132) (1982 5fg 6f 7fg⁴ 7g) Mar 25; 3,600F, 8,200Y; neat, strong individual; first foal; dam won in Norway; 1¼ lengths fourth of 20 behind Freedom Glory in seller at Redcar in September, best effort; sold 3,400 gns Doncaster November Sales and exported to Norway. *R. Hollinshead.*   **60**

RUSWARP 4 b.g. Gold Form 108–Lady Cortina 80 (Cortachy 107) (1981 7d 5d 5f 5f² 5f² 5f² 6g 5f 5fg 5f 1982 5f 5f 8fg 6f) sprint handicapper; poorish form here in 1982, including in a seller, but won twice in Belgium; form only on firm ground; got loose and had to be withdrawn when tried in blinkers once; sold 1,750 gns Ascot November Sales, reportedly for export to Italy. *D. Garraton.*   **—**

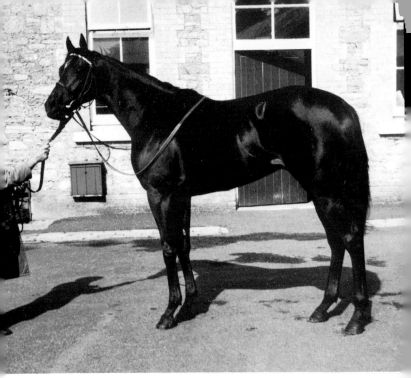

Mr R. G. Percival's "Rutland"

RUSWICK 2 b.f. Lucky Leaprechaun–Arabella Miller (pedigree unknown) — (1982 10d 5d) Apr 14; compact non-thoroughbred filly; first known foal; dam never ran; of no account. *T. Fairhurst.*

RUTH GIBSON 4 b.f. Beatic–My Moonshine (Pannier 106) (1981 NR 1982 — 12.2f) compact, plain filly; third living foal; dam never ran; needed race when tailed-off last of 9 behind Dangerous Moonlite in maiden race at Catterick in July, first outing. *J. Townson.*

RUTH POP 3 b.f. Wishing Star 117–Gardinella (Tanavar 118) (1981 5f 7f 7f — 1982 13.8f) small, compact filly; of no account; has worn blinkers and bandages. *J. Doyle.*

RUTLAND 2 b.c. Mummy's Pet 125–Rennet 109 (King's Bench 132) (1982 **107** 5fg* 5f* 5g* 5f² 6d3) Apr 2; 23,000Y; rather lightly-made, attractive colt; good mover; brother to 4 winners, including high-class sprinter Runnett and very useful 1979 2-y-o 5f performer Cala-Vadella, and half-brother to 3 more; dam stayed 1¼m; followed up impressive win in newcomers race at Goodwood in May with smooth successes the month afterwards in 2 minor events at Lingfield; upgraded after that, and though running well was no match at all for Kafu in Molecomb Stakes at Goodwood nor for Top o'the North (rec 3 lb) in Champion Two Yrs Old Trophy at Ripon; suited by 6f; seems to act on any going. *J. Dunlop.*

RYECROFT 4 b.g. Condorcet-Moonlight Story (Narrator 127) (1981 12s⁴ — 12g 16s 1982 13.8d) lightly raced and little sign of ability in varied company on flat, but is a winner over hurdles. *F. Watson.*

S

SABA 2 b.f. Mill Reef 141–Vestal Virgin 91 (Hail to Reason) (1982 7fg 8fg **88** 8fg*) Mar 12; small, quite attractive filly; first foal; dam, winner over 1m and 1¼m, is out of half-sister to Irish classic winners Reindeer, Santa Tina and Atherstone Wood; favourite, stayed on well after coming under pressure long way out when winning 13-runner maiden race at Beverley in September by 1½ lengths from Nebiha; will be suited by 1¼m+. *I. Balding.*

SABA NEJD 4 b.c. Malacate 131–Padova (Forli) (1982 12v 12g³ 12d 12g **76** d 12d* 12g⁴ 13d 1982 12v 10v 10s 12f² 12.2d³ 12g 12fg 12d 16f⁴ 13fg³) neat, strong, attractive colt; good walker and mover; quite a modest handicapper; seems to stay 2m; probably acts on any going; sweated up and ran poorly in blinkers once. *T. Marshall.*

SABHAN 2 b.c. Blakeney 126–Idiot's Delight (Bold Ruler) (1982 7g 7s 8d) **66** p Mar 8; strong, compact colt; half-brother to fairly useful Irish 7f winner Van Lingen (by Bustino) and successful Belgian sprinter Muff Diver (by Deep Diver); dam unraced daughter of Musidora winner Fool's Gold; modest sixth in 16-runner minor 1m event at Redcar in November, best effort; will be better suited by 1¼m+. *G. Harwood.*

SABINA PARK 2 b.g. So Blessed 130–Miss Caribbean 74 (Sea Hawk II 131) **—** (1982 5fg 5fg 5.8f) Apr 15; 13,000Y; first foal; dam, half-sister to very smart 1973 2-y-o Welsh Harmony, won over 1½m; soundly beaten in maiden and minor events; gelded after final outing. *J. Sutcliffe.*

SABIR 6 ch.g. Sallust 134–Mrs Binks (Whistling Wind 123) (1981 NR 1982 **—** 8g) moderate performer in 1980; best form at up to 1m; acts on any going; good mount for an apprentice; bandaged only outing of 1982; sold 460 gns Doncaster September Sales. *W. Stubbs.*

SABI STAR 2 b. or br.f. Monsanto 121–Balandra Star 92 (Blast 125) (1982 **72** 6fg 5f 6g 5.8g 7.6v) May 14; workmanlike filly; half-sister to 3-y-o Barnaby Sam, fairly useful stayer Another Sam and useful sprinter Middleton Sam (all by Comedy Star), and to another winner; dam won over 5f at 2 yrs; quite a modest handicapper; will stay 1m; acts on heavy going. *R. Hannon.*

SABLE PRINCESS 2 gr.f. Young Emperor 133–Chinchilla II (Sicambre 135) **67** (1982 5.1f 5f² 6fg 6g) Apr 3; IR 3,700F, 5,000Y; short-coupled filly; sister to a poor animal, and half-sister to 3 winners, including fairly useful 1971 2-y-o 5f winner La Cilla (by Milesian); dam never ran; ½-length second to Amber Wind in 13-runner maiden race at Folkestone in August; last on both subsequent starts. *D. Morley.*

SABLE ROYALE (USA) 2 ch.f. Real Value–Tiddlywinks (Court Martial) **—** (1982 7d 7g) Mar 6; $75,000Y; leggy filly; half-sister to 2 winners by Go Marching, notably very smart French miler Brinkmanship; dam unraced daughter of Irish 1,000 Guineas third Banri an Oir; behind in maiden races at Leicester (dwelt) and Newmarket in October. *N. Callaghan.*

SABRE DANCE 3 b.c. Dance In Time–Sarissa (Reform 132) (1981 **105** 7d 1982 10.1fg² 10.1fg* 10.1fg* 10fg* 10.1g* 12fg* 12g) big, rangy, good-looking colt; had a fine year and put up good effort when beating Father Rooney by a length in well-contested minor event at Doncaster in September, finding a rare turn of foot when switched to outside after appearing not to be going all that well; had earlier won 3 minor events at Windsor and an amateur riders event at Newmarket; very well suited by 1½m; acts on a firm surface. *H. Cecil.*

SABUTAI (USA) 3 b.c. Mr Leader–Osprey (Beau Gar) (1981 8d⁴ 7.6s* **83** 7.3s 1982 7d² 10f³ 10.4fg 9g 8f⁴ 8f⁴ 8fg* 9d) well-made colt; poor walker; readily won amateur riders event at Goodwood in September; had earlier run well in Salisbury 2,000 Guineas Trial in April, keeping on to be 3 lengths second of 14 to impressive winner Hays; stays 1¼m; suited by some give in the ground. *I. Balding.*

SACHA'S SONG 4 ch.g. Crooner 119–Bouleversee (Napoleon Bonaparte **—** 114) (1981 12g 11.7g⁴ 11.7s* 1982 16d) big gelding; suited by 1½m; acts on soft going. *R. Hannon.*

SACKFORD (USA) 2 b.c. Stop the Music–Bon Fille (Ben Lomond) (1982 **114** p
7.6v³ 7s* 7s*)

Just four days after their outstanding four-year-old Kalaglow had ended
his career on a disappointing note in the Dubai Champion Stakes Messrs Bodie
and Ward must have been cheered by the impressive performance of their
two-year-old Sackford in the Granby Stakes, a minor event at Sandown. He
improved greatly on his initial effort, when third of seventeen to Telephone
Numbers at Lingfield a fortnight earlier, and looked potentially a smart colt.
After moving into the lead about a quarter of a mile from home, still travelling
very easily, he ran right away from his opponents with the minimum of urging
from his rider and won very comfortably by four lengths from the favourite
Gay Lemur. Better was to follow in the Pytchley Stakes at Leicester early in
November, where the opposition included the well-bred Elite Syncopation,
successful on his latest start, and the useful and consistent Lofty. Sackford
justified favouritism in a style which suggests that he'll make a fine three-year-
old even if he falls short of Kalaglow's class. He loomed alongside the front-
running Lofty two furlongs out, still hard on the bridle, and then quickly built
up an eight-length lead in effortless fashion. Although eased well before the
line he still had six lengths to spare over Lofty, who was conceding 5 lb. This
was a smart performance, one which in our opinion gives Sackford a first-rate
chance on 8-2 in the Ladbroke Free Handicap. Our main reservation about
his prospects is whether he'll be suited by the fast ground on which the
Free Handicap is often run—in five of the last ten years the ground has been
on the firm side and only once was it run on the soft going which clearly suits
Sackford well. He may eventually prove suited by firm going but he has a
round action, the type usually associated with a soft-ground performer.

		Stop the Music	Hail to Reason	Turn-to
Sackford (USA)		(b 1970)	(br 1958)	Nothirdchance
(b.c. Mar 2, 1980)			Bebopper	Tom Fool
			(b 1962)	Bebop II
		Bon Fille	Ben Lomond	Alycidon
		(ch 1962)	(ch 1954)	Phaetonia
			En Casserole	War Relic
			(ch 1952)	Beanie M.

Although well made and quite attractive Sackford gives the impression he
will improve physically from two to three. Indeed his trainer described him
late in the summer as 'a very backward sort' who 'needs plenty of time'.
Perhaps his immaturity was one of the reasons why Sackford was a fairly
cheap yearling by American standards, fetching only 95,000 dollars at the
Keeneland Select Sale where the average was over 250,000 dollars. He's a
half-brother to six winners including Blacksmith (by Jacinto), a very useful
French winner at up to a mile, and the very useful American miler Good John
(by Prince John). His dam Bon Fille won only a couple of claiming races
over sprint distances but she is a half-sister to two stakes winners in High
Tribute, successful in the Jerome Handicap over a mile, and Royal Spirit,
a good Canadian filly who twice won the nine-furlong Tattling Handicap.
Bon Fille was herself a granddaughter of Beanie M, one of the best two-year-
old fillies of 1935. Sackford's sire Stop the Music won over a mile and a quarter
and his maternal grandsire Ben Lomond was a brother to the high-class middle-
distance stayer High Perch so he should eventually stay at least a mile and a
quarter. He's an interesting prospect. *G. Harwood.*

SACRED PATH 2 b.g. Godswalk 130–Crepe Rose (Crepello 136) (1982 6f⁴ 7fg **71**
7fg³ 7.2f 8s) May 8; 21,000F, 38,000Y; quite attractive, good sort; good walker;
third foal; dam, placed in France, is half-sister to very smart performers Cistus
and Lancastrian; quite a modest maiden; stays 7f; acts on firm going; gelded after
final outing. *J. Bethell.*

SADDLE ROCK ROAD (USA) 4 b.g. Elocutionist–Lay In (Turn-to) (1981 —
8g 8g² 8g² 8g 7fg* 8.3fg 10fg 8f³ 8d⁴ 7fg 1982 10f) plater; stays 1m; probably
acts on any going; wears blinkers; sold 200 gns Ascot July Sales. *D. Jermy.*

SADEDAB 9 br.h. Badedas 81–June Clare (Fairwell) (1981 12s 10.6s 10f³ —
1982 16d) plater; stays 2m; acts on any going; sometimes wears blinkers;
suitable mount for an apprentice. *J. Edmunds.*

SAENREDAM 3 b.c. Malacate 131–Exmoor Lass 86 (Exbury 138) (1981 7f —
7fg⁴ 7fg² 7d² 7fg³ 8.2fg² 8d 1982 10s 10f 10f 10g) neat, well-made colt; good

walker and mover; second in maiden races and a nursery in 1981; soundly beaten in varied company at 3 yrs; should stay middle distances; sold to M. Naughton 1,100 gns Newmarket Autumn Sales. *J. Dunlop.*

SAFE HOUSE 3 b.f. Lyphard 132–Manor (Round Table) (1981 6g 6g 1982 7g 8f 7f 8g 10f³ 10fg² 10.8fg* 12g 10.6f) small, lengthy filly; good mover; landed odds in handicap at Warwick in July; looked thoroughly temperamental subsequently and whipped round at start final outing; stays 1¼m well; yet to race on a soft surface; wears blinkers; one to leave severely alone; sold 12,000 gns Newmarket December Sales. *H. Wragg.*   **81 §**

SAFE PROCESS (USA) 2 b.f. Bold Forbes–Krassata 114 (Nijinsky 138) (1982 8.5g² 7fg²) Feb 17; second foal; dam fourth in Irish 1,000 Guineas and Irish Guinness Oaks, and was very useful winner at up to 9f in USA; second in maiden races in September, going down by 1½ lengths to Countess Candy at Galway and by ¾ length to Lady Dara at Leopardstown; will stay 1¼m+; entered in Oaks. *D. Weld, Ireland.*   **91**

SAFETY NET 3 b.f. Reliance II 137–Bonsella 68 (Carlemont 132) (1981 NR 1982 7fg 8g 7fg 10fg 7d 11.7fg² 11.7g 12f 11.7g 10fg 10g 10s³) lengthy, workmanlike filly; half-sister to a winning plater and a winner abroad; dam placed at up to 1¼m; only plating class; suited by 1½m and will stay further; blinkered last 2 starts. *R. Hannon.*   **59**

SAFFAR 3 ch.c. Sassafras 135–Night Vision 100 (Yellow God 129) (1981 5d 8d 1982 12f 8g 8fg 11g⁴ 10.6g) plating-class maiden; best run at 11f; sold 1,300 gns Newmarket Autumn Sales. *W. Elsey.*   **—**

SAGAMORE 3 b.c. Sagaro 133–Veruschka (Turn-to) (1981 5d 6g³ 6fg 8g* 7s⁴ 10g 1982 12fg² 12.3g 10f 16g³ 12fg 11s* 16s) rangy colt; won minor event at Hamilton in September; twice had stiff tasks earlier; stays well; acts on soft going; pulls hard and needs strong handling (bolted for apprentice when withdrawn before sixth intended outing); ran abysmally third start. *F. Durr.*   **78**

SAGARMATHA 2 b. or br.c. Shantung 132–Aberside (Abernant 142) (1982 6f 6fg³ 6f 6d 7s) Apr 15; 1,500F, 5,000Y; lengthy, useful-looking colt; poor mover; half-brother to 2 winners, including 5f performer Setmark (by Sharpen Up); dam never ran; no worthwhile form in varied company. *G. Balding.*   **—**

SAGA'S HUMOUR 3 ch.f. Bustino 136–Summer Day 117 (Golden Cloud) (1981 5fg³ 6f* 6fg⁴ 6f³ 5d⁴ 1982 6s³ 6g³ 6f 5fg) small filly; plater at 2 yrs; twice third in better company early in year; suited by 6f and will stay further; acts on any going; suitable mount for a boy; sold 8,800 gns Newmarket December Sales. *D. Smith.*   **51**

SAGE HAWK 3 ch.g. Sagaro 133–Gerfalcon 105 (Falcon 131) (1981 NR 1982 9fg) sturdy gelding; fourth foal; half-brother to winning sprinter Chinese Kung Fu (by Roan Rocket); dam best at 7f; well-backed second favourite though in need of run when seventh of 12 to Rel Tiger in newcomers event at Wolverhampton in April (apprentice ridden). *J. Dunlop.*   **—**

SAGE KING 4 b.g. Shantung 132–Lady Gaylord (Double Jump 131) (1981 10.6d 10.6s 12.3fg* 13fg* 14g 13d 1982 12.3g* 12.3fg* 13fg² 12fg⁴ 14g 13d) lengthy, quite attractive gelding who seems to carry quite a bit of condition; ran well in first half of season and won handicaps at Newcastle (in good style) and Chester (by a head from Lakenheath); suited by 1½m+; seems to act on any going; usually ridden up with pace; trained by J. W. Watts until after fifth outing. *C. Spares.*   **88 d**

SAILOR'S DANCE 2 b.c. Dance In Time–Pirogue 99 (Reliance II 137) (1982 7f* 8.2fg) Mar 28; well-made, attractive colt; not a good mover in his slower paces; fourth foal; half-brother to winning stayer Admiral's Barge (by Brigadier Gerard); dam, closely related to good stayer Torpid, won over 1m; put up a most promising display in 16-runner £3,700 event at Salisbury in August, still being among back-markers 3f out but then producing a strong run to win by 1½ lengths from Dancing Meg; short-priced favourite, dropped right away after being driven into challenging position 2f out when 10 lengths fifth of 8 behind The Noble Player in minor event at Haydock the following month; should stay at least 1¼m; acts on firm going. *R. Hern.*   **99**

SAILOR'S PRAYER 4 gr.c. Martinmas 128–Coral Mermaid (Silver Shark 129) (1981 6s 8.2g 7fg 6f 6f 5fg* 6s* 6d 5s⁴ 5s⁴ 1982 6f 5f 6fg 5.8f³ 6fg 5g² 6f⁴ 5fg* 5g 5fg 5fg 5d³ 6s 6s 5s) leggy colt; poor walker; sprint handicapper; beat Vorvados decisively by 1½ lengths in £4,500 event at Ascot in July; good third to Pusey Street at Ascot in September, best subsequent effort; acts on any going. *R. Thompson.*   **75**

SAILWITCH BOY 3 b. or gr.g. Grisaille 115–Paddyswitch (St Paddy 133) —
(1981 NR 1982 12.2f) leggy gelding; bandaged near-hind and blinkered
when tailed-off last in seller at Catterick in May. *Miss L. Siddall.*

SAINT AND SINNER 2 b.c. St Paddy 133–Bordello 91 (Crepello 136) (1982 **88**
7f 7g⁴ 8f*) Apr 18; good-bodied, quite attractive colt; second foal; dam, half-
sister to smart No Alimony, won twice over 1m; won 6-runner maiden race at
Brighton in September by ¾ length from Hi Easter; will be suited by 1¼m+.
H. Cecil.

SAINT CRESPIN BAY 3 ch.c. Bay Express 132–Crisp Piece 90 (Saint Crespin **58**
III 132) (1981 5s 5g³ 5g 5fg 5g 5.3d 5g* 1982 5d 5d 5fg² 5f³ 5.3g 5fg 5g 5d)
workmanlike colt; inconsistent sprint handicapper; acts on firm going; blinkered
seventh start (ran badly). *S. Matthews.*

SAINT CYNTHIA 3 b.f. Welsh Saint 126–Little Cynthia 76 (Wolver Hollow —
126) (1981 NR 1982 7g 10g 9g 9g) IR 8,000Y; attractive ex-English filly;
first foal; dam won over 1m; soundly beaten in maiden races; trained by B.
Hanbury first 3 starts. *N. Meade, Ireland.*

SAINT CYRIEN (FR) 2 b.c. Luthier 126–Sevres (Riverman 131) (1982 **128**
8g* 9d* 8s*)
Britain's female flat trainers have a long way to go before they prove Kipling
right in his claim that the female of the species is more deadly than the male but
one of their French counterparts, Christiane 'Criquette' Head, has established
herself as one of her country's outstanding trainers. In her first four seasons,
from 1978 to 1981, she sent out Sigy, Three Troikas, Lydian and others to
win over twenty pattern races, including the Prix de l'Abbaye de Longchamp,
the Poule d'Essai des Pouliches, the Prix Vermeille, the Prix de l'Arc de Triomphe
and three other Group 1 events in France, Germany and Italy. Even by her own
high standards Mme Head had an excellent year in 1982: Harbour won her the
Prix Saint-Alary and the Prix de Diane, and among the two-year-olds were Ma
Biche and Maximova, the top fillies in the International Classification, and the
best young colt in France, the unbeaten Saint Cyrien. Mme Head also became
only the second woman to train the winner of a Group 1 event in Britain—Mrs
Lomax, trainer of the 1970 Gold Cup winner Precipice Wood, was the first—
when Ma Biche took the William Hill Cheveley Park Stakes and, judging by
Saint Cyrien's sparkling win in the Grand Criterium at Longchamp in October,
she must have an excellent chance of becoming the first woman to train the
winner of the Derby.
Only once in the last twenty years has there been a smaller field for the
Grand Criterium but among Saint Cyrien's seven opponents were Deep Roots,
an impressive three-length winner of the Prix Morny who had also dead-heated
with Maximova in the Prix de la Salamandre; L'Emigrant who had looked
every inch a top-class colt when running out an easy winner of the Prix La
Rochette; and the improving English challenger The Noble Player, a three-
length third to Dunbeath in the Royal Lodge Stakes on his latest start. Saint
Cyrien had created such a favourable impression when winning both his races
that he was backed from 2/1 to 6/4, eventually displacing L'Emigrant as favourite.
He proved thoroughly worthy of the support. Freddie Head, who rides Longchamp so well, settled Saint Cyrien in last place as L'Emigrant's pacemaker Midford established a clear lead, asking him to move up only as the field approached
the straight. Saint Cyrien still had quite a lot to do as L'Emigrant took over
from his pacemaker, with The Noble Player and Deep Roots hot on his heels,
inside the last two furlongs. None, though, could match Saint Cyrien when
he came to challenge at the distance: he cut the leaders down in a matter of
strides, with a magnificent burst of speed, and won easing up by a length from

*Prix Saint-Roman, Longchamp—Saint Cyrien books his place
in the Grand Criterium*

*Grand Criterium, Longchamp—France's top two-year-old race falls to Saint Cyrien,
L'Emigrant just gets the better of the British challenger
The Noble Player for second*

L'Emigrant with The Noble Player running the race of his life to take third place, just a nose behind. Two of the next five home raced afterwards: L'Emigrant comfortably won the Criterium de Maisons-Laffitte, accounting for a strong field which included the pattern-race winners Bal des Fees and Crystal Glitters; and Ginger Brink, eleven lengths behind Saint Cyrien at Longchamp, won a good-class event on his next start before finishing a creditable fourth of sixteen behind L'Emigrant at Maisons-Laffitte. Incidentally the last two hundred metres of the Grand Criterium were covered in 11·90 seconds, a highly creditable time considering the very holding conditions, and Saint Cyrien is clearly one of that rare breed which possess stamina and acceleration.

Saint Cyrien had made his first appearance only four weeks earlier in the Prix de Lamballe, a newcomers race over a mile at Evry in September. He was made favourite to beat eight others and did so in splendid style, cantering home four lengths clear of Al Nasr's 290,000-guinea half-brother Jabal Tarik. Saint Cyrien confirmed the promise of this run with an even more impressive display against stronger opposition in the Prix Saint-Roman over nine furlongs at Longchamp less than three weeks later, for which he again started favourite. After being held up he produced a first-rate turn of foot early in the straight, sweeping into a five-length lead in the space of a hundred yards, and won easing up by two and a half lengths from the subsequent Prix de Conde winner Nile Hawk. Nile Hawk wasn't the only one to frank the form; Lovely Dancer, beaten five and a half lengths into fourth place, later reached the frame in both the Prix de Conde and the Criterium de Saint-Cloud; and Little Meadow, three quarters of a length behind Lovely Dancer, was beaten only half a length by Belka in the Prix des Reservoirs on her next outing. Incidentally the ground was on the soft side for the Saint-Roman, although not so soft as for the Grand Criterium, and Saint Cyrien has yet to race on a firm surface.

Saint Cyrien (Fr) (b.c. Apr 27, 1980)	Luthier (br 1965)	Klairon (b 1952)	Clarion III
			Kalmia
		Flute Enchantee (b 1950)	Cranach
			Montagnana
	Sevres (b 1974)	Riverman (b 1969)	Never Bend
			River Lady
		Saratoga II (b 1966)	Snob
			Sariegail

Saint Cyrien not only has the form of a potential Derby winner but also the looks—he's a tall, attractive, imposing individual—and the pedigree. His sire Luthier has been one of the mainstays of the French bloodstock industry in recent years, finishing among the top ten sires in every year from 1974, the year his first crop were three-year-olds, to 1982 with the single exception of 1979 when he finished fifteenth. Luthier never won over further than eleven furlongs, gaining his most important successes in the Prix Lupin over ten and a half furlongs and the Prix Jacques le Marois over a mile, but many of his best winners have won over a mile and a half or more, including Riverqueen, Guadanini, Ashmore, Condorcet, Montcontour, Galiani and Sing Softly. Two sons, Twig Moss and Bois de Grace, also stayed well enough to be placed in the Prix du Jockey-Club and a daughter, Leandra, finished a good second in the Prix Vermeille. Unfortunately Luthier died of a heart attack in September 1981 and, since he missed the 1980 breeding season because of a severe attack of laminitis, he has only one more crop still to reach the racecourse.

Oddly enough Saint Cyrien's dam Sevres, like Ma Biche's dam Madge, was once employed as a pacemaker, making the running for her stable-companion Beaune in the Poule d'Essai des Pouliches. A comparison of the stud careers of pacemaking mares with those for whom they laboured might reveal some interesting statistics. Sevres had previously won her only race as a two-year-old, a newcomers race over seven and a half furlongs. She later proved herself a very useful filly in her own right, winning over a mile and nine furlongs in addition to finishing a respectable fifth in three pattern events, including two over a distance around a mile and a quarter, the Prix Fille de l'Air and the Prix de Flore. Saint Cyrien is Sevres' first foal; her second is a yearling colt by Bellypha named Senateur. Sevres was one of six reported foals, all winners, bred by Saratoga II. Of the other five the Habitat filly Sinaia gained two of her four successes over a mile and a quarter, the Cadmus gelding Sasor won over a mile and a half, the Dike filly Sabbatine won the Prix de l'Elevage, a valuable handicap over twelve and a half furlongs, and the Targowice filly Satilla won at up to the same distance. Satilla had a remarkable record, developing into a smart performer after winning at Dieppe and Rouen and being sold out of Mme Head's stable after winning a claiming race at Longchamp. She later won two more races and reached the frame in four pattern events, including the Prix Niel and the Prix du Conseil de Paris. Saratoga, twice a winner over middle distances, was one of four winners in France produced by the English mile-and-a-quarter winner Sariegail. None of the four was out of the ordinary but one of her daughters who failed to win, Sea Queen, is the dam of the smart middle-distance performer Mariacho. Sariegail was a half-sister to Sarcelle, the top two-year-old of 1956, to Prefect, a tip-top handicapper, and to Samaria who bred the top-class sprinter Sammy Davis and the good middle-distance colt Super Sam. Saint Cyrien will stay a mile and a half but he's also likely to prove effective at shorter distances and he must take a deal of beating in the Poule d'Essai des Poulains, his early-season target. We look forward to seeing him at Epsom. *Mme C. Head, France.*

SAINT DUBASSOFF 3 b.g. Dubassoff–Saint Shari 81 (Saint Crespin III 132) (1981 7fg 7fg 7g 8s 1982 10.1fg 16fg) in rear in maiden and minor events; blinkered once in 1981. *J. Spearing.* —

SAINTE PARFAIT (FR) 2 b.f. Ben Trovato 128–Caecilia 76 (Skymaster 126) (1982 7g 8g 7d) workmanlike filly; half-sister to 1¼m winner Vartkez (by A Tempo) and a winner in France; dam placed from 5f to 1m; in rear in maiden and minor events at Newmarket (2) and Doncaster in October. *D. Morley.* —

SAINT GERAN 6 ch.g. Red Alert 127–Blue Shark (Silver Shark 129) (1981 NR 1982 10v* 11g² 12g 12fg 8fg) quite a moderate handicapper; ran in Belgium first 3 starts and decisively won small handicap at Groenendaal in March; well beaten on his return; stays 1½m; acts on any going; has worn blinkers; suited by forcing tactics; good mount for an amateur; sold 1,450 gns Ascot October Sales. *R. Smyth.* —

SAINT JULIE 2 b.f. Monsanto 121–Tanzanite (Marino) (1982 6g 8d) May 27; 1,600F, 1,200Y; tall, rather narrow filly; half-sister to 2 French middle-distance winners; dam won over 7f at 2 yrs in France; well beaten in maiden race at Newmarket and minor event at Redcar in the autumn. *C. Spares.* —

SAINTLY LADY 7 b.m. Saintly Song 128–Melody Lady 74 (Highland Melody 112) (1981 NR 1982 9g 8.2g 9g) poor plater; stays 1¼m; seems to act on any going; has run creditably for an apprentice; has worn bandages. *M. Reddan.* —

SAINT MIA 4 ch.f. Arch Sculptor 123–Blue Bleep (Bleep-Bleep 134) (1981 5s 5v 5h³ 5fg 1982 5g 5f 8g) strong, well-made filly; poor maiden; behind in sellers on occasions; has worn blinkers. *J. Hill.* —

SAINT MOTUNDE 9 ch.m. Tyrant–Saint Veronica (Saint Crespin III 132) (1981 8v 8g⁴ 6d 9.4g³ 8g 7f⁴ 8f² 10f 8f³ 8f* 7g* 7fg* 7f* 8.2fg³ 7fg 7.2v 1982 8fg 8g 8g³ 7fg 8fg) quite a modest handicapper; ran respectably on occasions; **59**

best at up to 1m; appears to act on any going but is suited by top-of-the-ground; sometimes blinkered in 1979. *B. McMahon.*

SAINT SIMBIR 2 ch.f. Simbir 130–I'm No Saint (St Chad 120) (1982 9v*)   **82 p**
Apr 11; IR 1,500F, IR 4,800Y; third living foal; half-sister to a minor winner in France by Sallust; dam poor Irish maiden; gambled on from 20/1 to 4/1 when winning 20-runner maiden race at Gowran Park in October by ½ length from Welsh Hooker; will probably stay 1½m. *N. Meade, Ireland.*

SAKLAWI 2 b.c. Sparkler 130–Princess Eboli 108 (Brigadier Gerard 144) (1982   **—**
6v) Mar 24; 8,000F, 21,000Y; first produce; dam won Cheshire Oaks and Lancashire Oaks; unquoted, seventh of 9 in maiden race at Folkestone in October. *M. Masson.*

SALABELLA 3 b.f. Sallust 134–Supreme Lady 86 (Grey Sovereign 128§) (1981   **64**
NR 1982 7fg 8d³ 11f⁴ 10g⁴ 10.4d 11d³) rather lightly-made, shallow-girthed filly; half-sister to several winners, including very useful 6f winner Chemin (by Steel Heart) and Irish St Leger winner M-Lolshan (by Levmoss); dam 2-y-o 5f performer; in frame in maiden races; stays 11f; seems to act on any going. *F. J. Houghton.*

SALDORO 3 ch.g. Cavo Doro 124–Salonica II (Ocarina 131) (1981 6g 7g 8g   **—**
1982 10.1fg 14g 16f³ 14fg 15.5f⁴ 15g 16.5fg³ 15.8d 14s) neat, good-bodied gelding; not the best of movers; staying maiden. *J. Winter.*

SALEAF 2 b. or br.f. Free State 125–Misfield 99 (Sahib 114) (1982 5fg 5d 5.1g³   **75**
6g³ 6fg 6fg 6g² 5s³) Apr 24; 3,200Y; lightly-built filly; second foal; sister to modest 1981 2-y-o 5f winner Honest Opinion; dam sprinter; placed in varied races, including when blinkered in October in a £2,700 seller at Newmarket and an apprentice nursery at Sandown; best run at 5f, but stays 6f; possibly needs some give in the ground. *B. Swift.*

SALIERI (USA) 2 ch.c. Accipiter–Hogan's Sister (Speak John) (1982 6fg*   **118**
6fg* 7fg² 6g*)
Just over a year after being bought as a foal for 37,000 dollars at the Keeneland November Breeding Stock Sale Salieri reappeared in the sales ring,

Rous Memorial Stakes, Goodwood—a simple task for Salieri

this time at Newmarket. According to his trainer 'nobody wanted him . . . he couldn't fetch his reserve' but the sales returns show him as being knocked down to J. T. Doyle for 8,800 guineas. Had Salieri returned to the sales at the end of his two-year-old career he would have prompted a very different response: as the winner of three of his four races, including the Mill Reef Stakes, he would surely have beaten Britain's record price for a two-year-old colt, the 145,000 guineas paid for Galaxy Libra in 1978.

The Mill Reef Stakes at Newbury in September was Salieri's last race and his first in pattern company. He had won his first two races with impressive ease, an eleven-runner maiden event at Newmarket in mid-July, where he strode right away in the final furlong to beat Sharpish by five lengths, and the fairly valuable Rous Memorial Stakes at Goodwood a fortnight later, where he so outclassed the two other runners that no starting prices were returned. Interestingly his trainer described him after his Newmarket success as 'by far the best of my two-year-olds in work', adding that he had a lot of backward animals with which he hadn't done much. When Salieri reappeared in the Acomb Stakes at York in August he started favourite at 2/1 on despite having to give 7 lb to his thirteen opponents, among them a beautifully-bred newcomer named Gorytus. Salieri's supporters knew their fate well before the finish: he was overwhelmed by Gorytus after leading for five furlongs. He wasn't given a hard time when defeat was inevitable, and crossed the line seven lengths adrift. Following this reverse Salieri was only second choice in the betting behind the unbeaten Horage in the five-runner Mill Reef. He was soon prominent on the outside as Horage made the running and went in pursuit as the Norfolk Stakes runner-up Krayyan took over the lead with less than a quarter of a mile to run. He battled on gamely under strong pressure, hitting the front inside the last furlong, and then held off Kafu, who was giving 4 lb, by three quarters of a length. Krayyan took third place, half a length further behind, with a below-par Horage only fourth. This was a game effort by Salieri, and a smart one, but the subsequent running of Krayyan and Kafu in the Middle Park, where they finished third and fourth, beaten four lengths and five lengths respectively by Diesis, suggests that Salieri is the best part of a stone behind the top colts. Perhaps he would have proved otherwise in the Horris Hill Stakes at Newbury in October, in which he had been forecast to start second favourite to Proclaim, had it not been abandoned.

*Mill Reef Stakes, Newbury—a hard race for these youngsters as Horage (rails)
loses his unbeaten record behind Salieri (centre of leading three),
Kafu (right) and Krayyan*

Mr C. A. B. St George's "Salieri"

Salieri, a lengthy, quite attractive colt, is the first foal of the unraced Hogan's Sister, who derived her name from the fact that she is a half-sister to the smart American colt Father Hogan. Father Hogan won eight of his fifty-three races, including stakes events over nine furlongs and a mile and a quarter, and finished second in ten more, notably the Grade 1 Brooklyn Handicap over

	Accipiter (b 1971)	Damascus (b 1964)	Sword Dancer / Kerala
Salieri (USA) (ch.c. Feb 14, 1980)		Kingsland (b or br 1965)	Bold Ruler / Landmark
	Hogan's Sister (b 1977)	Speak John (b 1958)	Prince John / Nuit de Folies
		Liz. Piet (b 1960)	Piet / Miss Elizabeth

a mile and a half. Hogan's Sister is a half-sister to six other winners, the best of them the very promising two-year-old Northern Adventure and the very useful Dixmart, a veteran of well over a hundred races. Their dam Liz. Piet also had an arduous racing career, running eighty-three times for six wins at up to nine furlongs, mainly in claiming company. Salieri's third dam Miss Elizabeth, bred by Prince Aly Khan in France, managed only two third places from twelve starts in the USA and none of her five winners was out of the ordinary. She was a well-bred filly though, having as her dam the July Stakes winner Hilla, a sister to the Eclipse and Champion Stakes winner Rustom Pasha. Salieri is the second good British performer by the mile stakes winner Accipiter who died from a twisted intestine in May 1982. The first, Beldale Flutter, was at his best over a mile and a quarter but Salieri strikes us as a speedier type who's likely to prove best at up to a mile. He has as yet raced only on a sound surface. *H. Cecil.*

Mr R. E. Sangster's "Salmon Leap"

SALINA (GER) 2 b.f. Arratos–Sarina (Dark Star) (1982 6f 7g 8f) Mar 15; — lengthy German-bred filly; good walker; dam daughter of German 1,000 Guineas second Sabrina and half-sister to dam of top 1973 German 3-y-o filly Sheba; showed only a little ability in maiden and minor events; sold BBA 5,400 gns Newmarket Autumn Sales. *M. Stoute.*

SALIX 2 b.g. Stradavinsky 121–Stipa (Silver Shark 129) (1982 6fg 6fg) — May 7; good sort; half-brother to several minor winners; dam won at up to 6.5f in France; 33/1, behind in big fields for minor events at Newmarket in August and Doncaster in September; subsequently gelded. *J. W. Watts.*

SALLAMETTI (USA) 4 b.f. Giacometti 130–Gay Sally (Sir Gaylord) (1981 **44** 12d⁴ 12.5f 13.8f 12f 16s 12d 1982 8f 8f 11g* 12d 12g² 11fg 12.2f⁴ 8.2s) lengthy, lightly-made filly; 20/1 when beating Target Path a short head in handicap at Hamilton in June (made all); seems best at middle distances; ran moderately in a seller when blinkered once. *W. Bentley.*

SALLWAH 3 b.f. Balidar 133–Welsh Jewel 72 (Welsh Pageant 132) (1981 — 5g 5g² 5f³ 5f 5g⁴ 6s 5s² 1982 6f 5f 5f 5f 5f) sparely-made filly; sprint plater; has worn blinkers; exported to Algeria. *C. Booth.*

SALMON LEAP (USA) 2 ch.c. Northern Dancer–Fish-Bar (Baldric II 131) **94** P (1982 8d*) closely related to top-class 1m and 1¼m colt Kings Lake (by Nijinsky) and half-brother to 3 winners, including top-class 1976 2-y-o Cloonlara (by Sir Ivor), herself dam of National Stakes winner Glenstal (by Northern Dancer); dam very useful French 1½m winner; looked particularly promising when winning 12-runner maiden race at Leopardstown in October, coming through in straight to score by 5 lengths from Koudou with rest well beaten off; will probably stay 1¼m; has scope and looks sure to make a very good 3-y-o. *V. O'Brien, Ireland.*

SALORA LADY 4 b.f. Sassafras 135–Rocaserena 104 (Jimmy Reppin 131) **88** (1981 12.2s* 10s 12g² 12d³ 13fg² 14.6g² 13d* 12s³ 14s 1982 16fg 14f 16.1f

15fg³ 14g 13d 16v² 12s) neat filly; developed into a useful performer as a 3-y-o; didn't run up to her best in 1982 but seldom had ideal conditions; gained only placings in rather slowly-run Tennent Trophy at Ayr in July (2 lengths third to Lusitanica) and fairly valuable handicap at Ascot in October (stayed on really well and finished ½-length second to Man of Spirit); suited by a test of stamina; has rather a round action and is well suited by some give in the ground; sold 26,000 gns Newmarket December Sales and sent to France. *E. Weymes.*

SALTATORE 2 b.c. Orange Bay 131–Sideshow 103 (Welsh Pageant 132) — (1982 8g 10.2s) May 11; 21,000F; strong, good-topped, quite attractive colt; first produce; dam, half-sister to Oaks second Vielle, won 4 times over 1¼m; backward, well beaten in late-season minor events at Newmarket and Doncaster. *B. Hobbs.*

SALTCOTE MOSS ROSE 2 gr.f. Tudor Rhythm 112–Persian Kitty (Quorum **70** 126) (1982 5s 5fg 5f 6fg⁴ 6fg 6s) Apr 3; smallish filly; third reported foal; dam ran only 3 times; 3 lengths fourth of 17 to Aditi in maiden race at Folkestone in August, best effort; will stay 7f. *M. Tompkins.*

SALTHOUSE 5 b.g. Blakeney 126–Grilse Run 94 (Stupendous) (1981 12s **61** 13s² 14g 12g² 12s 14g² 13fg³ 14f 12fg 12d 1982 11g* 11s* 11.1g 10g) attractive, neat, strong gelding; won maiden race at Edinburgh (made all) and apprentice handicap at Hamilton (easily) in April; behind both subsequent outings; stays 1¾m; needs some give in the ground. *N. Callaghan.*

SALTOKI 2 gr.f. Ballad Rock 122–Farmers Daughter (Red Slipper 126 or **86** Javelot 124) (1982 5fg⁴ 5f 5fg* 5g 5g² 7.5g² 6g* 8g²) Feb 22; IR 70,000Y; strong, compact, quite attractive ex-English filly; good mover; half-sister to several winners, including Irish 3-y-o Remanded (by Garda's Revenge), a fairly useful 1m winner at 2 yrs, and speedy 1979 2-y-o Titauri (by Wishing Star); dam ran only 3 times; made all to win 5-runner minor event at York in June by 3 lengths from Brave Ivy when trained by B. Hobbs; sent to France after fourth start, winning minor event at Bordeaux in October and finishing second in her 3 other races; seems to stay 1m. *M. Laborde, France.*

SALUTELY (USA) 4 b.c. Hoist the Flag–Politely (Amerigo 116§) (1981 **107** won 3 times in USA 1982 7s³ 10s³ 8g* 8f³ 8f 8g) lengthy ex-American colt; half-brother to American stakes winner Northerly (by Northern Dancer), successful at up to 1¼m; dam an outstanding handicapper, winner of 21 races and over $550,000; third 3 times from 4 starts in USA as a 2-y-o and won 3 races from 12 starts there in 1981; won more than $47,000 altogether; third in Gladness Stakes and Sean Graham Ballymoss Stakes at the Curragh in April, beaten 4 lengths by Golden Fleece in latter; beat Punctilio in Coolmore Gay Fandango Stakes at Leopardstown the following month and finished creditable 3½ lengths third to Tellurano in Kilruddery Stakes on same course in June; never a serious threat when remote sixth of 10 behind impressive Mr Fluorocarbon in Queen Anne Stakes at Royal Ascot later in June on fifth start; stayed at least 1¼m; stud in USA. *M. Kauntze, Ireland.*

SALVINIA 2 ch.f. Mount Hagen 127–Aswellas 93 (Le Levanstell 122) (1982 **93 p** 6f 7g*) Mar 22; 10,000F; good-bodied, quite attractive filly; half-sister to 3 winners, including fairly useful 1981 2-y-o 6f winner Manchesterskytrain (by Home Guard); dam won 3 times over 7f at 2 yrs; won 23-runner £4,500 event at Newbury in September by a length from Gaygo Lady, racing close up throughout and running on strongly; will stay 1m; a useful filly in the making. *B. Hobbs.*

SAMANDAR (USA) 2 b.c. Decidedly–Dreaming (Bailarin) (1982 8g) Mar 7; — 19,000Y; close-coupled, workmanlike colt; half-brother to numerous winners, including stakes winner Wayside Station (by Shady Fellow), successful at up to 9f; dam won at 6f in USA and is out of sister to good colts Hill Rise and Hill Run; unquoted and backward, behind in 18-runner maiden race at Newmarket in October. *P. Haslam.*

SAMISEN (USA) 2 b.c. The Minstrel 135–Bamboozle 118 (Alcide 136) (1982 **94 p** 7s*) Feb 8; $200,000Y; closely related to 3 winners, including 1974 Champion Stakes runner-up Northern Gem (by Northern Dancer), and half-brother to French 1m and 9f winner Bamboo God (by Wajima); dam smart 1¼m performer; 7/1, ran on strongly when winning 16-runner maiden race at the Curragh in October by 6 lengths from Sir Simon; will stay 1¼m; very promising and is sure to win more races. *D. O'Brien, Ireland.*

SAM JOHN 3 b.c. Malinowski 123–Star of Sierra (Quisling 117) (1981 6g **86** 1982 8fg 8.5f³ 7fg 9f⁴ 13f* 12g⁴ 14s 11s* 12d) good sort; ex-English; won maiden event at Dundalk in September and handicap at Punchestown in October; beat Me Bonny Lass easily by 5 lengths on latter; stays 13f; acts on any going; trained by R. Price first start. *M. Connolly, Ireland.*

SAMMY BEAR 4 gr.f. Rupert Bear 105–Samba 69 (Sammy Davis 129) (1981 **59** 5g² 5g 5g* 5d* 5f* 5g* 6g³ 5d 5g 1982 5d 5fg 6f 5f² 5g³ 5fg³ 5.6f 5fg 5g 5g⁴ 5fg 5d) strong, compact filly; speedy and seems best at 5f; probably acts on any going; sometimes sweats up; ran as if something was amiss seventh start. *W. Bentley.*

SAMMYDAMUS 3 b. or br.g. Mandamus 120–Sapele 73 (Decoy Boy 129) **—** (1981 NR 1982 7.6f 8d) second foal; dam stayed 6f; well beaten in maiden races at Lingfield and Salisbury in June. *R. Smyth.*

SAMMY WATERS 3 b.c. Rapid River 127–Sambell 71 (Sammy Davis 129) **66** (1981 5f* 5d 5f 5f* 1982 5fg 5fg⁴) compact colt; won maiden auction event and valuable seller in 1981; modest form in handicap at Carlisle in July, better effort at 3 yrs; will stay 6f; acts on firm going. *C. Booth.*

SAM'S TICKLE 2 b.g. Tickled Pink 114–Samoa Tan 89 (Pago Pago) (1982 **—** 6f 7.6v 6g 5d) Feb 18; second foal; dam 1¼m winner; well beaten in maiden races and a seller; blinkered second and fourth starts. *H. Beasley.*

SANA 3 ch.f. Sallust 134–Kinnerton Street (Accordant) (1981 NR 1982 **—** 8fg 7fg 8g 6d 6s) 31,000Y; quite a well-made filly; half-sister to several winners, including very smart 1976 2-y-o Avgerinos (by Welsh Pageant) and very useful American sprinter Relent (by Crimson Satan); dam unraced half-sister to 3 stakes winners; little better than plating class. *M. Albina.*

SANCTA 3 b.f. So Blessed 130–Soft Angels 124 (Crepello 136) (1981 6g³ 7g³ **106** 1982 8fg* 8g* 10f* 10fg 8fg⁴ 8g) well-made, quite attractive filly; won valuable maiden race at York, minor event at Ayr and £3,000 race at Newbury; ran on well to beat Queen's Home by 1½ lengths in last-named in July; beaten some way in varied company afterwards; suited by 1¼m; acts on firm going. *P. Walwyn.*

SANDAAN 3 b.c. Zeddaan 130–St Louisan 109 (St Chad 120) (1981 6s⁴ 5s **—** 1982 6s² 5fg 8f) tall, slightly narrow colt; little better than plating class on balance of form; stays 6f; suited by some give in the ground; sold 440 gns Ascot July Sales. *J. W. Watts.*

SANDALAY 4 ch.c. Sandford Lad 133–No Delay 72 (Never Say Die 137) (1981 **72** 10g³ 12g 12d 11g⁴ 12.3fg 12d* 12fg 14s³ 1982 16s² 12g* 13.3f* 16.1g* 18.4g² 18.8fg) big, rangy colt; stayed on well when winning minor race at Pontefract and handicaps at Newbury and Haydock; beat Baron Blakeney by ½ length on last-named course in July; suited by a test of stamina; acts on any going, but is well suited by some give in the ground; has often made running; benefits from strong handling; never going well in blinkers final outing; sold out of P. Rohan's stable 30,000 gns Doncaster May Sales after second start; genuine. *P. Cundell.*

SANDCRACKER 3 b.g. Sandford Lad 133–Bubbly 61 (Busted 134) (1981 NR **53** 1982 12.3f⁴ 12f 12d 12g⁴ 16.5f³ 16.5f* 13.8f⁴ 16d 16g 15.8d) 4,800Y; big, strong gelding; third living foal; brother to a winner in Scandinavia; dam placed at up to 1¾m; won 3-runner maiden race at Redcar in August; not disgraced several other starts; suited by a test of stamina; acts on firm going; blinkered nowadays. *J. Etherington.*

Vernons Stakes, York—a winning reappearance for Sancta who beats Apples of Gold

Waterford Crystal Mile, Goodwood—Sandhurst Prince makes most of the running

SANDHURST PRINCE 3 ch.c. Pampapaul 121–Blue Shark (Silver Shark 129) **128**
(1981 6fg* 6fg* 1982 8s⁴ 8f² 8fg* 8f³ 8s)

Although the Two Thousand Guineas attracted its biggest field since 1964 and one of its biggest this century, as many as four of the season's best milers were missing from the line-up: Green Forest, Melyno, Pas de Seul and Sandhurst Prince. The absence of Sandhurst Prince caused the most stir. He'd been ante-post favourite for the race on the strength of two highly impressive wins at Kempton from two starts as a two-year-old, the first over Silver Hawk in the Chertsey Lock Stakes and the second over Foam Bath and the subsequent Cheveley Park third Admiral's Princess in the Sirenia Stakes. The Easter Stakes on the same course in April on his reappearance seemed little more than a formality for him, but he was beaten nearly twenty lengths into fourth place behind the very easy winner Rare Gift and promptly disappeared from the Guineas betting, never to return. Eventually Hays took his place in the field at Newmarket. No excuses were made on Sandhurst Prince's behalf at the time for his poor performance. Much later on it was suspected that he might have been carrying the unidentified viral infection which kept him off the course subsequently until the last week in July, but the explanation was staring us in the face: he cannot act on soft going, as he confirmed with another poor performance on his final outing of the season in the Queen Elizabeth II Stakes at Ascot in September. On that occasion he finished only eighth of ten behind Buzzards Bay, again beaten a long way. In between Sandhurst Prince showed excellent form on firm going, doing enough in three successive races to indicate that at his best he would have been a force to reckon with in the Guineas.

When he returned from his long lay-off to contest the Sussex Stakes at Goodwood Sandhurst Prince looked magnificent. He was also strongly fancied to win and almost did so, going down by only half a length to On The House after an eventful passage. Thirteen runners are quite enough on the Old Mile at Goodwood. Sandhurst Prince found them all too many as he tried to hold his place in the middle of the field on the inside round the long home turn: he received a nasty buffeting which cost him ground and seemed to put him out of serious contention, especially as his only hope of making progress lay up the rail. However, he proved good enough to take advantage of a clear path offered him on the inside and pulled the leaders back until he came to Bel Bolide at the furlong pole and had to be switched to continue his run. Once round he kept on very strongly to the end, as indeed did the winner.

The Waterford Crystal Mile at Goodwood the following month gave Sandhurst Prince an opportunity of capitalizing on his misfortune in missing so many big races, or to be more precise on his not having won one. The penalties incurred by On The House gave Sandhurst Prince an 8 lb pull (reduced a pound by overweight) and he also received weight from the two pattern-winning three-year-old colts, 7 lb from Dara Monarch and 2 lb from Pas de Seul. The rest of the opposition amounted to Kareena (20/1), Beldale Lustre and Riyahi (both 50/1) and the five-year-old Milk Of The Barley (150/1). Dara Monarch started favourite, a quarter of a point ahead of Sandhurst Prince. Over the years we have become resigned to assuming that the better a horse's chance the more likely he is to be held up. How refreshing therefore to see Sandhurst Prince make virtually all. It was obvious very early on in the race that no-one particularly wanted to go on, so Starkey seized the initiative and set a good gallop. Passing the three-furlong marker he kicked Sandhurst Prince clear and nothing thereafter looked the least bit likely to get to him; the horse's superiority was such that Starkey felt able to indulge in the increasingly common practice on English racecourses of easing right up in the last hundred yards, so that Sandhurst Prince in the end had an advantage of only a length and a half over the runner-up

Milk Of The Barley when he might have had four or five permitted to stride on. Such a practice not only carries the risk of collision with those coming up fast behind, it makes results downright misleading and should be discouraged. We appreciate that the horse had another race in the offing but Sandhurst Prince would surely have been better served had he been allowed to win by four or five lengths: his reputation, and hence his stud value, would have been boosted. After all, a bare length-and-a-half beating of Milk Of The Barley at weight-for-age is not top form, and those not witness to the performance might well take it at face value.

There was no easy race for Sandhurst Prince next time. He took on three of the best French milers in the Prix du Moulin de Longchamp in September, starting favourite at 6/4 ahead of The Wonder, Green Forest and Melyno. The tactics that had served him well in the Waterford Crystal Mile proved ineffective against Green Forest who, on his running here, has sound claim to being the leading European miler of 1982. Sandhurst Prince went off at such a lick that the presence of Green Forest's pacemaker Samer became unnecessary; he held the lead until inside the last two furlongs where Green Forest challenged and settled the issue in a matter of strides. Although Sandhurst Prince looked tired after setting such a gallop that the course record went, he ran on well enough to stay within one and a half lengths of the second horse The Wonder and to keep Melyno out of third place. Green Forest beat him by four and a half lengths.

Sandhurst Prince, who has run only seven times so far, remains in training. With so many of his contemporaries retired he should make hay while the (metaphorically and literally) the sun shines. We don't particularly favour his chances once the next set of three-year-olds move up to take on their elders after mid-season since it's probable that there will be one or more at least as good as Green Forest among them; the three-year-old milers of 1982, the colts at any rate, weren't a vintage collection by any means. It's almost certain that Sandhurst Prince will continue to be raced at a mile. He's a very free-moving sort, slightly headstrong, inclined to sweat up, not really the type that would

Mr J. C. Thompson's "Sandhurst Prince"

encourage his trainer to think seriously at this stage about a good race for him at a mile and a quarter such as the Eclipse. Aspects of Sandhurst Prince's pedigree do hold out some encouragement. His sire, a remote seventh after running too freely in The Minstrel's Derby on his only attempt at a longer distance than a mile, was out of an Irish Oaks winner and was a full brother to a horse that stayed a mile and a quarter. His dam, who was retired after her two-year-old days, would probably have stayed middle distances; she is a daughter of the fair mile-and-a-half winner Well Armed. The first of the dam's two previous foals to have run, Saint Geran (by the sprinter Red Alert), has won at a mile and a quarter and stays a mile and a half; the second, Snake Hips (by Gay Fandango), has won at a fraction beyond a mile in the United States.

Sandhurst Prince (ch.c. 1979)	Pampapaul (b 1974)	Yellow God (ch 1967)	Red God / Sally Deans
		Pampalina (br 1964)	Bairam II / Padus
	Blue Shark (b 1970)	Silver Shark (gr 1963)	Buisson Ardent / Palsaka
		Well Armed (ch 1961)	Persian Gulf / Armentieres

Sandhurst Prince is a rangy, quite attractive colt with an excellent action. Although it's not true that all good-actioned horses are suited by a sound surface, Sandhurst Prince certainly belongs to the majority that are: he needs top-of-the-ground. Before leaving him it would be remiss not to point out that like so many in his stable over the past few years he was very well bought as a yearling, for 16,000 guineas at Goffs. *G. Harwood.*

SANDICLIFFE GIRL 2 b.f. Malinowski 123–Ballynixon (Ballyciptic 122) (1982 6g 5.8g⁴ 5d 8fg) May 18; IR 4,200F, 11,000Y; neat filly; half-sister to two 2-y-o winners in Ireland; dam unraced half-sister to smart sprinter Trasi Girl; plating-class maiden; stays 1m; sold German International Bloodstock 1,400 gns Newmarket Autumn Sales. *B. Hills.*   **66**

SANDIFOOT 3 ch.c. Hotfoot 126–Sandray's Palace (Royal Palace 131) (1981 8s 7g 1982 8s 9g 12fg³ 13g* 12g 14.6f³ 12fg 12v) rangy, attractive colt; stayed on well to win maiden race at Ayr in June; well beaten afterwards; should stay 1¾m; sold 6,800 gns Newmarket Autumn Sales. *J. W. Watts.*   **78 d**

SAND LADY 5 b.m. Sandford Lad 133–Ribocana (Molvedo 137) (1981 7s⁴ 8fg² 10f³ 8f 9f 9f³ 10f 9f⁴ 10g 1982 8fg 7g 10fg 8.3fg 8fg* 8g) ex-Irish mare; half-sister to 2 winners, including fairly useful 5f to 7f winner Soul Singer (by Saulingo); dam won over 1¼m in Ireland; placed in varied company in 1981; dropped in class, showed first form over here when winning selling handicap at Warwick in August (no bid); probably stays 11f; probably acts on any going; often blinkered in Ireland. *J. Jenkins.*   **43**

SANDMOOR COURT 4 b.g. Moulton 128–Queen Anne 88 (Faraway Son 130) (1981 12f 16.5fg 10fg 1982 14.7f) big gelding; behind in amateur riders event and maiden races. *N. Tinkler.*   **—**

SANDRA'S SECRET 5 b.m. Most Secret 119–Grovenka (Kibenka 119) (1981 5g⁴ 5g 5d⁴ 5fg 5g² 5f² 5fg 5g 5s³ 5g² 5g 1982 5f 5g³ 5.1g 5f) sprint handicapper; ran easily best race when 3 lengths third to Soba in Gosforth Park Cup at Newcastle in June; best at 5f; acts on any going; blinkered twice at 2 yrs; ridden for 4 successes by apprentice N. Connorton. *G. Huffer.*   **84**

SANDRA'S SOVEREIGN 3 b.f. Workboy 123–Ruritania (Pampered King 121) (1981 5g 6g 1982 8f 7f 8g) workmanlike filly; little sign of ability; trained part of season by R. Ward. *G. Huffer.*   **—**

SANDY BIGHT 3 br.f. Orange Bay 131–Sea Holly 93 (Larkspur 128) (1981 NR 1982 10fg 12d 12fg 16fg) workmanlike filly; half-sister to Italian 7f and 1¼m winner Piazza Navona (by Upper Case) and a winning plater; dam stayed 1m; has shown a little ability in varied company; promises to stay 1½m; sold 2,500 gns Ascot November Sales. *J. Dunlop.*   **63**

SANDY LOOKS 2 ch.f. Music Boy 124–Hannah Darling 108 (Match III 135) (1982 5fg 6h³ 7d) well-made filly; has a capped off-hock; half-sister to 2 winners, including 3-y-o Zertxuna (by Averof), successful at up to 11f in France; dam second in Irish 1,000 Guineas; quite a modest maiden; not raced after July; stays 6f; acts on hard going. *C. Brittain.*   **69**

SAN FERMIN 3 ch.g. Sallust 134–Ilsebill (Birkhahn) (1981 NR 1982 6s 7g 8fg) IR 22,000Y; compact gelding; half-brother to 3 winners, including   **—**

smart 7f to 9f winner Sin Timon (by Captain's Gig); dam won in Germany and is half-sister to 2 German classic winners; beaten some way in maiden races early in year; sold to J. Fitzgerald 3,900 gns Newmarket Autumn Sales. *T. Robson.*

SANGRADOR 2 b.c. Thatch 136–Shadow Rose 112 (Dancer's Image) (1982 **105** 5fg³ 6g² 6g* 7d* 7d) Feb 1; 20,000F; big, strong, good-bodied colt; first foal; dam very useful Irish sprinter from family of King of Spain; ran best race when winning Birdcage Nursery at Newmarket in October by 2½ lengths from Tysandi; had got up on line to dead-heat with Liberty Tree in minor event at Ayr the previous month; suited by 7f; bandaged in front second outing and wore a small bandage on near-hind at Ayr. *W. Hastings-Bass.*

SAN ISIDRO 3 ch.g. Sallust 134–Ladys View 109 (Tin Whistle 128) (1981 — 5f 7fg 7g 7.6s 7d 1982 6s 6d) workmanlike gelding; only plating class; stays 7f; blinkered final start; sold 850 gns Ascot July Sales. *R. Smyth.*

SANJARIDA 4 b.g. Sandford Lad 133–Caught In The Rye 97 (Manacle 123) **86** (1981 6g² 5g* 5g* 6fg 6d 5fg 1982 6fg 6f 6fg* 6fg² 6fg 6f³ 6f² 6fg* 6g 5d) leggy, lightly-made gelding; held up when winning handicap at Salisbury in May and Nottingham Stewards Cup in August, latter by ½ length from Tobermory Boy; placed 3 times in between; stays 6f; probably ideally suited by a sound surface; blinkered final start in 1981. *M. Smyly.*

SANNA'S POST 3 ch.g. Pieces of Eight 128–Santa Laura 64 (Canisbay 120) — (1981 6g 7.6s 1982 10.1fg 12f 10.1g 7s 10v) well beaten in varied company, including selling; has twice been blinkered. *M. Masson.*

SANS BLAGUE (USA) 3 ch.f. The Minstrel 135–Joking Apart 120 (Jimmy **108** Reppin 131) (1981 6fg 7d* 7s 1982 12g* 10f³ 12v) attractive, rangy filly; good mover; third foal; half-sister to very useful middle-distance filly Deadly Serious (by Queen's Hussar); dam very smart at up to 1m; jarred a cannon bone in spring and was having first outing for 10 months when coming with a steady run to peg back Oxslip and beat her ¾ length in 11-runner Galtres Stakes at York in August; outpaced when 3¾ lengths third of 5 to Dione in Twickenham Stakes at Kempton following month and finished well beaten behind Believer in Princess Royal Stakes at Ascot in October; suited by 1½m and will stay further; possibly unsuited by very soft going. *R. Hern.*

SANTA ROSEANNA 3 br.f. Caracol–Santa Vittoria 100 (Ragusa 137) (1981 **111** 7.5f* 6d² 7d² 1982 7s* 9s* 10s 12fg 12fg 12g⁴ 9fg⁴ 10fg 10g 12v²) smallish, rather lightly-made filly; sister to Santa Elena, second in Group 3 Grosser Preis der International Harvester over 10.5f, and half-sister to 5 winners, including good middle-distance winner San Vicente (by Priamos); dam, from good family, finished fourth in Irish 1,000 Guineas; beat Wollisa a head in Warmlife Race at Leopardstown in March and floored odds laid on Pilgrim by a length in The Minstrel Stakes on same course in April; ran creditably several subsequent outings, notably when fourth in Brownstown Stakes at the Curragh (to Miraflora) and Pacemaker International Whitehall Stakes at Leopardstown (behind Punctilio), when fifth to Time Charter in Sun Chariot Stakes at Newmarket and when ¾-length second to Believer in Princess Royal Stakes at Ascot; stays 1½m well; acts on any going but evidently goes well on soft; blinkered seventh to ninth starts; sold 175,000 gns Newmarket December Sales and is to race in USA. *J. Bolger, Ireland.*

SANTA TOMAS 2 b.c. Varano–Celtic Scandal 77 (Celtic Ash) (1982 7d 8.2fg — 8.2s) Apr 15; IR 600F; robust colt; half-brother to fair 6f winner King Alfred (by St Alphage) and a winner in Belgium; dam needed a test of stamina; bad plater; sold 400 gns Doncaster November Sales. *W. Haigh.*

SANTELLA KING (USA) 2 b.c. King Pellinore 127–Timing (Bold Ruler) **93** (1982 6fg 6f³ 7.2g⁴ 7f 8g 8g) Apr 3; $110,000Y; rangy, attractive colt; half-brother to a winner by Forli; dam, half-sister to champion handicap mare Relaxing, won over 6f; disappointed after running well in useful company at Royal Ascot and Haydock on second and third appearances; off course 2 months after fourth start; stays 7f; acts on firm going. *G. Harwood.*

SANTELLA MAN 3 ch.c. Nebbiolo 125–Belle Bretonne 90 (Celtic Ash) (1981 **108** 7fg* 7fg* 7g 8f³ 7.6g* 8s⁴ 1982 10f 12f⁴ 16fg² 16g* 14fg 14f* 18g³ 16d 18d) well-made colt; good mover; easily landed odds in minor event at Chepstow in June and showed much more resolution than runner-up when beating Father Rooney a short head in 6-runner March Stakes at Goodwood in August; also ran well to be 1½ lengths second of 14 to Evzon in Queen's Vase at Royal Ascot

Mr Roy Taiano's "Santella Man"

and under 2 lengths third of 8 to Ardross in Doncaster Cup; suited by a test of stamina; acts on any going; genuine; ran poorly last 2 starts. *G. Harwood.*

SANTELLAS 4 b.g. Arch Sculptor 123–Stop Thinking (Divine Gift 127) (1981 — 7s³ 8d* 8.5fg* 8d* 10.1d 8g 8.3fg 8fg 8fg² 8.2v 8d 1982 8g 8g) good-topped, attractive gelding; fair handicapper on his day as a 3-y-o; in rear twice at Doncaster in March; subsequently won over hurdles in Jersey; best form at around 1m; probably acts on any going; blinkered once in 1981. *M. Vautier, Jersey.*

SANU 4 b.c. Steel Heart 128–Light Link 99 (Tudor Music 131) (1981 6g 6g³ **99** 6f 5g* 5fg² 6fg² 5fg³ 5d 5d 6fg 6fg 1982 6f 6g 6fg³ 6f 5g 5f 5.3f* 5fg² 6f 5d 5v) very useful handicapper as a 3-y-o; sent to USA and finished last of 6 at Aqueduct in April on only start over there; none too consistent on his return but got up close home to beat Dawn Ditty a head in minor event at Brighton in August; stays 6f; acts well on firm going (far from disgraced once on dead however); ran in error as Steel Pass first outing on his return from USA. *G. Hunter.*

SAPPHIRE 3 b.f. Warpath 113–So Precious 100 (Tamerlane 128) (1981 6g **73** 1982 8d 12fg³ 12d* 14.7fg 13.8d³ 12d² 15d⁴) neat filly; good walker; has a round action; won maiden race at Ripon in August; placed afterwards in 2 handicaps, one of them a valuable seller; stays 1¾m; suited by some give in the ground; tended to hang and didn't look too keen penultimate start; sold 4,000 gns Newmarket December Sales. *C. Thornton.*

SAQQARA 2 b.f. Persian Bold 123–Ballinteskin (Busted 134) (1982 6fg 6g 6s²) **73** Apr 29; 2,700F; close-coupled, rather lightly-made filly; fourth living foal; half-sister to a winner in Scandinavia; dam never ran; 2¼ lengths second of 16 to Onaizah in maiden race at Leicester in November; will stay at least 7f; acts on soft going. *P. Makin.*

SARACEN 2 b.c. Sharpen Up 127–Awash (Busted 134) (1982 6s²) Apr 24;   **93** p
135,000Y; second living foal; half-brother to 3-y-o 1m winner Rare Gift (by
Rarity); dam modest daughter of smart 5f to 7f winner Fluke, a half-sister to
Buoy and Bireme; co-favourite, went down by ¾ length to Golden Souvenir
after disputing lead throughout in 13-runner maiden race at Naas in November;
will probably stay 1m; promising and will win races. *D. O'Brien, Ireland.*

SARAH COURT 2 b.f. Rhodomantade 110–High Meadow 105 (High Treason   —
126) (1982 5f 6fg 5fg 8f 8s) May 1; workmanlike filly; half-sister to 9f winner
Fabrica (by Supreme Sovereign); dam won at up to 7f; well beaten in maiden
races. *H. Westbrook.*

SARAH GILLIAN (USA) 2 b.f. Zen–Kim's Song (Journalist) (1982 8g)   — p
Mar 23; $18,000Y; lightly-made filly; third foal; sister to American 3-y-o Zen's
Gem; dam ran only 4 times; sire, son of Damascus, won from 5.5f to 1m, showing
smart form at 3 yrs; outpaced throughout in Hoover Fillies Mile at Ascot in
September. *P. Kelleway.*

SARAH'S VENTURE 3 br.f. Averof 123–Railway Hill (Guersant 129) (1981   **63**
5s 5d⁴ 5f³ 6g 5f 5h 5s 7d 1982 7.6f 7fg 10fg 10f 8g⁴ 8s²) small, fair sort; in
frame in seller and minor event in the autumn; stays 1m; acts on any going;
blinkered once at 2 yrs. *P. Mitchell.*

SARAJILL 3 b.f. High Line 125–Centro 86 (Vienna 127) (1981 7d 1982 12f⁴   —
12fg⁴ 14g) lengthy, workmanlike filly; good walker; did best work in closing
stages when fourth in maiden races won by Glowing Halo and Fitzwarren at
Salisbury in May; should stay 1¾m. *H. Candy.*

SARAK 3 br.g. Jolly Good 122–Sarasingh 93 (Mansingh 120) (1981 5s 5v 6f 6g   —
7f³ 6f 6f 8.2fg 1982 10s 7f 6fg) leggy, lengthy gelding; plater; suited by 7f but
has run poorly over further; sometimes blinkered; trained by D. Garraton first
start; sold 400 gns Doncaster August Sales. *R. Ward.*

SARANITA 3 b. or br.f. Thatch 136–Sarania 118 (Sassafras 135) (1981 NR   **70**
1982 7fg 8fg 8f 8s 9s 7s²) good sort; good walker; second foal; half-sister to
Irish 7f winner Rafael (by Habitat); dam won over 6f and 1¼m, including Blue
Seal Stakes and Sandleford Priory Stakes; runner-up to wide-margin winner
Open The Box in handicap at Leicester in November; stays 1m; acts on soft
going; blinkered last 2 starts. *J. Dunlop.*

SARATINO 2 ch.c. Bustino 136–Sarah Siddons (Reform 132) (1982 7.6v 7d)   **79**
Feb 12; 19,000Y; useful sort; second foal; dam French 8.5f winner; 4½ lengths
sixth of 13 to Joyful Dancer in maiden race at Lingfield in October; last of 13 in
Houghton Stakes at Newmarket later in month; should stay 1½m. *I. Balding.*

SARATOGA CHIP (USA) 4 b.f. Plenty Old–Saratoga Gal (Royal Orbit)   **42**
(1981 7.6d 9f 7f 7f 7f 7f 6fg⁴ 7s* 7g 7g 1982 8f 7fg³ 10.6f 8f 8.3fg 8.3g 7g⁴ 8s 8.2v)
lightly-made filly; plater; stays 1m; probably acts on any going; suitable mount
for an apprentice; blinkered sixth start; sold 660 gns Newmarket Autumn Sales.
R. Sheather.

SARATOGA JIM (USA) 3 b.g. Accipiter–Billiken (Herbager 136) (1981 7fg   —
7d 1982 9g) good-topped, useful sort; behind in maiden races; sent to
Singapore. *E. Eldin.*

SARENA PLASTICS 2 b.g. Saulingo 122–Good Court (Takawalk II 125)   **63**
(1982 5f⁴ 5fg 6s 7g 6d 6s) Apr 12; IR 4,600F, 8,400Y; strong, compact gelding;
third produce; half-brother to 1980 2-y-o 1m winner Santella Ascot (by Furry
Glen); dam poor Irish maiden; only plating class; best run on fifth outing; off
course 3 months before third start. *S. Harris.*

SARITAMER CITY 3 b.f. Saritamer 130–Carmine City 104 (Charlottesville   **49**
135) (1981 6g 1982 6d 8f 11.7g³ 10.1fg 10.2g 8.3g 10fg 10.1d 10.2f 10g)
plating-class maiden; stays 1½m; has worn blinkers; sold to BBA 3,400 gns
Newmarket Autumn Sales. *M. Smyly.*

SARKAN (USA) 2 b.c. Naskra–Myrtle Dee (Revoked) (1982 5fg 5f 7g) May   —
6; $12,000Y; small, strong, compact colt; half-brother to numerous winners in
USA, including smart 8.5f stakes winner Gray Bar (by Tudor Grey); dam won
at up to 1m at 2 yrs; in rear in maiden and minor events; wears blinkers; sold
1,150 gns Newmarket Autumn Sales. *D. Elsworth.*

SAROAN MEED 3 ch.f. Midsummer Night II 117–Glistening 84 (Aureole 132)   —
(1981 7g 6d 1982 11.7f 12f) leggy, rather sparely-made filly; behind in maiden
races and a seller. *D. Gandolfo.*

SASHAMEL 3 ch.c. Tower Walk 130–Misty Echo 58 (Mountain Call 125) (1981 57
7fg 6g⁴ 6g 7fg 8.2s 8s 7g⁴ 1982 8fg 8fg² 8f⁴ 7fg³ 8g⁴ 8g 8s) useful sort; plater;
in frame in better company on occasions; stays 1m; blinkered twice in 1981;
suitable mount for an apprentice; claimed £2,005 after final start. *G. Huffer.*

SASOL 3 ch.f. Bustino 136–Wrekinianne 96 (Reform 132) (1981 7.2f² 1982 —
12f) big, rangy filly; has plenty of scope; poor walker; creditable second of 6 to
Swiftfoot in Rose of Lancashire Stakes at Haydock at 2 yrs; ran only once in
1982, when 8½ lengths sixth of 15 to Snow Forecast in well-contested maiden
race at Haydock in May; promises to stay 1½m; hasn't looked happy on firm
going either start. *M. H. Easterby.*

SASSALA 3 gr.f. Sassafras 135–Key of the Kingdom 111 (Grey Sovereign 128§) —
(1981 8d 1982 12d) leggy, unfurnished filly; beaten a long way in maiden race
at Wolverhampton and minor event at Leicester; sold 2,500 gns Newmarket
July Sales; resold $17,000 Fasig-Tipton Kentucky Mixed November Sale. *R.
Boss.*

SATIN GRANGE 4 br.g. Satingo 129–Court Circular (Ambiorix 130) (1981 51
8d 10d 8d³ 8d 10fg 9f 10g⁴ 1982 8.2s² 8f² 8g 8g 8fg) poor handicapper; tended
to hang when second at Haydock (seller) and Salisbury in spring, best efforts;
probably stays 1¼m; acts on any going; blinkered once at 2 yrs. *C. James.*

SAUCY FLUSH 3 br.g. Meldrum 112–Lady Loveliness (Flush Royal 127) —
(1981 7g 7fg 8g 10.2g 1982 10f 10fg 12d 16g 14.7f³ 14.6g 16g 18d 14.7f) leggy
gelding; poor maiden; stays 1¾m; acts on firm going; blinkered nowadays.
W. Bentley.

SAUCY'S SISTER 3 ch.f. Malicious–Beryl's Song 86 (Sing Sing 134) (1981 —
5d 5s 5s 1982 8fg 7f 8g 12fg 7s) lightly-made filly; of little account. *W.
Wightman.*

SAUCY VENTURE 3 b.g. Young Emperor 133–Reina Isabel 69 (St Alphage 119) —
(1981 5d 5g 7fg 1982 13.8f) small gelding; probably of little account. *G.
Richards.*

SAULANN 4 b. or br.c. Saulingo 122–Lucerne 76 (Gun Shot) (1981 5d 6g 63
6g 6f 7g 7g⁴ 1982 7f² 8f² 8f² 7f 8f* 8.2g* 8f³ 8fg 8fg² 7g³ 7g 7f 8s) compact
colt; won handicaps at Edinburgh in June and Nottingham in July in decisive
fashion; stays 1m well; probably acts on any going; started slowly when blinkered
once; sold to BBA (Italia) 4,600 gns Newmarket Autumn Sales. *P. Calver.*

SAULINGO LAD 2 br.g. Saulingo 122–Terina (Bold Lad, Ire 133) (1982 5s —
5s) Apr 12; IR 1,500Y; brother to 3-y-o Pilot Flyer and half-brother to a
2-y-o winner, dam ran only 3 times; well beaten in minor event at Ayr in March
and maiden race at Haydock in October. *W. Stubbs.*

SAULINGO SONG 3 b. or br.c. Saulingo 122–Comino Song (Tudor Music 131) 47
(1981 5s 5g 5g 5fg 5.3f³ 5.3fg⁴ 5fg 6g 1982 6f 6f 5h² 7g 5g 5.3fg) fair sort;
plater; yet to prove he stays 6f; acts on hard going; blinkered nowadays. *R.
Hodges.*

SAUNSON BOY (USA) 2 br.c. Honey Jay–Rulassah (Fleet Nasrullah) —
(1982 6g) Apr 14; $19,000Y; tall, lengthy colt; half-brother to 2 winners;
dam never ran; unquoted, always behind after starting slowly in 19-runner maiden
race at Newmarket in October. *I. Walker.*

SAUVAGE 4 b.c. Wolver Hollow 126–Belle Affaire 96 (Elopement 125) (1981 99
8g* 8.2s³ 8f 7.2f³ 8fg 9f* 10.2fg 10g 1982 8d* 8g² 8f² 8fg 8g* 8f³ 7f 7s) strong,
good-bodied colt; good walker and an excellent mover; useful handicapper;
successful at Kempton in April and Sandown in July, beating Macmillion easily
by 2 lengths in £5,600 event on latter course after travelling very strongly
throughout; also placed on same 2 courses in between and at Goodwood (didn't
find much) afterwards; stays 9f; acts on any going; held up nowadays and isn't
the easiest of rides; probably best on a turning track nowadays; blinkered last 4
outings. *M. Stoute.*

SAVAHRA 3 b.f. Free State 125–Avahra 108 (Sahib 114) (1981 5g 7fg 6d 8s 10s 82
1982 10fg 12fg 11g⁴ 11d* 12g 13d* 12d³) neat filly; has a rather round action;
won maiden race at Wolverhampton in August (apprentice ridden) and handicap
at Nottingham in September; stays 13f; suited by some give in the ground.
P. Rohan.

Rockfel Stakes, Newmarket—a pleasing performance from newcomer Saving Mercy who beats Thessaloniki

SA-VEGAS 3 b.f. Star Appeal 133–Rotondo (Royal Buck) (1981 8fg 8fg 8d² 1982 10d* 12fg 12g³ 12g² 12g* 14.6g² 13.3g² 12v 14v) strong, deep-girthed, attractive filly; good walker; won maiden race at Salisbury in April and £4,600 handicap at Goodwood in August; didn't have best of runs but quickened well to beat Lyphard's Pride by a neck in latter; also ran well to be second to Balanchine in A.T.S. Trophy Handicap at Newbury, to odds-on Swiftfoot in Park Hill Stakes at Doncaster and to Fitzpatrick in Coral Autumn Cup at Newbury, but carried head high and didn't appear to go through with her effort after looking likely winner in last-named; stays 1¾m; suited by some give in the ground; sold 52,000 gns Newmarket December Sales. *J. Dunlop.* **99**

SAVERNAKE 2 b.f. Whitstead 125–Miss Gruckles 89 (Derring-Do 131) (1982 5fg 5fg 6d 5fg 6f) Apr 28; 3,400Y; lightly-made filly; second living foal; dam 2-y-o 5f winner; poor form, including in sellers; not seen out after July. *M. Blanshard.* **57**

Mr Moufid F. Dabaghi's "Sayyaf"

SAVIAL MIST 2 ch.c. Mr Bigmore 123–Eridantini (Indigenous 121) (1982 —
6f 7fg 7g 6d) Apr 28; lengthy, good sort; half-brother to prolific sprint winner
Offa's Mead (by Rathlin); dam never ran; behind in maiden races and a nursery,
twice last. *R. Thompson.*

SAVING GRACE 2 b. or br.f. Red Alert 127–Swinging Nun (Tudor Melody 129) —
(1982 5g⁴ 6f 7d) May 1; IR 2,000Y; lightly-made filly; well beaten in maiden
auction race and sellers; blinkered final start; sold 625 gns Ascot July Sales.
Sir Mark Prescott.

SAVING MERCY 2 b.f. Lord Gayle 124–Fair Darling 93 (Darling Boy 124) **101** p
(1982 7g*) Mar 17; 42,000Y; lengthy filly; good walker; half-sister to several
winners, including fairly useful 1980 2-y-o 6f winner Paradise Bird (by Sallust);
dam, best at up to 1m, is daughter of very good filly Fair Astronomer; 14/1, put
up a pleasing first effort in 7-runner Rockfel Stakes at Newmarket in October,
leading 1f out and striding clear to win by 1½ lengths from Thessaloniki; will
be suited by 1m+; promises to make a very useful 3-y-o. *J. Hindley.*

SAX 2 b.c. Anax 120–Spring Music (Silly Season 127) (1982 5fg² 6fg 5.8g⁴ 6f⁴ **80**
5fg⁴ 5s 5v) Apr 14; 3,000Y; leggy, narrow filly; half-sister to 2 winning stayers
and a winner in Malaya; dam never ran; ran creditably in better company after
finishing 2 lengths second to Leandros in seller at Salisbury in May, best effort
when 4¼ lengths fourth of 10 to Aldern Stream in £3,400 event at Goodwood in
September on fifth outing; stays 6f; acts on any going; blinkered final appearance.
S. Woodman.

SAXHAM BRECK 2 gr.c. Abwah 118–Double Blush 76 (Double-U-Jay 120) **67**
(1982 5f⁴ 5d 5fg 6d 5s) Mar 22; 6,400Y; strong colt; third foal; dam, half-sister
to smart sprinter Son of Shaka, won over 1m; plating-class maiden; should
stay 6f. *F. Durr.*

SAXON FARM 3 ch.c. Hittite Glory 125–Kemoening 78 (Falcon 131) (1981 **75**
5s 5s 5s 6fg 7fg⁴ 7g 8g³ 8d 1982 10d 12f 13g² 16d³ 13.4g² 12fg 14g* 16fg 14.7fg
16.1s) good-topped colt; won minor event at Haydock in August; stays well;
suited by some give in the ground; blinkered sixth and final starts; has sweated up.
S. Mellor.

SAXON FORT 2 b. or br.g. Manado 130–Thanks Edith (Gratitude 130) (1982 —
8.2s) May 18; 8,000Y; half-brother to 2 winners in Ireland, including 1½m
winner Rare Edition (by Caracolero); dam, unplaced 6 times in USA, is half-sister
to top-class filly Aunt Edith; weak in the market and backward, never out of
mid-division in 19-runner minor event at Nottingham in October; subsequently
gelded. *M. Jarvis.*

SAYFARI 4 b.g. Sayfar 116–Flying Nun 66 (Welsh Abbot 131) (1981 12fg —
10.5f³ 10f 10₅ 11.0f¹ 10f 10.5f 1982 13.8f 14g 12.3g) leggy gelding; seems a
very slow maiden; blinkered last 2 starts. *Mrs N. Macauley.*

SAYF EL ARAB (USA) 2 b.c. Drone–Make Plans (Go Marching) (1982 **110**
5f⁴ 5fg* 5f² 6g⁴ 6d² 5fg* 5f⁴) Feb 12; $37,000Y; small, attractive colt; good
walker but none too good a mover; half-brother to 3 minor winners; dam lightly-
raced daughter of smart 9f stakes winner Sister Antoine; readily landed the odds
in minor event at Newmarket in May; took on good horses subsequently and
gained only one more success, when getting up close home to beat Jonacris
(gave 12 lb) by 1¼ lengths in £3,800 race at Thirsk (blinkered first time) in
September; best form at 5f, and appears barely to stay 6f; probably acts on any
going. *W. O'Gorman.*

SAY PRIMULA 4 ch.c. Hotfoot 126–Renoir Picture 90 (Relko 136) (1981 **105**
8v* 9s* 9d³ 10g* 12f 10fg 10g* 10d* 10.2g⁴ 10d³ 12v³ 1982 10s⁴ 10.5f* 10f*
10fg 10g² 10.5fg 11d² 10v 10g) lengthy colt; held up when winning handicaps at
York (by 3 lengths from Indian Trail) and Redcar (beat Meeka Gold by a head in
Zetland Gold Cup) in May; had much stiffer tasks next 3 starts, best efforts
when about 6 lengths fifth of 7 behind Kind of Hush in Prince of Wales's Stakes
at Royal Ascot (would have finished even closer had he not stumbled when
hampered on home turn) and 3 lengths second to Castle Keep in Land of Burns
Stakes at Ayr; beaten neck by Cool Decision in quite valuable handicap at Ayr,
best effort in autumn; best form at around 1¼m; evidently acts on any going;
has a useful turn of foot, but sometimes hangs and isn't the easiest of rides.
J. W. Watts.

SAYYAF 5 b.h. Habitat 134–Pavello 94 (Crepello 136) (1981 6g⁴ 6fg 5fg* 5fg³ **117**
5g 6fg³ 5fg² 6fg 1982 6g* 6f* 5fg 6g 7.2h 6f⁴ 6g* 5s) small, quite attractive
horse; half-brother to 2 winners, including useful 1982 2-y-o 5f to 1m winner

Impudent Miss (by Persian Bold); dam 1m winner and half-sister to smart Rymer; very smart sprinter; was probably at his peak as a 3-y-o, when winning Gus Demmy Memorial Stakes at Haydock and Scarbrough Stakes at Doncaster; in good form in spring and won Cammidge Trophy at Doncaster (made virtually all and held off Great Eastern narrowly) and Thirsk Hall Stakes (beat Crofthall by ½ length after none too clear a run); ran most disappointingly fourth and fifth starts but returned to form; showed all his usual speed when less than 4 lengths fourth to Indian King in Vernons Sprint Cup at Haydock in September (first race for 3 months) and made all and put up an excellent performance to beat subsequently-demoted Mister Rock's by 3 lengths in Prix de Seine-et-Oise at Maisons-Laffitte later in month; stayed 6f; acted well on firm going (ran creditably on soft in Prix de l'Abbaye final start however); ran creditably in blinkers but was better without in his later days (wore them in 1982 only on fourth start); standing at Baroda Stud, Newbridge, Co. Kildare. *W. O'Gorman.*

SCARLET TOWN   4 b.c. Town Crier 119–Sindo 91 (Derring-Do 131) (1981 **69**
6v 6s³ 8g 6g 6g³ 8g³ 8.2s 9g⁴ 8f² 10.4fg⁴ 8.2fg* 8d³ 8f 8g 8.2v 8d⁴ 8g   1982 10.2g 8g³ 10f 8f³ 8f⁴ 10fg³ 9.4fg³ 10fg⁴ 10.2g⁴ 10d* 10g 10fg⁴ 10g² 10fg 10d² 8.2s² 8g* 8s)   small, lightly-made, quite attractive colt; good walker; ungenuine in a finish, but usually reaches frame and won handicaps at Beverley in July and Leicester (raced alone in closing stages) in October; stays 1¼m; acts on any going; suited by a strong gallop. *R. Hollinshead.*

SCARROWMANWICK   4 b.c. Tickled Pink 114–Almadena 73 (Dairialatan **110**
111) (1981 7g 7fg² 7g* 7.6g 8f 7.2f 6g* 6g⁴ 6fg 6g* 6d 6s   1982 6fg² 7fg 7g² 7f 6f 7.3g 6g⁴ 7s 6s² 6s)   quite a useful sort; good walker; better than ever as a 4-y-o but didn't manage to win; second in Ladbrokes Abernant Stakes and Van Geest Stakes at Newmarket (beaten 2½ lengths by Lightning Label and by Noalcoholic respectively), and in Coral Bookmakers Champion Sprint at York; led inside last furlong until line when short headed by Soba in last-named event in October; best form at distances short of 1m; acts on any going; usually blinkered at 3 yrs, but wore them in 1982 only on second start; occasionally disappoints, and ran miserably final start. *N. Vigors.*

SCHARADE   3 b.f. Lombard 126–Shura (Birkhahn) (1981 NR   1982 10fg* **74**
10.1fg³ 11g⁴ 13g³ 13s)   tall, lengthy, sparely-made filly; shows quite a bit of knee action; sister to fairly useful 1980 2-y-o 7f winner Sunion and useful Sharifa, and half-sister to several winners in Germany, including top 1973 3-y-o filly Sheba (by Dschingis Khan), smart middle-distance horse Schiwago (by Masetto) and German 1,000 Guineas and Oaks runner-up Shantoo (by Charlottown); dam won at up to 10.5f in Germany; beat Gouverno by 1½ lengths going away in 21-runner minor event at Nottingham in June; in frame in similar event and 2 handicaps afterwards; will stay 1¾m; apprentice ridden when successful but seems suited by strong handling; sold 11,500 gns Newmarket December Sales. *M. Stoute.*

SCHEMING   4 ch.g. Great Nephew 126–Look Out 84 (Vimy 132) (1981 8g **69** d
12g⁴ 14g⁴ 16fg² 16f³ 14fg² 16g* 16s   1982 18.8fg² 18.8fg 16s 17.1s)   smallish, deep-girthed gelding; showed only form and ran well when 3 lengths second to Baron Blakeney in handicap at Warwick in May; off course afterwards until September; suited by a test of stamina; probably acts on any going. *P. Cole.*

SCHOLAR'S RING   6 b.g. Continuation 120–Schull (Yorick II 127) (1981 —
14.6f 10f 8g 8.2d   1982 10.2g 15.5g)   strong gelding; poor performer; seems to stay well; probably acts on any going except heavy; has worn blinkers; sometimes bandaged. *Mrs J. Pitman.*

SCHULA   2 b.f. Kala Shikari 125–Golden Track (Track Spare 125) (1982 **81**
5g 5f³ 5f² 5f² 5fg³ 5fg*)   Apr 16; IR 550F, IR 3,100Y; well-made filly; good walker; third foal; half-sister to Irish 9f winner Just Touch (by Touch Paper); dam ran once; won 11-runner maiden auction event at Warwick in July by 1½ lengths from odds-on Prairie Saint; should stay 6f; yet to race on a soft surface. *S. Mellor.*

SCHUSS   2 b.c. High Top 131–Christiana 106 (Double Jump 131) (1982 6fg³) **82** p
Feb 29; rather lengthy, quite attractive colt; half-brother to several winners, including high-class middle-distance 3-y-o Electric (by Blakeney) and smart 7f to 1m winner Chalet (by Luthier); dam, half-sister to very smart 1m and 1¼m performer Calpurnius, won over 5f at 2 yrs; short-priced favourite, moved really well and shaped most promisingly when 3 lengths third of 21 behind Coquito's Friend in minor event at Newmarket in August, tracking leaders

throughout, joining issue on rising ground, and being eased slightly when chance had gone; clearly quite highly thought of and is sure to improve and win races. *R. Hern.*

SCHWEPPERUSSCHIAN 5 br.h. Take a Reef 127–Romanee Conti (Will **115** Somers 114§) (1981 10.5v 11s* 9.7g² 11v 8fg 8s* 10f 8g 9d² 10v² 9v² 1982 10s 9s 8s* 8d 8s 8s³ 8s) useful performer as a 2-y-o when trained by J. W. Watts, winner twice at Ayr; has raced in France since and gained easily his most important win there in 7-runner Prix du Muguet at Longchamp in May, making all and beating Big John by 2 lengths; gained only other placing when about 5 lengths third to Ya Zaman in Prix du Rond-Point on same course in September; successful at up to 11f, but races mainly at around 1m nowadays; suited by plenty of give in the ground; has worn blinkers (wore them when successful); inconsistent. *P. Biancone, France.*

SCOT BENNETT 4 b.g. Tarboosh–Hell's Mistress (Skymaster 126) (1981 **45** 12fg 10fg 10.8fg 12fg³ 12fg* 12.2g² 12d 10.2g 1982 10d 15.8f⁴ 12f 12f 10.6h 10d 10g⁴ 12d 15.5v*) fair sort; plater; attracted no bid when winning at Folkestone in October; stays well; seems to act on any going; sometimes wears blinkers (did at Folkestone) and isn't entirely genuine; trained until after seventh start by C. Brittain. *J. Jenkins.*

SCOTSEZO 5 br.h. Scottish Rifle 127–Spice Berry 63 (Tutankhamen) (1981 — NR 1982 12f) well-made horse; should stay beyond 1m; usually blinkered; probably none too genuine. *P. Brookshaw.*

SCOTTISCHE 2 b.f. Quiet Fling 124–Fatherless 63 (Ragusa 137) (1982 — 8fg 8s) Apr 3; 4,100Y; workmanlike filly; third foal; half-sister to 9f winner Nob (by Mansingh); dam in frame both outings; in rear in maiden races at Beverley (slowly away) and Wolverhampton (last of 11) in the autumn. *P. Haslam.*

SCOTTISH AGENT 6 gr.g. Porto Bello 138–Alys Grey 91 (Grey Sovereign **46** 128§) (1981 6g* 6g* 6fg² 6f 6fg* 6g 6.5f² 7g* 6fg 6fg 6s 6s 6d 6s⁴ 1982 6g 6d³ 6f 6f 5fg 6g 6f⁴ 7f⁴ 6fg 6d 7g⁴ 7f² 8fg 7g⁴ 7f 7fg 6f 6v 6v³ 8g 6s² 7s) tall gelding; in frame in several handicaps, including a claimer; stays 7f; probably acts on any going; occasionally blinkered; often bandaged behind nowadays; not particularly consistent. *M. Ryan.*

SCOTTISH BELLE 5 br.m. Scottish Rifle 127–Persian Belle 77 (Darius 129) — (1981 12s 12f 10fg 16d 1982 10fg 14fg 12f) leggy mare; poor performer nowadays; often blinkered and has worn a hood as well. *A. Moore.*

SCOTTISH BOY 3 b.g. Music Boy 124–Klontina (Klondyke Bill 125) (1981 — 5s 5g⁴ 5g⁴ 5g 5g⁴ 6fg 5g* 5g 6d⁴ 7d² 6d 7d 1982 8.2fg 7f 8f 6g) tall gelding; plater; better suited by 7f than shorter distances; acts on a soft surface; best in blinkers. *J. Berry.*

SCOTTISH GREEN 4 ch.g. Scottish Rifle 127–Nuque (Suceso) (1981 6fg 6g **46** 8f* 8.3fg* 8g³ 9d 7g 1982 8f 8.3fg 8fg² 8.3g) neat gelding; plater; stays 1m well; acts on firm going; probably best in blinkers (didn't wear them final start); sometimes sweats up; claimed out of P. Makin's stable £1,555 after third outing. *A. Turnell.*

SCOTT'S ENTERPRISE 3 b.c. Prince Regent 129–Zulu Queen (Sovereign — Path 125) (1981 6g 6fg 6fg⁴ 7.2d 1982 10s 14fg 13fg 10fg) stocky colt; poor form, including in a seller; sold, probably for export to Scandinavia, 400 gns Doncaster October Sales. *R. Williams.*

SCOUTSMISTAKE 3 b. or br.g. Prince Tenderfoot 126–Summer Serenade 96 — (Petingo 135) (1981 6fg 7.2fg* 7g 1982 8fg³ 8f 8f 8.3g 8d 8.2s 10.2s) lengthy, quite attractive gelding; poor performer nowadays; well beaten in sellers last 2 starts; seems to stay 1m; blinkered second start; sold out of P. Walwyn's stable 3,600 gns Ascot August Sales after third outing. *B. McMahon.*

SCRUMMAGE 4 b.f. Workboy 123–Broughton Flyer (Huntercombe 133) (1981 — NR 1982 8s 8fg 8d 11g 6g 8g 7f 8.2v) first foal; dam never ran; little worthwhile form, including in sellers. *J. Berry.*

SCRUMPTIOUS (USA) 3 b.f. Nijinsky 138–Queen Pot (Buckpasser) (1981 **69** 7g 1982 10s³ 11f 10.1fg³) big, rangy, attractive filly; has a slightly round action; quite moderate; will stay 1½m. *I. Balding.*

SDENKA ROYAL 3 b. or br.f. Queen's Hussar 124–Sdenka 79 (Habitat 134) **69** (1981 5g 5g 7g 1982 9f⁴ 10f² 10fg 10g² 10.2g²) fair sort; runner-up in maiden races; will stay 1½m; yet to race on soft ground; blinkered final start. *A. Hide.*

SDENKA'S HUSSAR 2 b.g. Queen's Hussar 124–Sdenka 79 (Habitat 134) —
(1982 6f 7g 8s) Mar 8; robust, heavy-bodied gelding; third foal; dam placed
over 7f; backward, well beaten in maiden events August onwards at Newmarket
and Leicester (2); gelded after final outing. *A. Hide.*

SEA AURA 4 b.f. Roi Soleil 125–Sinkit (Sing Sing 134) (1981 7g 8s³ 7g² 7g⁴ —
8g 7g 1982 7.2s 7f) sturdy, good sort; fair performer as a 3-y-o; towards rear
twice in spring, 1982; probably best at 7f; probably acts on any going. *P.
Cole.*

SEABATTLE (USA) 3 b.c. Cannonade–Smooth Siren (Sea-Bird II 145) (1981 **80**
7g 8g 1982 12fg 11.7f³ 11.7f² 12f* 12s) rangy colt; made much of running and
kept on strongly to win maiden race at Lingfield in June decisively from The
Governor; will stay 1¾m; acts on firm going; ran as though something was wrong
with him final start. *P. Walwyn.*

SEA CLAIRE 3 b.f. Seaepic 100–Act The Creep (Gala Performance) (1981 6g —
1982 10f) behind in 2 maiden races at Nottingham. *K. Bridgwater.*

SEA DART 2 ch.f. Air Trooper 115–Major Isle (Major Portion 129) (1982 8s —
7d 6s) Apr 3; workmanlike filly; first foal; dam poor half-sister to Cesarewitch
winner Centurion; behind in autumn maiden races at Wolverhampton and
Leicester (2). *B. Morgan.*

SEA EXPRESS 2 b. or br.c. Seaepic 100–Expresso 76 (Roan Rocket 128) (1982 —
8fg 8s) Apr 18; rangy colt; half-brother to 3-y-o 1¾m winner Rexribo (by
Riboboy) and winners here and in Belgium; dam ran twice; behind in maiden
races at Goodwood (backward) and Bath (last of 11) in the autumn. *Mrs J.
Reavey.*

SEAFLOW (USA) 3 ch.f. Little Current–Shahtash (Jaipur) (1981 NR 1982 **60**
6d²) $62,000Y; quite attractive, lengthy filly; sister to a minor winner over
1m in USA, and half-sister to 3 other winners; dam, daughter of Hollywood Oaks
winner Rose O'Neill, won at up to 7f; favourite when beaten 2 lengths by
Florencia in 20-runner maiden race at Nottingham in September; will be suited
by 7f+. *R. Hern.*

SEA FRET 2 gr.f. Habat 127–Fluke 117 (Grey Sovereign 128§) (1982 6g* 6fg² **96**
7fg) May 25; 32,000Y; quite attractive filly; half-sister to useful 3-y-o 7f and
1m winner Main Sail (by Blakeney) and fairly useful 1¼m winner Sextant (by
Star Appeal); dam won from 5f to 7f and is half-sister to high-class Buoy and
Oaks winner Bireme); impressive winner of maiden race at Haydock in July on
debut; took on very useful fillies at Newbury and Goodwood afterwards,
running well on first occasion and poorly on second; should stay 7f. *G. Hunter.*

SEAGAS JETS 3 br.c. Balidar 133–Rudella 95 (Raffingora 130) (1981 6f 8.2s —
1982 6s 8fg) strong colt; has a round action; poor plater; sometimes bandaged
in front. *W. Wharton.*

SEA HARRIER 3 ch.f. Grundy 137–Anchor 106 (Major Portion 129) (1981 7g —
1982 10.6s) smallish, sturdy filly; ran promisingly in maiden race at Newmarket
at 2 yrs but finished well beaten in minor event at Haydock in October; sold
15,000 gns Newmarket December Sales. *R. Hern.*

SEA HAVOC 3 ch.f. Busted 134–Sea Lichen 106 (Ballymoss 136) (1981 6f 5d² **72**
6d⁴ 1982 8d² 8f* 8f 10g 7.2f) sparely-made filly; won minor event at Warwick
in April; soundly beaten afterwards, including when acting as pacemaker for
Zinzara fourth start; will stay 1½m; acts well on firm going; sold 13,000 gns
Newmarket December Sales. *H. Wragg.*

SEAMAN'S LOVE 3 ch.f. Royben 125–Snotch (Current Coin 118) (1981 7g —
1982 11.5f 8d) lengthy filly; tailed off in maiden races; blinkered final start;
sold 500 gns Newmarket July Sales. *C. Brittain.*

SEA PAGO (USA) 2 ch.c. Pago Pago–Sea Gate (Sea Charger 129) (1982 6f **92**
5g* 5f⁴ 6g² 6s 6d² 6d⁴) Mar 19; $13,000F, $20,000Y, $40,000 2-y-o; smallish,
strong, good-quartered, attractive colt; half-brother to numerous winners in
USA; dam won at 2 yrs in USA; won 7-runner maiden race at Pontefract in
August; good second afterwards in 2 nurseries, wearing blinkers for first time
when chasing home 3-length winner Bumpkin in £9,000 14-runner Martini
Trophy at Newmarket in October on sixth outing; suited by 6f; best form on
an easy surface; exported to Hong Kong. *M. Jarvis.*

SEA REPPIN 2 b.g. Jimmy Reppin 131–Sonseeahray 67 (March Past 124) **79**
(1982 6d 6f 7f 6d³ 8f³ 8.2s⁴ 7s 8.2v* 8.2s⁴ 10.2s) Apr 2; 1,500Y, 1,500 2-y-o;
neat gelding; fourth foal; dam seemed best at sprint distances; won 8-runner nursery at Hamilton in October; third in £3,000 seller at Newcastle on fourth outing;

suited by 1m; acts on any going, but revels in the mud; wears blinkers; gelded after final appearance. *K. Stone.*

SEATELL 2 ch.g. Guillaume Tell 121–Sea Dike (Dike) (1982 6fg) Apr 30; — IR 1,800Y; second foal; dam won over 1¼m in Ireland; 50/1, modest sixth of 12 in newcomers event at Chepstow in August; will need further. *G. Thorner.*

SEBAL 2 b.c. Prince Tenderfoot 126–Coral Lee (Le Levanstell 122) (1982 5f³ 5fg* 6s 6s) Mar 20; IR 22,000Y; lengthy, quite attractive colt; fifth foal; dam, Irish 9f and 13f winner, is half-sister to very smart Ballyhot; won 18-runner maiden race at Windsor in May by a length from Briavan; off course for 5 months afterwards, and was well beaten off severe marks in nurseries on return; should stay 6f. *G. Hunter.* **77**

SECOND FLOWER 3 ch.f. Indian Ruler 104–First Flower (Floribunda 136) (1981 6d 1982 10f 9f 7g² 7fg) workmanlike ex-Irish filly; fourth living foal; half-sister to 1975 2-y-o 5f winner Butterfly Boy (by Veiled Wonder), subsequently a good winner in Malaya, and Irish 1¼m winner Jo-Bo (by Aglojo); dam won twice over 1¼m in France; plater; best run at 7f though should stay further. *D. Gandolfo.* **49**

SECOND ORBIT 2 b.f. Space King 115–Seven Sisters 88 (Supreme Court 135) (1982 5g 8.2fg 8d) May 5; small, lightly-made filly; sister to 3 winners, and half-sister to several more; dam won at 1¼m; no worthwhile form in sellers. *R. Hollinshead.* —

SECOND SERVICE 3 ch.f. Red Regent 123–Monte Rosa (Crepello 136) (1981 NR 1982 6f 7d 6f 6g) small, good-topped, short-legged filly; second foal; dam, Irish 1m winner, from same family as Marwell; in rear in varied company, including selling. *W. Hastings-Bass.* —

SECOND TIME LUCKY 7 ch.g. Shiny Tenth 120–Luscious Bit 87 (Ennis 128) (1981 7f 1982 11fg 8f) lightly raced nowadays and was behind in a seller on first outing; stays 1½m; acts on any going; sometimes blinkered; has worn bandages. *T. Fairhurst.* —

SECRET EXPRESS 6 gr.h. Most Secret 119–Empress Donna 48 (Don II 123) (1981 6s 6s³ 6fg 6g 5fg 6g⁴ 5g⁴ 6g 6f 6g³ 6f⁴ 5d 6s 6s 1982 6d 6s 6g 6f 6fg 6g 6g⁴ 6g 7f 8fg 7g 6s) lightly-made horse; sprint plater; acts on any going; wears blinkers and sometimes bandages; has been ridden in spurs; sold 360 gns Doncaster November Sales. *W. Stubbs.* —

SECRET FINALE 3 ro.g. Warpath 113–Fox Covert 82 (Gigantic 102) (1981 NR 1982 8g 10fg⁴ 10.2g 11.5f 13.8f 10g² 10g 8.2s⁴ 9s) sturdy gelding; not the best of movers; half-brother to fairly useful middle-distance stayer Secret Ace (by Averof); dam sprinter; plating-class maiden; stays 1½m. *M. Lambert.* **58**

SECRET GILL 5 gr.m. Most Secret 119–Gill Breeze (Farm Walk 111) (1981 7d* 7.2s* 7g* 8g² 8g 7fg² 7g² 7f² 7d³ 7s² 7d² 7g* 1982 7d 7.6g⁴ 7f² 7fg* 8fg³ 7f² 7f⁴ 7f² 7d* 7s* 7d) lengthy, rather unfurnished mare; successful in Tia Maria Handicap at Ayr in May, Holsten Diat Pils Handicap on same course in September and Carling Black Label Lager Handicap at York in October; in frame most other starts; stays 1m but has won only at 7f; acts on any going, but has done most of her winning on an easy surface; needs to be held up (finds little in front); apprentice ridden for all her successes; consistent. *Miss S. Hall.* **88**

SECRET LIGHTNING (USA) 2 ch.f. Secretariat–Flash Flooding (Salvo 129) (1982 6fg³ 7fg 8fg⁴ 8g* 8.2v) Mar 12; $300,000Y; close-coupled, fair sort; half-sister to a winner in USA; dam unraced half-sister to high-class sprinter Swing Easy; made all in 8-runner maiden race at Edinburgh in October; soundly beaten in nursery at Hamilton later in month; suited by 1m; possibly unsuited by heavy going. *M. Stoute.* **78**

SECRET MIRACLE 2 ch.c. Abwah 118–Petit Secret 64 (Petingo 135) (1982 5fg² 5.8f* 5f* 5fg* 6g² 6f²) Mar 15; 9,000Y; well-made colt; fourth foal; half-brother to a winner in Trinidad by Town Crier; dam placed over 1m; landed the odds in small fields at Bath in May and June and at Windsor in July; second in his 3 other races, on final outing running On Stage (gave 3 lb) to 3 lengths in 6-runner New Ham Stakes at Goodwood; will be suited by 7f; acts well on firm going; blinkered fifth start; sold to race in USA. *I. Balding.* **103**

SECRET PURSUIT 3 b.g. Ardoon 124–Shangara (Credo 123) (1981 6fg 1982 8f² 8f³ 9.4fg*) small gelding; good walker; decisively won handicap at Carlisle in July; not seen out again; will stay 1¼m+. *M. H. Easterby.* **75**

SECTORI (USA) 3 ch.c. Secretariat–Marie Curie 96 (Exbury 138) (1981 NR 1982 8fg 11f 11.5f² 12f³ 12f 14.6g²) 92,000Y; neat, attractive colt; half-brother **77**

to 3 winners, notably very smart Irish miler Crofter (by Habitat); dam, half-sister to very smart Mariel, won over 6f at 2 yrs; quite a modest maiden; suited by 1¾m: sold to BBA 5,800 gns Newmarket Autumn Sales. *M. Jarvis.*

SECURO 2 ch.c. Le Johnston 123–Quite Safe 74 (Quorum 126) (1982 5g 5f⁴) — Feb 24; 2,500F, 2,900Y; poor last in maiden auction event at Hamilton in May and minor race at Ripon (blinkered) in June; evidently of no account; sold 420 gns Ascot 2nd June Sales. *M. Tompkins.*

SEDRA 2 ch.f. Nebbiolo 125–Hispanica 85 (Whistling Wind 123) (1982 6f² 92 6f* 6fg² 6s² 7.2s⁴) Mar 30; 22,000Y; useful-looking filly; half-sister to several winners, including Irish 3-y-o 1m winner Katie Roche (by Sallust); dam 2-y-o 5f winner; won 7-runner maiden race at Brighton in August by 2½ lengths from Grub; second in 3 other races, running creditably (even though generally flattered by proximity to winner) when beaten 2½ lengths by Misguided in minor event at Goodwood in September on fourth start; stays 7f; acts on any going, but has shown best form on soft ground; genuine and consistent. *J. Dunlop.*

SEED MERCHANT 2 br.c. Moulton 128–Mallow 70 (Le Dieu d'Or 119) — (1982 5f 6f 6d 6f) May 19; strong, well-made colt; first foal; dam, winner twice over hurdles, is half-sister to smart sprinter Bream and very useful 2-y-o Meldrum; poor maiden; tenth of 14 in valuable seller at York in July on final outing. *M. W. Easterby.*

SEEMS A NICE BOY 5 ch.g. Fair Decision 93§–Jevington 102 (Fairey — Fulmar 124) (1981 NR 1982 10g 8g) lightly raced and no worthwhile form, including in a seller. *B. Wise.*

SEE TEE BEE 2 b.f. Royal Blend 117–Acland (Mandamus 120) (1982 8f 8s) — May 17; sparely-made filly; first foal; dam of no account; behind in autumn maiden events at Leicester and Wolverhampton. *J. Wilson.*

SEGESTA 3 b.g. Blue Cashmere 129–Ann's Beam (Bold and Free 118) (1981 — 6fg 5g 1982 7f) lightly-made gelding; bad plater. *J. Tierney.*

SELBORNE RECORD 4 ch.g. Record Run 127–Flatter Me (Palestine 133) 50 (1981 12.3g³ 12.3g 12d 12s³ 12d 10.2g² 1982 15.8g 13v* 12f³ 12.3fg 12fg⁴) leggy, narrow gelding; won maiden race at Hamilton in April; gives impression he'll stay well (although was soundly beaten on reappearance); acts on any going; ran poorly fourth start. *J. Etherington.*

SEL-BY-OYSTON 2 ch.g. Sagaro 133–I Don't Mind 97 (Swing Easy 126) 72 (1982 6f³ 6g⁴ 7g³ 7f 7d 8f) Mar 31; strong, good-topped gelding; first foal; dam won 10 races over 5f and 6f; in frame in maiden races at Carlisle, Haydock and Chester; will stay beyond 1m; acts on firm going; gelded after final outing. *J. Berry.*

SENANG HATI 3 b. or br.c. Nonoalco 131–Sweet Sound 74 (Sound Track 132) 57 (1981 6fg 8s 1982 8.2v 9.4f 7g 8g³ 10g 9fg³ 10fg⁴ 12.3g) big, strong colt; poor maiden; stays 9f. *D. Smith.*

SENIOR CITIZEN 3 br.c. Brigadier Gerard 144–Argent Soleil 68 (Silver Shark 110 129) (1981 8s 8d 8s 1982 8s* 7g² 10fg 8g* 9fg³) 7,200Y; third foal; dam won over 6f; won maiden race at the Curragh in April and accounted for Memento by 2½ lengths in 7-runner Coolmore Hello Gorgeous Stakes on same course in June; also ran well when length second to Dara Monarch in McCairns Trial at Fairyhouse and third, under a length behind Punctilio, when giving weight all round in Pacemaker International Whitehall Stakes at Leopardstown; stays 9f; seems to act on any going. *C. Collins, Ireland.*

SENORINA FRANCESCA 5 b.m. The Brianstan 128–Pamaloo 93 (Pall Mall — 132) (1981 NR 1982 10d 8d 9fg) small, strong mare; poor walker; plating class at 2 yrs; won 3 times in Belgium in 1980. *K. Bridgwater.*

SENORITA QUERIDA 3 b.f. Steel Heart 128–Senorita Rugby 86 (Forward 92 Pass) (1981 5g* 6f⁴ 5f 1982 7d 6g⁴ 6fg 7f³ 6g* 7d 7f 6f* 6fg³ 6g 5.6g) neat, attractive filly; has a round action; won handicaps at Hamilton in June and Folkestone in August; best at 6f; acts on firm going; has won for an apprentice; blinkered final outing; racing in USA. *N. Guest.*

SENSING 6 b.g. Saulingo 122–Calcine 75 (Roan Rocket 128) (1981 NR 1982 — 10s 11s 6f 8f) poor performer nowadays; stays 1m; acts on any going; sometimes blinkered. *M. Naughton.*

SENTRY MAN 2 ch.c. On Your Mark 125–Lady Huzzar (Laser Light 118) 73 (1982 6g 5d 6g 6v⁴) Apr 3; IR 720F, 5,600Y; strong, good-quartered colt;

second living foal; dam never ran; blinkered when 2 lengths sixth of 17 to Shoeblack in maiden race at Nottingham in September, second outing; well beaten subsequently in £2,700 seller at Newmarket and 4-runner maiden event (blinkered again) at Hamilton; should stay 6f; sold 1,250 gns Ascot December Sales. *B. Hanbury.*

SEPARATE BID 4 b.c. Auction Ring 123–Fellow's Eyot (Roan Rocket 128) —
(1981 8fg 6f 1982 7g 7f 6fg 6fg 6s 7s) lightly-raced maiden; behind in a seller final start; possibly better suited by 6f than 7f; has been tried in blinkers; sold 440 gns Ascot December Sales. *I. Walker.*

SEPT 2 ch.g. The Parson 119–Mind The Beat (Gulf Pearl 117) (1982 6fg 6g 7g **101**
5f* 7f* 7.5f² 7g 7fg³ 7.5g*) May 23; IR 8,000Y; neat, attractive gelding; second foal; brother to winning Irish 3-y-o stayer Nesreen; dam unraced half-sister to very smart Blue Yonder; had a good season, winning maiden race at Bellewstown and nursery at Galway in July and valuable Waterford Glass Nursery at Gowran Park in September, carrying top weight to a 1½-length victory over Simmay at Gowran; also ran well when neck second to Indian Giver in another nursery at Gowran in August; will stay well; yet to race on a soft surface; wears blinkers. *D. Weld, Ireland.*

SEPTAGON 4 b. or br.g. Condorcet–Septima 82 (Primera 131) (1981 12g —
1982 12fg 16g) dipped-backed gelding; lightly raced and apparently of little account. *J. Hindley.*

SERENA MARIA 2 ch.f. Dublin Taxi–Slick Chick 89 (Shiny Tenth 120) (1982 **55**
5fg 6h 5g 5g⁴) Feb 20; 7,000Y; good-bodied, workmanlike filly; second foal; half-sister to 7f winner Basil Boy (by Jimsun); dam stayed 13f; 5 lengths fourth to Babycham Sparkle in 7-runner minor event at Edinburgh in October; off course over 3 months after second start. *M. McCormack.*

SERENDIPITY (USA) 2 ch.c. Terete–Gaska 110 (Gilles de Retz 132) (1982 —
7d) Apr 24; $16,000F, $55,000Y; half-brother to several winners and to Moiety Bird (by Falcon), the dam of Sharpo; dam, half-sister to Yellow God and St Alphage, was useful 2-y-o sprinter; unquoted and decidedly burly, tailed off in 19-runner maiden race at Salisbury in June. *R. Smyth.*

SERHEED (USA) 2 b.c. Nijinsky 138–Native Partner (Raise A Native) (1982 **92 p**
8g) Apr 23; $600,000Y; tall, rangy, good sort; brother to useful French filly Bev Bev, a winner over 5.5f and 7f at 2 yrs, and half-brother to several winners, including very good 6f to 1m winner Formidable (by Forli), very smart French middle-distance stayer Fabuleux Jane (by Le Fabuleux) and 3-y-o American stakes winner Flying Partner (by Hoist the Flag); dam, stakes winner over 1m, is half-sister to Kentucky Derby second Jim French; 12/1, ran on quite nicely once getting hang of things when 3 lengths fifth of 10 behind Coming And Going in minor event at Newmarket in October; looks sure to win races over middle distances. *P. Cole.*

SET 2 b.g. On Your Mark 125–Lucybird (Sea-Bird II 145) (1982 5f 5f² 5f*) **62**
Apr 14; 4,800F; compact, fair sort; half-brother to 3-y-o 1¼m winner Steel Glow (by Steel Heart) and a winning hurdler; dam unraced daughter of Sun Chariot Stakes winner Lucaya; sold 3,600 gns after making all in 8-runner seller at Redcar in May; should be suited by 6f; acts on firm going; wears blinkers. *W. O'Gorman.*

SET SAIL 3 b.f. Alpenkonig–Sayonara (Birkhahn) (1981 6g 6f 8fg 8d 7g **60**
1982 7d 7fg⁴ 8fg³ 8g³ 10g⁴ 8fg 8.2s 10g) small filly; plating-class maiden; will be suited by 1¼m; has twice run respectably for an apprentice. *J. Toller.*

SETTIMINO (USA) 4 b.c. Exclusive Native–Lucretia Bori (Bold Ruler) (1981 **50 §**
10d 8f² 8fg³ 7.6fg³ 6f 6fg 8fg 1982 10fg⁴ 8g³ 8f³ 8f³ 8f* 7f 8fg) strong, short-legged colt; won maiden race at Beverley in May unchallenged after making all; stays 1¼m; acts on firm going; usually wears blinkers and has also worn a hood; has sometimes given impression he has his own ideas about the game; sold 3,700 gns Newmarket July Sales and later raced in USA. *F. J. Houghton.*

SETTLED 3 b.f. Blue Cashmere 129–Fair Helen (Hopeful Venture 125) (1981 —
5s* 5g* 5g* 5g 1982 5s 6v 6v) lengthy, rather leggy filly; won 2 sellers and a claiming race in 1981; in rear in 3 handicaps at 3 yrs; should stay 6f; sold 400 gns Newmarket Autumn Sales. *D. Wilson.*

SEVEN BRIDGES ROAD 3 ch.f. Malinowski 123–Welshpool 75 (Henry the **53**
Seventh 125) (1981 7d⁴ 7g 1982 8fg* 10fg 8fg 8.2s) won maiden race at Thirsk in April; off course 5 months afterwards and was well beaten in handicaps on return; should stay 1¼m; trained by H. Cecil first start. *M. Blanshard.*

SEVEN CLUBS 2 b.g. Some Hand 119–Sister Angelica (Song 132) (1982 6fg⁴ **95** 5d* 5s² 5s) Apr 8; 3,200Y; sturdy gelding; first foal; dam never ran; always going well when winning 17-runner maiden race at Nottingham in September a shade cleverly by 2 lengths from Flying Scotsman; caught close home after showing excellent speed when head second of 7 to Private Label in minor event at York the following month; likely to prove best at 5f; acts well on soft going. *W. Hastings-Bass.*

SEVEN HEARTS 6 ch.h. Some Hand 119–Vienna Love 68 (Vienna 127) (1981 **86** 8g³ 8s² 8f 8fg⁴ 8fg 8fg² 8f 10d 8d² 9s* 8.2s³ 1982 8g⁴ 8g* 8g 8g⁴ 8f³ 8fg 8d* 8g⁴ 8fg 8g 8.2f²) strong horse; good mover; clear most of way up straight when winning quite valuable handicaps at Newcastle in April (Newcastle Centenary Handicap, beat Buffavento a neck) and June (Dobson Peacock Handicap, from Ring Bidder); good second to Fandangle in similar race at Haydock in September; stays 9f; acts on any going but has done most of his winning when there's been some give in the ground; wears blinkers nowadays; suitable mount for an apprentice; a genuine and consistent front runner. *K. Brassey.*

SEVERN SOVEREIGN 3 b.c. Fischio–Nimble Star (Space King 115) (1981 — 5s 8d 1982 8g 8d 11.7f 8s 10g) poor plater; has worn blinkers. *D. Wintle.*

SEW NICE 3 br.f. Tower Walk 130–Sew and Sew 96 (Hard Tack 111§) (1981 **71** 5v 5v 5g 1982 5fg 7g 5d* 6g* 6g² 6g⁴ 5fg 6g³) fair sort; has capped hocks; made all to win handicap at Beverley and minor event at Ayr in July; stayed 6f but seemed better at 5f; best form with some give in the ground; covered by Nicholas Bill. *J. Etherington.*

SEYMOUR HICKS (FR) 2 b.c. Ballymore 123–Sarah Siddons 122 (Le **78 P** Levanstell 122) (1982 6fg³) Mar 15; IR 125,000Y; second foal; dam won Irish 1,000 Guineas and Yorkshire Oaks; easy in market and bit backward, looked very green and was among backmarkers until making up ground hand over fist under sympathetic handling in closing stages, when very promising 3½ lengths third of 13 to Castanet in newcomers event at Goodwood in September; will be much better suited by longer distances; sure to improve, and win races. *J. Dunlop.*

S G S GLAZING 2 ch.g. Gunner B 126–Cherry Burton 79 (Kalydon 122) **66** (1982 5fg 5f 6f⁴ 6f 7d 6f 7f 7f* 8fg⁴ 8.2s 8d) Feb 10; 7,200Y; small, close-coupled gelding; half-brother to several winners, including smart sprinter Tackerton (by Hard Tack); dam sprinter; attracted no bid after winning 14-runner seller at Redcar in August; ran well in nurseries immediately before and after; stays 1m; suited by a firm surface. *N. Tinkler.*

SHAADY 3 b.c. Habitat 134–L'Eaulne (Busted 134) (1981 5fg* 5f³ 1982 **105** 7g* 7f 7g 7f 8fg* 8g 8f* 8g) strong, compact, deep-bodied colt; not the best of movers; successful in £3,800 handicap at Newmarket in April and quite valuable ladies races at Ascot in July and Doncaster in September; ran respectably on his other starts, including when close fifth of 14 to Paterno in Ward Hill Bunbury Cup (Handicap) at Newmarket on fourth; stays 1m well; yet to race on a soft surface; blinkered nowadays. *M. Stoute.*

SHABNAM 2 br.f. Jimsun 121–Beychevelle (Sir Herbert 106) (1982 5g 5h³ **66** 6f² 6fg 6g 6g³ 7g 8fg 8.2d 7g⁴ 7.2s²) Apr 17; small filly; second foal; dam won over 7f and 9f in Ireland and also over hurdles; plater; ran easily best race when second in selling nursery at Haydock in October; suited by 7f; acts on any going; started none too well seventh and ninth outings. *D. Gandolfo.*

SHACKLE PIN (USA) 2 b.c. Sir Wimborne 118–Countess Babu (Bronze **117** Babu) (1982 6fg² 7.2g* 6g³ 8.2fg⁴ 8d 8d) Apr 2; $50,000Y; neat, quite attractive colt; brother to a winner and half-brother to another; dam unplaced in 6 starts; won minor event at Haydock in August by a neck from Miss Sinclair; apart from one unsuccessful venture in handicap company, took on good horses subsequently, and on final outing finished creditable sixth, 3½ lengths behind Dunbeath, in William Hill Futurity at Doncaster; will be suited by 1¼m; best form on a soft surface. *J. Hanson.*

SHADAN 2 b.c. Cawston's Clown 113–Tudor Tilly 63 (Will Somers 114§) (1982 **90** 5fg 5g³ 5f* 5fg* 6fg* 7f⁴ 7g⁴ 6f* 7g* 6g) Mar 10; 920F, 5,800Y; small, well-made colt; second foal; dam won sellers over 5f and 6f, bought in 3,700 gns after showing much improved form to win seller at Bath in May and did very well afterwards, winning minor event at Hamilton, well-contested seller at Brighton (cost no less than 10,200 gns to buy in this time) and nurseries at Salisbury and Yarmouth; not certain to stay beyond 7f; yet to race on a soft surface; game and genuine. *P. Haslam.*

SHADES OF RED 2 ch.g. Whistling Deer ¸117–Positioned (Status Seeker) **71 §**
(1982 6fg 7g 6f 7f⁴ 7f 8f 8fg 8.2s³ 10d) May 18; IR 800F, IR 2,700Y; leggy,
lightly-made gelding; ran best race on seventh outing, when close up under 9-7 in
selling nursery at Beverley in September; well below that form most of the time;
stays 1m; blinkered last 4 starts; gelded after final appearance; unreliable.
D. Morley.

SHADEY DOVE 8 b.m. Deadly Nightshade 107–Red Dove (All Red 110) **61**
(1981 12g⁴ 13.3s⁴ 16.1s* 22.2f 12.2fg 12.3fg 16fg 16h 16s 1982 16g 16f³ 16.1fg⁴
17f) staying handicapper; ideally suited by some give in the ground; game;
doesn't always impress in paddock. *G. Price.*

SHAFIC 2 b.c. Monsanto 121–Secret Song 83 (Tudor Melody 129) (1982 6fg) **—**
Mar 12; 22,000Y; fifth foal; half-brother to 3 winners, including very useful but
temperamental 1977 2-y-o 6f winner Royal Harmony (by Sun Prince) and useful
1¼m winner Humming (by Bustino); dam sprinter; behind in 20-runner minor
event at Lingfield in September; has been exported. *G. Huffer.*

SHALABY 2 ch.c. Mansingh 120–Shelby (Pall Mall 132) (1982 5fg² 5fg³ 7f) **68**
May 7; rather leggy colt; half-brother to 2 winners, including fairly useful 1m
and 1¼m winner Beirut (by Northfields); dam won at up to 1⅜m in Ireland;
placed in maiden races at Chester in May and Hamilton in June; not sure to
stay 7f. *A. Jarvis.*

SHALIMAR 4 ch.g. Amber Rama 133–Enchanting 83 (Behistoun 131) (1981 **—**
10.2f 13fg² 14.6f* 1982 12.3g 13fg 20.4g 16f) big, lengthy gelding; poor form
on flat in 1982 (blinkered final start); suited by 1¾m; sold 5,100 gns Doncaster
November Sales. *C. Thornton.*

SHALLAAL (USA) 3 ch.g. Honest Pleasure–Grass Court (Herbager 136) **—**
(1981 7fg⁴ 1982 10fg 10g) strong, well-made, deep-girthed gelding; ran most
promisingly only outing at 2 yrs but disappointed in 1982 in Heathorn Stakes
at Newmarket in April and minor event at Nottingham in September; ran as
though something was wrong with him in former and showed signs of temperament, running in snatches, in latter; should stay middle distances. *J. Dunlop.*

SHALLOT BOY 4 ro.g. Workboy 123–Shall Do (Passenger 122 or Derring-Do **—**
131) (1981 NR 1982 11g) no worthwhile form, including in sellers. *F.
Watson.*

SHALLUM GIRL 2 b.f. Sheshoon 132–Zaratella (Le Levanstell 122) (1982 5f) **—**
Mar 2; 440F; leggy filly; poor walker and mover; second produce; dam ran 3
times; last of 11 after starting slowly in maiden race at Catterick in July. *D.
Yeoman.*

SHAMROCK GIRL 4 b.f. Workboy 100 Whistlewych 46 (Whistler 129) **—**
(1981 7fg 8f 7.2f 7f 6g 6d 1982 8fg 8f 6fg 7f) strong filly; little worthwhile
form; needs further than 6f; blinkered final start. *J. Carr.*

SHAMROCK NAIL 3 b.c. He Loves Me 120–Come Aboard 82 (Whistler 129) **62**
(1981 5d 6d 6fg 6d 5fg 5d 5v 5d² 1982 7g 9fg⁴ 8f³ 8fg⁴ 8.2f 8g³ 8fg 8fg 7fg 8.2s)
rather leggy colt; in frame in handicaps; will be suited by 1¼m; seems to act on
any going; sometimes sweats up; raced alone when blinkered once in 1981.
R. Hollinshead.

SHAM'S PRINCESS (USA) 3 gr.f. Sham–Alert Princess (Raise A Native) **117**
(1981 NR 1982 10fg* 10.5d* 10g³ 10g³ 12f) fourth foal; half-sister to minor
winners in France and USA; dam showed smart form over sprint distances at
2 yrs in USA and is half-sister to smart sprinter Tumiga; won maiden race at
Chantilly and Prix Fille de l'Air at Saint-Cloud in June; held up when beating
Unknown Lady by a length in latter; third subsequently at Deauville in Prix de
Psyche (6½ lengths behind Zinzara) and Prix de la Nonette (over 4 lengths behind
Grease); stays 1¼m and would be suited by more (soundly beaten in Prix Vermeille at Longchamp over
1½m); best form with some give in the ground. *O. Douieb, France.*

SHAND 3 b.c. Saritamer 130–Stockingful (Santa Claus 133) (1981 NR 1982 **—**
7f 8s 9.4fg 10g 10fg 10d 12d 12v) strong, sturdy, good-bodied colt; sixth foal;
half-brother to 3 winners, including useful stayer Wesley (by High Top); dam
half-sister to smart miler Richboy; well beaten in varied company. *W. Bentley.*

SHANIPOUR 2 ch.c. Nishapour 125–Forlorn Chance (Fighting Don) (1982 **96**
7fg 8g²) May 15; 12,000Y; tall, lengthy, attractive colt; half-brother to several
winners here and abroad, including very useful French middle-distance winner
Dieter (by Lord Gayle); dam once-raced sister to Forlorn River; promising
length second of 21 to Polished Silver in £4,200 event at Newbury in September,

making running for long way and keeping on strongly; stays 1m well; sure to win races. *G. Harwood.*

SHANLEYS STYLE 2 b.c. Balidar 133–Blue Promise 95 (Red Alert 127) **84** (1982 5s* 5fg² 5fg⁴ 5h* 6fg⁴ 5g 6s 6s) Apr 30; 10,000Y; workmanlike colt; has a round action; first foal; dam won over 5f from 3 starts at 2 yrs; won small races at Kempton and Chepstow in first part of season without needing to show great merit in order to do so, and was making little impact in nurseries in the autumn; probably best at 5f; blinkered final outing; unlikely to train on. *Mrs J Reavey.*

SHANNIE 3 b.c. Sharpen Up 127–Tender Annie 122 (Tenerani 135) (1981 NR — 1982 12f 14f 12g 8g 8g) 3,700F, 6,600Y; big, strong, good-bodied colt; brother to modest 1¼m winner Thimblerigger, and half-brother to several minor winners here and in USA; dam third in 1962 Oaks; seems of little account; usually blinkered. *W. Musson.*

SHANOUSKA 2 b.c. He Loves Me 120–Khadija 69 (Habat 127) (1982 5fg **66** 5.3g³ 5fg 5fg 7fg 7fg 6s) May 15; 11,000Y; somewhat lightly-made, quite attractive colt; first foal; dam plating-class maiden; no better than his dam; stays 6f. *J. Benstead.*

SHAPAARA 3 b.f. Rheingold 137–Sharmeen (Val de Loir 133) (1981 NR **65** 1982 10.2g 12f⁴ 12g³) third foal; half-sister to 2 winners, including brilliant Shergar (by Great Nephew); dam, granddaughter of French 1,000 Guineas winner Ginetta, won over 10.5f in France; quite moderate; will stay 1¾m. *M. Stoute.*

SHARAD 2 b.c. Mummy's Pet 125–Autumn Breeze (King's Bench 132) (1982 **84** 5fg 5g 5fg² 5g) May 12; 30,000Y; neat colt; brother to 3-y-o Incestuous and fairly useful sprinters Coded Scrap and Touch of Salt; dam ran only once; 25/1, put up easily best effort when 1½ lengths second of 10 to African Tudor in minor event at Warwick in August; should stay 6f. *G. Lewis.*

SHARAZOUR 2 gr.c. Nishapour 125–Scentless 88 (Floribunda 136) (1982 — 5.8g 6v) May 27; IR 25,000Y; half-brother to 3 winners, notably Brer Rabbit (by Song), successful over 5f at 2 yrs in this country and later a very good winner in Italy and South Africa; dam stayed 1¼m; in rear in maiden races at Bath in July and Folkestone in October. *F. J. Houghton.*

SHARED SECRET 3 ch.g. Most Secret 119–Mountain Child 70 (Mountain Call — 125) (1981 6f 1982 6fg³ 6f) workmanlike gelding; third in seller at Thirsk in April; stays 6f; exported to Malaysia. *C. Booth.*

SHAREEF DANCER (USA) 2 b.c. Northern Dancer–Sweet Alliance (Sir Ivor **93 p** 135) (1982 6f* 6fg⁴) Mar 3; $3,300,000Y; neat, well-made, handsome colt; first foal; dam won Kentucky Oaks; evens favourite, wasn't impressive when winning 18-runner maiden race at Newmarket in August by ½ length from Dalmane but didn't look fully wound up and showed distinct signs of greenness after leading 1f out; favourite although drawn on possibly slower side of course, couldn't quicken in closing stages when 5 lengths fourth of 25 to Orixo in minor event at Doncaster the following month; likely to do better over longer distances. *M. Stoute.*

SHARLIE'S WIMPY 3 ch.c. Tumble Wind–Sweet Sharlie 77 (Fighting Charlie **86** 127) (1981 5.8g³ 5g* 6fg² 5g³ 5fg 6fg³ 7fg 6d 6g 1982 6fg 8f² 8fg 8f 7g 8.5fg 8s 8v⁴ 8s 7s³ 6s) strong, attractive colt; good mover; fair handicapper on his day; stays 1m; acts on any going; ran moderately in blinkers sixth start; trained by P. Cole first 6 outings. *J. Bethell.*

SHARP CELESTE 5 ch.m. Sharpen Up 127–Celeste 83 (Sing Sing 134) (1981 — 7fg³ 7.6g⁴ 8.5g 8fg 7g² 8d 7g* 1982 8d 7f 7fg 7fg 7fg 8fg 7fg⁴ 7fg 8d 8g) small mare; mainly disappointing in 1982; stays 1m; acts on a firm surface; suitable mount for a boy; trained much of season by A. Pitt. *D. Weeden.*

SHARPEN UP BOY 2 b.c. Impecunious–Sharpenella 72 (Sharpen Up 127) — (1982 8s) Mar 26; lengthy colt; first foal; dam won over 5.8f at 2 yrs; 33/1, missed break when behind in 14-runner maiden race at Leicester in November. *R. Simpson.*

SHARPISH 2 ch.c. Sharpen Up 127–Restive 96 (Relic) (1982 6fg² 6fg 6fg³ **86** 6d 6s) Mar 8; half-brother to Irish 5f winner Restless Dancer (by Saritamer); dam suited by 6f; beaten 5 lengths when second of 11 to Salieri in maiden race at Newmarket in July and when third of 25 to Orixo in minor event at Doncaster in September; ran moderately in his other races; stays 6f; suited by a firm surface. *B. Hobbs.*

754

SHARP MELODY 3 b.f. Hot Spark 126–Tulchan 95 (Tudor Melody 129) —
(1981 5s² 5d 5fg² 5d⁴ 5d 6f 7f 1982 10f) poor form, including in a seller;
has been blinkered. *R. Hoad.*

SHARPO 5 ch.h. Sharpen Up 127–Moiety Bird (Falcon 131) (1981 5g³ 5s* 5f **130**
5d* 5d² 7v 1982 5fg³ 6f* 5g* 6f 5s*)
      The sprinting scene was much the poorer in 1982 without Marwell and
Moorestyle who, along with Sharpo, had cleaned up nearly all of the top races
during the previous two seasons. A handful of new names emerged—Fearless
Lad, Indian King and Soba making as much impact as any—and a few of the
second division such as Great Eastern, Sayyaf and Tina's Pet remained, but
none was able to offer a serious threat to Sharpo. On his day Sharpo was head
and shoulders above them and he won two of the three most important sprints in
the Calendar, the William Hill July Cup at Newmarket and the William Hill
Sprint Championship at York, before going out in a blaze of glory in the Prix
de l'Abbaye de Longchamp.
      Sharpo had spent much of 1981 racing over five furlongs as his trainer
regarded Moorestyle superior over further; he was equally effective at six, so
with Moorestyle out of the way he had all the top sprints on his agenda in 1982
as long as suitable going could be found. Sharpo had jarred himself badly in
the 1981 King's Stand Stakes, and as far as possible running him on firm again
would be avoided. He was risked on fastish ground in the Palace House Stakes
at Newmarket on Guineas day (the going was officially returned as good), where
he was a shade-unlucky third to Lightning Label, but before he made his next
appearance in the July Cup engagements had frustratingly to be passed over in
the Duke of York Stakes, the Temple Stakes and the King's Stand Stakes on
account of the conditions. Come July Cup day the going was firm yet again;
this time, after much deliberation, Sharpo was allowed to take his chance. In a
field of sixteen, the biggest since 1966, Sharpo started a weak third favourite
behind the confirmed top-of-the-ground specialist Indian King and the erstwhile
classic horse Tender King. Sharpo was unquestionably the pick of the paddock
and his connections must have been relieved to see no sign of his feeling the
ground on the way to post. Eddery, who'd ridden Sharpo to his most
important successes, handled him superbly. He held him up for a long time,
reportedly fearing to let him down, bringing him with his challenge as the
leaders met the hill. There was very little room, and Sharpo had to be switched
to get through; he changed his legs without losing any momentum, finally saw
daylight and quickened up so well that Eddery was able to drop his hands a
couple of strides from the line. Despite this he still had three quarters of a
length to spare over Vaigly Star, with Indian King and Tender King third and
fourth respectively.
      Sharpo was clearly right back to form. Luckily running him at Newmarket
had no ill effects and the following month he won the William Hill Sprint
Championship at York most convincingly for the third year in succession, thus
equalling the record of the grey gelding Tag End who'd won it in 1928, 1929 and
1930, and surpassing that of Highborn II, Abernant, Royal Serenade and Right
Boy who'd all won it twice when it was known as the Nunthorpe Stakes. Tag
End must have been a grand sort—he also won the King's Stand and the Portland
Handicap (a far more important race in those days) and gained the last of his
twenty wins as a nine-year-old—but the Nunthorpe took a good deal less
winning then and he faced no more than four opponents each time. Few

*William Hill July Cup, Newmarket—Sharpo (centre of picture)
takes the race with his terrific late burst*

*William Hill Sprint Championship, York—a majestic performance
as Sharpo lifts the prize for the third year in a row*

therefore would argue that Sharpo's record in the race is second to none. Ridden by Cauthen for the first time, as Eddery was out of action with a hand injury sustained on the first day of the meeting, Sharpo was held up as usual before being produced with a terrific burst of acceleration that took him to the front inside the last furlong. He was soon clear and cruised home two lengths ahead of the filly Chellaston Park. Had he been ridden out he would certainly have surpassed the two-and-a-half-length margin by which he'd won in 1980, from Valeriga, and 1981, from Marwell and Moorestyle.

Since Sharpo had beaten nearly all the best sprinters in Europe on his last two outings it was difficult to see anything preventing him from going through the remainder of the season unbeaten. However, that was overlooking the fact that in previous years he had been inclined to lose the odd race he should have won. In his next, despite odds of 15/8 being laid on him in the Vernons Sprint Cup at Haydock in September, he was defeated. Eddery was once again unavailable—he was required at Leopardstown where all his five mounts were winners—and as Cauthen was retained for Jester the ride went to Rouse who'd been in the saddle when Sharpo had burst so dramatically on the scene in the 1980 Temple Stakes. The going was firm again, but although we are emphatic that Sharpo didn't go down to the start with the freedom he'd shown at Newmarket and York, the conditions weren't necessarily the cause of his defeat. Sharpo seemed to lose his chance on the bend, only a furlong or so from the start. He became involved in some scrimmaging as the runners jostled for position—Rouse claimed Sharpo was barged into by Fearless Lad, although this detail was not apparent from the stands or on the video recording—and after turning wide into the straight Sharpo was always fighting a losing battle. He had no chance with Indian King in the closing stages and came in fifth, beaten about four lengths. Arguably Sharpo's lack of experience of taking bends at full racing pace was as much to blame as anything; he'd only raced round a bend once before, in the Prix de la Foret at Longchamp.

Sharpo returned from Haydock with a cut on his near-fore which fortunately didn't prevent him from taking his place in the line-up for the Prix de l'Abbaye a month later nor gaining a decisive win so richly deserved after two seconds in the race. As in 1981 Sharpo was none too quickly into his stride in the Abbaye and at halfway he looked to have plenty to do. Such was his response when Eddery asked him that he was soon on terms with the leaders, and once in front

*Prix de l'Abbaye de Longchamp—an English 1-2
as Fearless Lad keeps Kind Music
out of second place*

the race was in safe-keeping, although Eddery took no chances. Sharpo passed the post a length ahead of the King's Stand winner Fearless Lad with the top French sprinter Kind Music third, as he'd been at York. Eddery reported Sharpo had been struck across the face when making his challenge otherwise he'd have won more easily. Sharpo's victory was the fourth consecutive one by a British-trained sprinter in the race.

Sharpo (ch.h. 1977)	Sharpen Up (ch 1969)	Atan (ch 1961)	Native Dancer
			Mixed Marriage
		Rocchetta (ch 1961)	Rockefella
			Chambiges
	Moiety Bird (ch 1971)	Falcon (b 1964)	Milesian
			Pretty Swift
		Gaska (ch 1961)	Gilles de Retz
			Sally Deans

Sharpo has been syndicated for £20,000 a share and is to stand at Lord Derby's Woodland Stud, Newmarket, at the competitive fee of £3,000, plus £3,000 (October 1st). With both he and Kris at stud here the departure to the United States of Sharpen Up, a success almost from the start and represented also by Diesis in 1982, no longer seems quite such a loss. Sharpo's dam Moiety Bird, an unraced daughter of the very useful two-year-old Gaska, has had only two other runners to date, Demi Feu (by Firestreak), a winner at up to a mile and a quarter who became thoroughly temperamental, and Kalami (by Averof), who has been lightly raced and shown no form on the flat or over hurdles. Moiety Bird has since had fillies by Tachypous and Formidable, the latter fetching 68,000 guineas when sold at the December Sales as a foal. Besides Sharpo the most significant members of the family to emerge in recent years are Yellow God, St Alphage and Redowa, all by Red God out of the third dam Sally Deans. Yellow God and St Alphage were successful both on the racecourse and at stud while Redowa, only a plater, is the dam of Red Regent.

Miss M. Sheriffe's "Sharpo"

Sharpo raced throughout his career in the colours of Miss Monica Sheriffe, who never has more than a couple of horses in training at a time yet has also owned the prolific sprint winner Constans, the smart two-year-old Prime Boy, the Observer Gold Cup winner The Elk and the Two Thousand Guineas winner Only for Life. The last-named reportedly had unattractive curby hocks but they gave so little trouble that Tree wasn't put off when he noticed Sharpo had the same defect and was able to buy him reasonably as a yearling for 10,000 guineas. Apart from when Sharpo incurred a hip injury as a two-year-old which almost resulted in his being sold the purchase can seldom have been regretted. Sharpo, an attractive, close-coupled horse with a relaxed manner of racing which was ideally suited to Eddery's style of riding, had a dazzling turn of finishing speed and was without question the champion sprinter of Europe in 1982. *J. Tree.*

SHARP SEA 2 b.f. Sharpen Up 127–Windy Sea 105 (Sea Hawk II 131) (1982 **94** 6g³ 6f² 6f* 7f³ 6g 7.6s² 7s² 7g³) Mar 26; robust, well-made filly; carries plenty of condition; second foal; dam won over 7f and 1¼m; won 11-runner maiden race at Yarmouth in August by a neck from Mavournski; showed much better form afterwards over 7f, finishing 3½ lengths third of 6 to Muscatite in Fitzroy House Stakes at Newmarket, short-head second to Ultimate Pride in Burr Stakes at Lingfield, length second to John French in nursery at York and 3 lengths third of 7 to Saving Mercy in Rockfel Stakes at Newmarket; will be well suited by 1m; acts on any going; needs holding up for a late run; the type to train on. *B. Hobbs.*

SHARP SINGER (USA) 3 b.c. The Minstrel 135–Cutty (Smart) (1981 8s* **120** 7d* 1982 9.7fg* 10.5fg³ 12fg 10s 10v) IR 100,000Y; strong, good-bodied, attractive ex-Irish colt; third foal; half-brother to 2 winners in USA; dam won 9 times from 3 yrs to 5 yrs in USA, including 8.5f Osunitas Stakes; beat What A Guest in good style by a length in 9-runner Prix de Guiche at Long-champ in April; could only keep on at one pace when 2½ lengths third of 10 to Persepolis in Prix Lupin at Longchamp in May; in rear all subsequent starts, including in Prix du Jockey-Club at Chantilly and La Coupe de Maisons-Laffitte; possibly didn't stay an extended 1¼m; seemed to act on any going; wore a tongue strap at 3 yrs; standing at Bluegrass Farm, Kentucky, $10,000 live foal. *O. Douieb, France.*

SHARP STAR 4 ch.g. Sharpen Up 127–Sara's Star 70 (Sheshoon 132) (1981 **—** 8d³ 7d⁴ 8g* 7g² 7fg⁴ 8fg 8fg 1982 8d 8f⁴ 10f⁴ 10fg 10f 8g) leggy gelding; suited by 1m; acts on any going; has worn blinkers. *G. Blum.*

SHARP VENITA 4 b.f. Sharp Edge 123–Miss Venus (Comedy Star 121) (1981 **—** 6g 6g* 7d 6f 6f 6g² 7g 1982 6f 6fg 8f⁴ 6fg 6g 7d) lengthy, rather unfurnished filly; walks and moves well; ran best race third start; possibly stayed 1m; acted on firm going; often apprentice ridden; missed break when blinkered second outing; in foal to Faraway Times. *W. Musson.*

SHASTA SAM 2 b.c. Dragonara Palace 115–Deva Rose 80 (Chestergate 111) **87** (1982 5f² 5g* 5g 5g 5g) May 27; well-made, attractive colt; third foal; half-brother to 1¼m winner Rio Deva (by Spanish Gold); dam won 4 times over 5f; made all to land the odds by 2 lengths from Air Command in 10-runner maiden race at Newcastle in August; beaten only 5 lengths when seventh of 8 to Cat O'Nine Tails in Prince of Wales's Stakes at York later in month, but didn't run up to that form in 2 nurseries at Newmarket in the autumn; a free-running colt not sure to stay 6f. *R. Hollinshead.*

SHAVES YOU CLOSE 2 ch.c. Swing Easy 126–Sharpway 79 (Good Bond **109** 122) (1982 5fg³ 5f* 5fg² 6d 6f* 6g* 6fg* 7g⁴ 6fg⁴) Apr 4; 4,000Y; strong colt; first foal; dam 2-y-o 5f winner; had an excellent season, winning maiden race at Wolverhampton, minor event at Catterick and nurseries at Haydock and Folkestone; beaten less than length when fourth of 13 under 9-7 in nursery won by Pentland Javelin at Redcar in September on final appearance; best at 6f; acts on any going; game and genuine. *K. Brassey.*

SHEARWALK 2 gr.c. Godswalk 130–Sairshea (Simbir 130) (1982 5fg* 5f³ **109** 7.2g² 7f³ 7g³) Apr 6; compact, deep-girthed colt; good mover; first foal; dam won 3 times over 1½m in Ireland; won 9-runner maiden race at Newmarket in May, bursting through to win comfortably by 2½ lengths from Prince Reymo; placed in good-class races subsequently, running on best of all when just over 3 lengths third of 5 to Krayyan in National Stakes at Sandown, failing by a length to catch Alchise in 6-runner Cock of the North Stakes at Haydock and then finishing third to All Systems Go in Lanson Champagne Stakes (beaten about 1½ lengths) at Goodwood and in 5-runner Seaton Delaval Stakes (beaten 2 lengths, receiving 3 lb) at Newcastle; will be very well suited by 1m; yet to race on a soft surface. *M. Stoute.*

SHEBA'S GLORY 4 br.g. Averof 123–Little Miss 92 (Aggressor 130) (1981 **62**
12fg³ 12d 12d 12d 12.5f 12g 12g 1982 12g² 10d² 12fg* 12f⁴ 11fg* 12f² 12fg
10fg³ 11g² 9g 12g 12g) small, compact gelding; beat Mount Magic when winning handicaps at Edinburgh in April and May; ran moderately seventh and last 3 starts; suited by 1½m; yet to race on very soft going but acts on any other; well beaten when blinkered once as a 2-y-o. *F. Watson.*

SHEEN CLEEN 2 ch.f. Tumble Wind–Mandorla (Aureole 132) (1982 5d **—**
5f) Mar 15; IR 1,000Y; third foal; dam second over 1m at 2 yrs in Ireland; in rear in auction event at Leicester in March and seller at Catterick in July; sold 540 gns Doncaster September Sales. *W. Stubbs.*

SHEER GRIT 4 b.c. Busted 134–Abettor 103 (Abernant 142) (1981 7d 10fg⁴ **101**
12g² 12d 12f² 14fg³ 11.1f 1982 12fg 12fg 10fg 16g 15fg 21f³ 16g 18g 16d 16d
12g*) rangy, attractive colt; has rather a round action; smart and genuine as a 2-y-o; ridden superbly by L. Piggott when gaining his first subsequent win in handicap at Newmarket in October, holding on by a head from Keelby Kavalier after being shot into lead about 2f out; had run very well when dead-heating for third, 2 lengths behind Heighlin, in Goodwood Cup in July (headed only inside last furlong), but often disappoints; stays very well; evidently acts on any going. *C. Brittain.*

SHEER MADNESS 2 ch.c. Wollow 132–Our Song 70 (Song 132) (1982 **—**
5d 6g) Feb 16; 7,600Y; lengthy, workmanlike colt; second foal; half-brother to prolific 6f to 11f winner Rocket Song (by Roan Rocket); dam, half-sister to Swiss Maid, won over 6f and 7f; well beaten in large fields of maidens at Nottingham (second favourite) in September and Newmarket (favourite) in October; sold to CBA 3,100 gns Ascot December Sales. *Sir Mark Prescott.*

Mr R. E. Sangster's "Shearwalk"

SHELDAN 2 b.c. African Sky 124–Stickpin 74 (Gulf Pearl 117) (1982 5g **91**
5fg² 5fg² 5g³ 5s² 6s²) Jan 24; 11,000Y; neat colt; brother to 6f and 1¼m
winner African Pearl, and half-brother to a winning plater; dam placed over
5f and 7f at 2 yrs; placed in 5 maiden races, on final outing caught on line when
beaten short head by Raashideah in 25-runner event at Doncaster in November;
should stay 7f; best form with some give in the ground; deserves to win a race.
S. Mellor.

SHENTON WAY (USA) 2 b.c. Silver Saber–Recia (Silver Moon III) (1982 —
8.2s) Apr 6; $25,000Y; rangy, quite attractive colt; second foal; brother to
American 3-y-o Chilly Boy; dam won Las Oaks in Chile; weak in the market,
no show in 19-runner minor event at Nottingham in October. *M. Jarvis.*

SHERBAZ 2 b.c. Wolver Hollow 126–Shelina 114 (Mill Reef 141) (1982 **113**
5.5d³ 7d* 8fg* 8f³ 9d) May 23; attractive colt; first foal; dam very useful
winner at up to 10.5f; successful in maiden race at Saint-Cloud in July and
valuable Prix des Foals at Deauville the following month, finishing well to
score by ½ length from My Madness in latter; beaten in pattern races at Longchamp subsequently, putting up a good effort under top weight when just
over 3 lengths third of 8 to L'Emigrant in Prix La Rochette in September;
should stay 1¼m; probably acts on any going. *F. Mathet, France.*

SHERCOL 2 ch.f. Monseigneur 127–Merette 63 (Runnymede 123) (1982 **74**
6d 7fg 7f 6g 5f³ 5s 6s) Apr 17; 4,000Y; leggy filly; third foal; half-sister to
middle-distance winner French Knot (by Take a Reef); dam second twice
over 1m; quite a modest maiden; best form at 5f; acts on firm going. *R.
Hollinshead.*

SHERIFF MUIR 2 b.c. Try My Best 130–First Round 97 (Primera 131) (1982 **105**
5f² 6f³ 7fg* 7g² 7f) May 23; quite attractive colt; excellent mover; half-brother
to several winners, including very useful 5f to 7f winner Glenturret (by Habitat)
and very useful sprinter Rollahead (by Tower Walk); dam won at up to 1½m;
wasn't impressive in winning well-contested event at Redcar in July, taking
a long time to get into top gear and scoring by only ½ length from Arrowood
Bob who gave 15 lb; looked sure to win when moving up strongly 2f out in
minor event at Leicester the following month but didn't find as much as expected
and went down by 1½ lengths to Game Dame; will be suited by 1m; possibly
best with some give in the ground; sweated up on second start and got a bit
warm at Redcar; has plenty of ability but finds little off bridle and looks a
difficult ride. *M. Stoute.*

SHERNIYA (USA) 2 b.f. Empery 128–Sherkala 116 (Crepello 136) (1982 **82**
7fg⁴ 7fg) Feb 17; first foal; dam smart at around 1½m in France; 50/1 and
ridden by 7-lb claimer, made good headway in final 2f when 3½ lengths fourth
of 16 to Mamunia in maiden race at Yarmouth in August; ran poorly, finishing
out of first 10 of 19, in similar event won by Liberty Tree at Chepstow later
in the month; should stay 1½m. *M. Stoute.*

SHERRIFS BOY 6 ch.g. Comedy Star 121–Grania (Map Maker) (1981 NR —
1982 12d) selling hurdler; bandaged when towards rear in amateur riders
race won by Big-Ed at Beverley in July, first outing on flat. *R. E. Peacock.*

SHERWOOD OAK 2 ch.c. No Loiterer 90–My Pal (Welsh Abbot 131) (1982 —
5g 5f) Feb 3; 1,900Y; neat colt; half-brother to minor winners by Richboy
and Cavo Doro; dam ran only twice; well beaten in minor event at Doncaster
in March and seller (blinkered) on same course in May; sent to Malaysia. *W.
Stubbs.*

SHE'S INCREDIBLE (USA) 3 ch.f. Le Fabuleux 133–Her Prerogative **93**
(Buckpasser) (1981 6fg³ 1982 8.5f* 8g* 10fg³ 10f⁴ 10fg) leggy, lightly-
made, attractive filly; won maiden race at Epsom and minor event at Doncaster
in June; quickened in good style to beat That's My Son 4 lengths in latter;
in frame afterwards in handicaps at Newbury and Redcar; will stay 1¼m;
acts on firm going. *J. Dunlop.*

SHE'S MISTY 2 gr.f. Dragonara Palace 115–Bourges (Luthier 126) (1982 **57**
5d³ 5g 5.8f 5f⁴ 5.3fg 5f) Apr 2; first living foal; dam placed over hurdles at 3 yrs
in France; plating-class maiden; should stay 6f; blinkered final start; sold 600 gns
Ascot September Sales. *M. Haynes.*

SHE'S MY GIRL 3 b. or br.f. Mandamus 120–Boston Flyer 57 (Mansingh 120) **54**
(1981 5s³ 5s² 5fg³ 5g⁴ 5g* 5fg 5.3f* 5fg 5f³ 6fg⁴ 5f⁴ 5g⁴ 5d* 5s* 5g 1982 5s³ 5s
6f 6fg 6g 8g 8.2fg) leggy, narrow, lightly-made filly; first past post 5 times at 2
yrs; below form in 1982 and ran badly third and final starts; best at sprint
distances; acts on any going; has worn bandages; exported to Algeria. *K. Ivory.*

SHICKLAH (USA) 2 ch.f. The Minstrel 135–Logette 79 (Forli) (1982 5f* **106**
5f* 5fg 6f 5fg² 6g* 6g) Mar 27; $310,000Y; short-coupled, attractive filly;
good walker; first foal; dam, from same family as Habitat and Northfields, won
over 7f at 2 yrs; put up easily best effort when winning valuable Moet and Chandon Zukunfts-Rennen at Baden-Baden in September, beating Cause Celebre 2
lengths after leading at halfway; had earlier won 3-runner event at Lingfield and
Uplands Park Acorn Stakes at Epsom; not disgraced when 2 lengths second of 5
to Jonacris in Horn Blower Stakes at Ripon in August, but was no match for top
fillies in Queen Mary Stakes, Cherry Hinton Stakes and Cheveley Park Stakes;
suited by 6f, and is bred to stay further; has won on firm going but is possibly
better with some give in the ground; sweated up a bit fourth and fifth outings.
H. T. Jones.

SHIFT SUPPORT 2 b.f. Malinowski 123–Pushpa Ji Rao (Sayajirao 132) **50**
(1982 5fg² 5h³ 6fg 5.8f 6g⁴ 8.2fg 7g) May 13; 1,300Y; half-sister to numerous
winners here and abroad; poor plater; blinkered fifth and sixth starts; sold
450 gns Doncaster October Sales. *D. H. Jones.*

SHIMAAL (USA) 3 ch.f. Foolish Pleasure–Chalk Face (Nearctic) (1981 6g —
1982 7g) neat filly; showed a little ability in maiden race at Newmarket at 2 yrs
but finished last in similar race at Sandown in June; dead. *H. T. Jones.*

SHINE FORTH 4 ch.g. Shiny Tenth 120–Furley 91 (Decoy Boy 129) (1981 —
5g 6g 7fg* 7f⁴ 7fg 7f² 8fg 1982 5fg 7fg 8.2s 9g 8s 8g) lengthy, plain gelding;
plater; stays 7f; cost 600 gns Doncaster June Sales. *J. Edmunds.*

SHINING FUTURE 3 b.c. Sun Prince 128–Destinee (Roan Rocket 128) —
(1981 NR 1982 8g 10f 10fg 12g 12f) lengthy colt; behind in maiden races and 2
sellers; dead. *B. Swift.*

SHINING OUT (USA) 2 b.c. Full Out–All Agleam (Gleaming) (1982 6fg⁴ 6g²) **93**
Jan 21; $63,000Y; strong, well-made, attractive colt; first foal; dam unraced
half-sister to champion 1979 American 3-y-o filly Davona Dale; favourite, ran
well until weakening in closing stages when in frame in 13-runner newcomers
race at Goodwood in September and 19-runner maiden event (3 lengths second
to Matou) at Newmarket in October; sure to win in maiden company. *G.
Harwood.*

SHINING START 3 b.f. Lord Gayle 124–Scintillation 55 (Ballyciptic 122) —
(1981 5d 5d 5fg⁴ 6g² 7g* 7.2fg³ 7d 1982 8f 10.2f⁴ 12.3d) rather lightly-made
filly; good mover; won £4,200 nursery at York in 1981; in rear all starts at 3 yrs;
should stay 1¼m; acts on a firm surface. *C. Booth.*

SHINY HOUR 3 ch.c. Shiny Tenth 120–Lizzylyn 84 (Tower Walk 130) (1981 **71**
5s⁴ 5d* 6g 5f³ 5f 6g 5g 1982 5d 6f* 6fg 6f³ 7fg 5.8g 5.8f 6f 6fg 6d 6g*) rangy,
workmanlike colt; decisively won apprentice handicap at Salisbury in May
and claiming handicap at Newmarket in October; suited by 6f; seems to act on
any going. *M. McCormack.*

SHINY PILGRIM 2 b.g. Sparkler 130–Mecca II 90 (Exbury 138) (1982 **65** p
6fg 7g) Mar 20; 3,300Y; fair sort; brother to modest 1¼m winner Embustera,
and half-brother to 3 winners, including good Spanish horse El Senor (by Taj
Dewan); dam won at 1¼m; not fully wound up, showed ability in maiden auction
event at Newcastle in July and minor event on same course in August; will
be suited by 1m; likely to improve. *W. A. Stephenson.*

SHIPLAKE 2 b.c. Monsanto 121–Marie Denise 68 (Dual 117) (1982 5fg 5g **63**
7fg³ 5.8f 7fg³ 8f 8g) Apr 29; 3,500F, 4,200Y; strong, good-bodied colt; half-
brother to 3 winners, including stayer Passerine (by My Swallow); dam a stayer
and fairly useful hurdler; modest plater; stays 1m; wears blinkers; sent to
Malaysia. *N. Vigors.*

SHIPSBOY 2 b.c. Decoy Boy 129–Saucy Arethusa 76 (Fighting Ship 121) —
(1982 6fg) May 1; 700Y; first reported foal; dam won over 15f; last of 12 in
newcomers race at Chepstow in August. *Mrs J. Reavey.*

SHIR KHAN 3 b.c. Bold Lad (Ire) 133–True Rocket 116 (Roan Rocket 128) **99**
(1981 5g² 5s 6f² 5fg* 5fg 1982 6f 5f* 5f 6f 6fg) brother to very smart Irish
sprinter Ballad Rock, and half-brother to 3 winners; dam very speedy 2-y-o;
beat The Primate by 4 lengths in minor event at Navan in May; showed speed 4f
when behind in Cork and Orrery Stakes won by Indian King at Royal Ascot
on third start; stays 6f; possibly not at his best on soft going; best in blinkers.
N. McGrath, Ireland.

SHMAIN 3 ch.c. Sheshoon 132–Maiden d'Or 87 (Songedor 116) (1981 7g **77**
1982 12f 16fg* 12g 16d³ 15.8f 19f² 16.5g* 16f⁴ 16g⁴) deep-girthed, useful sort;

won maiden race at Beverley in June and handicap at Redcar (made all) in August; suited by a thorough test of stamina; seems to act on any going; sold to G. Richards 8,000 gns Newmarket Autumn Sales. *S. Norton.*

SHOCK TREATMENT 3 ch.f. Hot Spark 126–Parez 67 (Pardao 120) (1981 5fg³ 5fg 1982 5fg² 6g 6g 8.5f³ 7g⁴ 7fg 9f³ 8fg 8f³) leggy, useful-looking filly; placed in maiden and minor races; stays 9f; yet to race on a soft surface; sold 2,700 gns Newmarket Autumn Sales. *P. Walwyn.* **52**

SHOEBLACK 2 gr.c. Hotfoot 126–Tranquility Base 112 (Roan Rocket 128) (1982 5fg 5fg³ 6fg 5d* 5s³ 5s) Feb 23; strong, lengthy colt; half-brother to 5f and 7f winner Lady of Man (by So Blessed); dam at her best at 2 yrs when 5f and 6f winner; kept on genuinely when winning 17-runner maiden race at Nottingham in September by ¾ length from Non-Wet; creditable third of 7, beaten just over 2 lengths, in minor event won by Private Label at York the following month; stays 6f; seems to act on any going; dwelt last 2 starts; the type to train on. *N. Gaselee.* **94**

SHOEBUTTON 3 ch.f. Habat 127–Forgotten Dreams 82 (Shoemaker 121) (1981 6g 6g 6g 8fg⁴ 1982 12.2g 10f 12.2f³ 12f 12g 11g 11fg) leggy filly; plating-class maiden; stays 1½m; acts on firm going; sold 1,150 gns Doncaster August Sales. *P. Calver.* **54**

SHOOLERBOY 6 b.h. Shoolerville 121–Lovely Lady II 81 (My Love 133) (1981 NR 1982 12g 16f³) poor maiden on flat; probably stays 2m; has worn bandages. *K. Stapleton.* **—**

SHOONBEAM 3 ch.g. Sheshoon 132–Dust Sheet (Silly Season 127) (1981 5s 6g 6fg 5f 7g 6s 7.6s 1982 7fg 8.3g 12f 7.6f 10.1fg 10f 10fg 8g) smallish, fair sort; poor plater; sometimes blinkered; sold 370 gns Ascot September Sales. *P. K. Mitchell.* **—**

SHOOTING BUTTS 4 b.g. Tycoon II–Charlies Double (Fighting Charlie 127) (1981 10fg⁴ 16s 16.9s* 16g⁴ 16f 16.9fg 16.1s 1982 12g 16d* 16fg 16d 17.1s 18d 18s) workmanlike gelding; beat Elsell by 1½ lengths in handicap at Warwick in April; showed only other form on fifth outing; suited by a test of stamina; acts well on soft going; trained until after third start by J. Smith. *B. McMahon.* **69**

SHOOTING HIGH 3 b.f. Busted 134–Regal Miss 90 (Sovereign Path 125) (1981 7d 6g⁴ 1982 10fg 10f² 12.2g 10.1fg) well-made filly; has shown ability in varied company, on second outing going down by 1½ lengths to More Kisses in £4,100 event at Newbury in June; stays 1¼m (well beaten over 1½m); ran moderately final start. *P. Walwyn.* **80**

SHOOTING MATCH 4 gr.g. Home Guard 129–Bundling (Petingo 135) (1981 6fg³ 7g³ 6g³ 8g³ 6d 8s 8fg³ 8fg² 8fg* 9g 11g 9d 1982 8s 8.2s 11fg 8fg⁴ 8g 8f 7g 8fg 6fg) workmanlike gelding; plater; stays 1m; probably acts on any going, but seems best on a sound surface; often blinkered; has run creditably for a boy. *Mrs A. Bell.* **—**

SHOOT THE RAPIDS 2 b.g. Rapid River 127–Weirdi 76 (Yrrah Jr) (1982 8f) June 7; fifth foal; dam placed over 1m at 2 yrs; ninth of 10 in maiden race at Edinburgh in September; subsequently gelded. *W. A. Stephenson.* **—**

SHORE LINE 2 b.f. High Line 125–Dark Finale (Javelot 124) (1982 6fg 6g²) Feb 20; robust, good sort; good mover; sister to several winners, notably Park Hill Stakes winner Quay Line and very useful French filly Ancholia, and closely related to a winner by High Hat; dam won at up to 1½m in Ireland; ran on really well after being outpaced when 4½ lengths fifth of 9 to Habibti in £6,000 newcomers race at Ascot in July; favourite for 16-runner maiden event at Newbury the following month but couldn't match Jemeela's finishing speed and went down by ¾ length; will do considerably better over 1¼m+; worth following. *H. Candy.* **88 p**

SHOUT 2 b.c. Balidar 133–Cedar Tree (Alcide 136) (1982 5s) June 3; 3,300Y; tall, close-coupled colt; half-brother to a winner in Norway and a winner over jumps; dam, half-sister to top-class stayer Hornbeam, ran only twice; 10/1, stayed on after being outpaced and pushed along most of way when 4½ lengths sixth of 15 to Dry Land in maiden race at Sandown in October; sure to do better over longer distances. *G. Harwood.* **76 p**

SHOW-A-LEG 4 b.c. Tumble Wind–Lovely Woman 81 (Primera 131) (1981 10fg 12g² 12s² 11d⁴ 10fg² 10fg 10g² 10g* 10.8s* 10.2g 1982 10fg 12fg 9f⁴ 12f 10d 10.4d³ 12fg² 10fg³ 12g² 10.8s³) shapely colt; didn't reproduce his 3-y-o **95**

form, best efforts on seventh to ninth starts when placed in handicaps at Beverley and Goodwood and in valuable race at Taby, Sweden; went down by ½ length to Shaftesbury in Stockholm Cup on last-named course in September; finds 9f too sharp and stays 1½m; has run creditably on firmish ground but is ideally suited by some give underfoot; acted as a pacemaker for Glint of Gold second and fourth outings; probably not an ideal mount for an apprentice (ran most disappointingly sixth start in apprentice event at Chester); sold privately out of I. Balding's stable after ninth start. *R. Atkins.*

SHOW BUSINESS 5 b.m. Auction Ring 123–Modern Miracle (St Chad 120) **48** (1981 NR 1982 10.1d 12.2fg* 12.2fg) attractive, lengthy mare; showed only form on flat since 1979 when winning handicap at Warwick in July; stays 1½m; seems to act on any going; has been tried in blinkers. *J. Webber.*

SHOW OF HANDS 6 b.g. Royal Prerogative 119–Lindylee 99 (Grey Sovereign **70** 128§) (1981 7g* 8g² 7g² 7g* 6fg³ 8.2g³ 8g³ 7f³ 7d 7v 1982 7fg* 7g* 8f⁴ 8fg* 8f³ 7g 7g 7g) tall gelding; goes extremely well at Edinburgh and won there in April, May and July, on each occasion making virtually all; stays 1m, but probably best at 7f; acts well on firm going; blinkered once in 1979; ridden by apprentice N. Connorton for last 5 wins; ideally suited by an easy, turning track. *J. W. Watts.*

SHOW TENT 3 ch.f. Abwah 118–Carmel Valley (Real Good Deal) (1981 — 6fg 6g 6d 1982 7f 6f 7f 6d) quite an attractive filly; plater; stays 6f; sold 700 gns Newmarket Autumn Sales. *G. Lewis.*

SHREE 4 b.f. Moulton 128–Garnette Rose 74 (St Paddy 133) (1981 NR 1982 — 7f) showed a little ability at 2 yrs; last in seller on only outing since; will stay at least 1m. *A. Bailey.*

SHURWIN 2 ch.f. Touch Paper 113–Windy Rush (Whistling Wind 123) (1982 — 5v 6s 5d) May 11; IR 1,000F (privately), IR 2,800Y; half-sister to 1m and 1¼m winner Court House (by My Swanee) and a winner in Belgium; dam moderate at 2 yrs in Ireland; showed a little ability in maiden event at Hamilton in October on first outing, but none in plating company afterwards. *W. Stubbs.*

SHUTLAR'S FLING (USA) 2 ch.c. Northern Fling–Nora Harvey (Le — Fabuleux 133) (1982 7g 7.6v) Apr 23; $20,000Y; third foal; brother to a winner in USA and half-brother to another; dam never ran; little sign of ability in maiden races at Yarmouth (eighth of 16) in August and Lingfield in October. *I. Walker.*

SHUTTLECOCK DARTER 2 b.f. Jimsun 121–Cut and Thrust 78 (Pardal — 120) (1982 7g 6s) May 13; big, strong filly; half-sister to middle-distance winner Abielle (by Abwah) and a winner in Holland; dam won over 8.5f; unquoted, behind in September in £4,500 event at Newbury and Blue Seal Stakes at Ascot. *R. Hannon.*

SHUTTLE CRAFT 5 b.m. Sole Mio–Cindy O'Dea (Cintrist 110) (1981 NR — 1982 8f 8d 6g 7f) strong non-thoroughbred mare; little worthwhile form. *R. Woodhouse.*

SHUTTLE D'OR 4 ch.g. Goldhill 125–Northern Flight (Borealis) (1981 8g — 8fg 10.1fg 1982 10d) little worthwhile form, although has yet to run in a seller. *M. Chapman.*

SHY MASTER 3 br.g. Saritamer 130–Harriny 94 (Floribunda 136) (1981 **57** NR 1982 8d 5fg 5fg² 5d 6s) 2,700Y; smallish, fair sort; third foal; dam stayed 7f; sprint maiden; best run at 5f on a firm surface; retained 420 gns Ascot December Sales. *I. Walker.*

SHY TALK 6 ch.m. Sharpen Up 127–Skymistress 91 (Skymaster 126) (1981 — 6s 5s 5f³ 5fg 5g² 6fg* 5d 5f² 5f³ 6f* 6fg 5g 1982 6f 6fg) leggy, unfurnished mare; sprint handicapper; behind both outings in 1982; suited by 6f; seems to act on any going; ran moderately when blinkered once; sometimes bandaged off-hind; suitable mount for an inexperienced rider. *A. W. Jones.*

SIAGNE (FR) 2 ch.f. Riverman 131–Cap D'Antibes (Better Boy 91) (1982 **?** 5fg*) third foal; half-sister to fairly useful 3-y-o 1m winner French Current (by Without Fear); dam won 2 of Australia's most important sprints, the 5f Lightning Stakes and 6f Newmarket Handicap, after finishing ½-length second in 12.5f VRC Oaks; wore down Protos to win 5-runner Prix Yacowlef at Deauville in August by 1½ lengths; found to have a small chip of bone in her off-fore and wasn't seen out again; will be suited by 1m; should make a decent filly if she recovers fully. *Mme C. Head, France.*

SICONDA 3 ch.f. Record Token 128–Quickmatch 89 (Match III 135) (1981   **53**
5s² 5h³ 5g 5d 5g 8fg 8d³ 8.2s 8d⁴ 1982 8d 8.2d 10f 11fg 9g 10fg 8fg 7g⁴ 8fg⁴ 6f 9fg*
8.2s⁴ 8d⁴) small filly; plater; attracted no bid after winning at Wolverhampton
in September (apprentice ridden); stays 9f; seems to act on any going. *R.
Hollinshead.*

SIDAB 2 b.c. Lochnager 132–Ritruda 95 (Roi Dagobert 128) (1982 5fg 6fg³   **92**
5f* 6f 5fg* 5g* 5g³ 5g 5s²) Feb 12; 3,100Y; strong, sturdy colt; moderate
walker and mover; second foal; half-brother to 7f winner Irish Commandment
(by Shiny Tenth); dam stayed 7f; won maiden auction event at Haydock in
June and nurseries at Nottingham and Goodwood in August; seems to stay 6f
but is evidently thought better at 5f; acts on any going; game and genuine.
W. Musson.

SID'S MOB 2 b.g. Mummy's Pet 125–Native Nymph 97 (Indigenous 121)   **60**
(1982 5f³ 5fg⁴ 5g³ 6g 6fg 5g*) May 28; 3,400Y; leggy gelding; half-brother to
winning sprinter Little Atom (by The Go-Between) and to 3 winners abroad;
dam 2-y-o 7f winner; backed from 7/1 to 4/1, returned to form after 2 poor efforts
when leading close home to win 14-runner seller at Wolverhampton (retained
1,150 gns) in August by a neck from Sofica; evidently best at 5f; blinkered third
to fifth starts and is evidently better when not. *J. Berry.*

SIGN DANCER (USA) 3 ch.c. Fifth Marine–Queen Magi (T. V. Commercial)   **64**
(1981 6f 6f³ 6g* 6fg 6fg 8g 1982 16.1h 12f 11.1fg⁴ 12s 11.7s⁴ 12s 12d) well-
made colt; middle-distance handicapper; acts on any going; has twice been
blinkered; sold 5,600 gns Newmarket Autumn Sales. *G. Hunter.*

SIKORSKY (USA) 2 b.c. Honest Pleasure–Regal Exception 126 (Ribot 142)   **– p**
(1982 8g) Feb 14; $275,000Y; half-brother to smart French 1m and 10.5f
winner Twilight Hour (by Raise A Native) and a winner in USA; dam won Irish
Guinness Oaks and was fourth in Arc de Triomphe; 20/1, behind in 21-runner
£4,200 event at Newbury in September; will do better in time. *J. Sutcliffe.*

SILARI 8 gr.g. Birdbrook 110–Ciao Ciao Bambina (Welsh Abbot 131) (1981   **–**
8fg 7f³ 8f 7g 7.6fg* 7fg 7f² 7fg² 7.6s 7h³ 8f 7g 8d 6s 1982 8g 7g) plater; stays
1m; acts on any going but is suited by a sound surface; sold 720 gns Ascot
November Sales. *J. Harris.*

SILCAKEY 5 b.m. High Line 125–Resurgence (Runnymede 123) (1981 12s⁴   **56**
11.7d 11.7v⁴ 9.4g 10f 12.2s 12g² 1982 13.1f* 12h⁴ 14fg³ 16fg³ 16d² 12.2fg 16fg⁴
16fg⁴ 16s² 12g² 18d 12s³) lengthy, light-framed mare; won handicap at Bath
in May; very good 1½ lengths second to Wollow Will in 1¼m handicap at
Newmarket in September; stays 2m; acts on any going; blinkered occasionally
in 1981. *D. Elsworth.*

SILCA STAR KEY (USA) 4 b.g. Majestic Prince–Who's to Know (Fleet   **–**
Nasrullah) (1981 8g 10s 7.6g* 8fg⁴ 7.3d* 8fg* 8d* 8v 8g* 8s 1982 8g 8d 7f⁴
10g 8.5f 8fg 8f 8g) strong, well-made, attractive gelding; fair handicapper as
a 3-y-o; mainly disappointing in 1982; stays 1m; probably unsuited by very
soft going; has raced with tongue tied down; blinkered sixth outing; sold 1,050
gns Ascot December Sales. *H. Westbrook.*

SILENCER 5 br.g. Pinsun 108–Roychateau (Royal Record II) (1981 8g 11g   **–**
8g 8g⁴ 10f 1982 8.2fg) neat gelding; plater; stays 1¾m; acts on firm going;
has worn blinkers; sometimes sweats up. *R. Allan.*

SILENCE RULES (USA) 3 b.f. Secretariat–Love of Learning (Hail to Reason)   **75**
(1981 6fg 6fg³ 8g⁴ 1982 8d² 10fg² 10f* 10.2f* 10g 9g⁴ 10fg⁴ 10.2f² 10g) lengthy
filly; landed odds in maiden race at Beverley in May and 3-runner apprentice
handicap at Bath in June; suited by 1¼m and will stay 1½m; seems to act on
any going. *I. Balding.*

SILENT POOL 2 b.f. Relkino 131–Idle Waters 116 (Mill Reef 141) (1982   **68**
7.6v 7d⁴ 8s³) Mar 16; small, quite well-made filly; first foal; dam won Park Hill
Stakes; in frame in maiden events at Leicester in October and November;
looks slow, and will probably need 1¼m+. *F. J. Houghton.*

SILENT TEARS 5 br.m. Weepers Boy 124–Skilla (Mexico III) (1981 5s 5fg   **–**
5d 5g 5fg³ 5fg* 5f 1982 5f 5fg 5f 5fg 5fg 6g 5fg³ 5fg 5fg 7.6d 8fg) small, strong
mare; stays 6f; acts on a firm and a soft surface; blinkered nowadays; has raced
with her tongue tied down; trained first 3 starts by M. Cousins. *M. James.*

SILK EMPRESS 3 gr.f. Young Emperor 133–Taking Silk (Shantung 132)   **–**
(1981 7f 5s 1982 14.6fg 10g) smallish, rather leggy filly; good walker; little
sign of ability in maiden races. *F. Durr.*

SILKEN ANNA 5 br.m. Scottish Rifle 127–Bar Gold 80 (Lucky Brief 128) — (1981 NR 1982 8fg) poor plater as a 3-y-o; will stay 1½m; possibly unsuited by soft going; has worn blinkers. *L. Kennard.*

SILK PYJAMAS 2 ch.f. Queen's Hussar 124–Silk Stocking 109 (Pardao 120) **107** (1982 6fg⁴ 6f³ 7f* 7fg⁴ 8g²) Mar 27; rangy, quite attractive filly; good mover; third foal; sister to 7f and 1m winner Blue Patrol and half-sister to 1m winner Organdy (by Blakeney); dam, who stayed 1¼m, is half-sister to good sprinter Shiny Tenth (by Queen's Hussar); gained a very smooth 3-length win over Lucy Raynalds in 11-runner maiden race at Sandown in July; also in frame in 3 much better races, failing by only a head and a neck to catch Crime of Passion in Cherry Hinton Stakes at Newmarket in July, finishing 7 lengths fourth of 9 to Flamenco, after being badly hampered 2f out, when favourite for Waterford Candelabra Stakes at Goodwood in August and going down by 5 lengths to all-the-way winner Bright Crocus in May Hill Stakes at Doncaster in September; stays 1m; yet to race on a soft surface. *R. Hern.*

SILK ROAD 2 b.c. Shantung 132–Golconda 84 (Matador 130) (1982 7fg 7g — 6g) Apr 20; sixth reported foal; dam lightly-raced half-sister to Eclipse winner Henry the Seventh; backward, behind in big fields of maidens at Newmarket in August and October (2). *A. Jarvis.*

SILK SARI (USA) 2 b.f. Raja Baba–Wisp O'Will (New Policy) (1982 5g **101** 5fg 5f* 6f³ 6fg² 6fg* 6g* 7.2f⁴ 7fg*) Mar 25; $190,000Y; neat, strong filly; half-sister to numerous winners in America, including champion sprinter Gallant Bob (by Gallant Romeo); dam won 4 sprint claiming races; developed into a useful filly, winning maiden race at Wolverhampton in May, minor event at Redcar in July, nursery under 9-7 at Windsor in August and well-contested race at Chepstow in September; stays 7f; yet to race on a soft surface; consistent. *G. Harwood.*

SILK SCREEN 3 ch.c. Relkino 131–Silken Way 103 (Shantung 132) (1981 **80** 8g 7g 1982 12f³ 12f² 12f 12f² 13.1f* 14g) rangy colt; landed odds in minor event at Bath in September; runner-up in maiden race at Kempton and minor event at Salisbury previously; stays 1¾m; acts on firm going; doesn't find a lot off bridle; sold to BBA 8,000 gns Newmarket Autumn Sales. *R. Hern.*

SILK'S SUGGESTION 3 b.f. Shantung 132–Lead Me On (King's Troop 118) — (1981 NR 1982 11.5g⁴ 10fg 10s) third foal; half-sister to a winning plater; dam never ran; little worthwhile form in maiden races. *J. Toller.*

SILLAGER 2 gr.c. Lochnager 132–Silly Sue 55 (Great Nephew 126) (1982 **85** 5g 6fg 5f⁴ 5d*) Apr 19; big, strong, good type of colt; good walker; third living foal; half-brother to a prolific winner in Italy by Northfields; dam lightly raced, looked fully fit for first time when winning 9-runner maiden event at Newcastle in August in good style by 3 lengths from Eastbrook; should stay 6f; best run on a soft surface; sure to win more races. *M. W. Easterby.*

SILLEY'S KNIGHT 6 b.g. Derring-Do 131–Silley's Maid 100 (Continuation **75** 120) (1981 8g³ 7g 7d 8f 7g 8d 7s 8g 1982 7g 7d 7.6g 7f³ 10f⁴ 8fg⁴ 8fg* 9f² 8g 8fg* 8fg 8fg⁴ 8g⁴ 8d⁴ 7d 8.2s) strong, good-bodied, attractive gelding; poor mover nowadays; fair handicapper on his day; won at Carlisle in June and Ayr in July; in frame on several other occasions, including Royal Hunt Cup at Royal Ascot; stays 9f; acts on any going; usually blinkered nowadays; sold to D. Chapman 6,300 gns Doncaster October Sales after final start. *J. Hanson.*

SILLY BOY 2 ch.g. Decoy Boy 129–Scilly Isles 54 (Silly Season 127) (1982 **66** 6d 7f 8f⁴) Apr 30; 600f; 1,900Y; strong gelding; half-brother to 2 winning jumpers; dam half-sister to smart miler Murrayfield; 3½ lengths fourth of 20 to Figure de Danse in maiden auction event at Redcar in September; evidently stays 1m. *N. Bycroft.*

SILLY CRACK 3 b.c. Silly Season 127–Crackle 74 (Nelcius 133) (1981 NR — 1982 8d) 740Y; second foal; dam placed twice over 1m; behind in 16-runner maiden race won by Breeze Hill at Warwick in April; sold 380 gns Doncaster September Sales. *L. Barratt.*

SILLY MOO 4 b.f. Silly Season 127–Rikis (Town Crier 119) (1981 10g 10fg — 10fg² 12fg 10f⁴ 10fg 10fg³ 10s 1982 11.7f) narrow, compact filly; plater; stays 1¼m. *T. Hallett.*

SILLY STEVEN 3 b.c. Silly Season 127–Super Anna (Super Sam 124) (1981 **112** 7g 6g³ 1982 7d 7fg* 8f² 8fg 7g 8f* 7fg² 7g 7fg* 7.3g 7g) big, lengthy colt; third foal; half-brother to a winner in Ireland; dam won at up to 1¼m in Ireland

and over hurdles; won maiden race at Newmarket in April, £4,000 event at Newbury in June and Beeswing Stakes at Newcastle in July; made most of running and rallied very gamely to beat Rebollino a short head in last-named; also ran well to be ½-length second to Merlins Charm in Jersey Stakes at Royal Ascot; stays 1m; needs a firm surface; very useful. *R. Hannon.*

SILMIRA 5 gr.m. Grey Mirage 128–Silent Post 70 (Dumbarnie 125) (1981 10s **55** 10g⁴ 10v 8fg* 12d* 8fg⁴ 8h 1982 8d 8g 8f 10d² 10g* 10g) plain mare; plater; bought in 1,500 gns after winning in good style at Nottingham in July; tended to put head in air previous start; stays 1¼m; probably acts on any going; has run respectably for an apprentice. *Mrs R. Lomax.*

SILOJOKA 3 br.f. Home Guard 129–Pereliance (Reliance II 137) (1981 **95** 5g 5s* 5g³ 5f⁴ 5g² 6fg² 6fg⁴ 7d⁴ 7fg⁴ 6g 1982 7d 8d 6fg³ 6f⁴ 6g* 5fg³ 6g* 6fg³ 7fg 6g 6g) strong, useful sort; won handicaps at Lingfield in June (beat Lindsey 1½ lengths) and Newmarket in August (by ¾ length from Azaam); best at 6f; acts on any going; suited by waiting tactics; genuine; below her best last 3 starts; retained 39,000 gns Newmarket December Sales. *J. Benstead.*

SILVER CREEK 4 b.c. English Prince 129–Corbalton 103 (Milesian 125) **—** (1981 12s⁴ 1982 12f) quite attractive colt; lightly-raced maiden; would have stayed beyond 1½m; dead. *I. Walker.*

SILVERDIP (USA) 2 br.f. The Minstrel 135–Royal Dilemma (Buckpasser) **— p** (1982 7f) Feb 9; closely related to smart 5f and 1¼m winner Imperial Fling (by Northern Dancer) and half-sister to 2 winners, including useful Imperial Dilemma (by Damascus), a winner here and in USA at up to 1m; dam stakes-placed winner at up to 6f and daughter of champion 1964 American 2-y-o filly Queen Empress; 7/1, 9 lengths fifth of 19 to Verbarium in maiden race at Salisbury in July; likely to do much better. *I. Balding.*

SILVER DREAMER 2 gr.g. Derrylin 115–Petingalyn (Petingo 135) (1982 7f) Mar 13; 3,000F, 6,000Y; lengthy gelding; third foal; half-brother to 1979 2-y-o 6f winner Sponsorship (by Sparkler); dam of no account; unquoted, behind in 18-runner maiden race at Catterick in August. *G. Richards.*

SILVER HAWK (USA) 3 b.c. Roberto 131–Gris Vitesse (Amerigo 116§) **123** (1981 6fg* 6fg² 7f* 8s² 1982 8g* 8fg 12f³ 12g²) .

As the home of the Derby, a race that many regard as the greatest in the world, Epsom has a number of drawbacks, the most important being that its mile-and-a-half course is not really suitable for the big fields that are usual for the race. Scrimmaging often takes place in the first two and a half furlongs or so as the runners first bear to the right, converging and bunching to cut the right-hand bend soon after the start, and then swing back to the left-hand rail for the rest of the ascent to the top of the hill; Glint of Gold and Kalaglow both suffered serious interference at around this point in the 1981 Derby. Much of the first mile is on the turn and practically everywhere the ground slopes, either along the track or across it and commonly in both directions, making it more likely than if the Derby were run on a flatter track that a horse's prospects of winning might be seriously affected by ill-luck in running. In the second half of the Derby in particular there is the risk of interference from beaten horses or horses which are unable to act on the downhill sections of the track:

Ladbrokes Craven Stakes, Newmarket—Silver Hawk shows a good turn of foot to beat dead-heaters Nioulargo (rails) and Wongchoi (centre); Simply Great is fourth

in the latest Derby Silver Hawk's rider reported that his mount was baulked at the top of the hill—he was squeezed out approaching Tattenham Corner too—and both Silver Hawk and the French-trained Persepolis met with trouble as they tried to make progress along the inside in the straight. Both Silver Hawk and Persepolis did really well to finish in the frame, Silver Hawk staying on very strongly in the closing stages to hold off the faster-finishing Persepolis by a head for the third place, beaten three lengths and a length by Golden Fleece and Touching Wood.

Silver Hawk cracked a cannon bone on the gallops in the summer, an injury which kept him out of the big middle-distance races after June, and he never really had the chance to show whether he was worthy of a higher placing in the Derby. It is almost certain that Silver Hawk was some way below his best—he sweated up beforehand—when beaten a long-looking eight lengths by Assert in the Irish Sweeps Derby at the Curragh on his only outing after Epsom; it was only by two and a half lengths that the hard-ridden Silver Hawk held off Patcher for second place in a poor field by classic standards. Silver Hawk's two races as a three-year-old before the Derby were over the Rowley Mile. He started 5/1 favourite for the Two Thousand Guineas on the strength of his smart two-year-old form—he won the Intercraft Solario Stakes at Kempton and came second in the Royal Lodge Stakes at Ascot—and his victory in the Ladbrokes Craven Stakes in April when he showed a good turn of speed up the final hill to beat the dead-heaters Nioulargo and Wongchoi by a length and a half with Simply Great fourth. Drawn one in a field of twenty-six for the Guineas Silver Hawk was in front of the stand-side group practically all the way but he could never get to the leaders in the centre of the course and finished fifth, beaten a little over five lengths by the winner Zino.

		Roberto (b 1969)	Hail to Reason (br 1958)	Turn-to
Silver Hawk (USA) (b.c. 1979)				Nothirdchance
			Bramalea (b 1959)	Nashua
				Rarelea
		Gris Vitesse (gr 1966)	Amerigo (ch 1955)	Nearco
				Sanlinea
			Matchiche II (gr 1956)	Mat de Cocagne
				Chimere Fabuleuse

A strong, well-made colt and a good mover, Silver Hawk has been retired to the Airdrie Stud in Kentucky where his fee for 1983 is 12,500 dollars (live foal). By a Derby winner out of a winner of the Prix Jacques le Marois (a Group 1 pattern race over a mile at Deauville), Silver Hawk has an excellent pedigree, one which we dealt with in considerable detail in *Racehorses of 1981*. Suffice to say here that Silver Hawk's dam has bred four other winners, the best of them Blast Off (by Graustark), a very useful winner from a mile to eleven furlongs in France, and the smart two-year-old of 1982 Kuwait Tower (by Little Current). Silver Hawk reputedly became a nervous racehorse as a three-year-old—he was sweating freely by the time he reached the start on Guineas day—but, interestingly, he survived the so-called Epsom 'ordeal', the preliminaries before the Derby, the effects of which, as we have said before, are generally much overestimated. Silver Hawk was suited by a mile and a half and acted on any going. *M. Albina.*

SILVER KNIGHT 2 gr.c. Ardoon 124–Abanilla 115 (Abernant 142) (1982 5g 6f 5f 5f) Apr 1; 1R 7,000F, 6,200Y; well-grown, rather leggy colt; no form, including when carrying low weight in nursery (blinkered) at Edinburgh in September. *J. Gilbert.*   —

SILVER LEO 4 br.g. Dubassoff–Fingerofortune 100 (Fortino II 120) (1981 12s 8.2fg 9.4g 13.8fg 13fg 7f 8fg 1982 8g) disappointing handicapper; suited by 7f and 1m as a 2-y-o; possibly needs a sound surface; has worn blinkers; bandaged only outing of 1982. *J. Harris.*   —

SILVER MANTLE 3 b.f. Bustino 136–Moonlight Night 112 (Levmoss 133) (1981 7g 8g 1982 11f 14f2 14g4 16.9g2 12f2 12v) big, strong, good sort; good walker; runner-up in maiden races; stays well; acts on firm going and ran poorly on heavy final start; sold 34,000 gns Newmarket December Sales. *H. Cecil.*   **70**

SILVER MARKET 2 ch.g. Native Bazaar 122–Silver Leg (Silver Cloud 121) (1982 5g4 5g3 5f4 5.3g2 6g 5f* 5.8f 6g) Mar 21; fair sort; fourth living foal; dam never ran; in frame in minor and maiden events prior to landing the odds by a neck from Kathleen's Money in 7-runner seller at Lingfield (no bid) in July; not raced after August; best form at 5f; dwelt third start. *R. Smyth.*   **62**

SILVER RIBBON 2 gr.f. Legal Eagle 126–Gold Ribbon 106 (Blast 125) (1982 **60**
5s³ 5d⁴ 5fg² 5f* 5f* 5f 5fg 6d) Mar 27; 400F, 500Y, resold 1,200Y; leggy filly;
half-sister to several winners including 1981 2-y-o 5f winner Super Bee Jay (by
Mummy's Pet); dam 2-y-o 7f and 1m winner; attracted no bid after accounting
for small fields in sellers at Newcastle and Ripon in May; off course nearly 2
months afterwards and wasn't disgraced in nursery on return; should stay 6f;
acts well on firm going; blinkered third to fifth outings; retained by trainer
800 gns Newmarket Autumn Sales. *J. Berry.*

SILVER RULER 4 b.c. Sovereign Path 125–Argentessa 80 (Sing Sing 134) **76**
(1981 7fg 7g* 7d 7d⁴ 7g 7f* 7f 8.3fg 8g 1982 8fg 7fg² 8fg² 8g² 8f* 8fg* 7f*)
strong, attractive colt; in very good form in summer and quickened up nicely
when winning handicaps at Kempton, Sandown and Newmarket; not seen
out after beating Cajolery by a neck on last-named course; stays 1m; well suited
by a sound surface; usually held up. *G. Harwood.*

SILVER SEASON 4 b.c. Martinmas 128–Silver Ray 70 (Skymaster 126) (1981 **109**
8g⁴ 8g*(dis) 10g* 8.2s* 12d 8f 10d 8d* 8fg² 8fg 9g 10g 1982 8g² 8d 8g⁴ 8f³ 10f²
10fg⁴ 10g 8fg² 8f 8g³ 8d² 10g 8s) lengthy colt; has a round action; very useful
performer; had stiff tasks when second in Doncaster Mile in March (1½ lengths
behind Princes Gate) and 1¼m in Brigadier Gerard Stakes at Sandown in May
(beaten 8 lengths by Kalaglow, but had some smart performers behind); also in
frame in good handicaps at Kempton, York (two), Ascot and Ripon, and in
Prince of Wales's Stakes at Royal Ascot (creditable fourth to Kind of Hush);
races mainly at up to 1¼m, but has run creditably over 1½m; acts on firm going
but is ideally suited by some give in the ground; nearly always makes running,
but ran well when held up eleventh start; game and genuine, although well
beaten on last 2 starts; has run well with his tongue tied down. *C. Brittain.*

SILVER SNOW 4 gr.f. Abwah 118–Silver Yarn (Peter's Yarn 106) (1981 **64**
8g 8f 8f⁴ 8.2f* 8fg³ 8.2d* 8f⁴ 10.6fg 8g 1982 9fg* 9fg³ 9f³ 8.2g 8fg⁴ 10f 8fg* 8s*
8.2s) long-backed filly; successful in handicaps at Hamilton in May (her third
win on course), Beverley in September and Newcastle in October; quickened
and beat Winart comfortably on last-named course; never going particularly
well final outing; acts on any going; ran respectably in blinkers fifth start. *N.
Tinkler.*

SILVER STONE 2 b.f. Derrylin 115–Chequered Flag 70 (King's Troop 118) —
(1982 6f 6fg⁴) Mar 8; 18,500Y; lengthy, good-bodied filly; half-sister to several
2-y-o winners, including fairly useful 1981 sprinter Fimi (by Tachypous); dam
won over 5f at 2 yrs; 6½ lengths fourth of 18 behind Liberty Tree in minor event
at Redcar in September. *B. Hobbs.*

SILVER STRINGS 2 b.g. Blakeney 126–Melody Hour 105 (Sing Sing 134) —
(1982 6f 6f⁴) Feb 3; rangy, attractive gelding; fourth foal; half-brother to 3 winners, including very useful middle-distance 3-y-o Sing Softly (by Luthier) and
fairly useful stayer Military Band (by Sassafras); dam useful 5f winner at 2 yrs;
last of 4 in maiden race at Yarmouth in August. *H. Cecil.*

SILVER SURPRISE 4 br.f. Son of Silver 123–Bunny Club 66 (Astec 128) —
(1981 8f 8fg 10fg* 10.6v 1982 14f) rangy filly; stays 1¼m; acts on a firm
surface. *M. Pipe.*

SILVER VENTURE 2 gr.g. Town Crier 119–Grecian Bridge 90 (Acropolis 132) —
(1982 7d) Mar 16; 11,000Y; compact, fair sort; closely related to 1¼m winner
Monemvasia (by Sovereign Path) and half-brother to 2 winners by March Past,
including good-class 1m to 1¼m performer Roy Bridge; dam from same family
as Ribocco and Ribero; remote ninth of 12 in maiden race at Leicester in
September. *H. Candy.*

SIMBAD 6 b.g. Simbir 130–Amsterdam Lassie (Arctic Storm 134) (1981 **36**
18g 1982 15.8g³ 11s 16.1s 15.8d) poor handicapper; evidently stays well.
R. Fisher.

SIMBOL EQUATION 4 b.c. Simbir 130–Golda 81 (Red God 128§) (1981 —
12fg 10.1g 13.1g 14s⁴ 1982 10.2g 12g 17f 18.8fg³ 16f⁴ 17f⁴ 16f³ 16g 16.9f) slow
maiden; in frame in handicaps. *D. Ancil.*

SIMBULA 3 b. or br.g. Simbir 130–Lavarna (Le Levanstell 122) (1981 5g⁴ **76**
6f 1982 7g⁴ 8d*) big, useful sort; good walker; stayed on well to win maiden
race at Beverley in July; would have been suited by 1¼m+; was suited by
some give in the ground; dead. *M. H. Easterby.*

SIMETTE 5 ch.g. Simbir 130–Machete (Macherio) (1981 12fg 12g⁴ 14s 13.1g **60** 13.3g³ 16g 16fg² 14g 16g³ 17.1d³ 12g³ 1982 14f 14fg² 13.3f⁴) quite well-made gelding; staying handicapper; appears to act on any going; often blinkered (not in 1982 however). *C. James.*

SIMMIES LOVE 3 ch.f. Record Token 128–Love Is Blind 90 (Hasty Road) **48** (1981 5g 5g 5d 6f 6d 1982 12.2g 8f 7f² 7g³ 8.2g⁴ 8g 8f* 7fg 8fg³ 9g 9g 8.2g 10f⁴ 8.2s) quite a well-made filly; plater; attracted no bid after winning at Leicester in July (apprentice ridden); stays 1m; acts on firm going. *R. Hollinshead.*

SIMPLY GREAT (FR) 3 b.c. Mill Reef 141–Seneca (Chaparral 128) (1981 **122** 7g* 7g 1982 8g⁴ 10.5f*)
The leg injury sustained on the gallops by Simply Great five days before the Derby left Lester Piggott without a mount in the race for the first time since 1962. Piggott's eight Derby wins—on Never Say Die (1954), Crepello (1957), St Paddy (1960), Sir Ivor (1968), Nijinsky (1970), Roberto (1972), Empery (1976) and The Minstrel (1977)—constitute a record unequalled by any jockey in the history of the race. Since his first ride in the Derby, on Zucchero in 1951, Piggott has had twenty-nine Derby rides (he has finished second four times) and has been without a mount on only three occasions; he was under suspension in 1962 and was left without a ride in 1961 after the defection of Pinturischio. Two of Piggott's Derby victories, on Crepello and St Paddy, were gained for Pinturischio's trainer Noel Murless who was succeeded at Warren Place stables by the present occupant Henry Cecil. According to Cecil, Simply Great represented his best hope so far of saddling a Derby winner. At the time of his injury Simply Great was ante-post favourite for the race, largely on the strength of his outstanding home reputation which he had gone some way towards vindicating when starting a short-priced favourite for Britain's most valuable Derby trial, the Mecca-Dante Stakes at York's May meeting. Quickening in good style to lead over three furlongs out, Simply Great had to be pushed along after seeming to idle in front to win by two and a half lengths from the subsequent Derby sixth Palace Gold. Palace Gold finished more than eight

Simply Great (Fr) (b.c. 1979)	Mill Reef (b 1968)	Never Bend (b 1960)	Nasrullah
			Lalun
		Milan Mill (b 1962)	Princequillo
			Virginia Water
	Seneca (b 1972)	Chaparral (b 1966)	Val de Loir
			Niccolina
		Schonbrunn (b 1966)	Pantheon
			Scheherezade III

lengths behind Golden Fleece at Epsom and the Mecca-Dante fourth Count Pahlen came ninth in the Derby, beaten almost three times as far by Golden Fleece as he had been by Simply Great at York. Simply Great's performance in the Mecca-Dante is easily his best from four racecourse appearances, consi-

Mecca-Dante Stakes, York—Simply Great wins Britain's most valuable Derby trial

derably better, in our view, than his fourth in the Ladbrokes Craven Stakes at Newmarket on his reappearance when he seemed to find a mile too sharp. If he comes back fit and well as a four-year-old Simply Great will no doubt be aimed at the top middle-distance races. His three-year-old form wasn't so good as some of those he is likely to meet in races such as the Coronation Cup and the Hardwicke Stakes but he gave the impression in the ten-and-a-half-furlong Mecca-Dante that he would be suited by a mile and a half plus.

A well-made, deep-girthed colt—and a really good mover—Simply Great is the second foal of Seneca who won at twelve and a half furlongs in France and is a daughter of the German One Thousand Guineas and Oaks winner Schonbrunn. Simply Great acts well on firm ground and has yet to race on a soft surface. *H. Cecil.*

SINGALONG JOE 4 ch.g. Sharpen Up 127–Captive Flower 99 (Manacle 123) **56**
(1981 8.2s 7f 8g⁴ 1982 10fg 8g⁴ 8f² 9f³ 8f 8g 8s²) leggy, light-framed gelding; in frame in sellers; probably stays 9f; acts on any going. *K. Bailey.*

SINGING DANDY 3 ch.g. Dynastic 105–Nottingham Belle 78 (Chanteur II —
135) (1981 6g 5fg² 6g 6g 5f 6fg⁴ 1982 11g 10d 8.2g) compact, plain gelding; plater; well beaten in better company at 3 yrs; should stay 1m; has had tongue tied down. *H. Bell.*

SINGING FOOL 6 gr.g. Singing Bede 122–Dilwyn 84 (Immortality) (1981 —
7g 8.5g 8f 12fg 10f² 8f 1982 10.1d 12fg) poor maiden; last in a seller final outing; stays 1¼m; acts on firm going; has twice worn blinkers. *D. Jermy.*

SINGING HIGH 2 b.f. Julio Mariner 127–Sing High 85 (Sound Track 132) **77** p
(1982 7d³) May 10; half-sister to several winners, including fairly useful 1970 2-y-o 6f and 7f winner Thief Lane (by Mandamus); dam raced 1m; 20/1 and just in need of race, shaped very well when 1¾ lengths third of 11 to Molokai in maiden race at Ayr in September, staying on in excellent style under considerate handling after being well behind early in straight; will probably stay at least 1¼m; sure to win a race. *J. Fitzgerald.*

SINGING SAILOR 3 br.c. Mansingh 120–Sealady (Seaepic 100) (1981 **89**
5s 5v³ 5d* 5d* 6s 5g² 5f* 6fg⁴ 6g² 5d 1982 5s³ 5fg 5f 5fg 5g 5fg 5g⁴ 5s 5v² 5s²
5s) small, quite well-made colt; fair handicapper; second at Ascot (5 lengths behind Bri-Eden in Bovis Stakes) and Sandown (beaten 1½ lengths by Ferryman) in October; best at 5f; acts on any going; blinkered fourth outing; sold out of C. Spares's stable 12,000 gns Newmarket July Sales after fourth start. *R. Thompson.*

SINGING SOPRANO 2 b.f. Music Boy 124–Vanity (Vimy 132) (1982 5g —
5fg 5d 6s) Apr 26; 4,200F, 3,100Y; half-sister to several winners in Ireland and Belgium by No Mercy; dam never ran; poor form, including in a £2,000 seller. *P. Bailey.*

SINGING TROOPER 3 ch.f. Air Trooper 115–Arne Melody (Romany Air 118) —
(1981 NR 1982 11.7g 12s 10s) third foal; dam of little account; well beaten in maiden races and a seller. *A. Andrews.*

SINGLETON (FR) 3 b.f. Sun Prince 128–One Only 77 (Sicambre 135) (1981 **76**
8g 8s 1982 8s 10d 8d 8f* 10.1fg² 10fg² 8g 8g) rangy, attractive ex-French filly; half-sister to several winners here and in France, including useful 1979 2-y-o 6f and 7f winner One No Trump (by Auction Ring); dam French 11f winner; pick of paddock when beating Elmar by 1½ lengths going away in 13-runner minor event at Newmarket in July; ran respectably next 2 outings; will be suited by 1½m; apparently needs a sound surface; blinkered third outing; trained by D. Smaga first 2 starts; sold 21,000 gns Newmarket December Sales. *R. Hern.*

SING SOFTLY 3 br.f. Luthier 126–Melody Hour 105 (Sing Sing 134) (1981 **112**
6fg* 1982 10fg* 10.5fg⁴ 12fg² 12g* 10fg⁴ 14.6g³) tall, lengthy filly; good mover; third foal; half-sister to fairly useful stayer Military Band (by Sassafras) and 1979 2-y-o 5f winner Bandsman (by So Blessed); dam useful 5f winner at 2 yrs; kept on strongly to beat Cornish Heroine by 2½ lengths in Pretty Polly Stakes at Newmarket in April and stable-companion Tants by 1½ lengths in Lancashire Oaks at Haydock in July; in frame on other starts in Musidora Stakes at York, Ribblesdale Stakes at Royal Ascot (strong-finishing neck second to Dish Dash), Nassau Stakes at Goodwood and Park Hill Stakes at Doncaster (2 lengths third

Lancashire Oaks, Haydock—Sing Softly (right) beats her stable-companion Tants (second right)

to Swiftfoot); stays 1¾m; yet to race on a soft surface; reluctant to go to post at Haydock and Goodwood; sold privately before fourth start; sent to USA. H. Cecil.

Mrs P. W. Harris' "Sing Softly"

SING SOMETHING 2 b.f. Music Maestro 119–Miss Lollypop (St Paddy 133) —
(1982 5f 5s 6s) May 19; 820Y; half-sister to 3 winners, including stayer Morlolly
(by Morston); dam unraced half-sister to some useful animals; behind in varied
races, one a claimer, in the autumn; sold Norsk Jockey Club 600 gns Doncaster
November Sales. *P. Calver.*

SINGULARITY 3 ch.f. Mansingh 120–Standoffish (Be Friendly 130) (1981 —
5g 5f 5fg 5g 5g3 6s 5g2 5s 1982 7f 6f) leggy filly; sprint plater. *H. Fleming.*

SINISTER SMILE (USA) 2 ch.c. Crimson Satan–Perfect Love (Cornish **90**
Prince) (1982 5fg* 5f3 5.3g) Feb 14; $50,000Y; neat colt; first foal; dam, who
never ran, is closely related to smart filly Loved; won 11-runner maiden race at
Windsor in July; put up easily better subsequent effort when creditable 1¼
lengths third of 10 to Grey Desire (after being taken down very steadily) in
nursery at Redcar in September; sent to USA. *H. Cecil.*

SIN NO MORE 7 b.g. So Blessed 130–Moghari 78 (Djebe) (1981 16fg 12.3g —
1982 16d) seems of little account; has worn blinkers. *M. Reddan.*

SIR ALCO 2 ch.c. Nonoalco 131–Verde Dimora (Sir Ivor 135) (1982 5d* **102 ?**
5f* 5f3 5f 6g2 7fg 6d) Mar 23; IR 7,200Y; narrow colt; poor walker; first foal;
dam useful winner in Italy; won small races at Nottingham and Thirsk in April;
ran well afterwards only when ½-length second to Domynsky in 3-runner minor
event at Pontefract in July; should stay 1m; seems to act on any going; trained
by A. Jarvis first 4 starts. *J. Hardy.*

SIR BLESSED 3 b.g. So Blessed 130–Morinda 87 (Matador 130) (1981 6d **71**
6fg 7g2 7g3 8d3 1982 8g 8fg 8.2f 10.4fg 8fg2 8g4 9s 8g2) lengthy, rather sparely-
made gelding; quite moderate; stays 1m; sold 4,800 gns Newmarket Autumn
Sales. *R. Williams.*

SIR BUTCH 2 b.c. Record Token 128–Acquire 105 (Burglar 128) (1982 6f 6g* **90**
6g 6g) May 20; strong, lengthy, good-quartered colt; good walker; brother to
tough and very speedy 3-y-o 5f performer Chellaston Park, and half-brother to
a winner; dam won twice over 5f at 2 yrs; won 12-runner maiden race at Epsom in
August; fair eighth of 12 behind Captivating Lady in nursery at Newmarket in
October, final outing and better subsequent effort; stays 6f. *J. Dunlop.*

SIR GERALD 3 ch.c. Roan Rocket 128–Sucu Sucu 73 (Tudor Jinks 121) —
(1981 5g 6fg 7fg 6fg 6g 1982 8g 7f 10g 10.1fg 8.2s 10d 10s) workmanlike,
slightly hollow-backed colt; carries plenty of condition; no worthwhile form in
varied company; trained part of season by J. Benstead. *M. Tompkins.*

SIR GIVENCHY 4 ch.g. High Line 125–Topolass 79 (Acropolis 132) (1981 **43**
12d 15fg 16.5fg 12fg 10g 1982 16d 15.8f2) leggy, sparely-made gelding;
plater; bandaged when second in non-selling handicap at Catterick in April; stays
well; winning hurdler. *W. Musson.*

SIR HUMPHREY 2 ch.c. High Line 125–Greek Money (Sovereign Path 125) —
(1982 7s) Apr 24; 19,000Y; first foal; dam Irish 1¼m and 1½m winner; 25/1,
showed speed to halfway when ninth of 12 in minor event at Chepstow in October.
B. Swift.

SIR JOHN FALSTAFF (USA) 3 br.g. True Knight–Laughing Allegra **62**
(His Majesty) (1981 5g 6fg 7g4 7f4 8.2fg* 8d 8.2s 8g2 8d2 1982 10f4 10f3 8.5f
8g2) neat, rather lightly-made, quite attractive gelding; plater; stays 1¼m;
seems to act on any going; has run well in blinkers; suitable mount for an
apprentice; does best when ridden up with pace; claimed £4,100 after final start.
P. Cole.

SIR KEVITA 3 b.g. Regal George–Ellie Mae IV (pedigree unknown) (1981 —
7fg 8.2d 8s 1982 12f) plain non-thoroughbred gelding; of little account.
R. Ward.

SIR LUCKY 3 ch.g. Bonne Noel 115–Mount Gay (Divine Gift 127) (1981 **50**
6d 8.2d 8d 1982 8f 12f4 12g 12fg4 11g 12d* 12d 12s4) lightly-made gelding;
plater; won claiming handicap at Leicester in September; stays 1½m; best run on a
soft surface; usually blinkered. *C. Crossley.*

SIR MALA MALA (USA) 2 b.c. Seattle Slew–Mama Kali (Tom Rolfe) —
(1982 6f) May 1; well-made, attractive colt; third foal; half-brother to a
stakes-placed winner by Forli; dam, smart winner at up to 1m, at her best at 4
yrs and 5 yrs; finished very lame and was found to have a severely ricked back
when tailed off in Chesham Stakes at Royal Ascot; had taken charge of his jockey
on the way down. *J. Sutcliffe.*

SIX

SIR MICHAEL 6 b.h. Manacle 123–Ragirl (Ragusa 137) (1981 NR 1982 16s —
14g⁴ 16fg 16.1fg) big horse; staying handicapper; respectable fourth to Military
Band at Newmarket in April; ideally suited by firm going; blinkered second
and third starts; suitable mount for an apprentice. *D. Thom.*

SIR MORDRED 5 br.h. Linacre 133–Morgan le Fay 80 (Milesian 125) (1981 **81**
10s 16d 12s 12g³ 12d³ 12d 1982 10.2g* 12f) ex-Irish horse; half-brother to 2
winners, including useful miler London Glory (by Pall Mall); dam won over 7f in
Ireland as a 2-y-o; ran creditably in varied company in 1981 when trained by
owner; put up quite an impressive performance when beating Battalion by 3
lengths in 29-runner amateur riders race at Doncaster in March; fractured a
leg in similar event at Thirsk in May and will not race again; stayed 1½m, but
possibly not 2m; acted on any going. *M. H. Easterby.*

SIR PATRICK 3 ch.c. Sir Ivor 135–Eltisley 82 (Grey Sovereign 128§) (1981 **71**
NR 1982 8fg 12f 12fg 13.3f 16d 12fg² 12.3fg) 9,000Y; strong, heavy-topped
colt; third foal; brother to useful 7f winner Applemint and half-brother to useful
sprinter Dare Me (by Derring-Do); dam 2-y-o 5f winner; quite moderate; runs as
if he should get further than 1½m; blinkered last 2 outings; trained by P. Mitchell
first 4 starts. *M. Ryan.*

SIR PRINCE JOHN 2 b.c. Prince Tenderfoot 126–Star of Sierra (Quisling 117) **88**
(1982 6f 6d² 6s²) Mar 13; half-brother to Irish 7f winner Sierra Boy (by African
Sky) and Irish 3-y-o 11f and 13.5f winner Sam John (by Malinowski); dam
Irish stayer; second twice in the autumn, going down by ½ length to Iron Leader
in 21-runner maiden race at Navan and by 2 lengths to Taoiseach in minor
event at Punchestown; will stay 1m; sure to win a race. *M. Connolly, Ireland.*

SIR ROBERT 2 b. or br.c. Cavo Doro 124–Flowering (Reform 132) (1982 6d) —
Mar 12; first foal; dam in frame over 1m in France; 33/1, last of 9 in minor
event at Windsor in September. *M. Haynes.*

SIR SHOSTAKOVICH 3 br.c. Rheingold 137–Sinful 72 (Grey Sovereign **99**
128§) (1981 7fg³ 7fg² 8.5g* 7d 1982 9g 9f² 10fg 14f⁴ 12f 12g 14g* 12f* 16f
11.5f³ 12fg 12fg 12d 10v⁴ 12s) IR 3,800Y; half-brother to numerous winners
here and abroad, including very useful sprinter Adams Pet (by Super Sam);
dam ran only at 2 yrs; ridden by 5-lb claimer when narrowly winning handicaps
at Leopardstown and Naas in July; creditable third to Steel Duke in valuable
handicap at Galway in August; saddle slipped when last of 8 to Cool Decision
in valuable gentleman riders race at Epsom later in August on twelfth start;
stays 1¾m; acts on firm going; blinkered seventh to ninth outings. *L. Browne,
Ireland.*

SISTER RESISTA 3 b.f. Record Token 128–Silk Willoughby (Plate King **46**
129) (1981 7.2f⁴ 6fg 1982 8d 8f 9g² 8.3fg 8fg) lightly-made filly; plater;
stays 9f; sold 1,600 gns Ascot August Sales. *B. Hills.*

SISTER SASSAFRAS 3 b.f. Sassafras 135–The Nun 99 (Saint Crespin III **82**
132) (1981 7d 1982 10f 12f* 12.2f⁴) well-made filly; made all and held on
by ¾ length from Pretty Picture despite wandering in closing stages in 12-runner
maiden race at Thirsk in May; well beaten in blinkers only subsequent start
in June; will stay 1¾m. *M. Stoute.*

SITEX 4 b.c. Record Run 127–Glorious Light 53 (Alcide 136) (1981 5s 6d² **45**
6fg 8fg 7g 6g³ 6d⁴ 5d² 6g 6fg 6fg 6s 6s 1982 5d 6g 5d 6fg 7g 7g 6fg³ 6g* 6g
6fg 6v 6s) sprint handicapper; bought in 1,150 gns after winning 21-runner
seller at Windsor in July; acts on a firm surface but is ideally suited by some
give in the ground; has run well in blinkers. *M. Bolton.*

SITICA 5 b.g. Siliconn 121–Time Call (Chanteur II 135) (1981 5s⁴ 5d 6g **69**
6g 6f 1982 7d²) narrow, fair sort; having first outing on flat for 15 months
when going down by a neck to Glorious in handicap at Doncaster in October
(showed plenty of speed); stays 7f; goes well on a soft surface and is unsuited
by really firm going. *E. Alston.*

SIX CLUBS (USA) 3 ch.g. Charles Elliott–Augusta J. (Lenso) (1981 6g⁴ **69**
7d 1982 11f 10.1f⁴ 8fg² 8fg 8s³ 8f* 10.1g² 8g² 9g 8.2g) strong, good sort;
good mover; made all to win maiden race at Kempton in July; ran respectably
several other starts; stays 1¼m; acts on any going but seems suited by top-
of-the-ground; has run creditably for an apprentice; sent to Hong Kong. *R.
Sheather.*

SIX MILE BOTTOM 4 b.c. Brigadier Gerard 144–Bamba 76 (Busted 134) **113**
(1981 9fg 12.3g³ 12g³ 10v 12f* 12f* 11g² 12d⁴ 11.1f 8g 10g 1982 10f 13.4fg*

Mr E. B. Moller's "Six Mile Bottom"

10fg³ 11g* 12g) neat, strong, attractive colt; very useful performer; successful in Ormonde Stakes at Chester in May and Grand Prix de Lyon at Parilly, Lyon, in June; came from behind in a very strongly-run race to beat Critique by 4 lengths on former and comfortably accounted for Singing Boy (rec 9 lb) by 1½ lengths on latter; outpaced in last 2f when 3 lengths third of 6 to Castle Keep in Clive Graham Stakes at Goodwood in between; not seen out after finishing ninth of 12 behind Karkour in Grand Prix de Vichy in August; suited by 1½m+; has won on a soft surface, but is suited by top-of-the-ground; sold 50,000 gns Newmarket December Sales. *H. Wragg.*

SIX O SIX AUCTION 2 b.c. Connaught 130–Honey Pot 111 (Hotfoot 126) **72** (1982 6g 6d 8f⁴ 8g) Mar 25; 5,200Y; neat colt; third foal; brother to 1979 2-y-o 5f winner Concession; dam very useful sprinting 2-y-o; quite a modest maiden; suited by 1m; probably acts on any going. *C. Thornton.*

SIZERS COURT 4 br.g. Lorenzaccio 130–Seam 100 (Nearula 132) (1981 — NR 1982 12f) 2,700F; rangy gelding; brother to a poor animal and half-brother to several winners, including smart 1966 staying 2-y-o Slip Stitch (by Parthia); dam a miler; 33/1 when distant seventh of 8 behind Cool Decision in minor event at Pontefract in July. *M. H. Easterby.*

SKEWSBY 6 b.g. Andrea Mantegna–Rogali 80 (Royal Avenue 123) (1981 — 18g 1982 10.2d 10d) staying handicapper; no worthwhile form on flat for a long time; probably acts on any going; bandaged behind on first outing. *M. W. Easterby.*

SKIN DEEP 9 b.m. Prevailing–Vanity Case 77 (Counsel 118) (1981 6s⁴ — 6s* 6s 8g 7g 8f 6f² 6f⁴ 6d 6g 6fg 6s 1982 11.7fg 8.3fg 8f⁴) fair handicapper at her best; probably stayed 1m; acted on any going; blinkered once; was a suitable mount for an apprentice; dead. *W. Musson.*

SKI RUN 7 b.g. Workboy 123–Snow Rum (Quorum 126) (1981 12s 10f 10g³ **78** 12f⁴ 10fg² 12g² 11fg² 10g* 11d² 10.5s³ 11d* 10.2g³ 8g 1982 12g² 10.6s* 12fg*

774

10.5f³ 10.2d 12s) middle-distance handicapper; successful twice at Haydock, quickening up well when asked and beating Regal Steel by ½ length on second occasion in May; acts on any going; usually races with his tongue tied down; has worn bandages; suitable mount for a claimer; most genuine and consistent; off course 5 months before fifth start. *P. Wigham.*

SKI SAILING (USA) 2 b.f. Royal Ski–Space Sailing (Sail On-Sail On) (1982 **97 p**
6v² 7g*) Apr 2; $53,000Y; tall, good-topped filly; first foal; dam won 5f maiden race at 2 yrs; sire second best 2-y-o in USA in 1976; 12/1, stayed on well to finish 1½ lengths second of 10 to Northern Adventure in Duke of Edinburgh Stakes at Ascot in October; won 21-runner maiden event at Newmarket later in the month by 1½ lengths from Amphitheatre; has plenty of scope, and promises to make up into useful 3-y-o. *B. Hills.*

SKI'S DOUBLE 6 br.g. Double-U-Jay 120–Some Poser (Will Somers 114§) **72**
(1981 12s* 12s* 12.5s*(dis) 12v 12.3d 12.3d⁴ 12g⁴ 12f² 12f² 12.3fg³ 12s⁴ 13fg
11fg³ 12fg² 12v* 12d⁴ 12.2s³ 12g 12d 1982 12s* 10.6s⁴ 13g 12.3fg 12f 12f⁴
13fg 12.3g² 12g 12.3fg 12g⁴ 12.3s 12g 12d⁴ 12s²) middle-distance handicapper;
won at Leicester in March; acts on any going, but is well suited by some give;
usually apprentice ridden; finds little off bridle and has shown tendency to
hang. *R. Hollinshead.*

SKISKELTER 2 b.g. Malinowski 123–Skelmorlie (Blakeney 126) (1982 8s **—**
8.2s) Apr 20; IR 31,000Y; strong, well-made gelding; fourth foal; brother
to Irish 3-y-o 1½m winner The Pawn; dam won over 1½m in Ireland; behind
in October in maiden race (dwelt) at Sandown and minor event at Nottingham;
subsequently gelded. *B. Hills.*

SKITTISH (USA) 2 b. or br.f. Far North 120–Bright Merry (Speak John) **69 p**
(1982 8s) Mar 21; $225,000Y; tall, rather leggy filly; closely related to 2
winners by Barachois, one of them stakes placed; dam, who never ran, comes
from same family as Nijinsky, The Minstrel and Far North; 16/1, looked very
green when about 5 lengths fifth of 18 to Oranella in maiden race at Wolverhampton in October; sure to do better. *M. Stoute.*

SKYBOOT 3 b.g. African Sky 124–Sans Sabots (Whistler 129) (1981 6g **78**
5s 6g 1982 6s² 6g 6d* 6g 6g) close-coupled, useful sort; quite a moderate
handicapper; won at Windsor in June; will stay 7f; well suited by
soft ground; ran creditably in blinkers final start; sold 6,400 gns Newmarket
Autumn Sales. *A. Pitt.*

SKYBRIGHT 4 b.f. The Brianstan 128–Sky Hostess 72 (Skymaster 126) (1981 **—**
8s 8d 8g 10s 8fg 8d 12fg⁴ 10d 12d 1982 12fg 10fg 12fg 11.5fg 12g 10d 12d)
leggy filly, plater, stays 1½m, sometimes sweats up. *C. Blum*

SKY HIGH GUY (USA) 3 b.g. Son Ange–Gay Minette (Sir Gaylord) (1981 **71**
7.6s 1982 10s² 11.7f² 12fg 12fg 13d 14g 12s) strong, good-looking gelding;
runner-up in maiden races early in year; ran poorly afterwards; stays 1½m; acts on
any going; blinkered final start. *J. Bethell.*

SKY JUMP 8 ch.g. Double Jump 131–Damascus Sky (Skymaster 126) (1981 **55**
6s 7d² 7d 7fg* 7d⁴ 7g 5.8f 7f 7fg 7fg 6s 1982 6d³ 6g 7f 7f² 7h 8f³ 7g 7f⁴ 7fg⁴ 8.3g*
7g*(dis)) selling handicapper nowadays; bought in 900 gns after winning by
5 lengths at Windsor in August; disqualified after passing post first at Yarmouth in September; stays 1m; acts on any going; has been tried in blinkers;
good mount for a boy. *B. Swift.*

SKYLANDER 3 b.c. African Sky 124–Lagosta (Ragusa 137) (1981 7g 6s **81**
1982 7.6f³ 7.6g 8f² 8f² 8fg³ 10.2f³ 8.2s* 8s²) quite attractive, well-made colt;
made all to win maiden race at Haydock in October; stays 1¼m; acts on any
going; bandaged near-fore both starts in 1981; looked none too keen in blinkers
sixth outing. *J. Dunlop.*

SKY LAWYER (FR) 4 b.c. Sea Lawyer–Medenine (Prudent II 133) (1981 6.5g² **119**
6.5s² 7.6g* 7g* 8s 8v 10g 10.6g 9g³ 10g 10.6g 1982 8g 6.5v³ 5s² 6g⁴ 8g 7.6g
6g* 6s³ 5fg 6s 5g* 6fg³ 6g 5v²) French colt; half-brother to 3 winners in France,
including Over The River (by Luthier), useful on flat and over jumps; dam
won over 7f; won handicaps at Marseille in April and Deauville in August, on
latter course beating Flying Melody by 1½ lengths in a well-contested event;
placed twice in better company, putting up a good effort on final start when ½-
length second of 14 behind Kind Music in Prix du Petit Couvert at Longchamp
in October; best at sprint distances, though stays further; acts on heavy going
and has run respectably on a firm surface; blinkered nowadays; trained until
after eighth start by A. Curelly. *R. Touflan, France.*

SKYMERIC 3 ch.f. Homeric 133–Skymarlin 75 (Skymaster 126) (1981 NR **58**
1982 8d 8d 8fg 7g 10.4fg 10fg* 10.1g⁴ 10.1fg 10d³ 10d) 1,000Y; leggy, plain
filly; fourth living foal; dam stayed 1m; plater; bought in 3,400 gns after winning
at Newmarket in July; suited by 1¼m; acts on a firm and a soft surface; has
run well for an apprentice. *N. Guest.*

SKYRAM 3 b.g. Sagaro 133–Molly Fay 69 (Faberge II 121) (1981 8g 8s 8g **73**
1982 14fg⁴ 13.8f² 12.3d² 12d 16g 12.2f*) strong, compact gelding; made all
to win 4-runner handicap at Catterick in July; had run dismally previous 2
starts; should stay long distances; seems to act on any going. *D. Morley.*

SKYTRAIN JETSET 3 b.c. Rheingold 137–Caramel 93 (Crepello 136) (1981 **65**
7fg 7d 7fg 8s 1982 10d³ 12s 16h 12fg³) lengthy colt; quite a modest maiden;
stays 1½m; has run respectably for an amateur rider; sold 5,800 gns Newmarket
Autumn Sales. *R. Smyth.*

SKYTRICK 3 b.c. African Sky 124–Fascinating Trick (Buckpasser) (1981 **95**
7fg* 8g² 1982 8g) fine, big, rangy, attractive colt; won maiden race at Yarmouth and ran well in nursery at Newmarket at 2 yrs; ran only once in 1982,
keeping on to be about 5½ lengths fifth of 9 to Silver Hawk in Ladbrokes Craven
Stakes at Newmarket in April; stays 1m well; wandered badly in front second
start in 1981. *L. Cumani.*

SKYWALKER 3 b.g. Tower Walk 130–Skyey 70 (Skymaster 126) (1981 —
NR 1982 8.2f 8.2f 8g) strong, lengthy gelding; half-brother to very useful
1978 2-y-o sprinter Eyelet (by Sharpen Up); dam won over 6f; well beaten in
maiden race and 2 minor events in the North; sold to S. Leadbetter 1,050 gns
Doncaster August Sales. *M. Jarvis.*

SLATE 3 gr.f. Ragstone 128–January (Sigebert 131) (1981 NR 1982 10f)
small, useful-looking filly; good mover; fourth foal; half-sister to quite moderate
1m winner Rifle Green (by Scottish Rifle); dam placed twice at around 11f in
France; 33/1 and ridden by apprentice unable to claim his allowance, made
some late headway to be over 5 lengths sixth of 11 to More Kisses in £4,100
event at Newbury in June, only outing; will be suited by 1½m. *J. Dunlop.*

SLEEPLINE PRINCESS 4 ch.f. Royal Palace 131–Tin Mary 96 (Tin King **§§**
126) (1981 8fg 8s 8fg 7f 6fg² 6fg 6f 6fg 7f 7fg 8f 7.3d 10g 11.7d 1982 16s 7fg 7f)
poor handicapper nowadays; best form at 6f (unlikely to get 2m); sometimes
blinkered; one to be wary of. *S. Matthews.*

SLEEPLINE PROMISE 3 b.f. Record Token 128–Herods Palace 95 (Palestine
133) (1981 5s 5s³ 5fg 5g 5d 1982 5d 7d 8g 8s 6s) useful sort; has been tubed;
poor plater nowadays; has worn blinkers; trained by P. Cundell first 3 starts.
R. Thompson.

SLEIGH QUEEN 4 b. or br.f. Comedy Star 121–Snow Rum (Quorum 126) —
(1981 9s 6f⁴ 6f 6f 5g 5s 5s 1982 5d 5d 5f) compact filly; sprint maiden; no
form in 1982, including in a seller; has been tried in blinkers; sold 675 gns Ascot
May Sales and resold 750 gns Ascot 2nd June Sales *P. Cundell.*

SLENDERHAGEN (GER) 6 b.h. Alpenkonig–Saxifraga (Alizier 131) (1981
7.2s 8fg³ 7g 8g³ 7fg 1982 8g 7f 6f) good-quartered, attractive ex-German
horse; successful 8 times in his native country; ran best race of 1981 when third
in Queen Anne Stakes at Royal Ascot; not fully wound up either outing in
spring, 1982, and was off course almost 5 months before only other start; stays
9f; probably acts on any going; may need strong handling. *K. Brassey.*

SLICK WILLIE 3 b.g. Red Alert 127–Kilcurley Lass (Huntercombe 133) **75**
(1981 6d 6g 1982 6s² 7g* 7f⁴ 7d 7g³ 8f 7.2s 7s 6s) lengthy, useful sort; good
walker; won maiden race at Newcastle in April; claimed after running fifth in
claiming handicap at Nottingham in October and is to race in Scandinavia;
stays 7f; acts on soft going. *M. Jarvis.*

SLIGHTLY DANGEROUS (USA) 3 b.f. Roberto 131–Where You Lead 120 **122**
(Raise A Native) (1981 6s* 1982 7.3g* 8fg 12f²)
The excellent band of broodmares Khaled Abdulla is building up suggests
that the next few years ought to see his already familiar colours enjoying even
greater success. Among the mares that raced for him were Abeer and Alia, while
private purchases include Aryenne, Devon Ditty, Infra Green, Miss Manon and
Sookera; on top of this, in October came news that in a sizeable deal the Ferrans
Stud in Ireland and Belair Farm in Kentucky had come into Mr Abdulla's
ownership along with bloodstock including sisters to those outstanding fillies
Numbered Account and Rose Bowl. Slightly Dangerous, acquired for an

*Fred Darling Stakes, Newbury—this Guineas trial goes to
Slightly Dangerous from Zinzara (left)
and Ecstatica*

undisclosed sum after winning her first start at three, will not be out of place in
this exalted company   she's a fine stud prospect whose second place in the Oaks
showed her one of the best middle-distance fillies in Britain.

A comfortable winner of the Duke of Edinburgh Stakes at Ascot on her
sole appearance as a two-year-old, Slightly Dangerous had all too brief a second
season.   She started off in grand style in an acknowledged Guineas trial, the
Fred Darling Stakes at Newbury in April for which there were four other contestants, including Stratospheric and Zinzara.   Slightly Dangerous didn't look
fully wound up and wore a bandage on her near-hind after being cast in her
box two days previously, but in a slowly-run race she found no difficulty coping
with the opposition, coming through to join issue a furlong and a half out then
lengthening her stride impressively to beat Zinzara by two lengths.   For a filly
who seemingly possessed too much pace for her rivals at Newbury, Slightly
Dangerous rather surprisingly ran as if the mile trip of the One Thousand Guineas
a fortnight later was altogether too sharp.   Second favourite to Play It Safe, she
lay towards the rear early on and after only three furlongs her jockey, looking
uneasy, started to push her along; under vigorous riding she gradually got into
top gear, picking off several of the others in the last two furlongs without ever
looking like troubling the leaders.   At the post she was almost seven lengths
behind On The House in fifth.

The Guineas indicated that Slightly Dangerous would be well suited by the
Oaks trip, but with the stable doubly-represented Cauthen decided to ride the
Musidora winner Last Feather with Cook taking the mount on Slightly Dangerous.
No doubt to Cauthen's chagrin he made the wrong choice.   In the middle of
the field for much of the race, Slightly Dangerous moved up to fifth rounding
Tattenham Corner and followed Last Feather through as the latter went to the
head of affairs.   Depriving her stable-companion of the lead about a furlong out,
Slightly Dangerous had all her opponents except one beaten; unfortunately
for her that one, Time Charter, travelling strongly on the outside, promptly

SLI

launched an attack that Slightly Dangerous had little hope of withstanding. The eventual margin of defeat was a length, with Last Feather another one and a half lengths further back. Following this display there was reason to suppose that Slightly Dangerous would be a strong contender in top fillies' races at a mile and a half during the rest of the year but regrettably she didn't race again. A pulled muscle prevented her participation in the Irish Guinness Oaks and with the problem persisting she was retired.

	Roberto (b 1969)	Hail to Reason (br 1958)	Turn-to / Nothirdchance
Slightly Dangerous (USA) (b.f. 1979)		Bramalea (b 1959)	Nashua / Rarelea
	Where You Lead (ch 1970)	Raise A Native (ch 1961)	Native Dancer / Raise You
		Noblesse (ch 1960)	Mossborough / Duke's Delight

By finishing runner-up in the Oaks Slightly Dangerous provided her sire Roberto with one of three second places in classics in the space of a week— Touching Wood and Real Shadai occupied the same position in the Derby and Prix du Jockey-Club respectively—and emulated her dam who ran second to Mysterious in the 1973 Oaks. Where You Lead, sold for 1,000,000 dollars at the 1981 Fasig-Tipton November Sales, foaled two winners in France before Slightly Dangerous, notably the smart middle-distance filly I Will Follow (by Herbager), successful in the Prix de Minerve, while the grandam Noblesse, whose five foals all won, put up a brilliant performance to win the 1963 Oaks in runaway fashion. One first and two seconds in the Epsom classic is a fine record for a family and it will be intriguing to see whether at stud Slightly Dangerous, who visits Star Appeal, manages to produce a filly capable of maintaining the tradition. A rangy, attractive individual and a good walker, she was well suited by a mile and a half and acted on any going. *B. Hills.*

SLIGHTLY RISKY 2 b.c. Take a Reef 127–Slightly Saucy 74 (Galivanter 131) — (1982 9fg) May 15; 560F, 1,700Y; fourth living foal; dam stayed well; unquoted, behind in 17-runner maiden race at Warwick in July; sent to Malaysia. *P. Ransom.*

SLIGO BAY 5 b.g. Sassafras 135–Sleat 112 (Santa Claus 133) (1981 NR 76 1982 16g 16fg³ 16.1f 20fg 16g⁴ 16fg² 16d 17.1s 18d) strong gelding; has been fired; good walker; staying handicapper; in frame at Newmarket, Sandown and Ascot; acts on any going; usually bandaged in front nowadays. *F. J. Houghton.*

SLIM BOY 5 b.g. Starch Reduced 112–Astec Anne 66 (Astec 128) (1981 — NR 1982 12d⁴ 13fg⁴ 16fg 18.8fg 16fg 15.5f) small, narrow gelding; poor maiden; running on over 2¼m on fourth start and probably stays the trip; blinkered second and third outings. *M. Haynes.*

SLINGS AND ARROWS 2 gr.f. Warpath 113–Maysting 62 (Maystreak 118) 64 (1982 5d⁴ 6g 6fg 6g 8.2s 8.2v) Apr 13; fair sort; poor walker; has a high knee action; first foal; dam placed over 1¼m; only plating class; should stay 1¼m. *W. A. Stephenson.*

SLIP UP 2 b.g. Quiet Fling 124–Artemis 91 (King Emperor) (1982 7s 7s) — Jan 24; 16,000Y; well-made, good sort; half-brother to 2 winners, including useful Italian filly Adolfina (by Gay Fandango); dam 2-y-o 7f winner; behind in races won by Sackford at Sandown and Leicester in the autumn; subsequently gelded. *I. Balding.*

SLIX 2 b.f. High Top 131–Herbary (Herbager 136) (1982 6fg 6s) Mar 6; 79 p smallish, quite attractive filly; third foal; half-sister to 2 seemingly temperamental animals; dam never ran; made good late progess without being punished unduly when beaten about 9 lengths in maiden race at Salisbury in September and Blue Seal Stakes at Ascot later in the month; will be suited by 7f+; one to keep an eye on. *J. Dunlop.*

SMACKOVER 7 ch.h. Pontifex (USA)–Atanya (Atan) (1981 8fg² 10fg 7.6g 58 7.6s 8d³ 7s 1982 8f⁴ 8f* 8f* 8f³ 8fg³) strong, lengthy horse; poor walker; not the force he was, but gained narrow wins in handicaps at Redcar and Wolverhampton in May when apprentice ridden; finished first on his side of course when third to Bombil in valuable seller at Doncaster in September on final start, first outing for 4 months; best at around 1m; acts on any going but is suited by top-of-the-ground; used to be blinkered and held up but isn't nowadays; has worn bandages in front. *B. McMahon.*

778

SMALLBOY (USA) 3 b.c. Honest Pleasure–Northern Alibi (Northern Dancer) **68**
(1981 NR 1982 6s³ 6d² 5f 7.6f 8f) $20,000Y; small, compact colt; has a slightly
round action; first foal; dam won over 1m; placed in maiden races early in year;
should stay at least 7f; probably needs some give in the ground; bandaged
near-fore final start. *L. Cumani.*

SMALL PRINCESS 2 gr.f. Godswalk 130–Stormy Princess 76 (Ballymoss —
136) (1982 5v) Apr 17; IR 4,200Y; second foal; dam won at up to 13f; unquoted, tailed-off last of 9 in maiden race at Hamilton in October. *S. Norton.*

SMART AMBITION 4 ch.c. Amber Rama 133–Ember Grill 84§ (Indigenous —
121) (1981 8g 10.1fg 10.1fg 1982 10.1fg 12fg 12h 11.7fg) no worthwhile
form in varied races, including a seller. *C. Wildman.*

SMART GAL 2 b.f. Martinmas 128–Galway Gate (Laser Light 118) (1982 —
6d 6g 7.2s) Apr 16; IR 2,200F, 2,000Y; plain filly; second foal; dam never
ran; no form, including in a seller. *Mrs J. Reavey.*

SMART GUARD 5 b.g. Shiny Tenth 120–Smartie Pants 69 (Galivanter 131) —
(1981 7s 8g² 8g 7d⁴ 7g 7f 8f 11.5d 1982 10fg) poor maiden; stays 1m; acts
on a soft surface; has been blinkered and bandaged. *W. Wharton.*

SMART MART 3 ch.g. Jimmy Reppin 131–Fochetta (Fortino II 120) (1981 **61**
6f 6f³ 7fg³ 7d 7fg* 1982 7f 8f² 8f 8f³ 8fg² 7f* 7fg² 8f⁴ 7f⁴ 7s) workmanlike,
sturdy gelding; plater at 2 yrs; ran in better company in 1982 and won handicap
at Leicester in July; stays 1m; acts very well on fast ground; consistent, but
doesn't find much off bridle. *M. Camacho.*

SMILE SOFTLY 3 b.f. Prince Tenderfoot 126–Farce (Bon Mot III 132) (1981 **65**
NR 1982 7d² 8s) rangy, attractive filly; half-sister to very useful middle-
distance winner Lindoro (by Sun Prince) and to Whitehall Bridge (by Auction
Ring), a useful winner over 1½m here and in France; dam unplaced 3 times in
France; promising 1½ lengths second of 12 to Apple Blossom in minor event at
Salisbury in June; didn't run up to that form only subsequent start in September;
should stay at least 1m; sold 7,000 gns Newmarket December Sales. *R. Hern.*

SMILING LAUREL 3 ch.c. Young Emperor 133–Tom's Delight (Tom Rolfe) **76**
(1981 NR 1982 6fg⁴ 5fg 5g³ 7.2s) IR 5,000Y; strong, lengthy, useful sort;
second foal; dam, second twice over 1¼m in France, is half-sister to smart 1973
2-y-o Dragonara Palace (by Young Emperor); quite a moderate maiden; should
stay 7f. *Mrs B. Waring.*

SMITHY LANE 4 b.g. Pitskelly 122–Seamstress (Sea Hawk II 131) (1981 —
10d 11.7s 10g 10fg 11.5d 12g 8d 5f 10.4s 15.5f 10.6s 1982 10fg 12d 10d 7.6f)
strong gelding; little worthwhile form in varied company; has been tried in
blinkers; trained by C. Wildman until after third start. *G. Balding.*

SMOKE SCREEN 6 b.g. Blakeney 126–Cigarette Case 89 (Faberge II 121) —
(1981 13s 18g 1982 16f 15.8d 16fg) good sort; has been fired; stays 1¾m;
acts on any going; blinkered twice at 3 yrs; tailed off in 1982. *R. Hollinshead.*

SMOKE SINGER 7 b.g. Crooner 119–Smokey Dawn 78 (March Past 124) **§§**
(1981 6f* 5.6fg 6d 6g 7g 6v⁴ 6d 6g 1982 6f 6fg 9d) neat, strong gelding; fair
performer in 1981; effective at sprint distances and stays 11f; acts on any going;
blinkered once at 5 yrs; seems temperamental nowadays and is best left alone.
K. Brassey.

SMOKEY BEAR 7 b.h. Gulf Pearl 117–Seul 69 (Faberge II 121) (1981 12g⁴ —
20fg 1982 14.6f⁴) fairly useful handicapper at his best; very lightly raced
nowadays; stays well; acts on any going; has run creditably for an amateur.
J. Hanson.

SMOKEY SHADOW 5 gr.g. Dragonara Palace 115–Camdamus 83 (Mandamus **75**
120) (1981 8s 8d⁴ 8g 8g 1982 8g 7f³ 7f* 7f⁴ 7f³ 7g³ 8f² 10fg⁴ 8g) fair sort;
made all in handicap at Brighton in May; in frame most other outings, although
ran moderately final start; seems to stay 1¼m; acts well on firm ground; often
blinkered; usually ridden by claimer E. Guest nowadays. *E. Eldin.*

SMOKY WONDER 2 ch.g. Royal Smoke 113–Honey Wonder (Winden 109) —
(1982 5f 6fg) Mar 30; workmanlike gelding; first foal; dam never ran; little
worthwhile form; sold 580 gns Newmarket Autumn Sales. *D. Elsworth.*

SMUGGLY (USA) 2 ch.f. Caro 133–Call Me Goddess (Prince John) (1982 **?**
8s³ 7.5s*) Jan 24; $95,000Y; half-sister to a winner by Exclusive Native;
dam, stakes-placed winner at up to 1m, is daughter of CCA Oaks winner Marshua;
favourite when winning 12-runner maiden race at Saint-Cloud in November

cleverly by a neck from Allicance; will stay at least 1¼m; engaged in 1,000 Guineas and Oaks. *O. Douieb, France.*

SNAP TIN 4 ch.f. Jimmy Reppin 131–Hunu (Hul a Hul 124) (1981 7g 8f⁴ — 8fg² 7f 6g 8fg 10f 11g 8s 6s 1982 8.2s 8f) leggy filly; plater; stays 1m; sometimes wears blinkers. *R. Ward.*

SNATCH AND RUN (USA) 2 b.c. Full Pocket–Running Fight (Degage) **108** (1982 5fg³ 5g⁴ 5fg* 5fg* 6fg²) Apr 13; $28,000Y; $60,000 2-y-o; well-made, quite attractive colt; half-brother to several winners in USA and Puerto Rico, 2 of them stakes placed; dam, unplaced in 7 starts, is daughter of very smart filly Whirlabout; improved with each outing in a campaign restricted to 5 races in midsummer, on last 3 appearances winning maiden race at Windsor and minor event at Ayr and finishing excellent second to Orange Squash in nursery at Goodwood; suited by 6f; has raced only on a sound surface. *M. Jarvis.*

SNIFFY 3 b.c. Saulingo 122–Alizarina (Ragusa 137) (1981 5d 5s 6f² 5fg 5fg **63** 1982 8g 8fg 8fg⁴ 8fg* 7f³ 8d 9g* 8f 10d⁴) good-topped colt; won apprentice handicaps at Redcar in July and Newcastle in August; stays 1¼m; seems to act on any going; blinkered twice in 1981. *A. Jarvis.*

SNITTERFIELD 4 b.g. Royal Match 117–Mile Cross 88 (Milesian 125) (1981 — 10g 6d 6d 8d 5fg 8.5f 5h³ 9.5f 1982 10fg 16d 16f) 5,200Y; ex-Irish gelding; half-brother to useful sprinter Puza (by Realm); dam best at up to 1m; poor form over a wide range of distances; sometimes blinkered. *D. Elsworth.*

SNOW FORECAST (USA) 3 ch.c. Far North 120–Promise You (Promised **87** Land) (1981 6fg² 6s² 1982 9fg 10fg 12f* 12fg⁴ 13.3f 10f 8g³) attractive, lengthy colt; has a round action; stayed on well to win maiden race at Haydock in May; needs further than 1m and will stay 1¾m; acts on any going; retained 3,600 gns Ascot December Sales. *G. Hunter.*

SNOWY RIVER 2 ch.c. Sagaro 133–Lydiate 77 (Tower Walk 130) (1982 **86** 7fg 8s²) May 16; short-coupled colt; first foal; dam 1¼m winner; 8/1, came from some way behind when creditable ¾-length second of 9 to High Cannon in maiden race at Newcastle in October; should stay 1½m. *R. D. Peacock.*

SOBA 3 ch.f. Most Secret 119–Mild Wind (Porto Bello 118) (1981 5g 5g 6f **121** 6fg 7fg 7fg 6d 6d 5g³ 1982 5f* 6fg* 6fg* 7f* 6f* 5g* 6g 6f* 5fg* 6g² 6g* 5g* 6g² 6s*)

In a sparkling season which saw her win eleven of her fourteen starts Soba proved handsomely that there is more to entertainment value in racing than success in one or two of the top weight-for-age events. Beaten off bottom weight in a nursery at Edinburgh on the last of nine outings at two, Soba subsequently made strides of which Gog or Magog might have been proud, developing into one of the best three-year-old sprinters in Europe, amassing over £81,000 in prize money and capturing the imagination of the racing public in much the same way as Raffingora did more than a decade ago.

No praise is too high for Soba's trainer, who kept her fit and enthusiastic during an arduous campaign with the pleasing result that he received the Derby Award as Flat trainer of the year. Yet it is possible that the filly's initial improvement took even him by surprise. Among the 33/1 outsiders for the seventeen-runner Millgate Maiden Stakes at Thirsk in May, Soba came through to lead two furlongs out and soon drew clear to account for High Realm by four lengths. Within the space of five and a half weeks Soba had added four more facile successes to her tally, in minor events at Hamilton and Catterick and handicaps at Catterick again and Thirsk. The aggregate margin of these wins came to thirteen lengths and each time Soba displayed the characteristic which became her trademark—tremendous pace from the outset that left her rivals floundering and virtually ensured victory before a quarter of a mile had been covered. Nowhere was this quality better seen than in Soba's first venture into good handicap company in the Gosforth Park Cup at Newcastle towards the end of June. Up against the likes of Blue Singh, Sweet Monday and Touch Boy, Soba put up a highly impressive display, soon having a decisive advantage and cruising home by three lengths from Touch Boy after being eased near the finish.

Soba's triumphant progress came to an abrupt end in the Tote Sprint Trophy at Ayr in July. An odds-on chance, she didn't manage to gain her customary clear lead and had nothing in reserve in the closing stages, eventually finishing a well-beaten fifth to Camisite. Soba walked away feeling her off-hind leg; it transpired she had trapped a nerve, and a fight to make her fit to run

William Hill Stewards' Cup, Goodwood—the remarkable Soba makes all;
Bracadale and Celestial Dancer are best of the far-side group

in the William Hill Stewards' Cup seventeen days later began immediately, involving the assistance of a physiotherapist from Harrogate. Allotted 7-9 in the long handicap for the Stewards' Cup, Soba had been installed ante-post favourite as soon as lists appeared at the start of the month but this performance, along with the disclosure about her lameness, understandably resulted in most firms taking her out of the betting. By the Thursday following the Tote Sprint Trophy reports were filtering through that Soba's leg had improved a little; four days later her name reappeared in the lists, though not as favourite, and on the day she started at 18/1 in a typically strong field of thirty containing most of the best sprint handicappers in training. With a 5-lb penalty for her Newcastle success and a general 4-lb rise in the weights as well Soba carried 8-4 and received weight from nearly half her rivals. Those rivals saw a great deal more of Soba than she did of them for she turned what is usually one of the season's most competitive handicaps into something of a procession, breaking the course record in the process. Fast away from her number-one draw, Soba opened up a definite lead in the space of a furlong and a half and never looked like surrendering the advantage, galloping on determinedly despite drifting slightly right to beat Bracadale by two and a half lengths with Celestial Dancer two lengths away third. Quite a lot had been said prior to the race concerning the supposed disadvantage of being drawn one on the Goodwood six-furlong course. This argument ignored two points; first, that for a front-running sprinter a draw on the rail is normally a considerable bonus since it helps prevent the horse wandering, and secondly, that two runners drawn one had in fact won the Stewards' Cup in the previous twenty-five years, namely Arcandy, who made all in 1957, and Jukebox, who made virtually all to defeat a horse drawn two in 1970. As a last word on the matter, our comments in the essay on Jukebox in *Racehorses of 1970* still apply: 'A high number in sprint races at Goodwood is desirable but it is not nearly so advantageous as some make it out to be'.

In the light of her achievements Soba could hardly expect any mercy from the handicapper; nonetheless eleven days after the Stewards' Cup she carried 10-1 to a decisive success over Russian Winter in the Coral Bookmakers Handicap at Haydock, again having her opponents in trouble by halfway and keeping on all too strongly for them. Nor was there any question of Soba's resting on her laurels; just a couple of days later she travelled to Newcastle to try and carry on the good work in the Northumberland Sprint Trophy. Trainer Chapman obviously believes strongly in the principle that racehorses exist to race no matter how great their talents, and it is perhaps a comment on the extent to which the best performers tend to be pampered now that such an approach should seem refreshing. Regrettable as it may be, the days are long gone when a horse like Virago could win the City and Suburban and Great Metropolitan within half an hour of each other, as she did in 1854, or one like Voltigeur could dead-heat in the 1850 St Leger, win the re-run two hours later and then collect

Coral Bookmakers Handicap, Haydock—Soba
defies her weight of 10-1

the Doncaster Cup forty-eight hours afterwards, and consequently the decision to run Soba at Newcastle caused a few raised eyebrows. Soba showed the doubters the error of their ways and struck a blow on behalf of the belief that modern racehorses are tougher than many give them credit for by putting up her best performance so far. Meeting Celestial Dancer on terms 12 lb worse than at Goodwood she went down by a short head after giving her all in a tremendous tussle over the last furlong.

Only a visionary might have forecast at the start of the year that Soba would pick up eight races by mid-August. Remarkably she continued to improve and it is arguable that the translation of a formula made famous in the 'twenties by the French doctor Émile Coué would have been an appropriate inscription on her box at Stillington: 'Every day, in every way, I am getting better and better'. Conceding weight to almost all her nine opponents in the Great St Wilfrid Handicap at Ripon proved not the slightest problem to Soba who beat Polly's Brother easing up by two and a half lengths having been in complete command from three furlongs out, and in the four-runner Scarbrough Stakes at the Doncaster St Leger meeting she landed the odds by three quarters of a length from the King's Stand third Blue Singh. By now it was apparent that Soba deserved a crack at the best sprinters around and her chance came in the Diadem Stakes at Ascot towards the end of September. The twelve-runner field included the high-class Indian King plus three that had run well in pattern races during the year, Blue Singh, Jester and Vaigly Star; Soba started second favourite to Indian King. Sensibly in a six-furlong contest in this company Soba's rider did all he could to conserve his mount's energy, sitting against her while still letting her make the running. She bowled along happily for over four furlongs whereupon Indian King loomed up, looking for all the world as if he would swamp her. Such an interpretation reckoned without Soba's fighting qualities; though visibly tired she buckled down to her task with the utmost courage, making Indian King fight harder than expected for his length-and-a-half success.

The Diadem proved Soba could give top sprinters a run for their money, but Chapman decided not to pit her against Sharpo and Fearless Lad in the

Scarbrough Stakes, Doncaster—number ten!

Prix de l'Abbaye, choosing instead as her farewell for the year the Coral Book-makers Champion Sprint at York on the Saturday following the French race. There were three other runners, the four-year-old Scarrowmanwick and the three-year-olds Hay Habit and The Dinmont; despite sweating up and giving the impression she might have been feeling the effects of her hard season, Soba started at odds on. She duly landed the spoils by a short head from Scarrow-manwick, achieving victory in an exhilarating style that brought to mind the postscript Sir Edward Elgar jotted down at the end of the manuscript of the *Enigma Variations:* 'Great is the art of beginning, but greater the art of ending'. Pinging out of the stalls as usual, Soba led by about two lengths at halfway without looking to be racing too comfortably, showing a tendency to hang. Gradually Scarrowmanwick, on the outside, whittled away the gap and when he gained the initiative inside the final furlong it seemed all up with Soba who went almost half a length down. Defeat appeared inevitable—to win Soba needed to come again, something she hadn't done before and something which, after thirteen races, she could be excused for not doing this time. Yet rally she did. With her jockey putting down his whip and chasing her along like a man inspired, Soba answered the call with commendable enthusiasm, inching her way back to snatch the race out of the fire in the last stride for a memorable and popular victory, one that provided a fitting conclusion to an equally memorable campaign.

Soba's pedigree is hardly fashionable and her success must have given great encouragement to small-scale breeders in these days of multi-million dollar yearlings. Her sire Most Secret died in 1981. A smart sprint handicapper who won six and gained places in twelve of his thirty starts, he was as tough, genuine and consistent as Soba and, like her, showed his best form in blinkers. Most Secret's first runners appeared on the track in 1976, and while he has sired the winners of nearly one hundred and fifty races he hasn't exactly hit the high-spots—Secret of Success, successful in the 1979 Gladness Stakes, is his sole pattern-race winner and when he covered Soba's dam Mild Wind his fee stood at just £350 no foal no fee. Mild Wind, a twin bought by Chapman for 360

Mrs M. Hills's "Soba"

guineas as a yearling at Doncaster, showed precious little ability in nine starts on the flat, seven of which were in sellers, and on her only outing over hurdles she finished tailed off in a seller at Southwell. As a matter of interest on her final appearance at two she was ridden by D. Nicholls, then a 7-lb claimer; Nicholls rode Soba with dash in all her starts at three. Mild Wind, whose two-year-old Jo-Andrew (by Joshua) joined Chapman unbroken in the autumn, is a half-sister out of the fair maiden Mile Cross to the useful five-furlong sprinter Puza and the disqualified five-furlong winner Sable Streak. As proof that if one goes back far enough almost any pedigree contains good performers, the third dam, though she ran only twice and produced a single winner over jumps in Italy, was a half-sister to the very smart stayer Almiranta and to Antalya, dam of the smart Attalus.

Soba (ch.f. 1979)	Most Secret (ch 1968)	Crocket (ch 1960)	King of the Tudors	Chandelier
		Parysatis (b 1960)	Darius	Leidenschaft
	Mild Wind (b 1972)	Porto Bello (ch 1965)	Floribunda	Street Song
		Mile Cross (br 1967)	Milesian	Cross Wind

As things stand Soba, a strong-quartered filly who acts on any going but is ideally suited by top-of-the-ground, stays in training. An attempt to purchase her for a sum reportedly in excess of £500,000 came to nothing, as did Robert Sangster's suggestion that she be covered by Golden Fleece with any resultant foal being shared between himself and Soba's owner. It will not be so easy to place Soba at four, but horses with her qualities aren't easily kept out of the winner's enclosure. Provided all goes well, the King George Stakes at Goodwood would be an ideal target—the course is perfect for a sprinter of her type and five furlongs is likely to suit her better in top company than six, excellent as her form is at the latter. Whatever she does in 1983 Soba has already left an enduring mark and afforded immense pleasure to thousands of racegoers; we take our hats off to her. *D. Chapman.*

SOCIAL DEMOCRAT 2 ch.f. Status Seeker–Deviation (Petingo 135) (1982 — 5g 5g) May 5; IR 3,100Y; half-sister to 1981 2-y-o 5f winner Kash-In (by Kashiwa); dam never ran; well beaten in sellers at Wolverhampton and Warwick in the spring; dead. *Mrs J. Reavey.*

SOCIETY BOY 2 b.c. Sir Gaylord–Miss Petard 113 (Petingo 135) (1982 **95** p 7fg* 7fg2) June 5; nice, rangy colt, with a good, long stride; closely related to useful miler Cracking Form and fair sprinter Kiss (both by Habitat) and half-brother to very useful middle-distance stayer Meistersinger (by Rheingold); dam, very useful at 2 yrs and 3 yrs, won at up to 1½m; came with a steady run to lead over 1f out when winning 12-runner minor event at Sandown in August by 2½ lengths from Conor's Rock; creditable 2½ lengths second of 12 to Zoffany in well-contested event at Goodwood the following month; will stay 1¼m; promises to make up into useful 3-y-o, and seems sure to win more races. *J. Tree.*

SOCKBURN 7 b.g. My Swallow 134–Blue Bird 84 (Majority Blue 126) (1981 — NR 1982 12g 12.3g 12g 16d 13.8d) big, strong gelding; one-time fair handicapper; showed signs of retaining a little ability; suited by a test of stamina; seems to act on any going but ideally suited by a sound surface; suitable mount for an apprentice; bandaged nowadays. *M. Camacho.*

SOCKS UP 5 ch.g. Sharpen Up 127–Mrs Moss 81 (Reform 132) (1981 6s* **82** 6g 6f 6fg 6g 7.3d 7s3 7g4 6s 1982 8g 7s 8f4 8fg 8g4 8g3 8fg2 8f2 8d4 9d 9s4 8.2s) leggy, somewhat lightly-made gelding; good mover; went down by only ½ length to Shaady in ladies race at Doncaster in September on eighth outing; ran respectably most other starts, including in Hunt Cup at Royal Ascot and William Hill Cambridgeshire at Newmarket (though unplaced in both); stays 9f; acts on any going; hung badly on occasions in 1980 and was blinkered twice. *F. J. Houghton.*

SOCRATIC (USA) 2 ch.c. Exclusive Native–La Jalouse (Nijinsky 138) (1982 **94** p 7f3) Feb 29; $330,000Y; strong, deep-girthed, attractive colt; second foal; brother to 8.5f stakes winner Exclusive One; dam useful stakes winner over 8.5f in Canada; 14/1 but fit, eventually got the hang of things after being chased along vigorously with hands and heels when strong-finishing length third of 17 to Hasty Flirt in maiden race at Newmarket in July; likely to have learnt good deal from the experience and has makings of useful 3-y-o. *F. Durr.*

SOFICA 2 b.f. Martinmas 128–Skymarlin 75 (Skymaster 126) (1982 5f³ 5fg **56** 6fg 6s³ 5g² 6f 6s 6s) May 16; 1,000Y; leggy, lightly-made filly; half-sister to winning plater Skymeric (by Homeric); dam stayed 1m; modest plater; best run at 5f; probably acts on any going. *M. Hinchliffe.*

SOFTLY DOWN (USA) 2 gr.f. First Landing–Sea Grey 91 (Sea Hawk II 131) **66** (1982 5f³ 6h 7g 7fg⁴) May 18; $50,000Y; rather leggy, attractive filly; half-sister to a winning plater and French 7.5f and 10.5f winner Flight Sergeant (by Ragusa); dam, winner over 7f, is half-sister to successful broodmares Godzilla and Greedy of Gain; plating-class maiden; stayed 7f; blinkered final outing; dead. *J. Hindley.*

SOFT TOP 3 b.g. High Top 131–Softly Glowing 90 (Tutankhamen) (1981 — 5s 1982 7.6f 10d) well behind in maiden races. *C. James.*

SOIE GENTILLE 2 ch.f. Shantung 132–Ma Reine 89 (Grand Roi 118) (1982 — 6fg 8s 7d) June 2; workmanlike filly; fourth foal; dam 2-y-o 1m winner; seventh of 18 in maiden race at Leicester in October, third outing and only sign of ability. *R. Baker.*

SOIE GRISE 6 gr.h. Town Crier 119–Floating Melody 101 (Tudor Melody 129) — (1981 NR 1982 8f) plater; stayed 10.6f; seemed to act on any going; dead. *A. Smith.*

SOIGNEUSE (USA) 2 ch.f. Tom Rolfe–Trim and Tidy (Sea-Bird II 145) **109** (1982 5s² 7fg* 7g² 7f) Apr 3; $250,000Y; half-sister to 2 winners in USA, including $100,000-earner Pledge of Honor (by Illustrious); dam, unplaced in 2 starts, is half-sister to top-class racehorse and sire Hoist the Flag (by Tom Rolfe); won maiden race at Chantilly in July in good style by 4 lengths; ran very well when ½-length second of 12 to Maximova, who gave 3 lb, in Prix du Calvados at Deauville the following month but was beaten 6 lengths when fifth of 6 to dead-heaters Deep Roots and Maximova in Prix de la Salamandre at Longchamp in September; will stay middle distances; very useful. *F. Boutin, France.*

SOLABOY (USA) 3 ch.c. The Minstrel 135–Seminar 113 (Don II 123) (1981 **100** 6g* 6fg 7g 1982 7fg 7g 10f4 10.5fg³ 8g) strong, well-made, full-quartered, attractive colt; has a round action; in frame in £3,000 race at Newbury in July and £5,700 event at York in August; dwelt when 4¾ lengths third to Yard Bird in latter; suited by 1¼m; yet to race an a soft surface; blinkered last 2 starts; has shown a tendency to hang and is ungenuine. *R. Hern.*

SOLARES 2 br.g. Free State 125–Indian Wells (Reliance II 137) (1982 5s 5f **61** 6fg 7g 8 9s 7 9s) Apr 24; big, strong, workmanlike gelding; first foal; dam well beaten both starts; little worthwhile form; blinkered in seller at Haydock in October on final appearance; subsequently gelded. *J. Berry.*

SOLAR GRASS 7 b.g. Veiled Wonder–Fair Marilyn (Macherio) (1981 6d — 6s 5s 6g 5d² 5s⁴ 5g³ 5fg 6g 5fg 6fg 1982 5fg 9fg 5f 5fg 6f³ 7.6f 6fg 5g 6d) strong, fair sort; sprint handicapper; third at Thirsk and Carlisle in June, best efforts; probably acts on any going; suitable mount for an inexperienced rider; often blinkered nowadays. *W. Charles.*

SOLARIUM 4 br.g. Scottish Rifle 127–Daydreamer 78 (Star Gazer 123) (1981 **39** 12g 12fg 12g² 13.8fg⁴ 1982 12d 15.5v² 10g⁴ 12g) poor plater; stays 2m; acts on heavy going; sometimes blinkered. *W. Musson.*

SOLAR LIGHT 2 br.c. Nonoalco 131–Madina 119 (Beau Prince II 131) (1982 **91** 8g⁴ 8g) May 4; strong, sturdy, good sort; brother to very smart French miler Nonoalca and a winner in Italy, and half-brother to 2 winners and to leading French hurdler Mazel Tov (by Sigebert); dam won Prix Morny; strong-finishing 3½ lengths fourth of 21 to Polished Silver in £4,200 event at Newbury in September; short-priced favourite, improved under pressure to have every chance 1f out when 4 lengths fifth of 18 behind Holy Spark in maiden race at Newmarket the following month. *J. Tree.*

SOLAR ROCK 2 ch.c. Ballad Rock 122–Solar Jinks (Immortality or Delirium **107** 126) (1982 5fg 5d* 5g² 6f² 6fg² 5fg 6s³ 6s) Mar 5; IR 9,800F, 35,000Y; good-bodied colt; good walker; closely related to 2 winners by Irish Love, including useful Irish 5f and 1¼m winner Jinkitis; dam ran once; won maiden race at Salisbury in June by 2 lengths from Both Ends Burning; placed 4 times subsequently in useful company, once beaten short head; stays 6f; acts on any going; ran poorly in blinkers sixth start; hung badly fifth and seventh outings; sold 26,000 gns Newmarket Autumn Sales for export to Hong Kong. *G. Harwood.*

SOLAR SYSTEM 2 ch.c. On Your Mark 125–Pagan Slipper (Red God 128§) **101**
(1982 5s² 5g* 5fg* 5f² 5fg 5fg³) May 10; IR 25,000Y; half-brother to 3 winners,
including Irish 1¼m winner Pagan Love (by Wishing Star); dam, placed over
6f at 2 yrs, is half-sister to Boldboy; favourite when successful in maiden race
at Navan in April (beat Cremation 2 lengths) and minor event at Leopardstown
in May (landed odds by a length from Reveal); later ran well in valuable races,
finishing 4 lengths second to Virginia Deer at Naas, 2¼ lengths sixth to same
horse at the Curragh and 3¼ lengths third of 11 to Sweet Emma, after showing
up throughout, in Heinz '57' Phoenix Stakes at Leopardstown; not seen out
after early-August; will stay 6f; blinkered final start. *D. Weld, Ireland.*

SOLAR TEMPTRESS 2 b.f. Status Seeker–Sundalgo 82 (Fidalgo 129) (1982 **58**
6fg 7f³ 7f 8.2g) Apr 14; IR 820F, 2,100Y; big filly; half-sister to 3 winners;
dam won over 7f at 2 yrs and probably stayed 2m; 7 lengths third of 9 to Commodore Bateman in maiden auction event at Catterick in July, best effort;
should stay 1¼m; retained 720 gns Doncaster October Sales. *D. Morley.*

SOLBELLA 2 b.f. Starch Reduced 112–Dear Sol (Dear Gazelle 113) (1982 —
6fg 6s) May 6; lightly-made filly; half-sister to 1976 2-y-o 5f seller winner
Solchella (by Welham); dam of little account; no worthwhile form in sellers at
Windsor in August and Haydock (slowly away) in October. *H. J. Jones.*

SOLDAN 4 br.c. Royalty 130–Mercilla 94 (Welsh Abbot 131) (1981 NR **88**
1982 8g 8f² 9f* 8fg 10g³ 8g) big colt; useful performer as a 2-y-o; reportedly
cracked a bone in a knee as a 3-y-o but evidently made a full recovery; beat
Don Presto by ½ length in minor event at Ripon in May and was placed in handicaps at Redcar and Ripon again; possibly finds 1¼m a bit far for him; acts on
any going; ran too freely, but wasn't disgraced, when blinkered final start;
sold to D. Smith 6,000 gns Newmarket Autumn Sales. *J. W. Watts.*

SOLDBY 2 b.g. Connaught 130–My Mary 93 (French Beige 127) (1982 6fg 6d **77**
8.2fg* 8.2s²) Apr 5; 4,100Y; useful-looking gelding; half-brother to numerous
winners here and abroad, including smart Bona Mia (by Good Bond), successful
at up to 1m; dam a stayer; landed a gamble in 14-runner seller at Haydock
(bought in 7,400 gns) in September, winning by 6 lengths; beaten short head
in nursery at Hamilton later in the month; suited by a test of stamina; seems
to act on any going; gelded after final outing. *M. H. Easterby.*

SOLDIER ANT 2 ch.c. Brigadier Gerard 144–Hants 111 (Exbury 138) (1982 —
6fg 6f) Apr 10; 19,000Y; strong colt; half-brother to 3 winners, including
3-y-o Tants (by Vitiges), a very useful winner at up to 1½m, and very useful
1978 2-y-o 6f to 1m winner Potemkin (by Sir Gaylord); dam won 4 times at
around 1¼m; little worthwhile form in minor event at Leicester in June and
Chesham Stakes at Royal Ascot. *C. Brittain.*

SOLDIER BIRD 3 ch.f. Shiny Tenth 120–Ibis 96 (Tamerlane 128) (1981 —
5d 6g 6fg 7.2v 1982 8.5f 8g 6fg) lengthy, rather sparely-made filly; poor plater;
sold 350 gns Ascot July Sales. *R. Hannon.*

SOLDIER ON 3 b.g. Queen's Hussar 124–Tegleaze 81 (Galivanter 131) (1981 —
7g 7fg 1982 10f 8d) strong, short-legged, attractive gelding; behind in maiden
races; blinkered final start. *B. Swift.*

SOLDIER'S JOY 2 b.f. Dance In Time–Major Barbara 90 (Tambourine II 133)
(1982 8fg 8s) Apr 18; fair sort; half-sister to several winners, including useful
3-y-o 13f winner Brevet (by Busted) and very smart 1975 2-y-o Dame Foolish
(by Silly Season); dam won at up to 7f as a 2-y-o; last but one in maiden races at
Beverley (slowly away) and Wolverhampton in the autumn; sold 2,600 gns
Doncaster October Sales. *E. Weymes.*

SOLEIL ETOILE 3 ch.f. Roi Soleil 125–Fair Measure (Quorum 126) (1981
NR 1982 12g 10f) 1,100F, 780Y, 520 2-y-o; fourth foal; half-sister to winning
stayer Gold Measure (by Goldhill); dam ran 3 times; in rear in maiden race at
Folkestone and minor event at Brighton in April. *R. Hoad.*

SOLERCO 2 br.g. Ercolano 118–Solvilium (Vilmorin) (1982 5f 8f) Feb 21; — §
3,000Y; neat gelding; half-brother to 2 winners and to several winners over
jumps; seems of no account and looks temperamental too; blinkered, swerved
at halfway and was virtually pulled up on second start; subsequently gelded.
Mrs N. Macauley.

SOLFORD (USA) 2 b.c. Nijinsky 138–Fairness (Cavan) (1982 6fg* 7fg*) **103** p
Jan 31; $1,300,000Y; half-brother to numerous winners, notably very smart
No Bias (by Jacinto), a winner at up to 1m; dam unraced half-sister to 3 stakes
winners, including top-class middle-distance stayer Prove Out; won only narrowly

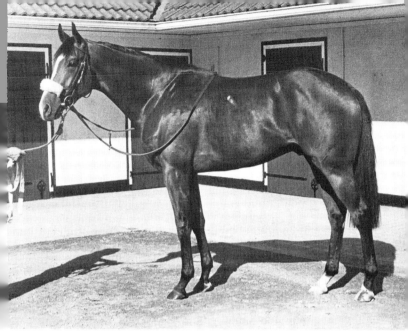

Mr R. E. Sangster's "Solford"

when 5/2 on for both his races, beating Winning Feature ¾ length in maiden race at the Curragh in August and Moral Leader a short head, giving him 5 lb, in minor event at Leopardstown in September; will be well suited by 1¼m⁺, should leave this form behind at 3 yrs. *V. O'Brien, Ireland.*

SOLIMILE 2 b.f. Solinus 130–Mile By Mile 92 (Milesian 125) (1982 5fg 5fg **84** 7g 6s³) Apr 24; 12,000Y; half-sister to fairly useful 1977 2-y-o 5f winner Speedometer (by Sharp Edge); dam won over 6f at 2 yrs; off course for 4 months after running at Royal Ascot on second outing, and returned to show fair form in maiden events at Newmarket and Doncaster (third of 25); stays 7f; capable of winning small race. *P. Kelleway.*

SOLITAIRE 2 br.f. Warpath 113–So Precious 100 (Tamerlane 128) (1982 — 6g 7d) Apr 10; rather lightly-made filly; sister to 3-y-o 1½m winner Sapphire and half-sister to 1½m winner Midsummer Madness (by Silly Season); dam won at up to 1¼m and stayed 1½m; 16/1, modest seventh of 14 in minor event at Catterick in October, second outing; should stay 1½m. *C. Thornton.*

SOLWAY WINDS 4 b.g. Windjammer (USA)–Maggie Mine 85 (Native Prince) — (1981 8g 8d⁴ 7g 8f* 7g 7d² 7f 7g³ 7d 7g 1982 7f 7f 9g 8d 7f) leggy gelding; fair handicapper as a 3-y-o; in rear all starts in 1982; stays 1m; seems to act on any going; trained until after second outing by N. Crump. *B. Wilkinson.*

SOMA 2 b.f. Gay Fandango 132–Yellow Ribbon (Shooting Chant) (1982 5g **59** 5fg 5fg) Mar 23; 16,000Y; useful-looking filly; third living foal; dam won over 7f and 1m in Ireland; poor form; off course 4 months after second outing; sold BBA 1,100 gns Newmarket Autumn Sales. *M. Masson.*

SOME BABY 5 b.m. Some Hand 119–Scottish Lullaby 92 (Aberdeen 109) — (1981 NR 1982 5g) of little account nowadays. *N. Kernick.*

SOME BOSS 2 b.g. Some Hand 119–Salambos (Doon 124) (1982 5f 7fg 6s) — Apr 17; 2,000Y; fair sort; third foal; dam behind in seller on only start; well beaten in maiden races and a seller. *P. Rohan.*

SOME CHERRY 6 br.m. Some Hand 119–Cherry Brandy (Tenerani 135) **41**
(1981 11g 8fg 8g² 7fg³ 8fg⁴ 8fg 8.2d 1982 10.2g 5f 5fg³ 5f 6s 6s⁴) unfurnished
mare; plater; stays 1m, but has run creditably at 5f; probably acts on any going;
sold 500 gns Doncaster November Sales. *T. Taylor.*

SOME GRANGE 3 b.f. Some Hand 119–Grange Park 73 (Derring-Do 131) —
(1981 5f 6f 1982 8d 9g 8fg) compact filly; behind in maiden races and a handicap. *R. Hollinshead.*

SOME JET 4 ch.g. Some Hand 119–Jetador 73 (Queen's Hussar 124) (1981 **43**
7.2s 8f 6g 7.6s²(dis) 6d 7s 1982 8f 8g 6g 7.6fg 8g⁴ 8fg⁴ 8.2v⁴) neat gelding;
plater; stays 1m. *C. Crossley.*

SOMERFOLDS 3 ch.f. Some Hand 119–Florica 80 (Floriana 106) (1981 8g **48**
7d 7g 7.6s 1982 8fg* 10f 8.3g 8g 10v) dipped-backed filly; plater; bought in
1,500 gns after winning at Wolverhampton in April; stays 1m. *H. O'Neill.*

SOMERFORD GLORY 4 b.f. Hittite Glory 125–Peregrine Peach 79 (Falcon **44**
131) (1981 7g 7f 1982 8f⁴ 7fg² 8f) small, workmanlike filly; second in seller
at Lingfield in May; stays 1m. *R. Baker.*

SOMERSDAY 3 b.f. Some Hand 119–Spring Day (Vic Day 126) (1981 7d **72**
7.6s 10s 1982 10d³ 12g 14f 14s) workmanlike filly; plating-class maiden;
best run at 1¼m on soft ground. *M. Francis.*

SOMERSET BRIDGE (USA) 2 b. or br.f. Advocator–Harbour Queen (Young **68**
Emperor 133) (1982 7d 8g³) Apr 12; $40,000F; third foal; half-sister to 3-y-o
1¼m winner Off The Reel (by Silent Screen) and fairly useful 7f and 1m winner
Ice Harbour (by Icecapade); dam, half-sister to very useful 1976 French staying
2-y-o El Criollo, won over 1m; placed in maiden race at Edinburgh in October;
will stay beyond 1m. *S. Norton.*

SOMERS HEIR 7 b.g. Will Somers 114§–Treatisan 67 (Milesian 125) (1981 —
7g 7v 8f 8f 8.2s⁴ 7d 1982 7s 8d 8f 9g 8g) poor handicapper nowadays; stays 1m;
goes well in the mud; occasionally wears blinkers; suitable mount for a boy.
D. Wintle.

SOME SPARE 3 b.c. Track Spare 125–Some Say (I Say 125) (1981 NR **70 d**
1982 8fg⁴ 8fg⁴ 10fg 9g 10d 8s) compact colt; first foal; dam apparently of little
account; quite a moderate maiden; should stay 1¼m; blinkered final start.
M. Smyly.

SOME SUNNY DAY 2 br.f. Radetzky 123–Derry Willow (Sunny Way 120) **77**
(1982 5fg 6fg 7f 7g 8f² 8s⁴ 8.2s) Apr 21; 1,000F, 4,600Y; compact filly; half-sister
to several winners, including 3-y-o 1m winner Hanabi (by Hittite Glory); dam
middle-distance maiden; in frame in nursery (1½ lengths second of 12 to Walton
Heath) at Bath in September and maiden race on same course the following
month; suited by 1m and will stay 1¼m; acts on any going. *J. Benstead.*

SOMETHING SPECIAL 5 b.h. Queen's Hussar 124–Calling The Tune 84 —
(Tudor Melody 129) (1981 8g 12s 12g 12f 12g 15fg* 13.8fg 15.8f 18f² 18.1d
17.1d 18g 1982 13g 16.1s) staying handicapper; ideally suited by fast ground;
blinkered once in 1980; suited by front-running tactics. *P. Bevan.*

SOME YOYO 2 b.g. Lochnager 132–Katira 83 (Paveh 126) (1982 5f 5fg³ **65**
5g² 6f 5f³ 5g 5g) May 3; 6,600Y; strong gelding; good walker; half-brother to a
winner in Belgium; dam, half-sister to high-class sprinter Royben, won over 2m;
placed in small races in Scotland; gelded after final outing; disappointing.
H. Bell.

SONADA 3 br.g. Reliance II 137–Sunsaly 75 (Sallymount 125) (1981 NR —
1982 11g 12g) 5,800Y; big, strong gelding; half-brother to fair 1m to 1¼m
performer Golden Vow (by Good Bond) and a winner in Austria; dam won 5f
seller at 2 yrs; in rear in maiden race at Newbury in April and minor event at
Kempton in May. *P. Mitchell.*

SON FILS 7 ch.h. Mon Fils 124–Crespinall 100 (Saint Crespin III 132) (1981 —
8s 12s⁴ 16d² 12f 1982 12fg 16fg) tall, narrow horse; really good mover;
very useful performer at his best, but only lightly raced nowadays; led to past
halfway when tenth of 11 behind Glint of Gold in John Porter Stakes at Newbury
in April (bandaged in front and having first race for more than 9 months);
not seen out after being pulled up at Ascot later in month; effective from 1½m to
2m; acts on any going but is best with some give in the ground; game and genuine.
M. Pipe.

SONG BOY 3 ch.g. Music Boy 124–Sorceress 72 (On Your Mark 125) (1981   —
5v 5g 5g⁴ 5g   1982 8f 10fg 8.3g 16h) workmanlike gelding; poor plater; has
worn blinkers. *R. Keenor.*

SONG MINSTREL 4 b.g. Song 132–Tribal Festival 65 (Tribal Chief 125)   **77**
(1981 5g 8f 7f 6fg* 6g* 6d² 6fg³ 6f 6d² 6d² 6d* 1982 6f 6fg 6fg 6f* 6s 6d 6d
6fg² 6f⁴ 7s 6s 7d*) strong, compact gelding; won handicaps at Redcar in May
(£4,500 race) and November, latter by 2½ lengths from O.I. Oyston; ran creditably
on 3 occasions in between but isn't particularly consistent; stays 7f; yet to prove
he acts on very soft going, but acts on any other; usually blinkered nowadays;
missed break sixth start. *M. Camacho.*

SONG MYDAD 3 b.g. Song 132–Sheinter (Sheshoon 132) (1981 5fg 5fg 7.2v   —
1982 5fg) compact gelding; in rear in maiden races and a seller; dead. *J.
Townson.*

SONGROID 2 b.f. Haveroid 122–Songs Jest (Song 132) (1982 5fg* 5fg 5f³   **93**
5f* 5g² 5d* 5g) Feb 1; 6,000Y; lengthy, workmanlike filly; first foal; dam, who
never ran, is closely related to very useful sprinter Jester; successful in maiden
race at Newmarket in April and in nurseries at Thirsk in July and Windsor in
September; not sure to stay 6f; probably acts on any going; sweated up and
didn't impress in paddock final start. *A. Jarvis.*

SONGS SLIPPER 3 b.f. Song 132–Warm Slipper (King's Company 124)   —
(1981 NR 1982 8f 7f 7fg⁴ 8.2v) 1,050Y; smallish, lightly-made filly; second
foal; half-sister to a winning plater; dam tailed off only start; plater; stays 7f;
blinkered last 2 starts; sold 1,050 gns Newmarket Autumn Sales. *C. Spares.*

SONG TO SINGO 2 b.f. Master Sing 109–Song Book 85 (Saintly Song 128)   **63**
(1982 5fd 5fd 5f 5g* 5d⁴ 5g 5d 6s² 5d⁴) Apr 8; small, lightly-made filly; first foal;
dam won 6f seller at 2 yrs; stuck on well to beat Rapid Lady a short head in
15-runner seller at Ripon (no bid) in August; stays 6f; suited by some give in the
ground. *J. Etherington.*

SONIC METEOR 2 b.c. Star Appeal 133–Knightside (Graustark) (1982   **72**
8s² 10s 8d⁴) Apr 14; close-coupled, workmanlike colt; half-brother to middle-
distance winner Justin Thyme (by Rheingold); dam won over 6f at 3 yrs in USA;
quite modest form in late-season maiden and minor events; stays 1m. *W.
Hastings-Bass.*

SON OF A GUNNER 2 ch.c. Gunner B 126–Swakara 92 (Porto Bello 118)   **61**
(1982 5fg 6d 5fg³ 7g 5d 6g) Apr 13; compact colt; first foal; dam won 10 sprint
races and was well suited by give in the ground; plating-class maiden; best run
at 5f. *S. Mellor.*

SON OF MANADO 2 b.c. Manado 100 Digny (Assagai) (1982 5fg 5fg⁵ 6f 7f)   **74**
May 10; leggy colt; fourth live foal; half-brother to a winner in USA; dam never
ran; placed in maiden race at Nottingham in June; should stay beyond 5f;
slowly away first outing and unruly at start second. *A. Jarvis.*

SON OF RAJA (USA) 2 ch.c. Raja Baba–Couronne de Fer (Iron Ruler)   **93**
(1982 5fg 5g² 5f² 6d 5fg²) Feb 18; $90,000Y; really strong colt; has a sharp
action; first foal; dam, 2-y-o 6f winner, is half-sister to very useful British performers Bass Rock and St Puckle; ran well, showing excellent speed, in quite
useful company at Kempton and Newbury in the spring, but disappointed in
his 2 races afterwards, second a maiden at Wolverhampton in August when
6/4 on; doubtful temperamentally. *P. Cole.*

SONSERI 3 b.f. Prince Tenderfoot 126–Domani 106 (Mourne 126) (1981 5s*   **95**
1982 6g* 6s* 7fg 8g 7s) good-bodied filly; fairly useful handicapper; won at
Doncaster in March and Kempton in April; not disgraced in quite valuable
events last 2 starts; stays 1m; needs some give in the ground. *R. Price.*

SOPHRETTO 3 ch.c. Hot Spark 126–Permutation 79 (Pinza 137) (1981   —
5s 6g 6g 8g 8s 1982 12d⁴ 16f 12fg⁴) strong, good-bodied colt; poor maiden;
stays 1½m. *J. Hardy.*

SOPRANO BOY 3 b.g. Tudor Music 131–Dovyalisa (Dike) (1981 NR 1982   **49**
8g 6s 8f⁴ 11.5fg 10v 15.5v³ 12s⁴ 12s) IR 2,100F, 3,800Y; fair sort; first produce;
dam, fourth 3 times at up to 1¼m in Ireland, is daughter of smart French filly
Arnica; plater; suited by a test of stamina; acts on heavy going; blinkered last 4
starts; trained part of season by C. Brittain. *R. Simpson.*

SORROW 3 b.f. Wolver Hollow 126–Penitent 85 (Sing Sing 134) (1981 5s   —
1982 5fg 8fg 12fg) lightly-made filly; poor maiden; sold 1,300 gns Ascot July
Sales. *G. Harwood.*

SO TRUE 2 b.f. So Blessed 130–Veracious 86 (Astec 128) (1982 5f² 5d* 7fg **92**
7v³ 6g) Apr 6; lengthy filly; second foal; dam effective from 1¼m to 2m; ran on
strongly to win in good style by 2 lengths from It's A Pleasure in 17-runner
maiden race at Salisbury in June; was respectably afterwards in valuable nurseries
at York and Lingfield; better suited by 7f than by shorter distances, and will
stay further; seems to act on any going. *G. Balding.*

SOULIEANA 2 br.f. Manado 130–Hip (Ragusa 137) (1982 5fg 5s 5d 6fg 6d 7d) **58**
Mar 4; sturdy filly; second live foal; dam, of little account, is half-sister to
Derby winner Larkspur and smart stayer Ballymarais; plating-class maiden;
will stay at least 1m. *W. Haigh.*

SOUND AND HAPPY 2 br.f. Diamonds Are Trump 108–Safe And Happy **—**
(Tudor Melody 129) (1982 6g 6fg 5v) May 5; 3,500Y; good-topped filly;
third foal; half-sister to a winner in Belgium; dam never ran; no worthwhile
form in maiden races. *G. Lewis.*

SOUND OF THE SEA 3 b.f. Windjammer (USA)–Running Cedar (Bryan G.) **65**
(1981 5g 5f 5s* 6s 1982 6f² 6f² 6g 5fg⁴ 6f 5fg 6fg 6f* 6s) lightly-made, fair
sort; made all to win handicap at Brighton in September; will stay 7f; acts on
any going; blinkered fifth and last 2 starts. *W. Wightman.*

SOUTH ATLANTIC 2 b.c. Mill Reef 141–Arkadina 121 (Ribot 142) (1982 **95 p**
8fg² 6s*) May 4; 640,000Y (record price for yearling sold in Europe to end
of 1981); well-made, medium-sized colt; half-brother to smart Irish middle-
distance winner Encyclopedia (by Reviewer) and useful 1979 Irish staying
2-y-o Forlene (by Forli); dam, placed in 3 classics, is sister to high-class stayer
Blood Royal and closely related to Gregorian; had field quite well strung out when
winning 20-runner maiden race at the Curragh in October by 2½ lengths from
Mr Big John; had previously gone down by a short head to Homeowner in 14-
runner maiden race at Leopardstown in September but would probably have
won had he not lost 3 or 4 lengths when forced to switch positions early in straight;
will be suited by middle distances; still has improvement in him and is sure to
make a good 3-y-o. *V. O'Brien, Ireland.*

SOUTHERNAIR 2 b.c. Derrylin 115–Port La Joie (Charlottown 127) (1982 **65**
7fg 7g 7fg) Apr 30; 13,500F, 17,500Y; quite attractive, well-made colt; first
foal; dam unraced daughter of 1,000 Guineas and Oaks second Spree; little
worthwhile form in quite useful company; should stay 1m. *J. Sutcliffe.*

SOUTHERN DANCER 3 b.c. Connaught 130–Polyandrist 92 (Polic 126) **74**
(1981 8g⁴ 8s 7s 1982 8g⁴ 8f⁴ 10f 12fg 7fg) tall, fair sort; quite moderate; should
stay middle distances but has run moderately over them; suited by some give
in the ground; sold to J. Parkes 9,600 gns Doncaster September Sales. *R.
Price.*

SOUTHERN MUSIC 4 ch.c. Music Boy 124–Wavetree (Realm 129) (1981 **104**
6s² 8s 7g³ 6g³ 7g³ 6s* 6s* 6fg* 6g⁴ 5g³ 6g 6d³ 1982 5g 8g⁴ 6fg³ 6g³ 8f⁴ 8f 6.3g²
7g² 6.3fg* 6fg² 7fg* 6f² 8g) workmanlike Irish colt; first foal; dam, unraced
half-sister to smart Imperial Dancer, successful at up to 1¼m; successful in
handicaps at the Curragh in July and August; in frame most other starts and
was second in valuable handicap at the Curragh, Ballycorus Stakes at Leopardstown, Seven Springs Sprint Stakes at the Curragh again (promoted from
third) and Herbertstown Stakes at Naas; remote eighth of 10 to Mr Fluorocarbon
in Queen Anne Stakes at Royal Ascot on sixth outing; has run respectably at
1m but best at shorter distances; probably acts on any going. *N. Meade,
Ireland.*

SOUTH FORK LASS 3 b.f. Pitcairn 126–Ballycancan (El Gallo 122) (1981 **—**
NR 1982 8g 8s 8s 8d 6s) IR 4,200F, resold 7,600Y; second foal; dam won from
7f to 1½m in Ireland; well beaten in 4 races at Cagnes-sur-Mer and maiden race
at Leicester in spring. *R. Baker.*

SOUTHFORK STAR 3 b.c. Malacate 131–Beatrice Frost 78 (Princely Gift 137) **—**
(1981 5f 1982 7g 12f 12f) strong colt; in rear in maiden races and a minor
event; sweated up badly second start. *R. Morris.*

SOVEREIGN CELLAR 4 gr.g. Sovereign Path 125–Kessella (Le Levanstell **—**
122) (1981 8f 10fg 11f 9g 9d 1982 12d) little worthwhile form. *Miss L. Siddall.*

SOVEREIGN FLAME 4 ch.f. Supreme Sovereign 119–Flaming Peace 104 **43**
(Queen's Hussar 124) (1981 7s 7g 6g 6g⁴ 6fg 5.3fg 6f 8d 1982 7g 8f²) poor
performer; bandaged when second in apprentice handicap at Redcar in July;
stays 1m; acts on any going; has been tried in blinkers. *A. Hide.*

SOVEREIGN ISLAND 3 gr.c. Supreme Sovereign 119–Practicality (Weavers' — Hall 122) (1981 7f 7g 6g 1982 8s 7g) tall, leggy colt; poor maiden. *N. Guest.*

SOVEREIGN LACE 2 gr. or ro.f. Oats 126–Sovereign Sunset 65 (Sovereign **76** Path 125) (1982 5f 5fg 6f 6fg 6d 6s⁴) May 15; IR 1,000F, 7,600Y; rather lightly-made, fair sort; fourth foal; dam temperamental maiden from family of Burwell and King of Spain; quite a moderate filly; should stay beyond 6f; appears to act on any going; inconsistent. *R. Hollinshead.*

SOVEREIGN NOTION 3 b.c. He Loves Me 120–Notonia 73 (Never Say Die **97** 137) (1981 5d 6s* 6fg 7f g³ 7f g² 8g³ 1982 7s 7g 7g* 8fg* 8f 7fg) IR 15,500Y; rangy colt; good mover; half-brother to 2 winners in France; dam, half-sister to Psidium, won over 1¼m; 3-length winner of 2 handicaps at Leopardstown in May, beating Hunters Delight on first occasion and Lattygar on second; well beaten in £4,000 race at Newbury (well-backed favourite) and Jersey Stakes at Royal Ascot afterwards; stays 1m; seems to act on any going; ran moderately in blinkers second start. *M. Kauntze, Ireland.*

SOVEREIGN PEARL (FR) 2 b.f. Nonoalco 131–Perla 107 (Young Emperor **82** 133) (1982 6g 6d² 7d²) May 15; 41,000Y; compact filly; first foal; dam speedy Irish 2-y-o, winner of Phoenix Stakes, from family of Lorenzaccio; runner-up in minor events at Pontefract (caught on line and beaten a short head by Stephalotus) and Doncaster in October; stays 7f; yet to race on a firm surface. *H. T. Jones.*

SOVEREIGN RING 3 b.f. Welsh Saint 126–Zulu Lady (Proud Chieftain 122) — (1981 5d 5d 5f 1982 10f 8fg 10d) leggy filly; plater; promises to stay 1m; has been tried in blinkers. *Miss L. Siddall.*

SOVEREIGN ROYAL 3 b.c. Sovereign King–Carmenta (Dumbarnie 125) — (1981 6fg 6f 7.2v 8d 1982 6g 7f⁴ 6f 5fg 5g 5f) plater; possibly stays 7f; usually wears blinkers. *H. Fleming.*

SOVEREIGNS IMAGE 3 gr.c. Grey Mirage 128–Sovereign Help 98 (Sovereign **52** Lord 120) (1981 5g 6g 6fg⁴ 7f 7g⁴ 8d* 8g 8g³ 8.2s* 7d 1982 8g 8fg 9f 8fg 9g 10fg² 13.8f³ 9g 13.8f² 12f² 10f² 13.8f² 12s 13.8d² 12s) small, strong colt; good walker and mover; plater; suited by 1¼m or more; acts on any going but has done his winning on soft ground; effective with or without blinkers; has twice given trouble in preliminaries; not the heartiest of battlers and is suited by strong handling. *R. Hollinshead.*

SOVEREIGN'S QUILL 3 gr. or ro.g. Young Emperor 133–Blissful Hour — (Hardicanute 130) (1981 7.2d 7g 1982 8f 8.2g 7.6d) leggy gelding; in rear in maiden and minor races. *C. Crossley.*

SOVEREIGN STEED 4 gr.g. Royalty 130–Green Sovereign (Sovereign Path **49** 125) (1981 8g 9s 10v³ 12d 1982 10g 12g 12fg 12g³ 15.8d⁴ 12g) compact colt; in frame in 2 handicaps in October, hanging badly on first occasion; well beaten in a valuable seller final start; stays well; often bandaged; sold 1,000 gns Newmarket Autumn Sales. *E. Eldin.*

SPACED 3 gr.c. Godswalk 130–Jaidlamour (Jaipur) (1981 5fg 6fg 6fg 1982 — 8fg 7fg 10fg 8fg 10f) good sort; plating-class maiden; possibly stays 1¼m; has twice worn blinkers. *R. Armstrong.*

SPACEMAKER BOY 2 br.c. Realm 129–Glounanarrig (Dike) (1982 5fg* **75** 5d² 5f³ 5f⁴ 7g 6fg 7g 5s 6g³ 6s) Mar 24; 700Y; strong colt; third foal; half-brother to a winning hurdler; dam unplaced 5 times in Ireland; won maiden auction event at Edinburgh in May; form a bit mixed afterwards; stays 7f; seems to act on any going. *G. Fletcher.*

SPACE ROCKET 2 gr.g. Roan Rocket 128–Davina (Darius 129) (1982 7g — 6g 7fg 8s) Apr 27; 2,100F, 4,200Y; half-brother to winners in Hungary and Italy; dam never ran; no worthwhile form; trained by A. Jarvis first 3 starts. *M. Pipe.*

SPANISH BAY 4 b.g. Roan Rocket 128–Spanish Sail 113 (Matador 131) **64** (1981 8fg* 10g⁴ 8f 7fg 7g 1982 10f 10d³ 10f⁴) attractive gelding; third in amateur riders race at Lingfield in June; stays 1¼m; ran moderately when blinkered once. *M. Masson.*

SPANISH BOLD 2 b.f. Tower Walk 130–Jill Somers 76 (Will Somers 114§) — (1982 8f 6d) fair sort; second foal; dam second over 5f at 2 yrs; behind in maiden race at Leicester and minor event at Pontefract in the autumn. *M. Ryan.*

SPANISH ESTATES 2 b.f. Firestreak 125–Lead Me On (King's Troop 118) — (1982 7g 7g) Mar 23; neat filly; fourth foal; sister to a winning plater; dam never ran; well beaten in maiden races at Newmarket in October. *J. Toller.*

SPANISH FURY 3 ch.f. Double Jump 131–Tweezer (Songedor 116) (1981   —
5s 5g 5fg³ 5fg⁴ 5fg³ 6d³ 5s² 5d* 5g²   1982 5fg 6fg 6d) lightly-made filly; fair
performer in 1981; soundly beaten in handicaps at 3 yrs; best form at 5f, and with
some give in the ground; sold only 390 gns Ascot November Sales. *M. Ryan.*

SPANISH PLACE (USA) 2 b.c. Greek Answer–Candy Aglo (Candy Spots)   **98 p**
(1982 6d*) Jan 24; $25,000Y, $51,000 2-y-o; rangy colt; half-brother to 4
minor winners in USA; dam unplaced in 11 starts; 12/1, put up a useful first
effort when finishing very strongly to win 21-runner maiden race at Newmarket in
October by a neck from Polka Princess; will stay 1m; has scope and looks certain
to win more races. *B. Hills.*

SPANISH POINT 3 ch.g. Malacate 131–Bracken Girl (Skymaster 126) (1981   **70 d**
7fg 7fg 7g 6s 6g 1982 5g 6.5g 6.5v 5s 5g³ 5d³ 5d³ 6fg 5f² 6g² 5fg* 5h³ 5g 5g
5.8f 6g 5d 5g⁴ 6s 5s) big, heavy-bodied gelding; won maiden race at Newcastle
in May; bred to stay 7f+ but is evidently regarded as a sprinter; seems to act on
any going; often blinkered (was when successful). *D. Sasse.*

SPANISH POOL 3 b.c. Gay Fandango 132–Watermark 83 (Henry the Seventh **116**
125) (1981 5g* 5g* 6fg³ 8fg³ 7s*   1982 8.2s² 8f* 10.4fg² 8.2f* 8f³ 8f 8d* 8g²)
   When Spanish Pool took the John Sutcliffe Trophy at Lingfield, the season's
most valuable nursery, on his final start at two years he had as many of his ten
rivals above him in the weights as he had below him.   Nevertheless he put up a
useful performance which augured well, particularly if he managed to maintain
the improvement he'd shown throughout his first season.   He did maintain it
and developed into a smart performer with three further successes, the last of
them in a pattern race, the Oettingen Rennen at Baden-Baden in August.
   Spanish Pool's victory at Baden-Baden caused little surprise as he'd run well
previously in pattern company.   His two earlier wins had been in handicaps, the
Esher Cup at Sandown and the valuable Cecil Frail Handicap at Haydock, both
times carrying big weights.   He put up a particularly useful performance at Haydock at the end of May, and a notably game one too.   After Spanish Pool had
quickened two or three lengths clear inside the last furlong one of his shoes
twisted and lamed him; although his stride shortened he held off First Phase,
who received 27 lb, by half a length.   Spanish Pool contested three pattern
races before the Oettingen Rennen.   In the Dee Stakes at Chester three weeks

*Cecil Frail Handicap, Haydock—Spanish Pool (right) and
First Phase fight it out; Gavo is third*

Mrs M. M. Haggas' "Spanish Pool"

before the Cecil Frail he ran Ivano to three quarters of a length, challenging throughout the last furlong and a half but hanging a little to his left; in the Queen Anne Stakes at Royal Ascot he finished a six-length third to Mr Fluorocarbon, running on really well at the finish; and in the Sussex Stakes at Goodwood he was beaten under three lengths into sixth place behind On The House. The finish of the Oettingen Rennen, a Group 3 race run over a mile, concerned only two of the fourteen runners. Spanish Pool, who had enjoyed a far from trouble-free run, caught the tiring Princes Gate close home and beat him by half a length, the pair finishing nearly three lengths clear of the remainder. Princes Gate and Spanish Pool met again the following month in a challenge match in aid of charity but this time Spanish Pool, 3 lb worse off, went down by a length and a half.

Spanish Pool (b.c. 1979)	Gay Fandango (ch 1972)	Forli (ch 1963)	Aristophanes Trevisa
		Gay Violin (b 1964)	Sir Gaylord Blue Violin
	Watermark (b 1967)	Henry the Seventh (ch 1958)	King of the Tudors Vestal Girl
		Filigrana (b 1953)	Niccolo Dell 'Arca Gamble in Gold

Spanish Pool cost 8,600 guineas in Ireland as a yearling. In terms of first prize-money won he's the most successful of Gay Fandango's runners to date, though in merit he's a little behind Irish Two Thousand Guineas runner-up Last Fandango and about the equal of Rasa Penang and Moomba Masquerade. Spanish Pool's dam Watermark, closely related to smart middle-distance performer Entanglement and half-sister to Cheveley Park Stakes winner Magic Flute and to Filiform, the dam of Heighlin and Goodbye Shelley, showed fair form and won over a mile at two years. Her dam raced only once due to injury but her

793

grandam, Gamble in Gold, won the Lowther Stakes and was grandam also of top Irish two-year-old Whistling Wind. Watermark has produced two winners besides Spanish Pool, Gin Game (by Red Alert), successful three times over six furlongs, and Balifine (by Balidar), who showed quite moderate form in England at two years before winning in Trinidad. Spanish Pool has also been exported, his destination South Africa. He was a most genuine and consistent performer with a good turn of foot who acted on any going. He stayed a mile and a quarter, though his best performance came at a mile. *J. Hindley.*

SPARE MAN 3 b.g. Track Spare 125–Cricket Bat 87 (Indigenous 121) (1981 — NR 1982 5fg 8s 8s) tall gelding; second foal; half-brother to 6f winner Mrs Leadbetter (by Birdbrook); dam 2-y-o 6f winner; behind in maiden races and a minor event. *R. Baker.*

SPARE THE ROD 4 gr.f. Sweet Revenge 129–Grisle Run 94 (Stupendous) — (1981 8d² 8d 10.2g 12g 11.7fg³ 12fg 10s 10s² 1982 12fg 11fg) narrow filly; placed in varied company as a 3-y-o, including selling; well beaten in non-sellers in 1982; evidently stays 1½m; seems to act on any going. *T. Marshall.*

SPARE WHEEL 3 ch.f. Track Spare 125–Lady Councillor (Privy Councillor **48** 125) (1981 8d 8s 8.2s² 1982 8g³ 8d⁴ 7d⁴ 11.7d 10.2g 10fg² 8fg 10d³ 12s*) lengthy filly; plater; sold to J. Baker 2,100 gns after winning readily at Wolverhampton in October; suited by 1½m; acts well on soft ground; has run respectably in blinkers and for an apprentice. *P. Cundell.*

SPARKING POST 5 ch.g. Picture Post 39–Bonnie Virginia (Virginia Boy 106) — (1981 NR 1982 12.2f) workmanlike gelding; first foal; dam a plater; last of 9 behind Another City in minor event at Catterick in July, first outing. *F. Watson.*

SPARKLER CLEAR 4 b.g. Double Jump 131–Fiery Flo 78 (Firestreak 125) — (1981 10fg 10g 10fg 10.1fg 15.5f 15.5fg³ 12fg 1982 18f 12f) plating-class maiden; probably stays 2m; has worn blinkers. *T. Gosling.*

SPARKLING BOY 5 br.h. Comedy Star 121–Tinsel 95 (Right Boy 137) (1981 **97** 7d 7.6g 6g 6s³ 7fg 5f 5fg 6g 6fg³ 6f⁴ 5.6fg 6g 5v⁴ 6s² 1982 5s 6g⁴ 6g 6g 6fg 6d 6f 6g 5g 6g 7s 6d²) useful sort; good mover; very useful performer at his best, winner of 4 races in 1980, including Ladbrokes (Ayr) Gold Cup; deteriorated and failed to win again, gaining only placing of 1982 when going down by ½ length to Dawn's Delight in handicap at Doncaster in October; was best at sprint distances; acted on any going; was often blinkered; standing at Benson Stud, Colchester, at £500 n.f.n.f. *P. Kelleway.*

SPARKLING FORM 3 ch.c. Gold Form 108–Light Spark 73 (Twilight Alley **66** 133) (1981 7fg 6fg 6s 1982 5f 7g⁴ 5g 5f³ 6fg⁴ 5f⁴ 5fg 5fg 6f 7f 5g* 6s* 5s 5d 6s) strong colt; won seller at Beverley (no bid) and minor event at York in the autumn; stays 6f; acts on any going. *R. Whitaker.*

SPARKLING GIRL 3 ch.f. Hot Spark 126–Lady Gaston 76 (Pall Mall 132) — (1981 5g 6fg 5.8h 1982 5fg 6g 5f 7fg⁴ 7f⁴ 8.5g 8f 10d) deep-girthed, workmanlike ex-English filly; fourth in handicap at Down Royal and maiden race at Galway in July; stays 7f; trained part of season by B. Swift; sold privately 500 gns Goffs November Sales. *M. Kauntze, Ireland.*

SPARKLING MOMENT 2 ch.c. Hot Spark 126–Parez 67 (Pardao 120) (1982 **94** 5fg 5.8g² 6f* 6f³ 6fg² 6fg* 6f* 6d 7d 6g) Feb 11; 4,500Y; small colt; brother to 3-y-o Shock Treatment, and half-brother to 3 winners; dam seemed not to stay 1m; won maiden auction event at Kempton in July and nurseries at Windsor in August and Kempton in September; suited by 6f; acts well on firm going and is possibly unsuited by dead; didn't handle track when ridden by 7-lb claimer at Catterick on fourth outing; has a useful turn of foot. *R. Armstrong.*

SPARKLING REFAIN 3 b.f. Song 132–Sparkling Jewel (Faberge II 121) — (1981 5s⁴ 5s³ 1982 7g 8f) lengthy, plain sort; poor plater; has worn a bandage on off-hind. *A. Smith.*

SPARKLING SIN 3 b. or br.c. Sparkler 130–Sinkit (Sing Sing 134) (1981 **70** 5v 5g² 6fg⁴ 7g 5d 8s² 8d⁴ 1982 10f⁴ 8f³ 8.2f* 8fg 8g 8d 8.2f* 8g³ 8.2g 8d⁴) tall, good-bodied colt; won maiden race at Haydock in June and handicap at Nottingham in July; stays 1¼m; acts on any going; game; sold 8,200 gns Newmarket Autumn Sales. *R. Boss.*

SPARKLING SUZIE 2 ch.f. Hot Spark 126–Jolisu 110 (Welsh Abbot 131) **96** (1982 5fg³ 5g* 6g⁴ 5f³ 5g 5g⁴ 5fg⁴ 5fg³) Apr 20; 2,700F, 3,700Y; small, workmanlike filly; good walker; closely related to 1981 2-y-o 5f winner Haycombe

Barn (by Hittite Glory) and half-sister to 2 winners, including fairly useful 1½m to 2¼m winner Jolimo (by Fortissimo); dam miler; made all to win maiden auction event at Kempton in May by 5 lengths; best subsequent efforts when 4 lengths seventh of 16 to Widaad in Queen Mary Stakes at Royal Ascot, 5½ lengths third of 4 to Kafu in Molecomb Stakes at Goodwood in July and 1¾ lengths third of 9 to Miss Anagram in minor event at Salisbury in September; doesn't stay 6f; yet to race on a soft surface; none too consistent. *R. Hannon.*

SPARKPLUG 2 ch.f. Hot Spark 126–My Ginny 83 (Palestine 133) (1982 **74** 6g 6fg 5g 6d⁴ 5v⁴ 6s) Mar 14; 10,000Y; well-made filly; third foal; half-sister to 1979 2-y-o 5f winner Auntie Bessie (by No Mercy); dam 2-y-o 6f winner; quite a modest filly; fourth in maiden races at Brighton and Folkestone in October; acts on heavy going. *R. Smyth.*

SPARKS 2 ch.g. Sparkler 126–Arethusa 94 (Acropolis 132) (1982 7f* 6g² **90** 7fg 8f) Feb 22; 9,000F; good-bodied, quite attractive gelding; half-brother to minor winners and a winner in Norway; dam stayed 1½m; won 8-runner maiden race at Yarmouth in August; had to be snatched up inside final 2f when 4 lengths second of 19 to Return To Paris in minor event at Windsor later in month, best subsequent effort; stays 7f; blinkered third outing; gelded after final appearance. *W. O'Gorman.*

SPARKY 2 ch.g. Sparkler 130–Nyota 97 (Reform 132) (1982 5f³ 5.8f 7f 7g) — Feb 20; first foal; dam won over 7f and 1½m; no worthwhile form; apprentice ridden at 7-0 when last of 9 in nursery at Bath in August; has worn a bandage on near-fore. *Dr A. Jones.*

SPARTAN ARROW 4 gr.g. Andrea Mantegna–Spartan Queen (Matador 131) — (1981 NR 1982 12f 16f 11.7f 12f) temperamental novice hurdler; behind in maiden races. *D. Wilson.*

SPATS 2 ch.c. Mansingh 120–Princely Maid 71 (King's Troop 118) (1982 5fg — 6g) Jan 17; brother to a plater and half-brother to several winners, including Lady Constance (by Connaught), very useful at up to 7f; dam 2-y-o 5f winner; behind in maiden races at Windsor and Yarmouth in August; exported to Malaysia. *M. Jarvis.*

SPEARGUN 8 ch.g. Deep Diver 134–Annie Oakley 106 (Big Game) (1981 — NR 1982 12d 10g 8g) big gelding; poor maiden; behind in a seller second start; seems to stay 1½m; probably acts on any going; has been tried in blinkers. *R. Atkins.*

SPECIAL LEAVE 2 b.c. Mill Reef 141–Light Duty 113 (Queen's Hussar 124) **105** p (1982 7g³ 7g³ 7v*) Mar 24; attractive, well-made colt; good mover; third

Hyperion Stakes, Ascot—a useful staying performance from Special Leave who beats Tivian (left) and the odds-on Lord Protector

foal; brother to Paradise Bay, a very useful performer at up to 1½m; dam, very useful middle-distance filly, is sister to 1,000 Guineas and Prix de Diane winner Highclere; quickened clear very smoothly 2f out and stayed on strongly to win 5-runner Hyperion Stakes at Ascot in October by 3 lengths from Tivian; previously third in 21-runner maiden race (beaten 6½ lengths by Zoffany) at Newbury in August and 5-runner Gilbey Champion Racehorse Futurity (beaten a head and the same by Now and Again and Goodbye Shelley) at York in September; will be suited by 1¼m+; yet to race on a firm surface; could be good horse, but has some way to go yet. *I. Balding.*

SPECIAL PLEASURE 3 b.f. Saulingo 122–Ordinary Fare (What A Pleasure) (1981 5d⁴ 6fg⁴ 5f* 5fg 5fg 5g⁴ 5g² 5g 1982 6g 5f⁴ 5fg² 5g³ 5fg* 5fg³ 5fg 5g³ 5fg 5g* 5d) tall, lightly-built filly; good mover; sprint handicapper; made most to win at Chester in July and Newbury in September; beat long-odds-on Chellaston Park by 2½ lengths in minor event on latter; best at 5f; acts on firm going; sometimes sweats up; a free-running filly who finds little off bridle; sold 35,000 gns Newmarket December Sales. *R. Armstrong.* **98**

SPECTACULAR SKY 4 b.c. African Sky 124–Orient Queen (King's Troop 118) (1981 6fg 5fg 1982 5fg3 6g 6f 6f 6g 5g) quite attractive, robust, well-made colt; only lightly raced and hasn't fulfilled his early promise; dead-heated for third in small handicap at Newmarket in May; unlikely to stay beyond sprint distances. *R. Armstrong.* **79 d**

SPECTRAL 3 b.c. Sharpen Up 127–Hurly Burly (Sing Sing 134) (1981 NR 1982 6s 6g 5f 7.6fg 7f 6g 6g 6f 6fg 5f) compact colt; has been fired on near-hind; beaten some way in varied company, including claiming; has sweated up, and was very coltish final start (blinkered); sold to K. Morgan 460 gns Doncaster September Sales. *C. Brittain.* **—**

SPEED BABY (USA) 2 b.f. Diplomat Way–Stormy Ruler (Sir Ruler) (1982 5g* 5f³ 6f 6f) Jan 16; tall, useful sort; half-sister to several minor winners in USA; dam modest sister to very smart 1m and 9f performer Swift Ruler; won 12-runner maiden race at Windsor in May at 20/1; showed little afterwards; should stay 6f; possibly not suited by firm ground. *P. Cole.* **76**

SPEED OF MUSIC (USA) 2 b.c. Pago Pago–Baby Lullaby (Royal Serenade 132) (1982 5s² 8s³) May 5; half-brother to several winners in USA, one a minor stakes winner; dam won 3 sprint races; placed in maiden races at Kempton (favourite) in April and at Bath (second favourite) in October; better run at 5f. *P. Cole.* **81**

SPEED OF SOUND (USA) 2 br.c. Super Concorde 128–Chatter Box 118 (Ribot 142) (1982 7g 7s⁴ 7g) Mar 23; strong, rangy colt; half-brother to 3 winners in France, including useful 1974 2-y-o 1m winner Gadfly (by Le Fabuleux); dam smart performer at up to 1¼m in France; staying-on 2 lengths fourth of 28 behind Jungle Romeo in maiden race at Redcar in October, best effort; appeared not to come down hill particularly well at Leicester on next appearance; will stay 1m; races with his tongue tied down. *B. Hanbury.* **86**

SPEEDWAY BELLE 3 b.f. Track Spare 125–Royal Camp 91 (Sovereign Path 125) (1981 NR 1982 6f 8fg 7fg 8d) 350 2-y-o; plain filly; sister to 2 winners, including fairly useful sprinter Royal Track, and half-sister to another; dam a sprinter; poor plater. *T. Taylor.* **—**

SPENDING CUT 2 b.c. Guillaume Tell 121–Riva Ring (Riva Ridge) (1982 6f² 6g⁴ 7g* 6.3g⁴ 7fg³ 7d) Jan 28; first foal; dam out of sister to top-class American horse Bold Bidder; won 15-runner maiden race at Leopardstown in July by a length from Bold Connection; in frame behind very promising colts subsequently, finishing just over 4 lengths fourth to Ancestral in Railway Stakes at the Curragh and 6¾ lengths third to Danzatore in minor event at Leopardstown; will stay 1½m; acts on a firm surface; blinkered last 2 starts. *D. Weld, Ireland.* **99**

SPIDERWOOD 3 b.g. Tudor Rhythm 112–Calibre (Caliban 123) (1981 6g⁴ 7g 7fg 6fg 1982 6f 6g 10.1d 8.2g 7d 10s³) rather leggy gelding; plater; best run at 1¼m on soft going in blinkers. *P. M. Taylor.* **—**

SPIKEY BILL 5 ch.h. Souvran 98–Whitton Lane (Narrator 127) (1981 10.1d* 8d 12s² 10d 1982 12d 10g³ 15.5f 10f) tall horse; plater; possibly stays 1½m; acts on soft going; blinkered third start (always behind); trained by P. Mitchell first 2 outings. *R. Simpson.* **—**

SPILT MILK 2 ro.f. The Go-Between 129–Dick's Yarn 80 (Peter's Yarn 106) (1982 5fg 5g 5f) Mar 22; 3,000F, 3,100Y; small filly; half-sister to 4 winners, including quite useful sprinter Fair Dandy (by Carnival Dancer); in rear in sellers; of no account. *D. Ringer.*

SPINDLE BERRY 2 gr.f. Dance In Time–Chokeberry (Crepello 136) **92** (1982 5fg² 5fg* 6f 5g 7.6s³ 7v⁴) Apr 27; 7,800Y; quite attractive, rather lightly-made filly; fourth foal; dam unraced sister to smart 1¼m filly Cranberry Sauce; made all and had only to be hand ridden when winning maiden race at Newbury in June by 4 lengths; 2¼ lengths third of 8 to Ultimate Pride in Burr Stakes at Lingfield in September, best subsequent effort; should stay 1¼m; seems to act on any going. *R. Price.*

SPINNER 3 b.f. Blue Cashmere 129–Penny Pincher 95 (Constable 119) (1981 **59** 6g 5s 1982 7f 5g³ 5fg* 5f² 5fg 5g 6s) sturdy non-thoroughbred filly; good mover; sprint handicapper; won at Warwick in July; best at 5f; acts on firm going. *S. Norton.*

SPIN OF A COIN 4 bl.c. Boreen (Fr) 123–Lovely Linan (Ballylinan 118) **88** (1981 12.3d* 10g³ 12d 14fg⁴ 11f* 12fg³ 12.5g* 12g² 12s 11f³ 14fg² 12fg* 12g 11f² 12g⁴ 12.5g² 12g 12s) strong, rangy, attractive colt; looked particularly keen and well when winning Bessborough Stakes (Handicap) at Royal Ascot in June, making strong headway from rear in straight and running on really well to beat Cannon King by ¾ length; had stiff tasks when good second in Grand Prix Prince Rose at Ostend in July (beaten 5 lengths by Castle Keep) and Grote Prijs der Nederlanden at Duindigt (finished well but failed by a nose to catch Ataxerxes and repeat his 1981 victory); suited by 1½m+ and a strongly-run race; acts on any going; fell on fifth start; below form last 2 outings. *R. Price.*

SPLENDID AGAIN 7 b.g. John Splendid 116–Maella (Traffic) (1981 16f — 12fg* 15fg² 20.4fg² 1982 12fg 15.8f) former plater; last both outings in 1982; stays well; acts on any going; good mount for an inexperienced rider; has worn bandages. *J. Parkes.*

SPLENDIDLY GAY 4 b.f. Lord Gayle 124–Splendidly (Luminary 132) (1981 — 10s 10.1s* 12f 16.5f 16.1d 14.6fg 12g 14s* 13s 1982 13f 16.1f 14.6g 16.1g 12d 16s) smallish, workmanlike ex-English filly; quite often faced stiff tasks; probably stays 2m; best form on soft going; trained until after fourth start by G. Hufter. *P. Norris, Ireland.*

SPLIT THE BREEZE 3 gr.g. Roan Rocket 128–First Flight 78 (Pirate King — 129) (1981 5g 6d 1982 10fg 12fg 16g 14f 15.5f) workmanlike gelding; beaten some way in maiden and minor events; sold 800 gns Doncaster August Sales. *S. Mellor.*

SPOILT FOR CHOICE 4 b.g. The Brianstan 120 Gong of May 70 (King King **48** 134) (1981 6f 7fg 6fg 5fg 7g³ 8s 7g² 7s 1982 6s* 6g³ 6fg 6f⁴ 6f² 7g 6g 6f³ 7f 7g 6f 6s 6g 7s³) neat gelding; poor mover; attracted no bid after winning seller at Ayr in March; placed afterwards, including in better company; probably best at distances short of 1m; acts on any going; blinkered last 2 outings at 3 yrs. *D. Chapman.*

SPOTSYLVANIA 4 b.c. Empery 128–First Draft (Tom Rolfe) (1981 10s **47** 8g 10d 8.5d 10fg 10fg³ 10fg³ 9g³ 10fg 7g² 1982 8d⁴ 10.6f* 10.6h 10f 12.2fg 10f⁴ 8fg 8fg 12d 7s) neat colt; plater; attracted no bid after winning at Haydock in May; stays 1¼m well; seems to act on any going; has worn blinkers; often bandaged. *D. H. Jones.*

SPOT THE PATCH (USA) 2 b.c. Mr Leader–Spotter (Double Eclipse 125) — (1982 6fg) May 25; $85,000Y; brother to stakes-placed winner Las Profesoras, and half-brother to numerous winners; dam ran 3 times; 33/1, moved moderately to start and made no show in 19-runner maiden race at Newmarket in July. *J. Sutcliffe.*

SPRIGHTLY WILLOW 3 b.f. Native Bazaar 122–Woodland Promise (Philemon **45** 119) (1981 5fg 1982 6f³ 5f 5fg 5fg 5fg) poor maiden; best run at 6f. *R. Baker.*

SPRING LANE 3 br.f. Forlorn River 124–Merry Cindy 63 (Sea Hawk II **61** 131) (1981 7h² 8g* 7g* 1982 9g 8f³ 8f² 8fg 7d⁴ 7g) fair performer at her best; stays 1m; seems to act on any going. *Sir Mark Prescott.*

SPRINGLASS 2 ch.f. Redundant 120–Olibanum 61 (Frankincense 120) (1982 — 5fg 6f) Mar 20; third foal; half-sister to winning sprinter Blochairn Skolar (by Most Secret); dam plater; tailed-off last in maiden races at Warwick in July and Brighton in August. *G. Thorner.*

SPRINGS ETERNAL 3 ch.f. Sagaro 133–Oudalia 107 (Gala Performance) **59**
(1981 6fg 1982 8fg 10h 10d 7.6d² 8.2g⁴ 8.2s 8s) small, close-coupled filly;
plating-class maiden; stays 1m; usually bandaged behind; sold 500 gns Ascot
December Sales. *M. Smyly.*

SPRING SURPRISE 5 b.g. Saritamer 130–A Deux 80 (Crepello 136) (1981 —
NR 1982 10fg 16g 16.5fg) strong gelding; stays 1m (well beaten over further);
suited by a sound surface; used to wear blinkers. *R. Williams.*

SPRINGWELL LANE (USA) 3 ch.g. Singh–Funny Comedienne (Bolinas —
Boy) (1981 7s 6g 1982 11g 11.7f 12fg 12f 14f) quite attractive gelding;
behind in maiden races and a handicap; blinkered last 2 starts (ran very freely
in them on second occasion). *R. Price.*

SPRITEBRAND 2 br.g. Workboy 123–Benedetta da Castello (St Paddy 133) **69**
(1982 5f⁴ 5f³ 5fg³ 7f 7f⁴ 7d 8f³ 8f) June 4; 2,000Y; strong gelding; half-brother
to 3 winners here and abroad; dam never ran; in frame in maiden auction events
and a nursery; stays 1m; blinkered sixth start. *M. H. Easterby.*

SPYLAW 3 br.g. No Mercy 126–La Dolce Vita 78 (Sallymount 125) (1981 —
6fg 7g 7f 8g 8s 1982 8f³ 7fg 7g 7fg 8g 8fg) plater; stays 1m; has run badly in
blinkers. *J. Douglas-Home.*

STAGE COACH 2 b.c. Luthier 126–Glass Slipper 100 (Relko 136) (1982 **78** p
7d) Jan 22; big colt; half-brother to 3 winners, including St Leger winner
Light Cavalry (by Brigadier Gerard) and 1,000 Guineas winner Fairy Footsteps
(by Mill Reef); dam staying half-sister to Royal Palace; second favourite,
faded after leading some way when 8 lengths sixth of 18 behind Northern
Adventure in minor event at Doncaster in October; sure to do better. *H.
Cecil.*

STAG'S HORN 3 b. or br.g. Blue Cashmere 129–Falling Gold 77 (High Echelon) —
(1981 6f 5g 7.2d 6fg 6f 6s 6s⁴ 1982 8s 6g 9.4f 6f 9v) small gelding; poor
performer; twice behind in valuable sellers; usually blinkered at 2 yrs. *E.
Weymes.*

STALY BELL 4 b.f. Porto Bello 118–Stalybridge 88 (The Brianstan 128) —
(1981 NR 1982 8fg 9f 8g 7f 7f 8g 5g 10g) fair sort; disappointing maiden;
in rear in sellers on 2 occasions; blinkered last 2 starts; trained most of season
by C. Thornton. *Hbt. Jones.*

STALY'S PET 3 b.f. Mummy's Pet 125–Stalybridge 88 (The Brianstan 128) **56**
(1981 5fg 5fg 5f 7v 7g 6d 6g 1982 5fg 5fg³ 6d 5d³ 7g 6f* 6g 6f 7d) strong
filly who carries plenty of condition; made much of running to win handicap
at Catterick in August; third in seller second start; stays 7f but is better at
shorter distances; seems to act on any going; best in blinkers. *Hbt Jones.*

STAND EASY 5 b.g. Connaught 130–Paresseuse 114 (Relko 136) (1981 —
10g⁴ 10fg³ 10s² 10s 10.4g 11.1s 1982 12d) big, strong gelding; will stay
beyond 1½m; seems to act on any going. *I. Wardle.*

STANDON ROCK 4 ch.g. Mansingh 120–Teenager 71 (Never Say Die 137) —
(1981 7s 7s 8.2fg 8fg 8s 10d* 9d 12g⁴ 12v⁴ 12g⁴ 12g 1982 15.5g) quite a moderate
handicapper; needed 1¼m+, but possibly didn't stay 2m; seemed to act on
any going; blinkered once in 1980; dead. *P. Kelleway.*

STANERRA 4 ch.f. Guillaume Tell 121–Lady Aureola (Aureole 132) (1981 **118**
10d* 7s 1982 10s² 10s 8g 10fg⁴ 10g* 10f⁴ 12f³ 12fg³ 12g³ 10fg⁴ 10g² 12v 12f⁴)
rangy Irish filly; half-sister to French middle-distance winners Loirolo (by
Val de Loir) and Padarek (by Sanctus II); dam won twice over 1¼m in France;
4-length winner of handicap at the Curragh in May; usually had stiffer tasks
and ran extremely well when 1¼ lengths third to Critique in Hardwicke Stakes
at Royal Ascot in June on seventh start, ¾-length second of 10 behind Time
Charter in Sun Chariot Stakes at Newmarket in October (tended to hang in
behind winner but finished clear of remainder) and 1½ lengths fourth of 15
behind Half Iced in Japan Cup at Tokyo in November; stays 1½m; acts on any
going, except possibly heavy; by no means disgraced considering an iron broke
sixth start; smart. *F. Dunne, Ireland.*

STAR ALLIANCE 4 b.f. Big Morton 85–Wet and Windy (Babu 117) (1981 **42**
8.2g 8g 7.2f 8fg 8d 1982 8.2s* 8f⁴ 7f 10.6f 9g) plater; attracted no bid when
winning at Hamilton in April by 10 lengths; stays 1m well; probably acts on
any going. *R. Morris.*

STAR ATTENTION 8 b.m. Northfields–Star Relation (Star Gazer 123) —
(1981 NR 1982 7g 8d) lightly raced and no form since 1977. *M. Reddan.*

STARAWAK   3 b.f. Star Appeal 133–Arawak 109 (Seminole II)   (1981 7fg   **68**
7g 7d   1982 7.6fg 9f⁴ 12d⁴ 12fg³ 10s⁴ 12d*)   close-coupled filly; won maiden
race at Redcar in November; suited by 1½m; seems to act on any going; blinkered
last 2 starts.   *C. Brittain.*

STAR BELLA   3 b.f. Star Appeal 133–Dobella (Sovereign Lord 120)   (1981   —
5fg 6fg 6g   1982 7d 8f 6g)   compact filly; little worthwhile form in varied
company; sweated up badly final start.   *M. Lambert.*

STAR BURST   5 b.g. Busted 134–Pearl Star 110 (Gulf Pearl 117)   (1981   **73**
12s 15g 14s² 12f² 12.3fg² 12g* 13d* 14.7fg² 15.8g 12g³ 13d* 14s² 12s* 12g²
16g   1982 13s² 12fg* 14fg 13g² 12fg 13fg 12g³ 13g³ 13fg⁴ 12fg 13d⁴)   quite
a modest handicapper; beat Aberfield by 5 lengths in apprentice event at Newmarket in April; probably ran best subsequent races when placed at Hamilton
(course specialist there), Haydock (Old Newton Cup) and Ayr; stays 1¾m;
acts on any going; good mount for a boy (usually ridden by N. Vaughan nowadays); game.   *D. Francis.*

STAR CHARTER   2 gr.c. Comedy Star 121–Charter Belle 60 (Runnymede 123)   **76** d
(1982 5f² 6f⁴ 8.2fg⁴ 7s 8d)   Apr 16; leggy colt; good mover; second foal;
dam won 1¼m seller; quite a moderate colt; at his best in first half of season,
and ran poorly, including in sellers, on last 3 appearances; should stay 1m;
possibly not suited by soft ground.   *J. Hardy.*

STAR COVE   3 ch.f. Porto Bello 118–Your Star (On Your Mark 125)   (1981   —
5s² 5g² 5fg² 5f² 6f* 5d*   1982 6g 6fg 6fg 5d)   workmanlike filly; plater; stays
6f; seems to act on any going; trained part of season by Mrs A. Bell and W. H. H.
Williams.   *A. Balding.*

STARELA   2 gr. or ro.f. Starch Reduced 112–Anthela 76 (Acropolis 132)   (1982   —
6d 8f 6fg 6d 5g)   Apr 13; 510F; lengthy, rather lightly-built filly; sister to
3-y-o Miss Starchy and 6f winner Fairmile Lad, and half-sister to a winning plater;
dam ran twice; no worthwhile form, including under low weight in nursery at
Edinburgh.   *J. Wilson.*

STARFINDER   5 b.h. Comedy Star 121–Delfina (Salvo 129)   (1981 10.5d 10g   **40**
9fg 10fg³ 10f² 11fg³ 10d 10g 10.5s 8.2d²   1982 12.2f⁴ 10.6f³ 15.8f)   compact
horse; stays 11f; seems to act on any going but is suited by a sound surface;
has worn blinkers but seems better without.   *M. Camacho.*

STAR FLEET   4 ch.g. Record Token 128–New Way 103 (Klairon 131)   (1981   —
8fg² 8g 6d 7s² 7g⁴ 5f 10fg² 10fg 8d 11.5fg² 12.3fg³ 16g² 14g   1982 11.5f 14g 16g)
compact, lightly-made gelding; has run well in varied company over a wide
range of distances, but is still a maiden; soundly beaten in amateur riders races
in summer; evidently stays 2m, seems to act on any going; inconsistent; front
runner.   *P. Kelleway.*

STAR GALLANT   2 ch.c. Star Appeal 133–Repel (Hardicanute 131)   (1982 8g)   —
Apr 18; sixth living foal; half-brother to a winning hurdler; dam never ran;
unquoted, behind in 18-runner maiden race at Newmarket in October.   *G.
Pritchard-Gordon.*

STARGAZE   2 b.c. Busted 134–Star of Bagdad 95 (Bagdad)   (1982 7d)   May   —
6; fourth foal; dam won over 1m and is half-sister to Malinowski and Gielgud;
unquoted and in need of race, not in first 9 of 18 in minor event at Doncaster in
October (ridden by lad in paddock).   *P. Calver.*

STAR HEADING   4 ch.f. Upper Case–Star Dell (Red God 128§)   (1981 6v   **42**
6s³ 8g 6fg 6g⁴ 6d 6f 7d   1982 6s 7fg 6fg³ 7f² 6g 6g³ 8.2fg² 8fg 8.2g)   poor maiden;
stays 1m; acts on any going; sometimes blinkered; unseated rider leaving stalls
fifth start.   *W. H. H. Williams.*

STARKY'S PET   4 gr.f. Mummy's Pet 125–Starkist 81 (So Blessed 130)   (1981   —
NR   1982 8f 5f 7f 5d)   500 3-y-o; lengthy, workmanlike filly; second foal;
dam won over 5f at 2 yrs; behind in varied races; wears bandages; trained
part of season by J. Doyle.   *A. Watson.*

STAR LIFE   2 ch.f. Star Appeal 133–Alive Alivo 77 (Never Say Die 137)   (1982   **61**
6f 6f 5f)   Apr 17; lightly-made filly; half-sister to several winners here and in
Italy, including Phoenix Stakes winner Areola (by Kythnos), the dam of Chalon;
dam showed ability at 2 yrs; poor form in maiden and minor events; bred to
need further.   *T. Fairhurst.*

STARLIT SKY   2 b.f. Radetzky 123–Young May Moon (Hopeful Venture 125)   —
(1982 6f)   Apr 7; 2,500F; rangy filly; first produce; dam unraced half-sister

to 1,000 Guineas second Abbeydale; unquoted and on backward side, behind in 20-runner maiden race at Newmarket in July. *J. Winter.*

STARLUST 3 br.f. Sallust 134–Welsh Star 102 (Welsh Abbot 131) (1981 **77** 5g 5f* 5f² 6g 6fg 1982 6s 5fg 5fg 6g 6g⁴) neat filly; sprint handicapper; best in blinkers; sometimes gave trouble at start; covered by Nicholas Bill. *S. Norton.*

STAR OF A GUNNER 2 ch.c. Gunner B 126–Starkist 81 (So Blessed 130) **71** (1982 5fg 5fg 6g⁴ 8fg 8.2g⁴ 7f 8.2d⁴ 7g⁴ 7g) Apr 24; fair sort; third reported foal; dam 2-y-o 5f winner; quite moderate form, mainly in nurseries; stays 1m; probably needs some give in the ground. *S. Mellor.*

STAR OF ANAX 2 b.f. Anax 120–Starlit Coach 66 (Sandstone 105) (1982 **67** 5.8f 5f³ 6fg⁴ 5g 5f² 5f² 5.3f³ 5g⁴ 5d³ 5fg 6s² 5v 6s* 6s) Apr 11; plain filly; third reported foal; dam won 5f seller at 2 yrs; plater; won 19-runner race at Haydock (no bid) in October by 4 lengths; far better suited to 6f than 5f; acts on any going, except perhaps heavy; blinkered eighth outing. *M. Blanshard.*

STAR OF ENZO 4 b.c. Comedy Star 121–Cry Help 94 (Martial 131) (1981 — 5g 5f 5fg² 5f 5fg 5g* 5fg* 5f 5s 5s³ 1982 5g 6.5v 5s 5g* 5s 5f 5f 5g 5fg 5.3fg) small, fair sort; beat Little Starchy in very close finish at Cagnes-sur-Mer in March; was suited by a sharp 5f; probably acted on any going; blinkered once as a 2-y-o; dead. *T. Marshall.*

STAR OF IRELAND 2 b.c. Star Appeal 133–Belligerent 74 (Roan Rocket **76** 128) (1982 6g 6f 7g) Apr 12; 10,000Y; half-brother to 3 winners, including useful sprinter Goldhills Pride (by Goldhill); dam half-sister to very good French miler Kenmare; kept on quite nicely when 2¾ lengths fifth of 18 to Shareef Dancer in maiden race at Newmarket in August, second start; 12/1, prominent 5f when out of first 9 of 30 in similar event won by Mandelstam on same course in October; should stay 7f. *A. Jarvis.*

STAR OF SALFORD 4 gr.c. Town Crier 119–False Evidence 53 (Counsel 118) — (1981 NR 1982 8d 10.1fg 10f 10.6f 8g 10.8fg) poor performer; beaten in sellers several times; not certain to stay 1¼m; sold 1,150 gns Ascot July Sales. *D. Nicholson.*

STAR OF SPRING 5 gr.m. Silly Season 127–Daystar 91 (Major Portion 129) — (1981 NR 1982 10.6h) of no account. *J. Gilbert.*

STAR OF TAURUS 2 b.f. Mansingh 120–Western Star 107 (Alcide 136) **73** p (1982 5f*) Feb 22; first living foal; dam, half-sister to very smart animals Western Jewel and Mr Fluorocarbon, won over 7f and 1¼m; 9/4, kept on very well when winning 5-runner maiden race at Carlisle in June by ½ length from Dollar Darling; will stay 6f. *Sir Mark Prescott.*

STARRY WAY 2 br.f. Star Appeal 133–Sorebelle 95 (Prince Tenderfoot 126) — (1982 7d) May 4; 13,000Y; quite well-made, attractive filly; first foal; dam best at up to 1m; 13/2 and in need of outing, moved badly to start when tailed off in maiden race at Leicester in October. *Sir Mark Prescott.*

STARS AND STRIPES 3 br.f. Royalty 130–America 112 (Buisson Ardent — 129) (1981 NR 1982 14fg 16fg) lengthy filly; half-sister to 7f and 1¼m winner Oklahoma Star (by Hotfoot), useful hurdler Mount Harvard (by High Top) and a winner in Norway; dam, very useful at 2 yrs, stayed 1m; soundly beaten in maiden races at Newmarket and Lingfield early in year; sold 560 gns Newmarket Autumn Sales; resold 440 gns Doncaster November Sales. *M. Jarvis.*

STARSKI 4 b.c. Margouillat 133–Poliphony (Polic 126) (1981 10.5g³ 11g* **115** 12g* 12g* 15fg 15.5g 15.5v⁴ 14s* 12g² 1982 15.5v 15.5fg* 20v 12.5d 15fg⁴) French colt; half-brother to 2 winners; dam, middle-distance maiden, is daughter of Prix Vanteaux winner Toscanella; successful 7 times in France, gaining most of his wins in Provinces; gained his most important win in very slowly-run 6-runner Prix Jean Prat at Longchamp in April, coming with a great run from back of field to beat El Badr by ½ length; ran easily best subsequent race when 2½ lengths fourth of 9 behind Valentinian in Prix Kergorlay at Deauville in August; stays well; acts on soft going but is possibly ideally suited by a sound surface (tailed off on heavy in Prix du Cadran on third start); wears blinkers. *A. de Royer Dupre, France.*

STARSPANGLED 2 b.g. Star Appeal 133–Katharina 105 (Frankincense — 120) (1982 5fg 5.8f) Apr 13; 2,500F, 15,000Y; first produce; dam useful at up to 1m; soundly beaten in minor event at Windsor in June and maiden race at Bath in July; gelded afterwards; sold 1,350 gns Ascot August Sales and exported to Malaysia. *A. Ingham.*

STARTERS IMAGE   3 ch.f. On Your Mark 125–Dame's Delight (Ballymoss 136)   (1981 5s 5d 5f⁴ 6f² 7g* 7fg* 7s 8d   1982 8fg 7fg 7fg 7d 6g)   quite a well-made filly; won valuable seller and nursery in 1981; well beaten in handicaps at 3 yrs; better suited by 7f than shorter distances but has yet to show she stays 1m; probably needs a sound surface; suited by forcing tactics; blinkered final start; sold 1,500 gns Newmarket December Sales. *W. Hastings-Bass.*

STAR VENTURE   6 br.g. Swing Easy 126–Street Vendor 60 (High Perch 126)   (1981 7fg⁴ 6f 7f³ 6f² 7f 6fg³ 6f 6d 6s   1982 6fg 8d 6f 8f 7.6fg 8fg 11.7fg)   strong gelding; ran poorly in 1982; suited by 7f and may stay 1m; acts on any going; has worn blinkers but is better without; suitable mount for an apprentice; has raced with tongue tied down. *M. Chapman.*

STATE BALL   2 b.f. Dance In Time–Crystal Palace 121 (Solar Slipper 131)   (1982 5f 5.3fg 6g)   May 22; medium-sized, sparely-made filly; half-sister to numerous winners, notably Royal Palace (by Ballymoss), Prince Consort (by Right Royal V), Selhurst (by Charlottesville) and Glass Slipper (by Relko), last-named the dam of Light Cavalry and Fairy Footsteps; dam smart from 7f to 1¼m; showed no ability; slowly away on debut and gave trouble at start when withdrawn on next intended appearance; sold 35,000 gns Ascot August Sales. *A. Ingham.*

STATE DUTY (USA)   2 ch.c. Stage Door Johnny–Oath Of Allegiance (Olden Times)   (1982 6fg⁴ 6fg2)   Apr 15; $115,000Y; strong, good-bodied colt; second foal; dam unraced half-sister to a stakes winner by Stage Door Johnny and to very smart 1975 French staying 2-y-o French Friend; in frame in June in minor event at Leicester and 6-runner maiden race at Ayr; will be better suited by much longer distances. *B. Hanbury.*   **84**

STATE HOUSE (USA)   3 ch.c. Full Pocket–Star Empress (Young Emperor 133)   (1981 6fg 6f   1982 5fg 6g 6g 7fg 6s)   lengthy, rather sparely-made colt; plater; stays 6f; blinkered last 2 starts; trained part of season by J. W. Watts. *M. Chapman.*   **—**

STATELY MAIDEN   2 b.f. Free State 125–Namur (Amber Rama 133)   (1982 5d⁴ 6f 5fg 7f² 7g 7.2s 8d)   May 15; 360Y; neat, strong filly; second live foal; dam never ran; poor plater; suited by 7f; acts on any going; races with her head high and looks none too genuine; blinkered final start. *D. Weeden.*   **51**

STATE ROMANCE   3 b. or br.f. Free State 125–Eastern Romance 73 (Sahib 114)   (1981 5.8g 5f 5fg 5f⁴ 5h 7d   1982 8g 8f* 8f 8g⁴ 7g* 7f* 8 3g² 8fg 7f)   lightly-made filly; plater; won at Brighton in May (no bid) and July (bought in 1,850 gns); won non-selling handicap at Bath later in July; stays 1m; acts well on firm going; suitable mount for an apprentice; below form third outing and last 2 starts. *R. Laing.*   **67**

STATES GENERAL   3 b.g. Swing Easy 126–Without Reproach 102 (Above Suspicion 127)   (1981 8s⁴ 7g   1982 8f)   workmanlike, lengthy gelding; seems only plating class; probably stays 1m; sold 950 gns Doncaster September Sales. *D. Smith.*   **—**

STATESMANSHIP (USA)   2 b.c. Quadratic–Ocracoke (Cyane)   (1982 7fg 8fg 8g*)   April 10; $110,000Y; deep-girthed colt; fourth foal; half-brother to 2 winners by Farewell Party, including stakes-placed Wake; dam, unplaced in 4 starts, is sister to smart Roanoke River, a winner at up to 9f; short-priced favourite and faced with easier task than previously, clear from 2f out when winning 10-runner maiden race at Beverley in September by 5 lengths from Wang Feihoong; will stay 1¼m. *G. Harwood.*   **82**

STATFOLD JOANNE   3 br.f. Baragoi 115–Pride of Statfold (Compensation 127)   (1981 NR   1982 16fg)   smallish, workmanlike filly; fourth live foal; half-sister to a winning hurdler; dam never ran; 100/1 and very much in need of run when last of 7 behind Boardman's Crown in maiden race at Nottingham in August. *W. Wharton.*   **—**

STAY SECRET   5 b.g. Most Secret 119–Savvanter (Galivanter 131)   (1981 6g 5g 6g² 5g 6g 5g 5f 5f 5f 5g 6d 8.2d   1982 6g 5f 6f 5f³ 5fg 5g 5d 5g)   poor mover; plater; stays 6f; acts on any going; best in blinkers. *W. Bentley.*   **—**

STAY SHARP   2 ch.c. Sharpen Up 127–Brevity 76 (Pindari 124)   (1982 6f* 6f³ 5.5g 7fg)   Mar 23; 15,000Y; rather leggy, lightly-made, useful-looking colt; brother to fair 1981 2-y-o Short and Sharp and half-brother to several   **95**

winners, including prolific 1975 2-y-o sprint winner Short Reign (by Tribal Chief); dam won over 7f at 2 yrs; hung quite badly all way up straight in 7-runner Woodcote Stakes at Epsom in June but was still good enough to come through and win by 2 lengths from Another Risk; out of his depth subsequently in Coventry Stakes at Royal Ascot, Prix Robert Papin at Maisons-Laffitte and Intercraft Solario Stakes at Sandown; should stay 7f; acts on firm going. *P. Kelleway.*

ST BONIFACE 2 ch.c. Halo–Joking Apart 120 (Jimmy Reppin 131) (1982 **109** 7f* 7f⁴ 8s) Mar 9; strong, well-made, quite attractive colt; half-brother to Galtres Stakes winners Sans Blague (by The Minstrel) and Deadly Serious (by Queen's Hussar); dam very smart at up to 1m; put up the performance of a potentially very useful colt in 15-runner maiden race at Newmarket in July, finding his stride in final 2f and running on strongly to win by ¾ length from Dunbeath; put up another pleasing display when 1¾ lengths fourth of 7 to All Systems Go in Lanson Champagne Stakes at Goodwood later in month, getting behind early on, probably through inexperience, but running on really well in closing stages; 4/1, every chance when 9 lengths sixth of 9 to Dunbeath in Royal Lodge Stakes at Ascot in September; should stay 1½m; probably acts on any going. *R. Hern.*

ST CONAL 3 ch.c. Status Seeker–Irish Picture (Dual 117) (1981 5s 7g 8s — 10s 1982 6.5g⁴ 8s 7d 6f⁴ 6g 7g³ 8fg 8fg) fair sort; poor maiden; stays 7f; blinkered once at 2 yrs. *G. Beeson.*

STEADY DUDLEY 2 br.g. Owen Dudley 121–Ready Steady Go 87 (On Your **73** Mark 125) (1982 7fg 7g) Mar 27; good-bodied, quite well-made gelding; first foal; dam second over 6f at 2 yrs and over 1m at 4 yrs; prominent in big fields of maidens at Newbury in July and August; may improve. *P. Cundell.*

STEADY MUSIC 2 b.f. Music Boy 124–Gin and French 71 (Poaching 115) **74** (1982 5f⁴ 5f⁴ 6f 6g* 5fg 6fg³ 6fg 7fg 6s) Apr 8; 4,100F, 6,000Y; close-coupled filly; half-sister to a winner in Austria; dam, a plater, won at up to 10.8f; won 7-runner maiden race at Hamilton in June; beaten in nurseries subsequently; suited by 6f; acts on firm going. *C. Nelson.*

STEADY THE BUFFS 3 b.f. Balidar 133–Dinant 114 (Abernant 142) (1981 **62** 6fg 7g 7g 1982 8d 8d 7f 7fg³ 8f 8fg 8s⁴ 10.8s 10s⁴ 10g³) big, rangy filly; poor walker; has a round action; in frame in maiden races; stays 1¼m. *M. McCourt.*

STEAL A GLANCE 2 b.c. Nishapour 125–Parthian Song (Parthia 132) (1982 **79** 6fg⁴ 7fg) Apr 17; 29,000Y; well-made, quite attractive colt; half-brother to 3 winners, including Piperhill (by Red God), a useful winner at up to 7f; dam unraced half-sister to Porto Bello; 2 lengths fourth of 16 to Behind The Lines in maiden race at Salisbury in September; will probably stay 1m. *B. Hills.*

STEAMBOAT BILL 3 ch.g. Bustino 136–Shoshoni 82 (Ballymoss 136) (1981 — NR 1982 10.2g) strong gelding; tenth of 17 of Woolf in maiden race at Doncaster in June; destroyed after getting loose and injuring himself before similar event at Newcastle in August. *C. Thornton.*

STEAUA ROMANA 2 b.f. Pitskelly 122–Makura (Pampered King 121) — (1982 6f 8fg) Mar 12; 43,000Y; useful-looking filly; half-sister to 2 winners, including very smart sprinter Abdu (by Balidar); dam well beaten on all her 3 starts; in rear in maiden races at Newmarket (last of 20) in July and Beverley in September. *W. Wharton.*

STEEL BAY 3 b.c. Red Alert 127–Spadilla 59 (Javelot 124) (1981 7.2d² **82** 7d² 1982 7d⁴ 8.5fg² 8fg 10f* 10g 8.2f² 8f 8f⁴ 10fg 10.6f 8g⁴) strong, quite attractive colt; has a round action; smoothly landed odds by 5 lengths from Hypnosis in 8-runner £4,500 event at Lingfield in May; had run well earlier when fourth to Hays in Salisbury 2,000 Guineas Trial and neck second of 7 to Count Pahlen (gave 10 lb) in Blue Riband Trial at Epsom; stays 1¼m; has won on firm going but gives impression he'll always be suited by some give in the ground. *P. Cole.*

STEEL CHARGER 5 b.h. Steel Heart 128–Belaying Pin (Iron Peg §§) (1981 **90** 5s² 5fg* 5g 5g* 5g 5f 5fg 5fg 5fg² 5fg* 5g 5g 1982 5f³ 5f* 5fg 5fg* 5f* 5fg) strong, compact, good sort; improved dramatically and had a fine season; won quite valuable handicaps at Doncaster (£7,800 event), Newmarket and Epsom; ran on strongly to head Pontin Lad inside last 100 yards and beat him a neck (pair clear) on last-named course in June; also ran creditably on his other starts, having a very stiff task on last (Royal Ascot); best at around 5f; has run respectably on soft going but is clearly well suited by top-of-the-ground conditions; blinkered once in 1980; genuine. *R. Boss.*

STEEL CHOICE 3 b.g. Comedy Star 121–Port Meadow 83 (Runnymede 123) **75**
(1981 5v 5d² 5s 6g 6g* 7g³ 7f⁴ 8f 8g 8d   1982 7g 8fg⁴ 8fg 12f 9.4fg 8g² 8f)   strong
gelding; quite a moderate handicapper; stays 1m but is unlikely to stay 1¼m; acts
on any going with possible exception of really soft; sometimes blinkered; has
shown a tendency to hang left and is possibly not particularly keen; exported to
Malaysia. *M. W. Easterby.*

STEEL COMMANDER 4 b.g. Steel Heart 128–Commander Ali (Bold Com- **84**
mander) (1981 10d 6d* 7d² 6d² 7f 6.3fg 6.3fg 7.5g 9d 8s   1982 8s 8s 6fg* 6.3g
5d 6.3fg 7fg 5fg⁴ 6f 7fg³ 6d³ 6d)   Irish gelding; beat Martialette decisively
by 2 lengths in handicap at Naas in May and ran creditably when in frame 3
times, but was disappointing most other outings; stays 7f; yet to show he acts on
extremes of going; usually blinkered nowadays; sold to BBA 2,800 gns
Newmarket Autumn Sales. *D. Weld, Ireland.*

STEEL DUKE 6 b.g. Calpurnius 122–Corrie Royal (Fury Royal 108) (1981 **108**
14g* 12g* 16fg* 11.5f* 13f* 11.5fg* 16d   1982 8s 8s 16fg* 16g³ 16fg 9g 14f*
11.5f* 12fg² 11.5g 10fg)   strong Irish gelding; second foal; dam won over
hurdles; put up an excellent performance when beating Ore by a head in Savel
Beg Stakes at Leopardstown in May; subsequently won a minor event and a
handicap at Galway in July, latter under 10·6; ran another fine race and finished
well clear of remainder when going down by a neck to Lords in Blandford Stakes
at the Curragh in August; didn't do himself justice when only tenth of 14 behind
Evzon in Queen's Vase at Royal Ascot on fifth start; stays well but has run
creditably at around 1m; acts on any going; most genuine; had stiff task final
outing. *N. Meade, Ireland.*

STEEL FLIGHT 9 ch.g. Grey Steel 90–Monkey Flight 59 (Flyover 109) (1981 **—**
NR 1982 7.6fg 8.2g)   successful at up to 1m in this country and Scandinavia
from 1976 to 1978; has since won over hurdles; still bit backward when seventh
of 18 to Eliza de Rich in selling handicap at Haydock in August. *M. Cousins.*

STEEL GLOW 3 b.c. Steel Heart 128–Lucybird (Sea-Bird II 145) (1981 6g **85**
7d⁴ 6g³   1982 8d 7g 8fg⁴ 8fg² 8fg 10fg³ 10fg* 8f³ 10.1g²)   strong, good sort;
landed odds in maiden race at Ripon in August; in frame in varied company
most other starts; stays 1¼m; acts on firm going. *B. Hills.*

STEEL KID (USA) 3 b.c. Caro 133–Gallant Trial (Gallant Man) (1981 7g 8g **82**
7g 7g   1982 14g 14d³ 12f⁴ 14f* 10.1g⁴ 10g* 12g³ 10.6f)   strong, stocky colt;
landed odds in slowly-run 4-runner maiden race at Yarmouth in August and
decisively won minor event at Ripon later in month; stays 1¾m; seems to act on
any going. *R. Armstrong.*

STEEL PART 4 ch.g. Steel Heart 128–Dalriada (Ribot 142) (1981 8s 6g 5v **—**
7f 5fg 6fg² 6g   1982 6fg 5f 8f 7f 8g 8fg)   very small gelding; plater; should
stay at least 7f. *D. Gandolfo.*

STEEL PASS 4 b.g. Steel Heart 128–Senorita Rugby 86 (Forward Pass) **92** d
(1981 7d 6g⁴ 6g 6d* 6g² 6fg² 6f* 6fg 6d 6fg   1982 6fg 6d 7f 6f 6f 6f⁴ 8g 8f 8g³
7s 7g)   good-bodied gelding; sent to USA in autumn, 1981, but didn't win there;
didn't recover his best form on his return, best efforts in handicaps at Newmarket
(3) and Yarmouth; stays 1m, but best form at shorter distances; acts on any
going; has often been blinkered; often pulls hard and is not the easiest of rides;
sold 6,800 gns Newmarket Autumn Sales. *F. Durr.*

STEELSTOCK 3 br.g. Tamerlane 128–Lady Talisman (Continuation 120) **—**
(1981 5d 6g³ 6fg³ 7f² 7g 7f³ 7fg² 8fg 8g 8s   1982 10s 16f 12f 12f 12fg 12fg⁴ 14.7f
12g)   useful sort; good walker; modest maiden at his best; fourth in seller
sixth outing; not certain to stay 2m; acts well on firm going; blinkered fourth
start; sold to W. Storey 1,250 gns Doncaster October Sales. *K. Stone.*

STEEL VENTURE 3 b.c. Full of Hope 125–Grove Star (Upper Case) (1981 **86**
8s   1982 8g* 12fg³ 12.3fg 10f 8g* 8d² 8f 9s)   rather lightly-made, lengthy
colt; awarded maiden race at Doncaster in March and got the better of Brookline
by ¾ length in handicap on same course in June; best at 1m and appears not to
stay 1½m; suited by some give in the ground; has run well when sweating up; has
a tendency to hang; blinkered seventh start (ran moderately); trained by B.
Hills first 7 outings. *M. Ryan.*

STEELWORKS 4 ch.c. Steel Heart 128–Hariota 73 (Hook Money 124) (1981 **72**
8fg⁴ 8fg* 8g 8fg* 8.5fg 8fg   1982 8d 7f 7.6g³ 8.5f 9fg* 10d 9f* 8f 8fg* 9g 9d³
8g 10.2f)   compact, sturdy colt; none too consistent, but won handicaps at
York in June and July and at Pontefract in August; suited by a strongly-run 1m
or 9f; acts on a soft surface, but is well suited by firm going; blinkered first 3

803

starts as a 3-y-o; has done all his winning on left-handed tracks; had a poor run twelfth start and form can be ignored. *B. Hills.*

STEEPLE BELL 6 b.g. Tower Walk 130–Nine Lessons 101 (Santa Claus 133) **91**
(1981 6g 7g 7.6g² 7fg² 7f 8g⁴ 7fg² 7g³ 7s⁴ 9s 1982 8d 8fg 7g* 7fg³ 8d* 8d 8s⁴)
lengthy, quite attractive gelding; good walker; won handicaps at Sandown in
July and Ripon in August narrowly, on latter course beating Silver Season most
gamely in slowly-run £5,600 Ripon Rowels Handicap; unlucky in running when
third to Basil Boy at Sandown in between and didn't have best of runs sixth
start; stays 1m; seems to act on any going; does best when ridden up with
pace (held up first 2 starts); genuine; often apprentice ridden nowadays (wasn't
at Ripon). *M. Stoute.*

STEERS 3 b.c. He Loves Me 120–Mile Cross 88 (Milesian 125) (1981 5g 5fg —
6fg 8s 6s 1982 6fg 6g 5f 6g) smallish, quite attractive colt; plater; stays 6f;
best in blinkers; has sweated up; sold 400 gns Ascot August Sales. *Peter Taylor.*

STEIN CHART 2 b.f. Native Bazaar 122–Ballycreek (Ballymoss 136) (1982 **57**
5fg 6fg⁴ 5g³ 6fg 8d) small filly; second foal; dam tailed-off last on only
start; plater; stays 1m; suited by an easy surface; blinkered last 3 starts; sold
400 gns Newmarket Autumn Sales. *D. H. Jones.*

STELLA'S PET 10 ch.g. Elvis 96–Fairworth 74§ (Fair Seller 126) (1981 8s **36**
8g² 1982 11fg³) plater; stayed 11f; appeared to act on any going, but was
particularly well suited by firm; dead. *W. Storey.*

STEP DANCE (USA) 3 ch.c. Dance Spell–Sealand (Luthier 126) (1981 **84**
8g 1982 11g* 13.3f 14f³ 14g 16g) rangy, quite attractive colt with plenty of
scope; kept on strongly to account for Heather's Reef by 3 lengths in 14-runner
maiden race at Newbury in April; respectable third in handicap at Salisbury
in August despite running rather in snatches; should stay 2m; yet to race on
a soft surface. *J. Tree.*

STEPHALOTUS 2 br.f. Coded Scrap 90–Stephandre 94 (Derring-Do 131) **82**
(1982 5fg 5s 6d* 6d⁴) Mar 4; big, rangy filly with scope; has a capped hock;
first foal; dam won from 5f to 1¼m; won 12-runner minor event at Pontefract
in October in finish of short heads with Sovereign Pearl and Rainbow Springs;
will probably stay 7f; seems suited by some give in the ground. *T. Fairhurst.*

STEPHANY'S DREAM 2 b.f. Reform 132–American Beauty 74 (Mill Reef **99**
141) (1982 7v 8.5v³ 8s² 7v² 7v*) May 5; 16,000Y; first foal; dam, second
twice over 1¼m, is daughter of Oaks second West Side Story; developed into
a useful filly and won 19-runner maiden race at Saint-Cloud in November by
2 lengths; had gone down by 1½ lengths to Mille Balles in similar event at Maisons-
Laffitte on previous start; will stay 1¼m+; entered in 1,000 Guineas. *R.
Collet, France.*

STEPOUT 3 b.f. Sagaro 133–Pepstep 66 (Polic 126) (1981 7d 7.6s⁴ 1982 **78**
10f 12f³ 12f* 12f 12g 10g² 11.7s* 12g) small, fair sort; good walker; won
maiden race at Lingfield in July and handicap at Bath in October; stays 1½m;
acts on any going. *M. Smyly.*

STEPS 2 b.f. Dance In Time–Miss Justice 87 (King's Bench 132) (1982 6fg³ **75**
6g³ 5.8g) May 3; 3,700Y; half-sister to numerous winners, including very
useful Obstacle (by Dike) and speedy Law and Impulse (by Roan Rocket);
dam 2-y-o 6f winner; quite a modest filly; disappointing favourite in maiden
race won by Broken Habit at Bath in July on final outing; stays 6f. *H. Candy.*

STERN 6 br.g. No Mercy 126–Rudder (Reliance II 137) (1981 7g 6g 6f* 5.6f³ **71**
6d 6f³ 6fg 1982 6f 6f 6fg 6g 6f 6g⁴ 7fg* 6fg* 6f² 7.2s* 7d) won handicaps
at Chepstow in August and September and at Haydock in October, last-named
by ½ length from Carriage Way; needs at least 6f and stays 1m; good mover
who evidently acts on any going; blinkered once at 3 yrs; tends to sweat up;
rider lost irons fifth start; genuine. *I. Walker.*

STEVIE CEE 2 ch.f. Roi Soleil 125–Senna (Sica Boy 132) (1982 5fg) April —
29; 1,200Y; half-sister to several winners, including sprinter My Jem (by My
Swallow); dam won over 11f in France; unquoted, eleventh of 12 maiden race
at Warwick in May. *S. Harris.*

STEWART'S RISE 5 ch.m. Good Bond 122–Devadara 74 (Royal Levee or **41**
Hill Clown) (1981 10.8d² 8d 10.8fg 10fg 10f* 10f⁴ 10f 10g² 10fg⁴ 10fg 1982
10fg 8d² 8f 12f* 10.6f 10fg* 10fg⁴ 10d 12fg 10.2s 12s) leggy, light-framed mare;
plater; attracted no bid after winning at Wolverhampton in May and Beverley
(apprentice event) in June; stays 1½m; acts on any going; tends to sweat up;
genuine; suitable mount for an apprentice. *B. McMahon.*

STICK IN THE MUD 3 ch.f. Wollow 132–Albercaro 88 (Hard Tack 111§) —
(1981 6fg 6f 6g 1982 7g 6g 5fg⁴ 5f) useful sort; soundly beaten all starts in
varied company; blinkered third outing; sold 1,000 gns Newmarket Autumn
Sales. *H. T. Jones.*

STICKY FINGERS 2 b.f. Octavo 115–Till 85 (Hook Money 124) (1982   **80 ?**
5.1g 6f 7f* 6g⁴ 7g) May 12; IR 3,000Y; smallish filly; half-sister to several
winners here and abroad; dam won over 1m; put up best effort when getting
home by a short head from Town Star in auction event at Thirsk in July; off
course 2 months after next outing; probably needs at least 7f. *H. T. Jones.*

STILL FREE 4 ch.g. Manacle 123–Shilly Shally 89 (Sallymount 125) (1981   —
8d 7d 8d⁴ 5f 8fg⁴ 6fg 8h⁴ 8fg 1982 8f 8f) lightly-made gelding; plating-class
maiden; stays 1m. *A. Turnell.*

STIMLER 5 b.h. Charlottown 127–Pardalina 69 (Pardal 130) (1981 7fg 8g⁴   **42** d
11.7fg 8g 7f 7fg 8fg 12g 1982 10fg 7.6f² 7f² 7g 8fg 9g) lightly-made horse;
plater; should stay beyond 1m; probably acts on any going; often blinkered;
suitable mount for an inexperienced rider. *M. Bolton.*

STINGO 3 b.c. Mansingh 120–Quita II 105 (Lavandin 128) (1981 5s⁴ 1982   —
7d 6fg 7fg 10g) plating-class maiden; unlikely to stay 1¼m. *R. Price.*

STIRABOUT 2 b.c. Oats 126–Magic Light (Tarqogan 125) (1982 7fg⁴ 7fg²   **92**
8.5g*) May 11; IR 4,200F, IR 10,000Y; half-brother to winning Irish stayer
Ailwee Caves (by Weavers' Hall); dam once-raced half-sister to high-class
Irish and American performer Spence Bay; looked a useful stayer in the making
when winning 13-runner maiden race at Galway in September by 1½ lengths
from Arrested; clear of 11 others when beaten short head by Branch Line in
similar event at Leopardstown the previous month. *D. Weld, Ireland.*

ST LYDIA 2 b.f. Martinmas 128–Lydja 75 (Hethersett 134) (1982 5f*) Mar   **71+**
15; IR 3,000Y; workmanlike filly; half-sister to winners here and abroad,
including Troms (by Wolver Hollow), a useful winner at up to 1¼m in France;
dam stayed 1¼m; 11/8, looked a cut above her 3 rivals in seller at Nottingham
in April and made all to win easily by 5 lengths; bought in 3,500 gns afterwards;
later won in Italy. *Mrs J. Reavey.*

ST MAWES BAY 3 ch.f. Jimmy Reppin 131–Terre Promise (Soderini 123)   **80**
(1981 6f 7d 6d⁴ 1982 8f³ 7.6fg 8fg³ 7fg² 7g 7f* 7f* 7d⁴ 7fg) leggy filly; poor
walker; won maiden race at Leicester and handicap at Thirsk in July; stays
1m; acts well on firm ground; sold 5,000 gns Newmarket Autumn Sales and sent
to Trinidad. *B. Hobbs.*

STOIC 3 b.c. Oats 126–Gentle Way 74 (Gentle Art 121) (1981 7fg 8s 7.6s   —
1982 12g) medium-sized, quite attractive gelding; poor plater; swerved badly
halfway once in 1981. *A. Moore.*

STOLFORD 2 ch.c. Dublin Taxi–Moonsprite (Ragusa 137) (1982 5.8f 6g   —
6f) Apr 12; third foal; dam lightly raced; well behind in maiden and minor
events; not raced after July. *G. Balding.*

STONEHENGE 5 gr.h. Great Nephew 126–Fairy Ring 91 (Quorum 126)   **48** d
(1981 NR 1982 10f 10fg 10.8fg 10d³ 11.7fg³ 10f 10g 10fg 10s 10.8s) strong,
compact horse; third in handicaps at Salisbury and Windsor in summer, best
efforts for quite a while; stays 11.7f; probably acts on any going. *P. Burgoyne.*

STONE OF SCONE 3 b.f. Ragstone 128–Linguistic 95 (Porto Bello 118)   —
(1981 NR 1982 7fg 10f⁴ 7.6d) quite attractive filly; first foal; dam won twice
over 5f at 2 yrs; in need of run, pulled hard when over 8 lengths fourth of 6
to Valiancy in maiden race at Nottingham in July, only glimmer of ability;
may stay 1¼m; sold 2,900 gns Newmarket Autumn Sales. *J. Dunlop.*

STONEY 2 ch.f. Balidar 133–Sweetstone (Honeyway 125) (1982 6f 6f⁴ 7f)   **73**
Feb 24; workmanlike filly; half-sister to 2 winners in Italy, notably Italian
1,000 Guineas winner Sinthesis (by Court Fool); dam unraced twin; 33/1, dwelt
badly and in circumstances did well when 2¾ lengths fourth of 18 to Shareef
Dancer in maiden race at Newmarket in August; modest sixth of 14 in similar
event won by Zariya at Brighton the following month; should stay 7f. *J. Winter.*

STOPOVER 3 b.f. Bruni 132–Cannon Ball 91 (By Thunder! 122) (1981 7fg⁴   —
7fg 1982 8fg⁴ 12fg 16d 12g) lightly-made, quite attractive filly; good walker;
little worthwhile form, including in a seller; claimed £3,100 after final start.
J. Berry.

STOP TALKING 2 b.c. Mount Hagen 127–Chit Chat (Baldric II 131) (1982   **85** d
6f⁴ 5d² 6f² 5fg 6d⁴ 6v⁴) Apr 3; IR 40,000Y; small, lengthy, quite attractive

colt; second foal; half-brother to 1980 2-y-o 5f winner Trina's Girl (by Nonoalco); dam, daughter of smart French filly Chatter Box, won over 7.5f at 2 yrs from only 2 starts in France; seemed sure to win a race after finishing good second at Windsor (24-runner maiden event) in June and Lingfield in July, but became disappointing; sold Susan Piggott Bloodstock 7,800 gns Newmarket Autumn Sales. *G. Harwood.*

STORMING 3 ch.g. Red Alert 127–Winbeam (Hornbeam 130) (1981 5fg 5g 7fg 7d² 8.2fg 8g 7g 1982 8s* 12fg 11.7d 11.7fg) strong gelding; plater; bought in 1,600 gns after winning at Leicester in March; stays 1m; acts on soft going; usually blinkered. *D. Dale.*   **48**

STORMY JIM 4 ch.c. Jimmy Reppin 131–Stormy Gal 71 (Rockavon 120) (1981 8g⁴ 7g 7g² 8f 8f⁴ 8g 7g 7g 7.2v 8v 7g⁴ 8s 8g 1982 7f 8f 9f 10f³ 10g* 12g 9g 11f⁴) strong colt; often disappointing since 1980, but beat Mills High by 1¼ lengths in handicap at Redcar in August; stays 1¼m; acts on any going; usually blinkered nowadays. *Hbt Jones.*   **67 d**

STORTON 3 b.g. Morston 125–Love Story 79 (Aureole 132) (1981 7fg 7g 7fg⁴ 7fg 8g³ 8d⁴ 8d² 1982 12f 12d² 16.9fg 16s) quite attractive gelding; fair maiden at his best; below form at 3 yrs and ran abysmally last 2 outings; should stay 1¾m+; evidently needs some give in the ground; blinkered last 3 starts; trained part of season by B. Hills. *P. Kearney.*   **—**

ST PADDY'S BABY 3 ch.g. St Paddy 133–Isomer 60 (Runnymede 123) (1981 5d 5d 5.3f⁴ 7f 6f 5d 5.3d 5s 1982 10d 10f 8f 8.5f 10g) leggy, lightly-made gelding; poor plater nowadays; has been tried in blinkers; sold 440 gns Newmarket July Sales. *O. Jorgensen.*   **—**

ST PEDRO 4 b.c. St Paddy 133–Jinkin (King's Troop 118) (1981 8g* 10.2g 8s⁴ 7d 1982 8g 8g⁴ 8f² 8g* 10d³ 8fg 9g 8f⁴ 8g³ 9d 8s³ 10g) quite an attractive, robust colt; took the eye when beating Little Mercy very gamely by 2 lengths in handicap at Sandown in June; ran creditably most other outings, including in William Hill Cambridgeshire at Newmarket on tenth start; stays 1¼m; probably acts on any going; genuine. *E. Eldin.*   **82**

STRADEY LYNN 2 ch.f. Derrylin 115–Stradey Park 103 (Murrayfield 119) (1982 5.1g 6f 5s) Apr 22; 5,200F, 2,500Y; fair sort; first produce; dam won over 5f and stayed 1¼m; poor form, including in maiden auction events; sold 1,600 gns Newmarket Autumn Sales. *J. Winter.*   **57**

STRAEKER 3 ch.c. Sharpen Up 127–Princess Tavi (Sea Hawk II 131) (1981 6fg³ 6f* 6d* 6f² 7g* 7g 1982 7fg 7f 6f 8f) compact, fair sort; fairly useful at 2 yrs; below form most starts in 1982; suited by 7f and should stay 1m; has won on firm going but is ideally suited by some give in the ground. *J. W. Watts.*   **—**

STRAFUI 3 ch.c. Home Guard 129–Nonsensical 99 (Silly Season 127) (1981 NR 1982 8d² 8f* 8f² 10fg⁴ 10f² 8d²) 6,000F, 6,600Y; useful-looking colt with some scope; half-brother to useful 1975 2-y-o Drop Of A Hat (by Midsummer Night II), successful at up to 7.2f; dam won at up to 1¼m; won maiden race at Beverley in April; runner-up on 4 of his other starts; stays 1¼m; seems to act on any going; has a tendency to hang, appears none too genuine and isn't an easy ride. *L. Cumani.*   **77**

STRAIGHT TO BED 2 b.f. Dominion 123–Burning Love 78 (Buisson Ardent 129) (1982 6g 7g) Apr 28; 720F; strong, fair sort; poor walker; closely related to fairly useful 1978 2-y-o 7f winner Deed I Do (by Derring-Do) and half-sister to numerous winners here and abroad; dam half-sister to very smart Le Cordonnier; behind in maiden races at Newmarket in September (last of 19) and October; bandaged in front on second occasion. *M. Smyly.*   **—**

STRAPLESS 3 b.f. Bustino 136–Dame Foolish 121 (Silly Season 127) (1981 6fg 6fg* 7d 7.2fg 1982 6fg 6f 8f 6h⁴ 7d 6s* 7d⁴) small, strong, well-made filly; good walker and mover; led near finish to win apprentice race at Nottingham in October; stayed 7f; acted on soft going; trained by M. Jarvis first 4 starts; visits Music Maestro. *M. Camacho.*   **74**

STRASS CHANDERLIER 3 b.g. Roi Soleil 125–Lochness Lass (Track Spare 125) (1981 6g 7fg 7fg 7g 1982 10d 10s 8fg) compact gelding; poor mover; poor plater. *C. Williams.*   **—**

STRATFORD PLACE 2 ch.c. Moulton 128–Wild Words 95 (Galivanter 131) (1982 6g³ 8d) Apr 8; 8,000Y; big, strong, rangy colt; half-brother to several winners, including useful 3-y-o sprinter Battle Hymn (by Music Boy) and useful 7f to 1m winner Chukaroo (by Kibenka); dam half-sister to very useful sprinter   **87+**

Sound Barrier; had 2 late-season outings in high-class company, running well behind On Stage and Alchise in Clarence House Stakes at Ascot and not so well (tailed off after being badly hampered in first 2f) behind Dunbeath in William Hill Futurity at Doncaster; obviously highly regarded, and could easily prove much better than we are able to rate him. *R. Laing.*

STRATFORD (USA) 2 b.c. Hoist the Flag–Thong (Nantallah) (1982 6d 7s*) Feb 29; $525,000Y; half-brother to 5 good winners, including top-class sprinter/miler Thatch (by Forli), top-class middle-distance colt King Pellinore (by Round Table) and high-class sprinter Marinsky (by Northern Dancer), and also to dam of Nureyev; dam stakes-placed sister to 3 high-class performers; 3/1, led 2f out when winning 15-runner maiden race at the Curragh in October by 2 lengths from Sunder, easily better effort; will be suited by 1m. *V. O'Brien, Ireland.* **89 p**

STRATHLEVEN 3 ro.f. My Swanee 122–Derreks Pet (Hop Bridge 87) (1981 NR 1982 12v 12d) half-sister to 2 winning jumpers; dam of little account; behind in maiden race and minor event in Scotland. *D. Smith.* **—**

STRATH OF ORCHY 3 br.f. Lochnager 132–Silver Teal 79 (Meldrum 112) (1981 5fg 5fg⁴ 5fg³ 6d³ 6d* 6s³ 6d* 1982 7s⁴ 7g 6fg³ 5fg 5fg³ 5fg 6f 5fg⁴ 6s 6s 5s³) compact filly; good walker; in frame in varied company; best at sprint distances; ideally suited by some give in the ground; hung left second start; blinkered last 3 outings; has worn blinkers in front. *K. Stone.* **80**

STRATOSPHERE 2 b.f. Solinus 130–Marsville (Trouville 125) (1982 5.5s*) Apr 7; IR 35,000Y; half-sister to 3 winners, including very smart Irish sprinter Springhill (by Sallust); dam won over 7f and 1m in Ireland; won 11-runner newcomers race at Maisons-Laffitte in June by ½ length from Palitana but wasn't seen out again; will stay 7f, possibly 1m; entered in 1,000 Guineas. *O. Douieb, France.* **98 p**

STRATOSPHERIC (USA) 3 b.f. Majestic Light–Clear Ceiling (Bold Ruler) (1981 7d 7fg* 8fg² 1982 7.3g⁴ 8fg) well-made, attractive filly; closely related to a modest filly, and half-sister to 1,000 Guineas winner Quick As Lightning (by Buckpasser); dam, sister to 5 winners including champion US sire What A Pleasure, won at up to 6f in USA; smart at 2 yrs when she won Waterford Candelabra Stakes at Goodwood; put up better effort at 3 yrs when sixth of 15 to On The House in 1,000 Guineas at Newmarket in April; subsequently broke blood vessels in training; would have been suited by middle distances; dead. *J. Dunlop.* **110**

STRAWBERRY SPECIAL 3 b.c. Bay Express 132–Square Acre (Palestine 133) (1981 5s 5g 7g 1982 7g) small colt; poor plater. *P. Bevan.* **—**

STRDAMON 3 b.f. Rapid River 127–Reignon 74 (Lucky Brief 128) (1981 6f 7f 1982 10.2g 8g) lengthy, lightly-made filly; beaten some way in varied company, including selling. *M. Camacho.* **—**

STREATLY 2 gr.f. Town Crier 119–Camusky 77 (Charlottown 127) (1982 5fg 6g⁴ 7fg³ 7g 7.2f 6s) Mar 20; strong, chunky filly; fourth foal; half-sister to 7.5f and 10.6f winner Lonely Signorita (by Hotfoot); dam placed over 1½m; in frame in July in maiden race at Haydock and minor event at Chester; soundly beaten in nurseries afterwards; suited by 7f; blinkered fifth outing. *W. Wharton.* **74**

STREET GIRL 7 b.m. Streetfighter 120–Brighton Girl 96 (Right Boy 137) (1981 NR 1982 8d) plater; ran respectably at Warwick in April on only outing on flat since 1979; has been tried in blinkers. *M. Bradley.* **—**

STREET MARKET 3 ch.g. Porto Bello 118–Balgreggan (Hallez 131) (1981 5.8g³ 5d² 5f* 5f² 5d³ 5d* 5g⁴ 5g 1982 6s 5g* 5f³ 5fg 6f 5fg 5g 5f² 5fg 5g 5g) well-made, good sort; sprint handicapper; beat To The Point by 4 lengths at Newbury in April; should stay 6f; probably acts on any going but goes well on firm; suitable mount for an apprentice; blinkered seventh and final starts; sometimes starts slowly; exported to Malaysia. *N. Vigors.* **99**

STREGGA 4 b.f. Roman Warrior 132–Mehir 59 (King's Company 124) (1981 7g 6g 6d 5.3f 5g 1982 6d⁴ 5g) small filly; poor maiden; ran respectably in a seller on first outing; stays 6f; blinkered last 3 outings as a 3-y-o. *M. Masson.* **—**

STRETCHEES 3 b.f. Full of Hope 125–Shy Meld 65 (Meldrum 112) (1981 8fg 8s 1982 12d 12.2f) big filly; in rear in maiden races and a minor event in the North. *S. Norton.* **—**

STRIDE 2 b.c. Tachypous 128–Span (Pan II 130) (1982 8g²) Apr 2; robust, good-bodied colt; half-brother to winning stayer Cantilever (by Crooner); **99 p**

dam placed over 1½m; second favourite, ran on very strongly after taking long time to get the hang of things when short-head second of 18 to Holy Spark in maiden race at Newmarket in October; will stay 1¼m; bound to win in similar company. *B. Hobbs.*

STRIKE ACTION 5 b.g. Tyrant–Corte (Alcide 136) (1981 12f 1982 8.2g) — poor walker; little worthwhile form in varied company; has worn blinkers. *R. Allan.*

STRIKE IT RICH (FR) 3 b. or br.f. Rheingold 137–Lucky For Me 116 **88** (Appiani II 128) (1981 8g² 1982 9g* 8f 10g 12fg 9f² 12d² 10g* 11.5g 10d² 12v 12g) quite attractive, lightly-made filly; third foal; half-sister to Euclid (by Lyphard), a very useful winner over 6f and 1m at 2 yrs in Ireland; dam smart middle-distance filly, and half-sister to smart Nor; won maiden race at Limerick Junction in May and apprentice handicap at Tralee in August; beat Uzonkopru by 5 lengths in latter; ran creditably on several other occasions but finished well beaten in Princess Royal Stakes won by Believer at Ascot in October on penultimate start; possibly unsuited by very soft going but acts on any other. *C. Collins, Ireland.*

STRIKE LUCKY 2 ch.c. Royal Match 117–Chance Belle 85 (Foggy Belle 108) **85** (1982 7g 6v⁴) Mar 30; 6,200Y; well-made colt; first foal; dam won over 1½m and 1¾m; 33/1; disputed lead until final furlong when 9½ lengths fourth of 10 to Northern Adventure in Duke of Edinburgh Stakes at Ascot in October. *A. Pitt.*

STRING OF STARS 4 ch.f. Jukebox 126–Lunar Star (Star Gazer 123) — (1981 6s 5g 5g 1982 5g 8f 8f 7f 5f 6g 6fg 5fg 6g 8g 5g) little worthwhile form, including in sellers; has been tried in blinkers. *D. Chapman.*

STRIP FAST 9 ch.m. Virginia Boy 106–Light Gail (Hill Gail) (1981 10t⁴ **51** 8f 8f* 8h⁴ 8f 8.3g 7h 1982 10fg* 10g 10f⁴ 8fg⁴ 10fg) neat mare; game winner of handicap at Nottingham in June; stays 1½m; probably needs a sound surface; game; excellent mount for a boy; has worn blinkers. *D. H. Jones.*

STROMBOLI 3 b.g. The Brianstan 128–Authorise 95 (Ribot 142) (1981 — 5g 6fg 7fg 7g 7d 1982 6d 7f 9g 10.1d 10.8fg³) plater; seemed to stay 10.8f; injured himself when winning over hurdles and was put down. *T. Marshall.*

ST TERRAMAR 7 b.h. St Alphage 119–Terramar Lass (Tom Rolfe) (1981 **53** d 6fg 5g 5d 5g 6f 5g³ 5d 6f 5fg 5.8g 5g 5s 5s 1982 6f 5.8f³ 5.8f 5g 6g³ 5g 5fg 7f 5s 6s) sprint handicapper; hasn't won since 1980, but runs respectably from time to time; appears to act on any going but is particularly well suited by a sound surface; acts on any track; suitable mount for a boy; best in blinkers; sometimes bandaged on off-fore; often starts slowly. *C. James.*

STUBBINGTON GREEN 5 br.g. Swing Easy 126–Lake Victoria 94 (Stupen- — dous) (1981 10g 10d 8g 10fg 7f² 8f² 10f² 8fg 10f⁴ 10f 1982 8f 8f) leggy gelding; plater; stays 1¼m; acts on any going; wears blinkers. *D. Yeoman.*

STUDENT VENTURE 2 br.g. Averof 123–Tropical Fruit (Tropique 128) **82** (1982 5s* 5f² 5f* 5f² 5fg 5fg) May 4; 680Y; leggy gelding; closely related to 3-y-o Hello Sunshine (by Song), successful at up to 7f and half-brother to several winners; won 4-runner maiden auction event at Hamilton in April and dead-heated with Forget Me Not in small race at Pontefract in May; bred to stay at least 1m; exported to Malaysia. *D. Smith.*

ST WILLIAM 5 b.h. St Paddy 133–Lower Slade (Solar Duke 103) (1981 NR — 1982 13.1g) big, tall horse; plating-class maiden in 1980; well beaten only outing since; best form at 1¼m though is bred to stay well; acts on firm going. *Mrs R. Lomax.*

STYLISH MISS 2 br.f. Solinus 130–Custom Maid (Big Joker) (1982 5d⁴ — 6g 6fg 6s) Mar 19; IR 8,600Y; second foal; dam placed over 9f in Ireland; no worthwhile form in maiden races; off course for 4 months after first outing. *G. Lewis.*

STYLISH MOVER 3 b.c. Martinmas 128–Fuiseog (Eudaemon 129) (1981 **62** 5fg 5d 5g 1982 7fg³ 6f⁴ 8fg 7f 6fg⁴ 8g* 7f 8fg²) close-coupled, fair sort; poor walker; won selling handicap at Newmarket in August (no bid); suited by 1m; best form on a sound surface; has run respectably for an amateur rider. *M. Haynes.*

STYREN (POL) 5 b.g. Szafir–Stoklosa (Deer Leap 125) (1982 10.2g) Polish- — bred gelding; evidently won abroad; blinkered when tailed off in amateur riders event at Doncaster in March; dead. *H. Bell.*

SUCHONG 4 b.f. No Mercy 126–Tea Leaf (Cracksman NZ) (1981 6g 7fg 1982 7fg 8fg) big, strong, quite attractive filly; behind in varied company, including selling. *G. Cottrell.* —

SUDDEN STAR 3 b.f. Grundy 137–Sudden Glory 98 (Luthier 126) (1981 7d 8d 1982 6g 7fg 6fg 12f 6d 8v 10s 6s) neat filly; soundly beaten in varied company; often blinkered. *C. Austin.* —

SUELIZELLE 2 b.f. Carnival Dancer 113–Cathro (Appiani II 128) (1982 5d 5d 5f² 6f³ 6f 6f 6d) June 6; lightly-made filly; fifth foal; dam bad plater; poor plater; probably stays 6f; usually blinkered. *J. Mason.* 54

SUE'S PRINCE 4 b.g. King Log 115–Fairy First 54§ (Fairey Fulmar 124) (1981 12d⁴ 10fg⁴ 1982 9fg 8fg 8.2g 7f³) plater; yet to prove he stays middle distances. *W. H. H. Williams.* 44

SUEZ 3 br.g. Scottish Rifle 127–Somalia 96 (Alcide 136) (1981 8d* 7v 7g 1982 11f 11.7g³ 11.7g) good-looking gelding; won maiden race at Bath in 1981; blinkered when soundly beaten in handicaps at 3 yrs; will stay 1½m. *R. Hern.* —

SUFFIELD PARK 4 b.f. Wolver Hollow 126–Jungle Princess (Native Prince) (1981 8fg 10g 10fg 1982 14.6g 15.8f) small filly; plating-class maiden; should stay at least 1¼m; sold 725 gns Ascot July Sales. *G. Harman.* —

SUFFRED 2 b.f. African Sky 124–Cariole 84 (Pardao 120) (1982 6fg⁴ 6f² 6g⁴ 6g² 7d) Mar 14; IR 38,000Y; robust, useful sort; half-sister to several winners, including useful 5f to 7f winner Marking Time (by On Your Mark); dam won over 7.6f; caught final furlong when second in maiden races at Goodwood in July and Epsom in August; ran poorly on final outing after absence of almost 2 months; should stay 7f; possibly not suited by a soft surface; none too consistent. *J. Benstead.* 86

SUGAR AND MINT (USA) 3 ch.f. Key To The Mint–Acidulee (Vitriolic) (1981 8g 8d* 1982 10fg 11.7g 12f) quite attractive filly; has a round action; won maiden race at Leicester in 1981; well beaten in handicaps in spring; should stay 1½m+; possibly needs some give in the ground; sweated up first start and wore blinkers on second. *M. Albina.* —

SUGAR COATED 4 b.f. Track Spare 125–Star Abbess 86 (Welsh Abbot 131) (1981 7g 6g 6f 6f 7f 8fg⁴ 8fg 7g 10s 10d 1982 8s⁴ 10g 8d 8.3g 10f² 7fg 10.1d 8f 10f) leggy, light-framed filly; plater; stays 1¼m; has worn blinkers. *C. Wildman.* 31

SUGAR LOCH 2 b.f. Lochnager 132–Quite Sweet 100 (Super Sam 124) (1982 7g 7d⁴ 6g) May 12; half-sister to fairly useful 5f to 7f winner Lucky Man (by Manado) and winning 0 y o stayer Quite Hot (by Hotfoot); dam best at up to 1¼m; quite a modest filly; stays 7f. *J. Hindley.* 73

SUGAR MELON 3 ch.f. Streak 119–Kenn Towy (Murrayfield 119) (1981 NR 1982 7.6f 10.1fg 14fg) 600Y; first foal; dam of no account; behind in maiden races and a minor event. *J. Bridger.* —

SUGARVILLE JET 2 b.f. Warpath 113–Conchita 113 (Matador 131) (1982 6fg 6s 6d) Apr 21; big, lengthy filly; half-sister to several winners, including fairly useful sprinter Fish and Chips (by Major Portion); dam won 5 times at 6f; no sign of ability in maiden and minor events; looks the type to do better. *P. Haynes.* —

SUGGESTIVE 3 b.f. Bold Lad (Ire) 133–Nighty Night (Sassafras 135) (1981 5fg 5g² 6f⁴ 6g² 7g 1982 8.5fg* 8f 10d* 10f⁴ 10fg² 11g² 10g 10g3) quite an attractive filly; good mover; won handicaps at Epsom in April and Leicester in June; stays 11f; seems to act on any going; has a useful turn of foot and is suited by waiting tactics. *J. Dunlop.* 80

SULA BULA 4 b.c. Midsummer Night II 117–Blue Ann 60 (Road House II) (1981 10.4d 9d 8g⁴ 8f³ 7g 8fg 1982 10.2f³ 9f³ 10.2g 8d) lengthy, quite useful-looking colt; hasn't won on flat since his 2-y-o days and is sometimes disappointing, but retains a fair bit of ability and finished third to Lafontaine under top weight in Sporting Chronicle Spring Handicap at Doncaster and to Soldan in minor event at Ripon in May; probably suited by 1¼m nowadays; acts on any going; smart hurdler. *M. H. Easterby.* 87

SUL-EL-AH 2 b.f. Tachypous 128–Anjonic 56 (Le Levanstell 122) (1982 6s3) Apr 1; 15,000Y; quite attractive, leggy, good-topped filly; half-sister to several winners, including speedy 1977 early-season 2-y-o Silk Lady (by Tribal Chief); dam of little account; 20/1, always in leading group and kept on quite 91 p well when 2¼ lengths third of 11 to Khaizaraan in Blue Seal Stakes at Ascot in September; sure to improve. *P. Kelleway.*

SULPHUR 4 ch.c. Simbir 130–Dazzling Hue (Double Jump 131) (1981 10d 10fg 1982 11.7fg 7.2f³) lightly-raced and rather disappointing maiden: possibly unsuited by firm going; sold 825 gns Ascot 2nd June Sales. *M. Smyly.* —

SULZANO 4 b.g. Rheingold 137–Ribasha (Ribot 142) (1981 10g² 10d² 10s² 10s⁴ 12s* 12fg* 12.3d 10fg 10fg⁴ 12fg³ 12g 1982 12fg² 16g³ 12fg⁴ 19f 16g 12s³ 12d) well-made gelding; placed in handicaps at Ascot (2, including an apprentice event) and Sandown; disappointing on his other starts, and ran atrociously on fifth outing; suited by 2m nowadays (never in race over 19f); probably acts on any going; blinkered when successful, but is effective without; inconsistent; sold 5,200 gns Newmarket Autumn Sales. *W. Hastings-Bass.* — §

SUMAIL 2 br.f. Mansingh 120–Harmony Thyme 73 (Sing Sing 134) (1982 5f 5fg 6g 5f⁴ 6fg) May 1; 1,700F, 5,800Y; leggy, fair sort; sister to 1979 2-y-o 5f winner Harlyn and a winner in the Isle of Man, and half-sister to fair 1976 5f winner Tribal King (by Tribal Chief); dam 2-y-o 5f winner; moderate plater; not raced after August; best at 5f; blinkered last 2 outings. *M. W. Easterby.* 56

SUMMARY 5 b.g. Mandamus 120–Abstract 73 (French Beige 127) (1981 9d 10f 1982 8f³ 9fg² 12f 10f 10fg² 10g 10g² 10f) well-made gelding; good walker; second at Ripon (twice, including in an amateur riders event) and Redcar; seemed to stay 1½m, but was probably best at shorter distances; acted on any going; was usually blinkered; dead. *M. H. Easterby.* 63

SUMMER HOUSE 3 gr.f. Habat 127–Autumn Double 72 (Double Jump 131) (1981 5f 6f 6fg³ 7g 1982 8d 6d 6s) big, lengthy filly; has shown no form since finishing third in seller at Doncaster at 2 yrs; blinkered final start. *J. Hardy.*

SUMMER IMPRESSIONS (USA) 2 ch.f. Lyphard 132–Roussalka 123 (Habitat 134) (1982 5fg) Apr 6; quite attractive filly; third foal; closely related to disqualified 11f winner Northern Supremo (by Northern Dancer); dam won 7 races at up to 1¼m, including Nassau Stakes twice; favourite, said to have pulled a muscle when never-dangerous 4 lengths sixth of 11 behind Miss Realm in maiden race at York in May. *H. Cecil.* — p

SUMMERLAND 2 b.g. Warpath 113–Croisette 95 (Sunny Way 120) (1982 6g) Apr 25; compact, quite well-made gelding; third foal; dam won 9 times from 6f to 11f; 20/1, ran on through beaten horses to finish remote sixth of 10 behind dead-heaters Liberty Tree and Sangrador in minor event at Ayr in September; will do better with time and longer distances. *C. Thornton.* — p

SUMMER LIGHTNING 2 b.f. Hot Spark 126–Carrigeen 94 (Royalty 130) (1982 7.6v 7s) May 25; good-topped filly; second foal; dam won 4 times from 1¼m to 1¾m; in mid-division in minor events at Lingfield and Sandown in October. *W. Wightman.* 66

SUMMER PATH 5 gr.m. Warpath 113–Summersoon 89 (Sheshoon 132) (1981 12g 12g³ 15.8g³ 12s* 12.3fg⁴ 11d 12v 11d 12d⁴ 1982 12g² 12f 12fg³ 12f³ 12.3g 10g⁴ 13.8f 16g² 15.8f* 18d 16g⁴ 15.8d) compact mare; former plater; won slowly-run non-selling handicap at Catterick in August; probably stays 2m, but has yet to prove it in a strongly-run race; acts on any going. *M. Camacho.* 45

SUMMER SILKS 3 ch.f. Shantung 132–Summer Love 60 (Silver Cloud 121) (1981 8g 1982 10f 11d³ 16.5fg² 16s 12d) staying maiden. *J. Toller.* —

SUMMER SINGER 2 b.c. Silly Season 127–La Scala (Royben 125) (1982 6s) June 14; strong colt; bad mover; first foal; dam poor plater; tailed-off last of 22 in valuable seller at York in October. *Mrs J. Reavey.* —

SUMMER'S LUCK 4 ch.f. Giacometti 130–Lucky Coloullah (Lucky Mel) (1981 NR 1982 10f 12fg) $10,500F; second produce; dam won over 1m; behind in maiden races at Beverley in May and Brighton in June; sold 475 gns Ascot July Sales. *T. Robson.* —

SUMMONS 3 b.g. Rouser 118–Silk II 102 (Counsel 118) (1981 NR 1982 12s* 12g 16d) useful-looking, deep-girthed gelding; half-brother to several winners; dam middle-distance performer; made most of running and stayed on strongly to beat Reef Glade by 6 lengths in 14-runner maiden race at Kempton in April; well beaten afterwards and didn't race after June; should stay 1¾m+. *B. Hobbs.* 90 d

SUNBURST (FR) 6 b.g. Sassafras 135–Miss Sunshine (Mourne 126) (1981 —
15.5d 1982 12fg 12d 16f 15.8d) big ex-French gelding; soundly beaten since
1980; stays 1½m; probably acts on any going but seems well suited by some give
in the ground; has been tried in blinkers. *J. Tierney.*

SUNDANCE KID 3 b.g. Star Appeal 133–Shady Side 82 (Pall Mall 132) **48**
(1981 8s 7d 7g 1982 10g 8.5fg 10v 8f² 9f² 10.1g 12fg 10v⁴ 15.5v) small, strong,
lengthy gelding; plater; stays 1¼m; acts on any going; sometimes blinkered;
sold out of W. Hastings-Bass's stable 4,200 gns Ascot May Sales after fifth
start; resold, probably for export to Italy, 3,100 gns same venue in November.
P. Mitchell.

SUNDHOPE LYNN 3 bl.g. Rapid River 127–Read Aloud 57 (Town Crier —
119) (1981 8.2d 8d 1982 6fg 8g 9fg) plater; stays 1m; has had tongue tied
down. *H. Bell.*

SUNFLOWER LAD 3 b.g. Jimsun 121–Floral Palm 69 (Floribunda 136) **58**
(1981 NR 1982 12.2f 12g³ 12.2f 10fg⁴ 10g³ 10.2d) 10,500Y; big, strong
gelding; brother to fairly useful 6f to 1¼m winner Jim's Tricks, and half-brother
to 2 winners, including very useful Italian sprinter Dublin Taxi (by Sharpen
Up); dam won 5f seller at 2 yrs; has shown a little ability in maiden races and
a minor event; will be suited by a return to 1½m; seems to act on any going;
sold to R. Holder 6,000 gns Newmarket Autumn Sales. *D. Morley.*

SUNLEY BUILDS 4 ch.c. Patch 129–Dance Mistress (Javelot 124) (1981 **97 d**
8g⁴ 12.3g² 12d 12f 10.8s 1982 16s³ 16fg⁴ 18.4fg⁴ 16.1f³ 20fg⁴ 16g 13.3g 12d²
18d 12s⁴) quite attractive, rangy colt; in frame most starts, including in Mono
Sagaro Stakes at Ascot, Ladbrokes Chester Cup, Lymm Stakes at Haydock,
Ascot Stakes at Royal Ascot and William Hill November Handicap at Doncaster; lacks pace and stays well; acts on any going; blinkered once at 3 yrs.
G. Hunter.

SUNLIT RIVER 5 br.m. Roi Soleil 125–River Moy (Niagara Falls 104) (1981 —
12.5s 1982 16f 12f) well-made mare; poor maiden; stays 9f well; suited by
some give in the ground; sometimes blinkered. *W. Haigh.*

SUNNY BEAM 2 b.f. Roi Soleil 125–Elbeam (Hornbeam 130) (1982 6f —
6g 7f 8.2fg) May 9; 3,100Y; smallish, strong filly; half-sister to Star Stroller
(by Tower Walk), successful at up to 7f in Ireland, and to a winner in Italy;
dam won in Sweden; no form in maiden event (last of 13) and 3 sellers. *P.
Rohan.*

SUNNY ISLAND (USA) 3 ch.g. Our Native–Gwinn Island (Groton) (1981 —
6g 6fg 1982 7fg 7f) plain gelding; poor maiden; exported to Malaysia. *E.
Eldin.*

SUNNY KING 2 b.g. Roi Soleil 125–Beamless 73 (Hornbeam 130) (1982 **64**
5g 5fg 6f 5g⁴ 6d 8.2fg) May 21; 600F, 2,400Y; fair sort; half-brother to 4
winners here and abroad, including quite useful sprinter Bill's Song (by Song);
dam stayed 1½m; close fourth of 15 to Song To Singo in seller at Ripon in August,
best effort; blinkered sixth outing. *M. W. Easterby.*

SUNNY LOOK 3 ch.f. Lombard 126–Sooner or Later (Sheshoon 132) (1981 **91**
8d² 10s* 1982 12f³ 12f³ 16.1h² 16fg* 15d² 18d) leggy, fair sort; won handicap
at Thirsk in September; stays very well; acts on any going; ran moderately
final start. *J. Hindley.*

SUNNY REEF 2 b.c. Take a Reef 127–Sunny Bloom 71 (Forlorn River 124) **47**
(1982 5fg 5f³ 7g 5fg 6g⁴ 6s) Mar 19; smallish, leggy colt; half-brother to 2
winners, including fairly useful 1979 2-y-o 5f winner Manacle (by Manacle);
poor form, including in a seller; sold out of H. Westbrook's stable 340 gns
Doncaster September Sales after fifth outing. *L. Barratt.*

SUNOAK 2 b.c. Averof 123–Blue Queen 54 (Majority Blue 126) (1982 7g) **— p**
Apr 22; 18,000Y; useful-looking colt; half-brother to several winners, notably
very useful middle-distance filly Reprocolor (by Jimmy Reppin); dam half-
sister to Sandford Lad; 20/1 and in need of race, noted running on promisingly
after very slow start when out of first 10 of 28 behind Tolomeo in maiden event
at Newmarket in October; bound to do a good deal better. *G. Harwood.*

SUN PRINCESS 2 b.f. English Prince 129–Sunny Valley (Val de Loir 133) **93 p**
(1982 6s²) May 18; rangy, quite attractive filly; good mover; second foal;
half-sister to smart 1m and 1¼m winner Dancing Shadow (by Dancer's Image);
dam won at up to 1½m in France; well-backed second favourite, ran on well

when $1\frac{1}{2}$ lengths second of 11 to Khaizaraan in Blue Seal Stakes at Ascot in September; will be much better suited by middle distances; sure to improve and win races. *R. Hern.*

SUNRULLAH   3 ch.g. Sun Prince 128 Fleet Serenade (Lorenzaccio 130)   (1981   —
NR   1982 12fg 12fg 8.2g 15d 12.2d)   tall, leggy gelding; poor maiden; possibly temperamental (tried to pull himself up fourth start). *W. H. H. Williams.*

SUNSHINE GAL   4 br.f. Alto Volante 109 Chinese Princess (Sunny Way   **67**
120)   (1981 8g 12fg 8fg 8fg 9fg 10s² 10d³   1982 12.2g 10.1fg⁴ 10f 8g 10.1fg*
10fg² 10g⁴ 12s* 10s³)   neat filly; bought in 2,100 gns after winning seller at Windsor in July; apprentice ridden when winning non-selling handicap at Haydock in October by 4 lengths from City's Sister; stays $1\frac{1}{2}$m; probably acts on any going, but seems well suited by soft. *N. Guest.*

SUPER ACT (USA)   3 b.f. Native Royalty Air Maid (Fleet Nasrullah)   (1981   **54**
5g² 5s⁴   1982 7f³ 10f⁴ 8g)   tall, sparely-made filly; in frame in maiden races and a minor event; stays $1\frac{1}{2}$m. *M. Albina.*

SUPER BRAT   3 b.g. Shiny Tenth 120 Mishabo (Royalty 130)   (1981 6g   —
1982 6s⁴ 7g 6f 6fg 7d)   workmanlike, good-quartered gelding; poor form, including in a valuable seller; has been tried in blinkers. *R. Carter.*

SUPERB SINGER   3 ch.f. Music Boy 124 Sinzinbra 112 (Royal Palace 131)   **52**
(1981 5s 5s⁴ 5s² 5g 5d 6f⁴ 6f 5f   1982 6s 5g 5f 5h 7g 5fg* 5fg 5f)   tall, leggy filly; plater; apprentice ridden when winning non-selling handicap at Windsor in July; stays 6f; has worn blinkers; usually bandaged on all legs; exported to Algeria. *K. Ivory.*

SUPER ENTENTE (USA)   2 b.f. Super Concorde 128 Evastrive (Restless   **115**
Native)   (1982 6g² 6g² 6g³)
   Super Concorde and Seattle Slew, the two outstanding sons of the short-lived Bold Reasoning, each retired to stud in 1979.   Seattle Slew, the American triple crown winner of 1977, has met with tremendous success with his first runners, siring Slewpy, winner of the 300,000-dollar Young American Stakes, and Landaluce who died tragically after winning all her five races in the style of a champion.   Super Concorde, the top French two-year-old of 1977, winner of the Prix Morny and Grand Criterium, stood his first season at a much lower fee than Seattle Slew after a disappointing three-year-old career.   He has made a very encouraging start though.   He sired eleven winners in all including the American stakes winner Jetta J., the Prix La Rochette runner-up Le Voleur, the smart Beldale Concorde, a creditable fifth in the William Hill Futurity, and other useful winners in Concorde Hero, Herodote and Conerton.   Oddly enough Super Concorde's best daughter, Robert Sangster's Super Entente, failed to win a race.   She was unlucky not to.   Lack of experience told against her when a well-backed favourite for a maiden race at Doncaster in June; she failed by the narrowest of margins to hold off her owner's other runner, Bright Cone, after looking sure to win when taking the lead two furlongs out.   Nearly two months went by before she next appeared in the valuable Firth of Clyde Stakes at Ayr.   This time the 1 lb overweight she carried for the services of stable-jockey Hide made the difference between victory and defeat; after appearing to have taken the measure of Myra's Best, another Sangster filly, she was again caught on the line as Myra's Best rallied.   Although Super Entente was clearly a useful filly she looked out of her depth in the William Hill Cheveley Park Stakes at Newmarket eleven days later in which she re-opposed Myra's Best on terms 7 lb worse.   She proved well worth her place in the field, keeping on so strongly after chasing Sweet Emma from the start that she took third place, beaten two and three quarter lengths by Ma Biche and two lengths by Favoridge.

Super Entente (USA) (b.f. Feb 27, 1980)	Super Concorde (br 1975)	Bold Reasoning (br 1968)	Boldnesian
			Reason to Earn
		Prime Abord (br 1967)	Primera
			Homeward Bound
	Evastrive (b or br 1969)	Restless Native (gr 1960)	Native Dancer
			Next Move
		Avie (b 1963)	Gallant Man
			Evilone

   Super Entente, a lightly-made filly, cost 82,000 dollars as a yearling.   She is the fourth foal of Evastrive, both of whose successes came in small sprint races as a four-year-old.   Evastrive's three previous foals appear to have been the subject of an experiment in inbreeding, being by the high-class one- to two-mile winner Jean-Pierre, a half-brother to Evastrive's dam Avie. None of the three won. Avie was also a half-sister to a very good filly in Tona, winner of the Vineland Handicap over nine furlongs and the Alabama Stakes over a mile and a quarter, and a sister to the very useful mile winner Lesjo. Avie won only once from twenty-four starts, in a six-furlong maiden event at two, but she has an excellent record as a broodmare, producing four winners in addition to Evastrive, three of them stakes winners. One, Lord Avie, was the best two-year-old of 1980 and later won the Florida Derby, and another, Evastrive's brother Jolly Johu, was a smart performer at up to a mile and a half. Super Entente should stay the distance of her only classic engagement, the One Thousand Guineas, but she needs to make further improvement if she's to beat the likes of Ma Biche and Habibti. Even if she falls short of classic standard she seems most unlikely to stay a maiden for long. *J. W. Watts.*

SUPERFLUOUS 2 b.c. Track Spare 125–Super Jennie 80 (Stephen George 102) (1982 6g 6s) Mar 26; 7,000Y; useful-looking colt; first foal; dam won at up to 14.7f; behind in big fields of maidens at Newmarket and Doncaster in the autumn. *Sir Mark Prescott.* —

SUPER GRASS 3 b.g. Thatch 136–Pepi Image 111 (National) (1981 6.3fg 6fg 1982 6g 7f 8f* 8f⁴ 8f² 8fg³ 8d) neat, quite attractive ex-Irish gelding; good mover; won maiden race at Pontefract in May; ran creditably in handicap fifth start; suited by 1m on fast ground; blinkered nowadays; suited by enterprising riding tactics; game; sold to S. Mellor 10,500 gns Newmarket Autumn Sales. *M. Stoute.* 76

SUPERIOR QUALITY 2 ch.f. Star Appeal 133–Lavington 64 (Ratification 129) (1982 6g 7.2s 8g) Apr 16; 11,000Y; big, lengthy filly; half-sister to disappointing 3-y-o Incandesce (by Wolver Hollow) and to 4 winners, including 1976 2-y-o 7f winner Bushy Pieces (by Ribero); dam, placed twice at 1m, is half-sister to top sprinters So Blessed and Lucasland; little worthwhile form in the North, but showed promise on one occasion; trained first outing by P. Rohan; may be worth keeping an eye on. *D. Garraton.* 67

SUPERIOR SAINT 4 b.c. Welsh Saint 126–Superina 62 (Super Sam 124) (1981 8s 7fg³ 7g² 7d⁴ 8d³ 7g 8.3fg² 8fg 6fg⁴ 8fg 8s 8s 8d 1982 16g 12f² 17.1f³ 11fg⁴ 12f² 12f³ 17.1f² 12d⁴ 15.5g³) strong, compact, short-legged individual; poor maiden; evidently stays well; blinkered occasionally; sold 380 gns Doncaster September Sales. *R. Hannon.* 47 d

SUPER RIVER (USA) 2 b.c. Super Concorde 128–Christmas Wishes (Northern Dancer) (1302 5g³ 5f 5f¹ 5.3g* 5f¹ 5fg¹ 5g) Mar 10; $105,000Y, 055,000Y, all made colt; half-brother to a winner in USA by Tom Rolfe; dam, stakes-placed winner at up to 1m, is sister to Canadian Oaks winner Cool Mood; won poor maiden race at Brighton in June; not raced after July; blinkered final outing; exported to Malaysia. *J. Hindley.* 74

SUPER SIOUX 2 ch.f. Mandrake Major 122–Siouxsie 90 (Warpath 113) (1982 5g² 5v* 5f* 5fg² 6f* 5fg³ 6d² 6g* 6fg⁴) Mar 18; 1,050Y, 2,600Y; sturdy filly; second foal; sister to 1981 2-y-o 6f seller winner Commissar, subsequently a useful winner in Italy; dam ran only at 2 yrs when 6f winner; won a maiden race at Hamilton, 2 minor events at Catterick and a quite well-contested race at Chester; also ran very well when beaten only ½ length by Arrowood Bob in 6-runner Chesters Stakes at Newcastle in June; not seen out after July; well suited by 6f and may stay further; acts on any going; tough and consistent. *J. Berry.* 86

SUPER SOX 2 ch.c. No Loiterer 90–Pinzamber (Pinicola 113) (1982 5.1g 6fg³ 5fg² 5.1fg 5.1d*) May 21; neat colt; brother to a poor animal and half-brother to Zamber Boy (by Weepers Boy), winner of a 6f seller and in Hong Kong; dam winning hurdler; plater; bought in 1,200 gns after winning 6-runner event at Yarmouth in August; best form at 5f on soft surface; ran moderately in blinkers fourth start. *A. Jarvis.* 73

SUPER SUNRISE 3 b.c. Sagaro 133–Lay Aboard (Sing Sing 134) (1981 7fg⁴ 7fg* 8d* 8d 1982 12fg 12.3g* 12f 15g 12g⁴ 11.1fg⁴ 12d⁴ 13d 11g) 4,600F; rangy colt; fourth foal; dam never ran; stayed on well to account for Father Rooney in workmanlike style by 1½ lengths in Chester Vase in May; respectable fourth in September Stakes at Kempton (4½ lengths behind Critique) and Cumberland Lodge Stakes at Ascot (beaten 3 lengths by Lafontaine) on sixth and seventh outings; soundly beaten in Derby and Grand Prix de Paris third 111

Chester Vase—Super Sunrise returns to form

and fourth starts; suited by 1½m and should stay further; acts on a firm and a soft surface; game; racing in USA. *G. Hunter.*

SUPER SUNSHINE (USA) 2 ch.c. Nodouble–On With It (On-and-On) **86**
(1982 5fg 6f 7d* 7g 7v) Mar 7; shapely, attractive colt; half-brother to several winners in USA, including Society Hill (by Exclusive Native), a very useful performer at up to 1¼m; dam, half-sister to 4 stakes winners, won small races at up to 1m; won 15-runner maiden race at Chester in August; well beaten under 8-8 in nursery at Ascot in October on final outing; will stay at least 1m. *G. Hunter.*

SUPERTRIM 2 ch.g. Continuation 120–Sassanian Queen 71 (Sassafras 135) **—**
(1982 5f 5f³ 6f) June 4; lengthy gelding; second foal; brother to winning 3-y-o sprinter Transonic; dam won 5f seller at 2 yrs; no worthwhile form; last of 11 in July seller at Doncaster on final outing. *J. Hardy.*

SUPER WARRIOR 2 b.g. Roman Warrior 132–Super Princess 84 (Falcon **61**
131) (1982 5g* 5g 5f 5fg⁴ 6f³ 6fg 6g 5f⁴ 5g 5.1fg²) Apr 30; 410Y; sparely-made gelding; won 3-runner maiden race at Doncaster in March; raced mainly in sellers thereafter, on final appearance going down by 2 lengths to Harp Song at Yarmouth in August; stays 6f; yet to race on a soft surface; blinkered third and seventh outings. *K. Ivory.*

SUPREME CHALLENGER 2 br.c. Coded Scrap 90–Celtic Gwen 60 (Celtic **51**
Ash) (1982 5d 5d 5d) June 11; second foal; dam bad plater; poor form in back-end sellers. *T. Fairhurst.*

SUPREME HARMONY 2 gr.f. Music Boy 124–Complex Girl (Entangle- **—**
ment 118) (1982 8s 6s) June 2; 940 2-y-o; third reported foal; half-sister to a winner over hurdles; dam won over hurdles and fences; well beaten in late-season seller and maiden event. *R. Hoad.*

SURAJ 2 b.c. Pitskelly 122–Miss Wittington (Red God 128§) (1982 6fg 6f⁴ **81**
8fg 8.2s³) Mar 18; IR 34,000Y; small, leggy, lightly-made colt; brother to very useful 1981 2-y-o 5f winner My Lover and half-brother to several winners here and abroad; dam ran at 3 yrs in Ireland; showed ability in maiden races, on final outing 5½ lengths third of 11 to Equanaid at Hamilton in September; stays 1m. *P. Haslam.*

SUSANNA 4 b.f. Warpath 113–Susan McIntyre 67 (Double Jump 131) (1981 **—**
9f 10d* 9d³ 12d* 10.2g 1982 13fg) tall, lengthy, lightly-made filly; last on only outing of 1982; stays 1½m; acts on a soft surface. *T. Craig.*

SUSAN'S SUNSET 4 br.f. Welsh Saint 126–Honi Soit (Above Suspicion **59**
127) (1981 7d 7g 7f 8.3d* 7f* 8h⁴ 8.2fg³ 8f 8d 1982 7f 8g 7f² 7fg* 8fg² 7fg³ 7g 7f 7f⁴ 7g³ 7f 7g 7fg 6fg³ 7f 7g) neat filly; former plater; won handicap at

Goodwood in May comfortably and ran creditably most other starts; effective from 6f to 1m; probably acts on any going. *S. Woodman.*

SUSARMA (USA) 6 gr.h. Tudor Grey 119–Maui Moon (Swoon's Son) (1981 **112** 6d 5d 7fg 1982 5g⁴ 5s 5fg* 5fg*) strong, short-legged horse; good mover; very useful handicapper; disappointed in 3 races in Ireland in 1981 and was sold out of J. Oxx's stable only 2,900 gns Newmarket Autumn Sales; proved himself a tremendous bargain by returning to form to win handicaps at Chester (got up in last strides) and York (made virtually all) in May; put up a tremendous performance under a 10-lb penalty in David Dixon Sprint Trophy on latter course, beating Ponchielli by 1½ lengths; speedy and best at 5f; acts on any going; occasionally blinkered (wore them at York); sent to South Africa. *W. O'Gorman.*

SUSIE LYNAM 7 b.m. Hipster 101–Diana Carlos 64 (Don Carlos) (1981 — NR 1982 12f) of no account; dead. *R. Whitaker.*

SUSIE'S BABY 2 b.f. Balidar 133–Game Girl 85 (Abernant 142) (1982 5d 5s) Apr 30; 1,900F, 4,200Y; small filly; half-sister to numerous winners here and abroad, including brilliantly speedy 1972 2-y-o The Go-Between (by Runnymede); dam ran only at 2 yrs; behind in maiden races at Wolverhampton in August (trained by D. H. Jones) and Sandown in October. *R. Laing.*

SUSSEX QUEEN 3 ch.f. Music Boy 124–Counsel's Opinion 83 (Counsel 118) **67** (1981 5fg² 5fg* 6f² 1982 6fg³ 6fg 6f 6fg 7fg³ 8d⁴ 8.2s⁴ 7d) fair sort; quite a moderate handicapper; suited by 1m; acts on any going; retained 3,100 gns Newmarket December Sales. *W. Musson.*

SUTTON AIRBOURNE 3 ch.f. Beau of Paree–Full Swing 71 (Ballyciptic — 122) (1981 NR 1982 5fg 6f 10fg 5fg 6v 10s) third reported living foal; dam, half-sister to smart Lord Helpus, won over 5f at 2 yrs; tailed off in varied company, including selling. *J. Long.*

SUTTY'S GIRL 2 ch.f. Jolly Good 122–Pegs Promise (Tumble Wind) (1982 **52** 5s⁴ 5f² 5f³ 5f⁴ 6f 6s² 6fg* 6g 7f⁴ 8fg 8fg 7g 6s) Apr 21; 500Y; fair sort; second foal; dam well beaten in 2 starts at 2 yrs; plater; bought in 1,700 gns after landing the odds by ¾ length from Philpet at Carlisle in July; stays 7f; acts on any going; wears blinkers; sold Susan Piggott Bloodstock 1,450 gns Doncaster November Sales for export to Norway. *K. Stone.*

SUWAINA (USA) 2 ch.c. The Irish Lord–Gin Score (Ballymartial 117) (1982 **76** 6fg⁴ 7g⁴ 8d²) rather leggy colt; brother to a minor winner and half-brother to 3 others; dam won 6f claiming race; 1½ lengths second of 6 to Helewise in maiden race at Edinburgh in November; stays 1m; sent to Malaysia. *J. Long.*

SUZY MARIE 2 b.f. Swing Easy 126–Betony 76 (Sovereign Path 125) (1982 — 5s 5fg) May 9, third foal; half-sister to 1980 2-y-o 5f seller winner Steel Lady (by Continuation); dam 2-y-o 5f winner; tailed-off last in early-season maiden races at Haydock and Chester. *R. Hollinshead.*

SVALBARD (USA) 5 b.g. Rheingold 137–Brent's Queen (Crozier USA) (1981 **56** 12f 12s 10d 10.5g 10.5d⁴ 12g² 12.2g 1982 9f² 8f³ 10f² 9fg* 10g³) ex-French gelding; won handicap at Hamilton in June and was placed in varied company; stayed 1½m; acted on any going; blinkered once in 1980; apprentice ridden first 3 starts; dead. *A. Jarvis.*

SWALEDALE (USA) 2 gr.c. Al Hattab–Door Star (Stage Door Johnny) **76** (1982 7d³ 8f) May 3; $25,000Y; close-coupled colt; half-brother to several winners, including fairly useful stayer Dawn Johnny (by Grey Dawn II) and a stakes winner in USA by Dewan; dam unraced half-sister to smart stakes winner Strong Strong; showed ability in maiden races at Yarmouth in August and Brighton in September; will stay 1¼m; appears to act on any going. *M. Stoute.*

SWEEPY 4 b.g. Caro 133–Sweet Ambre (Sicambre 135) (1981 8s* 8fg 10g³ — 12s² 1982 10.2s) big ex-French gelding; half-brother to 2 winners in France, including French Amber (by Jim French), successful over middle distances; dam won over 11f in France; won newcomers race at Evry and was second in claimer at Chantilly in first half of 1981 (trained by A. Head at time); behind in a seller on last day of 1982 season, only outing on flat since; stays 1½m; acts on soft going and wasn't disgraced on a firm surface second start at 3 yrs; winner over hurdles. *A. Jarvis.*

SWEET ANDY 3 br.c. Ardoon 124–Black Honey 91 (March Past 124) (1981 **49** 5g⁴ 5s 5s⁴ 6g⁴ 6fg 7f 6fg 7g 8f 8.2fg 6fg 5s 1982 6s 6d 9f 7.6fg⁴ 8.2f 8f 7f 7.6d 10g 12f³) neat colt; poor maiden; seems to stay 1¼m; usually wears blinkers; has been bandaged on off-fore; suitable mount for an apprentice; retained 2,700 gns Doncaster January Sales. *J. Gilbert.*

Heinz '57' Phoenix Stakes, Leopardstown—Sweet Emma wins this Group I race on her first outing for four months

SWEET AS SUGAR 3 ch.c. The Minstrel 135–Cappella 98 (Crepello 136) **89** (1981 6fg³ 7f⁴ 1982 10.5d 10f 10fg* 10d⁴ 13.3f 10f) neat colt; showed a tendency to hang when accounting for Duke of Dollis by short head in ladies race at Lingfield in June; out of depth first 2 starts and had very stiff task on fifth; will stay 1½m; sometimes sweats up and has looked coltish in paddock. *P. Kelleway.*

Mrs J. Ramos' "Sweet Emma"

SWEET DIANA 3 b.f. Bivouac 114–Easter Tinkle (Hot Brandy 119) (1981 —
NR 1982 12d) leggy, narrow filly; first foal; dam winning hurdler; unquoted
when staying-on fifth of 15 to Royal Insight, beaten over 11 lengths, in apprentice
race at Pontefract in October. *A. Bailey.*

SWEET DIPPER 5 br.g. Golden Dipper 119–Sharp and Sweet (Javelot 124) —
(1981 NR 1982 7fg 7fg 7fg 8.3g 9g 7d) poor handicapper nowadays; stays
7f; probably acts on any going; has run creditably for an apprentice; blinkered
last 2 starts. *W. Wightman.*

SWEET ECSTASY 3 ch.f. Rarity 129–Acrasia 74 (Bold Lad, Ire 133) (1981 **79**
5g⁴ 6fg⁴ 6f 6fg* 6d 1982 8fg 7d 10fg 10.8fg 10g 10g 11.7s² 12.2s* 10s 12g*)
small, close-coupled filly; good walker; won handicaps at Warwick and Newmarket in October; suited by 1½m and will get further; acts very well on soft
going. *W. Wightman.*

SWEET EMMA 2 b.f. Welsh Saint 126–Gang Plank 84 (Tower Walk 130) **108**
(1982 5s* 5s* 5fg* 6d⁴ 6g)
The winner of the Heinz '57' Phoenix Stakes at Leopardstown in August,
Sweet Emma, was sold for 220,000 guineas at the Newmarket December Sales
and will be trained in 1983 by Peter Walwyn. The Phoenix Stakes—the only
five-furlong Group 1 race in Europe restricted to two-year-olds—didn't take
a lot of winning for a race of its status: of the first three in the betting Treasure
Trove had been placed on his two starts, including third in the Curragh Stakes,
whilst the favourite Najran had run once and finished second in a maiden race;
only Flame of Tara, unbeaten in three runs including in a listed race, the Irish
Chorus Stakes at Navan, was a winner. Sweet Emma was the only other
unbeaten runner but she drifted in the betting from 4/1 to 12/1. Her victories
in a maiden race at Naas and a minor event at the Curragh had been gained
over four months earlier on different going and she had since been sold out of
M. Connolly's stable. She looked very well, however, and won in good style,
showing enough speed to overcome her disadvantageous draw then quickening
clear over a furlong out to beat Najran by three lengths. On her two subsequent
starts Sweet Emma appeared to find six furlongs beyond her: in the Moyglare
Stud Stakes at the Curragh she weakened inside the last furlong to finish fourth,
three lengths behind Habibti, and in the Cheveley Park Stakes she was eighth
of nine behind Ma Biche after leading for over four furlongs.

			Aureole
	Welsh Saint	St Paddy	Edie Kelly
	(b 1966)	(b 1957)	Abernant
Sweet Emma		Welsh Way	Winning Ways
(b.f. Mar 19, 1980)		(gr 1954)	
	Gang Plank	Tower Walk	High Treason
	(ch 1972)	(b 1966)	Lorrikeet
		Hunea	Hornbeam
		(ch 1967)	Appeal

Sweet Emma cost 8,200 guineas as a yearling in Ireland. Her sire Welsh
Saint had several other speedy produce representing him in the latest season,
notably Brondesbury and Welwyn. Sweet Emma's family is not exclusively
a speedy one although her year-older half-sister Love Me Do (by He Loves Me)
is a modest six-furlong winner. Their dam Gang Plank, who showed ability
at two years but disappointed subsequently, is a half-sister to four winners
including three over jumps, the best of them the fairly useful three-mile chaser
Katmandu, also successful over a mile and a half on the flat. Gang Plank's
dam ran only three times but her grandam, a half-sister to the top-class stayer
Exar and to the dam of Wollow, won twice at a mile and a half. Sweet Emma,
a lengthy, attractive filly, appears to act on any going but put up her best
performance on a firm surface. She was officially rated the best Irish-trained
two-year-old filly and is a very useful sprinter, but with her apparent stamina
limitations and with her liability to a penalty for her Group 1 success she is
likely to prove hard to place successfully in the future. *K. Prendergast, Ireland.*

SWEETHEART 2 b.f. Reform 132–Cupid's Delight 84 (St Paddy 133) (1982 **70**
8f 8g⁴) Apr 16; 2,600Y; compact filly; fifth foal; half-sister to Norfolk Arrow
(by Blakeney), successful over 2m and a useful hurdler; dam, half-sister to
good stayer Rangong, won twice over 1½m; staying-on 3½ lengths fourth to
Secret Lightning in 8-runner maiden race at Edinburgh in October; will be
suited by 1¼m+. *I. Jordon.*

SWEET JAPONICA 3 b.f. Native Bazaar 122–Edlin (Monet 127) (1981 —
5fg 6fg³ 6g 7g 6f 6f⁴ 6f³ 6f 6s 8g 7g   1982 8g⁴ 7f 6fg 6f 10f) leggy, lightly-made
filly; poor plater; has been tried in blinkers; sold 400 gns Doncaster September
Sales. *W. Stubbs.*

SWEET JUDICIARY 2 b.f. Legal Eagle 126–Sharp and Sweet (Javelot 124) —
(1982 6g 5fg) May 17; small, close-coupled filly; half-sister to 3 winners,
notably very useful Sweet Reclaim (by Compensation); dam half-sister to
Sweet Revenge; in rear in minor event at Windsor in August and £3,400 race
at Goodwood in September. *W. Wightman.*

SWEET KOE 5 b.m. Tycoon II–Khotso (Alcide 136) (1981 NR 1982 10.2s)
poor novice hurdler; tailed off in apprentice event at Bath in October, first
outing on flat. *J. Brennan.*

SWEET LUCY 2 ch.f. Status Seeker–Hataway (High Hat 131) (1982 6g 42
5g³ 5f) May 4; IR 800F; half-sister to three 2-y-o winners, including 1976
Irish 7f and 7.9f winner Pat's Swallow (by My Swallow); dam stayed 1¼m;
bad plater; not raced after July. *J. Holt.*

SWEET MILLION 2 ch.f. Sweet Revenge 129–Cendrillon (Sound Track —
132) (1982 6s) Mar 23; 12,500Y; lengthy filly; half-sister to 2 winners by
Laser Light, including very useful 1979 2-y-o 5f performer Lucinda Light;
dam poor Irish maiden; last of 11 in Blue Seal Stakes at Ascot in September.
R. Sheather.

SWEET MONDAY 4 b.c. Sweet Revenge 129–Solly Graham 82 (Romulus 111
129) (1981 6g² 6f 7s⁴ 6s² 6g   1982 5s 6d⁴ 5fg 6f² 6f 5g⁴ 5f 5g 6g* 6f 6g 5d)
lengthy colt; ran best race when chasing home Jester in Duke of York Stakes
in May, racing prominently throughout and going down by 1½ lengths; by no
means disgraced in top company on several other occasions and landed odds
when facing simple task in small race at Brighton in August; suited by 6f;
acts on any going; usually sweats up; didn't run particularly well in blinkers
final start. *J. Holt.*

SWEET REMARK 2 ch.f. On Your Mark 125–Judy O'Grady (Whistler 129) 81
(1982 5g* 5g² 5f² 5g³ 5.1f²) Mar 1; IR 3,700F, 2,500Y; sturdy, compact
filly; half-sister to 6f winner Grey Trilby (by Don II) and 3-y-o 7f winner
Jennyjo (by Martinmas); dam never ran; won maiden auction event at Catterick
in March; not raced after July; acts on firm going; blinkered third and final
starts. *W. O'Gorman.*

SWEET SATISFACTION 3 ch.f. Sweet Revenge 129–Pendula 76 (Tamerlane 48
128) (1981 5g 5g 6f 6g 6g³ 7.6s   1982 8fg 8f 5fg 6g 6g³ 7g² 7fg* 7d³ 7s) small
filly; plater; attracted no bid after winning at Newmarket in August; stays
7f; acts on a firm and a soft surface; blinkered third and fourth starts; suitable
mount for an apprentice; sold to Norsk Jockey Club 2,200 gns Doncaster
November Sales. *C. Spares.*

SWEET SAVAGE 2 ch.f. Gay Fandango 132–Cronk Bourne (Brigadier 74
Gerard 144) (1982 7fg 5f⁴ 6s) Apr 5; IR 11,500Y; first foal; dam won over
7f at 2 yrs in Ireland; 2 lengths fourth of 13 to Babybarn Sparkle in maiden
race at Catterick in September; should stay beyond 5f. *N. Callaghan.*

SWEET SIDE 3 b.f. Quayside 124–Sweet Delight (Klairon 131) (1981 5d* 96
5s 6v³ 5fg 5fg 5f 6d³ 5s²   1982 7s 8g 6f 7d 6fg 5g* 8d 8g 6v) IR 560F; small,
lightly-made filly; second foal; dam never ran; returned to form when accounting
for Americus by a neck in Philips Electrical Stakes (Handicap) at the Curragh
in August; well beaten most other starts, including in Goffs Irish 1,000 Guineas
at the Curragh and Cork and Orrery Stakes at Royal Ascot; best at sprint
distances; needs some give in the ground; sold 45,000 gns Goffs November Sales.
M. Quaid, Ireland.

SWEET SLEW (USA) 2 b.f. Seattle Slew–Trick Chick (Prince John) (1982 96
6fg 6g²) Apr 3; $300,000Y; lengthy, good-looking filly; good mover; half-
sister to several winners, notably On The Sly (by Roi Dagobert), a high-class
winner at up to 1½m; dam unraced sister to smart filly Fairway Fun and half-
sister to very smart animals Filiberto and White Star Line; third favourite,
ran as though needing further when 4 lengths second of 19 to What Lake in
maiden race at Newmarket in September; sure to win a similar event over
1m+, and could make up into quite a useful 3-y-o. *J. Sutcliffe.*

SWEET SMILE 2 b.f. Native Bazaar 122–Flaretown 63 (Town Crier 119) 71
(1982 5d 5d* 5d) Apr 28; lightly-made filly; first foal; dam, out of half-sister

to Cajun, was third over 5f and 6f at 2 yrs; attracted no bid after winning 17-runner seller at Catterick in October by 2 lengths from La Di Da; promises to stay 6f. *S. Matthews.*

SWEET SOLICITOR 3 ch.g. Legal Eagle 126–Sharp and Sweet (Javelot — 124) (1981 5g 5.8f 7g 8d 8s 6g 1982 5f 7.6f 10.8fg 10.1g 10.1g) smallish, workmanlike gelding; good mover; behind in varied company; blinkered first and fourth starts. *W. Wightman.*

SWEET SURPRISE (HOL) 4 b.f. Vesins-Fiery (Firestreak 125) (1981 — NR 1982 10.1d 10fg⁴) poor form over hurdles; staying-on fourth in minor event at Brighton in July, better effort; sold 750 gns Ascot September Sales. *D. Elsworth.*

SWEET VENGEANCE 4 b.f. Reliance II 137–Maddelena (Tudor Melody — 129) (1981 8s 10s 1982 8fg 10.1fg 10f 10.1d 10.1fg 8.3g) poor plater; blinkered last 2 starts. *C. James.*

SWELL SOUND 2 b.c. Undulate–Clatter 67 (Songedor 116) (1982 7s) Mar — 10; fourth foal; half-brother to 5f winner Burglar Tip (by Burglar); dam placed over 5f at 2 yrs; tenth of 12 in minor event at Chepstow in October. *M. McCormack.*

SWIFTBLADE 3 br.f. Tachypous 128–Swordblade 84 (Pall Mall 132) (1981 — 5.1f 5fg 7g 7h 7d 6g 1982 7fg) compact filly; in rear in varied company, including selling; has been tried in blinkers. *C. Mackenzie.*

SWIFT ENCOUNTER 3 b.c. Owen Dudley 121–Pop Gun 85 (King's Troop **52** 118) (1981 5g 7fg 7g 7fg 7g 8d⁴ 8d 1982 11s² 10d 11.7g 13.8f⁴ 14g 13.8f⁴ 16.5f) small colt; not the best of movers; plating-class maiden; stays 1¾m; suited by some give in the ground; blinkered last 2 starts. *R. Williams.*

SWIFTFOOT 3 b.f. Run The Gantlet–Whitefoot 108 (Relko 136) (1981 **119** 7.2f* 8s⁴ 1982 12.3fg* 12f 12fg* 12fg² 14.6g* 14s³)

In Swiftfoot the once-underrated stallion Run The Gantlet had another good stayer besides Ardross and another good filly besides April Run representing him in Europe in 1982; the odds against his being so well represented over here in future have been increased considerably by his repatriation to the United States from Ireland in 1980. Like Ardross, Swiftfoot was essentially

Irish Guinness Oaks, the Curragh—Swiftfoot makes all to beat Irish One Thousand Guineas winner Prince's Polly

Park Hill Stakes, Doncaster—Swiftfoot is well on top; Sa-Vegas (stripes) and Sing Softly follow her home

a stayer though quite capable of holding her own in top races at a mile and a half. She was the best of a handful of top fillies in this country to tackle long distances during the season and one of the best to tackle a mile and a half, similar to, though not the equal of, the stable's previous winner of the Park Hill Stakes, Irish Guinness Oaks and Cheshire Oaks, Shoot A Line who also won the Ribblesdale Stakes and Yorkshire Oaks.

Coincidentally both Swiftfoot and Shoot A Line ran badly in the Oaks after a fine trial at Chester. Swiftfoot won a slowly-run race there in good style by three lengths from Epithet, making all. Passed over in favour of Cut Above's sister Cut Loose by stable-jockey Carson, Swiftfoot finished last of thirteen behind Time Charter at Epsom, six places behind Cut Loose. Neither filly served the stable in the Ribblesdale—that task went to Main Sail —and Swiftfoot didn't race again until the middle of July, in the Irish Oaks at the Curragh where she faced the Goffs Irish One Thousand Guineas winner Prince's Polly, the Italian Guineas winner Rosananti and seven others with lesser form, of whom Santa Roseanna had been a useful staying two-year-old in Ireland. Since the Irish Guineas Prince's Polly had won the ten-furlong Pretty Polly Stakes and seemed certain to prove very difficult to beat, especially as she was bred to be suited by a mile and a half. Swiftfoot, second favourite to Prince's Polly, led all the way. She was always in command, too, and when Prince's Polly came away from the others to begin her challenge a quarter of a mile out Swiftfoot lengthened her stride so that her main rival never quite got to grips. At the end Swiftfoot was still striding out well, three lengths up on Prince's Polly and six on the third-placed Rosananti. The result provoked a stewards' inquiry into Swiftfoot's improved form compared with that at Epsom. Her trainer said that at Epsom she had been going well to the straight when Starkey, her jockey, reported she had choked up. The jockey, knowing that something was wrong, had eased her. Subsequent to the race blood samples had been taken which, in common with those taken from several horses in the yard, proved abnormal. The trainer was at a loss to explain why she had choked, as she had never done so before or since. Swiftfoot had worked well and was fancied for the Irish Oaks. The stewards accepted the explanation.

As so often Hern's stable housed a powerful string of middle-distance fillies. It provided three of the seven runners for the Yorkshire Oaks at York in August: Swiftfoot ridden by Carson, the Princess of Wales's Stakes winner Height of Fashion ridden by Starkey, and Cut Loose ridden by former stable-jockey Mercer; each had a chance of winning on her best form. Height of Fashion solved the intriguing question of which of several possible candidates in the field would make the running when she quickly took over in front followed by Swiftfoot. The race developed into a test primarily of stamina and courage. After Height of Fashion gave way to Swiftfoot early in the straight the latter had to face a challenge from her other five opponents as she battled to hang on. Never much up, Swiftfoot still held the lead running into the last furlong, strongly pressed by Awaasif and Dish Dash. The three continued to fight it out to the line, Swiftfoot being headed a hundred and fifty yards from home and eventually having to settle for second place, a neck behind Awaasif.

It was as plain as a pikestaff that Swiftfoot would be suited by a longer distance; so would the winner, come to that, and it was impossible to name two better qualified to contest the Park Hill Stakes three weeks hence, a race run over the St Leger course at Doncaster sometimes called the fillies' Leger. In the absence of Awaasif, who was sent for the Prix Vermeille, the field that faced Swiftfoot in the Park Hill was not a strong one—only five other runners, only Sing Softly, Tants and Sa-Vegas with a genuine chance. Swiftfoot started at 6/4 on. Carson's duty lay in making every yard count. There was no need to suppose that he wouldn't recognise this, of course: he's a sound tactician and he knew the filly as well as anyone. Swiftfoot dictated the gallop, a fairly slow one at first quickening gradually as the race developed, with Tants throwing down the gauntlet early in the straight. Tants pressed hard for two furlongs then began to fade. By now Swiftfoot had got into top gear and she was much too good for the others; the longer the race the further she would have won, and in the end Carson eased her by at least a length in winning by a length and a half from Sa-Vegas.

After this, there was a suggestion that Swiftfoot would have been better employed in Saturday's St Leger. Perhaps she would. Had she been started for the race after winning the Park Hill she would have been one of the favourites, that's certain. As things turned out Swiftfoot would surely have stood more chance of beating Touching Wood at that time than when she did meet him in October in the Jefferson Smurfit Memorial Irish St Leger, for she ran a long way below her best at the Curragh, dropping out to a modest third after failing to get on terms with Touching Wood in the first two furlongs of the straight. The way Father Rooney went by her, this couldn't have been the Swiftfoot we had come to appreciate. Perhaps she was over the top, but more likely the soft going was against her; she had shown all her form on a sound surface.

Swiftfoot might be bred to win a Park Hill Stakes. Her great grandam Mitrailleuse won it, so did a fairly close relative Reload, who was out of Fusil, a half-sister to Swiftfoot's dam Whitefoot. Whitefoot herself never had the opportunity of running in the race, for she was retired after finishing fifth in the Irish Oaks; earlier she'd finished a good eighth in the Oaks, handicapped by a slipped saddle, and won the Musidora Stakes at York. While not so successful at stud as Fusil (dam also of the One Thousand Guineas winner Full Dress II and the Park Hill runner-up Boulette), she has produced five other winners—Whitey (by Sassafras), Overlook (by Royal Palace), Santarelle

Lord Rotherwick's "Swiftfoot"

(by Jim French), Barrow (by Moulton) and the useful six-furlong winner Neenah
(by Bold Lad, Ire). Mitrailleuse was the dam of eleven winners, most of whom
were stayers; their number included that stout-hearted gelding Rally, a full
brother to Swiftfoot's grandam Mitraille, who between 1956 and 1958 won two
Brown Jack Stakes and a Queen Alexandra Stakes.

			Tom Rolfe	Ribot
Swiftfoot (b.f. 1979)	Run The Gantlet (b 1968)		(b 1962)	Pocahontas II
		First Feather (ch 1963)	First Landing
			Quill
		Relko	Tanerko
	Whitefoot (ch 1967)		(b 1960)	Relance III
		Mitraille (b 1953)	Big Game
			Mitrailleuse

Swiftfoot has been retired and visits Be My Guest. A well-made, attractive
filly, she was well suited by a test of stamina and forcing tactics, the two things
related, and top-of-the-ground conditions. She was genuine and consistent.
R. Hern.

SWIFT PALM 5 b.g. Some Hand 119–March Stone 84 (March Past 124) **67**
(1981 8s 8d 8d* 10g⁴ 8g* 10fg 8fg³ 10s³ 12.2s 8s³ 8g* 1982 8f³ 8g 8d³ 8f⁴ 8.3g²
8fg 8d² 9g 8.2s 8.2s⁴ 8s) lengthy gelding; quickened clear 1¼f out in apprentice
handicap at Ascot in September on seventh start, but drifted right under pressure
and was caught on line by Lion City; ran respectably afterwards (given too much
to do next time); stays 1¼m; acts on any going but is ideally suited by some give
in the ground; suitable mount for a boy; very slowly away second outing.
P. Cundell.

SWIFT SERVICE 2 ch.c. Captain James 123–November (Firestreak 125) (1982 **107**
8g⁴ 10g²) Feb 18; 11,000F, 16,000Y; smallish, fair sort; half-brother to 2
winners, including useful 7f and 9f winner Brands Hatch (by Track Spare);
dam of no account; unquoted, ran on strongly after getting well behind early
on when 2¾ lengths fourth of 18 behind Holy Spark in maiden race at Newmarket
in October; excellent ½-length second to John French in £8,300 race on same
course later in the month; will stay 1¼m; sure to win a race. *R. Williams.*

SWIFT TO CONQUER 2 b.f. Solinus 130–Wilhelmina (Proud Chieftain **79**
122) (1982 6g² 6d* 6fg³) Apr 12; 10,000F, IR 12,000Y; smallish, active
sort; half-sister to numerous winners, including very useful sprinter Burlington
Boy (by Whistling Wind) and useful 5f to 7f winner Dunmurry Boy (by Tudor
Music); dam stayed 9f; won 9-runner minor event at Chester in August; will
be suited by 7f. *R. Williams.*

SWIFT WING 3 b.f. Malinowski 123–Mear-Aille (Hard Ridden 131) (1981 **95**
6g 6f* 7h* 7.2fg⁴ 8g* 1982 10fg 10f³ 12.2g³ 10f²) quite attractive filly;
good mover; placed most starts, on final one being caught close home and
beaten a head by Even Banker in 9-runner handicap at Kempton in July;
seems to stay 1½m; yet to race on a soft surface; game and consistent; sent to
USA. *J. Dunlop.*

SWINGIN' COWBOY (USA) 2 b.c. Parade of Stars–Tara Blue (Bold Bidder) **92**
(1982 5f⁴ 6f* 6fg* 7f² 7fg 7fg 8.2d 8.2v) Mar 2; $65,000Y; strong, deep-girthed,
attractive colt; brother to useful American stakes winner Paradin' Cowboy,
and half-brother to 2 winners; dam ran 8 times unplaced; successful in small
races at Carlisle in June and July; also ran respectably under top weight in
nurseries at York in August and Nottingham in September; best form at up
to 7f; suited by a sound surface; blinkered fifth and final outings. *S. Norton.*

SWINGING BABY 3 br.f. Swing Easy 126–Hi-Baby 102 (High Treason **62**
126) (1981 5s⁴ 5d 5fg³ 5g² 5d 5d² 6d 1982 5v³ 5g* 5f² 6f⁴ 6f 6h³ 5fg 5s 7d)
lengthy, useful sort; won modest maiden race at Pontefract in April; in frame
in 3 handicaps afterwards; stays 6f; acts on any going; dwelt badly eighth
outing. *J. Fitzgerald.*

SWINGING MOON 3 ch.c. Swing Easy 126–Moon Gem (Moontrip) (1981 **63**
5d 5fg 7.6s 7d³ 1982 7fg 10.1fg 12f⁴ 10g⁴ 12v³ 12.2s⁴ 14s³) lengthy, shallow-
girthed colt; plating-class maiden; stays 1¾m; acts on any going; blinkered
last 3 starts; trained part of season by P. Cole. *A. Ingham.*

SWINGING REBEL 4 br.c. Swing Easy 126–Rebecca (Quorum 126) (1981 **84**
10d 10.1v³ 8.2s 8d⁴ 10fg 8.3fg* 7fg* 7g⁴ 7g* 7g* 7s 8s 1982 8fg 8g 7f 7f* 7g
7g* 8.2f 7f² 7s³) lengthy colt; won handicaps at Goodwood in July and Brighton

in August after having a soft palate operation; ran easily his best other races when narrowly beaten at Brighton and Ascot in September; has run respectably over 1¼m but seems best at 7f; acts on any going; usually held up; inconsistent. *N. Vigors.*

SWINGING RHYTHM   4 ch.g. Swing Easy 126–Soft Chinook (Hitting Away)   **75**
(1981 6fg 6d³ 6s 5d 7fg 8fg 7fg 6fg² 6s 6g   1982 7s 6d² 6g 7g⁴ 7f 6f 7f² 7g² 6s⁴ 7s² 7d) lengthy gelding; good mover; beat Never So Lucky by a short head in handicap at Salisbury in August but wandered in last furlong and placings were subsequently reversed; second twice at York afterwards; stays 7f; acts on any going; often sweats up and fails to impress in paddock. *J. Holt.*

SWINGING TRIO   6 ch.g. Swing Easy 126–Algarve 94 (Alcide 136)   (1981   —
8d 8d 7g 8fg   1982 12fg 8.3fg)   poor handicapper nowadays; stays 7f; acts on any going; blinkered once. *W. R. Williams.*

SWING SO EASY   2 b.f. Tudor Rhythm 112–Grande Merci 82 (Gratitude   —
130)   (1982 8s)   Mar 17; useful-looking filly; half-sister to 2 winners, including Queen Elizabeth II Stakes winner Buzzards Bay (by Joshua); dam, half-sister to very smart sprinter Jukebox, stayed 1m; no show in 18-runner maiden race at Wolverhampton in October. *H. Collingridge.*

SWING TO ME   2 br.c. Swing Easy 126–Françoise 109 (French Beige 127)   **85**
(1982 6fg³ 7f)   Mar 26; 2,500F, 10,000Y; big, rangy colt; half-brother to fair 1977 2-y-o 7f winner French Swallow (by My Swallow); dam middle-distance performer; 6 lengths fifth of 15 behind St Boniface in maiden event at Newmarket in July, better effort; stays 7f. *C. Brittain.*

SWORD EDGE   5 ch.g. Sharpen Up 127–Coulter Belle 80 (Quorum 126)   (1981   —
12s 8f   1982 13.8f 16fg)   compact gelding; poor form, including in a seller; has worn bandages. *W. C. Watts.*

SYCAMORE SAGA   2 b.f. Sagaro 133–Phoenix Rose 85 (Frankincense 120)   —
(1982 7s 9s)   Mar 9; lengthy filly; first foal; beaten well over sellers over 9f and 10.6f; in rear in £3,700 event at York and maiden race at Redcar late in season. *M. Jarvis.*

SYDETZKY   2 br.c. Radetzky 123–Sygnome 53 (Precipice Wood 123)   (1982   **65**
5g⁴ 5d 6fg 7g 7f 7g 7g 8g 8d 10.2s)   Mar 16; useful-looking colt; second foal; dam poor staying maiden; moderate plater; probably stays 1¼m; blinkered fifth and last 2 starts. *C. Brittain.*

SYLLOGIZER   3 gr.g. Godswalk 130–French Bird (Guersant 129)   (1981 6g   —
6fg 6f 5.1d 5v   1982 6g 5f 7g)   close-coupled gelding; soundly beaten in maiden races and a seller; has twice worn blinkers. *F. Durr.*

SYLVAN BARBAROSA   2 ch.c. Native Bazaar 122–The Silver Darling 75   **95**
(John Splendid 116)   (1981 5fg³ 5g⁴ 5s⁴ 6g* 6f⁴ 5fg² 6fg* 5f² 5d 5g 6g   1982 5f³ 6fg² 5f³ 6fg* 5fg 5g 6f 5.6g 6g)   quite well-made colt; backed from 10/1 to 11/2 when keeping on well to beat Travel On by 2 lengths in valuable 8-runner Leisure Stakes at Lingfield in June; ran creditably in King's Stand Stakes at Royal Ascot later in month, keeping on to be over 6 lengths sixth of 14 to Fearless Lad; effective at 5f and 6f; best form on a sound surface. *P. Mitchell.*

SYLVAN DANDY   2 ro.c. North Stoke 130–Janabelle 101 (Gentle Art 121)   **60**
(1982 5f 7g 7fg 7g 6s 5v)   May 1; 9,000F, 4,100Y; close-coupled colt; half-brother to 2 winners, including sprinter Kelso Belle (by Town Crier); only poor form; blinkered when last of 18 under top weight in selling nursery at Lingfield in October on final appearance; sold 740 gns Newmarket Autumn Sales. *P. Mitchell.*

SYLVAN NAVARRO   2 b.c. Raga Navarro 119–Tinsel 95 (Right Boy 137)   **87**
(1982 5f 5g 5g³ 5f² 5fg⁴ 5g³ 5f 6g⁴ 7fg 6g 7v 6s⁴)   May 1; 8,200F, 8,600Y; sturdy, useful-looking colt; half-brother to 4 winners here and abroad, including very useful sprinter Sparkling Boy (by Comedy Star); dam genuine 5f to 7f handicapper; showed ability most outings; top weight when creditable fourth of 8 to Leslie Stone in nursery at Windsor in July on eighth; stays 7f; blinkered final appearance. *P. Mitchell.*

SYLVIA'S SECRET   4 b.f. Most Secret 119–Princess Chesnut (King Chesnut   —
120)   (1981 8g 7f 7f³ 8fg 5g   1982 5f 6f 6fg)   small filly; plater; soundly beaten in 1982; suited by 6f; sold 680 gns Doncaster August Sales. *A. Smith.*

SYMPATIQUE   4 b.c. Simbir 130–Fun of the Fair (Skymaster 126)   (1981   — §
10d² 8s 10.1f³ 8f⁴ 10f⁴ 11.5d² 12f 11.5g² 10d*   1982 12fg² 10fg⁴ 12fg² 16s 12.2s)

strong, good sort; moves well; second in handicaps at Lingfield in May (hung badly) and June; stays at least 1½m (off course over 3 months before running respectably over 2m); seems to act on any going but is well suited by some give underfoot; not the most genuine of animals. *N. Gaselee.*

SYNCOPATE 6 br.m. Highland Melody 112–Manipulation 90 (Appiani II — 128) (1981 10.2d 10v* 12.5s*(dis) 12v³ 12.3d 12.5g* 12d³ 12d² 12s* 12g⁴ 13g⁴ 12.2g 15g 12v 1982 12g 18.4fg 12f 12.2f) neat mare; had a good season in 1981; lightly raced in 1982 and didn't recover her form; stays 13f; acts on any going, but is probably best with some give underfoot nowadays; good mount for an apprentice; very tough. *A. Smith.*

SZYMANOWSKI 3 ch.g. Malinowski 123–Ismene II (Silnet 131) (1981 7g⁴ — 1982 10s 10f 11.5g 10g) leggy ex-English gelding; showed ability only start at 2 yrs but has been well beaten since; should stay middle distances; blinkered final outing; trained by J. Hindley first 2 starts; sold 1,300 gns Goffs November Sales. *C. Collins, Ireland.*

T

TABASCO ROYAL 2 b.g. Royal Blend 117–Pensong 84 (Pendragon) (1982 **53** 5f 5f⁴ 5f 7fg 8.2fg⁴ 8fg 7.2s) June 4; rather leggy non-thoroughbred gelding; half-brother to 2 winners, including 6f to 1½m winner Streets Ahead (by Ovid); dam stayed 1m; quite a moderate plater; will be suited by 1¼m+ ; sweated up and very unruly fourth start. *J. Wilson.*

TABASCO STAR 2 ch.c. Grundy 137–Laxmi 108 (Palestine 133) (1982 5f 5f **54** 7fg 8s) May 1; 30,000Y; strong, short-coupled colt; half-brother to 1,000 Guineas winner Enstone Spark (by Sparkler); dam best at 5f; poor form in maiden races; blinkered third outing. *I. Balding.*

TABERNACLE 9 b.g. Manacle 123–Tabarka (Dicta Drake 126) (1981 10.2s 13fg — 9g 8fg 1982 8g 12fg 16g) poor plater; stays 1¼m; seems to act on any going. *K. Bridgwater.*

TACHYROS 2 b. or br.g. Tachypous 128–Russellia (Red God 128§) (1982 7g 7g) — Mar 25; 5,200Y; half-brother to 2 winners, including 7f and 1m winner Gallea (by Prince de Galles); dam placed at up to 10.5f in France; out of first 9 in maiden races at Newmarket and Yarmouth in August. *M. Ryan.*

TACTFUL BOY 2 b.c. Tachypous 128–Baggage 86 (Zeus Boy 121) (1982 6fg — 6g 5d) Mar 22; small colt; half-brother to 1981 2-y-o 7f winner Allan Wells (by Queen's Hussar) and fair sprinter Bunny Boy (by Right Boy); dam stayed 1m; in rear in minor events and a seller. *T. Craig.*

TACTIC 2 ch.c. Tachypous 128–Lively Lassie (Never Say Die 137) (1982 7g **83** 7fg 7d 8.2s³) May 25; 18,000Y; small colt; half-brother to a winning plater and a winner in Italy (both by Sweet Revenge); dam lightly-raced half-sister to Roan Rocket; 6 lengths third of 12 to Mitilini in maiden race at Haydock in October; suited by 1m; acts on soft going. *E. Eldin.*

TACTIQUE (FR) 2 ch.f. Anne's Pretender 124–Torre Blanca (Sailor) (1982 6fg) — Feb 13; 100,000 francs Y (approx £9,000); lengthy filly; half-sister to Irish 1½m winner Torestel (by Reliance II); dam French 1¼m winner; eleventh of 14 in valuable newcomers race at Ascot in June; likely to need 1¼m+. *P. Cole.*

TAFFY GIRL 2 b.f. Welsh Saint 126–Trixie Girl 86 (Bold Lad, Ire 133) (1982 **67** 5g 5fg 5d³ 5fg 5fg) Mar 31; lightly-made filly; half-sister to 3 winners abroad, notably Italian St Leger winner Lotar (by Sassafras); dam 2-y-o 5f performer; plating-class maiden; disappointing favourite at Beverley in July on third outing; blinkered final start; sold BBA (Italia) 6,800 gns Newmarket Autumn Sales. *H. T. Jones.*

TAFFY JONES 3 br.c. Welsh Pageant 132–Shallow Stream 100 (Reliance II **80** 137) (1981 7d 1982 8.2fg 8f² 10fg³ 10fg³ 10.2f³ 10f³ 11.7f* 12.2f 13.8f³ 12s²) good-bodied colt; won maiden race at Bath in July; probably stays 1¾m; acts on any going; blinkered sixth start; suitable mount for an inexperienced rider. *M. McCormack.*

TAGIO 2 b.g. Martinmas 128–Harford Belle 97 (Track Spare 125) (1982 6fg) **68** p Apr 27; IR 8,400F, 11,500Y; quite attractive gelding; third foal; brother to fair 1980 2-y-o 5f and 6f winner Mrs Palmer, and half-brother to American 3-y-o winner Fort Guard (by Home Guard); dam won over 5f at 2 yrs; 7 lengths fifth of 15 in newcomers race at Goodwood in September; gelded subsequently; likely to improve. *G. Hunter.*

TAI FAI WOOD   2 gr.f. Dragonara Palace 115–Meadow Wood (Meadow Court 129)   (1982 7f 5fg)   Apr 16; 2,700F, 2,000Y; light-framed filly; showed a great deal of temperament but no ability; unseated rider in paddock on second outing and at start when withdrawn on third (blinkered); sold 380 gns Ascot December Sales. *R. Ward.*   — §

TAI FU KWAI   3 gr.g. Sagaro 133–Rebecca ƒ(Quorum 126)   (1981 6fg 7f4 7fg 6g3 7g 7.2v2 8g   1982 10s 9f* 10f* 11g* 12h 11.7d4 10.8fg2 10fg3 10.1d3 10g)   compact gelding; won seller at Ripon (bought in 3,000 gns) in May; subsequently showed himself better than a plater, winning handicaps at Beverley and Hamilton; will stay 1¾m; acts on any going; best in blinkers; suited by waiting tactics; changed hands 10,500 gns Newmarket Autumn Sales. *C. Williams.*   71

TAI LEE   3 gr.g. No Mercy 126–Cansanta 96 (Canisbay 120)   (1981 5d4 5fg4 6g2 6g 6fg 7fg 5g 6s   1982 6s 6g3 6f 7fg2 7f4 8.5f2 8f 8g 9g* 9fg4 10f 10g2 10d2 12fg* 11s2 12.2s3)   sparely-made gelding; successful in handicaps at Hamilton in July and Beverley in September; beaten in 2 sellers earlier; stays 1½m; acts on any going; blinkered twice at 2 yrs; sold 6,800 gns Newmarket Autumn Sales. *R. Williams.*   67

TAI SING KUNG   3 b.f. Hot Spark 126–Miss Kung Fu 70 (Caliban 123)   (1981 NR   1982 10s 12f 12fg)   720Y; useful sort; first foal; dam won 7f seller; in rear in varied company. *C. Williams.*   —

TAI WING WAH   2 b.f. Music Boy 124–Resurgence (Runnymede 123)   (1982 5s* 5g2 5f3 5g 7s)   Apr 13; 6,000Y; rather lightly-made filly; half-sister to 3 winners, including 1981 2-y-o 7f winner Return To Power (by Relko) and very useful Reside (by Quayside), successful at up to 1½m; dam lightly raced and no sign of ability; won maiden race at Nottingham in April by 4 lengths; well beaten in autumn nurseries on last 2 outings after absence of over 4 months; sold BBA 3,000 gns Newmarket Autumn Sales. *R. Williams.*   70

TAJWIND   2 b.f. Windjammer (USA)—Taj Lady 77 (Prince Taj 123)   (1982 including 6g* 6g4 8v*)   Apr 21; IR 27,000 Y; half-sister to very useful 5f to 1m winner Lady Tan (by Red God); dam, placed twice over 5f at 2 yrs, is grand-daughter of Molecomb Stakes winner Crawley Beauty; put up a very useful effort when winning 14-runner Criterium Femminile at Rome in November by 3½ lengths from English filly Coming And Going with French challenger Little Meadow a neck back in third; had earlier been successful in 3 other races at Rome, the Premio Marguerite Vernaut, Premio Aurora and Criterium di Roma, making all to justify favouritism by 4 lengths in last named, second favourite for Criterium Nazionale at Milan in September but ran disappointingly to finish 6 lengths fourth of 5 to Faith Guest; well suited by 1m; a good filly who is sure to win more valuable races. *A. Botti, Italy.*   112 ?

TAKE A CARD   3 ch.g. Tachypous 128–Cigarette Case 89 (Faberge II 121)   (1981 6g4 7d   1982 7f*)   rangy, useful sort; good mover; not seen out after landing odds in maiden race at Leicester in April; will be suited by 1m+; acts on firm going. *M. Stoute.*   80

TAKEAFENCE   3 ch.g. My Swallow 134–Set Piece 69 (Firestreak 125)   (1981 10s4 10d 12g3 11.7g2 14f 16f 14g 12fg   1982 10.2s)   workmanlike gelding; disappointing maiden; stays 1½m. *R. Hannon.*   —

TAKE A STEP   2 b.f. Ashmore 125–Truly Thankful 111 (Majority Blue 126)   (1982 7v*)   half-sister to 1981 Irish 2-y-o 6f winner Toast of the Town (by Prince Tenderfoot); dam won at up to 6.5f, including Queen Mary Stakes; shaped very well when easily winning 17-runner maiden race at the Curragh in October by 1½ lengths from Clouded Issue, the pair 8 lengths clear; will stay at least 1m; sure to make a useful 3-y-o; entered in Oaks. *D. O'Brien, Ireland.*   96 p

TAKEN FOR GRANTED   4 b.g. Martinmas 128–Romanee Conti (Will Somers 114§)   (1981 10g3 10s 8fg* 8g3 8v* 8s   1982 8.3fg 8g)   tall, lengthy gelding; fair performer as a 3-y-o; stays 1¼m; acts on a firm surface but clearly revels in the mud. *R. Carter.*   —

TAKE TO FLIGHT   2 ch.c. Vitiges 132–Powerscourt (Salvo 129)   (1982 7fg 7d 8g4)   May 15; 12,000Y; rather sparely-made colt; half-brother to several winners in Germany; dam, daughter of very useful 2-y-o Kew, won over 1½m and 13f in Ireland; 4¾ lengths fourth of 11 to Triple Jump in £2,900 seller at Newmarket in October, final outing and first indication of merit; capable of winning a seller. *J. Sutcliffe.*   69

TAKHOS 3 b.c. Tachypous 128–Ribofleur 74 (Ribero 126) (1981 6fg 6g⁴ 7g **65**
5g 5fg⁴ 1982 7g² 7g³ 10f 8.2f⁴ 8.2fg³ 9g² 9.4fg 8.2g² 8fg 8fg) tall colt; good
mover; runner-up in maiden races in Scotland; bred to stay 1¼m but was well
beaten when tried at trip; twice blinkered and possibly none too genuine; dead.
D. Smith.

TAKING SILK (USA) 3 ch.f. Good Counsel–Yetive (Ribot 142) (1981 NR —
1982 8s) $65,000Y; half-sister to Irish 7f winner High Larch (by Bold Ruler)
and 2 winners in USA; dam unraced sister to top-class racehorse and sire Graustark and half-sister to champion American filly Bowl of Flowers; 20/1 and
in need of race when behind in 20-runner maiden event won by Wintergrace at
Pontefract in June. *L. Cumani.*

TAMARIND ST JAMES 2 b.f. Hot Spark 126–Peach Stone (Mourne 126) —
(1982 5g 5d 7fg 6fg 7fg 7g 6s) Apr 10; 1,500Y; of no account; sold 340 gns
Ascot November Sales. *S. Harris.*

TAMATORY 5 ch.m. Military 112–Tamborder (Tambourin) (1981 NR 1982 —
13.8f) leggy, lightly-made mare; half-sister to a winning point-to-pointer; last
of 17 behind Blakey Bank in maiden race at Catterick in May, first outing.
J. Yardley.

TAMDOWN FLYER 4 b.c. Hotfoot 126–Swing The Cat (Swing Easy 126) **84**
(1981 6fg* 6s³ 6fg* 6f⁴ 6f 7g 1982 7f* 7f⁴ 7f* 6fg* 7f³ 5.8f⁴ 7d 8.2f³ 7f* 9d 8s)
leggy, light-framed colt; had a good season and won handicaps at Thirsk in
April and May, Windsor in June and Doncaster in September; produced with a
storming late run when beating Secret Gill a head in valuable Battle of Britain
Stakes on last-named course; also ran very well when close third in quite valuable
events at Newmarket (to Paterno in Ward Hill Bunbury Cup) and Haydock;
effective at 6f and stays 1m well (not entirely disgraced over 9f in Cambridgeshire); has run respectably on soft going but is much better on firm; suited by
waiting tactics. *W. O'Gorman.*

Mrs Harold Phillips' "Tants"

TAMERCO 5 b. or br.g. Saritamer 130–Congola (Bold Lad, Ire 133) (1981 10g — 1982 10g 16d 16f) narrow gelding; poor maiden; well beaten in a seller on reappearance; unlikely to stay 1½m+; blinkered final start. *K. Cunningham-Brown.*

TAMER GRANGE 3 gr.f. Saritamer 130–Hornton Grange 101 (Hornbeam 130) — (1981 6s 1982 10f 11f 10f⁴ 11d 12v) quite attractive, well-made filly; beaten some way in varied company; best run at 1¼m on firm going. *H. Candy.*

TA MORGAN 4 b.g. Targowice 130–Sericana (Petingo 135) (1981 8s³ 7d 8.5d² **78** 7fg* 7f* 8.2g 7g 8.3fg² 8.3g* 8.3g* 8d² 8g 1982 6g* 7f* 7f* 7.6f² 8g) tall, lengthy gelding; did well during a short season; won apprentice handicaps at Folkestone and Epsom and £7,300 handicap at Lingfield in spring; effective at 6f and stays 1m well; acts on any going; successful with blinkers and without; genuine front runner. *G. Lewis.*

TAMPA BAY 6 b.h. Ickford 101–Tide and Time (Easter Island 101) (1981 6g 5f 7g — 6fg 1982 6fg) tall horse; plater; best form at sprint distances; seems to act on any going; blinkered once at 2 yrs. *D. Leslie.*

TAMPERO (FR) 3 br.c. Pharly 130–Bienvenida (Tom Rolfe) (1981 7d³ 6f **115** 8fg* 8s² 7.5s² 1982 8v⁴ 8fg² 10.5fg 9fg⁴ 9g² 10fg³ 10g⁴) small, strong, close-coupled colt; first foal; dam won over 9f at 2 yrs and 1¼m at 3 yrs in France; ran best races second to fourth starts, going down by 1½ lengths to Melyno in Poule d'Essai des Poulains at Longchamp, finishing 5 lengths fifth of 10 to Persepolis in Prix Lupin on same course (faded in closing stages) and 5 lengths fourth of 5 to Melyno again in Prix Jean Prat at Chantilly; stays 1¼m; seems to act on any going. *J. Cunnington, jnr, France.*

TANCRED WALK 3 b.g. Farm Walk 111–Darling Do (Derring-Do 131) (1981 — 7g 7.2fg⁴ 8g² 7d 1982 8fg) smallish, fair sort; quite moderate form in varied company; will be suited by 1¼m; has run respectably when sweating up; takes a good hold; not seen out after April. *Miss S. Hall.*

TANEENA (USA) 3 b.f. Chieftain–Haneena 118 (Habitat 134) (1981 raced — in USA 1982 7.6fg 9g) first foal; dam smart 2-y-o; ran twice unplaced in USA at 2 yrs; apprentice ridden when well beaten in maiden races at Lingfield in May and Wolverhampton in August; sold to BBA (Italia) 5,000 gns Newmarket Autumn Sales. *F. Durr.*

TANGMAN 2 b.c. Great Nephew 126–Silk Blend (Busted 134) (1982 6v 7s) **76** May 27; IR 24,000Y; neat colt; first foal; dam unraced sister to Silk Buds, a very useful performer at up to 1½m; showed up in Duke of Edinburgh Stakes at Ascot in October and minor event at Chepstow later in the month; dead. *G. Balding.*

TANTS 3 ch.f. Vitiges 132–Hants 111 (Exbury 138) (1981 7v² 7g* 1982 12fg* **111** 12f 12fg³ 12g² 14.6g 12v³) tall, useful-looking filly; half-sister to 2 winners, including very useful 1978 2-y-o 6f to 1m winner Potemkin (by Sir Gaylord), subsequently a stakes winner in USA; dam won 4 times at around 1¼m; shot into clear lead entering straight and never looked likely to be caught when beating Rockfest in good style by 4 lengths in 9-runner Esal Bookmakers Oaks Trial at Lingfield in May; placed afterwards in Ribblesdale Stakes at Royal Ascot (2¾ lengths third to Dish Dash), Lancashire Oaks at Haydock (1½ lengths second to stable-companion Sing Softly) and Princess Royal Stakes at Ascot (3½ lengths third to Believer); well beaten in Oaks (favourite) and possibly found 1¾m too far when fifth of 6 to Swiftfoot in Park Hill Stakes at Doncaster on penultimate outing; seems to act on any going. *H. Cecil.*

TANWEN 8 gr.m. Firestreak 125–Riccardi 68 (Roan Rocket 128) (1981 NR — 1982 17f 18.8fg 12s) poor stayer; lightly raced since 1977; acts on any going; has been tried in blinkers; has worn bandages. *K. Bridgwater.*

TAOISEACH (USA) 2 b.c. Northern Dancer–Millicent (Cornish Prince) (1982 **93** 6d³ 6s*) May 5; closely related to smart 1981 2-y-o 5f performer Peterhof (by The Minstrel) and half-brother to 3 other winners; dam unraced half-sister to Mill Reef; looked a useful colt when winning 13-runner minor event at Punchestown in October by 2 lengths from Sir Prince John, the pair 5 lengths clear; had previously started at 2/1 on for 20-runner maiden race at the Curragh but was beaten 2¾ lengths into third place behind 33/1-shot Lodina after having every chance; will probably stay 1m. *V. O'Brien, Ireland.*

TAPESTRY KING 5 b.g. Henry the Seventh 125–Petitpoint 77 (Petition 130) — (1981 NR 1982 12f) 3,100Y, 1,550 2-y-o; half-brother to 2 winners abroad; dam 1½m winner and half-sister to 2 smart performers; 20/1 when in rear behind Plaza Toro in 13-runner minor event at Carlisle in April. *R. E. Peacock.*

TAPIZ 2 b.c. Pitskelly 122–Santa Chiara 79 (Astec 128) (1982 6f 7fg 7g) — May 3; 1R 13,500F, 21,000Y; well-grown, fair sort; third live foal; half-brother to a winner in Jersey; dam, a stayer, is half-sister to dam of good French filly Pitasia (by Pitskelly); soundly beaten in maiden and minor events; trained first start by P. Mitchell. *C. James.*

TAP-O-STRATH 2 br.f. Mandrake Major 122–Duck Walk (Farm Walk 111) — (1982 6g) May 16; first foal; dam of little account on flat and over hurdles; last of 15 in minor event at Hamilton in September. *J. S. Wilson.*

TAQA 2 b.f. Blakeney 126–Gliding 94 (Tudor Melody 129) (1982 7.6v) Mar — 31; 40,000Y; third foal; half-sister to useful 7f and 8.5f winner Bay Street (by Grundy) and useful 3-y-o 7f winner Rose of Montreaux (by Habat); dam, winning sprinter, is half-sister to very smart 1973 2-y-o Splashing; in rear in 17-runner maiden race at Lingfield in October. *M. Masson.*

TARA'S CHIEFTAIN 4 b.g. African Sky 124–Hillberry Corner 70 (Atan) **45** (1981 8d 8d 8s 7f² 8f 8f* 8g 8.2d⁴ 8s 1982 8h 7f 7g 8g 8g³ 8.3fg 8g⁴ 10fg³ 10s) compact gelding; plater; stays 1¼m; often blinkered; sometimes starts slowly; trained most of season by J. Jenkins. *R. Atkins.*

TARGET PATH 4 b.c. Scottish Rifle 127–Florabette (Floribunda 136) (1981 **68** 8d 9d* 8.2d 10g⁴ 11.7s 11g* 10f⁴ 11fg* 12g⁴ 12f 11d 1982 11g² 12fg* 13s 12g 12v⁴) strong colt; off course 3 months after winning amateur riders handicap at Carlisle in June; stays 1½m; possibly not at his best on really soft going, but acts on any other; has worn blinkers but seems better without. *C. Nelson.*

TARIFA 2 gr.f. Pitskelly 122–Slap Up (Gala Performance) (1982 5g 5f 6d 6s*) **70** Apr 4; 9,400Y; good-topped filly; third foal; half-sister to 1981 Irish 2-y-o 5f winner Fade To Grey (by Gay Fandango); dam very useful winner at up to 13f in Ireland; well-backed favourite, showed first form when winning 19-runner claiming race at Nottingham in October by 4 lengths; claimed £3,000 afterwards; will stay 7f; acts on soft going. *J. Sutcliffe.*

TARLETON 5 b. or br.g. Workboy 123–Lady Jester 108 (Bleep-Bleep 134) — (1981 8.2g 6g 6d 6g 7f³ 6fg 6fg³ 6g 6fg 7g⁴ 7v 1982 8g 8fg 10fg 9fg³ 12f 8fg) plater; possibly stays 9f but seems better at shorter distances; acts on firm going; finds little off the bridle; dwelt second outing. *P. Rohan.*

TARLETON ELM (USA) 2 br.c. Tarleton Oak–Nuthatch (Young Emperor — 133) (1982 7fg) Mar 6; $20,000Y; workmanlike colt; fourth foal; closely related to a winner of over $100,000 by Northern Jove; dam won 1m claiming race at 4 yrs; sire, son of Northern Dancer, won small 6f race from 5 starts; eighth of 11 in maiden race at Yarmouth in July. *I. Walker.*

TARRYSTONE 3 br.f. So Blessed 130–Bajour 89 (Forlorn River 124) (1981 — 6g 1982 5f 7fg) rather lightly-made filly; soundly beaten in maiden races. *C. Nelson.*

TARSUS (FR) 3 ch.g. Hotfoot 126–Yole Tartare (Captain's Gig) (1981 6g — 7g 6g 1982 7fg 10fg 7f 10.1fg 10d 12f) medium-sized, attractive gelding; plating-class maiden; stays 1¼m; blinkered last 4 starts. *B. Swift.*

TASOMUDU 3 ch.g. Tachypous 128–High Ransom 88 (High Treason 126) **70** (1981 5f⁴ 6fg 6fg 6s 1982 10f 10.1fg 11.7g 10.6h² 13fg² 11.7d* 11g* 12g⁴ 12.2f³ 10fg² 10g) strong, compact gelding; won handicaps at Windsor in June and Edinburgh in July; runner-up in valuable seller fourth start; stays 13f; seems to act on any going; has run well when sweating up. *W. Musson.*

TATIBAH 2 b.c. Habitat 134–Three Tees (Tim Tam) (1982 6f* 6d 6s 5v*) **117**
As the man who trained Habitat to become Europe's champion miler and Double Form, a son of Habitat, to become one of Europe's best sprinters Fulke Johnson Houghton must have been delighted when Tatibah, a big, handsome, well-made Habitat colt, was sent to be trained by him in July. Tatibah had already raced twice for Newmarket trainer Ben Hanbury, looking potentially a high-class performer on his debut in the second division of the Kennett Maiden Stakes at Newbury in June. After travelling very easily from halfway he left his seventeen rivals standing in the last furlong, winning by six lengths from Harvest Boy. By the time Tatibah reappeared a fortnight later in the Chesters Stakes at Newcastle, Harvest Boy had finished a creditable fourth in the Chesham Stakes at Royal Ascot, and Tatibah started favourite at 2/1 on despite having to give weight to the five other runners, four of them winners. Everything seemed to be going as expected as Tatibah moved up smoothly after halfway

Cornwallis Stakes, Ascot—the end of a testing race for these two-years-olds: shown are Tatibah and third-placed Top O'The North

but hardly had he reached a challenging position than he was beaten. He found nothing under pressure and was eased right up, coming home the best part of twenty lengths behind Arrowood Bob. As Tatibah's impressive Newbury display had come on firm going there was a distinct possibility that his very disappointing performance at Newcastle has been caused by the softish ground. Subsequent events were to discount this possibility. He was beaten on softer ground on his first appearance for his new trainer, finishing seventh of sixteen to Worrell at 20/1 in the Golden Gates Nursery at Ascot, but he wasn't disgraced considering that he was carrying top weight, that he'd been off the course for three months and that he was hampered before halfway. Back at Ascot a fortnight later he proved beyond doubt his ability to handle soft ground, winning the Cornwallis Stakes in very testing conditions. Only County Broker of the nine runners started at longer odds than Tatibah in a market headed by What Lake, a filly from the Hanbury stable who had recently slammed a big field of maidens at Newmarket. Also in the field were Top O'The North, a smart winner of the Champion Two Yrs Old Trophy at Ripon, Miss Anagram, an excellent second under 10-0 in a valuable nursery at Newmarket last time out, Orange Squash, successful in five of his last six races, and the tough colts Wiki Wiki Wheels and Mac's Palace who had seven wins between them. With the exception of Mac's Palace and Miss Anagram the field raced up the middle of the course, with What Lake and Top O'The North moving through to dispute the lead with a quarter of a mile to run. As What Lake began to hang right, bumping Top O'The North, Tatibah's strong run took him into the lead inside the final furlong and by the line he'd gone a length and a half clear of Mac's Palace who ran on to take second place. This was one of the season's best performances by a two-year-old colt over five furlongs.

Tatibah (b.c. Feb 27, 1980)	Habitat (b 1966)	Sir Gaylord (b 1959)	Turn-to
			Somethingroyal
		Little Hut (b 1952)	Occupy
			Savage Beauty
	Three Tees (b 1962)	Tim Tam (b 1955)	Tom Fool
			Two Lea
		Teretania (ch 1944)	Stardust
			Teresina

Tatibah, who was foaled in Ireland, was sold as a yearling in Kentucky for 215,000 dollars. His yearling sister fetched only 5,000 dollars less in 1982 while another sister, the six-furlong winner Baby Diamonds, was sold for 410,000 dollars at Keeneland in November, carrying her first foal. Tatibah is the ninth winner produced by Three Tees, a two-year-old six-furlong winner. Easily best of the others was the very smart Vertee (by Vertex), who won two stakes races as a four-year-old in 1973, notably the Widener Handicap over a mile and a quarter. Teresina, Tatibah's great-grandam, was born as long ago as 1920. She was a fine stayer, winner of the Goodwood Cup and the Jockey Club Stakes, and later did well as a broodmare, producing several notable performers, including the Irish Oaks winner Theresina, besides Tatibah's grandam Teretania, the winner of a small race over a mile in Ireland. Teretania produced seven winners in all and one of them, Bravura, became the dam of the very smart middle-distance performer Hail the Pirates.

Tatibah has been entered in the Two Thousand Guineas. There's no reason on breeding why he shouldn't stay a mile except that Habitat now and again sires a good animal who stays nothing like so well as one would expect, Double Form, Hittite Glory and Sayyaf being prime examples. That Tatibah did so well over five furlongs in the Cornwallis, after three races over six furlongs, suggests he may be another. Whatever his distance turns out to be he needs to make further improvement if he's to reach the top but he's such a good sort of colt that he may well do so. *F. J. Houghton.*

TATTLE 2 b.f. St Paddy 133–Babble On 79 (Acropolis 132) (1982 7fg 7fg 7f) 61 Mar 25; smallish, quite well-made, useful sort; sister to useful middle-distance performer Kings General and half-sister to numerous winners, including very useful 1979 2-y-o 6f and 1m winner Home Ground (by No Mercy); dam, sister to Espresso, won at up to 11f; poor form in maiden events; may be capable of better. *B. Hobbs.*

TAVITA 2 b.f. Octavo 115–Martita 99 (Tacitus 124) (1982 6f 5fg⁴ 6fg 7g³ 7.2s) 55 May 17; IR 4,500Y; sparely-made filly; half-sister to 3 winners, including 1978 2-y-o 5f winner Rendition (by Song); dam won over 1m at 2 yrs; modest plater; will be suited by 1m; ran poorly in blinkers final outing; sold 400 gns Newmarket Autumn Sales and exported to Holland. *G. Hunter.*

TAWAAG (USA) 2 b.c. Hoist the Flag–Sarsar (Damascus) (1982 7d 8g 8d) 67 Mar 2; $440,000Y; strong, medium-sized, attractive colt; first living foal; dam very smart 3-y-o, when successful at up to 1m, and is half-sister to 3 stakes winners; not raced until October, and showed no form until finishing modest fifth of 16 behind High Cannon in minor event at Redcar on third outing; will probably stay 1¼m. *G. Harwood.*

TAW CROSSING 2 b.f. High Line 125–Taw Court 58 (Lear Jet 123) (1982 — 5.8g 6fg) Apr 14; unattractive filly; first foal; dam sprint plater; 19 lengths fifth of 6 to Royal Heroine in Princess Margaret Stakes at Ascot in July, second start. *J. Hill.*

TAWFIQ (USA) 3 ch.c. Blushing Groom 131–Manta (Ben Lomond) (1981 7g 86 8s³ 1982 8.2fg* 9f* 8f 10fg 12h* 12f 12fg 12fg* 13d³ 12g³ 12s) medium-sized, good-topped, quite attractive colt; good mover; successful in maiden race at Nottingham, minor event at Ripon and 2 handicaps at Chepstow; suited by 1½m or more; acts on any going but is ideally suited by fast ground; blinkered nowadays. *H. T. Jones.*

TAXODIUM 2 b.c. Sharpen Up 127–Lucent 117 (Irish Ball 127) (1982 7g 7f — 8.2s 8s 7s) Apr 28; 4,100Y; smallish colt; first foal; dam, daughter of very good sprinter Lucasland, was smart winner from 1m to 1½m from 2 yrs to 4 yrs; poor form, including in a maiden auction event. *T. Fairhurst.*

TAZLINA 2 b.f. Tarboosh–Holme Lacy 88 (March Past 124) (1982 5d 5fg⁴ 5g 54 6f 7.3g 8.2d) Apr 8; IR 1,000Y, IR 3,600Y; half-sister to several winners, including very useful miler Silver Steel (by Double-U-Jay); poor maiden. *C. Wildman.*

T. BELLE 3 br.f. Foggy Bell 108–Susan 88 (Hard Tack 111§) (1981 8g 8d 1982 62 8fg 10fg 10d⁴ 12.2f³ 12fg) sparely-made filly; plating-class maiden; suited by 1½m and will stay further; acts on firm going; sold to J. Yardley 1,500 gns Doncaster November Sales. *C. Spares.*

TCHOUPITOULAS 2 ch.c. Grundy 137–Fall to Pieces 101 (Forli) (1982 6fg* 86 7g³ 8g) Apr 23; 54,000Y; good-bodied colt; third foal; half-brother to 1980 2-y-o 6f winner Piece of the Realm (by Realm); dam won over 7f and 1m; won 11-runner maiden race at Doncaster in July; odds on when third to Game Dame and Sheriff Muir in 10-runner minor event at Leicester the following month, better subsequent effort; should stay at least 1m; possibly needs fast ground. *H. Cecil.*

TEA BISCUIT 2 ch.f. Cranley 75–Gay Desire (Dragonara Palace 115) (1982 —
5f 5f 5g) Mar 28; small filly; first foal; dam never ran; last in maiden races;
of no account. *J. Townson.*

TEA DANCE 2 ch.f. Vitiges 132–Rose Girl (Thatch 136) (1982 5d 7f 8fg 10s) —
May 11; 8,400Y; big, good-bodied filly; dam, poor maiden, is half-sister to smart
sprinter Rambling Rose and very smart French colt Rose Laurel; in rear in
maiden races, twice none too well away. *M. Blanshard.*

TEA HOUSE 2 ch.f. Sassafras 135–House Tie (Be Friendly 130) (1982 6g*) **95 p**
Mar 30; first foal; dam, Irish 1m winner, is daughter of high-class filly Meso-
tamia; 12/1, led before halfway when winning 11-runner maiden race at Listowel
in September by 2½ lengths from Hole In The Wall; will be suited by 1m+; a
well-bred filly who will go on to better things. *M. Kauntze, Ireland.*

TEAMWORK 5 br.h. Workboy 123–Affirmative 96 (Derring-Do 131) (1981 8s **94**
8fg² 8d² 8v³ 8f* 8fg² 8g* 8fg² 9g 1982 8g 8g 8g* 8f* 8f⁴ 8fg 8f⁴ 8fg³ 8f* 8g³ 8fg⁴
10.2g 9d) strong, good-bodied horse; won at Kempton and Thirsk in May and
at Thirsk again in July; won Thirsk Hunt Cup and an apprentice event on latter
course, both in very good style; needs a strongly-run race at 1m (never got into
race and ran moderately over 1¼m however); acts on any going but is very well
suited by top-of-the-ground; usually held up; consistent; ridden by apprentice
S. Jewell for all his wins in 1982. *R. Sheather.*

TEA-POT 6 ch.m. Ragstone 128–Desert Ash (Celtic Ash) (1981 14s* 16s² 16g **77**
15.5fg² 16fg 14fg 16g* 17.1d 18g 14g* 1982 15.5g³ 16g² 14f 14fg³ 14fg³ 16fg
16fg⁴ 16d³ 17f 15.8d² 14g⁴ 16d⁴ 17.1s³ 18d³ 18s*) workmanlike mare; gained a
well-deserved success in 20-runner handicap at Doncaster on penultimate day of
season, staying on strongly and beating Mayotte by 1½ lengths; in frame most
other starts and ran very well indeed when third of 28 to Mountain Lodge in
Tote Cesarewitch at Newmarket; needs a really stiff test of stamina; seems to act
on any going but is very well suited by soft; genuine. *M. Blanshard.*

TECORNO (USA) 2 b.c. Tentam–Nimble Deb (Lucky Debonair) (1982 6f **113**
7g² 7s²) Mar 5; $120,000Y; strong, good-bodied, attractive colt; has a high knee
action; half-brother to 3 minor winners; dam never ran; 1½ lengths second of 21
to Zoffany in maiden race at Newbury in August, holding a good place throughout
and drawing clear of remainder; favourite, well clear of rest when caught on line
and beaten short head by By Decree in 13-runner £5,900 event at Ascot the
following month; will stay 1¼m; acts on soft going; certain to win races. *R. Hern.*

TEDARI 3 b.g. Native Bazaar 122–Form (Reform 132) (1981 5d 5g⁴ 1982 5fg —
7fg 7g) lightly-made gelding; poor plater; sold 460 gns Ascot 2nd June Sales,
R. Hannon.

TEDDINGTON JEWEL 2 ch.c. Import 127–Welsh Cape (Abernant 142) —
(1982 6d 6f 5fg) Feb 6; 2,400Y; half-brother to Irish 1½m winner Evolution
(by Upper Case); dam ran only twice; no form, including in a maiden auction
event; not seen out after August. *H. O'Neill.*

TEEJAY 3 b.g. Jimmy Reppin 131–Billingsgate 82 (High Perch 126) (1981 6f **73**
6g 6g 7f 6s³ 1982 8g 7g⁴ 8g⁴ 8g* 8fg⁴ 8.2s² 8d²) compact gelding; won maiden
race at Beverley in August; runner-up in 2 handicaps afterwards; stays 1m;
suited by some give in the ground; has given trouble at start. *M. Camacho.*

TEENOSO (USA) 2 b.c. Youth 135–Furioso 116 (Ballymoss 136) (1982 6fg **86**
7g 8g⁴) Apr 7; rangy, useful-looking colt; half-brother to 2 winners, notably
very smart Topsy (by Habitat), successful at up to 1¼m; dam, half-sister to Irish
1,000 Guineas winner Favoletta, was second in Oaks; improved steadily, and
showed plenty of ability when 4¾ lengths fourth of 17 to Oula Owl in maiden race
at Newmarket in October, disputing lead 2f and not being given hard time once
winner quickened clear; will stay 1½m; has plenty of scope and promises to make
up into a useful 3-y-o. *H. Wragg.*

TEIGH 2 b.c. Gold Form 108–Palmural 111 (Palestine 133) (1982 5f 5g 5g 5d) **57**
May 21; 780F; compact, sturdy colt; brother to 1980 2-y-o 5f winner Artistry and
half-brother to 3 winners, including top-class German sprinter Pentathlon (by
Ennis); dam very useful over 5f and 6f at 2 yrs; poor plater; not raced after
August; blinkered final start. *J. Fitzgerald.*

TELEGRAMS AGAIN (HOL) 5 br.m. Pentathlon–Darling Caroline (Ilix)
(1981 10.2s 13fg⁴ 12.5s 10g* 15.5f⁴ 10.7d² 18s³ 1982 10.2g 15.5g 10d³ 15.5f 12.5g⁴
12fg 15.8f 12d² 12.5s³ 10s 9.5d² 9.5v 10s) big mare; poor form here, but was
placed several times in Holland; stays well; has worn blinkers; trained part of
season by M. Ryan. *J. Ives, Holland.*

TELEGRAPH BOY 4 b.c. Bay Express 132–Code of Love 99 (Bleep-Bleep 134) **55**
(1981 6fg 7fg 5fg 5d 5s 5s* 6s 1982 5f 5.8f 5g² 5fg² 5fg² 5fg² 5d 5s 5d) strong,
close-coupled colt; second in 4 handicaps; best form at 5f; acts on any going
with possible exception of very firm; often gets outpaced in early stages. *W.
Wightman.*

TELEPATHY 3 b.c. He Loves Me 120–Clear Belle (Klairon 131) (1981 6g —
1982 10.2g 9fg⁴ 8g 10fg) fair sort; poor form, including in a seller; sold to
W. A. Stephenson 800 gns Newmarket Autumn Sales. *R. Williams.*

TELEPHONE MAN 3 b. or br.c. Record Token 128–Needless 81 (Petingo 135) **95**
(1981 5s² 6fg⁴ 7fg² 7fg² 7g² 7s⁴ 8s 7g 7v² 1982 7d 8fg 10.4fg 8fg* 7fg 10g 8fg
12f 12g 10.5g 10d² 12d 16d) well-made colt; good walker and mover; gained
a well-deserved success when beating Steel Glow all out by ¾ length in 10-runner
£5,800 maiden race at York in June; had stiff tasks on a number of occasions,
including when sixth in Coral-Eclipse Stakes at Sandown in July on sixth start
(to Kalaglow) and in Cumberland Lodge Stakes at Ascot on twelfth (under 5
lengths behind Lafontaine); stays 1½m and should get further (ran as though
something was wrong with him when tried at 2m); acts well on heavy going;
often blinkered but goes just as well without; lacks pace. *P. Kelleway.*

TELEPHONE NUMBERS (USA) 2 b.c. Annihilate 'Em–Tims Flirt (Tim **93**
Tam) (1982 6g² 6f 6s² 7.6v*) Apr 13; $13,500F, 54,000 gns Y; rangy, attractive
colt; half-brother to 3 winners in USA; dam, half-sister to King's Stand Stakes
winner Flirting Around, ran 15 times unplaced in USA; favourite, made all
when winning 17-runner maiden race at Lingfield in October by a head from
One O'Clock Jump, with remainder well beaten; had run creditably previously,
including in Coventry Stakes at Royal Ascot; will be suited by 1m+; acts on
any going. *R. Price.*

TELEPROMPTER 2 b.g. Welsh Pageant 132–Ouija 104 (Silly Season 127) — p
(1982 7g) Apr 11; big, strong, useful-looking gelding; half-brother to useful 7f
and 1m winner Rosia Bay (by High Top); dam best at 1m; 10 lengths tenth
of 13 to Cock Robin in Ribero Stakes at Doncaster in September; gelded subsequently; sure to do better. *J. W. Watts.*

TELL TALE LASS 3 b. or br.f. Guillaume Tell 121–Shantung Lassie (Shantung **62**
132) (1981 5s 5g 5s 7fg 7d 7fg 10d⁴ 10g 8d 1982 12g 16f 12g³ 14g² 16.9fg³
16.5f³ 16fg⁴ 14g) small filly; plater at 2 yrs; ran respectably in better company
on occasions in 1982; suited by a test of stamina; sometimes blinkered; has given
trouble at start; does best when ridden up with pace. *W. Marshall.*

TELLURANO 4 ch.c. Guillaume Tell 121–Uranus (Manacle 123) (1981 7g* **116** d
10d 7f 8fg* 7fg* 8fg⁴ 6g² 8fg³ 1982 6g 8f* 10f 7g 6f) big, rangy colt; very
smart performer at his best; returned to form in 12-runner Kilruddery Stakes
at Leopardstown in June, belying his odds of 20/1 by beating slow-starting
3-y-o Memento a length with remainder quite well strung out; ran moderately
afterwards, and dropped right out in straight when last of 7 behind Kind of Hush
in 1¼m Prince of Wales's Stakes at Royal Ascot later in June; best form at 1m;
probably acts on any going, but evidently acts well on a firm surface; sometimes
sweats up. *K. Prendergast, Ireland.*

TELSMOSS 6 b.h. Levmoss 133–Elakonee Wind 110 (Restless Wind) (1981 **87**
10fg 11s 10fg 11.7fg 11.7fg 12g 11.7g* 12fg* 14fg² 13.3d* 1982 12g* 16s 12fg
12fg* 13.3f 12f 11.7d³ 13.3g 12g) small horse; poor walker; successful in hand-
caps at Doncaster in March and Lingfield in May, staying on very gamely to win
by 1½ lengths from Sympatique on latter course; had stiff tasks on several
occasions; stays 1¾m; acts on any going; genuine; suitable mount for an inexperienced rider; does best when ridden up with pace; moved poorly to start
and ran moderately sixth outing. *P. Mitchell.*

TEMPLE BAR MAID 2 ch.f. Decoy Boy 129–Razia 97 (Martial 131) (1982 **79**
6fg 5f 5fg³ 5f 5g 5fg⁴ 5v* 5v³ 5g) Feb 23; lengthy filly; half-sister to winners here
and abroad, including 1m and 1½m winner Tudorville (by Shoolerville); dam
won over 5f at 2 yrs; in frame in maiden races in the Midlands prior to running
out a 7-length winner from Princess Navarro in 18-runner selling nursery at
Lingfield (bought in 1,600 gns) in October; not sure to stay 6f; seems to act on
any going but clearly revels in the mud. *D. Wilson.*

TEMPTING LADY (USA) 3 b.f. L'Enjoleur–Sakti (Arts and Letters) (1981 —
NR 1982 7fg 10.2g 10.1fg) $65,000F, IR 165,000Y; good-bodied filly; third
produce; half-sister to a winner; dam unraced half-sister to brilliant American
horse Damascus; in rear in varied company; sold 42,000 gns Newmarket
December Sales. *T. Robson.*

TENDER BENDER 2 b.f. Prince Tenderfoot 126–Too Soon 73 (Sheshoon 132) **65**
(1982 6fg 6fg 7.6v 8.2s³) Apr 20; IR 16,000Y; smallish, quite attractive filly;
half-sister to 4 winners by Sterling Bay, including useful Irish 9f winner Bolton
Tom; dam stayer; showed ability only when 2½ lengths third of 8 to very easy
winner Hungarian Prince in maiden race at Haydock in October; suited by 1m;
blinkered last 2 outings. *G. Pritchard-Gordon.*

TENDER GIFT 2 b. or br.f. Prince Tenderfoot 126–Hung Pao 75 (Cumshaw **73**
111) (1982 6g 5s 6s) May 21; half-sister to 3 winners, including fairly useful
1980 Irish 2-y-o 5f winner Happy Reprieve (by Tower Walk); dam placed at
up to 1m; 3½ lengths fifth of 21 to Holy Day in 5f maiden race at Bath in October,
best effort; should be suited by 6f. *J. Benstead.*

TENDER GODESS 2 b.f. Prince Tenderfoot 126–Fairy Goddess (Yellow God **65**
129) (1982 5g 5fg 5fg 6d 5d) Apr 28; 2,300Y; compact filly; fourth living
foal; half-sister to a winning plater; dam never ran; moderate plater; acts on firm
going. *D. Whelan.*

TENDER KING 3 b.c. Prince Tenderfoot 126–Cider Princess (Alcide 136) **123**
(1981 5g² 5s* 5d 5g² 5f* 6fg² 6fg* 6f⁴ 6g⁴ 7g³ 1982 7s 7fg² 8fg³ 8g² 8.5f⁴ 8fg²
6f⁴ 8f⁴)
These days not many horses trained at Epsom are capable of putting up a
bold show in the classics, and by finishing third in the Two Thousand Guineas
and second in the Airlie/Coolmore Irish Two Thousand Guineas Tender King
came closer to success than any since Steel Pulse who won the Irish Sweeps
Derby in 1972. In many ways Tender King's career has been that of Right
Tack writ small. Both colts were trained by Sutcliffe and both followed similar
campaigns, yet while Right Tack won five top events Tender King usually
managed to find one or two to beat him. He has been sent to race in California
with the slightly unfortunate record of having been in the frame in twelve pattern
races only one of which, the 1981 Richmond Stakes, he won.
The races that showed Tender King to best advantage in 1982 were the two
classics and the St James's Palace Stakes at Royal Ascot, all three of which
Right Tack had won in 1969. Tender King ran twice before the Guineas, easily
the better effort a strong-finishing half-length second to Cajun after being boxed
in over a furlong out in the Clerical, Medical Greenham Stakes at Newbury.
At Newmarket he gradually threaded his way through from halfway, having had
trouble going the early pace, and kept on powerfully to finish just over two
lengths behind Zino. Tender King succeeded in reversing form with the Guineas
second Wind and Wuthering at the Curragh but he caught a tartar in the shape
of Dara Monarch, only eighth at Newmarket. The pace presented no problems
this time and with a quarter of a mile left Tender King could be seen travelling
smoothly on the bridle; hitting the front below the distance he looked set for
victory until Dara Monarch produced a storming run that took him three lengths
clear of the English colt by the post.
The difference between Dara Monarch and Tender King in Ireland was cut
to a length and a half at Royal Ascot where Tender King started fifth favourite
in a field of nine, probably because on his previous start he had put up a rather
lacklustre display behind Prima Voce in the Diomed Stakes at Epsom. Held
up as usual, he made steady headway to reach a challenging position halfway up
the straight and struggled on bravely to finish six lengths clear of third-placed
Ivano without making any impression on Dara Monarch whose turn of foot once
again proved decisive. Those who by now regarded Tender King as a professional
loser no doubt believed the colt's last two races, the William Hill July Cup and
the Sussex Stakes, provided further proof of the point. In fact there is no
reason to suppose that Tender King is quite up to winning a Group 1 race—
certainly not one over the six furlongs of the July Cup—and in finishing fourth
to Sharpo at Newmarket and to On The House at Goodwood, beaten about two
lengths each time, he ran somewhere near his best.

		⎧ Blue Prince	⎧ Princequillo
	⎧ Prince Tenderfoot	⎨ (b 1951)	⎨ Blue Denim
	⎨ (b 1967)	⎩ La Tendresse	⎩ Grey Sovereign
Tender King	⎨	(b 1959)	Isetta
(b.c. 1979)	⎨	⎧ Alcide	⎧ Alycidon
	⎩ Cider Princess	⎨ (b 1955)	⎨ Chenille
	(ch 1971)	⎩ Paris Princess	⎩ Prince Chevalier
		(br 1958)	⎩ Viviparus

Tender King ran moderately in blinkers once as a two-year-old; his sire, the sprinter Prince Tenderfoot, wore blinkers on all his starts at three. On the dam's side Tender King comes from a successful family and was well bought for 8,200 guineas as a yearling. His dam, who won over nine furlongs in Ireland, is a daughter of the National Stakes and Beresford Stakes winner Paris Princess, herself a half-sister to another winner of the Beresford Stakes, Viviptic, and to Vivi Tarquin, successful in the Ascot Gold Vase, out of a mare from the family of Musidora. There is no shortage of stamina here and since Prince Tenderfoot's sire ran second in the Gold Cup there's a chance Tender King will stay beyond a mile, especially as he doesn't waste his energy in the early stages of a race. A strong, quite attractive colt and a good mover, he is ideally suited by a sound surface. *J. Sutcliffe.*

TENDER NIECE 3 b. or br.f. Prince Tenderfoot 126–Nasty Niece (Great Nephew 126) (1981 5fg 8fg 5s 6d 6d 1982 6s 7d 7g 8f 9g 7fg² 8fg* 7.2s 8g 8s 7s) close-coupled filly; short-priced favourite when winning apprentice maiden race at Warwick in July; stays 1m; acts well on fast ground; best in blinkers. *J. Spearing.*   **66**

TENDER PET 2 b.c. Mummy's Pet 125–Tender Courtesan 90 (Primera 131) (1982 6d) Apr 6; 4,000Y; lengthy colt; brother to very useful 1977 2-y-o 6f performer Lambkin and half-brother to 2 winners, including very useful sprinter Overtown (by Raffingora); dam won twice over 7f at 2 yrs; thirteenth of 22 in maiden race at Doncaster in October. *D. H. Jones.*   —

TENDER SOVEREIGN 2 b.c. Prince Tenderfoot 126–Yellow Lotus (Majority Blue 126) (1982 5fg⁴ 5.3g 6v³) Apr 6; IR 4,800F; first produce; dam placed twice over 1¼m in Ireland and won over hurdles; 2 lengths third of 9 to Joy Hour in maiden race at Folkestone in October; will be suited by 7f; acts on heavy going. *G. Lewis.*   **86**

TENDER TRADER (USA) 3 ch.g. Our Michael–My Roue (Hilarious) (1981 5fg 5d² 5s 5.8d³ 5g 5d 6fg 6fg² 1982 7fg 7.6f 6f 5h* 6fg* 5.8g* 6g 6d 6f) strong, attractive gelding; good mover; landed odds in seller at Chepstow in May (bought in 5,000 gns); subsequently showed himself better than a plater, winning handicaps at Brighton and Bath; best at sprint distances; seems to act on any going; sometimes wears bandages or boots in front. *G. Lewis.*   **72**

TENDER VENTURE 3 br.g. Prince Tenderfoot 126–Hopeful Maid (Hopeful Venture 125) (1981 5s 6fg⁴ 7fg 7fg 7fg* 7fg 1982 7g 8fg 8fg 8fg 8fg) neat gelding; fair at his best; well beaten most starts at 3 yrs; not certain to stay beyond 7f unless he learns to settle; acts on a firm surface; best in blinkers. *G. Pritchard-Gordon.*   —

TENIST 3 b.f. Czarist 89–Ten Knots (Raise You Ten 125) (1981 NR 1982 10s) first foal; dam quite a moderate hurdler; tailed-off last in minor event at Leicester in November. *J. Brennan.*   —

TENNIS TUNE 2 ch.c. Music Boy 124–Bonny Bertha (Capistrano 120) (1982 5g² 5fg* 5d² 5g³ 6fg 5g³ 5g²) Mar 9; 8,800Y; smallish, strong colt; good walker; first foal; dam won over 12.5f in Ireland; sold out of P. Haslam's stable 6,800 gns after winning 6-runner seller at Ayr in July; ran most consistently in nurseries afterwards; stays 6f. *D. Garraton.*   **74**

TENTH OF OCTOBER 3 b.c. Shiny Tenth 120–Seam 100 (Nearula 132) (1981 5d³ 5d* 5g* 5s* 5g 6s⁴ 6fg 7d* 8fg 8s 7s 1982 8g 10.6fg 8fg³ 10f⁴) useful sort; fair handicapper; stays 1m (soundly beaten over 1¼m); acts on any going with possible exception of very firm; ran moderately in blinkers once at 2 yrs. *S. Mellor.*   **82**

TEN-TRACO 3 b.f. Forlorn River 124–Cithern 91 (Canisbay 120) (1981 5d*(dis) 5d* 5fg³ 6fg* 6d 7s 6fg² 6s* 7s⁴ 6s 1982 6g 7d 6f 6g 7.2g 8f³ 10.4d 10.2g 8s) small, workmanlike filly; consistent and very genuine at 2 yrs when she was first past post 4 times; below form most starts in 1982; best form at 6f and is unlikely to stay 1¼m; seems to act on any going; broke a blood vessel second outing; sold 4,000 gns Newmarket December Sales. *D. H. Jones.*   **65**

TENTWORT 5 ch.m. Shiny Tenth 120–Pinguicula (Pinza 137) (1981 12s⁴ 15g² 16g 16f² 15g³ 14.7fg⁴ 14d 17f 16s⁴ 18g³ 18g³ 1982 15g² 16fg⁴ 16fg 16fg² 16g* 16d³ 17.4d 16.1s³ 18d 18s) lengthy mare; in frame most outings and won small handicap at Newcastle in August; stays well; acts on any going but seems ideally suited by some give in the ground. *W. Elsey.*   **61**

TEPELENI 2 b.c. Averof 123–Starbright (Petingo 135) (1982 7fg³) Mar 18; rangy colt; third foal; half-brother to a winner in Italy; dam ran once at 2 yrs;   — p second favourite but on backward side and very green, ran well until tiring in closing stages when 7 lengths third of 5 to very easy winner On Stage in £4,100 race at Newmarket in July; gave trouble at stalls when withdrawn at York the previous month; has plenty of scope for improvement. *C. Brittain.*

TEQUILLA SUNRISE (FR) 3 b.f. Nonoalco 131–Treacle 85 (Hornbeam 130) **75** (1981 7g² 1982 9g³ 12f 10.2g 8g² 7d² 7g 8s) rather leggy, useful-looking filly; best at up to 1m; suited by forcing tactics; sold 7,200 gns Newmarket Autumn Sales. *P. Walwyn.*

TERRENO 4 gr.c. Vaguely Noble 140–Ileana 113 (Abernant 142) (1981 9d* **116** 10s⁴ 1982 10.5s* 10.5d³ 12s 10.5g* 12v* 12g* 12g³ 12v) half-brother to several winners, including very smart French 6f to 1¼m winner Antrona (by Royal Palace); dam very useful miler; had a far busier season than in 1981 and showed smart form; won minor event at Maisons-Laffitte and valuable handicap at Saint-Cloud (in good style) before graduating successfully to pattern-race company; gained his most important wins in La Coupe at Chantilly in June (beat Hard To Sing by a neck) and Gran Premio di Milano in July (won by 2 lengths from Capricorn Line); ran only twice afterwards, finishing 7¼ lengths third to Orofino in Grosser Preis von Berlin at Dusseldorf later in July and bad last of 6 to Friendswood in Gran Premio del Jockey Club at Milan in October; stays 1½m; acts well on soft and heavy ground (yet to race on a firm surface). *F. Boutin, France.*

TESTON LAD 5 b.g. Blast 125–Right On Time 78 (Right Boy 137) (1981 6d — 6d 7fg 7fg 1982 7f) lengthy, fair sort; plater; best at 6f or 7f; acts on any going; sold 460 gns Newmarket Autumn Sales. *P. K. Mitchell.*

TETRAROSE 3 b. or br.f. Orange Bay 131–Ardgowan Brownie 81 (Prince **67** Tenderfoot 126) (1981 NR 1982 8fg 12fg 12fg³) 4,100F; leggy, lightly-made filly; second produce; dam won over 1m at 2 yrs and is half-sister to dam of Oats; just over 3 lengths fifth of 19 to Always Welcome in Wood Ditton Stakes at Newmarket in April; soundly beaten afterwards in Esal Bookmakers Oaks Trial at Lingfield and Lupe Stakes at Goodwood; dead. *P. Kelleway.*

TETRON BAY 2 b.c. Nonoalco 131–Tanella 103 (Habitat 134) (1982 5f 5fg **94** 8fg 8.2s 7g² 7s²) May 14; 5,400Y; well-made colt; third foal; dam, closely related to smart 1¼m filly Nanticious, won over 5f and 6f at 2 yrs; showed little worthwhile form until placed in fair company at Leicester and Chepstow in October; suited by 7f; acts on soft going. *R. Hannon.*

TEUCER 2 ch.g. Dance In Time–Rose and the Ring (Welsh Pageant 132) (1982 — 5fg 5fg 8s) Feb 27; 37,000Y; lengthy gelding; first foal; dam, well beaten both starts, is daughter of unbeaten 2-y-o Golden Treasure; stayed on steadily when seventh of 19 to Full Rainbow in maiden race at Warwick in October, third outing and first sign of ability; evidently suited by test of stamina; gelded after final start. *G. Lewis.*

TEXAS GOLD 3 ch.g. Dragonara Palace 115–Concisely (Connaught 130) — (1981 5fg 6d 1982 6f 6f 8g 8.3fg 10.1fg⁴ 10f) big gelding; plater; possibly stays 1¼m; has worn blinkers; has been taken early to stable. *H. O'Neill.*

TEZ SHAHZADA 2 b.c. Mummy's Pet 125–Eastern Romance 73 (Sahib 114) — (1982 6fg) Apr 29; 7,000Y; rather lightly-made colt; second foal; half-brother to 3-y-o 7f and 1m winner State Romance (by Free State); dam won 6f seller at 2 yrs; behind in 19-runner maiden race at Newmarket in July. *P. Haslam.*

THAHUL (USA) 5 b.h. Nijinsky 138–Queen City Miss (Royal Union) (1981 **79** 15.5d 13.1g 14d* 16.1f* 16fg³ 16.1d 14fg 1982 16d 16f* 14fg* 14fg* 16g 12fg) deep-girthed, rangy horse; good walker; improved and won handicaps at Warwick, Salisbury (made all) and Goodwood; trotted up by 8 lengths from John O' Groats on last-named course in May; shade disappointing afterwards (not seen out after Royal Ascot); suited by 1¾m+; has won on a soft surface but is much better suited by top-of-the-ground; wears blinkers nowadays. *F. J. Houghton.*

THARALEOS (USA) 2 ch.c. Junction–Right About (Citation) (1982 7fg 7g) — Mar 5; $50,000Y; robust, heavy-topped colt; half-brother to numerous winners in USA, including Ruthie's Native (by Native Royalty), a very smart winner at up to 9f; dam 6f winner; sire, son of Never Bend, was very smart 7f to 9f winner at 3 yrs; behind in maiden races at Salisbury and Yarmouth in September; sold F. Watson 1,600 gns Newmarket Autumn Sales. *C. Brittain.*

THARSUS GIRL 3 br.f. Blakeney 126–Just Larking (Sea-Bird II 145) (1981 **70** 6f 6g 7fg 8fg 10s 1982 12f 17f 12f 16fg 12.3d* 13.8f³ 12g 12g³ 16fg² 17.4d 16s³ 15.8d³ 18s) workmanlike filly; showed improved form when winning handicap at Newcastle in June; not disgraced most subsequent starts; stays well; seems to act on any going; usually blinkered. *K. Stone.*

THAT'S INCREDIBLE 2 b.c. Oats 126–Lively (Run The Gantlet) (1982 — 6f 6f 6v) Mar 1; IR 16,000Y; neat, strong, quite attractive colt; second foal; dam never ran; little worthwhile form; trained by C. Williams first 2 starts, and off course 4 months subsequently. *P. Mitchell.*

THAT'S MAGIC 4 ch.f. Bay Express 132–Alumina 86 (Fortino II 120) (1981 — 6g 6g 7f* 7f 7f 7.2fg 7g 7g 6g 7g 1982 7g 10fg 7g 8f 6g 7f) neat filly; plater nowadays; suited by 7f; acts on any going; has been tried in blinkers; sold 750 gns Doncaster September Sales. *J. Parkes.*

THAT'S MY SON 3 b.c. Busted 134–Take a Chance (Baldric II 131) (1981 **99** 6f 7g 7fg 6g 7g³ 8d 1982 8s 10f 8f² 8fg² 8f 8g² 8fg* 7f* 8f* 8g 8g 7g) big, strong, attractive colt; excellent walker; landed the odds in maiden race at Yarmouth, 3-runner handicap at Sandown and minor event at Salisbury; beat Thorndown a shade cheekily by a neck on last-named; will stay 1¼m; acts on firm going; suited by waiting tactics and isn't easiest of rides; beaten a long way last 2 starts (out of depth on second occasion). *C. Brittain.*

THATS ODD 2 ro.g. Warpath 113–Broughton Flyer (Huntercombe 133) **70** (1982 5s³ 5fg 6fg 5g 5g 5d) May 15; 4,600Y; leggy gelding; good walker; third foal; brother to tough 1981 2-y-o 5f and 6f winner Houghton Weaver; 4 lengths fifth of 7 behind Sea Pago in maiden race at Pontefract in August, fourth outing and best effort; in front rank when hampered below distance in valuable seller at York on next appearance; should be suited by 6f. *J. Berry.*

THE ADRIANSTAN 7 ch.g. Sparkler 130–Riberta 89 (Ribot 142) (1981 10s — 11s 1982 8f 10f) one-time useful handicapper but is completely unreliable; stays 1¼m; acts on any going; has been tried in blinkers; sometimes starts slowly; not an easy ride; sold 1,025 gns Ascot 2nd June Sales. *D. Hanley.*

THE ARKESDEN AXE 5 ch.g. Redundant 120–Brocette (Brocade Slipper — 116) (1981 NR 1982 12g 16d) plater at 3 yrs; stays 1¼m; has worn blinkers. *R. Johnson.*

THE ASPEL 4 b.g. Pongee 106–Stephela (Young Stratford 92) (1981 NR — 1982 10g) workmanlike gelding; well behind in maiden races and sellers. *D. Chapman.*

THE BABE (USA) 2 b.f. Fleet Mel–Babe's Wind (Windy Sands) (1982 5fg **91** 6f³ 6f* 6g 7s) close-coupled filly; first foal; dam, placed twice from 5 starts in USA, is daughter of Balcony's Babe, a very useful winner at up to 9f; ran on gamely under very strong riding when winning 14-runner maiden race at Goodwood in July by ¾ length from Suffred; in rear subsequently in Lowther Stakes at York and nursery on same course; should be suited by 7f. *H. Wragg.*

THE BEGINNING 4 ro.f. Goldhill 125–Histoun (Behistoun 131) (1981 6g 5f — 7.2f 8g³ 9g 8f 8fg³ 8.2s³ 9s 1982 8.2s³ 8f 12f 9.4fg 12fg 15.8f 10d 12g⁴) fair sort; plater; probably stays 1½m; trained until after third start by C. Booth. *W. Storey.*

THE BONDERIZER 2 gr.g. Tennyson 124–Zeddenosa (Zeddaan 130) (1982 **57** 7g 7fg 8s) Apr 3; 6,000F; short-backed, plain gelding; second produce; dam French middle-distance winner; little worthwhile form; gelded after final outing. *M. Blanshard.*

THE BRADFORD 3 b.c. Connaught 130–Mockbridge 106 (Bleep-Bleep 134) — (1981 NR 1982 8.2f 9fg 5fg 8.2s 6s) big, strong, workmanlike colt; has a round action; brother to 1978 2-y-o 6f winner Haven Bridge and a half-brother to 2 winners; dam won over 5f and 7f at 2 yrs from four starts; plating-class maiden; stays 1m. *L. Barratt.*

THE BRU 2 b.g. Welsh Saint 126–Mrs Bizz (Status Seeker) (1982 5f⁴ 5fg 6f **60** 8d⁴ 10d) May 13; 200Y; unimpressive, leggy, dipped-backed gelding; first foal; dam Irish 1m and 9f winner; modest plater; suited by a test of stamina; blinkered final outing. *J. Fitzgerald.*

THE BUSINESS 3 b.f. Young Emperor 133–Shenan (Dunce) (1981 NR — 1982 7g 11.5fg) IR 3,100F, 11,500Y; strong, plain filly; half-sister to Irish middle-distance winner Double Century (by Double-U-Jay); dam won 4 races at up to 6f in USA, including a stakes race; behind in maiden races at Newmarket in April and Sandown in August. *P. Haslam.*

THE BYSTANDER 3 b.g. Owen Anthony 102–Pearl River (Bourbon Prince) — (1981 5d 1982 6d 7fg 6g³) smallish, lengthy gelding; little worthwhile form in varied company, including selling; best run at 6f when apprentice ridden. *J. Holt.*

THE CAIRNWELL 3 b.f. Mount Hagen 127–Deep Company 94 (Carnival —
Dancer 113) (1981 5s² 5g 5fg³ 5.8h² 5g⁴ 5s² 1982 5g 5g 5f) workmanlike
filly; sprint maiden; stays 6f; acts on any going; blinkered last 2 starts.
H. T. Jones.

THE CATISFIELD KID 3 br.c. Comedy Star 121–Pure Gold (Pieces of Eight —
128) (1981 NR 1982 6s 8d 7.6f 5f 10g) quite well-made colt; third living
foal; dam unraced half-sister to smart 1969 French 2-y-o Chatter Box; in rear
in maiden races and a minor event. *W. Wightman.*

THE CLIFTONIAN 4 b.g. Firestreak 125–Ile de France 84 (French Beige 127) —
(1981 10.1d* 10.1v* 10g 10.1f 10f⁴ 10g 1982 10g 12fg 10d 10.8s) won 2 minor
events at Windsor in 1981 but has become disappointing and is none too consistent; should stay 1½m; acts on heavy going. *J. Bethell.*

THE DICE MAN (USA) 3 ch.c. Key To The Mint–Bases Loaded (Northern **91**
Dancer) (1981 7g⁴ 1982 10f* 10.1fg³) shapely colt; landed odds narrowly
from Goumi in maiden race at Nottingham in April; ran respectably only subsequent start in May; stays 1¼m. *H. Cecil.*

THE DINMONT 3 b.c. Mummy's Pet 125–Veronique 96 (Matador 131) (1981 **100**
6fg⁴ 6g* 6fg 1982 7s 5d 6s³ 6d) rangy, quite attractive colt; has an enlarged
off-fore; won Rous Memorial Stakes at Goodwood in 1981 in fine style; fractured
a bone in off-fore next time and wasn't seen out at 3 yrs until September, putting
up respectable efforts on second and third starts when 2½ lengths fifth of 11 to
Ferryman in £4,600 race at Newmarket and 4 lengths third of 4 to Soba in Coral
Bookmakers Champion Sprint at York; likely to prove best at 6f; sold, probably
for export to South Africa, 10,000 gns Newmarket December Sales. *J. Dunlop.*

THE DIPLOMAT 4 gr.g. The Go-Between 129–Serene Thought (Burglar 128) —
(1981 NR 1982 8f 12f⁴ 11g) big gelding; brother to quite moderate 1979
2-y-o maiden Secret Agent; dam last on only outing; showed signs of a little
ability on first 2 starts; not certain to stay 1½m. *D. Ringer.*

THE DISCO DAGO 4 ch.g. Record Token 128–Repel (Hardicanute 130) —
(1981 10d² 10fg⁴ 12.2g³ 12s⁴ 1982 14.7f 16.5s) small, workmanlike gelding;
in frame in maiden and minor races as a 3-y-o; stays 1½m; sold 8,000 gns Ascot
December Sales, and is to be trained by R. Champion. *G. Pritchard-Gordon.*

THE ENID 2 b.f. Tudor Rhythm 112–Flora Leigh 94 (Floribunda 136) (1982 **53**
5fg 5fg 6g 5g 5.1f⁴) May 13; lengthy, good sort; half-sister to winners in Brazil
and Trinidad; dam, half-sister to smart fillies Weeber and Amicable, stayed
1¼m, poor form in maiden and minor events; not raced after July; blinkered
final start. *C. Mackenzie.*

THE FIREBIRD 3 b.f. Busted 134–Karsavina 89 (Silly Season 127) (1981 —
NR 1982 8fg 10fg) third foal; half-sister to fairly useful 1m and 9f winner
The Shrew (by Relko) and to Katharina (by Frankincense), a useful performer
at up to 1m; dam half-sister to very useful miler Boswellia; under 8 lengths
eighth of 18 to Photo in minor event at Thirsk in September, first outing and
better effort; should stay middle distances; sold 10,000 gns Newmarket December Sales. *E. Incisa.*

THE FLOORLAYER 4 b.g. Import 127–Lonely Nymph 60 (Forlorn River 124) — ·
(1981 5f 10.1fg 8fg 11.7h 1982 16d) little worthwhile form over a wide range
of distances. *D. Elsworth.*

THE FORT 2 ch.c. Sallust 134–Fortlin 95 (Fortino II 120) (1982 6fg³ 7g* **123**
7fg* 7s*)
    That The Fort is just 6 lb behind the top-rated Diesis in the International
Classification gives some idea of the impression the colt created when winning
the last three of his four races, none of them a pattern event. Although we
haven't rated The Fort quite so highly we too hold a good opinion of him and
feel sure he'll make a formidable three-year-old. The Fort first looked something out of the ordinary when proving far too good for twenty-two others in a
maiden race at Newmarket early in August; he drew away in the last two furlongs
to win easily by four lengths from Penybont, showing a great deal of improvement
on his modest third to Persian Glory in a similar event at York a month before.
He was similarly impressive against stiffer opposition in his other races, the
Intercraft Solario Stakes at Sandown later in August and the Limekiln Stakes
at Goodwood towards the end of September. At Sandown he started co-favourite
with Kuwait Tower, who had dead-heated with Muscatite at Ascot on his only
appearance, with the unbeaten Naar, winner of the Granville Stakes, next in the

Intercraft Solario Stakes, Sandown—another good two-year-old winner for Cecil as The Fort beats Kuwait Tower

betting. The Fort went straight into the lead, setting a pace which had nearly all his opponents in trouble with two furlongs still to race. The one exception, Kuwait Tower, threw down a dangerous-looking challenge but The Fort needed only a few reminders to stride away again for a three-length success, breaking the seven-furlong course record for two-year-olds in the process. The Fort showed here that he acts well on fast ground and he proved just as effective on soft going at Goodwood where he had to give 3 lb to the only other fancied runner, the dual-winner Zoffany. When Zoffany closed to within a length of him below the distance it looked for a moment as though the weight concession might sway the issue but The Fort had plenty in reserve, despite having led from the start, and shook him off in good style to win by two and a half lengths.

			┌ Palestine
		┌ Pall Mall	┤
	┌ Sallust	┤ (ch 1955)	└ Malapert
	┤ (ch 1969)	└ Bandarilla	┌ Matador
The Fort	┤	(ch 1960)	└ Interval
(ch.c. Apr 14, 1980)	┤	┌ Fortino II	┌ Grey Sovereign
	└ Fortlin	┤ (gr 1959)	└ Ranavalo
	(b 1966)	└ Creepy Crawley	┌ The Bug
		(br 1956)	└ Iverley Way

The Fort is a brother to the tip-top French filly Sanedtki, an 1,150-guinea yearling who went on to record ten victories, including one in the Prix du Moulin de Longchamp, two in the Prix de la Foret and one in the nine-furlong Santa Margarita Invitational Handicap. Once Sanedtki's merit became established her breeder wasted no time in returning her dam, the fairly useful two-year-old sprinter Fortlin, to Sallust. Fortlin produced three colts by him, all of whom sold far better as yearlings than Sanedtki had done. The first two, Cimon and Tony Tan, fetched 105,000 Irish guineas and 63,000 Irish guineas respectively before developing into fairly useful performers at up to a mile in Ireland. Cimon is now at stud in France. When The Fort appeared in the sales ring his pleasing appearance—he's a good-bodied, full-quartered colt—was marred by what his trainer described as 'the most enormous splint' on his near-fore. Cecil told us that he wasn't too worried by the splint, which has never caused The Fort any lameness, but it was sufficiently unsightly to limit The Fort's sale price to 42,000 Irish guineas. The Fort is also a half-brother to the Belgian winner Twister (by Double-U-Jay) and the French nine- to eleven-furlong winner

Mrs Harold Phillips' "The Fort"

Mrs Hippy (by Tudor Music), who incidentally foaled a chesnut filly by Sallust in 1982. Fortlin's most recent foal, a colt by General Assembly, was sold for 60,000 guineas at the 1982 Goffs Yearling Sale. The Fort's grandam Creepy Crawley didn't win, coming nearest to success when second twice over six furlongs in Ireland, but she was a half-sister to the high-class sprinter Vilmoray. The Fort will be well suited by a mile, although he's unlikely to stay much further. His trainer is a lucky man to have such an excellent reserve should anything go wrong with his Two Thousand Guineas favourite Diesis. *H. Cecil.*

THE FRIEND 4 ch.c. Run The Gantlet–Loose Cover 106 (Venture VII 129) **59** (1981 8d* 8.2s³ 10f 12fg 12fg 12g³ 13d 16s⁴ 1982 12s² 13d⁴ 12f³ 12f* 12fg) lightly-made, quite attractive colt; poor walker; won amateur riders race at Redcar in August; seems to stay 2m; evidently acts on any going; blinkered nowadays; not the most genuine of horses and seems to run well when fresh. *H. T. Jones.*

THE GOVERNOR (FR) 3 ch.c. Grundy 137–Cley 85 (Exbury 138) (1981 7d **73** 1982 12s 10f⁴ 12f² 14d 12f 12v) big colt; quite moderate; likely to need a stiff test of stamina; hung badly second start; sold to D. Ringer 7,200 gns Newmarket Autumn Sales. *J. Dunlop.*

THE GRADER 4 ch.f. Master Sing 109–Full Swing 71 (Ballyciptic 122) (1981 **—** 5fg 6f 5g 1982 7fg 10f 6fg 6g) seems of little account. *J. Long.*

THE GRASS (USA) 3 b.c. Raja Baba–Name Me Not (Pago Pago) (1981 NR **69** 1982 7g* 8f 7.6fg⁴ 8f 7fg 7.6g 7f⁴ 7g 7.2s) $75,000Y; robust, good-quartered colt;

839

first foal; dam, sister to 3 stakes winners, won over 6f; beat stable-companion Bombili by ½ length in 11-runner newcomers race at Doncaster in March; well beaten most subsequent starts; should stay 1m; best form on a sound surface; blinkered final start. *G. Balding.*

THE GREY BOMBER 3 gr.c. Scallywag 127–Halkissimo 61 (Khalkis 127) — (1981 NR 1982 16fg⁴ 12d³ 16g⁴ 14.6g) very big colt; half-brother to 3 winners, including 9f and 1¼m winner Mac's Delight (by Scottish Rifle); dam won over 1m; in frame in maiden races and a minor event in the North; one paced and was suited by a test of stamina; useful juvenile hurdler; dead. *D. Smith.*

THE HARLEQUIN (USA) 3 gr.c. Roberto 131–Belle de Nuit (Warfare) **70** (1981 NR 1982 11g*) half-brother to 3 winners, notably very smart French middle-distance winner Paint the Town (by Vaguely Noble) and very smart 1981 American 3-y-o filly Dame Mysterieuse (by Bold Forbes); dam, smart winner at up to 7f, is half-sister to top 1953 American 2-y-o Evening Out; favourite and coltish in paddock when beating King of Man easily by 2¼ lengths in 11-runner maiden race at Ayr in July; looked promising here but didn't race again; will stay 1½m. *C. Nelson.*

THE HOUSE BUILDER 2 b.c. Sharpen Up 127–Via Tritus 103 (Sovereign **79** Path 125) (1982 6v 5s³) May 12; 21,000 gns F, $63,000Y, $65,000 2-v-o; strong colt; half-brother to a winning plater and a winner in Belgium; dam won twice at around 1m; 3 lengths third of 15 to Dry Land in maiden race at Sandown in October; should stay at least 6f; may improve. *M. Jarvis.*

THE HUYTON GIRLS 4 ch.f. Master Sing 109–Artway 82 (Articulate 121) **53** (1981 6v³ 5d* 5g³ 5s* 5d* 6f 5fg 5fg 5d 5s 5s 5s 1982 6s 6s² 5fg 5f 6fg⁴ 5g 5d 5s) fair sort; sprint handicapper; off course 3 months with a back injury after sixth start and was well beaten on her return; ideally suited by some give in the ground; often apprentice ridden; out of her depth fourth start; usually blinkered in 1982. *M. James.*

THE IRISH RHINE 4 b.g. Ragapan 118–At The King's Side (Kauai King) — (1981 11g³ 7s 12fg 1982 12s³ 15.5fg 12f 12s) ex-Irish gelding; third foal; brother to Irish 1½m winner King Ragapan; dam won claiming races at up to 1m in USA; moderate third in maiden race at Haydock in April, best effort on flat over here; stays 1½m. *D. Wilson.*

THE KNIFE 4 b.g. Fine Blade 121–Mary Kanga 67 (Charlottesville 135) (1981 8fg 11.7g 11.7g 8f³ 8f² 8fg² 8.3fg 1982 15.5fg) small, lightly-made gelding; plater; should stay further than 1m; occasionally blinkered. *J. Bosley.*

THE LEGIONARY 2 ch.g. Roman Warrior 132–Trigonella (Balliol 125) (1982 — 5d 5fg 5d 6s 10s) Apr 24; 1R 1,900F, 720Y; strong gelding; first foal; dam never ran; of no account. *A. Potts.*

THE LIQUIDATOR 2 b.c. Busted 134–Teleflora 89 (Princely Gift 137) (1982 **104 p** 8d*) Mar 30; 31,000Y; half-brother to 1½m and 2¼m winner Baron Blakeney (by Blakeney), also a very useful winner over hurdles, and a winner in Hungary; dam sprinting half-sister to high-class stayer Grey Baron; third favourite, put up a very taking performance when winning 23-runner maiden race at Newmarket in October, making much of running and fighting off his challengers in fine style to score by 3 lengths from Herodote; will stay 1½m; a very useful colt in the making. *B. Hobbs.*

THE LYCANTHROPE 2 ch.f. Filiberto 123–Deep Lady 78 (Deep Diver 134) — (1982 5fg 7fg 6g) Apr 22; 800F; lightly-made filly; first produce; dam 2-y-o 5f winner; bad plater; sold 340 gns Doncaster November Sales. *P. Kelleway*

THE MAZALL 2 br.g. Persian Bold 123–Dance All Night 106 (Double-U-Jay — 120) (1982 7.2g 6g) May 19; 900Y; small gelding; half-brother to 2 winners, including useful 6f and 7f winner Dancing Sally (by Sallust); dam won from 5f to 9f; well beaten in minor events at Haydock and Ripon in August. *Miss L. Siddall.*

THE MINSTER (USA) 2 b.c. The Minstrel 135–Play at Home (Round Table) **94 p** (1982 6g² 7g²) Mar 26; $365,000Y; strong, good-looking colt; good walker and mover; fifth foal; half-brother to a winner; dam, winner at up to 1m in USA, is half-sister to high-class colts Home Guard and Boone's Cabin; looked unlucky when promising second of 20 in maiden race at Yarmouth in September, failing by only a short head to catch Asswan after hanging left when putting in a strong late run; drew well clear of remainder and again showed plenty of promise when 3 lengths second of 28 to odds-on Tolomeo in similar race at Newmarket the following month; will stay 1m; should have no difficulty in winning in maiden company and promises to make a useful 3-y-o. *M. Albina.*

THE NEUROLOGIST 4 ch.f. Ragstone 128–Flower Centre 98 (Jaipur) (1981 **103**
9d 14g³ 12s* 14f³ 12fg² 12fg 12d* 16d* 12d* 1982 10s 10s 16fg 16g* 22.2fg³ 12g
11.5g⁴ 20s² 16d⁴ 12g⁴) small, lightly-built filly; developed into a very useful filly
in 1981; ran well at times in 1982, particularly when 2 lengths second of 11
behind Kelbomec in Prix Gladiateur at Longchamp in September; ran respectably
when about 13 lengths fourth of 8 behind Little Wolf in Jockey Club Cup at
Newmarket the following month; had earlier won minor event at Limerick
Junction and had stayed on very strongly to be 6½ lengths third to Ore in Queen
Alexandra Stakes at Royal Ascot; stays extremely well (finds 1¼m too short for
her); acts on any going, but is particularly well suited by give in the ground.
E. O'Grady, Ireland.

THE NIDD 3 b.f. Rapid River 127–Molly Mayfield (Clear River 114) (1981 —
5g 1982 7f4 7g 6g⁴ 5f 6g) robust, lengthy filly; plater; possibly stays 7f; sold
510 gns Doncaster October Sales. *C. Thornton.*

THE NOBLE PLAYER (USA) 2 ch.c. The Minstrel 135–Noble Mark 120 (On **126**
Your Mark 125) (1982 5g³ 5f* 5f* 6f² 7.2g³ 6g² 8.2fg* 8s³ 8s³)
   Peterhof's two successes in five-furlong pattern races in 1981 perhaps set
trainers thinking that The Minstrel's offspring were, by and large, going to prove
speedier and more precocious than their sire, an outstanding mile-and-a-half
performer who didn't race until the September of his two-year-old days. Before
the season was three months old no fewer than ten of The Minstrel's British
two-year-olds, members of his second crop, were being entered in races. Two
of them, Shicklah and The Noble Player, did prove to have sufficient speed to
win over five furlongs but it wasn't until The Noble Player tackled a mile in the
autumn that he showed what a tough, high-class performer he is. He had by
then won two of his six races, a maiden at Sandown in April, which he took in
excellent style by three lengths from Prince Spy, and a three-runner event at Bath
when 9/1 on, but he had been beaten on his last three starts: in the Chesham
Stakes at Royal Ascot he had gone down by a short head to Right Dancer; in the
Cock of the North Stakes at Haydock he'd finished third, beaten a length and
a neck by Alchise and Shearwalk, after hanging left in the closing stages; and in

Mr R. E. Sangster's "The Noble Player" (S. Cauthen)

the Washington Singer Stakes at Newbury, when receiving 6 lb, he'd gone down by two and a half lengths to Horage, after giving him a good fight up to the final hundred yards. He first tackled a mile in the John Player New Grandstand Stakes at Haydock in September where the opposition included the impressive Salisbury winner Sailor's Dance, the useful maiden Montrevie, who'd been beaten only narrowly by Flamenco and Acclimatise on her last start, the Gimcrack third Shackle Pin and the six-length Sandown winner Beldale Concorde. The Noble Player and Beldale Concorde had the race to themselves in the last quarter mile and The Noble Player, who'd been going well from the start, proved easily the stronger, gaining the upper hand inside the final furlong to win by a length and a half, despite again hanging left.

The Noble Player followed this very smart display with two more excellent efforts in the Royal Lodge Stakes at Ascot and the Grand Criterium at Longchamp. At Ascot he came through to finish third of nine, three lengths behind Dunbeath, giving the strong impression he would have finished closer had he not had difficulty finding a clear passage in the straight. He proved at Longchamp that he's better than his Royal Lodge running suggests. Although up against very tough opposition in the French pattern-race winners Saint Cyrien, L'Emigrant and Deep Roots, The Noble Player was far from outclassed; he threw down a challenge as L'Emigrant, another colt by The Minstrel, hit the front inside the last two furlongs and then battled on so well, as Saint Cyrien swept by them both, that he failed by only a nose to snatch second place. Saint Cyrien beat him a length. The Noble Player was still clearly improving despite his long, hard season but he hasn't been given credit in the International Classification for this splendid effort; he has been rated 7 lb behind Saint Cyrien who gave him only a 2-lb beating, 3 lb behind L'Emigrant and 4 lb behind Deep Roots whom he beat by two lengths.

The Noble Player (USA) (ch.c. Apr 17, 1980)	The Minstrel (ch 1974)	Northern Dancer (b 1961)	Nearctic
			Natalma
		Fleur (b 1964)	Victoria Park
			Flaming Page
	Noble Mark (ch 1971)	On Your Mark (ch 1964)	Restless Wind
			Super Scope
		Noble Joan (ch 1963)	Pall Mall
			Rhena Belle

The Noble Player's trainer also trained his dam Noble Mark as a three-year-old, winning the Duke of York Stakes with her and also collecting third place in the Temple Stakes and the King's Stand Stakes. When trained in Ireland the previous season Noble Mark had won the Phoenix Stakes and three other five-furlong events, meeting her only defeat when an honourable second in the Lowther Stakes. She was later sent to the USA, racing five times without success. Noble Mark's three previous foals appeared to inherit little of her speed: Victor's Boast (by Roberto) and the three-year-old filly Traviata (by Youth) each gained their single success over a mile and a quarter, and Noble Dudley (by Giacometti) gained his four victories at nine furlongs to a mile and a half in the North. Noble Mark was one of three winners foaled by the unraced twin Noble Joan. The family is, on the whole, not a very distinguished one but that needn't concern us now that The Noble Player has proved himself a high-class performer. He's a well-made, attractive colt who should train on and he's sure to win good middle-distance events if he reproduces his Longchamp form. He has run well on all types of going but his best performance came in very testing conditions and it may be significant that he has twice shown a tendency to hang when racing on a sound surface. It bears repeating that he's admirably tough, and he's consistent too. *B. Hills.*

THE NUB 3 br.c. Mr Bigmore 123–Sun Queen 76 (Lucky Sovereign) (1981 7fg 7fg⁴ 8s³ 8d* 1982 8s 10f 11.5g 9.2g*) strong, workmanlike ex-English colt; has a round action; beaten a long way in Easter Stakes at Kempton and Guardian Classic Trial at Sandown in April; subsequently sent to France and won minor event at Rouen in October; should stay 1¼m; suited by some give in the ground; trained by F. Durr first 2 starts. *E. Bartholomew, France.*

THE OWLS 3 b. or br.g. Pieces of Eight 128–Keino (Kautokeino) (1981 6fg 6g 7fg⁴ 7.6fg⁴ 8.2s 8g 8d 1982 10d* 12f 11.7d³ 11g⁴ 10fg³ 13d² 12g 12d² 16s) narrow, workmanlike gelding; won maiden race at Folkestone in March; ran respectably most starts afterwards; stays 13f; acts on a firm and a soft surface; has run creditably for an apprentice; ran badly in blinkers once in 1981. *M. Tompkins.*

*Kiveton Park Steel Stakes, Doncaster—best run of the year from
The Quiet Bidder who beats Merlins Charm and Cajun*

THE PAIN BARRIER 3 b.g. Blakeney 126–Vilswitch 93 (Vilmorin) (1981 **78**
7fg⁴ 1982 8.2fg³ 8d³ 10fg³ 10f² 10fg 12s² 12v* 12g) quite attractive gelding;
drew clear to beat Quonset by 12 lengths in 12-runner minor event at Lingfield in
October (odds on); placed in maiden races and handicaps previously; suited by
1½m; acts on any going but revels in the mud; has shown a tendency to hang.
J. Sutcliffe.

THE PARROT 3 b.g. Pampapaul 121–Puka (Parthia 132) (1981 6d 7fg 7fg³ 7d³ **77**
1982 11.7d² 11.7fg) rangy, quite attractive gelding; quite moderate; will stay
1½m; sometimes blinkered but is effective without. *J. Tree.*

THE PAWN 3 b.c. Malinowski 123–Skelmorlie (Blakeney 126) (1981 NR **?**
1982 12f* 12f³ 10g 10g³ 16.5g³ 14f 12f* 13g 18d 12s 10s) IR 40,000Y; smallish ex-
Irish colt; third foal; dam Irish 1½m winner; narrowly won maiden race at Naas
in April and handicap at Sligo in August; placed several other starts but ran his
share of moderate races and finished well beaten in minor events at Doncaster and
Leicester and apprentice race at Chepstow on last 3 outings; stays well; acts on
firm going; blinkered fifth to eighth starts; sold out of A. Maxwell's stable IR
12,500 gns Goffs September Sales after eighth outing. *M. Ryan.*

THE QUIET BIDDER 4 b.c. Auction Ring 123–Capule (Middleground) (1981 **115**
7g² 8g 6s 7.2s³ 6f* 6.5fg 7.3fg 1982 5fg 6f 5f 7g⁴ 7g* 7g³) quite a useful sort
who did well over winter; none too good a mover in slower paces; a smart and
genuine performer as a 3-y-o who gained a well-deserved success in Cork and
Orrery Stakes at Royal Ascot; had stiff task and ran easily best race of 1982 in
9-runner Kiveton Park Steel Stakes at Doncaster in September, quickening up
well when a gap appeared to lead inside last furlong, and running on strongly to
beat Merlins Charm by ½ length; also ran creditably 3 times at Newmarket,
finishing about 3 lengths fifth of 12 behind Lightning Label in Palace House
Stakes on reappearance in May, 6½ lengths fourth of 14 to Noalcoholic in Van
Geest Stakes the following month and 3¾ lengths third of 8 to Noalcoholic again in
Bisquit Cognac Challenge Stakes in October; rather disappointing in good races
on other starts; suited by 7f and stayed 1m; acted on any going; retired to Haras
du Pin. *M. Stoute.*

THE QUIET DON (USA) 2 b.c. Caucasus 127–Softly (Solo Landing) (1982 **93**
6f 7d* 7f* 7f* 8fg) Mar 28; $115,000Y; quite well-made colt; half-brother to
2 winners by Rock Talk, including very useful stakes winner Rock Softly; dam,
sprinter, at her best at 2 yrs when very useful; won 18-runner maiden race at
Salisbury in June, minor event at Leicester in July and £3,900 nursery at Brighton
in August; sweated up quite badly and was never going well under top weight in
nursery at Thirsk in September; considered best on galloping track; sold 31,000
gns Newmarket Autumn Sales and subsequently raced in Italy. *G. Harwood.*

THE RANEE 2 b.f. Royal Palace 131–Gingerale (Golden Horus 123) (1982 6g **—**
7g) Jan 30; lengthy filly; half-sister to 3-y-o Gigondas and 2 winners, including

1m winner Countess Walewski (all by Brigadier Gerard); dam useful at up to 9.5f in France; well beaten in big fields of maidens at Newmarket in the autumn. *W. Holden.*

THE RED DUKE 3 ch.c. Red Alert 127–Dutchess of Man (Petingo 135) (1981 6g 8g⁴ 8s² 1982 9g 12.3f³ 12d) big, strong colt; poor mover; quite moderate at his best; not certain to stay 1¼m; sold 1,300 gns Doncaster November Sales. *R. D. Peacock.* —

THE RIDINGS 3 br.g. Town Crier 119–Grenfilt 83 (Sheshoon 132) (1981 NR 1982 8.2f 8.2fg 9fg 10d) half-brother to a winning plater; dam won over 7f at 2 yrs; poor maiden. *J. W. Watts.* —

THE RIPLEYITE 3 ch.c. Northfields–Red Ruby 113 (Tudor Melody 129) (1981 5g 6g 6g 7fg³ 6fg 6fg⁴ 6f⁴ 7g³ 7d 1982 7g⁴ 8g² 8f² 8fg* 8fg 8.5f³ 8f³ 8fg³ 8f² 8.5fg³ 8fg³ 8d² 8s 8s) lightly-made, quite attractive colt; fair handicapper; won at Goodwood in May; stays 1m; probably acts on any going; doesn't find much off bridle and is suited by waiting tactics. *G. Balding.* 82

THE RUGBY CLUB (USA) 5 ch.g. Giacometti 130–Blabla 118 (Lavandin 128) (1981 10g* 10d 9g⁴ 8.5f 8.5f* 10fg⁴ 10fg* 10g 1982 10fg 10fg⁴ 12.2fg 12f) robust, short-legged gelding; won 3 apprentice races in 1981, 2 of them handicaps; didn't recapture that form (blinkered final start); stays 1¼m; suited by top-of-the-ground; sold to BBA (Italia) 760 gns Newmarket Autumn Sales. *D. Morley.* —

THE SHINER 2 b.g. Julio Mariner 127–Wolver Valley 72 (Wolver Hollow 126) (1982 7f 7g 7g 8g) Mar 11; 7,800Y; narrow, leggy, unfurnished gelding; third foal; dam won 5 middle-distance races; blinkered, about 9 lengths eighth in big field of maidens at Newmarket in October, final outing and easily best effort; will be suited by 1¼m+. *D. Morley.* 83

THE SMALL MIRACLE 4 gr.g. Most Secret 119–Grey Aglow 89 (Aglojo 119) (1981 10.7d³ 12d⁴ 10d² 12fg² 11g 10g 10g² 9s² 12s³ 12g² 12d 1982 10d* 10d 12.3fg 10.5s 12d) workmanlike gelding; held up when winning handicap at Leicester in March; stays 1½m; has run respectably on a firm surface, but revels in the mud; has run creditably in blinkers; off course 5 months after third start. *N. Bycroft.* 63

THE SOLENT 6 ch.g. Exbury 138–West Side Story 127 (Rockefella) (1981 12g 12f 20.4fg 15.8g 19g 16f 8g 8g 12d 11d 1982 12g⁴ 15.8f 12fg² 12s 10g 10fg² 16d 8fg) workmanlike gelding; temperamental nowadays, although ran creditably when in frame in 3 handicaps (one of them a seller) at Pontefract in 1982; blinkered last 3 starts. *D. Chapman.* §§

THESSALONIKI 2 ch.f. Julio Mariner 127–Camina Bay 109 (Whistling Wind 123) (1982 6fg⁴ 8g 8f² 6g⁴ 7g² 7s) May 20; smallish, close-coupled filly; half-sister to several winners, including 1981 2-y-o 6f winner Aegean Beauty (by Sharpen Up) and Foveros (by Averof), a very smart winner at up to 1¼m here and in South Africa; dam useful sprinting 2-y-o; showed consistent form without winning in varied company, on penultimate outing finishing 1½ lengths second of 7 to Saving Mercy in Rockfel Stakes at Newmarket in October; needs at least 7f, and will stay beyond 1m; acts on any going. *C. Brittain.* 94

THE SURVEYOR 6 br.g. Goldhill 125–Shortino 71 (Fortino II 120) (1981 8.2g 1982 8.2s) plater; stays 1m; acts on firm going. *R. Hollinshead.* —

THE TEXEL 2 b.g. Coded Scrap 90–Jet Maiden (Star Gazer 123) (1982 6f² 6f 6f 7fg 6g) Mar 14; half-brother to a winning plater; short-head second to Cadasi in minor event at Carlisle in June; lost his form afterwards, and was soundly beaten in sellers last 2 outings; not sure to stay 7f; sold 340 gns Ascot October Sales. *R. Johnson.* 69 d

THE THUNDERER 2 gr.g. Town Crier 119–Fair Measure (Quorum 126) (1982 7s 8s) May 17; fifth foal; half-brother to 2m winner Gold Measure (by Goldhill); dam ran only 3 times; 5 lengths fifth to Rana Pratap in 12-runner minor event at Chepstow in October, first outing and better effort; stays 7f. *P. M. Taylor.* 69

THE TURNED REVENGE 5 ch.g. Sweet Revenge 129–Turnstone 83 (Sea Hawk II 131) (1981 10f 10.1g 12fg 1982 10.1fg 7f 16f 8fg 12fg) poor plater; has worn bandages in front. *J. Bridger.* —

THE WARRIOR 2 ch.c. Roman Warrior 132–Spanish Lantern 92 (Don Carlos) (1982 5.3g 5s) May 4; strong, rangy colt; poor walker; second foal; brother to 3-y-o Latin Light; dam stayed well; 6 lengths sixth of 9 behind Boy Trumpeter in minor event at Brighton in September, first outing and better effort; will be suited by 6f+. *G. Lewis.* 63

THE WAY SHE MOVES 2 b.f. North Stoke 130–Lovely Clare 106 (Sing Sing —
134) (1982 7fg 8s) Apr 19; 17,000 Y; fair sort; half-sister to 3 winners, including
3-y-o 1½m winner Favoloso (by Sun Prince) and fairly useful 1980 2-y-o 6f winner
Lord Clarence (by Prince Tenderfoot); dam 2-y-o 5f and 6f winner; behind in
sizeable fields of maidens at Chepstow in August and Wolverhampton in October.
P. Cole.

THE WONDER (FR) 4 br.c. Wittgenstein 123–The Lark (Lanark 123) (1981 **127**
10.5g* 10.5s² 12g 9.2s* 8f 8f³ 10g 1982 8v* 10v⁴ 8f⁴ 9.7fg² 9.2g² 8f 8g* 8f² 7v²)
   The Wonder was in the leading half dozen or so of his generation in France
throughout three busy seasons, yet was never the most straightforward of horses
to assess.   As a two-year-old he seemed extremely well suited by a test of
stamina and gained the last two of his four wins over a mile and a quarter in the
mud, in the Prix de Conde and the Criterium de Saint-Cloud.   At three however
he disappointed badly in the Prix du Jockey-Club over a distance we thought
would suit him and gained his most important win when beating Northjet in the
nine-furlong Prix d'Ispahan; he also ran well over a mile, finishing third to
Northjet in the Prix du Moulin.   By his third season he had clearly come to be
regarded by his connections as primarily a miler and was ridden for speed rather
than stamina: all but one of his nine races were over distances short of a mile
and a quarter and he showed on his final outing that he's reasonably effective
over seven furlongs, a trip he hadn't tried since his second outing at two.   His
assessment is further complicated by his failing to do himself justice in any of
his three appearances in Britain.   In 1981 he finished only sixth to Vayrann in
the Champion Stakes, and in 1982 he was only fourth to Motavato in the very
slowly-run Tote Lockinge Stakes at Newbury, not disgraced giving weight all
round, and only seventh to On The House when co-favourite for the Sussex
Stakes at Goodwood.
   As a four-year-old The Wonder was just about as good as ever and he added
the Prix Edmond Blanc at Saint-Cloud in March and the Prix Jacques le Marois
at Deauville in August to the six wins he'd already accumulated.   The former
race was weakly contested and The Wonder landed the odds from Vargas Llosa
and seven others without any fuss; the Jacques le Marois presented a far stiffer
test to The Wonder who was beaten five times in the meantime, running his best
races when a close second to Al Nasr at Longchamp in the Prix Dollar and the
Prix d'Ispahan.   His opponents in a field of nine included the Guineas winners
Zino and Melyno, Green Forest, the outstanding French two-year-old of 1981
who'd disappointed on both his previous starts, the improving Noalcoholic,
easy winner of the Prix Morridor last time out, and the filly Exclusive Order
who'd recently beaten Indian King in the Prix Maurice de Gheest.   The betting
was dominated by Melyno, Zino and Noalcoholic but with Melyno meeting with
a mishap and Noalcoholic and Exclusive Order dropping out of contention before
the distance the finish was dominated by The Wonder, Green Forest and Zino.
The Wonder, ridden for the first time by Eddery, was produced with a perfectly-
timed challenge which took him to the front inside the last furlong for a three-

*Prix Jacques le Marois, Deauville—The Wonder accounts for a
strong field: Green Forest and Zino chase him home*

Marquesa de Moratalla's "The Wonder" (P. Eddery)

quarter-length win over Green Forest. Green Forest undoubtedly still had some way to go to reach his peak but it was nevertheless a fine performance on The Wonder's part to win one of the season's most strongly-contested mile races.

The Wonder failed to confirm the form with Green Forest in the Prix du Moulin at Longchamp the following month, going down by three lengths in an extremely fast-run race on really firm going, and had only one more race, in the Prix de la Foret over seven furlongs on the same course in October. He looked exceptionally well before the Foret but was no match for another lightly-raced, late-improving three-year-old, Pas de Seul. The Wonder was possibly taken past Tres Gate into the lead too soon, and it was suggested in at least one quarter that Eddery timed his run for the first winning post instead of the second (the post used for the Foret is some way beyond that used in the Moulin); The Wonder was overwhelmed in the last furlong and beaten three lengths again.

The Wonder (Fr) (br.c. 1978)	Wittgenstein (br 1971)	Roi Dagobert (b 1964)	Sicambre Dame d'Atour
		Stavroula (b 1956)	Nasrullah Segula
	The Lark (gr 1972)	Lanark (gr 1963)	Grey Sovereign Vermilion O'Toole
		Norman Lass (b 1968)	Timmy Lad Golden Glory

The Wonder is a rangy, quite attractive colt bred by Alain du Breil, President of the Societe des Steeple-Chases. He's easily the best horse sired by the little-used stallion Wittgenstein, now dead, who won three of his ten races in Europe, including the Criterium de Maisons-Laffitte and La Coupe de Maisons-Laffitte, but failed to reach the frame in four outings in the United States. The dam The Lark ran thirty times on the flat, winning three races at up to a mile and three quarters in the French Provinces, and she was also second over hurdles at Rouen. The Wonder is her first foal; she has since produced The Fun (by Funny Hobby), second three times over middle distances in France in 1982. The second dam Norman Lass was a plating-class half-sister to the 1974 French Two Thousand Guineas winner Moulines who is now at stud in Japan.

The Wonder was already being advertised in the French Press as standing at the Haras de Clarbec for 1983 when it was announced that he was instead being sent to race in the United States. It is to be hoped he does better there than did his sire. He has joined the powerful stable of Charlie Whittingham who has done well with ex-European horses and has won big races with Erins Isle, Galaxy Libra, Kilijaro, Perrault, Providential and Queen to Conquer in the last two years. Whittingham also acquired the Prix du Jockey-Club second and third, Real Shadai and Bois de Grace, and the Irish St Leger runner-up Father Rooney at the end of the season. It will be interesting to see how they fare. *J. de Chevigny, France.*

THIEF OF TIME 2 ch.c. Dublin Taxi–Dracaena 62 (Double Jump 131) (1982 5d 6g 5g² 5f) May 12; 7,200Y; half-brother to 2 winners by Jimsun, including quite useful 1980 2-y-o 6f winner Veleso; dam won 7f seller at 2 yrs; poor plater; not raced after July. *P. Haslam.* **48**

THIJSSEN 3 ch.c. Habat 127–Kirisana 82 (Darius 129 or Kribi 110) (1981 7g 5s 6s 1982 6s⁴ 6fg* 7g) workmanlike colt; showed improved form when winning maiden race at Pontefract in May; suited by 6f on fast ground; blinkered at 3 yrs; sent to Singapore. *W. O'Gorman.* **68**

THINKLUCKYBELUCKY 2 b.f. Maystreak 118–Rugby Princess 82 (El Gallo 122) (1982 5v 6s) sister to 5f and 7f winner Par Pak; dam won 1¼m seller; well beaten in end-of-season maiden races at Hamilton and Leicester. *M. James.* **—**

THINK ON (USA) 2 b.c. Habitony–Native Mistress (Nearctic) (1982 6d 6f 6fg³ 6f⁴ 6g⁴ 5g 5g 6g) Mar 28; small, fair sort; first living foal; dam placed 5 times from 13 starts; disappointed after finishing ¾-length third of 6 to Pentland Javelin in £5,200 event at Ayr in July; probably needs 7f+; started very slowly when blinkered sixth outing. *M. Tompkins.* **91**

THIRD REALM 3 b.g. Realm 129–Such Moor 77 (Santa Claus 133) (1981 6fg 5d 6g 6g 1982 8f 7fg 12g⁴ 10fg) compact gelding; plating-class maiden; best run at 1½m; sold to M. Lambert 7,000 gns Newmarket Autumn Sales. *F. Durr.* **—**

THIRTLE 3 ch.g. Morston 125–Pearl Star 110 (Gulf Pearl 117) (1981 NR 1982 10fg 11fg) 18,000Y; sturdy gelding; half-brother to 3 winners, including middle-distance stayer Star Burst (by Busted); dam game performer at up to 7f; well behind in minor event at Nottingham and maiden race at Hamilton in June; sold 780 gns Newmarket July Sales. *M. Stoute.* **—**

THIS ONES FOR YOU 3 b.c. Malacate 131–Spoiled Wine (Pampered King 121) (1981 5s² 5v 6fg 5fg 6f⁴ 7f 6g 6f 1982 10f 12f 9g 9f² 8g² 9g⁴ 8g³) lengthy, fair sort; plater; stays 9f; acts on any going; a strong puller. *G. Toft.* **57**

THOMAS A BECKET 3 ch.c. Record Token 128–St Gay 77 (St Chad 120) (1981 NR 1982 8d 9f 8f² 10.1d 8fg 9f 9fg) 2,000Y; compact colt; third foal; dam won over 6f; plater; stays 1m; acts on firm going; wears blinkers; sold to Mrs N. Smith 550 gns Ascot October Sales. *C. Nelson.* **42**

THOMSON'S TENDER 2 b.g. Prince Tenderfoot 126–Layer Cake (Levmoss 133) (1982 7.6v 8g³) Mar 2; 12,000Y; first foal; dam won over 1¼m in Ireland and is half-sister to very useful 1975 Irish 2-y-o Icing (by Prince Tenderfoot); well-backed favourite and blinkered first time, beaten only ¾ length into third place behind Triple Jump after dwelling in good-class 11-runner seller at Newmarket in October; gelded subsequently; stays 1m; sent to Malaysia. *J. Sutcliffe.* **77**

THORBELL ARCH 3 br.g. Tarboosh–Larch (Busted 134) (1981 NR 1982 12f 15d 15.8d) big, lengthy gelding; no worthwhile form in varied company; blinkered final appearance; unruly at start when withdrawn on intended second outing. *J. Mason.* **—**

THORNDOWN 3 b.c. Busted 134–Sky Fever 108 (Skymaster 126) (1981 NR 1982 8fg² 8fg⁴ 8f* 8fg² 8f² 10fg* 10g) very attractive, well-made colt; closely related to smart 6f and 7f winner Kittyhawk (by Bustino) and half-brother to a winning hurdler; dam 5f sprinter; favourite when winning maiden race at Sandown in July and handicap on same course in August; stayed on well to beat Always Welcome by 2½ lengths going away in latter; ran creditably most other starts; pulled a muscle when below his best final outing; suited by 1¼m; yet to race on a soft surface. *R. Hern.* **94**

THORN PARK 2 ro.c. Sit In The Corner–Grey Charlotte (Fighting Charlie 127) (1982 5fg 7g 8g) May 25; tall, leggy colt; half-brother to 2 winning jumpers, including quite useful Orchard Park (by Precipice Wood); in rear in maiden and minor events, twice last. *G. Harman.*

THORNTON WALK 2 b.c. Farm Walk 111–Tula Star 62 (Comedy Star 121) — (1982 5d 5s 7s) Apr 26; small colt; first foal; dam sprint plater; tailed off in autumn maiden races. *R. Ward.*

THOROUGH 4 ch.f. Thatch 136–Polly Cotton (Vaguely Noble 140) (1981 **115** 8v 8g 10.5g² 10g 12f* 12d⁴ 12.5s 10.5v⁴ 9.7v 10.5s⁴ 1982 9s⁴ 10.5g 10.5d* 10s² 12g 10.5d³ 9g* 8d⁴ 8fg* 8s 8f 8s² 9.2s 8s) good-bodied French filly; first reported foal; dam, unplaced twice in France, is half-sister to high-class Real Good Deal, winner of both Hollywood and California Derbys; had a busy season and won 90,000 francs event at Saint-Cloud, minor event at Maisons-Laffitte and 7-runner Prix d'Astarte at Deauville; favoured by terms and favourite when beating Play It Safe by ½ length in last-named event in July; had stiff tasks afterwards, best effort when 5 lengths second of 13 behind Ya Zaman in Prix du Rond-Point at Longchamp in September; stays 1¼m, but races mainly at much shorter distances; acts on any going; often has a pacemaker. *D. Smaga, France.*

THOUGHTFUL 3 ch.f. Northfields–Wishful Thinking 104 (Petition 130) (1981 **86** 6s⁴ 1982 10fg⁴ 10fg* 10.2g 10g) well-made, robust filly; made all and stayed on strongly to land odds in maiden race at Ascot in July; soundly beaten in handicaps at Doncaster and Ascot (blinkered) in September; will stay 1½m. *R. Hern.*

THREE CROWNS 4 b.f. Connaught 130–Soverena 98 (Sovereign Lord 120) — (1981 7d* 12f 11s 1982 8f) won maiden race at Sandown as a 3-y-o (apprentice ridden); no other form, but has had stiff tasks; should stay at least 1m; acts on a soft surface. *P. Makin.*

THREE JOKERS 3 ch.g. Some Hand 119–Doubtful Request (Cheveley Lad 105) — (1981 5g 5fg 6d 5v 5d 5g 5d 1982 6s 6s 5fg 5f⁴ 6fg 8f⁴ 8g 6f 8.2v) fair sort; plater; best at 5f; acts on any going; has been tried in blinkers; has run respectably for a boy; sold 660 gns Newmarket Autumn Sales. *J. Berry.*

THREE LANES 2 ch.f. Great Nephew 126–Sharondor 84 (Matador 131) (1982 — 5g 7d) Feb 9; narrow, leggy, sparely-made filly; sister to a poor animal and half-sister to several winners, including useful 1972 2-y-o Altiora (by Taj Dewan); dam 6f sprinter; behind in maiden races at Windsor in July and Leicester in October; sold BBA 800 gns Newmarket Autumn Sales. *H. Candy.*

THRICE NIGHTLY 3 ch.f. Gallant Romeo–Zest (Crepello 136) (1981 6s 6s — 1982 11.7f 11.7f 10s 10s) lengthy filly; poor maiden. *B. Hills.*

THRILLING 6 b.m. So Blessed 130–Loop the Loop 81 (Hopeful Venture 125) **52** (1981 8g 8f² 8f² 8f 8.2d³ 8s 8.2d 1982 8s* 8.2s 8f* 8f⁴ 8 2g 8fg) workmanlike mare; decisively won selling handicaps at Ayr in March (bought in 2,000 gns) and Ripon in April (no bid); stays 1¼m; acts on any going; has worn blinkers. *C. Thornton.*

THROW ME OVER 2 ch.c. Roman Warrior 132–Sultry One (Tropique 128) — (1982 5g) May 31; 2,500F, 4,000Y; half-brother to several winners, notably very smart miler General Vole (by Songedor); dam ran twice; 10 lengths seventh of 10 to Shasta Sam in maiden race at Newcastle in August. *R. Whitaker.*

THUG 2 ch.c. Persian Bold 123–Spring Azure 98 (Mountain Call 125) (1982 7f*) **102** p Feb 7; 8,000Y; well-made, attractive colt; good walker; closely related to Irish 5f winner Belmullet (by Bold Lad, Ire); dam 2-y-o 5f winner; 6/1, won 6-runner Bernard van Cutsem Stakes at Newmarket in July by 2½ lengths from Ayman, leading approaching final furlong and running on strongly; met with minor setback afterwards, but has reportedly made full recovery; should win more races. *J. Hindley.*

THUNDERBRIDGE 3 br.g. Rapid River 127–Sayvanter (Galivanter 131) — (1981 5g* 6s 1982 5fg 6f 5fg³ 6s 6s 5g 5s) smallish, strong gelding; sprint handicapper; seems to stay 6f; blinkered last 2 starts. *S. Norton.*

TIBOUCHINA 3 br. or gr.f. Runnymede 123–Reproach Me Not (Connaught 130) — (1981 6g 6g 1982 5f) lengthy filly; has shown a little ability in maiden races; probably stays 6f. *M. Smyly.*

TICKER KHAN 3 gr.g. Brittany–Implacable (Never Say Die 137) (1981 NR — 1982 8.2s) 1,250F; third produce; dam French 1¼m winner; 25/1, dwelt when last of 14 finishers to Nonstop in maiden race at Haydock in October. *M. W. Easterby.*

Mrs B. Haggas' "Thug"

TICKY TACHS GIRL   2 b.f. Tachypous 128–Birthday Present 80 (Bleep-Bleep   —
134)   (1982 5g 5 1g 6f)   Mar 12; reportedly 220Y; leggy, lightly made filly;
half-sister to a winner in Hungary; dam, winner over 5f at 2 yrs, is sister to smart
sprinter Lazenby; in rear in maiden races in June and July, one an auction event
H. Westbrook.

TIDWORTH TATTOO (USA)   3 ch.c. Native Charger–Beautiful World (Dr   87
Fager)   (1981 5d 6d³ 6fg 7g² 7fg 7fg   1982 7d 12s⁴ 12fg 12f 10fg* 12d 10d)   tall,
long-striding colt; beat Miramar Reef by a length in valuable 17-runner maiden
race at Sandown in June; by no means disgraced previous start when eleventh of
18 to Golden Fleece in Derby; stays 1½m; has worn bandages.   *D. Elsworth.*

TIEBOLT   2 b.g. Native Bazaar 122–Contented Sole 77 (Gulf Pearl 117)   (1982   —
5fg 6g 7s)   Apr 23; lightly-made gelding; first foal; dam 2-y-o 5f winner; no
worthwhile form, including in valuable seller; blinkered final start.   *P. Burgoyne.*

TIGER SCOUT (USA)   2 b.f. Silent Screen–Indian Tigress (Terrible Tiger)   86
(1982 7f 7d⁴ 7fg* 7g⁴)   Mar 10; $120,000Y; quite attractive, well-made filly;
second foal; dam, winner of 7f claiming race at 4 yrs, is half-sister to high-class 6f
to 8.5f winner Screen King (by Silent Screen); finished well to win 19-runner
maiden race at Chepstow in August by short head from Midnight Flit; 4 lengths
fourth of 23 behind Salvinia in £4,500 event at Newbury the following month;
will stay 1m.   *I. Balding.*

TIGER TRAP (USA)   3 gr.f. Al Hattab–Polynesian Charm (What A Pleasure)   64
(1981 6fg 6fg³   1982 7g 8fg 6f 6g* 6fg²)   lengthy, useful-looking filly; a grand
mover; won handicap at Chepstow in June; ran respectably only subsequent
start; should stay 7f.   *I. Balding.*

TIGRANES (USA)   3 b.c. Decidedly–Hill Whisper (Hillary)   (1981 7.6s 8g 8g   73
1982 12fg 12fg² 13g⁴ 14.7f² 14fg³ 14s⁴)   big, rangy colt; good mover; in frame in
maiden races; will stay 2m; probably needs holding up and may be ungenuine;
sold 15,000 gns Newmarket Autumn Sales and has been sent to France.   *J.
Dunlop.*

TIGRETTA 2 ch.c. Persian Bold 123–One Rose (Pall Mall 132) (1982 5s 7d 6g 71
8.5g⁴ 10s 8s 8g) Feb 12; IR 25,000Y; ex-English colt; half-brother to several
winners here and abroad, including very useful Irish sprinter Shadow Rose (by
Dancer's Image); dam never ran; remote fifth of 7 to Shanleys Style in maiden
race at Kempton in April when trained by R. Simpson; raced in Ireland afterwards,
best effort when 5¾ lengths fourth of 13 to Stirabout in maiden race at Galway in
September; suited by 1m but isn't sure to stay 1¼m. *K. Prendergast, Ireland.*

TIJUCA 3 ch.g. Roi Soleil 125–Royal Message 57 (Town Crier 119) (1981 5g 7fg —
8g 8s 1982 10f) good-bodied gelding; well beaten in varied company, including
selling; sold 720 gns Ascot October Sales. *J. King.*

TIKAKI (USA) 3 b.f. Hawaii–Kushka (First Landing) (1981 7g 7g⁴ 7.3s² §§
1982 8fg⁴ 12fg 10f 9s) well-made, quite attractive filly; fairly useful at her best
but has become temperamental; should stay middle distances; acts well on soft
going; best in blinkers; one to leave severely alone; sold 25,000 gns Newmarket
December Sales. *R. Hern.*

TILKEY FRED 2 b.c. Fine Blade 121–Riberina (Ribero 126) (1982 7s) May 7; —
small, hollow-backed colt; fourth foal; dam unplaced at 2 yrs in France and at
3 yrs in Ireland; ran out and unseated rider when saddle slipped at halfway in
minor event at Sandown in October. *A. Moore.*

TILLMAN 3 b.g. Swing Easy 126–Spytra 64 (Spy Well 125) (1981 6g 6f⁴ 7fg 7f —
1982 10f 10f) tall gelding; quite a modest maiden at his best; not sure to stay 7f;
sent to France. *F. Durr.*

TILLYMOSS 3 b.f. Ascertain–Cliff's Daughter (Tudor Cliff) (1981 NR 1982 —
16.5fg 16.5s) leggy filly; third reported foal; dam never ran; well beaten in
2 minor events at Redcar in the autumn. *R. Woodhouse.*

TILLY SCOTT 3 b.f. Roi Soleil 125–Scottish Double (Dual 117) (1981 6fg 7d —
6d 1982 8g 10.1g³ 12f 12fg) little worthwhile form in maiden and minor events;
blinkered final start. *M. Masson.*

TIMARACK 6 ch.g. Double Act 94–Gondook 97 (Chamier 128) (1981 NR —
1982 12d) plater; stayed 1¼m; acted on any going; sometimes blinkered and
bandaged; dead. *Mrs M. Nesbitt.*

TIMBER CREEK 2 b.c. Hot Grove 128–Krafty Kate 73 (Klairon 131) (1982 91
5f 6f 6f 6f² 7fg³ 7f 7.6v⁴ 7s*) Mar 22; close-coupled colt; fourth reported foal;
half-brother to 2 winning platers; dam won over 1¼m; stayed on well to overhaul
11 Pontevecchio close home when winning 6-runner nursery under a low weight at
Sandown in October; will be well suited by 1m+; acts on any going but goes
particularly well on soft; saddle slipped sixth outing. *D. Whelan.*

TIMBER TRACK 5 b.g. Palm Track 122–Kindling (Psidium 130) (1981 82
12fg 13g³ 12g* 12d 14d 13g* 14s 1982 11g* 12g 11g* 12fg³ 12g 10g³ 13d 11s)
big, good-topped gelding; has a round action; fair handicapper; held up when
winning at Ayr in June and July, latter by ½ length from Sheba's Glory; had a
poor run fourth start; finds 1¼m on sharp side and stays 13f well; unsuited by
very soft going but acts on any other. *E. Weymes.*

TIMBER TYCOON 2 gr.c. Dragonara Palace 115–Sabala 93 (Tribal Chief 125) 94 p
(1982 6f2) Apr 21; 10,000Y; well-made colt; first living foal; dam 6f and 7f
winner; backed at long odds although on backward side, ran extremely well in
16-runner maiden race at Newmarket in July, putting in a strong late run and
failing by only a head to catch more-experienced Lofty; promises to stay 7f.
R. Armstrong.

TIME CHARTER 3 b.f. Saritamer 130–Centrocon 112 (High Line 125) (1981 131
5d³ 6fg* 6fg 7g* 7s 1982 8d* 8fg² 12f* 10fg² 10g* 10d*)
The unconventional mating of the sprinter Saritamer with the stayer
Centrocon produced in Time Charter one of the season's leading middle-distance
horses. She won four of her six races, including the Oaks by a length and the
Dubai Champion Stakes by seven lengths, and finished runner-up in the other
two, one of them the One Thousand Guineas. Her record was exceptional and
her manner of winning the Champion Stakes little short of brilliant. In any
review of the period since Petite Etoile last achieved the Oaks-Champion Stakes
double Time Charter must deserve serious consideration along with the likes
of Sweet Solera, Park Top, Highest Hopes, Dibidale, Mysterious and Highclere
for best English-trained middle-distance filly. The International Classification
grossly underestimates her merit both by rating her only seventh of her sex in
Europe in 1982, behind Akiyda, April Run, Awaasif, Harbour, All Along and

*Oaks Stakes, Epsom—Time Charter confirms her superiority over
Slightly Dangerous; Last Feather holds on to third from Awaasif*

River Lady, and in allotting her a mark 17 lb below the so-called 'norm' of 100 which only Alleged and Shergar have attained since the International Classification began in 1977.

Time Charter appears on her mark of 83 in the six-and-a-half-furlong to ten-and-a-half-furlong category in the International Classification, a handicap agreed jointly by the official handicappers of Great Britain, France and Eire; so presumably her form within those limits is considered her best. We should go along with that and should pick out her run in the Champion Stakes on her final appearance as better than the one which won her the Sun Chariot Stakes over the same course. How anyone could be so little impressed with her in the Champion Stakes as to place her 6 lb behind Akiyda or, perhaps more pertinently, as to place her where she is in relation to each of the last three fillies to have won the race, Cairn Rouge (85), Swiss Maid (91) and Flying Water (91) is impossible to understand; though it's perfectly true that Prima Voce, Noalto and Montekin who took the minor prizes aren't quite in the top bracket, and equally true that the favourite Kalaglow ran well below form. Time Charter didn't just beat her thirteen opponents, she slaughtered them; after running into trouble, too. Bunching occurred as the long-time leader Kalaglow began to tire on the stand rail going into the Dip. Time Charter, travelling strongest of all, had to switch round Kalaglow and force a passage between him and Montekin, finally getting in the clear on the hill inside the last furlong. From that point she sprinted clean away, with great enthusiasm and determination.

You will search the records in vain for as clear-cut a winner of the Champion Stakes in the last sixty years: Rose Royale II in 1957 and Dynamiter in 1951 on the first of his two victories had six lengths to spare, Rockfel five in 1938 and Cameronian four in 1932. Some could have won by more than they did, but so could Time Charter without interference. The race is as important now as it ever was, yet we are asked to believe that in the course of the European season there were many better performances than Time Charter's taking all ages and distances into account (twenty-seven horses are actually rated above her). And, far more serious since the reputation of European bloodstock is at stake, that such a performance was achieved by one nowhere near so good as the best race-horses of only a few years ago. The official handicappers are on record, through the spoken word and through the six International Classifications so far handed down, as of the view that our horses aren't what they used to be. They claim to have observed over the period a sharp decline in the number and quality of good horses about. We can't swallow this at all, it's nonsense, though we accept the number and quality is likely to vary from one year to another—it's only natural that it should. Since 1977 the 'norm', defined at first as the top rating in an average year then redefined as a rating to be achieved by a horse capable of dominating a crop of average ability, has not been surpassed, and animals that most racegoers would regard as outstanding by any reasonable standards such as Troy (96), Ardross (91), Moorestyle (91), Irish River (91), Le Moss (89) and Kris (89), were slighted. If these examples, by no means all that could be cited, on top of that of Time Charter whom arguably no horse ever

Sun Chariot Stakes, Newmarket—Time Charter remains in cracking form and gives weight all round

foaled could have beaten at 17 lb, can persuade some people to take the International Classification a little less seriously, they will have served a useful purpose; perhaps more people will now see the flaws inherent in handicapping by committee, and come to appreciate that on occasions the International Classification may say more about the compilers than the merits of the horses in it.

Twice in the same week Time Charter's trainer went near to winning his first classic—in the One Thousand Guineas with Time Charter, home bred from a family that has served the stable very well over the years, and in the Two Thousand Guineas with the cheaply-bought American-bred Wind and Wuthering. On two-year-old form the latter held much the better chance but Time Charter had run much the more encouraging trial, showing improvement and the necessary stamina as she led throughout and beat Epithet five lengths in the Masaka Stakes over a mile at Kempton. Time Charter was smartly away in the Guineas, too, and shared the lead until Hello Cuddles left her in front at halfway. Two furlongs later she'd lost the advantage to On The House; nevertheless she'd been running on strongly, and she continued to do so under pressure up the hill so that she finished clear of the others. On The House beat her by two and a half lengths.

Time Charter's stamina had to be taken on trust at Epsom, otherwise she'd have started much shorter than 12/1 in the absence of On The House; Slightly Dangerous whom she'd beaten decisively at Newmarket started at 10/1. Only three of Saritamer's foals, The Vic, Strathdearn and Swiss Maid's half-brother Birch Grove, had won at further than a mile; his winners averaged 6.7 furlongs. He himself had won over a mile as a two-year-old before being put exclusively to sprinting the following season, during which he'd won four six-furlong events, including the Cork and Orrery Stakes, July Cup and Diadem Stakes. The only other from the Guineas field in the thirteen-strong line-up for the Oaks was third-placed Dione: she seemed sure to get the trip, though events were to suggest that perhaps she didn't. Tants started favourite at 4/1, just preferred to On The House's stable-companion Zinzara, on the strength of an easy victory in the

Dubai Champion Stakes, Newmarket—Time Charter makes hacks of the opposition in this prestigious race

Esal Bookmakers Oaks Trial at Lingfield. The Musidora winner Last Feather was the better fancied of Hills's pair at 11/2 while another Lingfield winner Awaasif at 10/1 was better fancied than her stable-companion Dione. A third pair of stable-companions in the line-up held a fair chance: Hern's Cut Loose, a winning sister to the Leger winner Cut Above, and Swiftfoot, easy winner of the Cheshire Oaks. Apart from these only the sole French challenger All Along, the same odds as Time Charter, started at less than 40/1.

Time Charter got the trip really well. They didn't seem to go very fast early on and they were all in a bunch at the entrance to the straight but the time for the race was good, a shade better than that for the Derby. Swiftfoot turned for home in front, followed by Devon Air, Last Feather, Cadi Ha, Slightly Dangerous and Dione. Time Charter hardly surprisingly had been held up on this occasion; she wasn't asked to improve until three furlongs out. By then Swiftfoot had given way to Last Feather and Cadi Ha. When Cadi Ha in turn began to lose her place running to the two-furlong pole five or six seemed to have the race between them, but once Time Charter moved into top gear on the outside the number dropped fairly quickly, and well before she took the lead from Slightly Dangerous halfway through the final furlong she could be named the winner. Besides stamina she had shown a fine turn of foot, and Slightly Dangerous was powerless to prevent her going a length up by the line. Apart from the winner Awaasif finished strongest, coming through to deprive Zinzara of fourth, three parts of a length behind Last Feather who was beaten twice that distance by stable-companion Slightly Dangerous. Not only did Time Charter provide that first classic winner for her trainer, she also provided a first win in the Oaks for an apprentice since Joe Mercer partnered Ambiguity in 1953: stable-jockey Billy Newnes had the mount in all her races during the season and handled her well throughout, though he might not have got away with barging through in the Champion Stakes if others hadn't contributed to the trouble and if, dare we say it, his filly hadn't been manifestly so superior.

Time Charter ran only twice between the Oaks and the Champion Stakes. According to her trainer it's best not to race her hard, but the chief reason for her absence in the long period between her next race, the Nassau Stakes at Goodwood, and the Sun Chariot Stakes at Newmarket in the autumn was an infection: she would have run in either the Yorkshire Oaks or the Benson and Hedges Gold Cup at the Ebor meeting except for a dirty nose. Time Charter finished a game second to Dancing Rocks in the Nassau, succumbing to a well-timed challenge: she gave weight to all the field, 7 lb to Dancing Rocks who beat her by two lengths. On that performance Time Charter seemed to face a very stiff task indeed in a well-contested Sun Chariot, especially since she'd been off for so long. Again she had to give weight all round and here, unlike at Goodwood, there were some older fillies in the line-up. One of them Stanerra (receiving 3 lb) finished second. Time Charter, always going well, ran on strongly to beat her by three quarters of a length when smoothly taking the lead two furlongs out. The pair had the finish to themselves. Dish Dash was third, the favourite Cut Loose sixth, Dancing Rocks seventh. Because of the time of year the winner's performance tended to be viewed with suspicion. However she confirmed it with a vengeance in the Champion, through a display that led to her remaining in training for another year instead of, as was planned, her visiting Northern Dancer.

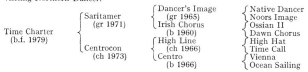

		Dancer's Image	Native Dancer
	Saritamer	(gr 1965)	Noors Image
	(gr 1971)	Irish Chorus	Ossian II
Time Charter		(b 1960)	Dawn Chorus
(b.f. 1979)		High Line	High Hat
	Centrocon	(ch 1966)	Time Call
	(ch 1973)	Centro	Vienna
		(b 1966)	Ocean Sailing

It hardly needs to be said that if Time Charter returns to the course as good as she left it she will win more top races. With a family like hers on the dam's side there must be a fair chance that she'll return even better! Centrocon won in each of the three seasons she ran. At three she won the Lancashire Oaks, made the frame in similar races and finished a good fifth to Pawneese in the Oaks. The following season she won her first two races, including the Paradise Stakes at Newbury from Shanganuzo, before being outclassed behind Sagaro in the Gold Cup. Centrocon has a well-known full brother who remained in training even longer, that good, honest stayer Nicholas Bill; she is also full sister to the 1981 Jockey Club Cup winner Centroline and the one-paced Athford. The next

Mr R. Barnett's "Time Charter"

dam, unusually for one of this family, was best as a two-year-old; less unusually, she managed to win. Time Charter's great-grandam Ocean Sailing, a useful mile-and-a-half handicapper with a good turn of foot, was still winning at the age of four. This marvellous family has provided other classic winners and even a Grand National winner this century. Time Charter and Grittar, no less, have a common ancestress in the mare Athasi who bred several important horses in the history of the Turf including the 1929 Derby winner Trigo, Harina (the grandam of Tulyar) and Avena (the great-grandam of Monteverdi).

Time Charter is Centrocon's first foal and only runner to date; the dam foaled a colt by Home Guard in 1981 and another by Tap On Wood in 1982. Strong and well-made, an excellent walker, Time Charter seems to act on any going (one race as a two-year-old suggested she might be unsuited by very soft). Though her best performances have been at a mile and a quarter none but a fool would rule her out of any race at a mile and a half on the score of distance. She shows an unmistakable enthusiasm for the game, and is a likeable filly in every way. *H. Candy.*

TIME FOR A LAUGH 2 b.c. Cawston's Clown 113–Picnic Time (Silly Season 127) (1982 5g³ 6fg 5g 5g 5d) Mar 12; neat, strong colt; modest plater; best form in non-sellers first 2 outings; possibly needs 6f+. *R. Hollinshead.* **61** d

TIME FOR PLEASURE 3 b.f. Tower Walk 130–Elope 68 (Jimmy Reppin 131) (1981 NR 1982 5fg 6g) compact filly; first reported foal; dam plating-class half-sister to top-class Blushing Groom; showed early speed when behind in minor event at Thirsk in April and £3,300 race at Kempton in May. *R. Boss.* **—**

TIME IS TIME 2 b.f. Broxted 120–As Time Goes By (Calpurnius 122) (1982 5f 5f² 5fg* 6fg* 6g³ 7f 7f⁴ 7g² 6g 7g 7f) Apr 11; 1,900Y; small, lightly-made filly; first foal; dam, who never ran, is closely related to **very smart stayer Sir** **77**

854

Montagu; 5-length winner of sellers at Warwick (bought in 1,550 gns) in May and Yarmouth (changed hands 2,600 gns) in June; went down by only a head to Shadan under 7-7 in nursery at Yarmouth in August; suited by 7f; has raced only on a sound surface. *W. Marshall.*

TIME'S TIME 2 ch.g. Whistling Deer 117–Needy (High Top 131) (1982 5fg⁴ **111**
5s² 5f* 5f* 5f* 5fg* 5fg* 5f* 5g) Mar 20; IR 1,100F, 4,600Y; compact, fair sort; second produce; dam fairly useful winner over 6f and 7f at 2 yrs in Ireland; put up a very useful performance in Star Stakes at Sandown in July when gaining sixth successive victory, making all and responding well under strong pressure to hold off Favoridge by a neck; had earlier won maiden auction events at Catterick and Redcar, small race at Catterick and well-contested events at Beverley and Ayr; faded in final 2f to finish last behind Cat O'Nine Tails when favourite for 8-runner Prince of Wales's Stakes at York in August; usually makes the running but should stay 6f; not disgraced on soft going on second start but is thought by trainer to need a sound surface; tough and genuine; appears flattered by his weight of 8-12 in Free Handicap. *W. Wharton.*

TIME TO REFLECT 3 gr.g. Roan Rocket 128–Game Girl 85 (Abernant 142)   —
(1981 5g⁴ 6g² 6g 6f 6s² 6s³ 1982 6f⁴ 6f 6fg 8g 8g 7f 8.2s 6s⁴) rather leggy gelding; not the best of movers; poor maiden nowadays; beaten in seller seventh start; stays 1m; suited by some give in the ground; has worn a bandage on near-fore. *M. Camacho.*

TIME WIND 3 b.f. Dance In Time—Schoolhouse Dale 72 (Reform 132) (1981 **68**
5d 5g 6s⁴ 6fg⁴ 7f 8f 8fg² 8d 8.2s² 8g 1982 8f 8f 9.4f² 9.4f² 9.4fg 9.4f² 10g³ 10fg
8g 9v* 10s) compact filly; decisively won maiden race at Hamilton in October; stays 1½m; acts on any going; effective with or without blinkers; sold 1,500 gns Newmarket December Sales. *W. Elsey.*

TIMMY BOY 2 ch.c. Timolin 81–Cabarita 88 (First Landing) (1982 7fg 5fg **48**
5g 5d 7fg 8d) May 23; workmanlike colt; has a round action; well beaten, including in sellers. *R. Cambidge.*

TIMONIER (FR) 5 b. or br.g. Satingo 129–Trelex (Exbury 138) (1981 10g³   —
12g⁴ 12.12fg 12f 15.8g 1982 12g 12g) tall gelding; plating-class maiden; stays 1½m; has run respectably for an apprentice. *D. Smith.*

TIMOTHY HOGAN 2 b.c. Mandrake Major 122–Love Seat (King's Bench 132) **57**
(1982 5g³ 5f³ 5f 7f² 8fg 8s) May 4; small colt; half-brother to 3 winners, including 1978 2-y-o 5f winner Flitterdale (by Abwah); plater; having first race for nearly 3 months when creditable 3 lengths second of 10 to Water Pistol at Beverley in July; off course again 2 months subsequently; stays 7f; best form on a sound surface; sold 700 gns Doncaster November Sales. *J. Etherington.*

TIMSAH 2 b.c. Solinus 130–Haco 104 (Tribal Chief 125) (1982 5g 5d 6f 6fg 6g⁴) **69**
Apr 14; 17,000Y; tall, quite attractive colt; first foal; dam, from excellent family, showed useful form at up to 1m without winning; plating-class maiden; stays 6f. *J. Benstead.*

Star Stakes, Sandown—six in a row for Time's Time who upsets the odds on Favoridge (centre); third is Another Risk (right)

King George Stakes, Goodwood—a well-deserved success for Tina's Pet, with (left to right) Crofthall, Ponchielli, Vaigly Star and Golden Green on his heels

TINA'S PET 4 b.c. Mummy's Pet 125–Merry Weather 69 (Will Somers 114§) **119**
(1981 7g³ 6g 5f 6g 5.6fg 6d² 6s⁴ 1982 5f³ 5fg⁴ 6f 5f* 5g⁴ 6d* 5s)
    The decision to persevere with Tina's Pet after his disappointing three-year-old campaign was rewarded with pattern-race wins in the King George Stakes at Goodwood in July and the Goldene-Peitsche at Baden-Baden in September. A runaway winner at Yarmouth, Ripon and Ayr as a two-year-old Tina's Pet had surprisingly gone through 1981 without a win although he'd showed he'd retained his ability with placings in the Tote European Free Handicap and the Ladbrokes (Ayr) Gold Cup.
    The King George provided Tina's Pet with his first clear-cut opportunity of the season, as he'd been on the burly side when third to Mummy's Game in the Temple Stakes at Sandown and had had stiffer tasks when fourth to Fearless Lad in the King's Stand Stakes at Royal Ascot and sixth to Sharpo in the William Hill July Cup at Newmarket. The fast downhill course and firm going were ideal for him as he's a quick-starting, free-running sort. He was always going well, disputing the lead, and when Piggott picked up his whip shortly before the furlong marker Tina's Pet quickened into a decisive lead. From there on he never looked likely to be caught and he came home two lengths clear of the 50/1-chance Golden Green with the short-priced favourite Vaigly Star only third; he smashed the course record that Stilvi had established when beating Deep Diver in the same race in 1972. Tina's Pet put up another good performance when just over two lengths fourth to Sharpo in the William Hill Sprint Championship at York the following month, where he was the pick of the paddock, and he started a hot favourite for the Goldene-Peitsche at Baden-Baden at the beginning of September, a six-furlong race run on easy going. For once Tina's Pet was none too well away and he came through only inside the last furlong to win by three quarters of a length and a length from his compatriots Milk Heart and Gabitat. On his only subsequent outing, in the Prix de l'Abbaye de Longchamp, Tina's Pet failed to do himself justice. He looked his usual bonny self in the preliminaries but dropped right out after showing prominently from his outside draw to around halfway.

			⎧ Sing Sing	⎧ Tudor Minstrel
	⎧ Mummy's Pet		⎨ (b 1957)	⎩ Agin the Law
	⎪ (b 1968)		⎩ Money for Nothing	⎧ Grey Sovereign
Tina's Pet	⎨		(br 1962)	⎩ Sweet Nothings
(b.c. 1978)	⎪		⎧ Will Somers	⎧ Tudor Minstrel
	⎩ Merry Weather		⎨ (br 1955)	⎩ Queen's Jest
	(br 1971)		⎩ Copper Sky	⎧ Hook Money
			(b 1964)	⎩ Eternal Goddess

    Tina's Pet is to stand alongside another King George Stakes winner Music Boy at his owners' Cheveley Park Stud, Newmarket, where his fee is £1,500 with the October 1st concession. By Mummy's Pet out of a Will Somers mare, he has a sprinting pedigree, though his dam Merry Weather managed to win a poor race over nine furlongs. His grandam Copper Sky and great-grandam Eternal Goddess were sprinters, the latter a very useful one. Merry Weather has produced only two other foals so far. Her first Indian Spring (by Mansingh) won a seven-furlong seller and was subsequently successful on the flat and over jumps in Belgium. After producing Tina's Pet she was barren twice and slipped once before producing another colt by Mummy's Pet. Tina's Pet, a strong, well-made, attractive colt who usually impressed in appearance, was well bought for 5,900 guineas as a yearling. He was tried in blinkers once when right out of form as a three-year-old, but raced most genuinely throughout 1982. *G. Huffer.*

TIN BOY 3 br.c. Welsh Pageant 132–Tin Mary 96 (Tin King 126) (1981 5g 6g* —
6g* 1982 7g 8f 8g 7fg 7f 6s 7g) quite a useful sort; fairly useful at 2 yrs; below form most starts in 1982; should stay 1m; should to sweat up and is usually taken quietly to start nowadays; sent to France. *W. Hastings-Bass.*

TINDERELLA 3 ch.f. Hot Spark 126–Flying Fancy (King of the Tudors 129) —
(1981 5d⁴ 6f 5d 6d 1982 7g 7d 7fg 8fg 8fg 8fg 8f) compact filly; poor maiden; well beaten in a seller final start; sometimes blinkered. *D. Elsworth.*

TINKER'S IMAGE 3 gr.f. Dancer's Image–Water Pageant 58 (Welsh Pageant **87**
132) (1982 5fg² 5f² 5fg* 6f 5f* 5f 6g) Mar 16; small, quite attractive filly; first foal; dam poor middle-distance maiden; successful in minor event at Pontefract in May and nursery at Folkestone in July; apparently best at 5f; acts on firm going; sold 6,200 gns Newmarket Autumn Sales. *P. Walwyn.*

TINOCO 2 b.c. Bustino 136–Consistent 90 (Connaught 130) (1982 7f 7.2g⁴ 7g **80**
8f³ 8f⁴) Feb 9; neat colt; third foal; half-brother to a winning plater and 3-y-o 1m winner Coley (by Morston); dam won over 5f on first outing; put up best effort when 2 lengths third of 11 to Axkernish in £5,700 nursery at Doncaster in September; ran wide on bend when favourite for nursery at Bath later in month and wasn't disgraced in finishing 3½ lengths fourth to Walton Heath; will stay beyond 1m; sold 9,200 gns Newmarket Autumn Sales. *R. Hern.*

TINTED BLONDE (USA) 2 ch.f. Charles Elliott–Color Me Blonde (Craigwood) —
(1982 5fg) 5,000Y; sister to 3 winners, including 1981 2-y-o 1m winner Colorwood Silk, and half-sister to several winners; dam placed at 2 yrs in USA; seventh of 12 in maiden race at Warwick in May. *D. Ringer.*

TINTERELLO 3 ch.c. Continuation 120–Polly Bellino 56 (Dadda Bert 95) **63**
(1981 5d 5fg 8g 8s 1982 8f 8fg² 8fg* 10fg) compact colt; plater; successful in better company at Beverley in June; suited by 1m on fast ground. *J. Hardy.*

TINY FEET 2 b.f. Music Maestro 119–Shianta 85 (St Paddy 133) (1982 5f) —
Apr 15; 400F, 320Y; very small but well-made filly; half-sister to 7f winner Olro's Folly (by African Sky); dam won over 5f at 2 yrs in this country and over 1m at 3 yrs in USA; last of 13 finishers in maiden race at Salisbury in August; sold 950 gns Ascot October Sales. *M. Smyly.*

TIPPERARY FIXER 4 b.c. Targowice 130–Rabisina (Alcide 136) (1981 12fg⁴ **116**
12d 12s² 15s* 15s² 15f* 15s* 15.5v 1982 15.5v 15.5fg³ 20v² 20f² 12.5d 12f 20s) big French colt; grand sort; developed into a high-class stayer as a 3-y-o and won 3 races, including Prix Kergorlay at Deauville; didn't win in 1982 but ran well on occasions in first half of season; looked to be struggling most of way in Prix du Cadran at Longchamp in May but ran on very well under pressure in straight and failed by only a short head to catch El Badr; had no chance with 3-length winner Ardross in Gold Cup at Royal Ascot in June but stuck on well in straight and got up close home to beat El Badr a neck for second; well beaten last 3 starts, but only once had the stiff test of stamina that suits him; acts on any going. *J. Fellows, France.*

TIPPI 3 br.g. Saritamar 130–Trigamy 112 (Tribal Chief 125) (1981 5fg⁴ 5fg —
5.1d 5s 6s 5g 5s 1982 5d 8fg) compact gelding; plater; has worn blinkers; sold 700 gns Ascot September Sales. *Mrs N. Macauley.*

TIPTONIAN 3 gr.g. Royalty 130–Pretty Fast 74 (Firestreak 125) (1981 NR —
1982 7fg 10s) first foal; dam won over 1¼m and also over hurdles; behind in maiden race at Edinburgh and minor event at Leicester. *T. Taylor.*

TIRAWA (USA) 3 b.c. Majestic Prince–Imalulu (Black Beard) (1981 6g **77**
1982 8f 10f³ 10f 11.7fg* 11fg* 12g³) good-looking, lengthy colt; not the best of movers; carries plenty of condition; favourite when successful in handicap at Windsor in July and small race at Ayr in August (long odds on); will stay 1¾m; yet to race on a soft surface but gives impression one may suit him. *M. Jarvis.*

TIRESOME 2 ch.f. Some Hand 119–Ratificate 77 (Ratification 129) (1982 —
6fg 6f 5d 8.2d 7g) Apr 21; 440F; strong filly; has enlarged off-fore knee; bad
plater. *P. Felgate.*

TIT FOR TAT 3 b.g. Warpath 113–Yours and Mine 83 (Tin Whistle 128) —
(1981 6d 6g 1982 9f 8.2f 8fg 12fg) small, strong gelding; poor form, including in
a seller; sweated up badly second start; blinkered final outing; sold to J. Harris
1,000 gns Doncaster October Sales. *C. Thornton.*

TIVIAN 2 b.c. Busted 134–Jovian 88 (Hardicanute 130) (1982 8g 7s³ 7v²) **98**
Apr 30; lengthy colt; fifth foal; dam won twice over 5f at 2 yrs; shaped well on all
outings, notably 5 lengths third of 6 to The Fort in £4,700 race at Goodwood in
September and 3 lengths second of 5 to Special Leave in Hyperion Stakes at
Ascot in October; should stay 1¼m; yet to race on a firm surface; sure to win
maiden event. *C. Brittain.*

TIVOLI GARDENS 3 b.f. Flashback 102–Jean's Joy 74 (Specific 102) (1981 —
NR 1982 12g 12fg 12v) good-topped, lengthy filly; third foal; dam won sellers
at up to 1¼m and also won over hurdles; in rear in maiden races and a minor event.
M. Bolton.

TOBERMORY BOY 5 b.g. Mummy's Pet 125–Penny Pincher 95 (Constable 119) **85**
(1981 5g 5d 5fg 5g4 5f³ 6f² 5.6f² 5g² 5.6fg 5g 5s 1982 5f³ 5g 5f* 6fg² 5fg 5fg 5.6g)
neat gelding; fair handicapper; stayed on under very hard driving to get up
close home and beat Cree Song a short head in £4,600 event at York in July;
good second at Nottingham the following month; stays 6f; acts on any going.
J. Hardy.

TOBINA'S GUEST 2 ch.c. Be My Guest 126–Happy Tobina (Tobin Bronze) **91**
(1982 7f 7g² 8s) Mar 30; IR 15,500F, IR 105,000Y; attractive colt; half-brother
to a winner in Italy; dam won 3 sprint races in USA, including a claiming event;
flattered by proximity to easy 4-length winner Dunbeath when second in 9-runner
event at York in September; always struggling in £3,400 event won by Proclaim
at Goodwood later in month; should stay 1m. *B. Hills.*

TOBY LEGER 2 br.c. Record Token 128–True Dresden 58 (Vilmoray 126) —
(1982 6fg 6f) Mar 13; 7,200F, 24,000Y; stocky colt; half-brother to several
minor winners; dam sprint maiden; in rear in maiden races at Doncaster in July
and Nottingham in August; sold 410 gns Ascot September Sales. *B. Hobbs.*

TO KAMARI MOU 3 ch.g. Moulton 128–Scala di Seta 85 (Shantung 132) **86**
(1981 7fg 1982 12fg 13.3f 14d² 16f² 14fg* 16g 14fg* 16g 14s) chunky gelding;
won maiden race at Sandown in July and apprentice handicap at Goodwood in
September; suited by a test of stamina; seems to act on any going; blinkered
nowadays; inconsistent and probably none too genuine; sold 9,400 gns Newmarket
Autumn Sales. *G. Harwood.*

TO KORITSI MAS 2 ch.f. Mansingh 120–Never Part (Never Say Die 137) **55**
(1982 5g 5d 5f 5h* 5fg³ 6fg4) May 9; 700Y; lengthy filly; half-sister to 3 winners,
including quite useful 1978 2-y-o 5f winner Tribal Princess (by Tribal Chief);
showed first sign of ability when winning 4-runner seller at Chepstow (bought in
1,600 gns) in June by ¾ length from Allergirl; stays 5f; acts on hard going;
claimed £3,000 at Yarmouth in July on sixth outing. *K. Ivory.*

TOLAYTALA 2 ch.f. Be My Guest 126–Night Vision 100 (Yellow God 129) —
(1982 5fg) May 1; 19,000Y; third foal; half-sister to 7f and 1m winner Lautrec
(by Wolver Hollow); dam, half-sister to high-class Take a Reef, won over 6f at
2 yrs; in rear in 17-runner maiden race at Folkestone in September. *M. Masson.*

TOLOMEO 2 b.c. Lypheor 118–Almagest 72 (Dike) (1982 7d² 7g² 7g*) May **101** p
10; IR 17,000Y; big colt; first foal; dam 1¼m winner; put up an excellent effort
in 28-runner maiden race at Newmarket in October, quickening smoothly to lead
1f out and winning by 3 lengths from The Minster with rest at least 6 lengths
further back; second to Polished Silver and to Lord Protector in 2 races at
Yarmouth previously; will stay 1¼m; the type to train on and win more races.
L. Cumani.

TOM DOWDESWELL 6 br.g. Balidar 133–Georgian Princess 75 (Tamerlane **52** d
128) (1981 5s 5d 5fg³ 5g 5f* 5f² 6fg 5.8f 5d 5f 1982 5d³ 5f 6f³ 5f 5fg 5g 5fg
5fg 5fg 5fg 5d) strong, good sort; sprint handicapper; ran best races in spring;
ideally suited by top-of-the-ground; often blinkered, but better without nowadays; trained until after sixth start by J. Berry. *C. Crossley.*

TOMKELLY 2 br.c. Heres 81–Tamblast (Tamerlane 128) (1982 6fg 7fg 6d 6s) —
Mar 30; half-brother to 6f winner Bluehill (by Blue Streak); dam lightly-raced
plater; in rear all outings, including in sellers. *P. Burgoyne.*

TOMMY GUNNER 2 b.g. Gunner B 126–Joan Doreen (Lucky Brief 128) **54**
(1982 6g 6f 6f 8.2s⁴ 8d⁴) Mar 22; lengthy gelding; first reported foal; dam of
little account; modest plater; will stay 1¼m; blinkered final outing. *S. Norton.*

TOMMY'S CHOICE 3 ch.c. Some Hand 119–Nikali 89 (Siliconn 121) (1981 —
5fg 5d 6fg 1982 8.2g 6fg) sturdy, compact colt; bad mover; poor plater; has
worn bandages. *J. Berry.*

TOMMY TUDOR 2 b.g. Tudor Rhythm 112–Wheatley (Town Crier 119) (1982 —
6f 6d 7fg 7fg 8d 8.2d 8s) Mar 21; 1,800Y; smallish, well-made gelding; bad
plater; has worn blinkers. *J. Douglas-Home.*

TOM NOEL (USA) 7 b.g. Tom Rolfe–Christmas Belle (Santa Claus 133) —
(1981 NR 1982 12g) poor handicapper nowadays; stays 1¾m; acts on any
going, but is probably best on a sound surface; sometimes sweats up. *C.
Pinkham.*

TOM OKKER (USA) 2 b.c. Tom Rolfe–Grass Court (Herbager 136) (1982 **75 p**
6f 7fg) May 17; $42,000Y; good-looking colt; third foal; half-brother to 3-y-o
Shallaal (by Honest Pleasure) and a winner by Secretariat; dam poor sister
to smart American stayer Outdoors; in mid-division in maiden races at
Newmarket and Ascot in July; will be better suited by 1¼m+. *L. Cumani.*

TOM'S BOY 5 b.g. Weepers Boy 124–Fleet Street Fifty 51 (I Say 125) (1981 —
NR 1982 11.7f) third foal; half-brother to a winning hurdler; dam poor
plater; pulled up in maiden event at Bath in July, first outing. *W. R. Williams.*

TOM SEYMOUR 2 b.c. Grundy 137–One Over Parr 114 (Reform 132) (1982 **83 p**
8g) Mar 11; third foal; half-brother to 3-y-o 1m winner Particular Miss (by
Luthier); dam, sister to Oaks winner Polygamy, won Cheshire Oaks and Lancashire Oaks; unquoted, put in best work in closing stages when pleasing 7 lengths
eighth of 21 to Polished Silver in £4,200 event at Newbury in September; sure
to do better. *M. Jarvis.*

TOM SHARP 2. b.g. Martinmas 128–Prellgo (El Gallo 122) (1982 8s 8.2s) —
Apr 27; IR 6,500Y; close-coupled gelding; third living foal; dam won over
2m in Ireland and also won over hurdles; behind in October in maiden race at
York and minor event at Nottingham. *W. Wharton.*

TO-NISAKI-MAS 2 ch.c. Sharpen Up 127–Skyey 70 (Skymaster 126) (1982 **70**
7f 7f 7g) Mar 23; 14,500Y; brother to very useful 1978 2-y-o 5f and 6f winner
Eyelet; dam won over 6f; plating-class maiden; stays 7f. *C. Brittain.*

TONY BATTLER 3 b.g. Owen Anthony 102–Battling 75 (Pinza 137) (1981 NR —
1982 9fg 12f 10f 12g) third foal; half-brother to winning middle-distance stayer
Peon Day (by Camo Hand), dam won sellers over 5f and 1m, and also won a
hurdle race and point-to-points; behind in varied company; sold 520 gns
Doncaster August Sales. *J. Tierney.*

TONY TAN 3 br.c. Sallust 134–Fortlin 95 (Fortino II 120) (1981 6d⁴ 6d² **94**
1982 7s 6fg² 8f 8g⁴ 7fg² 7g² 8.5g*) IR 63,000Y; brother to 3 winners, including
top-class French and American 6.5f to 9f winner Sanedtki and good 1982 2-y-o
The Fort, and half-brother to 2 winners; dam, winner of 4 races at 2 yrs, stayed
7f; landed odds by a head from Valley King in 12-runner maiden race at Galway
in September; in frame in varied company previously, running particularly well on
sixth start when going down by ½ length to Mirabeau in City of York Stakes in
August; stays 1m; acts on a firm and a soft surface. *D. Weld, Ireland.*

TOO DO 2 br.f. Manado 130–Topa (Dark Tiger) (1982 5f⁴ 5fg 6f 6fg 7g 7fg) **57**
Feb 1; IR 4,000F, IR 5,000Y; rather lightly-made filly; second reported produce;
half-sister to 1979 Irish 2-y-o 9.5f winner Santopa (by Sandford Lad); dam won
over 6.5f at 2 yrs in France and also over jumps; moderate plater; should stay 7f;
unseated 7-lb claiming rider when blinkered at Wolverhampton in July on final
appearance. *A. Jarvis.*

TOO FAMILIAR 2 ch.f. Oats 126–Born Friendly (Takawalk II 125) (1982 **52**
5fg 6d 5f 7f*) Apr 1; IR 2,600F, 3,000Y; half-sister to 3 winners, including
Irish 7f and 1m winner Matagouri (by Welsh Saint); dam ran 3 times; plater;
awarded 15-runner event at Catterick (bought in 2,700 gns) in August on disqualification of head winner Miandra for hampering another horse; needs at
least 7f, and should stay at least 1¼m; acts on firm going. *D. Ringer.*

TO-ONERO-MOU 2 br.c. Wolver Hollow 126–Emma Canute 93 (Hardicanute **78**
130) (1982 8d 8s⁴) Apr 27; 36,000Y; well-made, quite attractive colt; excellent
walker; brother to 1¼m winner Well Appraised, closely related to 2 winners by
Sovereign Path, including very useful 5f to 10.5f winner Everything Nice, and
half-brother to a winner; dam stayed 1¾m; second favourite, every chance when

8 lengths fourth of 26 to stable-companion Magic Rarity in maiden race at Sandown in October; the type to do better on faster ground. *G. Harwood.*

TO-PALLIKARI-MOU   2 ch.c. Record Token 128–Bouchette 76 (Current Coin   — 118) (1982 5g 6s 7g)   Apr 15; 6,200Y; lengthy colt; third foal; dam, half-sister to smart Lordedaw, won two 7f sellers; soundly beaten in maiden and minor events; sold M. Pipe 500 gns Ascot November Sales. *I. Walker.*

TOP CREATOR   3 b.c. High Line 125–Corneater (Skymaster 126) (1981 8g   **86** 1982 9fg 10fg⁴ 11f² 13.3f 10.1g³ 12g³ 12fg* 10d² 14g³) strong, rangy colt; won 10-runner maiden race at Goodwood in September very smoothly by 7 lengths from Hypnosis; finds 1¼m on sharp side and will stay 2m; yet to race on really soft going but acts on any other. *B. Hills.*

TOP GOLD   3 b.f. Supreme Sovereign 119–Dyna Bell 62 (Double Jump 131)   — (1981 5g 1982 6fg) behind in maiden races; sold 480 gns Doncaster October Sales. *R. Hartop.*

TOP HOPE   3 b.f. High Top 131–Port Ahoy 93 (Petingo 135) (1981 7fg* 7f² 7g*   **104** 1982 12fg⁴ 12g³ 10g⁴ 12g) small, lengthy, wiry filly; doesn't impress in her slower paces; in frame in Ribblesdale Stakes at Royal Ascot (4¼ lengths fourth to Dish Dash), Lancashire Oaks at Haydock (3 lengths third to Sing Softly), keeping on quite well each time, and Twickenham Stakes at Kempton (4½ lengths fourth of 5 to Dione); suited by 1½m; yet to race on a soft surface. *M. Stoute.*

TOP LAD   3 gr.c. Town Crier 119–Pinnacle 70 (High Perch 126) (1981 6d 5.3f   **87** 6s² 1982 8.2fg* 8f 8fg⁴ 8g*) small, quite attractive colt; good walker and mover; won maiden race at Nottingham in April and handicap at Wolverhampton in June; stayed 1m well; was ideally suited by some give in the ground; dead. *R. Price.*

TOP LADY (USA)   3 b.f. Bold Bidder–Matchless Native (Raise A Native)   **73** (1981 NR 1982 8fg² 10fg) $85,000Y; well-made, attractive filly with scope; sixth foal; closely related to a winner and half-sister to another; dam won 6f stakes event at 3 yrs; second favourite, caught close home when beaten a neck by Always Welcome in 19-runner Wood Ditton Stakes at Newmarket in April; ran much better than final position indicates when sixth of 9 to Sing Softly in Pretty Polly Stakes on same course later in month (would probably have been placed but for being badly squeezed out 2f from home); not seen out again; may stay 1½m. *B. Hills.*

TOPLEIGH   2 b.g. High Top 131–Nom de Plume 70 (Aureole 132) (1982 8s 9s³)   **91** Apr 28; rather small gelding; half-brother to 3 winners, including useful 1981 2-y-o 5f to 7f winner French Gent (by Sassafras); dam ran only at 2 yrs when winner over 7f; close-up third of 15 to Omar Ramsden in maiden race at Redcar in October; will stay 1¼m; should win a race. *Sir Mark Prescott.*

TOP MATCH   3 ch.c. Royal Match 117–Hilltop Chimes (Mountain Call 125)   — (1981 7fg 7g 7fg³ 7fg 7fg 1982 12f) leggy colt; quite modest at his best; broke a leg in minor event at Carlisle in April and was destroyed; would have stayed 1m. *H. Bell.*

TOP MOUSE   3 b.f. High Top 131–Field Mouse 108 (Grey Sovereign 128§)   — (1981 NR 1982 7.2g 7f) sister to smart 5f to 10.5f winner Triple First, and half-sister to several other winners; dam 5f sprinter; behind in maiden races at Haydock and Leicester in July. *H. T. Jones.*

TOP OF THE MARK   4 ch.g. On Your Mark 125–None-So-Pretty (Never Say   — Die 137) (1981 5s 6f 6f⁴ 6s 6f 7fg² 7fg⁴ 6f 1982 5.8f 8g 8fg 8g 5.8f 8f 8g) strong gelding; poor handicapper nowadays; suited by 7f; acts on any going but goes well on firm; has been tried in blinkers; possibly none too genuine; sold 550 gns Ascot October Sales. *G. Cottrell.*

TOPOLINO SAURO   3 ch.f. El-Birillo–Souris Francais (Decoy Boy 129)   — (1981 6s 6d 1982 8f 10fg 8.3g 10.1d 8.3fg) leggy, close-coupled filly; poor plater; sometimes blinkered. *Mrs R. Lomax.*

TOPORI   3 br.g. High Top 131–Lady Oriana 91 (Tudor Melody 129) (1981 6g   **69** d 1982 8d 8fg 8.5f* 8g 7f 8.3g 10fg 10v) sparely-made gelding; good mover; dropped in class when winning valuable seller at Epsom in June in good style; sold out of B. Hills's stable 5,400 gns afterwards; well beaten most starts afterwards; stays 1m well; acts well on firm going. *S. Woodman.*

TOP O'THE NORTH   2 b. or br.c. High Top 131–Gold Poulet 84 (Goldhill 125)   **112** (1982 5fg⁴ 5fg 6fg* 6g 6d* 7fg⁴ 5v³) Mar 4; big, strong, lengthy, attractive colt who carries plenty of condition; half-brother to 2 winners, including fairly useful 1978 2-y-o 5f winner Argentina Bound (by Amber Rama); dam ran only at 5f; showed vast improvement when winning 8-runner Champion Two Yrs Old Trophy at Ripon in August by 2½ lengths from Sayf El Arab; had previously beaten newcomer On Stage by 3 lengths in maiden race at Redcar; creditable 1¾ lengths third of 9 to Tatibah, after being bumped 1f out, in Cornwallis Stakes at Ascot in October, best other effort; way out of his depth behind Gorytus in Laurent Perrier Champagne Stakes at Doncaster; better suited by 6f than 5f; best form with some give in the ground. *M. W. Easterby.*

TOP O' TH' LANE 5 b.g. Palm Track 122–Poachings Folly (Poaching 115) **61** (1981 7d 7.2s 9fg⁴ 8fg 8fg² 8g 8g⁴ 7f² 7f* 7d 7v 1982 7.2f² 7fg⁴ 8fg 6f²) lengthy gelding; stays 9f but runs mainly at shorter distances; ideally suited by top-of-the-ground; ran moderately when blinkered once; not the most reliable of animals. *W. Haigh.*

TOP RATED 2 b. or br.f. Averof 123–Archaic 65 (Relic) (1982 5s 5s³ 5s 5f⁴ 5g* **105** 5fg 5fg⁴ 5fg 6f² 7.9g* 8fg³ 8s) Mar 5; 8,000Y; half-sister to very smart 1978 2-y-o 5f winner Schweppeshire Lad (by Decoy Boy); dam poor maiden; won 11-runner maiden race at Leopardstown in June by ½ length from Dermaleen and beat Push A Button by 2 lengths in 10-runner minor event at Dundalk in August; also ran well when 1½ lengths fourth of 9 to Virginia Deer in Curragh Stakes on seventh outing, when short-head second of 14 to Certain Something in Oldtown Stud Stakes at Naas and when narrowly-beaten third of 14 to Impudent Miss in Silken Glider Stakes at Leopardstown (looked sure to win 2f out but stride shortened in closing stages); sweated up when last of 16 in Queen Mary Stakes at Royal Ascot on sixth outing; stays 1m; blinkered fifth and sixth starts. *M. O'Toole, Ireland.*

TOP REEF 4 br.g. Take a Reef 127–Bienvenida 75 (Sheshoon 132) (1981 12s **—** 10s* 10s² 12g² 12d² 12d³ 11fg³ 13.8fg 11.7f⁴ 12fg 16.9fg 10.8fg 12g 13d 1982 15.5g 16s 17.1s 12v) small, lengthy gelding; poor handicapper; suited by 1⅛m; has run creditably on firm going, but is ideally suited by soft; suitable mount for an apprentice. *J. Jenkins.*

Mr P. Cameron's "Top O' The North"

TOPSEY'S SECRET 2 ch.f. Most Secret 119–Topsey Lorac (St Columbus 98) **69**
(1982 6fg 6d 7d) Apr 25; lengthy filly; first foal; dam never ran; 5 lengths
eighth of 12 to Stephalotus in minor event at Pontefract in October, second
outing; last of 14 at Catterick later same week. *W. Haigh.*

TOP SPADE 2 b.g. Precipice Star 90–Diddy Duck 53 (Dicta Drake 126) (1982 —
8d) fair sort; half-brother to 1976 2-y-o 7f winner What-A-Secret (by Most
Secret) and to a winner abroad; dam best at 1m; no show in 24-runner seller at
Leicester in September. *W. Turner.*

TOP TOUCH 2 b.g. Touch Paper 113–Candy Flake (Dionisio 126) (1982 5f2 **64**
5fg 5f 5fg 5g 5g) May 7; 9,200Y; well-grown gelding; brother to Irish 3-y-o 6f
winner Classic Touch, and half-brother to 2 winners, including fairly useful 5f to
7f winner Honey Flake (by Kelly); dam Irish 2-y-o winner; plating-class maiden;
blinkered last 2 outings; gelded after final appearance. *J. Berry.*

TOP TRAVELLER 7 ch.h. Galivanter 131–Apex 72 (Donore 119) (1981 8h 8h —
1982 8f 10.8fg 8g 8fg) poor handicapper; suitable mount for a boy. *G. Price.*

TORONTO STAR 2 b.c. Ardoon 124–Bristol Milk 88 (Raise You Ten 125) —
(1982 6g 6f 7.2s 6s 8d) May 26; stocky colt; half-brother to useful 3-y-o middle-
distance winner Corked (by Tumble Wind) and 1m to 1¼m winner Majestic Nurse
(by On Your Mark); dam stayed 1½m; no form, including in sellers. *A. Potts.*

TORREY (USA) 3 ch.c. Torsion–Deltaville (Delta Judge) (1981 5f2 6fg* 6d4 **92**
1982 7f 7d4) rather leggy, light-bodied colt; good walker and mover; fairly
useful at his best; creditable fourth to Paperetto in £4,000 handicap at Newmarket in October; stays 7f; blinkered final outing. *R. Hern.*

TORSION PRINCE (USA) 3 b.g. Torsion–Lucky Flirt (Lucky Debonair) **73**
(1981 5g2 7g2 7fg4 7d4 7fg 1982 8g* 10g2 8s2 10v2 10s 8.2s 8fg 8f4 8g3 8.2g2 10f)
lengthy, attractive gelding; good mover; won once and finished second three
times at Cagnes-sur-Mer in spring; twice ran respectably in handicaps afterwards;
stays 1¼m; seems to act on any going; has run respectably for an apprentice; has
given trouble at start on several occasions. *N. Callaghan.*

TOT 2 ch.g. Dragonara Palace 115–Silver Cygnet 71 (My Swanee 122) (1982 7f **60**
7g 7g) May 3; small, lengthy, lightly-made gelding; good walker; first foal;
dam won over 1m and stayed well; soundly beaten in useful company. *J. Carr.*

TO THE POINT 3 ch.f. Sharpen Up 127–Right as Rain 96 (King's Bench 132) **86**
(1981 5d* 5g2 5f 5fg4 5g2 5d* 5g 1982 5g2 5g) leggy, light-framed filly; creditable
4 lengths second of 6 to Street Market in handicap at Newbury in April; didn't
have best of runs only subsequent start in May; will be suited by 6f; best form with
some give in the ground; sent to USA. *G. Hunter.*

TOUCH BOY 6 b.h. Touch Paper 113–Hello Amy 70 (Forlorn River 124) **100**
(1981 5s 6g4 7.6g 5fg2 6g4 5fg 5f* 5fg 6f 5g* 5d3 5fg* 5.6fg* 6d 5s 6d 1982 5g
5s 5f 5fg 5g2 5g* 5fg* 6f 5fg 5fg3 5.6g3 5d 5d) compact, robust horse; useful
sprint handicapper; put up good efforts when winning at Haydock and Ayr in
July; held up when beating Little Starchy by a length under 10-8 on latter
course; unlucky in running and was subsequently moved up a place when fourth
to Vorvados in Portland Handicap at Doncaster in September on eleventh start;
acts on any going, but is possibly best on a sound surface nowadays; effective with
or without blinkers. *J. Berry.*

TOUCHING 2 br.c. Touch Paper 113–Rag Flowers (Tarqogan 125) (1982 5g2 **72**
5f4 6g2 5g* 7g 7d 6d) May 4; 4,900Y; quite well-made colt; good walker; half-
brother to 4 winners; dam lightly raced; made all to win maiden race at Hamilton
in June by ½ length from odds-on Brave Ivy; stays 6f; suited by some give in the
ground; careered across paddock and crashed into rails when withdrawn on
intended second outing; sold 4,000 gns Newmarket Autumn Sales. *T. Barron.*

TOUCHING WOOD (USA) 3 b.c. Roberto 131–Mandera 112 (Vaguely Noble **127**
140) (1981 7s3 1982 10fg2 12fg2 12f2 12fg* 12f2 12g3 14.6f* 14s*)
The decision, taken late in the year, to retire the dual St Leger winner
Touching Wood leaves the 1983 Cup races looking wide open. Judged on his
victories at Doncaster and the Curragh Touching Wood would have been first-
class Cup material, a natural successor to Ardross. He possessed good stamina
and showed himself to be a very game and determined racehorse capable of
showing his form on any going. Some time before the news of Touching Wood's
retirement his trainer had told us that the horse would have the Coronation Cup
as his first major objective in 1983. In our opinion, the distance of that race—
a mile and a half—wouldn't have been far enough for Touching Wood in top

St Leger Stakes, Doncaster—Touching Wood shows stamina his strong suit as he shakes off Zilos; the third horse Diamond Shoal is on the wide outside

company at four. Long-distance racing on the other hand would have been meat and drink to him. Touching Wood's lack of a good turn of finishing speed was disclosed on several occasions as a three-year-old and his best performances came in the Derby, the St Leger and the Jefferson Smurfit Memorial Irish St Leger, all of which were run at a hot pace from start to finish, conditions which made his deficiency in finishing speed less of a handicap and brought his stamina fully into play. To counter the possibility of Touching Wood's being tapped for speed, he was provided with a pacemaker at Doncaster and the Curragh and was sent into the lead more than three furlongs from home on each occasion, running on strongly to win the St Leger by a length and a half from Zilos and the Irish St Leger by two lengths from Father Rooney. The strong end-to-end gallop in the Derby undoubtedly favoured Touching Wood: pushed along throughout the last mile to hold a prominent position and strongly ridden in the straight, he finished a three-length second to Golden Fleece, ahead of Silver Hawk and Persepolis, both of whom met ill-luck in running.

Touching Wood was still a maiden when he lined up for the Derby, a 40/1 chance after receiving weight and a beating from Mr Fluorocarbon in the mile-and-a-quarter Heathorn Stakes at Newmarket in April, and from Peacetime in the mile-and-a-half Schroder Life Predominate Stakes at Goodwood in May, ridden for stamina on each occasion. Touching Wood's performance in the Derby, after which he landed the odds in the Welsh Derby at Chepstow, made him appear an outstanding prospect for the St Leger but defeat in the Gordon Stakes in July and the Great Voltigeur Stakes in August served to focus attention on other St Leger contenders and Touching Wood started 7/1 fourth favourite at Doncaster. There were, however, plausible explanations for Touching Wood's below-par showing at Goodwood and York: by the end of July he almost certainly needed a longer distance than a mile and a half to show to best advantage; and in the Gordon Stakes he was incorrectly ridden, held up at the back of the field for a long way, and readily outpaced by Electric at the end of a fairly slowly-run race; and when he was well beaten by Electric and Diamond Shoal in the Great Voltigeur he was known to be short of work. After York Touching Wood was tried in blinkers at home; he reportedly worked well in them and wore them at both Doncaster and the Curragh. The absence of the season's two best three-year-olds, the Derby winners Assert and Golden Fleece, led to an unusually large field turning out for the St Leger, the oldest of England's classics. There were fifteen runners, a number exceeded only once in the past twenty-five runnings of the race. The St Leger line-up included four others who had contested the Derby—Norwick (fifth at Epsom), Palace Gold (sixth), Rocamadour (eighth) and Jalmood (fourteenth)—but only four members of the field had won pattern races during the current season: Le Nain Jaune (Grand

Jefferson Smurfit Memorial Irish St Leger, the Curragh—Touching Wood and Father Rooney have the race between them

Prix de Paris), Electric (White Rose Stakes, Gordon Stakes and Great Voltigeur), Jalmood (Highland Spring Derby Trial), and Chem (Prix de l'Esperance). Credit for Touching Wood's victory lay chiefly with the extremely enterprising way in which he and his stable-companion Muslab were ridden to make the very most of Touching Wood's stamina. The blistering pace and the firm going resulted in the fastest time for the race—3m 3.53sec—since Bahram's 3m 1.80sec in 1935 (Chamossaire won a war-time St Leger at York in 2m 56.60sec). Some of Touching Wood's rivals were stone cold early in the straight while others, including the eventual third Diamond Shoal, were so far behind that they had practically no chance of overhauling him providing he kept up the gallop. Zilos put in a good challenge over the last three furlongs but Touching Wood held him off and drew away inside the final furlong. Of the others who had run in the Derby Norwick again came out best, finishing about five lengths fourth to Touching Wood with Rocamadour fifth and Jalmood sixth. The French challengers Chem and Le Nain Jaune finished tenth and twelfth while Electric came back tailed-off last.

There was talk of Touching Wood's running in the Prix de l'Arc de Triomphe but connections eventually decided to reserve him for the Irish St Leger which had its value raised sharply in 1982, although it was still worth less than half its English counterpart. The Irish St Leger was expected to be dominated by the two classic winners in the field, Touching Wood and the Irish Guinness Oaks winner Swiftfoot. Third-placed Swiftfoot never got on terms with Touching Wood in the straight but another British-trained challenger Father Rooney, going very easily on Touching Wood's tail, looked a serious threat with about a furlong and a half to go. However, not for the first time Father Rooney found little when let down and Touching Wood galloped on relentlessly, ridden right out as at Doncaster, to become the first horse to complete the English–Irish St Leger double since Trigo in 1929. Traditionally less well-contested than its English counterpart, the Irish St Leger had failed to attract a single St Leger winner in the period between Trigo's victory and that of Touching Wood, but the sponsorship of the Smurfit Group Ltd gave the race a much-needed shot in the arm and it should attract some stronger fields in the 'eighties, especially as the race is to follow the Prix Royal-Oak (French St Leger) and be opened in 1983 to horses above the age of three.

All of Ireland's classics are now sponsored but the British turf authorities have so far refused to permit commercial backing of the Two Thousand Guineas, the One Thousand Guineas, the Derby, the Oaks or the St Leger. Nine of the nineteen Group 1 pattern events in Britain had sponsors in 1982: the King George VI and Queen Elizabeth Diamond Stakes, the Coral-Eclipse Stakes, the Benson and Hedges Gold Cup, the Dubai Champion Stakes, the William Hill July Cup, the William Hill Cheveley Park Stakes, the William Hill Middle Park, the William Hill Dewhurst and the William Hill Futurity. It goes without saying that the five classics would be at least as attractive to sponsors so why has the Jockey Club so far regarded them as sacrosanct? One reason, the main one as we see it, is that sponsors expect a say in the way their money is spent—they want maximum publicity which usually means, for example, that they require the freedom to select the title of their race—and the Jockey Club would probably regard negotiation with sponsors as potentially jeopardizing its hold on the classics. The idea of adding the name of a sponsor to the title of a classic event is opposed on principle in some quarters though why the distaste should be selective, confined only to the classics, is difficult to fathom. Some also see it as desirable to avoid changes of race names, which would occur with changes of sponsor, so as to avoid possible confusion. In our view, the oft-stated disadvantages of sponsorship of the major races are more imagined than real. Racecourses staging important races have, by and large, been very successful in achieving continuity of sponsorship and the entertainment value of races which have had changes of sponsor (the William Hill Futurity was inaugurated as the Timeform Gold Cup in 1961 and has also been sponsored by *The Observer*) has been unaffected by the change in race name. The steep rise in sponsorship revenue over the past ten years or so has been an important benefit for racing, allowing Levy Board contributions to prize money to be spread more widely or used for other projects; for example, the sponsorship of the Champion

Maktoum Al-Maktoum's "Touching Wood"

Stakes in 1982 by the Al-Maktoum family freed £30,000 of Levy Board money which was reallocated to other pattern events. It seems nonsensical, especially in the present economic climate, for racing to turn its back on the additional money that could be secured through classic sponsorship.

	Roberto (b 1969)	Hail to Reason (br 1958)	Turn-to Nothirdchance
Touching Wood (USA) (b.c. 1979)		Bramalea (b 1959)	Nashua Rarelea
	Mandera (b 1970)	Vaguely Noble (b 1965)	Vienna Noble Lassie
		Foolish One (b 1957)	Tom Fool Miss Disco

A small, strong, attractive colt, and a fluent mover, Touching Wood is by the very successful 1972 Derby winner Roberto who stands at Darby Dan Farm, Lexington, Kentucky; Roberto was also represented in the most recent season in Europe by such as Real Shadai, Silver Hawk, Critique and the filly Slightly Dangerous, all of whom won pattern events. Touching Wood's dam Mandera wasn't raced at two but won two important races for fillies as a three-year-old, the Sandleford Priory Stakes at Newbury and the Princess Royal Stakes at Ascot, before being retired to the paddocks. Mandera was out of an unraced half-sister to Bold Ruler and was a half-sister to three winners in the United States including two stakes winners, Funny Fellow and Protanto. Until Touching Wood came along, however, Mandera had not lived up to her potential as a broodmare, her only offspring being the Irish mile-and-a-half winner and winning hurdler Mansky (by Nijinsky). Touching Wood will stand his first season at the Dalham Hall Stud, Newmarket, in 1983 at a fee of 7,000 guineas (live foal). *H. T. Jones.*

TOUCH SET 4 b.g. Touch Paper 113–Setaria (Sigebert 131) (1981 10s 9g 7.5g⁴ 8fg² 1982 10.1g) ex-Irish gelding; first living foal; plating-class French maiden; second in maiden race at Bellewstown as a 3-y-o when trained by W. Robinson; soundly beaten at Windsor in July; stays 9f; blinkered once at 2 yrs; sold 1,050 gns Ascot November Sales. *G. Kindersley.* —

TOUCH TENDER 2 b.c. Prince Tenderfoot 126–Touch of Dutch 54 (Goldhill 125) (1982 7fg 7g) Mar 8; 16,000Y; big, strong, good-bodied colt; first foal; dam sprint maiden; backward, behind in big fields of maidens at Redcar and Newmarket (last of 28) in the autumn. *P. Haslam.* —

TOUGH COMMANDER (USA) 2 b. or br.c. Bold Commander–She's Tuff **111 ?** (Royal Gem II) (1982 6f 6fg³ 7g 7g³) May 14; $35,000Y; quite attractive colt; half-brother to 2 winners by War Trouble, including minor stakes winner Stuff N' Nonsense; dam won 4 sprints; 200/1, far from disgraced but possibly flattered considerably when 7 lengths third of 4 to Diesis in William Hill Dewhurst Stakes at Newmarket in October; had previously shown up in 2 Newmarket maiden races, finishing 5¾ lengths third of 12 to Salieri in July and 10 lengths fifth of 28 to Tolomeo in October; will stay 1m. *R. Armstrong.*

TOUGH CUSTOMER 2 gr.g. Lucky Wednesday 124–Silver Swallow (My Swallow 134) (1982 5fg) Apr 15; third reported foal; dam ran once; behind in 18-runner maiden race at Lingfield in May. *H. Westbrook.* —

TOUJOURS VERT 3 ch.f. Northfields—Gently 95 (Grey Sovereign 128§) **73** (1981 6g 1982 8fg³ 7fg 8g² 8fg² 8f* 7fg³ 10.2f) attractive, well-made filly; made all to win maiden race at Thirsk in July; had earlier finished good third to Kareena in £5,100 event at Ascot; suited by 1m (ran as if something was wrong with her over 1¼m); has run respectably for an apprentice; didn't show much sparkle in blinkers on fourth outing. *M. Stoute.*

TOUR DE FORCE 2 ch.g. Reliance II 137–Set to Work (Workboy 123) (1982 **79 p** 7s³) May 5; first foal; dam never ran; 33/1, 6 lengths third of 12 to Dabdoub in minor event at Chepstow in October. *P. Makin.*

TOURNAMENT LEADER 2 ro.c. Dance In Time–Implacable (Never Say Die **75 p** 137) (1982 6fg²) Feb 29; 5,000F; fourth produce; dam French 1½m winner; 50/1, clear second best when beaten 3 lengths by Hossam in 12-runner newcomers event at Chepstow in August; will be suited by 7f+. *D. Marks.*

TOUSAN 3 b.f. Mandrake Major 122–Lochville 83 (Charlottesville 135) (1981 — 5f 5fg 5fg 1982 5f 7fg 6f⁴ 5f 8.2g 6g 6f 12s 8.2v) smallish, dipped-backed filly; plater; stays 6f; sometimes blinkered; sold out of D. Smith's stable 740 gns Doncaster August Sales after seventh start. *M. James.*

TOVERIS 2 gr.f. Homing 130–Smeralda 105 (Grey Sovereign 128§) (1982 7d **91** 7g*) Mar 31; 33,000Y; good-topped filly; good mover; half-sister to 3-y-o middle-distance winner Jorge Miguel (by Welsh Pageant) and 3 winners abroad; dam sprinter; won 22-runner maiden race at Newmarket in October by length from Current Raiser; badly away at Leicester earlier in the month; will stay 1m; promises to make quite a useful 3-y-o. *M. Stoute.*

TOWER-BIRD 10 b.g. Tower Walk 130–Misquote (Quorum 126) (1981 NR **—** 1982 10d) lightly raced on flat nowadays but is a fair chaser; stays 13f; acts on any going. *J. Webber.*

TOWERING 3 br.c. Tower Walk 130–Up And At It 72 (Tamerlane 128) (1981 **66** 5fg 6g 6g² 6g² 8f³ 7fg* 8d³ 8.2s* 1982 8g² 10fg 9g 8.2g 9g* 9s³ 8.2v*) big, good-topped colt; routed his opponents in handicap at Wolverhampton in October and accounted for Trade High by ½ length in similar event at Hamilton later in month; promises to stay 1¼m; acts on any going but is particularly well suited by soft; has run respectably for an apprentice and when sweating up; sold 14,000 gns Newmarket Autumn Sales. *Sir Mark Prescott.*

TOWER JOY 8 b.h. Tower Walk 130–Great Joy (Kythnos 126) (1981 6g 8g 7g³ **86** 7f* 8f⁴ 7f² 7fg 8fg³ 7fg³ 8fg 1982 8g 7fg 7f³ 8fg³ 7f 8g) strong, good-looking horse; fairly useful handicapper; third in apprentice event at Doncaster and Royal Hunt Cup at Royal Ascot; going on strongly at finish when beaten just over a length by Buzzards Bay on latter course in June; stays 1m; acts on any going; used to be an excellent mount for an apprentice but tends to get behind nowadays and sometimes has trouble getting through (did on second and fifth starts). *L. Cumani.*

TOWER OF STRENGTH 3 b.c. Tower Walk 130–Amberetta 72 (Supreme **70** Sovereign 119) (1981 NR 1982 5f* 6g 5f 6tg³ 6f 6f 6g 5fg³ 7d³ 8.2s) 17,500Y; quite attractive, well-made colt; not the best of movers; first foal; dam won 6 times at up to 9f; won maiden race at Sandown in April; not disgraced several subsequent starts; stays 7f; seems to act on any going. *J. Winter.*

TOWER WIN 5 ch.h. Tower Walk 130–Takawin 109 (Takawalk II 125) (1981 **49** 7d⁴ 8fg⁴ 8d³ 10v 8f⁴ 8f² 10f 8fg 8.3g³ 8f³ 8d* 10d 1982 8d 10f⁴ 8f³ 8g 10f 10f 10fg⁴ 8g* 10d³ 10d) quite attractive horse; won apprentice handicap at Yarmouth in September; stays 1¼m; acts on any going; blinkered 3 times in 1980; sometimes sweats up. *J. Benstead.*

TOWN FLIER 3 b.g. Town Crier 119–Go Baby Go 81 (Takawalk II 125) (1981 **78** 5fg 5s* 6d² 6s 1982 5f² 6g³ 6f* 6f 6g 6g 6f) compact gelding; good walker; quite a moderate handicapper; won at Haydock in May; will stay 7f; acts on any going; blinkered final start; exported to Malaysia. *N. Vigors.*

TOWNGATE CROSS 3 b.f. Royal Match 117–Blue Bleep (Bleep-Bleep 134) **—** (1981 6g 7f³ 7f⁴ 7g⁴ 7d² 8.2fg⁴ 1982 8fg 7f 12g 9f) poor mover; plater; ran moderately at 3 yrs; should stay 1m; blinkered last 2 starts. *M. H. Easterby.*

TOWN JENNY 4 b.f. Town Crier 119–Just Jenny 88 (Ennis 128) (1981 8d 7fg **—** 7f 5fg³ 5fg 7f 6fg 6f 5d 5s 1982 5fg 7s 6s 6g) plating-class maiden; not disgraced over 7f as a 3-y-o. *R. Hollinshead.*

TOWNLEY STONE 3 b.g. Legal Tender 94–Dream Isle (Indian Ruler 89) **—** (1981 7d 10.2g 1982 7f 8fg 12fg 13f) rangy gelding; has shown only a little ability; should stay middle distances. *J. Webber.*

TOWN PARADE 2 br.f. Creetown 123–Quick March 72 (March Past 124) **49** (1982 5d 5d³ 5g 6g 7fg) Mar 23; 3,100F; half-sister to a winner abroad; dam won 5f seller at 2 yrs; very poor form, including in a seller; sold 440 gns Ascot October Sales. *R. Smyth.*

TOWN ROCKET 3 b.g. Levanter 121–Town Girl 99 (Town Crier 119) (1981 **—** NR 1982 10s) tall, rangy, good sort; first foal; dam won twice over 6f; behind in 18-runner minor event won by Whenyourtrainsgone at Leicester in November. *R. Price.*

TOWN SPECIAL 3 ch.g. Town Crier 119–Come On Girl (Sheshoon 132) (1981 **—** 5s 5d 5fg⁴ 5fg² 5fg* 5g 6fg 5.3d 1982 7fg⁴ 7fg 6fg 6fg 6fg) quite attractive gelding; fair at his best; well beaten in claiming race final start (dwelt); stays 7f; suited by a firm surface; below form in blinkers once at 2 yrs. *P. Ashworth.*

TOWN STAR 2 gr.g. Town Crier 119–My Dearest Sarah 79 (Anwar 120) (1982 **85** 5f* 5f 5fg 6f 7f² 7f* 7g³ 7d³ 6g 7d) Apr 5; 1,600F, 1,800Y; strong gelding; half-brother to several winners here and abroad; dam sprint plater; ran moderately immediately after winning maiden auction event at Beverley in April but returned to form after being gelded in June, making all to win nursery at Redcar in July and being placed in auction event and 2 more nurseries; well suited by 7f; yet to race on very soft going but acts on any other; didn't keep a straight course under pressure fifth and sixth starts and ran rather wide into straight on seventh; blinkered in valuable seller third outing; exported to Hong Kong. *K. Stone.*

TRAA-DY-LIOOAR   2 b.c. Wollow 132–Parengeta 74 (So Blessed 130)   (1982   **74**
5g 5g³ 6f² 7g² 7d³ 6fg³)   Apr 5; 7,000F, 3,000Y; leggy colt; first foal; dam stayed 1¼m; quite a moderate maiden; not seen out after July; suited by 7f, and will stay further; seems to act on any going; sold 2,700 gns Newmarket Autumn Sales. *J. Mason.*

TRACK SECRET   3 b.f. Palm Track 122–Secret Folly 83 (Infatuation 129)   **41**
(1981 NR   1982 12.2f 12.2f 12d 10f³ 9f⁴ 12s² 12d)   lengthy filly; second foal; half-sister to 1¼m winner Pendle's Secret (by Le Johnstan); dam stayed 1½m; plater; suited by 1½m; acts on any going. *E. Weymes.*

TRACK TAMER   3 gr.f. Saritamer 130–Track Music 74 (Track Spare 125)   –
(1981 NR   1982 6f 5fg 8s 6s)   1,200Y; strong, robust filly; fifth foal; half-sister to a winner in Austria by Town Crier; dam won over 5f at 2 yrs; behind in maiden races and a claiming handicap. *J. Benstead.*

TRADE   2 b.c. Great Nephew 126–Grove Star (Upper Case)   (1982 8s)   Mar 6;   –
23,000Y; lightly-made, quite attractive colt; second foal; closely related to 3-y-o 1m winner Steel Venture (by Full of Hope); dam once-raced half-sister to smart Uncle Pokey; 14/1, no show in 14-runner maiden race at Leicester in November. *M. Ryan.*

TRADE HIGH   3 b.g. Tower Walk 130–Lucky Deal 93 (Floribunda 136)   (1981   **51**
5s⁴ 5g² 5g³ 5d⁴ 5g² 5g³ 6fg 7d 7g³   1982 8g 7f 7.6d 8.2g⁴ 8.2s³ 8.2v² 6s⁴)   lightly-made gelding; stays 1m; suited by some give in the ground; has run respectably for an apprentice; blinkered, gave trouble at start when withdrawn from seller fourth intended outing. *G. Richards.*

TRADESMAN   2 br.c. Workboy 123–Song of May 79 (Sing Sing 134)   (1982   **59**
5fg 5g 5g 5g 5f⁴ 7g)   Apr 8; neat, sturdy colt; half-brother to 3 winners, including 7f winner Song of Gold (by Goldhill); dam 5f sprinter; led over 4f when 5½ lengths fourth of 11 to Al Trui in nursery at Edinburgh in September, only sign of ability. *J. Haldane.*

TRADITIONAL MISS   7 ch.m. Traditionalist–Starboard Mist 81 (Right Boy   **90**
137)   (1981 8d 7g* 7v³ 8g⁴ 8f* 8fg* 8f³ 8h² 8fg 8h* 8h* 7fg²   1982 8fg 8fg* 11.7f* 12.2g² 11f 8h* 12h² 10h² 10.6g² 8g² 10f³ 8fg 10.6g 8g 10.2f⁴)   fairly useful handicapper; successful at Wolverhampton, Bath and Chepstow in first half of season; effective at 7f and 1½m; seems to act on any going but goes very well indeed on firm; good mount for an apprentice; extremely tough and genuine; sold 8,000 gns Newmarket December Sales. *J. Hill.*

TRAMPLER   5 br.h. Bustino 136–Chieftain Girl (Chieftain)   (1981 16g⁴ 14g   **53**
16g³ 16f 16fg 12s⁴ 18g   1982 16fg² 16d⁴ 15.8f³ 19f³ 17f³ 16.9fg⁴)   neat, well-made horse; staying handicapper; probably acts on any going. *A. Hide.*

TRANSFLASH   3 br.c. Auction Ring 123–Gwen Somers (Will Somers 114§)   **61**
(1981 6fg 6d   1982 5f 6g² 6f³ 7fg 8g 6v 6s³ 6s²)   leggy, useful-looking colt; stays 7f; acts on any going; blinkered third start; suitable mount for an apprentice. *I. Walker.*

TRANSIENT (USA)   3 gr.c. For The Moment–Cutalong (The Axe 115)   (1981   **84**
7v   1982 8fg 10.1fg 8d* 8d² 8f⁴ 8f 8.3g* 8fg⁴ 8s²)   lengthy, useful-looking colt; won maiden race at Salisbury in June and handicap at Windsor in August; stays 1m well; acts well on soft ground; blinkered fourth start; has shown a tendency to hang, isn't an easy ride and is suited by strong handling; sold 16,000 gns Newmarket Autumn Sales. *J. Tree.*

TRANSIT   3 b.f. Thatch 136–Bella Carlotta (Charlottesville 135)   (1981 7d   –
1982 9g 11.5g)   strong, good-bodied, short-legged filly; behind in maiden races. *B. Hills.*

TRANSONIC   3 br.f. Continuation 120–Sassanian Queen 71 (Baragoi 115)   **51**
(1981 5s 5f* 5f 5g   1982 5f* 5fg 7f 5f 6s)   lengthy, dipped-backed filly; sprint handicapper; won at Beverley in April; acts well on firm going. *J. Hardy.*

TRAPEZEY   4 ch.g. Red Alert 127–Floatingonair (Whistling Wind 123)   (1981   –
6s 5g 5v² 5g² 7g 6fg   1982 6g 5g)   light-framed gelding; plater; seems best in blinkers; sold 540 gns Ascot December Sales. *J. Gilbert.*

TRAVELGUARD   2 gr.c. Nishapour 125–Sequoia 87 (Sassafras 135)   (1982 6fg²   **108**
7fg³ 8s³ 7d* 7s*)   Apr 15; 7,600Y; well-made colt; second foal; dam 2-y-o 6f

winner; showed vastly improved form in late-season nurseries at Doncaster on last 2 outings, winning by long-looking 4 lengths on first occasion, and by ½ length from Greene Normandy, with remainder well beaten off, on the second; should stay 1¼m; acts well on soft ground. *J. W. Watts.*

TRAVEL ON 3 b.f. Tachypous 128–Chiltern Red (Red God 128§) (1981 5d² 5d² 5fg* 6fg² 6f* 6g² 7fg 8d 1982 6f 6fg² 6f 7f⁴) neat, strong, good-quartered filly; good mover; very useful in 1981; put up best effort at 3 yrs when going down by 2 lengths to Sylvan Barbarosa in valuable Leisure Stakes at Lingfield in June; soundly beaten in Duke of York Stakes, Cork and Orrery Stakes at Royal Ascot and Oak Tree Stakes at Goodwood on her other starts; should stay beyond 6f; best form on a sound surface; genuine. *P. Walwyn.* **94**

TRAVIATA (USA) 3 b.f. Youth 135–Noble Mark 120 (On Your Mark 125) (1981 NR 1982 10fg³ 10s³ 10.5d 11.5fg 11d² 10fg* 10.6s² 10s) $70,000F; lengthy ex-French filly; half-sister to middle-distance winners Noble Dudley (by Giacometti) and Victor's Boast (by Roberto), and good 2-y-o The Noble Player; dam very smart sprinter; kept on well when beating Caballo a neck in 18-runner maiden race at Beverley in September; will be suited by 1¼m; yet to race on really firm going, but acts on any other; trained by M. Zilber first 3 starts. *J. Dunlop.* **70**

TREASURE HUNTER 3 br.c. Full of Hope 125–Antigua 100 (Hyperion) (1981 NR 1982 7f 8d 9g) 72,000Y; quite attractive, strong colt; half-brother to Fiesta Fun (by Welsh Pageant), a useful winner at around 1¼m, and several other winners, including smart 6f and 7f winner Derrylin (by Derring-Do); dam won at 1½m; has shown a little ability in maiden races; will be suited by 1¼m+; sold 13,000 gns Newmarket Autumn Sales and is to be trained by J. Fitzgerald. *T. Robson.* **—**

TREASURE TROVE 2 gr.c. Try My Best 130–Turkish Treasure 111 (Sir Ivor 135) (1982 6g² 5fg³ 5fg 7fg* 6d*) Apr 12; second foal; half-brother to useful 1981 staying Irish 2-y-o Sun Worship (by Nonoalco), subsequently a stakes winner over 8.5f in USA; dam ran only at 2 yrs when very useful winner over 6f and 7f; favourite when successful twice at Naas in the autumn, winning maiden race by ¾ length before carrying top weight to a very narrow victory over Paladoon in Birdcatcher Nursery; had previously been placed twice at the Curragh, finishing well when 2 lengths second to stable-companion Caerleon in Tyros Stakes and being beaten a length when third of 9 to Virginia Deer in Curragh Stakes; blinkered when 5 lengths sixth of 11 to Sweet Emma in Heinz '57' Phoenix Stakes at Leopardstown in August (second favourite); needs further than 5f and will stay 1m. *V. O'Brien, Ireland.* **107**

TREBORO (USA) 3 b.c. Roberto 131–Costly Dream (Cohoes) (1981 5fg 5s 6f² 7f* 7g* 7fg* 1982 9fg) $240,000Y; well-made, good sort; good walker; second foal; dam smart winner of 15 races at up to 1m from 2 yrs to 4 yrs; very useful at 2 yrs when he won maiden race at Newmarket, Donnington Castle Stakes at Newbury (from Diamond Shoal) and Lanson Champagne Stakes at Goodwood (beat Telephone Man); subsequently had a set-back and needed run when modest ninth of 14 to Ivano in Gerry Feilden Memorial Stakes at Newmarket in April (beaten fully 3f out); would have stayed 1¼m+; usually an excellent mover but didn't go to post at all well at Newmarket; standing at Butterstocks Stud, Horsham, Sussex at £2,000 straight. *G. Harwood.* **—**

TREE FELLA 5 br.g. King Log 115–Gold Reid (Le Dieu d'Or 119) (1981 NR 1982 6f⁴ 5fg 5fg³ 6g³ 6f³ 6f 6g* 6f 6d 6fg 7.2s) leggy gelding; successful in handicap at Chester in July; possibly stays 7f; acts on any going; suitable mount for a boy. *C. Crossley.* **64**

TREE MALLOW 4 b.f. Malicious–Potentilla 89 (Nearula 132) (1981 10d 12f 12fg³ 12d² 12g⁴ 13d² 15.5s* 14g³ 1982 16f 12fg 12f 18d 13s) compact filly; suited by a test of stamina; well suited by some give in the ground; sometimes sweats up; bought out of M. Smyly's stable 7,000 gns Ascot March Sales and didn't run well for new connections; blinkered final start. *K. Morgan.* **—**

TRENDBUCKER (USA) 3 b.c. Far North 120–Sentimental Girl (Antonio Canale) (1981 7d⁴ 8g 1982 8g 9g² 9.4f³ 10f* 12.2f² 14fg 12.3d⁴ 12fg* 12.2f² 12f 12fg* 15f* 12g 15d) workmanlike colt; not the best of movers; won maiden race at Redcar in May and handicaps at Edinburgh in July and Wolverhampton (apprentices) and Edinburgh again in September; stays 15f; ideally suited by fast ground; blinkered fourth to sixth starts; suitable mount for an apprentice; game. *S. Norton.* **83**

TRENDY PHILLY 2 b. or br.f. Ballymore 123–Twaddle II (Tim Tam) (1982 7g 8s²) May 3; IR 57,000Y; fair sort; half-sister to several winners, including **85**

3-y-o 11f winner Corny Story (by Oats) and smart sprinter Petipa (by Habitat); dam placed at 1¼m in France; 33/1, made up ground hand over fist in closing stages, after being off bridle all way, when neck second to Running Melody, clear of remainder, in 11-runner maiden race at Wolverhampton in October; will be suited by 1¼m+; sure to win a race. *B. Hanbury.*

TRES GATE 5 b.h. Thatch 136–Setsu 117 (Shantung 132) (1981 2 wins and 2 places from 8 starts, including 6g* 5g* 6s³ 1982 6g³ 6v* 8g³ 7g³ 6.5fg 7s² 7v³ 8s³) 7,600Y; smallish horse; second living foal; dam one of best staying 2-y-o fillies of 1972; very smart performer in Italy, winner of 10 races; won Group 2 Premio Melton at Rome in May for second successive time, beating Vargas Llosa by 3 lengths; subsequently ran well when placed in Premio Emilio Turati at Milan (about a length third to Stifelius), Prix de la Porte Maillot at Longchamp (1¼ lengths third to Exclusive Order), Harroways Stakes at Goodwood (½-length second to shade comfortable winner Hays), Prix de la Foret at Longchamp (4¼ lengths third to Pas de Seul) and Prix Perth at Saint-Cloud (about 4 lengths third to Commodore Blake); effective at sprint distances and stayed 1m; acted on heavy going; often made running; stud in Italy. *L. Cumani.* **119**

TRESTLE 3 gr.f. Three Legs 128–Abbie West 112 (Abernant 142) (1981 5d 7d 1982 11.5f 12g 10g) leggy, quite attractive filly; excellent mover; only plating class; possibly stays 1½m. *L. Cumani.* **57**

TRI'AS 3 ch.f. Tyrant–Anoda (Amber Rama 133) (1981 NR 1982 7g 9f 9g) 1,850Y; sturdy filly; first foal; dam, placed in Italy, is half-sister to smart 1977 2-y-o Bolak; well beaten in varied company in the North. *P. Wigham.* **–**

TRICKSHOT 3 br.g. Workboy 123–Lemoncilla (Philemon 119) (1981 7g 7fg 7f 7fg³ 8g 8.2d* 7s³ 8.2d⁴ 8.2s² 1982 12f 12.3d 13g² 16f 12g 16d⁴ 17.4d 16s) useful sort; evidently stays 2m; best form on soft ground but has run respectably on a firm surface; blinkered sixth and final outings and didn't look too keen on fourth. *K. Stone.* **82 §**

Mr G. C. Forloni's "Tres Gate"

TRIFLING 3 b.f. Tower Walk 130–Whiffle 105 (King's Troop 118) (1981 6f⁴ **51**
1982 7fg 8g 8g² 7fg³ 7f⁴ 6g² 7s) smallish filly; plater; stays 1m; sold to BBA
1,400 gns Newmarket Autumn Sales. *J. W. Watts.*

TRIGGER POINT (USA) 2 b.c. Bold Bidder–Cornish Lady (Sir Ivor 135) **83**
(1982 7f 7g³ 7g² 7.6s 9s) Apr 16; $85,000Y; fair sort; good mover; first foal;
dam, sister to very successful Australasian stallion Sir Tristram, won at up to 1m
in USA; placed in maiden races at Ayr in July and Yarmouth in August; not
disgraced over 9f; appears to act on soft going. *M. Jarvis.*

TRIGOWEN 4 ch.g. Owen Anthony 102–Salvo of Conkers 79 (Salvo 129) (1981 —
7d 6d⁴ 8d 5f 1982 7h 8f) lightly-raced plater; probably stayed 7f; dead. *B.
Palling.*

TRIPLE ALLIANCE 3 b.c. Shantung 132–Rhodie Blake 101 (Blakeney 126) **88**
(1981 7g 1982 10d² 11.7f³ 12f* 12f* 16.1s² 16v) compact, attractive colt;
favourite when winning maiden race at Folkestone in May and handicap at
Leicester in September; stays well; acts on any going; has run creditably for
an apprentice; sold 8,800 gns Newmarket Autumn Sales. *G. Harwood.*

TRIPLE AXEL (USA) 3 b.c. Dance Spell–Shivering (Etonian) (1981 7fg 7fg* **98**
7.6g* 8s 1982 7s³ 8.5fg 10fg 8.2f 7.6f⁴ 8d) sturdy, good-looking colt; excellent
mover; fairly useful performer; in frame in slowly-run £3,000 event at Leicester
in March (2¾ lengths third of 5 to Mirabeau) and valuable handicap at Lingfield
in June; stays 1¼m; acts on any going; ran very freely in blinkers third and
fourth starts. *I. Balding.*

TRIPLE JUMP 2 ch.c. Orbit Dancer–Crisp Piece 90 (Saint Crespin III 132) **79**
(1982 6fg 6g 8.2fg³ 8g 8.2s² 8g* 8.2s) May 12; 800Y; workmanlike colt; half-
brother to 3 winners, including 1981 2-y-o 5f winner Saint Crespin Bay (by Bay
Express); dam placed over 6f and 7f; showed improved form when running on
gamely to win £2,900 seller at Newmarket (bought in 5,600 gns) in October by ½
length from American Boy; suited by 1m and will stay 1¼m. *R. Hannon.*

TRIPLE TIPPLE (USA) 3 b.f. Raise a Cup–Ameridouble (Nodouble) (1981 **111**
6fg² 6g 1982 7fg³ 8fg 7.6fg* 7fg* 7d* 7g* 10fg³ 10g² 7g* 8f* 10g) $34,000Y;

Fittocks Stud Limited's "Triple Tipple"

lengthy, attractive filly; good mover; third foal; half-sister to French 1¼m winner Ranan (by Ace of Aces) and very useful American 4-y-o stakes winner Pale Purple (by Verbatim); dam unraced half-sister to very useful middle-distance filly Trillionaire; won maiden race at Lingfield, minor events at Leicester, Salisbury and Folkestone, Strensall Stakes at York and £11,900 Sceptre Stakes at Doncaster; wasn't troubled to beat Fairy Tern by a length at York, and ran out a comfortable ¾-length winner over Perang Tejam at Doncaster; also ran well to be third in Ladbrokes Nell Gwyn Stakes at Newmarket (behind Chalon) and Nassau Stakes at Goodwood (to Dancing Rocks) and 2½ lengths second to Zinzara in Prix de Psyche at Deauville; stays 1¼m; acts on a firm and a soft surface; consistent. *L. Cumani.*

TRISKELION 3 b.c. Three Legs 128–Maynooth Belle (Busted 134) (1981 5f 7f¼ 5s 6g 1982 6f 6f 8f 7g³ 8.3g 8g) small, strong colt; plater; stays 7f; blinkered once at 2 yrs; has run respectably for an apprentice; sold 340 gns Ascot November Sales. *S. Woodman.* **44**

TROCADERO 3 b.g. Sagaro 133–True Love 89 (Princely Gift 137) (1981 6d 1982 10d² 11g 12f² 11fg³ 13g 8g² 9g 10d 8g) neat gelding; runner-up in maiden races; stays 1½m; seems to act on any going. *C. Thornton.* **63**

TROJAN KING 3 b.c. Free State 125–Shari (Rustam 127) (1981 6g 1982 8fg 7g 8f 8g² 8fg³ 8f) neat, attractive colt; plater; stays 1m; best in blinkers; sold 1,100 gns Newmarket Autumn Sales. *B. Swift.* **41**

TROJAN AVEROF 4 br.c. Averof 123–Camina Bay 109 (Whistling Wind 123) (1981 8f³ 10d 1982 12d 10.2g³ 10fg³ 10f 8g 8fg 8s) sparely-made colt; disappointing maiden; stays 1¼m. *C. Brittain.* **—**

TROLL LADY 5 b.m. Crisp and Even 116–Fire Hawk 70 (Firestreak 125) (1981 10g 10.1d 10s⁴ 12d 15.5fg⁴ 12g⁴ 12g* 12.2g 12d 1982 10.6f 12d 12fg 16.5f 12g⁴) leggy mare; plater; stays 1½m; probably needs some give in the ground; sometimes sweats up. *P. Feilden.* **—**

TROOPER SERGEANT 3 b.g. Queen's Hussar 124–Grass Widow (Thatch 136) (1981 6d 7g 7fg³ 6g 6fg³ 7g 1982 8.2fg⁴ 7f 7g 8f⁴ 8.5f³ 8d⁴ 7g* 6fg* 6f³ 6fg* 6d 6g) workmanlike gelding; sold out of M. Blanshard's stable 8,200 gns after easily winning valuable seller at Newmarket in June; subsequently showed himself a cut above a plater, winning handicaps at Windsor and Yarmouth; stays 1m but seems better at shorter distances; seems to act on any going; appears not to find much off bridle. *G. Huffer.* **77**

TROPICAL LOVE 4 ch.g. Red Alert 127–Luluna (Pinza 137) (1981 12d 8f⁴ 8.2g* 7g* 9g 8fg 1982 12s 10.2d) neat, strong gelding; well beaten in 1982 (not seen out until October); should stay beyond 1m. *J. King.* **—**

TROPICAL MIST (FR) 2 b. or br.c. Faraway Son 130–Tropical Cream (Creme dela Creme) (1982 8.2s³) Apr 20; half-brother to 2 winners in France, notably smart 1m winner Tropicaro (by Caro); dam, smart at 2 yrs and 3 yrs, won 10.5f Prix Cleopatre; very backward, made steady progress without being knocked about and had every chance until weakening in final furlong when 4½ lengths third of 19 to Holy Spark in minor event at Nottingham in October; certain to improve. *P. Walwyn.* **80 p**

TROPICAL RED 2 ch.c. Red Alert 127–Desert Pet 77 (Petingo 135) (1982 8s*) May 27; IR 2,000Y; second foal; half-brother to 3-y-o 6f and 7f winner Godly (by Godswalk); dam won over 1¼m; 50/1, put up a remarkable display after starting very slowly in 17-runner apprentice seller at Warwick in October, coming through to win easily by 2½ lengths; was bought in 1,050 gns; acts well on soft going; evidently useful in plating company, and probably quite capable of paying his way outside. *C. Wildman.* **72 p**

TROPINGAY 2 b.f. Cawston's Clown 113–Summer Sales 94 (Tropique 128) (1982 6fg 5s) Mar 26; sister to 1981 2-y-o 5f winner Vanity Fair; dam won over 6f at 2 yrs; well beaten in autumn maiden events at Goodwood and Bath. *D. Elsworth.* **—**

TROUBADOUR 2 b.c. Hotfoot 126–Beryl's Song 86 (Sing Sing 134) (1982 5f 5fg 5fg 5fg³ 6fg 6g 5g) Apr 2; well-made, strong-quartered colt; half-brother to 1978 2-y-o 6f winner Saucy Melody (by Malicious); dam fair 2-y-o; quite moderate; best race when sixth of 20 to Misguided in maiden event at Newbury in September on final start; should stay 6f. *W. Wightman.* **72**

TRUE SEASON 2 ch.f. Silly Season 127–True Course II (Sea Charger 129) (1982 7d 8fg 8.2s) Feb 3; 6,200Y; workmanlike filly; half-sister to numerous winners, including Lincoln winner Southwark Star (by Midsummer Night II); well beaten in maiden events, twice last; sold 750 gns Doncaster October Sales. *E. Carter.*

TRUMPERY 2 br.c. Diamonds Are Trump 108–Dorchester 50 (Connaught 130) **66**
(1982 5fg⁴ 5f² 5fg⁴ 5g² 6f⁴ 6g* 7d 7.2f) Apr 18; 3,800Y; slightly dipped-backed, quite attractive colt; first foal; dam placed second over 6f from only 3 starts; sold out of P. Walwyn's stable 3,500 gns after winning 8-runner seller at Haydock in August; in rear in nurseries subsequently; should stay 7f; exported to Malaysia. *R. Hollinshead.*

TRUMPS 2 ch.g. Grundy 137–Good Try 92 (Good Bond 122) (1982 6g 6g 7fg 6g) **—**
Feb 10; 25,000Y; strong, compact, attractive gelding; second foal; half-brother to 3-y-o 6f winner Hawk's Nest (by Moulton); dam 2-y-o 5f winner; little worthwhile form in maiden and minor events; blinkered final outing; subsequently gelded. *B. Swift.*

TRUPER GEE 4 b.g. Rheingold 137–Cappuccilli 111 (Lorenzaccio 130) (1981 **33**
8fg 10s 16s 12g 8fg 10f 7g 12fg* 9g 12fg 12f 12g⁴ 11d² 12d 12d² 1982 12g 12f 12f⁴ 10f⁴ 10fg 15g 12g³ 12f³ 12fg 12g 12d) small gelding; plater; well beaten after finishing third in non-selling handicap at Beverley in July on eighth start; suited by 1½m; probably acts on any going; blinkered once at 3 yrs; sold out of R. Whitaker's stable 1,850 gns Doncaster September Sales after tenth start and resold 1,000 gns Ascot December Sales. *W. Stubbs.*

TRUST SALLY 3 b.f. Sallust 134–Trust Sylvia (Linacre 133) (1981 5s 5g 5fg **50**
5f 5f* 5g 5f 5g³ 1982 5fg 5fg 5f² 5f 5g 5g) neat, sturdy filly; plater; acts on firm going; sold 1,250 gns Newmarket Autumn Sales. *B. McMahon.*

TRUSTY CATCHER (USA) 4 ch.g. Pass Catcher–In Trust (Buckpasser) **—**
(1981 8g 10f² 11fg⁴ 8g1 982 15.5fg) rangy gelding; in frame in maiden races as a 3-y-o; suited by middle distances; sold 740 gns Newmarket Autumn Sales. *G. Thorner.*

TRUSTY TROUBADOR (USA) 2 ch.c. The Minstrel 135–In Trust (Buck- **89**
passer) (1982 6f 7g³ 7s 7g 8s²) Apr 25; $275,000Y; lengthy, attractive colt; good walker; half-brother to 3 minor winners; dam, half-sister to dam of John Cherry, was placed in 4 of her 7 starts; ran well in fairly useful company, on last 2 appearances finishing 3 lengths fifth of 30 to Mandelstam in maiden race at Newmarket in October and 2½ lengths second of 19 to Full Rainbow in similar event at Warwick (found little off bridle); will stay beyond 1m; whipped round at start and unseated rider on debut; sure to win a race. *F. J. Houghton.*

TRY TO REMEMBER 2 b.f. Music Boy 124–Beech Tree 67 (Fighting Ship **—**
121) (1982 6g 7d) Apr 26; big filly; half-sister to 2 winners, including 7f winner Swing The Axe (by No Mercy), subsequently successful in Jersey and France; dam stayer; in rear in October in 15-runner seller at Newmarket and in 18-runner maiden race at Leicester. *B. Hanbury.*

TRY TO SMILE 5 b.h. Murrayfield 119—Teersaway 74 (Weepers Boy 124) **105**
(1981 6.5fg³ 6fg 5fg 8f³ 8f 1982 6.5g* 5g³ 6d² 8s⁴ 6g) very useful in this country and in France at 2 yrs; lightly raced since (raced for only around 2 months in both 1981 and 1982) but retains plenty of ability; won 60,000 francs event at Evry in July and was in frame on his next 3 starts; ran best race when deadheating for second, a head behind Great Eastern, in Prix de Meautry at Deauville in August; stays 1m but seems better at sprint distances; seems to act on any going. *O. Douieb, France.*

TRY TROFFEL 2 b.g. Golden Dipper 119–Floral 82 (Floribunda 136) (1982 **84**
5f⁴ 5f⁴ 5fg³ 5d³ 6f 5fg* 5d 5g 5s) May 16; strong, sturdy gelding; poor walker; half-brother to 2 minor winners; dam 2-y-o 7f winner; won maiden race at Sandown in July by ½ length from Grand Harbour; in rear in nurseries subsequently, dwelling on seventh outing; should stay 6f; gelded after final appearance. *P. Haynes.*

TRY YOUR BEST 2 b.c. Try My Best 130–Limuru 83 (Alcide 136) (1982 7s) **— p**
Mar 7; 83,000Y; half-brother to numerous winners, including Derby runner-up Cavo Doro (by Sir Ivor); dam, 1m and 1¼m handicapper, is half-sister to good miler Saintly Song; ninth of 13 behind By Decree in £5,900 race at Ascot in September. *P. Haslam.*

TUBES CARE 3 b.f. Moulton 128–Drury Lane 83 (Gala Performance) (1981 **60**
8fg 8s 8s 10.2g 1982 12fg 12f 16fg 12fg 9f* 9g²) big, strong filly; plater; won at Redcar in August (bought in 1,500 gns); should stay 1¼m; acts on firm going; best in blinkers; sometimes sweats up; didn't find much off bridle final outing. *Hbt Jones.*

TUDOR BELL STAR 3 b.g. Wishing Star 117–Affectionately 82 (Mark-Ye- —
Well) (1981 6h 7f 8s 1982 8fg 8f 9g 8.3fg 8fg 12g 10fg³ 9fg) lengthy, sparely-
made gelding; plater; stays 1¼m; sometimes blinkered. *D. Wintle.*

TUDOR CHIEF 6 b.g. Tudenham 118–Bally Girl (Ballyciptic 122) (1981 NR —
1982 12f³) ex-Irish gelding; quite moderate in 1980; had stiff task and needed
race when last of 3 behind Bedford in small race at Pontefract in September;
stays 9f; probably acts on any going; good mount for an inexperienced rider.
T. Craig.

TUDOR DREAM 4 b. or br.f. Averof 123–So Smooth (Pall Mall 132) (1981 —
7v⁴ 6g 6f 5g 8.2f 6d 1982 6f) leggy, lengthy filly; no worthwhile form since
1980, including in sellers; should stay 7f; usually apprentice ridden. *T. Cuthbert.*

TUDOR FANTASY 3 b.f. Welsh Pageant 132–Tadorna 82 (Sea-Bird II 145) **69**
(1981 6g 1982 10fg 12d 10fg4) small, quite attractive filly; has shown some
ability in varied company; should stay 1½m; sold 13,000 gns Newmarket
December Sales. *J. Dunlop.*

TUDOR GATE 2 b. or br.g. Tachypous 128–Shikra (Sea Hawk II 131) (1982 —
5f 7g 7g 7d) May 4; smallish, good-topped gelding; second live foal; dam placed
over 1½m in Ireland; behind in maiden and minor events; dwelt last 2 starts;
subsequently gelded. *M. Tompkins.*

TUDOR ROOT 2 br.f. Tudor Rhythm 112–Beetroot 89 (Psidium 130) (1982 **61**
7f⁴ 7fg 8s⁴ 8.2s⁴) Mar 19; 5,000Y; medium-sized, lengthy filly; closely related
to 1½m winner Salsafy (by Tudor Melody), and half-sister to 2 other winners;
dam stayed well; plating-class maiden; will stay middle distances. *R. Laing.*

TUDORVILLE 4 br.c. Shoolerville 121–Razia 97 (Martial 131) (1981 10v² **60**
10s⁴ 12d 12g 12d 12.3g 10g 10g 12f 12fg 13d 12s² 12d 1982 13s 12f 13g⁴ 12f*
12f 12s² 12.3g³ 12g* 12g 13g 12fg 13.8d 12v³ 12d 15d) rangy colt; good walker;
has rather a round action; successful in handicaps at Carlisle in May and Hamilton
in June; disappointed a few times; stays 13f; acts on any going; occasionally
blinkered (better without); has worn bandages. *K. Stone.*

TUDOR WYNK 9 b.g. Wynkell 88–Wandering Rose (Tudor Minstrel 144) **60**
(1981 13.1g³ 12.2fg 12g³ 14g² 1982 12fg³ 13.1f³ 14f⁴ 12fg⁴ 16s* 16v³) won
handicap at Lingfield in September by 3 lengths from stable-companion Silcakey;
stays well; acts on any going; was tried in blinkers once at 2 yrs; good mount
for an apprentice; consistent. *D. Elsworth.*

TUDY 2 b.f. Welsh Saint 126–Truly A Princess 90 (Prince Regent 129) (1982 **67**
6g 6f 6f) Feb. 16; strong, good-bodied filly; first foal; dam won twice over 7f
at 2 yrs; plating-class maiden; showed form only on second outing; not raced
after August. *G. Pritchard-Gordon.*

TUGAWAY 2 ch.c. Tug of War 117–Living Legend 88 (Derring-Do 131) (1982 —
5fg 7d 7fg 7f 8fg) Mar 31; small, closed-coupled colt; second foal; dam won twice
over 1m; behind in maiden and minor events; sweated up and raced very keenly
when blinkered final start. *D. Whelan.*

TUGOFLOVE 6 b.h. Tudor Rhythm 112–Speyside 84 (Live Spirit 121) (1981 **103**
8s⁴ 8g⁴ 7g 8g* 8fg³ 8fg² 8fg* 9g 1982 8g 8fg 8g* 8f* 8.5f 8fg* 8d 8g 8g 8g 10g
9d 8s) useful, well-made horse; useful handicapper; improved and won £14,100
Jubilee Stakes at Kempton (from Sauvage), £10,500 Hambleton Stakes (Limited
Handicap) at York (beat Bel Bolide) and £7,600 Ronaldshay Cup at Redcar (from
Polly's Brother) in first half of year; didn't show a great deal on his other starts,
but usually had pretty stiff tasks; suited by 1m; probably acts on any going;
does best when held up; can produce a good turn of foot, and is suited by a
strongly-run race. *R. Laing.*

TULA FANCY 4 b.g. Roan Rocket 128–Becassine (El Gallo 122) (1981 8g —
10g⁴ 11g⁴ 9d 12d 12f⁴ 9fg³ 11.5f³ 12g 1982 13v) ex-Irish gelding; in frame in
varied company in 1981; stays 1½m. *J. S. Wilson.*

TULA MUSIC 3 gr.f. Patch 129–Tula Melody 71 (Tudor Melody 129) (1981 **62**
NR 1982 12fg 12.2f 12.2f 12g² 13.8f* 12d⁴ 13.8d*) leggy, lightly-made filly;
half-sister to 2 minor winners here and abroad; dam won at 1m; plater; bought
in 1,750 gns after winning at Catterick in August; successful in better company on
same course in October; suited by 1¾m; seems to act on any going. *J.
Etherington.*

TULSA FLYER 3 b.c. He Loves Me 120–Happy Thought 57 (Kauai King) **85**
(1981 6d 6g* 7g* 7fg* 8s 7.3s 1982 8f* 10fg³ 8f³ 10g³ 8d⁴ 10fg³ 8g⁴ 7g² 8f 8g)
compact, rather hollow-backed colt; beat African Pearl by 2 lengths in £3,000 race
at Brighton in April; ran respectably in handicaps several times afterwards;

needs further than 7f and stays 1¼m; probably unsuited by very soft going but acts on any other; has run creditably for an apprentice; below form last 2 starts. *P. Cole.*

TUMBLEDOWNHILL 4 ch.g. Tumble Wind–Little Hills (Candy Cane 125)   — §
(1981 8.2fg 10.6d 8g 8.2s 7f 7.2f 6g³ 7g² 7.2g 7g 7g 1982 7f 7.2f⁴ 7f 8.2f) work-manlike gelding; rather a disappointing handicapper; best at up to 7f; occasion-ally blinkered; often starts slowly; trained first 2 starts by C. Crossley. *B. McMahon.*

TUMBLE JIM 3 b.g. Tumble Wind–Little Rastro (Above Suspicion 127)   —
(1981 5g 5.8g⁴ 6g 7d 7g 1982 7f 7f³ 7g 8.2g 7g 9fg 14.7f) rangy, quite attractive gelding; good mover; plater; stays 7f; blinkered fourth start (ran badly). *C. Pinkham.*

TUNGUSKA 3 b.f. Busted 134–Sunblast 108 (Roan Rocket 128) (1981 7v⁴ 7g 75
1982 12f⁴ 10f* 10fg³ 10.2d³) narrow, rather lightly-made filly; poor mover; won maiden race at Leicester in May; not disgraced subsequently; stays 1½m; seems to act on any going; sold to BBA 5,000 gns Newmarket December Sales. *H. Cecil.*

TUNKU (USA) 3 b.c. Jacinto–Avanti Girl (Royal Levee) (1981 5.1f 6fg 6g —
1982 8fg 7f 7f 7fg 8g) neat colt; poor maiden. *R. Armstrong.*

TUNSTALL 3 ch.c. Palm Track 122–Goldwis 94 (Golden Cloud) (1981 6d 72
1982 9.4f 9.4f 8.2s 8s²) big, strong colt; only plating class; best run at 1m on soft going. *Mrs A. Cousins.*

TURBULENCE (FR) 3 ch.f. Targowice 130–Rough Sea (Herbager 136) (1981 58
NR 1982 10s⁴ 12g 14d⁴ 12fg³ 14g 13d 12v 10g) 5,800F; tall filly; half-sister to several winners in France, including smart 9f and 10.5f winner North Sea (by Lyphard); dam, sister to Sea Hawk II, placed over 1¼m on only start; in frame in maiden races; stays 1¾m; blinkered last 2 starts. *M. Ryan.*

Elcotgrange Ltd's "Tugoflove"

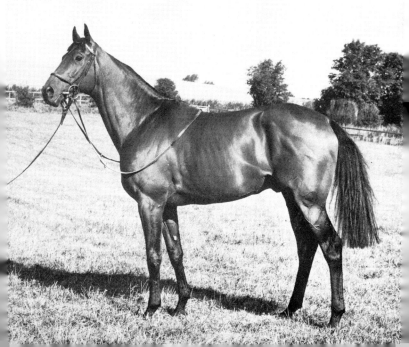

TURI 3 b. or br.c. Welsh Pageant 132–Turiana (Citation) (1981 5g 6fg 7g 7fg —
1982 7f 7f) compact colt; no worthwhile form in varied company, including
selling; has twice worn blinkers. *G. Toft.*

TURKOMAN 3 b.g. Patch 129–Arctrullah (Great Captain) (1981 5g 5.8g⁴ 6f **96**
7fg 7.2fg 7s⁴ 8s 8s 1982 9g 10fg 10s⁴ 10v* 10s* 12s* 10d* 12.3fg³ 10f⁴ 12g 10g
10v 10g 12s*) strong, compact gelding; inconsistent at 2 yrs but did little wrong
in 1982, winning 2 races at Cagnes-sur-Mer and handicaps at Chepstow and
Kempton early in year and William Hill November Handicap at Doncaster;
rallied to dead-heat with Double Shuffle after swerving 1½f out in last-named;
suited by 1½m; probably acts on any going, but revels in the mud; does best when
ridden up with pace; blinkered twice in 1981; game. *D. Sasse.*

TURN BACK THE TIME (USA) 4 b.c. Youth 135–Topolly (Turn-to) **97**
(1981 9fg³ 8.2s* 12s 1982 12g 12f³ 12.3fg 10fg* 16.1f 16.1f³ 17.1g²) tall,
lengthy, attractive colt; good mover; placed in handicaps at Thirsk, Newmarket
and Bath, finishing lame when 4 lengths second of 3 to Morgan's Choice on last-
named course in July; beat Rekal without much fuss in match at Newbury in
May; seems to stay quite well; acts on any going, but is probably suited by a
sound surface. *B. Hills.*

TURNBERRY 3 b.g. Sallust 134–Cherry Bird 68 (Abernant 142) (1981 5d 5fg —
6fg 5fg 5.1d⁴ 5s 1982 6s 8f 7f 7g) small gelding; poor plater; has worn blinkers;
sold 400 gns Doncaster August Sales. *M. Lambert.*

TURTLE HILL 3 b.f. Home Guard 129–Bantam 64 (Combat 123) (1981 5fg³ **73**
6g 6g 7g 1982 6f² 6g² 6fg² 5d 5f³ 5f² 5fg* 5fg*) workmanlike filly; poor
walker; won maiden race at Warwick in August and minor event at Beverley in
September (made all); best at sprint distances; needs top-of-the-ground. *J.
Etherington.*

TUTHILL BELLO 4 ch.f. Porto Bello 118–Grill Room 79 (Connaught 130) —
(1981 6g² 6s² 7fg⁴ 6d 6f 6f 1982 6s) strong filly; has some ability but was tailed
off in a seller on only outing of 1982; possibly doesn't quite stay 7f; ran moderately
in blinkers once at 3 yrs; usually apprentice ridden. *W. Stubbs.*

TUTHILL BOND 5 ch.g. Good Bond 122–Whirlibird 78 (The Pelican) (1981 —
10s 1982 11.7fg 11.1g 10d 8g 8s) leggy, narrow gelding; fairly useful at his best
but hasn't shown much on flat for a long time, including in a seller; stays 1m;
acts on any going; trained by N. Callaghan until after third start. *Mrs N.
Macauley.*

TWENTY DOWN 2 ch.c. Kinglet 98–Kipping Hill (Petition 130) (1982 5f **57**
6fg⁴ 7f 7g 7d⁴ 8.2g 8fg) May 1; 5,600Y; lengthy colt; half-brother to fairly useful
1m to 1¼m winner Alpaca (by Parthia) and to a winner in France; dam unraced
sister to smart American performer Day Court; modest plater; stays 1m; sold
NBA 1,500 gns Newmarket Autumn Sales. *P. Haslam.*

TWICE AS FRESH 3 ch.c. Free State 125–Rose Mullion 82 (Tudor Melody 129) **60**
(1981 7d 7d 1982 8g⁴ 10fg 8fg 8fg 10fg⁴ 15.8d) fair sort; plating-class maiden;
stays 1¼m; often blinkered; sold 4,000 gns Newmarket Autumn Sales. *J. Bethell.*

TWICE LUCKY 3 b.f. Condorcet–Fortuity (Fortino II 120) (1981 5fg 7d³ 8s **56**
7g 8d 1982 8d 8d 8fg* 8fg⁴ 9g³ 8fg 9g 8.3g 8g 8g 10v³ 10d 12s*) leggy, narrow
filly; plater; won narrowly at Newmarket in May (bought in 1,600 gns) and
hacked up in claiming handicap at Leicester in November; claimed £2,520 after
latter; stays 1½m; seems to act on any going but goes well on soft; often apprentice
ridden; blinkered ninth start. *N. Guest.*

TWICKENHAM 6 b.g. Martinmas 128–Ember Grill 84§ (Indigenous 121) **94**
(1981 8d 8g* 8.3fg 8fg 8f* 9fg² 8fg 8g² 1982 8g 8fg 8f* 8fg* 8g* 8fg* 8v² 8v* 8s)
leggy gelding; poor walker; in tremendous form in 1982 and won handicaps at
Salisbury (2), Sandown (apprentice event, making all) and Bath, and apprentice
race at Ascot; rallied gamely after being headed 2½f out to beat Ash Ridge by a
short head in last-named event in October; also ran well when close second to
Charlo Mio in Premio Mincio at Milan; stays 1½m; acts on any going; good mount
for a boy; sometimes starts slowly. *I. Balding.*

TWINACRE 6 b.g. Cumshaw 111–Saphir II (Rustam 127) (1981 NR 1982 —
12.2f) selling hurdler; needed race when behind in maiden event at Catterick in
July, first outing on flat; sold 3,200 gns Doncaster October Sales. *A. Smith.*

TWIST HOME (FR) 3 b.c. Homeric 133–Doctor's Choice 116 (Petingo 135) **91**
(1981 6d 8g 8s* 8s² 10.2g² 1982 12f² 16fg 16g) well-made, attractive colt;
good walker; went down by 4 lengths to Alpha Omega in 6-runner handicap at

Ripon in April; had stiff tasks afterwards; should stay beyond 1½m; acts on any going. *G. Harwood.*

TWO HIGH 3 b.f. High Top 131–Two's Company (Sheshoon 132) (1981 NR **89**
1982 7fg³ 8g³ 10.2g⁴ 10fg² 10f² 12fg* 12g* 12v* 12s² 10.2d²) quite attractive
filly; first foal; dam useful French 6.5f and 1½m winner; favourite when winning
maiden race at Folkestone and minor events at Beverley and Lingfield; ran
creditably last 2 starts, going down by ¾ length to Aura in handicap at York and
by ½ length to Lady Justice in £6,400 event at Doncaster; suited by 1½m; acts on
any going. *F. J. Houghton.*

TWO IN A ROW 3 br.f. Manado 130–Tekatrack 81 (Track Spare 125) (1981 —
NR 1982 5g) 7,600Y; quite attractive, well-made filly; first foal; dam lightly-
raced 2-y-o 5f winner; 20/1 when behind in valuable 15-runner maiden race
won by Zanubia at Sandown in June. *F. J. Houghton.*

TWO MINUTES 3 ch.g. High Line 125–Elm Park (Aberdeen 109) (1981 7f **71**
7f² 7fg² 8s 1982 9g 10fg³ 12d*) lightly-made, useful sort; readily won maiden
race at Redcar in November; suited by 1½m; possibly unsuited by very soft going
but acts on any other. *G. Pritchard-Gordon.*

TWO SHOTS 2 b.f. Dom Racine 121–Daffodil Girl (Blakeney 126) (1982 5v —
6s) Apr 18; 2,500Y; small, fair sort; good walker; third foal; dam modest half-
sister to smart 6f to 1¼m winner Escapologist; well beaten in autumn maiden
events at Folkestone and Leicester. *H. Westbrook.*

TWO STEP (FR) 4 b.c. Caracolero 131–Tap Dance (Baldric II 131) (1981 **116**
10d* 12fg³ 12s² 10.5g* 12g* 12g 12s² 12v² 1982 12fg³ 12s² 10s³ 12v² 12v⁴ 12v*)
French colt; second foal; dam, who won over 1¼m from 3 outings, is daughter of
very smart American filly Nasrina; ran consistently well as a 3-y-o and won at
Longchamp (on a disqualification), Maisons-Laffitte and Compiegne (Grand Prix);
gained only win of 1982 when beating Dago by 3 lengths in small race at Maisons-
Laffitte on last day of season; in frame on all other starts, notably on second when
short-neck second of 15 to Hard To Sing in Grand Prix d'Evry in May (off course
over 5 months afterwards); stays 1½m; probably acts on any going; genuine.
A. Head, France.

TYMAPALI 2 b.c. Native Bazaar 122–The Blessing (Yrrah Jr) (1982 5fg 5g 5d **72**
6s) May 24; lightly-made colt; second foal; dam never ran; 8 lengths sixth of 11
to African Tudor in small race at Wolverhampton in August, second outing and
only form. *J. Spearing.*

TYNDRUM 2 gr.t. Habat 127–Grilse Run 94 (Stupendous) (1982 5fg² 5g 6f³ 6g **80**
6f² 7f³ 7g) May 3; 1,500F; close-coupled, fair sort; half-sister to 111 winner
Salthouse (by Blakeney); dam 2-y-o 5f winner; modest maiden; stays 7f; acts on
firm going; ran well in blinkers fourth outing; retained by trainer 3,300 gns
Newmarket Autumn Sales. *R. Sheather.*

TYPECAST 3 br.g. Tachypous 128–Ile de France 94 (French Beige 127) (1981 **56**
5fg 5g 5d⁴ 5s 6g 6f 6f 5f² 5g³ 6g* 6g 5g 1982 7g 6f³ 6f 9f) workmanlike gelding;
good mover; made all to win selling nursery at Brighton in 1981; well beaten
most starts at 3 yrs; not sure to stay beyond 6f; suited by a sound surface;
blinkered twice at 2 yrs; sold out of Mrs J. Reavey's stable 1,050 gns Doncaster
August Sales after third start. *C. Pinkham.*

TYPESET 2 b.g. Status Seeker–Folle Remont (Prince Tenderfoot 126) (1982 **69**
5g 5f 5fg 6fg² 6g 5f* 6f² 6g³ 6f³ 6d³ 6g 7fg²) Apr 30; 5,600Y; strong, compact
gelding; first foal; dam never ran; bought in 2,300 gns after winning seller at
Leicester in July by 4 lengths; ran well afterwards including in nurseries; stays
7f; yet to race on really soft going but acts on any other; wears blinkers; ridden
by 7-lb claimer ninth and tenth outings; claimed £2,415 final start. *Mrs J.
Reavey.*

TYPHOON POLLY 3 ch.f. Lord Gayle 124–Polinesia (Takawalk II 125) (1981 **117**
6f 8s* 1982 8d³ 8g² 10v⁴ 9d) third foal; half-sister to Polly Pearl (by Gulf
Pearl), a winner up to 1m in France; dam useful winner at up to 1m in
France; placed twice behind impressive winner River Lady at Longchamp in
spring, finishing 4½ lengths third in Prix de la Grotte and 2½ lengths second in
Poule d'Essai des Pouliches; kept on at one pace to be about 5½ lengths fourth
of 8 to Harbour in Prix Saint-Alary at Longchamp again in May; stays 1¼m;
acts on heavy going; not seen out after July; to be trained by P. Walwyn.
C. Milbank, France.

TYRANNOS 9 ch.h. Tyrant–Orange Sash (Sica Boy 132) (1981 7g 8h³ 1982 —
8h 8fg 11.7g) lightly raced and apparently difficult to train, though has won
several times at up to 1¼m; seems to act on any going. *J. Baker.*

TYRANT PRINCE 3 b.g. English Prince 129–Little Trilby 107 (Tyrant) **44**
(1981 8g 8g 8d 1982 12.2f⁴ 10.6h 12g⁴ 13.8f) good sort; poor mover; plater;
suited by 1½m; has worn blinkers; sold 1,050 gns Ascot August Sales. *J. Fitzgerald.*

TYSANDI 2 ch.f. Sharpen Up 127–Tikki Tavi 92 (Honeyway 125) (1982 5fg³ **96**
5f* 5fg² 5fg 5fg 6g³ 6fg² 7d²) Apr 16; lightly-made filly; half-sister to several
winners, including useful 1m to 1¼m winner Duration (by Only for Life); dam
sprinter; odds on, quickened clear to beat Naive comfortably by 3 lengths in
maiden race at Thirsk in May; placed 4 times subsequently, best race when
2½ lengths second to Sangrador in nursery at Newmarket in October on final
appearance; suited by 7f; probably acts on any going; wore blinkers and was
slowly into stride fourth outing; trained by J. W. Watts first 4 starts. *W. Bentley.*

TYTHERINGTON CHANT 3 ch.f. Tachybrus 128–Gold Cypher 76 (Pardao **71**
120) (1981 6g⁴ 6d 1982 8fg 7s⁴ 7d* 8s* 7g) favourite and dropped in class
when decisively winning selling handicap at Brighton in October; attracted no
bid afterwards; won in better company at Chepstow later in month; stays 1m;
acts well on soft ground; has been bandaged in front; changed hands 4,600 gns
Newmarket Autumn Sales. *W. Hastings-Bass.*

TY-WITH-BELLE 3 b.f. Pamroy 99–Saucy Walk (Saucy Kit 76) (1981 5d
5d 5f 7g 8d 7g 6d 1982 7d 6g⁴ 8fg 7g 5fg) small, lengthy filly; good walker;
poor form, including in a seller; blinkered once in 1981. *B. Palling.*

U

ULTIMATE PRIDE (USA) 2 ch.c. Lyphard 132–Classicist (Princequillo) **93**
(1982 6fg 7.6s* 7d) Feb 25; $275,000Y; big, rangy, good-looking colt; excellent
mover; half-brother to numerous winners, including Proponent (by Gallant Man),
a smart stakes winner at up to 9f; dam won over 7f; accounted for some useful
animals when making much of running to win 8-runner Burr Stakes at Lingfield
in September by a short head from Sharp Sea; co-favourite, tailed off in quite
valuable nursery at Newmarket the following month; will stay 1m. *G. Harwood.*

ULTRASONIC 3 br.g. Prince Tenderfoot 126–Native Charm (Red God 128§) **52§**
(1981 5fg 6fg 6fg 5g⁴ 6g 5g 5g 6g 1982 7g 6s 5fg 6fg 5fg 5f³ 6f 5fg 5f 5fg 6s
6g) workmanlike gelding; plating-class maiden; best at 5f; best in blinkers;
headstrong and isn't one to rely on; sold to D. Chapman 1,850 gns Doncaster
November Sales. *R. Hollinshead.*

ULTRAVOX 2 gr.g. Town Crier 119–Aurea Vix (Aureole 132) (1982 8s) May —
23; 2,000Y; first foal; dam ran only once; tailed off in 14-runner maiden race at
Leicester in November; sold to Mrs B. Waring 525 gns Ascot December Sales.
R. Laing.

UNBEKNOWN 2 br.f. Most Secret 119–Wits End (Salerno) (1982 5g 5f² 5f) **58**
Mar 31; 310F; smallish, lengthy filly; first produce; dam never ran; 4 lengths
second of 11 to Prairie Saint in maiden race at Catterick in July, only form;
blinkered final outing. *R. Woodhouse.*

UNBRIDLED PLEASURE (USA) 2 b.f. Honest Pleasure–Hempens Song **70 p**
(Hempen) (1982 5f) Apr 8; $130,000Y; quite well-made filly; half-sister to
3 minor winners in USA; dam very useful winner of 8 sprint races, including
3 stakes events; made good late progress when 9 lengths sixth of 15 to Widaad in
maiden race at Sandown in May; should stay 1m. *I. Balding.*

UNCLE JOSEPH 3 b.c. Workboy 123–Ritratto (Pinturischio 116) (1981 NR —
1982 8f 8g) big, strong, heavy-topped colt; brother to 7f and 8.2f winner Italian
Master; dam never ran; well behind in maiden race at Beverley in May and minor
event at Doncaster in June. *M. H. Easterby.*

UNDEB 2 ch.c. Winden 109–Spanish Ruler (Indian Ruler 89) (1982 5fg 8s 7g) —
narrow, unimpressive-looking colt; of no account. *M. Bradley.*

UNDERBID 2 b.c. Sallust 134–Lady Minstrel (Tudor Music 131) (1982 7.6v) — p
May 14; 16,500Y; first foal; dam, placed over hurdles in Ireland, is half-sister to
Tap On Wood (by Sallust); ninth of 17 in maiden race at Lingfield in October;
should do better. *I. Balding.*

UNDER-RATED 4 b.g. Undulate–Ruffino 99 (Como 120) (1981 8fg 10.2f 12f —
12.3g 10fg 1982 12s) workmanlike gelding; little worthwhile form in varied

company, but has won over hurdles; sold out of M. W. Easterby's stable 2,400 gns Ascot June Sales. *R. Holder.*

UNDER THE HAMMER 2 b.c. Auction Ring 123–Threadneedlestreet (Bold **81** Lad, Ire 133) (1982 5.8f⁴ 5g 7d 6g³ 7.2s* 7v* 7d³) Mar 26; 3,000Y; stocky colt; first foal; dam never ran; showed much improved form when beating Triple Jump impressively by 6 lengths in seller at Haydock (bought in 3,300 gns) in October; won Tankerville Nursery at Ascot a week later in very close finish with Aragon and Ismore; will stay 1m; revels in the mud. *D. Arbuthnot.*

UNIT TENT 4 bl.g. Double-U-Jay 120–Signal Melody 70 (Bleep-Bleep 134) — (1981 6g 6d 7fg 10.1fg 8g 10.1fg 10s* 10d* 1982 11.7fg 12f⁴ 8.3g 10fg 10v 12v 10.2s) neat, quite attractive gelding; plater; little form in non-sellers in 1982; stays 1¼m; acts well on soft going. *G. Lewis.*

UNIVERSAL PENNY 4 ch.f. Royal Match 117–Rose of Damascus (Ommeyad — 120) (1981 10f 10.1f 12f 1982 8s 6fg) plater; no form since 1980; yet to show she stays middle distances; acts on any going; often blinkered; one to leave alone. *W. Marshall.*

UNKNOWN LADY (USA) 3 b. or br.f. Hoist the Flag–Unknown Heiress **116** (Bagdad) (1981 NR 1982 10fg* 10.5g 10.5d² 12d 10g⁴ 9d³ 9.2s² 10.5v³ 10g⁴ 10v) $350,000Y; third foal; dam won 8.5f stakes race; smoothly won new-comers race at Longchamp in April; in frame subsequently in 4 pattern races, namely Prix Fille de l'Air at Saint-Cloud (blinkered when length second to Sham's Princess), Prix de Psyche at Deauville (fourth to Zinzara), Prix de l'Opera at Longchamp (strong-finishing length second to Dione) and Prix de Flore at Saint-Cloud (close third to Buchanette); will stay 1½m (fell when tried at trip); seems to act on any going; smart. *F. Boutin, France.*

UPLANDS PARK 3 b.c. Rheingold 137–God Sent 75 (Red God 128§) (1981 **77** 7f 7fg 1982 10.4g² 11f 10.4fg³ 10g² 8f 9g² 8.5fg* 8f⁴ 8s⁴ 8s³ 8.2s) rangy colt; made all and kept on strongly to win 5-runner handicap at Epsom in August; stays 1¼m; seems to act on any going; ran moderately in blinkers fifth start; suited by forcing tactics. *C. Brittain.*

UPLANDS SO SO 2 b.c. Native Bazaar 122–So Unlikely 60 (Blast 125) — (1982 6f 5.3g 6f) May 4; leggy, workmanlike colt; brother to winning sprinter Casbar Lady and half-brother to a winner abroad; dam of no account; well beaten in maiden races; not seen out after July. *R. Baker.*

UP TEMPO 3 b.g. Dance In Time–Graceful 83 (Grey Sovereign 128§) (1981 **67** 6g 1982 6d 7f 7f 7fg* 7f) workmanlike gelding; plater; apprentice ridden; showed improved form to win at Newmarket in May (no bid); will stay 1m; sent to Singapore. *A. Hide.*

UP THE ANTE (USA) 2 b.c. Properantes–Mini Midi Maxi (Promised Land) **87** (1982 6f 7g 7fg³ 8s³ 7s) lengthy, quite attractive colt; has a round action; half-brother to 2 winners in USA; dam stakes winner at up to 1m; placed in quite useful company at Goodwood and York in the autumn, and ran well off 9-7 in nursery at Doncaster; will be suited by 1¼m+; should win a maiden race. *H. Wragg.*

UP THE NORTH 2 ro.f. Abwah 118–Miss Anabella 93 (The Brianstan 128) **55** (1982 5f⁴ 5f 5g* 5fg) Apr 21; 520Y; smallish, fair sort; good walker; first foal; dam sprinter; plater; ridden by 7-lb claimer at 3-lb overweight, made all to win 6-runner event at Hamilton (no bid) in June by ¾ length from Rahere Hussar; not raced after July. *J. Berry.*

UPTOP FASHION 2 gr.f. No Loiterer 90–Perspicacious (Young Emperor 133) — (1982 5f 5fg 6f) Mar 21; 650Y; first foal; dam never ran; of no account; sold 310 gns Doncaster August Sales. *J. Hardy.*

V

VACANI 3 b.f. Dance In Time–Italian Sky 94 (Skymaster 126) (1981 6d 7fg 6d — 1982 9s) leggy filly; poor maiden; has given trouble at start. *E. Incisa.*

VADROUILLE (USA) 3 b.f. Foolish Pleasure–Vincennes 111 (Vieux Manoir **111** 132) (1981 6g² 7g³ 1982 7g² 10f* 10.5fg³ 8v*) rather lightly-made filly; good mover; fourth live foal; dam second in Irish Guinness Oaks and daughter of Irish 1,000 Guineas and Epsom Oaks winner Valoris; won maiden race at Sandown in April and Marlborough House Stakes at Ascot in October; made most of running and drew clear to beat Kareena unchallenged by 8 lengths in latter; stays 1¼m; acts on any going but clearly revels in the mud; very useful; sold to Hesmonds Stud 230,000 gns Newmarket December Sales. *H. Cecil.*

VAGRANT MAID (USA) 2 b.f. Honest Pleasure–Vigia 115 (Tiziano) (1982   — p
7g) Mar 20; half-sister to Via Maris (by Dancer's Image), a very useful stakes winner at up to 9f in USA; dam, third in Prix Saint-Alary, is sister to Oaks and Irish 1,000 Guineas winner Valoris; joint-favourite but apparently backward, not persevered with once struggling, 2f out, in 22-runner maiden race won by Toveris at Newmarket in October; should improve. *H. Cecil.*

VAGUELY IMPRESSIVE (USA) 2 ch.f. Vaguely Noble 140–Impressive   —
Style (Ready Say Go) (1982 7g) Apr 22; $310,000Y; fourth foal; half-sister to 2 winners by Wajima, including a minor stakes winner; dam won 19 races at up to 1m, showing smart form from 2 yrs to 6 yrs; in rear in 15-runner maiden race at Yarmouth in September. *H. Cecil.*

VAGUELY JAMES 8 ch.g. Jimmy Reppin 131–Vaguely Hopeful 65 (Fortino   —
II 120) (1981 15.5d 1982 15.5g 16.5fg) poor stayer; needs some give in the ground; sometimes blinkered. *G. Beeson.*

VAIGLY REL 2 ch.c. Relkino 131–Dervaig 90 (Derring-Do 131) (1982 6g 5d)   **75**
May 10; useful sort; fourth foal; half-brother to 3 winners, including smart 3-y-o sprinter Vaigly Star (by Star Appeal) and high-class sprinter Vaigly Great (by Great Nephew); dam won over 5f at 2 yrs and became a leading sprinter in Trinidad; put up a pleasing first effort when 7 lengths fifth of 20 to Asswan in maiden race at Yarmouth in September; favourite, soon struggling when eighth of 17 behind Shoeblack in similar event at Nottingham later in month. *M. Stoute.*

VAIGLY STAR 3 b.f. Star Appeal 133–Dervaig 90 (Derring-Do 131) (1981   **118**
5s² 5fg* 6f 6f² 6d 6g* 1982 7fg⁴ 6f² 6f² 6f² 5f³ 5g 6f* 6g⁴ 5d²)
The *Trinidad and Tobago Racing Guide* is not required reading for British racegoers yet a browse through it can reveal interesting details about ex-English

Mr T. E. Sellier's "Vaigly Star"

horses. The editions covering the early 'seventies, for instance, show that Dervaig, a fairly useful performer at the minimum trip over here in 1969, won a dozen times at sprint distances during three seasons' racing in Trinidad. The races concerned weren't run-of-the-mill affairs, either, since she gained the title of champion sprinter at three after winning five successive events culminating in a facile pillar-to-post victory in the important six-furlong Stewards' Cup at Queen's Park Savannah, Port-of-Spain. Retired after two successes as a five-year-old Dervaig is doing as well at stud as she did on the track. Her first foal, Vaigly Great (by Great Nephew), developed into a high-class sprinter, winning the Ayr Gold Cup and Palace House Stakes besides twice finishing runner-up in the July Cup; the second, Vaigly Blue (by Blue Cashmere), won over a mile; and the third, Vaigly Star, is a smart filly who emulated Vaigly Great by running second in the William Hill July Cup.

In nine starts Vaigly Star finished out of the frame just once, in the William Hill Sprint Championship at York, but she won only a minor event at Brighton in September in which she easily justified long odds-on favouritism from Dawn Ditty. Vaigly Star usually faced much stiffer tasks and showed her best form at six furlongs—over the minimum trip, apart from her York performance, she couldn't cope with Tina's Pet and Golden Green in the King George Stakes at Goodwood or with Ferryman in a £4,600 event at Newmarket, and in the seven-furlong Ladbrokes Nell Gwyn Stakes she appeared to find the final furlong too much when a respectable fourth to Chalon. Vaigly Star arrived at Newmarket for the July Cup with two creditable runs immediately behind her, having finished second to Not For Show in the Gus Demmy Memorial Stakes at Haydock and to Indian King, beaten three quarters of a length, in the Cork and Orrery Stakes at Royal Ascot; in the latter she made up about a length on the winner in the last hundred yards without really looking capable of pegging him back. In a field of sixteen at Newmarket Vaigly Star started fifth favourite behind Indian King again, Tender King, Sharpo and Jester and ran the race of her life. Covered up and always going well, she came with an apparently perfectly-timed challenge to head Indian King under a furlong from home and seemed on the verge of victory until Sharpo pounced with fifty yards left for a three quarters of a length win. On her other outing Vaigly Star made some late headway without threatening the principals to be three lengths fourth to Indian King in the Diadem Stakes at Ascot, beaten also by Soba and Blue Singh.

			Appiani II		Herbager
	Star Appeal		(b 1963)		Angela Rucellai
	(b 1970)		Sterna		Neckar
Vaigly Star			(br 1960)		Stammesart
(b.f. 1979)			Derring-Do		Darius
	Dervaig		(br 1961)		Sipsey Bridge
	(b 1967)		Babucon		My Babu
			(ch 1956)		Conkers

The fact that Dervaig's foal by the sprinter Blue Cashmere stayed a mile well whereas those by the mile to mile-and-a-quarter horse Great Nephew and the Arc winner Star Appeal have had stamina limitations is a fine example of the unpredictability of breeding. Apart from Dervaig, the second dam Babucon foaled five winners one of whom, the useful sprinter Hi-Baby, has made her mark at stud in Italy by producing the good colt Hoche and the Criterium di Roma winner Travolta. Vaigly Star, a compact, good-quartered filly who acts on any going, stays in training and will probably face an uphill struggle in top company. Nonetheless, second, third and fourth prize money in the best sprints is not to be treated with disdain and there's every chance that Vaigly Star will add to her earnings, which already stand at over £45,000. *M. Stoute.*

VAIN DEB 3 b.f. Gay Fandango 132–Saint Mildred 89 (Saint Crespin III 132) **63** (1981 6g 6fg 7fg 1982 7fg 7g⁴ 8g* 8fg² 8.2fg* 8g⁴ 8d* 8fg 9s*) sparely-made filly; heavily-backed favourite when scoring in seller at Ayr in July; bought in 3,600 gns afterwards; ran well in better company afterwards, winning handicaps at Nottingham, Yarmouth and Redcar; suited by 9f; seems to act on any going; has run respectably for an apprentice and when sweating up; genuine and consistent. *P. Haslam.*

VAISSEAU (USA) 2 ch.c. Far North 120–Valhalla (New Chapter 106) (1982 **104** p 7d* 7d²) Jan 24; lengthy colt; first foal; dam, very useful French 1½m winner, is out of half-sister to Vitiges; challenged from 2f out and ran on in great style when winning 12-runner maiden race at Leicester in September by 1½ lengths from Mister Golden; put up an excellent effort giving weight to most of his 12 opponents in Houghton Stakes at Newmarket the following month, failing by only a short head to hold off Russian Roubles after wandering about in final furlong; will stay 1¼m; promises to make very useful 3-y-o. *H. Cecil.*

VAL BRILLIANT (USA) 3 b.f. Val de l'Orne 130–Funny Peculiar 106 (Funny Fellow) (1981 NR 1982 9fg) $100,000F; first produce; dam, winner over 5f and 7f in Ireland, showed smart form at up to 1m at 4 yrs and 5 yrs in USA; 12/1 and in need of run when always behind in 12-runner newcomers race won by Rel Tiger at Wolverhampton in April. *J. Dunlop.*   —

VAL CLIMBER (USA) 4 b.g. Val de l'Orne 130–Hardy Climber (Never Bend) (1981 10.5s 12fg² 10.5g³ 10f³ 12.5f 10.5s⁴ 10.5s³ 1982 12d 11.7d³ 16fg 12fg*) ex-French gelding; second foal; half-brother to a winner in USA; dam won at up to 7f; placed several times in France in 1981 when trained by A. Head, including in a seller final outing; well backed when winning maiden race at Redcar in September; stays 1½m; acts on any going. *A. Jarvis.*   **76**

VAL DE PONCE 3 b.c. Radetzky 123–Sovereigns Whistle 67 (Sovereign Path 125) (1981 NR 1982 8s 10v 8g 8f 9g 8d) big colt; poor mover; poor plater; often bandaged in front. *C. Brittain.*   —

VALEDICTION 2 b.f. Town Crier 119–Golden Thoughts 86 (Golden Cloud) (1982 6fg 6g) Apr 11; close-coupled, rather lightly-made filly; excellent mover; sister to fairly useful miler Dream Town and 3-y-o Colonel Mad, and half-sister to several winners, including useful 1980 2-y-o 7f winner Cocaine (by High Line); dam won over 5f at 2 yrs; little worthwhile form in big fields of maidens in September. *H. Candy.*   —

VALENTINIAN 4 ch.c. Morston 125–Appian Way 89 (Romulus 129) (1981 12g 13.3d⁴ 14g* 14g* 14g⁴ 12fg* 12g* 13.3d⁴ 1982 12fg⁴ 12f* 12g* 15fg* 13.5g)   **113**
Valentinian went from strength to strength as a three-year-old, winning four of his last six races, and his improvement continued at such a rate in 1982 that he successfully managed the step up from handicap to pattern company before being sold privately to race in the United States. His campaign got off to an unhappy start at York in May, where he had no luck in running and finished fourth to Karadar; to avoid a repetition his rider Carson adopted different tactics in their next three races, having Valentinian in the lead or disputing it. The change couldn't have worked out better. Next time out Valentinian beat Kings Parade comfortably by a length in the Newbury Summer Cup in June and he followed up with an extremely game half-length win over Military Band under 10-3 in the Old Newton Cup at Haydock in July, one of the handicap performances of the season. The Old Newton Cup was Valentinian's last run in a handicap and his last race in Britain too. Both his subsequent outings were at Deauville in August, in the Prix Kergorlay and the Grand Prix, and in the former he ran the race of his life. With the fast ground which

Old Newton Cup, Haydock—this valuable handicap goes to Valentinian from Military Band and Star Burst (second left)

Lord Scarbrough's "Valentinian"

suits him so well and opposition which was, to say the least, modest by Group 2 standards Valentinian started favourite and was always going well in the lead. He won without being hard pressed by a length and a half from the six-year-old Kelbomec who gave 4 lb. The Grand Prix de Deauville didn't go nearly so well for Valentinian. He missed the break and, faced with stiffer opposition, was never better than mid-division. He trailed in eighth of twelve behind the French Derby second Real Shadai, beaten a long way; given a better run Valentinian would have had to show further improvement to have coped successfully with classic horses.

Valentinian (ch.c. 1978)	Morston (ch 1970)	Ragusa (b 1960)	Ribot
			Fantan II
		Windmill Girl (b 1961)	Hornbeam
			Chorus Beauty
	Appian Way (b 1968)	Romulus (b 1959)	Ribot
			Arietta
		Polar Way (ch 1956)	Borealis
			Petticoat Lane

Valentinian is by Morston out of the Romulus mare Appian Way, a middle-distance handicapper who, unlike Valentinian, went particularly well in the soft. He is a brother to the Hungarian winner Appia and the Italian jumping winner Jonro, closely related to the mile-and-a-half winner By-Way (by Blakeney) and a half-brother to the two-mile winner Belfe (by Tachypous). Both Morston and Appian Way were trained by Arthur Budgett who also had the grandam Polar Way and Polar Way's most successful offspring, the useful middle-distance handicappers Polish Warrior and Chiltern Lass, as well as Petty Officer, a grandson of the third dam Petticoat Lane. The last-named was one of the two pillars of the highly successful breeding operation of the late Colonel P. L. M.

Wright; the other, Palais Glide, produced the good stayers Paul Jones and Peter Jones and is the grandam of Prominent, Dominion and Jeune Premier.

Valentinian was bought privately after the Grand Prix de Deauville by Dogwood Farm racing syndicates, who also bought the very useful two-year-old Domynsky and whose previous purchases from Europe include Dominion, Pipedreamer, Potemkin, Sea Chimes and Uncle Pokey. Valentinian, a strong colt who is effective at a mile and a half and stays well, is a most genuine top-of-theground front-runner and strikes us as the type who could do well in the States. *R. Hern.*

VALE OF BELVOIR 3 b.f. Steel Heart 128–Gables End (Roi Soleil 125) — (1981 6fg 5d³ 5d 5d 1982 5fg 5fg³ 5fg⁴ 6g 6s 5g) strong filly; carries plenty of condition; poor mover; sprint maiden; well beaten in seller final start; acts on a firm and a soft surface; blinkered third and fourth outings; sold to BBA 480 gns Newmarket Autumn Sales. *D. Smith.*

VALERIAN (USA) 2 ch.c. Medaille d'Or–Majestic Julie (Majestic Prince) 88 (1982 5g 5f* 5g 7f 7fg² 8g 8d) May 11; $45,000Y; sturdy, short-legged colt; first foal; dam, half-sister to dam of Godswalk, won 2 sprint races at 4 yrs; won maiden race at Bath in April by 2 lengths from Artist's Reel; ½-length second of 8 to Ridge Heights in nursery at Goodwood in August, best subsequent effort; off course 4 months after third outing; stays 7f; acts on firm going; sent to USA. *B. Hills.*

VALERIO (USA) 2 b.c. Raise a Cup–Erin O'Connell (Dondeen 123) (1982 7g) — p Mar 13; $42,000Y; attractive colt; closely related to useful French 1m and 10.5f winner Bakst and useful Irish sprinter Severiano (both by Native Royalty); dam won claiming races at up to 1m; 20/1 and carrying plenty of condition, shaped nicely when seventh of 23 to The Fort in maiden race at Newmarket in August, making up a lot of ground without being knocked about; sure to do better. *L. Cumani.*

VALIANCY 3 b.f. Grundy 137–Val's Girl 113 (Sir Ivor 135) (1981 6s³ 7.3s⁴ 77 1982 10f* 12g³) small, robust, deep-girthed filly; landed odds in maiden race at Nottingham in July; stays 1½m; gives impression she may always be suited by some give in the ground; sweated up final start; has shown a tendency to hang. *H. Cecil.*

VALLEY KING 3 br.c. Pitcairn 126–Bryn Du 81 (El Gallo 122) (1981 NR 75 1982 8s³ 7g⁴ 7fg 10d³ 7g 7fg 8.5g² 10fg 11s 8g⁴) IR 9,200F, IR 10,000Y; strong, workmanlike colt; third living foal; half-brother to a winner in Belgium by On Your Mark and a minor winner in France by Pitskelly; dam middle-distance winner; in frame in maiden races, including when head second of 12 to odds-on Tony Tan at Galway in September (apprentice ridden); twice out of depth, including in Jersey Stakes at Royal Ascot third outing; stays 1¼m; pulled very hard eighth start. *M. O'Toole, Ireland.*

VALLEY MILLS 2 ch.g. Red Alert 127–Haunting 79 (Lord Gayle 124) (1982 76 6g 6g 6fg⁴ 7d³ 6d² 7g 6s) Feb 16; 6,000Y; lengthy, strong gelding; third foal; dam stayed 1m; placed in September in claiming race at Yarmouth and nursery at Nottingham; stays 7f; acts on a soft surface; wears blinkers. *S. Wiles.*

VALOROSO 2 b.g. Young Emperor 133–My Plucky Lady 64 (Cash and Courage — 116) (1982 6g 6fg) Apr 15; 2,600F, 5,000Y; neat gelding; half-brother to several minor winners; dam won at up to 1m, including 2 sellers; soundly beaten when sixth of 13 in maiden race at Haydock in July and fifth of 7 in similar event at Ayr the following month; subsequently gelded. *C. Thornton.*

VAL'S DELIGHT 2 ch.f. Cawston's Clown 113–Sweet Hortense 71 (King's Troop — 118) (1982 5fg 5f 5fg 5fg) Mar 16; 4,500Y; leggy, well-grown filly; sister to 5f and 7f winner No Clown, and half-sister to a winner in Malaya; dam stayed 1m; in rear in maiden and minor events; not raced after July. *R. Ward.*

VALWYN 2 b.f. Streak 119–Quolanta 81 (Quorum 126) (1982 5g 5d 5f 5f) — May 18; 880Y; 1,600 2-y-o; small filly; bad plater. *D. Yeoman.*

VAMMELERTS QUILP 2 ch.f. Orange Bay 131–Friendly Chorus 71 (Be — Friendly 130) (1982 6f) Feb 12; 1,300Y; plain filly; second foal; dam, sister to top-class filly Be Tuneful, showed a little ability at 2 yrs; last of 19 in maiden race at Leicester in May. *D. Thom.*

VANRENOS 4 b.f. Gold Rod 129–Supafrag 55 (Track Spare 125) (1981 7f 8f 8s — 11s 10s 1982 6g 7f 8f 7fg³) small filly; plater; ran best race for a while on final start; suited by 7f and should stay 1m; form only on firm going; sold 350 gns Doncaster September Sales. *W. Clay.*

VARTKEZ (FR) 5 b.g. A Tempo 127–Caecilia 76 (Skymaster 126) (1981 10s —
12d 11.7v 12fg 1982 16fg⁴ 16d 16.1s 18d) strong, sturdy gelding; poor handicapper; probably acted on any going; trained first outing by C. Mackenzie; dead.
G. Huffer.

VASLAV (USA) 4 ch.c. Nijinsky 138–Waterloo 120 (Bold Lad, Ire 133) (1981 —
7d² 8g* 1982 10.5f) big, strong, rangy colt; an extremely well-bred colt who
was only very lightly raced but showed quite useful form; won at Yarmouth as a
3-y-o; clear leader until stopping very quickly in straight when remote fifth of 6
behind Say Primula in handicap at York in May on only outing of 1982; should
have stayed beyond 1m; sent to stud in Australia. *H. Cecil.*

VATICAN WAY (USA) 2 br.f. J. O. Tobin 130–Gayway (Sir Gaylord) (1982 **74**
6fg³ 7.6v³ 7d³) lengthy filly; half-sister to 6 winners in USA, notably very useful
sprinter Robalea (by Roberto) and very useful Introductivo
(by Sensitivo), a winner at up to 1m; dam stakes-placed sprint winner; placed in
biggish fields in maiden and minor events in the autumn; stays 7.6f; appears to
act on any going. *M. Stoute.*

VAYRANN 4 br.c. Brigadier Gerard 144–Val Divine (Val de Loir 133) (1981 **123**
10s* 12d² 12d* 15s³ 10s* 10g* 1982 10.5g⁴ 12.5d)
Without quite rivalling *The Mousetrap* the so-called 'Vayrann case' is having
quite a run. At the time of writing, more than a year after Vayrann passed the
post first at Newmarket, the result of the 1981 Champion Stakes is still in some
doubt: the owner of the second Cairn Rouge is in the process of seeking a High
Court ruling that the Jockey Club did not abide by its own regulations when
allowing Vayrann to keep the race after traces of a prohibited substance, anabolic
steroids, were found in his routine urine sample. The racing public had already
remained in doubt for almost eight months about which horse had won the 1981
Champion Stakes when the Disciplinary Committee of the Jockey Club met on
June 7th 1982 to consider the analysis of the sample taken from Vayrann. After
a seven-hour inquiry, conducted in private with reportedly more than two dozen
British and French lawyers and scientists in attendance, the Disciplinary Committee concluded that Estrane-3,17-Diol, a breakdown product of anabolic
steroids which had been found in Vayrann, could be self-produced on occasions by
a colt or entire horse. Racecourse Security Services had been unable to find any
evidence that steroids had been administered to Vayrann and the Disciplinary
Committee accordingly held that no breaches of rules 53, 180 (ii) and 200 of the
Rules of Racing had been committed and ordered that the placings should
remain unchanged.

The claim that the Jockey Club did not abide by its rules is to be a matter for
legal decision and it would be pointless for us to offer any view on the matter.
The particular rule at issue is 180 (ii) which states that a horse *shall* be disqualified
if *any* quantity is found of any substance which is either a prohibited substance
or a substance the origin of which cannot be traced to normal and ordinary
feeding and which could by its nature affect the racing performance of the horse.
It is true to say that many regarded the disqualification of Vayrann as a formality
once the result of the dope test became known. However, the Rules of Racing
define a prohibited substance as 'a substance which originates externally', a point
which seems sure to figure prominently if and when the Jockey Club has to defend
its judgement on Vayrann in the law-court.

The use of drugs on racehorses is not in itself illegal—the rules are only
transgressed if traces of drugs are found at the time of racing—and anabolic
steroids are used legitimately to help horses who have difficulty in obtaining the
benefit they need from their food, for example when they are convalescing after
illness; it helps them to put on weight. The administration of anabolic steroids
over a long period is also a proven aid to muscular development: it has been used
to improve performance in human athletes, particularly with such as weight-lifters
and athletes competing in some of the 'heavy' field events where the weight of a
competitor can be a vital factor. Although it is not clear whether putting on
extra muscle enables an athlete to run faster, some runners use steroids because
they have found them an aid to recovery after hard training thus enabling the
athlete to withstand a more strenuous training regime. The use of anabolic
steroids as an integral part of a long training schedule can help to promote better
performance in a racehorse in a similar way, although the operation has to be
timed well and the use of the drug discontinued some time before the race for
which the horse is being prepared so as to ensure that no residue is left in the
horse's system; the use of diuretic drugs may help to clear the system but some of
these drugs also contain substances which are regarded as illegal. Anabolic

steroids are found naturally in the male horse in the form of the sex hormone testosterone, but prior to the Vayrann case it had been assumed that Estrane-3,17-Diol could be derived only from anabolic steroids administered externally. However, tests performed by a top French veterinary expert at the instigation of Vayrann's connections showed that testosterone itself produces a small amount of Estrane-3,17-Diol; this was subsequently confirmed in independent tests carried out by Jockey Club experts. The positive dope test on Vayrann did not, therefore, necessarily indicate guilt—trainer Mathet had protested his innocence from the start—and the Jockey Club was unable to prove that Vayrann had been injected with anabolic steroids. Some of the comments passed on the Jockey Club's decision were singularly ill-informed. It is an elementary principle of British justice that a man is presumed innocent until proven guilty and those who evidently believed that the onus should have been put on Mathet to prove his innocence should be ashamed. At one time it was presumed, in cases of doping, that a trainer was guilty of negligence, dereliction of duty or complicity in doping in the absence of proof to the contrary: in the decade following the 1939-45 war a dozen trainers lost their licences—without a shred of evidence being produced to justify even suspicion of complicity—because of the barbaric rules in force at the time. Thankfully, the Jockey Club is now much less uncompromising towards trainers than it used to be.

After the Jockey Club inquiry Vayrann was widely referred to as 'the horse that doped itself', which was used for the title of a television documentary on the case. But such a description is misleading: the Jockey Club accepted that Vayrann *could have* produced his own Estrane-3,17-Diol, not that he *did* so. One of the questions left unanswered by the case was why Estrane-3,17-Diol had not been discovered in Vayrann after any of the races in which he was tested in France. One reason advanced by the French authorities was that their dope test is less sensitive than the British one and therefore less likely to pick up the smaller amounts of naturally produced Estrane-3,17-Diol. There is another puzzling question to which no satisfactory answer has so far come to light. The breakthrough which enabled the Jockey Club's chemists to detect anabolic steroids was made in November 1977 but apart from a spate of positive tests in the spring of 1978 (mostly on geldings) there have been very few doping inquiries involving anabolic steroids. As a large proportion of winners are automatically tested it is intriguing, to say the least, that in the best part of four years there were less than a handful of positive tests on colts and entires. Are we expected to believe that Vayrann is such a rarity? Or does the case perhaps indicate that the method used in horse racing to analyse dope samples is at fault in some way? Whatever the answer, the Vayrann judgement leaves a grey area in the hitherto very strict doping rules: argument is now permissible in any case involving the discovery of traces of anabolic steroids in a colt or entire which, theoretically at least, gives a greater incentive for the drug to be used more freely by trainers on such animals. Racecourse Security Services are thought to be conducting research into the levels of anabolic steroids that can be self-produced and are also working on a test to distinguish between the hormones which are naturally produced and those administered externally. The latter represents the only satisfactory way that we can see of restoring the unequivocality of the doping rules. Any acceptance of a permitted level or value or anabolic steroids would inevitably lead to pressure, difficult to resist, for relaxation of the rules in other cases, such as those involving accidental contaminations of foodstuffs. The more the rules are relaxed the more likely it becomes that the use of drugs on racehorses will increase.

Vayrann (br.c. 1978)	Brigadier Gerard (b 1968)	Queen's Hussar (b 1960)	March Past / Jojo
		La Paiva (ch 1956)	Prince Chevalier / Brazen Molly
	Val Divine (b 1971)	Val de Loir (b 1959)	Vieux Manoir / Vali
		Pola Bella (br 1965)	Darius / Bella Paola

What of Vayrann himself? Alas, he broke down on his off-fore in the Grand Prix de Saint-Cloud in July on his second outing as a four-year-old and has been retired to the Haras de Bonneval. He had looked in need of the race when finishing a most creditable fourth in the Prix Ganay at Longchamp in May on his reappearance, beaten about two and a half lengths by the winner Bikala. Vayrann is an attractive colt, as we said in *Racehorses of 1981* one of the nicest of Brigadier Gerard's offspring yet seen out. Vayrann is easily the best produce of Val Divine who was a fair racemare, a winner at ten and a half furlongs in France. Val Divine is a daughter of a Prix du Moulin and Poule d'Essai des Pouliches winner in Pola Bella and a granddaughter of a One Thousand Guineas, Oaks, Prix Vermeille and Champion Stakes winner in Bella Paola. Vayrann stayed a mile and a half and had a good turn of foot. He acted well on soft going and never raced on a firm surface. *F. Mathet, France.*

Postscript: French racing lost one of its most distinguished figures when Francois Mathet died in his sleep in January 1983. He was one of the most successful trainers in racing history and his final season was among many in the past thirty years or so in which he topped the trainers' table in France. Akiyda gave him his fourth victory in the Prix de l'Arc de Triomphe (following Tantieme in 1950 and 1951 and Sassafras in 1970), Melyno his seventh in the Poule d'Essai des Poulains (French Two Thousand Guineas) and Le Nain Jaune his ninth in the Grand Prix de Paris. Mathet also trained six winners of the Prix du Jockey-Club (French Derby): Reliance II, Tapalque, Sassafras, Rheffic, Crystal Palace and Top Ville. Among the many other famous racehorses that passed through Mathet's care and will be well-known to British readers were the Epsom Derby winners Phil Drake and Relko, the much-travelled Match III who won the King George VI and Queen Elizabeth Stakes, the Oaks winner Sicarelle and Vayrann's great-grandam Bella Paola. Mathet's successor is to be A. de Royer Dupre.

VEE BEE 3 b.c. High Award 119–Ritual 79 (Right Royal V 135) (1981 NR 1982 8g 5g 6f 5fg 6f 5s 6s 6s) robust colt; poor mover; third foal; half-brother to useful 7f to 9f winner Malin Court (by Major Portion); dam won over 7f at 2 yrs; sprint maiden; withdrawn under orders fourth start. *D. Leslie.* —

VELESO 4 b.g. Jimsun 121–Dracaena 62 (Double Jump 131) (1981 8s 7.3g 7.6fg 8fg 10.1fg 8s 10d 1982 15.5fg 14fg 10.2s⁴) quite useful at 2 yrs; mainly disappointing on flat since, although was running on at finish and not entirely disgraced final start (first outing for 5 months); stays 1¼m; acts on a soft surface; sometimes sweats up; blinkered first 2 starts of 1982. *J. King.* —

VELOCIDAD 2 ch.f. Balidar 133–Sun Lamp 76 (Pall Mall 132) (1982 5g² 6f 5fg² 5fg⁴ 5g) rangy, quite attractive sort; first foal; dam 7f winner; second in 15-runner maiden races at Windsor in the summer; should stay 6f; acts on a firm surface; ran poorly in blinkers on final appearance. *M. Ryan.* 80

VENETIAN JOY 3 br.f. Windjammer (USA)–Veneziana 91 (Tiger 125) (1981 5g⁴ 5d² 5g² 5fg³ 5g⁴ 5d⁴ 5d³ 5g 1982 5fg 5g⁴ 5fg⁴ 8f⁴ 7f 9s³ 6s² 6s) fair sort; ex-English; inconsistent maiden; suited by 1m; acts on any going; sometimes blinkered; gives strong impression she's not genuine and isn't to be trusted; trained by M. W. Easterby first 5 starts. *C. Guest, Holland.* —

VENJA 4 ch.c. Native Bazaar 122–Avengeress 73 (Aggressor 130) (1981 7fg² 6d 7s* 7fg⁴ 7fg² 7f 7fg² 7d* 1982 11.7fg 7g 7.6g³) leggy, light-framed, lengthy colt; successful as 2 sellers as a 3-y-o; third in non-selling handicap at Lingfield in June; stays 1m; probably acts on any going. *A. Moore.* 39

VENT ARRIERE (FR) 6 b.h. Tennyson 124–Vahinee (Mourne 126) (1981 NR 1982 11fg 12g 9f 8fg) sturdy horse; half-brother to numerous winners in France, notably very smart Dragoon (by Le Fabuleux); dam won at 2 yrs; behind in maiden and minor races and a seller, 3 times finishing last. *R. Morris.* —

VENT SOLAIRE 2 ch.c. Vitiges 132–Voie Lactee (Amber Rama 133) (1982 7f 7fg 8f³ 8s) Mar 13; 8,000F; tall colt; has a nice, easy action; first produce; dam, out of sister to high-class sprinter Polic and brilliant broodmare Relance III, won 2 small 11f races at 4 yrs in France; quite a modest maiden; stays 1m; acts on firm going. *P. Walwyn.* 79

VENUS STAR (USA) 3 b.f. Barachois–Final Word (Final Ruling) (1981 6g 6g 6d² 1982 10f 10.2g⁴ 10s 10fg) rather lightly-made filly; has a round action; has shown little form since final outing at 2 yrs; possibly doesn't stay 1¼m; had tongue tied down final outing. *M. Albina.* —

VERAMENTE 7 b.g. Sassafras 135–Quelle Blague (Red God 128§) (1981 10s 1982 10.6f 12fg 16d 10f) lightly raced on flat nowadays; poor form in 1982, including in a seller; best over middle distances; seems to act on any going; has been tried in blinkers; suitable mount for an inexperienced rider; has worn a tongue strap; changed hands 1,700 gns Ascot June Sales. *S. Mellor.* —

VERBARIUM (USA) 2 br.c. Verbatim–Havre (Mister Gus) (1982 7g³ 7f* 7fg⁴ 7f 8g) Mar 23; $34,000Y; close-coupled, workmanlike colt; half-brother to 85 several winners in USA, including a minor stakes winner; dam once-raced half-sister to very smart middle-distance filly Bold Reply; won 19-runner maiden race at Salisbury in July by 1½ lengths from Zorn; should stay 1¼m; acts on firm going; played up badly in stalls and reared as they opened on third start. *P. Cole.*

VERILY JANE 2 ch.f. Royben 125–Swannery 94 (My Swanee 122) (1982 5d 5fg **53** 5fg 5f⁴ 5f 6s 5v³ 5s³ 6s) Feb 15; 560Y; half-sister to 2 winners by Tudor Rhythm, including useful 1979 2-y-o 6f winner Atlantic City; dam 2-y-o 5f winner; third in October in 18-runner selling nursery at Lingfield and 20-runner maiden auction event at Warwick; best form at 5f; appears to need the mud. *C. Wildman.*

VERNHAM STREET 4 b.g. Streetfighter 120–Bois Le Duc (Kalydon 122 or **53** March Past 124) (1981 8d 9s 11.7g 8fg* 7f 8fg 6fg* 6g* 7g⁴ 1982 6fg 6fg 6fg⁴ 5g³ 5fg 6g 6fg 6f 6v 6v) strong, lengthy gelding; rather disappointing, best effort when third to Pontin Lad in £6,300 handicap at Lingfield in June; effective at 5f and stays 1m; acts on a firm surface; often apprentice ridden; blinkered last 2 starts. *H. Candy.*

VERRIA (USA) 2 ch.f. Blushing Groom 131–Via Venise (Shoemaker 121) **112 p** (1982 8f* 8s⁴) third foal; sister to American 3-y-o Vie en Rose and half-sister to very useful 1980 French 2-y-o 6f to 1m winner Vorias (by Cannonade); dam, useful winner at up to 1¼m in France, comes from same family as Val de Loir; had a lot to do entering straight in 6-runner Prix de Toutevoie at Longchamp in September but quickened well to win by ¾ length from Escaline; 7/1, finished well when about 1¼ lengths fourth of 9 to Belka in Prix des Reservoirs on same course the following month; will stay 1¼m; likely to improve further; in 1,000 Guineas and Oaks. *F. Boutin, France.*

VERSAILLES PRINCE 9 br.g. Versailles–Villarrica (Dan Cupid 132) (1981 — NR 1982 7g 10d) poor handicapper nowadays; probably best at 7f or 1m; acts on any going but is well suited by soft; best in blinkers; excellent mount for an inexperienced rider. *P. Haynes.*

VERY SHARP 2 b.c. Sharpen Up 127–Vivante 87 (Bold Lad, Ire 133) (1982 **?** including 6v⁴) Mar 21; 16,000F; half-brother to 3 winners, including Majestic Star (by Star Appeal), a useful winner at up to 1¼m here and in Ireland; dam stayed 1m; won his first 3 races, all at Milan, gaining most valuable success in 5f Premio Bimbi in May; favourite for all-aged Premio Umbria at Rome in November but faded after disputing lead for 3½f and finished remote fourth of 17 to French filly Bold Apparel; should stay 1m; entered in 2,000 Guineas. *V. Bignami, Italy.*

VESTAL TELEGRAPH 3 b.g. Sayfar 116–Flying Nun 66 (Welsh Abbot 131) — (1981 5d⁴ 5d 6fg 6g 8.2d 1982 10.1d 8f 10.8fg) poor plater; cost 540 gns Doncaster May Sales. *P. Allingham.*

VICEROY PRINCESS 2 gr.f. Godswalk 130–Black Crow 72 (Sea Hawk II **65** 131) (1982 5f 5f 7d 7fg* 8d) Mar 6; 1,400Y and 4,800Y; neat filly; first produce; dam won over 9f and 1½m; favourite and running in seller for first time, attracted no bid after winning 15-runner event at Chepstow in September by 2 lengths from Frontlet; showed nothing otherwise; suited by 7f; acts on a firm surface. *C. Williams.*

VICTOR HUGO 5 b. or br.h. Vaguely Noble 140–Anna Karenina (Princely Gift — 137) (1981 10d 8fg 1982 12v 12s) compact horse; poor form, including in a seller; has worn blinkers. *R. Atkins.*

VICTORIAN PRINCE 2 ch.g. English Prince 129–Victorian Habit 101 **61** (Habitat 134) (1982 5s² 5f³ 6d 7f 5s 8d 7s) Mar 22; IR 1,000Y; short-coupled gelding; third foal; half-brother to French 3-y-o 1m winner Ya Sater (by Sassafras); dam 2-y-o 5f winner; placed in auction races in April; no form afterwards; should stay 1m; blinkered fourth outing. *A. Jarvis.*

VICTORIA PALACE 3 br.f. Prince Tenderfoot 126–Gull (Fleet Nasrullah) — (1981 6fg 6g 1982 6fg 7.6f 10.1g² 10fg) good work; little worthwhile form in varied company; exported to Algeria. *N. Guest.*

VICTORY HOUSE 3 ch.c. Habitat 134–Star Court 102 (Aureole 132) (1981 **79** 5g³ 1982 6g*) neat colt; ran on well to beat Gavo by ¾ length in 15-runner maiden race at Newmarket in April; not seen out again and is presumably difficult to train; will stay at least 7f. *H. Cecil.*

VICTORY WARRANT 2 b.g. Pitskelly 122–Woo 72 (Stage Door Johnny) — (1982 7f 7.2g 10s) Mar 30; IR 2,500F; 6,200Y; well-grown gelding; half-brother to Irish 3-y-o Moreda (by Mount Hagen), successful at up to 1½m, and fairly useful 1980 Irish 2-y-o 5f winner Ring of Steel (by Steel Heart); dam middle-distance maiden; little worthwhile form in maiden and minor events; retained by trainer 6,200 gns Newmarket Autumn Sales, and subsequently gelded. *C. Williams.*

VIDEO KING 3 b.c. Blue Cashmere 129–Florintina 104 (Floribunda 136) **82** (1981 6fg³ 5fg 7fg 7f 7s 1982 7d² 6s² 8fg* 7.3fg* 8fg* 8f* 8fg⁴ 7fg⁴) rangy, quite attractive colt; won handicaps at Newmarket, Newbury, Salisbury and Leicester; beat Rel Tiger in good style by 1½ lengths on last-named in May; ran respectably last 2 starts; suited by 7f and 1m; ideally suited by a sound surface; genuine and consistent. *C. Brittain.*

VIDEO MAN 2 b.c. Guillaume Tell 121–Pennycress 99 (Florescence 120) (1982 **83** 5f⁴(dis) 6d 6g⁴ 7fg² 7f*) Mar 6; IR 4,600F, 8,400Y; half-brother to winners here and abroad, including useful sprinter Ponchielli (by Pitskelly); dam won twice over 5f at 2 yrs; showed improved form over 7f, finishing excellent second to Ashmolean in maiden race at Warwick in July and running on strongly to beat Charlotte's Dunce 1½ lengths in nursery at Beverley 3 days later; will stay 1m; acts well on firm ground. *G. Huffer.*

VIDOR (USA) 3 br.f. Vaguely Noble 140–Prestissimo (Bold Reasoning) (1981 **115** 8v* 1982 9fg² 8g³ 10v 10.5fg* 10.5v⁴ 11f 12f 9.2s³ 10s* 10f 11f) $150,000Y; good-bodied filly; first foal; dam, stakes-placed winner at up to 6f, is half-sister to high-class Jalmood; made all to beat Épithet by 2 lengths in Prix de Royaumont at Chantilly in June and accounted for Trevira readily by 4 lengths in E. P. Taylor Stakes at Woodbine, Canada, in October; in frame several other starts, including when 4½ lengths third to River Lady in Poule d'Essai des Pouliches at Longchamp, 4¾ lengths fourth to Harbour in Prix de Diane Hermes at Chantilly and 2½ lengths third to Dione in Prix de l'Opera at Longchamp again; stays 1¼m well; seems to act on any going; ran moderately sixth start. *M. Zilber, France.*

VIENNESE WALTZ 3 b.f. High Top 131–Austria 93 (Henry the Seventh 125) **85** (1981 NR 1982 10.2g* 12fg 13d⁴ 16.5s* 18d² 18s) rangy filly; fourth live foal; half-sister to a winner in Malaya; dam stayed 1½m; won maiden race at Doncaster in June and minor event at Redcar in October; creditable ½-length second to Bajan Sunshine (pair clear) in minor event at Doncaster on penultimate start; suited by a test of stamina; suited by some give in the ground. *J. W. Watts.*

VIGOROUS VIGORS (USA) 2 gr.c. Vigors–Libelinha 123 (Hodell 120) **78** (1982 7f 7g 7s) May 14; well-made, quite attractive colt; half-brother to French 1½m winner Deauville Deal (by Le Fabuleux); dam smart winner over 5f and 7f in France; fifth of 13 finishers behind easy winner Sackford in minor event at Sandown in October, final outing and best effort; second favourite in 30-runner maiden event at Newmarket on second appearance; acts on soft going. *R. Armstrong.*

VIKING CENTRE 2 ch.g. Owen Dudley 121–Another Clare (Blason 109) **71** (1982 5.8g 6f 6f³ 6f*) Apr 27; 2,900F, 3,900Y; small, short-legged, strong-quartered gelding; half-brother to 3 winners here and abroad, including 1981 2-y-o 5f and 6f seller winner Tiger Town (by Town Crier); dam of no account; dropped in class and blinkered first time, looked useful for a plater when winning easing up by 2 lengths from Five Jacks in 8-runner seller at Thirsk in July; surprisingly attracted no bid; will probably stay 7f. *P. Haslam.*

VILLACANA 3 b.f. Lord Gayle 124–Etoile Freda (Florescence 120) (1981 7d —
7f 1982 10f 11.7fg 8fg 8d) close-coupled filly; poor maiden; sold 460 gns Newmarket Autumn Sales. *I. Walker.*

VILLAGE SCENE 3 br.c. Blakeney 126–Hayloft 111 (Tudor Melody 129) —
(1981 NR 1982 8.2f 8fg) 92,000Y; neat, attractive colt; first foal; dam, daughter of Coronation Stakes and Nassau Stakes winner Haymaking, won Molecomb Stakes; well beaten in minor event at Haydock in May and maiden race at Ayr in July; blinkered on latter; sold to W. A. Stephenson 4,500 gns Newmarket Autumn Sales. *T. Robson.*

VILLA MILL 6 b.g. Porto Bello 118–Amante 121§ (Tehran) (1981 NR 1982 —
8f) plater nowadays; stays 1¼m; suited by some give in the ground; has been tried in blinkers; inconsistent. *C. Crossley.*

VILLARS 2 ch.f. Home Guard 129–Telamonia (Ballymoss 130) (1982 7f 7s³) **81** June 14; 4,100F, 2,500Y; well-grown, rangy filly; third foal; dam unraced half-sister to high-class 1m to 1¾m filly Calaba; 7 lengths third of 13 finishers behind Sackford in minor event at Sandown in October; will be suited by further; should win a race. *J. Winter.*

889

VINCENZA 3 ch.f. Grundy 137–Lady Vincent 75 (High Hat 131) (1981 NR — 1982 10g 12g 10.4d 12fg) half-sister to 2 winners, notably very smart stayer Vincent (by Busted); dam 13f winner; only plating class; sold 1,550 gns Newmarket December Sales. *J. Winter.*

VINDICATION (USA) 2 b.f. Advocator–Jani Nasrullah (Amastar) (1982 **70** 5fg² 6fg³ 5g⁴ 5f 7f³ 8.2s 7g² 8s 7d³) Apr 22; $30,000Y; neat, strong, attractive filly; third foal; half-sister to 2 winners, one a minor stakes winner; dam won 4 sprint races; plating-class maiden; suited by 7f; best form on an easy surface; ran moderately in blinkers fourth outing. *S. Norton.*

VINO ROSSO 2 b.g. Nebbiolo 125–Magic Quiz (Quisling 117) (1982 5fg³) **76 p** Mar 21; IR 24,000Y; half-brother to 2 winners by Northfields, including very useful Irish 1978 2-y-o 7f winner Magic North, successful subsequently at up to 10.5f in France; dam won three 7f races in Ireland; easy 9/2-shot, kept on well when 2 lengths third of 11 to Sinister Smile in maiden race at Windsor in July; gelded subsequently; will be suited by 6f+; should do better. *H. Candy.*

VIN ST BENET 3 b.c. The Brianstan 128–Hopeful Gift 95 (Bounteous 125) **109** (1981 5g 5g 5fg* 7fg² 7fg³ 7fg⁴ 7f 8g² 1982 8.5fg³ 8fg 7fg 7g 7g³ 8g² 7f 8g*) useful-looking colt; odds on when gaining a smooth success in 6-runner minor event at Newbury in September; ran creditably most other starts, including when 1¾ lengths third to Count Pahlen in Blue Riband Trial at Epsom, tenth of 26 to Zino in 2,000 Guineas at Newmarket, 2 lengths third to Mirabeau in City of York Stakes and short-head second to Paperetto in Northern Goldsmiths' Handicap at Newcastle; stays 1m well; acts on firm going; tough, genuine and consistent; racing in California. *M. Tompkins.*

VIOLET BOUQUET (USA) 2 gr.f. Vigors–Boheme (Exbury 138) (1982 7g) — p Mar 22; big, strong, lengthy filly; closely related to 1½m and 13f winner Green Dawn (by Grey Dawn II) and half-sister to 2 winners in USA; dam, half-sister to high-class 1962 French 2-y-o Quiqui, won over middle distances in France; noted going on at finish when out of first 10 of 21 behind Ski Sailing in maiden race at Newmarket in October; certain to improve. *R. Armstrong.*

VIOLETTA 3 b.f. Royben 125–Top Soprano 89 (High Top 131) (1981 NR — 1982 8f 8s) 4,000Y; first foal; dam 2-y-o 5f winner; tailed off in maiden race at Kempton and minor event at Warwick; sold 525 gns Ascot November Sales. *R. Hannon.*

VIOLINO DORO 3 b. or br.f. Cavo Doro 124–Morning Cloud 79 (Hard Tack — 111§) (1981 7f 7.9f 9d 7s 1982 7s 10s 12f 12.2f) neat ex-Irish filly; half-sister to fair 1978 2-y-o 7f winner River Canyon (by Rheingold); dam placed at up to 9f in England and Ireland; beaten some way in varied company, including selling; trained by C. Collins first 2 starts; retained 580 gns Doncaster October Sales. *E. Carter.*

VIOLINO FANDANGO 4 b.c. Gay Fandango 132–Parkhurst (Sing Sing 134) — (1981 10fg 6s 7g 7f 7f² 7fg 8f 1982 8g 7f 10fg 8g 10fg 8.3g 6f) tall colt; poor handicapper nowadays; last in a seller on fifth start and was well beaten when tried in blinkers next time; stays 7f well; acts on any going. *H. O'Neill.*

VIRGINIA DEER 2 b.c. Auction Ring 123–Via Mala 81 (Pall Mall 132) (1982 **115** 5fg 5g² 6g* 5f* 5f 5fg* 6.3fg 6.3g² 5f 5d* 5s) Apr 1; IR 4,300Y; well-grown colt; third living foal; brother to 3-y-o Bold Fort, a useful winner over 5f and 6f in 1981; dam 1½m winner; one of the leading 2-y-o sprinters in Ireland, winning minor event at the Curragh, Marwell Stakes at Naas, Group 3 Curragh Stakes and Goffs Stakes at the Curragh again; got home by a short head from Gormanstown Prince after disputing lead throughout in Curragh Stakes in July, and accounted for Rock 'N' Roller by a head in Goffs Stakes in September; met his last 5 defeats in good races, including Windsor Castle Stakes at Royal Ascot on fifth start (5 lengths fifth to Prince Reymo) and Flying Childers Stakes at Doncaster on ninth (moved short to post, finished 5¾ lengths last of 5 to Kafu); stays 6f; acts on any going except perhaps very soft; usually ridden by apprentice K. O'Brien, often when he's unable to claim his allowance; sold 100,000 gns Newmarket December Sales and is to race in France. *P. Flynn, Ireland.*

VIRTUOSO 3 br.g. So Blessed 130–Virginia (Pirate King 129) (1981 NR — 1982 7f 9.4f³ 11g 8fg 9s) leggy gelding; half-brother to 2 winners, including 1m and 9.4f winner Nun (by Amber Rama); dam lightly-raced sister to very useful stayer Avast; poor form, including in a seller; sold 2,100 gns Doncaster November Sales. *C. Thornton.*

VISIBLE ASSET 3 b.f. Vitiges 132–Look Out 84 (Vimy 132) (1981 NR — 1982 12d 12d 10.2g 10f 10.1fg) workmanlike filly; half-sister to several winners, including 2m winner Scheming (by Great Nephew) and out-and-out French stayer Second Watch (by Paveh); dam half-sister to very smart stayer Raise You Ten; poor maiden. *N. Vigors.*

VISITOR 2 b.f. Be My Guest 126–Sarania 118 (Sassafras 135) (1982 7fg) — Apr 15; IR 38,000Y; small, quite attractive, short-backed filly; third foal; half-sister to 3-y-o Saranita (by Thatch) and to Irish 7f winner Rafael (by Habitat); dam won over 6f and 1¼m, including Blue Seal Stakes and Sandleford Priory Stakes; 33/1, eleventh of 12 to Zoffany in minor event at Goodwood in September. *J. Dunlop.*

VITALE 3 ch.f. Vitiges 132–Fire Dance (Habitat 134) (1981 NR 1982 16fg) — 9,200Y; second foal; half-sister to 1980 2-y-o 5f winner Disco Dancing (by Record Token), subsequently a winner in Italy; dam never ran; 8/1 when remote eighth of 11 to Ariadne in maiden race at Lingfield in May; sold 680 gns Newmarket July Sales. *J. Hindley.*

VITAL INTERESTS 2 ch.c. Sagaro 133–Rosalina 71 (Porto Bello 118) — (1982 7fg 7s) May 6; 4,400Y; compact colt; third foal; half-brother to fair 1980 2-y-o 5f performer Fire Mountain (by Dragonara Palace); dam won over 7f and 1m; behind in maiden races at Redcar in September (last of 26) and October; refused to enter stalls intended debut. *B. Wilkinson.*

VITAL SPIRIT 3 b.f. Tachypous 128–Vital Error 105 (Javelot 124) (1981 **49** 5fg 6f³ 5fg⁴ 6fg 5d 1982 7g 7f² 7f³ 8g 7f) leggy filly; only plating class; stays 7f; acts on firm going; blinkered once at 2 yrs; has run respectably when sweating up; sold 5,000 gns Newmarket December Sales. *J. Etherington.*

VITIGESON 2 ch.c. Vitiges 132–Piccadilly Etta 76 (Floribunda 136) (1982 **77** 5f 5fg³ 6g 5f 5f 5g² 5s) May 5; 14,000Y; strong colt; half-brother to 2 winning sprinters, including fairly useful Jose Collins (by Singing Bede); dam won from 1½m to 2m; ran respectably in nurseries fifth and sixth outings, on latter finishing clear when ½-length second of 8 to Best Bidder at Beverley in September; should be suited by 6f; ran moderately in blinkers third and fourth outings, and poorly on soft going final start. *T. Fairhurst.*

VITINGO 3 ch.c. Vitiges 132–Petlady 81 (Petingo 135) (1981 7fg 8d 1982 10s — 9g 10f 8f 8s 10.1d⁴ 11fg⁴ 12f 10f 12.2f 10fg 10d) fair sort; has shown only a little ability in varied company; stays 11f; sometimes blinkered; sold to Miss S. Morris 1,300 gns Newmarket Autumn Sales. *C. Brittain.*

VITO'S GIRL 3 b.f. Some Hand 119–Keep At It (Larkspur 128) (1981 NR — 1982 10f) half-sister to a winning hurdler and a winner in Trinidad; dam won over 9.5f at 2 yrs in Ireland; 50/1 and very burly when last of 9 behind My Maravilla in minor event at Salisbury in August. *J. Old.*

VITTEL 2 b.g. Vitiges 132–Klaxonette 88 (Klairon 131) (1982 7f) Apr 27; — first foal; dam won over 5f and 6f; in rear in 15-runner maiden race at Newmarket in July. *J. Winter.*

VIVIAN'S PARK 3 b.f. Porto Bello 118–Paddy's Tern 59 (St Paddy 133) — (1981 NR 1982 8fg 8g) first foal; dam suited by a test of stamina; well behind in maiden races at Warwick in August and Yarmouth in September. *E. Eldin.*

VIVIEN'S DELIGHT 2 b.c. Monseigneur 127–Wild Bee (Hill Gail) (1982 **49** 7fg 7f 7g⁴ 8.2fg) May 5; IR 2,000Y; big, strong, rangy colt; half-brother to several winners, including quite useful sprinter Laseroy (by Laser Light); dam fair Irish sprinter; poor plater; dead. *Mrs J. Reavey.*

VIVRE POUR VIVRE (ITY) 2 ch.g. Great Nephew 126–Velatura (Acropolis — 132) (1982 6fg 7g) May 29; IR 10,500Y; short-coupled gelding; good walker; half-brother to 2 winners in Italy, including useful Verde Dimora (by Sir Ivor), and to Irish 1m winner Voice (by Habitat); dam winning sister to champion 1969 Italian 2-y-o Viani; well beaten in quite useful company at York in June and September; subsequently gelded. *P. Kelleway.*

VOCIFEROUS 3 ch.f. Vitiges 132–Too Much 100 (Major Portion 129) (1981 — 7f 1982 9g 12g⁴ 12f) rangy, good sort; poor maiden; stays 1½m; sold 1,600 gns Newmarket Autumn Sales. *I. Walker.*

VODKATINI 3 b.g. Dubassoff–Olympic Visualise 84 (Northfields) (1981 NR — 1982 14s) 2,000 3-y-o; big, strong gelding; first foal; dam won over 1m; un-quoted when about 6 lengths fifth of 12 to Royal Agnes in maiden race at Sandown in October. *P. Haynes.*

*Portland Handicap, Doncaster—the event's customary close finish as Vorvados
bursts through on the rails to catch subsequently-disqualified
My Dear Fellow with Famous Star (No. 7)
and Touch Boy next*

VOICE OF PROGRESS 4 b.g. Matahawk 127–La Crima 63 (Runnymede 123) **73**
(1981 12d 12fg⁴ 12f⁴ 12g² 12g* 1982 12d 12d²) quite a moderate handicapper;
pulled hard when second at Leicester in October; will stay beyond 1½m; trained
by R. Hannon first outing. *P. Bailey.*

VORACITY 3 ch.c. Vitiges 132–Wolverene 114 (Relko 136) (1981 7g 1982 **94**
8fg 10f³ 10f² 11.5fg* 12g* 12g⁴) tall, good-looking colt; won maiden race at
Sandown in August and minor event at York in September; beat Line Slinger
a shade comfortably by 1½ lengths in latter; suited by 1½m and will stay further;
yet to race on a soft surface. *J. Winter.*

VORVADOS 5 gr.h. The Go-Between 129–Keravnos 64 (Ionian 128) (1981 **94**
5s⁴ 6s 6fg 5g⁴ 6d² 6g 5.3f 6fg* 6g* 6fg 6fg 6g 6s³ 6d 1982 6d* 6d² 7fg 6f 6f 6g
5g* 5fg² 6f* 5.6g* 6g 6g*) lightly-built horse; improved and had a highly
successful time; tends to get behind, and finished very strongly indeed when
winning handicaps at Salisbury in April, Sandown and Newmarket in July,
Doncaster in September and Newmarket again in October; beat subsequently-
disqualified My Dear Fellow by a neck in Portland Handicap at Doncaster and
Off The Hook by a length in Phantom House Handicap at Newmarket; suited
by 6f, or by 5f on a stiff track; acts on any going; occasionally blinkered in 1981;
has a terrific turn of foot; has run creditably for an apprentice but has had
particularly strong handling on last 7 occasions when successful (W. Carson 5
times and L. Piggott twice). *M. Haynes.*

VOUSSAC 2 b.c. Great Nephew 126–Orange Squash 78 (Red God 128§) **?**
(1982 10v*) Feb 17; 36,000Y; first foal; dam, sister to very useful Irish colt
Matuno God, won 3 times at around 1m; came through in closing stages to win
10-runner maiden race at Saint-Cloud in November by a short neck from Baly;
evidently stays quite well; bound to go on to better things. *J. C. Cunnington,
France.*

VOX 2 br.g. Quiet Fling 124–Pollster 101 (Majority Blue 126) (1982 7f 7f 7g) **—**
May 8; 11,500Y; smallish, quite well-made gelding; half-brother to 3 winners
here and abroad, including 6.5f and 1m winner Speed Bonnie Boat (by Swing
Easy); dam won 3 races over 5f at 2 yrs; soundly beaten in maiden and minor
events; blinkered first start. *W. O'Gorman.*

VOYANT 3 ch.c. Star Appeal 133–Vernier 94 (High Hat 131) (1981 7fg² 7.6g **104**
7g² 1982 10s* 14fg³ 16g 14f³ 12g* 12fg³ 12g³) smallish, rather lightly-built
colt; won maiden race at Leicester in March (odds on) and Great Yorkshire
Handicap at York in August; put up an improved display in latter, leading 2f
out and staying on really well to beat Nauteous by 3 lengths; stays 1¾m; seems
to act on any going. *B. Hobbs.*

VRESIA 3 b.f. Vitiges 132–Zantedeschia 91 (Zimone) (1981 NR 1982 8g⁴ 7fg **78**
10.2g³ 10f* 10g) useful-looking, close-coupled filly; a twin; half-sister to 3
winners, notably 2,000 Guineas fourth Cut Throat (by Sharpen Up); dam fairly
useful miler; kept on gamely to beat Two High by 1½ lengths in 8-runner maiden

race at Nottingham in August; suited by 1¼m and will stay further; acts on firm going. *H. Candy.*

VRONDI 10 ch.h. Welsh Rake 118–Jevington 102 (Fairey Fulmar 124) (1981 NR 1982 10f) modest handicapper at his best; behind in a seller at Brighton in April, first outing on flat since 1979; stays 1¼m, but best form at up to 1m; seems to act on any going; suitable mount for an apprentice; has been tried in blinkers; has been at stud. *B. Wise.* —

VRONSKY 6 gr.g. Warpath 113–Janabelle 101 (Gentle Art 121) (1981 12.5s 12s 9fg 10.6s 8g 14.6f 1982 12f² 12.2f²) former plater; close second in handicaps at York (apprentice event) and Catterick in May, best efforts on flat for a while; stays 1½m; seems to act on any going; sometimes wears blinkers. *C. Gray.* **38**

VYNZ GIRL 2 b.f. Tower Walk 130–Mayo Girl 110 (Connaught 130) (1982 7g 7d⁴ 8s³ 7d 10.2s³) May 16; 5,600Y; rangy filly; first living foal; dam ran well in top company but failed to win; modest form in maiden and minor events; stays 1¼m; acts on soft going; has shown a tendency to hang. *C. Booth.* **82**

VYNZ SUPREME 2 b.c. Supreme Sovereign 119–High Drama 90 (Hill Clown) (1982 6s⁴) Apr 9; useful-looking colt; second foal; dam stayed well; 12 lengths last of 4 to Domynsky in £3,400 event at York in October; should do better in time. *W. Haigh.* — p

W

WAGONER 2 b.c. Rheingold 137–Tranquilly (Sea-Bird II 145) (1982 8s) Apr 2; 6,000F; second live foal; dam Irish 1¼m winner; no show in 21-runner maiden race at Leicester in November. *P. Walwyn.* —

WAHED 7 gr.g. Red God 128§–Welsh Crest 86 (Abernant 142) (1981 7f* 7f 8g 8f³ 7g 8f² 7g⁴ 8fg² 1982 8g⁴ 7fg² 8f 8f³ 8fg 8g 10f* 10g 10g* 10g 10g² 10d) strong gelding; won handicaps at Redcar in July (poorish race) and Newcastle in August; evidently suited by 1¼m; probably acts on any going; has worn blinkers; suitable mount for an inexperienced rider; inconsistent and ungenuine. *D. Smith.* **61 §**

WALDRON HILL 2 ch.c. Hotfoot 126–Ankole 85 (Crepello 136) (1982 6f 7d 6d 6v³) Mar 1; fair sort; good walker and mover; half-brother to numerous winners, including useful miler Horbury (by Sing Sing); dam won at up to 13f; only plating class on form in maiden and minor events; may be capable of a little improvement at 1¼m+. *S. Norton.* **62**

WALJAT 2 b.c. Bay Express 132–Giglet (Frankincense 120) (1982 5.1f³ 5d 5g⁴ 6g³) May 12; 13,500Y; fair sort; half-brother to disappointing 3-y-o Match Master (by Roman Warrior) and a minor winner; dam showed no form; showed only quite modest form until finishing just over ½-length third of 12 behind 66/1 stable-companion Captivating Lady in nursery at Newmarket (backed from 7/1 to 11/2) in October; suited by 6f; sure to win a race. *W. Musson.* **89**

WALK ALONG 3 ch.g. Farm Walk 111–Leger Bar 63 (French Beige 127) (1981 7d⁴ 7f 1982 10f 12d) lightly-made gelding; little worthwhile form in varied company; doesn't look an easy ride. *W. Haigh.* —

WALLY'S FOLLY 3 br.c. Goldhill 125–Golden Palermo 70 (Dumbarnie 125) (1981 NR 1982 8d 7fg) compact colt; tailed-off last in maiden race and seller at Beverley in summer. *J. Mulhall.* —

WALTHAM TERRACE 3 b.f. Auction Ring 123–Dandy Brush 82 (Will Somers 114§) (1981 5s 5d 5fg 5f 6fg 1982 8f 7f 8f 5f⁴ 5fg 5d 5f) compact filly; poor maiden. *C. Gray.* **50**

WALTON HEATH 2 b. or br.g. Persian Bold 123–Faa Paa (Skymaster 126) (1982 5d 5fg⁴ 5f⁴ 7d² 7g 7g 7fg 8f* 7g) Apr 11; 15,500Y; lightly-made gelding; half-brother to several winners, including useful 7f performer The Yellow Girl (by Yellow God); dam 2-y-o 7f winner in Ireland; blinkered first time when winning 12-runner nursery at Bath in September by 1½ lengths from Some Sunny Day; other form very mixed to say the least; suited by 1m; seems to act on any going; inconsistent; gelded after final outing. *A. Ingham.* **78**

WALTZ 3 ch.f. Jimmy Reppin 131–Strip The Willow 79 (Native Dancer) (1981 6s³ 1982 8d 8g 7.6fg³ 8f 8g* 7.2f³ 8d) workmanlike filly; won maiden race at Goodwood in August; ran creditably in handicap next start but moderately in blinkers on final appearance; suited by 1m. *I. Balding.* **75**

WANCHAI GIRL 3 ch.f. Lombard 126–Double Mint 82 (Double-U-Jay 120) —
(1981 NR 1982 10.1fg 10fg) third foal; dam won at 1½m and was also successful
over hurdles; blinkered when behind in 2 sellers; sold 600 gns Newmarket Autumn
Sales and has been sent to Holland. *P. Feilden.*

WANGANUI 2 ro.c. Grey Mirage 128–Vilmainder 78 (Remainder 106) (1982 —
5f 6g 6s) Mar 23; leggy, lightly-made colt; half-brother to successful 6f to 1¼m
plater Whangarei (by Gold Rod); dam won over 5f at 2 yrs; soundly beaten in
Northern sellers. *B. McMahon.*

WANGAROO (USA) 3 b.g. Charles Elliott–Saratoga Gal (Royal Orbit) (1981 —
5s 6g 6g 6d³ 7fg 8.2fg⁴ 10s 1982 10g) sturdy gelding; plating-class maiden;
stays 1m; blinkered once in 1981. *R. Hartop.*

WANG FEIHOONG 2 b.c. Sagaro 133–Tulchan 95 (Tudor Melody 129) (1982 **71**
6fg 7f 8g²) Apr 24; 6,000Y; fourth foal; dam won over 6f and 1¼m; 5 lengths
second of 10 to Statesmanship in maiden race at Beverley in September; will stay
at least 1¼m. *P. Haslam.*

WAR AND PEACE 3 br.g. Red Alert 127–Swinging Nun (Tudor Melody 129) —
(1981 NR 1982 7.6f 10.2g 10.1fg 7g) poor mover; poor form, including in a
seller; sold 700 gns Ascot August Sales. *R. Sheather.*

WARBIOLA 2 ch.f. Nebbiolo 125–War Lass 100 (Whistler 129) (1982 5d) —
May 22; 6,400Y; half-sister to several winners, including useful 1976 2-y-o
Tamariscifolia (by Ridan); dam won twice over 5f at 2 yrs; eighth of 12 in maiden
race at Warwick in April. *W. Musson.*

WARBURY DELL 3 br.f. Warpath 113–Slightly Saucy 74 (Galivanter 131) —
(1981 6f⁴ 7d³ 7fg 8g 8g 1982 8.2fg 10.4fg 10.4d 10.6s 12v 10s 12s) leggy,
lightly-made filly; seems no longer of any account; sometimes bandaged. *R. E.
Peacock.*

WARESLEY 4 gr.c. Town Crier 119–Nasca 81 (King's Bench 132) (1981 6d **61**
6g 5f 5fg³ 5fg 5f² 5f* 5g²(dis) 1982 6f 5f² 5f² 5fg⁴ 6f 5fg 5.6f⁴) neat, strong
colt; second in handicaps at Thirsk in May and Redcar in June; sometimes had
stiff tasks; best at 5f; acts well on firm going; blinkered nowadays; sometimes
sweats up. *G. Huffer.*

WARFLIGHT 3 b.c. Warpath 113–Brief Flight 108 (Counsel 118) (1981 6d **66**
8.2d 1982 9g 10.6fg 9.4fg 9g* 8.2g* 8f² 8d³ 10.6s² 12v* 12g 12s) big, useful-
looking colt; won seller at Newcastle (bought in 4,200 gns) in August; subsequently ran well in better company, picking up handicaps at Hamilton (made
all) and Ascot (gentleman riders); stays 1½m well; acts on any going but goes
well in the mud; blinkered third start; suitable mount for an amateur rider;
wears a tongue strap; sold 10,000 gns Doncaster November Sales. *C. Thornton.*

WARGAME 2 ch.c. Warpath 113–Sunshine Holyday 96 (Three Wishes 114) **95**
(1982 6fg 7g* 7s 7d³) Apr 20; rangy, good sort; good walker; half-brother to 2
winners, including fairly useful 1977 2-y-o 1m winner Westwood Boy (by Saintly
Song); dam stayer; 100/1, wore down odds-on Magnetic Field inside final furlong to win 18-runner minor event at Newcastle in August by a head; good
third of 4 to Bright Cone at Catterick 2 months later; will be suited by 1¼m + ;
likely to develop into a useful 3-y-o. *C. Gray.*

WARM HEARTED 3 b. or br.f. Steel Heart 128–Tamarisk Way 92 (Tamerlane **97**
128) (1981 5fg* 6g* 6g* 6fg* 6d* 1982 7fg 8fg 6f 6g) neat filly; unbeaten
in five races at 2 yrs, gaining easily most important success in Firth of Clyde
Stakes at Ayr; not disgraced first 2 starts in 1982 in Ladbrokes Nell Gwyn Stakes
at Newmarket (seventh of 12 to Chalon) and 1,000 Guineas on same course
(ninth of 15 to On The House); seems to stay 1m; probably acts on any going;
ran miserably third outing; sold 56,000 gns Newmarket December Sales. *F.
Durr.*

WARM ORDER 3 b.c. Hot Spark 126–Canaan (Santa Claus 133) (1981 5s **71**
5.1f⁴ 5fg³ 6fg* 7g 8d 1982 8.2d³ 7f² 8f* 10f 10.6f² 11.7fg 12fg² 12fg⁴ 11.5fg 10fg)
strong, compact colt; awarded handicap at Redcar in May; stays 1½m; goes well
on fast ground; effective with or without blinkers; suitable mount for an inexperienced rider; sold 5,800 gns Newmarket Autumn Sales and sent to Malaysia.
P. Feilden.

WARM WIND 3 b.f. Tumble Wind–Unsuspected 95 (Above Suspicion 127) **84**
(1981 6fg 7g* 7fg 8d⁴ 1982 7d² 8f² 8f 8g 9g* 10g² 10f³ 10d*) neat filly; won
apprentice races at Ripon in August and Newmarket (handicap) in October;
will stay 1½m; seems to act on any going; ran poorly third and fourth starts and
wore blinkers afterwards. *P. Rohan.*

WARNER'S PRIDE 2 b.g. Sweet Revenge 129–Sheila's Pearl (Javelot 124) **54** (1982 6fg 6fg 7g 5g 5.1d) Apr 17; IR 3,400F, 6,800Y; compact gelding; has rather a round action; poor plater; blinkered final start; sold 320 gns Doncaster September Sales. *P. Haslam.*

WAROOKA 5 gr.g. Veiled Wonder–Grey Parrot (Abernant 142) (1981 6d **—** 6v⁴ 5.8g 5g* 5g³ 5d* 5h 5s 6d 6g 1982 6g 5d 5g 5.8f 6fg 7.6g 6g 5g 5fg 5fg) strong gelding; has a round action; rather disappointing sprint handicapper; suited by some give in the ground; blinkered last 2 starts. *J. O'Donoghue.*

WARREN GORSE 8 b.g. Lucky Sovereign–Dunoon Court (Dunoon Star 110) **—** (1981 NR 1982 12d 11.5f) winner over hurdles and fences; behind in amateur riders races at Beverley and Yarmouth in July. *J. Leigh.*

WARRENICE LAD 3 gr.g. Abwah 118–Broadway Lass 70 (March Past 124) **51** (1981 5g 5g⁴ 6g⁴ 6f 7fg* 7d⁴ 8f 8fg 8.2d⁴ 8d⁴ 8d⁴ 8d 1982 10s 10g 9f 12.2f² 13.8f 10d 12g* 12g) narrow, plain gelding; bad mover; plater; bought in 1,050 gns after winning at Pontefract in July; stays 1½m; seems to act on any going; wears blinkers. *K. Stone.*

WARRI 3 b.c. Rolfe 77–Lotto 83 (Derring-Do 131) (1981 5.8d 7g** 7fg 8g 8.2s **82** 1982 10d³ 10f* 10f⁴ 12f⁴ 10g³ 10f 11g) strong colt; ridden with confidence when winning handicap at Epsom in April; not disgraced most subsequent outings; stays 1¼m; seems to act on any going; blinkered sixth start; exported to Malaysia. *D. Arbuthnot.*

WARRIORS DELIGHT 2 b.f. Roman Warrior 132–Deaney's Delight 63 (Sahib **—** 114) (1982 7g) Apr 29; first foal; dam won seller over 5.8f; slow-starting last of 13 in seller at Thirsk in July. *Miss S. Hall.*

WAR TRACK 3 b.c. Warpath 113–Miss O'Brien 67 (Gulf Pearl 117) (1981 **—** 5g 7fg 7fg 7fg 8g 10g⁴ 8.2s 1982 8fg 10f 7f 10.8fg) neat colt; plater; will be suited by 1½m; sometimes blinkered. *Mrs C. Lloyd-Jones.*

WAR WAR 2 ch.c. Tachypous 128–Top Line 99 (Saint Crespin III 132) (1982 **—** 7g 7g 8d) Feb 20; 21,000Y; brother to 3-y-o Dutch Romantic, and half-brother to a winning plater and a winning hurdler; dam won at 1m and 1½m and is out of smart Reel In; little worthwhile form in maiden events. *P. Haslam.*

WARWICK BLUE 2 b.g. Raga Navarro 119–Allegretto (Preciptic 122) (1982 **40** 5fg 7g 5g) May 11; 3,100Y; leggy, close-coupled gelding; half-brother to several minor winners; bad plater; not raced after August. *J. Holt*

WARWICK STAR 2 b.f. Comedy Star 121–Maid of Warwick 96 (Warwick 110) **88** (1982 5f 5f³ 5.3fg⁴ 5g³ 5.8g⁴ 5g³ 5d 7fg 5f* 5s* 5s) Apr 6; compact, deep-girthed filly; third foal; dam sprinter; improved in the autumn, making much of running when winning maiden race at Bath by a neck and nursery at Warwick by a head; best at 5f; acts on any going; blinkered sixth and eighth outings but is better without; genuine. *R. Hannon.*

WASSL 2 b.c. Mill Reef 141–Hayloft 111 (Tudor Melody 129) (1982 6fg*) **93 p**
It is a pity that no more was seen of the very well-bred Wassl as a two-year-old than his gaining a three-length success in the Duchess of Kent Stakes at York in June. Although the form of the race is no better than good maiden-race form—the runner-up All Systems Go, also making his debut, had a neck and two lengths respectively to spare over Cash or Carry and Faites Vite, both of whom ended the year still maidens—the manner of Wassl's victory marked him out as a very interesting prospect indeed. An attractive colt, Wassl looked fit and started a well-backed second favourite in the nine-horse field. He appeared to struggle early on after an indifferent break and by halfway had a great deal to do, but he was really making ground approaching the two-furlong marker and produced such a good turn of foot that he won impressively in the end, eased down at the finish. Wassl looked sure to hold his own in much stronger company after this but unfortunately an injury sustained when he was cast in his box a fortnight later proved very slow in clearing up and he wasn't seen out again. Wassl was bought for 300,000 guineas as a yearling. He is the second foal of Hayloft, the winner of the Molecomb Stakes in 1975 who trained on quite well and showed she stayed a mile. Her first foal, Village Scene (by Blakeney), realised 92,000 guineas as a yearling but fetched only 4,500 guineas at Newmarket Autumn Sales after failing to show any form in two races at three years. Hayloft's dam Haymaking was a smart performer who numbered the Coronation Stakes and Nassau Stakes among her six victories. She has produced four

Duchess of Kent Stakes, York—300,000-guinea Wassl wins in smart style on his only racecourse appearance

other winners besides Hayloft, including Hay Reef, a close relative to Wassl who won over a mile and a quarter. Wassl's fifth dam New Moon was a half-sister to Hyperion. Wassl looked as though he'd be suited by further than six furlongs at York and he'll stay the distance of the Two Thousand Guineas,

		Never Bend (b 1960)	Nasrullah / Lalun
	Mill Reef (b 1968)	Milan Mill (b 1962)	Princequillo / Virginia Water
Wassl (b.c. Apr 27, 1980)		Tudor Melody (br 1956)	Tudor Minstrel / Matelda
	Hayloft (b 1973)	Haymaking (br 1963)	Galivanter / Haytime

reportedly his first major objective bar further set-backs. He is also likely to stay beyond a mile but whether he'll get a mile and a half only time will tell. What is certain is that we've yet to see the best of Wassl. *J. Dunlop.*

WATCH IT COME DOWN 2 b. or br.f. Panama Canal 105–Quick Return (The Bo'sun 114) (1982 5f) Mar 16; third reported foal; dam showed no ability at 2 yrs; well beaten in seller at Lingfield in July; sold 260 gns Ascot August Sales. *P. Mitchell.* —

WATERHEAD 2 b.c. High Top 131–Djimbaran Bay (Le Levanstell 122) (1982 7s⁴) June 7; lengthy colt; fifth foal; half-brother to fairly useful 1¼m winner Bettyknowes (by Satingo); dam won at up to 1¼m in France; third favourite, made excellent progress in straight, without being hard ridden, when promising 7 lengths fourth of 14 behind Sackford in minor event at Sandown in October; will be suited by 1m+; sure to do better, and win races. *J. Tree.* **84 p**

WATER PISTOL 2 br.g. Scottish Rifle 127–Jane Bond 59 (Good Bond 122) (1982 6d 6f² 7f* 7fg³ 7g² 8g 8.2s) Apr 22; 620F, 1,050Y; compact, lightly-made gelding; first foal; dam won 5f seller at 2 yrs; justified favouritism in good style in seller at Beverley in July but surprisingly failed to attract a bid afterwards; placed in nurseries at York (£5,000 event) and Beverley the following month; suited by 7f; acts well on firm going; slowly away on final appearance. *M. Lambert.* **76**

WATET KHET (FR) 3 b.f. Wittgenstein 123–Abamira (Abdos 134) (1981 7g 1982 10s² 12fg 12.3f* 11fg⁴ 13.1g 12fg⁴ 12g²) rangy filly; made much of run-

896

ning and kept on strongly to win minor event at Catterick in June; in frame in 3 handicaps afterwards; ran out fifth start; stays 1½m well; acts on any going. *B. Hills.*

WATT BRIDGE 4 b.f. Mandamus 120–Blasllyn 88 (Blast 125) (1981 NR 1982 8f 8g 10g 8s 8s 7d) 2,600Y; big, strong filly; half-sister to 3 minor winners; dam won over 6f at 2 yrs and stayed 1½m; wasn't disgraced when 10 lengths fifth of 7 behind Bancario in minor event at Newcastle in August on second appearance; started slowly first two outings. *Miss L. Siddall.* —

WATTLEFIELD 3 b.c. Red God 128§–Short Commons 109 (Hard Tack 111§) (1981 6fg 6d* 6f* 6d 6g3 1982 8g 7.2h) a grand individual; walks well and moves with an extravagant, light action; smart performer at 2 yrs; didn't run up to his best in Ladbrokes Craven Stakes at Newmarket in April or John of Gaunt Stakes at Haydock in June and was subsequently found to have a hairline fracture of a knee; may prove best at distances short of 1m; has won on a soft surface but needs a sound surface to show to best advantage; has a good turn of foot. *M. Stoute.* —

WAULKMILL 2 ch.f. Grundy 137–Guiding Light 78 (Crepello 136) (1982 7fg 8g) Mar 21; 35,000F; rangy, attractive filly; half-sister to several winners, including fairly useful 1977 3-y-o 5f winner Princess Zena (by Habitat) and useful 1m to 1½m performer La Dolce (by Connaught); dam middle-distance maiden; 20/1, made little show in minor event at Goodwood in September and maiden race at Newmarket in October; will do better in time if looks count for anything. *J. Dunlop.* — p

WAYWARD KATE 3 b.f. Cornuto 111–Kit-O-Kate 61 (Raccolto 120) (1981 NR 1982 10.2g 10fg 10.6s) workmanlike filly; fourth foal; dam poor maiden; well behind in maiden races and a minor event. *M. Scudamore.* —

WAYWARD POLLY 2 br.f. Lochnager 132–Trigamy 112 (Tribal Chief 125) (1982 5fg 5f 5f3 5g 5d* 5g) May 14; 5,200F; smallish, lengthy filly; good walker; third foal; half-sister to 1980 2-y-o 5f winner Rathmoy's Sparkle (by Sparkler); dam 5f performer; dropped in class, ridden with more restraint than previously when winning 17-runner seller at Ripon in August (bought in 4,600 gns) by 1½ lengths from Little Vagabond; evidently suited by a soft surface. *M. W. Easterby.* 63

WEAVERS' PIN 5 b.g. Weavers' Hall 122–Priceless Pin (Saint Crespin III 132) (1981 8s 12g3 9g 12f2 10fg* 12.5fg 11f2 12d 16f* 8fg 14.6fg 15g3 11s 11d 15.8g2 14g 1982 13fg2 16g4 14f 12f* 12fg3) small, light sort; favourite when winning amateur riders race at Redcar in June easily by 8 lengths from Cool Decision; had difficulty getting a run when 1½ lengths third of 16 behind Spin of a Coin in Bessborough Stakes (Handicap) at Royal Ascot later in month; effective at middle distances and stays 2m; needs top-of-the-ground; retained by trainer 7,200 gns Newmarket July Sales. *M. Francis.* 88

WEAVERS WAY 2 b.c. Weavers' Hall 122–Corneater (Skymaster 126) (1982 8d) Apr 11; 5,500Y; has rather a round action; third foal; half-brother to 3-y-o 1½m winner Top Creator (by High Line); dam ran once; behind in 23-runner maiden race at Newmarket in October. *H. Collingridge.* —

WEBBS JEWEL 3 b.f. Shiny Tenth 120–Prompt Delivery (Catullus) (1981 5fg 5.3f 5d 5s 8d3 1982 6s* 6f 7f* 6fg 7d 7f 7fg 6f4 6d 8s) fair sort; won seller at Haydock in April (bought in 1,650 gns) and handicap at Brighton in May; stays 1m; acts on any going. *D. Marks.* 65

WEDDED BLISS 6 b.m. Relko 136–True Love 89 (Princely Gift 137) (1981 16s* 15.8g3 16g 12g 16g 15.8g* 12fg* 16g2 15.8fg 16fg* 12.2g 16g2 13d 12d 18g 1982 13s4 16.1s 12f4 18f4 15.8f4 13.8f 14g4 15.8f2 15.8d* 16d) sturdy mare; beat Tea-Pot by a head in handicap at Chester in August; stays well; seems to act on any going; suited by a strong pace and waiting tactics; has given trouble on way to post. *D. Chapman.* 49

WEDDING GUEST 3 gr.f. Sanbal–Albatross (Petros 118) (1982 5d) Mar 6; third reported foal; dam never ran; behind in 24-runner maiden race at Windsor in June. *K. Bridgwater.* —

WEDNESDAY BOY 3 ch.c. Lucky Wednesday 124–Hutton Barns 92 (Saintly Song 128) (1981 5d 5s 6g 6f 7f4 7.2v 6s 1982 6s 6g* 6g 7fg 6fg3 7fg3 6d) plater; attracted no bid after winning at Pontefract in April; will be suited by 1m; acts on any going; has been tried in blinkers. *S. Norton.* 45

WEDNESDAY REDHEAD 2 ch.f. Lucky Wednesday 124–Redhead 66 (Hotfoot 126) (1982 5fg 6fg 7f 7fg2 8.2fg2 8fg) Apr 29; 1,700Y; fair sort; second foal; dam won 9f seller; plater; second to wide-margin winners Lady Tut and Soldby at Wolverhampton in July and Haydock in September; will stay 1¼m. *P. Haslam.*

WEDNESDAY'S CHASE 3 ch.g. Lucky Wednesday 124–Royal Huntress — (Royal Avenue 123) (1981 6fg 7f⁴ 7g 7d 1982 10.6s 8f 9fg 11g 10g) tall, narrow gelding; poor form, including in a seller; sold out of W. Elsey's stable 1,000 gns Doncaster August Sales after fourth start; resold 575 gns Ascot November Sales. *R. Carter.*

WELD MAIN 3 b.c. Mansingh 120–Sarong 97 (Taj Dewan 128) (1981 8g — 1982 8.2fg 10fg 8fg 8g 8.2g 7.6d 9fg 8s) fair sort; poor plater; sometimes blinkered; sold out of M. Jarvis' stable 2,000 gns Newmarket July Sales after fourth outing. *L. Barratt.*

WELL GREASED 5 b. or br.m. Workboy 123–Jolly Smooth 84 (Jolly Jet 111) **33** (1981 10.8d 10g 8f 8.3g 8fg³ 8s 1982 10g2) lengthy mare; poor handicapper; second in seller at Folkestone in April; stayed 1¼m; acted well on firm going; was a good mount for a boy; dead. *W. Holden.*

WE'LL MEET AGAIN 5 b.h. Song 132–Coaster 61 (Right Tack 131) (1981 **70** 7d³ 8fg² 8d* 8v* 10s⁴ 10d* 10f* 10d 10fg 10d² 10s* 1982 10s 10g 10fg 10fg 10s⁴ 10v² 12s) workmanlike horse; rather disappointing in 1982, best effort when head second to Aldenham in handicap at Lingfield in October; stays 1¼m; acts on any going but goes well on soft; has run creditably for a boy; usually held up. *J. Benstead.*

WELSH CLOUD 3 b.f. Welsh Saint 126–Treble Cloud (Capistrano 120) (1981 — 5g* 5g 6fg⁴ 6d 6fg 6f 7f* 1982 7f 7fg 7f) well-made filly; plater; beaten some way at 3 yrs; suited by 7f; acts on firm going; blinkered last 4 starts in 1981; has won for an apprentice. *A. Jarvis.*

WELSH DIAMOND 4 b.f. High Top 131–Camarina 62 (Aureole 132) (1981 — 12.5f 12fg 10f 8g 1982 10.6g 8fg 10d) plater; one paced and should stay 1½m; probably unsuited by soft going; has worn blinkers; sold 450 gns Ascot November Sales. *D. H. Jones.*

WELSH GLORY 2 ch.c. Welsh Pageant 132–Fairy Fans (Petingo 135) (1982 **82 p** 7s³) Apr 14; rather sparely-made but quite attractive colt; second foal; dam unraced daughter of very useful Jolie Fleur, a half-sister to Connaught; favourite, close-up third of 11 behind more experienced colts Ice Patrol and Burley Griffin in maiden race at Redcar in October; will stay 1¼m; will do better. *H. Cecil.*

WELSH IDOL 2 gr.c. Welsh Pageant 132–Idover 95 (Fortino II 120) (1982 7f) — Feb 1; 18,000Y; rangy, good-bodied colt; brother to 5f to 7f winner Hamdani and half-brother to several winners; dam sprinter; last of 15 in maiden race at Newmarket in July. *P. Kelleway.*

WELSH KERNEL 3 ch.g. Kernel Rose–Tenby Lady (Kadir Cup 97§) (1981 — 5fg 5f 6g 1982 9g) small gelding; of no account. *Miss A. Hill-Wood.*

WELSH LOCH 2 b. or br.c. Lochnager 132–La Gallia 70 (Welsh Saint 126) **77** (1982 5f² 5fg² 6f³) June 1; 3,000Y; second live foal; brother to 1981 2-y-o sprint winner Nagalia; dam won 3 times over 1¼m and also won over hurdles; won 13-runner maiden auction event at Beverley in May; not seen out after early June; exported to Hong Kong. *K. Stone.*

WELSH NOBLE 4 b.c. Welsh Saint 126–Just A Glimmer 75 (Dumbarnie 125) **52** (1981 6s² 8s⁴ 6f 6fg² 6d³ 7fg 7f³ 6f 6f 6d* 7g 1982 6fg² 6f² 6fg⁴ 6fg² 6fg) good-topped colt; won seller at Ayr as a 3-y-o; second in 3 non-selling handicaps in spring; runs mainly over sprint distances, but probably stays 1m; acts on any going; suitable mount for an apprentice; in rear in blinkers final start (June). *A. Balding.*

WELSH PARTNER 3 b.f. Welsh Saint 126–King's Mate 91 (King's Bench 132) **87** (1981 5f² 6d* 6f³ 1982 8f³ 6fg³ 6h 5fg) lengthy filly; good walker; fair third in Timeform Race Card Stakes at Thirsk in April (behind Full Extent) and valu-able handicap at Newmarket in May (made most when beaten 1½ lengths by Admiral's Princess); may prove best at distances short of 1m; seems to act on any going; not raced after June. *H. T. Jones.*

WELSH RAFFLES 3 b.f. Welsh Saint 126–Colour Bar (Majority Blue 126) — (1981 NR 1982 7fg 10d) 4,500Y; 1,200 3-y-o; half-sister to winners in Belgium and Austria; dam won over 5f at 2 yrs in Ireland; backward when well beaten in maiden race won by Fanny's Cove at Ripon in August; unseated rider in seller first start. *Hbt Jones.*

WELSH TERM 3 b.c. Welsh Pageant 132–Trinity Term 100 (Primera 131) **119**
(1981 NR 1982 8.5v* 8v² 10.5fg 12s* 12s*) 29,000F; tall, well-made, attractive
colt; brother to Coronation Stakes winner Orchestration and half-brother to
2 winners, including useful Irish middle-distance winner Bishop of Orange (by
English Prince); dam 2-y-o 6f winner; won newcomers race at Maisons-Laffitte in
March, Prix Jacques Papin at Saint-Cloud in October (beat Maiymad 3 lengths)
and Grand Prix de Bordeaux in November; dead-heated for second with Gipsy
Road, ½-length behind subsequently-disqualified Balitou, in last-named; also ran
well to be 3 lengths second to Melyno in Prix de Fontainebleau at Longchamp
but ran dismally in Prix Lupin on same course on third start; stays 1½m; needs
some give in the ground. *R. Collet, France.*

WELSH WARRIOR 2 ch.g. Welsh Pageant 132–Brave Lass 114 (Ridan) — p
(1982 6f) Mar 21; rangy gelding; first foal; dam won 4 of her 5 starts at 2 yrs,
over 5f and 6f, but ran only once afterwards; well-backed favourite, sixth of 11
behind 10-length winner Princely Fighter in maiden race at Yarmouth in June;
gelded subsequently. *H. Cecil.*

WELWYN 3 b.f. Welsh Saint 126–Takawin 109 (Takawalk II 125) (1981 5g 5fg **92**
6fg⁴ 5fg⁴ 5g* 5g 1982 5g 6fg* 6fg 5g² 5fg 6f* 6f* 6g* 6g 6g) robust, quite
attractive filly; a game and consistent filly who won handicaps at Lingfield (2)
and Goodwood (2); beat Copper Beeches by ½ length for final success at Goodwood
in August; suited by 6f; acts well on firm going; retained 76,000 gns Newmarket
December Sales. *J. Benstead.*

WESLEY 6 b.g. High Top 131–Stockingful (Santa Claus 133) (1981 NR 1982 **78**
14g 16fg² 16.1g) rangy gelding; useful staying handicapper in 1980; has
reportedly had suspensory trouble and was having only second outing since May,
1980, when ¾-length second to Cheka in handicap at Newmarket in April (made
running and stuck on gamely); didn't run up to his best on only subsequent start;
acts on any going; usually blinkered; bandaged in front nowadays. *J. W. Watts.*

WESLEY BOAT 8 b.m. Forlorn River 124–Ever Grateful 95 (King's Bench 132) —
(1981 NR 1982 8d) plater; stays 1m; acts on any going. *M. Bradley.*

WESTAMIST 3 ch.f. Malacate 131–Clearing Mist 62 (Double Jump 131) (1981 —
6f 7v 8s 1982 8f 8fg 7f 12d 10s 12d) strong, short-coupled filly; shows a bit of
knee action; poor maiden; trained part of season by M. Camacho. *D. Chapman.*

WESTERING BREEZE 4 gr.c. Windjammer (USA)–Inishanier (Prevailing) **47**
(1981 6g 5g 5g 5g 6f 5fg 5f 5d⁴ 5d⁴ 7g 1982 6g 6g 5f 5f* 5fg 5f³ 6g 6r 5f 5d² 6g
5g 5d) leggy, lightly-made on Irish colt, sprint plater; bought in 980 gns after
winning apprentice seller at Carlisle in April; yet to race on really soft ground but
acts on any other; best in blinkers; sold 800 gns Doncaster November Sales.
W. Bentley.

WESTERN CIRCUIT 2 br.f. Undulate–Quick Draw 70 (Kalydon 122) (1982 —
5d) Apr 4; 1,050F, 500Y; neat filly; fourth foal; dam, 1¼m winner, is closely
related to very smart Ksar; always in rear in 9-runner minor event at Beverley
in July; bred to need 7f+. *J. Mason.*

WESTERN HERO 3 ch.g. Scottish Rifle 127–Cheyenne Queen 87 (Yellow God **64** d
129) (1981 6f 6g 7f 7d 1982 6fg² 5fg 6g³ 6f³ 7g 5g³ 6g⁴ 7f 6g 6f 6g) rangy,
workmanlike gelding; placed in varied company; will be suited by 1m; acts on
firm going; blinkered fifth and eighth starts, not looking particularly keen on
latter; has run respectably for an apprentice; sold to J. Baker 2,000 gns Ascot
November Sales. *M. Naughton.*

WESTERN WENDY 2 ch.f. Young Emperor 133–Maggie Mine 85 (Native **50**
Prince) (1982 5d 6g* 7g 7.2s) May 22; tall, lengthy filly; half-sister to 2 winners,
including fair 6f and 1m winner Solway Winds (by Windjammer); dam 2-y-o 5f
winner; won seller (bought in 2,300 gns) at Warwick in June; stays 6f well;
retained 740 gns Doncaster October Sales. *D. H. Jones.*

WESTER ROSS 5 b.g. Shoolerville 121–Huna 84 (Doutelle 128) (1981 NR —
1982 13.1f) little sign of ability on flat; has been tried in blinkers. *W. R.
Williams.*

WEST FAILTE (USA) 3 b.g. West Coast Scout–Rubye Brooks (Bold Hour) **50**
(1981 7fg 7fg⁴ 7f 7fg 1982 8f 8fg 9fg² 8f) leggy gelding; excellent mover but is
only a plater; will stay 1¼m; blinkered final start; has run respectably when
sweating up. *B. Hills.*

WESTGATE STAR 3 b.g. He Loves Me 120–Sea Swallow 90 (Dan Cupid 132) **63**
(1981 6g 6g 6d 1982 7g⁴ 10f⁴ 11g³ 10.1fg 11g 8fg³ 9g⁴ 8f³ 10.6s 8s) rangy

gelding; ran easily best races when third to Shaady in quite valuable ladies races at Ascot and Doncaster; best at 1m on firm ground. *C. Booth.*

WESTON BAY 5 b.g. Mon Fils 124–Mineral 67 (Tarqogan 125) (1981 8f 8.3fg⁴ **39** 8g 1982 10.1fg² 12f³) plater; possibly doesn't stay 1½m; acts on any going; wears blinkers nowadays. *M. Pipe.*

WESTWAY LAD 3 b.g. Firestreak 125–Groupi Girl 66 (Goupi 120) (1981 — NR 1982 9fg 8fg 7f 5g 7s) 2,400Y; lengthy gelding; half-brother to 1977 2-y-o 5f seller winner Young Toby (by Sayfar), subsequently successful in Malaya; dam poor handicapper; only plating class; stays 9f. *M. Hinchliffe.*

WEST WELLOW 2 ch.g. Red Alert 127–Jodees Gift (On Your Mark 125) **85** (1982 5f 5f 5d 6f⁴ 6fg 6f⁴ 6g⁴ 6fg* 7v) Apr 1; IR 7,200Y; robust, useful-looking gelding; first foal; dam never ran; won 12-runner nursery at Salisbury in September by a length from Ardrox Lad; creditable fifth of 10 behind Under the Hammer in £5,400 nursery at Ascot the following month; stays 7f; probably acts on any going; gelded at end of season. *G. Balding.*

WESTWOOD DANCER 3 b.f. Home Guard 129–Great Bounty (Tarqogan 125) **59** (1981 5s 5d* 7g 7f 6fg 7s 7g 8.2d 7d 1982 10s 8fg³ 10f³ 8f³ 11g 8f 8fg 7f² 7f⁴ 9g 8.2g 7f² 7d 7g² 6s) strong, quite well-made filly; placed in handicaps and an apprentice race; doesn't stay 11f; seems to act on any going; best in blinkers. *T. Fairhurst.*

WET BOB 4 ch.c. Run The Gantlet–River Craft (Reliance II 137) (1981 8d⁴ — 10.1fg 11.7f⁴ 1982 11.7fg 12d 12fg 12fg 16d 15.8d) small, stocky colt; plating-class maiden; stays 1½m; seems to act on any going; often blinkered; trained first outing by R. Baker. *C. James.*

WHANGAREI 4 b.f. Gold Rod 129–Vilmainder 78 (Remainder 106) (1981 7s **50** 6d* 7f 8.2f 8.2g³ 8f³ 8fg* 8g* 8.2s* 1982 7g 8fg 8g 8fg 8fg 8.2g 8g² 8fg 10d* 8.2s 10g³) plain filly; plater; bought in 1,350 gns after winning decisively at Nottingham in September; stays 1¼m; acts on any going. *B. McMahon.*

WHAT A BLESSING 3 b.f. So Blessed 130–Delfina (Salvo 129) (1981 NR — 1982 9f 13g) fourth foal; half-sister to 9f and 1¼m winner Starfinder (by Comedy Star); dam unplaced 3 times in France; behind in minor event at Ripon in April and maiden race at Ayr in June. *E. Weymes.*

WHAT A GUEST 3 ch.c. Be My Guest 126–Princess Tiara 111 (Crowned **119** Prince 128) (1981 NR 1982 7s* 9.7fg² 8d* 10v⁴ 9d² 10g* 8g) 40,000F; quite a good-looking colt; first foal; dam won over 7f at 2 yrs and appeared to stay 1¼m at 3 yrs; a very smart performer who won newcomers race at Evry, Prix de la Jonchere at Longchamp (beat Floriano a short head) and Prix Eugene Adam at Saint-Cloud (held renewed challenge of Bon Sang by short head); also ran well to be in frame in Prix de Guiche at Longchamp (length second to Sharp Singer), Prix La Force on same course (fourth to Be My Native) and Prix Daphnis at Evry (went down by ¾ length to General Holme); broke down in Prix Jacques le Marois at Deauville final start; stayed 1¼m; seemed to act on any going; wore blinkers; genuine and consistent; standing at Kilfrush Stud, Co. Limerick, at a fee of IR £7,500 (Oct. 1st). *R. Collet, France.*

WHAT EXCITEMENT 2 gr.f. Dragonara Palace 115–Gold of the Day 72 **69** (Bing II) (1982 5f 5.3g³ 5s⁴) May 25; 740Y, 5,000 2-y-o; half-sister to 1978 2-y-o 5f winner Ergo (by Song) and a winner in Italy; dam won at up to 1m; in frame in minor event at Brighton in September and maiden auction race, after being hampered at distance, at Warwick in October; will be suited by 6f. *C. Williams.*

WHAT LAKE (USA) 2 b.f. What Luck–Placid Lake (Terrang) (1982 5g² **107** 6g* 5v⁴) Mar 4; $25,000F, $53,000 2-y-o; well-made, quite attractive filly; half-sister to a winner in USA and another in France; dam, placed once from 19 starts, is daughter of smart filly Kootenai; justified favouritism in fine style in 19-runner maiden race at Newmarket in September, leading 2f out and drawing away to win by 4 lengths from Sweet Slew; didn't help her chance by hanging at distance but wasn't at all disgraced when 2½ lengths fourth of 9 to Tatibah in Cornwallis Stakes at Ascot the following month; will stay beyond 6f; yet to race on a firm surface. *B. Hanbury.*

WHAT NONSENSE (USA) 2 b.c. Foolish Pleasure–Ivorona (Sir Ivor 135) — (1982 6fg) Apr 12; medium-sized colt; first foal; dam, half-sister to very useful Irish 1m to 1¼m performer Opachisco, won 6f maiden race at 4 yrs; favourite, pushed along at halfway when never-dangerous 6 lengths sixth of 9 behind House

Guest in maiden race at Pontefract in August; sold 4,000 gns Newmarket Autumn Sales. *H. Cecil.*

WHEELS DISCO 2 ch.g. Artaius 129–Tristan Da Cunha (Sir Ivor 135) (1982 — 7d 7g 6f 5d 5d 6s) Apr 13; 6,000F; short-coupled gelding; of no account; blinkered final start. *A. Smith.*

WHEEL SPIN (USA) 3 b. or br.c. Northerly–Hot Wheels (Tulyar 134) (1981 — 5f 1982 10f 10.1g 11.5g 10fg) small, quite attractive colt; well beaten in maiden races. *M. Albina.*

WHENEVER 2 bl.f. Arctic Kanda 111–Sealac 81 (Sea Wolf 116) (1982 6g 7d) — Jan 23; workmanlike filly; sister to winning hurdler Bulging Pockets; dam stayed 1m; last in summer maiden races at Lingfield and Sandown. *A. Davison.*

WHENYOURTRAINSGONE 3 b. or br.c. Free State 125–Great Blue White **84** 73 (Great Nephew 126) (1981 7g 8s* 1982 9fg² 8fg² 10f 10d* 10f 9g² 8g 9d 8.2s 10s*) fair sort; won handicap at Nottingham in June and minor event at Leicester in November; suited by 1¼m; ideally suited by some give in the ground; blinkered fifth start. *R. Boss.*

WHERE YOU WILL 2 gr.f. Great Nephew 126–Bundling (Petingo 135) (1982 — p 7g) Apr 1; half-sister to 3 winners, including 1m and 10.6f winner Boltingo (by Bold Lad, Ire); dam, half-sister to dam of Enstone Spark, won over 5f in Ireland; never-dangerous seventh of 21 behind Ski Sailing in maiden race at Newmarket in October; should do better. *I. Balding.*

WHIFFLING 2 br.f. Balidar 133–Whiffle 105 (King's Troop 118) (1982 6g 6f) — Apr 18; neat filly; half-sister to 1m and 1¼m winner Windpipe (by Leander); dam stayed 1m; remote sixth of 12 to Fenny Rough in minor event at Pontefract in September; unseated rider leaving stalls on debut; sold 460 gns Newmarket Autumn Sales and exported to Holland. *J. W. Watts.*

WHINSTONE 2 ch.c. Great Nephew 126–Irma Flintstone 110 (Compensation — 127) (1982 5g 6fg) Mar 30; fourth foal; dam 5f performer; little worthwhile form in minor events at Newcastle in April and Carlisle in July. *T. Fairhurst.*

WHISKAWAY 3 b.f. He Loves Me 120–Coming-of-Age 93 (Majority Blue 126) **61** (1981 NR 1982 10.5fg 11g² 10g 11fg² 8fg 8g 8g² 8g) 36,000Y; tall, leggy, sparely-made filly; half-sister to 2 winners, including fairly useful 5f to 1½m winner Oriental Star (by Falcon), and useful maiden Scigueta (by Prince Tenderfoot); dam 2-y-o 6f winner; second in maiden races and a minor event in Scotland; may stay 1½m; blinkered fifth start; sold to BBA 5,200 gns Newmarket December Sales. *J. Hindley.*

WHISKEY GO GO 6 ch.g. Grey Mirage 128–My Nan (Pampered King 121) — (1981 12s 12g³ 12g* 12g 13g 12fg 12.2s 1982 12g³ 11s) compact gelding; stays 1½m. *R. Morris.*

WHISKY TALK 2 b. or br.c. Wolverlife 115–Little Hills (Candy Cane 125) **91** p (1982 6d³) Mar 15; IR 72,000Y; tall, quite attractive colt; good walker; half-brother to 2 winners, notably top-class 7f to 1¼m winner Cairn Rouge (by Pitcairn); dam won over 1½m in Ireland and also over hurdles; 25/1, showed deal of promise when 2¼ lengths third of 13 behind comfortable winner Lyphard's Special in Champagne Stakes at Salisbury in June, running on in fine style from halfway; met with a set-back afterwards; will be suited by 7f+; sure to win a race. *I. Balding.*

WHISPER A WORD 5 ch.g. Most Secret 119–Wordrone (Worden II 129) **43** (1981 NR 1982 16fg 16fg 15.8f 12f² 15.8d) rangy gelding; poor maiden; seems to stay 2m; acts on firm going; used to wear blinkers. *G. Lockerbie.*

WHISPERED WISHES 2 br.f. High Top 131–Twill 89 (Crocket 130) (1982 **87** 5f* 5g³ 6s) Mar 23; 1,800Y; sturdy, good-bodied filly; half-sister to 2 winners, including successful 1m to 1½m performer Corduroy (by Hotfoot); dam stayed 1¼m; quickened clear to beat Ampersand by 1½ lengths after starting slowly in 11-runner maiden race at Newbury in July; 1½ lengths third of 6 to Broken Habit in nursery at Lingfield the following month; will stay 1m; acts on firm going; sold BBA (Italia) 9,600 gns Newmarket Autumn Sales. *H. Candy.*

WHISPER GENTLY 5 b.m. Pitskelly 122–Muraka (Off Key 121) (1981 12g — 12f 12fg 1982 10.2g 10fg 14fg 10fg 16.1g⁴) lightly-made mare; poor performer nowadays; stays 1½m; probably acts on any going; has worn blinkers; sold out of M. Francis' stable 680 gns Newmarket July Sales after fourth start. *D. Morrill.*

WHISTLE HILL 2 b.c. So Blessed 130–Sera Sera 88 (Hill Clown) (1982 6fg 6d **75** 7fg⁴ 8s) Feb 13; 5,400Y; third foal; half-brother to 11f winner Willerby (by

Great Nephew); dam 7f winner; 5 lengths fourth of 26 to Zaheendar in maiden race at Redcar in September; suited by 7f. *C. Thornton.*

WHISTLEPATH 4 ch.g. Warpath 113–Gentle Spring 118 (Gentle Art 121) — (1981 NR 1982 12f) 2,500Y; leggy gelding; half-brother to a minor winner; dam, a sprinter, at her best at 2 yrs; needed race when tailed-off last of 11 behind Dollymixture Boy in minor event at Thirsk in June. *J. Townson.*

WHITBY HIGH LIGHT 3 ro.f. Roan Rocket 128–Alive Alivo 77 (Never Say — Die 137) (1981 5fg 5fg 5f⁴ 5d 8f 7g 7d⁴ 1982 8fg⁴ 8f 7f 8f 13.8f 12g 8g 8.2v) sturdy filly; poor mover; poor maiden; blinkered third and fourth starts. *J. Calvert.*

WHITE MORNING 3 ch.f. Swing Easy 126–Carina Janie 88 (Silver Cloud 121) — (1981 5fg 5.8h 6fg 5g⁴ 5d 1982 8f 8g 8fg) poor form, including in sellers; has worn blinkers. *J. Cann.*

WHITE NILE (USA) 2 b.c. Upper Nile–Popaway (Cyclotron) (1982 5fg³ 7d) **73** Feb 18; $500,000Y; neat, strong, quite attractive colt; half-brother to numerous winners, including Sarasota Bay (by Allen Adair), a very useful colt at around 1m, and a minor stakes winner; dam never ran; sire, son of Nijinsky, was very smart winner at up to 1¼m at 4 yrs; 7½ lengths third of 7 to Fine Edge in maiden race at Newmarket in April; favourite, not persevered with after being hampered 2f out when 6½ lengths ninth of 18 behind The Quiet Don in similar event at Salisbury 2 months later; will be suited by 1m+. *F. Durr.*

WHITEOUT (USA) 2 b.f. It's Freezing 122–Indistinct (To Market) (1982 5fg **74** 7f 7g³ 8f 7f 8fg 7d) Feb 24; lengthy, quite useful sort; half-sister to 3 minor winners in USA; dam never ran; quite a moderate filly; stays 1m; disappointing; sold 3,600 gns Newmarket Autumn Sales. *G. Harwood.*

WHITE ROSAIRE 2 ch.f. Music Boy 124–Lady of York 75 (Double-U-Jay 120) — (1982 6fg) Mar 7; 3,300F, 6,800Y; first foal; dam won 3 times over 1½m; no show in 18-runner minor event at Redcar in September. *J. Winter.*

WHITE SPADE 2 b.c. Brigadier Gerard 144–Mattinata 90 (Matador 131) **119** (1982 5g² 5.5s² 6fg² 6.5g³ 8d* 10v⁴ 10v²) Jan 27; 9,400 gns F, 100,000 francs Y (approx £9,000); half-brother to several winners, including useful 1978 2-y-o 7f winner Chalumeau (by Relko); dam 5f sprinter; put up best effort when 9/1-shot for 12-runner Criterium de Saint-Cloud in November on final start, finishing strongly to take second place, 1½ lengths behind Escaline; had previously run consistently well, winning 15-runner minor event at Maisons-Laffitte in September by 2½ lengths from Un Monsieur and finishing about 5 lengths fourth to Nile Hawk in Prix de Conde at Longchamp in October; improved with distance and may well stay 1½m; acts well on heavy ground. *D. Smaga, France.*

WHITE VALLEY (USA) 2 b.f. Far North 120–Pink Valley 112 (Never Bend) **?** (1982 8s*) Jan 30; first foal; dam, half-sister to Green Dancer and Ercolano, was very useful winner over 7f and 1m in France; always prominent when winning 11-runner newcomers event at Longchamp in October gamely by ¾ length from Luth Enchantee; will probably stay 1¼m; a very well-bred filly who should go on to better things. *A. Head, France.*

WHITEWALLS 2 b.c. Pitskelly 122–More The Perrier (Rarity 129) (1982 **71** 5f 5g 6f 5g 5d⁴ 6s 5d³) Apr 26; 3,000F; sturdy colt; poor walker and mover; second produce; dam never ran; in frame in the autumn in maiden race at Nottingham and seller at Catterick; should stay at least 6f. *G. Toft.*

WHITSTAR 2 b.f. Whitstead 125–Reita 87 (Gilles de Retz 132) (1982 8g 10.2s*) **93 p** Apr 24; 8,600Y; strong, well-made filly; half-sister to several winners, including fair 3-y-o 1¼m winner Hill's Pageant (by Welsh Pageant) and very useful 6f and 1¼m winner Homeboy (by King's Troop); dam miler; stepped up considerably on debut effort 3 weeks previously when winning 15-runner minor event at Doncaster in November by 4 lengths from Holy Spark; stays well; acts on soft going; promises to make a useful 3-y-o. *M. Jarvis.*

WHITTINGTON (USA) 4 b.g. Best Turn–Novee (Judgable) (1981 12g **42** 10.1f 10.1fg 10f 8.2f³ 8f 9g 1982 8g 8g³ 12fg⁴) workmanlike gelding; in frame in sellers; stays 1¼m; acts on any going. *G. Balding.*

WHITTON 3 b.g. Kemal 120–Star Clipper (Polly's Jet) (1981 5s 5s⁴ 5g³ 5g 6g 1982 13.8f) light-framed gelding; poor form, including in a seller; has had tongue tied down. *J. Mason.*

Queen Mary Stakes, Ascot—Widaad accounts for twelve previous winners;
Crime of Passion is second, Annie Edge dead-heats for third

WHITWORTH   4 ch.g. Hot Spark 126–Clarity 98 (Panaslipper 130)   (1981 14g   **68**
12f 13.8fg* 13fg² 12.3fg³ 13.8g² 16f⁴ 13.8g⁴ 13fg* 16g   1982 12f 12.3fg² 12f³
14f² 12fg³ 15.8f⁴ 12f⁴ 12f³ 11.7g³ 12fg³)   rangy gelding; has been hobdayed; in
frame in handicaps on most outings; looks short of pace when racing over 1¼m
and stays 2m; probably acts on any going but is evidently well suited by firm;
possibly requires a strong gallop; blinkered last start. *D. Morley.*

WIBIS RANGE   3 b.c. Wolver Hollow 126–Polonaise (Takawalk II 125)   (1981   **76**
6g 7.2d 6fg² 7f*   1982 7g* 8fg⁴ 10f 8.2f 8d 7.2g⁴ 8g 7fg⁴ 10f³ 8g⁴ 10.6f)   tall colt;
beat Houghton Weaver by a length in Northern Free Handicap at Newcastle in
April; not disgraced in handicaps several subsequent starts; stays 1¼m; acts on
firm going. *M. Naughton.*

WICKED WAVE (USA)   3 b.f. North Sea–Simply Furious (Delta Judge) · ?
(1981 5g? 7.0g* 8g 8f₅ 8f₅ 8fg³ 8g³ 7.9s   1982 including 6g 6fg 5.8f⁴ 7f*)   sturdy
ex-English filly; good walker; fairly useful at 2 yrs; soundly beaten first 3 starts
in 1982 when trained by M. Francis but did well after being sent to USA, winning
at least 3 times including Caesar's Wish Handicap at Bowie in September;
evidently stays 7f; seems to act on any going. *G. Wilson, USA.*

WICKWELL   9 b.g. Wolver Hollow 126–Wise Counsel (Counsel 118)   (1981 12g⁴   —
10.6s* 9g 10f 12fg³ 10.6s   1982 12fg)   poor handicapper; stays 1½m; acts on any
going; good mount for an inexperienced rider; inconsistent and doesn't find much
off bridle. *A. W. Jones.*

WIDAAD (USA)   2 b.f. Mr Prospector–Attache Case (Diplomat Way)   (1982   **109**
5f* 5fg* 6f 5f³ 6g⁴)
    Widaad's win in the Queen Mary Stakes at Royal Ascot was as good as any-
thing she achieved although it came on only the second of her five appearances.
Widaad started favourite on the strength of a very easy success in a maiden race
at Sandown the previous month where she had looked fit, impressed in her
slower paces and had beaten Myra's Best by four lengths. The main dangers
to Widaad in a field that included twelve other winners appeared to be Shicklah,
Deportment and Crime of Passion, each undefeated in two runs, and Annie Edge,
runner-up to Crime of Passion in a minor event at Newbury. These filled four of
the first five places behind Widaad who won with authority. She was never
far off the pace, went slightly to her right when sent to challenge over a furlong
out and stayed on to beat Crime of Passion by a length and a half. Widaad
had to concede weight all round in the Cherry Hinton Stakes at Newmarket
the following month but even so was below her best in finishing fifth, about
five and a half lengths behind Crime of Passion. She hung to her left this time
when asked to quicken and her response was disappointing. Widaad was next
seen out in the autumn and wasn't disgraced in the Flying Childers Stakes and the
William Hill Cheveley Park Stakes, running on to finish over two lengths third
to Kafu and under five lengths fourth to Ma Biche respectively. Those were

Maktoum Al-Maktoum's "Widaad"

Widaad's last appearances on a racecourse for she was retired afterwards. We're not particularly surprised at that as she appeared nervous in her races after Royal Ascot, sweating up beforehand on each occasion, and the best had probably been seen of her already. She took a strong hold on the way to the start of the Cherry Hinton Stakes and was taken down very steadily before the Cheveley Park.

		Raise A Native (ch 1961)	Native Dancer
	Mr Prospector (b 1970)		Raise You
		Gold Digger (b 1962)	Nashua
Widaad (USA) (b.f. Mar 28, 1980)			Sequence
		Diplomat Way (b 1964)	Nashua
	Attache Case (b 1970)		Jandy
		Old Bess (b 1948)	Vincentive
			Movie Lass

Widaad is by the popular American stallion Mr Prospector, sire of Conquistador Cielo and successful European performers Miswaki, Hello Gorgeous, Diamond Prospect and Proclaim. She cost 220,000 dollars as a yearling and comes from a successful line of broodmares: she is the fifth winner from as many foals of racing age for her dam Attache Case, herself one of twelve winners from Old Bess's thirteen foals to race including stakes winners in the United States and Puerto Rico. The third dam Movie Lass produced ten winners from twelve foals. Widaad, a quite attractive filly, is her dam's first pattern or stakes winner. A good mover, she stayed six furlongs and raced only on a sound surface. *M. Stoute.*

WIDD 5 b.g. Derring-Do 131–Tin Mary 96 (Tin King 126) (1981 6g 7.6g³ 7g* 8.5g 7f 8f 1982 7fg 7g 8fg⁴) workmanlike gelding; poor handicapper nowadays; well suited by 7f and should stay 1m; seems to act on any going; blinkered once at 3 yrs. *M. Masson.*

WIDE MISSOURI 2 br.c. Warpath 113–Shenandoah 88 (Mossborough 126)   — p
(1982 6d 6s) May 16; small, lengthy colt; good walker; brother to 2 minor
winners; dam won over 14.7f, and is half-sister to very useful Sovereign Edition;
missed break when soundly beaten in late-season maiden events at Doncaster;
will be much better suited by 1¼m + ; should improve. *C. Thornton.*

WIDOW BIRD 2 ch.f. Vitiges 132–Grass Widow (Thatch 136) (1982 5f*   **84**
6fg³ 5g 5s) Apr 8; neat filly; second foal; half-sister to 3-y-o 6f and 7f winner
Trooper Sergeant (by Queen's Hussar); dam unraced half-sister to high-class
1973 2-y-o The Blues; made all to win 13-runner maiden race at Nottingham
in April by 3 lengths from Winning Tender; creditable 2½ lengths third of 12 to
West Wellow in nursery at Salisbury in September, only subsequent form;
suited by 6f; acts well on firm going. *H. Candy.*

WIKI WIKI WHEELS 2 ch.c. Import 127–Falcrello 51 (Falcon 131) (1982   **98**
6d⁴ 5.8g* 6fg* 6fg 5g* 6f² 5g* 5v) Mar 25; 3,500Y; strong, quite attractive colt;
first foal; dam won 11f seller; had a fine season, winning maiden auction event at
Bath, minor race at Hamilton, nursery at Newcastle and valuable Champagne
Louis Roederer Trophy (nursery) at Newbury; out of his depth in Cornwallis
Stakes at Ascot on final appearance; effective at 5f and 6f; acts on firm going;
genuine and consistent. *C. Nelson.*

WILD COAST 2 b.g. African Sky 124–No Such Luck (Prince Regent 129)   **92**
(1982 5fg⁴ 5fg² 5fg³ 5g² 5s² 5d*) Apr 2; 7,400Y; smallish gelding; first foal;
dam never ran; runner-up in maiden races and a nursery prior to winning
8-runner maiden auction event at Catterick in October by a length from Kynaston; will stay 6f; has run respectably on a firm surface but is better on soft
ground; sold 5,000 gns Newmarket Autumn Sales. *R. Armstrong.*

WILDHORN 2 ch.g. Midsummer Night II 117–She's the One (Sword Dancer)   **81**
(1982 6fg 7d 7fg³ 7g² 7g) May 25; 6,600Y; well-made gelding; first foal; dam,
daughter of very smart Fall In Love, won small races over 7f and 9f in France;
placed in maiden race and a nursery in the summer; will be suited by 1m; not
particularly consistent; gelded after final outing. *H. Candy.*

WILD PRINCESS 3 b.f. Free State 125–Marita (Right Royal V 135)   **69**
6fg 6g 10fg 10fg 12v² 12d) smallish filly; second in maiden race at Hamilton
in October; reportedly struck into when virtually pulled up in valuable seller
at Doncaster later in month; suited by 1½m; sold 4,200 gns Newmarket December
Sales. *B. Hills.*

WILD PUMPKIN 5 b.m. Auction Ring 123–Wild Thyme 63 (Galivanter 131)   —
(1981 8f 10f 16fg⁴ 16 5f 12g³ 16fg 1002 12g) lengthy, narrow mare; plating-
class maiden; stays well. *P. Ashworth.*

WILDRUSH 3 b.g. Free State 125–Ribble Reed 75 (Bullrush 106) (1981 5fg   —
6fg 7g³ 7fg 1982 8g 8.2v 8f 10fg) big gelding; poor maiden on balance of form;
best run at 7f though should stay further; sometimes sweats up. *W. C. Watts.*

WILLAWAY 4 b.f. Willipeg 112–Pontesbury (Falls of Clyde 126) (1981 6fg   —
5fg 5g 5s 5s 1982 5fg 6g 5fg 5g⁴ 12d) rather plain filly; showed first form when
fourth in all-aged seller at Beverley in September; usually to stay 1½m; blinkered
third and fourth outings; usually bandaged in front. *D. Ancil.*

WILL BE WANTON 2 b.f. Palm Track 122–Immodest Miss 73 (Daring Display   **64**
129) (1982 6f 6f 6fg 8fg 7.2s 6s 6s³ 6s 6s) Apr 14; small filly; first foal; dam
won 1¼m seller; plater; ran best race on sixth start when 5½ lengths fifth of 22
to Blue Nantucket in £3,600 event at York in October; evidently best at 6f;
inconsistent. *R. Hollinshead.*

WILLERBY 5 b.g. Great Nephew 126–Sera Sera 88 (Hill Clown) (1981 10.2fg   **39**
10f 10f 11d 8g 1982 11fg* 13fg 8f³ 11g 12fg⁴ 11fg 10fg) neat gelding; bought
in 2,100 gns after winning selling handicap at Edinburgh in April; had stiff tasks
on occasions afterwards; stays 11f; acts on firm going. *T. Craig.*

WILL GEORGE 3 br.g. Abwah 118–Grey Miss 72 (Grey Sovereign 128§) (1981   **75**
5v 5g³ 5g 5g 5fg 5f 6g⁴ 5f² 5f 5f² 5fg⁴ 5f* 5d* 5g 1982 5f 5f 5f 5f 5fg³ 5fg 5g 5f
5fg* 6f 5s*) leggy gelding; poor mover; plater; made all to win in better company at Windsor in August and Doncaster in November; best at 5f; acts on any
going; usually blinkered; suitable mount for an apprentice; sold out of K.
Stone's stable 3,500 gns Ascot August Sales after ninth start and ran for Mrs N.
Smith next time. *R. Akehurst.*

WILL GULF 5 ch.g. Gulf Pearl 117–Gwen Somers (Will Somers 114§) (1981   —
10d 12s 1982 12d 12s) strong gelding; plater; stays 1m well; acts on firm
going; often blinkered; sold 440 gns Doncaster August Sales. *T. Kersey.*

WILLIE GAN 4 ch.g. McIndoe 97–Queen's Bay 73 (King's Troop 118) (1981   **56**
6s² 5g* 5f 5f 5fg⁴ 5g 5g² 5fg* 6s 8d   1982 11s 7f³ 6f* 6fg* 6f⁴ 6g) quite a useful
sort; made most in handicaps at Thirsk (apprentice event) and Newcastle (in
really good style by 5 lengths from Welsh Noble), best efforts; not seen out after
May; stays 7f; acts on any going, but seems well suited by a sound surface;
suitable mount for an apprentice. *D. Smith.*

WILLOWBED 2 gr.f. Wollow 132–Abergrove 103 (Abernant 142) (1982 6d)   – p
Apr 22; 20,000Y; half-sister to 2 winners, including fairly useful stayer Marzook
(by Blakeney); dam best at 6f; never-dangerous seventh of 9 in maiden race at
Brighton in October. *J. Dunlop.*

WILLOWBROOK WORLD 3 ch.g. Free State 125–Jantu 81 (Deep Diver 134)   —
(1981 5fg 7g 8s   1982 10f 10f 10d 10.8fg) small, good-bodied gelding; poor
maiden; sold 800 gns Doncaster October Sales. *W. Wharton.*

WILLOW RED 6 ch.g. Red Alert 127–Willow Bird 74 (Weepers Boy 124)   **55**
(1981 NR 1982 11.7fg² 10fg 10fg³ 8d) workmanlike gelding; poor handicapper
nowadays; stays 1½m, and finds 1m on short side; acts on any going but is very
well suited by some give in the ground; usually blinkered; not the easiest of
rides. *G. Thorner.*

WILLSPAL 4 ch c. Firestreak 125–Beauklarion (Klairon 131) (1981 10s* 12g⁴   —
12.5f³ 10g³ 10f 12.3g³ 10g 10d 11d⁴ 10s   1982 10g 12.3fg) plater; stays 1½m; .
seems to act on any going; occasionally blinkered. *W. Barrett.*

WILLY JAMES 2 br.c. Blue Cashmere 129–Seadora 68 (Sea Hawk II 131)   **82**
(1982 5fg⁴ 5f² 5.1g* 5fg³ 5fg³ 5fg⁴ 6d 7s) Mar 12; 4,600Y; rangy, attractive
colt; not a good mover in his slower paces; third foal; dam stayed 1½m; won
maiden auction event at Yarmouth in June; placed subsequently in nurseries
at Wolverhampton and Nottingham; should be suited by 6f; apparently not at
his best on a soft surface. *R. Armstrong.*

WILLYPOUS 2 b.c. Tachypous 128–Daughter of Song 73 (Song 132) (1982   **56**
6d 6fg 7d 7g 5d 7g 6d) Apr 21; 6,800Y; sturdy colt; third foal; half-brother
to 5f winner Gorgeous Girl (by Dragonara Palace); dam won 5f seller; plating-
class maiden; best run at 7f. *R. Hollinshead.*

WILLY WITEFOOT ESQ 3 ch.g. Hotfoot 126–Mountain of Mourne 87   —
(Mountain Call 125) (1981 7g 7d 1982 10d 12.3fg⁴ 10f) rather lightly-made
gelding; middle-distance handicapper. *M. Jarvis.*

WILTON BEACON 6 br.g. Goldhill 125–Daylight 92 (Princely Gift 137)   —
(1981 NR 1982 15.8g) poor performer; best run at 1m; blinkered final start
in 1980. *J. Harris.*

WILTSHIRE YEOMAN 2 ch.c. Derrylin 115–Ribo Pride 77 (Ribero 126)   **82 p**
(1982 8s³) May 5; third foal; dam won over 1½m; 33/1, stuck on well when
3 lengths third of 14, clear of remainder, to Broad Beam in maiden event at
Leicester in November; capable of winning small race. *J. Fox.*

WIMBLEDON'S PET 3 b.f. Mummy's Pet 125–Wimbledon 105 (Abernant   —
142) (1981 5d⁴ 5f 6f 6d 5s   1982 8fg 7f 6d 6s 6s) compact filly; poor maiden;
blinkered second start. *Miss A. Hill-Wood.*

WIMPY FRANKHART 2 b.g. Relkino 131–Colony 93 (Constable 119) (1982   —
7g 6g 7fg) Mar 9; rangy gelding; half-brother to several winners, including
useful French sprinter Porto (by Klairon); dam 2-y-o 5f winner; behind in
maiden and minor events. *T. Gosling.*

WIMSEY 5 b.g. Run The Gantlet–Bell Song 101 (Tudor Melody 129) (1981   —
15.5d 15.5d 16d   1982 15.5fg 12d) staying handicapper; sometimes blinkered;
sold 1,250 gns Ascot November Sales. *R. Hoad.*

WINART 4 br.c. Scottish Rifle 127–Alice (Parthia 132) (1981 8.2s* 10s² 10.4g⁴   **77**
9s³ 8d³ 8d* 10d³   1982 8g³ 8fg³ 8f 8g² 8s² 8.2s) neat colt; poor mover; fair
handicapper; in frame in William Hill Lincoln at Doncaster, Newbury Spring
Cup and quite valuable races at Ascot and Newcastle; stays 1¼m; acts on a
firm surface but is well suited by some give underfoot; possibly not the most
genuine of colts. *G. Pritchard-Gordon.*

WIND AND WUTHERING (USA) 3 br.c. No Robbery–J.A's Joy (Johns Joy) **127**
(1981 5fg* 5g* 6fg 6fg⁴ 7f⁴ 7.6g² 7g* 7g* 1982 7fg⁴ 8fg² 8g 8fg)
   The time for the Two Thousand Guineas was a fast one, the fastest since
My Babu equalled the course record in 1948, thanks in no small measure to
Wind and Wuthering's presence in the field. He set a gallop up the centre of

Mr R. M. Cyzer's "Wind and Wuthering"

the course that quickly had the opposition well strung out, and he sustained it right to the end after coming under the whip fully two furlongs from home. Of those who attempted to stick close from the race's early stages only Zino didn't run himself out; even he required almost the full length of the Rowley Mile to get his head in front, with Wind and Wuthering still strong enough at the finish to hold off Tender King by two lengths for second place.

Here we saw the best of Wind and Wuthering once again after a disappointing fourth to Cajun in the Clerical, Medical Greenham Stakes on his seasonal re-appearance which his trainer attributed to a lack of fitness. His form in his last two races as a two-year-old, particularly in his last, the William Hill Dewhurst Stakes, had been a revelation. Wind and Wuthering won the Dewhurst by the staggering margin of seven lengths from Be My Native and Tender King, making all with obvious enthusiasm; as a result he received second top weight behind the Grand Criterium winner Green Forest in the International Classification and came strongly into the reckoning for the Guineas. Having signalled his return to form in such an admirable fashion in the Guineas, giving one of the most genuine performances we'd seen for a long time, the way looked clear for Wind and Wuthering to gain compensation in the Airlie/Coolmore Irish Two Thousand Guineas and to enjoy the kind of season that had been widely predicted for him the previous autumn. In fact, he was retired to stud at the end of the year with nothing more to show; he ran only in the Irish Guineas and the St James's Palace Stakes at Royal Ascot. He missed fourth-place money by only a short head in Ireland but didn't give his running; he was nowhere near so strong at the finish as at Newmarket, despite having shown no sign whatever of his hard race there in the paddock beforehand, and although he took over in the lead from Full Extent halfway up the straight the writing was soon on the wall as Anfield, Red Sunset, Tender King and then Dara Monarch came at him. A most convincing winner beat him by five lengths. When the two horses met again at Royal Ascot the result went even more emphatically in Dara Monarch's favour. Wind and Wuthering, who again couldn't be faulted in appearance, set a good pace until quickly overwhelmed by Red Sunset, Ivano and Dara Monarch two furlongs out; he had dropped out to seventh of nine by the finish.

Wind and Wuthering remained in training, and as late as October was said to be a possible starter for the Dubai Champion Stakes but that same month it was announced he had been sold to America and would be standing at Mint Lane Farm near Lexington in 1983.

		Swaps	Khaled
	No Robbery	(ch 1952)	Iron Reward
	(b 1960)	Bimlette	Bimelech
Wind and Wuthering (USA)		(b 1944)	Bloodroot
(br.c. 1979)		Johns Joy	Bull Dog
	J.A's Joy	(br 1946)	My Auntie
	(b or br 1965)	Belle Rebelle	Count Fleet
		(br 1950)	Gala Belle

Since Wind and Wuthering's breeding will be considerably more familiar in America than in Britain that's perhaps where his best prospects of becoming established as a stallion lie. He was the ninth North American-bred winner of the Dewhurst Stakes in fourteen years, not a blue-blooded individual like his predecessors who included Nijinsky, The Minstrel and Storm Bird, but tolerably well bred nevertheless. His sire, due to stand at 15,000 dollars live foal at the age of twenty-three in 1983, had actually sired a higher percentage of winners to foals (69% against 64%) by the end of 1981 than the great Northern Dancer whose stud career has spanned the same period as his own. The percentage of stakes winners (10% against 21%) puts a different complexion on things, but No Robbery did have another good horse representing him in the latest season, the American mare Track Robbery whose earnings have now topped the million-dollar mark; No Robbery's best previous winner in England, almost the only one, was the John Smith's Magnet Cup winner Bold Pirate, a very useful horse at up to a mile and a quarter. Wind and Wuthering's dam produced five previous winners, all in the United States, including the stakes-winning sprinting filly Mitos Joy (by Mito), and her two-year-old is the useful English colt Joy Hour. The next dam was a winning half-sister to several good horses, one of them the very successful sire Revoked, another the Kentucky Oaks runner-up Galarullah.

Wind and Wuthering would have been an interesting candidate for the Champion Stakes. He wasn't certain to stay a mile and a quarter, particularly if asked to force the pace in the way that suited him at seven furlongs and a mile, but he would have had softish ground for the first time in his career. Though he ran such a fine race in the Guineas on top-of-the-ground he often gave us the impression that he would be seen to better advantage on soft; to tell the truth, we were looking forward all summer and autumn to taking a big price about him when he reappeared in a good race on soft. Wind and Wuthering was a tall, quite attractive, lengthy colt, a particularly good walker. While his courage was never in doubt, his consistency left something to be desired. *H. Candy.*

WINDIER 3 b.f. Luthier 126–Winden (Worden II 129) (1981 6fg 7d 1982 **64** 8f 12f³ 12f³ 12g⁴ 14d³ 12fg) tall, rather narrow filly; third in maiden races; will stay 2m; one paced; sold to BBA 10,000 gns Newmarket December Sales. *P. Walwyn.*

WINDMILLS 3 ch.c. Red Alert 127–Nice Tack 106 (Hard Tack 111§) (1981 — 5g⁴ 5d 5g* 6d 6fg 5fg⁴ 5.1d² 5d 6fg 5g 6s 1982 5f 5.8f 7.3fg 7f) smallish, sturdy colt; fair in 1981; beat only one horse home in his 4 races at 3 yrs and is one to be wary of; form only at 5f; blinkered second outing. *S. Matthews.*

WINDPIPE 4 ch.g. Leander 119–Whiffle 105 (King's Troop 118) (1981 8g* **64** 8g* 8g³ 10g* 11g³ 10fg 10f 8g* 1982 8f 8g² 8f 8fg² 8fg² 8d³ 8d² 7s) workmanlike gelding; quite a moderate handicapper; close second 4 times at Ayr; well beaten third start; may well prove suited by a return to 1¼m; occasionally blinkered (has won in them). *J. W. Watts.*

WINDSOR BRIDGE 3 b.f. Swing Easy 126–Grecian Bridge 90 (Acropolis 132) — (1981 6fg 6fg 6fg³ 6g 6d 7d 1982 7d 7f) attractive, good-bodied filly; good walker; quite moderate at her best; probably stays 7f; blinkered nowadays; sold 6,000 gns Goffs September Sales. *H. T. Jones.*

WINDYHAUGH 2 b. or br.g. Porto Bello 118–Carolinda 63 (Grand Roi 118) — (1982 5d 7g 6g) June 3; 2,000 2-y-o (privately); first foal; dam ran only 4 times; behind in maiden and minor events, twice last. *M. Haynes.*

WINDY LAD 3 ch.c. Tumble Wind–Bold Bird (Bold Lad, Ire 133) (1981 5s* — 5d⁴ 5fg 5g 5v* 5s⁴ 6f 5fg⁴ 5d 5d 5s 1982 5d 5d 8f 5.3g 5fg 5d) compact colt;

poor handicapper nowadays; unlikely to stay 1m; revels in the mud; has twice worn blinkers; trained by J. Jenkins first 4 starts and was sold out of R. Price's stable 2,200 gns Doncaster September Sales after fifth. *S. Matthews.*

WINGED DAGGER 13 b.g. Falcon 131–Gay Natasha 105 (Prince Chevalier)   —
(1981 12d 12g³ 12d 1982 11.7f⁴ 12fg² 12fg) middle-distance handicapper; in lead when eased up close home (jockey thought he'd gone lame) when fourth in race won by Traditional Miss at Bath in April; acts on any going but is suited by a sound surface; has worn blinkers; suitable mount for an apprentice. *J. Old.*

WINGSOFTHEMORNING 5 b. or br.g. Solar Topic 97–Narratus 94 (Narrator   —
127) (1981 NR 1982 18d) lightly-made gelding; half-brother to winning stayer Blue Chrome (by Hot Brandy); dam won Chester Cup; novice hurdler; faded in last 3f when eighth of 13 behind Bajan Sunshine in minor event at Doncaster in October. *A. Madwar.*

WINKING FIELDS 6 ch.g. Northfields–Winky Joe (Eudaemon 129) (1981   —
11d 1982 12fg) poor plater; has worn blinkers; wears a tongue strap; sold to E. Alston 520 gns Doncaster November Sales. *D. Weeden.*

WINK (USA) 3 b.f. Forli–Glisk (Buckpasser) (1981 6g* 7d 6fg² 6g³ 6d* **101**
1982 7fg 8g² 8.5f² 7f² 8fg² 8f⁴) rangy filly; runner-up 4 times, going down by 2¼ lengths to ready winner Chalon in International Fillies Stakes at Kempton, by ½ length to Dalmally in NMT Ebbisham Stakes (Handicap) at Epsom, by ¾ length to Chalon again in Oak Tree Stakes at Goodwood and by 8 lengths to Main Sail in £4,400 event at Sandown; will stay 1¼m; seems to act on any going; suited by waiting tactics. *J. Dunlop.*

WINNER TAKES ALL 5 b.h. Singing Bede 122–Julita 87 (Rockavon 120)   **48**
(1981 6s 6s 6d³ 5s² 6d 7s⁴ 5fg 6f 7f 6f 6g² 6f 6g* 7g 1982 6s 5fg⁴ 5g⁴ 7f³ 6g 7fg 6f 6v 5s) poor handicapper; third in a seller fourth start; stays 7f; acts on any going; blinkered nowadays; has run respectably for a boy. *D. Marks.*

WINNINGS THE GAME 4 b.f. Workboy 123–Pams Choice 87 (Mandamus 120)   —
(1981 5g 5g 8.2d 7g 8g 8f 8.2f 1982 8fg 6fg 9f 8g 10g) poor plater; yet to prove she stays beyond sprint distances; sold 400 gns Doncaster November Sales. *T. Taylor.*

WINNING TENDER 2 br.f. Mansingh 120–Godhood 86 (Green God 128)   **66** d
(1982 5fg⁴ 5f² 5g 6f 5.8f 5g² 5.1d⁴ 5g) Apr 13; 1,150F, 1,500Y; small, narrow, lightly-made filly; first foal; dam 2-y-o 6f winner; only 3 lengths off the winner in maiden events at Newmarket and Nottingham on first 2 appearances, but couldn't win sellers; seems best at 5f; acts on firm going; trained by R. Boss first 4 outings; sold 330 gns Ascot October Sales. *M. Blanshard.*

WINOLA (USA) 3 b.f. Windsor Ruler–Omalio (Restless Wind) (1981 7g 6g   —
1982 7d 8g 8fg 8fg 8f 6v 6g) $15,000 2-y-o; narrow, lightly-made ex-Irish filly; half-sister to 2 minor winners in USA by Gladwin; dam won over 6f; behind in varied company; trained by T. Conroy first 2 starts. *D. Wilson.*

WIN SHOON PLEASE 3 gr.f. Sheshoon 132–Windsor Walk (Sovereign Path   —
125) (1981 NR 1982 10s 8g 10f 12fg 10d 12s) leggy, plain filly; fifth foal; dam unraced half-sister to speedy Song of Songs; poor plater. *M. Ryan.*

WINTERGRACE (USA) 3 ch.f. Northern Dancer–Stylish Pattern (My Babu   **69**
136) (1981 6fg² 6d³ 1982 8fg 8s* 8f³) lengthy, unfurnished filly; short-priced favourite when narrowly winning maiden race at Pontefract in June; will stay middle distances; acts on any going. *H. Cecil.*

WINTER QUEEN 3 ch.f. Welsh Pageant 132–Snow Habit (Habitat 134)   **60**
(1981 NR 1982 7fg 7.6fg 8d 10.1fg 8f 9g³ 12s²) 17,500Y; deep-girthed, workmanlike ex-English filly; third foal; half-sister to 7f winner Snow Maid (by High Top) and a winner in Scandinavia; dam placed over 6f at 2 yrs in France; placed in maiden races at Gowran Park and Thurles in the autumn; neck behind Standing Ovation on latter; suited by 1½m; acts on soft going; blinkered fifth start; trained by D. Whelan first 5 outings. *J. Oxx, Ireland.*

WINTERREISE 4 b.g. Fine Blade 121–Pouilly Fuse (Tudor Music 131) (1981   **55**
8g 8g 10.2g 9s 13g 12.3g 10fg 9s³ 1982 12g 11f 12d 12f³ 11g* 12g) strong gelding; showed improved form when winning minor event at Hamilton in July; looked as if he might need race and moved badly to start when well beaten only subsequent start; stays 1½m. *W. Bentley.*

WINTER WIND 6 b.h. Tumble Wind–Northern Beauty (Borealis) (1981 5s³   **96**
6s* 6g 6g* 6s² 6fs 6g⁴ 6fg 6v 6g 1982 6g* 6d* 6f 6d* 6g 6s) very attractive horse; good mover with a nice, easy action; sprint handicapper; won at Catterick and Nottingham (twice); dead-heated with Camisite in £6,400 Home Ales Gold

Tankard on latter in June for last win; towards rear on his other starts but was hampered on last occasion; acts on any going but seems suited by some give in the ground nowadays; blinkered once at 3 yrs; needs to be held up and goes well for B. Raymond; trained until after third start by D. Kent; sold 15,000 gns Newmarket Autumn Sales. *P. Haynes.*

WINTER WORDS 3 b.c. Wollow 132–Prinia 77 (On Your Mark 125) (1981 5f⁴   **92** 5f² 6fg* 6fg⁴ 6g² 6g 7g 1982 7g³ 7fg³ 7f 7g) close-coupled, quite useful sort; none too good a mover; creditable third in handicaps at Newmarket in April and May, making running each time and being beaten a length by Shaady and 4¼ lengths by Chalon respectively; will stay 1m; yet to race on a soft surface; sold to Mrs C. Lloyd-Jones 3,500 gns Ascot October Sales. *G. Pritchard-Gordon.*

WIPPIN CRUST (USA) 3 ch.c. Balompie 122–Song of Life (Personality)   **72** (1981 7f 7fg 8g 1982 12s² 16f* 16.1h 17fg 19f) compact colt; won maiden race at Beverley in April; ran poorly afterwards; was suited by a test of stamina; acted on any going; sometimes raced with tongue tied down; dead. *I. Walker.*

WISE CHOICE 3 b.f. Sagaro 133–Light Duty 113 (Queen's Hussar 124) (1981   — 7g 1982 11.7g) leggy, rather plain filly; beaten a long way in 2 maiden races; sold 44,000 gns Newmarket December Sales. *R. Hern.*

WISE OWL 5 ch.h. Crowned Prince 128–Tawny Owl 123 (Faberge II 121)   **72** (1981 10g² 10g⁴ 10.1fg² 10.6d² 10d⁴ 1982 10d⁴ 8f 10.1d² 9g) good-looking horse; disappointing and ungenuine maiden; stays 1¼m; acts on a firm and a soft surface. *H. Wragg.*

WISE SOLUTION 3 ch.g. Solution–Miss Worden 40 (Worden II 129) (1981   — 5d 6f 1982 8f³ 10g 10v) plater; best run at 1m on firm going; has been tried in blinkers. *B. Wise.*

WISE SPECULATION (USA) 2 ch.f. Mr Prospector–Wisdom (Hail to Reason)   — (1982 5d 5fg) Apr 15; useful-looking filly; first foal; dam, winner of 6f maiden race at 3 yrs, is daughter of Taken Aback, a very smart winner at up to 9f; well beaten in maiden races at Nottingham in June and Edinburgh in July. *P. Calver.*

WISH YOU LUCK 2 b.f. Faraway Son 130–Wow 106 (Baldric II 131) (1982   **94** 6g 6f² 6d* 6s⁴) Apr 19; half-sister to useful 1979 2-y-o 5f and 6f winner Why Not (by Dancer's Image); dam won over 1¼m; won 14-runner maiden race at Navan in September by a length from Blue Image; evens favourite, slowly away when 3 lengths fourth of 13 to subsequently-demoted Bay Empress in minor event at Punchestown the following month; will be suited by 1m+. *D. O'Brien, Ireland.*

WITCH'S POINT 3 br.c. Lochnager 132–Vacation 102 (Remainder 106) (1981   **68** 5v³ 5g*(dis) 5g² 5g³ 6f⁴ 5g² 6g 5fg² 5g 6s³ 1982 5f 5f 7f² 8fg 7f⁴ 7g³ 7fg* 7f³ 7g 7fg 7d 7d) useful sort; won handicap at Redcar in July; stays 7f; acts on any going; often blinkered (was at Redcar). *M. H. Easterby.*

WITCHY WOMAN 2 br.f. Broxted 120–Minibus 77 (John Splendid 116)   — (1982 6s) Mar 16; poor walker; second foal; dam won over 6f; well beaten after slow start in 19-runner maiden race at Leicester in November. *C. Crossley.*

WITHERIDGE HILL 4 b.f. Porto Bello 118–Bud's Promise 68 (Runnymede   — 123) (1981 NR 1982 12f 7g) sturdy, compact filly; third foal; dam plating class at 2 yrs; gave trouble at start and was tailed off in minor events at Thirsk and Folkestone in June; sold 480 gns Ascot August Sales. *D. Dale.*

WIVETON 4 br.g. Blakeney 126–Wolverene 114 (Relko 136) (1981 8fg* 13.3g³   **90** 14d² 14g 10d³ 10d³ 1982 10.6g* 11.5f² 10.6g* 12g² 12fg* 12g 10g) useful-looking gelding; fairly useful handicapper; won at Haydock in July and August and at Doncaster in September, beating Keelby Kavalier gamely by a head on latter course; also a very close second at Sandown and Epsom (apprentice event); stays 1¾m but is effective at much shorter distances; yet to race on very soft going, but acts on any other. *W. Hastings-Bass.*

WOE BETIDE 2 ch.g. Lucky Wednesday 124–Fear Not 106 (Faubourg II 127)   **73** (1982 7.2g 7g⁴ 7fg 8.2v⁴ 7d) June 19; short-coupled gelding; fourth reported live foal; dam won at up to 1m; fourth in £3,600 event at York in September and nursery at Hamilton in October; stays 1m; acts on heavy going; blinkered final outing; subsequently gelded. *W. Elsey.*

WOJO 2 b.g. Royal Palace 131–Spring Running 91 (Nearula 132) (1982 6f 7f   **67** 8.2fg 6g⁴ 10d² 10s⁴) June 7; sturdy, good sort; half-brother to several winners, including useful 1m to 1¼m winner Ring Time II (by Pardal); dam won at up to 1½m; plater; ¾-length second to Pledgdon Green at Pontefract in

October; good fourth in maiden race at Nottingham later in the month; suited by 1¼m, and will stay further; acts on soft going; wears blinkers; gelded at end of season. *M. Ryan.*

WOLFIE 3 ch.g. Wolverlife 115–Apair (Red Slipper 126) (1981 NR 1982 8g⁴ 8f³ 9.4f³ 8fg) leggy, unfurnished gelding; seldom impresses in appearance; second foal; dam Irish middle-distance winner; in frame in Northern maiden races; stays 9f. *R. Woodhouse.* **63**

WOLLOTTEEN 3 ch.f. Wollow 132–Charlotteen 96 (Charlottown 127) (1981 5d 7fg² 7g 6d 1982 8fg 7fg* 9f³) lengthy, lightly-built ex-English filly; beat odds-on Taniwa by a neck in 7-runner handicap at Leopardstown in August; will stay 1¼m; sold out of G. Hunter's stable 1,700 gns Newmarket July Sales after first start. *D. Weld, Ireland.* **66**

WOLLOW MAID 2 ch.f. Wollow 132–Maid In Love (Sky Gipsy 117) (1982 6d 7g; 4,700f; second produce; dam never ran; 3½ lengths sixth to Foil 'Em in 22-runner maiden race at Doncaster in October, first outing and better effort; should stay 7f. *M. Ryan.* **73**

WOLLOW WILL 3 b.c. Wollow 132–Ready and Willing 82 (Reliance II 137) (1981 7g 8g 1982 10fg 10g* 10.6f*(dis) 10g* 12g*) narrow, rather leggy colt; a progressive sort who was first past post in maiden race at Pontefract in August and handicaps at Haydock (hung violently and was disqualified), Newbury and Newmarket in September; made all and again wandered around when beating Silcakey by 1½ lengths on last-named; stays 1¼m; yet to race on a soft surface; evidently not an easy ride. *B. Hills.* **90**

WOLL STAR 2 b.f. Wollow 132–Southwark Star 97 (Midsummer Night II 117) (1982 5fg 5d 6fg 5.8f³ 6g* 5fg 6g 7g) Apr 28; IR 10,500Y; well-grown, leggy filly; third foal; half-sister to French 3-y-o Busted Etoile (by Busted); dam won Lincoln; blinkered first time, won 15-runner seller at Lingfield (bought in 3,000 gns) in August; showed form subsequently only on the occasion not blinkered; should stay 1m; inconsistent; sold BBA 3,500 gns Newmarket Autumn Sales. *D. Elsworth.* **62**

WOLVERBEE 3 b.g. Wolverlife 115–Beelet (Royal Hamlet 115) (1981 5v² 5s² 1982 6v² 6s² 7g* 6f 5fg 6g² 6f 7fg 5g 6d) neat, quite attractive gelding; half-brother to several winners, including useful sprinter Major Bee (by Majority Blue); dam winning sprinter; won maiden race at Fairyhouse in April; also runner-up in similar events at Naas and the Curragh and in handicap at the Curragh again, going down by ¾ length to Hay Habit in last-named; ran creditably in Jersey Stakes at Royal Ascot on eighth start, keeping on strongly to be 2½ lengths sixth of 21 to Merlins Charm; suited by 7f; seems to act on any going; blinkered nowadays. *J. Bolger, Ireland.* **89**

WONDERFUL SURPRISE 5 b.h. Run The Gantlet–Ashling's Lass 89 (Levmoss 133) (1981 12f 13.3s 12s 12v 14s 1982 12.3g⁴ 12fg 13fg⁴ 14.6fg² 12fg* 14f* 12f* 14f* 12g* 14.6g 12s 12g 12s) quite attractive horse; was in tremendous form in summer and was gaining his fifth successive win when beating Middlin Thrang by ¾ length in handicap at Ripon; had earlier won similar events at Chepstow, Yarmouth (2) and Carlisle, last 2 in good style by 5 lengths; not disgraced in a more strongly-contested race on tenth start, but lost his form afterwards; stays 1¾m well; acts on any going; blinkered once at 3 yrs; bandaged in front nowadays; suitable mount for an apprentice. *E. Eldin.* **83**

WONDER WOOD 3 ch.g. High Line 125–Alice (Parthia 132) (1981 8g 8s 1982 12fg 12fg² 12f* 13.8f 13d 12.2d² 16s⁴ 15d³) strong, lengthy gelding; made all and kept on strongly to win maiden race at Edinburgh in June; ran respectably most subsequent starts; stays 2m; acts on any going; has run respectably for an apprentice. *Sir Mark Prescott.* **67**

WONGCHOI 3 b.c. Bustino 136–Lady of Chalon (Young Emperor 133) (1981 7g² 7s⁴ 7.3s⁴ 1982 8g² 8fg 12f 7fg 7g⁴ 7fg⁴ 8fg 8.2s 7g² 7d) tall, most attractive colt; good mover; good equal second, 1½ lengths behind Silver Hawk, in 9-runner Ladbrokes Craven Stakes at Newmarket in April; didn't reproduce that form and has become disappointing; stays 1m; suited by some give in the ground; blinkered seventh start. *E. Eldin.* **104** d

WOODCOTE 2 b. or br.c. Blakeney 126–Fragrant Air 94 (Frankincense 120) (1982 6f 7fg 7g⁴ 8g) Apr 25; neat, attractive colt; third foal; half-brother to a winner in Norway by Ragstone; dam won at up to 7f; 5 lengths fourth of 8 to Ominous in minor event at Epsom in August; beaten about 9 lengths when tenth of 21 behind Polished Silver in £4,200 race at Newbury the following month; will stay 1¼m+; sold 16,000 gns Newmarket Autumn Sales. *D. Whelan.* **82**

WOODCOTE BELLE 2 ch.f. Connaught 130–Pamagilan 89 (Pall Mall 132) **89**
(1982 6g 7g⁴ 7f³ 7.6v*) Mar 15; half-sister to several winners, including fairly
useful 1979 2-y-o 5f winner Pam's Song (by Song); dam 2-y-o 5f winner; showed
much improved form when making all to win 21-runner maiden race at Lingfield
in October by 6 lengths from Mavournski; will stay 1m; clearly revels in the
mud; sold BBA 17,000 gns Newmarket Autumn Sales. *R. Smyth.*

WOODEN SPOON 2 ch.f. Sagaro 133–Hazor 74 (Joshua 129) (1982 6g 8.2fg —
8d 6s) Mar 8; 820F, 620 2-y-o; small filly; first produce; dam 2-y-o 5f winner; in rear in sellers. *J. Wilson.*

WOODLAND MAID (USA) 2 b.f. Our Native–Who Lives Here (No Fear 104) —
(1982 7.6v) Apr 7; $40,000Y; half-sister to winners in USA and Puerto Rico,
one stakes placed; dam placed at 2 yrs; behind in 21-runner maiden race at
Lingfield in October; sold 940 gns Newmarket Autumn Sales and sent to Trinidad.
Sir Mark Prescott.

WOODSTREAM (USA) 3 ch.f. Northern Dancer–Rule Formi (Forli) (1981 **108**
6fg* 7fg* 6d* 6g* 1982 8g² 8fg)
Although the Coronation Stakes at Royal Ascot clearly heralded the arrival
of a high-class performer in Chalon it also marked a sad end to the careers of
two of the top fillies in the previous year's Free Handicap, Woodstream and
Circus Ring, who occupied the last two places in a field of eight. Woodstream,
successful in all four of her starts in 1981, looked none too happy beforehand,
sweating up badly, and having pulled hard for the first half mile she found little
once put under strong pressure early in the straight, eventually finishing nine
lengths behind Chalon, a neck ahead of Circus Ring. The announcement soon
followed that Woodstream had been retired; she visits the young American
stallion Alydar whose yearlings were highly sought after during the year, one
of them fetching 2,200,000 dollars.
Woodstream was the fourth Cheveley Park Stakes winner in the last decade
to have run without winning as a three-year-old, following Gentle Thoughts,
Cry of Truth and Pasty, but unlike the other three she did at least show she
had retained the ability that had enabled her to beat On The House decisively
at Newmarket. Indeed, after taking time to come to hand and thus missing

Mr R. E. Sangster's "Woodstream"

the opportunity of a rematch with On The House in the One Thousand Guineas, Woodstream again accounted for the English filly, who admittedly ran below her best, in the Goffs Irish One Thousand Guineas at the Curragh. Even so, she couldn't win the race. Having made ground to take fourth place a quarter of a mile from home she tended to hang in behind Prince's Polly, failed to muster any extra pace and went down by a length, depriving On The House of second by a short head in the shadow of the post. Considering how well she ran here Woodstream's display at Royal Ascot—where she started joint favourite with Chalon—seemed all the more disappointing.

	Northern Dancer	Nearctic	Nearco
	(b 1961)	(br 1954)	Lady Angela
Woodstream (USA)		Natalma	Native Dancer
(ch.f. 1979)		(b 1957)	Almahmoud
	Rule Formi	Forli	Aristophanes
	(ch 1969)	(ch 1963)	Trevisa
		Miss Nasrullah	Nasrullah
		(ch 1958)	Not Afraid

Woodstream took as strong a hold at the Curragh as at Royal Ascot and this style of racing suggests she might have had difficulty getting the trip of the Oaks, a race in which her trainer originally planned to run her. Woodstream is not the only one of her dam's progeny to have shown this trait—Indian Lore (by Apalachee) was a headstrong sort who didn't stay so far as expected, winning over six and seven furlongs. Rule Formi's two other successful foals have been Jaazeiro (by Sham), a high-class miler who won the Irish Two Thousand Guineas and Sussex Stakes, and the two-year-old Ankara, a brother to Woodstream, who won a seven-furlong maiden race at Leopardstown in October. Rule Formi didn't reach the racecourse; nor did the next two dams, though both did well at stud. Miss Nasrullah produced six winners and Not Afraid's five winners included the high-class staying two-year-old and good stallion Prince John and the smart stayer Brave Lad. With this pedigree and her looks—she is a strong, very attractive filly and a good mover who acted on a firm and a soft surface—Woodstream has the right credentials to make a grand broodmare. *V. O'Brien, Ireland.*

WOOLF (FR) 3 b. or br.f. Roi Dagobert 128–Stavroula (Nasrullah) (1981 NR 1982 8fg 10.2g* 12f2 14f4 12g 15.5fg4 10g3 11.7s 16s) big, rangy filly with scope; sister to 2 winners, notably very smart French 7f to 1¼m winner Wittgenstein, and half-sister to 2 minor winners in USA; dam unraced sister to Nashua; stayed on very well to win maiden race at Doncaster in June; in frame in varied company afterwards; stays well; form only on a sound surface; swerved away from whip third start but has run respectably for an amateur rider. *B. Hills.* **73**

WOOLMANS 3 b.g. Dawn Review 105–Highland Night (Night Thought 83) (1981 NR 1982 8fg 15.5fg) second foal; dam tailed off in a selling hurdle; tailed off in maiden races at Yarmouth and Folkestone in summer. *J. Scallan.* **—**

WOOLOOWARE 2 br.g. Wollow 132–Regency Gold (Prince Regent 129) (1982 7d 7f3 7f4 6,200Y; quite well-made, attractive gelding; closely related to 1m winner Mianach Oir (by Wolver Hollow); dam won from 7f to 2m in Ireland; in frame in maiden events at Salisbury and Goodwood in July and at Leicester in November; should stay 1¼m; best form on firm ground; gelded at end of season. *G. Balding.* **77**

WORD OF MOUTH 3 ch.g. Town Crier 119–Valdesta 106 (Persian Gulf) (1981 6d 7g 6g 1982 10fg 10.1d 6g 8fg) neat gelding; poor plater; has worn blinkers. *P. Kearney.* **—**

WORDSWORTH 2 br.c. Warpath 113–April 107 (Silly Season 127) (1982 7s) Feb 17; neat, strong colt; first foal; dam won 4 times over 1¼m; tenth of 11 in maiden race at Redcar in October. *C. Thornton.* **—**

WORK MATE (USA) 3 ch.c. Secretariat–Wedding (Noholme II) (1981 7g 8g 1982 11f 12fg3 13.3f3 14f2 14fg3 12g2 14fg* 16g4) big, strong, heavy-bodied colt; stuck on well to beat Master Boatman decisively by 4 lengths in 16-runner maiden race at Haydock in September; placed in similar events previously; one paced and is suited by a test of stamina; yet to race on a soft surface; sold to P. Bailey 18,000 gns Newmarket Autumn Sales. *R. Hern.* **84**

WORLEY BIRD 2 b.f. Lochnager 132–Disa 55 (Dike) (1982 5s4 5fg3 5fg 6f4 6f4 5g 5g3 6g* 7d* 5g 6s4 7g) May 10; 1,600Y; neat filly; fourth foal; dam of little account; plater; attracted no bid after winning at Hamilton and Ripon (nursery) in August; better suited by 6f than 5f (dwelt when tried over 7f); seems suited by some give in the ground; also dwelt tenth start; sold 1,100 gns Doncaster October Sales. *K. Stone.*

WORLINGFOOT 2 br.g. Hotfoot 126–Taormina (Windjammer) (1982 7g 7d) — Apr 14; strong gelding; good mover; second foal; dam never ran; showed signs of ability in maiden races at Newmarket in June and Yarmouth in August; gelded subsequently; unseated rider on way to start when withdrawn on intended debut and was ridden by lad in paddock at Newmarket. *M. Ryan.*

WORLINGWORTH 3 ch.c. Jimmy Reppin 131–Derring Maid (Derring-Do 131) 98 (1981 5d 5f 5fg 5.1d* 6d 6g 6s² 1982 5g* 6s 5f 5f 6fg 6g² 6h² 6fg 6g 6fg 6d 5.6g 6g³ 7s* 6g 8s 8s*) short-backed colt; won handicaps at Doncaster, Lingfield and Sandown; beat Bold Hawk decisively by 1½ lengths on last-named in October; stays 1m; acts on any going but revels in the mud; blinkered eleventh start. *M. Ryan.*

WORLINGWORTH WALTZ 3 b.g. Connaught 130–My Polyanna 81 (Polyfoto 59 124) (1981 NR 1982 8f 12f 8s 8fg 8f 8g 10fg⁴ 10s 7g 8s³) compact gelding; second foal; dam, thoroughly genuine and consistent performer, stayed 1¼m; plater; promises to stay middle distances; sweated up fourth start; claimed £1,800 after final outing. *F. Durr.*

WORRELL (USA) 2 gr.g. Cougar–Lily Marlene 76 (Drone) (1982 5s 5f³ 7g 6fg 91 6fg² 7fg² 6fg⁴ 6s*) Feb 17; $45,000Y; neat, attractive gelding; first foal; dam won over 5f and 7f; won Golden Gates Nursery at Ascot in September by short head from Razor Sharp, disputing lead all way and responding well to hard riding; gelded subsequently; stays 7f; acts on any going. *G. Lewis.*

WORTH AVENUE 6 ch.h. Busted 134–Lavenham Rose 85 (Floribunda 136) 66 (1981 13s* 16g* 13fg* 14s⁴ 16d* 15.8g 1982 16.1s² 16fg 16g⁴ 16d) staying handicapper; second at Haydock in April, best effort of 1982; acts on any going. *I. Walker.*

WOT THE DICKINS 4 gr.g. Runnymede 123–Gardenia (Cagire II 122) (1981 — 8d 7d 10.8fg 12fg 1982 12g) tall gelding; quite a moderate maiden; probably stays 1½m; sold 950 gns Ascot December Sales. *S. Mellor.*

WYKE 4 b.g. No Mercy 126–Harvest Melody 103 (Tudor Minstrel 144) (1981 8g — 8d 8s 1982 10fg) workmanlike gelding; little worthwhile form, including in a seller. *J. Hardy.*

WYNFIELD GILL 3 b.f. Maystreak 118–Rantzesther 66 (Bally Russe 113) — (1981 8d 1982 8fg⁴ 8.2f 8fg) compact, lightly-made filly; little worthwhile form, including in a seller; sold to W. Barrett 520 gns Doncaster June Sales. *D. McCain.*

WYNNWITH BOY 3 ch.g. Music Boy 124–Blaskette 99 (Blast 125) (1981 NR 69 1982 8fg 8fg² 7.6f² 8s⁴ 8g² 7.6g*) 4,000Y; good-bodied gelding; second foal; half-brother to middle-distance winner D'Lo (by Sovereign Path); dam successful middle-distance handicapper; made all and kept on strongly to beat Rossett in good style by 4 lengths in handicap at Chester in July; not seen out again; stays 1m; seems to act on any going. *N. Vigors.*

WYNNWITH STAR (USA) 3 b.c. Silent Screen–Finest Star (Pia Star) (1981 — 6g 7d 1982 8g 7.6f 10fg 10.1fg 10.1d 9fg) small, lengthy colt; little worthwhile form, including in a seller; sometimes blinkered; trained by N. Vigors first 5 starts. *J. Peacock.*

X

XENIA 4 b.f. High Line 125–Zugela 90 (Zucchero 133§) (1981 12g 12s 12f³ 12d³ 41 12fg 12g 13.1g 1982 16d 12.2g 17.1f 12f 12g³ 12.2fg 12fg⁴ 14fg 12d 17.1s 15.8d) lengthy filly; poor maiden; should stay well; blinkered third start; sold to D. Elsworth 1,600 gns Newmarket Autumn Sales. *W. Wightman.*

Y

YABANA 3 ch.c. Thatch 136–Ananiyya (Faristan 123) (1981 NR 1982 8f⁴ — 12fg 8fg 8f) workmanlike colt; second foal; dam French 2-y-o 1m winner; only plating class; not certain to have stayed 1½m; ran freely in blinkers final start; dead. *M. Jefferson.*

YAFEFIA (ISR) 2 b.f. Verre Dore–Tudor Doxie (Burglar 128) (1982 6g 6g **76**
5fg² 5s 5g 6v) Mar 3; big, useful-looking filly; half-sister to 1979 2-y-o 5f winner
Queensbury Kate and a winner in Sweden (both by Streetfighter); dam never
ran; ran best race when short-head second to Grub in 14-runner maiden event at
Wolverhampton in September, and would have won but for hanging badly left
inside last furlong. *Mrs B. Waring.*

YAHARA 3 b.f. Reliance II 137–Swan Ann 84 (My Swanee 122) (1981 NR **46**
1982 7g 8fg 7.2g³ 7f 5fg³ 6d 6s) 28,000Y; smallish, lengthy filly; half-sister to
2 winners, namely useful 6f and 7f winner Poyle Crusher (by Sweet Revenge) and
speedy Swan Princess (by So Blessed); dam won over 6f; poor maiden; stays 7f;
blinkered final start; sold 16,000 gns Newmarket Autumn Sales. *C. Brittain.*

YAMAMOTO 4 b.g. Deep Diver 134–Amber Goddess 50 (Yellow God 129) **—**
(1981 7s 7fg 8g² 8g 8g* 10s 8d 7g 1982 8s 8d) plater; didn't run well in 1982;
stays 1m; wears blinkers. *R. Hoad.*

YANGTSE-KIANG 2 ro.g. Rapid River 127–Au Pair 68 (Runnymede 123) **70**
(1982 5f 5f⁴ 5fg² 5fg 6fg* 6g 5g) May 11; 1,800Y; first foal; dam placed at up to
1¼m; won maiden auction event at Newcastle in July; stays 6f well; yet to race
on a soft surface. *J. Carr.*

YANGTZE 3 b.f. Galivanter 131–Nanking 90 (Above Suspicion 127) (1981 NR **—**
1982 9g 10.6s 10s 12d) small filly; first foal; dam won 3 times around 2m;
soundly beaten in maiden races and a minor event. *W. Elsey.*

YANKEE HONEY 2 gr.f. Yankee Gold 115–Honey For Tea 70 (Hul a Hul 124) **—**
(1982 6g 5fg) May 28; IR 800Y; second living foal; dam second 4 times at up to
7f in Britain and Ireland; well beaten in sellers at Hamilton in July. *W. Stubbs.*

YARD BIRD 3 ch.c. Busted 134–Final Orders (Prince John) (1981 7g³ 10.2g* **109**
1982 12d* 12fg² 12v⁴ 12f* 10.5fg* 11d⁴) medium-sized, fair sort; won minor
event at Leicester in March (from Rajhaan), £3,400 race at Newmarket in July
(battled on well to beat Inviting by a neck) and High Line Stakes at York in

Mrs J. Bricken's "Yard Bird"

August; beat Father Rooney in workmanlike style by ¾ length in last-named; also ran creditably in 2 races won by Old Country, going down by ¾ length in Warren Stakes at Epsom and coming home 5½ lengths fourth in Derby Italiano at Rome; will be suited by 1¾m; seems to act on any going; a likeable and genuine individual who races with zest; racing in USA with J. Weipert. *B. Hobbs.*

YASMEEN 2 b.f. Mansingh 120–Western Vale (Milesian 125) (1982 6g 6f 5fg **67** 5f 5v 5d³) Mar 20; 5,200F; smallish, lengthy filly; half-sister to 3 winners, including fairly useful 1979 5f performer Westburg (by Burglar); dam ran only at 2 yrs; 2 lengths third of 20 to Master Broker in seller at Redcar in November; blinkered fourth outing. *C. Spares.*

YASU NAFTI 2 b.g. Octavo 115–Russalka (Emerson) (1982 5d 5d 5f³ 5f 6f 7g **64** 8.2g 8f 8.2d³ 10d⁴ 10d) Feb 10; IR 2,900F, 6,000Y; smallish, fair sort; third in maiden race at Bath in April and 17-runner seller at Nottingham in September; stays 1¼m; seems to act on any going; blinkered last 3 starts, on final outing running badly; subsequently gelded. *D. Sasse.*

YAWA 2 ch.c. Luthier 126–Lucky For Me 116 (Appiani II 128) (1982 8.2s) — p Mar 4; IR 61,000Y; quite attractive colt; half-brother to Irish 3-y-o 9f and 1¼m winner Strike It Rich (by Rheingold) and very useful 1980 Irish 2-y-o 6f and 1m winner Euclid (by Lyphard); dam smart middle-distance filly; 25/1, not given hard race when ninth of 19 in minor event won by Holy Spark at Nottingham in October. *G. Lewis.*

YA ZAMAN (USA) 5 b.h. Gallant Man–Irish Exchange (Swaps) (1981 10.5v* **122** 10d 8g* 8f 12v⁴ 12s⁴ 1982 8g² 10g 8s* 7v 8v³) big horse; smart performer; won 70,000 francs event and Prix Messidor at Maisons-Laffitte in 1981; tried to make all when 1½ lengths second of 6 behind Big John in Prix du Chemin de Fer du Nord at Chantilly in June on reappearance; ran easily best subsequent race when impressive 5-length winner from Thorough in 13-runner Prix du Rond-Point at Longchamp in September (off course over 2½ months beforehand); never a factor in Coral-Eclipse Stakes at Sandown (eighth of 9 to Kalaglow) and Prix de la Foret at Longchamp, and was beaten nearly 10 lengths when third to Commodore Blake in Premio Ribot at Rome; ran respectably over 1½m, but best form at shorter distances; was suited by plenty of give in the ground; standing at Athgarvan Stud, the Curragh, at £IR 2,500 (Oct 1st). *M. Saliba, France.*

YEARS AHEAD 6 b.g. Sweet Revenge 129–Warrior Queen 95 (King's Bench — 132) (1981 NR 1982 8d) poor performer in 1980; in rear in a seller on only start of 1982; best form at up to 7.6f; acts on heavy going; often wears blinkers. *M. Tate.*

YELED 4 br.g. Youth 135–Lalibela 123 (Honeyway 125) (1981 8g 10fg 10g 12s² **78** 12d 12f⁴ 1982 12g 13d* 12fg³ 12f* 12f* 12fg 12d² 12fg 14g 12fg* 10.6s) big, lengthy gelding; won amateur riders events at Nottingham in April and Thirsk in May and ladies races at Ripon in June and Chepstow in September; suited by 1½m+; acts on any going; front runner; didn't look at his best and ran moderately eighth and ninth starts. *P. Kelleway.*

YEOMAN 13 b.g. Queen's Hussar 124–Freeholder 95 (Pinza 137) (1981 NR — 1982 8fg) does little racing on flat nowadays and is probably no longer of much account; has worn blinkers. *C. James.*

YO-HO 3 b.g. Mansingh 120–Unclaimed Treasure 81 (Nice Guy 123) (1981 — 5s 5fg 5f 6fg 5fg 7fg³ 7fg 8.2fg 1982 10d 8f 10f⁴ 13fg 12fg) strong, workmanlike gelding; plating-class maiden; stays 1¼m; acts on firm going; effective with or without blinkers. *J. Hardy.*

YOLANSO 6 ch.g. Lauso–Yolancar 65 (Kibenka 119) (1981 15.8g 12g 14.6f 12f⁴ — 13.8fg 12d 18g 1982 15.8g) plain gelding; poor performer; stays 1⅞m; acts on soft going. *P. Asquith.*

YONDER HE GOES 7 b.g. Gulf Pearl 117–Hark Hark 75 (Sing Sing 134) — (1981 NR 1982 12d 19f) poor plater; seems to stay 1½m; acts on firm going; sometimes wears blinkers; occasionally sweats up. *H. Fleming.*

YOOHOO 8 ch.g. Mountain Call 125–Dreamy Idea 68 (Double Jump 131) **58** (1981 5s 6g 6d 6g 7g 5f 6f 5fg 1982 6f² 6f³ 6g 6g² 6d⁴ 6fg 7f 6s) sprint handicapper; acts on any going; usually wears blinkers; had stiffish task third start and carried overweight fifth and sixth. *C. Booth.*

YORKSHIRE MOORES 2 ch.c. Sagaro 133–Taffytina 106 (Caerdeon 98) — (1982 6g) Apr 29; 30,000Y; second foal; dam, useful 2-y-o 5f and 7f winner, is half-sister to smart animals Ovaltine and Guillotina; no show in 19-runner maiden race at Newmarket in October. *R. Armstrong.*

YORK TERRACE 5 b.g. Derring-Do 131–Slipperty 99 (Hardicanute 130) (1981 12g 14g 11.7g 1982 12g 17.1f) small, good sort; no form since 1980; stays 1¼m; acts on any going; bandaged and blinkered final start (finished last). *T. Marshall.* —

YOUNG ATHENA 4 br.f. Young Emperor 133–Alea-Yacta (Javelot 124) (1981 8d 12.2g 13g 12f 10fg 10f 9g⁴ 1982 12f 12.2f 12f 10g) small filly; plater; stays 1¼m; usually wears blinkers. *C. Booth.* —

YOUNG CROFTIE 5 b.g. Sit In The Corner–Open Arms 77 (Dignitary 121) (1981 6s 7d 8g 6g 6g 6g 6g² 8.2g 7h 6f 1982 6g 7g 7f 8fg 6fg 8fg) poor handicapper; last in a seller final outing; stays 7f; acts on firm going; effective with or without blinkers; has worn a bandage on his off-hind; sweating third start; usually ridden by apprentice N. Vaughan and often carries overweight (around 7-13). *D. Francis.* —

YOUNG DANIEL 4 b.c. Dragonara Palace 115–Pepperita 79 (Nelcius 133) (1981 7fg 8fg 10d 7fg* 7fg* 7fg³ 8fg² 8f* 7f 1982 8d 7fg⁴ 8g 7fg 8g 8fg 8fg 7f 7fg²) well-made colt; in frame in handicaps at Ascot in April (Autobar Victoria Cup) and Lingfield in September (short-head second to Egnoussa); most disappointing in between; stays 1m; probably needs a firm surface; has won for an apprentice. *R. Armstrong.* 78

YOUNG INCA 4 gr.g. Young Emperor 133–Sunny Eyes (Reliance II 137) (1981 7fg 6g 7d 7g 6f 5.3f³ 6f² 6f 7f* 10.1fg 7g 1982 7fg³ 8fg 7h 5fg 5.8f 5g⁴ 5fg* 5fg 5.8f² 5d²) leggy gelding; won handicap at Chepstow in August; close second at Bath and Ascot afterwards; stays 7f; acts on really soft going, but acts on any other; often blinkered, but is effective without; unseated rider leaving stalls eighth outing. *G. Cottrell.* 56

YOUNG ROBIN 5 ch.g. High Line 125–Goldilocks II (Pinza 137) (1981 15.8s 16s 16g⁴ 15.8g⁴ 16f 17.4g 16.5g* 16.1s 1982 13fg* 12.3g) leggy non-thoroughbred gelding; beat Weavers' Pin by 2½ lengths in handicap at Nottingham in April; well beaten shortly afterwards and not seen out again; unimpressive in paddock both times; stays well. *W. Haigh.* 51

YUHZURU 2 b.f. Thatch 136–Joie de France (Reliance II 137) (1982 7g) Apr 21; 12,500Y; lengthy, angular filly; half-sister to 1¼m winner Belmont Blue (by Kashmir II) and a good winner in Mexico; dam won over 1½m in Ireland; no show in 22-runner maiden race at Newmarket in October. *Sir Mark Prescott.* —

YUKON FLASH 8 b.h. Yukon Eric–Headliner (Pampered King 121) (1981 NR 1982 16d) poor plater; stays middle distances; goes well in the mud. *A. Davison.* —

YUKON STAR 2 gr.f. Nebbiolo 125–Tiepoless (Tiepolo II 121) (1982 5g³ 5d² (dis) 5fg* 5fg⁴ 5fg 5f³ 5fg² 5g 5fg) Apr 21; neat, sharp sort; good mover; second living produce; dam won from 9f to 1½m in Ireland; made all to land the odds by 6 lengths from Maurmax in maiden race at Epsom in April; reached the frame afterwards in a 21-runner minor event and 2 nurseries; not seen out after August, having run poorly on last 2 outings; unlikely to train on. *B. Swift.* 78

<h1 style="text-align:center">Z</h1>

ZABEEL 2 b.c. Habitat 134–Never So Lovely 87 (Realm 129) (1982 6fg³ 6f³ 6g⁴) Apr 3; 145,000Y; a grand individual, who walks well and gallops with extremely long, raking stride; second foal; half-brother to 3-y-o No Contest (by Nonoalco), a fair winner at up to 7.2f; dam won at 6f; shaped with deal of promise when placed in quite useful company at Ascot in July and Salisbury in August; subject of an inquiry after being handled very tenderly in maiden race at Nottingham the following month, the stewards accepting jockey's explanation that the colt was still green and gets unbalanced; looks and moves like a high-class horse, and must be kept on the right side. *F. J. Houghton.* 89+

ZACCIO 4 ch.g. Lorenzaccio 130–Hepash 81 (Henry the Seventh 125) (1981 10s 12fg 7g 8g⁴ 8f* 10f² 10f² 8.3fg 8h 8fg 8f 1982 12d 15.5fg) poor handicapper; unplaced in sellers on occasions in 1981; promises to stay beyond 1¼m; has run creditably on a soft surface but seems well suited by firm going; blinkered third start in 1981. *D. Grissell.*

ZAGATO 2 b.c. Octavo 115–Bee In Bonnet (Track Spare 125) (1982 5fg 5fg³ **60**
5.1g) June 25; IR 800F, 1,000Y; small colt; 2 lengths third of 7 to Leandros in
seller at Salisbury in May; not seen out after June; sold 340 gns Doncaster
September Sales. *P. Haslam.*

ZAHEENDAR 2 gr.c. Welsh Saint 126–Zaheen (Silver Shark 129) (1982 6fg⁴ **87**
6f² 6g² 7g³ 7fg* 7d) May 8; lengthy, workmanlike colt; good mover; third foal;
half-brother to 3-y-o 7f winner Zaynala (by Habat); dam, half-sister to top-class
Zeddaan, won over 5f at 2 yrs in France; made all and was eased inside last
furlong when winning 26-runner maiden race at Redcar in September by 4
lengths from Holmbury; co-favourite, appeared to have stiffish task and was
beaten over 1f out when eighth of 14 in nursery won by Sangrador at Newmarket
the following month; suited by 7f; acts on firm going. *M. Stoute.*

ZAHEER 2 b.c. Nonoalco 131–Red Berry 115 (Great Nephew 126) (1982 7fg **81**
7g 7g³) Mar 26; 58,000Y; big, rangy colt; half-brother to useful French 3-y-o
1¼m winner Strong Blake (by Blakeney) and very useful 1m to 10.5f winner New
Berry (by Sir Gaylord); dam at her best at 2 yrs when second in Cheveley Park
Stakes; well-backed second favourite, ridden along most of way when about 7
lengths third of 15 to Herodote in maiden race at Leicester in October; will be
better suited by 1m+. *G. Lewis.*

ZALATAIA (FR) 3 ch.f. Dictus 126–Tapioquerie (Tapioca 123) (1981 7f 9d **121**
10v² 10g² 1982 10d² 12d* 12s* 11fg³ 10.5g² 12d² 13.5fg* 12f) fifth reported
foal; half-sister to a minor winner in France by Sole Mio; dam placed from 1m
to 11.2f in France; a tough and thoroughly consistent filly who won maiden race
at Saint-Cloud, handicap at Maisons-Laffitte and Prix de Pomone at Deauville;
beat Akiyda by ½ length in last-named in August; also ran well to be second in
Prix Cleopatre at Saint-Cloud (beaten ½ length by Paradise) and Prix de Minerve
at Evry (went down by a short head to Perlee); will stay 1¾m; seems to act on any
going. *A. Fabre, France.*

ZANUBIA 3 ch.f. Nonoalco 131–Russian Princess 99 (Henry the Seventh 125) **81**
(1981 6s 1982 7g* 8g² 8fg 7fg 8g 8v) rangy filly with scope; kept on well to
beat Egnoussa by 2 lengths in valuable 15-runner maiden race at Sandown in
June; twice ran creditably afterwards; will stay 1¼m. *J. Winter.*

ZARIYA (USA) 2 ch.f. Blushing Groom 131–Zahra (Habitat 134) (1982 6g³ 7fg **88**
7f* 7d*) Mar 7; close-coupled, fair sort; first foal; dam, daughter of brilliant filly
Petite Etoile, was placed from 1m to 1¼m in France; won maiden race at Brighton
in September and minor event at Catterick the following month; will be suited by
1m; probably acts on any going; disappointed second outing. *M. Stoute.*

ZARNINA 2 b.f. The Brianstan 128–Cham-Ol Bazaar 85 (Native Bazaar 122) **56**
(1982 5d³ 5fg* 5f⁴ 5f² 5g⁴) Mar 17; 310Y; small, lengthy, lightly-made filly;
first foal; dam 2-y-o 5f winner; bought in 1,300 gns after winning 10-runner seller
at Nottingham in April; not seen out after May. *C. Wildman.*

ZAYNALA 3 gr.f. Habat 127–Zaheen (Silver Shark 129) (1981 6d² 1982 5f⁴ **69**
7f* 7f⁴) lightly-made filly; justified short-priced favouritism in maiden race at
Redcar in June; well beaten only subsequent start later in month; suited by 7f.
M. Stoute.

ZE AVATAR 2 b.g. Whitstead 125–Miss Venus (Comedy Star 121) (1982 6fg **—**
8g 8s) Apr 1; neat gelding; third foal; half-brother to fairly useful sprinter Sharp
Venita (by Sharp Edge); dam never ran; little worthwhile form; gelded after final
appearance. *W. Musson.*

ZEEZA (USA) 2 b.f. His Majesty–Azeez (Nashua) (1982 7g 7s) Mar 23; neat, **76 p**
attractive filly; sister to Obraztsovy, a very smart performer at up to 1¾m here
and in USA, and half-sister to several winners, including smart stakes winners
Azirae (by Raise A Native) and Emperor Rex (by Warfare); dam winning sister
to very smart Guillaume Tell; showed promise without being knocked about over
1m; certain to improve, and is one
to note. *J. Dunlop.*

ZENA MARINA 2 b.f. Julio Mariner 127–Princess Zena 96 (Habitat 134) **—**
(1982 6g) Mar 27; second foal; half-sister to very useful 1981 French 2-y-o
sprinter Lulworth Cove (by Averof); dam won over 5f at 2 yrs; slipped up in
maiden race at Doncaster in June and had to be destroyed. *C. Brittain.*

ZENYATTA 2 ro.g. Town Crier 119–Soldier Girl (Queen's Hussar 124) (1982 **80**
5g² 5fg* 5f²) Apr 7; 580F, 1,800Y; rangy gelding; half-brother to 1m winner
Bionic Bill (by Sovereign Bill); dam of little account; won 6-runner maiden race

at Chester in May by 4 lengths from Shalaby; had no chance with sole opponent Brondesbury at Thirsk later in month. *D. Smith.*

ZERO OPTION 2 ch.f. Privy Seal 108–Destarte (Royal Levee) (1982 7.6v 5v 6s); second foal; dam tailed off only start; well beaten in autumn maiden races at Lingfield, Folkestone and Leicester. *R. Hannon.* —

ZERO READER 3 ch.f. Track Spare 125–Harvest Reap (Majority Blue 126) (1981 5s 7g 1982 8g 6f 6fg 5fg 5fg) plain filly; behind in varied races, including a valuable seller; dwelt first outing and ran wide on second; has worn blinkers; sold out of P. Cundell's stable 480 gns Ascot May Sales after second start. *D. H. Jones.* —

ZETA (USA) 2 gr.f. Zen–Aries Kiss (Power Ruler) (1982 8s) Mar 18; $20,000Y; second foal; half-sister to a winner in USA; dam won 4 sprint claiming races; no show in 21-runner maiden race at Leicester in November. *A. Hide.*

ZHUKOV 3 br.c. Malinowski 123–Star Set (Sunny Way 120) (1981 5g 5fg 7.6s 1982 8f 10.1fg 14f) small colt; in rear in varied company; blinkered once in 1981; sold 1,500 gns Ascot 2nd June Sales. *P. Mitchell.* —

ZILOS 3 b.c. Grundy 137–Sandarey 94 (Darius 129) (1981 6d* 6fg 7g* 8s **124** 1982 10f⁴ 12.3g⁴ 12f 12fg 14fg³ 14f³ 14.6f² 15.5v)

Make a note of Zilos for the Yorkshire Cup in May. The conditions of the race favour horses that have not won a pattern race since their two-year-old days—Zilos has not won since the 1981 Seaton Delaval Stakes—and if Zilos reproduces his St Leger form he should take a lot of beating at York. A sound surface, which evidently suits him best, and the prospect of a strong gallop, which we regard as essential for him at the Yorkshire Cup distance, would help his cause. If he comes through his early-season programme successfully Zilos could also represent Britain's best chance of warding off the strong challenge likely to be mounted by the French on the Gold Cup at Royal Ascot.

Zilos ran easily the best race of his career to date in the St Leger on his seventh outing in 1982, keeping up a strong challenge to Touching Wood from three furlongs out and beating the rest of a big Leger field decisively, finishing only a length and a half behind Touching Wood. The searching gallop set for a long way by Touching Wood's stable-companion Muslab undoubtedly suited Zilos. Like Touching Wood, Zilos is a thorough stayer without much turn of foot and a fast-run race is very much in his favour—at up to two miles at any rate—because it diminishes the possibility of his being beaten for speed over the last furlong or two. Zilos hasn't the pace to win top races at a mile and a half; a mile and three quarters, the distance of the Yorkshire Cup, is the minimum for him in good company. We can take it for granted that Zilos will be ridden as a four-year-old in the manner calculated to get the best out of him. He was up front all the way at Doncaster and was sent on early in the straight when third under top weight to Broken Rail and Crusader Castle in the Melrose Handicap over a mile and three quarters at York's August meeting. It was apparent as early as the spring that Zilos would almost certainly need distances beyond a mile and a half as a three-year-old: in both the Guardian Classic Trial at Sandown and the Chester Vase he kept on gamely, maintaining a good gallop to the end, without ever threatening to reach the front rank, being just beaten out of a place on each occasion. Zilos had the opportunity twice before the St Leger to display his ability at a mile and three quarters: after his performances in the Melrose Handicap and the March Stakes at Goodwood, in which he was beaten a short head and two lengths in a truly-run race by Santella Man and Father Rooney, Zilos could be given only an outside chance (he started at 40/1) in the St Leger. On his only outing after Doncaster Zilos finished a well-beaten seventh, one position behind the best-placed British challenger Little Wolf, in the Prix Royal-Oak on heavy going at Longchamp in October, and it has to be said that his overall three-year-old record is a poor one for a horse good enough to finish second in a classic. The fact that Zilos wore blinkers in his last four races may lead some to conclude that connections entertain doubts about his trustworthiness, but he has never given us the impression of being a shirker. He stuck to his task in good style in most of his races, and in all probability was a fast-improving horse in the autumn whose running in the Prix Royal-Oak can be put down to the appalling underfoot conditions.

A big, well-made colt, Zilos is not certain to stay the Gold Cup distance judging him upon his pedigree antecedents alone. His sire Grundy, who was also represented on the racecourse in the most recent season by another good stayer in Little Wolf, never raced beyond a mile and a half while Zilos' dam

Sandarey, a genuine racemare who won at a mile and at eleven furlongs, seemed best at distances short of a mile and a half. Sandarey has bred numerous other winners, two of the best of them before Zilos being the fairly useful handicappers Good Courage (by Never Say Die) and Sousa (by March Past), both of whom showed their best form at up to a mile and a quarter. Sandarey comes from a family with plenty of speed. Sandarey's great-grandam Golden Way did produce a Cesarewitch winner in Whiteway but her grandam Weighbridge was a sharp sort who didn't get a yard beyond five furlongs and her dam San Luis Rey,

Zilos (b.c. 1979)	Grundy (ch 1972)	Great Nephew (b 1963)	Honeyway Sybil's Niece
		Word from Lundy (b 1966)	Worden II Lundy Princess
	Sandarey (b 1964)	Darius (b 1951)	Dante Yasna
		San Luis Rey (b 1955)	Hard Sauce Weighbridge

a useful sprinter and half-sister to Libra, the dam of Ribocco and Ribero, was also a half-sister to the top-class sprinter Edmundo and to the best two-year-old filly of 1954 Gloria Nicky who was at her best over a mile as a three-year-old. How far will Zilos stay? Well, his general character as a racehorse is very much that of an out-and-out stayer and we should say that there is no room for doubt that Zilos will stay at least two miles, and every chance that he will get two and a half miles at the pace at which the Gold Cup is usually run nowadays. *B. Hobbs.*

ZIMAM 2 b.f. Free State 125–Once For All (Quorum 126) (1982 5fg 5fg² 5.3fg) **62**
Feb 18; 5,000F; small, quite well-made filly; half-sister to several winners; dam never ran; 3 lengths second of 10 to Myra's Best in maiden race at Sandown in June; ran badly in similar event at Brighton later in the month; will be suited by 6f. *J. Winter.*

ZIMBABWE 3 br.f. Home Guard 129–Matoa (Tom Rolfe) (1981 NR 1982 **81**
8d 8f² 10h² 12fg³ 12f* 11.7g² 13.1g 12f² 12g) third foal; half-sister to fairly useful 1m to 13f winner Prince Spruce (by Big Spruce) and a useful winner in Italy; dam won twice at up to 1m in USA; won handicap at Folkestone in August; ran creditably on several other occasions; suited by 1½m; acts on hard going; sold 16,500 gns Newmarket December Sales. *G. Harwood.*

ZINGO 7 b.g. Petingo 135–Tamarisk Way 92 (Tamerlane 128) (1981 NR 1982 —
17.1f) plater; stayed 1¼m; probably acted on any going; dead. *D. Wintle.*

ZINO 3 b.c. Welsh Pageant 132–Cyriana (Salvo 129) (1981 5.5g² 7s* 7f* 7s² **127**
7v* 1982 7s* 8fg* 9fg² 8g³ 10d)
Zino's record bears close inspection. He was a genuine and most consistent racehorse who until he failed in the Dubai Champion Stakes on his final outing didn't run a single moderate race. That said, he wasn't one of the better Guineas winners of recent years; afterwards the Poule d'Essai des Poulains winner Melyno beat him easily in the Prix Jean Prat, and The Wonder and Green Forest beat him conclusively enough, if less easily, in the Prix Jacques le Marois. He has now been retired to the Haras du Logis with a valuation of around £1.3 million on him, and will be standing alongside the promising Dom Racine.
Zino looked particularly well in what was not a very distinguished-looking field of twenty-six for the Two Thousand Guineas. He possessed excellent credentials for the race, among the best, and started co-third favourite at 8/1 with Wind and Wuthering behind the Ladbrokes Craven Stakes winner Silver Hawk and the Tetrarch Stakes winner Achieved. In France he'd been rated second to Green Forest in the Handicap Libre of 1981 after winning three of his last four races as a two-year-old, including the important Criterium de Maisons-Laffitte; in between he'd finished a good second to Green Forest in the Prix de la Salamandre. His performance in the classic trial at Maisons-Laffitte in April, the Prix Djebel, could hardly be faulted since he'd trotted up by six lengths from Pampabird, a more-than-useful colt the previous season. His ability to act on the firmish ground was not in doubt, nor was his ability to get the mile though he hadn't up to that time tackled the trip. His trainer Boutin, a staunch supporter of English racing through thick and thin, had sent over Nonoalco to win the Guineas in 1974 and Nureyev to pass the post first in 1980.

Two Thousand Guineas Stakes, Newmarket—Zino (far side) gets up from Wind and Wuthering in the last strides; Tender King is third

In the end the Guineas turned out very much a two-horse affair; many of those that had boosted the field to above-average proportions as a result of a number of inconclusive trials confirmed their suspected unworthiness to be contesting a classic. Wind and Wuthering, whose own early-season form had been a let-down after his superb seven-length win in the William Hill Dewhurst Stakes, set out to lead all the way as he'd done the previous autumn. He maintained so strong a gallop that most of those attempting to match it were burned out long before the finish. All the significant action came from the runners drawn in the middle to high numbers, for the smaller stand-side group, led practically all the way by Silver Hawk who eventually finished a creditable fifth, was always fighting a losing battle. Zino tracked Wind and Wuthering from the start up the middle of the course, and two furlongs out looked a certain winner; he was moving easiest of any in the field while the leader gave the impression he had come to the end of his tether. However, appearances were very deceptive, and although Zino ran on very gamely indeed he took until fifty yards out to master the equally-game Wind and Wuthering; eventually he got home by a head. Tender King, unable to keep up in the early stages, made good progress over the last two furlongs and stayed on into third place two lengths further back. The strong gallop, firmish ground and stiff following breeze contributed to a winning time of 1m 37.13sec, the fastest since My Babu's record-equalling 1m 37.00sec in 1948. Judging the pace can't have been easy for the jockeys, but it was done beautifully by Freddie Head who also rode a fine finish on the winner. Head, an outstanding French jockey, hasn't always been seen to such advantage in this country for one reason or another; regular visitors to Longchamp will know just how well he can ride. Remarkably he hadn't ridden a winner in England since Green Dancer in the Observer Gold Cup in 1974. Zino was his first English classic winner but is unlikely to be the last, and he has a very promising mount for 1983 in Ma Biche, his William Hill Cheveley Park Stakes filly.

The general appearance of the field in the paddock, the presence of Roca-madour in fourth place at the finish and the subsequent turn-round in the form in the Airlie/Coolmore Irish Two Thousand Guineas where Dara Monarch easily beat Tender King, with Wind and Wuthering only fifth, suggested that the Guineas might have been a substandard one. By the end of the season only Dara Monarch and Vin St Benet of the first ten home at Newmarket had managed to win afterwards; yet when Zino turned out for the Prix Jean Prat at Chantilly early in June for his next run there was no telling that he would be beaten. He'd been a better two-year-old than Melyno, the length-and-a-half winner from Tampero of the Poule d'Essai des Poulains, the French Guineas, in which Green Forest had finished an unlucky fourth. These three, plus the English horse Be My Native provided the opposition in the Jean Prat. Zino started favourite at 6/4, Green Forest started 2/1, Melyno 21/10, Be My Native 8/1 and Tampero 10/1. Zino adopted the role of Wind and Wuthering, setting a fast pace; evidently no doubts were entertained about his getting the additional furlong. Melyno, in Zino's former role, tracked the leader until unleashing a finishing burst that Zino couldn't hold, and he went away over the final furlong to win most convincingly by four lengths. Be My Native finished third, Tampero fourth and Green Forest only last of five. A change of strategy brought Zino a pacemaker, Spoleto, in the Prix Jacques le Marois at Deauville in August, though one hardly seemed necessary in the strongest-contested mile race of the French season to that time, especially with a horse like Noalcoholic present. Covered up for a

Mr G. Oldham's "Zino" (F. Head)

long way Zino produced a good finish without threatening another strong finisher, The Wonder. He was catching Green Forest close home but was beaten three parts of a length and half a length into third. This was probably Zino's form or pretty near it: he was a good miler but not an outstanding one.

Zino (b.c. 1979)	Welsh Pageant (b 1966)	Tudor Melody (br 1956)	Tudor Minstrel Matelda
		Picture Light (b 1954)	Court Martial Queen of Light
	Cyriana (gr 1972)	Salvo (ch 1963)	Right Royal V Manera
		Cynara (gr 1958)	Grey Sovereign Ladycroft

Looking at Zino's pedigree he might, on balance, have been expected to stay a mile and a quarter. There are significant sprinting elements in it though, notably in the form of the second dam Cynara, a high-class filly over five furlongs, a five-length winner of the Queen Mary Stakes at two and runner-up to Flori-bunda in the Nunthorpe at three; she was by Grey Sovereign out of a Portlaw mare. Cynara bred several winners, including some who stayed middle distances such as the Derby third Stintino, the Chester Vase and Ormonde Stakes winner Ormindo and Tempio, a close fifth in the Prix du Jockey-Club. Zino's dam Cyriana, twice third over a mile and a quarter in France, is a sister to Tempio. She previously foaled Sargo (by Caracolero), a winner over nine furlongs in France as a two-year-old, and Livorno (by Satingo), a winner over seven furlongs in Ireland at the same age and later a winner in Malaya under the name of Man of Action. Her two-year-old of 1982 Leventina (by Sagaro) hasn't yet run. Zino's sire Welsh Pageant was a top-class miler: he finished third in the Two Thousand Guineas. He wasn't disgraced when tried over a mile and a quarter as a five-year-old in the Eclipse (third to Mill Reef) and the Champion Stakes (third to Brigadier Gerard). Welsh Pageant's only previous Group 1 winner was the Champion Stakes winner Swiss Maid. When Zino's turn in the same race came along he ran unaccountably badly. Just about the pick of the paddock, he was moved into a good position half a mile out after being held up but his challenge came to nothing and he dropped away rapidly to finish last of fourteen.

Zino is a tall, good-looking colt, and a good walker. He acted on any going. He was, as we said at the beginning, a notably genuine and consistent sort. *F. Boutin, France.*

ZINZARA (USA) 3 b.f. Stage Door Johnny–Old Gypsy (Olden Times) (1981 **119** 6g* 8fg³ 7g 1982 7.3fg² 10fg* 12f 10g⁴ 10g* 10f²)

Trainer Harry Wragg's retirement was announced early in 1983, some six months after he had celebrated his eightieth birthday. He had a long and significant career in racing. As a jockey he rode the first of his 1,762 winners as long ago as 1919 and signed off with a treble at Manchester on the last day of the 1946 season; in between he was successful in all five classics, riding thirteen individual winners, and rode for most of the well-known owners and trainers of his day. Although he was champion jockey only once, in 1941, this was already the era of Gordon Richards and anyway Wragg's career as a jockey had a much more significant effect than can be summarised by facts and figures alone. Nick-named the 'Head Waiter', he revolutionised race-riding theories and his influence on riding tactics is quite evident today. His first classic success, on Felstead in the 1928 Derby, was gained with a well-timed late challenge which defied the convention that one had to lead most of the way to win. Wragg never became champion trainer in England but his training career, which started auspiciously with sixteen winners of twenty-five races in 1947 and the Chester Cup winner the following year, was a glorious one. He took his first classic, the Irish Derby, with Fraise du Bois II in 1951. Ireland became a happy hunting-ground, for he saddled a further eight classic winners there and his three in 1956 made him champion trainer in Ireland that year. Wragg's first winner of an English classic was Darius in the 1954 Two Thousand Guineas and Darius was followed by Abermaid, Full Dress II and On The House (One Thousand Guineas), Psidium (Derby) and Intermezzo (St Leger). Nor was Wragg slow to appreciate the opportunities for his horses on the Continent and he was one of the first British trainers regularly to visit Germany and Italy: in the mid-'sixties for example, he saddled four winners in five consecutive runnings of the Grosser Preis von Baden; Milan's Gran Premio del Jockey Club fell three times between 1958 and 1968 to Wragg-trained runners.

On Oaks day Zinzara had the opportunity, the last opportunity as it turned out, of giving Wragg a place in racing history that might never have been seriously challenged: winner of all five English classics both as a trainer and as a jockey. She seemed to have an excellent opportunity, too, and started second favourite following good runs at Newbury in the Fred Darling Stakes, in which she was two lengths second to Slightly Dangerous, and the 3lb Charles Clore Memorial Stakes, which she won very comfortably by two and a half lengths from Dreaming Away. She ran creditably in the Oaks, beaten under five lengths into fifth by Time Charter, just lacking the necessary turn of foot after holding every chance well below the distance. Insufficient pace also contributed to Zinzara's downfall in the Prix de Malleret at Longchamp later in June, in which she finished under four lengths fourth to Grease after the race had developed into a sprint in the closing stages. When she contested the Group 3 Prix de Psyche at Deauville in August, Zinzara was given a pacemaker from her stable, Sea Havoc, who made the early gallop a good one. Zinzara was sent on early in the straight, and she stayed on strongly to account for Triple Tipple by two and a half lengths. In view of the manner of this success it was rather surprising to see Zinzara ridden for speed on her final appearance in the Twickenham Stakes at Kempton in September. She never looked like catching all-the-way winner Dione when asked for her effort and was eventually eased up to finish a three-length second. She wasn't disgraced in the circumstances, giving

Prix de Psyche, Deauville—Zinzara beats Triple Tipple comfortably

Dione 6 lb. Zinzara was subsequently sent to the USA to be trained by Charlie Whittingham.

Zinzara (USA) (b.f. 1979)	Stage Door Johnny (ch 1965)	Prince John (ch 1953)	Princequillo
			Not Afraid
		Peroxide Blonde (ch 1960)	Ballymoss
			Folie Douce
	Old Gypsy (b 1968)	Olden Times (b 1958)	Relic
			Djenne
		Gypsy Life (b 1960)	Khaled
			Leventina

Zinzara is a very attractive filly and a good mover. She impressed in appearance every time we saw her. Bought for 46,000 dollars as a foal, she is a half-sister to two minor winners by Knight in Armor; her dam was a stakes winner at up to a mile. The next three dams were well-bred winners: Gypsy Life is a half-sister to Irish One Thousand Guineas winner Fiorentina and Leventina, four times a winner at two years in England, was a sister to Palestine out of a half-sister to the Oaks winner Udaipur. The fifth dam Uganda won the French Oaks and French St Leger. Zinzara, a smart and consistent performer, stays a mile and a half. She did all her racing in Europe on a sound surface. *H. Wragg.*

ZIPARIB 4 ch.g. Ribston 104–Zaraspar 70 (Zarathustra 131) (1981 9.4g⁴ 9s 12g 10f 13.8fg 12f 13fg 8d 1982 10.1fg 10f 8.3fg) strong gelding; plater; stays 9f. *M. Hinchliffe.*

ZIRCON'S SUN 3 b.g. Roi Soleil 125–Zircon (Pall Mall 132) (1981 6fg 7fg 7f 8d 1982 11.7f 12f 11.7d 14f 15.5fg* 13.1g 16fg) lightly-made gelding; showed improved form when making all to win modest maiden race at Folkestone in August; suited by a test of stamina. *R. Laing.* **66**

ZOFFANY (USA) 2 b.c. Our Native–Grey Dawn Girl (Grey Dawn II 132) **114** (1982 6f² 6g* 7fg* 7s²)
When Zoffany made his first appearance in a seventeen-runner maiden race at Newmarket in July he put up one of the most extraordinary displays we saw all season. After disputing the lead from the start he quickened clear in a matter of strides with a quarter of a mile to run, looking as though he would come home alone. Hardly had he done so than he started to veer very badly left, defying all his rider's attempts to keep him straight. In the end Starkey decided to let him drift right over to the far rails, no doubt hoping their lead would see them home, but Zoffany had by then lost much of his momentum and he lost the race to Hasty Flirt in the last strides. Zoffany would obviously have little difficulty winning races provided his actions were the result of nothing more serious than greenness, and he started a short-priced favourite to beat a big field of maidens at Newbury in August on his next start. His supporters must have feared the worst when he swerved left leaving the stalls but that proved to be the only blemish on his display: he quickened nicely in the final furlong to win easily by a length and a half from Tecorno, with the newcomer Special Leave a further five lengths away third. After another smooth victory in a minor event at Goodwood a month later, where he again showed a fine turn of foot to beat Society Boy by two and a half lengths, Zoffany was returned to Goodwood later in September for the six-runner Limekiln Stakes. As the betting suggested, the race developed into a match between Zoffany and The Fort, winner of the Intercraft Solario Stakes. When Zoffany, receiving 3 lb, moved up to within a length of The Fort inside the last two furlongs he looked about to make a race of it but in the end he faded to finish two and a half lengths behind.

Zoffany (USA) (b.c. May 14, 1980)	Our Native (b or br 1970)	Exclusive Native (ch 1965)	Raise A Native
			Exclusive
		Our Jackie (gr 1964)	Crafty Admiral
			Rakahanga
	Grey Dawn Girl (gr 1970)	Grey Dawn II (gr 1962)	Herbager
			Polamia
		Hoi Polloi (b 1956)	Princequillo
			Mondaine

Zoffany, a tall, good-bodied colt, was bought for 80,000 dollars at the Keeneland September Yearling Sale. Like those other good British performers Be My Native and Orixo he is a son of the American stallion Our Native, the winner of the Flamingo Stakes, the Ohio Derby and the Monmouth Invitational Handicap, all valuable nine-furlong events. His dam Grey Dawn Girl was also a

Mr Anthony Speelman's "Zoffany"

stakes winner, showing useful form when taking the Heirloom Handicap over eight and a half furlongs, but she had earlier won in claiming company carrying a claiming price of only 10,000 dollars. Zoffany is her fourth foal and third winner, following the fillies Dewan Diddy (by Dewan) and Dawning Heroine (by Our Hero). Grey Dawn Girl comes from an undistinguished family, being the best of the three winners produced by Hoi Polloi, a filly who failed to reach the first three in thirteen starts. The next dam Mondaine was no better, finishing unplaced in all her five starts, and none of her six winning foals managed to win more than 18,000 dollars. One of the six, Destiny's Turn, did however produce the very useful fillies Wings of Destiny and Destiny's Twist. Zoffany promises to become the best winner from his family in recent generations, even though his form at two suggests he needs to make more than normal improvement if he's to reach classic standard. As with so many American-bred animals it's difficult to say how far he will stay but his connections have entered him in the Derby, and not the Guineas, so they must regard him as a middle-distance performer. *G Harwood.*

ZOILO 4 b.g. Workboy 123–L'Elita 83 (Porto Bello 118) (1981 5s 5f 5f 5fg 5fg 6f 5fg² 5fg 5g³ 5g 1982 6f³ 6fg³ 6f 5fg 5fg 6d 7g³ 6f 6fg 8g) big, strong gelding; plater nowadays; stays 7f; probably not at his best on soft going; usually band-aged in front nowadays; sometimes blinkered; sold 510 gns Doncaster September Sales. *M. W. Easterby.* ... **58** d

ZOIROS (GR) 3 ch.c. Tachypous 128–Sils Maria (Midsummer Night II 117) (1981 NR 1982 10g 8fg² 8fg*) attractive, well-made colt; first foal; dam, half-sister to Count Pahlen, won a selling hurdle; smoothly justified favouritism by 1½ lengths from Caballo in 20-runner maiden race at Chepstow in August; had run well in similar event at Sandown previous start; worth trying at 1¼m again. *B. Hobbs.* ... **87**

ZOLA 2 br.c. Guillaume Tell 121–Blonda (Exbury 138) (1982 7s 8s) May 11; 8,200F, 5,000Y; half-brother to smart French 1½m winner La Toulzanie (by ... **—**

Sanctus II); dam, daughter of top-class filly and broodmare Bella Paola, won over 10.5f in France; behind in £5,900 race at Ascot in September and in maiden race at Bath the following month; sold D. Smith 2,200 gns Newmarket Autumn Sales. *D. Sasse.*

ZORN 2 ch.c. Riboboy 124–Pearlemor 93 (Gulf Pearl 117) (1982 7f² 7d 8s* 8g³) **87** Apr 16; fourth foal; narrow, useful-looking colt; half-brother to 2 winners in Italy, notably smart Alpherat (by Amber Rama), and to another winner; dam won 3 times over 5f and is half-sister to Steel Heart; won 12-runner maiden race at Bath in October; 5½ lengths third of 9 to Ashmolean in minor event at Leicester later in month; suited by 1m; acts on any going; looked unsuited by course when running poorly at Chester on second outing. *J. Dunlop.*

ZUBEDAH 2 ch.f. Red Alert 127–Icaza (Go Marching) (1982 5fg⁴ 5fg 5.1f³ 6g **79** 5f 6fg³ 7g⁴ 7fg) Feb 16; 9,200F; strong, smallish filly; second produce; dam, daughter of high-class Hidden Meaning, won over 1½m and 13f in Ireland; in frame in maiden races and nurseries, carrying 4-lb overweight when just over 2 lengths fourth of 10 to Shadan at Yarmouth in August on penultimate appearance; suited by 7f; blinkered fourth outing; sold London Thoroughbred Services 2,800 gns Newmarket Autumn Sales. *J. Winter.*

ZULAIKA HOPWOOD 4 b.f. Royalty 130–Zulaika 75 (Worden II 129) (1981 — 8g 10.2g⁴ 12f* 14g 12g 12d 1982 12s³ 13f 11.1g) tall, leggy, rather unfurnished filly; only raced in spring, best effort on first outing; suited by 1½m; probably acts on any going. *W. Holden.*

ZULU WARRIOR 3 ch.g. Cawston's Clown 113–Miss Taurus 79 (Bullrush 106) — (1981 5d⁴ 6fg 6d 7.2v 1982 11fg 7f 8g 9g 7g 6g 12g) workmanlike, dipped-backed gelding; poor plater; sometimes blinkered. *A. W. Jones.*

Whatever your betting requirements, you can always count on, Immediate acceptance, Courtesy, Promptness of payment. Plus the privacy you expect from your Banker

Open a Credit Account now

Speak to Alf Johntsone, "Members' Rails" or 'phone . . .

041-332 2861

Dan Flynn

1 Lynedoch Street, Glasgow, G3.

NIZON
(PREMIO ROMA 1978
GROUP ONE)

POLICEMAN
(FRENCH DERBY 1980
GROUP ONE)

ARGUMENT
(WASHINGTON D.C.I 1980
PRIX GANAY 1981
BOTH GROUP ONE)

DEEP ROOTS
(PRIX MORNY 1982
PRIX DE LA SALAMANDRE
1982
BOTH GROUP ONE)

Photo: Bernard Gourier

Buy Black Type before it is printed . . .

CONTACT: **Patrick Barbe**
Bloodstock Agent

 259, avenue Charles de Gaulle
60260 LAMORLAYE-FRANCE
24h/24: (4) 421.23.51 Telex: BARBE 150980 F

TIMEFORM
CHAMPIONS OF 1982

HORSE OF THE YEAR (RATED AT 134)
ARDROSS
6 b.h. Run The Gantlet—Le Melody (Levmoss)
Owner Mr C. A. B. St George   **Trainer** H. Cecil

BEST TWO-YEAR-OLD COLT (RATED AT 133)
DIESIS
2 ch.c. Sharpen Up–Doubly Sure (Reliance II)
Owner Lord Howard de Walden   **Trainer** H. Cecil

BEST TWO-YEAR-OLD FILLY (RATED AT 123)
MA BICHE (USA)
2 b. or br.f. Key To The Kingdom–Madge (Roi Dagobert)
Owner Mme A. Head   **Trainer** Mme C. Head

BEST SPRINTER (RATED AT 130)
SHARPO
5 ch.h. Sharpen Up–Moiety Bird (Falcon)
Owner Miss M. Sheriffe   **Trainer** J. Tree

BEST MILER (RATED AT 134)
GREEN FOREST (USA)
3 ch.c. Shecky Greene–Tell Meno Lies (The Axe)
Owner Mr M. Fustok   **Trainer** M. Saliba

BEST MIDDLE-DISTANCE HORSE (RATED AT 134)
ASSERT
3 b.c. Be My Guest–Irish Bird (Sea-Bird II)
Owner Mr R. E. Sangster   **Trainer** D. O'Brien

BEST STAYER (RATED AT 134)
ARDROSS
6 b.h. Run The Gantlet–Le Melody (Levmoss)
Owner Mr C. A. B. St George   **Trainer** H. Cecil

1982 STATISTICS

The following tables show the leading owners, trainers, breeders, jockeys, horses and the sires of winners during the 1982 season. Except for the list of sires, which relates to racing in both Great Britain and Ireland, the statistics refer only to racing under Jockey Club rules. Some of the tables are reproduced by permission of *The Sporting Life*.

OWNERS

	Horses	Races Won	Stakes £
1. R. Sangster ..	27	38	397,749
2. A. P. Ward ..	3	7	246,500
3. C. A. B. St George ..	12	27	229,169
4. R. Barnett ..	1	4	209,159
5. Sir P. Oppenheimer	8	10	177,132
6. M. Riordan ..	2	10	169,717
7. Sheikh Mohammed..	20	30	142,760
8. Maktoum Al-Maktoum	6	9	130,559
9. Lord Howard de Walden ..	11	23	128,287
10. A. Rachid ..	1	9	104,188
11. J. Levy ..	2	7	104,176
12. D. Wildenstein	8	10	90,725

TRAINERS

	Horses	Races Won	Stakes £
1. H. Cecil ..	58	111	872,614
2. G. Harwood..	59	120	708,540
3. M. Stoute ..	62	103	381,542
4. J. Dunlop ..	51	87	351,739
5. W. Hern ..	30	44	300,873
6. H. Candy ..	19	32	262,170
7. H. Wragg ..	20	30	259,572
8. B. Hills ..	40	55	245,029
9. H. Thomson Jones ..	30	45	214,305
10. C. Brittain ..	28	53	192,466
11. W. O'Gorman ..	22	49	192,314
12. R. Armstrong	20	43	183,103

BREEDERS

	Horses	Races Won	Stakes £
1. Someries Stud ..	4	7	265,525
2. W. and R. Barnett Ltd ..	2	6	236,727
3. Hascombe and Valiant Studs ..	7	9	169,120
4. Moyglare Stud Farm Ltd ..	2	7	160,436
5. Late P. Prendergast ..	3	8	152,347
6. Mr and Mrs. Paul Hexter ..	1	1	146,720
7. Lord Howard de Walden ..	13	27	137,396
8. J. M. Egan ..	1	9	104,188
9. Gaines-Johnson ..	1	5	98,776
10. Eaton Farms and Red Bull Stable	3	6	93,844
11. H. H. Aga Khan ..	15	31	88,494
12. Dayton Ltd ..	5	6	84,183

JOCKEYS

		1st	2nd	3rd	Unpl	Total Mts	Per Cent
1.	L. Piggott ..	188	87	94	329	698	26·93
2.	W. Carson ..	145	124	87	471	827	17·53
3.	S. Cauthen ..	107	104	89	445	745	14·36
4.	G. Starkey ..	103	89	74	315	581	17·72
5.	G. Duffield ..	91	85	73	429	678	13·42
6.	P. Eddery ..	83	95	72	340	590	14·06
7.	P. Cook	83	88	92	440	703	11·80
8.	T. Ives	82	72	68	342	564	14·53
9.	B. Raymond ..	74	69	79	379	601	12·31
10.	M. Birch	69	69	54	365	557	12·38
11.	E. Hide	65	66	69	325	525	12·38
12.	W. R. Swinburn ..	64	48	44	281	437	14·64

HORSES

		Races Won	Stakes £
1.	Kalaglow (4 yrs) gr.c. Kalamoun—Rossitor..	4	242,304
2.	Time Charter (3 yrs) b.f. Saritamer—Centrocon	4	209,159
3.	Golden Fleece (3 yrs) b.c. Nijinsky—Exotic Treat	1	146,720
4.	Ardross (6 yrs) b.h. Run The Gantlet—Le Melody	6	141,866
5.	On The House (3 yrs) b.f. Be My Guest—Lora	2	130,294
6.	Horage (2 yrs) b.c. Tumble Wind—Musicienne	9	104,189
7	Indian King (4 yrs) b.c. Raja Baba—Protest	5	98,776
8.	Dunbeath (2 yrs) b.c. Grey Dawn II—Priceless Fame	4	91,081
9.	Touching Wood (3 yrs) b.c. Roberto—Mandera	2	90,059
10.	Diesis (2 yrs) ch.c. Sharpen Up—Doubly Sure	3	88,649
11.	Assert (3 yrs) b.c. Be My Guest—Irish Bird	1	81,800
12.	Zino (3 yrs) b.c. Welsh Pageant—Cyriana ..	1	80,080

SIRES OF WINNERS

		Horses	Races Won	Stakes £
1.	Be My Guest (1974) by Northern Dancer	18	28	392,075
2.	Nijinsky (1967) by Northern Dancer..	12	23	275,816
3.	Kalamoun (1970) by Zeddaan ..	7	12	268,598
4.	Habitat (1966) by Sir Gaylord ..	22	45	262,736
5.	Sharpen Up (1969) by Atan	19	30	250,356
6.	Run The Gantlet (1968) by Tom Rolfe	10	24	249,068
7.	Saritamer (1971) by Dancer's Image..	3	7	212,879
8.	Roberto (1969) by Hail To Reason ..	10	14	206,727
9.	Tumble Wind (1964) by Restless Wind	16	35	158,740
10.	Blakeney (1966) by Hethersett ..	14	30	157,801
11.	Realm (1967) by Princely Gift ..	15	26	157,050
12.	Welsh Pageant (1966) by Tudor Melody	13	17	147,113

GILBEY
RACING

congratulate their Champion Racehorses of 1982

ARDROSS
Champion Racehorse of the Year

ARDROSS
Champion Racehorse of Europe

ARDROSS
Champion Stayer

GLINT OF GOLD
Middle Distance Champion

THE WONDER
Champion Miler

SHARPO
Champion Sprinter

Gilbey Racing
Cletex House
83 Charlotte Street, London W.1
01-580 0459

Fine art inspired by the best in racing

AN INTERNATIONAL CLASSIFICATION 1982

The following ratings for horses which ran in France, Great Britain or Ireland were allotted jointly by the official Handicappers concerned and published on 2nd December. The rating given to each horse represents the official assessment of its merit against a norm of 100.

TWO-YEAR-OLDS, 1982

Diesis	87	Crystal Glitters	78	On Stage	76
Saint Cyrien	86	Habibti	78	Pluralisme	76
Danzatore	85	Krayyan	78	Prince Reymo	76
Gorytus	85	Nile Hawk	78	Ameraken	75
Deep Roots	83	Proclaim	78	American Stress	75
Dunbeath	83	Salieri	78	Bal des Fees	75
Horage	83	Time's Time	78	Beldale Concorde	75
L'Emigrant	82	Allverton	77	Belka	75
Ma Biche	81	Bold Bob	77	Escaline	75
Orixo	81	Bright Crocus	77	Flamenco	75
The Fort	81	Cat O'Nine Tails	77	Glenstal	75
Caerleon	80	Goodbye Shelley	77	Go Jogging	75
Cock Robin	80	Mysterieuse Etoile	77	Jonacris	75
Kafu	80	Acclimatise	76	Kuwait Tower	75
Maximova	80	All Systems Go	76	Polished Silver	75
Brondesbury	79	Crime of Passion	76	Royal Heroine	75
Favoridge	79	Lovely Dancer	76	Sherbaz	75
Lyphard's Special	79	Muscatite	76	Super Entente	75
The Noble Player	79				

THREE-YEAR-OLDS, 1982

Golden Fleece	94	Dara Monarch	83	Chalon	81
Assert	93	General Holme	83	On The House	81
Green Forest	90	Sandhurst Prince	83	What A Guest	81
Akiyda	89	Simply Great	83	Coquelin	80
Awaasif	87	Time Charter	83	Diamond Shoal	80
Harbour	87	Zilos	83	Fearless Lad	80
All Along	86	Zino	83	Height of Fashion	80
Touching Wood	86	Electric	82	Kind Music	80
Melyno	85	Grease	82	Norwick	80
Pas de Seul	85	Real Shadai	82	Old Country	80
River Lady	85	Wind and		Peacetime	80
Persepolis	84	Wuthering	82	Perlee	80
Silver Hawk	84	Achieved	81	Zalataia	80
Bon Sang	83				

FOUR-YEAR-OLDS AND UPWARDS, 1982

Kalaglow	93	Glint of Gold	87	Vayrann	81
Ardross	91	Lancastrian	86	Amyndas	80
April Run	88	The Wonder	86	Easter Sun	80
Bikala	88	Critique	84	Karkour	80
Sharpo	88	Indian King (USA)	82	Lafontaine	80
Al Nasr (Fr)	87	Buzzards Bay	81	Ya Zaman	80

THE FREE HANDICAPS

TWO-YEAR-OLDS OF 1982

The following are the weights allotted in the Ladbroke European Free Handicap published on 2nd December. The race is to be run over seven furlongs at Newmarket on 13th April, 1983.

Diesis ..	..	9	7	Bal des Fees ..	8	9	Annie Edge ..	8 3
Saint Cyrien	..	9	6	Beldale Concorde	8	9	Carolside ..	8 3
Danzatore	..	9	5	Belka	8	9	Fine Edge ..	8 3
Gorytus	..	9	5	Escaline ..	8	9	Key Tothe	
Deep Roots	..	9	3	Flamenco ..	8	9	Minstrel ..	8 3
Dunbeath	..	9	3	Glenstal ..	8	9	Shearwalk ..	8 3
Horage	..	9	3	Go Jogging ..	8	9	Boom Town	
L'Emigrant	..	9	2	Jonacris ..	8	9	Charlie ..	8 2
Ma Biche	..	9	1	Kuwait Tower ..	8	9	Rutland ..	8 2
Orixo ..	..	9	1	Polished Silver	8	9	Sackford ..	8 2
The Fort	..	9	1	Royal Heroine ..	8	9	St Boniface ..	8 2
Caerleon	..	9	0	Sherbaz ..	8	9	Shaves You	
Cock Robin	..	9	0	Super Entente..	8	9	Close ..	8 2
Kafu ..	..	9	0	Drumalis ..	8	8	Shicklah ..	8 2
Maximova	..	9	0	Northern Secret	8	8	Special Leave ..	8 2
Brondesbury	..	8	13	Now And Again	8	8	The Liquidator	8 2
Favoridge	..	8	13	Shackle Pin ..	8	8	Tolomeo ..	8 2
Lyphard's				Tatibah ..	8	8	Another Risk ..	8 1
Special	..	8	13	Arrowood Bob	8	7	Ayman	8 1
The Noble				Fire Thatch ..	8	7	Boy Trumpeter	8 1
Player	..	8	13	Gallant Special	8	7	Holy Spark ..	8 1
Crystal Glitters	..	8	12	Johnny Nobody	8	7	Misguided ..	8 1
Habibti..	..	8	12	Sayf El Arab ..	8	7	Octavia Girl ..	8 1
Krayyan	..	8	12	Top O'The			Tough	
Nile Hawk	..	8	12	North ..	8	7	Commander..	8 1
Proclaim	..	8	12	Wassl	8	7	Accused ..	8 0
Salieri ..	..	8	12	Zoffany.. ..	8	7	Castle Guard ..	8 0
Time's Time	..	8	12	Cause Celebre	8	6	Domynsky ..	8 0
Allverton	..	8	11	John French ..	8	6	Lofty	8 0
Bold Bob	..	8	11	Silk Pyjamas ..	8	6	Miss Anagram..	8 0
Bright Crocus	..	8	11	Alchise ..	8	5	Northern	
Cat O'Nine Tails		8	11	By Decree ..	8	5	Adventure ..	8 0
Goodbye Shelley		8	11	Gordian ..	8	5	Prince Spy ..	8 0
Mysterieuse				Henry's Secret	8	5	Saving Mercy ..	8 0
Etoile	..	8	11	Mac's Palace ..	8	5	Rare Event ..	7 13
Acclimatise	..	8	10	Orange Squash	8	5	Rocky Marriage	7 13
All Systems Go		8	10	Sailor's Dance..	8	5	Solar Rock ..	7 13
Crime of Passion		8	10	Tecorno ..	8	5	What Lake ..	7 13
Lovely Dancer		8	10	Thug	8	5	Aragon	7 12
Muscatite	..	8	10	Widaad.. ..	8	5	Bid Again ..	7 12
On Stage	..	8	10	Dancing Meg ..	8	4	Naar	7 12
Pluralisme	..	8	10	Lord Protector	8	4	Persian Glory ..	7 12
Prince Reymo	..	8	10	Myra's Best ..	8	4	Right Dancer ..	7 12
Ameraken	..	8	9	Able Albert ..	8	3	Vaisseau ..	7 12
American Stress		8	9	Alligatrix ..	8	3		

THREE-YEAR-OLDS OF 1982

The following handicap, published on 2nd December, is for information only. The figures shown against each horse represent the official assessment of its merit against a norm of 100.

Golden				Silver Hawk	84	9	4	Zilos	83 9 3
Fleece	94	10	0	Dara				Zino	83 9 3
Assert	93	9	13	Monarch	83	9	3	Electric	82 9 2
Awaasif	87	9	7	Sandhurst				Grease	82 9 2
Touching				Prince	83	9	3	Wind and	
Wood	86	9	6	Simply Great	83	9	3	Wuthering	82 9 2
Pas de Seul	85	9	5	Time Charter	83	9	3	Achieved	81 9 1

Chalon	81	9	1
On The House	81	9	1
Diamond Shoal	80	9	0
Fearless Lad	80	9	0
Height of Fashion	80	9	0
Kind Music	80	9	0
Norwick	80	9	0
Old Country	80	9	0
Peacetime	80	9	0
Tender King	79	8	13
Be My Native	78	8	12
Ivano	78	8	12
Montekin	78	8	12
Prima Voce	78	8	12
Jalmood	77	8	11
Slightly Dangerous	77	8	11
Spanish Pool	77	8	11
Swiftfoot	77	8	11
Beldale Lustre	76	8	10
Count Pahlen	76	8	10
Criterion	76	8	10
Cut Loose	76	8	10
Dancing Rocks	76	8	10
Mr Fluoro-carbon	76	8	10
Open Day	76	8	10
Soba	76	8	10
Dione	75	8	9
Last Feather	75	8	9
Lords	75	8	9
Zinnara	75	8	9
Chellaston Park	74	8	8
Dish Dash	74	8	8
Jester	74	8	8
Rose of Montreaux	74	8	8
Mummy's Game	73	8	7
Sing Softly	73	8	7
Tants	73	8	7
Vaigly Star	73	8	7
Hays	72	8	6
Lobkowiez	72	8	6
Full Extent	71	8	5
Farioffa	70	8	4
Lyphmas	70	8	4
Rajhaan	70	8	4
Rocamadour	70	8	4
Rosananti	70	8	4
Super Sunrise	70	8	4
Triple Tipple	70	8	4
Khairpour	69	8	3
Broken Rail	68	8	2
Cajun	68	8	2
Clare Island	68	8	2
Mary Mitsu	68	8	2
Match Winner	68	8	2
Merlins Charm	68	8	2
Not For Show	68	8	2
Palace Gold	68	8	2
Perang Tejam	68	8	2
Silly Steven	68	8	2
Celestial Dancer	67	8	1
Diamond Cutter	67	8	1
Rebollino	67	8	1
Sans Blague	67	8	1
Admiral's Princess	66	8	0
Believer	66	8	0
Cadi Ha	66	8	0
Century City	66	8	0
Favoloso	66	8	0
Knave of Trumps	66	8	0
Top Hope	66	8	0
Busaco	65	7	13
Kareena	65	7	13
Lucky Hunter	65	7	13
Main Sail	65	7	13
Mennea	65	7	13
Mirabeau	65	7	13
Padalco	65	7	13
Santa Roseanna	65	7	13
Vadrouille	65	7	13
Vin St Benet	65	7	13
Yard Bird	65	7	13
Father Rooney	64	7	12
Macmillion	64	7	12
Never Talk	64	7	12
Santella Man	64	7	12
Fairy Tern	62	7	10
First Mint	62	7	10
Noble Gift	62	7	10
Bancario	61	7	9
Patcher	61	7	9
Sabre Dance	61	7	9
Voyant	61	7	9
Bali Dancer	60	7	8
Boxberger Speed	60	7	8
Brady	60	7	8
Cyril's Choice	60	7	8
Mubarak of Kuwait	60	7	8
Wink	60	7	8

FOUR-YEAR-OLDS AND UPWARDS, 1982

The following handicap, published on 2nd December, is for information only. The figures shown against each horse represent the official assessment of its merit against a norm of 100.

Kalaglow	93	10	0
Ardross	91	9	12
Sharpo	88	9	9
Glint of Gold	87	9	8
Critique	84	9	5
Indian King (USA)	82	9	3
Buzzards Bay	81	9	2
Amyndas	80	9	1
Easter Sun	80	9	1
Lafontaine	80	9	1
Kind of Hush	79	9	0
Bel Bolide	78	8	13
Commodore Blake	78	8	13
Motavato	78	8	13
Noalcoholic	78	8	13
Noalto	78	8	13
Princes Gate	78	8	13
Ring The Bell	78	8	13
Castle Keep	76	8	11
Little Wolf	76	8	11
Prince Bee	75	8	10
Stanerra	75	8	10
Tina's Pet	75	8	10
Tres Gate	74	8	9
Baffin	73	8	8
Blue Singh	73	8	8
Capstan	73	8	8
Susarma	72	8	7
The Quiet Bidder	72	8	7
Great Eastern	71	8	6
Lightning Label	70	8	5
Milk of the Barley	70	8	5
Sayyaf	70	8	5
Crofthall	68	8	3
Ore	68	8	3
Sweet Monday	68	8	3
Valentinian	68	8	3
Fine Sun	67	8	2
Capricorn Line	66	8	1
Heighlin	66	8	1
Six Mile Bottom	66	8	1
Centurius	65	8	0
El Badr	65	8	0
Tipperary Fixer	65	8	0
Castelnau	64	7	13
Gabitat	64	7	13
Scarrowman-wick	63	7	12
Camisite	60	7	9
I'll See You	60	7	9
Say Primula	60	7	9
Silver Season	60	7	9

AN IRISH CLASSIFICATION 1982

THE TWO-YEAR-OLDS

Published on 2nd December, for information only.

Danzatore	..	9	7	Certain				Butlers Bridge	7 10
Caerleon	..	9	2	Something	..	8	1	Laois Princess	7 10
Habibti	..	9	0	Najran ..	..	8	1	Mothers Word	7 10
Glenstal	..	8	11	Persian Polly ..		8	1	Out Of The	
Ancestral	..	8	10	Putney Bridge		8	1	Question ..	7 10
Beaudelaire	..	8	10	Samisen	..	8	1	Swordlestown	
Virginia Deer	..	8	10	Ankara	..	8	0	Miss ..	7 10
Gormanstown				Curravilla	..	8	0	Tea House ..	7 10
Prince	..	8	7	Hot Princess ..		8	0	Kimbernic ..	7 9
Heron Bay	..	8	7	Solar System ..		8	0	Push A Button	7 9
Rock 'N' Roller		8	7	Top Rated ..		8	0	Arrested ..	7 8
Sweet Emma	..	8	7	Committed	..	7	13	Art Class ..	7 8
Burslem	..	8	6	Nadasdy	..	7	13	Branch Line ..	7 8
Countess Candy		8	6	Sept ..	..	7	13	Carlingford	
Lomond	..	8	6	Stormy Fellow		7	13	Castle ..	7 8
Solford	..	8	6	Ballydoyle	..	7	12	El Kantaoui ..	7 8
Beat The Drum		8	5	Fighting Falcon		7	12	Evening M'Lord	7 8
Homeowner	..	8	5	Green Lucia ..		7	12	Hole In The	
Minnelli	..	8	5	Manhatten Miss		7	12	Wall	7 8
South Atlantic..		8	5	Tagrag ..		7	12	Paladoon ..	7 8
Treasure Trove		8	5	Taoiseach ..		7	12	Safe Process ..	7 8
Avalanche Way		8	4	Ashanti ..		7	11	Take A Step ..	7 8
Bon Marche	..	8	4	Go Alone ..		7	11	Aras An	
Flame of Tara..		8	2	Indian Giver ..		7	11	Uachtarain ..	7 7
Impudent Miss		8	2	Lady Dara ..		7	11	Evening Belle ..	7 7
Red Rudy ..		8	2	Moral Leader ..		7	11	Mink Goddess..	7 7
Salmon Leap	..	8	2	Spending Cut ..		7	11	Mr Big John ..	7 7
Autumn Sunset		8	1	Be My Love ..		7	10	Roof	7 7
				Burrow Hill ..		7	10	Wish You Luck	7 7

THREE-YEAR-OLDS OF 1982

The following ratings were published on 2nd December, for information only.
The rating given to each horse represents the official assessment of its merit
against a norm of 100.

Golden Fleece	..	94	Swiftfoot ..	..	77	Condell ..	..	68
Assert ..	..	93	Lords ..	..	75	Pilgrim ..	..	68
Touching Wood ..		86	Anfield ..	..	74	Prince's Polly ..		68
Pas de Seul	..	85	Red Sunset	..	74	Raconteur	..	67
Silver Hawk	..	84	Day Is Done	..	72	Woodstream	..	67
Dara Monarch	..	83	Punctilio ..	..	72	Afghan ..	..	66
Wind and			Longleat ..	..	71	Princess Seal	..	66
Wuthering	..	82	Americus	..	70	Santa Roseanna	..	65
Achieved ..	..	81	Peterhof ..	..	70	Senior Citizen	..	65
Tender King	..	78						

FOUR-YEAR-OLDS AND UPWARDS, 1982

The following ratings were published on 2nd December, for information only.
The rating given to each horse represents the official assessment of its merit
against a norm of 100.

Belted Earl	..	77	Royal Hobbit	..	69	Clanjolly ..	..	65
Stanerra ..	..	75	Noelino ..	..	68	Majestic Star	..	65
Tellurano	..	71	Jasmine Star	..	67	Salutely ..	..	65
Kilian ..	..	70	Steel Duke	..	67			

THE FRENCH FREE HANDICAPS

TWO-YEAR-OLDS, 1982

The following are the weights allotted in the Handicap Libre, published on 16th December.

Horse	st	lb	Horse	st	lb	Horse	st	lb
Saint Cyrien ..	9	12	Belka	9	1	Bold Apparel ..	8	10
Deep Roots ..	9	10	Escaline ..	9	1	Dona Gaylord	8	10
L'Emigrant ..	9	8	Go Jogging ..	9	1	Le Voleur ..	8	10
Ma Biche ..	9	7	Sherbaz ..	9	1	Manola ..	8	10
Maximova ..	9	6	Dancing Display	9	0	My Madness ..	8	10
The Noble			Drumalis ..	9	0	Pajalski ..	8	10
Player	9	5	L'Attrayante ..	9	0	Prince Kebir ..	8	10
Crystal Glitters	9	4	Little Meadow	9	0	Rose de Bagdad	8	10
Nile Hawk ..	9	4	Northern Fashion	9	0	Soigneuse ..	8	10
Allverton ..	9	3	White Spade ..	9	0	Tarte Chaude ..	8	10
Cat O'Nine Tails	9	3	Air Distingue ..	8	13	Afsarjaan ..	8	9
Goodbye Shelley	9	3	Alluvia ..	8	13	Bid for Bucks ..	8	9
Mysterieuse			Alma Ata ..	8	13	Blue River ..	8	9
Etoile	9	3	Ginger Brink ..	8	13	Brillante ..	8	9
Crime of Passion	9	2	Interco ..	8	13	Forlore ..	8	9
Lovely Dancer	9	2	Rhapsodien ..	8	13	Honey Stage ..	8	9
On Stage ..	9	2	Verria ..	8	13	Jeu de Paille ..	8	9
Pluralisme ..	9	2	Alzao ..	8	11	Mille Balles ..	8	9
Ameraken ..	9	1	Flying Sauce ..	8	11	Pietru ..	8	9
American Stress	9	1	Insolent ..	8	11	Riverba ..	8	9
Bal des Fees ..	9	1	Ask the Wind ..	8	10	Un Monsieur ..	8	9

THREE-YEAR-OLDS, 1982

The following are the weights allotted in the Handicap Libre, published on 16th December.

Horse	st	lb	Horse	st	lb	Horse	st	lb
Assert	10	5	Typhoon Polly	9	4	Doubling Time	9	0
Green Forest ..	10	2	Alfred's Choice	9	3	Evening Bleu	9	0
Akiyda ..	10	1	Denel	9	3	Le Monastere ..	9	0
Awaasif ..	9	13	Dreaming Away	9	3	Lichine.. ..	9	0
Harbour ..	9	13	Kaiserblume ..	9	3	Mistretta ..	9	0
All Along ..	9	12	Vidor ..	9	3	Tampero ..	9	0
Melyno.. ..	9	11	Welsh Term ..	9	3	Unknown Lady	9	0
Persepolis ..	9	11	Beldale Lustre..	9	2	Bell Tempo ..	8	13
River Lady ..	9	11	Brezzo ..	9	2	Bright Dick ..	8	13
Bon Sang ..	9	10	Ideal Point ..	9	2	Criterion ..	8	13
Dara Monarch..	9	10	Jester ..	9	2	Epithet ..	8	13
General Holme	9	10	Nabirpour ..	9	2	Maniches ..	8	13
Sandhurst Prince	9	10	Noble Bloom ..	9	2	Phebis ..	8	13
Zino ..	9	10	Parannda ..	9	2	Rienzi ..	8	13
Grease ..	9	8	Rudolfina ..	9	2	Sabr Ayoub ..	8	13
Real Shadai ..	9	8	Sharp Singer ..	9	2	Saronic ..	8	13
What A Guest..	9	7	Un Etendard ..	9	2	Top Ivory ..	8	13
Coquelin ..	9	6	Anfield ..	9	1	Comtal ..	8	11
Fearless Lad ..	9	6	Chem ..	9	1	Darly ..	8	11
Kind Music ..	9	6	Dear Patrick ..	9	1	Egalite ..	8	11
Perlee ..	9	6	Dione ..	9	1	Estere ..	8	11
Zalataia ..	9	6	Dom Donizetti	9	1	Flower Prince ..	8	11
Balitou ..	9	4	Floriano ..	9	1	Freeway Folly ..	8	11
Be My Native ..	9	4	Gipsy Road ..	9	1	Gold Bird ..	8	11
Bois de Grace ..	9	4	Pasadoble ..	9	1	Ma Mere L'Oie	8	11
Cadoudal ..	9	4	Sham's Princess	9	1	Miss Summer ..	8	11
Exclusive Order	9	4	Zinzara ..	9	1	Mulaz Palace ..	8	11
Le Nain Jaune	9	4	Beau Pretender	9	0	Palace Tower ..	8	11
Oak Dancer ..	9	4	Buchanette ..	9	0	Radiance ..	8	11
Paradise ..	9	4	Day Is Done ..	9	0	Rhoecus ..	8	11
Play It Safe ..	9	4	Dom Cimarosa	9	0	Valiyar ..	8	11
Prima Voce ..	9	4						

FOUR-YEAR-OLDS AND UPWARDS, 1982

The following are the weights allotted in the Handicap Libre, published on 16th December.

Ardross	..	10	3	Bylly the Kid	..	9	3	Ledmir	..	9	0
April Run	..	10	0	Little Wolf	..	9	3	Lou Piguet	..	9	0
Bikala	..	10	0	Blue Courtier	..	9	2	Mariacho	..	9	0
Sharpo	..	10	0	First Prayer	..	9	2	Ranapour	..	9	0
Al Nasr (Fr)	..	9	13	Great Substence		9	2	Thorough	..	9	0
Glint of Gold	..	9	13	King James	..	9	2	Two Step	..	9	0
Lancastrian	..	9	12	Le Mamamouchi		9	2	Valentinian	..	9	0
The Wonder	..	9	12	Lord Jack	..	9	2	Arc d'Or	..	8	13
Critique	..	9	11	Marasali	..	9	2	Cesario	..	8	13
Indian King				Ponchielli	..	9	2	Fin Gourmet	..	8	13
(USA)	..	9	8	Protection				La Pompadour		8	13
Vayrann	..	9	7	Racket	..	9	2	Sayyaf	..	8	13
Karkour	..	9	6	Water Melon	..	9	2	Votre Altesse	..	8	13
Ya Zaman	..	9	6	Mondino	..	9	1	La Hougue	..	8	11
Commodore				Music Streak	..	9	1	Mourtazam	..	8	11
Blake	..	9	5	Schwepperuss-				Prince du Bourg		8	11
Kelbomec	..	9	5	chian..		9	1	Prospero	..	8	11
Noalcoholic	..	9	5	Sky Lawyer	..	9	1	Rubino	..	8	11
Tres Gate	..	9	5	Sno Bird	..	9	1	Sardos ..	..	8	11
El Badr	..	9	4	Starski ..	..	9	1	This Man	..	8	11
Hard to Sing	..	9	4	Terreno	..	9	1	Tonar ..	..	8	11
No Attention	..	9	4	Tipperary Fixer		9	1	Vieux Carre	..	8	11
Big John	..	9	3							

Anthony Penfold Bloodstock

International Bloodstock Investment and Management

Tithe Barn Oving Chichester Sussex PO20 6DE

Telephone: Chichester (0243) 774992 (office) 789278 (home)
Telex: 86402 (attn Penfold)

FEDERATION OF BLOODSTOCK AGENTS (GB)

Airlie....*for*
the best selection of stallions in Europe and the best care that money can buy

The studs under the control of Captain A. D. D. Rogers comprise over 1,500 acres of fenced and watered lands. Each of the four main studs have a completely separate staff and are run independently. Of the two smaller studs one is used completely for isolation and the other for the resident yearlings. There are three private veterinary surgeons and a private laboratory staffed seven days a week during the covering season.

For the convenience of overseas patrons we can offer accommodation for mares prior to the start of the covering season. This enables mares visiting the stallions **ARTAIUS, BALLAD ROCK, CUT ABOVE, DARA MONARCH, DOUBLE FORM, ELA-MANA-MOU, HABITAT, HENBIT, PRINCE BEE,** and **TUMBLE WIND** to settle in their new surroundings.

Under the management of Captain A. D. D. Rogers

Airlie Stud
Lucan, Co. Dublin

Grangewilliam Stud
Maynooth, Co. Kildare

Loughmore Stud
Killeen, Dunsany, Co. Meath

Loughtown Stud
Donadea, Co. Kildare

Simmonstown Stud
Celbridge, Co. Kildare

Williamstown Stud
Clonsilla, Co. Dublin

939

THE BROWNSTOWN STUD

CURRAGH, CO. KILDARE

One of the World's Great Breeding Establishments

Brownstown is the only stud farm to have bred the winners of all the Irish classics—as well as the Prix de l'Arc de Triomphe, Epsom Derby, Ascot Gold Cup (3 times), French Oaks, Champion Stakes etc; Breeders of the most individual winners in 1978 and 1979; 2nd Leading Irish stud (money earnings) in 1978.

BROWNSTOWN mares have produced many top horses including 16 individual Group 1 winners:

Levmoss
(8 races, £143,483, including Prix de l'Arc de Triomphe, Prix du Cadran and Ascot Gold Cup)

Sweet Mimosa
(Prix de Diane, 1970, £76,407)

Arctic Prince
(Derby Stakes; leading broodmare sire)

Panaslipper
(Irish Derby; a leading sire)

Solar Slipper
(Champion Stakes, broodmare sire of Royal Palace)

Royal Danseuse
(Irish 1000 Guineas)

Allangrange
(Irish St Leger)

Mart Lane
(St Simon Stakes 1976)

Ballad Rock
(Champion Irish sprinter)

Le Moss
(Ascot Gold Cup twice, Goodwood Cup twice, Doncaster Cup twice and 2nd St Leger)

Captain James
(Waterford Crystal Mile)

Weavers' Hall
(Irish Sweeps Derby and £67,757)

Silken Glider
(Irish Oaks, 2nd Epsom Oaks)

Feevagh
(Yorkshire Oaks; dam of Feemoss; grandam of LEVMOSS, LE MOSS and SWEET MIMOSA)

Sixpence
(leading two-year-old; dam of Four-and-Twenty, won Santa Anita and Hollywood Derbys)

Arctic Sun
(leading two-year-old; dam of Arctic Prince)

Le Levanstell
(Queen Elizabeth II Stakes; a leading sire and grandsire)

Nikoli
(Irish 2000 Guineas)

Bog Road
(Gallinule Stakes, Ballymoss Stakes and £37,419)

El Badr
(Prix du Cadran)

Spence Bay
(Century Handicap USA)

All enquiries to The Manager, Brownstown Stud, Curragh, Co. Kildare. Tel. Curragh 41303

EUROPEAN GROUP 1 PATTERN RACES 1982

1   PREMIO PARIOLI (3y c) 1m
£21,349   Rome   12 April
  Sorabancies 9-2 GDettori ..**1**
  How To Go 9-2 PPerlanti.. ½.**2**
  Realistic Boy 9-2
    RFestinesi ns.**3**
  Ma No 9-2 RSannino....1½.4
  Crawford 9-2 AParravani.. ½.5
  Danilo Petrovich 9-2
    LBietolini 3.6
  Cric Crac 9-2 SDettori....2.7
  Luthier's Bonnet 9-2
    J-PLefevre 4.8
  Logar 9-2 SFancera.......3.9
  Jammer 9-2 CWigham...2.10
4/5 How To Go, 5/2 SORABAN-
CIES and Logar, 4/1 Danilo
Petrovich and Luthier's Bonnet,
5/1 Realistic Boy, 10/1 Cric Crac,
20/1 Jammer, 25/1 Ma No, 28/1
Crawford.
  Scuderia Gabriella (E. Camici)
10 ran 1m 41.2 (Good).

2   POULE D'ESSAI DES   1m
     POULAINS   (3y c)
£36,397   Longchamp   25 April
  Melyno 9-2 YSaint-Martin..**1**
  Tampero 9-2
    MPhilipperon 1½.**2**
  Day Is Done 9-2
    LPiggott   , , , , ,ns.**3**
  Green Forest 9-2
    AGibert s.nk.4
  Dear Patrick 9-2 SGorli...¾.5
  Rollins 9-2 GDoleuze.....1.6
  Telephone Man 9-2
    SCauthen 3.7
  Abraje 9-2 AGoldsztejn..20.8
  Volonte de Fer 9-2
    PLagoutte s.nk.9
Evens Green Forest and Abraje,
17/10 MELYNO, 13/2 Dear Patrick
and Volonte de Fer, 10/1 Day Is
Done, 17/1 Tampero, 24/1 Tele-
phone Man, 26/1 Rollins.
  S. Niarchos (F. Mathet) 9ran
1m 38.6 (Good to Firm).

3   PREMIO REGINA ELENA
     (3y f)   1m
£21,496   Rome   25 April
  Rosananti 8-11 WCarson...**1**
  Ilenia 8-11 GDettori....2½.**2**
  Smageta 8-11 GStarkey.. ½.**3**
  Delices 8-11 SDettori......2.4
  Deux Aout 8-11 GPLigas..2.5
  Maria Stuarda 8-11
    PPerlanti ½.6
  Astorga 8-11 SFancera....3.7

  Dewanadance 8-11 JReid.2½.8
  Maria Cignaroli 8-11
    OPessi 4.9
  Wolver Maid 8-11
    WSwinburn ½.10
  Miss Eleonora 8-11
    MMassimi ½.11
  Dark Angel 8-11
    LBietolino ½.12
9/4 ROSANANTI, 5/2 Ilenia and
Dewanadance, 3/1 Astorga, 7/2
Maria Stuarda, 6/1 Smageta, 13/2
Delices, 20/1 Dark Angel, 25/1
Wolver Maid, 50/1 Maria Cignaroli,
66/1 Deux Aout, 100/1 Miss
Eleonora.
  R. More O'Ferrall (J. Dunlop)
12ran 1m 39.7 (Dead).

4   ONE THOUSAND
     GUINEAS STAKES (3y f) 1m
£75,630   Newmarket   29 April
  On The House 9-0 JReid...**1**
  Time Charter 9-0
    WNewnes 2½.**2**
  Dione 9-0 JMercer 2.**3**
  Play It Safe 9-0 LPiggott..nk.4
  Slightly Dangerous 9-0
    SCauthen 2.5
  Stratospheric 9-0
    WCarson hd.6
  Celestial Path 9-0
    DGillespie 4.7
  Exclusive Order 9-0
    MPhilipperon ½.8
  Warm Hearted 9-0
    GStarkey 1½.9
  Merlins Charm 9-0
    PEddery 1½.10
  Triple Tipple 9-0 TIves.½.11
  Glancing 9-0 EHide....1½.12
  God Bless 9-0
    WRSwinburn 3.13
  Panatella 9-0 NHowe....½.14
  Hello Cuddles 9-0 SPerks..15
5/2 Play It Safe, 4/1 Slightly
Dangerous, 7/1 Merlins Charm,
10/1 Stratospheric, 11/1 Exclusive
Order, Time Charter, 20/1 Triple
Tipple, 25/1 Celestial Path, Dione,
33/1 ON THE HOUSE,
Warm Hearted, 100/1 Hello
Cuddles, 200/1 God Bless, Panatella.
  Sir P. Oppenheimer (H. Wragg)
15ran 1m 40.45 (Good to Firm).

5   TWO THOUSAND   1m
     GUINEAS STAKES
     (3y c+f)
£80,080   Newmarket   1 May
  Zino 9-0 FHead...........**1**

Wind and Wuthering 9-0
   SCauthen hd.**2**
Tender King 9-0
   YSaint-Martin 2.**3**
Rocamadour 9-0
   WRSwinburn 2¼.4
Silver Hawk 9-0 AMurray.¾.5
Achieved 9-0 PEddery...2½.6
Final Strike 9-0
   GDuffield ½.7
Dara Monarch 9-0
   PWaldron 1.8
Rebollino 9-0 EHide......1½.9
Vin St Benet 9-0 RCurant.1.10
Montekin 9-0
   WCarson s.hd.11
Prima Voce 9-0 BTaylor.1½.12
Nioulargo 9-0
   BRaymond hd.13
Silly Steven 9-0
   RCochrane ½.14
Cornish Gem 9-0
   PTulk s.hd.15
Wongchoi 9-0 TIves......½.16
Hays 9-0 GStarkey......¼.17
Royal Rendevouz 9-0
   ALequeux hd.18
Come On The Blues 9-0
   PBradwell s.hd.19
Full Extent 9-0 JLowe..½.20
Rare Gift 9-0 LPiggott...¾.21
Steel Bay 9-0 RWeaver..1½.22
Macmillion 9-0 GBaxter.½.23
Mirabeau 9-0 BCrossley.hd.24
Bold Fort 9-0 SPerks....3.25
Regent Leisure 9-0
   SDawson t.o.26
5/1 Silver Hawk, 15/2 Achieved,
8/1 Wind and Wuthering, ZINO,
11/1 Hays, Tender King, 12/1 Full
Extent, Rare Gift, 20/1 Mirabeau,
Montekin, Nioulargo, 25/1 Rebol-
lino, 33/1 Dara Monarch, 40/1
Macmillion, Wongchoi, 50/1 Come
On The Blues, Cornish Gem,
Prima Voce, 66/1 Final Strike, Vin
St Benet, 100/1 Silly Steven,
Royal Rendevouz, Silly Steven,
Steel Bay, 200/1 Bold Fort, Regent
Leisure.
   G. Oldham (F. Boutin) 26ran
1m 37.13 (Good to Firm).

6 POULE D'ESSAI DES 1m
   POULICHES   (3y f)
£36,530   Longchamp   2 May
   River Lady 9-2 LPiggott...**1**
   Typhoon Polly 9-2
     GDubroeucq 2½.**2**
   Vidor 9-2 ALequeux.....2.**3**
   Parannda 9-2
     YSaint-Martin ¾.4
   Mac Rhefna 9-2
     GGuignard 1½.5
   Estere 9-2 SGorli 6.6
   Princely Penny 9-2 FHead.4.7

Star Guide 9-2
   MPhilipperon 5.8
Pasadoble 9-2
   OMongelluzzo 3.9
4/10 RIVER LADY and Pasadoble,
6/1 Parannda, Vidor, 8/1 Estere,
17/1 Princely Penny, 19/1 Typhoon
Polly, 24/1 Star Guide, 52/1 Mac
Rhefna.
   R. Sangster (F. Boutin) 9ran
1m 39.6 (Good).

7 PRIX GANAY   1m 2½f
£36,530   Longchamp   2 May
   Bikala 4-9-2 SGorli........**1**
   Lancastrian 5-9-2 FHead.½.**2**
   Al Nasr (Fr) 4-9-2
     AGibert 2.**3**
   Vayrann 4-9-2
     YSaint-Martin s.nk.4
   Lord Jack 5-9-2 HSamani.nk.5
   Protection Rocket 4-9-2
     ALequeux ¾.6
   Kalaglow 4-9-2
     GStarkey s.nk.7
   April Run 4-8-13
     LPiggott 5.8
   Maraway 6-9-2 PLagoutte.15.9
   Marasali 4-9-2 ABadel......10
16/10 BIKALA and Maraway, 3/1
Vayrann, 7/2 April Run, 8/1
Kalaglow, 11/1 Protection Racket
and Marasali, Al Nasr, Lancastrian,
34/1 Lord Jack.
   J. Ouaki (P-L. Biancone) 10ran
2m 9.7 (Good).

8 DERBY ITALIANO
     (3y c+f)   1½m
£42,863   Rome   9 May
   Old Country 9-2 PEddery..**1**
   Teofane 9-2 WCarson...3.**2**
   Bater 9-2 GDettori......2.**3**
   Yard Bird 9-2 GBaxter....½.4
   Torbrak 9-2 MDepalmas.hd.5
   Rajhaan 9-2 J Reid......2½.6
   Alan Huth 9-2 RFestinesi.8.7
   Green Ray 9-2 SFancera..1½.8
   Big Hit 9-2 ASauli.........9
   Conte Rualp 9-2 PPerlanti..10
   Barba di Becco 9-2
     EBietolini 11
   Hiregote 9-2 SDettori.....12
16/10 Rajhaan, 18/10 OLD
COUNTRY, 47/10 Bater, 48/10
Yard Bird, 12/1 Green Ray, 20/1
Teofane, 27/1 Torbrak, 28/1 Barba
di Becco, 72/1 Conte Rualp, 75/1
Hiregote, 120/1 Alan Huth, 237/1
Big Hit.
   Mrs O. Abegg (L. Cumani)
12ran 2m 35.8 (Heavy).

9 AIRLIE/COOLMORE
IRISH TWO THOUSAND
GUINEAS (3y c+f) 1m
£63,671 The Curragh 15 May

5 **Dara Monarch** 9-0
  MJKinane **1**
5³ **Tender King** 9-0 EHide. . 3.**2**
  Red Sunset 9-0 GCurran. ½.**3**
  Anfield 9-0 CRoche. 1½.4
5² Wind and Wuthering 9-0
  PWaldon s.hd.5
5 Achieved 9-0 GMcGrath. 1½.6
  Raconteur 9-0 PEddery. . . 2.7
  Barbender 9-0 RCarroll. . . 3.8
  Cajun 9-0 LPiggott. 5.9
  Gouverno 9-0 MNikki. . . . 2.10
  Chivalry 9-0 VRossiter. . . 2½.11
  Philip Martin 9-0 SCraine. . 12
5 Full Extent 9-0 JLowe. 13
  Malspin 9-0 FSkelly. 14

2/1 Wind and Wuthering, 4/1
Cajun, Raconteur, 7/1 Anfield,
Tender King, 16/1 Achieved, 20/1
DARA MONARCH, 25/1 Full
Extent, 33/1 Red Sunset, 40/1
Barbender, 50/1 Gouverno, 100/1
Chivalry, Malspin, Philip Martin.
 Mrs L. Browne (L. Browne) 14ran
1m 41.8 (Good).

10 PRIX LUPIN 1m 2½f
  (3y c+f)
£45,872 Longchamp 16 May

  Persepolis 9-2 LPiggott. . . . **1**
  Alfred's Choice 9-2
  GDoleuze 2.**2**
  Sharp Singer 9-2
  ALequeux ½.**3**
  Le Monastere 9-2 SGorli. . . 2.4
2² Tampero 9-2
  MPhilipperon ½.5
  Epoc Chance 9-2
  J-YGuerrier 7
  Terson 9-2 AGibert. 2.8
  Welsh Term 9-2 FHead. . . . 8.9
  Academic 9-2 ABadel. 2.10
  Garibaldi 9-2
  GDubroeucq . . . . disq

6/4 Sharp Singer and Academic,
18/10 PERSEPOLIS, 23/4
Tampero, 10/1 Garibaldi, 11/1
Alfred's Choice, 13/1 Welsh Term,
20/1 Le Monastere, 54/1 Terson,
68/1 Epoc Chance.
Garibaldi finished sixth, 2 lengths
behind Tampero and ½ length in
front of Epoc Chance, but was
disqualified and placed last.
 S. Niarchos (F. Boutin) 10ran
2m 9.8 (Good to Firm).

11 OAKS D'ITALIA 1m 3f
  (3y f)
£25,729 Milan 16 May
3² **Ilenia** 8-11 GDettori. **1**
3* **Rosananti** 8-11 WCarson. 1.**2**

3³ **Smageta** 8-11 GStarkey. . 1.**3**
  Friendswood 8-11
  AParravani nk.4
  American Baby 8-11
  MDepalmas ½.5
  Berbera 8-11 AMarcialis. . 2.6
3 Delices 8-11 SDettori. . . . ½.7
  Marduchea 8-11 ADiNardo. 3.8
  Sygne 8-11 JReid. 4.9
3 Maria Stuarda 8-11
  SFancera 10
  Spitinfia 8-11 PPerlanti. . . . 11
  Gold Desire 8-11 EHide. . . . 12

6/4 Rosananti, 7/2 ILENIA and
Sygne, 4/1 Smageta and Spitinfia,
5/1 Delices, 6/1 Friendswood,
15/1 Maria Stuarda, 40/1 American
Baby, 45/1 Berbera, 50/1 Marduchea,
100/1 Gold Desire.
 Scuderia Cieffedi (A. Botti)
12ran 2m 17.9 (Good).

12 GOFFS IRISH ONE
THOUSAND GUINEAS
  (3y f) 1m
£41,777 The Curragh 22 May

  Prince's Polly 9-0
  WSwinburn **1**
  Woodstream 9-0 PEddery. 1.**2**
4* **On The House** 9-0
  JReid s.hd.**3**
  Kazankina 9-0 SCraine. . . . ½.4
  Mary Mitsu 9-0
  WCarson 2½.5
  Legal Expertise 9-0
  DGillespie hd.6
  Miss Lilian 9-0 AMurray. . 1½.7
  Bonnie Bess 9-0 JDeegan. 1¾.8
  More Heather 9-0
  MJKinane ½.9
  Quite Shy 9-0 GCurran. . . ½.10
  Murcot 9-0 NByrne. 11
  Sweet Side 9-0 JVSmith. . . . 12
  Oileann Carrig 9-0 RCarroll. 13
  Fly Start 9-0 CRoche. 14
  Tumble Belle 9-0
  PVGilson 15
  Cooliney Princess 9-0
  GMcGrath 16
  Salmette 9-0 WRSwinburn. 17
  Ounavarra 9-0 DParnell. . . . 18
  Bustereen 9-0 EHide 19
  Beechmount Lass 9-0
  JGO'Neill. 20
  Batwoman 9-0
  JoannaMorgan 21
  Turk O Witz 9-0 PLowry. . . 22
  Ogamissa 9-0 MDuffy. 23
  Royal Suite 9-0
  MPDwyer 24

3/1 On The House, 7/2 Wood-
stream, 8/1 Mary Mitsu, 10/1 Miss
Lilian, 12/1 PRINCE'S POLLY,
14/1 Cooliney Princess, Fly Start,
Salmette, 16/1 Oileann Carrig, 20/1
More Heather, 25/1 Bustereen,
Kazankina, 33/1 Quite Shy, 50/1

943

Legal Expertise, Royal Suite, Sweet Side, 66/1 Bonnie Bess, 100/1 Batwoman, Beechmount Lass, Murcot, Ogamissa, Ounavarra, Tumble Bell, Turk O Witz.
K. Fitzpatrick (D. Weld) 24ran 1m 40.5 (Good).

13 PRIX SAINT-ALARY
        (3y f)   1¼m
£37,140   Longchamp   23 May
    Harbour 9-2 FHead.......**1**
    All Along 9-2 SGorli.....**4.2**
    Perlee 9-2 AGibert......1½.**3**
6² Typhoon Polly 9-2
        GDubroeucq s.nk.4
    Grease 9-2 CAsmussen....6.5
6³ Vidor 9-2 ALequeux.....nk.6
4   Play It Safe 9-2 LPiggott.nk.7
    Wild Run 9-2 PLagoutte...8.8
7/10 All Along and Wild Run, 17/4 Play It Safe, 11/2 HARBOUR, 15/2 Grease, 11/1 Perlee, 16/1 Typhoon Polly, 18/1 Vidor.
    Ecurie Aland (Mme C. Head) 8ran 2m 20.1 (Heavy).

14 PRIX DU CADRAN   2½m
£27,855   Longchamp   23 May
    El Badr 7-9-2 AGibert.....**1**
    Tipperary Fixer 4-9-2
        MPhilipperon s.hd.**2**
    Halsbury 4-9-2 JMercer ..2.**3**
    Hereas 5-9-2
        YSaint-Martin 4.4
    Starski 4-9-2 FHead....dist.5
12/10 EL BADR, 3/1 Halsbury, 13/4 Starski, 4/1 Hereas, 19/4 Tipperary Fixer.
    M. Fustok (M. Saliba) 5ran 5m 19.1 (Heavy).

15 PREMIO PRESIDENTE
        DELLA REPUBBLICA 1¼m
£21,692   Rome   23 May
    Maffei 3-8-6 OPessi.......**1**
1* **Sorabancies** 3-8-6
        GDettori **4.2**
    Dentz 4-9-7 SFancera....hd.**3**
    Efidanville 4-9-7
        RSannino............3½.4
    Seiorlando 4-9-7
        MMassimi.............4.5
    Buonamico 4-9-7 ASauli...3.6
    Great Pretense 3-8-6
        RFestinesi 3.7
8   Torbrak 3-8-6 BJovine....3.8
5/6 Dentz, 7/2 MAFFEI, 9/2 Sorabancies, 7/1 Buonamico, 18/1 Torbrak, 25/1 Efidanville, 33/1 Seiorlando, 66/1 Great Pretense.
    Razza Dormello-Olgiata (U. Pandolfi) 8ran 2m 2.4 (Good).

16 GRAN PREMIO
        D'ITALIA   (3y c+f)   1½m
£25,773   Milan   30 May
    Oui Mon Capitaine 9-2
        MDepalmas **1**
8³ **Bater** 9-2 LPiggott.......3.**2**
    Tirak 9-2 AParravani....2½.**3**
8² Teofane 9-2 WCarson....5.4
    Johnny Logan 9-2
        PPerlanti 3.5
8   Green Ray 9-2 SFancera...4.6
11* Ilenia 8-13 GDettori......6.7
    Baran 9-2 CCastaldi......10.8
6/5 Ilenia, 6/4 Bater, Tirak and Baran, 9/2 Teofane, 6/1 OUI MON CAPITAINE, 13/2 Johnny Logan, 33/1 Green Ray.
    R. Scully (J. Fellows) 8ran 2m 31.2 (Good).

17 DERBY STAKES   1½m
        (3y c+f)
£146,720   Epsom   2 June
    Golden Fleece 9-0 PEddery.**1**
    Touching Wood 9-0
        PCook 3.**2**
5   **Silver Hawk** 9-0 AMurray.1.**3**
10* Persepolis 9-0
        YSaint-Martin hd.4
    Norwich 9-0 GStarkey....1½.5
    Palace Gold 9-0 TIves.....3.6
    Peacetime 9-0 JMercer....4.7
5   Rocamadour 9-0
        WRSwinburn 4.8
    Count Pahlen 9-0
        GBaxter..............1½.9
    Fitzwarren 9-0 RWeaver..2.10
    Tidworth Tattoo 9-0
        BRouse hd.11
    Super Sunrise 9-0
        EHide hd.12
    Father Rooney 9-0
        SCauthen s.hd.13
    Jalmood 9-0 WCarson....8.14
    Lobkowiez 9-0 BTaylor...4.15
    Reef Glade 9-0 PWaldron...16
5   Wongchoi 9-0 DBrosnan...17
    Florida Son 9-0 EJohnson..18
3/1 GOLDEN FLEECE, 4/1 Jalmood, Persepolis, 6/1 Peacetime, 14/1 Silver Hawk, 20/1 Rocamadour, Super Sunrise, 25/1 Palace Gold, 28/1 Father Rooney, 33/1 Count Pahlen, Norwich, 40/1 Touching Wood, 150/1 Wongchoi, 200/1 Lobkowiez, 250/1 Fitzwarren, Florida Son, Reef Glade, 300/1 Tidworth Tattoo.
    R. Sangster (V. O'Brien, Ireland) 18ran 2m 34.27 (Firm).

18 CORONATION CUP   1½m
£43,176   Epsom   3 June
    Easter Sun 5-9-0
        BRaymond **1**

944

Glint of Gold 4-9-0
JMatthias.............½.2
Critique 4-9-0 LPiggott..2¼.3
Castle Keep 5-9-0
PEddery.............1½.4
Prince Bee 5-9-0 WCarson.2.5
7² Lancastrian 5-9-0 FHead.nk.6
7 Protection Racket 4-9-0
ALequeux..............7
Show-A-Leg 4-9-0 PCook...8
7/4 Glint of Gold, 9/2 Lancastrian,
7/1 Castle Keep, Critique, Prince
Bee, 14/1 Protection Racket, 20/1
EASTER SUN, 100/1 Show-A-
Leg.
Lady Beaverbrook (M. Jarvis)
8ran 2m 35.05 (Firm).

19 OAKS STAKES (3y f) 1½m
£97,034 Epsom 5 June
4² **Time Charter** 9-0
WNewnes..............1
4 **Slightly Dangerous** 9-0
PCook 1.2
Last Feather 9-0
SCauthen............1½.3
Awaasif 9-0 PWaldron.....¾.4
Zinzara 9-0 PEddery.....1½.5
13² All Along 9-0
YSaint-Martin 1.6
Cut Loose 9-0 WCarson...2.7
Cadi Ha 9-0 GBaxter......4.8
Tants 9-0 LPiggott.......2.9
4³ Dione 9-0 JMercer......12.10
Devon Air 9-0 BRouse....¾.11
Brummendelle 9-0
DDineley 12
Swiftfoot 9-0 GStarkey.....13
4/1 Tants, 9/2 Zinzara, 11/2 Last
Feather, 10/1 Awaasif, Cut Loose,
Slightly Dangerous, 12/1 All Along,
TIME CHARTER, 14/1 Dione,
15/1 Swiftfoot, 40/1 Cadi Ha, 66/1
Devon Air, 750/1 Brummendelle.
R. Barnett (H. Candy) 13ran 2m
34.21 (Firm).

20 PRIX DU JOCKEY-
CLUB (3y c+f) 1½m
£81,008 Chantilly 6 June
Assert 9-2 CRoche........1
Real Shadai 9-2
MPhilipperon 3.2
Bois de Grace 9-2
HSamani..............2.3
10² Alfred's Choice 9-2
GDoleuze ½.4
Noble Bloom 9-2 AGibert...¾.5
10 Le Monastere 9-2
YSaint-Martin 1.6
Beau Pretender 9-2 FHead.½.7
Cadoudal 9-2
J-LKessas hd.8
Criterion 9-2 GStarkey....½.9
River Sand 9-2
J-CDesaint 3.10

Ekaha 9-2 MPlanard........0
10³ Sharp Singer 9-2 ALequeux..0
Newjdar 9-2 SGorli.........0
Marcao 9-2 CAsmussen.....0
22/10 ASSERT, 7/2 Cadoudal,
11/2 Real Shadai, 27/4 Le Mona-
stere and Newjdar, 13/1 Bois de
Grace, 14/1 Sharp Singer, 15/1
Noble Bloom, 20/1 Beau Pretender,
22/1 Alfred's Choice, 26/1 Criterion,
Ekaha, 27/1 Marcao, 28/1 River
Sand.
R. Sangster (D. O'Brien, Ireland)
14ran 2m 29.5 (Good to Firm).

21 PREMIO EMILIO
TURATI 1m
£21,186 Milan 6 June
Stifelius 4-9-3 PPerlanti....1
Vargas Llosa 9-2
MDepalmas............1.2
Tres Gate 5-9-3
WCarson.............hd.3
15² Sorabancies 3-8-7
GDettori ¾.4
Pian del Lupo 5-9-3
OPessi ½.5
Charlo Mio 4-9-3 GFois...½.6
Star Melody 3-8-7
AParravani 1.7
11 Delices 3-8-4 SDettori.....3.8
Kings Envoy 3-8-7
APerrotta ....p.u
9/4 STIFELIUS, 11/4 Soraban-
cies, 5/1 Pian del Lupo, 7/1 Vargas
Llosa, 15/2 Tres Gate, 10/1 Star
Melody, 12/1 Delices, 13/1 Charlo
Mio, 14/1 Kings Envoy.
Scuderia Reheati (A. Botti) 9ran
1m 38.8 (Good).

22 PRIX DE DIANE HERMES
(3y f) 1m 2¼f
£59,322 Chantilly 13 June
13* **Harbour** 9-2 FHead......1
Akiyda 9-2 YSaint-Martin.2.2
Paradise 9-2
GDubroeucq 2.3
13 Vidor 9-2 ALequeux......¾.4
19 All Along 9-2 SGorli.......1.5
Buchanette 9-2 HSamani..2½.6
Pomme d'Ebene 9-2
MPhilipperon 8.7
Airmail 9-2 GGuignard...hd.8
13³ Perlee 9-2 AGibert.......10.9
6 Pasadoble 9-2
OMongelluzzo 10.10
Santa Musica 9-2 PBruneau..0
Ash Ridge 9-2 PEddery.....0
Ninoushka 9-2 CAsmussen...0
6* River Lady 9-2 LPiggott...p.u
12/10 HARBOUR and Santa
Musica, 2/1 River Lady, Pasadoble
and Ninoushka, 31/4 Akiyda, 35/4
Paradise and Vidor, 13/1 All Along,

16/1 Perlee, 21/1 Ash Ridge, Buchanette, 29/1 Pomme d'Ebene, 65/1
Airmail.
Ecurie Aland (Mme C. Head)
14ran 2m 16.8 (Heavy).

23 GOLD CUP   2½m
£42,649   Ascot   17 June
    Ardross 6-9-0 LPiggott.....**1**
14² **Tipperary Fixer** 4-9-0
        MPhilipperon 3.**2**
14* **El Badr** 7-9-0 AGibert...nk.**3**
    Noelino 6-9-0
        GCurran s.hd.4
    Dzudo 5-9-0 PEddery....10.5
1/5 ARDROSS, 10/1 El Badr,
Tipperary Fixer, 25/1 Noelino,
66/1 Dzudo.
C. St George (H. Cecil) 5ran
4m 35.24 (Firm).

24 KING'S STAND STAKES
              5f
£36,006   Ascot   18 June
    Fearless Lad 3-8-9 EHide..**1**
    Chellaston Park 3-8-6
        GBaxter 2.**2**
    Blue Singh 4-9-0
        WRSwinburn 1.**3**
    Tina's Pet 4-9-3 JMercer..hd.4
    Jester 3-8-9 SCauthen.....¾.5
    Sylvan Barbarosa 3-8-9
        BRouse 2½.6
    Peterhof 3-8-9 PEddery...nk.7
    Lucky Hunter 3-8-9
        WCarson nk.8
    Clanjolly 4-9-3 CRoche...hd.9
    Lightning Label 6-9-3
        GStarkey nk.10
9   Cajun 3-8-9 LPiggott....½.11
    Steel Charger 5-9-3 TIves ¾.12
    Crofthall 5-9-3 SPerks ...1.13
    My Lover 3-8-9 BRaymond
                          6.14
9/4 Jester, 6/1 Lightning Label, 8/1
Cajun, Peterhof, Tina's Pet, 10/1
Chellaston Park, FEARLESS LAD,
12/1 Lucky Hunter, 20/1 Crofthall,
My Lover, 25/1 Blue Singh, Clanjolly, Steel Charger, Sylvan Barbarosa.
G. Soulsby (R. D. Peacock)
14ran 1m 1.39 (Good to Firm)

25 IRISH SWEEPS DERBY
           (3y c+f)   1½m
£104,516   The Curragh 26 June
20* **Assert** 9-0 CRoche **1**
17³ **Silver Hawk** 9-0 AMurray 8.**2**
    Patcher 9-0 GCurran...2¼.**3**
    Favoloso 9-0 PEddery.....8.4
    Condell 9-0 DGillespie...hd.5
9   Raconteur 9-0
        WSwinburn 3.6
    Bruckner 9-0 GMcGrath..1.7

    Remanded 9-0
        RCarroll s.hd.8
5   Royal Rendevouz 9-0
        SCraine ½.9
    Grateful Heir 9-0
        MJKinane 2¼.10
4/7 ASSERT, 3/1 Silver Hawk,
11/1 Condell, 20/1 Royal Rendevouz, 25/1 Raconteur, 28/1 Patcher,
50/1 Bruckner, Favoloso, 66/1
Grateful Heir, 100/1 Remanded.
R. Sangster (D O'Brien) 10ran
2m 33.2 (Good).

26 GRAND PRIX DE PARIS
           (3y c+f)   1m 7f
£37,879   Longchamp   27 June
    Le Nain Jaune 8-11
        HSamani **1**
    Chem 8-11 ALequeux....2.**2**
    Rhoecus 8-11 PEddery...2.**3**
    Hollytino 8-11 FHead....1½.4
    Un Etendard 8-11
        CAsmussen ns.5
    Flower Prince 8-11
        MPhilipperon ¾.6
16* Oui Mon Capitaine 8-11
        YSaint-Martin 4.7
17   Super Sunrise 8-11 PCook.½.8
    My Midway 8-11
        GDubroeucq nk.9
20   Ekaha 8-11 MPlanard....5.10
    Petit Montmorency 8-11
        GDoleuze 11
5/2 Petit Montmorency and Oui
Mon Capitaine, 13/4 Chem, 37/10
LE NAIN JAUNE, 13/2 Super
Sunrise, 15/2 Flower Prince, 14/1
Hollytino, 17/1 My Midway, Un
Etendard, 21/1 Ekaha, 23/1 Rhoecus.
Baron G. de Rothschild (F.
Mathet) 11ran 3m 18.4 (Good).

27 PRIX D'ISPAHAN   1m 1½f
£37,879   Longchamp   27 June
7³ **Al Nasr (Fr)** 4-9-6
        ALequeux **1**
    The Wonder 4-9-6 FHead.¾.**2**
2* **Melyno** 3-8-9
        YSaint-Martin nk.**3**
    Big John 4-9-6 AGibert...2.4
    Mourtazam 4-9-6
        DVincent............2½.5
    Rattling Wind 4-9-3
        PEddery 8.6
6/10 Melyno, 9/4 The Wonder, 7/2
AL NASR and Mourtazam, 9/1
Big John, 19/1 Rattling Wind.
M. F. Dabaghi (A. Fabre) 6ran
1m 54.3 (Good).

28 CORAL-ECLIPSE
    STAKES   1¼m
£84,140   Sandown   3 July
7   **Kalaglow** 4-9-7 GStarkey...**1**
17   **Lobkowiez** 3-8-8 TIves....4.**2**

17 **Rocamadour** 3-8-8
  GSexton 1.3
17 Peacetime 3-8-8
  PEddery ¾.4
  Kind of Hush 4-9-7
  SCauthen 2.5
2 Telephone Man 3-8-8
  PWaldron hd.6
5 Prima Voce 3-8-8
  BRaymond s.hd.7
  Ya Zaman 5-9-7 AMurray 12.8
  Silver Season 4-9-7
  BRouse 2.9
11/10 KALAGLOW, 3/1 Peacetime, 7/1 Kind of Hush, 11/1 Lobkowiez, 14/1 Prima Voce, 25/1 Rocamadour, Ya Zaman, 50/1 Silver Season, 100/1 Telephone Man.
  A. Ward (G. Harwood) 9ran 2m 8.83 (Good)

29 GRAND PRIX DE   1m 4½f
  SAINT-CLOUD
£67,340   Saint-Cloud   4 July
18² **Glint of Gold** 4-9-8
  PEddery 1
18 **Lancastrian** 5-9-8
  ALequeux hd.2
20² **Real Shadai** 3-8-9
  MPhilipperon 3.3
20 Alfred's Choice 3-8-9
  GDoleuze 2½.4
7 Vayrann 4-9-8
  YSaint-Martin 3.5
26 Ekaha 3-8-9 MPlanard...2½.6
17 Persepolis 3-8-9 LPiggott..6.7
23² Tipperary Fixer 4-9-8
  FHead 20.8
20 Beau Pretender 3-8-9
  GGuignard 2.9
22/10 GLINT OF GOLD, 11/4 Persepolis, 7/2 Vayrann, 6/1 Real Shadai, 17/2 Beau Pretender, 11/1 Alfred's Choice, 12/1 Lancastrian, 31/1 Tipperary Fixer, 55/1 Ekaha
  P. Mellon (I. Balding) 9ran 2m 41.40 (Dead).

30 GRAN PREMIO DI   1½m
  MILANO
£41,580   Milan   4 July
  Terreno 4-9-6 CAsmussen..1
  Capricorn Line 4-9-6
  WCarson 2.2
16² **Bater** 3-8-8 GDettori..1½.3
  Mulberry 5-9-6
  J-PGoddard 2.4
26★ Oui Mon Capitaine 3-8-8
  MDepalmas 4.5
  Turbo 4-9-6 BRaymond.1½.6
  Solero 4-9-6 SDettori.....3.7
  Scouting Miller 5-9-6
  ASauli 8
8 Hiregote 3-8-8 ADiNardo...9
6/4 TERRENO, 5/2 Capricorn Line, 3/1 Oui Mon Capitaine, 4/1 Turbo, 5/1 Bater, 6/1 Mulberry, 10/1 Solero, 25/1 Scouting Miller, 100/1 Hiregote.
  G. A. Oldham (F. Boutin) 9ran 2m 31.8 (Good).

31 WILLIAM HILL JULY
  CUP   6f
£39,988   Newmarket   8 July
  Sharpo 5-9-6 PEddery.....1
  Vaigly Star 3-8-8
  WRSwinburn ¾.2
  Indian King (USA) 4-9-6
  GStarkey 1.3
9² Tender King 3-8-11
  BRaymond nk.4
  Gabitat 4-9-6 RCurant....¾.5
24 Tina's Pet 4-9-6
  BCrossley 3.6
  Not For Show 3-8-11
  JMercer hd.7
  Diamond Cutter 3-8-11
  RCochrane 2½.8
24 Crofthall 5-9-6 SPerks.....2.9
24 Jester 3-8-11 SCauthen..nk.10
  Kind Music 3-8-11
  AMurray hd.11
24³ Blue Singh 4-9-3 EHide..nk.12
  Blue Courtier 5-9-6
  ABredillet 1½.13
24 Lucky Hunter 3-8-11
  WCarson 1.14
  Molly 3-8-8 PCook......3.15
  Prince Echo 4-9-6
  LPiggott ½.16
2/1 Indian King, 3/1 Tender King, 13/2 SHARPO, 8/1 Jester, 9/1 Vaigly Star, 20/1 Not For Show, Prince Echo, Tina's Pet, 25/1 Diamond Cutter, 33/1 Molly, 40/1 Kind Music, Lucky Hunter, 50/1 Blue Courtier, Blue Singh, Crofthall, Gabitat.
  Miss M. Sheriffe (J. Tree) 16ran 1m 11.74 (Firm).

32 IRISH GUINNESS
  OAKS   (3y f)   1½m
£46,607   The Curragh   17 July
19 **Swiftfoot** 9-0 WCarson.....1
12★ **Prince's Polly** 9-0
  WSwinburn 3.2
11² **Rosananti** 9-0 PEddery...3.3
  Miss Connaught 9-0
  GCurran 2.4
  Santa Roseanna 9-0
  DGillespie 1½.5
12 Cooliney Princess 9-0
  GMcGrath hd.6
12 More Heather 9-0
  PVGilson 4.7
  Cairi Bai 9-0 CRoche....2½.8
  London Gal 9-0 JCoogan.1½.9
  Strike It Rich 9-0
  PShanahan 1½.10
Evens Prince's Polly, 4/1 SWIFT-FOOT, 13/2 Santa Roseanna, 8/1

Rosananti, 14/1 Cooliney Princess,
20/1 More Heather, 33/1 Miss
Connaught, Strike It Rich, 66/1
Cairi Bai, 200/1 London Gal.
Lord Rotherwick (R. Hern)
10ran 2m 33.8 (Good to Firm).

33 KING GEORGE VI AND
QUEEN ELIZABETH
DIAMOND STAKES 1½m
£126,472 Ascot 24 July
28* Kalaglow 4-9-7 GStarkey...1
25* Assert 3-8-8 CRoche....nk.2
29* Glint of Gold 4-9-7
PEddery 3.3
18³ Critique 4-9-7 LPiggott...nk.4
7* Bikala 4-9-7 SGorli.....nk.5
18* Easter Sun 5-9-7
BRaymond 10.6
Height of Fashion 3-8-5
WCarson.............8.7
Lafontaine 5-9-7 SCauthen.2.8
Dronacharya 6-9-7
JMercer t.o.9

10/11 Assert, 11/2 Bikala, 13/2
KALAGLOW, 9/1 Height of
Fashion, 10/1 Glint of Gold,
13/1 Critique, Easter Sun, 100/1
Lafontaine, 750/1 Dronacharya.
A. Ward (G. Harwood) 9ran
2m 31.88 (Good to Firm).

34 PRIX ROBERT PAPIN 5½f
(2y c+f)
£25,359 Maisons-Laffitte 25 July
Ma Biche 8-9 FHead......1
Deep Roots 8-11
YSaint-Martin 1½.2
Crime of Passion 8-9
WNewnes s.nk.3
American Stress 8-11
BPizzorni 1.4
Interco 8-11 GWMoore...½.5
Bal des Fees 8-11
JDupin s.hd.6
Stay Sharp 8-11 SCauthen.6.7
Targhese 8-9 ALequeux...5.8
Faith Guest 8-11
ADiNardo 3.9

Evens Deep Roots, 43/10 MA
BICHE, 9/2 Crime of Passion,
9/1 Targhese, 10/1 Interco, 12/1
American Stress, 15/1 Faith Guest,
26/1 Bal des Fees, 33/1 Stay Sharp.
Mme A. Head (Mme C. Head)
9ran 1m 5.3 (Good).

35 GROSSER PREIS VON
BERLIN 1½m
£28,302 Dusseldorf 25 July
Orofino 4-9-6 PAlafi.......1
Little Wolf 4-9-6
WCarson 1½.2
30* Terreno 4-9-6
OMongelluzzo 12.3
30 Turbo 4-9-6 PRemmert...3.4

Czubaryk 6-9-7 LMäder...2.5
Fall 3-8-5 ESchindler....12.6
Nephrit 7-9-7 JOrihuel......7

4/5 OROFINO, 22/10 Little Wolf,
3/1 Terreno, 17/1 Turbo, 20/1
Fall, 28/1 Czubaryk, 33/1 Nephrit.
Gestüt Zoppenbroich (S. von
Mitzlaff) 7ran 2m 34.6 (Good).

36 SUSSEX STAKES 1m
£54,664 Goodwood 28 July
12³ On The House 3-8-7 JReid..1
Sandhurst Prince 3-8-10
GStarkey ½.2
9 Achieved 3-8-10 PEddery.¾.3
31 Tender King 3-8-10
WCarson..............1.4
Bel Bolide 4-9-7
BRouse s.hd.5
Spanish Pool 3-8-10
BTaylor ½.6
27² The Wonder 4-9-7
LPiggott nk.7
Riyahi 3-8-10 EHide......1.8
Motavato 4-9-7 JMatthias..½.9
9³ Red Sunset 3-8-10
JMercer 4.10
Noalto 4-9-7 PCook......3.11
4 Merlins Charm 3-8-7
SCauthen ¾.12
28 Silver Season 4-9-7
BRaymond 3.13

4/1 Sandhurst Prince, Tender King,
The Wonder, 9/1 Merlins Charm,
11/1 Achieved, 12/1 Spanish Pool,
14/1 Noalto, 20/1 Bel Bolide,
40/1 Red Sunset, 50/1 Silver
Season, 66/1 Riyahi.
Sir P. Oppenheimer (H. Wragg)
13ran 1m 37.65 (Firm).

37 HEINZ "57" PHOENIX
STAKES (2y) 5f
£13,171 Leopardstown 7 August
Sweet Emma 8-11
GCurran 1
Najran 9-0 PGilson.......3.2
Solar System 9-0
WSwinburn nk.3
Flame of Tara 8-11
DGillespie 1.4
Red Rose Bowl 8-11
SCraine ¾.5
Treasure Trove 9-0
PEddery s.hd.6
Shapely Test 8-11
MKinane 1.7
Top Rated 8-11 CRoche...¾.8
Baton Charge 9-0
Joanna Morgan 3.9
Hot Princess 8-11
DParnell 3½.10
The Bould James 9-0
RCarroll 11

11/4 Najran, 3/1 Treasure Trove,
7/2 Flame of Tara, 12/1 Shapely

948

Test, SWEET EMMA, Top Rated, 16/1 Solar System, Red Rose Bowl, 20/1 Hot Princess, 50/1 Baton Charge, The Bould James.
Mrs J. Ramos (K. Prendergast) 11ran 1m 0.2 (Good to Firm).

38   PRIX JACQUES
     LE MAROIS   1m
£29,338   Deauville   15 August
36   **The Wonder** 4-9-2
         PEddery 1
2   **Green Forest** 3-8-9
         AGibert ½.2
5*   **Zino** 3-8-9 FHead ½.3
4   Exclusive Order 3-8-6
         MPhilpperon 2½.4
     Noalcoholic 5-9-2
         GDuffield 2.5
     What A Guest 3-8-9
         LPiggott 1½.6
     Phydilla 4-8-13 ALequeux.2.7
27³ Melyno 3-8-9 HSamani...20.8
     Spoleto 4-9-2 GWMoore...5.9
5/2 Melyno, 7/2 Noalcoholic, 13/4 Zino and Spoleto, 23/4 Exclusive Order, 62/10 THE WONDER, 35/4 Green Forest, 20/1 Phydilla, What A Guest.
Marquesa de Moratalla (J. de Chevigny) 9ran 1m 35.5 (Good).

39   ARAL-POKAL   1½m
£23,474 Gelsenkirchen-Horst
                        15 August
35* **Orofino** 4-9-6 PAlafi.......1
     Ataxerxes 5-9-2 ATylicki.3.2
     Ti Amo 4-9-2
         BRaymond 3.3
     Elektrant 4-9-2 GHuber...3.4
     Revlon Boy 6-9-2
         LMäder hd.5
     Maivogel 5-9-2
         HHorwart 2½.6
     Alex 5-9-2 SEccles.........7
     Areopag 5-9-2
         DRichardson 8
     Lützow 3-8-3 ESchindler....9
     Maldix 3-8-3
         Manfred Hofer 10
35   Nephrit 7-9-2 JOrihuel....11
     Kai 5-9-2 PRemmert......12
3/10 OROFINO, 3/1 Ataxerxes, 12/1 Ti Amo, 20/1 Maldix, 25/1 Lützow, 33/1 Maivogel, Revlon Boy, 37/1 Elektrant, 43/1 Kai, 60/1 Nephrit, 80/1 Alex, 85/1 Areopag.
Gestüt Zoppenbroich (S. von Mitzlaff) 12ran 2m 35.7 (Soft).

40   BENSON AND HEDGES
     GOLD CUP   1m 2½f
£81,800   York   17 August
33² **Assert** 3-8-10 PEddery.....1
17   **Norwick** 3-8-10
         GStarkey 6.2

     Amyndas 4-9-6 GBaxter.nk.3
18   Castle Keep 5-9-6
         WCarson 1½.4
     Mr Fluorocarbon 3-8-10
         LPiggott s.hd.5
     Be My Native 3-8-10
         BRaymond 1½.6
     Say Primula 4-9-6 EHide.10.7
4/5 ASSERT, 9/4 Mr Fluorocarbon, 10/1 Amyndas, Castle Keep, 16/1 Norwick, 25/1 Be My Native, 100/1 Say Primula.
R. Sangster (D. O'Brien, Ireland) 7ran 2m 9.09 (Good to Firm).

41   YORKSHIRE OAKS   1½m
                      (3y f)
£40,564   York   17 August
19   **Awaasif** 9-0 LPiggott......1
32* **Swiftfoot** 9-0 WCarson..nk.2
     Dish Dash 9-0
         BRaymond hd.3
     Dancing Rocks 9-0 EHide.2½.4
19   Cut Loose 9-0 JMercer....3.5
19³ Last Feather 9-0
         SCauthen 3.6
33   Height of Fashion 9-0
         GStarkey 12.7
11/4 Swiftfoot, 4/1 AWAASIF, Dancing Rocks, 5/1 Last Feather, 11/2 Height of Fashion, 10/1 Cut Loose, 25/1 Dish Dash.
Sheikh Mohammed (J. Dunlop) 7ran 2m 30.57 (Good to Firm).

42   PRIX MORNY (2y c+f) 6f
£25,021   Deauville   22 August
34² **Deep Roots** 8-11
         WCarson 1
     On Stage 8-11 TIves......3.2
34* **Ma Biche** 8-8 FHead.s.nk.3
34   Bal des Fees 8-11
         AGibert hd.4
     Gormanstown Prince 8-11
         GWMoore 8.5
     Gallant Special 8-11
         LPiggott 6.6
7/4 Ma Biche, 11/4 Gallant Special, 9/2 On Stage, 69/10 DEEP ROOTS, 12/1 Bal des Fees, 15/1 Gormanstown Prince.
Mme P. Barbe (P. Bary) 6ran 1m 11.1 (Good to Firm).

43   PRIX DU MOULIN DE 1m
     LONGCHAMP
£33,223 Longchamp 5 September
38² **Green Forest** 3-8-12
         AGibert 1
38* **The Wonder** 4-9-2
         FHead 3.2
36² **Sandhurst Prince** 3-8-12
         GStarkey 1½.3
38   Melyno 3-8-12 HSamani.1½.4
     Lichine 3-8-12 LPiggott...1.5

949

Prospero 5-9-2 CRamonet..¾.6
21² Vargas Llosa 6-9-2
ALequeux 1½.7
Thorough 4-8-13 WCarson..¾.8
Samer 4-9-2 AGoldsztejn.15.9
6/4 Sandhurst Prince, 2/1 The
Wonder, 7/2 GREEN FOREST
and Samer, 15/4 Melyno and
Lichine, 21/1 Prospero, Vargas
Llosa, 27/1 Thorough.
M. Fustok (M. Saliba) 9ran
1m 34.9 (Firm).

44   GROSSER PREIS   1½m
     VON BADEN
£40,888 Baden-Baden 5 September
33³ Glint of Gold 4-9-6
     PEddery 1
39★ Orofino 4-9-6 PAlafi....2½.2
39³ Ti Amo 4-9-6 MHofer....5.3
30   Mulberry 5-9-6
     J-PGodard s.hd.4
     Index 4-9-6 GBocskai..dist.5
39   Maivogel 5-9-6
     DRichardson 2½.6
39   Elektrant 4-9-6 GHuber..6.7
3/5 GLINT OF GOLD, 9/5 Orofino, 8/1 Ti Amo, 13/1 Index, 17/1
Mulberry, 20/1 Elektrant, Maivogel.
P. Mellon (I. Balding) 7ran
2m 29.1 (Good).

45   ST LEGER   1¾m 127y
     STAKES   (3y c+f)
£80,120 Doncaster 11 September
17² Touching Wood 9-0 PCook.1
     Zilos 9-0 GBaxter......1½.2
     Diamond Shoal 9-0
     JMatthias 2½.3
40² Norwick 9-0 GStarkey....¾.4
28³ Rocamadour 9-0 EHide....2.5
17   Jalmood 9-0 LPiggott...nk.6
     Khairpour 9-0 JReid..s.hd.7
17   Palace Gold 9-0 TIves..2½.8
     Broken Rail 9-0 WCarson.5.9
26² Chem 9-0 ALequeux....2.10
     Born Hero 9-0 WNewnes.1½.11
26★ Le Nain Jaune 9-0
     HSamani 5.12
     Rivellino 9-0 EJohnson.nk.13
     Muslab 9-0 TRogers...3.14
     Electric 9-0
     WRSwinburn t.o.15
100/30 Electric, 5/1 Jalmood, 13/2
Le Nain Jaune, 7/1 TOUCHING
WOOD, 8/1 Broken Rail, 17/2
Chem, 9/1 Diamond Shoal, 10/1
Norwick, 28/1 Khairpour, Roca-
madour, 30/1 Born Hero, 40/1
Palace Gold, Zilos, 66/1 Rivellino,
100/1 Muslab.
Maktoum Al-Maktoum (H. T.
Jones) 15ran 3m 3.53 (Firm).

46   PRIX VERMEILLE   1½m
                          (3y f)
£49,423 Longchamp 12 September
22   All Along 9-2 GStarkey 1
22² Akiyda 9-2
     YSaint-Martin 1½.2
13   Grease 9-2 GWMoore..hd.3
22★ Harbour 9-2 FHead.....¾.4
22   Perlee 9-2 AGibert......½.5
     Zalataia 9-2
     WRSwinburn nk.6
41★ Awaasif 9-2 LPiggott....1½.7
22   Vidor 9-2 GDubroeucq...8.8
22³ Paradise 9-2 J-CDesaint..¾.9
     Sham's Princess 9-2
     ALequeux ½.10
     Kawarah 9-2 HSamani......0
     Dish Dash 9-2 WCarson....0
     Hanna Alta 9-2 PBruneau...0
5/4 Harbour and Hanna Alta, 4/1
Grease, 21/4 Akiyda and Kawarah,
73/10 ALL ALONG, 10/1 Awaasif,
14/1 Zalataia, 15/1 Paradise and
Vidor, 21/1 Perlee, 40/1 Dish
Dash, 46/1 Sham's Princess.
D. Wildenstein (P-L. Biancone)
13ran 2m 29.9 (Firm).

47   JOE MCGRATH   1¼m
     MEMORIAL STAKES
£16,790   Leopardstown
                        18 September
40★ Assert 3-8-11 CRoche.....1
28   Kind of Hush 4-9-5
     SCauthen 3.2
     Punctilio 3-8-11
     PEddery 1½.3
     Stanera 4-9-2 WSwinburn.5.4
25   Royal Rendevouz 3-8-11
     GCurran 2½.5
     Steel Duke 6-9-5 SCraine.nk.6
32   Santa Roseanna 3-8-8
     DGillespie nk.7
     Northern Glory 4-9-5
     MJKinane 8.8
     Honest Broker 3-8-11
     RCarroll 9
     Valley King 3-8-11
     GMcGrath 10
1/4 ASSERT, 8/1 Kind of Hush,
Punctilio, 12/1 Steel Duke, 16/1
Royal Rendevouz, 20/1 Santa
Roseanna, Stanera, 100/1 Honest
Broker, Northern Glory, Valley
King.
R. Sangster (D. O'Brien) 10ran
2m 6.3 (Good to Firm).

48   PRIX DE LA
     SALAMANDRE
                (2y c+f)   7f
£24,793 Longchamp 19 September
42★ Deep Roots 8-11 WCarson..1
     Maximova 8-8
     FHead d-ht.1

Crystal Glitters 8-11
AGibert..............3.3
34 Interco 8-11 J-LKessas...1¼.4
Soigneuse 8-8 LPiggott...1½.5
Ginger Brink 8-11
ALequeux..........1½.6

6/4 DEEP ROOTS, MAXIMOVA, 11/4 Crystal Glitters, 17/4 Interco, 19/4 Soigneuse, 26/1 Ginger Brink. DEEP ROOTS, Mme P. Barbe (P. Bary). MAXIMOVA, Haras D'Etreham (Mme C. Head) 6ran 1m 23.2 (Firm).

49 **WILLIAM HILL CHEVELEY PARK STAKES** (2y f)   6f
£39,118 Newmarket 29 September
42³ **Ma Biche** 8-11 FHead......1
Favoridge 8-11 PEddery..¾.2
Super Entente 8-11
EHide 2.3
Widaad 8-11
WRSwinburn..........2.4
Myra's Best 8-11
SCauthen.............¾.5
Shicklah 8-11 PCook.....2½.6
Fairlawne 8-11 JReid.....nk.7
37* Sweet Emma 8-11
LPiggott 1½.8
Evening Belle 8-11
WCarson 3.9

13/8 Favoridge, 11/4 MA BICHE, 8/1 Sweet Emma, Widaad, 14/1 Evening Belle, Myra's Best, Shicklah, 25/1 Super Entente, 66/1 Fairlawne.
Mme A. Head (Mme C. Head) 9ran 1m 14 63 (Good).

50 **WILLIAM HILL MIDDLE PARK STAKES** (2y c+f)   6f
£39,268 Newmarket 30 September
Diesis 9-0 LPiggott........1
Orixo 9-0 WCarson......2½.2
Krayyan 9-0
BRaymond 1½.3
Kafu 9-0 GStarkey........1.4
Ancestral 9-0 PEddery.....¾.5

10/11 DIESIS, 7/2 Ancestral, 5/1 Kafu, 6/1 Krayyan, 16/1 Orixo.
Lord H. de Walden (H. Cecil) 5ran 1m 13.36 (Good).

51 **PREMIO LYDIA TESIO** (Gr 1) (3+4y f) 1¼m
£20,695   Rome   2 October
11 **Friendswood** 3-8-10
OPessi..................1
11³ **Smageta** 3-8-10
PPerlanti 4.2
Stately Girl 3-8-10
SFancera 7.3

Tanapa 3-8-10
LFicuciello 1.4
Black Nobility 4-9-0
RSannino..............1.5
Saimore 3-8-10
LBietolini ½.6
16 Ilenia 3-8-10 GDettori.....2.7
Oltremare 3-8-10 BPanico...2.8
11 Sygne 3-8-10 RFestinesi...4.9

5/6 Ilenia and Sygne, 7/2 Smageta, 9/2 FRIENDSWOOD, 6/1 Saimore, 8/1 Stately Girl, 18/1 Tanapa, 33/1 Black Nobility, 100/1 Oltremare.
N. B. Hunt (L. Turner) 9ran 2m 0.4 (Soft).

52 **PRIX MARCEL BOUSSAC** (2y f)   1m
£24,752 Longchamp 3 October
Goodbye Shelley 8-9
JLowe.................1
Mysterieuse Etoile 8-9
AGibert s.hd.2
L'Attrayante 8-9
ALequeux..............3
48² Maximova 8-9 FHead.......4
Alma Ata 8-9
GDubroeucq ½.5
Rose de Bagdad 8-9
FPegurri ½.6
Air Distingue 8-9
CAsmussen 1½.7
37 Top Rated 8-9 PEddery....4.8
Tarte Chaude 8-9 RBriard..4.9
Arta 8-9 SGorli.........10.10
Solidarite 8-9 PBruneau....11

1/2 Maximova and Solidarite, 17/4 Air Distingue, 13/2 Mysterieuse Etoile, 12/1 Alma Ata, 17/1 Top Rated, 29/1 Tarte Chaude, 31/1 Arta, L'Attrayante, 36/1 GOODBYE SHELLEY, 54/1 Rose de Bagdad.
Maximova finished third, a length behind Mysterieuse Etoile and ¾ length in front of L'Attrayante, but after an objection and a stewards' inquiry was placed fourth. L'Attrayante was promoted to third place.
Mrs S. Brook (S. Norton) 11ran 1m 47.4 (Soft).

53 **PRIX DE L'ABBAYE DE LONGCHAMP**   5f
£24,752 Longchamp 3 October
31* **Sharpo** 5-9-11 PEddery....1
24* **Fearless Lad** 3-9-11
EHide 1.2
31 **Kind Music** 3-9-11
FHead..............hd.3
31 Blue Courtier 5-9-11
ABredillet 2.4
31 Jester 3-9-11
SCauthen..........s.hd.5
Music Streak 4-9-11
LPiggott ¾.6

Sayyaf 5-9-11 TIves.......1.7
Exclusive Order 3-9-7
  MPhilipperon........s.nk.8
24 Lightning Label 6-9-11
  PWaldron 1¼.9
Dear Prince 3-9-11
  AGibert.............6.10
Chart Topper 3-9-11
  ALequeux..............0
Conversion 3-9-11 AMurray.0
31 Tina's Pet 4-9-11 MMiller...0
4/5 SHARPO, 23/4 Sayyaf, 31/4
Chart Topper and Kind Music, 10/1
Exclusive Order, 12/1 Fearless Lad,
15/1 Tina's Pet, 17/1 Jester, 20/1
Lightning Label, 24/1 Music Streak,
32/1 Blue Courtier, 64/1 Dear
Prince, 86/1 Conversion.
  Miss M. Sheriffe (J. Tree) 13ran
1m 00.2 (Soft).

54 TRUSTHOUSE FORTE
  PRIX DE L'ARC DE
  TRIOMPHE   1½m
£165,016 Longchamp 3 October
46² Akiyda 3-8-8
  YSaint-Martin..........1
23* Ardross 6-9-4 LPiggott..hd.2
46 Awaasif 3-8-8 WCarson...½.3
7 April Run 4-9-1
  CAsmussen...........hd.4
29³ Real Shadai 3-8-11
  MPhilipperon.........4.5
No Attention 4-9-2
  ALequeux.............1.6
20 Cadoudal 3-8-11
  J-LKessas............1½.7
33 Critique 4-9-4 JMercer....¾.8
46 Harbour 3-8-8 FHead...s.hd.9
20 Newjdar 3-8-11
  GGuignard ¾.10
47* Assert 3-8-11 PEddery..hd.11
33 Bikala 4-9-4 SGorli.....1½.12
Bon Sang 3-8-11
  AGibert.............1½.13
41 Last Feather 3-8-8
  SCauthen............2.14
46* All Along 3-8-8 GStarkey...15
Mariacho 4-9-4
  GDubroeucq...........16
Kastet 3-8-11 AChavouev..17
5/2 Assert, 11/2 Bon Sang, 25/4
Ardross, Harbour, 13/2 Bikala, 11/1
AKIYDA, 15/1 April Run, 17/1
All Along, 22/1 Real Shadai, 26/1
Kastet, 39/1 No Attention, 54/1
Cadoudal, 56/1 Mariacho, 58/1 Last
Feather, 69/1 Critique, 90/1 Awaa-
sif, 99/1 Newjdar.
  H. H. Aga Khan (F. Mathet)
17ran 2m 37.0 (Soft).

55 JEFFERSON SMURFIT
  MEMORIAL IRISH
  ST LEGER   1¾m
  (3y c + f)
£35,956 The Curragh 9 October

45* Touching Wood 9-0
  PCook 1
17 Father Rooney 9-0
  SCauthen 2.2
41² Swiftfoot 8-11 WCarson..8.3
Future Spa 9-0 GMcGrath.5.4
45 Muslab 9-0 TRogers....s.hd.5
Sam John 9-0 CRoche....1.6
Home And Dry 8-11
  SCraine 3½.7
Konigin Kate 8-11
  MKinane 1.8
25³ Patcher 9-0 GCurran....2½.9
Nolan 9-0 WSwinburn..t.o.10
5/4 TOUCHING WOOD, 6/4
Swiftfoot, 8/1 Patcher, 10/1 Future
Spa, 14/1 Father Rooney, 50/1
Sam John, 100/1 Home And Dry,
Konigin Kate, Muslab, Nolan.
  Maktoum Al-Maktoum (H. T.
Jones) 10ran 3m 10.2 (Soft).

56 GRAND CRITERIUM 1m
  (2y c + f)
£41,220 Longchamp 10 October
  Saint Cyrien 8-11 FHead..1
  L'Emigrant 8-11
  CAsmussen............1.2
  The Noble Player 8-11
  SCauthen ns.3
48* Deep Roots 8-11 WCarson.2.4
Insolent 8-11
  YSaint-Martin 5.5
48 Ginger Brink 8-11
  AGibert 3.6
Prince Kebir 8-11 SGorli...1.7
Midford 8-11
  OMongelluzzo 8.8
6/4 SAINT CYRIEN, 9/4 L'Emi-
grant and Midford, Deep Roots,
12/1 Insolent, 13/1 The Noble
Player, 24/1 Prince Kebir, 35/1
Ginger Brink.
  Mme A. Head (Mme C. Head)
8ran 1m 46.5 (Soft).

57 PREIS VON EUROPA 1½m
£69,767 Cologne 10 October
39² Ataxerxes 5-9-2 ATylicki...1
54 No Attention 4-9-2
  ALequeux ¾.2
45³ Diamond Shoal 3-8-7
  PCook ns.3
Arszlan 4-9-2 ESchindler....4
Pageno 3-8-7 EHide.......7.5
35 Turbo 4-8-7 PRemmert... 7
Razdel 3-8-11
  ATschugujevez 8
Ideal Point 3-8-7
  J-LKessas 9
Ludovico 5-9-2 LMader....10
Eliara 3-8-7 WJakowlew....11
Winslow 4-9-2 RSuerland..12
Rheinsteel 5-9-2 PAlafi.....13
Sharp End 4-9-2 GBocskai..14

45 Norwick 3-8-7 GStarkey..disq
39 Kai 5-9-2 DRichardson.....f
5/2 Diamond Shoal, 7/2 Norwick,
4/1 No Attention, 10/1 ATAX-
ERXES, 11/1 Sharp End, 17/1
Turbo, 18/1 Eliara, Winslow, 19/1
Ideal Point, 22/1 Rheinsteel, 25/1
Ludovico, 30/1 Kai, 33/1 Pageno,
Razdel, 40/1 Arszlan.
  Norwick finished fourth, three
lengths behind Diamond Shoal and
a head in front of Arszlan, but
after a stewards' inquiry was
disqualified and placed last.
  Gestut Schlenderhan (H. Jentzch)
15ran 2m 39.8 (Heavy).

58 GRAN CRITERIUM   1m
          (2y c+f)
£20,492   Milan   10 October
    Anguillo 8-11 GDettori.....1
    Beldale Concorde 8-11
        LPiggott 2.2
    My Top 8-11 PPerlanti...5.3
    Bigwood Cay 8-11
        BRaymond 1½.4
34 Faith Guest 8-11
        ADiNardo 2½.5
    Conan 8-11 AMarcialis...3½.6
    Charlie Yelverton 8-11
        AParravani 2½.7
    Maladonte 8-11 SDettori...3.8
3/5 Faith Guest, Evens Beldale
Concorde, 10/1 ANGUILLO, 12/1
Bigwood Cay, 14/1 Conan, 20/1
Maladonte, 30/1 Charlie Yelverton,
33/1 My Top.
  Scuderia Cieffedi (A. Botti) 8 ran
1m 13.1 (Soft).

59 WILLIAM HILL
    DEWHURST STAKES   7f
          (2y c+f)
£46,228   Newmarket   15 October
50★ **Diesis** 9-0 LPiggott.......1
    Gordian 9-0 GStarkey....5.2
    Tough Commander 9-0
        SCauthen 2.3
    Gorytus 9-0 WCarson....30.4
1/2 Gorytus, 2/1 DIESIS, 33/1
Gordian, 200/1 Tough Commander.
  Lord H de Walden (H. Cecil)
4ran 1m 27.46 (Good).

60 DUBAI CHAMPION
    STAKES   1¼m
£85,400   Newmarket   16 October
19★ **Time Charter** 3-8-7
        WNewnes 1
28 **Prima Voce** 3-8-10
        BRaymond 7.2
36 **Noalto** 4-9-3 WCarson..nk.3
5   Montekin 3-8-10 BTaylor.1½.4
    Princes Gate 5-9-3 PCook.½.5
8   Rajhaan 3-8-10 JReid....1½.6

17 Count Pahlen 3-8-10
        GBaxter 2¼.7
33★ Kalaglow 4-9-3 GStarkey..¾.8
47 Kind of Hush 4-9-3
        SCauthen ½.9
40³ Amyndas 4-9-3 AMurray...10
20 Criterion 3-8-10 LPiggott...11
28² Lobkowiez 3-8-10 TIves....12
    Buzzards Bay 4-9-3
        WRSwinburn 13
38³ Zino 3-8-10 FHead.......14
6/4 Kalaglow,   9/2   TIME
CHARTER, 7/1 Zino, 11/1 Buzzards Bay, 12/1 Criterion, 20/1
Count Pahlen, Kind of Hush, 22/1
Princes Gate, 25/1 Amyndas, 40/1
Noalto, 50/1 Lobkowiez, Montekin,
Prima Voce, 66/1 Rajhaan.
  R. Barnett (H. Candy) 14ran
2m 10.76 (Dead).

61 GRAN PREMIO DEL
    JOCKEY CLUB   1½m
£40,816   Milan   17 October
51★ **Friendswood** 3-8-8
        MJerome 1
30 **Solero** 4-9-3 SDettori.....4.2
    Karkour 4-9-3 GDettori..4.3
54 Cadoudal 3-8-11 JLKessas.2.4
15 Efidanville 4-9-3 LBietolini.8.5
35³ Terreno 4-9-3 LPiggott.....6
Evens Terreno, 6/5 Cadoudal,
2/1 Karkour, 15/1 FRIENDS-
WOOD, 20/1 Solero, 50/1 Efidanville.
  N. B. Hunt (L. Turner) 6ran
2m 36.9 (Heavy).

62 WILLIAM HILL
    FUTURITY STAKES   1m
          (2y c+f)
£50,842   Doncaster   23 October
    Dunbeath 9-0 LPiggott.....1
    Cock Robin 9-0
        WRSwinburn 1½.2
    Lyphard's Special 9-0
        BRaymond s.hd.3
    Muscatite 9-0 BTaylor...1½.4
58² Beldale Concorde 9-0
        SCauthen hd.5
    Shackle Pin 9-0 EJohnson.nk.6
    Neorion 9-0 PRobinson..2½.7
    Stratford Place 9-0 EHide....8
4/7 DUNBEATH, 6/1 Lyphard's
Special, Muscatite, 9/1 Cock Robin,
14/1 Beldale Concorde, 22/1
Neorion, 66/1 Stratford Place,
100/1 Shackle Pin.
  M. Riordan (H. Cecil) 8ran
1m 44.05 (Dead).

63 PRIX LA FORET   7f
£24,814   Longchamp   24 October
    Pas de Seul 3-9-11 CRoche.1
43² The Wonder 4-9-12
        PEddery 3.2

953

21³ **Tres Gate** 5-9-12
LPiggott 1½.3
27 Big John 4-9-12 FHead...nk.4
9★ Dara Monarch 3-9-11
MJKinane 1.5
28 Ya Zaman 5-9-12
AGibert s.nk.6
53 Jester 3-9-11 SCauthen...6.7
Dancing Devil 6-9-12
ABredillet 5.8
Valrant 3-9-11 YVasseur..8.9
Evens The Wonder, 5/4 Jester and
PAS DE SEUL, 5/2 Ya Zaman,
6/1 Big John, 13/1 Dara Monarch,
17/1 Tres Gate, 36/1 Valrant, 95/1
Dancing Devil.
R. Sangster (D. O'Brien, Ireland)
9ran 1m 27.7 (Heavy).

64 PRIX ROYAL-OAK 1m 7½f
£24,814 Longchamp 24 October
Denel 3-8-12 YSaint-Martin.1
57 **Ideal Point** 3-8-12
J-LKessas nk.2
Rienzi 3-8-12 SGorli.....3.3
No Attention 4-9-3 FHead.1.4
Balitou 3-8-12 AGibert..s.hd.5
35² Little Wolf 4-9-3 WCarson.1.6
45² Zilos 3-8-12 GBaxter.....4.7
Campero 5-9-3 ABadel....5.8
55 Muslab 3-8-12 PCook...1½.9
45 Le Nain Jaune 3-8-12
HSamani 5.10
7 Marasali 4-9-3 ALequeux...0

20 Le Monastere 3-8-12
GGuignard 0
45 Chem 3-8-12 LPiggott......0
2/1 Little Wolf, 3/1 No Attention,
23/4 Le Nain Jaune, 25/4 Zilos,
79/10 DENEL and Ideal Point,
33/4 Chem and Marasali, 14/1
Rienzi and Le Monastere, Balitou,
46/1 Campero, 88/1 Muslab.
Mme S. Nathan (B. Secly) 13ran
3m 44.2 (Heavy).

65 PREMIO ROMA (Gr1) 1¾m
£41,271 Rome 14 November
64 **Campero** 5-9-0 ALequeux..1
15³ **Dentz** 4-9-0 SFancera....15.2
30 **Scouting Miller** 5-9-0
GDettori 3.3
Rouge Oiseau 4-9-0
ASauli s.hd.4
Crusader Castle 3-8-10
JMatthias 4.5
Sa-Vegas 3-8-7 WCarson...2.6
61² Solero 4-9-0 AParravani...3.7
Haul Knight 6-9-0
AGibert 10.8
Sassonger 3-8-10
SDettori 6.9
6/4 Crusader Castle, 5/2 Sa-Vegas,
7/2 Dentz, 5/1 CAMPERO, 6/1
Solero, 7/1 Rouge Oiseau and
Scouting Miller, 18/1 Haul Knight,
33/1 Sassongher.
I. Correas (D. Smaga) 9ran 3m
14.5 (Heavy).

INDEX

954

An invaluable contribution to bloodstock data

PEDIGREES OF LEADING WINNERS
1960-1980

Compiled by Martin Pickering & Michael Ross

The first time as many as 1,056 four generation pedigrees have been published in one book. It contains the pedigrees and summarised racing records, with number of wins and places, total earnings, and the names of the Pattern Races in which wins or places were achieved, for the winners of every Group 1 race in Great Britain, Ireland, France and Italy, from 1966 to 1980 inclusive. Also the winners of 12 of the British Group 2 races, and 9 top races in the U.S.A.—a grand total of 85 races.

Many other important horses which did not win qualifying races have also been included.

In addition it also incorporates all 214 pedigrees which appeared in the 1960-1965 edition of **Pedigrees of Leading Winners,** published by the Thoroughbred Breeders' Association, with racing updates and the pedigrees of the overseas winners increased to four generations.

There is also a really comprehensive index, listing not only the winners themselves but also their parents, their grandparents and their third and fourth dams.

Invaluable for reference to pedigrees or racing records in the major racing countries of the world. 6 Pedigrees to the page. Cloth Bound £25.00, postage £1.00 extra per copy. Obtainable from J. A. Allen & Co., The Horseman's Bookshop Ltd., 1 Lower Grosvenor Place, London SW1W 0EL.

Telephone : 01-834 5606

957

Come racing at
LONGCHAMP
CHANTILLY
DEAUVILLE

Principal races in 1983 *season:*

Longchamp	April 4	Prix d'Harcourt (Gr 2)
	April 10	Prix Greffulhe (Gr 2)
	April 17	Prix Noailles (Gr 2)
	April 24	Poule d'Essai des Poulains (Gr 1) and Prix Jean Prat (Gr 2)
	May 1	Prix Ganay (Gr 1) and Poule d'Essai des Pouliches (Gr 1)
	May 8	Prix Hocquart (Gr 2)
	May 15	Prix Lupin (Gr 1)
	May 22	Prix Saint-Alary (Gr 1) and Prix du Cadran (Gr 1)
	May 29	Prix Dollar (Gr 2)
	June 26	Grand Prix de Paris (Gr 1) and Prix d'Ispahan (Gr 1)
	Sept. 5	Prix du Moulin de Longchamp (Gr 1)
	Sept. 11	Prix Vermeille (Gr 1)
	Sept. 18	Prix de la Salamandre (Gr 1)
	Sept. 25	Prix du Rond Point (Gr 3) and Prix Gladiateur (Gr 3)
	Oct. 2	Trusthouse Forte Prix de l'Arc de Triomphe (Gr 1), Prix de l'Abbaye de Longchamp (Gr 1) and Prix Marcel Boussac (Gr 1)
	Oct. 9	Grand Criterium (Gr 1)
	Oct. 16	Prix du Conseil de Paris (Gr 2)
	Oct. 23	Prix de la Foret (Gr 1)
	Oct. 30	Prix Royal Oak (Gr 1)
Chantilly	June 5	Prix du Jockey-Club (Gr 1)
	June 12	Prix de Diane Hermes (Gr 1)
Deauville	Aug. 7	Prix Maurice de Gheest (Gr 2) and Prix Kergorlay (Gr 2)
	Aug. 14	Prix Jacques le Marois (Gr 1)
	Aug. 21	Prix Morny (Gr 1)
	Aug. 28	Grand Prix de Deauville (Gr 2)

**Enquiries: Societe d'Encouragement,
11 Rue du Cirque, 75008 Paris
Tel: 266-92-02   Telex: 280 071**

TRAINERS

The figure in brackets are the number of winners each trainer has had over the past five seasons, from 1978 to 1982 inclusive. Quarters and telephone numbers are given after the trainer's name.

Akehurst, R. P. J. (15:14:9:1:1)
Lambourn
Lambourn (0488) 71850
Albina, M. H. (—:—:0:10:5)
Newmarket
Newmarket (0638) 661998
Allan, A. R. (0:1:0:3:3)
St Boswells
St Boswells (083 52) 2403
Allingham, P. B. (0:0:0:0:0)
Luton Offley (046 276) 337
Alston, E. J. (—:—:—:—:0)
Preston Longton (0772) 612120
Ancil, D. I. (2:2:2:0:0)
Banbury Banbury (0295) 711006
Andrews, A. M. (—:—:—:0:0)
Taunton
Bishops Lydeard (0823) 432 632
Arbuthnot, D. W. P. (—:—:—:—:4)
Newbury Lambourn (0488) 72637
Armstrong, R. W. (30:38:29:45:43)
Newmarket
Newmarket (0638) 663333/4
Armytage, R. C. (0:0:0:0:0)
East Ilsley
East Ilsley (063 528) 203
Arnold, A. T. (0:0:0:0:0)
Bridgnorth Quatt (0746) 780400
Ashworth, P. H. (6:0:1:3:4)
Epsom Epsom (037 27) 20336
Asquith, P. (12:9:6:5:7)
Wetherby Wetherby (0937) 62122
Atkins, R. A. L. (1:2:0:0:0)
Elstead Elstead (0252) 702028
Atkinson, W. (0:0:0:0:0)
Carlisle Carlisle (0228) 25649
Austin, C. A. (2:2:4:2:2)
Wokingham
Wokingham (0734) 786 425

Bailey, A. (—:—:6:4:11)
Newmarket
Newmarket (0638) 661537
Bailey, K. C. (0:0:0:0:0)
East Ilsley
East Ilsley (063 528) 253
Bailey, P. G. (0:0:0:0:0)
Salisbury
(Home) Amesbury (0980) 22964
and (Office) 22682
Baker, J. H. (0:1:0:0:0)
Dulverton
Dulverton (0398) 820508
Baker, R. J. (—:—:—:6:6)
Marlborough
Marlborough (0672) 54739
Balding, A. (2:5:4:8:7)
Doncaster
Doncaster (0302) 710221
or (stables) 0777-818407

Balding, G. B. (16:17:26:14:18)
Weyhill Weyhill (026 477) 2278
Balding, I. A. (39:39:49:39:58)
Kingsclere
Kingsclere (0635) 298210
Barnes, T. A. (5:3:1:0:0)
Ousby Langwathby (076 881) 379
Barons, D. H. (0:0:0:0:0)
Kingsbridge
Loddiswell (054 855) 326
Barratt, L. J. (3:2:1:0:0)
Oswestry
Queens Head (069 188) 209
Barrett, W. A. (—:—:—:0:0)
Lincoln
Fenton Claypole (063684) 413
Barron, T. D. (—:0:0:5:11)
Thirsk Thirsk (0845) 587 435
Beasley, H. R. (—:—:—:—:0)
Lewes Lewes (07916) 6619
Beeson, E. E. G. (2:8:6:5:3)
Lewes
Lewes (079 16) 4581 and 5654
Bell, Mrs A. M. (—:—:—:1:2)
Biggar Skirling (089 96) 273
Bell, C. H. (0:0:6:6:2)
Hawick Denholm (045 087) 278
Benstead, C. J. (18:17:17:19:13)
Epsom Ashtead (037 22) 71512
Bentley, W. (—:7:6:11:8)
Middleham
Wensleydale (0969) 22289
Berry, J. (20:11:15:19:26)
Lancaster Forton (0524) 791179
Bethell, J. D. W. (14:15:19:14:15)
Didcot Abingdon (0235) 834333
Bevan, P. J. (0:0:0:0:0)
Kingstone
Dapple Heath (088 921) 647
or 670
Bill, T. T. (—:—:—:—:1)
Ashby-de-la-Zouch
Ashby-de-la-Zouch (0530) 415881
Blakeney, R. E. (0:0:0:0:0)
Devizes Cannings (038 086) 243
Blanshard, M. T. W. (—:0:4:5:8)
Lambourn
Lambourn (0488) 71091
Blum, G. (5:7:6:5:7)
Newmarket
Newmarket (0638) 662734
Blundell, J. W. (—:—:—:0:0)
Grimsby
North Thoresby (047 287) 256
Bolton, M. J. (2:1:5:0:1)
East Grinstead
Dormans Park (034 287) 403
Booth, C. B. B. (1:5:1:6:6)
Flaxton
Whitwell-on-the-Hill (065 381) 586
or 239 (stables)

Bosley, J. R.   (—:2:1:4:7)
Bampton
    Bampton Castle (0993) 850 212
Boss, R.   (18:14:21:9:16)
Newmarket
    Newmarket (0638) 661335
Bradley, J. M.   (7:4:2:0:0)
Chepstow
    Chepstow (029 12) 2486
Brassey, K. M.   (—:—:—:0:12)
Lambourn
    Lambourn (0488) 71508
Brennan, J. J.   (—:—:—:—:0)
Cheltenham
    Withington (024 289) 238
Brennan, O.   (0:0:0:0:0)
Newark   Caunton (063 686) 332
Bridger, J. J.   (—:—:—:0:0)
Chichester
    Eastergate (024368) 3525
Bridgwater, K. S.   (4:2:1:0:0)
Solihull   Knowle (056 45) 77026
Brittain, C. E.   (52:34:25:54:53)
Newmarket
    Newmarket (0638) 663739
    and 664347
Brookshaw, P. T.   (—:—:—:0:2)
    Melton Mowbray (0664) 813161
Bulgin, T. S. M.   (—:—:—:—:0)
Shaftesbury
    Fontmell Magna (0747) 811 648
Burgoyne, P. V. J. P. (—:—:—:—:0)
Wantage   Childrey (023 559) 623
Butler, P.   (0:0:0:0:0)
Lewes   Plumpton (0273) 890124
Bycroft, N.   (—:—:—:0:2)
Brandsby   Brandsby (034 75) 641

Callaghan N. A.   (40:34:14:29:15)
Newmarket
    Newmarket (0638) 664040
Calver, P.   (2:7:2:2:5)
Ripon   Ripon (0765) 700313
Calvert, J. B.   (3:0:5:3:3)
Hambleton   Thirsk (0845) 597373
Camacho, M. J. C.   (17:13:7:16:16)
Malton   Malton (0653) 4901
Cambidge, B. R.   (0:0:0:0:1)
Shifnal
    Weston-under-Lizard (095 276) 249
Candy, H. D. N. B. (35:39:28:30:32)
Wantage   Uffington (036 782) 276
Cann, J. F.   (1:0:0:0:0)
Cullompton
    Kentisbeare (088 46) 356
Carr, E. J.   (11:4:3:4:4)
Hambleton
    Thirsk (0845) 597 288
Carter, E.   (2:2:0:3:6)
Malton   Malton (0653) 3522
Carter, R.   (0:0:2:0:0)
Swaffham
    Gooderstone (036 621) 226
Cecil, H. R. A. (108:128:84:107:111)
Newmarket
    Newmarket (0638) 662192 or
    (home) 662387

Chamberlain, N.   (—:—:0:0:0)
West Auckland
    Bishop Auckland (0388) 832 465
Champion, R.   (—:—:—:—:0)
Swindon
    Broad Hinton (079 373) 329
Chapman, D. W.   (2:2:5:11:22)
Stillington
    Easingwold (0347) 21683
Chapman, M. C.   (0:0:0:0:0)
Market Harborough
    Clipston (085 886) 255
Charles, W.   (0:1:3:0:1)
Warwick   Warwick (0926) 493878
Charlton, J. I. A.   (—:—:—:0:0)
Stocksfield
    Stocksfield (0661) 843 247
Clay, W.   (0:0:2:0:0)
Uttoxeter   Uttoxeter (088 93) 2068
Cole, P. F. I.   (56:61:48:50:39)
Lambourn
    Lambourn (0488) 71632
Cole, S. N.   (0:0:0:0:0)
Newport Pagnell
    Northampton (0604) 870330
Collingridge, H. J.   (3:9:3:7:4)
Newmarket
    Newmarket (0638) 665454
Cottrell, L. G.   (0:2:2:2:4)
Cullompton
    Kentisbeare (088 46) 320
Cousins, M. A.   (1:0:1:1:0)
Tarporley
    Little Budworth (082 921) 260
    or 316
Cousins, Mrs S. A.   (—:—:1:0:0)
Carnforth
    Carnforth (052 473) 3058
Craig, T.   (16:10:5:5:5)
Dunbar   Dunbar (0368) 62583
Crawford, W. H.   (—:—:—:—:0)
Haddington
    Haddington (062 082) 2229
Cross, R. F.   (0:0:0:0:0)
Alnwick   Chatton (066 85) 247
Crossley, C. C.   (8:7:12:4:8)
Wirral   (051 648) 1546
Crump, N. F.   (4:3:2:3:1)
Middleham
    Wensleydale (0969) 23269
Cumani, L. M.   (53:19:26:30:25)
Newmarket
    Newmarket (0638) 661569
    and 665432
Cundell, P. D.   (10:10:10:10:8)
Compton
    Compton (063 522) 267/8
Cunningham-Brown, K. O.
     (—:—:—:0:0)
Stockbridge
    Wallop (026 478) 611
Cuthbert, T. A.   (—:—:0:0:0)
Carlisle   Carlisle (0228) 60822

Dale, D.   (0:4:4:7:7)
Newmarket
    Newmarket (0638) 661586

Davison, A. R. (2:6:0:0:0)
Caterham
　　　Caterham (0883) 43857
Dickinson, M. W. (—:—:1:1:0)
Harewood
　(Office) Harewood (0532) 886536
　(Home) Harewood (0532) 886346
Dodds, J. P. (0:0:0:0:0)
Alnwick　　　Chatton (066 85) 216
Douglas-Home, J. T. A.
　　　　　　(—:0:0:1:1)
Wantage
　　　East Hendred (023588) 247
Doyle, J. C. M. (—:—:5:0:0)
Wetherby
　(Home) Wetherby (0937) 63855
　　　or (Stable) 65051
Dudgeon, I. M. (1:0:0:0:0)
Warminster
　　　Codford St Mary (09855) 477
Duggins, P. H. (—:—:—:0:0)
Shepton Mallet
　　　Upton Noble (074 985) 527
Dunlop, J. L. (73:96:91:67:87)
Arundel
　(Office) Arundel (0903) 882194
　(Home) Arundel (0903) 882106
Durr, F. (—:38:51:42:13)
Newmarket
　　　Newmarket (0638) 662090

Easterby, M. H. (50:74:63:37:43)
Malton
　　　Kirby Misperton (065 386) 600
Easterby, M. W. (12:31:17:26:17)
Sheriff Hutton
　　　Sheriff Hutton (03477) 368
Eckley, M. W. (—:—:—:0:0)
Ludlow　　Brimfield (058 472) 372
Edmunds, J. (1.0.0.0.0)
Birmingham
　　　Wythall (0564) 822334
Edwards, J. A. C. (0:0:0:0:0)
Ross-on-Wye
　　　Harewood End (098987) 259
Eldin, E. (—:0:11:11:27)
Newmarket
　　　Newmarket (0638) 662036
　　　or 663217
Elsey, C. W. C. (18:12:26:11:18)
Malton　　Malton (0653) 3149
Elsworth, D. R. C. (—:10:12:10:17)
Fordingbridge
　(Home) Rockbourne (07253) 220
　　　or (Office) 528
Etherington, J. (22:24:20:20:22)
Malton　　Malton (0653) 2842

Fairhurst T. (34:20:11:13:13)
Middleham
　　　Wensleydale (0969) 23362
Feilden, P. J. (—:3:3:4:3)
Newmarket　Exning (063877) 637
Felgate, P. S. (0:0:1:0:7)
Melton Mowbray
　　　Melton Mowbray (0664) 812019

Finch, Mrs P. A. (0:0:0:0:0)
Shaftesbury
　　　East Knoyle (074 783) 305
Fisher, A. L. (0:0:0:0:0)
Melton Mowbray
　　　Leicester (0533) 605907
Fisher, R. F. (—:—:—:—:0:0)
Ulverston
　　　Ulverston (0229) 55664
Fitzgerald, J. G. (9:15:13:14:10)
Malton　　Malton (0653) 2718
Fleming, H. (0:0:1:2:0)
Cleethorpes
　　　Cleethorpes (0472) 695215
Fletcher, G. G. (—:2:3:4:2)
Newmarket
　　　Newmarket (0638) 668826
Forsey, B. (—:—:0:0:0)
Crowcombe
　　　Crowcombe (098 48) 270
Forster, T. A. (0:0:0:0:0)
Letcombe Bassett
　　　Wantage (023 57) 3092
Fox, J. C. (—:—:—:0:0)
Amesbury
　　　Shrewton (0980) 620 861
Francis, M. E. D. (2:3:3:3:1)
Lambourn
　　　Lambourn (0488) 71700
Francis, W. D. (2:4:2:4:3)
Malpas　　Tilston (082 98) 208

Gandolfo, D. R. (3:4:2:3:0)
Wantage　Wantage (023 57) 3242
Garraton, D. T. (—:—:1:3:3)
Malton　　Rillington (094 42) 506
Gaselee, N. A. D. C. (3:2:5:6:1)
Lambourn
　　　Lambourn (0488) 71503
Gifford, J. T. (0.5.1.0.0)
Findon　　Findon (090 671) 2226
Gilbert, J. A. (—:—:1:1:1)
Oakham
　　　Edenham (077832) 226 or 330
Gosling, T. (4:2:4:1:0)
Epsom　　Epsom (037 27) 22080
Gray, C. W. (—:—:1:4:4)
Beverley　Beverley (0482) 882490
Grissell, D. M. (—:—:—:0:1)
Heathfield
　　　Brightling (042 482) 241
Gubby, B. (—:2:4:2:4)
Bagshot　Bagshot (0276) 63282
Guest, W. N. (5:14:11:4:12)
Newmarket
　　　Newmarket (0638) 661680

Haigh, W. W. (10:6:9:13:5)
Malton　　Malton (0653) 4428
Haldane, J. S. (—:—:—:0:0)
Kelso　　　Kelso (0573) 24956
Hall, N. (0:0:2:0:0)
Burton-on-Trent
　　　Barton-under-Needwood (028 371)
　　　　　　2279

961

Hall, Miss S. E. (7:15:7:12:22)
Middleham
    Wensleydale (0969) 40223
Hallett, T. B. (0:0:0:0:0)
Saltash   Saltash (075 55) 2064
Hanbury, B. (18:8:25:21:22)
Newmarket
(Stables) Newmarket (0638) 663193
(Home) Wickhambrook
    (044 082) 396
Hanley, D. L. (2:0:0:2:2)
Lambourn
Lambourn (0488) 72169 and 72219
Hannon, R. M. (47:30:37:29:28)
Marlborough
Collingbourne Ducis (026 485) 254
Hanson, J. (12:8:13:5:7)
Wetherby
    Wetherby (0937) 62841
Hardy, J. (31:14:17:10:4)
Staunton
Long Bennington (0400) 81212
Harman, G. R. (—:—:—:2:1)
Helmsley   Helmsley (0439) 70838
Harris, J. L. (0:2:1:0:0)
Melton Mowbray
    Harby (0949) 60671
Harris, S. T. (—:0:1:0:1)
Amersham
    Amersham (02403) 21718
Hartop, R. W. (—:—:0:0:0)
Cheltenham
    Andoversford (024 282) 448
Harwood, G. (59:48:69:97:120)
Pulborough
    Pulborough (079 82) 2335
Haslam, P. C. (10:25:38:35:29)
Newmarket
    Newmarket (0638) 664525
    and 664523
Hastings-Bass, W. E. R. H.
    (27:27:26:44:22)
Newmarket
    Newmarket (0638) 662024
Haynes, M. J. (12:16:12:9:8)
Epsom
    Burgh Heath (073 73) 51140
Haynes, P. D. (—:—:—:—:9)
Chichester
    West Ashling (024 358) 231
Head, R. A. (0:0:0:0:0)
Lambourn
    Lambourn (0488) 71411
Henderson, N. J. (0:0:0:0:0)
Lambourn
    Lambourn (0488) 72259
Hern, W. R. (74:16:65:64:44)
West Ilsley
East Ilsley (063 528) 219 and 251
Hide, A. G. (4:5:4:8:10)
Newmarket
    Newmarket (0638) 662063
Hill, C. J. (12:13:7:6:8)
Barnstaple
    Barnstaple (0271) 2048
Hills, B. W. (86:56:61:82:55)
Lambourn
    Lambourn (0488) 71548

Hill-Wood, Miss A. K. (—:—:0:0:0)
Grantham Knipton (0476) 870 226
Hinchliffe, M. J. (—:—:0:0:0)
Lambourn
    Marlborough (0672) 40755 and
    Chaddleworth (04882) 586
Hindley, J. J. (42:41:46:32:39)
Newmarket
    Newmarket (0638) 664141/2
Hoad, R. P. C. (—:—:2:1:3)
Lewes   Lewes (07916) 77124
Hobbs, B. R. (43:42:60:50:42)
Newmarket
    Newmarket (0638) 662129
Hobson, R. (13:5:4:0:2)
Worksop
(Home) Mansfield (0623) 822 835
(Stable) Worksop (0909) 475 962
    or 475425
Hodges, R. J. (—:—:—:—:0)
Langport
    Long Sutton (045 824) 340
Holden, W. (15:8:4:5:4)
Newmarket   Exning (063 877) 384
Holder, R. J. (—:—:—:—:3)
Portbury
    Bristol (0272) 9881 and 2192
Hollinshead, R. (50:25:26:57:36)
Upper Longdon
    Armitage (0543) 490298
Holt, L. J. (6:12:9:10:9)
Tunworth
    Long Sutton (025 681) 376
Houghton, R. F. J. (47:39:42:29:38)
Blewbury
    Blewbury (0235) 850480
Huffer, G. A. (—:23:11:18:22)
Newmarket
    Newmarket (0638) 730391
    and 667997
Hunter, G. H. (24:22:30:29:18)
East Ilsley
    East Ilsley (063 528) 250

Incisa, D. E. (—:—:—:0:0)
Leyburn
    Wensleydale (0969) 40653
Ingham, A. P. (16:9:3:3:3)
Headley   Ashtead (037 22) 72859
Ivory, K. T. (11:15:9:19:10)
Radlett   Radlett (092 76) 6081

James, C. J. (5:3:10:3:1)
Newbury
    Great Shefford (048 839) 280
James, M. B. C. (—:—:0:3:0)
Whitchurch
    Whitchurch (0948) 3155 or 4067
Jarvis, A. P. (13:5:6:24:34)
Royston
(Office) Royston, Herts (0763) 47444
(Home) Royston, Herts (0763) 46611
Jarvis, M. A. (31:39:30:35:31)
Newmarket
    Newmarket (0638) 661702
    and 662519